WEBSTER'S
SHORTER SCHOOL
DICTIONARY

A Merriam-Webster

BASED UPON
WEBSTER'S NEW INTERNATIONAL
DICTIONARY

MANY ILLUSTRATIONS

REG. U.S. PAT. OFF.

AMERICAN BOOK COMPANY

NEW YORK   CINCINNATI   CHICAGO

PREFACE

Webster's Shorter School Dictionary here presented is condensed from the somewhat larger Elementary School Dictionary. The problem of presenting in so moderate a compass that part of the English language likely to be of most service to the schoolchild is one of unusual difficulty. There is the constant temptation to include so large a vocabulary that the definitions must be left imperfect and perfunctory, with the result that the dictionary fails in school use. An equally insidious danger is that of attaining condensation by running together in single paragraphs definitions of separate, though related, words. It is the almost universal testimony of teachers that words so grouped are not readily found by the pupil.

Webster's Shorter School Dictionary has resolutely steered clear of these two common failings of small dictionaries, and at the same time has succeeded in presenting a carefully chosen vocabulary of more than 35,000 words, a number ample for the purpose intended.

Another feature, shared by the Shorter School Dictionary with others of the Merriam series, and with none beside, is that no word is used in a definition that is not itself defined or explained in the dictionary itself. To make a dictionary thus self-contained is a task requiring special attention in editing and entails no small additional expense. The result does not lend itself to advertising exploitation, but does save the consulter of the dictionary from definitions that cannot be explained save by consulting other dictionaries. If it be remembered that a few experiences with such definitions will shake the student's faith in the utility of dictionaries in general, it will be seen that the importance of this sort of unity cannot well be exaggerated.

The Editors have kept constantly in mind the needs of the schoolboy and schoolgirl, and the Shorter School Dictionary is designed expressly to meet them. While primarily and fundamentally a school dictionary, it is sufficiently broad in its vocabulary to be of value in the general field. As a working tool for school use no dictionary of similar size and price approaches the utility and quality of Webster's Shorter School Dictionary.

Vocabulary. Over 35,000 words and phrases are defined in simple and clear terms. Not only in ordinary words, but in technical and scientific terminology, the vocabulary is remarkably complete, while its up-to-date character is shown by the inclusion of such terms as *aileron, airplane, dictograph, hangar, radio, sabotage, zoom,* etc.

Definitions. Clearness is the keynote. The language is at all times as simple as the nature of the word will allow, a safe course being steered between brevity and ambiguity.

Capitalization. The correct use of capital letters is taught by the simple plan of using initial capitals only where such capitalization is essential. Thus, *Christian, Christmas, Easter, Halloween, Labor Day, Spartan, Sunday, January*, etc., are capitalized, while all ordinary words are begun with small letters.

Pronunciation. The simple and well-established Webster system of respelling, with one symbol only for each sound, renders the Shorter School Dictionary an infallible guide to correct pronunciation. The key is placed for convenience at the foot of each page.

Grammar. The Shorter School Dictionary is unique among smaller dictionaries in removing grammatical difficulties from the path of the learner. Thus:

Plurals. The plurals of all difficult and irregular words are given in the vocabulary; as, *ebony*, pl. EBONIES; *echo*, pl. ECHOES; *fish*; *minutia*, pl. MINUTIÆ; *miscellany*, pl. MISCELLANIES; *radius*, pl. Latin RADII, English RADIUSES; *son-in-law*, pl. SONS-IN-LAW; *tomato*, pl. TOMATOES; *tonneau*, pl. TONNEAUX.

Adjectives. The comparison of adjectives is a valuable innovation: those usually compared with *-er* and *-est* and those with *more* and *most* being carefully distinguished, while the irregular forms are given in full; e. g., *easy, happy, hard, safe, sage*, etc., are marked [3] to indicate the form of comparison with *-er* and *-est* (final *y* changing into *i*); *capricious, hapless, radical, sarcastic*, etc., are marked [4] to indicate the form of comparison with *more* and *most*; adjectives whose comparatives and superlatives are irregular, as *bad, fit, good, little, much*, etc., have the forms indicated in every instance.

Verbs. The principal parts of verbs are given or indicated, irregularities of inflection being noted without exception; e. g., *alienate, capitalize, capsize, saddle*, and other words ending in silent *e*, are marked [1] to indicate that the *e* is dropped before *-ed* and *-ing*; as, *live*, LIVED, LIVING; *carry, defy*, and other words ending in *-y* are marked [2] to indicate that the *y* is changed into *i* before *-ed*; as, *carry*, CARRIED, CARRYING. Irregular inflections are given in full; as, *come*, pret. CAME, p. p. COME, p. pr. & vb. n. COMING; *eat, go, lay, lie, sag*, etc. Many people have difficulty in remembering whether or not to double the final letter in such verbs as *differ, level, prefer, refer, skim, wrap*, etc. The Shorter School Dictionary makes all such matters plain.

Illustrations. Wherever an illustration can add clearness to the definition or replace a long description it has been inserted. There are numbers of such illustrations, which for correctness of drawing and fullness of detail leave nothing to be desired.

Appendices. Tables of measures, weights, metric system, decimal equivalents, foreign coinage, etc., are set out clearly, with a view to rapid memorizing or ready reference.

SYMBOLS USED TO INDICATE PRONUNCIATION

ACCENTS AND HYPHENS. The principal accent is indicated by a heavy mark (′), and the secondary accent by a lighter mark (′), at the end of the syllable. Syllabic division is indicated by a light hyphen, except where this is replaced by an accent mark, or by a heavier hyphen used to join the members of words written or printed with a hyphen.

FOREIGN SOUNDS for which no special symbols are provided are represented by the nearest English equivalents.

PRONUNCIATIONS OMITTED. The accentuation only is given for some compound words, and for some derivatives ending in common suffixes like *-ess, -est, -ing, -ist, -less, -like, -ness, -ship*, if the pronunciation is perfectly regular and can therefore easily be learned from the separate parts. In other cases where a part or the whole of a pronunciation is omitted, it is the same as that of a word immediately preceding, and may be supplied from this preceding entry.

ā, as in āle, fāte, lā′bor, chā′os.

ȧ, „ „ sen′ȧte, pref′ȧce, leg′is-lȧ-tive.

â, „ „ câre, pâr′ent, com-pâre′.

ă, „ „ ăm, ădd, ăc-cept′, re′ăd-mit′.

ä, „ „ ärm, fär, fä′ther, äh, pälm.

à, „ „ àsk, gràss, dànce, stàff, pàth.

a̍, „ „ so′fa̍, i-de′a̍, a̍-bound′, mo′la̍r.

b, „ „ baby, be, bit, bob, but.

ch, „ „ chair, chew, much.

d, „ „ day, do, add′ed.

dụ̄ : for du as in ver′dure.

ē, as in ēve, mēte, se-rēne′.

ė, „ „ ė-vent′, dė-pend′, crė-ate′.

ĕ, as in ĕnd, ĕx-cuse′, ĕf-face′, car′pĕt.

ĕ, „ „ re′cĕnt, de′cĕn-cy, nov′ĕl.

ẽ, „ „ ev′ẽr, pẽr-vert′; ru′mor (rōo′mẽr).

f, as in fill, feel, ful-fill′.

g (always "hard"), as in go, begin.

gz : for x as in ex-ist′, ex-act′, ex-am′ple.

h, as in hat, hot, hurt, oho.

hw : for wh as in what, why, where.

ī, as in īce, sīght, in-spīre′, ī-de′a.

ĭ, „ „ ĭll, ad-mĭt′, dĭ-vide′, pity (pĭt′ĭ).

j, „ „ joke, jolly, prej′u-dice.

k, „ „ keep, kick.

ᴋ (small capital) : for ch as in Ger. ich, ach.

ks : for x as in vex, exit, perplex, dextrous.

kw : for qu as in queen, quit, quality.

l, as in late, leg, lip, lot, lull, holly.

m, „ „ man, men, hum, hammer.

n, as in ɴo, nine, man, manner.

ɴ (small capital) : indicates nasal tone (as in French) of preceding vowel, as in bon (bôɴ).

ŋ (like ng) : for n before the sound of k or of "hard" g, as in bank, junction, linger.

ng, as in long, sing, sing′er.

ō, as in ōld, nōte, bōld, he′rō, cal′i-cō.

ȯ, „ „ ȯ-bey′, tȯ-bac′co, a-nat′ȯ-my.

ô, „ „ ôrb, lôrd; law (lô), saw (sô), all (ôl).

ŏ, „ „ ŏdd, nŏt, fŏr′est, hŏr′ror.

ǒ, „ „ cǒn-nect′, cǒn-trol′, cǒm-bine′.

ǭ, „ „ sǭft, dǭg, clǭth.

oi, „ „ oil, nois′y, a-void′, goi′ter.

ōō, „ „ fōōd, mōōn; rude (rōōd).

ŏŏ, „ „ fŏŏt, wŏŏl; put (pŏŏt), pull (pŏŏl).

ou, „ „ out, thou, de-vour′.

p, „ „ papa, pen, pin, pop, put.

r, „ „ rap, red, rip, rod.

s (always voiceless, or "sharp"), as in so, this, haste.

sh, as in she, ship, shop, hush.

t, as in time, talk; also for ed as in baked.

th (voiceless), as in thin, through, wealth.

th (voiced) : for th as in then, this, smooth.

tụ̄ : for tu as in cul′ture, na′ture, pic′ture.

ū, as in ūse, pūre, dū′ty.

ů, as in û-nite′, for′mů-late, hů-mane′.

û, „ „ ûrn, fûrl; her (hûr), fir (fûr).

ŭ, as in ŭp, tŭb, stŭd′y, ŭp-hill′.

ŭ, „ „ cir′cŭs, cau′cŭs, cir′cŭm-stance.

ü : for French u, as in menu (mē-nü′); for German ü, as in grün, Sün′de.

v, as in van, vent, vote, revoke.

w, „ „ want, win, weed, wood.

y, „ „ yard, yet, yellow, beyond.

z, „ „ zone, haze, la′zy.

zh : for z as in azure; for s as in pleasure; etc.

′ as in pardon (pär′d'n), eaten (ēt′n), evil (ē′v'l) : indicates the elision of a vowel, or a slight vowel sound amounting to a mere vocal murmur.

ADDITIONAL SYMBOLS FOR USE IN INDICATING PRONUNCIATION WITHOUT RESPELLING

For indicating PRONUNCIATION BY RESPELLING, the table on page iv. is complete in itself and is alone used throughout this Dictionary. To indicate PRONUNCIATION WITHOUT RESPELLING, the table below may be used in connection with that on page iv. The table here given is to be used only when any letter of a word has a sound that is represented in the other table by a different letter. Thus, in the *respelling*, s is used for one sound only, that in sin or so, never for that in his (hĭz), is (ĭz). To show the pronunciation of his, therefore, *without respelling*, the s is marked with a diacritic; thus: hĭṣ; the first two letters (hĭ) being from the table on page iv., and the ṣ from the table below. In this table, the symbols in parentheses are the equivalent symbols from the respelling table.

In digraphs, mark only the letter that is to be regarded as sounded, as in brĕāk, brĕad, yĭēld, vĕil, etc. Ce, ci, sci, se, si, and ti, before a vowel and immediately after an accented syllable, usually have the sound of sh, and need not be marked. Silent e at the end of a syllable, as in fate, etc., need not be marked. When desirable, a silent letter may be shown as an unmarked italic. In a few words, the pronunciation can be indicated only by respelling.

ā (= ĕ), . . . as in li'ār, cow'ārd, mus'tārd.
a̤ (= ŏ), . . . ,, ,, what, wa̤s, qua̤l'i-ty.
a̤ (= ô), . . . ,, ,, a̤ll, a̤we, swa̤rm, ta̤lk.
au, aw (= ô), ,, ,, ,, Au Sable, au'thor, law.
ę (= ā), . . . ,, ,, ęight, pręy, vęin; or (= ä), as in os'pręy.
ê (= â), . . . ,, ,, thêre, hêir, whêrein'.
ẽ (= û), . . . ,, ,, ẽr'mine, e-tẽr'nal.
ee (= ē), . . . ,, ,, eel, feet, fee'ble, un-seen'.
ew (= ū), . . . ,, ,, ewe, dew, hewn; or (= o͞o), as in brew.
ï (= ē), . . . ,, ,, pïque, ma-chïne', po-lïce'; or (= ĕ), as in fï-as'co.
ī (= ē), . . . ,, ,, vīr-gin'i-ty, e-lix'īr; or (= û), as in īrk'some, fīr.
ǫ (= o͞o), . . ,, ,, wǫlf, wǫm'an, wǫl'ver-ine'.
ǫ (= o͞o), . . ,, ,, ǫoze, dǫ, whǫ, tǫmb.
ô (= ŭ), . . . ,, ,, ôth'er, sôn; or (= ŭ), as in wel'côme.

ŏ (= ĕ), . . . ,, ,, sail'ŏr, mi'nŏr; or (= û), as in wŏrk, wŏrth.
ow (= ou), . as in owl, cow'ard, vow'el.
oy (= oi), . . ,, ,, oys'ter, boy, roy'al.
u̇ (= o͞o), . . ,, ,, fu̇ll, pu̇t, pu̇sh, joy'fu̇l.
u̇ (= o͞o), . . ,, ,, ru̇de, ru̇'mor, in-tru̇de'.
ȳ (= ī), . . . ,, ,, flȳ, skȳ, stȳle, de-fȳ', dȳ'ing.
y̆ (= ĭ), . . . ,, ,, hy̆mn, ly̆r'ic.
ỹ (= ē), . . . ,, ,, sat'ỹr; or (= û), my̆rrh
e (= k), . . . ,, ,, eat, eon-eur'.
ç (= s), . . . ,, ,, çell, viçe.
eh (= k), . . ,, ,, eho'rus, eeh'o, ep'oeh
çh (= sh), . ,, ,, çhaise, ma-çhine'.
ġ (= g), . . . ,, ,, ġet, be-ġin', an'ġer.
ġ (= j), . . . ,, ,, ġem, en'ġine.
dġ (= j), . . ,, ,, edġe, bridġe, badġ'er.
ṣ (= z), . . . ,, ,, iṣ, haṣ, wiṣ'dom.
x (ks), ... ,, ,, vex, ex'it.
x̱ (= gz), . . ,, ,, ex̱-ist', ex̱-am'ple.
ph (= f), . . ,, ,, phan'tom, sul'phur.
qu (= kw), . . ,, queen, con'quest.
wh (= hw), ,, ,, when, what.

Capital letters may be marked with the same symbols as the small letters, as in Charles, Çhar'le-magne, €ha'ron, Ẽr'skine, Ĭt'a-ly, etc.

RULES FOR SPELLING CERTAIN CLASSES OF WORDS
FOUNDED ON THE ORTHOGRAPHY OF DR. WEBSTER

FINAL CONSONANTS.

§ 1. The letters f, l, and s at the end of monosyllables, and standing immediately after single vowels, are generally doubled; as in *staff*, *cliff*, *doff*, *puff*, *all*, *bell*, *hill*, *toll*, *null*, *grass*, *press*, *hiss*, *moss*, *truss*.

EXCEPTIONS : *Clef*, *if*, *of*, *pal*, *as*, *gas*, *yes*, *his*, *this*, *pus*, *plus*, *bus* (for *omnibus*), *thus*, and *us*. The s is not doubled when (as in *o's*, *spade's*, *tones*, *loves*, *has*, *is*, *was*, etc.) it is used to form the possessive case or the plural of a noun, or the third person singular of a verb.

§ 2. C, h, j, k, q, v, w, and y are never doubled when final. **B, d, g, m, n, p, r, t,** and z, when final, are doubled in only a few words, the most important being *ebb*, *add*, *odd*, *egg*, *Ann*, *inn*, *Finn*, *Lapp*, *err*, *shirr*, *butt*, *fizz*, *buzz*, *fuzz*.

§ 3. Monosyllables ending with the sound of k, and having *c* following the vowel, usually have *k* added after the *c ;* as in *black*, *fleck*, *click*, *knock*, and *buck*.

EXCEPTIONS: *Lac*, *sac*, *arc*.

§ 4. Words of more than one syllable, ending in -ic or -iac, are now written (except *derrick*) without the *k;* as, *maniac*, *elegiac*, *zodiac*, *cubic*, *music*, *public*. **Words of more than one syllable, in which c is preceded by other vowels than i or ia,** commonly end in *ck ;* as, *barrack*, *hammock*, *hillock*, *wedlock*.

EXCEPTIONS: *Almanac*, *zebec*, *manioc*, *havoc*.

FORMATION OF DERIVATIVES.

§ 5. Words ending in c have a k inserted when adding a termination beginning with *e*, *i*, or *y*, so that the *c* shall not be pronounced like *s ;* as, *colic*, *colicky ; traffic*, *trafficked*, *trafficking*, *trafficker ; physic*, *physicked*, *physicking ; zinc*, *zincked*, *zincking*, *zincky*.

§ 6. Final consonant doubled. Words accented on the last syllable (including words of one syllable) if they end in a single consonant (except *h* or *x*) preceded by a single vowel, double the consonant before a suffix beginning with a vowel ; as, *clan*, *clan'nish; plan*, *planned*, *plan'ning*, *plan'ner; bag*, *bag'gage ; hot*, *hot'ter*, *hot'test ; wit*, *wit'ty ; cabal'*, *cabal'ling; abel'*, *abel'ted*, *abel'ting*, *abel'tor; begin'*, *begin'ning*, *begin'ner ; infer'*, *inferred'*, *infer'ring*. The consonant is doubled to preserve the short sound of the vowel. Thus, *plănned*, *hŏttest* and *abĕtted*, would naturally be pronounced *plāned*, *hōtest*, and *abēted*, if the consonant were not doubled.

EXCEPTIONS : *Gaseous*, *inferable*, *transferable*, and derivatives in which the accent of the primitive is thrown back upon another syllable ; as, *prefer'*, *pref'erence*, *refer'*, *ref'erence*, etc.

§ 7. Final consonant not doubled. Words accented on any syllable except the last, words ending in more than one consonant, and words ending in a single consonant preceded by more than one vowel, do not double the final consonant before a suffix beginning with a vowel ; as, *daub*, *daubed*, *daub'er ; need*, *need'y ; brief*, *brief'er*, *brief'est; trav'ail*, *trav'ailed*, *trav'ailing ; trav'el*, *trav'eling*, *trav'eler ; prof'it*, *prof'ited; act*, *act'ed*, *ac'tor; perform'*, *perform'er; stand*, *stand'ing*.

EXCEPTIONS : In *humbug* and a few other words ending in *g*, the *g* is doubled (*humbugged*, *humbugging*) before *e* or *i*, so that the *g* shall not be pronounced like *j*. Derivatives of *kidnap* are preferably spelled with one *p*, but the forms *kidnapper*, *kidnapping*, *kidnapped* are not uncommon. The form *woolen*, with one *l*, is usual in the United States, but British usage prefers two *l's*.

§ 8. Double consonant retained. Words ending in a double consonant generally retain both consonants when adding suffixes; as, *ebb*, *ebbing ; odd*, *oddly ; stiff*, *stiffness ; tell*, *teller ; skill*, *skillful*, *skillfulness ; will*, *willful*, *willfulness ; dull*, *dullness ; full*, *fullness*. So also the double *l* is retained in the words *installment*, *enthrallment*, *thralldom*, and *enrollment* (from *install*, *enthrall*, *thrall*, and *enroll*).

EXCEPTIONS : *Illy ; dully ; fully*.

§ 9. Silent e retained. Words ending with silent *e* generally retain this *e* before suffixes beginning with a consonant ; as, *pale*, *paleness ; hate*, *hateful ; incite*, *incitement ; chaste*, *chastely*, *chasteness ; move*, *movement ;* and their derivatives.

EXCEPTIONS : *Wholly*, *nursling*, *abridgment*, *acknowledgment*, *lodgment*, *judgment*, and, often, certain words (as, *due*, *duly ; argue*, *argument ; true*, *truly ; awe*, *awful*) in which the final *e* of the primitive is preceded by another vowel.

§ 10. Silent e omitted. Words ending with silent *e* generally drop the *e* before suffixes beginning with a vowel ; as, *bride*, *bridal ; guide*, *guidance ; plume*, *plumage ; use*, *usable*, *usage; grieve*, *grievance ; come*, *coming ; shape*, *shaping ; move*, *movable ; sale*, *salable ; fleece*, *fleecy ; force*, *forcible ; true*, *truism*.

EXCEPTIONS : The *e* is retained in *hoeing*, *shoeing*, and *toeing* (from *hoe*, *shoe*, and *toe*), to guard against mispronunciation, but is generally excluded from *shoer*. It is retained in *dyeing*, *singeing*, *swingeing*, *tingeing* (from *dye*, *singe*, *swinge*, *tinge*), to distinguish them from *dying*, *singing*, *swinging*, etc. (from *die*, *sing*, *swing*, etc.). The word *mileage*, as commonly written, does not omit the *e*. Words ending in *ce* or *ge* retain the *e* before suffixes beginning with *a* or *o*, so that the *c* or *g* shall not be pronounced with the "hard" sound ; as, *peace*, *peaceable ; notice*, *noticeable ; manage*, *manageable ; change*, *changeable ; advantage*, *advantageous ; outrage*, *outrageous*. *Mortgagor*, pronounced *mor'ga-jor'*, from *mortgage*, is the form preferred in usage. In derivatives in *-able*, as *usable*, *useable*, *salable*, *saleable*, etc., usage is divided.

§ 11. Ending -ing added to -ie. Words ending in *ie* generally drop the *e* and change *i* to *y* when adding *-ing*, so as to prevent two *i's* from coming together ; as, *die*, *dying ; hie*, *hying ; lie*, *lying ; tie*, *tying ; vie*, *vying*.

§ 12. y preceded by a consonant. Words

ending in *y* preceded by a consonant usually change *y* to *i* before any suffix except one beginning with *i* ; as, *icy, iciest, icily ; mercy, merciless ; tidy, tidiness ; modify, modifies ; foggy, fogginess ; earthy, earthiness ; pity, pitiful.*

The derivatives of adjectives of one syllable generally retain the *y* ; as, *shy, shyness ; sly, slyest ; dry, dryly ; wry, wryness.* But *sprier, spriest, drier* and *driest*, from *spry* and *dry*, are commonly written with *i* instead of *y* ; and *drily, shily, slily*, are not uncommon. Before -*ship* and -*like*, as *secretaryship, suretyship, ladyship, citylike, countrylike*, and in derivatives formed from *baby* and *lady*, the *y* is retained. The *y* also is retained in the possessive case of nouns, when formed by adding *s* with the apostrophe; as, *country's, everybody's.*

§ 13. *y* preceded by a vowel. Words ending in *y* preceded by a vowel generally retain the *y* unchanged before all suffixes; as, *gay, gayety, gayly ; play, player, plays ; sway, swayed ; obey, obeying ; joy, joyful ; enjoy, enjoyed ; buy, buying ; gluey, glueyness.*

EXCEPTIONS: *Daily, laid, paid, said, saith, slain,* and *staid* (from *day, lay, pay, say, slay*, and *stay*), with their compounds; *dewiness.*

§ 14. Adding a vowel to a vowel ending. Words ending with a vowel sound generally retain the letter or letters representing such sound before a suffix beginning with a vowel ; as, *huzza, huzzaed ; agree, agreeable, agreeing ; weigh, weighing ; dough, doughy ; echo, echoed ; woo, wooer ; bow, bowed.* Sometimes *cooes, wooes* (from the verbs, *coo, woo*) are found; but *coos, woos*, like *taboos, shampoos*, are preferable. *Cooed* and *wooed* are proper, like other participles in -*ed*.

PLURALS.

☞ For irregular plurals, as of *man, foot, brother, ox, deer*, and for plurals of foreign words, as of *datum, genus, index, crisis*, consult the individual words in the Vocabulary. See also the *Note* under the word PLURAL, *n.*, in the Vocabulary.

§ 15. The plural of English nouns regularly ends in *s*, or, in certain classes of words, in *es*.

When the singular ends in a sound with which *s* can unite and be pronounced without forming a separate syllable, *s* only is added in forming the plural ; as, *bay, bays ; shah, shahs ; sea, seas ; tree, trees ; pie, pies ; Hindu, Hindus; woe, woes; canto, cantos ; virtue, virtues ; purlieu, purlieus ; claw, claws; cab, cabs; panic, panics; bead, beads; chief, chiefs ; bag, bags ; path, paths ; ache, aches ; plague, plagues ; lock, locks ; bell, bells ; gem, gems ; fan fans; cup, cups; ear, ears; act, acts.* **Singulars ending in *o*** generally add *s* only to form their plurals. Certain words (as, *echo, echoes ; cargo, cargoes ; motto, mottoes ; potato, potatoes*, etc.) ending in *o* preceded by a consonant add *es* to form their plurals. Other nouns ending thus generally form their plurals regularly, though usage differs with regard to some of them. As to **nouns ending in *i*** usage differs, though, as a rule, their plurals are preferably written with the termination *is ;* as, *rabbi, rabbis.*

When the singular ends in a sound (as that of *ch* in *much, sh, j, s, x,* or *z*) with which *s* cannot unite in pronunciation, *e* is inserted before the *s* in

forming the plural, unless the word ends with silent *e*, which then forms a separate syllable with the *s* ; as, *church, churches ; rush, rushes ; age, ages ; edge, edges ; lace, laces ; gas, gases ; class, classes; alias, aliases; marquis, marquises; case, cases; loss, losses; box, boxes; maze, mazes.*

§ 16. Singulars ending in *y* preceded by a consonant form their plurals by adding *es* and changing *y* into *i* ; as, *mercy, mercies; lady, ladies; sky, skies; army, armies; pity, pities; Mary, Maries* (sometimes *Marys*) *; colloquy, colloquies.*

Singulars ending in *y* preceded by a vowel (except *u* having the power of *w*), form their plurals by adding *s* only ; as, *day, days ; key, keys ; money, moneys ; monkey, monkeys ; attorney, attorneys ; alloy, alloys ; guy, guys.*

§ 17. The plurals of a few nouns ending in *f* or *fe* are irregularly formed by changing *f* or *fe* into *ves*. Typical examples are: *life, lives ; knife, knives ; leaf, leaves ; sheaf, sheaves ; loaf, loaves ; beef, beeves; thief, thieves; calf, calves; half, halves; elf, elves ; shelf, shelves ; self, selves ; wolf, wolves.* See STAFF, WHARF, SCARF, in the Vocabulary. Other nouns ending in *f, fe,* or *ff*, form the plural regularly by adding *s* only.

§ 18. Plural of a letter, figure, sign, etc. To express the plural of a letter, a figure, or any character or sign, or of a word mentioned without regard to its meaning, the letter *s*, generally preceded by the apostrophe, is appended, as : " The two *l's* in *all;* " " The two *0's* in *400* ;" " Two **'s* in Orion ; " " He uses too many *if's*." Some omit the apostrophe in such cases.

MISCELLANEOUS RULES.

§ 19. -er or -re. Some words ending in -*er* are written by many authors with the termination -*re;* as, *center, meter, theater*, etc., often written *centre, metre, theatre,* etc. *Acre, lucre, nacre, massacre,* and *ogre* retain the termination -*re*, in order to preserve the hard sound of the *c* and *g*.

§ 20. -ize or -ise. Certain words ending, as pronounced, with the sound of long *i*, followed by *z*, are written with either -*ize* or -*ise ;* as, *criticize* or *criticise; civilize* or *civilise; naturalize* or *naturalise ; patronize* or *patronise.* But the latter spelling being now less often used, only the form in -*ize* is given in this book. Words still retaining the spelling -*ise* are : those derived from the French verb *prendre* (participle *pris* or *prise*), as *apprise, comprise, enterprise, surprise ;* and, also, *advertise, advise, arise, chastise, circumcise, compromise, demise, despise, devise, disfranchise, disguise, enfranchise, exercise, exorcise, franchise, merchandise, premise, revise, supervise, surmise.*

§ 21. mold or mould. The words *mold* and *molt*, and their compounds and derivatives, are written in this Dictionary with *o* instead of *ou*, in analogy with the words *bold, bolt, colt, gold,* etc., from which the *u* has been dropped. Many authors, however, write these words *mould* and *moult*, and their derivatives in like manner.

§ 22. -or or -our. There is a numerous class of words almost universally written in the United States with the termination -*or*, many of which are also written, esp. in England, with the termination -*our;* as, *candor, favor, honor, labor, rumor, vigor.* The English usage, however, is not uniform.

SPECIAL EXPLANATORY NOTES, SIGNS, AND ABBREVIATIONS

EXPLANATORY NOTES

Numbers in brackets. The small numbers, [1], [2], [3], etc., attached to certain words in this Dictionary (as **mate**, *v. t.* [1]) refer to the following paragraphs:

[**1.**] Verbs that are referred by number to this paragraph end in a silent *e* which is dropped before the endings *ed* and *ing* in forming the preterit, or past tense, and the present participle; thus, *mate, mated, mating; range, ranged, ranging.*

[**2.**] Verbs that are referred by number to this paragraph end in *y* preceded by a consonant. The *y* is changed to *i* before the ending *ed* in forming the preterit, or past tense; thus, *carry, carried, carrying.*

[**3.**] Adjectives that are referred by number to this paragraph are usually compared by adding *er* and *est.* See RULES FOR SPELLING, § 6. Those that end in silent *e* drop the *e* before these endings; thus, *late, later, latest.* Those that end in *y* preceded by a consonant change the *y* to *i* before the endings; thus, *sunny, sunnier, sunniest.* Adjectives usually compared by adding *er* and *est* are : **a** Those of one syllable; as, *big, gay, small.* **b** Those of two syllables accented on the final and not ending in a consonant group; as, *polite, severe, serene.* **c** Many adjectives of two syllables accented on the first, especially such as end in *w, y,* or *le ;* as, *narrow, happy, simple.* Many adjectives that are usually compared by adding *er* and *est* are often compared with *more* and *most* for euphony, emphasis, etc. Adjectives like *complete, perfect, universal,* etc., strictly speaking do not admit of comparison. When we say that a thing is *more perfect* than another we mean that it approaches nearer to perfection.

[**4.**] Adjectives that are referred by number to this paragraph are usually compared with *more* and *most.* They are : **a** Those of more than two syllables; as, *ignorant, amiable, prodigal.* **b** Those of two syllables ending in a consonant group ; as, *distinct, correct, ancient, frequent.* But some such adjectives, often used in comparison, as *pleasant, cunning,* usually take *er* and *est.* **c** Those ending in *ful ;* as, *mournful, careful ;* those ending in *ive ;* as, *active ;* many ending in *ed* and *ing ;* as, *wretched, daring.*

[**5.**] Words ending in *or* that are referred by number to this paragraph (as *favor, honor, labor*) are by many, especially in England, written with *our* (as *favour, honour, labour*). Also, usually, derivatives, as *honorable (honourable), honorably (honourably),* etc.

[**6.**] Words ending in *er* that are referred by number to this paragraph (as *meter, center, theater*) are by many written with *re* (as *metre, centre, theatre*).

[**7.**] Words referred by number to this paragraph are such as are accented on a syllable other than the last, and preferably *do not double* the final consonant in adding an ending beginning with a vowel ; as, *bevel, beveled, beveling ; bias, biased, biasing ; travel, traveled, traveling, traveler ; wainscot, wainscoted, wainscoting,* etc. By many writers, however, the final consonant is doubled, unnecessarily and contrary to analogy. These words, which form a large class, mostly end in *l.*

[**8.**] A word that is referred by number to this paragraph is entered without definition because it ends with one of the common suffixes *-able, -er,* or *-or, -ess, -ish, -less, -ly, -ness.* The meaning of any such word can readily be gathered from the definition of the main word to which it is attached, or of which it is a derivative, in connection with the definition of the proper suffix given below.

-able, -ible. A suffix used to form adjectives meaning: 1. *Capable of being, fit to be, worthy to be* (acted upon in a certain way); as in lov*able, fit to be,* or *worthy to be,* loved ; break*able, capable of being broken;* renew*able,* mov*able,* etc. 2. *Able to, capable of causing, productive of, characterized by;* also, *inclined to, subject to, liable to ;* as in dur*able, able to* endure; pleasur*able, capable of causing* pleasure ; peace*able, inclined to* peace ; perish*able, liable to* perish.

-er. A suffix used to form nouns meaning : 1. *One who has to do with* (something indicated), esp. *by way of trade* or *occupation ;* as in hat*ter, one who makes* or *deals in* hats; slav*er, one who deals in* slaves; tinn*er, potter,* etc. 2. *A native* or *inhabitant of* (a place indicated); as in London*er, a native* or *inhabitant of* London; British*er,* New York*er,* etc. 3. *A person* or *thing that does* (something indicated); *one who ; a thing that ;* as in bind*er, one* *that* binds; plead*er*, *one who* pleads; reap*er*, sink*er*, fight*er*, etc.

-ess. A suffix denoting the *female* corresponding to the male named by the noun to which the suffix is added; as in author*ess*, *a female* author; hunt*ress*, *a female* hunter; govern*ess* (for gover*noress*), lion*ess*, etc. See **-ER** and **-OR**.

-ish. A suffix used to form adjectives meaning: 1. *Belonging to*, *of the nature of*, *like;* as in book*ish*, *of the nature of*, or *characteristic of*, a book; girl*ish*, *belonging to*, or *like*, a girl. *-ish* often lends a derogatory force, as in boy*ish*, woman*ish*, etc., *like* a boy, woman, etc., *in their faults or weaknesses.* 2. *Like to a limited extent ; somewhat;* as in dull*ish*, *somewhat* dull ; tall*ish*, *somewhat* tall.

-less. A suffix that is added: 1. To nouns, to form adjectives meaning: *without, destitute of;* as in wit*less*, father*less*, etc., *without* wit, a father, etc. 2. To verbs to form adjectives meaning: *unable* or *powerless* (to be acted on or to act as indicated); as in resist*less*, daunt*less*, quench*less*, etc., *unable* to be resisted, daunted, quenched, etc.; cease*less*, *unable* to cease.

-like. A suffix used to form adjectives. It is from the word *like* and as a suffix has the same meaning as *like* the adjective; as in man*like*, *like* a man.

-ly. A suffix used to form adverbs meaning: **a** *In*, *at*, or *during* (an indicated) *time* or *period;* hence, *every* (so often), *by the* . . . , *once a* . . . ; as in late*ly* or recent*ly*, *in*, *at*, or *during* a late or recent *time* or *period ;* year*ly*, week*ly*, etc., *every* year, week, etc., *by the*, or *once a*, year, week, etc. **b** *In*, *at*, *through*, or the like (an indicated) *place*, *part*, or *direction*, etc.; as in low*ly*, easter*ly*, inward*ly*, etc., *in* or *at a place*, *part*, or *direction* that is low, eastern, etc. ; wide*ly*, *through a region* that is wide. **c** *In* (an indicated) *way*, *manner*, *method*, *mode*, or the like ; as in slow*ly*, tru*ly*, possib*ly*, etc., *in a* slow, true, etc., *way*, *manner*, *method*, *mode*, or the like. **d** *In* or *to* (an indicated) *degree*, *number*, *measure*, *extent*, *amount*, *quantity*, or the like; as in great*ly*, entire*ly*, part*ly*, etc., *in* or *to a* great, etc., *degree*, *number*, *measure*, *extent*, *amount*, *quantity*, or the like.

-ness. A suffix used to form nouns meaning: 1. Primarily, *state*, *condition*, or *quality of being ;* as in good*ness*, *state* or *quality of being* good ; sick*ness*, *condition of being* sick ; white*ness*, *quality of being* white. 2. Secondarily, *a* (particular) *thing* or *act that is an instance* of, or that *exhibits* or *embodies* (the state, condition, or quality denoted by the word in its primary sense); as in kind*ness*, *an act that is* kind ; foul*ness*, *a thing that is* foul.

-or. A suffix used to form nouns meaning: *One who*, *one that;* as in elevat*or*, *one that* elevates;

act*or*, *one who* acts; surviv*or*, *one who* survives, etc. It is appended chiefly to words from the Latin, and is equivalent to **-ER**, 3.

Pronunciation. See p. v.

Preferred Forms of Spelling or Pronunciation. When two or more forms of spelling or of pronunciation are recorded, the general rule has been to place first the one that has been selected as preferable. When instead of a definition there is a cross reference (introduced by =, by ***Var. of***, or by *See*) to another spelling, the form referred to is the one preferred.

Capitalization. When a word should begin with a capital letter in writing or print, the vocabulary word itself begins with a capital. Where, in a specific use, a different style from that shown by the vocabulary entry is to be followed, [*cap.*] (meaning a capital initial) or [*l.c.*] (meaning a lower case, or small, initial) is inserted at the definition affected. Thus *Italic*, *a.* in sense 1 should begin with a capital, but in sense 2 a small letter is preferred.

Hyphened Words. Words that are to be written or printed with a hyphen have this hyphen indicated by a mark (–) longer and heavier than the short, light hyphen (-) used to show division into syllables ; as in **ab′sent–mind′ed, light′–heart′edness.**

Principal parts of verbs are given in small capitals after the vocabulary titles, except when the parts are regularly formed by the simple addition of **ed** and **ing**. Regular verbs ending in silent *e* are referred to § 1, above. Regular verbs ending in *y* are referred to § 2, above.

Plurals are given whenever they are irregular in form or when, from analogy, an irregular form might be expected. For the regular formation of plurals see RULES FOR SPELLING, pp. vi–vii.

See PLURAL, after such words as *blackfish*, *deer*, *quail*, *trout*, etc., refers to the Note under the word *plural*, *n.*, in the Vocabulary, for information as to the two plural forms in use and the differences in their meanings.

The comparative and superlative forms of adjectives are given in small capitals after the vocabulary word except where these forms are made by the simple addition of *er* and *est* or by the use of *more* and *most*. See §§ 3, 4, above.

Music, Scot., Archaic, Colloq., or a similar "label," when preceding the first numbered definition of a word, applies to all of the definitions; when preceding a group of definitions distinguished by **a, b, c,** etc., it applies to the entire group (see SUE, SUITE). Otherwise, such a "label" applies only to the definition to which it is joined. ***Both*** or ***All*** may precede a "label" (as, *Both Colloq.*) to

x SPECIAL EXPLANATORY NOTES, SIGNS, AND ABBREVIATIONS

show that it applies to two or more parts of speech, as a noun and a verb, defined under one vocabulary title (see SPLUTTER).

‖ prefixed to a vocabulary word indicates that this word is from a foreign language and that it would ordinarily be printed in italic letters when used in English; as, ‖ **mas′seur′**.

X 2, X 6, ½, ⅙, or the like, inserted at an illus-

tration indicates that a picture is twice, six times, one half, one sixth, etc., as long and as high as the original.

= preceding a word in small capitals indicates that the vocabulary word has the same meaning as the word in small capitals and that the latter is the preferred form, under which the consulter will find the definition.

ABBREVIATIONS USED IN THIS WORK

a. ....Adjective.
ab. ....About.
abbr. .....Abbreviation.
A. D. ....Anno Domini (L., in the year of our Lord).
adv. ....Adverb.
aft. ....After.
Amer. ....American.
Anat. ....Anatomy.
Anc. ....Ancient.
Anthropol. .....Anthropology.
Antiq. ......Antiquities.
Arch. .....Architecture.
Archæol. ...Archæology.
Arith. ....Arithmetic.
Astrol. .....Astrology.
Astron. ......Astronomy.
av. ....Avoirdupois.

B. C. .....Before Christ.
bet. ....Between.
Biol. ....Biology.
Bot. ....Botany.
Brit. ....British.

cap. .....Capital, capitalize; that is, make the initial letter a capital.
Carp. ....Carpentry.
cf. .....Confer (L., compare).
Ch. ...Charles, Church.
Chem. ....Chemistry.
Ch. of Eng. ...Church of England.
Class. ....Classical.
Col. ...Colonel, Colossians.
Colloq. ....Colloquial.
com. ....Commonly.
Com. ....Commerce.
comp. ....Composition.
compar. ...Comparative.
conj. .....Conjunction.
contr., contract. Contraction.
corrupt. ....Corruption.
cu. ....Cubic.

dat. ....Dative.
def. ....Definition.
deriv. ....Derivative.
Dial. ....Dialectic.
dim. ....Diminutive.
disting. ..Distinguished.
dr. ....Dram.
dwt. ..Pennyweight (denarius weight).

E. ....English, East.
Eccl. ....Ecclesiastical.
Elec. ....Electricity.
Eng. .England, English.
Engin. ....Engineering.
equiv. ......Equivalent.
esp. ......Especially.
etc. ....Et cetera (L., and so forth).
Ex. ....Exodus.
exc. ....Except.
excl. ....Excluding.

F. ....French.
fem. ....Feminine.
fig. ....Figuratively.
form. ....Formerly.
Fort. ....Fortification.
fr. ....From.
ft. ....Foot, feet.

G. ....German.
Gen. ....Genesis.
Geog. ......Geography.
Geol. ....Geology.
Geom. ....Geometry.
Gram. ....Grammar.
Gr. ....Greek.

Her. ....Heraldry.
Hist. ...History, historic.

i. e. ..Id est (L., that is).
Illust. .....Illustration.
imp. ....Imperative.
in. ....Inch, inches.
incho. ......Inchoative.
incor. ......Incorrectly.
indic. ....Indicative.
inf. ....Infinitive.
intens. ....Intensive.

interj. .....Interjection.
It. ....Italian.

L. ....Latin.
lb., lbs. ..Pound, pounds.
l. c. ..Lower case; that is, make the initial a small letter, not a capital.
lit. ....Literally.

Mach. ......Machinery.
masc. ....Masculine.
Math. ....Mathematics.
Matt. ....Matthew.
Mech. .....Mechanics.
Med. ....Medicine.
Mil. ....Military.
Min. ....Mineralogy.
Myth. ......Mythology.

n. ....Noun.
N. ....North.
Nat. Hist. ..Natural History.
Naut. ....Nautical.
Nav. ....Naval.
neut. ....Neuter.

obj., object. ..Objective.
Obs. ....Obsolete.
Obsoles. ...Obsolescent.
opp. .Opposed, opposite.
Org. ....Organic.
oz. ....Ounce, ounces.

p. a. ...Participial adjective.
perh. ....Perhaps.
pers. ....Person.
pert. ....Pertaining.
Pharm. .....Pharmacy.
Philol. .....Philology.
Philos. .....Philosophy.
Phon. ....Phonetics.
Photog. ..Photography.
Phys. ....Physical.
Physiol. ....Physiology.
pl. ....Plural.
Poet. ....Poetic.
Port. ....Portuguese.
possess. ....Possessive.

p. p. ...Past participle.
p. pr. .....Present participle.
prep. ......Preposition.
pres. ....Present.
pret. ....Preterit.
prin. ....Principal.
prob. ....Probably.
pron. ....Pronoun.
prop. ....Properly.
Pros. ....Prosody.
Ps. ....Psalm.

R. ....Rare.
R. C. Ch. ...Roman Catholic Church.
Ref. Sp. ....Reformed Spelling.
Relig. ....Religion.
Rev. ....Revelation.
Rhet. ....Rhetoric, rhetorical.

Sam. ....Samuel.
sc. ....Scilicet (L., to wit, namely).
Scot. ....Scottish.
Shak. .....Shakespeare.
sing. ....Singular.
Sp. ....Spanish.
specif. ...Specifically.
subj. .....Subjunctive.
superl. .....Superlative.
Surg. ....Surgery.
Surv. ....Surveying.
syn. ....Synonym.

Teut. ....Teutonic.
Theol. ....Theology.
Tim. ....Timothy.

U. S. ....United States.
usu. ....Usually.

var. ....Variant.
vb. n. ....Verbal noun.
v. i. ..Verb intransitive.
v. t. ....Verb transitive.

yd. ....Yard, yards.

Zoöl. ....Zoölogy.

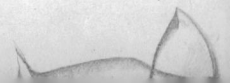

A

DICTIONARY

OF THE

ENGLISH LANGUAGE

A (unstressed, ǎ ; emphatic, ā), adj., or indefinite article. **1.** The shortened form of AN, signifying one or any, and commonly used before words beginning with a consonant sound. See AN. **2.** In each; to or for each; per; as, a dollar a yard.

a (ǎ), prep., **a-, a–** (ǎ-), prefix. On; in; at; as in afloat, asleep, once a year, a hunting.

A 1 (ā wŭn). A registry mark given to ships in first-class condition. Hence, prime; first-class.

a-back' (ǎ-băk'), adv. Back; backward; as, a sail is aback when pressed back by the wind, or a ship is taken aback when so checked; — often used figuratively.

ab'a-cus (ăb'ǎ-kŭs), n.; pl. E. -CUSES (-ĕz), L. ABACI (-sī). **1.** A frame for reckoning by means of sliding balls. **2.** The uppermost division of the capital of a column.

Abacus, 1.

a-baft' (ǎ-bȧft'), prep. Naut. Behind; toward the stern from. — adv. Toward or at the stern; aft.

a-ban'don (ǎ-băn'dŭn), v.t. **1.** To give up wholly; forsake or renounce utterly. **2.** To yield (one's self) without restraint; as, to abandon one's self to vice.

A Abacus, 2.

a-ban'doned (-dŭnd), p. a. [4] **1.** Forsaken; deserted. **2.** Given up to evil; utterly bad; wicked; corrupt; dissolute.

a-ban'don-ment (-dŭn-mĕnt), n. Act of abandoning; abandoned state; absence of self-restraint.

a-base' (ǎ-bās'), v.t. [1] To cast down or reduce, as in rank or estimation; to degrade.

a-base'ment (-mĕnt), n. An abasing; humiliation.

a-bash' (ǎ-băsh'), v.t. To destroy the self-possession of; confuse; put to shame; embarrass.

a-bate' (ǎ-bāt'), v.t. [1] To reduce in amount, number, degree, intensity, etc.; lessen; moderate. — v. i. To be abated; grow less; decrease.

a-bate'ment (-mĕnt), n. An abating; state of being abated; also, amount abated; decrease.

‖ **a-bat'toir'** (ȧ'bȧ'twär'), n. [F.] A slaughterhouse.

ab'bess (ăb'ĕs), n. A female superior or governess of a nunnery.

ab'bey (-ĭ), n.; pl. -BEYS (-ĭz). **1.** A society of persons who live by themselves, as in a monastery, remain unmarried, and devote themselves to religion; also, the building or buildings in which they live; monastery. **2.** The church of a monastery.

ab'bot (-ŭt), n. The head of an abbey of monks.

ab-bre'vi-ate (ǎ-brē'vĭ-āt), v.t. [1] To make briefer; shorten, esp. by contraction or omission, as words.

ab-bre'vi-a'tion (-ā'shŭn), n. Act or result of abbreviating; abbreviated form of a word.

ab'di-cate (ăb'dĭ-kāt), v. t. [1] To surrender sovereign power; renounce; give up, as a trust, right, etc. — v. i. To renounce a throne or high office.

ab'di-ca'tion (-kā'shŭn), n. Act of abdicating.

ab-do'men (ăb-dō'mĕn), n. That part of the body which contains the stomach, bowels, etc.

ab-dom'i-nal (ăb-dŏm'ĭ-năl), a. Of or pertaining to the abdomen.

ab-duct' (-dŭkt'), v. t. **1.** To take away stealthily by force; kidnap. **2.** Physiol. To draw away from a part or axis. — **ab-duc'tor** (-tĕr), n. [8].

ab-duc'tion (-dŭk'shŭn), n. Act of abducting.

a-beam' (ǎ-bēm'), adv. Naut. On a line at right angles with the ship's keel; opposite the middle of the ship's side.

a-bed' (ǎ-bĕd'), adv. In bed or on the bed.

ab'er-ra'tion (ăb'ĕr-ā'shŭn), n. **1.** A wandering; deviation, esp. from what is right, natural, or typical. **2.** Mental disorder.

a-bet' (ǎ-bĕt'), v. t.; -BET'TED; -BET'TING. — To encourage; uphold; aid, as by approval; — now chiefly in a bad sense; as, to abet one in a crime.

a-bet'ment (-mĕnt), n. Act of abetting.

a-bet'ter, a-bet'tor (ǎ-bĕt'ĕr), n. One who abets.

a-bey'ance (ǎ-bā'ăns), n. Temporary inactivity.

ab-hor' (ăb-hôr'), v.t.; AB-HORRED' (-hôrd') ; -HOR'RING. To shrink with shuddering from ; detest.

ab-hor'rence (-hŏr'ĕns), n. Act or state of abhorring.

ab-hor'rent (-ĕnt), a. [4] **1.** Contrary or repugnant; as, crime was abhorrent to him. **2.** Hateful; detestable; as, pride is abhorrent.

a-bide' (ǎ-bīd'), v. i.; pret. & p. p. A-BODE' (-bōd') ; p. pr. & vb. n. A-BID'ING (-bīd'ing). **1.** To continue in a place; dwell. **2.** To remain stable or *f*ixed in some state ; continue. —*v. t.* **1.** To await ; watch for ; as, I will *abide* his coming. **2.** To endure ; submit to ; bear patiently ; tolerate ; as, she could not *abide* him.

a-bil'i-ty (*à*-bĭl'ĭ-tĭ), *n. ; pl.* -TIES (-tĭz). Quality or state of being able ; power to perform ; capacity ; skill ; in *pl.*, faculty, talent.

ab'ject (ăb'jĕkt), *a.* [4] Sunk to a low condition ; cast down in spirit or hope. — **ab'ject-ly**, *adv.* [8] — **ab'ject-ness**, *n.* [8].

ab'ju-ra'tion (ăb'jŏŏ-rā'shŭn), *n.* Act of abjuring, or forswearing.

ab-jure' (ăb-jŏŏr'), *v. t. & i.* [1] **1.** To renounce upon oath ; forswear ; disavow ; as, to *abjure* allegiance to a king. **2.** To renounce solemnly ; recant ; repudiate ; as, to *abjure* errors.

a-blaze' (*à*-blāz'), *adv. & a.* On fire ; gleaming ; brilliant ; ardent.

a'ble (ā'b'l), *a.* [3] **1.** Having sufficient power, force, skill, etc. ; competent ; as, an *able* workman. **2.** Having strong mental powers ; talented ; clever.

ab-lu'tion (ăb-lū'shŭn), *n.* A washing or cleansing ; washing of the person, as a religious rite.

a'bly (ā'blĭ), *adv.* In an able manner ; with ability.

ab'ne-ga'tion (ăb'nĕ-gā'shŭn), *n.* A denial ; a renunciation ; self-denial.

ab-nor'mal (ăb-nôr'măl), *a.* [4] Not according to rule ; unnatural ; irregular. — **-mal-ly**, *adv.* [8].

ab'nor-mal'i-ty (ăb'nôr-măl'ĭ-tĭ), *n.* **1.** Abnormal state or quality. **2.** Something abnormal.

a-board' (*à*-bōrd'), *adv.* On board ; into or within a boat or railroad car. — *prep.* On board of.

a-bode' (*à*-bōd'), *pret. & p. p.* of ABIDE.

a-bode', *n.* **1.** Stay or continuance in a place ; sojourn. **2.** Abiding place ; dwelling ; residence.

a-bol'ish (*à*-bŏl'ĭsh), *v. t.* To do away with wholly ; put an end to.

ab'o-li'tion (ăb'ō-lĭ'sh'ŭn), *n.* Act of abolishing ; state of being abolished.

ab'o-li'tion-ist, *n.* One who favors abolition, esp., *Hist.*, of negro slavery.

a-bom'i-na-ble (*à*-bŏm'ĭ-n*à*-b'l), *a.* [4] Worthy of or causing abomination ; detestable ; loathsome. — **a-bom'i-na-bly**, *adv.* [8].

a-bom'i-nate (-nāt), *v. t.* [1] To regard with extreme disgust or aversion ; abhor ; loathe.

a-bom'i-na'tion (-nā'shŭn), *n.* **1.** Feeling of extreme disgust and hatred ; abhorrence ; loathing ; detestation. **2.** Anything hateful or vile ; pollution. **3.** A cause of wickedness.

ab'o-rig'i-nal (ăb'ō-rĭj'ĭ-năl), *a.* **1.** First ; original ; indigenous. **2.** Of or pert. to aborigines. — *n.* One of the aborigines.

ab'o-rig'i-nes (-nēz), *n. pl. ; sing.* AB'O-RIG'I-NE (-nē). The earliest known inhabitants of a country ; native races.

a-bor'tion (*à*-bôr'shŭn), *n.* **1.** A premature birth ; miscarriage. **2.** Something (as a fruit) that fails to mature ; hence, any failure to attain completion of perfection in what has been begun.

a-bor'tive (-tĭv), *a.* [4] Born prematurely ; unsuccessful ; fruitless. — **-ly**, *adv.* [8] — **-ness**, *n.* [8].

a-bound' (*à*-bound'), *v. i.* **1.** To be in great plenty or very prevalent. **2.** To be copiously supplied ; — followed by *in* or *with*.

a-bout' (*à*-bout'), *adv.* **1.** On all sides ; here and there ; around ; as, to look *about ;* wandering *about.* **2.** In circuit ; around the outside ; as, at the waist he is one yard *about.* **3.** Nearly ; approximately ; as, *about* 400. **4.** To a reversed position ; half around ; as, to face *about.* **5.** In rotation ; as, turn *about* is fair play. — *prep.* **1.** Around ; on every side of. **2.** In the immediate neighborhood of ; near ; by or on (one's person). **3.** Over or upon different parts of ; here and there in ; throughout ; as, wandering *about* the world. **4.** Near ; not far from ; as, *about* this time yesterday. **5.** Engaged in ; intent on ; as, to be *about* one's business. **6.** On the point or verge of ; as, he was *about* to leap. **7.** Concerning ; touching ; as, to talk *about* politics. **8.** Appertaining to ; in connection with ; as, there is something pleasing *about* him.

a-bove' (*à*-bŭv'), *adv.* **1.** In a place above something ; overhead. **2.** Earlier in order. **3.** Higher in rank or power. — *prep.* In or to a higher place than ; higher than ; surpassing ; beyond ; more than. — *a.* Being above ; that is, situated, placed, said, written, mentioned, or the like, above.

a-bove'board' (-bōrd'), *adv. & a.* [4] Above the board or table ; hence, in open sight ; without trick or concealment.

ab-rade' (ăb-rād'), *v. t.* [1] To rub off ; wear away by friction ; as, to *abrade* rocks.

ab-ra'sion (ăb-rā'zhŭn), *n.* Act of abrading ; also, an abraded place.

a-breast' (*à*-brĕst'), *adv.* **1.** Side by side. **2.** Up to a certain level or line ; equally advanced.

a-bridge' (*à*-brĭj'), *v. t.* [1] To shorten ; lessen ; diminish ; condense ; as, to *abridge* a dictionary.

a-bridg'ment (-mĕnt), *n.* **1.** Act of abridging ; state of being abridged. **2.** Something produced by abridging ; diminution ; reduction ; compend.

a-broad' (*à*-brôd'), *adv.* **1.** At large ; widely ; broadly ; as, "the fox roams far *abroad.*" **2.** Out-doors ; outside a country ; in foreign countries.

ab'ro-gate (ăb'rō-gāt), *v. t.* [1] To annul by an authoritative act.

ab'ro-ga'tion (-gā'shŭn), *n.* Act of abrogating.

ab-rupt' (ăb-rŭpt'), *a.* [4] **1.** Rising or descending sharply from a given surface or level. **2.** Sudden ; hasty. **3.** Having sudden transitions ; unconnected ; broken. — **-ly**, *adv* [8] — **-ness**, *n.* [8].

ab'scess (ăb'sĕs), *n.* collection of pus in the body, usually due to injury or infection.

ab-scond' (ăb-skŏnd'), *v. i.* To depart stealthily ; steal off and secrete one's self. — **-er**, *n.* [8].

ab'sence (ăb'sĕns), *n.* **1.** State or time of being absent. **2.** Want ; lack. **3.** Inattention.

ab'sent (-sĕnt), *a.* [4] **1.** Being away ; not present ; lacking. **2.** Inattentive ; absent-minded.

ab-sent' (ăb-sĕnt'), *v. t.* To withdraw (one's self) to such a distance as to prevent intercourse.

ab'sen-tee' (ăb'sĕn-tē'), *n.* One absent, as from his country, office, post, or the district where he owns an estate. — **ab'sen-tee'ism** (-ĭz'm), *n.*

ab'sent-ly, *adv.* In an absent or inattentive way.

ab'sent-mind'ed (ăb'sĕnt-mīn'dĕd), *a.* [4] Being in a state of mind in which one fails to pay attention to what is going on about one.

ab'so-lute (-sō-lūt), *a.* **1.** Perfect ; complete ; as, *absolute* purity. **2.** Free from limit, restriction, or qualification ; as, *absolute* monarch. — **-ly**, *adv.* [8].

āle, senāte, câre, ăm, ăccount, ärm, ȧsk, sofȧ ; ēve, ĕvent, ĕnd, recĕnt, makēr ; īce, ĭll ; ōld, ōbey, ôrb, ŏdd, sŏft, cŏnnect ; ūse, ūnite, ûrn, ŭp, circŭs ; fōōd, fŏŏt ; out, oil ;

ab'so-lu'tion (ăb'sŏ-lū'shŭn), *n.* Act of absolving.

ab'so-lut'ism (-lūt'ĭz'm), *n.* State or quality of being absolute, or without limitation or condition.

ab-solve' (ăb-sŏlv'), *v. t.* [1] **1.** To set free, or release, as from obligation or the consequences of guilt. **2.** To free from a penalty; pardon.

ab-sorb' (ăb-sôrb'), *v. t.* To swallow up; engulf; suck up; drink or take in; engross; occupy fully.

ab-sorb'ent (-sôr'bĕnt), *a.* [4] Absorbing; having power to absorb, or suck up; as, *absorbent* earth. — *n.* Anything that absorbs.

ab-sorp'tion (-sôrp'shŭn), *n.* Act of absorbing; fact or state of being absorbed.

ab-stain' (-stān'), *v. i.* To do without or give up voluntarily; refrain; — with *from.* — *er*, *n.* [8].

ab-ste'mi-ous (-stē'mĭ-ŭs), *a.* [4] Sparing in diet; temperate; abstinent. — *ly*, *adv.* — *ness*, *n.* [8].

ab'sti-nence (ăb'stĭ-nĕns), *n.* Act or practice of abstaining, esp. from indulgence of appetite.

ab'sti-nent (-nĕnt), *a.* [4] Refraining from indulgence, esp. of appetite; abstemious. — *ly*, *adv.* [8.]

ab'stract (ăb'străkt), *a.* [4] **1.** Considered apart from any object; as, *abstract* numbers. Hence: Hard to understand; difficult; as, an *abstract* subject. **2.** Expressing a quality apart from any particular subject. — *n.* That which comprises in itself the essential qualities of a larger thing or of several things; summary; epitome, as of a book.

ab-stract' (ăb-străkt'), *v. t.* **1.** To withdraw; separate; take away; as, to *abstract* one's attention. **2.** To take secretly or dishonestly; purloin; as, to *abstract* a watch from a person's pocket.

ab-stract'ed, *p. a.* [4] Absent in mind; as, an *abstracted* scholar. — **ab-stract'ed-ly**, *adv.* [8].

ab-strac'tion (-străk'shŭn), *n.* **1.** Act of abstracting; state of being abstracted; as, the sensation of cold is due to an *abstraction* of heat from our bodies. **2.** That which is abstracted; hence, an abstract idea; loosely, a theory. **3.** Absence of mind.

ab'stract-ly (ăb'străkt-lĭ), *adv.* In an abstract state or manner; separately; by itself.

ab-struse' (ăb-strōōs'), *a.* [4] Hard to understand; obscure; difficult. — *ly*, *adv.* [8] — *ness*, *n.* [8].

ab-surd' (ăb-sûrd'), *a.* [4] Contrary to reason or propriety; obviously and flatly opposed to truth; nonsensical; ridiculous. — *ly*, *adv.* — *ness*, *n.* [8].

ab-surd'i-ty (ăb-sûr'dĭ-tĭ), *n.; pl.* -TIES (-tĭz). **1.** Quality or state of being absurd. **2.** That which is absurd.

a-bun'dance (ȧ-bŭn'dȧns), *n.* An overflowing fullness; great plenty; profusion.

a-bun'dant (-dȧnt), *a.* [4] Overflowing; more than sufficient; plentiful; ample. — *ly*, *adv.* [8].

a-buse' (ȧ-būz'), *v. t.* [1] **1.** To put to a wrong or bad use; misuse. **2.** To use ill; maltreat; as, to *abuse* prisoners. **3.** To revile; reproach coarsely.

a-buse' (-būs'), *n.* **1.** Improper treatment or use; misuse. **2.** Physical ill treatment; injury. **3.** Evil practice or custom; offense; fault. **4.** Coarse, insulting speech.

a-bu'sive (-bū'sĭv), *a.* [4] **1.** Practicing or given to abuse, as by insulting words. **2.** Containing, or serving for, abuse; insulting; scurrilous. — **a-bu'sive-ly**, *adv.* [8] — **a-bu'sive-ness**, *n.* [8].

a-but' (-bŭt'), *v. i.; -*BUT'TED; -BUT'TING. To end or border; touch on; — with *on, upon,* or *against.*

a-but'ment (-mĕnt), *n.* **1.** Act or state of abutting. **2.** That on which a body abuts; part of a buttress, wall, pier, etc., that receives lateral pressure; in a bridge, the support at either end of the entire bridge.

a-bys'mal (ȧ-bĭz'mȧl), *a.* [4] Pertaining to or resembling an abyss; bottomless; fathomless.

a-byss' (-bĭs'), *n.* A bottomless gulf, or hollow place in the earth; any space of vast depth.

a-ca'cia (ȧ-kā'shȧ), *n.* Any of a genus (*Acacia*) of trees and shrubs of warm regions.

ac'a-dem'ic (ăk'ȧ-dĕm'ĭk) | *a.* [4] Belonging or
ac'a-dem'i-cal (-Ĭ-kȧl) | pertaining to an academy or higher institution of learning; scholarly; literary or classical, rather than technical or scientific. — **ac'a-dem'i-cal-ly**, *adv.* [8].

a-cad'e-mi'cian (ȧ-kăd'ē-mĭsh'ȧn), *n.* A member of an academy. See ACADEMY, *n.*, 2.

a-cad'e-my (-kăd'ē-mĭ), *n.; pl.* -MIES (-mĭz). **1.** A school ranking between a common school and a college. **2.** A society of learned men.

a-can'thus (-kăn'thŭs), *n.* Any of a genus (*Acanthus*) of prickly herblike plants.

ac-cede' (ăk-sēd'), *v. i.* [1] **1.** To enter on an office or dignity; attain. **2.** To agree; assent.

ac-cel'er-ate (ăk-sĕl'ĕr-āt), *v. t. & i.* [1] **1.** To move faster; quicken; — opposed to *retard.* **2.** To quicken the natural progression or process of. **3.** To hasten, as the occurrence of an event.

ac-cel'er-a'tion (-ā'shŭn), *n.* Act of accelerating; state of being accelerated; — opp. to *retardation.*

ac-cel'er-a-tive (-sĕl'ĕr-ȧ-tĭv), *a.* [4] Relating to, or tending to cause, acceleration.

ac-cel'er-a'tor (-ā'tēr), *n.* One who or a thing that accelerates or increases speed.

ac'cent (ăk'sĕnt), *n.* **1.** Emphasis or stress given to certain syllables of words or phrases. **2.** A mark used to regulate pronunciation; esp. : a mark to indicate the place of the spoken accent. **3.** Modulation of the voice in speaking; manner of pronouncing; tone. **4.** A word; *pl.*, language; speech.

ac-cent' (ăk-sĕnt'), *v. t.* **1.** To utter or mark with accent. **2.** To emphasize.

ac-cen'tu-al (-sĕn'tū-ȧl), *a.* Of or pert. to accent.

ac-cen'tu-ate (-āt), *v. t.* [1] To pronounce or mark with an accent or with accents; emphasize.

ac-cen'tu-a'tion (-ā'shŭn), *n.* An accentuating.

ac-cept' (-sĕpt'), *v. t.* **1.** To receive or take willingly (a thing offered). **2.** To receive with favor; approve. **3.** To assent or agree to.

ac-cept'a-bil'i-ty (-sĕp'tȧ-bĭl'ĭ-tĭ), **ac-cept'a-ble-ness**, *n.* The quality of being acceptable.

ac-cept'a-ble (-sĕp'tȧ-b'l), *a.* [4] Capable, worthy, or sure of being accepted; agreeable; welcome.

ac-cept'a-bly, *adv.* In an acceptable manner.

ac-cept'ance (-tȧns), *n.* **1.** Act of accepting; esp., favorable reception; approval; acceptableness. **2.** An accepted bill of exchange.

ac'cep-ta'tion (ăk'sĕp-tā'shŭn), *n.* The accepted meaning of a word, or that which it generally has.

ac-cept'er (ăk-sĕp'tēr), *n.* One who accepts.

ac-cep'tor (-sĕp'tēr - tôr), *n.* One who accepts; in commerce, one who accepts a bill of exchange.

ac'cess (ăk'sĕs; ăk-sĕs'), *n.* **1.** Act of coming to or near; admission; accessibility; as, to gain *access.* **2.** Means, place, or way of approach.

---

chair; go; sing, iŋk; then, thin; nature, verdure; yet; zh = z in azure. Numbers refer to §§ in the Special Notes which, with Abbreviations, Signs, etc., precede the Vocabulary.

ac-ces'sa-ry (ăk-sĕs'á-rĭ), *a. & n.* Accessory.

ac-ces'si-bil'i-ty (-ĭ-bĭl'ĭ-tĭ), *n.* Condition or quality of being accessible or approachable.

ac-ces'si-ble (-ĭ-b'l), *a.* [4] Easy of access.

ac-ces'sion (-sĕsh'ŭn), *n.* **1.** Increase by something added ; that which is added. **2.** Act of coming to a throne, office, or dignity.

ac-ces'so-ry (-sĕs'ŏ-rĭ), *a.* Accompanying as a subordinate ; aiding or contributing in a secondary way; esp., of persons, uniting in, or contributing to, a crime, but not as the chief actor.— *n.; pl.* **-ries** (-rĭz). **1.** Something additional and subordinate; adjunct. **2.** *Law.* One who, not being present, contributes to the commission of an offense, or one who aids or shelters the offender to defeat justice.

ac'ci-dence (ăk'sĭ-dĕns), *n.* The inflections of words ; the rudiments of grammar.

ac'ci-dent (-dĕnt), *n.* **1.** An unforeseen or unexpected event, usually unfortunate; chance ; mishap. **2.** A nonessential.

ac'ci-den'tal (-dĕn'tăl), *a.* **1.** Happening by chance or accident, or unexpectedly. **2.** Not essential; incidental. — **-tal-ly,** *adv.* [8].

ac-claim' (ă-klām'), *v. t.* **1.** To applaud. **2.** To declare or proclaim by acclamations. **3.** To shout.

ac'cla-ma'tion (ăk'lá-mā'shŭn), *n.* **1.** Act of acclaiming ; loud applause. **2.** Act or method of voting orally.

ac-cli'mate (ă-klī'mát), *v. t. & i.* [1] To accustom, or to become accustomed, or hardened, to a new climate ; acclimatize.

ac'cli-ma'tion (ăk'lĭ-mā'shŭn), *n.* Process of acclimating ; state of being acclimated.

ac-cli'ma-ti-za'tion (ă-klī'má-tĭ-zā'shŭn), *n.* Acclimation.

ac-cli'ma-tize (-tīz), *v. t. & i.* [1] To acclimate.

ac-cliv'i-ty (ă-klĭv'ĭ-tĭ), *n.; pl.* **-ties** (-tĭz). A slope of the earth, as a hill, considered as ascending ; ascent ; — opposed to *declivity.*

ac'co-lade' (ăk'ŏ-lād'; -läd'), *n.* A salutation used in conferring knighthood, now usually, a tap on the shoulders with the blade of a sword.

ac-com'mo-date (ă-kŏm'ŏ-dāt), *v. t.* [1] **1.** To render fit or correspondent ; adapt ; conform ; as, to *accommodate* ourselves to circumstances. **2.** To furnish with something desired or needed; oblige.

ac-com'mo-dat'ing, *p. a.* [4] Affording, or disposed to afford, accommodation ; obliging.

ac-com'mo-da'tion (-dā'shŭn), *n.* **1.** Act of accommodating ; state of being accommodated ; adaptation ; adjustment. **2.** Willingness to accommodate. **3.** Whatever supplies a want ; often, in *pl.*, lodgings and food. **4.** Adjustment of differences.

ac-com'pa-ni-ment (ă-kŭm'pá-nĭ-mĕnt), *n.* That which accompanies as a circumstance, or by way of ornament, or to give symmetry ; *Music,* a subsidiary part, vocal or instrumental, accompanying another to enrich or support it.

ac-com'pa-nist (-nĭst), *n. Music.* The performer who takes the accompanying part.

ac-com'pa-ny (-nĭ), *v. t.* [2] **1.** To attend as a companion ; go along or consort with. **2.** *Music.* To play or sing an accompaniment to or for.

ac-com'plice (ă-kŏm'plĭs), *n.* Associate in guilt.

ac-com'plish (-plĭsh), *v. t.* **1.** To get (something) done ; bring about. **2.** Formerly, to equip thoroughly ; hence, to render accomplished.

ac-com'plished (-plĭsht), *p. a.* [4] **1.** Completed; effected ; as, an *accomplished* fact. **2.** Complete in acquirements, esp. as the result of training.

ac-com'plish-ment (-plĭsh-mĕnt), *n.* **1.** Accomplishing; completion; fulfillment. **2.** That which completes, or equips thoroughly; that which constitutes an excellence of mind or an elegance of manners, acquired by education or training.

ac-cord' (-kôrd'), *v. t.* To grant as suitable or proper; concede; award; as, to *accord* due praise to any one. — *v. i.* To agree ; correspond ; harmonize. — *n.* **1.** Agreement; harmony ; consent ; assent. **2.** Harmony of sounds; concord. **3.** Voluntary or spontaneous motion or impulse.

ac-cord'ance (-kôr'dăns), *n.* Agreement; harmony. — **ac-cord'ant** (ă-kôr'dănt), *a.*

ac-cord'ing, *p. a.* Agreeing ; harmonious. — **according as,** precisely as ; the same as.

ac-cord'ing-ly, *adv.* **1.** Agreeably ; suitably ; conformably. **2.** Consequently; so.

ac-cor'di-on (-kôr'dĭ-ŭn), *n.* A small, keyed wind instrument in which the wind is forced upon the metallic reeds by means of a bellows.

ac-cost' (-kŏst'), *v. t.* To speak to first; address.

ac-count' (-kount'), *v. t.* To value ; estimate ; judge ; deem. — *v. i.* **1.** To render, or state the terms of, an account, as of money expended. **2.** To answer in judgment or explanation ; — with *for;* as, we must *account* for our opportunities. **3.** To give a satisfactory reason ; explain ; — with *for.* — *n.* **1.** A reckoning ; computation. **2.** A statement of business dealings subjected to a reckoning or review ; hence, a claim the items of which make up such a statement. Abbr. *acct., a/c.* **3.** A statement of reasons ; explanation. Hence : Reason, ground, motive, or the like; as, on no *account.* **4.** A statement of facts; narrative ; report. **5.** Importance ; worth ; value.

ac-count'a-bil'i-ty (-koun'tá-bĭl'ĭ-tĭ), *n.* The state or condition of being accountable.

ac-count'a-ble (-koun'tá-b'l), *a.* [4] **1.** Liable to be called to account ; answerable. **2.** Capable of being accounted for ; explicable. — **-ness,** *n.* [8].

ac-count'ant (ă-koun'tănt), *n.* One who is skilled in, or who keeps or adjusts, accounts.

ac-cou'ter (-kōō'tẽr), *v. t.* [6] To furnish with dress or equipments, esp. military ; equip.

ac-cou'ter-ment (-mĕnt), *n.* [6] **1.** *pl.* Dress ; equipment. **2.** Act or process of accoutering ; state of being accoutered.

ac-cred'it (-krĕd'ĭt), *v. t.* **1.** To bring into credit or esteem ; establish the authority of. **2.** To send with credentials ; authorize.

ac-cre'tion (-krē'shŭn), *n.* **1.** Growth ; also, increase by addition from the outside ; as, the *accretion* of particles so as to form a mass. **2.** Result of such growth ; the matter added.

ac-crue' (-krōō'), *v. i.* [1] **1.** To increase. **2.** To come or be added as increase, esp. as the produce of money lent.

ac-cu'mu-late (-kū'mŭ-lāt), *v. t.* [1] To heap up; pile up ; amass; collect ; aggregate. — *v. i.* To increase ; collect.

addressing one's self or one's words. **2.** A formal communication, application, or statement; speech; petition. **3.** Direction or superscription of a letter, or the name, title, and place of residence or business of the one addressed. **4.** Manner of speaking to another; delivery; as, a man of good *address.* **5.** Suit; courtship; — usually in *pl.* **6.** Skillful management; dexterity; adroitness; as, he has both *address* and courage.

ad-dress′ee′ (ă-drĕs′ē′), *n.* One to whom anything, as a letter, is addressed.

ad-duce′ (ă-dūs′), *v. t.* [1] To offer, as a reason; cite. — **ad-duc′i-ble** (-dūs′ĭ-b'l), *a.* [8].

ad′e-noid (ăd′ē-noid), *a.* Like or pertaining to a gland. — *n.* An enlargement of the adenoid tissue in the cavity back of the mouth; — usually in *pl.*

a-dept′ (ă-dĕpt′), *n.* One fully skilled or well versed; a proficient. — *a.* [4] Proficient. — **a-dept′ness,** *n.* [8].

ad′e-qua-cy (ăd′ē-kwå-sĭ), *n.* Sufficiency.

ad′e-quate (-kwăt), *a.* Equal to or sufficient for some (specific) requirement; fully sufficient; as, an *adequate* definition. **—ly,** *adv.* [8]— **-ness,** *n.* [8].

ad-here′ (ăd-hēr′), *v. i.* [1] **1.** To stick fast as if glued; become joined or united. **2.** To hold; be attached or devoted (*to*); as, men *adhere* to a party.

ad-her′ence (-hēr′ĕns), *n.* Quality, act, or state of adhering; steady attachment or support; devotion.

ad-her′ent (-ĕnt), *a.* [4] Sticking; clinging; adhering. — *n.* One who adheres; follower; partisan.

ad-he′sion (-hē′zhŭn), *n.* Act or state of adhering; a sticking together of substances in contact.

ad-he′sive (-sĭv), *a.* [4] **1.** Sticky; tenacious; of the nature of adhesion. **2.** Apt or tending to adhere; clinging. — **ad-he′sive-ness,** *n.* [8].

a-dieu′ (ă-dū′), *interj. & adv.* Good-by; farewell; — a parting expression of kind wishes. — *n. ; pl.* E. ADIEUS (-dūz′), F. ADIEUX (á-dyŭ′). A farewell; commendation to the care of God at parting.

ad′i-pose (ăd′ĭ-pōs), *a.* Of or pertaining to fat; fatty. — *n.* Fat.

ad-ja′cence (ă-jā′sĕns)
ad-ja′cen-cy (-sĕn-sĭ) } *n.* **1.** Quality or state of being adjacent; contiguity. **2.** That which is adjacent.

ad-ja′cent (-sĕnt), *a.* Lying near; close; contiguous; neighboring.

ad′jec-ti′val (ăj′ĕk-tī′văl; ăj′ĕk-tĭv-ăl), *a.* Of or relating to, or of the nature of, an adjective.

ad′jec-tive (ăj′ĕk-tĭv), *n. Gram.* A word used with a noun, or substantive, to express a quality of the thing named, or something attributed to it, or to limit, define, specify, or describe it. — *a.* Added to a substantive as an attribute; of the nature of an adjunct. — **ad′jec-tive-ly,** *adv.* [8].

ad-join′ (ă-join′), *v. t.* To join or unite to; lie next to, so as to touch; also, to attach; append. — *v. i.* To lie or be next, or contiguous.

ad-join′ing, *p. a.* Joining to; adjacent.

ad-journ′ (ă-jûrn′), *v. t.* To put off or defer to another day, or indefinitely; to close or suspend for the day, as a legislative meeting. — *v. i.* To suspend business for a time, esp. public business, as of legislatures, courts, etc.

ad-journ′ment (-mĕnt), *n.* Act of adjourning; state of being adjourned; also, the interval for which a body adjourns.

ad-judge′ (-jŭj′), *v. t.* [1] **1.** To decide judicially; order; decree. **2.** To sentence; condemn. **3.** To award judicially in a case of controversy.

ad-ju′di-cate (-jōō′dĭ-kāt), *v. t. & i.* [1] To hear or try, as in a court, and decide according to the law; adjudge; as, to *adjudicate* a claim.

ad-ju′di-ca′tion (-kā′shŭn), *n.* Act or process of adjudicating.

ad-ju′di-ca′tor (-kā′tẽr), *n.* One who adjudicates.

ad′junct (ăj′ŭnkt), *a.* Connected or added (to); subordinate. — *n.* Something joined or added to a thing, but subordinate to it; auxiliary.

ad′ju-ra′tion (-ōō-rā′shŭn), *n.* Act of adjuring.

ad-jure′ (ă-jōōr′), *v. t.* [1] To charge, bind, or command, solemnly, as if under oath; entreat earnestly.

ad-just′ (-jŭst′), *v. t.* **1.** To settle or arrange; free from differences or discrepancies. **2.** To make exact; fit; make correspondent or conformable. **3.** To put in order; regulate. — **ad-just′a-ble,** *a.* [8]— **ad-just′er,** *n.* [8].

ad-just′ment, *n.* Act of adjusting, or state of being adjusted.

ad′ju-tan-cy (ăj′ōō-tăn-sĭ), *n.* Office of an adjutant.

ad′ju-tant (-tănt), *n.* **1.** A helper. **2.** A staff officer who assists a commander in the details of duty.

ad-min′is-ter (ăd-mĭn′ĭs-tẽr), *v. t.* **1.** To manage or conduct, as public affairs; direct the execution, application, or conduct of. **2.** To dispense; serve out; supply. **3.** To give or apply, as medicine or a remedy. **4.** To tender or impose, as an oath. **5.** *Law.* To settle, as the estate of one who dies intestate. — *v. i.* To contribute; conduce.

ad-min′is-tra′tion (-trā′shŭn), *n.* Act of administering (in any sense); *Law & Politics,* the action of the state in the exercise of its political powers; usually, the action of the executive alone; also, collectively, those having executive powers; the term of office of an administrative officer or body.

ad-min′is-tra-tive (-mĭn′ĭs-trā-tĭv), *a.* Of or pertaining to administration; executive.

ad-min′is-tra′tor (-trā′tẽr), *n.* One who administers; *Law,* one legally vested with the right of administration of an estate. See ADMINISTER, 5.

ad-min′is-tra′trix (-trā′trĭks), *n. fem. ; L. pl.* -TRATRICES (-trā-trī′sēz). A female administrator.

ad′mi-ra-ble (ăd′mĭ-rá-b'l), *a.* [4] Having qualities that excite admiration. — **-ra-bly,** *adv.* [8].

ad′mi-ral (-răl), *n.* Commander in chief of a navy. **2.** Naval officer of the highest rank. See NAVY.

ad′mi-ral-ty (-răl-tĭ), *n. ; pl.* -TIES (-tĭz). **1.** Office or jurisdiction of an admiral. **2.** The department or officers having authority over naval affairs. **3.** The court or the law dealing with maritime questions and offenses.

ad′mi-ra′tion (-rā′shŭn), *n.* **1.** Wondering or marveling approbation or delight. **2.** Something that excites wonder; a prodigy.

ad-mire′ (ăd-mīr′), *v. t.* [1] To regard with wonder and delight. — **ad-mir′er** (-mīr′ẽr), *n.* [8].

ad-mis′si-bil′i-ty (-mĭs′ĭ-bĭl′ĭ-tĭ), *n.* The quality of being admissible.

ad-mis′si-ble (-mĭs′ĭ-b'l), *a.* Entitled or worthy to be admitted; allowable.

ad-mis′sion (-mĭsh′ŭn), *n.* **1.** Act or practice of admitting; admittance; access. **2.** The granting of an argument not fully proved. **3.** A fact or statement admitted. **4.** Price of entrance.

ad-mit′ (ăd-mĭt′), *v. t.; -mit′ted; -mit′ting.* **1.** To allow to enter; receive. **2.** To give a right of entrance to. **3.** To concede as true; grant. **4.** To be capable of; allow; permit.

ad-mit′tance (-ăns), *n.* **1.** Act of admitting. **2.** Permission to enter; admission; entrance.

ad-mix′ture (-mĭks′tụ̇r), *n.* A mixing; mixture.

ad-mon′ish (-mŏn′ĭsh), *v. t.* **1.** To warn of a fault; give warning advice to. **2.** To instruct; direct.

ad′mo-ni′tion (ăd′mọ̇-nĭsh′ŭn), *n.* An admonishing; expression of advice or warning.

ad-mon′i-to-ry (ăd-mŏn′ĭ-tọ̇-rĭ), *a.* Conveying admonition; as, "a raised *admonitory* finger."

a-do′ (ȧ-dōō′), *n.* Doing; trouble; fuss; bustle.

a-do′be (ȧ-dō′bĕ), *n.* An unburnt brick dried in the sun; a house or structure of such bricks. *Sp. Amer.*

ad′o-les′cence (ăd′ọ̇-lĕs′ĕns), *n.* Process or period of growing from childhood to maturity; youth.

ad′o-les′cent (-ĕnt), *a.* Growing to maturity; in a state of adolescence. — *n.* A youth.

a-dopt′ (ȧ-dŏpt′), *v. t.* **1.** To take by choice into a relationship, esp. that of a child or an heir. **2.** To take or receive as one's own (what is not so naturally). — **a-dopt′ed**, *p. a.* — **a-dopt′er**, *n.* [8].

a-dop′tion (-dŏp′shŭn), *n.* Act of adopting.

a-dor′a-ble (ȧ-dōr′ȧ-b'l), *a.* [4] Worthy to be adored. — **ness**, *n.* [8] — **bly**, *adv.* [8].

ad′o-ra′tion (ăd′ọ̇-rā′shŭn), *n.* Act of adoring.

a-dore′ (ȧ-dōr′), *v. t.* [1] **1.** To worship with profound reverence. **2.** To love in the highest degree. — **a-dor′er**, *n.* [8] — **a-dor′ing**, *p. a.*

a-dorn′ (ȧ-dôrn′), *v. t.* To deck with ornaments.

a-dorn′ment (-mĕnt), *n.* An adorning; decoration.

a-drift′ (ȧ-drĭft′), *adv. & a.* Floating at random.

a-droit′ (ȧ-droit′), *a.* [4] Dexterous in the use of the hands or in the exercise of the mental faculties; ready in invention. — **ly**, *adv.* [8] — **ness**, *n.* [8].

ad′u-la′tion (ăd′ụ̇-lā′shŭn), *n.* Servile flattery.

ad′u-la-to-ry (ăd′ụ̇-lȧ-tọ̇-rĭ), *a.* Servilely flattering.

a-dult′ (ȧ-dŭlt′), *a.* Having attained full size and strength; matured. — *n.* An adult person, animal, or plant.

a-dul′ter-ant (ȧ-dŭl′tẽr-ănt), *n.* That which adulterates.

a-dul′ter-ate (-āt), *v. t.* [1] **1.** To corrupt, debase, or make impure by admixture of a foreign or a baser substance. — **a-dul′ter-a′tor** (-ā′tẽr), *n.* [8].

a-dul′ter-a′tion (-ā′shŭn), *n.* Act of adulterating; state of being adulterated; an adulterated product.

a-dul′ter-er (ȧ-dŭl′tẽr-ẽr), *n.* One, esp. a man, who commits adultery. — **ess** (-ĕs), *n. fem.* [8].

a-dul′ter-ous (-ŭs), *a.* [4] Guilty of, given to, or pertaining to, adultery. — **ly**, *adv.* [8].

a-dul′ter-y (-ĭ̆), *n.; pl.* -teries (-ĭz). Unfaithfulness of a married person to the marriage bed.

ad-um′brate (ăd-ŭm′brāt), *v. t.* [1] **1.** To give a shadowy or slight representation of; shadow forth. **2.** To overshadow; shade.

ad′um-bra′tion (ăd′ŭm-brā′shŭn), *n.* An adumbrating; also, a faint sketch; imperfect representation.

ad va-lo′rem (ăd vȧ-lō′rĕm). [L.] Literally, according to the value; — used of a duty or charge on goods at a certain rate per cent on their value.

ad-vance′ (ăd-vȧns′), *v. t.* [1] **1.** To move forward.

---

2. To raise to a higher rank; elevate; promote; as, he was *advanced* to captain. **3.** To accelerate or help in growth or progress; further; aid; as, to *advance* one's interests. **4.** To bring to view or notice; offer; address; as, to *advance* an argument. **5.** To make or place earlier, as an event or date; hasten. **6.** To furnish, as money, before it is due, or in aid of an enterprise. **7.** To raise to a higher point; raise in rate; as, to *advance* prices. — *v. i.* **1.** To move forward; proceed. **2.** To increase or make progress in any respect. **3.** To rise as in rank or office; be promoted. — *n.* **1.** An advancing; progress. **2.** Improvement or progression. **3.** A rise in price or value. **4.** Approach made to gain favor, adjust a dispute, etc.; overture; tender; — usually in *pl.* **5.** A furnishing of something before an equivalent is received; money or value supplied beforehand.

ad-vance′ment (-mĕnt), *n.* Act of advancing; state of being advanced; progression; promotion; also, that which is advanced.

ad-van′tage (-văn′tăj), *n.* **1.** Any condition, circumstance, opportunity, or means, particularly favorable to some desired end; benefit. **2.** Superiority; mastery; — with *of* or *over.* **3.** Superiority of state, or that which gives it; gain; profit. — *v. t.* [1] To give an advantage to; benefit.

ad′van-ta′geous (ăd′văn-tā′jŭs), *a.* [4] Being of advantage; gainful; beneficial. — **ad′van-ta′geous-ly**, *adv.* [8] — **ness**, *n.* [8].

Ad′vent (ăd′vĕnt), *n.* **1.** The period including the four Sundays before Christmas. **2.** The first, or the expected second, coming of Christ. **3.** [*l. c.*] Coming; arrival; approach.

ad′ven-ti′tious (-vĕn-tĭsh′ŭs), *a.* Added from without and not essentially inherent; additional; accidental; foreign. — **ad′ven-ti′tious-ly**, *adv.* [8].

ad-ven′ture (ăd-vĕn′tụ̇r), *n.* **1.** Chance of danger or loss. **2.** The encountering of risks; a bold undertaking. **3.** A remarkable occurrence or experience; a stirring incident. **4.** A mercantile or speculative venture. — *v. t.* [1] **1.** To risk; hazard; venture. **2.** To venture upon; dare. — *v. i.* To try the chance; take the risk.

ad-ven′tur-er (-ẽr), *n.* One who adventures; esp. : **a** One who engages in new and hazardous enterprises. **b** A soldier of fortune. **c** One who seeks an unmerited position by trickery. — **ess**, *n. fem.*

ad-ven′tur-ous (-ŭs), *a.* [4] Characterized by, or of the nature of, adventure: **a** Inclined to adventure; rashly daring; — applied to persons. **b** Full of hazard; rash; — applied to acts. — **ly**, *adv.* [8] — **ness**, *n.* [8].

ad′verb (ăd′vûrb), *n.* A part of speech used to qualify esp. verbs, adjectives, and other adverbs.

ad-ver′bi-al (ăd-vûr′bĭ-ăl), *a.* Of, pertaining to, or of the nature of, an adverb. — **al-ly**, *adv.* [8].

ad′ver-sa-ry (ăd′vẽr-sȧ-rĭ), *n.; pl.* -ries (-rĭz). One turned against another or others to oppose or resist them; antagonist.

ad′verse (ăd′vẽrs), *a.* [4] **1.** Acting against, or in a contrary direction; opposed; as, *adverse* winds. **2.** In hostile opposition; unfavorable; unfortunate; as, *adverse* circumstances. — **ly**, *adv.* [8].

ad-ver′si-ty (ăd-vûr′sĭ-tĭ), *n.; pl.* -ties (-tĭz). A state or circumstance of adverse fortune.

āle, senăte, câre, ăm, ȧccount, ärm, ȧsk, sofȧ; ēve, ĕvent, ĕnd, recĕnt, makẽr; īce, ĭll; ōld, ȯbey, ôrb, ŏdd, sŏft, cŏnnect; ūse, ŭnite, ûrn, ŭp, circŭs; fōōd, fŏŏt; out, oil;

ad-vert′ (ăd-vûrt′), *v. i.* To turn the mind or attention; refer; allude; — with *to*.

ad′ver-tise′ (ăd′vẽr-tīz′; ăd′vẽr-tīz′),*v. t.* [1] **1.** To give notice to ; inform ; hence, to warn. **2.** To announce publicly, esp. by a printed notice. — *v. i.* To give notice, esp. in printed announcements. — **ad′ver-tis′er** (-ẽr), *n.* [8].

ad-ver′tise-ment (ăd-vûr′tĭz-mĕnt; ăd′vẽr-tīz′mĕnt), *n.* A public notice, esp. in public print.

ad′ver-tize, -ment Vars. of ADVERTISE, -MENT.

ad-vice′ (ăd-vīs′), *n.* **1.** An opinion recommended or offered to be followed ; counsel. **2.** Information or notice given ; — commonly in *pl.*

ad-vis′a-bil′i-ty (ăd-vīz′á-bĭl′ĭ-tĭ), *n.* The quality of being advisable ; expediency ; propriety.

ad-vis′a-ble (-vīz′á-b'l), *a.* [4] Proper to be advised or to be done ; expedient.

ad-vis′a-ble-ness, *n.* Advisability.

ad-vise′ (-vīz′), *v. t.* [1] **1.** To give advice to ; counsel ; warn. **2.** To inform ; notify ; apprise ; as, we were *advised* of the risk. — *v. i.* To take counsel ; consult. — **ad-vis′er** (-vīz′ẽr), *n.* [8].

ad-vis′ed-ly (-ĕd-lĭ), *adv.* Deliberately ; after consideration.

ad-vise′ment (-vīz′mĕnt), *n.* Consideration ; deliberation.

ad-vi′so-ry (-vī′zō-rĭ), *a.* Having power to advise ; pertaining to or containing advice.

ad′vo-ca-cy (ăd′vō-ká-sĭ), *n.* An advocating or pleading for ; intercession.

ad′vo-cate (-kāt), *n.* One who pleads the cause of another, as a lawyer or counselor in court ; pleader ; intercessor. — (-kāt), *v. t.* [1] To plead in favor of ; support publicly.

adz, adze (ădz), *n.* A cutting tool having a blade set at right angles to the handle.

æ′on, e′on (ē′ŏn),*n.* An immeasurable or indefinite period of time ; an age.

a′ẽr-ate (ā′ẽr-āt), *v. t.* [1] To supply or combine or charge with a gas, as carbon dioxide or air.

a′ẽr-a′tion (-ā′shŭn), *n.* Act or process of aërating, or state of being aërated.

a-ē′ri-al (a-ē′rĭ-ǎl), *a.* [4] **1.** Of or pertaining to the air ; inhabiting, produced by, or done in, the air. **2.** Consisting of air, of the nature of air. Hence: Unsubstantial ; unreal. **3.** Reaching high into the air ; lofty. — **a-ē′ri-al-ly,** *adv.* [8].

ae′rie (ē′rĭ; ā′ẽr-ĭ), *n.* The nest of certain birds of prey, as the eagle ; also, a brood of such birds ; eyrie.

a′ẽr-i-form (ā′ẽr-ĭ-fôrm), *a.* [4] Of the nature of air ; gaseous ; hence, unreal.

a′ẽr-o-drome′ (-ō-drōm′), *n.* A ground or field used for flying purposes.

a′ẽr-o-gram (-grăm), *n.* A message sent by wireless telegraphy.

a′ẽr-o-lite (-līt), *n.* A meteorite ; a meteoric stone.

a′ẽr-o-naut (-nôt), *n.* A balloonist or aviator.

a′ẽr-o-nau′tic (-nō′tĭk), **a′ẽr-o-nau′ti-cal** (-tĭ-kǎl), *a.* Pertaining to aëronautics.

a′ẽr-o-nau′tics (-nō′tĭks),*n.* The science or art of navigating or floating in the air.

a′ẽr-o-plane′ (ā′ẽr-ō-plān′), *n.* An airplane. *Brit.*

a′ẽr-o-plan′ist (-plān′ĭst), *n.* One who operates or flies in an airplane.

a′ẽr-o-stat′ic (-stăt′ĭk), **a′ẽr-o-stat′i-cal** (-ĭ-kǎl), *a.* Of or pertaining to aërostatics.

a′ẽr-o-stat′ics (-stăt′ĭks), *n.* The science that treats of the equilibrium of elastic fluids, or of that of bodies sustained in them.

a′ẽr-y (ā′ẽr-ĭ), *a.* Aërial ; ethereal.

æs′thete (ĕs′thēt), *n.* One who makes much or overmuch of the sense of the beautiful.

æs-thet′ic (ĕs-thĕt′ĭk), *a.* [4] Of or pertaining to æsthetics ; appreciative of the beautiful, or in accord with its principles.

æs-thet′i-cal (-ĭ-kǎl), *a.* [4] Æsthetic. — **æs-thet′i-cal-ly,** *adv.* [8].

æs-thet′ics (-ĭks), *n.* Theory or philosophy of taste ; science of the beautiful.

æ′ther, æ-the′re-al. Vars. of ETHER, ETHEREAL.

a-far′ (á-fär′), *adv.* At, to, or from a distance.

af′fa-bil′i-ty (ăf′á-bĭl′ĭ-tĭ), *n.* Affable quality or stat ; ease and graciousness in conversation.

af′fa-ble (ăf′á-b'l), *a.* [4] **1.** Easy to be spoken to ; courteous ; sociable. **2.** Gracious ; mild. — **af′fa-ble-ness,** *n.* [8] — **af′fa-bly,** *adv.* [8].

af-fair′ (ă-fâr′), *n.* **1.** That which is, or is being, or is to be, done ; concern ; business. **2.** A material object (vaguely designated).

af-fect′ (ă-fĕkt′), *v. t.* **1.** To fancy ; be fond of. **2.** To make a display of liking, adopting, or following after. **3.** To feign ; counterfeit. **4.** To act on ; produce an effect on ; touch.

af′fec-ta′tion (ăf′ĕk-tā′shŭn), *n.* An attempt to assume or exhibit what is not natural or real ; false display ; artificial show.

af-fect′ed (ă-fĕk′tĕd), *p. p. & p. a.* [4] **1.** Assumed ; not natural. **2.** Given to false show. **3.** Inclined ; disposed. **4.** Afflicted or tainted, as by disease. **5.** Impressed ; moved. — **af-fect′ed-ly,** *adv.* [8].

af-fect′ing, *p. a.* [4] Moving the emotions.

af-fec′tion (-fĕk′shŭn), *n.* **1.** Act of affecting. **2.** A settled good will ; kind feeling ; love. **3.** A bodily state ; esp., disease.

af-fec′tion-ate (-āt), *a.* [4] Having, proceeding from, or indicating, warm regard ; loving ; fond ; tender ; attached. — **af-fec′tion-ate-ly,** *adv.* [8].

af-fi′ance (ă-fī′ăns), *v. t.* [1] To pledge in or for marriage ; betroth.

af′fi-da′vit (ăf′ĭ-dā′vĭt), *n.* A sworn statement in writing, esp. one made before an authorized officer.

af-fil′i-ate (ă-fĭl′ĭ-āt), *v. t.* [1] To attach (*to*) or unite (*with*) ; receive into a society as a member. — *v. i.* To associate one's self ; — followed by *with*.

af-fil′i-a′tion (-ā′shŭn), *n.* Act of affiliating ; state or relation of being affiliated.

af-fin′i-ty (ă-fĭn′ĭ-tĭ), *n. ; pl.* -TIES (-tĭz). **1.** Relationship by marriage ; hence, kinship generally ; relation ; connection. **2.** A spiritual relationship or attraction held to exist between some persons ; also, one who exerts such attraction.

af-firm′ (-fûrm′), *v. t. & i.* **1.** To confirm, or ratify. **2.** To assert positively ; aver.

af′fir-ma′tion (ăf′ẽr-mā′shŭn), *n.* **1.** Confirmation ; ratification. **2.** Assertion.

af-firm′a-tive (ă-fûr′má-tĭv), *a.* That affirms ; answering "yes" to a question. — *n.* **1.** That which affirms ; that side of a question which affirms the proposition stated. **2.** A word or phrase expressing assent. — **-tive-ly,** *adv.* [8].

af-fix′ (ă-fĭks′), *v. t.* **1.** To fix or fasten (*to, on,* or *upon*). **2.** To attach or join (*to*).

---

chair ; go ; sing, iŋk ; then, thin ; nature, verdure ; yet ; zh = z in azure. Numbers refer to §§ in the Special Notes which, with Abbreviations, Signs, etc., precede the Vocabulary.

af-flict' (ă-flĭkt'), v. t. To inflict some great injury or hurt on, causing continued pain or distress.

af-flic'tion (-flĭk'shŭn), n. State of being afflicted; cause of pain, distress, or grief; a pain; a grief.

af'flu-ence (ăf'lōō-ĕns), n. An abundant supply, as of thought or words; profusion; also, abundance of property; wealth; plenty; opulence.

af'flu-ent (-ĕnt), a. [4] 1. Flowing to; flowing abundantly. 2. Abundant; copious; hence, wealthy. — n. A tributary stream.

af-ford' (ă-fōrd'), v. t. 1. To give forth; yield, furnish, or the like, as the natural result, fruit, or issue; as, the sea affords fish. 2. To incur, stand, or bear, or manage without serious harm (as to financial condition, health, reputation, etc.)

af-fray' (ă-frā'), n. A riotous quarrel; brawl.

af-fright' (ă-frīt'), v. t. To frighten or terrify.—n. 1. An affrighting. 2. Sudden fear; terror.

af-front' (ă-frŭnt'), v. t. To offend by disrespect; treat with marked rudeness; also, to cause to feel affront.—n. Rude treatment; a deliberately offensive act or word; an offense to one's dignity.

af'ghan (ăf'găn), n. A kind of worsted blanket or wrap.

a-field' (ă-fēld'), adv. 1. To, in, or on, the field. 2. Out of the way; astray.

a-fire' (ă-fīr'), adv. & a. On fire.

a-float' (ă-flōt'), adv. & a. 1. Floating; on board ship. 2. Moving; in circulation; as, a rumor is afloat. 3. Adrift. 4. Flooded.

a-foot' (ă-fŏŏt'), adv. On foot; in motion; astir.

a-fore'said (ă-fōr'sĕd'), a. Said or named before.

a-fore'time (-tīm'), adv. Formerly.

a-foul' (ă-foul'), adv. & a. In collision; fouled.

a-fraid' (ă-frād'), p. a. [4] In a state of fear or apprehension; alarmed; frightened.

a-fresh' (ă-frĕsh'), adv. Anew; again; newly.

aft (ăft), adv. & a. Naut. Near, toward, or in, the stern of a vessel; astern; abaft.

aft'er (ăf'tĕr), adv. & conj. Subsequently in time or place; behind; later than. — prep. 1. Behind in place. 2. Following the course of; in search or pursuit of; hence, with a view to; concerning; in respect of. 3. Later in time; subsequent to. 4. Subsequent to and in view of. 5. Below in rank. 6. In imitation of. 7. According to.— a. 1. Next; later in time; subsequent. 2. Hinder; nearer the rear.

aft'er-clap' (ăf'tĕr-klăp'), n. An unexpected subsequent event.

aft'er-damp' (-dămp'), n. A choking gas remaining after an explosion of fire-damp in a mine.

aft'er-glow' (-glō'), n. A glow or refulgence remaining where a light has disappeared, as in the sky after sunset.

aft'er-math (-măth), n. A second mowing; second crop of grass.

aft'er-most (-mōst), a. superl. Hindmost; last.

aft'er-noon' (-nōōn'), n. The part of the day between noon and evening.

aft'er-thought' (-thôt'), n. Reflection after an act.

aft'er-wards (-wĕrdz) } adv. At a later time; subsequently.

aft'er-ward (-wĕrd) }

a-gain' (ă-gĕn'), adv. 1. In return; back. 2. Another time; anew. 3. Once repeated; as, as large again. 4. On the other hand. 5. Moreover; besides; further.

a-gainst' (ă-gĕnst'), prep. 1. From an opposite direction and so as to strike or touch; in contact with. 2. In opposition to; counter to; adverse to.

a-gape' (ă-gāp'; -gāp'), adv. & a. Gaping, as with wonder, expectation, or eager attention.

ag'ate (ăg'āt), n. A kind of stone with colors in stripes, clouds, etc.

a-ga've (ă-gā'vē), n. Any of a genus (Agave) of plants including the century plant.

age (āj), n. 1. That part of the duration of a being or a thing between its beginning and any given time. 2. The whole duration of a being; lifetime. 3. The time of life at which some particular qualification, power, or capacity arises; as, to be of school age. 4. One of the stages of life; mature age; old age. 5. A particular period of time, esp. with reference to civilization or the earth's history; as, the stone age. 6. The people who live at a particular period; hence, a generation. 7. A long time (indefinitely). Colloq.— v. i. & t.; AGED (ăjd); AG'ING, AGE'ING (āj'ĭng). To grow or make old; mature.

aged (āj'ĕd; ājd; in compounds, ājd), a. 1. That has grown (more or less) old; esp., advanced in years; old. 2. Pert. to old age; as, "aged cramps."

a'gen-cy (ā'jĕn-sĭ), n.; pl. -CIES (-sĭz). 1. Faculty or state of acting; action; instrumentality. 2. Office or business of an agent. 3. Place of business or district of an agent.

a'gent (ā'jĕnt), a. 1. One that exerts power, or has power to act; one that acts; as, the bee is an agent of fertilization. 2. One who acts for, or in the place of, another by authority from him; deputy.

ag-glom'er-ate (ă-glŏm'ĕr-āt), v. t. & i. [1] To gather into a mass; cluster; mass.

ag-glom'er-ate (-ăt), n. 1. A collection or mass. 2. Geol. A mass of volcanic fragments united haphazard.

ag-glom'er-a'tion (-ā'shŭn), n. 1. Act of agglomerating. 2. A mass of agglomerated things; cluster.

ag-glu'ti-nate (-glōō'tĭ-nāt), v. t. [1] To unite, or cause to adhere, as with glue; unite by adhesion.

ag-glu'ti-na'tion (-nā'shŭn), n. 1. Act of agglutinating. 2. Anything formed by agglutination.

ag'gran-dize (ăg'răn-dīz), v. t. [1] To make great or greater; to exalt.

ag-gran'dize-ment (ă-grăn'dĭz-mĕnt), n. Act or result of aggrandizing; exaltation.

ag'gra-vate (ăg'rā-vāt), v. t. [1] 1. To make worse, or more severe; intensify. 2. To exasperate; provoke; irritate. Colloq.

ag'gra-va'tion (-vā'shŭn), n. 1. Act of aggravating; state of being aggravated. 2. An additional circumstance that increases the guilt of a crime or the hardship of a misfortune. 3. Provocation; irritation. Colloq.

ag'gre-gate (ăg'rē-gāt), v. t. [1] 1. To bring together; collect; accumulate. 2. To amount to. Colloq. — (-găt), a. Formed by aggregation; collective. — n. A mass, assemblage, or sum.

ag'gre-ga'tion (-gā'shŭn), n. Act of aggregating.

ag-gres'sion (ă-grĕsh'ŭn), n. A first or unprovoked attack, or act of hostility or encroachment.

ag-gres'sive (ă-grĕs'ĭv), a. [4] Tending or disposed to aggression; characterized by aggression. — ag-gres'sive-ly, adv. [8] — -ness, n. [8].

āle, senåte, câre, ăm, ăccount, ärm, ăsk, sofá; ēve, ĕvent, ĕnd, recĕnt, makĕr; īce, ĭll; ōld, ŏbey, ôrb, ŏdd, sŏft, cŏnnect; ūse, ûnite, ûrn, ŭp, circŭs; fōōd, fŏŏt; out, oil;

ag-gres'sor (ă-grĕs'ẽr), *n.* One making an aggression; an assailant.

ag-grieve' (-grēv'), *v. t.* [1] To grieve; afflict; hence, to oppress or injure.

a-ghast' (á-gȧst'), *a. & p. p.* Terrified.

ag'ile (ăj'ĭl), *a.* Apt or ready to move; lively. — **ag'ile-ly**, *adv.* [8].

a-gil'i-ty (á-jĭl'ĭ-tĭ), *n.* Quality of being agile.

ag'i-tate (ăj'ĭ-tāt), *v. t.* [1] **1.** To move with a violent, irregular action. **2.** To stir up; disturb; perturb. **3.** To discuss earnestly; debate. **4.** To revolve in the mind; devise; plot. — *v. i.* To make an agitation; stir up discussion.

ag'i-ta'tion (-tā'shŭn), *n.* Act of agitating.

ag'i-ta'tor (ăj'ĭ-tā'tẽr), *n.* One that agitates.

a-glow' (á-glō'), *adv. & a.* Glowing.

ag-nos'tic (ăg-nŏs'tĭk), *n.* One who professes agnosticism. — *a.* Professing ignorance; pertaining to or involving agnosticism.

ag-nos'ti-cism (-tĭ-sĭz'm), *n.* **1.** The doctrine that neither the nature nor the existence of God can be known. **2.** Any doctrine which affirms that all knowledge is relative and uncertain.

a-go' (á-gō'), *a. & adv.* Past; gone by.

a-gog' (-gŏg'), *a. & adv.* In eager desire; eager.

ag'o-nize (ăg'ō-nīz), *v. t.* [1] To cause to suffer agony; torture. — *v. i.* **1.** To suffer anguish. **2.** To struggle or strive desperately.

ag'o-ny (ăg'ō-nĭ), *n.; pl.* -NIES (-nĭz). **1.** Extreme pain of mind or body; anguish. **2.** Death struggle.

a-gra'ri-an (á-grā'rĭ-ăn), *a.* Of or pertaining to fields or lands, or their tenure.

a-gree' (-grē'), *v. i.; A-GREED' (á-grēd'); A-GREE'-ING.* **1.** To yield assent; consent; accede. **2.** To harmonize in opinion, statement, or action; concur. **3.** To come to terms or to a common resolve (with another or one another); to promise. **4.** To be conformable; resemble; coincide; correspond. **5.** To suit or be adapted in its effects; do well. **6.** *Gram.* To be alike in gender, number, case, or person.

a-gree'a-ble (-á-b'l), *a.* [4] **1.** Pleasing, either to the mind or senses; pleasant; grateful. **2.** Willing; ready to agree or consent. *Colloq.* **3.** Agreeing or suitable; conformable. — **a-gree'a-ble-ness**, *n.* [8] — **a-gree'a-bly** (-blĭ), *adv.* [8].

a-gree'ment (-mĕnt), *n.* State or act of agreeing.

ag'ri-cul'tur-al (ăg'rĭ-kŭl'tŭr-ăl), *a.* Of or pertaining to or engaged in agriculture.

ag'ri-cul'ture (ăg'rĭ-kŭl'tŭr), *n.* Art or science of cultivating the ground; husbandry; farming.

ag'ri-cul'tur-ist (-kŭl'tŭr-ĭst), *n.* One engaged in, or skilled in, agriculture; a husbandman.

a-ground' (á-ground'), *adv. & a.* On the ground; stranded; as, the ship is *aground*.

a'gue (ā'gū), *n.* **1.** A malarial fever. **2.** A chill, or state of shaking, as with cold.

ah (ä), *interj.* An exclamation, expressive of pity, contempt, triumph, etc.

a-ha' (á-hä'), *interj.* An exclamation expressing triumph mixed with derision, or simple surprise.

a-head' (á-hĕd'), *adv.* In or to the front; onward.

a-hoy' (-hoi'), *interj. Naut.* A term used in hailing; as, "Ship *ahoy!*"

aid (ād), *v. t.* To help. — *n.* **1.** Help. **2.** One that helps; assistant; a military or naval officer acting as confidential assistant to a superior.

aid'–de–camp' ⎱ (ād'dĕ-kămp'; ād'dĕ-kän'), *n.;*
aide'–de–camp' ⎰ *pl.* AIDS-DE-CAMP, *or* AIDES- (ādz'-). An officer attached to the person of a general or a sovereign to assist him.

ai-grette' (ā-grĕt'; ā'grĕt), **ai'gret** (ā'grĕt), *n.* A plume or tuft for the head, to ornament hats, etc., composed of feathers, gems, or the like. See EGRET.

ail (āl), *v. t.* To affect with pain or uneasiness; trouble; as, what *ails* you? — *v. i.* To be affected with pain or uneasiness.

ai'le-ron (ā'lĕ-rŏn; *F.* ĕl'rôN'), *n. Aëronautics.* A small accessory plane or surface capable of being manipulated so as to preserve lateral balance.

ail'ment (āl'mĕnt), *n.* Indisposition; disease.

aim (ām), *v. i.* **1.** To point or direct a weapon toward an object with the intent of hitting it. **2.** To direct the intention or purpose; try; endeavor. — *v. t.* To direct or point (as a weapon, a blow, a remark, a proceeding) at, or so as to hit or affect, a particular object. — *n.* **1.** Act of aiming something. **2.** Intention; design.

aim'less, *a.* [4] Without aim or purpose. — **aim'-less-ly**, *adv.* [8] — **aim'less-ness**, *n.* [8].

air (âr), *n.* **1.** The invisible, odorless, and tasteless mixture of gases, chiefly nitrogen and oxygen, surrounding the earth; the atmosphere. **2.** Air in motion; gentle wind. **3.** *Music.* A melody; tune. **4.** Outward appearance; manner; style. **5.** Bearing; demeanor or manner. **6.** An artificial or affected manner. — *v. t.* **1.** To expose to the air; ventilate. **2.** To expose for notice; display.

air'craft' (âr'krȧft'), *n.; pl.* AIRCRAFT. A craft for navigating the air, as a balloon, airplane, or airship.

air'i-ly (âr'ĭ-lĭ), *adv.* In an airy manner; lightly.

air'i-ness, *n.* Quality of being airy; lightness.

air'ing (âr'ĭng), *n.* **1.** An exposure to air, as for drying. **2.** A walk or a ride in the open air.

air'man (-măn), *n.; pl.* -MEN. A man who ascends in a balloon, or flies in an airship or airplane.

air'plane' (-plān'), *n.* A form of aircraft, heavier than air, driven by a screw propeller; an aëroplane.

air'port' (âr'pōrt'), *n.* A field prepared for aircraft to land and receive or discharge passengers, etc.

air'ship' (âr'shĭp'), *n.* Any large machine for navigating the air; now, often a dirigible balloon.

air'–tight', *a.* So tight as to admit no air.

air'way' (âr'wā'), *n.* A designated route along which aircraft may ply.

air'y (-ĭ), *a.* [3] **1.** Pert. to air. **2.** Open to a free current of air. **3.** Airlike; unsubstantial. **4.** Light of heart; gay. **5.** Light; delicate.

aisle (īl), *n.* **1.** A passage into which the pews of a church or seats of an assembly room open. **2.** An aislelike space or passage, esp. in a forest.

a-jar' (á-jär'), *adv.* Slightly turned or open.

a-jar', *adv.* In discord; out of harmony.

a-kim'bo (á-kĭm'bō), *a. & adv.* With a crook or bend; with hand on hip and elbow turned out.

a-kin' (á-kĭn'), *a.* **1.** Of the same kin. **2.** Allied by nature; of the same kind.

al'a-bas'ter (ăl'á-bás'tẽr), *n.* A gypsum of fine texture and usually white and translucent; also, a variety of calcite.

‖ **à la carte'** (à lä kärt'). [F.] According to the carte, or bill of fare, esp. according to a bill of fare with the price given for each dish.

---

chair; go; sing, iŋk; then, thin; nature, verdure; yet; zh = z in azure. Numbers refer to §§ in the Special Notes which, with Abbreviations, Signs, etc., precede the Vocabulary.

a-lac′ri-ty (ȧ-lăk′rĭ-tĭ), n. A cheerful willingness or promptitude; briskness.

a-larm′ (ȧ-lärm′), n. **1.** A summons to arms. **2.** Any sound or signal notifying of danger. **3.** A mechanical contrivance for rousing persons. **4.** Sudden surprise with fear; fright. — v. t. **1.** To call to arms for defense; notify of danger; rouse to vigilance. **2.** To excite with sudden fear.

a-larm′ist, n. One prone to sound or excite alarms, esp. needlessly.

a-las′ (ȧ-lås′), interj. An exclamation expressive of sorrow, pity, or apprehension of evil.

Alb.

alb (ălb), n. Eccl. A kind of white linen vestment.

al′ba-tross (ăl′bȧ-trŏs), n. Any of several large web-footed birds.

al-bi′no (ăl-bī′nō), n.; pl. -nos (-nōz). **1.** A person born with deficiency of pigment in the skin, hair, and eyes. **2.** An animal or plant similarly deficient in pigment.

al′bum (ăl′bŭm), n. **1** A register for visitors' names. **2.** A blank book in which to insert autographs, sketches, photographs, etc.

Wandering Albatross. (₁⁄₇)

al-bu′men (ăl-bū′mĕn), n. The white of an egg.

al-bu′min (-mĭn), n. Any of a class of proteids forming the most important constituent of blood serum and found also in milk, muscle, etc.

al-bu′mi-nous (-mĭ-nŭs), a. Pertaining to, containing, or of the nature of, albumen or albumin.

al′che-mist (ăl′kĕ-mĭst), n. One given to the study or practice of alchemy.

al′che-my (-mĭ), n. The medieval chemical science, the great objects of which were to transmute baser metals into gold and to find a panacea and a means of indefinitely prolonging life.

al′co-hol (ăl′kȯ-hŏl), n. △ colorless, volatile, inflammable liquid, which is the intoxicating principle in fermented and distilled liquors.

al′co-hol′ic (-hŏl′ĭk), a. [4] Of or pertaining to alcohol; containing alcohol.

al′co-hol-ism (ăl′kȯ-hŏl-ĭz′m), n. A diseased condition due to excessive use of alcoholic liquors.

al′cove (ăl′kōv), n. A recessed portion of a room, as for a bed, or a small room opening into a larger one.

al′der (ôl′dĕr), n. Any of a certain genus of trees or

Alder, showing Leaves and Fruiting Aments; Staminate Ament.

shrubs, the wood of which is used by turners and the bark by dyers and tanners.

al′der-man (-măn), n.; pl. -men (-mĕn). **1.** In England and Ireland: **a** Formerly, a city or borough magistrate ranking next to the mayor. **b** A member of the smaller of the two classes composing the town or county council. **2.** A member of a city governing body, usually of the upper one of two legislative chambers. U. S.

ale (āl), n. A fermented liquor made from an infusion of malt, usually with the addition of hops.

a-lee′ (ȧ-lē′), adv. Naut. On or toward the lee.

ale′house′ (āl′hous′), n. House where ale is sold.

a-lert′ (ȧ-lûrt′), a. [3] **1.** Watchful; vigilant. **2.** Brisk; nimble. — n. Mil. An alarm; warning signal. — **-ly**, adv. [8] — **-ness**, n. [8].

ale′wife′ (āl′wīf′), n.; pl. -wives (-wīvz′). A certain fish of the herring family.

al-fal′fa (ăl-făl′fȧ), n. A forage plant with clover-like leaves, and bluish purple flowers in loose heads.

al′ga (ăl′gȧ), n.; pl. -gæ (-jē). A seaweed.

al′ge-bra (-jĕ-brȧ), n. That branch of mathematics which investigates the relations and properties of quantity by means of letters and other symbols.

al′ge-bra′ic (-brā′ĭk), **al′ge-bra′i-cal** (-ĭ-kăl), a. Of or pertaining to algebra. — **-cal-ly**, adv. [8].

a′li-as (ā′lĭ-ăs), adv. Otherwise; otherwise called — n. Another name; assumed name.

al′i-bi (ăl′ĭ-bī), n. The plea, or the fact, of having been, at the time of the commission of an act, elsewhere than at the place of commission.

al′ien (āl′yĕn), a. [4] **1.** Of another country; foreign; as, an alien race. **2.** Wholly different in nature; incongruous. — n. A person of another family, race, or nation; a foreigner.

al′ien-a-ble (-ȧ-b'l), a. That may be alienated.

al′ien-ate (-āt), v. t. [1] **1.** To transfer, as property. **2.** To withdraw, as the affections; estrange.

al′ien-a′tion (-ā′shŭn), n. **1.** Act of alienating. **2.** Mental derangement; insanity.

a-light′ (ȧ-līt′), v. i. To spring down; get down; descend; dismount.

a-light′, a. & adv. Lighted; aflame.

a-lign′ (-līn′), v. t. & i. To adjust or form to a line; range in line.

a-lign′ment (ȧ-līn′mĕnt), n. Act of aligning; formation in a straight line.

a-like′ (ȧ-līk′), a. [4] Having resemblance; similar. — adv. In the same manner, form, or degree; in common; equally.

al′i-ment (ăl′ĭ-mĕnt), n. Food; nutriment. Hence, sustenance; means of support.

al′i-men′tal (-mĕn′tăl), a. Supplying food; nourishing.

al′i-men′ta-ry (-mĕn′tȧ-rĭ), a. Of or pertaining to aliment or nutrition; nutritious.

al′i-mo-ny (ăl′ĭ-mȯ-nĭ), n. Law. An allowance made to a woman out of the property of him who is or was her husband, on legal separation or divorce, or during a suit for it.

a-line′, v. t. & i. [1] Var. of ALIGN. — **-ment**, n.

al′i-quot (ăl′ĭ-kwŏt), a. Designating a part of a number that will divide the number without a remainder; as, 5 is an aliquot part of 15.

a-live′ (ȧ-līv′), a. [4] **1.** Living. **2.** Being in a state of action, force, or operation. **3.** Full of, or swarming with, beings or things in motion. **4.** Sprightly; lively. **5.** Susceptible ; sensitive.

al′ka-li (ăl′kȧ-lĭ ; -lī), *n. ; pl.* -LIES or -LIS (-līz ; -lĭz). *Chem.* Any of various substances, as soda, potash, and ammonia, esp. soda, having a peculiar taste, and forming salts with acids.

al′ka-line (-lĭn), *a.* [4] Of, pertaining to, or having the properties of, an alkali or alkalies.

al′ka-loid (-loid), *n. Chem.* An organic substance, esp. one occurring naturally in plants or animals, and having alkaline properties.

all (ôl), *a.* **1.** The whole quantity, extent, duration, amount, quality, or degree of; the whole; any whatever; every. **2.** Only; alone; nothing but; as, it was *all* profit and no loss. — *adv.* Wholly; entirely ; quite ; very. — *n.* The whole; totality ; hence, everything or every person.

al-lay′ (ă-lā′), *v. t.* **1.** To make quiet or put at rest ; pacify; quell ; calm, as a tumult. **2.** To alleviate ; abate ; mitigate, as pain.

al′le-ga′tion (ăl′ē-gā′shŭn), *n.* Act of alleging ; that which is alleged; positive assertion.

al-lege′ (ă-lĕj′), *v. t.* [1] **1.** To bring forward with positiveness ; declare ; assert. **2.** To produce or urge as a reason, plea, or excuse.

al-le′giance (-lē′jăns), *n.* **1.** The relation of a feudal vassal to his superior, or liege lord ; duty of fidelity to one's king, government, or sovereign state. **2.** Devotion or loyalty where obedience or service and respect are due.

al′le-gor′ic (ăl′ē-gŏr′ĭk), *a.* Allegorical.

al′le-gor′i-cal (-gŏr′ĭ-kăl), *a.* Belonging to, or consisting of, allegory ; figurative. — -ly, *adv.* [8].

al′le-go-ry (-gŏ-rĭ), *n. ; pl.* -RIES (-rĭz). Representation by a figurative story of something metaphorically suggested, but not expressly stated ; also, an instance of such representation.

∥**al′le-gret′to** (ăl′lā-grĕt′tō), *a. & adv.* [It.] *Music.* Quicker than *andante*, but not so quick as *allegro.*

∥**al-le′gro** (äl-lā′grō), *a. & adv.* [It.] *Music.* Brisk ; lively.   [HALLELUJAH.

al′le-lu′ia, -lu′iah (ăl′ē-lōō′yȧ), *n. & interj.* =

al-le′vi-ate (ă-lē′vĭ-āt), *v. t.* [1] To lighten or lessen ; make easier to bear, as sorrow, pain, etc. — **al-le′vi-a′tion** (ă-lē′vĭ-ā′shŭn), *n.*

al-le′vi-a-tive (-ā-tĭv), *a.* Tending to alleviate.

al′ley (ăl′ĭ), *n. ; pl.* -LEYS (-ĭz). A choice marble.

al′ley, *n.* A narrow passage ; esp. : **1.** A bordered walk as in a park. **2.** A narrow way in a city.

al-li′ance (ă-lī′ăns), *n.* State of being allied ; act of allying or uniting ; union of interests, esp. between families by marriage, or states by treaty.

al-lied′ (-līd′), *p. p. & p. a.* from ALLY, *v.*

al-lies′ (-līz′), *n. pl.* of ALLY.

al′li-ga′tor (ăl′ĭ-gā′tẽr), *n.* Any of several reptiles in which the snout is shorter and broader than in the crocodiles. They are mainly American.

al-lit′er-a′tion (ă-lĭt′ẽr-ā′shŭn), *n.* Repetition of the same letter or sound at the beginning of words succeeding each other immediately, or at short intervals, as in one form of verse.

al-lit′er-a-tive (ă-lĭt′ẽr-ȧ-tĭv), *a.* Pertaining to, or characterized by, alliteration.

al′lo-path (ăl′ō-păth), **al-lop′a-thist** (ă-lŏp′ȧ-thĭst), *n.* One who practices allopathy.

al′lo-path′ic (ăl′ō-păth′ĭk), *a.* Pert. to allopathy.

al-lop′a-thy (ă-lŏp′ȧ-thĭ), *n.* System of medical practice combating disease by remedies producing effects different from those of the disease treated. Cf. HOMEOPATHY.

al-lot′ (ă-lŏt′), *v. t. ;* -LOT′TED ; -LOT′TING. **1.** To distribute by lot. **2.** To distribute in portions; assign or set apart as a share, lot, or part.

al-lot′ment (-mĕnt), *n.* Act of allotting or that which is allotted; apportionment.

al-low′ (ă-lou′), *v. t.* **1.** To grant ; give; to let one have. **2.** To own or acknowledge, as a claim ; accept as true ; concede. **3.** To grant as a deduction or an addition; esp., to abate or deduct. **4.** To grant license to ; permit. — *v. i.* To admit ; concede ; make allowance or abatement.

al-low′a-ble (-ȧ-b′l), *a.* [4] Permissible. — **al-low′a-bly,** *adv.* [8].

al-low′ance (-ăns), *n.* Act of allowing ; that which is allowed ; a share or portion allotted ; a limited or stated amount, as of income or food.

al-loy′ (-loi′), *v. t.* **1.** To reduce the purity of by mixing with a less valuable metal. **2.** To mix so as to form an alloy. **3.** To lessen in value, excellence, or the like, by mixture. — *n.* **1.** A substance composed of two or more metals, or of a metal and a nonmetal, united or blended, usually by fusing ; also, the state of union of the components. **2.** A baser metal mixed with a finer, esp. a precious one. **3.** A mixture of a baser metal with a finer one. **4.** An element in a mixture which lessens the value or excellence of the whole.

all′spice (ôl′spĭs′), *n.* The berry of the pimento; also, the spice prepared from it.

al-lude′ (ă-lūd′), *v. i.* [1] To refer indirectly or by suggestion ; — followed by *to.*

al-lure′ (-lūr′), *v. t.* [1] To tempt or draw by a lure or bait ; entice ; attract.

al-lure′ment (-mĕnt), *n.* Act of alluring ; that which allures ; temptation; attraction ; lure.

al-lur′ing, *p. a.* [4] That allures ; tempting.

al-lu′sion (ă-lū′zhŭn), *n.* Act of alluding ; hint.

al-lu′sive (-sĭv), *a.* [4] Making or containing allusion. — -ly, *adv.* [8] — -ness, *n.* [8].

al-lu′vi-al (-vĭ-ăl), *a.* Of, pertaining to, or contained in, alluvium.

al-lu′vi-um (-ŭm), *n. ; pl.* E. -VIUMS (-ŭmz), L. -VIA (-ȧ). A deposit of earth, sand, or other material, made by the action of running water.

al-ly′ (-lī′), *v. t. & t.* [2] To unite or join by alliance; to connect. — *n. ; pl.* ALLIES (ă-līz′). One united or bound to another by a league or treaty ; — used esp. of rulers or states united by treaty ; one allied to another in any way ; a helper.

al′ma-nac (ôl′mȧ-năk), *n.* A calendar of days, weeks, and months, to which astronomical data and various statistics are often added.

al-might′y (-mīt′ĭ), *a.* Omnipotent ; all-powerful. — The Almighty, the omnipotent God. *Rev.* i. 8.

al′mond (ä′mŭnd), *n.* A small tree related to the peach ; also, its fruit, esp. its nut-like kernel.

al′mon-er (ăl′mŭn-ẽr), *n.* One who distributes alms for another.

al′most (ôl′mōst; *emphatic* ôl′mōst′), *adv.* Nearly ; for the greatest part.

alms (ämz), *n. sing. & pl.* Anything given gratuitously to relieve the poor ; a gift of charity.

---

alms'house' (ämz'hous'), *n.* A house for paupers.

al'oe (ăl'ō), *n.; pl.* -oes (-ōz). **1.** In *pl.* A kind of fragrant resin or wood. **2.** Any of a large genus of succulent plants, of the lily family, several of which yield a medicinal juice; also, usually in *pl.*, the thickened juice.

a-loft' (á-lŏft'), *adv.* **1.** On high; high above the earth. **2.** *Naut.* In the top; over head.

a-lone' (á-lōn'), *a.* **1.** Quite by one's self or itself; solitary. **2.** Of or by itself; only. **3.** Unique; matchless; rare; unequaled.
☞ The adj. *alone* commonly follows its noun.

a-lone', *adv.* Solely; simply; exclusively.

a-l o n g' (á-lŏng'), *adv.* **1.** By the length; lengthwise. **2.** In a line, or progressively; onward. **3.** In company; together. — *prep.* Lengthwise of.

Aloe. *a* Entire plant (much reduced). *b* Single flower (⅓).

a-long'side' (-sīd'), *adv. & prep.* Along or by the side; side by side with; — often with *of*.

a-loof' (á-lōōf'), *adv.* At or from a distance; apart; away. — **a-loof'ness,** *n.* [8].

a-loud' (á-loud'), *adv.* Loudly; audibly.

al-pac'a (ăl-păk'á), *n.* A kind of domesticated llama with fine long woolly hair; also, its hair or a thin kind of cloth made wholly or chiefly of it.

al'pen-stock' (ăl'pĕn-stŏk'), *n.* An iron-pointed staff used in mountain climbing.

al'pha-bet (ăl'fá-bĕt), *n.* The letters of a language in their usual order; a set of letters or signs which form the elements of a written language.

al'pha-bet'ic (-bĕt'ĭk) } *a.* Of or pertaining to,
al'pha-bet'i-cal (-ĭ-kăl) } or in the order of, the letters of the alphabet. — **-i-cal-ly,** *adv.* [8].

al'pha-bet-ize (ăl'fá-bĕt-īz), *v. t.* [1] To arrange alphabetically.

al-read'y (ôl-rĕd'ĭ), *adv.* Prior to some specified time; previously.

al'so (ôl'sō), *adv. & conj.* In the same manner (as something else); likewise; in addition; too.

al'tar (ôl'tĕr), *n.* **1.** A raised structure, or any structure or place, on which sacrifices are offered or incense is burned in religious worship. **2.** In the Christian church, the Communion table.

al'ter (-tĕr), *v. t.* To make otherwise; make different without changing into something else; vary; modify. — *v. i.* To become different; change.

al'ter-a-ble (-á-b'l), *a.* Capable of being altered.

al'ter-a'tion (-ā'shŭn), *n.* **1.** Act of altering; state of being altered. **2.** Result of altering; change.

al'ter-cate (ăl'tĕr-kāt; ôl'-), *v. i.* [1] To contend warmly in words; dispute; wrangle.

al'ter-ca'tion (-kā'shŭn), *n.* Warm contention in words; controversy; wrangle.

al-ter'nate (ăl-tûr'nát; ăl'tĕr-), *a* **1.** Occurring or succeeding by turns; one after the other; first one and then the other by turns; reciprocal. **2.** Every other; every second.— *n.* A substitute; one designated to take the place of another.

al'ter-nate (ăl'tĕr-nāt; ôl'-), *v. t.* [1] To perform by turns, or in succession; interchange regularly. — *v. i.* **1.** To happen, succeed, act, or the like, by turns, or in alternation. **2.** *Elec.* Of a current, to reverse periodically and rapidly in direction of flow.

al-ter'nate-ly (ăl-tûr'nát-lĭ ; ăl'tĕr-), *adv.* In an alternate manner; by alternation.

al'ter-na'tion (ăl'tĕr-nā'shŭn; ôl'-), *n.* Act of alternating; alternate succession, performance, etc.

al-ter'na-tive (ăl-tûr'ná-tĭv; ôl-), *a.* Offering a choice (strictly a necessary one) of two (or, loosely, several) things; offering for choice a second thing or proposition. — *n.* **1.** An offer or statement of two things, one of which may (or strictly must) be chosen, but not both; also, either of the things offered. **2.** A choice or offer of choice between more than two things or courses; hence, any of the things so offered. — **al-ter'na-tive-ly,** *adv.* [8].

al-tho' (ôl-thō'), *conj.* Var. of ALTHOUGH.

al-though' (-thō'), *conj.* Grant all this; notwithstanding; though.

al'ti-tude (ăl'tĭ-tūd), *n.* Extent upward; height.

al'to (-tō), *n. ; pl.* -ros (-tōz). *Music.* **a** The part sung by the lowest female, or contralto; voice. **b** An alto voice or singer.

al'to-geth'er (ôl'tōō-gĕth'ẽr), *adv.* Without exception; wholly; completely.

al'tru-ism (ăl'trōō-ĭz'm), *n.* Regard for the interests of others, as a principle of conduct.

al'tru-ist, *n.* One who practices altruism.

al'tru-is'tic (-ĭs'tĭk), *a.* [4] Of or pert. to altruism; actuated by regard for the welfare of others.

al'um (ăl'ŭm), *n.* An astringent mineral salt.

a-lu'mi-na (á-lū'mĭ-ná), *n.* The oxide of aluminium. *Alumina* is the chief constituent of all clays.

al'u-min'i-um (ăl'ŭ-mĭn'ĭ-ŭm), *or, in commerce,* **a-lu'mi-num** (á-lū'mĭ-nŭm), *n.* A bluish silverwhite malleable metal, noted for lightness and resistance to oxidation.

a-lum'nus (á-lŭm'nŭs), *n. masc. ; pl.* -ni (-nī) ;
a-lum'na (-ná), *n. fem. ; pl.* -næ (-nē). A graduate of a college or other institution of learning.

al'way (ôl'wā; ôl'wā'), *adv.* Always. *Archaic.*

al'ways (ôl'wāz; -wăz), *adv.* At all times; ever; continually; invariably; uniformly.

a-lys'sum (á-lĭs'ŭm), *n.* Any of various plants, especially the sweet alyssum.

am (ăm). The first person singular present indicative of the verb *be.*

a-main' (á-mān'), *adv.* **1.** With might; violently. **2.** At full speed ; also, at once.

a-mal'gam (á-măl'găm), *n.* **1.** An alloy of mercury with another metal or metals. **2.** A mixture, compound, or union of different things.

a-mal'ga-mate (-gá-māt), *v. t. & i.* [1] To unite or mix so as to form an amalgam.

a-mal'ga-ma'tion (-mā'shŭn), *n.* Act or process of amalgamating ; state of being amalgamated.

a-man'u-en'sis (á-măn'ŭ-ĕn'sĭs), *n.; pl.* -ses (-sēz). One employed to write what another dictates, or to copy what another has written.

am'a-ranth (ăm'á-rănth), *n.* **1.** An imaginary unfading flower. *Poetic.* **2.** Any of various plants, including several cultivated for their flowers.

am'a-ran'thine (-răn'thĭn), *a.* **1.** Of or pertaining to the amaranth. **2.** Unfading; undying.

āle, senāte, câre, ăm, ăccount, ärm, ȧsk, sofȧ; ēve, ĕvent, ĕnd, recĕnt, makĕr; īce, ĭll; ōld, ȯbey, ôrb, ŏdd, sŏft, cŏnnect; ūse, ŭnite, ûrn, ŭp, circŭs; fōōd, fŏŏt; out, oil;

a-mass′ (ȧ-mȧs′), *v. t. & i.* To collect into a mass or heap; accumulate.

am′a-teur′ (ăm′ȧ-tûr′; ăm′ȧ-tūr), *n.* **1.** One following a particular pursuit, study, or science, but not as a means of making a living. **2.** In sports and esp. athletics, one not rated as a professional. **— -ish,** *a.* [8] **— -ish-ness,** *n.* [8].

am′a-to-ry (-tŏ-rĭ), *a.* [4] Pertaining to, causing, or expressing, sexual love.

a-maze′ (ȧ-māz′), *v.t.* [1] To confound or bewilder, as by fear or wonder; astound.

a-maze′ment (-mĕnt), *n.* State of being amazed.

a-maz′ing (-māz′ĭng), *p. a.* [4] Astounding; astonishing. **— a-maz′ing-ly,** *adv.* [8].

Am′a-zon (ăm′ȧ-zŏn), *n.* **1.** *Gr. Myth.* One of a race or nation of female warriors. **2.** [*Often l. c.*] A tall, strong, masculine woman.

am-bas′sa-dor (ăm-băs′ȧ-dĕr), *n.* **1.** A minister of high rank sent by one sovereign or state to another. **2.** A minister of the highest rank sent to a foreign court to reside there and represent his sovereign or country. **—am-bas′sa-dress** (-drĕs), *n. fem.* [8].

am-bas′sa-do′ri-al (-dŏ′rĭ-ăl), *a.* Of or pertaining to an ambassador.

am′ber (ăm′bĕr), *n.* **1.** A yellowish translucent fossil resin. **2.** Amber color, or something amber-colored. **—** *a.* Amber-colored.

am′ber-gris (-grēs), *n.* A waxy substance secreted by the sperm whale. It is highly valued in perfumery.

am′bi-dex-ter′i-ty (ăm′bĭ-dĕks-tĕr′ĭ-tĭ), *n.* Quality or faculty of being ambidextrous.

am′bi-dex′trous (-dĕks′trŭs), *a.* [4] **1.** Using both hands with equal ease. **2.** Double-dealing.

am′bi-ent (ăm′bĭ-ĕnt), *a.* Inclosing on all sides.

am′bi-gu′i-ty (-gū′ĭ-tĭ), *n.; pl.* -TIES (-tĭz). Quality of being ambiguous; an ambiguous expression.

am-big′u-ous (ăm-bĭg′ū-ŭs), *a.* [4] Doubtful; uncertain, esp. as to meaning; capable of being understood in either of two or more senses. **— am-big′u-ous-ly,** *adv.* [8] **—ness,** *n.* [8].

am-bi′tion (-bĭsh′ŭn), *n.* Eager or excessive desire for preferment, honor, superiority, power, or attainment; also, an object of such desire.

am-bi′tious (-ŭs), *a.* [4] **1.** Possessing, or controlled by, ambition. **2.** Strongly desirous. **3.** Springing from, characterized by, or indicating, ambition. **— -ly,** *adv.* [8].

am′ble (ăm′b′l), *v. i.* [1] To go at an amble. **—** *n.* A gait of a horse like the pace; any easy gait.

am-bro′si-a (ăm-brō′zhĭ-ȧ; -zĭ-ȧ), *n. Class. Myth.* The substance which, with nectar, formed the food and drink of the gods, and which made immortal those who partook of it.

am′bu-lance (ăm′bū-lȧns), *n.* A covered vehicle for conveying the sick or injured, as to a hospital.

am′bus-cade′ (-bŭs-kād′), *n.* A lying in wait to attack an enemy by surprise; ambush.

am′bush (ăm′bŏŏsh), *v.t.* **1.** To station in ambush. **2.** To attack by ambush; waylay. **—** *n.* **1.** Arrangement of troops in concealment to attack an enemy unexpectedly. **2.** A station where troops or enemies lie in wait to attack by surprise.

a-meer′ (ȧ-mēr′), *n.* A Mohammedan noble, esp. a ruling prince of Afghanistan or of Sind.

a-mel′io-rate (ȧ-mēl′yŏ-rāt), *v. t. & i.* [1] To improve; meliorate.

a-mel′io-ra′tion (-rā′shŭn), *n.* Act or result of ameliorating; improvement.

a′men′ (ā′mĕn′; ä′mĕn′), *adv. & interj.* So be it; verily; — a term of solemn ratification, esp. in religious ceremony.

a-me′na-bil′i-ty (ȧ-mē′nȧ-bĭl′ĭ-tĭ), *n.* Quality of being amenable; tractableness.

a-me′na-ble (ȧ-mē′nȧ-b′l), *a.* [4] **1.** Liable to be brought to account or punishment; answerable; accountable. **2.** Responsive; tractable.

a-mend′ (ȧ-mĕnd′), *v. t.* **1.** To reform or correct, as conduct; to mend; repair. **2.** To improve; better. **3.** In parliamentary procedure, to alter formally in any way.

a-mend′a-to-ry (ȧ-mĕn′dȧ-tŏ-rĭ), *a.* Corrective.

a-mend′ment (ȧ-mĕnd′mĕnt), *n.* Act of amending; a thing done or a change made or suggested by way of amending; correction.

a-mends′ (ȧ-mĕndz′), *n. sing. & pl.* Compensation for a loss or injury; recompense.

a-men′i-ty (ȧ-mĕn′Ĭ-tĭ), *n.; pl.* -TIES (-tĭz). Quality or state of being agreeable; civility; suavity.

am′ent (ăm′ĕnt; ā′mĕnt), *n.* A flower cluster of certain trees, as the willow or poplar; a catkin.

a-merce′ (ȧ-mûrs′), *v. t.* [1] **1.** To punish by a fine the amount of which is not fixed by law but by the court. **2.** To fine; punish.

A-mer′i-can (ȧ-mĕr′ĭ-kăn), *a.* Of or pertaining to America or the United States. **—** *n.* **a.** A native of America; orig., an American aborigine; now, a person of European descent born in America. **b.** A citizen of the United States.

Aments, or Catkins.

A-mer′i-can-ism (-ĭz′m), *n.* **1.** Attachment to the United States. **2.** A custom, word, or phrase peculiar to America or to the United States.

am′e-thyst (ăm′ē-thĭst), *n.* A purple or bluish violet quartz much used in jewelry.

a′mi-a-bil′i-ty (ā′mĭ-ȧ-bĭl′ĭ-tĭ), *n.* Quality of being amiable; sweetness of disposition.

a′mi-a-ble (ā′mĭ-ȧ-b′l), *a.* [4] Having those qualities, as good nature, kind-heartedness, and friendliness, which cause one to be liked. **— a′mi-a-ble-ness,** *n.* [8]. **— a′mi-a-bly,** *adv.* [8].

am′i-ca-bil′i-ty (ăm′ĭ-kȧ-bĭl′ĭ-tĭ), *n.* Quality or state of being amicable.

am′i-ca-ble (ăm′ĭ-kȧ-b′l), *a.* [4] Friendly; arising from or exhibiting friendliness. **— am′i-ca-ble-ness,** *n.* [8] **— am′i-ca-bly,** *adv.* [8].

a-mid′ (ȧ-mĭd′), *prep.* In the midst of; amidst.

a-mid′ships (-shĭps), *adv. Naut.* In or toward the middle of a ship, esp. with regard to her length.

a-midst′ (ȧ-mĭdst′), *prep.* In or into the midst of.

a-mir′ (ȧ-mēr′). Var. of AMEER.

a-miss′ (ȧ-mĭs′), *adv.* Astray; faultily; improperly. **—** *a.* Wrong; faulty; as, what is *amiss?*

am′i-ty (ăm′Ĭ-tĭ), *n.; pl.* -TIES (-tĭz). Friendship; friendly relations.

am'me'ter (ăm'mē'tēr), *n.* *Elec.* An instrument for measuring the amperage of a current.

am-mo'ni-a (ă-mō'nĭ-ȧ), *n.* **1.** A colorless gas with a strong and choking smell and taste. **2.** A solution of ammonia gas in water.

am-mo'ni-ac (ă-mō'nĭ-ăk), **am'mo-ni'a-cal** (ăm'-ŏ-nī'ȧ-kăl), *a.* Of or pertaining to or like ammonia.

am'mu-ni'tion (ăm'ū-nĭsh'ŭn), *n.* **1.** The materials, as powder, shot, balls, bombs, etc., with which firearms are charged. **2.** Any stock of missiles.

am'nes-ty (ăm'nĕs-tĭ), *n.; pl.* -TIES (-tĭz). An act of the sovereign power granting a general pardon for a past offense or offenses.

a-mœ'ba (ȧ-mē'bȧ), *n.;* *pl.* E. -BAS (-băz), L. -BÆ (-bē). A tiny animal common in stagnant fresh water. It is one of the simplest forms of animal life, consisting of a single cell, and can be seen only through a microscope.

a-mong' (ȧ-mŭng'), Amœba. 1 Nucleus.

a-mongst' (ȧ-mŭngst'), *prep.* **1.** In or into the midst of; surrounded by; in connection with. **2.** In the number or class of. **3.** To each of by way of dispersion or distribution. **4.** By the joint action, consent, or knowledge of.

am'o-rous (ăm'ŏ-rŭs), *a.* [4] **1.** Inclined to love; loving; fond. **2.** Affected with love; in love. **3.** Of or relating to love; produced by love. — **am'o-rous-ly**, *adv.* [8] — **am'o-rous-ness**, *n.* [8].

a-mor'phous (ȧ-môr'fŭs), *a.* Having no determinate form; shapeless; not crystallized.

a-mount' (ȧ-mount'), *v. i.* To rise, reach, or extend (*to*) in quantity, number, effect, substance, or influence. — *n.* **1.** Sum total of two or more sums or quantities; aggregate. **2.** Effect, substance, value, significance, or result.

a'mour' (ȧ'mōōr'), *n.* [F.] A love affair.

am-per'age (ăm-pâr'ăj; ăm'pēr-), *n.* Strength of a current of electricity measured in amperes.

am-pere' (ăm-pâr'), *n.* The practical unit of electrical current; the current produced by one volt acting through a resistance of one ohm.

am-pere'me'ter (-mē'tēr), *n.* An ammeter.

am'per-sand' (ăm'pēr-sănd), *n.* The character &, &, or &. See *and so forth*, under AND.

am-phib'i-an (ăm-fĭb'ĭ-ăn), *a.* Amphibious.

am-phib'i-an, *n.* **1.** An amphibian animal or plant. **2.** An airplane designed to alight on or arise from either land or water.

am-phib'i-ous (-ŭs), *a.* Able to live both on land and in water, as frogs.

am'phi-the'a-ter (ăm'fĭ-thē'ȧ-tēr), *n.* [6] **1.** An oval or circular building with rising tiers of seats about an arena. **2.** Anything resembling an amphitheater in form.

am'ple (ăm'p'l), *a.* [3] **1.** Large; big; spacious. **2.** Fully sufficient; abundant; liberal.

am'pli-fi-ca'tion (-plĭ-fĭ-kā'shŭn), *n.* An amplifying; that by which a thing or statement is amplified.

am'pli-fi'er (ăm'plĭ-fī'ēr), *n.* One that amplifies, or increases; in a radio receiving set, a vacuum tube for magnifying feeble electric impulses.

am'pli-fy (-plĭ-fī), *v. t.* [2] **1.** To render larger, more intense, or the like; — used esp. of telescopes, microscopes, etc. **2.** To enlarge (as a statement) by adding particulars, illustrations, etc. — *v. i.* To employ amplification; expatiate.

am'pli-tude (-tūd), *n.* State or quality of being ample; largeness; breadth; abundance; fullness.

am'ply (-plĭ), *adv.* In an ample manner.

am'pu-tate (-pū-tāt), *v. t.* [1] To cut off (a limb, part of a limb, or projecting part).

am'pu-ta'tion (-tā'shŭn), *n.* Act of amputating.

a-muck' (ȧ-mŭk'), *a.* Possessed with murderous frenzy. — *adv.* In a frenzied, murderous manner.

am'u-let (ăm'ū-lĕt), *n.* Some small object worn as a charm against evil.

a-muse' (ȧ-mūz'), *v. t.* [1] To entertain or occupy pleasurably; divert; excite to mirth.

a-muse'ment (-mĕnt), *n.* State of being amused; also, that which amuses.

a-mus'ing (ȧ-mūz'ĭng), *p. a.* [4] Giving amusement.

an (ăn), *or* **a**, *a.,* or *indefinite article.* One or any, — without emphasis on the number.
☞ In present usage *an* is used before words beginning with a vowel sound; *a* is used before words beginning with a consonant sound.

an-ach'ro-nism (ăn-ăk'rŏ-nĭz'm), *n.* **1.** An error in recording by which events are misplaced in order, esp. one by which an event is placed too early. **2.** Anything out of keeping with its surroundings in regard to time.

an'a-con'da (ăn'ȧ-kŏn'dȧ), *n.* Any large snake that crushes its prey, esp. a species of boa.

a-næ'mi-a, a-ne'mi-a (ȧ-nē'mĭ-ȧ), *n.* Condition of having poor blood or not enough blood.

a-næ'mic, a-ne'mic (-nē'mĭk; -nĕm'ĭk), *a.* [4] Of, pertaining to, or affected with, anæmia.

an'æs-the'si-a, an'es-the'si-a (ăn'ĕs-thē'sĭ-ȧ; -zhĭ-ȧ), *n.* Entire or partial loss of feeling.

an'æs-thet'ic, an'es-thet'ic (-thĕt'ĭk), *a.* [4] Capable of rendering insensible. — *n.* Something, as ether, that renders insensible to pain.

an-æs'the-tize, an-es'- (ăn-ĕs'thē-tīz), *v. t.* [1] To render insensible to pain, as by an anæsthetic.

an'a-gram (ăn'ȧ-grăm), *n.* The change of one word or phrase into another by the transposition of its letters.

a'nal (ā'năl), *a.* Pert. to, or situated near, the anus.

an'al-ge'si-a (ăn'ăl-jē'sĭ-ȧ; -zĭ-ȧ), *n.* *Med.* Insensibility to pain. — **an'al-ges'ic** (-jĕs'ĭk), *a.*

an'a-log'ic (-ȧ-lŏj'ĭk), **an'a-log'i-cal** (-lŏj'ĭ-kăl) *a.* **1.** Founded on, or of the nature of, or implying, analogy. **2.** Having analogy; analogous. — **an'a-log'i-cal-ly**, *adv.* [8].

a-nal'o-gous (ȧ-năl'ŏ-gŭs), *a.* Having analogy; bearing some resemblance. — **-gous-ly**, *adv.* [8]

an'a-logue (ăn'ȧ-lŏg), *n.* That which is analogous to, or corresponds with, some other thing.

a-nal'o-gy (ȧ-năl'ŏ-jĭ), *n.; pl.* -GIES (-jĭz). Agreement or likeness between things in some ways but not in others.

an'a-lyse, *v.,* **-lys'er**, *n.,* etc. Vars. of ANALYZE, etc.

a-nal'y-sis (ȧ-năl'ĭ-sĭs), *n., pl.* -SES (-sēz). **1.** The separation of anything into elements, or the parts that compose it; an examination of component parts separately, or in relation to the whole. **2.** A table of the heads of a discourse.

an'a-lyst (ăn'ȧ-lĭst), *n.* One who analyzes.

an'a-lyt'ic (ăn'ă-lĭt'ĭk)) a. [4] Of or pert. to analy-
an'a-lyt'i-cal (-ĭ-kăl)) sis. — **-i-cal-ly**, adv. [8].

an'a-lyze (-ă-līz), v. t. [1] To resolve into elements
or constituent parts ; to separate or discriminate
the parts of in relation to the whole and to one another; to subject to analysis. — **an'a-lyz'er**, n. [8].

a-nar'chic (ă-när'kĭk)) a. [4] Of or pertaining
a-nar'chi-cal (-kĭ-kăl)) to anarchy.

an'arch-ism (ăn'är-kĭz'm), n. 1. The principles
underlying anarchy ; especially, the theory that
all government is an evil. 2. Advocacy or practice of anarchistic principles.

an'arch-ist (-kĭst), n. An advocate of anarchy or
anarchism.

an'arch-y (-kĭ), n. 1. State of society where
there is no law or supreme power ; hence, a state
of lawlessness. 2. Confusion ; disorder.

a-nath'e-ma (ă-năth'ĕ-mă), n. ; pl. -MAS (-măz).
1. A solemn ban or curse pronounced by ecclesiastical authority, esp. with excommunication. 2. A
curse. 3. Any person or thing anathematized.

a-nath'e-ma-tize (-tīz), v. t. & i. [1] To pronounce an anathema against ; to curse.

an'a-tom'ic (ăn'ă-tŏm'ĭk)) a. Of or relating to
an'a-tom'i-cal (-ĭ-kăl)) anatomy. — **an'a-
tom'i-cal-ly**, adv. [8].

a-nat'o-mist (ă-năt'ō-mĭst), n. A person skilled
in anatomy.

a-nat'o-mize (-mīz), v. t. [1] To dissect ; analyze.

a-nat'o-my (-mĭ), n. ; pl. -MIES (-mĭz). 1. Art of
dissecting an animal or plant to discover the situation, structure, and economy of its parts. 2. The
science of the structure of animals or plants.
3. Structure or organization of an animal or plant.

an'ces-tor (ăn'sĕs-tŏr), n. One from whom a person is descended; a progenitor. — **-tress**, n. fem.

an-ces'tral (ăn-sĕs'trăl), a. Of, pert. to, derived
from, or possessed by, an ancestor or ancestors.

an'ces-try (ăn'sĕs-trĭ), n. Ancestral lineage ;
hence, birth ; honorable descent.

an'chor (ăn'kẽr), n. 1. An appliance attached to
a ship or other vessel by a line or
cable so that when cast overboard
it will lay hold of the earth by a
fluke or hook and hold the vessel
in place; also, anything similarly
used. 2. Something suggestive of
a ship's anchor in its use. — v. t.
1. To place at anchor; secure by an
anchor. 2. To fix; fasten. — v. i.
To cast anchor; come to anchor.

Anchor. Com-
mon Anchor ;
aa Stock ; b
Shank ; cc
Flukes ; d d
Arms.

an'chor-age (-âj), n. 1. A place
suitable for anchoring. 2. A toll for anchoring.

an'cho-ress (-kŏ-rĕs), n. A female anchoret.

an'cho-ret (-rĕt), an'cho-rite (-rīt), n. One who
renounces the world to live in seclusion ; hermit.

an-cho'vy (ăn-chō'vĭ; ăn'chŏ-), n. ; pl. -VIES (-vĭz).
Any of various small herring-like fishes of the Mediterranean, used for pickling or making a sauce.

an'cient (ān'shĕnt), a. [4] 1. Old ; antique ; old-
fashioned. 2. Belonging to times long past. — n.
1. An aged being. 2. One who lived in antiquity ; pl., the civilized peoples of antiquity, esp.
the classical nations. — **an'cient-ly**, adv. [8] —
an'cient-ness, n. [8].

and (ănd), conj. 1. A particle expressing the gen-

eral relation of connection or addition, and used to
conjoin word with word, clause with clause, or sentence with sentence. 2. In order to ; — used after
try, come, go, send ; as, try *and* do it.
and **so forth**, and others or more of the same or of
similar kind; and the rest. The abbreviation *etc.*
(*et cetera*) or *&c.* is usually read *and so forth*.

‖ **an-dan'te** (än-dän'tā; ăn-dăn'tā), a. [It.] *Music.*
Moderately slow, but distinct and flowing.

and'i'ron (ănd'ī'ûrn), n. A utensil for supporting wood in a fireplace; a firedog.

an'ec-dot'al (ăn'ĕk-dōt'ăl), an'ec-dot'ic (-dŏt'ĭk),
a. Of or pertaining to anecdotes.

an'ec-dote (ăn'ĕk-dōt), n. A short account of a single incident or fact of an interesting nature, esp. in
the life of a well-known person.

a-ne'mi-a (ă-nē'mĭ-á), a-ne'mic (-mĭk), etc. Vars.
of ANÆMIA, ANÆMIC, etc.

an'e-mom'e-ter (ăn'ĕ-mŏm'ĕ-tẽr), n. An instrument for measuring the velocity of the wind.

a-nem'o-ne (ă-nĕm'ō-nē), n. 1. Any of various
plants, related to the buttercup, having white, red,
blue, or, some-
times, yellow
flowers. 2. A
sea anemone.

an'er-oid (ăn'ẽr-
oid), a. Contain-
ing no liquid ; —
said of a kind of
barometer regis-
tering by the at-
mospheric pres-
sure on a me-
tallic box par-
tially exhausted
of air. — n. An aneroid barometer.

Aneroid Barometer. *a* Exhausted
Box connected with Levers *b* and *c*
to actuate Pointer *d*.

an'es-the'sia, an'es-thet'ic. Vars. of ANÆSTHESIA,
ANÆSTHETIC.

a-new' (ă-nū'), adv. Over again; in a new form.

an'gel (ān'jĕl), n. 1. A supernatural messenger
of God ; a spiritual, celestial being, superior to
man in power and intelligence. 2. A person like
an angel in goodness or loveliness. 3. A former
English gold coin bearing the image of the archangel Michael. 4. Attendant spirit ; genius ; demon.

an-gel'ic (ăn-jĕl'ĭk)) a. [4] Belonging to angels.
an-gel'i-cal (-ĭ-kăl)) characteristic of or like an
angel; heavenly; divine. — **-i-cal-ly**, adv. [8].

an'ger (ăŋ'gẽr), n. A strong passion or emotion
of displeasure or antagonism excited by what is
regarded as an injury or insult done by another
or by the intent to do such injury. — v. t. To excite to anger; enrage; provoke.

an'gle (ăŋ'g'l), n. A fish-
hook or fishing tackle.
— v. i. [1] 1. To fish
with hook and line. 2. To
use a bait or artifice;
intrigue; scheme.

an'gle, n. 1. The inclosed
space near the point
where two lines meet;
corner; nook. 2. a The
figure formed by two
meeting lines. b Dif-

Angle (2). *ABD* and *ABC*
Right Angles ; *F* (or *F'*,
F'', *F'''*) *B D* Acute An-
gle; *E* (or *E'*, *E''*,*E'''*)*BD*
Obtuse Angle.

ference in direction of two lines. **3.** An angular part, object, or space; sharp corner.

an'gled (ăn'g'ld), *a.* Having an angle or angles.

an'gler (-glēr), *n.* **1.** One who angles. **2.** A kind of fish having a very large mouth and fleshy outgrowths on the head, by which latter it is said to lure fish within reach.

an'gle-worm' (-g'l-wŭrm'), *n.* An earthworm.

An'gli-can (ăn'glĭ-kăn), *a.* English; esp., of or pert. to the Church of England and churches in communion with it. — *n.* A member of an Anglican church or of the Anglican party.

An'gli-ci-za'tion (-sĭ-zā'shŭn), *n.* The action or process of Anglicizing, or making English.

An'gli-cize (ăn'glĭ-sīz), *v. t. & i.* [1] To make or become English.

An'glo-ma'ni-a (-glŏ-mā'nĭ-à), *n.* Extreme prejudice in favor of English customs, institutions, etc.

An'glo-ma'ni-ac (-ăk), *n.* One affected with Anglomania.

an'gri-ly (ăn'grĭ-lĭ), *adv.* In an angry manner.

an'gry (ăn'grĭ), *a.* [3] **1.** Affected with anger; enraged. **2.** Showing, or proceeding from, anger.

an'guish (-gwĭsh), *n.* Extreme pain of body or mind; agony; torture; torment.

an'gu-lar (-gŭ-lẽr), *a.* [4] **1.** Of or pertaining to an angle or angles; having or forming an angle; sharp-cornered. **2.** Fig. : Lean; lank ; sharp and stiff in character. — **an'gu-lar-ly**, *adv.* [8].

an'gu-lar'i-ty (-lär'ĭ-tĭ), *n.; pl.* -TIES (-tĭz). Quality of being angular.

an'i-line (ăn'ĭ-lĭn; -lēn), *n.* An oily poisonous liquid used in making dyes.

an'i-mad-ver'sion (-măd-vŭr'shŭn), *n.* Remark by way of criticism and, usually, of censure ; adverse criticism ; blame ; reproach ; stricture.

an'i-mad-vert' (-vûrt'), *v. i.* To consider or remark by way of criticism or censure.

an'i-mal (ăn'ĭ-măl), *n.* **1.** A living being having sensation, or feeling, and the power to move at will, as distinguished from a *plant*. **2.** One of the lower animals ; a brute or beast, as distinguished from man. — *a.* **1.** Of, pertaining to, or derived from, animals; as, *animal* life or courage. **2.** Pertaining to the merely physical part of a creature; as, *animal* passions or appetites.

an'i-mal'cule (ăn'ĭ-măl'kūl), *n.* A minute animal, invisible, or nearly so, to the naked eye.

an'i-mate (-māt), *v. t.* [1] **1.** To make alive ; quicken. **2.** To give spirit or vigor to; rouse; inspire. — (-măt), *a.* Alive; living ; animated.

an'i-mat'ed (-māt'ĕd), *p. a.* [4] Alive; full of life or spirit; lively. — **an'i-mat'ed-ly**, *adv.* [8].

an'i-ma'tion (-mā'shŭn), *n.* Act of animating; state of being animate or animated.

an'i-mos'i-ty (-mŏs'ĭ-tĭ), *n.; pl.* -TIES (-tĭz). Violent hatred leading to active opposition.

an'i-mus (ăn'ĭ-mŭs), *n.* Mind ; animating spirit ; inclination ; bad or malicious intention.

an'i-on (ăn'ī-ŏn), *n. Chem.* **a** The product evolved at the anode in electrolysis. **b** A negative ion.

an'ise (-ĭs), *n.* A small plant cultivated for its aromatic seeds; also, the seeds.

an'i-seed (-ĭ-sēd), *n.* The seed of the anise.

an'kle (ăŋ'k'l), *n.* The joint between the foot and the leg; also, the region of this joint.

an'klet (-klĕt), *n.* Something encircling the ankle.

an'nal-ist (ăn'ăl-ĭst), *n.* A writer of annals.

an'nals (-ălz), *n. pl.* **1.** A record of events in the order in which they take place, each under the year in which it happened. **2.** Chronicles; history.

an-neal' (ă-nēl'), *v. t.* To subject to high heat and then cool ; to soften and render less brittle.

an-nex' (ă-nĕks'), *v. t.* **1.** To join (one thing, usually something smaller or subordinate, to another). **2.** To attach as a consequence, condition, etc.

an-nex' (ă-nĕks'; ăn'ĕks), *n.* Something annexed.

an'nex-a'tion (ăn'ĕk-sā'shŭn), *n.* **1.** Act of annexing; addition. **2.** A thing or things annexed.

an-ni'hi-late (ă-nī'hĭ-lāt), *v. t.* [1] **1.** To reduce to nothing; make void. **2.** To destroy the form or essential character of, as an army.

an-ni'hi-la'tion (-lā'shŭn), *n.* Act of annihilating; state of being annihilated.

an'ni-ver'sa-ry (ăn'ĭ-vûr'sà-rĭ), *a.* **1.** Returning with the year ; annual. **2.** Of or pertaining to an anniversary. — *n.; pl.* -RIES (-rĭz). **1.** The annual return of the day of a past event, esp. a notable event. **2.** An anniversary celebration.

|| **an'no Do'mi-ni** (ăn'ō dŏm'ĭ-nī). [L., in the year of [our] Lord.] In the (specified) year of the Christian Era. Abbr., *A.D.*; as, A.D. 1887.

an'no-tate (ăn'ŏ-tāt), *v. t.* [1] To explain or criticize by notes. — *v. i.* To make notes or comments.

an'no-ta'tion (-tā'shŭn), *n.* An annotating ; note made in annotating. — **an'no-ta'tor**, *n.* [8].

an-nounce' (ă-nouns'), *v. t.* [1] **1.** To give public notice, or first notice, of ; publish ; proclaim. **2.** To give notice of the arrival or presence of.

an-nounce'ment (-mĕnt), *n.* Act of announcing; that which announces ; publication ; declaration.

an-noy' (ă-noi'), *v. t.* **1.** To disturb or irritate, esp. by repeated acts; tease. **2.** To molest, or injure.

an-noy'ance (ă-noi'ăns), *n.* **1.** Act of annoying; state of being annoyed. **2.** That which annoys.

an'nu-al (ăn'ū-ăl), *a.* **1.** Of or pertaining to a year; coming or happening once a year; yearly. **2.** Done in a year ; reckoned by the year. **3.** Lasting only a year or, of plants, one growing season. — *n.* **1.** A thing happening or recurring yearly; esp., a literary work published once a year. **2.** Anything that lasts but one year or season. — **al-ly**, *adv.* [8].

an-nu'i-ty (ă-nū'ĭ-tĭ), *n. ; pl.* -TIES (-tĭz). An amount payable yearly; the right to such payments.

an-nul' (ă-nŭl'), *v. t.; -* NULLED' (-nŭld'), -NUL'LING. To nullify ; abolish ; avoid.

an'nu-lar (ăn'ū-lär), *a.* Ring-shaped.

an-nul'ment (ă-nŭl'mĕnt), *n.* Act of annulling.

an-nun'ci-ate (-nŭn'shĭ-āt), *v. t.* [1] To announce.

an-nun'ci-a'tion (-sĭ-ā'shŭn ; -shĭ-ā'shŭn), *n.* Act of announcing ; announcement.

an-nun'ci-a'tor (-nŭn'shĭ-ā'tẽr), *n.* A signaling device which shows, as by a pointer, bell, or light, the place where attendance is required.

an'ode (ăn'ōd), *n. Elec.* The positive terminal of an electric source. Cf. CATHODE.

an'o-dyne (-ŏ-dĭn), *a.* [4] Serving to ease pain; soothing. — *n.* An anodyne drug or agent.

a-noint' (ă-noint'), *v. t.* To smear or rub over with oil or an oily or greasy substance; also, to spread over, as oil. — **a-noint'er**, *n.* [8].

a-noint'ment (-mĕnt), *n.* Act of anointing.

āle, senāte, câre, ăm, ăccount, ärm, àsk, sofà; ēve, ĕvent, ĕnd, recĕnt, makĕr; īce, ĭll; ōld, ŏbey, ôrb, ŏdd, sŏft, cŏnnect; ūse, ŭnite, ûrn, ŭp, circŭs; fōōd, fŏŏt; out, oil;

a-nom′a-lous (á-nŏm′á-lŭs), a. [4] Deviating from a general rule, method, or analogy; abnormal; irregular. — **-ly**, adv. [8] — **-ness**, n. [8].

a-nom′a-ly (-lĭ), n.; pl. **-LIES** (-lĭz). Deviation from common rule; irregularity; anything anomalous.

a-non′ (-nŏn′), adv. **1.** At once. *Archaic.* **2.** Soon; in a little while. **3.** At another time; again.

an′o-nym′i-ty (ăn′ó-nĭm′ĭ-tĭ), n. Quality or state of being anonymous; also, that which is anonymous.

a-non′y-mous (á-nŏn′ĭ-mŭs), a. Nameless; of unknown name; also, of unknown or unavowed authorship. — **a-non′y-mous-ly,** adv. [8].

an-oth′er (ă-nŭth′ĕr), pron. & a. **1.** One more; an additional one. **2.** Not the same; different. **3.** Any or some other; any one else; some one else.

an′swer (ăn′sẽr), n. **1.** A reply to a charge, question, call, argument, etc. ; defense ; also, a correct or adequate reply. **2.** An action by way of reply or response; as, the enemy's *answer* was a shot. **3.** A solution, the result of a mathematical operation. — v. i. **1.** To make an answer; respond. **2.** To render account; be responsible. **3.** To be or act in return. Hence: **a** To serve the purpose. **b** To be or act as an equivalent, or as adequate or sufficient. **c** To conform; correspond; suit. — v. t. **1.** To speak in defense against; reply to in defense. **2.** To make answer to; reply to. **3.** To be or act in return or response to or in satisfaction of.

an′swer-a-ble (ăn′sẽr-á-b′l), a. **1.** Liable to be called to account; accountable; responsible. **2.** Capable of being answered, or refuted.

ant (ănt), n. Any of certain small insects related to the bees, wasps, etc. The ants are social, living in communities.

an-tag′o-nism (ăn-tăg′ó-nĭz′m), n. Opposition of action; mutual opposition of two forces.

an-tag′o-nist (-nĭst), n. One who contends with another, esp. in combat; adversary; opponent.

an-tag′o-nis′tic (-nĭs′tĭk), a. [4] Opposing in combat; contending or acting against.

an-tag′o-nize (-tăg′ó-nīz), v. t. & i. [1] To contend with; oppose actively.

ant-arc′tic (ănt-ärk′tĭk), a. Opposite to the north, or arctic, pole; — applied esp. to a circle, or parallel of latitude, 23° 28′ from the south pole.

ant′eat′er (ănt′ēt′ẽr), n. Any of several mammals that feed largely or entirely on ants.

an′te-ced′ence (ăn′tè-sēd′ẽns), n. Act, fact, or state of going before; precedence; priority.

an′te-ced′ent (-ĕnt), a. Going before in time. — n. **1.** That which goes before in time. **2.** pl. The earlier events of one's life. **3.** *Gram.* A noun or clause referred to by a pronoun. **4.** *Math.* The first of the two terms of a ratio. — **ced′ent-ly,** adv.

an′te-cham′ber (ăn′tè-chām′bẽr), n. A chamber leading into the chief apartment; outer chamber.

an′te-date′ (-dāt′), n. Prior date. — v. t. [1] **1.** To date before the true time; assign to, or put at, an earlier date. **2.** To precede in time or date.

an′te-di-lu′vi-an (-dĭ-lū′vĭ-ăn), a. [4] Of or relating to the period before the Deluge; hence, antiquated. — n. An antediluvian person.

an′te-lope (ăn′tè-lōp), n. Any of a group of animals of the same family as the oxen, sheep, and goats, light and graceful in form and having horns that are directed upward and backward.

an-ten′na (ăn-tĕn′á), n.; L. pl. **-NÆ** (-ē). **1.** A movable organ of feeling on the head of insects, spiders, lobsters, etc.; a feeler. **2.** A wire or wires supported in the air for directly transmitting or receiving electric waves.

an-te′ri-or (ăn-tē′rĭ-ẽr), a. Being before in time or place; antecedent. — **-ly,** adv. [8].

an′te-room′ (ăn′tè-room′), n. A room forming an entrance to another; a waiting room.

an′them (ăn′thĕm), n. **1.** A prose composition, usually a selection from the Psalms, set to sacred music. **2.** A song of praise or gladness.

an′ther (-thẽr), n. In seed plants, the part of the stamen that bears the pollen.

an-thol′o-gy (ăn-thŏl′ó-jĭ), n.; pl. **-GIES** (-jĭz). A collection of poems or epigrams.

an′thra-cite (ăn′thrá-sīt), n. A hard coal containing less volatile matter than bituminous coal.

an′thro-poid (-thrò-poid), a. Resembling man; — esp. of certain apes. — n. An anthropoid ape.

an′thro-po-log′ic (-pò-lŏj′ĭk)) a. Of or pert. to **an′thro-po-log′i-cal** (-lŏj′ĭ-kăl)) anthropology.

an-thro-pol′o-gy (-pŏl′ò-jĭ), n. The science of man, esp. in relation to physical character, distribution, culture, etc.

an′thro-po-mor′phic (-pò-môr′fĭk), a. Of or pertaining to anthropomorphism.

an′thro-po-mor′phism (-pò-môr′fĭz′m), n. Representation of the Deity, or of a polytheistic deity, with human attributes; also, ascription of human characteristics to things not human.

an′tic (ăn′tĭk), a. Odd; fantastic. — n. **1.** A buffoon. **2.** A grotesque trick; piece of buffoonery.

an-tic′i-pate (ăn-tĭs′ĭ-pāt), v. t. [1] **1.** To do, take up, or deal with, before another; forestall. **2.** To take up, use, or introduce before the proper time; as, he has *anticipated* a part of his argument. **3.** To foresee (a wish, command, etc.) and execute (it) beforehand. **4.** To foretaste or foresee; as, to *anticipate* a pleasure.

an-tic′i-pa′tion (-pā′shŭn), n. Act of anticipating; expectation; foretaste; foresight; forethought.

an-tic′i-pa-tive (-tĭs′ĭ-pă-tĭv), a. Anticipatory.

an-tic′i-pa-to-ry (-pá-tò-rĭ), a. Anticipating; of the nature of anticipation.

an′ti-cli′max (ăn′tĭ-klī′măks), n. A sentence or passage in which the ideas fall off in dignity or importance at the close; — the opposite of *climax*.

an′ti-dot′al (ăn′tĭ-dōt′ăl), a. Acting as, or of the nature of, an antidote.

an′ti-dote (-dōt), n. **1.** A remedy for poison. **2.** Whatever tends to prevent or counteract evil.

an′ti-im-pe′ri-al-ism (ăn′tĭ-ĭm-pē′rĭ-ăl-ĭz′m), n. Opposition to imperialism.

an′ti-mo-ny (ăn′tĭ-mò-nĭ), n. A hard and brittle, tin-white metal, used chiefly in making alloys. It is an element.

an′ti-pa-thet′ic (ăn′tĭ-pá-thĕt′ĭk), a. [4] Naturally contrary; marked by antipathy.

an-tip′a-thy (ăn-tĭp′á-thĭ), n.; pl. **-THIES** (-thĭz). **1.** Opposition or disagreement in feeling; repugnance. **2.** Disagreement in nature, incompatibility.

an-tip′o-dal (ăn-tĭp′ò-dăl), a. **1.** Pertaining to the antipodes. **2.** Diametrically opposite.

an′ti-pode (ăn′tĭ-pōd), n. One of the antipodes; a direct opposite.

an-tip'o-des (ăn-tĭp'ŏ-dēz), *n. pl.* **1**. Those who live on the diametrically opposite side of the globe. **2**. The regions or country of the antipodes. **3**. The direct opposite or contrary.

an'ti-qua'ri-an (ăn'tĭ-kwā'rĭ-ăn), *a.* Of or pert. to antiquaries or antiquities. — *n.* An antiquary.

an'ti-qua-ry (ăn'tĭ-kwā-rĭ), *a.* Antiquarian. — *n. ; pl.* -RIES (-rĭz). A student of antiquities.

an'ti-quate (-kwāt), *v. t.* [1] To make old, antique, or out of date.

an'ti-quat'ed (-kwāt'ĕd), *p. a.* [4] Grown old; hence, bygone ; old-fashioned.

an-tique' (ăn-tēk'), *a.* [4] **1**. Old ; belonging to antiquity, esp. to ancient Greece or Rome. **2**. Old, as respects the present time; antiquated ; old-fashioned. — *n.* Anything very old; esp., a relic or object of ancient art.

an-tiq'ui-ty (ăn-tĭk'wĭ-tĭ), *n. ; pl.* -TIES (-tĭz). **1**. Quality of being old or ancient ; oldness ; ancientness. **2**. Ancient times, esp. those before the Middle Ages. **3**. A relic, monument, etc., of ancient times ; — usually in *pl.*

an'ti-sep'tic (ăn'tĭ-sĕp'tĭk), *a.* **1**. Tending to prevent putrefaction, pus formation, etc. **2**. Using antiseptics. — *n.* An antiseptic substance.

an'ti-slav'er-y (-slăv'ēr-ĭ), *a.* Opposed to slavery.

an-tith'e-sis (ăn-tĭth'ē-sĭs), *n. ; pl.* -SES (-sēz). **1**. An opposition or contrast of words or ideas. **2**. Opposition ; contrast ; an opposite.

an'ti-thet'ic (ăn'tĭ-thĕt'ĭk), **an'ti-thet'i-cal** (-ĭ-kăl), *a.* [4] Of or pertaining to antithesis; opposing ; contrasted. — **thet'i-cal-ly**, *adv.* [8].

an'ti-tox'in (ăn'tĭ-tŏk'sĭn), *n.* Any of certain substances formed in the blood of animals, either naturally or by inoculation, and having the power of neutralizing some specific poison, esp. a specific poison produced in the body by bacteria.

an'ti-trade' (ăn'tĭ-trād'), *n.* An upper tropical wind blowing steadily in a direction opposite to the trade wind, beyond which, in the north temperate and the south temperate zones, it becomes a surface wind.

ant'ler (ănt'lēr), *n.* The entire horn, or any branch of the horn, of an animal of the deer family.

an'to-nym (ăn'tō-nĭm), *n.* A word which is the opposite, in meaning, of another word.

a'nus (ā'nŭs), *n.* The posterior opening of the alimentary canal.

an'vil (ăn'vĭl), *n.* A block, usually of iron faced with steel, on which metal is shaped, as by hammering.

anx-i'e-ty (ăng-zī'ē-tĭ), *n. ; pl.* -TIES (-tĭz). Anxious state or condition; painful uneasiness about a future or uncertain event.

Anvil. *a* Horn: *b, c* Holes for Set Chisels, Swage Blocks, etc.

anx'ious (ăngk'shŭs), *a.* [4] **1**. Disquieted over a possible or impending ill; concerned or solicitous, esp. as to a future or unknown thing. **2**. Accompanied with or causing anxiety ; worrying. **3**. Earnestly desirous. — **-ly**, *adv.* [8] — **-ness**, *n.* [8].

an'y (ĕn'ĭ), *a. & pron.* One indifferently out of a number ; one (or, as *pl.*, some) indiscriminately of whatever kind or quantity. — *adv.* To any extent ; in any degree ; at all.

an'y-bod-y (-bŏd-ĭ), *n. & pron.* Any person.

an'y-how (-hou), *adv. & conj.* In any way or manner whatever ; at any rate ; in any event.

an'y-thing (-thĭng), *n.* Any object, act, state, event, or fact whatever ; a thing of any kind.

a-pace' (á-pās'), *adv.* At a quick pace ; quick; fast.

a-part' (á-pärt'), *adv.* **1**. Separately as to space or company ; aside. **2**. Separately as to purpose, use, character, etc. ; independently. **3**. Aside ; away. **4**. In two or more parts ; asunder.

a-part'ment (-mĕnt), *n.* **1**. A suite, or set, of rooms. **2**. A room in a building.

ap'a-thet'ic (ăp'á-thĕt'ĭk), *a.* [4] Void of feeling; passionless; indifferent. — **i-cal-ly**, *adv.* [8].

ap'a-thy (ăp'á-thĭ), *n. ; pl.* -THIES [(-thĭz). **1**. Want of feeling or emotion. **2**. Indifference to what ordinarily stirs the feelings or activities.

ape (āp), *n.* **1**. Any monkey, esp. one of the larger tailless Old World forms. **2**. An imitator; mimic. — *v. t.* [1] To mimic.

a-peak' (á-pēk'), *adv. & a. Naut.* In a vertical line.

a-pe'ri-ent (-pē'rĭ-ĕnt), *a. & n. Med.* Laxative.

ap'er-ture (ăp'ēr-tûr), *n.* An opening; gap; hole.

a'pex (ā'pĕks), *n. ; pl.* E. APEXES (-pĕk-sĕz), L. API-CES (ăp'ĭ-sēz). The tip or point of anything.

a-phel'ion (á-fĕl'yŭn), *n.* That point of a planet's or comet's orbit farthest from the sun.

a'phid (ā'fĭd; ăf'ĭd), *n.* A plant louse.

a'phis (ā'fĭs), *n.; pl.* APHIDES (ăf'ĭ-dēz). An aphid.

aph'o-rism (ăf'ō-rĭz'm), *n.* A sentence stating a general truth briefly and aptly.

a'pi-a-ry (ā'pĭ-ā-rĭ), *n. ; pl.* -RIES (-rĭz). Place where bees are kept for their honey.

ap'i-ces (ăp'ĭ-sēz), *n., Lat. pl.* of APEX.

a'pi-cul'ture (ā'pĭ-kŭl'tûr), *n.* Rearing of bees.

a-piece' (á-pēs'), *adv.* To or for each by itself; each ; as the share of each.

ap'ish (āp'ĭsh), *a.* [4] Having the qualities of an ape; given to servile imitation; hence, fantastically silly or affected.

a-poc'a-lypse (á-pŏk'á-lĭps), *n.* **1**. [*cap.*] The last book of the New Testament ; Revelation. **2**. Anything viewed as a revelation ; a disclosure.

A-poc'ry-pha (-rĭf-á), *n. pl.* Certain writings not part of the Hebrew Bible and rejected by Protestants as not inspired sources of doctrine.

a-poc'ry-phal (-făl), *a.* [4] **1**. Of or like the Apocrypha. **2**. Not canonical ; fictitious ; false.

ap'o-gee (ăp'ō-jē), *n.* **1**. *Astron.* That point in the moon's orbit which is farthest from the earth. **2**. The farthest or highest point ; culmination.

ap'o-log-et'ic (á-pŏl'ō-jĕt'ĭk), **a-pol'o-get'i-cal** (-ĭ-kăl), *a.* [4] Defending by discourse ; of the nature of an apology. — **i-cal-ly**, *adv.*

a-pol'o-gist (-jĭst), *n.* One who makes an apology.

a-pol'o-gize (-jīz), *v. i.* [1] To make an apology.

ap'o-logue (ăp'ō-lŏg), *n.* A fictitious story intended to convey a moral truth.

āle, senāte, câre, ăm, ăccount, ärm, ȧsk, sofả ; ēve, ĕvent, ĕnd, recĕnt, makĕr ; īce, ĭll ; ōld, ŏbey, ôrb, ŏdd, sŏft, cŏnnect ; ūse, ũnite, ûrn, ŭp, circŭs ; fŏŏd, fŏŏt ; out, oil ;

a-pol'o-gy (*ā-pŏl'ō-jĭ*), *n.; pl.* -GIES (-jĭz). **1.** Something said or written by way of defense or justification. **2.** An acknowledgment intended as an atonement for an improper or injurious remark or act. **3.** What serves as an excuse for the absence of something; a makeshift.

ap'oph-thegm (*ăp'ō-thĕm*). Var. of APOTHEGM.

ap'o-plec'tic (-plĕk'tĭk), *a.* Of or pertaining to apoplexy.— *n.* An apoplectic person.

ap'o-plex'y (-plĕk'sĭ), *n.* *Med.* Sudden diminution or loss of consciousness, sensation, and voluntary motion, usually due to effusion of blood or serum into the brain or spinal cord.

a-port' (*ā-pōrt'*), *adv.* *Naut.* On or toward the port, or left, side ;— said esp. of the helm.

a-pos'ta-sy (*ā-pŏs'tā-sĭ*), *n.; pl.* -TASIES (-sĭz). Abandonment of what one has voluntarily professed ; a total desertion from one's faith, principles, party, or, esp., from one's religion.

a-pos'tate (-tāt), *n.* One who has abandoned his faith, party, or, esp., religion.

a-pos'ta-tize (-tā-tīz), *v. i.* To commit apostasy.

a-pos'tle (*ā-pŏs''l*), *n.* **1.** One of the 12 disciples of Christ, sent forth to preach the gospel; also, any of various others sent forth by Christ or sent forth soon after His death to preach the gospel. **2.** The first Christian missionary in any region; one who initiates any new principle or system.

a-pos'tle-ship, *n.* Office or position of apostle.

ap'os-tol'ic (*ăp'ŏs-tŏl'ĭk*), **ap'os-tol'i-cal** (-ĭ-kăl), *a.* **1.** Of or pertaining to an apostle, or the apostles, their times, or their spirit. **2.** Papal.

a-pos'tro-phe (*ā-pŏs'trō-fē*), *n.* **1.** Act of suddenly breaking off in a discourse and addressing, in the second person, some person or thing, absent or present. **2.** *Gram.* Omission of a letter or letters from a word. **3.** The mark ['] used to indicate the possessive case, the close of a quotation.

a-pos'tro-phize (-fīz), *v. t. & i.* [1] To address by or in an apostrophe.

a-poth'e-ca-ry (-pŏth'ē-kā-rĭ), *n.; pl.* -RIES (-rĭz). One who prepares and sells drugs or compounds for medicinal purposes. — **apothecaries' weight**, a system of weights used for compounding medical prescriptions. See TROY, *a.*

ap'o-thegm (*ăp'ō-thĕm*), *n.* A short, pithy, and instructive saying; a maxim.

ap'o-the'o-sis (*ăp'ō-thē'ō-sĭs; ā-pŏth'ē-ō'sĭs*), *n.; pl.* -OSES (-sēz). **1.** Act of deifying, or making a god of. **2.** Exaltation, as of a person or an ideal.

ap-pall' (*ā-pôl'*), *v. t.* To overcome, depress, or discourage with fear or horror ; dismay.

ap'pa-nage (*ăp'ā-nāj*), *n.* **1.** Provision made by a sovereign or prince for the younger members of his family. **2.** That which belongs by custom or right ; a natural endowment.

ap'pa-ra'tus (-rā'tŭs), *n. ; pl.* -RATUS ; -RATUSES (-tŭs-ĕz). **1.** Things provided as means to an end. **2.** A set of implements or utensils for a given work; a complex instrument or appliance ; mechanism.

ap-par'el (*ā-păr'ĕl*), *n.* Dress; garb; raiment. — *v. t.* **1.** To equip. **2.** To clothe.

ap-par'ent (*ā-pâr'ĕnt ;ā-păr'-*), *a.* [4] **1.** Open to view ; visible. **2.** Clear or manifest to the understanding ; plain ; evident; obvious. **3.** Appearing as actual; seeming. — **ap-par'ent-ly**, *adv.* [8].

ap'pa-ri'tion (*ăp'ā-rĭsh'ŭn*), *n.* **1.** Act of becoming apparent ; appearance. **2.** The thing appearing ; visible object ; form. **3.** A preternatural or unexpected appearance ; ghost ; specter ; phantom.

ap-peal' (*ā-pēl'*), *v. t.* *Law.* To take an appeal of. — *v. i.* **1.** *Law.* To make or take an appeal. **2.** To call on another to decide a matter controverted ; to call on one for aid or sympathy; — with *to.* — *n.* **1.** *Law.* A proceeding by which a cause is brought to a superior court for reëxamination ; also, right of taking such proceeding. **2.** A call on a person, or any kind of authority, for proof or decision in one's favor ; a call for help or a favor ; entreaty.

ap-pear' (-pēr'), *v. i.* **1.** To come or be in sight; become visible. **2.** To attend before some authority or tribunal, either in person or by attorney. **3.** To come before the public. **4.** To become visible or clear to the mind; be obvious or manifest. **5.** To seem ; look.

ap-pear'ance (-ăns), *n.* **1.** Act of appearing. **2.** Semblance ; external show. **3.** Manner of appearing ; look ; aspect ; air. **4.** A thing seen; phenomenon ; apparition.

ap-peas'a-ble (*ā-pēz'ā-b'l*), *a.* Capable of being appeased.

ap-pease' (-pēz'), *v. t.* [1] To make quiet; pacify.

ap-pel'lant (*ā-pĕl'ănt*), *a.* Appealing. — *n.* One who appeals.

ap-pel'late (-āt), *a.* Pertaining to, or taking cognizance of, appeals ; as, an *appellate* court.

ap'pel-la'tion (*ăp'ĕ-lā'shŭn*), *n.* **1.** Act of calling by a name. **2.** An appellative.

ap'pel'la-tive (*ā-pĕl'ā-tĭv*), *n.* **1.** A common name or noun. **2.** The word by which a person or thing is called; appellation; descriptive name. — *a.* **1.** Of or pertaining to a common name ; denominative. **2.** *Gram.* Common, as opposed to *proper.*

ap'pel-lee' (*ăp'ĕ-lē'*), *n.* *Law.* The person against whom an appeal is taken.

ap-pend' (*ā-pĕnd'*), *v. t.* **1.** To attach, as by a string, so as to suspend. **2.** To add as accessory; annex.

ap-pend'age (-pĕn'dāj), *n.* Something appended to a principal or greater thing ; an appurtenance.

ap-pen'di-ces (*ā-pĕn'dĭ-sēz*), *n., L.pl.* of APPENDIX.

ap-pen'di-ci'tis (-sī'tĭs), *n.* Inflammation of a little tubelike part of the bowels called the *vermiform appendix.* See VERMIFORM APPENDIX.

ap-pen'dix (*ā-pĕn'dĭks*), *n.; pl.* E. -DIXES (-dĭk-sēz), L. -DICES (-dĭ'-sēz). **1.** Matter added to a book but not necessarily essential. **2.** *Anat.* An appendage ; esp., the vermiform appendix.

ap'per-tain' (*ăp'ēr-tān'*), *v. i.* To belong or pertain by right, nature, appointment, or custom; relate.

ap'pe-tite (*ăp'ē-tīt*), *n.* **1.** An inherent or habitual desire or propensity for some personal gratification of body or mind; craving ; longing. **2.** Desire for, or relish of, food or drink; hunger.

ap'pe-tiz'er (-tīz'ēr), *n.* That which stimulates appetite.

ap'pe-tiz'ing (-tīz'ĭng), *p.a.* [4] Exciting appetite.

ap-plaud' (*ā-plôd'*), *v. i.* To express approbation loudly, emphatically, or significantly. — *v. t.* **1.** To show approval of by clapping the hands, acclamation, etc. **2.** To praise; approve; extol; magnify.

ap-plause' (-plôz'), *n.* Act of applauding ; public approbation; acclaim ; commendation.

---

ap′ple (ăp′'l`, *n.* **1.** The well-known round or oblong fruit of any of certain trees related to the quince, pear, etc. **2.** A tree that bears apples.

ap-pli′ance (ă-plī′ăns), *n.* **1.** Act of applying. **2.** Thing applied; device.

ap′pli-ca-bil′i-ty (ăp′lĭ-kȧ-bĭl′ĭ-tĭ), *n.* The quality of being applicable; pertinence.

ap′pli-ca-ble (ăp′lĭ-kȧ-b'l), *a.* [4] Capable of being applied; fit, suitable, or right to be applied.

ap′pli-cant (-kănt), *n.* One who applies for something.

ap′pli-ca′tion (-kā′shŭn), *n.* **1.** Act of applying. **2.** A thing applied; a means. **3.** Capacity or fact of being practically applied or used; relevancy.

ap-plied′ (ă-plīd′), *p. a.* Put to use; — said of various sciences, and distinguished from *pure*.

ap-ply′ (ă-plī′), *v. t.* [2] **1.** To put on or close to; adjust (one thing *to* another). **2.** To use for a particular purpose; devote (*to*). **3.** To make use of as fitting to some person or thing; as, to *apply* an epithet to a person. **4.** To fix closely; employ diligently; as, to *apply* one's mind to a problem. — *v. i.* **1.** To have connection (*with*) or relevancy (*to*). **2.** To make request; go (*to*) with a view to gain something; as, to *apply* for money.

ap-point′ (ă-point′), *v. t.* **1.** To fix firmly; establish. **2.** To fix by a decree, order, or mutual agreement; ordain. **3.** To assign, designate, or set apart, by authority. **4.** To furnish in all points. — *v. i.* To ordain; determine.

ap-point′ee′ (ă-point′tē′), *n.* A person appointed.

ap-poin′tive (ă-poin′tĭv), *a.* That is filled by appointment; as, an *appointive* position.

ap-point′ment (ă-point′mĕnt), *n.* **1.** Act of appointing; as : **a** An engagement for a meeting. **b** Designation of a person to hold an office, etc. **2. a** Agreement; compact. **b** An office, station, or position; an assigned duty or service. **c** Equipment; furniture; outfit; — usually in *pl.*

ap-por′tion (ă-pōr′shŭn), *v. t.* To assign in just proportion; portion out; allot.

ap-por′tion-ment (-mĕnt), *n.* Act of apportioning; that which is apportioned.

ap′po-site (ăp′ō-zĭt), *a.* [4] Very applicable; well adapted. — **-ly**, *adv.* [8] — **-ness**, *n.* [8].

ap′po-si′tion (ăp′ō-zĭsh′ŭn), *n.* **1.** Fact or condition of being placed near or beside. **2.** *Gram.* The setting of a word or phrase beside another, that is, in a parallel construction, without a connective, as in "John, the apostle."

ap-prais′al (ă-prāz′ăl), *n.* Act of appraising; also, the value fixed in appraising.

ap-praise′ (ă-prāz′), *v. t.* [1] **1.** To set a value on; estimate the worth of, esp. officially. **2.** To estimate; conjecture. — **ap-prais′er** (-ẽr), *n.* [8].

ap-pre′ci-a-ble (ă-prē′shĭ-ȧ-b'l), *a.* [4] Capable of being appreciated; perceptible. — **-bly**, *adv.* [8].

ap-pre′ci-ate (-āt), *v. t.* [1] **1.** To value; estimate justly; recognize or feel the worth of; esteem duly. **2.** To raise the value of. **3.** To be sensible of; distinguish. — *v. i.* To rise in value.

ap-pre′ci-a′tion (-ā′shŭn), *n.* Act of appreciating; as: **a** A valuation; estimate; esp., due recognition of worth. **b** A rise in value.

ap-pre′ci-a-tive (ă-prē′shĭ-ȧ-tĭv), *a.* [4] Having or showing appreciation.

ap′pre-hend′ (ăp′rē-hĕnd′), *v. t.* **1.** To arrest. **2.** To become conscious or sensible of as existing; to anticipate, esp. with fear. **3.** To lay hold of with the understanding; interpret the meaning of. — *v. i.* **1.** To think, believe, or be of opinion; understand; suppose. **2.** To be apprehensive; fear.

ap′pre-hen′si-ble (-hĕn′sĭ-b'l), *a.* [4] That may be apprehended or conceived.

ap′pre-hen′sion (-hĕn′shŭn), *n.* **1.** Act of apprehending. **2.** Opinion; conception. **3.** The faculty by which ideas are conceived; understanding.

ap′pre-hen′sive (ăp′rē-hĕn′sĭv), *a.* [4] **1.** Capable of apprehending, or quick to apprehend; apt; discerning. **2.** Anticipative; fearful. — **ap′pre-hen′sive-ly**, *adv.* [8] — **-hen′sive-ness**, *n.* [8].

ap-pren′tice (ă-prĕn′tĭs), *n.* One bound to serve another for a certain time in consideration of instruction in an art or trade, and formerly, usually, of maintenance. — *v. t.* [1] To bind or indenture as an apprentice.

ap-pren′tice-ship, *n.* Service or state of an apprentice; time during which an apprentice serves.

ap-prise′ (ă-prīz′), *v. t.* [1] To give notice; inform; acquaint; advise.

ap-prize′, *v. t.* [1] **1.** To appraise. **2.** To apprise.

ap-proach′ (ă-prōch′), *v. i. & t.* To come or go near; draw nigh; approximate; also, to make advances to. — *n.* **1.** Act of approaching. **2.** *pl.* Maneuvers toward securing personal relations; advances. **3.** A way by which a place can be approached; access. — **ap-proach′a-ble**, *a.* [8].

ap′pro-ba′tion (ăp′rō-bā′shŭn), *n.* Act of approving; approval; commendation.

ap-pro′pri-ate (ă-prō′prĭ-ăt), *a.* [4] Belonging peculiarly; suitable; fit; proper. — (-āt), *v. t.* [1] **1.** To take to one's self or to claim in exclusion of others. **2.** To assign to a specific person or use. — **-ly**, *adv.* [8] — **-ness**, *n.* [8].

ap-pro′pri-a′tion (-ā′shŭn), *n.* **1.** Act of appropriating. **2.** That which is appropriated; esp., money set apart by formal action to a specific use.

ap-prov′al (-prōōv′ăl), *n.* Act of approving; approbation; sanction.

ap-prove′ (ă-prōōv′), *v. t.* [1] **1.** To make proof of; demonstrate. **2.** To sanction officially; ratify; confirm. **3.** To regard as good; commend. — *v. i.* To pass or judge favorably.

ap-prox′i-mate (ă-prŏk′sĭ-măt), *a.* **1.** Approaching; proximate; resembling nearly. **2.** Near to correctness; nearly exact. — (-māt), *v. t.* [1] **1.** To carry near to; cause to approach. **2.** To come near to. — *v. i.* To approach. — **-ly**, *adv.* [8].

ap-prox′i-ma′tion (-mā′shŭn), *n.* **1.** Act or result of approximating. **2.** An approach to a correct estimate, or conception, etc.

ap-pur′te-nance (ă-pûr′tē-năns), *n.* That which appertains to something; adjunct; something incident to a principal or more important thing.

ap-pur′te-nant (-nănt), *a.* Accessory; incident.

a′pri-cot (ā′prĭ-kŏt; ăp′rĭ-), *n.* The oval, orange-colored fruit of a certain tree of the plum family; also, the tree.

A′pril (ā′prĭl), *n.* The fourth month of the year.

a′pron (ā′prŭn), *n.* **1.** An article of dress worn on the fore part of the body as a covering or to protect the clothes. **2.** Something like an apron.

ap'ro-pos' (ăp'rô-pō'), *adv. & a.* [4] **1.** Opportunely; opportune; seasonable. **2.** To the purpose; suitably.

apse (ăps), *n.; pl.* APSES (ăp'sĕz). *Arch.* A projecting part of a building, esp. of a church, usually semicircular in plan.

apt (ăpt), *a.* [3] **1.** Fit or suited; suitable; appropriate. **2.** Having a habitual tendency. **3.** Ready; quick to learn; expert.

apt'i-tude (ăp'tĭ-tūd), *n.* **1.** Natural or acquired capacity for a particular purpose, or tendency to a particular action or effect. **2.** General fitness; adaptation. **3.** Readiness in learning; aptness.

apt'ly (ăpt'lĭ), *adv.* In an apt manner.

apt'ness, *n.* Quality or state of being apt.

a'qua-ma-rine' (ä'kwȧ-mȧ-rēn'), *n.* A transparent stone, commonly bluish green, used as a gem.

a-qua'ri-um (ȧ-kwā'rĭ-ŭm), *n.; pl.* E. -RIUMS (-ŭmz), L. -RIA (-ȧ). **1.** An artificial pond, or a vessel of water, in which living aquatic animals or plants are kept. **2.** A place for the care and exhibition of such aquatic collections.

a-quat'ic (ȧ-kwăt'ĭk), *a.* Of or pertaining to water; growing in or frequenting water. — *n.* **1.** An aquatic animal or plant. **2.** *pl.* Sports or exercises practiced in or on the water.

aq'ue-duct (ăk'wē-dŭkt), *n.* **1.** Any conduit for water, esp. a large one. **2.** A structure for conveying a canal over a river or hollow.

a'que-ous (ā'kwē-ŭs), *a.* [4] **1.** Of, or of the nature of, water, or abounding with it; watery. **2.** Produced by water.

aq'ui-line (ăk'wĭ-lĭn;-lĭn), *a.* [4] Curving; prominent, like the beak of an eagle; — esp. of the nose.

ar'a-besque' (ăr'ȧ-bĕsk'), *n.* A kind of ornamentation consisting of a fantastic pattern of plants or fruits, foliage, etc., and usually in combination with a geometric design.

ar'a-ble (ăr'ȧ-b'l), *a.* [4] Fit for, or cultivated by, plowing or tillage.

ar'bi-ter (ăr'bĭ-tẽr), *n.* **1.** A person having power to decide a dispute; arbitrator. **2.** Any person having absolute power of judging and determining.

ar-bit'ra-ment (är-bĭt'rȧ-mĕnt), *n.* Act of deciding as an arbiter; an arbitration.

ar'bi-tra-ry (är'bĭ-trä-rĭ), *a.* [4] Exercised according to, or based on, one's own will or caprice; despotic or tyrannical; capricious; uncertain.—**ar'bi-tra-ri-ly** (-trä-rĭ-lĭ), *adv.* [8] — **-ri-ness,** *n.* [8].

ar'bi-trate (-trāt), *v. t. & i.* [1] **1.** To hear and decide, or to act, as arbitrator; hence, to decide; determine. **2.** To submit to arbitration.

ar'bi-tra'tion (-trā'shŭn), *n.* Act of arbitrating; esp., the hearing and determining of a cause in controversy by an arbitrator.

ar'bi-tra'tor (är'bĭ-trä'tẽr), *n.* **1.** A person chosen or appointed to settle a difference between parties in controversy; an arbiter. **2** One who has absolute power of deciding. = ARBITER, **2**.

ar'bor (-bẽr), *n.* [5] A kind of latticework formed of, or covered with, vines, branches of trees, or other plants, for shade; a bower.

ar'bor, *n.* *Mech.* **a** A main shaft or beam. **b** A spindle or axle.

ar-bo're-al (är-bō'rē-ăl), *a.* **1.** Of or like a tree or trees. **2.** Attached to or frequenting trees.

ar'bor vi'tæ, *or* **ar'bor-vi'tæ** (är'bŏr-vī'tē), *n.* Any of certain trees of the pine family.

ar'bu-tus (är'bū-tŭs; är-bū'tŭs), *n.* A trailing plant of the heath family; the Mayflower.

arc (ärk), *n.* **1.** *Geom.* A portion of a curved line. **2.** An object of an arclike curvature. **3.** *Elec.* A sustained luminous glow formed under certain conditions when a break is made in an electric circuit. It is used in various kinds of lights, called arc lights. — *v. i. ;* ARCKED or ARCED (ärkt); ARCK'ING or ARC'ING (är'kĭng). *Elec.* To form an electric arc.

ar-cade' (är-kād'), *n.* **1.** *Architecture.* **a** A series of arches with their columns or piers. **b** A long, arched building or gallery. **2.** An arched or covered way or avenue, as between shops.

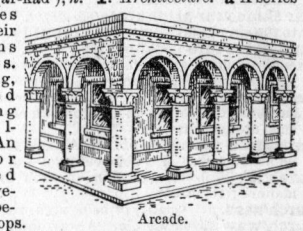

Arcade.

ar-ca'num (-kā'nŭm), *n. ; L. pl.* -CANA (-nȧ). **1.** A secret; mystery; — usually in *pl.* **2.** In alchemy, an elixir; hence, a secret remedy or nostrum.

arch (ärch), *n.* **1.** *Architecture.* A structural member, usually curved and made up of separate wedge-shaped solids with their joints at right angles to the curve. **2.** Any place covered by an arch; archway. **3.** Any curve in the form of an arch. — *v. t. & v. i.* **1.** To cover or provide with an arch or arches. **2.** To form into an arch.

arch (ärch), *a.* **1.** Chief; eminent. **2.** Cunning; sly; esp., sportively mischievous; roguish.

ar'chæ-o-log'ic (är'kē-ô-lŏj'ĭk), **-log'i-cal** (-ĭ-kăl), *a.* Relating to archæology or antiquities.

ar'chæ-ol'o-gist (-ŏl'ô-jĭst), *n.* A specialist in archæology.

ar'chæ-ol'o-gy, ar'che-ol'o-gy (är'kē-ŏl'ô-jĭ), *n.* The study of antiquities ; the study of the art, customs, etc., of ancient peoples.

ar-cha'ic (är-kā'ĭk), *a.* [4] Very old; antiquated; of language, no longer in common use.

ar'cha-ism (är'kȧ-ĭz'm), *n.* An old-fashioned word, expression, or the like, no longer in common use.

arch'an'gel (ärk'ān'jĕl), *n.* A chief angel.

arch'bish'op (ärch'bĭsh'ŭp), *n.* A chief bishop; a prelate at the head of an ecclesiastical province.

arch'bish'op-ric (-rĭk), *n.* Jurisdiction or office of an archbishop; see or province of an archbishop.

arch'dea'con (-dē'k'n), *n.* A chief deacon.

arch'du'cal (-dū'kăl), *a.* Of or pertaining to an archduke or an archduchy.

arch'duch'y (-dŭch'ĭ), *n. ; pl.* -DUCHIES (-ĭz). Territory of an archduke or archduchess.

arch'duke' (-dūk'), *n.* A prince of the imperial family of Austria.—**arch'duch'ess** (-dŭch'ĕs), *n. fem.*

arched (ärcht), *a.* Made with an arch ; curved.

arch'en'e-my (ärch'ĕn'ē-mĭ), *n.* Chief enemy.

ar'che-ol'o-gy (är'kē-ŏl'ô-jĭ), **ar'che-o-log'i-cal,** etc. Vars. of ARCHÆOLOGY, etc.

arch′er (är′chẽr), *n.* A bowman; one who uses the bow and arrow, esp. in war.

arch′er-y (-ĭ), *n.* **1.** Art or practice of shooting with bow and arrows. **2.** Archers collectively.

ar′che-type (är′kē-tīp), *n.* The original pattern or model of a work.

arch′fiend′ (ärch′fēnd′), *n.* The chief fiend; Satan.

ar′chi-pel′a-go (är′kĭ-pĕl′á-gō), *n.; pl.* -GOES, -GOS (-gōz). Any sea or broad sheet of water interspersed with islands.

ar′chi-tect (är′kĭ-tĕkt), *n.* A person skilled in architecture; one who plans and oversees the construction of buildings, etc.

ar′chi-tec′tur-al (är′kĭ-tĕk′tŭr-ăl), *a.* Of or pert. to the art of building. — **-tec′tur-al-ly**, *adv.* [8].

ar′chi-tec′ture (är′kĭ-tĕk′tŭr), *n.* **1.** Art or science of building, esp. for the purposes of civil life. **2.** Construction, in general; structure.

ar′chi-trave (-trāv), *n.* The lower division of an entablature, resting on the column, esp. in classical architecture.

ar′chives (-kīvz), *n. pl.* **1.** A place for keeping public records. **2.** Public records; — also in *sing.*

arch′ly (ärch′lĭ), *adv.* In an arch or roguish manner; roguishly.

arch′ness, *n.* Quality of being arch; roguishness.

arch′way′ (ärch′wā′), *n.* A way under an arch.

arc′tic (ärk′tĭk), *a.* Pertaining to, or characteristic of, the north polar regions; frigid. — *n.* A kind of waterproof overshoe. *U. S.* — **arctic circle,** a circle or parallel of latitude 23° 28′ from the north pole.

ar′den-cy (är′dĕn-sĭ), *n.* Ardent quality or state.

ar′dent (-dĕnt), *a.* [4] **1.** Hot or burning; fiery; glowing. **2.** Passionate; fervent. — **-ly,** *adv.* [8].

ar′dor (-dẽr), *n.* [5] **1.** Burning heat; fire; flame. **2.** Warmth or heat of passion or affection; zeal.

ar′du-ous (-dū-ŭs), *a.* [4] **1.** Steep and lofty; hard to climb. **2.** Laborious; difficult. — **ar′du-ous-ly,** *adv.* [8] — **ar′du-ous-ness,** *n.* [8].

are (âr), *n. Metric System.* The area of a square of which each side is ten meters in length (about 119.6 square yards, or .025 acre).

are (är), *n.* The pres. indicative pl. of the verb *to be.*

a′re-a (ā′rē-á), *n.* **1.** Any plane surface. **2.** The sunken space or court affording access and light to a basement. **3.** A particular extent of surface; region. **4.** *Geom.* The amount of surface included within the lines of a figure.

a-re′na (á-rē′ná), *n.; pl.* Ē. -NAS (-náz), L. -NÆ (-nē). **1.** *Roman Antiq.* The area, usually sanded, for the spectacles in an amphitheater. **2.** Place of public contest; sphere of action.

ar′gent (är′jĕnt), *n.* **1.** Silver, or money. *Archaic.* **2.** *Fig. & Poet.* Whiteness; anything white. — *a.* Silver; silvery; white.

ar′gon (-gŏn), *n. Chem.* A colorless, odorless gas occurring in small amount in the air.

ar′go-sy (är′gō-sĭ), *n.; pl.* -SIES (-sĭz). A large ship; esp., a merchant vessel of the largest size.

ar′gue (-gū), *v. i.* [1] **1.** To offer reasons for or against something; reason. **2.** To contend in argument; dispute. — *v. t.* **1.** To debate; discuss; as, to *argue* a case. **2.** To manifest by reasoning; prove. **3.** To persuade by reasons.

ar′gu-ment (-gū-mĕnt), *n.* **1.** A reason or reasons offered for or against something; reasoning. **2.** Dis-

cussion; debate. **3.** An abstract or summary of the subject matter of a book, poem, etc.

ar′gu-men-ta′tion (-mĕn-tä′shŭn), *n.* **1.** Argument. **2.** Debate; discussion.

ar′gu-men′ta-tive (-mĕn′tá-tĭv), *a.* [4] Pertaining or given to argument.

a′ri-a (ä′rĭ-á; ä′rĭ-á), *n. Music.* A melody; esp., an elaborate solo sung in opera.

ar′id (är′ĭd), *a.* [3] Dry; barren.

a-rid′i-ty (á-rĭd′ĭ-tĭ), *n.* Arid state or quality.

a-right′ (á-rīt′), *adv.* Rightly; correctly.

a-rise′ (-rīz′), *v. i.; pret.* A-ROSE′(-rōz′); *p.p.* A-RIS′EN (-rĭz′'n). **1.** To ascend; rise. **2.** To come into action, being, or notice; become operative, sensible, or visible. **3.** To proceed; issue.

ar′is-toc′ra-cy (är′ĭs-tŏk′rá-sĭ), *n.; pl.* -CIES (-sĭz). **1.** Rule by the best; hence, government by a relatively small, privileged class. Also, a state thus governed, or the governing body. **2.** The nobles or chief persons in a state; a privileged class; popularly, those regarded as superior to the rest of the community, as in rank, fortune, or intellect.

a-ris′to-crat (á-rĭs′tō-krăt), *n.* A member of an aristocracy; a person of high birth; patrician.

ar′is-to-crat′ic (är′ĭs-tō-krăt′ĭk; á-rĭs′-), *a.* [4] Of or pert. to an aristocracy; characteristic of an aristocracy or of aristocrats.—**crat′i-cal-ly,** *adv.* [8].

a-rith′me-tic (á-rĭth′mē-tĭk), *n.* Science of numbers; art of computation by figures.

ar′ith-met′i-cal (är′ĭth-mĕt′ĭ-kăl), *a.* Of or pertaining to arithmetic. — **-cal-ly,** *adv.* [8].

a-rith′me-ti′cian (á-rĭth′mē-tĭsh′ăn; är′ĭth-), *n.* One skilled in arithmetic.

ark (ärk), *n.* **1.** A chest or coffer. **2.** The vessel in which Noah and his family were preserved during the Deluge; hence, any place of refuge.

arm (ärm), *n. Mil.* A branch of the military service, as the infantry. **b** A weapon. Cf. ARMS.

arm (ärm), *v. t.* **1.** To furnish with weapons. **2.** To cover with a strengthening or protective covering. — *v. i.* To provide one's self with arms.

arm, *n.* **1.** A human upper limb, esp. the part between shoulder and wrist. **2.** Something suggestive of an arm; a projecting part.

ar-ma′da (är-mä′dá), *n.* A fleet of armed ships.

ar′ma-dil′lo (är′má-dĭl′ō), *n.; pl.* -LOS (-ōz). A small burrowing animal of South and tropical America, having the body and head incased in an armor of small bony plates.

Armadillo.

ar′ma-ment (är′má-mĕnt), *n.* **1.** A body of forces equipped for war. **2.** All the guns, torpedoes, small arms, etc., of a ship, a fortification, etc.

ar′ma-ture (-tŭr), *n.* **1.** Armor to protect the body, as in battle. Hence, a covering suggestive of such armor. **2.** *Magnetism.* A piece of soft iron or steel used to connect the poles of a magnet or magnets. **3.** *Elec.* That part of a dynamo-electric machine carrying the conductors.

arm′chair′ (ärm′châr′), *n.* A chair with arms.

arm′ful (ärm′fŏŏl), *n.; pl.* -FULS. As much as the arm, or both arms, can hold.

āle, senăte, câre, ăm, *ă*ccount, ärm, ȧsk, sofȧ; ēve, ĕvent, ĕnd, recĕnt, makēr; īce, ĭll; ōld, ōbey, ôrb, ŏdd, sŏft, cŏnnect; ūse, ŭnite, ûrn, ŭp, circŭs; fōōd, fŏŏt; out, oil;

arm′hole (ärm′hōl′), n. **1.** The armpit. **2.** A hole for the arm in a garment.

ar′mi-stice (är′mĭ-stĭs), n. A brief suspension of hostilities by agreement; a truce.

Armistice Day. The 11th of November, on which day, in 1918, an armistice was declared in the World War.

arm′let (ärm′lĕt), n. A bracelet for the upper arm.

ar′mor (är′mẽr), n. [5] **1.** A defensive clothing or covering worn to protect one's person in battle. **2.** Steel or iron plating on ships or forts. **3.** Any similar protective covering, as a diver's suit. — v. t. To equip with armor.

ar′mor-er (-ẽr), n. **1.** One who makes or repairs armor or arms. **2.** One in charge of arms and armor.

ar-mo′ri-al (är-mō′rĭ-ăl), a. Pertaining to armor or to (heraldic) arms.

ar′mor-y (är′mẽr-ĭ), n.; pl. -IES (-ĭz). **1.** A place where arms are deposited; esp., U. S., a large building including also a drill hall. **2.** A factory where rifles, pistols, etc., are made. U. S.

Plate Armor. a Helmet; b Throat piece; c Shoulder piece; d Armpit plate; e Breastplate; f Arm piece; g Elbow piece; h Skirt; i Thigh plate; k Gauntlet; l Thigh piece; m Knee piece; n. Shin piece; o Shoe.

arm′pit (ärm′pĭt), n. The hollow, or pit, beneath the arm, at the shoulder.

arms (ärmz), n. pl. **1.** Instruments of offense or defense. **2.** Exploits of war; military service. **3.** Any of certain devices formed of figures of animals or of other objects, combined with various colors, granted to families of rank as in England, from feudal times for use on shields, banners, documents, etc.; also, similar devices adopted by a government.

ar′my (är′mĭ), n.; pl. -MIES (-mĭz). **1.** A body, esp. an organized body, of men armed for war. In the United States Army the commissioned officers rank as follows: general, lieutenant general, major general, brigadier general, colonel, lieutenant colonel, major, captain, first lieutenant, and second lieutenant; the noncommissioned officers: sergeant, and corporal. **2.** A large body of persons organized to advance a cause. **3.** A great number.

ar′ni-ca (-nĭ-kȧ), n. An herb of the aster family, or a medicinal preparation from its roots.

a-ro′ma (ȧ-rō′mȧ), n. The distinctive fragrance of a substance; agreeable odor.

ar′o-mat′ic (ăr′ō-măt′ĭk), a. [4] Pertaining to aroma; fragrant. — n. An aromatic plant or drug.

a-rose′ (ȧ-rōz′), pret. of ARISE.

a-round′ (ȧ-round′), adv. **1.** Circularly; on every side; round. **2.** In a circuit; all about. **3.** Near; in the neighborhood. Colloq., U. S. — prep. **1.** Encircling; about; so as to make the circuit of. **2.** From one part to another of; at random through; about. Colloq., U. S.

a-rouse′ (-rouz′), v. t. & i. [1] To excite to action from a state of rest; stir; rouse.

‖ **ar-peg′gio** (är-pĕd′jō), n. [It.] Music. The production of the tones of a chord in rapid succession, as in playing the harp; a chord thus played.

ar-raign′ (ă-rān′), v. t. **1.** Law. To call (a prisoner) to the bar of a court to answer to a charge. **2.** To call to account, or accuse, before any tribunal.

ar-raign′ment (ă-rān′mĕnt), n. An arraigning, or state of being arraigned.

ar-range′ (-rānj′), v. t. [1] **1.** To put in proper order; dispose in the manner intended, or best suited for the purpose. **2.** To adjust; settle; prepare.

ar-range′ment (-mĕnt), n. **1.** Act of arranging, or the way in which things are arranged; disposition. **2.** Preparatory proceeding; preparation.

ar′rant (ăr′ănt), a. [4] Originally, wandering; vagrant; hence, notoriously bad; as, an arrant thief.

ar′ras (-ăs), n. Tapestry; a screen or hangings of tapestry.

ar-ray′ (ă-rā′), v. t. **1.** To dispose in order, as troops; marshal; draw up. **2.** To deck; dress. — n. **1.** Order; a regular and imposing arrangement; hence, order of battle. **2.** The body of persons placed in order; hence, a body of soldiers. **3.** An imposing series of things. **4.** Dress; rich or beautiful apparel.

ar-rear′ (ă-rēr′), n. That which is unpaid but due; — usually in pl.

ar-rear′age (-āj), n. **1.** State of being in arrear or behindhand. **2.** Arrears.

ar-rest′ (-rĕst′), v. t. **1.** To stop; check; as, to arrest decay; arrest the current of a river. **2.** To take or keep in custody by authority of law. **3.** To hold; catch; seize on and fix the attention of; as, the display arrested his attention. — n. Act of arresting. — **ar-rest′er**, n. [8].

ar-riv′al (ă-rīv′ăl), n. **1.** Act of arriving. **2.** The person or thing arriving or that has arrived.

ar-rive′ (-rīv′), v. i. [1] **1.** To come to the end of a journey; reach a destination; come upon the scene. **2.** To gain or compass an object or attain a state by effort, study, etc.; — with at. **3.** To come; — said of time.

ar′ro-gance (ăr′ō găns), n. Act or habit of arrogating; quality of being arrogant.

ar′ro-gan-cy (-găn-sĭ), n. Arrogance.

ar′ro-gant (-gănt), a. [4] **1.** Making, or disposed to make, exorbitant claims of rank, estimation, or importance; assuming; haughty. **2.** Containing, or marked with, arrogance. — -ly, adv. [8].

ar′ro-gate (-gāt), v. t. [1] To assume or claim unduly, proudly, or presumptuously.

ar′ro-ga′tion (-gā′shŭn), n. An arrogating.

ar′row (ăr′ō), n. The missile used with a bow, a long, slender shaft with pointed head.

ar′row-root′ (-rōōt′), n. A West Indian plant having tuberous roots; starch made from them.

ar′row-y (-ĭ), a. Resembling or suggestive of an arrow; swift; darting.

ar′se-nal (är′sĕ-năl), n. A public establishment for storing or making arms and military equipments.

ar′se-nic (-nĭk), n. **1.** One of the elements, a solid, brittle, poisonous substance of grayish color and metallic luster. **2.** An oxide of arsenic, a violent poison, — called also white arsenic.

ar′son (är′sŭn), *n.* The malicious burning of a building or other structure, esp. the burning of a dwelling house or outhouse of another.

art (ärt), *n.* **1.** Skill in performance; knack. **2.** Human contrivance or ingenuity, as in adapting natural things to man's use. **3.** A branch of learning; a science; specifically: *pl.* Those branches of learning taught in the academical course of colleges. **4.** The principles or rules of any branch of learning or of any craft. **5.** Systematic application of knowledge or skill in effecting a desired result. Also, an occupation requiring such knowledge or skill; a craft. **6.** Application of skill and taste to production according to æsthetic principles; such application to the production of beauty by imitation or design, as in painting and sculpture. **7.** Skillful plan; device; also, cunning; artifice.

art. *v.* 2d pers. indicative sing. of the verb BE.

ar-te′ri-al (är-tē′rĭ-ăl), *a.* Of or pertaining to an artery or arteries.

ar′ter-y (är′tēr-ĭ), *n.; pl.* -TERIES (-ĭz). *Anat.* One of the tubular branching vessels which distribute the blood from the heart through the body.

artesian well (är-tē′zhăn). **a** A well made by boring till water is reached which, from internal pressure, flows without pumping. **b** Loosely, any deep, bored well. *U. S.*

art′ful (ärt′fŏŏl), *a.* [4] **1.** Using or showing much art; dexterous. **2.** Cunning; crafty. — **-ly,** *adv.*

ar′ti-choke (är′tĭ-chōk), *n.* **1.** A certain tall plant of the aster family; also, its flower head, eaten as a vegetable. **2.** The Jerusalem artichoke, a species of sunflower, or its tuber, often eaten like potatoes.

ar′ti-cle (-k′l), *n.* **1.** A clause in a contract, treaty, or the like. **2.** A literary composition forming an independent part of a periodical, cyclopedia, etc. **3.** Something considered by itself; also, a thing of a particular class or kind; as, an *article* of diet. **4.** *Eng. Gram.* Any of the words, *a*, *an*, *the*, used before nouns to define or limit their application. — *v. t.* [1] To bind by articles of agreement.

ar-tic′u-lar (är-tĭk′ū-lår), *a.* Of or pertaining to a joint or joints; as, an *articular* disease.

ar-tic′u-late (-lăt), *a.* [4] **1.** Jointed; formed with joints. **2.** Characterized by division into words and syllables; spoken intelligibly. **3.** Expressed or formulated clearly and logically. — (-lāt), *v. i. & t.* [1] **1.** To join by articulation. **2.** To utter, or utter in, articulate sounds. — **-ly,** *adv.* [8].

ar-tic′u-la′tion (-lā′shŭn), *n.* **1.** A joint or juncture between the bones of an animal. **2.** *Bot.* A node or thickened portion of a stem, or the interval between two such portions. **3.** Any meeting of parts in a joint. **4.** Utterance of articulate sounds, as in pronunciation. **5.** An articulate utterance or an elementary sound; esp., a consonant.

ar′ti-fice (är′tĭ-fĭs), *n.* **1.** Artful or skillful contrivance; ingenuity. **2.** Crafty device; an artful, ingenious, or elaborate trick.

ar-tif′i-cer (är-tĭf′ĭ-sẽr), *n.* **1.** A skilled or artistic worker; craftsman. **2.** One who makes or contrives.

ar′ti-fi′cial (är′tĭ-fĭsh′ăl), *a.* [4] **1.** Made or contrived by art; — opposed to *natural*. **2.** Feigned; fictitious. — **ar′ti-fi′cial-ly,** *adv.* [8].

ar′ti-fi′ci-al′i-ty (-ĭ-ăl′ĭ-tĭ), *n.* Artificial state, quality, or appearance; that which is artificial.

ar-til′ler-ist (är-tĭl′ẽr-ĭst), *n.* A person skilled in artillery or gunnery; a gunner.

ar-til′ler-y (-ĭ), *n.* **1.** Mounted guns; cannon; ordnance. **2.** That branch of the army handling the artillery. **3.** The science of artillery or gunnery.

ar′ti-san (är′tĭ-zăn), *n.* One trained in some mechanic art; craftsman; mechanic.

art′ist (-tĭst), *n.* **1.** One who professes and practices one or more of the fine arts, as painting or sculpture; a painter, sculptor, or the like. **2.** One who shows trained skill or rare taste in any art or occupation, as a highly skilled cook, an expert barber, etc.

ar-tis′tic (är-tĭs′tĭk), *a.* [4] Of or pertaining to art or artists; showing taste or skill; as, an *artistic* design. — **ar-tis′ti-cal-ly,** *adv.* [8].

ar′ti-zan. Var. of ARTISAN.

art′less (ärt′lĕs), *a.* [4] **1.** Without art or skill; uncultured; rude. **2.** Free from art, guile, or craft; frank; open; honest. — **art′less-ly,** *adv.* [8] — **art′less-ness,** *n.* [8].

as (ăz), *adv., conj., & rel. pron.* **1.** Like; in the same way or degree; equally; no less than. **2.** In the idea, character, or condition, of. **3.** While; when. **4.** Because; since. **5.** Expressing concession; — often nearly equal. to *though.* **6.** That: **a** Expressing a result; as, "Be so good *as* to come." **b** As a relative pronoun; as, give such *as* you have. **7.** For instance; thus.

as′a-fet′i-da } (ăs′å-fĕt′ĭ-då), *n.* The fetid gum
as′a-fœt′i-da } resin of various Oriental plants.

as-bes′tos } (ăs-bĕs′tŏs; ăz-) } *n.* A certain fibrous
as-bes′tus } (ăs-bĕs′tŭs; ăz-) } mineral used in fireproof clothing, curtains, roofing, etc.

as-cend′ (ă-sĕnd′), *v. i. & t.* To move upward; mount; rise.

as-cend′ance (ă-sĕn′dăns) } *n.* Act of ascending;
as-cend′ence (ă-sĕn′dĕns) } also, ascendancy.

as-cend′an-cy (-dăn-sĭ) } *n.* Controlling influence;
as-cend′en-cy (-dĕn-sĭ) } domination; power.

as-cend′ant (-dănt) } *n.* Ascendancy. — *a.* **1.** Ris-
as-cend′ent (-dĕnt) } ing toward the zenith; hence, rising; ascending. **2.** Superior; dominant.

as-cen′sion (ă-sĕn′shŭn), *n.* Act of ascending; ascent.

as-cent′ (ă-sĕnt′), *n.* **1.** Act of rising; rise. **2.** Way or means by which one ascends. **3.** An eminence; hill; upward slope.

as′cer-tain′ (ăs′ẽr-tān′), *v. t.* To learn for a certainty, by trial, examination, or experiment; get to know. — **as′cer-tain′a-ble,** *a.* [8].

as′cer-tain′ment (-mĕnt), *n.* Act of ascertaining.

as-cet′ic (ă-sĕt′ĭk), *a.* [4] Of or pertaining to ascetics or their practices; austere. — *n.* One who practices extreme rigor and self-denial, as by seclusion. — **as-cet′i-cal-ly,** *adv.* [8].

as-cet′i-cism (-ĭ-sĭz′m), *n.* **1.** Condition, practice, or mode of life, of ascetics. **2.** Doctrine that the carnal or material world is evil, and that salvation is gained by mortification of the flesh.

as-cribe′ (ăs-krīb′), *v. t.* [1] **1.** To attribute, refer, or assign, as to a cause or source. **2.** To attribute, as a quality; consider or allege to belong. — **as-crib′a-ble** (-å-b′l), *a.* [8].

āle, senāte, câre, ăm, ăccount, ärm, àsk, sofà; ēve, ĕvent, ĕnd, recĕnt, makẽr; īce, ĭll; ōld, ŏbey, ôrb, ŏdd, sŏft, cŏnnect; ūse, ûnite, ûrn, ŭp, circŭs; fŏŏd, fŏŏt; out. oil;

as-crip'tion (ăs-krĭp'shŭn), n. Act of ascribing; also, that which is ascribed.

a-sea' (á-sē'), adv. On or toward the sea; at sea.

a-sep'tic (á-sĕp'tĭk), a. Free from harmful organisms, as germs or bacteria; — said of wounds, surgical instruments, etc. — n. An antiseptic substance or preparation.

ash (ăsh), n. A common timber and shade tree of the olive family, or its wood.

ash. n., sing. of ASHES.

☞ *Ash* is rare in the singular except in naming a chemical or geological product, or as a qualifying or combining word.

a-shamed' (á-shāmd'), p. a. [4] Affected by shame.

ash'en (ăsh'ĕn), a. Of or pertaining to the ash tree or its wood.

ash'en, a. [4] Consisting of or resembling ashes; ash-colored; gray; pale.

Ash Leaf and Fruit.

ash'es (-ĕz), n. pl. **1.** The earthy or mineral parts of anything that will burn, left after the thing itself is burned. **2.** The remains of the human body when burned, or when "returned to dust" by natural decay. **3.** Fine lava thrown out in a volcanic eruption.

ash'lar (-lẽr), n. Hewn or squared stone.

a-shore' (á-shōr'), adv. To, or toward, the shore; on the shore.

ash'y (ăsh'ĭ), a. [3] **1.** Of, pertaining to, or filled with, ashes. **2.** Ash-colored; ashen.

A'si-at'ic (ā'shĭ-ăt'ĭk; ā'zhĭ-), a. Of, pertaining to, or characteristic of, Asia or its inhabitants. — n. A native of Asia.

a-side' (á-sīd'), adv. **1.** On or to one side; out of the way; apart. **2.** So as not to be heard by others; privately. — n. Something spoken aside, as an actor's remark which the other players are supposed not to hear.

as'i-nine (ăs'ĭ-nīn), a. [4] Pertaining to the ass; hence, stupid; obstinate; — because the ass is commonly thought to be so.

as'i-nin'i-ty (-nĭn'ĭ-tĭ), n. Asinine quality.

ask (ȧsk), v. t. **1.** To inquire of; question; as, *ask* him the way. **2.** To request; solicit; as, he *asked* for a drink. **3.** To demand, claim, or expect; as, he *asks* a high price. **4.** To invite; as, *ask* her to come. — v. i. **1.** To request; petition. **2.** To make inquiry; as, to *ask* after one's health.

a-skance' (á-skăns') } adv. Sideways; obliquely;
a-skant' (á-skănt') } hence, with disdain, envy, or suspicion; as, to eye one *askance.*

a-skew' (á-skū'), adv. & a. Awry.

a-slant' (á-slȧnt'), adv. & a. Slanting; obliquely. — prep. In a slanting direction over; athwart.

a-sleep' (á-slēp'), a. & adv. **1.** In or into a state of sleep or inactivity; dormant. **2.** Dead. **3.** Numbed.

a-slope' (á-slōp'), adv. & a. Slopingly; aslant.

asp (ăsp), n. A small venomous snake of Egypt.

as-par'a-gus (ăs-păr'á-gŭs), n. **1.** Any of a large genus of perennial plants. **2.** The tender shoots of one species, used as food.

as'pect (ăs'pĕkt), n. **1.** *Astrol.* The situation of planets or stars with respect to one another. **2.** Position facing a particular direction, or the part so facing. **3.** Look; mien; air; appearance.

asp'en (ăs'pĕn), n. Any of several poplars, esp. one the leaves of which are swayed by a breath of air. — a. Like the aspen; tremulous.

as-per'i-ty (ăs-pĕr'ĭ-tĭ), n.; pl. -TIES (-tĭz). Roughness; unevenness; harshness; severity.

as-perse' (-pûrs'), v. t. [1] To slander; spread false charges against (a person or his character).

as-per'sion (-pûr'shŭn), n. **1.** Act of aspersing, or slandering; calumny. **2.** A slanderous report.

as'phalt (ăs'fȧlt), n. **1.** A brown to black bitumen found in natural beds; mineral pitch. **2.** An asphaltic composition used in paving, etc. — (ăs'-fȧlt; ăs-fȧlt'), v. t. To cover with asphalt.

as-phal'tic (ăs-făl'tĭk), a. Pertaining to, of the nature of, or containing, asphalt.

as-phal'tum (ăs-făl'tŭm), n. Var. of ASPHALT.

as'pho-del (ăs'fō-dĕl), n. Any of several plants of the lily family; also, in poetry, a narcissus.

as-phyx'i-a (ăs-fĭk'sĭ-á), n. Suspended animation due to lack of oxygen and excess of carbon dioxide in the blood.

as-phyx'i-ate (-āt), v. t. [1] To bring to a state of asphyxia; suffocate.

as-phyx'i-a'tion (-ā'shŭn), n. Action of producing asphyxia; condition of being asphyxiated.

as-pir'ant (ăs-pīr'ănt), a. Aspiring. — n. One who aspires.

as'pi-rate (ăs'pĭ-rāt), v. t. [1] To utter with a breathing, or aspirate. — (-răt), n. **1.** The sound of *h*; the letter *h.* **2.** A sound followed by, or combined with, an *h* sound.

as'pi-rate (ăs'pĭ-rāt) } a. Pronounced with, or ac-
as'pi-rat'ed (-rāt'ĕd) } companied by, an *h* sound.

as'pi-ra'tion (-rā'shŭn), n. **1.** Act of breathing; a breath. **2.** Act of aspiring; a desiring ardently. **3.** Pronunciation of an aspirate; also, the aspirate.

as-pire' (ăs-pīr'), v. i. [1] **1.** To desire with eagerness; seek; long. **2.** To rise; tower; soar.

a-squint' (á-skwĭnt'), adv. & a. With the eye askance, or directed to one side.

ass (ăs), n. **1.** Any of several quadrupeds of the horse kind, smaller than the horse, and having longer ears, a shorter mane, and shorter hair on the tail. **2.** A dull, stupid fellow; a dolt.

as-sail' (ă-sāl'), v. t. To attack violently; assault.

as-sail'ant (-ănt), a. Assailing. — n. One that assails.

as-sas'sin (ă-săs'ĭn), n. One who kills by surprise or secret assault.

as-sas'si-nate (-I-nāt), v. t. [1] To kill by surprise or secret assault.

as-sas'si-na'tion (-nā'shŭn), n. Act of assassinating; a killing by treacherous violence.

as-sault' (-sôlt'), n. A violent onset or attack; onslaught. — v. t. To make an assault on; attack.

as-say' (ă-sā'), n. Analysis, as of an ore, to determine the amount of one or more components.

as-say' (ă-sā'), v. t. & i. To subject to assay or analysis. — **as-say'er** (-ēr), n. [8].

as-sem′blage (ă-sĕm′blăj), *n.* **1.** Act of assembling ; state of being assembled. **2.** A collection of individuals, or of particular things. **3.** The fitting together of parts, as of machinery.

as-sem′ble (-b'l), *v. t.* [1] **1.** To collect into one place or body ; convene ; congregate. **2.** To fit together the parts of, as a machine. — *v. i.* To meet together ; convene ; congregate.

as-sem′bly (-blĭ), *n. ; pl.* -BLIES (-blĭz). **1.** A gathering of persons, esp. for deliberation and legislation, for worship, or for entertainment. **2.** Act of assembling ; state of being assembled. **3.** A signal, as by drum, for troops to assemble.

as-sem′bly-man (-măn), *n. ; pl.* -MEN (-mĕn). A member of an assembly.

as-sent′ (ă-sĕnt′), *v. i.* To admit a thing as true ; express agreement ; acquiesce ; concur. — *n.* Act of assenting ; consent ; acquiescence.

as-sert′ (ă-sûrt′), *v. t.* **1.** To maintain or defend, as a cause or a claim ; vindicate or insist upon a claim or title to. **2.** ~~To~~ affirm ; state positively. — **as-sert′er, as-ser′tor** (ă-sûr′tẽr), *n.* [8].

as-ser′tion (ă-sûr′shŭn),*n.* Act of asserting ; thing asserted.

as-ser′tive (-tĭv), *a.* [4] Positive ; dogmatic.

as-sess′ (-sĕs′), *v. t.* **1.** To fix the rate or amount of. **2.** To apportion (a sum to be paid) in the nature of a tax, fine, etc. ; impose according to an apportionment. **3.** To tax. **4.** To value, esp. for taxation.

as-sess′ment (-mĕnt), *n.* Act of assessing ; value or amount assessed.

as-ses′sor (-ẽr), *n.* One appointed to assess property for taxation.

as′set (ăs′ĕt), *n.* Any article or part of one's assets.

as′sets (-ĕts), *n. pl.* The entire property of a person, corporation, or estate, applicable or subject to the payment of his or its debts.

as-sev′er-ate (ă-sĕv′ẽr-āt), *v. t.* [1] To affirm or aver positively or solemnly.

as-sev′er-a′tion (-ā′shŭn), *n.* Act of asseverating.

as′si-du′i-ty (ăs′ĭ-dū′ĭ-tĭ), *n. ; pl.* -TIES (-tĭz). Quality or state of being assiduous ; diligence.

as-sid′u-ous (ă-sĭd′ū-ŭs), *a.* [4] Constant in application or attention ; devoted. — **-ly,** *adv.* [8].

as-sign′ (-sīn′), *v. t.* **1.** To appoint ; allot. **2.** To specify ; designate ; point out authoritatively or exactly. **3.** *Law.* To transfer or make over (property) to another, as for the benefit of creditors. — *v. i.* To make over property to another, as for the benefit of one's creditors. — *n.* One assigned, as : **a** An agent. **b** An assignee. — **ment,** *n.*

as′sig-na′tion (ăs′ĭg-nā′shŭn), *n.* **1.** An appointment for a meeting. **2.** Assignment.

as′sign-ee′ (ăs′ĭ-nē′), *n. Law.* A person to whom an assignment is made.

as-sign′er (ă-sīn′ẽr), *n.* One who assigns.

as-sign′ment (-mĕnt), *n.* Act of assigning ; a written transfer to title or interest, esp. for the benefit of creditors ; that which is assigned.

as′sign-or′ (ăs′ĭ-nôr′), *n. Law.* An assigner.

as-sim′i-late (ă-sĭm′ĭ-lāt), *v. t.* [1] **1.** To bring to a likeness or to conformity. **2.** To absorb, or take in, and make part of itself ; as, the body *assimilates* food. — *v. i.* To be or become assimilated.

as-sim′i-la′tion (-lā′shŭn), *n.* Act or process of assimilating.

as-sim′i-la-tive (-lā-tĭv), *a.* Tending to assimilation ; characterized by assimilation.

as-sist′ (ă-sĭst′), *v. t.* To give support to ; help ; aid ; succor. — *v. i.* To lend aid ; help.

as-sist′ance (-sĭs′tăns), *n.* Help ; aid.

as-sist′ant (-tănt), *a.* That assists ; helping ; acting as a subordinate.—*n.* One that assists ; helper.

as-size′ (ă-sīz′), *n.* [*Usually in pl.*] **a** The periodical sessions of the judges of the superior courts in every county of England. **b** The time or place of holding a court of assize ; the court itself.

as-so′ci-ate (ă-sō′shĭ-āt), *v. t.* [1] **1.** To join as a friend, companion, partner or accomplice. **2.** To join ; connect ; combine. — *v. i.* To unite in company or action ; keep company ; — implying intimacy. — (-ăt), *a.* **1.** Closely joined with some other, as in interest, action, etc. **2.** Admitted to some, but not to all, rights and privileges. — (-ăt) *n.* **1.** One often in company with another ; — implying intimacy or equality ; companion. **2.** One having an interest in common with another, as a partner, an accomplice, etc. **3.** Anything closely or usually connected with another.

as-so′ci-a′tion (ă-sō′sĭ-ā′shŭn ; -shĭ-ā′shŭn), *n.* **1.** Union ; connection. **2.** Mental connection, or that which is mentally associated with a thing **3.** Union of persons in a company or society for some purpose ; a society.

as-so′ci-a-tive (ă-sō′shĭ-ă-tĭv), *a.* Tending or leading to, or characterized by, association.

as-sort′ (ă-sôrt′), *v. t.* To distribute into classes ; classify. — *v. i.* **1.** To agree ; suit ; fall into a class or place. **2.** To consort or associate (with).

as-sort′ment (-mĕnt), *n.* **1.** Act of assorting ; assorted condition. **2.** That which is formed by assorting, as a group or class.

as-suage′ (ă-swāj′), *v. t. & i.* [1] To allay ; soothe.

as-sume′ (ă-sūm′), *v. t.* [1] **1.** To take or adopt ; take to or on one's self, as without authority. **2.** To pretend to possess. **3.** To take upon one's self (to do) ; undertake. **4.** To take for granted ; suppose

as-sum′ing (ă-sūm′ĭng), *p. a.* [4] Pretentious ; presumptuous ; arrogant.

as-sump′tion (ă-sŭmp′shŭn), *n.* Act of assuming ; the thing assumed ; arrogance.

as-sur′ance (-shōōr′ăns), *n.* **1.** Act of assuring **2.** Insurance. **3.** Security ; certainty. **4.** Firmness of mind ; self-reliance. **5.** Impudence ; audacity.

as-sure′ (ă-shōōr′), *v. t.* [1] **1.** To insure. **2.** To give confidence to ; convince ; make sure, or certain. **3.** To declare solemnly (to a person).

as-sured′ (ă-shōōrd′), *p. a.* [4] Made sure ; insured ; certain. — *n.* A person whose life or property is insured. — **-ed-ly** (-shōōr′ĕd-lĭ), *adv.* [8].

as′ter (ăs′tẽr), *n.* Any of various garden plants, related to the thistle.

as′ter-isk (-ĭsk), *n.* A figure of a star [*], used in printing and writing as a reference mark.

a-stern′ (ă-stûrn′), *adv.* **1.** Backward ; to the rear. **2.** Behind a vessel ; in the rear.

as′ter-oid (ăs′tẽr-oid), *n. Astron.* A starlike body ; esp., one of the many small planets mostly having orbits between Mars and Jupiter.

asth′ma (ăz′mà ; ăs′mà), *n.* A disease characterized by difficult breathing, a sense of constriction in the chest, a cough, and expectoration.

---

asth-mat′ic (ăz-măt′ĭk; ăs-), *a.* Pertaining to or affected with asthma. — *n.* An asthmatic person.

a-stig′ma-tism (à-stĭg′mà-tĭz′m), *n.* A defect of the eye or a lens because of which rays from one point do not focus at a point.

a-stir′ (-stûr′), *adv. & a.* Stirring ; in activity.

as-ton′ish (ăs-tŏn′ĭsh), *v. t.* To strike with sudden wonder or surprise ; amaze ; surprise greatly.

as-ton′ish-ing, *p. a.* [4] Wonderful ; amazing.

as-ton′ish-ment (-mĕnt), *n.* **1.** State of one who is astonished ; esp., amazement. **2.** The object causing such an emotion.

as-tound′ (ăs-tound′), *v. t.* To astonish. — **astound′ing,** *p. a.* [4] — **ing-ly,** *adv.* [8].

a-strad′dle (à-străd′l), *adv.* Straddling ; astride.

as′tra-khan (ăs′trà-kăn), *n.* The skin, or pelt, of young lambs of Astrakhan, the curly wool of which resembles fur ; also, a rough cloth imitating it.

as′tral (ăs′trăl), *a.* Pertaining to the stars.

a-stray′ (à-strā′), *adv. & a.* Wandering ; straying.

a-stride′ (-strīd′), *adv.* With one leg on each side.

as-trin′gen-cy (ăs-trĭn′jĕn-sĭ), *n.* Quality or state of being astringent.

as-trin′gent (-jĕnt), *a.* [4] Drawing together the tissues ; binding ; contracting. — *n.* An astringent medicine or other substance.

as-trol′o-ger (ăs-trŏl′ō-jẽr), *n.* A practicer of astrology.

as′tro-log′ic (ăs′trō-lŏj′ĭk), **-log′i-cal** (-ĭ-kăl), *a.* Of or pertaining to astrology. — **-ly,** *adv.* [8].

as-trol′o-gy (ăs-trŏl′ō-jĭ), *n.* The science of the stars, esp. with reference to their formerly supposed influence on human affairs.

as-tron′o-mer (ăs-trŏn′ō-mẽr), *n.* One versed in astronomy.

as′tro-nom′i-cal (ăs-trō-nŏm′ĭ-kăl), *a.* Of or pertaining to astronomy. — **-i-cal-ly,** *adv.* [8].

as-tron′o-my (ăs-trŏn′ō-mĭ), *n.* The science which treats of the heavenly bodies.

as-tute′ (ăs-tūt′), *a.* [3] Critically discerning ; sagacious ; shrewd. — **-ly,** *adv.* [8] — **-ness,** *n.* [8].

a-sun′der (à-sŭn′dẽr), *adv.* Apart ; into parts.

a-sy′lum (-sī′lŭm), *n.* **1.** An inviolable sanctuary, as a temple, altar, etc., where, in olden times, criminals and debtors found shelter. **2.** Any place of retreat and security. **3.** An institution for the relief of destitute or afflicted persons ; as, a blind *asylum.*

at (ăt), *prep.* Primarily *at* expresses the relation of *presence or contact in space or time,* or of *direction toward.* Hence it implies : **1.** Simple presence or position in, on, by, or near, or the like ; as, *at* the door. **2.** Position, object, or end directed toward ; as, aim *at* a mark. **3.** A relation of action in, or occupation with ; as, to pull *at* an oar. **4.** In a posture, circumstance, or mode of ; as, *at* war. **5.** Because of as a source, cause, or occasion ; as, sad *at* the sight. **6.** Position or order in time ; as, *at* present.

ate (āt ; *in England usually* ĕt), *preterit of* EAT.

‖ **a tem′po** (ä tĕm′pō). [It.] *Music.* In time ; — used to direct a return to the original time.

a′the-ism (ā′thẽ-ĭz′m), *n.* **1.** Disbelief in, or denial of, the existence of God. **2.** Godlessness.

a′the-ist, *n.* One who disbelieves, or denies, the existence of God. — **a′the-is′tic** (-ĭs′tĭk), **-is′ti-cal** (-tĭ-kăl), *a.*

ath′e-næ′um (ăth′ē-nē′ŭm), *n.; pl.* E. **-ums** (-ŭmz), **ath′e-ne′um** ‖ L. **-næa** (-à). **1.** A literary or scientific association. **2.** A building where a library, periodicals, and newspapers are kept for use.

a-thirst′ (à-thûrst′), *a.* Thirsty.

ath′lete (ăth′lēt), *n.* One trained to contend in exercises requiring great physical agility and strength.

ath-let′ic (ăth-lĕt′ĭk), *a.* [4] **1.** Of or pertaining to athletes or athletics. **2.** Befitting an athlete ; strong ; robust. — **ath-let′i-cal-ly,** *adv.* [8].

ath-let′ics (-ĭks), *n.* Art of training by athletic exercises ; the games and sports of athletes.

a-thwart′ (à-thwôrt′), *adv.* Across, esp. obliquely. — *prep.* **1.** Across. **2.** *Naut.* Across the length, direction, or course of.

At-lan′tic (ăt-lăn′tĭk), *a.* Designating, or pertaining to, the ocean between Europe and Africa on the east and America on the west.

at′las (ăt′lăs), *n.* **1.** *Anat.* The first vertebra of the neck. **2.** A collection of maps in a volume.

at′mos-phere (ăt′mŏs-fēr), *n.* **1.** The whole mass of air surrounding the earth. **2.** Any surrounding or pervading influence. **3.** The air in any place. **4.** *Physics.* The pressure of the air at the sea level, used as a unit.

at′mos-pher′ic (-fẽr′ĭk), *a.* Of or pertaining to the atmosphere.

a-toll′ (à-tŏl′; ăt′ŏl), *n.* A coral island consisting of a coral reef surrounding a central lagoon.

at′om (ăt′ŭm), *n.* **1.** In the atomic theory, the smallest particle of an element which can exist. See ATOMIC THEORY. **2.** A particle ; jot.

a-tom′ic (à-tŏm′ĭk), *a.* **1.** Of or pertaining to atoms. **2.** Very minute ; tiny. — atomic theory *or* hypothesis, the theory that all material substances consist of minute indivisible particles, or atoms, of a few kinds, all of the same kind being uniform in size, weight, and other properties.

at′om-ize (ăt′ŭm-īz), *v. t.* [1] To reduce to atoms, or to fine spray. — **at′om-iz′er** (-īz′ẽr), *n.* [8].

a-tone′ (à-tōn′), *v. i.* [1] To make amends for an offense. — *v. t.* To expiate.

a-tone′ment (à-tōn′mĕnt), *n.* **1.** Reconciliation ; concord. *Archaic.* **2.** Satisfaction or reparation : expiation ; amends ; — with *for.*

a-tro′cious (à-trō′shŭs), *a.* [4] Savagely brutal ; outrageously cruel or wicked. — **-ly,** *adv.* [8] — **-ness,** *n.* [8].

a-troc′i-ty (à-trŏs′ĭ-tĭ), *n. ; pl.* **-ties** (-tĭz). Quality of being atrocious ; also, an atrocious deed.

at′ro-phy (ăt′rō-fĭ), *n.* A wasting away, or failure of normal growth, from want of nourishment. — *v. t. & i.* [2] To cause, or to undergo, atrophy.

at-tach′ (ă-tăch′), *v. t.* **1.** To take by legal authority, esp. under a writ as a means of enforcing a debt. **2.** To bind ; fasten ; tie ; connect. **3.** To assign by authority ; appoint. **4.** To connect by ties of love or self-interest ; attract. **5.** To ascribe or attribute. — *v. i.* To adhere ; be attached.

‖ **at′ta-ché′** (à′tà′shā′), *n.* [F.] A person attached as a member to a suite or staff, esp. to an embassy.

at-tach′ment (ă-tăch′mĕnt), *n.* **1.** Act of attaching ; state of being attached ; close adherence or affection ; fidelity. **2.** That by which one thing is attached to another ; connection. **3.** Something attached ; adjunct of a machine or other object.

---

at-tack′ (ă-tăk′), *v. t.* **1.** To fall upon or set upon with force; assault. **2.** To assail with unfriendly speech or writing; censure; as, to *attack* one's reputation. **3.** To set to work on, as on a task or problem. **4.** To begin to affect; begin to act upon injuriously. — *v. i.* To make an onset or attack. — *n.* Act of attacking; onset; assault.

at-tain′ (ă-tān′), *v. t.* **1.** To reach or come to by motion; arrive at. **2.** To achieve; accomplish; gain; compass. — *v. i.* To come or arrive by motion, growth, or effort; reach. — **-a-ble** (-ă-b'l), *a.* [8] — **-a-ble-ness,** *n.* [8]. — **at-tain′a-bil′i-ty** (-ă-bĭl′ĭ-tĭ), *n.*

at-tain′der (-dẽr), *n.* Extinction of the civil rights of a person, on sentence of death or outlawry.

at-tain′ment (-mĕnt), *n.* **1.** Act of attaining. **2.** That which is attained; accomplishment.

at-taint′ (ă-tānt′), *v. t.* **1.** *Law.* To affect by attainder. **2.** To taint; corrupt. — *n.* **1.** A touch; a touch in tilting. *Archaic.* **2.** Stain; disgrace.

at′tar (ăt′är), *n.* A perfume extracted from flowers, esp. from rose petals.

at-tempt′ (ă-tĕmpt′), *v. t.* **1.** To make trial or experiment of; try; assay. **2.** To attack; assail, esp. in *to attempt the life of,* that is, to try to kill. — *n.* Act of attempting; trial; endeavor.

at-tend′ (ă-tĕnd′), *v. t.* **1.** To care for; take charge of; as, to *attend* a machine. **2.** To go with or stay with as a companion, nurse, or servant; serve; accompany; escort. **3.** To accompany; as, an act *attended* with ill effects. **4.** To be present at; as, to *attend* church. — *v. i.* **1.** To pay attention or regard; heed; listen. **2.** To accompany or be near at hand in pursuance of duty. **3.** (With *to*) To look (after); as, to *attend* to one's business.

at-tend′ance (ă-tĕn′dăns), *n.* **1.** Act or fact of attending. **2.** The persons attending; retinue.

at-tend′ant (-dănt), *a.* Attending; accompanying. — *n.* **1.** One who attends. **2.** An accompaniment.

at-ten′tion (-tĕn′shŭn), *n.* **1. a** Act or state of attending, or heeding; earnest consideration, thought, or regard, esp. in *to pay* or *give attention.* **b** The mental power or faculty of paying attention or considering or regarding earnestly. **2.** *Mil.* Attitude of readiness for action on receiving orders. **3.** An act of civility or courtesy.

at-ten′tive (-tĭv), *a.* [4] **1.** Heedful; observant. **2.** Heedful of the comfort of others; courteous; regardful. — **-ly,** *adv.* [8] — **-ness,** *n.* [8].

at-ten′u-ate (-ū-āt), *v. t.* [1] To make thin or slender by hunger or disease.

at-ten′u-a′tion (-ā′shŭn), *n.* Act or process of attenuating; state of being attenuated.

at-test′ (-tĕst′), *v. t.* **1.** To bear witness to; authenticate by signing as a witness or officially. **2.** To afford proof of; manifest. — *n.* Witness; attestation.

at′tes-ta′tion (ăt′ĕs-tā′shŭn), *n.* Act of attesting.

at′tic (ăt′ĭk), *n.* The room or space of rooms immediately below the roof in a house; a garret.

at-tire′ (ă-tīr′), *v. t.* [1] To dress; array; esp., to clothe elegantly or splendidly; apparel. — *n.* Dress; clothes; esp., elegant or splendid clothing.

at′ti-tude (ăt′ĭ-tūd), *n.* **1.** Posture; position assumed or studied to serve a purpose. **2.** Position or bearing as indicating action, feeling, or mood.

at-tor′ney (ă-tûr′nĭ), *n.; pl.* **-neys** (-nĭz). A legal

agent, esp. one (an **attorney at law**) qualified to act for suitors and defendants in legal proceedings.

at-tract′ (ă-trăkt′), *v. t.* **1.** To draw to or toward one's self or itself; esp., to cause to approach, adhere, or combine. **2.** To draw by influence of a moral or emotional kind; invite; allure.

at-trac′tion (ă-trăk′shŭn), *n.* **1.** Act or power of attracting. **2.** That which attracts; charm.

at-trac′tive (-tĭv), *a.* [4] Having the power or quality of attracting. — **-ly,** *adv.* — **-ness,** *n.* [8].

at-trib′ute (ă-trĭb′ūt), *v. t.* [1] To ascribe; impute; consider as due or appropriate (to); assign. — **at-trib′ut-a-ble,** *a.* [8].

at′tri-bute (ăt′rĭ-būt), *n.* That which is attributed; essential or necessary property.

at′tri-bu′tion (-bū′shŭn), *n.* Act of attributing.

at-trib′u-tive (ă-trĭb′ū-tĭv), *a.* Attributing; pert. to, or of the nature of, an attribute. Specif.: *Gram.* Designating an adjective when standing with its qualified noun; as, *yellow* gold, *village* school. — *n.* *Gram.* An attributive word. — **-tive-ly,** *adv.* [8].

at-tri′tion (ă-trĭsh′ŭn), *n.* Act of rubbing together; a wearing or grinding down by rubbing.

at-tune′ (ă-tūn′), *v. t.* [1] To tune; harmonize.

au′burn (ô′bûrn), *a.* Reddish brown.

auc′tion (ôk′shŭn), *n.* A public sale of property to the highest bidder, esp. by an auctioneer; as, to sell, or put up, at *auction.* — *v. t.* To sell at auction.

auc′tion-eer′ (-ēr′), *n.* One who sells, or makes a business of selling, at auction. — *v. t.* To auction.

au-da′cious (ô-dā′shŭs), *a.* [4] **1.** Daring; adventurous. **2.** Bold in indecorum, wickedness, or the like. **3.** Committed with, or proceeding from, audacity. — **au-da′cious-ly,** *adv.* [8].

au-dac′i-ty (-dăs′ĭ-tĭ), *n.* Quality of being audacious; boldness; assurance; impudence.

au′di-bil′i-ty (ô′dĭ-bĭl′ĭ-tĭ), *n.* Audible quality.

au′di-ble (ô′dĭ-b'l), *a.* [4] Capable of being heard; actually heard. — **au′di-bly** (-blĭ), *adv.* [8].

au′di-ence (-ĕns), *n.* **1.** Act or state of hearing. **2.** Opportunity of being heard; admittance to a hearing. **3.** A formal hearing or interview. **4.** An assembly of hearers.

au′di-o (ô′dĭ-ō), *a. Radio.* Of or pert. to electric currents or phenomena of frequencies corresponding to audible sound waves.

au′dit (ô′dĭt), *n.* An examination; esp., an official examination and confirmation of accounts; an account as adjusted by auditors. — *v. t.* To examine and adjust, as an account.

au′di-tor (ô′dĭ-tẽr), *n.* **1.** A hearer; listener. **2.** A person appointed to audit an account or accounts.

au′di-to′ri-um (-tō′rĭ-ŭm), *n.* The part of a church, theater, or the like assigned to the audience.

au′di-to-ry (ô′dĭ-tŏ-rĭ), *a.* Of or pertaining to hearing or the sense or organs of hearing. — *n.* **1.** An audience. **2.** An auditorium.

au′ger (ô′gẽr), *n.* A carpenter's tool for boring holes larger than those bored by a gimlet.

aught (ôt), *n.* Also **ought.** **1.** Anything; any part. **2.** A cipher; hence, a naught, a nothing. — *adv.* At all; to any extent.

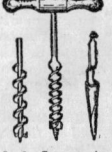

1, 2, Screw Augers; 3 Tapering Pod Auger.

aug-ment' (ôg-mĕnt'), *v. t. & i.* To increase.

aug'men-ta'tion (ôg'mĕn-tā'shŭn), *n.* Act of augmenting; increase; addition.

au'gur (ô'gŭr), *n.* One who foretells events by omens; soothsayer. — *v. t.* To predict or foretell, as from omens; portend. — *v. i.* **1.** To make an augury; predict. **2.** To foretell how a thing will turn out; as, it *augurs* well for our success.

au'gu-ry (ô'gû-rĭ), *n.; pl.* -RIES (-rĭz). **1.** A foreseeing or foretelling of future events. **2.** An omen; prediction; indication of the future.

au-gust' (ô-gŭst'), *a.* [4] Having an aspect of solemn dignity or grandeur; majestic; also, exalted in birth, character, state, or authority.

Au'gust (ô'gŭst), *n.* The eighth month of the year, having 31 days.

auk (ôk), *n.* Any of certain diving sea birds with short wings and tail and a heavy body.

auld (ôld; äld), *a.* Old. *Scot. & Dial. Eng.* — auld lang syne (lăng zīn), old long since; hence, old times; the (good) old times.

aunt (änt), *n.* The sister of one's father or mother; also, an uncle's wife.

au'ra (ô'rá), *n.; L. pl.* AURÆ (-rē). Any delicate, invisible emanation or exhalation, as the odor from flowers, or something likened to it.

au'ral (ô'răl), *a.* Of or pertaining to the ear or the sense of hearing.

au'ri-cle (ô'rĭ-k'l), *n.* **1.** The external ear. **2.** One of the two chambers of the heart that receive the blood from the veins.

au-ric'u-lar (ô-rĭk'ŭ-lár), *a.* **1.** Pertaining to the ear. **2.** Addressed to the ear.

au-rif'er-ous (ô-rĭf'ẽr-ŭs), *a.* Gold-bearing.

au'rist (ô'rĭst), *n.* One skilled in diseases of the ear.

au-ro'ra (ô-rō'rá), *n.* **1.** The light of dawn; dawn. **2.** The aurora borealis. — au-ro'ra bo're-a'lis (bō'rē-ā'lĭs), an atmospheric phenomenon consisting, usually, of streams of light radiating upward and outward toward the east and west from the north polar region, visible at night; northern lights.

au-ro'ral (ô-rō'răl), *a.* Of, or like, the aurora.

aus'pice (ôs'pĭs), *n.* **1.** An omen; sign; an auspicious indication as to the future. **2.** Protection; patronage and care; — usually in *pl.*

aus-pi'cious (ôs-pĭsh'ŭs), *a.* [4] **1.** Giving promise of success; propitious. **2.** Prosperous; fortunate. **3.** Favoring. — **-ly**, *adv.* [8] — **-ness**, *n.* [8].

aus-tere' (ôs-tēr') *a.* [3] **1.** Severe or strict; rigorous; stern. **2.** Unadorned; severely simple. — **aus-tere'ly**, *adv.* [8].

aus-ter'i-ty (-tẽr'ĭ-tĭ), *n.; pl.* -TIES (-tĭz). Quality of being austere; an austere or ascetic practice.

aus'tral (ôs'trăl), *a.* Southern.

Aus-tra'li-an (ôs-trā'lĭ-ăn), *a.* Of or pertaining to Australia. — *n.* **1.** One of the original native race of Australia. They are rather tall, and brown or black in color. **2.** A native or citizen of the Australian commonwealth.

au-then'tic (ô-thĕn'tĭk), *a.* [4] **1.** Having a genuine original or authoritative source; genuine; real; as, an *authentic* paper. **2.** Of approved authority; true; credible. — **au-then'ti-cal-ly**, *adv.* [8].

au-then'ti-cate (-tĭ-kāt), *v. t.* [1] **1.** To render authentic; give authority to, as by legal formalities. **2.** To prove authentic or genuine.

au-then'ti-ca'tion (-kā'shŭn), *n.* Act of authenticating; state of being authenticated; confirmation.

au'then-tic'i-ty (ô'thĕn-tĭs'ĭ-tĭ), *n.* Quality or state of being authentic.

au'thor (ô'thẽr), *n.* **1.** The beginner of anything; hence, creator; originator. **2.** One who composes or writes something, as a book; a composer; also, an author's writings. — **au'thor-ess**, *n. fem.* [8].

au-thor'i-ta-tive (ô-thôr'ĭ-tă-tĭv), *a.* [4] **1.** Having, or proceeding from, authority; entitled to obedience or credit. **2.** Having an air of authority; dictatorial. — **-ly**, *adv.* [8] — **-ness**, *n.* [8].

au-thor'i-ty (-tĭ), *n.; pl.* -TIES (-tĭz). **1.** Rightful power; right to command or to act; jurisdiction. **2.** Government; those in power or command; — usually in *pl.* **3.** Power due to character, station, superiority, or the like. **4.** One appealed or referred to in support of opinions, actions, etc.

au'thor-i-za'tion (ô'thôr-ĭ-zā'shŭn), *n.* Act of authorizing; sanction; warrant.

au'thor-ize (ô'thôr-īz), *v. t.* [1] **1.** To clothe with authority; empower. **2.** To give legal sanction to. **3.** To establish by authority, as by usage.

au'thor-ship, *n.* **1.** Quality, state, or function of being an author. **2.** Source; origin.

au'to-bi'o-graph'ic (ô'tô-bī'ô-grăf'ĭk), **-i-cal** (-ĭ-kăl), *a.* Pertaining to or containing autobiography.

au'to-bi-og'ra-phy (-bī-ŏg'rá-fĭ), *n.; pl.* -PHIES (-fĭz). A biography written by the subject of it; memoirs of one's life written by one's self.

au'to-bus' (ô'tô-bŭs'), *n.* An automobile omnibus.

au-toc'ra-cy (ô-tŏk'rá-sĭ), *n.; pl.* -CIES (-sĭz). **1.** Absolute supremacy. **2.** Supreme governing power in an individual; authority of an autocrat.

au'to-crat (ô'tô-krăt), *n.* An absolute sovereign; a monarch ruling by claim of absolute right; despot.

au'to-crat'ic (-krăt'ĭk), *a.* [4] Of or pertaining to an autocrat. — **au'to-crat'i-cal-ly**, *adv.* [8].

au'to-graph (ô'tô-grăf), *n.* That written with one's own hand; a person's own signature.

au'to-graph'ic (-grăf'ĭk), *a.* Pertaining to, or of the nature of, an autograph.

au'to-mat'ic (ô'tô-măt'ĭk), *a.* **1.** Having an inherent power of action. **2.** Self-acting or self-regulating; — applied esp. to machinery. **3.** Not voluntary. — **au'to-mat'i-cal-ly**, *adv.* [8].

au-tom'a-ton (ô-tŏm'á-tŏn), *n.; pl.* L. -ATA (-tá), E. -TONS. **1.** A self-moving machine, esp. one made to imitate the motions of men, birds, etc. **2.** A living being acting in a mechanical manner.

au'to-mo'bile (ô'tô-mō'bĭl), *a.* Containing means of propulsion within itself; self-propelling.

au'to-mo'bile (-mō'bĭl; -mô-bēl'), *n.* An automobile vehicle or mechanism; esp., a self-propelled vehicle suitable for use on a street or roadway. — **au'to-mo'bil-ist**, *n.*

au-ton'o-mous (ô-tŏn'ô-mŭs), *a.* Self-governing.

au-ton'o-my (-mĭ), *n.* Quality or state of being self-governing; power or right of self-government.

au'top-sy (ô'tŏp-sĭ), *n.; pl.* -SIES (-sĭz). *Med.* Dissection of a dead body to learn the cause, seat, or nature of a disease, or the cause of death.

au'tumn (ô'tŭm), *n.* The season between summer and winter, often called *fall*.

au-tum'nal (ô-tŭm'năl), *a.* Of, belonging to, or peculiar to, autumn.

---

aux-il'ia-ry (ôg-zĭl' yȧ-rĭ), *a.* Conferring aid or help; assistant. — *n.; pl.* -RIES (-rĭz). **1.** One that aids or helps. **2.** *Mil.* (*pl.*) Foreign troops in the service of a nation at war. **3.** *Gram.* A verb (as, *have, be, may, do, shall* and *will, can, must*) which helps to form the moods, tenses, etc., of other verbs.

a-vail' (ȧ-vāl'), *v. i.* To be of use; to have strength, force, or efficacy sufficient to accomplish the object in mind. — *v. t.* To benefit; help. — **to avail one's self of,** to make use of; take advantage of. — *n.* **1.** Effective advantage; as, of no *avail.* **2.** *pl.* Proceeds.

a-vail'a-ble (ȧ-vāl'ȧ-b'l), *a.* [4] Such as one may avail one's self of; usable. — **a-vail'a-bil'i-ty** (-ȧ-bĭl'ĭ-tĭ), *n.*

av'a-lanche (ăv'ȧ-lȧnch), *n.* A large mass of snow and ice, or of earth, rocks, etc., sliding swiftly down a mountain side, or falling down a precipice.

av'a-rice (-rĭs), *n.* Excessive desire of gain; greediness for wealth; covetousness; cupidity.

av'a-ri'cious (-rĭsh'ŭs), *a.* [4] Moved by avarice; greedy of gain.

a-vast' (ȧ-vȧst'), *interj. Naut.* Cease! Stop! Stay!

a-vaunt' (-vȯnt'; -vänt'), *interj.* Begone! Depart!

a-venge' (ȧ-věnj'), *v. t.* [1] To take vengeance for; exact satisfaction for. — **a-veng'er,** *n.* [8].

av'e-nue (ăv'ĕ-nū), *n.* **1.** A way of approach or of exit. **2.** Any broad passageway bordered on each side by trees. **3.** A broad street.

a-ver' (ȧ-vûr'), *v. t.; -*VERRED* (-vûrd'); -*VER'RING.'* To affirm confidently; declare positively.

av'er-age (ăv'ẽr-ȧj), *n.* **1.** A sum or quantity got by adding together unequal sums or quantities and dividing the result by the number of quantities added. **2.** Any medial estimate based on a comparison of different cases; a medium or usual size, quantity, quality, rate, etc. — *a.* Pertaining to an average; medial; ordinary; usual; as, the *average* man. — *v. t.* [1] **1.** To find the average of; reduce to a mean. **2.** To divide among a number according to a given proportion. **3.** To do, accomplish, get, etc., on an average.

a-verse' (ȧ-vûrs'), *a.* Having an aversion; reluctant; opposed. — **a-verse'ness,** *n.* [8].

a-ver'sion (-vûr'shŭn), *n.* **1.** A state of mind in which attention to an object is coupled with dislike of it and desire to turn from it. **2.** An object of dislike or repugnance.

a-vert' (ȧ-vûrt'), *v. t.* To turn aside or away; ward off or prevent the occurrence or effects of.

a'vi-a-ry (ā'vĭ-ȧ-rĭ), *n.; pl.* -RIES (-rĭz). A place, as a house, for keeping birds confined.

a'vi-ate (-āt), *v. i.* [1] To fly, or navigate the air, in an airplane.

a'vi-a'tion (-ā'shŭn), *n.* Art or science of locomotion by airplanes.

a'vi-a'tor (ā'vĭ-ā'tẽr), *n.* One who is occupied with, or expert in, aviation. — **a'vi-a'trix, a'vi-a'-trice** (-ā'trĭks; -ā'trĭs), *n. fem.*

a-vid'i-ty (ȧ-vĭd'ĭ-tĭ), *n.* Greediness; eagerness.

av'o-ca'tion (ăv'ô-kā'shŭn), *n.* **1.** A subordinate occupation. **2.** [*Usually in pl.*] Vocation.

a-void' (ȧ-void'), *v. t.* **1.** To make void, as a contract; annul; vacate. **2.** To keep away from; shun; abstain from. — **a-void'a-ble,** *a.* [8].

a-void'ance (-ăns), *n.* Act of avoiding.

av'oir-du-pois' (ăv'ẽr-dŭ-poiz'), *n.* Avoirdupois weight. — **avoirdupois weight,** the common system in English-speaking countries. In it 16 drams (dr.) make 1 ounce (oz.); 16 ounces, or 7,000 grains, make 1 pound (lb.).

a-vouch' (ȧ-vouch'), *v. t.* To maintain as true.

a-vow' (ȧ-vou'), *v. t.* To declare openly. — **a-vowed'** (ȧ-voud'), *p. a.* — **a-vow'ed-ly,** *adv.* [8].

a-vow'al (ȧ-vou'ăl), *n.* An open declaration.

a-wait' (ȧ-wāt'), *v. t.* **1.** To wait for; stay for; expect. **2.** To be in store for; be in waiting for.

a-wake' (-wāk'), *v. i. & t.; pret.* A-WOKE' (ȧ-wōk'), A-WAKED' (ȧ-wākt') ; *p. p.* A-WAKED' ; *p. pr. & vb. n.* A-WAK'ING. To cease to sleep; rouse from sleep or, fig., a sleeplike state; wake. — *a.* Not sleeping or dull; roused from sleep; vigilant.

a-wak'en (ȧ-wāk''n), *v. t. & i.* To rouse from sleep; awake.

a-ward' (ȧ-wôrd'), *v. t.* To adjudge; to grant or give after due deliberation, consideration of relative merits, etc. — *n.* **1.** A judgment; a granting or giving after due deliberation or a consideration of relative merits. **2.** That which is awarded.

a-ware' (ȧ-wâr'), *a.* Conscious; informed; having knowledge (of). — **a-ware'ness,** *n.*

a-wash' (ȧ-wŏsh'), *adv. & a.* **1.** Washed by the waves or tide. **2.** Floating in the water.

a-way' (ȧ-wā'), *adv.* **1.** From a place; hence, aside; from one's possession. **2.** From a state of being into extinction or termination; out of existence; as, to sleep the day *away.* **3.** On; without intermission or delay; as, sing *away. Colloq.*

awe (ô), *n.* Reverential fear such as is felt for the Divine Being; profound reverence; solemn wonder. — *v. t.* [1] To strike or inspire with awe.

awe'some (ô'sŭm), *a.* [4] Causing, or expressive of, awe or terror. — **awe'some-ness,** *n.*

aw'ful (ô'fŏol), *a.* [3] **1.** Filling with awe; appalling. **2.** Frightful; exceedingly bad; — used intensively. *Slang.* — **-ly,** *adv.* [8] — **-ness,** *n.* [8].

a-while' (ȧ-hwīl'), *adv.* For a while or a short time.

awk'ward (ôk'wẽrd), *a.* [4] **1.** Not dexterous; clumsy; ungraceful. **2.** Not easily managed or effected; embarrassing; as, an *awkward* affair. — **awk'ward-ly,** *adv.* [8] — **-ness,** *n.* [8].

awl (ôl), *n.* A pointed instrument for piercing small holes, as in leather or wood.

awn (ôn), *n.* One of the bristle-like hairs that form the beard of a head of barley, oats, etc.

awn'ing, *n.* A rooflike cover, esp. of canvas, extended over or before a place.

a-woke' (ȧ-wōk'), *pret. & p. p.* of AWAKE.

a-wry' (ȧ-rī'), *adv. & a.* Turned to one side; not straight or true; perverse or perversely.

ax, axe (ăks), *n. ; pl.* AXES (ăk'sěz). A common tool for hewing, chopping, or splitting wood.

ax'i-al (ăk'sĭ-ăl), *a.* Of or pertaining to an axis.

ax'i-om (-sĭ-ŭm), *n.* **1.** A self-evident truth. **2.** An established principle in some art or science.

ax'i-o-mat'ic (-ô-măt'ĭk), *a.* Pertaining to an axiom. — **ax'i-o-mat'i-cal-ly,** *adv.* [8].

ax'is (-sĭs), *n. ; pl.* AXES (-sēz). A straight line, real or imaginary, passing through a body that actually or supposedly revolves on it; a line passing through a body or system around which the parts are symmetrically arranged.

āle, senāte, câre, ăm, ăccount, ärm, ȧsk, sofȧ; ēve, ĕvent, ĕnd, recĕnt, makēr; īce, ĭll; ōld, ŏbey, ôrb, ŏdd, sŏft, cŏnnect; ūse, ŭnite, ûrn, ŭp, circŭs; fŏŏd, fŏŏt; out, oil;

ax′le (ăk′s′l), *n.* **1.** The pin or spindle on which a wheel revolves, or which revolves with a wheel. **2.** The bar or shaft connecting the opposite wheels of a car or carriage; axletree.

ax′le-tree′ (-trē′), *n.* The bar or shaft on the ends of which opposite wheels of a vehicle revolve.

aye, *or* **ay** (ā), *adv.* Always; ever.

aye, *or* **ay** (ī), *adv.* Yes; yea. — *n.* An affirmative vote.

a-za′le-a (á-zā′lē-á), *n.* Any of various shrubs closely related to the rhododendron.

az′ure (ăzh′ŭr), *n.* **1.** Azure color; the clear blue of the sky; also, a pigment or dye of this color. **2.** The unclouded sky. — *a.* Sky-blue; cloudless.

B

baa (bä), *v. i.* To cry "baa"; to bleat as a sheep. — *n.* The cry of a sheep; bleat.

bab′ble (băb′′l), *v. i.* [1] **1.** To utter words indistinctly or without sense; utter indistinct sounds. **2.** To chatter; prate. **3.** To murmur, as a brook. — *v. t.* **1.** To utter indistinctly or senselessly. **2.** To disclose by too free talk, as a secret. — *n.* **1.** Idle talk; prattle. **2.** Indistinct speech; a confused murmur. — **bab′bler** (-lẽr), *n.* [8].

babe (bāb), *n.* An infant; baby.

ba-boon′ (bă-boon′), *n.* Any of certain large apes.

ba′by (bā′bĭ), *n.; pl.* -BIES (-bĭz). An infant; child in arms; babe. — *v. t,* [2] To treat as a baby; humor; fondle. — **ba′by-ish**, *a.* [8].

ba′by-hood (-hŏŏd), *n.* Condition or period of being a baby.

bac′ca-lau′re-ate (băk-á-lô′rē-ăt), *n.* The degree of bachelor, conferred by universities and colleges.

bac′cha-na′li-an (băk′á-nā′lĭ-ăn), *a.* Of or pertaining to drunkenness and revelry.

bach′e-lor (băch′ē-lẽr), *n.* **1.** One who has taken his first degree at a college, school, or university. **2.** A man of any age who has not married.

bach′e-lor-hood, *n.* State of being a bachelor.

bach′e-lor′s–but′ton, *n.* Any of several flowers with buttonlike heads, esp. the cornflower.

ba-cil′lus (bá-sĭl′ŭs), *n.; pl.* -CILLI (-ī). Any of certain tiny rod-shaped vegetable organisms or germs (bacteria), some of which are harmless while others cause disease. See BACTERIA.

back (băk), *n.* **1.** The hinder part of the human body, or, of animals, the upper part. from the neck to the end of the spine. **2.** The hinder or rear part of anything. **3.** The upper part of something. **4. a** The part of a cutting tool opposite its edge. **b** The part of a book or its leaves where it is sewed when bound. **c** The upright hinder part of a chair or sofa above the seat. — *v. t.* **1.** To furnish with a back; also, to form the back of; be at the back of. **2.** To support or help; second; — often with *up.* **3.** To bet on the success of. **4.** To get on the back of; mount. **5.** To drive, force, or cause to move or act, backward.

back, *adv.* **1.** To or toward the rear. **2.** In or into time past. **3.** To or toward a former place, condition, or station. **4.** In withdrawal from a statement, promise, or undertaking. **5.** In concealment or reserve; in one's own possession. **6.** In return, repayment, or requital. — *a.* **1.** Being at the back or rear. **2.** Being in arrears; overdue; as, *back* rent. **3.** Moving or operating backward. **4.** No longer current.

back′bite′ (-bīt′), *v. t. & i.* To censure meanly or spitefully (one absent); slander. — **-bit′er**, *n.* [8].

back′bone′ (băk′bōn′), *n.* **1.** The spine. **2.** Firmness; moral principle.

back′er (-ẽr), *n.* One who backs a person or thing.

back′gam-mon (băk′găm-ŭn), *n.* A certain well-known game of chance and skill.

back′ground′ (-ground′), *n.* **1.** Ground or surface that is in the rear or behind. **2.** In a painting, etching, etc., that part of the scene farthest from the spectator; also, the general surface on which any pattern, design, etc., is represented. **3.** That which is back of anything and against which it is viewed. **4.** A place in obscurity.

back′hand′ed (-hănd′ĕd), *a.* **1.** Made with the back of the hand, or with the back of the hand turned in the direction of the stroke. **2.** Indirect; awkward; insincere; as, a *backhanded* compliment.

back′ing, *n.* **1.** The act of one that backs. **2.** That which forms the back of anything.

back′log′ (băk′lŏg′), *n.* A large log of wood forming the back of a fire on the hearth. *U. S.*

back′slide′ (băk′slīd′; băk′slīd′), *v. i.; for prin. parts see* SLIDE. To slide back; esp., to abandon gradually a religion once professed.

back′ward (-wẽrd), *adv.* **1.** Toward the back or rear. **2.** With the back in advance or foremost. **3.** On the back, or with the back downward; as, to fall over *backward.* **4.** From better to worse. — *a.* [4] **1.** Directed or turned back. **2.** Slow in action or progress; dull; as, a *backward* child. — **-ward-ly**, *adv.* [8] — **-ward-ness**, *n.* [8].

back′wards (-wẽrdz), *adv.* Var. of BACKWARD.

back′woods′ (-wŏŏdz′), *n. pl.* The forests or partly cleared grounds o the frontiers or remote from civilization. — **-man**, *n.*

ba′con (bā′k′n), *n.* The back and sides of a pig, salted and smoked.

bac-te′ri-a (băk-tē′rĭ-á), *n. pl.* A remarkable group of widely distributed vegetable organisms so tiny that they can be seen only through a microscope. Some convert dead matter into food materials for plants; some are active in fermentation; and many cause disease.

bac-te′ri-al (-ăl), *a.* Relating to bacteria.

bac-te′ri-cide (-sīd), *n.* A substance that destroys bacteria.

bac-te′ri-ol′o-gist (-ŏl′ō-jĭst), *n.* An expert in bacteriology.

bac-te′ri-ol′o-gy (-ŏl′ō-jĭ), *n.* The science which deals with bacteria.

bad (băd), *a.; compar.* WORSE (wûrs); *superl.* WORST (wûrst). **1.** Of the nature of evil; wicked. **2.** Injurious; hurtful. **3.** Offensive; disagreeable; annoying. **4.** Inadequate; unfit. **5.** Defective; faulty; not good legally; invalid. **6.** Ill; sick. **7.** Severe; aggravated; as, a *bad* case of mumps.

bade (băd), *pret.* of BID.

badge (băj), *n.* **1.** A distinctive mark, token, or sign, worn on the person. **2.** A mark or token.

badg'er (băj'ẽr), *n.* A flesh-eating burrowing animal with long claws on the forefeet. — *v. t.* To tease or annoy persistently; worry.

bad'ly (băd'-lĬ), *adv.* In a bad manner.

Badger.

bad'ness, *n.* Quality or state of being bad.

baf'fle (băf'l), *v. t.* [1] **1.** To check or defeat by perplexing; thwart; foil. **2.** To beat about; check or turn in its course; as, a ship *baffled* by the wind.

bag (băg), *n.* **1.** A sack or pouch. **2.** Any of various pouchlike objects, as the udder of a cow. — *v. i.;* BAGGED (băgd); BAG'GING. To swell or bulge like a full bag. — *v. t.* **1.** To swell out; distend. **2.** To put into a bag. **3.** To put (game) into a bag; hence, to kill or capture in or as in hunting.

bag'a-telle' (băg'à-tĕl'), *n.* **1.** A trifle. **2.** A game played with a cue and balls on an oblong board.

bag'gage (băg'åj), *n.* **1.** The trunks, valises, etc., which one takes on a journey; luggage. **2.** The clothes, tents, utensils,etc.,of an army. **3.** A worthless woman; hence, playfully, any young woman.

bag'ging (-Ĭng), *n.* Material for bags.

bag'gy (-Ĭ), *a.* [3] Like a bag; loose; flabby.

bag'pipe' (-pīp'), *n.* A kind of musical wind instrument, of which one pipe sounds the air and the others are drones. — **bag'pip'er** (-pīp'ẽr), *n.* [8].

bail (bāl), *n.* A scoop or other vessel used in bailing out water. — *v. t. & i.* **1.** To lade; dip and throw. **2.** To dip or lade water from.

bail, *v. t. Law.* To set (a person) free temporarily on the agreement of another to be responsible for the due appearance of the person set free ; to procure the release of by giving such an agreement with security. — *n. Law.* The security given, the person or persons giving it, or the temporary delivery or release.

bail (bāl), *n.* **1.** A hoop; ring. **2.** The arched handle of a kettle, pail, etc.

bail'a-ble (bāl'á-b'l), *a.* Capable of being bailed.

bail'iff (-Ĭf), *n.* **1.** In England, the steward of the lord of a manor, etc.; also, a sheriff's deputy. **2.** In the U. S.,sometimes,a sheriff's officer or constable.

bait (bāt), *n.* **1.** Anything, esp. food, used as a lure in catching fish, or other animals. **2.** A lure.

bait, *v. t.* **1.** To worry (an animal) by setting on dogs to harass or torment (it) for sport; as, to *bait* a bear. **2.** To persecute, harass, or torment, wantonly. **3.** To give food and drink to, esp. on the road; feed (an animal). **4.** To cover with bait, as a hook. **5.** To allure or entice with bait.

bake (bāk), *v. t.* [1] **1.** To prepare, as food, by cooking in a dry heat. **2.** To dry or harden (anything) by subjecting to heat. — *v. i.* **1.** To do the work of baking something. **2.** To become baked. — *n.* Act, process, or result of baking.

bak'er (bāk'ẽr), *n.* One that bakes; esp., a person whose business it is to bake bread, pastry, etc.

bak'er-y (-Ĭ), *n.; pl.* -ERIES (-Ĭz). A place for baking bread, pastry, etc.

bak'ing (-Ĭng), *n.* **1.** Act or process of baking. **2.** The quantity baked at once, as of bread; batch.

bal'ance (băl'ăns), *n.* **1.** An instrument for weighing, being, in its simplest form, a beam or lever balanced in the middle and supporting a scale or pan at each end. **2.** A vibrating wheel operating with a hairspring to regulate the movement of a timepiece. **3.** A counterpoise used in weighing. **4.** Equipoise between the weights in opposite scales; hence, equipoise; equilibrium; fig.: composure; steadiness. **5.** An equality between the sums total of the two sides of an account; also, the excess on either side. — *v. t.* [1] **1.** To weigh in a balance. **2.** To weigh (two things) by each other; compare. **3.** To counterbalance; set off. **4.** To bring to an equipoise, as the scales of a balance; hence, to poise or keep in equilibrium. **5.** To bring about an equality in the debits and the credits of. — *v. i.* **1.** To be in equipoise. **2.** To be an equal counterpoise; be equal. **3.** To be equal in debits and credits, as accounts.

bal-brig'gan (băl-brĬg'ăn), *n.* A cotton fabric for either hosiery or underwear.

bal'co-ny (băl'kŏ-nĬ), *n.; pl.* -NIES (-nĬz). A projecting platform inclosed by a parapet or railing.

bald (bôld), *a.* **1.** Destitute of the natural or common covering on the head or top, as of hair. **2.** Destitute of ornament; bare. — **bald eagle,** the common eagle of North America; — from the white feathers of the head and neck of bald eagles several years old.

bal'der-dash (bôl'dẽr-dăsh), *n.* A senseless jumble of words: nonsense.

bald'ly, *adv.* In a bald manner.

bald'ness, *n.* Quality or state of being bald.

bal'dric (bôl'-drĬk), *n.* A belt worn over the shoulder and across the body to hold a sword, bugle, etc.

Bald Eagle.

bale (bāl), *n.* Evil; an evil influence. *Poetic.*

bale, *n.* A large bundle for storage or transportation. — *v. t.* [1] To put up in a bale or bales.

bale'ful (-fōōl), *a.* [4] Full of bale, or evil influence; destructive; painful; woeful.

balk (bôk), *n.* A hindrance; disappointment; check.

balk, *v. t.* To check; frustrate; foil. — *v. i.* To stop short and refuse to go, as a horse.

balk'y (bôk'Ĭ), *a.* [3] Apt to balk, as a horse.

ball (bôl), *n.* **1.** Any roundish body; a sphere or globe. **2.** The globe, or earth; any celestial body. **3.** A game in which a ball is thrown, kicked, or knocked; esp., now, baseball. **4.** A round missile; now, esp., any round or elongated solid missile for a firearm.

ball, *n.* A social assembly for dancing.

bal'lad (băl'l̇ăd), *n*. **1.** A simple song of any kind; specifically, a romantic song. **2.** A popular kind of short narrative poem.

bal'last (-ȧst), *n*. **1.** *Naut.* Any heavy substance put into the hold of a vessel to steady her, or to determine her trim in the water. **2.** Gravel, broken stone, etc., such as is laid in a roadbed to make it solid. — *v. t.* **1.** To steady or equip, as a vessel, with ballast. **2.** To fill in, as the bed of a railroad, with gravel, stone, etc.

bal'let' (băl'lā'), *n*. **1.** An artistic dance performed as a theatrical entertainment, or an interlude, usually by women. **2.** Those who perform the dance.

bal-loon' (bȧ-lōōn'), *n*. A bag or envelope, as of silk, filled with a gas lighter than air, as hydrogen, so as to rise and float in the atmosphere.

bal-loon'ist, *n*. One who sails a balloon; aëronaut.

bal'lot (băl'ŭt), *n*. **1.** Any object, esp. a printed ticket, used in secret voting. **2.** Act or system of secret voting (or, loosely, open voting) by tickets, or ballots. **3.** The whole number of votes so cast. — *v. i. & t.* To vote or decide by ballot.

balm (bäm), *n*. **1.** Any of several plants of the mint family, of which one is a common garden herb. **2. a** = BALSAM, 1 a. **b** Any fragrant ointment. **3.** Anything that heals or soothes.

balm'i-ness, *n*. Quality or state of being balmy.

balm'y (bäm'ĭ), *a*. [3] Aromatic; soothing; mild.

bal'sam (bôl'săm), *n*. **1. a** A fragrant substance flowing from certain plants or trees. **b** Any of various preparations with a balsamic odor. **2.** Any of several balsam-yielding trees, as a kind of fir.

bal-sam'ic (bŏl-săm'ĭk; bâl-), *a*. Containing, resembling, or having the qualities of, balsam.

bal'us-ter (băl'ŭs-tẽr), *n*. An upright support of the rail of a balustrade.

bal'us-trade' (-trād'), *n*. A row of balusters topped by a rail.

bam-boo' (băm-bōō'), *n*. A woody or treelike tropical plant of the grass family.

ban (băn), *n*. **1.** A public proclamation or edict. **2.** *pl.* See BANNS. **3.** A prohibition or curse pronounced by the church. **4.** A curse, bringing evil. **5.** An authoritative prohibition. — *v. t.; BANNED* (bănd); *BAN'NING*. **1.** To curse. **2.** To forbid.

ban'al (băn'ăl; bā'năl), *a*. Commonplace; trite; trivial; as a *banal* remark.

ba-nal'i-ty (bȧ-năl'ĭ-tĭ), *n.; pl.* -TIES (-tĭz). Something banal; a commonplace.

ba-na'na (bȧ-nä'nȧ; bȧ-năn'ȧ), *n*. *Bot.* A treelike tropical plant, often reaching a height of 20 feet, with large simple leaves; also, its finger-shaped fruit, an important article of food.

band (bănd), *n*. **1.** Anything used to confine the body or limbs, as a fetter. *Archaic or Fig.* **2.** A cord, string, or ligament, as for tying or holding something in place. **3.** That which figuratively unites or restrains; a bond or tie; as, the *bands* of matrimony. **4.** A thin flat strip of any material. **5.** A company of persons, as of musicians, working together; a troop. — *v. t. & i.* **1.** To bind, tie, or mark with a band. **2.** To unite in a troop or company, or in a conspiracy.

band'age (băn'dĕj), *n*. A strip, usually of cloth, used in dressing wounds, etc. — *v. t.* [1] To bind, dress, or cover with a bandage.

ban-dan'na } (băn-dăn'ȧ), *n*. A handkerchief hav-
ban-dan'a } ing a uniform ground, usually of red or blue, with simple white or yellow figures.

band'box' (bănd'bŏks'), *n*. A light box of pasteboard or wood for collars, caps, bonnets, etc.

ban'dit (-dĭt), *n.; pl.* -DITS (-dĭts), *or* -DITTI (-dĭt'ĭ). An outlaw; hence, a brigand; lawless marauder.

ban'dy (-dĭ), *n*. The game of hockey. — *v. t.* [2] To beat to and fro, as a ball; exchange. — *v. i.* To contend; give and take.

ban'dy, *a*. [3] Curved laterally, esp. with the convex side outward, as a leg.

bane (bān), *n*. Any cause of ruin or of injury.

bane'ful (-fōōl), *a*. [3] Poisonous; deadly; injurious.

bang (băng), *v. t. & i.* **1.** To beat or thump with a resounding blow. — *n.* **1.** A resounding blow; thump; whack. **2.** A sudden noise, as from a heavy blow or an explosion. — *adv.* With a violent blow, clap, or noise; also, all of a sudden. *Colloq.*

bang (băng), *v. t.* To cut squarely across, as the tail of a horse. — *n.* The front hair cut short and even and worn hanging down over the forehead.

ban'gle (băng'g'l), *n*. An ornamental ring, as of glass, gold, or silver, worn around the wrist or ankle; also, a solid bracelet, generally with small ornaments hanging from it.

ban'ish (băn'ĭsh), *v. t.* **1.** To condemn to leave a country by sovereign authority. **2.** To drive out from, or as from, a home, accustomed place, etc.

ban'ish-ment (-mĕnt), *n*. Act of banishing, or state of being banished.

ban'is-ter (-ĭs-tẽr), *n*. A baluster; *pl.*, the balustrade of a staircase.

ban'jo (-jō), *n.; pl.* -JOS (-jōz). A kind of stringed musical instrument having a body like a tambourine. — **ban'jo-ist**, *n*.

bank (băŋk), *n*. **1.** A mound or ridge of earth; anything shaped like such a mound or ridge; as, a *bank* of clouds. **2.** A shoal, shelf, or shallow in the sea bottom. **3.** A steep slope, as of a hill. **4.** The margin of a watercourse; the ground bordering a river, ditch, lake, pond, etc. — *v. t.* **1.** To raise or form a bank about. **2.** To heap or pile up. **3.** *Aëronautics.* To incline (an airplane) sidewise, to prevent skidding when rounding a curve.

bank, *n*. A bench for rowers in a galley; also, a tier of oars.

bank, *n*. **1.** An office for banking purposes. **2.** An establishment for the custody, loan, exchange, or issue of money. — *v. i.* **1.** To do business as a banker. **2.** To deposit money in a bank. — *v. t.* To deposit in a bank. — **bank'a-ble** (-ȧ-b'l), *a*.

bank discount. A sum equal to the interest at a given rate on the principal (face) of a bill or note from the time of discounting until it becomes due.

bank'er (-ẽr), *n*. One that conducts a bank.

bank'ing, *n*. The business consisting in the custody, loaning, exchange, or issue of money.

bank note. A promissory demand note issued by a banker and intended to circulate as money.

bank'rupt (-rŭpt), *n*. One who becomes unable to pay his debts; an insolvent person. — *a.* Being a bankrupt; unable to pay, or discharged from paying, one's debts. — *v. t.* To make bankrupt.

bank'rupt-cy (-sĭ), *n.; pl.* -CIES (-sĭz). State of being or becoming bankrupt.

ban'ner (băn'ẽr), n. 1. A piece of cloth attached by its edge to a pole or staff and used as a standard. 2. An ensign displaying some distinctive device.

ban'nock (-ŭk), n. A kind of round flat oatmeal or barley cake or bread. *Scot. & North. Eng.*

banns (bănz), n. pl. Notice of a proposed marriage, proclaimed as in a church.

ban'quet (băn'kwĕt), n. A feast; esp., an elaborate feast with speeches. — *v. t. & i.* To feast.

ban'tam (băn'tăm), n. A fowl of small breeds.

ban'ter (-tẽr), v. t. To address with jest or ridicule; rally. — n. Good-humored raillery; pleasantry.

ban'yan (băn'yăn), n., or **banyan tree**. An East Indian tree whose branches send out many roots that grow downward and form additional trunks.

ban'zai' (băn'zā'ĕ), interj. A cry used in Japan in saluting the emperor and in battle, meaning "May you live ten thousand years."

bap'tism (băp'tĭz'm), n. 1. Act of baptizing, esp. as a Christian sacrament. 2. Any act or experience by which one is purified, initiated, etc.

bap-tis'mal (-tĭz'măl), a. Of or pert. to baptism.

bap'tis-ter-y (băp'tĭs-tẽr-ĭ), **bap'tis-try** (-trĭ), n.; pl. -TERIES (-ĭz), -TRIES (-trĭz). A separate building, or part of a church, used for baptism.

bap-tize' (băp-tīz'), v. t. [1] 1. To immerse in water, or to sprinkle water on, as a religious ceremony. 2. To christen; name.

bar (bär), n. 1. A slender piece of wood, metal, etc., esp. one used for a lever, fastening, etc. 2. A piece of some substance like a bar (sense 1) in shape; as a bar of soap. 3. A broad band or stripe, as of color. 4. *Music.* A vertical line across the staff, before the initial metrical accent. 5. Anything that obstructs or hinders; barrier. 6. A bank, as of sand, esp. at the mouth of a river or harbor, obstructing navigation. 7. *Law.* **a** The railing that incloses the place where prisoners are placed, or where the business of the court is transacted. **b** Hence, the court itself. **c** The whole body of lawyers in any jurisdiction; also, the profession of a lawyer. 8. Any tribunal; as, the bar of public opinion. 9. A counter over which liquor or food is passed to customers; hence, the part of the room behind the counter. — v. t.; BARRED (bärd); BAR'RING. 1. To fasten or obstruct by a bar or bars. 2. To shut out; hinder; prevent. 3. To mark with bars; stripe.

1, 2 Bars : 3 Double Bar.

bar (bär), prep. Except; but; as, bar none.

barb (bärb), n. The point that projects backward in an arrow, fishhook, etc. — v. t. To furnish with barbs, as an arrow, etc.

barb, n. One of a race of horses noted for speed and endurance, brought to Spain by the Moors.

bar-ba'ri-an (bär-bā'rĭ-ăn), n. 1. A foreigner, esp. in speech and manners. 2. **a** A rude, uncivilized person. **b** A person devoid of culture. — a. 1. Foreign. 2. Uncivilized; savage.

bar-bar'ic (-bǎr'ĭk), a. [4] 1. Barbarian; foreign. 2. Of or resembling uncivilized people.

bar'ba-rism (bär'bǎ-rĭz'm), n. 1. A word or expression not in standard usage. 2. Uncivilized state; ignorance of arts, learning, and literature.

bar-bar'i-ty (bär-bǎr'ĭ-tĭ), n.; pl. -TIES (-tĭz). 1. Cruelty; inhumanity; also, a cruel act. 2. Barbaric style, or violation of good taste, in art.

bar'ba-rous (bär'bǎ-rǔs), a. [4] 1. Not classical or pure; — said of language. 2. Uncivilized. 3. Cruel; inhuman. 4. Harsh-sounding, like barbarian speech. — **bar'ba-rous-ly**, adv. [8].

bar'be-cue (bär'bė-kū), n. A social entertainment at which one or more large animals are roasted or broiled whole. *U. S.*

bar'bel (bär'bĕl), n. A slender outgrowth, or "feeler," on the lips of certain fishes.

bar'ber (bär'bẽr), n. One whose business is to shave, trim beards, cut the hair, etc. — v. t. To shave, trim, or dress the beard or hair of.

bar'ber-ry (-bẽr-ĭ), n.; pl. -RIES (-ĭz). Any of a genus of shrubs, of which one bears oblong red berries often made into a preserve; also, the berry.

bard (bärd), n. 1. A professional poet and singer, as in ancient Britain. 2. A poet.

bare (bâr), a. [3] 1. Naked; nude. 2. With head bare. 3. Without ornament or the like; plain. 4. Without the usual furnishing, contents, or the like. 5. Mere; unaccompanied by anything else or more. — v. t. [1] To make bare.

bare'back' (-băk'), adv. &a. On a horse's bare back.

bare'faced' (-fāst'), a. 1. With the face uncovered; not masked. 2. Without concealment; hence, shameless; audacious; as, a barefaced lie.

bare'foot (bâr'fŏŏt), a. & adv. With the feet bare.

bare'foot-ed, a. With the feet bare.

bare'ly, adv. 1. Nakedly. 2. Without concealment or disguise. 3. But just; scarcely; hardly.

bare'ness, n. State or quality of being bare.

bar'gain (bär'gĕn), n. 1. An agreement between parties settling what each shall give and receive in a transaction; agreement. 2. A thing got by bargaining; a purchase, esp. an advantageous purchase. — v. i. 1. To negotiate over an agreement; haggle. 2. To make or strike a bargain; — followed by with and for; as, the Dutch bargained with the Indians for Manhattan island. — v. t. To transfer for a consideration; barter; trade.

barge (bärj), n. Any of various boats; esp., a roomy flat-bottomed boat designed to be towed.

bar'i-tone (băr'ĭ-tōn). Var. of BARYTONE.

bark (bärk), n. The tough outside covering of the stem, branches, and roots of trees, shrubs, and perennial plants. — v. t. 1. To strip the bark from. 2. To skin; strip the skin from.

bark, v. i. 1. To utter a short, explosive cry; — said of a dog, fox, etc. 2. To clamor. — n. The short, explosive cry of a dog, or a sound like it.

bark (bärk), n. 1. A vessel, or boat. *Poetical.* 2. *Naut.* A kind of three-masted vessel.

bar'ley (bär'lĭ), n. A hardy bearded cereal; also, its seed or grain, used as food.

barn (bärn), n. 1. A building for storing grain, hay, etc., and for stables. 2. A building in which to keep horses, wagons, etc. *U. S.*

Bark, 2.

bar'na-cle (bär'nǎ-k'l), n. Any of numerous small marine shellfish growing on rocks, etc.

barn′yard′ (bärn′yärd′), *n.* A yard or inclosure around a barn.

ba-rom′e-ter (bȧ-rŏm′e-tẽr), *n.* Instrument for determining the weight or pressure of the atmosphere. — **bar′o-met′ric** (băr′ŏ-mĕt′rĭk), **-met′ri-cal,** *a.*

bar′on (băr′ŭn), *n.* In Great Britain and various other countries, a nobleman, now only of the lowest grade; also, the grade or rank itself.

bar′on-age (-ȧj), *n.* The whole body of barons or peers; the dignity or rank of baron.

bar′on-ess (-ĕs), *n.* A baron′s wife; also, a lady who holds the baronial title in her own right.

bar′on-et (-ĕt), *n.* A dignity or degree of honor next below a baron and above a knight; also, a holder of this dignity. British baronets are commoners.

bar′on-et-cy (băr′ŭn-ĕt-sĭ), *n.; pl.* **-CIES** (-sĭz). Rank or dignity of a baronet.

bar′o-ny (băr′ŏ-nĭ), *n.; pl.* **-NIES** (-nĭz). Domain or rank of a baron. — **ba-ro′ni-al** (bȧ-rō′nĭ-ăl), *a.*

ba-rouche′ (bȧ-rōōsh′), *n.* A kind of four-wheeled carriage with a folding top.

barque (bärk). Var. of BARK (vessel).

bar′rack (băr′ăk), *n.* [*Usually in pl.*] *Mil.* A building or group of buildings for lodging soldiers.

‖**bar′rage′** (bȧ′räzh′), *n.* [F.] A barrier to the advance or retreat of an enemy, established by rapid and continuous artillery or machine-gun fire concentrated upon a narrow area.

bar′rel (băr′ĕl), *n.* **1.** A round bulging vessel or cask having flat ends or heads. **2.** The quantity constituting a full barrel. **3.** A drum or cylinder or similarly round part, hollow or solid. — *v. t.* [7] To put or pack in a barrel or barrels.

bar′ren (-ĕn), *a.* [3] Incapable of producing offspring; sterile; not fruitful; unprofitable. — *n.* A tract of barren land. — **bar′ren-ness,** *n.* [8].

bar′ri-cade′ (-ĭ-kād′), *n.* **1.** *Mil.* A fortification, as in a street, hastily made of anything that will obstruct progress. **2.** Any bar or obstruction. — *v. t.* [7] To fortify or close with a barricade.

bar′ri-er (băr′ĭ-ẽr), *n.* **1.** A fence or railing to mark the limits of a place, or to keep back a crowd. **2.** Any obstruction; as, a *barrier* to friendship.

bar′ring (bär′ĭng), *prep. or conj.* Excluding by exception; excepting; as, *barring* accident.

bar′ris-ter (băr′rĭs-tẽr), *n.* Counselor at law.

bar′row (băr′ō), *n.* A support having handles, and with or without a wheel, on which things can be transported by hand.

bar′ter (bär′tẽr), *v. i. & t.* To traffic or trade, or traffic or trade in, by exchange of commodities. — *n.* Act or practice of bartering. — **ter-er,** *n.* [8].

bar′y-tone, bar′i-tone (băr′ĭ-tōn), *n.* A male voice intermediate between the bass and the tenor; a person having such a voice. — *a. Music.* Grave and deep in tone; having the compass of a barytone.

bas′al (bās′ăl), *a.* Pertaining to the base.

ba-salt′ (bȧ-sôlt′; băs′ôlt), *n.* Any of several dark-colored rocks of volcanic origin.

base (bās), *n.* **1.** That on which a thing rests for support; foundation; bottom. **2.** The chief or necessary part of a thing; ground work. **3.** The point or line from which a start is made in any action or operation. **4.** A station or goal in various games. **5.** A protected place from which the operations of an army proceed.

base, *v. t.* [1] To put on a base or basis; found.

base (bās), *a.* [3] **1.** Deep or grave in sound. See BASS. **2.** Inferior in quality; mean; as, a *base* imitation. **3.** Of small comparative value, as metals inferior to the noble or precious metals (esp. gold and silver). **4.** Alloyed with inferior metal; debased; as, *base* coin. **5.** Morally low; ignoble; as, a *base* man. **6.** Suitable to, or characteristic of, an inferior person or position; as, *base* service.

base′ball′ (-bôl′), *n.* A certain well-known game of ball; also, the ball used in the game.

base′board′ (bās′bōrd′), *n.* A board situated at or forming the base of something.

base′born′ (-bôrn′), *a.* **1.** Of low parentage; plebeian. **2.** Born out of wedlock; illegitimate.

base′less, *a.* Without a base; groundless.

base′ly, *adv.* In a base manner.

base′ment (-mĕnt), *n.* **1.** *Arch.* The lower part of the wall or walls of a building; also, the story behind this part. **2.** Popularly, the floor in a building next below the principal floor.

base′ness (-nĕs), *n.* Quality or state of being base.

bash′ful (băsh′fŏŏl), *a.* [4] Very or excessively modest; indicating excessive modesty; shy; retiring. — **-ly,** *adv.* [8] — **-ness,** *n.* [8].

bas′ic (bās′ĭk), *a.* [4] Of or pertaining to the base or a base; fundamental.

ba′sin (bā′s′n), *n.* **1.** A wide hollow utensil, usually circular and with sloping sides. **2.** The quantity a basin holds. **3.** A hollow or inclosed place containing water, as a pond. **4.** The tract of country drained by a river and its tributaries.

bas′i-net (băs′ĭ-nĕt), *n.* A light steel helmet.

ba′sis (bā′sĭs), *n.; pl.* BASES (-sēz). **1.** Foundation; base. **2.** Chief component. **3.** Groundwork.

bask (bȧsk), *v. i.* To lie in warmth; to be exposed to genial heat.

bas′ket (băs′kĕt), *n.* **1.** A vessel made of osiers, rushes, splints, or other flexible material, interwoven. **2.** The contents of a basket.

basket ball, *or* **bas′ket-ball′,** *n.* An indoor game played with an inflated ball and elevated basket-like goals. Also, the ball used.

bas′ket-ry (băs′kĕt-rĭ), *n.* Art of making baskets; also, baskets collectively.

basque (băsk), *n.* A kind of bodice; now, often, a fitted waist.

bas′–re-lief′ (bä′-), *n.* Sculpture in low relief.

bass (bȧs), *n.* (see PLURAL, *n.,* Note). Any of numerous edible spiny-finned fishes.

bass (bās), *n.* **1.** A bass, or deep, sound or tone. **2.** *Music.* **a** The lowest part in the harmony of a composition, or a male voice that sings this part. **b** A singer or instrument having a bass voice, part, or compass. — *a.* Deep or grave in tone.

bas-soon′ (bȧ-sōōn′), *n. Music.* A wind instrument of the double-reed kind.

bass viol (bās). *Music.* An instrument of the viol family used for playing bass.

bass′wood′ (bȧs′wŏŏd′), *n.* A certain tree of the linden family, or its wood.

bast (băst), *n.* The strong woody fiber from the phloëm of various trees, esp. the linden.

bas′tard (băs′tãrd), *n.* An illegitimate child. — *a.* **1.** Illegitimate by birth. **2.** Not genuine; spurious.

bas′tar-dy (-tãr-dĭ), *n.* Illegitimacy.

baste (bāst), *v. t.* [1] **1.** To beat; cudgel. **2.** To wet (roasting meat, etc.) with melted butter, fat, etc.

baste. *v. t.* To sew loosely, or with long stitches, esp. temporarily.

bast′ing (bās′tĭng), *n.* Act of one who bastes, or stitches loosely; also, the thread so used.

bas′tion (băs′chŭn), *n.* *Fort.* A work projecting from the main inclosure, with two flanks.

bat (băt), *n.* A stout, solid stick; club; a club with one end thicker or broader than the other, used in baseball, cricket, etc.— *v. t.*; BAT′TED (-ĕd); BAT′TING. To strike or hit with or as with a bat. — *v. i.* To use, or hit a ball with, a bat.

bat, *n.* Any of numerous small animals with soft furry bodies and having the fore limbs modified to form wings. They fly by night.

batch (băch), *n.* **1.** Quantity of bread baked at one time; a baking. **2.** A quantity of material for one operation, as of dough for a baking. **3.** A quantity produced at one operation or taken at a time; lot; as, a *batch* of letters.

bate (bāt), *v. t. & i.* [1] To abate; deduct.

bath (bàth), *n.; pl.* BATHS (bàthz). **1.** Act of subjecting the body, or part of it, to water, vapor, hot air, or the like, for cleanliness, health, etc. **2.** A quantity or supply of water or other medium prepared for bathing. **3.** A receptacle, room, or place for bathing. **4.** A building arranged for bathing, or (usually *pl.*) a building containing a series of apartments so arranged. **5.** Any liquid in which objects are dipped to be acted on by it; also, the vessel holding the liquid.

bathe (bāth), *v. t.* [1] **1.** To wash by immersion, as in a bath. **2.** To lave; wet. **3.** To surround, or envelop, as water does a person immersed in it. — *v. i.* To bathe one's self; take a bath. — **bath′er** (bāth′ẽr), *n.* [8].

ba-tiste′ (bȧ-tēst′), *n.* A kind of fine cotton muslin.

ba′ton′ (bȧ′tŏn′; băt′ŭn), *n.* **1.** A staff or truncheon borne as a symbol of office. **2.** *Music.* The stick with which a leader beats time.

bats′man (băts′mȧn), *n.; pl.* -MEN (-mĕn). The one who wields the bat in baseball, cricket, etc.

bat-tal′ion (bă-tăl′yŭn), *n.* Any considerable division of an army organized to act together; in *pl.*, forces.

bat′ten (băt′'n), *v. i. & t.* To thrive; fatten in ease and luxury.

bat′ten, *n.* **1.** A strip of sawed timber used for flooring, etc. **2.** A strip of wood for nailing across two other pieces, for covering a crack. — *v. t.* To furnish or fasten with battens.

bat′ter (-ẽr), *v. t. & i.* To beat with successive blows; beat so as to bruise, shatter, or demolish. — *n.* *Cookery.* A semiliquid mixture, as of flour, eggs, milk, etc., beaten together.

bat′ter, *n.* A batsman.

bat′ter-ing-ram′, *n.* A military engine of antiquity, usually consisting of a huge iron-tipped beam mounted so as to be used to beat down walls.

bat′ter-y (băt′ẽr-ĭ), *n.; pl.* -TERIES (-ĭz). **1.** *Law.* The unlawful beating of another. **2.** *Mil.* **a** Any emplacement where artillery is mounted. **b** Two or more pieces of artillery under a single command. **c** A division, usually of from 4 to 6 guns, of artillery organized as a unit of command. **3.** *Naval.*

The guns, or any group of the guns, of a warship. **4.** *Elec.* **a** An apparatus of one or more cells for generating voltaic electricity. **b** Any combination of apparatus for producing a united electrical effect.

bat′ting (-ĭng), *n.* **1.** Act of one who bats; use of a bat. **2.** Cotton in sheets, for making quilts, etc.

bat′tle (-'l), *n.* **1.** A general encounter between armies or ships; engagement. **2.** A combat between two individuals. **3.** Fighting of armed forces; war. — *v. i.* [1] To contend in battle; fight.

bat′tle-ax ⎱ *n.* *Mil.* A kind of broadax formerly
bat′tle-axe ⎰ used as an offensive weapon.

bat′tle-dore (-dōr), *n.* A kind of light flat bat used in striking a shuttlecock to and fro.

bat′tle-ment (-mĕnt), *n.* A parapet with open spaces, at the top of ancient fortified buildings.

bat′tle-ship (-shĭp′), *n.* *Naval.* One of a class of the largest, most heavily armed and armored vessels.

bau′ble (bô′b'l), *n.* A trifling piece of finery.

bawl (bôl), *v. i. & t.* **1.** To cry out with a loud, full sound; to shout. **2.** To cry loudly, as from pain; howl. — *n.* A loud, prolonged cry; outcry.

bay (bā), *n.* *Geog.* An inlet of the sea, similar to, smaller than, a gulf.

bay, *n.* A window with its usual setting or framing, as jambs, window seat, etc. **2.** In a barn, a compartment, as for storing hay or grain in the stalk.

bay, *n.* **1.** The laurel tree. **2.** Leaves or sprigs of the laurel, esp. as woven into an honorary wreath or crown; hence, figuratively, fame; renown, esp. of a poet or victor; — usually in *pl.* Cf. LAUREL.

bay, *v. i.* To bark, esp. with deep, prolonged tones, as a dog in the chase. — *v. t.* **1.** To bark at; beset with barking. **2.** To bring or drive to bay. — *n.* **1.** The baying of dogs. **2.** State or position of one obliged to face an antagonist or a difficulty, when escape is impossible; — in *at*, or *to*, *bay*.

bay, *a.* Reddish brown; — used chiefly of horses. — *n.* A bay animal; esp., a bay horse.

bay′o-net (-ṓ-nĕt), *n.* *Mil.* A weapon of the dagger kind made to fit on the muzzle end of a musket or rifle. — *v. t.* To stab with a bayonet.

bay′ou (bī′ṓṓ), *n.* An inlet from the Gulf of Mexico, from a lake, or from a large river. *Southern U. S.*

bay window. A windowed bay or recess in a room.

ba-zaar′ (bȧ-zär′), *n.* **1.** In the East, an exchange, market place, or assemblage of shops. **2.** A spacious hall or suite of rooms for the sale of goods, as at a fair; also, a fair for the sale of fancy wares, etc., commonly for a charitable object.

ba-zar′, *n.* Var. of BAZAAR.

be (bē), *v. i.; pret.* WAS (wŏz); *p. p.* BEEN (see BEEN, *in vocabulary*); *p. pr. & vb. n.* BE′ING. The forms of **be** are as follows: Indicative: present, sing., 1st person, am; 2d art, [you] are; 3d, is. Pl., 1st, 2d, and 3d persons, are. Preterit, sing., 1st and 3d persons, was; 2d, wast. Pl., 1st, 2d, and 3d persons, were. Subjunctive: present, sing. and pl., 1st, 2d, and 3d persons, be. Preterit, sing. and pl., 1st and 3d persons, were; 2d sing. wert. **1.** To hold or obtain as true with respect to some condition, thing, or quality; as, "Blessed *are* the merciful." **2.** To exist; have place as a fact

1

2

Bayonets 1 Triangular; 2 Trowel

among facts; specifically, to live; as, "To be or not to be." **3. a** To come to pass; happen; as, the bride to be. **b** To continue in existence; last; as, this cannot be forever. **4.** To exist with reference to a certain place or condition; as, to be here; to be at ease. **5.** To signify; mean; as, what is it to you? **6.** To belong or pertain; befall;— usually with to or unto; as, woe be unto you!

beach (bēch), n. The shore of the sea or of a lake washed by the waves, esp. the sandy or pebbly part; strand. — v. t. & i. To run or drive (as a boat) on to a beach; strand.

bea'con (bē'k'n), n. **1.** A signal, esp., a signal fire on a pole or other eminence. **2.** A watchtower or signal station. **3.** A signal or mark erected on an eminence near the shore to guide mariners.

bead (bēd), n. **1.** A little perforated ball to be strung on a thread and used (1) in a rosary or (2) for ornament. **2.** Any small globular body. **3.** Arch. A small projecting molding of rounded surface. — v. t. & i. To ornament or provide with, or to form, beads or beading.

bea'dle (bē'd'l), n. An inferior parish officer in England having various duties.

bead'y (bēd'ĭ), a. [3] Beadlike; as, beady eyes.

bea'gle (bē'g'l), n. A small, short-legged, smooth-coated hound, with pendulous ears.

beak (bēk), n. **1.** The bill or nib of a bird, or of some other animals, as the turtle. **2.** Anything like or suggestive of a beak.— **beaked** (bēkt), a.

beak'er (-ēr), n. **1.** A large wide-mouthed drinking cup, supported on a standard. **2.** A deep, open-mouthed vessel used by chemists, etc.

beam (bēm), n. **1.** Any large and relatively long piece of timber or metal prepared for use. **2.** A principal horizontal timber or metal support of a building or ship. **3.** The extreme breadth of a vessel. **4.** The bar of a balance, from which hang the scales. **5.** A ray emitted from the sun or other luminous body. — v. t. To send forth; emit, as light. — v. i. To emit beams, as of light.

beam'ing (bēm'ĭng), p. a. [4] Emitting beams; radiant. — **-ly**, adv. [8].

bean (bēn), n. **1. a** The seed of any of certain leguminous plants. **b** Any of various beanlike seeds or fruits. **2.** Any plant that yields beans.

bear (bâr), v. t.; pret. BORE (bōr); p. p. BORN (bôrn), BORNE (bōrn), (see Note, below); BEAR'ING. **1.** To support and move; carry. **2.** To render or give, as testimony. **3.** To carry (one's self); behave. **4.** To possess or have; wear. **5.** To hold in the mind; harbor. **6.** To support or sustain; hold up. **7.** To sustain, or be answerable for, as blame, expense, etc. **8.** To be capable of; to suffer or sustain without injurious change. **9.** To endure; tolerate. **10.** To sustain, or have on. **11.** To press; thrust; drive. **12.** To bring forth or produce; yield.

☞ In the passive form of this verb, the best usage restricts the past participle born to the sense of given birth to. In the active form, borne alone is used as the past participle.

— v. i. **1.** To endure with patience. **2.** To press. **3.** To relate; refer. **4.** To be situated, as to the point of compass, with respect to something else; to have or take a certain bearing or direction. **5.** To produce fruit.

bear, n. **1.** A large, heavy animal, with long shaggy hair, and very short tail. **2.** An animal likened to a bear. **3.** [cap.] Astron. See URSA MAJOR, URSA MINOR. **4.** A brutal, coarse, uncouth, or morose person. **5.** Stock Exchange. A person who sells securities for future delivery in hopes of a fall in price. — v. t. Stock Exchange. To endeavor to depress the price of, or prices in.

bear'a-ble (-â-b'l), a. [4] Capable of being borne.

beard (bērd), n. **1.** The hair on the chin, lips, and adjacent parts of a man. **2.** Any of certain appendages likened to a man's beard; as, a goat's beard, the beard of grain. — v. t. **1.** To take by the beard; pluck the beard of (a man), in anger or contempt. **2.** To oppose to the face; defy.

beard'ed (bēr'dĕd), a. Having a beard.

beard'less, a. Having no beard.

bear'er (bâr'ēr), n. **1.** One that bears. **2.** One who holds a check, note, draft, or the like.

bear'ing, n. **1.** Act or process of one that bears **2.** The manner in which one bears one's self; carriage. **3.** Any single emblem in a coat of arms; — usually in pl. **4.** An object, surface, or point that supports; in machines, a part in which a journal, pivot, pin, or the like, turns or revolves. **5.** Purport; meaning. **6.** The situation or direction of one point or object with respect to another or to the points of the compass.

bear'ish (bâr'ĭsh), a. [4] Like a bear in manner, feeling, etc.; hence, rough; surly; gruff.

beast (bēst), n. **1.** Any four-footed animal, as distinguished from birds, reptiles, fishes, and in sects. **2.** A brutal or degraded person.

beast'ly (-lĭ), a. [3] **1.** Of, pertaining to, or having the form, nature, or habits of a beast. **2.** Brutal; filthy. — **beast'li-ness,** n. [8].

beat (bēt), v. t.; pret. BEAT; p. p. BEAT, BEAT'EN (bēt'n); p. pr. & vb. n. BEAT'ING. **1.** To strike repeatedly. **2.** To punish by blows; thrash. **3.** To overcome in a contest, game, etc.; vanquish; surpass. **4.** To measure or mark off by strokes. **5.** To range over in the chase, striking bushes, etc., to rouse game. **6.** Mil. To give the signal for by beat of drum or other instrument. — v. i. **1.** To strike repeatedly. **2.** To come, act, dash, or fall with force. **3.** To move with pulsation or throbbing **4.** Naut. To make progress to windward by tacking or wearing. **5.** To make a sound when struck **6.** To win the victory. Colloq. — n. **1.** A stroke blow. **2.** A recurring stroke; throb; pulsation **3.** Music. The rise or fall of the hand, baton, foot, etc., marking the divisions of time and the accent a division of the measure so marked, or the accent **4.** A round or course often gone over. — **beat'er,** n. [8].

beat'en (bēt''n), p. a. **1.** Wrought, or worked upon, by beating. **2.** Vanquished; baffled.

be'a-tif'ic (bē'â-tĭf'ĭk), a. [4] Having power to impart blissful enjoyment; making blessed.

be-at'i-fi-ca'tion (bē-ăt'ĭ-fĭ-kā'shŭn), n. Act of beatifying, or state of being beatified.

be-at'i-fy (bē-ăt'ĭ-fī), v. t. [2] To bless with celestial enjoyment.

beat'ing, p. pr. & vb. n. of BEAT.

be-at'i-tude (bē-ăt'ĭ-tūd), n. **1.** Felicity of the highest kind; blessedness. **2.** Any of the declara-

---

chair; go; sing, iŋk; then, thin; nature, verdure; yet; zh = z in azure. Numbers refer to §§ in the Special Notes which, with Abbreviations, Signs, etc., precede the Vocabulary.

tions (*the Beatitudes*) made in the Sermon on the Mount (*Matt.* v. 3–12).

beau (bō), *n. ; pl.* F. BEAUX (*E. pron.* bōz), E. BEAUS (bōz). **1.** A man who dresses with great care in the latest fashion; a dandy. **2.** A man who escorts, or pays attentions to, a lady; escort; lover.

beau'te-ous (bū'tē-ŭs), *a.* [4] Full of beauty; beautiful to see. — **-ly,** *adv.* [8] — **-ness,** *n.* [8].

beau'ti-ful (-tĭ-fŏŏl), *a.* [4] Having beauty; full of beauty. —*n.* That which is beautiful. — **beau'-ti-ful-ly,** *adv.* [8] — **beau'ti-ful-ness,** *n.* [8].

beau'ti-fy (-fī), *v. t. & i.* [2] To make, or to become, beautiful; adorn; embellish.

beau'ty (bū'tĭ), *n. ; pl.* -TIES (-tĭz). **1.** That quality or combination of qualities which gratifies the eye or ear, or which delights the intellect or moral sense by its grace or fitness; the beautiful. **2.** A particular grace or excellence; anything beautiful.

beaux (bōz), *n. pl.* See BEAU.

bea'ver (bē'vẽr), *n.* **1.** A valuable fur-bearing animal, chiefly of North America, about two feet in length, with small fore feet, large webbed hind feet, and a broad, flat tail. It fells trees by gnawing, and builds "houses" and dams. **2.** Fur of the beaver. **3.** A heavy woolen cloth.

Beaver. 1/18

bea'ver, *n.* Armor for the lower face.

be-calm' (bē-käm'), *v. t.* **1.** To calm. **2.** *Naut.* To keep from motion or progress by lack of wind.

be-came' (-kām'), *pret.* of BECOME.

be-cause' (-kôz'), *adv. & conj.* By or for the cause that ; for the reason that ; since.

beck, *n.* A significant nod, or motion of the head or hand, esp. as a call or command.

beck'on (bĕk'′n), *v. i. & t.* To signal, or call, by or as by a motion of the hand, finger, or head.

be-cloud' (bē-kloud'), *v. t.* To obscure ; cloud.

be-come' (-kŭm'), *v. i. ; pret.* -CAME' (-kām') ; *p. p.* -COME' ; *p. pr. & vb. n.* -COM'ING (-kŭm'ĭng). To pass from one state to another; come to be. — *v. t.* To suit or be suitable to ; befit ; accord with.

be-com'ing (-kŭm'ĭng), *p. a.* [4] Suitable; proper; appropriate or fit. — **be-com'ing-ly,** *adv.* [8].

bed (bĕd), *n.* **1. a** That upon or within which one sleeps or rests. **b** A bedstead. *Colloq. or Cant.* **2.** A plat, or level piece, of ground in a garden. **3.** A mass or heap suggestive of a bed (sense 1) ; as, a *bed* of rock. **4.** The bottom of any body of water; as, the *bed* of the ocean. **5.** A foundation for a machine, or a solid support on which its work is done; as, the *bed* of a press. **6.** The earthwork or ballast of a railroad. — *v. i. ;* BED'DED ; BED'-DING. **1.** To go to bed. **2.** To lie on or as on a bed. — *v. t.* **1.** To put to bed; furnish with a bed or bedding. **2.** To plant or arrange, as plants, in a bed or beds. **3.** To embed ; to rest.

be-dab'ble (bē-dăb''l), *v. t.* [1] To dabble.

be-daub' (-dôb'), *v. t.* To daub over.

be-daz'zle (-dăz''l), *v. t.* [1] To dazzle completely

bed'bug' (bĕd'bŭg'), *n.* A wingless, bloodsucking insect, sometimes infesting houses and esp. beds

bed'cham'ber (-chām'bẽr), *n.* A bedroom.

bed'clothes' (-klōthz'), *n. pl.* Coverings for a bed.

bed'ding (-ĭng), *n.* Bedclothes; materials for beds.

be-deck' (bē-dĕk'), *v.t.* To deck out; adorn; grace.

be-dew' (-dū'), *v. t.* To wet with or as with dew.

be-dim' (bĕ-dĭm'), *v. t.* To make dim ; becloud.

be-diz'en (-dĭz''n; -dī'z'n), *v. t.* To dress out ; esp., to adorn tawdrily.

bed'lam (bĕd'lăm), *n.* **1.** A lunatic asylum. **2.** Any place of uproar and confusion.

be-drag'gle (bē-drăg''l), *v. t.* [1] To draggle.

bed'rid'den (bĕd'rĭd''n), *a.* Confined to the bed by sickness or infirmity; decrepit; worn out.

bed rock. The solid rock below the surface.

bed'room', *n.* A room for a bed ; lodging room.

bed'stead (-stĕd), *n.* Framework of a bed.

bee (bē), *n.* **1.** Any of certain small insects of many species. They store up pollen for food, and often also honey. **2.** A neighborly gathering to work for some one, or for some coöperative purpose. *U. S.*

beech (bēch), *n.* A common hardwood tree of various species. The beeches have smooth gray bark and bear a sweet edible nut (**beech'nut'**). — **beech'en** (-'n), *a.*

beef (bēf), *n.* **1.** *pl.* BEEVES (bēvz), *or, esp. in U. S.,* BEEFS. Any animal, esp. an adult of the domestic species, of the genus including the bull, cow, and ox ; esp., an ox or cow, fatted for food. **2.** The flesh of a beef used for food.

beef'y (-ĭ), *a.* [3] Having much beef ; brawny.

bee'hive' (bē'hīv'), *n.* A hive for bees.

been (bĭn; bēn). Past participle of BE.

beer (bēr), *n.* **1.** A brewed liquor made with malted grain, commonly barley, and flavored with hops. **2.** Any of various fermented but undistilled liquors.

bees'wax' (bēz'wăks'), *n.* Wax secreted by bees.

beet (bēt), *n.* A certain biennial plant extensively cultivated; also, its large edible root.

bee'tle (bē't'l), *n.* A heavy hammering or ramming instrument, usually with a wooden head or entirely of wood.

bee'tle, *n.* **1.** Any of certain insects having four wings, the outer pair being stiff cases covering the others when folded. **2.** Popularly, an insect more or less like a beetle (in sense 1).

bee'tle, *a.* Projecting ; lowering. —*v. i.* To project so as to overhang ; jut.

beeves (bēvz), *n., pl.* of BEEF.

be-fall' (bē-fôl'), *v.i. ;* for parts see FALL. To happen.

be-fit' (-fĭt'), *v. t. ;* BE-FIT'TED ; -FIT'TING. To be suitable to ; become. — **be-fit'ting-ly,** *adv.* [8].

be-fog' (-fŏg'), *v. t. ;* -FOGGED' (-fŏgd') ; -FOG'GING. To involve in fog ; hence, to confuse ; mystify.

be-fore' (bē-fōr'), *adv.* **1.** On the fore part; in front. **2.** In advance. **3.** In time past ; previously. **4.** Earlier; sooner. — *prep.* **1.** In front of; preceding. **2.** Farther onward, in place or time. **3.** In presence or sight of ; face to face with. — *conj.* **1.** Previous to the time when. **2.** Sooner than ; rather than.

be-fore'hand' (-hănd'), *adv.* In advance, as by way of forethought. — *a.* Forehanded.

be-friend' (bĕ-frĕnd'), *v. t.* To act as a friend to.

be-fud'dle (-fŭd''l), *v. t.* [1] To becloud and confuse, as with liquor.

beg (bĕg), *v. t.;* BEGGED (bĕgd) ; BEG'GING. **1.** To ask for as a charity, esp. habitually ; as, he *begs* his bread. **2.** To supplicate for ; beseech ; entreat. — *v. i.* **1.** To ask alms or charity, esp. habitually. **2.** To make petition ; supplicate.

be-gat' (bĕ-găt'). Archaic pret. of BEGET.

be-get' (bĕ-gĕt'), *v. t.; pret.* -GOT' (-gŏt'), *Archaic* -GAT' (-găt') ; *p. p.* -GOT', GOT'TEN (-gŏt''n) ; *p. pr. & vb. n.* -GET'TING. To procreate as a father or sire ; generate ; cause to exist.

beg'gar (bĕg'ẽr), *n.* One who begs. — *v. t.* **1.** To reduce to beggary ; impoverish. **2.** To cause to seem poor or inadequate ; as, to *beggar* description.

beg'gar-ly (-lĭ), *a.* [4] Like, or suitable for, a beggar; extremely indigent; mean. — **-li-ness,** *n.*

beg'gar-y (-ĭ), *n.* Act of begging ; state or condition of a beggar ; indigence ; penjury.

be-gin' (bĕ-gĭn'), *v. i.; pret.* BE-GAN' (-găn') ; *p. p.* BE-GUN' (-gŭn') ; *p. pr. & vb. n.* -GIN'NING. **1.** To do the first act or take the first step ; start ; as, let us *begin.* **2.** To come into existence ; commence. — *v. t.* To set about ; commence ; as, they *began* to get dinner. — **be-gin'ner,** *n.* [8].

be-gin'ning (-ĭng), *n.* **1.** Commencement of an action or state. **2.** The first cause ; origin ; source.

be-gone' (-gŏn'), *interj.* Go away ! Depart !

be-go'ni-a (-gō'nĭ-à), *n.* *Bot.* Any plant of a genus (*Begonia*) of tropical flowering herbs or low shrubs, much cultivated.

be-got' (-gŏt'), **be-got'ten** (-'n). See BEGET.

be-grime' (bĕ-grīm'), *v. t.* [1] To soil with grime.

be-grudge' (-grŭj'), *v. t.* [1] To grumble at ; envy the possession of.

be-guile' (-gīl'), *v. t.* [1] **1.** To delude by guile or craft ; deceive. **2.** To deprive by guile ; cheat. **3.** To charm ; divert ; amuse. **4.** To while away.

be-gun' (bĕ-gŭn'), *p. p. & p. a.* of BEGIN.

be-half' (-häf'), *n.* Side ; part ; interest ; affair ; defense ; — only in phrases ; as in *in behalf of.*

be-have' (-hāv'), *v. t.* [1] To carry; conduct;—used reflexively.— *v. i.* To act; conduct one's self or itself ; often, to conduct one's self well or properly.

be-hav'ior (-hāv'yẽr), *n.* [5] Act or manner of behaving ; conduct ; bearing ; deportment.

be-head' (-hĕd'), *v. t.* To sever the head from.

be-held' (-hĕld'), *pret. & p. p.* of BEHOLD.

be-hest' (-hĕst'), *n.* An order ; command.

be-hind' (-hīnd'), *adv.* **1.** Back in place or time. **2.** Not yet produced or exhibited to view; remaining; still to come. **3.** After the set or proper time; late; slow, as a watch. **4.** Toward the back; as, to look *behind.* — *prep.* **1.** In a place, state, or time departed from by (the one referred to). **2.** Inferior to in dignity, attainments, etc. **3.** Of time, after; later than. **4.** On or at the back side of; in the rear of.

be-hind'hand' (-hānd'), *adv. & a.* **1.** In arrears financially ; in debt. **2.** Behind the times; late.

be-hold' (-hōld'), *v. t. & i.; pret.* -HELD' (-hĕld') ; *p. p.* -HELD', *Archaic* -HOLD'EN (-hōl'd'n) ; *p. pr. & vb. n.* -HOLD'ING. To see ; gaze upon ; view. — *interj.* Lo ! Look ! — used to call attention.

be-hold'en (-hōl'd'n), *p. a.* Obliged ; indebted.

be-hold'er (-dẽr), *n.* A spectator; looker-on.

be-hoof' (bĕ-hōōf'), *n.* Advantage ; benefit; use.

be-hoove' (-hōōv'), *v. t.* [1] To be proper for or incumbent on ; as, it *behooves* you to go.

be-hoove (-hōōv'; -hŏv'). Var. of BEHOOVE.

be'ing (bē'ĭng), *p. pr. & p. a.* of BE. Existing. — *n.* **1.** Existence ; life. **2.** That which exists.

be-la'bor (-lā'bẽr), *v. t.* [5] To beat soundly.

be-lat'ed (-lāt'ĕd), *p. a.* [4] Overtaken by night; delayed.

belch (bĕlch), *v. i.* **1.** To eject wind or gas spasmodically from the stomach through the mouth ; eructate. **2.** To eject its contents, as a gun; issue spasmodically, as fire from a volcano. — *v. t.* **1.** To eject (gas) from the stomach. **2.** To eject, esp. violently; vent forcibly; emit. — *n.* An eructation. *All now Vulgar* when referring to eructation from the stomach.

be-lea'guer (bĕ-lē'gẽr), *v. t.* To surround with an army ; hence, to beset ; encompass.

bel'fry (bĕl'frĭ), *n. ; pl.* -FRIES (-frĭz). A tower, or the like, for a bell or bells.

be-lie' (bĕ-lī'), *v. t.;* -LIED' (bĕ-līd') ; -LY'ING (-lī'ĭng). **1.** To tell lies about; slander. **2.** To misrepresent. **3.** To be false to. **4.** To show or prove to be false.

be-lief' (-lēf'), *n.* **1.** A state or habit of mind in which trust is placed in some person or thing; trust; confidence. **2.** A persuasion of the truths of religion; faith. **3.** Thing believed ; doctrine ; creed.

be-liev'a-ble (-lēv'à-b'l), *a.* [4] Capable of being believed ; credible.

be-lieve' (-lēv'), *v. i.* [1] **1.** To have faith or confidence. **2.** To exercise belief or faith, esp. as to the truths of religion. **3.** To think; judge.— *v. t.* To regard, accept, or hold as true; also, to think; consider. — **be-liev'er,** *n.* [8].

be-lit'tle (-lĭt''l), *v. t.* [1] To make little or less ; speak of in a depreciatory way.

bell (bĕl), *n.* **1.** A hollow, often cup-shaped, metallic vessel, giving forth a ringing sound when struck. **2. a** A bell rung to tell the hours ; also, a stroke of such a bell, esp. on shipboard. **b** The time so indicated ; *Naut.,* a half hour. **3.** Anything in the form of a bell, as the corolla of a flower. — *v. t.* To provide with a bell.

bel'la-don'na (bĕl'à-dŏn'à), *n.* A European poisonous plant, of the nightshade family.

belle (bĕl), *n.* A beautiful girl or woman.

bel'li-cose (bĕl'ĭ-kōs), *a.* [4] Inclined to fight; pugnacious ; warlike. — **bel'li-cose-ly,** *adv.* [8].

bel-lig'er-ence (bĕ-lĭj'ẽr-ĕns) } *n.* Quality of be-
bel-lig'er-en-cy (-lĭj'ẽr-ĕn-sĭ) } ing belligerent; status of a belligerent; act or state of waging war.

bel-lig'er-ent (-ĕnt), *a.* [4] **1.** Waging war. **2.** Pertaining to war; warlike. — *n.* A belligerent nation, state, or person. — **-ly,** *adv.* [8].

bel'low (bĕl'ō), *v. i.* To make a hollow, loud noise, as a bull; hence, to bawl; clamor. — *v. t.* To emit with a bellow. — *n.* A noise as of a bull; roar.

bel'lows (-ōz ; -ŭs), *n. sing. & pl.* A device which, by alternate expansion and contraction, draws in air through a hole and blows it out through a tube.

bell'weth'er (bĕl'wĕth'ẽr), *n.* A wether which leads the flock, with a bell on his neck.

bel'ly (bĕl'ĭ), *n. ; pl.* -LIES (-ĭz). **1.** The part of the human body between the thorax, or breast, and the thighs; also, the cavity of this part; abdo-

---

chair; go; sing, iŋk; then, thin; nature, verdure; yet; zh = z in azure. Numbers refer to §§ in the Special Notes which, with Abbreviations, Signs, etc., precede the Vocabulary.

men. **2.** The under part of the body of an animal. **3.** A part suggestive of the belly. — *v. t. & i.* [2] To swell or bulge out.

be-long' (bĕ-lŏng'), *v. i.* [Usually construed with *to.*] **1.** To be connected (with) as a part, quality, duty, office, or the like. **2.** To be the property (of). **3.** To be bound (to) or connected (with) by some relation, as of birth or residence.

be-long'ing (-ĭng), *n.* A thing that belongs to one; — usually in *pl.* : Goods; effects.

be-loved' (*as p. p.* -lŭvd' ; *as adj. & n.* -lŭv'ĕd *or* -lŭvd'), *p. p. & p. a.* Loved. — *n.* A loved one.

be-low' (-lō'), *adv.* In a lower place, with respect to any object ; beneath. — *prep.* Under, or lower than, in place, rank, value, etc. ; not so high as.

belt (bĕlt), *n.* **1.** A broadish strip of leather, cloth, or the like, used to girdle the person. **2.** Any stripe, or series of things, suggestive of a belt (sense 1). **3.** *Mach.* A broad, flexible, usually endless, leather band passing round two or more pulleys, or the like, for communicating motion. —*v. t.* To encircle or invest with or as with a belt.

be-moan' (-mōn'), *v. t. & i.* To express grief for by moaning ; bewail ; lament.

bench (bĕnch), *n.* **1.** A long seat. **2.** The seat where the judges sit in court; judge's seat; hence, office or dignity of judge. **3.** The judges collectively, or a judge, sitting in court ; also, a court. **4.** A long worktable.

bend (bĕnd), *v. t.* ; BENT (bĕnt) *or* BEND'ED ; BEND'-ING. **1.** To strain into a state of tension by means of a band or string;—used of the bow. **2.** To strain, stretch, or move out of a straight line ; to crook or curve. **3.** To cause to bow, stoop, or yield; subdue. **4.** To turn; deflect; hence, incline; dispose.—*v. i.* **1.** To be moved or strained out of a given line ; curve ; incline. **2.** To bend the body, as in prayer; bow; fig., to yield; submit. — *n.* **1.** Act of bending; a turn from a straight line or direction; state of being bent. **2.** A bent thing or part ; curve ; crook.

be-neath' (bĕ-nēth'; -nĕth'), *adv.* In a lower place; below. — *prep.* Lower than in place, rank, dignity, excellence, power, etc. ; below.

ben'e-dict (bĕn'ĕ-dĭkt), *n.* A married man; usually, a man newly married, esp. one long a bachelor.

ben'e-dic'tion (-dĭk'shŭn), *n.* A blessing.

ben'e-dic'to-ry (-tō-rĭ), *a.* Expressing benediction; blessing.

ben'e-fac'tion (-făk'shŭn), *n.* Act of benefiting or a benefit conferred, esp. in charity; gift; donation.

ben'e-fac'tor (-tẽr), *n.* One who confers a benefaction or benefits. — **-fac'tress** (-trĕs), *n. fem.*

ben'e-fice (bĕn'ĕ-fĭs), *n.* A church living; an estate or endowment providing an income to maintain a clergyman in his official position; also, the income thus provided.

be-nef'i-cence (bĕ-nĕf'ĭ-sĕns), *n.* **1.** Active goodness, kindness, or charity. **2.** A benefaction.

be-nef'i-cent (-sĕnt), *a.* [4] Doing good; actively kind. — **be-nef'i-cent-ly**, *adv.* [8].

ben'e-fi'cial (bĕn'ĕ-fĭsh'ăl), *a.* [4] Conferring benefits; helpful; advantageous. — **-ly**, *adv.* [8].

ben'e-fi'ci-a-ry (-ĭ-ă-rĭ), *n.; pl.* -RIES (-rĭz). One who receives anything as a gift; one who receives a benefit or advantage, as the person who is to receive the proceeds of an insurance policy.

ben'e-fit (bĕn'ĕ-fĭt), *n.* **1.** Act of kindness; favor; gift. **2.** Whatever promotes prosperity and personal happiness ; advantage ; profit. — *v. t. & i.* To give, or to receive, benefit ; profit.

be-nev'o-lence (bĕ-nĕv'ō-lĕns), *n.* **1.** Quality of being benevolent; disposition to do good ; charitableness. **2.** An act of kindness ; good done.

be-nev'o-lent (-lĕnt), *a.* [4] Having a disposition to do good; charitable. — **-ly**, *adv.* [8].

be-night'ed (-nit'ĕd), *a.* [4] **1.** Overtaken by night or darkness. **2.** Involved in, or due to, moral darkness or ignorance.

be-nign' (-nīn'), *a.* [3] **1.** Kind or gentle in disposition; gracious. **2.** Showing kindness, gentleness, etc. ; kindly. **3.** Of a mild kind.

be-nig'nan-cy (-nĭg'năn-sĭ), *n.* Benignant quality or state; kindliness.

be-nig'nant (-nănt), *a.* [4] Kindly (to inferiors or dependents) ; gracious. — **-ly**, *adv.* [8].

be-nig'ni-ty (-nĭ-tĭ), *n.; pl.* -TIES (-tĭz). **1.** Quality or state of being benign. **2.** A kind deed.

be-nign'ly (-nīn'lĭ), *adv.* In a benign manner.

ben'i-son (bĕn'ĭ-z'n), *n.* Blessing ; benediction.

bent (bĕnt), *pret. & p. p.* of BEND, *v.* ; used also adjectivally.

bent, *n.* **1.** A leaning or bias; tendency of mind; disposition. **2.** Power of endurance ; capacity.

bent, *n.* Any of numerous stiff, wiry grasses.

be-numb' (bĕ-nŭm'), *v. t.* To deprive of sensation or sensibility, as by cold ; deaden.

ben'zene (bĕn'zēn; bĕn-zēn'), *n.* A volatile, inflammable, colorless liquid got by distilling coal.

ben'zine (bĕn'zĭn; -zēn), *n.* **1.** A volatile inflammable liquid derived from petroleum. **2.** An inflammable liquid obtained from coal tar.

be-queath' (bĕ-kwēth'), *v. t.* **1.** To give or leave by will. **2.** To hand down ; transmit.

be-quest' (-kwĕst'), *n.* Act of bequeathing ; also, that which is left by will.

be-rate' (-rāt'), *v. t.* [1] To rate or chide vehemently ; scold.

be-reave' (bĕ-rēv'), *v. t.* ; -REAVED' (-rēvd'), -REFT' (-rĕft'); -REAV'ING. To deprive; dispossess.

be-reave'ment (-mĕnt), *n.* State of being bereaved.

berg (bûrg), *n.* Short for ICEBERG.

ber'ry (bĕr'ĭ), *n.; pl.* -RIES (-ĭz). **1.** Any pulpy fruit of small size, as the strawberry, raspberry, checkerberry, hagberry, hip of the rose, etc. **2.** *Bot.* Any simple fruit having a pulpy or fleshy pericarp, as the currant, grape, cranberry, or banana. **3.** The dry seed or kernel of certain plants, as the coffee *berry.* — *v. i.* [2] **1.** To produce berries. **2.** To gather berries.

berth (bûrth), *n.* **1.** The place where a ship lies at anchor or at a wharf. **2.** An allotted place; situation. **3.** A shelflike sleeping place on the side of a ship's cabin, a stateroom, or a railroad car.

ber'yl (bĕr'ĭl), *n.* A mineral or gem, of which the aquamarine and emerald are varieties.

be-seech' (bĕ-sēch'), *v. t.* ; *pret. & p. p.* -SOUGHT' (-sôt') ; *p. pr. & vb. n.* -SEECH'ING. **1.** To ask or entreat with urgency; supplicate. **2.** To ask earnestly for; beg. — **be-seech'ing**, *p. a.* [4] — **be-seech'ing-ly**, *adv.* [8].

be-seem' (-sēm'), *v. i.* To befit; become.

be-set' (-sĕt'), *v. t.* ; *pret. & p. p.* BE-SET' ; *p. pr. &*

vb. n. -SET′TING. **1.** To stud with prominences. **2.** To set upon on all sides; to harass. **3.** To hem in; surround.

be-side′ (bĕ-sīd′), *adv.* = BESIDES, *adv.* — *prep.* **1.** At or by the side of; near by; hence, compared with. **2.** Over and above. = BESIDES, *prep.*, 2.

be-sides′ (-sīdz′), *adv.* In addition; else. — *prep.* **1.** At or by the side of. =BESIDE, *prep.*, 1. **2.** Over and above; in addition to; other than.

be-siege′ (bĕ-sēj′), *v. t.* [1] To beset with armed forces; lay siege to. — **be-sieg′er** (-sēj′ẽr), *n.* [8].

be-sot′ (bĕ-sŏt′), *v. t.; -*SOT′TED (-ĕd); -SOT′TING. To make sottish, dull, or stupid; stupefy.

be-sought′ (-sôt′), *pret. & p. p.* of BESEECH.

be-spat′ter (-spăt′ẽr), *v. t.* To spatter over; soil by spattering.

be-speak′ (-spēk′), *v. t. ;* for prin. parts see SPEAK. **1.** To speak for beforehand; engage in advance. **2.** To betoken; indicate, as by appearances.

best (bĕst), *a. ; superl.* of GOOD. **1.** Having good qualities in the highest degree ; most excellent. **2.** Most productive of good; most advantageous, serviceable, etc. **3.** Most; largest.—*adv.; superl.* of WELL. **1.** In the best way; to the most advantage. **2.** In the best or highest degree; to the fullest extent ; most. — *n.* That which is best ; the best part. — *v. t.* To get the better of. *Colloq.*

bes′tial (bĕs′chăl), *a.* [4] Belonging to a beast; animal; brutish ; irrational; beastly.

bes-tial′i-ty (bĕs-chăl′ĭ-tĭ ; bĕs′chĭ-ăl′ĭ-tĭ), *n. ; pl.* -TIES (-tĭz). Bestial state or quality or practice.

be-stir′ (bĕ-stûr′), *v. t. & i.* To stir up; rouse.

be-stow′ (-stō′), *v. t.* **1.** To deposit ; stow. **2.** To give or confer, as in marriage.

be-stow′al (-stō′ăl), *n.* Act of bestowing; disposal.

be-strew′ (-strōō′), *v. t.* To strew or scatter over.

be-stride′ (-strīd′), *v. t. ;* BE-STRODE′ (-strōd′); -STRID′DEN (-strĭd′n). **1.** To stand or sit astride of ; straddle. **2.** To stride over or across.

bet (bĕt), *n.* Something staked, or pledged, upon the outcome of some contest, future event, or other contingency; act of giving such a pledge ; wager. — *v. t. & i. ;* BET, also BET′TED (-ĕd) ; BET′TING. To stake or hazard (as money, etc.) on the outcome of an event ; to wager.

be-take′ (bĕ-tāk′), *v. t.;* for prin. parts see TAKE. To have recourse or resort to ; — used reflexively.

be-think′ (bĕ-thĭnk′), *v. t.* To call to mind ; recall ; think ; consider ; as, to *bethink* one's self.

be-thought′ (-thôt′), *pret. & p. p.* of BETHINK.

be-tide′ (-tīd′), *v. i.* [1] To befall ; come to pass.

be-times′ (-tīmz′), *adv.* In good season ; early.

be-to′ken (-tō′k'n), *v. t.* To foreshow by present signs ; presage ; signify ; evidence.

be-took′ (bĕ-tŏŏk′), *pret.* of BETAKE.

be-tray′ (bĕ-trā′), *v. t.* **1.** To deliver to the enemy by treachery or fraud. **2.** To fail or desert in need. **3.** To mislead ; lead into error, sin, or danger. **4.** To disclose or reveal. — **be-tray′er**, *n.* [8].

be-tray′al (-ăl), *n.* Act of betraying.

be-troth′ (-trŏth′; -trōth′), *v. t.* To contract or engage (to any one) for marriage.

be-troth′al (-ăl), *n.* Act of betrothing; espousal.

bet′ter (bĕt′ẽr), *n.* One who bets, or lays a wager.

bet′ter, *a. ;* used as *compar.* of GOOD. **1.** Having good qualities in a greater degree than another. **2.** Preferable. **3.** Larger ; greater. **4.** Improved in health.—*adv. ;* used as *compar.* of WELL. **1.** In a superior or more excellent manner. **2.** In a higher or greater degree; more.—*n.* **1.** That which is better. **2.** A superior, as in merit, rank, etc. ; — now only in *pl.* **3.** Advantage or victory; — chiefly in *to get the better of.* — *v. t.* **1.** To improve in condition, as morally, physically, socially. **2.** To surpass in excellence ; excel.

bet′ter-ment (-mĕnt), *n.* A making better; improvement ; permanent improvement, as of property.

bet′tor (bĕt′ẽr), *n.* One who bets ; a better.

be-tween′ (bĕ-twēn′), *prep.* **1.** In the space which separates ; betwixt. **2.** From one to another of. **3.** In common to; in the joint possession of; by the united action of. **4.** In connection with the mutual action or interaction of. **5.** In point of comparison of.—*adv.* In an intermediate position or relation in space or time ; in the interval.

be-twixt′ (-twĭkst′), *prep., adv., & b.* Between.

bev′el (bĕv′ĕl), *n.* **1.** The angle which one surface or line makes with another when not at right angles. **2.** An instrument for drawing angles or for adjusting the surfaces of work to a given inclination. — *v. t.* [7] To cut or shape to a bevel angle. — *v. i.* To incline; slant. — *a.* Having the slant of a bevel; slanting ; oblique ; as, a *bevel* edge.

bev′er-age (-ẽr-ăj), *n.* Liquid for drinking; drink.

bev′y (-ĭ), *n. ; pl.* BEVIES (-ĭz). A company; — of girls or ladies, quails, larks, etc.

be-wail′ (bĕ-wāl′), *v. t. & i.* To lament ; bemoan.

be-ware′ (-wâr′), *v. i.* To be on one's guard ; to take care. — *v. t.* To have a care for.

be-wil′der (-wĭl′dẽr), *v.t.* **1.** To cause to lose one's bearings; to confuse. **2.** To daze ; dumfound.

be-wil′der-ment (-mĕnt), *n.* State or fact of being bewildered;also;a bewildering tangle or confusion.

be-witch′ (-wĭch′), *v. t.* **1.** To affect (esp. to injure) by witchcraft. **2.** To charm ; fascinate.

be-witch′ing, *p. a.* [4] Fascinating ; enchanting. — **be-witch′ing-ly**, *adv.* [8].

be-witch′ment (-mĕnt), *n.* Act or power of bewitching ; state of being bewitched.

be-yond′ (bĕ-yŏnd′), *adv.* Farther away; at a distance; yonder. — *prep.* **1.** Of space or time : On or to the farther side of ; farther on or away than. **2.** Out of the reach or sphere of; greater than; further than. **3.** Above, as in dignity, excellence, etc. — *n.* That which is on the farther side or beyond, esp. beyond the present life.

bi-an′nu-al (bī-ăn′ū-ăl), *a.* Semiannual.

bi′as (bī′ăs), *n.;pl.* BIASES (-ĕz). **1.** A diagonal or slant, esp. across a fabric. **2.** A natural inclination of the mind ; bent. — *a.* Slanting ; diagonal to the texture or outline ; — applied to fabrics. — *adv.* In a slanting manner ; obliquely. — *v.t.* [7] To give a bias to ; incline ; prejudice.

bib (bĭb), *n.* A small protective piece of cloth worn over the breast, esp. by children.

Bi′ble (bī′b'l), *n.* **1.** The book of writings accepted by Christians as inspired of God ; the Scriptures. **2.** A book of the sacred writings of any religion.

Bib′li-cal (bĭb′lĭ-kăl), *a.* Of, pertaining to, derived from, or in accord with, the Bible.

bib-li-og′ra-pher (bĭb′lĭ-ŏg′rȧ-fẽr), *n.* One who writes, or is versed in, bibliography.

---

chair; go; sing, iŋk; then, thin; nature, verdure; yet; zh = z in azure. Numbers refer to §§ in the Special Notes which, with Abbreviations, Signs, etc., precede the Vocabulary.

bib'li·og'ra·phy (bĭb'lĭ-ŏg'ra-fĭ), n.; pl. **-PHIES** (-fĭz). **1.** The history or description of books. **2.** A list of books relating to a given subject.

bib'u·lous (bĭb'ū-lŭs), a. [4] **1.** Absorbent; as, *bibulous* paper. **2.** Inclined to drink; given to tippling.

bi·cam'er·al (bī-kăm'ēr-ăl), a. Of or including two chambers, or legislative branches.

bi'ceps (bī'sĕps), n. The large muscle of the front of the upper arm.

bick'er (bĭk'ēr), v. i. **1.** To wrangle; chatter. **2.** To flow noisily, as a brook; flicker; quiver. — n. Contention; wrangle.

bi·cus'pid (bī-kŭs'pĭd), n. Either of the two double-pointed teeth on each side of each jaw.

bi'cy·cle (bī'sĭ-k'l), n. A light vehicle having two wheels one behind the other and propelled by the rider's feet acting on treadles. — v. i. [1] To ride a bicycle. — **bi'cy·clist** (-klĭst), n.

bid (bĭd), v. t.; pret. BADE (băd), BID; p. p. BIDDEN (bĭd'n), BID; p. pr. & vb. n. BID'DING. **1.** To offer to pay (a certain price, as for a thing put up at auction), or to take (a certain price, as for work to be done under a contract). **2.** To order; command. **3.** To invite; request to come. **4.** To express or utter, as a wish, a greeting, etc. — v. i. To make a bid. — n. Act of one who bids something; an offer.

bid'der (bĭd'ēr), n. One who bids.

bid'ding, n. **1.** Act of making bids; a bid. **2.** Command; order. **3.** An invitation; summons.

bide (bĭd), v. i.; pret. BODE (bōd); pret. & p. p. BID'ED (bĭd'ĕd); p. pr. & vb. n. BID'ING (bĭd'ĭng). To continue in a place, state, or action; stay; continue to be. — v. t. **1.** To wait for; now only in to *bide one's time*, that is, to await one's opportunity, etc. **2.** To encounter; withstand; abide.

bi·en'ni·al (bī-ĕn'ĭ-ăl), a. **1.** Taking place once in two years. **2.** Continuing or lasting for two years; — n. **1.** Something that takes place once in two years. **2.** A plant that lasts only two years. — **bi·en'ni·al·ly**, adv. [8].

bier (bēr), n. The frame on which a corpse is placed, or borne to the grave.

bi·fur'cate (bī-fûr'kāt; bī'fŭr-kāt), v. i. To divide into two branches.

bi·fur·ca'tion (bī'fŭr-kā'shŭn), n. A forking.

big (bĭg), a.; BIG'GER (-ēr); BIG'GEST. **1.** Large in size, bulk, or extent. **2.** Pregnant. **3.** Having greatness, fullness, inflation, or the like.

big'a·mist (-ȧ-mĭst), n. One who commits bigamy.

big'a·mous (-mŭs), a. Guilty of bigamy.

big'a·my (-mĭ), n. Act of marrying one person when already legally married to another.

big'ger (-ēr), a., compar. of BIG.

big'horn' (-hôrn'), n. The wild sheep of the Rocky Mountains.

bight (bīt), n. **1.** A bend or curve, as in a river; esp., a sharp bend in a coast, forming an open bay. **2.** Naut. A loop in a rope.

big'ness, n. Quality or state of being big.

big'ot (bĭg'ŭt), n. One obstinately and blindly devoted to his own church, party, etc.

Head of Bighorn.

big'ot·ed (-ĕd), a. [4] Obstinately and blindly attached to some creed, or the like; intolerant.

big'ot·ry (-rĭ), n.; pl. **-RIES** (-rĭz). State of mind of a bigot; intolerance.

big tree. See SEQUOIA.

bi·lat'er·al (bī-lăt'ēr-ăl), a. Having two sides.

bile (bīl), n. **1.** The yellow, or greenish, fluid secreted by the liver. **2.** Peevishness; ill humor.

bilge (bĭlj), n. The lower part of a ship's underwater body. — v. i. [1] To spring a leak in the bilge; to rest on the bilge; — said of a vessel. — v. t. Naut. To fracture or stave in the bilge or bottom of (a vessel).

bil'i·a·ry (bĭl'ĭ-ȧ-rĭ; -yȧ-rĭ), a. Physiol. Pertaining to or conveying bile; as, *biliary* acids or ducts.

bi·lin'gual (bī-lĭŋ'gwȧl), a. Using two languages.

bil'ious (bĭl'yŭs), a. [4] **1.** Disordered in respect to the bile. **2.** Peevish; ill-tempered. — **bil'ious·ly**, adv. [8] — **bil'ious·ness**, n. [8].

bill (bĭl), n. **1.** The beak of a bird. **2.** A similar beak in other animals, as the turtles. — v. i. To join bills, as doves; caress fondly.

bill, n. **1.** A kind of old military weapon having a hook-shaped blade. **2.** A cutting instrument with a hook-shaped point, used in pruning, etc.

bill, n. **1.** A document containing a petition. **2.** A draft of a law presented to a legislature for enactment. **3.** Law. A declaration in writing stating the wrong complained of in an action. **4.** A placard; poster; handbill. **5.** a=BILL OF EXCHANGE. **b** A promissory note. **c** A bank note, treasury note, or silver certificate; as, a ten-dollar *bill*. U. S. **6.** An account of goods sold or services rendered, with the price or charge. **7.** Any paper containing a statement of particulars; as, a *bill* of fare. — *bill of exchange*, an unconditional written order from one person to another to pay to some person designated a certain sum therein named. — **b.** of lading, an account of goods shipped by any one. — **b.** of sale, a written instrument for the transfer of personal property. — v. t. **1.** To make a bill, or list, of; as, to *bill* goods. **2.** To advertise by bills, or posters; placard with bills.

bil'let (bĭl'ĕt), n. **1.** A note; short letter. **2.** A written order or ticket. **3.** Quarters or place to which one is assigned; berth; position; place.

bil'let, n. A small stick of wood; a bar of metal.

bill'head' (bĭl'hĕd'), n. A blank form, usually with the address, etc., of a business house at the top, used for rendering accounts, etc.

bil'liards (bĭl'yȧrdz), n. Any of several games played on an oblong table, surrounded by an elastic ledge or cushion, with balls impelled by a cue.

bil'lion (-yŭn), n. In French and American numeration, a thousand millions (1,000,000,000); in English and German, a million millions (1,000,-000,000,000). — **bil'lion·aire'** (-âr'), n.

bil'low (bĭl'ō), n. A wave; esp., a great wave. — **bil'low·y** (-ō-ĭ), a. [4].

bin (bĭn), n. A box, frame, crib, or inclosed place, used as a receptacle; as, a coal *bin*.

bind (bīnd), v. t.; pret. & p. p. BOUND; p. pr. & vb. n. BIND'ING. **1.** To tie or confine with a cord, band, chain, or the like. **2.** To confine, restrain, or hold by physical force or influence of any kind. **3.** To cover as with a bandage; bandage. **4.** To

---

āle, senāte, câre, ăm, ăccount, ärm, ȧsk, sofȧ; ēve, ēvent, ĕnd, recĕnt, makēr; īce, ĭll; ōld, ŏbey, ôrb, ŏdd, sŏft, cŏnnect; ūse, ŭnite, ûrn, ŭp, circŭs; fōōd, fŏŏt; out, oil;

fasten (a thing *about* or *upon* something) by or as by tying. **5.** To protect or strengthen by a band or binding. **6.** To sew or fasten together and inclose in a cover, as a book. — *v. i.* **1.** To perform the act of tying something. **2.** To cohere. **3.** To be restrained from motion or in action, as by friction. **4.** To exert a binding or restraining influence.

bind'er (bīn'dẽr), *n.* One that binds.

bind'er·y (-ĭ), *n.; pl.* -ERIES (-ĭz). A place where books, etc., are bound; a bookbinder's shop.

bind'ing, *p. a.* [4] That binds or serves to bind. — *n.* **1.** Act or process of one that binds. **2.** A thing that binds, as the fastening of the sections of a book, esp. this fastening with the cover.

bin·oc'u·lar (bĭn-ŏk'ū-lȧr), *a.* Pert. to or using both eyes at once; also, adapted to the use of both eyes. — *n.* A binocular glass, as an opera glass.

bi'o·graph (bī'ō-grȧf), *n.* A cinematograph.

bi·og'ra·pher (bī-ŏg'rȧ-fẽr), *n.* One who writes biography.

bi'o·graph'ic (bī'ō-grăf'ĭk), **bi'o·graph'i·cal** (-ĭ-kȧl), *a.* Of or pertaining to biography; containing biography. — **bi'o·graph'i·cal·ly,** *adv.* [8].

bi·og'ra·phy (bī-ŏg'rȧ-fĭ), *n.; pl.* -PHIES (-fĭz). **1.** The written history of a person's life. **2.** Biographical writings or composition in general.

bi'o·log'i·cal (bī'ō-lŏj'ĭ-kȧl), **bi'o·log'ic** (-ĭk), *a.* Of or pertaining to biology. — **i·cal·ly,** *adv.* [8].

bi·ol'o·gist (bī-ŏl'ō-jĭst), *n.* One versed in biology.

bi·ol'o·gy (bī-ŏl'ō-jĭ), *n.* Science of life; science which treats of plants and animals.

bi'ped (bī'pĕd), *n.* A two-footed animal, as man.

bi'plane' (bī'plān'), *n.* An aëroplane having two supporting planes.

birch (bûrch), *n.* **1.** Any of various species of valuable timber trees. **2.** A birch rod for flogging. — *v. t.* To whip with a birch.

birch'en (bûr'ch'n), *a.* Of or relating to birch.

bird (bûrd), *n.* Any of a class of warm-blooded egg-laying animals having the body more or less completely covered with feathers and the fore limbs modified into wings.

bird'man' (-măn'), *n.; pl.* -MEN. An airman.

bird's'-eye' (bûrdz'ī'), *a.* Seen from above, as if by a flying bird; hence, general; not minute.

birth (bûrth), *n.* **1.** Act or fact of coming into life, or of being born; also, act of bringing forth. **2.** Lineage; descent; sometimes, noble descent.

birth'day' (-dā'), *n.* **1.** Day of birth, origin, or commencement. **2.** The anniversary of one's birth.

birth'mark' (-märk'), *n.* Some peculiar mark or blemish on the body at birth.

birth'place' (-plās'), *n.* Place of birth or origin.

birth'right' (-rīt'), *n.* Any right belonging by birth.

bis'cuit (bĭs'kĭt), *n.; pl.* -CUIT (-kĭt) or -CUITS (-kĭts). **1.** A kind of unraised bread, baked hard in flat cakes; — usually called *cracker* in the U. S. **2.** A small cake of bread raised and shortened, or made light with soda or baking powder. *U. S.*

bi·sect' (bī-sĕkt'), *v. t.* To divide into two parts or, *Geom.*, into two equal parts. — **bi·sec'tor,** *n.* [8].

bi·sec'tion (-sĕk'shŭn), *n.* Act of bisecting.

bish'op (bĭsh'ŭp), *n.* A clergyman of the highest order in various Christian churches.

bish'op·ric (-rĭk), *n.* **1.** A diocese. **2.** The office of bishop.

bi'son (bī'sŭn), *n.* A large quadruped of the ox kind with massive shaggy fore quarters and head.

bisque (bĭsk), *n.* A kind of rich soup.

bit (bĭt), *n.* **1.** The biting or cutting edge or part of a tool. **2.** A tool for drilling or boring. **3.** The part of a bridle, usually of steel, inserted in a horse's mouth. **4.** Anything that curbs or restrains. — *v. t.;* BIT'TED; BIT'TING. To put a bridle or bit on; curb; check.

bit, *n.* **1.** A part of anything such as may be bitten off; morsel; bite. **2.** A small part of anything; little; jot.

bitch (bĭch), *n.* Female of the dog, wolf, or fox.

bite (bīt), *v. t.; pret.* BIT; *p. p.* BIT'TEN (bĭt'n), BIT; *p. pr. & vb. n.* BIT'ING (bīt'ĭng). **1.** To seize with or as with the teeth so as to enter, nip, or grip the thing seized. **2.** To cut, gash, or pierce. **3.** To cause sharp pain or smarting to. **4.** To act on chemically; to corrode; eat. — *v. i.* **1.** To bite something. **2.** To be pungent. **3.** To take a bait; take a tempting offer. — *n.* **1.** Act of biting; a biting; manner of biting. **2.** A morsel; as much as is taken at a bite. **3.** Food; victuals. **4.** A wound made by biting. **5.** A smarting or penetrating effect. — **bit'er** (bīt'ẽr), *n.* [8].

bit'ing, *p. a.* [4] That bites; sharp; cutting; sarcastic; caustic. — **bit'ing·ly,** *adv.* [8].

bitt (bĭt), *n.* On a ship, a fixed vertical timber or iron casting, usually one of a pair, for securing hawsers, ropes, etc.

bit'ten (bĭt'n), *p. p.* of BITE.

bit'ter (-ẽr), *a.* **1.** Having or designating a peculiar, characteristically disagreeable taste, as of hops. **2.** Painful; distressful. **3.** Characterized by severity or cruelty; harsh; caustic. — *v. t. & i.* To make or become bitter. — **bit'ter·ly,** *adv.* [8].

bit'tern (bĭt'ẽrn), *n.* Any of certain birds of the heron family, noted for their booming cry.

bit'ter·ness, *n.* Quality or state of being bitter.

bit'ters (-ẽrz), *n. pl.* A liquor, generally spirituous, in which a bitter herb, leaf, or root is steeped.

bit'ter·sweet' (-ẽr-swēt'), *a.* Mingling bitter and sweet. — *n.* **1.** A climbing poisonous plant with red berries. **2.** A climbing shrub the yellow capsule of which opens and discloses a red seed.

bi·tu'men (bī-tū'mĕn; bĭt'ū̇-), *n.* Originally, mineral pitch, or asphalt. Hence, any of a number of inflammable mineral substances.

bi·tu'mi·nous (bī-tū'mĭ-nŭs), *a.* Having the qualities of, compounded with, or containing, bitumen.

bi'valve (bī'vălv), *n.* A mollusk having a shell consisting of a right and a left valve connected by a hinge, as an oyster.

biv'ouac (bĭv'wăk; bĭv'ōō-ăk), *n.* An encampment with only an improvised shelter, if any. — *v. i.;* -OUACKED (-wăkt; -ōō-ăkt); -OUACKING. To encamp without tents or housing.

bi'week'ly (bī'wēk'lĭ), *a.* Occurring or appearing every two weeks; also, semiweekly. — *n.* A biweekly publication. — **bi'week'ly,** *adv.*

bi·zarre' (bĭ-zär'), *a.* [3] Characterized by unnatural or sensational contrasts; fantastical.

blab (blăb), *v. t. & i.;* BLABBED (blăbd); BLAB'BING. **1.** To talk foolishly or idly; chatter; babble. **2.** To speak, talk, or tell unnecessarily or thoughtlessly. — *n.* **1.** One who blabs; a telltale. **2.** Idle talk.

---

chair; go; sing, ink; then, thin; nature, verdure; yet; zh = z in azure. Numbers refer to §§ in the Special Notes which, with Abbreviations, Signs, etc., precede the Vocabulary.

black (blăk), *a.* [3] **1.** Destitute of light, or incapable of reflecting it. **2.** Having very dark skin and, usually, dark hair and eyes. **3.** Soiled with dirt; foul. **4.** Dismal, gloomy, or forbidding, like darkness. **5.** Destitute of moral light or goodness; wicked. — *n.* **1.** The darkest color. **2.** A black pigment or dye. **3.** A Negro; loosely, one of any dark-skinned race.— *v. t.* **1.** To make black; sully. **2.** To make black and shining, as boots.

black'ber-ry (-bĕr-ĭ), *n.; pl.* -RIES (-ĭz). The fruit, black or very dark purple when ripe, of any of many species of brambles; also, any of the plants.

black'bird (-bûrd), *n.* Any of a number of birds largely or entirely black.

black'board' (-bōrd'), *n.* Any dark smooth surface prepared for writing on, drawing on, etc., with chalk or crayons.

biack'en (blăk'n), *v. t.* **1.** To make black; darken. **2.** To defame; sully.—*v. i.* To grow black or dark.

black'fish' (-fĭsh'), *n.; pl.* -FISH *or* -FISHES (see PLURAL, *n., Note*). **1.** Any of several small, toothed whales. **2.** Any of a number of fishes so called from their dark color, as the tautog, the black sea bass of the Atlantic coast, etc.

black'guard (blăg'ärd), *n.* A person of low character, esp. one who is scurrilous or abusive; a scoundrel. — *v. t.* To revile or abuse scurrilously. — *a.* Low; abusive; scurrilous.

black'ing, *n.* A preparation for giving a black luster to boots and shoes, or to stoves.

black lead. Graphite or plumbago.

black'leg' (-lĕg'), *n.* A swindler, esp. in gambling.

black'ly (-lĭ), *adv.* In a black manner; gloomily.

black'mail' (-māl'), *n.* Extortion by threats of public accusation or exposure. — *v. t.* To exact blackmail from. — **black'mail'er,** *n.* [8].

black'ness, *n.* State or quality of being black.

black'smith' (-smĭth'), *n.* A smith who works in iron with a forge.

blad'der (blăd'ĕr), *n.* *Anat. & Zoöl.* A membranous sac serving as a receptacle of a fluid or containing gas; often, specifically, the urinary bladder.

blade (blād), *n.* **1.** A leaf of a plant; the flat or expanded portion of a leaf, esp. of grass. **2.** The thin cutting part of an instrument. **3.** A sword; also, one who bears an edged weapon. **4.** An object or part likened to the blade of a leaf, sword, etc. **5.** A dashing, wild, or reckless fellow.

olam'a-ble (blām'à-b'l), *a.* Faulty; culpable. — **blam'a-ble-ness,** *n.* [8] — **-bly** (-blĭ), *adv.* [8].

blame (blām), *v. t.* [1] To censure; find fault with; reproach. — *n.* **1.** Expression of disapproval; censure. **2.** Fault; culpability.

blame'less, *a.* Free from blame or fault. — **blame'less-ly,** *adv.* [8] — **blame'less-ness,** *n.* [8].

blame'wor'thy (-wûr'thĭ), *a.* Deserving blame.

blanch (blânch), *v. t.* To take the color out of; make white; bleach. — *v. i.* To become white.

blanc-mange' (blä-mänzh'), *n.* A dessert made of gelatinous or starchy substances and milk.

bland (blănd), *a.* [3] Smooth and soothing; gentle; suave. — **bland'ly,** *adv.* [8] — **bland'ness,** *n.* [8]

blan'dish (blăn'dĭsh), *v. t. & i.* To flatter; cajole.

blan'dish-ment (blăn'dĭsh-mĕnt), *n.* A word or act expressive of gentle flattery, affection, or kindness, and tending to win the heart; cajolery.

blank (blăngk), *a.* [3] **1.** Free from writing, printing, or marks. **2.** Empty; void; fruitless. **3.** Lacking variety or interest. **4.** Expressionless; vacant. — *n.* **1.** Any space left to be filled in later, as in a check, etc. **2.** A paper with spaces to be filled in. **3.** A piece of metal prepared to be made into something, as a coin, key, screw, etc.

blan'ket (blăn'kĕt), *n.* **1.** A heavy, loosely woven covering, usually of wool, used for beds. **2.** Any piece of cloth similar in appearance or use. — *v. t.* To cover with or as with a blanket.

blank'ly (blăngk'lĭ), *adv.* In a blank manner.

blank'ness, *n.* State or quality of being blank.

blare (blâr), *v. i. & t.* [1] To sound loud and harsh, as a trumpet; hence, to proclaim loudly. — *n.* The harsh noise of, or one like that of, a trumpet.

blar'ney (blär'nĭ), *n.* Smooth, wheedling talk; flattery. *Colloq.* — *v. t.* To influence by, or subject to, blarney; wheedle.

blas-pheme' (blăs-fēm'), *v. t.* [1] To speak of, or address, with impious irreverence. — *v. i.* To utter blasphemy. — **blas-phem'er,** *n.* [8].

blas'phe-mous (blăs'fē-mŭs), *a.* [4] Uttering blasphemy; profane. — **blas'phe-mous-ly,** *adv.* [8].

blas'phe-my (blăs'fē-mĭ), *n.; pl.* -MIES (-mĭz). Indignity offered to God in words, writing, or signs.

blast (blàst), *n.* **1.** A violent gust of wind. **2.** A forcible stream of air or other gas from an orifice. **3.** The sound made by a wind instrument. **4.** A sudden pernicious effect; blight. **5.** Act of rending masses of rock, earth, etc., by an explosive; also, the charge used. — *v. t.* **1.** To wither; blight; ruin. **2.** To rend by an explosive.

blat (blăt), *v. i.* To cry, as a calf or sheep; bleat.

bla'tan-cy (blā'tăn-sĭ), *n.* Blatant quality.

bla'tant (-tănt), *a.* [4] **1.** Bellowing, as a calf; bawling. **2.** Offensively obtrusive; coarse.

blaze (blāz), *n.* **1.** A glowing flame; a fire. **2.** Intense, direct light accompanied with heat. **3.** An active display of any quality; outburst. **4.** Splendor; effulgence. — *v. i.* [1] **1.** To burn with bright flame; glow. **2.** To be resplendent or conspicuous, as with light.

blaze, *n.* **1.** A white mark on the face of an animal. **2.** A mark made on trees by chipping off a piece of the bark. — *v. t.* [1] To mark (a tree, path, etc.) by blazes.

blaz'er (blāz'ĕr), *n.* A light jacket, usually bright-colored, for wear at tennis, cricket, or other sport.

bla'zon (blā'z'n), *n.* A heraldic shield; a coat of arms.—*v. t.* **1.** To depict in colors; publish far and wide. **2.** To describe (heraldic or armorial bearings); popularly, to delineate (armorial bearings).

bla'zon-ry (-rĭ), *n.* **1.** An armorial bearing or armorial bearings. **2.** Brilliant display.

bleach (blēch), *v. t.* To make white or whiter; blanch; whiten. — *v. i.* To grow white or lose color; whiten.

bleach'er (-ĕr), *n.* **1.** One that bleaches. **2.** A roofless seat for spectators at outdoor games; — usually in *pl. U. S.*

bleak (blēk), *a.* [3] **1.** Exposed and, usually, desolate; swept by cold winds. **2.** Cold and cutting; as, a *bleak* blast. — **-ly,** *adv.* [8] — **-ness,** *n.* [8].

blear (blēr), *a.* Dim or sore with water or rheum; — said of the eyes. — *v. t.* To make blear.

āle, senáte, cåre, ăm, ăccount, ärm, ásk, sofá; ēve, ĕvent, ĕnd, recĕnt, makẽr; īce, ĭll; ōld, ŏbey, ôrb, ŏdd, sôft, cŏnnect; ūse, ŭnite, ûrn, ŭp, circŭs; fōōd, fŏŏt; out, oil;

blear'y (blēr'ĭ), *a.* [3] Somewhat bleary; blear-eyed.

bleat (blēt), *v. i.* To make the cry of, or one like that of, a sheep, goat, or calf. — *n.* The cry of a sheep, goat, or calf, or a sound resembling it.

bleb (blĕb), *n.* A vesicle; blister; bubble.

bled (blĕd), *pret. & p. p.* of BLEED.

bleed (blēd), *v. i.; BLED (blĕd); BLEED'-ING.* **1.** To emit blood; to lose or shed one's blood. **2.** To exude water or sap, as a tree. — *v. t.* **1.** To let blood from. **2.** To exude or let drop, as blood or sap. **3.** To draw or extort money from (one). *Colloq.*

blem'ish (blĕm'ĭsh), *v. t.* To injure; mar; sully. — *n.* Any mark of deformity or injury.

blench (blĕnch), *v. i.* To shrink; start back.

blench. *v. i. & t.* To pale; whiten.

blend (blĕnd), *v. t.* **1.** To mix or mingle so that the separate things mixed, or the line of demarcation, cannot be distinguished. **2.** Of whisky, coffee, etc., to prepare by mingling different varieties. — *v. i.* To unite intimately, esp. so as to form a uniform or harmonious mixture or whole; merge. — *n.* A thorough mixture of things; blending.

bless (blĕs), *v. t.; BLESSED (blĕst), BLEST; BLESS'-ING.* **1.** To consecrate or hallow by religious rite or word. **2.** To pray for the happiness of. **3.** To make happy; confer prosperity or happiness on. **4.** To praise or glorify.

bless'ed (blĕs'ĕd), *p. a.* [4] **1.** Hallowed; holy. **2.** Favored with blessings; happy. **3.** Enjoying spiritual happiness. — **bless'ed-ness,** *n.*

bless'ing, *n.* **1.** Act of one who blesses; benediction. **2.** A means of happiness or welfare.

blest (blĕst), *pret. & p. p.* of BLESS. — *p. a.* Blessed.

blew (blōō), *pret.* of BLOW.

blight (blīt), *v. t. & i.* To affect, or be affected, with blight; blast; hence, to ruin; frustrate. — *n.* **1.** Any disease or injury of plants resulting in withering or decay. **2.** Anything that causes blights.

blimp (blĭmp), *n.* A small dirigible balloon, often used for aërial observation.

blind (blīnd), *a.* [3] **1.** Sightless. **2.** Not having or not using discernment or judgment. **3.** Difficult or impossible to see; dim; hidden. **4.** Having no opening for light or passage, as a wall; blank. **5.** Having but one opening, as an alley. **6.** Unintelligible; also, illegible. — *v. t.* **1.** To make blind. **2.** To dazzle. **3.** To obscure; dim. — *n.* **1.** Something to hinder sight or keep out light; screen. **2.** A place or means of concealment; ambush. **3.** Something to mislead, or to conceal a covert design; subterfuge.

blind'er (blīn'dĕr), *n.* One that blinds; a blinker.

blind'fold' (blīnd'fōld'), *v. t.* To cover the eyes of, as with a bandage. — *a.* Having the eyes covered.

blind'ly, *adv.* In a blind manner.

blind'ness (-nĕs), *n.* The state of being blind.

blink (blĭnk), *v. i.* **1.** To look with eyes half shut; see indistinctly. **2.** To wink. **3.** To look evasively or indifferently. **4.** To shine intermittently; twinkle. — *v. t.* To shut out of sight; ignore. — *n.* A glimpse or glance; glimmer; sparkle.

blink'er (blĭnk'ĕr), *n.* **1.** One that blinks. **2.** Either of two flaps on a horse's bridle to prevent sight of objects at his side or behind him.

bliss (blĭs), *n.* Exalted happiness; heavenly joy.

bliss'ful (-fŏŏl), *a.* [4] Full of, characterized by, or causing, bliss. — **-ful-ly,** *adv.* [8] — **-ful-ness,** *n.* [8].

blis'ter (blĭs'tĕr), *n.* **1.** A vesicle of the skin containing watery matter. **2.** Any cavity resembling a blister (sense 1). — *v. t. & i.* To affect or be affected with a blister or blisters.

blithe (blīth), *a.* [3] Jocund in disposition; joyous; glad; cheerful. — **blithe'ly,** *adv.* [8].

blithe'some (-sŭm), *a.* [4] Cheery; gay.

bliz'zard (blĭz'ard), *n.* A dry, cold, violent storm, with high wind and fine driving snow.

bloat (blōt), *v. t.* **1.** To cause to swell up, as with air, water, etc. **2.** To puff up; inflate; make vain. — *v. i.* To puff out; swell.

bloat'er, *n.* The common herring when cured by being salted, smoked, and half dried.

‖**bloc** (blŏk), *n.* A combination of political groups or parties, or of members of different parties, willing to work for a certain object regardless of party.

block (blŏk), *n.* **1.** A bulky piece of wood, stone, or the like, usually with one or more flat faces. **2.** The wooden piece on which condemned persons are beheaded. **3.** A grooved pulley or sheave in a frame or shell. **4.** A row of houses or shops, esp. when built so as to form one building. **5.** A city square; also, the length of one of its sides. **6.** A hindrance; obstacle. — *v. t.* **1.** To stop by obstructing; blockade. **2.** To sketch or plan without working up details. **3.** To support with blocks.

block-ade' (blŏk-ād'), *n.* **1.** The shutting up of a place by troops or ships so as to prevent ingress or egress. **2.** An obstruction to passage. — *v. t.* [1] To subject to a blockade.

block'head' (blŏk'hĕd'), *n.* A stupid fellow; dolt.

block'house' (-hous'), *n.* A structure of heavy timbers for military defense, with sides pierced for gun fire and, often, a projecting upper story.

blond, blonde (blŏnd), *a.* [3] **1.** Of a fair color. **2.** Having yellowish brown or light auburn hair, blue or gray eyes, and pale or rosy white skin.

blond, *fem.* **blonde,** *n.* A blond person.

blood (blŭd), *n.* **1.** The fluid, commonly red, which circulates in the heart, arteries, and veins of animals. **2.** The shedding of blood; act of killing. **3.** Kinship; kindred; race. **4.** Descent; esp., honorable birth; royal lineage. **5.** Temper; state of the passions; hence, anger. **6.** A man of fire or spirit. **7.** The juice of anything, esp. if red.

blood'ed (blŭd'ĕd), *a.* Having (such) blood; of approved breed; of the best stock.

blood'hound' (-hound'), *n.* One of a breed of large dogs noted for their sense of smell.

blood'i-ly, *adv.* In a bloody manner.

blood'i-ness, *n.* **1.** Bloody state or condition. **2.** Disposition to shed blood.

blood'less, *a.* **1.** Without blood. **2.** Not attended with bloodshed. **3.** Without spirit or activity. — **-ly,** *adv.* [8].

blood'root' (-rōōt'), *n.* A plant of the poppy family having a red root and red sap.

Bloodroot. (⅓)

blood′shed′ (blŭd′shĕd′), n. The shedding of blood; slaughter.

blood′shot′ (-shŏt′), a. Red and inflamed; suffused with blood ; — said of the eye.

blood′suck′er (-sŭk′ẽr), n. **1.** Animal that sucks blood ; esp., a leech. **2.** Extortioner.

blood′thirst′y (-thŭrs′tĭ), a. [3] Eager to shed blood ; cruel.

blood′y (-Ĭ), a. [3] **1.** Of, containing, or like, blood. **2.** Smeared or stained with blood. **3.** Given to bloodshed; murderous. **4.** Attended with blood-shed.—v. t. [2] To make bloody; stain with blood.

bloom (blōōm), n. **1. a** A blossom; flower. **b** The flowering state. **2.** A state or time of beauty, fresh-ness, and vigor. **3.** The delicate powdery coating on some fruits and leaves; any surface coating sug-gestive of this.—v. i. **1.** To blossom ; flower. **2.** To be in a state of vigorous, growing youth.

bloom′er (blōōm′ẽr), n. **1.** A woman's costume consisting of a short dress and loose trousers gath-ered at the ankles. **2.** pl. Loose trousers gathered near the knee, worn by women in exercising, etc.

bloom′ing, p. a. [4] **1.** Blossoming ; flowering. **2.** Thriving in health, beauty, and vigor.

blos′som (blŏs′ŭm), n. **1.** The flower of a seed plant; bloom. **2.** A blooming period or stage of development. — v. i. To flower.; bloom.

blot (blŏt), n. A spot ; stain. — v. t. ; BLOT′TED (-ĕd); -TING. **1.** To spot or stain. **2.** To obliterate, as writing with ink ; cancel ; — generally with out. **3.** To dry, as writing with blotting paper. — v. i. **1.** To make a blot or blots. **2.** To take a blot.

blotch (blŏch), n. **1.** A blot or spot, as of ink. **2.** A large pustule, as on the face. — v. t. & i. To cover with blotches ; make or cause a blotch.

blot′ter (blŏt′ẽr), n. **1.** One that blots; esp., a piece of blotting paper. **2.** A book in which en-tries of transactions or events are made as they occur, as in recording accounts, arrests, etc.

blotting paper. A spongy paper for absorbing ink from fresh manuscript.

blouse (blouz ; blous), n. A loose shirtlike over-garment of various lengths and styles.

blow (blō), v. i. ; pret. BLEW (blōō) ; p. p. BLOWN (blōn); p. pr. & vb. n. BLOW′ING. To flower; bloom. — n. Blossom ; flower ; bloom.

blow, n. **1.** A forcible stroke with the hand, fist, or some instrument. **2.** A sudden or forcible act or effort; assault. **3.** A sudden calamity.

blow, v. i. ; pret. BLEW (blōō) ; p. p. BLOWN (blōn); p. pr. & vb. n. BLOW′ING. **1.** To move, as air, esp. rapidly or with power. **2.** To send forth a forci-ble current of air or gas, as from a bellows. **3.** To sound on being blown into, as a trumpet. **4.** To pant; puff. **5.** Of whales and other cetaceans, to eject the moisture-laden air from the blowhole or blowholes in the head. **6.** To be carried or moved by the wind. — v. t. **1.** To force a current of air upon or through, as with the mouth. **2.** To drive by a current of air ; impel. **3.** To form by inflating, as with air; as, to blow glass. **4.** To clear of contents by forcing air through. **5.** To burst, shatter, or de-stroy by an explosion; — with up, open, etc. **6.** To put out of breath. — n. Act of blowing ; blowing.

blow′er (-ẽr), n. One that blows ; specifically, a device for producing a current of air.

blow′hole′ (-hōl′), n. **1.** A hole for the escape of air or gas; esp., a nostril in the top of the head of whales, etc. **2.** A hole in the ice to which whales, seals, etc., come to breathe.

blown (blōn), p. p. & p. a. from BLOW, v.

blowz′y (blouz′Ĭ), a. [3] Coarse and ruddy-faced; fat and ruddy ; frowzy ; slovenly.

blub′ber (blŭb′ẽr), n. The fat of whales or other large marine mammals. It yields oil. — v. i. To weep noisily, or so as to disfigure the face.

bludg′eon (blŭj′ŭn), n. A short club with one end weighted, or thick and heavier than the other.

blue (blōō), a. [3] **1.** Having the color of the clear sky, or a hue resembling it. **2.** Low in spirits; melancholy. **3.** Tending to produce low spirits. Colloq. **4.** Severe or overstrict in morals; suiting one overstrict in morals.—n. **1.** A certain color of the spectrum; blue color. **2.** A pigment or dye that colors blue. **3.** A person dressed in blue, as a Union soldier in the Civil War. **4.** pl. Low spirits; melan-choly. Colloq. — v. t. & i. · BLUED (blōōd); BLU′-ING or BLUE′ING. To make or turn blue.

blue′bell′ (-bĕl′), n. Any of various plants bear-ing blue bell-shaped flowers.

blue′ber-ry (-bĕr-Ĭ), n.; pl. -RIES (-Ĭz). The small edible, blue or blackish berry of a certain shrub; also, the shrub.

blue′bird′ (-bûrd′), n. A small song bird of the northern United States.

blue blood. The blood of noble or aristocratic families; also, a person of such a family.

blue′bot′tle (-bŏt′'l), n. **1.** The cornflower. **2.** Any of several species of large flies.

blue′fish′ (-fĭsh′), n. (see PLURAL, n., Note). A certain voracious marine food fish of wide distri-bution; also, any of various other fishes.

blue′ing, n. Var. of BLUING.

blue′jack′et (-jăk′ĕt), n. An enlisted man in the navy ; — often as distinguished from a marine.

blu′et (blōō′ĕt), n. A delicate plant of the United States with bluish flowers and tufted stems.

bluff (blŭf), a. [3] **1.** Having a broad, flattened front. **2.** Rising steeply with a flat or rounded front, as a coast. **3.** Abrupt ; roughly frank ; brusque; blunt; crusty. — n. A high, steep bank.

bluff, v. t. To deceive by an assumed confidence of manner, speech, or expression. — v. i. To bluff an opponent.— n. Act of bluffing.

bluff′ly (blŭf′lĬ), adv. In a bluff manner.

bluff′ness, n. Quality of being bluff ; bluntness.

blu′ing (blōō′Ĭng), n. Something to give a bluish tint, as a preparation of indigo used in laundering.

blu′ish, a. Somewhat blue.

blun′der (blŭn′dẽr), v. i. **1.** To move clumsily ; stumble. **2.** To make a gross error or mistake. — v. t. To utter awkwardly ; — usually with out. — n. A gross error. — **blun′der-er,** n. [8].

blun′der-buss (-bŭs), n. **1.** A kind of short gun, with a large bore and flaring muzzle, formerly in use. **2.** A stupid, blundering fellow.

blunt (blŭnt), a. [3] **1.** Not sensitive; obtuse in feeling or perception. **2.** Dull-witted; stupid. **3.** Having a thick edge or point, as an instrument; dull. **4.** Abrupt in speech or manners. — v. t. & i. **1.** To make or become blunt. **2.** To repress, or weaken. — **-ly,** adv. [8] — **-ness,** n. [8].

---

blur (blûr), *v. t.; *BLURRED (blûrd); BLUR'RING. **1.** To make indistinct and confused. **2.** To cause imperfect vision in; dim.—*v. i.* To become blurred or obscure.—*n.* **1.** A stain; blot. **2.** A dim, confused appearance; indistinctness.

blurt (blûrt), *v. t.* To utter suddenly and indiscreetly;—commonly with *out*.

blush (blŭsh), *v. i.* **1.** To become red, esp. in the cheeks or face, as from modesty, shame, or confusion; flush. **2.** To grow or be red or rosy.—*n.* **1.** Act of blushing. **2.** A red or rosy tint.

blus'ter (blŭs'tẽr), *v. i.* **1.** To blow fitfully and noisily, as the wind; be windy and boisterous, as the weather. **2.** To talk with noisy violence; swagger.—*n.* **1.** Fitful noise and violence, as of a storm. **2.** Noisy, boastful language.—**-er,** *n.* [8].

bo'a (bō'à), *n.; pl.* BOAS (bō'àz). **1.** Any large snake that crushes its prey. **2.** A long, round scarf of fur, feathers, etc., for the neck.

boa constrictor. A large boa of tropical America.

boar (bōr), *n.* The male of swine; the wild hog.

board (bōrd), *n.* **1.** A piece of timber sawed thin, relatively broad, and long. **2.** A table; esp., a table for food; hence, what is served on a table; provision, usually as furnished for pay. **3.** A table at which a council or court is held; hence, a council, or authorized assembly. **4.** Pasteboard. **5.** *pl.* The stage in a theatre;—on board. **a** On shipboard. **b** In or into a railway car or similar vehicle.—*v. t.* **1.** To cover with boards or boarding. **2.** To go on board of, as a ship. **3.** To furnish with regular meals, or with meals and lodgings, for pay. **4.** To place at board, for pay.—*v. i.* To obtain or have meals, or meals and lodgings, for pay.

board'er (bōr'dẽr), *n.* **1.** One who boards at another's table or house. **2.** One who boards a ship.

board'ing, *p. pr. & vb. n.* of BOARD, *v.* Hence: *n.* Boards collectively; a covering of boards.

boast (bōst), *v. i.* To vaunt one's self; brag.—*v. t.* To speak of or display ostentatiously or vaingloriously.—*n.* **1.** Boasting; bragging. **2.** The cause of boasting.—**boast'er,** *n.* [8].

boast'ful (-fŏŏl), *a.* [4] Given to, or full of, boasting; inclined to boast.—**-ly,** *adv.* [8]—**-ness,** *n.* [8].

boat (bōt), *n.* **1.** A small open vessel, or water craft, usually moved by oars or paddles; any vessel for navigating the water. **2.** A vehicle or utensil suggestive of a boat.—*v. t.* To transport or place in a boat.—*v. i.* To go or row in a boat.

boat'swain (bōt'swān; *naut.* bō's'n), *n.* On a war vessel, a warrant officer in charge of the rigging, anchors, cables, cordage, etc.

bob (bŏb), *n.* **1.** A knob or weight at the end of a rod or line. **2.** A short, jerking motion; act of bobbing.—*v. t. & i.;* BOBBED (bŏbd); BOB'BING. To move or cause to move in a short, jerking way.

bob'bin (-ĭn), *n.* A spool or reel used to hold yarn, thread, or wire.

bob'o-link (-ŏ-lĭŋk), *n.* A common American song bird related to the blackbirds.

bob'tail' (-tāl'), *a.* Having the tail cut short; hence, deficient; abbreviated.—**bob'tailed',** *a.*

bob'white' (-hwīt'), *n.* A quail. See QUAIL, *n.,* 2.

bode (bōd), *v. t. & i.* [1] To portend; presage.

bod'ice (bŏd'ĭs), *n.* **1.** A close-fitting outer waist of a woman's dress. **2.** A wide belt or girdle.

bod'i-less (-ĭ-lĕs), *a.* Having no body.

bod'i-ly (-ĭ-lĭ), *a.* Of or pertaining to the body.—*adv.* **1.** In bodily form; in the body. **2.** In respect to the whole body; all at once; completely.

bod'kin (-kĭn), *n.* **1.** Dagger. *Obs.* **2.** *Needle-work.* A sharp-pointed implement for making holes.

bod'y (bŏd'ĭ), *n.; pl.* BODIES (-ĭz). **1.** The whole material organism of an animal or plant. **2.** The central or main part. **3.** A person; a human being. **4.** A number of individuals or things united, as for some purpose. **5.** That part of a garment covering the body. **6.** A mass or portion of matter; as, a moving *body.* **7.** Consistency; thickness; substance; strength.—*v. t.* [2] To embody.

bod'y-guard (-gärd'), *n.* A guard for the person.

bog (bŏg), *n.* A piece of wet spongy earth consisting chiefly of decayed vegetable matter; marsh; morass.—*v. t. & i.* To sink, as into a bog; mire.

bo'gey (bō'gĭ), *n.; pl.* -GEYS (-gĭz). Var. of BOGY.

bog'gle (bŏg''l), *v. i.* [1] To hesitate; to bungle.

bog'gy (-ĭ), *a.* [3] Like or containing a bog.

bo'gus (bō'gŭs), *a.* Spurious; sham. *Colloq.*

bo'gy (-gĭ), *n.; pl.* -GIES (-gĭz). Specter; bugbear.

boil (boil), *v. i.* **1.** To be agitated by the generation and rising of bubbles of vapor;—said of a liquid. **2.** To be agitated like boiling water; to seethe. **3.** To be excited with passion. **4.** To be in boiling water, as food in cooking.—*v. t.* **1.** To heat to the boiling point. **2.** To heat in a boiling liquid.—*n.* Act or state of boiling.

boil, *n.* **1.** A hard, inflamed, painful lump or small swelling formed in the skin by inflammation of the tissue beneath and having a "core" of dead tissue.

boil'er (-ẽr), *n.* **1.** A vessel in which anything is boiled. **2.** A strong metallic vessel in which steam is generated for driving engines. **3.** A hot-water tank.

boil'ing, *a.* Heated to the point of bubbling; seething; swelling with heat, ardor, or passion.

bois'ter-ous (bois'tẽr-ŭs), *a.* [4] Tumultuously violent; rough; turbulent; loud; violent; tumultuous.—**-ly,** *adv.* [8]—**-ness,** *n.* [8].

bold (bōld), *a.* [3] **1.** Forward to meet danger; brave. **2.** Exhibiting or requiring spirit and contempt of danger; daring. **3.** Too forward; rude; impudent. **4.** Somewhat overstepping usual bounds. **5.** Steep; abrupt; prominent.

bold'ly, *adv.* In a bold manner or state.

bold'ness, *n.* State or quality of being bold.

bole (bōl), *n.* The trunk of a tree.

boll (bōl), *n.* The pod or capsule of a plant, esp. flax or cotton.—*v. i.* To form a boll; go to seed.

Bol'she-vik', *or* **bol'-** (bŏl'shĕ-vĕk'), *n.; pl.* -SHE-VIKI; (-vĕ-kē'; -vē'kē), -SHEVIKS (-vĕks'). In Russian politics, a member or adherent of the radical wing (the **Bolsheviki**) of the Social Democratic party, so called. The Bolsheviki aim to overthrow private property and establish communism. Hence, often, any extreme radical of similar aims.

Bol'she-vism, *or* **bol'-** (bŏl'shĕ-vĭz'm), *n.* Doctrines, tactics, or practices of, or like those of, the Bolsheviki.—**-vist,** *a. & n.*—**vis'tic,** *a.*

bol'ster (bōl'stẽr), *n.* **1.** A long pillow or cushion for a bed.—*v. t.* **1.** To support with a bolster or pillow. **2.** To support, hold up, or maintain, esp. with difficulty;—often with *up.*

bolt (bōlt), *n.* **1.** A short, stout, blunt-headed

arrow. **2.** Lightning ; thunderbolt. **3.** A sliding catch or fastening. **4.** A strong pin used to fasten or hold something in place, often having a head at one end and a screw thread on the other. **5.** A package or roll of cloth. **6.** Act of bolting. — *v. t.* **1.** To swallow without chewing. **2.** *U. S. Politics.* To refuse to support, as a policy or a nominee of one's party. **3.** To fasten with or as with a bolt or bolts. — *v. i.* **1.** To start forth like a bolt, or arrow ; dart off. **2.** *U. S. Politics.* To refuse to support the nominee, policy, etc., of one's party. — *adv.* Like a bolt.

bolt (bōlt), *v. t.* To sift (flour from bran) with a bolter; hence, to separate, assort, refine, or purify.

bolt′er (bōl′tẽr), *n.* One that bolts ; a cloth, sieve, or machine for sifting flour from bran.

bomb (bŏm ; bŭm), *n.* **1.** *Mil.* A shell ; esp., a spherical shell. **2.** Any similar missile or device.

bom-bard′ (-bärd′), *v. t.* **1.** To attack with artillery; esp., to throw shells, shot, etc., at or into. **2.** To assail vigorously or persistently. — **-er,** *n.* [8].

bom-bard′ment (-mĕnt), *n.* Act of bombarding.

bom′bast (bŏm′bȧst), *n.* High-sounding words.

bom-bas′tic (bŏm-bȧs′tĭk), *a.* [4] Characterized by bombast.

bom′ba-zine′ (bŏm′bȧ-zēn′), *n.* A dress fabric.

bomb′shell′ (-shĕl′), *n.* A bomb.

‖ **bo′na fi′de** (bō′nȧ fī′dē). [L.] In or with good faith ; without fraud or deceit ; as, a *bona fide* sale.

bo-nan′za (bȯ-năn′zȧ), *n.* In mining, a rich ore body; hence, anything that yields a large income. *Colloq., U. S.*

bon′bon′ (bŏn′bŏn′ ; bŏn′bŏn′), *n.* A sweetmeat.

bond (bŏnd), *a.* In servitude; captive.

bond, *n.* **1.** That which binds ; band ; shackle ; manacle. **2.** *pl.* State of being bound; imprisonment. **3.** A binding force or influence. **4.** A binding agreement ; covenant. **5. a** *Law.* A writing under seal by which a person binds himself to pay a certain sum, usually only in the event that some condition is not fulfilled. **b** *Finance.* Such an instrument, or, loosely, an interest-bearing certificate, issued by a government or corporation. **6.** A timber, stone, or the like, overlapping another, or the connection thus formed. — *v. t.* To place under a bond ; mortgage.

bond′age (bŏn′dȧj), *n.* Involuntary servitude ; slavery ; captivity.

bond′ed (bŏn′dĕd), *p. a.* Placed under, or covered by, a bond, as for payment of customs duties.

bond′maid′ (bŏnd′mād′), *n.* A female slave.

bond′man (-mȧn), *n.; pl.* **-men** (-mĕn). A man slave ; serf.

bonds′man (bŏndz′mȧn), *n.; pl.* **-men** (-mĕn). **1.** A bondman. **2.** *Law.* A surety on a bond.

bond′wom′an (bŏnd′wŏŏm′ȧn),*n.* A woman slave.

bone (bōn), *n.* **1.** One of the pieces or parts of a vertebrate's skeleton. **2.** Any of various other hard animal substances or structures, as whalebone. **3.** *pl.* The skeleton; body. **4.** A bone with meat adhering to it, as used for food. **5.** Something originally or usually made of bone, ivory, or the like. — *v. t.* [1] To take out bones from the flesh of. — **bone′less,** *a.* [8].

bon′fire′ (bŏn′fīr′), *n.* A large fire built in the open air as an expression of public joy, for sport, etc.

bon′net (bŏn′ĕt), *n.* **1.** A soft woolen cap without brim or visor, worn by men in Scotland. **2.** A head covering, worn by women and children out of doors, usually tied on with strings.

bon′nie. Var. of BONNY.

bon′ny (-ĭ), *a.* [3] **1.** Good-looking ; comely. **2.** Gay ; cheerful ; blithe.

bo′nus (bō′nŭs), *n.; pl.* **-nuses** (-ĕz). Something given beyond what is usual or strictly due.

bon′y (bōn′ĭ), *a.* [3] Like, consisting of, full of, or pertaining to, bones ; having conspicuous bones.

boo (bōō), *interj.* An exclamation used to indicate contempt, disapproval, etc., or to frighten.

boo′by (bōō′bĭ), *n.; pl.* **-bies** (-bĭz). **1.** A dunce; a stupid fellow. **2.** In card playing, etc., the player whose score is lowest.

book (bŏŏk), *n.* **1.** A literary composition of considerable length. **2.** A collection of sheets of paper bound together; usually, a printed and bound volume. **3.** A subdivision of a literary work.—*v. t. & i.* To enter or register (as one's name) in a book or list, esp. so as to engage service or accommodation.

book′ish, *a.* [4] **1.** Fond of, or learned in, books. **2.** Characterized by literary form ; hence, formal ; pedantic. — **book′ish-ness,** *n.* [8].

book′keep′er (-kēp′ẽr),*n.* One who keeps accounts.

book′keep′ing, *n.* Art or practice of keeping a systematic record of business transactions.

book′let, *n.* A little book.

book′worm′ (-wûrm′), *n.* **1.** An insect larva that injures books. **2.** One unusually devoted to books.

boom (bōōm), *n.* **1.** *Naut.* A long spar used esp. to extend the bottom of a sail. **2.** A line of connected floating timbers used to confine logs, etc.

boom, *v. i.* **1.** To make a hollow sound, as waves or cannon. **2.** To have a rapid growth in market value, resources, etc. — *v. t.* **1.** To give forth with a resonant or booming sound. **2.** To cause a rapid growth or increase of in favor, price, etc. — *n.* **1.** A hollow roar, as of waves or cannon. **2.** A strong and rapid increase in market value, etc.

boom′er-ang (bōōm′ẽr-ăng),*n.* **1.** A curved or angular club used, mainly by the natives of Australia, as a missile weapon. It can be hurled so that its flight will bring it back near to the place from which it was thrown. **2.** Any story or scheme that reacts to the damage of its originator.

boon (bōōn),*n.* A thing asked, granted, or enjoyed, as a benefit or favor ; a gift.

boon, *a.* Jovial; convivial; as, a *boon* companion.

boor (bōōr), *n.* **1.** A peasant; esp., an awkward, ill-bred countryman. **2.** A rude, ill-bred person.

boor′ish (bōōr′ĭsh), *a.* [4] Like a boor; uncultured. — **boor′ish-ly,** *adv.* [8] — **-ness,** *n.* [8].

boost (bōōst),*v. t. & i.* To lift or push from behind ; give a boost to ;hence,to assist or advance. *Colloq., U. S.* — *n.* A push or shove (literally or fig.) that aids one in rising or advancing. *Colloq., U. S.*

boot (bōōt),*n.* Something to equalize an exchange.

boot, *n.* **1.** A covering, usually of leather, for the foot and leg. **2.** Something suggestive of a boot (sense 1). — *v. t.* To put boots on.

boot′black′ (bōōt′blăk′), *n.* One who polishes boots.

booth (bōōth; bŏŏth), *n.* **1.** A frail temporary house or shed. **2.** A covered stall or temporary structure in a fair, at a polling place, etc.

brist

boot'jack' (boot'jăk'), *n.* A boot-pulling device.

boot'leg' (-lĕg'), *v. t. & i.* To make, transport, or sell illegally, as liquor; to smuggle. — **boot'leg'-ger** (-lĕg'ẽr), *n.* — **leg'ging**, *n.*

boot'less, *a.* Unavailing; useless; unprofitable.

boo'ty (boo'tĭ), *n.; pl.* -TIES (-tĭz). **1.** Spoil, esp. that taken in war; plunder. **2.** Any rich gain.

bo'rax (bō'răks), *n.* A crystalline, slightly alkaline, substance used as a cleansing agent, flux, etc.

bor'der (bôr'dẽr), *n.* **1.** The outer part or edge; margin. **2.** A boundary or frontier. — *a.* Pertaining to a boundary district or frontier. — *v. t.* **1.** To furnish with a border. **2.** To touch or be touched, as by a border; bound. — *v. i.* [With *on* or *upon.*] **1.** To touch at the edge or boundary. **2.** To approach; come near to.

bor'der-land' (-lănd'), *n.* Land on a border.

bore (bōr), *v. t.* [1] **1.** To penetrate (a body), as with an auger; to pierce. **2.** To make (a hole, well, passage, etc.) with or as with an auger. **3.** To weary by dullness, or by forcing one's presence upon. — *v. i.* **1.** To bore a hole. **2.** To be pierced by a boring instrument. — *n.* **1.** A hole made by boring. **2.** A round internal cavity, as of a pipe or tube. **3.** Size of a hole; interior diameter of a tube; caliber. **4.** A tiresome person or affair.

born (bôrn), *p. a.* of BEAR, *v. t.* Having from birth a certain character; inborn; as, a *born* artist.

borne (bōrn), *p. p.* of BEAR. Supported; carried; brought forth (by the mother), etc.

bor'ough (bŭr'ō), *n.* **1.** In England: **a** A town that sends a member or members to Parliament. **b** An incorporated town with special privileges conferred by royal charter. **2.** A form of municipal corporation corresponding in general to an incorporated town or village. *Local, U. S.*

bor'row (bŏr'ō), *v. t.* **1.** To receive with the intention of returning; — opposite of *lend.* **2.** To copy; imitate. — *v. i.* To borrow something.

bosh (bŏsh), *n.* Empty talk; trash. *Colloq.*

bos'om (booz'ŭm), *n.* **1.** The breast of a human being. **2.** The breast as the seat of the passions, affections, and thoughts. **3.** Any thing or place suggestive of the breast. **4.** That part of a garment which is worn over the breast. — *a.* **1.** Of or pertaining to the bosom. **2.** Intimate; trusted.

boss (bŏs), *n.* A round projecting part or body. — *v. t.* To ornament with bosses; stud.

boss, *n.* A master workman; superintendent; manager; political dictator. — *v. t.* To be master over; direct. — *v. i.* To be master. *All Colloq.*

bo-tan'ic (bō-tăn'ĭk)) *a.* Of or pertaining to bot-**bo-tan'i-cal** (-ĭ-kăl)) any. — **i-cal-ly**, *adv.* [8].

bot'a-nist (bŏt'á-nĭst), *n.* One who is a specialist in, or a student of, botany.

bot'a-nize (-nīz), *v. i.* [1] To collect plants for botanical investigation; to study plants in the field.

bot'a-ny (-nĭ), *n.* Science of plants and plant life.

botch (bŏch), *n.* **1.** A patch clumsily put on. **2.** Clumsy work; bungle. — *v. t.* **1.** To mark with or as with botches. **2.** To mend; repair; esp., to patch clumsily. **3.** To combine, express, or do in a bungling way; to mar. — **botch'er**, *n.* [8].

both (bōth), *a.* or *pron.* The one and the other; the two. — *conj. & adv.* **1.** As well; not only; equally; — used with *and.* **2.** As well; also; too.

both'er (bŏth'ẽr), *v. t.* To annoy; worry; perplex. — *v. i.* To feel care or anxiety. — *n.* One who or that which bothers; embarrassment; worry.

both'er-some (-sŭm), *a.* [4] Causing bother.

bot'tle (bŏt'l), *n.* **1.** A hollow vessel, usually of glass or earthenware, with a narrow neck or mouth and without handles. **2.** The contents of a bottle; fig., intoxicating liquor. — *v. t.* [1] To inclose in or as in a bottle or bottles.

bot'tom (-ŭm), *n.* **1.** The part of anything under and supporting the contents or bulk; under surface; foot; base; foundation. **2.** Bed of a body of water. **3.** Low alluvial land along a river. **4.** *Naut.* The part of a ship ordinarily under water; hence, a ship. **5.** Power of endurance. — *a.* Of or pertaining to the bottom; lowest. — *v. t.* **1.** To furnish with a bottom, as a chair. **2.** To found or build; to base; — with *on* or *upon.* — *n.* — **bot'tom-less**, *a.* [8].

bou'doir' (boo'dwär'), *n.* A lady's private room.

bough (bou), *n.* An arm or branch of a tree.

bought (bôt), *pret. & p. a.* of BUY.

bouil'lon (boo'yŏn'; bool'yŏn'), *n.* [F.] A kind of clear beef or other meat soup or broth.

boul'der (bōl'dẽr), *n.* Var. of BOWLDER.

bou'le-vard (boo'lē-värd), *n.* A broad avenue.

bounce (bouns), *v. t.* [1] To cause to bound or rebound. — *v. i.* **1.** To strike so as to rebound. **2.** To leap or spring suddenly; bound. — *n.* A sudden leap or bound; rebound.

boun'cer (boun'sẽr), *n.* **1.** One who bounces. **2.** Something big; as, a *bouncer* of a fish.

bounc'ing (-sĭng), *a.* Stout; buxom; big.

bound (bound), *n.* **1.** The limiting line; limit; confine; — usually in *pl.* **2.** *pl.* Borderland; domain. — *v. t.* **1.** To limit; terminate; inclose; restrain; confine. **2.** To name the boundaries of. — *v. i.* To have its boundary (on); adjoin.

bound, *v. i.* **1.** To move with a sudden spring or leap. **2.** To rebound, as a ball. — *v. t.* To cause to rebound; bounce. — *n.* **1.** A quick leap; a spring; jump. **2.** A rebound.

bound (bound), *a.* Prepared; ready to go; going.

bound, *p. a.* **1.** Restrained or fastened by a band, bond, or the like; tied; confined. **2.** Inclosed in a binding or cover, as a book. **3.** Under legal or moral restraint or obligation. **4.** Constrained or compelled; destined; certain.

bound'a-ry (boun'dá-rĭ), *n.; pl.* -RIES (-rĭz). That which indicates or fixes a limit, as of a territory.

bound'en (-d'n), *p. p. & a.* **1.** Under obligation, as for a favor. **2.** Made obligatory; binding.

bound'less, *a.* Without bounds; infinite.

boun'te-ous (boun'tē-ŭs), *a.* [4] **1.** Characterized by bounty; liberal; munificent. **2.** Liberally bestowed; plentiful. — **ly**, *adv.* [8] — **ness**, *n.* [8].

boun'ti-ful (boun'tĭ-fool), *a.* [4] **1.** Free in giving; liberal. **2.** Plentiful. — **ly**, *adv.* [8] — **ness**, *n.* [8].

boun'ty (-tĭ), *n.; pl.* -TIES (-tĭz). **1.** Liberality in giving. **2.** That which is given liberally. **3.** A reward; a premium to encourage an industry.

bou-quet' (boo-kā'), *n.* **1.** A nosegay; a bunch of flowers. **2.** A perfume; aroma, as of wine.

bourn (bōrn; boorn), *n.* Bound; boundary.

bout (bout), *n.* A conflict; contest; trial.

bo'vine (bō'vīn; -vĭn), *a.* Of or like animals of the ox kind; sluggish and patient; dull.

---

bow (bou), *v. i.* **1.** To bend the head, knee, or body in reverence, submission, civility, or assent. **2.** (*pron.* bō) To bend; curve. — *v. t.* **1.** To cause (anything) to incline; bend. **2.** To bend or incline, as the head or body, in respect, assent, or condescension. **3.** To prostrate; depress; crush. **4. a** To express by bowing. **b** To usher (*in* or *out*) with bowing. **5.** (*pron.* bō) To cause to become curved, or bow-shaped.—*n.* An inclination of the head, or a bending of the body, in respect, submission, etc.

bow (bou), *n.* **1.** The forward part of a vessel, or of an airship or dirigible balloon. **2.** One who rows in the bow of a boat.

bow (bō), *n.* **1.** Anything bent, or curved, as the rainbow; a bend. **2.** A weapon made of elastic material, as a strip of wood, with a cord to connect the two ends when bent, by which an arrow is propelled. **3.** Anything shaped like a bow.

bow'el (bou'ĕl), *n.* **1.** An intestine; entrail, esp. of man; gut; — usually in *pl.* **2.** *pl.* The interior of anything, as of the earth. **3.** *pl.* The seat of pity or kindness; tenderness; compassion.

bow'er (-ẽr), *n.* **1.** A rustic cottage. **2.** A chamber; esp., a lady's private apartment. *Now only Poetic.* **3.** A leafy or wooded shelter or arbor.

bowl (bōl), *n.* **1.** A concave vessel to hold liquids, etc. **2.** A part suggestive of a bowl (sense 1).

bowl, *n.* **1.** A ball used in playing bowls, tenpins, etc. **2.** *pl.* **a** A game that is played with balls on a level greensward. **b** Ninepins, skittles, or tenpins.— *v. i.* **1.** To play with or at bowls. **2.** To roll a ball, as in the game of bowls. **4.** *Cricket.* To serve the ball to the batsman. **4.** To move rapidly and smoothly, as a ball.—*v. t.* **1.** To roll or deliver, as a bowl or cricket ball. **2.** *Cricket.* To put out (a batsman) by bowling; — often with *out.*

bowl'der, boul'der (bōl'dẽr), *n.* A rounded or worn mass of rock, larger than a cobblestone.

bow'leg' (bō'lĕg'), *n.* A crooked leg, esp. one bowed outward. — **bow'-leg'ged** (-lĕg'ĕd; -lĕgd'), *a.*

bowl'er (bōl'ẽr), *n.* One who bowls.

bowl'ing (bōl'ĭng), *n.* The sport of playing bowls, or tenpins, or the game itself.

bow'man (bō'măn),*n.; pl.* -MEN (-mĕn). An archer.

bow'sprit (bō'sprĭt; bou'-), *n. Naut.* A spar projecting forward from the stem of a vessel.

bow window (bō). *Arch.* A bay window.

box (bŏks), *n.* A blow on the head or ear with the hand. — *v. i.* To fight with the fist; to spar with gloves. — *v. t.* To strike with the hand or fist.

box, *n.* An evergreen shrub or small tree widely used for hedges and borders.

box, *n.* **1.** A case or other receptacle usually having a lid or cover. **2.** Driver's seat on a carriage. **3.** A limited compartment in a public place, as in a theater, or its occupants. — *v. t.* **1.** To furnish with boxes, or inclose like a box. **2.** To inclose in or as in a box; confine; stow.

box'er (bŏk'sẽr), *n.* One who boxes.

box'ing, *n.* Act of fighting with the fists; sparring.

boy (boi), *n.* **1.** A male child from birth to about 14 years of age; a youth. **2.** A male servant.

boy'cott (boi'kŏt), *v. t.* **1.** To subject to a boycott. **2.** To refrain from the use of; keep aloof from. — *n.* A combining to withhold business or social relations from a tradesman, etc.

boy'hood(-hŏŏd), *n.* State or period of being a boy.

boy'ish, *a.* [4] Like, or in the manner of, a boy.

boy scout. Originally, a member of an organization founded in England in 1908 to promote good citizenship by creating in boys a spirit of duty and usefulness. Hence, a member of any of many similar organizations, now world-wide, as "The Boy Scouts of America" (incorporated, 1910).

brace (brās), *n.* **1.** A curved line connecting two or more words or lines; thus, $\begin{cases} boll \\ bowl \end{cases}$; or, in music, connecting staves. **2.** A curved handle for holding and turning boring implements. **3.** A rod, piece of timber, or the like, to strengthen something, or hold it firmly. **4.** A pair; couple. — *v.t.* [1] **1.** To bind, support with or as with braces. **2.** To give tone, vigor, or firmness to; — often with *up.* **3.** To hold firmly.—*v.i.* To get tone or vigor; rouse one's energies; — often with *up. Colloq.*

brace'let (brās'lĕt), *n.* An ornamental band worn about the wrist or arm, chiefly by women.

brac'er (brās'ẽr), *n.* That which braces; a tonic.

brac'ing (brās'ĭng), *p. a.* [4] Strengthening.

brack'en (brăk'n), *n.* A brake, or large fern.

brack'et (-ĕt),*n.* **1.** A projecting supporting piece. **2.** In writing and printing, either of the characters [ ], used to set something off from the context. — *v. t.* To place within brackets; connect by, or furnish with, a bracket or brackets.

brack'ish (-ĭsh), *a.* [4] Saltish; distasteful.

brad (brăd), *n.* A kind of thin, small nail.

brag (brăg), *v. i.; BRAGGED* (brăgd); *BRAG'GING.* To talk boastfully; boast. — *v. t.* To boast of; vaunt. — *n.* **1.** Boasting. **2.** Thing bragged of. **3.** One who brags; braggart. — **brag'ger** (-ẽr), *n.* [8].

brag'gart (brăg'ạrt),*n.* A boaster. — *a.* Boastful.

Brah'man (brä'mǎn), *n.; pl.* -MANS. A Hindu of the highest caste. — **Brah'min** (-mĭn), *n.*

braid (brād), *v. t.* **1.** To interlace; plait. **2.** To bind (the hair) as with a braid. **3.** To trim with braid. — *n.* **1.** A plait formed by intertwining strands. **2.** A narrow fabric for binding, etc.

brain (brān), *n.* **1.** The large mass of nerve tissue inclosed in the cranium, regarded as the seat of consciousness. **2.** Understanding; intellect; — often in the *pl.* — *v. t.* To dash out the brains of.

brain'less, *a.* Without understanding; witless.

braise (brāz), *v. t.* [1] *Cookery.* To stew or broil in a covered kettle or pan.

brake (brāk), *n.* Any of various large ferns.

brake, *n.* Any device for retarding or stopping by friction. — *v. t.* [1] To apply a brake to.

brake'man (-mǎn), *n.; pl.* -MEN (-mĕn). A man in charge of a brake or brakes, as on a railroad car.

bram'ble (brăm'b'l), *n.* The raspberry, blackberry, etc.; hence, any rough, prickly shrub.

bran (brăn), *n.* The broken coat of the seed of grain separated from flour by sifting or bolting.

branch (brànch), *n.* **1.** A shoot growing from the main stem of a plant or from one of the main divisions of the stem. **2.** Any division extending like a branch; ramification. **3.** A division of a family, descended from a particular ancestor. **4.** A member, part, section, or the like, of any complex body or work. — *a.* **1.** Diverging from, or tributary to, a main stock, line, way, theme,etc. **2.** Of or pert. to a branch.— *v. i.* To shoot or spread in or as in branches; ramify; diverge.

brand (brănd), *n.* **1.** A piece of partly burnt wood. **2.** A mark put on criminals with a hot iron; a stigma. **3.** A mark made with a hot iron, as to designate ownership, quality, etc.; any mark made for such a purpose; hence, grade; sort; class; make. — *v. t.* To make a brand upon; to stigmatize.

bran'dish (-dĭsh), *v. t.* To wave or flourish, as a weapon. — *n.* A flourish, as with a weapon.

brand'-new', *a.* Perfectly new; quite new.

bran'dy (brăn'dĭ), *n.; pl.* -DIES (-dĭz). A spirituous liquor distilled from wine or, sometimes, from the fermented juice of peaches, cherries, or apples. — *v. t.* [2] To flavor or treat with brandy.

brass (brás), *n.* **1.** An alloy of copper and zinc, and, sometimes, tin. **2.** *pl.* Brass utensils, ornaments, musical instruments, etc.

brass'y (brás'ĭ), *a.* [3] **1.** Of, pertaining to, or like, brass. **2.** Impudently bold; brazen. — **brass'i-ly**, *adv.* [8] — **brass'i-ness**, *n.* [8].

brat (brăt), *n.* A child; — now contemptuous.

bra-va'do (brá-vä'dō; -vā'dō), *n.; pl.* -DOES or -DOS (-dōz). Boastful behavior or parade of bravery.

brave (brāv), *a.* [3] **1.** Courageous. **2.** Making a fine show or display. — *n.* **1.** A brave person. **2.** A North American Indian warrior. — *v. t.* [1] To dare. — **brave'ly**, *adv.* [8].

brav'er-y (brāv'ĕr-ĭ), *n.; pl.* -ERIES (-ĭz). **1.** Quality of being brave; courage. **2.** Brave show; fine dress. **3.** A fine thing; an adornment.

bra'vo (brä'vō, brä'vō), *n.; pl.* -VOES or -VOS (-vōz). A daring villain; a bandit or professional assassin.

bra'vo (brä'vō), *interj.* Well done! Excellent!

brawl (brôl), *v. i.* **1.** To quarrel noisily. **2.** To make a loud confused noise. — *n.* Noisy quarrel.

brawn (brôn), *n.* **1.** Full, strong muscles, esp. of arm or leg; muscular strength. **2.** Boar's flesh.

brawn'y (brôn'ĭ), *a.* [3] Muscular; fleshy; strong.

bray (brā), *v. t.* To pound, beat, rub, or grind small or fine, usually in a mortar.

bray, *v. i.* To utter a harsh cry; — chiefly of the ass or donkey. — *v. t.* To make or utter harshly.— *n.* A harsh noise; esp., the cry of an ass.

braze (brāz), *v. t.* [1] To solder with hard solder.

bra'zen (brā'z'n), *a.* [3] **1.** Pertaining to, made of, or resembling, brass. **2.** Sounding harsh and loud, like resounding brass. **3.** Impudent; shameless. — *v. t.* To face brazenly; carry (*out* or *through*) impudently or shamelessly. — **bra'zen-ly**, *adv.* [8] — **bra'zen-ness**, *n.* [8].

bra'zier (brā'zhēr), *n.* A skilled worker in brass.

bra'zier, *n.* A pan or tray for holding burning coals.

Bra-zil' nut (brá-zĭl'). An oily 3-angled nut, the seed of a certain tree of Brazil.

Brazil Nut. 1 Fruit showing arrangement of nuts; 2 Nut.

breach (brēch), *n.* **1.** Act of breaking; gap or opening made by breaking; break. **2.** A breaking or infraction of a law, obligation, or tie. **3.** A breaking up of amicable relations; rupture.

bread (brĕd), *n.* **1.** A common article of food made from flour or meal. **2.** Food; sustenance. — *v. t. Cookery.* To cover with bread crumbs.

bread'fruit' (-frōōt'), *n.* The large round fruit of a certain Polynesian tree; also, the tree.

bread'stuff' (brĕd'stŭf'), *n.* That of which bread is made; also, bread; biscuit; — used chiefly in the *pl.*

breadth (brĕdth), *n.* **1.** Distance or measure from side to side of any surface or thing; width. **2.** Anything considered with reference to its width, or breadth. **3.** Largeness; liberality, as of ideas.

break (brāk), *v. t.; pret.* BROKE (brōk); *p. p.* BRO'KEN (brō'k'n); *p. pr. & vb. n.* BREAK'ING. **1.** To separate into parts or fragments as by a blow or strain; shatter; crush. **2.** To destroy the completeness, continuity, or arrangement of. **3.** **a** To reduce to subjection. **b** To bankrupt; ruin. **c** To degrade; dismiss. **d** Togo beyond or exceed (a record). **4.** To lay open by or as by breaking. **5.** **a** To transgress or violate. **b** To impart, as news, esp. bad news. **6.** To cause (one) to discontinue (a habit or practice).— *v. i.* **1.** To come apart, usually with suddenness and violence; curl over and fall in foam, as waves. **2.** To give way; fail. **3.** To burst forth or burst in violently or forcibly. **4.** To come suddenly (into sight or notice) ; of the day, to dawn. **5.** To make an abrupt or sudden change. **6.** To cease to have relations.— *n.* **1.** Act or action of breaking; rupture. **2.** A gap, rent, or breach; interruption; pause. — **-a-ble** (-á-b'l), *a.* [8].

break'age (brāk'ăj), *n.* Act or result of breaking; articles broken; allowance for things broken.

break'down' (-doun'), *n.* **1.** A breaking down; failure. **2.** A noisy, rapid, shuffling dance.

break'er (-ēr), *n.* **1.** One that breaks. **2.** A wave breaking into foam, as on rocks.

break'fast (brĕk'fást), *n.* The first meal of the day, or the food then eaten. — *v. i.* To eat breakfast.

break'neck' (brāk'nĕk'), *a.* Involving danger of a broken neck; as, a *breakneck* pace.

break'wa'ter (-wô'tēr), *n.* A structure for breaking the force of waves, as a sea wall.

bream (brēm), *n.* Any of various fishes.

breast (brĕst), *n.* **1.** The fore part of the body below the neck. **2.** A mammary gland. **3.** Something like the human breast. — *v. t.* To meet with the breast; struggle with bravely.

breast'plate' (-plāt'), *n.* A plate or the like covering the breast, esp., as defensive armor.

breast'work' (-wûrk'), *n. Fort.* A defensive work of moderate height, hastily thrown up.

breath (brĕth), *n.* **1.** An odor, esp. a fragrant one, given off by some object or objects; as, a *breath* of flowers. **2.** Air drawn into and forced out of the lungs in breathing; a single effort of breathing; hence, an instant; as, all at one *breath.* **3.** A very slight breeze. **4.** Power of breathing; hence, life; strength. **5.** Act or power of breathing freely; also, time to breathe; pause. **6.** Something produced by the breath; utterance; word.

breathe (brēth), *v. i.* [1] **1.** To give off an odor or perfume. **2.** To take breath; rest; also, to live. **3.** To blow gently. — *v. t.* **1.** To give forth. **2.** To inject by breathing; infuse. **3.** To respire. **4.** To whisper. **5.** To suffer to recover natural breathing; rest. **6.** To put out of breath; exhaust.

breath'less (brĕth'lĕs), *a*. [4] **1**. Without breath; hence, dead. **2**. Out of breath. **3**. Holding the breath from fear, expectation, or intense interest.

bred (brĕd), *pret. & p. p.* of BREED.

breech (brēch), *n*. **1**. The buttocks. **2**. The hinder or lower part; esp., the rear part of a firearm.

breech'es (brĭch'ĕz), *n. pl.* **1**. A kind of short trousers worn by men. **2**. Trousers. *Colloq.*

breech'ing (brĭch'ĭng ; brēch'-), *n*. A part of a harness that passes round the breech of a horse.

breed (brēd), *v. t.;* BRED (brĕd); BREED'ING. **1**. To produce as offspring; bear; beget. **2**. To bring up; train. **3**. To produce; be the native place of. **4**. To propagate.—*v. i.* **1**. To bear and nourish young, be with young. **2**. To have birth; originate. —*n*. **1**. A race or variety related by descent; stock; strain. **2**. Class; sort; kind.—**breed'er**, *n*. [8].

breed'ing, *n*. **1**. Act of one that breeds. **2**. Nurture; bringing up. **3**. Deportment; manners.

breeze (brēz), *n*. A gentle wind.

breez'y (brēz'ĭ), *a*. [3] **1**. Having breezes; airy. **2**. Fresh; brisk; vivacious. *Colloq.*

breth'ren (brĕth'rĕn), *n., pl.* of BROTHER; — used in solemn address, and of religious sects or their members or of professional relationship.

breve (brēv), *n*. A curved mark [◡] used commonly to indicate a short vowel or syllable.

bre-vet' (brē-vĕt'), *n*. *Mil.* A commission giving an officer higher nominal rank than that for which he receives pay.—*v. t.;* -VET'TED; -VET'TING. To confer rank on by brevet.

brev'i-ty (brĕv'ĭ-tĭ), *n. ; pl.* -TIES (-tĭz). Shortness; conciseness; quality of being brief.

brew (broo), *v. t.* **1**. To prepare, as beer, by steeping and fermentation, or infusion and fermentation. **2**. To foment; plot.—*v. i.* **1**. To brew beer or the like. **2**. To be forming or gathering.—*n*. That which is brewed.—**brew'er** (-ēr), *n*. [8].

brew'er-y (-ēr-ĭ), *n.; pl.* -ERIES (-ĭz). An establishment for brewing.—**brew'house** (-hous'), *n*.

bri'ar (brī'ēr). Var. of BRIER.

bribe (brīb), *n*. A price, gift, or favor bestowed or promised to corrupt a person in a position of trust, as an official.—*v. t.* [1] To give, promise, influence, or gain by a bribe.—*v. i.* To practice bribery.—**brib'a-ble** (brīb'á-b'l), *a*. [8].

brib'er (-ēr), *n*. One who gives or offers a bribe.

brib'er-y (-ĭ), *n.; pl.* -ERIES (-ĭz). Act or practice of giving or taking bribes.

bric'-a-brac' (brĭk'á-brăk'), *n*. Curious or antique articles of artistic character.

brick (brĭk), *n*. **1**. A building and paving material made from clay molded into blocks and baked in the sun or by fire; also, one of these blocks. **2**. Any of various oblong rectangular masses.

brid'al (brīd'ăl), *n*. A wedding. —*a*. Of or pertaining to a bride or a wedding; nuptial.

bride (brīd), *n*. A woman newly married, or about to be married.

bride'groom (-groom'), *n*. A man newly married, or about to be married.

brides'maid (brīdz'mād'), *n*. A maid or woman who attends a bride at her wedding.

bridge (brĭj), *n*. **1**. A structure erected over a depression or an obstacle, as a river, railroad, etc., carrying a passageway. **2**. *Naut.* A platform ele-

vated above the rail and extending across or over the deck of a vessel. **3**. Anything like, or suggestive of, a bridge. **4**. A card game resembling whist. — *v. t.* [1] **1**. To build a bridge or bridges on or over. **2**. To open or make (a passage, way, etc.) by a bridge.

bri'dle (brī'd'l), *n*. **1**. The headgear with which a horse is governed. **2**. A restraint ; curb ; check. — *v. t.* [1] **1**. To equip with a bridle. **2**. To restrain, guide, or govern with or as with a bridle. — *v. i.* To hold up the head and draw in the chin, as an expression of pride, scorn, or resentment.

brief (brēf), *a*. [3] Short, of short duration. — *n*. *Law.* A concise statement of a client's case for the instruction of counsel, or of the points of a legal argument.—*v.t.* To make an abstract of.—**brief'ly**, *adv*. [8] —**brief'ness**, *n*. [8].

bri'er (brī'ēr), *n*. Any plant with a woody stem bearing thorns or prickles, as the blackberry.

bri'er, *n*. A heath of southern Europe, the root of which is used in making tobacco pipes.

bri'er-y (-ĭ), *a*. [4] Full of briers.

brig (brĭg), *n*. A two-masted, square-rigged vessel.

bri-gade' (brĭ-gād'), *n*. **1**. *Mil.* A body of troops consisting of two or more regiments. **2**. Any body of persons organized to act or march together.

brig'a-dier' (brĭg'á-dēr'), *n*. *Mil.* One in command of a brigade ; a brigadier general.

brigadier general. An officer in command of a brigade, ranking next above a colonel.

brig'and (brĭg'ănd), *n*. One who lives by plunder.

brig'and-age (-ăn-dăj), *n*. Life and practices of brigands ; pillage ; also, brigands collectively.

brig'an-tine (-ăn-tēn ; -tīn), *n*. A two-masted, square-rigged vessel differing from a brig in not carrying a square mainsail.

bright (brīt), *a*. [3] **1**. Shining ; filled with light ; not dark ; clear. **2**. Keen; intelligent. **3**. Illustrious; glorious. — *adv*. Brightly.

bright'en (-'n), *v. t. & i.* To make or grow bright.

bright'ly, *adv*. In a bright manner.

bright'ness (brīt'nĕs), *n*. Quality of being bright.

Bright's' dis-ease' (brīts'). *Med.* Any of several forms of kidney disease.

bril'liance (brĭl'yăns), *n*. Brilliancy.

bril'lian-cy (-yăn-sĭ), *n.; pl.* -CIES (-sĭz). Quality or state of being brilliant; glitter; great brightness.

bril'liant (-yănt), *a*. [4] **1**. Sparkling, very bright. **2**. Distinguished by admirable qualities; splendid; shining. — *n*. A diamond or other gem cut in a particular form with numerous facets; also, the form itself. — **bril'liant-ly**, *adv*. [8].

bril'lian-tine (-yăn-tēn), *n*. A dress fabric, as of mohair, glossy on both sides.

brim (brĭm), *n*. **1**. Edge or margin; brink; border. **2**. Rim or upper edge of a dish or other vessel. **3**. The projecting edge or rim of a hat. — *v. t. & i.;* BRIMMED (brĭmd); BRIM'MING. To fill, or be full, to the brim.

brim'stone (-stōn), *n*. Sulphur.

brin'dled (brĭn'd'ld), *a*. Having dark streaks or spots on a gray or tawny ground.

brine (brīn), *n*. **1**. Water strongly impregnated with salt; salt water; fig., tears. **2**. The ocean; water of an ocean, sea, etc.

bring (brĭng), *v. t.; pret. & p. p.* BROUGHT (brôt),

āle, senāte, câre, ăm, ăccount, ärm, ȧsk, sofȧ; ēve, ĕvent, ĕnd, recĕnt, makēr; īce, ĭll; ōld, ōbey, ôrb, ŏdd, sŏft, cŏnnect; ūse, ŭnite, ûrn, ŭp, circŭs; fōōd, fŏŏt, out, oil.

p. pr. & vb. n. BRING′ING. **1.** To convey from a more distant to a nearer place. **2.** To procure in or as in exchange; fetch; produce. **3.** To present; *Law*, to prefer, as a charge; begin, as an action. **4.** To cause to come or to become.—**bring′er,** *n.* [8].

brink (brĭŋk), *n.* Edge, margin, or border.

brin′y (brĭn′ĭ), *a.* [3] Like brine; salty.

bri-quette′ (brĭ-kĕt′), *n.* A brick-shaped mass, of fine stuff (as coal) with a cementing material.

brisk (brĭsk), *a.* [3] Full of activity; lively.—*v. t. & i.* To make or become brisk.—**brisk′ly,** *adv.* [8] —**brisk′ness,** *n.* [8].

bris′ket (brĭs′kĕt), *n.* The breast of an animal.

bris′tle (brĭs′'l), *n.* A short, stiff, coarse hair. —*v. i.* [1] **1.** To stand erect, like bristles. **2.** To appear as if covered with bristles. **3.** To show defiance or indignation.

bris′tly (brĭs′lĭ), *a.* [3] Bristlelike; rough.

Brit′ish (brĭt′ĭsh), *a.* Of or pert. to Great Britain or its inhabitants.—*n.* **1.** Language of the ancient Britons. **2.** The people of Great Britain.

Brit′on (-ŭn), *n.* **1.** A member of one of the tribes inhabiting Britain in ancient times. **2.** A native of Great Britain, esp. an Englishman.

brit′tle (brĭt′'l), *a.* [4] Breaking easily and suddenly, like glass; fragile.—**-ness,** *n.* [8].

broach (brōch), *n.* Any of various pointed tools —*v. t.* To tap, as a cask to draw liquor. **2.** To make public; introduce in conversation.

broad (brôd), *a.* [3] **1.** Wide; extended in breadth, **2.** Spacious; vast. **3.** Clear; full. **4.** Plain; evident; obvious. **5.** Indelicate; coarse. **6.** Liberal; catholic, as in ideas. **7.** Main and essential; general.

broad′ax ⎱ (brôd′ăks), *n.* An ax with a broad
broad′axe ⎰ blade, as a kind of ax for hewing.

broad′cast (-kȧst′), *n.* A casting of seed in all directions.—*a.* Cast or scattering in all directions. —*v.* To scatter broadcast; spread abroad; send out from a central station, as in radio communication.—*adv.* So as to spread widely.

broad′cloth (-klôth), *n.* A kind of fine smooth woolen cloth, usually of double width.

broad′en (-'n), *v. i. & t.* To grow, or to make, broad.

broad′ly, *adv.* In a broad manner; widely.

broad′ness, *n.* State or quality of being broad.

broad′side′ (brôd′sīd′), *n.* **1.** *Naut.* The side of a ship above the water line, from bow to quarter. **2.** A broad surface. **3.** All the guns, collectively, than can be trained to fire to one side of a ship, or their simultaneous discharge.

broad′sword′ (-sōrd′), *n.* A broad-bladed sword.

bro-cade′ (brō-kād′), *n.* Silk stuff woven with gold and silver threads, or ornamented with raised flowers, foliage, etc.—**bro-cad′ed** (-kād′ĕd), *p. a.*

bro′gan (brō′găn), *n.* A kind of stout, coarse shoe.

brogue (brōg), *n.* **1.** A brogan. **2.** A dialect pronunciation or accent, esp. one such as often characterizes the Irish pronunciation of English.

broil (broil), *n.* A confused disturbance; a brawl.

broil, *v. t.* **1.** To cook by direct exposure to heat over a fire. **2.** To subject to great heat.—*v. i.* To be subjected to heat, as meat over the fire.—*n.* Act of broiling; also, something broiled.

broil′er (broil′ẽr), *n.* **1.** A utensil used in broiling. **2.** A chicken or other bird fit for broiling.

broke (brōk), *pret.* of BREAK.

bro′ken (brō′k'n), *p. a.* **1. a** Violently separated or fractured; sundered. **b** Subdued; crushed. **c** Violated, as a vow. **2.** Rough; uneven, as a surface. **3.** Imperfectly spoken; as, *broken* English.

bro′ker (brō′kẽr), *n.* A dealer in money, notes, drafts, stocks, etc.

bro′ker-age (-ăj), *n.* Business or fee of a broker.

bro′mide (-mid; -mĭd), *n.* A compound of bromine and another element.

bro′mine (-mĭn; -mēn), *n. Chem.* An element which ordinarily is a deep reddish brown, ill-smelling, caustic liquid, emitting a brown vapor.

bron′chi (brŏn′kī), *n., pl.* of BRONCHUS.

bron′chi-al (-ăl), *a.* Of or pert. to the bronchi.

bron-chi′tis (brŏn-kī′tĭs), *n. Med.* Inflammation of the bronchi.

bron′cho, bron′co (brŏn′kō), *n.; pl.* -CHOS, -COS (-kōz). A small hardy horse or pony of the plains of western North America.

bron′chus (-kŭs), *n.; pl.* -CHI (-kī). *Anat.* One of the subdivisions of the trachea, or windpipe, esp. either of the two primary divisions.

bronze (brŏnz), *n.* **1.** An alloy chiefly of copper and tin. **2.** A statue, bust, or the like, of bronze. **3.** Yellowish or reddish brown; bronze color. —*v. t.* [1] To give the appearance of bronze to.

brooch (brōch; brōōch), *n.* An ornamental clasp.

brood (brōōd), *n.* **1.** Progeny or young, esp. of such as breed from eggs; specifically, those hatched or cared for at one time. **2.** Species; kind; breed. —*v. t.* **1.** To sit on or incubate (eggs); hatch. **2.** To think anxiously or moodily upon; ponder. —*v. i.* **1.** To sit on and cover eggs or young to hatch or protect them. **2.** To have the mind dwell continuously or moodily on a subject.—*a.* Kept for breeding from; as, a *brood* mare.

brook (brōōk), *n.* A natural stream of water smaller than a river or creek.

brook, *v. t.* To bear; endure.

brook′let, *n.* A little brook.

broom (brōōm), *n.* **1.** Any of several European shrubs. **2.** An implement for sweeping.

broom corn. A variety of sorghum bearing a stiff-branched panicle of which brooms are made.

broth (brôth), *n.* Liquid in which flesh (or, sometimes, barley or rice) has been boiled; thin soup.

broth′er (brŭth′ẽr), *n.; pl.* -ERS (-ẽrz) or BRETHREN (brĕth′rĕn). See BRETHREN. **1.** A male considered in his relation to another having the same parents (whole brother), or one parent in common (half brother). **2.** One of a common family or race; fellow man. **3.** One closely united to another by a common tie or interest, as of rank or profession.

broth′er-hood (-hŏŏd), *n.* **1.** State of being brothers or a brother; brotherliness. **2.** A body of associates, as in a society, profession, etc.

broth′er-in-law′, *n.; pl.* -ERS-IN-LAW. Brother of one's husband or wife, or husband of one's sister.

broth′er-ly, *a.* Pert., or becoming, to brothers. —*adv.* Like a brother. —**-li-ness,** *n.* [8].

brough′am (brōō′ŭm), *n.* A form of light, close carriage. See *Illust.*

Brougham.

brought (brôt), *pret. & p. p.* of BRING.

brow (brou), *n.* **1.** The eyebrow. **2.** The forehead. **3.** Expression; mien. **4.** Edge of a steep place.

brow′beat′ (brou′bēt′), *v. t.* To bear down with stern looks or arrogant speech ; bully.

brown (broun), *a.* [3] Of any of various shades of dusky color between black and red or yellow. — *n.* **1.** A brown color. **2.** Any pigment or dye that colors brown. — *v. t. & i.* To make or become brown.

brown′stone′ (-stōn′), *n.* A reddish brown sandstone, used for building.

browse (brouz), *n.* **1.** Tender shoots or twigs, fit for food of cattle ; green food. **2.** A browsing. — *v. t.* [1] **1.** To eat or nibble off, as tender branches. **2.** To feed on, as pasture ; graze. — *v. i.* To browse the shoots of shrubs or trees.

bru′in (brōō′ĭn), *n.* A bear ; — so called in popular tales and often [*cap.*] personified.

bruise (brōōz), *v. t.* [1] **1.** To injure, as by a blow, without laceration ; contuse. **2.** To batter or indent, as with the fists. **3.** To break, as in a mortar; crush ; triturate. — *v. i.* To fight with the fists. — *n.* An injury without laceration, as from a blow with a blunt or heavy instrument ; a contusion.

bru-net′ (brōō-nĕt′), *a.* Having brown or olive skin and dark hair and eyes. — *n.* A brunet person.

bru-nette′ (-nĕt′), *n.* A brunet girl or woman.

bru-nette′, *a. fem.* Brunet.

bruut (brŭnt), *n.* The force of a blow ; shock or greatest violence as of an onset or a struggle.

brush (brŭsh), *n.* **1.** An implement composed of bristles, or the like, set in a back or handle. **2.** The bushy tail of some animals, esp. of the fox. **3.** Something suggestive of a brush (in sense 1). **4.** Act of brushing, rubbing, or grazing. — *v. t.* **1.** To rub, smooth, clean, paint, etc., with a brush. **2.** To graze lightly or quickly. **3.** To remove with or as with a brush. — *v. i.* To move so as to graze, skim over, or sweep, anything.

brush, *n.* **1.** Branches of trees lopped off; brushwood. **2.** A thicket; underbrush.

brush, *n.* **1.** A short, brisk encounter. **2.** A short contest, trial, or spurt of speed.

brush′wood (-wŏŏd), *n.* A thicket of shrubs and small trees; also, small branches cut off.

brusque (brŏŏsk; brŭsk), *a.* [3] Rough and short in manner; abrupt; bluff. — **brusque′ly,** *adv.* [8] — **brusque′ness,** *n.* [8].

bru′tal (brōō′tăl), *a.* [4] Of, like, or pertaining to, a brute; brutish; savage; inhuman. — **-ly,** *adv.* [8].

bru-tal′i-ty (-tăl′ĭ-tĭ),*n.; pl.* -TIES. **1.** State or quality of being brutal ; savageness. **2.** A brutal act.

bru′tal-ize (brōō′tăl-īz), *v. t. & i.* [1] To make or become brutal.

brute (brōōt), *a.* **1.** Irrational ; unthinking. **2.** Without life or sensibility; inanimate; soulless. **3.** Brutal ; savage ; coarse; sensual. — *n.* **1.** A beast. **2.** A brutal person.

brut′ish (brōō′tĭsh), *a.* [4] Of, pertaining to, or resembling, a brute ; irrational ; stupid; coarse. — **-ish-ly,** *adv.* [8] — **-ness,** *n.* [8].

bub′ble (bŭb″l), *n.* **1.** A thin film of liquid inflated with air or gas. **2.** A small body of air or gas within a liquid or a transparent solid. **3.** Anything that wants firmness, solidity, or reality; a false show; a delusive scheme. — *v. i.* [1] **1.** To

rise in or form bubbles. **2.** To run with a gurgling noise, as if forming bubbles ; to gurgle.

buc′ca-neer′ (bŭk′ȧ-nēr′), *n.* A pirate.

buck (bŭk), *n.* **1.** The male of deer, antelopes, goats, hares, rabbits, etc. **2.** A dashing young fellow ; a dandy. *Archaic.* — *v. i.* To spring with a quick plunging leap; — of a horse or mule.— *v. t.* To throw by bucking. — *n.* Act of bucking.

buck′board′ (-bōrd′), *n.* A four-wheeled vehicle with a long elastic board or frame bearing the seat.

buck′et (-ĕt), *n.* **1.** A vessel for drawing, holding, or carrying something, as water, coal, etc. **2.** The quantity a bucket will hold.

buck′eye′ (-ī′), *n.* Any of several American trees of the horse-chestnut family.

buck′le (-′l), *n.* **1.** A certain device for uniting two loose ends, as of a belt or strap. **2.** A distortion, as a bend or twist in a metal tube. — *v.t.* [1] **1.** To fasten with a buckle. **2.** To bend permanently; distort by bending.— *v. i.* **1.** To prepare for a contest, as, orig., by buckling on armor; hence, to apply one's self with vigor; as, to *buckle* down to work. **2.** To bend permanently or so as to distort, as a wheel.

buck′ler (-lẽr), *n.* A kind of shield worn on the arm. — *v. t.* To shield ; defend.

buck′ram (-răm), *n.* A coarse cloth of linen, hemp, or cotton, stiffened with size or glue.

buck′saw′ (-sô′), *n.* A saw set in a frame and used for sawing wood on a sawbuck, or sawhorse.

buck′shot′ (-shŏt′), *n.* A coarse leaden shot.

buck′skin′ (bŭk′skĭn′), *n.* A strong, soft dressed leather, usually yellowish or grayish.

buck′wheat′ (-hwēt′), *n.* A plant cultivated for its triangular seeds, which are ground into flour. Also, the seed, or the flour.

bu-col′ic (bū-kŏl′ĭk), *a.* [4] Pastoral; rustic.

bud (bŭd), *n.* **1.** One of the small growths that appear on trees and plants and later become leaves, blossoms, or branches; a flower or leaf not yet fully opened. **2.** A similar growth on some part of the body of certain plants and animals, as the coral, which develops into a new organism. — *v. i. ;* BUD′DED; -DING. To put forth buds, begin to develop.— *v.t.* To graft by inserting a bud from one plant into an opening in the bark of another.

Bud′dha(bŏŏd′ȧ),*n.* A deified religious teacher of the Buddhists, on whose teachings a religion (**Bud′dhism** [-Iz′m]) is based. — **Bud′dhist** (-Ist), *n.*

budge (bŭj), *v. i. & t.* [1] To move ; stir.

budg′et (bŭj′ĕt), *n.* **1.** A stock ; store; accumulation; as, a *budget* of news. **2.** The annual financial statement and estimate of expenditure and revenue made, for the ensuing year, in the British House of Commons. **3.** A similar statement in other countries or bodies.

buff (bŭf), *n.* **1.** A sort of superior leather. **2.** The color of buff; a dull yellowish orange. — *a.* Made of or like buff ; of the color of buff.

buf′fa-lo (bŭf′ȧ-lō), *n. ; pl.* -LOES or -LOS (-lōz). Any of several species of wild ox, as the American bison.

buff′er (-ẽr), *n.* Anything that serves to deaden a shock or bear the brunt of opposing forces.

buf-fet′ (bŏŏ-fā′; F. bü/fě′), *n.* **1.** A cupboard or set of shelves for displaying silver, china, etc. **2.** A counter for refreshments ; a restaurant.

buf'fet (bŭf'fĕt), *n.* A blow, as with the hand; a slap; hence, any blow or stroke. — *v. t.* **1.** To strike with the hand or fist; box; cuff. **2.** To strike repeatedly; strive with or contend against.

buf-foon' (bŭ-fōon'), *n.* A man who makes a practice of amusing others by tricks, antics, etc.; clown.

buf-foon'er-y (-ẽr-ĭ), *n.; pl.* -ERIES (-ĭz). Arts and practices of a buffoon.

bug (bŭg), *n.* An insect of almost any kind; esp., a beetle or an insect that crawls like one.

bug'a-boo' (bŭg'á-bōo'), *n.* An imaginary object of fright; a bugbear.

bug'bear' (-bâr'), *n.* A bugaboo.

bug'gy (-ĭ), *n.; pl.* -GIES (-ĭz). A light vehicle or carriage.

bu'gle (bū'g'l), *n.* **1.** A huntsman's horn. **2.** A brass or copper wind instrument, shorter than the trumpet, curved, and sometimes keyed. — *v. t. & i.* [1] To sound with or like a bugle; also, to summon by a bugle call. — **bu'gler** (bū'glẽr), *n.* [8].

build (bĭld), *v. t.; pret. & p. p.* BUILT (bĭlt); *p. pr. & vb. n.* BUILD'ING. **1.** To erect or construct, as a house; fabricate; make. **2.** To fashion; create. **3.** To settle or establish. — *v. i.* **1.** To perform the act, or follow the business, of building something. **2.** To rest or depend, as on a foundation; rely. — *n.* Form of construction; figure; make.

build'er (bĭl'dẽr), *n.* One who builds; one whose occupation is to build, as a carpenter.

build'ing, *n.* **1.** Act of making, erecting, or establishing. **2.** That which is built, as a house, barn, factory, etc. **3.** Art of constructing edifices.

bulb (bŭlb), *n.* **1.** A large bud, usually underground, sending out roots from below, and bearing overlapping, scalelike leaves. **2.** A fleshy tuber or a short fleshy stem (corm) resembling a true bulb (sense 1). **3.** An expansion or part resembling a bulb.

bulb'ous (bŭl'bŭs), *a.* Having or containing bulbs; bulblike in shape or structure.

bulge (bŭlj), *n.* A swelling, protuberant part, as in a wall. — *v. i. & t.* [1] To swell or jut out.

bulk (bŭlk), *n.* **1.** Magnitude or volume; size; esp., great or considerable size. **2.** Body; mass; aggregate. **3.** The main body; largest part.

bulk'head' (-hĕd'), *n.* **1.** *Naut.* Any upright partition separating the compartments of a vessel. **2.** A structure to resist the pressure of earth or water.

bulk'y (bŭl'kĭ), *a.* [3] Of great bulk; large; massive. — **bulk'i-ly,** *adv.* [8] — **bulk'i-ness,** *n.* [8].

bull (bōōl), *n.* A grotesque blunder in language.

bull, *n.* A formal letter, or edict, of the Pope.

bull, *n.* **1.** The male of any bovine or of certain other animals, as of the seal, etc. **2.** *Stock Exchange.* One expecting or trying to effect a rise in price. — *v. t.* To try to raise the price of (stocks).

bull'dog' (bōōl'dŏg'), *n.* One of a variety of short-haired, powerful, courageous dogs. — *a.* Characteristic of or like a bulldog; stubborn.

bull'doze' (-dōz'), *v. t.* [1] To frighten or bully (a person) into doing or not doing something; intimidate. *Colloq., U. S.*

bul'let (bōōl'ĕt), *n.* **1.** A small ball. **2.** A missile, usually of lead, to be shot from a firearm.

bul'le-tin (-ĕ-tĭn), *n.* **1.** A brief statement of news to the public. **2.** A periodical publication, esp. of a society. — *v. t.* To state in a bulletin.

bull'finch' (-fĭnch'), *n.* Any of several song birds.

bull'frog' (-frŏg'), *n.* A large North American frog.

bull'head' (-hĕd'), *n.* Any of various fishes, so called from their large head.

bul'lion (bōōl'yŭn), *n.* Gold or silver considered merely as so much metal; uncoined gold or silver, in bars or ingots.

bull'ock (bōōl'ŭk), *n.* An ox or steer.

bull's'-eye' (bōōlz'ī'), *n.* **1.** A disk of glass in a deck, floor, etc., to let in light. **2.** A lens of short focal distance, or a lantern with such a lens. **3.** The center of a target; also, a shot that hits it.

bul'ly (bōōl'ĭ), *n.; pl.* -LIES (-ĭz). A blustering fellow, more insolent than courageous. — *a.* [3] Fine; excellent. *Slang.* — *interj.* Good! *Slang.* — *v. t.* [2] To intimidate by manner or threats.

bul'rush (-rŭsh'), *n.* A kind of large rush.

bul'wark (-wãrk), *n.* **1.** A solid, wall-like, defensive structure; rampart. **2.** Any means of defense or protection. **3.** The side of a ship above the upper deck; — usually in *pl.*

bum'ble-bee' (bŭm'b'l-bē'), *n.* Any of various species of true bees, mostly of large size.

bump (bŭmp), *v. t.* To strike, as against anything big or solid or with such a thing; thump. — *v.i.* To come into violent contact with something. — *n.* A thump; heavy blow; also, a swelling due to a bump.

bump'er (bŭm'pẽr), *n.* **1.** A cup or glass filled to the brim, esp. in drinking a toast. **2.** Anything unusually large or great. *Colloq.*

bump'kin (bŭmp'kĭn), *n.* A country lout.

bump'tious (-shŭs), *a.* [4] Self-conceited; forward. — -**tious-ly,** *adv.* [8] — -**tious-ness,** *n.* [8].

bun (bŭn), *n.* A kind of cake or bread; commonly, a sweetened, often spiced, raised cake or biscuit.

bunch (bŭnch), *n.* **1.** A protuberance; hump; knob. **2.** A cluster, as of grapes. **3.** A group or number of things of the same kind, as of cattle. — *v. i. & t.* To swell out or form into a bunch.

bun'combe (bŭn'kŭm), *n.* Speechmaking to gratify constituents, or to gain public applause; anything said, written, or done for mere show. *U. S.*

bun'dle (bŭn'd'l), *n.* **1.** A number of things bound together; a loose package; roll. **2.** A given quantity of some commodity bound together so as to form a unit. **3.** A number or group considered together; a lot. — *v. t.* [1] **1.** To tie or bind in a bundle or roll. **2.** To hustle or hurry.

bung (bŭng), *n.* The stopper of the hole in the bilge of a cask by which it is filled; also, the bung-hole. — *v. t.* To stop with a bung; — often with *up*

bun'ga-low (bŭn'gá-lō), *n.* A kind of one-storied house or cottage, usually with a wide veranda and widely over-hanging eaves.

bung'hole' (bŭng'hōl'), *n.* Hole stopped by a bung.

Bungalow.

bun'gle (bŭn'g'l), *v. i. & t.* [1] To act, work, make, or perform in a clumsy or awkward manner. — *n.* A clumsy or awkward performance; botch. — **bun'gler** (-glẽr), *n.* [8] — **bun'gling,** *p. a.* — **bun'gling-ly,** *adv.* [8].

---

bun′ion (bŭn′yŭn), n. An inflamed swelling on the foot, usually on the first joint of the great toe.

bunk (bŭnk), n. A case or frame attached to a wall to serve as a bed, as in a ship's forecastle. — v. i. To go to bed, or to sleep, in a bunk. Colloq.

bunk′er (bŭnk′ẽr), n. **1.** A large bin; esp., one of several large compartments for coal on shipboard. **2.** Golf. Any rough, hazardous ground on the links; esp., an artificial hazard with built-up faces.

bun′ko (bŭn′kō), n. A swindling game or scheme. — v. t. To swindle by a bunko game.

bun′ny (bŭn′ĭ), n. pl.; -NIES (-ĭz). A rabbit or a squirrel; — a pet name.

Bun′sen burn′er (bōōn′sĕn). A kind of burner for gas in which the air and gas mix and burn with intense heat and a blue sootless flame.

bunt (bŭnt), v. t. & i. To butt or push with or as with the horns. — n. Act of bunting.

bun′ting (-tĭng), n. Any of various small birds.

bun′ting, n. A thin woolen stuff, used for flags.

buoy (boi; bōō′ĭ; bwoi), n. **1.** Naut. A float; esp., a floating object moored to the bottom to mark a channel, anchor, rock, etc. **2.** A buoyant float to prevent one from drowning; — usually life buoy. — v. t. & i. **1.** To keep from sinking in a fluid; float; hence, to support; sustain; — with up. **2.** To mark by or as by a buoy or buoys.

buoy′an·cy (-ăn-sĭ), n.; pl. -CIES (-sĭz). **1.** Property of floating on the surface of a liquid, or in a fluid, as in the air. **2.** Power of a fluid to bear up a body in it, or the upward pressure exerted by the fluid on the body. **3.** Cheerfulness; vivacity.

buoy′ant (-ănt), a. [4] **1.** Having the quality of rising or floating in a fluid. **2.** Bearing up, as a fluid. **3.** Light-hearted.—**buoy′ant·ly**, adv. [8].

bur (bûr). Var. of BURR.

bur, n. **1.** Any rough or prickly envelope of a fruit, as of the chestnut; also, any weed bearing burs. **2.** Something that clings like a bur.

bur′bot (bûr′bŏt), n. Either of two fresh-water fishes, of the cod family.

bur′den (bûr′d'n), n. **1.** The verse repeated in a song; chorus; refrain. **2.** The main topic; gist.

bur′den, n. **1.** Thing borne; load; hence, care; responsibility; burdensome lot; grievous fate. **2.** Capacity of a vessel for carrying cargo; also, the weight of the cargo. — v. t. To load; overload; hence, to oppress.

bur′den·some (-sŭm), a. [4] Hard to bear.

bur′dock (bûr′dŏk), n. Any of various coarse biennial plants with burlike heads.

bu′reau (bū′rō; bū-rō′), n.; pl. E. -REAUS (-rōz), F. -REAUX (E. pron. -rōz). **1.** A government department or office, or subdivision thereof. **2.** A chest of drawers for clothes, often with a mirror.

bu-reau′cra-cy (bū-rō′krȧ-sĭ), n.; pl. -CIES (-sĭz). **1.** Government by bureaus; loosely, officialism. **2.** Government officials collectively.

bur′glar (bûr′glẽr), n. One guilty of burglary.

bur-gla′ri-ous (bûr-glā′rĭ-ŭs), a. [8] Pertaining to or involving burglary.

bur′gla-ry (bûr′glȧ-rĭ), n.; pl. -RIES (-rĭz). Law. Breaking and entering the dwelling house of another, especially in the nighttime, with intent to commit a felony therein.

bur′i-al (bĕr′ĭ-ăl), n. Act of burying; interment.

bur′lap (bûr′lăp), n. A fabric of jute or hemp, used for bagging, coverings, etc.

bur-lesque′ (bûr-lĕsk′), a. Tending to excite laughter or contempt by extravagant treatment of a subject. — n. Burlesque representation; also, an instance of it. — v. t. [1] To mock or make ludicrous by burlesque.

bur′ly (bûr′lĭ), a. [3] **1.** Large or stout of body; bulky. **2.** Coarse and rough; boisterous; bluff. — **bur′li-ness**, n. [8].

burn (bûrn), v. t.; BURNED (bûrnd) or BURNT (bûrnt); BURN′ING. **1.** To consume by fire. **2.** To injure by fire or heat. **3.** To bake. **4.** To make or produce by fire or heat. **5.** To affect as if by the action of fire or heat. — v. i. **1.** To be on fire; undergo combustion. **2.** To undergo some change, esp. some injury, by fire or heat. **3.** To feel, or to appear, as if on fire or excessively heated. — n. **1.** A hurt, injury, or effect caused by burning. **2.** Process, operation, or result of burning.

burn′er, n. **1.** One that burns anything. **2.** Part of a lamp, etc., where the flame is produced.

bur′nish (bûr′nĭsh), v. t. To make smooth and bright; polish. — -**nish-er**, n.

burnt (bûrnt), pret., p. p., & p. a. of BURN.

burr, bur (bûr), n. **1.** A thin ridge or roughness left by a tool in cutting metal, etc. **2.** A trilled pronunciation of the letter r. **3.** A whir.

bur′ro (bŏŏr′ō; bûr′ō), n.; pl. -ROS (-ōz). A donkey, or ass. Southwestern U. S.

bur′row (bûr′ō), n. A hole in the ground made by certain animals, as rabbits, for shelter and habitation. — v. i. To excavate a hole, as in the earth, esp. one to lodge in. — v. t. To make burrows in or to construct by burrowing.

bur′sar (bûr′sẽr), n. A treasurer, or cash keeper, as of a college; a purser.

burst (bûrst), v. i.; BURST; BURST′ING. **1.** To fly apart or in pieces; break open; explode. **2.** To appear or depart suddenly and unexpectedly; — usually with forth, out, upon, etc.— v. t. To cause to burst.— n. **1.** Act of bursting; also, that which bursts forth or out. **2.** Any brief violent activity or effort; a spurt. **3.** Result of bursting; a breach.

bur′y (bĕr′ĭ), v. t. [2] **1.** To deposit (a corpse) in its resting place, with funeral ceremonies; inter. **2.** To put away finally as if in the grave.

bus (bŭs), n.; pl. BUSSES. An omnibus. Colloq.

bush (bŏŏsh), n. **1.** A shrub; esp., a thick, densely branched shrub or a cluster of shrubs. **2.** Uncleared or uncultivated country, esp. woodland or land covered with shrubby vegetation.

bush′el (bŏŏsh′ĕl), n. **1.** A dry measure containing 4 pecks, or 32 quarts. Abbr., bu. **2.** A vessel or measure holding a bushel. **3.** A weight assumed as the equivalent of the bushel measure.

bush′el, v. t. Tailoring. To repair or put in order, as men's garments.—v. i. To repair garments. U.S.

bush′y (-ĭ), a. [3] **1.** Full of, or overgrown with, bushes. **2.** Thick and spreading like a bush.

bus′i-ly (bĭz′ĭ-lĭ), adv. In a busy manner.

busi′ness (bĭz′nĕs), n. **1.** That which engages one's time, attention, or labor, as a serious employment; work. **2.** That which one has to do or should do; duty; mission. **3.** Affair; matter; — used indefinitely. **4.** Mercantile transactions; tra[?]

fic in general ; trade. **5.** A commercial or industrial establishment or enterprise.

bust (bŭst), *n.* **1.** A piece of sculpture representing the upper part of the human body. **2.** The part of the human body between head and waist.

bus′tard (bŭs′tȧrd), *n.* Any of a family of large game birds, related to the cranes.

bus′tle (-'l), *v. i.* [1] To move about busily and noisily or with commotion. — *n.* Act of one who bustles; stir. — *n.* A kind of pad or form worn by women to expand the skirt behind.

bus′y (bĭz′ĭ), *a.* [3] **1.** Engaged in some business; hard at work. **2.** Constantly or actively at work; active. **3.** Crowded with business or activities. **4.** Characteristic of, or indicating, diligence. — *v. t. & i.* [1] To make, keep, or be, busy ; to employ ; occupy.

bus′y-bod′y (-bŏd′ĭ), *n.; pl.* -BODIES (-ĭz). One of ficious in the affairs of others; a meddling person.

but (bŭt), *prep. & conj.* **1.** Outside of ; without; except ; save ; that. **2. a** Only ; no more than. **b** No more or less than ; just. **3.** If not. **4.** On the contrary ; yet ; however.

butch′er (bŏŏch′ẽr), *n.* **1.** One whose business is to slaughter animals, or dress their flesh, for market; a dealer in meat. **2.** One who kills in large numbers or brutally. — *v. t.* **1.** To slaughter as a butcher does. **2.** To botch; mangle.

butcher bird. Any of certain species of shrikes that impale their prey on thorns.

butch′er-y (-ẽr-ĭ), *n.; pl.* -ERIES (-ĭz). Murder or manslaughter, esp. when extensive or brutal; great or cruel slaughter.

but′ler (bŭt′lẽr), *n.* A manservant in charge of the wines and liquors.

butt (bŭt), *n.* **1.** A large cask or vessel, esp. for wine or beer. **2.** As a measure, two hogsheads.

butt, *n.* **1.** The thicker end (of anything) or the part at the bottom. **2. a** A target. **b** A range for target practice ; — called also *the butts*. **3.** A person at whom ridicule, jest, or contempt is directed. **4.** A sudden blow given by the head of an animal. — *v. i.* To strike or thrust, now esp. with the head or horns; hence, to go or drive headfirst. — *v.t.* **1.** To strike, esp. with the head or horns; drive or push by butting. **2.** To join end to end, as two timbers.

butte (būt), *n.* A conspicuous isolated steep hill or small mountain. *Western U. S. & Canada.*

but′ter (bŭt′ẽr), *n.* **1.** The fatty substance got from milk or cream by agitation, as by churning. **2.** Any butterlike substance. — *v. t.* To cover or spread with butter.

but′ter-cup′ (-kŭp′), *n.* Any of various yellow-flowered species of crowfoot.

but′ter-fish′ (-fĭsh′), *n.* Any of several fishes.

but′ter-fly′ (-flī′), *n.; pl.* -FLIES (-flīz′). **1.** Any of various insects, often brightly colored, having very large wings. **2.** One like a butterfly.

but′ter-ine (-ēn; -ĭn), *n.* Oleomargarine.

but′ter-milk′ (-mĭlk′), *n.* The liquid left from cream or milk from which butter has been churned.

but′ter-nut′ (-nŭt′), *n.* The edible nut of a certain American walnut tree ; also, the tree.

but′ter-y (-ĭ), *a.* Like butter; containing, or spread with, butter.

but′ter-y (bŭt′ẽr-ĭ; *colloq.* bŭt′rĭ), *n. ; pl.* -TERIES (-ĭz). A room or rooms where liquors or other provisions are kept; a pantry.

but′tock (bŭt′ŭk), *n.* The part at the back of the hip ; in *pl.*, rump.

but′ton (-'n), *n.* **1.** A knob, disk, or the like, to be sewn on an article of dress, usually as a catch. **2.** A small fastening, knot, or piece suggestive of a button. — *v. t.* To furnish or fasten with a button or buttons. — *v. i.* To admit of being buttoned.

but′ton-hole′ (-hōl′), *n.* The hole or loop for a button. — *v. t.* **1.** To hold by the button, as for conversation. **2.** To furnish with buttonholes.

but′ton-wood′ (-wŏŏd′), *n.* The plane tree or sycamore of America ; — from the buttonlike fruits.

but′tress (-rĕs), *n.* A projecting structure to support a wall or building. — *v. t.* To furnish or support with a buttress; prop.

bux′om (bŭk′sŭm), *a.* [3] Having health, vigor, and comeliness and a gay, lively manner; jolly.

buy (bī), *v. t. & i. ; pret. & p. p.* BOUGHT (bôt); *p. pr. & vb. n.* BUY′ING (bī′ĭng). **1.** To acquire (property) by giving a price; purchase ; — opposed to *sell.* **2.** To hire; bribe. — **buy′er**, *n.* [8].

buzz (bŭz), *v. i.* To make a low, continuous, humming sound, as that made by bees. — *v. t.* To utter with a buzz; spread as a rumor. — *n.* **1.** A confused murmur; hum. **2.** A rumor.

buz′zard (bŭz′ȧrd), *n.* **1.** Any of numerous heavy, slow-flying hawks. **2.** Any of various other birds of prey ; esp., *Southern U. S.*, the turkey buzzard.

by (bī), *prep.* **1.** In proximity to ; near. **2.** Along, over, or through. **3.** In, on, or at. **4.** Past; near to and then on beyond. **5.** In the course of; at; in; — of time; also, not later than. **6.** To the amount of ; — in expressions involving comparison. **7.** In conformity to. **8.** With respect to. **9.** Through the medium or means of. **10.** With the witness or sanction of; — used in oaths. — *adv.* **1.** Near; near by. **2.** Near in passing ; past; beyond. **3.** Aside.

bye (bī), *n.* Something aside or secondary. *Obs.*, except in : **by the bye**, by the way.

by′gone′ (bī′gŏn′), *a.* Past ; gone by. — *n.* Something gone by or past.

by′-law′, *n.* A law made by a society or the like for the regulation of its own affairs.

by′path′ (bī′pȧth′), *n. ; pl.* BYPATHS (-pȧthz′). A private, indirect, or retired path or way.

by′play′ (-plā′), *n.* Action carried on aside or apart from the main action, as on the stage.

by′-prod′uct, *n.* Something produced, as in manufacture, in addition to the principal product.

by′stand′er (-stăn′dẽr), *n.* One standing near ; one present but not taking part.

by′way′ (-wā′), *n.* Unfrequented way; side path.

by′word′ (-wûrd′), *n.* **1.** A proverb. **2.** An object of scorn or derision.

---

chair; go; sing, iŋk; then, thin; nature, verdure; yet; zh = z in azure. Numbers refer to §§ in the Special Notes which, with Abbreviations, Signs, etc., precede the Vocabulary.

C

cab (kăb), *n.* **1**. A kind of close carriage; a cabriolet. **2**. The covered part of a locomotive.

ca-bal' (kȧ-băl'), *n.* **1**. The secret schemes of a few persons united in a design or plot; intrigue. **2**. A junto. — *v. i.;* -**BALLED'** (-băld') ; -**BAL'LING**. To unite in a cabal; plot; intrigue.

cab'a-lis'tic (kăb'ȧ-lĭs'tĭk), *a.* Having a mystic sense; mysterious; occult.

cab'bage (kăb'ăj), *n.* A common vegetable in which the thick leaves are crowded into a dense head; also, one of the heads.

cab'in (-ĭn), *n.* **1**. A small house, esp. a rude one. **2**. A room in a ship for officers or passengers.

cab'i-net (kăb'ĭ-nĕt), *n.* **1**. A case, set of drawers, or cupboard to contain jewels, specimens, or other articles. **2**. A small room or retired apartment. **3**. A body of advisers, esp. the advisory council of the sovereign or chief executive.—*a.* **1**. Private; secret. **2**. Suitable, as to size, value, etc., for a small room. **3**. Of or pertaining to a political cabinet.

ca'ble (kā'b'l), *n.* **1**. A strong rope of 10 or more inches in circumference; hence, a very strong wire rope or a chain. **2**. A waterproof insulated bundle of wires, as for submarine telegraphy. **3**. A cablegram. *Colloq.* — *v. t. & i.* [1] To transmit or communicate by a submarine cable.

ca'ble-gram (-grăm'), *n.* A message sent by a submarine telegraphic cable.

ca-boose' (kȧ-bōōs'), *n.* **1**. *Naut.* A deck room for cooking; galley. **2**. A car on freight or construction trains for workmen or the train crew. *U. S.*

cab'ri-o-let' (kăb'rĭ-ŏ-lā'), *n.* A kind of light one-horse carriage with two seats and, often, a top.

ca-ca'o (kȧ-kā'ō; kȧ-kā'ō), *n.* **1**. A certain South American tree, now cultivated also in the West Indies, Mexico, etc., for its seeds. **2**. The seeds of this tree, used in making cocoa and chocolate.

cache (kăsh), *n.* A hiding or storing place, as for goods, treasure, or provisions; esp., a hole or mound for hiding stores of provisions, ammunition, etc.; also, that which is hidden in a cache. — *v. t. & i.* [1] To put, hide, or store in a cache.

Cacao. 1 Leaves ; 2 Pod ; 3 Single Seed.

cack'le (kăk''l), *v. i.* [1] **1**. To make the sharp, broken noise or cry of a hen. **2**. To laugh or chatter with a noise like a hen's cackle. — *n.* Act or noise of cackling; idle talk; prattle.

cac'tus (kăk'tŭs), *n.; pl.* E. -**TUSES** (-ĕz), L. **CACTI** (-tī). Any of a large family of plants having fleshy stems and branches with scales or spines.

cad (kăd), *n.* A lowbred, presuming person ; a mean, vulgar fellow. *Colloq.*

ca-da'ver (kȧ-dā'vēr),*n.* A dead body, esp. human.

ca-dav'er-ous (-dăv'ēr-ŭs), *a.* [4] Of or pertaining to, or like, a cadaver ; esp., pale ; ghastly.

cad'die (kăd'ĭ), *n.* An attendant who carries a golf player's clubs, etc.

cad'dish (-ĭsh), *a.* [4] Like a cad; lowbred.

cad'dy (kăd'ĭ). Var. of CADDIE.

cad'dy, *n.; pl.* -**DIES** (-ĭz). A small box for tea.

ca'dence (kā'dĕns), *n.* **1. a** Rhythmical flow of sound; rhythm. **b** The measure or beat of any rhythmical motion, as music. **2**. The close or conclusion of a musical strain.

ca-det' (kȧ-dĕt'), *n.* **1**. A younger brother or son. **2**. A youth in training for military or naval service.

cad'mi-um (kăd'mĭ-ŭm), *n.* *Chem.* A tin-white, malleable, ductile metallic element.

cæ'cum (sē'kŭm), *n.; L. pl.* -**CA** (-kȧ). The blind pouch or sac in which the large intestine begins.

‖**ca-fé'** (kȧ/fā'), *n.* [F.] **1.** A coffeehouse; restaurant; often, in the U. S., erroneously, a barroom.

caf'e-te'ri-a (kăf'ĕ-tē'rĭ-ȧ), *n.* A café or restaurant where patrons serve themselves with food kept at a counter, taking the food to small tables. *U. S.*

caf'fe-ine (kăf'ē-ĭn ; -ēn), *n.* A stimulant alkaloid occurring in coffee, tea (*theine*), etc.

cage (kāj), *n.* **1**. A box or inclosure, wholly or partly of openwork, for birds or other animals. **2**. That which confines ; place or state of imprisonment. **3**. Something suggestive of a cage.—*v. t.* [1] To confine in or as in a cage.

cairn (kârn), *n.* A heap of stones for a memorial or mark. — **cairned** (kârnd), *a.*

cais'son (kā'sŏn), *n.* **1**. *Mil.* **a** A chest to hold ammunition. **b** An ammunition wagon for mobile artillery. **2**. A water-tight chamber within which submarine construction or the like is carried on.

cai'tiff (kā'tĭf), *a.* Base ; wicked and mean; despicable. — *n.* A mean, despicable person.

ca-jole' (kȧ-jōl'), *v. t. & i.* [1] To deceive with, or persuade by, fair words or the like ; wheedle.

ca-jol'er-y (-jōl'ēr-ĭ), *n.* Act of cajoling ; deceit.

cake (kāk), *n.* **1**. A sweetened mixture of flour and other ingredients baked in a loaf or mass. **2**. A griddlecake; pancake. **3**. Matter congealed or molded into a solid mass, esp. into a rather flat form.—*v. t. & i.* [1] To form or harden into a cake or mass.

cal'a-bash (kăl'ȧ-băsh), *n.* **1**. The hard-shelled fruit of a certain tropical American tree (calabash tree). **2**. A utensil made from a calabash.

ca-lam'i-tous (kȧ-lăm'ĭ-tŭs), *a.* [4] Producing, or attended with, calamity ; making wretched. — **-tous-ly**, *adv.* [8] — **-tous-ness**, *n.* [8].

ca-lam'i-ty (-tĭ), *n.; pl.* -**TIES** (-tĭz). **1**. A state of deep distress or misfortune ; misery. **2**. Any great misfortune.

cal'a-mus (kăl'ȧ-mŭs), *n.* The sweet flag or its aromatic root.

ca-lash' (kȧ-lăsh'), *n.* A kind of light, low-wheeled carriage with a top or hood.

cal-ca′re-ous (kăl-kā′rē-ŭs), *a.* Of the nature of, or containing, calcite or calcium carbonate.

cal′ci-mine (-sĭ-mĭn ; -mĭn), *n.* A kind of white or colored wash for a ceiling or other plastering. — *v. t.* [1] To wash or cover with calcimine.

cal′ci-na′tion (-nā′shŭn), *n.* Act of calcining.

cal-cine′ (kăl-sīn′; kăl′sĭn), *v. t. & i.* [1] To make or become powdery or friable by heat.

cal′cite (kăl′sīt), *n.* Native calcium carbonate, including chalk, marble, etc.

cal′ci-um (-sĭ-ŭm), *n.* A soft silver-white metal, occurring only in combination.— **calcium carbide,** a crystalline, usually gray, solid, used for the generation of acetylene.— **c. carbonate,** a solid occurring in nature chiefly as calcite (limestone, marble, etc.) ; carbonate of lime. — **c. light.** See LIMELIGHT.

cal′cu-la-ble (-kŭ-lá-b'l),*a.* That may be calculated.

cal′cu-late (-lāt),*v.t.* [1] 1. To determine by mathematical processes ; reckon ; compute ; estimate. 2. To adjust, adapt, arrange, design, or fit for a purpose ; — now only in passive. — *v. i.* To count or rely ; — with *upon* or *on*.

cal′cu-la′tion (-lā′shŭn), *n.* 1. Act, process, or result of calculating ; reckoning ; estimate. 2. An expectation based on circumstances ; forecast.

cal′cu-la-tive (kăl′kŭ-lá-tĭv), *a.* Of or pert. to calculation ; involving, or inclined to, calculation.

cal′cu-la′tor (-lā′tẽr), *n.* One that calculates.

cal′cu-lus (-lŭs), *n. ; pl.* -LI (-lī). A solid concretion formed in the body, as in the bladder.

cal′dron (kôl′drŭn), *n.* A large kettle or boiler.

cal′en-dar (kăl′ĕn-dár), *n.* 1. An orderly arrangement of the divisions of time, as years, months, etc. 2. A table showing the divisions of a given year. 3. *Law.* A list of causes to be tried.

cal′en-der (-dẽr), *n.* A machine for calendering cloth, etc. — *v. t.* To press, as cloth, paper, etc., between rollers so as to glaze or to water it.

calf (kȧf),*n.; pl.* CALVES (kȧvz). The fleshy hinder part of the leg below the knee.

calf, *n. ; pl.* CALVES (kȧvz). 1. The young of the cow or of some other large mammals, as of the elephant. 2. Leather made of calfskin.

calf′skin′ (-skĭn′),*n.* 1. Skin of a calf. 2.= CALF,2.

cal′i-ber (kăl′ĭ-bẽr), *n.* [6] 1. The diameter of a bullet or other projectile or of the bore of a firearm. 2. Capacity of mind.

cal′i-co (-kō), *n. ; pl.* -COES or -COS (-kōz). A kind of cheap figured cotton cloth.

cal′i-per (kăl′ĭ-pẽr), *n.* [*Usually in pl.*] An instrument with two legs, usually bent and joined with a hinge or spring, for measuring the thickness of objects or the distance between surfaces. — *v. t. & i.* To measure with calipers.

ca′liph (kā′lĭf ; kăl′ĭf), *n.* A title of the successors of Mohammed.

Calipers : 1 Outside; 2 Inside.

cal′is-then′ics (kăl′ĭs-thĕn′ĭks), *n.* Science, art, or practice of bodily exercise to promote strength and gracefulness. — **-ic** (-ĭk), *a.*

calk (kôk), *v. t.* To drive oakum, cotton, etc., into the seams of (a boat, etc.) to prevent leaking.

calk, *n.* A metal projection on a horseshoe to prevent slipping. — *v. t.* To furnish with calks.

call (kôl), *v. t.* 1. To utter in a loud or distinct voice. 2. To announce, esp. with authority. 3. To summon ; invite. 4. To invite or command to meet (a meeting or assembly). 5. To name ; address. 6. To regard as ; to estimate as being. 7. To demand payment of.— *v. i.* 1. To speak in a loud tone ; shout. 2. To make a brief visit. — *n.* 1. Act of calling ; shout ; cry. 2. Summons ; invitation. 3. A claim ; appeal. 4. A short visit. 5. The cry of a bird or other animal.

cal′la (kăl′á), *n.,* or **calla lily.** A familiar cultivated plant the flowers of which form a fleshy yellow spike (*spadix*) surrounded by a pure white sheathing leaf (*spathe*).

call′er (kôl′ẽr), *n.* One who calls.

cal-lig′ra-phy (kă-lĭg′rá-fĭ), *n.* 1. Beautiful penmanship. 2. Handwriting in general.

call′ing (kôl′ĭng), *n.* 1. Act of one that calls ; as : **a** A crying aloud. **b** An invitation ; summons. 2. Vocation ; business.

cal-li′o-pe (kă-lī′ô-pē), *n.* A musical instrument comprising a set of steam whistles played by keys.

cal-los′i-ty (kă-lŏs′ĭ-tĭ),*n.; pl.* -TIES-(-tĭz). 1. State or quality of being callous. 2. A hard or thickened place on the skin, or on the bark of a plant.

cal′lous (kăl′ŭs), *a.* [4] 1. Hardened ; having a callosity or callosities. 2. Insensible ; unfeeling. — **cal′lous-ly,** *adv.* [8] — **cal′lous-ness,** *n.* [8].

cal′low (kăl′ō), *a.* [3] Immature ; green.

cal′lus (-ŭs), *n. ; L. pl.* CALLI (-ī). A callosity.

calm (käm), *n.* Freedom from motion or disturbance ; quiet ; serenity. — *v. t.* To make or become calm.— *a.* [3] 1. Not stormy ; still ; quiet ; serene. 2. Undisturbed by passion or emotion ; tranquil. — **calm′ly,** *adv.* [8] — **calm′ness,** *n.* [8].

ca-lor′ic (ká-lŏr′ĭk), *a.* Of or pert. to heat.

cal′u-met (kăl′ū-mĕt), *n.* The ceremonial pipe, or pipe of peace, of the North American Indians.

ca-lum′ni-ous (ká lŭm′nĭ-ŭs), *a.* [4] Containing or implying calumny ; slanderous ; libelous.

cal′um-ny (kăl′ŭm-nĭ), *n. ; pl.* -NIES (-nĭz). False and malicious accusation or report ; slander.

calve (käv), *v. i.* [1] To give birth to a calf.

calves, *n., pl.* of CALF.

ca′lyx (kā′lĭks ; kăl′ĭks), *n.; pl.* E. CALYXES (-ĕz), L. CALYCES (kăl′ĭ-sēz). *Bot.* The external, usually green or foliaceous, part of a flower.

cam (kăm), *n.* A rotating or sliding piece or projection, as on a wheel, for moving, or to receive motion from, a roller, pin, etc., moving against it.

cam′bi-um (-bĭ-ŭm), *n.* Soft tissue from which new wood and bark originate in shrubs and most trees.

cam′bric (kām′brĭk), *n.* 1. A fine, thin, white linen fabric. 2. A similar cotton fabric, often figured.

came (kām), *pret.* of COME.

cam′el (kăm′ĕl), *n.* Either of two large animals used in the desert regions of Africa and Asia to carry burdens and to ride upon.

A Cam.

ca-mel′li-a (ká-mĕl′ĭ-á ; -mĕl′yá),*n.* A greenhouse shrub with red or white roselike flowers.

cam′e-o (kăm′ē-ō),*n.; pl.* -EOS (-ōz). A gem carved in relief, or relief carving ; — opposed to *intaglio.*

cam′er-a (-ẽr-á), *n.* 1. A chamber. 2. An apparatus for taking photographs, so arranged that the scene to be reproduced is focused by a lens on a surface sensitive to light.

cam'o-mile (kăm'ō-mĭl), *n.* A plant of the aster family, having very strong-scented foliage.

|| **ca'mou'flage'** (kȧ'mōō'flȧzh'), *n.* The act or art of concealing, or disguising the nature of, objects, esp. in warfare. — **ca'mou'fleur'** (-flûr'), *n.*

camp (kămp), *n.* **1.** A place where tents, huts, etc., are erected for shelter. **2.** A tent or a collection of tents, huts, etc.; encampment. **3.** The body of persons in camp. — *v. i.* To lodge in a camp ; stay or live temporarily in a camp ; — often with *out.*

cam-paign' (kăm-pān'), *n.* **1.** A series of military operations forming a distinct stage in a war. **2.** Any similar undertaking. — *v. i.* To serve in, or go on, a campaign. — **paign'er**, *n.* [8].

cam'phor (kăm'fēr), *n.* A well-known gumlike, crystalline substance obtained from a tree found chiefly in Japan and Formosa.

cam'pus (kăm'pŭs), *n.* The grounds of a college or school. *U. S.*

can (kăn), *v. t. & i. ; pres. sing., 1st & 3d pers.* CAN, *2d* CANST (kănst), *pl.* CAN; *pret.* COULD (kŏŏd); the participles are now lacking in standard English. As an auxiliary : To be able (to do, accomplish, etc. what is indicated by the verb — expressed or understood — with which *can* is used).

can, *n.* A vessel of sheet metal of various forms; as, a milk *can ;* oil *can ; can* of tomatoes. — *v. t. ;* CANNED (kănd); CAN'NING. To put in a can or cans; preserve by sealing up in a can or cans. Cf. TIN.

Ca-na'di-an (kȧ-nā'dĭ-ăn), *a.* Of or pertaining to Canada or her people. — *n.* A native of Canada.

ca-nal' (kȧ-năl'), *n.* An artificial channel filled with water for navigation, irrigation, etc.

ca-nal'ize (kȧ-năl'ĭz ; kăn'ȧ-lĭz), *v. t.* [1] To provide with canals; to make like a canal.

ca-nard' (kȧ-närd'), *n.* An absurd report set afloat to hoax the public.

ca-na'ry (kȧ-nā'rĭ), *n.; pl.* -RIES (-rĭz). **1.** A canary bird. **2.** A light yellow color.

canary bird. A small finch native of the Canary Islands, the Azores, etc., now a common cage bird.

can'cel (kăn'sĕl), *v. t.* [7] **1.** To cross and deface, as a word ; hence, to annul; destroy; revoke. **2.** *Math.* To strike out (as a common factor from the numerator and denominator of a fraction).

can'cel-la'tion (-sĕ-lā'shŭn), *n.* The act, process, or result of canceling.

can'cer (kăn'sẽr), *n.* **1.** [*cap.*] The fourth sign of the zodiac. **2.** *Med.* A malignant tumor.

can'cer-ous (-ŭs), *a.* Like a cancer; having cancer.

can'de-la'brum (-dĕ-lā'brŭm), *n.; pl.* L.-BRA (-brȧ) (CANDELABRA is often used as a singular, with *pl.* CANDELABRAS), E. -BRUMS (-brŭmz). A large ornamental candlestick, with several branches.

can'did (kăn'dĭd), *a.* [4] **1.** Fair ; just; impartial. **2.** Open; frank. — **-ly**, *adv.* [8] — **-ness**, *n.* [8].

can'di-da-cy (-dĭ-dȧ-sĭ), *n.* Position of a candidate ; state of being a candidate.

can'di-date (-dĭ-dāt), *n.* One who offers himself, or is put forward, as a contestant for an office, etc.

can'di-da-ture (-dȧ-tụr), *n.* Candidacy.

can'died (-dĭd), *p. a.* **1.** Preserved in or with sugar, as fruit. **2.** Converted into sugar or candy.

can'dle (kăn'd'l), *n.* A slender rounded body of tallow, wax, or the like, containing a wick, burned to give light.

can'dle-light' (-līt'), *n.* **1.** Light of a candle or candles ; artificial light. **2.** Nightfall ; twilight.

candle power. Illuminating power, reckoned in terms of the light of a standard candle.

can'dle-stick' (-stĭk'), *n.* A support for a candle.

can'dor (kăn'dẽr), *n.* [5] A disposition to treat subjects fairly ; impartiality ; frankness.

can'dy (-dĭ), *n. ; pl.* -DƖES (-dĭz). A preparation, usually flavored, made of sugar or molasses boiled down and crystallized ; any sweetmeat made of, or coated with, sugar or molasses. — *v. t.* [2] **1.** To conserve or preserve by boiling with sugar. **2.** To form into sugar crystals. — *v. i.* To become coated with, or to form, sugar crystals.

can'dy-tuft' (-tŭft'), *n.* Any of various plants cultivated for their white, pink, or purple flowers.

cane (kān), *n.* **1.** *Bot.* Any hollow or pithy jointed stem, usually slender and more or less flexible, as the stem (called *rattan*) of certain palms, the stem of the sugar cane, of bamboos, etc. **2.** A walking stick. — *v. t.* [1] **1.** To beat with a cane. **2.** To make or furnish with cane or rattan, as chairs.

cane'brake' (kān'brāk'), *n.* A thicket of canes.

ca-nine' (kȧ-nīn'; kā'nīn), *a.* **1.** Of or pertaining to the family consisting of the dogs, wolves, jackals, and foxes ; doglike. **2.** *Anat.* Pertaining to or designating the pointed tooth next to the incisors, or one of like shape. — *n.* **1.** *Anat.* A canine tooth. **2.** A dog. *Colloq. or Humorous.*

can'is-ter (kăn'ĭs-tẽr), *n.* **1.** A small box or case for tea, coffee, etc. **2.** *Mil.* A kind of case shot.

can'ker (kăn'kẽr), *n.* **1.** A corroding or sloughing ulcer. **2.** A cankerworm. **3.** That which corrodes, corrupts, or destroys. — *v. t.* To affect with canker or as a canker ; eat away.

can'ker-ous (-ŭs), *a.* Like a canker.

can'ker-worm' (-wûrm'), *n.* Any of various insect larvæ injurious to plants.

can'na (kăn'ȧ), *n.* Any of several tropical American plants with large leaves and irregular flowers.

canned (kănd), *p. a.* Preserved in cans.

can'nel coal, *or* **can'nel** (kăn'ĕl), *n.* A kind of soft coal that burns with a bright flame.

can'ner-y (-ẽr-ĭ), *n. ; pl.* -NERIES (-ĭz). A place where the business of canning fruit, meat, etc., is carried on.

can'ni-bal (-ĭ-băl), *n.* A human being that eats human flesh. — **can'ni-bal**, *a.*

can'ni-bal-ism (-ĭz'm), *n.* Act or practice of cannibals ; hence, bloodthirsty barbarity.

can'ni-ly, *adv.* In a canny manner.

can'non (-ŭn), *n. ; pl.* -NONS (-ŭnz), collectively -NON. A piece of artillery; a gun discharged from a carriage or mount.

can'non-ade' (-ād'), *n.* Act of discharging cannon to destroy an army, or to batter a town, fort, etc. — *v. t.* [1] To attack with heavy artillery.

can'non-eer' (kăn'ŭn-ēr'), *n.* An artillery gunner.

can'not (kăn'nŏt). Am, is, or are, not able; — the more usual form of *can not.*

can'ny, can'nie (kăn'ĭ), *a.* [3] **1.** Prudent; cautious. *Archaic or Scot.* **2.** Shrewd ; sharp.

ca-noe' (kȧ-nōō'), *n. ; pl.* -NOES (-nōōz'). A light

boat propelled and guided by paddling. — *v. t.* ; **-NOED'** (**-nōōd'**) ; **-NOE'ING**. To paddle, sail in, or voyage in, a canoe. — **ca-noe'ist**, *n.*

Birch-bark Canoe.

can'on (kăn'ŭn), *n.* **1.** A law or rule of church doctrine or discipline. **2.** A general rule, law, or truth. **3.** The collection or list of Biblical books received as genuine and inspired.

can'on, *n.* In the Church of England, one of a body of dignitaries now usually charged with the management of a cathedral church and the (formal) election of the bishop.

ca'ñon (kăn'yŭn), **can'yon** (kăn'yŭn), *n.* A valley with high, steep sides. *Western U. S. & Mexico.*

ca-non'i-cal (ká-nŏn'ĭ-kăl), *a.* Of, or conforming to, a canon or canons. — **ca-non'i-cal-ly**, *adv.* [8].

ca-non'i-cals (-kălz), *n. pl.* The dress prescribed by canon to be worn by an officiating clergyman.

can'on-i-za'tion (kăn'ŭn-ĭ-zā'shŭn), *n.* Act of canonizing ; state of being canonized.

can'on-ize (kăn'ŭn-īz), *v. t.* [1] **1.** To declare (a deceased person) a saint. **2.** To make canonical.

can'o-py (-ŏ-pĭ), *n. ; pl.* **-PIES** (-pĭz). **1.** A covering fixed over a bed, dais, or the like, or carried on poles over an exalted personage or a sacred object, etc., chiefly as a mark of honor. **2.** An overhanging shelter or shade ; a covering. — *v. t.* [2] To cover with or as with a canopy ; as, " yon gray clouds, which *canopy* the skies."

can't (känt ; kănt). Contr. of CANNOT. *Colloq.*

cant (kănt), *n.* An inclination or slope ; tilt. — *v. t.* To give a cant to ; bevel. — *v. i.* To lean ; tilt.

cant, *n.* **1.** The idioms of speech in any sect, class, or occupation. **2.** The affected use of religious or pious language ; hypocrisy. — *v. i.* To use, or speak in, cant.

can'ta-loupe, can'ta-loup (kăn'tá-lōōp ; -lōp), *n.* A variety of muskmelon having a hard furrowed rind and reddish flesh ; loosely, any muskmelon.

can-tan'ker-ous (kăn-tăn'kĕr-ŭs), *a.* [4] Showing ill nature ; quarrelsome. — **-ly**, *adv.* [8].

can-ta'ta (kăn-tä'tá), *n.* A religious poem, a story, or a drama set to music to be sung by a chorus, but not intended to be acted.

can-teen' (kăn-tēn'), *n.* **1.** A sort of store or shop connected with a military post, or camp, for supplying extra provisions, drinks, etc., to the enlisted men. **2.** A small vessel or flask used by soldiers, travelers, etc., for carrying liquids.

can'ter (kăn'tĕr), *n.* A gait resembling the gallop, but moderate and easy. — *v. i. & t.* To move, or cause to go, in or as in a canter.

an'ti-le'ver (kăn'tĭ-lē'vĕr ; -lĕv'ĕr), *n.* Either of two beams or trusses projecting from piers so that when joined they form a span of a bridge.

Part of Cantilever Bridge over the Firth of Forth.

can'to (kăn'tō), *n. ; pl.* **-TOS** (-tōz). One of the chief divisions of a long poem ; a book.

can'ton (kăn'tŏn ; kăn-tŏn'), *n.* **1.** A division, part, or section. **2.** A small territorial division.

Can'ton flan'nel (kăn'tŏn). A stout cotton fabric with long fleecy nap.

can'ton-ment (kăn'tŏn-měnt ; kăn-tōōn'-), *n.* The place, as in a town, assigned to troops for quarters.

can'vas (kăn'vás), *n.* **1.** A strong cloth of hemp, flax, or cotton, used for tents, sails, etc. **2.** Something made of canvas or on canvas, as a painting.

can'vas-back' (-băk'), *n.* A kind of wild duck.

can'vass (-vás), *v. t.* **1.** To examine in detail mentally ; scrutinize ; sift ; discuss ; as, they *canvassed* the matter thoroughly. **2.** To go through (a district), or go to (persons), in order to solicit orders, votes, etc. — *v. i.* To solicit or seek orders, support. votes, etc. ; to solicit ; as, to *canvass* for a book. — *n.* Act of canvassing. — **-er**, *n.* [8].

can'yon (kăn'yŭn). Var. of CAÑON.

caout'chouc (kōō'chŏŏk ; kou'-), *n.* A tenacious, elastic substance got from the milky juice of many tropical plants ; India rubber.

cap (kăp), *n.* **1.** A brimless covering for the head. **2.** Anything like, or suggestive of, a cap. — *v. t. ;* CAPPED (kăpt) ; CAP'PING. **1.** To cover with or as with a cap ; to cover the top or end of ; crown. **2.** To match ; furnish an equal to.

ca'pa-bil'i-ty (kā'pá-bĭl'ĭ-tĭ), *n. ; pl.* **-TIES** (-tĭz). Quality of being capable ; capacity, esp. intellectual.

ca'pa-ble (kā'pá-b'l), *a.* [4] **1.** Able to receive ; having capacity. **2.** Having ability ; efficient ; competent. — **-bly** (-blĭ), *adv.* [8] — **-ness**, *n.* [8].

ca-pa'cious (ká-pā'shŭs), *a.* [4] Able to contain much ; large ; spacious. — **-ness**, *n.* [8].

ca-pac'i-tate (-păs'ĭ-tāt), *v. t.* [1] To render capable ; enable ; qualify.

ca-pac'i-ty (-păs'ĭ-tĭ), *n. ; pl.* **-TIES** (-tĭz). **1.** Power of receiving or containing ; extent of room or space ; content. **2.** Power of receiving and holding ideas, knowledge, etc. ; active mental power. **3.** Capability.

ca-par'i-son (ká-păr'ĭ-sŭn), *n.* **1.** An ornamental covering, or housing, for a horse. **2.** The clothing or dress and ornaments of men or women ; outfit. — *v. t.* To cover with caparisons ; hence, to dress richly.

cape (kāp), *n.* A sleeveless garment, or part of a garment, hanging from the neck over the back, arms, and shoulders.

cape, *n.* A point or extension of land jutting out into a sea, lake, or river.

ca'per (kā'pĕr), *v. i.* To leap or jump about in a sprightly way. — *n.* A frolicsome leap ; skip.

ca'per (kā'pĕr), *n.* A low prickly shrub with greenish flower buds, which are pickled and used in sauces, etc. ; *pl.,* the flower buds themselves.

cap'il-lar'i-ty (kăp'ĭ-lăr'ĭ-tĭ), *n.* **1.** Quality or state of being capillary. **2.** *Physics.* The action, best observed in capillary tubes, by which the surface of a liquid, where in contact with a solid, is elevated or depressed.

cap'il-la-ry (kăp'ĭ-lā-rĭ), *a.* **1.** Resembling a hair ; very slender. **2.** Pertaining to capillary tubes, or to capillarity. — *n. ; pl.* **-RIES** (-rĭz). **1.** A capillary tube or vessel. **2.** *Anat.* A minute, thin-walled vessel ; esp., one of the minute blood vessels connecting arteries and veins.

chair ; go ; sing, iṇk ; then, thin ; nature, verdure ; yet ; zh = z in azure. Numbers refer to §§ in the Special Notes which, with Abbreviations, Signs, etc., precede the Vocabulary.

cap′i-tal (kăp′ĭ-tăl), *a.* **1.** Involving, or punishable with, death. **2.** Of primary importance; vital. **3.** Chief, in a political sense, as being the seat of government. **4.** Of first-rate quality; excellent. **capital letter,** a letter of the kind used at the beginning of a sentence and as the first letter of certain words, of different form and larger size than the small letters.— c. **stock. a** The assets of a corporation at a given time. **b** The amount represented by the face value of the total shares of a corporation. — *n.* **1.** A capital letter. **2.** A capital city. **3.** A stock of accumulated wealth; esp., the amount of property owned at a specified time, or the amount of property used in a business. **4.** Anything that serves to increase one's power or influence.

cap′i-tal, *n.* The head, or uppermost member, of a column, pilaster, etc.

cap′i-tal-ism (-ĭz′m), *n.* State of having capital, or wealth; concentration of capital; power of capital, as when in the control of a few persons.

cap′i-tal-ist, *n.* One who has capital; esp., a person of large property which is or may be employed in business.

cap′i-tal-is′tic (-ĭs′tĭk), *a.* Of or pertaining to, or accomplished by, capitalists.

cap′i-tal-i-za′tion (-ĭ-zā′shŭn), *n.* Act of capitalizing; amount resulting from capitalizing.

cap′i-tal-ize (-īz), *v. t.* [1] **1.** To convert into, or use as, capital. **2.** To write or print with an initial capital, or in capital letters.

cap′i-tal-ly, *adv.* In a capital manner.

cap′i-ta′tion (-tā′shŭn), *n.* A poll tax.

Cap′i-tol (kăp′ĭ-tŏl), *n.* The edifice at Washington

The Capitol at Washington.

in which Congress holds its sessions; also [*often l. c.*], a statehouse. *U. S.*

ca-pit′u-late (ká-pĭt′ū-lāt), *v. i.* [1] To surrender on certain conditions; make terms of surrender.

ca-pit′u-la′tion (-lā′shŭn), *n.* **1.** A summary of the heads of a subject. **2.** Act of capitulating.

ca′pon (kā′pŏn), *n.* A castrated cock, esp. when fattened for the table.

ca-price′ (ká-prēs′), *n.* **1.** An abrupt change in feeling, opinion, or action due to a whim or fancy; a freak; whim. **2.** Capricious disposition or state.

ca-pri′cious (-prĭsh′ŭs), *a.* [4] Governed or characterized by caprice; freakish; changeable.— **ca-pri′cious-ly,** *adv.* [8] — **ness,** *n.* [8].

cap-size′ (kăp-sīz′), *v. t. & i.* [1] To upset or overturn, as a vessel.

cap′stan (kăp′stăn), *n.* A vertical revolving drum

or cylinder much used, esp. on shipboard, **as in** hoisting the anchor.

cap′sule (-sūl), *n.* **1.** *Anat.* A membrane or saclike structure inclosing a part or organ. **2.** *Bot.* Any closed vessel containing spores or seeds. **3.** *Med.* A small cylindrical or spherical envelope for offensive doses of medicine.

cap′tain (-tĭn), *n.* **1.** A chief or leader. **2.** *Mil.* An officer of the army or marine corps. See ARMY. **3.** *Nav.* A naval officer entitled to command a man-of-war. See NAVY. **4.** *Naut.* The commanding officer, or master, of a vessel. — *v. t.* To act as captain of; to lead.

cap′tain-cy (-sĭ), **cap′tain-ship,** *n.* Action, rank, post, or commission, etc., of a captain.

cap′tion (-shŭn), *n.* The heading of a chapter, section, page, or article.

cap′tious (-shŭs), *a.* [4] Apt to catch at faults; caviling; carping. — **-ly,** *adv.* [8] — **-ness,** *n.* [8].

cap′ti-vate (-tĭ-vāt), *v. t.* [1] To acquire ascendancy over by art or attraction; fascinate; charm.

cap′tive (kăp′tĭv), *n.* A prisoner, esp. in war — *a.* Made or held prisoner, esp. in war.

cap-tiv′i-ty (kăp-tĭv′ĭ-tĭ), *n.* State of being a captive; bondage; imprisonment; confinement.

cap′tor (kăp′tŏr), *n.* One who takes or holds captive.

cap′ture (-tŭr), *n.* **1.** Act of seizing by force or stratagem; seizure. **2.** Thing captured; prize; prey.— *v. t.* [1] To take captive; seize by force.

car (kär), *n.* **1.** A vehicle moved on wheels; as: **a** An automobile. **b** A vehicle for use on a railroad. **2.** An elevator cage. **3.** The basket of a balloon.

car′a-mel (kär′á-mĕl), *n.* **1.** Burnt sugar, used for coloring and flavoring. **2.** A kind of confection.

car′at (-ăt), *n.* **1.** A unit of weight for precious stones, as diamonds, being 200 milligrams, or about 3⅕ grains troy. **2.** A 24th part; — used in stating the proportionate fineness of gold.

car′a-van (kär′á-văn, kär′á-văn′), *n.* **1.** A company traveling together, esp. through a desert or dangerous country. **2.** A van; covered vehicle.

car′a-van′sa-ry (-văn′sá-rĭ), *n.; pl.* -RIES (-rĭz). **1.** A kind of rude inn, in the East, where caravans rest. **2.** A large hotel or inn.

car′a-vel (kär′á-vĕl), *n.* *Naut.* Any of several kinds of vessels, usually small sailing vessels.

car′a-way (-wā), *n.* A biennial plant, of the celery family, having aromatic, pungent seeds.

car′bide (kär′bīd, -bĭd), *n.* A compound of carbon and another element; calcium carbide.

car′bine (-bīn), *n.* A short, light rifle or musket.

car′bo-hy′drate (kär′bō-hī′drāt), *n.* *Chem.* Any of a group of compounds, including the sugars, starches, celluloses, etc., composed of carbon, hydrogen, and oxygen.

car-bol′ic (kär-bŏl′ĭk), *a.* Designating an acid derived from coal tar, etc. See PHENOL.

car′bon (kär′bŏn), *n.* **1.** *Chem.* An elementary substance occurring native as the diamond and as graphite, and forming a constituent of coal and carbonates and of all organic compounds. **2.** *Elec.* A piece or stick of carbon used in an arc lamp, or as an element of a voltaic battery.

car′bo-na′ceous (-bō-nā′shŭs), *a.* Pertaining to, containing, or composed of, carbon.

āle, senáte, câre, ăm, *ă*ccount, ärm, ȧsk, sofá; ēve, ĕvent, ĕnd, recĕnt, makẽr; īce, ĭll; ōld, ŏbey, ôrb, ŏdd, sŏft, cŏnnect; ūse, ûnite, ûrn, ŭp, circŭs; fōōd, fŏŏt; out, oil;

car'bon-ate (kär'bŏn-āt), n. Chem. A salt or ester of carbonic acid. — v. t. [1] To convert into a carbonate ; impregnate with carbonic acid.

carbon dioxide. A heavy colorless and odorless gas, which extinguishes flame and is unfit for breathing. See CARBONIC ACID.

car-bon'ic (kär-bŏn'ĭk), a. Chem. Of, pertaining to, or obtained from, carbon.—**carbonic acid,** Chem., an acid, composed of hydrogen, carbon, and oxygen, and existing only in solution. It breaks up readily into water and carbon dioxide (often called carbonic acid or carbonic acid gas).

car'bon-if'er-ous (kär'bŏn-ĭf'ẽr-ŭs), a. Producing or containing carbon or coal.

car'bon-ize (kär'bŏn-īz), v. t. [1] 1. To convert into carbon, as by fire. 2. To coat with carbon. — **car'bon-i-za'tion** (-ĭ-zā'shŭn), n.

car'bo-run'dum (-bŏ-rŭn'dŭm), n. A compound of carbon and silicon, harder than emery, used for grinding, polishing, etc.

car'boy (kär'boi), n. A large globular glass bottle, esp. one inclosed in wickerwork or a box.

car'bun-cle (-bŭn-k'l), n. 1. The garnet cut in convex form without facets. 2. A painful tumor, like a boil, but having no central core.

car'bu-ret (-bŭ-rĕt), v. t. [7] To mix or charge with an easily vaporizing compound of carbon, as air with the vapor of gasoline.

car'bu-ret'or (-rĕt'ẽr), n. [7] An apparatus for carbureting ; esp. one by which air is mingled with the vapor of a light petroleum oil, as in the gasoline engine.

car'cass (-kás), n.; pl. -CASSES (-ĕz). 1. A dead body of a beast. 2. The human body. Now Contemptuous.

card (kärd), n. 1. A playing card. 2. pl. A game or games played with cards ; card playing. 3. A flat, stiff, usually rectangular, piece of paper or thin pasteboard, variously used ; as, a post card.

card, n. 1. An implement for raising a nap on cloth. 2. An instrument for combing cotton, wool, flax, etc. — v. t. To comb with or as with a card.

card'board' (kärd'bôrd'), n. A stiff compact pasteboard of various qualities, for making cards, etc.

car'di-ac (kär'dĭ-ăk), a. Anat. Of, pertaining to, or situated near, the heart.

car'di-nal (-năl), a. 1. Of fundamental importance ; chief ; principal. 2. Of or pertaining to a cardinal or the cardinals. 3. Of a bright red color. — **cardinal number** or **numeral,** a primary number or numeral used in simple counting, etc.; as, one, two, etc.

car'di-nal, n. R. C. Ch. One of the ecclesiastical princes appointed by the Pope, and constituting his council.

car'di-nal-ate (-āt), n., **car'di-nal-ship,** n. Office, rank, or dignity of a cardinal.

care (kâr), n. 1. A burdensome sense of responsibility ; anxiety ; concern. 2. Serious attention of mind ; heed. 3. Charge, oversight. 4. A person or thing that is an object of care, or concern.

care, v. i. [1] 1. To have, feel, or exercise, care (for, about, etc.). 2. a To have an inclination or wish (to). b To have a fondness or affection.

ca-reen' (kȧ-rēn'), v. t. Naut. To cause (a vessel) to lean over on one side. — v. i. To lie or heel over, as a ship under a breeze.

ca-reer' (-rēr'), n. 1. A running ; course, esp. a swift one ; speed ; full speed. 2. General course of action or conduct, esp. when notable. — v. i. To move or run rapidly.

care'ful (kâr'fŏŏl), a. [4] 1. Taking care or heed ; cautious. 2. Marked by care ; done with care. — **care'ful-ly,** adv. [8] — **-ness,** n. [8].

care'less (-lĕs), a. [4] Free from care ; having no care ; thoughtless ; negligent ; inattentive. — **care'less-ly,** adv. [8] — **care'less-ness,** n. [8].

ca-ress' (kȧ-rĕs'), n. An act of endearment ; an embracing or touching with tenderness. — v. t. To touch, stroke, or handle endearingly ; fondle ; pet.

car'et (kăr'ĕt ; kā'rĕt), n. A mark [∧] used to indicate that something (written above or in the margin) belongs in the place marked.

care'worn' (kâr'wôrn'), a. [4] Worn with care.

car'go (kär'gō), n.; pl. -GOES or -GOS (-gōz). The freight of a ship or other vessel ; load ; freight.

car'i-bou (kär'ĭ-bōō), n. (see PLURAL, n., Note). Any of several species of reindeer.

car'i-ca-ture (kär'ĭ-kȧ-tụr), n. 1. A distortion by exaggeration, producing a grotesque or ridiculous effect. 2. A picture, figure, or description showing such exaggeration. — v. t. [1] To make a caricature of. — **car'i-ca-tur'ist** (-tū'rĭst), n.

ca'ri-es (kā'rĭ-ēz), n. Decay of the bones or teeth.

car'il-lon (kär'ĭ-lŏn), n. [F.] Music. 1. A set of bells played by machinery or by finger keys. 2. An instrument imitating a carillon of bells. 3. A composition adapted to a carillon.

ca'ri-ous (kā'rĭ-ŭs), a. Affected with caries.

car'mine (kär'mĭn ; -mĭn), n. The coloring matter of cochineal, having a rich red, crimson, or purplish red color, also, this color. [ter.]

car'nage (-nȧj), n. Great destruction of life ; slaughter.

car'nal (-năl), a. [4] Of or pert. to the body as the seat of the appetites ; animal ; fleshly ; hence, material ; temporal ; — opp. to spiritual. — **-nal-ly,** adv.

car-na'tion (kär-nā'shŭn), n. 1. A light rosy pink, or, often, a deeper crimson color ; a shade of red. 2. Any of numerous cultivated, usually doubleflowered, varieties of the pink.

car-nel'ian (-nēl'yăn), n. A reddish variety of chalcedony, often used for seals.

car'ni-val (kär'nĭ-văl), n. 1. The season just before Lent ; also, the festivity of this season. 2. Any merrymaking, feasting, etc.

Car-niv'o-ra (kär-nĭv'ŏ-rȧ), n. pl. An order of mammals, mostly carnivorous, including the dogs, cats, bears, seals, etc.

car'ni-vore (kär'nĭ-vōr), n. One of the Carnivora.

car-niv'o-rous (kär-nĭv'ŏ-rŭs), a. 1. Eating flesh. 2. Of or pertaining to the Carnivora.

car'ol (kăr'ŭl), n. A song, usually of joy, exultation, or mirth ; a lay. — v. i. [7] To sing, esp. joyfully. — v. t. To praise or celebrate in song.

car'om (-ŭm), n. 1. Billiards. A shot in which the cue ball strikes each of two object balls. 2. Any similar shot or stroke. — v. i. To make a carom.

ca-rous'al (kȧ-rouz'ăl), n. Revelry ; a carouse.

ca-rouse' (-rouz'), n. A drinking match or bout ; carousal. — v. i. [1] To drink deeply ; take part in a carousal. — **ca-rous'er,** n. [8].

carp (kärp), v. i. To talk complainingly ; find fault.

carp, n. A kind of soft-finned fish.

car'pel (kär'pĕl), *n.* *Bot.* In seed plants, a spore-bearing organ considered as part of the pistil.

car'pen-ter (-pĕn-tẽr), *n.* An artisan who frames and builds houses, ships, etc.

car'pen-try (-trĭ), *n.* The work of a carpenter.

carp'er (kär'pẽr), *n.* One who carps; a faultfinder.

car'pet (kär'pĕt), *n.* **1.** A heavy woven or felted fabric; esp., a floor covering made in breadths to be sewed together and nailed to the floor. **2.** A covering suggestive of a carpet; as, a *carpet* of leaves. — *v. t.* To cover with or as with a carpet.

car'pet-bag' (-băg'), *n.* A traveler's portable bag, originally made of carpet.

car'pet-bag'ger (-băg'ẽr), *n.* One traveling with a carpetbag; — a term of contempt, esp. for Northerners who went South after the Civil War to live, esp. to seek profit under the often corrupt Reconstruction governments.

car'pet-ing, *n.* Material for carpets; carpets.

carp'ing (kär'pĭng), *p. a.* Faultfinding; captious.

car'riage (kär'rĭj), *n.* **1.** Act of carrying; conveyance, esp. of goods. **2.** The price or expense of carrying. **3.** Manner of carrying one's body or self; bearing. **4.** That which carries or conveys, as, a wheeled vehicle for persons, esp. one designed for elegance and comfort.

car'ried (kär'ĭd), *pret. & p. p.* of CARRY.

car'ri-er (-ĭ-ẽr), *n.* One that carries, as: **a** A bearer; messenger. **b** One who carries goods for hire. **c** A carrying mechanism.

car'ri-on (-ŭn), *n.* The dead and putrefying body or flesh of an animal. — *a.* Of or pertaining to carrion; feeding on carrion.

car'rot (-ŭt), *n.* A biennial plant related to the celery; also, its edible yellow or orange-red, usually tapering, root. — **car'rot-y** (-ĭ), *a.*

car'ry (kär'ĭ), *v. t.* [2] **1.** To convey or transport; to bear; transfer; take. **2.** To conduct; lead; guide; impel; move; extend. **3.** To get or obtain, as by effort or force; capture. **4.** To succeed in; win; secure the adoption or passage of, as a motion. **5.** To bear (one's self); behave. **6.** To sustain the weight of; support. **7.** To bear the charges or burden of having. — *v. i.* **1.** To act as a bearer. **2.** To have or exert propulsive power. — *n.; pl.* -RIES (-ĭz). **1.** Range, as of a gun or projectile. **2.** A portage between navigable waters. *U. S. & Canada.*

car'ry-all' (-ôl'), *n.* A kind of light, covered carriage for four or more persons. *U. S.*

cart (kärt), *n.* **1.** A two-wheeled vehicle for transporting bulky or heavy articles. **2.** A light business wagon. — *v. t.* To carry in a cart.

cart'age (kär'tåj), *n.* **1.** Act of carrying in a cart. **2.** The price paid for carting.

‖ carte' blanche' (kärt' blänsh'). [F.] Unconditional terms or power.

car'tel (kär'tĕl; kär-tĕl'), *n.* **1.** A letter of defiance or challenge; as to a duel. **2.** A written agreement between opposing nations.

cart'er (kär'tẽr), *n.* A teamster.

car'ti-lage (kär'tĭ-låj), *n.* *Anat.* **1.** A firm, elastic and flexible, whitish tissue composing most of the skeleton of very young vertebrate animals, and mostly converted into bone later; gristle. **2.** A part or structure composed of cartilage.

car'ti-lag'i-nous (-lăj'ĭ-nŭs), *a.* [4] Composed of, containing, or pertaining to, cartilage.

car'ton (kär'tŏn), *n.* A pasteboard box.

car-toon' (kär-tōōn'), *n.* A pictorial caricature. — *v. t.* To make a cartoon of. — **car-toon'ist,** *n.*

car'tridge (kär'trĭj), *n.* **1.** A case, shell, or bag, as of metal or pasteboard, holding an explosive charge, esp. for a firearm. In small arms and some cannon it contains also the projectile. **2.** A roll of protected films for use in a camera.

carve (kärv), *v. t.* [1] **1.** To cut; esp., to cut artistically; sculpture. **2.** To cut into pieces or slices, as meat at table. — *v. i.* To cut up meat, as at table.

carv'er (kär'vẽr), *n.* One that carves.

carv'ing, *n.* **1.** Act or art of one who carves. **2.** Carved work; decorative sculpture.

cas-cade' (kăs-kād'), *n.* A fall of water over a precipice; a waterfall less than a cataract.

case (kās), *n.* **1.** An instance of the kind; a special state of affairs. **2.** Condition; actual state of things or affairs. **3.** *Med. & Surg.* A patient under treatment; an instance of sickness or injury. **4.** *Law.* A suit or action; a cause. **5.** *Gram.* One of the forms, or of the inflectional changes in form, of a noun, pronoun, or adjective which indicate its sense relation to other words.

case, *n.* **1.** A box, sheath, or covering. **2.** A box and its contents; quantity in a box; hence, set. **3.** An inclosing frame or framework; a casing. — *v. t.* [1] To inclose or put in a case; incase.

case'hard'en (kās'här'd'n), *v. t.* To harden the surface or outside of, as iron or steel.

case knife. A knife such as is kept in a sheath or case; hence, a table knife.

case'mate (kās'māt), *n.* **1.** A well-protected chamber, as for cannon. **2.** In ships of war, an armored inclosure where guns are mounted.

case'ment (-mĕnt), *n.* A window sash opening on hinges; a window with such a sash or sashes.

ca'se-ous (kā'sẽ-ŭs), *a.* Of or like cheese.

case shot. A collection of small projectiles contained in a case.

cash (kăsh), *n.* **1.** Money, esp. ready money. **2.** Money or its equivalent paid promptly after purchasing. — *v. t.* To pay or receive cash for.

cash'book' (kăsh'bōōk'), *n.* *Bookkeeping.* A book in which is kept a record of all money either received or paid out.

cash-ier' (kă-shēr'), *n.* **1.** One who has charge of money. **2.** One who has charge of payments and receipts (moneys, checks, notes, etc.), as in a bank.

cash-ier', *v. t.* To discharge; to dismiss with ignominy from military service or from a place of trust.

cash'mere (kăsh'mēr; kăsh'mēr'), *n.* A rich stuff for shawls, scarfs, etc., originally made from soft wool of goats; also, a dress fabric imitating it.

cas'ing (kās'ĭng), *n.* Something that incases, or material for incasing; a case; as, a window *casing*.

ca-si'no (kå-sē'nō), *n.; pl.* -NOS (-nōz). A building or room for social meetings, amusements, etc.

cask (kásk), *n.* A barrel-shaped vessel made of staves, hoops, etc., and varying in size from a keg to a hogshead.

cas'ket (kås'kĕt), *n.* **1.** A small chest or box, as for jewels. **2.** A coffin, esp. an expensive one. *U. S.*

casque (kásk), *n.* *Armor.* A helmet.

cas'se-role (kăs'ĕ-rōl; kăs'ĕ-rōl'), n. **1.** A saucepan. **2.** *Cookery.* A mold of boiled rice, mashed potato, or paste, baked, and filled with vegetables or meat. **3.** A covered earthenware baking dish, often with an ornamental metal container.

cas'si-mere (kăs'ĭ-mēr), n. A thin twilled woolen cloth, used for men's garments.

cas-si'no (kă-sē'nō), n. A certain game at cards.

cas'sock (kăs'ŭk), n. A long close-fitting garment worn by certain clergy under their surplices.

cas'so-wa-ry (-ō-wă-rĭ), n.; pl. -WARIES (-rĭz). Any of several large birds related to the emu.

cast (kȧst), v. t.; pret. & p. p. CAST; p. pr. & vb. n. CAST'ING. **1.** To throw; fling; hurl; as, to *cast* dice ; to *cast* stones. **2.** To project or impel as if by throwing ; as, to *cast* a shadow. **3.** To deposit or place, esp. in a decisive or violent manner ; as, to *cast* a man into prison. **4.** To direct or bestow; as, to *cast* a glance around. **5.** To throw off, out, or away; shed ; as, the horse *cast* a shoe; a snake *casts* its skin. **6.** To compute; reckon; calculate; as, to *cast* accounts. **7.** To allot (as parts of a play) ; allot or assign the parts of (a play) ; also, to assign (an actor for a part). **8.** To form (liquid material) by pouring it into a mold and letting it harden ; to found ; as, to *cast* iron. — v. i. **1.** To add figures. **2.** To receive form or shape in a mold. —**to cast about.** a *Naut.* To change the course; tack. **b** To consider ; lay plans ; as, he *cast about* in his mind for a reply. — n. **1.** Act or manner of casting; a throw. **2.** Distance to which a thing can be thrown. **3.** A turn or twist; as, a *cast* of the eye, that is, a slight squint. **4.** Assignment of parts in a play to the actors; the actors themselves. **5.** An impression or mold. **6.** Thing formed in a mold or form. **7.** A tendency to any color; a tinge; hue. **8.** Form; appearance; style; as, a peculiar *cast* of countenance.

cas'ta-net (kăs'tȧ-nĕt ; kăs/tȧ-nĕt'), n. An instrument consisting of two small ivory or wooden shells clicked together in accompaniment to dances and music ; — usually in pl.

cast'a-way' (kȧst'ȧ-wā'), a. Thrown away; cast adrift. — n. A shipwrecked person ; outcast.

caste (kȧst), n. **1.** One of the hereditary classes into which the native society of India is divided. **2. a** Any similar division or class of society. **b** The position conferred by the caste system.

cast'er (kȧs'tẽr), n. **1.** One that casts. **2.** A vial for condiments at the table; a cruet ; also, a stand to hold a set of cruets. **3.** A small wheel on a swivel, on which furniture is supported.

cas'ti-gate (kăs'tĭ-gāt), v. t. [1] To punish; chastise, as with words or blows. — **-ga'tor,** n. [8].

cas'ti-ga'tion (-gā'shŭn), n. Punishment, esp. severe punishment or reproof.

cast'ing, n. **1.** Act of one that casts. **2.** That which is cast in a mold.

cast iron. See IRON.

cast'-i'ron, a. Made of cast iron ; hard ; rigid.

cas'tle (kȧs/'l), n. **1.** A large fortified building or set of buildings; fortress ; citadel; stronghold, esp. of a prince or nobleman. **2.** Anything resembling, or likened to, a castle. **3.** *Chess.* = ROOK.

cas'tor (kȧs'tẽr), n. A hat, esp. of beaver fur ; a beaver.

cas'tor, n. = CASTER, 2 & 3.

cas'tor-oil' plant. A tropical plant yielding castor beans, from which a cathartic oil, **castor oil,** is expressed or extracted.

cas'trate (kăs'trāt), v. t. [1] To emasculate; geld.

cas-tra'tion (kăs-trā'shŭn), n. Act of castrating.

cas'u-al (kăzh'ū-ăl ; kăz'-), a. [4] **1.** Happening without design and unexpectedly ; coming by chance; as, a *casual* meeting. **2.** Coming without regularity; incidental; as, *casual* expenses. **3.** Having the air of a chance occurrence ; often, with assumed indifference. — **cas'u-al-ly,** adv. [8].

cas'u-al-ty (-tĭ), n.; pl. -TIES (-tĭz). **1.** Chance; accident ; contingency. **2.** An unfortunate occurrence ; a mishap. **3.** pl. *Mil. & Nav.* Losses caused by death, wounds, discharge, or desertion.

cas'u-ist (kăzh'ū-ĭst ; kăz'-), n. One skilled in, or given to, casuistry.

cas'u-is'tic (-ĭs'tĭk), **-is'ti-cal** (-tĭ-kăl), a. [4] Of or pert. to casuists or casuistry.—**-cal-ly,** adv. [8].

cas'u-ist-ry (-ĭs-trĭ), n. ; pl. CASUISTRIES (-trĭz). **1.** Science or doctrine dealing with questions of right or wrong in conduct. **2.** Sophistical, equivocal, or false reasoning as to duties and morals.

cat (kăt), n. A well-known domestic animal which is the type of the family including the lion, tiger, leopard, puma, various species of tiger cats, wild cats, lynxes, etc.; also, any member of the family.

cat'a-clysm (kăt'ȧ-klĭz'm), n. **1.** A flood of water; deluge. **2.** Any violent change involving sudden and great alterations of the earth's surface; hence, figuratively, an upheaval, esp. social or political.

cat'a-comb (kăt'ȧ-kōm), n. A subterranean place of burial, esp. one consisting of passages with side recesses for tombs ; — commonly in pl.

cat'a-lep'sy (-lĕp'sĭ), n. *Med.* A sudden loss of consciousness with stiffening of the muscles.

cat'a-lep'tic (-lĕp'tĭk), a. Pertaining to catalepsy ; affected with catalepsy.

cat'a-log, -loger. Vars. of CATALOGUE, -LOGUER.

cat'a-logue (-lŏg), n. A list; esp., a list of names, titles, or articles arranged, usually, alphabetically. — v. t. [1] To make a catalogue of; insert in a catalogue. — **cat'a-logu'er** (-lŏg'ẽr), n. [8].

ca-tal'pa (kȧ-tăl'pȧ), n. Any of several broadleaved trees bearing long pods.

cat'a-ma-ran' (kăt'ȧ-mȧ-răn'), n. **1.** A kind of raft or float made of logs or pieces of wood lashed together, and moved by paddles or sails. **2.** Any vessel with twin hulls side by side.

cat'a-mount (kăt'ȧ-mount), n. Any of various wild animals of the cat family ; in America, usually, the cougar or a lynx.

cat'a-pult (-pŭlt), n. An engine used in ancient time to throw stones, arrows, spears, etc. — v. t. & i. To throw from or as from a catapult.

cat'a-ract (-răkt), n. **1.** A waterfall. **2.** A deluge; flood. **3.** *Med.* A disease of the eye, characterized by opacity of the lens.

ca-tarrh' (kȧ-tär'), n. *Med.* An inflammatory affection of a mucous membrane, esp. of the nose.

ca-tarrh'al (-ăl), a. Pertaining to catarrh.

ca-tas'tro-phe (kȧ-tăs'trō-fẽ), n. **1.** A final event or conclusion, generally unfortunate ; hence, any great calamity or disaster, esp. if sudden. **2.** The final event in a romance, drama, etc.; dénouement.

---

chair; go; sing, iŋk; then, thin; nature, verdure; yet; zh = z in azure. Numbers refer to §§ in the Special Notes which, with Abbreviations, Signs, etc , precede the Vocabulary.

cat′bird′ (kăt′bûrd′), *n.* An American song bird allied to the mocking bird.

cat′boat′ (-bōt′), *n.* A sailboat rigged with a single mast set far forward and a single large sail with gaff and boom.

Catbird.
(⅛)

catch (kăch), *v. t.; pret. & p. p.* CAUGHT (kôt); *p. pr. & vb. n.* CATCH′ING. **1.** To capture or seize, as after pursuit; overtake; take; as, to *catch* a thief; to *catch* a fish. **2.** Hence: **a** To insnare; entangle; as, "to *catch* him in his words" (*Mark* xii. 13). **b** To come on by surprise; detect; as, to *catch* one stealing. **3.** To take or contract by or as if by contagion, infection, or exposure, as a disease. **4.** To lay hold on, as if capturing; as, the fire *caught* the woodwork; to *catch* a ball. **5.** To arrest the attention, fancy, etc., of; please; charm; as, the picture *caught* his eye. **6.** To apprehend mentally; as, to *catch* one's meaning. — *v. i.* **1.** To make captures. **2.** To take hold, as fire; spread. **3.** To take and retain hold, as a hook. **4.** To be impeded by entanglement or obstruction; as, the door *catches.* — *n.* **1.** Act or fact of catching. **2.** That which catches, as an insnaring question, a device for fastening, or one for checking motion, etc. **3.** That which is, or is to be, caught or taken; as, a good *catch* of fish. — **catch′er,** *n.* [8].

catch′all′ (kăch′ôl′), *n.* A general receptacle.

catch′ing, *p. a.* [4] **1.** That catches; of diseases, infectious; contagious. **2.** Captivating; taking.

catch′pen-ny (-pĕn-ĭ), *a.* Made for getting small sums of money, as from the unwary; as, a *catchpenny* book or show. — *n.* A catchpenny thing.

catch′up (kăch′ŭp), *n.* A table sauce made of tomatoes, mushrooms, or walnuts.

catch′y (-ĭ), *a.* [3] Catching; taking; fitful.

cat′e-chism (kăt′ē-kĭz′m), *n.* **1.** Instruction by question and answer. **2.** A book containing a summary of principles, esp. religious, in the form of questions and answers. **3.** A set of questions put to candidates, etc. — **cat′e-chist** (-kĭst), *n.*

cat′e-chize (-kīz), *v. t.* [1] **1.** To instruct by catechism, esp. in religion. **2.** To question in detail.

cat′e-gor′i-cal (-gŏr′ĭ-kăl), *a.* [4] **1.** Of, pertaining to, or in the form of, a category. **2.** Without condition or exception; positive; unconditional; as, a *categorical* reply. — **-i-cal-ly,** *adv.* [8].

cat′e-go-ry (kăt′ē-gō-rĭ), *n.; pl.* -RIES (-rĭz). **1.** A class to which a certain statement or assertion applies; a class or division in any general plan of classification.

ca′ter (kā′tẽr), *v. i.* **1.** To provide food; to buy, procure, or prepare provisions. **2.** To supply what is needed or desired; — followed by *for* or *to.*

ca′ter-er, *n.* One who caters; esp., one who furnishes the provisions and service at banquets, etc.

cat′er-pil′lar (kăt′ẽr-pĭl′ẽr), *n.* The wormlike larva of a butterfly or moth, or any similar larva.

cat′er-waul (-wôl), *v. i.* Of cats, to make a kind of harsh cry; hence, to cry as cats.

cat′fish′ (kăt′fĭsh′), *n.* (see PLURAL, *n.*, *Note*). Any of various fishes.

cat′gut′ (-gŭt′), *n.* A tough cord variously used, made from the intestines of animals, esp. of sheep.

ca-thar′tic (kå-thär′tĭk), *a.* Cleansing the bowels; purgative. — *a.* A cathartic medicine; purgative.

ca-the′dral (kå-thē′drål), *n.* Designating, or pert. to, the bishop's church, which is the head church of a diocese. — *n.* The head church of a diocese; improperly, any large church.

cath′ode (kăth′ōd), *n. Elec.* The negative terminal of an electric source; — opposed to *anode.*

cathode rays. Rays projected from the cathode of a vacuum tube in which an electric discharge takes place. By impinging on solids they generate Röntgen rays.

cath′o-lic (kăth′ō-lĭk), *a.* [4] **1.** Universal or general in human interests; affecting mankind as a whole. **2.** Not narrow-minded or bigoted; liberal. **3.** Of or pert. to the church universal (the whole body of Christians). Hence: [*cap.*] Designating, or pertaining to, the Roman Catholic Church, or Roman Catholics. — *n.* [*cap.*] A member of the Catholic church.

ca-thol′i-cism (kå-thŏl′ĭ-sĭz′m), *n.* Catholic faith, practice, or system.

cath′o-lic′i-ty (kăth′ō-lĭs′ĭ-tĭ), *n.* **1.** Quality of being catholic; liberality. **2.** Catholicism.

cat′i-on (kăt′ĭ-ŏn), *n.* **a** The product evolved at the cathode in electrolysis. **b** A positive ion.

cat′kin (-kĭn), *n.* An ament.

cat′like′ (-līk′), *a.* Like a cat; stealthy; noiseless.

cat′nip (-nĭp), *n.* A plant of the mint family for which cats have a peculiar fondness.

cat′-o′-nine′-tails (kăt′ō-nīn′tālz′), *n.* An implement used in flogging.

cat′s′-paw′, *n.* A dupe; tool.

cat′sup (kăt′sŭp). Var. of CATCHUP.

cat′-tail′, *n.* A tall marsh plant with long, flat leaves, and flowers in a close cylindrical spike.

cat′tle (kăt′'l), *n.* Like stock kept as property or for use; esp., bovine animals.

Cau-ca′sian (kô-kā′shăn, -kăsh′ăn), *a.* Designating, or pertaining to, the white race. — *n.* A member of the white race.

cau′cus (kô′kŭs), *n.* A meeting of the members or leaders of a party or faction to decide on policies or candidates to be supported. *U. S.*

cau′dal (-dăl), *a.* Like, or pertaining to, a tail.

caught (kôt), *pret. & p. p.* of CATCH.

caul (kôl), *n.* **1.** The great omentum. **2.** A membrane sometimes covering the head of a child at birth.

caul′dron. Var. of CALDRON.

cau′li-flow′er (kô-lĭ-flou′ẽr), *n.* A variety of cabbage, in which the head consists of the thick flower cluster; also, the head.

caulk, caulk′er, etc. Vars. of CALK, CALKER, etc.

caus′al (kôz′ăl), *a.* Relating to, implying, containing, or of the nature of, a cause or causes.

cau-sal′i-ty (kô-zăl′ĭ-tĭ), *n.* **1.** Causal quality or agency. **2.** The relation of cause and effect; the operation of cause as a principle or fact of nature.

cau-sa′tion (-zā′shŭn), *n.* **1.** Act of causing; also, act or agency producing an effect. **2.** Causality.

caus′a-tive (kôz′å-tĭv), *a.* Acting as a cause.

āle, senāte, câre, ăm, năccount, ärm, àsk, sofá; ēve, ēvent, ĕnd, recĕnt, makēr; īce, ĭll; ōld, ōbey, ôrb, ŏdd, sôft, cönnect; ūse, ūnite, ûrn, йp, circûs; fōŏd, fŏŏt; out, oil;

cause (kôz), *n.* **1.** That which produces an effect or result. **2.** The person or thing that brings about or does something; reason; motive. **3.** *Law.* A ground of action; also, a suit or action in court; case. **4.** Any subject of discussion or debate. **5.** The side of a question advocated and upheld by a person or party. — *v. t.* [1] To be the cause of ; effect ; bring about. — **cause′less**, *a.* [8].

cause′way (kôz′wā), *n.* **1.** A raised way across wet ground. **2.** A highway or paved way. *Hist.*

caus′tic (kôs′tĭk), *a.* [4] **1.** Capable of destroying, or eating away, by chemical action; corrosive. **2.** Severe; stinging; cutting; as, a *caustic* remark. — *n.* A caustic substance. — **-ti-cal-ly**, *adv.* [8].

cau′ter-i-za′tion (kô′tẽr-ĭ-zā′shŭn), *n.* Act of cauterizing; result of cauterizing.

cau′ter-ize (kô′tẽr-īz), *v. t.* [1] To burn or sear with or as with a cautery or caustic.

cau′ter-y (-ĭ), *n. ; pl.* -TERIES (-ĭz). *Med.* A searing, as with a hot iron or a caustic substance; the instrument or substance used in cauterizing.

cau′tion (-shŭn), *n.* **1.** A warning against evil ; a word, act, or the like, that conveys a warning. **2.** Prudence in regard to danger ; cautiousness ; heedfulness. — *v. t.* To notify of danger ; warn.

cau′tion-a-ry (-ã-rĭ), *a.* Of, pertaining to, or of the nature of, a caution ; cautioning ; warning.

cau′tious (kô′shŭs), *a.* [4] Attentive to examine probable consequences of acts so as to avoid danger; wary. — **-ly**, *adv.* [8] — **-ness**, *n.* [8].

cav′al-cade′ (kăv′ăl-kād′), *n.* A procession of persons on horseback, esp. by way of parade.

cav′a-lier′ (-á-lēr′), *n.* **1.** A horseman; esp., a knight. **2.** A gay, sprightly military man; hence, a gallant. **3.** [*cap.*] One of the court party in England in the time of King Charles I. (reigned 1625–49). — *a.* **1.** Gay; easy; frank. **2.** Disdainful ; haughty; supercilious. **3.** [*cap.*] Of or relating to the Cavaliers. — **-lier′ly**, *adv.* [8].

cav′al-ry (kăv′ăl-rĭ), *n. ; pl.* -RIES (-rĭz). *Mil.* The part of a military force that serves on horseback. — **cav′al-ry-man**, *n.*

cave (kāv), *n.* A hollow place in the earth ; cavern ; den. — *v. t.* [1] To hollow out. *Obs.*, exc. in : **to cave in**, to cause to cave or fall in ; hence, also, to fall in or down.

cav′ern (kăv′ẽrn), *n.* An underground cavity ; a cave, esp. a large cave.

cav′ern-ous (-ẽr-nŭs), *a.* Full of caverns ; of the nature of, or like, a cavern ; hollow. — **-ly**, *adv.*

cav′i-ar′ (kăv′ĭ-är′; kä′vyär′), *n.* The salted roe of the sturgeon or other large fish, used as a relish.

cav′il (kăv′ĭl), *v. i.* [7] To find fault or make objection without good reason. — *n.* A frivolous objection ; a quibble. — **cav′il-er**, *n.* [7, 8].

cav′i-ty (-ĭ-tĭ), *n.; pl.* -TIES (-tĭz). A hollow place.

ca-vort′ (ká-vôrt′), *v. i.* To prance; caper; — said of a horse or its rider. *Colloq., U. S.*

caw (kô), *v. i.* Of crows, rooks, ravens, etc., to utter their call or cry. — *n.* The cry made in cawing.

cay′man (kā′măn), *n.; pl.* -MANS (-mănz). A kind of alligator of tropical America.

ca-yuse′ (kī-ūs′), *n.* An Indian pony. *West. U. S.*

cease (sēs), *v. i.* [1] To come to an end ; stop. — *v. t.* To leave off; discontinue.

cease′less, *a.* Without stop; incessant.

ce′dar (sē′dẽr), *n.* Any of various trees, chiefly of the pine family, having fragrant, durable wood.

cede (sēd), *v. t.* [1] To yield; surrender; give up.

ce-dil′la (sē-dĭl′á), *n.* A mark under the letter *c* [thus, *ç*], to show that it is to be sounded like *s*.

ceil (sēl), *v. t.* To furnish with a ceiling.

ceil′ing, *n.* **1.** Act of one who ceils a room, etc. **2.** The lining of a room, esp. that overhead.

cel′an-dine (sĕl′ăn-dīn), *n.* An herb of the poppy family, with yellow flowers.

cel′e-brant (sĕl′ē-brănt), *n.* One who celebrates a religious rite; the officiating priest at the Mass.

cel′e-brate (-brāt), *v. t.* [1] **1.** To perform publicly and with appropriate rites ; solemnize ; as, to *celebrate* Mass. **2.** To observe with solemn rites, ceremonies of joy and respect, or refraining from business ; to keep, as a holiday. **3.** To extol, or publish the fame of ; make known publicly.

cel′e-brat′ed (-brāt′ĕd),*p.a.* [4] Distinguished; renowned; illustrious.

cel′e-bra′tion (-brā′shŭn), *n.* Act or process of celebrating, or state of being celebrated.

ce-leb′ri-ty (sē-lĕb′rĭ-tĭ),*n.; pl.* -TIES (-tĭz). **1.** Celebrated state; renown. **2.** A celebrated person.

ce-ler′i-ty (-lĕr′ĭ-tĭ),*n.* Rapidity of motion; speed.

cel′er-y (sĕl′ẽr-ĭ), *n.* A widely cultivated plant, the blanched leaf-stalks of which are eaten.

ce-les′tial (sē-lĕs′chăl),*a.* **1.** Of or pertaining to the sky or visible heavens. **2.** Heavenly; divine. **3.** Of or pertaining to the Chinese, or Celestial, Empire, or, *Humorously*, the Chinese people ; Chinese. — *n.* [*cap.*] A native of China; a Chinese. *Colloq.*

cel′i-ba-cy (sĕl′ĭ-bá-sĭ ; sē-lĭb′á-), *n.* The state of being or living unmarried ; single life.

cel′i-bate (sĕl′ĭ-bāt), *n.* An unmarried person — *a.* Unmarried ; single.

cell (sĕl), *n.* **1.** A very small close apartment, as in a prison. **2.** A small hollow receptacle, as in a honeycomb. **3.** *Elec.* A receptacle containing a liquid, in which two plates or pieces of different substances, as carbon and zinc, are immersed to generate electricity, etc. **4.** *Biol.* The structural unit of which animals and plants are built up.

cel′lar (sĕl′ẽr), *n.* A room or set of rooms below the surface of the ground, generally under a building, used esp. for keeping provisions and other stores.

cel′lar-age (-ăj), *n.* Cellar space, or a charge for it.

cel′lo (chĕl′ō), *n. ; pl.* -LOS (-ōz). A violoncello — **cel′list** (-ĭst), *n.* Also **′cel′lo, ′cel′list.**

cel′lu-lar (sĕl′ū-lär), *a.* Consisting of, characterized by, or pertaining to, a cell or cells.

cel′lu-loid (-loid), *n.* A substance, essentially soluble guncotton and camphor, resembling ivory in texture and color, but often variously colored.

cel′lu-lose (-lōs), *n.* The chief component of the solid part of plants and of linen, paper, etc.

ce-ment′ (sē-mĕnt′; sĕm′ĕnt), *n.* **1.** A substance used in a soft state to join bricks in building, cover floors, etc., which afterwards becomes hard like stone. **2.** Any substance used to make bodies adhere to each other, as glue, paste, etc. — (sē-mĕnt′), *v. t.* To unite by, or overlay with, cement.

cen′en-ta′tion (sĕm′ĕn-tā′shŭn; sē′mĕn-), *n.* Act or process of cementing ; state of being cemented.

cem′e-ter-y (sĕm′ē-tẽr-ĭ), *n. ; pl.* -TERIES (-ĭz). A place set apart for burial of the dead ; graveyard.

cen′ser (sĕn′sẽr), *n.* A vessel to burn incense in.

cen′sor (-sŏr ; -sẽr), *n.* **1.** An official who examines books, plays, or the like, in order to forbid publication or presentation if objectionable. **2.** A faultfinder ; critic.

cen-so′ri-ous (sĕn-sō′rĭ-ŭs), *a.* [4] **1.** Given to censure ; apt to condemn. **2.** Implying or expressing censure. — **-ly**,*adv.* [8] — **-ness**, *n.* [8].

cen′sor-ship (sĕn′sŏr-shĭp ; sĕn′sẽr-), *n.* The office or function of a censor.

cen′sur-a-ble (-shŭr-a̍-b′l), *a.* Deserving of, or subject to, censure ; blamable.

cen′sure (-shŭr), *n.* Act of finding fault with, or condemning as wrong ; hostile criticism ; blame ; condemnation. — *v. t. & i.* [1] To find fault with or condemn as wrong ; criticize adversely ; blame.

cen′sus (-sŭs), *n.* An official enumeration of the population of a country, city, or other place.

cent (sĕnt), *n.* **1.** A hundred ; — used only in *per cent* (see PER CENT). **2.** The 100th part of the unit in various monetary systems,or a coin of this value.

cen′taur (sĕn′tôr), *n.* *Gr. Myth.* One of a race, half man and half horse.

cen′te-na′ri-an (sĕn′tē-nā′rĭ-ăn), *a.* Of or pert. to a hundred years. — *n.* A person 100 years old.

cen′te-na-ry (sĕn′tē-nā-rĭ), *a.* Of or pertaining to a period of 100 years ; centennial. — *n.; pl.* -RIES (-rĭz). **1.** A century. **2.** A centennial.

cen-ten′ni-al (sĕn-tĕn′ĭ-ăl), *a.* **1.** Of, pertaining to, or completing, a space of 100 years. **2.** Lasting, or aged, 100 years. — *n.* A hundredth anniversary or its celebration ; a centenary.

cen′ter (sĕn′tẽr), *n.* [6] **1.** Middle point of a circle or sphere. **2.** Middle or central point or part of anything. **3.** A point about which influences, etc., concentrate, or from which they proceed ; as, a religious *center*. — *v. t.* **1.** To place or fix in or at the center. **2.** To collect to a point ; concentrate. — *v. i.* To be centered.

cen′ter-board (-bōrd′), *n.* [6] *Naut.* A device, usually a broad board or slab, that can be lowered to increase the area of lateral resistance.

cen′ti-grade (sĕn′tĭ-grād), *a.* See THERMOMETER.

cen′ti-gram (-grăm), *n.* A weight equal to one 100th of a gram.

cen′ti-li′ter (-lē′tẽr), *n.* [6] A measure of volume equal to one 100th of a liter.

cen′time′ (sän′tēm′ ; sän′tēm),*n.* The hundredth part of a franc.

cen′ti-me′ter (sĕn′tĭ-mē′tẽr), *n.* [6] A measure of length equal to one 100th of a meter.

cen′ti-pede (-pēd), *n.* Any of numerous small, many-legged animals,with jointed flattened worm-like body.

cen′tral (-trăl), *a.* [4] Relating to, situated in or near, or containing, the center. — **-ly**, *adv.* [8].

cen′tral-i-za′tion (-ĭ-zā′shŭn), *n.* Act or process of centralizing, or state of being centralized.

cen′tral-ize (-īz), *v. t.* [1] To bring to a central point ; bring under one system or control.

cen′tre (sĕn′tẽr). Var. of CENTER.

cen-trif′u-gal (sĕn-trĭf′ŭ-găl),*a.* Proceeding from the center ; designating a force (centrifugal force) directed outward when a body is made to move in a curved path.

cen-trip′e-tal (-trĭp′ē-tăl), *a.* Proceeding or di-

rected toward the center ; designating a force (centripetal force) directed toward the center.

cen′tu-ple (sĕn′tṳ-p′l), *a.* Hundredfold.

cen-tu′ri-on (sĕn-tū′rĭ-ŭn), *n.* *Roman Hist.* A captain in the army.

cen′tu-ry (sĕn′tṳ-rĭ), *n.; pl.* -RIES (-rĭz). **1.** Any body of 100 men, or of 100 things. **2.** A period of 100 years.

century plant. A species of agave which does not flower until at least eight years old.

ceph′a-lo-pod (sĕf′a̍-lō-pŏd), *n.* Any of the highest class of mollusks, containing the squids, cuttle-fishes, octopuses, etc.

ce-ram′ic (-răm′ĭk), *a.* Of or pertaining to pottery.

ce-ram′ics (-ĭks), *n.* Art of making things of baked clay, as pottery, tiles, etc.

ce′rate (sē′rāt), *n.* A kind of thick ointment.

ce′re-al (sē′rē-ăl), *a.* Of or pertaining to grain or the grasses producing it. — *n.* Any grass yielding grain used for food, as wheat, rice, etc.; also, the grain, or a foodstuff prepared from it.

cer′e-bel′lum (sĕr′ē-bĕl′ŭm),*n.* A large lobe of the hinder part of the brain. — **cer′e-bel′lar** (-ăr), *a.*

cer′e-bral (sĕr′ē-brăl), *a.* Of or pertaining to the brain ; also, of or pertaining to the cerebrum.

cer′e-brum (-brŭm), *n.* The hemispheres of the brain, constituting the part most concerned in the voluntary and conscious mental processes.

cere′ment (sēr′mĕnt), *n.* A shroud for the dead ; — usually in *pl.*

cer′e-mo′ni-al (sĕr′ē-mō′nĭ-ăl), *a.* [4] Of or pertaining to ceremony ; characterized by, or of the nature of, ceremony. — *n.* **1.** A system of rules and ceremonies, as in worship ; ritual. **2.** A ceremonial usage or formality ; a rite. — **cer′e-mo′ni-al-ly** (sĕr′ē-mō′nĭ-ăl-ĭ), *adv.* [8].

cer′e-mo′ni-ous (-ŭs), *a.* [4] Ceremonial ; punctilious. — **-ly**, *adv.* [8] — **-ness**, *n.* [8].

cer′e-mo-ny (sĕr′ē-mō-nĭ), *n.; pl.* -MONIES (-nĭz). **1.** A formal act or series of acts, often symbolical, prescribed by law, custom, or authority in matters of religion, of state, etc. **2.** A rite regarded as a mere form ; anything done ceremoniously.

ce-rise′ (sē-rēz′), *a.* Of the color of the bright red cherry. — *n.* A cerise color.

cer′tain (sûr′tĭn), *a.* [4] **1.** Fixed ; stated ; settled. **2.** Sure or dependable ; reliable. **3.** Not to be doubted or denied ; indubitable. **4.** Assured in mind ; sure ; as, I am *certain* of it. **5.** One or some specific (thing or person not further described) ; as, a *certain* town.

cer′tain-ly, *adv.* With certainty ; surely.

cer′tain-ty (-tĭ), *n.; pl.* -TIES (-tĭz). **1.** A fact unquestionably established. **2.** Quality, state, or fact of being certain.

cer-tif′i-cate (sûr-tĭf′ĭ-kāt), *n.* A certified statement ; a written testimony to the truth of any fact ; anything that certifies. — (-kāt), *v. t.* [1] To verify, authorize, or attest by certificate ; to furnish with a certificate.

cer′ti-fi-ca′tion (sûr′tĭ-fĭ-kā′shŭn), *n.* Act of certifying ; certificate.

cer′ti-fy (sûr′tĭ-fī), *v. t.* [2] **1.** To attest authoritatively ; verify. **2.** To testify to in writing. **3.** To assure. **4.** *Banking.* To guarantee (a check ; hence, **certified check**) by writing across its face "good"

āle, senāte, câre, ăm, ăccount, ärm, ȧsk, sofȧ ; ēve, ĕvent, ēnd, recĕnt, makẽr ; īce, ĭll ; ōld, ȯbey, ôrb, ŏdd, sŏft, cŏnnect ; ūse, ŭnīte, ûrn, ŭp, circŭs ; fōōd, fŏŏt ; out, oil ;

or the like and the signature of the cashier or paying teller of the bank on which it is drawn.

cer′ti-tude (sẽr′tĭ-tūd), *n.* State of being mentally certain ; mental assurance as to a belief.

ce-ru′le-an (sē-rōō′lē-ăn), *a. & n.* Azure.

ces-sa′tion (sĕ-sā′shŭn), *n.* A ceasing, as of action or motion ; a stop ; pause ; intermission.

ces′sion (sĕsh′ŭn), *n.* A surrender, as of rights, to another ; ceding.

cess′pool (sĕs′pōōl′), *n.* A cistern or receptacle at the end of a drain to collect sewage.

ce-ta′cean (sē-tā′shăn), *n.* Any of an order of aquatic, mostly marine, mammals, consisting of the whales, dolphins, porpoises, etc.

chafe (chāf), *v. t.* [1] **1.** To rub in order to stimulate and warm. **2.** To rub so as to wear away ; fret ; gall. **3.** To anger ; fret ; irritate. — *v. i.* **1.** To rub ; move, as one body on or against another, so as to cause friction. **2.** To be vexed.

chaff (chȧf), *n.* **1.** The husks of grains and grasses separated from the seed by threshing, winnowing, etc. **2.** Anything light and worthless ; refuse. **3.** Light, jesting talk ; banter ; raillery.— *v. t. & i.* To banter ; rally ; tease.

chaf′finch (chȧf′ĭnch ; chȧf′-), *n.* A kind of finch.

chaff′y (chȧf′ĭ), *a.* [3] Abounding in or like chaff.

chaf′ing dish (chāf′ĭng). A vessel for cooking on the table, or for keeping food hot, as by a lamp.

cha-grin′ (shȧ-grĭn′), *n.* Vexation or annoyance due to wounded pride, failure, etc.; mortification.

chain (chān), *n.* **1.** A series of links or rings, usually of metal, joined together. **2.** That which confines, fetters, or binds ; bond ; fetter ; hence, esp. in *pl.*, imprisonment ; bondage. **3.** A series of things connected as if in a chain (sense 1). — *v. t.* **1.** To fasten, secure, or connect with or as with a chain. **2.** Hence : To fetter ; restrain ; enslave.

chair (châr), *n.* **1.** A movable single seat with a back. **2.** A seat of authority, state, or dignity ; an office of authority, dignity, etc. **3.** A chairman. — *v. t.* To place in a chair.

chair′man (-măn), *n.; pl.* -MEN. The occupant of a chair of authority ; esp., a presiding officer.

chair′man-ship, *n.* The office of chairman or presiding officer.

chair′wom′an (-wŏŏm′ăn), *n.* A woman occupying a chair of office, or serving as a presiding officer.

chaise (shāz), *n.* **1.** A two- or four-wheeled, usually one-horse, carriage with a top. **2.** A post chaise.

Chaise.

chal-ced′o-ny (kăl-sĕd′ō-nĭ), *n.* A kind of quartz, commonly pale blue or gray, with waxlike luster.

cha-let′ (shȧ-lā′), *n.* **1.** A herdsman's cabin, or a small wooden cottage, of the Alpine regions. **2.** A cottage built in the style of the Swiss chalets.

chalk (chôk), *n.* **1.** *Min.* A soft limestone, white, gray, or buff in color. **2.** Chalklike material, esp. that used in crayons ; a piece of such material. — *v. t.* **1.** To mix with chalk ; whiten with chalk. **2.** To write or outline with chalk.

chalk′y (-ĭ), *a.* [3] Consisting of or like chalk.

chal′lenge (chăl′ĕnj), *v. t.* [1] **1.** *Mil.* To question, and demand the countersign from. **2.** To object to ; take exception to ; dispute. **3.** To claim as due, as respect, etc. **4.** To defy ; dare. — *v. i.* To challenge a person, act, or the like. — *n.* Act of challenging ; that which is done in challenging. — **chal′leng-er** (-ĕn-jẽr), *n.* [8].

chal′lis (shăl′ĭ ; chăl′ĭs), *n.* A lightweight cotton or wool dress fabric, usually figured.

cha-lyb′e-ate (kȧ-lĭb′ē-āt), *a.* Impregnated or flavored with iron, as certain mineral waters.

cham′ber (chām′bẽr), *n.* **1.** A room in a house ; esp., a bedroom. **2.** *pl.* Rooms for single persons in a lodging house or tenement, or arranged in sets for offices, etc. **3.** A hall for deliberative meetings. **4.** A deliberative body. **5.** That part of the bore of a gun which holds the charge.

cham′ber-lain (-bẽr-lĭn), *n.* **1.** An attendant on a monarch or nobleman ; hence, one of the high officers of a court. **2.** A steward or treasurer.

cham′ber-maid (-mād′), *n.* A maidservant who has the care of chambers, making the beds, etc.

cham′bray (shăm′brā), *n.* A gingham woven in plain colors with linen finish.

cha-me′le-on (kȧ-mē′lē-ŭn), *n.* Any of various lizards notable for changing their color.

cham′ois (shăm′ĭ ; shȧ′mwä′), *n.* **1.** A small goatlike antelope of the mountain ridges of Europe and southwestern Asia. **2.** A soft, pliant leather.

champ (chămp), *v. t. & i.* To bite and chew with force and noise ; munch.

cham-pagne′ (shăm-pān′), *n.* A white sparkling wine made in the old province of Champagne, France ; also, any wine of this type.

cham′pi-on (chăm′pĭ-ŭn), *n.* **1.** A contestant or fighter, esp. in behalf of another or of a cause ; defender ; advocate. **2.** One acknowledged supreme in a branch of athletics or game of skill. — *v. t.* To attend or defend as champion.

cham′pi-on-ship′, *n.* Act of championing ; position of champion ; supremacy.

chance (chȧns), *n.* **1.** The happening of events ; fortune ; hap. **2.** Something that happens ; an unexpected event. **3.** A possibility or likelihood of anything happening ; probability. **4.** Opportunity. — *v. i.* [1] To happen, come, or arrive, without design or expectation ; happen ; come to pass. — *v. t.* To risk ; — usually with *it*. *Colloq.* — *a.* Happening by chance ; casual.

chan′cel (chȧn′sĕl), *n.* That part of a church reserved for the clergy, where the altar, or communion table, is placed.

chan′cel-lor (-ẽr), *n.* **1.** [*cap.*] The chief chancery judge in England. **2.** The head of some universities. **3.** The chief minister of state in Austria-Hungary and in the German Empire. **4.** A judge in a court of chancery. *U. S.*

chan′cer-y (chȧn′sẽr-ĭ), *n.* **1.** A court of equity. **2.** Chancery practice or principles ; equity.

chan′de-lier (shăn′dē-lēr′), *n.* A branched candlestick, lamp stand, gas fixture, or the like.

chan′dler (chȧn′dlẽr), *n.* **1.** A maker or seller of candles. **2.** A dealer in groceries, provisions, small wares, etc.; as, a ship *chandler*.

chan′dler-y (-ĭ), *n.; pl.* -IES (-ĭz). A place where candles, etc., are kept ; a chandler's shop.

---

change (chānj), *v. t.* [1] **1.** To alter by substituting something for, or by giving up for something else. **2.** To give and take reciprocally; exchange. **3.** To make different; turn; convert. — *v. i.* **1.** To be altered. **2.** To make a change of place or circumstances; shift; — often with *about.* — *n.* **1.** Act or fact of changing; substitution of one thing for another; variety. **2.** Any variation; alteration. **3. a** Money given in exchange for that of a higher denomination. **b** The balance returned when payment is made by a coin or note exceeding the sum due.

change′a-bil′i-ty (chān′já-bĭl′ĭ-tĭ), *n.* Changeable quality; changeableness.

change′a-ble (chān′já-b'l), *a.* [4] **1.** Capable of changing; variable. **2.** Appearing different in different lights or circumstances. — **change′a-ble-ness,** *n.* [8] — **change′a-bly** (-blĭ), *adv.* [8].

change′ling (chānj′lĭng), *n.* One left or taken in place of another; esp., in popular superstition, a child (usually deformed or ugly) supposed to have been exchanged for another by fairies or elves.

chang′er (chān′jẽr),*n.* One who changes anything.

chan′nel (chăn′ĕl), *n.* **1.** The bed of a natural stream. **2.** The deeper part of a waterway. **3.** A strait, or narrow sea. **4.** A closed course or conduit, as a tube. **5.** That through which anything passes; means or medium of passing, conveying, or transmitting. **6.** A long gutter, groove, or furrow. — *v. t.* [7] To form a channel in; groove.

chant (chȧnt), *v. t.* **1.** To sing. **2.** *Music.* To sing or recite after the manner of a chant; intone. — *v. i.* **1.** To sing. **2.** *Music.* To sing a chant; intone. — *n.* **1.** Song; melody. **2.** *Music.* A short, simple melody or phrase characterized by the reciting of an indefinite number of syllables to one tone, used in public worship. **3.** A composition chanted or for chanting. — **chant′er,** *n.* [8].

cha′os (kā′ŏs), *n.* **1.** The unorganized state of matter before the creation of orderly forms in the universe. **2.** Any confused state of things.

cha-ot′ic (kȧ-ŏt′ĭk), *a.* [4] Of or like chaos.

chap (chăp), *v. t. & i.*; CHAPPED (chăpt) or CHAPT; CHAP′PING. To open or crack in slits or chinks; cause the skin of to crack or be rough. — *n.* A crack or fissure, esp. in the skin, due to exposure.

chap (chŏp; chăp), *n.* One of the jaws or the fleshy covering of a jaw; — usually in *pl.*

chap (chăp), *n.* A man; boy; fellow. *Colloq.*

chap′ar-ral′(-ȧ-răl′),*n.* Thicket of dwarf evergreen ′oaks; a dense thicket of stiff or thorny shrubs, etc.

chap′el (chăp′ĕl) , *n.* **1.** A subordinate place of worship. **2.** A room, recess, or cell, in a church, containing an altar and separately dedicated.

chap′er-on (shăp′ẽr-ōn), *n.* A person, esp. a matron, who accompanies a young unmarried lady for propriety. — *v. t.* To attend as a chaperon.

chap′fall′en (chŏp′fôl′'n), *a.* [4] Crestfallen.

chap′lain (chăp′lĭn), *n.* **1.** A clergyman officially attached to the army or navy, a public institution, family, or court. **2.** A clergyman or layman chosen to conduct religious exercises for a society, etc.

chap′lain-cy (-sĭ), *n.* The office of a chaplain.

chap′let (-lĕt), *n.* **1.** A garland or wreath for the head. **2.** A string of beads.

chap′ter (chăp′tẽr), *n.* **1.** A main division of a book, treatise, or the like. **2.** A regular meeting of the canons of a church, or the like; also, **a** body of those who hold such a chapter.

char (chär), *v. t.*; CHARRED (chärd); CHAR′RING. **1.** To reduce to charcoal or carbon by heat. **2.** To burn partially; scorch.

char′ac-ter (kăr′ăk-tẽr),*n.* **1.** A distinctive mark; a brand or stamp. **2.** A symbol used in writing or print; a letter, figure, or sign. **3.** A distinguishing trait or characteristic or the sum of such traits; kind; sort; nature. **4.** Quality, position, rank, or capacity; status. **5.** Reputation; repute. **6.** A person regarded as embodying peculiar or notable traits. **7.** One of the persons of a drama or novel. **8.** Distinctive character; individuality.

char′ac-ter-is′tic (-ĭs′tĭk), *a.* [4] Pertaining to, or serving to constitute, the character; distinctive; typical. — *n.* A distinguishing trait, quality, or property. — **char′ac-ter-is′ti-cal-ly,** *adv.* [8].

char′ac-ter-i-za′tion (-ĭ-zā′shŭn), *n.* Act, process, or result of characterizing.

char′ac-ter-ize (kăr′ăk-tẽr-īz), *v. t.* [1] **1.** To indicate or delineate the character of; describe. **2.** To be a characteristic of; mark the character of.

cha-rade′ (shȧ-rād′), *n.* A verbal or acted enigma based on a word with two or more significant parts, each of which, as well as the word itself, is to be guessed from the representations.

char′coal′ (chär′kōl′), *n.* Carbon made from vegetable or animal substance; esp., coal made by charring wood in a kiln, retort, etc.

charge (chärj), *v. t.* [1] **1.** To load; lade; to task or load (with) mentally. **2.** To place a charge, as of powder, electricity, or gas within or upon. **3.** To command, instruct, or exhort with authority. **4.** To accuse; lay to one's charge; impute. **5.** To fix or demand as a price. **6.** To place something as a debt to the account of; to debit. **7.** To bring (a weapon) to a position of attack. **8.** To bear down on; attack. — *v. i.* **1.** To deliver or make a charge. **2.** To squat on its belly, with head on its fore paws, and be still; — said of a dog. — *n.* **1.** A load; burden. **2.** Quantity, as of powder, which an apparatus, bore, etc., holds at one time. **3.** A heraldic bearing. **4.** Pecuniary burden; expense; — usually in *pl.* **5.** Price demanded. **6.** An entry or account of something due. **7.** A duty or task laid on a person; responsibility; trust. **8.** An order; mandate. **9.** An accusation of a wrong. **10.** An impetuous onset or attack, as of troops.

charge′a-ble (chär′jȧ-b'l), *a.* That may be charged.

charg′er (chär′jẽr), *n.* A large platter for meat.

charg′er, *n.* One that charges; esp., a war horse.

char′i-ly (châr′ĭ-lĭ), *adv.* In a chary manner.

char′i-ness, *n.* Quality of being chary; caution.

char′i-ot (chăr′ĭ-ŏt), *n.* Among the ancients, a two-wheeled car or vehicle for war, racing, etc.

char′i-ot-eer′ (-ēr′), *n.* One who drives a chariot.

char′i-ta-ble (chăr′ĭ-tȧ-b'l), *a.* [4] **1.** Liberal in benefactions; generous. **2.** Of or pertaining to charity. **3.** Liberal in judging others; lenient; forgiving. — **ness,** *n.* [8] — **ta-bly,** *adv.* [8].

char′i-ty (-tĭ), *n.* ; *pl.* -TIES (-tĭz). **1.** Christian love and benevolence. **2.** Liberality in judging men or actions. **3.** Good will to the poor or suffering ; generosity ; almsgiving ; hence, public relief of the poor. **4.** Whatever is given to the needy ; alms. **5.** A gift, as by a person's will, for some beneficial public use ; also, an institution founded by such a gift, as a hospital, a school, etc.

char′la-tan (shär′là-tăn), *n.* One who makes unwarrantable pretensions ; a quack.

char′la-tan-ry (shär′là-tăn-rĭ), **char′la-tan-ism** (-ĭz′m), *n.* Undue pretension to skill ; quackery.

charm (chärm), *n.* **1.** Originally, the reciting of a magic verse ; hence, any action, process, or thing believed to have magic power ; spell. **2.** Anything worn to avert ill, or to secure good fortune ; amulet. **3.** That which fascinates. — *v. t.* **1.** To affect by or as by a charm ; fascinate ; enchant. **2.** To protect as by a charm. — *v. i.* **1.** To use charms or magic. **2.** To act as a charm ; to be fascinating. — **charm′er,** *n.* [8].

charm′ing, *p. a.* [4] Working a charm or charms ; fascinating. — **-ing-ly,** *adv.* [8].

chart (chärt), *n.* **1.** A map ; esp. : **a** A map for navigators. **b** An outline geographical map. **2.** A graphic representation, as by curves, of fluctuations, as of temperature, prices, etc. **3.** A sheet, as of paper, on which information is given in tabular form. — *v. t.* To lay down in a chart ; map.

char′ter (chär′tẽr), *n.* **1.** An instrument in writing from the sovereign power of a state or country, granting or guaranteeing rights. **2.** A writing from the authorities of an order or society creating a lodge or branch. — *v. t.* **1.** To grant a charter to. **2.** To hire. *Colloq.*

char′wom′an (chär′wŏŏm′ăn; chär′-), *n. ; pl.* **-women** (-wĭm′ĕn). A woman hired for odd jobs of domestic work, or for such work by the day.

char′y (chār′ĭ ; chã′rĭ), *a.* [3] **1.** Held, regarded, or done cautiously or with reserve or deliberation ; careful ; cautious. **2.** Reserved ; shy ; fastidious.

chase (chās), *v. t. & i.* [1] **1.** To cause to flee ; put to flight. **2.** To follow (that which flees) in order to, or as if to, harm it ; to hunt. — *n.* **1.** Act of chasing or pursuing ; pursuit ; hunting ; specifically, *the chase,* the hunting of wild beasts. **2.** That which is hunted, as an animal.

chase, *v. t.* To ornament (a metal surface) by embossing, engraving, or the like.

chas′er (chās′ẽr), *n.* One that chases.

chasm (kăz′m), *n.* A deep breach, as in the earth.

chas′sis (shà′sē), *n. ; pl.* **chassis** (-sēz). The under part of an automobile, consisting of the frame under the body with the wheels and machinery.

chaste (chāst), *a.* [3] **1.** Virtuous ; pure ; modest. **2.** Pure in design and expression ; refined, as art.

chas′ten (chās′'n), *v. t.* **1.** To discipline ; chastise ; — usually of divine chastisement. **2.** To keep from excess ; subdue ; temper.

chaste′ness (chāst′nĕs), *n.* Chastity ; purity.

chas-tise′ (chăs-tīz′), *v. t.* [1] To punish ; inflict punishment, esp. corporal punishment. — **chas-tis′er** (-tīz′ẽr), *n.* [8].

chas′tise-ment (chăs′tĭz-mĕnt), *n.* Punishment.

chas′ti-ty (-tĭ-tĭ), *n.* Chaste state or quality.

chat (chăt), *v. i. ;* **chat′ted** ; **chat′ting.** To talk in a light and familiar manner. — *n.* Light, familiar talk ; gossip.

‖ **châ′teau′** (shä′tō′), *n. ; pl.* **-teaux** (-tōz′ ; *F.* -tō′).

[F.] **1.** A feudal castle in France. **2.** A manor house or a gentleman's countryseat.

chat′e-laine (shăt′ē-lān), *n.* **1.** Mistress of a château. **2.** An ornamental clasp or brooch worn as at a woman's waist, with a chain for keys, etc.

chat′tel (chăt′'l), *n.* **1.** *Law.* Any item of property except real estate. **2.** A slave.

chat′ter (-ẽr), *v. i.* **1.** To utter rapid, inarticulate, but speechlike sounds. **2.** To jabber ; prate. **3.** To make a noise by rapid collisions, as the teeth. — *v. t.* To utter rapidly, idly, or indistinctly. — *n.* Act or noise of chattering. — **chat′ter-er,** *n.* [8].

chat′ty (-ĭ), *a.* [3] Given to chat ; talkative.

‖ **chauf′feur′** (shō′fûr′), *n.* [F.] One who manages the running of an automobile, esp. one who does so for hire. — ‖ **chauf′feuse′** (-fûz′), *n. fem.*

cheap (chēp), *a.* [3] **1.** Of small cost or price. **2.** Of comparatively small value ; of slight esteem. — *adv.* Cheaply. — **-ly,** *adv.* [8]. — **-ness,** *n.* [8].

cheap′en (chēp′'n), *v. t.* To beat down the price of ; depreciate. — *v. i.* To become cheap.

cheat (chēt), *n.* **1.** A deception ; fraud ; imposture. **2.** A swindler ; impostor. — *v. t. & i.* **1.** To deceive, esp. so as to defraud ; trick ; as, to *cheat* a person out of money. **2.** To beguile. — **cheat′er,** *n.* [8].

check (chĕk), *n.* **1.** *Chess.* A word of warning denoting that the king is in immediate danger. **2.** Interruption of progress ; a sudden arrest or stop ; setback. **3.** Whatever arrests progress, or limits action ; restraining influence. **4.** A mark to show that something has been examined. **5.** A written order directing a banker to pay money. **6.** A ticket or token by which a thing may be identified. **7.** A crack or small chink, as in timber. **8.** A pattern in squares, like those of a checkerboard ; a square in such a design. — *v. t.* **1.** *Chess.* To put (a king) in check. **2.** To put a sudden restraint on. **3.** To restrain ; curb. **4.** To verify by a token or other check. **5.** To make checks, or chinks, in (timber). **6.** To mark with a check pattern ; checker. — **check′er,** *n.* [8].

check′er (chĕk′ẽr), *n.* **1.** [In form **checkers,** construed as *sing.*] A game played on a checkerboard by two persons **2.** A piece in the game of checkers. **3.** A square or spot suggestive of those of a checkerboard. — *v. t.* **1.** To mark with small squares like a checkerboard. **2.** To variegate or diversify.

check′er-ber′ry (-bĕr′ĭ), *n. ; pl.* **-ries** (-ĭz). The spicy red fruit of the wintergreen ; also, the plant.

check′er-board′ (-bōrd′), *n.* A board with (usually) 64 squares of alternate colors.

check′ers (-ẽrz), *n.* See **checker,** *n.*, 1.

check′mate (-māt), *n.* **1.** *Chess.* Act of checkmating an opponent's king ; a mate. **2.** A complete check ; utter defeat. — *v. t.* [1] **1.** *Chess.* To check (an adversary's king) so that escape is impossible ; mate. **2.** To defeat completely.

check′rein′ (-rān′), *n.* A short rein fastened to the saddle of a harness to keep a horse's head up.

cheek (chēk), *n.* **1.** The side of the face below the eye and above and to the side of the mouth. **2.** Saucy talk ; assurance ; impudence. *Colloq. or Slang.* **3.** Something likened to the human cheek.

cheek′y (chēk′ĭ), *a.* [3] Impudent. *Colloq.*

cheep (chēp), *v. i.* To peep ; squeak, as a young bird. — *n.* A peep ; squeak. — **cheep′er,** *n.* [8].

---

cheer (chēr), *n.* **1.** Feeling; state of mind or heart. **2.** Gayety; animation. **3.** That which cheers or gladdens; that which is provided for entertainment, esp. at table; food. **4.** A shout of joy, applause, etc. — *v. t.* **1.** To infuse good cheer or hope into; enliven. **2.** To urge on or encourage, now esp. by shouts or cheers. **3.** To salute with shouts of approval, welcome, or the like. — *v. i.* **1.** To grow or be cheerful; — with *up.* **2.** To shout applause, triumph, etc. — **cheer′er,** *n.* [8].

cheer′ful (-fōol), *a.* [4] Having or showing good spirits. — **-ly,** *adv.* [8].

cheer′ful-ness, *n.* Quality of being cheerful.

cheer′less (-lĕs), *a.* [4] Without cheer; joyless; comfortless. — **-ly,** *adv.* [8] — **-ness,** *n.* [8].

cheer′y (chēr′ĭ), *a.* [3] Cheerful; lively; gay. — **cheer′i-ly** (-ĭ-lĭ), *adv.* [8] — **i-ness,** *n.* [8].

cheese (chēz), *n.* The compressed curd of milk, used as food; also, a cake of this.

cheese′cloth′ (-klŏth′), *n.* A thin, unsized, loose-woven cotton cloth.

chees′y (-ĭ), *a.* [3] Having the taste, consistency, or appearance of cheese.

chee′tah (chē′tä), *n.* An animal of the cat family.

∥chef (shĕf), *n.* [F.] A chief; esp., a head cook.

∥chef—d′œu′vre (shā′dû′vr′), *n.; pl.* CHEFS- (shā′-). [F.] A masterpiece, as in art, literature, etc.

chem′i-cal (kĕm′ĭ-kăl), *a.* **1.** Of or pertaining to chemistry; used in the processes of chemistry. **2.** Acting by chemical agency. — *n.* A substance got by chemical process, or used to produce chemical effect. — **chem′i-cal-ly,** *adv.* [8].

che-mise′ (shē-mēz′), *n.* An undergarment worn by women.

chem′ist (kĕm′ĭst), *n.* **1.** One versed in chemistry. **2.** A druggist. *British.*

chem′is-try (-ĭs-trĭ), *n.* **1.** Science of the composition of substances, and of their transformations. **2.** An application of chemical theory and method to a particular subject; as, the *chemistry* of iron.

che-nille′ (shē-nēl′), *n.* A kind of tufted cord used for trimming, fringes, etc.

cheque (chĕk), *n.* Var. of CHECK.

cher′ish (chĕr′ĭsh), *v. t.* **1.** To hold dear; treat with tenderness; to protect and aid. **2.** To harbor in the mind; cling to. — **cher′ish-er,** *n.* [8].

che-root′ (shē-rōot′; chē-), *n.* A kind of cigar cut off square at both ends.

cher′ry (chĕr′ĭ), *n.; pl.* -RIES (-ĭz). A common fruit tree, related to the plum; also, its fruit.

cher′ub (chĕr′ŭb), *n.; pl.* CHERUBS (-ŭbz); but in senses 1 & 2 the Heb. *pl.* CHERUBIM (-ŭ-bĭm; -ōo-bĭm) is also used. **1.** A mysterious composite being described in Ezekiel i. and x. Also, a representation of a cherub. **2.** One of an order of angels. **3.** A beautiful child.

che-ru′bic (chē-rōo′bĭk), *a.* [4] Like a cherub.

chess (chĕs), *n.* A well-known game played on a chessboard, a board like a checkerboard, with pieces called **chessmen.**

chest (chĕst), *n.* **1.** A large box, esp. one with a lid, as for keeping valuables. **2.** The place for the keeping of the money of a public institution; treasury; also, the fund itself. **3.** The part of the body inclosed by the ribs and sternum; thorax.

chest′nut (chĕs′nŭt), *n.* **1.** The edible nut of cer-

tain trees of the beech family; also, any of the trees or the wood of any of them. **2.** Chestnut color; a bright reddish brown.

chev′a-lier′ (shĕv′á-lēr′), *n.* A member of certain orders of knighthood; also, in France, a member of an order of merit.

chev′i-ot (chĕv′ĭ-ŭt), *n.* **1.** A kind of woolen fabric. **2.** A cotton fabric, used for waists, shirts, etc.

chev′ron (shĕv′rŭn), *n.* A device of two bands meeting at an angle, used in heraldry, or worn on the sleeve as a mark of military rank, etc.

chew (chōo), *v. t. & i.* **1.** To bite and grind with the teeth; masticate. **2.** To meditate or plan. — *n.* Act of chewing; also, that which is chewed.

che-wink′ (chē-wĭnk′), *n.* A common North American bird of the sparrow family.

∥chic (shĕk), *n.* [F.] Artistic cleverness; good form; style. — *a.* Characterized by chic. *Both Colloq.*

chi-can′er-y (shĭ-kān′ĕr-ĭ), *n.; pl.* -ERIES (-ĭz). Sharp practice; trickery.

chick (chĭk), *n.* **1.** A chicken, esp. a young one. **2.** A child or young person.

chick′a-dee′ (chĭk′á-dē′), *n.* Any of various titmice.

chick′en (-ĕn), *n.* **1.** A young cock or hen; also, the young of various other birds. **2.** A young or inexperienced person; child.

chicken pox. A mild, contagious disease, chiefly of children, characterized by an eruption of the skin.

chick′weed′ (-wēd′), *n.* Any of various weeds of the pink family, the seeds and young foliage of which are eaten by birds.

Chickadee.

chic′o-ry (chĭk′ō-rĭ), *n.* A common perennial plant with bright blue flowers; also, its root, which is roasted and mixed with coffee.

chide (chīd), *v. i. & t.; pret.* CHID (chĭd), sometimes CHID′ED (chĭd′ĕd); *p. p.* CHID (chĭd), CHID′DEN (chĭd′'n), CHID′ED; *p. pr. & vb. n.* CHID′ING (chĭd′-ĭng). To find fault; scold; make, or effect with, a noise as of scolding or brawling.

chief (chēf), *n.* The head or leader of any body of men; one in authority; the principal actor. — *a.* **1.** Highest in office or rank. **2.** Principal or most eminent; foremost.

chief′ly (-lĭ), *adv.* **1.** In the first place; above all; especially. **2.** For the most part; mostly.

chief′tain (-tĭn), *n.* A chief; commander.

chief′tain-cy (-sĭ), *n.; pl.* -CIES (-sĭz). The rank, dignity, office, or rule of a chieftain.

chif′fon (shĭf′fŏn), *n.* A soft gauzy silk material.

chif′fo-nier′ (-ŏ-nēr′), *n.* An ornamental cabinet; esp., a high chest of drawers, often having a mirror.

chil′blain (chĭl′blān′), *n.* An inflammatory swelling, due to exposure of the feet or hands.

child (chīld), *n.; pl.* CHILDREN (chĭl′drĕn). **1.** An infant; baby. **2.** A young person of either sex. **3.** A son or daughter; offspring. **4.** Any descendant; — used in *pl.*

child′hood (-hōod), *n.* State or time of being a child.

child′ish, *a.* **1.** Of or like a child. **2.** Puerile; trifling; weak. — **-ly,** *adv.* [8] — **-ness,** *n.* [8].

child′less, *a.* Having no child. — **-ness,** *n.* [8].

āle, senāte, câre, ăm, *a*ccount, ärm, ȧsk, sofá; ēve, ĕvent, ĕnd, recĕnt, makĕr; īce, ĭll; ōld, ŏbey, ôrb, ŏdd, sŏft, cŏnnect; ūse, ŭnite, ûrn, ŭp, circ*u*s; fōod, fŏŏt: out. oil;

child'like', *a.* Resembling or becoming to a child.

chil'dren (chĭl'drĕn), *n., pl.* of CHILD.

chil'i (chĭl'ĭ), *n. ; pl.* CHILIES (-ĭz). The red pepper.

chill (chĭl), *n.* **1.** A sensation of cold attended with convulsive shaking. **2.** A moderate but disagreeable degree of cold. **3.** A check to enthusiasm ; discouragement. — *a.* **1.** Moderately cold; chilly. **2.** Affected by cold ; shivering. **3.** Cool in manner; formal. **4.** Discouraging; depressing. — *v.i.* **1.** To cool. **2.** To become surface-hardened by sudden cooling, as cast iron. — *v. t.* **1.** To strike with a chill; make chilly. **2.** To check, as enthusiasm; dispirit. **3.** *Metal.* To cool suddenly at the surface so as to harden.

chill'y (chĭl'ĭ), *a.* [3] Moderately or disagreeably cold. — **chill'i-ly**, *adv.* [8] — **chill'i-ness**, *n.* [8].

chime (chīm), *n.* **1** Mechanical arrangement for chiming a bell or set of bells. **2.** A set of bells musically attuned. **3.** The music from such a set of bells; — usually in *pl.* **4.** Music ; melody; harmony. — *v. i.* [1] **1.** To sound musically or harmoniously, as bells. **2.** To sound, or sound in, chimes. **3.** To harmonize ; agree. — *v. t.* To strike, as a bell, so as to produce a musical sound; to cause to sound in harmony.

chi-me'ra (kĭ-mē'rȧ ; kī-), *n. ; pl.* -RAS (-rȧz). A frightful, foolish, or incongruous fancy.

chi-mer'i-cal (-mĕr'ĭ-kăl), *a.* Merely imaginary.

chim'ney (chĭm'nĭ), *n. ; pl.* -NEYS (-nĭz). **1.** An upright flue, as of brick or stone, for smoke. **2.** A tube, usually of glass, placed around a flame, as of a lamp, to create a draft.

chim-pan'zee (chĭm-păn'zē; chĭm'păn-zē'), *n.* An ape of equatorial Africa, smaller than the gorilla.

chin (chĭn), *n.* The lower extremity of the face, below the mouth; the point of the under jaw.

chi'na (chī'nȧ), *n.* Porcelain ware, originally made in China. Loosely, crockery.

Chi'na-man (-măn), *n.; pl.* -MEN. A male Chinese.

chi'na-ware (-wâr'), *n.* China.

chin-chil'la (chĭn-chĭl'ȧ), *n.* **1.** A small rodent, with soft pearly gray fur, of Peru and Chile. Also, its fur. **2.** A kind of heavy, tufted, woolen cloth.

chine (chīn), *n.* The backbone ; also, a piece of the backbone of an animal with adjoining parts, cut for cooking.

Chi-nese' (chī-nēz' ; -nēs'), *a.* Of or pertaining to China. — *n. sing. & pl.* **1.** A native of China. **2.** The language of the Chinese.

chink (chĭngk), *n.* A small narrow cleft or fissure; crack. — *v. t.* To crack; also, to fill the chinks of.

chink, *n.* **1.** A short, sharp sound, as of metal lightly struck. **2.** Coin; money. *Slang.* — *v. t. & i.* To make, or cause to make, a chink.

chin'qua-pin (chĭng'kȧ-pĭn), *n.* **1.** The dwarf chestnut; also, its sweet nut. **2.** A related tree of California and Oregon, or its nut.

chintz (chĭnts), *n.* Cotton cloth printed with flowers, etc., and often glazed.

chip (chĭp), *v. t.; * CHIPPED (chĭpt); CHIP'PING. **1.** To cut or hew with an ax, chisel, etc. **2.** To break or crack off a bit or bits of, as of a piece of crockery. — *v. i.* To break or fly off in bits. — *n.* **1.** A fragment or bit, as of wood, etc., chopped, cut, or broken off. **2.** Anything valueless or trivial; also, anything dried up or without flavor.

chip'munk (chĭp'mŭngk), *n.* Any of many small striped rodents of the squirrel family.

Chipmunk.
(¼)

chi-rog'ra-phy (kĭ-rŏg'rȧ-fĭ), *n.* Art of writing or engrossing ; handwriting. — **-ra-pher** (-fẽr), *n.*

chi-rop'o-dist (kī-rŏp'ō-dĭst), *n.* One who treats the feet ; esp., one who treats corns and bunions.

chi'ro-prac'tic (kī'rō-prăk'tĭk), *n.* A system, or the practice, of adjusting by hand the joints, esp. of the spine, for the curing of disease. — **chi'ro-prac'tor** (-tẽr), *n.*

chirp (chûrp), *v. i.* To make a short, sharp sound, as small birds or crickets. — *v. t.* To utter by chirping. — *n.* A short, sharp note, as of some birds.

chir'rup (chĭr'ŭp), *v. i.* **1.** To chirp, esp. repeatedly and with a lively effect. **2.** Of persons, to make a similar sound, as with the lips to urge on a horse. — *n.* Act or sound of chirruping.

chis'el (chĭz'ĕl), *n.* A tool with a cutting edge at the end of a blade, used in shaping wood, etc. — *v. t. & i.* [7] To cut or work with a chisel.

chit (chĭt), *n.* A child ; also, a pert, forward girl.

chit'chat (-chăt), *n.* Light, familiar talk.

chiv'al-ric (shĭv'ăl-rĭk), *a.* [4] Chivalrous.

chiv'al-rous (shĭv'ăl-rŭs), *a.* [4] Pertaining to chivalry ; valiant; also, gallant; courteous; brave and generous. — **chiv'al-rous-ly**, *adv.* [8].

chiv'al-ry (shĭv'ăl-rĭ), *n.* **1.** A body of knights. **2.** The system, spirit, usages, or manners, of knighthood. **3.** The traditional qualities of the ideal knight, as honor, protection of the weak, generosity to foes, and gallantry.

chlo'ride (klō'rīd ; -rĭd), *n.* A compound of chlorine with another element or radical.

chlo'rine (klō'rĭn ; -rēn), *n.* A poisonous, greenish yellow gas of a suffocating odor, got esp. from chlorides, as common salt. It is an element.

chlo'ro-form (-rō-fôrm), *n.* A colorless sweetish liquid smelling like ether and evaporating rapidly. It is used to produce unconsciousness, for dissolving various substances, etc. — *v. t.* To make insensible with chloroform.

chlo'ro-phyll, chlo'ro-phyl (-fĭl), *n.* The green coloring matter of plants.

chock (chŏk), *n.* **1.** A wedge or block to fill in a space or to prevent motion, as of a cask. **2.** *Naut.* A form of casting or wooden piece for hawsers to run through. — *v. t.* To fasten, or wedge, with a chock. — *adv.* As close or tight as possible.

choc'o-late (chŏk'ō-lăt), *n.* **1.** A preparation of roasted cacao seeds, or a beverage made with it. **2.** The color of chocolate ; dark brown.

choice (chois), *n.* **1.** Act of choosing ; preference; also, right of choosing ; option. **2.** Best part; the pick. **3.** A sufficient number to choose among. **4.** Thing or person chosen. — *a.* [3] **1.** Worthy to be chosen. **2.** Selected with care. **3.** Preserving or using with care ; — with *of.* — **-ly**, *adv.*

choir (kwīr), *n.* **1.** An organized company of

singers, esp. in church service. **2.** That part of a church appropriated to the singers.

choke (chōk), *v. t.* [1] **1.** To stifle or to strangle; suffocate. **2.** To check the growth, progress, or action of. **3.** To obstruct by filling up or clogging. — *v. i.* **1.** To suffocate; strangle. **2.** To be obstructed; stick. — *n.* Act or sound of choking.

choke'cher'ry (-chĕr'ĭ), *n. ; pl.* -RIES. Any of several wild cherries, or their small astringent fruit.

chok'y, chok'ey (chōk'ĭ), *a.* [3] Tending or inclined to choke, as with emotion.

chol'er (kŏl'ĕr), *n.* Irascibility ; irritability.

chol'er-a (-á), *n. Med.* Any of several diseases; esp.,a kind of infectious, and usually fatal, disease, more fully called *Asiatic cholera*. — **chol'er-a in-fan'tum** (ĭn-făn'tŭm), a disease of infants, attended with vomiting and diarrhea.—**c. mor'bus** (môr'bŭs), acute inflammation of the digestive tract, with vomiting and cramps.

chol'er-ic (-ĭk), *a.* [4] **1.** Characterized by choler ; irritable; irascible. **2.** Angry; wrathful.

choose (chōoz), *v. t. ; pret.* CHOSE (chōz) ; *p. p.* CHO'SEN (chō'z'n) ; *p. pr. & vb. n.* CHOOS'ING. **1.** To make choice of. **2.** To think proper ; be pleased; as, he did not *choose* to go. — *v. i.* To make a selection. — **choos'er,** *n.* [8].

chop (chŏp), *v. t. ;* CHOPPED (chŏpt) ; CHOP'PING. To cut by striking, esp. repeatedly, with a sharp instrument. — *v. i.* To make a quick stroke, or repeated strokes, as with an ax. — *n.* **1.** Act of chopping ; a cutting stroke. **2.** A piece chopped off; a slice or small piece, as of meat. **3.** Of waves, etc., a short, abrupt motion.

chop, *v. i.* To shift suddenly, as the wind ; veer.

chop, *n.* **1.** A jaw ;—usually in *pl.* **2.** *pl.* The jaws with the space between them; the fleshy parts about the mouth ; mouth cavity ; fauces.

chop'per (chŏp'ĕr), *n.* One that chops.

chop'py (chŏp'ĭ), *a.* [3] Rough, with short, tumultuous waves ; as, a *choppy* sea.

chop'py, *a.* [3] Variable;—said of the wind.

chop'stick' (-stĭk'), *n.* One of two small sticks or slips of wood, ivory, etc. used by the Chinese and some others in taking food.

cho'ral (kō'răl), *a.* Pertaining to, or of the nature of, a choir or chorus ; adapted to be sung in chorus.

chord (kôrd), *n.* **1.** String of a musical instrument. **2.** *Anat.* A cord. **3.** *Math.* A straight line joining the extremities of an arc. **4.** *Music.* A combination of tones sounding simultaneously and in harmonic relation. — *v. i. Music.* To accord ; harmonize.

chore (chōr), *n.* A small or odd job ; *pl.*, the daily light work of a household or farm.

cho-re'a (kō-rē'á), *n.* St. Vitus's dance, a disease attended with convulsive twitchings, etc.

cho'ric (kō'rĭk ; kŏr'ĭk),*a.* Of or pert. to a chorus.

chor'is-ter (kŏr'ĭs-tẽr), *n.* **1.** A singer in a choir; esp., a choir boy. **2.** One who leads a church choir.

cho'rus (kō'rŭs), *n.* **1.** *Music.* A company of singers singing in concert ; choir. **b** The simultaneous song of a number of persons. **c** A composition to be sung by voices in concert. **d** A part of a song recurring at the end of stanzas. **2.** Utterance by a number simultaneously.

chose (chōz), *pret.* of CHOOSE.

cho'sen (chō'z'n), *p. p. & p. a.* of CHOOSE.

chow'chow' (chou'chou'), *n.* A mixture; esp., chopped mixed pickles.

chow'der (-dẽr), *n.* A dish of fresh fish or clams, biscuit, onions, etc., stewed together.

chrism (krĭz'm), *n.* Consecrated oil used in baptism, confirmation, etc.

chris'om (-ŭm), *n.* **1.** = CHRISM. **2.** A white cloth, robe, or mantle thrown over a child when baptized.

Christ (krīst), *n.* **1.** The Messiah, whose coming was prophesied by the Jews. **2.** Jesus, as fulfilling this expectation.

chris'ten (krĭs'n), *v. t.* To baptize; also, to name at baptism, or as at baptism.

Chris'ten-dom (-dŭm), *n.* **1.** Christians as a body; the church. **2.** The Christian world.

Chris'tian (krĭs'chăn),*n.* One who believes in Jesus Christ. — *a.* **1.** Professing, or belonging to, Christianity. **2.** Pertaining to Christ or His religion. **3.** Characteristic of or becoming Christian people. **4.** Of or pertaining to a Christian or Christians. **Christian name,** name given in baptism, as distinct from the family name; first name ; given name. — **C. Science,** a system of healing disease of mind and body teaching that all cause and effect is mental.

Chris'ti-an'i-ty (krĭs'chĭ-ăn'ĭ-tĭ ; krĭs-chăn'-), *n.* **1.** The religion of Christians. **2.** State or fact of being a Christian ; Christian character.

Chris'tian-ize (-chăn-īz), *v. t.* To make Christian.

Christ'mas (krĭs'măs), *n.* An annual festival (December 25) in memory of Christ's birth.

Christ'mas-tide' (-tīd'), *n.* The Christmas season.

chro-mat'ic (krō-măt'ĭk), *a.* **1.** Of or pertaining to color or colors. **2.** *Music.* Proceeding by the smaller intervals (semitones) of the scale.

chrome (krōm), *n.* Chromium.

chro'mi-um (krō'mĭ-ŭm), *n.* A grayish white metal, hard, brittle, and difficult to fuse.

chro'mo (-mō), *n. ; pl.* -MOS (-mōz). A chromolithograph, or lithographic picture printed in colors.

chron'ic (krŏn'ĭk), *a.* [4] Continuing a long time.

chron'i-cle (-ĭ-k'l), *n.* **1.** A historical account of events in the order of time ; a history. **2.** *pl.* [*cap.*] Two books of the Old Testament. — *v. t.* [1] To record in or as in a chronicle. — **chron'i-cler** (-klẽr), *n.* [8].

chron'o-log'i-cal (krŏn'ō-lŏj'ĭ-kăl), *a.* Pert. to or in accordance with chronology.—**-cal-ly,** *adv.* [8].

chro-nol'o-gy (krō-nŏl'ō-jĭ), *n. ; pl.* -GIES (-jĭz). Science of measuring time by regular periods, and dating and arranging events.

chro-nom'e-ter (-nŏm'ĕ-tẽr), *n.* A timepiece, esp. one of a very exact portable kind.

chrys'a-lis (krĭs'á-lĭs), *n. ; pl.* E. -LISES (-lĭs-ĕz), L. -SALIDES (krĭ-săl'ĭ-dēz). The pupa stage of insects (esp. butterflies).

chrys-an'the-mum (krĭs-ăn'thē-mŭm), *n.* Any of many species of perennials of the aster family. The cultivated species have large double flowers.

chrys'o-lite (krĭs'ō-līt), *n.* A mineral, usually olive-green, often used as a gem.

chub (chŭb), *n.* A fresh-water fish of the carp kind.

chub'by (chŭb'ĭ), *a.* [3] Like a chub ; short, plump, and round.—**chub'bi-ness** (-ĭ-nĕs), *n.* [8].

chuck (chŭk), *n.* **1.** A part of a side of dressed beef, including most of the neck and the parts ad-

āle, senāte, cãre, ăm, ăccount, ärm, ȧsk, sofȧ ; ēve, ĕvent, ĕnd, recĕnt, makẽr ; īce, ĭll ; ōld, ȯbey, ôrb, ŏdd, sŏft, cȯnnect ; ūse, ŭnite, ûrn, ŭp, circŭs ; fōod, fŏot ; out, oil ;

jacent. **2.** A contrivance for holding work or a tool in a machine, esp. in a lathe.

chuck (chŭk), *v. t.* **1.** To strike gently; tap. **2.** To throw, esp. with a short action of the arm. — *n.* **1.** A pat under the chin. **2.** A toss or jerk.

chuck′le (chŭk′'l), *v. i.* [1] To laugh in a suppressed manner, as from inward satisfaction. — *n.* Act or sound of chuckling.

chum (chŭm), *n.* A roommate, esp. at college; also, an intimate friend.—*v.i.;* CHUMMED (chŭmd), CHUM′MING. To live or associate as a chum or chums. — **chum′my** (-ĭ), *a.* [3] *All Colloq.*

chunk (chŭngk), *n.* A short, thick piece, person, or horse.—**chunk′y** (-ĭ),*a.* [3] *Both Colloq.,U.S.*

church (chûrch), *n.* **1.** A building for public Christian worship. **2.** Christians collectively. **3.** A body of Christian believers of the same creed; a denomination. **4.** Organized Christianity, as in a nation. **5.** The clerical profession. **6.** Church service; divine worship.

church′ly,*a.* Pertaining to, or suitable for, church.

church′man (-măn), *n.; pl.* -MEN. **1.** An ecclesiastic; clergyman. **2.** An adherent of the church, esp. an established church.

church′ward′en (-wôr′d′n),*n.* Lay officer in Anglican churches who cares for the church property.

church′yard′ (-yärd′), *n.* The inclosure about a church, often, esp. formerly, used as a burial place.

churl (chûrl), *n.* **1.** A freeman without rank. *Now Hist.* **2.** A rustic; boor; ill-bred fellow.

churl′ish (chûr′lĭsh), *a.* [4] Of or like a churl; surly. — **-ly**, *adv.* [8] — **-ness**, *n.* [8].

churn (chûrn), *n.* A vessel in which milk or cream is agitated in making butter. — *v. t.* **1.** To agitate (milk or cream) in a churn. **2.** To agitate violently; to make, as foam, by so doing. — *v. i.* To perform the operation of churning.

chute (shoot), *n.* **1.** A quick or steep descent, as in a river; a rapid. **2.** An inclined plane, channel, or trough for sliding things down; a flume.

chyle (kīl), *n. Physiol.* A modification of lymph occurring in the lacteals, or the lymphatics leading from the small intestine.

chyme (kīm), *n. Physiol.* The pulpy semi-digested food in the small intestines.

ci-ca′da (sĭ-kā′dȧ), *n.; pl.* E. -DAS (-dȧz), L. -DÆ (-dē). Any of several large insects, called also locusts, noted for the shrill sound made by the male.

ci-ca′trix (sĭ-kā′trĭks; sĭk′ȧ-), *n.; L. pl.* -TRICES (sĭk′ȧ-trī′sēz). The skin or film which forms over a wound, later contracting to form the scar; a scar.

cic′a-trize (sĭk′ȧ-trīz), *v. t. & i.* [1] To heal by the formation of a cicatrix.—**-tri-za′tion** (-trĭ-zā′-),*n.*

ci′der (sī′dẽr), *n.* The expressed juice of apples, used for drinking, making vinegar, etc.

ci-gar′ (sĭ-gär′),*n.* A roll of tobacco for smoking.

cig′a-rette′ (sĭg′ȧ-rĕt′), *n.* A little roll of finely cut tobacco or the like for smoking, usually wrapped in paper.

cinch (sĭnch), *n.* **1.** A strong girth for a pack or saddle. *Western U. S.* **2.** A tight grip; also, a sure or easy thing. *Slang, U. S.* — *v. t.* **1.** To girth tightly. **2.** To get a sure hold on. *Slang, U. S.*

cin-cho′na (sĭn-kō′nȧ), *n.* Peruvian bark.

cinc′ture (sĭngk′tụr), *n.* That which surrounds, as a belt or a girdle. — *v. t.* [1] To gird or girdle.

cin′der (sĭn′dẽr), *n.* **1.** Slag from a metal furnace; dross. **2.** A partly burned coal; ember. **3.** *pl.* Loosely, ashes. — **cin′der-y** (-ĭ), *a.*

cin′e-ma (sĭn′ē-mȧ),*n.* A moving picture; a moving-picture theater. *Originally British.*

cin′e-mat′o-graph (sĭn′ē-măt′ō-grȧf),*n.* **1.** A machine for throwing on a screen a series of pictures succeeding each other so rapidly as to produce the appearance of continuous motion. **2.** A camera to take pictures for use in this machine.

cin′er-a-ry (sĭn′ẽr-ȧ-rĭ), *a.* Pertaining to, or used for, ashes, esp. of the cremated dead, as an urn.

cin′na-bar (-ȧ-bär), *n.* **1.** The chief ore of mercury. **2.** A chemical compound of mercury and sulphur used as a red pigment.

cin′na-mon (-mŭn), *n.* **1.** The bark of any of several trees of the laurel family, much used as a spice. **2.** Any tree that yields cinnamon.

cinque′foil (sĭngk′foil′),*n.* **1.** Any of several plants of the rose family having leaves with five leaflets. **2.** A decorative design likened to the leaf or flower of the cinquefoil.

ci′pher (sī′fẽr),*n.* **1.** A symbol (written 0) denoting naught; zero. **2.** A nonentity. **3.** An alphabet, contrived for secret writing. **4.** A device or monogram. — *v. i.* To use figures in a mathematical process. — *v. t.* To calculate; figure.

cir′cle (sûr′k′l), *n.* **1.** A closed plane curve exactly alike throughout, all its points being equidistant from a point within called the *center*. **2.** The surface bounded by such a curve. **3.** Something circular, as a ring, a set of seats in a theater, etc. **4.** A set of connected series; cycle; round, as of pleasures. **5.** A company bound by a common tie; a coterie; set.—*v.t. & i.* [1] **1.** To encompass by or as by a circle; surround.**2.**To revolve around.

Circle: *AB* Diameter; *C* Center; *CD, CA, CB* Radii; *EKF* Arc on Chord *EF*; *ELFK* (area) Segment on Chord *EF*; *ACD* (area) Sector; *GH* Secant; *TPM* Tangent at point *P*; *EKFBPDA* Circumference.

cir′clet (-klĕt), *n.* A little circle; esp., an ornament such as a ring, bracelet, or bangle.

cir′cuit (-kĭt),*n.* **1.** The circumference of any space; compass. **2.** Act of moving or revolving round, as in a circle or orbit. **3.** A route over, or district through, which one periodically journals. **4.** In electricity, the path of a current. — *v. i. & t.* To go or go around in a circuit.

cir-cu′i-tous (sẽr-kū′ĭ-tŭs), *a.* [4] Going round in a circuit; roundabout. — **cir-cu′i-tous-ly**, *adv.*

cir′cu-lar (sûr′kū-lár), *a.* **1.** Of or pertaining to a circle; in the form of, bounded by, or moving in, a circle; round. **2.** Circuitous; roundabout; indirect. **3.** Addressed to or pertaining to a circle, or coterie of persons. — *n.* A letter, note, or paper, usually printed and distributed to various persons. — **cir′cu-lar-ly**, *adv.* [8].

cir′cu-late (-lāt), *v. i. & t.* [1] **1.** To move or revolve in a circle or circuit, as the blood. **2.** To pass or cause to pass about, as money.

cir′cu-la′tion (-lā′shŭn), *n.* **1.** Act of circulating. **2.** The movement of the blood in the vessels of the body. **3.** Circulating coin, notes, or bills.

---

cir′cu-la-to-ry (sûr′kṵ-lá-tṓ-rĭ), *a.* Of or pertaining to circulation, as of the blood, air, etc.

cir′cum-am′bi-ent (sûr′kŭm-ăm′bĭ-ĕnt), *a.* Surrounding; inclosing; encompassing.

cir′cum-am′bu-late (-bṵ-lāt), *v. t. & i.* [1] To walk around or about.

cir-cum′fer-ence (sẽr-kŭm′fẽr-ĕns), *n.* The outer boundary, or perimeter, of a circle; hence, circuit.

cir′cum-flex (sûr′kŭm-flĕks), *n.* A mark (^, ˆ, later ˜) now used to mark length, contraction, etc. — *a.* **1.** Designating, or relating to, the circumflex. **2.** Flexed; bent or bending round.

cir′cum-lo-cu′tion (-lṓ-kū′shŭn), *n.* Use of many words where but few are necessary.

cir′cum-nav′i-gate (-năv′ĭ-gāt), *v. t.* [1] To sail round. — **cir′cum-nav′i-ga′tion** (-gā′shŭn), *n.* — **cir′cum-nav′i-ga′tor** (-năv′ĭ-gā′tẽr), *n.*

cir′cum-scribe′ (-skrĭb′), *v. t.* [1] **1.** To draw a line around; bound; hence, to limit, esp. narrowly. **2.** *Geom.* To draw, or be drawn, round so as to touch at as many points as possible.

cir′cum-scrip′tion (-skrĭp′shŭn), *n.* Act of circumscribing; limitation; restraint.

cir′cum-spect (sûr′kŭm-spĕkt), *a.* [4] Watchful on every side; cautious; prudent; wary. — **cir′cum-spect-ly**, *adv.* [8] — **cir′cum-spect-ness**, *n.* [8].

cir′cum-spec′tion (-spĕk′shŭn), *n.* Circumspect action or behavior; caution; prudence.

cir′cum-stance (sûr′kŭm-stăns), *n.* **1.** A condition, fact, or event accompanying or determining the occurrence of another fact or event. **2.** *pl.* Condition in regard to worldly estate or means. **3.** The sum of the essential conditions or attendant facts of a matter or subject; significant state of affairs. **4.** Hence, formality; ceremonial. **5.** An event, detail, or incident. — *v. t.* [1] To provide with circumstances.

cir′cum-stan′tial (-stăn′shăl), *a.* [4] **1.** Consisting in, pertaining to, or dependent on, circumstances; as, *circumstantial* evidence, that is, evidence tending to prove a fact in issue by establishing other facts which in common experience are usually attended by the fact in issue. **2.** Incidental; having relation, but not essential; as, this is important, all else is *circumstantial* and secondary. **3.** Abounding with circumstances; particular as to details; as, a *circumstantial* story. — **-ly**, *adv.* [8].

cir′cum-stan′ti-ate (-shĭ-āt), *v. t.* [1] To support with particulars; exhibit in detail.

cir′cum-vent′ (-vĕnt′), *v. t.* [1] To gain advantage over by craft; to get round; delude.

cir′cum-ven′tion (-vĕn′shŭn), *n.* Act of circumventing.

cir′cus (sûr′kŭs), *n.* An inclosure for exhibition of feats by horsemen, acrobats, etc. Hence, the company of performers, or the performance.

cir′ro-cu′mu-lus (sĭr′ṓ-kū′mṵ-lŭs), *n.* A cloud form of small, white, rounded masses at a high elevation, usually forming the *mackerel sky.*

cir′ro-stra′tus (-strā′tŭs), *n.* A fairly uniform layer of high stratus haze, darker than cirrus.

cir′rus (sĭr′ŭs), *n.; pl.* CIRRI (-ī). A white, filmy variety of cloud, formed at a very high elevation.

cis′tern (sĭs′tẽrn), *n.* An artificial reservoir or a tank for water or other liquids.

cit′a-del (sĭt′á-dĕl), *n.* A fortress.

ci-ta′tion (sī-tā′shŭn), *n.* **1.** A summons to appear before a court of justice. **2.** Act of citing a passage, as from a book, or the passage cited.

cite (sīt), *v. t.* [1] **1.** To summon before a court. **2.** To quote, as a passage or book, in support of a statement. **3.** To bring forward, or refer to.

cit′i-zen (sĭt′ĭ-zĕn), *n.* **1.** An inhabitant of a city or town. **2.** A member of a state; one who owes allegiance to a government.

cit′i-zen-ship′, *n.* State or quality of being a citizen; the status of a citizen.

cit′ric (sĭt′rĭk), *a.* Pertaining to or designating an acid extracted from lemons, currants, etc.

cit′ron (-rŭn), *n.* The fruit of a tree related to the lemon and the orange; also, the tree; also, the thick rind of the fruit, used in preserves, etc.

cit′rous (-rŭs), *a.* Of or pertaining to the genus (*Citrus*) including the orange, citron, lemon, etc.

cit′rus (-rŭs), *a.* Citrous; as, *citrus* fruit. *U. S.*

cit′y (sĭt′ĭ), *n.; pl.* CITIES (-ĭz). **1.** A town, esp. a large or noted town. **2.** In the United States, an incorporated municipality, variously governed.

civ′et (sĭv′ĕt), *n.* **1.** A yellowish musky secretion of civet cats. It is used in some perfumes. **2.** = CIVET CAT.

civet cat. Any of various catlike animals.

civ′ic (-ĭk), *a.* Of or pertaining to a citizen, or a city, or citizenship; civil.

civ′ics (-ĭks), *n.* Science of civil government.

civ′il (-ĭl), *a.* [3] **1.** Of, pertaining to, or made up of, citizens. **2.** Characteristic of or befitting a citizen; civilized; courteous. **3.** Pertaining to civic life, in distinction from military, ecclesiastical, etc. **4.** *Law.* Relating to private rights.

ci-vil′ian (sĭ-vĭl′yăn), *n.* One whose pursuits are those of civil life.

ci-vil′i-ty (sĭ-vĭl′ĭ-tĭ), *n.; pl.* -TIES (-tĭz). Good breeding; civil conduct; politeness; courtesy.

civ′i-li-za′tion (sĭv′ĭ-lĭ-zā′shŭn), *n.* Act of civilizing; an advanced condition of social culture.

civ′i-lize (sĭv′ĭ-līz), *v. t.* [1] To reclaim from savagery; educate; refine; humanize.

civ′il-ly (-lĭ), *adv.* In a civil manner.

clack (klăk), *v. i.* **1.** To talk rapidly; chatter. **2.** To cackle; cluck, as a hen. — *n.* A sharp, abrupt noise, or succession of noises. — **-er**, *n.* [8].

clad (klăd), *pret. & p. p.* of CLOTHE.

claim (klām), *v. t.* **1.** To demand as due. **2.** To assert as a fact which ought to be conceded. **3.** To require; demand. — *n.* **1.** A demand of a right; assertion of a right or fact. **2.** A right or title to a thing. **3.** Thing claimed; as, a mining *claim.* — **claim′a-ble**, *a.* [8] — **claim′er**, *n.* [8].

claim′ant (-ănt), *n.* One who asserts a right or title.

clair-voy′ance (klâr-voi′ăns), *n.* A power of discerning objects concealed from sight or at a distance, of reading thought, etc.

clair-voy′ant (-ănt), *a.* [4] Having or pertaining to clairvoyance. — *n.* A clairvoyant person.

clam (klăm), *n.* Any of numerous shellfish having a hinged shell in two parts like the oyster and mussel, but of various shapes.

clam′ber (klăm′bẽr), *v. i. & t.* To climb, as by scrambling.

clam′my (-ĭ), *a.* [3] Soft and sticky; coldly damp and adhesive. — **clam′mi-ness**, *n.* [8].

āle, senāte, câre, ăm, ăccount, ärm, ȧsk, sofᴀ; ēve, ĕvent, ĕnd, recĕnt, makĕr; īce, ĭll; ōld, ōbey, ôrb, ŏdd, sŏft, cŏnnect; ūse, ūnite, ûrn, ŭp, circᴜs; fōod, fo͝ot; out, oil;

clam′or (klăm′ẽr), *n.* [5] **1.** A great shouting or outcry. **2.** Popular outcry. **3.** Any loud, esp. continued, noise. — *v. i.* To make a clamor.

clam′or-ous (-ŭs), *a.* [4] Full of clamor; vociferous; noisy. — **-ly**, *adv.* [8] — **-ness**, *n.* [8].

clamp (klămp), *n.* Something rigid that holds things together. — *v. t.* To fasten with a clamp.

clan (klăn), *n.* **1.** A social group comprising a number of households the heads of which claim descent from a common ancestor. **2.** A social group all the members of which are of common descent, traced in but one line.

clan-des′tine (klăn-dĕs′tĭn), *a.* [4] Conducted with secrecy; underhand. — **-ly**, *adv.* [8].

clang (klăng), *v. i.* To give out a clang; resound. — *v. t.* To strike together with a clang. — *n.* A loud sound like that made by pieces of metal struck together.

clan′gor (klăn′gẽr; klăng′ẽr), *n.* A sharp, harsh resonant sound; clang.

clank (klăngk), *n.* A sharp, brief, ringing sound. — *v. i.* To make, or sound or move with, a clank. — *v. t.* [1] To cause to sound with a clank.

clan′nish (klăn′ĭsh), *a.* [4] Of, pert. to, or characteristic of, a clan. — **-ly**, *adv.* [8] — **-ness**, *n.* [8].

clans′man (klănz′măn), *n.; pl.* **-MEN.** One of a clan.

clap (klăp), *v. i. ;* CLAPPED or CLAPT; CLAP′-PING. **1.** To make a clap or clatter. **2.** To clap the hands in applause. — *v. t.* **1.** To strike resoundingly. **2. a** To strike (the hands) together to express applause. **b** To applaud by clapping. **3.** To put, thrust, etc., vigorously and effectually. — *n.* **1.** A loud noise made by the striking together of hard surfaces ; esp., a peal of thunder. **2.** The sound made by striking the hands together, or the act of so doing, esp. to express applause. **3.** A resounding blow, as with the hand.

clap′board (klăp′bôrd ; *colloq.* klăb′ôrd, -ẽrd), *n.* A narrow board, thicker at one edge than at the other, for weatherboarding frame buildings. *U. S.*

clap′per (klăp′ẽr), *n.* That which claps or makes a noise, as the tongue of a bell.

clap′trap′ (-trăp′), *n.* A trick, device, or expression, or language or show, designed to gain applause.

clar′et (-ĕt), *n.* **1.** Any of various red wines. **2.** The color of claret ; a purplish red.

clar′i-fi-ca′tion (-ĭ-fĭ-kā′shŭn), *n.* Act or process of clarifying.

clar′i-fy (klăr′ĭ-fī), *v. t. & i.* [2] To make or become pure and clear; clear. — **-fi′er** (-fī′ẽr), *n.* [8].

clar′i-net′ (-nĕt′), *n. Music.* A wind instrument having a bell-mouthed tube with a single reed.

clar′i-on (-ŭn), *n.* Kind of trumpet with clear shrill tones ; also, the sound of a clarion. *Poetic.*

clar′i-ty (-ĭ-tĭ), *n.* Clearness.

clash (klăsh), *v. i.* **1.** To make a clash. **2.** To collide ; come into conflict. — *v. t.* To strike with a clash. — *n.* **1.** A loud noise resulting from collision; a collision. **2.** Opposition; conflict.

clasp (klăsp), *v. t.* **1.** To fasten together with a clasp. **2.** To cling or entwine about ; embrace. **3.** To seize with or in the hand. — *n.* **1.** Any of various forms of catch or hook. **2.** An embrace; grasp.

class (klås), *n.* **1.** A group or division of persons or things of the same rank, or having common characteristics. **2.** A rank or grade of society ;

social rank, esp. high rank. **3. a** A body of students graduating in the same year. **b** An assembling of students, as for recitation. — *v. t.* To place in a class or its class. — *v. i.* To be classed.

clas′sic (klăs′ĭk), *n.* A work, esp. in literature or art, of the highest class and of acknowledged excellence, or its author ; — used esp., usually in *pl.*, of Greek and Latin works or authors.

clas′sic (klăs′ĭk) ⎱ *a.* [4] **1.** Of or relating to
clas′si-cal (-ĭ-kăl) ⎰ the first class or rank, esp. in literature or art; standard. **2.** Of or pertaining to the ancient Greeks and Romans or their culture, esp. their authors, artists, etc. — **-ly**, *adv.* [8].

clas′si-cism (-ĭ-sĭz′m), *n.* Conformity to, or practice of, classical style.

clas′si-cist (-sĭst), *n.* **1.** An advocate of classical style, etc. **2.** One learned in the classics.

clas′si-fi-ca′tion (-fĭ-kā′shŭn), *n.* **1.** Act of classifying. **2.** A systematic arrangement in classes.

clas′si-fy (-fī), *v. t.* [2] To distribute into classes; arrange in classes. — **-fi′a-ble** (-fī′à-b′l), *a.* [8].

class′mate′ (klås′māt′), *n.* One belonging to the same class with another, as at school or college.

clat′ter (klăt′ẽr), *v. i. & t.* To make a clatter; cause to clatter; rattle. — *n.* A rattling noise.

clause (klôz), *n.* **1.** A single passage of a discourse or writing ; a distinct article in a formal document. **2.** In grammar, a simple sentence forming part of a complex or compound sentence.

clav′i-cle (-k′l), *n. Anat.* A bone joined to the breastbone and the shoulder blade; the collar bone.

claw (klô), *n.* **1.** A sharp nail on the finger or toe of an animal, esp. when slender and curved. **2.** One of the pincerlike organs forming the end of certain limbs of lobsters, crabs, etc. **3.** Something suggestive of an animal's claw. — *v. t. & i.* [1] To tear, scratch, etc., with or as with claws.

clay (klā), *n.* **1.** A widely distributed earth, plastic and tenacious when moist and hardening when baked, and hence used in making pottery, brick, etc. **2.** Loosely, earth ; mud.

clay′ey (-ĭ), *a.* [3] Composed of, or like, clay.

clean (klēn), *a.* [3] **1.** Free from what defiles; untarnished; unsoiled. **2.** Habitually clean; cleanly. **3.** Free from obstructions or imperfections. **4.** Shapely ; trim. — *adv.* **1.** Cleanly. **2.** Quite; wholly. — *v. t.* To render clean; purify. — *v. i.* To undergo or perform the process of cleaning.

clean′ly (klĕn′lĭ), *a.* [3] Habitually clean or kept clean. — **clean′li-ness**, *n.* [8].

clean′ly (klēn′lĭ), *adv.* In a clean manner.

clean′ness (-nĕs), *n.* Quality or state of being clean.

cleanse (klĕnz), *v. t.* [1] To render clean; clean. — **cleans′er**, *n.* [8].

clear (klēr), *a.* [3] **1.** Free from all that dims, blurs, or obscures. **2.** Free from contamination or admixture; clean; pure. **3.** Distinctly heard, seen, or understood. **4.** Keen ; discriminating. **5.** Free from doubt; certain; sure; — used of persons. **6.** Free from burden, charges, encumbrance, debt, etc. — *adv.* Clearly. — *v. t.* **1.** To make clear ; free from muddiness, impediment, obligation, etc. **2.** To free from imputation, as of guilt. **3.** To remove so as to leave something clear. **4.** To leap or pass by or over without touching. **5.** To gain without deduction. — *v. i.* **1.** To become clear. **2.** *Naut.* To get permission to leave port, or to discharge cargo. **3.** *Banking.* To exchange checks and bills and settle balances.

clear'ance (klēr'ăns), *n.* **1.** Act of clearing. **2.** The distance by which one object clears another.

clear'ing, *n.* **1.** Act or process of one that clears. **2.** A tract of land cleared of wood, as for cultivation. **3.** A method adopted by bankers for making an exchange of checks and settling differences of accounts. — *clearing house,* an institution for carrying on the business of clearing.

clear'ly, *adv.* In a clear manner or degree.

clear'ness (-nĕs),*n.* Quality or state of being clear.

cleat (klēt), *n.* **1.** A device, usually having two arms, used to secure a line. **2.** A strip fastened across something to strengthen or hold in position.

cleav'a-ble (klēv'ả-b'l), *a.* [4] That can be cleft.

cleav'age (-ăj), *n.* **1.** Act of cleaving, or splitting ; division. **2.** The quality or peculiarity of structure of many crystallized substances and rocks of splitting readily in certain directions.

cleave (klēv), *v. i.* To adhere closely ; cling.

cleave, *v. t. ; pret.* CLEFT (klĕft), CLEAVED (klēvd); *p. p.* CLEFT, CLEAVED, or CLO'VEN (klō'v'n); *p. pr. & vb. n.* CLEAV'ING. **1.** To part or divide by force, as by cutting. **2.** To sever by cutting or splitting. — *v. i.* **1.** To part ; separate. **2.** To make a way by or as by cutting.

cleav'er (klēv'ẽr), *n.* One that cleaves, as a butcher's instrument for cutting up carcasses.

clef (klĕf), *n.* A character used in musical notation to determine the position and pitch of the scale on the staff.

G. Treble, or Violin, Clef.

F, or Bass, Clef.

Clef.

cleft (klĕft), *pret. & p. p.* from CLEAVE, to part.

cleft, *n.* A space or opening made by splitting.

clem'a-tis (klĕm'ả-tĭs), *n.* Any of various flowering vines or erect herbs of the crowfoot family.

clem'en-cy (-ĕn-sĭ),*n.;pl.*-CIES(-sĭz). **1.** Disposition to forgive and spare ; leniency or an act or instance of it. **2.** Mildness (of the weather, climate).

clem'ent (-ĕnt), *a.* [4] Compassionate ; lenient.

clench (klĕnch), *v. t.* **1.** To clinch. **2.** To set closely together, as the teeth or hands. **3.** To grasp firmly ; grip. — *n.* A thing that clenches ; a clinch. — **clench'er,** *n.* [8].

cler'gy (klûr'jĭ), *n. ; pl.* -GIES (-jĭz). The body of men formally ordained to the service of God.

cler'gy-man (-măn), *n.; pl.* -MEN (-mĕn). A member of the clergy ; an ordained minister.

cler'ic (klĕr'ĭk), *n.* A clergyman.

cler'i-cal (-ĭ-kăl), *a.* [4] **1.** Of or pert. to the clergy. **2.** Of or pert. to a clerk or copyist.

clerk (klûrk; *in England commonly* klärk), *n.* **1.** A layman who performs some minor ecclesiastical office. **2.** One employed to keep records, have charge of correspondence, etc. **3.** A salesman or saleswoman, esp. at retail. *U.S.*—**clerk'ly,***a.* [8].

clerk'ship, *n.* The office or business of a clerk.

clev'er (klĕv'ẽr), *a.* [3] **1.** Possessing quickness of intellect, skill, dexterity, or talent. **2.** Showing skill. —**-ly,** *adv.* [8] —**-ness,** *n.* [8].

clew, clue (kloo), *n.* **1.** A ball of thread, yarn,

or cord. **2.** That which guides in any doubtful or intricate matter. **3.** *Naut.* A lower corner of a square sail, or the after lower corner of a fore-and-aft sail. — *v. t.* To haul (a sail) up to a yard or mast, as for furling ; — with *up.*

click (klĭk), *n.* A pawl or ratchet.

click (klĭk), *n.* A slight sharp noise. — *v. i. & t.* To make, or cause to make, a click.

cli'ent (klī'ĕnt), *n.* One who consults a legal adviser or submits his cause to his management; also, one who consults any expert.

cli'en-tele (klī'ĕn-tēl'; -tēl'),*n.* A body of clients ; clients collectively ; hence, a body of customers.

cliff (klĭf), *n.* A high, steep face of rock.

cli'mate (klī'mȧt), *n.* The average condition of a place or locality as to temperature, moisture, etc.

cli-mat'ic (klī-măt'ĭk), *a.* Pertaining to climate.

cli'ma-tol'o-gy (klī'mȧ-tŏl'ỏ-jĭ), *n.* Science of climates and their phenomena.

cli'max (klī'măks), *n.* **1.** A figure of speech in which ideas in a sentence or paragraph are so arranged that each succeeding idea exceeds its predecessor in force. **2.** The last or highest member of a rhetorical climax ; highest point ; acme.

climb (klīm), *v. i. & t.* **1.** To ascend or mount, esp. by using the hands and feet; ascend. **2.** *Bot.* To ascend in growth by twining or by tendrils, aërial roots, etc. — *n.* Act of climbing ; a place to be climbed. — **-er,** *n.* [8].

clime (klīm), *n.* A region or climate.

clinch (klĭnch), *v. t.* **1.** To fix securely, esp. by bending over the point of (something driven through) so as to hold fast; to fasten in this way. **2.** To make conclusive, as an argument ; clench. — *v. i.* **1.** To clinch something. **2.** To seize one another firmly, or to seize another firmly, as in wrestling or fighting. *U. S.* — *n.* **1.** Act or process of clinching. **2.** A clinched fastening ; that which clinches. — **clinch'er,** *n.* [8].

cling (klĭng), *v. i. ; pret.* CLUNG (klŭng) ; CLING'ING. **1.** To adhere closely, as a wet garment; stick or hold fast, as by embracing. **2.** To keep near.

clin'ic (klĭn'ĭk), *n. Med.* **a** Instruction of a class by examination and treatment of patients in its presence. **b** The class itself.

clin'i-cal (-ĭ-kăl), *a. Med.* Of or pert. to a clinic.

clink (klĭngk), *v. i.* [1] To make, or to move with, a clink, or tinkling sound. — *v. t.* To cause to clink. — *n.* A slight, sharp, tinkling sound.

clink'er (klĭngk'ẽr), *n.* Vitrified stony matter, as in a furnace ; slag.

clip (klĭp), *v. t. & i. ;* CLIPPED (klĭpt) or CLIPT ; CLIP'PING. To clutch ; hold tightly. — *n.* Any of various devices for clasping.

clip, *v. t.* **1.** To cut, cut off, or snip ; esp., to cut the hair or fleece of ; shear. **2.** To curtail ; cut short; as, to *clip* one's words. — *v. i.* To move swiftly. *Colloq.* — *n.* **1.** A clipping ; the product of a single shearing of sheep. **2.** A sharp blow, as with the hand. *Colloq.* **3.** A rapid gait. *Colloq.*

clip'per (klĭp'ẽr), *n.* **1.** One that clips something; esp., in *pl.*, an instrument or machine for clipping hair. **2.** One that clips, or goes fast, as a horse, a sled, etc. ; esp., a kind of fast-sailing vessel.

clip'ping,*n.* **1.** Act of cutting or trimming. **2.** That which is clipped off or out of something.

āle, senāte, cȧre, ăm, ȧccount, ärm, ȧsk, sofả ; ēve, ĕvent, ĕnd, recĕnt, makẽr; īce, ĭll; ōld, ỏbey, ôrb, ŏdd, sôft, cỏnnect ; ūse, ŭnite, ûrn, ŭp, circŭs; fōōd, fŏŏt; out. oil;

clipt (klĭpt), *pret. & p. p.* of CLIP.

clique (klēk), *n.* A small, exclusive set or coterie.

cloak (klōk), *n.* 1. A loose outer garment. 2. That which conceals; disguise; mask. — *v. t.* To cover with or as with a cloak; hide; conceal.

clock (klŏk), *n.* An ornamental figure or figured work on the ankle or side of a stocking.

clock (klŏk), *n.* Any of various devices for measuring and indicating time; a timepiece, not intended to be carried on the person.

clock'work′ (-wûrk′),*n.* The machinery of a clock, or machinery suggestive of that of a clock.

clod (klŏd), *n.* 1. A lump or mass, esp. of earth. 2. The soil; earth. 3. That which is earthy, as the body in relation to the soul. 4. Stupid fellow.

clod′hop′per (-hŏp′ẽr), *n.* 1. A rude, rustic fellow. 2. *pl.* Heavy and clumsy work shoes.

clog (klŏg), *n.* 1. A weight, as a log, on an animal or a vehicle, to hinder motion. 2. Impediment; encumbrance. 3. A kind of wooden-soled shoe; also, a light form of this used in dancing. 4. A dance by one wearing clogs. — *v. t.;* CLOGGED (klŏgd) CLOG′GING. To encumber; hamper; obstruct; choke up. — *v. i.* To become clogged.

clois′ter (klois′tẽr), *n.* 1. A monastery or nunnery. 2. A covered passage, usually having one side an open arcade or colonnade. — *v. t.* [1] To confine in a cloister; seclude.

clois′tral (-trăl), *a.* Pertaining to a cloister.

close (klōs), *a.* [3] 1. Shut fast; closed. 2. Narrow; confined. 3. Strictly confined; guarded. 4. Out of the way of observation; hidden. 5. Secretive; reticent. 6. Oppressive; causing lassitude. 7. Near in space, time, or thought. 8. Dense; compressed. 9. Short. 10. Intimate, confidential. 11. Parsimonious; stingy. 12. Accurate; precise. 13. Closed to public competition or admission. 14. Closed to hunters or fishermen; — of a season when game or fish may not lawfully be taken. 15. Nearly equal or balanced. — *adv.* Closely.

close (klōz), *v. t.* [1] 1. To stop up; shut. 2. To bring to an end; conclude. 3. To bring together the parts of; unite; as, to *close* the ranks. — *v. i.* 1. To come together; unite, as parts separated. 2. To come close; hence, to engage at close quarters. 3. To end; terminate. 4. To agree. — *n.* Conclusion; ending; end.

close (klōs), *n.* An inclosed place.

close′fist′ed (klōs′fĭs′tĕd), *a.* [4] Stingy.

close′ly (klōs′lĭ), *adv.* In a close manner.

close′ness, *n.* State or quality of being close.

clos′et (klŏz′ĕt), *n.* 1. A close small room for privacy. 2. A potentate's private chamber for counsel or devotions. 3. A small room or recess for clothing, etc. 4. A water-closet. — *v. t.* To take into a closet for a secret interview.

clo′sure (klō′zhụr), *n.* 1. That which incloses or confines; inclosure. 2. Conclusion; close. 3. A proceeding for closing parliamentary debate.

clot (klŏt), *n.* A mass; lump, as of coagulated matter. — *v. i. & t.;* CLOT′TED; CLOT′TING. To coagulate, thicken, or form into a clot.

cloth (klŏth), *n.; pl.* CLOTHS (klŏ̵t̵hz; klŏths), except in the sense of garments, when it is CLOTHES (klō̵t̵hz). 1. A pliable fabric for garments, etc.;

esp.,a woolen fabric. 2. *pl.* (CLOTHES). See CLOTHES. 3. The distinctive dress of any profession, esp. of the clergy; hence, with *the*, the clergy.

clothe (klō̵t̵h), *v. t.;* CLOTHED (klō̵t̵hd) or CLAD (klăd); CLOTH′ING (klō̵t̵h′ĭng). 1. To provide with garments, or clothes; to dress. 2. To cover or invest as with a garment.

clothes (klō̵t̵hz), *n. pl.* 1. Covering for the body; dress. 2. Bedclothes.

cloth′ier (klō̵t̵h′yẽr), *n.* One who makes or sells cloths or clothes.

cloth′ing (-ĭng), *n.* Garments in general; clothes.

cloud (kloud), *n.* 1. A visible mass of fog or haze suspended at some distance above the surface of the earth. 2. A mass or volume of smoke or flying dust. 3. A dark or opaque vein or spot, as in marble. 4. Something having a dark, lowering, or threatening aspect. — *v. t.* 1. To overspread or hide with a cloud or clouds. 2. To darken; obscure; render gloomy. — *v. i.* To grow cloudy.

cloud′-burst′, *n.* A sudden copious rainfall.

cloud′less, *a.* Clear; bright.

cloud′y (kloud′ĭ), *a.* [3] 1. Consisting of, or pertaining to, a cloud or clouds. 2. Overcast with clouds. 3. Confused; obscure; not clear. — **cloud′i-ly**, *adv.* [8] — **cloud′i-ness**, *n.* [8].

clove (klōv), *pret. & archaic p. p.* of CLEAVE.

clove, *n.* The dried flower bud of a certain tropical tree of the myrtle family, used as a spice.

clo′ven (klō′v'n), *p. p. & p. a.* from CLEAVE, *v. t.*

clo′ver (klō′vẽr), *n.* A certain low herb having leaves of three leaflets and flowers in dense heads.

clown (kloun), *n.* 1. A rustic; ill-bred fellow; boor. 2. The buffoon in a play, circus, etc.

clown′ish (kloun′ĭsh), *a.* [4] Of or resembling a clown; ill-bred. — **-ly**, *adv.* [8] — **-ness**, *n.* [8].

cloy (kloi), *v. t.* To glut, or satisfy; surfeit.

club (klŭb), *n.* 1. A heavy staff of wood; cudgel. 2. A stick or bat used in various games with a ball. 3. *Playing cards.* Any card of the suit (called *clubs*) having a figure like the clover leaf. 4. An association of persons to promote a common object. 5. The house, or rooms of a club (sense 4). — *v. t. & i.;* CLUBBED (klŭbd); CLUB′BING. 1. To beat with a club. 2. To unite in a club.

club′foot′ (-fŏŏt′), *n. Med.* **a** (*pl.* CLUBFEET.) A short, distorted foot. **b** The deformity which such a foot exhibits. — **club′foot′ed** (-fŏŏt′ĕd), *a.*

cluck (klŭk), *v. i.* To utter the call of a brooding hen. — *n.* The call of a hen to her chickens.

clue (klōō), *n. & v.* Clew. See CLEW.

clump (klŭmp), *n.* A lump; cluster; group.

clump, *v. i.* To tread clumsily or heavily.

clum′sy (klŭm′zĭ), *a.* [3] Without skill or grace; awkward; hence, ill-made or inappropriate. — **-si-ly**, *adv.* [8] — **-si-ness**, *n.* [8].

clung (klŭng), *pret. & p. p.* of CLING.

clus′ter (klŭs′tẽr), *n.* A number of similar things growing or grouped together; bunch; group. — *v. i. & t.* To grow, gather, or unite, in a cluster.

clutch, *v. t.* To seize or gripe with the hand, hands, or claws. — *v. i.* To reach (at something) as if to grasp; snatch. — *n.* 1. A claw, talon, or hand in the act of grasping firmly. 2. A gripe; grasp. 3. A coupling for connecting two working parts; any device for gripping.

chair; go; sing, iŋk; ŧhen, thin; nature, verdure; yet; zh = z in azure. Numbers refer to §§ in the Special Notes which, with Abbreviations, Signs, etc., precede the Vocabulary.

clut'ter (klŭt′ẽr), n. A confused collection; hence, crowded confusion; disorder. — v. t. To crowd together in disorder; disarrange.

coach (kōch), n. 1. A kind of large, close, four-wheeled carriage. 2. *Colloq.* a One who coaches a student. b An instructor in athletics. 3. A passenger car. — v. t. To prepare (another) for examination, or for a contest, privately. *Colloq.*

coach'man (kōch′măn), n.; pl. -MEN (-mĕn). A man whose business is to drive a coach or carriage.

co'ad-ju'tor (kō′ă̇-jōō′tẽr), n. One who aids.

co-ag'u-late (kọ̈-ăg′ū-lāt), v. t. & i. [1] To curdle or congeal, esp. by chemical action.

co-ag'u-la'tion (-lā′shŭn), n. Action of coagulating; state of being coagulated; curdling; clotting.

coal (kōl), n. 1. A piece of glowing carbon or charred wood or the like; ember. 2. = CHARCOAL. 3. A black, or brownish black, solid, combustible mineral. — v. t. To supply, as a steamship, with coal. — v. i. To take in coal.

co'a-lesce' (kō′ȧ-lĕs′), v. i. [1] 1. To grow together. 2. To unite in one body or product.

co'a-les'cence (-ĕns),n. Act or state of coalescing.

co'a-les'cent (-lĕs′ĕnt), a. Growing together.

co'a-li'tion (kō′ȧ-lĭsh′ŭn), n. A union; combination; alliance, as of parties.

coal oil. Petroleum; esp., kerosene.

coal tar. Tar distilled from bituminous coal.

coarse (kōrs), a. [3] 1. Common; of inferior quality or appearance. 2. Large in bulk, or composed of large particles; gross. 3. Harsh or rude; vulgar. — **ly,** adv. [8] — **ness,** n. [8].

coars'en, v. t. & i. To make or turn coarse.

coast (kōst), n. The seashore, or land near it. — v. i. 1. To sail along a coast. 2. To slide, as on a sled, or glide, as on a bicycle, down a hill. — v. t. To sail along the coast of. — **coast'al,** a.

coast'er, n. One that coasts; esp., a coastwise vessel.

coast'wise' (-wīz′), adv. & a. By way of or along the coast; as, to sail *coastwise* ; *coastwise* trade.

coat (kōt), n. 1. An outer garment fitting the upper part of the body. 2. The natural covering of animals (as fur, hair, etc.). 3. A covering layer of anything. — v. t. To cover with a coat. — **coat of arms,** the heraldic emblems of a person, taken together.

coat'ing (kōt′ĭng), n. A coat, or covering.

coax (kōks), v. t. 1. To influence by gentle courtesy, flattering, or fondling; wheedle. 2. To obtain, induce, or effect by such acts. — v. i. To coax a person; use coaxing. — **coax'er,** n. [8].

cob (kŏb), n. 1. = CORNCOB. 2. A short-legged, stocky, rather small horse.

co'balt (kō′bôlt), n. A tough, lustrous, reddish white metal occurring with iron and nickel.

cob'ble (kŏb′'l), n. A cobblestone.

cob'ble, v. t. & i. To make or mend coarsely; patch, as shoes.

cob'bler (-lẽr), n. 1. A mender of shoes. 2. A clumsy workman; botcher.

cob'ble-stone' (-'l-stōn′), n. A naturally rounded stone larger than a pebble, often used in paving.

co'bra (kō′brȧ), n. A very venomous snake of the warm parts of Asia, esp. India.

cob'web (kŏb′wĕb′), n. 1. The network, or a single thread of it, spun by a spider. 2. Anything suggestive of a spider web as being flimsy, clogging, entangling, etc. — v. t.; -WEBBED′ (-wĕbd′); -WEB-BING. To cover with cobwebs.

co'ca (kō′kȧ), n. A certain South American shrub or its dried leaves, which yield cocaine.

co'ca-ine (kō′kȧ-ĭn; -ēn ; *colloq. and commonly* kō-kān′), n. A bitter crystalline alkaloid got from coca leaves and used as a local anæsthetic.

coc'cyx (kŏk′sĭks), n.; L. pl.-CYGES (-sī′jēz). *Anat.* The lower end of the spinal column.

coch'i-neal (kŏch′ĭ-nēl), n. A dyestuff consisting of the dried bodies of females of a certain insect.

cock (kŏk), n. A small conical pile, esp. of hay. — v. t. To put into a cock or cocks, as hay.

cock, n. 1. The male of the common barnyard fowl or of any of various birds. 2. A weathercock. 3. A chief person; leader. 4. A faucet, tap, valve, etc. 5. The hammer in the lock of a firearm or the cocked position of the hammer. — v. t. & i. To draw the hammer of (a firearm) fully back and set it for firing.

cock, v. t. & i. To set, turn, or stick up, esp. in a pert or defiant way; as, to *cock* the ears, or a hat. — n. Act of cocking or the tilt so given.

cock-ade' (-ād′), n. A rosette, knot, or the like, worn on the hat as a badge.

cock'a-too' (-ȧ-tōō′), n. Any of various parrots.

cock'chaf'er (-chāf′ẽr), n. A large European stout-bodied beetle often destructive to vegetation.

cock'er-el (-ẽr-ĕl), n. A young domestic cock.

cock'le (kŏk′'l), n. Any of several plants growing in grainfields, as the darnel.

cock'le, n. 1. A kind of shellfish having a shell composed of two ribbed, somewhat heart-shaped, parts, joined by a hinge. 2. A cockleshell. 3. A small light boat. — **cockles of the heart,** depths of the heart; inmost feelings.

Cockle.

cock'le, v. t. & i. [1] To pucker; wrinkle. — n. Pucker; wrinkle.

cock'le-shell' (-'l-shĕl′), n. 1. One of the shells of a cockle. 2. A light boat.

cock'ney (-nĭ), n.; pl. -NEYS (-nĭz). A native or a long-established resident of London, esp. of the East End, talking with a certain characteristic dialect. — a. Of or relating to, or like, cockneys.

cock'pit' (-pĭt′), n. *Naut.* a In old sailing war vessels, the quarters for junior officers, occupied by the wounded in engagements. b In small vessels, a space aft lower than the deck.

cock'roach' (-rōch′), n. A well-known nocturnal insect of flattened form.

cocks'comb' (kŏks′kōm′), n. 1. a A cock's comb or crest. b = COXCOMB. 2. A garden plant of the amaranth family, cultivated for its showy blossoms.

cock'swain. Var. of COXSWAIN.

co'co (kō′kō), n., *or* **coco palm.** A tall palm of the tropics; also, its fruit, the coconut.

co'coa (kō′kō), n. 1. = CACAO, 1. 2. Pulverized seeds of the cacao or the beverage from them.

co'coa-nut' (kō′kō-nŭt′). Var. of COCONUT.

co'co-nut' (-kȧ-nŭt′), n. The fruit of the coco.

co-coon' (kọ̈-kōōn′), n. The silky envelope in which many insects pass the pupa stage.

cod (kŏd), *n.* A fish of the colder parts of the North Atlantic. It is one of the chief food fishes.

cod'dle (kŏd''l), *v. t.* [1] **1.** To parboil; stew. **2.** To treat with excessive tenderness; pamper.

code (kōd), *n.* **1.** A systematic body of law; digest. **2.** Any system or collection of principles or rules relating to one subject. **3.** A system of signals for communication, as in telegraphy; also, a system of words or other symbols arbitrarily used.

cod'fish' (kŏd'fĭsh'), *n.* The cod.

codg'er (kŏj'ẽr), *n.* A singular or odd person.

cod'i-cil (kŏd'ĭ-sĭl), *n.* *Law.* A supplement to a will, modifying it in some respect.

co·di-fi-ca'tion (kō'dĭ-fĭ-kā'shŭn; kŏd'ĭ-), *n.* Act, process, or result of codifying.

co'di-fy (kō'dĭ-fī; kŏd'ĭ-), *v. t.* [2] To reduce to a code, as laws.

co-ed'u-ca'tion (kō-ĕd'ŭ-kā'shŭn), *n.* Joint education of both sexes at one institution. — **-al** (-ăl), *a.*

co·ef-fi'cient (kō'ĕ-fĭsh'ĕnt), *n.* *Math.* Any symbol or group of symbols placed before another or others as a multiplier; as, in 6 *x* the *coefficient* is 6.

co·e'qual (kō-ē'kwăl), *a.* Being equal, as in rank, age, or extent. — *n.* One coequal with another.

co-erce' (kō-ûrs'), *v. t.* [1] To constrain or restrain by force, esp. by authority; repress; compel; force. — *v. i.* To use coercion.

co-er'cion (-ûr'shŭn), *n.* Act or power of coercing.

co-er'cive (-sĭv), *a.* Serving or intended to coerce.

co-e'val (kō-ē'văl), *a.* Of the same age. — *n.* A contemporary.

co'ex-tend' (kō'ĕks-tĕnd'), *v. t. & i.* To extend through the same space or time with another.

co'ex-ten'sive (-tĕn'sĭv), *a.* Having the same or equal extent in space or time; having the same limits.

cof'fee (kŏf'ĭ), *n.* **1.** A drink made from the seeds of a certain shrub of the madder family. **2.** The seeds of the shrub; also, the shrub.

cof'fee-house' (-hous'), *n.* A restaurant where coffee and other refreshments are served.

cof'fer (-ẽr), *n.* **1.** A casket, chest, or trunk, esp. one for valuables. **2.** Fig.: Treasure or funds; — usually in *pl.*

Coffee. 1 Flowering Branch with Leaves ($\frac{1}{4}$) : 3 Fruit in section ($\frac{1}{2}$) : 4 Seeds ($\frac{1}{2}$).

cof'fer-dam' (-dăm'), *n.* A water-tight inclosure from which the water is pumped to expose the bottom (of a river, etc.).

cof'fin (kŏf'ĭn), *n.* A chest or case for a corpse.

cog (kŏg), *n.* **1.** *Carp.* A tenon or projection on a beam or timber to be received into a notch or mortise in another. **2.** *Mach.* A tooth, cam, or the like, for transmitting motion.

co'gen-cy (kō'jĕn-sĭ), *n.* Quality of being cogent.

co'gent (kō'jĕnt), *a.* [4] Compelling or constraining; esp., convincing. — **-ly**, *adv.* [8].

cog'i-tate (kŏj'ĭ-tāt), *v. t. & i.* [1] To think; ponder over; plan.

cog'i-ta'tion (-tā'shŭn), *n.* Act of cogitating.

co'gnac (kō'nyăk), *n.* A superior French brandy.

cog'nate (kŏg'nāt), *a.* **1.** Allied by blood. **2.** Of the same stock; allied. **3.** Of the same or similar nature. — *n.* One cognate with another.

cog-ni'tion (kŏg-nĭsh'ŭn), *n.* Act or fact of knowing; also, knowledge.

cog'ni-za-ble (kŏg'nĭ-zȧ-b'l; kŏn'ĭ-), *a.* **1.** Knowable. **2.** Subject to judicial cognizance.

cog'ni-zance (kŏg'nĭ-zăns; kŏn'ĭ-zăns; *the second is still common in legal usage*), *n.* **1.** Knowledge; hence, heed; notice. **2.** *Law.* **a** Jurisdiction. **b** The judicial hearing of a matter.

cog'ni-zant (-zănt), *a.* [4] Having cognizance (of)

cog-no'men (kŏg-nō'mĕn), *n.* A surname.

cog'wheel' (kŏg'hwēl'), *n.* A wheel with cogs.

co-hab'it (kō-hăb'ĭt), *v. i.* To live together as husband and wife.

co-hab'i-ta'tion (-ĭ-tā'shŭn), *n.* Act of cohabiting

co-heir' (kō-âr'), *n.* A joint heir. — **-ess**, *n. fem.*

co-here' (kō-hēr'), *v. i.* [1] To stick together; cleave; be united.

co-her'ence (-hēr'ĕns) } *n.* **1.** A sticking together; **co-her'en-cy** (-ĕn-sĭ) } cohesion. **2.** Connection; congruity; consistency.

co-her'ent (-ĕnt), *a.* [4] **1.** Sticking together, cleaving. **2.** Following logical order, connection, or arrangement; consistent. — **-ly**, *adv.* [8].

co-he'sion (-hē'zhŭn), *n.* Act or state of cohering; specifically, that form of attraction by which the particles of a body are held united.

co-he'sive (-sĭv), *a.* [4] Sticking together; marked by cohesion. — **-ly**, *adv.* [8] — **-ness**, *n.* [8].

co'hort (kō'hôrt), *n.* **1.** In the Roman army, one of the ten divisions of a legion. **2.** Any band of warriors; fig., a company; band.

coif (koif), *n.* A close-fitting cap, like a small hood

coif'fure' (kwä'fūr'; koif'ūr), *n.* A headdress, or manner of dressing the hair.

coign (koin), *n.* Var. of COIN, QUOIN, a projecting corner, wedge, etc.; — chiefly used in **coign of vantage**, an advantageous position.

coil (koil), *v. t. & i.* To wind cylindrically or spirally. — *n.* **1.** A series of rings, or a spiral; also, a single ring of such a series. **2.** A series of connected pipes in rows, layers, or windings. **3.** *Elec.* A spiral of wire, or an instrument composed of such a spiral and its accessories.

coin (koin), *n.* **1.** A corner, corner stone, or wedge. See QUOIN. **2.** A piece of metal officially stamped and authorized to be used as money; also, such pieces collectively. — *v. t.* **1.** To make (coins) by stamping. **2.** To invent, as a word.

coin'age (-ăj), *n.* A coining; that which is coined.

co'in-cide' (kō'ĭn-sīd'), *v. i.* [1] **1.** To occupy the same place in space or the same period in time. **2.** To correspond exactly; agree; concur.

co-in'ci-dence (kō-ĭn'sĭ-dĕns), *n.* **1.** Condition or fact of coinciding. **2.** An instance of coinciding.

co-in'ci-dent (-dĕnt), *a.* Having coincidence.

coin'er (koin'ẽr), *n.* One who coins.

coir (koir), *n.* Prepared fiber of coconut husk, used in making cordage, matting, etc.

coke (kōk), *n.* Bituminous coal deprived of its volatile constituents by heating in a retort or oven.

col'an-der (kŭl'ăn-dẽr), *n.* A perforated vessel used as a sieve or strainer.

cold (kōld), *a.* [3] **1.** Of a temperature sensibly

lower than that of the body; frigid; chilly. **2.** Deficient in emotion or cordiality. **3.** Having the sensation of cold. — *n.* **1.** The relative absence of heat or warmth; chilliness. **2.** *Med.* A disordered state, generally infectious, and often following exposure ; catarrh. **3.** Cold weather ; frost.

cold'ly (kōld'lĬ), *adv.* In a cold manner.

cold'ness, *n.* State of being cold ; cold quality.

cole (kōl), *n.* A plant related to the cabbage, turnip, etc.; esp., the rape.

cole'wort (-wûrt'), *n.* **1.** = COLE. **2.** A variety of cabbage not forming a compact leafy head.

col'ic (kŏl'ĭk), *n.* A paroxysmal abdominal pain.

col-lab'o-rate (kŏ-lăb'ō-rāt), *v. i.* [1] To labor together ; work or act jointly. — **-ra'tor**, *n.* [8].

col-lab'o-ra'tion (-rā'shŭn), *n.* Act of collaborating ; united labor.

col-lapse' (kŏ-lăps'), *v. i.* [1] **1.** To fall or shrink together abruptly. **2.** To break down or fail abruptly. — *n.* An act or instance of collapsing. — **col-laps'i-ble** (-lăp'sĬ-b'l), *a.* [8].

col'lar (kŏl'ẽr), *n.* **1.** A band, chain, or the like, worn or placed round the neck for dress, restraint, etc. **2.** An encircling strap or band. — *v. t.* To put a collar on ; to seize by the collar.

collar bone. The clavicle.

col-late' (kŏ-lāt'), *v. t.* [1] To compare critically, as books or writings.

col-lat'er-al (-lăt'ẽr-ăl), *a.* **1.** Subordinate; indirect. **2.** Designating an obligation or security attached to another to secure its performance; hence, secured by additional obligation or security. **3.** Parallel; concomitant; coördinate. **4.** Belonging to the same ancestral stock, but not in a direct line of descent. — *n.* Collateral security. — **-ly**, *adv.* [8].

col-la'tion (kŏ-lā'shŭn), *n.* **1.** Any light meal or repast. **2.** Act of comparing, as manuscripts.

col'league (kŏl'ēg), *n.* An associate in a profession, office, or employment.

col'lect (kŏl'ĕkt), *n.* Any of certain short ritual prayers used in some churches.

col-lect' (kŏ-lĕkt'), *v. t.* **1.** To gather into one body or place; assemble. **2.** To demand and obtain payment of, as a bill. **3.** To gather (specimens or examples), as for study or ornament. **4.** To regain command of (one's self, one's powers); rally. — *v. i.* To assemble; accumulate.

col-lec'tion (-lĕk'shŭn), *n.* **1.** Act or process of collecting. **2.** That which is collected; accumulation.

col-lec'tive (-tĬv), *a.* **1.** Formed by gathering or collecting; gathered into one mass, sum, or body; united. **2.** Characteristic of, derived from, or relating to, a group of individuals; common. **3.** *Gram.* Treating a number of objects as a group, whole, or aggregate: thus, a **collective noun** names a collection of individuals by a singular form, as *assembly, army, jury,* etc., and takes a singular verb when the aggregate is thought of as a whole, but may take a plural verb when the individuals are in mind. — *n.* *Gram.* A collective noun or name. — **col-lec'tive-ly**, *adv.* [8].

col-lec'tor (-tẽr), *n.* **1.** One that collects. **2.** An official whose duty is to collect; as, tax *collector*.

col'lege (kŏl'ĕj), *n.* **1.** A body of persons engaged

in common pursuits, or having common **interests,** and sometimes, by charter, special **rights and** privileges. **2.** A society of scholars incorporated for study or instruction, esp. in the liberal **arts ;** also, a building or buildings used by them.

col-le'gi-an (kŏ-lē'jĬ-ăn), *n.* Member of a college.

col-le'gi-ate (-āt), *a.* Of or pertaining to a college.

col-lide' (kŏ-līd'), *v. i.* [1] To strike or dash against each other; come into collision.

col'lie (kŏl'Ĭ), *n.* The Scotch shepherd dog.

col'lier (-yẽr), *n.* **1.** A coal miner. **2.** A vessel for carrying coal.

col'lier-y (-Ĭ), *n. ; pl.* -LIERIES (-Ĭz). Place where coal is dug ; a coal mine with its buildings, etc.

col-li'sion (kŏ-lĬzh'ŭn), *n.* Act or instance of colliding ; clash; conflict; opposition.

col'lo-cate (kŏl'ō-kāt), *v. t.* [1] To set or place, esp. side by side.

col'lo-ca'tion (-kā'shŭn), *n.* Act of collocating.

col-lo'di-on (kŏ-lō'dĬ-ŭn), *n.* *Chem.* A sticky solution of guncotton in a mixture of alcohol and ether, used by evaporation to form films, as for photographic use, on wounds, etc.

col-lo'qui-al (kŏ-lō'kwĬ-ăl), *a.* Pertaining to, or used in, conversation, esp. familiar conversation ; hence, informal. — **col-lo'qui-al-ly**, *adv.* [8].

col-lo'qui-al-ism (-Ĭz'm), *n.* Colloquial style or quality; a colloquial expression.

col'lo-quy (kŏl'ō-kwĬ), *n. ; pl.* -QUIES (-kwĬz). Mutual discourse ; dialogue ; conference.

col-lude' (kŏ-lūd'), *v. i.* [1] To share secretly in an action, esp. a fraudulent or deceitful one.

col-lu'sion (-lū'zhŭn), *n.* Act of colluding ; deceit.

col-lu'sive (-sĬv), *a.* [4] Characterized by, or of the nature of, collusion. — **-ly**, *adv.* [8].

co-logne' (kŏ-lōn'), *n.* An aromatic toilet water.

co'lon (kō'lŏn), *n. ; pl.* E. -LONS (-lŏnz), L. -LA (-lȧ). *Anat.* That part of the large intestine extending from cæcum to rectum.

co'lon, *n.* Punctuation. The character [:] used to separate parts of a sentence that are complete in themselves and nearly independent.

colo'nel (kûr'nĕl), *n.* The commanding officer of a regiment. See ARMY.

colo'nel-cy (-sĬ), *n.; pl.* -CIES (-sĬz). The office, rank, or commission of a colonel.

co-lo'ni-al (kŏ-lō'nĬ-ăl), *a.* Of or pertaining to a colony or colonies, specifically the thirteen British colonies which formed the United States.

col'o-nist (kŏl'ō-nĭst), *n.* A member of a colony.

col'o-ni-za'tion (-nĬ-zā'shŭn), *n.* Formation of a colony or colonies.

col'o-nize (-nīz), *v. t.* [1] **1.** To establish a colony or colonies in. **2.** To gather or establish in a colony. — *v. i.* To make or establish a colony; settle. — **col'o-niz'er** (-nīz/ẽr), *n.* [8].

col'on-nade' (kŏl'ō-nād'), *n.* *Arch.* A series or range of columns placed at regular intervals.

col'o-ny (kŏl'ō-nĬ), *n. ; pl.* -NIES (-nĬz). **1.** A company of people who settle in a remote country, but remain subject to the parent state. **2.** The district colonized ; loosely, any distant territory dependent on a ruling power. **3.** A group so situated as to resemble a colony.

col'or (kŭl'ẽr), *n.* [5] **1.** A property of visible objects, distinct from form and from light and shade,

---

āle, senāte, câre, ăm, ȧccount, ärm, ȧsk, sofȧ; ēve, ėvent, ĕnd, recĕnt, makẽr; īce, Ĭll; ōld, ȯbey, ôrb, ŏdd, sŏft, cŏnnect; ūse, ûnite, ûrn, ŭp, circŭs; fŏŏd, fŏŏt; out, oil;

depending on the kind of light reflected from their surfaces. **2.** A particular variety of the above quality; — strictly, excluding black and white. **3.** Complexion; esp., the hue of good health; blush. **4.** A paint; pigment. **5.** *pl.* A distinguishing colored badge, dress, or device. **6.** A national flag, ensign, etc.; — usually in *pl.* **7.** Outward semblance; aspect. — *v. t.* **1.** To give color to; dye; paint; stain. **2.** To misrepresent or disguise. **3.** To imbue with a quality likened to color. — *v. i.* To acquire or change color.

col'or-a-ble (kŭl'ẽr-ȧ-b'l), *a.* [4, 5] **1.** Capable of being colored. **2.** Specious; deceptive.

col'or-a'tion (kŭl'ẽr-ā'shŭn; kŏl'ŏ-rā'-), *n.* Act or art of coloring; state of being colored; arrangement, combination, or use of colors.

col'ored (kŭl'ẽrd), *a.* [5] **1.** Having color. **2.** Having a skin other than white, as a negro.

col'or-ing, *n.* [5] **1.** Act of applying color, the effect so produced, or that which produces color. **2.** Change of appearance, as by color.

col'or-ist, *n.* [5] One who colors; an artist who excels in the use of color.

col'or-less, *a.* [5] Without color.

co-los'sal (kŏ-lŏs'ăl), *a.* [4] Of the size of a colossus; gigantic.

Col'os-se'um (kŏl'ŏ-sē'ŭm), *n.* An amphitheater built at Rome about 80 A. D.

Colosseum.

co-los'sus (-lŏs'ŭs), *n.; pl.* L. -SI (-ī), E. -SUSES (-sŭs-ĕz). **1.** A statue of gigantic size. **2.** Anything of gigantic size or overawing greatness.

col'por'tage (kŏl'pōr'tàj; kŏl'pŏr'tàzh'), *n.* A colporteur's work.

col'por'teur (kŏl'pōr'tẽr; kŏl'pŏr'tûr'), *n.* A hawker; esp., one who goes about distributing religious tracts or books.

colt (kōlt), *n.* **1.** The young of the horse. **2.** One like a colt, esp. in youth and inexperience.

col'ter (kōl'tẽr), *n.* A cutter on a plow, to cut the sward.

colt'ish, *a.* [4] Like a colt; frisky.

col'um-bine (kŏl'ŭm-bīn; -bĭn), *a.* Of or pertaining to a dove; dovelike.

col'um-bine (-bĭn), *n.* A certain flowering plant of the crowfoot family.

Columbine. (⅓)

Columbus Day. October 12, on which day, in 1492, Columbus discovered America.

col'umn (kŏl'ŭm), *n.* **1.** *Arch.* A kind of supporting pillar; esp., a pillar with shaft, base, and capital, the shaft being round. **2.** Anything like or suggestive of such a column; as, a *column* of air, water, etc.; spinal *column; column* of figures. **3.** *Print.* One of two or more upright sections separated by a rule or blank. **4.** A formation of soldiers or ships placed one behind another.

co-lum'nar (kŏ-lŭm'nȧr), *a.* **1.** Formed in columns; like a column. **2.** Pertaining to, or characterized by, columns.

co'ma (kō'mȧ), *n.* A state of deep insensibility, due to disease, injury, or poison.

co'ma, *n.; pl.* COMAE (kō'mē). **1.** *Astron.* A cloudlike mass around the nucleus of a comet. **2.** *Bot.* A tuft or bunch, as on the seed of the cotton.

com'a-tose (kŏm'ȧ-tōs; kō'mȧ-), *a.* [4] Relating to or like coma; lethargic. — **-ly,** *adv.* [8].

comb (kōm), *n.* **1. a** A toothed instrument for adjusting, cleaning, or confining the hair, or for adornment. **b** A currycomb. **2.** Any of various instruments like or suggestive of a comb (sense 1), as one for carding wool. **3.** The fleshy crest on the head of the domestic fowl, etc. **4.** Something resembling a cock's comb, as the crest of a wave. **5.** A honeycomb. — *v. t.* To smooth out or adjust with or as with a comb. — *v. i. Naut.* To roll over or break, as a wave crest.

com'bat (kŏm'băt), *v. i.* To contend, as with an opposing force; fight. — *v. t.* To oppose by force, argument, etc.; resist. — *n.* A fight; contest.

com'bat-ant (kŏm'băt-ănt), *a.* [4] Contending, or disposed to contend. — *n.* One who combats.

com'ba-tive (kŏm'bȧ-tĭv; kŏm-băt'ĭv), *a.* [4] Disposed to combat; pugnacious. — **-ness,** *n.* [8].

comb'er (kōm'ẽr), *n.* One that combs, as a wave.

com'bi-na'tion (kŏm'bĭ-nā'shŭn), *n.* **1.** Act or process of combining; state of being combined. **2.** A union or aggregate made by combining one thing with another.

com-bine' (kŏm-bīn'), *v. t. & i.* [1] To unite or join. — (kŏm-bīn'; *commonly* kŏm'bīn), *n.* A combination, esp. of persons. *Colloq., U. S.*

com-bus'ti-ble (-bŭs'tĭ-b'l), *a.* [4] **1.** Capable of combustion; inflammable. **2.** Easily kindled or excited; fiery. — *n.* A thing that is combustible. — **com-bus'ti-bil'i-ty** (kŏm-bŭs'tĭ-bĭl'ĭ-tĭ), *n.*

com-bus'tion (-chŭn), *n.* Act or instance of burning; chemical combination of a substance with, usually, oxygen so rapidly as, generally, to produce heat and light.

come (kŭm), *v. i.; pret.* CAME (kām); *p. p.* COME (kŭm); *p. pr. & vb. n.* COM'ING (kŭm'ĭng). **1.** To

Column. 1 Cornice ; 2 Frieze ; 3 Architrave ; 4 Capital ; 5 Shaft ; 6 Base ; 7 Pedestal.

approach ; as, he *came* to me ; — opposed to *go*.
2. To arrive at, or appear on, a scene of action ;
as, he *came* to the rescue ; his case *came* to trial.
3. To approach or arrive in time, sequence, or order ; as, to *come* of age ; after joy *comes* sadness ;
also, to approach in kind or quality ; as, brute pain
comes near to human. **4.** To appear in the course
of development or change ; to emanate ; result ;
also, to happen ; befall ; as, to *come* into bloom ;
no harm will *come* to you ; an idea *came* into his
head ; to *come* untied ; *come* true ; to *come* into
fashion. **5.** To extend or reach from point to point
or along a space ; as, breeches *coming* to the knees.

¢o-me'di-an (kǒ-mē'dǐ-ǎn), *n.* **1.** An actor in
comedy. **2.** A writer of comedy.

com'e-dy (kǒm'ē-dǐ), *n. ; pl.* -DIES (-dǐz). **1.** An
amusing drama, typically having a happy ending ;
also, the dramatic quality characteristic of comedies. **2.** Matter suitable for comedy.

come'ly (kǔm'lǐ), *a.* [3] Pleasing or agreeable to
the sight ; good-looking.— **-li-ness** (lǐ-něs),*n.* [8].

com'er (kǔm'ẽr), *n.* One that comes, or has come.

com'et (kǒm'ět), *n.* A kind of heavenly body,
often having a long nebulous train, or tail.

com'fit (kǔm'fǐt), *n.* A dry sweetmeat or confection, esp. one containing a seed, bit of root, etc.

com'fort (kǔm'fẽrt), *n.* **1.** Strengthening aid ;
solace ; consolation. **2.** State or feeling of having
relief, cheer, or consolation ; freedom from pain,
want, or anxiety. **3.** That which gives or brings
comfort. — *v. t.* To impart strength and hope
to ; to relieve of mental distress ; console.

com'fort-a-ble (-fẽr-tá-b'l), *a.* [4] **1.** Affording
comfort. **2.** In a state of comfort ; at ease.
3. Marked by an appearance of comfort. — *n.* A
stuffed or quilted cover for a bed. — **com'for-
ta-bly,** *adv.* [8].

com'fort-er (-tẽr), *n.* **1.** One that gives comfort,
as aid, consolation, cheer, etc. **2.** [*cap.*] In the
Bible, the Holy Spirit. **3.** = COMFORTABLE, *n. U. S.*

com'fort-less, *a.* Having no comfort or comforts ;
forlorn ; desolate ; cheerless ; miserable.

com'ic (kǒm'ǐk), *a.* [4] **1.** Relating to comedy,
as distinct from tragedy. **2.** Causing mirth.

com'i-cal (-ǐ-kǎl),*a.* [4] **1.** Belonging to comedy.
2. Exciting mirth ; laughable. — **-ly,** *adv.* [8].

com'i-cal'i-ty (-ǐ-kǎl'ǐ-tǐ), *n.* Quality of being
comical ; something comical.

com'ing (kǔm'ǐng), *p. a.* That comes ; approaching. — *n.* Act of approaching.

com'i-ty (kǒm'ǐ-tǐ), *n. ; pl.* -TIES (-tǐz). Mildness
and suavity of manners ; courtesy ; good breeding.

¢om'ma (kǒm'á), *n.* *Punctuation.* A point [,] used
to separate the smallest members of a sentence.

¢om-mand' (kǒ-mȧnd'), *v. t.* **1.** To direct authoritatively ; charge ; enjoin. **2.** To have at command ;
have command over ; have under control or at disposal. **3.** To dominate in situation, as by height ;
overlook. — *v. i.* To have or exercise direct authority ; be commander. — *n.* **1.** Act of commanding ; bidding. **2.** A thing commanded ; as :
a An order ; a commandment. **b** A force under
a commander. **c** A position in which one commands, as a military post. **3.** Faculty or power of
commanding ; mastery ; as, a *command* of language.

com'man-dant' (kǒm'ȧn-dȧnt'),*n.* A commander.

com'man-deer' (-dēr'), *v. t.* **1.** *Mil.* To force into
military service. **2.** To seize arbitrarily or forcibly. *Colloq.*

com-mand'er (kǒ-mȧn'dẽr), *n.* **1.** One who commands ; hence, a chief or leader. **2.** *Navy.* An
officer ranking next below a captain. See NAVY.

com-mand'ing, *p. a.* [4] That commands ; authoritative ; imperative ; imperious. — **-ly,** *adv.* [8].

com-mand'ment (-mȧnd'měnt), *n.* Act of commanding ; what is commanded, esp. one of the
Ten Commandments. See *Exodus* xx. 1-17.

com-mem'o-rate (-měm'ō-rāt), *v. t.* [1] To call
to remembrance ; to serve as a memorial of.

com-mem'o-ra'tion (-rā'shŭn), *n.* Act of commemorating ; a memorial.

com-mem'o-ra-tive (-měm'ō-rȧ-tǐv), *a.* Intended
to commemorate ; as, a *commemorative* chapel.

com-mence' (kǒ-měns'), *v. i. & t.* [1] To originate ; start ; begin.

com-mence'ment (-měnt),*n.* **1.** Act, fact, or time,
of commencing. **2.** The day when, or the ceremonies at which, degrees are conferred by colleges
and universities ; — now also applied to the graduating exercises of academies and schools.

com-mend' (-měnd'), *v. t.* **1.** To commit, intrust,
or give in charge for care or preservation. **2.** To
recommend as worthy of confidence or regard. —
com-mend'a-ble (-měn'-dá-b'l), *a.* [8] — **com-
mend'a-bly,** *adv.* [8].

com'men-da'tion (kǒm'ěn-dā'shŭn), *n.* Act of
commending or that which commends.

com-mend'a-to-ry (kǒ-měn'dá-tō-rǐ), *a.* [4] Of,
pertaining to, or serving for, commendation.

com-men'su-ra-bil'i-ty (kǒ-měn'shǒō-rá-bǐl'ǐ-tǐ),
n. Quality of being commensurable.

com-men'su-ra-ble (kǒ-měn'shǒō-rá-b'l), *a.* [4]
1. Exactly measurable by the same quantity.
2. Proportionable. — **-su-ra-bly,** *adv.* [8].

com-men'su-rate (-rȧt), *a.* **1.** Equal in measure
or extent ; also, proportionate. **2.** Commensurable. — *v. t. & i.* [1] To make, or to be, commensurate. — **com-men'su-rate-ly,** *adv.* [8].

com'ment (kǒm'ěnt ; kǒ-měnt'), *v. i.* To make
comments ; — with *on* or *upon*. — (kǒm'ěnt), *n.*
1. An explanatory, illustrative, or critical note on
a writing, book, etc. ; annotation. **2.** A remark
or criticism.

com'men-ta-ry (kǒm'ěn-tá-rǐ), *n. ; pl.* -RIES. A
series of comments or memorandums ; exposition.

com'men-ta'tor (kǒm'ěn-tā'tẽr), *n.* One who
writes a commentary ; annotator.

com'merce (kǒm'ẽrs), *n.* **1.** Business intercourse ;
the buying and selling of commodities, esp. on a
large scale ; trade. **2.** Personal intercourse.

com-mer'cial (kǒ-mûr'shǎl), *a.* [4] Of or pertaining to commerce ; mercantile. — **-ly,** *adv.* [8].

com-mer'cial-ism (-ǐz'm), *n.* Commercial spirit
or practices ; a commercial practice or expression

com-mer'cial-ize (-īz), *v. t.* [1] To render commercial ; to subject to commercialism.

com-min'gle (kǒ-mǐn'g'l), *v. t. & i.* [1] To mingle together.

com'mi-nute (kǒm'ǐ-nūt), *v. t.* [1] To reduce to
minute particles ; pulverize.

com-mis'er-ate (kǒ-mǐz'ẽr-āt), *v. t.* [1] To feel or
express sorrow or compassion for ; condole with

com-mis′er-a′tion (kŏ-mĭz′ẽr-ā′shŭn), *n.* Compassion for another's wants or sufferings.

com-mis′er-a-tive (-mĭz′ẽr-ā-tĭv), *a.* [4] Given to commiseration.

com′mis-sa′ri-at (kŏm′ĭ-sā′rĭ-ăt), *n.* In an army, the department charged with the duty of providing food and other daily necessaries.

com′mis-sa-ry (kŏm′ĭ-sā-rĭ), *n. ; pl.* -RIES (-rĭz). 1. A deputy ; commissioner. 2. A military officer charged with providing food for forces.

com-mis′sion (kŏ-mĭsh′ŭn), *n.* 1. A formal warrant giving certain powers or privileges and authorizing or requiring certain acts. 2. A certificate conferring military or naval rank and authority. 3. Authorization or command made by or as if by such a warrant. 4. A body of commissioners. 5. *Commerce.* **a** A thing to be done as agent for another. **b** The allowance made to an agent for transacting business. 6. Act of committing, doing, or performing. — *v. t.* To give a commission to ; appoint and authorize.

com-mis′sion-er (-ẽr), *n.* 1. One commissioned. 2. An officer in charge of some department or bureau of the public service. 3. A member of a commission, such as now governs many cities.

com-mit′ (kŏ-mĭt′), *v. t.; -*MIT′TED; -MIT′TING. 1. To give in trust ; intrust ; consign. 2. To consign (for preservation) ; — in phrases: as, *to commit to memory* (also, simply, *to commit*). 3. To imprison. 4. To refer, as a bill to a committee. 5. To do ; perpetrate, as a sin. 6. To pledge ; bind ; — often reflexive ; as, *to commit* one's self.

com-mit′ment(-mĕnt),*n.* Act of committing; state of being committed ; consignment, esp. to prison.

com-mit′tal (-ǎl), *n.* Commitment.

com-mit′tee (-ē), *n.* 1. A person to whom some trust or charge is intrusted. 2. A body of persons appointed to deal with some matter.

com-mode′ (kŏ-mōd′), *n.* A kind of washstand which contains below an inclosed compartment and, usually, one or more drawers.

com-mo′di-ous (-mō′dĭ-ŭs), *a.* [4] Convenient ; serviceable ; esp., conveniently roomy; spacious ; as, a *commodious* house. — **-ly,** *adv.* — **-ness,** *n.*

com-mod′i-ty (-mŏd′ĭ-tĭ),*n.; pl.* -TIES (-tĭz). That which affords convenience or advantage, esp. in commerce, including everything movable that is bought and sold (except animals).

com′mo-dore′ (kŏm′ō-dōr′), *n. Naval.* An officer next above a captain. See NAVY.

com′mon (kŏm′ŭn), *a.* [3] 1. Shared equally or similarly by two or more individuals. 2. Of frequent occurrence; familiar. 3. Hence : **a** Of the usual type or standard ; ordinary. **b** Below the ordinary standards. 4. Habitual, professed, or confessed ; as, a *common* nuisance. — **common council,** in a city, the representative (legislative) body, or its lower branch. — **c. divisor** (of two or more numbers), a number that divides them without remainder. — **c. multiple,** a multiple of each of two or more numbers. — **c. noun,** *Gram.,* a noun or name noting any one of a class; an appellative ; as, *man, whip, day.* — **c. sense,** good, sound, ordinary sense ; normal intelligence. — **c. stock,** ordinary capital stock not sharing the privileges of preferred stock. — *n.* Land held as a common possession, as by all members of a community.

com′mon-al-ty (-ăl-tĭ), *n.* 1. The common people ; commons. 2. The general membership of a corporation.

com′mon-er (-ẽr), *n.* 1. One of the commonalty. 2. A member of the House of Commons.

com′mon-ly, *adv.* In a manner or degree that is common ; usually ; ordinarily.

com′mon-ness, *n.* Quality of being common.

com′mon-place′ (-plās′), *n.* 1. Anything common or trite ; esp., a trite remark. 2. That which is commonplace.—*a.* [4] Common ; ordinary; trite.

com′mons (kŏm′ŭnz), *n. pl.* 1. The mass of the people, as distinguished from the nobility ; commonalty. 2. [*cap.*] The House of Commons ; — usually with *the.* 3. Provisions for a common table, as in colleges ; fare.

com′mon-weal′ (kŏm′ŭn-wēl′), *n., or* **common weal.** Commonwealth ; the general good.

com′mon-wealth′ (-wĕlth′),*n.* The people constituting a state ; a state, as England under Cromwell, any of the States of the United States, etc.

com-mo′tion (kŏ-mō′shŭn), *n.* Disturbed or violent motion ; agitation; tumult.

com′mu-nal (kŏm′ū-nǎl ; kŏ-mū′nǎl), *a.* [4] Of or pertaining to a commune ; hence, belonging to a simple social life.

com′mune (kŏm′ūn), *n.* The smallest administrative district in France ; a similar district elsewhere.

com-mune′ (kŏ-mūn′), *v. i.* [1] 1. To confer; converse intimately. 2. To receive the Communion.

com-mu′ni-ca-ble (kŏ-mū′nĭ-kà-b'l),*a.* [4] Capable of being communicated.

com-mu′ni-cant (-kǎnt), *n.* 1. One who is entitled to partake of the Communion; a church member. 2. One who communicates.

com-mu′ni-cate (-kāt), *v. t.* [1] 1. To impart; convey. 2. To make known ; recount, as a secret. — *v. i.* 1. To have intercourse; be connected. 2. To take part in the Communion ; commune. — **com-mu′ni-ca′tor** (-kā′tẽr), *n.* [8].

com-mu′ni-ca′tion (-kā′shŭn), *n.* 1. Act of communicating. 2. That which is communicated ; message. 3. Means of communicating ; passage.

com-mu′ni-ca-tive (-mū′nĭ-kà-tĭv), *a.* [4] Inclined to communicate. — **-ness,** *n.* [8].

com-mun′ion (-mūn′yŭn), *n.* 1. Act of sharing ; community. 2. Intercourse, esp. intimate, between persons ; fellowship. 3. A body of Christians of a common faith and discipline. 4. [*cap.*] The celebration of the Lord's Supper.

‖**com′mu′ni′qué′** (kŏ′mü′nē′kā′), *n.* [F.] A piece of information given out officially.

com′mu-nism (kŏm′ū-nĭz'm), *n.* 1. A system of social organization in which goods are held in common. 2. A system of social organization involving common ownership of the means of production, and some equality in the distribution of the products of industry. — **-nist** (-nĭst), *n.* — **-nis′tic** (-nĭs′tĭk), *a.* [4].

com-mu′ni-ty (kŏ-mū′nĭ-tĭ), *n. ; pl.* -TIES (-tĭz). 1. A body of people or animals living in the same place under the same conditions. 2. The body of people living in the same locality. 3. Society at large ; the public ; the people of a country as a whole. 4. Joint ownership or participation.

---

com-mut′a-ble (kŏ-mūt′ȧ-b'l), *a.* [4] Capable of being commuted, or interchanged.

com′mu-ta′tion (kŏm′ū-tā′shŭn), *n.* Act of commuting ; substitution.

com′mu-ta′tor (kŏm′ū-tā′tẽr), *n.* A part of a direct-current dynamo for changing the induced alternating current into a direct current.

com-mute′ (kŏ-mūt′), *v. t.* [1] To exchange; substitute; esp., to substitute for (one obligation) a less one. — *v. i.* To pay in gross, at a reduced rate, instead of part by part. — **com-mut′er**, *n.* [8].

com′pact (kŏm′păkt), *n.* An agreement; contract.

com-pact′ (kŏm-păkt′), *a.* [3] **1.** Closely united or packed; solid; dense; also, arranged in narrow compass ; close. **2.** Brief ; pithy ; not diffuse. — *v. t.* **1.** To press closely together ; join firmly ; consolidate. **2.** To form by connecting firmly. — **-ly**, *adv.* [8] — **-ness**, *n.* [8].

com-pan′ion (kŏm-păn′yŭn), *n.* One that accompanies, or is associated with, another or others; associate ; fellow. — *v. t.* To attend ; accompany.

com-pan′ion-a-ble (-ȧ-b'l), *a.* [4] Fitted to be a companion ; sociable. — **-ness**, *n.* [8].

com-pan′ion-ship (kŏm-păn′yŭn-shĭp), *n.* State or relation of being a companion ; fellowship.

com-pan′ion-way′ (-wā′), *n.* A set of steps leading below from the deck ; the passageway occupied by them.

com′pa-ny (kŭm′pȧ-nĭ), *n.* ; *pl.* -NIES (-nĭz). **1.** Fellowship ; society ; companionship. **2.** An assemblage of individuals ; band. **3.** A companion or companions. **4.** People assembled for social intercourse. **5.** Guests or visitors. **6.** An association of persons for a joint purpose, esp. for carrying on business. **7.** A body of actors in a theater or play. **8.** *Mil.* A body of soldiers ; specifically, a subdivision of a regiment of infantry under a captain. **9.** Crew of a ship, including the officers.

com′pa-ra-ble (kŏm′pȧ-rȧ-b'l), *a.* [4] Capable or worthy of being compared. — **-ra-bly**, *adv.* [8].

com-par′a-tive (kŏm-păr′ȧ-tĭv), *a.* **1.** Of or pertaining to comparison. **2.** Proceeding from or by comparison. **3.** *Gram.* Of an adjective or adverb, expressing. an increased (or, with a negative, a less) degree of the quality denoted by the simple form. **4.** Estimated by comparison ; relative. — *n.* *Gram.* The comparative degree or the form denoting it. — **-ly**, *adv.* [8].

com-pare′ (kŏm-pâr′), *v. t.* [1] **1.** To represent as similar ; liken. **2.** To examine in order to discover resemblances or differences. **3.** *Gram.* To inflect or otherwise modify (an adverb or adjective) so as to denote degrees of quality, quantity, or relation; to state the positive, comparative, and superlative forms of. — *v. i.* To be like or equal ; to be compared; vie. — *n.* Comparison ; — now chiefly in *beyond,* or *past, compare.*

com-par′i-son (-păr′ĭ-sŭn), *n.* **1.** Act of comparing. **2.** A relation between things which admits of their being compared.

com-part′ment (-pärt′mĕnt), *n.* One of the parts into which an inclosed space is divided; a separate division, as of a structure.

com′pass (kŭm′pȧs), *n.* **1.** Boundary ; circumference; circuit. **2.** An inclosed space; area ; extent; hence, limits; reach; bounds; esp., moderate

bounds. **3.** *Music.* The range of tones within the capacity of a voice or instrument. **4.** An instrument for describing circles, etc., consisting essentially of two pointed branches or legs, joined at the top by a pivot ; — usually in *pl.* **5.** An instrument for determining directions by means of a magnetized needle or bar which indicates the magnetic north and south. — *v. t.* **1.** To make the circuit of. **2.** To inclose; encircle; surround. **3.** To reach ; obtain; accomplish.

com′pass-es (-ĕz), *n. pl.* See COMPASS, *n.,* 4.

com-pas′sion (kŏm-păsh′ŭn), *n.* Literally, suffering with another ; pity for another; sympathy.

com-pas′sion-ate (-ŭn-āt), *a.* [4] Disposed to pity; sympathizing ; pitiful. — **-ly**, *adv.* [8].

com-pat′i-bil′i-ty (kŏm-păt′ĭ-bĭl′ĭ-tĭ), *n.* Quality of being compatible; as, *compatibility* of tempers.

com-pat′i-ble (kŏm-păt′ĭ-b'l), *a.* [4] Capable of existing together in harmony; congruous. — **-ness**, *n.* [8] — **com-pat′i-bly**, *adv.* [8].

com-pa′tri-ot (-pā′trĭ-ŭt), *n.* A fellow countryman.

com-peer′ (kŏm-pēr′), *n.* An equal; a peer; also, a companion ; associate.

com-pel′ (kŏm-pĕl′), *v. t.; -*PELLED′ (-pĕld′); -PEL′- LING. **1.** To drive or urge irresistibly; constrain. **2.** To exact ; command.

com′pend (kŏm′pĕnd), *n.* A compendium.

com-pen′di-ous (kŏm-pĕn′dĭ-ŭs), *a.* [4] Containing the substance in small compass; abridged; summarized; — esp. of literary work. — **com-pen′di-ous-ly**, *adv.* [8] — **-ness**, *n.* [8].

c o m-p e n′di-u m (kŏm-pĕn′dĭ-ŭm), *n.* ; *pl.* E. -DIUMS (-ŭmz), L. -DIA (-ȧ). A condensed summary of the main heads of a subject or work; epitome.

com′pen-sate (kŏm′pĕn-sāt), *v. t.* [1] **1.** To be equivalent to ; make amends for. **2.** To make equal return to; requite suitably. — *v. i.* To make amends ; supply an equivalent.

com′pen-sa′tion (kŏm′pĕn-sā′shŭn), *n.* **1.** Act or principle of compensating. **2.** That which compensates; equivalent ; recompense ; amends.

com′pen-sa′tor (kŏm′pĕn-sā′tẽr), *n.* One that compensates ; — of various mechanical devices.

com-pen′sa-to-ry (kŏm-pĕn′sȧ-tō-rĭ), *a.* [4] Serving for, or to give, compensation; making amends.

com-pete′ (-pēt′), *v. i.* [1] To contend in rivalry.

com′pe-tence (kŏm′pē-tĕns)) *n.* **1.** Means suffi-
com′pe-ten-cy (-tĕn-sĭ)) cient for comfort without superfluity. **2.** State of being competent.

com′pe-tent (-tĕnt), *a.* [4] **1.** Answering to all requirements; adequate; fit; capable. **2.** Legally qualified or capable. — **com′pe-tent-ly**, *adv.* [8].

com′pe-ti′tion (-tĭsh′ŭn), *n.* Act of competing; emulous contest; rivalry.

com-pet′i-tive (kŏm-pĕt′ĭ-tĭv), *a.* [4] Of, pert. to, or based on, competition. — **-tive-ly**, *adv.* [8].

com-pet′i-tor (-tẽr), *n.* One who competes ; rival.

com′pi-la′tion (kŏm′pĭ-lā′shŭn), *n.* **1.** Act of compiling. **2.** That which is compiled.

com-pile′ (kŏm-pīl′), *v. t.* [1] To compose out of existing materials, esp. from other books or documents. — **com-pil′er** (-pīl′ẽr), *n.* [8].

com-pla′cence (-plā′sĕns)) *n.* Calm contentment;
com-pla′cen-cy (-sĭ)) esp., self-satisfaction.

com-pla′cent (-sĕnt), *a.* [4] Satisfied; esp., self-satisfied. — **com-pla′cent-ly**, *adv.* [8].

com-plain′ (kŏm-plān′), *v. i.* **1.** To give utterance to grief, pain, discontent, or the like. **2.** To make accusation. — **com-plain′er**, *n.* [8].

com-plain′ant (-ănt), *n.* One who makes complaint.

com-plaint′ (-plānt′), *n.* **1.** Expression of grief, pain, or resentment. **2.** *Law.* A formal charge against a party. **3.** Cause or subject of complaint. **4.** Ailment; disease; disorder; malady.

com′plai-sance′ (kŏm′plā-zăns′; kŏm-plā′zăns), *n.* Disposition to please; obliging compliance.

com′plai-sant′ (-zănt′; -zănt), *a.* [4] Disposed to please; courteous; obliging. — **-ly**, *adv.* [8].

com′ple-ment (kŏm′plĕ-mĕnt), *n.* **1.** The quantity or number required to fill or complete a thing; full allowance. **2.** That which is required to supply a deficiency. **3.** The amount of angle or arc by which a given angle or arc falls short of 90°.

com′ple-ment′ (kŏm′plĕ-mĕnt′; kŏm′plĕ-mĕnt′), *v. t.* To supply a lack.

com′ple-men′ta-ry (-tå-rĭ), *a.* [4] **1.** Forming a complement. **2.** Mutually completing.

com-plete′ (kŏm-plēt′), *a.* [3] **1.** Filled up; with no part lacking; completed. **2.** Perfectly equipped or skilled. — *v. t.* [1] To bring to entirety; perfect; fulfill; finish. — **-ly**, *adv.* [8] — **-ness**, *n.* [8]. — **com-ple′tion** (-plē′shŭn), *n.*

com′plex (kŏm′plĕks), *a.* [4] **1.** Composed of two or more parts; not simple. **2.** Complicated; intricate. — *n.* **1.** A whole made up of complicated or interrelated parts. **2.** *Psychol.* An association of mental elements which tend to act in the mind and to enter consciousness together.

com-plex′ion (kŏm-plĕk′shŭn), *n.* **1.** Disposition; temperament. **2.** Hue of the skin, esp. of the face. **3.** General appearance; character.

com-plex′ioned (kŏm-plĕk′shŭnd), *a.* Having a (specified) complexion; as, dark-*complexioned*.

com-plex′i-ty (-sĭ-tĭ), *n.; pl.* -TIES (-tĭz). **1.** State of being complex. **2.** That which is complex.

com′plex-ly, *adv.* In a complex manner.

com-pli′ance (kŏm-plī′ăns), *n.* Act of complying; yielding; conformity. — **com-pli′an-cy** (-ăn-sĭ).

com-pli′ant (-ănt), *a.* [4] Disposed to comply; complaisant. — **com-pli′ant-ly**, *adv.* [8].

com′pli-cate (kŏm′plĭ-kāt), *v. t.* [1] To combine so as to make intricate or difficult.

com′pli-ca′tion (-kā′shŭn), *n.* Act of complicating; state of being complicated; intricate or confused relation of parts; complexity.

com-plic′i-ty (kŏm-plĭs′ĭ-tĭ), *n.; pl.* -TIES (-tĭz). **1.** State of being an accomplice. **2.** Complexity.

com-pli′er (-plī′ẽr), *n.* One who complies.

com′pli-ment (kŏm′plĭ-mĕnt), *n.* **1.** An expression of approbation, civility, or admiration. **2.** A ceremonious greeting; — usually in *pl.*

com′pli-ment′ (kŏm′plĭ-mĕnt′; kŏm′plĭ-mĕnt′), *v. t.* **1.** To make or pay a compliment to. **2.** To present (one with something) by way of compliment. — *v. i.* To employ compliments.

com′pli-men′ta-ry (kŏm′plĭ-mĕn′tå-rĭ), *a.* [4] Expressive of compliment.

com-ply′ (kŏm-plī′), *v. i.* [2] To yield or acquiesce; consent; conform; as, to *comply* with a request.

com-po′nent (-pō′nĕnt), *a.* Serving or helping to form; constituent. — *n.* A component part.

com-port′ (-pōrt′), *v. t.* To carry; conduct; — with a reflexive pronoun; as, to *comport* one's self with dignity. — *v. i.* To agree, accord, or suit (with).

com-port′ment (-mĕnt), *n.* Behavior; deportment.

com-pose′ (-pōz′), *v. t.* [1] **1.** To form by putting together; fashion or construct. **2.** To constitute; in the *passive*, to be made up (of). **3.** *Print.* To set (type). **4.** To adjust or arrange. **5.** To calm; quiet. — *v. i.* To practice composition, as of literary or musical work, or in printing.

com-posed′ (-pōzd′), *p.a.* [4] Free from agitation. — **com-pos′ed-ly** (-pōz′ĕd-lĭ), *adv.* [8].

com-pos′er (-pōz′ẽr), *n.* One who composes; specifically, an author; esp., a writer of music.

com-pos′ite (kŏm-pŏz′ĭt; kŏm′pŏ-zĭt), *a.* [4] **1.** Made up of distinct parts or elements; compounded. **2.** *Bot.* Having florets borne in dense heads resembling single flowers, as the daisy, aster, etc. — *n.* A composite thing. — **-ly**, *adv.* [8].

com′po-si′tion (kŏm′pŏ-zĭsh′ŭn), *n.* **1.** Act or art of composing; as: **a** Art or practice of writing. **b** *Print.* The setting up of type. **2.** Manner of being composed; make-up. **3.** Composite substance. **4.** A literary, musical, or artistic production; often, an essay done as an educational exercise. **5.** An agreement, esp. to settle differences.

com-pos′i-tor (kŏm-pŏz′ĭ-tẽr), *n.* One who sets type.

com′post (kŏm′pōst), *n.* A fertilizing mixture, esp. one composed of leaf mold, manure, etc.

com-po′sure (kŏm-pō′zhŭr), *n.* Calmness; repose.

com′pote (kŏm′pōt), *n.* A preparation of fruit in whole, halves, etc., in sirup.

com′pound (-pound), *n.* In the East Indies, etc., an inclosure containing a house, outbuildings, etc.

com-pound′ (kŏm-pound′), *v. t. & i.* **1.** To put or unite together into a whole; combine; mix. **2.** To adjust by agreement; compromise, as a dispute, a debt.

com′pound (kŏm′pound), *a.* Composed of, or formed by union of, two or more elements or parts; composite. — *n.* **1.** That which is formed by union or mixture of elements or parts; a composition. **2.** A substance formed by chemical union of ingredients. **3.** A word formed of two or more distinct words, as *homesick, steamboat.*

com′pre-hend′ (-prē-hĕnd′), *v. t.* **1.** To apprehend the meaning of; understand. **2.** To contain; embrace; include.

com′pre-hen′si-bil′i-ty (-hĕn′sĭ-bĭl′ĭ-tĭ), *n.* Quality of being comprehensible.

com′pre-hen′si-ble (-hĕn′sĭ-b'l), *a.* [4] Capable of being comprehended; intelligible.

com′pre-hen′sion (-shŭn), *n.* **1.** Act of comprehending, containing, or comprising. **2.** Power or act of grasping with the intellect; understanding.

com′pre-hen′sive (-sĭv), *a.* [4] **1.** Including much; extensive; full. **2.** Characterized by mental comprehension. — **-ly**, *adv.* [8] — **-ness**, *n.* [8].

com-press′ (kŏm-prĕs′), *v. t.* To press or squeeze together; condense.

com′press (kŏm′prĕs), *n.* A folded cloth or pad applied to some part of the body, esp. with a bandage to give due pressure.

com-press′i-bil′i-ty (kŏm-prĕs′ĭ-bĭl′ĭ-tĭ), *n.* Quality of being compressible.

com-press′i-ble (kŏm-prĕs′ĭ-b'l), *a.* [4] Capable of being compressed.

com-pres′sion (-prĕsh′ŭn), *n.* Act of compressing; state of being compressed.

com-pres′sive (-prĕs′ĭv), *a.* [4] Tending to or having power to compress.

com-prise′ (-prīz′), *v. t.* [1] To comprehend or include.

com-prize′, *v. t.* Var. of COMPRISE.

com′pro-mise (kŏm′prō-mīz), *n.* **1.** A settlement reached by mutual concessions. **2.** An endangering; exposure to risk or suspicion. **3.** The result of concession or adjustment; hence, *Colloq.*, a thing intermediate between two different things. — *v. t.* [1] **1.** To adjust and settle by mutual concessions. **2.** To imperil or injure (the reputation, etc., of a person) by exposure to suspicion, discredit, or evil.—*v. i.* To come to agreement by concession.

comp-trol′ler (kŏn-trōl′ẽr), *n.* A public officer who examines and certifies accounts.

com-pul′sion (kŏm-pŭl′shŭn), *n.* Act of compelling; state of being compelled; subjection to force.

com-pul′so-ry (-sō-rĭ), *a.* [4] **1.** Obligatory; enforced. **2.** Compelling. — **-so-ri-ly,** *adv.* [8].

com-punc′tion (-pŭngk′shŭn), *n.* Pricking or uneasiness of the conscience; remorse; now often, mere regret for slight wrong.

com′pu-ta′tion (kŏm′pū-tā′shŭn), *n.* **1.** Act or process of computing. **2.** The amount computed.

com-pute′ (kŏm-pūt′), *v. t. & i.* [1] To determine by calculation; reckon.— **-put′er** (-pūt′ẽr), *n.* [8].

com′rade (kŏm′rād ; -rǎd), *n.* A mate ; companion. — **com′rade-ship,** *n.*

con (kŏn), *v. t.;* CONNED (kŏnd) ; CON′NING. To study; commit to memory.

con, *adv.* Against ; on the negative side ; — the opposite of *pro.* — *n.* The opposing argument, voter, etc. See PRO.

con-cat′e-nate (kŏn-kăt′ē-nāt), *v. t.* [1] To link together ; unite in a series or chain.

con-cat′e-na′tion (-nā′shŭn), *n.* Union in a series.

con′cave (kŏn′kāv), *a.* [4] Hollow and curved or rounded ; — said of the interior of a curved surface or line. — *n.* A concave line or surface. — *v. t.* [1] To make concave.

con-cav′i-ty (kŏn-kăv′ĭ-tĭ), *n.; pl.* -TIES (-tĭz). Quality or state of being concave; a concave.

con-ceal′ (kŏn-sēl′), *v. t.* To hide or withdraw from observation or sight; withhold knowledge of.

con-ceal′ment (-mĕnt), *n.* Act or fact of concealing ; also, state of being concealed.

con-cede′ (-sēd′), *v. t.* [1] **1.** To admit to be true; acknowledge. **2.** To grant, as a privilege.

con-ceit′ (-sēt′), *n.* **1.** Conception; personal judgment or opinion. **2.** An overweening pride; vanity. **3.** A fanciful, odd, or extravagant notion; a witty thought or turn of expression; whim; quip.

con-ceit′ed (kŏn-sēt′ĕd), *a.* [4] Having a flattering opinion of one's self ; vain. — **-ly,** *adv.* [8].

con-ceiv′a-ble (-sēv′ȧ-b'l), *a.* Capable of being conceived or imagined. — **-a-bly,** *adv.* [8].

con-ceive′ (-sēv′), *v. t.* [1] **1.** To become pregnant with. **2.** To form a conception of ; imagine.

con-ceive′ (-sēv′), *v. i.* **1.** To become pregnant. **2.** To have a conception, idea, or opinion ; think.

con′cen-trate (kŏn′sĕn-trāt), *v. t. & i.* [1] **1.** To bring to or towards, or to approach, a common center ; gather into one body or force. **2.** To increase in strength as by reducing bulk ; condense.

con′cen-tra′tion (-trā′shŭn), *n.* **1.** Act of concentrating ; state of being concentrated. **2.** Specifically, close mental application.

con-cen′tric (kŏn-sĕn′trĭk) } *a.* Having a com-
con-cen′tri-cal (-trĭ-kǎl) } mon center.— **con-cen′tri-cal-ly,** *adv.* [8].

con′cept (kŏn′sĕpt), *n.* A notion, thought, or idea.

con-cep′tion (kŏn-sĕp′shŭn), *n.* **1.** Act of becoming pregnant. **2.** The action or faculty of forming an idea of anything. **3.** An image or idea.

con-cern′ (-sûrn′), *v. t.* **1.** To relate or belong to; to affect the interest of. **2.** To engage; make anxious ; interest ; — usually reflexive or passive. — *n.* **1.** That which relates or belongs to one ; business ; affair. **2.** That which affects the welfare or happiness; interest. **3.** Interest; anxiety. **4.** A business organization. **5.** A contrivance or thing, esp. a complicated or cumbrous one.

con-cern′ing, *prep.* Pertaining to ; regarding.

con-cert′ (-sûrt′), *v. t. & i.* **1.** To plan together; settle by agreement. **2.** To plan; devise; arrange.

con′cert (kŏn′sẽrt), *n.* **1.** Agreement in a design or plan ; simultaneous action. **2.** A musical entertainment in which several voices or instruments take part.

con′cer-ti′na (kŏn′sẽr-tē′nȧ), *n.* A small musical instrument on the principle of the accordion.

con-ces′sion (kŏn-sĕsh′ŭn), *n.* **1.** Act of conceding or yielding ; admission. **2.** A thing yielded ; acknowledgment ; grant.

conch (kŏngk), *n.* Any of various large, spiral, marine shells.

Concertina.

con-chol′o-gy (kŏn-kŏl′ō-jĭ), *n.* Branch of zoölogy dealing with shells or mollusks.

con-chol′o-gist (-jĭst), *n.* One versed in conchology.

con-cil′i-ate (kŏn-sĭl′ĭ-āt), *v. t.* [1] To reconcile; win over from hostility; gain the good will of.

con-cil′i-a′tion (kŏn-sĭl′ĭ-ā′shŭn), *n.* Act of conciliating ; state of being conciliated.

con-cil′i-a′tor (-ā′tẽr), *n.* One that conciliates.

con-cil′i-a-to-ry (-ȧ-tō-rĭ), *a.* [4] Tending to conciliate ; showing a spirit of conciliation.

con-cise′ (-sīs′), *a.* [3] Expressing much in few words; condensed; brief. — **-ly,** *adv.* —**-ness,** *n.*

con′clave (kŏn′klāv), *n.* **1.** A set of rooms in which the Roman Catholic cardinals are secluded while choosing a pope. **2.** The meeting of cardinals to choose a pope. **3.** A private meeting.

con-clude′ (kŏn-klood′), *v. t.* [1] **1.** To bring to an end ; close; finish. **2.** To come to a conclusion. **3.** To bring about as a result; effect. — *v. i.* To come to an end; terminate.

con-clu′sion (kŏn-kloo′zhŭn), *n.* **1.** The last part of anything; close; end. **2.** Final decision; result; outcome. **3.** The summing up of a discourse. **4.** An inference ; a judgment reached by reasoning.

con-clu′sive (-sĭv), *a.* [4] Putting an end to debate or question ; decisive ; final ; as, a *conclusive* argument. — **-ly,** *adv.* [8] — **-ness,** *n.* [8].

āle, senāte, câre, ăm, *ă*ccount, ärm, ȧsk, sof*ȧ* ; ēve, ĕvent, ĕnd, recĕnt, makĕr; īce, ĭll ; ōld, ŏbey, ôrb, ŏdd, sôft, cŏnnect ; ūse, ŭnĭte, ûrn, ŭp, circŭs; fo͞od, fo͝ot : out, oil.

con-coct′ (kŏn-kŏkt′), *v. t.* To prepare, as food, by combining ingredients; to make up, as a story.

con-coc′tion (-kŏk′shŭn), *n.* Act of concocting; that which is concocted.

con-com′i-tant (-kŏm′ĭ-tănt), *a.* Accompanying; attending; as, *concomitant* circumstances. — *n.* That which accompanies. — **-ly**, *adv.* [8].

con′cord (kŏn′kôrd; kŏn′-), *n.* State of agreement; harmony; — opp. to *discord.*

con-cord′ance (kŏn-kôr′dăns), *n.* **1.** Agreement: harmony; as, *concordance* of opinion. **2.** An alphabetical index of the principal words in a book, citing the passages in which they occur.

con-cord′ant (-dănt), *a.* [4] Agreeing; correspondent ; harmonious. — **con-cord′ant-ly**, *adv.* [8].

con′course (kŏŋ′kōrs; kŏn′-), *n.* **1.** A flocking together, as of people. **2.** An assemblage ; gathering.

con′crete (kŏn′krēt; kŏn-krēt′), *a.* [4] **1.** Formed into a mass by union of particles. **2.** Belonging to actual things or events ; not abstract, ideal, or general. **3.** Specific in application ; particular. — *n.* A mixture of sand, gravel, or the like, with cement or tar, etc., used for sidewalks, buildings, etc. — **-ly**, *adv.* [8] — **-ness**, *n.* [8].

con-crete′ (kŏn-krēt′), *v. t.* [1] **1.** To form into a mass, as by cohesion or coalescence ; solidify. **2.** To cover with, or form of, concrete.

con-cre′tion (-krē′shŭn), *n.* Act or process of concreting ; also, a concreted mass.

con′cu-bine (kŏŋ′kū-bīn), *n.* A woman who cohabits with a man without being his wife.

con-cur′ (kŏn-kûr′), *v. i.; -*curred*′ (-kûrd′); -*cur**-ring. **1.** To combine in action; coöperate. **2.** To agree (in opinion, etc.) ; accord.

con-cur′rence (-kŭr′ĕns), *n.* Act of concurring.

con-cur′rent (-ĕnt), *a.* **1.** Running together ; associate ; existing or happening at the same time. **2.** Agreeing ; coöperating. — **-ly**, *adv.* [8].

con-cus′sion (-kŭsh′ŭn), *n.* A shaking; agitation; the shock caused by the collision of two bodies.

con-demn′ (-dĕm′), *v. t.* **1.** To pronounce to be wrong, as an act; censure. **2.** To pronounce guilty; also, to sentence ; doom. **3. a** To pronounce to be unfit for use; as, to *condemn* a bridge. **b** To adjudge to be forfeited, or taken for public use by right of eminent domain ; as, to *condemn* land. — **con-demn′er** (-dĕm′ēr ; -dĕm′nēr), *n.* [8].

con′dem-na′tion (kŏn′dĕm-nā′shŭn), *n.* Act of condemning ; state of being condemned.

con-dem′na-to-ry (kŏn-dĕm′nả-tō-rĭ), *a.* [4] Expressing condemnation.

con-den′sa-ble (-dĕn′sả-b'l), *a.* [4] That can be condensed.

con′den-sa′tion (kŏn′dĕn-sā′shŭn), *n.* Act or process of condensing ; state of being condensed ; also, a product of condensation.

con-dense′ (kŏn-dĕns′), *v. t. & i.* [1] To make or become more close, compact, or dense ; compress ; concentrate. — **con-dens′er**, *n.* [8].

con′de-scend′ (kŏn′dẻ-sĕnd′), *v. i.* To stoop or descend; waive the privilege of rank or dignity ; — often ironical. — **-ing-ly**, *adv.* [8].

con′de-scen′sion (-sĕn′shŭn), *n.* Act of condescending ; affability, or patronizing attitude, toward or as toward inferiors.

con-dign′ (kŏn-dīn′), *a.* [3] Deserved; suitable *Archaic,* exc. of punishment. — **-dign′ly**, *adv.*[8].

con′di-ment (kŏn′dĭ-mĕnt), *n.* Something used as a relish; a pungent appetizer, as pepper; seasoning.

con-di′tion (kŏn-dĭsh′ŭn), *n.* **1.** Something necessary or essential to the doing or taking effect of something else ; a prerequisite. **2.** That which limits or modifies something ; a qualification **3.** A mode or state of being ; social estate ; rank **4.** State of being fit, as for work. — *v. t.* **1.** To stipulate ; agree. **2.** To limit by, or subject to conditions.

con-di′tion-al (kŏn-dĭsh′ŭn-ăl), *a.* Of or pertaining to a condition ; not absolute. — **-ly**, *adv.* [8]

con-di′tioned (-ŭnd), *p.a.* Subjected to conditions

con-dole′ (-dōl′), *v. i.* [1] To express or feel sympathetic sorrow ; — usually with *with.*

con-do′lence (-dō′lĕns), *n.* Expression of sympathetic sorrow or grief.

con′do-na′tion (kŏn′dỏ-nā′shŭn), *n.* Act of condoning.

con-done′ (kŏn-dōn′), *v. t.* [1] To forgive (an offense), esp. tacitly, as by ignoring it.

con′dor (kŏn′dŏr), *n.* A very large American vulture of the highest Andes.

con-duce′ (kŏn-dūs′), *v. i.* [1] To lead or tend, esp. to a favorable result ; contribute;— with *to* or *toward.*

con-du′cive (-dū′sĭv), *a.* [4] Leading or tending; contributive. — **-cive-ness**, *n.* [8].

con′duct (kŏn′dŭkt), *n.* **1.** Act or method of conducting ; guidance. **2.** Act or manner of carrying on, as a business; management; direction. **3.** Manner of conducting or carrying one's self; behavior.

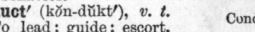

Condor.

con-duct′ (kŏn-dŭkt′), *v. t.* **1.** To lead ; guide; escort. **2.** To manage ; carry on. **3.** To behave (one's self himself, etc.). **4.** To be a channel or medium for

con-duct′ance (-dŭk′tăns), *n. Elec.* Conducting power ; — the reciprocal of resistance.

con-duc′tion (-dŭk′shŭn), *n.* **1.** Transmission, as of heat or electricity. **2.** The transfer of soluble foods, etc., from one part of a plant to another.

con-duc′tive (-tĭv), *a.* [4] Having conductivity.

con′duc-tiv′i-ty (kŏn′dŭk-tĭv′ĭ-tĭ), *n. ; pl.* -ties (-tĭz). Quality or power of conducting, or of receiving and transmitting, as heat, electricity, etc

con-duc′tor (kŏn-dŭk′tēr), *n.* **1.** One that conducts. **2.** A guide; director. **3.** One in charge of a public conveyance, as a street car. **4.** A substance or body capable of readily transmitting electricity, heat, etc.

con′duit (kŏn′dĭt), *n.* **1.** A channel, as a pipe or a natural passage, for conveying fluid; canal. **2.** A tube, trough, or subway for electric wires.

cone (kōn), *n.* **1.** A solid body, tapering uniformly to a point from a circular base. **2.** In certain trees, as the pine, a mass of ovule-bearing or pollen-bearing scales.

Cone, 1.

con-fab'u-late (kŏn-făb'ū-lāt), *v. i.* [1] To talk familiarly together; chat.

con-fab'u-la'tion (-lā'shŭn), *n.* Familiar talk.

con-fec'tion (-fĕk'shŭn), *n.* **1.** A making by combining ingredients. **2.** A sweetmeat; preserve.

con-fec'tion-a-ry (-ā-rĭ), *a.* Of or pertaining to confections or their making.

con-fec'tion-er (-ẽr), *n.* One whose occupation it is to make or sell confections, candies, etc.

con-fec'tion-er-y (-ẽr-ĭ ; -ẽr-ĭ), *n. ; pl.* -ERIES (-ĭz). Sweetmeats; confections; candies.

con-fed'er-a-cy (-fĕd'ẽr-à-sĭ), *n. ; pl.* -CIES (-sĭz). **1.** A league or compact for mutual support or common action; alliance. **2.** The body formed by persons, states, etc., united by a league; confederation. **3.** [*cap.;* and with *the*] *Hist.* The Confederate States of America.

con-fed'er-ate (-ăt), *a.* **1.** United in a league; confederated. **2.** [*cap.*] Of or pertaining to the Confederate States of America. — *n.* **1.** An ally; also, an accomplice, in a bad sense. **2.** [*cap.*] An adherent of the Confederate States of America. — (-ăt), *v. t. & i.* [1] To unite in a league.

con-fed'er-a'tion (-ā'shŭn), *n.* Act of confederating ; league ; alliance ; confederacy.

con-fer' (-fûr'), *v. t. ;* -FERRED' (-fûrd') ; -FER'RING. **1.** To grant ; bestow. **2.** To compare ; — abbr. *cf.* — *v. i.* To converse ; consult ; deliberate.

con'fer-ee' (kŏn'fẽr-ē'), *n.* One taking part in a conference.

con'fer-ence (kŏn'fẽr-ĕns), *n.* **1.** Act of conferring ; serious consultation or discussion. **2.** A meeting for consultation or discussion.

con-fess' (kŏn-fĕs'), *v. t.* **1.** To acknowledge, own, or admit. **2.** To admit as true ; assent to ; concede. **3.** To profess belief in. **4.** Of a priest, to hear or receive confession from. — *v. i.* **1.** To make confession ; also, of a priest, to hear confession. **2.** To make acknowledgment.

con-fess'ed-ly (-ĕd-lĭ), *adv.* By confession.

con-fes'sion (-fĕsh'ŭn), *n.* **1.** Act of confessing ; acknowledgment, esp. of sin to a priest or of belief in religion. **2.** What one confesses.

con-fes'sion-al (-ăl), *n.* The place where a priest hears confessions.

con-fes'sor (-fĕs'ẽr), *n.* **1.** One who confesses, as a fault. **2.** One who avows belief, esp. in religion or in Christ. **3.** A priest who hears confessions.

‖**con-fet'ti** (kŏn-fĕt'tē), *n. pl.* [It.] Bonbons; confections ; also, plaster or paper substitutes for bonbons, often thrown at carnivals, etc.

con'fi-dant', *n. masc.*, **con'fi-dante'**, *n. fem.* (kŏn'fĭ-dànt'). One to whom secrets are confided.

con-fide' (kŏn-fīd'), *v. i.* [1] To put or have faith (in); trust. — *v. t.* **1.** To tell or impart confidentially. **2.** To intrust ; commit ; — with *to.*

con'fi-dence (kŏn'fĭ-dĕns), *n.* **1.** Act of confiding ; trust ; belief. **2.** State of feeling sure ; assurance. **3.** Relation or state of trust or intimacy. **4.** A confidential communication.

con'fi-dent (-dĕnt), *a.* [4] Having confidence. — *n.* A confidant.

con'fi-den'tial (-dĕn'shăl), *a.* [4] **1.** Communicated in confidence; secret. **2.** Indicating close intimacy. **3.** Enjoying, or treated with, confidence. — **con'fi-den'tial-ly**, *adv.* [8].

con'fi-dent-ly, *adv.* With confidence.

con-fig'u-ra'tion (kŏn-fĭg'ū-rā'shŭn), *n.* Relative disposition of parts ; figure ; contour.

con'fine (kŏn'fīn), *n.* A boundary ; limit ; also, a frontier ; — now in *pl.*

con-fine' (kŏn-fīn'), *v. t.* [1] **1.** To restrain within limits; imprison ; restrict ; secure. **2.** To keep within doors, esp. by sickness, as from childbirth.

con-fine'ment (-mĕnt), *n.* **1.** Act of confining ; state of being confined ; restraint. **2.** Restraint within doors, esp. by sickness, as from childbirth.

con-firm' (-fûrm'), *v. t.* **1.** To establish ; strengthen. **2.** To sanction ; ratify. **3.** To administer the rite of confirmation to. **4.** To corroborate ; verify.

con'fir-ma'tion (kŏn'fẽr-mā'shŭn), *n.* **1.** Act of confirming. **2.** A church rite supplemental to baptism and admitting to full church privileges.

con-firm'a-tive (kŏn-fûr'mȧ-tĭv), *a.* [4] Serving to confirm ; corroborative.

con-firm'a-to-ry (-tō-rĭ), *a.* [4] Confirmative.

con-firmed' (-fûrmd'), *p. a.* [4] Firmly established ; habitual.

con'fis-cate (kŏn'fĭs-kāt ; kŏn-fĭs'-), *v. t.* [1] To appropriate to the public use.

con'fis-ca'tion (kŏn'fĭs-kā'shŭn), *n.* Act of confiscating ; appropriation.

con'fis-ca'tor (-kā'tẽr), *n.* One who confiscates.

con-fis'ca-to-ry (kŏn-fĭs'kȧ-tō-rĭ), *a.* [4] Of the nature of confiscation.

con'fla-gra'tion (kŏn'flȧ-grā'shŭn), *n.* A fire ; esp., a large, destructive fire.

con-flict' (kŏn-flĭkt'), *v. i.* To contend ; fight ; clash; be contradictory ; as, duty and desire *conflict*.

con'flict (kŏn'flĭkt), *n.* **1.** A strife ; fight ; battle ; esp., a prolonged contest. **2.** Opposing action.

con'flu-ence (kŏn'flōō-ĕns), *n.* **1.** A flowing together ; junction of streams ; place of meeting. **2.** Act of flocking, or coming together ; concourse.

con'flu-ent (-ĕnt), *a.* Flowing together.

con-form' (kŏn-fôrm'), *v. t.* To make like ; bring into harmony or agreement, as with law. — *v. i.* **1.** To be in accord or harmony ; comply ; — with *to* or *with.* **2.** To be a conformist.

con-form'a-ble (-fôr'mȧ-b'l), *a.* [4] **1.** That conforms; similar ; consistent ; proper. **2.** Tractable ; submissive ; compliant. — **-a-bly**, *adv.* [8].

con'for-ma'tion (kŏn'fôr-mā'shŭn), *n.* State of being conformed; agreement; structure as depending on the arrangement of parts ; form.

con-form'er (kŏn-fôr'mẽr), *n.* One who conforms.

con-form'ist (-mĭst), *n.* A conformer ; esp., in England, one who conforms to the Established Church.

con-form'i-ty (-mĭ-tĭ), *n. ; pl.* -TIES (-tĭz). **1.** Correspondence in form, manner, or character; agreement. **2.** Action of conforming to something established; compliance ; esp., in England, compliance with Established Church usages.

con-found' (-found'), *v. t.* **1.** To damn ; — used as a mild imprecation ; as, *Confound* you ! **2.** To put to shame ; abash. **3.** To throw into confusion or disorder ; perplex ; dismay. **4.** To mix up ; to mistake for another ; confuse.

con-front' (kŏn-frŭnt'), *v. t.* **1.** To face, esp. hostilely ; oppose. **2.** To cause to face or meet.

con-fuse' (-fūz'), *v. t.* [1] **1.** To perplex ; disconcert. **2.** To throw into disorder ; mix or blend indiscriminately. **3.** To mistake for another.

con-fu′sion (kŏn-fū′zhŭn), n. **1.** State of being disconcerted ; discomfiture ; embarrassment. **2.** Act of confusing ; state of being confused.

con′fu-ta′tion (kŏn′fū-tā′shŭn), n. **1.** Act of confuting. **2.** That which confutes.

con-fute′ (kŏn-fūt′), v. t. [1] To overwhelm by argument ; prove false ; silence ; refute.

con-geal′ (kŏn-jēl′), v. t. To change from a fluid to a solid state, as by cold ; freeze. — v. i. To grow hard, stiff, or thick, as from cold or coagulation. — **con-geal′a-ble**, a. [8].

con-gen′ial (kŏn-jēn′yăl), a. [4] **1.** Partaking of the same nature ; kindred ; sympathetic. **2.** Naturally adapted ; agreeable. — **-ly**, adv. [8].

con-ge′ni-al′i-ty (-jē′nĭ-ăl′ĭ-tĭ), n. Quality of being congenial.

con-gen′i-tal (-jĕn′ĭ-tăl), a. Existing at, or dating from, birth ; inborn. — **con-gen′i-tal-ly**, adv. [8].

con′ger (kŏn′gẽr), n. A kind of large sea eel.

con-gest′ (kŏn-jĕst′), v. t. **1.** To cause overfullness of the blood vessels of (an organ or part). **2.** To make overcrowded. — v. i. To become congested.

con-ges′tion (-jĕs′chŭn), n. Congested state.

con-glom′er-ate (-glŏm′ẽr-āt), a. [4] Gathered into a ball or a mass, or consisting of parts so collected. — n. A mass formed of fragments ; a rock composed of gravel or shingle cemented together. — v. t. [1] To gather into a coherent mass.

con-glom′er-a′tion (-ā′shŭn), n. Coherent mass.

con-grat′u-late (-grăt′ū-lāt), v. t. [1] To address with expressions of pleasure at some event happily affecting the person addressed ; felicitate.

con-grat′u-la′tion (-lā′shŭn), n. A congratulating ; an expression of sympathetic pleasure.

con-grat′u-la-to-ry (-grăt′ū-la-tō-rĭ), a. [4] Expressive of, or disposed to, congratulations.

con′gre-gate (kŏn′grē-gāt), v. t. & i. [1] To collect into a crowd, mass, or assemblage ; assemble.

con′gre-ga′tion (-gā′shŭn), n. **1.** Act of congregating. **2.** An assemblage of separate things. **3.** An assembly of persons, esp. for worship.

con′gre-ga′tion-al (-ăl), a. Pertaining to a congregation.

con′gre-ga′tion-al-ism (-ĭz′m), n. Church organization which vests all ecclesiastical power in the assembled brotherhood of each local church.

con′gress (kŏn′grĕs), n. **1.** A gathering or assembly, as of delegates or representatives. **2.** [cap.] The body of senators and representatives of the United States. **3.** Any similar national legislative body.

con′gress boot or **gaiter** (kŏn′grĕs). A high shoe having elastic material in the sides.

con-gres′sion-al (kŏn-grĕsh′ŭn-ăl), a. Of or pert. to a congress, esp. [cap.] the Congress of the U. S.

Con′gress-man (kŏn′grĕs-măn), n. ; pl. -MEN. A member of Congress, esp. of the House of Representatives. — **Con′gress-wom′an** (-wŏŏm′ăn), n.

con′gru-ence (-grŏŏ-ĕns), n. Congruity ; harmony.

con′gru-ent (-ĕnt), a. [4] Possessing congruity ; suitable ; agreeing. — **con′gru-ent-ly**, adv. [8].

con-gru′i-ty (kŏn-grŏŏ′ĭ-tĭ), n. ; pl. -TIES (-tĭz). Quality of being congruous ; agreement ; correspondence ; also, an instance of being congruous.

con′gru-ous (kŏn′grŏŏ-ŭs), a. [4] **1.** Suitable ; harmonious. **2.** Accordant with what is proper, reasonable, or right. — **-ly**, adv. [8].

con′ic (kŏn′ĭk) } a. In the form of, like, or pert.
con′i-cal (-ĭ-kăl) } to, a geometrical cone.

co′ni-fer (kō′nĭ-fẽr), n. Any tree or shrub of an order of mostly evergreen trees including those of the pine and yew families.

co-nif′er-ous (kō-nĭf′ẽr-ŭs), a. **1.** Bearing cones. **2.** Pertaining to a conifer.

con-jec′tur-al (kŏn-jĕk′tūr-ăl), a. [4] Of or pertaining to conjecture. — **-ly**, adv. [8].

con-jec′ture (-tūr), n. Inference from defective or presumptive evidence ; a surmise ; guess. — v. t. [1] To arrive at by conjecture ; infer ; surmise. — v. i. To form conjectures. — **con-jec′tur-a-ble** (-tūr-á-b′l), a. [8] — **con-jec′tur-er**, n. [8].

con-join′ (-join′), v. t. & i. To join together.

con-joint′ (-joint′), a. United. — **-ly**, adv. [8].

con′ju-gal (kŏn′jŏŏ-găl), a. Pertaining to marriage ; connubial. — **con′ju-gal-ly**, adv. [8].

con′ju-gate (-gāt), v. t. [1] Gram. To inflect (a verb), or give in order its forms in the several voices, moods, tenses, numbers, and persons.*

con′ju-ga′tion (-gā′shŭn), n. **1.** Act of joining together ; union. **2.** Gram. **a** Inflection of a verb. **b** Class of verbs having the same type of inflection.

con-junc′tion (kŏn-jŭngk′shŭn), n. **1.** Act of conjoining ; state of being conjoined ; union. **2.** The position of two or more heavenly bodies when they are in the same, or nearly the same, direction as seen from the earth. **3.** Gram. An indeclinable word, as and, but, or, if, as, since, etc., which joins sentences, clauses, phrases, or words.

con′junc-ti′va (kŏn′jŭngk-tī′vá), n. The mucous membrane lining the eyelids and covering the eye.

con-junc′tive (kŏn-jŭngk′tĭv), a. [4] **1.** Connective. **2.** Conjoined ; united. — **-ly**, adv. [8].

con-junc′ture (-tūr), n. A combination of events.

con′ju-ra′tion (kŏn′jŏŏ-rā′shŭn), n. Act of conjuring ; esp., the practice of magic ; incantation.

con′jure (kŭn′jẽr), v. i. [1] To summon or command a devil, spirit, etc., by invocation or a spell ; practice magic ; juggle. — v. t. **1.** (kŏn-jŏŏr′) To entreat earnestly ; implore. **2.** To summon or constrain, as a devil, by invocation or a spell. **3.** To call forth or send away by magic.

con′jur-er, **con′jur-or** (kŭn′jẽr-ẽr), n. A magician

con′nate (kŏn′āt ; kŏ-nāt′), a. **1.** Congenital ; in born. **2.** Born together. **3.** Agreeing in nature

con-nect′ (kŏ-nĕkt′), v. t. To join together ; asso ciate ; combine. —v. i. To join, unite, or cohere.

con-nec′tion (-nĕk′shŭn), n. **1.** Act of connect ing ; union ; relationship. **2. a** Continuity or co herence of words or ideas. **b** Context. **c** Relation of things mutually involved. **3.** That which con nects ; bond ; tie. **4.** A person connected with others by some tie.

con-nec′tive (-nĕk′tĭv), a. [4] Connecting, or adapted to connect. — n. That which connects, as, Gram., a conjunction.

con-niv′ance (-nīv′ăns), n. Act of conniving.

con-nive′ (-nīv′), v. i. [1] **1.** To feign ignorance ; pretend not to look (at something distasteful or irregular). **2.** To have a secret understanding (with). — **-niv′er** (-ẽr), n. [8].

con'nois-seur' (kŏn'ĭ-sûr'; -sūr'), *n.* One competent to act as a critical judge of an art.

con'no-ta'tion (kŏn'ō-tā'shŭn), *n.* Act of connoting; that which is connoted.

con-note' (kŏ-nōt'), *v. t.* [1] To suggest, denote, or mean along with, or in addition to, the essential or primary meaning.

con-nu'bi-al (-nū'bĭ-ăl), *a.* Of or pertaining to marriage; conjugal; nuptial.

con'quer (kŏn'kĕr), *v. t.* **1.** To gain or acquire by or as by force; subjugate; vanquish; overcome. **2.** To gain in war, or by overcoming obstacles; win. — *v. i.* To be victorious. —**-a-ble**, *a.* [4,8].

con'quer-or (kŏn'kĕr-ẽr), *n.* One who conquers.

con'quest (-kwĕst), *n.* Act or process of conquering, or that which is conquered.

con'san-guin'e-ous (kŏn'săŋ-gwĭn'ē-ŭs), *a.* Of the same blood; akin.

con'san-guin'i-ty (-ĭ-tĭ), *n.* Blood relationship.

con'science (kŏn'shĕns), *n.* Consciousness of the moral goodness or badness of one's own conduct or motives, together with a feeling of obligation to do or be good. — **con'science-less**, *a.* [8].

con'sci-en'tious (-shĭ-ĕn'shŭs), *a.* [4] **1.** Influenced by conscience. **2.** Done according to conscience. —**-ly**, *adv.* [8] —**-ness**, *n.* [8].

con'scious (kŏn'shŭs), *a.* [4] **1.** Aware or sensible. **2.** Self-conscious. **3.** Mentally awake. **4.** Involving consciousness of something; as, *conscious* guilt. — **-ly**, *adv.* [8].

con'scious-ness, *n.* **1.** Direct knowledge or perception of the presence of any object, state, or sensation. **2.** State or faculty of recognizing one's own existence, sensations, actions, etc.

con'script (kŏn'skrĭpt), *a.* Enlisted by compulsion, as a soldier. — *n.* A recruit so secured.

con-scrip'tion (-skrĭp'shŭn), *n.* Compulsory enlistment for military or naval service; draft.

con'se-crate (kŏn'sē-krāt), *v. t.* [1] **1.** To make or declare sacred; dedicate or devote to God's service or worship. **2.** To hallow; sanctify.

con'se-cra'tion (-krā'shŭn), *n.* Act of consecrating; state of being consecrated.

con-sec'u-tive (kŏn-sĕk'ủ-tĭv), *a.* Following in regular order; with no interval; successive. — **con-sec'u-tive-ly**, *adv.* [8] —**-ness**, *n.* [8].

con-sen'sus (kŏn-sĕn'sŭs), *n.* Agreement in opinion, custom, or function.

con-sent' (-sĕnt'), *v. i.* **1.** To agree together. **2.** To give approval; comply. — *n.* **1.** Voluntary agreement or yielding to what is done by another; assent. **2.** Agreement as to action or opinion.

con'se-quence (kŏn'sē-kwĕns), *n.* **1.** That which follows something on which it depends; result. **2.** Importance; value; social distinction.

con'se-quent (-kwĕnt), *a.* Following as a result, inference, or effect; resulting. — *n.* **1.** An event or phenomenon which follows another; —opposed to *antecedent.* **2.** *Math.* The second term of a ratio.

con'se-quen'tial (-kwĕn'shăl), *a.* [4] **1.** Of the nature of a consequence. **2.** Important. **3.** Self-important. — **-ly**, *adv.* [8].

con'se-quent-ly (kŏn'sē-kwĕnt-lĭ), *adv.* By consequence; accordingly.

con'ser-va'tion (kŏn'sẽr-vā'shŭn), *n.* A conserving, preserving, or protecting; preservation.

con-serv'a-tism (kŏn-sûr'vå-tĭz'm), *n.* Conservative principles, practices, or disposition.

con-serv'a-tive (-tĭv), *a.* [4] **1.** Conserving; preservative. **2.** Tending or disposed to maintain existing institutions or views; opposed to change or innovation. — *n.* A conservative person or thing.

con'ser-va'tor (kŏn'sẽr-vā'tẽr), *n.* One who preserves from injury; keeper; custodian.

con-serv'a-to-ry (kŏn-sûr'vå-tō-rĭ), *n.; pl.* -RIES (-rĭz). **1.** A greenhouse; esp., one attached to a dwelling. **2.** A music school or art school.

con-serve' (kŏn-sûrv'), *v. t.* [1] To keep in a safe or sound state; preserve. — (kŏn-sûrv'; kŏn'sûrv), *n.* A sweetmeat; *pl.*, preserves.

con-sid'er (kŏn-sĭd'ẽr), *v. t. & i.* **1.** To think; ponder; study. **2.** To heed or regard; treat with consideration or sympathetic regard. **3.** To view, as in a certain relation; look upon.

con-sid'er-a-ble (-å-b'l), *a.* [4] **1.** Worthy of consideration; of importance; notable. **2.** Rather large in amount, extent, etc. — **-a-bly**, *adv.* [8].

con-sid'er-ate (-ăt), *a.* [4] Thoughtful of consequences; careful, esp. of others' rights, feelings, etc. — **con-sid'er-ate-ly**, *adv.* [8].

con-sid'er-a'tion (-ā'shŭn), *n.* **1.** Act or process of considering. **2.** Attentive respect or notice; sympathetic regard. **3.** Claim to notice or regard; importance. **4.** Result of considering; matured opinion. **5.** That which is, or should be, considered as a ground of opinion or action; reason. **6.** A recompense, as for a service; compensation.

con-sign' (-sīn'), *v. t.* **1.** To give, transfer, or deliver, formally. **2.** To give in charge; intrust. **3.** *Commerce.* To send or address (as by bill of lading) to an agent, to be used, cared for, or sold.

con-sign'er, *n.* A consignor.

con'sign-ee' (kŏn'sĭ-nē'; -sĭ-nē'), *n.* One to whom something is consigned or shipped.

con-sign'ment (kŏn-sīn'mĕnt), *n.* **1.** Act of consigning; also, that which is consigned. **2.** The writing by which anything is consigned.

con-sign'or (kŏn-sīn'ẽr; kŏn'sĭ-nôr'), *n.* One who consigns something.

con-sist' (kŏn-sĭst'), *v. i.* **1.** To be comprised (*in*); to inhere (*in*). **2.** To be composed or made up (*of*).

con-sist'ence (-sĭs'tĕns), *n.* Consistency.

con-sist'en-cy (-tĕn-sĭ), *n.; pl.* -ENCIES. **1.** Firmness or degree of firmness. **2.** Harmony, esp. the correspondence of a person's acts with his professions, or of his conduct at various times.

con-sist'ent (-tĕnt), *a.* [4] **1.** Having agreement with itself or with something else; having harmony among its parts; congruous; —used with *with.* **2.** Living or acting conformably to what one believes or professes. — **-ly**, *adv.* [8].

con-sol'a-ble (kŏn-sōl'å-b'l), *a.* Capable of being consoled or comforted.

con'so-la'tion (kŏn'sō-lā'shŭn), *n.* Act of consoling; state of being consoled; one that consoles.

con-sol'a-to-ry (kŏn-sōl'å-tō-rĭ), *a.* [4] Consoling.

con-sole' (-sōl'), *v. t.* [1] To cheer in distress or depression; comfort; soothe.

con'sole (kŏn'sōl), *n.* *Arch.* A bracketlike member for support or ornament.

con-sol'i-date (kŏn-sōl'ĭ-dāt), *v. t. & i.* [1] To

make or become solid ; bring or come into close union. — **con-sol′i-da′tor** (-dā′tĕr), *n*. [8].

con-sol′i-da′tion (-dā′shŭn), *n*. Act or process of consolidating ; state of being consolidated.

|| **con′som-mé′** (kŏN′sŏ′mā′ ; kŏn′sŏ-mā′), *n*. [F.] Concentrated broth of meat and vegetables ; often, a thin soup made by dilution of this.

con′so-nance (kŏn′sŏ-năns), *n*. Agreement or congruity ; harmony ; accord ; consistency.

con′so-nan-cy (-năn-sĭ), *n*. Consonance.

con′so-nant (-nănt), *a*. [4] **1**. Having agreement ; consistent ; according. **2**. Harmonizing ; accordant, as tones. **3**. Consonantal. — *n*. A sound which in utterance is usually combined with a vowel. Also, a letter representing such a sound.

con′so-nan′tal (-năn′tăl), *a*. Pert. to consonants.

con′so-nant-ly, *adv*. In a consonant manner.

con′sort (kŏn′sôrt), *n*. **1**. A wife or husband ; spouse ; mate. **2**. A ship accompanying another.

con-sort′ (kŏn-sôrt′), *v. i. & t*. To unite ; associate.

con-spec′tus (-spĕk′tŭs), *n*. A general survey ; esp., a sketch or outline of a subject ; synopsis.

con-spic′u-ous (-spĭk′ū-ŭs), *a*. Obvious to the eye or mind ; manifest ; striking ; eminent ; remarkable. — **-ly**, *adv*. [8] — **-ness**, *n*. [8].

con-spir′a-cy (-spĭr′à-sĭ), *n.; pl*. -CIES (-sĭz). Act of conspiring ; combination for an evil purpose.

con-spir′a-tor (-tĕr), *n*. One engaged in a conspiracy ; a plotter.

con-spire′ (-spīr′), *v. i*. [1] **1**. To make an agreement, esp. a secret one to do something wrong ; plot together. **2**. To work to one end ; agree. — *v. t*. To plot ; plan. — **con-spir′er** (kŏn-spīr′ĕr), *n*. [8].

con′sta-ble (kŭn′stà-b'l), *n*. **1**. A high medieval court officer. **2**. Orig., a military officer ; now, any of various police officers.

con′sta-ble-ship′, *n*. The office of constable.

con-stab′u-la-ry (kŏn-stăb′û-lā-rĭ), *a*. Of or pertaining to constables. — *n.; pl*. -RIES (-rĭz). **1**. Constables collectively. **2**. An armed force of a civil government, distinct from the regular army.

con′stan-cy (kŏn′stăn-sĭ), *n*. **1**. Steadfastness ; fidelity. **2**. State of being constant ; stability.

con′stant (-stănt), *a*. [4] **1**. Firm or steadfast ; resolute ; also, faithful ; true. **2**. Fixed ; invariable ; unchanging. **3**. Invariable under given conditions. **4**. Continually recurring ; regular. — *n*. That which is unchanging or invariable.

con′stant-ly, *adv*. In a constant manner.

con-stel-la′tion (kŏn′stĕ-lā′shŭn), *n*. Any of various arbitrary groups of fixed stars, or a division of the sky including such a group.

con′ster-na′tion (-stĕr-nā′shŭn), *n*. Amazement or horror that confounds the faculties ; dismay.

con′sti-pate (kŏn′stĭ-pāt), *v. t*. [1] To affect with constipation.

con′sti-pa′tion (-pā′shŭn), *n*. A state of the bowels in which evacuations are infrequent and difficult ; costiveness.

con-stit′u-en-cy (kŏn-stĭt′û-ĕn-sĭ), *n.; pl*. -CIES (-sĭz). A body of constituents.

con-stit′u-ent (-ĕnt), *a*. **1**. Serving to form or make up ; component. **2**. Having power to elect or appoint. — *n*. **1**. One of those who elect a representative to a legislature. **2**. That which constitutes ; component ; element.

con′sti-tute (kŏn′stĭ-tūt), *v. t*. [1] **1**. To appoint to the office or function of. **2**. To set up ; establish, as a law, a proceeding, etc. **3**. To form ; make up ; make (a person or thing) what it is.

con′sti-tu′tion (-tū′shŭn), *n*. **1**. Act or process of constituting, esp. of enacting, establishing, or appointing. **2**. Natural structure, or conformation. **3**. The aggregate of the physical and vital powers of an individual. **4**. The fundamental law or principles of government of a nation, society, etc.

con′sti-tu′tion-al (-ăl), *a*. **1**. Of or affecting the constitution (of body or mind). **2**. In accordance with, or relating to, the constitution of a state or a society. — *n*. An exercise ; esp., a walk for one's health or constitution. *Colloq*.

con′sti-tu′tion-al′i-ty (-ăl′ĭ-tĭ′), *n*. Quality or state of being constitutional (esp. in sense 2). — **con′sti-tu′tion-al-ly**, *adv*. [8].

con′sti-tu′tive (kŏn′stĭ-tū′tĭv), *a*. [4] Tending or assisting to constitute, or compose ; essential.

con-strain′ (kŏn-strān′), *v. t*. **1**. To compel ; force. **2**. To secure by bonds ; confine ; restrain.

con-strained′ (-strānd′), *p. a*. Marked by constraint ; forced. — **con-strain′ed-ly**, *adv*. [8].

con-straint′ (-strānt′), *n*. **1**. Act of constraining ; compulsion. **2**. Repression ; embarrassment.

con-strict′ (-strĭkt′), *v. t*. To draw together ; bind.

con-stric′tion (-strĭk′shŭn), *n*. Act of constricting ; anything that constricts or is constricted.

con-stric′tive (-tĭv), *a*. Of, pertaining to, or marked by, constriction.

con-stric′tor (-tĕr), *n*. **1**. That which constricts. **2**. A serpent that crushes its prey in its coils.

con-struct′ (-strŭkt′), *v. t*. To put together the constituent parts of (something) ; build ; devise.

con-struc′tion (-strŭk′shŭn), *n*. **1**. Process or art of constructing ; composition ; structure. **2**. Form or manner of constructing. **3**. *Gram*. Arrangement and connection of words in a sentence. **4**. Interpretation or explanation.

con-struc′tion-al (-ăl), *a*. Pert. to construction.

con-struc′tive (-tĭv), *a*. [4] **1**. Qualified for, or given to, constructing. **2**. Pert. to construction. **3**. Derived from, or depending on, construction, or interpretation. — **-ly**, *adv*. [8] — **-ness**, *n*. [8].

con-struc′tor (-tĕr), *n*. One who constructs.

con-strue (kŏn′strŏo ; kŏn-strŏo′), *v. t*. [1] **1**. *Gram*. To apply the rules of syntax to (a sentence or clause) ; also, to translate. **2**. To interpret.

con′sul (kŏn′sŭl), *n*. **1**. *Roman Hist*. Either of the two joint chief magistrates of the republic. **2**. A government official residing in some foreign country to care for the commercial interests of the citizens of his government.

con′su-lar (kŏn′sŭ-lár), *a*. Of, pertaining to, or of the nature of, a consul.

con′su-late (-sŭ-lăt), *n*. Consular government, jurisdiction, or term of office ; also, the official premises of a consul.

con′sul-ship, *n*. The office of consul.

con-sult′ (kŏn-sŭlt′), *v. i*. To seek another's opinion or advice ; confer. — *v. t*. **1**. To ask the advice or opinion of ; refer to. **2**. To have regard to ; consider. — **con-sult′er**, *n*. [8].

con′sul-ta′tion (kŏn′sŭl-tā′shŭn), *n*. Act of consulting or conferring ; a council or conference.

---

con-sume′ (kŏn-sūm′), *v. t.* [1] **1.** To destroy, as by decomposition, or fire. **2.** To use up; expend; devour; waste; dissipate. — *v. i.* To waste away or suffer destruction. — **-sum′er** (-sūm′ĕr), *n.* [8].

con-sum′mate (kŏn-sŭm′ăt), *a.* [4] Complete; perfect. — **con-sum′mate-ly**, *adv.* [8].

con′sum-mate (kŏn′sŭ-māt), *v. t. & i.* [1] To bring to, or arrive at, completion; finish; perfect.

con′sum-ma′tion (-mā′shŭn), *n.* Act of consummating ; state of being consummated; perfection.

con-sump′tion (kŏn-sŭmp′shŭn), *n.* **1.** Act or process of consuming ; state of being consumed; waste. **2.** Progressive wasting of the body, esp. from pulmonary tuberculosis ; tuberculosis.

con-sump′tive (-tĭv), *a.* Of or pert. to wasting; affected with, or inclined to, consumption. — *n.* One affected with consumption. — **-ly**, *adv.* [8].

con′tact (kŏn′tăkt), *n.* A touching or meeting of bodies, as of two electric conductors.

con-ta′gion (kŏn-tā′jŭn), *n.* **1.** Transmission of a disease. **2.** A contagious disease. **3.** A medium transmitting disease.

con-ta′gious (-jŭs), *a.* [4] **1.** Communicable or spreading by contagion. **2.** Conveying contagion; hence, noxious. — **-ly**, *adv.* [8] — **-ness**, *n.* [8].

con-tain′ (-tān′), *v. t.* **1.** To hold within fixed limits; include. **2.** To be equivalent to. **3.** To restrain; — used reflexively. **4.** To be divisible by, (generally) without a remainder. — **-er**, *n.* [8].

con-tam′i-nate (-tăm′ĭ-nāt), *v. t.* [1] **1.** To soil, stain, or corrupt by contact ; defile ; pollute.

con-tam′i-na′tion (-nā′shŭn), *n.* Act or process of contaminating ; that which contaminates.

con-temn′ (-tĕm′), *v. t.* To view or treat with contempt; scorn.

con′tem-plate (kŏn′tĕm-plāt), *v. t.* [1] **1.** To view or consider with continued attention; meditate on. **2.** To look forward to; intend; plan; purpose. — *v. i.* To ponder ; meditate.

con′tem-pla′tion (-plā′shŭn), *n.* Act of contemplating ; meditation ; expectation ; intention.

con-tem′pla-tive (kŏn-tĕm′plă-tĭv), *a.* [4] Pert. to, of the nature of, or addicted to, contemplation. — **-ly**, *adv.* — **-ness**, *n.*

con′tem-pla′tor (kŏn′tĕm-plā′tĕr), *n.* One who contemplates.

con-tem′po-ra′ne-ous (kŏn-tĕm′pŏ-rā′nē-ŭs), *a.* Contemporary. — **-ly**, *adv.* [8] — **-ness**, *n.* [8].

con-tem′po-ra-ry (-tĕm′pŏ-rā-rĭ), *a.* **1.** Living, occurring, or existing at the same time ; contemporaneous. **2.** Of the same age ; coeval. — *n.* ; *pl.* -RIES (-rĭz). One contemporary with another.

con-tempt′ (-tĕmpt′), *n.* **1.** Act of contemning or despising ; disdain ; scorn. **2.** State of being despised ; disgrace. **3.** *Law.* Willful disobedience to, or open disrespect of, a court of justice.

con-tempt′i-ble (-tĕmp′tĭ-b'l), *a.* [4] Worthy of, or held in, contempt ; despicable. — **con-tempt′-i-ble-ness**, *n.* [8] — **con-tempt′i-bly**, *adv.* [8].

con-temp′tu-ous (-tĕmp′tŭ-ŭs), *a.* [4] Expressing contempt or disdain. — **con-tempt′u-ous-ly**, *adv.* [8] — **con-tempt′u-ous-ness**, *n.* [8].

con-tend′ (-tĕnd′), *v. i.* To strive in opposition or rivalry ; compete ; also, to strive in debate ; argue. — *v. t.* To maintain ; assert. — **-er**, *n.* [8].

con′tent (kŏn′tĕnt ; kŏn-tĕnt′), *n.* ; *usually in pl.,*

CONTENTS. **1.** That which is contained, as in a cask, bale, or room ; the matter treated in a document or the like. **2.** Extent ; size. **3.** Area or volume contained within certain limits.

con-tent′ (kŏn-tĕnt′), *a.* [4] **1.** Having the desires limited by what one has ; satisfied. **2.** Willing ; assenting. — *n.* State of being content. — *v. t.* To make content.

con-tent′ed, *p. a.* [4] Content. — **con-tent′ed-ly**, *adv.* [8] — **con-tent′ed-ness**, *n.* [8].

con-ten′tion (-tĕn′shŭn), *n.* **1.** Act or instance of contending. **2.** A position taken in arguing.

con-ten′tious (-shŭs), *a.* [4] Given to or involving contention. — **-ly**, *adv.* [8] — **-ness**, *n.* [8].

con-tent′ment (-tĕnt′mĕnt), *n.* Act or process of contenting ; state or fact of being contented.

con-test′ (kŏn-tĕst′), *v. t.* **1.** To contend about or for ; oppose ; dispute. **2.** To strive earnestly to gain, hold, or maintain. **3.** *Law.* To litigate. — *v. i.* To engage in contention ; to contend.

con′test (kŏn′tĕst), *n.* Earnest struggle for superiority, victory, etc. ; competition ; strife ; an encounter, as in arms. — **con-test′a-ble**, *a.* [4, 8].

con-test′ant (kŏn-tĕs′tănt), *n.* One who contests.

con′text (kŏn′tĕkst), *n.* The part or parts of a discourse that precede, follow, or are intimately associated with any particular passage or word and determine its meaning.

con-ti-gu′i-ty (kŏn′tĭ-gū′ĭ-tĭ), *n.* ; *pl.* -TIES (-tĭz). **1.** State of being contiguous. **2.** A continuous mass ; a stretch.

con-tig′u-ous (kŏn-tĭg′ũ-ŭs), *a.* In contact; touching ; also, loosely, near, though not in contact ; adjoining. — **-ly**, *adv.* [8] — **-ness**, *n.* [8].

con′ti-nence (kŏn′tĭ-nĕns), *n.* Self-command; self-restraint in regard to desires and passions.

con′ti-nent (-nĕnt), *a.* [4] Exercising continence : temperate. — *n.* **1.** A continuous extent or mass, esp. of land ; mainland. **2.** One of the grand divisions of land on the globe. — **the Continent**, the mainland of Europe.

con′ti-nen′tal (-nĕn′tăl), *a.* **1.** Of, pertaining to, or characteristic of, a continent. **2.** [*cap.*] Of or pert. to the mainland of Europe. **3.** [*cap.*] *Amer. Hist.* Of or pert. to the confederated colonies in the time of the Revolution. — *n. Amer. Hist.* [*cap.*] A soldier in the Continental army.

con-tin′gen-cy (kŏn-tĭn′jĕn-sĭ), *n.* ; *pl.* -CIES (-sĭz). Quality of being contingent ; a chance event.

con-tin′gent (-jĕnt), *a.* [4] **1.** Liable, but not certain, to occur ; possible. **2.** Happening from unforeseen causes ; chance. **3.** Conditional. — *n.* That which falls to one in a division or apportionment ; quota ; esp., a quota of troops.

con-tin′u-al (-tĭn′ū-ăl), *a.* **1.** Marked by continuity ; continuous. **2.** Occurring in steady and rapid succession; frequent ; often repeated. — **-ly**, *adv.* [8].

con-tin′u-ance (-ăns), *n.* **1.** A continuing in a state or course ; duration ; stay. **2.** Uninterrupted succession ; continuation. **3.** *Law.* Adjournment to a fixed future day.

con-tin′u-a′tion (-ā′shŭn), *n.* **1.** Act or state of continuing. **2.** Act of resuming after interruption ; also, that which extends and carries on.

con-tin′ue (-tĭn′ū), *v. i.* [1] **1.** To remain in a given place or condition; abide; stay. **2.** To be con-

āle, senāte, câre. ăm, ŏccount, ärm, ásk, sofà ; ēve, ĕvent, ĕnd, recĕnt, makĕr; īce, ĭll ; ōld, ŏbey, ôrb, ŏdd, sŏft, cónnect ; ūse, ûnite, ûrn, ŭp, circŭs; fōōd, fŏŏt ; out, oil ;

stant in any course; persist; persevere. —*v.t.* **1.** To protract or extend in duration; persist in. **2.** To carry onward; extend; of a legal proceeding, to keep on the calendar or undecided. **3.** To retain; suffer or cause to remain.

con·ti·nu′i·ty (kŏn-tĭ-nū′Ĭ-tĬ), *n.* Quality or state of being continuous.

con·tin′u·ous (kŏn-tĬn′ū-ŭs), *a.* Without break, cessation, or interruption; unbroken; continued. — **-ly**, *adv.* [8].

con·tort′ (-tôrt′), *v. t.* To twist; twist together; turn away; bend; distort.

con·tor′tion (-tôr′shŭn), *n.* Act of contorting or state of being contorted; a twisting or writhing.

con·tor′tion·ist (kŏn-tôr′shŭn-ĭst), *n.* An acrobat who contorts his body into unnatural postures.

con′tour′ (kŏn′tōōr′; kŏn′tōōr′), *n.* The outline of a figure or body; esp., the outline of a coast, mountain, or the like.

con′tra (kŏn′trȧ), *adv.* On the opposite side; to the contrary; in the opposite direction.

con′tra-band (-bănd), *n.* **1.** Illegal or prohibited traffic. **2.** Contraband or smuggled goods. — *a.* Prohibited or excluded by law or treaty; forbidden.

con·tract′ (kŏn-trăkt′), *v. t.* **1.** To undertake by contract. **2.** To betroth; affiance. **3.** To bring on; incur; acquire. **4.** To draw together; reduce; lessen. — *v. i.* **1.** To make a contract. **2.** To be contracted, or reduced.

con′tract (kŏn′trăkt), *n.* An agreement between parties to do or forbear something; covenant; also, the written evidence of such an agreement.

con·tract′ed (kŏn-trăk′tĕd), *p. a.* [4] **1.** Drawn together; shrunken; shortened. **2.** Narrow; illiberal. — **-ly**, *adv.* [8] —**-ness**, *n.* [8].

con·tract′i·ble (-tĬ-b′l), *a.* [4] Capable of contraction.

con·trac′tile (kŏn-trăk′tĬl), *a.* [4] Contractive.

con′trac·til′i·ty (kŏn′trăk-tĬl′Ĭ-tĬ), *n.* The quality or property of being contractile.

con·trac′tion (-trăk′shŭn), *n.* **1.** Act or process of contracting; contracted state. **2.** The shortening of a word, or words, as *ne′er* for *never*.

con·trac′tive (-tĬv), *a.* [4] Tending or able to contract; pertaining to or causing contraction.

con·trac′tor (-tẽr), *n.* **1.** One who contracts to do something for another, esp. to perform work or supply articles on a large scale at a certain price or rate. **2.** One that contracts, shortens, etc.

con′tra-dict′ (kŏn′trȧ-dĬkt′), *v. t.* To assert the contrary of; deny the truth of; impugn. — *v. i.* To oppose in words. — **con′tra-dict′er**, *n.* [8].

con′tra-dic′tion (-dĬk′shŭn), *n.* **1.** An assertion of the contrary. **2.** Inconsistency.

con′tra-dic′to·ry (-tō-rĬ), *a.* [4] Tending to contradict; of the nature of contradiction. — **-ri-ly** (-Ĭ-lĬ), *adv.* [8] — **-to-ri-ness**, *n.* [8].

con′tra-dis-tinc′tion (-dĬs-tĬngk′shŭn), *n.* Distinction by contrast.

con-tral′to (kŏn-trăl′tō), *n.; pl.* E. -TOS (-tōz), It. -TI (-tē). *Music.* **a** The part sung by the lowest female voice, intermediate between tenor and soprano. **b** The voice or singer performing this part.

con′tra-ri′e-ty (kŏn′trȧ-rī′ĕ-tĬ), *n.; pl.* -TIES (-tĬz). **1.** State or quality of being contrary. **2.** Something contrary; an inconsistency; discrepancy.

con′tra-ri·ly (kŏn′trȧ-rĬ-lĬ), *adv.* In a contrary manner.

con′tra-ri·ness (-nĕs), *n.* Contrariety.

con′tra-ri·wise′ (-wīz′), *adv.* **1.** On the contrary. **2.** Conversely. **3.** Perversely; contrarily.

con′tra-ry (kŏn′trȧ-rĬ), *a.* [4] **1.** Opposed; contradictory; inconsistent. **2.** Opposed to one's interests or desires; unfavorable. **3.** Opposite in direction. **4.** Given to opposition; perverse. — *n.; pl.* -RIES (-rĬz). **1.** Either of two things or objects having contrary qualities. **2.** The opposite of what has been already said or asserted.

con·trast′ (kŏn-trȧst′), *v. i.* To form a contrast. — *v. t.* To put in, or set off by, contrast.

con′trast (kŏn′trȧst), *n.* **1.** Opposition or unlikeness of associated things or qualities, esp. as shown by placing them together or by comparison. **2.** A thing or quality in such contrast to another.

con′tra-vene′ (kŏn′trȧ-vēn′), *v. t.* [1] **1.** To go or act contrary to; infringe, as a law. **2.** To oppose in principle or effect; defeat.

con′tra-ven′tion (-vĕn′shŭn), *n.* Act of contravening; transgression; violation.

con·trib′ute (kŏn-trĬb′ūt), *v. t.* [1] To give in common with others. — *v. i.* To give a part to a common stock; lend aid to a common purpose.

con′tri-bu′tion (kŏn′trĬ-bū′shŭn), *n.* Act of contributing; that which is contributed.

con·trib′u·tive (kŏn-trĬb′ū-tĬv), *a.* [4] Contributing, or tending to contribute. — **-ly**, *adv.* [8].

con·trib′u·tor (-tẽr), *n.* One who contributes; one who writes articles for a newspaper or periodical.

con·trib′u·to·ry (-tō-rĬ), *a.* [4] **1.** Contributing making contribution. **2.** Of the nature of a contribution; bearing a share toward any result.

con′trite (kŏn′trīt), *a.* [4] **1.** Humbly penitent. **2.** Proceeding from contrition. — **con′trite-ly**, *adv.* [8] — **con′trite-ness**, *n.* [8].

con·tri′tion (kŏn-trĬsh′ŭn), *n.* Contrite state.

con·triv′ance (-trīv′ăns), *n.* **1.** Act or faculty of contriving. **2.** An ingenious device or expedient.

con·trive′ (-trīv′), *v. t.* [1] **1.** To form or make ingeniously; devise. **2.** To effect; bring about by device, scheme, or stratagem. —*v. i.* To make devices; scheme; plot. — **-triv′er** (-trīv′ẽr), *n.* [8]

con·trol′ (-trōl′), *v. t.; ·* TROLLED (-trōld′); ·TROL′LING. To exercise restraining or directing influence over. — *n.* **1.** Power or authority to control. **2. a** Reserve; restraint. **b** A controller.

con·trol′la-ble (-ȧ-b′l), *a.* Capable of being controlled.

con·trol′ler (-ẽr), *n.* **1.** An officer for checking expenditure. **2.** One that controls or governs, as a device for controlling an electric circuit.

con′tro-ver′sial (kŏn′trō-vûr′shăl), *a.* [4] Pertaining to controversy. — **-ly**, *adv.* [8].

con′tro-ver′sial-ist, *n.* A disputant.

con′tro-ver′sy (kŏn′trō-vûr′sĬ), *n.; pl.* -SIES (-sĬz) Act or instance of controverting; discussion; dispute; debate; quarrel.

con′tro-vert (kŏn′trō-vûrt; kŏn′trō-vûrt′), *v. t.* To debate, dispute, or oppose in words; contest; oppose. — **con′tro-vert′er**, *n.* [8].

con·tu·ma′cious (kŏn′tū-mā′shŭs), *a.* [4] Exhibiting contumacy; obstinate; stubborn; perverse; refractory. — **-ly**, *adv.* [8] — **-ness**, *n.* [8].

con'tu-ma-cy (kŏn'tū-mȧ-sĭ), *n. ; pl.* -CIES (-sĭz). Pertinacious resistance to authority; obstinacy.

con'tu-me'li-ous (-mē'lĭ-ŭs), *a.* [4] Exhibiting contumely. — **con'tu-me'li-ous-ly**, *adv.* [8].

con'tu-me-ly (kŏn'tū-mē-lĭ), *n. ; pl.* -LIES (-lĭz). 1. Haughty contempt; scornful insolence. 2. An instance or exhibition of contumely; insult.

con-tuse' (kŏn-tūz'), *v. t.* [1] To bruise.

con-tu'sion (kŏn-tū'zhŭn), *n.* 1. Act or process of contusing; state of being contused. 2. A bruise.

co-nun'drum (kȯ-nŭn'drŭm), *n.* 1. A riddle of which the answer is a pun. 2. A puzzling thing.

con'va-lesce' (kŏn'vȧ-lĕs'), *v. i.* [1] To recover health and strength after sickness.

con'va-les'cence (-lĕs'ĕns), *n.* Recovery, esp. gradual recovery, of health after disease ; also, the period during which such recovery takes place.

con'va-les'cent (-ĕnt), *a.* 1. Recovering from sickness or debility. 2. Of or pertaining to convalescence. — *n.* One in a convalescent state.

con-vec'tion (kŏn-vĕk'shŭn), *n.* Transfer, as of heat, by means of currents in liquids or gases.

con-vene' (kŏn-vēn'), *v. i.* [1] To come together, as in one body; assemble; meet; congregate. — *v. t.* To cause to assemble ; convoke.

con-ven'ience (kŏn-vēn'yĕns), *n.; pl.* -CES (-sĕz). 1. State or quality of being convenient; fitness or suitableness, as of place, time, etc. 2. Freedom from discomfort or trouble ; ease. 3. A convenient condition or time. 4. That which promotes comfort or advantage; esp., an appliance or utensil for personal ease or comfort.

con-ven'ien-cy (-yĕn-sĭ), *n. ; pl.* -CIES (-sĭz). Convenience.

con-ven'ient (-yĕnt), *a.* [4] Suited to or affording ease, comfort, or advantage ; saving trouble. — **con-ven'ient-ly**, *adv.* [8].

con'vent (kŏn'vĕnt), *n.* 1. A community of recluses, as monks, friars, or esp. (popularly) nuns, devoted to a religious life. 2. A monastery or nunnery ; esp. (popularly), a nunnery.

con-ven'tion (kŏn-vĕn'shŭn), *n.* 1. Act of convening. 2. A body of persons met for a common purpose. 3. Agreement; contract; covenant. 4. General consent as the basis of any custom, opinion, or the like ; fixed custom or usage.

con-ven'tion-al (-ăl), *a.* [4] 1. Of the nature of convention or custom; customary; formal. 2. *Fine Arts.* Following conventions or set rules in design or technique. — *-ly*, *adv.* [8].

con-ven'tion-al-ism (-ĭz'm), *n.* 1. Regard for or adherence to that which is conventional. 2. A conventional practice, usage, or the like.

con-ven'tion-al'i-ty (-ăl'ĭ-tĭ), *n. ; pl.* -TIES (-tĭz). State or quality of being conventional; also, a conventional usage, practice, or thing.

con-ven'tion-al-ize (-vĕn'shŭn-ăl-īz), *v. t.* [1] To make conventional.

con-verge' (kŏn-vûrj'), *v. i.* [1] To tend to one point or line; incline and approach nearer together. — *v. t.* To cause to converge.

con-ver'gence (-vûr'jĕns), *n.* Act of converging.

con-ver'gen-cy (-jĕn-sĭ), *n.* Convergence.

con-ver'gent (-jĕnt), *a.* Tending to one point or focus or line; approaching each other.

con'ver-sant (kŏn'vẽr-sănt), *a.* [4] Having frequent or familiar intercourse ; intimately acquainted ; familiar by use or study.

con'ver-sa'tion (-sā'shŭn), *n.* Familiar talk or discourse ; interchange of thoughts by means of spoken words.

con'ver-sa'tion-al (-ăl), *a.* [4] 1. Ready to converse; given to conversation. 2. Of, pertaining to, or appropriate to, conversation. — *-al-ly*, *adv.* [8].

con'ver-sa'tion-al-ist, *n.* One who converses much or well.

con-verse' (kŏn-vûrs'), *v. i.* [1] To interchange thoughts and opinions in informal speech ; talk.

con'verse (kŏn'vûrs), *n.* 1. Intercourse; intimate association. 2. Familiar discourse; conversation.

con'verse, *a.* Turned about; reversed or opposite in order or relation; acting contrarily. — *n.* Something that is opposite to something else.

con'verse-ly (kŏn'vẽrs-lĭ ; kŏn-vûrs'-), *adv.* In a converse manner.

con-vers'er (kŏn-vûr'sẽr), *n.* One who converses.

con-ver'sion (-shŭn), *n.* 1. Act of converting ; state of being converted. 2. A spiritual and moral change attending a change of belief from what is false or worldly to what is true or godly.

con-vert' (-vûrt'), *v. t.* 1. To change or turn from one belief or course to another. 2. To produce spiritual conversion in (any one). 3. To transform; transmute. 4. To exchange for an equivalent.

con'vert (kŏn'vûrt), *n.* A person converted in opinion or practice; proselyte.

con-vert'er (kŏn-vûr'tẽr), *n.* One that converts, as, *Electricity*, a device for changing electrical energy from one form to another.

con-ver'ti-bil'i-ty (-vûr'tĭ-bĭl'ĭ-tĭ), *n.* Quality of being convertible.

con-vert'i-ble (-tĭ-b'l), *a.* [4] Capable of being converted. — **con-vert'i-bly**, *adv.*

con'vex (kŏn'vĕks), *a.* [4] Rising or swelling into a spherical or rounded form. — *-ly*, *adv.* [8].

con-vex'i-ty (kŏn-vĕk'sĭ-tĭ), *n.* Convex state.

con-vey' (kŏn-vā'), *v. t.* 1. To bear from one place to another ; carry ; transport. 2. To serve as a medium or conduit for; transmit. 3. To impart, as by language. 4. To transfer or deliver to another, as the title to property by a deed. — **con-vey'er** (-ẽr), **con-vey'or** (-ẽr), *n.* [8].

con-vey'ance (-ăns), *n.* 1. Act of conveying. 2. Means or way of conveying ; esp.: a A deed or mortgage. b A vehicle ; carriage.

con-vict' (kŏn-vĭkt'), *v. t.* To prove or find guilty.

con'vict (kŏn'vĭkt), *n.* One convicted of, and under sentence for, a serious crime; criminal; felon.

con-vic'tion (kŏn-vĭk'shŭn), *n.* 1. A convicting; state of being convicted. 2. Act of convincing of error, or compelling the admission of a truth 3. State of being convinced; strong belief.

con-vince' (-vĭns'), *v. t.* [1] To persuade by argument;satisfy by proof. — **con-vinc'ing-ly**,*adv.*[8]

con-viv'i-al (-vĭv'ĭ-ăl), *a.* [4] Relating to a feast or entertainment; festive. — *-ly*, *adv.* [8].

con-viv'i-al'i-ty (-ăl'ĭ-tĭ), *n.* Convivial spirit or humor ; festivity.

con'vo-ca'tion (kŏn'vȯ-kā'shŭn), *n.* 1. Act of convoking. 2. An assembly convoked.

con-voke' (kŏn-vōk'), *v. t.* [1] To call together ; assemble by summons ; convene.

āle, senāte, cãre, ăm, ȧccount, ärm, ȧsk, sofȧ; ēve, ĕvent, ĕnd, recĕnt, makẽr; īce, ĭll ; ōld, ȯbey, ôrb, ŏdd, sŏft, cȯnnect ; ūse, ŭnite, ûrn, ŭp, circŭs ; fōōd, fŏŏt ; out, oil ;

con'vo-lute (kŏn'vŏ-lūt), *a.* Rolled together, one part on another. — **con'vo-lut'ed** (-lūt'ĕd), *a.*

con'vo-lu'tion (-lū'shŭn), *n.* **1.** A rolling or coiling together; a winding. **2.** A fold or coil.

con-voy' (kŏn-voi'), *v. t.* To accompany for protection, by sea or land; escort.

con'voy (kŏn'voi), *n.* **1.** Act of convoying. **2.** One that convoys another. **3.** One that is convoyed, as a wagon train having an armed escort.

con-vulse' (kŏn-vŭls'), *v. t.* [1] To shake violently; agitate greatly.

con-vul'sion (-vŭl'shŭn), *n.* **1.** A violent and involuntary contraction or series of contractions of the muscles; spasm; — usually in *pl.* **2.** Any violent irregular agitation; tumult.

con-vul'sive (-sĭv), *a.* Of the nature of a convulsion. — **-ly**, *adv.* [8] — **-ness**, *n.* [8].

co'ny (kō'nĭ), *n.; pl.* -NIES (-nĭz). A rabbit; esp., the European rabbit.

coo (kōō), *v. i.* **1.** To make the characteristic cry of the pigeon, or a sound suggestive of it. **2.** To converse in a loving way; as, billing and *cooing.* — *n.* The cry or call of one that coos.

cook (kŏok), *n.* One who prepares food for the table by cooking. — *v. t.* **1.** To prepare (food) by boiling, roasting, baking, broiling, etc.; prepare or treat (anything) by heat. **2.** To prepare; hence, tamper with; falsify. *Colloq.* — *v. i.* **1.** To do the work of a cook. **2.** To be cooked.

cook'er, *n.* One that cooks something; esp., a special vessel or apparatus for cooking something.

cook'er-y (-ĭ), *n.; pl.* -ERIES (-ĭz). **1.** Art, process, or practice of cooking. **2.** A place for cooking.

cook'ie (-ĭ), *n.* Var. of COOKY.

cook'y (-ĭ), *n.; pl.* -IES (-ĭz). A small flat cake.

cool (kōōl), *a.* [3] **1.** Moderately cold; lacking in warmth. **2.** Not retaining or admitting heat. **3.** Not ardent or passionate; deliberate; self-possessed. **4.** Manifesting coldness or dislike. **5.** Quietly impudent; audacious. **6.** Stated, estimated, or the like, without exaggeration. — *n.* **1.** Something that is cool; cool time, place, etc. **2.** Coolness. — *v. i. & t.* **1.** To become or make cool. **2.** To calm; allay; moderate.

cool'er (kōōl'ẽr), *n.* One that cools something, as a vessel used to cool liquids, etc.

coo'lie (kōō'lĭ), *n.* In India, China, etc., a native unskilled laborer or porter; also, elsewhere, a cheap laborer from the Orient.

cool'ly (kōōl'lĭ), *adv.* In a cool manner.

cool'ness, *n.* State of being cool.

coon (kōōn), *n.* A raccoon.

coop (kōōp), *n.* A cage or small inclosure, as for poultry. — *v. t.* To confine in or as in a coop.

coop'er (kōōp'ẽr), *n.* One who makes or repairs barrels, casks, etc.

coop'er-age (-ăj), *n.* Work done by a cooper, or the pay for it; also, a cooper's shop.

co-öp'er-ate (kō-ŏp'ẽr-āt), *v. i.* [1] **1.** To act jointly with another or others. **2.** To join in coöperation (sense 2). — **a'tor** (-ā'tẽr), *n.* [8].

co-öp'er-a'tion (-ā'shŭn), *n.* **1.** A joint effort or labor. **2.** The association, or collective action, of persons for their common benefit.

co-öp'er-a-tive (-ă-tĭv), *a.* [4] Coöperating; of or pertaining to coöperation. — **-ly**, *adv.* [8].

co-ör'di-nate (-ôr'dĭ-nāt), *a.* Equal in rank, order, or importance; not subordinate. — *n.* One that is coördinate. — (-nāt), *v. t. & i.* [1] **1.** To make or become coördinate. **2.** To adjust; harmonize. — **co-ör'di-nate-ly**, *adv.* [8].

co-ör'di-na'tion (-nā'shŭn), *n.* Act of coördinating; harmonious adjustment.

coot (kōōt), *n.* **1.** Any of certain ducklike birds of the rail family. **2.** A scoter.

co'pal (kō'păl), *n.* A resin from various tropical trees, used in making varnishes.

co-part'ner (kō-pärt'nẽr), *n.* Joint associate; partner. — **co-part'ner-ship**, *n.*

cope (kōp), *v. i.* [1] To contest hostilely; struggle; now, usually, to contend on equal terms or with some success; match; — followed by *with.*

cope, *n.* **1.** A kind of ecclesiastical hooded cloak. **2.** A vault or canopy; esp., the vault of heaven.

cop'i-er (kŏp'ĭ-ẽr), *n.* **1.** One who copies, as from an original; copyist. **2.** An imitator.

cop'ing (kōp'ĭng), *n.* The highest course of a wall.

co'pi-ous (kō'pĭ-ŭs), *a.* [4] **1.** Having or yielding an abundance; abounding (*in*); also, profuse in words. **2.** Large in amount; plentiful; abundant. — **-ly**, *adv.* [8] — **-ness**, *n.* [8].

cop'per (kŏp'ẽr), *n.* **1.** A common metal, reddish, ductile, malleable, and tenacious, an excellent conductor of heat and electricity. **2.** Something made of copper, as: **a** A copper (or bronze) coin, as the cent. **b** A vessel, esp. a large boiler.

cop'per-as (-ăs), *n.* A sulphate of iron, a green substance used in ink, in dyeing black, etc.

cop'per-head' (-hĕd'), *n.* **1.** A poisonous snake of the eastern U. S. **2.** [*cap.*] A Northerner who sympathized with the South during the Civil War.

cop'per-plate', *n.* An engraved plate of copper; also, an engraving made from it.

cop'per-y (-ĭ), *a.* [4] Containing or like copper.

cop'pice (-ĭs), *n.* A thicket or grove of small trees.

cop'ra (kŏp'rä), *n.* Dried coconut meat.

copse (kŏps), *n.* A coppice.

cop'u-la (kŏp'ū-lä), *n.; pl.* -LAS (-läz). A word (esp. a form of the verb *be*) used as expressing simply the relation between subject and predicate.

cop'u-la-tive (-lā-tĭv), *a.* Serving to connect. — **copulative verb**, an intransitive verb taking a noun complement, as in, John *became* king.

cop'y (kŏp'ĭ), *n.; pl.* COPIES (-ĭz). **1.** An imitation or reproduction of an original work. **2.** That which is to be imitated or reproduced; pattern. **3.** Manuscript or printed matter to be set up in type. **4.** An individual one of a number of books, engravings, etc., reproducing the same composition or work. — *v. t. & i.* [2] **1.** To make a copy or copies of; reproduce. **2.** To imitate.

cop'y-ist, *n.* A copier; transcriber; imitator.

cop'y-right' (-rīt'), *n.* The exclusive right for a term of years to reproduce, publish, sell, etc., a literary or artistic work. — *v. t.* To secure a copyright on.

co-quet' (kō-kĕt'), *n.* A coquette. — *v. t. & i.* To treat or act as, or like, a coquette; flirt.

co'quet-ry (kō'kĕt-rĭ), *n.; pl.* -RIES (-rĭz). Conduct or appearance of, or like that of, a coquette.

co-quette' (kō-kĕt'), *n.* A woman who seeks to attract men's admiration or affection for mere self-gratification, as to gratify vanity ; a flirt. — **co-quet'tish** (kŏ-kĕt'ĭsh), a. [8] — **-ly**, adv. [8].

co-qui'na (-kē'ná), n. A soft, whitish stone, formed of broken shells and corals.

cor'al (kŏr'ăl), n. A hard stony substance of various colors, composed of the combined skeletons of colonies of tiny sea animals; also, one of these minute animals, or a piece of coral. — a. Having a red color, like coral.

End of a Branch of Red Coral with expanded Polyps.

cor'bel (kŏr'bĕl), n. Supporting projection from a wall.

cord (kŏrd), n. **1.** A string or small rope; also, such string as a material. **2.** A tendon or nerve. **3.** A cubic measure used esp. for cut wood, a pile 8 ft. by 4 ft. by 4 ft. (128 cu. ft.). — v. t. **1.** To bind with cord. **2.** To pile up (wood, etc.) in cords.

cord'age (kŏr'dăj), n. Cords or ropes collectively; esp., the ropes in a ship's rigging.

cor'date (-dāt), a. Heart-shaped; — esp. of leaves.

cor'dial (kŏr'jăl; kŏrd'yăl), a. [4] **1.** Tending to revive, cheer, or invigorate. **2.** Hearty ; sincere ; warm. — n. **1.** Any invigorating preparation. **2.** A liqueur. — **cor'dial-ly**, adv. [8].

cor-dial'i-ty (kŏr-jăl'ĭ-tĭ; kŏr/dĭ-ăl'-), n. Cordial quality ; warmth of regard ; heartiness.

cor'don (kŏr'dŏn), n. **1.** A line as of sentinels or guards, or military posts, around a place. **2.** A cord or ribbon worn as a badge or decoration.

cor'do-van (-dŏ-văn), n. A soft, fine-grained, colored leather.

cor'du-roy (kŏr'dŭ-roi'), n. A durable cotton fabric with velvetlike surface raised in ridges. — a. **1.** Made of or like corduroy. **2.** Designating a road, bridge, or the like, formed of logs laid side by side transversely.

core (kōr), n. **1.** The hard central part in fruits of the apple family. **2.** The central part of anything. **3.** The portion of a mold which shapes the interior of a hollow casting. — v. t. [1] To take out the core of.

co're-op'sis (kō/rē-ŏp'sĭs ; kŏr/ē-), n. Any of various plants (genus *Coreopsis*) of the aster family.

co'ri-an'der (kō/rĭ-ăn'dēr), n. A certain herb of the celery family, having aromatic seeds.

cork (kôrk), n. **1.** The thick light bark of an oak of southern Europe. **2.** A piece of cork, or an object made of cork; esp., a stopper, as for a bottle. — v. t. To furnish, fit, or stop with cork or a cork ; hence, to hold in reserve, as if sealed ; restrain ; confine ; — often with *up*.

cork'screw (kŏrk'skrōō'), n. An instrument with a screw or a spiral for drawing corks from bottles.

cork'y (kŏr'kĭ), a. [3] Of the nature of or like cork.

corm (kôrm), n. *Bot.* A short, bulblike fleshy stem, as in the crocus.

cor'mo-rant (kŏr'mŏ-rănt), n. **1.** A voracious sea bird having under the beak a sac in which it holds captured fish. **2.** Hence : A greedy or gluttonous person.

corn (kôrn), n. **1.** A small, hard seed, esp. of a cereal grass, as wheat, rye, etc. **2.** Collectively, the seeds of any cereal grass used for food; grain ; in the U. S., usually, Indian corn ; maize. **3.** Any plant that produces corn. — v. t. To salt slightly, as in brine; as, to *corn* beef.

corn, n. A horny thickening and hardening of the epidermis, or outer layer of skin, at some point, esp. on the toes, due to friction or pressure.

corn'cob' (-kŏb'), n. The chaffy axis on which the kernels of Indian corn, or maize, are arranged. *U.S.*

corn cockle. An annual weed of the pink family, with bright red flowers, common in grainfields.

cor'ne-a (kŏr'nē-á), n. The transparent part of the coat of the eyeball covering the iris and pupil.

cor'nel (kŏr'nĕl), n. Any herb or shrub of the genus including the dogwood.

cor'ner (-nēr), n. **1.** The point or place where two converging lines, sides, or edges meet; angle. **2.** A position from which retreat is impossible. **3.** A secluded place; a nook. **4.** An edge or extremity. **5.** The state of things produced by persons who buy up the whole or the available part of any stock or property, and thus compel those who need such stock or property to buy of them at their own price. — v. t. **1.** To drive into a corner (sense 2). **2.** To bring about a " corner " in ; as, to *corner* wheat.

corner stone. **1.** A stone in a corner. **2.** Hence ; Something of fundamental importance.

cor'ner-wise (-wīz'), adv. So as to form a corner; also, from corner to corner ; diagonally.

cor'net (kŏr'nĕt; kŏr-nĕt'), n. **1.** *Music.* A brass wind instrument resembling the trumpet. **2.** A hollow cone formed of a sheet of paper rolled up, as to hold candy, etc.; a cornucopia.

cor'net-ist, n. [7] A player on the cornet.

corn'flow'er (kŏrn'flou'ēr), n. **1.** The corn cockle. **2.** The bachelor's-button, or bluebottle, a plant of the aster family having flower heads with blue, pink, or white bottle-shaped rays.

cor'nice (kŏr'nĭs), n. A horizontal part (usually ornamented by a molding and projecting) which crowns, or finishes, a building or part of a building, as a column (see COLUMN); hence, the top course of a wall when treated as a crowning member.

corn'starch' (-stärch'), n. Starch made from Indian corn, esp. a fine white flour for puddings, etc.

cor'nu-co'pi-a (kŏr'nŭ-kō'pĭ-á), n. **1.** The "horn of plenty," emblem of abundance. **2.** = CORNET, 2.

co-rol'la (kŏ-rŏl'á), n. *Bot.* The inner, usually bright-colored, series of leaves of a flower.

cor'ol-la-ry (kŏr'ŏ-lá-rĭ), n. ; pl. -RIES (-rĭz). An obvious deduction, consequence, or inference.

co-ro'na (kŏ-rō'ná), n. ; pl. L. -NÆ (-nē), E. -NAS (năz). **1.** A crown. **2.** A circle or halo sometimes seen around a luminous body, as the sun or moon.

cor'o-na'tion (kŏr'ŏ-nā'shŭn), n. Act or solemnity of crowning a sovereign.

cor'o-ner (kŏr'ŏ-nēr), n. A public officer whose duty is to inquire, by an inquest, into any death supposedly not due to natural causes.

cor'o-net (-nĕt), n. **1.** A crown worn as the mark of high rank lower than sovereignty. **2.** An ornamental fillet or wreath worn round the temples.

Coronet of Prince of Wales.

cor′po-ral (kôr′pŏ-răl), *n.* The lowest noncommissioned officer. See ARMY.

cor′po-ral, *a.* Bodily; personal. — **cor′po-ral-ly,** *adv.* [8].

cor′po-rate (-pŏ-rāt), *a.* **1.** Combined into one body; united. **2.** *Law.* Incorporated. **3.** Belonging to a corporation.

cor′po-ra′tion (-rā′shŭn), *n.* Any body consisting of one or more individuals treated by the law as a unit; esp., such a body consisting of persons and endowed by law with the right to perpetual succession and to act as a single person.

cor-po′re-al (kôr-pō′rē-ăl), *a.* Of the nature of, consisting of, or pertaining to, matter or a material body; physical. — **cor-po′re-al-ly,** *adv.* [8].

cor-po′re-al′i-ty (-ăl′ĭ-tĭ), *n.* Corporeal quality.

corps (kōr; *pl.,* kōrz), *n. sing. & pl.* A body of persons organized or under common direction; esp., such a military division; as, the Marine *Corps.*

corpse (kôrps), *n.* The dead body of a human being.

cor′pu-lence (kôr′pū-lĕns), *n.* Largeness or bulkiness of body; excessive fatness.

cor′pu-len-cy (-lĕn-sĭ), *n.* Corpulence.

cor′pu-lent (-lĕnt), *a.* [4] Bulky; very fat; obese.

cor′pus-cle (-pŭs-'l), *n.* **1.** A minute particle. **2.** A protoplasmic cell, as in the blood.

cor-pus′cu-lar (kôr-pŭs′kŭ-lär), *a.* Of or pertaining to corpuscles or particles.

cor-ral′ (kŏ-răl′), *n.* An inclosure for confining or capturing animals, as cattle; also, one for defense and security. — *v. t.; -*RALLED′; -RAL′LING. To confine in or as in a corral; form into a corral.

cor-rect′ (-rĕkt′), *a.* **1.** Conforming to a just, acknowledged, or conventional standard. **2.** Conforming to fact or truth. — *v. t.* **1.** To make or set right; amend. **2.** To reprove or punish for faults. **3.** To counteract by opposite qualities or tendencies; neutralize.

cor-rec′tion (-rĕk′shŭn), *n.* **1.** A correcting. **2.** That which is substituted for something wrong.

cor-rec′tion-al (-ăl), *a.* Of or pertaining to correction; reformatory.

cor-rec′tive (-tĭv), *a.* [4] Tending to rectify or amend. — *n.* A corrective agent.

cor-rect′ly, *adv.* In a correct manner.

cor-rect′ness, *n.* State of being correct.

cor-rec′tor (-rĕk′tẽr), *n.* One that corrects.

cor′re-late′ (kŏr′ē-lāt′; kŏr′ē-lāt), *v. i.* [1] To have correlation. — *v. t.* To connect by disclosure of a mutual relation.

cor′re-la′tion (-lā′shŭn), *n.* Mutual or reciprocal relation, as of part to part or of a part to a whole; act of bringing into or determining such relation.

cor-rel′a-tive (kŏ-rĕl′ă-tĭv), *a.* Having, indicating, or involving a reciprocal relation; mutually related. — *n.* One that stands in a reciprocal relation to something else. — **ly,** *adv.* [8].

cor′re-spond′ (kŏr′ē-spŏnd′), *v. i.* **1.** To answer in character, function, amount, etc.; to suit, agree, or match; — followed by *with* or *to.* **2.** To have intercourse, esp. by sending and receiving letters.

cor′re-spond′ence (-spŏn′dĕns), *n.* **1.** Act or state of corresponding; mutual adaptation. **2.** Intercourse by letters; also, the letters.

cor′re-spond′en-cy (-sĭ), *n.; pl.* -CIES (-sĭz). Correspondence (now only in sense 1).

cor′re-spond′ent (-dĕnt), *a.* Answering (to something) in fitness, quality, size, function, etc.; corresponding. — *n.* **1.** Something that corresponds, or answers; a correlative. **2.** One with whom intercourse is carried on by letters. **3.** A person who contributes news regularly to a periodical. **4.** One who has regular commercial relations with another, esp. with a business house at a distance.

cor′re-spond′ing, *p. a.* **1.** Correspondent. **2.** Communicating by letters. — **ly,** *adv.* [8].

cor′ri-dor (kôr′ĭ-dôr), *n.* A gallery or passageway connecting several apartments.

cor′ri-gi-ble (-jĭ-b'l), *a.* [4] Capable of, or submissive to, correction.

cor-rob′o-rate (kŏ-rŏb′ŏ-rāt), *v. t.* [1] To make more certain; confirm.

cor-rob′o-ra′tion (-rā′shŭn), *n.* Confirmation.

cor-rob′o-ra-tive (-rŏb′ŏ-rá-tĭv; -rá-tĭv), *a.* Tending to corroborate; confirmatory.

cor-rob′o-ra-to-ry (-rá-tŏ-rĭ), *a.* Corroborative.

cor-rode′ (kŏ-rōd′), *v. t.* [1] **1.** To diminish gradually by chemical action or the like. **2.** To consume; wear away.

cor-ro′sion (kŏ-rō′zhŭn), *n.* Act, process, or effect of corroding.

cor-ro′sive (-sĭv), *a.* [4] **1.** Corroding, as an acid. **2.** Having the quality of fretting or vexing. — *n.* That which corrodes.

cor′ru-gate (kôr′ŏŏ-gāt), *v. t. & i.* [1] To form or shape in alternate ridges and grooves.

cor′ru-ga′tion (-gā′shŭn), *n.* Act of corrugating; also, a wrinkle or groove of a corrugated surface.

cor-rupt′ (kŏ-rŭpt′), *a.* [4] Changed from a state of uprightness, correctness, truth, etc., to a bad state. — *v. t.* **1.** To change from good to bad; debase. **2.** To draw aside from rectitude and duty; pervert.

cor-rupt′i-bil′i-ty (-rŭp′tĭ-bĭl′ĭ-tĭ), *n.* Quality of being corruptible; corruptibleness.

cor-rupt′i-ble (-rŭp′tĭ-b'l), *a.* Capable of being corrupted; liable to corruption. — **ness,** *n.* [8].

cor-rup′tion (-shŭn), *n.* Act of corrupting; state of being corrupt.

cor-rup′tive (-tĭv), *a.* [4] Corrupting or vitiating.

cor-rupt′ly, *adv.* In a corrupt manner.

cor-rupt′ness, *n.* Quality of being corrupt.

cor′sage (kôr′sáj; *F.* kôr′sázh′), *n.* The waist or bodice of a woman's dress.

cor′sair (kôr′sâr), *n.* A privateer; a pirate.

corse (kôrs), *n.* Corpse. *Archaic.*

corse′let, cors′let (kôrs′lĕt), *n.* A piece of defensive armor for the body.

cor′set (kôr′sĕt), *n.* A woman's inner laced bodice or waist, used chiefly to shape or support the body; stays; — often in *pl.*

‖ **cor′tège′** (kôr′tĕzh′), *n.* [F.] A train of attendants; procession.

cor′tex (kôr′tĕks), *n.* **1.** *Bot.* Bark. **2.** The outer layer of gray matter of the brain.

co-run′dum (kŏ-rŭn′dŭm), *n.* Native alumina, the hardest mineral except the diamond.

cor′us-cate (kôr′ŭs-kāt), *v. t.* [1] To glitter or gleam in flashes.

cor′us-ca′tion (kôr′ŭs-kā′shŭn), *n.* A coruscating.

cor′vet (kôr′vĕt) } *n.* A war vessel ranking
cor-vette′ (kôr-vĕt′) } next below a frigate in the old sailing navies.

cos-met′ic (kŏz-mĕt′ĭk), *a.* Beautifying, esp. the complexion or hair.—*n.* Any external application to beautify the complexion or hair.

cos′mic (kŏz′mĭk), *a.* Of or relating to the cosmos or something similarly vast and systematic. — **cos′mi-cal** (-mĭ-kăl), *a.* [8].

cos′mo-pol′i-tan (-mŏ-pŏl′ĭ-tăn), *a.* [4] **1.** Belonging to all, or most of, the world; not local. **2.** At home in any country. — *n.* A cosmopolite.

cos-mop′o-lite (kŏz-mŏp′ŏ-līt), *n.* A cosmopolitan person, plant, or animal.

cos′mos (kŏz′mŏs), *n.* The universe as an orderly and harmonious system; — opposed to *chaos.*

cos′set (kŏs′ĕt), *n.* A pet lamb; a pet.— *v. t.* To pet; pamper.

cost (kŏst), *v. i. ; pret. & p. p.* COST; *p. pr. & vb. n.* COST′ING. **1.** To be of the price of; to cause the expenditure, relinquishment, or loss of. **2.** To require or cause to be borne or suffered.—*n.* **1.** The amount or equivalent paid, given, or charged, for anything. **2.** Outlay, as of money, time, labor, etc. **3.** *pl. Law.* Expenses incurred in litigation.

cos′ter-mon′ger (kŏs′tĕr-mŭn′gĕr), *n.* A hawker of fruit or vegetables. *Chiefly Eng.*

cos′tive (-tĭv), *a.* [4] Constipated or causing constipation. — **cos′tive-ness**, *n.* [8].

cost′ly (kŏst′lĭ), *a.* [3] Of great cost; expensive. — **cost′li-ness**, *n.* [8].

cos′tume (kŏs′tūm; kŏs-tūm′), *n.* **1.** Dress in general, including ornaments and the style of wearing the hair. **2.** A dress of a particular period or locality, worn in the drama, etc. **3.** A suit or dress of outer garments, esp. for a woman.

cos-tume′ (kŏs-tūm′), *v. t.* [1] To provide with, or to put on, a costume.

cos-tum′er (-tūm′ĕr), *n.* A dealer in costumes.

co′sy (kō′zĭ), *a.* [3] Var. of COZY.

cot (kŏt), *n.* **1.** A cottage. **2.** A sheath.

cot, *n.* A portable or small bed.

cote (kōt), *n.* A shed or inclosure for small domestic animals, as sheep or doves.

co′te-rie (kō′tĕ-rĭ), *n.* A set or circle of persons who meet familiarly, as for social purposes.

co-til′lion (kō-tĭl′yŭn), *n.* A series of round dances interspersed with fanciful evolutions ; a german.

cot′tage (kŏt′ăj), *n.* A small house; also, any house at a summer resort.

cot′tag-er (-ă-jĕr), *n.* One who lives in a cottage.

cot′ter, *n.* A pin to fasten together parts of a machine or structure.

cot′ton (kŏt′'n), *n.* **1.** A soft, white, fibrous substance composed of the hairs clothing the seeds of various plants of the mallow family. **2.** The cotton plant or crop. **3.** Fabric made of cotton. **4.** Thread spun from cotton.

Cotton. 1 Flowering Branch ; 2 Fruit ; 3 Seed. (⅔)

cot′ton-tail′ (-tāl′),*n.* The common American rabbit.

cot′ton-wood′ (-wŏŏd′),*n.* Any of several American species of poplar having a cottony tuft about the seeds.

cot′ton-y (kŏt′'n-ĭ). *a.* [4] Like cotton ; downy.

cot′y-le′don (kŏt′ĭ-lē′dŭn), *n. Bot.* The first leaf, or one of the first pair or whorl of leaves, developed in seed plants ; — called also *seed leaf.*

couch (kouch), *n.* **1.** A structure, as a bed or lounge, for repose or sleep. **2.** Any place for repose, as the lair of a beast, etc.— *v. t.* **1.** To lay upon a bed or resting place. **2.** To lower ; bend down ; depress, as some part of the body, a lance, etc. **3.** To put into language ; express ; phrase. — *v. i.* **1.** To lie in a place or position of rest ; repose. **2.** To lie in ambush ; be concealed.

cou′gar (kōō′gär), *n.* A large tawny American quadruped of the cat family.

cough (kŏf), *v. i.* To expel air, or obstructing or irritating matter, from the lungs or air passages in a sudden noisy manner. — *v. t.* To expel by coughing ; — with *up* or *out.* — *n.* **1.** Act of coughing. **2.** The more or less frequent repetition of coughing, a symptom of disease.

could (kŏŏd), *pret.* of CAN. Was, should be, or would be, able ; — used as an auxiliary.

cou′lee (kōō′lĭ, *F.* kōō′lā′), *n.* [F.] The bed of a ‖ **cou′lée′** ‖ stream when deep and having inclined sides. *Western U. S.*

cou-lomb′ (kōō-lŏm′), *n.* Practical unit of quantity in electrical measurements; quantity transferred by a current of one ampere in one second.

coul′ter (kōl′tĕr), Var. of COLTER.

coun′cil (koun′sĭl), *n.* **1.** An assembly convened for consultation, advice, or agreement. **2.** A body constituted as an advisory or legislative body.

coun′cil-man (-măn), *n. ; pl.* -MEN. A member of a council, esp. of the common council of a city.

coun′ci-lor (-sĭ-lĕr), *n.* [7] A member of a council, as of a council advisory to a chief magistrate.

coun′sel (-sĕl), *n.* **1.** Mutual advising ; deliberation together. **2.** Advice. **3.** One who gives advice; a lawyer; collectively, the legal advocates united in managing a case.— *v. t.* [7] **1.** To advise. **2.** To recommend, as an act or course.

coun′se-lor (-sĕ-lĕr), *n.* [7] **1.** One who counsels; an adviser. **2.** A counsel, or barrister.

count (kount), *v. t.* **1.** To tell or name one by one, or by groups ; number ; enumerate. **2.** To take into account ; include in reckoning. **3.** To name the numerals in order up to and including(a specified numeral). **4.** To esteem ; consider. — *v. i.* **1.** To count articles ; also, to name numerals in order. **2.** To reckon ; rely ; depend. **3.** To be of account or value. — *n.* **1.** Act of numbering, or the number ascertained by counting. **2.** *Law.* A particular charge, in a declaration or indictment, stating the cause of action or prosecution.

count, *n.* A nobleman on the continent of Europe, corresponding in rank to an English earl.

coun′te-nance (koun′tĕ-năns), *n.* **1.** Look or expression of the face ; the face ; visage. **2.** Approving bearing or facial aspect; hence, favor; support; aid.— *v. t.* [4] To give countenance to ; favor.

count′er (koun′tĕr), *n.* **1.** A device, as a piece of metal, used in reckoning. **2.** A kind of table, as in a shop, over which business is transacted.

count′er, *n.* One that counts.

coun′ter (koun′tẽr), *adv.* **1.** In the wrong way. **2.** Contrary; contrariwise. — *a.* Contrary; opposite; opposed. — *n.* The leather that stiffens or supports the heel part of a boot or shoe upper.

coun′ter, *v. t.* To encounter, oppose, combat, or the like. — *v. i.* To deliver a counter (blow). — *n.* Act of giving a blow when receiving or parrying one, as in boxing; also, the blow given.

coun′ter-act′ (-ăkt′), *v. t.* To act in opposition to.

coun′ter-ac′tion (-ăk′shŭn), *n.* Contrary action.

coun′ter-ac′tive (-ăk′tĭv), *a.* Tending to counteract. — *n.* That which counteracts.

coun′ter-bal′ance (-băl′ăns), *v. t.* To oppose with an equal weight or power. — *n.* **1.** A weight that balances another; a counterpoise. **2.** Influence or power which offsets another.

coun′ter-claim′ (-klām′), *n.* An opposing claim.

coun′ter-feit (koun′tẽr-fĭt), *a.* Given or assuming the appearance of something genuine or original; spurious. — *n.* That which is made in imitation of something else with intent to deceive. — *v. t.* To imitate, esp. for deceiving; to make a counterfeit of. — *v. i.* **1.** To dissemble; pretend. **2.** To make counterfeits, esp. of money. — **coun′ter-feit′er** (-fĭt′ẽr), *n.* [8].

coun′ter-ir′ri-tant (-ĭr′ĭ-tănt), *n.* An irritant to cause irritation to relieve an existing irritation elsewhere.

coun′ter-mand′ (-mȧnd′), *v. t.* To revoke (a command); cancel (an order) by a contrary order.

coun′ter-mand (koun′tẽr-mȧnd; koun′tẽr-mȧnd′), *n.* A contrary order; a revoking order or act.

coun′ter-march′ (koun′tẽr-märch′), *n.* A marching back; retrocession.

coun′ter-march′ (koun′tẽr-märch′; koun′tẽr-märch′), *v. i. & t.* To execute a countermarch.

coun′ter-mine′ (koun′tẽr-mīn′), *n. Mil.* An underground gallery to intercept an enemy's mine. — **coun′ter-mine′** (-mīn′), *v. t. & i.* [1].

coun′ter-pane′ (-pān′), *n.* A coverlet for a bed.

coun′ter-part′ (-pärt′), *n.* **1.** A part or thing corresponding to another; a copy; facsimile. **2.** A person closely resembling another. **3.** A thing that serves to complete or complement something else.

coun′ter-poise′ (-poiz′), *n.* **1.** A counterbalance. **2.** An equal opposing power or force. **3.** Equilibrium. — *v. t.* [1] **1.** To counterbalance. **2.** To weigh (one thing) against another.

coun′ter-sign′ (koun′tẽr-sīn′; koun′tẽr-sīn′), *v. t.* To sign in addition to the signature of another. — *n.* **1.** The signature of a person to a writing already signed by another, as to authenticate it. **2.** A secret signal which must be given by any one wishing to pass a sentry.

coun′ter-sink′ (koun′tẽr-sĭŋk′),*v. t.;* for prin. parts see SINK. **1.** To enlarge (a hole) to receive the head of a screw, bolt, etc. **2.** To cause (a screw, bolt, etc.) to sink even with or below the surface.

count′ess (koun′tĕs), *n.* Wife or widow of an earl (British or Irish), or of a count (on the Continent); also, a lady of the same rank in her own right.

count′ing-house′ (koun′tĭng-hous′)) *n.* Place **count′ing-room′** (koun′tĭng-rōōm′)) where a merchant, trader, or manufacturer keeps his books and transacts business.

count′less, *a.* Incapable of being counted.

coun′tri-fied (kŭn′trĭ-fīd), *p. a.* [4] Having a rustic look and manners; rustic.

coun′try (-trĭ), *n. ; pl.* -TRIES (-trĭz). **1.** A region or tract of land of undefined extent; a district. **2.** An inhabited region of more or less definite limits, or the people of a region. **3.** The territory of a nation; a state distinct as to name and people; also, the people. **4.** Land of one's birth, allegiance, or citizenship. **5.** Rural regions as opposed to city or town. — *a.* Of or pertaining to the country, or rural regions; also, rustic; unpolished.

coun′try-man (-măn), *n.; pl.* -MEN. **1.** An inhabitant of a (certain) country; also, a compatriot. **2.** A rustic; farmer.

coun′try-seat′ (-sēt′), *n.* A country residence.

coun′try-side′ (-sīd′), *n.* A country neighborhood.

coun′try-wom′an (-wŏŏm′ăn), *n.; pl.* -WOMEN. A woman of the country, or of the same country.

coun′ty (koun′tĭ), *n. ; pl.* -TIES (-tĭz). In the U. S., the largest division for local government in all States but Louisiana, where it is called *parish.*

‖**coup** (kōō), *n.* [F.] Lit., a stroke; blow; esp., a sudden or unexpected stroke, device, or stratagem.

cou-pé′ (kōō′pā′), *n.* A four-wheeled closed carriage for two persons inside, with an outside seat for the driver.

cou′ple (kŭp′'l), *n.* **1.** That which links two things together; tie; leash. **2.** Two of the same kind considered together; pair; brace. **3.** A man and woman married or betrothed, or partners at a dance, etc. — *v. t.* [1] To link or tie; join. — *v. i.* To come together, forming a pair or pairs.

cou′pler (-lẽr), *n.* One that couples; a coupling.

cou′plet (-lĕt), *n.* Two successive riming lines of verse, esp. two of the same length.

cou′pling (-lĭng), *n.* **1.** Act of one that couples. **2.** *Mach.* A contrivance or device to couple adjacent parts or objects.

cou′pon (kōō′pŏn), *n.* **1.** A certificate of interest due, to be cut from transferable bonds, and presented for payment. **2.** A section of a ticket, showing the holder to be entitled to something.

cour′age (kŭr′ăj), *n.* That quality of mind which enables one to encounter danger and difficulties with firmness, or without fear; valor.

cou-ra′geous (kŭ-rā′jŭs), *a.* [4] Having, or characterized by, courage; brave. — **-ly,** *adv.* — **-ness,** *n.*

cou′ri-er (kōō′rĭ-ẽr), *n.* **1.** A special, swift messenger. **2.** An attendant on travelers who looks out for their convenience at hotels and on the way.

course (kōrs), *n.* **1.** Act of moving from one point to another; progress; passage; direction. **2.** Ground or path traversed; track; way. **3.** Method of procedure; conduct. **4.** A series of acts or proceedings arranged in order or at regular intervals. **5.** That part of a meal served at one time. **6.** A horizontal row of bricks or stones in a wall.

course, *v. t.* [1] **1.** To pursue. **2.** To cause, as dogs, to pursue game. **3.** To run through or over. — *v. i.* **1.** To take or follow a course. **2.** To run as in a race or in hunting.

cours′er (kōr′sẽr), *n.* A swift or spirited horse; a racer or a war horse. *Poetic.*

court (kōrt), *n.* **1.** An uncovered area partly or wholly inclosed as by buildings. **2.** An inclosed open space like a short street. **3.** A space for

playing any of various games with a ball, as tennis.
4. The residence of a sovereign or other dignitary;
palace. **5.** The retinue of a sovereign or person
high in authority; also, a prince or sovereign and his
ministers and officials as a political body. **6.** Any
formal assembling of the retinue of a sovereign.
7. Attention or homage directed to one whose
favor, affection, or interest is sought. **8. a** The
place where justice is administered. **b** A judicial
tribunal, or those constituting it. **c** The session of
a judicial assembly. — *v. t.* **1.** To seek the favor of
by attention or flattery. **2.** To seek the affections
of ; woo. **3.** To attempt to gain ; solicit ; seek.

cour′te-ous (kûr′tĕ-ŭs ; kōrt′yŭs), *a.* [4] Of
courtlike manners ; characterized by courtesy. —
-ly, *adv.* [8] —**ness**, *n.* [8].

cour′te-sy (kûr′tĕ-sĭ ; kōrt′tĕ-sĭ), *n.; pl.* -SIES (-sĭz).
1. Politeness ; civility ; courtliness. **2.** An act
of civility or respect. **3.** Favor or indulgence,
as distinguished from right ; as, a title given by
courtesy.

court′house′ (kōrt′hous′),*n.* A building for courts
(see COURT, *n.*, 8) and public meetings.

court′ier (-yẽr), *n.* **1.** An attendant at the court
of a prince. **2.** One who courts favor ; flatterer.

court′ly, *a.* [3] Elegant ; polite. — *adv.* Politely ;
elegantly. — **court′li-ness** (-lĭ-nĕs), *n.* [8].

court′-mar′tial (kōrt′mär′shăl), *n.; pl.* COURTS-
MARTIAL. A court of military or naval officers
for the trial of one belonging to the army or navy,
or of offenses against military or naval law.— *v. t.*
[7] To subject to trial by a court-martial.

court′-plas′ter, *n.* Sticking plaster, as of silk.

court′ship (kōrt′shĭp), *n.* The act or process of
paying court ; esp., wooing.

court′yard′ (-yärd′), *n.* A court or inclosure attached to a house, castle, or palace.

cous′in (kŭz′'n), *n.* The son or daughter of one's
uncle or aunt (more fully *own, first,* or *full, cousin*) ; also, a relative descended the same number
of steps by a different line from a common ancestor (as in *second cousin, third cousin,* etc.).

cous′in-ger′man (-jûr′măn), *n. ; pl.* COUSINS-GER-
MAN. A first cousin.

cove (kōv),*n.* A retired nook, esp. a sheltered inlet.

cov′e-nant (kŭv′ĕ-nănt),*n.* An agreement between
two or more persons or parties ; a compact. — *v. i.
& t.* To agree ; contract ; bargain.

cov′er (-ẽr), *v. t.* **1.** To place a covering over ;
also, to overspread or envelop ; clothe. **2.** To hide
from sight ; conceal. **3** To brood or sit on ; incubate. **4.** To extend thickly over. **5.** To shelter, as
from evil ; protect. **6.** To be sufficient for ; include ; embrace. **7.** To pass over (a distance), as
a train. **8.** To bring or hold within range, as of a
gun. — *n.* **1.** Something laid, set, or spread on,
about, or over another thing. **2.** Anything that
veils or conceals ; cloak. **3.** Shelter ; protection.
4. Covert for game. **5.** The table furniture or
service, esp. for one person, at a meal.

cov′er-ing (-ĭng), *n.* Anything that covers.

cov′er-let (-lĕt), *n.* The uppermost cover of a bed.

cov′er-lid (-lĭd), *n.* A coverlet.

cov′ert (-ẽrt), *a.* [4] Covered over ; secret ; dis-
guised. — *n.* **1.** A place that covers and protects ;
esp., a thicket affording cover for game. **2.** One of

the special feathers covering the bases of the quills
of the wings and tail of a bird. — **-ly**, *adv.* [8].

cov′et (-ĕt), *v. t. & i.* To wish for, or desire, with
eagerness or inordinately, esp. wrongly.

cov′et-ous (-ĕ-tŭs), *a.* [4] Excessively eager to get
(esp. money) ; avaricious. — **-ly**, *adv.* —**ness**, *n.*

cov′ey (-ĭ), *n. ; pl.* COVEYS (-ĭz). **1.** A brood of
birds ; small flock, as of partridges, grouse, etc.
2. A company ; bevy.

cow (kou), *n.; pl.* COWS (kouz). The mature female
of any bovine animal, or of any other animal the
male of which is called *bull.* See BULL.

cow, *v. t.* To depress with fear.

cow′ard (kou′ẽrd), *a.* [4] **1.** Destitute of courage ;
cowardly. **2.** Due to base fear, or expressive of
such fear. — *n.* A person who lacks courage ;
poltroon ; craven ; dastard.

cow′ard-ice (-ẽr-dĭs), *n.* Want of courage ; faint-
heartedness ; cowardliness.

cow′ard-ly, *a.* [4] **1.** Wanting courage. **2.** Befitting a coward. —**li-ness** (-lĭ-nĕs), *n.* [8].

cow′boy′ (-boi′), *n.* A cattle herder, esp. one of the
mounted herdsmen of the western United States.

cow′catch′er (-kăch′ẽr), *n.* A strong frame in
front of a locomotive, to throw aside obstructions.

cow′er (-ẽr), *v. i.* To stoop by bending the knees ;
crouch ; hence, to quail.

cow′herd′ (-hûrd′), *n.* One who tends cows at
pasture.

cow′hide′ (-hīd′), *n.* **1.** A cow's hide, or leather
from it. **2.** A heavy whip of rawhide or of braided
leather. — *v. t.* [1] To flog with a cowhide.

cowl (koul), *n.* A monk's hood.— *v. t.* To cover
with or as with a cowl. — **cowled** (kould), *p. a.*

cow′lick′ (kou′lĭk′), *n.* A tuft of hair turned up
or awry (usually in front), as if licked by a cow.

co′work′er (kō′wûr′kẽr), *n.* One who works with
another.

cow′pea′ (kou′pē′), *n.* A plant of the bean family ;
also, its edible seed.

cow′pox′ (kou′pŏks′), *n.* A pustular disease of a
cow's udder, which, when communicated to man,
as by vaccination, protects from smallpox.

cow′rie (-rĭ), *n.; pl.* -RIES (-rĭz). A kind of small
cow′ry } porcelain-like sea shell sometimes used
as money in parts of Africa and Asia.

cow′slip′ (-slĭp′), *n.* **1.** A kind of common primrose. *Great Britain.* **2.** The marsh marigold. *U.S.*

cox′comb′ (kŏks′kōm′), *n.* A vain fellow ; fop.

cox′swain, cock′swain (kŏk′swān ; *naut.* -s'n),*n.*
The steersman of a ship's boat, a racing shell, etc.

coy (koi), *a.* [3] Shrinking from approach or familiarity ; reserved ; shy ; modest ; bashful ; demure.
See SHY. — **coy′ly**, *adv.* [8] —**ness**, *n.* [8].

coy-o′te (kī-ō′tĕ ; kī′ōt), *n.* The prairie wolf.

coz (kŭz), *n.* Cousin ; — used in familiar address.

coz′en (kŭz′'n), *v. t. & i.* To cheat ; deceive.

co′zy (kō′zĭ), *a.* [3] Snug ; comfortable. — **co′zi-
ly**, *adv.* [8] —**ness**, *n.* [8].

crab (krăb), *n.* **1.** A crustacean having a broad
and usually flattened shell, a small abdomen, and
short antennæ. **2.** [*cap.*] *Astron.* The zodiacal
sign Cancer.

crab, *n.* **1.** A crab apple. **2.** A crabbed person.

crab apple. 1. A small, wild, sour apple. **2.** Any
of several cultivated apples with small acid fruit.

āle, senāte, câre, ăm, ăccount, ärm, ȧsk, sofȧ ; ēve, ĕvent, ĕnd, recĕnt, makẽr ; īce, ĭll ;
ōld, ȯbey, ôrb, ŏdd, sŏft, cŏnnect ; ūse, ŭnite, ûrn, ŭp, circŭs ; fōōd, fŏŏt ; out, oil ;

crab′bed (krăb′ĕd),*p. a.* [3] **1**. Characterized by, or manifesting, peevishness, moroseness, or sourness; cross. **2**. Obscure or intricate, as a book or author. **3**. Cramped; irregular, as writing. — **crab′- bed-ly**, *adv.* [8] — **crab′bed-ness**, *n.* [8].

crack (krăk), *v. i.* **1**. To make a sharp, sudden sound in or as in breaking. **2**. To break with or without quite separating into parts. **3**. To become cracked; — said of the voice. — *v. t.* **1**. To break or burst with a sharp sound. **2**. Hence : To rend or burst, as the heart with grief ; make unsound ; to craze. **3**. To utter smartly, as a joke. **4**. To snap, as a whip. **5**. To impair the musical quality or clearness of ; — said of the voice. **6**. To laud; extol ; praise; — with *up*. *Colloq.* — *n.* **1**. A sharp, sudden sound ; the sound of anything suddenly burst or broken. **2**. A sharp, resounding blow. *Colloq.* **3**. A partial separation of parts ; chink ; crevice. — *a.* Of superior excellence. *Colloq.*

crack′-brained′ (krăk′brānd′), *a.* [4] Crazy.

crack′er (-ēr), *n.* **1**. One that cracks. **2**. A firecracker. **3**. One of the lower class of rural whites of the southern States; — a nickname. **4**. A thin hard biscuit. *U. S.*

crack′le (-′l), *v. i.* [1] To make small, sharp, sudden noises, frequently repeated ; crepitate. — *v. t.* To crack or break with slight crushing rapidly repeated. — *n.* **1**. A crackling noise. **2**. *Fine Arts.* A peculiar cracked surface, as in certain kinds of pottery, etc.

crack′ling (-lĭng), *n.* **1**. The making of repeated small, sharp cracks, or reports. **2**. The crisp rind of roasted pork.

crack′nel (-nĕl), *n.* A dry, brittle kind of biscuit.

cra′dle (krā′d′l), *n.* **1**. A bed for a baby, usually on rockers or pivots ; hence, place of origin. **2**. Something suggestive of a baby's cradle, as a rocking device used in washing out gold-bearing earth, etc. — *v. t.* [1] **1**. To lay to rest or rock in or as in a cradle. **2**. To nurse or train in infancy.

craft (kráft), *n.* **1**. Art or skill ; hence, an occupation requiring this ; a manual art. **2**. A power; faculty ; knack. **3**. Artifice ; guile. **4**. Those engaged in any trade, collectively; guild. **5**. *Naut.* A vessel; vessels, collectively.

crafts′man (kráfts′măn), *n. ; pl.* -MEN (-mĕn). One who practices some trade or manual occupation.

crafts′man-ship. *n.* Occupation or performance of a craftsman.

craft′y (kráf′tĭ),*a.* [3] Skillful at deceiving others; wily. — **craft′i-ly**, *adv.* [8] — **-ness**, *n.* [8].

crag (krăg), *n.* A steep, rugged, broken cliff or projecting rock.

crag′gy (-ĭ), *a.* [3] Full of, or marked by, crags; rugged ; rough. — **crag′gi-ness**, *n.* [8].

crake (krāk), *n. Zoöl.* Any of various rails, especially of the short-billed kind.

cram (krăm), *v. t. ;* CRAMMED (krămd); CRAM′MING. **1**. To press, esp. in filling, or in thrusting one thing into another ; stuff. **2**. To fill to satiety with or as with food. **3**. To prepare in a subject by hurried study, as for an examination ; also, to get a knowledge of by cramming. *Colloq.* — *v. i.* **1**. To eat greedily and to satiety ; stuff. **2**. To cram a subject (see CRAM, *v. t.*, 3). *Colloq.*

cramp (krămp), *n.* **1**. Any of various holding

devices, esp. a frame with a tightening screw. **2**. Cramped state or part ; a constraint. **3**. *Med.* **a** Spasmodic and painful involuntary contraction of a muscle or muscles. **b** A paralysis of certain muscles due to excessive use ; as, writer's *cramp*. — *v. t.* **1**. To affect with cramp. **2**. To compress ; restrain ; hamper. **3**. To fasten or hold with or as with a cramp.

Cramp, 1.

cran′ber-ry (krăn′bĕr-ĭ), *n.; pl.* -RIES (-ĭz). The bright red, acid berry of a certain plant of the heath family ; also, the plant.

crane (krān), *n.* **1**. Any of several tall wading birds resembling the herons. **2**. The great blue heron. **3**. A machine for handling heavy weights, commonly by a projecting swinging arm. **4**. Any arm which swings about a vertical axis at one end, for supporting a weight. — *v. t.* **1**. To lift by or as by a crane. **2**. To stretch (the neck) as a crane does. — *v. i.* To stretch out the neck, as to see better.

cra′ni-al (krā′nĭ-ăl), *a.* Pert. to the cranium.

cra′ni-um (krā′nĭ-ŭm), *n.; pl.* E. -NIUMS (-ŭmz), L. -NIA (-*à*). *Anat.* **a** The skull of a vertebrate. **b** The part of the skull inclosing the brain.

crank (krănk), *n.* **1**. *Mach.* A part or arm at right angles to a shaft to impart or receive motion. **2**. A fanciful or eccentric twist or turn in speech, thought, or action ; crotchet ; caprice ; also, a person having a crank. *Colloq.* — *v. t.* To bend into the shape of, or to move or operate by, a crank.

crank, *a.* [3] **1**. Out of gear; loose; shaky. **2**. *Naut.* Of a vessel, very easily inclined by any external force, as that of the wind on the sails.

crank shaft, *or* **crank′shaft′**, *n.* A shaft turning, or driven by, a crank.

crank′y (krănk′ĭ), *a.* [3] **1**. Ill-tempered ; irritable; also, eccentric; crotchety. **2**. *Naut.* Crank. — **crank′i-ly** (-ĭ-lĭ), *adv.* [8] — **-i-ness**, *n.* [8].

cran′ny (krăn′ĭ), *n.; pl.* -NIES (-ĭz). A small, narrow opening; crevice.

crape (krāp), *n.* **1**. A kind of thin, crimped stuff, usually of silk. **2**. A mourning band of this stuff.

crash (krăsh), *v. t. & i.* To break violently and noisily ; strike with a crash. — *n.* **1**. A loud, sudden, confused sound ; the shock of collision and breaking. **2**. Ruin; failure, as of a business.

crash, *n.* Coarse, heavy linen cloth, as for towels.

crass (krăs), *a.* [3] Gross; very stupid or coarse. — **crass′ly**, *adv.* [8] — **crass′ness**, *n.* [8].

crate (krāt), *n.* **1**. A large wickerwork basket. **2**. A case usually of wooden slats, with interspaces. — *v. t.* [1] To pack in a crate.

cra′ter (krā′tēr), *n.* The funnel-shaped opening of a volcano or a geyser.

cra-vat′ (krá-văt′), *n.* A neckcloth, chiefly for men.

crave (krāv), *v. t.* [1] **1**. To ask earnestly ; beg. **2**. To long for ; need. — *v. i.* To desire strongly.

cra′ven (krā′v′n), *a.* [3] Avowedly defeated or afraid ; cowardly. — *n.* An avowed coward.

craw (krô), *n.* The crop of a bird or insect.

craw′fish′ (krô′fĭsh′), **cray′fish′** (krā′-), *n.* (see PLURAL, *n.*, *Note*). Any of numerous fresh-water shellfish resembling the lobster, but smaller.

crawl (krôl), *v. i.* To move slowly by drawing the body along the ground, as a worm; to creep.

chair; go; sing, iŋk; then, thin; nature, verdure; yet; zh = z in azure. Numbers refer to §§ in the Special Notes which, with Abbreviations, Signs, etc., precede the Vocabulary.

cray'fish' (krā'físh'), *n.* Var. of CRAWFISH.

cray'on (krā'ŏn), *n.* **1.** A stick of chalk, clay, or the like used in drawing. **2.** A crayon drawing.

craze (krāz), *v. t. & i.* [1] To render or become insane. — *n.* **1.** A mania, or temporary passion or infatuation. **2.** Craziness; insanity. **3.** In pottery, a crack in the glaze or enamel.

cra'zy (krā'zĭ), *a.* [3] **1.** Full of cracks or flaws; unsound. **2.** Insane.— **cra'zi-ly** (-ĭ-lĭ), *adv.* [8] — **cra'zi-ness**, *n.* [8].

creak (krēk), *v. i.* To make a prolonged sharp, squeaking sound.— *v. t.* To cause to creak.— *n.* The sound of creaking.

creak'y (-ĭ), *a.* [3] Marked by creaking.

cream (krēm), *n.* **1.** The rich, oily, and yellowish part of milk. **2.** A fancy dish, or sweet, made from cream, etc., or so as to resemble cream. **3.** The choicest part of a thing. **4.** The color of cream. — **cream of tartar**, purified tartar. See TARTAR, 1. — *v. i.* To form, or become covered with, cream; hence, to mantle; froth.— *v. t.* **1.** To skim the cream from. **2.** To furnish with or as with cream.

cream'er-y (krēm'ẽr-ĭ), *n.; pl.* -ERIES (-ĭz). An establishment where butter is made.

cream'y (-ĭ), *a.* [3] Containing or resembling cream; creamlike; luscious.

crease (krēs), *n.* A line or mark made by folding any pliable substance; any similar mark. — *v. t.* [1] To make a crease in or on; wrinkle. — *v. i.* To become creased.

cre-ate' (krē-āt'), *v. t.* [1] **1.** To cause to exist; produce; originate. **2.** To invest with a new form, office, etc.; appoint; as, to *create* a man king.

cre-a'tion (-ā'shŭn), *n.* **1.** Act of creating; fact of being created. **2.** That which is created.

cre-a'tive (-tĭv), *a.* [4] **1.** Having the power or quality of creating; originative. **2.** Productive.

cre-a'tor (-tẽr), *n.* One that creates; [*cap.*] the Supreme Being.

crea'ture (krē'tŭr), *n.* **1.** Anything created; esp., a living created being. **2.** A servile dependent.

cre'dence (krē'dĕns), *n.* Belief; credit.

cre-den'tial (krē-dĕn'shăl), *n.* **1.** That which gives a title to credit or confidence. **2.** *pl.* Testimonials accrediting a person.

cred'i-bil'i-ty (krĕd'ĭ-bĭl'ĭ-tĭ), *n.* Quality of being credible, or an instance of it.

cred'i-ble (krĕd'ĭ-b'l), *a.* [4] Capable of being believed; trustworthy. — **-i-bly** (-blĭ), *adv.* [8].

cred'it (-ĭt), *n.* **1.** Reliance on the truth or reality of something; belief; faith. **2.** Quality of being generally believed; trustworthiness. **3.** Reputation; esp., good reputation. **4. a** That which procures, or adds to, reputation. **b** A source of honor. **5.** *Commerce.* Trust given or received. **6.** *Bookkeeping.* **a** Entry, in an account, of a payment or other value received. **b** The side (right-hand) of an account on which such entries are made. **7.** Balance in a person's favor in an account. — *v. t.* **1.** To confide in the truth of; believe. **2.** *Bookkeeping.* To enter on the credit side; give credit for. **3.** To give credit for; attribute or ascribe.

cred'it-a-ble (-á-b'l), *a.* [4] Deserving or possessing esteem; estimable. — **cred'it-a-bly**, *adv.* [8].

cred'i-tor (-ĭ-tẽr), *n.* **1.** One who gives mercan-

tile credit; one to whom money is due; — opposed to *debtor.* **2.** *Bookkeeping.* The credit side of an account. Abbr. *Cr.*

cre-du'li-ty (krē-dū'lĭ-tĭ), *n.* Belief; esp., a disposition to believe on insufficient evidence.

cred'u-lous (krĕd'ů-lŭs), *a.* [4] Inclined to believe, esp. on slight evidence. — **-ly**, *adv.* [8].

creed (krēd), *n.* An authoritative formula, as of the essential articles of Christian faith.

creek (krēk), *n.* **1.** A small inlet or bay, narrower and extending farther inland than a cove. **2.** A stream of water, smaller than a river; rivulet.

creel (krēl), *n.* A wicker basket, as for fish.

creep (krēp), *v. i.;* CREPT (krĕpt); CREEP'ING. **1.** To move along with the body prone or close to the ground or floor; crawl. **2.** To move slowly, stealthily, or timorously. **3.** Of plants, to spread by means of prostrate or clinging stems. **4.** To have a sensation as of insects creeping on the skin. — *n.* **1.** Act of creeping. **2.** A distressing creeping sensation; — often *colloq.* in *pl., the creeps.*

creep'er (krēp'ẽr), *n.* One that creeps; as: **a** Any of various (mostly small) birds that creep about on trees, bushes, etc. **b** A creeping plant.

creep'y (krēp'ĭ), *a.* [3] **1.** Marked by creeping, or slow motion. **2.** Having or producing a creeping sensation. — **creep'i-ness** (-ĭ-nĕs), *n.* [8].

cre-mate' (krē-māt'; krē'māt), *v. t.* [1] To burn; incinerate, as a corpse.

cre-ma'tion (krē-mā'shŭn), *n.* A burning; esp., the cremating of the dead.

crem'a-to-ry (krĕm'á-tō-rĭ; krē'má-), *n.* A furnace or a building for cremating dead bodies or refuse.

‖ **crème** (krâm), *n.* [F.] Cream.

cre'ole (krē'ōl), *n.* [*Usually cap.*] **a** A white descendant of the French or Spanish settlers of Louisiana, preserving their speech and culture. **b** The French patois spoken in Louisiana.

cre'o-sote (krē'ō-sōt), *n.* An oily, antiseptic liquid got by distillation of tar.

‖ **crêpe** (krâp; *E.* krāp), *n.* [F.] Crape. — **crêpe de Chine** (d'shēn'), a soft silk fabric, of a close texture and wavy appearance.

crep'i-tate (krĕp'ĭ-tāt), *v. i.* [1] To crackle; snap.

crept (krĕpt), *pret. & p. p.* of CREEP.

cre-scen'do (krē-shĕn'dō; -sĕn'dō), *a. & adv. Music.* Gradually increasing in force and fullness of tone; — indicated by the mark <, or by *cresc.*

cres'cent (krĕs'ĕnt), *n.* **1.** The increasing moon, or new moon, or a representation of it. **2.** A crescent-shaped figure or object; hence, this figure as emblem of the former Turkish sultans.— *a.* **1.** Increasing; growing. **2.** Shaped like the new moon.

cress (krĕs), *n.* Any of numerous plants with pungent leaves used in garnishing, etc.

cres'set (krĕs'ĕt), *n.* An iron vessel for holding burning oil, pitchy wood, or the like, for lighting.

crest (krĕst), *n.* **1.** A tuft, comb, or similar process on the head of a bird or animal. **2.** The plume, or other decoration, worn on a helmet; hence, a helmet. **3.** *Heraldry.* A bearing or device worn, not upon the shield, but usually above it or separately. **4.** A crestlike part; top; as, the *crest* of a hill. — *v. t.* To furnish with, or surmount as, a crest.

crest'fall'en (krĕst'fôl'n), *a.* [4] With drooping crest; hence, dispirited; dejected; cowed.

cre-ta'ceous (krḗ-tā'shŭs), a. [4] Having the qualities of, or abounding in, chalk.

cre-tonne' (krḗ-tŏn'), n. A strong unglazed cotton cloth, used to cover furniture, for curtains, etc.

cre-vasse' (krḗ-vàs'), n. A deep crevice, as in a glacier or embankment; U. S., a break in a levee.

crev'ice (krĕv'ĭs), n. A narrow opening resulting from a split or crack.

crew (krōō), pret. of CROW.

crew, n. **1.** Any band or force of armed men. **2.** A company; assemblage. **3.** Those who man a ship, collectively. **4.** Any small body of men regarded as associated.

crew'el (-ĕl), n. Worsted yarn slackly twisted.

crib (krĭb), n. **1.** A manger or rack for feeding animals. **2.** A small bedstead with high sides, for a child. **3.** A box, bin, or building for storing grain, salt, etc.

crib'bage (krĭb'âj), n. A certain game at cards.

crick (krĭk), n. A painful spasmodic affection of the muscles, as of the back.

crick'et (krĭk'ĕt), n. A low stool.

crick'et, n. A kind of leaping insect allied to the locust, noted for the chirping notes of the male.

crick'et, n. A certain outdoor game played with bats, ball, wickets, etc. — **crick'et-er,** n. [8].

cried (krīd), pret. & p. p. of CRY.

cri'er (krī'er), n. One who cries or proclaims.

crime (krīm), n. **1.** An omission of a duty commanded, or the commission of an act forbidden, by law; — commonly used only of grave offenses. **2.** Gross violation of law. **3.** An offense; a sin.

crim'i-nal (krĭm'ĭ-nǎl), a. [4] **1.** Involving, or of the nature of, a crime. **2.** Relating to crime or its punishment. **3.** Guilty of crime. — n. One who has committed a crime. — **ly,** adv. [8].

crim-i-nal'i-ty (-nǎl'ĭ-tĭ), n. Quality or fact of being criminal.

crim'i-nate (-nāt), v. t. [1] To accuse of a crime; incriminate. — **crim-i-na'tion** (-nā'shŭn), n.

crimp (krĭmp), n. One whose business it is to lure, entrap, or force men into nautical or, formerly, military service.

crimp, v. t. **1.** To fold or plait in small regular undulations. **2.** To entrap into military or sea service. — n. Act or product of crimping; a small wrinkle or a series of them. — **crimp'er,** n. [8].

crimp'y (krĭm'pĭ), a. [3] Frizzly.

crim'son (krĭm'z'n), n. A deep red color tinged with blue; also, red color in general. — a. Of the color crimson; deep red; hence, bloody. — v. t. & i. To make or become crimson.

cringe (krĭnj), v. i. [1] To draw one's self together in fear or servility; wince; to show servile deference; fawn. — n. Servile civility; fawning.

crin'kle (krĭŋ'k'l), v. i. & t. [1] **1.** To turn or wind in and out; also, to move in waves; ripple. **2.** To rustle, as stiff cloth. — n. A winding; wrinkle. — **crin'kly** (-klĭ), a. [8].

crin'o-line (krĭn'ō-lĭn; -lĕn), n. **1.** A kind of stiff cloth. **2.** A woman's skirt of any stiff material; also, a hoop skirt.

crip'ple (krĭp'p'l), n. One who creeps, halts, or limps; a lame person; one partially disabled. — v. t. [1] To deprive of the proper use of a limb, esp. of a leg; to lame; disable.

cri'sis (krī'sĭs), n.; pl. CRISES (-sēz). **1.** That change in a disease which indicates whether the result is to be recovery or death. **2.** Decisive moment; turning point; time of difficulty or danger.

crisp (krĭsp), a. [3] **1.** Curly; in curls or ringlets. **2.** Crinkled. **3.** Brittle; friable. **4.** Having characteristics of crisp substances; sharp and clear. — v. t. & i. **1.** To form into curls; ripple. **2.** To make or become crisp or brittle, as in cooking. — **ly,** adv. [8] — **ness,** n. [8].

crisp'y (krĭs'pĭ), a. [3] **1.** Formed into short, close ringlets; curly. **2.** Crisp; brittle.

criss'cross (krĭs'krŏs), a. Crossed; marked by crossings. — adv. In a way to cross something else.

cri-te'ri-on (krī-tē'rĭ-ŭn), n.; pl. L. -RIA (-ǎ), E. -RIONS (-ŭnz). A standard of judging; rule; test.

crit'ic (krĭt'ĭk), n. One who expresses a judgment on any matter with respect to its value, truth, beauty, literary or artistic merit, etc.

crit'i-cal (-ĭ-kǎl), a. [4] **1.** Inclined to criticize; esp., captious; censorious. **2.** Exercising, or qualified to exercise, careful judgment. **3.** Of the nature of criticism or critics. **4.** Pertaining to or indicating a crisis, or turning point; decisive; crucial. — **ly,** adv. [8] — **ness,** n. [8].

crit'i-cism (-ĭ-sĭz'm), n. **1.** A critical judgment; esp., an unfavorable judgment or opinion; censure. **2.** The art of critical judging.

crit'i-cize, crit'i-cise (krĭt'ĭ-sīz), v. i. & t. [1] To judge as a critic; esp., to find fault.

cri-tique' (krĭ-tēk'), n. **1.** A critical essay; criticism; review. **2.** Act or art of criticism.

croak (krōk), v. i. & t. **1.** To make, or utter with, a croak, or similar hoarse, dismal sound. **2.** To grumble; forebode (evil), esp. habitually. — n. The hoarse, harsh cry of a frog or a raven.

croak'er (-ẽr), n. One that croaks.

cro-chet' (krō-shā'), n. A kind of knitting done with a single hooked needle. — v. t. & i.; -CHETED' (-shăd'); -CHET'ING (-shā'ĭng). To knit with a crochet needle or hook.

crock (krŏk), n. **1.** Soot; smut. **2.** Coloring matter which rubs off from cloth. — v. t. To soil with crock. — v. i. To give off crock.

crock, n. A piece of crockery, esp. of coarse earthenware; an earthen pot, jar, or pitcher.

crock'er-y (-ẽr-ĭ), n. Earthenware; crocks collectively.

croc'o-dile (krŏk'ō-dĭl), n. Any of several large, thick-skinned, long-tailed, aquatic reptiles.

croc'o-dil'i-an (-dĭl'ĭ-ăn), a. Of or pertaining to an order of reptiles including the crocodiles, gavials, and alligators. — n. A crocodilian animal.

cro'cus (krō'kŭs), n. Any of a large genus (Crocus) of bulbous plants, of the iris family, with solitary flowers.

Crocus. (½)

crone (krōn), n. A withered old woman.

cro'ny (krō'nĭ), n.; pl. -NIES (-nĭz). An intimate companion; a familiar friend; chum.

crook (krŏŏk), *n.* **1.** A bent or hooked contrivance or implement. **2.** Act of crooking ; a bend or turn. **3.** A sharper, swindler, thief, or the like. *Cant.* — *v. t. & i.* To turn from a straight line; bend.

crook'ed (krŏŏk'ĕd), *a.* [3] **1.** Characterized by a crook, or curve ; bent. **2.** Not straightforward ; wicked. **3.** False; dishonest ; fraudulent. — **-ly,** *adv.* [8] — **-ness,** *n.* [8].

crook'neck' (krŏŏk'nĕk'), *n.* Either of two varieties of squash with tapering curved "necks."

croon (krōōn), *v. i. & t.* To hum or sing in a low tone. — *n.* The sound made in crooning.

crop (krŏp), *n.* **1.** A pouchlike enlargement of the gullet of many birds ; craw. **2.** The handle of a whip; a riding whip with a loop instead of a lash. **3.** Of grain or fruit, that which is cropped, cut, or gathered ; the product of the field; harvest. Also fig.; as, a *crop* of ice; a *crop* of lies. **4.** Act or product of cropping, as hair cut short. — *v. t. ;* CROPPED (krŏpt) ; CROP'- PING. **1.** To cut off the tops or tips of ; to bite or pull off; pluck ; reap. **2.** To clip the ears, hair, etc., of. — *v. i.* To come or appear, as from concealment ; — usually with *out* or *up.*

cro-quet' (krŏ-kā'), *n.* A familiar game played with balls, mallets, and arches.

cro-quette' (-kĕt'), *n.* A fried ball of minced meat, rice, etc.

cro'sier, cro'zier (krō'zhĕr),*n.* The staff of a bishop or abbot.

cross (krŏs), *n.* **1.** A gibbetlike structure, anciently used in crucifying; specifically, with *the,* the cross on which Christ was crucified. **2.** A representation of the cross as the symbol of Christ's death ; also, the emblem and symbol of Christianity. **3.** Something like, or suggestive of, a cross. **4.** Affliction or trial as a test of Christian patience or virtue. **5.** Two lines crossing. **6.** A mixing of breeds; crossbreed ; hybrid. — *v.t.* **1.** To put or lay across or athwart; also, to lie or pass across ; intersect. **2.** To make the sign of the cross on or over. **3.** To cancel by marking crosses on or over;—usually with *out* or *off.* **4.** To draw or write something, as a line, across. **5.** To move across or past. **6.** To meet and pass. **7.** To cause to interbreed ; hybridize. — *v. i.* **1.** To lie or be athwart. **2.** To move or pass, or to extend, from side to side, or from place to place ; — often with *over.* **3.** To meet and pass. **4.** To interbreed ; hybridize. — *adv. & prep.* Across. — *a.* [3] **1.** Not parallel ; lying, falling, or passing athwart; transverse. **2.** Contrary or adverse. **3.** Peevish ; ill-humored.

cross'bar' (krŏs'bär'), *n.* Transverse bar or line.

cross'bill' (-bĭl'), *n.* Any of several finches having mandibles curved and crossing each other.

cross'bones' (-bōnz'), *n. pl.* Two leg or arm bones placed or depicted crosswise.

cross'bow' (-bō'), *n.* A medieval weapon formed of a bow set crosswise on a stock.

cross'breed' (-brēd'), *n.* A hybrid.

cross'–bun', *n.* A bun or cake marked with a cross, commonly eaten on Good Friday.

cross'–ex-am'i-na'tion, *n.* A cross-examining.

cross'–ex-am'ine, *v. t. & i.* [1] *Law.* To question,

Crosier.

especially as a check to a previous examination. — **cross'–ex-am'in-er,** *n.* [8].

cross'–eye', *n.* See STRABISMUS. — **-eyed'** (-īd'),*a.*

cross'–fer'ti-li-za'tion, *n. Bot.* Fertilization by cross-pollination. — **cross'–fer'ti-lize,** *v. t.*

cross'–grained', *a.* [4] **1.** Having the grain transverse or irregular. **2.** Perverse ; contrary.

cross'ing, *n.* **1.** A point of intersection. **2.** A place where anything, as a street, is crossed.

cross'ly, *adv.* In a cross manner.

cross'ness, *n.* State or quality of being cross.

cross'–pol'li-na'tion, *n. Bot.* Deposition of pollen from one flower on the stigma of another, as by insects. — **cross'–pol'li-nate,** *v. t.* [1].

cross'–pur'pose, *n.* An opposing purpose.

cross'–ques'tion, *v. t.* To cross-examine ; question closely. — *n.* A question in cross-examination.

cross reference. A reference made from one part of a book or register to another part.

cross'road' (krŏs'rōd'), *n.* **1.** A road that crosses a main road or connects main roads. **2.** Place where roads intersect ; — often in *pl.*

cross'trees' (-trēz'),*n. pl. Naut.* Two horizontal pieces supported by trestletrees at a masthead.

cross'way' (krŏs'wā'), *n.* A crossroad.

cross'wise' (-wiz'), *adv.* In the form of a cross ; also, athwart; across ; perversely; contrarily.

crotch (krŏch), *n.* **1.** A fork; esp., a forked pole or stake to prop something. **2.** The angle formed by the parting of two legs or branches ; fork.

crotched (krŏcht), *a.* Having a crotch ; forked.

crotch'et (krŏch'ĕt), *n.* **1.** A small hook or hooklike instrument. **2.** A perverse fancy ; whim.

crotch'et-y (-ĭ), *a.* [4] Given to crotchets.

crouch (krouch), *v. i.* **1.** To bend or stoop low, with bent legs, as an animal waiting for prey, or in fear. **2.** To bend servilely ; fawn ; cringe.

croup (krōōp), *n.* The rear part of the back of a quadruped, esp. the horse.

croup, *n. Med.* A disease of children characterized by a hoarse, ringing cough and difficult breathing.

croup'ous (-ŭs), *a.* [4] Characteristic of croup.

croup'y (-ĭ), *a.* [3] Croupous.

crow (krō), *v. i.; pret.* CREW (krōō), chiefly in sense 1, or CROWED (krōd) ; *p. p.* CROWED ; *p. pr. & vb. n.* CROW'ING. **1.** To make the loud shrill sound characteristic of a cock. **2.** To utter an expression of joy, exultation, or defiance.

crow, *n.* **1.** Any of various species of large, usually entirely glossy black, birds with harsh unmusical notes. **2.** The cry of the cock ; crowing.

crow'bar' (-bär'), *n.* A bar of iron, usually wedgeshaped at the working end, used as a lever, etc.

crowd (kroud), *v. i.* **1.** To urge forward ; force one's self. **2.** To collect in numbers ; throng. — *v. t.* **1.** To shove or push. **2.** To press, force, or thrust, as into a smaller space or time; cram. **3.** To fill or occupy to excess or obstruction. — *n.* **1.** A large number of persons or things closely massed together. **2.** A great number of persons ; esp., the people; populace.

crow'foot' (krō'fŏŏt'), *n.; pl.* -FOOTS (-fŏŏts'). Any of a genus of herbs having lobed leaves and fivepetaled flowers. See BUTTERCUP.

crown (kroun), *n.* **1.** A garland or fillet for the head, esp. as a reward of victory or a mark of distinction; hence, reward. **2.** A royal headdress. **3.** Hence: a Dominion of a ruler; sovereignty. **b** A sovereign;—used with *the.* **4.** Something suggestive of a crown; the top part. **5.** A crowning ornament; also, the highest state or quality of anything. **6.** Top of the head; the head. **7.** An English coin worth 5 shillings. — *v. t.* **1.** To invest with a crown, as a sovereign. **2.** To bestow something on as a mark of honor, dignity, or recompense; adorn. **3.** To top, cap, or surmount. **4.** To form the topmost or finishing part of; perfect; glorify.

Crown of England.

crown prince. The heir apparent to a crown.

crown princess. The wife of a crown prince.

crow's-foot′, *n. ; pl.* -FEET. One of the wrinkles that come with age at the outer corners of the eyes.

crow's nest. *Naut.* A lookout box or perch near the top of a mast, esp. in whalers.

cro′zier (krō′zhẽr), *n.* Var. of CROSIER.

cru′cial (krōō′shăl), *a.* [4] Of the nature of, or pert. to, a supreme trial or final choice; decisive.

cru′ci-ble (-sĭ-b'l), *n.* **1.** A pot, as of clay, for melting metals, ores, etc. **2.** A severe trial or test.

cru′ci-fix (krōō′sĭ-fĭks), *n.* A representation of Christ on the cross; loosely, the cross itself.

cru′ci-fix′ion (-fĭk′shŭn), *n.* **1.** Act of crucifying; [*cap.*] the execution of Christ on the cross. **2.** Death on a cross. **3.** Intense suffering; agony.

cru′ci-form (krōō′sĭ-fôrm), *a.* Cross-shaped.

cru′ci-fy (-fī), *v. t.* [2] **1.** To put to death by fastening to a cross of execution. **2.** Fig., to subdue; mortify; as, to *crucify* the flesh or passions.

crude (krōōd), *a.* [3] **1.** In a natural state; not prepared, refined, etc. **2.** Wanting finish, grace, tact, taste, etc. — **-ly,** *adv.* [8] — **-ness,** *n.* [8].

cru′di-ty (krōō′dĭ-tĭ), *n. ; pl.* -TIES (-tĭz). State or quality of being crude; that which is crude.

cru′el (krōō′ĕl), *a.* [3] **1.** Disposed to give pain; savage; merciless. **2.** Causing or attended by pain, grief, or misery. — **-ly,** *adv.* [8].

cru′el-ty (-tĭ), *n. ; pl.* -TIES (-tĭz). **1.** Quality or state of being cruel. **2.** A cruel deed.

cru′et (-ĕt), *n.* A bottle; esp., a small glass bottle for vinegar, pepper, or the like, for the table.

cruise (krōōz), *v. i.* [1] To sail about or to and fro, as for pleasure. — *n.* A sailing to and fro.

cruis′er (krōōz′ẽr), *n.* One that cruises; a man-of-war less powerful than a battleship.

crul′ler (krŭl′ẽr), *n.* A small sweet cake of a rich egg batter, twisted and fried brown in deep fat.

crumb (krŭm), *n.* **1.** A small fragment or piece, as of bread. **2.** A little; bit. **3.** The soft part of bread. — *v. t. & i.* To break into crumbs.

crum′ble (krŭm′b'l), *v. t. & i.* [1] To break into small pieces; hence, to fall to decay.

crum′bly (-blĭ), *a.* [3] Easily crumbled; friable.

crum′my (krŭm′ĭ), *a.* [3] Full of crumb or crumbs, or soft, as the crumb of bread.

crump′et (-pĕt), *n.* A kind of light griddle cake.

crum′ple (-p'l), *v. t. & i.* [1] To press into wrinkles or folds; rumple. — *n.* A wrinkle, fold, or crease made by crumpling; a crumpled part.

crunch (krŭnch), *v. i. & t.* To chew, grind, or press, noisily. — *n.* Act or noise of crunching.

crup′per (krŭp′ẽr; krŏŏp′ẽr), *n.* A loop passing under a horse's tail to hold the harness saddle.

cru-sade′ (krōō-sād′), *n.* **1.** Any of various military expeditions undertaken between 1096 and 1270 by Christian powers to recover the Holy Land from the Mohammedans. **2.** An enterprise undertaken with zeal and enthusiasm. — *v. i.* [1] To engage in a crusade. — **cru-sad′er** (krōō-sād′ẽr), *n.* [8].

cruse (krōōs; krōōz), *n.* A vessel for water, oil, etc.

crush (krŭsh), *v. t.* **1.** To compress so as to bruise or squeeze out of the natural shape. **2.** To reduce to fine particles by pounding or grinding. **3.** To overwhelm; conquer. — *v. i.* To be or become crushed. — *n.* **1.** Act of crushing. **2.** Violent crowding, or a great crowd. — **crush′er,** *n.* [8].

crust (krŭst), *n.* **1.** The hardened surface of bread; also, a piece of this or of any hard bread. **2.** The cover or case of a pie. **3.** A hard external covering; shell. — *v. t. & i.* To incrust; become incrusted.

crus-ta′cean (krŭs-tā′shăn), *a.* Of or pert. to a class of mostly aquatic animals including the lobsters, shrimps, crabs, barnacles, etc. — *n.* A crustacean animal.

crust′y (krŭs′tĭ), *a.* [3] **1.** Having the nature of crust, or a hard covering. **2.** Having a short, rough manner; harshly curt. — **crust′i-ly** (-tĭ-lĭ), *adv.* [8] — **crust′i-ness,** *n.* [8].

crutch (krŭch), *n.* A staff with a crosspiece at the top, used to support the lame in walking.

crux (krŭks), *n. ; pl.* E. CRUXES (-ĕz), L. CRUCES (krōō′sēz). A perplexing difficulty.

cry (krī), *v. i.* [2] **1.** To make a loud call or cry, as in prayer, pain, anger, etc.; shout. **2.** To lament audibly; shed tears with or without sound; weep. **3.** Of an animal, to utter its characteristic call. — *v. t.* To utter loudly; shout; proclaim. **2.** To affect, effect, or cause to be, by weeping. — *n. ; pl.* CRIES (krīz). **1.** A loud utterance expressing strong emotion. **2.** A loud calling out of words. **3.** A characteristic call of an animal. **4.** A fit of weeping.

cry′ing (krī′ĭng), *p. a.* [4] That cries; hence, compelling attention; notorious; as, a *crying* evil.

crypt (krĭpt), *n.* A vault wholly or partly under ground; esp., a vault under a church.

cryp′tic (krĭp′tĭk), *a.* [4] Hidden; secret; occult.

cryp′to-gam (-tṓ-găm), *n.* Any of the plants that do not produce flowers or seeds.

cryp′to-gam′ic (-găm′ĭk), *a.* Pert. to cryptogams.

cryp-tog′a-mous (krĭp-tŏg′ȧ-mŭs), *a.* Of the nature of a cryptogam.

cryp′to-gram (krĭp′tṓ-grăm), *n.* A writing in cipher.

crys′tal (krĭs′tăl), *n.* **1.** Quartz transparent or nearly so, or a piece of it. **2.** A body formed by a substance solidifying so that it has plane surfaces symmetrically arranged. **3.** Glass of superior brilliancy. **4.** The glass over a watch dial. — *a.* Resembling crystal; clear.

crys′tal-line (-ĭn; -īn), *a.* [4] **1.** Consisting, or of the nature, of crystal. **2.** Resembling crystal; pure; transparent. — **crystalline lens,** a lens in the eye, which serves to focus the rays of light.

crys′tal-li-za′tion (-ĭ-zā′shŭn), *n.* Act or process of crystallizing; also, a crystallized formation.

crys′tal-lize (-īz), *v. t.* [1] **1.** To cause to form crystals or assume crystalline form. **2.** To cause to assume a fixed and definite form. — *v. i.* **1.** To become crystalline. **2.** To become settled and fixed in form.

cub (kŭb), *n.* The young of the fox, bear, wolf, lion, tiger, etc., or, sometimes, of the whale.

cub′by–hole′ (kŭb′ĭ-hōl′), *n.* A snug place.

cube (kūb), *n.* **1.** *Geom.* The regular solid of six equal square faces. **2.** *Math.* The product got by taking a number or quantity three times as a factor. — *v. t.* [1] To form the cube of.

cu′beb (kū′bĕb), *n.* The pungent berry of a climbing shrub, native of Java and Borneo.

cube root. That factor of a quantity which when cubed produces the quantity.

cu′bic (kū′bĭk), *a.* **1.** Having the form or properties of a cube. **2.** Three-dimensional; esp., as used with a unit of length, denoting the volume of a cube one edge of which has the length of that unit; as, a *cubic* foot. Abbr. *c.* or *cu.*

cu′bi-cal (kū′bĭ-kăl), *a.* Cubic.

cu′bit (kū′bĭt), *n.* An old linear measure, from 18 to 21 inches.

cuck′oo (kŏŏk′ŏŏ), *n.* **1.** A European bird that lays its eggs in the nests of other birds for them to hatch. **2.** The call of the cuckoo.

cu′cum-ber (kū′kŭm-bēr), *n.* The fruit of a vine of the same genus as the muskmelon, cultivated as a garden vegetable; also, the vine.

cud (kŭd), *n.* A portion of food brought up into the mouth from the first stomach by a ruminating animal, to be chewed a second time.

cud′dle (kŭd′'l), *v. t.* [1] To embrace closely; fondle. — *v. i.* To lie close or snug; nestle.

cud′dy (kŭd′ĭ), *n.; pl.* -DIES (-ĭz). A small cabin, or the galley of a small vessel.

cudg′el (kŭj′ĕl), *n.* A short club. — *v.t.* [7] To beat with a cudgel.

cue (kū), *n.* **1.** A queue. **2.** A tapering rod used to impel the balls in billiards, etc.

cue, *n.* **1.** The last words of a speech in a play, as a warning for the next speaker. **2.** A hint.

cuff (kŭf), *v. t.* To strike with or as with the flat of the hand; buffet; slap. — *n.* A blow so made.

cuff, *n.* An ornamental band covering the wrist.

cui-rass′ (kwē-răs′),*n.* A piece of armor, originally of leather, covering the body; also, the breastplate of such a piece.

cui′ras-sier′ (kwē′rȧ-sēr′), *n.* A mounted soldier wearing a cuirass.

‖ **cui-sine′** (kwē-zēn′), *n.* [F.] Kitchen; culinary department; style of cooking.

‖ **cul′–de–sac′** (kŭl′d′-săk′; kŭl′dĕ-săk′), *n.; pl.* CULS-DE-SAC (kŭ′-; kŭlz′-). [F.] A passage with only one outlet, as a blind alley.

cu′li-na-ry (kū′lĭ-nȧ-rĭ), *a.* Of, pertaining to, or suited for, the kitchen or cookery.

cull (kŭl), *v. t.* **1.** To select; choose; pick out. **2.** To subject to culling. — *n.* Something, esp. something inferior, culled out.

culm (kŭlm), *n.* Refuse coal or coal dust.

culm, *n.* Jointed stem of a grass.

cul′mi-nate (kŭl′mĭ-nāt), *v. i.* [1] To reach its highest altitude, point, or degree.

cul′mi-na′tion (kŭl′mĭ-nā′shŭn),*n.* Act of culminating; also, culminating position; summit; crown.

cul′pa-bil′i-ty (-pȧ-bĭl′ĭ-tĭ), *n.; pl.* -TIES (-tĭz). Quality of being culpable.

cul′pa-ble (kŭl′pȧ-b′l), *a.* [4] Deserving censure or moral blame; censurable.—**cul′pa-bly,***adv.*[8].

cul′prit (-prĭt), *n.* **1.** One arraigned for a crime, as in court. **2.** One guilty of a crime or a fault.

cult (kŭlt), *n.* **1.** Worship. **2.** Devotion to a person, idea, or thing, esp. by a body of admirers.

cul′ti-vate (kŭl′tĭ-vāt), *v. t.* [1] **1.** To prepare (land) for the raising of crops; till. **2.** To raise, or foster the growth of (a plant), by tillage. **3.** To civilize; refine. **4.** To devote time and thought to; cherish. **5.** To seek the society of.

cul′ti-va′tion (-vā′shŭn), *n.* Art or act of cultivating; state of being cultivated; culture.

cul′ti-va′tor (kŭl′tĭ-vā′tēr), *n.* **1.** One who cultivates. **2.** An implement or machine to loosen the earth and kill weeds between the rows of crops.

cul′ture (-t̶u̶r), *n.* **1.** Cultivation; tillage. **2.** Act of improving or developing by education, discipline, etc. **3.** The enlightenment and discipline acquired by mental training; refinement.

cul′tured (-t̶u̶rd), *p. a.* [4] Cultivated; refined.

cul′vert (-vẽrt), *n.* A transverse drain under a road, railroad, etc.; an arched drain or sewer.

cum′ber (-bẽr), *v. t.* To hinder or burden.

cum′ber-some(-sŭm),*a.* [4] Cumbrous; unwieldy.

cum′brous (-brŭs), *a.* [4] Rendering action or motion difficult; unwieldy; burdensome.

cu′mu-late (kū′mū-lāt),*v. t.* [1] To heap together; accumulate.

cu′mu-la′tion (-lā′shŭn), *n.* Act of cumulating; a gathered mass; a heap.

cu′mu-la-tive (-lȧ-tĭv), *a.* [4] **1.** Formed or increasing by additions. **2.** Subject to cumulation; that is to be added to something else.

cu′mu-lus (kū′mū-lŭs), *n.; pl.* -LI (-lī). **1.** A heap. **2.** A kind of massy cloud form.

cu-ne′i-form (kū-nē′ĭ-fôrm), *a.* Wedge-shaped; — applied esp. to the characters anciently used in writing in Persia, Assyria, etc., or to the writing itself.

Cuneiform Writing.

cun′ner (kŭn′ēr),*n.* Any of several small, edible, dark marine fishes.

cun′ning (-ĭng), *a.* [3] **1.** Skillful; dexterous. **2.** Wrought with or exhibiting skill or ingenuity.

Cunner.

3. Crafty, sly, or artful. **4.** Prettily or piquantly interesting. *U. S.* — *n.* **1.** Skill; dexterity. *Archaic.* **2.** Faculty or act of using stratagem; deceit; craft. — **cun′ning-ly,** *adv.* [8].

cup (kŭp), *n.* **1.** A small drinking vessel or its containing part. **2.** A thing suggestive of a cup (in sense 1). **3.** A drinking vessel and its contents; a cupful. **4.** *pl.* Repeated potations; indulgence in intoxicating drinks.

cup′board (kŭb′ērd), *n.* A closet with shelves for dishes, food, etc.; a small closet.

cup'ful (kŭp'fŏŏl), *n.; pl.* CUPFULS (-fŏŏlz). As much as a cup will hold; in cookery, a half pint.

Cu'pid (kū'pĭd), *n. Roman Myth.* The god of love, represented as a naked, winged boy with bow and arrow.

cu-pid'i-ty (kū-pĭd'ĭ-tĭ), *n.* Eager desire, esp. for wealth; avarice.

cu'po-la (kū'pō-lȧ), *n.; pl.* -LAS (-lȧz). 1. A roof, less often a ceiling, hemispherical or nearly so. 2. A small structure on top of a roof or building. 3. A furnace for melting metals, as in foundries.

cur (kûr), *n.* 1. A mongrel or inferior dog. 2. A worthless, snarling fellow. *Contemptuous.*

cur'a-bil'i-ty (kûr'ȧ-bĭl'ĭ-tĭ), *n.* Curable quality.

cur'a-ble (kûr'ȧ-b'l), *a.* [4] Capable of being cured.

cu'ra-çao' (kū'rȧ-sō'; kŏŏ'rȧ-sō'), *n.* A liqueur flavored with the dried peel of bitter oranges.

cu'ra-cy (kū'rȧ-sĭ), *n.; pl.* -CIES (-sĭz). The office or employment of a curate.

cu'rate(kū'rȧt),*n.* A rector's or a vicar's assistant.

cur'a-tive (kûr'ȧ-tĭv), *a.* [4] Relating or tending to the cure of diseases. — *n.* A remedy.

cu-ra'tor (kū-rā'tēr), *n.* One having the care of anything; esp., a custodian of a museum, library, etc.

curb (kûrb), *v. t.* 1. To guide and manage, or restrain, as with a curb; restrain; confine. 2. To furnish with a curb, as a sidewalk. — *n.* 1. A chain or strap attached to the upper part of the branches of a bit, to check the horse. 2. That which restrains or subdues;check. 3. Inclosing border,as of upright stones, along the outer limit of a sidewalk.

curb'stone',*n.* A stone set as a curb (see CURB,*n.*, 3).

cur-cu'li-o (kûr-kū'lĭ-ō), *n.* Any snout beetle, esp. any of certain forms that injure fruit.

curd (kûrd), *n.* The coagulated substance that is formed from milk, as distinguished from the *whey.* — *v. t. & i.* To coagulate or thicken; curdle.

cur'dle (kûr'd'l), *v. t. & i.* [1] 1. To change into curd; coagulate. 2. To congeal; thicken.

cur'dy (-dĭ), *a.* [3] Like curd; full of curd.

cure (kūr), *n.* 1. Spiritual charge; care of souls; hence, a curacy. 2. Medical care; method of medical treatment. 3. Act of healing, or state of being healed. 4. Means of removing disease or evil; remedy. — *v. t.* [1] 1. To heal (a sick person); restore to health, soundness, or sanity. 2. To remove (an ailment) by remedial means; heal. 3. To prepare (meat, fish, tobacco, etc.) for keeping, by salting, drying, etc.— *v. i.* To become cured, as hay.

‖ cu'ré' (kü'rā'), *n.* [F.] A parish priest.

cure'-all', *n.* A remedy for all diseases or ills.

cur'few (kûr'fū), *n.* 1. In the Middle Ages, a regulation that fires be covered or put out on the ringing of a bell at a fixed hour in the evening; hence, the ringing, or the time of ringing, or the bell itself. 2. The ringing of an evening bell as a signal, as for children to retire from the streets.

cu'ri-o (kū'rĭ-ō), *n.; pl.* CURIOS (-ōz). A curiosity, or object of art, bit of bric-a-brac, or the like.

cu'ri-os'i-ty (-ŏs'ĭ-tĭ), *n.; pl.* -TIES (-tĭz). 1. Disposition, often a meddling disposition, to inquire into anything. 2. That which is curious, or fitted to excite or reward attention.

cu'ri-ous (kū'rĭ-ŭs), *a.* [4] 1. Exhibiting nicety; artfully or elaborately constructed; as, a *curious* cabinet. *Archaic.* 2. Careful or anxious to learn;

inquisitive. 3. Exciting attention or inquiry; strange; rare. — **-ly**, *adv.* [8] — **-ness**, *n.* [8].

curl (kûrl), *v. t. & i.* 1. To twist, bend, or form into ringlets, as the hair. 2. To form into a curved shape; twist; coil. — *n.* 1. A spiral lock of hair; ringlet. 2. A spiral or winding form, as of smoke; coil. 3. Act of curling; state of being curled.

cur'lew (kûr'lū), *n.* Any bird of the snipe family with long downwardly curved bill.

curl'ing (kûr'lĭng), *n.* 1. Act or state of one that curls. 2. A game in which rounded stones are hurled along ice toward a mark.

curl'y (kûr'lĭ), *a.* [3] Curling; having curls.

cur-mudg'eon (kūr-mŭj'ŭn), *n.* A niggard; miser.

cur'rant (kûr'ȧnt), *n.* 1. A small seedless raisin. 2. The acid berry of a shrub of the gooseberry family; also, the shrub.

cur'ren-cy (-ĕn-sĭ), *n.; pl.* -CIES (-sĭz). 1. State of being current; circulation, as of bank notes. 2. A circulating medium of exchange, including coin, government notes, and bank notes.

cur'rent (-ĕnt), *a.* [4] 1. Now passing, as time; belonging to the present time. 2. Passing from person to person, or from hand to hand; circulating. 3. Commonly acknowledged or accepted; in vogue. — *n.* 1. A flowing or passing; onward motion. Hence: A body of fluid moving in a certain direction; stream. 2. General course or movement. 3. *Elec.* A movement of electricity likened to the motion of a stream of liquid, or the rate of such a movement. — **cur'rent-ly**, *adv.* [8].

cur-ric'u-lum (kŭ-rĭk'ū-lŭm), *n.; pl.* E. **-LUMS** (-lŭmz), L. **-LA** (-lȧ). A specified or regular course of study, as in a university.

cur'ri-er (kûr'ĭ-ēr), *n.* One who curries leather.

cur'rish (kûr'ĭsh), *a.* [4] Pert. to or like a cur; quarrelsome; also, base; ignoble. — **-ly**, *adv.* [8].

cur'ry (kûr'ĭ),*v. t.* [2] 1. To dress the hair or coat of a (horse, ox, etc.) with a currycomb. 2. To dress (leather) by scraping, coloring, etc.

cur'ry (kûr'ĭ),*n.; pl.* -RIES (-ĭz). 1. A kind of highly spiced condiment introduced from India. 2. A stew, as of fowl, fish, or game, cooked with curry.

cur'ry-comb' (-kōm'), *n.* A comb for grooming a horse. — *v. t.* To comb with a currycomb.

curse (kûrs), *v. t.; pl.* CURSED (kûrst) or CURST; CURS'-ING. 1. To call on divine or supernatural power to send injury upon; swear at. 2. To use profanely insolent language against; blaspheme. 3. To bring great evil on; harass; torment. — *v. i.* To utter curses; swear. — *n.* 1. A prayer or invocation for injury to come upon one, malediction; oath. 2. That which is cursed or accursed. 3. Evil coming as if in response to imprecation, or as retribution. 4. The cause of great harm, evil, or misfortune.

curs'ed (kûr'sĕd), *p. a.* [3] 1. Being under a curse; damned. 2. Deserving a curse; execrable.

cur'sive (kûr'sĭv), *a.* Of writing, running; having the letters joined and the angles often rounded.

cur'so-ry (kûr'sō-rĭ), *a.* [4] Characterized by haste; superficial; careless. — **cur'so-ri-ly** (-rĭ-lĭ), *adv.* [8] — **-ri-ness**, *n.* [8].

curt (kûrt), *a.* [3] 1. Short; abbreviated. 2. Short or brief in language; esp., short to a fault; rudely concise. — **curt'ly**, *adv.* [8] — **curt'ness**, *n.* [8].

---

chair; go; sing, iŋk; then, thin; nature, verdure; yet; zh = z in azure. Numbers refer to §§ in the Special Notes which, with Abbreviations, Signs, etc., precede the Vocabulary.

cur-tail′ (kŭr-tāl′), *v. t.* To cut off the end, or any part, of; shorten.

cur-tail′ment (-mĕnt), *n.* A shortening.

cur′tain (kŭr′tĭn), *n.* A hanging screen, usually admitting of being drawn back or up at pleasure. — *v. t.* To furnish or inclose with a curtain or curtains.

curt′sy } (kŭrt′sĭ); *pl.* -SIES, -SEYS (-sĭz). An act **curt′sey** } of civility performed by women, consisting of a slight depression of the body with bending of the knees. — *v. i.;* -SIED, -SEYED (-sĭd); -SY-ING, -SEY-ING. To make a curtsy.

cur′va-ture (kŭr′vá-tūr), *n.* Act of curving; state of being curved; a bend; curve.

curve (kŭrv), *n.* A curving; that which is curved; flexure. — *v. t. & i.* [1] To bend; crook.

cur′vet (kŭr′vĕt; kŭr-vĕt′), *n.* A certain leap of a horse.

cur-vet′ (kŭr-vĕt′; kŭr′vĕt), *v. i.;* -VET′TED or -VET-ED; -VET′TING or -VET-ING. To make a curvet; leap; bound. — *v. t.* To cause to curvet.

cur′vi-lin′e-al (kŭr′vĭ-lĭn′ē-ăl), *a.* Curvilinear.

cur′vi-lin′e-ar (-ár), *a.* Made up of curved lines.

cush′ion (kŏosh′ŭn), *n.* **1.** A soft pillow or pad. **2.** Something like a cushion. — *v. t.* **1.** To seat or place on or as on a cushion. **2.** To furnish with cushions.

cusp (kŭsp), *n.* A pointed end; apex; peak.

cus′pid (kŭs′pĭd), *n.* A canine tooth.

cus′pi-date (-pĭ-dāt), *a.* Having a cusp or cusps.

cus′pi-dor (-dôr; -dôr), *n.* A spittoon.

cus′tard (-tárd), *n.* A sweetened mixture of milk and eggs, baked or boiled.

cus-to′di-al (kŭs-tō′dĭ-ăl), *a.* Relating to custody.

cus-to′di-an (-ăn), *n.* One who has custody, as of a public building; a keeper.

cus′to-dy (kŭs′tō-dĭ), *n.* **1.** A keeping or guarding. **2.** Judicial or penal safe-keeping. **3.** State of being guarded; restraint; confinement.

cus′tom (-tŭm), *n.* **1.** A habitual or usual course of action. **2.** The body of practices or conventions which regulate social life. **3.** *pl.* Duties, tolls, or imposts imposed on commodities imported or (rarely) exported. **4.** Habitual buying of goods; business patronage.—*a.* **1.** Made or done to order. **2.** Dealing in things made to order, or doing work only when it is ordered.

cus′tom-a-ry (-á-rĭ), *a.* [4] Agreeing with, or established by, custom; habitual. — **-a-ri-ly** (-rĭ-lĭ), *adv.* [8] — **-ri-ness**, *n.* [8].

cus′tom-er (-ẽr), *n.* **1.** One who regularly or repeatedly deals in business with a tradesman or business house; a purchaser. **2.** A fellow; chap; — usually with qualifying adjective, as *queer, ugly,* etc.

cus′tom-house′ (kŭs′tŭm-hous′), *n.* The building where customs and duties are paid.

cut (kŭt), *v. t.; pret. & p. p.* CUT; *p. pr. & vb. n.* CUT′TING. **1.** To penetrate, divide, or sever with or as with an edged instrument; cleave; gash. **2.** To reduce, as if by cutting off some part. **3.** To intersect; cross, as lines. **4.** To form by cutting, as a garment, etc. **5.** To strike sharply, as with a whip. **6.** Fig., to hurt the feelings of. **7.** To ignore socially. *Colloq.* **8.** To absent one's self from. *Colloq.* — *v. i.* **1.** To do the work of an edged tool. **2.** To admit of being cut. **3.** To

use a cutting instrument. **4.** To go across something; make a short cut; — usually with *across.* **5.** To make a stroke as with a sword or whip. — *n.* **1.** An opening made with an edged instrument; gash; slash. **2.** An excavated notch or passage; furrow; groove. **3.** A straight or easy course. **4.** Manner in which a thing is cut or formed; style; fashion. **5.** That which is cut or cut off; a severed portion. **6.** An engraved block or plate for printing or the impression therefrom. **7.** Act of cutting; as: **a** A blow with a knife, whip, etc. **b** Act of removing a part as if by use of a knife; also, the part removed. **8.** That which wounds the feelings; a slight. **9.** One of several pieces, as of straw, as used in drawing lots.

cu-ta′ne-ous (kū-tā′nē-ŭs), *a.* Of, pertaining to, or affecting, the skin.

cute (kūt), *a.* [3] *Colloq.* **1.** Clever or shrewd. **2.** Attractive by reason of daintiness or picturesqueness, as a child.—**cute′ly**, *adv.* [8] — **-ness**, *n.* [8].

cu′ti-cle (kū′tĭ-k'l), *n.* The epidermis.

cu′tis (kū′tĭs), *n.* The derma, or deeper layer of the skin.

cut′lass (kŭt′lás), *n.* A short, heavy, curved sword, used esp. by sailors.

cut′ler (-lẽr), *n.* One who makes or sells cutlery.

cut′ler-y (-ĭ), *n.* Edged instruments collectively.

cut′let (-lĕt), *n.* A small piece of meat, as of veal, cut from the ribs or leg, for broiling or frying.

cut′-off′, *n.* **1.** That which shortens, as a nearer road. **2.** Act of shutting off the working fluid, as steam, from an engine cylinder; also, the point at which this occurs, or the mechanism effecting it.

cut′-out′, *n.* **1.** *Elec.* A device by which a circuit or a portion of a circuit may be disconnected; a circuit breaker. **2.** A device for allowing an internal-combustion engine that regularly exhausts through a muffler to exhaust directly into the air.

cut′ter (kŭt′ẽr), *n.* **1.** One that cuts. **2. a** A broad, square-sterned boat, used by ships of war. **b** A one-masted vessel rigged much like a sloop, and having a deep, often heavily weighted, keel. **c** A small armed steam vessel in the Revenue Cutter Service. *U. S.* **3.** A small, light sleigh.

cut′throat′ (kŭt′thrōt′), *n.* One who cuts throats; murderer. — *a.* Murderous; cruel.

cut′ting (kŭt′ĭng), *n.* **1.** Act or process of one that cuts. **2.** Something cut, cut off, or cut out. — *a.* [4] **1.** Adapted to cut. **2.** Chilling; piercing; as, a *cutting* wind. **3.** Severe; sarcastic.

cut′tle-fish′ (kŭt′'l-fĭsh′), *n.* A ten-armed shellfish related to the squids, but having a light, easily powdered internal shell, known in commerce as **cuttle bone**, valued for its lime and salts.

cut′worm′ (-wûrm′), *n.* A caterpillar which eats off young plants of cabbage, corn, etc.

cy′a-nide (sĭ′á-nĭd; -nĭd), *n.* A compound of cyanogen with an element or radical.

cy-an′o-gen (sĭ-ăn′ō-jĕn), *n.* *Chem.* A radical composed of carbon and nitrogen.

cyc′la-men (sĭk′lá-mĕn), *n.* Any of various plants (genus *Cyclamen*) of the primrose family, having pretty, nodding, white or pink flowers.

cy′cle (sī′k'l), *n.* **1.** A period of time occupied by one round or course of events. **2.** A complete course of operations returning to the original state;

circle; round. **3.** An age; long period. **4.** A body of literature, esp. poetry and romance, treating of the exploits of a hero or heroes. **5.** A shortened form of *bicycle, tricycle,* etc. — *v. i.* [1] To ride a cycle. — **cy'cler** (sī'klẽr), *n.* [8].

cy'cle-car' (sī'k'l-kär'), *n.* A light four-wheeled vehicle propelled by an engine of the motor-cycle type.

cyc'lic (sĭk'lĭk; sī'klĭk), *a.* Of or pertaining to a cycle or circle; moving in cycles; as, *cyclic* time.

cyc'li-cal (sĭk'lĭ-kăl; sī'klĭ-), *a.* Cyclic.

cy'clist (sī'klĭst), *n.* One who rides a cycle.

cy'cloid (-kloid), *n.* Geom. A curve traced by a point on the radius of a circle rolling in a plane along a line in the plane.

Common Cycloid. *p* Tracing point.

cy-cloi'dal (sī-kloi'dăl), *a.* Pertaining to or resembling a cycloid.

cy-clom'e-ter (sī-klŏm'ē-tẽr), *n.* A device for indicating the distance traveled by a bicycle.

cy'clone (sī'klōn), *n.* **1.** A violent storm characterized by high winds rotating about a calm center of low atmospheric pressure. This center moves onward, often rapidly. **2.** A tornado. *Middle U. S.* — **cy-clon'ic** (sī-klŏn'ĭk), *a.* [4].

cy'clo-pæ'di-a, cy'clo-pæ'dic. Var. of CYCLOPEDIA, CYCLOPEDIC.

cy'clo-pe'di-a (sī'klō-pē'dĭ-á), *n.* Encyclopedia. — **-pe'dic** (-pē'dĭk), *a.* [4].

cyg'net (sĭg'nĕt), *n.* A young swan.

cyl'in-der (sĭl'ĭn-dẽr), *n.* Geom. **a** The surface traced by one side of a rectangle rotated round the parallel side as axis. **b** The volume generated by a rectangle so rotated. **2.** Any body having the form of a cylinder, as the piston chamber in an engine, the barrel of a pump, etc.

Cylinder.

cy-lin'dric (sī-lĭn'drĭk), **cy-lin'dri-cal** (-drĭ-kăl) *a.* Having the form or properties of a cylinder.

cym'bal (sĭm'băl), *n.* Music. One of a pair of brass half globes or plates for clashing together.

cyme (sīm), *n.* Bot. **a** A flower cluster in which the primary, as well as each secondary, stem has a flower at the end, the central flower opening first. **b** Hence, any flat or convex flower cluster of this type containing many flowers, as that of forget-me-not. — **cy'mose** (sī'mōs), *a.*

Cyme.

cyn'ic (sĭn'ĭk), *n.* One who believes human conduct to be directed wholly by self-interest or self-indulgence.

cyn'i-cal (-ĭ-kăl), *a.* [4] Of the character of a cynic; given to sneering at virtue and morality. — **-ly,** *adv.* [8].

cyn'i-cism (sĭn'ĭ-sĭz'm), *n.* Cynical quality.

cy'no-sure (sī'nō-shōōr), *n.* **1.** [*cap.*] The constellation Ursa Minor. **2.** A center of attraction.

cy'press (-prĕs), *n.* **1.** A tree of the pine family having dark evergreen scalelike leaves; also, its wood. **2.** Any of various related trees, as the bald cypress, a tree with light green feathery foliage.

cyst (sĭst), *n.* Med. A closed abnormally developed sac containing morbid fluid or semi-fluid.

czar (zär; tsär), *n.* A king; an emperor; formerly, the popular title of the emperor of Russia.

cza-ri'na (zä-rē'ná; tsä-), *n.* Formerly, wife of the czar of Russia.

Czech (chĕk), *n.* A member of the most westerly branch of the Slavs. Also, their language.

Czech'o-slo-vak' (chĕk'ō-slō-vǎk'), *n.* **1.** A native of Czechoslovakia. **2.** Language of Czechoslovaks.

D

dab (dăb), *v. t. & i.;* DABBED (dăbd); DAB'BING. To strike or touch gently, as with a soft or moist substance; tap. — *n.* **1.** A gentle blow or pat; also, a peck, thrust, or sharp slap. **2.** A small soft or moist mass, portion, or the like.

dab'ble (dăb'l), *v. t.* [1] To wet by splashing; spatter. — *v. i.* **1.** To paddle or splash in water, as with the hands. **2.** To work at without serious application. — **dab'bler** (-lẽr), *n.* [8].

dab'ster (-stẽr), *n.* A dabbler at anything.

dace (dās), *n.* Any of various fishes of the carp family.

dachs'hund' (däks'hŏŏnt'), *n.* One of a certain breed of hounds with a long body and very short, crooked legs.

Dachshund. (¹⁄₂₀)

dac'tyl (dăk'tĭl), *n.* A poetical foot of three syllables (-⌣⌣), one accented, followed by two unaccented, as in *mer'ci-ful.*

dad (dăd), **dad'dy** (-ĭ), *n.* Father. *Familiar.*

daddy longlegs. The harvestman (an insect).

da'do (dā'dō; dä'dō), *n.; pl.* -DOES (-dōz). **1.** That part of an architectural pedestal between base and surbase. **2.** The lower part of the wall of an apartment when specially decorated.

daf'fo-dil (dăf'ō-dĭl), *n.* A species of narcissus, with large yellow single or double flowers.

daft (dȧft), *a.* [3] Foolish; imbecile; insane.

dag'ger (dăg'ẽr), *n.* **1.** A short weapon for stabbing. **2.** In printing, a mark of reference [†].

da-guerre'o-type (dá-gĕr'ō-tīp), *n.* An early kind of photograph, or the process used.

dahl'ia (dăl'yá; *often* dāl'- *or* däl'-), *n.* **1.** Any of several tuberous-rooted plants of the aster family. **2.** A flower or tuber of these plants.

dai'ly (dā'lĭ), *a.* Happening, belonging to, done, or issued, each or every day. — *n.; pl.* -LIES (-lĭz). A daily newspaper. — *adv.* Every day; day by day.

dain'ty (dān'tĭ), *n.; pl.* -TIES (-tĭz). Something that arouses favor or pleasure; now esp., a delicacy. — *a.* [3] **1.** Delicious to the taste; toothsome. **2.** Of a delicate beauty or charm. **3.** Having or showing delicate taste, esp. as to food or material comforts. — **dain′ti-ly** (dān′tĭ-lĭ), *adv.* [8] — **dain′ti-ness,** *n.* [8].

dai′ry (dā′rĭ ; dâr′ĭ), *n. ; pl.* -RIES (-rĭz). **1.** A place, as a room or building, where milk is kept and made into butter or cheese. **2.** The business of producing milk, butter, and cheese.

dai′ry-man (-măn), *n.; pl.* -MEN. A man who keeps, or works in, a dairy; also, one who sells dairy produce. — **dai′ry-wom′an,** *n. fem.*

da′is (dā′ĭs ; dās), *n.* A raised platform in a hall.

dai′sy (dā′zĭ), *n. : pl.* -SIES (-zĭz). Any of various plants of the aster family. The common daisy of the U. S. is a rather tall leafy-stemmed plant, bearing flowers having a yellow disk surrounded by long white rays.

dale (dāl), *n.* A vale ; valley. *Chiefly Poetical.*

dalles (dălz), *n. pl.* A rapid, esp. one in a rocky gorge. *Northwestern U. S. & Canada.*

dal′li-ance (dăl′ĭ-ăns), *n.* Act of dallying; trifling.

dal′ly (dăl′ĭ), *v. i.* [2] **1.** To act playfully ; to sport. **2.** To trifle, play, or be light (with a person or matter). **3.** To waste time ; idle.

dam (dăm), *n.* A bank or wall across a watercourse to keep back water. — *v. t. ;* DAMMED (dămd) ; DAM′MING. To obstruct or restrain by or as by a dam.

dam, *n.* A female parent ; — used of beasts.

dam′age (dăm′ȧj), *n.* **1.** Loss or detriment due to injury ; hurt ; harm. **2.** *pl. Law.* The estimated reparation in money for detriment or injury sustained. — *v. t.* [1] To harm ; impair.

dam′ask (dăm′ȧsk), *n.* **1.** Silk woven with an elaborate pattern of flowers, etc. **2.** Linen with a pattern made by difference in direction of threads of uniform color. **3.** A deep rose color.

dame (dām), *n.* **1.** A title equivalent to *Lady, Madam, Mistress, Miss,* used in address. *Obs. or Archaic,* except in personifications; as, *Dame* Nature etc. **2.** A matron; elderly woman.

damn (dăm), *v.t.;* DAMNED (dămd) ; DAMN′ING (dăm′-ĭng ; dăm′nĭng). **1.** To adjudge guilty; sentence; doom. *Archaic.* **2.** To doom to eternal punishment. **3.** To condemn as a failure ; pronounce adverse judgment on (a work of art or literature, esp. a play). **4.** To bring ruin upon ; be the ruin of. — *v. i.* To curse ; swear.

dam′na-ble (dăm′nȧ-b'l), *a.* [4] **1.** Deserving to be condemned or damned. **2.** Detestable ; execrable. — **dam′na-bly,** *adv.* [8].

dam-na′tion (-nā′shŭn), *n.* **1.** Act of damning; state of being damned. **2.** A cause of being damned.

dam′na-to-ry (dăm′nȧ-tō-rĭ), *a.* [4] Expressing, imposing, or causing condemnation or damnation.

damned (dămd; *poet. or rhetorical,* dăm′nĕd), *p.p. & p. a.* from DAMN ; — now chiefly profane.

dam′o-sel′ (dăm′ō-zĕl′). Var. of DAMSEL. *Archaic.*

damp (dămp), *n.* **1.** A gaseous product formed in coal mines, etc. See FIRE DAMP. **2.** Moisture ; humidity. **3.** Dejection ; depression of spirits. — *a.* [3] Moist; humid. — *v.t.* **1.** To choke; stifle, as a fire or a sound. **2.** To depress; discourage; restrain, as action. **3.** To make damp; moisten. — **ly,** *adv.* [8] — **ness,** *n.* [8].

damp′en (dăm′p'n), *v. t.* **1.** To depress or deaden; to damp; as, to *dampen* one's ardor. **2.** To make damp or moist. — **damp′en-er,** *n.* [8].

damp′er (-pẽr), *n.* One that damps or checks, as a valve or plate to regulate the draft in a stove, etc.

dam′sel (dăm′zĕl), *n.* A girl ; maiden.

dam′son (-z'n), *n.,* or **damson plum.** A small dark purple plum ; also, the tree producing it.

dance (dȧns), *v. i.* [1] **1.** To perform a regulated and rhythmical series of movements, commonly to music. **2.** To move nimbly or merrily. — *v.t.* **1.** To perform, or take part in, as a dancer. **2.** To cause to dance; to dandle. — *n.* **1.** A measured leaping, tripping, or stepping in unison with music or rhythmic beats. **2.** A round of dancing; also, a social assembly for dancing; a ball. **3.** A tune for dancing. — **danc′er** (dȧn′sẽr), *n.* [8].

dan′de-li′on (dăn′dē-lī′ŭn), *n.* A common weed of the chicory family, with bright yellow flowerheads.

dan′der (-dẽr), *n.* Anger or temper; — used esp. in **to have one's dander up.** *Colloq.*

dan′dle (-d'l), *v. t.* [1] **1.** To move up and down in affectionate play, as an infant ; also, to fondle.

dan′druff (-drŭf), *n.* A scurf that forms on the head and comes off in small scales or particles.

dan′dy (-dĭ), *n. ; pl.* -DIES. A man who gives excessive attention to dress; fop. — **dan′dy-ish,** *a.*

dan′ger (dān′jẽr), *n.* Exposure or liability to loss, pain, or other evil ; risk ; also, a case or cause of such exposure or liability ; in *pl.,* perils ; risks.

dan′ger-ous (dān′jẽr-ŭs), *a.* [4] Attended with danger; perilous. — **ly,** *adv.* [8] — **ness,** *n.* [8].

dan′gle (dăn′g'l), *v. i.* [1] **1.** To hang loosely with a swinging or jerking motion. **2.** To be a hanger-on or dependent; to hang about any one. — *v. t.* To cause to dangle. — **dan′gler** (-glẽr), *n.* [8].

dank (dăngk), *a.* [3] Damp ; wet ; esp., disagreeably moist or wet.

dap′per (dăp′ẽr), *a.* [4] Little and active; spruce; trim; neat in dress and personal appearance.

dap′ple (-'l), *n.* **1.** Dappled state or appearance; spotting ; clouding. **2.** A dappled animal, as a horse. — *v. t.* [1] To variegate with spots.

dare (dâr), *v. i. ; pret.* DURST (dûrst) or DARED (dârd) ; *p. p.* DARED ; *p. pr. & vb. n.* DAR′ING. To have sufficient courage for a purpose ; not to be afraid; venture. — *v. t.* [1] **1.** To have courage for; venture to undertake. **2.** To meet defiantly; challenge. — *n.* Act of daring ; challenge. — **dar′ing** (dâr′ĭng), *p. a.* [4].

dark (därk), *a.* [3] **1.** Destitute, or partially destitute, of light ; not receiving, reflecting, or radiating light ; not light-colored. **2.** Destitute of moral or spiritual light; wicked. **3.** Destitute of sunniness or cheer; gloomy. **4.** Not clear to the understanding; obscure. **5.** Reticent; secretive; silent. **6.** Not enlightened; destitute of knowledge: in intellectual obscurity. — **Dark Ages** (ā′jĕz). See MIDDLE AGES.

dark, *n.* **1.** Absence of light ; darkness ; dark place; time, or color. **2.** State of being secret or obscure, often, understood meaning; also; ignorance.

dark′en (där′k'n), *v. i.* **1.** To grow dark ; become obscure. — *v. t.* **1.** To make dark or black ; obscure. **2.** To dim; blind. **3.** To obscure or perplex. **4.** To cast a gloom on. **5.** To make foul; sully.

dark′ey (där′kĭ), *n.* Var. of DARKY.

dark′ling (därk′lĭng), *adv.* In the dark.

dark′ly, *adv.* In a dark manner.

---

dark′ness (därk′nĕs), *n.* State or quality of being dark; as: **a** Blackness; gloom. **b** Dark quality in color. **c** State of ignorance or error; sin.

dark′some (-sŭm), *a.* Darkish; gloomy. *Poetic.*

dark′y (där′kĭ), *n.; pl.* -IES (-kĭz). A negro. *Colloq.*

dar′ling (där′lĭng), *n.* One dearly beloved.— *a.* Dearly beloved; favorite.

darn (därn), *v. t.* To mend with interlacing stitches. — *v. i.* To do darning. — *n.* Act or result of darning; place darned.

dar′nel (där′nĕl),*n.* A common weed in grainfields.

darn′ing, *n.* Things darned or to be darned, collectively. — **darning needle. a** A long strong needle used in darning. **b** A dragon fly.

dart (därt), *n.* **1.** A short lance or javelin; hence, any sharp-pointed missile weapon, as an arrow. **2.** A darting movement. — *v. t.* To throw with a sudden effort or thrust (as a dart, etc.); cast; emit; shoot out. — *v. i.* To move like a dart; shoot rapidly along.

dash (dăsh), *v. t.* **1.** To strike violently; hence, to shatter; crush. **2.** To knock, throw, hurl, or thrust violently or suddenly. **3.** To hurl against so as to splash; hence, to throw on roughly, as color on a canvas; splash. **4.** To ruin; bring to naught, as one's hopes. **5.** To abash; depress. **6.** To form, write, or sketch rapidly or carelessly. — *v. i.* To rush; to hurl itself or one's self so as to strike violently.— *n.* **1.** Violent collision of two bodies; crash. **2.** A sudden or discouraging check. **3.** The striking or breaking of a liquid in violent motion, or the sound of this. **4.** A small quantity dashed, or appearing as if dashed, into or on anything. **5.** A stroke or mark [—] used to denote a sudden pause, an omission, etc. **6.** A sudden onset or rush. **7.** Energy in style or action; spirit.

dash′board (dăsh′bōrd′), *n.* A screen on the fore part of a vehicle, to intercept mud, etc.

dash′er (-ĕr), *n.* One that dashes.

das′tard (dăs′tärd), *n.* A coward; poltroon; esp., one who is sly and malicious. — *a.* [4] Dastardly.

das′tard-ly, *a.* [4] Like a dastard; marked by despicable cowardice.

da′ta (dā′tà), *n.*, *pl.* of DATUM.

date (dāt), *n.* The oblong, single-seeded, sweet, edible fruit of a lofty species of palm of northern Africa and western Asia; also, the tree.

date, *n.* **1.** That statement affixed to a writing, coin, etc., which specifies the time, and often the place, of making. **2.** A given point or period of time. **3.** A time to which anything is referred as present, as to usage, style, knowledge, etc.; — chiefly in: out of date, obsolete; antiquated; and up, *or* down, to date, up to the modern or present standard of style. — *v. t.* [1] **1.** To express the time of execution in; as, to *date* a letter, bond, etc. **2.** To ascertain, estimate, or give the date or period of. — *v. i.* To be dated.

date′less (dāt′lĕs), *a.* Having no date.

da′tive (dā′tĭv),*a.* *Gram.* Designating that case of a noun or pronoun which expresses the relation of indirect object; as, *him* in *I gave him the book* is in the *dative* case.— *n.* The dative case, or a word in it.

da′tum (dā′tŭm), *n.; pl.* DATA (-tà). Something given or admitted, as a fact or principle on which an inference is based.

da-tu′ra (dà-tū′rà), *n.* The thorn apple.

daub (dôb), *v. t.* **1.** To cover, coat, or smear with soft, adhesive matter, as plaster, mud, pitch, etc.; plaster. **2.** To paint unskillfully. — *v. i.* To do daubing; apply paint,etc., coarsely and unskillfully. — *n.* **1.** Anything, as plaster; daubed on; a smear. **2.** A picture unskillfully painted.—**daub′er**,*n.* [8].

Branch of Datura.
a Section of Capsule.

daugh′ter (dô′tĕr), *n.* **1.** A human female considered with reference to her parents or either of them, or, more remotely, to any ancestor or ancestors; a female descendant; also, a woman of a given country, faith, etc. **2.** A daughter-in-law.

daugh′ter-in-law′, *n.; pl.* DAUGHTERS-IN-LAW. The wife of one's son.

daugh′ter-ly, *a.* [4] Becoming a daughter; filial.

daunt (dänt; dônt), *v. t.* To repress or subdue the courage of; cow; intimidate.

daunt′less, *a.* [4] Not to be daunted; undaunted — **daunt′less-ly**, *adv.* [8] — **-ness**, *n.* [8].

dau′phin (dô′fĭn), *n.* *French Hist.* From 1349 to 1830, title of the eldest son of the king of France

dav′it (dăv′ĭt; dā′vĭt), *n.* *Naut.* One of a pair of curved arms having a tackle to hoist or lower boats, stores, etc.

daw (dô), *n.* **1.** A jackdaw. **2.** A simpleton.

daw′dle (-d'l), *v. i. & t.* [1] To waste time, or to waste, in trifling employment; trifle. — **daw′dler** (dô′dlĕr), *n.* [8].

dawn (dôn), *v. i.* **1.** To begin to grow light in the morning. **2.** To begin to appear, develop, or give promise. **3.** To begin to make a mental impression (on or upon) as, the fact *dawned* upon him. — *n.* **1.** Daybreak **2.** First appearance; rise.

a a Davits *b.*

day (dā), *n.* **1.** The time of light between one night and the next; hence, the light; sunshine. **2.** The period of the earth's revolution on its axis. **3.** The mean (average) solar day of 24 hours, generally used in reckoning time. **4.** The hours allotted by usage or law for work; as, a *day's* work. **5.** The conflict or contention of the day; as, to win the *day*. **6.** A specified time or period; age.

day′book (-bòòk′), *n.* *Bookkeeping.* A book in which accounts of the day are recorded.

day′break (-brāk′), *n.* The first appearance of light in the morning, or the time of it; dawn.

day′dream (-drēm′), *n.* A pleasant reverie.

day′light (dā′līt′), *n.* The light of day; daytime.

day′time (-tīm′), *n.* Time of daylight.

daze (dāz), *v. t.* [1] To stupefy with excess of light, with a blow, with cold, or with fear, grief, etc.; stun; dazzle. — *n.* State of being dazed.

daz′zle (dăz′'l), *v. t.* [1] **1.** To confuse the vision of by excess of light, by moving lights, etc. **2.** To bewilder or surprise with brilliancy or display. — *n.* Act of dazzling; state of being dazzling.

dea'con (dē'k'n), *n.* An officer performing varying subordinate functions in Christian churches. — **dea'con-ess**, *n. fem.* [8].

dead (děd), *a.* [3] **1.** Deprived or destitute of life. **2.** Hence, extinct; extinguished; disused. **3.** Resembling the dead as being devoid of motion, activity, power, effect, etc. **4.** Entire; absolute. **5.** Sure as death; certain; exact; direct. — **dead letter. a** That which has lost its force or authority. **b** A letter which is undeliverable because of defective address, lack of postage, or contravention of some postal regulation.

dead, *n.* **1.** One who is dead; usually, collectively (with *the*), those who are dead. **2** The most quiet or deathlike time. — *adv.* **1.** Absolutely; utterly. **2.** With sudden and entire, or almost entire, stoppage of motion or action. **3.** Directly; exactly.

dead'en (děd'n), *v. t.* **1.** To make as dead; impair in vigor or sensation. **2.** To make vapid or spiritless. **3.** To deprive of gloss or brilliancy. **4.** To render impervious to sound.

dead'lock (-lŏk'), *n.* A complete obstruction of action by the counteraction of persons or events.

dead'ly (-lĭ), *a.* [3] **1.** Causing, or capable of causing, death. **2.** Aiming or willing to destroy; implacable. **3.** Like or pertaining to death; deathly. — **li-ness,** *n.* [8].

dead'ness (-nĕs), *n.* Quality or state of being dead.

deaf (děf), *a.* **1,** Wanting, or deprived of, the sense of hearing, wholly or in part. **2.** Unwilling to hear; willfully inattentive. — **ness,** *n.* [8].

deaf'en (děf'n), *v. t.* **1.** To make deaf. **2.** To make inaudible; drown; — said of sounds.

deaf'–mute', *n.* A person both deaf and dumb.

deal (dēl), *n.* **1.** A portion; share; indefinite amount. **2.** A good or great deal. *Colloq.*

deal, *v. t.; DEALT* (dĕlt); DEAL'ING. **1.** To give in portions or as one's portion; distribute; apportion. **2.** To deliver, as blows. — *v. i.* **1.** To contend (*with*); or strive to treat (*with*) in opposition. **2.** To have to do, be concerned, or be occupied (*with* or *in*). **3.** To do a distributing or retailing business (*in*). — *n.* Act of dealing; hence : **a** Apportionment. **b** An act of buying and selling; a bargain. *Colloq.* **c** A secret arrangement, as in political bargains. *Cant, U. S.*

deal, *n.* A board of fir or pine, cut to any of several specified sizes; also, the wood.

deal'er (-ēr), *n.* **1.** One who deals, as the player who distributes the cards. **2.** A trader; esp., one who buys and sells goods without altering their condition; as, a retail *dealer.*

deal'ing, *n.* **1.** Intercourse; traffic; — usually in *pl.* **2.** Method of business or manner of conduct.

dean (dēn), *n.* **1.** In a cathedral church, or any church having a chapter of canons, the head of the chapter. **2.** The chief administrative officer, under the president, of a college or university faculty or department. **3.** The chief or senior of a body, as of a diplomatic corps; — so called by courtesy.

dean'er-y (dēn'ēr-ĭ), *n.; pl.* -ERIES (-ĭz). Office, jurisdiction, or official residence of a dean.

dean'ship, *n.* The office, position, or rank of dean.

dear (dēr), *a.* [3] **1.** Highly valued or esteemed; loved; — in forms of address merely an expression of politeness; as, *dear* sir. **2.** Costly; expensive; high-priced; also, marked by high prices. **3.** Heartfelt; earnest. — *n.* A dear one; darling. — *adv.* Dearly; at a high price; fondly. — **dear'ly,** *adv.* [8] — **dear'ness,** *n.* [8].

dearth (dûrth), *n.* Scarcity which renders dear; want; lack; esp., famine.

death (děth), *n.* **1.** Total cessation of life, as in animals or plants; act or fact of dying. **2.** Personified [*often cap.*]: The destroyer of life. **3.** State of being dead. **4.** Anything so dreadful as to be like death. **5.** Total privation or loss; extinction; annihilation. **6.** Cause or occasion of loss of life.

death'bed' (-bĕd'), *n.* The bed in which a person dies; hence, closing hours of life; last sickness.

death cup. A common very poisonous mushroom.

death'less, *a.* Not subject to death; immortal.

death'like', *a.* [4] Like death; deathly.

death'ly, *a.* [3] **1.** Deadly; mortal. **2.** Like death. — *adv.* Deadly; as, *deathly* pale.

death's'–head' (děths'hěd'), *n.* A human skull as the emblem of death.

death'watch (děth'wŏch'), *n.* The guard set over a criminal before his execution.

de-bar' (dḗ-bär'), *v. t.; -BARRED* (-bärd'); -BAR'RING. To cut off from entrance, as if by a bar; to exclude; deny; — usually with *from.*

de-bark' (-bärk'), *v. t. & i.* To disembark.

de-base' (dḗ-bās'), *v. t.* [1] To reduce to a lower state or grade of worth, dignity, purity, etc.; degrade; depreciate. — **de-bas'er** (-bās'ẽr), *n.* [8]

de-base'ment (-mĕnt), *n.* Act of debasing.

de-bat'a-ble (-bāt'á-b'l), *a.* [4] Liable to be debated; disputable; as, a *debatable* question.

de-bate' (-bāt'), *v. i.* [1] To dispute; hence, to deliberate; consider; to discuss or examine by argument. — *v. t.* To strive to maintain by reasoning dispute. — *n.* Contention; discussion; controversy. — **de-bat'er** (-bāt'ẽr), *n.* [8].

de-bauch' (-bôch'), *v. t.* To lead away from purity, virtue, or excellence; corrupt; seduce. — *n.* **1.** An act or occasion of debauchery. **2.** Debauchery. — **er,** *n.* — **de-bauched'** (-bôcht'), *p. a.* [4]

deb'au-chee' (dĕb'ō-shē'), *n.* One given to debauchery.

de-bauch'er-y (dḗ-bôch'ẽr-ĭ), *n.; pl.* -ERIES (-ĭz) **1.** Excessive indulgence of the sensual appetites **2.** Corruption of fidelity; seduction from virtue.

de-ben'ture (dḗ-bĕn'tụr), *n.* A writing or certificate serving as a voucher for a debt.

de-bil'i-tate (-bĭl'ĭ-tāt), *v. t.* [1] To weaken.

de-bil'i-ty (-tĭ), *n.; pl.* -TIES (-tĭz). Weakened or feeble condition; weakness; feebleness.

deb'it (dĕb'ĭt), *n. Bookkeeping.* An entry, in an account, of something owed; also, the left-hand, or debtor, side of an account. — *v. t.* To charge with, or as, a debt.

deb'o-nair' (dĕb'ō-nâr'), *a.* [4] **1.** Of good disposition; kindly. **2.** Affable and courteous; characterized by grace and light-heartedness.

de-bouch' (dḗ-bōōsh'), *v. i.* **1** *Mil.* To march out from a confined spot. **2.** To emerge; issue.

|| **dé'bris'** (dā'brē'), *n.* [F.] Rubbish, esp. such as results from destruction; ruins.

debt (dĕt), *n.* **1.** That which is due from one to another; obligation; liability. **2.** A sin; trespass.

debt/or (-ẽr), *n.* **1.** One who owes a debt. **2.** The debit side of an account, or an entry there made.

‖ **dé/but/** (dā/bü/; dĕ-bū/), *n.* [F.] A beginning; hence, a first appearance before the public, as of an actor; entrance into society.

‖ **dé/bu/tant/** (dā/bü/täɴ/; dĕb/ū/tänt/), *n.* [F.] One making a début. — ‖ **dé/bu/tante/** (-tänt/ ; -tänt/), *n. fem.*

dec/ade (dĕk/ād), *n.* A group of ten; esp., a period of ten years.

de-ca/dence (dĕ-kā/dĕns; dĕk/á-), *n.* A falling away; decay; decline. — **de-ca/den-cy** (-sĭ), *n.*

de-ca/dent (dĕ-kā/dĕnt; dĕk/á-), *a.* [4] Characterized by decadence.—*n.* One that is decadent.

dec/a-gon (dĕk/á-gŏn), *n.* A polygon of ten sides. — **de-cag/o-nal** (dĕ-kăg/ō-nȧl), *a.*

dec/a-gram (dĕk/á-grăm), *n.* A metric measure of weight equal to 10 grams, or 0.3527 oz.

dec/a-he/dron (-hē/drŏn), *n. ; pl.* E. **-DRONS** (-drŏnz), L. **-DRA** (-drȧ). A polyhedron of ten faces. — **dec/a-he/dral** (-drȧl), *a.*

dec/a-li/ter (dĕk/á-lē/tẽr), *n.* [6] A metric measure of volume containing 10 liters, or 2.64 gallons.

Dec/a-logue (-lŏg), *n.* [*Sometimes l. c.*] The Ten Commandments.

dec/a-me/ter (dĕk/á-mē/tẽr), *n.* [6] A metric measure of length equal to 10 meters, or 32.809 ft.

de-camp/ (dĕ-kămp/), *v. i.* **1.** To break up a camp, esp. secretly. **2.** To depart suddenly.

de-cant/ (dĕ-kănt/), *v. t.* To pour off gently, as liquor, so as not to roil.

de/can-ta/tion (dē/kăn-tā/shŭn), *n.* Act or process of decanting.

de-cant/er (dĕ-kăn/tẽr), *n.* A vessel used to decant liquors, or to receive decanted liquors.

de-cap/i-tate (-kăp/ĭ-tāt), *v. t.* [1] To behead.

dc-cap/i ta/tion (-tā/shŭn), *n.* Act of decapitating; fact of being decapitated.

dec/a-pod (dĕk/á-pŏd), *a.* Having ten feet or legs.

de-car/bon-ize (dĕ-kär/bŏn-īz), *v. t.* [1] To deprive of carbon. — **de-car/bon-i-za/tion**, *n.*

dec/a-syl/la-ble (dĕk/á-sĭl/á-b'l), *n.* A line of ten syllables. — **dec/a-syl-lab/ic** (-sĭ-lăb/ĭk), *a.*

de-cath/lon (dĕ-kăth/lŏn), *n.* In the modern Olympian games, a contest consisting of a 400-meter run, broad jump, putting the shot, running high jump, 100-meter run, throwing the discus, 100-meter hurdle race, pole vaulting, throwing the javelin, and 1500-meter run.

de-cay/ (dĕ-kā/), *v. i.* **1.** To fail gradually; decline. **2.** To decrease in numbers, volume, or intensity, or in health or vigor. **3.** To rot. — *n.* **1.** Gradual failure; corruption; rottenness. **2.** Ruin; dilapidation. **3.** A decline in health.

de-cease/ (dĕ-sēs/), *n.* Death. — *v. i.* To die.

de-ceased/ (dĕ-sēst/), *a.* Dead; esp., lately dead. — the deceased, the dead person.

de-ce/dent (dĕ-sē/dĕnt), *n.* A deceased person.

de-ceit/ (-sēt/), *n.* An attempt to deceive; disposition to deceive; a trick; fraud.

de-ceit/ful (-fŏŏl), *a.* [4] Full of deceit; fraudulent; insincere. — **-ly**, *adv.* [8] — **-ness**, *n.* [8].

de-ceive/ (-sēv/), *v. t.* [1] To lead into error; impose upon; mislead. — **de-ceiv/er**, *n.* [8].

De-cem/ber (-sĕm/bẽr), *n.* The 12th and last month of the year, having 31 days.

de/cen-cy (dē/sĕn-sĭ), *n. ; pl.* **-CIES** (-sĭz). **1.** Quality or state of being decent in words or behavior; modesty. **2.** That which is decent, or proper.

de-cen/ni-al (dĕ-sĕn/ĭ-ȧl), *a.* Consisting of or happening every ten years. — **de-cen/ni-al**, *n.*

de/cent (dē/sĕnt), *a.* [3] **1.** Suitable in words, behavior, etc.; becoming; fit; modest. **2.** Moderate, but competent; hence, respectable; fairly good. — **de/cent-ly**, *adv.* [8] — **-ness**, *n.* [8].

de-cen/tral-ize (dĕ-sĕn/trȧl-īz), *v. t.* [1] To deprive of centralization; —esp. said of authority. — **de-cen/tral-i-za/tion** (-ĭ-zā/shŭn), *n.*

de-cep/tion (-sĕp/shŭn), *n.* **1.** Act of deceiving; fact of being deceived. **2.** That which deceives or is intended to deceive; fraud.

de-cep/tive (-tĭv), *a.* [4] Tending to deceive. — **-ly**, *a.* — **-ness**, *n.* [8].

dec/i-are (dĕs/ĭ-âr/; dĕs/ĭ-âr/), *n.* A metric measure of surface equal to $\frac{1}{10}$ are, or 11.96 sq. yd.

de-cide/ (dĕ-sīd/), *v. t. & i.* [1] To determine; settle; conclude.

de-cid/ed (-sīd/ĕd), *p. a.* [4] **1.** Free from ambiguity; clear. **2.** Free from doubt or wavering; determined. — **-ly**, *adv.* [8] — **-ness**, *n.* [8].

de-cid/u-ous (-sĭd/ū-ŭs), *a.* **1. a** *Bot. & Zoöl.* Falling off at maturity, or at certain seasons, as the antlers of deer, or leaves, fruits, etc. **b** *Bot.* Having leaves of this type; —opposed to *evergreen*. **2.** Transitory; fleeting.

dec/i-gram (dĕs/ĭ-grăm), *n.* A metric weight, equal to .1 gram, or 1.5432 grains.

dec/i-li/ter (-lē/tẽr), *n.* [6] A metric measure of volume, containing $\frac{1}{10}$ liter.

dec/i-mal (dĕs/ĭ-mȧl), *a.* Numbered or proceeding by tens, each unit being ten times the unit next smaller.—**decimal fraction**, a fraction in which the denominator is some power of 10, usually signified by a point or dot (**decimal point**) placed at the left of the numerator, as $.2 = \frac{2}{10}$, $.25 = \frac{25}{100}$.—*n.* A decimal fraction. — **dec/i-mal-ly**, *adv.* [8].

dec/i-mate (-māt), *v. t.* [1] **1.** To take the tenth part of. **2.** To select by lot and punish with death every tenth man of. **3.** To destroy a considerable part of.

dec/i-ma/tion (-mā/shŭn), *n.* Act of decimating.

dec/i-me/ter (dĕs/ĭ-mē/tẽr), *n.* [6] A metric measure of length, equal to .1 meter, or 3.937 in.

de-ci/pher (dĕ-sī/fẽr), *v. t.* **1.** To translate from secret characters, or ciphers, into intelligible terms. **2.** To find out the meaning of; make out, as words partly obliterated. — **-a-ble**, *a.* [8].

de-ci/sion (-sĭzh/ŭn), *n.* **1.** Act of deciding; settlement; conclusion. **2.** A report or a conclusion; as, a *decision* of the Supreme Court. **3.** Quality of being decided; ready determination.

de-ci/sive (-sī/sĭv), *a.* [4] **1.** Able to decide a question; final; conclusive. **2.** Marked by prompt decision. — **de-ci/sive-ly**, *adv.* [8] — **de-ci/sive-ness**, *n.* [8].

deck (dĕk), *v. t.* **1.** To dress; array; adorn. **2.** To furnish with a deck, as a vessel. — *n.* **1.** One of the platforms extending from side to side of a ship or part of a ship and forming a covering for the space below and also serving as a floor. **2.** A flat space or floor likened to a ship's deck. **3.** A pack of playing cards.

de-claim' (dĕ-klām'), *v. i. & t.* To speak or deliver rhetorically; make, or utter in, a formal speech; harangue. — **de-claim'er**, *n.* [8].

dec'la-ma'tion (dĕk'lă-mā'shŭn), *n.* **1.** Act or art of declaiming. **2.** A set speech or harangue.

de-clam'a-to-ry (dĕ-klăm'á-tô-rĭ), *a.* **1.** Pertaining to declamation. **2.** Pretentiously rhetorical.

dec'la-ra'tion (dĕk'lá-rā'shŭn), *n.* **1.** Act of declaring. **2.** That which is declared or proclaimed, or the document containing it.

de-clar'a-tive (dĕ-klăr'á-tĭv), **-a-to-ry** (-tô-rĭ), *a.* Making declaration; explanatory; affirmative.

de-clare' (-klâr'), *v. t.* [1] **1.** To make known explicitly and plainly; proclaim. **2.** To make declaration of; assert; affirm. **3.** To make full statement of (goods, etc., subject to duties, etc.) as being in one's possession or ownership. —*v. i.* To make a declaration; proclaim one's self.

de-clen'sion (-klĕn'shŭn), *n.* **1.** Descent; declination; decline. **2.** Act of declining; refusal. **3.** *Gram.* Inflection of nouns, adjectives, etc., according to the grammatical cases; also, the inflectional class of a word that is declined by cases.

de-clin'a-ble (-klīn'á-b'l),*a.* That can be declined.

dec'li-na'tion (dĕk'lĭ-nā'shŭn), *n.* **1.** Act of declining; as: deviation or swerving; decay or decline; refusal. **2.** *Astron.* The angular distance of any object north or south from the celestial equator. **3.** The angle made by the magnetic needle with the true north and south line.

de-cline' (dĕ-klīn'), *v. i.* [1] **1.** To draw toward a close or extinction; fail; diminish; decay. **2.** To bend downward; hang down. **3.** To refuse; reject with thanks. —*v. t.* **1.** To bend downward; depress. **2.** To put or turn aside; to refuse; reject. **3.** *Gram.* To inflect (a noun or adjective). —*n.* **1** A falling off; diminution or decay; also, the period when a thing nears extinction. **2.** a A gradual sinking and wasting away. **b** Any wasting disease; esp., pulmonary consumption.

de-cliv'i-ty (-klĭv'ĭ-tĭ), *n.; pl.* **-TIES** (-tĭz). **1.** Deviation from the horizontal; gradual descent; slope. **2.** A descending surface; slope.

de-coc'tion (-kŏk'shŭn), *n.* An extract got from a substance by boiling it in water.

|| **dé'col'le-té'** (dā'kŏ'l'-tā'), *a.* [4] [F.]. **1.** Leaving the neck and shoulders uncovered. **2.** Wearing a décolleté gown.

de'com-pose' (dē'kŏm-pōz'), *v. t. & i.* [1] To separate into the constituent parts; to resolve into original elements or into simpler compounds; rot; decay. — **de'com-pos'a-ble** (-pōz'á-b'l), *a.* [8].

de-com'po-si'tion (dē-kŏm'pô-zĭsh'ŭn), *n.* Act or process of decomposing; decomposed state; decay.

de'com-pound' (dē'kŏm-pound'), *a.* *Bot.* Having divisions themselves compound; — said of leaves.

dec'o-rate (dĕk'ō-rāt), *v.t.* [1] **1.** To deck; adorn; embellish. **2.** To award a decoration of honor to.

dec'o-ra'tion (-rā'shŭn), *n.* **1.** Act of adorning; decorating. **2.** An embellishment; ornament. **3.** A mark or badge of honor, as a medal.

Decoration Day. = MEMORIAL DAY. *U. S.*

dec'o-ra-tive (dĕk'ō-rā-tĭv),*a.* [4] Suited to decorate; adorning. — **-ly**, *adv.* [8] — **-ness**, *n.* [8].

dec'o-ra'tor (-rā'tẽr), *n.* One who decorates; an artist or artisan whose business is the decoration, esp. the interior decoration, of houses.

de-co'rous (dĕ-kō'rŭs; dĕk'ô-rŭs), *a.* [4] Suitable to a character, or to the time, place, and occasion; proper. — **-ly**, *adv.* [8] — **-ness**, *n.* [8].

de-co'rum (dĕ-kō'rŭm), *n.; pl.* E. **-RUMS** (-rŭmz), L. **-RA** (-rá). **1.** Propriety of manner or conduct; dignity; seemliness. **2.** A seemly and fitting act.

de-coy' (dĕ-koi'), *n.* **1.** A place into which wild fowl, esp. ducks, are enticed. **2.** Anything intended to lead into a snare: lure; bait; esp., a fowl, or likeness of one, used to entice birds within gunshot. **3.** One employed to lead a person into a position where he may be swindled or the like. —*v. t.* To lead into danger by artifice; entice.

de-crease' (-krēs'), *v. i. & t.* [1] To diminish gradually, in size, degree, number, duration, etc., or in strength or quality.

de-crease' (dĕ-krēs'; dē'krēs),*n.* A becoming less; gradual diminution; amount of diminution.

de-cree' (dĕ-krē'), *n.* An authoritative order or decision determining what is done, or is to be done; edict; law; ordinance. —*v. t. & i.* [1] To command authoritatively; appoint by decree; ordain.

de-crep'it (-krĕp'ĭt), *a.* [4] Broken down with age; infirm; worn-out.

de-crep'i-tude (-I-tūd), *n.* Decrepit state.

de-cri'al (dĕ-krī'ăl), *n.* A crying down; decrying.

de-cry' (-krī'), *v. t.* [2] To cry down; censure as faulty, mean, or worthless. — **de-cri'er**, *n.* [8].

de-cum'bent (-kŭm'bĕnt), *a.* *Bot.* Reclining on the ground, but with ascending apex or extremity; — said of stems or shoots.

ded'i-cate (dĕd'I-kāt), *v. t.* [1] **1.** To set apart and consecrate; devote solemnly; as, to *dedicate* a church. **2.** To devote, as one's self, to a duty or service. **3.** To inscribe by way of compliment, as a book. — **ded'i-ca'tor** (-kā'tẽr), *n.* [8].

ded'i-ca'tion (-kā'shŭn), *n.* Act of dedicating.

ded'i-ca-to-ry (dĕd'I-ká-tô-rĭ), *a.* Constituting, or serving as, a dedication.

de-duce' (dĕ-dūs'), *v. t.* [1] To obtain or arrive at, as a truth, by reasoning; derive; infer.

de-duc'i-ble (-dūs'I-b'l), *a.* That can be deduced.

de-duct' (-dŭkt'), *v. t.* To take away in number ing or calculating; subtract.

de-duc'tion (-dŭk'shŭn), *n.* **1.** Act or process of deducing; — opp. to *induction.* **2.** Act of deducting, or taking away; subtraction. **3.** That which is deduced; abatement. **4.** That which is deduced; inference; conclusion.

de-duc'tive (-tĭv), *a.* Pertaining to deduction.

deed (dēd), *n.* **1.** That which is done; act; action. **2.** Illustrious act; exploit; feat. **3.** A sealed instrument in writing, duly executed and delivered, containing some transfer, bargain, or contract. **4.** Performance; action, esp. as contrasted with words. — **in deed**, in fact; in truth. See INDEED. —*v. t.* To convey, or transfer, by deed (see *n.*, def. 3). *U. S.*

deem (dēm), *v. t. & i.* To think; esteem; suppose.

deep (dēp), *a.* [3] **1.** Extending comparatively far below the surface; of great, or a specified, perpendicular dimension (measured downward). **2.** Extending far back, or a specified distance, from the

---

āle, senāte, cāre, ăm, ăccount, ärm, ȧsk, sofá; ēve, ĕvent, ĕnd, recĕnt, makēr; īce, ĭll; ōld, ŏbey, ôrb, ŏdd, sŏft, cŏnnect; ūse, ūnite, ûrn, ŭp, circŭs; fōod, foŏt; out, oil;

front or outer part. **3.** Hard to comprehend; profound; mysterious. **4.** Serious; grave; also, intense; heavy; profound. **5.** Penetrating; sagacious; cunning; as, a *deep* person. **6.** Of colors: strong; intense. **7.** Of low tone; grave; heavy. **8.** Heavy; extreme; excessive. Also, of persons, acting, feeling, etc., profoundly. **9.** Immersed; absorbed; involved.

deep, *n.* **1.** That which is deep; esp., the sea or ocean. **2.** The middle, or intense, part. — *adv.* **1.** To a great depth; profoundly. **2.** Far on (in time); as, *deep* in the night. — **deep′ly** (dēp′lĭ), *adv.* [8] — **deep′ness,** *n.* [8].

deep′en (dēp′n), *v. t. & i.* To make or become deep or deeper.

deer (dēr), *n. sing. & pl.* (see PLURAL, *n.*). Any of numerous ruminant mammals, distinguished chiefly by the peculiar type of horns, called *antlers,* borne by the males and shed and renewed annually.

de-face′ (dē-fās′), *v. t.* [1] To destroy or mar the face or appearance of; disfigure.

de-face′ment (-měnt), *n.* **1.** Act of defacing; state of being defaced. **2.** That which disfigures.

de fac′to (dē făk′tō). [L.] Actually; in fact.

de-fal′cate (dē-făl′kāt),*v.i.* [1] To embezzle money held in trust. — **def′al-ca′tor** (děf′ăl-kā′tẽr), *n.*

de′fal-ca′tion (dē′făl-kā′shŭn; děf′ăl-), *n.* An abstraction or misappropriation of money, etc., in breach of trust; embezzlement.

def′a-ma′tion (děf′á-mā′shŭn; dē′fá-), *n.* Act of defaming another; calumny; libel; slander.

de-fam′a-to-ry (dē-făm′á-tō-rĭ), *a.* Containing defamation; slanderous; as, *defamatory* words.

de-fame′ (-fām′), *v. t.* [1] To harm or destroy the good fame or reputation of; speak evil of maliciously. — **de-fam′er** (-fām′ẽr), *n.* [8].

de-fault′ (-fôlt′), *n.* **1.** A failing or failure; neglect to do what duty or law requires. **2.** Fault; offense. — *v. i.* **1.** To fail in fulfilling an agreement, obligation, or duty, esp. a financial obligation; specifically, to fail to account properly for property held in trust. **2.** To fail to appear in court; let a case go by default. — *v. t.* To fail to perform or pay. — **de-fault′er,** *n.* [8].

de-feat′ (-fēt′), *v. t.* **1.** To bring to naught; render null and void; frustrate, as hope. **2.** To overcome; vanquish; overthrow. — *n.* Act of defeating or bringing to naught (plans, hopes, etc.); overthrow, as of an army; — opposed to *victory.*

def′e-cate (děf′ē-kāt), *v. i.* [1] To void excrement.

def′e-ca′tion (-kā′shŭn), *n.* Act of defecating.

de-fect′ (dē-fěkt′), *n.* **1.** Want of something necessary to completeness; deficiency. **2.** Failing; fault; imperfection.

de-fec′tion (-fěk′shŭn), *n.* Failure in duty or allegiance; desertion; apostasy.

1e-fec′tive (-tǐv), *a.* [4] **1.** Incomplete; imperfect; faulty. **2.** *Gram.* Lacking one or more of the usual forms of inflection. — **de-fec′tive-ly,** *adv.* [8] — **de-fec′tive-ness,** *n.* [8].

de-fence′. Var. of DEFENSE.

de-fend′ (-fěnd′), *v. t.* **1.** To repel danger or harm from; protect; uphold. **2.** To oppose or resist, as a claim at law; contest. — **de-fend′er,** *n.* [8].

de-fend′ant (dē-fěn′dănt), *n.* One required to make answer in a legal action.

de-fense′ (-fěns′), *n.* **1.** Act of defending; state of being defended. **2.** That which defends or protects; guard. **3.** Protecting plea; vindication; justification. **4.** *Law.* The defendant's denial, answer, or plea. — **de-fense′less,** *a.* [8].

de-fen′si-ble (-fěn′sĭ-b'l), *a.* [4] Capable of being defended, or of offering defense.

de-fen′sive (-sĭv), *a.* **1.** Serving to defend or protect. **2.** Carried on by resisting attack or aggression. **3.** In a state or posture of defense; as, a *defensive* attitude. — *n.* That which defends; a defensive position, as in to be, *or* stand, on the defensive, to be or stand in a defensive state or posture. — **de-fen′sive-ly,** *adv.* [8].

de-fer′ (-fûr′), *v. t. ; -FERRED′* (-fûrd′) ; *-FER′RING.* To put off; postpone; withhold. — *v. i.* To wait; procrastinate.

de-fer′, *v. t. & i.* To yield to the opinion or wishes of another, or to authority; — with *to.*

def′er-ence (děf′ẽr-ěns), *n.* Act of deferring; courteous or complaisant regard for another's wishes.

def′er-en′tial (-ěn′shăl), *a.* [4] Marked by deference.

de-fi′ance (dē-fī′ăns),*n.* **1.** Act of defying. **2.** Disposition to resist; contempt of opposition.

de-fi′ant (-ănt), *a.* [4] Full of defiance; bold; insolent. — **de-fi′ant-ly,** *adv.* [8].

de-fi′cien-cy (dē-fĭsh′ĕn-sĭ), *n. ; pl.* -CIES (-sĭz). State of being deficient; inadequacy; defect.

de-fi′cient (-ěnt), *a.* [4] Lacking some element of completeness; insufficient; defective; incomplete.

def′i-cit (děf′ĭ-sĭt), *n.* A falling short, esp. of income; deficiency; as, a *deficit* of a hundred dollars.

de-fi′er (dē-fī′ẽr), *n.* One who defies.

de-file′ (dē-fīl′), *v. t. & i.* [1] To march off in a line, file by file.

de-file′, *n.* A long pass or gorge.

de-file′, *v. t.* To make foul; corrupt; tarnish, as reputation. — **de-fil′er** (-fīl′ẽr), *n.* [8].

de-file′ment (-měnt), *n.* Act of defiling; state of being defiled; pollution; uncleanness.

de-fin′a-ble(-fīn′á-b'l),*a.* Capable of being defined.

de-fine′ (-fīn′), *v. t.* [1] **1.** To determine the boundaries or limits of ; hence, to fix clearly and authoritatively. **2.** To fix the meaning of; explain; interpret. — **de-fin′er** (-fīn′ẽr), *n.* [8].

def′i-nite (děf′ĭ-nĭt), *a.* [4] **1.** Having certain or distinct limits; fixed. **2.** Having certain limits in meaning; precise; exact. **3.** Limiting; determining; as, the **definite article,** *Gram.,* the article *the,* used to designate a particular person or thing or class of persons or things. — **def′i-nite-ly** (děf′ĭ-nĭt-lĭ), *adv.* [8] — **def′i-nite-ness,** *n.* [8].

def′i-ni′tion (-nĭsh′ŭn), *n.* **1.** Act of defining; esp., act of making definite or clear. **2.** Distinctness. **3.** A description of a thing by its properties; an explanation of the meaning of a word or term.

de-fin′i-tive (dē-fĭn′ĭ-tĭv), *a.* [4] **1.** Determinate; positive; final; express. **2.** Limiting; determining; as, a *definitive* word. — *n.* A word used to define or limit the extent of the signification of a common noun, such as the definite article and some pronouns.—-**ly,** *adv.* [8]—-**ness,** *n.* [8].

de-flate′ (dē-flāt′), *v. t.* [1] To reduce from inflation by releasing the air or gas. — **de-fla′tion** (-flā′shŭn), *n.*

de-flect' (dĕ-flĕkt'), v.t. & i. To turn aside; deviate.

de-flec'tion (-flĕk'shŭn), n. A turning, or state of being turned, aside; deviation.

de-flow'er (dĕ-flou'ẽr), v.t. To violate or ravish; desecrate; spoil.

de-for'est (-fŏr'ĕst), v. t. To clear of forests. — **de-for'est-a'tion** (-fŏr'ĕs-tā'shŭn), n.

de-form' (-fôrm'), v. t. **1.** To distort; disfigure. **2.** To deprive of beauty, grace, or perfection.

def'or-ma'tion (dĕf'ôr-mā'shŭn; dē'fôr-), n. Act of deforming; state of being deformed.

de-form'i-ty (dĕ-fôr'mĭ-tĭ), n.; pl. -TIES (-tĭz). **1.** State of being deformed; distortion. **2.** Something that deforms or disfigures; esp., a malformation of some part of the body.

de-fraud' (-frôd'), v. t. To deprive of some right, interest, or property, by deceit; cheat; — with of.

de-fray' (-frā'), v. t. To pay or discharge, as a debt, costs, etc. — **de-fray'er,** n. [8].

de-fray'al (-ăl), n., **de-fray'ment** (-mĕnt), n. Act of defraying; payment.

deft (dĕft), a. [3] Apt; dexterous; neat in action. — **deft'ly,** adv. — **deft'ness,** n.

de-funct' (dĕ-fŭnkt'), a. Dead; deceased. — n. A dead person; generally, one recently deceased.

de-fy' (-fī'), v.t. [2] **1.** To provoke to strife; challenge. **2.** To challenge to do something. Hence, of things, to withstand completely; resist successfully.

de-gen'er-a-cy (dĕ-jĕn'ẽr-á-sĭ), n. Act of becoming, or state of being, degenerate; deterioration.

de-gen'er-ate (-āt), a. [4] Having become worse than one's kind, or one's former state; degraded; low. — n. One having the characteristics of degeneracy, esp. by birth. — (-āt), v. i. [1] To become or grow worse than one's kind, or than one was originally; deteriorate. — **ly,** adv. [8].

de-gen'er-a'tion (-ā'shŭn), n. A growing or a being worse; degeneracy; deterioration.

deg'lu-ti'tion (dĕg'lōō-tĭsh'ŭn; dē'glōō-), n. Act, process, or power of swallowing.

deg'ra-da'tion (dĕg'rá-dā'shŭn), n. Act of degrading; state of being degraded; abasement; disgrace.

de-grade' (dĕ-grād'), v. t. [1] **1.** To reduce from a higher to a lower rank or degree; deprive of office, dignity, or position. **2.** To reduce in character or reputation; debase; disgrace.

de-gree' (-grē'), n. **1.** A step or station in a series; point or stage of advancement or retrogression. **2.** Relative quantity, quality, or intensity. **3.** Gram. One of the three grades — positive, comparative, superlative — in comparing an adjective or adverb. **4.** Relative rank; station in life. **5.** Academical rank or grade. **6.** A remove in the chain of relationship. **7.** Math. A 360th part of the circumference of a circle.

de-hisce' (dĕ-hĭs'), v. i. [1] To gape open; to open by dehiscence.

de-his'cence (-hĭs'ĕns), n. A gaping open; esp., in Botany, the bursting open of fruits, capsules, etc., to discharge their ripened contents.

de-his'cent (-ĕnt), a. Characterized by dehiscence.

de-horn' (dē-hôrn'), v. t. To deprive of horns.

de'i-fi-ca'tion (dē'ĭ-fĭ-kā'shŭn), n. Act of deifying; state of being deified; apotheosis.

de'i-fy (dē'ĭ-fī), v. t. [2] To make a god of; treat as an object of supreme regard.

deign (dān), v. i. To think fit; vouchsafe; condescend. — v. t. To condescend to give or bestow; vouchsafe.

de'ism (dē'ĭz'm), n. **1.** Belief in a personal God, with disbelief in Christian revelation. **2.** Doctrine that God exists apart from the physical universe. — **de-is'tic** (dĕ-ĭs'tĭk), **-ti-cal** (-tĭ-kăl), a.

de'ist, n. A believer in deism.

de'i-ty (dē'ĭ-tĭ), n.; pl. -TIES (-tĭz). **1.** Divinity; godhead. **2.** A god or goddess. — **the Deity,** God; the Supreme Being.

de-ject' (dĕ-jĕkt'), v. t. To cast down the spirits of; dishearten.

de-ject'ed (-jĕk'tĕd), p.a. [4] Cast down; depressed; sad. — **de-ject'ed-ly,** adv. [8] — **ness,** n. [8].

de-jec'tion (-jĕk'shŭn), n. Lowness of spirits; depression; melancholy.

‖ **de ju're** (dē jōō'rē). [L.] By right or lawful title.

de-lay' (dĕ-lā'), v. t. & i. **1.** To put off; postpone; defer; linger; tarry. **2.** To retard; to stop, detain, or hinder for a time. — n. A putting off or deferring; stop; detention. — **de-lay'er,** n. [8].

de-lec'ta-ble (dĕ-lĕk'tá-b'l), a. [4] Highly pleasing; delightful. — **ness,** n. — **ta-bly,** adv. [8].

de'lec-ta'tion (dē'lĕk-tā'shŭn), n. Great pleasure; delight.

del'e-gate (dĕl'ē-gāt), n. One sent and empowered to act for another; deputy; representative. — (-gāt), v. t. [1] **1.** To send as one's representative; commission; depute. **2.** To intrust to another's care or management; commit.

del'e-ga'tion (-gā'shŭn), n. **1.** Act of delegating. **2.** One or more persons commissioned to represent others, as in a convention; a body of delegates.

de-lete' (dĕ-lēt'), v. t. [1] To erase; cancel.

del'e-te'ri-ous (dĕl'ē-tē'rĭ-ŭs), a. [4] Hurtful; noxious; pernicious. — **ly,** adv. [8] — **ness,** n.

de-le'tion (dĕ-lē'shŭn), n. Act of deleting; that which is deleted; extinction.

delf (dĕlf), n. Delftware.

delft'ware' (dĕlft'wâr'), or **delft,** n. Pottery made at Delft (formerly Delf), in Holland; esp., a kind of brown pottery covered with an opaque, decorated white glaze.

de-lib'er-ate (dĕ-lĭb'ẽr-āt), a. [4] **1.** Carefully considered; not sudden or rash; as, a deliberate opinion. **2.** Weighing facts and arguments; careful and slow in determining; as, a deliberate man. **3.** Not hasty or sudden; slow; as, deliberate speech. — (-āt), v. t. [1] To weigh in the mind; reflect on; ponder. — v. i. To take counsel; reflect; also, to weigh matters in deciding. — **de-lib'er-ate-ly,** adv. [8] — **de-lib'er-ate-ness,** n. [8] — **de-lib'-er-a'tor,** n. [8].

de-lib'er-a'tion (-ā'shŭn), n. **1.** Act of deliberating; consideration of the reasons for and against a measure. **2.** Quality or state of being deliberate.

de-lib'er-a-tive (-lĭb'ẽr-á-tĭv), a. [4] Pertaining to, or characterized by, deliberation; deliberating.

del'i-ca-cy (dĕl'ĭ-ká-sĭ), n.; pl. -CIES (-sĭz). **1.** A luxury; dainty, as for food. **2.** Nicety or fineness of form, constitution, etc.; tenderness; hence, frailty or weakness; as, the delicacy of a thread or a watch. **3.** Nicety of touch; as, the delicacy of the painter's stroke; also, quality or state of requiring delicate or tactful management. **4.** Nice perception; sensitiveness. **5. Refinement of feel-**ing; consideration.

del′i-cate (dĕl′ĭ-kāt), a. [4] **1.** Characterized by daintiness, softness, or effeminacy; hence, tender; frail. **2.** Characterized by nice appreciation or discrimination; exquisitely sensitive; hence, refined; considerate. **3.** Hence, of instruments: showing very slight changes; as, a *delicate* thermometer. **4.** Pleasing to a nice or cultivated taste; of a mild or subtle quality; not strong. **5.** Of a quality opposed to coarse, rough, gross, etc.; fine; graceful. **6.** Marked by or requiring ingenuity or fine skill. **— del′i-cate-ly,** adv. [8].

del′i-ca-tes′sen (-kȧ-tĕs′ĕn), n. pl. Prepared foods, as cooked meats, preserves, relishes, etc.

de-li′cious (dē-lĭsh′ŭs), a. [4] Affording exquisite pleasure; delightful; esp., very pleasing to the taste. **— de-li′cious-ly,** adv. [8] **— -ness,** n. [8].

de-light′ (-līt′), n. **1.** A state of extreme satisfaction; joy. **2.** Anything that gives delight; an object of delight. **— v. t.** To give delight to; please highly. **— v. i.** To be greatly pleased or rejoiced.

de-light′ful (-fŏŏl), a. [4] Highly pleasing; giving delight. **— -ly,** adv. [8] **— -ness,** n. [8].

de-lin′e-ate (dē-lĭn′ē-āt), v. t. [1] **1.** To sketch out; portray. **2.** To set forth in words; describe. **— de-lin′e-a′tor,** (-ā′tẽr), n. [8].

de-lin′e-a′tion (-ā′shŭn), n. **1.** A representing, portraying, or describing, as by lines, sketches, etc. **2.** A sketch; verbal description.

de-lin′quen-cy (-lĭn′kwĕn-sĭ), n.; pl. -cies (-sĭz). Failure, omission, or violation, of duty; offense.

de-lin′quent (-kwĕnt), a. [4] Failing in, or neglectful of, duty. **— n.** One who is delinquent.

del′i-quesce′ (dĕl′ĭ-kwĕs′), v. i. [1] To become liquid gradually by absorbing moisture from the air, as do certain salts, acids, and alkalies.

del′i-ques′cence (-kwĕs′ĕns), n. Act, state, or process of deliquescing.

del′i-ques′cent (-ĕnt), a. Deliquescing.

de-lir′i-ous (dē-lĭr′ĭ-ŭs), a. Having a delirium; raving. **— -ly,** adv. [8] **— -ness,** n. [8].

de-lir′i-um (-ŭm), n.; pl. E. -iums (-ŭmz), L. -ia (-ȧ). **1.** A more or less temporary state of mental disturbance. **2.** Strong excitement.

delirium tremens (trē′mĕnz), violent delirium induced by excessive and prolonged use of intoxicants, and characterized by terrifying hallucinations and by tremor of the hands and tongue.

de-liv′er (dē-lĭv′ẽr), v. t. **1.** To set at liberty; save. **2.** To give or transfer; part with (to); surrender; resign. **3.** To disburden (a woman) of young. **4.** To give; utter; communicate; impart. **5.** To give forth in action or exercise; discharge (a blow, etc.). **— -er,** n. [8].

de-liv′er-ance (-ăns), n. **1.** Act of delivering; state of being delivered, as from restraint, peril, etc.; release. **2.** Anything delivered or communicated.

de-liv′er-y (dē-lĭv′ẽr-ĭ), n.; pl. -eries (-ĭz). **1.** Act of delivering, or being delivered; as: **a** Rescue; release. **b** Parturition. **c** Utterance. **d** Act or manner of discharging, throwing, or the like. **2.** That which is delivered.

dell (dĕl), n. A small, retired valley; vale.

del′ta (dĕl′tȧ), n. An alluvial deposit at the mouth of a river.

de-lude′ (dē-lūd′), v. t. [1] To lead from truth or into error; impose upon. **— de-lud′er** (-lūd′ẽr), n. [8].

del′uge (dĕl′ūj), n. **1.** An overflowing of the land by water; [cap.], the great flood in the days of Noah (Gen. vii.). **2.** Something that overwhelms, or causes great destruction. **— v. t.** [1] To overflow; inundate; overwhelm.

de-lu′sion (dē-lū′zhŭn), n. **1.** Act of deluding. **2.** False belief; misconception.

de-lu′sive (dē-lū′sĭv), a. [4] Apt or fitted to delude; deceptive. **— -ly,** adv. [8] **— -ness,** n. [8].

∥ de luxe′ (dē lüks′). [F.] Literally, of luxury; sumptuous.

delve (dĕlv), v. t. [1] To dig. Now Chiefly Scot. **— v. i.** To labor with or as with a spade; to seek laboriously for information. **— delv′er,** n. [8].

dem′a-gog′ic (dĕm′ȧ-gŏj′ĭk) a. [4] Pert. to or **dem′a-gog′i-cal** (-gŏj′ĭ-kăl) ∫ like a demagogue.

dem′a-gogue (dĕm′ȧ-gŏg), n. An insincere politician or popular orator or leader who stirs up popular prejudice to gain office or influence.

de-mand′ (dē-mȧnd′), v. t. **1.** To ask or call for with authority or peremptorily; claim as due. **2.** To inquire authoritatively or earnestly; question. **3.** To call for; require; need. **— v. i.** To make a demand; inquire. **— n.** **1.** Act of demanding; requisition. **2.** Desire to possess; manifested want; a call (for a commodity). **3.** Economics. Quantity of an article demanded at a given price. **4.** That which one demands or has a right to demand; claim. **— de-mand′er,** n. [8].

de′mar-ca′tion (dē′mär-kā′shŭn), n. A marking by bounds; ascertaining and settling of a limit.

de-mean′ (dē-mēn′), v. t. To debase, lower, or degrade (one's self). Colloquial.

de-mean′, v. t. To behave or comport (one's self).

de-mean′or (-ẽr), n. [5] Behavior; carriage.

de-ment′ed (-mĕn′tĕd), p. a. Insane; mad.

de-men′ti-a (-shĭ-ȧ), n. Insanity, esp. that characterized by more or less apathy or indifference.

de-mer′it (-mĕr′ĭt), n. Merit; desert; — now only in a bad sense: that which deserves blame; fault.

de-mesne′ (-mān′; -mēn′), n. **1.** Possession (of land) as one's own. **2. a** Formerly, an estate or land possessed. **b** Now, a lord's chief manor place, with its adjoining lands.

dem′i-god′ (dĕm′ĭ-gŏd′), n. An inferior deity; hero.

dem′i-john (-jŏn), n. A large bottle, of glass or earthenware, usually inclosed in wickerwork.

de-mise′ (dē-mīz′), n. **1.** Law. The conveyance of an estate, usually by will or lease. **2.** Decease of a royal or princely person; hence, grandiloquently, decease.**—v. t. & i.** [1] Law. To convey or pass, as an estate, by will or lease; esp., to lease.

∥ de-mi′-tasse′ (dē-mē′täs′; E. dĕm′ĭ-tás′), n. [F.] A small cup for, or of, black coffee.

de-mo′bi-li-za′tion (dē-mō′bĭ-lĭ-zā′shŭn), n. A demobilizing; change from war to peace footing.

de-mo′bi-lize (dē-mō′bĭ-līz; -mŏb′ĭ-), v. t. [1] Mil. To disband, as troops.

de-moc′ra-cy (dē-mŏk′rȧ-sĭ), n.; pl. -cies (-sĭz). **1.** Government by the people, as in a republic; — opposed to aristocracy. **2.** A community or state so governed. **3.** [cap.] The principles and policy of the Democratic party, so called; also, that party, or its members. U. S.

dem'o-crat (děm'ō-krăt), *n.* **1.** An adherent of democracy. **2.** [*cap.*] A member of the Democratic party. *U. S.*

dem'o-crat'ic (-krăt'ĭk), *a.* [4] **1.** Pert. to or of the nature of democracy. **2.** Designating or pert. to a political party called *democratic*, esp. [*cap.*] *U. S. Politics*, one of the two great political parties since 1828. — **dem'o-crat'i-cal-ly**, *adv.* [8].

de-mol'ish (dē-mŏl'ĭsh), *v. t.* To throw or pull down ; to ruin ; destroy. — **de-mol'ish-er**, *n.* [8].

dem'o-li'tion (děm'ō-lĭsh'ŭn), *n.* Act of demolishing or state or fact of being demolished.

de'mon (dē'mŏn), *n.* **1.** A supernatural being intermediate between a man and a deity ; hence, a familiar spirit or genius. **2.** An evil spirit ; devil.

de-mon'e-ti-za'tion (dē-mŏn'ĕ-tĭ-zā'shŭn), *n.* Act of demonetizing ; state of being demonetized.

de-mon'e-tize (dē-mŏn'ĕ-tīz), *v. t.* [1] To deprive of standard value as money.

de-mo'ni-ac (-mō'nĭ-ăk), *n.* One supposedly possessed by an evil spirit.

de-mo'ni-ac (-mō'nĭ-ăk), **de'mo-ni'a-cal** (dē'mō-nī'á-kál), *a.* [4] **1.** Influenced, produced, or possessed, by a demon. **2.** Pert. to or characteristic of a demon ; devilish. — **de'mo-ni'a-cal-ly**, *adv.* [8].

de-mon'stra-bil'i-ty (dē-mŏn'strá-bĭl'ĭ-tĭ), *n.* Quality of being demonstrable.

de-mon'stra-ble (dē-mŏn'strá-b'l), *a.* [4] Capable of being demonstrated. — **-bly** (-blĭ), *adv.* [8].

dem'on-strate (děm'ŏn-strāt), *v. t.* [1] **1.** To make evident ; prove. **2.** To exhibit by way of proof.

dem'on-stra'tion (-strā'shŭn), *n.* **1.** Act of demonstrating ; proof. **2.** An expression, as of the feelings, by outward signs ; manifestation ; show.

de-mon'stra-tive (dē-mŏn'strá-tĭv), *a.* [4] **1.** Making evident ; exhibiting clearly. **2.** *Gram.* Serving to point out the thing referred to ; as, a *demonstrative* pronoun or adjective, as *this* or *that.* **3.** Given to the display of feeling or sentiment. — *n. Gram.* A word having a demonstrative function. — **-ly**, *adv.* [8] — **-ness**, *n.* [8].

dem'on-stra'tor (děm'ŏn-strā'tẽr), *n.* One who makes a demonstration ; one who demonstrates.

de-mor'al-i-za'tion (dē-mŏr'ăl-ĭ-zā'shŭn), *n.* Act of demoralizing ; state of being demoralized.

de-mor'al-ize (dē-mŏr'ăl-īz), *v. t.* [1] **1.** To corrupt in morals ; pervert or deprave. **2.** To render untrustworthy in discipline, efficiency, spirit, or the like. **3.** Hence, to disorganize ; confuse.

de-mount'a-ble (dē-moun'tá-b'l), *a.* Permitting of removal from the wheel without separation from the tire ; — said of some automobile wheel rims.

de-mul'cent (dē-mŭl'sĕnt), *a.* Softening ; mollifying; soothing. — *n. Med.* A demulcent substance.

de-mur' (-mûr'), *v. i.* ; -MURRED' (-mûrd') ; -MUR'RING. To scruple or object ; take exception. — *n.* Objection ; scruple.

de-mure' (dē-mūr'), *a.* [3] **1.** Of sober or serious mien ; staid ; grave. **2.** Affectedly modest, serious, or grave. — **-ly**, *adv.* [8] — **-ness**, *n.* [8].

de-mur'rage (-mŭr'ăj), *n.* **1.** Detention of a vessel, a railroad car, etc., by the freighter beyond the time allowed for loading, unloading, etc. **2.** Allowance made for such detention.

den (děn), *n.* **1.** A lair, esp. of a beast of prey ; hence, a cavern as a place of resort or concealment.

2. A squalid place of resort ; haunt. **3.** Any snug and private retreat, as for reading.

de-na'ture (dē-nā'tụ̄r), *v. t.* [1] To change the nature of ; to render unfit for eating or drinking, without impairing usefulness for other purposes. — **de-na'tur-a'tion** (-ā'shŭn), *n.*

de-ni'al (dē-nī'ăl), *n.* **1.** Refusal to grant ; rejection of a request ; an instance of such denying. **2.** Refusal to admit the truth, or assertion of the untruth, of a thing stated ; contradiction. **3.** Refusal to acknowledge ; disavowal ; disowning.

de-ni'er (dē-nī'ẽr), *n.* One who denies.

den'im (děn'ĭm), *n.* A coarse cotton drilling.

den'i-zen (děn'ĭ-zěn), *n.* An inhabitant ; occupant. — *v. t.* To provide with denizens.

de-nom'i-nate (dē-nŏm'ĭ-nāt), *v. t.* [1] To give a name to. — *a.* Having a specific name ; concrete.

de-nom'i-na'tion (-nā'shŭn), *n.* **1.** Act of denominating. **2.** A name, designation, or title ; esp., a general name for a class. **3.** A class or society having a specific name ; sect. **4.** One of a series of related units or values denoted by special names ; as, the *denominations* of U. S. money ($1, $2, $5, etc.).

de-nom'i-na'tion-al (-ăl), *a.* Pertaining to a denomination, esp. a sect ; sectarian.

de-nom'i-na'tor (-nā'tẽr), *n.* Part of a fraction below the horizontal line. In simple fractions it shows into how many equal parts the unit is divided.

de'no-ta'tion (dē'nō-tā'shŭn), *n.* **1.** A sign or token ; designation. **2.** Meaning or signification.

de-note' (dē-nōt'), *v. t.* [1] **1.** To mark out plainly ; indicate. **2.** To betoken ; signify.

‖ **dé-noue'ment** (dā-nōō'män ; dā'nōō'män'), *n.* [F.] **1.** The unraveling or solving of a plot, esp. that of a drama or a romance. **2.** Outcome.

de-nounce' (dē-nouns'), *v. t.* [1] To invoke censure on ; also, to inform against.

dense (děns), *a.* [3] **1.** Having its parts crowded together ; compact ; close ; thick. **2.** Of ignorance, etc., impenetrable ; hence, of persons, stupid. — **dense'ly**, *adv.* [8] — **dense'ness**, *n.* [8].

den'si-ty (děn'sĭ-tĭ), *n. ; pl.* -TIES (-tĭz). **1.** Quality or state of being dense. **2.** The ratio of mass to bulk or volume ; ratio of the mass of any volume of a substance to the mass of an equal volume of some standard substance.

dent (děnt), *n.* A slight depression as from a blow or pressure ; indentation. — *v. t.* To make a dent on ; indent. — *v. i.* To become indented.

den'tal (děn'tăl), *a.* **1.** Pertaining to the teeth or to dentistry. **2.** Articulated with the tip of the tongue applied to the back of the upper front teeth, or to the gum above ; — said of certain consonants, as *t, d,* n. — *n.* A dental consonant.

den'tate (-tāt), *a.* Having a toothed margin or toothlike projections ; as, a *dentate* leaf.

den'ti-frice (-tĭ-frĭs), *n.* A tooth powder, paste, or wash.

den'tine (-tĭn), *n.* A calcareous material composing the main part of a tooth ; ivory.

den'tist (-tĭst), *n.* One whose profession it is to treat the teeth ; a dental surgeon.

den'tist-ry (-tĭs-trĭ), *n.* Dentist's art or profession.

den-ti'tion (děn-tĭsh'ŭn), *n.* **1.** The development of teeth ; teething. **2.** The number, kind, and arrangement of teeth of an animal.

āle, senāte, câre, ăm, ăccount, ärm, ȧsk, sofá; ēve, ēvent, ĕnd, recĕnt, makẽr; īce, ĭll; ōld, ȯbey, ôrb, ŏdd, sŏft, cŏnnect; ūse, ŭnite, ûrn, ŭp, circŭs; fōōd, fŏŏt; out, oil;

den'u·da'tion (dĕn'ū-dā'shŭn ; dē'nū-), *n.* Act of denuding ; state of being denuded.

de·nude' (dĕ-nūd'), *v. t.* [1] To divest of all covering ; strip ; to lay bare (as rocks, etc.) by erosion, or wearing away of overlying material.

de·nun'ci·a'tion (dĕ-nŭn'sĭ-ā'shŭn ; -shĭ-ā'shŭn), *n.* **1.** Act of denouncing. **2.** A threat of evil ; a public accusation or condemnation.

de·nun'ci·a·tive (-nŭn'shĭ-ā-tĭv ; -sĭ-ā-tĭv), *a.* [4] Denunciatory ; apt to denounce. — **-ly**, *adv.* [8].

de·nun'ci·a·to·ry (-ā-tō-rĭ),*a.* [4] Pert. to, characterized by, or given to, denunciation ; threatening.

de·ny' (dĕ-nī'), *v. t.* [2] **1.** To declare not to be true ; contradict. **2.** To disclaim connection with ; disown. **3.** To refuse to grant or gratify, as a request, or one requesting.

de·o'dor·ant (dē-ō'dẽr-ănt), *n.* A deodorizer ; substance that removes offensive odors.

de·o'dor·i·za'tion (-ī-zā'shŭn), *n.* A deodorizing.

de·o'dor·ize (dē-ō'dẽr-īz), *v. t.* [1] To deprive of odor, esp. offensive odor. — **de·o'dor·iz'er**, *n.* [8].

de·ox'i·dize (-ŏk'sĭ-dīz), *v. t.* [1] To deprive of oxygen ; reduce from the state of an oxide.

de·part' (dĕ-pärt'), *v. i.* **1.** To go forth or away ; leave. **2.** To pass away ; die. **3.** To turn aside.

de·part'ment (-mĕnt), *n.* **1.** A part or subdivision. **2.** A distinct division or course of something, as of action, study, etc. ; sphere ; province. **3.** A subdivision of business or official duty ; esp., a division of governmental administration. **4.** A district, as one under military regulation. — **department store**, a store keeping a great variety of goods arranged in departments.

de'part·men'tal (dē'pärt-mĕn'tăl), *a.* Pertaining to a department.

de·par'ture (dĕ-pär'tụr), *n.* **1.** A departing, or going away. **2.** A setting out or beginning. **3.** Death.

de·pend' (-pĕnd'), *v. i.* **1.** To hang down. **2.** To rely for support ; to be conditioned or contingent. **3.** To trust ; rely.

de·pend'a·ble (-pĕn'dȧ-b'l), *a.* [4] Trustworthy.

de·pend'ant (-dănt). Var. of DEPENDENT.

de·pend'ence (-dĕns), *n.* **1.** State of being influenced and determined by, or of being conditional on, something else. **2.** State of depending ; subjection ; inability to provide for one's self. **3.** Reliance ; assured confidence or trust. **4.** That on which one depends or relies.

de·pend'en·cy (-dĕn-sĭ),*n.; pl.* -CIES (-sĭz). **1.** State of being dependent ; dependence. **2.** A subject territory, esp. a distinct, often remote, province.

de·pend'ent (-dĕnt), *a.* [4] **1.** Hanging down. **2.** Relying on something else for support ; conditioned; subordinate. — *n.* **1.** That which depends; dependency. **2.** One sustained by another, or relying on another for support or favor.

de·pict' (-pĭkt'), *v. t.* **1.** To represent by a picture. **2.** To portray in words ; describe.

de·pic'tion (-pĭk'shŭn),*n.* A depicting; description.

de·pic'ture (-tụr), *v. t.* To picture ; depict.

de·plete' (dĕ-plēt'), *v. t.* [1] **1.** To empty or unload, as the vessels of the body by purgation. **2.** To exhaust, as of strength.

de·ple'tion (-plē'shŭn), *n.* Act of depleting.

de·plor'a·ble (-plōr'ȧ-b'l), *a.* [4] To be deplored; sad ; grievous. — **de·plor'a·bly**, *adv.* [8].

de·plore' (dĕ-plōr'), *v. t.* [1] To feel or express deep grief for ; lament ; mourn.

de·ploy' (dĕ-ploi'), *v. t. & i. Mil.* To extend the front of a body of troops ; spread out in front.

de·ploy'ment (-mĕnt), *n.* Act of deploying.

de·po'nent (-pō'nĕnt), *n.* One who testifies under oath, usually in writing.

de·pop'u·late (-pŏp'ū-lāt), *v. t.* [1] To deprive of inhabitants, wholly or in part.

de·pop'u·la'tion (-lā'shŭn), *n.* Act of depopulating ; state of being depopulated.

de·port' (-pōrt'), *v. t.* **1.** To behave (one's self). **2.** To banish ; transport ; exile.

de'por·ta'tion (dē'pōr-tā'shŭn), *n.* Act of deporting; state of being deported; esp., the removal from a country of an alien considered undesirable.

de·port'ment (dĕ-pōrt'mĕnt), *n.* Manner of deporting one's self; behavior ; demeanor ; bearing.

de·pose' (dĕ-pōz'), *v. t.* [1] **1.** To remove from a throne ; deprive of office. **2.** To say under oath, esp. by an affidavit. — *v. i.* To bear witness.

de·pos'it (-pŏz'ĭt),*v. t.* **1.** To lodge for safe-keeping or as a pledge ; intrust ; put on deposit in a bank. **2.** To lay down; place ; to let fall or throw down (as sediment). — *n.* **1.** Something intrusted to another ; esp. : **a** Money lodged with a banker, subject to order. **b** A pledge or security. **2.** That which is deposited. **3.** State of being deposited.

de·pos'i·ta·ry (-ĭ-tȧ-rĭ),*n.; pl.* -RIES (-rĭz). **1.** One receiving a deposit. **2.** Storehouse ; depository.

dep'o·si'tion (dĕp'ô-zĭsh'ŭn ; dē'pô-), *n.* **1.** Act of deposing, a sovereign. **2.** Testimony under oath, esp. in writing ; evidence. **3.** A depositing ; precipitation. **4.** That which is deposited ; deposit.

de·pos'i·tor (dĕ-pŏz'ĭ-tẽr), *n.* One who deposits.

de·pos'i·to·ry (-tō-rĭ),*n.; pl.* -RIES (-rĭz). **1.** = DEPOSITARY, 1. **2.** Place where anything is deposited.

de'pot (dē'pō), *n.* **1.** *Mil.* **a** A place where ammunition, provisions, etc., are kept. **b** A station where recruits are assembled and trained. **2.** A warehouse; storehouse. **3.** A railroad station. *U.S.*

de·prave' (dĕ-prāv'), *v. t.* [1] To vitiate; corrupt; pervert ; — chiefly with reference to morals.

de·praved' (-prāvd'), *p. a.* [4] Characterized by debasement, corruption, or degeneration.

de·prav'i·ty (-prăv'ĭ-tĭ),*n.; pl.* -TIES (-tĭz). **1.** State of being depraved. **2.** A depraved act or practice.

dep're·cate (dĕp'rḗ-kāt), *v. t.* [1] To express disapproval of. — **dep're·cat'ing·ly**, *adv.* [8].

dep're·ca'tion (-kā'shŭn), *n.* Act of deprecating.

dep're·ca·to·ry (dĕp'rḗ-kȧ-tō-rĭ), *a.* Serving to deprecate; seeking to avert disfavor; apologetic.

de·pre'ci·ate (dĕ-prē'shĭ-āt),*v. t. & i.* [1] To lessen in price or estimated value; also, to disparage.

de·pre'ci·a'tion (-ā'shŭn), *n.* Act of depreciating; state of being depreciated.

de·pre'ci·a·tive (-prē'shĭ-ā-tĭv), *a.* [4] Intended or tending to depreciate or express depreciation.

de·pre'ci·a·to·ry (-ȧ-tō-rĭ), *a.* [4] Tending to depreciate or disparage.

dep're·date (dĕp'rḗ-dāt), *v. t. & i.* [1] To plunder. — **dep're·da'tor**, *n.* [8].

dep're·da'tion (-dā'shŭn), *n.* Act of depredating; a despoiling or destructive operation.

de·press' (dĕ-prĕs'), *v. t.* **1.** To press down ; let fall; lower. **2.** To lessen the activity, value, or the like, of; make dull, as trade, etc. **3.** To lower the pitch of, as the voice. **4.** To sadden.

de-pres'sion (dĕ-prĕsh'ŭn), *n.* **1.** Act of depressing, state of being depressed. **2.** That which is depressed or is made by depressing, as a hollow.

de-pres'sive (-prĕs'ĭv), *a.* [4] Tending to depress.

de-pres'sor (dĕ-prĕs'ẽr), *n.* One that depresses.

dep'ri-va'tion (dĕp'rĭ-vā'shŭn), *n.* Act of depriving; state of being deprived; privation.

de-prive' (dĕ-prīv'), *v. t.* [1] To take away from; strip; hinder from possessing.

depth (dĕpth), *n.* **1.** That which is deep; esp., a deep part of the sea, or of any body of water. **2.** The innermost part of anything. **3.** Quality of being deep; deepness; also, distance from the point of view, as upward from the surface or backward from the front. **4.** Profoundness; degree of intensity. **5.** Lowness of pitch.

dep'u-ta'tion (dĕp'ū-tā'shŭn), *n.* **1.** Act of deputing; appointment; delegation. **2.** A person or persons deputed to act in one's behalf; a delegation.

de-pute' (dĕ-pūt'), *v. t.* [1] **1.** To appoint as deputy, delegate. **2.** To assign as to a deputy.

dep'u-tize (dĕp'ũ-tiz), *v. t.* [1] To depute.

dep'u-ty (-tĭ), *n.; pl.* -TIES (-tĭz). One appointed to act for another, a substitute in office; delegate.

de-rail' (dē-rāl'), *v. t.* To cause to run off the rails. — **de-rail'ment** (-mĕnt), *n.*

de-range' (dē-rānj'), *v. t.* [1] **1.** To disarrange; disorder, confuse. **2.** To render insane.

de-ranged' (-rānjd'), *p. a.* [4] Disordered; insane.

de-range'ment (-rānj'mĕnt), *n.* Act of deranging; state of being deranged; esp., mental disorder.

der'by (dûr'bĭ), *n.* A stiff felt hat usually with a dome-shaped crown.

der'e-lict (dĕr'ē-lĭkt), *a.* [4] **1.** Abandoned by the natural owner or guardian. **2.** Unfaithful; neglectful. *Chiefly U. S.* — *n.* A thing voluntarily abandoned, esp. a vessel at sea.

der'e-lic'tion (-lĭk'shŭn), *n.* **1.** A forsaking; abandonment. **2.** A failure in duty.

de-ride' (dē-rīd'), *v. t.* [1] To laugh at with contempt; mock; taunt. — **de-rid'er**, *n.* [8].

de-ri'sion (-rĭzh'ŭn), *n.* **1.** Act of deriding; state of being derided; mockery. **2.** An object that is derided.

de-ri'sive (-rī'sĭv), *a.* [4] Expressing, or serving for, derision. — **-ly**, *adv.* [8] — **-ness**, *n.* [8].

de-ri'so-ry (dē-rī'sō-rĭ), *a.* [4] Derisive.

de-riv'a-ble (-rĭv'ȧ-b'l), *a.* That can be derived.

der'i-va'tion (dĕr'ĭ-vā'shŭn), *n.* **1.** Act or process of deriving anything from a source. **2.** That from which a thing is derived; origin. **3.** Development of a word from its more original elements; also, a statement of the origin and history of a word.

de-riv'a-tive (dē-rĭv'ȧ-tĭv), *a.* Derived; not original or fundamental. — *n.* That which is derived.

de-rive' (-rīv'), *v. t.* [1] **1.** To receive, as from a source; obtain by descent or transmission; deduce. **2.** To trace the origin, descent, or derivation of, as of a word.

der'ma (dûr'mȧ), *n.* The sensitive layer of the skin beneath the epidermis. — **der'mal** (-mᾰl), *a.*

der'ma-tol'o-gy (-mᾱ-tŏl'ō-jĭ), *n.* Science treating of the skin. — **der'ma-tol'o-gist** (-jĭst), *n.*

der'mis (dûr'mĭs), *n.* The derma.

der'o-gate (dĕr'ō-gāt), *v. t.* [1] To lessen in value, rank, influence, etc.; detract from. — *v. i.* To take away; detract; — usually with *from.*

der'o-ga'tion (-gā'shŭn), *n.* Act of derogating; disparagement; detraction; depreciation.

de-rog'a-to-ry (dē-rŏg'ȧ-tō-rĭ), *a.* [4] Tending to derogate, detracting; — with *from* or *to.* — **-to-ri-ly** (-rĭ-lĭ), *adv.* [8] — **-ri-ness**, *n.* [8].

der'rick (dĕr'ĭk), *n.* A hoisting apparatus employing a tackle rigged at the end of a spar or beam.

der'rin-ger (dĕr'ĭn-jẽr), *n.* A short-barreled pocket pistol, of large caliber.

der'vish (dûr'vĭsh), *n.* A member of any of various Mohammedan orders taking vows of poverty and austerity, and living in monasteries or wandering as friars.

des-cant' (dĕs-kănt'), *v. i.* To discourse with fullness and particularity; discourse at large.

de-scend' (dē-sĕnd'), *v. i.* **1.** To pass or come down from a higher to a lower place, station, scale, etc.; to come or go down. **2.** To make an attack or incursion, esp. suddenly or with violence. **3.** To come down, as from a source or stock; fall or pass by inheritance. — *v. t.* To go down upon or along.

de-scend'ant (dē-sĕn'dᾰnt), *a.* Descendent. — *n.* One who descends, as offspring.

de-scend'ent (-dĕnt), *a.* **1.** Descending; falling. **2.** Proceeding from an ancestor or source.

de-scent' (-sĕnt'), *n.* **1.** Act of descending; change from higher to lower. **2.** Incursion; sudden attack. **3.** Progress downward, as in station, virtue, etc. **4.** Derivation, as from an ancestor; lineage. **5.** Transmission of an estate by inheritance. **6.** Inclination downward; slope; a descending way.

de-scrib'a-ble (-skrĭb'ȧ-b'l), *a.* That can be described; capable of description.

de-scribe' (-skrīb'), *v. t.* [1] **1.** To represent by words written or spoken; give an account of. **2.** To trace or traverse the outline of. — **de-scrib'er** (-skrīb'ẽr), *n.* [8].

de-scrip'tion (-skrĭp'shŭn), *n.* **1.** Act or result of describing. **2.** A class; kind; sort.

de-scrip'tive (-tĭv), *a.* Serving to describe; characterized by description. — **-ly**, *adv.* [8].

de-scry' (-skrī'), *v. t.* [2] To spy out or discover.

des'e-crate (dĕs'ē-krāt), *v. t.* [1] To divert from a sacred purpose; violate; profane. — **-cra'tor**, *n.*

des'e-cra'tion (-krā'shŭn), *n.* Act of desecrating.

de-sert' (dē-zûrt'), *n.* **1.** Worthiness of reward or punishment; merit or demerit. **2.** That which is deserved; due reward or punishment.

des'ert (dĕz'ẽrt), *n.* **1.** A deserted region; solitary place. **2.** A barren tract almost destitute of moisture and vegetation.

des'ert, *a.* [4] Of or pertaining to a desert; waste; barren; wild.

de-sert' (dē-zûrt'), *v. t.* **1.** To leave (esp. something which one should stay by); abandon. **2.** *Mil.* To abandon (the service) without leave. — *v. i.* To abandon a service without leave. — **de-sert'er**, *n.* [8].

de-ser'tion (-zûr'shŭn), *n.* **1.** Act of deserting. **2.** State of being forsaken; desolation.

de-serve' (-zûrv'), *v. t.* [1] To earn by service; merit; be entitled to. — *v. i.* To be worthy of recompense. — **de-serv'er**, *n.* [8].

āle, senᾱte, cᾱre, ᾰm, ᾰccount, ᾰrm, ᾰsk, sofᾱ; ēve, ĕvent, ĕnd, recĕnt, makẽr; īce, ĭll; ōld, ōbey, ôrb, ŏdd, sŏft, cŏnnect; ūse, ūnite, ûrn, ŭp, circŭs; fōōd, fŏŏt; out, oil;

de-serv'ed-ly (dĕ-zûr'vĕd-lĭ), *adv.* According to desert.

de-serv'ing (-vĭng), *n.* Desert ; merit. — *p. a.* [4] Meritorious ; worthy. — **de-serv'ing-ly**, *adv.* [8].

des'ha-bille' (dĕz'ȧ-bēl'), *n.* See DISHABILLE.

des'ic-cate (dĕs'ĭ-kāt), *v. t. & i.* [1] To dry up ; preserve by drying, as fish.—**des'ic-ca'tor**, *n.* [8].

des'ic-ca'tion (-kā'shŭn), *n.* Act of desiccating.

des'ic-ca-tive (dĕs'ĭ-kā-tĭv ; dĕ-sĭk'ȧ-tĭv), *a.* [4] Drying up ; tending to dry up.

de-sid'er-a'tum (dĕ-sĭd'ẽr-ā'tŭm), *n. ; pl.* -ATA (-tȧ). A thing desired ; a recognized want.

de-sign' (-zīn'), *v. t.* **1.** To intend or purpose. **2.** To draw in outline ; sketch. **3. a** To plan or devise. **b** To make a design or pattern for. — *v. i.* To produce a plan for anything. — *n.* **1.** A plan or scheme ; purpose ; aim. **2.** A preliminary sketch of something to be executed, as of a picture ; a pattern ; a plan. **3.** Arrangement of details. **4.** A piece of art considered as to its form, colors, etc.

des'ig-nate (dĕs'ĭg-nāt ; dĕz'-),*v.t.* [1] **1.** To make known ; indicate ; specify. **2.** To name.

des'ig-na'tion (-nā'shŭn), *n.* **1.** Act of designating. **2.** That which designates ; distinctive title.

des'ig-na-tive (dĕs'ĭg-nā-tĭv ; dĕz'-), *a.* Serving to designate ; pointing out.

des'ig-na'tor (-nā'tẽr), *n.* One who designates.

de-sign'ed-ly (dĕ-zīn'ĕd-lĭ), *adv.* Purposely.

de-sign'er (-ẽr), *n.* **1.** One who designs ; contriver. **2.** One who produces original works of art.

de-sign'ing, *n.* Act or art of one who designs. — *a.* [4] Planning ; esp., artful ; scheming.

de-sir'a-bil'i-ty (-zĭr'ȧ-bĭl'ĭ-tĭ), *n.* Quality of being desirable.

de-sir'a-ble (-zĭr'ȧ-b'l), *a.* [4] Worthy of desire or longing ; pleasing ; agreeable. — **de-sir'a-ble-ness**, *n.* [8] — **de-sir'a-bly** (-ȧ-blĭ), *adv.* [8].

de-sire' (dĕ-zīr'), *v. t.* [1] **1.** To long for ; covet. **2.** To express a wish for ; ask. — *n.* **1.** Act of desiring ; longing. **2.** Anything desired.

de-sir'ous (-zĭr'ŭs), *a.* [4] Feeling, or characterized by, desire ; solicitous ; covetous.

de-sist' (-zĭst'), *v. i.* To cease to act ; stop.

desk (dĕsk), *n.* A table, frame, or case with a sloping or a flat top for the use of writers or readers.

des'o-late (dĕs'ō-lāt), *a.* [4] **1.** Destitute or deprived of inhabitants ; deserted ; hence, gloomy. **2.** Laid waste ; in a ruinous or neglected state. **3.** Left alone ; forsaken. — (-lāt), *v. t.* [1] **1.** To make desolate ; ravage. **2.** To forsake ; leave alone. — **-ly**, *adv.* — **-ness**, *n.* [8] — **lat'er** (-lāt'-ẽr), **-la'tor** (-lā'tẽr), *n.* [8].

des'o-la'tion (-lā'shŭn), *n.* **1.** Act of desolating ; state of being desolated. **2.** A place wasted and forsaken ; waste ; destruction. **3.** Loneliness ; sadness.

de-spair' (dĕ-spâr'), *v. i.* To be hopeless ; give up hope.—*n.* **1.** Loss of hope ; hopelessness. **2.** That which is despaired of, or which causes despair.

de-spair'ing, *p. a.* [4] Feeling or expressing despair ; hopeless. — **de-spair'ing-ly**, *adv.* [8].

des'per-a'do (dĕs'pẽr-ā'dō), *n. ; pl.* -DOES or -DOS (-dōz). A reckless criminal or ruffian.

des'per-ate (dĕs'pẽr-ăt), *a.* [4] **1.** Beyond or almost beyond hope or cure ; causing despair. **2.** Proceeding from, or expressing, despair. — **-ly**, *adv.* [8] — **-ness**, *n.* [8].

des'per-a'tion (-ā'shŭn), *n.* Act of despairing ; hopelessness leading to extreme recklessness.

des'pi-ca-ble (dĕs'pĭ-kȧ-b'l), *a.* [4] Fit to be despised ; contemptible. — **des'pi-ca-bly**, *adv.* [8].

de-spise' (dĕ-spīz'), *v. t.* [1] To look down upon with disfavor or contempt ; scorn.

de-spite' (-spīt'),*n.* **1.** Scorn ; contempt ; malice. **2.** An act of insult, malice, or defiance.—*v. t.* [1] To despise. — *prep.* In spite of ; notwithstanding.

de-spite'ful (-fŏŏl), *a.* [4] Full of despite ; insulting ; malicious. — **-ly**, *adv.* [8] — **-ness**, *n.* [8].

de-spoil' (dĕ-spoil'), *v. t.* To strip of belongings ; plunder ; rob ; divest (*of*). — **de-spoil'er**, *n.* [8].

de-spond' (-spŏnd'),*v.i.* To be much disheartened.

de-spond'ence (-spŏn'dĕns), *n.* Despondency.

de-spond'en-cy (-dĕn-sĭ), *n.* Loss of hope and cessation of effort ; discouragement ; dejection.

de-spond'ent (-dĕnt), *a.* [4] Marked by, or given to, despondency. — **de-spond'ent-ly**, *adv.* [8].

de-spond'ing,*p.a.* [4] Despondent.—**-ly**,*adv.* [8].

des'pot (dĕs'pŏt), *n.* An absolute ruler ; tyrant.

des-pot'ic (dĕs-pŏt'ĭk), *a.* [4] Having the character of, or pertaining to, a despot ; tyrannical ; arbitrary. — **des-pot'i-cal-ly**, *adv.* [8].

des'pot-ism (dĕs'pŏt-ĭz'm), *n.* The power, spirit, principles, or government of a despot ; tyranny.

des-sert' (dĕ-zûrt'), *n.* A service of fruits, pastry, puddings, etc., at the close of a repast.

des'ti-na'tion (dĕs'tĭ-nā'shŭn), *n.* **1.** Act of destining, or appointing. **2.** The place set for the end of a journey, or to which something is sent.

des'tine (dĕs'tĭn), *v. t.* [1] **1.** To decree beforehand, as by divine will ; predetermine ; foreordain. **2.** To appoint (to) or design (for a given end, use, or purpose) ; specif., *passive*, to be bound (for).

des'ti-ny (-tĭ-nĭ), *n. ; pl.* -NIES (-nĭz). **1.** That to which any person or thing is destined ; lot ; doom. **2.** The predetermined course of events, often conceived as a resistless power ; fate.

des'ti-tute (-tūt), *a.* [4] Bereft or not in possession (of something needed or desired) ; lacking.

des'ti-tu'tion (-tū'shŭn), *n.* State of being destitute ; lack ; utter want.

de-stroy' (dĕ-stroi'), *v. t.* **1.** To unbuild ; break up the structure and organic existence of ; demolish. **2.** To kill ; slay. **3.** To counteract ; nullify.

de-stroy'er (-stroi'ẽr), *n.* One that destroys.

de-struct'i-ble (-strŭk'tĭ-b'l), *a.* [4] Liable to destruction.

de-struc'tion (-shŭn), *n.* **1.** Act of destroying ; demolition ; ruin. **2.** State of being destroyed. **3.** A destroyer ; cause of ruin.

de-struc'tive (-tĭv), *a.* [4] **1.** Causing destruction ; ruinous. **2.** Designed or tending to destroy.

des'ue-tude (dĕs'wē-tūd), *n.* State of disuse.

des'ul-to-ry (dĕs'ŭl-tō-rĭ), *a.* [4] **1.** Jumping, or passing, from one thing to another, without rational connection ; aimless. **2.** Constituting a digression. — **-to-ri-ly** (-rĭ-lĭ), *adv.* [8] — **-to-ri-ness**, *n.* [8].

de-tach' (dĕ-tăch'), *v. t.* To part ; separate ; disunite ; disengage. — **de-tach'a-ble**, *a.* [8].

de-tached' (-tăcht'), *p. a.* Separate ; unconnected.

de-tach'ment (-tăch'mĕnt), *n.* **1.** Act of detaching ; state of being detached. **2.** That which is detached, as troops sent out from the main body.

---

chair ; go ; sing, ink ; then, thin ; nature, verdure ; yet ; zh = z in azure. Numbers refer to §§ in the Special Notes which, with Abbreviations, Signs, etc., precede the Vocabulary.

de-tail′ (dĕ-tāl′; dē′tāl), *n.* **1.** A particular; item; — chiefly in *pl.* **2.** *Mil.* Act of detailing; the person or the body of men detailed. — in detail, item by item; circumstantially. — (dĕ-tāl′), *v. t.* **1.** To report minutely and distinctly. **2.** *Mil.* To appoint for a particular service, as an officer.

de-tain′ (dĕ-tān′), *v. t.* To keep back; restrain from proceeding; delay. — **de-tain′er**, *n.* [8].

de-tect′ (-tĕkt′), *v. t.* To discover (something obscure); find out; expose. — **de-tect′er**, *n.* [8].

de-tec′tion (-tĕk′shŭn), *n.* A detecting; state of being detected.

de-tec′tive (-tĭv), *a.* **1.** Serving to detect. **2.** Relating to detectives or detection.— *n.* One whose occupation is to detect concealed matters, as crimes.

de-tec′tor (-tĕr), *n.* One that detects; a detecter; esp., *Radio*, any of various devices for detecting the presence of electric waves.

de-tent′ (dĕ-tĕnt′), *n. Mech.* That which locks or unlocks a movement, as a pawl.

de-ten′tion (-tĕn′shŭn), *n.* **1.** Act of detaining; state of being detained. **2.** Confinement; custody.

de-ter′ (-tûr′), *v. t.; -TERRED′* (-tûrd′); *-TER′RING*. To turn aside, discourage, hinder, or prevent by fear of consequences.

de-ter′gent (-tûr′jĕnt), *a.* [4] Cleansing; purging. — *n.* A cleansing substance, esp. for the skin.

de-te′ri-o-rate (-tē′rĭ-ō-rāt), *v. t. & i.* [1] To make or grow worse; impair; degenerate. — **de-te′ri-o-ra′tion** (-rā′shŭn), *n.*

de-ter′mi-na-ble (-tûr′mĭ-ná-b'l), *a.* Capable of being determined, or definitely ascertained.

de-ter′mi-nate (-nát), *a.* Having defined limits; fixed, as by a rule; definite; decisive.

de-ter′mi-na′tion (-nā′shŭn), *n.* **1.** Act of determining; state of being determined. **2.** Decision of character; resoluteness.

de-ter′mine (-mĭn), *v. t.* [1] **1.** To limit; bound. **2.** To bring to a conclusion; decide. **3.** To resolve; decide definitely. **4.** To fix the form or character of beforehand; establish. **5.** To obtain knowledge of as to character, location, quantity, etc. — *v. i.* **1.** To end; terminate. **2.** To decide; resolve.

de-ter′mined (-mĭnd), *p.a.* [4] Decided; resolute; as, a *determined* man.

de-ter′rent (-tĕr′ĕnt; -tûr′ĕnt), *a.* [4] Serving to deter. — *n.* That which deters or prevents.

de-test′ (-tĕst′), *v. t.* To hate intensely; abhor.

de-test′a-ble (-tĕs′tá-b'l), *a.* [4] Worthy of being detested; abominable; odious; hateful. — **de-test′a-ble-ness**, *n.* [8] — **-a-bly**, *adv.* [8].

de′tes-ta′tion (dē′tĕs-tā′shŭn; dĕt′ĕs-), *n.* **1.** Act of detesting; loathing. **2.** That which is detested.

de-throne′ (dĕ-thrōn′), *v. t.* [1] To depose from a throne. — **de-throne′ment**, *n.*

det′o-nate (dĕt′ō-nāt), *v. i. & t.* [1] To explode with a sudden report.

det′o-na′tion (-nā′shŭn), *n.* Explosion with a sudden report; as, the *detonation* of guncotton.

de-tour′ (dĕ-tōōr′),*n.* A turning; roundabout course.

de-tract′ (dĕ-trăkt′), *v. t.* To withdraw; subtract; as, the defect *detracts* something from the beauty of the picture.— *v. i.* To take away a part, or something, esp. from one's credit or reputation; as, this habit *detracts* from his influence.

de-trac′tion (dĕ-trăk′shŭn), *n.* A taking away or

withdrawing; esp., a taking away from the reputation of another; depreciation; calumny.

de-trac′tor (-tĕr), *n.* One who detracts.

det′ri-ment (dĕt′rĭ-mĕnt), *n.* Injury or damage, or that which causes it; mischief; harm.

det′ri-men′tal (-mĕn′tăl), *a.* [4] Hurtful or harmful; injurious. — **det′ri-men′tal-ly**, *adv.* [8].

de-tri′tus (dĕ-trī′tŭs), *n. Geol.* Alluvial material worn off from the exposed surfaces of solid bodies.

deuce (dūs), *n.* **1.** Two; a card or a die with two spots. **2.** A certain tie score in lawn tennis. **3.** Bad luck; the devil; — an expletive.

dev′as-tate (dĕv′ăs-tāt), *v. t.* [1] To lay waste; desolate. — **dev′as-ta′tor** (-tā′tĕr), *n.*

dev′as-ta′tion (-tā′shŭn), *n.* Act of devastating.

de-vel′op (dĕ-vĕl′ŏp), *v. t.* [1] **1.** To lay open or unfold by degrees or in detail; disclose; reveal. **2.** To open up and expand the possibilities of. **3.** To form or expand by or as by a process of growth. **4.** *Photog.* To subject to the action of chemicals to bring out the latent image on a sensitized surface; also, to render visible in this way. — *v. i.* **1.** To advance to a more complex form; expand. **2.** To become apparent gradually, as a photographic image. — **de-vel′op-er**, *n.* [8].

de-vel′op-ment (-mĕnt), *n.* Act of developing; also, result of developing, or a developed state.

de′vi-ate (dē′vĭ-āt), *v. i.* [1] To turn aside, as from a course or method; stray; digress; wander.

de′vi-a′tion (-ā′shŭn), *n.* Act of deviating; turning aside, as from a way, rule, position, etc.

de-vice′ (dĕ-vīs′), *n.* **1.** That which is devised, or formed by design; contrivance; scheme; stratagem. **2.** An emblematic design, esp. one used as a heraldic bearing. **3.** Will; desire. *Obs.*, except in phrases; as, left to his own *devices*.

dev′il (dĕv′'l), *n.* **1.** [*cap. or l. c.*] In theology, the personal supreme spirit of evil and wickedness. **2.** A lesser evil or malignant spirit; fiend; demon. **3.** A human fiend. **4.** Jocosely, a dashing, reckless person. **5.** A wretched fellow; — usually with *poor*. — *v. t.* [7] To season highly in cooking.

dev′il-fish′ (-fĭsh′), *n.* (see PLURAL, *n.*, *Note*). **1.** Any of several large rays of warm seas. **2.** An octopus.

dev′il-ish, *a.* [4] Resembling, or characteristic of, the Devil; diabolical. — *adv.* Excessively; extremely. *Colloq.* — **-ly**, *adv.* [8] — **-ness**, *n.* [8].

dev′il-ry (-rĭ), *n.; pl.* -RIES (-rĭz). Devilish magic or action; reckless or wicked conduct; mischief.

dev′il-try (dĕv′'l-trĭ), *n.; pl.* -TRIES (-trĭz). Deviltry; esp., malicious or wanton mischief.

de′vi-ous (dē′vĭ-ŭs), *a.* [4] **1.** Out of a straight line; winding; sinuous. **2.** Going out of the right or common course. — **-ly**, *adv.* [8] — **-ness**, *n.* [8].

de-vise′ (dĕ-vīz′), *v. t. & i.* [1] **1.** To form in the mind by new combinations of ideas, etc.; contrive; invent; scheme. **2.** *Law.* To give by will; — now esp. of real estate. — *n.* **1.** Act of disposing of property by will; — now esp. of real property. **2.** Property devised. — **de-vis′er** (-vīz′ēr), *n.* [8].

dev′i-see′ (dĕv′ĭ-zē′; dĕ-vīz′ē′), *n. Law.* One to whom a devise is made.

de-vi′sor (dĕ-vī′zŏr), *n.* One who devises property.

de-vi′tal-ize (dē-vī′tăl-īz), *v. t.* [1] To deprive of vitality.

---

de-void′ (dĕ-void′), *a.* Destitute (of); not in possession; entirely without; — with *of*.

de-voir′ (dĕ-vwär′; -vwôr′), *n.* Duty; hence, due act of civility or respect; — now in *pl.*

de-volve′ (dĕ-vŏlv′), *v. i.* [1] To pass or be transferred from one person to another, as by succession; to be handed over or down.

de-vote′ (dĕ-vōt′), *v. i.* [1] **1.** To appropriate or dedicate by a vow; consecrate; also, to doom. **2.** To give up wholly; addict; attach; apply.

de-vot′ed (-vōt′ĕd), *p. a.* [4] **1.** Consecrated to a purpose; strongly attached. **2.** Dedicated; also, doomed. — **-ly,** *adv.* [8] — **-ness,** *n.* [8].

dev′o-tee′ (dĕv′ō-tē′), *n.* One zealously devoted, esp. to religious duties and ceremonies.

de-vo′tion (dĕ-vō′shŭn), *n.* **1.** State of being devoted; zeal; esp., feelings toward God expressed in worship; devoutness. **2.** An act of worship; prayer. **3.** Consecration; dedication.

de-vo′tion-al (-ăl), *a.* [4] Pert. to, suited to, or used in, devotion; as, a *devotional* exercise. — **-ly,** *adv.*

de-vour′ (-vour′), *v. t.* **1.** To eat up greedily or ravenously; to prey upon. **2.** To seize and destroy, or appropriate greedily or wantonly; consume; waste; annihilate. **3.** To take in eagerly by the senses. — **de-vour′er,** *n.* [8].

de-vout′ (-vout′), *a.* [3] **1.** Devoted to religion; pious; religious. **2.** Expressing devotion or piety. **3.** Warmly devoted; sincere; as, a *devout* friend. — **-ly,** *adv.* [8] — **-ness,** *n.* [8].

dew (dū), *n.* **1.** Moisture condensed on the surfaces of cool bodies, esp. at night. **2.** Fig., something that falls lightly or refreshingly. **3.** An emblem of morning, or fresh vigor.

dew′ber-ry (dū′bĕr-ĭ), *n.; pl.* -RIES (-ĭz). Any of certain species of blackberry.

dew′claw′ (-klô′), *n.* A short rudimentary digit on the foot of a quadruped, or a claw or hoof terminating such a digit.

dew′drop′ (dū′drŏp′), *n.* A drop of dew.

dew′lap′ (-lăp′), *n.* The hanging fold of skin under the neck of various animals, esp. bovines.

dew′y (dū′ĭ), *a.* [3] Of or pert. to dew; hence, suggestive of, consisting of, or moist with, dew.

dex′ter (dĕks′tĕr), *a.* **1.** Pertaining to, or situated on, the right hand; — opp. to *sinister*. **2.** *Heraldry.* Pertaining to the side of a shield, or escutcheon, at the right of the person wearing it.

dex-ter′i-ty (dĕks-tĕr′ĭ-tĭ), *n.* Readiness and grace in physical or in mental activity; adroitness.

dex′ter-ous (dĕks′tĕr-ŭs), *a.* [4] **1.** Skillful and active physically or mentally; ready. **2.** Done with dexterity; skillful; artful. — **dex′ter-ous-ly,** *adv.* [8] — **dex′ter-ous-ness,** *n.* [8].

dex′trin (-trĭn), *n.* A certain gummy substance formed from starch by heat, acids, or ferments, used as a substitute for gums, for sizing, etc.

dex′trous (-trŭs), *a.,* **dex′trous-ly,** *adv.,* **dex′trous-ness,** *n.* = DEXTEROUS, etc.

dey (dā), *n.* **1.** The governor of Algiers (before the French conquest in 1830). **2.** A ruler or pasha of Tunis or Tripoli, as in the 16th century.

di′a-be′tes (dī′a-bē′tēz ; -tĭs), *n.* A disease attended with an excessive discharge of urine.

di′a-bol′ic (-bŏl′ĭk) } *a.* [4] **1.** Of or pertain-
di′a-bol′i-cal (-ĭ-kăl) } ing to the Devil or devils.

2. Appropriate to devils; devilish. — **di′a-bol′-i-cal-ly,** *adv.* [8].

di′a-crit′ic (dī′a-krĭt′ĭk), *a.* Diacritical. — *n.* A diacritical mark or point.

di′a-crit′i-cal (-ĭ-kăl), *a.* Serving to separate or distinguish, as a point or sign applied to a letter to distinguish it in form or sound. — **-ly,** *adv.* [8].

di′a-dem (dī′a-dĕm), *n.* **1.** A crown; specifically, an ornamental headband or fillet worn by Eastern monarchs. **2.** Regal power or dignity.

di-ær′e-sis, di-er′e-sis (dī-ĕr′ĕ-sĭs), *n.; pl.* -ESES (-sēz). A mark, consisting of two dots [¨], placed over a vowel to indicate its pronunciation in a separate syllable, as in *zoölogy*.

di′ag-nose′ (dī′ăg-nōs′), *v. t. & i.* [1] To ascertain by, or to make, a diagnosis.

di′ag-no′sis (-nō′sĭs), *n.; pl.* -NOSES (-sēz). **1.** Art or act of recognizing disease from its symptoms. **2.** A critical scrutiny and judgment.

di-ag′o-nal (dī-ăg′ō-nạl), *a.* **1.** Running across from corner to corner, as a straight line joining either pair of opposite angles, or corners, of any four-sided figure bounded by straight lines. **2.** Having an oblique direction or extension. **3.** Having diagonal parts or markings. — *n.* **1.** A diagonal line or plane. **2.** A diagonal direction, row, or arrangement, or a part of a structure placed diagonally. — **di-ag′o-nal-ly,** *adv.* [8].

Diagonal, *n.,* 1.

di′a-gram (dī′a-grăm), *n.* **1.** A drawing composed of lines, or in outline, as for scientific purposes. **2.** Any graphic representation; a scheme, chart, or plan.— *v. t.* [7] To represent by a diagram or put into the form of a diagram.

di′a-gram-mat′ic (-gră-măt′ĭk), *a.* [4] Pertaining to a diagram; of the nature of a diagram.

di′al (dī′ạl), *n.* **1.** A sundial. **2.** The graduated face of a timepiece. **3.** A plate or face having a pointer or pointers for indicating something; as, the *dial* of a speedometer. — *v. t.* [7] To measure with a dial.

di′a-lect (-ă-lĕkt), *n.* **1.** Language; tongue; phraseology. **2.** A form of speech marked by local peculiarities; esp., a local form of a language differing from the standard, or literary, form. **3.** The cant or jargon of a class, profession, trade, or the like.

di′a-lec′tal (dī′a-lĕk′tạl), *a.* Relating or pertaining to a dialect. — **di′a-lec′tal-ly,** *adv.* [8].

di′a-lec′tic (-lĕk′tĭk) } *a.* Pertaining to, or of
di′a-lec′ti-cal (-tĭ-kạl) } the nature of, a dialect.

di′a-logue (dī′a-lŏg), *n.* **1.** A written composition representing two or more persons as conversing or reasoning; as, Plato's *Dialogues*. **2.** A colloquy or conversation between two or more.

di-am′e-ter (dī-ăm′ē-tĕr), *n.* **1.** *Geom.* Any chord passing through the center of a figure or body. **2.** The length of a straight line through the center of an object from side to side; width; thickness.

di-am′e-tral (-trạl), *a.* Pertaining to a diameter.

di′a-met′ric (dī′a-mĕt′rĭk), *a.* **1.** Of or pertaining to a diameter, or being a diameter. **2.** As remote as possible; opposite; adverse. — **di′a-met′ri-cal,** *a.* — **cal-ly,** *adv.* [8].

di′a-mond (dī′a-mŭnd), *n.* **1.** Native crystallized carbon, highly valued as a precious stone when transparent and free from flaws; also, a piece of this material. **2.** A rhombus ; a lozenge. **3.** *Playing Cards.* A red lozenge stamped on a card; a card, or (in *pl.*) the suit, so marked. **4.** *Baseball.* The space within the lines connecting the bases.

di'a-per (dī′ȧ-pẽr), *n.* **1.** A fabric of linen, cotton, or the like, usually white, with a small uniform pattern; also, the pattern. **2.** A cloth for an infant's breech.

di-aph'a-nous (dī-ăf′ȧ-nŭs), *a.* [4] Translucent or transparent; as, *diaphanous* clouds.

di'a-phragm (dī′ȧ-frăm), *n.* **1.** A dividing membrane or thin partition. **2.** *Anat.* The muscular tendinous partition separating the chest from the abdomen. **3.** A vibrating disk or membrane, as in a telephone. **4.** In an optical instrument, a perforated plate to regulate the amount of light received, or reduce the field of view.

di'ar-rhe'a (dī′ȧ-rē′ȧ), *n.* A morbid purging or looseness of the bowels.— **di'ar-rhe'al** (-ăl), *a.*

di'ar-rhœ'a (-rē′ȧ), *n.* Var. of DIARRHEA.

di'a-ry (dī′ȧ-rǐ), *n. ; pl.* -RIES (-rǐz). A daily record ; esp., a book of personal notes or memoranda.

di'a-ton'ic (-tŏn′ĭk), *a.* *Music.* Pert. to or designating a standard major or minor scale of 8 tones to the octave without chromatic modification.

di'a-tribe (dī′ȧ-trīb), *n.* A prolonged discussion ; esp., a bitter or violent speech criticizing some person or work.

dib'ble (dĭb′′l), *n.* A pointed implement to make holes in the ground, esp. for plants or seeds.—*v.t.* [1] To plant, or make holes in (soil), with or as with a dibble.

dice (dīs), *n. ; pl.* of DIE. Small cubes marked, usually, with spots from one to six, used in gaming; also, gaming with dice.—*v. i.* [1] To play games with dice.— **dic'er** (dīs′ẽr), *n.* [8].

dick'er (dĭk′ẽr), *v. i. & t.* To barter. *U. S.*—*n.* A petty bargain, trade, or deal. *U. S.*

dic'tate (dĭk′tāt ; dĭk-tāt′), *v. t.* [1] **1.** To tell or utter so that another may write down. **2.** To utter authoritatively ; deliver (a command) to a subordinate ; declare with authority ; impose. —*v. i.* To practice dictation. — (dĭk′tāt), *n.* A statement delivered with authority ; a rule ; command.

dic-ta'tion (dĭk-tā′shŭn), *n.* **1.** Act of dictating. **2.** That which is dictated.

dic-ta'tor (-tẽr), *n.* **1.** One appointed to exercise, or one exercising, absolute authority in government, esp. in a republic. **2.** Hence, one vested with supreme authority in any line.

dic'ta-to'ri-al (dĭk′tȧ-tō′rĭ-ăl), *a.* [4] Pertaining or suited to a dictator. — **-ly,** *adv.* [8].

dic-ta'tor-ship, *n.* **1.** Office or position of dictator. **2.** Absolute authority.

dic'tion (dĭk′shŭn), *n.* Choice of words for expression of ideas ; mode of verbal expression.

dic'tion-a-ry (-ā-rǐ), *n. ; pl.* -RIES (-rǐz). A book containing the words of a language, or of any system or province of knowledge, usually arranged alphabetically, with their meanings ; a lexicon.

dic'to-graph (dĭk′tȯ-grȧf), *n.* A telephonic instrument in which a sound-magnifying device replaces the ordinary mouthpiece. *A trade name.*

dic'tum (-tŭm), *n. ; pl.* L. -TA (-tȧ), E. -TUMS

(-tŭmz). An authoritative statement ; dogmatic saying ; a judicial opinion on a point immaterial to the matter being decided.

did (dĭd), *pret.* of DO.

di-dac'tic (dĭ-dăk′tĭk ; dī-).*a.* [4] Fitted or intended to teach ; instructive.— **di-dac'ti-cal-ly,** *adv.* [8].

didst (dĭdst), *2d pers. sing. pret.* of DO.

die (dī), *v. i. ; pret. & p. p.* DIED (dīd) ; *p. pr. & vb. n.* DYING (dī′ĭng). **1.** To become dead ; perish ; expire ; — said of any living organism. **2.** To pass out of existence ; cease. **3.** To sink, faint, or pine away ; languish.

die (dī), *n. ; pl.*, in senses 1 and (usually) 2 and (rarely) 3, DICE (dīs) ; in 4, DIES (dīz). **1.** One of the small cubes used in gaming. **2.** Any small cubical body. **3.** That which is, or might be, determined by a throw of the die ; hazard ; chance. **4.** *Mech.* A metal block or plate so shaped as to give a certain desired form or shape to an object by pressure or a blow, as in coining, etc.

di-er'e-sis (dī-ĕr′ē-sĭs). Var. of DIÆRESIS.

die'sink'er (dī′sĭnk′ẽr), *n.* An engraver of dies.

di'et (dī′ĕt), *n.* **1.** Course of living ; also, what is eaten and drunk habitually ; fare. **2.** A course of food selected with reference to a particular state of health. —*v.t.* To cause to eat and drink sparingly or by prescribed rules. —*v. i.* To eat according to prescribed rules ; eat sparingly.

di'et (dī′ĕt), *n.* A formal public assembly.

di'et-a-ry (-â-rǐ), *a.* Pertaining to diet, or to the rules of diet. — *n. ; pl.* -RIES (-rǐz). A rule of, or a treatise on, diet; also, a fixed allowance of food.

di'e-tet'ic (dī′ė-tĕt′ĭk), *a.* Pert. to diet ; dietary.

di'e-tet'ics (-ĭks), *n.* Medical or hygienic art relating to diet.

dif'fer (dĭf′ẽr), *v. i.* To be or stand apart ; be unlike ; be of unlike or opposite opinion ; disagree.

dif'fer-ence (-ẽns), *n.* **1.** State, quality, or measure of being different ; dissimilarity or unlikeness, or an instance of such. **2.** Mental discrimination ; —in *to make a difference*, that is, to discriminate. **3.** Disagreement in opinion ; dissension ; hence, cause of dissension ; matter in controversy.

dif'fer-ent (-ĕnt), *a.* [4] **1.** Of various or contrary nature, form, or quality ; unlike ; dissimilar. **2.** Distinct ; separate ; other. — **dif'fer-ent-ly,** *adv.* [8].

dif'fer-en'tial (-ĕn′shăl), *a.* [4] Relating to or indicating difference ; discriminating.—*n.* A small difference, esp. one between the rates, as of a railroad, over two routes between the same points.

dif'fer-en'ti-ate (-shĭ′āt), *v. t.* [1] **1.** To make or render different ; to distinguish or mark. **2.** To ascertain or state the difference of ; discriminate. — *v. i.* **1.** To acquire a distinct and separate character. **2.** To recognize or mark the difference.

dif'fer-en'ti-a'tion (-ā′shŭn), *n.* Act, process, or result of differentiating.

dif'fi-cult (dĭf′ĭ-kŭlt), *a.* [4] **1.** Hard to do or to make ; beset with difficulty ; also, hard to understand ; obscure. **2.** Hard to manage or to please ; exacting. — **-ly,** *adv.* [8].

dif'fi-cul-ty (-kŭl-tǐ), *n. ; pl.* -TIES (-tǐz). **1.** Quality or state of being difficult. **2.** A thing hard to do or to understand. **3.** Reluctance ; objection, demur. **4.** Embarrassment of affairs.

dif'fi-dence (dĭf′ĭ-dĕns), *n.* State of being diffident.

dif'fi-dent (-dĕnt), a. [4] Wanting confidence, esp. in one's self; not self-reliant; timid; modest; shrinking, bashful. — **dif'fi-dent-ly,** adv. [8].

dif-fuse' (dĭ-fūz'), v. t. & i. [1] To pour out and spread, as a fluid; spread; disseminate.

dif-fuse' (-fūs'), a. [3] Poured out; widespread; copious; full; of speech or writing, verbose; wordy; prolix. — **ly,** adv. [8] — **ness** (-nĕs), n.

dif-fus'i-bil'i-ty (dĭ-fūz'ĭ-bĭl'ĭ-tĭ), n. Capacity of being diffused.

dif-fus'i-ble (-fūz'ĭ-b'l), a. [4] Capable of diffusing, or of being diffused.

dif-fu'sion (-fū'zhŭn), n. Act of diffusing; state of being diffused; a spreading; dispersion.

dif-fu'sive (-sĭv), a. [4] Tending to diffuse; marked by diffusion; diffuse. — **ly,** adv. — **ness,** n.

dig (dĭg), v. t.; pret. & p. p. DUG (dŭg) or DIGGED (dĭgd); p. pr. & vb. n. DIG'GING (dĭg'ĭng). 1. To turn up, or delve in (earth), with a spade, hoe, etc.; pierce, open, or loosen with or as if with a spade. 2. To bring to the surface or get by digging; exhume. 3. To form or hollow out by or as by digging. — v. i. 1. To dig anything; delve. 2. To work hard; drudge. Colloq. — n. A thrust. Colloq.

di-gest' (dĭ-jĕst', dī-), v. t. 1. To distribute methodically; classify. 2. To arrange methodically in the mind; comprehend. 3. To convert (food) in the stomach or intestines into the form in which it is assimilated by the system. — v. i. 1. To digest food. 2. To undergo digestion.

di'gest (dī'jĕst), n. A body of information or written matter that is digested, or classified.

di-gest'i-bil'i-ty (dĭ-jĕs'tĭ-bĭl'ĭ-tĭ), n. Quality of being digestible.

di-gest'i-ble (dĭ-jĕs'tĭ-b'l), a. [4] Capable of being digested.

di-ges'tion (-jĕs'chŭn), n. Act or process of digesting; also, power or faculty of digesting food.

di-ges'tive (-tĭv), a. [4] Pertaining to digestion.

dig'ger (dĭg'ẽr), n. One that digs.

dig'it (dĭj'ĭt), n. 1. A finger or toe. 2. Math. Any of the ten figures or symbols, 0, 1, 2, 3, 4, 5, 6, 7, 8, 9, by which all numbers may be expressed. Many authorities do not include 0 with the digits.

dig'it-al (-ĭ-tăl), a. Of, pertaining to, or resembling a digit (sense 1) or digits.

dig'i-ta'lis (-tā'lĭs), n. The leaves of the purple foxglove, an important drug.

dig'i-tate (dĭj'ĭ-tāt), a. Resembling a finger or fingers, as some leaves.

dig'i-ti-grade' (-tĭ-grād'), a. Walking on the digits; — opposed to plantigrade; as, the cat is a digitigrade animal.

dig'ni-fied (dĭg'nĭ-fīd), p. a. [4] Marked with dignity.

dig'ni-fy (-fī), v. t. [2] 1. To invest with dignity; honor. 2. To give a semblance of dignity to.

Digitate Leaf.

dig'ni-ta-ry (-tā-rĭ), n.; pl. -RIES (-rĭz). One exalted in rank or in a position of dignity or honor.

dig'ni-ty (-tĭ), n.; pl. -TIES (-tĭz). 1. Quality of being worthy or honorable; worth; nobleness. 2. Elevated rank; also, an office, rank, or title of honor. 3. Nobleness of manner, aspect, or style.

di'graph (dī'gráf), n. A group of two letters representing a single simple speech sound, as ea in head (hĕd), or th in bath.

di-gress' (dĭ-grĕs'; dī-), v. i. To turn aside; deviate, esp. from the main subject of discourse.

di-gres'sion (-grĕsh'ŭn), n. Act of digressing, or an instance of digressing.

di-gres'sive (-grĕs'ĭv), a. [4] Digressing, or of the nature of digression. — **sive-ly,** adv. [8].

dike (dīk), n. 1. A ditch; channel dug for water. 2. A bank of earth thrown up from a ditch; hence, a causeway. 3. A bank, as of earth, thrown up to form a barrier, line of demarcation, or the like; esp., a levee. — v. t. [1] 1. To surround with a dike or dikes. 2. To drain by a dike or ditch.

di-lap'i-date (dĭ-lăp'ĭ-dāt), v. t. [1] To bring (a building) into decay or partial ruin. — v. i. To fall into decay or partial ruin.

di-lap'i-da'tion (-dā'shŭn), n. Act of dilapidating; also, condition of being in ruins, disrepair, etc.

di-lat'a-ble (dĭ-lāt'á-b'l; dī-), a. [4] Capable of dilation.

dil'a-ta'tion (dĭl'á-tā'shŭn; dī-lá-), n. Act of dilating; state of being dilated; also, a dilated part.

di-late' (dĭ-lāt'; dī-), v. t. [1] To enlarge or extend in bulk or size; expand. — v. i. 1. To dwell in narration; expatiate. 2. To expand.

di-la'tion (dĭ-lā'shŭn; dī-), n. Act of dilating; state of being dilated; dilatation.

dil'a-to-ry (dĭl'á-tō-rĭ), a. [4] 1. Designed to cause delay; as, a dilatory policy. 2. Characterized by, or given to, procrastination; tardy; slow. — **dil'a-to-ri-ly** (-rĭ-lĭ), adv. — **to-ri-ness,** n.

di-lem'ma (dĭ-lĕm'á; dī-), n. A vexatious predicament; difficult choice or position.

dil'et-tan'te (dĭl'ĕ-tän'tĕ; It. dē'lĕt-tän'tä), n.; pl. It. -TANTI (-tē), E. -TANTES (-tēz). A lover of the fine arts; esp., one who follows an art or a branch of knowledge desultorily, or for amusement only.

dil'i-gence (dĭl'ĭ-jĕns; F. dē'lē'zhäns'), n. A public stagecoach; — now only of Continental ones.

dil'i-gence (dĭl'ĭ-jĕns), n. Quality of being diligent; persevering effort; assiduity.

dil'i-gent (-jĕnt), a. [4] 1. Assiduous; industrious; persevering. 2. Prosecuted with careful attention and effort. — **ly,** adv. [8].

dill (dĭl), n. A European herb. Its seeds are used for flavoring pickles, etc.

dil'ly-dal'ly (-ĭ-dăl'ĭ), v. i. [2] To loiter or trifle.

di-lute' (dĭ-lūt'; dī-), v. t. [1] To make thinner by admixture; weaken by mixing, esp. with water; as, to dilute acid. — a. [3] Diluted; weak.

di-lu'tion (-lū'shŭn), n. Act of diluting, or state of being diluted; something diluted.

di-lu'vi-al (dĭ-lū'vĭ-ăl), **di-lu'vi-an** (-ăn), a. [4] Of or pert. to a flood or deluge, esp. the Deluge.

dim (dĭm), a.; DIM'MER (-ẽr); DIM'MEST. 1. Not bright or distinct; obscure; faint; dull. 2. Of obscure vision; hence, dull of apprehension. — v. t. & i.; DIMMED (dĭmd); DIM'MING. To render or become dim; dull; obscure.

dime (dīm), n. A U. S. silver coin, worth ten cents.

di-men'sion (dĭ-mĕn'shŭn), n. 1. Measure in a single line; usually, in pl., measure in length and breadth, or in length, breadth, and thickness; size. 2. pl. Extent; importance.

---

di-men′sion-al (dĭ-mĕn′shŭn-ăl), *a.* Of or pertaining to dimension; having dimensions (usually specified in number); as, three-*dimensional*.

di-min′ish (dĭ-mĭn′ĭsh), *v. t. & i.* To make smaller or less; lessen; reduce in size or importance.

di-min′u-en-do (dĭ-mĭn′ŭ-ĕn′dō; *It.* dē-mē-nwĕn′-), *a. & adv. Music.* With gradually diminishing volume; — a direction noted by *Dim.*, or *Dimin.*, or the sign, ⟍.

dim′i-nu′tion (dĭm′ĭ-nū′shŭn), *n.* Act of diminishing; state of being diminished; reduction.

di-min′u-tive (dĭ-mĭn′ŭ-tĭv), *a.* [4] **1.** Expressing diminution, as a word. **2.** Below the average size; very small; little. — *n.* **1.** *Gram.* A derivative word denoting something small or young of the kind denoted by the primitive; as, *gosling*, *lambkin*. **2.** A diminutive form or variety. — **di-min′u-tive-ly**, *adv.* [8] — **-ness**, *n.* [8].

dim′i-ty (dĭm′ĭ-tĭ), *n.; pl.* -TIES (-tĭz). A kind of cotton fabric with raised stripes.

dim′ly, *adv.* In a dim or obscure manner.

dim′ness, *n.* Quality or state of being dim.

dim′ple (dĭm′p'l), *n.* A slight natural indentation in the body, esp. in the cheek or chin. — *v. i. & t.* [1] To form, or mark with, dimples.

din (dĭn), *n.* Loud, confused, or clanging noise; clamor.—*v. t.;* DINNED (dĭnd); DIN′NING. To assail, or to utter, with a din. — *v. i.* To make a din.

dine (dīn), *v. i.* [1] To take dinner. — *v. t.* To give a dinner to; feed.

din′er (dīn′ēr), *n.* One who dines; a guest at dinner.

ding (dĭng), *v. i. & t.* **1.** To ring, as a bell. **2.** To talk with vehemence, importunity, or reiteration. *Colloq.* — *n.* The noise of dinging.

ding′dong′ (dĭng′dŏng′), *n.* The sound of or as of repeated strokes on a metallic body, as a bell.

din′ghy, din′gey (dĭng′gĭ), *n.; pls.* -GHIES, -GEYS (-gĭz). A small boat, of various kinds.

din′gle (-g'l), *n.* A dell, esp. a small one.

din′gy (dĭn′jĭ), *a.* [3] Dark; dusky; grimy; soiled.— **-gi-ly** (-jĭ-lĭ),*adv.* [8]— **-gi-ness**,*n.* [8].

din′ner (dĭn′ēr), *n.* The chief meal of the day, or a formal repast or feast answering to this.

dint (dĭnt), *n.* **1.** Force; power; — esp. in *by dint of.* **2.** A dent. — *v. t.* To dent.

di-oc′e-san (dī-ŏs′ē-săn), *a.* Of or pert. to or governing a diocese.—*n.* **1.** One in charge of a diocese. **2.** One of the clergy or the people of a diocese.

di′o-cese (dī′ō-sēs; -sĕs), *n.* The district in which a bishop has authority.

di-ox′ide (dī-ŏk′sĭd; -sĭd), *n.* An oxide having two atoms of oxygen in each molecule.

dip (dĭp), *v. t.;* DIPPED (dĭpt) or DIPT; DIP′PING. **1.** To plunge or immerse, esp. temporarily or partly into or in a liquid or the like. **2.** To take out as by lading. **3.** To lower and raise quickly, as a flag. — *v. i.* **1.** To immerse one's self, as in a liquid, and emerge quickly. **2.** To drop down, as if into water; sink. **3.** To plunge a ladle or the like into a liquid or other soft substance and remove a part. **4.** To go; to enter, esp. slightly or cursorily. **5.** To incline downward; slope. — *n.* **1.** Act of dipping or immersing. **2.** Inclination downward; pitch. **3.** A candle made by repeated dipping of a wick in a fat or wax. *Colloq.* **4.** Any liquid prep-

aration into which objects may be dipped, as for cleansing, coloring, etc.

diph-the′ri-a (dĭf-thē′rĭ-à), *n.* A febrile infectious disease in which the air passages, esp. the throat, become coated with a false membrane.

diph′the-rit′ic (dĭf′thē-rĭt′ĭk), *a.* Pertaining to, or of the nature of, diphtheria.

diph′thong (dĭf′thŏng), *n.* **1.** A union of two vowels forming a compound sound pronounced in one syllable, as *ou* in *out*, *oi* in *oil*. **2.** A vowel digraph, as *ea* in *head*; — often called an *improper diphthong.*

diph-thon′gal (dĭf-thŏn′găl), *a.* Pertaining to a diphthong.

di-plo′ma (dĭ-plō′mà), *n.; pl.* E. -MAS (-màz), L. -MATA (-mà-tà). A writing conferring some privilege, honor, or power; esp., an official record of graduation.

di-plo′ma-cy (-mà-sĭ), *n.; pl.* -CIES (-sĭz). **1.** Art of conducting negotiations between nations. **2.** Dexterity in securing advantages; tact.

dip′lo-mat (dĭp′lō-măt), *n.* One employed or skilled in international diplomacy; a diplomatist.

dip′lo-mat′ic (-măt′ĭk), *a.* [4] **1.** Of or pert. to international diplomacy. **2.** Characterized by, or skilled in, diplomacy; tactful.

dip′lo-mat′i-cal-ly, *adv.* In a diplomatic manner.

di-plo′ma-tist (dĭ-plō′mà-tĭst), *n.* **1.** A diplomat. **2.** One tactful or crafty in affairs.

dip′per (dĭp′ēr), *n.* **1.** One that dips; esp., a ladle for water or other liquid. **2.** Any of various diving birds. **3.** [*cap.*] The group comprising the seven principal stars in the constellation of the Great Bear; — from their arrangement.

dip′so-ma′ni-a (dĭp′sō-mā′nĭ-à), *n.* A morbid uncontrollable craving for alcoholic liquor.

dire (dīr), *a.* [3] Fearful; dreadful; horrible.

di-rect′ (dĭ-rĕkt′), *a.* [4] **1.** Straight; leading by the shortest way to a point or end. **2.** Straightforward; not swerving from truth and openness. **3.** Express; plain; unambiguous. **4.** In the line of descent; lineally related, not collaterally. — *direct current, Elec.,* a current flowing in one direction only; — distinguished from *alternating current.* — *adv.* Directly.— *v. t.* **1.** To put a direction or address on, as on a letter. **2.** To direct or point straight to or toward a place; aim. **3.** To show to (any one), as the right way; guide, as by pointing out the way. **4.** To determine the course of; guide; govern. **5.** To instruct as a superior; order.—*v. i.* To give direction; point out a course.—**di-rect′er**, *n.* [8].

di-rec′tion (-rĕk′shŭn), *n.* **1.** Act of directing; guidance; management. **2.** Instruction; order; command. **3.** The superscription or address, as of a letter. **4.** The line on which anything is moving or aimed to move, or in which anything is lying or pointing.

di-rect′ly (-rĕkt′lĭ), *adv.* **1.** In a direct manner or line. **2.** Without delay; immediately.

di-rect′ness, *n.* Quality or state of being direct.

di-rec′tor (dĭ-rĕk′tēr), *n.* **1.** One that directs; a manager. **2.** One of a body appointed to manage the affairs of a company or corporation.

di-rec′to-rate (-tō-rāt), *n.* Office of director; a body of directors.

āle, senāte, câre, ăm, *ă*ccount, ärm, ȧsk, sofȧ; ēve, ĕvent, ênd, recĕnt, makēr; īce, ĭll; ōld, ȯbey, ôrb, ŏdd, sŏft, cŏnnect; ūse, ūnite, ûrn, ŭp, circŭs; fōod, fŏot; out, oil;

di-rec'to-ry (dĭ-rĕk'tŏ-rĭ), n. ; pl. -RIES (-rĭz).
1. That which directs ; esp., a body of directions or rules. **2.** A book or list containing the names and addresses of the inhabitants of any place, or of classes of them.

dire'ful (dĭr'fŏŏl), a. [3] Dire ; terrible. — **dire'-ful-ly**, adv. [8].

dire'ly (dĭr'lĭ), adv. In a dire manner.

dirge (dûrj), n. A piece of music, esp. a mournful song, to accompany funeral or memorial rites.

dir'i-gi-ble (dĭr'ĭ-jĭ-b'l), a. [4] That can be directed or steered, as a balloon. — n. A dirigible airship.

dirk (dûrk), n. A kind of dagger.

dirt (dûrt), n. **1.** Any foul substance, as mud, dust, etc. **2.** Loose earth or soil. Colloq.

dirt'i-ly (dûr'tĭ-lĭ), adv. In a dirty manner.

dirt'i-ness, n. State or quality of being dirty.

dirt'y (-tĭ), a. [3] **1.** Soiled with dirt ; unclean. **2.** Of color, sullied ; clouded. **3.** Base ; sordid ; as, a dirty deed. **4.** Foggy ; stormy ; as, dirty weather. — v. t. [2] **1.** To foul ; soil. **2.** To tarnish ; sully.

dis'a-bil'i-ty (dĭs'ă-bĭl'ĭ-tĭ), n. ; pl. -TIES (-tĭz). State of being disabled ; absence of competent power, etc.

dis-a'ble (dĭs-ā'b'l), v. t. [1] To render unable or incapable ; disqualify ; unfit ; incapacitate.

dis-a'bled (-ā'b'ld), p. a. [4] Incapable ; crippled.

dis-a'ble-ment (-b'l-mĕnt), n. Act of disabling, or state of being disabled.

dis'a-buse' (dĭs'ă-būz'), v. t. [1] To undeceive.

dis'ad-van'tage (-ăd-văn'tăj), n. **1.** That which hinders success, or causes loss or injury. **2.** Loss ; detriment ; injury ; prejudice to fame, profit, or other good. — v. t. [1] To injure the interest of.

dis-ad'van-ta'geous (dĭs-ăd'văn-tā'jŭs), a. [4] Attended with disadvantage ; unfavorable ; prejudicial. — **-ly**, adv. [8] — **-ness**, n. [8].

dis'af-fect' (dĭs'ă-fĕkt'), v. t. To diminish the affection of ; to fill with discontent.

dis'af-fec'tion'(-fĕk'shŭn), n. State of being disaffected ; unfriendliness ; disloyalty ; hostility.

dis'a-gree' (-ă-grē'), v. i. ; -GREED' (-grēd') ; -GREE'-ING. **1.** To fail to agree ; be unlike. **2.** To differ in opinion. **3.** To be unsuited.

dis'a-gree'a-ble (-ă-b'l), a. [4] Exciting repugnance ; offensive ; unpleasant in temper or mood. — **-a-ble-ness**, n. [8] — **-a-bly**, adv. [8].

dis'a-gree'ment (-mĕnt), n. Act or state of disagreeing ; difference ; dissension ; discord.

dis'al-low' (-ă-lou'), v. t. To refuse to allow.

dis'al-low'ance (-ăns), n. Refusal to admit or permit ; rejection ; disapprobation.

dis'ap-pear' (-ă-pēr'), v. i. **1.** To cease to appear ; pass from view ; vanish. **2.** To cease to be ; be lost.

dis'ap-pear'ance (-ăns), n. Act of disappearing.

dis'ap-point' (-point'), v. t. **1.** To defeat of expectation or hope ; balk. **2.** To frustrate ; foil ; defeat. — **dis'ap-point'ed**, p. a. [4].

dis'ap-point'ment (-mĕnt), n. **1.** Act of disappointing ; state or emotion of being disappointed ; frustration. **2.** That which disappoints.

dis'ap'pro-ba'tion (dĭs-ăp'rŏ-bā'shŭn), n. Act, state, or fact of disapproving ; disapproval.

dis'ap-prov'al (-prŏŏv'ăl), n. Disapprobation.

dis'ap-prove' (dĭs'ă-prŏŏv'), v. t. [1] **1.** To pass

unfavorable judgment on ; censure. **2.** To refuse official approbation to. — v. i. To feel or express disapprobation (of).

dis-arm' (dĭs-ärm'), v. t. **1.** To deprive of arms or weapons. **2.** To deprive of means or disposition to harm ; render harmless.

dis-ar'ma-ment (-är'mă-mĕnt), n. Act of disarming ; esp., reduction of an army or navy approximately to a peace footing.

dis'ar-range' (dĭs'ă-rānj'),v. t. [1] To disturb the arrangement of ; disorder.

dis'ar-range'ment (-mĕnt),n. Act of disarranging.

dis'ar-ray' (-ă-rā'), v. t. **1.** To throw into disorder. **2.** To strip of personal array ; disrobe ; undress. — n. **1.** Disorder. **2.** Confused or incomplete attire.

dis-as'ter (dĭz-ås'tẽr), n. An unfortunate event ; esp., a sudden extraordinary misfortune ; calamity.

dis-as'trous (-trŭs), a. [4] Attended with disaster ; calamitous. — **dis-as'trous-ly**, adv. [8].

dis'a-vow' (dĭs'ă-vou'), v. t. To refuse to own or acknowledge ; disclaim ; disown ; deny.

dis'a-vow'al (-ăl), n. Repudiation.

dis-band' (dĭs-bănd'), v. t. To break up the organization of, as of an army. — v. i. To disperse; esp., to quit military service by breaking up organization.

dis-band'ment, n. Act or fact of disbanding.

dis-bar' (-bär'), v. t. ; DIS-BARRED' (-bärd') ; DIS-BAR'RING. Law. To deprive of the status and privileges of a member of the bar.

dis'be-lief' (dĭs'bē-lēf'), n. Act or state of disbelieving ; refusal of assent or credence.

dis'be-lieve' (-lēv'), v. t. & i. [1] To refuse credence to.

dis-bur'den (-bûr'd'n), v. t. **1.** To rid of a burden ; disencumber. **2.** To put off (a burden) ; discharge.

dis-burse' (-bûrs'), v. t. [1] To pay out ; expend.

dis-burse'ment (-mĕnt), n. Act of disbursing ; also, that which is disbursed.

disc (dĭsk), n. Var. of DISK.

dis-card' (dĭs-kärd'), v. t. To cast off as useless ; throw or lay aside ; turn away ; reject.

dis-cern' (dĭz-zûrn'), v. t. **1.** To perceive as distinct ; to recognize the difference between. **2.** To see by the eye or by the understanding ; perceive and recognize. — v. i. To make distinction ; distinguish. — **-er**, n. [8].

dis-cern'i-ble (-zûr'nĭ-b'l), a. [4] Capable of being discerned. — **-ness**, n. [4] — **-cern'i-bly**, adv. [8].

dis-cern'ing, p. a. [4] Acute ; shrewd.

dis-cern'ment (-zûrn'mĕnt), n. Act or faculty of discerning ; discrimination ; insight.

dis-charge' (dĭs-chärj'),v. t. [1] **1.** To relieve of a charge, or burden ; unload, as a vessel. **2.** To let fly, as an arrow ; shoot ; fire off, as a gun. **3.** To relieve, as of a debt, responsibility, accusation, etc. **4.** To send away from service ; dismiss ; release. **5.** To remove, as a charge or burden. **6.** To throw off the obligation of, esp. by performance ; hence, to perform, as a duty ; pay, as a debt. **7.** To give forth ; emit. — v. i. To throw off or deliver a load, charge, or burden. — n. **1.** Act of discharging ; unloading, as of a cargo. **2.** Firing off, as of artillery. **3.** Act of relieving, or state of being relieved, of an obligation or other burden ; acquittance. **4.** Act of getting rid of an obligation, liability, etc. **5.** Release or dismissal, as from office or custody. **6.** A

---

chair ; go ; sing, ink ; then, thin ; nature, verdure ; yet ; zh = z in azure. Numbers refer to §§ in the Special Notes which, with Abbreviations, Signs, etc., precede the Vocabulary.

flowing or issuing out or a rate of flow ; emission. **7.** That which is discharged or emitted.

dis-charg'er (-chär'jẽr), *n.* One that discharges.

dis-ci'ple (dĭ-sī'p'l), *n.* A pupil ; now esp., a follower who believes in the doctrine of his teacher.

dis-ci'ple-ship, *n.* State or function of a disciple.

dis'ci-plin-a'ri-an (dĭs'ĭ-plĭn-â'rĭ-ăn), *n.* One who disciplines, esp., excellently or rigorously.

dis'ci-plin-a-ry (-â-rĭ), *a.* [4] Pert. to discipline.

dis'ci-pline (-plĭn), *n.* **1.** The treatment suited to a learner ; education ; training ; drill. **2.** Subjection to rule ; habit of obedience. **3.** Correction ; chastisement by way of correction and training. — *v. t.* [1] **1.** To develop by instruction and exercise ; train. **2.** To accustom to regular and systematic action ; drill. **3.** To improve by corrective methods ; chastise.

dis-claim' (dĭs-klām'), *v. t.* To disavow any connection with ; repudiate ; disown.

dis-claim'er (dĭs-klām'ẽr), *n.* Act of disclaiming ; a denial or disavowal of claim.

dis-close' (dĭs-klōz'), *v.t.* [1] To lay open or expose to view ; reveal ; expose ; divulge.

dis-clo'sure (dĭs-klō'zhŭr), *n.* Act of disclosing or revealing : exposure ; thing disclosed.

dis-col'or (dĭs-kŭl'ẽr), *v. t.* [5] To alter the natural color of, esp. for the worse ; stain.

dis-col'or-a'tion (-ä'shŭn), *n.* **1.** Alteration of color. **2.** A discolored spot ; a stain.

dis-com'fit (-kŭm'fĭt), *v. t.* **1.** To defeat ; rout. *Archaic.* **2.** To balk ; throw into dejection.

dis-com'fi-ture (-fĭ-tŭr), *n.* Act of discomfiting.

dis-com'fort (-fẽrt), *v. t.* To disturb the comfort of ; make uneasy ; pain. — *n.* **1.** Want of comfort ; pain ; distress. **2.** An inconvenience.

dis'com-mode' (dĭs'kŏ-mōd'), *v. t.* [1] To incommode ; inconvenience.

dis'com-pose' (-kŏm-pōz'), *v.t.* [1] To destroy the composure of ; agitate ; disarrange ; disturb.

dis'com-po'sure (-pō'zhŭr), *n.* Discomposed state.

dis'con-cert' (-kŏn-sûrt'), *v. t.* **1.** To throw into disorder or confusion. **2.** To disturb; confuse.

dis'con-nect' (-kŏ-nĕkt'), *v. t.* To undo the connection of ; disunite.

dis'con-nect'ed (-nĕk'tĕd), *p. a.* [4] Disjoined ; not connected. — **-ly,** *adv.* [8] — **-ness,** *n.* [8].

dis'con-nec'tion (-nĕk'shŭn), *n.* Act of disconnecting, or state of being disconnected.

dis'con'so-late (dĭs-kŏn'sô-lȧt), *a.* [4] **1.** Destitute of consolation ; deeply dejected ; sad. **2.** Inspiring dejection ; cheerless. — **-ly,** *adv.* [8].

dis'con-tent' (dĭs'kŏn-tĕnt'), *a.* [4] Not content ; dissatisfied. — *n.* Want of content ; uneasiness ; dissatisfaction. — *v. t.* To dissatisfy ; displease.

dis'con-tent'ed (-tĕn'tĕd), *p. a.* [4] Dissatisfied ; uneasy in mind. — **-ly,** *adv.* [8] — **-ness,** *n.* [8].

dis'con-tent'ment (-tĕnt'mĕnt), *n.* State, fact, or feeling of discontent.

dis'con-tin'u-ance (-tĭn'û-ăns), *n.* A discontinuing ; state of being discontinued ; interruption.

dis'con-tin'ue (-tĭn'ū), *v.t. & i.* [1] To interrupt the continuance of ; break off ; stop ; leave off.

dis'con-tin'u-ous (-û-ŭs), *a.* [4] Not continuous ; broken off. — **dis'con-tin'u-ous-ly,** *adv.* [8].

dis'cord (dĭs'kôrd), *n.* **1.** Want of concord or agreement ; disagreement. **2.** A combination of

musical sounds which strikes the ear harshly. **3.** A harsh or confused noise ; uproar.

dis-cord'ance (dĭs-kôr'dăns), *n.* **1.** State or quality of being discordant. **2.** A discord.

dis-cord'an-cy (-dăn-sĭ), *n.* Discordance.

dis-cord'ant (-dănt), *a.* [4] Characterized by discord. — **dis-cord'ant-ly,** *adv.* [8].

dis'count (dĭs'kount ; dĭs-kount'), *v. t.* **1.** To deduct from an account, debt, charge, or the like. **2.** To lend money on, deducting in advance the discount. **3.** To take into consideration beforehand ; diminish by anticipation. **4.** To make allowance for exaggeration in (a tale, etc.). — (dĭs'kount), *n.* **1.** Act of discounting ; esp.: **a** A deduction from a gross sum on an account. **b** A deduction for interest in advancing money on or purchasing a bill or note not due. Cf. BANK DISCOUNT. **2.** The rate of interest charged in discounting. — **dis-count'a-ble** (dĭs-koun'tȧ-b'l), *a.* [8].

dis-coun'te-nance (dĭs-koun'tê-năns), *v. t.* [1] **1.** To put out of countenance ; abash. **2.** To refuse to countenance, or approve.

dis-cour'age (dĭs-kŭr'ĕj), *v.t.* [1] **1.** To lessen the courage of ; dishearten ; deject. **2.** To dishearten one with respect to ; deter one from.

dis-cour'age-ment (-mĕnt), *n.* **1.** Act of discouraging ; state of being discouraged ; depression. **2.** That which discourages ; a deterrent.

dis-course' (dĭs-kōrs'), *n.* **1.** Conversation; talk. **2.** Consecutive speech, written or unwritten ; treatise; dissertation. — *v. i.* [1] To express one's self in discourse; speak; converse. — *v. t.* To utter or give forth, as music. — **dis-cours'er,** *n.* [8].

dis-cour'te-ous (-kŭr'tē-ŭs; -kōrt'yŭs), *a.* [4] Uncivil; wanting in courtesy. — **-ly,** *adv.* [8].

dis-cour'te-sy (-kŭr'tĕ-sĭ), *n.* Lack of courtesy.

dis-cov'er (-kŭv'ẽr), *v.t.* **1.** To lay open to view; reveal. *Archaic.* **2.** To obtain sight or knowledge of, for the first time, as of a thing already existing, but hitherto not known; detect ; descry. — **-a-ble** (-ȧ-b'l), *a.* [8] — **-er** (-ẽr), *n.* [8].

dis-cov'er-y (-ẽr-ĭ), *n. ; pl.* **-ERIES** (-ĭz). **1.** Act of discovering. **2.** That which is discovered.

dis-cred'it (dĭs-krĕd'ĭt), *n.* **1.** Lack of credit or reputation ; disesteem. **2.** Lack of belief or confidence ; disbelief. — *v. t.* **1.** To refuse credence to; disbelieve. **2.** To destroy confidence in. **3.** To deprive of credit or good repute ; bring reproach upon. — **dis-cred'it-a-ble** (-ȧ-b'l), *a.* [8] — **-it-a-bly,** *adv.* [8].

dis-creet' (-krēt'), *a.* [3] Possessed of discernment, esp. in avoiding error or evil; circumspect; prudent. — **-ly,** *adv.* [8] — **-ness,** *n.* [8].

dis-crep'an-cy (-krĕp'ăn-sĭ), *n. ; pl.* **-CIES** (-sĭz). State or quality of being discrepant.

dis-crep'ant (-krĕp'ănt), *a.* [4] Discordant ; at variance ; disagreeing ; contrary ; different.

dis-crete' (dĭs-krēt' ; dĭs'krēt), *a.* [3] **1.** Separate; distinct. **2.** Composed of distinct parts.

dis-cre'tion (dĭs-krĕsh'ŭn), *n.* **1.** Freedom to decide or act; unrestrained exercise of choice or will. **2.** Quality of being discreet ; prudence.

dis-cre'tion-a-ry (-â-rĭ), *a.* Pert. to discretion; kept back only by discretion.

dis-crim'i-nate (krĭm'ĭ-nāt), *v. t.* [1] **1.** To constitute a difference in or between; differentiate.

āle, senāte, câre, ăm, ăccount, ärm, ȧsk, sofȧ ; ēve, ĕvent, ĕnd, recĕnt, makẽr ; īce, ĭll ; ōld, ȯbey, ôrb, ŏdd, sŏft, cȯnnect ; ūse, ŭnite, ûrn, ŭp, circŭs ; fo͝od, fo͝ot ; out, oil ;

2. To separate by discerning differences; distinguish. — *v. i.* **1.** To make a difference or distinction; distinguish. **2.** To make a difference in treatment or favor (of one as compared with others).

dis-crim'i-na'tion (-nā'shŭn), *n.* **1.** Act of discriminating; state of being discriminated. **2.** Quality of being discriminating; acute discernment.

dis-crim'i-na-tive (-krĭm'ĭ-nā-tĭv), *a.* [4] **1.** Distinctive. **2.** Discerning; discriminating.

dis-cur'sive (-kûr'sĭv), *a.* [4] Passing from one thing to another; digressive; desultory. — **-ly**, *adv.* [8] — **-ness**, *n.* [8].

dis'cus (dĭs'kŭs), *n.; pl.* E. **-cuses** (-ĕz), L. **DISCI** (dĭs'ī). A heavy circular plate, or quoit, to be thrown or hurled as a trial of strength and skill.

dis-cuss' (dĭs-kŭs'), *v. t.* To examine or investigate by disputation; debate.

dis-cus'sion (dĭs-kŭsh'ŭn), *n.* Act of discussing; debate; investigation by arguments.

dis-dain' (-dān'), *n.* A feeling of contempt and aversion; scorn; arrogance; pride. — *v. t.* **1.** To think unworthy; deem unsuitable or unbecoming. **2.** To reject as not deserving one's notice; scorn.

dis-dain'ful (-dān'fŏŏl), *a.* [4] Full of disdain; scornful. — **-ly**, *adv.* [8] — **-ness**, *n.* [8].

dis-ease' (dĭ-zēz'), *n. Med.* Any departure from health presenting marked symptoms; malady; illness; disorder. — *v. t.* [1] To afflict with disease or sickness; disorder; — chiefly in p. p., *diseased.*

dis'em-bark' (dĭs'ĕm-bärk'), *v. t. & i.* To remove or go ashore from on board a vessel; land.

dis'em-bar'rass (dĭs'ĕm-băr'ăs), *v. t.* To free from embarrassment; clear.

dis'em-bod'y (-ĕm-bŏd'ĭ), *v. t.* [2] To divest of the body or corporeal existence.

dis'em-bogue' (-bōg'), *v. t. & i.* [1] To discharge at the mouth, as a stream.

dis'em-bow'el (-bou'ĕl), *v. t.* [7] To take or let out the bowels of; eviscerate.

dis'en-chant' (dĭs'ĕn-chȧnt'), *v. t.* To free from enchantment, or delusion. — **-ment** (-mĕnt), *n.*

dis'en-cum'ber (-kŭm'bēr), *v. t.* To disburden.

dis'en-gage' (-gāj'), *v. t.* [1] To release from that with which anything is engaged; extricate.

dis'en-gage'ment (-mĕnt), *n.* Act of disengaging.

dis'en-tan'gle (-tăn'g'l), *v. t.* [1] To free from entanglement; disengage; extricate.

dis'es-tab'lish (-ĕs-tăb'lĭsh), *v. t.* To break up (anything established). — **-ment** (-mĕnt), *n.*

dis'es-teem' (dĭs'ĕs-tēm'), *n.* Want of esteem; disfavor. — *v. t.* To hold in disesteem; to slight.

dis-fa'vor (dĭs-fā'vēr), *n.* [5] **1.** Want of favor or favorable regard; disesteem. **2.** State of being regarded unfavorably. — *v. t.* To withhold or withdraw favor from; regard with disesteem.

dis-fig'ure (-fĭg'ŭr), *v. t.* [1] To mar the figure or appearance of.

dis-fig'ure-ment (-mĕnt), *n.* Act of disfiguring, or state of being disfigured; a defacement.

dis-fran'chise (dĭs-frăn'chĭz), *v. t.* [1] To deprive of a franchise, as suffrage.

dis-fran'chise-ment (-chīz-mĕnt), *n.* Act of disfranchising, or state of being disfranchised.

dis-gorge' (-gôrj'), *v. t. & i.* [1] **1.** To discharge by the throat and mouth; vomit. **2.** To give up, esp. unwillingly, something wrongfully held.

dis-grace' (-grās'), *n.* **1.** Condition of being out of favor. **2.** State of being dishonored; shame; ignominy. **3.** Cause of dishonor or shame. — *v. t.* [1] **1.** To put out of favor; dismiss with dishonor. **2.** To bring reproach or shame on; dishonor.

dis-grace'ful (-fŏŏl), *a.* [4] Bringing or involving disgrace; shameful. — **-ly**, *adv.* — **-ness**, *n.* [8].

dis-grun'tle (-grŭn't'l), *v. t.* [1] To put in bad humor; render dissatisfied.

dis-guise' (-gīz'), *v. t.* [1] **1.** To change the appearance of so as to conceal or mislead. **2.** To hide or obscure by a counterfeit appearance; cloak; conceal; mask. — *n.* **1.** A dress put on for concealment or deception. **2.** Any concealment of real by ostensible character; also, that which serves to disguise. — **dis-guis'er** (-gīz'ēr), *n.* [8].

dis-gust' (-gŭst'), *v. t.* To provoke disgust or strong distaste in. — *n.* Aversion or repugnance produced by something loathsome. — **dis-gust'ing**, *p. a.* [4] — **dis-gust'ing-ly**, *adv.* [8].

dis-gust'ful (-fŏŏl), *a.* [4] Disgusting.

dish (dĭsh), *n.* **1.** A vessel, as a platter, plate, or bowl, used for serving food at table. **2.** The food served in a dish; hence, any particular food; as, a dainty *dish.* **3.** The contents or capacity of a dish. — *v. t.* **1.** To put into a dish or dishes. **2.** To make concave like a dish.

dis'ha-bille' (dĭs'ȧ-bēl'; -bĭl'), *n.* Loose, unceremonious attire; negligee.

dis-heart'en (dĭs-här't'n), *v. t.* To discourage.

di-shev'el (dĭ-shĕv'ĕl), *v. t.* [7] To permit or cause (the hair) to hang loosely or disorderly; to put in disorder (one's costume, etc.); to tousle.

dis-hon'est (dĭs-ŏn'ĕst), *a.* [4] **1.** Wanting in honesty or integrity. **2.** Characterized by fraud; knavish. — **dis-hon'est-ly**, *adv.* [8].

dis-hon'es-ty (-ĕs-tĭ), *n.* **1.** Want of honesty, probity, or integrity. **2.** *pl.* **-TIES.** A dishonest act.

dis-hon'or (-ŏn'ēr), *n.* [5] **1.** Disgrace; shame; ignominy. **2.** Indignity; insult. — *v. t.* **1.** To disgrace; bring reproach or shame upon. **2.** To refuse to accept or pay (a draft, check, etc.).

dis-hon'or-a-ble (-ȧ-b'l), *a.* [5] **1.** Wanting in honor; base. **2.** Wanting in honor or esteem; disesteemed. — **dis-hon'or-a-ble-ness**, *n:* [5, 8] — **dis-hon'or-a-bly**, *adv.* [5, 8].

dis'il-lu'sion (dĭs'ĭ-lū'zhŭn), *n.* Act of freeing from an illusion. — *v. t.* To free from illusion.

dis-in'cli-na'tion (dĭs-ĭn'klĭ-nā'shŭn), *n.* State of being disinclined; unwillingness; repugnance.

dis'in-cline' (dĭs'ĭn-klīn'), *v. t.* To deprive of inclination; make unwilling.

dis'in-fect' (-fĕkt'), *v. t.* To free from infection; treat with a disinfectant.

dis'in-fect'ant (-fĕk'tȧnt), *n.* A substance for destroying the germs of infectious disease.

dis'in-fec'tion (-shŭn), *n.* Act of disinfecting.

dis'in-gen'u-ous (-jĕn'ū-ŭs), *a.* [4] Not ingenuous; artful. — **-ly**, *adv.* [8] — **-ness**, *n.* [8].

dis'in-her'it (-hĕr'ĭt), *v. t.* To cut off from, or deprive of, an inheritance.

dis-in'te-grate (dĭs-ĭn'tē-grāt), *v. t. & i.* [1] To separate into component parts.

dis-in'te-gra'tion (-grā'shŭn), *n.* Act of disintegrating; esp., the wearing away or falling to pieces of rocks by action of rain, frost, etc.

---

dis′in-ter′ (dĭs′ĭn-tûr′), v. t.; DIS/IN-TERRED/ (-tûrd′); DIS/IN-TER/RING. To take out of the grave or tomb; exhume. — **dis′in-ter′ment** (-mĕnt), n.

dis-in′ter-est-ed (dĭs-ĭn′tẽr-ĕs-tĕd), a. [4] Not influenced by self-interest; free from selfish motive. — **-ed-ly,** adv. [8] — **-ed-ness,** n. [8].

dis-join′ (-join′), v. t. & i. To disunite or prevent the joining of; separate; sunder; disconnect.

dis-joint′ (-joint′), v. t. & i. **1.** To separate the joints of; separate at the joints. **2.** To break the natural order and relations of; make incoherent.

dis-junc′tive (dĭs-jŭṇk′tĭv), a. [4] Tending to disjoin. — n. A conjunction that expresses an alternative or adversative relation between the words or clauses which it connects, as *either, or, neither, nor, although,* etc. — **-ly,** adv.

disk (dĭsk), n. **1.** A flat circular plate. **2.** *Astron.* The seemingly flat figure of a celestial body, as the moon. **3.** The central portion of the flower head in daisies, asters, etc.

dis-like′ (dĭs-līk′), v. t. [1] To regard with dislike; disapprove. — n. Aversion to something uncongenial or offensive; repugnance; distaste.

dis′lo-cate (dĭs′lō-kāt), v. t. [1] **1.** To displace (esp. a bone from its natural connections); disjoint. **2.** To disarrange, as plans.

dis′lo-ca′tion (-kā′shŭn), n. Displacement.

dis-lodge′ (dĭs-lŏj′), v. t. [1] To drive from a place of rest, hiding, or defense. — **dis-lodg′ment,** n.

dis-loy′al (-loi′ăl), a. [4] Not loyal; false where allegiance is due; faithless. — **-al-ly,** adv. [8].

dis-loy′al-ty (-tĭ), n. Quality of being disloyal.

dis′mal (dĭz′măl), a.; DIS/MAL-LER; DIS/MAL-LEST. Gloomy; dreary. — **dis′mal-ly,** adv.

dis-man′tle (dĭs-măn′t'l), v. t. [1] **1.** To strip of dress or covering. **2.** To strip of furniture and equipments, guns, etc., as a house or a fort.

dis-mast′ (-mȧst′), v. t. To deprive of masts.

dis-may′ (-mā′), v. t. To depress the spirits of; daunt; appall. — n. Loss of spirit through fear.

dis-mem′ber (-mĕm′bẽr), v. t. To tear limb from limb; to tear or cut in pieces, as a body; divide.

dis-mem′ber-ment (-mĕnt), n. A dismembering.

dis-miss′ (-mĭs′), v. t. **1.** To send away; cause or permit to go. **2.** To remove from office, etc.; discharge. **3.** To put out of consideration.

dis-miss′al (-ăl), n. Act of dismissing; state or fact of being dismissed.

dis-mount′ (-mount′), v. i. To alight from a horse. — v. t. **1.** To throw or remove from the carriage, or mount;—said of artillery. **2.** To unhorse. **3.** To remove from a setting, as a jewel.

dis′o-be′di-ence (dĭs′ō-bē′dĭ-ĕns), n. Neglect or refusal to obey; violation of a command.

dis′o-be′di-ent (-ĕnt), a. [4] Neglecting or refusing to obey; refractory. — **be′di-ent-ly,** adv. [8].

dis′o-bey′ (-ō-bā′), v. t. & i. To refuse or neglect to obey.

dis′o-blige′ (dĭs′ō-blīj′), v. t. [1] To refuse to oblige; be unaccommodating to.

dis′o-blig′ing (-blīj′ĭng), p. a. [4] That disobliges; unaccommodating. — **dis′o-blig′ing-ly,** adv. [8].

dis-or′der (dĭs-ôr′dẽr), n. **1.** Want of order; confusion; disarray. **2.** Breach of public order; tumult. **3.** Disease; ailment; illness; sickness. — v. t. To disturb the order or functions of; disarrange.

dis-or′der-ly (-lĭ), a. [4] Characterized by, or contributing to, disorder; disarranged; confused; unruly; lawless. — adv. In a disorderly manner; confusedly. — **dis-or′der-li-ness** (-lĭ-nĕs), n. [8].

dis-or′gan-i-za′tion (-găn-ĭ-zā′shŭn), n. Act of disorganizing, or state of being disorganized.

dis-or′gan-ize (-găn-iz), v. t. [1] To destroy the organization of; throw into disorder; disarrange.

dis-own′ (-ōn′), v. t. To refuse to acknowledge as belonging to or concerning one's self; repudiate.

dis-par′age (-păr′ầj), v. t. [1] To dishonor by bringing discredit or reproach upon; speak slightingly of; depreciate. — **dis-par′ag-ing-ly,** adv.

dis-par′age-ment (-mĕnt), n. **1.** Diminution of esteem or standing. **2.** Act of speaking slightingly; derogation; detraction.

dis-par′i-ty (dĭs-păr′ĭ-tĭ), n.; pl. -TIES (-tĭz). Inequality; difference in age, rank, condition, etc.

dis-pas′sion-ate (dĭs-păsh′ŭn-ȧt), a. [4] Free from passion; not moved by passion. — **-ly,** adv. [8].

dis-patch′ (-păch′), v. t. **1.** To send off or away, as a message or messenger. **2.** To put to death. **3.** To dispose of speedily, as business; execute quickly; finish. — n. **1.** A dispatching. **2.** Prompt disposal; esp., the speedy finishing up of a business; hence, diligence; haste. **3.** A message dispatched or sent with speed. — **dis-patch′er,** n. [8].

dis-pel′ (-pĕl′), v. t.; -PELLED′ (-pĕld′); -PEL′LING. To drive away by scattering; banish; dissipate.

dis-pen′sa-ble (dĭs-pĕn′sȧ-b'l), a. [4] Capable of being dispensed with.

dis-pen′sa-ry (-rĭ), n.; pl. -RIES (-rĭz). A place where medicines are dispensed, esp. without charge or at a small price.

dis′pen-sa′tion (dĭs′pĕn-sā′shŭn), n. **1.** Act of dispensing; distribution; hence, esp., distribution of good and evil by God to man. **2.** That which is dispensed or appointed; esp., a religious system. **3.** A specific arrangement; provision. **4.** A dispensing with some requirement; exemption.

dis-pen′sa-to-ry (dĭs-pĕn′sȧ-tō-rĭ), n.; pl. -RIES (-rĭz). A book of systematic descriptions of drugs.

dis-pense′ (dĭs-pĕns′), v. t. [1] **1.** To deal out; distribute. **2.** To apply, as laws; administer. — v. i. To grant dispensation. — **to dispense with,** to permit the neglect or omission of, as a form; to give up or do without; forgo. — **dis-pens′er,** n. [8].

dis-perse′ (-pûrs′), v. t. [1] **1.** To cause to break apart and go different ways; scatter. **2.** To distribute; dispense; disseminate. — v. i. To separate; hence, be dissipated; vanish.

dis-per′sion (-pûr′shŭn), n. Act of dispersing; state of being dispersed.

dis-pir′it (-pĭr′ĭt), v. t. To deprive of cheerful spirits; dishearten; discourage. — **ed-ly,** adv.

dis-place′ (-plās′), v. t. [1] **1.** To remove from its place. **2.** To crowd out; take the place of. **3.** To remove from an office or the like; discharge.

dis-place′ment (-mĕnt), n. **1.** Act of displacing; state or being displaced. **2.** The volume or weight of a fluid, as water, displaced by a floating body.

dis-play′ (-plā′), v. t. **1.** To unfold; spread out. **2.** To spread before the view; manifest. **3.** In printing, to make conspicuous by large type or varying length of lines. — n. **1.** An unfolding; exhibition. **2.** Ostentatious show; parade.

dis-please' (dĭs-plēz'), v. t. [1] To incur the disapproval of. — v. t. To give displeasure.

dis-pleas'ure (-plĕzh'ūr), n. **1.** The feeling of one who is displeased. **2.** That which displeases.

dis-port' (-pōrt'), n. Sport or diversion. *Archaic.* — v. t. To divert or amuse; make merry; — used reflexively, as in *to disport one's self, itself,* etc.

dis-pos'al (-pōz'ăl), n. **1.** A disposing; transfer or conveyance of anything, as of property. **2.** Power or authority to dispose of; command; control.

dis-pose' (-pōz'), v. t. [1] **1.** To arrange. **2.** To give a tendency to; incline the mind of. — v. i. To arrange or settle matters finally; make disposition. — **to dispose of,** to get rid of; part with; as, *to dispose of* rubbish or property. — **dis-pos'er** (dĭs-pōz'ẽr), n. [8].

dis'po-si'tion (dĭs'pŏ-zĭsh'ŭn), n. **1.** Act or power of disposing. **2.** Tendency; inclination. **3.** Natural or prevailing spirit, or temper of mind.

dis'pos-sess' (-pŏ-zĕs'), v. t. To put out of possession, esp. of land; eject; oust.

dis'pos-ses'sion (-zĕsh'ŭn), n. Act of dispossessing, or state of being dispossessed.

dis-praise' (dĭs-prāz'), n. Act of dispraising; detraction; disparagement.

dis-proof' (-prōōf'), n. A proving to be other than is maintained; confutation; refutation.

dis'pro-por'tion (dĭs'prŏ-pōr'shŭn), n. Want of proportion, symmetry, or due relation. — v. t. To make unsuitable in quantity, form, or fitness.

dis'pro-por'tion-ate (-ăt), a. [4] Not proportioned; unsuitable to something else in bulk, form, value, or extent. — **-ate-ly,** adv. [8] — **-ate-ness,** n. [8].

dis-prove' (dĭs-prōōv'), v. t. To prove to be false.

dis'pu-ta-ble (dĭs'pū-tá-b'l; dĭs-pūt'á-b'l), a. [4] Liable to be disputed, controverted, or contested.

dis'pu-tant (dĭs'pū-tănt), a. [4] Disputing; engaged in controversy. — n. One who disputes.

dis'pu-ta'tion (dĭs'pū-tā'shŭn), n. Act of disputing; controversy; debate.

dis'pu-ta'tious (-shŭs), a. [4] Inclined to dispute.

dis-pute' (dĭs-pūt'), v. i. [1] To contend in argument; discuss; debate; often, to argue irritably; wrangle. — v. t. **1.** To make (something) a subject of disputation; discuss. **2.** To oppose by argument or assertion; controvert. **3.** To contend about; contest. — n. Verbal controversy; controversial discussion; debate.

dis-qual'i-fi-ca'tion (dĭs-kwŏl'ĭ-fĭ-kā'shŭn), n. **1.** Act of disqualifying, or state of being disqualified. **2.** That which disqualifies.

dis-qual'i-fy (dĭs-kwŏl'ĭ-fī), v. t. [2] **1.** To render unfit; incapacitate. **2.** To deprive of some power, right or privilege, as by law.

dis-qui'et (-kwī'ĕt), v. t. To render unquiet; disturb. — n. Want of quiet; uneasiness.

dis-qui'e-tude (-ē-tūd), n. Want of quiet; disquiet.

dis'qui-si'tion (dĭs'kwĭ-zĭsh'ŭn), n. A formal inquiry or discussion; an elaborate dissertation.

dis're-gard' (dĭs're-gärd'), v. t. Not to regard, notice, or observe; hence, to slight as unworthy of regard. — n. A disregarding; neglect.

dis-rel'ish (dĭs-rĕl'ĭsh), n. Want of relish; distaste. — v. t. Not to relish; to feel disgust at.

dis're-pair' (dĭs're-pâr'), n. State of being in need of repair.

dis-rep'u-ta-ble (dĭs-rĕp'ū-tá-b'l), a. [4] Not reputable; dishonorable; low. — **-ta-bly,** adv. [8].

dis're-pute' (dĭs're-pūt'), n. Loss or want of reputation; disesteem; discredit; dishonor.

dis're-spect' (-spĕkt'), n. Want of respect.

dis're-spect'ful (-fŏŏl), a. [4] Wanting in respect; uncivil. — **dis're-spect'ful-ly,** adv. [8].

dis-robe' (dĭs-rōb'), v. t. & i. [1] To divest of a robe; undress.

dis-rupt' (-rŭpt'), v. t. & i. To break asunder; rend.

dis-rup'tion (-rŭp'shŭn), n. Act of rending asunder, or state of being rent asunder.

dis-rup'tive (-tĭv), a. [4] Causing disruption.

dis-sat'is-fac'tion (dĭs-săt'ĭs-făk'shŭn), n. State of being dissatisfied, unsatisfied, or discontented.

dis-sat'is-fy (-săt'ĭs-fī), v. t. [2] To render unsatisfied; displease by lack of something.

dis-sect' (dĭ-sĕkt'), v. t. **1.** To divide into separate parts, as an animal, esp. for examination; anatomize. **2.** To analyze; examine minutely.

dis-sec'tion (-sĕk'shŭn), n. **1.** Act of dissecting. **2.** Anything dissected.

dis-sec'tor (-tẽr), n. One who dissects.

dis-sem'ble (-sĕm'b'l), v. t. [1] **1.** To hide under a false semblance; disguise; mask. **2.** To pass as if unnoticed; ignore. — v. i. To conceal the real fact or sentiments by pretense. — **sem'bler** (-blẽr), n. [8].

dis-sem'i-nate (-ĭ-nāt), v. t. & i. [1] To sow broadcast or as seed; spread abroad; diffuse; disperse; scatter. — **dis-sem'i-na'tor** (-nā'tẽr), n.

dis-sem'i-na'tion (-nā'shŭn), n. A scattering; dispersion; diffusion.

dis-sen'sion (-sĕn'shŭn), n. Disagreement in opinion; contention; discord; quarrel.

dis-sent' (-sĕnt'), v. i. To differ in opinion; disagree; — with *from.* — n. **1.** Act of dissenting; disagreement. **2.** Nonconformity to an established church, esp. that of England. — **dis-sent'er,** n. [8].

dis'ser-ta'tion (dĭs'ẽr-tā'shŭn), n. A formal or elaborate argumentative discourse; a disquisition.

dis-sev'er (dĭ-sĕv'ẽr), v. t. & i. To sever thoroughly; disunite.

dis'si-dence (dĭs'ĭ-dĕns), n. Disagreement; dissent.

dis'si-dent (-dĕnt), a. [4] Not agreeing; different. — n. One who dissents; a dissenter.

dis-sim'i-lar (dĭ-sĭm'ĭ-lár), a. [4] Not similar; unlike. — **dis-sim'i-lar-ly,** adv. [8].

dis-sim'i-lar'i-ty (-lăr'ĭ-tĭ), n.; pl. **-ties** (-tĭz). Difference in appearance or nature; unlikeness.

dis-sim'u-late (dĭ-sĭm'ū-lāt), v. t. & i. [1] To dissemble; feign; pretend.

dis-sim'u-la'tion (dĭ-sĭm'ū-lā'shŭn), n. Act of dissembling; hypocrisy.

dis-sim'u-la-tive (-sĭm'ū-lá-tĭv), a. [4] Pertaining to, or of the nature of, dissimulation.

dis-sim'u-la'tor, n. One who dissimulates.

dis'si-pate (dĭs'ĭ-pāt), v. t. [1] **1.** To break up and drive off; disperse; dispel. **2.** To scatter aimlessly or foolishly. — v. i. **1.** To pass away; vanish. **2.** To be extravagant, wasteful, or dissolute in pursuit of pleasure.

dis'si-pat'ed (-pāt'ĕd), p. a. [4] **1.** Scattered; esp., wasted. **2.** Characterized by dissipation; dissolute; intemperate.

dis'si-pa'tion (-pā'shŭn), n. **1.** Act of dissipating; state of being dissipated; dispersion; diffusion;

---

chair; go; sing, iṅk; then, thin; nature, verdure; yet; zh = z in azure. Numbers refer to §§ in the Special Notes which, with Abbreviations, Signs, etc., precede the Vocabulary.

also, wasteful expenditure. **2.** Diversion or distraction, esp. in frivolity. **3.** A dissolute course of life; dissoluteness.

dis-so'ci-ate (dĭ-sō'shĭ-āt), *v. t. & i.* [1] To separate; disunite; disjoin.

dis-so'ci-a'tion (-shĭ-ā'shŭn ; -sĭ-ā'shŭn), *n.* Act of dissociating; state of being dissociated.

dis'so-lu-ble (dĭs'ŏ-lū-b'l ; dĭ-sŏl'ū-b'l), *a.* [4] Capable of being dissolved; dissolvable.

dis'so-lute (dĭs'ŏ-lūt), *a.* [4] Loose in morals; profligate. — **-ly**, *adv.* [8] — **-ness**, *n.* [8].

dis'so-lu'tion (dĭs'ŏ-lū'shŭn), *n.* Act or process of dissolving or breaking up; disintegration; death.

dis-solv'a-ble (dĭ-zŏl'và-b'l), *a.* [4] Capable of being dissolved.

dis-solve' (-zŏlv'), *v. t. & i.* [1] **1.** To separate into component parts; break up; disintegrate; hence, to destroy. **2.** To break the continuity of; disunite; sunder. **3.** To cause to pass, or to pass, into solution. **4.** To bring or come to an end by dispersion, as an assembly.

dis'so-nance (dĭs'ŏ-nặns), *n.* Discord.

dis'so-nant (-nặnt), *a.* [4] **1.** Marked by dissonance; discordant. **2.** Disagreeing; incongruous; as, *dissonant* faiths. — **dis'so-nant-ly**, *adv.* [8].

dis-suade' (dĭ-swād'), *v. t.* [1] To divert by persuasion; turn from a purpose.

dis-sua'sion (-swā'zhŭn), *n.* Act of dissuading.

dis-sua'sive (-sĭv), *a.* [4] Tending to dissuade.

dis'syl-lab'ic (dĭs'ĭ-lăb'ĭk), *a.* Consisting of two syllables.

dis-syl'la-ble (dĭ-sĭl'à-b'l), *n.* A word of two syllables, as *paper.*

dis'taff (dĭs'tȧf), *n.* The staff for holding the bunch of flax, tow, or wool in spinning.

dis'tance (-tặns), *n.* **1.** The space between two objects. **2.** Quality or condition of being distant; remoteness. — *v. t.* [1] **1.** To place or keep at a distance. **2.** To outstrip; to surpass greatly.

dis'tant (-tặnt), *a.* [4] **1.** Separated; away. **2.** Far off; remote. **3.** Reserved or repelling in manners; not cordial. — **-ly**, *adv.* [8].

dis-taste' (dĭs-tāst'),*n.* **1.** Dislike of food or drink; disrelish. **2.** Aversion; dislike; repugnance.

dis-taste'ful (-fŏŏl), *a.* [4] **1.** Unpleasant to the taste. **2.** Displeasing to the feelings; disagreeable. — **-ful-ly**, *adv.* [8] — **-ful-ness**, *n.* [8].

dis-tem'per (-tĕm'pẽr), *n.* **1.** Ill humor. **2.** Illness; malady; esp., any of various infectious diseases of animals. — *v. t.* To derange or sicken.

dis-tend' (-tĕnd'), *v. t. & i.* To stretch out in all directions; expand; enlarge; swell. — **dis-ten'si-ble** (-tĕn'sĭ-b'l), *a.* [4].

dis-ten'tion, dis-ten'sion (-tĕn'shŭn), *n.* Act of distending, or state of being distended.

dis'tich (dĭs'tĭk),*n.* Two lines of verse; a couplet.

dis-till', dis-til' (dĭs-tĭl'), *v. i. ; -TILLED'** (-tĭld') ; -TILL'ING. To drop; trickle. — *v. t.* **1.** To let fall in drops; let fall (drops). **2.** To obtain by or as by distillation. **3.** To subject to distillation.

dis-till'ate (dĭs-tĭl'ȧt ; dĭs'tĭ-lȧt), *n.* A product of distillation; specifically, a hydrocarbon intermediate between kerosene and gasoline.

dis'til-la'tion (dĭs'tĭ-lā'shŭn), *n.* **1.** Act or process of distilling; that which is formed by distilling. **2.** Specifically, the operation of driving off

gas or vapor from liquids or solids, as by heat, in a retort and condensing the products in a receiver.

dis-till'er (-tĭl'ẽr), *n.* One that distills.

dis-till'er-y (-ĭ), *n. ; pl.* **-ERIES** (-ĭz). Works where distilling is carried on.

dis-tinct' (-tĭngkt'), *a.* [3] **1.** Distinguished by nature; not the same; individual; distinctive. **2.** That may be clearly seen or discerned.

dis-tinc'tion (-tĭngk'shŭn), *n.* **1.** Act of distinguishing; discrimination; also, a difference. **2.** State or quality of being distinguishable or distinct. **3.** A distinguishing quality or mark. **4.** A special recognition; eminence; honor.

dis-tinc'tive (-tĭv), *a.* [4] Marking distinction; distinguishing. — **-ly**, *adv.* [8] — **-ness**, *n.* [8].

dis-tinct'ly (-tĭngkt'lĭ), *adv.* With distinctness.

dis-tinct'ness, *n.* Quality of being distinct.

dis-tin'guish (-tĭn'gwĭsh), *v. t.* **1.** To set apart by visible marks; mark off. **2.** To recognize or discriminate (one thing among or from others) by marks, signs, or characteristics. **3.** To perceive clearly; discern, esp. by a physical sense, as sight or hearing. **4.** To make eminent; confer distinction upon. — *v. i.* To make distinctions; discriminate; — commonly with *between.* — **-a-ble**, *a.* [8].

dis-tin'guished (-gwĭsht), *p. a.* [4] Marked; notable; famous; celebrated.

dis-tort' (-tôrt'), *v. t.* **1.** To twist out of shape; deform. **2.** To pervert in meaning.

dis-tor'tion (-tôr'shŭn), *n.* Act of distorting.

dis-tract' (-trăkt'), *v. t.* **1.** To draw (the sight, mind, or attention) to a different object or in different directions; divert. **2.** To agitate by conflicting passions; harass. **3.** To unsettle the reason of; craze. — **dis-tract'ed-ly** (-trăk'tĕd-lĭ), *adv.* [8].

dis-trac'tion (-trăk'shŭn), *n.* **1.** Act of distracting; confusion; disorder; violent agitation. **2.** That which diverts attention; a diversion.

dis-traught' (dĭs-trôt'), *p. a.* [4] Distracted.

dis-tress' (-trĕs'), *n.* **1.** Extreme suffering of body or mind; anguish. **2.** That which occasions suffering; misfortune. — *v. t.* To affect with distress; pain; afflict.

dis-tress'ful (dĭs-trĕs'fŏŏl), *a.* [4] Full of distress; causing or involving distress.

dis-trib'ute (-trĭb'ūt), *v. t.* [1] **1.** To divide among several or many; allot. **2.** To spread out. **3.** To separate; classify. — **dis-trib'ut-er**, *n.* [8].

dis'tri-bu'tion (dĭs'trĭ-bū'shŭn), *n.* **1.** Act of distributing; disposal. **2.** That which is distributed.

dis-trib'u-tive (dĭs-trĭb'ŭ-tĭv), *a.* [4] **1.** Tending or serving to distribute. **2.** *Gram.* Expressing separation among or into individuals or individual groups; as, a *distributive* adjective, as *either, every.* — *n.* A distributive word. — **-ly**, *adv.* [8].

dis-trib'u-tor (-ŭ-tẽr), *n.* One that distributes.

dis'trict (dĭs'trĭkt), *n.* **1.** A defined portion of a state, city, etc. **2.** A region; quarter; tract.

dis-trust' (dĭs-trŭst'), *v. t.* To feel a lack or the absence of trust in; mistrust. — *n.* Lack of trust.

dis-trust'ful (-fŏŏl), *a.* [4] Wanting confidence or trust; suspicious. — **dis-trust'ful-ly**, *adv.* [8].

dis-turb' (-tûrb'), *v. t.* **1.** To throw into disorder or confusion; stir up; unsettle. **2.** To agitate the mind of; disquiet. **3.** To turn from a regular or designed course; to cause to shift, stop, or go awry.

āle, senȧte, câre, ăm, *ă*ccount, ärm, ȧsk, sof*à* ; ēve, ĕvent, ĕnd, recĕnt, makẽr; īce, ĭll; ōld, ȯbey, ôrb, ŏdd, sŏft, cŏnnect ; ūse, ŭnite, ûrn, ŭp, circŭs; fŏŏd, fŏŏt ; out, oil ;

dis-turb′ance (-tûr′băns), *n.* Act of disturbing; state or fact of being disturbed; uproar; confusion.

dis-turb′er (-bẽr), *n.* One that disturbs; troubler.

dis-un′ion (-ūn′yŭn), *n.* Separation; dissension.

dis′u-nite′ (dĭs′ū-nīt′), *v. t.* [1] To destroy the unity of; divide. — *v. i.* To part; fall asunder.

dis-use′ (dĭs-ūs′), *n.* Cessation of use; desuetude.

dis-use′ (-ūz′), *v. t.* [1] To cease to use.

ditch (dĭch), *n.* A trench dug in the earth, as for drainage. — *v. t.* **1.** To dig a ditch in or around. **2.** To throw into a ditch. *U. S.* — **ditch′er,** *n.* [8].

dit′to (dĭt′ō), *n.; pl.* -TOS (-ōz). The aforesaid thing; the same (as before); — often contracted to *do.*, or represented by two "turned commas" (''), or small marks. Used in bills, tables, etc., to save repetition. — *adv.* As aforesaid; in the same way.

dit′ty (-ĭ), *n.; pl.* -TIES (-ĭz). A song; a little simple poem, intended to be sung.

di′u-ret′ic (dĭ′ū-rĕt′ĭk), *a.* [4] Tending to increase the secretion of urine. — *n.* A diuretic medicine.

di-ur′nal (dī-ûr′nǎl), *a.* **1.** Daily. **2.** Relating to the daytime. —**nal-ly,** *adv.* [8].

di-van′ (dĭ-văn′; *commonly* dī′văn), *n.* A cushioned seat, or a large, low sofa or couch.

dive (dīv), *v. i.; DIVED* (dīvd); *DIV′ING* (dīv′ĭng); *Colloq. pret., chiefly U. S.,* DOVE (dōv). **1.** To plunge into water, esp. headforemost. **2.** To penetrate into anything with the body or hand, esp. hastily or suddenly. **3.** To plunge deeply into any subject, business, etc. — *n.* **1.** Act of one who dives. **2.** A place of low resort. *Chiefly U. S.*

div′er (dīv′ẽr), *n.* One that dives.

di-verge′ (dĭ-vûrj′), *v. i.* [1] To extend from a common point in different directions; to deviate.

di-ver′gence (dĭ-vûr′jĕns), *n.* Act of diverging; state of being divergent; deviation.

di-ver′gen-cy (-jĕn-sĭ), *n.; pl.* -GENCIES (-sĭz). Divergence.

di-ver′gent (-jĕnt), *a.* [4] **1.** That diverges. **2.** Relating to, or characterized by, divergence.

di′vers (dī′vẽrz), *a.* Several; various; — in *pl.*

di-verse′ (dĭ-vûrs′; dī′vẽrs), *a.* [4] Different; unlike. — **di-verse′ly,** *adv.* [8].

di-ver′si-fi-ca′tion (dĭ-vûr′sĭ-fĭ-kā′shŭn), *n.* Act of diversifying, or state of being diversified.

di-ver′si-fy (dĭ-vûr′sĭ-fī), *v. t.* [2] To make diverse, or various, in form or quality; variegate.

di-ver′sion (-shŭn), *n.* **1.** Act of diverting. **2.** That which diverts, or amuses; pastime; entertainment.

di-ver′si-ty (-sĭ-tĭ), *n.; pl.* -TIES (-tĭz). A state of difference; a difference; a variety.

di-vert′ (-vûrt′), *v. t.* **1.** To turn aside (from or to); deflect. **2.** To amuse; entertain.

di-vest′ (-vĕst′), *v. t.* **1.** To unclothe; strip. **2.** To deprive; dispossess, as of rights.

di-vide′ (-vīd′), *v. t.* [1] **1.** To part asunder (a whole); separate into parts. **2.** To cause to be separate; keep apart. **3.** To make partition of among a number; apportion. **4.** To disunite; set at variance. — *v. i.* To be separated; undergo division; branch. — *n.* A dividing ridge between two drainage areas; a watershed.

div′i-dend (dĭv′ĭ-dĕnd), *n.* **1.** A sum or quantity to be divided and distributed, or the share that falls to each individual. **2.** *Math.* A number or quantity that is to be divided.

di-vid′er (dĭ-vīd′ẽr), *n.* **1.** One that divides. **2.** Compasses; — usually in *pl.*

div′i-na′tion (dĭv′ĭ-nā′shŭn), *n.* **1.** Act of divining; a foreseeing or foretelling of future events. **2.** An augury; prediction.

di-vine′ (dĭ-vīn′), *a.* [3] **1.** Of or pertaining to God. **2.** Proceeding from God. **3.** Addressed or appropriated to God; religious. **4.** Of the nature of God; godlike; heavenly. — *n.* A priest; clergyman; theologian. — *v. t.* [1] To perceive through reasoning, sympathy, or intuition; detect; surmise. — *v. i.* **1.** To use or practice divination; prophesy. **2.** To feel a foreboding. **3.** To conjecture. —**-ly,** *adv.* [8] —**-ness,** *n.* [8] — **di-vin′er** (-vĭn′ẽr), *n.* [8].

di-vin′i-ty (dĭ-vĭn′ĭ-tĭ), *n.; pl.* -TIES. **1.** State or quality of being divine; deity. **2.** A deity; a god. **3.** Supernatural power or virtue. **4.** Theology.

di-vis′i-bil′i-ty (dĭ-vĭz′ĭ-bĭl′ĭ-tĭ), *n.* Quality of being divisible.

di-vis′i-ble (-vĭz′ĭ-b'l), *a.* Capable of being divided.

di-vi′sion (-vĭzh′ŭn), *n.* **1.** Act or process of dividing; state of being divided. **2.** A section; compartment. **3.** Disunion; dissension; discord. **4.** *Math.* Process of, or rule for, finding how many times one number or quantity is contained in another. The sign of division is ÷, read *divided by.* **5.** *Mil.* Two or more brigades under a general officer.

di-vi′sion-al (-ăl), *a.* Pert. to division or a division.

di-vi′sor (dĭ-vī′zẽr), *n.* *Math.* The number by which the dividend is divided.

di-vorce′ (-vōrs′), *n.* **1.** A legal dissolution of marriage. **2.** Separation; disunion. — *v. t.* [1] **1.** To put away or separate by divorce. **2.** To disunite.

di-vor′cee′ (dĭ-vōr′sē′), *n.* A person divorced.

di-vorce′ment (dĭ-vōrs′mĕnt), *n.* Divorce.

di-vulge′ (dĭ-vŭlj′), *v. t.* [1] To make public; reveal; disclose; tell; as, to *divulge* a secret.

diz′zy (dĭz′ĭ), *a.* [3] **1.** Giddy; hence, mentally confused or unsteady. **2.** Causing, or tending to cause, giddiness. — *v. t.* [2] To make dizzy. —**-zi-ly** (-ĭ-lĭ), *adv.* [8] —**-ness,** *n.* [8].

do (dō), *n.* *Music.* The first tone of the scale.

do (dōō), *v. t.* or *auxiliary; pret.* DID (dĭd); *p. p.* DONE (dŭn); *p. pr. & vb. n.* DO′ING (dōō′ĭng). **1.** To bring about; produce, as an effect or result; render; pay; as, to *do* him reverence. **2.** To perform, as an action; execute; transact. **3.** To bring to an end by action; finish; — used in the p. p.; as, I have *done* weeping. **4.** To put forth; exert; as, to *do* one's best. **5.** To treat or deal with; as, to *do* one's hair. **6.** To serve; suit; suffice. *Colloq.* **7.** To put or bring into a form or state; — esp. in : **to do to death, to put to death; to do away** (often **do away with**), to put away : **to do for,** etc.

☞ *Do* is often used to add emphasis: as. but I *do* see; *do* help me. It is often substituted for verbs, to save repetition; as. he thinks as we *do.*

— *v. i.* **1.** To act or behave; conduct one's self. **2.** To fare; prosper; as, how do you *do?* **3.** To act; work; achieve. **4.** To suffice: avail; serve.

dob′bin (dŏb′ĭn), *n.* A farm horse; a gentle family horse; sometimes, a worn-out horse.

doc′ile (dŏs′ĭl), *a.* [4] Disposed to be taught or trained; tractable; easily managed. —**-ly,** *adv.* [8].

do-cil′i-ty (dŏ-sĭl′ĭ-tĭ), *n.* Tractableness.

---

dock (dŏk), *n.* Any of various weeds of the buckwheat family, usually with long taproots.

dock, *n.* **1.** An artificial basin to receive vessels, having gates to keep in, or shut out, the water. **2.** A slip or waterway, as between two piers, for the reception of ships, sometimes including the piers themselves. — *v. t.* To haul (a ship) into a dock. — *v. i.* To come or go into dock.

dock, *n.* The place in court where a prisoner is placed.

dock (dŏk), *n.* The solid part of an animal's tail. — *v. t.* **1.** To cut off, as the end of a thing; clip. **2.** To shorten; deduct from; as, to *dock* one's wages.

dock'age (-ăj), *n.* **1.** A charge for the use of a dock. **2.** Docking facilities.

dock'et (-ĕt), *n.* **1.** *Law.* An abridged entry of a proceeding in an action, or a register of such entries. **2.** A schedule of matters for action in an assembly. *U. S.* — *v. t.* **1.** To indorse with an abstract of contents, as a letter or a bill. **2.** *Law.* To enter in a docket.

dock'yard/ (-yärd/), *n.* A storage place for naval stores and timber, with facilities to repair ships.

doc'tor (dŏk'tẽr), *n.* **1.** One holding the highest degree conferred by a university or college. **2.** One licensed to practice medicine; a physician or surgeon.—*v.t.* **1.** To treat as a physician does. *Colloq.* **2.** To tamper with; falsify. *Slang.*

doc'tor-ate (-ăt), *n.* Doctor's degree or rank.

ioc'tri-nal (-năl), *a.* [4] Pert. to doctrine.

doc'trine (-trĭn), *n.* A principle, or the body of principles, in any branch of knowledge; tenet.

doc'u-ment (-ŭ-mĕnt), *n.* A writing conveying information, esp. an original or official paper.

doc'u-men'ta-ry (-mĕn'tȧ-rĭ), *a.* [4] Consisting of, or of the nature of, documents.

dod'der (dŏd'ẽr), *n.* A kind of leafless parasitic plant with yellow or whitish threadlike stem.

do-dec'a-gon (dṓ-dĕk'ȧ-gŏn), *n.* A polygon of twelve sides.

dodge (dŏj), *v. i. & t.* [1] **1.** To start suddenly aside, or evade by so doing. **2.** To evade, as a duty, by craft. — *n.* Act of dodging; also, an artful device. — **dodg'er** (-ẽr), *n.* [8].

io'do (dṓ'dṓ), *n.; pl.* -DOES *or* -DOS (-dṓz). A very large flightless bird of Mauritius. It is now extinct.

ioe (dṓ), *n.* The female of the deer, rabbit, etc.

do'er (dōō'ẽr), *n.* One who does; actor; agent.

does (dŭz), *3d pers. sing. pres.* of DO.

doe'skin/ (dṓ'skĭn/), *n.* **1.** The skin of the doe, or a leather made of it. **2.** A soft, firm woolen cloth.

doff (dŏf), *v. t.* To put off, as dress; remove or lift (the hat or cap); fig., to get rid of.

dog (dŏg), *n.* **1.** A flesh-eating domestic animal related to the wolves, jackals, and foxes; also, any member of the family to which these animals belong. **2.** Any of various devices for holding, gripping, or fastening something. — *v. t.;* DOGGED (dŏgd); DOG'GING (dŏg'ĭng). To hunt or track like a hound; to worry as if by dogs.

dog'cart/ (-kärt/), *n.* A kind of light one-horse carriage with two seats set back to back.

dog days. A sultry, oppressive period variously placed between early July and early September.

doge (dṓj), *n.* The chief magistrate in the former republics of Venice and Genoa.

dog'-ear/, *n.* = DOG'S-EAR.

dog'fish/ (-fĭsh/), *n.* Any of various small sharks.

dog'ged (dŏg'ĕd), *a.* [3] Obstinately persistent. — **dog'ged-ly**, *adv.* [8].

dog'ger-el (-ẽr-ĕl), *a.* Of verse, low in style and often irregular in measure; trivial.—*n.* A sort of loose or irregular verse, esp. burlesque or comic.

dog'gish (-ĭsh), *a.* [4] Like a dog; snarling.

dog'ma (dŏg'mȧ), *n.; pl.* E.-MAS (-mȧz), L.-MATA (-mȧ-tȧ). That which is held as an opinion; tenet; doctrine, esp. one laid down by a church.

dog-mat'ic (dŏg-măt'ĭk), **dog-mat'i-cal** (-ĭ-kăl), *a.* [4] **1.** Of or pertaining to dogma. **2.** Characterized by dogmatism. — **-i-cal-ly**, *adv.* [8].

dog'ma-tism (dŏg'mȧ-tĭz'm), *n.* Positive assertion in matters oi opinion, esp. when unwarranted.

dog'ma-tist (-tĭst), *n.* A dogmatic person.

dog'ma-tize (-tīz), *v. i.* [1] To speak or write dogmatically.

dog's'-ear/ (dŏgz'-), *n.* The corner of a leaf, in a book, turned down. — **dog's-eared**/ (-ẽrd/), *a.*

Dog Star. Sirius, the brightest star in the heavens.

dog'tooth/ **vi'o-let.** A plant of the lily family bearing a nodding yellow or white flower.

dog'trot/, *n.* A gentle trot.

dog'wood/ (-wŏŏd/), *n.* Any of various plants, esp. a flowering tree or shrub with a very hard wood.

doi'ly (doi'lĭ), *n.; pl.* -LIES (-lĭz). A small fancy napkin or piece of linen, lace, etc., for a table.

do'ing (dōō'ĭng), *n.* Anything done; hence, conduct; —usually in *pl.*

dol'drums (dŏl'drŭmz), *n. pl.* **1.** Dullness; the dumps. **2.** *Naut.* A part of the ocean, near the equator, abounding in calms.

dole (dōl), *n.* **1.** A part; share; lot. **2.** A distribution, esp. of gifts of charity; also, that which is distributed. — *v. t.* [1] To deal out in small portions; distribute, as a dole.

dole'ful (-fŏŏl), *a.* [4] Full of grief; sad; gloomy. — **dole'ful-ly**, *adv.* [8].— **ness**, *n.* [8].

doll (dŏl), *n.* A child's puppet or toy baby.

dol'lar (dŏl'ẽr), *n.* **1. a** A United States silver coin of the legal value of 100 cents; also, a gold coin (no longer issued) worth 100 cents, the monetary unit of the U. S. (symbol, $). **b** A bank note, treasury note, or the like, of the legal value of 100 cents. **2.** Any of various other coins, as the Mexican peso.

do'lor (dṓ'lẽr), *n.* [5] Grief; distress; pain. *Poet.*

dol'or-ous (dŏl'ẽr-ŭs), *a.* [4] **1.** Grievous; painful. **2.** Full of grief; sad. — **dol'or-ous-ly**, *adv.* [8].

Dogtooth Violet. (⅛)

Dolphin, 1. ¹⁄₄₅

dol'phin (-fĭn), *n.* **1.** Any of various small-toothed cetaceans, some being commonly called *porpoises*. **2.** Either of two ocean fishes esteemed as food.

---

dolt (dōlt), *n.* A heavy, stupid fellow. — **-ish**, *a.*

do-main' (dŏ-mān'), *n.* **1.** An estate held in possession; landed estate. **2.** The territory or region over which dominion is exerted; scope; range.

dome (dōm), *n.* A cupola, esp. a large one.

do-mes'tic (dŏ-mĕs'tĭk), *a.* [4] **1.** Of or pertaining to one's house, home, or family. **2.** Of or pertaining to one's own country; native. **3.** Remaining much at, or devoted to, home. **4.** Living in association with man; domesticated; not wild.—*n.* A hired household assistant.

do-mes'ti-cate (-tĭ-kāt), *v. t. & i.* [1] To make or become domestic.

do-mes'ti-ca'tion (-kā'shŭn), *n.* Act of domesticating, or state of being domesticated.

do'mes-tic'i-ty (dō'mĕs-tĭs'ĭ-tĭ), *n.* State or character of being domestic.

dom'i-cile (dŏm'ĭ-sĭl), *n.* A dwelling place; residence. — *v. t. & i.* [1] To establish in a domicile, or fixed residence.

dom'i-nance (dŏm'ĭ-năns), *n.* Quality or state of being dominant.

dom'i-nant (-nănt), *a.* Ruling; prevailing; controlling.

dom'i-nate (-nāt), *v. t.* [1] To control; rule; govern.—*v. i.* To control; predominate.

dom'i-na'tion (-nā'shŭn), *n.* Act of dominating; supremacy; often, arbitrary or insolent sway.

dom'i-na'tor (-nā'tẽr), *n.* One who dominates.

dom'i-neer' (dŏm'ĭ-nēr'), *v. i. & t.* To rule insolently or arbitrarily; tyrannize; swagger.

dom'i-neer'ing, *p. a.* [4] That domineers; tyrannical. —**-ly**, *adv.* [8].

dom'i-nie (dŏm'ĭ-nĭ; dō'mĭ-nĭ), *n.* **1.** A schoolmaster. **2.** A clergyman.

do-min'ion (dŏ-mĭn'yŭn), *n.* **1.** Supreme authority; sovereignty. **2.** A territory governed.

dom'i-no (dŏm'ĭ-nō), *n.; pl.* -NOS or (esp. the pieces for a game) -NOES (-nōz). **1.** A masquerade costume consisting of a robe, with adjustable hood, and a light half mask. **2.** A kind of mask, esp. a half mask. **3.** *pl.* A game played with, usually, flat, oblong pieces dotted on one side after the manner of dice. Also, *sing.*, one of these pieces.

don (dŏn), *n.* **1.** [*cap.*] Sir; Mr.;—a title in Spain, now common to all classes. **2.** A Spanish nobleman or gentleman. **3.** A grand personage.

don, *v. t.;* DONNED (dŏnd); DON'NING. To put on.

do'nate (dō'nāt), *v. t.* [1] To make a donation of.

do-na'tion (dŏ-nā'shŭn), *n.* Act of giving, or that which is given, as a present.

don'a-tive (dŏn'á-tĭv), *n.* A gift; largess; present. — *a.* [4] Of the nature of, or subject to, donation.

done (dŭn), *p. p.* of DO.

don'jon (dŭn'jŭn; dŏn'jŏn), *n.* A massive chief tower in medieval castles.

don'key (dŏn'kĭ), *n.; pl.* -KEYS (-kĭz). **1.** The ass. **2.** A stupid or obstinate fellow; an ass.

do'nor (dō'nŏr), *n.* One who gives, or presents.

don't (dōnt). Colloq. contr. of *do not*.

doom (dōōm), *n.* **1.** Judgment; sentence. **2.** That to which one is doomed; destiny or fate; hence, ruin; death. — *v. t.* **1.** To pronounce judgment upon; condemn. **2.** To destine; fix; ordain.

dooms'day' (dōōmz'dā'), *n.* **1.** The day of the final judgment of mankind. **2.** A day of judgment.

door (dōr), *n.* **1.** The movable hinged or sliding frame or barrier by which an entrance, as into a house, may be closed. **2.** A doorway.

door'way' (-wā'), *n.* Passage such as a door closes.

dor'man-cy (dôr'măn-sĭ), *n.* Dormant state.

dor'mant (-mănt), *a.* [4] Sleeping; asleep; hence, inactive; in abeyance.

dor'mer (dôr'mẽr), *n.* A dormer window, or window vertical in a roof; also, the projecting part in which it is contained.

dor'mi-to-ry (-mĭ-tŏ-rĭ), *n.; pl.* -RIES (rĭz). A sleeping room; building containing a series of sleeping rooms.

Dormer window.

dor'mouse' (-mous'), *n.; pl.* -MICE (-mīs'). Any of several small Old World rodents somewhat resembling small squirrels.

dor'sal (-săl), *a.* Pertaining to the back.

do'ry (dō'rĭ), *n.; pl.* -RIES (-rĭz). A kind of flat-bottomed boat.

Dories.

dose (dōs), *n.* The measured quantity of a medicine to be taken at one time. — *v. t.* [1] To give a dose or doses to.

dost (dŭst), 2*d pers. sing. pres. indic.* of DO.

dot (dŏt), *n.* A small point or spot; a speck. — *v.t.;* DOT'TED, DOT'TING. To mark with or as with dots.

dot, *n.* A woman's marriage portion, or dowry.

dot'age (dōt'ăj), *n.* Feebleness of mind, esp. in old age; senility.

do'tard (dō'tärd), *n.* A foolish or imbecile person; esp., one whose mind is impaired by age.

dote (dōt), *v. i.* [1] **1.** To be weak-minded, esp. from age. **2.** To be foolishly fond; love to excess; — with *on* or *upon*. — **dot'ing-ly**, *adv* [8].

doth (dŭth), 3*d pers. sing. pres.* of DO. *Archaic.*

dou'ble (dŭb''l), *a.* **1.** Twofold; doubled: made or being twice as great, as large, as much, as many, as strong, as valuable, etc. **2.** Being in pairs; coupled. **3.** Twofold in relation, character, or action. **4.** *Bot.* Having the floral leaves considerably increased beyond the natural number.—*n.* **1.** Twice as much; twice the number, quantity, value, or the like. **2.** The counterpart of another; duplicate. **3.** A sharp turn in running, or in a river. — *adv.* Doubly; in a pair. — *v. t.* [1] **1.** To multiply by two; make twice as great. **2.** To make of two thicknesses by bending together; fold. **3.** To amount to twice as much as. **4.** To pass around or by. — *v. i.* **1.** To be doubled. **2.** To return on one's track.

dou'ble-quick', *a.* Of, or performed in, the fastest time or step in marching, next to a run. — *n.* Double-quick time, step, or march.

dou'blet (dŭb'lĕt), *n.* **1.** A close-fitting body garment for men, worn from about the 15th to the 17th century. **2.** One of a pair. **3.** A pair.

dou-bloon' (dŭb-lōōn'), *n.* A Spanish gold coin, no longer issued, originally worth about $16, later $5.

dou'bly (dŭb'lĭ), *adv.* In twice the quantity; to twice the degree; in a twofold manner; twice.

doubt (dout), *v. i.* To waver in opinion; hesitate in belief. — *v. t.* **1.** To hold questionable; be inclined not to believe; distrust. **2.** To be apprehensive of; fear; also, to suspect; surmise. — *n.* **1.** Uncertainty of mind arising from insufficient knowledge or evidence; hesitation; uncertainty. **2.** Uncertainty of condition.— **doubt'er**, *n.* [8].

doubt'ful (dout'fŏŏl), *a.* [4] **1.** Admitting of doubt; not obvious, or certain. **2.** Of questionable character. **3.** Not settled in opinion; undetermined; hesitating. **4.** Of uncertain issue or event. — **-ly**, *adv.* [8] — **-ness**, *n.* [8].

doubt'less, *a.* Free from doubt.— *adv.* Undoubtedly. — **doubt'less-ly**, *adv.* [8].

douche (dōōsh), *n.* A jet of water or vapor directed upon or into a part of the body; also, a bath taken by means of a douche.

dough (dō), *n.* **1.** Paste of bread, pie, or the like. **2.** Something of the consistency of such paste.

dough'nut' (-nŭt'), *n.* A small cake usually sweetened, often made with yeast, fried in deep fat.

dough'ty (dou'tĭ), *a.* [3] Able; strong; valiant. *Now Archaic, or somewhat Humorous.*— **dough'ti-ly** (-tĭ-lĭ), *adv.* [8] — **dough'ti-ness**, *n.* [8].

dough'y (dō'ĭ), *a.* [3] Like dough; pasty.

Doug'las spruce (dŭg'lăs). A valuable Western timber tree of the pine family.

douse (dous), *v. t. & i.* [1] To duck; immerse; also, to drench; as, to *douse* one in, or with, water.

dove (dōv), *colloquial pret.* of DIVE. *v. i.*

dove (dŭv), *n.* A pigeon.

dove'cot' (dŭv'kŏt')) *n.* An elevated box, with
dove'cote (-kōt';-kŏt)) compartments, for doves.

dove'tail' (-tāl'),*n. Carpentry.* A flaring tenon or a mortise making an interlocking joint. — *v. t.* **1.** *Carpentry.* **a** To cut to a dovetail. **b** To join by dovetails. **2.** To fit in or connect strongly or nicely.

Dovetails.

dow'a-ger (dou'ā-jẽr),*n.* **1.** A widow who has a title or property that came from her deceased husband. **2.** A dignified elderly woman. *Colloq.*

dow'dy (-dĭ), *a.* [3] Shabbily dull; not smart or bright and tidy; as, a *dowdy* bonnet.

dow'el (-ĕl), *n.* A pin fitting into a hole in an abutting piece to prevent motion or slipping.

dow'er (-ẽr), *n.* **1.** That portion of, or interest in, the real estate of a deceased husband which the law gives for life to his widow. **2.** Dowry. **3.** Personal endowment; natural gifts. — *v. t.* To supply with a dower or dowry; endow.

down (doun), *n.* **1.** Soft fluffy feathers, as those of young birds or those under the ordinary feathers of adult birds. **2.** A soft hairy outgrowth.

down, *n.* [*Usually in pl.*] **1.** A hill; esp., a hillock of sand cast up by the wind along the shore. **2.** A tract of open upland.

down, *adv.* **1.** In the direction of gravity; toward or in a lower place or position; below. **2.** From a past or remote time or period. **3.** From a greater to a less bulk, amount, or strength, or from a thinner to a thicker consistence. **4.** On or upon a table or counter; hence, (paid) in cash or on the spot. — *prep.* In a descending direction along; from a higher to a lower place, on or within. — *v. t.* To put or bring down. *Archaic or Colloq.* — *a.* Downward; descending; sloping; as, a *down* grade. — *n.* A descent; a reverse of fortune.

down'cast' (-kȧst'), *a.* [4] Cast down; directed downward; dejected; as, *downcast* eyes.

down'fall' (-fôl'), *n.* A fall or descent; hence, ruin. — **down'fall'en** (-fôl'n), *a.* [4].

down'heart'ed (-härt'ĕd), *a.* [4] Dejected; low-spirited. — **-ed-ly**, *adv.* [8] — **-ed-ness**, *n.* [8].

down'hill' (-hĭl'), *adv.* Down the slope of a hill; downward. — (doun'hĭl'), *a.* Sloping.

down'right' (doun'rīt'; doun'rīt'), *adv.* Thoroughly; completely.—(doun'rīt'), *a.* **1.** Directed vertically downward. **2.** Plain; direct; positive. **3.** Absolute; thorough.

down'stairs' (-stärz'), *adv.* Down the stairs; on or to a lower floor.— (doun'stärz'), *a.* Below stairs.

down'trod'den (-trŏd'n), *a.* [4] Trodden down; abused by superior power.

down'ward (-wẽrd), *adv.* **1.** From a higher to a lower place, condition, etc. **2.** From an earlier time. — *a.* Descending; inclined downward.

down'wards (-wẽrdz), *adv.* = DOWNWARD.

down'y (doun'ĭ), *a.* [3] **1.** Covered with down. **2.** Made of or resembling down; downlike; soft.

dow'ry (dou'rĭ), *n.; pl.* -RIES (-rĭz). **1.** The money, goods, or estate which a woman brings to her husband in marriage; dot. **2.** Gift of nature; talent.

dox-ol'o-gy (dŏk-sŏl'ŏ-jĭ), *n.; pl.* -GIES (-jĭz). A kind of hymn or formula expressing praise to God.

doze (dōz), *v. i.* [1] To sleep lightly; be drowsy or dull. — *n.* A light sleep; drowse.

doz'en (dŭz''n), *n.; pl.* DOZEN (before another noun), DOZENS (-'nz). A collection of twelve objects.

doz'y (dōz'ĭ), *a.* [3] Drowsy.

drab, *n.* A dull brownish yellow or yellowish gray. — *a.* Of the color of drab.

drab'ble (drăb''l), *v. t. & i.* [1] To draggle.

drachm (drăm), *n.* Var. of DRAM, the weight.

draft (drȧft), *n.* **1.** Act of drawing, or hauling a load. **2.** Act of drinking or inhaling, as liquor, smoke, etc.; also, a drink; potion; inhalation. **3.** A current of any sort; current of air. **4.** A preliminary sketch or outline. **5.** A drawing of money from a fund or stock; an order directing the payment of money. **6.** The detaching or selecting of individuals from a mass, or those so detached or selected. **7.** Depth of water necessary to float a ship. — *v. t.* **1.** To draw the preliminary sketch or plan of. **2.** To detach for service.

drafts'man (drȧfts'mȧn), *n.; pl.* -MEN. One who makes mechanical plans or sketches, etc.

draft'y (drȧf'tĭ), *a.* [3] Having a draft, or current of air; abounding in drafts; as, a *drafty* room.

drag (drăg),*v. t.*; DRAGGED (drăgd); DRAG'GING (-ĭng). **1.** To draw slowly or heavily; haul. **2. a** To dredge or search by means of a drag, grapnel, or the like. **b** To harrow. **3.** To continue tediously; — usually with *on* or *out*. — *v. i.* **1.** To be drawn along on the ground; trail. **2.** To move onward heavily or slowly. **3.** To hang or lag behind. — *n.* **1.** Act of dragging; anything dragged. **2.** A kind of heavy harrow. **3.** A device for dragging along the bottom under water, for dredging, etc. **4.** A kind of heavy coach with seats on top. **5.** Anything that retards; a clog.

drag'gle (drăg''l), *v. t.* [1] To wet and soil by dragging on the ground or in the wet; drabble. — *v. i.* **1.** To be draggled. **2.** To follow slowly; straggle.

ᾱie, senᾱte, cȧre, ăm, *ȧ*ccount; ȧrm, ȧsk, sofᾱ; ēve, ĕvent, ĕnd, recĕnt, makẽr; Ice, Ĭll; ōld, ōbey, ôrb, ŏdd, sôft, cŏnnect; ūse, ūnite, ûrn, ŭp, circŭs; fōōd, fŏŏt; out, oil;

drag'net' (-nĕt'), *n.* Net to be drawn along the bottom of water or over ground to catch something.

drag'o-man (drăg'ô-măn), *n. ; pl.* -MANS (-mănz). An interpreter; — so called in the East.

drag'on (drăg'ŭn), *n.* A fabulous animal, generally a monstrous, crested, winged, scaly reptile.

dragon fly. Any of several large harmless insects that feed on gnats, mosquitoes, etc.

dra-goon' (dra-gōōn'), *n.* Orig., a mounted infantryman; now, a cavalryman, usu. heavily equipped.

drain (drān), *v. t. & i.* **1.** To draw or flow off by degrees; draw off utterly; exhaust. **2.** To make or become gradually dry or empty. — *n.* **1.** A draining. **2.** A channel, trench, or the like by which liquid is drained.

drain'age (-ăj), *n.* **1.** Act or process of draining; that which is drained off. **2.** System of drains.

drake (drāk), *n.* The male of the duck; a male duck.

ram (drăm), *n.* **a** A weight; in *apothecaries' weight*, 1-8th of an ounce, or 60 grains (3.888 grams); in *avoirdupois weight*, 1-16th of an ounce, or 27.34 grains (1.77 grams). **b** Short for FLUID DRAM. **2.** A small drink or draft.

dra'ma (drä'mä), *n.* **1.** A composition intended to portray life or character, esp. one designed to be performed on the stage. **2.** Dramatic art, literature, or affairs.

dra-mat'ic (dra-măt'ĭk), *a.* [4] Of or pertaining to the drama; suited to the drama. — **-i-cal-ly**, *adv.*

dra-mat'ics, *n. pl.* Dramatic writings; plays.

dram'a-tist (drăm'a-tĭst), *n.* A playwright.

dram'a-ti-za'tion (-tĭ-zā'shŭn), *n.* Act of dramatizing; a dramatized version.

dram'a-tize (-tīz), *v. t.* [1] **1.** To make into a drama, as a story. **2.** To represent dramatically.

drank (drăngk), *pret.* of DRINK.

drape (drāp), *v. t.* [1] **1.** To cover or adorn with or as with drapery. **2.** To arrange in folds; hang.

dra'per (drā'pẽr), *n.* A dealer in cloths.

ra'per-y (-ĭ), *n. ; pl.* -PERIES (-ĭz). **1.** Cloth, or woolen stuffs in general. **2.** A textile fabric for decoration, esp. hangings, or loose vestments.

dras'tic (drăs'tĭk), *a.* [4] Acting rapidly and violently; extreme in effect; as, a *drastic* remedy.

draught (drȧft), *n. & v. t.* See DRAFT, *n. & v. t.*

draughts (drȧfts), *n.* Checkers, the game.

draw (drô), *v. t.; pret.* DREW (drōō) ; *p. p.* DRAWN (drôn); *p. pr.& vb.n.* DRAW'ING. **1.** To pull so as to cause to follow; haul; drag. **2.** To attract; allure; induce. **3.** To inhale; also, to utter or produce with inhalation. **4.** To cause to come out; extract; bring forth. **5.** To deduce or infer, as from premises; also, to derive or take, as from a source, a fund, etc. **6.** To disembowel; eviscerate. **7.** To lengthen, protract, or stretch. **8.** To produce by or as by tracing a pen or pencil over a surface. **9.** To write in due form; as, to *draw* a deed. **10.** To require (such a depth) to float; — of a vessel. **11.** To leave (a contest) undecided.

draw (drô), *v. i.* **1.** To move; come or go; — with prepositions and adverbs of direction; as, to *draw on*, to advance; to *draw* near, etc. **2.** To pull; move something by pulling. **3.** To contract; shrink. **4.** To attract; entice. **5.** To act as a blistering agent; — said of a plaster, poultice, etc. **6.** To be drawn or pulled; admit of being drawn. **7.** To deline-

ate; sketch; practice drawing. **8.** To make a demand for money deposited or due, or for supplies, etc. **9.** To produce, or admit of, a draft, or current, as a chimney. — *n.* **1.** Act or process of drawing. **2.** The result of drawing ; state of being drawn; a drawn battle, game, etc. **3.** The movable part of a drawbridge. *U. S.* **4.** A ravine. *Western U. S.*

draw'back' (-băk'), *n.* **1.** Money paid back after collection. **2.** Hindrance; objectionable feature.

draw'bridge' (-brĭj'), *n.* A bridge of which all or part is made to be raised, drawn, or moved aside, to admit or hinder passage.

Swing Drawbridge.

draw-ee' (drô-ē'), *n.* The person on whom an order or bill of exchange is drawn.

draw'er (drô'ẽr), *n.* **1.** One who draws. **2.** One who issues a draft. **3.** A boxlike receptacle as in a table, arranged to be drawn out. **4.** *pl.* An undergarment for the legs and lower body.

draw'ing, *n.* **1.** Act of one that draws. **2.** A picture or representation made by lines or, loosely, by shading or color; sketch.

draw'ing-room', *n.* A room for the reception or company.

drawl (drôl), *v.t. & i.* To speak in a slow, lengthened tone. — *n.* A drawling utterance. — **-er**, *n.* [8]

dray (drā), *n.* A strong low cart or wagon, without fixed sides.

dray'age (drā'ăj), *n.* **1.** Use of a dray. **2.** Charge, or sum paid, for the use of a dray.

dread (drĕd), *v. t. & i.* To fear greatly; regard or look forward to with great apprehension. — *n.* **1.** Great fear, esp. of impending evil. **2.** Reverential or respectful fear; awe. **3.** An object of fear or awe. — *a.* [3] Dreadful.

dread'ful (drĕd'fŏŏl), *a.* [4] **1.** Fearful; inspiring dread; terrible; as, a *dreadful* storm. **2.** Awful; inspiring reverence; as, *dreadful* majesty. — **-ful-ly**, *adv.* [8] — **-ful-ness**, *n.* [8].

dread'nought' (-nôt'), *n.* A type of very heavily armed and armored battleship.

dream (drēm), *n.* **1.** A series of thoughts, images, or emotions occurring during sleep. **2.** A visionary creation of the imagination.

dream (drēm), *v. i.; pret.* DREAMED (drēmd) or DREAMT (drĕmt) ; DREAM'ING. **1.** To have a dream or dreams. **2.** To indulge in daydreams or reverie. **3.** To conceive (of), esp. as a plan or possibility. — *v. t.* **1.** To have a dream of. **2.** To fancy or think of as if in a dream. — **dream'er**, *n.* [8].

dream'land' (-lănd'), *n.* An unreal, delightful country such as is sometimes pictured in dreams.

dreamt (drĕmt), *pret. & p. p.* of DREAM.

dream'y (drēm'ĭ), *a.* [3] **1.** Abounding in dreams; given to dreaming. **2.** Like a dream; soft; languid. — **dream'i-ly** (-ĭ-lĭ), *adv.* [8] — **-i-ness**, *n.* [8].

drear (drēr), *a.* [3] Melancholy; gloomy.

drear'y (-ĭ), *a.* [3] Comfortless; dismal; gloomy. — **drear'i-ly** (-ĭ-lĭ), *adv.* [8] — **-i-ness**, *n.* [8].

dredge (drĕj), *n.* **1.** A machine for scooping up or removing mud or wet earth. **2.** A device for dragging over the sea bottom, as to gather shellfish.

— *v. t.* [1] To gather with a dredge; to excavate or deepen with a dredge.— **dredg'er** (drĕj'ẽr), *n.* [8].

dredge (drĕj), *v. t.* To sprinkle (as a roast) with flour, etc.; also, to sift or sprinkle (flour, etc.).

dredg'er, *n.* A box to sprinkle flour, etc.

dreg (drĕg), *n.* Grounds or lees of a liquid; most worthless part of anything ; — usually in *pl.*

drench (drĕnch), *v. t.* **1.** To cause to drink; esp., to dose by force. **2.** To wet through and through; soak. — *n.* **1.** A draft, or potion, esp. one given to an animal. **2.** Act of drenching. **3.** Something that drenches.

dress (drĕs), *v. t.* **1.** To arrange in exact line, as soldiers; align. **2.** To make ready; prepare (food, lumber, stone, etc.) for use, for the market, etc. **3.** To clothe ; to clothe in formal dress ; array ; deck. **4.** To treat with remedies, bandages, etc., as a wound. **5.** To rebuke; scold; beat; — often with *down.*— *v. i.* **1.** *Mil.* To form alignment. **2.** To clothe one's self, esp. in formal dress.— *n.* **1.** Act of dressing. **2.** Attire ; clothes ; costume ; esp., fine or distinctive apparel. **3.** A lady's gown.

dress'er (drĕs'ẽr), *n.* One that dresses.

dress'er, *n.* A chest of drawers, or bureau, with a mirror.

dress'ing, *vb. n.* **1.** Act of one that dresses. **2.** That which is used to dress anything. **3.** A scolding ; castigation ; — often with *down.*

dress'mak'er (-māk'ẽr), *n.* A maker of dresses.

dress'y (-ĭ), *a.* [3] **1.** Attentive to dress. **2.** Of garments, etc., stylish. *Colloq.*

drew (drōō), *pret.* of DRAW.

drib'ble (drĭb'l), *v. i. & t.* [1] **1.** To trickle. **2.** To slaver; drivel.— *n.* A trickling stream.

drib'let (drĭb'lĕt), *n.* A small piece or quantity.

dried (drīd), *pret. & p. p.* of DRY.

dri'er (drī'ẽr), *n.* **1.** One that dries. **2.** A substance mixed with the oil for paints, varnishes, etc., to make it dry more quickly.

dri'er, *compar.*, **dri'est**, *superl.*, of DRY, *a.*

drift (drĭft), *n.* **1.** That which is forced, or urged along, esp. by wind, water, or ice. **2.** State of being driven; act or motion of drifting. **3.** Tendency of an act or process or esp. of an argument or the like ; purport ; meaning; aim.— *v. i. & t.* **1.** To float or drive along by or as by water or air. **2.** To heap up by the force of wind; also, to cover, or be covered, with drifts.

drill (drĭl), *n.* **1.** An instrument for boring holes in hard substances. **2.** Act or exercise of training soldiers. **3.** Any exercise, physical or mental, enforced with regularity.— *v. i. & t.* **1.** To pierce or bore with a drill. **2.** To train in the military art, as soldiers. **3.** To instruct or train thoroughly in any art or subject; discipline.

drill, *v. t.* **1.** To sow, as seeds, in drills, or light furrows. **2.** To sow (ground) in drills.

drill, *n.* **1.** An implement for making holes or furrows into which it sows seeds. **2.** A light furrow into which seed is sown, or the row of sown seed.

drill'er (-ẽr), *n.* One that drills.

drill'ing, *n.* A heavy twilled linen or cotton fabric.

dri'ly (drī'lĭ). Var. of DRYLY.

drink (drĭnk), *v. t.; pret.* DRANK (drănk), formerly DRUNK (drŭnk); *p. p.* DRUNK and (chiefly used as an adjective) DRUNK'EN (-'n); *p. pr. & vb. n.* DRINK'-ING. **1.** To swallow (a liquid); imbibe. **2.** To absorb (a liquid); suck up. **3.** To take in through the senses; inhale, hear, see, etc. — *v. i.* **1.** To swallow anything liquid ; imbibe. **2.** To drink alcoholic liquors, esp. to excess. — *n.* **1.** Liquid to be swallowed. **2.** Alcoholic liquor. **3.** Excessive drinking. **4.** A potion ; draft.

drink'a-ble (-ȧ-b'l), *a.* [4] Suitable for drinking.

drink'er (-ẽr), *n.* One who drinks, esp. habitually of intoxicants ; as, a hard *drinker*.

drip (drĭp), *v. t.; DRIPPED* (drĭpt) or DRIPT ; DRIP'-PING. To let fall in drops. — *v. i.* **1.** To let fall drops of moisture or liquid. **2.** To fall in drops. — *n.* Act of dripping ; that which drips.

drip'ping, *vb. n.* **1** A falling in drops. **2.** That which falls in drops.

drive (drīv), *v. t.; pret.* DROVE (drōv); *p. p.* DRIV'EN (drĭv''n); *p. pr. & vb. n.* DRIV'ING (drīv'ĭng). **1.** To urge or push onward ; press forward. **2.** To urge on and direct the motions of, as horses or a vehicle; to convey in a vehicle. **3.** To urge, press, or bring to a point or state. — *v. i.* **1.** To rush and press with violence. **2.** To be forced along ; be driven. **3.** To go by, or pass in, a vehicle whose course is wholly or partly under one's direction. **4.** To aim, or tend, to a point; to mean ; — usually with *at.* — *n.* **1.** Act of driving ; esp., a trip in a vehicle wholly or partly under one's control. **2.** A road esp. for driving. **3.** Urgent pressure of work. **4.** A collection of objects driven, as of floating logs.

driv'el (drĭv''l), *v. i.* [7] **1.** To slaver or slobber like a child or an idiot. **2.** To flow from the mouth like spittle. **3.** To be silly in speech. — *n.* **1.** Slaver or slobber. **2.** Foolish talk. — **-el-er**, *n.* [7, 8].

driv'en (drĭv''n), *p. p.* of DRIVE.

driv'er (drĭv'ẽr), *n.* One that drives, as a coachman, an overseer, etc.

drive'way (drĭv'wā'), *n.* A passage or way along which vehicles or animals are driven.

driz'zle (drĭz''l), *v. i.* [1] To rain in minute drops.— *n.* Fine rain like mist. — **driz'zly** (-lĭ),*a.*

droll (drōl), *a.* [3] Queer, and fitted to provoke laughter; ludicrous from oddity.

droll'er-y (drōl'ẽr-ĭ), *n. ; pl.* -ERIES (-ĭz). **1.** Something droll. **2.** Droll quality ; quaint humor.

drom'e-da-ry (drŭm'ê-dā-rĭ ; drŏm'-), *n. ; pl.* -RIES (-rĭz). Originally, a fleet camel bred esp. for riding ; now, more often, the one-humped camel.

drone (drōn), *n.* **1.** The male of bees, esp. the male of the honeybee, which has no sting and gathers no honey. **2.** A sluggard. — *v. i. & t.* [1] To idle.

drone, *v. i. & t.* [1] To make, or sound with, a low, dull, monotonous, murmuring sound; to speak monotonously. — *n.* **1.** A bagpipe, or one of the lowest tubes of a bagpipe, or its tone. **2.** A humming or deep murmuring sound.

drool (drōōl), *v. i.* To drivel.

droop (drōōp), *v. i.* **1.** To sink or hang down, as from exhaustion. **2.** To be dispirited ; languish. — *v. t.* To let droop or sink. — *n.* A drooping.

drop (drŏp), *n.* **1.** The quantity of fluid that falls in one spherical mass; liquid globule. **2.** **a** A small quantity of drink. **b** *pl.* Any medicine measured by drops. **3.** That which resembles a liquid drop, as an earring, a sugarplum, etc. **4.** A sudden fall; descent. **5.** Whatever is arranged to drop or fall from an elevated position. **6.** Depth to which one drops. **7.** An abrupt fall in level.—*v. t.;* DROPPED (drŏpt) or DROPT; DROP′PING. **1.** To let fall in a drop or drops. **2.** To release to a downward motion. **3.** To let go; dismiss; also, to quit. **4.** To omit (as a letter) in writing or speaking. **5.** To fell or bring down, as by a blow. **6.** To lower, as one's eyes, voice, etc.—*v. i.* **1.** To fall in drops. **2.** To fall, or fall away; sink. **3.** To lower, as the voice. **4.** To come unexpectedly or casually. **5.** To cease. **6.** To move (easily) with the current or tide.—**drop′per** (-ẽr), *n.* [8].

drop′si·cal (drŏp′sĭ-kăl), *a.* [4] Affected with, or subject to, dropsy; pertaining to dropsy.

drop′sy (drŏp′sĭ), *n.; pl.* -SIES (-sĭz). An unnatural accumulation of serous fluid in the body.

drosh′ky (drŏsh′kĭ), *n.; pl.* -KIES (-kĭz). A low, four-wheeled, open carriage, used in Russia.

dross (drŏs), *n.* **1.** The scum or refuse matter from molten ore or metal. **2.** Waste; refuse.

drought (drout), *n.* Dryness; want of rain or water.

drouth (drouth). Var. of DROUGHT.

drove (drōv), *n.* **1.** A collection of cattle driven or collected for driving. **2.** Any collection of animals, or a crowd of people.

drove, *pret.* of DRIVE.

dro′ver (drō′vẽr), *n.* One who drives domestic animals to market; hence, a dealer in cattle.

drown (droun), *v. i.* To be suffocated in water or other liquid.—*v. t.* **1.** To immerse in water or other liquid, or to kill by so doing. **2.** To overwhelm; overpower; as, cheers *drowned* his voice.

drowse (drouz), *v. i. & t.* [1] To be or make heavy with sleepiness; doze.—*n.* A doze

drow′sy (drou′zĭ), *a.* [3] Inclined to drowse; dozy.—**-si·ly** (-zĭ-lĭ), *adv.*—**-si·ness,** *n.*

drub (drŭb), *v. t.;* DRUBBED (drŭbd); DRUB′BING. To beat, as with a stick; thrash; cudgel.—*n.* A blow with a cudgel; thump.

drudge (drŭj), *v. i.* [1] To perform drudgery.—*n.* One who drudges; servant; hack.

drudg′er·y (-ẽr-ĭ), *n.* Work or toil that is mean, irksome, or distasteful.

drug (drŭg), *n.* **1.** Any substance used medicinally. **2.** A commodity of slow sale, or in no demand. —*v. t.;* DRUGGED (drŭgd); DRUG′GING (drŭg′ĭng). To affect with drugs; esp., to stupefy by a narcotic.

drug′get (-ĕt), *n.* A kind of coarse woolen cloth.

drug′gist (-ĭst), *n.* An apothecary.

dru′id (drōō′ĭd), *n.* One of a religious order among the ancient Britons.

dru·id′ic (drōō-ĭd′ĭk), **dru·id′i·cal** (-ĭ-kăl), *a.* Pertaining to, or resembling, the druids.

drum (drŭm), *n.* **1.** A musical instrument having a stretched skin or vellum head or heads, played by beating with a stick or pair of sticks. **2.** The sound of this instrument. **3.** Anything suggestive of a drum, as the tympanum of the ear.—*v. i.;* DRUMMED (drŭmd); DRUM′MING. **1.** To play on a drum. **2.** To make a noise like that of a beaten drum.—*v. t.* **1.** To assemble by beat of drum; to collect;—with *up.* **2.** To drive or force by reiteration. **3.** To strike or thump as in beating a drum.

drum major. The marching leader of a band.

drum′mer (drŭm′ẽr), *n.* **1.** One who plays the drum, as in a band. **2.** A commercial traveler. *U. S.*

drunk (drŭngk), *a.* [3] Intoxicated with drink.

drunk′ard (-ạrd), *n.* One who often gets drunk.

drunk′en (-'n), *a.* [3] **1.** Drunk. **2.** Pert. to intoxication.—**-ly,** *adv.* [8]—**-ness,** *n.* [8].

drupe (drōōp), *n.* A fruit consisting of an outer covering and a woody inner shell, or stone, as in the plum, cherry, and peach.

dry (drī), *a.; ;* DRI′ER (drī′ẽr), DRI′EST. **1.** Free from moisture; not wet or moist. **2.** Not having the usual supply of liquid; as: **a** Of animals, not giving milk. **b** Thirsty; needing drink. **c** Not shedding, or accompanied by, tears. **d** Of commodities, solid, as opposed to liquid. **3.** Not showing feeling; impassive. **4.** Lacking sweetness;—said of wines. **5.** Deficient in interest; dull.—**a** A prohibitionist.—**dry goods,** textile fabrics;—in distinction from *groceries. Chiefly U. S.*—**dry measure,** a system of measures of volume for dry or coarse articles, esp. that in which 2 pints =1 quart, 8 quarts = 1 peck, 4 pecks = 1 bushel.

dry, *v. t. & i.* [2] To make or become dry.

dry′ad (-ăd), *n.* A wood nymph.

dry′er. Var. of DRIER.

dry′ly (drī′lĭ), *adv.* In a dry manner.

dry′ness, *n.* State or quality of being dry.

dry′-shod′, *a.* Without wetting the feet.

du′al (dū′ăl), *a.* **1.** Pertaining to two. **2.** Twofold.

du′al-ism (-ĭz'm), *n.* State of being twofold; any system recognizing two independent principles.

du′al-is′tic (-ĭs′tĭk), *a.* Pert. to dualism or duality.

du·al′i·ty (dū-ăl′ĭ-tĭ), *n.* Dual quality or state.

dub (dŭb), *v. t.;* DUBBED (dŭbd); DUB′BING. **1.** To confer knighthood on. See ACCOLADE. **2.** To call; style;—now usually jocular.

du′bi·ous (dū′bĭ-ŭs), *a.* [4] **1.** Occasioning doubt; doubtful; undetermined; uncertain. **2.** Of questionable character.—**-ly,** *adv.* [8]—**-ness,** *n.* [8].

du′bi·ta·ble (-tȧ·b'l), *a.* [4] Liable to be doubted.

du′cal (-kăl), *a.* Pertaining to a duke or dukedom.

duc′at (dŭk′ăt), *n.* A former gold coin worth about $2.28, first coined in Venice in 1284.

duch′ess (dŭch′ĕs), *n.* The wife or widow of a duke; also, a lady who has the sovereignty of a duchy in her own right.

duch′y (-ĭ), *n.; pl.* DUCHIES (-ĭz). The territory of a duke or a duchess; a dukedom.

duck (dŭk), *n.* A linen (or sometimes cotton) fabric, finer and lighter than canvas.

duck, *n.* **1.** Any of numerous flat-billed swimming birds. **2.** A female duck.

duck, *v. t. & i.* **1.** To thrust or plunge momentarily under water or other liquid. **2.** To bow; to bob down, as one's head.—*n.* A sudden inclination, as of the head; a dip or quick plunge.

duck′ling, *n.* A young duck.

duct (dŭkt), *n.* **1.** *Anatomy.* A tube or vessel. **2.** Any tube or canal by which a fluid flows.

duc′tile (dŭk′tĭl), *a.* [4] **1.** Capable of being permanently drawn, as into wire. **2.** Tractable.

duc-til′i·ty (dŭk-tĭl′ĭ-tĭ), *n.* Ductile quality.

dud (dŭd), *n.* An article of clothing;—usually in *pl.*, clothes; esp., old or cast-off clothes. *Colloq.*

dude (dūd), *n.* A dandy; a fop. *Colloq.*

dudg′eon (dŭj′ŭn), *n.* Anger; ill humor.

due (dū), *a.* **1.** Owed or owing as a debt. **2.** Capable of satisfying an obligation; sufficient; regular. **3.** Owing or attributable (*to* something).

---

chair; go; sing, iŋk; then, thin; nature, verdure; yet; zh = z in azure. **Numbers refer to §§ in the Special Notes which, with Abbreviations, Signs, etc., precede the Vocabulary.**

4. Appointed to arrive (at a given time). — *n.* That which is due. — *adv.* Directly; as, *due* east.

du'el (dū'ĕl), *n.* A combat between two persons, fought with deadly weapons by agreement, usually before witnesses (*seconds*) on each side. — *v. i.* [7] To fight in a duel. — **du'el-ist,** *n.* [7, 8].

du-en'na (dū-ĕn'ȧ), *n.* A governess; chaperon.

du-et' (-ĕt'), *n.* *Music.* A composition for two performers.

dug (dŭg), *pret. & p. p.* of DIG.

dug, *n.* A teat; pap.

dug'out' (-out'), *n.* **1.** Boat made by hollowing out a log. **2.** Rude shelter, as one dug in a hillside.

duke (dūk), *n.* **1.** A sovereign prince, ruler of a duchy. **2.** A nobleman of the highest hereditary rank after that of prince.

duke'dom (-dŭm), *n.* A duchy or the title of a duke.

dul'cet (dŭl'sĕt), *a.* [4] Sweet; melodious.

dul'ci-mer (-sĭ-mẽr), *n.* A musical instrument having wire strings, played with two light hammers.

dull (dŭl), *a.* [3] **1.** Slow of understanding; stupid. **2.** Slow in action; sluggish; listless; inert. **3.** Furnishing little pleasure or variety; uninteresting. **4.** Not sharp. **5.** Not bright or clear to the eye; dim. **6.** Muffled; not clear, as sounds. — *v. t. & i.* To make or become dull. — **dul'ly** (-lĭ), *adv.* [8] — **dull'ness,** *n.* [8].

dull'ard (dŭl'ȧrd), *n.* A stupid person; a dunce.

du'ly (dū'lĭ), *adv.* In a due or becoming manner.

du'ma (dōō'mä), *n.* In Russia, a council; specif. [*cap.*], the Russian parliament (since 1905).

dumb (dŭm), *a.* [3] **1.** Destitute of speech; mute; silent. **2.** Dull; stupid. *Colloq. U. S.* — **dumb'ly,** *adv.* [8] — **dumb'ness,** *n.* [8].

dumb'-bell', *n.* A kind of weight used (esp. in pairs) in gymnastic exercise.

dumb'found'. Var. of DUMPFOUND.

dumb'-wait'er, *n.* **1.** A portable serving table or stand. **2.** A kind of lift or elevator for dishes, etc.

dum'found' (dŭm'found'), *v. t.* To strike dumb, as with astonishment.

dum'my (dŭm'ĭ), *a.* Fictitious or sham. — *n.; pl.* -MIES (-ĭz). **1.** One dumb. **2.** Dolt. *Colloq.* **3.** One ostensibly acting for himself, but really acting for another. **4.** A sham; hence, a model or lay figure on which clothing is exhibited.

dump (dŭmp), *n.* A dull, gloomy state of the mind; low spirits; — now only in *pl.* and often humorous.

dump, *v. t.* To drop or throw down; hence, to unload, as coal from a cart by tilting it. — *n.* A place for dumping anything, as rubbish or refuse; also, that which is dumped.

dump'ish (dŭmp'ĭsh), *a.* [4] Sad; dejected.

dump'ling (-lĭng), *n.* A roundish mass of dough boiled in soup, or as a sort of pudding.

dump'y (dŭm'pĭ), *a.* [3] Short and thick; of relatively low stature.

dun (dŭn), *v. t. & i.;* DUNNED (dŭnd); DUN'NING. To ask or beset for payment; importune. — *n.* **1.** One who duns. **2.** An urgent request for payment.

dun, *a.* Yellowish or grayish brown.

dunce (dŭns), *n.* A stupid person.

dune (dūn), *n.* A hill or ridge of drifted sand.

dung (dŭng), *n.* Manure; feces.

dun'geon (dŭn'jŭn), *n.* A donjon; A close, dark prison or vault, commonly underground.

‖ **du'o** (dōō'ō), *n.; pl.* It. DUI (-ē), E. DUOS (-ōz). [It.] A duet, esp. instrumental.

du'o-dec'i-mo (dū'ō-dĕs'ĭ-mō), *a.* Having 12 leaves to a sheet, as a book. — *n.; pl.* -MOS (-mōz). A size (about 5×7½ inches) of a book, or of its pages, resulting from folding each sheet into 12 leaves; also, a book of such size; — often written 12mo or 12°.

du'o-de'num (dū'ō-dē'nŭm), *n.* The part of the small intestine next below the stomach.

dupe (dūp), *n.* One who has been deceived or who is easily deceived; a gull. — *v. t.* [1] To deceive.

du'plex (dū'plĕks), *a.* Double; twofold.

du'pli-cate (-plĭ-kát), *a.* Double; twofold; also, that is a counterpart or double of something. — *n.* A copy; counterpart. — (-kāt), *v. t.* [1] **1.** To double; render double. **2.** To make a duplicate of (something).

du'pli-ca'tion (-kā'shŭn), *n.* **1.** Act of duplicating. **2.** A duplicate; counterpart.

du-plic'i-ty (dū-plĭs'ĭ-tĭ), *n.; pl.* -TIES (-tĭz). AD insincere mode of conduct; deceitfulness.

du'ra-bil'i-ty (dū'rȧ-bĭl'ĭ-tĭ), *n.* Quality of being durable.

du'ra-ble (dū'rȧ-b'l), *a.* [4] Able to endure; lasting; enduring; as, a *durable* cloth. — **du'ra-ble-ness,** *n.* [8] — **du'ra-bly,** *adv.* [8].

dur'ance (dūr'ȧns), *n.* Imprisonment; duress.

du-ra'tion (dū-rā'shŭn), *n.* State or quality of lasting; continuance.

du'ress (dū'rĕs), *n.* Imprisonment; constraint.

dur'ing (dūr'ĭng), *prep.* In the time of; as long as the action or existence of.

durst (dŭrst), *pret.* of DARE.

dusk (dŭsk), *a.* [3] Moderately dark; dusky. — *n.* **1.** The darker part of twilight or dawn. **2.** Quality of being, or that which is, dusk; shade; duskiness.

dusk'y (-kĭ), *a.* [3] Somewhat dark, as in color or from lack of light. — **dusk'i-ness,** *n.* [8].

dust (dŭst), *n.* **1.** Fine, dry, powdery particles of earth; hence, any fine powder. **2.** The earthy remains of bodies once alive, esp. of human bodies. **3.** Fig., something worthless, or a low or mean condition. **4.** A cloud of dust in the air. — *v. t.* **1.** To make dusty; soil with dust. **2.** To free from dust. **3.** To strew or sprinkle as dust.

dust'er (dŭs'tẽr), *n.* **1.** One that dusts. **2.** A light overgarment to protect clothing from dust.

dust'y (dŭs'tĭ), *a.* [3] **1.** Filled, abounding, or covered, with dust; clouded with dust. **2.** Like dust in color or nature. — **dust'i-ness,** *n.* [8].

Dutch (dŭch), *a.* Of or pert. to the Netherlands, esp. Holland. — *n.* **1.** The Dutch language. **2.** *pl.* The people of the Netherlands, esp. Holland.

du'te-ous (dū'tē-ŭs), *a.* [4] Fulfilling duty; dutiful; obedient. — **-ly,** *adv.* [8] — **-ness,** *n.* [8].

du'ti-a-ble (-tĭ-ȧ-b'l), *a.* Subject to a duty (tax).

du'ti-ful (-fŏŏl), *a.* [4] **1.** Performing duties; obedient, as to parents. **2.** Controlled by a sense of duty. — **-ly,** *adv.* [8] — **-ness,** *n.* [8].

du'ty (-tĭ), *n.; pl.* -TIES (-tĭz). **1.** Conduct due to parents or superiors, as shown in obedience or submission; respect or an act of respect. **2.** That which is required by one's station or occupation. **3.** That which a person is morally obliged to do or forbear. **4.** A payment to the government, esp.

āle, senāte, câre, ăm, ŏccount, ärm, ȧsk, sofȧ; ēve, ēvent, ĕnd, recĕnt, makẽr; īce, ĭll; ōld, ōbey, ôrb, ŏdd, sôft, cŏnnect; ūse, ūnite, ûrn, ŭp, circŭs; fōōd, fŏŏt; out, oil;

dwarf (dwôrf), *n.* A person much below the average size ; a pygmy ; also, an animal or a plant much below the usual size of its kind. — *v. t.* To stunt ; hence, to make to seem small in comparison. — *a.* Of less than the usual or normal size ; stunted. — **dwarf′ish** (dwôr′fĭsh), *a.* [8].

dwell (dwĕl), *v. i. ; pret. & p. p.* DWELT (dwĕlt), DWELLED (dwĕld) ; *p. pr. & vb. n.* DWELL′ING. To abide as a resident ; live ; reside. — **er** (-ẽr), *n.* [8].

dwell′ing, *n.* Habitation ; abode.

dwelt (dwĕlt), *pret. & p. p.* of DWELL.

dwin′dle (dwĭn′d'l), *v. i.* [1] To diminish ; become less ; waste away.

dye (dī), *n.* **1.** Color produced by dyeing. **2.** Material for dyeing ; dyestuff. — *v. t. ;* DYED (dīd) ; DYE′ING. **1.** To stain ; color, esp. with dyestuffs. **2.** To impart (a given color) by dyeing. — *v. i.* To take or impart color in dyeing. — **dye′ing** (dī′ĭng), *n.* — **dye′er** (dī′ẽr), *n.* [8].

dye′stuff′ (-stŭf′), *n.* A dye ; stuff yielding a dye.

dy′ing (dī′ĭng), *p. a.* **1.** In the act of dying ; moribund. **2** Of or pertaining to dying or death.

dy-nam′ic (dī-năm′ĭk ; dĭ-), *a.* [4] **1.** *Physics.* **a** Of or pertaining to physical forces or energy. **b** Of or pert. to dynamics ; active. **2.** Energetic ; active ; forceful.

dy-nam′i-cal (-ĭ-kăl), *a.* [4] Dynamic. — **dy-nam′i-cal-ly**, *adv.* [8].

dy-nam′ics (-ĭks), *n.* Mechanics treating of the motion of bodies and of the action of forces in producing or changing their motion.

dy′na-mite (dī′nà-mīt), *n.* An explosive consisting of nitroglycerin absorbed in a porous material. — *v. t.* [1] To shatter with dynamite.

dy′na-mo (-mō), *n. ; pl.* -MOS (-mōz). A machine for converting mechanical energy into electrical energy by magneto-electric induction.

dy′na-mo-e-lec′tric (-ĕ-lĕk′trĭk)) *a.* Pert. to **dy′na-mo-e-lec′tri-cal** (-trĭ-kăl)) conversion, by induction, of mechanical into electrical energy or vice versa ; as, a *dynamo-electric* machine.

dy′na-mom′e-ter (dī′nà-mŏm′ĕ-tẽr ; dĭn′à-), *n.* An apparatus for measuring force.

dy-nas′tic (dī-năs′tĭk ; dĭ-), *a.* Of or relating to a dynasty.

dy′nas-ty (dī′năs-tĭ ; dĭn′ăs-tĭ), *n. ; pl.* -TIES (-tĭz). A race or succession of kings of the same line or family, or their continued lordship.

dys′en-ter-y (dĭs′ĕn-tẽr-ĭ), *n.* An inflammatory disease of the large intestine characterized by griping pains and a discharge of mucus and blood.

dys-pep′si-a (dĭs-pĕp′sĭ-à ; -shà), *n.* Indigestion.

dys-pep′tic (-tĭk), *a.* [4] Pertaining to or having dyspepsia. — *n.* A person having dyspepsia.

E

each (ēch), *a. or a. pron.* Every (individual of two or more) considered separately.

ea′ger (ē′gẽr), *a.* [4] **1.** Spirited or strenuous. **2.** Keenly desirous to pursue, perform, or obtain ; ardent. — **ly**, *adv.* [8] — **ness**, *n.* [8].

ea′gle (ē′g'l), *n.* **1.** Any of various large birds of prey of the falcon family. **2.** A gold coin of the U. S., of the value of ten dollars. There are also a gold **double eagle** ($20), **half eagle** ($5), and **quarter eagle** ($2.50).

ea′glet (ē′glĕt), *n.* A young eagle.′

ear (ēr), *n.* **1.** The organ of hearing. **2.** The external ear of man and most mammals. **3.** The sense or act of hearing ; also, a refined or acute sense of hearing. **4.** That which resembles an ear. **5.** Attention, esp. favorable attention.

ear, *n.* The fruiting spike of any cereal (as Indian corn, or maize, rye, etc.), including the kernels, or grains. — *v. i.* To put forth ears.

ear′drum′ (ēr′drŭm′), *n.* A thin membrane closing externally the cavity of the middle ear.

eared (ērd), *a.* Having ears ; as, long-*eared.*

earl (ûrl), *n.* In Great Britain, a nobleman next below a marquis.

earl′dom (-dŭm), *n.* Rank or domain of an earl.

ear′ly (ûr′lĭ), *adv.* In a time or position near the beginning of a period or a series ; betimes. — *a.* [3] Coming early ; of remote past time. — **ear′li-ness** (-lĭ-nĕs), *n.* [8].

ear′mark′ (ēr′märk′), *n.* A mark of identification on the ear ; any mark of identification.

earn (ûrn), *v. i.* To merit, or to acquire, by labor or performance, as wages.

ear′nest (ûr′nĕst), *n.* **1.** Something of value given by a buyer to a seller, to bind the bargain. **2.** Something given beforehand as a pledge.

ear′nest (ûr′nĕst), *n.* An aroused and intent mental state ; — chiefly in the phrase *in earnest.* — *a.* [4] **1.** Characterized by, or proceeding from, an intense and serious state of mind. **2.** Important ; not trivial. — **ly**, *adv.* [8] — **ness**, *n.* [8].

earn′ing (ûr′nĭng), *n.* Act or process of earning, or what is earned ; esp., *pl.*, money earned.

ear′shot′ (-shŏt′), *n.* Hearing distance.

earth (ûrth), *n.* **1.** The globe or planet which we inhabit ; the world. **2.** The land, in distinction from the air or water. **3.** The softer part of the land, in distinction from rock ; soil or dirt.

earth′en (ûr′th'n), *a.* Made of earth or clay.

earth′en-ware′ (-wâr′), *n.* Vessels, ornaments, etc., of baked clay, esp. the coarser kinds.

earth′i-ness (-thĭ-nĕs), *n.* Quality of being earthy.

earth′ly (-lĭ), *a.* [3] **1.** Of, like, or pertaining to, the earth ; not heavenly or spiritual. **2.** Possible ; as, of what *earthly* use is it ?

earth′quake′ (-kwāk′), *n.* A trembling of the earth's surface, due chiefly to faulting of rocks and volcanic explosions.

earth′worm′ (-wûrm′), *n.* Any of numerous worms found in damp soil.

earth′y (ûr′thĭ), *a.* [3] **1.** Consisting of or resembling earth. **2.** Of or pertaining to the earth ; terrestrial ; esp., worldly. **3.** Gross ; unrefined.

ear′wig′ (ēr′wĭg′), *n.* Any of numerous harmless beetle-like insects, popularly supposed to creep into the human ear.

ease (ēz), *n.* **1.** State of being comfortable; freedom from pain, effort, trouble, etc. **2.** Freedom from constraint, formality, difficulty, etc.; naturalness, as of manner. — *v. t. & i.* [1] **1.** To free from anything that pains, disquiets, or oppresses; relieve. **2.** To render less painful or oppressive; alleviate. **3.** To lessen the pressure or tension of.

ea′sel (ē′zĕl), *n.* A frame to hold a painter's canvas upright, or on which to stand a picture.

ease′ment (ēz′mĕnt), *n.* **1.** That which gives ease. **2.** *Law.* Any of several rights which one person may have in the land of another.

eas′i-ly (ēz′ĭ-lĭ), *adv.* In an easy manner; readily.

eas′i-ness (-nĕs), *n.* Condition of being easy.

east (ēst), *n.* **1.** The direction of sunrise. **2.** [*cap.*] Regions, countries, or peoples, lying to the east; esp., the Asiatic countries; the Orient. — *a.* Toward or at the east; also, from the east, as a wind. — *adv.* Eastward.

East′er (ēs′tēr), *n.* An annual church festival commemorating Christ's resurrection, occurring on a Sunday between March 21 and April 26.

east′er-ly, *a. & adv.* Situated, directed, or moving toward the east; of winds, blowing from the east.

east′ern (ēs′tērn), *a.* **1.** [*cap.*] Pertaining to the East; Oriental. **2.** East or easterly.

east′ern-er (-tēr-nēr), *n.* A native or inhabitant of the east, esp. [*cap.*] of the eastern part of the U. S.

east′ward (ēst′wērd), *adv.* Toward the east; in the direction of east from some point or place. — *a.* Moving or looking toward the east; in an eastern part. — **east′ward-ly,** *adv. & a.* [8].

east′wards (-wĕrdz), *adv.* Var. of EASTWARD.

eas′y (ēz′ĭ), *a.* [3] **1.** At ease; free from trouble, pain, care, anxiety, constraint, etc. **2.** Causing, or attended with, little difficulty or discomfort. **3.** Of persons, moods, etc.: **a** Not difficult to influence; tractable. **b** Not harsh or exacting; lenient. **4.** Supportable with ease; not burdensome or oppressive. **5.** Giving ease or comfort.

eat (ēt), *v. t.; pret.* ATE (āt); *p. p.* EAT′EN (ēt′′n); *p. pr. & vb. n.* EAT′ING. **1.** To take in through the mouth as food; ordinarily, to chew and swallow, as solid food. **2.** To devour; consume; destroy, as by eating. **3.** To consume gradually; waste away; corrode. **4.** To gnaw, perforate, or bore into. — *v. i.* **1.** To take food or a meal; to board. **2.** To wear or waste away; corrode. — *er, n.* [8].

eat′a-ble (ēt′á-b'l), *a.* Fit to be eaten; edible. — *n.* Something fit to be eaten — usually in *pl.*

eaves (ēvz), *n. pl.* Projecting lower edges of a roof.

eaves′drop′ (ēvz′drŏp′), *v. i.* To listen secretly. — **drop′per** (-ēr), *n.* [8] — **drop′ping,** *n.*

ebb (ĕb), *n.* **1.** Flowing back of the tide toward the sea; — opposed to *flood.* **2.** Low state; decline. — *v. i.* **1.** To flow back; return, as of a tide toward the ocean; — opposed to *flow.* **2.** To decrease; wane; decline; sink; as, his *ebbing* fortunes.

eb′on (ĕb′ŭn), *a.* [4] Consisting of or like ebony; esp., black; dark. — *n.* Ebony. *Poetic.*

eb′on-ize (-īz), *v. t.* [1] To make black, or stain black, in imitation of ebony. — *ized* (-īzd), *p. a.*

eb′on-y (-ĭ), *n.; pl.* -ONIES (-ĭz) A hard, heavy wood, generally black, yielded by various trees of Asia and Africa; also, any tree yielding this wood.

e-bul′lience (ē-bŭl′yĕns) } *n.* A boiling up or
e-bul′lien-cy (-yĕn-sĭ) } over; effervescence.
e-bul′lient (ē-bŭl′yĕnt), *a.* Boiling up.

eb′ul-li′tion (ĕb′ŭ-lĭsh′ŭn), *n.* Act or state of boiling or bubbling up; agitation or excitement.

ec-cen′tric (ĕk-sĕn′trĭk), *a.* [4] **1.** Not having the same center; — opposed to *concentric.* **2.** Deviating from circular form, as an orbit. **3.** Deviating from stated methods, usual practice, or established forms; irregular; odd. — *n.* **1.** One that is eccentric, as in conduct. **2.** *Mach.* A device consisting of a disk through which a shaft is keyed eccentrically so that the disk gives a reciprocating motion to an attached rod. — **ec-cen′tri-cal-ly,** *adv.* [8].

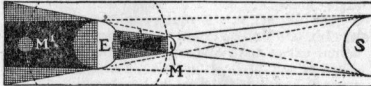
Eccentric, 2. *a* Eccentric; *c* Rod.

ec′cen-tric′i-ty (ĕk′sĕn-trĭs′ĭ-tĭ), *n.; pl.* -TIES (-tĭz). State of being eccentric; oddity.

ec-cle′si-as′tic (ĕ-klē′zĭ-ăs′tĭk), *a.* Ecclesiastical — *n.* A clergyman; priest.

ec-cle′si-as′ti-cal (-tĭ-kăl), *a.* Pert. to the church

ech′o (ĕk′ō), *n.; pl.* -OES (-ōz). **1.** Repetition of a sound due to the reflection of the sound waves **2.** Any repetition; also, one who repeats another's words, ideas, etc. — *v. t.* **1.** To send back or repeat (a sound). **2.** To repeat or imitate, as words or thoughts. — *v. i.* To give an echo.

é′clair′ (ā′klâr′), *n. Cookery.* A small oblong glazed or frosted cake with a cream filling.

é′clat′ (ā′klä′), *n.* **1.** Ostentation. **2.** Brilliancy of success or effort; glory.

ec-lec′tic (ĕk-lĕk′tĭk), *a.* **1.** Choosing from various sources. **2.** Consisting of what is selected — *n.* One who follows a selective method.

ec-lec′ti-cism (-tĭ-sĭz′m), *n.* The use of an eclectic method; an eclectic method or system.

e-clipse′ (ē-klĭps′), *n.* **1.** *Astron.* The interposition of a dark celestial body between a luminous

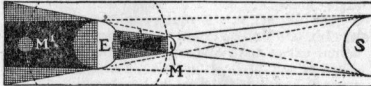

Diagram of Eclipses, showing the Sun, *S,* Earth, *E,* and Moon, the latter being at *M* in a Solar, and at *M¹* in a Lunar, Eclipse.

one and the eye, or the passing of a luminous body into the shadow of another body. **2.** An obscuration; esp., a temporary one; as, an *eclipse* of one's powers. — *v. t.* [1] To cause obscuration of.

e-clip′tic (ē-klĭp′tĭk), *a.* Pertaining to an eclipse or the ecliptic. — *n.* The great circle which is the apparent path of the sun among the stars.

ec′logue (ĕk′lŏg), *n.* A bucolic; idyl.

e′co-nom′ic (ē′kŏ-nŏm′ĭk; ĕk′ō-), *a.* [4] Of or pertaining to economy (senses 1 & 3) or economics.

e′co-nom′i-cal (-ĭ-kăl), *a.* Of, or characterized by, economy; avoiding waste; frugal; thrifty. — *ly,* *adv.* [8].

e′co-nom′ics (-ĭks), *n.* The science that investigates the production, distribution, and consump-

 āle, senāte, câre, ăm, ăccount, ärm, ȧsk, sofȧ; ēve, ėvent, ĕnd, recĕnt, makēr; īce, ĭll; ōld, ȯbey, ôrb, ŏdd, sŏft, cȯnnect; ūse, ŭnite, ûrn, ŭp, circŭs; fōōd, fŏŏt; out, oil;

tion of wealth, or the material means of satisfying human desires; political economy.

e-con'o-mist (ĕ-kŏn'ō-mĭst), *n.* **1.** A manager, esp. a frugal one; one who economizes money, time, labor, etc. **2.** One versed in economics.

e-con'o-mize (-mīz), *v. t.* [1] To manage with economy; to use prudently, frugally, or the like. — *v. i.* To expend prudently; be frugal.

e-con'o-my (-mǐ), *n.; pl.* -MIES (-mǐz). **1.** Management of the business of a household, estate, community, etc., esp. in regard to income and expenses. **2.** Thrifty management; also, an act or means of saving; disposition or ability to save. **3.** The system by which anything is managed or operated; organization; as, the *economy* of nature. **é'cru** (ā'krōō; ĕk'rōō), *a.* [F.] Having the pale brown color of raw silk, linen, or the like.

ec'sta-sy (ĕk'stà-sǐ), *n.; pl.* -SIES (-sǐz). State of being beyond all reason and self-control, as from fear, passion, etc. **2. a** A prophetic or poetic trance. **b** State of overpowering feeling; rapture. **ec-stat'ic** (ĕk-stăt'ĭk), *a.* [4] Pertaining to, or in a state of, ecstasy. — **ec-stat'i-cal-ly**, *adv.* [8].

ec'ze-ma (ĕk'zĕ-mà), *n.* An inflammatory itching disease of the skin.

ed'dy (ĕd'ǐ), *n.; pl.* -DIES (-ǐz). A current of air or water running contrary to the main current, esp. one moving circularly; a whirlpool. — *v. i. & t.* [2] To move as an eddy, or as in an eddy.

e'del-weiss (ā'dĕl-vīs), *n.* A kind of small plant, thickly covered with white hairs, growing in the mountains of central Europe.

E'den (ē'd'n), *n.* The garden where Adam and Eve first dwelt; paradise. See *Gen.* ii. 8.

edge (ĕj), *n.* **1.** The thin cutting side of the blade of an instrument. **2.** Sharpness; keenness. **3.** Any sharp terminating border; margin. —*v. t. & i.* [1] **1.** To furnish with an edge. **2.** To move along edgeways; advance by repeated slight movements. **edge'ways'** (-wāz') ⎱ *adv.* With the edge towards **edge'wise'** (-wīz') ⎰ or foremost; on, by, or with, the edge; as if by the edge.

edg'ing (ĕj'ĭng), *n.* That which forms an edge or border, as lace or embroidery trimming.

ed'i-ble (ĕd'ǐ-b'l), *a.* Fit to be eaten as food; eatable. — *n.* Anything edible.

e'dict (ē'dĭkt), *n.* A public notice or ordinance issued by official or state authority.

ed'i-fi-ca'tion (ĕd'ǐ-fǐ-kā'shŭn), *n.* Act of edifying; state of being edified.

ed'i-fice (ĕd'ǐ-fĭs), *n.* A building; structure; esp., a large or elegant building.

ed'i-fy (ĕd'ǐ-fī), *v. t.* [2] To instruct and improve, esp. morally, spiritually, or religiously; teach.

ed'it (ĕd'ĭt), *v. t.* To superintend or direct the publication of; revise for publication.

e-di'tion (ē-dǐsh'ŭn), *n.* **1.** The form in which a literary work or group of works is published. **2.** All the copies of a work published at one time.

ed'i-tor (ĕd'ǐ-tẽr), *n.* One who edits (a book, etc.). **ed'i-to'ri-al** (-tō'rǐ-ăl), *a.* Of or pertaining to an editor. — *n.* An article in a newspaper or magazine giving the views of the editor.

ed'u-cate (ĕd' û-kāt), *v. t.* [1] To develop and cultivate mentally or morally; train; instruct; teach. **ed'u-ca'tion** (-kā'shŭn), *n.* **1.** Act or process of

educating. **2.** The sum of the qualities acquired through instruction and training.

ed'u-ca'tion-al (-ăl), *a.* [4] Of or pertaining to education. — **ed'u-ca-tive** (ĕd'û-kà-tĭv), *a.* [4].

ed'u-ca'tor (ĕd'û-kā'tẽr), *n.* One who educates.

e-duce' (ē-dūs'), *v. t.* [1] To draw forth; elicit.

eel (ēl), *n.* Any of numerous voracious, elongated, snakelike fishes with smooth slimy skin.

eel'grass' (ēl'gràs'), *n.* An aquatic plant with very long narrow leaves, abundant in shallow bays.

e'en (ēn), *adv.* Even; — a contraction.

e'er (âr ; ār), *adv.* Ever; — a contraction.

ee'rie ⎱ (ē'rĭ), *a.* **1.** Affected with fear, as of **ee'ry** ⎰ ghosts; timid. **2.** Serving to inspire fear, as of ghosts; weird; uncanny.

ef-face' (ĕ-fās'), *v. t.* [1] To rub out or erase.

ef-face'ment (-mĕnt), *n.* Process of effacing.

ef-fect' (-fĕkt'), *n.* **1.** That which is produced by an agent or cause; immediate result. **2.** Purport; intent. **3.** State or fact of being operative; execution; performance. **4.** Reality; fact. **5.** *pl.* Goods; personal estate. — *v. t.* **1.** To produce; do; make. **2.** To bring about; execute.

ef-fec'tive (ĕ-fĕk'tĭv), *a.* [4] Able to produce an effect; active; efficient; operative. — **ef-fec'tive-ly**, *adv.* [8] — **ef-fec'tive-ness**, *n.* [8].

ef-fec'tu-al (-tû-ăl), *a.* [4] Producing, or able to produce, an intended effect. — **-al-ly**, *adv.* [8].

ef-fem'i-na-cy (-fĕm'ĭ-nà-sĭ), *n.* Womanish quality, as softness or weakness, unbecoming a man.

ef-fem'i-nate (-nàt), *a.* [4] Having womanlike traits to an inappropriate degree. — **-ly**, *adv.* [8].

ef'fer-vesce' (ĕf'ẽr-vĕs'), *v. i.* [1] **1.** To bubble and hiss, as fermenting liquors. **2.** To exhibit liveliness or exhilaration ; be gay, merry, etc.

ef'fer-ves'cence (-vĕs'ĕns), *n.* Action or state of effervescing.

ef'fer-ves'cent (-ĕnt), *a.* [4] Effervescing.

ef-fete' (ĕ-fēt'), *a.* [3] Worn out; exhausted.

ef-fi-ca'cious (ĕf'ĭ-kā'shŭs), *a.* [4] Productive of, or powerful to produce, the effect intended. — **ef-fi-ca'cious-ly**, *adv.* [8] — **-ness**, *n.* [8].

ef'fi-ca-cy (ĕf'ĭ-kà-sĭ), *n.* Power to produce effects ; efficient action.

ef-fi'cien-cy (ĕ-fĭsh'ĕn-sĭ), *n.* Quality or degree of being efficient ; efficient power or action.

ef-fi'cient (-ĕnt), *a.* [4] **1.** Productive of effects; effective. **2.** Characterized by energetic and useful activity; as, an *efficient* officer. — **-ly**, *adv.* [8].

ef'fi-gy (ĕf'ĭ-jĭ), *n. ; pl.* -GIES (-jĭz). An image or representation, esp. of a person.

ef-flu'vi-um (ĕ-flōō'vĭ-ŭm), *n. ; pl.* -VIA (-à). An exhalation or odor, esp. one that is offensive.

ef'fort (ĕf'ôrt ; -ẽrt), *n.* **1.** Exertion of power, physical or mental. **2.** A production, as of oratory.

ef-front'er-y (ĕ-frŭn'tẽr-ĭ), *n.* Impudent transgression of the bounds of duty or decorum.

ef-ful'gence (ĕ-fŭl'jĕns), *n.* Splendor ; radiance.

ef-ful'gent (-jĕnt), *a.* [4] Diffusing a flood of light; shining; splendid; radiant. — **-ly**, *adv.* [8].

ef-fu'sion (ĕ-fū'zhŭn), *n.* **1.** Act of pouring out or forth. **2.** That which is poured out or forth; esp., an unrestrained utterance.

ef-fu'sive (-sĭv), *a.* [4] Unduly emotional or demonstrative. — **-ly**, *adv.* [8] — **-ness**, *n.* [8].

eft (ĕft), *n.* A newt.

---

chair; go; sing, iŋk; then, thin; nature, verdure; yet; zh = z in azure. Numbers refer to §§ in the Special Notes which, with Abbreviations, Signs, etc., precede the Vocabulary.

egg (ĕg), *v. t.* To urge (on).

egg, *n.* **1.** The oval or roundish body, covered with a shell or firm membrane, laid by birds and many reptiles; esp., in common usage, that of the domestic hen. **2.** Something egglike, as in form.

egg′plant′ (-plȧnt′), *n.* A plant allied to the potato, producing a large ovoid edible fruit; also, the fruit.

eg′lan-tine (ĕg′lȧn-tīn), *n.* The sweetbrier.

e′go-ism (ē′gō-ĭz′m; ĕg′ō-), *n.* Excessive love and thought of self; — opp. to *altruism.* — **e′go-ist**, *n.*

e′go-tism (-tĭz′m), *n.* The practice of too often using the word *I ;* hence, self-praise.

e′go-tist (-tĭst), *n.* One who speaks much of himself or his own deeds or affairs.

e′go-tis′tic (-tĭs′tĭk) | *a.* [4] Addicted to or
e′go-tis′ti-cal (-tĭ-kȧl) | manifesting egotism. —
e′go-tis′ti-cal-ly, *adv.* [8].

e-gre′gious (ē-grē′jŭs ; -jĭ-ŭs), *a.* [4] Remarkable for bad quality ; flagrant ; gross. — **e-gre′gious-ly**, *adv.* [8] — **e-gre′gious-ness**, *n.* [8].

e′gress (ē′grĕs), *n.* **1.** Act of going out, or leaving; power to leave ; exit. **2.** A way of exit ; outlet.

e′gret (ē′grĕt), *n.* **1.** Any of various herons which during the breeding season bear long plumes (the aigrettes of commerce). **2.** An aigrette.

eh (ā; ĕ), *interj.* Expression of inquiry or surprise.

ei′der (ī′dẽr), *n.,* or **eider duck.** Any of several large northern sea ducks. The female lines the nest with very soft down plucked from her body.

eight (āt), *a.* Seven plus one. — *n.* **1.** The number greater by a unit than seven. **2.** A symbol denoting eight units, as 8 or viii. **3.** Something having as a feature eight units or members.

eight′een′ (ā′tēn′; ā′tēn′), *a.* Eight plus ten. — *n.* **1.** The number greater by a unit than seventeen. **2.** A symbol denoting eighteen units.

eight′eenth′ (ā′tēnth′; ā′tēnth′), *a.* Next in order after the seventeenth ; also, constituting one of eighteen equal parts into which a (whole) thing may be divided. — *n.* **1.** An eighteenth part. **2.** An eighteenth unit or object.

eighth (ātth), *a.* Next in order after the seventh; also, constituting one of eight equal parts into which a (whole) thing may be divided.—*n.* **1.** An eighth part. **2.** An eighth unit or object.

eight′i-eth (ā′tĭ-ĕth), *a.* Next in order after the seventy-ninth; constituting one of eighty equal parts into which a (whole) thing may be divided. — *n.* **1.** An eightieth part. **2.** An eightieth unit or object.

eight′y (ā′tĭ), *a.* Eight times ten. — *n.* **1.** The number equal to the sum of eight tens. **2.** A symbol representing eighty units, as 80 or lxxx.

ei′ther (ē′thẽr ; ī′thẽr), *a. & pron.* **1.** Each of two ; the one and the other. **2.** One of two ; the one or the other.— *conj.* A disjunctive connective, used : **a** Before two or more words or phrases joined by the correlative *or ;* as, *either* he is busy *or* he is away. **b** After an alternative to emphasize a negation ; as, nor you, *either.*

e-jac′u-late (ē-jăk′ū-lāt), *v. t.* [1] To throw out, as an exclamation ; utter by a brief, sudden impulse.

e-jac′u-la′tion (-lā′shŭn), *n.* An ejaculating ; an ejaculated utterance, as of exclamation.

e-jac′u-la-to-ry (-lá-tō-rĭ), *a.* Like, or of the nature of, an ejaculation, or sudden utterance.

e-ject′ (ē-jĕkt′), *v. t.* To throw, push, or drive out.

e-jec′tion (-jĕk′shŭn), *n.* Act of ejecting ; state of being ejected; ejected matter.— **e-jec′tor**, *n.* [8].

e-ject′ment (ē-jĕkt′mĕnt), *n.* An ejecting; ejection.

eke (ēk), *v. t.* [1] To add to, or piece out, by a laborious, inferior, or scanty addition ; — with *out.*

e-lab′o-rate (ē-lăb′ō-rāt), *a.* [4] Wrought out with great care or detail; complicated.—(-rāt), *v. t.* [1] To produce with labor ; work out in detail or with painstaking care.— **-ly**, *adv.* [8] — **-ness**, *n.* [8].

e-lab′o-ra′tion (-rā′shŭn), *n.* Act of elaborating.

e-lapse′ (ē-lăps′), *v. i.* [1] To pass away, as time.

e-las′tic (ē-lăs′tĭk), *a.* [4] **1.** Springing back ; springy. **2.** Of temperaments, etc., able to recover quickly ; buoyant. — *n.* Fabric made elastic by the use of India rubber; also, India rubber in cords, strings, or bands. — **e-las′ti-cal-ly**, *adv.* [8].

e′las-tic′i-ty (ē′lăs-tĭs′ĭ-tĭ), *n.* Elastic quality.

e-late′ (ē-lāt′), *v. t.* [1] To fill with elation.

e-la′tion (ē-lā′shŭn), *n.* A lifting up of the mind or spirit by success, or hope of success; exaltation.

el′bow (ĕl′bō), *n.* **1.** The joint or bend of the arm. **2.** Any bend like an elbow.— *v. t. & i.* To hit, jostle, or force with or as with the elbows.

eld (ĕld), *n. Obs. or Poetic.* **1.** Age ; esp., old age. **2.** Antiquity ; old times.

eld′er (ĕl′dẽr), *a.* Older ; prior ; senior; — used chiefly of persons. — *n.* **1.** A senior; — chiefly in *pl.* **2.** Any of various church officers.

el′der (ĕl′dẽr), *n.* A shrub, of the honeysuckle family, bearing broad clusters of white or pink flowers, and black or red berries.

el′der-ber′ry (-bẽr′ĭ), *n.* The berry of the elder

eld′er-ly (-lĭ), *a.* [4] Somewhat old.

eld′est (-dĕst), *a.* Oldest ; — used chiefly of persons.

e-lect′ (ē-lĕkt′), *a.* **1.** Chosen; picked. **2.** Chosen to an office, but not inducted. **3.** *Theol.* Chosen by election. — *n.* **1.** One chosen or set apart. **2.** *Theol.* One who is elect ; — now only as a collective; as, the *elect.*— *v. t.* **1.** To choose ; select. **2.** To select for an office by vote.

e-lec′tion (ē-lĕk′shŭn), *n.* **1.** Act of choosing ; selection ; choice. **2.** A choosing by vote, as to an office. **3.** *Theol.* Divine choice; predestination.

e-lec′tion-eer′ (-ēr′), *v. i.* To work for, or in behalf of, a person, ticket, or the like, in an election.

e-lec′tive (ē-lĕk′tĭv), *a.* **1.** Appointed or bestowed by election. **2.** Exerting a power of choice. **3.** Pertaining to, or consisting in, choice; electoral.— *n.* A study or course of study which a student may choose from several alternatives. *U. S.*

e-lec′tor (-tẽr), *n.* **1.** One who elects. **2.** One of the persons chosen, by popular vote, to a body(the "electoral college") which elects the president and vice president. *U. S.*

e-lec′to-ral (-tō-rȧl), *a.* Pertaining to election, electors, or an elector ; consisting of electors.

e-lec′to-rate (-tō-rāt), *n.* The persons entitled to vote in an election; also, an electoral district.

e-lec′tric (ē-lĕk′trĭk) | *a.* **1.** Pert.to, producing,
e-lec′tri-cal (-trĭ-kȧl) | or produced or operated by, electricity. **2.** Designating any of several fishes capable of giving an electric shock. — **e-lec′tri-cal-ly**, *adv.* [8].

e-lec-tri′cian (ē-lĕk-trĭsh′ȧn), *n.* One versed in the science or uses of electricity.

āle, senāte, câre, ăm, ẚccount, ärm, ȧsk, sofȧ ; ēve, ĕvent, ĕnd, recĕnt, makẽr ; īce, ĭll ; ōld, ōbey, ôrb, ŏdd, sŏft, cŏnnect ; ūse, ûnite, ûrn, ŭp, circŭs ; fōōd, fŏŏt ; out, oil ;

e-lec'tric'i-ty (ē-lĕk-trĭs'ĭ-tĭ), *n.* **1.** The agency or force to which are due numerous physical phenomena, as the electric spark, lightning, electro-magnetism, etc. **2.** Electrical science.

e-lec'tri-fi-ca'tion (ē-lĕk'trĭ-fĭ-kā'shŭn), *n.* Act of electrifying; state of being electrified.

e-lec'tri-fy (ē-lĕk'trĭ-fī), *v. t.* [2] **1.** To charge or shock with electricity. **2.** To equip for using electric power. **3.** To thrill.

e-lec'tro-cute (ē-lĕk'trŏ-kūt), *v.t.* [1] To execute (a criminal) by electricity.

e-lec'tro-cu'tion (-kū'shŭn), *n.* An electrocuting.

e-lec'trode (ē-lĕk'trōd), *n.* Either terminal of an electric source; esp., either conductor by which the current enters or leaves an electrolyte.

e-lec-trol'y-sis (ē-lĕk-trŏl'ĭ-sĭs), *n.* Chemical decomposition by the action of the electric current.

e-lec'tro-lyte (ē-lĕk'trŏ-līt), *n.* A compound subjected to decomposition by an electric current.

e-lec'tro-mag'net (ē-lĕk'trŏ-măg'nĕt), *n.* A core of magnetic material, in practice soft iron, surrounded by a coil of wire through which an electric current is passed to magnetize it by induction. — **mag-net'ic** (-măg-nĕt'ĭk), *a.* — **mag'net-ism,** *n.*

e-lec'tro-mo'tive (-mō'tĭv), *a.* Producing, or tending to produce, electricity or an electric current.

e-lec'tron (ē-lĕk'trŏn), *n.* One of the supremely minute particles projected from the cathode of a vacuum tube as the cathode rays. Electrons are probably the ultimate constituents of all atoms.

e-lec'tro-plate' (ē-lĕk'trŏ-plāt'), *v. t.* To plate, as with silver, by electrolysis. — *n.* Ware produced by this process.

e-lec'tro-type (ē-lĕk'trŏ-tīp), *n.* A facsimile plate for printing made by electroplating a wax impression; also, a print from such a plate. — *v. t.* To make an electrotype or electrotypes of.

el'ee-mos'y-na-ry (ĕl'ē-mŏs'ĭ-nā-rĭ; ĕl'ē-ē-), *a.* **1.** Relating or devoted to charity or alms. **2.** Given in charity or alms. **3.** Supported by charity.

el'e-gance (ĕl'ē-găns) *n.; pl.* -GANCES (-găn-sĕz),
el'e-gan-cy (-găn-sĭ) *)* -GANCIES (-sĭz). **1.** State or quality of being elegant. **2.** That which is elegant.

el'e-gant (-gănt), *a.* [4] **1.** Marked by niceties of manner, dress, or the like. **2.** Characterized by grace, propriety, and refinement. **3.** Neat or simple and apt. **4.** Keenly appreciative of what is elegant. — **ly,** *adv.* [8].

e-le'gi-ac (ē-lē'jĭ-ăk; ĕl'ē-jī'ăk), *a.* **1.** Pertaining to elegies; mournful. **2.** Used in elegies.

el'e-gy (ĕl'ē-jĭ), *n.; pl.* -GIES (-jĭz). A mournful or plaintive poem; a funeral song.

el'e-ment (-mĕnt), *n.* **1.** One of the simple substances (generally earth, air, fire, and water) formerly believed to compose the physical universe. **2.** *pl.* Conditions of weather, usually implying violent weather. **3.** One of the four elements (def. 1) viewed as a natural habitat; hence, the sphere suited to any person or thing. **4.** A substance not separable into substances different from itself, at least by ordinary chemical processes, as carbon, copper, gold, iron, lead, mercury, oxygen, sulphur, tin, etc. **5.** One of the constituent parts of anything. **6.** *pl.* **a** The fundamental principles of any system in philosophy, science, or art; rudiments. **b** The bread and wine used in the Eucharist.

el'e-men'tal (-mĕn'tăl), *a.* [4] **1.** Pert. to the phenomena of physical nature in general. **2.** Pert. to rudiments; elementary. **3.** Forming a constituent part. — **el'e-men'tal-ly,** *adv.* [8].

el'e-men'ta-ry (ĕl'ē-mĕn'tà-rĭ), *a.* [4] **1.** Consisting of a single element. **2.** Treating of the first principles of anything; introductory.

el'e-phant (ĕl'ē-fănt),*n.* Any of various well-known mammals, of Africa and India, having long tusks and the snout prolonged into a prehensile proboscis. They are the largest existing land animals.

el'e-phan'tine (-făn'tĭn; -tīn), *a.* [4] Like, or suggestive of, an elephant; hence, huge; heavy.

el'e-vate (ĕl'ē-vāt), *v. t.* [1] **1.** To lift up; raise; exalt; ennoble. **2.** To exhilarate; raise the spirits of.

el'e-va'tion (-vā'shŭn), *n.* **1.** Act of elevating; height; exaltation. **2.** An elevated place. **3.** Height above sea level. **4.** A drawing of an object that shows its vertical or upright parts.

el'e-va'tor (ĕl'ē-vā'tẽr), *n.* One that raises anything; as: **a** A contrivance, as an endless chain with buckets, for raising grain to a loft. **b** A cage or platform for conveying persons, goods, etc., to or from different levels; a lift. **c** A building for elevating, storing, and discharging grain.

e-lev'en (ē-lĕv''n), *a.* One more than ten. — *n.* **1.** The sum of ten and one. **2.** A symbol representing eleven units, as 11 or xi. **3.** *Sports.* Eleven players forming a team or side, as in cricket or football.

e-lev'enth (-'nth), *a.* **1.** Next after the tenth. **2.** Constituting one of eleven equal parts into which a (whole) thing may be divided. — *n.* **1.** An eleventh part. **2.** An eleventh unit or object.

elf (ĕlf), *n.; pl.* ELVES (ĕlvz). **1.** A mythical being, esp. a sprite; fairy. **2.** An elflike human being.

elf'in (ĕl'fĭn), *a.* [4] Pertaining to or resembling elves; produced or ruled by elves. — *n.* An elf.

elf'ish (-fĭsh), *a.* [4] Of, pert. to, or like, elves; mischievous; impish. — **elf'ish-ly,** *adv.* [8].

e-lic'it (ē-lĭs'ĭt), *v. t.* To draw out or forth; educe, to draw or entice forth; evoke.

e-lide' (ē-līd'), *v. t.* [1] To cut off or omit.

el'i-gi-bil'i-ty (ĕl'ĭ-jĭ-bĭl'ĭ-tĭ),*n.* Quality of being eligible; fitness; as, the *eligibility* of a candidate.

el'i-gi-ble (ĕl'ĭ-jĭ-b'l), *a.* Fitted or qualified to be chosen. — *n.* One that is eligible. — **gi-bly,** *adv.*

e-lim'i-nate (ē-lĭm'ĭ-nāt), *v. t.* [1] **1.** To throw out; expel; exclude. **2.** To ignore as unimportant or inapplicable. **3.** To cause (an unknown quantity) to disappear from an equation.

e-lim'i-na'tion (-nā'shŭn), *n.* Act of eliminating.

e-li'sion (ē-lĭzh'ŭn), *n.* An eliding or cutting off, as of a vowel or syllable, a passage in a book, etc.

é'lite' (ā'lēt'), *n.* [F.] A choice or select body.

e-lix'ir (ē-lĭk'sẽr), *n.* **1.** A supposed essence or substance with the power to prolong life indefinitely, sought by the alchemists. **2.** An aromatic, sweetened, alcoholic preparation of a drug.

E-liz'a-be'than (ē-lĭz'à-bē'thăn), *a.* Pertaining to Queen Elizabeth (1533-1603) or her times.

elk (ĕlk), *n.* **1.** The largest existing deer of Europe and Asia, having broad palmate antlers. **2.** In America, the wapiti.

ell (ĕl), *n.* A measure, chiefly for cloth, now little used, varying from 27 to 48 inches.

---

el·lipse' (ĕ-lĭps'), *n.; pl.* -LIPSES (-sĕz). A plane curve which is the path of a point the sum of whose distances from two fixed points (foci) is constant.

el·lip'sis (ĕ-lĭp'sĭs), *n.; pl.* -LIPSES (-sēz). *Gram.* Omission of a word or words obviously understood, but necessary to make the construction complete.

el·lip'tic (-tĭk), **el·lip'ti·cal** (-tĭ-kăl), *a.* **1.** Pertaining to, or having the form of, an ellipse. **2.** *Gram.* Pertaining to ellipsis; having a part omitted. — **el·lip'ti·cal·ly**, *adv.* [8].

Ellipse. F F' Foci ; P P' P'' any point in bounding curve. FP + PF' = FP'' + P''F' = FP' + P'F'.

elm (ĕlm), *n.* **1.** Any of various well-known shade trees. **2.** The hard, tough wood of the elm.

el'o·cu'tion (ĕl'ō-kū'shŭn), *n.* The art of public speaking or reading, esp. with reference to the graces of intonation, gesture, etc.

el'o·cu'tion·a·ry (-â-rĭ), *a.* Pert. to elocution.

el'o·cu'tion·ist, *n.* One versed in elocution.

e·lon'gate (ē-lŏn'gāt), *v. t. & i.* [1] To lengthen; extend. — (-gāt), *a.* —**gat'ed** (-gāt'ĕd), *p. a.*

e'lon·ga'tion (ē'lŏn-gā'shŭn), *n.* **1.** Act of elongating. **2.** That which lengthens out; continuation.

e·lope' (ē-lōp'), *v. i.* [1] To run away from one's spouse or home with a lover. — **e·lop'er**, *n.* [8].

e·lope'ment (ē-lōp'mĕnt), *n.* Act of eloping.

el'o·quence (ĕl'ō-kwĕns), *n.* Discourse characterized by force, art, and persuasiveness; also, the art or power of employing such discourse.

el'o·quent (-kwĕnt), *a.* [4] Expressing or able to express one's self eloquently; marked by eloquence. — **el'o·quent·ly**, *adv.*

else (ĕls), *a., pron.* Other; other one. — *adv.* **1.** In a different place, time, or respect. **2.** In another or a contrary case; otherwise.

else'where' (-hwâr'), *adv.* In or to another place.

e·lu'ci·date (ē-lū'sĭ-dāt), *v. t.* [1] To make clear or manifest; illustrate.

e·lu'ci·da'tion (-dā'shŭn), *n.* A making clear; act of elucidating, or that which elucidates.

e·lude' (ē-lūd'), *v. t.* [1] To avoid by dexterity or stratagem; evade; baffle.

e·lu'sion (ē-lū'zhŭn), *n.* Act of eluding; evasion.

e·lu'sive (-sĭv), *a.* [4] Tending to elude; adroitly evading; of ideas, etc., not easily understood or defined; baffling. —**ly**, *adv.* [8] —**ness**, *n.* [8].

e·lu'so·ry (ē-lū'sō-rĭ), *a.* [4] Elusive; evasive.

elves (ĕlvz), *n., pl.* of ELF.

elv'ish (ĕl'vĭsh), *a.* [4] Elfin; elfish.

E·ly'sian (ē-lĭzh'ăn; ē-lĭz'ĭ-ăn), *a.* Pertaining to Elysium; delightful.

E·ly'si·um (-ĭ-ŭm), *n. Class. Myth.* **1.** The dwelling place of happy souls after death. **2.** Any similarly conceived place or state of delight; a paradise.

e·ma'ci·ate (ē-mā'shĭ-āt), *v. t.* [1] To cause to lose flesh so as to become very lean.

e·ma'ci·a'tion (-ā'shŭn), *n.* Process of emaciating; emaciated condition.

em'a·nate (ĕm'á·nāt), *v. i.* [1] To issue forth from a source.

em'a·na'tion (-nā'shŭn), *n.* **1.** Act of emanating. **2.** That which emanates.

e·man'ci·pate (ē-mǎn'sĭ-pāt), *v. t.* [1] To set free; esp. from bondage; liberate. —**pa'tor**, *n.* [8].

e·man'ci·pa'tion (-pā'shŭn), *n.* Act or process of freeing; liberation; release; freedom.

e·mas'cu·late (-mǎs'kū-lāt), *v. t.* [1] To deprive of virile power or masculine vigor or spirit; weaken. — (-lǐt), *a.* [4] Deprived of virility or vigor.

e·mas'cu·la'tion (-lā'shŭn), *n.* Act or process of emasculating; state of being emasculated.

em·balm' (ĕm-bäm'), *v. t.* **1.** To treat (a dead body), as with aromatic oils, etc., so as to prevent decay. **2.** To keep in memory. — **em·balm'er**, *n.* [8].

em·bank' (-bǎngk'), *v. t.* To protect or confine by a bank or banks, as of earth.

em·bank'ment (-mĕnt), *n.* **1.** Act of embanking. **2.** A raised structure of earth, gravel, etc., to retain or hold back water, carry a roadway, etc.

em·bar'go (-bär'gō), *n.; pl.* -GOES (-gōz). **1.** An edict of a government prohibiting the departure or entry of ships of commerce at a port or ports. **2.** Any prohibition imposed by law on commerce.

em·bark' (ĕm-bärk'), *v. t. & i.* **1.** To put or go on shipboard for a voyage. **2.** To engage, enlist, or invest (as persons, money, etc.) in any affair.

em'bar·ka'tion (ĕm'bär-kā'shŭn), *n.* Act of embarking; as, the *embarkation* of troops.

em·bar'rass (ĕm-bǎr'ǎs), *v. t.* **1.** To confuse; disconcert; nonplus. **2.** To impede; complicate. **3.** To involve in financial difficulties.

em·bar'rass·ment (-mĕnt), *n.* Embarrassed condition; that which embarrasses.

em·bas'sa·dor (-bǎs'á-dẽr). Var. of AMBASSADOR.

em'bas·sy (ĕm'bá-sĭ), *n.; pl.* -SIES (-sĭz). **1.** Function or position of an ambassador; the sending of ambassadors. **2.** An ambassador and his suite. **3.** The residence or office of an ambassador.

em·bat'tle (ĕm-bǎt''l), *v. t.* [1] To arrange in order of battle; to prepare for battle.

em·bed' (-bĕd'), *v. t.* To lay or inclose in surrounding matter.

em·bel'lish (-bĕl'ĭsh), *v. t.* **1.** To make beautiful or elegant, as by ornaments. **2.** To set out with fanciful enlargements; to heighten, as a story.

em·bel'lish·ment (-mĕnt), *n.* **1.** Act of embellishing. **2.** That which embellishes; ornament.

em'ber (ĕm'bẽr), *n.* A lighted coal smoldering in ashes; *pl.*, smoldering ashes.

em'ber, *a. R. C. & Eng. Ch.* Designating, or pertaining to, certain days (ember days) in each season, set apart for fasting and prayer.

em·bez'zle (ĕm-bĕz''l), *v. t.* [1] To appropriate (property) fraudulently to one's own use. — **em·bez'zler** (-lẽr), *n.* [8].

em·bez'zle·ment (-mĕnt), *n.* Act of embezzling.

em·bit'ter (-bĭt'ẽr), *v. t.* To make bitter or more bitter.

em·bla'zon (-blā'z'n), *v. t.* To depict (heraldic bearings); hence, to display brilliantly or conspicuously. — **em·bla'zon·ry** (-rĭ), *n.*

em'blem (ĕm'blĕm), *n.* A visible sign of an idea; a figurative representation; a symbol.

em'blem·at'ic (-ǎt'ĭk) } *a.* Pertaining to an **em'blem·at'i·cal** (-ĭ-kǎl) } emblem; symbolic.

em·bod'i·ment (ĕm-bŏd'ĭ-mĕnt), *n.* An embodying; thing embodying or embodied.

em·bod'y (-ĭ), *v. t.* [2] **1.** To give a body to, as

▲ spirit; incarnate. 2. Hence, to render concrete and definite. **3.** To cause to become a body or part of a body; incorporate.

em-bold'en (-bōl'd'n), *v. t.* To make bold.

em-bos'om (ĕm-bŏŏz'ŭm), *v. t.* **1.** To take into the bosom; cherish. **2.** To inclose; shelter closely.

em-boss' (-bŏs'), *v. t.* **1.** To ornament with raised work. **2.** To raise in relief. — **-er,** *n.* [8].

em-bow'er (-bou'ẽr),*v.t.&i.* To shelter or seclude, as in a bower; as, a cottage *embowered* with roses.

em-brace' (-brās'), *v. t.* [1] **1.** To clasp in the arms. **2.** To encircle; inclose. **3.** To take up; accept; adopt. **4.** To include as parts of a whole; comprehend. — *v. i.* To join in an embrace. — *n.* An encircling with the arms; clasp; hug.

em-bra'sure (-brā'zhŭr), *n.* **1.** A splay of a door or window. **2.** *Fort.* An opening in a wall for cannon, with sides flaring outward.

em-bro-ca'tion (ĕm/brō-kā'shŭn), *n.* Act of moistening and rubbing (a diseased part) with a lotion, as liniment; also, the liquid or lotion so used.

em-broid'er (ĕm-broid'ẽr),*v.t.&i.* To ornament or make ornamentally with the needle. — **-er,** *n.* [8].

em-broid'er-y (-ĭ), *n.; pl.* -ERIES (-ĭz) **1.** Needlework to enrich fabrics, etc. **2.** Ornamentation, esp. by contrasted figures and colors.

em-broil' (-broil'), *v. t.* To confuse or stir up by discord; involve in difficulties by strife.

em-broil'ment, *n.* Act of embroiling; quarrel.

em'bry-o (ĕm/brĭ-ō), *n.; pl.* -os (-ōz). **1.** An animal in the earliest stages of development, as before hatching from an egg. **2.** The rudimentary plant contained in the seed. **3.** A beginning stage of anything. — *a.* Rudimentary.

em'bry-on'ic (-ŏn'ĭk),*a.* Of or pert. to an embryo.

e-meer' (ĕ-mēr'). Var. of EMIR.

e-mend' (ĕ-mĕnd'), *v. t.* To free from faults; esp., to correct (a literary work).

e/men-da'tion (ē/mĕn-dā'shŭn; ĕm/ĕn-), *n.* A mending; correction, esp. of a literary text.

e/men-da'tor (-tẽr), *n.* One who emends.

e-mend'a-to-ry (ĕ-mĕn'dȧ-tō-rĭ), *a.* Of or pertaining to emendation.

em'er-ald (ĕm/ẽr-ȧld), *n.* A gem: **a** A variety of beryl, of various shades of green. **b** The Oriental emerald, a green variety of transparent corundum. — *a.* Of a rich green color.

e-merge' (ĕ-mûrj'), *v. i.* [1] To rise from or as from an enveloping fluid; come out into view.

e-mer'gence (ĕ-mûr'jĕns), *n.* Act of emerging.

e-mer'gen-cy (ĕ-mûr'jĕn-sĭ), *n.; pl.* -CIES (-sĭz). An unforeseen occurrence or condition calling for immediate action; exigency.

e-mer'i-tus (-mĕr'ĭ-tŭs),*a.* Retired without change of rank from active duty because of age, infirmity, or long service; — esp. of a clergyman or professor.

e-mer'sion (ĕ-mûr'shŭn), *n.* Act of emerging.

em'er-y (ĕm/ẽr-ĭ), *n.* A very hard dark mineral used, esp. powdered or crushed, for polishing and grinding. It is a variety of corundum.

e-met'ic (ĕ-mĕt'ĭk), *a.* Tending to cause vomiting. — *n.* An emetic agent.

em'i-grant (ĕm/ĭ-grȧnt), *a.* Removing from one country to another. — *n.* One who emigrates.

em'i-grate (-grāt), *v. i.* [1] To remove from one country or state to another.

em'i-gra'tion (-grā'shŭn),*n.* **1.** Act of emigrating. **2.** A body of emigrants; emigrants collectively.

em'i-nence (ĕm/ĭ-nĕns), *n.* **1.** That which is eminent; a height. **2.** An elevated station; high rank; distinction. **3.** [*cap.*] A title of honor, now applied only to cardinals.

em'i-nen-cy (-nĕn-sĭ), *n.* Eminence; elevation.

em'i-nent (-nĕnt), *a.* [4] **1.** Lofty; prominent. **2.** Being above others by birth, merit, etc.; virtue; distinguished. **3.** Conspicuous. — **-ly,** *adv.* [8].

e-mir' (ĕ-mēr'; ē'mēr), *n.* An Arabian chieftain or ruler; also, a title of certain Turkish officials.

em'is-sa-ry (ĕm/ĭ-să-rĭ), *n.; pl.* -RIES (-rĭz). An agent employed to advance certain interests or to gain information; esp., a secret agent.

e-mis'sion (ĕ-mĭsh/ŭn), *n.* **1.** Act of emitting. **2.** That which is emitted; discharge; emanation.

e-mit' (ĕ-mĭt'), *v. t.; -MIT'TED ; -MIT'TING.* **1.** To throw or give out or off. **2.** To issue, as currency.

e-mol'lient (ĕ-mŏl'yĕnt ; -ĭ-ĕnt), *a.* Softening; making supple. — *n.* A softening or soothing application to allay soreness, etc.

e-mol'u-ment (-ū-mĕnt), *n.* Profit from office, employment, or labor; perquisites, fees, or salary.

e-mo'tion (ĕ-mō'shŭn), *n.* A feeling of joy, grief, fear, hate, love, awe, etc.

e-mo'tion-al (-ăl), *a.* **1.** Characterized by emotion. **2.** Appealing to or arousing emotion.

em'per-or (ĕm/pẽr-ẽr), *n.* The sovereign or monarch of an empire.

em'pha-sis (ĕm/fȧ-sĭs), *n.; pl.* -SES (-sēz). **1.** In reading or speaking, a force or stress of utterance given to important words or syllables. **2.** Special impressiveness of expression or weight of thought.

em'pha-size (-sīz), *v. t.* [1] To give emphasis to.

em-phat'ic (ĕm-făt'ĭk), *a.* [4] **1.** Uttered with emphasis; forcibly expressive ; as, an *emphatic* tone or word. **2.** Impressive; striking; as, an *emphatic* gesture. **3.** Marked by emphasis of voice, gesture, or language ; — of persons. — **--i-cal-ly,** *adv.* [8].

em'pire (ĕm/pīr), *n.* **1.** A group of nations or states under a single sovereign power. **b** A state including broad territories and various peoples, or having its ruler styled *emperor*. **2.** Imperial organization, rule, or domain ; hence, dominion.

em-pir'ic (ĕm-pĭr'ĭk), *n.* One who follows an empirical method; quack; charlatan. — *a.* Empirical.

em-pir'i-cal (-ĭ-kăl), *a.* [4] **1.** Pertaining to, or founded on, experiment or experience. **2.** Depending on observation alone, without due regard to theory. — **em-pir'i-cal-ly,** *adv.* [8].

em-pir'i-cism (-ĭ-sĭz'm), *n.* Method or practice of an empiric, esp. in medicine ; hence, quackery.

em-place'ment (-plās/mĕnt), *n.* **1.** Space in a fortification assigned to a gun or group of guns. **2.** The gun platform, parapet, and accessories.

em-ploy' (-ploi'), *v. t.* **1.** To make use of ; use. **2.** To occupy ; devote. **3.** To give work to. — *n.* State of being employed ; employment.

em-ploy-ee' (ĕm-ploi-ē'), *n.* One employed by another, as a clerk, workman, etc.

em-ploy'er (ĕm-ploi'ẽr), *n.* One who employs another or others.

em-ploy'ment (-mĕnt), *n.* **1.** Act of employing; state of being employed. **2.** That which engages or occupies; occupation.

---

em-po′ri-um (ĕm-pō′rĭ-ŭm), *n.; pl.* E. -RIUMS (-ŭmz), L. -RIA (-ä). A place of trade; commercial center; often, esp., a principal center of trade.

em-pow′er (-pou′ẽr), *v. t.* To give power to.

em′press (ĕm′prĕs), *n.* The consort of an emperor; a female sovereign of an empire.

emp′ti-ness (ĕmp′tĭ-nĕs), *n.* State of being empty.

emp′ty (-tĭ), *a.* [3] **1.** Containing nothing; without contents; vacant. **2.** Without substance, effect, sense, feeling, sincerity, etc. — *v. t. & i.* [2] To make or become empty; of a river, or the like, to discharge (itself).

em-pyr′e-al (ĕm-pĭr′ē-ăl; ĕm′pĭ-rē′ăl), *a.* Of or pertaining to the empyrean; celestial.

em′py-re′an (ĕm′pĭ-rē′ăn), *n.* The highest heaven. — *a.* Empyreal.

e′mu (ē′mū), *n.* An Australian bird related to the ostrich.

em′u-late (ĕm′ů-lāt), *v.t.* [1] To strive to equal or excel (another); vie with; rival.

em′u-la′tion (-lā′-shŭn), *n.* Endeavor to equal or excel; rivalry.

em′u-la-tive (ĕm′ů-lā-tĭv), *a.* Pertaining to emulation; rivaling.

em′u-la′tor (-lā′tẽr), *n.* One who emulates.

em′u-lous (-lŭs), *a.* Ambitious to equal or excel another. — **em′u-lous-ly**, *adv.* [8].

e-mul′si-fy (ē-mŭl′sĭ-fī), *v. t.* [2] To convert into an emulsion; form an emulsion with.

e-mul′sion (ē-mŭl′shŭn), *n.* A liquid preparation having the color and consistency of milk.

en-a′ble (ĕn-ā′b′l), *v. t.* [1] To make able; give (one) power or ability (to be or do something).

en-act′ (-ăkt′), *v. t.* **1.** To make into an act or law; decree. **2.** To act the part of; represent.

en-act′ment (-mĕnt), *n.* **1.** Act of enacting; state of being enacted. **2.** Thing enacted; law; decree.

en-am′el (-ăm′ĕl), *v. t.* [7] **1.** To lay enamel on; decorate with enamel. **2.** To form a glossy surface like enamel on. — *n.* **1.** A glassy composition, usually opaque, for coating the surface of metal, glass, or pottery. **2.** Any of various enamellike varnishes, etc. **3.** The very hard outer layer or surface of the teeth. — **en-am′el-er**, *n.* [7, 8].

en-am′or (-ăm′ẽr), *v. t. & i.* [5] To inflame with love.

‖en′ bloc′ (äN′ blŏk′). [F.] In a block; as a whole.

en-camp′ (ĕn-kămp′), *v. i. & t.* To form, or form into, a camp. — **en-camp′ment** (-mĕnt), *n.*

en-caus′tic (-kôs′tĭk), *a. Fine Arts.* Prepared by heat; having decorations burned in, as on pottery.

en-chain′ (-chān′), *v. t.* **1.** To bind with, or hold in, chains; fetter. **2.** To hold fast; confine.

en-chant′ (-chȧnt′), *v. t.* **1.** To act on by charms; bewitch. **2.** To delight greatly. — **-er**, *n.* [8].

en-chant′ment (-mĕnt), *n.* Act of enchanting; state of being enchanted; that which enchants.

en-chant′ress (-chȧnt′rĕs), *n.* A sorceress; also, a fascinating woman.

en-cir′cle (-sûr′k′l), *v. t.* [1] To circle, or form a circle, about; surround.

en-co′mi-um (-kō′mĭ-ŭm), *n.* High praise.

en-com′pass (-kŭm′pȧs), *v. t.* To surround.

en′core′ (äN′kōr′; äN′kōr′), *adv. & interj.* Once more; again; — used as a call for a repetition of a part of a play, concert, etc. — (*pron.* äN′kōr′; äN′kōr), *n.* The demand for repetition, as by applause; also, the repetition.

en-core′ (äN-kōr′; äN′kōr), *v. t.* [1] To call for a repetition of or from.

en-coun′ter (ĕn-koun′tẽr), *v. t. & i.* To meet, esp. in opposition or with hostile intent. — *n.* A meeting, esp. with hostile purpose; a combat; battle.

en-cour′age (ĕn-kŭr′ăj), *v. t.* [1] **1.** To inspire with courage, spirit, or hope; inspirit. **2.** To give help or patronage to, as an industry; foster.

en-cour′age-ment (-ăj-mĕnt), *n.* **1.** State of being encouraged. **2.** That which encourages.

en-cour′ag-ing (-ā-jĭng), *p.a.* [4] Giving hope or courage; inspiriting. — **-cour′ag-ing-ly**, *adv.* [8].

en-croach′ (-krōch′), *v. i.* To enter gradually or by stealth into the rights of another; trespass.

en-croach′ment, *n.* Act or process of encroaching.

en-cum′ber (-kŭm′bẽr), *v.t.* **1.** To impede in motion or action; retard; embarrass. **2.** To render awkward, obstructive, or disagreeable, by superfluous parts, etc. **3.** To place a burden on, as a debt or legal claim.

en-cum′brance (-brȧns), *n.* **1.** That which encumbers. **2.** *Law.* A claim or lien on an estate.

en-cyc′li-cal (-sĭk′lĭ-kȧl; -sĭ′klĭ-), *a.* Sent to many persons or places; general. — *n.* An encyclical letter, esp. from the Pope.

en-cy′clo-pæ′di-a (-sī′klō-pē′dĭ-ȧ), *n.*, **-pæ′dic** (-dĭk), *a.* Vars. of ENCYCLOPEDIA, ENCYCLOPEDIC.

en-cy′clo-pe′di-a, *n.* A work in which the branches of learning are treated in separate articles.

en-cy′clo-pe′dic (-pē′dĭk), *a.* Pertaining to an encyclopedia; embracing a wide range of subjects.

end (ĕnd), *n.* **1.** A limit or boundary; esp., an extreme region or part. **2.** Extreme or last point or part; conclusion. **3.** Issue; result; also, final state. **4.** Death; destruction. **5.** The object aimed at in any effort; purpose; aim. **6.** That which is left; remnant; scrap. — *v. t. & i.* **1.** To bring or come to an end; finish. **2.** To form or be at the end of. **3.** To destroy; die.

en-dan′ger (ĕn-dān′jẽr), *v. t.* To bring into danger.

en-dear′ (-dēr′), *v. t.* To make or hold dear.

en-dear′ment (-mĕnt), *n.* Act of endearing; that which endears; caress.

en-deav′or (-dĕv′ẽr), *v. t. & i.* [5] To strive to achieve or reach; try; attempt. — *n.* A systematic or continuous attempt; an effort; a trial. — **en-deav′or-er**, *n.* [5, 8].

en-dem′ic (-dĕm′ĭk), *a.* Peculiar to a district or particular locality, or class of persons; as, an *endemic* disease. — *n.* That which is endemic.

end′ing (ĕn′dĭng), *n.* **1.** Termination; conclusion; also, death. **2.** *Gram.* The final syllable or letter of a word, esp. when inflectional.

en′dive (ĕn′dĭv; -dīv), *n.* An herb related to chicory. Its leaves are used for salads.

end′less (ĕnd′lĕs), *a.* **1.** Without end or ends; boundless; eternal; infinite. **2.** Continuous by reason of the ends being united; as, an *endless* chain. — **-ly,** *adv.* [8] — **-ness,** *n.* [8].

en-dorse′ (ĕn-dôrs′), *v. t.,* **en-dorse′ment,** *n.,* etc. See INDORSE, etc.

en-dow′ (-dou′),*v.t.* **1.** To furnish with a permanent source of income. **2.** To furnish with anything of the nature of a gift, as a quality or faculty.

en-dow′ment, *n.* **1.** Act of endowing. **2.** Property with which a person or an institution is endowed. **3.** Talents; gifts; — usually in *pl.*

en-due′ (ĕn-dū′), *v. t.* [1] To endow; indue.

en-dur′a-ble (ĕn-dūr′a̍-b'l), *a.* Capable of being endured.

en-dur′ance (-ăns), *n.* **1.** State, quality, or act of enduring. **2.** Ability to endure.

en-dure′ (-dūr′), *v. i.* [1] **1.** To continue in existence; last. **2.** To remain firm, as under trial; to suffer or bear up patiently. — *v. t.* **1.** To remain firm under; sustain. **2.** To put up with; tolerate; as, to *endure* a nuisance.

end′ways (ĕnd′wāz′), **end′wise** (-wīz′), *adv.* **1.** On end. **2.** With the end forward.

en′e-ma (ĕn′e̍-må; ĕ-nē′må), *n.; pl.* E. -MAS (-måz), L. ENEMATA (ĕ-nĕm′å-tå). *Med.* A liquid injected into the rectum.

en′e-my (ĕn′e̍-mĭ), *n.; pl.* -MIES (-mĭz). **1.** One who is hostile to another; hence, whatever does injury to one. **2.** A military foe.

en′er-get′ic (ĕn′ẽr-jĕt′ĭk), *a.* [4] Having energy; active; forceful; vigorous. — **-i-cal-ly,** *adv.* [8].

en′er-gize (ĕn′ẽr-jīz), *v. i.* [1] To put forth energy. — *v. t.* To impart energy to.

en′er-gy (ĕn′ẽr-jĭ), *n.; pl.* -GIES (-jĭz). Power to act; vigor; force of action; as, a man of *energy*.

en′er-vate (ĕn′ẽr-vāt),*v. t.* [1] To deprive of nerve, force, strength, or courage.

en′er-va′tion (ĕn′ẽr-vā′shŭn), *n.* Action or process of enervating; state of being enervated.

en-fee′ble (ĕn-fē′b'l), *v. t.* [1] To make feeble; weaken. — **en-fee′ble-ment,** *n.*

en′fi-lade′ (ĕn′fĭ-lād′), *n.* A firing along a trench, a line of troops, etc.; a raking fire. — *v. t.* [1] To rake, or be in a position to rake, with gun fire.

en-fold′ (ĕn-fōld′), *v. t.* Enwrap. = INFOLD.

en-force′ (-fōrs′), *v. t.* [1] **1.** To force; compel. **2.** To put in force or effect, as a law. **3.** To lay stress upon; emphasize.

en-force′a-ble, *a.* Capable of being enforced.

en-force′ment (-mĕnt), *n.* Act of enforcing.

en-fran′chise (-frăn′chĭz), *v. t.* [1] **1.** To set free. **2.** To endow with a franchise; admit to citizenship.

en-fran′chise-ment (-chĭz-mĕnt), *n.* Act of enfranchising; state of being enfranchised.

en-gage′ (-gāj′), *v. t.* [1] **1.** To put under pledge; pledge, as by a promise. **2.** To betroth. **3.** To secure or bespeak (services, etc.). **4.** To win and attach; draw. **5.** To employ the attention and efforts of. **6.** To enter into contest with; also, to join or interlock (weapons). **7.** *Machinery.* To come into gear with; interlock with. — *v. i.* **1.** To promise or pledge one's self. **2.** To embark in a business; to take a part. **3.** To enter into conflict. **4.** *Machinery.* To interlock and interact.

en-gaged′ (ĕn-gājd′),*p. a.* **1.** Occupied; employed. **2.** Pledged; esp., betrothed.

en-gage′ment (-gāj′mĕnt), *n.* **1.** Act of engaging; state of being engaged; as: **a** Betrothal. **b** Hostile encounter. **c** *Machinery.* State of being in gear. **2.** An occupation, obligation, or enterprise. **3.** An appointment.

en-gag′ing (-gāj′ĭng),*p. a.* [4] Attracting the attention or affections; attractive. — **-ly,** *adv.* [8].

en-gen′der (-jĕn′dẽr), *v. t.* **1.** To beget. **2.** To bear; bring forth; occasion, excite.

en′gine (ĕn′jĭn), *n.* **1.** Any mechanical instrument. **2.** A machine for converting physical force, as heat, into mechanical power. **3.** A locomotive.

en′gi-neer′ (-jĭ-nēr′), *n.* **1.** One skilled in engineering. **2.** One who manages a stationary or a locomotive engine.

en′gi-neer′, *v. t.* **1.** To lay out or manage as an engineer. **2.** To guide the course of; manage.

en′gi-neer′ing, *n.* The art and science by which the mechanical properties of matter are utilized in structures and machines.

Eng′lish (ĭŋ′glĭsh), *a.* **1.** Of, pertaining to, or characteristic of, England or its inhabitants or citizens. **2.** In, or belonging to, the English language. — *n.* **1.** *pl.* The people of England. **2.** The language of the English, and of the people of the U. S. and most of the British colonies. — *v. t.* To translate into English.

Eng′lish-man (-măn), *n.; pl.* -MEN (-mĕn). A native-born or a naturalized citizen of England.

en-graft′ (ĕn-gràft′), *v. t.* To graft; ingraft.

en-grave′ (-grāv′), *v. t.* [1] **1.** To carve figures, letters, or devices on. **2.** To form by incisions, as on wood, stone, or metal, esp. for printing. **3.** To impress deeply. — **en-grav′er** (-grāv′ẽr), *n.* [8]

en-grav′ing (-ĭng), *n.* **1.** Act or art of producing incised or raised figures on metal, wood, etc. **2.** An engraved plate or block. **3.** An impression from an engraving; a print

en-gross′ (-grōs′), *v. t.* **1.** To copy or write in a large hand; write a perfect copy of, as of a decree. **2.** To take the whole of; absorb; monopolize. —

en-gross′er, *n.* [8] — **en-gross′ment** (-mĕnt), *n.*

en-gulf′ (-gŭlf′), *v. t.* To swallow up as in a gulf.

en-hance′ (-håns′), *v. t. & i.* [1] To advance, augment, or elevate; heighten; intensify.

en-hance′ment (-mĕnt), *n.* Increase; advance.

e-nig′ma (e̍-nĭg′må), *n.* **1.** An obscure or inexplicable saying; riddle. **2.** Anything inexplicable

e′nig-mat′ic (ē′nĭg-măt′ĭk; ĕn′ĭg-), **e′nig-mat′i-cal** (-ĭ-kăl), *a.* Relating to or resembling an enigma; obscure; puzzling. — **-i-cal-ly,** *adv.* [8].

en-join′ (ĕn-join′), *v. t.* **1.** To command; charge. **2.** To forbid; prohibit.

en-joy′ (-joi′), *v. t.* **1.** To take pleasure in. **2.** To have and use with satisfaction.— **en-joy′er,** *n.* [8].

en-joy′a-ble, *a.* Capable of being enjoyed, or of giving joy. — **en-joy′a-bly,** *adv.* [8].

en-joy′ment (-ĕn-joi′mĕnt), *n.* Act or state of enjoying anything; possession and use.

en-kin′dle (-kĭn′d'l), *v. t. & i.* [1] To kindle.

en-large′ (-lärj′), *v. t. & i.* [1] To increase in quantity, capacity, dimensions, or extent; extend.

en-large′ment (-mĕnt), *n.* **1.** An enlarging; state of being enlarged. **2.** That which enlarges or is enlarged; *Photog.*, an enlarged photograph.

en-light′en (-līt′'n), *v. t.* **1.** To instruct; also, to give insight to. — **en-light′en-er,** *n.* [8].

en-light'en-ment (ĕn-līt″n-mĕnt), *n.* Act of enlightening ; state of being enlightened.

en-list' (-lĭst′), *v. t. & i.* **1.** To enter on a list ; enroll. **2.** To engage for military or naval service. **3.** To engage one's support and aid in behalf of.

en-list'ment (-mĕnt), *n.* Act of enlisting ; state of being enlisted.

en-liv'en (-lĭv′n), *v. t.* **1.** To give life, action, or motion to ; quicken. **2.** To give spirit or vivacity to ; animate. — **en-liv'en-er**, *n.* [8].

en'mi-ty (ĕn′mĭ-tĭ), *n.; pl.* -TIES (-tĭz). Quality or state of being hostile ; hatred ; animosity.

en-no'ble (ĕ-nō′b′l; ĕn-nō′-), *v. t.* [1] **1.** To make noble ; elevate ; dignify. **2.** To raise to the nobility.

en-no'ble-ment, *n.* Act of ennobling ; noble rank.

en'nui' (äN-nwē′; äṅ-nwē′), *n.* A feeling of weariness and dissatisfaction from want of occupation or lack of interest ; tedium.

e-nor'mi-ty (ē-nôr′mĭ-tĭ), *n.; pl.* -TIES (-tĭz). Extreme or monstrous wickedness ; an atrocious offense or crime.

e-nor'mous (-mŭs), *a.* **1.** Exceeding the usual rule, norm, or measure ; monstrous. **2.** Greatly exceeding the usual size, number, or degree ; immense. — **e-nor'mous-ly**, *adv.* [8] — **-ness**, *n.* [8].

e-nough' (ē-nŭf′), *a.* Satisfying desire ; giving content ; adequate ; sufficient. — *adv.* In a degree or quantity that satisfies ; sufficiently ; hence, tolerably. — *interj.* Short for *it is enough.* — *n.* A sufficiency ; an adequate quantity.

e-now' (ē-nou′), *a. & adv.* Enough. *Archaic.*

en-quire', **en-quir'y**, etc. Vars. of INQUIRE, etc.

en-rage' (-rāj′), *v. t.* [1] To fill with rage ; madden.

en-rap'ture (-răp′tụ̇r), *v. t.* [1] To transport, or delight beyond measure ; fascinate.

en-rich' (ĕn-rĭch′), *v. t.* **1.** To make rich or richer. **2.** To ornament ; adorn. **3.** To fertilize.

en-rich'ment (-mĕnt), *n.* Act of enriching ; that which enriches.

en-roll' (-rōl′), *v. t.* To insert in a roll, list, or catalogue ; hence, to record;also,to enlist (one's self).

en-roll'ment (-mĕnt), *n.* **1.** Act of enrolling. **2.** A writing in which anything is enrolled.

¶ en′ route' (äN′ rōōt′). [F.] On the way or road.

en-sconce' (ĕn-skŏns′), *v. t.* [1] **1.** To shelter, as with a fort ; conceal. **2.** To establish snugly.

en-shrine' (-shrīn′), *v. t.* [1] To inclose in a shrine ; to cherish as sacred. — **-ment** (-mĕnt), *n.*

en-shroud' (-shroud′), *v. t.* To shroud.

en'sign (ĕn′sīn), *n.* **1.** A flag ; banner ; esp., a national flag or banner. **2.** Badge of office, rank, or power. **3.** **a** In the British army, prior to 1871, the standard bearer of a company or regiment. **b** A commissioned officer in the U. S. navy. See NAVY.

en'si-lage (-sĭ-lāj), *n.* Preservation of green fodder (as cornstalks) by compressing it in a silo ; also, fodder so preserved ; silage.

en-slave' (ĕn-slāv′), *v. t.* [1] To reduce to slavery.

en-slave'ment (-mĕnt), *n.* Act of enslaving ; state of being enslaved ; bondage.

en-sue' (ĕn-sū′), *v. t. & i.* [1] To follow; pursue; come afterward or as a consequence.

en-tab'la-ture (-tăb′lȧ-tụ̇r), *n. Arch.* The wall resting on the capitals of the columns and consisting of the architrave, frieze, and cornice. See COLUMN.

en-tail' (-tāl′), *v. t.* **1.** To settle or bestow, as land

on a person and his descendants so that it cannot be bequeathed at pleasure by any possessor. **2.** To impose as a necessary accompaniment or result. — *n.* An entailing; something, as an estate, entailed ; also, the rule by which the descent is fixed.

en-tan'gle (-tăṅ′g′l), *v. t.* [1] **1.** To tangle. **2.** To involve ; insnare ; hence, to perplex ; bewilder.

en-tan'gle-ment, *n.* Act of entangling ; state of being entangled ; that which entangles.

¶ en-tente' (äN′täNt′), *n.* [F.] An understanding; esp. [cap.], the alliance between France, Great Britain, and Russia, dating from 1907, commonly called the *Triple Entente.*

en'ter (ĕn′tẽr), *v. i.* **1.** To go, or come in, to a place or condition. **2.** To consider or treat fully, as in discussion;— with *into.* **3.** To make a beginning; engage ; start. **4.** To make one's self a party ;— with *into.* **5.** To form a constituent part ; become a part or partaker. — *v. t.* **1.** To come or go into; penetrate ; of time, to pass within the limits of. **2.** To make a beginning in; take up ; begin. **3.** To become a member of ; join. **4.** To cause to go (into), or to be admitted ; insert ; enroll; record.

en-ter'ic (ĕn-tĕr′ĭk), *a. Anat.* Intestinal.

en'ter-prise (ĕn′tẽr-prīz), *n.* **1.** That which is, or is to be, undertaken ; project ; esp., a bold or arduous attempt; undertaking ; venture. **2.** Readiness to engage in bold or arduous projects.

en'ter-pris'ing (-prīz′ĭng), *p. a.* [4] Having a disposition for enterprise; having initiative.

en'ter-tain' (-tān′), *v. t.* **1.** To give hospitable reception or maintenance to. **2.** To receive and take into consideration. **3.** To harbor, as a grudge. **4.** To amuse; divert. — *v. i.* To receive, or provide entertainment for, guests. — **-er**, *n.*

en'ter-tain'ing, *p. a.* [4] Affording entertainment ; amusing ; pleasing. — **-ly**, *adv.* [8].

en'ter-tain'ment (-mĕnt), *n.* **1.** Act of entertaining; reception;esp.,act of receiving as host. **2.** State of being entertained. **3.** That which entertains, or diverts, or that with which one is entertained.

en-thrall' (-thrôl′), *v. t.* **1.** To hold in thrall; enslave. **2.** To charm; hold spellbound.— **-ment**,*n.*

en-throne' (-thrōn′), *v. t.* [1] To seat on or as on a throne ; to invest with sovereignty. — **-ment**,*n.*

en-thu'si-asm (-thū′zĭ-ăz′m), *n.* Great eagerness on behalf of a cause or a subject ; fervor.

en-thu'si-ast (-ăst),*n.* One filled with enthusiasm.

en-thu'si-as'tic (-ăs′tĭk), *a.* [1] Filled with enthusiasm ; zealous; ardent.— **-ti-cal-ly**, *adv.* [8].

en-tice' (-tīs′),*v.t.* [1] To draw on by exciting hope or desire ; lure ; allure. — **en-tic'ing-ly**,*adv.* [8].

en-tice'ment (-mĕnt), *n.* **1.** Act of enticing; state of being enticed. **2.** That which entices.

en-tire' (-tīr′), *a.* **1.** Complete in all parts; whole. **2.** Complete in one piece; continuous. — **-ly**, *adv.*

en-tire'ty (-tĭ), *n. ; pl.* -TIES (-tĭz). State of being entire ; completeness ; also, that which is entire.

en-ti'tle (ĕn-tī′t′l), *v. t.* [1] **1.** To give a title to; style ; call. **2.** To give a right or title to.

en'ti-ty (ĕn′tĭ-tĭ), *n. ; pl.* -TIES (tĭz). Something that has a real existence ; being ; existence.

en-tomb' (-tōōm′), *v. t.* To put in or as in a tomb.

en'to-mol'o-gy (ĕn′tô-mŏl′ō-jĭ), *n.; pl.* -GIES (-jĭz). Zoölogy that treats of insects. — **-mol'o-gist**, *n.*

en'trails (ĕn′trālz), *n. pl.* Intestines ; viscera.

en'trance (ĕn'trăns), *n.* **1.** Act of entering; ingress. **2.** Means or place for entering, as a door, gate, etc. **3.** Power or permission to enter; entrée.

en-trance' (ĕn-trâns'), *v. t.* [1] **1.** To put into a trance. **2.** To enrapture. — **-tranc'ing-ly,** *adv.*

en-trap' (ĕn-trăp'), *v. t.* To catch in or as in a trap.

en-treat' (-trēt'), *v. t.* To ask earnestly; beseech. — *v. i.* To make entreaty; plead.

en-treat'y (-trēt'ĭ), *n.; pl.* -TREATIES (-ĭz). Act of entreating; earnest petition; supplication.

en'trée (än'trā'), *n.* **1.** Entrance. **2.** *Cookery.* A dish usually served between the fish and roast.

en'try (ĕn'trĭ), *n.; pl.* -TRIES (-trĭz). **1.** Act of entering; entrance. **2.** Act of making or entering a record, or an item entered. **3.** That by which entrance is made: a vestibule, hallway, or the like.

en-twine' (ĕn-twīn'), **en-twist'** (-twĭst'), *v. t.* [1] To twine or twist together or round.

e-nu'mer-ate (ê-nū'mẽr-āt), *v. t.* [1] To count or name over; number; count. — **-a'tor** (-ā'tẽr), *n.* [8].

e-nu'mer-a'tion (-ā'shŭn), *n.* Act of enumerating.

e-nun'ci-ate (ê-nŭn'shĭ-āt; -sĭ-āt), *v. t.* [1] **1.** To announce; declare. **2.** To utter articulately; pronounce. — **e-nun'ci-a'tor** (-ā'tẽr), *n.* [8].

e-nun'ci-a'tion (-sĭ-ā'shŭn; -shĭ-), *n.* **1.** Act or manner of enunciating. **2.** Announcement.

en-vel'op (ĕn-vĕl'ŭp), *v. t.* To wrap up or in.

en've-lope (ĕn'vê-lōp), **en-vel'op** (ĕn-vĕl'ŏp; ĕn'-vê-lōp), *n.* That which envelops, surrounds, or wraps; a wrapper; cover, esp. of a letter, etc.

en-vel'op-ment (ĕn-vĕl'ŭp-mĕnt), *n.* Act of enveloping; state of being enveloped; a covering.

en-ven'om (-vĕn'ŭm), *v. t.* To taint with venom; poison; imbue with bitterness or hate.

en'vi-a-ble (ĕn'vĭ-à-b'l), *a.* Fitted to excite envy.

en'vi-ous (-ŭs), *a.* [4] Feeling envy; jealously pained by the excellence or good fortune of another; — with *of, at,* or *against.* — **-ly,** *adv.* [8].

en-vi'ron (ĕn-vi'rŭn), *v. t.* To surround; envelop.

en-vi'ron-ment (-mĕnt), *n.* **1.** Act of environing. **2.** Surrounding conditions, influences, or forces.

en-vi'rons (ĕn-vi'rŭnz), *n. pl.* The parts or places that surround another place; suburbs.

en'voy (ĕn'voi), *n.* **1.** One dispatched on an errand or mission; messenger. **2.** A short stanza concluding certain metrical forms.

en'vy (ĕn'vĭ), *n.; pl.* -VIES (-vĭz). **1.** A feeling of discontent and ill will at another's excellence or good fortune. **2.** An object of envious notice. — *v. t.* [2] **1.** To be envious of. **2.** To feel envy on account of; begrudge. **3.** To long after; covet. — *v. i.* To be filled with envious feelings.

en'zyme (ĕn'zīm), *n.* A soluble ferment, as pepsin.

e'on (ē'ŏn), *n.* An immeasurable space of time; an age.

ep'au-let (ĕp'ô-lĕt), *n.* A shoulder ornament, chiefly military or naval.

e-phem'er-al (ê-fĕm'ẽr-ăl), *a.* [4] **1.** Beginning and ending in a day; existing only a day. **2.** Short-lived.

ep'ic (ĕp'ĭk), *a.* Of or pertaining to that kind of poetry which celebrates in the form of a continuous story the achievements of one or more heroes or demigods. — *n.* An epic poem.

ep'i-cure (-ĭ-kūr), *n.* One devoted to dainty and luxurious enjoyments, esp. of the table.

ep'i-cu-re'an (-kū-rē'ăn), *a.* Devoted to luxurious enjoyments; esp., pertaining to good eating. — *n.* One given to epicurean indulgence.

ep'i-dem'ic (-dĕm'ĭk), *a.* [4] Common to, or affecting at the same time, many in a community; general. — *n.* An epidemic disease.

ep'i-der'mis (-dûr'mĭs), *n.* Outer layer of the skin

ep'i-glot'tis (-glŏt'ĭs), *n.* A thin plate of elastic cartilage in front of the glottis, which folds back over and protects the latter during swallowing.

ep'i-gram (ĕp'ĭ-grăm), *n.* **1.** A short poem treating pointedly of a single thought or event, and now usually ending with a witticism, and often satirical. **2.** A witty thought tersely expressed; also, concise and pointed expression.

ep'i-gram-mat'ic (-grā-măt'ĭk), **-mat'i-cal** (-ĭ-kăl), *a.* [4] Suited to, characterized by, or of the nature of, epigram. — **-i-cal-ly,** *adv.* [8].

ep'i-lep'sy (ĕp'ĭ-lĕp'sĭ), *n.* A nervous disease characterized by fits, occurring at intervals.

ep'i-lep'tic (-lĕp'tĭk), *n.* One having epilepsy.— *a.* Pertaining to, having, or of the nature of, epilepsy

ep'i-logue (ĕp'ĭ-lŏg), *n.* **1.** The conclusion of a discourse. **2.** A speech or short poem recited by an actor after a play.

e-pis'co-pa-cy (ê-pĭs'kô-pá-sĭ), *n.* **1.** Government of the church by bishops, priests, and deacons. **2.** State of being a bishop; episcopal rank. **3.** = EPISCOPATE, 2 & 3.

e-pis'co-pal (-păl), *a.* Of or pertaining to bishops, governed by bishops; episcopalian. — **e-pis'co-pal-ly,** *adv.* [8].

e-pis'co-pa'li-an (-pā'lĭ-ăn), *a.* Pertaining to bishops, or government by bishops; episcopal. — *n.* One who belongs to an episcopal church or adheres to episcopal church government.

e-pis'co-pate (-pāt), *n.* **1.** A bishopric. **2.** The collective body of bishops. **3.** Bishop's term of office

ep'i-sode (ĕp'ĭ-sōd), *n.* **1.** In narration, a digression, separable from the main subject, but naturally arising from it. **2.** A prominent occurrence or incidental experience; as, an *episode* in one's life.

e-pis'tle (ê-pĭs''l), *n.* **1.** A letter addressed to one or more persons. **2.** [*Usually cap.*] One of the letters from the Apostles, included in the New Testament

e-pis'to-la-ry (-tô-lâ-rĭ), *a.* **1.** Pert. or suitable to letters. **2.** Contained in, or carried on by, letters

ep'i-taph (ĕp'ĭ-tȧf), *n.* An inscription on or at a tomb or grave in memory of the one buried there

ep'i-thet (ĕp'ĭ-thĕt), *n.* An adjective that fitly or aptly describes the noun it modifies.

e-pit'o-me (ê-pĭt'ô-mê), *n.; pl.* -OMES (-mēz). **1.** A brief statement of the contents of a literary work. **2.** A compact representation of anything.

e-pit'o-mize (-mīz), *v. t.* [1] To make an epitome of; abridge; summarize.

ep'i-zo-öt'ic (ĕp'ĭ-zō-ŏt'ĭk), *a.* Epidemic among animals. — *n.* An epizoötic disease.

ep'och (ĕp'ŏk; ē'pŏk), *n.* **1.** Any event or time or an event marking the beginning of a relatively new development. **2.** A period characterized by a distinctive development or by memorable events.

e'qua-bil'i-ty (ē'kwȧ-bĭl'ĭ-tĭ; ĕk'wȧ-), *n.* Quality or condition of being equable.

e'qua-ble (ē'kwȧ-b'l; ĕk'wȧ-), *a.* Uniform; even, not varying; tranquil. — **-bly** (-blĭ), *adv.* [8].

---

e′qual (ē′kwăl), *a.* **1.** Exactly the same or equivalent in measure, amount, number, degree, value, quality, etc. **2.** Uniform; equable. **3.** Evenly balanced or proportioned. **4.** Adequate. — *n.* One having the same or a similar age, station, talents, or other quality or condition. — *v. t.* [7] To have the same quantity, value, degree, rank, or the like, with.

e-qual′i-ty (ē-kwŏl′ĭ-tĭ), *n.; pl.* -TIES (-tĭz). Character or condition of being equal.

e′qual-i-za′tion (ē′kwăl-ĭ-zā′shŭn), *n.* Act of equalizing, state of being equalized.

e′qual-ize (ē′kwăl-īz), *v. t.* [1] **1.** To make equal. **2.** To make uniform; as, to *equalize* motion.

e′qual-ly (-ĭ), *adv.* In an equal manner or degree.

e′qua-nim′i-ty (ē′kwȧ-nĭm′ĭ-tĭ), *n.* Evenness of mind; composure; calmness; serenity.

e-quate′ (ē-kwāt′), *v. t.* [1] To make equal, or to represent as equal or equivalent, as two propositions; put into the form of an equation.

e-qua′tion (ē-kwā′shŭn; -zhŭn), *n.* **1.** Act or process of making equal; state of being equal. **2.** *Math.* An expression of equality between two magnitudes.

e-qua′tor (-tŏr), *n.* **1.** An imaginary great circle on the earth, everywhere equally distant from the poles. **2.** *Astron.* The great circle of the celestial sphere, in the same plane as the earth's equator.

e′qua-to′ri-al (ē′kwȧ-tō′rĭ-ăl), *a.* Of, pertaining to, or near, the equator.

e-ques′tri-an (ē-kwĕs′trĭ-ăn), *a.* **1.** Of or pertaining to horses or horsemen. **2.** Mounted; of a statue or a portrait, representing a person as on horseback. — *n.* One who rides on horseback; a rider.

e-ques′tri-enne′ (-ĕn′), *n.* A female equestrian.

e′qui-an′gu-lar (ē′kwĭ-ăn′gū-lȧr), *a.* Having equal angles.

e′qui-dis′tant (-dĭs′tănt), *a.* Equally distant.

e′qui-lat′er-al (-lăt′ēr-ăl), *a.* Having all the sides equal. — **e′qui-lat′er-al-ly**, *adv.* [8].

e′qui-li′brate (ē′kwĭ-lī′brāt), *v. t.* [1] **1.** To balance, as two scales. **2.** To be balanced with; counterbalance. — **e′qui-li′bra-tor** (-lī′brā-tēr), *n.* [8].

e′qui-li-bra′tion (-lĭ-brā′shŭn), *n.* Act of keeping a balance; state of being balanced.

e′qui-lib′ri-um (-lĭb′rĭ-ŭm), *n.* Balance between opposing forces, influences, actions, etc.

e′quine (ē′kwīn), *a.* Of or pertaining to a horse.

e′qui-noc′tial (ē′kwĭ-nŏk′shăl), *a.* Pertaining to the equinoxes, or to the time of equal day and night (see EQUINOCTIAL LINE, below). — **equinoctial line**, the celestial equator (=EQUATOR, 2). When the sun is on it night and day are equal all over the world. — **e. points**, the two points where the celestial equator and ecliptic cross.

e′qui-nox (ē′kwĭ-nŏks), *n.* The time when the sun's center crosses the celestial equator, about March 21 or September 22.

e-quip′ (ē-kwĭp′), *v. t.*; E-QUIPPED′ (-kwĭpt′); E-QUIP′PING. **1.** To furnish for service; fit out. **2.** To dress; array.

eq′ui-page (ĕk′wĭ-pȧj), *n.* **1.** Furniture or outfit, as of a camp, an army, or a soldier. **2.** A carriage with its horses, liveried servants, etc.; hence, a carriage.

e-quip′ment (ē-kwĭp′mĕnt), *n.* **1.** Act of equipping; state of being equipped. **2.** Anything used in equipping.

e′qui-poise (ē′kwĭ-poiz), *n.* **1.** Equality of weight or force; hence, equilibrium. **2.** Counterpoise.

eq′ui-ta-ble (ĕk′wĭ-tȧ-b'l), *a.* [4] Possessing or exhibiting equity; fair; just; reasonable. — **eq′ui-ta-ble-ness**, *n.* [8] — **eq′ui-ta-bly**, *adv.* [8].

eq′ui-ty (-tĭ), *n.; pl.* -TIES (-tĭz). **1.** State or quality of being equal or fair; fairness. **2.** *Law.* An equitable claim or right.

e-quiv′a-lence (ē-kwĭv′ȧ-lĕns), *n.* Condition or fact of being equivalent.

e-quiv′a-len-cy (-lĕn-sĭ), *n.* Equivalence.

e-quiv′a-lent (-lĕnt), *a.* Equal in power, meaning, etc. — *n.* Something equivalent. — **-ly**, *adv.* [8].

e-quiv′o-cal (-ŏ-kăl), *a.* **1.** Having two or more significations equally applicable; ambiguous; hence, suspicious; dubious. **2.** Uncertain as an indication or sign; doubtful. — **-ly**, *adv.*

e-quiv′o-cate (-kāt), *v. i.* [1] To use equivocal language with the purpose of misleading.

e-quiv′o-ca′tion (-kā′shŭn), *n.* Use of equivocal expressions, esp. so as to mislead; prevarication.

e-quiv′o-ca′tor (-kā′tēr), *n.* One who equivocates.

e′ra (ē′rȧ), *n.* **1.** A point of time from which a series of years is reckoned; epoch. **2.** A period of time reckoned from a given date as a basis. **3.** A period of time during which certain influences, social conditions, or the like, prevail.

e-rad′i-ca-ble (ē-răd′ĭ-kȧ-b'l), *a.* That can be eradicated.

e-rad′i-cate (-kāt), *v. t.* [1] To pluck up by the roots; hence, to destroy utterly; extirpate.

e-rad′i-ca′tion (-kā′shŭn), *n.* An eradicating.

e-rase′ (ē-rās′), *v. t.* [1] To rub or scrape out, as written characters, etc.; efface. — **e-ras′er**, *n.* [8].

e-ra′sure (ē-rā′zhŭr), *n.* Act of erasing.

ere (âr), *prep. & conj.* **1.** As a preposition: Before. **2.** As a conjunction: **a** Before. **b** Sooner than; rather than.

e-rect′ (ē-rĕkt′), *a.* [3] Upright; not leaning, bent, or prone. — *v. t.* **1.** To raise and place in an upright position. **2.** To raise, as a building; construct. Hence, *Machinery*, to put together for use; set up. **3.** To set up or establish; found; institute. — **e-rect′ly**, *adv.* [8] — **e-rect′ness**, *n.* [8] — **e-rec′tor** (-tēr), *n.* [8].

e-rec′tion (ē-rĕk′shŭn), *n.* **1.** Act of erecting; state of being erected. **2.** Anything erected.

ere′long′ (âr′lŏng′), *adv.* Before long; soon.

er′e-mite (ĕr′ē-mīt), *n.* A hermit; religious recluse.

ere′while′ (âr′hwīl′), *adv.* Some time ago; a little while before; heretofore. *Archaic.*

‖ **er′go** (ûr′gō), *conj. & adv.* [L.] Therefore; hence.

er′got (ûr′gŏt), *n.* **1.** A fungous disease of rye and other cereals. **2.** One of the growths due to this disease, used medicinally.

er′mine (ûr′mĭn), *n.* **1.** Any of several species of weasels of northern regions, which assume a pure white coat in winter, except for the black tip of the tail; also, the fur when white. **2.** The office or functions of a judge, whose state robe (in European countries), lined with ermine, is emblematic of purity.

Ermine in Winter Pelage. (⅛)

āle, senáte, câre, ăm, ŭccount, ärm, ȧsk, sofȧ; ēve, ĕvent, ênd, recênt, makêr; īce, ĭll; ōld, ŏbey, ôrb, ŏdd, sôft, cŏnnect; ūse, ŭnite, ûrn, ŭp, circŭs; fōod, foot; out, oil;

e-rode′ (ĕ-rōd′), *v. t.* [1] To eat into or away ; corrode ; to wear away, as land by the action of water ; to form (as a valley) by such action.

e-ro′sion (ĕ-rō′zhŭn), *n.* Act of eroding.

e-ro′sive (-sĭv), *a.* [4] That erodes ; eroding.

e-rot′ic (ĕ-rŏt′ĭk), *a.* [4] Amorous ; amatory.

err (ûr), *v. i.* To go astray ; fall into error.

er′rand (ĕr′ănd), *n.* **1.** A special business intrusted to a messenger ; a commission. **2.** A trip to carry a message or do some special business.

er′rant (-ănt), *a.* [4] **1.** Wandering, esp. for adventure ; adventurous ; chivalric. **2.** Erring.

er-rat′ic (ĕ-răt′ĭk), *a.* [4] **1.** Having no fixed course ; irregular. **2.** Eccentric ; queer.

er-rat′i-cal-ly, *adv.* In an erratic manner.

er-ro′ne-ous (ĕ-rō′nē-ŭs), *a.* [4] Containing error ; incorrect. — **-ly,** *adv.* [8] — **-ness,** *n.* [8].

er′ror (ĕr′ẽr), *n.* **1.** Belief in what is untrue. **2.** A moral offense ; fault. **3.** A mistake.

erst (ûrst), *adv. Archaic.* **1.** First ; in the first place. **2.** Erstwhile.

erst′while (ûrst′hwīl′; fûrst′hwīl′), *adv.* At a time past ; formerly. *Archaic.* — *a.* Former.

e-ruct′ (ĕ-rŭkt′), **e-ruc′tate** (ĕ-rŭk′tāt), *v. t. & i.* To belch. — **e-ruc-ta′tion** (ē′rŭk-tā′shŭn), *n.*

er′u-dite (ĕr′ōō-dīt), *a.* [4] Characterized by extensive knowledge ; scholarly. — **-ly,** *adv.* [8].

er′u-di′tion (-dĭsh′ŭn), *n.* Learning ; scholarship.

e-rupt′ (ĕ-rŭpt′), *v. i.* To burst forth ; break out. — *v. t.* To cause to burst forth, as lava.

e-rup′tion (ĕ-rŭp′shŭn), *n.* **1.** Act of bursting out or forth ; as : **a** Ejection of lava, etc., from a volcano. **b** A violent commotion ; outbreak. **2.** That which bursts forth. **3.** A rash, as on the skin.

e-rup′tive (-tĭv), *a.* Attended by eruption.

er′y-sip′e-las (ĕr′ĭ-sĭp′ĕ-lăs), *n.* An acute, infectious disease marked by inflammation of the skin.

es′ca-drille′ (ĕs′kȧ-drĭl′), *n.* 1. *Naval.* A squadron of war vessels, usually eight. **2.** *Mil.* In European air forces, esp. in France, a unit of, usually, six airplanes, as during the World War.

es′ca-lade′ (ĕs′kȧ-lād′), *n.* A mounting by ladders. — *v. t.* [1] To scale by means of ladders.

es′ca-la′tor (ĕs′kȧ-lā′tẽr), *n.* A moving stairway or incline arranged like an endless belt so that the steps or treads ascend or descend continuously.

es′ca-pade′ (ĕs′kȧ-pād′), *n.* **1.** Act of escaping from confinement or control ; runaway excursion. **2.** An adventure involving the breaking loose from restraint or rules of propriety ; prank.

es-cape′ (ĕs-kāp′), *v. i.* [1] **1.** To get away, as by flight. **2.** To issue from confinement or inclosure of any sort. **3.** To avoid a threatened ill ; to pass safely through peril. — *v. t.* To issue from (one) involuntarily. **2.** To get or be out of the way of ; succeed in averting ; avoid ; elude. **3.** To fail of (notice) ; fail of being noticed or recalled by (a person). — *n.* **1.** Act of escaping ; evasion of harm or notice ; deliverance from evil ; also, means of escape. **2.** Something that has escaped. **3.** Leakage ; outflow.

es-cape′ment (-mĕnt), *n.* The contrivance in a timepiece through which the wheels impart the impulse to the pendulum or balance.

One Form of Escapement.

es-cheat′ (ĕs-chēt′), *n. Law.* Reversion of land to the crown, or to the state in the U. S., by failure of persons legally entitled to hold the same. — *v. i. Law.* To revert or pass by escheat.

es-chew′ (-chōō′), *v. t.* To avoid ; shun.

es′cort (ĕs′kôrt), *n.* **1.** A person or body of persons accompanying or attending another or others for protection, or as a mark of honor or courtesy. **2.** Protection, care, or safeguard on a journey.

es-cort′ (ĕs-kôrt′), *v. t.* To attend with a view to guard or to show civility.

es′cri-toire′ (ĕs′krĭ-twär′), *n.* A writing desk.

es′cu-lent (ĕs′kū-lĕnt), *a.* Suitable for use by man as food ; edible.

es-cutch′eon (ĕs-kŭch′ŭn), *n. Heraldry.* The surface, usually a shield, on which armorial bearings are depicted.

Es′ki-mo (ĕs′kĭ-mō), *n.; pl.* -mos (-mōz). One of a race whose main habitat is the Arctic coasts of America. Eskimos have short to medium stature, yellow complexion, straight eyes, and prominent cheek bones.

e-soph′a-gus (ĕ-sŏf′ȧ-gŭs), *n.* The tube that leads from the pharynx to the stomach ; gullet.

es′o-ter′ic (ĕs′ō-tĕr′ĭk), *a.* [4] Designed for, and understood by, the initiated only ; secret ; private.

es-pe′cial (ĕs-pĕsh′ăl), *a.* Distinguished among others of the same class or kind ; special ; particular. — **es-pe′cial-ly,** *adv.* [8].

es-pi′al (ĕs-pī′ăl), *n.* Act of espying or spying.

es′pi-o-nage (ĕs′pĭ-ō-nâj; ĕs-pī′-), *n.* The practice of spying on others, or the employment of spies.

es′pla-nade′ (ĕs′plȧ-nād′), *n.* Any clear, level space, esp. one for public walks or drives.

es-pous′al (ĕs-pouz′ăl), *n.* **1.** *pl.* "The plighting of troth" between a man and a woman ; a wedding ; also, a betrothal ceremony. **2.** Act of espousing, or taking up as a supporter ; adoption.

es-pouse′ (-pouz′), *v. t.* [1] **1.** To marry. **2.** To adopt, as a cause or a theory.

es-py′ (ĕs-pī′), *v. t.* [2] To catch sight of ; descry ; spy ; discern ; discover ; detect.

es-quire′ (ĕs-kwīr′), *n.* **1.** Originally, a shield bearer ; esp., in chivalry, a candidate for knighthood attendant on a knight. **2.** A man of the English rank of gentry next below a knight. **3.** [*cap.*] A title of courtesy, now written after the surname (usually in form *Esq.*) with no title prefixed.

es′say (ĕs′ā), *n.* **1.** An effort ; trial ; attempt. **2.** A literary composition dealing with its subject from a more or less limited or personal standpoint.

es-say′ (ĕ-sā′), *v. t.* To exert one's power or faculties on ; attempt ; endeavor ; test.

es′say-ist (ĕs′ā-ĭst), *n.* A writer of essays.

es′sence (-ĕns), *n.* **1.** That which makes a thing what it is ; a necessary constituent ; element. **2.** A substance having in a high degree the qualities or virtues of a plant, drug, etc., from which it is extracted. **3.** Perfume, or the volatile matter constituting it.

es-sen′tial (ĕ-sĕn′shăl), *a.* [4] **1.** Having the character of an essence. **2.** Most important ; indispensable. — *n.* That which is essential. — **-ly,** *adv.* [8].

es-tab′lish (ĕs-tăb′lĭsh), *v. t.* **1.** To put on a firm basis ; settle ; found. **2.** To make a national or state institution of (a church).

---

chair ; go ; sing, iŋk ; then, thin ; nature, verdure ; yet ; zh = z in azure. Numbers refer to §§ in the Special Notes which, with Abbreviations, Signs, etc., precede the Vocabulary.

es-tab′lish-ment (ĕs-tăb′lĭsh-mĕnt), n. **1.** Act of establishing; permanent arrangement or constitution; organization. **2.** That which is established; as: **a** A permanent military or commercial force or organization. **b** Permanent place of residence or business. **c** Household.

es-tate′ (-tāt′), n. **1.** State or condition of being. **2.** Social standing or rank. **3.** A social or political class. **4.** A person's property in lands or tenements or both; loosely, fortune; possessions.

es-teem′ (-tēm′), v. t. **1.** To appreciate the worth of; to value. **2.** To set a high value on; prize. **3.** To consider; think; hold (a thing to be so and so). — n. **1.** Opinion of merit or value; estimation. **2.** High estimation; great regard.

es-thete′, es-thet′ic, etc. Vars. of ÆSTHETE, etc.

es′ti-ma-ble (ĕs′tĭ-ma-b'l), a. [4] **1.** That may be estimated. **2.** Worthy of esteem or respect; deserving good opinion. — **es′ti-ma-bly,** adv. [8].

es′ti-mate (-māt), v. t. [1] **1.** To form an opinion of; gauge; judge. **2.** To fix the worth, size, etc., of, esp. roughly; appraise. **3.** To calculate approximately. — (-măt), n. **1.** A valuing or rating, esp. from incomplete data. **2.** A statement by one who wishes to do certain work of the amount for which he will do it. **3.** A judgment or opinion.

es′ti-ma′tion (ĕs′tĭ-mā′shŭn), n. **1.** Act of estimating. **2.** Result of estimating; a rough calculation. **3.** Favorable opinion; esteem.

es-trange′ (-trānj′), v. t. [1] **1.** To cause to be strange; to keep at a distance; withdraw. **2.** To make indifferent or hostile; alienate.

es-trange′ment (-mĕnt), n. Act of estranging.

es-tray′ (-trā′), n. Law. Any valuable animal, not wild, found wandering from its owner.

es′tu-a-ry (ĕs′tụ̄-ā-rĭ), n.; pl. -RIES (-rĭz). A narrow arm of the sea at the lower end of a river where tide and current meet; a firth.

et cet′er-a, or **et cæt′er-a** (ĕt sĕt′ẽr-à). Others of the like kind; and so on; and so forth; — sometimes written as one word; usually abbr., etc. or &c.

etch (ĕch), v. t. **1.** To produce, as designs, on metal, glass, etc., by lines eaten in by a corrosive. **2.** To subject to etching, as a plate. — v. i. To practice etching.

etch′ing, vb. n. The art or process by which designs or pictures are etched; a picture or design made by impression from an etched plate.

e-ter′nal (ê-tûr′năl), a. **1.** Of infinite duration; everlasting. **2.** Incessant; perpetual. — n. [cap.] (With the) God. — **-ly,** adv. [8].

e-ter′ni-ty (ê-tûr′nĭ-tĭ), n.; pl. -TIES (-tĭz). **1.** Character or quality of being eternal; infinite duration. **2.** Condition which begins at death; immortality. **3.** Seeming endlessness; an age, or very long time.

e′ther (ē′thẽr), n. **1.** The upper regions of space or the rarefied element supposed to fill them. **2.** A medium supposed to fill all space, even that occupied by fluids and solids. **3.** A volatile liquid, chiefly used as an anæsthetic.

e-the′re-al (ê-thē′rê-ăl), a. [4] **1.** Heavenly; celestial. **2.** Formed of ether; hence, exceedingly light or delicate. **3.** Pert. to, containing, or resembling, ether (sense 3). — **-al-ly,** adv. [8].

e-the′re-al-ize (ê-thē′rê-ăl-īz), v. t. [1] To render ethereal or spiritlike; spiritualize.

e′ther-ize (ē′thẽr-īz), v. t. [1] To render insensible with ether. — **e′ther-i-za′tion** (-ĭ-zā′shŭn), n.

eth′i-cal (ĕth′ĭ-kăl), a. [4] Of or pertaining to moral action, motive, or character; also, treating of moral feelings or conduct; moral. — **-ly,** adv.

eth′ics (-ĭks), n. **1.** Science of moral duty. **2.** Moral principles, quality, or practice.

eth′nic (ĕth′nĭk) } a. Pertaining or peculiar to
eth′ni-cal (-nĭ-kăl) } race; pertaining to groups of mankind discriminated by common customs and characters. — **eth′ni-cal-ly,** adv. [8].

eth-nol′o-gy (ĕth-nŏl′ȯ-jĭ), n. The science which treats of races and peoples, their origin, distribution, relations, and peculiarities. — **eth′no-log′i-cal**(ĕth′nȯ-lŏj′ĭ-kăl),a.— **eth-nol′o-gist** (-jĭst),n.

et′i-quette (ĕt′ĭ-kĕt), n. The system of conventional forms required by good breeding, or to be observed in official or social life.

||é′tude′ (ā′tüd′), n. [F.] A study; Music, a piece for practice of some special point of technique.

et′y-mo-log′i-cal (ĕt′ĭ-mȯ-lŏj′ĭ-kăl), a. Pertaining to etymology. — **-cal-ly,** adv. [8].

et′y-mol′o-gy (ĕt′ĭ-mŏl′ȯ-jĭ), n.; pl. -GIES (-jĭz). **1.** The origin or derivation of a word as shown by its analysis or by referring it to an earlier form or word; also, an account of such origin or derivation. **2.** Branch of philology dealing with etymologies.

eu′ca-lypt (ū′kà-lĭpt), n. A eucalyptus.

eu′ca-lyp′tus (-lĭp′tŭs), n.; pl. -TI (-tī). Any of various trees of the myrtle family, including the most important timber trees of Australia.

Eu′cha-rist (ū′kà-rĭst), n. The sacrament of the Lord's Supper; the Communion; also, the consecrated elements, esp. the bread.

eu′chre (ū′kẽr), n. **1.** A certain game at cards. **2.** Failure to take three tricks in a hand at euchre by a player who made the trump. — v. t. [1] To defeat in a hand at euchre (an opponent who named the trump); hence, Slang, to defeat by scheming.

eu-gen′ics (ū-jĕn′ĭks), n. The science of improving offspring, esp. that of the human race.

eu′lo-gist (ū′lȯ-jĭst), n. One who eulogizes.

eu′lo-gis′tic (-jĭs′tĭk) } a.[4] Of,pert.to,or char-
eu′lo-gis′ti-cal (-tĭ-kăl) } acterized by, eulogy.

eu-lo′gi-um (ū-lō′jĭ-ŭm), n. pl.; E. -UMS (-ŭmz), L. -GIA (-à). A eulogy; also, eulogy.

eu′lo-gize (ū′lȯ-jīz), v. t. [1] To speak or write in strong commendation of; praise.

eu′lo-gy (-jĭ), n.; pl. -GIES (-jĭz). A composition, esp. an oration, in commendation of something, as of the character of a deceased person; praise.

eu′nuch (ū′nŭk), n. A castrated male person, orig. one in charge of a harem or employed in a palace as chamberlain; hence, formerly, a chamberlain.

eu′phe-mism (ū′fê-mĭz′m), n. A figure of speech in which an inoffensive word or expression is substituted for one considered unpleasant.

eu′phe-mis′tic (-mĭs′tĭk), a. [4] Pertaining to euphemism; softened in expression.

eu-phon′ic (ū-fŏn′ĭk), a. Of or pert. to euphony.

eu-pho′ni-ous (ū-fō′nĭ-ŭs),a.[4] Pleasing or sweet in sound; smooth-sounding. — **-ous-ly,** adv. [8].

eu′pho-ny (ū′fȯ-nĭ), n.; pl. -NIES (-nĭz). A pleasing or sweet sound; the effect produced by words uttered so as to please the ear.

eu-re′ka (ū-rē′kà), interj. "I have found (it)!"

— an exclamation attributed to Archimedes on finding a method of determining the purity of the gold in Hiero's crown.

Eu'ro-pe'an (ū'rŏ-pē'ăn), *a.* Of or pert. to Europe or its people. — *n.* A native of Europe.

Eu-sta'chi-an (ŭ-stā'kĭ-ăn), *a.* Pert. to the Eustachian tube, a tube between the ear and the pharynx.

e-vac'u-ate (ĕ-văk'ū-āt), *v. t.* [1] **1.** To empty. **2.** To discharge; void. **3.** To withdraw from; quit (a country, town, etc.); — said of an army, etc.

e-vac'u-a'tion (-ā'shŭn), *n.* **1.** Act of evacuating. **2.** That which is evacuated.

e-vade' (ĕ-vād'), *v. t. & i.* [1] To get away from by artifice; escape from cleverly; slip away; elude.

ev'a-nes'cence (ĕv'ă-nĕs'ĕns), *n.* **1.** Act or fact of vanishing. **2.** Quality of being evanescent.

ev'a-nes'cent (-ĕnt), *a.* [4] Liable to vanish or pass away like vapor; vanishing; fleeting.

e-van'gel (ĕ-văn'jĕl), *n.* **1.** The message, or "good news" of salvation through Christ; hence [*cap.*], any one of the four Gospels. **2.** Good news.

e'van-gel'ic (ē'văn-jĕl'ĭk; ĕv'ăn-jĕl'ĭk), *a.* Evangelical.

e'van-gel'i-cal (-ĭ-kăl), *a.* **1.** Contained in, or relating to, the four Gospels. **2.** Belonging to, agreeable to, or contained in, the gospel, or the teachings in the New Testament. — **-ly,** *adv.* [8].

e-van'gel-ism (ĕ-văn'jĕl-ĭz'm), *n.* Preaching or spreading of the gospel.

e-van'gel-ist (-ĭst), *n.* A bringer of the gospel: **a** [*cap.*] A writer of any of the four Gospels. **b** A preacher of the gospel: (1) In the early church, a traveling missionary or teacher. (2) In modern times, a traveling preacher; a revivalist.

e-van'gel-is'tic (-ĭs'tĭk), *a.* Pert. to evangelists.

e-van'gel-ize (-īz), *v. t.* [1] To instruct in the gospel; convert to Christianity.

e-vap'o-rate (ĕ-văp'ŏ-rāt), *v. i.* [1] To pass off in vapor or change to vapor, as a fluid; hence, to pass off like vapor, or without effect. — *v. t.* **1.** To cause to evaporate. **2.** To expel moisture from, as by heat, leaving the solid portion; as, to *evaporate* fruit. — **e-vap'o-ra'tor** (-rā'tẽr), *n.* [8].

e-vap'o-ra'tion (-rā'shŭn), *n.* **1.** Act, change, or process of evaporating. **2.** Result of evaporating.

e-va'sion (ĕ-vā'zhŭn), *n.* Act of evading; also, a means of evading; a subterfuge.

e-va'sive (-sĭv), *a.* [4] Tending to, or marked by, evasion; elusive. — **-ly,** *adv.* — **-ness,** *n.* [8].

eve (ēv), *n.* **1.** Evening. *Poetic.* **2.** The evening before a holiday, a saint's day, etc.; as, Christmas *Eve*; also, the period just before some (more or less) important event; as, on the *eve* of the battle.

e'ven (ē'v'n), *n.* Evening. *Poetic.*

e'ven, *a.* [3] **1.** Without elevation or depression; level. **2.** Free from inequality, irregularity, or fluctuation; uniform; equable; calm. **3.** Hence: Fair; equitable; impartial. **4.** Equal in size, number, or quantity. **5.** In the same plane, or in line (*with*). **6.** Of numbers, not odd; divisible by two without a remainder. — *adv.* **1.** In an even manner; evenly. **2. a** Precisely; just. **b** Fully; quite. **c** Of time: just; at the very time. **3.** As an intensive particle: **a** Emphasizing identity; as, I have debated *even* in my soul. **b** Serving to indicate what might not be expected; as, his work

is admired *even* by his enemies. — *v. t. & i.* To make, be, or become, even; level.

eve'ning (ēv'nĭng), *n.* The latter part and close of the day and early part of darkness or night.

e'ven-ly, *adv.* In an even manner, spirit, etc.

e'ven-ness, *n.* Quality or state of being even.

e-vent' (ĕ-vĕnt'), *n.* **1.** The fact of taking place; occurrence. **2.** That which happens; any incident, esp. one of importance or note. **3.** The consequence of anything; result; conclusion.

e-vent'ful (ĕ-vĕnt'fŏol), *a.* [4] Full of events; also, momentous. — **-ful-ly,** *adv.* [8] — **-ness,** *n.*

e'ven-tide' (ē'v'n-tīd'), *n.* Evening. *Archaic.*

e-ven'tu-al (ĕ-vĕn'tū-ăl), *a.* **1.** Belonging to, or determined by, the outcome or issue; ultimate. **2.** Dependent on events; contingent.

e-ven'tu-al'i-ty (-ăl'ĭ-tĭ), *n.; pl.* -TIES (-tĭz). The coming as a consequence; a contingency.

e-ven'tu-al-ly (ĕ-vĕn'tū-ăl-ĭ), *adv.* Finally.

e-ven'tu-ate (ĕ-vĕn'tū-āt), *v. i.* [1] To result.

ev'er (ĕv'ẽr), *adv.* **1.** At all times; always. **2.** At any time; as, seldom if *ever*. **3.** In any case; at all.

ev'er-glade (-glād), *n.* A low tract of swampy land.

ev'er-green (-grēn'), *a. Bot.* Remaining verdant through the winter, or retaining leaves unwithered until the next season. — *n.* **1.** An evergreen plant. **2.** *pl.* Twigs and branches of evergreen plants.

ev'er-last'ing (ĕv'ẽr-làs'tĭng), *a.* **1.** Lasting forever. **2.** Continuing long or indefinitely; hence, wearisome from repetition. — *n.* **1.** Eternity. **2.** Any of various plants whose flowers dry without losing form or color. — **-ly,** *adv.* [8].

ev'er-more' (-mōr'; ĕv'ẽr-mōr'), *adv.* Forever.

ev'er-y (ĕv'ẽr-ĭ), *a. & a. pron.* Each (one), without exception, of a group; as, his every word. — **every other,** each alternate; as, *every other* day.

ev'er-y-bod'y (-bŏd'ĭ), *n.* Every person.

ev'er y-day' (-dā'; -dā'), *a.* Used or fit for, or coming, every day; usual; as, *everyday* affairs.

ev'er-y-thing' (-thĭng'), *n.* All that pertains to the subject under consideration; all things.

ev'er-y-where' (-hwâr'), *adv.* In every place; in all places; hence, in every part; thoroughly.

e-vict' (ĕ-vĭkt'), *v. t. Law.* To put out or dispossess (a person) by legal process, or by virtue of a paramount right; eject; as, to *evict* a tenant.

e-vic'tion (ĕ-vĭk'shŭn), *n.* An evicting.

ev'i-dence (ĕv'ĭ-dĕns), *n.* **1.** State of being evident; clearness. **2.** That which makes evident; proof. — *v. t.* [1] To render evident or clear.

ev'i-dent (-dĕnt), *a.* [4] Clear to the vision; satisfactory to the judgment. — **-ly,** *adv.* [8].

e'vil (ē'v'l), *a.* **1.** Injurious or mischievous; not good. **2.** Bad morally; wicked; vicious. **3.** Producing or threatening pain, injury, or calamity; calamitous. **4.** Arising from bad character, actual or imputed. — *n.* **1.** Anything impairing happiness or welfare; affliction; misfortune. **2.** Moral badness or offense; wickedness; sin. — *adv.* In an evil manner; badly. — **e'vil-ly,** *adv.* [8].

e-vince' (ĕ-vĭns'), *v. t.* [1] To show clearly; make evident.

e-vis'cer-ate (ĕ-vĭs'ẽr-āt), *v. t.* [1] To disembowel.

e-voke' (ĕ-vōk'), *v. t.* [1] To call forth.

ev'o-lu'tion (ĕv'ŏ-lū'shŭn), *n.* **1.** An unfolding; hence, a process of developing something contained or implied in something else; specifically, the development of a race, species, etc. **2.** A thing evolved. **3.** A prescribed movement, or one of a series. — **ev′o-lu′tion-al** (ĕv′ō-lū′shŭn-ăl), **ev′o-lu′tion-a-ry** (-ă-rĭ), *a.*

e-volve′ (ē-vŏlv′), *v. t.* [1] To exhibit or produce by evolution; develop; deduce. — *v. i.* To become open, disclosed, or developed; unfold.

ewe (ū), *n.* The female of the sheep.

ew′er (ū′ẽr), *n.* A kind of wide-mouthed pitcher or jug, esp. one to hold water for the toilet.

ex-act′ (ĕg-zăkt′), *a.* [4] **1.** Strict; undeviating; rigorous. **2.** Marked by agreement with fact or a standard; precise or correct. **3.** Capable of great nicety; as, *exact* instruments. — *v. t.* **1.** To require peremptorily; compel to yield or furnish; extort. **2.** To call for; require; as, gray hairs *exact* reverence. — **-ly**, *adv.* [8] — **-ness**, *n.* [8].

ex-ac′tion (-zăk′shŭn), *n.* **1.** Act or process of exacting; hence, extortion. **2.** That which is exacted.

ex-act′i-tude (-tĭ-tūd), *n.* Quality of being exact.

ex-ac′tor (-zăk′tẽr), *n.* One who exacts.

ex-ag′ger-ate (-zăj′ẽr-āt), *v. t.* [1] **1.** To enlarge beyond the truth; overstate. **2.** To enlarge beyond the normal; as, an *exaggerated* development.

ex-ag′ger-a′tion (-ā′shŭn), *n.* Act of exaggerating; state of being exaggerated; overstatement.

ex-ag′ger-a-tive (-ā-tĭv), *a.* Tending to exaggerate; involving exaggeration.

ex-ag′ger-a′tor (-ā′tẽr), *n.* One who exaggerates.

ex-alt′ (ĕg-zôlt′), *v. t.* **1.** To elevate; dignify; glorify. **2.** To lift up with joy, pride, or success; elate; stimulate (powers, imagination, etc.).

ex′al-ta′tion (ĕg′zôl-tā′shŭn), *n.* An exalting; state of being exalted; elevation.

ex-am′i-na′tion (ĕg-zăm′ĭ-nā′shŭn), *n.* Act of examining; state of being examined; investigation.

ex-am′ine (ĕg-zăm′ĭn), *v. t.* [1] **1.** To inquire or search into; investigate. **2.** To interrogate closely, as in a judicial proceeding; try or test, as by question, as a student. — **ex-am′in-er**, *n.* [8].

ex-am′ple (-zăm′p'l; -zám′p'l), *n.* **1.** One or a portion taken to show the quality of all; a sample. **2.** Something to be followed; pattern. **3.** A precedent; parallel case. **4.** A warning case, esp. of punishment. **5.** An instance illustrating a rule; a problem to be solved, as in algebra.

ex-as′per-ate (ĕg-zăs′pẽr-āt), *v. t.* [1] **1.** To excite the anger of; irritate. **2.** To aggravate.

ex-as′per-a′tion (-ā′shŭn), *n.* Act of exasperating.

ex′ca-vate (ĕks′ká-vāt), *v. t.* [1] **1.** To hollow out by cutting or digging; to cut or dig out. **2.** To form by hollowing, as a cellar. **3.** To expose by digging. — **ex′ca-va′tor** (-vā′tẽr), *n.* [8].

ex′ca-va′tion (-vā′shŭn), *n.* Act of excavating; a cavity formed by excavating.

ex-ceed′ (ĕk-sēd′), *v. t. & i.* **1.** To go or be beyond the limit of; overdo; as, to *exceed* one's authority. **2.** To be greater than or superior to; surpass.

ex-ceed′ing, *a.* Extraordinary. — *adv.* In a very great degree. *Archaic.* — **ex-ceed′ing-ly**, *adv.*[8].

ex-cel′ (ĕk-sĕl′), *v. t. & i.; -celled′ (-sĕld′); -cel′-ling.** To go beyond or surpass, esp. in merit.

ex′cel-lence (ĕk′sĕ-lĕns), *n.* **1.** Quality of being excellent; great merit. **2.** An excellent quality; a virtue. **3.** [*Usually cap.*] Excellency (sense 2).

ex′cel-len-cy (-lĕn-sĭ), *n.; pl.* -cies (-sĭz). **1.** Excellence; virtue; worth. **2.** [*Usually cap.*] A title of honor given to certain high dignitaries.

ex′cel-lent (-lĕnt), *a.* [4] Very good of its kind; first-class; of great worth. — **-ly**, *adv.* [8].

ex-cel′si-or (ĕk-sĕl′sĭ-ŏr), *a.* More lofty; still higher; ever upward; — motto of the State of New York. — *n.* A material of curled shreds of wood used for stuffing, packing, etc.

ex-cept′ (-sĕpt′), *v. t.* To take or leave out (anything) from a number or a whole as not belonging to it; exclude; omit. — *v. i.* To take exception; object. — *prep.* With exclusion of; excepting. — *conj.* Unless; if it be not so that.

ex-cept′ing, *prep. & conj.* With exception of; excluding; except.

ex-cep′tion (ĕk-sĕp′shŭn), *n.* **1.** Act of excepting; exclusion. **2.** That which is excepted. **3.** Objection; hence, disapproval; complaint.

ex-cep′tion-a-ble (-à-b'l), *a.* [4] Liable to exception.

ex-cep′tion-al (-ăl), *a.* [4] Forming an exception; rare; hence, superior. — **-al-ly**, *adv.* [8].

ex′cerpt (ĕk′sẽrpt), *n.* An extract; a selected or copied passage.

ex-cess′ (ĕk-sĕs′), *n.* **1.** State of exceeding or going beyond limits; that which exceeds what is usual or proper. **2.** Undue indulgence; intemperance. **3.** The amount or degree by which one thing or number exceeds another. — *a.* More than or above the usual or specified amount.

ex-ces′sive (-sĕs′ĭv), *a.* [4] Characterized by or showing excess; very great. — **-ly**, *adv.* [8].

ex-change′ (ĕks-chānj′), *n.* **1.** Act of giving or taking one thing in return for another regarded as an equivalent. **2.** a Amount paid for the collection of a draft, check, etc. **b** Interchange of the money of two countries, with allowance for difference in value. **3.** Act of substituting one thing for another. **4.** A place where things or services are exchanged; esp.: **a** The place where brokers, merchants, or others meet to do business; as, a stock *exchange*. **b** A headquarters or central office. — *v. t.* [1] To transfer to another for an equivalent. — *v. i.* To make an exchange, or to pass in exchange. — **ex-change′a-ble**, *a.* [8].

ex-cheq′uer (-chĕk′ẽr), *n.* **1.** [*Often cap.*] In the United Kingdom of Great Britain and Ireland, the department of state in charge of the national revenue; hence, the national banking account or purse. **2.** A treasury, esp. of a nation. **3.** Pecuniary resources; purse; finances.

ex-cise′ (-sīz′), *n.* An inland duty levied on the manufacture, sale, or consumption of commodities within the country.

ex-cise′ (ĕk-sīz′), *v. t.* [1] To cut out or off.

ex-cise′man (-măn), *n.* An officer who collects excise taxes and enforces excise laws. *British.*

ex-ci′sion (-sĭzh′ŭn), *n.* Act or operation of cutting out or off; hence, destruction; extirpation.

ex-cit′a-bil′i-ty (-sĭt′á-bĭl′ĭ-tĭ), *n.* Quality of being readily excitable.

ex-cit′a-ble (-sĭt′à-b'l), *a.* [4] Capable of being excited; easily stirred up. — **-ness**, *n.* [8].

ex-cit′ant (-zĭnt), *a.* Tending to excite; exciting. — *n.* Something that excites.

ex'ci-ta'tion (ĕk'sĭ-tā'shŭn), *n.* Act of exciting; state of being excited; excitement; specif., production of a magnetic field in a dynamo or the like.

ex-cite' (ĕk-sīt'), *v. t.* [1] To call or stir to activity in any way; esp., to move to strong emotion.

ex-cite'ment (-mĕnt), *n.* 1. Act of exciting; state of being excited. 2. That which excites.

ex-cit'er (-sīt'ẽr), *n.* One that excites.

ex-claim' (-klām'), *v. i. & t.* To cry out, utter, or speak in strong or sudden emotion.

ex'cla-ma'tion (ĕks'klå-mā'shŭn), *n.* 1. Act of exclaiming; a sharp utterance of strong feeling. 2. *Punctuation.* A sign [!] by which outcry is marked; — called also **exclamation point.**

ex-clam'a-to-ry (ĕks-klăm'å-tō-rĭ), *a.* Containing, expressing, using, or pertaining to, exclamation.

ex-clude' (ĕks-klōōd'), *v. t.* [1] To shut out; refuse enjoyment, consideration, or inclusion, to.

ex-clu'sion (-klōō'zhŭn), *n.* Act of excluding; state of being excluded; debarring; rejection.

ex-clu'sive (-sĭv), *a.* [4] 1. Enjoyed to the exclusion of others. 2. Inclined to exclude outsiders. 3. Excluding; not comprising. — **-ly,** *adv.* [8] — **-ness,** *n.* [8].

ex'com-mu'ni-cate (ĕks'kŏ-mū'nĭ-kāt), *v. t.* [1] To cut off, or shut out, from communion with the church, by ecclesiastical sentence.

ex'com-mu'ni-ca'tion (-kā'shŭn), *n.* Act of excommunicating.

ex-co'ri-ate (ĕks-kō'rĭ-āt), *v. t.* [1] To flay; skin.

ex-co'ri-a'tion (-ā'shŭn), *n.* Act of excoriating.

ex'cre-ment (ĕks'krē-mĕnt), *n.* Waste discharged from the body, esp. from the alimentary canal.

ex-cres'cence (ĕks-krĕs'ĕns), *n.* An outgrowth; esp., an abnormal outgrowth, as a wart.

ex-cres'cent (-ĕnt), *a.* [4] Forming an outgrowth, esp. an abnormal or useless one; superfluous.

ex-crete' (-krēt'), *v. t.* [1] To separate and eliminate or discharge (waste or harmful material) from the blood or tissues.

ex-cre'tion (-krē'shŭn), *n.* 1. Act or process of excreting. 2. That which is excreted.

ex'cre-to-ry (ĕks'krē-tō-rĭ; ĕks-krē'-), *a.* Pert. to, or serving for, excretion; as, *excretory* organs.

ex-cru'ci-ate (ĕks-krōō'shĭ-āt), *v. t.* [1] To inflict agonizing pain on; torture; rack.

ex-cru'ci-a'tion (-ā'shŭn), *n.* Agony; torture.

ex-cul'pate (ĕks-kŭl'pāt; ĕks'kŭl-), *v. t.* [1] To relieve of blame; declare free from guilt.

ex'cul-pa'tion (ĕks'kŭl-pā'shŭn), *n.* Act of exculpating; that which exculpates; excuse.

ex-cul'pa-to-ry (ĕks-kŭl'på-tō-rĭ), *a.* Clearing, or tending to clear, from blame or a charge of guilt.

ex-cur'sion (-kûr'shŭn), *n.* 1. A going forth; expedition; sally. 2. A journey chiefly for recreation. 3. Deviation; digression.

ex-cur'sion-ist, *n.* One who goes on an excursion.

ex-cur'sive (-sĭv), *a.* [4] Digressive; wandering.

ex-cus'a-ble (-kūz'å-b'l), *a.* That may be excused.

ex-cuse' (-kūz'), *v. t.* [1] 1. To offer excuse for; apologize for. 2. To serve as excuse for; justify. 3. To pardon (a fault); forgive; overlook. 4. To release (from an obligation or duty).

ex-cuse' (ĕks-kūs'), *n.* 1. Act of excusing. 2. Reason offered for being excused; apology. 3. That which excuses.

ex'e-cra-ble (ĕk'sē-krå-b'l), *a.* 1. Deserving execration. 2. Bad; wretched. — **-bly,** *adv.* [8].

ex'e-crate (-krāt), *v. t.* [1] To curse; abominate.

ex'e-cra'tion (-krā'shŭn), *n.* 1. Act of execrating; a curse. 2. That which is execrated.

ex'e-cute (ĕk'sē-kūt), *v. t.* [1] 1. To follow out or through to the end; complete; perform. 2. To produce by carrying out a design; to perform, as music. 3. To give effect to; do what is provided or required by. 4. To put to death in conformity to a legal sentence.

ex'e-cut'er (ĕk'sē-kūt'ẽr), *n.* One who executes.

ex'e-cu'tion (ĕk'sē-kū'shŭn), *n.* 1. Act or process of executing. 2. Act, manner, or style of making a work of art, of performing on a musical instrument, etc. 3. Effective, esp. destructive, action. 4. The infliction of capital punishment.

ex'e-cu'tion-er (-ẽr), *n.* One who puts to death, esp. in conformity to legal warrant.

ex-ec'u-tive (ĕg-zĕk'ŭ-tĭv), *a.* Designed or fitted for execution, or carrying into effect; qualified for, or pertaining to, the execution of the laws or the conduct of affairs. — *n.* 1. Executive branch of a government. 2. Any person charged with administrative or executive work.

ex-ec'u-tor (ĕg-zĕk'ŭ-tẽr; *in sense* 1, ĕk'sē-kū'tẽr), *n.* 1. An executer. 2. One named in a person's will as the one who is to execute it.

ex-ec'u-trix (-trĭks), *n.; pl.* L. **-trices** (-trī'sēz), E. **-trixes** (-trĭk'sēz). A woman executor.

ex'e-ge'sis (ĕk'sē-jē'sĭs), *n.; pl.* **-geses** (-sēz). Explanation or interpretation; esp., critical explanation of Scripture. — **ex'e-get'ic** (-jĕt'ĭk), *a.*

ex-em'plar (ĕg-zĕm'plår), *n.* 1. One that serves as a model or pattern; esp., an ideal model. 2. An example; specimen.

ex'em-pla-ry (ĕg'zĕm-plå-rĭ; ĕg-zĕm'plå-rĭ), *a.* [4] 1. Serving as a pattern; deserving imitation. 2. Serving as a warning; monitory; as, *exemplary* justice. — **ex'em-pla-ri-ly** (-rĭ-lĭ), *adv.* [8].

ex-em'pli-fi-ca'tion (ĕg-zĕm'plĭ-fĭ-kā'shŭn), *n.* Act of exemplifying; an example.

ex-em'pli-fy (-zĕm'plĭ-fī), *v. t.* [2] To show or illustrate by example; illustrate.

ex-empt' (-zĕmpt'), *a.* Free or released from some liability to which others are subject; excepted. — *v. t.* To release from some liability.

ex-emp'tion (-zĕmp'shŭn), *n.* Act of exempting; state of being exempt; immunity; privilege.

ex'er-cise (ĕk'sẽr-sīz), *n.* 1. Act of exercising; a putting into action, use, or practice. 2. Exertion for the sake of training or improvement; also, that which gives practice, training, etc. 3. Performance, as of an office, ceremony, or the like. — *v. t.* [1] 1. To employ actively; use; train; exert repeatedly. 2. To practice in order to develop. 3. To occupy the attention and effort of; task; worry. — *v. i.* To drill; take exercise. — **ex'er-cis'er** (-sīz'ẽr), *n.* [8].

ex-ert' (ĕg-zûrt'), *v. t.* To put forth, as strength, ability, etc.; put in vigorous action.

ex-er'tion (-zûr'shŭn), *n.* Act of exerting; exercise of any power; effort.

|| **ex'e-unt** (ĕk'sē-ŭnt). [L.] They go out.

ex'ha-la'tion (ĕks'hå-lā'shŭn; ĕks'så-), *n.* Act of exhaling; also, that which is exhaled; emanation.

---

chair; go; sing, ink; then, thin; nature, verdure; yet; zh = z in azure. Numbers refer to §§ in the Special Notes which, with Abbreviations, Signs, etc., precede the Vocabulary.

ex-hale′ (ĕks-hāl′ ; ĕgz-), *v. t.* [1] **1.** To breathe out; emit, as vapor. **2.** To draw out; evaporate; as, the sun *exhales* the dew. — *v. i.* **1.** To rise or pass off as vapor. **2.** To emit breath or vapor.

ex-haust′ (ĕg-zôst′), *v. t.* **1.** To draw or drain off completely. **2.** To empty by drawing out the contents; esp., to create a vacuum in. **3.** To use up completely; tire or wear out. **4.** To develop completely or discuss thoroughly. — *n.* **1.** The escape of the working fluid, as steam, from an engine cylinder at the end of the stroke. **2.** Material exhausted, as from an engine. — **ex-haust′i-ble** (-zôs′tĭ-b'l), *a.* [8].

ex-haust′i-bil′i-ty (-bĭl′ĭ-tĭ), *n.* Quality of being exhaustible; capability of being exhausted.

ex-haus′tion (-zôs′chŭn), *n.* Act or process of exhausting; state of being exhausted.

ex-haus′tive (-tĭv), *a.* [4] Serving or tending to exhaust ; hence, thorough. — -**ly**, *adv.* [8].

ex-hib′it (-zĭb′ĭt), *v. t.* To hold forth or present to view; show; display; manifest. — *v. i.* To make a public exhibition. — *n.* **1.** An article, or articles, exhibited; display. **2.** A document identified in court for use as evidence. — -**it-er**, -**i-tor** (-ĭ-tẽr), *n.*

ex′hi-bi′tion (ĕk′sĭ-bĭsh′ŭn), *n.* **1.** Act of exhibiting. **2.** That which is exhibited; also, any public show; a display, as of works of art.

ex-hil′a-rant (ĕg-zĭl′á-rănt), *a.* [4] Exciting joy, mirth, or pleasure. — *n.* That which exhilarates.

ex-hil′a-rate (-rāt), *v.t.* [1] To make merry; enliven; cheer.

ex-hil′a-ra′tion (-rā′shŭn), *n.* Act of exhilarating; state of being exhilarated ; high spirits.

ex-hort′ (ĕg-zôrt′), *v. t. & i.* To incite by words or advice; urge strongly, as to a good deed; hence, to advise; warn; caution. — **ex-hort′er**, *n.* [8].

ex′hor-ta′tion (ĕk′sôr-tā′shŭn), *n.* **1.** Act or practice of exhorting ; incitement to that which is good. **2.** Language used in exhorting; advice ; counsel.

ex-hor′ta-tive (ĕg-zôr′tá-tĭv), **ex-hor′ta-to-ry** (-tō-rĭ), *a.* Of or pertaining to exhortation.

ex-hume′ (ĕks-hūm′), *v. t.* [1] To dig out of the ground; disinter. — **ex′hu-ma′tion**, *n.*

ex′i-gence (ĕk′sĭ-jĕns), *n.* Exigency.

ex′i-gen-cy (ĕk′sĭ-jĕn-sĭ), *n.; pl.* -**cies** (-sĭz). State or quality of being exigent; urgent want; a case demanding immediate action or remedy.

ex′i-gent (-jĕnt), *a.* [4] Requiring immediate aid or action; pressing ; critical; exacting.

ex′ile (ĕk′sĭl), *n.* **1.** Forced separation or expulsion from one's native country; banishment. **2.** One expelled from his country; also, one who abandons his home. — *v. t.* [1] To banish or expel from one's own country or home; drive away.

ex-ist′ (ĕg-zĭst′), *v. i.* **1.** To have being ; to be. **2.** To continue to be; to live.

ex-ist′ence (-zĭs′tĕns), *n.* **1.** Continuance in life; life. **2.** Actual occurrence. **3.** That which exists.

ex-ist′ent (-tĕnt), *a.* Having existence or being. ‖ **ex′it** (ĕk′sĭt). [L.] He (or she) goes out, or retires from the scene ; as, *exit* Macbeth.

ex′it, *n.* **1.** Departure of a player from the stage. **2.** Any departure; death. **3.** A passage out.

ex′o-dus (ĕk′sō-dŭs), *n.* **1** A going out; esp. (the **Exodus**), the journey of the Israelites from Egypt

under Moses; hence, any large migration. **2.** [*cap.*] The second book of the Old Testament.

‖ **ex of-fi′ci-o** (ĕks ŏ-fĭsh′ĭ-ō); *pl.* **ex officiis** (-ĭs). [L.] From office; by virtue of an office.

ex-on′er-ate (ĕg-zŏn′ẽr-āt), *v. t.* [1] To relieve, as of a charge; clear; free from blame; absolve.

ex-on′er-a′tion (-ā′shŭn), *n.* Act of exonerating.

ex-or′bi-tance (-zôr′bĭ-tăns), *n.; pl.* -**tances** (-sĕz). An exorbitant action, procedure, state, quality; esp., excessiveness of demands, charges, prices, etc.

ex-or′bi-tant (-tănt), *a.* [4] Going beyond established limits of right or propriety; grossly excessive. — **ex-or′bi-tant-ly**, *adv.* [8].

ex′or-cise (ĕk′sôr-sīz), *v. t.* [1] To drive off (an evil spirit) by adjuration ; hence, to deliver from an evil spirit. — **ex′or-cis′er**, *n.* [8].

ex′or-cism (ĕk′sôr-sĭz′m), *n.* Act or process of exorcising; also, a formula used in exorcising.

ex-or′di-um (ĕg-zôr′dĭ-ŭm), *n.; pl.* **E.** -**diums** (-ŭmz), L. -**dia** (-á). A beginning : introduction, esp. of a discourse, treatise, etc.

ex′o-ter′ic (ĕk′sō-tẽr′ĭk), *a.* [4] External; public; easily comprehended.

ex-ot′ic (ĕg-zŏt′ĭk), *a.* Introduced from a foreign country; foreign. — *n.* An exotic thing.

ex-pand′ (ĕks-pănd′), *v. t. & i.* **1.** To lay open by extending; open wide. **2.** To make to occupy more space ; dilate; distend. **3.** To express in greater detail; develop, as an argument.

ex-panse′ (ĕks-păns′), *n.* That which is expanded or its extent; spread ; a wide extent.

ex-pan′si-ble (-păn′sĭ-b'l), *a.* [4] Capable of being expanded.

ex-pan′sion (-shŭn), *n.* **1.** Act or process of expanding; state of being expanded ; enlargement. **2.** Extent of expansion; an expanded thing or part.

ex-pan′sive (-sĭv), *a.* [4] Having a capacity or tendency to expand ; also, of wide expanse; wide-extending. — **-ly**, *adv.* [8] — **-ness**, *n.* [8].

ex-pa′ti-ate (ĕks-pā′shĭ-āt), *v. i.* [1] To enlarge in discourse or writing; to be copious in discussion or description ; as, he *expatiated* on her charms.

ex-pa′ti-a′tion (-ā′shŭn), *n.* Act of expatiating.

ex-pa′tri-ate (ĕks-pā′trĭ-āt), *v. t.* An exile. — (-āt), *v. t.* To exile.

ex-pa′tri-a′tion (-ā′shŭn), *n.* Act of expatriating.

ex-pect′ (-pĕkt′), *v. t.* To look for (mentally); look forward to ; to look for with some confidence.

ex-pect′an-cy (-tăn-sĭ), *n.* **1.** Act or state of expecting; expectation. **2.** That which is expected.

ex-pect′ant (-tănt), *a.* Expecting ; having expectations ; prospective. — **ex-pect′ant-ly**, *adv.* [8].

ex′pec-ta′tion (ĕks′pĕk-tā′shŭn), *n.* **1.** Act or state of expecting; anticipation. **2.** That which is expected. **3.** The prospect of anything good to come, esp. [*pl.*] of property or rank.

ex-pec′to-rant (ĕks-pĕk′tō-rănt), *a.* Promoting discharges of mucus, etc., from the lungs or throat. — *n.* An expectorant drug or medicine.

ex-pec′to-rate (-rāt), *v. t. & i.* [1] To eject from the trachea or lungs, as phlegm, by coughing, or hawking, and spitting.

ex-pec′to-ra′tion (-rā′shŭn), *n.* Act of expectorating, or that which is expectorated.

ex-pe′di-ence (-pē′dĭ-ĕns), *n.* Expediency.

ex-pe′di-en-cy (-pē′dĭ-ĕn-sĭ), *n.* **1.** Quality or condition of being expedient; fitness. **2.** Cultivation of expedient methods; subordination of moral principle to what is politic or advantageous.

ex-pe'di-ent (-ĕnt), *a.* [4] Fit or suitable to the end in view; advisable under the circumstances. — *n.* Means devised in an exigency; shift.

ex'pe-dite (ĕks'pĕ-dīt), *v. t.* [1] To hasten the process or progress of; facilitate; quicken.

ex'pe-di'tion (-dĭsh'ŭn), *n.* **1.** Efficient promptness; dispatch; speed. **2.** An important journey or excursion for a particular purpose, as for war, trade, or exploration; also, the body of persons, etc., making such an excursion.

ex'pe-di'tion-a-ry (-ă-rĭ), *a.* Of, pertaining to, or constituting, an expedition.

ex'pe-di'tious (-dĭsh'ŭs), *a.* [4] Characterized by efficiency and rapidity; speedy; as, *expeditious* measures. — **-ly,** *adv.* [8] — **-ness,** *n.* [8].

ex-pel' (ĕks-pĕl'), *v. t.;* -PELLED' (-pĕld'); -PEL'LING. To drive or force out or away; eject.

ex-pend' (-pĕnd'), *v. t.* To lay out, put forth, or distribute so as to use up or consume; spend.

ex-pend'i-ture (-pĕn'dĭ-tụr), *n.* Act of expending; disbursement; expense.

ex-pense' (-pĕns'), *n.* **1.** That which is expended; outlay; hence, charge; cost. **2.** A source of expenditure.

ex-pen'sive (-pĕn'sĭv), *a.* [4] Occasioning expense; costly. — **-ly,** *adv.* [8] — **-ness,** *n.* [8].

ex-pe'ri-ence (-pē'rĭ-ĕns), *n.* **1.** The actual living through an event or events; actual enjoyment or suffering. **2.** Skill or practical wisdom gained by personal knowledge, feeling, or action. **3.** Something experienced. — *v. t.* [1] To have the lot or fortune of; undergo; feel.

ex-pe'ri-enced (-ĕnst), *p. a.* [4] Having experience; esp., made skillful or wise by experience.

ex-per'i-ment (-pĕr'ĭ-mĕnt), *n.* **1.** A trial made to confirm or disprove something doubtful; practical test; proof. **2.** The conducting of a test or of tests; experimenting. — *v. i.* To make experiment. — **ex-per'i-ment-er,** *n.* [8].

ex-per'i-men'tal (-mĕn'tăl), *a.* **1.** Relating to, or based on, experience, as distinct from theory. **2.** Of the nature of, pertaining to, or founded on, experiment. — **-ly,** *adv.* [8].

ex-pert' (-pûrt'), *a.* [3] Knowing and ready from much practice; clever. — **ex-pert'ly,** *adv.* [8] — **ex-pert'ness,** *n.* [8].

ex'pert (ĕks'pûrt), *n.* An expert or experienced person; hence, a specialist.

ex'pi-ate (-pĭ-āt), *v. t.* [1] To atone for, as a sin.

ex'pi-a'tion (-ā'shŭn), *n.* Act of expiating; atonement; expiatory sacrifice.

ex'pi-a-to-ry (ĕks'pĭ-ă-tŏ-rĭ), *a.* Having power or intended to make expiation; atoning.

ex'pi-ra'tion (-rā'shŭn), *n.* **1.** Act of expiring; a breathing out. **2.** A coming to a close; end.

ex-pir'a-to-ry (ĕk-spīr'ă-tŏ-rĭ), *a.* Pertaining to, or employed in, expiration of air from the lungs.

ex-pire' (ĕk-spīr'), *v. t.* [1] To breathe out; emit from the lungs. — *v. i.* **1.** To emit the breath. **2.** To die. **3.** To come to an end; cease.

ex-plain' (ĕks-plān'), *v. t.* To make plain; clear of obscurity; expound. — *v. i.* To give an explanation. — **-a-ble,** *a.* [8].

ex'pla-na'tion (ĕks'plȧ-nā'shŭn), *n.* **1.** Act or process of explaining. **2.** That which explains.

ex-plan'a-to-ry (ĕks-plăn'ȧ-tŏ-rĭ), *a.* Serving to explain; as, *explanatory* notes.

ex'ple-tive (ĕks'plĕ-tĭv), *a.* Filling up; hence, superfluous; redundant. — *n.* Something added merely as a filling, as a word; also, an oath.

ex'pli-ca-ble (-plĭ-kȧ-b'l),*a.* That can be explained.

ex'pli-ca'tion (-kā'shŭn), *n.* Explanation.

ex-plic'it (ĕks-plĭs'ĭt), *a.* [4] Distinctly stated so as to leave nothing to be implied; express; unequivocal. — **-ly,** *adv.* [8] — **-ness,** *n.* [8].

ex-plode' (ĕks-plōd'), *v. t.* [1] **1.** To drive from notice and acceptance, as a theory. **2.** To cause to burst noisily; detonate, as powder. — *v. i.* To burst or burst forth violently and noisily.

ex-ploit' (-ploit'), *n.* A deed or act; esp., a heroic act; a deed of renown. — *v. t.* **1.** To utilize; get the value out of. **2.** To draw an illegitimate profit from.

ex'ploi-ta'tion (ĕks'ploi-tā'shŭn), *n.* **1.** Act of exploiting. **2.** Selfish or unfair utilization.

ex'plo-ra'tion (-plŏ-rā'shŭn),*n.* Act of exploring.

ex-plore' (-plōr'), *v. t.* [1] To search through or range over for discovery, as new countries or seas. — **ex-plor'er** (-plōr'ĕr), *n.* [8].

ex-plo'sion (ĕks-plō'zhŭn), *n.* **1.** Act of exploding. **2.** A violent outburst of feeling.

ex-plo'sive (-sĭv), *a.* [8] **1.** Pertaining to explosion. **2.** Characterized in pronunciation by a slight explosion of breath, as the consonants *p, b, t, d, k, g.* — *n.* **1.** An explosive agent. **2.** An explosive consonant; a stop. — **-ly,** *adv.* [8] — **-ness,** *n.* [8].

ex-po'nent (-pō'nĕnt), *n.* **1.** *Algebra.* A symbol written above another symbol and on the right, denoting how many times the latter is taken as a factor. **2.** One who expounds or explains, or that which explains. **3.** One who or that which stands as a type or index. — **-nen'tial** (-pŏ-nĕn'shăl), *a.*

ex-port' (ĕks-pōrt'; ĕks'pōrt), *v. t.* To carry or send abroad in the way of commerce. — **-er,** *n.* [8].

ex'port (ĕks'pōrt), *n.* **1.** Act of exporting; exportation. **2.** That which is exported; — chiefly in *pl.*

ex'por-ta'tion (-pŏr-tā'shŭn),*n.* Act of exporting.

ex-pose' (ĕks-pōz'), *v. t.* [1] **1.** To lay open, as to attack, danger, test; to leave without shelter, protection, or care; hence, to subject to any action or influence. **2.** To lay open to, or set out for, inspection; disclose.

‖ **ex'po-sé'** (ĕks'pŏ'zā'), *n.* [F.] An exposure of something discreditable.

ex'po-si'tion (ĕks'pŏ-zĭsh'ŭn), *n.* **1.** An explanation in detail; interpretation. **2.** A public exhibition; as, the Paris *Exposition.*

ex-pos'i-tor (ĕks-pŏz'ĭ-tĕr), *n.* One that expounds.

ex-pos'i-to-ry (-tŏ-rĭ), *a.* Of, pertaining to, or containing exposition, or explanation.

ex-pos'tu-late (-pŏs'tụ̇-lāt), *v. i.* [1] To reason earnestly with a person in friendly protest against something that he has done, or intends to do.

ex-pos'tu-la'tion (-lā'shŭn), *n.* Act of expostulating; remonstrance; earnest and kindly protest.

ex-po'sure (-pō'zhụr), *n.* **1.** Act of exposing; state of being exposed. **2.** Position as to points of compass, influences of climate, etc.

---

chair; go; sing, iṇk; then, thin; nature, verdure; yet; zh = z in azure. **Numbers refer to §§ in the Special Notes** which, with Abbreviations, Signs, etc., precede the Vocabulary.

ex-pound' (ĕks-pound'), *v. t.* **1.** To set forth, as a theory. **2.** To interpret; as, to *expound* the Scriptures. — **ex-pound'er,** *n.* [8].

ex-press' (-prĕs'), *a.* **1.** Directly and distinctly stated; definite; explicit. **2.** Specific. **3.** Dispatched with special speed; as, an *express* train. **4.** Exact; precise. — *adv.* Expressly; by express. — *n.* **1.** A messenger or a dispatch specially sent. **2.** A company or system for the transportation of money or goods. **3.** An express train. — *v. t.* **1.** To press or press out, as fruit or its juice. **2.** To delineate; make known, esp. by words. **3.** To make known the opinions or feelings of. **4.** To represent by a sign or symbol. **5.** To send by express. — **ex-press'i-ble** (-ĭ-b'l), *a.* [8].

ex-press'age (ĕks-prĕs'ăj), *n.* The carrying of parcels by express; the charge for such carrying.

ex-pres'sion (-prĕsh'ŭn), *n.* **1.** Act or product of pressing or squeezing out. **2.** Act or process of representing, esp. by language. **3.** That which expresses a thought, feeling, or quality. **4.** Manner, means, or act of expressing; esp., expressive utterance; as, to read with *expression*.

ex-pres'sive (-prĕs'ĭv), *a.* [4] **1.** Serving to express; indicative. **2.** Full of expression. — **expres'sive-ly,** *adv.* [8] — **ness,** *n.* [8].

ex-press'ly, *adv.* **1.** In an explicit manner. **2.** For the particular purpose.

ex-pul'sion (-pŭl'shŭn), *n.* Act of expelling; state of being expelled; a driving or forcing out.

ex-pul'sive (-sĭv), *a.* Serving to expel.

ex-punge' (-pŭnj'), *v. t.* [1] To blot out, as with a pen; rub out; cancel.

ex'pur-gate (ĕks'pŭr-gāt), *v. t.* [1] To clear or cleanse, as a book, by taking out what is thought to be objectionable. — **ex'pur-ga'tion** (-gā'shŭn), *n.*

ex'qui-site (ĕks'kwĭ-zĭt), *a.* [4] **1.** Exciting intense delight or admiration by reason of rare beauty, excellence, or perfection. **2.** Keen; intense. **3.** Keenly appreciative; delicate. — *n.* One overnice in dress, etc.; a fop. — **ex'qui-site-ly,** *adv.* [8] — **ex'qui-site-ness,** *n.* [8].

ex'tant (ĕks'tănt), *a.* In existence or still existing; not destroyed, lost, or out of use; as, *extant* writings.

ex-tem'po-ra'ne-ous (ĕks-tĕm'pō-rā'nē-ŭs), *a.* Extemporary. — **ly,** *adv.* [8] — **ness,** *n.* [8].

ex-tem'po-ra-ry (-rā-rĭ), *a.* Composed, performed, or uttered on the spur of the moment; impromptu, as a speech. — **ri-ly** (-rĭ-lĭ), *adv.* — **ri-ness,** *n.*

ex-tem'po-re (-rē), *adv.* Extemporarily. — *a.* Extemporary; extemporaneous.

ex-tem'po-rize (-rīz), *v. t. & i.* [1] To do, make, speak or perform extempore, or offhand; improvise. — **ex-tem'po-riz'er** (-rīz'ẽr), *n.* [8].

ex-tend' (ĕks-tĕnd'), *v. t.* **1.** To stretch or draw out; hence, to lengthen in space or time. **2.** To straighten out, as a limb. **3.** To enlarge; expand, as a surface, or as power, etc. **4.** To hold out or reach forth. — *v. i.* To stretch or stretch out; reach; be broad or comprehensive.

ex-ten'si-ble (-tĕn'sĭ-b'l), *a.* [4] Capable of being extended; extensile.

ex-ten'sile (-sĭl), *a.* [4] Capable of being extended.

ex-ten'sion (-shŭn), *n.* **1.** Act of extending; state of being extended. **2.** That property of a body by which it occupies a portion of space.

ex-ten'sive (-sĭv), *a.* [4] Having wide extent; wide; far-reaching. — **ly,** *adv.* [8] — **ness,** *n.* [8].

ex-ten'sor (-sŏr), *n.* A muscle that serves to extend or straighten a limb or part.

ex-tent' (-tĕnt'), *n.* **1.** Space or amount to which a thing is extended; hence, compass; size; length. **2.** Degree; measure; proportion.

ex-ten'u-ate (-tĕn'ū-āt), *v. t.* [1] **1.** To diminish; weaken. **2.** To treat or represent (a fault, crime, or the like) as less than it appears; excuse.

ex-ten'u-a'tion (-ā'shŭn), *n.* Act of extenuating.

ex-te'ri-or (-tē'rĭ-ẽr), *a.* **1.** External; outward. **2.** Being or occurring without; external. — *n.* The outward part of a thing; the outside.

ex-ter'mi-nate (-tûr'mĭ-nāt), *v. t.* [1] To destroy utterly; annihilate. — **na'tor** (-nā'tẽr), *n.* [8].

ex-ter'mi-na'tion (-nā'shŭn), *n.* Act of exterminating; total destruction.

ex-ter'nal (-tûr'năl), *a.* Outward; exterior; superficial. — *n.* Something external. — **ly,** *adv.* [8].

ex-tinct' (-tĭŋkt'), *a.* **1.** Extinguished; gone out. **2.** No longer living or active; obsolete.

ex-tinc'tion (-tĭŋk'shŭn), *n.* **1.** Act of extinguishing. **2.** Destruction; suppression.

ex-tin'guish (-tĭŋ'gwĭsh), *v. t.* To put out, as a light or fire; hence, to cause to die out; destroy; obscure. — **ex-tin'guish-a-ble,** *a.* — **er,** *n.* [8].

ex-tin'guish-ment, *n.* Act of extinguishing.

ex'tir-pate (ĕks'tẽr-pāt), *v. t.* [1] To pluck up by the root; eradicate. — **ex'tir-pa'tor** (-pā'tẽr), *n.*

ex'tir-pa'tion (-pā'shŭn), *n.* Act of extirpating; eradication; total destruction.

ex-tol' (ĕks-tŏl'; -tōl'), *v. t.;* **-TOLLED'** (-tŏld'; -tōld'); **-TOL'LING.** To elevate by praise; laud; glorify.

ex-tort' (-tôrt'), *v. t.* To obtain (something, as money or a confession) from a person by force, threats, violence, etc.; wring; exact. — **ex-tort'er,** *n.* [8].

ex-tor'tion (-tôr'shŭn), *n.* Act of extorting.

ex-tor'tion-ate (-āt), *a.* Oppressive; exorbitant.

ex-tor'tion-er (-ẽr), *n.* One who practices extortion.

ex'tra (ĕks'trà), *a.* or *adv.* Beyond what is due, usual, or necessary; additional; hence, superior. — *n.* **1.** Something in addition to what is due, expected, or usual. **2.** An edition of a newspaper other than a regular one.

ex-tract' (ĕks-trăkt'), *v. t.* **1.** To draw out or forth; deduce. **2.** To withdraw by expression, distillation, etc. **3.** To select, as a passage from a book. — **ex-tract'a-ble,** *a.* [8].

ex'tract (ĕks'trăkt), *n.* **1.** Something extracted; esp., something prepared by decoction, or the like. **2.** A selection from a writing; a quotation.

ex-trac'tion (ĕks-trăk'shŭn), *n.* **1.** Act of extracting, or drawing out. **2.** Origin; descent; birth.

ex-trac'tive (-tĭv), *a.* Of the nature of an extract.

ex-trac'tor (-tẽr), *n.* One that extracts.

ex'tra-di'ta-ble (ĕks'trà-dī'tà-b'l), *a.* Subject to extradition; also, making liable to extradition.

ex'tra-dite (ĕks'trà-dīt), *v. t.* [1] To make or procure extradition of.

ex'tra-di'tion (-dĭsh'ŭn), *n.* Surrender of an alleged criminal by one state to another; surrender of a prisoner by one authority to another.

ex-tra'ne-ous (ĕks-trā'nē-ŭs), *a.* Not belonging to, or dependent on, a thing; not essential; foreign. — **ly,** *adv.* [8] — **ness,** *n.* [8].

āle, senāte, cāre, ăm, ăccount, ärm, àsk, sofà; ēve, ēvent, ĕnd, recĕnt, makĕr; īce, ĭll; ōld, ōbey, ôrb, ŏdd, sŏft, cŏnnect; ūse, ŭnite, ûrn, ŭp, circŭs; fōōd, fŏŏt; out, oil;

ex-traor′di-na-ry (ĕks-trôr′dĭ-nă-rĭ), *a.* [4] **1.** Beyond what is common or ordinary; uncommon; remarkable. **2.** Employed on a special service, as an ambassador. — **-na-ri-ly** (-rĭ-lĭ), *adv.* [8].

ex-trav′a-gance (-trăv′á-găns), *n.; pl.* **-gances** (-găn-sĕz). The quality, or an instance, of being extravagant, esp. in the expenditure of money.

ex-trav′a-gan-cy (-găn-sĭ), *n.; pl.* **-cies** (-sĭz). Extravagance.

ex-trav′a-gant (-gănt), *a.* [4] **1.** Excessive; unrestrained. **2.** Profuse in expenditure; prodigal. **3.** Excessively high; exorbitant. — **-trav′a-gant-ly**, *adv.* [8].

ex-trav′a-gan′za (-găn′ză), *n.* A wildly irregular musical or dramatic composition.

ex-treme′ (-trēm′), *a.* [3] **1.** Utmost; most remote. **2.** Last; final. **3.** Greatest in degree; such as cannot be exceeded. **4.** Very great; hence, excessive; immoderate; radical. — *n.* **1.** The utmost point; extremity. **2.** Utmost limit; highest degree; hence, an extreme case; esp., *pl.*, things removed as far as possible from each other, as in position, nature, or condition. **3.** An excessive degree, measure, step, or the like. **4.** *Math.* The first or the last term of a proportion or series. — **ex-treme′ly**, *adv.* [8].

ex-trem′ist (-trĕm′ĭst), *n.* A supporter of extreme measures; one who holds extreme opinions.

ex-trem′i-ty (-trĕm′ĭ-tĭ), *n.; pl.* **-ties** (-tĭz). **1.** The utmost limit, point, or part. **2.** A limb of the body, or, esp., the end part of a limb; — chiefly in *pl.*, the hands and feet. **3.** Highest degree; most intense form. **4.** Utmost point of adversity, suffering, danger, pain, or the like. **5.** An extremely severe act or measure; — usually in *pl.*

ex′tri-ca-ble (ĕks′trĭ-ká-b′l), *a.* That may be extricated.

ex′tri-cate (-kāt), *v. t.* [1] To free, as from difficulties; disentangle.

ex-tri-ca′tion (-kā′shŭn), *n.* An extricating or disentangling; disentanglement.

ex-trin′sic (ĕks-trĭn′sĭk), *a.* Not in or of a body; belonging to what is foreign to, or outside of, that which is under consideration; external; unessential. — **ex-trin′si-cal-ly**, *adv.* [8].

ex-trude′ (-trōōd′), *v. t. & i.* [1] To press out.

ex-tru′sion (-trōō′zhŭn), *n.* Act of extruding.

ex-u′ber-ance (ĕgz-ū′bĕr-ăns), *n.* **1.** State or quality of being exuberant; copious supply. **2.** An instance of exuberant action, growth, or the like.

ex-u′ber-an-cy (-ăn-sĭ), *n.* Exuberance.

ex-u′ber-ant (-ănt), *a.* Characterized by abundance or superabundance. — **ex-u′ber-ant-ly**, *adv.* [8].

ex′u-da′tion (ĕks′ū-dā′shŭn), *n.* Act of exuding; that which is exuded.

ex-ude′ (ĕks-ūd′; ĕgz-), *v. t. & i.* [1] To discharge from a body through pores or incisions, as sweat.

ex-ult′ (ĕg-zŭlt′), *v. i.* To be in high spirits; rejoice exceedingly; triumph. — **ex-ult′ing-ly**, *adv.* [8].

ex-ult′ant (-zŭl′tănt), *a.* [4] Characterized by or expressing exultation. — **ex-ult′ant-ly**, *adv.* [8].

ex′ul-ta′tion (ĕk′sŭl-tā′shŭn; ĕg′zŭl-), *n.* Act of exulting.

eye (ī), *n.* **1.** The organ of sight or vision. **2. a** Vision. **b** Look; glance; close regard; oversight; discernment; judgment; estimation. **3.** Something like, or suggestive of, the organ of sight; as: the bull's-eye of a target, a bud of a plant, the hole through a needle, etc. — *v. t.; pl.* EYED (īd); EY′ING (ī′ĭng) or EYE′ING. To view; watch narrowly.

eye′ball′ (ī′bôl′), *n.* The ball, or globe, of the eye.

eye′brow′ (ī′brou′), *n.* The arch or ridge over the eye; also, the hair growing on this ridge.

eyed (īd), *a.* Having eyes or eyelike spots.

eye′glass′ (ī′glás′), *n.* **1.** A lens of glass or rock crystal used to correct defects of vision. **2.** An eyepiece.

eye′lash′ (ī′lăsh′), *n.* The fringe of hair that edges the eyelid; also, a single hair of this fringe.

eye′less (ī′lĕs). *a.* Without eyes; blind.

eye′let (ī′lĕt), *n.* **1.** A small hole to receive a cord. **2.** A metal ring used to line an eyelet hole

eye′lid′ (ī′lĭd′), *n.* The lid or cover of the eye.

eye′piece′ (ī′pēs′), *n.* The lens, or combination of lenses, at the eye end of an optical instrument.

eye′sight′ (ī′sīt′), *n.* Sight; view; observation.

eye′sore′ (ī′sōr′), *n.* A thing offensive to the sight

eye′tooth′ (ī′tōōth′), *n.* An upper canine tooth.

eye′wink′er, *n.* An eyelash.

eye′wit′ness (ī′wĭt′nĕs), *n.* One who sees something done or happen and can testify to it.

ey′rie, ey′ry (ā′rĭ; ē′rĭ). Vars. of AERIE.

F

fa (fä), *n.* The fourth tone of the scale.

fa-ba′ceous (fá-bā′shŭs), *a.* Belonging to an immense family of plants (*Fabaceæ*, or bean family), the fruit of which is a true pod, or legume.

fa′ble (fā′b′l), *n.* **1.** A fictitious narrative or statement; untruth. **2.** A story with a moral, esp. one in which animals speak and act like human beings. — *v. t.* [1] To fabricate; invent, as a story.

fab′ric (făb′rĭk), *n.* **1.** A structure. **2.** Texture. **3.** Cloth woven or knit from fibers.

fab′ri-cate (-rĭ-kāt), *v. t.* [1] **1.** To construct; manufacture. *Archaic.* **2.** To invent (a tale, etc.); devise falsely. — **fab′ri-ca′tor** (-kā′tẽr), *n.* [8].

fab′ri-ca′tion (-kā′shŭn), *n.* **1.** A fabricating. **2.** That which is fabricated.

fab′u-list (făb′ū-lĭst), *n.* One who invents fables.

fab′u-lous (-lŭs), *a.* **1.** Feigned, as a fable; fictitious. **2.** Like a fable, esp. in exaggeration; astonishing. — **-ly**, *adv.* [8] — **-ness**, *n.* [8].

fa-çade′ (fá-säd′), *n.* *Arch.* Front of a building.

face (fās), *n.* **1.** The front part of the head; of man, the part of the head including from forehead to chin. **2.** Expression; look. **3.** Boldness; effrontery. **4.** Presence; view. **5.** The physical features of a country. **6.** The surface of anything; front. **7.** Any bounding plane of a polyhedron. **8.** The exact amount expressed on a note, bond, etc. — *v. t.* [1] **1.** To confront impudently. **2.** To meet in front; oppose firmly; resist. **3.** To stand with the face toward. **4.** To cause to present a face, as in a certain direction. **5**. To cover with anything, as for ornament or protection; put a face or facing on. — *v. i.* To present a face (in a certain direction).

fac′et (făs′ĕt), *n.* A little face; esp., one of the small plane surfaces of a cut gem, as a diamond.

fa-ce′tious (fȧ-sē′shŭs), *a.* Given to pleasantry; jocose; jocular. — **-ly,** *adv.* [8] — **-ness,** *n.* [8].

fa′cial (fā′shăl), *a.* Of or pertaining to the face.

fac′ile (făs′ĭl), *a.* **1**. Easily done; not difficult. **2**. Ready; fluent. — **-ly,** *adv.* [8] — **-ness,** *n.* [8].

fa-cil′i-tate (fȧ-sĭl′ĭ-tāt), *v. t.* [1] To make easy or less difficult.

fa-cil′i-ty (-tĭ), *n.; pl.* **-ties** (-tĭz). **1**. Quality of being easily done; ease. **2**. Readiness from skill or practice; dexterity. **3**. That which facilitates any action; aid; as, *facilities* for trade.

fac′ing (fās′ĭng), *n.* **1**. A covering in front, for ornament or protection; exterior covering. **2**. A lining near the edge of a garment.

fac-sim′i-le (făk-sĭm′ĭ-lē), *n.* An exact copy or likeness.

fact (făkt), *n.* **1**. A thing done or that comes to pass; event; occurrence; act; circumstance. **2**. The quality of being actual or real.

fac′tion (făk′shŭn), *n.* **1**. A combination or clique in a state, political party, etc. **2**. Party in general; party tumult.

fac′tion-al (-ăl), *a.* [4] Characterized by faction.

fac′tious (-shŭs), *a.* [4] **1**. Given to faction, or dissension; seditious. **2**. Due to, or characterized by, faction. — **-ly,** *adv.* [8] — **-ness,** *n.* [8].

fac-ti′tious (făk-tĭsh′ŭs), *a.* [4] Artificial; not natural. — **-ly,** *adv.* [8] — **-ness,** *n.* [8].

fac′tor (făk′tẽr), *n.* **1**. One who does business for another; agent. **2**. *Math.* Any of the quantities which, multiplied together, form a product. **3**. One of the elements that contribute to produce a result. — *v. t.* To resolve into factors.

fac′to-ry (făk′tō-rĭ), *n.; pl.* **-ries** (-rĭz). **1**. A trading station. **2**. A building, or collection of buildings, for the manufacture of goods.

fac-to′tum (făk-tō′tŭm), *n.* One employed to do all kinds of work.

fac′ul-ty (făk′ŭl-tĭ), *n.; pl.* **-ties** (-tĭz). **1**. Ability to act or do. **2**. Special endowment; knack; talent. **3**. One of the powers of mind or sense. **4**. A department of instruction in a university. **5**. The teachers in a university or college.

fad (făd), *n.* A hobby; craze.

fade (fād), *v. i.* [1] **1**. To decay; wither. **2**. To lose freshness; grow dim. **3**. To vanish. **4**. *Radio.* To diminish in strength or intensity; — said of received waves. — *v. t.* To cause to fade.

fade′less, *a.* Unfading. — **-less-ly,** *adv.* [8].

fag (făg), *v. t.; FAGGED (făgd); FAG′GING (făg′ĭng).* **1**. To labor to weariness; drudge. **2**. To act as a fag. — *v. t.* **1**. To exhaust. **2**. To use or treat as a fag. — *n.* In English schools, a boy who performs certain services for another of a higher form.

fag′-end′, *n.* The end of a web of cloth, of a rope, etc.; an end of poorer quality; remnant.

fag′ot, fag′got (făg′ŭt), *n.* A bundle of sticks or twigs, as for fuel or a fascine.

Fah′ren-heit (fä′rĕn-hīt), *a.* See THERMOMETER.

fail (fāl), *v. i.* **1**. To be wanting; fall short; come

to an end. **2**. To lose vigor, resources, etc.; become weaker. **3**. To be found wanting; fall short. **4**. To become bankrupt or insolvent. — *v. t.* To be wanting to; disappoint; desert. — *n.* Failure. *Rare,* except in *without fail.*

fail′ing, *vb. n.* A falling short; failure; fault.

fail′ure (fāl′ūr), *n.* **1**. A failing; default; deficiency. **2**. Omission to perform. **3**. Want of success; state of having failed. **4**. Breaking down; decline; decay. **5**. A becoming insolvent or bankrupt. **6**. One that has failed.

fain (fān), *a.* **1**. Well-pleased; glad. **2**. Relatively contented. — *adv.* With joy.

faint (fānt), *a.* [3] **1**. Lacking in courage or spirit; timorous. **2**. Lacking strength; weak; languid. **3**. Lacking distinctness; hardly perceptible. — *n.* Act or state of fainting; swoon. — *v. i.* **1**. To sink into dejection; lose courage or spirit. **2**. To swoon; — often with *away.* **3**. To decay; grow dim. — **faint′ly,** *adv.* [8] — **faint′-ness,** *n.* [8].

faint′-heart′ed (fānt′här′tĕd), *a.* [4] Cowardly.

fair (fâr), *a.* [3] **1**. Pleasing to the eye; beautiful. **2**. Free from spots, specks, dirt, or imperfection; unblemished. **3**. Distinct; legible, as writing. **4**. Characterized by frankness, honesty, or impartiality; open; just. **5**. Open to legitimate pursuit; — chiefly in *fair game.* **6**. Light; blond. **7**. Without marked merit or defect; average; middling. **8**. Not stormy; favorable; also, clear; cloudless. **9**. Unobstructed; clear; as, a *fair* view. — *adv.* In a fair manner.

fair, *n.* **1**. A gathering of buyers and sellers at a stated season. **2**. A festival, and sale of fancy articles, etc., esp. for charity. **3**. A competitive exhibition of wares, etc.; as, an agricultural *fair.*

fair′ly, *adv.* In a fair manner; justly, plainly, etc.

fair′ness, *n.* State or quality of being fair.

fair′-spo′ken (-spō′kĕn), *a.* [4] Using fair speech; uttered with fairness; courteous; plausible.

fair′y (fâr′ĭ), *n.; pl.* **FAIRIES** (-ĭz). An imaginary supernatural being, supposed to assume a human form (usually diminutive), and to meddle in human affairs; a fay. — *a.* Of or like fairies.

fair′y-land (fâr′ĭ-lănd′), *n.* The abode of fairies.

faith (fāth), *n.* **1**. Firm belief or trust (in a person, thing, doctrine, etc.). **2**. Recognition of spiritual realities and moral principles as supreme. **3**. That which is believed; esp., a system of religious beliefs. **4**. Fidelity; loyalty.

faith′ful (-fŏol), *a.* [4] **1**. Firm in adherence to promises and other engagements. **2**. True in affection or allegiance. **3**. Worthy of confidence; accurate, as a story. — **-ly,** *adv.* [8] — **-ness,** *n.*

faith′less, *a.* [4] **1**. Not believing. **2**. False to promises; disloyal. **3**. False to duty or service. — **faith′less-ly,** *adv.* [8] — **-ness,** *n.* [8].

fake (fāk), *v. t.* [1] To do, make, or work upon in some way, esp. so as to invent fictitiously, falsify, or the like. — *v. i.* To practice faking anything. — *n.* Any person or thing not as purported to be. *All Colloq. or Slang.*

fak′er (fāk′ẽr), *n. Slang.* One who fakes; as: **a** A peddler at fairs, etc. **b** A fraud; petty swindler.

fa-kir′ (fȧ-kēr′; fā′kẽr), *n.* A dervish; loosely, esp. in India, a beggar or itinerant wonder worker.

fal'chion (fôl'chŭn; -shŭn), *n.* A broad-bladed medieval sword, slightly curved; any sword.

fal'con (fô'k'n; fôl'-), *n.* Any of various hawks, formerly used in the sport of hawking.

fal'con-er (-ẽr), *n.* A breeder or trainer of falcons.

fal'con-ry (fô'k'n-rĭ), *n.* Art of training falcons to pursue game; also, hunting with falcons.

fall (fôl), *v. i.; pret.* **FELL** (fĕl); *p. p.* **FALL'EN** (fôl'n); *p. pr. & vb. n.* **FALL'ING.** **1.** To pass downwards freely; drop; hence, to hang freely. **2. a** To lose dignity, character, or the like. **b** To come to pass as if by descending; as, night *falls.* **c** To be uttered, as words. **d** To be lowered, as the glance. **e** To sound less loud or high. **3.** To become prostrate. **4. a** To die, esp. by violence. **b** To be captured or destroyed. **5.** To move or extend downward. **6. a** To subside, abate, decline, as flame; to ebb, as the tide. **b** To decline in activity, strength, price, etc., as stocks. **c** To become or appear dejected; — said of the face. **7.** To strike; impinge; as, music *falls* on the ear. **8.** To pass somewhat suddenly and passively into a new state; as, to *fall* asleep; hence, to begin; as, to *fall* to work. **9.** To happen; as, *fallen* on evil days. **10.** To come, pass, or be transferred, as by lot or inheritance. **11.** To be arranged or divisible (into). — *n.* **1.** Act of falling; a dropping; descent. **2.** Downfall; ruin. **3.** A thing or quantity that falls or has fallen. **4.** A dropping or shedding, as of leaves. **5.** Autumn. **6.** A sinking; subsidence, as of the tide. **7.** Descent of water; a cascade. **8.** A downward direction; declivity. **9.** Distance which anything falls. **10.** Decrease in price or value; depreciation. **11.** Lapse from goodness; spiritual ruin. **12.** Surrender of a besieged place. **13.** That part of the rope of a tackle to which the power is applied in hoisting.

fal-la'cious (fă-lā'shŭs), *a.* [4] Embodying a fallacy; misleading; as, *fallacious* arguments. — **fal-la'cious-ly**, *adv.* [8] — **-ness**, *n.* [8].

fal'la-cy (făl'á-sĭ), *n.; pl.* **-cies** (-sĭz). A false reasoning or idea; also, fallaciousness.

fall'en (fôl'n), *p. a.* Dropped; prostrate; degraded; ruined; shrunken; decreased; dead; etc.

fal'li-bil'i-ty (făl'ĭ-bĭl'ĭ-tĭ), *n.* Fallible state.

fal'li-ble (făl'ĭ-b'l), *a.* [4] **1.** Liable to err or to be deceived. **2.** Liable to be erroneous, as rules.

falling star. = METEOR.

fal'low (făl'ō), *n.* **1.** Land, ordinarily used for crops, when allowed to lie idle during the growing season. **2.** The tilling of land without sowing it for a season. — *a.* Left untilled or unsowed after plowing. — *v. t.* To plow, harrow, and break up (land) without seeding.

fal'low, *a.* Pale; pale yellow.

false (fôls), *a.* [3] **1.** Uttering falsehood; untruthful; dishonest. **2.** Not faithful or loyal; treacherous. **3.** Not according with truth or reality; not true. **4.** Not genuine or real; artificial; feigned. **5.** Not well founded; erroneous; wrong. **6.** Not essential or permanent, as temporary structures. — *adv.* Falsely.

false'hood (fôls'hŏŏd), *n.* Untruth; falsity; a lie.

false'ly, *adv.* In a false manner; erroneously.

false'ness, *n.* State or quality of being false; inaccuracy; deceitfulness.

fal-set'to (fôl-sĕt'ō), *n.; pl.* **-tos** (-ōz). A false or artificial voice; esp., that voice of a man which lies above his natural voice.

fal'si-fi-ca'tion (fôl'sĭ-fĭ-kā'shŭn), *n.* A falsifying.

fal'si-fy (-fī), *v. t.* [2] To make false; also, to prove false; disprove. — *v. i.* To lie. — **fal'si-fi'er**, *n.*

fal'si-ty (-tĭ), *n.; pl.* **-ties** (-tĭz). **1.** State or quality of being false. **2.** That which is false.

fal'ter (fôl'tẽr), *v. i.* To move or act unsteadily or waveringly; hesitate. — *v. t.* To utter hesitatingly or brokenly; — often with *out* or *forth.*

fame (fām), *n.* **1.** Public report; common talk. **2.** General opinion; reputation; renown.

famed (fāmd), *a.* Famous; celebrated.

fa-mil'iar (fá-mĭl'yár), *a.* [4] **1.** Closely acquainted; intimate. **2.** Like an intimate friend; not formal. **3.** Well-known; common; frequent. — *n.* An intimate; companion.

fa-mil'i-ar'i-ty (-ĭ-ăr'ĭ-tĭ), *n.; pl.* **-ties** (-tĭz). **1.** State of being familiar; intimacy; close acquaintance. **2.** Something said or done familiarly.

fa-mil'iar-ize (-mĭl'yár-īz), *v. t.* [1] **1.** To make well known or familiar. **2.** To make (a person or one's self) familiar or intimate (with).

fa-mil'iar-ly, *adv.* In a familiar manner.

fam'i-ly (făm'ĭ-lĭ), *n.; pl.* **-lies** (-lĭz). **1.** The body of persons who live in one house, and under one head; a household. **2. a** Those descended from a common progenitor; a tribe, clan, or race; kindred. **b** Lineage; esp., honorable lineage; noble stock; as, a man of *family.* **3.** A group comprising immediate kindred, esp. of parents and children. **4.** A group of kindred things; as, a *family* of languages. **5.** *Biol.* A group of related plants or animals ranking above a genus and below an order.

fam'ine (-ĭn), *n.* **1.** General scarcity of food; dearth; destitution. **2.** Extreme scarcity of something; as, a coal *famine.* **3.** Starvation.

fam'ish (-ĭsh), *v. t.* To starve, destroy, or distress with hunger. — *v. i.* **1.** To die of hunger; starve. **2.** To suffer extreme hunger or deprivation.

fa'mous (fā'mŭs), *a.* [4] **1.** Celebrated in fame; renowned. **2.** Excellent. *Colloq.* — **-ly**, *adv.* [8].

fan (făn), *n.* **1.** An instrument for producing currents of air by the motion of a broad surface. **2.** Something fan-shaped. — *v. t.;* **FANNED** (fănd); **FAN'NING.** **1.** To winnow. **2.** To move or impel with a fan. **3.** To direct a current of air upon with a fan, as upon a fire; hence, to stimulate.

fa-nat'ic (fá-năt'ĭk), *a.* [4] Excessively enthusiastic, esp. on religious subjects. — *n.* A fanatic person; a visionary zealot.

fa-nat'i-cal (-ĭ-kăl), *a.* [4] Fanatic. — **-ly**, *adv.*

fa-nat'i-cism (-sĭz'm), *n.* Excessive enthusiasm or unreasoning zeal, esp. as to religion.

fan'ci-er (făn'sĭ-ẽr), *n.* One who fancies, or has a special interest in, something, as birds or dogs.

fan'ci-ful (-fŏŏl), *a.* [4] **1.** Full of, or based on, fancy; whimsical. **2.** Curiously shaped or constructed. — **-ly**, *adv.* [8] — **-ness**, *n.* [8].

fan'cy (făn'sĭ), *n.; pl.* **-cies** (-sĭz). **1.** The faculty by which the mind forms images of things not present; imagination. **2.** An image formed in the mind; thought; idea. **3.** A caprice; whim; impression. **4.** Inclination; liking formed by caprice. — *a.* [3] **1.** Adapted to please the fancy; not plain; as, *fancy* goods. **2.** Above real value; as, a *fancy* price. **3.** Bred for special points, as an animal. **4.** Based on or dependent on fancy; whimsical; irregular. **5.** Superior; selected; — as fruits, etc. — *v. t.* [2] **1.** To form a conception of; imagine. **2.** To have a fancy for; like. **3.** To believe without being certain. — *v. i.* To imagine something without proof.

fan-dan′go (făn-dăn′gō), *n.; pl.* -gos (-gōz). A lively Spanish dance, or a tune with its rhythm.

fane (fān), *n.* A temple; church. *Archaic.*

fan′fare′ (făn′fâr′), *n.* A flourish of trumpets, etc.

fang (făng), *n.* A long sharp tooth by which an animal's prey is seized and held; any long pointed tooth; esp., one of the hollow or grooved teeth of venomous snakes.

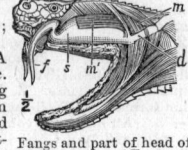
Fangs and part of head of Rattlesnake. *f* Fangs ; *s* Poison Bag or Sac ; *d* Its Duct ; *m m′* Muscles.

fan-tas′tic (făn-tăs′tĭk), *a.* [4] Grotesque; quaint; whimsical ; fanciful.

fan-tas′ti-cal (-tĭ-kăl), *a.* [4] Marked by fantasy; given to fantasies. — **-ti-cal-ly**, *adv.* [8].

fan′ta-sy (făn′tá-sĭ), *n.; pl.* -sies (-sĭz). **1.** Imagination ; fancy. **2.** A product of imagination, as : **a** A mental image; phantasm; hallucination. **b** An ingenious or fanciful design or invention. **3.** Whimsical or capricious mood.

far (fär), *adv.* **1.** At or to a great extent or distance of space or time ; widely ; remotely. **2.** In or to a great degree. **3.** In a great proportion; by a great interval ; greatly. **4.** To or at a definite distance, point, or degree; as, so *far* I will go; much; decidedly. — *a.;* FAR′THER (fär′thẽr) ; FAR′-THEST (-thĕst). **1.** Distant; hence, remote or widely different. **2.** Long; protracted. **3.** The more distant.

farce (färs), *n.* **1.** A light dramatic composition intended to excite laughter by absurdly extravagant incident. **2.** Ridiculous or empty show; mockery.

far′ci-cal (fär′sĭ-kǎl), *a.* [4] Pertaining to farce; ludicrous; unreal. — **far′ci-cal-ly**, *adv.* [8].

fare (fâr), *v. i.* [1] **1.** To go; pass; esp., to journey. **2.** To happen, well or ill ; turn out. **3.** To be in any state, or pass through any experience. **4.** To be treated at table, or with bodily comforts ; live. — *n.* **1. a** The price of transportation for a person. **b** The passenger or passengers hiring a public vehicle. **2.** Food ; provisions.

fare′well′ (fâr′wĕl′), *interj.* Go well ; good-by. — *n.* **1.** A wish of welfare at parting ; a good-by. **2.** Departure; leave-taking.

fare′well′ (fâr′wĕl′; fär′wĕl′), *a.* Parting ; final.

far′-fetched′, *p. a.* [4] Not naturally deduced or introduced ; forced ; as, a *far-fetched* joke.

fa-ri′na (fá-rī′ná; -rē′ná), *n.* A kind of fine flour or meal of starchy material, as cereals, nuts, etc.

far′i-na′ceous (făr′ĭ-nā′shŭs), *a.* **1.** Consisting or made of, or yielding, meal or flour. **2.** Mealy.

farm (färm), *n.* A tract of land devoted to agriculture ; — often qualified; as, a chicken *farm.* — *v. t.* **1.** To take, or to give up to another, the revenue, profits, etc. of (taxes, a business, or the

like), for a fixed sum. **2.** To devote (land) to agriculture ; to till, as a farm. — *v. i.* To till the soil ; to manage a farm. — **farm′er** (fär′mẽr), *n.* — **farm′house′** (-hous′), *n.* — **farm′ing**, *p. a.* & *n.*

far′ri-er (făr′ĭ-ẽr), *n.* A horseshoer.

far′row (-ō), *n.* A litter of pigs. — *v.t.* & *i.* To bring forth (young); — of swine.   [of cows.

far′row, *a.* Not bearing young in a given year; —|

far′see′ing (fär′sē′ĭng; fär′sē′ĭng), *a.* [4] **1.** Able to see far; farsighted. **2.** Having foresight.

far′sight′ed (-sīt′ĕd), *a.* [4] **1.** Seeing to a great distance; sagacious. **2.** Able to see distant objects more clearly than near ones. — **-sight′ed-ness,** *n.*

far′ther (-thẽr), *a., compar.* of FAR. **1.** Beyond a certain point; additional; further. **2.** More distant or remote. — *adv.* **1.** At or to a greater distance; more remotely. **2.** More completely; to a greater degree. **3.** Moreover. See *Note* under FURTHER.

far′ther-most (-mōst), *a.* Most remote; farthest.

far′thest (fär′thĕst), *a., superl.* of FAR. **1.** Most distant or remote. **2.** Longest. — *adv.* At or to the greatest distance.

far′thing (-thĭng), *n.* A fourth of a penny (English); small British bronze coin.   [petticoat.|

far′thin-gale (fär′thĭn-gāl), *n.* Hoop skirt or hoop|

fas′ci-nate (făs′ĭ-nāt), *v.t.* & *i.* [1] **1.** To influence by some powerful charm. **2.** Captivate.

fas′ci-na′tion (-nā′shŭn), *n.* Act of fascinating; enchantment; charm. — **fas′ci-na′tor,** *n.*

fas-cine′ (fă-sēn′), *n.* A long fagot for raising batteries, filling ditches, etc.

||**Fa-sci′sta** (fä-shē′stä), *n.; pl.* FASCISTI (-stē). A member of an Italian organization formed in 1919 for opposing Communists, Bolshevists, and other radicals. Each local branch is called a **Fa′scio** (fä′shō). — **Fas′cism** (făs′ĭz′m), *n.* — **Fas′cist,** *n.*

fash′ion (făsh′ŭn), *n.* **1.** The make or form of anything. **2.** The prevailing mode or style, esp. of dress. **3.** Polite, fashionable, or genteel life or, collectively, persons. **4.** Something fashionable; a fad. — *v. t.* To form; mold ; shape; construct.

fash′ion-a-ble (-á-b'l), *a.* [4] **1.** Conforming to the fashion. **2.** Of or pertaining to the world of fashion. — **-a-bly** (-blĭ), *adv.* [8].

fash′ion-er, *n.* One who fashions or forms.

fast (fȧst), *v. i.* **1.** To abstain from food or to eat sparingly, as by way of religious discipline. — *n.* **1.** Abstinence from food, or from certain kinds of food. **2.** A time of fasting.

fast, *a.* [1] **1.** Firmly fixed ; securely attached. **2.** Firm in adherence ; steadfast ; faithful ; as, *fast* friends. **3.** Permanent; not liable to fade, as a color. **4.** Not easily disturbed; sound, as a sleep. **5.** Moving, or capable of moving, rapidly ; rapid ; swift. **6.** Indicating the time of day as more advanced than it is ; — said of a timepiece. **7.** Making quick action possible ; as, a *fast* track. **8.** Occupying comparatively little time ; as, a *fast* trip. **9.** Pleasure-seeking; dissipated. — *adv.* **1.** In a fast or fixed manner. **2.** Rapidly ; swiftly ; also, extravagantly ; dissipately.

fast day. A day for fasting, humiliation, and religious services, to invoke divine favor.

fas′ten (făs′'n), *v. t.* **1.** To fix firmly ; secure, as by a knot, lock, etc. **2.** To cause to hold fast; attach firmly. **3.** To hold steadily and intently ; as, to

---

āle, senāte, câre, ăm, *a*ccount, ärm, ȧsk, sofá; ēve, ĕvent, ĕnd, recĕnt, makẽr; īce, ĭll; ōld, ŏbey, ôrb, ŏdd, sŏft, cŏnnect; ūse, ūnite, ûrn, ŭp, circŭs; fŏŏd, fŏŏt; out, oil;

fasten the eyes on something. — *v. i.* **1.** To fix one's self; seize; cling;— with *on*. **2.** To become fast or fixed. **3.** To become firm. — **fas'ten-er**, *n.* [8].

fas'ten-ing, *n.* That which makes fast, as a lock.

fas-tid'i-ous (făs-tĭd'ĭ-ŭs), *a.* [4] Difficult to please; dainty; finical. — **-ly**, *adv.* [8] — **-ness**, *n.* [8].

tast'ness, *n.* **1.** State of being fast. **2.** A stronghold.

fat (făt), *a.; *FAT'TER (-ĕr); -TEST. **1.** Abounding with fat; as: **a** Fleshy; plump. **b** Oily; rich; resinous. **2.** Dull; slow-witted. **3.** Profitable. — *n.* **1.** Any animal tissue containing much greasy or oily matter, or such matter itself. **2.** The best or richest productions; best part. — *v. t. & i.;* FAT'TED; FAT'TING. To make or grow fat.

fa'tal (fā'tăl), *a.* [4] **1.** Fateful. **2.** Causing death; deadly; mortal.

fa'tal-ism (-ĭz'm), *n.* **1.** The doctrine that all things are subject to fate. **2.** Submission to fate.

fa'tal-ist, *n.* One who believes in fatalism.

fa'tal-is'tic (-ĭs'tĭk), *a.* [4] Relating to fatalism.

fa-tal'i-ty (fă-tăl'ĭ-tĭ), *n.; pl.* -TIES (-tĭz). **1.** State of being fatal. **2.** That which is decreed by fate; destiny. **3.** Fatal influence; mortality. **4.** A calamity; disaster, esp. one resulting in death.

fa'tal-ly, *adv.* In a fatal manner.

fate (fāt), *n.* **1.** The necessity, or compelling principle, of nature; destiny. **2.** Appointed lot, or a predetermined event; ruin; death. **3.** Fortune.

fat'ed (fāt'ĕd), *a.* [4] Decreed by fate; destined; doomed; also, controlled by fate.

fate'ful (-fŏŏl), *a.* [4] **1.** Fraught with fate; momentous. **2.** Significant of fate; ominous. **3.** Fated. — **fate'ful-ly**, *adv.* [8] — **fate'ful-ness**, *n.* [8].

fa'ther (fä'thĕr), *n.* **1.** A male parent. **2.** A forefather; *pl.*, ancestors. **3.** A producer, author, or contriver. **4.** [*cap.*] The Supreme Being and Creator; God. **5.** As a title: **a** A dignitary of the church, as a bishop. **b** A confessor;—called also *father confessor*. **c** A priest. — *v. t.* **1.** To beget. **2.** To originate. **3.** To care for as a father; adopt; hence, to assume as one's own work.

fa'ther-hood (-hŏŏd), *n.* State of being a father.

fa'ther-in-law', *n.; pl.* FATHERS-IN-LAW (fä'-thĕrz-). The father of one's husband or wife.

fa'ther-land' (-lănd'), *n.* One's native land.

fa'ther-less, *a.* Destitute of a living father.

fa'ther-ly, *a.* [4] Like a father, as in affection or care; paternal. — **-li-ness** (-lĭ-nĕs), *n.* [8].

fath'om (făth'ŭm), *n.* A measure of length containing six feet, used chiefly to measure cables, cordage, and depth of water. — *v. t.* To measure by sounding; sound; get to the bottom of; comprehend. — **fath'om-a-ble**, *a.* [8].

fath'om-less, *a.* Incapable of being fathomed.

fa-tigue' (fà-tēg'), *n.* Weariness from labor or exertion; also, a cause of weariness; labor. — *v. t.* [1] To weary; tire.

fat'ling (făt'lĭng), *n.* A calf, lamb, kid, or other young animal fattened for slaughter.

fat'ness, *n.* Quality or state of being fat.

fat'ten (făt'n), *v. t. & i.* To make or become fat.

fat'ty (făt'ĭ), *a.* [3] Containing fat; like fat.

fa-tu'i-ty (fà-tū'ĭ-tĭ), *n.; pl.* -TIES (-tĭz). Stupidity; folly; self-complacent dullness.

fat'u-ous (făt'ŭ-ŭs), *a.* [4] Silly; often, self-complacently stupid. — **-ly**, *adv.* [8] — **-ness**, *n.* [8].

fau'ces (fô'sēz), *n. pl.* *Anat.* The narrow passage from mouth to pharynx.

fau'cet (-sĕt), *n.* A tap; cock; spigot. *U. S.*

faugh (fô), *interj.* An exclamation of disgust, etc.

fault (fôlt), *n.* **1.** A defect; an imperfection; a failing; flaw. **2.** A moral failing less serious than a vice. **3.** Negligence; also, culpability; responsibility; blame. **4.** *Geol.* A dislocation caused by a slipping of rock masses along a plane of fracture, or the resulting dislocated structure. — *v. t.* *Geol.* To produce a fault in.

fault'less, *a.* Without fault; not defective. — **fault'less-ly**, *adv.* [8] — **fault'less-ness**, *n.* [8].

fault'y (fôl'tĭ), *a.* [3] Of the nature of, or marked by, a fault or faults; imperfect. — **fault'i-ly**, *adv.* [8] — **fault'i-ness**, *n.* [8].

faun (fôn), *n.* In mythology, one of a class of rural deities represented as of human shape, with pointed ears, small horns, and sometimes a goat's tail, or as half goat and half man.

fau'na (fô'nà), *n.; pl.* E. -NAS (-nàz), L. -NÆ (-nē). The animals of a given region or geologic period.

fa'vor (fā'vĕr), *n.* [5] **1.** Kind regard; commendation; approving disposition. **2.** Act of countenancing; state of being countenanced. **3.** A kind act; kindness. **4.** Partiality. **5.** A gift or present; token, as of one's favor. **6.** A letter;—complimentary and now chiefly in business correspondence. — *v. t.* **1.** To regard with favor; show partiality to. **2.** To be advantageous to; facilitate. **3.** To tend to confirm or sustain. **4.** To resemble in features. **5.** To oblige; show favor to.

fa'vor-a-ble (-à-b'l), *a.* [4,5] **1.** Full of favor; favoring; propitious. **2.** Advantageous; tending to promote or facilitate. — **fa'vor-a-ble-ness**, *n.* — **fa'vor-a-bly**, *adv.*

fa'vored (-vĕrd), *a.* [4,5] **1.** Countenanced; aided. **2.** Of a (certain) appearance; as, ill-*favored*.

fa'vor-ite (-ĕr-ĭt), *n.* [5] One regarded with peculiar favor. — *a.* [4] Regarded with peculiar affection.

fa'vor-it-ism (-ĭt-ĭz'm), *n.* [5] The disposition to favor one to the neglect of others; partiality.

fawn (fôn), *n.* **1.** A young deer. **2.** A fawn color. — *a.* Of the color of a fawn; light yellowish brown.

fawn, *v. i.* **1.** To show delight or fondness by crouching, wagging the tail, etc.;— said of dogs. **2.** To court favor by a cringing and servile demeanor.

fay (fā), *n.* A fairy; elf.

fe'al-ty (fē'ăl-tĭ), *n.* Fidelity; faithfulness.

fear (fēr), *n.* **1.** The painful emotion caused by a sense of impending danger or evil; dread. **2.** The dread reverence felt toward God.

fear, *v. t.* **1.** To be afraid of. **2.** To have a reverential awe of (God). — *v. i.* To be afraid.

fear'ful (fēr'fŏŏl), *a.* [4] **1.** Full of fear; afraid. **2.** Inclined to fear; timid. **3.** Inspiring fear; dreadful. — **-ly**, *adv.* [8] — **-ness**, *n.* [8].

fear'less, *a.* [8] Free from fear; betraying no fear. — **-ly**, *adv.* [8] — **-ness**, *n.* [8].

fear'some (-sŭm), *a.* [4] Frightful; causing fear.

fea'si-bil'i-ty (fē'zĭ-bĭl'ĭ-tĭ), *n.* Quality of being feasible.

fea'si-ble (fē'zĭ-b'l), *a.* [4] Capable of being done, or effected; practicable. — **fea'si-ble-ness**, *n.* [8] — **fea'si-bly**, *adv.* [8].

feast (fēst), *n.* **1.** A festival; esp., a religious festival. **2.** Act or occasion of making an elaborate meal. **3.** An abundant and delicious meal, or repast; any rich treat. — *v. i.* To eat of a feast. — *v. t.* **1.** To entertain with sumptuous provisions. **2.** To delight; gratify.

feat (fēt), *n.* **1.** A noble deed; exploit. **2.** A striking act of strength, skill, or cunning.

feath′er (fĕth′ẽr), *n.* **1.** One of the light, horny outgrowths of the skin which make up the external covering, or plumage, of birds. **2.** A projecting strip, rib, fin, or flange. — *v. t.* **1.** To furnish with a feather or feathers, as an arrow. **2.** To clothe or deck, as with feathers. **3.** *Rowing.* To turn (an oar) after a stroke so that the blade is almost horizontal. — *v. i.* **1.** To grow feathers; become feathered. **2.** To feather oars in rowing.

feath′er-y (-ĭ), *a.* [4] Pertaining to or resembling feathers; covered with or as with feathers.

fea′ture (fē′tũr), *n.* **1.** The cast or appearance of the human face, esp. of a part of it; *pl.*, the face. **2.** Any marked characteristic.

fea′tured (-tũrd), *a.* Having, formed into, or expressed by, features.

fea′ture-less, *a.* Having no marked feature.

feb′ri-fuge (fĕb′rĭ-fūj), *n.* A remedy for fever.

fe′brile (fē′brĭl; fĕb′rĭl), *a.* [4] Feverish.

Feb′ru-a-ry (fĕb′rōō-ā-rĭ), *n.* The second month in the year, having 28 days, or, in leap year, 29.

fe′cal (fē′kăl), *a.* Relating to or containing feces.

fe′ces (fē′sēz), *n. pl.* Excrement.

fec′und (fĕk′ŭnd; fē′kŭnd), *a.* [4] Fruitful.

fec′un-date (fĕk′ŭn-dāt), *v. t.* [1] To fertilize or impregnate. — **fec′un-da′tion** (-dā′shŭn), *n.*

fe-cun′di-ty (fē-kŭn′dĭ-tĭ), *n.* Fruitfulness.

fed (fĕd), *pret. & p. p.* of FEED.

fed′er-al (fĕd′ẽr-ăl), *a.* **1.** Pertaining to a state consolidated of several states retaining limited powers; as, a *federal* government. **2.** Of or pertaining to, or loyal to, the United States in the Civil War (1861-65). — *n.* [*cap.*] *U.S. Hist.* A supporter of the United States in the Civil War (1861-65).

fed′er-ate (-āt), *a.* [4] Confederate. — (-āt), *v. t. & i.* [1] To unite in a league or federation; to organize under a federal government.

fed′er-a′tion (-ā′shŭn), *n.* A confederation; esp., act of uniting to form a state so that each of the uniting states remains locally self-governing.

fee(fē), *n.* **1.** A fief. **2.** An estate of inheritance in land, being an absolute fee (fee simple) or a fee limited to a class of heirs (fee tail). **3.** A charge fixed by law for certain services or privileges. **4.** Reward for services, esp. professional; pay. **5.** A payment for admission, as to a club. **6.** A gratuity; tip. — *v. t.; * FEED (fēd); FEE′ING. To give a fee to.

fee′ble (fē′b'l), *a.* [3] **1.** Weak physically. **2.** Wanting force, vigor, or efficiency. — **fee′ble-ness**, *n.* [8] — **fee′bly**, *adv.* [8].

feed (fēd), *v. t.; * FED (fĕd); FEED′ING. **1.** To give food to. **2.** To gratify, as a sense, talent, or desire. **3.** To supply with that which is used or wanted. **4.** To nourish; to foster. **5.** To produce, or serve as, food for. **6.** To give for food. **7.** To supply (material to be operated on) to a machine. — *v. i.* **1.** To take food; eat. **2.** To feed one's self; prey; — with *on* or *upon.* **3.** To be nourished or satisfied, as if by food. **4.** To pasture, as cattle; graze. — *n.* **1.** Act of eating; hence, a meal. *Archaic or Colloq.* **2.** That which is eaten; esp., fodder. **3. a** The act of carrying forward the stuff to be operated on, as in a machine. **b** Mechanism for feeding, as in a machine. — **feed′er**, *n.* [8].

feel (fēl), *v. t.; * FELT (fĕlt); FEEL′ING. **1.** To perceive by touch. **2.** To examine by touching; to test. **3.** To be conscious of; experience. — *v. i.* **1.** To have perception by touch. **2.** To have the sensibilities affected. **3.** To have a sense of being (in a certain state). **4.** To grope; search. **5.** To appear; seem. — *n.* **1.** Sense of touch; as, soft to the *feel.* **2.** A quality perceived by touch; the sensation produced.

feel′er, *n.* **1.** One that feels; esp., a tactile organ of an animal, as a tentacle. **2.** Anything, as a remark, etc., put forth to ascertain the views of others.

feel′ing, *p. a.* [4] **1.** Sentient; that can feel; sensitive; sympathetic. **2.** Having or expressing great sensibility. — *n.* **1.** Act or condition of one that feels. **2.** That sense of which sensations of touch, temperature, pressure, etc., are characteristic; esp., touch. **3.** A sensation; perception; consciousness. **4.** Any emotional state; emotion; *pl.*, general susceptibility. **5.** Susceptibility to emotion; sentiment. — **feel′ing-ly**, *adv.* [8].

feet (fēt), *n., pl.* of FOOT.

feign (fān), *v. t.* **1.** To imagine; hence, to pretend to form mentally and relate as if true. **2.** To sham; as, to *feign* illness. — *v. i.* To pretend; dissemble.

feint (fānt), *n.* **1.** That which is feigned; stratagem. **2.** A mock attack to disguise the real object of attack. — *v. i.* To make a mock attack.

feld′spar′ (fĕld′spär′), *n.* Any of a group of crystalline minerals. The feldspars are essential constituents of granite, gneiss, and most kinds of basalt.

fe-lic′i-tate (fē-lĭs′ĭ-tāt), *v. t.* [1] To congratulate.

fe-lic′i-ta′tion (-tā′shŭn), *n.* Act of felicitating.

fe-lic′i-tous (fē-lĭs′ĭ-tŭs),*a.* [4] Happily expressed; apt. — **fe-lic′i-tous-ly**, *adv.* [8].

fe-lic′i-ty (-tĭ), *n.; pl.* -TIES (-tĭz). **1.** State of being happy; blessedness. **2.** That which promotes happiness. **3.** A pleasing faculty or quality, esp. in art or language; aptness; grace.

fe′line (fē′lĭn), *a.* **1.** Of or pertaining to the cat family. **2.** Catlike; sly; stealthy; treacherous.

fell (fĕl), *pret.* of FALL.

fell, *n.* A skin or hide; pelt.

tell, *v. t.* **1.** To cut, beat, or knock down. **2.** To sew or hem down in a certain way. See *Illust.* — *n.* **1.** Timber cut down in one season. **2.** A seam formed by felling.

fell,*a.* [3] **1.** Cruel; fierce; savage; as, "his *fell* design." **2.** Deadly; dire; destructive; very painful; as, *fell* disease. *Poetic.*

Fell, 2. *a* Original Seam joining pieces *A* and *B*; *b* Hemmed-down Fold.

fel′loe (fĕl′ō), *n.* Var. of FELLY.

fel′low (fĕl′ō), *n.* **1.** A companion; comrade; associate; contemporary. **2.** An equal in power, rank, character, etc. **3.** One of two things used together. **4.** A person; individual. **5.** A man of low breeding or of little worth. **6. a** A member of a college corporation. **b** The holder of a fellowship. **7.** A

member of a literary or scientific society. — *a.* Being a companion ; associated.

fel'low-ship (-shǐp),*n.* **1.** State or relation of being a fellow, or associate. **2.** Partnership ; membership (in a society). **3.** Companionship ; comradeship. **4.** *Universities.* A foundation to maintain a scholar called a *fellow;* position of a fellow.

fel'ly (fĕl'ĭ),*n.; pl.* -LIES (-ĭz). The exterior wooden rim of a wheel, supported by the spokes.

fel'on (fĕl'ŭn), *n.* A kind of whitlow.

fel'on, *n.* One guilty of a felony ; criminal; convict.

fe-lo'ni-ous (fĕ-lō'nǐ-ŭs), *a.* Of, pertaining to, or of the nature of, a felony. — **-ly,** *adv.* [8].

fel'o-ny (fĕl'ŏ-nǐ), *n.; pl.* -NIES (-nǐz). Any of various crimes more serious than *misdemeanors.*

felt (fĕlt), *pret. & p. p.* of FEEL.

felt, *n.* **1.** A stuff of matted wool, or wool and fur or hair, compacted by rolling and pressure. **2.** Any article of felt, esp. a hat. —*v.t.* **1.** To make into felt ; to mat. **2.** To cover with or as with felt.

felt'ing, *n.* The material of felt ; also, felted cloth or the process by which it is made.

fe'male (fē'māl), *n.* A female human being ; also, a female animal or plant. — *a.* **1.** Of or pert. to the sex that brings forth young or fruit. **2.** Characteristic of woman ; feminine.

fem'i-nine (fĕm'ĭ-nǐn), *a.* **1.** Female ; of the female sex. **2.** Of or pert. to a woman or women. **3.** *Gram.* Conforming, or denoting conformity, to the class of words distinguished primarily as denoting females. — *n. Gram.* A word or inflectional form of the feminine gender.

fem'i-nin'i-ty (-nǐn'ǐ-tǐ), *n.* Womanliness.

fem'i-nism (fĕm'ǐ-nǐz'm), *n.* Advocacy of changes in laws and social conditions to remove undue restrictions upon women.

fem'o-ral (fĕm'ŏ-rǎl), *a.* Pertaining to the femur.

fe'mur (fē'mŭr), *n.; pl.* E. -MURS (-mŭrz), L. FEM-ORA (fĕm'ŏ-rà). The thigh bone.

fen (fĕn), *n.* Low swampy or boggy land.

fence (fĕns), *n.* **1.** Art of fencing, or use of the sword. **2.** An inclosing barrier, as of pickets, wire, stone, etc., as around a field. — *v.t.* [1] **1.** To fend off danger from; protect; guard. **2.** To inclose with or as with a fence. — *v. i.* **1.** To guard. **2.** To practice fencing. — **fenc'er** (fĕn'sẽr), *n.*

fenc'ing (fĕn'sĭng), *vb. n.* **1.** Art or practice of attack and defense with the sword or foil. Hence, evasive or equivocating argument or debate. **2. a** Materials for fences. *U. S.* **b** Fences collectively.

fend (fĕnd), *v. t.* To keep or ward off. — *v. i.* To act on the defensive ; resist ; parry.

fend'er, *n.* One that fends; as : **a** A cushion or pad to deaden a shock. **b** A device in front of locomotives, electric cars, etc., to throw off obstructions.

fen'nel (fĕn'ĕl), *n.* An aromatic perennial plant of the celery family, with yellow flowers.

fen'ny (-ĭ), *a.* [3] Of or pert. to a fen ; boggy.

fer'ment (fûr'mĕnt), *n.* **1.** A substance producing fermentation, as yeast. **2.** Tumult ; agitation.

fer-ment' (fẽr-mĕnt'), *v. i.* **1.** To undergo fermentation; work. **2.** To be agitated or excited.—*v.t.* To cause fermentation in.

fer'men-ta'tion (fûr'mĕn-tā'shŭn), *n.* **1.** A chemical change in organic matter accompanied with effervescence. **2.** Agitation ; excitement.

fern (fûrn), *n.* A kind of plant which resembles seed plants in having a root, stem, and leaves (fronds) but which produces no seeds.

fern'y (fûr'nǐ), *a.* [3] Of, or abounding in, ferns.

fe-ro'cious (fĕ-rō'shŭs), *a.* [4] Fierce ; savage; cruel. — **-ly,** *adv.* [8] — **-ness,** *n.* [8].

fe-roc'i-ty (-rŏs'ǐ-tǐ), *n.* Savage fierceness; cruelty.

fer'ret (fĕr'ĕt), *n.* An animal, of the weasel family, bred for hunting rabbits, etc. — *v. t.* To hunt out of a lurking place ; search out.

fer'ri-age (-ĭ-āj), *n.* Fare for passage over a ferry.

fer-ru'gi-nous (fĕ-rōō'jǐ-nŭs), *a.* [4] Of, pertaining to, or containing, iron.

fer'rule (fĕr'ōōl ; -ĭl), *n.* A metal ring or cap on a cane, tool handle, or the like, to strengthen it.

fer'ry (fĕr'ĭ), *v. t.* [2] To transport over a river, strait, etc., in a boat. — *v. i.* To pass over water in a boat or by a ferry. — *n.; pl.* -RIES (-ĭz). A place where, or a vessel in which, persons or things are carried across a river, etc. — **fer'ry-boat'**, *n.*

fer'tile (fûr'tǐl), *a.* [4] **1.** Producing in abundance; fruitful; prolific. **2.** Capable of producing offspring, seed, or fruit.

fer-til'i-ty (fẽr-tǐl'ǐ-tǐ), *n.* State or quality of being fertile; richness ; fertile invention.

fer'ti-li-za'tion (fûr'tǐ-lǐ-zā'shŭn), *n.* Act or process of making fertile.

fer'ti-lize (fûr'tǐ-līz), *v. t.* [1] To make fertile.

fer'ti-liz'er (-līz'ẽr), *n.* One that fertilizes ; esp., a commercial manure, as guano, bone dust, etc.

fer'ule (fĕr'ōōl ; -ĭl), *n.* A piece of wood, as a ruler, for striking children, esp. on the hand, in punishment. — *v. t.* [1] To punish with a ferule.

fer'ven-cy (fûr'vĕn-sǐ), *n.* State of being fervent.

fer'vent (-vĕnt), *a.* [4] **1.** Hot ; glowing ; burning. **2.** Warm in feeling; zealous. — **-ly,** *adv.* [8].

fer'vid (fûr'vǐd), *a.* [4] Ardent ; burning. — **-ly,** *adv.* [8] — **-ness,** *n.* [8].

fer'vor (-vẽr), *n.* [5] **1.** Heat ; excessive warmth. **2.** Intensity of feeling or expression ; ardor.

fes'tal (-tăl), *a.* Of or pertaining to a holiday or a feast ; joyous ; festive. — **fes'tal-ly,** *adv.* [8].

fes'ter (fĕs'tẽr), *n.* A small suppurating sore ; pustule. — *v. i.* **1.** To suppurate. **2.** To cause increasing inflammation of surrounding parts ; rankle. **3.** To putrefy; rot. — *v. t.* To cause to fester.

fes'ti-val (-tǐ-văl), *a.* [4] Of or pertaining to a festival. — *n.* **1.** A time of feasting or celebration. **2.** A periodical season of entertainment.

fes'tive (-tǐv), *a.* [4] Pertaining to, or befitting, a feast ; festal. — **fes'tive-ly,** *adv.* [8].

fes-tiv'i-ty (fĕs-tǐv'ǐ-tǐ),*n.; pl.* -TIES (-tǐz). **1.** State of being festive ; gayety. **2.** A festive celebration.

fes-toon' (-tōōn'), *n.* A garland hanging in a curve. — *v. t.* To form in, or adorn with, festoons.

fetch (fĕch), *v. t.* **1.** To bring, or to go and bring ; get. **2.** To perform ; hence, to draw (a breath) ; heave (a sigh). **3.** To attain; reach. **4.** To bring as price or equivalent ; sell for.—*v. i.* To get and bring things. — *n.* Act of fetching.

fetch'ing, *p. a.* [4] Pleasing ; fascinating.

‖ **fête** (fāt; *F.* fât), *n.* [F.] A festival ; esp., an outdoor entertainment on a more or less lavish scale.

fête (fāt), *v. t.* [1] To feast ; to honor with a fête.

fet'id (fĕt'ǐd), *a.* [4] Having a bad smell; stinking.

fe'tish (fē'tǐsh; fĕt'ǐsh), *n.* **1.** Among savages, an inanimate object, supposed to have magic powers. **2.** Hence, any object of unreasoning devotion.

fet′lock (fĕt′lŏk), *n.* The cushionlike projection above the hoof of the horse and similar animals ; also, the tuft of hair or the joint at this point.

fet′ter (fĕt′ẽr), *n.* A chain or shackle for the feet; a shackle ; — usually in *pl.* — *v. t.* To put fetters on ; shackle ; enchain.

fet′tle (-′l), *n.* Condition ; trim ; as, in fine *fettle.*

feud (fūd), *n.* A quarrel ; esp., an inveterate strife between families, clans, or the like.

feu′dal (fū′dăl), *a.* Of or pertaining to the feudal system. — **feudal system**, the political system in Europe, in the Middle Ages, based on the relation of lord to vassal ; feudalism.

feu′dal-ism (-ĭz′m), *n.* The feudal system.

fe′ver (fē′vẽr), *n.* **1.** A disease marked by increased heat, quickened pulse, and general derangement of the functions. **2.** Excessive excitement. — *v. t.* To put into, or affect with, a fever.

fe′ver-few (-fū), *n.* A perennial plant having finely divided leaves and small white flowers.

fe′ver-ish, *a.* [4] **1.** Having, pertaining to, or causing, fever. **2.** Disordered as by fever ; excited. — **fe′ver-ish-ly,** *adv.* [8] — **-ness,** *n.* [8].

few (fū), *a.* [3] Not many ; of small number. — **few′ness,** *n.* [8].

fez (fĕz), *n.; pl.* FEZZES (fĕz′ĕz). A form of cap, the headdress of the Turks.

‖ **fi′an-cé′** (fē′äN′sā′), *n. masc.;*
fi′an′cée′ (-sā′), *n. fem.* [F.]
A betrothed person.

fi-as′co (fĉ-ăs′kō), *n.; pl.* -COES or -COS (-kōz). A complete or ridiculous failure, as of a play.

fi′at (fī′ăt), *n.* An authoritative command or proclamation.

fib (fĭb), *n.* A falsehood concerning a trivial matter. — *v. i. ;* FIBBED (fĭbd) ; FIB′BING. To tell a fib.

Turkish Fez.

fi′ber (fī′bẽr), *n.* [6] **1.** A thread or threadlike substance. **2.** *Bot.* One of the elongated thick-walled cells forming the bast. **3.** Any tough threadlike substance capable of being spun and woven. **4.** Fibrous structure; texture ; sinew. **5.** A tough cotton or wood pulp substance, chemically treated and used for making trunks, boxes, etc.

fi′brin (-brĭn), *n.* A white insoluble fibrous proteid, formed esp. in the coagulation of blood.

fi′brous (-brŭs), *a.* [4] Containing or like fibers.

fib′u-la (fĭb′ů-là), *n.; L. pl.* -LÆ (-lē). The outer, and smaller, of the two bones of the human leg.

fick′le (fĭk′′l), *a.* [4] Changeable; inconstant; as, *fickle* princes, winds, etc. — **-ick′le-ness,** *n.* [8].

fic′tile (fĭk′tĭl), *a.* [4] Molded, or moldable, into form by art ; relating to pottery, etc.

fic′tion (-shŭn), *n.* **1.** A feigning or imagining. **2.** That which is feigned or imagined. **3.** Fictitious literature ; esp., novels and romances.

fic-ti′tious (fĭk-tĭsh′ŭs), *a.* [4] **1.** Feigned ; pretended. **2.** Pert. to or like fiction. — **-ly,** *adv.*

fid′dle (fĭd′′l), *n.* A violin ; — now familiar or contemptuous. — *v. i. & t.* [1] **1.** To play on a fiddle. **2.** To make aimless or idle motions, as with the fingers; hence, to trifle. — **fid′dler** (-lẽr), *n.* [8].

fid′dle-stick′ (fĭd′′l-stĭk′), *n.* **1.** The bow used in

playing the fiddle. **2.** A mere nothing ; — used, esp. in *pl.*, as an interjection.

fi-del′i-ty (fĭ-dĕl′ĭ-tĭ ; fī-), *n.* **1.** Faithfulness ; careful observance of duty or obligations ; esp. : **a** Loyalty. **b** Exactness ; accuracy.

fidg′et (fĭj′ĕt), *v. i.* To move about uneasily, as if restless. — *v. t.* To cause to fidget; make nervous. — *n.* **1.** Uneasiness; restlessness. **2.** *pl.* A general nervous restlessness.

fidg′et-y (-ĭ), *a.* [4] Restless; inclined to fidget.

fi-du′ci-a-ry (fĭ-dū′shĭ-à-rĭ), *a.* [4] **1.** Held in trust. **2.** Involving confidence or trust.

fie (fī), *interj.* An exclamation of disgust, etc.

fief (fēf), *n.* *Law.* A feudal estate ; a fee.

field (fēld), *n.* **1.** Cleared land ; land suitable, and often inclosed, for tillage or pasture. **2.** A piece of land put to a special use or yielding particular products ; as, gold *fields.* **3.** A place where a battle is fought ; also, the battle. **4.** A piece of land, usually inclosed, devoted to some sport, esp. the part used by the players; in *Baseball,* the infield and the outfield, esp. the latter. **5.** Collectively, all competitors in a contest, or all except one or more specified. **6.** A sphere or range of activity, influence, etc. **7.** An open space ; extent; expanse. **8.** The region or space throughout which an exerted force is felt, as that exerted by a magnetic pole or electric current (magnetic force). — *v. t. & i.* *Baseball & Cricket.* To catch, stop, throw, etc., the ball.

field day. **1.** A day when troops are exercised in field evolutions. **2.** Open air athletic meeting.

field′er (fēl′dẽr), *n.* Player stationed in the field.

field glass. A small compact telescope, to be carried about, so made that both eyes are used at once.

field marshal. In some armies, an officer next in rank below the commander in chief.

field′piece′ (fēld′pēs′), *n.* A gun mounted on wheels, for use in field campaigns.

fiend (fēnd), *n.* A diabolically wicked person; the Devil ; a demon. [or cruel.]

fiend′ish, *a.* [4] Like a fiend; diabolically wicked

fierce (fērs), *a.* [3] **1.** Furious ; violent ; impetuous. **2.** Vehement in anger ; ferocious. — **fierce′ly,** *adv.* [8] — **-ness,** *n.* [8].

fi′er-y (fī′ẽr-ĭ), *a.* [3] **1.** Consisting of, or like fire. **2.** Ardent; impetuous. **3.** Heated ; inflamed.

fife (fīf), *n.* A small shrill musical pipe, resembling the piccolo flute. — *v. i. & t.* [1] To play a fife. — **fif′er** (fīf′ẽr), *n.* [8].

fif′teen′ (fĭf′tēn′ ; fĭf′tēn′), *a.* Five and ten. — *n.* **1.** The sum of five and ten; fifteen units or objects. **2.** A symbol representing fifteen units, as 15 or xv.

fif′teenth′ (fĭf′tēnth′ ; fĭf′tēnth′), *a.* Next in order after the fourteenth; constituting one of fifteen equal parts into which a (whole) thing may be divided. — *n.* **1.** A fifteenth part. **2.** A fifteenth unit or object.

fifth (fĭfth), *a.* Next in order after the fourth; constituting one of five equal parts into which a (whole) thing may be divided. — *n.* **1.** A fifth part. **2.** A fifth unit or object. — *ly, adv.*

fif′ti-eth (fĭf′tĭ-ĕth), *a.* Next in order after the forty-ninth; constituting one of fifty equal parts into which a (whole) thing may be divided. — *n.* **1.** A fiftieth part. **2.** A fiftieth unit or object.

fif′ty (fĭf′tĭ), *a.* Five times ten. — *n.; pl.* -TIES

āle, senāte, câre, ăm, ăccount, ärm, ȧsk, sofȧ ; ēve, ĕvent, ĕnd, recĕnt, makẽr; īce, ĭll ; ōld, ȯbey, ôrb, ŏdd, sŏft, cŏnnect ; ūse, ŭnite, ûrn, ŭp, circŭs ; fōōd, fŏŏt ; out, oil ;

(-tĭz). **1**. The sum of five tens; fifty units. **2**. A symbol for fifty units, as 50 or l.

fig (fĭg), *n*. **1**. A small pear-shaped fruit, pulpy when ripe, and eaten raw or preserved or dried with sugar ; also, the tree which bears this fruit. **2**. The value of a fig, almost nothing.

fight (fīt), *n*. **1**. A battle ; combat. **2**. Any contest. **3**. Strength or disposition for fighting; pugnacity. — *v. i. ;* FOUGHT (fôt) ; FIGHT′ING. **1**. To attempt to defeat or destroy an enemy, by either blows or weapons. **2**. To act in opposition to anything. — *v. t.* **1**. To carry on or wage, as a conflict ; sustain, win, or gain by fighting. **2**. To contend with in battle ; war against. — **fight′er** (-ẽr), *n*. [8].

fig′ment (fĭg′mĕnt), *n*. An invented statement, doctrine, etc. ; a fiction.

fig′u·ra′tion (-û-rā′shŭn), *n*. **1**. Act of giving figure, or definite form. **2**. Form ; shape.

fig′ur·a·tive (fĭg′ûr-ȧ-tĭv), *a*. [4] **1**. Emblematical ; typical. **2**. Not literal ; also, abounding in figures of speech ; florid. — **-ly**, *adv.* — **-ness**, *n*.

fig′ure (fĭg′ûr), *n*. **1**. A numerical symbol; numeral; digit ; as, 1, 2, 3, etc. **2**. Value as expressed in numbers; price. *Colloq.* **3**. Form ; shape ; outline. **4**. An object having shape or form. **5. a** Appearance or impression made by a person's conduct or career. **b** A personage ; character. **6**. A drawing or likeness : a diagram ; a pattern or design. **7**. A type or symbol. **8**. A form of expression that differs from ordinary language and by means of which pictures or images are suggested to the mind ; pictorial language. **9**. *Dancing.* A set of evolutions in a dance. — *v. t.* [1] **1**. To represent by a figure. **2**. To embellish with figures, or designs. **3**. To indicate by numerals; also, to compute. **4**. To express by a metaphor; symbolize. — *v. i.* **1**. To make a figure ; be conspicuous; appear. **2**. To calculate; esp., to reckon in figures. *Colloq.* — **fig′ur·er**, *n*. [8].

fig′ure-head′ (-ûr-hĕd′), *n*. **1**. The figure on the prow of a ship. **2**. A merely nominal head.

fil′a·ment (fĭl′ȧ-mĕnt), *n*. A thread or threadlike object ; specif., *Bot.*, the anther-bearing stalk of a stamen. — **fil′a·men′tous** (-mĕn′tŭs), *a*.

fil′bert (fĭl′bẽrt), *n*. Either of two European hazels or their sweet-flavored nut.

filch (fĭlch), *v. t.* To pilfer ; steal. — **filch′- er**, *n*. [8].

file (fīl), *n*. **1**. A line, wire, or other contrivance by means of which papers may be kept in order. **2**. An orderly collection of papers. **3**. A row of persons, animals, or things arranged one behind the other. — *v. t.* [1] To arrange, or lay away, as papers, methodically ; place on file. — *v. i.* To march in a file, as soldiers, one after another.

file (fīl), *n*. A steel instrument with cutting ridges, or teeth, for abrading or smoothing substances. — *v. t.* **1**. To rub, smooth, cut, or sharpen with a file. **2**. To remove with a file ; — with *off*, *away*.

fil′ial (fĭl′yăl; -ĭ-ăl), *a*. [4] Of or pertaining to a son or daughter ; as, *filial* obedience.

fil′i·bus′ter (-ĭ-bŭs′tẽr), *n*. **1**. An irregular military adventurer. **2**. A legislator who filibusters. *U.S.* — *v. i.* To delay legislation by extreme dilatory tactics. *U.S.*

fil′i·gree (-grē), *n*. Ornamental work of fine wire. — *a*. Relating to, composed of, or like filigree.

fil′ing (fīl′ĭng), *n*. A bit filed off ; as, iron *filings*.

Fil′i·pi′no (fĭl′ĭ-pē′nō), *n. ; pl.* -NOS (-nōz). *Fem.* **Fil′i·pi′na** (-nä) ; *pl.* -NAS (-näz). A member of a native tribe, esp. of a Christianized tribe, of the Philippine Islands.

fill (fĭl), *v. t.* **1**. To make full. **2**. *Naut.* (1) To dilate ; distend, as a sail. (2) To trim (a yard) to the wind. **3**. To furnish an abundant supply to; to pervade. **4**. To feed ; satisfy. **5. a** To execute (a business order). **b** *Med.* To compound (a prescription). *U.S.* **6**. To have and perform the duties of ; hold, as an office. **7**. To supply with an incumbent, as an office. — *v. i.* **1**. To become full; be filled. **2**. To fill a cup or glass for drinking. — *n*. **1**. A full supply; as much as supplies a want or need. **2**. That which fills; also, the place to be filled.

fill′er (fĭl′ẽr), *n*. One that fills ; a filling.

fil′let (-ĕt), *n*. **1**. A little band, esp. one to encircle the hair. **2**. A thin, narrow strip of any material, or a narrow, flat part or ornament. **3**. *Cookery.* A piece of lean meat without bone; also, a long strip rolled up and tied. — *v. t.* To bind, furnish, or make, with or as with a fillet.

fill′ing (fĭl′ĭng), *vb. n.* That which is used to fill an empty space, or supply a deficiency.

fil′lip (-ĭp), *v. t. & i.* **1**. To strike or snap in a certain quick way with the finger. **2**. To snap as by a fillip. — *n*. **1**. A smart blow or tap with the finger. **2**. Something serving to rouse or excite.

fil′li·peen′ (-ĭ-pēn′), *n*. See PHILOPENA.

fil′ly (fĭl′ĭ), *n. ; pl.* -LIES. A female foal or colt.

film (fĭlm), *n*. **1**. A thin skin. **2**. Any thin, slight covering or layer, as the layer holding the sensitized salts of photographic plates, or a flexible sheet on which this layer is mounted. **3**. A flexible strip of photographic film, used in making a motion picture. — *v. t. & i.* **1**. To cover, or become covered, with or as with a film.

film′y (fĭl′mĭ), *a*. [3] Of, resembling, or covered with, a film. — **film′i-ness**, *n*. [8].

fil′ter (fĭl′tẽr), *n*. Anything porous through which liquid is passed to cleanse or strain it, or an apparatus containing such substance. — *v. t.* To pass through, or remove by, a filter ; strain. — *v. i.* To pass through or as through a filter ; percolate.

filth (fĭlth), *n*. **1**. Foul matter ; repulsive dirt; nastiness. **2**. Moral defilement ; corruption.

filth′y (fĭl′thĭ), *a*. [3] Defiled with filth ; foul; impure. — **filth′i·ly**, *adv.* [8] — **-i·ness**, *n*. [8].

fil′trate (fĭl′trāt), *v. t. & i.* [1] To filter. — *n*. The liquid which has been filtered.

fil·tra′tion (fĭl-trā′shŭn), *n*. **1**. Act or process of filtering. **2**. Percolation.

fin (fĭn), *n*. **1**. A membranous winglike or paddle-like process of a fish or other aquatic animal, used in propelling, balancing, or guiding the body. **2**. A finlike organ, attachment, or part.

fi′nal (fī′năl), *a*. **1**. Pertaining to, or occurring at, the end ; last. **2**. Conclusive; decisive. — *n*. That which is final.

fi·na′le (fē-nä′lā), *n*. Termination; concluding part.

fi·nal′i·ty (fī-năl′ĭ-tĭ), *n.; pl.* -TIES (-tĭz). **1**. State of being final, finished, or settled. **2**. That which is final ; a final action or state.

---

fi′nal-ly (fī′năl-ĭ), *adv.* **1.** At the end; ultimately; lastly. **2.** Conclusively; beyond recovery.

fi-nance′ (fĭ-năns′; fī-), *n.* **1.** Pecuniary resources, esp. of a ruler or of a state; — usually in *pl.* **2.** The conduct of monetary affairs. — *v. t.* [1] To conduct the finances of; provide the capital for.

fi-nan′cial (fĭ-năn′shăl), *a.* Pertaining to finance, or money matters. — **fi-nan′cial-ly**, *adv.* [8].

fin′an-cier′ (fĭn′ăn-sēr′), *n.* **1.** One having the administration of finance. **2.** One skilled in financial operations.

fin′back′ (fĭn′băk′), *n.* Any of various whalebone whales having a prominent dorsal fin; a rorqual.

finch (fĭnch), *n.* Any of a numerous family of singing birds, including the sparrows, grosbeaks, etc.

find (fīnd), *v. t.; pret. & p. p.* FOUND (found); *p. pr. & vb. n.* FIND′ING. **1.** To meet with, come upon, or light upon; as: **a** To discover by study or experiment. **b** To gain; get; procure. **c** To attain to; arrive at; reach. **2.** To arrive at, as a conclusion. **3.** To learn by experience; perceive. **4.** To gain, or regain, the use of. **5.** To provide; supply; maintain. — **to find fault**, to discover and proclaim some defect or fault; to criticize unfavorably. — *n.* A finding, or something found.

find′er (fīn′dēr), *n.* One that finds; specifically, a camera attachment which shows in miniature the view thrown on the photographic plate.

find′ing, *vb. n.* **1.** That which is found; esp., *pl.*, that which a journeyman artisan provides for himself, as tools, trimmings, etc. **2.** *Law.* The result of a judicial inquiry, esp. into some matter of fact.

fine (fīn), *a.* [3] **1.** Finished; refined; free from impurity. **2.** Not coarse or gross. **3.** Of delicate or nice perception. **4.** Of marked excellence. — **fine art**, art concerned with the creation of objects of imagination and taste for their own sake without relation to utility. — **f. arts**, painting, drawing, architecture, and sculpture; poetry, music, dancing, and dramatic art are often included.

fine, *n.* End. *Obs.*, except in : **in fine**, in conclusion. **2.** A sum exacted as penalty for an offense. — *v. t.* To set a fine on by judgment of a court.

fine′ly, *adv.* In a fine manner or degree.

fine′ness (fīn′něs), *n.* **1.** Quality or condition of being fine. **2.** The proportion of pure silver or gold in coins, etc., expressed in parts per thousand.

fin′er-y (fīn′ēr-ĭ), *n.; pl.* -ERIES (-ĭz). Ornament; decoration; esp., showy dress.

fi-nesse′ (fĭ-něs′), *n.* **1.** Delicate skill. **2.** Cunning; stratagem. — *v. i.* [1] To use finesse or artifice.

fin′ger (fĭŋ′gēr), *n.* **1.** One of the digits of the hand, esp. one other than the thumb. **2.** Something like, or suggestive of, a finger, as a pointer. **3.** A part of a glove into which a finger is inserted. — *v. t. & i.* To touch with the fingers; handle.

fin′ger-print′ (-prĭnt′), *n.* An imprint made by a finger or thumb, used as a means of identification. — *v. t.* To make a fingerprint of.

fin′i-cal (fĭn′ĭ-kăl), *a.* [4] Affectedly fine; unduly fastidious. — **fin′i-cal-ly**, *adv.* [8].

fi′nis (fī′nĭs), *n.* An end; conclusion.

fin′ish (fĭn′ĭsh), *v. t.* **1.** To arrive at the end of; end; terminate. **2.** To complete; perfect. **3.** To dispose of completely. — *v. i.* To come to an end; cease. — *n.* **1.** The conclusion; end. **2.** That which finishes, completes, or perfects. **3.** Condition resulting from completed labor; style of finishing. — **fin′ish-er**, *n.* [8].

fi′nite (fī′nīt), *a.* **1.** Having definable limits. **2.** Determinable; neither infinite nor infinitesimal. — **-ly**, *adv.* — **-ness**, *n.* [8].

fin′nan had′die (fĭn′ăn). A smoked haddock.

fin′ny (fĭn′ĭ), *a.* [3] Having or resembling fins; hence, pertaining to, or abounding in, fishes.

fiord (fyôrd), *n.* A narrow inlet of the sea, between high banks or rocks.

fir (fûr), *n.* Any of various evergreen trees of the pine family.

fire (fīr), *n.* **1.** The principle of combustion as manifested in light and heat, esp. flame, formerly regarded as one of the elements. **2.** Fuel in combustion, as on a hearth. **3.** A destructive burning, as of a house. **4.** Lightning; a thunderbolt. *Archaic.* **5.** An inflammable composition or a device for producing a fiery display; as, red *fire.* **6.** **a** Liveliness of imagination or fancy. **b** Ardor of passion. **c** Ardor of spirit or temperament; fervor. **7.** Brilliancy; hence, a glowing object, as a star. **8.** The discharge of firearms; firing. — **on fire**, burning; hence, ardent; passionate; eager; zealous. — *v.t.* [1] **1.** To set on fire; kindle; ignite. **2.** Hence: **a** To subject to intense heat; bake, as pottery. **b** To tend the fire of. **3.** **a** To animate; give life to. **b** To inflame; irritate. **4.** To cause to explode, as a mine; discharge, as a gun. **5.** To propel from or as from a gun. — *v. i.* **1.** To take fire; redden. **2.** To be inflamed with passion. **3.** To discharge artillery or firearms.

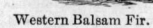

Western Balsam Fir.

fire′arm′ (-ärm′), *n.* A weapon, esp. a portable one, from which a shot is discharged by an explosive.

fire′brand′ (-brănd′), *n.* **1.** A piece of burning wood. **2.** One who inflames factions or causes contention.

fire′crack′er (fīr′krăk′ēr), *n.* A paper cylinder containing an explosive, fired to make a noise.

fire damp. A gas formed esp. in coal mines; also, the explosive mixture formed by this gas with air.

fire′dog′ (fīr′dôg′), *n.* An andiron.

fire engine. An apparatus for throwing a stream of water to extinguish fires.

fire escape. Any device for escape from a burning building.

fire′fly′ (-flī′), *n.; pl.* -FLIES (-flīz′). Any nocturnal winged light-producing insect.

fire′man (-măn), *n.; pl.* -MEN. **1.** A man employed to put out fires. **2.** A man who tends fires; stoker.

fire′place′ (-plās′), *n.* The part of a chimney below the fire, usually an open recess in a wall; a hearth.

fire′proof′ (-prōōf′), *a.* Proof against fire; relatively incombustible. — *v. t.* To render fireproof.

fire ship. A vessel carrying combustibles sent among the enemy's ships to set them on fire.

āle, senāte, câre, ăm, ăccount, ärm, ȧsk, sofȧ; ēve, évent, ĕnd, recênt, makêr; īce, ĭll; ōld, ŏbey, ôrb, ŏdd, sŏft, cŏnnect; ūse, ŭnite, ûrn, ŭp, circŭs; fŏŏd, fŏŏt; out, oil;

fire′side′ (-sĭd′), *n.* Place near the fire; home.

fire′weed′ (-wēd′), *n.* Any of several weeds troublesome in clearings or burned districts.

fire′wood′ (-wŏŏd′), *n.* Wood for fuel.

fire′work′ (-wûrk′), *n.* **1.** A device for producing a display of light or a figure in fire; — usually in *pl.* **2.** *pl.* A pyrotechnic exhibition.

fir′kin (fûr′kĭn), *n.* **1.** A small wooden vessel or cask, for butter, lard, etc. **2.** A measure of capacity, usually the fourth of a barrel.

firm (fûrm), *a.* [3] **1.** Fixed; hence, closely compressed; unyielding; as, *firm* flesh or wood. **2.** Not easily moved; established; loyal. **3.** Solid; — opposed to *fluid.* **4.** Indicating firmness; as, a *firm* voice. **5.** Steady; not fluctuating;— of prices, etc.

firm (fûrm), *n.* The name under which a company transacts business; partnership; commercial house.

fir′ma-ment (fûr′mȧ-mĕnt), *n.* The vault or arch of the sky; the heavens.

firm′ly, *adv.* In a firm manner.

firm′ness, *n.* State or quality of being firm.

first (fûrst), *a.* Preceding all others, as in time or rank. — *adv.* **1.** Before any or some other person or thing in time, space, rank, etc. **2.** For the first time. **3.** In preference to anything else. — **at first,** at the first, at the beginning. — *n.* Anything that is first.

first′-class′ (fûrst′klȧs′), *a.* Of the best or highest class, rank, or quality. — *adv.* By a first-class conveyance ; as, to travel *first-class.*

first′-hand′ (-hănd′), *adv.* Directly from the original source. — *a.* Obtained first-hand.

first′ling (-lĭng), *n.* The first of a class or kind ; the first produce, offspring, or result of anything.

first′ly (-lĭ), *adv.* In the first place; first; — commonly used in connection with *secondly,* etc. Many prefer *first* in this use.

first′-rate′ (-rāt′), *a.* Of the first rate; hence, very efficient or good. — *adv.* Very well. *Colloq.*

firth (fûrth), *n.* A narrow arm of the sea; a frith.

fis′cal (fĭs′kăl), *a.* **1.** Pertaining to the public treasury or revenue. **2.** Financial.— **-ly,** *adv.* [8].

fish (fĭsh), *n.; pl.* FISHES (-ĕz), *or, collectively,* FISH. **1.** Broadly, any animal living in the water. **2.** Any completely aquatic, water-breathing vertebrate having the limbs (when present) developed as fins and, usually, a scaly body. **3.** The flesh of fish, used as food.— *v. i.* **1.** To attempt to catch fish, as by angling or drawing a net. **2.** To search (for anything submerged or hidden) with hook, dredge, extended arm, etc. **3.** To seek to get by artifice, or indirectly. — *v. t.* **1.** To catch; draw (out or up). **2.** To fish in, as a stream. — **fish′er,** *n.* [8].

fish′er-man (-ẽr-măn), *n.* One whose occupation is to catch fish.

fish′er-y (fĭsh′ẽr-ĭ), *n.; pl.* -ERIES (-ĭz). Act, process, occupation, or place of fishing.

fish hawk. The osprey.

fish′hook′ (fĭsh′hŏŏk′),*n.* A hook for catching fish.

fish′ing, *vb. n.* Act of one who fishes.

fish′mon′ger (-mŭn′gẽr), *n.* A dealer in fish.

fish′wife′ (fĭsh′wīf′), *n.; pl.* -WIVES (-wīvz′). A woman who sells fish at retail.

fish′y (fĭsh′ĭ), *a.* [3] **1.** Consisting of, or having the qualities, taste, or odor of fish. **2.** Improbable. *Colloq.* **3.** Dull; lusterless, as an eye.

fis′sion (-ŭn), *n.* A cleaving into parts.

fis′sure (-ŭr), *n.* A narrow opening made by separation of parts; cleft.

fist (fĭst), *n.* The hand clenched, esp. for a blow.

fist′ic (fĭs′tĭk),*a.* [4] Pertaining to boxing. *Colloq.*

fist′i-cuffs′ (-tĭ-kŭfs′),*n.pl.* A fight with the fists.

fis′tu-la (fĭs′tṗ-lȧ), *n. ; pl.* E. -LAS (-lȧz), L. -LÆ (-lē). An abnormal opening or narrow cavity in a normal canal, organ, or other part of the body.

fit (fĭt), *a. ;* FIT′TER (-ẽr) ; FIT′TEST. **1.** Adapted to an end, object, or design; qualified. **2.** Becoming; seemly; proper. **3.** Prepared; ready. — *v. t. ;* FIT′TED (-ĕd) ; FIT′TING. **1.** To be suitable to ; to conform to the shape of. **2.** To make fit. **3.** To cause to conform; to adapt; adjust. **4.** To supply with something fit. — *v. i.* To conform to the wearer, as a coat. — *n.* The quality or condition of being fit or of fitting.

fit, *n.* **1.** A sudden violent attack of a disorder ; a convulsion. **2.** A sudden transitory outburst.

fit′ful (fĭt′fŏŏl), *a.* [4] Spasmodic; impulsive and unstable.— **fit′ful-ly,** *adv.* [8] — **-ness,** *n.* [8].

fit′ly (-lĭ), *adv.* In a fit manner or at a fit time.

fit′ness, *n.* State or quality of being fit or fitted.

fit′ter (fĭt′ẽr), *n.* One who fits or makes to fit.

fit′ting, *n.* Anything used in fitting up; esp., *pl.,* fixtures. — *a.* [4] Fit; suitable. — **-ly,** *adv.* [8].

five (fĭv), *a.* Four and one added. — *n.* **1.** The number greater by a unit than four. **2.** A symbol for this number, as 5 or v. **3.** Something having as an essential feature five units or members.

fix (fĭks), *v. t.* **1.** To make firm, stable, or fast. **2.** To render permanent or lasting. **3.** To set or place definitely ; establish. **4.** To repair. *Colloq.* — *v. i.* To become fixed, firm, or stable. — *n.* A predicament; dilemma. *Colloq.*— **fix′a-ble,***a.* [8].

fix-a′tion (fĭk-sā′shŭn), *n.* Act of fixing.

fix′i-ty (fĭk′sĭ-tĭ), *n.* State of being fixed.

fix′ture (fĭks′tṗr), *n.* **1.** Thing or person firmly fastened or established. **2.** That which is fixed or attached permanently or firmly ; as, a gas *fixture.*

fizz, fiz (fĭz), *v. i.; a.;* FIZZED (fĭzd); FIZZ′ING. To hiss, as a burning fuse.— *n.* A hissing sound.

fiz′zle (fĭz′'l), *v. i.* [1] **1.** To fizz. **2.** To burn with a fizz and then go out; hence, to fail ignominiously after a good beginning. *Colloq.*— *n.* **1.** A hissing. **2.** A failure. *Colloq.*

flab′by (flăb′ĭ), *a.* [3] Wanting firmness; flaccid; weak. — **-bi-ly,** *adv.* [8] — **-bi-ness,** *n.* [8].

flac′cid (flăk′sĭd), *a.* [4] Lacking stiffness; soft and weak; flabby. — **-ly,** *adv.* [8].

flac-cid′i- ty (-sĭd′ĭ-tĭ), *n.* Flaccid quality or state.

flag (flăg), *n.* Any of various plants having long, sword-shaped leaves; esp., an iris.

flag, *n.* Flagstone. — *v. t.* To lay with flagstones.

The United States Flag.

flag, *n.* A light cloth bearing a device or devices to indicate nationality, party, etc., or to give or ask information; a standard; banner; ensign. — *v. t.* ; FLAGGED (flăgd); FLAG'GING. **1.** To put a flag on. **2.** To signal with a flag.

flag (flăg), *v. i.* **1.** To hang loose; be limp. **2.** To grow spiritless; lose vigor; lag; droop.

flag'el-lant (flăj'ĕ-lănt; flá-jĕl'ănt), *n.* One who flagellates; especially, a fanatic who tortures himself by scourging.

flag'el-late (flăj'ĕ-lāt), *v. t.* [1] To whip; scourge.

flag'el-la'tion (-lā'shŭn), *n.* A beating; scourging.

flag'eo-let' (flăj'ō-lĕt; flăj'ō-lĕt), *n. Music.* A small shrill-sounding wooden pipe.

flag'ging (flăg'ĭng), *n.* A pavement or sidewalk of flagstones; flagstones, collectively.

fla-gi'tious (flá-jĭsh'ŭs), *a.* [4] Grossly wicked; villainous. — **-ly**, *adv.* [8] — **-ness**, *n.* [8].

flag officer. *Naval.* An officer entitled to display a flag; an admiral, vice-admiral, or rear admiral.

flag'on (flăg'ŭn), *n.* A vessel for liquors.

fla'gran-cy (flā'grăn-sĭ), *n.; pl.* -CIES (-sĭz). State or quality of being flagrant.

fla'grant (-grănt), *a.* [4] Flaming into notice; notorious; glaringly wicked. — **-ly**, *adv.* [8].

flag'ship' (flăg'shĭp'), *n. Naval.* The ship that carries the commander of a fleet and flies his flag.

flag'staff' (-stàf'), *n.; pl.* -STAFFS (-stàfs') or -STAVES (-stāvz'). A staff on which a flag is hoisted.

flag'stone' (-stōn'), *n.* Flat stone for paving; a flag.

flail (flāl), *n.* An instrument for threshing grain by hand. — *v. t. & i.* To beat with or as with a flail.

flake (flāk), *n.* A loose filmy mass or a thin chiplike layer of anything. — *v. t. & i.* [1] To form or separate into, or to cover or mark with, flakes.

flak'y (flāk'ĭ), *a.* [3] Consisting of, lying in, or cleaving off in, flakes, or layers. — **-i-ness**, *n.* [8].

flam'beau (flăm'bō), *n.; pl.* -BEAUX (-bōz) or -BEAUS (-bōz). A flaming torch.

flam-boy'ant (flăm-boi'ănt), *a.* [4] **1.** *Arch.* Marked by waving or flamelike curves, as the tracery of certain windows. **2.** Gorgeous; showy.

flame (flām), *n.* **1.** A body of burning gas or vapor. **2.** State of blazing combustion; blaze; glow. **3.** Burning zeal; passion; ardor. **4.** A sweetheart. — *v. i.* [1] **1.** To burn with a flame. **2.** To burst forth like flame, or with zeal or ardor. **3.** To have a flamelike appearance; glow.

fla-min'go (flá-mĭn'gō), *n.; pl.* -GOS or -GOES (-gōz). Any of several long-legged tropical or semi-tropical aquatic birds.

Flamingo.
(⅒)

flange (flănj), *n.* A rib or rim for strength, for a guide, or for attachment to another object.

flank (flăngk), *n.* **1.** The side of an animal, between the ribs and the hip. **2.** Hence, the side of anything. **3.** The right or left of an army, fleet, or fort. — *v. t.* **1.** To guard, or to be situated at, the flank of. **2.** To pass around, or turn, the flank of; as, to *flank* the enemy.

flan'nel (flăn'ĕl), *n.* **1.** A soft woolen cloth, of loose texture. **2.** *pl.* Flannel clothing.

flap (flăp), *n.* **1.** Anything broad and limber or flat and thin, that hangs loose. **2.** The motion of anything broad and loose, or a stroke or sound

made with it; as, the *flap* of wings. — *v. t. & i.*; FLAPPED (flăpt); FLAP'PING. **1.** To beat or rouse with a flap. **2.** To move with a beating motion.

flap'jack' (flăp'jăk'), *n.* A griddlecake.

flap'per (flăp'ẽr), *n.* **1.** One that flaps. **2.** A girl or young woman. *Slang.*

flare (flâr), *v. i.* [1] **1.** Tc burn or blaze out with a sudden unsteady light. **2.** To open or spread outward. — *v. t.* To display; also, to signal by flares. — *n.* **1.** An unsteady glaring light. **2.** A spreading outward, or a place or part that spreads.

flash (flăsh), *v. i.* **1.** To break forth in or like a sudden flame; to gleam. **2.** To come or pass like a flash. **3.** To break suddenly into action. — *v. t.* To send out in or as in, or by, flashes. — *n.* **1.** A sudden burst or blaze of light. **2.** A sudden brilliant burst, as of wit. **3.** The duration of a flash; a brief time. — *a.* **1.** Showy; cheap, pretentious, and vulgar. **2.** Pert. to thieves, vagrants, etc.

flash light. A light that flashes or that can be made to flash; esp., a small portable electric light that can be made to flash.

flash'y (flăsh'ĭ), *a.* [3] **1.** Flashing; dazzling for a moment. **2.** Showy; gaudy. — **flash'i-ly** (-ĭ-lĭ), *adv.* [8] — **flash'i-ness**, *n.* [8].

flask (flàsk), *n.* A narrow-necked or bottle-shaped vessel, variously used; as, a powder *flask*; oil *flask.*

flat (flăt), *n.* A story or a suite of rooms in one story, forming a complete residence.

flat, *a.*; FLAT'TER (-ẽr); FLAT'TEST. **1.** Having a surface level and smooth. **2.** Lying spread out; prostrate; hence, laid low; ruined. **3.** Having broad smooth surfaces and little thickness. **4.** a Positive; downright. Hence, unvarying; esp., without discount; as, a *flat* rate. **b** Dull; uninteresting; insipid, as a drink. **5.** *Music.* Below the true pitch; lower by a half step; as, A *flat.* — *adv.* **1.** Flatly. **2.** Without excess; exactly. — *n.* **1.** A level surface; a plain. **2.** A shoal; shallow. **3.** Something flat or the flat part of anything, as of a blade. **4.** *Music.* A flat tone or note; also, a character [♭] indicating a flat tone or pitch. — *v. t. & i.* ; FLAT'-TED; FLAT'TING. To make or become flat. — **flat'-ly**, *adv.* [8] — **flat'ness**, *n.* [8].

flat'fish' (flăt'fĭsh'), *n.* Any of a large group of flat fishes, including the flounder, halibut, etc.

flat'i'ron (-ī'ŭrn), *n.* An iron for ironing clothes.

flat'ten (-'n), *v. t. & i.* To make or become flat.

flat'ter (-ẽr), *v. t.* **1.** To treat with flattery. **2.** To represent too favorably, as a portrait. — *v. i.* To use flattery. — **-ter-er**, *n.* — **ter-ing-ly**, *adv.*

flat'ter-y (-ĭ), *n.; pl.* -TERIES (-ĭz). Act of pleasing by artful compliments; false or insincere praise; also, blandishment.

flat'u-lence (flăt'ū-lĕns) ⎫ *n.* State or quality ot
flat'u-len-cy (-lĕn-sĭ) ⎭ being flatulent.

flat'u-lent (-lĕnt), *a.* [4] Generating gas in the alimentary canal.

flat'ways' (flăt'wāz'), **flat'wise'** (-wīz'), *a. or adv.* With the flat side down, or next to another object.

flaunt (flänt; flônt), *v. i. & t.* To wave, flutter, or move ostentatiously; parade or display obtrusively. — *n.* Act of flaunting. — **flaunt'ing-ly**, *adv.* [8].

flau'tist (flô'tĭst), *n.* A flutist.

fla'vor (flā'vẽr), *n.* [5] **1.** Odor; fragrance. **2.** That quality of anything which affects the taste; relish; savor. **3.** A flavoring substance. **4.** A characterizing quality of anything. — v. t. To give flavor or savor to.

fla′vor·ing, n. [5] Anything, as an essence or extract, used to give a particular flavor.

flaw (flô), n. **1.** A crack; gap; fissure. **2.** A defect; fault. — v. t. To make a flaw in. — **flaw′less,** a. [8].

flaw, n. A sudden gust of wind.

flax (flăks), n. A slender erect annual plant, with blue flowers, commonly cultivated for its fiber and seed; also, its fiber prepared for spinning.

flax′en (flăk′s'n), a. Made of or resembling flax; of a light straw color.

flax′seed′ (flăks′sēd′; flăk′sēd′), n. The seed of flax, widely used in medicine, and yielding an oil called *linseed oil.*

flay (flā), v. t. To strip off the skin or surface of; fig., to criticize severely.

flea (flē), n. Any of certain hard-bodied wingless bloodsucking insects with great powers of leaping.

fleck (flĕk), n. A spot, as a freckle; a streak; speckle. — v. t. To spot, or streak; to dapple.

flec′tion (flĕk′shŭn), n. A flexing or bending.

fled (flĕd), pret. & p. p. of FLEE.

fledge (flĕj), v. i. [1] To acquire the feathers necessary for flight. — v. t. To provide with feathers.

fledg′ling (flĕj′lĭng), n. A bird just fledged.

flee (flē), v. i. ; FLED (flĕd); FLEE′ING. **1.** To run away, as from danger. **2.** To pass away swiftly; vanish. — v. t. To run away from; shun.

fleece (flēs), n. **1.** The coat of wool that covers a sheep; the wool shorn from a sheep at one time. **2.** A fleecelike covering. — v. t. [1] **1.** To shear (sheep). **2.** To strip of money or other property.

fleec′y (-Ĭ), a. [3] Like, or covered with, a fleece.

fleer (flēr), v. i. & t. To laugh or grin coarsely; mock; gibe. — n. A derisive word or look.

fleet (flēt), n. **1.** A number of war vessels under one command. **2.** Any group of vessels in company.

fleet, v. i. To fly swiftly; hasten. — a. [3] Swift in motion; quick; nimble; hence, evanescent; fleeting. — **-ly,** adv. [8] —**ness,** n. [8].

fleet′ing, p. a. [4] Passing swiftly.

flesh (flĕsh), n. **1.** The softer parts of an animal body; animal food; meat. **2.** The human body in distinction from the soul; the carnal or sinful nature of man. **3.** Mankind in general. **4.** Kindred; race. **5.** The pulpy substance of fruit.

flesh′i·ness (-Ĭ-nĕs), n. State of being fleshy.

flesh′ly (-lĬ), a. [4] Of or pertaining to the flesh or body; corporeal; carnal; sensual.

flesh′pot′ (-pŏt′), n. A pot or vessel in which flesh is cooked; hence, pl., plenty; high living.

flesh′y (-Ĭ), a. [3] Of, pertaining to, or resembling flesh; marked by abundant flesh; plump; fat.

∥ **fleur′–de–lis′** (flûr′dĕ-lē′), n.; pl. FLEURS-DE-LIS (flûr′-). [F.] **1.** The iris. **2.** A conventionalized flower, perhaps suggested by the iris.

flew (flo͞o), pret. of FLY.

flex (flĕks), v. t. & i. To bend.

flex′i·bil′i·ty (flĕk′sĬ-bĬl′Ĭ-tĬ), n. State or quality of being flexible.

flex′i·ble (-b'l), a. [4] **1.** Capable of being flexed; pliable; not stiff. **2.** Ready to yield;

Fleur-de-lis, 2.

tractable; compliant. **3.** Capable of being molded; plastic. — **flex′i·bly,** adv. [8].

flex′ile (flĕk′sĬl), a. [4] Flexible; pliant.

flex′or (-sŏr), n. A muscle which bends a limb.

flex′ure (-shŭr), n. **1.** A flexing, or state of being flexed; flexion. **2.** A turn; bend.

flick (flĭk), v. t. **1.** To whip lightly or with a quick jerk. **2.** To snap or toss with a jerk; flirt. — n. A flicking stroke, or the sound of it.

flick′er (flĭk′ēr), v. i. **1.** To flutter. **2.** To waver unsteadily like a dying flame; flutter. — n. A flickering. — **flick′er·ing·ly,** adv. [8].

flick′er, n. A well-known woodpecker of eastern North America; — called also *yellow-hammer.*

Flicker, male.

fli′er (flī′ēr), n. One that flies. = FLYER.

flight (flīt), n. **1.** Act or mode of flying; as, the *flight* of a bird, of time, etc. **2.** Power of flying or distance covered at a flight. **3.** A passing above or beyond ordinary bounds; as, a *flight* of wit. **4.** A number of beings or things passing through the air together; as, a *flight* of arrows. **5.** Stairs from one landing to the next.

flight′y (flīt′Ĭ), a. [3] **1.** Indulging in flights, or sallies,of fancy, caprice,etc.; volatile. **2.** Mildly insane.—**flight′i·ly** (-Ĭ-lĬ),adv.—**flight′i·ness,** n.

flim′sy (flĬm′zĬ), a. [3] Weak; slight; unsubstantial. — **-si·ly,** adv. — **ness,** n.

flinch (flĬnch), v. i. To draw back, as from pain; wince. — n. Act of flinching.

flin′ders (flĬn′dẽrz), n. Splinters; fragments.

fling (flĬng), v. t. ; pret. & p. p. FLUNG (flŭng); p. pr. & vb. n. FLING′ING. **1.** To cast from or as from the hand; throw; hurl. **2.** To throw off or down. **3.** To send forth; emit. **4.** To throw aside; cast off.—v. i. To throw one's self violently or hastily; rush. — n. **1.** A throw; flounce; kick. **2.** A contemptuous remark. **3.** A kind of lively dance. **4.** A time of unrestrained indulgence.

flint (flĬnt), n. **1.** A very hard kind of quartz, which strikes fire with steel. **2.** A piece of flint for striking fire. **3.** Anything hard, like flint.

flint′lock′ (flĬnt′lŏk′), n. **1.** A gunlock with a flint in the cock, or hammer,for striking a spark to ignite the charge. **2.** A firearm with such a lock.

flint′y (flĬn′tĬ), a. [3] Consisting of, abounding in, or resembling flint. — **flint′i·ness,** n.

flip (flĬp), n. A beverage of spiced and sweetened liquor heated, as with a hot iron.

flip, v. t. ; FLIPPED (flĬpt); FLIP′PING. **1.** To toss; fillip; as, to *flip* a coin. **2.** To flick; flirt. — v. i. To move with a jerk or flirt. — n. Act of flipping.

flip′pan·cy (flĬp′ăn-sĬ), n. State of being flippant.

flip′pant (flĭp′ănt), *a.* [4] Speaking confidently without knowledge or respect. — **-ly,** *adv.* [8].

flip′per (-ẽr), *n.* A broad flat limb adapted for swimming, as of seals, whales, etc.

flirt (flŭrt), *v. t.* **1.** To throw with a jerk; fling suddenly; fillip. **2.** To toss about jerkily. — *v. i.* **1.** To move jerkily; dart; hence, to trifle. **2.** To play at courtship; coquet. — *n.* **1.** A sudden jerk; quick throw. **2.** One who flirts.

flir-ta′tion (flẽr-tā′shŭn), *n.* A flirting; coquetry.

flir-ta′tious (-shŭs), *a.* [4] Inclined to flirt.

flit (flĭt), *v. i.;* FLIT′TED; FLIT′TING. **1.** To move rapidly; dart along. **2.** To flutter; rove on the wing.

flitch (flĭch), *n.* The side of a hog salted and cured; side of bacon.

float (flōt), *n.* **1.** Anything that floats on a fluid. **2.** A flat-topped vehicle without sides for carrying a display; also, the vehicle with the display. — *v. i.* **1.** To rest on the surface of a fluid. **2.** To move quietly or gently on or as on the water; drift along; also, to be suspended within a fluid. — *v. t.* **1.** To cause to float. **2.** To get (a scheme or company) started.

float′er (flōt′ẽr), *n.* **1.** One that floats. **2.** *U. S.* **a** A voter who shifts from party to party, esp. one whose vote can be bought. **b** One who votes illegally in various places.

float′ing, *p. a.* **1.** Buoyed on or in a fluid. **2.** Shifting from place to place; not permanent. **3.** Variable; not funded; as, a *floating* debt.

floc′cu-lent (flŏk′ū-lĕnt), *a.* [4] **1.** Like wool. **2.** Containing, or covered with, flocks of wool.

flock (flŏk), *n.* **1.** A lock of wool or hair. **2.** Woolen refuse, etc., used in upholstering, etc.

flock, *n.* **1.** A number of birds or of animals, as geese or sheep, of one kind living or herded together. **2.** All Christians in their relation to Christ, the "Good Shepherd," or a congregation in their relation to the pastor.

flock (flŏk), *v. i.* To gather or move in companies.

floe (flō), *n.* A field of floating ice.

flog (flŏg), *v. t.;* FLOGGED (flŏgd); FLOG′GING (flŏg′ĭng). To beat or strike with a rod or whip; whip.

flood (flŭd), *n.* **1.** A great flow of water; body of water overflowing land not usually covered; a deluge; inundation. **2.** The flowing in of the tide. **3.** The watery element. **4.** A great stream of or as of any fluid; a great quantity widely diffused; a superabundance. — **the Flood,** the Deluge (*Gen.* vii.). — *v. t.* **1.** To overflow; deluge. **2.** To cause to be inundated; fill to excess. — *v. i.* To issue like a flood.

flood′gate′ (flŭd′gāt′), *n.* A gate to shut out, admit, or release, a body of water; — often figurative.

floor (flōr), *n.* **1.** The bottom of a room, on which one treads. **2.** Hence, any ground surface, as of the sea. **3.** The structure dividing a building horizontally into stories; hence, a story of a building. **4.** The right to occupy the floor of a legislative chamber. — *v. t.* **1.** To furnish with a floor. **2.** To lay level with the floor; knock down; hence, to silence or defeat.

floor′ing, *vb. n.* A floor or material for a floor.

floor′walk′er (flōr′wôk′ẽr), *n.* One who walks about in a large retail store as an overseer. *U. S.*

flop (flŏp), *v. i.;* FLOPPED (flŏpt); FLOP′PING. *Colloq.*

1. To strike about, as does a fish with its tail; rise and fall loosely, as the brim of a hat. **2.** To throw one's self heavily. **3.** To change over suddenly, as from one party to another. — *v. t.* **1.** To flap or strike heavily or clumsily. **2.** To turn or drop suddenly and heavily. — *n.* Act or sound of flopping.

flo′ral (-rǎl), *a.* Of or pertaining to flowers.

flo′ret (flō′rĕt), *n.* A small flower; esp., one of the flowers of a composite inflorescence.

flo′ri-cul′ture (flō′rĭ-kŭl′tṳr; flōr′ĭ-), *n.* Cultivation of ornamental flowering plants.

flor′id (flŏr′ĭd), *a.* [4] **1.** Embellished with flowers of rhetoric; excessively ornate. **2.** *Music.* Flowery; embellished. **3.** Bright in color; flushed with red. — **flor′id-ly,** *adv.* [8] — **-ness,** *n.* [8].

flor′in (flŏr′ĭn), *n.* Any of several coins, esp. : **a** The Dutch gulden. **b** A British silver coin worth 2 shillings (48.7 cents).

flo′rist (flō′rĭst; flōr′ĭst), *n.* A cultivator of, or dealer in, flowers.

floss (flŏs), *n.* **1.** Waste silk fibers. **2.** The "silk" of certain plants, as corn. **3.** = FLOSS SILK.

floss silk. Lustrous untwisted silk thread of short and fine fiber used in embroidery, etc.

floss′y (flŏs′ĭ), *a.* [3] Of or like floss; downy.

flo′tage (flō′tăj), *n.* **1.** Act or state of floating; capacity for buoying up. **2.** That which floats.

flo-ta′tion (flō-tā′shŭn), *n.* Act of floating.

flo-til′la (-tĭl′ä), *n.* Small fleet; fleet of small boats

flot′sam (flŏt′săm), *n.* Wreckage of a ship or its cargo found floating on the sea. Cf. JETSAM.

flounce (flouns), *v. i.* [1] To throw the limbs and body one way and the other; to flop, often as in displeasure. — *n.* A sudden fling of the body.

flounce, *n.* A strip gathered and sewed on by its upper edge only, as on a woman's skirt. — *v. t.* To deck with a flounce or flounces.

floun′der (floun′dẽr), *n.* Any of various flatfishes.

floun′der, *v. i.* To struggle, as a horse in mire, or a fish on land. — *n.* A floundering.

flour (flour), *n.* Finely ground meal of grain; esp., fine meal separated by bolting; hence, any fine soft powder. — *v. t.* **1.** To grind and bolt; convert into flour. **2.** To sprinkle with flour.

flour′ish (flŭr′ĭsh), *v. i.* **1.** To grow luxuriantly; thrive. **2.** To increase in wealth, honor, etc.; to be in one's prime. **3.** To make ornamental strokes with the pen. — *v. t.* To swing about; brandish. — *n.* **1.** Flourishing condition; prosperity. **2.** Ostentatious embellishment; parade; show. **3.** A fanciful stroke, as of the pen. **4.** A fantastic or showy musical passage. **5.** A waving, as of a weapon. — **-er,** *n.* [8].

flour′y (flour′ĭ), *a.* Of, like, or covered with, flour.

flout (flout), *v. t.* To mock; insult. — *v. i.* To practice mocking; sneer. — *n.* An insult; jeer; mockery. — **flout′er,** *n.* [8] — **flout′ing-ly,** *adv.* [8].

flow (flō), *v. i.* **1.** To move or circulate, as a liquid; to run. **2.** To proceed; issue forth. **3.** To glide along smoothly; sound smoothly. **4.** To hang loose and waving. **5.** To rise, as the tide. — *n.* **1.** Act or manner of flowing or streaming. **2.** The type of motion characteristic of fluids. **3.** A stream of water or other fluid. **4.** The quantity that flows in a certain time, as of water. **5.** The tidal flood. **6.** A gentle movement of thought, music, etc.

āle, senāte, câre, ăm, ăccount, ärm, ȧsk, sofä; ēve, ĕvent, ĕnd, recĕnt, makẽr; īce, ĭll; ōld, ȯbey, ôrb, ŏdd, sŏft, cŏnnect; ūse, ŭnite, ûrn, ŭp, circŭs; fōōd, fŏŏt; out, oil;

flow'er (flou′ẽr), *n.* **1.** A bloom or blossom. **2.** Any plant cultivated or esteemed for its blossoms. **3.** *Bot.* That part of a plant destined to produce seed. **4.** An ornament, as a floral design; hence, a figure of speech. **5.** The choicest part of anything; state or time of freshness, bloom, or vigor; prime. — *v. i.* **1.** To blossom; produce flowers. **2.** To come into the finest or fairest condition. — *v. t.* To adorn with or as with flowers.

flow'er-et (-ĕt), *n.* A small flower; a floret.

flow'er-pot′ (-pŏt), *n.* A vessel, esp. of pottery, for earth in which to grow plants.

flow'er-y (-ĭ), *a.* [4] **1.** Full of flowers or blossoms. **2.** Of language, florid. — **flow′er-i-ness,** *n.* [8].

flown (flōn), *p. p.* of FLY.

fluc′tu-ate (flŭk′tū-āt), *v. i.* [1] **1.** To move as a wave; roll back and forth. **2.** To waver; vacillate.

fluc′tu-a′tion (-ā′shŭn), *n.* A fluctuating.

flue (flōō), *n.* An inclosed passage for a current of air, gases, etc., as in a chimney, organ, etc.

flu′en-cy (flōō′ĕn-sĭ), *n.* Quality of being fluent.

flu′ent (-ĕnt), *a.* [4] **1.** Flowing, or capable of flowing; unstable. **2.** Ready in the use of words; voluble; hence, flowing; smooth. — **-ly,** *adv.* [8].

fluff (flŭf), *n.* Nap; down, as from cotton, fur, etc. **fluff′y** (flŭf′ĭ), *a.* [3] Soft and downy; also covered with fluff. — **fluff′i-ness** (-ĭ-nĕs), *n.* [8].

flu′id (flōō′ĭd), *a.* [4] Liquid or gaseous.
fluid dram, *or* **f. drachm,** ½ fluid ounce. — **f. ounce,** a measure for liquid medicines, etc. ; 8 fluid drams. In the U.S. it equals 1⁄16 pint (29.6 c. c.).

flu′id, *n.* A fluid substance; a liquid or gas.

flu-id′i-ty (flōō-ĭd′ĭ-tĭ), *n.* Quality of being fluid.

fluke (flōōk), *n.* **1.** A flatfish or flounder. **2.** Any of various flattish, parasitic worms.

fluke, *n.* **1.** That part of an anchor which fastens in the ground. **2.** A lobe of a whale's tail.

fluke, *n.* An accidentally successful stroke, as at billiards; hence, any chance advantage. *Cant.*

flume (flōōm), *n.* An inclined channel to convey water from a distance.

flum′mer-y (flŭm′ẽr-ĭ), *n.; pl.* -MERIES (-ĭz). Trash; nonsense.

flung (flŭng), *pret. & p. p.* of FLING.

flunk′y (flŭnk′ĭ), *n.; pl.* FLUNKIES (-ĭz). **1.** A liveried servant; esp., a footman. **2.** One who is obsequious or cringing; a toady.

flu′or (flōō′ôr), *n.* Fluorite.

flu′o-res′cence (-ŏ-rĕs′ĕns), *n.* That property which some bodies have of emitting light while exposed to the action of certain rays of the spectrum, or of Röntgen rays, etc.; also, the light so produced.

flu′or-ine (flōō′ôr-ĭn; -ēn), *n.* A greenish yellow gas of a sharp odor, irritating to the nose and eyes. It is one of the elements, but is never found free in nature, being always combined, esp. with calcium as the mineral **flu′or-ite** (-ĭt), or **flu′or spar.**

flur′ry (flŭr′ĭ), *n.; pl.* -RIES (-ĭz). **1.** A sudden, brief commotion of the air. **2.** A light shower or snowfall with wind. **3.** Nervous commotion; flutter. — *v. t.* [2] To agitate; excite, as by haste.

flush (flŭsh), *v. i.* **1.** To flow and spread suddenly and freely; as, blood *flushes* into the face. **2.** To turn red or hot; blush; glow. — *v. t.* **1.** To animate; encourage. **2.** To cleanse by a rush of water. **3.** To make red, rosy, or glowing. — *n.* **1.** A sudden flowing; a rush, as of water, which fills or overflows. **2.** A sudden rush of feeling; a thrill. **3.** Any tinge of red, as due to blushing; glow; vigor.

flush, *v. i.* To start up suddenly; fly like a startled bird. — *v. t.* To cause to start up and fly.

flush, *a.* [3] **1.** Fully supplied; affluent. **2.** Full of vigor; hence, ruddy. **3.** Abundant; lavish; prosperous. **4.** Level with the adjacent surface. — *adv.* So as to be level or even.

flus′ter (flŭs′tẽr), *v. t.* To make hot and rosy, as with drinking; confuse. — *v. i.* To be agitated. — *n.* Heat or glow, as from drinking.

flute (flōōt), *n.* **1.** *Music.* A wind instrument. See *Illust.* **2.** A groove or channel of curved section.

Flute.

— *v. i.* [1] To play on or as on a flute. — *v. t.* **1.** To play, whistle, or sing, with a flute-like note. **2.** To form flutes in, as in a column.

flut′ing (flōōt′ĭng), *n.* Decoration with flutes or channels, as in architecture; flutes collectively.

flut′ist (flōōt′ĭst), *n.* A performer on the flute.

flut′ter (flŭt′ẽr), *v. i.* **1.** To flap the wings rapidly, without flying. **2.** To move with quick vibrations. **3.** To move about agitatedly, with little result. — *v. t.* **1.** To vibrate or move quickly. **2.** To throw into confusion. — *n.* **1.** A fluttering. **2.** Agitation; confusion. — **flut′ter-er,** *n.* [8].

flu′vi-al (flōō′vĭ-ăl), *a.* Of or pertaining to rivers.

flux (flŭks), *n.* **1.** An excessive and morbid fluid discharge, as from the bowels. **2.** A flowing; constant succession; change. **3.** Inflow of the tide. **4.** Any substance, as borax, lime, an alkali, etc., used to promote fusion of metals or minerals.

fly (flī), *v. i.; pret.* FLEW (flōō); *p. p.* FLOWN; *p. pr. & vb. n.* FLY′ING. **1.** To move in the air with wings. **2.** To be driven through the air, as before the wind. **3.** To move or pass swiftly. **4.** To float, wave, or soar, in the air, as a kite or flag. **5.** To flee. — *v. t.* **1.** To cause to fly, as a kite, flag, etc. **2.** To fly or flee from; shun; avoid. — *n.; pl.* FLIES (flīz). **1.** The course through the air of anything projected, as, esp., a batted ball; also, the ball in flight. **2.** A public covered one-horse carriage. *Eng.* **3.** A lap on a garment, to conceal buttons. **4.** *pl.* Space over a stage with mechanism for handling scenery.

fly, *n.* **1.** A two-winged insect of a family typified by the house fly; popularly, any flylike insect. **2.** A fish-hook dressed to imitate a fly.

fly'a-way′ (flī′ȧ-wā′), *a.* [4] Flighty; unrestrained.

fly'catch'er (-kăch′ẽr), *n.* Any of numerous small birds that feed on insects taken on the wing.

fly'er (flī′ẽr), *n.* One that flies.

fly'ing, *p. pr. & vb. n.* of FLY, *v.* — flying fish, any of certain fishes having winglike pectoral fins, and capable of moving some distance through the

Flying Fish

⅛

air. — flying jib, *Naut.,* a sail set outside the standing jib.

fly'leaf' (flī'lēf'), *n.* An unprinted leaf at the beginning or the end of a book.

fly'speck' (-spĕk'), *n.* A spot made by the excrement of a fly. — *v. t.* To soil with flyspecks.

fly'wheel' (-hwēl'), *n.* A heavy wheel for equalizing the speed of machinery with which it revolves.

foal (fōl), *n.* The young of the horse family ; a colt. — *v. t. & i.* To bring forth (a colt or foal).

foam (fōm), *n.* The white substance, of minute bubbles, formed on liquids by agitation, fermentation, etc.; froth; spume. — *v. i.* To gather or form foam ; to froth. — **foam'less,** *a.* [8].

foam'y (-ĭ), *a.* [3] Covered with foam ; frothy.

fob (fŏb), *n.* **1.** A little pocket in men's trousers for a watch, etc. **2.** A short watch chain or ribbon.

fo'cal (fō'kăl), *a.* Of or pertaining to a focus.

fo'cal-ize (-īz), *v. t.* [1] To focus.

fo'cus (-kŭs), *n. ; pl.* E. **-cuses** (-ĕz), L. **-ci** (-sī). **1.** A point in which rays, as of light, heat, sound, etc., meet, after being reflected or refracted ; the point at which an image is formed. **2. a** Focal length, that is, distance of its focus from a lens or mirror. **b** Adjustment, as of the eye or an eyepiece, necessary to give distinct vision. **3.** *Math.* Either of two certain points on the principal axis of an ellipse. See ELLIPSE. **4.** A central point ; point of concentration. — *v. t.* [7] **1.** To bring to a focus. **2.** To adjust the focus of (the eye, etc.).

fod'der (fŏd'ẽr), *n.* Coarse food for cattle, horses, and sheep, as hay, vegetables, etc.

foe (fō), *n.* **1.** One who has personal enmity, hatred, or malice, against another ; an enemy. **2.** An enemy in war ; adversary.

foe'man (fō'măn), *n. ; pl.* **-men** (-mĕn). A foe in war.

fog (fŏg), *n.* **1.** Vapor condensed to fine particles of water near the ground. **2.** Any murky condition of the atmosphere, or any substance causing it. **3.** State of mental confusion. — *v. t.* To envelop as with fog ; hence, to perplex. — *v. i.* To become obscured as with fog.

fog'gy (fŏg'ĭ), *a.* [3] **1.** Filled with fog ; misty. **2.** Beclouded; muddled. — **fog'gi-ness,** *n.* [8].

fog'horn' (-hôrn'), *n.* Horn sounded as a fog signal.

fo'gy (fō'gĭ), *n. ; pl.* **-gies** (-gĭz). A person with antiquated notions ; one behind the times. *Colloq.*

foi'ble (foi'b'l), *n.* A failing; weak point; frailty.

foil (foil), *v. t.* To defeat; baffle; frustrate; thwart. — *n.* Light blunt sword with a button at the point, for fencing.

foil, *n.* **1.** A very thin sheet of metal. **2.** Anything that adorns or sets off by contrast. **3.** A rounded or leaflike ornament in windows, etc.

foist (foist), *v. t.* To insert surreptitiously; interpolate ; pass off (something spurious) as genuine.

fold (fōld), *v. t.* **1.** To lap or lay in plaits or folds. **2.** To lay or clasp together; lay close to the body. **3.** To envelop; embrace. — *v. i.* To become folded or doubled. — *n.* **1.** A doubling; plait. **2.** That which is folded, or which infolds ; embrace.

fold, *n.* **1.** An inclosure for sheep. **2.** A flock of sheep; fig., the church or a church. — *v. t.* To confine in a fold, as sheep.

fold'er (fōl'dẽr), *n.* **1.** One that folds. **2.** A circular, as a time-table, of one or more folded sheets.

fo'li-age (fō'lĭ-ăj), *n.* The leaves of a plant collectively ; leafage. — **fo'li-a'ceous** (fō'lĭ-ā'shŭs), *a.*

fo'li-ate (-āt), *a.* Leafy ; having leaves.

fo'li-at'ed (-āt'ĕd), *a.* [4] Having leaves or leaflike projections ; separable into thin plates.

fo'li-a'tion (-ā'shŭn), *n.* **1.** Process of forming into a leaf or leaves. **2.** Ornamentation with foils, or with foliage ; also, one of these ornaments.

fo'li-o (fō'lĭ-ō), *n. ; pl.* **-os** (-ōz). **1.** A leaf of a book or manuscript. **2.** A sheet of paper once folded. **3. a** A book of the largest-sized pages. **b** The size or form of a folio book. Abbr. *fol.* **4.** A page of a book. — *a.* Formed of sheets each folded once.

folk (fōk), *n.* **1.** A group of kindred people, forming a tribe or nation. **2.** *pl.* People in general or of a special class ; as, *folks* say ; fine *folks.* *Colloq.* **3.** *pl.* Persons of one's family ; relatives. *Colloq.*

folk dance. A dance common among the people of a country ; also, the music for it.

folk'lore' (fōk'lōr'), *n., or* **folk lore.** Traditional customs, beliefs, etc., esp. such as are superstitious or legendary, current among the uneducated.

folk song. A song handed down among the people of a country from generation to generation.

fol'li-cle (fŏl'ĭ-k'l), *n.* **1.** *Bot.* A one-celled simple fruit, opening only by one suture. **2.** *Anat.* A small nearly or entirely closed cavity, or gland.

fol'low (fŏl'ō), *v. t.* **1.** To go or come after; attend. **2.** To succeed in order of time, rank, etc. **3.** To result from. **4.** To walk in, or proceed along; attend on closely, as a calling. **5.** To endeavor to overtake; pursue; strive after. **6.** To accept as authority; obey. **7.** To watch, as a receding object. — *v. i.* **1.** To go or come after a person or thing; hence, to attend. **2.** To result or occur as a consequence. **3.** To pursue.

fol'low-er, *n.* One who follows ; pursuer ; adherent ; retainer.

fol'low-ing, *vb. n.* One's followers collectively. — *p. a.* **1.** Next after ; succeeding ; as, the *following* day. **2.** That now follows.

fol'ly (fŏl'ĭ), *n. ; pl.* **-lies** (-ĭz). **1.** Want of good sense ; levity. **2.** A foolish act or idea.

fo-ment' (fō-mĕnt'), *v. t.* **1.** To apply a warm lotion, heated cloths, or the like, to. **2.** To stir up by excitements; rouse; instigate. — **fo-ment'er,** *n.*

fo'men-ta'tion (fō'mĕn-tā'shŭn), *n.* Act of fomenting ; a lotion used in fomenting.

fond (fŏnd), *a.* [3] **1.** Foolishly tender and loving; weakly indulgent. **2.** Affectionate; tender; — in a good sense. **3.** Greatly pleased; prizing highly; desirous ; — followed by *of.* **4.** Cherished.

fon'dle (fŏn'd'l), *v. t.* [1] To treat or handle tenderly or lovingly ; caress.

fond'ly (fŏnd'lĭ), *adv.* **1.** Affectionately ; tenderly. **2.** In a willingly credulous manner.

fond'ness, *n.* Doting affection; appetite; relish.

font (fŏnt), *n.* A full assortment of type of one size and style.

font, *n.* **1.** A vessel to hold water for baptizing. **2.** A fountain ; spring.

food (fōōd), *n.* **1.** Nutriment taken into an organism for growth or repair and to maintain life. **2.** Nutriment in solid form, as opposed to *drink.*

food'stuff' (fōōd'stŭf'), *n.* Anything used as food.

fool (fōōl), *n.* **1.** One deficient in judgment; a simpleton. **2.** A professional jester, formerly dressed in motley with cap and bells. **3.** One made to appear foolish; butt; dupe. — *v. i.* To play the fool; jest; trifle. — *v. t.* To make a fool of; dupe.

fool'er·y (fōol'ẽr-Ĭ), *n. ; pl.* -ERIES (-Ĭz). Practice of fooling; behavior of a fool; foolish act or thing.

fool'har'dy (-här'dĬ), *a.* [4] Daring without judgment ; foolishly bold. —**-di·ness**, *n.* [8].

fool'ish, *a.* [4] **1.** Exhibiting foily ; unwise. **2.** Proceeding from folly. —**fool'ish·ly**, *adv.* [8] —**fool'ish·ness**, *n.* [8].

fools'cap' (fōolz'kăp'), *n.* In sense 1 often **fool's cap.** **1.** A cap or hood, usually with bells, worn by fools (see FOOL, *n.*, 2). **2.** Paper for writing or printing in sheets about 13 × 16 or 17 inches.

foot (fōot), *n. ; pl.* FEET (fēt). **1.** Terminal part of the leg; that part of an animal on which it stands or moves. **2.** Soldiers who go on foot; infantry. **3.** Lowest part or base; also, the last of a row. **4.** That which is at the bottom. **5.** A measure of length; in English-speaking countries, ⅓ of a yard, or 12 inches, 30.48 cm. **6.** A group of syllables forming a metrical unit of verse. — *v. i.* To tread to measure or music ; dance ; also, to walk ; — usually with *it*. — *v. t.* **1.** To tread on, over, or through. **2.** To sum up, as the numbers in a column. **3.** To pay (a bill, etc.). *Colloq.*

foot'ball' (fōot'bôl'), *n.* **1.** An inflated ball to be kicked in sport. **2.** A game played with a football.

foot'board' (-bōrd'), *n.* **1.** A board to support the feet. **2.** A board across the foot of a bedstead.

foot'bridge' (-brĬj'), *n.* A bridge for pedestrians.

foot'ed, *a.* Having feet, or (such or so many) feet.

foot'fall' (-fôl'), *n.* A footstep ; sound of a footstep.

foot'hill' (-hĬl'), *n.* A hill at the foot of mountains.

foot'hold' (-hōld'), *n.* A hold for the feet ; footing.

foot'ing, *n.* **1.** Standing; stable position of the feet. **2.** Place for the foot to rest on. **3.** Relative position; condition; as, on a friendly *footing*. **4.** Act of adding up, or amount of, a column of figures.

foot'lights' (-lĬts'), *n. pl.* A row of lights at the front of the stage, in a theater, etc.

foot'man (-măn), *n. ; pl.* -MEN (-mĕn). A male servant who attends the door, carriage, table, etc.

foot'note' (-nōt'), *n.* A note at the foot of a page.

foot'pad' (-păd'), *n.* Highwayman or robber on foot.

foot'path' (-păth'), *n.* A path for pedestrians only.

foot pound. *Mech.* A unit of energy ; the work done in raising one pound avoirdupois against the force of gravity to the height of one foot.

foot'print' (-prĬnt'), *n.* An impression of the foot.

foot'sore' (-sōr'), *a.* [4] Having sore or tender feet, as from walking.

foot'step' (-stĕp'), *n.* **1.** Footfall. **2.** Footprint.

foot'stool' (-stōol'), *n.* A stool to support the feet.

fop (fŏp), *n.* A coxcomb; dandy.

fop'per·y (-ẽr-Ĭ), *n. ; pl.* -PERIES (-Ĭz). Behavior, dress, or other indication of a fop.

fop'pish (-Ĭsh), *a.* [4] Like a fop; dandyish. — **fop'pish·ly** (fŏp'Ĭsh-lĬ), *adv.* [8] — **-ness**, *n.* [8].

for (fôr), *prep.* In the most general sense, indicating that with reference to which anything is, is done, or takes place; as: **1.** With reference to (something) as an end or goal. **2.** Instead of; in requital of. **3.** In behalf of; in support of; in honor of. **4.** As being; as, to take *for* granted. **5.** Because of; on account of; also, because of the lack of. **6.** Notwithstanding; in spite of; — usually with *all.* **7.** In equality or proportion to. **8.** As regards concerning. **9.** Throughout. — *conj.* Because.

for'age (fôr'ăj), *n.* **1.** Food for horses and cattle **2.** A search for provisions. — *v. t.* [1] **1.** To collect forage from; ravage; as, they *foraged* the district. **2.** To supply with forage. **3.** To get by foraging. — *v. i.* To search for, or secure, forage; ravage; raid. — **for'ag·er** (fôr'ă-jẽr), *n.* [8].

for'as·much' (fôr'ăz-mŭch'), *conj.* Used with *as* to denote : In consideration that; seeing that; since.

for'ay (fôr'ă), *v. t. & i.* To ravage for spoils; pillage. — *n.* An incursion for war or spoils; a raid.

for·bade', for·bad' (fôr-băd'), *pret.* of FORBID.

for·bear' (fôr-bâr'; fôr'bâr), *n.* An ancestor.

for·bear' (fôr-bâr'), *v. t. ; pret.* -BORE' (-bōr'), *Archaic* -BARE' (-bâr'); *p. p.* -BORNE' (-bōrn'); *p. pr. & vb. n.* -BEAR'ING. To do without; give up; abstain or refrain from. — *v. i.* **1.** To refrain; abstain; hold back. **2.** To control one's self; be patient.

for·bear'ance (fôr-bâr'ăns), *n.* **1.** Act of forbearing; exercise of patience. **2.** A refraining from enforcement of what is due. **3.** Long-suffering.

for·bid' (-bĬd'), *v. t. ; pret.* -BADE' (-băd'), -BAD' *p. p.* -BID'DEN (-bĬd'n); *Archaic p. p.* -BID'; *p. pr. & vb. n.* -BID'DING. **1.** To command (a person) not to do (something); prohibit. **2.** To exclude from, or warn off, by command. **3.** To oppose or prevent; make impossible.

for·bid'ding, *p. a.* [4] Repellent; repulsive.

for·bore' (-bōr'), *pret., p. pr.,* of FORBEAR.

force (fōrs), *n.* **1.** Strength or energy; active power; vigor. **2.** A body of soldiers or sailors; — often in the *pl.* Hence, a body of men prepared for action; as, the police *force* (*colloq.* "the force"). **3.** Violence, compulsion, or constraint exerted on a person or thing. **4.** *Physics.* Any action between two bodies which tends to change their relative condition as to rest or motion. — *v. t.* [1] **1.** To constrain or compel; coerce. **2.** To compel to violent effort; urge. **3.** To get by strength or violence; pass through by force. **4.** To impel, wrest, extort, etc., by violence. **5.** To impose (something) upon. **6.** To cause (flowers or fruits) to develop by artificial means.

forced (fôrst), *p. a.* [4] **1.** Compelled by force; compulsory; as, *forced* labor. **2.** Done or produced laboriously; strained; as, a *forced* march.

force'ful (fôrs'fōol), *a.* [4] Full of force; forcible.

force'meat' (fôrs'mēt'), *n.* Meat chopped fine and highly seasoned, served alone or used as a stuffing.

for'ceps (fôr'sĕps), *n. ; pl.* -CEPS. A pair of pincers or tongs, esp. for delicate operations.

force pump. A pump with a solid plunger for drawing and forcing a liquid through the valves.

for'ci·ble (fôr'sĬ-b'l), *a.* [4] **1.** Effected by force. **2.** Characterized by force, efficiency, or energy; strong; powerful. — **for'ci·bly**, *adv.* [8].

ford (fōrd), *n.* A place where a river, or other water, may be crossed by wading. — *v. t.* To cross by a ford. — **ford'a·ble** (fôrd'dă-b'l), *a.* [8].

fore (fōr), *adv.* In the part that precedes or goes first; — as opp. to *aft.* — **fore and aft**, *Naut.,* from stem to stern; lengthwise of the vessel. — *a.* Toward the front; earlier; forward. — *n.* The front

fore'-and-aft', *a.* Lying, running, or acting lengthwise of a vessel ; as, *fore-and-aft* sails.

fore'arm' (fōr'ärm'), *n.* The part of the arm between the elbow and the wrist.

fore-arm' (fōr-ärm'), *v. t.* To arm beforehand.

fore-bode' (fōr-bōd'), *v. t. & i.* [1] **1.** To foretell; portend. **2.** To have a premonition or presentiment of; augur despondingly.

fore-bod'ing (-bōd'ĭng), *vb. n.* Presage, prediction, or presentiment, esp. of coming evil; portent.

fore-cast' (-kăst'), *v. t. & i. ;* -CAST', also -CAST'ED ; -CAST'ING. **1.** To plan beforehand; project. **2.** To foresee , calculate beforehand. **3.** To predict.

fore'cast' (fōr'kăst'), *n.* **1.** Foresight. **2.** A prophecy or estimate of a future event or condition.

fore'cas-tle (fōr'kȧs-'l ; *naut.* fōk's'l), *n.* *Naut.* **a** The upper deck of a vessel forward of the foremast. **b** In merchant vessels, the forward part or compartment where the sailors live.

fore-close' (fōr-klōz'), *v. t.* [1] To subject, as a mortgage, to foreclosure.

fore-clo'sure (-klō'zhŭr), *n.* A proceeding which destroys a right to redeem a mortgaged property.

fore'fa'ther (fōr'fä'thĕr), *n.* An ancestor.

fore'fin'ger (-fĭn'gĕr), *n.* Finger next the thumb.

fore'foot' (-fŏŏt'), *n. ; pl.* -FEET (-fēt'). One of the front feet of a quadruped.

fore'front' (-frŭnt'), *n.* Foremost part or place.

fore-go' (fōr-gō'), *v. t. & i.;* for prin. parts see GO. To go before ; precede. — **fore-go'er,** *n.* [8].

fore-gone' (-gŏn'), *p. a.* That has gone before; previous. — foregone conclusion. **a** A predetermined conclusion. **b** A result that was inevitable.

fore'ground' (fōr'ground'), *n.* That part of a scene nearest to, and in front of, the spectator.

fore'hand'ed, *a.* [4] Mindful of the future; thrifty; well-to-do. — **-ness,** *n.* [8].

fore'head (fōr'ĕd), *n.* The part of the face above the eyes ; the brow.

for'eign (fōr'ĭn), *a.* [4] **1.** Outside of a place or country, esp. of one's own country. **2.** Not native or domestic. **3.** Not naturally related; not appropriate. — **-ness,** *n.* [8].

for'eign-er (-ẽr), *n.* One not native, or not naturalized in the country under consideration ; alien.

fore-know' (fōr-nō'), *v. t. ;* for prin. parts see KNOW. To know beforehand. — **knowl'edge,** *n.*

fore'land (fōr'lănd), *n.* A promontory; headland.

fore'lock' (-lŏk'), *n.* The lock of hair growing from the fore part of the head.

fore'man (fōr'măn), *n. ; pl.* -MEN (-mĕn). The chief man; as : **a** The chairman of a jury. **b** The superintendent of a set of workmen. — **-ship,** *n.*

fore'mast (fōr'mȧst), *n.* The mast nearest the bow.

fore'most (-mōst), *a.* First in time or place; most advanced , chief in rank or dignity.

fore'noon' (fōr'nōōn'), *n.* The early part of the day, from morning to noon.

fo-ren'sic (fȯ-rĕn'sĭk), *a.* [4] Belonging to law courts or to public debate ; rhetorical.

fore'or-dain' (fōr'ȯr-dān'), *v. t.* To ordain beforehand , predestinate.

fore'or-di-na'tion (-dĭ-nā'shŭn), *n.* Predetermination ; predestination.

fore-run' (fōr-rŭn'), *v. t. ;* for prin. parts see RUN. To come before ; precede ; announce.

fore-run'ner (-ẽr), *n.* **1.** A messenger to give notice of the approach of others. **2.** A predecessor.

fore'sail' (fōr'sāl' ; *naut.* fōr's'l or fō's'l), *n.* The lowest sail on the foremast of a vessel.

fore-see' (fōr-sē'), *v. t. ;* for prin. parts see SEE. To see or have knowledge of beforehand.

fore-shad'ow (-shăd'ō), *v. t.* To shadow or typify beforehand ; to prefigure.

fore-short'en (fōr-shôr't'n), *v. t. Fine Arts.* To represent (an object) in the shortened form which it appears to have when viewed obliquely.

fore'sight' (fōr'sīt'), *n.* **1.** Act or power of foreseeing. **2.** Care or provision for the future.

for'est (fŏr'ĕst), *n.* A large tract of woodland.

fore-stall' (fōr-stôl'), *v. t.* To get ahead of ; anticipate. — **fore-stall'er,** *n.* [8].

for'est-a'tion (fŏr'ĕs-tā'shŭn), *n.* **1.** The practical application of the study of forestry. **2.** Establishment of new forest.

for'est-er (fŏr'ĕs-tẽr), *n.* **1.** One trained in forestry. **2.** A denizen of a forest.

for'est-ry (fŏr'ĕst-rĭ), *n.* The science and art of forming, caring for, or cultivating forests.

fore'taste' (fōr'tāst'), *n.* A taste beforehand.

fore-taste' (fōr-tāst'), *v. t.* [1] To taste before hand; anticipate.

fore-tell' (fōr-tĕl'), *v. t. & i.* To tell beforehand prophesy ; foreshow. — **fore-tell'er,** *n.* [8].

fore'thought' (fōr'thôt'), *n.* A thinking or planning beforehand ; premeditation ; provident care.

fore'to'ken (-tō'k'n), *n.* A prognostic ; omen.

fore-to'ken (fōr-tō'k'n), *v. t.* To be a foretoken of.

for-ev'er (fōr-ĕv'ẽr), *adv.* **1.** Through eternity; eternally. **2.** At all times; incessantly.

for-ev'er-more (-mōr), *adv.* Forever; — emphatic.

fore-warn' (fōr-wôrn'), *v. t.* To warn beforehand.

fore'word' (fōr'wŭrd'), *n.* A preface.

for'feit (fōr'fĭt), *n.* **1.** A thing forfeited ; a fine; penalty. **2.** Forfeiture. — *a.* Forfeited. — *v. t.* To lose, or lose the right to, by error, fault, or offense. — **for'feit-a-ble,** *a.* [8] — **for'feit-er,** *n.* [8].

for'fei-ture (fōr'fĭ-tụr), *n.* **1.** Act of forfeiting. **2.** That which is forfeited ; a penalty; fine.

for-fend' (fōr-fĕnd'), *v. t.* To prohibit; forbid ; also, to avert ; prevent. *Archaic.*

for-gath'er (fōr-găth'ẽr), *v. i.* **1.** To convene ; assemble. **2.** To meet. **3.** To fraternize.

for-gave' (-gāv'), *pret.* of FORGIVE.

forge (fōrj; fôrj), *n.* A furnace, or a place with its furnace, where metal is wrought by heating and hammering ; a smithy. — *v. t.* [1] **1.** To form by heating and hammering, as a metal. **2.** To form; invent ; to devise, as evil. **3.** To make or imitate falsely ; counterfeit. — *v. i.* **1.** To forge metals. **2.** To commit forgery. **3.** To move forward ; — esp. in *to forge ahead.* — **forg'er** (fōr'jẽr ; fôr'-), *n.*

for'ger-y (fōr'jẽr-ĭ ; fôr'-), *n. ; pl.* -GERIES (-ĭz). **1.** Act of forging, fabricating, or producing falsely. **2.** That which is forged.

for-get' (fōr-gĕt'), *v. t. ; pret.* -GOT' (-gŏt'), *p. p.* -GOT'TEN (-gŏt'n), -GOT'; *p. pr. & vb. n.* -GET'TING. **1.** To lose remembrance of ; be unable to recall. **2.** To omit or disregard unintentionally; hence, to neglect; slight. — *v. i.* To cease remembering.

for-get'ful (-fōŏl), *a.* [4] **1.** Apt to forget. **2.** Heedless ; neglectful. — **-ly,** *adv.* — **-ness,** *n.* [8].

āle, senāte, cãre, ăm, *ȧ*ccount, ärm, ȧsk, sofȧ; ēve, ēvent, ĕnd, recĕnt, makẽr; īce, ĭll; ōld, ȯbey, ôrb, ŏdd, sŏft, cŏnnect; ūse, ŭnite, ûrn, ŭp, circ*ŭ*s; fōōd, fŏŏt; out, oil;

for-get′—me-not′ (fŏr-gĕt′mē-nŏt′), *n.* A small herb having bright blue or white flowers.

forg′ing (fōr′jĭng; fôr′j′ĭng), *n.* **1.** Act of one that forges. **2.** A piece of forged work, as in iron.

for-give′ (fŏr-gĭv′), *v. t.; for prin. parts see* GIVE. **1.** To give up resentment or claim to requital for (an offense or wrong); pardon. **2.** To cease to feel resentment against(a person)for a wrong; pardon. — *v. i.* To grant forgiveness.

for-give′ness, *n.* Act of forgiving.

for-giv′ing, *p. a.* [4] That forgives or shows forgiveness; placable. —**-ly**, *adv.* — **-ness**, *n.*

for-go′ (fŏr-gō′), *v. t.; for prin. parts see* GO. To abstain from; renounce. — **for-go′er**, *n.* [8].

for-got′, for-got′ten. See FORGET.

fork (fôrk), *n.* **1.** An implement having two or more prongs, or tines, for piercing, holding, taking up, or pitching anything. **2.** Anything like, or suggestive of, a fork. **3.** One of the parts into which anything divides; the place where anything branches.—*v. i.* To divide into branches. — *v. t.* To raise, pitch, dig, or turn over, with a fork.

for-lorn′ (fŏr-lôrn′), *a.* [3] Deserted; forsaken; miserable; wretched; almost hopeless; desperate. —**for-lorn′ly**, *adv.* [8] —**-ness**, *n.* [8].

forlorn hope. A body of men selected for very perilous service; a desperate case or enterprise.

form (fôrm), *n.* **1.** The shape and structure of anything; configuration; figure. **2.** A body, esp. of a human being. **3.** A kind; species; variety. **4.** A manner or method. **5.** *a* Conduct regulated by custom, etiquette, etc. ; a formality, ceremony, or conventionality. **b** Manner of performing something. **6.** Orderly arrangement; also, a particular species of such arrangement; as, the sonnet is a poetical *form.* **7.** A long seat; bench. **8.** A rank of students in a school; class. **9.** That by which shape is given; mold; pattern.—*v. t.* **1.** To give form to ; make ; fashion. **2.** To train. **3.** To develop ; contract, as a habit. **4.** To act as constituent of.—*v. i.* **1.** To become formed or shaped. **2.** To take a definite shape.

for′mal (fôr′măl), *a.* [4] **1.** Conventional; often, having the form without the substance. **2.** Done in due form or order; regular. **3.** Devoted to forms or rules ; orderly ; exact. —**for′mal-ly**, *adv.* [8].

form-al′de-hyde (fôr-măl′dē-hīd), *n.* A pungent gaseous compound used for preserving and disinfecting, commonly prepared in aqueous solution.

for′mal-ism(fôr′măl-ĭz′m), *n.* Practice or doctrine of strict adherence to prescribed forms.

for′mal-ist, *n.* One characterized by formalism.

for-mal′i-ty(fŏr-măl′ĭ-tĭ),*n.;pl.*-TIES(-tĭz). **1.** Condition or quality of being formal. **2.** Form without substance ; external form. **3.** A ceremony.

for′mal-ize (fôr′măl-īz),*v. t.* [1] **1.** To give definite form to ; shape. **2.** To render formal.

for-ma′tion (fôr-mā′shŭn), *n.* **1.** Act of forming, or shaping. **2.** That which is formed. **3.** Conformation; structure; as, cloud *formations.*

form′a-tive (fôr′mȧ-tĭv), *a.* [4] **1.** Giving form; plastic. **2.** *Gram.* Serving to form words, as a suffix. — *n. Gram.* A formative element.

form′er (fôr′mẽr), *n.* One that forms.

for′mer (fôr′mẽr), *a.* Preceding in time or order ; previous ; prior ; foregoing.

for′mer-ly (-lĭ), *adv.* In time past; heretofore.

for′mi-da-ble (-mĭ-dȧ-b'l), *a.* [4] Exciting fear or dread; alarming. — **-ble-ness**,*n.* — **-bly**, *adv.*

form′less, *a.* Without determinate form; wanting regularity of shape. — **-ly**,*adv.* [8]—**-ness**,*n.* [8].

for′mu-la(fôr′mū-lȧ),*n.; pl.* E. -LAS (-lȧz), L. -LÆ (-lē). **1.** A set form ; established rule. **2.** A recipe, esp. for a medicinal compound. **3.** *Math.* A rule or principle expressed in algebraic symbols.

for′mu-la-ry (fôr′mū-lȧ-rĭ),*n.; pl.* -RIES (-rĭz). A collection of prescribed forms.

for′mu-late (-lāt),*v. t.* [1] To express in or as in a formula; state definitely and clearly.

for′mu-la′tion (-lā′shŭn),*n.* Act of formulating.

for-sake′ (fŏr-sāk′),*v.t.; pret.* -SOOK′ (-sŏŏk′); *p. p.* -SAK′EN (-sāk′'n); *p. pr. & vb. n.* -SAK′ING. To desert; abandon.

for-sooth′ (-sŏŏth′), *adv.* In truth; indeed ; — now used in irony or contempt.

for-swear′ (-swâr′),*v.t.* **1.** To reject or renounce on oath ; to renounce earnestly. **2.** To deny on oath.

for-syth′i-a (fŏr-sĭth′ĭ-ȧ; -sĭ′thĭ-ȧ), *n.* A plant of a genus (*Forsythia*) of the olive family, cultivated for its yellow, bell-shaped flowers.

fort (fōrt), *n.* A strong or fortified place, esp. one occupied only by troops ; a fortification.

forte, *n.* Strong point ; that in which one excels.

|| **for′te** (fōr′tā), *a. & adv.* [It.] *Music.* Loud.

forth (fōrth), *adv.* **1.** Forward ; onward in time, place, or order. **2.** Out, as from concealment.

forth′com′ing (fōrth′kŭm′ĭng ; fōrth′kŭm′-), *p. a.* About to appear; making appearance; approaching.

forth′with′ (fōrth′wĭth′ ; -wĭth′), *adv.* Immediately ; directly ; with reasonable dispatch.

for′ti-eth (fôr′tĭ-ĕth), *a.* Next in order after the thirty-ninth ; constituting one of forty equal parts into which a (whole) thing may be divided. — *n.* **1.** A fortieth part. **2.** A fortieth unit or object.

for′ti-fi-ca′tion (-fĭ-kā′shŭn), *n.* Act of fortifying or that which fortifies; a work erected for defense.

for′ti-fy (fôr′tĭ-fī), *v. t.* [2] **1.** To strengthen; invigorate. **2.** To strengthen by forts or batteries.

|| **for-tis′si-mo** (fôr-tĭs′ĭ-mō),*a. & adv.* [It.] *Music.* Very loud.

for′ti-tude (fôr′tĭ-tūd),*n.* Firmness in confronting danger or enduring trouble.

fort′night (fôrt′nīt ; -nĭt), *n.* The space of fourteen days; two weeks.

fort′night-ly (-nīt-lĭ), *a.* Occurring or appearing once in a fortnight. — *adv.* Once in a fortnight.

for′tress (fôr′trĕs), *n.* A fortified place ; a fort.

for-tu′i-tous (fŏr-tū′ĭ-tŭs), *a.* [4] Happening by chance. — **-ly**, *adv.* [8] —**-ness**, *n.* [8].

for-tu′i-ty (-tĭ), *n.; pl.* -TIES (-tĭz). Accident; chance ; casualty.

for′tu-nate (fôr′tū̇-nȧt), *a.* [4] **1.** Coming by or bringing good fortune. **2.** Favored by fortune ; lucky. — **for′tu-nate-ly**, *adv.* [8].

for′tune (-tūn), *n.* **1.** The arrival of something, or that which arrives or happens, in a sudden or unexpected manner; luck; hap. **2.** That which is to befall one ; destiny. **3.** Condition in life as indicated by wealth ; wealth.

for′ty (fôr′tĭ), *a.* Four times ten. — *n.; pl.* -TIES (-tĭz). **1.** The sum of four tens. **2.** A symbol expressing forty units, as 40 or xl.

---

chair; go; sing, iṅk; then, thin; nature, verdure; yet; zh = z in azure. Numbers refer to §§ in the Special Notes which, with Abbreviations, Signs, etc., precede the Vocabulary.

fo'rum (fō'rŭm), *n.; pl.* E. **-rums** (-rŭmz), L. **-ra** (-rä). **1.** *Roman Antiq.* The market place of a city. It was the center of public business, and a place of popular assembly. **2.** Tribunal; court.

for'ward (fôr'wẽrd), *a.* [3] **1.** Near, at, or belonging to, the fore part. **2.** Moving or leading to the front; onward. **3.** Advanced; precocious. **4.** Ready; prompt; also, over-ready. **5.** Ardent; eager; also, bold; pert. — *adv.* Toward what is before or in front; on or onward. — *v. t.* **1.** To help onward; advance; promote; also, hasten. **2.** To send forward; transmit. — *n.* [8].

for'ward-ness, *n.* Quality of being forward.

for'wards (fôr'wẽrdz), *adv.* Forward.

fos'sil (fŏs'Il), *a.* **1.** Of the nature of a fossil. **2.** Antiquated; dead to progress. — *n.* **1.** Any remains or trace of an animal or plant preserved esp. in a stratified deposit and from a past geological age. **2.** A person with antiquated opinions.

fos'sil-if'er-ous (-If'ẽr-ŭs), *a.* Containing fossils.

fos'sil-ize (fŏs'Il-īz), *v. t.* [1] **1.** To convert into a fossil; petrify. **2.** To make antiquated.

fos'ter (fŏs'tẽr), *a.* Affording, receiving, or sharing nourishment or nurture, though not related by blood; as, *foster* parent, child, brother, nurse, etc. — *v. t.* **1.** To nourish; support; rear. **2.** To cherish; sustain and promote. — **fos'ter-er**, *n.* [8].

fought (fôt), *pret. & p. p.* of FIGHT.

foul (foul), *a.* [3] **1.** Very offensive to the senses; loathsome; charged with filth. **2.** Covered with or containing dirt, etc.; soiled; smeared. **3.** Hateful; odious. **4.** Scurrilous; obscene. **5.** Unfavorable; stormy, as weather. **6.** Entangled, as a rope; — opp. to *clear.* **7.** Not conforming to the rules of a game, test, etc.; also, unfair; dishonorable. — **foul play**, unfair play, conduct, or dealing; specif., implying murder, as in *to meet with foul play.* — *n.* **1.** That which is foul. **2.** A foul hit, play, or the like. See FOUL, *a.*, 7. — *v. t.* **1.** To make foul; soil. **2.** To entangle, as a rope; collide with. — *v. i.* **1.** To become foul. **2.** To become entangled, as ropes; to collide, as boats **3.** To make a foul (see FOUL, *n.*, 2).

fou-lard' (foo-lärd'; F. foo'lár'), *n.* A thin, soft material of silk, or silk and cotton.

foul'ly (foul'lI), *adv.* In a foul manner.

foul'ness, *n.* Quality or state of being foul.

found (found), *pret. & p. p.* of FIND.

found, *v. t.* To melt and pour into a mold, or to form thus; to cast; as, to *found* metal, a bell.

found, *v. t.* **1.** To set or place, as on something solid, for support; ground; establish; fix. **2.** To take first steps in erecting; to furnish material for beginning. — *v. i.* To be founded or based.

foun-da'tion (foun-dā'shŭn), *n.* **1.** Act of founding. **2.** That on which anything is founded; groundwork. **3.** An endowment. **4.** An endowed institution or charity.

found'er, *n.* One who founds, or establishes.

found'er, *n.* One who founds, or casts, metals.

foun'der (foun'dẽr), *v. i.* **1.** To fall; stumble; go lame, as a horse. **2.** To fill with water and sink, as a ship. — *v. t.* To cause (a horse) to founder.

found'ling (found'lĬng), *n.* An infant found after its (unknown) parents have deserted it.

found'ry (foun'drĬ), *n.; pl.* **-RIES** (-drĬz). **1.** Proc-

ess or art of casting metals. **2.** A building or establishment where founding is done.

fount (fount), *n.* Fountain; source.

foun'tain (foun'tĬn), *n.* **1.** A spring of water. **2.** An artificial jet of water or the structure from which it flows. **3.** A reservoir for a liquid, as ink. **4.** Spring; source; as, a *fountain* of wisdom.

foun'tain-head' (-hĕd'), *n.* **1.** The source of a stream. **2.** Primary or principal source.

four (fōr), *a.* One more than three; twice two. — *n.* **1.** Sum of four units; four units or objects. **2.** Symbol representing four units, as 4 or iv.

four'fold' (-fōld'), *a.* Consisting of four things or parts; quadruple. — *adv.* Quadruple; four times.

four'-in-hand', *a.* **1.** Consisting of, or drawn by, four horses driven by one person. **2.** Designating a kind of necktie tied with a slipknot. — *n.* **1.** A four-in-hand team. **2.** A four-in-hand necktie.

four'square' (-skwâr'), *a. & adv.* Square.

four'teen' (fōr'tēn'; fōr'tēn'). *a.* Four plus ten. — *n.* **1.** The number greater by a unit than thirteen. **2.** A symbol for fourteen, as 14 or xiv.

four'teenth' (fōr'tēnth'; fōr'tēnth'), *a.* Next in order after the thirteenth; constituting one of fourteen equal parts into which a (whole) thing may be divided. — *n.* **1.** A fourteenth part. **2.** A fourteenth unit or object.

fourth (fōrth), *a.* Next in order after the third; constituting one of four equal parts into which a (whole) thing may be divided. — *n.* **1.** A fourth part. **2.** A fourth unit or object. — **-ly**, *adv.* [8].

fowl (foul), *n.; pl.* FOWLS, or, collectively, FOWL. **1.** The domestic cock or hen; sometimes, any bird; as, *fowls* of the air; wild *fowl.* **2.** The flesh of a fowl, esp. of the domestic fowl of mature age. — *v. i.* To take or kill wild fowl. — **-er** (foul'ẽr), *n.* [8].

fox (fŏks), *n.* Any of certain animals of the dog family, noted for craftiness.

fox'glove (fŏks'glŭv), *n.* Any species of digitalis. The common foxglove has racemes of dotted white or purple tubular flowers.

fox'y (fŏk'sĬ), *a.* [3] Like or pertaining to the fox; esp., wily; cunning. — **fox'i-ness**, *n.* [8].

|| foy'er' (fwä'yā') *n.* [F.] A lobby, as in a theater.

fra'cas (frā'kás; F. frá'kä'), *n.* Uproar; brawl.

frac'tion (frăk'shŭn), *n.* **1.** A fragment; scrap. **2.** One or more aliquot parts of a unit, as the *fraction* ¾ (read "three fourths," or "3 divided by 4").

frac'tion-al (-ăl), *a.* **1.** Of or pert. to fractions or a fraction. **2.** Relatively small; inconsiderable.

frac'tious (-shŭs), *a.* [4] Cross; ugly; unruly; peevish; irritable. — **frac'tious-ness**, *n.* [8].

frac'ture (-tŭr), *n.* **1.** Act of breaking; breach. **2.** The breaking of a bone. **3.** That which is produced by breaking; crack. — *v. t. & i.* [1] To break.

frag'ile (frăj'Il), *a.* [4] Easily broken; frail.

fra-gil'i-ty (frá-jĬl'Ĭ-tĬ), *n.* Quality of being fragile.

frag'ment (frăg'mĕnt), *n.* A part broken off.

frag'men-ta-ry (frăg'mĕn-tá-rĬ), *a.* [4] Composed of fragments; not complete.

fra'grance (frā'gráns), *n.* Quality of being fragrant; a pleasing odor.

fra'grant (-gránt), *a.* [4] Sweet-smelling; of an agreeable perfume. — **fra'grant-ly**, *adv.* [8].

frail (frāl), *a.* [3] **1.** Fragile; weak. **2.** Liable to be led into sin. — **-ly**, *adv.* [8] — **-ness**, *n.* [8].

āle, senāte, câre, ăm, ŏccount, ärm, ȧsk, sofá; ēve, ĕvent, ĕnd, recĕnt, makẽr; īce, Ĭll; ōld, ōbey, ôrb, ŏdd, sôft, cŏnnect; ūse, ûnite, ûrn, ŭp, circŭs; fōōd, fŏŏt; out, oil;

frail'ty (-tǐ),*n.*;*pl.* **-ties** (-tǐz). **1.** Quality of being frail. **2.** A fault or sin due to weakness.

frame (frām), *v. t.* [1] **1.** To shape or fashion. **2.** To construct; make. **3.** To plan, devise, or compose. **4.** To provide with a frame, as a picture. — *n.* **1.** Something composed of parts fitted together; a structure. **2.** The bodily structure. **3.** A kind of open case or structure for inclosing or supporting something, as a window, picture, etc. **4.** Form; shape. **5.** Particular state or disposition, as of the mind. — **fram'er** (frām'ẽr), *n.* [8].

frame'work/ (frām'wûrk/),*n.* The work of framing, or the completed work; the frame or skeleton.

franc (frăŋk), *n.* A silver coin and the monetary unit of France, now worth 19.3 cents.

fran'chise (frăn'chĭz; -chīz), *n.* **1.** Freedom; exemption; privilege. **2.** A constitutional or statutory right or privilege, as the right to vote.

fran'gi-ble (frăn'jĭ-b'l), *a.* Easily broken; fragile.

frank (frăŋk), *a.* [3] Free in uttering one's real sentiments; candid; open.

frank, *v. t.* To send by public conveyance free of expense, as a letter, telegram, etc. — *n.* The signature, mark, or sign of a franked letter, etc.

frank'in-cense (frăŋk'ĭn-sĕns),*n.* A fragrant gum resin, burned as incense.

frank'ly (-lǐ), *adv.* In a frank manner; freely.

frank'ness, *n.* Quality or state of being frank.

fran'tic (frăn'tĭk), *a.* [4] Frenzied; distracted.

fran'ti-cal-ly (-tǐ-kăl-ǐ), *adv.* In a frantic manner.

fra-ter'nal (frà-tûr'năl),*a.* [4] Of, pertaining to, or involving brethren; brotherly; of or pert. to a fraternity. — **-ly**. [8] — **-ism** (-ĭz'm),*n.*

fra-ter'ni-ty (-nǐ-tǐ), *n.*;*pl.* **-ties** (-tǐz). **1.** Brotherhood. **2.** A society of men, often secret, for religious, social, or business purposes, or for mutual aid; a brotherhood.

frat'er-nize (frăt'ẽr-nīz),*v.i.* & *t.* [1] To associate, or bring into fellowship, as brothers.

frat'ri-cid'al (frăt'rǐ-sīd'ăl; frā'trǐ-), *a.* [4] Of, pertaining to, or of the nature of fratricide.

frat'ri-cide (-sīd), *n.* **1.** Act of one who kills his own brother. **2.** One who kills his own brother.

fraud (frôd), *n.* **1.** Deceitfulness; trickery. **2.** Artifice by which the right of another is injured.

fraud'u-lence (frôd'ū-lĕns),*n.* Quality or state of being fraudulent; deliberate deceit; trickishness.

fraud'u-len-cy (-lĕn-sǐ), *n.* Fraudulence.

fraud'u-lent (-lĕnt), *a.* [4] **1.** Using fraud; deceitful. **2.** Characterized by, or proceeding from, fraud. — **fraud'u-lent-ly**, *adv.* [8].

fraught (frôt), *p. a.* Freighted; laden.

fray (frā), *n.* A commotion; affray; fight.

fray, *v. t.* & *i.* To rub; wear, wear off, or wear into shreds, by rubbing. — *n.* A frayed place.

freak (frēk), *n.* **1.** A whim; fancy; vagary; caprice. **2.** An abnormal product; a monstrosity.

freak'ish, *a.* [4] Full of freaks; capricious; queer. — **freak'ish ly**, *adv.* [8] — **ness**, *n.* [8].

freck'le (frĕk'l), *n.* A small yellow or brown spot in the skin. — *v. t.* & *i.* [1] To mark, or become marked, with freckles. — **freck'ly**, *a.*

free (frē), *a.*; **fre'er** (-ẽr); **fre'est**. **1.** Not in bondage to another; enjoying liberty; independent. **2.** Exempt or released, as from a tax or duty. **3.** Not combined with anything else; unattached.

4. Not strict in respect to form or expression. **5.** Spontaneous. — *adv.* Freely. — *v. t.*; **freed** (frēd); **free'ing**. To make free; set at liberty; exempt; relieve; disengage; clear.

free'board/ (frē'bōrd/), *n.* A vessel's side, or the distance, between water line and gunwale.

free'boot'er (frē'boot'ẽr), *n.* One who goes about plundering as a pirate; buccaneer.

freed'man (frēd'măn), *n.*; *pl.* **-men.** A man who has been freed from slavery. — **-wom'an**, *n. fem.*

free'dom (frē'dŭm), *n.* Quality or state of being free; as : **a** Liberty; independence. **b** Frankness; unreservedness. **c** Facility. **d** Boldness of conception or performance. **e** Exemption; immunity. **f** Right to certain privileges; unrestricted use.

free'-hand/, *a.* Done by the hand without support, instruments, measurements, etc.; — said of drawing.

free'hold/ (frē'hōld/), *n. Law.* A right to hold land for life or so it descends to one's heirs. — **-hold'er**, *n.* [8].

free'ly (frē'lǐ), *adv.* In a free manner.

free'man (-măn),*n.*;*pl.* **-men** (-mĕn). One who enjoys liberty, esp. civil or political liberty.

free'stone/ (frē'stōn/), *n.* Stone, esp. sandstone or limestone, that may be cut freely without splitting.

free'think'er (-thĭŋk'ẽr), *n.* One who forms opinions independently of the authority of the church.

free trade. Trade or commerce free from any governmental influences, as duties or bounties, intended to change its natural course. — **free trader**, *or* **free'trad'er** (frē'trād'ẽr), *n.* [8].

freeze (frēz), *v. i.*; *pret.* FROZE (frōz); *p. p.* FRO'ZEN (frō'z'n); *p. pr.* & *vb. n.* FREEZ'ING. **1.** To become congealed or solidified by cold; harden into ice. **2.** To become greatly chilled. **3.** To adhere, by freezing. — *v. t.* **1.** To congeal; harden into ice. **2.** To chill; paralyze as with fear. **3.** To harden, damage, kill, or the like, by frost. — *n.* Act of freezing; state of being frozen. — **freez'er**, *n.*

freight (frāt), *n.* **1.** The compensation paid for the transport of goods. **2.** That with which anything is laden for or as for transportation; lading; cargo. **3.** Freight transportation, or freight line. — *v. t.* **1.** To load with goods for transportation; to load or burden. **2.** To transport by freight.

freight'age (-åj), *n.* **1.** Charge for transportation. **2.** Freight; cargo. **3.** Transportation of freight.

freight'er (-ẽr),*n.* **1.** One who loads a ship. **2.** One who handles freight. **3.** A vessel to carry freight.

French (frĕnch), *a.* Of or pert. to France or its inhabitants; like the French people. — *n.* **1.** *pl.* The people of France. **2.** The language of the French people. — **French'man**, *n.* — **woman**, *n. fem.*

fren'zy (frĕn'zǐ), *n.*; *pl.* **-zies** (-zǐz). Any violent mental agitation approaching to distraction. — *v. t.* [2] To affect with frenzy. — **zied** (-zǐd),*p. a.*

fre'quence (frē'kwĕns), *n.* Frequency.

fre'quen-cy (-kwĕn-sǐ) *n.*; *pl.* **-cies** (-sǐz). **1.** Fact or condition of returning or occurring frequently. **2.** Number of complete cycles of current produced by an alternating current generator per second.

fre'quent (-kwĕnt),*a.* [4] **1.** Often met with; happening at short intervals. **2.** Habitual; persistent.

fre-quent/ (frē-kwĕnt/),*v.t.* To visit often; resort to often or habitually. — **fre-quent'er**, *n.* [8].

fre′quent-ly(frē′kwĕnt-lĭ),*adv.* At short intervals.

fres′co (frĕs′kō), *n. ; pl.* -COES or -COS (-kōz). Art or method of painting on plaster, esp. when not yet dried. — *v. t.* To paint in fresco. — **-er,** *n.*

fresh (frĕsh), *a.* [3] **1.** Newly produced, gathered, or made. **2.** Not salt. **3.** Pure; refreshing; brisk. **4.** Having the qualities unimpaired, as by age, use, fatigue, etc. **5.** Full of vigor, etc. ; newly made ready for use. **6.** Novel; recent; lately made public; hence, additional; further.

fresh′en (frĕsh′'n), *v. t.* To make fresh; esp., to refresh; revive. — *v. i.* To grow or become fresh, brisk, or strong.

fresh′et (-ĕt), *n.* A flood of a stream.

fresh′ly, *adv.* In a fresh manner.

fresh′man (frĕsh′mǎn), *n. ; pl.* -MEN (-mĕn). A student during his first year, as in a college.

fresh′ness, *n.* State or quality of being fresh.

fret (frĕt), *v. t. ;* FRET′TED; FRET′TING. **1.** To eat or wear away; rub. **2.** To agitate; disturb; irritate ; vex. — *v. i.* To be worn away; to chafe ; fray. **2.** To be agitated or irritated; to utter peevish expressions. — *n.* Agitation of mind marked by complaint and impatience; irritation.

fret, *n.* **1.** Any of the ridges, as of wire, fixed across the finger board of a guitar or similar instrument. **2.** Fretwork. **3.** An ornamental pattern characterized by lines or bars. — *v. t.* **1.** To adorn with interlacing lines or figures. **2.** To enrich or furnish with frets.

fret′ful(frĕt′fŏŏl), *a.* [4] Disposed to fret, or such as to cause fretting ; irritable ; peevish. — **fret′-ful-ly,** *adv.* [8] — **ness,** *n.* [8].

fret′work′ (-wŭrk′), *n.* Ornamental openwork or work in relief, esp. when elaborate.

fri/a-bil′i-ty (frī′ȧ-bĭl′ĭ-tĭ), *n.* Friable quality.

fri′a-ble (frī′ȧ-b'l), *a.* [4] Easily crumbled.

fri′ar (-ẽr), *n. R. C. Ch.* A brother of a religious order, esp. of a mendicant order.

fri′ar-y (frī′ẽr-ĭ), *n. ; pl.* -ARIES (-ĭz). A convent or brotherhood of friars.

fric/as-see′ (frĭk′ȧ-sē′), *n.* A dish composed of meat cut into pieces, and stewed in a gravy. — *v. t. ;* FRIC′A-SEED′ ; -SEE′ING. To cook as a fricassee.

fric′a-tive (frĭk′ȧ-tĭv), *a.* Characterized by friction of the breath in utterance ; — of certain consonants, as *f, v, s, z,* etc. — *n.* A fricative consonant.

fric′tion (-shŭn), *n.* **1.** Act of rubbing one body on another. **2.** A resistance to motion between two surfaces in contact. **3.** A clashing between persons or parties in opinions or work.

fric′tion-al (frĭk′shŭn-ăl), *a.* Pert. to friction.

Fri′day (frī′dā), *n.* The sixth day of the week.

fried (frīd), *pret. & p. p.* of FRY.

friend (frĕnd), *n.* **1.** One attached to another by esteem and affection. **2.** One of the same nation, party, kin, etc. **3.** A favorer; promoter. **4.** [*cap.*] One of a religious sect popularly called *Quakers.* — **-less,** *a.* [8] — **less-ness,** *n.* [8].

friend′ly (frĕnd′lĭ), *adv.* Amicably.

friend′ly, *a.* [3] Favorable; not hostile; propitious. — **friend′li-ness,** *n.* [8].

friend′ship, *n.* State of being friends; amity.

frieze (frēz), *n.* A kind of coarse woolen cloth, with a shaggy nap on one side.

frieze, *n.* **1.** That part of an entablature be-

tween the architrave and the cornice. See COL-UMN, *Illust.* **2.** An ornamental band, as on a wall.

frig′ate (frĭg′ȧt), *n.* A ship-rigged war vessel, ranking next below a ship of the line in the old sailing navies.

Frigate (1800-40).

fright (frīt), *n.* **1.** Sudden violent fear; sudden alarm. **2.** A thing that frightens; something ugly or shocking. — *v. t.* To frighten.

fright′en (frīt′'n), *v. t.* To throw into a state of alarm or fright; affright; terrify. — **-en-er,** *n.*

fright′ened (-'nd), *p. a.* [4] Alarmed.

fright′ful (-fŏŏl), *a.* [4] Terrifying; shocking ; dreadful; awful. — **-ly,** *adv.* [8] — **ness,** *n.* [8].

frig′id (frĭj′ĭd), *a.* [4] **1.** Very cold. **2.** Wanting warmth, vivacity, etc.; stiff and formal. — **-ly,** *adv.*

fri-gid′i-ty (frĭ-jĭd′ĭ-tĭ), *n.* Frigid quality or state.

frill (frĭl), *n.* **1.** A border or edging usually fluted or crimped. **2.** A showy or unpractical accomplishment. — *v. t.* To decorate with a frill.

fringe (frĭnj), *n.* **1.** A trimming consisting of projecting ends of a fabric twisted or plaited together, or of loose threads or strips, etc. **2.** Something suggestive of a fringe ; a border. — *v. t.* [1] To furnish with or serve as a fringe.

frip′per-y (frĭp′ẽr-ĭ), *n. ; pl.* -PERIES (-ĭz). Secondhand finery ; cheap tawdry ornament; ostentation.

frisk (frĭsk), *n.* A frolic ; fit of wanton gayety. — *v. i.* To skip, dance, or gambol, as in frolic.

frisk′y (frĭs′kĭ), *a.* [3] Inclined to frisk; frolicsome. — **frisk′i-ly,** *adv.* [8] — **frisk′i-ness,** *n.* [8].

frith (frĭth), *n.* An estuary; firth.

frit′ter (frĭt′ẽr), *n.* A little cake of batter (often inclosing fruit or meat), fried in fat.

frit′ter (frĭt′ẽr), *v. t.* To waste piecemeal; spend (as time, energy, etc.) on trifles; — with *away.*

fri-vol′i-ty (frĭ-vŏl′ĭ-tĭ), *n.; pl.* -TIES (-tĭz). **1.** Condition or quality of being frivolous. **2.** An act or thing that is frivolous.

friv′o-lous (frĭv′ȯ-lŭs), *a.* [4] **1.** Of little weight or importance. **2.** Given to trifling or levity; interested esp. in trifles. — **-ly,** *adv.* — **ness,** *n.*

friz, frizz (frĭz), *v. t. & i. ;* FRIZZED (frĭzd) ; FRIZZING. To curl closely, as hair; to crisp. — *n.* State of being frizzed; something frizzed, as a wig.

friz′zle (frĭz′'l), *v. t. & i.* [1] To cook with a sputtering or sizzling noise.

friz′zle (frĭz′'l), *v. t. & n.* [1] Friz.

friz′zly (-lĭ), *a.* [3] Crisped; crinkled, as hair.

fro (frō), *adv.* From; away; back; — in *to and fro.*

frock (frŏk), *n.* **1.** A monk's coarse gown, having a hood and girded by a cord. **2.** A gown; dress.

frock coat A body coat for men, usually double-breasted, having long skirts before and behind.

frog (frŏg), *n.* **1.** Any of numerous well-known

āle, senāte, câre, ăm, ăccount, ärm, ȧsk, sofȧ ; ēve, ĕvent, ĕnd, recĕnt, makẽr, ĭce, ĭll ; ōld, ȯbey, ôrb, ŏdd, sŏft, cŏnnect; ūse, ŭnite, ûrn, ŭp, circŭs; fōōd, fŏŏt; out, oil ;

web-footed tailless amphibians of aquatic habits. **2.** The triangular elastic horny pad in the middle of the sole of a horse's foot. **3.** *Railroads.* A device for connecting one track with another branching from or crossing it. **4.** An oblong covered button fastening into a loop. **5.** The loop, as on a belt, for a sword, bayonet, etc.

frol′ic (frŏl′ĭk), a. Frolicsome; merry.— n. **1.** A prank; flight of gayety or mirth. **2.** A merry-making.— v. i. ; -ICKED (-ĭkt) , -ICK-ING. To play pranks; make merry.— **frol′ick-er,** n. [8].

frol′ic-some (-sŭm), a. [4] Full of gayety; sportive. — **-some-ly,** adv. [8] — **ness,** n. [8].

from (frŏm), prep. Forth out of; away from contact with or proximity to; out of.

frond (frŏnd), n. *Bot.* **a** A leaflike expansion not differentiated into stem and foliage. **b** Specif., the leaf of a fern, including both stipe and blade.

front (frŭnt), n. **1.** The forehead or brow; sometimes, the whole face. **2.** The countenance or personal bearing, as expressive esp. of boldness. **3.** A part that is foremost or that faces in a given direction. **4.** A position directly before one. **5.** A thing attached in front. — a. Of or pertaining to the front or forward part; foremost. — v. t. **1.** To oppose face to face; confront. **2.** To face toward. **3.** To give a front to. — v. i. To have or turn the face or front (in a named direction); face.

front′age (frŭn′tåj), n. The front part of a building or lot; extent of front, as of land along a road.

fron′tal (frŭn′tăl), a. Belonging to the front part or the forehead; being in front.

fron′tier (frŏn′tēr; frŭn′tēr), n. That part of a country facing another country or an unsettled region. — a. **1.** Lying on the exterior part; bordering. **2.** Of or relating to a frontier.

fron′tiers-man, n. A man living on the frontier.

fron′tis-piece (frŭn′tĭs-pēs), n. An illustration fronting the first page, or title-page, of a book.

front′let (frŭnt′lĕt), n. A band for the forehead.

frost (frŏst), n. **1.** Temperature which occasions freezing. **2.** Frozen dew. — v. t. **1.** To injure by frost; freeze. **2.** To cover with hoarfrost; produce a frostlike surface on.

frost′bite′ (-bīt′), v. t. ; -BIT′TEN (-bĭt′'n); -BIT′ING. To blight or nip with frost. — n. The freezing, or effect of a freezing, of some part of the body.

frost′ed (frŏs′tĕd), p. a. Covered with hoarfrost; ornamented with frosting; also, frostbitten.

frost′i-ly (frŏs′tĭ-lĭ), adv. In a frosty manner.

frost′ing, n. **1.** A composition of sugar, as with beaten egg, used to cover or ornament cake, pudding, etc. **2.** A lusterless finish of metal or glass.

frost′work′ (-wûrk′), n. Delicate figures formed by frost, esp. on glass, or an imitation of it.

frost′y (frŏs′tĭ), a. [3] **1.** Attended with or producing frost; freezing. **2.** Covered with frost. **3.** Without warmth of feeling; as, a *frosty* manner.

froth (frŏth), n. **1.** Bubbles collected on liquids from fermentation, agitation, etc.; spume; foam; esp., a spume of saliva from disease or excitement. **2.** Something light or unsubstantial, as empty words. — v. t. & i. To cause to foam; to foam.

froth′y (-ĭ), a. [3] **1.** Full of or consisting of froth; foamy. **2.** Like froth; unsubstantial; as, a *frothy* speech. — **i-ly,** adv. [8] — **i-ness,** n. [8].

fro′ward (frō′wẽrd), a. [3] Perverse; obstinately willful. — **-ly,** adv. [8] — **ness,** n. [8].

frown (froun), v. i. **1.** To contract the brow, as in displeasure or sternness; scowl. **2.** To look with disfavor. — v. t. To affect, express, or drive, by a frown. — n. A wrinkling of the brow, as in anger; a scowl.

frow′zy (frou′zĭ), a. [3] Offensive to the smell or sight; musty; slovenly; unkempt.

froze, pret. of FREEZE.

fro′zen (frō′z'n), p. a. Congealed with cold.

fruc′ti-fi-ca′tion (frŭk′tĭ-fĭ-kā′shŭn), n. Action of bearing fruit; also, the fruit of a plant.

fruc′ti-fy (frŭk′tĭ-fī), v. i. [2] To bear fruit. — v. t. To make fruitful; fertilize.

fru′gal (frōō′găl), a. [4] **1.** Economical; saving; sparing. **2.** Got by, or appropriate to, economy; as, a *frugal* meal. — **fru′gal-ly,** adv. [8].

fru-gal′i-ty (frōō-găl′ĭ-tĭ), n. ; pl. -TIES (-tĭz). Quality of being frugal; thrift.

fruit (frōōt), n. **1.** Any useful product of plant growth. **2.** The edible product of a perennial or woody plant. **3.** *Bot.* The ripened ovary of a seed plant and its contents, as the pod of a pea, a nut, grain, berry, etc. **4.** Effect; consequence; product. — v. t. & i. To bear or cause to bear fruit.

fruit′age (frōōt′åj), n. **1.** Fruit collectively. **2.** The state or process of bearing fruit.

fruit′er-er, n. One who deals in fruit.

fruit′ful (-fōōl), a. [4] Full of fruit; producing fruit abundantly; bearing results; prolific. — **-ly,** adv. [8] — **ness,** n. [8].

fru-i′tion (frōō-ĭsh′ŭn), n. Use or possession of anything; pleasure from possession or use.

fruit′less, a. [4] Not bearing fruit; barren; unprofitable; as, *fruitless* effort. — **-ly,** adv. — **ness,** n.

fruit′y (frōōt′ĭ), a. [3] Of or resembling fruit.

fru′men-ty (frōō′mĕn-tĭ), n. Hulled wheat boiled in milk, with sugar, plums, etc.

frus′trate (frŭs′trāt), a. Frustrated. — v. t. [1] **1.** To defeat the purpose of; balk. **2.** To bring to naught; nullify, as a plan.

frus-tra′tion (frŭs-trā′shŭn), n. A frustrating.

frus′tum (frŭs′tŭm), n. ; pl. E. -TUMS (-tŭmz), L. -TA (-tá). *Geom.* The part of a solid next the base, formed by cutting off the top; or the part of any solid between any two cutting planes.

Frustum (C) of Cone.

fry (frī), n. **1.** *Chiefly collective.* The young of fishes. **2.** A crowd of young or small things; — often in *small fry.*

fry, v. t. [2] To cook in a pan or on a griddle (esp. with fat or oil) over a fire; cook in boiling fat; — disting. from *broil.* — v. i. To undergo the process of frying. — n. ; pl. FRIES (frīz). A dish of anything fried.

fuch′si-a (fū′shĭ-å; fū′shá), n. Any of a genus (*Fuchsia*) of plants, having handsome nodding flowers, usually red or pink.

Fuchsia.

fud'dle (fŭd''l), v. t. [1] To make foolish, as with drink; muddle. *Colloq.*

fudge (fŭj), n. 1. Nonsense; bosh; — often an exclamation of contempt. 2. A kind of soft candy.

fu'el (fū'ĕl), n. Anything that feeds fire; hence, that which increases passion or the like.

fu'gi-tive (fū'jĭ-tĭy), a. [4] 1. Fleeing, as from danger. 2. Not durable; liable to fade. 3. Of fleeting interest. — n. 1. One who flees from pursuit, danger, service, etc. 2. A refugee.

fugue (fūg), n. A musical composition in which the different parts in turn repeat the same theme.

ful'crum (fŭl'krŭm), n.; pl. E. -CRUMS (-krŭmz), L. -CRA (-krȧ). 1. A prop. 2. The support, as a wedge, about which a lever turns.

ful-fill', **ful-fil'** (fŏŏl-fĭl'), v. t.; -FILLED' (-fĭld'); -FILL'ING. To accomplish or carry out, as a promise; satisfy, as a desire; perform; bring to pass.

ful-fill'ment, **ful-fil'ment** (-mĕnt), n. Act of fulfilling; accomplishment, as of a prophecy.

full (fŏŏl), v. t. & i. To thicken by moistening, heating, and pressing, as cloth.

full, a. [3] 1. Filled; abundantly supplied. 2. Satisfied in appetite; sated; also, satisfying. 3. Absorbed in, and enthusiastic over (something); — with *of*. 4. Occupying completely the space or accommodation. 5. Complete; entire. 6. Rounded or plump. 7. Of sounds, having volume or depth. 8. Having so much material that it hangs in folds. **full** (fŏŏl), n. Complete measure; highest degree. — adv. 1. Quite; entirely. 2. To the utmost.

full'er, n. One whose occupation is to full cloth.

full'er's earth (-erz). A soft claylike substance used in cleansing cloth and wool of grease.

full'ness, n. State or quality of being full.

ful'ly (fŏŏl'ĭ̄; -lĭ̄), adv. In a full manner or degree.

ful'mi-nate (fŭl'mĭ-nāt), v. i. & t. [1] 1. To detonate; explode violently. 2. To issue (decrees, etc.) authoritatively; thunder forth (menaces). — n. A violently explosive powder.

ful'mi-na'tion (-nā'shŭn), n. 1. Act of fulminating. 2. That which is fulminated, as a menace.

ful'some (fŭl'sŭm), a. [4] Offensive, esp. from excess of display or from insincerity; as, *fulsome* praise. — **ful'some-ly**, adv. [8] — **-ness**, n. [8].

fum'ble (fŭm'b'l), v. i. [1] To feel or grope about clumsily. — v. t. To handle or manage awkwardly. — n. Act of fumbling. — **-bler** (-blĕr), n. [8].

fume (fūm), n. Smoke, vapor, or the like, arising as from incense or tobacco and having a strong odor, either fragrant or, esp., offensive; as, sulphurous *fumes*. — v. i. [1] 1. To smoke; throw off fumes; rise up, as vapor. 2. To show anger or irritation. — v. t. To treat with fumes.

fu'mi-gate (fū'mĭ-gāt), v. t. [1] To apply smoke or vapor to, esp. for disinfecting.

fu'mi-ga'tion (-gā'shŭn), n. Act of fumigating.

fun (fŭn), n. Sport; playful action or speech.

func'tion (fŭnk'shŭn), n. 1. The proper action of anything; office; duty. 2. A religious, public, or social ceremony or gathering, esp. if elaborate or formal. — v. i. To fulfill a function; act; operate.

func'tion-al (-ăl), a. Of or pert. to a function.

func'tion-a-ry (-ȧ-rĭ̄), n.; pl. -RIES (-rĭz). One charged with the performance of a function.

fund (fŭnd), n. 1. An accumulation or deposit of resources; stock; supply. 2. A sum of money, esp. one for a specific object; pl., pecuniary resources. — v. t. 1. To convert (a floating debt) into a more or less permanent debt at interest. 2. To place in a fund; accumulate.

fun'da-men'tal (fŭn'dȧ-mĕn'tȧl), a. [4] Of or pert. to the foundation; essential; basal. — n. Anything that serves as the groundwork of a system; an essential part. — **fun'da-men'tal-ly**, adv. [8].

fu'ner-al (fū'nĕr-ăl), n. Ceremonies in connection with a burial; obsequies. — a. Pertaining to or befitting a funeral.

fu-ne're-al (fū-nē'rē-ăl), a. [4] Appropriate to a funeral; sad and solemn.

fun'gi (fŭn'jĭ), n., L. pl. of FUNGUS.

fun'gi-cide (-jĭ-sīd), n. Any substance that destroys fungi.

fun'gous (fŭn'gŭs), a. Pertaining to or resembling a fungus, its texture, or its growth.

fun'gus (-gŭs), n.; pl. L. -GI (fŭn'jĭ), E. -GUSES (fŭn'-gŭs-ĕz). Any of a group of plants comprising the molds, mildews, rusts, smuts, mushrooms, etc.

funk (fŭnk), v. i. To shrink back through fear; flinch. — n. Cowering fear. *Both Colloq.*

fun'nel (fŭn'ĕl), n. 1. A vessel shaped like a hollow cone, tapering into a tube, through which liquids, powders, etc., may be run into another vessel. 2. A flue; smokestack.

Funnel.

fun'ny (-ĭ), a. [3] 1. Droll; comical; laughable. 2. Strange; queer; odd. *Colloq.* — **fun'ni-ly** (-ĭ-lĭ), adv. [8].

fur (fûr), v. t.; FURRED (fûrd); FUR'RING. Common 1. To line, face, cover, or clothe with fur. 2. *Arch.* To apply furring to. — n. 1. A piece of the dressed pelt of any of certain animals (as the seal, beaver, mink, etc.); hence, such a dressed pelt or pelts. 2. An article of clothing made of, or trimmed or lined with, fur. 3. The hairy coat of a mammal, when fine, soft, and thick. 4. pl. Skins of animals with the fur. 5. Any coating suggesting fur.

fur'be-low (fûr'bē-lō), n. A plaited or gathered flounce; hence, any showy or fussy trimming.

fur'bish (-bĭsh), v. t. To burnish; renovate.

fu'ri-ous (fū'rĭ-ŭs), a. [4] 1. Full of passion or fury; raging. 2. Moving with violence or impetuosity; rushing. — **-ly**, adv. [8] — **-ness**, n. [8].

furl (fûrl), v. t. To roll, as a sail, close to a spar.

fur'long (fûr'lŏng), n. A measure, ⅛ of a mile.

fur'lough (-lō), n. Leave of absence, esp. to a soldier. — v. t. To grant a furlough to.

fur'nace (-nȧs), n. An apparatus in which heat is produced for reducing ores, warming a house, etc.

fur'nish (-nĭsh), v. t. 1. To equip; supply with furniture. 2. To provide; supply. — **-er**, n.

fur'nish-ings, n. pl. Furniture, fixtures, etc.

fur'ni-ture (fûr'nĭ-tûr), n. 1. That with which anything is furnished. 2. Household furnishings.

fu'ror (fū'rŏr), n. 1. Fury; frenzy. 2. A prevalent and excited admiration; a "rage"; "craze."

fur'ri-er (fûr'ĭ-ẽr), n. A dealer in furs.

fur'ri-er-y (-ĭ), n.; pl. -ERIES (-ĭz). 1. Furs in general. 2. The business of a furrier; trade in furs.

fur'ring (fûr'ĭng), n. 1. Fur trimmings or lining. 2. *Arch.* **a** The placing of thin strips to level a surface for lathing, etc. **b** The strips so applied.

---

fur'row (fŭr'ō), n. **1.** A trench made by or as by a plow. **2.** Any narrow channel, or groove; a wrinkle. — v. t. & i. To cut furrows (in); to plow.

fur'ry (fŭr'ĭ), a. [3] **1.** Covered with fur; dressed in fur; furred. **2.** Consisting of or resembling fur.

fur'ther (fŭr'thẽr), a. compar.; positive wanting; superl. FUR'THEST. **1.** More remote; farther. **2.** Additional. — adv. **1.** To or at a greater distance; to a greater extent or degree. **2.** In addition; furthermore. — v. t. To promote; forward.

☞ Further usually refers to time, quantity, or degree; farther, to space.

fur'ther-ance (-ăns), n. Act of furthering, or helping forward; promotion; advancement; progress.

fur'ther-more' (-mōr'), adv. & conj. Moreover.

fur'ther-most (-mōst), a. Most remote; furthest.

fur'thest (-thĕst), a. & adv. superl. Most remote.

fur'tive (·tĭv), a. [4] Done by stealth; hence, sly; stealthy. — **fur'tive-ly,** adv. [8] — **ness,** n. [8].

fu'ry (fū'rĭ), n.; pl. -RIES (-rĭz). **1.** Violent anger; rage. **2.** Fierceness; violence. **3.** Overmastering agitation or enthusiasm; frenzy. **4.** [cap.] Class. Myth. An avenging spirit. **5.** A turbulent person, esp. a woman; virago.

furze (fûrz), n. A spiny evergreen shrub, with yellow flowers, common in Europe.

fuse (fūz), v. t. & i. [1] **1.** To liquefy by heat; melt. **2.** To unite or blend, as if melted together.

fuse (fūz), n. **1.** A tube, cord, or the like, filled or impregnated with a combustible matter, for igniting an explosive. **2.** A strip or piece of fusible metal inserted in an electric circuit. When the current increases beyond safety, the metal melts, thus interrupting the circuit.

fu-see' (fū-zē'), n. A kind of friction match.

fu'sel (fū'zĕl), n., or **fusel oil.** An acrid, oily liquid, often occurring in alcoholic liquors.

fu'se-lage (fū'zē-lāj), n. The car of an airplane, designed to hold the engine, passengers, etc.

fu'si-ble (fū'zĭ-b'l), a. [4] That can be fused.

fu'sil-iers' (-zĭ-lērz'), n. pl. A title borne by some British regiments.

fu'sil-lade' (-lād'), n. A simultaneous or rapidly repeated discharge of firearms.

fu'sion (fū'zhŭn), n. **1.** A melting. **2.** State of fluidity or flowing from heat. **3.** Union or blending of things melted, or as if melted, together.

fuss (fŭs), n. A commotion; unnecessary ado. — v. i. To be unduly anxious about trifles.

fuss'y (fŭs'ĭ), a. [3] **1.** Disposed to fuss; overnice; fidgety. **2.** Showing much detail or nicety.

fus'tian (fŭs'chăn), n. **1.** A coarse twilled cotton stuff, as corduroy, velveteen, etc. **2.** Inflated style of discourse or writing; bombast.

fust'y (fŭs'tĭ), a. [3] Moldy; musty.

fu'tile (fū'tĭl), a. **1.** Useless; vain. **2.** Of no importance; trifling. — **ly,** adv. [8].

fu-til'i-ty (fū-tĭl'ĭ-tĭ), n. Quality of being futile.

fu'ture (fū'tŭr), a. **1.** That is to be. **2.** Expressing futurity; as, the future tense. — n. **1.** Time to come. **2.** Future state. **3.** Gram. The future tense.

fu-tu'ri-ty (fū-tū'rĭ-tĭ), n.; pl. -TIES (-tĭz). **1.** State of being yet to come; future state. **2.** Future time; posterity. **3.** An event to come.

fuze, n., **fu-zee',** n. Vars. of FUSE, FUSEE.

fuzz (fŭz), n. Fine, light particles or fibers.

fuzz'y (fŭz'ĭ), a. [3] **1.** Having fuzz; downy; fluffy; as, fuzzy cloth. **2.** Frizzly; as, fuzzy hair.

G

gab (găb), n. & v. Prate; chatter. Colloq.

gab'ble (găb'l), v. i. & t. [1] **1.** To chatter; jabber. **2.** To cackle, as geese. — n. Act or sound of gabbling. — **gab'bler** (-lẽr), n. [8].

gab-er-dine', gab'ar-dine' (găb'ẽr-dēn'; găb'ẽr-dēn), n. A coarse loose frock or coat.

ga'bi-on (gā'bĭ-ŭn), n. A cylinder to be filled with earth and used in temporary fortifications.

ga'ble (-b'l), n. A vertical triangular portion of the end of a building.

gad (găd), n. A goad.

gad, v. i. To wander about idly. — **gad'der,** n. [8].

gad'fly' (-flī'), n.; pl. -FLIES (-flīz'). A fly that bites or annoys cattle.

Gable.

gadg'et (găj'ĕt, -ĭt), n. A contrivance or device; — often used when the correct name is not known.

gaff (găf), n. **1.** A barbed spear or a hook used in landing heavy fish. **2.** The upper spar of a fore-and-aft sail. — v. t. To secure with a gaff, or hook.

gag (găg), v. t.; GAGGED (găgd); GAG'GING (-ĭng). To stop the mouth of; hence, to prevent from free speech. — n. Something thrust into the mouth to hinder speaking; — often figurative.

gage (gāj), n. **1.** A security; pledge. **2.** A pledge (as a glove, cast on the ground) of one's intention to fight to support one's claims; hence, a challenge; defiance. — v. t. [1] To deposit as a pledge; wager.

gage, gag'er (gāj'ẽr). Vars. of GAUGE, GAUGER.

gai'e-ty, n., **gai'ly,** adv. Vars. of GAYETY, GAYLY.

gain (gān), n. Increase or addition to what one has of advantage or benefit; profit; — opposed to loss. — v. t. **1.** To get; acquire. **2.** To win, as a battle. **3.** To win to an interest or a party. **4.** To reach; arrive at. — v. i. **1.** To secure advantage or profit. **2.** To move faster than. — **gain'er,** n. [8].

gain'ful (-fool), a. [4] Profitable; advantageous.

gain'say' (gān'sā'; gān'sā'), v. t.; for prin. parts see SAY. To contradict; forbid. — **say'er,** n. [8].

gait (gāt), n. Manner of walking or going on foot.

gai'ter (gā'tẽr), n. **1.** A covering for the ankle and instep, or for the leg from knee to instep. **2.** A shoe with elastic straps at the sides. U. S.

ga'la (gā'là), n. **1.** Festive dress; — now only in in gala. **2.** A festival; — chiefly in gala day, etc.

gal'ax-y (găl'ăk-sĭ), n.; pl. -AXIES (-sĭz). **1.** [cap.] The Milky Way. **2.** An assemblage of brilliant or noted persons or things; as, a galaxy of beauty.

gale (gāl), n. **1.** A wind stronger than a stiff breeze, but not so strong as a hurricane. **2.** A state of excitement or hilarity. [sulphide.]

ga-le'na (gà-lē'nà), n. The chief ore of lead; lead]

gall (gôl), n. **1.** A bitter fluid secreted by the

liver; bile, esp. that from the ox. **2.** The gall bladder. **3.** Anything bitter to endure; as, the *gall* of disappointment. **4.** Bitterness of spirit; hate.

gall (gôl), *n.* A sore in the skin from chafing, esp. on a horse's back; hence, a cause or a state of irritation. — *v. t.* To chafe; hence, to vex.

gall, *n.* A swelling or excrescence on plants, caused by certain insects, etc.

gal'lant (găl'ănt; *see sense* 4), *a.* [4] **1.** Showy; gay, esp. in dress. **2.** Stately; grand. **3.** Noble in bearing or spirit; brave. **4.** (*Usually* gă-lănt') Polite and attentive to ladies. — (gă-lănt'; găl'-ănt), *n.* **1.** A gay, fashionable man. **2.** One gallant to ladies. — (gă-lănt'), *v. t.* To bestow gallant attentions on (a lady); escort (her). — *v. i.* To act the gallant; make love.

gal'lant-ly (găl'ănt-lĭ; gă-lănt'lĭ), *adv.* In a gallant manner.

gal'lant-ness, *n.* The quality of being gallant.

gal'lant-ry (găl'ănt-rĭ), *n.; pl.* -RIES (-rĭz). **1.** Bravery; a gallant action or speech. **2.** Civility or polite attention to ladies.

gall bladder. The sac which receives the bile.

gal'le-on (găl'ē-ŭn), *n.* A sailing vessel of the 15th and following centuries, used esp. by the Spaniards.

gal'ler-y (găl'ĕr-ĭ), *n.; pl.* GAL-LERIES (-ĭz). **1.** A

Galleon.

long narrow room, hall, or passage; hence, a room for showing pictures, shooting, taking photographs, etc.; also, an important collection, as of pictures. **2.** In an auditorium, a platform supported on brackets or columns, usually for part of the audience; in a theater, the highest of such platforms. **3.** The occupants of a gallery (sense 2); any body of spectators.

gal'ley (-ĭ), *n.; pl.* -LEYS (-ĭz). **1.** An ancient or medieval vessel, usually low and one-decked, propelled by oars, or by oars and sails. **2.** A large rowboat. **3.** Cookroom of a vessel. **4.** An oblong tray to hold type set but not made up into pages.

gall'fly (gôl'flī'), *n.; pl.* -FLIES (-flīz'). An insect that deposits its eggs in plants, causing galls.

gal'li-na'ceous (găl'ĭ-nā'shŭs), *a.* Resembling domestic fowls; of or pertaining to an order (*Gallinæ*) of birds, including the barnyard fowl, pheasants, turkeys, grouse, partridges, quails, etc.

gal'li-pot (găl'ĭ-pŏt), *n.* A small earthen pot, esp. for medicines, etc.; a nickname for a druggist.

gall'nut (gôl'nŭt'), *n.* A nutlike gall.

gal'lon (găl'ŭn), *n.* A measure of capacity, containing four quarts. The United States standard gallon contains 231 cubic inches. Abbr. *gal.*

gal-loon' (gă-loon'), *n.* A narrow binding or trimming, esp. of rich material.

gal'lop (găl'ŭp), *v. i.* To go or ride at a gallop. — *v. t.* To cause to gallop. — *n.* **1.** A springing

gait of various quadrupeds, esp. the horse. **2.** A ride on a galloping animal. — **gal'lop-er,** *n.* [8].

gal'lows (găl'ōz; -ŭs), *n.* **1.** A frame, in simplest form a crossbar on two posts, on which criminals are hanged. **2.** Any similar frame.

gall'stone' (gôl'stōn'), *n.* A stonelike concretion formed in the gall bladder or biliary passages.

gal'op (găl'ŭp; găl'ō), *n.* A kind of lively dance.

ga-lore' (gá-lōr'), *adv.* In abundance; plentifully.

ga-losh' (-lŏsh'), *n.* An overshoe, now of rubber.

gal-van'ic (găl-văn'ĭk), *a.* Of or pertaining to or exhibiting galvanism; hence, affected or affecting as by an electric shock or stimulus.

gal'va-nism (găl'vá-nĭz'm), *n.* Electricity produced by chemical action.

gal'va-nize (-nīz), *v. t.* [1] **1.** To affect with galvanism; hence, to excite as if by an electric shock. **2.** To electroplate; to coat (iron) with zinc.

gal'va-nom'e-ter (-nŏm'ē-tēr), *n.* An instrument to determine the intensity of an electric current or its presence or direction, usually by deflection of a magnetic needle.

gam'bit (găm'bĭt), *n.* A chess opening in which the first player loses a man for advantage in position.

gam'ble (-b'l), *v. i.* [1] To game; hazard something on a chance; wager. — *v. t.* To lose by gaming; — usually *with* away. — **gam'bler,** *n.* [8].

gam'bling (-blĭng), *n.* The act of playing or gaming for stakes; hence, any wagering.

gam-boge' (găm-bōj'; -boōj'), *n.* A gum resin used as a yellow pigment and in medicine.

gam'bol (găm'bŏl), *n.* A skipping or leaping about in frolic; a hop. — *v. i.* [7] To bound or frisk.

game (gām), *n.* **1.** Sport of any kind; fun; also, playful ridicule. **2.** A contest according to set rules for amusement or for a stake. **3.** A single contest lasting until a definite limit is reached. **4.** A scheme; plan. **5.** Wild animals or birds that are hunted; also, their flesh considered as food. — *v. i.* [1] To play, as with cards, dice, etc., for a wager or bet; to gamble. — *a.* Resolute; plucky. — **-ly,** *adv.* [8] — **-ness,** *n.* [8].

game'keep'er (-kēp'ēr), *n.* One in charge of game.

game'some (-sŭm), *a.* [3] Gay; playful; merry.

game'ster (-stēr), *n.* A habitual gambler.

gam'in (găm'ĭn), *n.* A neglected, untrained city boy.

gam'mon (-ŭn), *n.* A smoked or dried ham.

gam'mon, *n.* Nonsense. — *v. t.* To influence with gammon. *Both Colloq.*

gam'ut (găm'ŭt), *n.* **1.** The whole series of recognized musical notes; the major scale. **2.** Hence, an entire range or series.

gam'y (gām'ĭ), *a.* [3] **1.** Plucky; spirited; game. **2.** Having the flavor of game, esp. when "high."

gan'der (găn'dĕr), *n.* A male goose.

gang (găng), *n.* **1.** A group; company. **2.** A set of similar implements arranged to act together.

gan'gli-on (găn'glĭ-ŏn), *n.; L. pl.* -GLIA (-á). A nerve center; as : **a** An aggregation of nerve cells forming an enlargement on a nerve or on two or more nerves where they join or separate. **b** A mass of gray matter in the brain or spinal cord.

gang'plank' (găng'plănk'), *n.* A portable platform or bridge, used in entering or leaving a vessel.

gan'grene (găn'grēn), *n.* The dying of tissue due to interference with local nutrition.

gang′way (găng′wā′), n. A passageway from one place to another; esp., a temporary way of planks.

gan′net (găn′ĕt), n. Any of several large sea birds related to the pelicans.

gant′let (gănt′lĕt; gănt′lĕt), n. A gauntlet, or glove.

gant′let, n. An old form of punishment, wherein the offender was made to run between two rows of men, who struck him with switches, clubs, etc.

gaol (jāl), n. Vars. of JAIL, etc.

gaol′er, gaol′er, etc. Vars. of JAIL, etc.

gap (găp), n. **1.** An opening in anything made by or as by breaking or parting; any breach of continuity. **2.** A mountain pass, cleft, or ravine.

gape (gāp; găp; colloq. gāp), v. i. [1] **1.** To open the mouth wide, as in surprise or yawning ; to open widely. **2.** To stare with open mouth. — n. A gaping ; stare ; also, a gap or break.

ga′rage′ (gȧ′räzh′; găr′äj), n. A place for housing automobiles, or an airship or flying machine.

garb (gärb), n. Fashion or style of dress ; clothing ; dress. — v. t. To clothe.

gar′bage (gär′bȧj), n. Animal or vegetable refuse.

gar′ble (-b'l), v. t. [1] To pick out such parts of as may serve a (usually unfair) purpose; mutilate.

gar′den (gär′d'n), n. Ground used for cultivating herbs, fruits, flowers, or vegetables ; hence, a very fertile region. — v. i. & t. To cultivate, or labor in, a garden. — **gar′den-er**, n. [8].

gar′den-ing, n. Making and cultivating a garden.

gar′fish (gär′fĭsh′), n. Any of certain fishes having a long pikelike body, and long and narrow jaws.

gar′gle (gär′g'l), v. t. [1] To rinse, as the throat, agitating the liquid by expulsion of the breath. — v. i. To use a gargle. — n. Liquid used in gargling.

gar′goyle (-goil), n. A waterspout, often grotesquely carved, projecting at the upper part of a building.

gar′ish (gâr′ĭsh), a. [4] Showy ; dazzling ; glaring. — **-ly**, adv. [8].

gar′land (gär′lănd), n.

Gargoyle.

A wreath, as of flowers ; chaplet. — v. t. To deck with a garland.

gar′lic (-lĭk), n. A European plant of the lily family. Also, its pungent bulb, used in cooking.

gar′ment (gär′mĕnt), n. Any article of clothing.

gar′ner (-nẽr), n. A granary ; hence, a collection; store. — v. t. To gather for preservation; store.

gar′net (-nĕt), n. **1.** A hard mineral or gem of several varieties. **2.** Its deep red color.

gar′nish (-nĭsh), v. t. **1.** To decorate ; adorn. **2.** Law. To garnishee. — n. A decoration ; esp., something set round a dish as an embellishment.

gar′nish-ee′ (gär′nĭsh-ē′), n. Law. One who has been garnished, or served with a notice of garnishment. — v.t.; -EED′(-ēd′); -EE′ING. **1.** To make (one) a garnishee. **2.** To attach (property) by garnishment.

gar′nish-ment (gär′nĭsh-mĕnt), n. **1.** Ornament; embellishment. **2.** Law. **a** A notice to a third party to appear in a suit. **b** Warning to a person holding another's attached property, not to deliver it to him, but to account for it in court.

gar′ret (găr′ĕt), n. That part of a house which is immediately under or within the roof.

gar′ri-son (-ĭ-s'n), n. A body of troops stationed in a fortified place; also, a place where troops are thus stationed. — v. t. **1.** To furnish with soldiers, as a fort. **2.** To place on duty in a garrison.

gar-rote′ (gȧ-rōt′), n. **1.** Execution by strangulation; the instrument for strangling. **2.** Throttling, esp. for robbery. — v. t. [1] To strangle with or as with the garrote. — **gar-rot′er**, n. [8].

gar-ru′li-ty (gă-rōō′lĭ-tĭ), n. Talkativeness.

gar′ru-lous (găr′ōō-lŭs), a. [4] Talking much, esp. about trifles. — **-ly**, adv. [8] — **-ness**, n. [8].

gar′ter (gär′tẽr), n. **1.** A band or strap to hold up a stocking. **2.** [Cap.] The badge of the Order of the Garter, the highest order of British knighthood; also, the order or membership in it.

gas (găs), n. **1.** An aëriform, elastic fluid. Cf. VAPOR. **2.** Hence, any gaseous mixture except atmospheric air; as : **a** Laughing gas. **b** Any combustible gaseous mixture for illumination or for fuel.

gas′con-ade′ (găs′kŏn-ād′), n. A boast ; bravado.

gas engine. An internal-combustion engine using gaseous fuel; broadly, any internal-combustion engine.

gas′e-ous (găs′ē-ŭs), a. Of, pert. to, or like, gas.

gash (găsh), v. t. To make a gash in. — n. A deep long cut, esp. in flesh.

gas′ket (găs′kĕt), n. **1.** Naut. A line or band used to lash a furled sail securely. **2.** A packing for a joint, or between sliding parts, as for a piston.

gas′o-line (găs′ō-lēn ; -lĭn), **gas′o-lene** (-lēn), n. A volatile inflammable liquid distilled from petroleum, used esp. to produce heat and motive power.

gas-om′e-ter (găs-ŏm′ē-tẽr), n. A tank or apparatus for holding gas ; properly, one for holding and measuring gas.

gasp (gȧsp), v. i. To catch the breath convulsively; labor for breath. — n. Act of one that gasps.

gas′sy (găs′ĭ), a. [3] Full of or like gas.

gas′tric (-trĭk), a. Of or pertaining to the stomach. — gastric juice, the acid digestive fluid secreted by the stomach glands.

gas-tri′tis (găs-trī′tĭs), n. Med. Inflammation of the stomach, esp. of its mucous membrane.

gas-tron′o-my (-trŏn′ō-mĭ), n. Art of good eating.

gas′tro-nom′ic (găs′trō-nŏm′ĭk), **gas′tro-nom′i-cal**, a. Pertaining to gastronomy.

gas′tro-pod (găs′trō-pŏd), n. Any of a class of mollusks including snails, whelks, and slugs.

gate (gāt), n. **1.** An opening for passage in an inclosing wall, fence, or barrier, esp. such an opening with a movable frame or door to close it; also, the frame or door. **2.** A door, valve, etc., for stopping a dam, pipe, etc.

gate′way′ (-wā′), n. **1.** A gate. **2.** A passage.

gath′er (găth′ẽr), v. t. **1.** To bring together ; assemble ; collect ; accumulate. **2.** To infer; conclude. **3.** To compress; draw up together, as one's limbs, the brow, etc. ; to bring together in folds, plaits, or puckers, as a garment or cloth. — v. i. **1.** To come together; collect; congregate. **2.** To grow larger by accretion; increase. **3.** To come to a head, as a sore, and generate pus. — n. A plait or fold, as in cloth.

gath′er-ing, vb. n. A crowd ; assembly; abscess.

Gat′ling gun (găt′lĭng). A kind of machine gun.

gaud (gôd), n. A showy ornament ; trinket.

gaud′y (-ĭ), a. [3] Ostentatiously fine ; showy. — **gaud′i-ly** (-ĭ-lĭ), adv. [8] — **i-ness**, n. [8].

---

gauge, gage(gāj),*v. t.* [1] To measure accurately or limit by or as by a gauge. — *n.* **1.** An instrument for measuring or gauging; as, a wire *gauge ;* wind *gauge.* **2.** A standard of measurement; dimensions.

gaug'er, gag'er (gāj'ẽr), *n.* One that gauges; hence, an officer who gauges casks ; an exciseman.

gaunt (gänt; gônt), *a.* [3] Emaciated, as with fasting ; lean. — **gaunt'ness**, *n.* [8].

gaunt'let (gänt'lĕt ; gônt'-), *n.* = 2d GANTLET.

gaunt'let, *n.* A glove to defend the hand from wounds ; a stout glove, covering part of the arm.

gauze (gôz), *n.* A very thin, slight, transparent stuff, generally of silk ; also, a fabric resembling it.

gauz'y (gôz'ĭ), *a.* [3] Like gauze; thin and slight as gauze. — **gauz'i-ness**, *n.* [8].

gave (gāv), *pret.* of GIVE.

gav'el (găv'ĕl), *n.* Mallet of a presiding officer.

ga-vot' (ga-vŏt' ; găv'ŏt)) *n.* A lively dance of
ga-votte' (gȧ-vŏt')) French peasant origin.

gawk (gôk), *n.* A simpleton ; booby. — *v. i.* To act like a gawk. *Colloq.*

gawk'y (-ĭ), *a.* [3] Foolish and awkward; clumsy. — *n.; pl.* -IES. A gawk. — **gawk'i-ness**, *n.* [8].

gay (gā), *a.* [3] **1.** Excited with merriment; merry. **2.** Bright; brilliant. **3.** Given to social pleasures or indulgence; hence, loose; licentious. — **gay'ly, gai'ly** (-lĭ), *adv.* [8].

gay'e-ty, gai'e-ty (gā'ĕ-tĭ), *n. ; pl.* -TIES (-tĭz). **1.** State of being gay; merriment. **2.** Finery; show.

gaze (gāz), *v. i.* To fix the eyes in a steady and intent look. — *n.* A fixed, intent look.

ga-zelle' (gȧ-zĕl'), *n.* Any of various small graceful and very swift antelopes.

ga-zette' (-zĕt'), *n.* **1.** A newspaper. **2.** An official journal containing lists of honors, bankrupts, etc. — *v. t.* [1] To publish in a gazette.

gaz'et-teer' (găz'ĕ-tēr'), *n.* A geographical dictionary.

gear (gēr), *n.* **1.** Clothing ; dress; accouterments. **2.** Harness. **3.** Tools; implements. **4.** a A piece of mechanism for a specific use. **b** A cogwheel. **c** Working relation or adjustment. **5.** Goods; things; as, household *gear.* **6.** *Naut.* Rigging. — *v. t. Machinery.* To provide with gear or gearing; put into gear. — *v. i.* To be in, or come into, gear.

gear'ing (gēr'ĭng), *vb. n.* The parts, collectively, by which motion is transmitted in machinery.

gee (jē), *interj.* In driving oxen, etc., a word usually meaning : Turn to the right.

geese (gēs), *n., pl.* of GOOSE.

gei'sha (gā'shȧ), *n. ; pl.* GEISHA (-shȧ), GEISHAS (-shȧz). A Japanese singing and dancing girl.

gel'a-tin, gel'a-tine (jĕl'ȧ-tĭn), *n.* A sticky glue-like substance got by boiling bones, calves' feet, and other parts of animals for a long time. It dissolves easily in hot water and forms a jelly on cooling, and is used in making glue, as a food, etc.

ge-lat'i-nous (jĕ-lăt'ĭ-nŭs), *a.* [4] Of, like, or containing, gelatin.

geld (gĕld), *v. t.* To castrate ; — said esp. of horses.

geld'ing (gĕl'dĭng), *n.* A castrated horse.

gem (jĕm), *n.* **1.** A precious stone, esp. when cut and polished ; a jewel. **2.** Something prized for beauty, perfection, etc., esp. when small or brief. — *v. t.;* GEMMED (jĕmd) GEM'MING. To adorn with or as with gems ; — esp. in p. p. GEMMED.

‖**gen'darme'** (zhän'därm' ; jĕn-därm'), *n. ; pl* -DARMES (-därm' ; -därmz'). [F.] One of a body of military police, esp. in France.

gen-darm'er-y (jĕn-därm'ẽr-ĭ),‖**gen'dar'me-rie'** (zhän'där'mē-rē'), *n.* [F.] The body of gendarmes.

gen'der (jĕn'dẽr), *n.* Distinction of a word or words according to sex; also, the distinctive form itself, or a class so distinguished.

gen'e-al'o-gist (jĕn'ē-ăl'ō-jĭst ; jē'nĕ-), *n.* One who traces or studies genealogies.

gen'e-al'o-gy (jĕn'ē-ăl'ō-jĭ ; jē'nĕ-), *n.; pl.* -GIES (-jĭz). A history of the descent of an individual or family from an ancestor; pedigree ; lineage. — **gen'e-a-log'i-cal** (-ȧ-lŏj'ĭ-kăl), *a.*

gen'e-ra (jĕn'ẽr-ȧ), *n., pl.* of GENUS.

gen'er-al (-ăl), *a.* [4] **1.** Of or pertaining to the whole, or all; not local, or particular. **2.** Not limited in meaning or application; not specific, or in detail. **3.** Common to many; prevalent; extensive. though not universal. **4.** Not special or specialized. **5.** Chief ; superior ; — in titles ; as, attorney-*general*, etc. — *n.* **1.** The whole ; hence, a general fact, principle, etc. **2.** One of the chief military officers of a country. See ARMY.

gen'er-al'i-ty (-ăl'ĭ-tĭ), *n.; pl.* -TIES(-tĭz). **1.** State or quality of being general. **2.** A vague statement. **3.** Main body; bulk; as, the *generality* of mankind.

gen'er-al-i-za'tion (-ăl-ĭ-zā'shŭn), *n.* **1.** Act or process of generalizing. **2.** A general inference.

gen'er-al-ize (jĕn'ẽr-ăl-īz), *v. t.* [1] To make general; reduce to general laws. — *v. i.* To form or state general views. — **-iz'er** (-īz'ẽr), *n.* [8].

gen'er-al-ly (-ĭ), *adv.* **1.** In general; commonly; extensively. **2.** In a general way; on the whole.

gen'er-al-ship' (-ĕl'ĭp'), *n.* **1.** The office of general. **2.** Military skill; leadership; management.

gen'er-ate (-āt), *v. t.* [1] **1.** To beget; produce (offspring). **2.** To originate, esp. by a vital or chemical process. **3.** *Math.* To trace out, as a figure, by the motion of a point.

gen'er-a'tion (-ā'shŭn), *n.* **1.** Act of generating. **2.** A step in natural descent; those of the same stage in descent from an ancestor, or living at one period; also, the average lifetime of man.

gen'er-a-tive (-ȧ-tĭv), *a.* Pert. to generation.

gen'er-a'tor (-ā'tẽr), *n.* One that generates; apparatus for generating gas, steam, or electricity.

ge-ner'ic (jē-nĕr'ĭk), *a.* **1.** *Biology.* Pertaining to a genus. **2.** Pertaining to things of the same kind or class; characteristic of, or dealing with, groups rather than individuals; — opposed to *specific*. — **ge-ner'i-cal** (-ĭ-kăl), *a.* — **-i-cal-ly**, *adv.* [8].

gen'er-os'i-ty (jĕn'ẽr-ŏs'ĭ-tĭ), *n.; pl.* -TIES (-tĭz). Quality of being generous.

gen'er-ous (jĕn'ẽr-ŭs), *a.* [4] **1.** Liberal ; munificent. **2.** Marked by generosity; ample; as, a *generous* table. — **-ly**, *adv.* [8] — **-ness**, *n.* [8].

gen'e-sis (-ĕ-sĭs), *n.* **1.** [*cap.*] The first book of the Bible, narrating the creation of the world. **2.** Origin; mode of coming into existence.

ge-net'ic (jē-nĕt'ĭk), *a.* Pertaining to genesis.

ge'ni-al (jē'nĭ-ăl; jĕn'yăl), *a.* [4] Favorable to growth or comfort; hence, sympathetically cheerful and cheering; jovial ; kindly. — **-ly**, *adv.* [8].

ge'ni-al'i-ty (jē'nĭ-ăl'ĭ-tĭ ; jĕn-yăl'-), *n.* Quality of being genial ; cheerfulness ; warmth.

āle, senāte, câre, ăm, ŏccount, ärm, ȧsk, sofȧ ; ēve, ĕvent, ĕnd, recĕnt, makēr; īce, ĭll ; ōld, ȯbey, ôrb, ŏdd, sôft, cŏnnect; ūse, ŭnite, ûrn, ŭp, circǔs; fōōd, fŏŏt; out, oil;

ge′nie (jē′nĭ), n. A genius. = GENIUS, 2 **b.**

ge′ni-i (jē′nĭ-ī), n. L. pl. of GENIUS.

gen′i-tal (jĕn′ĭ-tăl), a. Pertaining to generation.

gen′i-tive (-tĭv), a. Gram. Designating the case (as in Latin and Greek) that expresses source or possession. — n. The genitive case or a word in it.

gen′ius (jēn′yŭs or, esp. in 1 & 2, jē′nĭ-ŭs), n.; pl., senses 1–2, L. GENII (jē′nĭ-ī), senses 3–6, E. GENIUSES (-ĕz). **1.** [Often cap.] Roman Relig. An attendant or protecting spirit or deity. **2. a** An imaginary spirit presiding over the destiny of a person or place. **b** An imaginary spirit of nature, esp. of fire or air; a jinni. **3.** Natural disposition or bent. **4.** Peculiar character, as of a nation. **5.** Uncommon intellectual power, esp. in invention. **6.** One endowed with genius.

gen-teel′ (jĕn-tēl′), a. [4] **1.** Polite; well-bred. **2.** Suited to the position of a lady or gentleman. — **gen-teel′ly**, adv. [8].

☞ Genteel as now used by careful writers has a humorous or sarcastic significance.

Gentian.

gen′tian (jĕn′shăn), n. **1.** Any of various herbs prized for their handsome flowers, usually blue. **2.** The bitter root of a species of gentian.

gen′tile (jĕn′tīl), n. One not Jewish; — in Biblical use usually capitalized. — a. [Often cap.] Belonging to nations other than the Jews.

gen-til′i-ty (jĕn-tĭl′ĭ-tĭ), n. **1.** Gentle birth. **2.** The qualities appropriate to those well born.

gen′tle (jĕn′t'l), a. [3] **1.** Well-born; of good, though not noble, family. **2.** Of or appropriate to good birth or position. **3.** Tamed; docile. **4.** Soft; soothing; refined. **5.** Moderate.

gen′tle-folk (-fōk′), **gen′tle-folks** (-fōks′), n. pl. Persons of gentle, or good, family and breeding.

gen′tle-man (-măn), n.; pl. -MEN (-mĕn). **1.** A man of good family. Chiefly Historical. **2.** A man of gentle or refined manners. **3.** A man, irrespective of condition; — esp. in pl., in address.

gen′tle-man-like } a. [4] Pertaining to or becom-
gen′tle-man-ly } ing a gentleman; courteous.

gen′tle-ness, n. Quality or state of being gentle.

gen′tle-wom′an (jĕn′t'l-wŏom′ăn), n.; pl. -WOMEN (-wĭm′ĕn). A woman of good family or breeding; also, Hist., a woman who attends a lady of rank.

gen′tly (-tlĭ), adv. In a gentle manner.

gen′try (-trĭ), n. Collective. **1.** People of education and breeding. **2.** People; persons of a class; — usually contemptuous or humorous.

gen′u-flec′tion (jĕn′ũ-flĕk′shŭn), n. Act of bending the knee, esp. in worship.

gen′u-ine (jĕn′ũ-ĭn), a. [4] **1.** Actually from the reputed source or author; authentic; real. **2.** Of or pertaining to the original stock. **3.** Sincere; frank. — **gen′u-ine-ly**, adv. [8] — **-ness**, n. [8].

ge′nus (jē′nŭs), n.; pl. GENERA (jĕn′ẽr-ȧ). A class divided into subordinate classes or species.

ge′ode (jē′ōd), n. Geol. A nodule of stone having a cavity lined with crystals or mineral matter.

ge-og′ra-pher (jē-ŏg′rȧ-fẽr), n. One versed in geography.

ge′o-graph′ic (jē′ō-grăf′ĭk) } a. Of or pertaining
ge′o-graph′i-cal (-ĭ-kăl) } to geography. — **-i-cal-ly**, adv.

ge-og′ra-phy (jē-ŏg′rȧ-fĭ), n.; pl. -PHIES (-fĭz). The description of the earth, its climate, products, inhabitants, etc.

ge′o-log′ic (jē′ō-lŏj′ĭk), **ge′o-log′i-cal** (-ĭ-kăl), a. Of or pertaining to geology. — **-i-cal-ly**, adv. [8].

ge-ol′o-gist (jē-ŏl′ō-jĭst), n. One learned in geology; one engaged in geological investigations.

ge-ol′o-gize (-ŏl′ō-jīz), v. i. [1] To study geology or make geological investigations.

ge-ol′o-gy (-jĭ), n.; pl. -GIES (-jĭz). The science of the history of the earth and its life.

ge-om′e-ter (jē-ŏm′ē-tẽr), n. A geometrician.

ge′o-met′ric (jē′ō-mĕt′rĭk), **-ri-cal** (-rĭ-kăl), a. Pertaining to, or determined by, geometry.

ge-om′e-tri′cian (jē-ŏm′ē-trĭsh′ăn), n. Geometer.

ge-om′e-try (-trĭ), n.; pl. -TRIES (-trĭz). The branch of mathematics treating of the relations and properties of solids, surfaces, lines, and angles.

ge-ra′ni-um (jē-rā′nĭ-ŭm), n. **1.** Any of various plants with, usually, pink or purple flowers, and leaves of pungent odor. **2.** Any of numerous cultivated plants of an allied genus, mostly with red, pink, or white flowers.

germ (jûrm), n. **1.** The earliest form of an organism; bud; seed; embryo. **2.** Any microscopic organism, especially one that causes disease; microbe. **3.** That from which anything springs; beginning.

Ger′man (jûr′măn), n.; pl. -MANS. **1.** A native or one of the people of Germany. **2.** The language of the Germans. **3.** [l. c.] A kind of intricate dance; cotillion; also, a party at which it is danced. — a. Of or pert. to Germany or the Germans. — German silver, a silver-white alloy, of copper, zinc, and nickel.

ger′man, a. Near of kin; as: **a** Of the same parentage; — in brother-german and sister-german. **b** Own, or first; — now only in cousin-german.

ger-mane′ (jẽr-măn′; jûr′măn), a. [4] **1.** = GERMAN, akin. **2.** Appropriate; relevant.

Ger-man′ic (jẽr-măn′ĭk), a. German; Teutonic.

ger′mi-cid′al (jûr′mĭ-sĭd′ăl), a. Destructive to germs, esp. disease germs.

ger′mi-cide (-sĭd), n. Any germicidal substance.

ger′mi-nal (-năl), a. Pert. to a germ; incipient.

ger′mi-nate (-nāt), v. i. & t. To sprout.

ger′mi-na′tion (-nā′shŭn), n. Process of germinating, beginning of growth.

ger′ry-man′der (gĕr′ĭ-măn′dẽr), v. t. To divide (a State, county, etc.) into civil divisions in an unnatural and unfair way. Political Cant, U. S. — (gĕr′ĭ-măn′dẽr), n. Act or result of gerrymandering.

ges-ta′tion (jĕs-tā′shŭn), n. Pregnancy.

ges-tic′u-late (-tĭk′ũ-lāt), v. i. To gesture, esp. when speaking. — **ges-tic′u-la′tor**, n. [8].

ges-tic′u-la′tion (-lā′shŭn), n. A gesture, esp. an undignified one.

ges′ture (jĕs′tũr), n. A bodily motion or posture intended to express or emphasize something.

ges′ture, v. i. To make gestures; gesticulate.

get (gĕt), v. t.; pret. GOT (gŏt), Archaic GAT (găt):

---

chair; go; sing, iŋk; then, thin; nature, verdure; yet; zh = z in azure. Numbers refer to §§ in the Special Notes which, with Abbreviations, Signs, etc., precede the Vocabulary.

p. p. GOT, or, *esp. in U. S.*, GOT'TEN (gŏt'n); *p. pr. & vb. n.* GET'TING. **1.** To come by; come to have; hence, to obtain, ascertain, learn, gain, win, etc. **2.** With *have* and *to*, to be obliged to; as, he has *got* to do it. *Collog.* **3.** To procure or cause to be (in some position or condition); as, to *get* one's feet wet. **4.** To induce; persuade; as, *get* him to come. **5.** To betake or remove one's self; as, *get* away! **6.** To beget; — now usually of animals. — *v. i.* **1.** To arrive, or bring one's self; become; — with a modifying word or phrase; as, to *get* home, *get* tree, *get* to sleep. **2.** To gain; profit. — **get'ter,** *n.* [8].

gew'gaw (gū'gô), *n.* A showy trifle; a toy.

gey'ser (gī'sẽr; gī'zẽr), *n.* A spring that, at intervals, throws forth jets of heated water and steam.

ghast'ly (gȧst'lĭ), *a.* [3] **1.** Horrible; shocking; as, *ghastly* wounds. **2.** Ghostlike in appearance; deathly; pale; as, a *ghastly* face. — *adv.* In a ghastly or deathlike manner. — **-li-ness,** *n.* [8].

gher'kin (gûr'kĭn), *n.* A kind of small, prickly cucumber; also, the immature garden cucumber.

ghet'to (gĕt'ō), *n.; pl.* It. -TI (-tē), E. -TOS (-ōz). A quarter to which Jews are restricted for residence, or where they live in greatest numbers.

ghost (gōst), *n.* **1.** The soul; also, a disembodied soul; spirit; hence, an apparition; specter. **2.** Any faint shadowy semblance; a phantom.

ghost'ly (gōst'lĭ), *a.* [3] **1.** Spiritual; as, *ghostly* comfort. **2.** Pert. to or like a ghost or apparition.

ghoul (gōōl), *n.* Among Eastern nations, an evil being supposed to rob graves and feed on corpses. — **ghoul'ish,** *a.* [4].

gi'ant (jī'ănt), *n.* **1.** A mythical manlike being or monster of huge stature. **2.** A person, or an animal, plant, or thing, of extraordinary size or power. — *a.* [4] Gigantic. — **gi'ant-ess,** *n. fem.* [8].

gib'ber (jĭb'ẽr; gĭb'ẽr), *v. i. & t.* To speak rapidly and inarticulately; chatter.

gib'ber-ish (gĭb'ẽr-ĭsh), *n.* Rapid, inarticulate talk.

gib'bet (jĭb'ĕt), *n.* A kind of gallows. — *v. t.* To execute by hanging; hang on a gibbet; hence, to hold up to public scorn.

gib'bon (gĭb'ŭn), *n.* Any of several tailless, arboreal apes of southeastern Asia and the East Indies.

gib-bos'i-ty (gĭ-bŏs'ĭ-tĭ), *n.; pl.* -TIES (-tĭz). **1.** State or quality of being gibbous. **2.** A protuberance.

gib'bous (gĭb'ŭs), *a.* [4] **1.** Protuberant; convex, as the moon when nearly full. **2.** Hunched.

gibe (jīb), *v. i.* [1] To utter taunting, sarcastic words; jeer. — *v. t.* To reproach contemptuously; mock. — *n.* An expression of sarcastic scorn; sneer. — **gib'er** (jīb'ẽr), *n.* [8].

gib'lets (jĭb'lĕts), *n. pl.;* sometimes used in *sing.* The edible portions of a fowl that are removed before cooking, esp. the liver, gizzard, and heart.

gid'dy (gĭd'ĭ), *a.* [3] **1.** Having a sensation of whirling in the head; dizzy. **2.** Inducing giddiness. **3.** Marked by inconstancy; flighty. — **gid'-di-ly** (-ĭ-lĭ), *adv.* [8]. — **gid'di-ness,** *n.* [8].

gift (gĭft), *n.* **1.** The act, right, or power of giving. **2.** Anything given; a present. **3.** Endowment given to man by God; special talent.

gift'ed, *p. a.* Endowed with a gift; talented.

gig (gĭg), *n.* **1.** A light two-wheeled, one-horse carriage. **2.** A light ship's boat for oars or sail; also, a kind of rowboat.

gi-gan'tic (jī-găn'tĭk), *a.* [4] Like a giant.

gig'gle (gĭg'l), *v. i.* [1] To laugh with short catches of the breath; laugh in an affected or silly manner. — *n.* Act of giggling. — **gig'gler** (-lẽr), *n.* [8].

gild (gĭld). Var. of GUILD.

gild (gĭld), *v. t. ;* GILD'ED or GILT (gĭlt); GILD'ING. **1.** To overlay thinly with gold; cover or tinge with a golden color. **2.** To make attractive; embellish; as, to *gild* a falsehood. — **gild'er** (gĭl'dẽr), *n.* [8].

gild'ing, *vb. n.* **1.** Art of overlaying with gold or gilt, or the material used. **2.** A golden surface.

gill (jĭl), *n.* A liquid measure; ¼ of a pint.

gill (gĭl), *n.* An organ for respiration under water, as in fishes.

gil'ly-flow'er (jĭl'ĭ-flou'ẽr), *n.* **1.** The wallflower or the common stock. **2.** A purplish red variety of apple.

gilt (gĭlt), *n.* Gold or goldlike material spread over a surface; gilding. — *p. a.* Gilded.

gim'bals (gĭm'bălz; jĭm'bălz), *n. pl.* A contrivance for suspending anything, as a compass, so that it will remain level when its support is tipped.

gim'crack' (jĭm'krăk'), *n.* A fanciful trifle; a toy.

gim'let (gĭm'lĕt), *n.* A small boring tool with a screw point and cross handle.

gimp (gĭmp), *n.* A narrow trimming, having often a wire or a coarse cord running through it.

gin (jĭn), *n.* A strong distilled alcoholic liquor flavored with juniper berries.

gin (jĭn), *n.* **1.** A trap. **2.** A machine for moving heavy weights.

gin'ger (jĭn'jẽr), *n.* A tropical plant with pungent, aromatic rootstock; also, the rootstock.

gin'ger-bread' (-brĕd'), *n.* **1.** A kind of plain cake flavored with ginger. **2.** Something tawdry and unsubstantial.

gin'ger-ly (-lĭ), *adv.* Cautiously; timidly. — *a.* [4] Cautious; wary. [vored with ginger.

gin'ger-snap' (-snăp'), *n.* A thin, brittle cake fla-

ging'ham (gĭng'ăm), *n.* A cotton or linen cloth, woven of dyed yarn, usually in stripes or checks.

gin'seng (jĭn'sĕng), *n.* A plant, the root of which is valued in China as a drug; also, the root.

gip'sy. Var. of GYPSY.

gi-raffe' (jĭ-ráf'), *n.* A large cud-chewing animal of Africa with a very long and rather stiff neck; the cameleopard. It is the tallest of all animals.

gird (gûrd), *v. t. ; pret. & p. p.* GIRT (gûrt) or GIRD'ED ; *p. pr. & vb. n.* GIRD'ING. **1.** To encircle as with a belt; to make fast or secure, as clothing with a cord. **2.** To surround; encompass.

gird'er (gûr'dẽr), *n.* A horizontal beam to span an opening or carry a weight.

gir'dle (gûr'd'l), *n.* That which girds or encircles; esp., a belt or sash about the waist. — *v. t.* [1] **1.** To bind with or as with a belt. **2.** To remove a ring of bark around (a tree, etc.).

girl (gûrl), *n.* **1.** A female child ; a maiden. **2.** A female servant. — **-hood** (-hōōd), *n.* — **-ish,** *a.* [8].

girt (gûrt), *pret. & p. p.* of GIRD.

girth (gûrth), *n.* **1.** A band around an animal, to fasten a saddle, etc., on its back. **2.** A girdle. **3.** Measure around the body ; circumference.

gist (jĭst), *n.* The main point ; pith.

give (gĭv), *v. t.; pret.* GAVE (gāv) ; *p. p.* GIV'EN (gĭv'n) ; *p. pr. & vb. n.* GIV'ING. **1.** To bestow freely without a return. **2.** To deliver in exchange for something; pay, as money. **3.** To proffer, present, or furnish. **4.** To deliver, or execute by bodily action; as, to *give* a blow. **5.** To produce; emit; yield; as, the cow *gives* milk. **6.** To cause or occasion. **7.** To communicate; as, to *give* a cold to another. — *n.* Act of giving way or yielding.

giv'en (gĭv'n), *p. a.* **1.** Addicted; — with *to*; as, *given* to drink. **2.** Stated; as, in a *given* time. — given name, the Christian name. *Colloq.*

giv'er (-ẽr), *n.* One who gives; donor; grantor.

giz'zard (gĭz'ẽrd), *n.* The second stomach of birds, having a horny lining for grinding food.

|| **gla'cé'** (glà'sā'), *a.* [F.] Coated with icing; iced.

gla'cial (glā'shǎl), *a.* Pertaining to ice or its action; esp., pertaining to glaciers.

gla'ci-ate (-shǐ-āt), *v. t.* [1] To subject to glacial action, as rocks. — **gla'ci-a'tion** (-ā'shŭn), *n.*

gla'cier (glā'shẽr; glā'ī-ẽr), *n.* A body of ice, formed in a region of perpetual snow, and moving slowly down a mountain slope or valley, as in the Alps, or over an extended area, as in Greenland.

Glacier.

gla'cis (glā'sĭs; glā'ĭs), *n.* A gentle slope of earth, esp. one in front of a fortification.

glad (glăd), *a.*; **GLAD'DER** (-ẽr); **-DEST**. **1.** Characterized by joy or pleasure; pleased; happy. **2.** Expressive of, or exciting gladness. **3.** Characterized by brightness and beauty.

glad'den (glăd'n), *v. t. & i.* To make, be, or become, glad.

glade (glād), *n.* An open space in a forest.

glad'i-a'tor (glăd'ĭ-ā'tẽr), *n. Roman Hist.* One who fought with a weapon for the amusement of the people, as at a festival.

glad'i-a-to'ri-al (-à-tō'rĭ-ǎl), *a.* Of or pertaining to gladiators.

gla-di'o-lus (glà-dī'ō-lŭs; glăd'ĭ-ō'lŭs), *n.; pl.* L. **-OLI** (-lī), E. **-OLUSES** (-lŭs-ĕz). A plant, of the iris family, with erect sword-shaped leaves and spikes of brilliant flowers; a flower of this plant.

glad'ly (glăd'lĭ), *adv.* With gladness; cheerfully.

glad'ness, *n.* State or quality of being glad.

glad'some (-sŭm), *a.* [4] Causing joy; expressive of gladness; pleased; cheerful. — **-ly,** *adv.* [8].

glair (glâr), *n.* White of egg; also, any similar adhesive substance. — **glair'y** (glâr'ĭ), *a.* [3].

glaive (glāv), *n.* A sword; esp., a broadsword.

glam'our (glăm'ẽr), *n.* Magic; a spell; a charm.

glance (glȧns), *v. i.* [1] **1.** To strike obliquely and fly off or turn aside. **2.** To flash; gleam. **3.** To look with a sudden, rapid cast of the eye. — *n.* **1.** A sudden movement causing a flash of light; flash so produced. **2.** Quick look; glimpse.

gland (glănd), *n.* A secreting organ of the body.

glan'ders (glăn'dẽrz), *n.* An infectious and destructive disease of horses, asses, etc.

glan'du-lar (-dṳ-lȧr), *a.* Of, or pert. to, a gland.

glare (glâr), *v. i.* [1] **1.** To shine dazzlingly. **2.** To stare with fierce or piercing eyes. — *v. t.* To shoot out or express with a glare; as, he *glared* defiance. — *n.* **1.** A dazzling light; showiness. **2.** A fierce or piercing stare.

glare, *n.* A bright, glassy surface, as of ice. *U. S.*

glar'ing (glâr'ĭng), *p. a.* [4] **1.** Fierce or piercing; — said of eyes. **2.** Dazzling. **3.** Open and bold; notorious; as, a *glaring* crime.

glass (glȧs), *n.* **1.** A hard, brittle, and, usually, transparent substance made by fusing together silica, as sand, an alkali, as potash or soda, and some other ingredient, as lime or lead oxide. **2.** Collectively, articles made of glass. **3.** Anything of glass; as: **a** A glass vessel, a tumbler; goblet; hence, the contents of such a vessel, as liquor; a drink. **b** An hourglass. **c** A mirror. **d** An optical glass; a lens; telescope; microscope; *pl.* eyeglasses; spectacles. **e** A barometer; thermometer.

glass'ful (glȧs'fŏŏl), *n.; pl.* **-FULS** (-fŏŏlz). The contents of a glass; as much as a glass will hold.

glass'i-ly (-ĭ-lĭ), *adv.* In a glassy manner.

glass'i-ness, *n.* Quality or state of being glassy.

glass'ware (glȧs'wâr'), *n.* Articles of glass.

glass'y (-ĭ), *a.* [3] **1.** Resembling glass, as in smoothness. **2.** Dull; — of the eye or look.

glaze (glāz), *v. t.* [1] **1.** To furnish or fit (a window, etc.) with glass. **2.** To overlay with a surface of or like glass. — *v. i.* To become glazed. — *n.* **1.** A smooth, glossy surface or coating, esp. one that is transparent. **2.** A substance for glazing. — **glaz'er** (glāz'ẽr), *n.* [8].

gla'zier (glā'zhẽr; -zĭ-ẽr), *n.* One whose business is to set glass in window frames, etc.

glaz'ing (glāz'ĭng), *vb. n.* **1.** Act of furnishing or fitting with glass. **2.** Act of laying on glaze; also, the glaze applied.

gleam (glēm), *n.* A moderate brightness; a beam; glow. — *v. i.* To dart, as rays of light; send out gleams. — *v. t.* To emit (flashes of light, etc.).

glean (glēn), *v. t.* **1.** To gather (as grain) after a reaper or the like. **2.** To gather from (a field or vineyard) what has been left, as by reapers. **3.** To collect with patient labor; pick out. — *v. i.* **1.** To gather what is left by reapers. **2.** To pick up or gather anything by degrees. — **glean'er,** *n.* [8].

glebe (glēb), *n.* **1.** Soil; ground; sod. **2.** A piece of land assigned to a clergyman as part of his benefice.

glee (glē), *n.* **1.** *Music.* An unaccompanied vocal piece for three or more voices (usually men's), with one voice to a part. **2.** Joy; merriment.

glee'ful (glē'fŏŏl), *a.* Full of glee; merry; gay.

glee'some (-sŭm), *a.* [3] Merry; joyous; gleeful.

glen (glĕn), *n.* A secluded, narrow valley.

glib (glĭb), *a.* [3] Flippantly smooth; fluent. — **-ly,** *adv.* [8] — **-ness,** *n.* [8].

glide (glīd), *v. i.* [1] **1.** To move smoothly; pass silently and easily. — *n.* Act of gliding.

glid'er (glīd'ẽr), *n.* One who, or that which, glides; a form of airplane having no power plant.

glid'ing (glīd'ĭng), *p. pr. & vb. n.* of GLIDE. — **gliding boat,** a hydroplane. — **g. machine,** a glider.

glim'mer (glĭm'ẽr), *v. i.* To give out feeble or scattered rays of light. — *n.* A faint, unsteady light; a gleam; shimmer.

---

glim′mer-ing (glĭm′ẽr-ĭng), *vb. n.* A faint, unsteady light; hence, a faint view or idea; inkling.

glimpse (glĭmps), *n.* **1.** A faint appearance. **2.** A short, hurried view. — *v. i.* [1] **1.** To shine faintly or unsteadily; glimmer. **2.** To take a glimpse; glance. — *v. t.* To catch a glimpse of.

glint (glĭnt), *v. i. & t.* To flash; gleam; glitter. — *n.* A gleam; flash.

glis′ten (glĭs′n), *v. i.* To sparkle or shine; esp., to shine with a fitful luster. — *n.* A glistening; a shining brightness.

glis′ter (-tẽr), *v. i.* To glitter. — *n.* Glitter.

glit′ter (glĭt′ẽr), *v. i.* **1.** To sparkle with light; gleam. **2.** To be showy, or striking, and hence attractive. — *n.* A bright, sparkling light.

gloam′ing (glōm′ĭng), *n.* Twilight; dusk.

gloat (glōt), *v. i.* To gaze or to meditate, esp. with malign satisfaction, or avarice.

globe (glōb), *n.* **1.** A spherical body; ball; sphere; orb. **2.** The earth; — with *the.* **3.** A spherical representation of the earth or heavens.

glo′bose′ (glō′bōs′), *a.* [4] Globular, or nearly so.

glob′u-lar (glŏb′û-lär), *a.* [4] **1.** Globe-shaped; spherical. **2.** Composed of globules.

glob′ule (-ūl), *n.* A little globe; a spherical particle.

gloom (glōom), *n.* Partial or total darkness; deep shade; hence, low spirits. — *v. i.* To become dark or threatening, as the sky; appear gloomy.

gloom′y (glōom′ĭ), *a.* [3] **1.** Dusky; dim. **2.** Affected with or expressing gloom; melancholy. **3.** Producing, or marked by, gloom; dismal. — **gloom′i-ly** (-ĭ-lĭ), *adv.* [8] — **-ness**, *n.* [8].

glo′ri-fi-ca′tion (glō′rĭ-fĭ-kā′shŭn), *n.* A glorifying, or state of being glorified.

glo′ri-fy (glō′rĭ-fī), *v. t.* [2] **1.** To make glorious; bestow honor and distinction upon. **2.** To render homage to; adore. — **glo′ri-fi′er**, *n.* [8].

glo′ri-ous (-ŭs), *a.* [4] **1.** Exhibiting qualities that deserve glory; illustrious. **2.** Splendid. **3.** Delightful. *Colloq.* — **-ly**, *adv.* [8].

glo′ry (glō′rĭ), *n.; pl.* -RIES (-rĭz). **1.** Praise, admiration, or distinction, accorded by common consent; renown. **2.** That which secures praise or renown. **3.** Brilliancy; radiant beauty. **4.** Celestial honor or splendor; heaven. **5.** Height of prosperity or splendor. — *v. i.* [2] To exult; rejoice; also, to be proud or boastful.

gloss (glŏs), *n.* **1.** Luster; polish. **2.** A fair, but deceptive, appearance; superficial quality or show. — *v. t.* **1.** To give luster or gloss to; glaze. **2.** To give a gloss, or specious appearance, to; — often with *over.*

gloss (glŏs), *n.* An interlinear, marginal, or other note of explanation or interpretation. — *v. t. & i.* To furnish with glosses; annotate.

glos′sa-ry (glŏs′à-rĭ), *n.; pl.* -RIES (-rĭz). A collection of glosses; a partial dictionary of a work, explaining the hard words, etc.

gloss′y (glŏs′ĭ), *a.* [3] **1.** Smooth and shining; polished. **2.** Smooth; plausible. — **gloss′i-ly** (-ĭ-lĭ), *adv.* [8] — **-i-ness**, *n.* [8].

glot′tis (glŏt′ĭs), *n.* The opening from the pharynx into the larynx. — **glot′tal** (glŏt′ăl), *a.*

glove (glŭv), *n.* A cover for the hand with a separate sheath for each finger. — *v. t.* [1] To cover with or as with a glove.

glov′er (-ẽr), *n.* One who makes or sells gloves.

glow (glō), *v. i.* **1.** To shine with an intense heat. **2.** To exhibit a strong, bright color; be brilliant or red, as the sky, at sunset. **3.** To feel hot; burn. **4.** To feel the heat of passion; be animated. — *n.* **1.** White or red heat as of a solid body; incandescence. **2.** Redness. **3.** Earnestness; ardor. **4.** Bodily warmth, as from exercise.

glow′er (glou′ẽr), *v. i.* To stare angrily.

glow′worm′ (glō′wûrm′), *n.* Any of various luminous insects or insect larvæ.

gloze (glōz), *v. t.* To smooth over; to palliate.

glu′cose (glōō′kōs), *n.* **1.** A sugar about half as sweet as cane sugar, usually made from starch. **2.** A sirup got by imperfect conversion of starch into glucose.

glue (glōō), *n.* **1.** A brownish gelatin, got by boiling skins, hoofs, etc., of animals, and used when heated with water as a cement. **2.** Any of various sticky substances. — *v. t.* [1] To join or fix with or as with glue; fasten. — **glu′ey** (-ĭ), *a.* [3].

glum (glŭm), *a.;* GLUM′MER (-ẽr); GLUM′MEST. Moody; sullen; gloomy. — **glum′ly**, *adv.* [8] — **glum′ness**, *n.* [8].

glume (glōōm), *n.* One of the chaffy scales of the spikelet in sedges and grasses.

glut (glŭt), *v. t.;* GLUT′TED; GLUT′TING. To swallow greedily; gorge; gulp.

glut, *v. t.* **1.** To fill to satiety; satiate; overload; surfeit. **2.** To overstock. — *v. i.* To eat gluttonously or to satiety. — *n.* **1.** A full supply; often, a surfeit. **2.** A supply of mercantile goods in excess of the demand at the seller's price.

glu′ten (glōō′tĕn), *n.* The sticky, tenacious, nutritious substance giving adhesiveness to dough.

glu′ti-nous (-tĭ-nŭs), *a.* [4] Of the nature of or resembling glue; sticky; gluey.

glut′ton (glŭt′n), *n.* **1.** A voracious eater; gormandizer. **2.** A wolverene.

glut′ton-ous (-ŭs), *a.* [4] Given to gluttony; voracious. — **glut′ton-ous-ly**, *adv.* [8].

glut′ton-y (-ĭ), *n.* Excess in eating.

glyc′er-in, glyc′er-ine (glĭs′ẽr-ĭn), *n.* A sweet, sirupy, colorless liquid obtained from fats and oils.

gnarl (närl), *n.* A knot in wood, esp. a large or hard knot, or the like, on a tree. — **gnarled** (närld), *a.* [4] — **gnarl′y** (när′lĭ), *a.* [4].

gnash (năsh), *v. t. & t.* To grind or strike (the teeth) together, as in anger or pain.

gnat (năt), *n.* Any of various small two-winged flies, esp. such as bite.

gnaw (nô), *v. t. & i.* **1.** To bite with repeated effort, esp. so as to wear away. **2.** To corrode; fret away. — **gnaw′er** (nô′ẽr), *n.* [8].

gneiss (nis), *n.* A rock resembling granite.

gnome (nōm), *n.* One of an imaginary race of dwarfs dwelling in the inner parts of the earth.

gno′mon (nō′mŏn), *n.* The style, pin, or the like of a sundial that, by its shadow, shows the time.

gnu (nōō; nū), *n.* An African antelope, with oxlike head, long mane, curved horns, and flowing tail.

go (gō), *v. i.; pret.* WENT (wĕnt); *p. p.* GONE (gŏn); *p. pr. & vb. n.* GO′ING. **1.** To pass from one place to another; proceed. **2.** To depart. **3.** To be habitually; as, to *go* unpunished. **4.** To pass away; be lost, spent, sold, etc. **5.** To be suited, as a song to a tune. **6.** To have recourse or resort. **7.** To extend; lead; reach; run.

☞ *Go* is used with many prepositions and adverbs in which, and not in the verb, lies the chief force of the expression; as, to *go against*, *into*, etc.

☞ The present participle **going** is specially used with an infinitive to express a future of intention; as, I was *going* to answer; we are *going* to play ball. — *n. Colloq. in all senses.* **1.** Energy; spirit. **2.** A turn of affairs, esp. an embarrassing one. **3.** A chance; turn. **4.** Something that is successful; an agreement. **5.** With *the*, the fashion; the rage.

goad (gōd), *n.* **1.** A pointed rod used to urge on a beast. **2.** Something like, or suggestive of, a goad, esp. in its effect. — *v. t.* To prick; drive with or as with a goad; — often with *on*, *to*, or *into*.

goal (gōl), *n.* **1.** The bound or point where a race or journey is to end. **2.** The final purpose, end, or aim. **3.** In various games, a bound which must be passed or gone through to score. **4.** The winning of a goal, or the score so made.

goat (gōt), *n.* Any of certain hollow-horned cud-chewing animals closely allied to the sheep.

goat′ee (gō′tē′), *n.* A beard on the chin, trimmed in a tuft like the beard of a he-goat.

gob′ble (gŏb′'l), *v. t.* [1] To swallow greedily; gulp.

gob′ble, *v. t. & i.* To utter (the cry of a turkey cock). — *n.* The characteristic noise made in the throat by the turkey cock.

gob′bler (gŏb′lẽr), *n.* A turkey cock.

go′-be-tween′, *n.* One that goes between persons with messages, etc.; an intermediary.

gob′let (gŏb′lĕt), *n.* **1.** A wine cup. *Archaic.* **2.** A drinking glass with a foot and stem.

gob′lin (-lĭn), *n.* A sprite usually conceived as ugly or grotesque and as mischievous or evil.

go′cart′ (gō′kärt′), *n.* A kind of baby carriage.

god (gŏd), *n.* **1.** A being of more than human attributes and powers; a deity, esp. a male deity. **2.** Any object thought to be endowed with divine powers; an idol. **3.** [*cap.*] The Supreme Being.

god′child′ (-chīld′), *n.* One for whom a person becomes sponsor at baptism.

god′daugh′ter (-dô′tẽr), *n.* A female godchild.

god′dess (gŏd′ĕs), *n.* A female god.

god′fa′ther (-fä′thẽr), *n.* A male sponsor, as for a child at baptism.

god′head (-hĕd), *n.* **1.** Deity; divinity; godhood. **2.** [*cap.*] The Deity; God.

god′hood (-hŏŏd), *n.* Godhead.

god′less, *a.* [4] Having or acknowledging no God; impious. — **god′less-ness**, *n.* [8].

god′like′ (-līk′), *a.* [4] Like a god or God; divine.

god′ly (-lĭ), *a.* [3] Pious; reverencing God; devout; righteous. — **god′li-ness** (-lĭ-nĕs), *n.* [8].

god′moth′er (-mŭth′ẽr), *n.* A woman sponsor at baptism.

god′par′ent (-pâr′ĕnt), *n.* Godfather or godmother.

god′send′ (gŏd′sĕnd′), *n.* Some desirable or needed thing coming unexpectedly, as if sent by God.

god′son′ (-sŭn′), *n.* A male godchild.

God′speed′ (-spēd′), *n.* Success; prosperous journeying; — contraction of "*God speed* you."

go′er (gō′ẽr), *n.* One that goes; a runner or walker.

gog′gle (gŏg′'l), *v. i.* [1] To squint; roll the eyes. — *n. pl.* A kind of spectacles with the lenses set in short tubes or collars to protect the eyes from dust, etc. — *a.* Protruding; staring; — of the eyes.

go′ing (gō′ĭng), *vb. n.* **1.** Departure. **2.** Condition of the ground or of a road, etc., as for traveling.

goi′ter (goi′tẽr), *n.* [6] An enlargement of a certain gland of the neck.

gold (gōld), *n.* **1.** A precious metal of yellow color, — the most malleable and ductile metal, and one of the heaviest substances known. **2.** Gold coin; riches. **3.** The yellow color of the metal.

gold′beat′er (-bēt′ẽr), *n.* One who beats or hammers gold into gold leaf. — **gold′beat′ing**, *n.*

gold′en (gōl′d'n), *a.* **1.** Of or pertaining to gold. **2.** Of the color of gold. **3.** Precious; excellent. **4.** Prosperous and happy. — **-ly**, *adv.* [8].

gold′en-rod′ (-rŏd′), *n.* Any of various plants of the aster family with heads of yellow flowers.

gold′-filled′ (-fĭld′), *a.* Jewelry. Covered with a layer of gold of appreciable thickness.

gold′finch′ (gōld′fĭnch′), *n.* Any of various yellow or partly yellow finches.

gold′fish′ (-fĭsh′), *n.* A small fish, of golden color.

gold′smith′ (gōld′smĭth′), *n.* A worker in gold.

golf (gŏlf), *n.* A game in which a small, hard ball is struck with clubs so as to drive it into a series of holes. — *v. i.* To play golf. — **golf′er**, *n.* [8].

gon′do-la (gŏn′dô-là), *n.* A kind of boat used in the canals of Venice.

gon′do-lier′ (-lēr′), *n.* A

Gondola.

man who propels a gondola, by rowing or by poling.

gone (gŏn), *p. p. & p. a.* of GO.

gong (gŏng), *n.* **1.** A metallic disk with upturned rim, producing, when struck, a harsh, resounding tone. **2.** A kind of saucer-shaped bell.

good (gŏŏd), *a.; compar.* BET′TER (bĕt′ẽr); *superl.* BEST (bĕst). **1.** Having desirable qualities; sufficient or satisfactory. **2.** Beneficial; fortunate. **3.** Agreeable; pleasant; cheerful. **4.** Morally excellent; virtuous; well-behaved. **5.** Reliable or genuine; as, *good* money. **6.** Ample; full. **7.** Considerable; — esp. in *a good deal*, *a good while*, etc. — **Good Friday**, the Friday of Holy Week, kept as the anniversary of Christ's crucifixion. — *n.* **1.** That which is good. **2.** Welfare; benefit. — *interj.* An expression of satisfaction; — often with *very*.

good′-by′ } (gŏŏd′bī′), *n. or interj.* Farewell; —
good′-bye′ } contraction of *God be with ye*.

good′-hu′mored, *a.* [4, 5] Having a good humor.

good′ly (-lĭ), *a.* **1.** Of pleasing appearance, or quality; comely; excellent. **2.** Large; considerable. — **good′li-ness** (gŏŏd′lĭ-nĕs), *n.* [8].

good nature, Kindly nature or disposition. — **-na′tured** (-nā′tũrd), *a.* [4] — **-ly**, *adv.* [8].

good′ness, *n.* Quality or state of being good; excellence; virtue; kindness; beneficence.

goods (gŏŏdz), *n. pl.* Wares; chattels; property.

good′-tem′pered, *a.* [4] Having a good temper.

good will, *or*, *esp. in sense* 2, **good′will′**, *n.* **1.** Benevolence; kindly feeling; heartiness. **2.** The custom or popularity which a business has acquired beyond the mere value of what it sells.

good'y, *n.*; *pl.* GOODIES (-ĭz). A bonbon, cake, etc.; — usually in *pl. Colloq.* — *a.* Sentimentally or affectedly good; — often in the form **good'y-good'y**. *Colloq.*

good'y, *n.* An appellation of civility for a woman, esp. a lowly one; hence, such a woman.

goose (gōōs), *n.*; *pl.* GEESE (gēs), *n.* **1.** Any of various web-footed birds, larger than ducks but smaller than swans. **2.** A simpleton. **3.** (*pl.* GOOSES.) A tailor's smoothing iron; — from its bent handle.

goose'ber-ry (gōōz'bĕr-ĭ; gōōs'-), *n.*; *pl.* -RIES (-ĭz). The acid, usually hairy berry of any of several species of shrubs; also, any of these shrubs.

goose flesh. The peculiar roughness of the skin often produced by cold or fear.

go'pher (gō'fẽr), *n.* **1.** Any of certain American burrowing rodents having very large outside cheek pouches. **2.** Any of numerous small, striped ground squirrels of the North American prairies.

gore (gōr), *n.* Blood; esp., clotted blood.

gore, *n.* Any triangular piece of cloth used in a garment, sail, etc., to vary the width. — *v. t.* [1] To cut into, or provide with, a gore.

gore, *v. t. & i.* To pierce or wound as with a horn.

gorge (gôrj), *n.* **1.** A hawk's crop; hence, stomach; maw. *Archaic.* **2.** A meal, esp. a full meal. *Archaic.* **3.** A narrow passage; a defile; pass; steep, rocky ravine. — **to have the gorge rise** (at), to be filled with extreme disgust or resentment. — **to rouse** (*or* **stir**) **the gorge**, to make very angry. — *v. i.* [1] To fill the gorge, or stomach; eat greedily. — *v. t.* **1.** To fill the stomach of; glut. **2.** To swallow, esp. greedily.

gor'geous (gôr'jŭs), *a.* [4] Imposing through splendid or various coloring; magnificent; dazzling. — **-ly**, *adv.* [8] — **-ness**, *n.* [8].

go-ril'la (gō-rĭl'á), *n.* The largest anthropoid ape.

gor'mand-ize (gôr'mặn-dīz), *v. i. & t.* [1] To eat greedily or ravenously. — **-iz'er**, *n.* [8].

gorse (gôrs), *n.* Furze. *Eng.* —

gors'y, *a.* [3].

gor'y (gōr'ĭ), *a.* [3] Covered with gore; murderous.

gos'hawk (gŏs'hôk), *n.* Any of certain rather large short-winged hawks.

gos'ling (gŏz'lĭng), *n.* A young goose.

gos'pel (gŏs'pĕl), *n.* **1.** The teachings of Christ and the apostles. **2.** [*Usually cap.*] One of the four New Testament narratives of the life of Jesus: "Matthew," "Mark," "Luke," and "John." **3.** [*Usually cap.*] A selection from one of the four Gospels, used in a religious service. — *a.* Accordant with, or relating to, the gospel.

gos'sa-mer (gŏs'á-mẽr), *n.* **1.** A film of cobwebs,

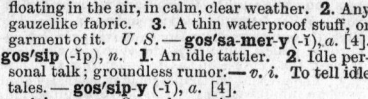

Gorilla.

floating in the air, in calm, clear weather. **2.** Any gauzelike fabric. **3.** A thin waterproof stuff, or garment of it. *U. S.* — **gos'sa-mer-y** (-ĭ), *a.* [4].

gos'sip (-ĭp), *n.* **1.** An idle tattler. **2.** Idle personal talk; groundless rumor. — *v. i.* To tell idle tales. — **gos'sip-y** (-ĭ), *a.* [4].

gos'sip-er, *n.* One who gossips.

got (gŏt), *pret. & p. p.* of GET.

Goth'ic (gŏth'ĭk), *a.* Pertaining to or designating a style of architecture characterized by pointed arches and steep roofs. — *n.* Gothic style or decoration.

got'ten (gŏt''n), *p. p.* of GET. See GET.

gouge (gouj), *n.* **1.** A kind of chisel. **2.** A cavity made with or as with a gouge. *Colloq., U. S.* — *v. t.* [1] To scoop out as with a gouge. — **goug'er**, *n.* [8].

gourd (gōrd), *n.* Any of various fleshy, many-seeded fruits, allied to the pumpkin, melon, etc.; also, any of the plants bearing these fruits or the dried hard shell of the fruit, used as a bottle, cup, etc.

gour'mand (gōōr'mănd), *n.* A luxurious eater.

gout (gout), *n.* **1.** A drop; clot. **2.** A disease marked by painful inflammation of the joints, esp. the joint of the great toe.

gout'y (gout'ĭ), *a.* [3] **1.** Diseased with the gout. **2.** Swollen as if from gout. **3.** Of, like, or causing, gout. — **gout'i-ness**, *n.* [8].

gov'ern (gŭv'ẽrn), *v. t.* **1.** To direct; control; restrain; manage. **2.** *Gram.* To require to be (in a particular case or mood); to require (a particular case or mood). — **gov'ern-a-ble**, *a.* [8]. — *v. i.* To administer the laws; to rule.

gov'ern-ess (-ẽr-nĕs), *n.* A woman teacher, esp. in a private household.

gov'ern-ment (-ẽrn-mĕnt), *n.* **1.** A governing; control; direction of affairs of state. **2.** Mode or system of governing; as, a democratic *government*. **3.** A country governed. **4.** The person or persons authorized to administer the laws; the administration. — **gov'ern-men'tal** (-mĕn'tặl), *a.*

gov'er-nor (-ẽr-nẽr), *n.* **1.** One who governs; esp., the chief executive of a State. **2.** An automatic attachment to an engine for controlling its speed. — **gov'er-nor-ship'**, *n.*

gown (goun), *n.* A loose, flowing outer garment; as: **a** The ordinary outer dress of a woman. **b** A nightgown. **c** The official or distinctive robe of office, profession, or the like. — *v. t.* To clothe in, or invest with, a gown.

A Form of Governor, 2.

grab (grăb), *v. t. & i.*; GRABBED (grăbd); GRAB'BING. To snatch; seize; hence, to take unscrupulously. — *n.* Act of grabbing.

grace (grās), *n.* **1.** Good will; favor; disposition to show mercy, etc. **2.** The mercy of God; enjoyment of divine favor. **3.** A blessing asked, or thanks rendered, at a meal. **4.** [*Usually cap.*] Title given to a duke, duchess, or archbishop. **5.** A sense of right; as, he had the *grace* to return. **6.** A pleasing or attractive characteristic; attractiveness; charm. — *v. t.* [1] To adorn; honor.

grace'ful (-fŏŏl), *a.* [4] Displaying grace; elegant; felicitous; tactful. — **grace'ful-ly**, *adv.* [8].

grace'less, *a.* [4] Lacking in grace; depraved.

gra'cious (grā'shŭs), *a.* [4] **1.** Attractive; acceptable. **2.** Abounding in grace, or mercy; kindly; merciful. — **-ly**, *adv.* [8] — **-ness**, *n.* [8].

grack'le (grăk'l), *n.* Any of certain birds of the family including the American blackbirds, etc.

gra-da'tion (gra-dā'shŭn), *n.* **1.** A series forming successive stages or grades. **2.** Any degree or relative position in an order or series.

grade (grād), *n.* **1.** A step or degree in any series or order; a class of things of the same relative quality or value. In elementary schools, a division of the course; also, the pupils working in any division. **2.** Rate of ascent or descent of a road, etc.; also, an incline. — *v.t.* [1] **1.** To arrange in grades; class; sort. **2.** To reduce to a level, or to an evenly progressive grade, as a road. — *v.i.* To be graded; be of a grade.

gra'di-ent (grā'dĭ-ĕnt), *a.* A part of a road which slopes upward or downward; a grade.

grad'u-al (grăd'ū-ăl), *a.* Proceeding by steps or degrees. — **-al-ly**, *adv.* [8] — **-al-ness**, *n.* [8].

grad'u-ate (-āt), *n.* One who has been graduated. — (-āt), *v.t.* [1] **1.** To admit to a certain grade or degree, as at the close of a course of study, to a standing defined by a diploma. **2.** To mark with, or divide into, degrees or grades; grade. — *v.i.* **1.** To become a graduate, as of a college. **2.** To pass or change by degrees. — *a.* That has been graduated; of or pertaining to graduates.

grad'u-a'tion (-ā'shŭn), *n.* **1.** A graduating; state of being graduated. **2.** A mark or marks on an instrument or vessel to indicate degrees or quantity.

graft (gràft), *n.* **1.** A small shoot of a tree inserted in or attached to another tree so as to become a living part of it; also, a branch or portion of a tree growing from such a shoot. **2.** Acquisition of money, position, etc., by dishonest, unjust, or parasitic methods; also, anything so gained. *Colloq.* — *v.t.* **1.** To insert (a graft) in or on; to join as if by grafting. **2.** To get by graft. *Colloq.* — *v.i.* **1.** To be or become grafted. **2.** To insert or implant as a graft. — **graft'er** (gràf'tĕr), *n.* [8].

Grafts.

Gra'ham flour (grā'ăm). Unbolted wheat flour.

grail (grāl), *n.* A platter; a chalice; — used only [*cap.*] of the *Holy Grail*, in medieval legends, the platter, or the chalice, used by Christ at the Last Supper, and later brought to England.

grain (grān), *n.* **1.** The seed or seedlike fruit of any cereal grass, as wheat, maize, oats, rice, etc. **2.** Collectively: The seeds or fruits of cereal grasses; also, the plants themselves. **3.** Any small, hard particle, as of sand, sugar, etc.; hence, any minute portion. **4.** The unit of the English system of weights. The pound avoirdupois contains 7,000 grains. A grain = .0648 gram. **5.** Texture; fiber, as of wood, etc. **6.** Temper; natural disposition. — *v.i. & t.* **1.** To form grains or into grains; granulate. **2.** To paint in imitation of the grain of wood, etc. — **grain'er.** *n.* [8].

gram (grăm), *n.* The unit of weight in the metric system. It is equivalent to 15.432 grains.

gra-min'e-ous (gra-mĭn'ē-ŭs), *a.* Grasslike.

gram'i-niv'o-rous (grăm'ĭ-nĭv'ō-rŭs), *a.* Feeding on grass and like food.

gram'mar (grăm'ĕr), *n.* **1.** The science or art treating of the classes of words, their inflections, syntax, etc. **2.** Manner of speaking or writing, in reference to conformity to grammatical rules. — **gram-ma'ri-an** (gra-mā'rĭ-ăn), *n.* — **gram-mat'i-cal** (gra-măt'ĭ-kăl), *a.* **1.** Of or pertaining to grammar. **2.** According to the rules of grammar. — **gram-mat'i-cal-ly**, *adv.* [8].

gramme. Var. of GRAM.

gram'pus (grăm'pŭs), *n.* A small whale allied to the blackfish.

gran'a-ry (grăn'a-rĭ), *n.; pl.* -RIES (-rĭz). A storehouse for grain, esp. after it is threshed.

grand (grănd), *a.* [3] **1.** Preëminent; chief; hence, great; prominent. **2.** Marked by great magnificence, display, or formality; possessing wealth or high social standing. **3.** Fine or imposing; magnificent; sublime. — **grand'ly**, *adv.* [8].

grand'child (grănd'chīld'), *n.* Child of one's son or daughter.

grand'daugh'ter (-dô'tĕr), *n.* A female grandchild.

gran-dee' (grăn-dē'), *n.* In Spain and Portugal, a nobleman of the first rank; hence, any man of high rank or station.

gran'deur (grăn'dūr), *n.* State or quality of being grand; magnificence.

grand'fa'ther (grănd'fä'thĕr), *n.* Father of one's father or mother; any forefather. — **-ly**, *a.* [8].

gran-dil'o-quence (grăn-dĭl'ō-kwĕns), *n.* Quality of being grandiloquent; bombast.

gran-dil'o-quent (grăn-dĭl'ō-kwĕnt), *a.* [4] Speaking in, or marked by, a lofty style; pompous.

gran'di-ose (grăn'dĭ-ōs), *a.* [4] **1.** Impressive or elevating in effect. **2.** Affectedly grand or splendid; pompous. — **-ly**, *adv.* [8].

grand'moth'er (grănd'mŭth'ĕr), *n.* Mother of one's father or mother; any female ancestor more remote than a mother. — **grand'moth'er-ly**, *a.*

grand'par'ent (-pâr'ĕnt), *n.* A parent's parent.

grand'sire' (-sīr'), *n.* A grandfather. *Archaic.*

grand'son' (-sŭn'), *n.* A son's or daughter's son.

grange (grānj), *n.* **1.** A farm; esp., a farmhouse with its outbuildings. **2.** *U. S.* **a** One of the lodges of the "Patrons of Husbandry," an association of farmers. **b** [*cap.*] Popularly, the association itself.

gran'ite (grăn'ĭt), *n.* A very hard crystalline granular rock, consisting of quartz, feldspar, and mica.

granite ware. A kind of enameled ironware.

gra-nit'ic (grā-nĭt'ĭk), *a.* Of or like granite.

grant (grànt), *v.t.* **1.** To agree to; accord. **2.** To give. **3.** To admit; concede. — *n.* **1.** Act of granting; concession. **2.** Thing or property granted; gift. **3.** A transfer of property by deed or writing.

gran-tee' (grán-tē'), *n.* *Law.* One to whom a grant is made.

grant'or (grán'tŏr; grán-tôr'), *n.* *Law.* One by whom a grant is made.

gran'u-lar (grăn'ū-lår), *a.* Consisting of grains or granules; granulated.

gran'u-late (-lāt), *v.t. & i.* [1] **1.** To form or collect into grains or granules. **2.** To raise in granules; make rough. — **gran'u-lat'ed** (-lāt'ĕd), *p. a.*

gran'u-la'tion (-lā'shŭn), *n.* **1.** A granulating;

state of being granulated. **2.** One of the grains of a granulated surface.

gran'ule (grăn'ūl), *n.* A little grain ; pellet.

grape (grāp), *n.* **1.** The berry of the grapevine. **2.** A grapevine. **3.** Grapeshot.

grape'fruit' (grāp'frōōt'), *n.* A tropical fruit with bitter rind and acid pulp.

grap'er-y (grāp'ẽr-ĭ), *n. ; pl.* -ERIES. An inclosure for cultivation of grapes.

grape'shot' (grāp'shŏt'), *n.* A cluster of small iron balls, to be shot from a cannon.

grape'vine' (grāp'vīn'), *n.* A vine bearing smooth berries in clusters.

graph'ic (grăf'ĭk)) *a.* [4] **1.** Of or pertaining to
graph'i-cal (-ĭ-kăl)) the arts of painting, drawing, and writing. **2.** Well delineated ; vividly described. **3.** Pertaining to or designating representation by diagrams, lines, etc. — **-i-cal-ly**, *adv.* [8].

graph'ite (-īt), *n.* Soft black carbon of metallic luster, used for lead pencils, as a lubricator, etc.

graph'o-phone (-ŏ-fōn), *n.* A kind of phonograph. *Trade-mark Name.*

grap'nel (grăp'nĕl), *n.* **1.** An instrument for grappling something, as a ship's rigging. **2.** A kind of small anchor.

grap'ple (-'l), *n.* **1.** A grapnel. **2.** A seizing or seizure ; close hug in contest. — *v. t.* [1] To seize, hold, or fasten, as with a grapnel ; lay fast hold of. — *v. i.* To use a grapple ; contend in close fight; seize one another.

Grapnel, 2.

grasp (gråsp), *v. i.* To make the motion of seizing ; clutch. — *v. t.* **1.** To seize and hold by or as by clasping ; catch. **2.** To lay hold of with the mind ; comprehend. — *n.* **1.** A grasping ; embrace. **2.** Reach; power of seizing and holding physically or mentally. **3.** Forcible holding; possession. **4.** Mental hold, or comprehension. — **grasp'er**, *n.* [8].

grasp'ing, *p. a.* Avaricious; greedy.

grass (gràs), *n.* Green herbage affording food for grazing animals; esp., the true grasses, plants having jointed stems, and narrow sheathing leaves.

grass'hop'per (-hŏp'ẽr), *n.* A leaping insect allied to the cricket, etc.

grass'y (gràs'ĭ), *a.* [3] **1.** Covered with grass. **2.** Resembling grass; green.

grate (grāt), *v. t.* [1] **1.** To reduce to particles by rubbing with something rough. **2.** To produce (a harsh sound) as by grinding. — *v. i.* To make a harsh sound; have a harsh or rasping effect.

grate, *n.* **1.** A frame of parallel or crossed bars, as in a window. **2.** Frame of iron bars to hold burning fuel. — *v. t.* To furnish with a grate or grates.

grate'ful (-fŏŏl), *a.* **1.** Having a due sense of benefits received. **2.** Affording pleasure ; pleasing; gratifying. — **-ly**, *adv.* [8] — **-ness**, *n.* [8].

grat'er (grāt'ẽr), *n.* One that grates; esp., a utensil with a rough surface, for grating a substance.

grat'i-fi-ca'tion (grăt'ĭ-fĭ-kā'shŭn), *n.* **1.** A gratifying, or state of being gratified. **2.** Something that gratifies ; a reward ; recompense; gratuity.

grat'i-fy (grăt'ĭ-fī), *v. t.* [2] To give or afford pleasure or satisfaction to; hence, to oblige; favor.

grat'ing (grāt'ĭng), *n.* A partition, covering, or frame of parallel or cross bars; a grate.

gra'tis (grā'tĭs), *adv.* For nothing; freely.

grat'i-tude (grăt'ĭ-tūd), *n.* State of being grateful ; thankfulness.

gra-tu'i-tous (grá-tū'ĭ-tŭs), *a.* [4] **1.** Given without recompense or pay; free. **2.** Not based upon reason, cause, or proof; groundless; uncalled-for. — **-ly**, *adv.* [8] — **-ness**, *n.* [8].

gra-tu'i-ty (-tĭ), *n.; pl.* -TIES (-tĭz). Something given without recompense, or in return for a favor or service ; a gift ; a tip.

grave (grāv), *a.* [3] **1.** Deserving serious consideration. **2.** Not light or gay; somber.

grave, *v. t.; pret.* GRAVED (grāvd) ; *p. p.* GRAV'EN (grāv'n) or GRAVED ; *p. pr. & vb. n.* GRAV'ING (grāv'ĭng). **1.** To engrave ; carve with a chisel; sculpture. **2.** To impress deeply (on the mind).

grave, *n.* An excavation in the earth as a place of burial; a tomb; sepulcher. — **grave'less**, *a.* [8].

grav'el (grăv'ĕl), *n.* **1.** Small stones and pebbles, often mingled with sand. **2.** Small concretions in the kidneys or bladder; also, the disease indicated by them. — *v. t.* [7] To cover with gravel.

grav'el-ly (-ĭ), *a.* [4] Of or like gravel.

grave'ly, *adv.* In a grave manner.

grav'en (grāv'n), *p. p.* of GRAVE. — **graven image**, an idol.

grave'ness, *n.* State or quality of being grave.

grav'er (-ẽr), *n.* **1.** Any of various cutting or shaving tools. **2.** An engraver or a sculptor.

grave'stone' (-stōn'), *n.* A stone marking a grave.

grave'yard' (-yärd'), *n.* A cemetery.

grav'i-tate (grăv'ĭ-tāt), *v. i.* [1] To obey the law of gravitation ; tend toward any object.

grav'i-ta'tion (-tā'shŭn), *n.* **1.** Act or process of gravitating. **2.** The attraction by which all bodies or particles of matter tend toward each other.

grav'i-ty (-tĭ), *n.; pl.* -TIES (-tĭz). **1.** State of being grave; seriousness. **2.** Gravitation; esp., the attraction of bodies toward the center of the earth.

gra'vy (grā'vĭ), *n.; pl.* -VIES (-vĭz). **1.** A liquid dressing for meat, etc. **2.** The juice that drips from flesh during and after cooking.

gray (grā), *a.* [3] **1.** Of the color gray; hence, dull; not bright. **2.** Gray-haired; hence, elderly or mature. — gray matter. Nerve tissue (esp. of the brain and spinal cord) which contains nerve cells as well as fibers, and so is brownish gray. — *n.* Any color formed by blending white and black. — **gray'ly**, *adv.* [8] — **gray'ness**, *n.* [8].

gray'beard' (-bērd'), *n.* An old man.

gray'hound', *n.* Greyhound.

gray'ling (grā'lĭng), *n.* Any of several fishes allied to the trouts.

graze (grāz), *v. t.* [1] **1.** To feed (cattle, etc.) on pasturage. **2.** To feed on (growing herbage); browse. **3.** To tend while grazing. — *v. i.* To feed on growing herbage. — **graz'er** (-ẽr), *n.* [8].

graze, *v. t.* **1.** To touch lightly in passing. **2.** To scratch or scrape; as, he *grazed* his arm. — *v. i.* To touch or rub against something in passing. — *n.* A scraping, or an abrasion made by scraping.

gra'zier (grā'zhẽr), *n.* One who grazes cattle.

grease (grēs), *n.* Animal fat; hence, oily matter. — (grēz; grēs), *v. t.* [1] To smear with grease.

greas'er (grēz'ẽr; grēs'ẽr), *n.* **1.** One that greases. **2.** A Mexican or a Spanish American. *Slang, U. S.*

greas'y (grēz'ĭ; grēs'ĭ), a. [3] Smeared with, containing, or like, grease; slippery. — **greas'i-ly** (-ĭ-lĭ), adv. [8] — **-ness**, n. [8].
great (grāt), a. **1.** Large in size; big. **2.** Numerous. **3.** Long continued. **4.** Considerable in degree. **5.** Eminent; important; distinguished. **6.** More remote, by one generation. — **Great Bear, Ursa Major.** — g. circle of a sphere, a circle the plane of which passes through the center of the sphere.
great'coat' (grāt'kōt'), n. An overcoat.
great'-grand'child', n., **great'-grand'daugh'ter**, n., **-grand'fa'ther**, n., etc. See GREAT, a., 6.
great'ly, adv. In a great manner or degree.
great'ness, n. State or quality of being great.
greave (grēv), n. Armor for the leg below the knee; — usually in pl.
grebe (grēb), n. A bird related to the loons.
Gre'cian (grē'shăn), a. Greek. — n. **1.** A Greek. **2.** One versed in Greek or Greek literature.
greed (grēd), n. Eager desire; greediness.
greed'y (-ĭ), a. [3] **1.** Having a keen appetite; ravenous; voracious. **2.** Having eager desire; avaricious. — **greed'i-ly**, adv. [8] — **-i-ness**, n. [8].
Greek (grēk), n. **1.** A native or citizen of Greece; specifically, one of the people of ancient Greece. **2.** The language of the Greeks, specifically of the classical Greeks. — a. Of or pertaining to Greece, the Greeks, or their language.
green (grēn), a. [3] **1.** Of the color green. **2.** Characterized by green growth; verdant. **3.** Full of life and vigor; fresh. **4.** Not ripened or matured. **5.** Young; not trained; hence, ignorant. **6.** Having a sickly color. — n. **1.** The color of growing herbage; color between yellow and blue. **2.** A grassy plot. **3.** a Fresh leaves or branches; — usually in pl. b pl. Green vegetables boiled for food.
green'back' (grēn'băk'), n. Any United States legal-tender note having the back printed in green.
green'er-y (-ēr-ĭ), n.; pl. -ERIES (-ĭz). Verdure.
green'gage' (grēn'gāj'), n. A kind of plum.
green'gro'cer (-grō'sẽr), n. A retailer of fresh vegetables and fruit. — **green'gro'cer-y** (-ĭ), n.
green'horn' (-hôrn'), n. An inexperienced person.
green'house' (-hous'), n. A building constructed chiefly of glass and used for growing tender plants.
groon'ing, n. Any of several kinds of green-skinned apples.
green'ish, a. Somewhat green.
green'ly, adv. With green; in a green manner.
green'ness, n. State or quality of being green.
green'room', n. Retiring room in a theater.
green'sward' (-swôrd'), n. Turf green with grass.
Green'wich (grĭn'ĭj), n. A borough of London in which is situated the Royal Observatory, from whose meridian longitude is usually counted.
green'wood' (grēn'wŏŏd'), n. A forest in foliage.
greet (grēt), v. t. To address, esp. with kind words; accost. — v. i. To meet and give salutations.
greet'ing (grēt'ĭng), n. Salutation; compliment.
gre-ga'ri-ous (grē-gā'rĭ-ŭs), a. [4] Habitually living or moving in flocks or herds; tending to flock together. — **gre-ga'ri-ous-ly**, adv. [8].
gre-nade' (grē-nād'), n. **1.** Mil. A shell filled with an explosive, to be thrown by hand and explode on impact. **2.** A flask, containing chemicals, to be thrown and burst, as for extinguishing fire.

gren'a-dier' (grĕn'ȧ-dēr'), n. A soldier of a special regiment or corps; originally, one who carried and threw grenades.
gren'a-dine (grĕn'ȧ-dēn), n. A dress fabric of silk or wool.
grew (grōō), pret. of GROW.
grey (grā), a. & n. Var. of GRAY.
grey'hound' (-hound'), n. One of a breed of slender dogs, swift and keen of sight.
grid (grĭd), n. A grating or gridiron; esp., in a vacuum tube, a device of wires or metal between the plate and the filament.
grid'dle (grĭd'l), n. A plate for cooking thin cakes of batter (griddlecakes) over a fire.
grid'i'ron (-ī'ŭrn), n. **1.** A grated iron utensil to broil food on. **2.** Something likened to a gridiron.
grief (grēf), n. **1.** Mental suffering, as from affliction, etc., or a cause of it. **2.** A mishap; disaster; failure; — esp. in to come, or bring, to grief.
griev'ance (grēv'ăns), n. A cause of complaint.
grieve (grēv), v. t. [1] To occasion grief to; afflict. — v. i. To feel grief; sorrow; mourn.
griev'ous (grēv'ŭs), a. [4] **1.** Distressing; hence, severe. **2.** Atrocious. **3.** Full of or expressing grief. — **-ly**, adv. [8] — **-ness**, n. [8].
grif'fin (grĭf'ĭn) }n. A fabulous monster, half
grif'fon (grĭf'ŏn) } lion and half eagle.
grill (grĭl), n. A gridiron. — v. t. & i. To broil on or as on a grill. Hence, grill'room', n.
grille (grĭl), n. A grating, esp. of wrought iron.
grim (grĭm), a.; GRIM'MER (-ẽr); -MEST. Savage and merciless; fierce; stern; harsh and forbidding.
gri-mace' (grĭ-mās'),n. A distortion of the countenance; a wry face. — v. i. [1] To make grimaces.
gri-mal'kin (grĭ-măl'kĭn; -môl'kĭn), n. A cat.
grime (grīm), n. Soot or dirt, rubbed in. — v. t [1] To soil deeply; begrime.
grim'ly (grĭm'lĭ), adv. In a grim manner.
grim'ness, n. State or quality of being grim.
grim'y (grīm'ĭ), a. [3] Full of grime; begrimed; dirty. — **-i-ly** (-ĭ-lĭ), adv. [8] — **-i-ness**, n. [8].
grin (grĭn),v. i.; GRINNED (grĭnd); -NING. To show the teeth, as in a smile of merriment, derision, etc. — n. An act of grinning.
grind (grīnd), v. t.; pret. & p. p. GROUND (ground); p. pr. & vb. n. GRIND'ING. **1.** To powder by friction; crush into bits. **2.** To wear down, polish, or sharpen, by friction. **3.** To rub together with a grating noise; grate; grit. **4.** To operate or produce by turning a crank. **5.** To oppress; harass — v. i. **1.** To perform the operation of grinding. **2.** To become ground.—n. **1.** Act of grinding. **2.** Severe continuous work. Colloq.
grind'er (grīn'dẽr), n. **1.** One that grinds, as an emery wheel. **2.** A molar tooth.
grind'stone' (grīnd'stōn'),n. A flat, circular stone, revolving on an axle, for grinding tools, etc.
grip (grĭp), n. **1.** A strong grasp; also, a mode of grasping the hand, as among members of a secret society. **2.** A handle or device for grasping. **3.** A gripsack. Colloq., U. S. — v. t. & i.; GRIPPED (grĭpt) or GRIPT; GRIP'PING. To grasp firmly; gripe.
gripe (grīp), v. t. [1] **1.** To grasp; esp., to clasp closely; hence, to distress; afflict. **2.** To cause spasmodic pain in the bowels of. — n. **1.** Act of griping; fast hold; control; hence, affliction; distress. **2.** Spasmodic intestinal pain;—chiefly in pl.

grippe (grĭp), *n.* Influenza, or epidemic catarrh.

grip′sack′ (-săk′),*n.* A traveler's hand bag. *Colloq.*

gris′ly (grĭz′lĭ), *a.* [3] Horrible; grim and ghastly. — **gris′li-ness** (-lĭ-nĕs), *n.* [8].

grist (grĭst), *n.* Grain to be, or that is, ground.

gris′tle (grĭs′'l), *n.* Cartilage.— **-tly** (-lĭ), *a.* [3].

grist′mill′ (grĭst′mĭl′),*n.* A mill for grinding grain.

grit (grĭt), *n.* **1.** Sand; gravel; rough, hard particles. **2.** A hard, coarse-grained sandstone. **3.** Firmness; courage. — *v. t. & i.;* GRIT′TED; GRIT′TING. To grind; grate.

grits (grĭts),*n.pl.* Grain, esp. oats or wheat, hulled and (usually) coarsely ground.

grit′ty (grĭt′ĭ),*a.* [3] **1.** Containing or resembling sand, or grit. **2.** Plucky. *Colloq., U. S.*

griz′zle (grĭz′'l), *n.* Gray. — *v. t. & i.* [1] To make or become grizzly.

griz′zled (-'ld), *a.* [4] Gray.

griz′zly (-lĭ),*a.* [3] Somewhat gray; grizzled. — grizzly bear, a large powerful bear of western N o r t h America. It is usually brownish yellow.— *n.; pl.* -ZLIES (-lĭz). A grizzly bear.

Grizzly Bear. ($\frac{1}{60}$)

groan (grōn), *v. i.* **1.** To utter a d e e p, moaning sound. **2.** To be afflicted to the point of groaning; hence, of things, to creak, as from a burden.—*v. t.* To utter with groans. — *n.* A sound uttered in groaning.

groat (grōt; grŏt), *n.* An old English silver coin worth fourpence.

groats (grōts; grŏts), *n. pl.* Grits.

gro′cer (grō′sẽr), *n.* A dealer in tea, coffee,sugar, spices, fruits, and other foodstuffs.

gro′cer-y (-sẽr-ĭ), *n.; pl.* -CERIES (-ĭz). **1.** The commodities sold by grocers; — usually in *pl.* **2.** A retail grocer's shop. *U. S.*

grog (grŏg),*n.* An unsweetened mixture of spirit and water; hence, any intoxicating liquor.

grog′gy (-ĭ),*a.* [3] Tipsy; hence, unsteady. *Colloq.*

grog′ram (grŏg′răm), *n.* A coarse stuff of silk and mohair, or of silk alone.

groin (groin), *n.* **1.** The junction of the lower part of the abdomen and the thigh, or the region about it. **2.** *Arch.* The angle formed by the meeting of two vaults. — *v. t.* To build with groins.

groom (grōōm), *n.* **1.** A manservant, now, esp., one in charge of horses. **2.** A bridegroom.— *v. t.* To tend (a horse), as by currying, feeding, etc.

grooms′man (grōōmz′măn), *n.; pl.* -MEN. A male friend who attends a bridegroom at his wedding.

groove (grōōv), *n.* **1.** A channel; furrow; rut. **2.** A fixed routine.— *v. t.* [1] To form a groove in.

grope (grōp), *v. i. & t.* [1] To search out by feeling, as in the dark; feel one's way. — **grop′er**, *n.*

gros′beak′ (grōs′bēk′),*n.* Any of various finches, or allied birds, with large, stout conical bill.

gros′grain′ (grō′grān′), *a.* Of large grain or cord, as certain silks.— *n.* Grosgrain silk or ribbon.

gross (grōs), *a.* [3] **1.** Big; thick; bulky; coarse. **2.** Rank; dense; heavy. **3.** Whole; entire; total. **4.** Wanting delicacy; coarse; vulgar. **5.** Flagrant; serious. — **-ly**, *adv.* [8] — **-ness**, *n.* [8].

gross (grōs), *n.* **1.** The main body; bulk; mass. **2.** *sing. & pl.* Twelve dozen.—in gross, in the bulk.

gro-tesque′ (grō-tĕsk′), *a.* **1.** Characterized by fantastic exaggeration or combination, esp. of human and animal figures. **2.** Absurdly incongruous or awkward. — *n.* That which is grotesque. — **gro-tesque′ly**, *adv.* [8] — **-ness**, *n.* [8].

grot′to (grŏt′ō), *n.; pl.* -TOES or -TOS (-ōz). A cave; also, an artificial recess or cavernlike apartment.

grouch (grouch), *n.* A fit of ill temper or sulkiness. *Slang.* — **grouch′y** (-ĭ), *a.* [3] *Slang.*

ground (ground), *pret. & p. p.* of GRIND.

ground (ground), *n.* **1.** The surface of the earth. **2.** A region, territory, or piece of land. **3.** Land; estate; esp., *pl.*, the gardens, lawns, etc., of a homestead. **4.** Basis; foundation; reason. **5.** The surface or background on which anything is wrought or displayed, as in painting, etc. **6.** *pl.* Sediment; dregs; lees. — *v. t.* **1.** To found; fix firmly; hence, to instruct in first principles. **2.** To place on, or cause to touch, the ground. — *v. i.* To run aground.

ground hog. The woodchuck.

ground′less, *a.* Without foundation or reason.

ground′ling (-lĭng), *n.* One that keeps close to the ground.

ground′work′ (-wûrk′), *n.* Foundation; basis.

group (grōōp), *n.* An assemblage of persons or things considered as a unit; cluster; aggregation. — *v. t.* To arrange or combine in a group.

grouse (grous), *n.* (see PLURAL, *n.*, *Note*.) Any of numerous game birds related to the domestic fowls; as, the ruffed *grouse* (partridge).

grout (grout), *n.* **1.** Thin mortar. **2.** A kind of plaster or cement.

grout′y (grout′ĭ),*a.* [3] Cross; sullen. *Colloq.,U.S.*

grove (grōv), *n.* A group of trees without underwood; a small wood.

grov′el (grŏv′'l), *v. i.* [7] **1.** To creep; lie flat, face downward; crawl; cringe. **2.** To delight in what is low or base. — **grov′el-er**, *n.* [7, 8]

grow (grō), *v. i.; pret.* GREW (grōō); *p. p.* GROWN (grōn); *p. pr. & vb. n.* GROW′ING. **1.** To spring up and mature; be developed; thrive; increase. **2.** To increase by gradual assimilation of new matter into the living organism, as animals, plants, etc. **3.** To come to be; become. **4.** To become united by or as by growth. — *v. t.* To cause to grow; cultivate; produce. — **grow′er**, *n.* [8].

growl (groul), *v. i. & t.* To utter or express with a growl or growls. — *n.* The deep, threatening sound made by a surly dog, a wolf, etc.; hence, a muttering complaint.

grown (grōn), *p. a.* Full-grown; matured.

growth (grōth), *n.* **1.** Act of growing; development. **2.** That which has grown or is growing.

grub (grŭb), *v. i.; pret.* GRUBBED (grŭbd); GRUB′BING. **1.** To dig; root. **2.** To drudge. — *v. t.* **1.** To clear or break up (land) by digging. **2.** To root out by digging; — followed by *up.* — *n.* Any thick wormlike larva, esp. of a beetle. — **grub′ber**, *n.*

grudge (grŭj), *v. t.* [1] To give or allow reluctantly; begrudge; envy. — *n.* A feeling of sullen malice or ill will. — **grudg'ing-ly**, *adv.* [8].

gru'el (grōō'ĕl), *n.* A kind of porridge made by boiling meal or flour in water or milk.

gru'el-ing, gru'el-ling (grōō'ĕl-ĭng), *a.* Requiring extreme and exhausting effort.

grue'some (grōō'sŭm), *a.* [4] Inspiring fear or horror; horrid. — **-ly**, *adv.* [8] — **-ness**, *n.* [8].

gruff (grŭf), *a.* [3] Of rough manner, speech, or countenance; surly. — **-ly**, *adv.* — **-ness**, *n.* [8].

grum'ble (grŭm'b'l), *v. i. & t.* [1] To murmur with discontent; to growl; mutter. — *n.* A grumbling; rumble. — **-bler**, *n.* — **-bling-ly**, *adv.*

grump'y (-pĭ), *a.* [3] Surly; dissatisfied; grouty. — **grump'i-ly**, *adv.* [8] — **-i-ness**, *n.* [8].

grunt (grŭnt), *v. i. & t.* To make, or utter with, a grunt. — *n.* A deep guttural sound, as of a hog:

gua'no (gwä'nō), *n.; pl.* -NOS (-nōz). A fertilizer composed chiefly of the excrement of sea fowl.

guar'an-tee' (găr'ăn-tē'), *n.; pl.* -TEES (-tēz'). **1.** A person to whom a guaranty is made; also, a guarantor. **2.** A guaranty. — *v. t.;* -TEED' (-tēd'); -TEE'ING. **1.** To undertake to answer for a payment or a duty, by (another person); warrant. **2.** To give security to; secure. [guaranty.|

guar'an-tor' (găr'ăn-tôr'), *n.* One who gives a

guar'an-ty (-tĭ), *n.; pl.* -TIES (-tĭz). **1.** An undertaking or agreement by which a person guarantees something. **2.** Something given to secure the existence, performance, or fulfillment of something; a security. — *v. t.* [2] To guarantee.

guard (gärd), *v. t.* To protect; defend; shelter; watch over; restrain. — *v. i.* To watch; stand guard; take precautions. — *n.* **1.** The state, act, or duty of keeping watch. **2.** An attitude of defense, as in fencing or boxing. **3.** One that guards; a watch; sentinel. **4.** A device or attachment for protection or security.

guard'house' (gärd'hous'), *n.* A building occupied by a guard; a military lockup.

guard'i-an (gär'dĭ-ăn), *n.* **1.** One who guards or secures; a warden. **2.** *Law.* One who has, or is entitled to, the care of the person or property, or both, of another. — **guard'i-an-ship'**, *n.*

guard'room' (gärd'rōōm'), *n.* A room occupied by a guard on duty, or where prisoners are confined.

guards'man (gärdz'mǎn), *n.; pl.* -MEN (-měn). **1.** One who guards; a guard. **2.** A member of any military body called *Guards.*

gua'va (gwä'và), *n.* A tropical American tree bearing a mildly acid fruit; also, the fruit.

gu'ber-na-to'ri-al (gū'bĕr-nà-tō'rĭ-ǎl), *a.* Pertaining to a governor or government.

gud'geon, *n.* A pivot or journal.

guer'don (gûr'dŭn), *n.* Reward; recompense.

guern'sey (gûrn'zĭ), *n.* A kind of close-fitting knitted woolen vest or shirt.

guer-ril'la (gĕ-rĭl'à), *n.* One who carries on irregular warfare.

guess (gĕs), *v. t. & i.* **1.** To form an opinion of without certain knowledge; judge of at random; conjecture. **2.** To hit on or solve by conjecture. **3.** To suppose; believe. *Colloq.* — *n.* A conjecture; surmise. — **-er**, *n.*

guess'work' (gĕs'wûrk'), *n.* Work done, or results obtained, by guess; conjecture.

guest (gĕst), *n.* **1.** A visitor; a person received and entertained in one's house. **2.** Any person who lodges, boards, or receives refreshment, for pay, at a hotel, etc.

guf-faw' (gŭ-fô'), *n.* A loud burst of laughter.

guid'ance (gīd'ǎns), *n.* A guiding; direction.

guide (gīd), *v. t.* [1] To act as a guide to; conduct; lead; pilot; regulate and manage; direct. — *n.* One who leads or directs another; also, that which guides; guidebook. — **guid'er** (-ēr), *n.* [8].

guide'book', *n.* Handbook of information for travelers, etc.

guide'post' (gīd'pōst'),*n.* A post to direct travelers.

guild (gĭld), *n.* An association of persons with kindred pursuits or common interests, formed for furthering some common purpose.

guil'der (gĭl'dĕr), *n.* The gulden.

guile (gīl), *n.* Crafty cunning; deceit.— **guile'ful** (-fŏŏl), *a.* — **guile'less**, *a.* [8].

guil'lo-tine (gĭl'ô-tēn), *n.* A machine with a heavy blade sliding in guides, for beheading persons. — (-tēn'), *v. t.* [1] To behead with the guillotine.

guilt (gĭlt), *n.* The fact of having committed a breach of conduct, esp. such as violates law and incurs a penalty; also, guilty conduct or state.

guilt'less, *a.* [4] Innocent.

guilt'y (gĭl'tĭ), *a.* [3] **1.** Having incurred guilt; justly chargeable with a delinquency, crime, or sin. **2.** Evincing, indicating, or involving guilt; sensible of guilt. — **-i-ly**, *adv.* — **-i-ness**, *n.* [8].

guin'ea (gĭn'ĭ), *n.* **1.** An English gold coin, no longer issued, worth 21 shillings. **2.** Sum of 21 shillings ($5.11).

Guinea Fowl.

guinea fowl, guinea hen. A bird related to the common barnyard fowl, having a dark slaty plumage finely speckled.

guinea pig. A short-eared rodent, of S. American origin, usually black, white, and tawny.

Guinea Pig.

guise (gīz), *n.* **1.** Customary way of speaking or acting; fashion; behavior. **2.** Appearance, esp. as to dress; aspect.

gui-tar' (gĭ-tär'), *n.* A musical instrument with long neck and six strings plucked with the fingers.

gulch (gŭlch), *n.* A cleft with steep sides, esp. the bed of a stream; ravine. *Western U. S.*

gul'den (gŏŏl'dĕn), *n.* Dutch coin = 40.2 cents.

gulf (gŭlf), *n.* **1.** A portion of an ocean or sea extending into the land. **2.** A hollow place in the earth; abyss; hence, a wide separation.

gull (gŭl), *v. t.* To deceive; cheat; defraud. — *n.* **1.** One easily cheated; a dupe. **2.** A trick; fraud.

gull, *n.* Any of numerous web-footed water birds.

gul'let (gŭl'ĕt), *n.* The esophagus.

gul′li-bil′i-ty (gŭl′ĭ-bĭl′ĭ-tĭ), *n.* Quality of being gullible.

gul′li-ble (gŭl′ĭ-b'l), *a.* [4] Easily gulled.

gul′ly (-ĭ), *n.; pl.* -LIES (-ĭz). A miniature valley or gorge, esp. one cut by a temporary stream. — *v. t. & i.* [2] To wear a gully or gullies in.

gulp (gŭlp), *v. t.* To swallow eagerly, or at one swallow. — *n.* A large swallow; mouthful.

gum (gŭm), *n.* The dense tissues which envelop the bases of the teeth.

gum, *n.* A viscid secretion of many trees or plants that hardens on exposure to the air. — *v. t.* To smear, unite, or stiffen with gum. — *v. i.* To exude or form gum; become gummy.

gum ar′a-bic. A well-known gum, variously used, got from either of two species of *Acacia.*

gum′bo (gŭm′bō), *n.* A soup thickened with okra pods; also, the okra plant or its pods.

gum′boil′ (-boil′), *n.* A small abscess on the gums.

gum′drop′ (-drŏp′), *n.* A confection of sweetened gum arabic, gelatin, or the like, molded in drops.

gum′my (-ĭ), *a.* [3] Consisting of, or covered with, gum; viscous. — **gum′mi-ness,** *n.* [8].

gump′tion (gŭmp′shŭn), *n.* Shrewdness; common sense; cleverness. *Colloq.*

gum tree. **1.** In the United States, any of several gum-yielding trees. **2.** In Australia, any eucalyptus.

gun (gŭn), *n.* **1.** A cannon. **2.** Any portable firearm, esp. a rifle, carbine, or shotgun. **3.** A discharge of a cannon, as in a salute. **4.** A revolver. *Colloq.*—*v. i.;* GUNNED (gŭnd); GUN′NING. To hunt with a gun.

gun′boat′ (-bōt′), *n.* An armed vessel of light draft.

gun′cot′ton (-kŏt′'n), *n.* An explosive substance got by soaking cotton in nitric and sulphuric acids.

gun′lock′ (gŭn′lŏk′), *n.* In some firearms, the mechanism by which the charge is ignited.

gun′ner (-ẽr), *n.* **1.** A cannoneer. **2.** One who hunts with a gun.

gun′ner-y (-ĭ), *n.* **1.** Science of the flight of projectiles and use of guns. **2.** Practical use of guns.

gun′ny (-ĭ), *n.* A kind of coarse jute sacking.

gun′pow′der (-pou′dẽr), *n.* An explosive used in guns, etc., and commonly a mixture of saltpeter, charcoal, and sulphur.

gun′shot′ (-shŏt′), *n.* **1.** Act of firing a gun; a shot. **2.** Distance to which a missile can be shot from a gun effectively; as, within *gunshot.*

gun′smith′ (-smĭth′), *n.* One whose occupation is to make or repair small firearms; an armorer.

gun′wale (gŭn′ĕl; *formally* gŭn′wāl), *n.* The upper edge of a vessel's or boat's side.

gur′gle (gûr′g'l), *v. i.* [1] To flow in a broken, noisy current, as water from a bottle; make a sound like gurgling liquid. — *v. t.* To utter with a gurgle. — *n.* Act or sound of gurgling.

gur′nard (gûr′nãrd), *n.* Any of certain spiny marine fishes having the head armored.

gush (gŭsh), *v. i.* **1.** To issue or pour forth copiously or violently, as a fluid. **2.** To show effusive affection, enthusiasm, etc. *Colloq.* — *v. t.* To emit freely. — *n.* **1.** A gushing. **2.** Effusive display of affection, enthusiasm, etc. *Colloq.*

gus′set (gŭs′ĕt), *n.* A small tapering piece inserted in a garment, glove, etc., to give width or strength.

gust (gŭst), *n.* **1.** A sudden blast of wind. **2.** A sudden outburst, esp. of temper.

gus′ta-to-ry (gŭs′tá-tō-rĭ), *a.* Pertaining to the sense of taste.

gus′to (-tō), *n.* Taste; keen appreciation; zest.

gust′y (-tĭ), *a.* [3] Windy; stormy.

gut (gŭt), *n.* **1.** An intestine; the alimentary canal, or a part of it; *pl.*, bowels; entrails; — not now in dignified use. **2.** Prepared entrail of an animal; as, cat*gut.* **3.** A narrow passage, as of water. — *v. t.;* GUT′TED (-ĕd); GUT′TING. **1.** To disembowel. **2.** To destroy or remove the interior or contents of, as by fire; also, to plunder.

gut′ta-per′cha (gŭt′á-pûr′chá), *n.* A thick juice, nearly white when pure, yielded by various Malaysian trees. In many ways it resembles caoutchouc.

gut′ter (gŭt′ẽr), *n.* **1.** A channel at the eaves of a house for carrying away rain. **2.** A small channel at a roadside to lead off surface water. **3.** Any narrow channel or groove. — *v. t.* To form gutters in. — *v. i.* **1.** To flow in streams. **2.** To become channeled, as a flaring candle.

gut′tur-al (gŭt′ẽr-ăl), *a.* [4] Of or pert. to the throat; made, or thought to be made, in the throat. — *n.* A guttural sound or its symbol.—**-ly,** *adv.* [8].

guy (gī), *n.* A rope, chain, or rod attached to a thing to steady it. — *v. t.* To steady with a guy.

guy (gī), *n.* A person of grotesque appearance.— *v.t.* To make (a person) an object of ridicule. *Colloq.*

guz′zle (gŭz′'l), *v. i. & t.* [1] To drink to excess or overfrequently. — **guz′zler** (-lẽr), *n.* [8].

gybe (jīb), *v. i.* [1] **1.** To shift from one side to the other; — said of a fore-and-aft sail or its boom. **2.** To change the course (of a vessel) so that the sail gybes. — *v. t.* To cause to gybe.

gym-na′si-um (jĭm-nā′zĭ-ŭm), *n.; pl.* E. -SIUMS (-ŭmz), L. -SIA (-á). A place or building for athletic exercises; a school for gymnastics.

gym′nast (jĭm′năst), *n.* A teacher of, or expert in, gymnastic exercises.

gym-nas′tics (jĭm-năs′tĭks), *n. pl.* Bodily exercises performed in, or adapted to performance in, a gymnasium. — **gym-nas′tic** (-tĭk), *a.* [4].

gyp′sum (jĭp′sŭm), *n.* Hydrous sulphate of calcium, used for making plaster of Paris, etc.

gyp′sy (-sĭ), *n.; pl.* -SIES (-sĭz). **1.** [*Often cap.*] One of a wandering Caucasian race, originally from India. **2.** [*cap.*] The language of the gypsies.

gypsy moth. A moth whose caterpillars do great damage to trees.

gy′rate (jī′rāt), *v. i.* [1] To revolve round a center; move spirally about an axis, as a tornado.

gy-ra′tion (jī-rā′shŭn), *n.* Act of turning or whirling, as around a center; rotation.

gy′ra-to-ry (jī′rá-tō-rĭ), *a.* [4] Whirling.

gyr′fal′con (jûr′fô′k'n; -fôl′k'n), *n.* Any of certain large falcons which are found in northern regions.

gy′ro-scope (jī′rŏ-skōp), *n.* An apparatus consisting of a heavy-rimmed fly-wheel usually mounted in a ring; — used to illustrate the laws of rotating bodies, etc.

gyve (jīv), *n.* A shackle, esp. for the legs; a fetter; — usually in *pl.*

Gyroscope.

H

ha (hä), *interj. & n.* An exclamation of surprise, joy, or grief, or, repeated, of laughter or triumph.

hab'er-dash'er (hăb'ẽr-dăsh'ẽr), *n.* A dealer in men's furnishings.

ha-bil'i-ment (há-bĭl'ĭ-měnt), *n.* Dress; attire; clothes; — chiefly in *pl.*

hab'it (hăb'ĭt), *n.* **1.** Dress; garb; clothes. **2.** a A costume indicative of rank, profession; esp., the dress of a religious order. **b** A lady's riding costume. **3.** Bodily appearance, form, or condition. **4.** A custom or practice. — *v. t.* To dress; clothe.

hab'it-a-ble (-á-b'l), *a.* [4] Capable of being inhabited.

hab'i-tat (hăb'ĭ-tăt), *n.* Natural abode of a plant or animal; dwelling place.

hab'i-ta'tion (-tā'shŭn), *n.* **1.** Act of inhabiting; occupancy. **2.** Place of abode; a residence.

ha-bit'u-al (há-bĭt'ū̇-ăl), *a.* [4] **1.** Of the nature of a habit; according to habit; customary. **2.** Doing or acting by force of habit. **3.** Usual; commonly used; accustomed. — **ha-bit'u-al-ly**, *adv.* [8].

ha-bit'u-ate (-āt), *v.t.* [1] To accustom; familiarize.

hab'i-tude (hăb'ĭ-tūd), *n.* **1.** Native character; habitual attitude. **2.** Habit of body or of action.

ha-bit'u-é' (há-bĭt'ū̇-ā'; F. á/bē'tü-ā'), *n.* One who habitually frequents a place or class of places.

ha-cien'da (ä-syěn'dä; hä/sĭ-ěn'dä), *n.* A large estate, or a works or establishment. *Sp. Amer.*

hack (hăk), *v. t.* To cut irregularly; haggle. — *v. i.* To cough in a short, broken manner. — *n.* A notch; cut; nick.

hack (hăk), *n.* **1.** a A horse for common hire. **b** A saddle horse, for the road. **2.** A carriage for hire; a hackney. **3.** One who hires out, esp. for literary work; drudge. — *a.* Hackneyed; hired.

hack'le (-'l), *n.* A hatchel. — *v. t.* [1] To hatchel.

hack'le, *v. t. & i.* To hack; haggle.

hack'ma-tack' (hăk'má-tăk'), *n.* The American larch, or tamarack; also, its wood.

hack'ney (-nĭ), *n.; pl.* -NEYS (-nĭz). **1.** A horse for ordinary riding or driving. **2.** A hired carriage. — *a.* Let out for hire. — *v. t.* To devote to, or wear out in, common or frequent use, as a horse; hence, to make trite or stale.

hack'neyed (-nĭd), *p. a.* [4] **1.** Commonplace; trite. **2.** Habituated.

had (hăd), *pret. & p. p.* of HAVE.

had'dock (hăd'ŭk), *n.* An important Atlantic food fish allied to, but smaller than, the cod.

Ha'des (hā'dēz), *n.* The abode of the dead.

hæ'mo-glo'bin (hē'mȯ-glō'bĭn), *n.* The coloring matter of the red blood corpuscles of vertebrates.

haft (hăft), *n.* A handle; hilt of a knife, sword, or dagger. — *v. t.* To set in, or furnish with, a haft.

hag (hăg), *n.* **1.** A witch. **2.** An ugly old woman.

hag'gard (-ârd), *a.* [4] Having the look of one wasted by want, suffering, etc.

hag'gle (-'l), *v. t.* [1] To cut roughly; hack. — *v. i.* To dispute; stickle. — *n.* Act of haggling.

hail (hāl), *n.* **1.** Small roundish masses of ice precipitated from the clouds. **2.** A shower of any-

thing like, or suggestive of, bail. — *v. i. & t.* To precipitate hail, or as hail.

hail, *v. t.* **1.** To salute; greet. **2.** To call loudly to or after; accost. — *v. i.* To call out. — *n.* Act of hailing; salutation.

hail'stone' (-stōn'), *n.* A pellet of hail.

hair (hâr), *n.* **1.** A slender threadlike outgrowth of an animal; esp., one of the filaments of the coat of mammals; also, this coat or a part of it, esp that of the human head. **2.** *Bot.* A very slender, flexible outgrowth of a plant. **3.** A hairbreadth.

hair'breadth' (-brĕdth'), *n.* Also **hair's breadth** (hârz). Diameter of a hair; very small distance.

hair'breadth', *a.* Very narrow or close.

hair'cloth' (-klŏth'), *n.* A fabric made of camel's hair or horsehair, used to cover furniture, etc.

hair'i-ness (hâr'ĭ-něs), *n.* Condition of being hairy.

hair'split'ting, *a.* Making overnice distinctions. — **hair'split'ting**, *n.*

hair'spring' (-spring'), *n.* The fine spring which regulates the motion of the balance in a watch.

hair trigger. A trigger so adjusted that a slight pressure on it actuates the firing mechanism.

hair'y (hâr'ĭ), *a.* [3] Bearing, or covered with, hair; hirsute; made of hair.

hake (hāk), *n.* Any of several fishes allied to the cods.

hal'berd (hăl'bẽrd), **hal'bert** (-bẽrt), *n.* A kind of old-time long-handled weapon.

hal'cy-on (hăl'sĭ-ŭn), *a.* Calm; peaceful; as, *halcyon* days.

hale (hāl), *v. t.* [1] To haul; pull; drag.

hale, *a.* [3] Free from defect, disease, or infirmity; sound; healthy; robust.

half (hăf), *a.* **1.** Consisting of one of two equal parts. **2.** Consisting of about a half; partial; imperfect. — *adv.* In an equal part or degree; partially; imperfectly. — *n.; pl.* HALVES (hävz). One of two equal parts of a (whole) thing.

half'-breed', *n.* Offspring of parents of different races, esp. of the American Indian and the white.

half brother. A brother by one parent only.

half'-heart'ed, *a.* Wanting in heart, spirit, etc.

half'-mast', *v.* A point some distance, not necessarily halfway, below the top of a mast or staff.

half'pen-ny (hā'pěn-ĭ; hăf'pěn'ĭ), *n.; for pl. see* PENNY. Half a penny, or a coin of this value. *Eng.*

half sister. A sister by one parent only.

half tone, *or* **half'-tone'**, *n.* **1.** An intermediate tone in a painting, engraving, etc., not very dark nor very light. **2.** A half-tone photo-engraving.

half'-tone', *a. Photo-engraving.* Designating a plate, process, or picture, in which the gradations of tone in the photograph are reproduced by spots produced by a screen.

half'way' (hăf'wā'; hăf'wā'), *adv.* In the middle; partially. — *a.* Midway.

half'-wit'ted, *a.* Mentally deficient; imbecile.

hal'i-but (hăl'ĭ-bŭt), *n.* Largest species of flatfish.

Head of
Halberd
(1670).

hall (nôl), *n.* **1.** The residence of a landed proprietor. *Chiefly British.* **2.** A building of considerable size or stateliness and usually containing a place of assembly; as, a town *hall.* **3.** An assembly room. **4.** A university building. **5.** Entrance room of a building; a corridor or passage.

hal'le-lu'jah } (hăl'ē-loo'yä), *interj.* Praise ye Je-
hal'le-lu'iah } hovah (*or* the Lord) ! — *n.* A song or exclamation of gratitude or praise to God.

hall mark, *or* **hall'mark'**, *n.* An official stamp of purity put on articles of gold and silver. *British.*

hal-lo', **-loa'** (hă-lō'), *n., v., & interj.* See HOLLO.

hal-loo' (hă-loo'), *interj. & n.* An exclamation or call to incite an animal or attract attention; shout. — *v. i. & t.* To shout a halloo.

hal'low (hăl'ō), *v. t.* To set apart for holy or religious use; consecrate.   [31.

Hal'low-een' (-ēn'), *n.* The evening of October

hal-lu'ci-na'tion (hă-lū'sĭ-nā'shŭn), *n.* Perception of objects with no reality, or experience of sensations with no external cause; illusion.

ha'lo (hā'lō), *n.; pl.* -LOS, -LOES (-lōz). **1.** A circle of light appearing to surround a luminous body, as around the moon. **2.** *Art.* A circle or disk of light around the head; a form of nimbus.

halt (hôlt), *n.* A stop, as in marching; arrest of progress. — *v. i. & t.* To cease progress; stop.

halt, *a.* Lame. — *v. i.* **1.** To limp. **2.** To hesitate.

hal'ter (hôl'tẽr), *n.* A strong strap or cord ; esp.:
a A rope or strap for leading or tying an animal.
b A rope for hanging criminals.

halve (häv), *v. t.* [1] To divide into halves.

halves (hävz), *n. ; pl.* of HALF.

hal'yard (hăl'yẽrd), *n.* A rope or tackle for hoisting or lowering sails, flags, etc.

ham (hăm), *n.* **1.** The region back of the knee joint; in quadrupeds, the hock. **2.** The thigh and buttock ; — esp. in *pl.* **3.** Thigh of an animal, esp. a hog, prepared for food.

hame (hām), *n.* Either of two curved pieces (bearing on the collar) to which the traces are fastened.

ham'let (hăm'lĕt), *n.* A small village.

ham'mer (-ẽr), *n.* **1.** An implement for pounding, beating, driving nails, etc. **2.** Something like, or suggestive of, a hammer. — *v. t. & i.* To strike with a hammer; beat with heavy blows.

ham'mer-head' (-hĕd'), *n.* Any of certain sharks having a hammer-shaped head.

ham'mock (-ŭk), *n.* A hanging couch or bed, consisting of a wide strip of canvas, of netting, or the like, suspended by cords at both ends.

ham'per (-pẽr), *n.* A large covered basket.

ham'per, *v. t.* To fetter ; embarrass ; encumber. — *n.* A shackle; anything which impedes.

ham'string' (-strĭng'), *n.* In man, either of the great tendons back of the knee. In quadrupeds, the large tendon above and behind the hock. — *v. t.* To cut the hamstring or hamstrings of; disable.

hand (hănd), *n.* **1.** The terminal part of the arm adapted, as in man and apes, as a grasping organ. **2.** Personal possession ; ownership ; hence, control ; — usually in *pl.* **3.** Handwriting. **4.** A hired worker at manual labor. **5.** Side; direction. **6.** Source, as of knowledge. **7.** Something like, or suggestive of, a hand, as a pointer on a dial, etc. **8.** A hand's breadth, or 4 inches. **9.** *Card Playing.*

a A player. **b** A single round in a game. **c** The cards received by a player at one deal. — *v. t.* **1.** To lead or assist with the hand; conduct. **2.** To give or pass with the hand.

hand'bill' (-bĭl'), *n.* Printed sheet to be handed out

hand'book' (-book'), *n.* A manual ; guidebook.

hand'breadth' (hănd'brĕdth'), *n.* A linear measure varying from about 2½ to 4 inches.

hand'cuff' (-kŭf'), *n.* A manacle ; — usually in *pl* — *v. t.* To manacle.

hand'ed, *a.* Having a hand or hands, esp. of a specified sort or number.

hand'ful (-fool), *n.; pl.* -FULS (-foolz). **1.** As much or many as the hand will grasp. **2.** A small quantity or number.

hand'i-cap (hăn'dĭ-kăp), *n.* **1.** A race or contest in which chances are equalized by imposing a disadvantage on a superior contestant, as by differences of start, etc.; also, the condition imposed or granted. **2.** Any disadvantage that renders achievement more difficult. — *v. t. ;* -CAPPED (-kăpt); -CAP'PING. To assign a handicap to.

hand'i-craft (-krăft), *n.* **1.** Manual skill. **2.** A trade requiring skill of hand. — **-crafts'man,** *n.*

hand'i-ly (hăn'dĭ-lĭ), *adv.* In a handy manner.

hand'i-ness (-nĕs), *n.* Quality of being handy.

hand'i-work' (-wûrk'), *n.* Work done with the hands; hence, any work done personally.

hand'ker-chief (hăn'kẽr-chĭf), *n.* **1.** A piece of cloth, usually square, carried for wiping the face, nose, etc. **2.** A kerchief; neckerchief.

han'dle (hăn'd'l), *v. t.* [1] **1.** To touch, feel, hold, take up, move, etc., with the hand. **2.** To manage; manipulate. **3.** To deal with ; treat. **4.** To deal or trade in. — *v. i.* To use the hands. — *n.* That part of a vessel, instrument, etc., to be held in the hand; — often *fig.*

hand'maid' (hănd'mād'), *n.* A female servant or attendant : — often figuratively.

hand'saw' (hănd'sô'), *n.* A saw used with one hand.

hand'some (hăn'sŭm), *a.* [3] **1.** Ample. **2.** Gracious ; liberal; generous. **3.** Having a pleasing appearance, with dignity and symmetry. — **hand'some-ly,** *adv.* [8] — **-ness,** *n.*

hand'spike' (hănd'spīk'), *n.* A bar, as of wood, used as a lever, as in a capstan.

hand'writ'ing (-rĭt'ĭng), *n.* Form of writing peculiar to a particular hand or person.

hand'y (hăn'dĭ), *a.* [3] **1.** Ready to hand ; convenient. **2.** Skillful with the hand ; dexterous **3.** *Naut.* Easily managed; as, the yacht is *handy.*

hang (hăng), *v. t. ; pret. & p. p.* HUNG (hŭng) or, in sense 2, HANGED (hăngd) ; *p. pr. & vb. n.* HANG'-ING. **1.** To fasten to a point above without support from below ; suspend. **2.** To put to death by suspending from a cross, gibbet, or gallows ; esp., to suspend by the neck till dead. **3.** To fasten so as to allow free motion. **4.** To droop ; incline. **5.** To cover or decorate by suspending something. — *v. i.* **1.** To dangle. **2.** To die by hanging. **3.** To lean or incline over or downward. **4.** To hover; impend. **5.** To depend. **6.** To be in rapt attention; — often with *on.* **7.** To cling; stick. **8.** To be in suspense; linger; loiter. — *n.* **1.** Manner in which a thing hangs. **2.** Meaning; method of use; knack. *Colloq., U. S.*

āle, senāte, câre, ăm, ăccount, ärm, ȧsk, sofȧ; ēve, ĕvent, ĕnd, recĕnt, makēr; īce, ĭll; ōld, ȯbey, ôrb, ŏdd, sŏft, cȯnnect; ūse, ŭnite, ûrn, ŭp, circŭs; fōōd, fŏŏt ; out, oil;

han′gar′ (hän′gär′; *F.* än′gär′), *n.* [F.] A shelter or shed, esp. for a coach or aircraft.

hang′bird′ (häng′bûrd′), *n.* The Baltimore oriole.

hang′dog′ (-dŏg′), *n.* A despicable person. — *a.* [4] Sneaking; base.

hang′er (-ĕr), *n.* **1.** One that hangs; a short, usually slightly curved sword. **2.** A hanging device.

hang′er-on′, *n.; pl.* HANGERS-ON. A dependent; one who stays longer than he is wanted.

hang′ing (häng′ĭng), *n.* **1.** A suspending or state of being suspended. **2.** Execution by hanging. **3.** That which is hung, as drapery, tapestry, wall paper, etc. ; — chiefly in *pl.*

hang′man (häng′mǎn), *n.; pl.* -MEN (-měn). One who executes a condemned person by hanging.

hang′nail′ (nāl′), *n.* A sliver of skin which hangs loose at the side of a finger nail.

hank (hăngk), *n.* A coil or skein, as of yarn.

han′ker (hǎn′kēr), *v. i.* To long (for).

Hansom.

han′som (hăn′-sŭm), *n.* A kind of carriage. See *Illust.*

hansom cab. A hansom.

hap (hăp), *n.* Chance ; happening ; luck. — *v. i.* ; HAPPED (hăpt) ; HAP′PING. To happen.

hap′haz′ard (hăp′hăz′ärd), *n.* Chance; accident; — chiefly in *at*, or *by*, *haphazard*.— *a.* [4] Chance; accidental. — *adv.* In a haphazard manner.

hap′less, *a.* [4] Unfortunate ; unlucky.

hap′ly, *adv.* By chance ; perhaps ; it may be.

hap′pen (hăp′'n), *v. i.* **1.** To occur by chance or without previous design ; fall out ; hence, to come to pass. **2.** To come (on) by chance.

hap′pen-ing, *n.* An occurrence ; event.

hap′pi-ly (-ĭ-lĭ), *adv.* **1.** Luckily. **2.** In a happy manner. **3.** With dexterity ; gracefully ; aptly.

hap′pi-ness (-něs), *n.* **1.** Good fortune ; prosperity. **2.** A state of pleasurable content with one's condition of life. **3.** Graceful aptitude ; felicity.

hap′py (hăp′ĭ), *a.* [3] **1.** Favored by hap, or fortune ; lucky ; prosperous. **2.** Contented ; joyous. **3.** Apt ; felicitous. **4.** Expressing happiness.

hap′py-go-luck′y, *a.* Easy-going.

ha′ra-ki′ri (hä′rä-kē′rē), *n.* Suicide by piercing the abdomen. *Japanese.*

ha-rangue′ (há-răng′), *n.* A loud address ; a noisy, ranting speech. — *v. i. & t.* [1] To make, or address in, a harangue.

har′ass (hăr′ăs), *v. t.* To weary or distress with importunity, care, etc., or by repeated attacks.

har′bin-ger (här′bĭn-jēr), *n.* A forerunner.

har′bor (-bēr), *n.* [5] **1.** A place of security and comfort. **2.** A portion of a body of water so protected as to afford a refuge for vessels ; port ; haven. — *v. t.* To give shelter to ; to indulge or cherish (a thought or feeling, esp. an ill thought).

har′bor-age (-ȧj), *n.* [5] Shelter; harbor.

hard (härd), *a.* [3] **1.** Not easily penetrated; firm; solid. **2.** Difficult to impress or influence ; unfeeling. **3. a** Severe or oppressive. **b** Arduous or troublesome. **4.** Having difficulty in doing something ; as, rather *hard* of hearing. **5.** Persevering, violent ; intense. **6.** Not agreeable; harsh. Specif.: **a** Acid; sour, as liquors. **b** Strong; spirituous, as distilled liquors. *U. S.* **7.** Containing mineral salts that interfere with the action of soap ; — said of water. **8. a** Explosive in utterance; — said of certain consonant sounds, as *c* in *came*, and *g* in *go*. **b** Voiceless, or surd, as *p*, *t*, *k*; — contrasted with "*soft*," that is, voiced, or sonant, as *b*, *d*, *g*. — *adv.* **1.** With pressure, tension, or strain ; with energy ; earnestly ; vigorously. **2.** Severely ; cruelly. **3.** With difficulty. **4.** Tightly ; firmly ; fast. **5.** So as to be hard. **6.** Close or near.

hard′en (här′d'n), *v. t. & i.* **1.** To make or become hard or harder, or hardy. **2.** To confirm, or to become confirmed, esp. in disposition.

hard′-head′ed, *a.* [4] Of sound judgment ; shrewd.

hard′-heart′ed, *a.* [4] Unfeeling ; cruel.

har′di-hood (här′dĭ-hŏod), *n.* Boldness with firmness, intrepidity ; also, impudence.

har′di-ly, *adv.* In a hardy manner ; boldly ; stoutly.

har′di-ness, *n.* **1.** Physical vigor. **2.** Hardihood.

hard′ly (härd′lĭ), *adv.* **1.** Severely ; harshly. **2.** With difficulty. **3.** Scarcely ; not probably.

hard′ness, *n.* Quality or state of being hard.

hard′pan′ (-păn′), *n.* Earth that is hard to dig into or excavate, as a firm clay subsoil. *Chiefly U. S.*

hard′ship (-shĭp), *n.* That which is hard to bear, as privation, injury, etc.

hard′-tack′, *n.* A kind of hard biscuit or sea bread.

hard′ware′ (-wâr′), *n.* Metal ware, as cutlery.

hard wood, or **hard′wood′**, *n.* **1.** Any wood which is heavy, close-grained, and resistant. **2.** The wood of any broad-leaved tree as distinguished from that of a conifer ; hence, any broad-leaved tree.

har′dy (här′dĭ), *a.* [3] **1.** Bold ; audacious. **2.** Inured to fatigue or hardships ; robust. **3.** Able to bear the cold of winter ; — of plants.

hare (hâr), *n.* A swift, timid rodent having a divided upper lip.

hare′bell′ (hâr′běl′), *n.* A small, slender plant with blue bell-shaped flowers ; — often called *bluebell.*

hare′brained′ (-brānd′), *a.* [4] Giddy ; heedless.

hare′lip′ (-lĭp′), *n.* A congenital deformity of the lip, commonly the upper one, marked by a split.

ha′rem (hā′rěm), *n.* The women's apartments in a Mohammedan residence ; also, the occupants.

har′i-cot (hăr′ĭ-kŏ; -kŏt), *n.* **1.** A ragout of meat with vegetables. **2.** The seed or unripe pod of the string bean.

Harebell.

hark (härk), *v. i.* To listen ; hearken. *Rare* except in imperative used as an interj., *Hark!* listen !

Har′le-quin (här′lĕ-kwĭn ; -kĭn), *n.* **1.** A character in comedy and pantomime with shaven head, and party-colored tights. **2.** [*l. c.*] A buffoon.

---

chair ; go ; sing, ink ; then, thin ; nature, verdure ; yet ; zh = z in azure. Numbers refer to §§ in the Special Notes which, with Abbreviations, Signs, etc., precede the Vocabulary.

harm (härm), n. 1. Injury; hurt; misfortune. 2. Evil; wrong.—v. t. To hurt; damage.

harm'ful (härm'fŏŏl), a. [4] Hurtful; mischievous.

harm'less, a. Free from harm; not harmful.

har-mon'ic (här-mŏn'Ĭk), a. 1. Concordant; consonant. 2. Relating to harmony as distinguished from melody or rhythm.

har-mon'i-ca (-Ĭ-ká), n. *Music.* A harmonicon.

har-mon'i-con (-kŏn), n.; *L. pl.* HARMONICA (-ká). A small wind instrument, played by the mouth; a "mouth organ."

har-mon'ics (-Ĭks), n. Science of musical sounds.

har-mo'ni-ous (-mō'nĬ-ŭs), a. 1. Symmetrical; congruous; in accord. 2. Marked by harmony.

har'mo-nize (här'mŏ-nīz), v. i. & t. [1] To be or make harmonious.

har'mo-ny (här'mŏ-nĬ), n.; pl. -NIES (-nĬz). 1. Just adaptation of parts to each other, giving unity or a pleasing whole; agreement; congruity. 2. Concord in facts, opinions, manners, interests, etc. 3. *Music.* **a** Tuneful sound. **b** Combination of tones into a chord. **c** Structure of a piece of music in relation to its chords. **d** Science of chords.

har'ness (här'nĕs), n. 1. The complete dress, armor, or trappings, of a warrior or a horse. *Hist.* 2. The gear (other than a yoke) of a draft animal, as of a horse.—v. t. 1. To accouter; arm. *Archaic.* 2. To put harness on, as a horse.

harp (härp), n. 1. A stringed instrument having the strings set in an open frame and plucked with the fingers. 2. Any contrivance like, or suggestive of, a harp.—v. i. 1. To play the harp. 2. To dwell on a subject tediously. — **harp'er**, n. [8].

harp'ist, n. A harp player.

har-poon' (här-pōōn'), n. A barbed spear or javelin, to which a rope is attached, used to strike large fish, whales, etc.—v. t. To strike, catch, or kill with a harpoon. — **har-poon'er**, n. [8].

harp'si-chord (härp'sĬ-kôrd), n. A harp-shaped wire-stringed instrument, precursor of the piano.

Har'py (här'pĬ), n.; pl. -PIES (-pĬz). 1. *Class. Myth.* A rapacious monster having a woman's head and body and a bird's wings, tail, legs, and claws. 2. [l. c.] A rapacious person; extortioner.

har'ri-dan (här'Ĭ-dăn), n. A vixenish woman; hag.

har'ri-er (här'Ĭ-ĕr), n. 1. One who harries. 2. A hawk that feeds on small animals and insects.

har'ri-er, n. One of a breed of small hounds used for hunting hares.

har'row (här'ō), n. An implement of agriculture set with iron or wooden teeth and drawn over plowed land to break the clods, etc.—v. t. 1. To draw a harrow over (land). 2. To torment or distress; lacerate; as, to *harrow* one's feelings.

har'ry (här'Ĭ), v. t. & i. [2] 1. To ravage; pillage; plunder. 2. To harrow; harass.

harsh (härsh), a. [3] 1. Offensive to sense or feeling as being coarse, rough, discordant, astringent, sour, severe, etc.; rasping; repellent. 2. Unfeeling; severe; cruel. — **-ly**, adv. [8] — **-ness**, n. [8].

hart (härt), n. A stag; male red deer.

harts'horn' (härts'hôrn'), n. The horn of a hart, or stag; hence, ammonia, or **spirit of hartshorn**, of which such horns were formerly the chief source.

har'um-scar'um (här'ŭm-skär'ŭm), a. [4] Reckless; wild; heedless; rash. *Colloq.*

har'vest (här'vĕst), n. 1. Season of gathering grain and fruits; also, the gathering of a crop or crops. 2. Crop; yield, as of grain, fruit, etc.—v. t. To reap or gather, as a crop.—**har'vest-er**, n. [8].

harvest home. The gathering and bringing home of the harvest; also, a feast made at the close of the harvest; hence, the song sung by the reapers.

har'vest-man (här'vĕst-măn), n.; pl. -MEN. Any of various harmless spiderlike insects.

has (hăz), 3d pers. sing. pres. of HAVE.

hash (hăsh), v. t. To mince and mix; mangle. — n. 1. That which is hashed; meat and vegetables, esp. when already cooked, minced, and mixed. 2. A mixture; jumble; mess.

hash'ish (hăsh'ēsh; há-shēsh'), n. A narcotic preparation of hemp used in the Orient for its intoxicating effect when chewed or smoked.

hasp (hăsp), n. A clasp or fastening, as for a door; esp., a hinged metal strap secured by a staple and pin or padlock.

has'sock (hăs'ŭk), n. 1. A rank tuft of sedge; tussock. 2. A cushion footstool.

hast (hăst), 2d pers. sing. pres. of HAVE.

haste (hāst), n. 1. Quickness of motion; swiftness; dispatch; — applied to voluntary action. 2. Undue celerity; hurry.

haste, v. t. & i. [1] To hasten; hurry. *Now Chiefly Literary.*

has'ten (hās'n), v. t. To drive or urge forward; expedite; hurry. — v. i. To make haste; hurry.

hast'y (hās'tĬ), a. [3] 1. Done or made quickly; swift; hurried. 2. Not deliberative or cautious; precipitate. 3. Having, proceeding from, or indicating a quick temper. — **hast'i-ly**, adv. [8] — **-i-ness**, n. [8].

hasty pudding. 1. A batter or pudding of flour or oatmeal. 2. Indian meal mush.

hat (hăt), n. A covering for the head, esp. one with a crown and brim.

hatch (hăch), v. t. 1. To mark with hatching. 2. To inlay in fine lines.

hatch, v. t. 1. To produce (young) from an egg or eggs; as, to *hatch* a chicken; also, to produce young from (an egg or eggs); as, to *hatch* an egg. 2. To contrive, as a plot. — v. i. To produce young; — said of eggs; to come from the egg; — of the young. — n. Act of hatching; also, that which is hatched.

hatch, n. 1. The covering of an opening in the deck of a vessel, in a floor, etc. 2. A hatchway.

hatch'el (hăch'ĕl), n. A toothed instrument for combing flax or hemp; hackle; heckle. — v. t. [7] To dress with a hatchel.

hatch'et (-ĕt), n. A small ax used with one hand.

hatch'ing, n. In drawing, etc., the process or result of making close fine lines, to give shading.

hatch'way' (-wā'), n. An opening in a deck, floor, roof, etc.; hatch.

hate (hāt), v. t. [1] To dislike intensely; detest; in a weakened sense, to dislike; as, to *hate* to write. — n. Intense aversion. — **hat'er**, n. [8].

hate'ful (hāt'fŏŏl), a. [4] 1. Full of ill will. 2. Exciting hate. — **-ly**, adv. [8] — **-ness**, n. [8].

hath (hăth). = HAS, 3d pers. sing. pres. of HAVE. *Archaic.*

ha'tred (hā'trĕd), n. Strong aversion with ill will.

hat'ter (hăt'ĕr), n. One who makes or sells hats.

hau'berk (hô'bẽrk), n. A coat of ring or chain mail.

haugh'ty (hô'tĭ), a. [3] Disdainfully proud; arrogant. — **haugh'ti-ly** (-tĭ-lĭ), adv. [8] — **haugh'ti-ness**, n. [8].

haul (hôl), v. t. & i. **1.** To pull; drag; transport by drawing. **2.** To shift the course of (a ship), esp. so as to sail closer to the wind. — n. **1.** A violent pull; a tug. **2.** A single draft of a net. **3.** That which is caught or gained at once, as by a net. **4.** Distance through which anything is hauled, as freight. — **haul'er**, n. [8].

haul'age (-ăj), n. Process of, or charge for, hauling.

haunch (hänch; hônch), n. **1.** The hip; loosely, in pl., the hind quarters. **2.** Of meats, the leg and loin taken together.

haunt (hänt; hônt), v. t. **1.** To frequent; visit persistently. **2.** To inhabit or frequent as a ghost. **3.** To recur to (the mind, etc.) often; as, haunted by regrets. — v. i. To resort habitually. — n. A place to which one often resorts; resort.

hau-teur' (hō-tûr'), n. Haughtiness.

have (hăv), v. t.; pret. & p. p. HAD (hăd); p. pr. & vb. n. HAV'ING. **1.** To hold in possession or control; possess; own. **2.** To possess mentally; know; understand. **3.** To be compelled; as, he had to leave. **4.** To keep or cherish in the mind. **5.** To be in a certain relation to; as, we have trouble in store. **6.** To give expression to, or to exercise (a feeling, opinion, or the like). **7.** To perform; experience; engage in; — in the widest sense; as, to have to do with. **8.** To maintain; assert; as, rumor had it so. **9.** To obtain or get; accept; take; as, he must have food. **10.** To obtain an advantage over; hold in one's power. Often Colloq. **11.** To cause to go into a place or state; cause (something) to be done.

☞ Have, as an auxiliary, is used with the past participle of any other verb to form its "perfect tenses," or to express completed action; as, I have loved; I shall have eaten. Had is used for would or would have with adjectives, adverbs, or phrases of comparison (as, as lief, rather, better) to indicate preference or advisability.

ha'ven (hā'v'n), n. Harbor; port; place of safety.

hav'er-sack (hăv'ẽr-săk), n. A bag or case, usually of cloth, for carrying provisions on a march.

hav'oc (hăv'ŏk), n. Destruction, esp. wide and general destruction; waste.

haw (hô), n. The hawthorn or its fruit.

haw, v. i. & t. To turn (a team, etc.) to the left.

haw, n. & interj. A certain hesitation of speech, or its sound. — v. i. To hesitate in speaking, as with a sound like haw; — esp. in to hum (or hem) and haw.

Ha-wai'ian (hä-wī'yăn), a. Pert. to Hawaii or the Hawaiians. — n. A native of Hawaii.

hawk (hôk), n. Any diurnal bird of prey (except the eagle and the vulture) of the family including the falcons, buzzards, harriers, and kites; esp., any of a certain genus of these birds, which pursue their prey with swift turns and dodges. — v. t. To pursue birds by means of trained hawks.

Hawk.

hawk (hôk), v. i. To clear the throat noisily. — v. t. To raise by hawking; — often with up.

hawk, v. t. To offer for sale by outcry; peddle.

hawk'er (hôk'ẽr), n. One who hawks wares.

hawk'er, n. One who follows the sport of hawking.

hawk'ing, n. Falconry.

hawse (hôz; hôs), n. A hawse hole; or, that part of the bow where the hawse holes are.

hawse hole. A hole in a ship's bow, through which a cable passes.

haw'ser (hô'zẽr; -sẽr), n. A large rope for towing or securing a ship.

haw'thorn (-thôrn), n. Any of various shrubs or trees having shining, often lobed, leaves, fragrant flowers, and small red fruits called haws.

hay (hā), n. Grass mowed or ready for mowing, grass cut and cured for fodder. — v. i. To cut and cure grass for hay.

hay fever. A catarrhal affection of the eyes and respiratory tract caused by inhaled pollen of certain plants.

hay'mow (hā'mou'), n. A mow of hay laid up in a barn; also, the part of a barn where hay is kept.

hay'rick (-rĭk'), n. A haystack.

hay'stack (-stăk'), n. A pile, or stack, of hay.

haz'ard (hăz'ạrd), n. **1.** Chance; accident. **2.** Risk; danger; peril. — v. t. To venture; risk.

haz'ard-ous (-ạr-dŭs), a. [4] Exposed to hazard; dangerous; risky. — **haz'ard-ous-ly**, adv. [8].

haze (hāz), n. Light vapor or smoke in the air; hence, figuratively, obscurity; dimness.

haze, v. t. [1] **1.** To harass with labor. Chiefly Naut. **2.** To play abusive or ridiculous tricks on; — used esp. of college students. — **haz'er** (hāz'ẽr), n. [8].

ha'zel (hā'z'l), n. **1.** Any of various shrubs or small trees bearing nuts, called hazelnuts, which are inclosed in a leafy involucre. **2.** A light reddish brown color. — a. Of the color hazel.

ha'zy (hā'zĭ), a. [3] Characterized by haze; obscure; vague. — **-ly**, adv. [8] — **-i-ness**, n. [8].

he (hē), pron.; nom. HE; poss. HIS (hĭz); obj. HIM (hĭm); pl. nom. THEY (thā); poss. THEIR (thâr) or THEIRS (thârz); obj. THEM (thĕm). **1.** The man or male being previously designated. **2.** Any man, any one; as, "He that hath ears to hear."

head (hĕd), n. **1.** The part of the body containing the brain, mouth, etc. **2.** The hair of the head. **3.** Intellect; understanding. **4.** Leader; chief. **5.** Chief position; front; the upper or the principal end of various things. **6.** An individual; — often used as a plural; as, ten head of cattle. **7.** The top part of a plant, esp. when compact. **8.** A heading; a separate part, or topic. **9.** Source, as of a stream; height of the surface, as of water, above a given place. **10.** Culminating point or crisis. — a. **1.** Principal; chief; leading. **2.** Situated at the head. **3.** Coming from in front. — v. t. **1.** To lop off the top branches of; poll. **2.** To fit or furnish with a head. **3.** To put something at the head of. **4.** To act as leader of. **5.** To get in front of; hence, to check; restrain; — often with off. **6.** To shape the course of. — v. i. **1.** To form a head, as a cabbage. **2.** To go or have direction; tend.

head'ache' (hĕd'āk'), *n.* Pain in the head.

head'band' (-bănd'), *n.* A band for the head; a fillet. [for the head.

head'dress' (-drĕs'), *n.* A covering or ornament

head'er (hĕd'ẽr), *n.* **1.** A fall or plunge headforemost. **2.** One that heads nails, rivets, etc.

head'first' (-fûrst'), **head'fore'most** (-fōr'mōst), *adv.* With the head foremost; headlong.

head'gear' (-gēr'), *n.* Headdress.

head'ing, *n.* **1.** Act or state of one that heads; formation of a head. **2.** A head; title.

head'land (-lănd), *n.* A cape or promontory.

head'light' (hĕd'līt'), *n.* A light at the head.

head'line' (-līn'), *n.* The title, etc., at the top of a page; a title in a newspaper, etc.

head'long (hĕd'lông), *adv.* **1.** Headforemost. **2.** Rashly; impetuously. — *a.* **1.** Rash; precipitate. **2.** Plunging headforemost.

head'piece' (-pēs'), *n.* **1.** A covering or fitting for the head, as a helmet, etc. **2.** An engraved ornament at the head of a chapter or page.

head'quar'ters (-kwôr'tẽrz), *n. pl.;* sometimes used as a *sing.* Quarters or residence of a chief officer; place from which orders are issued.

head'ship, *n.* Chief authority or place; primacy.

heads'man (hĕdz'mǎn), *n.; pl.* -MEN. Executioner.

head'stone' (-stōn'), *n.* Stone at head of a grave.

head'strong (-strông), *a.* [4] **1.** Not easily restrained; stubborn; self-willed. **2.** Proceeding from or marked by willfulness.

head'wa'ter (hĕd'wô'tẽr), *n.* The source or upper part of a stream; — chiefly in *pl.*

head'way' (hĕd'wā'), *n.* **1.** Motion forward, as of a ship. **2.** Clear space under an arch, etc.

head'y (hĕd'ĭ), *a.* [3] **1.** Willful; rash. **2.** Apt to affect the head; intoxicating.

heal (hēl), *v. t. & i.* **1.** To make or grow sound or whole; cure. **2.** To restore to purity or integrity; free from guilt. — **-er,** *n.* [8].

health (hĕlth), *n.* **1.** State of being hale or sound; esp., freedom from physical disease. **2.** A wish of health and happiness; as, to drink a *health.*

health'ful (-fool), *a.* [4] Promoting health; wholesome. — **-ful-ness,** *n.* [8].

health'y (hŏl'thĭ), *a.* [3] **1.** Enjoying health. **2.** Indicating or characteristic of health. **3.** Conducive to health; wholesome; salutary. — **health'-i-ly** (-thĭ-lĭ), *adv.* [8] — **-i-ness,** *n.* [8].

heap (hēp), *n.* **1.** A pile; mass. **2.** A great number or quantity. *Chiefly Colloq.* — *v. t.* **1.** To put in a heap; pile. **2.** To bestow large quantities upon. **3.** To fill more than even full.

hear (hēr), *v. t.; * HEARD (hûrd); HEAR'ING. **1.** To perceive by the ear; to gain knowledge of by hearing. **2.** To listen to; heed. **3.** To hear for examination or judgment. **4.** To grant, as a prayer. — *v. i.* **1.** To have the faculty of perceiving sound. **2.** To attend; listen. **3.** To receive information.

heard (hûrd), *pret. & p. p.* of HEAR.

hear'er (hēr'ẽr), *n.* One who hears; auditor.

hear'ing, *n.* **1.** Act or power of perceiving sound; the sense by which sound is perceived. **2.** Attention; audience; as, to get a *hearing.* **3.** A listening to evidence for adjudication. **4.** Earshot.

heark'en, hark'en (här'k'n), *v. i.* To listen; esp., to give heed.

hear'say' (hēr'sā'), *n.* Report; rumor.

hearse (hûrs), *n.* Formerly, a bier; now, a kind of wagon for conveying the dead to the grave.

heart (härt), *n.* **1.** *Anat.* The organ which keeps the blood circulating. **2.** The seat of life or strength; hence, mind; soul; spirit. **3.** Hence: **a** The emotional nature; affection; kindly feeling. **b** Courage; spirit; ardor. **c** The understanding; also, memory; — now chiefly in *by heart.* **d** Temperament; mood. **4.** Inmost, central, or vital part. **5.** Something resembling a heart in shape; hence, one of a suit (called *hearts*) of playing cards marked by such a figure.

heart'ache' (härt'āk'), *n.* Sorrow; anguish of mind.

heart'bro'ken (-brō'k'n), *a.* [4] Intensely grieved.
Heart, 5.

heart'burn' (-bûrn'), *n.* Burning sensation in the stomach, often with inclination to vomit.

heart'burn'ing, *n.* Discontent; secret enmity.

heart'ed, *a.* Having a heart; chiefly in combination; as, warm-*hearted*; faint-*hearted.*

heart'en (här't'n), *v. t.* To give heart to; encourage.

heart'felt' (härt'fĕlt'), *a.* [4] Deeply felt; sincere

hearth (härth), *n.* **1.** The floor of a fireplace. **2.** The fireside; hence, the house or home itself.

hearth'stone' (härth'stōn'), *n.* Stone forming the hearth; hence, fireside; home.

heart'i-ly (här'tĭ-lĭ), *adv.* **1.** From the heart; sincerely. **2.** With zest or zeal; warmly. **3.** Abundantly; completely; as, *heartily* tired of a thing.

heart'i-ness (-nĕs), *n.* Quality of being hearty.

heart'less, *a.* [4] **a** Without heart or a heart; as a Spiritless. **b** Unsympathetic; cruel.

hearts'ease' (härts'ēz'), *n.* Also **heart's'-ease'.** **1.** Peace of mind or feeling. **2.** Any of several plants; esp., the pansy.

heart'sick' (härt'sĭk'), *a.* [4] Sick at heart.

heart'strings' (-strĭngz'), *n. pl.* Deepest emotions or affections.

heart'wood' (härt'wŏŏd'), *n.* The hard tough wood in the center of a tree trunk.

heart'y (här'tĭ), *a.* [3] **1.** Proceeding from the heart; cordial; sincere. **2.** Strong; sound; firm. **3.** Promoting strength; nourishing; abundant. — *n.; pl.* HEARTIES (-tĭz). Comrade; good fellow; — used esp. to or of a sailor. *Archaic.*

heat (hēt), *n.* **1.** A form of energy appearing in the effects of fire, the sun's rays, friction, etc. **2.** High temperature; also, a period of heat. **3.** Condition, or color as indicating temperature; degree to which a thing is heated. **4.** Intensity of feeling or action. **5.** A single effort; also, single course in a race. — *v. t. & i.* To make or grow hot; hence, to excite; inflame. — **heat'er,** *n.* [8].

heath (hēth), *n.* **1.** A tract of waste land; esp., in Great Britain, an open, level area with a characteristic vegetation of heath or heather. **2.** Any of various evergreen shrubs growing on heaths.

hea'then (hē'th'n), *n.; pl.* -THENS (-th'nz) or *collectively* -THEN. **1.** An unconverted individual of a people that do not acknowledge the God of the Bible; in the Bible, an idolater or a Gentile. **2.** An unenlightened or irreligious person. — *a.* [4] Gentile; pagan. Hence, unenlightened; irreligious. — **hea'then-ish,** *a.* [4, 8].

ālé, senāte, câre, ăm, *ă*ccount, ärm, ásk, sof*à*; ēve, ĕvent, ênd, recênt, makēr; īce, ĭll; ōld, ōbey, ôrb, ŏdd, sŏft, cŏnnect; ūse, ŭnite, ûrn, ŭp, circ*ŭ*s; fōōd, fŏŏt; out, oil;

hea′then-dom (-dŭm), *n.* **1.** Heathenism. **2.** Heathens collectively; the heathen world.

hea′then-ism (-ĭz′m), *n.* The rites of heathens; idolatry; also, heathenlike manners or morals.

heath′er (hĕth′ẽr), *n.* Any of several British heaths (see *Illust.* and HEATH, 2).

heath′er-y (-ĭ), *a.* Abounding in or like heather.

heave (hēv), *v. t. ; pret. & p. p.* HEAVED (hēvd), HOVE (hōv); *p. pr. & vb. n.* HEAV′ING. **1.** To lift; raise, usually with exertion. **2.** To cause to swell or rise, as the breast. **3.** To force from the breast; utter with effort, as a groan. **4.** To throw; cast. *Chiefly Naut. or Colloq.* **5.** *Naut.* To draw or pull; haul on. — *v. i.* **1.** To be thrown up or raised; rise. **2.** To rise and fall alternately, as the waves. **3. a** To pant. **b** To retch. — **to heave to,** to stop a vessel by bringing her head into the wind, with a sail or sails aback; — said also of the vessel. — *n.* **1.** An effort to raise something. **2.** Upward motion, esp. if rhythmical.

Heather. Reduced.

heav′en (hĕv′n), *n.* **1.** The firmament; sky; — chiefly in *pl.* **2.** The dwelling place of the Deity; place or state of the blessed dead. **3.** Any place of supreme happiness; also, felicity; bliss; a sublime or exalted condition.

heav′en-ly (-lĭ), *a.* [4] Of, pertaining to, or appropriate to, heaven; celestial; divine. — **heav′en-li-ness**, *n.* [8].

heav′en-ly, *adv.* In a heavenly manner or degree.

heav′en-ward (-wẽrd), *a. & adv.* Toward heaven.

heav′er (hĕv′ẽr), *n.* One that heaves or lifts.

heaves (hēvz), *n.* A disease, esp. of horses, accompanied with heaving of the flanks and coughing.

heav′i-ly (hĕv′ĭ-lĭ), *adv.* In a heavy manner.

heav′i-ness (-nĕs), *n.* Quality of being heavy.

heav′y (hĕv′ĭ), *a.* [3] **1.** Lifted with labor; weighty. **2.** Burdensome; oppressive. **3.** Profound; intense; severe. **4.** Burdened; bowed down, as with care. **5.** Slow or dull; sluggish; stupid; drowsy; also, doleful. **6.** Of more than the usual amount or quantity. **7. a** Violent. **b** Gloomy; overcast. **c** Clayey; impeding motion; as, a *heavy* road. **d** Grave; loud; deep. **e** Thick; massive. **f** Oppressive; as, a *heavy* odor. **g** Steep; as, a *heavy* grade. **8. a** Of foods, etc., not easily digested. **b** Of wines, etc., strong. **c** Not raised or light, as bread. — *adv.* Heavily.

heav′y-weight′ (hĕv′ĭ-wāt′), *n.* One of more than average weight, as a boxer of the heaviest class.

heb-dom′a-dal (hĕb-dŏm′à-dăl), *a.* Consisting of seven days, or occurring at weekly intervals.

He-bra′ic (hê-brā′ĭk), *a.* Pertaining to the Hebrews or to Hebrew.

He′brew (hē′bro͞o), *n.* **1.** A member of one of a group of northern Semitic tribes including the Israelites of the Bible. *Cf.* JEW. **2.** The original language of the Hebrews, not now in common use. **3.** *pl.* The New Testament Epistle to the Hebrews. — **He′brew**, *a.*

hec′a-tomb (-tŏm; -toͦom), *n. Antiq.* A sacrifice of a hundred oxen; hence, a great slaughter.

heck′le (hĕk′'l), *v. t.* [1] **1.** = HACKLE. **2.** To badger with questions. — *n.* = HACKLE.

hec′tic (hĕk′tĭk), *a.* [4] **1.** Having a fever characteristic of tuberculosis; consumptive. **2.** Symptomatic of this fever; as, a *hectic* flush.

hec′to- (hĕk′tŏ-), **hect-**. A combining form fr. Greek, meaning *hundred;* as in : **hec′tare** (-târ), 100 ares; **hec′to-gram**, 100 grams; **hec′to-li′ter** (-lē′tẽr) [6], 100 liters; **hec′to-me′ter** (-mē′tẽr) [6], 100 meters; **hec′to-stere** (-stēr), 100 steres.

hec′to-graph (-tŏ-gráf), *n.* A manifolding device using a slab of gelatin to print from.

hec′tor (hĕk′tẽr), *v. t. & i.* To bully; bluster.

hedge (hĕj), *n.* **1.** A thicket, esp. when planted as a fence or boundary. **2.** A barrier; a limit. — *v. t.* [1] **1.** To inclose or separate with a hedge. **2.** To confine or protect as with a hedge. — *v. i.* To shift; dodge; avoid committing one's self.

hedge′hog′ (hĕj′hŏg′), *n.* **1.** Any of certain small Old World insect-eating animals having hair mixed with spines which stick out in all directions when they roll themselves up. **2.** In America, popularly, the porcupine.

hedge′row′ (hĕj′rō′), *n.* A row of shrubs or trees planted for inclosure or separation of fields.

heed (hēd), *v. t.* To regard with care; take notice of. — *v. i.* To pay attention. — *n.* Attention.

heed′ful (-fooͦl), *a.* [4] Full of heed; mindful.

heed′less, *a.* [4] Without heed; careless.

heel (hēl), *v. t. & i.* To tilt or incline, as a ship.

heel, *n.* **1.** The hinder part of the foot, or of a shoe, sock, etc. **2.** Something like, or suggestive of, the human heel.

heel′er (hēl′ẽr), *n.* One who follows at the heels; esp., a hanger-on of a politician. *Polit. Cant, U. S.*

heft (hĕft), *n.* **1.** Weight; heaviness. *Colloq.* **2.** Greater part; bulk. *Colloq., U. S.* — *v. t.* To try the weight of by raising. *Colloq.*

heif′er (hĕf′ẽr), *n.* A young cow that has not calved.

heigh (hī; hā), *interj.* An exclamation used to attract attention, to encourage, etc.; hey.

height (hīt), *n.* **1.** Condition of being high. **2.** Altitude; stature. **3.** A hill or mountain. **4.** Highest part; summit; hence, an extreme.

height′en (-'n), *v. t.* **1.** To make higher; elevate. **2.** To augment; intensify; as, a price, or a flavor.

hei′nous (hā′nŭs), *a.* [4] Hateful; odious; atrocious. — **-ly**, *adv.* [8] — **-ness**, *n.* [8].

heir (âr), *n.* One who inherits, or is entitled to inherit. — **heir apparent**, an heir whose right cannot be annulled if he survives the ancestor; — disting. from **heir presumptive**, whose right may be annulled by the birth of a nearer heir.

heir′ess (âr′ĕs), *n.* A female heir.

heir′loom′ (âr′loͦom′), *n.* Any piece of personal property owned by a family for several generations.

held, *pret. & p. p.* of HOLD.

hel′i-cal (hĕl′ĭ-kăl), *a.* Like a helix; spiral.

hel′i-cop′ter (hĕl′ĭ-kŏp′tẽr), *n.* A flying machine in which the lifting force is furnished by horizontal propellers.

he′li-o-graph′ (hē′lĭ-ŏ-gráf′), *n.* An apparatus for signaling by reflecting the sun's rays. — *v. t. & i.* To signal by means of the heliograph.

he′li-o-trope (hē′lǐ-ō-trōp), *n.* **1** Any of certain herbs bearing small, fragrant white or purple flowers in spikes. **2.** A light tint of purple.

he′li-um (hē′lǐ-ŭm), *n.* A rare gas first detected in the sun's atmosphere and later found in certain minerals and mineral waters on the earth. It is one of the elements.

he′lix (hē′lǐks; hĕl′ĭks), *n.; pl.* L. **HELICES** (hĕl′ĭ-sēz), E. **HELIXES** (hē′lǐk-sĕz; hĕl′ĭk-). Something spiral in form, as a volute or a screw thread.

hell (hĕl), *n.* **1.** Place of the dead, or of souls after death; abode of evil spirits. **2.** Hence, any place or state of misery or wickedness.

hel′le-bore (hĕl′ē-bōr), *n.* **1.** Any of a genus of herbs, of the crowfoot family, with showy flowers; *black,* or *fetid, hellebore.* Also, the powdered root, used as a cathartic. **2.** Any of various plants, called *white,* or *false, hellebore,* with poisonous rootstocks. Also, the powdered root, used as an insecticide.

Hel-len′ic (hĕ-lĕn′ĭk ; -lē′nĭk), *a.* Greek.

Hel′len-ism (hĕl′ĕn-ĭz′m), *n.* **1.** A Greek phrase or idiom. **2.** Greek character, spirit, or civilization; esp., the culture of the classical Greeks.

hell′gra-mite (hĕl′grȧ-mīt), *n.* The aquatic larva of a lace-winged insect, used as a bait for fish.

hell′ish, *a.* [4] Pertaining to hell; diabolical.

hel-lo′ (hĕ-lō′), *interj., n., & v. i.* Var. of **HOLLO**.

helm (hĕlm), *n.* The apparatus for steering a vessel, comprising rudder, tiller, wheel, etc.; commonly, the tiller or wheel alone.

helm, *n.* A helmet. *Archaic or Poetic.*

hel′met (hĕl′mĕt), *n.* **1.** A defensive covering for the head. **2.** Something resembling a helmet.

helms′man (hĕlmz′mǎn), *n.; pl.* **-MEN** (-mĕn). The man who steers a vessel; a steersman.

help (hĕlp), *v. t.; pret. & p. p.* **HELPED** (hĕlpt) ; *p. pr. & vb. n.* **HELP′ING.** **1.** To aid ; assist. **2.** To furnish with relief, as from distress; succor. **3.** To aid in bringing about. **4.** To prevent; avoid. **5.** To forbear; refrain from. **6.** To serve with food. — *v. i.* To lend aid ; avail; assist. — *n.* **1.** Aid; assistance; also, one furnishing aid. **2.** Remedy; relief. **3. a** A helper; assistant, esp. a hired one. **b** A force of hired helpers. **c** A domestic servant or farm hand. *Local, U. S.* — **help′er,** *n.* [8].

help′ful (hĕlp′fŏŏl), *a.* [4] Furnishing help; useful; salutary. — **ly,** *adv.* [8] — **ness,** *n.* [8].

help′less, *a.* [4] Destitute of help or strength; unable to help one's self. — **ly,** *adv.* — **ness,** *n.*

help′mate′ (-māt′), *n.,* **help′meet′** (-mēt′), *n.* Helper; companion, esp., a wife.

hel′ter-skel′ter (hĕl′tẽr-skĕl′tẽr), *adv.* In hurry and confusion. *Colloq.* — *a.* Characterized by confused hurry. — *n.* That which is helter-skelter.

helve (hĕlv), *n.* The handle of a tool or weapon, as an ax, hatchet, or adz.

hem (hĕm), *interj.* A word used to call attention, to express hesitation, etc., or to represent a clearing of the throat. — *n.* An uttering of "hem." — *v. i.; hemmed* (hĕmd) ; **HEM′MING.** To utter "hem"; hence, to hesitate in speaking. *Cf.* **HAW.**

hem, *n.* The edge or border of a garment or cloth, esp. when formed by doubling back the cloth and sewing it. — *v. t.* **1.** To fold and sew down the edge of ; hence, to border ; edge. **2.** To inclose and confine ; surround ; — usu. with *in* or *about.*

hem′i-sphere (hĕm′ĭ-sfēr), *n.* **1.** A half sphere. **2.** Half of the terrestrial globe, esp. either half north or south of the equator (*Northern* or *Southern Hemisphere*), or either of the halves containing Europe, Asia, and Africa (*Eastern Hemisphere*) and N. and S. America (*Western Hemisphere*).

hem′i-spher′i-cal (-sfĕr′ĭ-kǎl), *a.* Of, pertaining to, or resembling, a hemisphere.

hem′lock (-lŏk), *n.* **1.** Any of several poisonous herbs of the celery family. **2.** The *hemlock spruce,* a valuable tree of the pine family.

he′mo-glo′bin. Var. of **HÆMOGLOBIN.**

hem′or-rhage (hĕm′ō-rǎj), *n.* Any discharge of blood from the blood vessels.

hem′or-rhoid (-roid), *n.* [*Usually in pl.*] A painful swelling formed by dilatation of a blood vessel at the anus ; (*pl.*) piles.

hemp (hĕmp), *n.* **1.** A tall Asiatic herb, cultivated for its tough fiber and as the source of hashish. **2.** The fiber of this plant, prepared for use.

hemp′en (hĕm′p'n), *a.* Of, pert. to, or like, hemp.

hem′stitch′ (hĕm′stǐch′), *v. t.* To ornament at the head of a hem by drawing out a few parallel threads and fastening the cross threads in small groups. — *n.* Ornamental needlework done by hemstitching, or the stitch used in it.

hen (hĕn), *n.* The female of the domestic fowl, or of any of various other birds.

hen′bane′ (hĕn′bān′), *n.* A fetid poisonous Old World herb of the nightshade family.

hence (hĕns), *adv.* **1.** From this place ; away ; from this world or life. **2.** From this time. **3.** From this reason ; therefore. **4.** From this source.

hence′forth′ (hĕns′fōrth′ ; hĕns′fōrth′), **hence′for′ward** (-fôr′wẽrd), *adv.* From this time forward.

hench′man (hĕnch′mǎn), *n.; pl.* **-MEN** (-mĕn). A trusted follower ; esp. (*U. S.*), a venal follower.

hen′na (hĕn′ȧ), *n.* An Asiatic thorny tree or shrub with fragrant white flowers. From its leaves are made a reddish orange dye and a cosmetic.

hen′ner-y (-ẽr-ĭ), *n.* A place for keeping hens.

hen′peck′ (hĕn′pĕk′), *v. t.* To subject to petty attempts to rule ; — said of a wife who thus treats her husband.

he-pat′ic (hē-păt′ĭk), *a.* Of or pert. to the liver.

he-pat′i-ca (-ĭ-kȧ), *n.; pl.* L. **-CÆ** (-sē), E. **-CAS** (-kȧz). A plant or flower of the crowfoot family, having white, pink, or purplish flowers.

hep′ta-gon (hĕp′tȧ-gŏn), *n.* Polygon of seven sides.

hep-tag′o-nal (hĕp-tăg′ō-nǎl), *a.* Seven-sided.

hep′tarch-y (hĕp′tär-kĭ), *n.; pl.* **-TARCHIES** (-kĭz). A government by seven persons ; also, a country under seven rulers.

her (hûr), *pron. & a.* The objective and the possessive case of *she.*

her′ald (hĕr′ǎld), *n.* **1.** In olden times, an officer who bore messages between rulers or commanders, made announcements, officiated in tourneys, etc. **2.** One who proclaims ; a messenger ; forerunner. — *v. t.* To proclaim ; announce ; usher in.

he-ral′dic (hē-rǎl′dǐk), *a.* Pertaining to heralds or heraldry.

her′ald-ry (hĕr′ǎld-rǐ), *n.; pl.* **-RIES** (-rǐz). **1.** The science of genealogies and of armorial bearings. **2.** A heraldic symbol or symbols.

herb (ûrb ; hûrb), *n.* **1.** A seed plant whose stem

does not develop woody tissue, but persists only long enough to bear fruit. **2.** A plant valued for medicinal properties, scent, flavor, etc.

her-ba′ceous (hẽr-bā′shŭs), *a.* Pertaining to, or having the characteristics of, an herb; herblike.

herb′age (ûr′bȧj ; hûr′-), *n.* Herbaceous vegetation; green plants used for pasturage.

herb′al (hûr′băl), *a.* Of or pertaining to herbs.

herb′al-ist, Originally, a botanist; now, a collector of, or dealer in, herbs, esp. medicinal herbs.

her-ba′ri-um (hẽr-bā′rĭ-ŭm), *n. ; pl.* E. **-riums** (-ŭmz), L. **-ria** (-ȧ). A collection of dried plants.

her-biv′o-rous (-bĭv′ô-rŭs), *a.* Eating plants.

herb′y (ûr′bĭ ; hûr′bĭ), *a.* [3] **1.** Abounding in herbaceous vegetation; grassy. **2.** Pertaining to or resembling an herb.

her-cu′le-an (hẽr-kū′lē-ăn), *a.* [4] Requiring or having great strength; hence, very great, difficult, or dangerous.

herd (hûrd), *n.* **1.** A number of beasts, esp. large ones, assembled together. **2.** A crowd of common people ; esp., with *the,* the rabble. — *v. i.* To unite or associate in a herd. — *v. t.* To form or put into a herd.

herd, *n.* A herdsman. — *v. t.* To tend, lead, or drive as a herdsman. — **herd′er,** *n.*

herds′man (hûrdz′măn), *n. ; pl.* **-men** (-mĕn). One who owns, keeps, or tends a herd or herds.

here (hēr), *adv.* **1.** In this place. **2.** In the present life or state. **3.** To or into this place; hither. **4.** At this point of time ; now.

here′a-bout′ (-ȧ-bout′)) *adv.* About this place ;
here′a-bouts′ (-bouts′)) in this vicinity.

here-aft′er (hēr-ȧft′ẽr), *adv.* In some future time or state. — *n.* A future existence or state.

here-at′ (-ăt′), *adv.* At, or by reason of, this.

here-by′ (-bī′), *adv.* By this means.

he-red′i-ta-ry (hē-rĕd′ĭ-tȧ-rĭ), *a.* **1.** Descended, or capable of legally descending, from ancestor to heir. **2.** Having title or possession by inheritance. **3.** Transmitted or transmissible by heredity, as diseases, instincts, etc. **4.** Pertaining to inheritance or heredity.

he-red′i-ty (-tĭ), *n.* Hereditary transmission of the characteristics of parents to offspring.

here-in′ (hēr-ĭn′), *adv.* In this.

here-of′ (-ŏv′), *adv.* Of this ; from this ; hence.

here-on′ (-ŏn′), *adv.* On or upon this ; hereupon.

her′e-sy (hĕr′ĕ-sĭ), *n. ; pl.* **-sies** (-sĭz). **1.** Unorthodox religious opinion tending to promote schism. **2.** An opinion opposed to the commonly received doctrine, and tending to dissension.

her′e-tic (hĕr′ĕ-tĭk), *n.* One who holds to a heresy.

he-ret′i-cal (hē-rĕt′ĭ-kăl), *a.* [4] Of the nature of, or marked by, heresy.

here-to′ (hēr-tōō′), *adv.* To this ; hereunto.

here′to-fore′ (hēr′tōō-fōr′), *adv.* In time past.

here′un-to′ (hēr′ŭn-tōō′), *adv.* Unto this.

here′up-on′ (-ŭ-pŏn′), *adv.* On this ; hereon.

here-with′ (hēr-wĭth′), *adv.* With this.

her′it-a-bil′i-ty (hĕr′ĭt-ȧ-bĭl′ĭ-tĭ), *n.* Quality of being heritable.

her′it-a-ble (hĕr′ĭt-ȧ-b'l), *a.* **1.** Inheritable. **2.** Capable of inheriting.

her′it-age (hĕr′ĭ-tȧj), *n.* That which is inherited ; inheritance ; birthright.

her-maph′ro-dite (hẽr-măf′rô-dīt), *n.* An individual having both male and female reproductive organs or characteristics.

her-met′ic (hẽr-mĕt′ĭk), *a.* Made air-tight by fusion or soldering. — **her-met′i-cal** (-ĭ-kăl), *a.* — **her-met′i-cal-ly,** *adv.* [8].

her′mit (hûr′mĭt), *n.* One who retires from society and lives in solitude.

her′mit-age (-mĭ-tăj), *n.* Habitation of a hermit

her′ni-a (hûr′nĭ-ȧ), *n. Med.* Protrusion of an organ or part through some opening in the walls of its cavity ; rupture. — **her′ni-al** (-ăl), *a*

he′ro (hē′rō), *n.; pl.* **-roes** (-rōz). **1.** *Myth. & Relig.* **a** A man of superior powers, esp. a warrior. **b** A man honored after death by public worship, for his good deeds ; a demigod. **2.** The principal male personage in a poem, story, or the like. **3.** A man who exhibits distinguished valor or fortitude.

he-ro′ic (hē-rō′ĭk), *a.* [4] **1.** Pertaining to, like, or marked by, a hero or heroes. **2.** Worthy of a hero ; brave ; illustrious. **3.** *Fine Art.* Larger than life size, but smaller than colossal.— *n.* **1.** A heroic verse or poems. **2.** *pl.* Extravagant expression ; bombast. — **he-ro′i-cal** (-ĭ-kăl), *a.* [4] — **-i-cal-ly,** *adv.* [8].

he-ro′in (hē-rō′ĭn), *n.* A sedative substance derived from morphine.

her′o-ine (hĕr′ô-ĭn), *n.* A woman like a hero.

her′o-ism (-ĭz′m), *n.* Heroic qualities ; display of such qualities.

her′on (-ŭn), *n.* Any of certain wading birds with long neck and legs and soft plumage. Cf. **egret.**

her′ring (hĕr′ĭng), *n.* A small food fish caught in great numbers in the North Atlantic Ocean.

hers (hûrz), *pron.* The form of the possessive *her* used absolutely, that is, with no following noun.

her-self′ (hẽr-sĕlf′), *pron.* An emphasized form for *her, she.*

hes′i-tan-cy (hĕz′ĭ-tăn-sĭ), *n.* Hesitation.

hes′i-tant (-tănt), *a.* [4] Hesitating.

hes′i-tate (hĕz′ĭ-tāt), *v. i.* [1] **1.** To stop; pause; be in uncertainty. **2.** To falter in speaking.—*v. t.* To utter with, or intimate by, hesitation.

hes′i-ta′tion (hĕz′ĭ-tā′shŭn), *n.* **1.** Act of hesitating; doubt; vacillation. **2.** A faltering in speech.

Hes′sian (hĕsh′ăn), *a.* Of or pertaining to Hesse, in Germany, or the Hessians.— *n.* **1.** A native or inhabitant of Hesse. **2.** A mercenary or venal person ;— alluding to Hessian mercenaries in the British army in the Revolutionary War. *U. S.*

hest (hĕst), *n.* Command ; behest. *Archaic.*

het′er-o-dox (hĕt′ẽr-ô-dŏks), *a.* Differing from some acknowledged standard ; not orthodox.

het′er-o-dox′y (-dŏk′sĭ), *n. ; pl.* **-doxies** (-sĭz). **1.** Quality of being heterodox. **2.** A heterodox opinion, doctrine, etc.

het′er-o-ge′ne-ous (-jē′nē-ŭs), *a.* [4] Differing in kind ; dissimilar ;— opposed to *homogeneous.*

hew (hū), *v. t. ; pret.* **hewed** (hūd) ; *p. p.* **hewed, hewn** (hūn) ; *p. pr. & vb. n.* **hew′ing. 1.** To cut by blows with an ax or other sharp instrument ; chop. **2.** To fell, as trees, by cutting. **3.** To form or shape by blows with a sharp instrument ; as, to *hew* stone or timber.— *v. i.* To make cutting blows, as with an ax.— **hew′er,** *n.* [8].

hex′a-gon (hĕk′sȧ-gŏn), *n.* Polygon of six sides.

hex-ag′o-nal (hĕk-săg′ō-năl), *a.* Six-sided.

hex′a-he′dron (hĕk′sà-hē′drŏn), *n.* A polyhedron of six faces.

hex-am′e-ter (hĕk-săm′ė-tẽr), *n.* A poetic verse of six measures. — *a.* Having six metrical feet.

hey (hā), *interj.* An exclamation, as of interrogation, joy, surprise, or encouragement.

hey′day′, *n.* Time of highest strength, vigor, or bloom ; acme ; as, the *heyday* of youth.

hi-a′tus (hī-ā′tŭs), *n. ; pl.* L. **-TUS**, E. **-TUSES** (-ĕz). **1.** A gap ; a break with a part missing. **2.** Concurrence of two vowels in two successive words or syllables without contraction, as in *coöperate.*

hi′ber-nate (hī′bẽr-nāt), *v. i.* [1] To winter ; esp., to pass the winter in torpor as do many animals.

hi′ber-na′tion (-nā′shŭn), *n.* A hibernating.

hic′cough (hĭk′ŭp). Var. of HICCUP.

hic′cup (hĭk′ŭp), *n.* A spasmodic inspiration with closure of the glottis, producing a characteristic sound. — *v. i.* To have hiccups ; make a hiccup.

hick′o-ry (hĭk′ō-rĭ), *n. ; pl.* **-RIES** (-rĭz). Any of various American trees of the walnut family, or their wood ; esp., the shagbark.

hid (hĭd), *pret. & p. p.* of HIDE.

hi-dal′go (hĭ-dăl′gō), *n. ; pl.* **-GOS** (-gōz). A Spanish nobleman of the lower class.

hid′den (hĭd′'n), *p. a.* [4] Concealed ; secret.

hide (hīd), *n.* The skin of an animal, either raw or dressed. — *v. t.* [1] To flog, as with a cowhide. *Colloq.*

hide (hīd), *v. t. ; pret.* HID (hĭd) ; *p. p.* HID′DEN (hĭd′'n), HID ; *p. pr. & vb. n.* HID′ING (hīd′ĭng). **1.** To conceal ; put out of view ; secrete. **2.** To withhold from knowledge ; keep secret. — *v. i.* To lie concealed ; stay out of view.

hide′bound′ (hīd′bound′), *a.* [4] Obstinately or stupidly narrow in thought.

hid′e-ous (hĭd′ē-ŭs), *a.* [4] Revolting ; horribly ugly or discordant ; morally shocking or detestable. — **hid′e-ous-ly**, *adv.* [8] — **-ness**, *n.* [8].

hie (hī), *v. i. ;* HIED (hīd) HY′ING (hī′ĭng). To hasten ; go in haste.

hi′er-arch′y (hī′ẽr-är′kĭ), *n. ; pl.* **-ARCHIES** (-kĭz). A body of officials (esp. ecclesiastical) in successive ranks, or government by such a body.

hi′er-o-glyph′ (hī′ẽr-ō-glĭf′), *n.* A hieroglyphic.

hi′er-o-glyph′ic (-glĭf′ĭk), *a.* Pertaining to a hieroglyph or hieroglyphics ; also, inscribed with hieroglyphics. — *n.* **1.** A sacred character; esp., chiefly in *pl.*, a character in the picture writing of the ancient Egyptians, Mexicans, etc., or the mode of writing in such characters. **2.** A symbol of hidden significance ; *pl.*, humorously, illegible writing.

The name *Cleopatra* in Egyptian Hieroglyphics.

hig′gle (hĭg′'l), *v. i.* [1] To stickle for advantage.

hig′gle-dy-pig′gle-dy (-dĭ-pĭg′'l-dĭ), *adv.* In confusion ; topsy-turvy. — *a.* [4] Jumbled.

high (hī), *a.* [3] **1.** Lifted up ; lofty ; tall ; elevated. **2.** *Geog.* Far toward one of the poles ; — chiefly in *high latitude.* **3.** Of season or time : **a** Advanced to or toward its acme or fullness ; as, *high* noon, etc. **b** Ancient ; remote ; as, *high* antiquity. **4.** Of

sound : Loud ; shrill ; in music, acute ; sharp ; — opposed to *grave* or *low.* **5.** Chief ; as : **a** Exalted in rank, dignity, etc. **b** Grave ; serious ; as, *high* crimes. **6.** Elevated in character ; as, *high* thinking. **7. a** Arrogant ; boastful ; angry ; as, *high* words. **b** Showing elation ; as, *high* spirits. **c** Extreme, esp. in doctrine or ceremony ; as, *High* Church. **8.** Strong ; powerful ; intense, etc. ; of great degree ; as, *high* winds, explosives, etc. **9.** Strong-scented ; slightly tainted ; as, the venison is *high.* **10.** *Biol.* Complex in organization ; as, the *higher* apes. **11.** Dear ; costly ; of price, great. — *adv.* **1.** At or to a high altitude or degree. **2.** At or to a high pitch. **3.** Richly ; luxuriously.

high′born′ (hī′bôrn′), *a.* Of noble birth.

high′-flown′, *a.* [4] Extravagant ; bombastic.

high′-hand′ed (hī′hăn′dĕd), *a.* [4] Overbearing.

high′land (hī′lănd), *n.* Elevated or mountainous land ; often, in *pl.*, an elevated region.

high′land-er (-lăn-dẽr), *n.* An inhabitant of highlands, esp. [*cap.*] of the Highlands of Scotland.

high′ly, *adv.* In a high degree ; very much.

high′-mind′ed, *a.* [4] **1.** Proud ; arrogant. **2.** Having honorable pride ; of lofty principles.

high′ness (hī′nĕs), *n.* **1.** Elevation ; loftiness. **2.** [*cap.*] A title of honor given to princes.

high′road′ (hī′rōd′), *n.* A highway ; main road.

high′-spir′it-ed, *a.* [4] Bold or lofty in spirit.

high′-strung′, *a.* [4] In a state of tense or quick sensibility ; highly sensitive or nervous.

high′way′ (hī′wā′), *n.* A main road or thoroughfare ; any way open to the public.

high′way′man (-măn), *n.* A highway robber.

hike (hīk), *v. t. ;* HIKED (hīkt) ; HIK′ING (hīk′ĭng). To move with a swing, throw, jerk, or the like. — *v. i.* To tramp ; march laboriously. — *n.* Act of hiking. — *All Dial. or Colloq.*

hi-la′ri-ous (hi-lâ′rĭ-ŭs ; hī-), *a.* [4] Mirthful ; noisy ; merry. — **hi-la′ri-ous-ly**, *adv.* [8].

hi-lar′i-ty (hĭ-lăr′ĭ-tĭ ; hī-), *n.* Boisterous mirth.

hill (hĭl), *n.* **1.** A natural elevation of land, less than a mountain. **2.** An artificial heap or mound, as of earth, raised about a plant or cluster of plants.

hill′i-ness (hĭl′ĭ-nĕs), *n.* State of being hilly.

hill′ock (hĭl′ŭk), *n.* A small hill.

hill′y (-ĭ), *a.* [3] **1.** Abounding with hills. **2.** Of the nature of a hill ; steep.

hilt (hĭlt), *n.* A handle, esp. of a sword, etc.

him (hĭm), *pron.* Objective case of *he.*

him-self′ (hĭm-sĕlf′), *pron.* An emphasized form for *he, him.*

hind (hīnd), *n.* A farm workman or assistant as in Scotland or England ; a rustic ; boor.

hind (hīnd), *n.* Female of the red deer. Cf. STAG.

hind (hīnd), *a. ;* HIND′ER ; HIND′MOST, or HIND′ERMOST. In the rear ; — opposed to *front ;* pertaining to the part or end that follows, or is behind.

hind′er (hīn′dẽr), *a.* Hind.

hin′der (hĭn′dẽr), *v. t.* **1.** To keep back or behind ; check ; obstruct. **2.** To prevent ; embarrass ; shut out. — *v. i.* To interpose obstacles.

hind′er-most (hīn′dẽr-mōst)) *a.* Farthest in the **hind′most** (hīnd′mōst)) rear ; last.

hin′drance (hĭn′drăns), *n.* A hindering ; state of being hindered ; that which hinders ; impediment.

Hin′du (hĭn′dōō ; hĭn-dōō′), *n.* A member of one

āle, senâte, câre, ăm, ŏccount, ärm, ȧsk, sofȧ ; ēve, ĕvent, ĕnd, recĕnt, makẽr ; īce, ĭll ; ōld, ōbey, ôrb, ŏdd, sŏft, cŏnnect ; ūse, ŭnite, ûrn, ŭp, circŭs ; fōōd, fŏŏt ; out, oil ;

of the native races of Hindustan ; esp., an adherent of Hinduism. — **Hin′du,** *a.*

Hin′du-ism (hĭn′dōō-ĭz′m), *n.* The polytheistic religion of the Hindus.

hinge (hĭnj), *n.* The joint on which a door, etc., turns or swings. — *v. t.* [1] To attach by, or furnish with, hinges. — *v. i.* To hang or turn as on a hinge ; as, the argument *hinges* on one point.

hin′ny (hĭn′ĭ), *n. ; pl.* -NIES (-ĭz). The offspring of a stallion and a she-ass.

hint (hĭnt), *n.* A remote allusion ; a suggestion or reminder without a full declaration. — *v. t.* To bring to mind by a hint, or indirectly. — *v. i.* To make an indirect allusion.

hip (hĭp), *n.* The projecting region at each side of the body below the waist ; thigh joint ; haunch.

hip, *n.* The ripened fruit of a rosebush.

hip′po-drome (hĭp′ŏ-drōm), *n.* **1.** *Gr. Antiq.* An oval track for horse races, with tiers of seats for spectators. **2.** An arena for equestrian performances ; circus.

hip′po-pot′a-mus (hĭp′ŏ-pŏt′ȧ-mŭs), *n. ; pl.* E. -MUSES (-ĕz), L. -MI (-mī). A large animal common in the rivers of Africa. It spends part of the time on land, and feeds on plants.

hire (hīr), *n.* **1.** The price paid for the use of a thing or a place, or for service or labor ; pay. **2.** Act of hiring something. — *v. t.* [1] **1.** To engage the labor or services of for hire. **2.** To procure for temporary use for a compensation. **3.** To grant temporary use of for compensation.

hire′ling (-lĭng), *n.* One who is hired ; a mercenary. — *a.* Serving for hire, esp. mercenarily.

hir′sute (hŭr′sūt ; hẽr-sūt′), *a.* [4] Rough with hair or bristles ; shaggy. — **hir′sute-ness,** *n.* [8].

his (hĭz), *pron. & a.* Belonging or pertaining to him ; of him ; — used as the possessive case of *he,* or as a possessive adjective.

hiss (hĭs), *v. i.* To make a hiss. — *v. t.* **1.** To condemn by hissing. **2.** To utter with a hiss. — *n.* A prolonged sound like that of *s,* esp. as a token of anger, contempt, etc. ; sound made in hissing.

hist (hĭst), *interj.* Hush ! Be silent !

his-to′ri-an (hĭs-tō′rĭ-ăn), *n.* A writer of history.

his-tor′ic (-tŏr′ĭk)) *a.* [4] **1.** Of, pertaining **his-tor′i-cal** (-ĭ-kăl)) to, or of the nature of, history ; true to history. **2.** Constituting history ; associated with, or famous in, history. **3.** *Gram.* Used in telling past events ; as, the *historical* tenses. — **his-tor′i-cal-ly,** *adv.* [8].

his′to-ry (hĭs′tŏ-rĭ), *n. ; pl.* -RIES (-rĭz). **1.** A narrative of events ; esp., a systematic written account of events affecting a nation, etc. **2.** The branch of knowledge that records and explains past events ; the study of such records. **3.** The events that form the subject of a history.

his′tri-on′ic (hĭs′trĭ-ŏn′ĭk), *a.* Pertaining to the stage or to actors ; theatrical.

hit (hĭt), *v. t. ; pret. & p. p.* HIT ; *p. pr. & vb. n.* HIT′TING. **1.** To come upon (esp. a thing sought) ; meet with ; reach ; find. **2.** To strike or touch (esp. an object aimed at). **3.** To affect to one's detriment or discomfiture. — *v. i.* **1.** To succeed, often with implied luck. **2.** To strike. — *n.* **1.** A blow striking the object aimed at. **2.** A stroke of success. **3.** An apt or telling remark.

hitch (hĭch), *v. i.* **1.** To move with jerks ; hobble. **2.** To become entangled or caught ; catch ; cling. — *v. t.* **1.** To move (something) with jerks. **2.** To catch or fasten as by a hook or knot ; make fast ; unite. — *n.* **1.** A sudden movement or pull ; jerk. **2.** A hobble ; limp. **3.** A stop or sudden halt ; impediment ; obstacle. **4.** *Naut.* A knot or noose.

hith′er (hĭth′ẽr), *adv.* To this place. — *a.* On the side toward the person speaking.

hith′er-to′ (-tōō′ ; hĭth′ẽr-tōō′), *adv.* Up to this time ; as yet ; until now.

hith′er-ward (-wẽrd), *adv.* Toward this place.

hith′er-wards (-wẽrdz). Var. of HITHERWARD.

hit′ter (hĭt′ẽr), *n.* One that hits.

hive (hīv), *n.* **1.** A beehive ; also, a hived swarm of bees. **2.** Something suggestive of a beehive, as a place swarming with busy occupants. — *v. t.* [1] **1.** To collect into, or cause to enter, a hive. **2.** To store up in a hive, as honey ; lay up in store. — *v. i.* To enter a hive together, as bees ; reside in a body.

hives (hīvz), *n. pl. Med.* Nettle rash.

ho (hō), *interj.* Stop ! Stand still ! Hold ! Cf. WHOA.

ho, *interj.* **1.** A cry of surprise, delight, etc., or, repeated, of derisive laughter. **2.** Halloo ! Attend !

hoar (hōr), *a.* **1.** White, or grayish white. **2.** Gray or white with age ; hoary ; venerable.

hoard (hōrd), *n.* A store laid up ; hidden supply ; treasure. — *v. t.* To collect and lay up. — *v. i.* To lay up a store, as of money. — **hoard′er,** *n.* [8].

hoard′ing (hōr′dĭng), *n.* Act of one who hoards, also (in *pl.*), that which is hoarded.

hoar′frost′ (hōr′frŏst′), *n.* White frost ; rime.

hoarse (hōrs), *a.* [3] **1.** Harsh ; discordant. **2.** Having a grating voice ; as, *hoarse* from a cold.

hoar′y (hōr′ĭ), *a.* [3] **1.** White or whitish ; white or gray with age. **2.** Ancient ; as, *hoary* antiquity.

hoax (hōks), *n.* A mocking or mischievous deception or story. — *v. t.* To deceive by a hoax.

hob′ble (hŏb′'l), *v. i.* [1] To walk lame ; limp. — *v. t.* To fetter ; hopple ; clog. — *n.* **1.** An unequal gait ; limp. **2.** A fetter ; hopple ; clog.

hob′ble-de-hoy′ (-dĕ-hoi′), *n.* An awkward youth.

hob′by (hŏb′ĭ), *n.* A subject to which one constantly reverts ; favorite pursuit.

hob′by-horse′ (-hôrs′), *n.* A rocking horse, or other toy horse. [2. A bogy ; bugbear.|

hob′gob′lin (-gŏb′lĭn), *n.* **1.** A mischievous sprite.|

hob′nail′ (hŏb′nāl′), *n.* A short large-headed nail, for studding shoe soles.

hob′nob′ (-nŏb′), *v. i. ;* -NOBBED′ (-nŏbd′) ; -NOB′BING. To drink or associate familiarly (with).

hock (hŏk), *n.* A white Rhine wine.

hock, *n.* The joint in the hind limb of quadrupeds, as the horse, about midway between hoof and thigh, which bends backward.

hock′ey (-ĭ), *n.* A well-known game played by driving a ball or disk with a bent stick.

ho′cus-po′cus (hō′kŭs-pō′kŭs), *n.* **1.** A formula used by jugglers. **2.** A juggler's trick.

hod (hŏd), *n.* **1.** A trough with a handle for carrying mortar, bricks, etc. **2.** A coal scuttle.

hodge′podge′ (hŏj′pŏj′), *n.* A mixture ; medley.

hoe (hō), *n.* A long-handled implement, with a thin, flat blade set crosswise at one end, for weeding, etc. — *v. t. & i. ;* HOED (hōd) ; HOE′ING. To dig, cut, etc., with a hoe.

---

chair ; go ; sing, iṅk ; then, thin ; nature, verdure ; yet ; zh = z in azure. Numbers refer to §§ in the Special Notes which, with Abbreviations, Signs, etc., precede the Vocabulary.

hoe′cake (hō′kāk′), *n.* A cake of Indian meal.

hog (hŏg), *n.* A swine, esp. an adult one.

hog′gish (-ĭsh), *a.* [4] Gluttonous; filthy; selfish.

hogs′head (hŏgz′hĕd), *n.* **1.** A large cask. **2.** A liquid measure, usually 63 wine gallons.

hoist (hoist), *v. t.* To raise; elevate; esp., to lift with tackle. — *n.* **1.** Act of hoisting; lift; boost. *Colloq.* **2.** A lifting apparatus.

hoi′ty-toi′ty (hoi′tĭ-toi′tĭ), *a.* Thoughtless; giddy; also, haughty. — *interj.* An exclamation of surprise, with some degree of contempt.

hold (hōld), *n. Naut.* The interior of a vessel, esp. below the lower deck, where cargo is stowed.

hold, *v. t.; pret. & p.p.* HELD (hĕld); *p. pr. & vb. n.* HOLD′ING. **1.** To keep in a given situation, relation, or the like; retain; sustain; support. **2.** To contain; have capacity for. **3.** To maintain possession of, or authority over. **4.** To own or occupy. **5.** To detain; restrain; keep. **6.** To have or join in, as a meeting, etc. **7.** To entertain or accept, as an opinion. **8.** To consider; judge. — *v. i.* **1.** To maintain a grasp on, or a connection with, something. **2.** To endure; continue; last; persist. **3.** To remain steadfast or faithful. **4.** To be valid. **5.** To forbear; — mostly in imperative; as, "*Hold*, enough!" — *n.* **1.** Act of holding; grasp; possession. **2.** Authority to take or keep; claim. **3.** Something that may be grasped. **4.** A stronghold.

hold′er (hōl′dẽr), *n.* **1.** One that holds. **2.** A tenant. **3.** The person legally entitled to receive payment of a bill, note, or check.

hold′ing, *vb. n.* **1.** Land held, esp. of a superior. **2.** Property owned, as bonds or stocks.

hole (hōl), *n.* **1.** An opening; aperture. **2.** A hollow place; excavation; pit. **3.** A den or burrow.

hol′i-day (-dā), *n.* A day of exemption from work. — *a.* Festive; gay; as, *holiday* attire.

ho′li-ness (hō′lĭ-nĕs), *n.* **1.** State or character of being holy. **2.** [*cap.*] A title of the Pope.

hol′land (hŏl′ănd), *n.* A kind of linen; a fabric of cotton or linen, glazed or unglazed.

hol′lo (hŏl′ō; hŏ-lō′; *interj. usually* hŏ-lō′), *interj. & n.* Ho there! stop! attend! hence, a call to attract attention, etc.; also, an exclamation of greeting, now commonly *hello.* — (hŏl′ō), *v. i.* To call out or exclaim; halloo.

hol′low (hŏl′ō), *a.* [3] **1.** Having a cavity within a solid substance; not solid. **2.** Depressed; concave; sunken. **3.** Reverberated from or as from a cavity. **4.** Deceitful. — *n.* **1.** A cavity; hole. **2.** A depressed part of a surface; concavity; basin, or valley. — *v. t. & i.* To make or become hollow. — **hol′low-ness**, *n.* [8].

hol′ly (hŏl′ĭ), *n.; pl.* -LIES (-ĭz). **1.** Any tree or shrub of a certain genus having glossy, spiny-margined leaves and bright red berries. **2.** The foliage or branches of the holly.

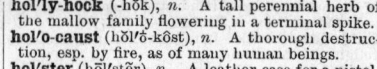

European Holly. Reduced.

hol′ly-hock (-hŏk), *n.* A tall perennial herb of the mallow family flowering in a terminal spike.

hol′o-caust (hŏl′ō-kôst), *n.* A thorough destruction, esp. by fire, as of many human beings.

hol′ster (hōl′stẽr), *n.* A leather case for a pistol.

ho′ly (hō′lĭ), *a.* [3] **1.** Set apart to the service of deity; hallowed; sacred; — opp. to *profane.* **2.** Spiritually perfect, whole, or sound; pure in heart; godly. — **Holy Ghost**, *or* **H.** Spirit. third person of the Trinity, the Comforter. — **H. Land**, Palestine. — **H. Week**, the week before Easter; Passion Week.

ho′ly, *n.; pl.* -LIES (-lĭz). A holy thing or place.

ho′ly-day′ (-dā′), *n., or* **holy day.** A religious festival.

ho′ly-stone′ (-stōn′), *n. Naut.* Sandstone used to scrub decks. — *v. t. & i.* To scrub with a holystone.

hom′age (hŏm′ăj), *n.* **1.** A ceremony by which a man, in feudal times, acknowledged himself the vassal of a lord; relation so established. **2.** Respect or reverential regard; deference; esp., obeisance.

home (hōm), *n.* **1.** One's dwelling place; abode of one's family. **2.** One's native place or land. **3.** The locality where a thing is usually or naturally abundant; habitat; seat. **4.** An asylum. **5.** In various games, the goal. — *a.* **1.** Of or pertaining to one's home; domestic. **2.** Poignant; intimate; effective; as, a *home* thrust. — *adv.* **1.** To one's home or country. **2.** To the heart or core; intimately. **3.** To the point or limit aimed at; as, to drive a nail *home.*

home′like′ (hōm′līk′), *a.* [4] Like a home; comfortable; cheerful; cozy; friendly.

home′li-ness (-lĭ-nĕs), *n.* Quality of being homely.

home′ly (-lĭ), *a.* [3] **1.** Characteristic of home life; simple; plain. **2.** Not comely.

ho′me-o-path (hō′mē-ō-păth; hŏm′ē-), *n.* A practitioner of homeopathy.

ho′me-op′a-thy (-ŏp′ȧ-thĭ), *n. Med.* The theory that disease is cured by remedies which produce on a healthy person effects similar to the symptoms of the malady to be cured, the remedies being usually given in minute doses; the practice based on this theory. — **-o-path′ic** (-ō-păth′ĭk), *a.*

home′sick′ (hōm′sĭk′), *a.* [4] Pining for home. — **home′sick′ness**, *n.* [8].

home′spun′ (-spŭn′), *a.* Spun or wrought at home; coarse; plain. — *n.* Cloth made at home, or of yarn spun at home, or like that of home make.

home′stead (-stĕd), *n.* The home place; a home and the ground immediately connected with it.

home′ward (-wẽrd), **-wards** (-wẽrdz), *adv.* Toward home. — *a.* Being in the direction of home.

hom′i-cid′al (hŏm′ĭ-sīd′ăl), *a.* [4] Murderous.

hom′i-cide (hŏm′ĭ-sīd), *n.* The killing of one human being by another.

hom′i-let′ics (-lĕt′ĭks), *n.* Art of preaching.

hom′i-ly (hŏm′ĭ-lĭ), *n.; pl.* -LIES (-lĭz). A discourse or sermon delivered to an audience.

hom′ing (hōm′ĭng), *p. a.* Home-returning.

hom′i-ny (hŏm′ĭ-nĭ), *n.* Maize hulled and often, also, broken, for food. *U. S.*

ho′mo-ge′ne-ous (hō′mō-jē′nē-ŭs; hŏm′ō-), *a.* [4] Of the same kind or nature; of similar elements.

ho-mol′o-gous (hō-mŏl′ō-gŭs), *a.* Having the same relative position, proportion, value, or structure.

hom′o-nym (hŏm′ō-nĭm; hō′mō-), *n.* Any of two

or more words alike in sound but differing in meaning; as, *bare* and *bear*.

hone (hōn), *n.* A fine whetstone, esp. one for razors. — *v. t.* [1] To sharpen or set with a hone.

hon'est (ŏn'ĕst), *a.* [4] **1**. Fair and straightforward in conduct, thought, etc. **2**. Free from deception or fraud. **3**. Open; frank. **4**. Chaste; virtuous. *Archaic.* — **hon'est-ly**, *adv.* [8].

hon'es-ty (-ĕs-tĭ), *n.* Quality or state of being honest; freedom from guile or fraud.

hon'ey (hŭn'ĭ), *n.* A sweet sticky fluid, the nectar of flowers as collected and worked up for food by certain insects, esp. bees.

hon'ey-bee' (-bē'), *n.* Any of certain social honey-producing bees.

hon'ey-comb' (-kōm'), *n.* **1**. The mass of six-sided cells of wax built by bees. **2**. Something likened to a bee's honeycomb. — *v. t. & i.* To make or become full of cavities like a honeycomb.

hon'eyed (hŭn'ĭd), *a.* [4] Abounding with honey; sweetened as with honey; sweet; dulcet.

honey locust. A North American tree bearing spines on the trunk and producing large flat pods.

hon'ey-moon' (-mōōn'), *n.* The first month or so after marriage; esp., the holiday spent by a couple after marriage, before settling down.

hon'ey-suck'le (-sŭk''l), *n.* **1**. Any of various climbing plants, having tubular fragrant flowers. **2**. Any of several other fragrant-flowered shrubs.

honk (hŏngk), *n.* The cry of the wild goose, or a sound likened to it. — *v. i.* To utter a honk.

hon'or (ŏn'ẽr), *n.* [5] **1**. Esteem due or paid to worth; renown; fame; high position. **2**. High moral worth; nobleness. **3**. A nice sense of what is right, just, and true, with strict conformity thereto. **4**. A token of esteem paid to worth. **5**. A title given to the holders of certain civil offices, as a mayor or judge; — with *his* or *your*. **6**. A cause of respect, fame, or glory; an ornament. **7**. *pl.* Academic distinctions. — *v. t.* **1**. To regard or treat with honor or respect. **2**. To bestow honor on. **3**. To accept and pay when due.

hon'or-a-ble (-a-b'l), *a.* [5] **1**. Worthy of honor; noble; illustrious. **2**. Actuated by, or consistent with, honor. **3**. Conferring honor. **4**. [*cap.*] A title of distinction prefixed to the names of those holding certain offices, etc. Abbr. *Hon.* — **hon'or-a-bly** (-blĭ), *adv.* [8].

hon'o-ra'ri-um (ŏn'ô-rā'rĭ-ŭm), *n.; pl.* -RIA (-ȧ). An honorary payment or reward, usually for services on which a price may not be set.

hon'or-a-ry (ŏn'ẽr-ȧ-rĭ), *a.* [4] **1**. Done or conferred as a token of honor. **2**. Designating or holding a title or place without rendering service or receiving the usual emoluments or privileges.

hood (hŏŏd), *n.* **1**. A flexible protective covering for the head and neck, as on a robe. **2**. Something like, or suggestive of, a hood in shape or use. — *v. t.* To provide with a hood.

hood'lum (hŏŏd'lŭm), *n.* A young rowdy. *Colloq.*

hoo'doo (hōō'dōō), *n.* **1**. = VOODOO. **2**. One that brings bad luck; hence, bad luck. *Colloq.*

hood'wink (hŏŏd'wĭngk), *v. t.* To deceive; humbug.

hoof (hōōf), *n.* The covering of horn which protects the front of the digits of horses, oxen, etc. Also, the foot as a whole, esp. of a horse.

hook (hŏŏk), *n.* **1**. A curved or bent piece, as for catching something. **2**. An implement for cutting or lopping, as a sickle. **3**. Something curved or bent like a hook. **4**. An act of hooking. — *v. t. & i.* **1**. To give the form of a hook to; crook. **2**. To catch, or draw, with or as with a hook; hence, to steal; pilfer. **3**. To gore (with the horns).

hook'ah, hook'a (hŏŏk'ȧ), *n.* A tobacco pipe in which the smoke passes through water.

hook'-up' (hŏŏk'ŭp'), *n.* Apparatus used in radio transmission or reception, or its plan.

hook'worm' (hŏŏk'wûrm'), *n.* A parasitic intestinal worm, with hooks or spines about the mouth.

hoop (hōōp), *n.* **1**. A circular band to hold together the staves of a cask, tub, etc. **2**. A circle, or set framework of circles, to expand skirts; — usually in *pl.* — *v. t.* To bind with hoops; encircle.

hoot (hōōt), *v. i.* **1**. To utter a loud shout; usually, to cry out in contempt. **2**. Of an owl, to utter its cry. — *v. t.* To assail with contemptuous cries. — *n.* **1**. A loud inarticulate shout or noise; esp., a derisive shout. **2**. The cry of an owl.

hop (hŏp), *v. i.; pret.* HOPPED (hŏpt); HOP'PING. **1**. To move, as a bird, by short brisk leaps; also, to jump on one foot. **2**. To dance. *Colloq.* — *v. t.* To hop about or over. — *n.* **1**. A short brisk leap, esp. on one leg. **2**. An informal dance or ball. *Colloq.*

hop, *n.* A twining vine with greenish flowers, the pistillate flowers growing in cones, or strobiles. **2.** *pl.* The dried ripe strobiles of the hop, used in making beer, etc.

hope (hōp), *n.* **1**. Desire, with expectation of getting what is desired or belief that it is obtainable. **2**. Trust. **3**. Ground of hope. **4**. That which is hoped for. — *v. i.* [1] To entertain hope; with *for.* — *v.t.* **1**. To cherish hope of. **2**. To desire; wish.

Hop Leaves and Strobiles.

hope'ful (-fŏŏl), *a.* [4] **1**. Full of hope; sanguine. **2**. Having qualities which excite hope; promising. — **hope'ful-ly**, *adv.* [8] — **-ful-ness,** *n.* [8].

hope'less, *a.* [4] **1**. Without hope. **2**. Affording no hope. — **-ly,** *adv.* [8] — **-ness,** *n.* [8].

hop'per (hŏp'ẽr), *n.* **1**. One that hops. **2**. A chute or receptacle, usually funnel-shaped, for feeding any material, as to a machine.

hop'ple (-'l), *v. t. & n.* [1] Hobble; fetter.

horde (hōrd), *n.* **1**. A clan or tribal group of nomad Mongolians; hence, any loosely organized nomadic group. **2**. A crowd; pack.

hore'hound' (hōr'hound'), *n.* **1**. A bitter mint with hoary leaves. **2**. Confection flavored with this plant.

ho-ri'zon (hô-rī'zŭn), *n.* The apparent junction of earth and sky. Fig., limit or bounds.

hor'i-zon'tal (hŏr'ĭ-zŏn'tăl), *a.* Parallel to the plane of the horizon. — *n.* A horizontal thing, esp. a horizontal line or plane. — **-tal-ly,** *adv.*

---

horn (hôrn), *n.* **1.** One of the hard, projecting processes borne on the head of many hoofed mammals, as cattle, sheep, etc. **2.** A wind instrument of music. **3.** One of the ends of a crescent. **4.** The material of which horns are composed.

horn′blende′ (-blĕnd′), *n.* A widely distributed mineral, commonly black, dark green, or brown.

horned (hôrnd, *or, esp. poetic or rhetorical,* hôr′nĕd), *a.* Having a horn or horns; as, *horned* cattle.

hor′net (hôr′nĕt), *n.* Any of several large, pugnacious wasps.

horn′pipe′ (hôrn′pīp′), *n.* A lively dance popular among sailors.

horn′y (hôr′nĭ), *a.* [3] **1.** Of horn or a hornlike substance. **2.** Hard or translucent like horn.

ho-rol′o-gy (hŏ-rŏl′ō-jĭ), *n.* Science or art of measuring time or of constructing timepieces.

hor′o-scope (hôr′ō-skōp), *n.* **1.** The representation of the aspect of the heavens at the moment of one's birth, used by the astrologer; esp., the zodiacal sign then rising. **2.** The diagram of 12 "houses," or signs of the zodiac, into which the circuit of the heavens is divided for such prediction.

hor′ri-ble (-ĭ-b'l), *a.* [4] Exciting horror; dreadful; hideous. — **hor′ri-bly,** *adv.* [8].

hor′rid (-ĭd), *a.* [4] Hideous; shocking. — **-ly,** *adv.* [8] — **ness,** *n.* [8].

hor-rif′ic (hŏ-rĭf′ĭk), *a.* [4] Horrifying; frightful.

hor′ri-fy (hôr′ĭ-fī), *v. t.* [2] To strike with horror.

hor′ror (hôr′ẽr), *n.* **1.** A painful emotion of fear and abhorrence; also, great aversion and repugnance. **2.** That which is horrible.

horse (hôrs), *n.; pl.* HORSES (hôr′sĕz), or collectively (in sense 3), HORSE. **1.** A well-known hoofed quadruped. **2.** The male of the genus horse; usually, a gelding. **3.** Cavalry; — a collective; — disting. from *foot.* **4.** A supporting frame, usually with legs. — *v. t.* [1] To provide with a horse or horses; mount on or as on a horse.

horse′back′ (hôrs′băk′), *n.* The back of a horse. — *adv.* On horseback; mounted on a horse.

horse′-chest′nut (hôrs′chĕs′nŭt), *n.* The large nutlike seed of a tree common in the temperate zones; also, the tree.

horse′fly′ (-flī′), *n.; pl.* -FLIES (-flīz′). Any of numerous flies (some large) annoying to horses.

horse′man (hôrs′măn), *n.; pl.* -MEN (-mĕn). A rider on horseback; one skilled in the management or care of horses.

horse′man-ship (-shĭp), *n.* Act or art of riding or of managing or training horses.

horse′play′ (plā′), *n.* Rude, boisterous play.

horse power *or* **horse′pow′er** (pou′ẽr), *n. Mechanics.* A unit of power, numerically equal to a rate of 33,000 foot pounds of work per minute.

horse′-rad′ish (-răd′ĭsh), *n.* A plant of the cabbage family, whose root is used as a condiment.

horse′shoe′ (hôrs′shōō′), *n.* **1.** A shoe for horses. **2.** Something shaped like a horseshoe.

horse′tail′ (-tāl′), *n.* **1.** The tail of a horse. **2.** Any of various plants allied to the ferns.

horse′wom′an (-wŏŏm′ăn), *n.; pl.* -WOMEN. A woman who rides on horseback.

hor′ta-tive (hôr′tà-tĭv), *a.* [4] Hortatory.

hor′ta-to-ry (-tō-rĭ), *a.* [4] Giving, or characterized by, exhortation; exhortative; hortative.

hor′ti-cul′tur-al (hôr′tĭ-kŭl′tūr-ăl), *a.* Pertaining to horticulture.

hor′ti-cul′ture (hôr′tĭ-kŭl′tūr), *n.* Cultivation of a garden or orchard; art or science of growing fruits, vegetables, or ornamental plants.

hor′ti-cul′tur-ist (-kŭl′tūr-ĭst), *n.* One who practices horticulture.

ho-san′na (hŏ-zăn′à), *interj. & n.* A Hebrew exclamation of praise to the Lord.

hose (hōz), *n.; pl.* HOSE. **1.** A stocking, or stockings. **2.** A flexible pipe for conveying fluids.

ho′sier-y (hō′zhẽr-ĭ), *n.* Stockings; goods knit or woven like hose.

hos′pice (hŏs′pĭs), *n.* An inn for travelers or strangers, esp. one belonging to a religious order.

hos′pi-ta-ble (-pĭ-tà-b'l), *a.* [4] Extending, or marked by, hospitality. — **-ta-bly,** *adv.* [8].

hos′pi-tal (-tăl), *n.* An institution in which the sick or injured are given medical or surgical care.

hos′pi-tal′i ty (-tăl′ĭ-tĭ), *n.; pl.* -TIES (-tĭz). Kind and generous reception of strangers or guests.

host (hōst), *n.* **1.** An army. **2.** A multitude.

host, *n.* **1.** One who receives or entertains another; landlord. **2.** Any animal or plant affording lodgment or food to a parasite.

Host, *n. R. C. Ch.* The consecrated wafer used in the Mass; also, the bread before consecration.

hos′tage (hŏs′tàj), *n.* **1.** A person given as a pledge. **2.** Any pledge or guarantee.

hos′tel-ry (-tĕl-rĭ), *n.; pl.* -RIES (-rĭz). Place of lodging; inn; lodging house. *Archaic.*

host′ess (hōs′tĕs), *n.* A female host.

hos′tile (hŏs′tĭl), *a.* [4] Like an enemy; showing ill will. — *n.* An enemy. — **-ly,** *adv.* [8].

hos-til′i-ty (hŏs-tĭl′ĭ-tĭ), *n.; pl.* -TIES (-tĭz). **1.** State of being hostile; enmity. **2.** An act of open enmity; hostile deed; esp., *pl.,* acts of warfare.

hos′tler (hŏs′lẽr; ŏs′-), *n.* One in charge of horses at an inn or stable; groom.

hot (hŏt), *a.,* HOT′TER (-ẽr) ; -TEST. **1.** Much above normal temperature; characterized by great or unusual heat. **2.** Characterized by violent activity or emotion. **3. a** Pressing hard; as, a *hot* chase. **b** Biting; pungent; as, *hot* as mustard. **4.** Strong; clear, as, in hunting, a trail or scent.

hot′bed′ (hŏt′bĕd′), *n.* **1.** *Hort.* A bed of earth inclosed in glass and prepared for growing plants. **2.** A place favoring rapid growth.

hotch′potch′ (hŏch′pŏch′), *n.* A hodgepodge.

ho-tel′ (hŏ-tĕl′), *n.* A house for entertaining strangers or travelers; inn.

hot′-head′ (hŏt′hĕd′), *n.* A hot-headed person.

hot′-head′ed, *a.* [4] Fiery; impetuous; hasty.

hot′house′ (-hous′), *n.* A greenhouse warmed for growing or keeping tender plants.

hot′ly, *adv.* In a hot or fiery manner ; hastily.

hot′ness, *n.* State of being hot ; heat.

hound (hound), *n.* **1.** A dog of any of certain breeds used in hunting. **2.** A despicable person. — *v. t.* **1.** To hunt with hounds; fig., to pursue unrelentingly. **2.** To incite to pursuit ; — often with *on.*

hour (our), *n.* **1.** The 24th part of a day ; 60 minutes. **2.** Time of day. **3.** Set or particular time or occasion. **4.** *pl. R. C. Ch.* Times of the day set for prayer, or the prayers to be said.

hour′glass′ (our′glás′), *n.* An instrument for measuring time, esp. the interval of an hour, as by sand running through an aperture.

hour'ly (our'lǐ), *adv.* Every hour; hour by hour; frequently; continually. — *a.* Happening or done hourly.

house (hous), *n.* **1.** A structure for human habitation. **2.** With qualifying term, a building for some other purpose; as, hen*house*, ware*house*, etc. **3.** A household. **4.** A family of kindred; esp., a noble family. **5.** A legislative or deliberative assembly; also, the place where it meets. **6.** A firm or commercial establishment. **7.** A theater; hence, an audience. **8.** See HOROSCOPE.—**House of Commons**, the lower house of the British Parliament, the upper house being the H. of Lords. — **H. of Representatives**, the lower branch of a legislature, as of the U. S. Congress. — (houz), *v. t.* [1] **1.** To take or put into a house; harbor. **2.** *Naut.* To stow safely.

house'break'ing, *n.* Act of breaking open and entering another's dwelling with felonious intent. — **house'break'er**, *n.* [8].

house'hold (-hōld), *n.* Those who dwell as a family; family. — *a.* Pert. to a household; domestic.

house'hold'er (-hōl'dẽr), *n.* The head of a family; one who occupies a house with his family or alone.

house'keep'er (-kēp'ẽr), *n.* One who does, or oversees, the work of keeping house.

house'keep'ing, *n.* Management of a house and home affairs.

house'maid' (hous'mād'), *n.* A female domestic servant, esp. one who takes care of the rooms.

house'room' (-rōōm'), *n.* Room in a house.

house'warm'ing (-wôr'mǐng), *n.* A festivity upon the occasion of occupying a new home.

house'wife' (-wīf'), *n.* Female head of a household.

hous'ing (houz'ǐng), *n.* **1.** Act of sheltering; dwelling in a house. **2.** That which shelters.

hous'ing, *n.* A cover, esp. of cloth for a horse's saddle; *pl.*, trappings.

hove (hōv), *pret. & p. p.* of HEAVE.

hov'el (hŏv'ĕl), *n.* A shed; mean house; hut.

hov'er (hŭv'ẽr), *v. i.* **1.** To hang fluttering in the air, or on the wing. **2.** To hang about.

how (hou), *adv.* **1.** In what manner or way. **2.** To what degree, extent, number, or amount. **3.** In what state or condition. **4.** For what reason; why.

how-be'it (hou-bē'ĭt), *conj. or adv.* Be it as it may; nevertheless; although; yet; but; however.

how'dah (hou'dä), *n.* A seat or pavilion, usually covered, on the back of an elephant.

how'ev'er (hou'ĕv'ẽr), *adv.* Contracted **how'e'er** (-âr'; -ār'). In whatever manner; by whatever means. — *conj.* Nevertheless; notwithstanding.

how'itz-er (hou'ĭt-sẽr), *n.* A short, light cannon used to throw shells.

howl (houl), *v. i.* **1.** To utter a loud, long, mournful cry, as of a dog or a wolf. **2.** To lament; wail. **3.** To make a wailing noise. — *v. t.* **1.** To utter with howling or outcry. **2.** To affect, effect, or bring by howling. — *n.* **1.** The cry of a dog or wolf in howling, or a like sound. **2.** A prolonged cry of distress, rage, etc. — **howl'er** (-ẽr), *n.* [8].

how'so-ev'er (hou'sō-ĕv'ẽr), *adv. & conj.* In what manner soever ; to whatever extent ; however.

hoy'den (hoi'd'n), *n.* A rude, bold girl; a romp. — *a.* [4] Rude; roistering.

hub (hŭb), *n.* Central part of a wheel; nave.

hub'bub (hŭb'ŭb), *n.* An uproar; tumult.

huck'a-back (hŭk'à-băk), *n.* A rough fabric of linen, or linen and cotton, much used for towels.

huck'le-ber'ry (hŭk'l-bĕr'ĭ), *n.; pl.* -RIES (-ĭz). **1.** The edible black or dark blue berry of any of several American shrubs; also, the shrub bearing this fruit. **2.** Erroneously, a blueberry. *U. S.*

huck'ster (-stẽr), *n.* A peddler; hawker. — *v. i. & t.* To deal pettily; haggle.

hud'dle (hŭd'l), *v. i. & t.* [1] **1.** To crowd together, as from confusion, fear, etc. **2.** To draw (one's self) into a heap; — esp. with *up.* **3.** To do, make, or put, in haste or roughly. — *n.* A jumble; disorder; confusion.

hue (hū), *n.* Color; tint.

hue, *n.* A shouting, esp. in the chase. *Obs.*, except in: hue and cry, a clamor of alarm, pursuit, etc.

huff (hŭf), *n.* · A fit of petulance or resentment; a sulky passion. — **huff'ish**, *a.* [4, 8].

huff'y (hŭf'ĭ), *a.* [3] Easily offended; pettish.

hug (hŭg), *v. t.;* HUGGED (hŭgd); HUG'GING (-ĭng). **1.** To embrace. **2.** To hold fast; cherish, as an opinion, etc. **3.** To keep very close to, as a shore in sailing. — *n.* A close embrace.

huge (hūj), *a.* [3] Very large; immense; vast. — **-ly**, *adv.* [8] — **-ness**, *n.* [8].

hulk (hŭlk), *n.* **1.** A ship; now, a heavy clumsy ship. **2.** The body of an old vessel laid by as unseaworthy. **3.** A bulky or unwieldy object.

hulk'ing, *a.* Bulky; unwieldy; loutish.

hull (hŭl), *n.* **1.** The outer covering or husk of a fruit or seed. **2.** The body of a ship. — *v. t.* To strip off the hulls of, as kernels of corn.

hul'la-ba-loo' (hŭl'ȧ-bȧ-lōō'), *n.* A clamor; uproar.

hum (hŭm), *v. i.* **1.** To utter a sound suggestive of *m* prolonged, without opening the mouth. **2.** To drone; buzz. **3.** To sing with closed lips. **4.** To give forth an indistinct sound, as of many voices; (*Colloq.*) to be all astir; as, he made things *hum.* — *n.* Act of humming, or sound made by humming.

hu'man (hū'măn), *a.* [4] Belonging or relating to man; characteristic of man.

hu-mane' (hū-mān'), *a.* [4] **1.** Having feelings and inclinations creditable to man; benevolent. **2.** Humanizing; refining. — *-ly*, *adv.* [8] — *-ness*, *n.* [8].

hu'man-ist (hū'măn-ĭst), *n.* One devoted to the humanities; a classical scholar. — **hu'man-ism** (-ĭz'm), *n.* — **hu'man-is'tic**, *a.*

hu-man'i-ta'ri-an (hū-măn'ĭ-tā'rĭ-ăn), *a.* [4] Pertaining to, or characteristic of, humanitarians. — *n.* A philanthropist; one actively concerned in promoting the welfare of humanity.

hu-man'i-ta'ri-an-ism (-ĭz'm), *n.* Philanthropy; active concern in the interests of humanity.

hu-man'i-ty (hū-măn'ĭ-tĭ), *n.; pl.* -TIES (-tĭz). **1.** Quality or condition of being human; human nature. **2.** Quality of being humane; kind feelings, dispositions, and sympathies. **3.** [*Usually in pl.,* with *the.*] The branches of polite learning, esp. the ancient classics. **4.** Mankind; the human race.

hu'man-ize (hū'măn-īz), *v. t.* [1] **1.** To make human. **2.** To render humane; soften; refine.

hu'man-ly, *adv.* In a human manner.

hum'ble (hŭm'b'l), *a.* [3] **1.** Not proud or assertive; lowly; meek. **2.** Of lowly condition, rank, etc.; unpretentious. — *v. t.* [1] **1.** To bring low; humiliate. **2.** To make humble in mind.

hum'bly (-blǐ), *adv.* In a humble manner.

hum'bug' (-bŭg'), *n.* **1.** An imposture; a fraud. **2.** Imposture. **3.** An impostor. — *v. t. ;* -BUGGED (-bŭgd'); -BUG'GING (-bŭg'ǐng). To deceive; impose on; hoax. — *v. i.* To play the humbug.

hum'drum' (-drŭm'), *a.* [4] Monotonous; dull.

hu'mer-us (hū'mẽr-ŭs), *n. ; pl.* -MERI (-ī). The bone of the upper part of the arm or fore limb.

hu'mid (hū'mǐd), *a.* [4] Damp; moist.

hu-mid'i-ty (hū-mǐd'ǐ-tǐ), *n.* Moisture; dampness.

hu-mil'i-ate (-mǐl'ǐ-āt), *v. t.* [1] To lower the dignity of; to humble; mortify.

hu-mil'i-a'tion (-ā'shǎn), *n.* Act of humiliating, or state of being humiliated; mortification.

hu-mil'i-ty (-mǐl'ǐ-tǐ), *n. ; pl.* -TIES (-tǐz). State or quality of being humble; lowliness; meekness.

hum'ming (hŭm'ǐng), *p. a.* Droning ; buzzing. — **humming bird,** any of numerous American, mostly tropical birds, of remarkably small size and brilliant plumage. Their wings produce a humming sound.

5/12
Ruby-and-Topaz Humming Bird.

hum'mock (-ŭk), *n.* **1.** A rounded knoll or hillock. **2.** A ridge of ice on an ice field.

hu'mor (hū'mẽr; ū'-), *n.* [5] **1.** An animal or vegetable fluid or juice. *Now R. or Archaic.* **2.** Disposition; temperament; mood. **3.** A chronic skin affection. **4.** A caprice. **5. a** The faculty of seeing the funny side of things and of expressing it to others. **b** That quality in a situation, or an expression, which appeals to a sense of the ludicrous. — *v. t.* To comply with the humor of; indulge; as, to *humor* a child.

hu'mor-ist (-ǐst), *n.* One who displays humor in speaking or writing; humorous talker or writer.

hu'mor-ous (-ŭs), *a.* [4] Characterized by humor; funny; facetious. — **-ly,** *adv.* [8] — **-ness,** *n.* [8].

hump (hŭmp), *n.* A rounded protuberance, as that on the back of the camel, bison, etc. — *v. t.* To make hump-shaped ; hunch.

hump'back' (-băk'), *n.* **1.** A humped back. **2.** A hunchback. **3.** Any of various whales.

hump'backed' (-băkt'), *a.* Having a humped back.

humph (hŭmf), *interj.* An exclamation of doubt, contempt, etc.

hu'mus (hū'mŭs), *n.* Vegetable mold.

hunch (hŭnch), *v. t.* To thrust out in a hump. — *n.* A hump; protuberance.

hunch'back' (-băk'), *n.* A back with a hunch or hump ; also, a hunchbacked person.

hunch'backed' (-băkt'), *a.* Humpbacked.

hun'dred (hŭn'drĕd), *n.* The product of ten multiplied by ten; five score. Also, a symbol for one hundred units, as 100 or ℅. — *a.* Ten times ten.

hun'dredth (-drĕdth), *a.* **1.** Forming one of a hundred equal parts into which a (whole) thing may be divided. **2.** Coming last in a series of a hundred individuals or units. — *n.* **1.** A hundredth part. **2.** A hundredth unit or object.

hun'dred-weight' (hŭn'drĕd-wāt'), *n.* An avoirdupois weight, commonly 112 lbs. In England, and 100 lbs. in the United States. Abbr. *cwt.* Cf. TON.

hung (hŭng), *pret. & p. p.* of HANG.

Hun-ga'ri-an (hŭn-gā'rǐ-ǎn), *a.* Of or pert. to Hungary or its people. — *n.* A native of Hungary.

hun'ger (hŭn'gẽr), *n.* **1.** A craving for food. **2.** Any strong or eager desire. — *v. i.* To feel hunger.

hun'gry (-grǐ), *a.* [3] **1.** Feeling or showing hunger. **2.** Poor; barren; as soil. — **-gri-ly,** *adv.* [8].

hunk (hŭngk), *n.* A chunk; lump. *Colloq.*

hunt (hŭnt), *v. t.* **1.** To follow or search for (game); pursue (game). **2.** To seek; pursue; follow; as, to *hunt* up evidence. **3.** To drive; chase; persecute. **4.** To use or traverse in pursuit of game; search carefully. — *v. i.* **1.** To follow the chase; pursue game. **2.** To seek; pursue; — with *for* or *after.* — *n.* **1.** Act or practice of hunting; chase; pursuit. **2.** An association of huntsmen.

hunt'er (hŭn'tẽr), *n.* **1.** A huntsman. **2.** A seeker. **3.** A dog or a horse trained for hunting.

hunt'ress (hŭn'trĕs), *n.* A woman who hunts.

hunts'man (hŭnts'mǎn), *n. ; pl.* -MEN (-mĕn). **1.** A man who hunts; hunter. **2.** Manager of a hunt.

hur'dle (hûr'd'l), *n.* **1.** A movable frame, for folding sheep, for gates, etc. **2.** Artificial barrier to be leaped in a race ; *pl.* (with *the*), a race in which hurdles are leaped. — *v. t. & i.* [1] To leap over while running, as a hurdle. — **-dler** (-dlẽr), *n.* [8].

hur'dy-gur'dy (-dǐ-gûr'dǐ), *n. ; pl.* -DIES (-dǐz). An instrument, esp. of street music, played by turning a crank.

hurl (hûrl), *v. t.* **1.** To throw or cast violently. **2.** To overthrow. **3.** To utter vehemently. — *n.* A violent throw; cast. — **hurl'er,** *n.* [8].

hurl'y-burl'y (hûr'lǐ-bûr'lǐ), *n. ; pl.* -LIES (-lǐz). Tumult; uproar; confusion.

hur-rah' (hŏo-rä'; hŭ-rä'), *interj.* A word used as a shout of joy, triumph, applause, etc. — *n.* A cheer; shout of joy, etc.

hur'ri-cane (hûr'ǐ-kān), *n.* A violent whirlwind, generally with rain, thunder, and lightning.

hur'ry (-ǐ), *v. t.* [2] To hasten; urge on; quicken. — *v. i.* To move or act hastily. — *n. ; pl.* -RIES (-ǐz). **1.** Quick, hurried motion; rush. **2.** Act of hurrying; undue haste; need of haste.

hurt (hûrt), *v. t. ;* HURT; HURT'ING. **1.** To pain; wound or bruise painfully; distress. **2.** To damage; injure; harm. — *v. i.* To cause pain or injury. — *n.* **1.** A wound, bruise, or the like, or the pain caused by it. **2.** Injury; harm.

hurt'ful (hûrt'fŏol), *a.* [4] Tending to impair or damage; injurious. — **-ly,** *adv.* [8] — **-ness,** *n.* [8].

hur'tle (hûr't'l), *v. i.* [1] **1.** To meet with a shock; clash. **2.** To rush suddenly. **3.** To make a sound as of clashing. — *v. t.* To drive violently ; fling.

hus'band (hŭz'bǎnd), *n.* A man who has a wife. — *v. t.* To direct and manage with frugality.

hus'band-man (-mǎn), *n. ; pl.* -MEN. A farmer.

hus'band-ry (-rǐ), *n.* **1.** Care of domestic affairs; domestic economy; hence, thrift. **2.** Farming.

hush (hŭsh), *v. t.* **1.** To make quiet, still, or calm. **2.** To allay; soothe. **3.** To procure silence concerning;— usually with *up.* — *v. i.* To become or keep quiet. — *n.* Stillness.

hush money. Money paid to hush up something.

husk (hŭsk), *n.* **1.** The outer coating of various seeds or fruits; *U. S.,* the envelope of an ear of Indian corn. **2.** Outside covering, esp. when rough or worthless. — *v. t.* To strip the husk from.

husk′ing, *vb. n.* A meeting of neighbors or friends to husk corn; — called also **husking bee.**

husk′y (hŭs′kĭ), *a.* [3] **1.** Abounding with, consisting of, or resembling, husks. **2.** Rough in tone; hoarse. — **husk′i-ly,** *adv.* [8] — **-ness,** *n.* [8].

hus-sar′ (hŏŏ-zär′), *n.* One of a class of light cavalry in European armies.

hus′sy (hŭz′ĭ), *n. ; pl.* -SIES (-ĭz). **1.** A worthless woman or girl. **2.** A pert girl; — used jocosely.

hus′tings (hŭs′tĭngz), *n. pl.,* construed as *sing.* The platform from which candidates for Parliament were nominated; also, election proceedings.

hus′tle (hŭs′'l), *v. t. & i.* [1] **1.** To push or crowd rudely. **2.** To force on or onward rapidly or roughly. *Colloq.* **3.** To move or work rapidly and tirelessly. *Colloq.* — *n.* The act of one who hustles. — **hus′tler** (hŭs′lẽr), *n.* [8].

hut (hŭt), *n.* A rude small house, hovel, or cabin.

hutch (hŭch), *n.* **1.** A chest, bin, coop, etc.; as, a rabbit *hutch.* **2.** A hut; shanty.

huz-za′ (hŭ-zä′; hŏŏ-), *interj.* Hurrah! — *n.* A shout of *huzza.* — *v. i. & t.* To shout *huzza;* cheer.

hy′a-cinth (hī′á-sĭnth), *n.* **1.** A transparent red or brownish zircon sometimes used as a gem. **2.** A well-known plant of the lily family, with spikes of bell-shaped flowers; also, its bulb or flower.

hy′brid (-brĭd), *n.* **1.** The offspring of two animals or plants of different species or races. **2.** Anything of mixed origin or composition. — *a.* **1.** Bred of two species or races. **2.** From unlike sources. — **hy′brid-ize,** *v. t. & i.*

Hy′dra (-drá), *n. ; pl.* E. -DRAS (-dráz), L. -DRÆ (-drē). **1.** *Gr. Myth.* A serpent or monster with nine heads; if one was cut off, two took its place, unless the wound was cauterized. **2.** [*l. c.*] An evil having many sources, or difficult to eradicate.

hy-dran′ge-a (hī-drăn′jē-á), *n.* Any of a genus (*Hydrangea*) of shrubs or small trees cultivated for their white or tinted flowers.

hy′drant (hī′drănt), *n.* A discharge pipe with a valve and spout at which water may be drawn.

hy′drate (-drāt), *n.* *Chem.* A compound formed by the union of water with another substance. — *v. t. & i.* [1] To become, or cause to be, a hydrate.

hy-drau′lic (hī-drô′lĭk), *a.* **1.** Of or pertaining to hydraulics; conveying or operated by water. **2.** Hardening or setting under water, as cement.

hy-drau′lics (-lĭks), *n.* The science dealing with water or other fluid in motion.

hy′dro-air′plane′ (hī′drŏ-âr′plăn′), **hy′dro-a′ẽr-o-plane′** (-ā′ẽr-ṓ-plăn′), *n.* An airplane designed to rise from and land on the water; a seaplane.

hy′dro-car′bon (-kär′bŏn), *n.* A compound of hydrogen and carbon only, as acetylene, gasoline, etc.

hy′dro-chlo′ric (-klṓ′rĭk), *a.* Pertaining to or designating an acid containing chlorine.

hy′dro-gen (hī′drṓ-jĕn), *n.* An inflammable gas, without taste, color, or (when pure) odor. It is an element, and is the lightest known substance.

hy-drog′ra-phy (hī-drŏg′rá-fĭ), *n.* Art of describing the sea and other waters, and mapping or charting them. — **hy-drog′ra-pher** (-fẽr), *n.* [8] — **hy′dro-graph′ic** (hī′drṓ-grăf′ĭk), *a.*

hy-drom′e-ter (hī-drŏm′ê-tẽr), *n.* A floating instrument for determining the specific gravities, and so the strength, of liquors, solutions, etc.

hy′dro-pho′bi-a (hī′drṓ-fṓ′bĭ-á), *n. Med.* **a** Morbid dread of water. **b** An infectious disease occurring chiefly among carnivorous animals; rabies.

hy′dro-plane (hī′drṓ-plān), *n.* A projecting plane or fin on a gliding boat to lift the moving boat on the water; also, a gliding boat. [statics.]

hy′dro-stat′ic (-stăt′ĭk), *a.* Of or pert. to hydro-

hy′dro-stat′ics (-stăt′ĭks), *n.* Science of the pressure and equilibrium of liquids, as water, etc.

hy′drous (hī′drŭs), *a.* Containing water; specifically, containing water chemically combined.

hy-drox′ide (hī-drŏk′sĭd; -sīd), *n. Chem.* A compound of an element or radical with hydrogen and oxygen, not regarded as containing water.

hy-e′na (hī-ē′ná), *n.* Any of several large, but cowardly, flesh-eating animals of Asia and Africa.

hy′gi-ene (hī′jĭ-ēn; hī′jēn), *n.* Science of preserving health. [hygiene; sanitary.]

hy′gi-en′ic (-jĭ-ĕn′ĭk), *a.* [4] Of or pertaining to

hy-grom′e-ter (hī-grŏm′ê-tẽr), *n.* An instrument for measuring the degree of moisture in the air.

hy′la (hī′lá), *n.* A tree frog.

hy′me-ne′al (hī′mē-nē′ăl), *a.* Pert. to marriage.

hymn (hĭm), *n.* A song of praise or adoration of God, a deity, etc. — *v. t. & i.;* HYMNED (hĭmd); HYMN′ING (hĭm′ĭng; hĭm′nĭng). To praise in song.

hym′nal (hĭm′năl), *n.* A hymn book.

hy-per′bo-la (hī-pûr′bṓ-lá), *n. Geom.* A curve formed by a section of a cone, when the cutting plane makes a greater angle with the base than the cone's side makes.

hy-per′bo-le (-lē), *n.* A figure of speech in which the expression is an evident exaggeration.

hy′per-bol′ic (hī′pẽr-bŏl′ĭk), *a.* [4] Relating to, containing, or like, hyperbole.

hy′per-bol′i-cal (-ĭ-kăl), *a.* [4] Hyperbolic.

hy′per-crit′i-cal (-krĭt′ĭ-kăl), *a.* [4] Too critical; captious. — **hy′per-crit′i-cal-ly,** *adv.* [8].

hy-per′tro-phy (hī-pûr′trṓ-fĭ), *n. Med.* A condition of excessive development of an organ or part.

hy′phen (hī′fĕn), *n.* A mark [-] placed between syllables of a divided word or between parts of a compound word. — *v. t.* To connect with a hyphen.

☞ In this Dictionary a heavy-faced hyphen [- or -] is used in compound words, and a light hyphen [-] in syllabication, as in for-get-me-not.

hy′phen-ate (-āt), *v. t.* [1] To hyphen.

hyp-no′sis (hĭp-nṓ′sĭs), *n.* See HYPNOTISM.

hyp-not′ic (-nŏt′ĭk), *a.* [4] **1.** Soporific. **2.** Pertaining to hypnotism. — *n.* **1.** An agent for producing sleep. **2.** One subject to hypnotism.

hyp′no-tism (hĭp′nṓ-tĭz′m), *n.* Induction of a state (called hypnosis, or hypnotic sleep) resembling sleep or somnambulism; loosely, hypnosis.

hyp′no-tist (-tĭst), *n.* One who practices, or advocates the use of, hypnotism.

hyp′no-tize (-tīz), *v. t.* [1] To induce hypnosis in. — **hyp′no-tiz′er** (-tīz′ẽr), *n.* [8].

hyp′o-chon′dri-a (hĭp′ṓ-kŏn′drĭ-á; hī′pṓ-), *n.* Morbid depression of mind or spirits.

---

chair; go; sing, iṅk; then, thin; nature, verdure; yet; zh = z in azure. Numbers refer to §§ in the Special Notes which, with Abbreviations, Signs, etc., precede the Vocabulary.

hyp'o-chon'dri-ac(hĭp'ô-kŏn'drĭ-ăk;hĭ'pô-),*a.* [4]
Affected by hypochondria.—*n.* One affected with
hypochondria.

hy-poc'ri-sy (hĭ-pŏk'rĭ-sĭ), *n.; pl.* -sies (-sĭz).
Act or practice of feigning to be what one is not;
esp., false assumption of an appearance of virtue.

hyp'o-crite (hĭp'ô-krĭt), *n.* One who feigns to be
other and better than he is; a dissembler.

hyp'o-crit'i-cal (-krĭt'ĭ-kăl), *a.* [4] Of or pert.
to a hypocrite or hypocrisy.—**-ly**, *adv.* [8].

hy'po-der'mic (hĭ'pô-dûr'mĭk; hĭp'ô-), *a.* Of or
pertaining to the parts under the skin.

hy-pot'e-nuse (hĭ-pŏt'ē-nūs; hĭ'-), *n.* The side opposite the right angle in a right-angled triangle.

hy-poth'e-cate (-pŏth'ê-kāt; hĭ-), *v.t.* [1] *Law.* To
pledge without delivery; mortgage.

hy-poth'e-ca'tion (-kā'shŭn), *n.* Act of hypothe-
cating.

hy-poth'e-nuse (-pŏth'ê-nūs). Var. of HYPOTENUSE.

hy-poth'e-sis (-pŏth'ê-sĭs; hĭ'-), *n.; pl.* -ses (-sēz).
A principle or theory not proved, but assumed
for argument, or to explain certain facts.

hy'po-thet'i-cal (hĭ'pô-thĕt'ĭ-kăl), *a.* [4] Con-
jectural; conditional; as, a *hypothetical* question.

hys'sop (hĭs'ŭp), *n.* An aromatic European mint.

hys-te'ri-a (hĭs-tē'rĭ-à), *n.* A nervous affection
marked by loss of control over the emotions, by
imaginary sensations, and, often, paroxysms.

hys-ter'ic (-tĕr'ĭk), *a.* [4] Hysterical.

hys-ter'i-cal (-ĭ-kăl), *a.* [4] Of or pertaining to
hysteria.—**hys-ter'i-cal-ly**, *adv.* [8].

hys-ter'ics (-ĭks), *n. pl.* Hysteria.

I

I (ī), *pron.; poss.* MY (mī) or MINE (mīn); *object.*
ME (mē); *pl. nom.* WE (wē); *poss.* OUR (our) or OURS
(ourz); *object.* US (ŭs). The nominative case of the
pronoun of the first person (by which a person denotes himself).

i-am'bus (ī-ăm'bŭs), *n.; pl.* L. -BI (-bī), E. -BUSES
(-bŭs-ĕz). A poetic foot consisting of a short (or
unaccented) syllable followed by a long (or accented) one, as in *amáze* or *invént*.

i'bex (ī'bĕks), *n.; pl.* E. IBEXES (-bĕk-sĕz), L. IBICES
(ĭb'ĭ-sēz; ī'bĭ-). A European wild mountain goat.

i'bis (ī'bĭs), *n.* A large wading bird of warm regions, related to the herons.

ice (īs), *n.* **1.** Frozen water. **2.** A sweetened mixture, usually fruit juice and water, artificially frozen. **3.** A substance looking like ice; as, camphor
ice. **4.** Icing; frosting.—*v.t.* [1] **1.** To cover
or supply with ice; convert into ice. **2.** To frost
(cakes, etc.). **3.** To chill; cool.

ice'berg' (īs'bûrg'), *n.* A large floating mass of
ice, detached from a glacier.

ice boat. A skeleton boat
or frame on three runners
propelled on ice by sails.

ice cream. Sweetened
cream or custard flavored,
beaten, and frozen.

ich-neu'mon (ĭk-
nū'mŏn), *n.* A
mongoose.

i'ci-cle (ī'sĭ-k'l), *n.*
A hanging taper-
ing mass of ice
formed from drip-
ping water.

i'ci-ly (-lĭ), *adv.* In an icy manner.

i'ci-ness (-nĕs), *n.* State of being icy; icy quality.

ic'ing (īs'ĭng), *n.* An icelike frosting, as for cake.

i-con'o-clasm (ī-kŏn'ô-klăz'm), *n.* Image breaking.

i-con'o-clast (-klăst), *n.* **1.** A breaker of images;
an enemy of image worship. **2.** One who attacks
cherished beliefs as shams. — **i-con'o-clas'tic**
(-klăs'tĭk), *a.*

i'cy (ī'sĭ), *a.* [3] **1.** Pertaining to, resembling, or

abounding in, ice; cold; frosty. **2.** Characterized
by coldness, as of manner, etc.; chilling; frigid.

i-de'a (ī-dē'à), *n.; pl.* IDEAS (-àz). **1.** A pattern,
standard, or ideal; hence, a plan or intention.
2. A mental image or picture. **3.** A notion, opinion,
or impression.

i-de'al (-ăl), *a.* [4] **1.** Existing in idea, or as a perfect pattern. **2.** Visionary; unreal. **3.** Pertaining to ideas or idealism.—*n.* A standard of
perfection, beauty, or excellence; a perfect type.

i-de'al-ism (-ĭz'm), *n.* **1.** A theory that makes
everything to consist of ideas. **2.** The practice of
idealizing; tendency to idealize. **3.** In literature
and art, the theory or practice which emphasizes
the value of imagination as compared with the
faithful copying of nature.

i-de'al-ist, *n.* **1.** One who holds a doctrine of idealism. **2.** One who idealizes, or who seeks the ideal.

i-de'al-is'tic (-ĭs'tĭk), *a.* Of or pert. to idealism.

i-de'al-i-za'tion (-ĭ-zā'shŭn), *n.* Act or product
of idealizing.

i-de'al-ize (ī-dē'ăl-īz), *v.t.* [1] To make ideal; attribute ideal characteristics to. — *v.i.* To form
or conceive ideals.

i-de'al-ly (-ĭ), *adv.* In an ideal manner; perfectly.

i-den'ti-cal (ī-dĕn'tĭ-kăl), *a.* **1.** The same; the
very same. **2.** Exactly alike or equal. — **i-den'ti-
cal-ly**, *adv.* [8] —**-ness**, *n.* [8].

i-den'ti-fi-ca'tion (-fĭ-kā'shŭn), *n.* Act of identi-
fying, or state of being identified.

i-den'ti-fy (-fī), *v.t.* [2] **1.** To make to be the
same. **2.** To establish the identity of.

i-den'ti-ty (-tĭ), *n.; pl.* -TIES (-tĭz). Absolute likeness; sameness; individuality.

ides (īdz), *n. pl.* In ancient Rome, the 15th day
of March, May, July, and October, and the 13th of
other months.

id'i-o-cy (ĭd'ĭ-ô-sĭ), *n.* Extreme deficiency in intelligence; imbecility.

id'i-om (-ŭm), *n.* **1.** A tongue or dialect. **2.** Mode
of expression peculiar to a language. **3.** An expression the meaning of which cannot be gathered
from the meanings of the separate words.

id'i-o-mat'ic (ĭd'ĭ-ô-măt'ĭk), *a.* Of, pertaining to,
or conforming to, idioms.—**i-cal-ly**, *adv.* [8].

Ice Boat.

āle, senāte, câre, ăm, ăccount, ärm, ásk, sofá; ēve, ēvent, ĕnd, recĕnt, makēr; īce, ĭll;
ōld, ôbey, ôrb, ŏdd, sôft, cŏnnect; ūse, ũnite, ûrn, ŭp, circŭs; fōōd, fŏŏt; out, oil;

id′i-o-syn′cra-sy (-sĭn′krà-sĭ), *n.; pl.* -SIES (-sĭz). A peculiarity of constitution, temperament, view, feeling, etc.; an eccentricity.

id′i-ot (ĭd′ĭ-ŏt), *n.* **1.** A person afflicted with idiocy. **2.** A fool; simpleton; — in reproach.

id′i-ot′ic (ĭd′ĭ-ŏt′ĭk), *a.* Pertaining to or like an idiot. — **id′i-ot′i-cal-ly,** *adv.* [8].

i′dle (ī′d′l), *a.* [3] **1.** Without worth or basis; groundless; useless; vain. **2.** Not occupied or employed; inactive. — *v. i.* [1] To spend time in idleness.

i′dle-ness, *n.* Quality or state of being idle.

i′dler (ī′dlẽr), *n.* One who idles; a lazy person.

i′dly (ī′dlĭ), *adv.* In an idle manner; lazily.

i′dol (ī′dŏl), *n.* **1.** An image; object of worship. **2.** Object of strong affection or devotion.

i-dol′a-ter (ī-dŏl′à-tẽr), *n.* A worshiper of idols. — **i-dol′a-tress** (-trĕs), *n. fem.* [8].

i-dol′a-trous (-trŭs), *a.* Of or pert. to idolatry.

i-dol′a-try (-trĭ), *n.; pl.* -TRIES (-trĭz). **1.** Worship of idols. **2.** Excessive veneration for anything.

i′dol-ize (ī′dŏl-īz), *v. t.* [1] To made an idol of.

i′dyl (ī′dĭl), *n.* A short pastoral poem; also, any simple description of rustic life.

i-dyl′lic (ī-dĭl′ĭk), *a.* Of or pertaining to an idyl.

if (ĭf), *conj.* **1.** In case that; granting, allowing, or supposing that. **2.** Whether.

ig′loo, ig′lu (ĭg′lōō), *n.* An Eskimo hut, as of snow blocks.

ig′ne-ous (-nē-ŭs), *a.* [4] **1.** Pertaining to, like, or containing, fire. **2.** *Geol.* Resulting from the action of intense heat; as, *igneous* rocks.

‖ **ig′nis fat′u-us** (ĭg′nĭs făt′ū-ŭs), *pl.* IGNES FATUI (ĭg′nēz făt′ū-ī). [L.] **1.** A phosphorescent light appearing at night over marshy grounds; will-o′-the-wisp. **2.** Something misleading.

ig-nite′ (ĭg-nīt′), *v. t.* [1] To set on fire; light; kindle. — *v. i.* To take fire. — **ig-nit′er,** *n.* [8].

ig-ni′tion (-nĭsh′ŭn), *n.* Act of igniting; state of being ignited; also, means of igniting.

ig-no′ble (-nō′b′l), *a.* [3] Of low birth; not noble; base; mean. — **ig-no′bly,** *a.* [8].

ig′no-min′i-ous (ĭg′nō-mĭn′ĭ-ŭs), *a.* [4] Marked with or deserving ignominy. — **ly,** *adv.* [8].

ig′no-min-y (ĭg′nō-mĭn-ĭ), *n.; pl.* -IES (-ĭz). **1.** Disgrace or dishonor; infamy. **2.** Infamous conduct.

ig′no-ra′mus (-rā′mŭs), *n.; pl.* -MUSES (-ĕz). An ignorant person; a dunce.

ig′no-rance (ĭg′nō-rǎns), *n.* State or fact of being ignorant; want of knowledge.

ig′no-rant (-rǎnt), *a.* [4] **1.** Destitute of knowledge. **2.** Unaware (of). **3.** Resulting from ignorance; as, an *ignorant* statement. — **ly,** *adv.*

ig-nore′ (ĭg-nōr′), *v. t.* [1] To refuse to notice; disregard willfully.

i-gua′na (ĭ-gwä′nà), *n.* A large tropical American lizard. The best-known species is five or six feet in length, but is harmless, living chiefly on leaves and blossoms, and is esteemed as food.

il′e-um (ĭl′ē-ŭm), *n.* The division of the small intestine between the jejunum and large intestine.

i′lex (ī′lĕks), *n.* **1.** An evergreen oak of southern Europe. **2.** Holly.

ill (ĭl), *a.; compar.* WORSE (wûrs); *superl.* WORST (wûrst). **1.** Unjust; unkind; harsh. **2.** Harmful; bad; evil. **3.** Incorrect; improper. **4.** Sick; in-disposed; unwell. — *adv.* In an ill manner; badly. — *n.* Whatever impairs happiness or prevents success; an evil; evil; misfortune, etc.

ill′-bred′, *a.* [4] Badly brought up; impolite; rude.

il-le′gal (ĭ-lē′gǎl), *a.* [4] Unlawful; illicit. — **il-le′gal-ly,** *adv.* [8].

il′le-gal′i-ty (ĭl′ē-gǎl′ĭ-tĭ), *n.; pl.* -TIES (-tĭz). Quality of being illegal; also, an illegal act.

il-leg′i-bil′i-ty (ĭ-lĕj′ĭ-bĭl′ĭ-tĭ), *n.; pl.* -TIES (-tĭz). State or quality of being illegible.

il-leg′i-ble (ĭ-lĕj′ĭ-b′l), *a.* [4] Not legible. — **il-leg′i-bly,** *adv.* [8].

il′le-git′i-ma-cy (ĭl′ē-jĭt′ĭ-mà-sĭ), *n.; pl.* -CIES (-sĭz). State or quality of being illegitimate.

il′le-git′i-mate (-mǎt), *a.* [4] **1.** Not according to law; unlawful; improper. **2.** Born out of wedlock. **3.** Illogical. — **ly,** *adv.* [8].

ill′-fa′vored (ĭl′fā′vẽrd), *a.* [4] **1.** Ugly; ill-looking. **2.** Offensive; unpleasant.

ill′-hu′mored (-hū′mẽrd), *a.* Cross; morose.

il-lib′er-al (ĭ-lĭb′ẽr-ǎl), *a.* [4] Not liberal; mean; narrow-minded; bigoted; stingy. — **ly,** *adv.* [8].

il-lib′er-al′i-ty (-ǎl′ĭ-tĭ), *n.* State or quality of being illiberal.

il-lic′it (ĭ-lĭs′ĭt), *a.* [4] Not allowed; improper; unlawful. — **ly,** *adv.* [8] — **ness,** *n.* [8].

il-lim′it-a-ble (ĭ-lĭm′ĭt-à-b′l), *a.* Boundless.

il-lit′er-a-cy (ĭ-lĭt′ẽr-à-sĭ), *n.; pl.* -CIES (-sĭz). Illiterate quality or state; inability to read.

il-lit′er-ate (-ǎt), *a.* [4] Ignorant of letters or books; uneducated; esp., unable to read. — *n.* One who is illiterate.

ill′ness (ĭl′nĕs), *n.* Sickness; indisposition.

il-log′i-cal (ĭ-lŏj′ĭ-kǎl), *a.* [4] Contrary to logic or sound reasoning. — **ly,** *adv.* [8].

ill′-tem′pered, *a.* [4] Morose; quarrelsome.

ill′treat′ (ĭl′trēt′), *v. t.* To treat badly.

il-lu′mi-nant (ĭ-lū′mĭ-nǎnt), *n.* That which gives light, as gas or petroleum.

il-lu′mi-nate (-nāt), *v. t.* [1] **1.** To make light; light up; enlighten. **2.** To make plain or clear. **3.** To decorate with artificial lights. **4.** To adorn with ornamental lettering or borders, in colors and gold, as in medieval manuscripts.

il-lu′mi-na′tion (-nā′shŭn), *n.* Act of illuminating; state of being illuminated; enlightenment.

il-lu′mi-na-tive (-lū′mĭ-nǎ-tĭv), *a.* [4] Tending to illuminate.

il-lu′mi-na′tor (-nā′tẽr), *n.* One that illuminates.

il-lu′mine (ĭ-lū′mĭn), *v. t.* [1] To illuminate.

il-lu′sion (ĭ-lū′zhŭn), *n.* **1.** A deceptive appearance. **2.** State or fact of being deceived; false impression.

il-lu′sive (-sĭv), *a.* [4] Deceiving by false show; unreal. — **il-lu′sive-ly,** *adv.* [8] — **ness,** *n.* [8].

il-lu′so-ry (-sō-rĭ), *a.* [4] Deceiving; illusive.

il-lus′trate (ĭ-lŭs′trāt; ĭl′ŭs-trāt), *v. t.* [1] **1.** To make clear or explain, as by figures or examples. **2.** To provide or adorn, as a book, with pictures, etc.; also, to make clear or adorn.

il′lus-tra′tion (ĭl′ŭs-trā′shŭn), *n.* **1.** Act of illustrating; state of being illustrated. **2.** That which illustrates; an example or a picture.

il-lus′tra-tive (ĭ-lŭs′trà-tĭv; ĭl′ŭs-trā-tĭv), *a.* [4] Tending or designed to illustrate. — **ly,** *adv.* [8].

il-lus′tra-tor (-tẽr), *n.* One that illustrates.

il·lus'tri·ous (ĭ-lŭs'trĭ-ŭs), *a.* [4] Great, noble, or the like; famous. — **-ly,** *adv.* [8] — **-ness,** *n.* [8].

im'age (ĭm'āj), *n.* **1.** A representation; effigy; statue. **2.** A symbol; also, a type. **3.** Picture drawn by the fancy; as, an *image* of farm life. **4.** A picture formed by reflection or refraction, as in a mirror or through a lens.

im'age (ĭm'āj), *v. t.* [1] **1.** To represent or form an image of; reflect. **2.** To conceive; *imagine.* **3.** To describe; also, to typify.

im'age·ry (-rĭ), *n.* **1.** Images collectively, esp. mental images. **2.** Use of ornate language.

im·ag'i·na·ble (ĭ-măj'ĭ-nà-b'l), *a.* [4] Capable of being imagined; conceivable. — **-na·bly,** *adv.* [8].

im·ag'i·na·ry (-nà-rĭ), *a.* [4] Existing only in imagination or fancy; not real; fancied; ideal.

im·ag'i·na'tion (-nā'shŭn), *n.* **1.** The power or process of forming images or pictures in the mind. **2.** A mental image; a fanciful or vain notion.

im·ag'i·na·tive (-nà-tĭv), *a.* [4] **1.** Pertaining to or characterized by imagination. **2.** Given to imagining. — **-ly,** *adv.* [8] — **-ness,** *n.* [8].

im·ag'ine (ĭ-măj'ĭn), *v. t.* [1] **1.** To form a mental picture of; conceive. **2.** To suppose; fancy. — *v. i.* To fancy; think.

i·ma'go (ĭ-mā'gō), *n.; pl.* E. **-goes** (-gōz), L. **imag-ines** (ĭ-măj'ĭ-nēz). Final adult stage of an insect.

im'be·cile (ĭm'bē-sĭl), *a.* [4] **1.** Feeble; esp., feeble-minded. **2.** Stupid; idiotic. — *n.* A person of weak or feeble mind.

im'be·cil'i·ty (-sĭl'ĭ-tĭ), *n.; pl.* **-ties** (-tĭz). **1.** Quality of being imbecile. **2.** Foolishness.

im·bed', *v. t.* To lay as in a bed.

im·bibe' (ĭm-bīb'), *v. t.* [1] **1.** To receive or absorb into the mind and retain; as, to *imbibe* knowledge. **2.** To drink or drink in; absorb; assimilate.

im'bri·cate (ĭm'brĭ-kāt) } *a.* [4] Lying lapped
im'bri·cat'ed (-kāt'ĕd) } over each other, as scales, in regular order like tiles.

im'bri·ca'tion (-kā'shŭn), *n.* An overlapping of the edges like that of tiles or shingles.

im·bro'glio (ĭm-brōl'yō), *n.; pl.* **-glios** (-yōz). An intricate or complicated situation; also, a confused state of things; serious misunderstanding.

im·bue' (ĭm-bū'), *v. t.* [1] To dye; saturate.

im'i·ta·ble (ĭm'ĭ-tà-b'l), *a.* Capable of being imitated or copied.

im'i·tate (-tāt), *v. t.* [1] **1.** To copy, or strive to copy; to assume the form or likeness of. **2.** To be or appear like; resemble externally.

im'i·ta'tion (-tā'shŭn), *n.* **1.** Act of imitating. **2.** That which is produced as a copy; a likeness; a counterfeit.

im'i·ta·tive (ĭm'ĭ-tā-tĭv), *a.* [4] **1.** Marked by imitation. **2.** Inclined to imitate; not original.

im'i·ta'tor (-tā'tēr), *n.* One who imitates.

im·mac'u·late (ĭ-măk'û-lāt), *a.* [4] **1.** Spotless; pure. **2.** Without flaw or fault. — **-ly,** *adv.* [8].

im'ma·nence (ĭm'à-něns), **im'ma·nen·cy** (-něn-sĭ), *n.* Immanent state or quality.

im'ma·nent (ĭm'à-něnt), *a.* [4] Inherent; intrinsic; subjective.

im'ma·te'ri·al (ĭm'à-tē'rĭ-ăl), *a.* [4] **1.** Not consisting of matter; spiritual. **2.** Unimportant.

im'ma·te'ri·al'i·ty (-ăl'ĭ-tĭ), *n.* State or quality of being immaterial.

im'ma·ture' (-tūr'), *a.* [4] Not mature; not developed; crude. — **im'ma·ture'ly,** *adv.* [8].

im'ma·tu'ri·ty (-tū'rĭ-tĭ), *n.* State or quality of being immature; unripeness.

im·meas'ur·a·ble (ĭ-mĕzh'ûr-à-b'l), *a.* [4] Incapable of being measured; boundless. — **-ness,** *n.*

im·me'di·ate (ĭ-mē'dĭ-āt), *a.* [4] **1.** With nothing between; acting without the intervention of anything; direct. **2.** Not distant or separated; adjoining; hence, occurring without delay; done at once.

im·me'di·ate·ly, *adv.* **a** Without anything between; directly; closely. **b** Without delay.

im'me·mo'ri·al (ĭm'ē-mō'rĭ-ăl), *a.* Ancient beyond memory or record. — **-ly,** *adv.* [8].

im·mense' (ĭ-mĕns'), *a.* [4] Immeasurable; hence, vast; huge. — **-ly,** *adv.* [8].

im·men'si·ty (ĭ-mĕn'sĭ-tĭ), *n.; pl.* **-ties**. State or quality of being immense; hugeness; vastness.

im·merse' (ĭ-mûrs'), *v. t.* [1] **1.** To plunge into (a fluid, etc.); dip; sink. **2.** To baptize by immersion. **3.** To absorb; as, *immersed* in thought.

im·mer'sion (ĭ-mûr'shŭn), *n.* **1.** An immersing. **2.** Baptism by plunging the whole person in water.

im'me·thod'i·cal (ĭm'ē-thŏd'ĭ-kăl), *a.* [4] Not methodical; confused.

im'mi·grant (ĭm'ĭ-grănt), *n.* One who immigrates.

im'mi·grate (-grāt), *v. i.* [1] To come into a country for permanent residence. Cf. **emigrate.**

im'mi·gra'tion (-grā'shŭn), *n.* An immigrating.

im'mi·nence (ĭm'ĭ-něns), *n.* Condition or quality of being imminent.

im'mi·nent (-něnt), *a.* [4] Threatening to happen immediately; impending; — usually of danger.

im·mo'bile (ĭ-mō'bĭl), *a.* [4] Immovable; fixed; also, motionless.

im'mo·bil'i·ty (ĭm'ŏ-bĭl'ĭ-tĭ), *n.* Condition or quality of being immobile; fixedness.

im·mod'er·ate (ĭ-mŏd'ēr-āt), *a.* [4] Not moderate; extreme. — **-ly,** *adv.* [8].

im·mod'est (ĭ-mŏd'ĕst), *a.* [4] Not modest; forward; bold; indecent; indelicate. — **-ly,** *adv.* [8].

im·mod'es·ty (-ĕs-tĭ), *n.* Want of modesty.

im'mo·late (ĭm'ŏ-lāt), *v. t.* [1] To sacrifice, or kill as a sacrificial victim. — **-la'tor** (-lā'tēr), *n.* [8].

im'mo·la'tion (-lā'shŭn), *n.* Act of immolating, or state of being immolated; a sacrifice.

im·mor'al (ĭ-mŏr'ăl), *a.* [4] Not moral; wicked; licentious. — **im·mor'al·ly,** *adv.* [8].

im'mo·ral'i·ty (ĭm'ŏ-răl'ĭ-tĭ), *n.; pl.* **-ties** (-tĭz). State or quality of being immoral; vice; wickedness; unchastity; also, an immoral act or practice.

im·mor'tal (ĭ-mŏr'tăl), *a.* [4] **1.** Not mortal; undying; everlasting. **2.** Of or pertaining to immortality. — *n.* **1.** An immortal being; esp., *pl.,* in classical mythology, the gods. **2.** One whose fame is lasting. — **im·mor'tal·ly,** *adv.* [8].

im'mor·tal'i·ty (ĭm'ŏr-tăl'ĭ-tĭ), *n.* Quality or state of being immortal; unending life or existence.

im·mor'tal·ize (ĭ-mŏr'tăl-īz), *v. t.* [1] To render immortal.

im'mor·telle' (ĭm'ŏr-tĕl'), *n.* = **everlasting,** *n.,* 3.

im·mov'a·bil'i·ty (ĭ-mōōv'à-bĭl'ĭ-tĭ), *n.* Quality or state of being immovable.

im·mov'a·ble (ĭ-mōōv'à-b'l), *a.* [4] Incapable of being moved; as **a** Stationary. **b** Steadfast; un-

---

Charlotte

yielding. **c** Emotionless. — *n.* **1.** That which cannot be moved. **2.** *pl. Law.* Lands and things attached thereto.—**-ness**, *n.* [8] —**-a-bly**, *adv.* [8].

im-mune′ (ĭ-mūn′), *a.* [4] Exempt; esp., protected against a particular disease, as by inoculation. — *n.* One that is immune.

im-mu′ni-ty (ĭ-mū′nĭ-tĭ), *n.* ; *pl.* -TIES (-tĭz). **1.** Freedom or exemption. **2.** State of resisting the development of disease.

im-mun′ize (ĭ-mūn′ĭz ; ĭm′ū-nĭz), *v.t.* [1] To render immune.

im-mure′ (ĭ-mūr′), *v.t.* [1] To inclose within walls.

im-mu′ta-bil′i-ty (ĭ-mū′tá-bĭl′ĭ-tĭ), *n.* State or quality of being immutable.

im-mu′ta-ble (ĭ-mū′tá-b'l), *a.* [4] Not changeable; unalterable. — **-ness**, *n.* [8] — **-bly**, *adv.* [8].

imp (ĭmp), *n.* **1.** A young or inferior devil; a little, malignant spirit. **2.** Mischievous child or urchin.

im′pact (ĭm′păkt), *n.* A striking together ; collision ; forcible contact.

im-pair′ (ĭm-pâr′), *v.t.* To make worse; diminish in quantity, value, excellence, or strength.

im-pair′ment (ĭm-pâr′mĕnt), *n.* An impairing; state of being impaired.

im-pale′ (-pāl′), *v.t.* [1] To pierce as with a stake.

im-pale′ment (-mĕnt), *n.* An impaling.

im-pal′pa-bil′i-ty (ĭm-păl′pá-bĭl′ĭ-tĭ), *n.* Quality or state of being impalpable.

im-pal′pa-ble (ĭm-păl′pá-b'l), *a.* [4] That cannot be felt; intangible; also, extremely fine.

im-pan′el (-păn′ĕl), *v.t.* [7] To enter in or on a panel (list) ; enroll.

im-part′ (-pärt′), *v.t.* **1.** To bestow a share of; share ; communicate. **2.** To make known.

im-par′tial (-pär′shăl), *a.* [4] Not partial; unbiased ; fair; just. — **im-par′tial-ly**, *adv.* [8].

im-par′ti-al′i-ty (ĭm-pär′shĭ-ăl′ĭ-tĭ ; ĭm′pär-shăl′-ĭ-tĭ), *n.* Quality of being impartial; fairness.

im-pass′a-ble (ĭm-pås′á-b'l), *a.* [4] Incapable of being passed or crossed; not admitting a passage. — **im-pass′a-ble-ness**, *n.* [8] — **im-pass′a-bly**, *adv.* [8].

im-pas′si-bil′i-ty (-păs′ĭ-bĭl′ĭ-tĭ), *n.* Quality or state of being impassible.

im-pas′si-ble (-păs′ĭ-b'l), *a.* [4] Unfeeling; impassive. — **im-pas′si-bly**, *adv.* [8].

im-pas′sion (-păsh′ŭn), *v.t.* To fill or affect strongly with passion.

im-pas′sive (-păs′ĭv), *a.* [4] Insensible to pain or suffering. — **-ly**, *adv.* [8] — **-ness**, *n.* [8].

im-pa′tience (-pā′shĕns), *n.* State or quality of being impatient.

im-pa′tient (-shĕnt), *a.* [4] Not patient ; uneasy. — **-ly**, *adv.* [8].

im-peach′ (-pēch′), *v.t.* **1.** To bring an accusation against; accuse. **2.** To impute some fault to; call in question.

im-peach′ment (-mĕnt), *n.* Act of impeaching.

im-pec′ca-bil′i-ty (ĭm-pĕk′á-bĭl′ĭ-tĭ), *n.* Quality of being impeccable.

im-pec′ca-ble (ĭm-pĕk′á-b'l), *a.* [4] Not liable to sin or wrongdoing ; free from fault or error.

im′pe-cu′ni-os′i-ty (ĭm′pē-kū′nĭ-ŏs′ĭ-tĭ), *n.* Lack of money; poverty.

im′pe-cu′ni-ous (ĭm′pē-kū′nĭ-ŭs), *a.* [4] Not having money; habitually without money; poor.

im-pede′ (ĭm-pēd′), *v.t.* [1] To obstruct; hinder.

im-ped′i-ment (-pĕd′ĭ-mĕnt), *n.* **1.** That which impedes ; hindrance; obstruction. **2.** An organic obstruction to speech.

im-pel′ (-pĕl′), *v.t.* ; -PELLED′ (-pĕld′) ; -PEL′LING. To urge forward or on ; give an impulse to; drive ; force. — **im-pel′ler**, *n.* [8].

im-pend′ (ĭm-pĕnd′), *v.i.* To hang over or be suspended (over) ; threaten ; be imminent.

im-pen′e-tra-bil′i-ty (-pĕn′ĕ-trá-bĭl′ĭ-tĭ), *n.* Quality or state of being impenetrable.

im-pen′e-tra-ble (-pĕn′ĕ-trá-b'l), *a.* [4] **1.** Incapable of being pierced. **2.** Incomprehensible. **3.** Not open, as to reason, sympathy, etc.—**-ness**, *n.* [8] — **im-pen′e-tra-bly**, *adv.* [8].

im-pen′i-tence (ĭm-pĕn′ĭ-tĕns), *n.* Fact, quality, or condition of being impenitent.

im-pen′i-tent (-tĕnt), *a.* [4] Not penitent ; not contrite ; having no sorrow for sin.—**-ly**, *adv.* [8].

im-per′a-tive (-pĕr′á-tĭv), *a.* **1.** *Gram.* Expressive of command, entreaty, or exhortation. **2.** Authoritative. **3.** Not to be avoided or evaded ; obligatory ; binding.—*n.* **1.** *Gram.* The imperative mood ; also, a verb or verbal form denoting it. **2.** Something imperative ; a command.—**-ly**, *adv.* [8] —**-ness**, *n.* [8].

im′per-cep′ti-ble (ĭm′pĕr-sĕp′tĭ-b'l), *a.* [4] Not perceptible; hence, very slight, gradual, or subtle. — **im′per-cep′ti-bly**, *adv.* [8].

im-per′fect (ĭm-pûr′fĕkt), *a.* [4] Not perfect; defective; incomplete. — **imperfect tense**, *Gram.*, a tense expressing action or state (esp. past) as going on but not completed at the time denoted ; as in, I *was choosing*. — *n.* *Gram.* The imperfect tense, or a verb or verbal form denoting it. — **im-per′fect-ly**, *adv.* [8] — **-ness**, *n.* [8].

im′per-fec′tion (ĭm′pĕr-fĕk′shŭn), *n.* Quality or state of being imperfect; deficiency ; fault.

im-pe′ri-al (ĭm-pē′rĭ-ăl), *a.* [4] **1.** Of or pertaining to an empire or emperor. **2.** Of or pert. to a state as sovereign, and supreme over colonies, etc. **3.** Of superior size or excellence. — *n.* **1.** An article of superior size or excellence. **2.** A pointed tuft of hair on a man's chin. — **-ly**, *adv.* [8].

im-pe′ri-al-ism (-ĭz'm), *n.* **1.** Imperial rule or system. **2.** The policy or practice of seeking to extend the control or empire of a nation.

im-pe′ri-al-ist, *n.* An adherent of an emperor; an advocate of imperialism. — **-is′tic** (-ĭs′tĭk), *a.* [4].

im-per′il (-pĕr′ĭl), *v.i.* [7] To endanger.

im-pe′ri-ous (-pē′rĭ-ŭs), *a.* [4] **1.** Arrogant; overbearing. **2.** Imperative; urgent; as, an *imperious* demand. — **-ly**, *adv.* [8] — **-ness**, *n.* [8].

im-per′ish-a-ble (ĭm-pĕr′ĭsh-á-b'l), *a.* [4] Not perishable. — **im-per′ish-a-bly**, *adv.* [8].

im-per′me-a-bil′i-ty (ĭm-pûr′mē-á-bĭl′ĭ-tĭ), *n.* Quality or state of being impermeable.

im-per′me-a-ble (ĭm-pûr′mē-á-b'l), *a.* [4] Not permeable ; impervious.

im-per′son-al (-sŏn-ăl), *a.* [4] Not personal; as : **a** *Gram.* Of verbs, used with no subject or an indefinite one ; as, it *snows*. **b** Not connected with any particular person. **c** Not having personality. — **-ly**, *adv.* [8].

im-per′son-ate (-āt), *v.t.* [1] **1.** To personify ; typify. **2.** To act the character of ; personate.

im-per'son-a'tion (ĭm-pûr'sŭn-ā'shŭn), *n.* An impersonating; personification; acting.

im-per'son-a'tor, *n.* One who impersonates.

im-per'ti-nence (ĭm-pûr'tĭ-nĕns), *n. ; pl.* -NENCES (-nĕn-sĕz). **1.** Fact, state, or quality of being impertinent. **2.** That which is impertinent.

im-per'ti-nent (-nĕnt), *a.* [4] **1.** Not pertinent; not to the point; irrelevant. **2.** Guilty of, or prone to, rudeness; insolent. —**ly**, *adv.* [8].

im'per-turb-a-bil'i-ty (ĭm'pẽr-tûr'bà-bĭl'ĭ-tĭ), *n.* State or quality of being imperturbable.

im'per-turb'a-ble (-tûr'bà-b'l), *a.* [4] Incapable of being disturbed; calm; serene.

im-per'vi-ous (ĭm-pûr'vĭ-ŭs), *a.* [4] Not pervious. — **im-per'vi-ous-ly**, *adv.* [8] —**ness**, *n.* [8].

im-pet'u-os'i-ty (ĭm-pĕt'ū-ŏs'ĭ-tĭ), *n. ; pl.* -TIES (-tĭz). Impetuous state or quality; vehemence.

im-pet'u-ous (-pĕt'ū-ŭs), *a.* [4] **1.** Rushing with violence; furious; violent. **2.** Hastily or rashly energetic. —**ly**, *adv.* [8] —**ness**, *n.* [8].

im'pe-tus (ĭm'pē-tŭs), *n.* **1.** Force or energy of motion; momentum. **2.** Impulse; incentive.

im-pi'e-ty (ĭm-pī'ē-tĭ), *n.; pl.* -TIES(-tĭz). **1.** Quality of being impious; ungodliness. **2.** An impious act.

im-pinge' (-pĭnj'), *v. i.* **1.** To strike or dash (on, upon, against), esp. with sharp collision; of waves of sound, light, etc. **2.** To encroach or infringe.

im'pi-ous (ĭm'pĭ-ŭs), *a.* [4] Not pious; profane; irreverent. —**ly**, *adv.* [8] —**ness**, *n.* [8].

imp'ish (ĭm'pĭsh), *a.* [4] Like an imp; esp., mischievous. —**ly**, *adv.* [8] —**ness**, *n.* [8].

im-pla'ca-ble (ĭm-plā'kà-b'l), *a.* [4] That cannot be appeased; inexorable.

im-plant' (-plănt'), *v. t.* To plant or set securely or deeply; instill or inculcate thoroughly.

im'ple-ment (ĭm'plē-mĕnt), *n.* An instrument, tool, or utensil. [*implicate* one in a crime.

im'pli-cate (-plĭ-kāt), *v. t.* [1] To involve; as, to

im'pli-ca'tion (ĭm'plĭ-kā'shŭn), *n.* **1.** Act of implicating; state of being implicated. **2.** That which is implied or involved; entanglement.

im-plic'it (ĭm-plĭs'ĭt), *a.* [4] **1.** Fairly to be understood, though not expressed; implied. **2.** Unquestioning. —**ly**, *adv.* [8] —**ness**, *n.* [8].

im-plore' (ĭm-plōr'), *v. t.* [1] To call upon or for earnestly; beseech; entreat.— **im-plor'er**, *n.* [8].

im-ply' (-plī'), *v. t.* [2] **1.** To involve or include as a necessary logical consequence (something not expressly stated). **2.** To express indirectly.

im'po-lite' (ĭm'pŏ-līt'), *a.* [4] Not polite; uncivil; rude. —**ly**, *adv.* [8] —**ness**, *n.* [8].

im-pol'i-tic (ĭm-pŏl'ĭ-tĭk), *a.* [4] Not politic; unwise; inexpedient; as, an *impolitic* law.

im-pon'der-a-ble (ĭm-pŏn'dẽr-à-b'l), *a.* [4] Not ponderable; without sensible weight.

im-port' (ĭm-pōrt'), *v. t.* **1.** To mean; signify; imply. **2.** To introduce from without; bring (wares) into a place from a foreign country in commerce.

im'port (ĭm'pōrt), *n.* **1.** Meaning. **2.** Importance. **3.** Merchandise imported;—esp. in *pl.*

im-por'tance (ĭm-pōr'tăns), *n.* Quality or state of being important; consequence; significance.

im-por'tant (-tănt), *a.* [4] **1.** Having consequence; significant; weighty. **2.** Consequential; pompous.

im'por-ta'tion (ĭm'pŏr-tā'shŭn), *n.* Act of importing; that which is imported.

im-port'er (ĭm-pōr'tẽr), *n.* One who imports.

im-por'tu-nate (-pōr'tū-nāt), *a.* Troublesomely urgent; pressing in demand. —**ly**, *adv.* [8].

im'por-tune' (ĭm'pŏr-tūn'; ĭm-pōr'tūn), *a.* [4] Importunate. —*v. t.* [1] To urge persistently.

im'por-tu'ni-ty (ĭm'pŏr-tū'nĭ-tĭ), *n.; pl.* -TIES (-tĭz). Troublesome pertinacity.

im-pose' (ĭm-pōz'), *v. t.* [1] **1.** To lay on(the hands), as in confirmation. **2.** To lay as a charge, tax, penalty, etc.; inflict; levy. —*v. i.* **1.** To take advantage of; presume. **2.** To deceive by false representation. —**im-pos'er** (ĭm-pōz'ẽr), *n.* [8].

im-pos'ing (-ĭng), *p.a.* [4] Impressive; commanding.

im'po-si'tion (ĭm'pō-zĭsh'ŭn), *n.* **1.** Act of imposing or laying on. **2.** That which is imposed; as: **a** A burden; tax. **b** An unwarranted requirement. **c** A trick; imposture.

im-pos/si-bil'i-ty (ĭm-pŏs'ĭ-bĭl'ĭ-tĭ), *n. ; pl.* -TIES (-tĭz). **1.** Quality of being impossible. **2.** An impossible thing.

im-pos'si-ble (-pŏs'ĭ-b'l), *a.* [4] **1.** Not possible. **2.** Impracticable. **3.** Hopelessly unsuitable; as, an *impossible* hat. *Colloq.* —**si-bly**, *adv.* [8].

im'post (ĭm'pŏst), *n.* **1.** A tax; excise. **2.** The top part of a pillar, etc., supporting an arch.

im-pos'tor (ĭm-pŏs'tẽr), *n.* An imposer on others.

im-pos'ture (-tūr), *n.* Act or conduct of an im postor; fraud or imposition.

im'po-tence (ĭm'pō-tĕns)) *n.* Impotent quality

im'po-ten-cy (-tĕn-sĭ)) or state; weakness.

im'po-tent (-tĕnt), *a.* [4] Wanting in power, strength, or vigor; weak; infirm. —**ly**, *adv.* [8].

im-pound' (ĭm-pound'), *v. t.* To shut up in or as in a pound; hence, to seize and hold in legal custody.

im-pov'er-ish (-pŏv'ẽr-ĭsh), *v. t.* To make poor.

im-pov'er-ish-ment (-mĕnt), *n.* An impoverishing.

im-prac'ti-ca-bil'i-ty (ĭm-prăk'tĭ-kà-bĭl'ĭ-tĭ), *n.* State or quality of being impracticable.

im-prac'ti-ca-ble (ĭm-prăk'tĭ-kà-b'l), *a.* [4] Incapable of being practiced or used; unserviceable. —**ness**, *n.* [8] —**ca-bly**, *adv.* [8].

im'pre-cate (ĭm'prē-kāt), *v. t.* [1] To call down or invoke by prayer (usually some evil); curse.

im'pre-ca'tion (-kā'shŭn), *n.* A curse.

im-preg-na-bil'i-ty (ĭm-prĕg'nà-bĭl'ĭ-tĭ), *n.* State or quality of being impregnable.

im-preg'na-ble (-prĕg'nà-b'l), *a.* [4] Able to resist attack; unconquerable. —**na-bly**, *adv.* [8].

im-preg'nate (-nāt), *v. t.* [1] **1.** To make pregnant; fertilize. **2.** To saturate; imbue.

im'preg-na'tion (ĭm'prĕg-nā'shŭn), *n.* An impregnating; fertilization; mixture of parts; infusion.

im'pre-sa'ri-o (ĭm'prä-sä'rē-ō), *n. ; pl.* E.-RIOS (-ōz) It. -SARI (-sä'rē). The projector or manager of an opera or concert company.

im'press (ĭm'prĕs), *n.* Impressment.

im-press' (ĭm-prĕs'), *v. t.* To levy for public service; esp., to force into the army or navy.

im-press', *v. t.* **1.** To press, stamp, or print something in or upon. **2. a** To cause a vivid impression of; stamp; imprint. **b** To affect or influence, esp. deeply.

im'press (ĭm'prĕs), *n.* **1.** Act of impressing. **2.** A mark made by pressure; impression. **3.** Characteristic. [ity of being impressible.

im-press'i-bil'i-ty (ĭm-prĕs'ĭ-bĭl'ĭ-tĭ), *n.* Qual-

im-press′i-ble (-prĕs′ĭ-b'l), a. [4] Capable of being impressed; susceptible; sensitive.

im-pres′sion (-prĕsh′ŭn), n. 1. Act of impressing; state of being impressed. 2. Effect of impressing, as an indentation, stamp, or figure. 3. Influence or effect, as on the mind, senses, or feelings. 4. An indistinct notion.

im-pres′sion-a-bil′i-ty (-ă-bĭl′ĭ-tĭ), n. Quality of being impressionable.

im-pres′sion-a-ble (-ă-b'l), a. [4] Liable to impression, susceptible.

im-pres′sion-ism (-ĭz′m), n. The theory and practice of a school of painting which aims to render the immediate sense impression of the artist. — im-pres′sion-ist (-ĭst), n. & a.

im-pres′sive (-prĕs′ĭv), a. [4] Making, or tending to make, an impression; as, an impressive speech, scene, etc. —ly, adv. [8] —ness, n. [8].

im-press′ment (-prĕs′mĕnt), n. Act of seizing for public use, or of impressing into public service.

im-print′ (-prĭnt′), v. t. 1. To impress; stamp. 2. To stamp or mark, as letters on paper, by means of type, stamps, etc. 3. To fix, as on the mind.

im′print (ĭm′prĭnt), n. 1. Whatever is imprinted; impress. 2. The name of the publisher or printer, as on a title-page or on any printed sheet.

im-pris′on (-prĭz′'n), v. t. To put in prison; confine.

im-pris′on-ment (-mĕnt), n. Confinement.

im-prob′a-bil′i-ty (-prŏb′ă-bĭl′ĭ-tĭ), n.; pl. -TIES (-tĭz). Quality or state of being improbable; unlikelihood, also, that which is improbable.

im-prob′a-ble (-prŏb′ă-b'l), a. [4] Not probable; unlikely to be true or to occur. — -a-bly, adv. [8].

im-promp′tu (-prŏmp′tū), adv. or a. Offhand; extempore. —n. Something made or done offhand.

im-prop′er (-prŏp′ẽr), a. [4] Not proper; specifically: a Not suitable or appropriate. b Incorrect. c Not normally formed, or not properly so called; as: improper fractions, fractions in which the numerator is greater than the denominator. d Not fitting, unbecoming, or indecent. — im-prop′er-ly, adv. [8].

im′pro-pri′e-ty (ĭm′prŏ-prī′ē-tĭ), n.; pl. -TIES (-tĭz). 1. Quality or fact of being improper. 2. An improper act, use, sense, etc.

im-prove′ (-prōōv′), v. t. [1] 1. To make good use of. 2. To make better. —v. i. 1. To rise in value. 2. To grow better 3. To make improvements.

im-prove′ment (ĭm-prōōv′mĕnt), n. 1. Act of improving, or state of being improved. 2. A result of improving, or that which constitutes it.

im-prov′i-dence (-prŏv′ĭ-dĕns), n. Quality of being improvident.

im-prov′i-dent (-prŏv′ĭ-dĕnt), a. [4] Not provident; thoughtless; thriftless; wasteful. —ly, adv.

im-prov′i-sa′tion (ĭm-prŏv′ĭ-sā′shŭn; -zā′shŭn), n. Act or art of improvising; that which is improvised.

im′pro-vise′ (ĭm′prŏ-vīz′), v. t. & i. [1] 1. To compose, recite, sing, etc., without preparation; extemporize. 2. To make, do, or provide offhand.

im-pru′dence (ĭm-prōō′dĕns), n. Quality, state, or instance of being imprudent; want of caution.

im-pru′dent (-dĕnt), a. [4] Not prudent; indiscreet. — im-pru′dent-ly, adv. [8].

im′pu-dence (ĭm′pū-dĕns), n. Quality of being impudent; insolence; effrontery; impertinence.

im′pu-dent (-dĕnt), a. [4] Bold or pert; impertinent; insolent. —ly, adv. [8].

im-pugn′ (ĭm-pūn′), v. t. To attack by words or arguments; call in question. — im-pugn′er, n. [8].

im′pulse (ĭm′pŭls), n. 1. Act of impelling; motion so produced. 2. A sudden inclination; an impelling force or natural tendency.

im-pul′sion (-pŭl′shŭn), n. An impelling; impulse.

im-pul′sive (-sĭv), a. [4] Actuated or marked by impulse. —ly, adv. [8] —ness, n. [8].

im-pu′ni-ty (-pū′nĭ-tĭ), n. Freedom from punishment, harm, or loss.

im-pure′ (-pūr′), a. [3] Not pure: as: a Containing something unclean; dirty, unwholesome. b Adulterated. c Defiled; unholy. d Unchaste. —ly, adv. [8] —ness, n. [8].

im-pu′ri-ty (-pū′rĭ-tĭ), n.; pl. -TIES (-tĭz). 1. A being impure. 2. That which is or renders impure.

im′pu-ta′tion (ĭm′pū-tā′shŭn), n. Act of imputing; thing imputed; censure; insinuation.

im-pute′ (-pūt′), v. t. [1] To charge or credit, as a fault or virtue; attribute.

in (ĭn), prep. Primarily, in denotes situation or position with respect to surrounding or inclosure; as · 1. Indicating inclusion in space, time, or physical surrounding; as, to travel in France in September. 2. Indicating inclusion, surrounding, or engrossment as to scope, influence, character, activity, etc.; as, to be in difficulties. —in as much as, or in-asmuch as, in the degree that; in like manner as; since. — in that, because.

in, adv. 1. Indicating a direction of entering; as, come in. 2. Indicating a position as to surroundings, inclosure, etc. — a. Inward; as, an in curve. —n. One that is in, esp. one in office

in′a-bil′i-ty (ĭn′ă-bĭl′ĭ-tĭ), n. Want of ability.

in′ac-ces′si-ble (ĭn′ăk-sĕs′ĭ-b'l), a. [4] Not accessible. — -si-bly, adv. [8] — -si-bil′i-ty, n.

in-ac′cu-ra-cy (ĭn-ăk′ū-rā-sĭ), n.; pl. -CIES (-sĭz). Quality or fact of being inaccurate, mistake: error.

in-ac′cu-rate (-rāt), a. [4] Not accurate; inexact; incorrect; erroneous. —ly, adv. [8].

in-ac′tion (-ăk′shŭn), n. Lack of action. idleness.

in-ac′tive (-tĭv), a. [4] Not active; as · a Having no power to move; inert. b Indisposed to action; sluggish. —ly, adv. [8] —ness, n. [8].

in-ac-tiv′i-ty (ĭn′ăk-tĭv′ĭ-tĭ), n. State or quality of being inactive; idleness. [inadequate.]

in-ad′e-qua-cy (ĭn-ăd′ē-kwá-sĭ), n. State of being

in-ad′e-quate (ĭn-ăd′ē-kwăt), a. [4] Not adequate; insufficient. —ly, adv. [8] —ness, n. [8].

in′ad-mis′si-ble (ĭn′ăd-mĭs′ĭ-b'l), a. [4] Not admissible; as, inadmissible evidence.

in′ad-vert′ence (-ăd-vûr′tĕns); pl. -CES (-sĕz) } n. in′ad-vert′en-cy (-tĕn-sĭ); pl. -CIES (-sĭz) } 1. Inattention; negligence. 2. An oversight.

in′ad-vert′ent (-tĕnt), a. [4] Not turning the mind to a matter; negligent. —ly, adv. [8].

in-al′ien-a-ble (ĭn-āl′yĕn-á-b'l), a. [4] Incapable of being alienated. — -a-bly, adv. [8].

in-ane′ (ĭn-ān′), a. [3] Without contents; empty; esp., void of sense or intelligence; silly. —ly, adv.

in-an′i-mate (ĭn-ăn′ĭ-măt), a. Not animate; lifeless; dull. —ly, adv. [8] —ness, n. [8].

in′a-ni′tion (ĭn′á-nĭsh′ŭn), n. State of being inane; emptiness; exhaustion from lack of food.

chair; go; sing, iŋk; then, thin; nature, verdure; yet; zh = z in azure. Numbers refer to §§ in the Special Notes which, with Abbreviations, Signs, etc., precede the Vocabulary.

in-an'i-ty (ĭn-ăn'ĭ-tĭ), *n.* ; *pl.* -TIES (-tĭz). **1.** State or quality of being inane. **2.** An inane thing.

in-ap'pli-ca-ble (-ăp'lĭ-kå-b'l), *a.* Not applicable.

in'ap-pre'ci-a-ble (ĭn'å-prē'shĭ-å-b'l), *a.* [4] Not appreciable ; too small to be perceived.

in'ap-pro'pri-ate (-prō'prĭ-ăt), *a.* [4] Not appropriate. — **-ly,** *adv.* [8] — **-ness,** *n.* [8].

in-ar-tic'u-late (ĭn'ar-tĭk'ū-låt), *a.* [4] **1.** Of sounds, words, etc., uttered without the articulations of intelligible speech. **2.** Unable to articulate ; dumb. — **-ly,** *adv.* [8] — **-ness,** *n.*

in'ar-tis'tic (ĭn'ar-tĭs'tĭk) *a.* [4] Not artistic.
in'ar-tis'ti-cal (-tĭ-kål) } — **-cal-ly,** *adv.* [8].

in'as-much' (ĭn'ăz-mŭch'), *adv.* In as much , — with *as.* See *in as much as,* under IN, *prep.*

in'at-ten'tion (ĭn'å-tĕn'shŭn), *n.* Want of attention ; disregard ; heedlessness.

in'at-ten'tive (-tĭv), *a.* [4] Not attentive , heedless , negligent. — **-ly,** *adv.* [8] — **-ness,** *n.* [8].

in-au'di-ble (ĭn-ô'dĭ-b'l), *a.* [4] Not audible. — **in-au'di-bly,** *adv.* [8].

in-au'gu-ral (-gû-rål), *a.* Pertaining to an inauguration. — *n.* An inaugural address. *U. S.*

in-au'gu-rate (-rāt), *v. t.* [1] **1.** To admit or induct into an office formally. **2.** To celebrate the first public use of. **3.** To commence or enter upon; set in motion. — **-ra'tor** (-tẽr), *n.* [8].

in-au'gu-ra'tion (-rā'shŭn), *n.* An inaugurating.

in'aus-pi'cious (ĭn'ôs-pĭsh'ŭs), *a.* [4] Not auspicious; unfavorable. — **-ly,** *adv.* — **-ness.** *n.* [8].

in'born' (ĭn'bôrn'), *a.* Born in or with one.

in'bred' (ĭn'brĕd'), *a.* **1.** Bred within; innate. **2.** (*pron.* ĭn-brĕd') Subjected to inbreeding.

in-breed' (ĭn-brēd'), *v. t.* ; -BRED (-brĕd', *cf. the adj.*) ; -BREED'ING. **1.** To produce within **2.** To breed with each other (animals closely related).

in-cal'cu-la-ble (ĭn-kăl'kŭ-lå-b'l), *a.* [4] Not to be calculated ; very great. — **-la-bly,** *adv.* [8].

in'can-des'cence (ĭn'kăn-dĕs'ĕns), *n.* Glowing due to heat, as of the filament of an electric lamp.

in'can-des'cent (-ĕnt), *a.* [4] White or glowing with intense heat ; hence, clear ; shining; brilliant.

in-can-ta'tion (-tå'shŭn), *n.* The use of magical spells or charms; also, the formula of words used.

in-ca'pa-bil'i-ty (ĭn-kā'på-bĭl'ĭ-tĭ), *n.* Quality or state of being incapable ; incapacity.

in-ca'pa-ble (-kā'på-b'l), *a.* [4] **1.** Not capable. **2.** Not susceptible. **3.** Not to be brought to do.

in'ca-pac'i-tate (ĭn'kå-păs'ĭ-tāt), *v. t.* [1] To deprive of capacity, disable ; disqualify.

in'ca-pac'i-ty (-tĭ), *n.* Want of capacity, inability ; disability.

in-car'cer-ate (ĭn-kär'sẽr-āt), *v. t.* [1] To imprison.

in-car'cer-a'tion (-å'shŭn), *n.* Imprisonment.

in-car'nate (-nåt), *a.* [4] Clothed with flesh; embodied in human form. — (-năt), *v. t.* [1] To make incarnate ; embody.

in'car-na'tion (ĭn'kär-nā'shŭn), *n.* **1.** Act or fact of incarnating. **2.** Of Christ, the union of Godhead with manhood. **3.** An incarnated being or idea.

in-case' (ĭn-kās'), *v. t.* [1] To inclose in a case or in something solid. — **in-case'ment** (-mĕnt), *n.*

in-cau'tious (ĭn-kô'shŭs), *a.* [4] Not cautious ; heedless ; rash. — **-ly,** *adv.* [8] — **-ness,** *n.* [8].

in-cen'di-a-rism (ĭn-sĕn'dĭ-å-rĭz'm), *n.* Incendiary action or practice.

in-cen'di-a-ry (ĭn-sĕn'dĭ-å-rĭ), *a.* [4] **1.** Of or pertaining to the malicious burning of property. **2.** Tending to excite quarrels; seditious. — *n.; pl.* -RIES (-rĭz). **1.** One who maliciously sets fire to a building. **2.** One who excites strife.

in'cense (ĭn'sĕns'), *n.* Perfume from spices or gums burned in religious rites ; any pleasing fragrance, also, the material used to produce such perfume.

in-cense' (ĭn-sĕns'), *v t.* [1] To inflame with anger

in-cen'tive (-sĕn'tĭv), *a.* [4] Inciting. — *n.* That which incites ; motive.

in-cep'tion (-sĕp'shŭn), *n.* Beginning , initiation.

in-cer'ti-tude (-sûr'tĭ-tūd), *n.* Doubtfulness.

in-ces'sant (ĭn-sĕs'ănt), *a.* [4] Continuing without interruption ; unceasing. — **-ly,** *adv.* [8].

inch (ĭnch), *n.* A measure of length, 1-12th of a foot (= 2.54 centimeters).

in'cho-ate (ĭn'kô-åt), *a.* [4] Recently, or just, begun; incipient ; incomplete. — **-ly,** *adv.* [8].

in'ci-dence (ĭn'sĭ-dĕns), *n.* *Physics.* The falling of a projectile, ray of light, etc., on a surface.

in'ci-dent (-dĕnt), *a.* [4] **1.** Liable to happen; happening or belonging, esp. as a subordinate feature. **2.** Falling or striking, as a light ray on a surface. — *n.* **1.** That which happens , event. **2.** An accidental or minor action or event.

in'ci-den'tal (-dĕn'tål), *a.* [4] Happening, or liable to happen, without design or as a chance feature of something else ; casual ; subordinate. — *n.* That which is incidental ; esp., *pl.,* minor or incidental items not particularized. — **-ly,** *adv.* [8].

in-cin'er-ate (ĭn-sĭn'ẽr-āt), *v. t. & i.* [1] To burn to ashes , cremate.

in-cin'er-a'tion (-å'shŭn), *n.* Cremation.

in-cin'er-a'tor (-å'tẽr), *n.* One that incinerates.

in-cip'i-ence (-sĭp'ĭ-ĕns) *n.* **1.** State of being incipient. **2.** Beginning.
in-cip'i-en-cy (-ĕn-sĭ) } ient ; beginning.

in-cip'i-ent (-ĕnt), *a.* Beginning to be, or to appear ; as, *incipient* madness. — **-ly,** *adv.* [8].

in-cise' (-sīz'), *v. t.* [1] To cut in or into , carve

in-ci'sion (-sĭzh'ŭn), *n.* **1.** Act of incising. **2** A cut ; gash.

in-ci'sive (-sī'sĭv), *a.* [4] Cutting , sharp; hence, acute; clear-cut. — **-ly,** *adv.* [8] — **-ness,** *n.* [8]

in-ci'sor (-sī'zẽr; -sẽr), *n.* A tooth adapted for cutting ; esp., one of the teeth in front of the canines

in'ci-ta'tion (ĭn'sĭ-tā'shŭn), *n.* Act of inciting , incitement.

in-cite' (ĭn-sīt'), *v. t.* [1] To spur or urge on. — **in-cit'er** (-ẽr), *n.* [8].

in-cite'ment (-mĕnt), *n.* An inciting ; that which incites ; incentive.

in'ci-vil'i-ty (ĭn'sĭ-vĭl'ĭ-tĭ), *n.; pl.* -TIES (-tĭz). **1.** Quality of being uncivil. **2.** Any uncivil act.

in-clem'en-cy (ĭn-klĕm'ĕn-sĭ), *n.; pl.* -CIES (-sĭz) State, quality, or fact of being inclement.

in-clem'ent (-ĕnt), *a.* [4] Not clement ; severe harsh ; stormy. [ably disposed.|

in-clin'a-ble (-klĭn'å-b'l), *a.* [4] Inclined, favor

in'cli-na'tion (ĭn'klĭ-nā'shŭn), *n.* **1.** A leaning; propensity. **2.** Act of inclining; nod. **3.** Amount of deviation from the vertical or horizontal; slant; slope.

in-cline' (ĭn-klīn'), *v. i.* [1] **1.** To bow the head or body forward; bend. **2.** To be disposed. **3.** To deviate from a line, direction, or course. — *v. t.*

1. To cause to incline. **2.** To turn; dispose. — *n.* An inclined plane; grade; slope.

in-close′ (-klōz′), *v. t.* [1] **1.** To shut up or in. **2.** To insert (something) in the same parcel or envelope with another. **3.** To surround.

in-clo′sure (ĭn-klō′zhŭr), *n.* **1.** Act of inclosing; state of being inclosed. **2.** That which is inclosed. **3.** That which incloses, as a fence.

in-clude′ (ĭn-klōōd′), *v. t.* [1] To comprise; contain; comprehend; embrace.

in-clu′sion (-klōō′zhŭn), *n.* Act of including.

in-clu′sive (-sĭv), *a.* [4] **1.** Inclosing; surrounding; containing. **2.** Including the stated limit or extremes. — **-ly**, *adv.* [8] — **-ness**, *n.* [8].

in-cog′ni-ta (-nĭ-tȧ), *a. & n.* Fem. of *incognito*.

in-cog′ni-to (-nĭ-tō), *a. or adv.* With (one's) identity concealed under an assumed name or title. — *n.; pl.* **-tos** (-tōz). One appearing or living incognito ; also, state or disguise of such a one.

in′co-her′ence (ĭn′kō-hēr′ĕns) } *n. ; pl.* **-ences**
in′co-her′en-cy (-ĕn-sĭ) } (-ĕn-sēz), **-en-cies** (-sĭz). **1.** Quality or fact of being incoherent. **2.** That which is incoherent.

in′co-her′ent (-ĕnt), *a.* [4] Not coherent; as : **a** Wanting cohesion. **b** Wanting agreement or connection; rambling. — **-ly**, *adv.* [8].

in′com-bus′ti-ble (ĭn′kŏm-bŭs′tĭ-b'l), *a.* [4] Not combustible.

in′come (ĭn′kŭm), *n.* Gain from labor, business, or property; revenue; receipts; wages or salary.

in′com′ing, *a.* Coming in; accruing, as profit; taking possession, as a tenant; about to begin, as a year; entering. — *n.* A coming in; arrival.

in′com-men′su-ra-ble (ĭn′kŏ-mĕn′shŏō-rȧ-b'l), *a.* [4] Having no common measure or basis of comparison; *Arith.*, having no common divisor but 1.

in′com-men′su-rate (-rȧt), *a.* [4] Not commensurate; as : **a** Incommensurable. **b** Inadequate.

in′com-mode′ (ĭn′kŏ-mōd′), *v. t.* [1] To give inconvenience; discommode; inconvenience.

in′com-mo′di-ous (-mō′dĭ-ŭs), *a.* [4] Not commodious; inconvenient. — **-ness**, *n.* [8].

in′com-mu′ni-ca-ble (-mū′nĭ-kȧ-b'l), *a.* [4] Incapable of being communicated or told.

in′com′pa-ra-ble (ĭn-kŏm′pȧ-rȧ-b'l), *a.* [4] **1.** Beyond comparison; matchless. **2.** Not suitable for comparison. — **in′com′pa ra bly**, *adv.* [8].

in′com-pat′i-bil′i-ty (ĭn′kŏm-păt′ĭ-bĭl′ĭ-tĭ), *n.* A being incompatible ; as, *incompatibility* of temper.

in′com-pat′i-ble (-păt′ĭ-b'l), *a.* [4] Incapable of uniting or of acting together; discordant.

in-com′pe-tence (ĭn-kŏm′pē-tĕns), **-ten-cy** (-tĕn-sĭ), *n.* Quality, state, or fact of being incompetent.

in-com′pe-tent (-tĕnt), *a.* [4] Not competent; not legally qualified. — **-ly**, *adv.* [8].

in′com-plete′ (ĭn′kŏm-plēt′), *a.* [4] Not complete; imperfect. — **-ly**, *adv.* [8] — **-ness**, *n.* [8].

in-com′pre-hen′si-ble (ĭn-kŏm′prē-hĕn′sĭ-b'l), *a.* [4] Not capable of being understood; unintelligible. — **in-com′pre-hen′si-bly**, *adv.* [8].

in′con-ceiv′a-ble (ĭn′kŏn-sēv′ȧ-b'l), *a.* [4] Not conceivable; unthinkable; incredible; unbelievable. — **-ness**,*n.* [8] — **in′con-ceiv′a-bly**,*adv.* [8].

in′con-clu′sive (-klōō′sĭv), *a.* [4] Not leading to a definite conclusion. — **-ly**, *adv.* [8] — **-ness**, *n.* [8].

in′con-gru′i-ty (ĭn′kŏn-grōō′ĭ-tĭ), *n.; pl.* **-ties** (-tĭz). **1.** Quality or state of being incongruous; inconsistency. **2.** That which is incongruous.

in-con′gru-ous (ĭn-kŏn′grōō-ŭs), *a.* [4] Not congruous; inconsistent; improper. — **-ly**, *adv.* [8].

in-con′se-quence (ĭn-kŏn′sē-kwĕns), *n.* Quality or state of being inconsequent; irrelevance.

in-con′se-quent (-kwĕnt), *a.* [4] **1.** Illogical. **2.** Disconnected; irrelevant. — **-ly**, *adv.* [8].

in-con′se-quen′tial (-kwĕn′shăl), *a.* [4] Not strictly logical; irrelevant; hence, unimportant.

in′con-sid′er-a-ble (ĭn′kŏn-sĭd′ĕr-ȧ-b'l), *a.* [4] Not considerable; trivial. — **-a-bly**, *adv.* [8].

in′con-sid′er-ate (-ăt), *a.* [4] Not considerate; thoughtless. — **-ly**, *adv.* [8] — **-ness**, *n.* [8].

in′con-sist′en-cy (-sĭs′tĕn-sĭ), *n.; pl.* **-cies** (-sĭz). **1.** Quality or state of being inconsistent; incompatibility. **2.** That which is inconsistent.

in′con-sist′ent (-tĕnt), *a.* [4] Not consistent: **a** Contradictory; illogical. **b** Changeable; fickle. — **in′con-sist′ent-ly**, *adv.* [8].

in′con-sol′a-ble (nŏl′ȧ b'l), *a.* [4] Incapable of being consoled; disconsolate. — **-a-bly**, *adv.* [8].

in′con-spic′u-ous (-spĭk′ū-ŭs), *a.* [4] Not conspicuous; hardly discernible. — **-ness**, *n.* [8].

in-con′stan-cy (ĭn-kŏn′stăn-sĭ), *n.* Want of constancy; fickleness; want of uniformity.

in-con′stant (ĭn-kŏn′stănt), *a.* [4] Not constant; fickle; changeable. — **-ly**, *adv.* [8].

in′con-test′a-ble (ĭn′kŏn-tĕs′tȧ-b'l), *a.* [4] Not contestable. — **in′con-test′a-bly**, *adv.* [8].

in-con′ti-nence (ĭn-kŏn′tĭ-nĕns), *n.* Quality or state of being incontinent. [*adv.* [8].]

in-con′ti-nent (-nĕnt),*a.* [4] Not continent. — **-ly**, **in′con-tro-vert′i-ble** (ĭn-kŏn′trŏ-vûr′tĭ-b'l), *a.* [4] Not controvertible; indisputable.

in′con-ven′ience (ĭn′kŏn-vēn′yĕns), *n.* **1.** Quality or state of being inconvenient; discomfort. **2.** That which is inconvenient. — *v. t.* [1] To incommode. [— **-ly**, *adv.* [8].]

in′con-ven′ient (-yĕnt), *a.* [4] Not convenient.

in′con-vert′i-ble (ĭn′kŏn-vûr′tĭ-b'l), *a.* [4] Not convertible; not exchangeable for something else.

in-cor′po-rate (ĭn-kôr′pō-rāt), *a.* [4] **1.** Closely united or blended. **2** Incorporated. — (-rāt), *v. t.* [1] **1.** To form into a body; combine into one mass or uniform substance. **2.** To blend. **3.** To form into a corporation. — *v. i.* To unite in or as one body.

in-cor′po-ra′tion (-rā′shŭn), *n.* **1.** An incorporating; state of being incorporated. **2.** A corporation.

in′cor-po′re-al (ĭn′kôr-pō′rē-ăl), *a.* [4] **1.** Not formed of matter. **2.** Pertaining to, or characteristic of, spiritual beings. — **-al-ly**, *adv.* [8].

in′cor-rect′ (ĭn′kŏ-rĕkt′), *a.* [4] **1.** Not correct; faulty. **2.** Unbecoming; improper. **3.** Untrue; inaccurate. — **-ly**, *adv.* [8] — **-ness**, *n.* [8].

in-cor′ri-gi-bil′i-ty (ĭn-kŏr′ĭ-jĭ-bĭl′ĭ-tĭ), *n.* State or quality of being incorrigible.

in-cor′ri-gi-ble (-kŏr′ĭ-jĭ-b'l), *a.* [4] Not corrigible; bad beyond correction. — *n.* One who is incorrigible. — **-ness**, *n.* [8] — **-gi-bly**, *adv.* [8].

in′cor-rupt′i-bil′i-ty (ĭn′kŏ-rŭp′tĭ-bĭl′ĭ-tĭ), *n.* Quality of being incorruptible.

in′cor-rupt′i-ble (-rŭp′tĭ-b'l), *a.* [4] Not corruptible; incapable of being bribed. — **-i-bly**, *adv.* [8].

---

in-crease′ (ĭn-krēs′), *v. i.* [1] **1.** To become greater; grow; advance; wax. **2.** To be fertile or prolific. — *v. t.* To make greater; enhance.

in′crease (ĭn′krēs), *n.* **1.** Act of increasing; growth; multiplication. **2.** That which results from increasing; addition; produce.

in-cred′i-ble (ĭn-krĕd′ĭ-b′l), *a.* [4] Not credible; beyond belief. — **in-cred′i-bly**, *adv.* [8].

in′cre-du′li-ty (ĭn′krē-dū′lĭ-tĭ), *n.* State, quality, or fact of being incredulous.

in-cred′u-lous (ĭn-krĕd′ū-lŭs), *a.* [4] **1.** Not credulous. **2.** Indicating disbelief. — **-ly**, *adv.* [8].

in′cre-ment (ĭn′krē-mĕnt), *n.* An increase.

in-crim′i-nate (ĭn-krĭm′ĭ-nāt), *v. t.* [1] To charge with, or involve in, a crime or fault; accuse.

in-crust′ (-krŭst′), *v. t.* To cover with a crust.

in′crus-ta′tion (ĭn′krŭs-tā′shŭn), *n.* **1.** An incrusting. **2.** A crust or hard coating.

in′cu-bate (ĭn′kŭ-bāt), *v. t.* [1] To sit on (eggs) to hatch them; brood; maintain (eggs, bacteria, etc.) under conditions favorable to development, as in an incubator. — *v. i.* To sit on eggs; brood.

in′cu-ba′tion (-bā′shŭn), *n.* **1.** Act or process of incubating. **2.** A brooding or brooding upon.

in′cu-ba′tor (ĭn′kŭ-bā′tẽr), *n.* One that incubates; esp., an apparatus for hatching eggs.

in′cu-bus (ĭn′kŭ-bŭs), *n. ; pl.* E. **-BUSES** (-ĕz), L. **-BI** (-bī). **1.** Nightmare. **2.** Any person or thing that oppresses or burdens.

in-cul′cate (ĭn-kŭl′kāt ; ĭn′kŭl-), *v. t.* [1] To teach and impress by repetition. — **-ca-tor**, *n.*

in′cul-ca′tion (ĭn′kŭl-kā′shŭn), *n.* A teaching and impressing by repetitions or admonitions.

in′cul-pate (ĭn′kŭl-pāt ; ĭn-kŭl′pāt), *v. t.* [1] To impute guilt to ; blame.

in′cul-pa′tion (ĭn′kŭl-pā′shŭn), *n.* Blame;censure.

in-cul′pa-to-ry (-kŭl′pá-tō-rĭ), *a.* Imputing blame.

in-cum′ben-cy (-kŭm′bĕn-sĭ), *n. ; pl.* **-CIES** (-sĭz). State of holding an office or benefice.

in-cum′bent (-bĕnt), *a.* [4] Required as a duty. — *n.* One holding an office.

in-cur′ (ĭn-kûr′), *v. t.; -*CURRED′ (-kûrd′) ; -RING. To become liable to ; bring down upon one's self.

in-cur′a-ble (ĭn-kūr′á-b′l), *a.* [4] Not capable of being cured. — *n.* One diseased beyond cure.

in-cur′sion (-kûr′shŭn), *n.* A hostile entrance into a territory ; raid.

in-curve′ (ĭn-kûrv′), *v. t. & i.* [1] To curve, esp. inwards. [or under obligation.]

in-debt′ed (ĭn-dĕt′ĕd), *p. a.* [4] Brought into debt

in-debt′ed-ness, *n.* **1.** State of being indebted. **2.** Sum owed; debts collectively.

in-de′cen-cy (-dē′sĕn-sĭ), *n. ; pl.* **-CIES** (-sĭz). **1.** Quality of being indecent. **2.** Indecent act.

in-de′cent (-sĕnt), *a.* [4] Not decent; offensive to modesty and delicacy. — **-ly**, *adv.* [8].

in′de-ci′sion (ĭn′dē-sĭzh′ŭn), *n.* Want of decision.

in′de-ci′sive (-sĭ′sĭv), *a.* [4] **1.** Not decisive. **2.** Undetermined ; wavering. — **-ly**, *adv.* [8].

in′de-clin′a-ble (-klīn′á-b′l), *a.* Not declinable.

in′de-co′rous (ĭn′dē-kō′rŭs; ĭn-dĕk′ō-rŭs), *a.* [4] Not decorous. — **-ly**, *adv.* [8] — **-ness**, *n.* [8].

in′de-co′rum (ĭn′dē-kō′rŭm),*n.* Want of decorum.

in-deed′ (ĭn-dēd′), *adv.* In reality; truly; to be sure.

in′de-fat′i-ga-bil′i-ty (ĭn′dē-făt′ĭ-gá-bĭl′ĭ-tĭ), *n.* Quality of being indefatigable.

---

in′de-fat′i-ga-ble (-făt′ĭ-gá-b′l), *a.* [4] Not yielding to fatigue; tireless. — **-bly**, *adv.* [8].

in′de-fea′si-ble (-ĭē′zĭ-b′l),*a.* [4] That cannot be made void or forfeited. — **-si-bly**, *adv.* [8].

in′de-fen′si-ble (-fĕn′sĭ-b′l), *a.* [4] Not defensible ; unjustifiable. — **-ness**, *n.* [8].

in′de-fin′a-ble (-fĭn′á-b′l), *a.* [4] Incapable of being defined. — **-ness**, *n.* [8] — **-a-bly**, *adv.* [8].

in-def′i-nite (ĭn-dĕf′ĭ-nĭt), *a.* [4] **1.** Not definite; undetermined or indeterminate. **2.** *Gram.* Not defining. — **indefinite article,** the word *a* or *an*. — **-ly**, *adv.* [8] — **-ness**, *n.* [8].

in′de-his′cent (ĭn-dē-hĭs′ĕnt), *a.* Not dehiscent.

in-del′i-ble (ĭn-dĕl′ĭ-b′l), *a.* [4] That cannot be removed, or effaced. — **-bly**, *adv.* [8].

in-del′i-ca-cy (-ká-sĭ), *n.; pl.* **-CIES** (-sĭz). Quality of being indelicate ; that which is indelicate.

in-del′i-cate (-kāt), *a.* [4] Not delicate; offensive to good manners ; rude. — **-ly**, *adv.* [8].

in-dem′ni-fi-ca′tion (-dĕm′nĭ-fĭ-kā′shŭn),*n.* **1.** An indemnifying. **2.** That which indemnifies.

in-dem′ni-fy (-dĕm′nĭ-fī), *v. t.* [2] **1.** To secure against loss or damage. **2.** To repay or compensate, as for loss, damage, etc.

in-dem′ni-ty (-tĭ), *n.; pl.* **-TIES** (-tĭz). **1.** Protection or exemption from loss or damage. **2.** Compensation for loss or injury sustained.

in-dent′ (-dĕnt′),*v.t.* **1.** To make a notch or a series of notches in the border of. **2.** To set (a line or lines) with indention. **3.** To indenture.

in-dent′ (ĭn-dĕnt′), *v. t.* To dent ; impress.

in′den-ta′tion (ĭn′dĕn-tā′shŭn), *n.* An indenting; state of being indented.

in-den′tion (ĭn-dĕn′shŭn),*n.* **1.** An indenting. **2.** In printing and writing : **a** Act of setting a line or lines (esp. the first line of a paragraph) in from the margin. **b** The blank space so left.

in-den′ture (-tūr), *n.* **1.** An indenting ; state of being indented. **2.** *Law.* An agreement in writing ; esp. (usually in *pl.*), a contract binding an apprentice to a master, a servant to service in a colony, etc. — *v. t.* [1] To bind by an indenture.

in′de-pend′ence (ĭn′dē-pĕn′dĕns), *n.* **1.** State or quality of being independent. **2.** Independent means ; a competency.

in′de-pend′ent (-dĕnt), *a.* [4] **1.** Not dependent; free from external control; self-governing. **2.** Not dependent for support ; hence : **a** Obtained by one's own exertion. **b** Affording a comfortable livelihood. **3.** Not subject to bias or influence. **4.** *Politics.* Not bound by party; exercising a free choice in voting.— *n.* One who exercises independence, esp. in religion or politics. — **-ly**, *adv.* [8].

in′de-scrib′a-ble (-skrīb′á-b′l), *a.* [4] Incapable of being described. — **in′de-scrib′a-bly**, *adv.* [8].

in′de-struct′i-bil′i-ty (-strŭk′tĭ-bĭl′ĭ-tĭ),*n.* Quality of being indestructible. [structible.]

in′de-struct′i-ble (-strŭk′tĭ-b′l), *a.* [4] Not destructible. — **-ly**, *adv.* [8].

in′de-ter′mi-na-ble (-tûr′mĭ-ná-b′l), *a.* [4] Impossible to be definitely known or defined.

in′de-ter′mi-nate (-nāt), *a.* [4] Not determinate; indefinite; vague. — **-ly**,*adv.* [8] — **-ness**, *n.* [8].

in′dex (ĭn′dĕks), *n. ; pl.* E. **INDEXES** (-dĕk-sĕs), L. **INDICES** (ĭn′dĭ-sēz). **1.** The forefinger. **2.** A pointer or indicator. **3.** That which points out or discloses ; indication. **4.** [*pl.* commonly *in-*

āle, senāte, câre, ăm, ăccount, ärm, àsk, sofá ; ēve, ĕvent, ĕnd, recĕnt, makẽr ; īce, ĭll ; ōld, ŏbey, ôrb, ŏdd, sŏft, cŏnnect ; ūse, ŭnite, ûrn, ŭp, circŭs ; fōod, foŏt ; out, oil ;

dexes.] A table or list for facilitating reference to names, etc., in a book. **5.** [*pl.* always *indices.*] *Math.* The figure, letter, or expression showing the power or root of a quantity. — *v. t.* To provide with an index; put into an index.

In′di-an (ĭn′dĭ-ăn), *a.* **1.** Of or pertaining to, or characteristic of, India, the Indies, or the Indians. **2.** Of, pertaining to, or designating the aborigines, or Indians, of America. — **Indian corn,** a North American cereal (called *corn* in the U. S.); maize; also, the meal (**Indian meal**) made from it. — **I.** file, single file. — **I. summer,** a period of mild weather in late autumn or early winter. — *n.* **1.** A native of India (Hindustan) or Indo-China; a Hindu. **2.** A member of any aboriginal American stock other than an Eskimo.

India rubber, *or* **In′di-a-rub′ber,** *n.* A tough elastic substance got from the milky juice of various tropical plants. See CAOUTCHOUC *and* RUBBER.

in′di-cate (-kāt), *v. t.* [1] **1.** To point out or to; make known; betoken. **2.** In medicine, to show by symptoms; point to as the proper remedy.

In′di-ca′tion (-kā′shŭn), *n.* **1.** Act of indicating. **2.** That which serves to indicate; mark; sign.

in-dic′a-tive (ĭn-dĭk′ȧ-tĭv), *a.* [4] **1.** Designating that mood of the verb which states something as an undoubted fact. **2.** Pointing out; suggestive. — *n.* *Gram.* The indicative mood, or a verbal form denoting it.

in′di-ca′tor (ĭn′dĭ-kā′tẽr), *n.* One that shows or points out; esp., a device for indicating something.

in′di-ces (ĭn′dĭ-sēz), *n., L. pl.* of INDEX.

in-dict′ (-dīt′), *v. t.* To charge with an offense; find an indictment against. — **-er, -or,** *n.* [8].

in-dict′a-ble (-ȧ-b'l), *a.* [4] Liable to be indicted.

in-dict′ment (-dīt′mĕnt), *n.* **1.** An indicting. **2.** *Law.* The formal written statement of an offense as found by the grand jury.

in-dif′fer-ence (ĭn-dĭf′ẽr-ĕns), *n.* Quality, state, or fact of being indifferent; apathy; unimportance.

in-dif′fer-ent (-ĕnt), *a.* [4] **1.** Without choice or interest; unconcerned; heedless. **2.** Having no marked tendency; neutral. **3.** Neither very good nor very bad; passable; mediocre. **4.** Unimportant. — *n.* An indifferent person. — **-ly,** *adv.* [8].

in′di-gence (ĭn′dĭ-jĕns), *n.* Poverty; want.

in-dig′e-nous (ĭn-dĭj′ē-nŭs), *a.* [4] Produced naturally in a place or climate; native; not exotic or imported. — **-ly,** *adv.* [8].

in′di-gent (ĭn′dĭ-jĕnt), *a.* [4] Needy; poor.

in′di-gest′i-ble (-jĕs′tĭ-b'l), *a.* [4] Not digestible; not readily digested. [dyspepsia.]

in′di-ges′tion (-ʼĕs′chŭn), *n.* Lack of digestion;

in-dig′nant (ĭn-dĭg′nȧnt),*a.* [4] Affected with indignation. — **-ly,** *adv.* [8].

in′dig-na′tion (ĭn′dĭg-nā′shŭn), *n.* Anger with contempt or loathing.

in-dig′ni-ty (ĭn-dĭg′nĭ-tĭ), *n. ; pl.* -TIES (-tĭz). Any action toward another which shows contempt for him.

in′di-go (ĭn′dĭ-gō),*n.; pl.* -GOS *or* -GOES (-gōz). **1.** A blue dyestuff. **2.** A deep violet-blue color.

in′di-rect′ (-rĕkt′), *a.* [4] Not direct; as : **a** Not straight; roundabout, as a road. **b** Not straightforward. **c** Not resulting directly from an act or cause, although more or less connected with it. — **-ly,** *adv.* — **-ness,** *n.*

in′di-rec′tion (-rĕk′shŭn), *n.* Indirect course or means; unfair or dishonest practices.

in′dis-cern′i-ble (-zûr′nĭ-b'l),*a.*[4] Imperceptible.

in′dis-creet′ (ĭn′dĭs-krēt′), *a.* [4] Lacking discretion. — **-ly,** *adv.* [8] — **-ness,** *n.* [8].

in′dis-cre′tion (ĭn′dĭs-krĕsh′ŭn), *n.* Quality or state of being indiscreet; an indiscreet act.

in′dis-crim′i-nate (-krĭm′ĭ-nāt), *a.* [4] Confused; promiscuous. — **-ly,** *adv.* [8] — **-ness,** *n.* [8].

in′dis-crim′i-na′tion (-nā′shŭn), *n.* Want of discrimination, or of distinguishing clearly.

in′dis-pen′sa-ble (-pĕn′sȧ-b'l), *a.* [4] Not dispensable; absolutely necessary. — **-bly,** *adv.* [8].

in′dis-pose′ (-pōz′), *v. t.* [1] **1.** To render unfit or indisposed. **2.** To render unwilling or unfavorable.

in′dis-posed′ (-pōzd′), *p. a.* [4] **1.** Sick; ill, often, slightly out of health. **2.** Disinclined; unwilling. [being indisposed.]

in-dis′po-si′tion (ĭn-dĭs′pŏ-zĭsh′ŭn), *n.* State of

in-dis′pu-ta-ble (ĭn-dĭs′pū-tȧ-b'l), *a.* [4] Not disputable; unquestionable. — **-bly,** *adv.* [8].

in-dis′so-lu-ble (ĭn-dĭs′ō-lū-b'l; ĭn′dĭ-sŏl′ū-b'l), *a.* [4] Not dissoluble; not capable of being dissolved. — **-ness,** *n.* [8] — **-bly,** *adv.* [8].

in′dis-tinct′ (ĭn′dĭs-tĭngkt′),*a.* [8] **1.** Not clear; difficult to distinguish; confused. **2.** Not separate or separable; not readily distinguishable.

in′dis-tin′guish-a-ble (-tĭn′gwĭsh-ȧ-b'l), *a.* [4] Not distinguishable. — **-a-bly,** *adv.* [8].

in-dite′ (ĭn-dīt′),*v. t.* [1] To compose; put in writing. — **in-dit′er,** *n.* [8].

in′di-vid′u-al (ĭn′dĭ-vĭd′ū-ȧl), *a.* [4] **1.** Existing as a distinct entity; particular; single. **2.** Having marked individuality. **3.** Arising from, belonging to, or used by, an individual. — *n.* **1.** A person. **2.** A thing that cannot be divided without losing its identity.

in′di-vid′u-al-ism (-ĭz'm), *n.* **1.** The being individual; individuality. **2.** Selfishness; egoism.

in′di-vid′u-al′i-ty (-ăl′ĭ-tĭ), *n.; pl.* -TIES (-tĭz). **1.** Individual character. **2.** Separate existence

in′di-vid′u-al-ize (-vĭd′ū-ăl-īz), *v. t.* [1] **1.** To make individual. **2.** To treat or notice individually; particularize. [**2.** Personally.]

in′di-vid′u-al-ly,adv. **1.** In an individual manner.

in′di-vis′i-bil′i-ty (-vĭz′ĭ-bĭl′ĭ-tĭ), *n.* Quality or state of being indivisible.

in′di-vis′i-ble (-vĭz′ĭ-b'l), *a.* [4] Not divisible into parts. — **in′di-vis′i-bly** (-blĭ), *adv.* [8].

in′do-lence (ĭn′dō-lĕns), *n.* Quality or state of being indolent; habitual idleness.

in′do-lent (-lĕnt), *a.* [4] Habitually idle; as, an *indolent* fellow. — **-ly,** *adv.*

in-dom′i-ta-ble (ĭn-dŏm′ĭ-tȧ-b'l), *a.* Not to be subdued; unconquerable. — **-ta-bly,** *adv.* [8].

in′door′ (ĭn′dōr′), *a.* Pertaining to the interior of a building; done, living, or given, within doors.

in′doors′ (ĭn′dōrz′),*adv.* In or into the house.

in-dorse′ (ĭn-dôrs′),*v. t.* [1] **1.** To inscribe something on the back of (a document). **2.** To write one's name on the back of (a paper), in order to transfer it, or to secure its payment or performance; certify something upon the back of (a draft, writ, etc.). **3.** To sanction. — **in-dors′a-ble,** *a.* [8]. [bill is indorsed.]

in′dor-see′ (ĭn′dŏr-sē′), *n.* One to whom a note or

---

chair; go: sing, ink; ~~then~~, thin; nature, verdure; yet; zh = z in azure. Numbers refer to §§ in the Special Notes which, with Abbreviations, Signs, etc., precede the Vocabulary.

in-dorse′ment (ĭn-dôrs′mĕnt), n. **1.** Act of writing on the back of a note, bill, etc., or that which is so written. **2.** Sanction, support, or approval.

in-dors′er (-dôr′sẽr), n. One who indorses.

in-dor′sor, n. An indorser.

in-du′bi-ta-ble (-dū′bĭ-tá-b'l), a. [4] Not dubitable, or doubtful; unquestionable. — **bly,** adv.

in-duce′ (-dūs′), v. t. [1] **1.** To lead on; influence, as by argument. **2.** To bring on or about; cause. **3.** To produce by induction, as an electric current.

in-duce′ment (-dūs′mĕnt), n. **1.** Act of inducing; state of being induced. **2.** That which induces.

in-duct′ (-dŭkt′), v. t. To put formally in possession of a benefice or office; install.

in-duc′tance (ĭn-dŭk′tăns), n. Elec. That property of an electric circuit by virtue of which a varying current induces an electromotive force in that circuit or a neighboring one.

in-duc′tion (-shŭn), n. **1.** An inducting, or bringing in; initiation. **2.** Logic. Act or process of reasoning from particular facts to general truths; the conclusion so reached. **3.** Act or process by which an electrical conductor or a magnetizable body becomes itself electrified or magnetized in the proximity of an electrified or magnetized body.

in-duc′tive (-dŭk′tĭv), a. [4] **1.** Leading or drawing; persuasive; — usually with to. **2.** Of or pertaining to induction. — **ive-ly,** adv. [8].

in-due′ (-dū′), v. t. [1] **1.** To assume; put on. **2.** To clothe; invest; endow, as with intelligence.

in-dulge′ (ĭn-dŭlj′), v. t. [1] To yield to the wishes of; humor. — v. i. To indulge one's self; esp., to give one's self up (to).

in-dul′gence (-dŭl′jĕns), n. **1.** Act, fact, or practice of indulging; gratification; esp., self-gratification. **2.** Favor granted.

in-dul′gent (-jĕnt), a. [4] Indulging or prone to indulge; compliant. — **in-dul′gent-ly,** adv. [8].

in′du-rate (ĭn′dū-rāt), a. [4] Hardened; indurated. — (-rāt), v. t. & i. [1] **1.** To harden. **2.** To make unfeeling or stubborn. **3.** To become fixed.

in′du-ra′tion (-rā′shŭn), n. **1.** A growing or being hard; a hardened formation. **2.** Want of pliancy or feeling; callousness.

in-dus′tri-al (-dŭs′trĭ-ăl), a. [4] **1.** Engaged in, or derived from, industries. **2.** Devoted to industrial training. — **ly,** adv. [8].

in-dus′tri-ous (-ŭs), a. [4] Given to, or marked by, industry; busy; assiduous. — **ly,** adv. [8].

in′dus-try (ĭn′dŭs-trĭ), n. ; pl. **-TRIES** (-trĭz). **1.** Steady application to labor or business. **2.** Systematic labor. **3.** Any branch of business.

in′dwell′ (ĭn′dwĕl′), v. t. & i. To dwell in; abide within; inhabit. — **in′dwell′er,** n. [8].

in-e′bri-ate (ĭn-ē′brĭ-āt), v. t. [1] To intoxicate. — (-āt), a. [4] Intoxicated. — n. One who is intoxicated; esp., a habitual drunkard.

in-e′bri-a′tion (-ā′shŭn), n. Intoxication; drunkenness. [being inebriated.]

in′e bri′e-ty (ĭn′ē-brī′ē-tĭ), n. State or habit of

in-ed′i-ble (ĭn-ĕd′ĭ-b'l), a. [4] Not edible.

in-ef′fa-ble (-ĕf′ă-b'l), a. [4] Unutterable; — usually in a pleasing sense. — **bly,** adv. [8].

in′ef-face′a-ble (ĭn′ĕ-fās′á-b'l), a. Not effaceable.

in′ef-fec′tive (-fĕk′tĭv), a. [4] Not effective; ineffectual. — **ly,** adv. [8] — **ness,** n. [8].

in′ef-fec′tu-al (-tū̇-ăl), a. [4] Not effectual; not producing the proper effect. — **ly,** adv. [8] — **ness,** n. [8]. [ficacious. — **ly,** adv. [8].

in-ef′fi-ca′cious (ĭn-ĕf′ĭ-kā′shŭs), a. [4] Not ef-

in-ef′ri-ca-cy (-ĕf′ĭ-ká-sĭ), n. Want of power to produce the proper or desired effect.

in′ef-fi′cien-cy (ĭn′ĕ-fĭsh′ĕn-sĭ), n. Want of efficiency; inability or failure to do something.

in′ef-fi′cient (ĭn′ĕ-fĭsh′ĕnt), a. [4] **1.** Not efficient; inefficacious. **2.** Not fully capable.

in′e-las′tic (-ē-lăs′tĭk), a. [4] Not elastic.

in-el′e-gance (ĭn-ĕl′ē-găns), **in-el′e-gan-cy** (-găn-sĭ), n. ; pl. **-GANCES** (-găn-sĕz), **-GANCIES** (-sĭz). **1.** Want of elegance. **2.** Anything inelegant.

in-el′e-gant (-ĕl′ē-gănt), a. [4] Not elegant.

in-el′i-gi-bil′i-ty (ĭn-ĕl′ĭ-jĭ-bĭl′ĭ-tĭ), n. Quality or fact of being ineligible.

in-el′i-gi-ble (ĭn-ĕl′ĭ-jĭ-b'l), a. [4] Not eligible.

in-ept′ (-ĕpt′), a. [4] **1.** Not apt or fit; unsuited. **2.** Absurd; foolish. — **ly,** adv. [8] — **ness,** n. [8].

in-ept′i-tude (-ĕp′tĭ-tūd), n. Quality of being inept.

in′e-qual′i-ty (ĭn′ē-kwŏl′ĭ-tĭ), n.; pl. **-TIES** (-tĭz). Want of equality or proportion; unevenness.

in-eq′ui-ta-ble (-ĕk′wĭ-tá-b'l), a. Not just.

in-e-rad′i-ca-ble (ĭn′ē-răd′ĭ-ká-b'l), a. [4] Incapable of being rooted out. — **bly,** adv. [8].

in-ert′ (-ûrt′), a. [4] **1.** Powerless to move itself, or to resist motion actively. **2.** Powerless for a desired effect, as a drug. **3.** Inactive; sluggish. — **ly,** adv. [8] — **ness,** n. [8].

in-er′ti-a (ĭn-ûr′shĭ-á), n. **1.** Physics. That property of matter by which it tends to remain in an existing state of rest, or of motion in the same direction. **2.** Inertness; want of energy.

in-es′ti-ma-ble (-ĕs′tĭ-má-b'l), a. [4] Incapable of being estimated; esp., too valuable or excellent to be measured. — **in-es′ti-ma-bly,** adv. [8].

in-ev′i-ta-ble (ĭn-ĕv′ĭ-tá-b'l), a. [4] That cannot be avoided or shunned; unavoidable. — **in-ev′i-ta-ble-ness,** n. [8] — **in-ev′i-ta-bly,** adv. [8].

in-ex-act′ (ĭn′ĕg-zăkt′), a. [4] Not exact; inaccurate

in-ex-cus′a-ble (-ĕks-kūz′á-b'l), a. [4] Not excusable; unpardonable. — **in′ex-cus′a-bly,** adv [8].

in′ex-haust′i-ble (-ĕg-zôs′tĭ-b'l), a. [4] Incapable of being exhausted. — **ness,** n. — **i-bly,** adv.

in-ex′o-ra-ble (ĭn-ĕk′sŏ-rá-b'l), a. [4] Not to be persuaded by entreaty or prayer; unyielding; relentless. — **in-ex′o-ra-bly,** adv. [8].

in′ex-pe′di-en-cy (ĭn′ĕks-pē′dĭ-ĕn-sĭ), n. Quality or state of being inexpedient.

in′ex-pe′di-ent (-ĕnt), a. [4] Not expedient.

in′ex-pen′sive (-pĕn′sĭv), a. [4] Not expensive.

in′ex-pe′ri-ence (-pē′rĭ-ĕns), n. Want or absence of experience. [ting of expiation.]

in′ex-pi-a-ble (ĭn-ĕks′pĭ-á-b'l), n. [4] Not admit-

in-ex′pli-ca-ble (-plĭ-ká-b'l), a. [4] Incapable of being explained. — **in-ex′pli-ca-bil′i-ty** (ĭn-ĕks-plĭ-ká-bĭl′ĭ-tĭ), n. — **in-ex′pli-ca-bly,** adv. [8].

in′ex-press′i-ble (-prĕs′ĭ-b'l), a. [4] That cannot be expressed; indescribable. — **bly,** adv. [8].

in′ex-tin′guish-a-ble (ĭn′ĕks-tĭn′gwĭsh-á-b'l), a. [4] Not extinguishable; unquenchable.

in-ex′tri-ca-ble (ĭn-ĕks′trĭ-ká-b'l), a. [4] Not extricable; incapable of being disentangled. — **in-ex′tri-ca-bly,** adv. [8]. [being infallible.]

in-fal′li-bil′i-ty (ĭn-făl′ĭ-bĭl′ĭ-tĭ), n. Quality of

in-fal′li-ble (ĭn-făl′lĭ-b'l), *a.* [4] Not fallible; unerring; certain. — **-bly**, *adv.* [8].

in′fa-mous (ĭn′fā-mŭs), *a.* [4] **1.** Notoriously vile. **2.** Causing infamy. — **-ly**, *adv.* [8].

in′fa-my (-mĭ), *n.; pl.* -MIES (-mĭz). **1.** Evil fame or reputation; public disgrace, dishonor, or reproach. **2.** Extreme vileness; an infamous act.

in′fan-cy (-făn-sĭ), *n.* **1.** Early childhood. **2.** *Law.* The status of one under 21 years.

in′fant (-fănt), *n.* **1.** A child in the first period of life; a babe. **2.** *Law.* A person not of full age; a minor. — *a.* **1.** Pertaining to, or being in, infancy; immature. **2.** Intended for young children.

in′fan-ti-cide (ĭn-făn′tĭ-sĭd), *n.* **1.** The killing of a recently born child. **2.** One guilty of infanticide.

in′fan-tile (ĭn′făn-tĭl; -tĭl)) *a.* [4] Of or pertaining to infancy
in′fan-tine (ĭn′făn-tĭn; -tĭn)) or an infant; childish.

in′fan-try (-trĭ), *n.* A body of foot soldiers.—**in′fan-try-man** (-măn), *n.; pl.* -MEN.

in-fat′u-ate (ĭn-făt′ū-āt), *v. t.* [1] To deprive of sound judgment; inspire with a foolish passion.

in-fat′u-a′tion (-ā′shŭn), *n.* Act of infatuating; state of being infatuated; that which infatuates.

in-fect′ (-fĕkt′), *v. t.* **1.** To taint with any disease-producing substance or bacteria. **2. a** To corrupt; deprave. **b** To imbue with some feeling.

in-fec′tion (-fĕk′shŭn), *n.* **1.** An infecting, esp. with disease. **2.** That which infects, or causes a disease. **3.** State of being infected; epidemic. **4.** = CONTAGION, *n.*, 2.

in-fec′tious (-shŭs), *a.* [4] **1.** Having qualities that may infect. **2.** Capable of being easily spread. — **-ly**, *adv.* [8] — **-ness**, *n.* [8].

in′fe-lic′i-tous (ĭn′fĕ-lĭs′ĭ-tŭs), *a.* [4] Not felicitous; unhappy; not well expressed.—**-ly**, *adv.* [8].

in′fe-lic′i-ty (-tĭ), *n.; pl.* -TIES (-tĭz). **1.** Quality of being infelicitous. **2.** That which is infelicitous.

in-fer′ (-fûr′), *v. t.; -*FERRED′ (-fûrd′); -FER′RING. **1.** To conclude; *Colloq.*, to surmise. **2.** To lead to as a conclusion; imply; indicate. — *v. i.* To draw inferences. — **in-fer′a-ble** (-à-b'l), *a.* [4].

in′fer-ence (ĭn′fẽr-ẽns), *n.* **1.** Act or process of inferring. **2.** That which is inferred; conclusion.

in′fer-en′tial (-ĕn′shăl), *a.* [4] Deduced or deducible by inference. — **in′fer-en′tial-ly**, *adv.* [8].

in-fe′ri-or (ĭn-fē′rĭ-ẽr), *a.* [4] **1.** Situated lower down; lower. **2.** Of lower rank. **3.** Of less importance or merit. **4.** Of poor quality. — *n.* One that is inferior to another.

in-fe′ri-or′i-ty (-ŏr′ĭ-tĭ), *n.* State of being inferior.

in-fer′nal (-fûr′năl), *a.* [4] **1.** Of or pertaining to the lower regions. **2.** Of or pertaining to hell; hellish; diabolical; fiendish. — **-ly**, *adv.* [8].

in-fer′no (-nō), *n.; pl.* -NOS (-nōz). Hell.

in-fest′ (ĭn-fĕst′), *v. t.* To trouble by numbers or by frequency of presence; as, fleas *infest* dogs.

in′fi-del (ĭn′fĭ-dĕl), *a.* [4] **1.** Not holding to the faith; esp., non-Christian. **2.** Of or pertaining to infidels or infidelity; as, *infidel* writings. — *n.* A disbeliever; one not a Christian.

in′fi-del′i-ty (-dĕl′ĭ-tĭ), *n.; pl.* -TIES (-tĭz). **1.** Want of faith or belief in (a certain) religion. **2.** Breach of trust; deceit; also, an unfaithful act.

in′field′ (ĭn′fēld′), *n. Baseball.* The diamond; also, the players on the infield. — **in′field′er**, *n.* [8].

in-fil′trate (ĭn-fĭl′trāt), *v. t.* [1] **1.** To cause to penetrate gradually. **2.** To pass through or into as in filtering. — *v. i.* To filter into or through.

in′fil-tra′tion (ĭn′fĭl-trā′shŭn), *n.* Act or process of infiltrating, as of water into a porous substance

in′fi-nite (ĭn′fĭ-nĭt), *a.* Unlimited; immeasurable. — *n.* **1.** Boundless space or duration. **2.** [*cap.*] God; — with *the.* — **-ly**, *adv.* [8] — **-ness**, *n.* [8]

in′fin-i-tes′i-mal (-fĭn-ĭ-tĕs′ĭ-măl), *a.* [4] Infinitely small; very minute. — **i-mal-ly**, *adv.*

in-fin′i-tive (-fĭn′ĭ-tĭv), *a. Gram.* Unlimited, as to person or number; undefined.— *n. Gram.* That form of the verb which simply names the action without affirming it of a subject; as, *to write*.

in-fin′i-tude (ĭn-fĭn′ĭ-tūd), *n.* Infinity.

in-fin′i-ty (-tĭ), *n.; pl.* -TIES (-tĭz). **1.** Quality of being infinite. **2.** Infinite quantity or number.

in-firm′ (-fûrm′), *a.* [4] **1.** Not firm or sound physically; feeble. **2.** Weak; irresolute. — **in-firm′ly**, *adv.* [8]. [hospital.]

in-fir′ma-ry (-fûr′mà-rĭ), *n.; pl.* -RIES (-rĭz). A

in-fir′mi-ty (-mĭ-tĭ), *n.; pl.* -TIES (-tĭz). Disease; failing; defect.

in-fix′ (-fĭks′), *v. t.* **1.** To fasten or fix by thrusting in. **2.** To implant; instill; as, to *infix* ideas.

in-flame′ (-flām′), *v. t.* [1] **1.** To kindle or intensify, as passion. **2.** To incense; enrage. **3.** *Med.* To cause inflammation in.

in-flam′ma-bil′i-ty (-flăm′à-bĭl′ĭ-tĭ), *n.* State or quality of being inflammable.

in-flam′ma-ble (-flăm′à-b'l), *a.* [4] **1.** Easily set on fire; combustible. **2.** Excitable; irritable.

in′flam-ma′tion (ĭn′flă-mā′shŭn), *n.* **1.** Act of inflaming. **2.** *Med.* A diseased condition marked by redness and swelling, with heat and pain, accompanied by overfilling of the blood vessels.

in-flam′ma-to-ry (ĭn-flăm′à-tō-rĭ), *a.* [4] **1.** Tending to inflame, irritate, or excite. **2.** *Med.* Accompanied with, or tending to cause, inflammation.

in-flate′ (-flāt′), *v. t. & i.* [1] To swell with air or gas; distend. [pompous.]

in-flat′ed (-ĕd), *p. a.* [4] Affected with inflation;

in-fla′tion (-flā′shŭn), *n.* An inflating; inflated condition; as: **a** Swelling. **b** State of being puffed up, as with pride. **c** Undue expansion or increase, as in prices, paper currency, etc.

in-flect′ (-flĕkt′), *v. t.* **1.** To bend. **2.** *Gram.* To vary (a word) by inflection.

in-flec′tion (-flĕk′shŭn), *n.* **1.** Act of inflecting; a bending or bend. **2.** Change in pitch or tone of the voice. **3.** *Gram.* A variation in form which words undergo to mark case, gender, number, tense, person, mood, voice, etc. **b** An inflectional form, suffix, or element. [by, inflection]

in-flec′tion-al (-ăl), *a.* Pertaining to, or marked

in-flex′i-ble (-flĕk′sĭ-b'l), *a.* [4] **1.** Not capable of being bent. **2.** Resolute. — **in-flex′i-bil′i-ty** (ĭn-flĕk-sĭ-bĭl′ĭ-tĭ), *n.* — **in-flex′i-bly**, *adv.* [8].

in-flict′ (-flĭkt′), *v. t.* To cause to bear or suffer

in-flic′tion (-flĭk′shŭn), *n.* Act of inflicting; something inflicted, as punishment, disgrace, etc.

in′flo-res′cence (ĭn′flō-rĕs′ĕns), *n.* **1.** A flowering. **2.** A flower cluster.

in′flow′ (ĭn′flō′), *n.* Act of flowing in; influx.

in′flu-ence (ĭn′floō-ĕns), *n.* **1.** An insensible or indirect altering of anything, or power to effect this

2. Power due to position, wealth, etc. **3.** That which exerts influence; an influential person.

in-flu-ence (ĭn'flŏŏ-ĕns), *v. t.* [1] To exert influence upon; as: **a** To alter or move; sway; persuade. **b** To affect; modify.

in-flu-en'tial (ĭn'flŏŏ-ĕn'shăl), *a.* [4] Exerting or possessing influence; powerful. **—ly,** *adv.*

in-flu-en'za (-zä), *n.* An epidemic disease characterized by acute catarrh; grippe.

in'flux (ĭn'flŭks'), *n.* A flowing in; inflow.

in-fold' (ĭn-fōld'), *v. t.* **1.** To wrap up or cover with folds; envelop; inclose. **2.** To embrace.

in-form' (-fôrm'), *v. t.* **1.** To animate; inspire. **2.** To communicate knowledge to; acquaint. **—** *v. i.* To give information, esp. in accusation.

in-for'mal (ĭn-fôr'măl), *a.* [4] Not in the usual form; hence, without ceremony. **—ly,** *adv.* [8].

in'for-mal'i-ty (ĭn'fôr-măl'ĭ-tĭ), *n.; pl.* -TIES (-tĭz). State or quality of being informal; an informal proceeding. [formation.]

in-form'ant (ĭn-fôr'mănt), *n.* One who gives in-

in'for-ma'tion (ĭn'fôr-mā'shŭn), *n.* **1.** Act of informing. **2.** Knowledge; intelligence; news.

in-form'a-tive (ĭn-fôr'mà-tĭv), *a.* [4] Instructive.

in-form'er (-fôr'mẽr), *n.* **1.** One who imparts knowledge or news. **2.** One who informs of breaches of law.

in-frac'tion (ĭn-frăk'shŭn), *n.* Act of breaking; breach, esp. of a law or obligation; infringement.

in-fre'quence (-frē'kwĕns), **-quen-cy** (-kwĕn-sĭ), *n.* State of rarely happening; rareness.

in-fre'quent (ĭn-frē'kwĕnt), *a.* [4] Seldom happening; rare; uncommon. **—ly,** *adv.* [8].

in-fringe' (-frĭnj'), *v. t.* [1] To commit a breach of. **—** *v. i.* To encroach; trespass; **—** with *on* or *upon.* **— in-fring'er** (-frĭn'jẽr), *n.* [8].

in-fringe'ment (-mĕnt), *n.* **1.** Act of infringing. **2.** A breach of, or an encroachment on, a right or privilege, as of a patent or a copyright.

in-fu'ri-ate (-fū'rĭ-āt), *v. t.* [1] To enrage; madden.

in-fuse' (-fūz'), *v. t.* [1] **1.** To instill, as principles or qualities; introduce. **2.** To inspire or imbue (with); fill. **3.** To steep without boiling.

in-fu'si-ble (-fū'zĭ-b'l), *a.* [4] Not fusible.

in-fu'sion (-zhŭn), *n.* Act or process of infusing; also, that which is infused or is got by infusing.

in-gen'ious (ĭn-jēn'yŭs), *a.* [4] **1.** Possessed of ingenuity; inventive. **2.** Showing cleverness or ingenuity. **—ly,** *adv.* [8] **— -ness,** *n.* [8].

in'ge-nu'i-ty (ĭn'jē-nū'ĭ-tĭ), *n.; pl.* -TIES (-tĭz). Quality of being ingenious; **as: a** Inventiveness. **b** Cleverness of design or contrivance.

in-gen'u-ous (-jĕn'ū-ŭs), *a.* [4] Free from reserve, disguise, or pretense; open; frank; artless. **—ly,** *adv.* [8] **— -ness,** *n.* [8].

in-glo'ri-ous (ĭn-glō'rĭ-ŭs), *a.* [4] Not glorious. **2.** Shameful. **—ly,** *adv.* **— -ness,** *n.* [8].

in'got (ĭn'gŏt; ĭn'-), *n.* A mass of metal cast into a convenient shape, as a bar, block, etc.

in-graft' (ĭn-gráft'), *v. t.* To graft, as a bud or a tree; fig., to infix; as, *ingraft* in him a love of art.

in'grain (ĭn'grān'; ĭn-grān'), *v. t.* **1.** To dye in the grain, or before manufacture. **2.** To saturate; infix deeply. **—** (ĭn'grān'), *a.* **1.** Dyed before manufacture or in the fiber; as, an *ingrain* carpet. **2.** Thoroughly inwrought; ingrained.

in'grained' (ĭn'grānd'; ĭn-grānd'), *p. a.* [4] Wrought into the grain or fiber; deep-seated.

in'grate (ĭn'grāt), *a.* [4] Showing ingratitude; ungrateful. **—** *n.* An ingrate person.

in-gra'ti-ate (ĭn-grā'shĭ-āt), *v. t.* [1] To bring into favor. [tude; ungratefulness.]

in-grat'i-tude (ĭn-grăt'ĭ-tūd), *n.* Want of grati-

in-gre'di-ent (-grē'dĭ-ĕnt), *n.* A component part of a combination or mixture; element; constituent.

in'gress (ĭn'grĕs), *n.* **1.** Act of entering; entrance. **2.** Power or liberty of access.

in-hab'it (-hăb'ĭt), *v. t.* To live in; occupy.

in-hab'it-a-ble (-à-b'l), *a.* [4] Capable of being inhabited.

in-hab'it-ant (-tănt), *n.* A permanent resident.

in'ha-la'tion (ĭn'hà-lā'shŭn), *n.* Act of inhaling.

in-hale' (ĭn-hāl'), *v. t.* [1] To breathe in; draw into the lungs; inspire; **—** opp. to *exhale.*

in-hal'er (-hāl'ẽr), *n.* **1.** One who inhales. **2.** An apparatus for administering a vapor or gas, etc.

in'har-mo'ni-ous (-här-mō'nĭ-ŭs), *a.* [4] Not harmonious; discordant. **—ly,** *adv.* **— -ness,** *n.*

in-here' (ĭn-hēr'), *v. i.* [1] To be inherent.

in-her'ence (-ĕns)   *n.* State or fact of inhering;

in-her'en-cy (-ĕn-sĭ)   quality of being inherent.

in-her'ent (-ĕnt), *a.* [4] Permanently existing as an attribute in something; belonging by nature; inseparable; essential. **— in-her'ent-ly,** *adv.* [8].

in-her'it (-hĕr'ĭt), *v. t. & i.* **1.** To take by descent or inheritance. **2.** To come into possession of.

in-her'it-a-ble (-à-b'l), *a.* [4] **1.** Capable of being inherited, as a title. **2.** Capable of inheriting.

in-her'it-ance (-ĭ-tăns), *n.* **1.** An inheriting. **2.** That which is or may be inherited; heritage. **3.** A valuable possession or blessing, esp. one received by gift; benefaction.

in-her'i-tor (-ĭ-tẽr), *n.* One who inherits; an heir. **— in-her'i-tress** (-trĕs), **-trix** (-trĭks), *n. fem.*

in-hib'it (-hĭb'ĭt), *v. i.* To check; restrain, as in activity. **— in-hib'i-to-ry** (-ĭ-tō-rĭ), *a.* [4].

in'hi-bi'tion (ĭn'hĭ-bĭsh'ŭn), *n.* An inhibiting.

in-hos'pi-ta-ble (-hŏs'pĭ-tà-b'l), *a.* [4] **1.** Not hospitable. **2.** Affording no shelter or food; barren; wild. **— -ness,** *n.* [8] **—bly,** *adv.* [8].

in-hos'pi-tal'i-ty (-tăl'ĭ-tĭ), *n.* Quality of being inhospitable.

in-hu'man (-hū'măn), *a.* [4] Destitute of human kindness; cruel; unfeeling. **—ly,** *adv.* [8].

in'hu-man'i-ty (ĭn'hū-măn'ĭ-tĭ), *n.; pl.* -TIES (-tĭz). Quality or state of being inhuman; cruelty.

in-im'i-cal (-ĭm'ĭ-kăl), *a.* [4] **1.** Like an enemy; unfriendly. **2.** Antagonistic. **—ly,** *adv.* [8].

in-im'i-ta-ble (-tà-b'l), *a.* [4] That cannot be imitated. **— -ness,** *n.* [8] **—bly,** *adv.* [8].

in-iq'ui-tous (-ĭk'wĭ-tŭs), *a.* [4] Characterized by iniquity; unjust; wicked. **—ly,** *adv.* [8].

in-iq'ui-ty (-tĭ), *n.; pl.* -TIES (-tĭz). **1.** Unrighteousness; wickedness. **2.** A sin; crime.

in-i'tial (ĭn-ĭsh'ăl), *a.* **1.** Of or pertaining to the beginning. **2.** Standing at the beginning; first. **—** *n.* The first letter of a word or name. **—** *v. t.* [7] To mark with initials. **—ly,** *adv.* [8].

in-i'ti-ate (-ĭ-āt), *v. t.* [1] **1.** To originate; begin. **2.** To instruct in rudiments or principles. **3.** To introduce into a society, club, etc., as by formal rites.

in-i'ti-ate (-āt), *a.* Initiated. **—** *n.* One initiated.

āle, senâte, câre, ăm, ăccount, ärm, ȧsk, sofȧ; ēve, ĕvent, ĕnd, recĕnt, makẽr; īce, ĭll; ōld, ȯbey, ôrb, ŏdd, sŏft, cŏnnect; ūse, ûnite, ûrn, ŭp, circŭs; fŏŏd, fŏŏt; out, oil;

in-i'ti-a'tion (-ā'shŭn), n. 1. An initiating. 2. The rites, ceremonies, or instructions, with which one is made a member of a society, etc.

in-i'ti-a-tive (-ĭsh'ĭ-ā-tĭv), a. Of or pertaining to initiation; introductory; preliminary. — n. 1. An introductory step. 2. The right or power to introduce a new measure or course of action.

in-i'ti-a'tor, n. One who initiates.

in-i'ti-a-to-ry (-ă-tō-rĭ), a. [4] 1. Initial; introductory. 2. Tending or serving to initiate.

in-ject' (-jĕkt'), v. t. 1. To throw or force in. 2. To throw in by way of suggestion, etc.

in-jec'tion (-jĕk'shŭn), n. 1. An injecting. 2. That which is injected, as an enema.

in-jec'tor (-tẽr), n. One that injects, esp., a device for injecting water into a steam boiler.

in'ju-di'cious (ĭn'jŏŏ-dĭsh'ŭs), a. [4] Not judicious; unwise. —ly, adv. [8] —ness, n. [8].

in-junc'tion (ĭn-jŭnk'shŭn), n. 1. An enjoining. 2. An order; precept. 3 Law. Judicial writ or process requiring a party to do or forbear some act.

in'jure (ĭn'jŏŏr), v. t. [1] To do harm to; hurt; wrong; offend. — in'jur-er (-ẽr), n. [8].

in-ju'ri-ous (ĭn-jŏŏ'rĭ-ŭs), a. [4] Inflicting or tending to inflict injury; hurtful. —ly, adv. [8] —ness, n. [8].

in'ju-ry (ĭn'jŏŏ-rĭ), n.; pl. -ries (-rĭz). 1. Damage or hurt done or suffered. 2. An injustice; wrong. [2. An unjust act.

in-jus'tice (ĭn-jŭs'tĭs), n. 1. Want of justice.

ink (ĭnk), n. A fluid or sticky material used for writing and printing. — v. t. To put ink upon.

ink'ling (ĭnk'lĭng), n. An intimation; a hint.

ink'stand' (-stănd'), n. A small vessel for holding ink, to dip the pen into.

ink'well' (-wĕl'), n. A reservoir for ink.

ink'y (ĭnk'ĭ), a. [3] Consisting of, using, or resembling, ink; soiled with ink; black.

in'land (ĭn'lănd), a. [4] 1. Interior; not bordering the sea. 2 Confined to a country; domestic. — adv. Away from the frontier or coast.

in'land (ĭn'lănd), n. The interior of a country, the parts away from the coast.

in-lay' (ĭn-lā'), v. t., in-laid (-lād', or, esp. as p.a., ĭn'lād') ; in-lay'ing. To set into the body of a surface, also, to adorn (a surface) by inlaying

in'lay' (ĭn'lā'), n. Material inlaid, inlaid work.

in'let (ĭn'lĕt), n. 1. A passage for entering, entrance. 2. A recess in a shore, a narrow strip of water running into the land or between islands

in'mate (ĭn'māt), n. One of a family or community occupying a single dwelling, an occupant, also, one kept in an asylum, prison, etc.

in'most (-mōst), a Deepest within, innermost.

inn (ĭn), n. A public house for lodging and entertaining travelers, hotel, hostelry.

in'nate (ĭn'nāt, ĭn-nāt'), a [4] Inborn, native, natural. —ly, adv. [8] —ness, n. [8].

in'ner (ĭn'ẽr), a. 1. Farther in, interior, internal 2. Mental or spiritual, as, the inner life.

in'ner-most (-mōst), a. Farthest inward; inmost.

in'ning (ĭn'ĭng), n. In baseball, cricket, etc. one of the turns of a side or a player to bat.

inn'keep'er (ĭn'kēp'ẽr), n One who keeps an inn.

in'no-cence (ĭn'ō-sĕns), n. 1. State or quality of being innocent. 2. The bluet

in'no-cent (-sĕnt), a. [4] 1. a Of persons : Guiltless ; sinless ; pure ; also, blameless. b Of actions and things: Without evil influence or effect; harmless. 2. Guileless, ignorant, or simple. 3. Devoid (of); without; — usually jocular; as, to be innocent of clothes. — n. 1. a An innocent one ; esp., a young child. b A simpleton; also, a natural fool 2. pl. Bluets. See innocence, 2. —ly, adv. [8]

in-noc'u-ous (ĭ-nŏk'ū-ŭs), a. [4] Harmless; producing no ill effect. — ly, adv. [8] —ness, n. [8].

in'no-vate (ĭn'ō-vāt), v. i. [1] To make changes — in'no-va'tor (-vā'tẽr), n. [8].

in'no-va'tion (-vā'shŭn), n. 1. Act of innovating 2. A change, esp. in customs, manners, or rites.

in'nu-en'do (ĭn'ū-ĕn'dō), n.; pl. -does (-dōz). A side allusion, usually detracting ; an insinuation.

in-nu'mer-a-ble (ĭ-nū'mẽr-á-b'l), a. Too many to be counted ; numberless. —a-bly, adv. [8].

in-oc'u-late (ĭn-ŏk'ū-lāt), v. t. [1] 1. To infect with a disease by inserting its virus in the flesh, esp. so as to induce a mild form to secure future immunity. 2. To imbue (with something, esp. harmful ideas). [of inoculating.

in-oc'u-la'tion (-lā'shŭn), n. Act, process, or art

in-o'dor-ous (-ō'dẽr-ŭs), a. Odorless.

in-of-fen'sive (ĭn'ō-fĕn'sĭv), a. [4] Giving no offense ; harmless. —ly, adv. [8] —ness, n. [8].

in-op'er-a-tive (ĭn-ŏp'ẽr-á-tĭv), a. [4] Not operative ; not active ; producing no effect.

in-op'por-tune' (-ŏp'ŏr-tūn'), a. [4] Not opportune; unseasonable. —ly, adv. [8] —ness, n. [8]

in-or'di-nate (-ôr'dĭ-nát), a. [4] Not limited to rules or to usual bounds; excessive. —ly, adv [8] —ness, n. [8].

in-or-gan'ic (ĭn'ŏr-găn'ĭk), a. [4] Not organic, designating, or composed of, matter other than animal or vegetable ; as, inorganic nature.

in'quest (ĭn'kwĕst), n. 1. Judicial or official inquiry, esp. before a jury, as, a coroner's inquest 2. A body of men holding such an inquiry.

in-qui'e-tude (ĭn-kwī'ē-tūd), n. Disturbed state, uneasiness; restlessness; pl. disquieting thoughts

in-quire' (ĭn-kwīr'), v. t. [1] To ask about or ask — v. i. 1. To ask a question ; ask. 2. To examine; investigate. — in-quir'er (ĭn-kwir'ẽr), n. [8]

in-quir'ing (ĭn-kwir'ĭng), p. a. [4] Inquisitive.

in-quir'y (ĭn-kwir'ĭ), n.; pl. -quiries (-ĭz) An inquiring a Search for truth or knowledge. b A question or questioning

in'qui-si'tion (ĭn'kwĭ-zĭsh'ŭn), n. 1. Act of inquiring, search, examination. 2. A judicial inquiry before a jury, also, the finding of the jury 3. [cap.] R. C. Church. A tribunal for the discovery, examination, and punishment of heretics

in-quis'i-tive (ĭn-kwĭz'ĭ-tĭv), a. [4] 1 Given to inquiry. 2. Disposed to ask questions, esp. about matters which do not concern the inquirer — ly adv. [8] —ness, n. [8]

in-quis'i-tor (-tẽr), n. One who inquires or makes inquisition, esp. officially, as a coroner, etc.

in-quis'i-to'ri-al (-tō'rĭ-ăl), a. [4] Of or like an inquisitor; searching, prying — ly, adv. [8].

in'road (ĭn'rōd), n. A hostile incursion or invasion. raid, hence, forcible entrance or encroachment.

in'rush' (ĭn'rŭsh'), n. A rush inwards, influx.

in-sane' (ĭn-sān'), a. [4] 1. Not sane, mad; de

ranged. **2.** Used by, or set apart for, insane persons. **3.** Utterly foolish; senseless. — **-ly**, *adv.*

in-san'i-ty (ĭn-săn'ĭ-tĭ), *n.* **1.** State of being insane. **2.** Extravagant foolishness or folly.

in-sa'ti-a-ble (-sā'shĭ-à-b'l; -shà-b'l), *a.* [4] Not satiable. — **-ness**, *n.* [8] — **-a-bly**, *adv.* [8].

in-sa'ti-ate (-ăt),*a.* [4] Insatiable. — **-ly**, *adv.* [8].

in-scribe' (-skrīb'), *v. t.* **1.** To write or engrave (words or characters); also, to mark or engrave (as a tablet) with characters. **2.** Hence, to impress. **3.** To address; dedicate informally. **4.** *Geom.* To draw (one figure within another) so that as many points as possible of the inner figure lie in the boundary of the outer figure.

in-scrip'tion (-skrĭp'shŭn), *n.* **1.** That which is inscribed. **2.** A dedication, as of a book.

in-scru'ta-bil'i-ty (-skrŏō'tá-bĭl'Ĭ-tĭ), *n.* Quality or state of being inscrutable.

in-scru'ta-ble (-skrŏō'tá-b'l), *a.* [4] Incapable of being searched into and understood; incomprehensible. — **-ness**, *n.* [8] — **in-scru'ta-bly**, *adv.* [8].

in'sect (ĭn'sĕkt), *n.* Any of numerous small invertebrate animals belonging to a class (*Insecta*) comprising beetles, bugs, bees, flies, etc. Popularly, *insect* is applied also to the spiders, mites, ticks, centipedes, etc.

in-sec'ti-cide (ĭn-sĕk'tĭ-sīd),*n.* A powder or other agent used to destroy insects.

in'sec-tiv'o-ra (ĭn'sĕk-tĭv'ô-rà), *n. pl. Zoöl.* An order of mammals, including moles, shrews, hedgehogs, and related animals. They are mostly small, active at night, and feed on insects, etc.

in'sec-tiv'o-rous (-rŭs), *a.* Feeding on insects.

in'se-cure' (ĭn'sê-kūr'), *a.* [4] Not secure; unsafe.

in'se-cu'ri-ty (-kū'rĭ-tĭ), *n.* ; *pl.* **-ties** (-tĭz). State or quality of being insecure; want of safety.

in-sen'sate (ĭn-sĕn'sāt), *a.* [4] **1.** Without sensation; inanimate. **2.** Without sense; foolish; as, *insensate* ambition. **3.** Unfeeling; brutal.

in-sen'si-bil'i-ty (ĭn-sĕn'sĭ-bĭl'Ĭ-tĭ), *n.* State or quality of being insensible; want of sensibility.

in-sen'si-ble (-sĕn'sĭ-b'l),*a.* [4] **1.** Incapable or bereft of sensation. **2.** Imperceptible; inappreciable; gradual. **3.** Devoid or incapable of emotion or passion; indifferent. — **in-sen'si-bly**, *adv.* [8].

in-sep'a-ra-bil'i-ty (-sĕp'á-rá-bĭl'Ĭ-tĭ), *n.* Quality or state of being inseparable.

in-sep'a-ra-ble (-sĕp'á-rá-b'l), *a.* [4] Not separable. — **in-sep'a-ra-bly**, *adv.* [8].

in-sert' (-sûrt'), *v. t.* To set or put into.

in'sert (ĭn'sûrt), *n.* A thing inserted.

in-ser'tion (ĭn-sûr'shŭn), *n.* **1.** An inserting. **2.** That which is inserted.

in'set (ĭn'sĕt), *n.* An insertion ; insert.

in'shore' (ĭn'shōr' ; ĭn'shōr'), *a.* Near, or directed toward, the shore. — *adv.* (*pron.* ĭn'shōr') In toward the shore.

in'side' (ĭn'sīd' ; ĭn'sīd'), *n.* **1.** The inner side, surface, or part; interior. **2.** Inward nature.

in'side' (ĭn'sīd'), *a.* Internal ; interior ; as, *inside* decoration. — (ĭn'sīd'; ĭn'sīd'),*adv.* Within ; internally. — *prep.* Inside of ; within.

in'sid'er (ĭn'sĭd'ẽr), *n.* A person inside; hence, one in a position to have first-hand information.

in-sid'i-ous (ĭn-sĭd'Ĭ-ŭs),*a.* [4] Treacherous; sly; crafty. — **-ly**, *adv.* [8] — **-ness**, *n.* [8].

in'sight' (ĭn'sīt'), *n.* **1.** Discernment. **2.** Apprehension of the inner nature of things.

in-sig'ni-a (ĭn-sĭg'nĭ-à), *n. pl.; sing.* **insigne** (-nē). Distinguishing marks ; badges ; emblems.

in'sig-nif'i-cance (ĭn'sĭg-nĭf'Ĭ-kǎns), *n.* Want of significance.

in'sig-nif'i-cant (-kǎnt), *a.* [4] Meaningless; unimportant; trifling; small; mean. — **-ly**, *adv.* [8].

in'sin-cere' (ĭn'sĭn-sēr'), *a.* [3] Not sincere; deceitful. — **-ly**, *adv.* [8]. [fulness.

in'sin-cer'i-ty (-sĕr'Ĭ-tĭ), *n.* Hypocrisy; deceit-

in-sin'u-ate (ĭn-sĭn'û-āt), *v. t.* [1] **1.** To introduce gently, slowly, or artfully. **2.** To work or introduce (a person or one's self) gently or artfully as into some relation; ingratiate. **3.** To hint indirectly; imply maliciously. — **in-sin'u-a'tor**, *n.*

in-sin'u-a'tion (-ā'shŭn), *n.* **1.** Act or process of insinuating. **2.** That which is insinuated.

in-sip'id (-sĭp'Ĭd), *a.* [4] **1.** Without savor; tasteless; flat. **2.** Wanting in animation; uninteresting; dull. — **-ly**, *adv.* [8] — **-ness**, *n.* [8].

in'si-pid'i-ty (ĭn'sĭ-pĭd'Ĭ-tĭ), *n.* Quality or state of being insipid; also, something insipid.

in-sist' (ĭn-sĭst'), *v. i.* To hold to something firmly; be persistent.

in-sist'ence (-sĭs'tĕns), *n.* Act of insisting ; state or quality of being insistent; persistence; urgency.

in-sist'en-cy (-tĕn-sĭ), *n.* Insistence.

in-sist'ent (-tĕnt), *a.* [4] Disposed to insist; persistent; compelling attention. — **-ly**, *adv.* [8].

in-snare' (-snâr'), *v. t.* To catch in or as in a snare.

in'sole' (ĭn'sōl'), *n.* Inside sole of a boot or shoe; also, a strip, as of leather, placed inside a shoe.

in'so-lence (-sō-lĕns), *n.* **1.** Quality of being insolent; insulting behavior. **2.** An insult.

in'so-lent (-lĕnt), *a.* [4] Haughty and contemptuous ; impertinently insulting. — **in'so-lent-ly**, *adv.* [8]. [being insoluble.

in-sol'u-bil'i-ty (ĭn-sŏl'û-bĭl'Ĭ-tĭ), *n.* Quality of

in-sol'u-ble (-sŏl'û-b'l), *a.* [4] Not soluble; as: **a** Not to be solved. **b** Incapable or very difficult of being dissolved. — **-ness**, *n.* [8].

in-sol'ven-cy (-vĕn-sĭ), *n.* State of being insolvent.

in-sol'vent (-vĕnt), *a.* Not solvent; unable to pay one's debts. — *n.* An insolvent debtor.

in-som'ni-a (-sŏm'nĭ-à), *n.* Sleeplessness.

in'so-much' (ĭn'sō-mŭch'), *adv.* So much; to such a degree ; so ;— usually followed by *that* or *as.*

in-spect' (ĭn-spĕkt'), *v. t.* **1.** To view critically ; examine. **2.** To view and examine officially.

in-spec'tion (-spĕk'shŭn), *n.* Act of inspecting.

in-spec'tor (-tẽr), *n.* **1.** One who inspects ; overseer. **2.** A police officer having charge of a certain number of precincts.

in'spi-ra'tion (ĭn'spĭ-rā'shŭn),*n.* **1.** Act of breathing in. **2.** In theology, a supernatural influence fitting men to receive and communicate divine truth; also, the truth so communicated. **3.** Act, power, or result of stimulating the intellect or emotions ; as, the *inspiration* of art.

in-spire' (ĭn-spīr'), *v. t.* [1] **1.** To inhale. **2.** To give inspiration to. **3.** To produce as by inspiration. — **in-spir'er**, *n.* [8].

in-spired' (ĭn-spīrd'), *p. a.* [4] **1.** Breathed in. **2.** Animated or affected as by a supernatural influence. **3.** Suggested by some one in power.

āle, senãte, cãre, ãm, ắccount, ãrm, àsk, sofà ; ēve, ĕvent, ĕnd, recĕnt, makẽr; īce, ĭll ; ōld, ŏbey, ôrb, ŏdd, sŏft, cŏnnect; ūse, ūnite, ûrn, ŭp, circŭs; fŏŏd, fŏŏt; out, oil ;

in-spir'it (ĭn-spĭr'ĭt), *v. t.* To infuse life or spirit into; animate. [as by evaporation.

in-spis'sate (-spĭs'āt), *v. t. & i.* [1] To thicken,

in-sta-bil'i-ty (ĭn/stă-bĭl'ĭ-tĭ), *n. ; pl.* -TIES (-tĭz).
1. Want of firmness or security. 2. Inconstancy.

in-stall' (-stôl'), *v. t.* 1. To place formally in office. 2. To set in a seat, give a place to. 3. To set up or fix in position for use or service.

in/stal-la'tion (ĭn/stŏ-lā'shŭn), *n.* Act of installing; state of being installed.

in-stall'ment, in-stal'ment (ĭn-stôl'mĕnt), *n.*
1. Installation. 2. Any of the portions of a debt or sum paid or payable at different times. 3. A portion of something produced or furnished apart from the remainder; as, an *installment* of a serial story.

in/stance (ĭn/stăns), *n.* 1. Request. 2. An illustrative example. 3. Step in an action; occasion.
— *v. t.* [1] To mention as a case, or example; cite.

in'stant (-stănt), *a.* [4] 1. Pressing; urgent; earnest. 2. Present; current. *Archaic*, exc. as used with dates to indicate the current month. 3. Immediate, without delay. — *n.* A moment.

in/stan-ta/ne-ous (ĭn/stăn-tā/nē-ŭs), *a.* [4] Done or occurring in an instant. — *ly*, *adv.* [8].

in-stan'ter (ĭn-stăn'tẽr), *adv.* Immediately.

in'stant-ly (ĭn'stănt-lĭ), *adv.* Without delay, at once. — *conj.* As soon as.

in-state' (ĭn-stāt'), *v. t.* [1] To install, as in office.

in-stead' (-stĕd'), *adv.* 1. In the place or room; in lieu, — esp. with *of.* 2. In its stead; rather.

in/step (ĭn/stĕp), *n.* The arched part of the human foot in front of the ankle joint.

in/sti-gate (-stĭ-gāt), *v. t.* [1] To urge forward; set on, incite; — chiefly with reference to evil actions. — **in/sti-ga/tor**, *n.* [8].

in/sti-ga/tion (-gā/shŭn), *n.* Incitement.

in-still', in-stil' (ĭn-stĭl'), *v. t.; -*STILLED' (-stĭld'); -STILL'ING. To drop in; pour in drop by drop; hence, to impart gradually, infuse slowly.

in/stil-la'tion (ĭn/stĭ-lā'shŭn), *n.* Act of instilling.

in-still'ment, in-stil'ment, *n.* Instillation.

in-stinct' (ĭn-stĭŋkt'), *a.* [4] Imbued or filled.

in'stinct (ĭn'stĭŋkt), *n.* 1. Natural inward impulse; involuntary prompting to any action. 2. A natural aptitude; as, an *instinct* for order.

in-stinc'tive (-stĭŋk'tĭv), *a.* [4] Derived from, or prompted by, instinct; involuntary. — *ly*, *adv.*

in'sti-tute (ĭn'stĭ-tūt), *v. t.* [1] To set up; originate and establish; hence, to inaugurate. — *n.* That which is instituted, as. **a** An authoritative precept or rule. **b** An institution, an organization to promote learning, art, etc.

in'sti-tu'tion (-tū'shŭn), *n.* 1. Act or process of instituting, establishment, foundation. 2. That which is instituted, or established; as: **a** An established social, political, or national law, custom, etc. **b** An organized society or corporation.

in'sti-tu'tion-al (-ăl), *a.* Of, pertaining to, or of the nature of, an institution; organized.

in'sti-tu'tor (ĭn'stĭ-tū'tẽr), *n.* One who institutes.

in-struct' (-strŭkt'), *v. t.* 1. To impart knowledge to; teach. 2. To give directions to, direct.

in-struc'tion (-strŭk'shŭn), *n.* 1. Act of instructing or teaching. 2. That which instructs; as: **a** Knowledge given. **b** A teaching; thing taught. 3. [*In pl.*] Orders, esp. as to duty or procedure.

in-struc'tive (-strŭk'tĭv), *a.* [4] Conveying knowledge; serving to instruct or inform. — **in-struc'tive-ly**, *adv.* [8] — *-ness*, *n.* [8].

in-struc'tor (-tẽr), *n.* One who instructs; a teacher — **in-struc'tress** (-trĕs), *n. fem.* [8].

in'stru-ment (ĭn'strōō-mĕnt), *n.* 1. That by means of which something is done; medium; a means. 2. A device for doing work or producing an effect; tool, implement. 3. A contrivance by which musical sounds are produced. 4. A legal writing, as a deed, writ, etc.

in'stru-men'tal (ĭn'strōō-mĕn'tăl), *a.* [4] 1. Acting as an instrument, helpful. 2. Of or pertaining to an instrument, esp. a musical instrument.

in'stru-men-tal'i-ty (-mĕn-tăl'ĭ-tĭ), *n. ; pl.* -TIES (-tĭz). Quality or state of being instrumental. means, agency.

in'sub-or'di-nate (-sŭb-ôr'dĭ-nāt), *a.* [4] Disobedient; mutinous. — **-or'di-na'tion** (-nā'shŭn), *n.*

in'sub-stan'tial (ĭn'sŭb-stăn'shăl), *a.* [4] Not substantial; as: **a** Not real. **b** Flimsy; frail.

in-suf'fer-a-ble (ĭn-sŭf'ẽr-à-b'l), *a.* [4] That cannot be endured; intolerable. — *-a-bly*, *adv.* [8].

in'suf-fi'cien-cy (ĭn'sŭ-fĭsh'ĕn-sĭ), *n.* Insufficient quality or state. [quate.

in'suf-fi'cient (-ĕnt), *a.* [4] Not sufficient; inade-

in'su-lar (ĭn'sū-lăr), *a.* [4] 1. Of, pert. to, or like, an island. 2. Standing alone; isolated. 3. Pert. to islanders; illiberal. [sular.

in'su-lar'i-ty (-lăr'ĭ-tĭ), *n.* Quality of being in-

in'su-late (ĭn'sū-lāt), *v. t.* [1] To isolate; esp., *Physics*, to separate by nonconductors, as to prevent transfer of electricity or heat.

in'su-la'tion (-lā'shŭn), *n.* Act of insulating; state of being insulated; material used in insulating.

in'su-la'tor (ĭn'sū-lā'tẽr), *n.* One that insulates.

in-sult' (ĭn-sŭlt'), *v. t.* To treat with insolence. — **in-sult'er**, *n.* [8]. [other; an affront.

in'sult (ĭn'sŭlt), *n.* Gross indignity offered to an-

in-su'per-a-bil'i-ty (ĭn-sū/pẽr-à-bĭl'ĭ-tĭ), *n.* Quality or state of being insuperable.

in-su'per-a-ble (ĭn-sū'pẽr-à-b'l), *a.* [4] Incapable of being surmounted. — **in-su'per-a-ble-ness**, *n.* [8] — **in-su'per-a-bly**, *adv.* [8].

in'sup-port'a-ble (ĭn'sŭ-pōr'tà-b'l), *a.* [4] Not supportable, insufferable. — *-a-bly*, *adv.* [8].

in-sur'a-ble (ĭn-shōōr'à-b'l), *a.* Capable of being insured against loss, damage, death, etc.

in-sur'ance (-ăns), *n.* 1. An insuring against loss, the business of making insurance contracts. Called also *assurance.* 2. Premium paid for insuring anything. 3. Sum for which anything is insured.

in-sure' (-shōōr'), *v. t.* [1] 1. To make sure or secure, guarantee. 2. To secure against loss (as from fire, accident, death, etc.), on certain conditions, or at a given premium. — *v. i.* To contract to give insurance, to procure insurance.

in-sured' (-shōōrd'), *n.* One who is insured.

in-sur'er (-shōōr'ẽr), *n.* One that insures.

in-sur'gence (-sûr'jĕns), *n.* An uprising; revolt.

in-sur'gent (-jĕnt), *a.* [4] Rising against authority, rebellious. — *n.* One who revolts; rebel.

in'sur-mount'a-ble (ĭn'sŭr-moun'tà-b'l), *a.* [4] Incapable of being surmounted; insuperable.

in'sur-rec'tion (-sŭ-rĕk'shŭn), *n.* A rising against civil or political authority.

in'sur-rec'tion-a-ry (ĭn'sŭ-rĕk'shŭn-ă-rĭ), a. Rebellious.

in'sus-cep'ti-bil'i-ty (ĭn'sŭ-sĕp'tĭ-bĭl'ĭ-tĭ), n. Quality of being insusceptible. [tible.

in'sus-cep'ti-ble (-sĕp'tĭ-b'l), a. [4] Not susceptible.

in-tact' (ĭn-tăkt'), a. [4] Untouched; left entire.

in-tagl'io (ĭn-tăl'yō; It. ēn-täl'yō), n.; pl. E.-TAGLIOS (ĭn-tăl'yōz), It. -TAGLI (ēn-täl'yē). 1. An engraving; esp., a figure depressed below the surface of the material. 2. Anything, esp. a gem, carved in intaglio. Cf. CAMEO.

in'take' (ĭn'tāk'), n. 1. A taking in; thing taken in. 2. Place where a fluid is taken into a channel, etc.

in-tan'gi-bil'i-ty (ĭn-tăn'jĭ-bĭl'ĭ-tĭ), n. Quality or state of being intangible.

in-tan'gi-ble (ĭn-tăn'jĭ-b'l), a. [4] Not tangible; impalpable. — n. [8] —**bly**, adv. [8].

in'te-ger (ĭn'tĕ-jẽr), n. A whole number.

in'te-gral (-grăl), a. [4] 1. Essential to completeness. 2. Complete; entire. 3. Math. Not fractional. — n. A whole; a whole number.

in'te-grate (-grāt), v. t. & i. [1] 1. To form into one whole; make entire; perfect. 2. To indicate the whole of; give the sum or total of.

in'te-gra'tion (-grā'shŭn), n. An integrating.

in-teg'ri-ty (ĭn-tĕg'rĭ-tĭ), n. 1. State or quality of being complete. 2. Unimpaired state; soundness; uprightness. [ment; coat; skin.

in-teg'u-ment (-ū-mĕnt), n. A covering; invest-

in'tel-lect (ĭn'tĕ-lĕkt), n. 1. Power or faculty of knowing; the understanding. 2. A mind or intelligence; person of intellectual power.

in'tel-lec'tu-al (-lĕk'tū-ăl), a. [4] 1. Belonging or relating to, or performed by, the intellect or understanding. 2. Endowed with intellect, esp. in a high degree. — **ly**, adv. [8].

in'tel-lec'tu-al'i-ty (-ăl'ĭ-tĭ), n.; pl. -TIES (-tĭz). Intellectual powers; quality of being intellectual.

in-tel'li-gence (ĭn-tĕl'ĭ-jĕns), n. 1. The intellect. 2. Mental quickness; sagacity. 3. Information communicated; news; advice; knowledge.

in-tel'li-gent (-jĕnt), a. [4] 1. Endowed with intelligence or intellect. 2. Possessed of a high degree of understanding. — **ly**, adv. [8].

in-tel'li-gi-bil'i-ty (ĭn-tĕl'ĭ-jĭ-bĭl'ĭ-tĭ), n. Quality or state of being intelligible.

in-tel'li-gi-ble (ĭn-tĕl'ĭ-jĭ-b'l), a. [4] Capable of being understood; comprehensible. — **bly**, adv.

in-tem'per-ance (-tĕm'pẽr-ăns), n. Want of temperance; any excess; esp., excessive indulgence in intoxicating liquors.

in-tem'per-ate (-āt), a. [4] Not temperate; as: **a** Immoderate. **b** Indulging any appetite or passion to excess. **c** Esp., given to the excessive use of intoxicating liquors. — **ly**, adv. [8] — **ness**, n. [8].

in-tend' (-tĕnd'), v. t. To have in mind as a purpose; mean; plan; as, to intend to go to Europe.

in-tend'ed (ĭn-tĕn'dĕd), p. p. of INTEND. Betrothed. Colloq. — n. An affianced lover. Colloq.

in-tense' (-tĕns'), a. [3] 1. Extreme in degree; excessive; immoderate. 2. Strained or straining; high-wrought; profoundly earnest or intent. — **in-tense'ly**, adv. [8] — **ness**, n. [8].

in-ten'si-fy (-tĕn'sĭ-fī), v. t. [2] To render intense or more intense. — **in-ten'si-fi'er** (-fī'ẽr), n. [8]. — v. i. To become intense or more intense.

in-ten'sion (-shŭn), n. 1. Intentness; determination. 2. Increase of power or energy; intensity.

in-ten'si-ty (-sĭ-tĭ), n.; pl. -TIES (-tĭz). 1. State or quality of being intense; extreme or high degree. 2. Degree or amount; strength; energy.

in-ten'sive (-sĭv), a. [4] 1. Of, pertaining to, or marked by, intensity. 2. Gram. Serving to give force or emphasis; as, an intensive verb. 3. Designed to increase the productiveness of land by expenditure of more capital and labor on it. — n. That which intensifies; Gram., an intensive word, prefix, etc. — **in-ten'sive-ly**, adv. [8].

in-tent' (-tĕnt'), a. [3] Directed with, or giving, keen attention; hence, earnest; intense; also, closely occupied.

in-tent', n. 1. Intention; purpose. 2. Meaning; import. — **to all intents and purposes**, practically.

in-ten'tion (-tĕn'shŭn), n. 1. That which is, or is intended to be, conveyed to the understanding; meaning; import. 2. Purpose; design; pl., Colloq., purpose as to marriage.

in-ten'tion-al (-ăl), a. [4] Done by intention; designed. — **ly**, adv. [8].

in-tent'ly (-tĕnt'lĭ), adv. In an intent manner.

in-tent'ness, n. Quality or state of being intent.

in-ter' (-tûr'), v. t.; -TERRED' (-tûrd'); -TER'RING. To deposit (a corpse) in a grave or tomb; bury.

in'ter-act' (ĭn'tẽr-ăkt'), v. i. To act upon each other.

in'ter-ac'tion (-ăk'shŭn), n. Reciprocal action.

in'ter-breed' (-brēd'), v. i. & t. To breed by crossing different stocks, varieties, or species.

in-ter'ca-la-ry (ĭn-tûr'kd-lā-rĭ), a. 1. Intercalated in the calendar. 2. Inserted; interpolated.

in-ter'ca-late (-lāt), v. t. [1] 1. To insert, as a day, in a calendar. 2. To interpolate.

in-ter'ca-la'tion (-lā'shŭn), n. Act of intercalating; that which is intercalated; interpolation.

in'ter-cede' (ĭn'tẽr-sēd'), v. i. [1] To plead in favor of another or others; interpose; mediate.

in'ter-cept' (-sĕpt'), v. t. 1. To take or seize by the way; stop; check. 2. To interrupt communication with; cut off from view, approach, etc.

in'ter-cep'tion (-sĕp'shŭn), n. An intercepting.

in'ter-ces'sion (-sĕsh'ŭn), n. Act of interceding; petition or entreaty in favor of another or others.

in'ter-ces'sor (-sĕs'ẽr), n. One who intercedes.

in'ter-change' (-chānj'), v. t. [1] 1. To put each in the place of the other; exchange. 2. To alternate; vary.

in'ter-change' (ĭn'tẽr-chānj'), n. 1. Mutual exchange. 2. Alternation.

in'ter-change'a-bil'i-ty (ĭn'tẽr-chān'jà-bĭl'ĭ-tĭ), n. Quality of being interchangeable.

in'ter-change'a-ble (-chān'jà-b'l), a. [4] Capable of being interchanged. — **ness**, n. [8] — **bly**, adv. [8]. [leges.

in'ter-col-le'gi-ate (-kŏ-lē'jĭ-āt), a. Between col-

in'ter-com-mu'ni-cate (-kŏ-mū'nĭ-kāt), v. t. & i. [1] To communicate mutually.

in'ter-com-mu'ni-ca'tion (-kā'shŭn), n. An intercommunicating.

in'ter-cos'tal (-kŏs'tăl), a. Between the ribs.

in'ter-course (ĭn'tẽr-kōrs), n. Communication; commerce; interchange of thought and feeling.

in'ter-de-pend'ence (-dē-pĕn'dĕns), -**pend'en-cy** (-dĕn-sĭ), n. Mutual dependence. — **pend'ent**, a.

in′ter-dict (ĭn′tẽr-dĭkt), *n.* A prohibitory decree.
in′ter-dict′ (-dĭkt′), *v. t.* To forbid, esp., authoritatively; debar. [also, an interdict.]
in′ter-dic′tion (-dĭk′shŭn),*n.* Act of interdicting;
in′ter-est (ĭn′tẽr-ĕst), *n.* **1**. Share in advantage, profit, and responsibility; as, an *interest* in a store. **2**. Advantage; profit; benefit. **3**. Those interested in any particular affair taken collectively. **4**. Excitement of feeling accompanying special attention to some object; concern. **5**. Premium paid by a borrower for the use of what he borrows. — *v. t.* **1**. To cause or induce to have a share or interest. **2**. To engage the attention of.
in′ter-est-ing, *p. a.* [4] Engaging the attention; exciting, or adapted to excite, interest or emotion.
in′ter-fere′ (-fēr′),' *v. i.* [1] **1**. To collide; clash. **2**. To take part in the concerns of others; meddle.
in′ter-fer′ence (-fẽr′ĕns), *n.* An interfering.
in′ter-im (ĭn′tẽr-ĭm), *n.* The meantime; interval between events, etc.
in-te′ri-or (ĭn-tē′rĭ-ẽr), *a.* [4] **1**. Being within; inside; inner; internal; inward. **2**. Remote from the limits, frontier, or shore; inland.— *n.* **1**. The internal or inner part of a thing; inside. **2**. The inland part of a country. **3**. The domestic affairs of a nation; as, the Department of the *Interior*. — **-ly**, *adv.* [8].
in′ter-ject′ (-jĕkt′), *v. t. & i.* To insert; interpose.
in′ter-jec′tion (-jĕk′shŭn), *n.* **1**. An interjecting; also, that which is interjected. **2**. *Gram.* A word or form thrown in without grammatical connection, as *O! Alas! Ha ha!* etc. Cf. EXCLAMATION.
in′ter-lace′ (-lās′), *v. t. & i.* [1] To unite as by lacing together; interweave. [versify.]
in′ter-lard′ (-lärd′), *v. t.* To mix or mingle; diversify.
in′ter-leave′ (-lēv′), *v. t.* [1] To insert a leaf or leaves in; bind with blank leaves inserted.
in′ter-line′ (-līn′), *v. t.* [1] To write or insert between lines; insert something between the lines of.
in′ter-lin′e-ar (-lĭn′e-ȧr), *a.* Contained between lines; inserted between lines.
in′ter-lock′ (-lŏk′), *v. i. & t.* To unite or engage with one another; lock into one another.
in′ter-loc′u-tor (ĭn′tẽr-lŏk′ū-tẽr), *n.* One who takes part in conversation; talker; questioner.
in′ter-lop′er (ĭn′tẽr-lōp′ẽr), *n.* One who interferes wrongfully or officiously; intruder.
in′ter-lude (-lūd), *n.* **1**. An entertainment between the acts of a play. **2**. A piece of music played between the parts of a song, of a church service, etc.
in′ter-mar′riage (-măr′ĭj), *n.* **1**. Marriage as between two families, tribes, etc. **2**. Marriage between blood relations.
in′ter-mar′ry (-măr′ĭ), *v. i. & t.* [2] To become connected by marriage between their members.
in′ter-med′dle (-mĕd′'l), *v. i.* [1] To meddle with others' affairs; interfere; — **-dler** (-lẽr), *n.* [8].
in′ter-me′di-a-ry (-mē′dĭ-ȧ-rĭ), *a.* [4] Intermediate.— *n.; pl.* -RIES. One intermediate; go-between.
in′ter-me′di-ate (-ȧt), *a.* Being in the middle; coming between. — *n.* **1**. Something intermediate. **2**. An intermediary. [between.]
in′ter-me′di-a′tion (-ā′shŭn), *n.* Act of coming
in′ter-ment (ĭn-tûr′mĕnt), *n.* Burial.
in-ter′mi-na-ble (ĭn-tûr′mĭ-nȧ-b'l),*a.* [4] Without termination; endless. — **-na-bly**, *adv.* [8].

in′ter-min′gle (ĭn′tẽr-mĭn′g'l), *v. t. & i.* [1] To mingle together.
in′ter-mis′sion (-mĭsh′ŭn), *n.* **1**. Act or state of intermitting; state of being intermitted; interruption. **2**. A pause; interval.
in′ter-mit′ (-mĭt′), *v. t. & i.; * -MIT′TED; -MIT′TING. To discontinue; interrupt.
in′ter-mit′tent (-ĕnt), *a.* Having periods of interruption or cessation. — **-ly**, *adv.* [8].
in′ter-mix′ (-mĭks′), *v. t. & i.* To intermingle.
in′ter-mix′ture (-mĭks′tụ̄r), *n.* A mixing together; also, a mass of ingredients mixed.
in-tern′ (ĭn-tûrn′), *v. t.* To confine to one locality.
in-ter′nal(-tûr′nȧl),*a.* [4] **1**. Inclosed; inward; interior; also, designating that which is to be inwardly applied; as, *internal* medicine. **2**. Pertaining to the inner nature; intrinsic. **3**. Domestic, as opposed to *foreign*. — **-ly**, *adv.* [8].
in-ter′nal-com-bus′tion, *a.* *Mach.* Designating, or pertaining to, any engine (**internal-combustion engine**) in which power is developed by the explosion or combustion of fuel in the engine cylinder. Gas, gasoline, and oil engines are of this type.
in′ter-na′tion-al (ĭn′tẽr-năsh′ŭn-ȧl), *a.* Between or among nations. — **-ly**, *adv.* [8].
in′ter-ne′cine (ĭn′tẽr-nē′sĭn; -sĭn), *a.* [4] Deadly; mutually destructive. [fluence.]
in′ter-play′ (ĭn′tẽr-plā′), *n.* Mutual action or in-
in-ter′po-late (ĭn-tûr′pŏ-lāt), *v. t.* [1] To alter or corrupt, esp. a text, by inserting new or foreign matter. — **in-ter′po-la′tor** (-lā′tẽr), *n.* [8].
in-ter′po-la′tion (-lā′shŭn),*n.* Act of interpolating; that which is interpolated.
in′ter-pose′ (-pōz′), *v. t.* [1] **1**. To place between. **2**. To thrust in; intrude; also, to interject. — *v. i.* **1**. To be or come between; as, hills *interpose*. **2**. To mediate; intervene. **3**. To interrupt.
in′ter-po-si′tion (-pŏ-zĭsh′ŭn),*n.* Act of interposing; state of being interposed; thing interposed.
in-ter′pret (ĭn-tûr′prĕt), *v. t.* To explain or tell the meaning of; translate; make clear.— *v. i.* To act as an interpreter; translate.
in-ter′pre-ta′tion (-prĕ-tā′shŭn), *n.* **1**. An interpreting. **2**. Explanation given; rendering.
in-ter′pre-ta-tive (-tā-tĭv), *a.* [4] Explanatory.
in-ter′pret-er (-prĕt-ẽr), *n.* One who interprets.
in′ter-reg′num (ĭn′tẽr-rĕg′nŭm), *n.; L. pl.* -NA (-nȧ). **1**. The time during which a throne is vacant between two reigns. **2**. A pause; interval.
in′ter-re-la′tion (-rĕ-lā′shŭn), *n.* Mutual or reciprocal relation. — **-re-lat′ed** (-lāt′ĕd), *p. a.*
in-ter′ro-gate (ĭn-tĕr′ŏ-gāt),*v. t. & i.* [1] To examine by questioning; question.
in-ter′ro-ga′tion (-gā′shŭn), *n.* **1**. An interrogating; inquiry. **2**. A mark [?] indicating that the preceding sentence is interrogatory; — called also *interrogation point*.
in-ter′rog′a-tive (ĭn′tẽ-rŏg′ȧ-tĭv), *a.* [4] Interrogatory. — *n.* A word used in asking questions, as *who*, *what*, *which*. — **-ly**, *adv.* [8].
in-ter′ro-ga′tor (ĭn-tĕr′ŏ-gā′tẽr), *n.* One who interrogates.
in′ter-rog′a-to-ry (ĭn′tẽ-rŏg′ȧ-tŏ-rĭ), *a.* [4] Containing, expressing, or implying a question. — *n.; pl.* -TORIES (-rĭz). A formal question or inquiry.
in′ter-rupt′ (ĭn′tẽ-rŭpt′), *v. t.* **1**. To break into

or between, interfere with the course, current, or motion of. **2.** To break the continuity or uniformity of. — *v. i.* To break in on, esp. with questions or remarks. — **·rupt′er, ·rup′tor** (-tẽr), *n.* [8].

in′ter-rup′tion (ĭn′tẽr-rŭp′shŭn), *n.* **1.** An interrupting. **2.** A break; stoppage; check; hindrance.

in′ter-sect′ (ĭn′tẽr-sĕkt′), *v. t. & i.* To divide, or cut by passing through or athwart ; cut across.

in′ter-sec′tion (-sĕk′shŭn), *n.* An intersecting.

in′ter-space (ĭn′tẽr-spās′), *n.* Intervening space.

in′ter-sperse′ (-spũrs′), *v. t.* [1] **1.** To scatter among other things. **2.** To place something at intervals in or among.

in′ter-sper′sion (-spũr′shŭn),*n.* An interspersing.

in′ter-state′ (ĭn′tẽr-stāt′), *a.* Existing between or including different states; as, *interstate* commerce.

in′ter-stice (ĭn-tûr′stĭs), *n.* ; *pl.* -STICES (-stĭ-sēz). An intervening space, esp. when small or narrow, chink ; crevice. — **·sti′tial** (ĭn-tẽr-stĭsh′ăl), *a.*

in′ter-twine′ (ĭn′tẽr-twīn′),*v. t. & i.* [1] To twine one with another.

in′ter-ur′ban (-ûr′băn),*a.* Between cities or towns.

in′ter-val (ĭn′tẽr-văl), *n.* **1.** A space or gap between things. **2.** Intervening space of time. **3.** *Music.* Difference in pitch between two tones.

in′ter-vene′ (-vēn′), *v. i.* [1] **1.** To come in (between, or among). **2.** To occur, fall, or come, between points of time or events. **3.** To occur or lie (between). — **in′ter-ven′er** (-vēn′ẽr), *n.* [8].

in′ter-ven′tion (-vĕn′shŭn), *n.* **1.** Act or fact of intervening. **2.** An interference, esp. one by a state in the affairs of another state.

in′ter-view (ĭn′tẽr-vū), *n.* A meeting face to face; conference , esp. , a meeting between a representative of the press and another person to get information for publication, also, the published account of such meeting. — *v. t.* To have an interview with. — **in′ter-view′er** (-vū′ẽr), *n.* [8].

in′ter-weave′ (-wēv′),*v.t. & i.* [1] To unite by or as by weaving together, intertwine, intermingle.

in-tes′tate (ĭn-tĕs′tāt), *a.* **1.** Not having made a will. **2.** Not disposed of by will. — *n.* One who dies intestate.   [intestine.|

in-tes′ti-nal (-tĭ′năl), *a.* Of or pertaining to the

in-tes′tine (-tĭn), *a.* Internal, domestic. — *n.* The tubular convoluted portion of the alimentary canal , the bowels, — usually in *pl.*

in′ti-ma-cy (ĭn′tĭ-mà-sĭ),*n.*, *pl.* -CIES (-sĭz) State or fact of being intimate, friendship.

in′ti-mate (ĭn′tĭ-măt), *a.* [4] **1.** Deep-seated , innermost. **2.** Close in association or acquaintance; familiar, also, thorough. **3.** Closely united. — *n.* An intimate friend or associate , a confidant. — **in′ti-mate-ly**, *adv.* [8]

in′ti-mate (ĭn′tĭ-māt), *v. t.* [1] To announce or suggest, esp. indirectly.

in′ti-ma′tion (-mā′shŭn), *n.* Act of intimating, also, the thing intimated; hint.

in-tim′i-date (ĭn-tĭm′ĭ-dāt), *v. t.* [1] To make timid or fearful; esp., to deter, as by threats, overawe ; cow. — **in-tim′i-da′tor** (-dā′tẽr), *n.* [8].

in-tim′i-da′tion (-dā′shŭn), *n.* Act of intimidating, or state of being intimidated.

in′to (ĭn′tōō), *prep.* To the inside of. See IN.

in-tol′er-a-ble (ĭn-tŏl′ẽr-à-b′l), *a.* [4] Not tolerable , insufferable. — **in-tol′er-a-bly**, *adv.* [8].

in-tol′er-ance (-ăns), *n.* State of being intolerant.

in-tol′er-ant (-ănt), *a.* [4] **1.** Unable to endure. **2.** Not tolerant ; not tolerating difference of opinion, esp. as to religion ; bigoted. — **·ly**, *adv.* [8].

in′to-na′tion (ĭn′tŏ-nā′shŭn), *n.* **1.** An intoning. **2.** Manner of playing or uttering tones.

in-tone′ (ĭn-tōn′), *v. t. & i.* [1] To utter with musical or prolonged tones, recite in monotone.

in-tox′i-cant (-tŏk′sĭ-kănt), *n.* That which in toxicates ; an intoxicating agent, as whisky.

in-tox′i-cate (-kāt), *v. t.* [1] **1.** To make drunk; excite or stupefy by strong drink or a narcotic **2.** To excite to enthusiasm, frenzy, or madness.

in-tox′i-ca′tion (-kā′shŭn), *n.* **1.** *Med.* A poisoning. **2.** State of being intoxicated, or drunk; act of intoxicating. **3.** A high excitement of mind.

in-trac′ta-bil′i-ty (ĭn-trăk′tà-bĭl′ĭ-tĭ),*n.* Quality of being intractable.

in-trac′ta-ble (ĭn-trăk′tà-b′l), *a.* [4] Not tractable; not easily governed, managed, or directed, obstinate; refractory. — **·ness**, *n.* [8]— **in-trac′ta-bly**, *adv.* [8].

in-tran′si-tive (-trăn′sĭ-tĭv), *a.* Not transitive ; expressing an action or state as limited to the agent or subject, or as ending in itself ; as, an *intransitive* verb, e. g., the bird *flies*, the dog *barks*. — **in-tran′si-tive-ly**, *adv.* [8].

in-trench′ (-trĕnch′), *v. t.* To surround with a trench or intrenchments.—*v. i.* To encroach ; infringe , — usually with *on* or *upon*.

in-trench′ment (-mĕnt), *n.* **1.** An intrenching, state of being intrenched. **2.** *Mil.* Any defensive work consisting of at least a trench and a parapet of the earth thrown up.

in-trep′id (ĭn-trĕp′ĭd), *a.* [4] Not trembling with fear; fearless; brave; undaunted. — **·ly**, *adv.* [8].

in′tre-pid′i-ty (ĭn′trĕ-pĭd′ĭ-tĭ),*n.* Fearless bravery; valor.

in′tri-ca-cy (ĭn′trĭ-kà-sĭ), *n.* ; *pl.* -CIES (-sĭz). Intricate state or quality ; that which is intricate.

in′tri-cate (-kăt), *a.* [4] Entangled ; involved ; difficult to understand, follow, etc.— **·ly**,*adv.* [8].

in-trigue′ (ĭn-trēg′), *v. i. & t.* [1] **1.** To carry on a secret and improper love affair. **2.** To plot , scheme — (ĭn-trēg′ , ĭn′trēg),*n.* **1.** A plot ; conspiracy **2.** A secret love affair. — **in-tri′guer** (-trē′gẽr), *n.* [8].

in′tro-duce′ (ĭn′trŏ-dūs′),*v t.* [1] **1.** To bring into knowledge of something **2.** To bring into practice or use. **3.** To lead, bring, or usher in. **4.** To put (something into a place); insert. **5.** To open to notice , begin. **6.** To cause to be acquainted, esp. in a formal manner.

in′tro-duc′tion (-dŭk′shŭn), *n.* **1.** An introducing. **2.** a Preface. **b** Formal preliminary treatise ; guide. **3.** Act of formally making persons known to each other.   [prefatory.|

in′tro-duc′to-ry (-tŏ-rĭ),*a.* Serving to introduce;|

in′tro-spect′ (ĭn′trŏ-spĕkt′), *v. t.* To look into or within ; examine introspectively.

in′tro-spec′tion (-spĕk′shŭn), *n.* A looking in ward ; a self-examination.

in′tro-spec′tive (-spĕk′tĭv), *a.* Looking within ; seeing inwardly. — **in′tro-spec′tive-ly**, *adv.* [8]

āle, senāte, câre, ăm, ȧccount, ärm, ȧsk, sofȧ; ēve, ĕvent, ĕnd, recĕnt, makẽr; īce, ĭll; ōld, ōbey, ôrb, ŏdd, sŏft cȯnnect, ūse, ŭnite, ûrn, ŭp, circŭs; fōͦd, fŏŏt; out, oil,

in-trude' (ĭn-trōōd'), v. t. [1] To thrust or force in or on ; esp., to force (one's self) in without leave or welcome. — **in-trud'er** (-trōōd'ẽr), n. [8]. — v. i. To thrust one's self in ; trespass.

in-tru'sion (ĭn-trōō'zhŭn), n. Act of intruding ; esp., act of forcing one's self in without right.

in-tru'sive (-sĭv), a. [4] 1. Apt to intrude. 2. Intruded, or thrust in, as a foreign element. — **-ly**, adv. [8] — **-ness**, n. [8].

in-trust' (-trŭst'), v. t. To confer a trust on ; esp., to deliver something in trust to (another).

in'tu-i'tion (ĭn'tū-ĭsh'ŭn), n. 1. Knowledge obtained without conscious reasoning ; ready insight. 2. Anything known by intuition.

in'tu-i'tion-al (-ăl),a. Pertaining to, derived from, or perceived by, intuition; intuitive.—-**ly**,adv. [8].

in-tu'i-tive (ĭn-tū'ĭ-tĭv),a. [4] Perceiving, or perceived by, intuition. — **-ly**, adv. [8] — **-ness**, n. [8]. [overflow ; flood.

in'un-date (ĭn'ŭn-dāt; ĭn-ŭn'dāt), v. t. [1] To inundate ; overflow ; flood.

in'un-da'tion (ĭn'ŭn-dā'shŭn), n. An inundating; state of being inundated ; overflow ; flood.

in-ure' (ĭn-ūr'), v. t. [1] To accustom ; harden.

in-vade' (ĭn-vād'), v. t. [1] 1. To enter for conquest or plunder. 2. To infringe ; encroach on. — **in-vad'er** (-vād'ẽr), n. [8].

in'va-lid (ĭn'vȧ-lĭd), n. A person weak and infirm, esp. one in chronic ill health.— a. 1. Not well; infirm. 2. Adapted for a sick person. — v.t. To classify or enroll, or dismiss from duty, as an invalid.

in-val'id (ĭn-văl'ĭd), a. [4] Not valid; of no force or cogency ; void ; null. [or null.

in-val'i-date (-ĭ-dāt), v.t. [1] To render invalid.

in-val'i-da'tion (-dā'shŭn), n. Act of invalidating.

in'va-lid'i-ty (ĭn'vȧ-lĭd'ĭ-tĭ), n. Want of validity.

in-val'u-a-ble (ĭn-văl'ū-ȧ-b'l), a. [4] Valuable beyond estimation ; inestimable ; precious. — **in-val'u-a-bly** (-blĭ), adv. [8].

in-va'ri-a-bil'i-ty (ĭn-vā'rĭ-ȧ-bĭl'ĭ-tĭ), n. Fact or quality of being invariable ; uniformity.

in-va'ri-a-ble (ĭn-vā'rĭ-ȧ-b'l), a. [4] Not variable; uniform. — **-ness**, n. [8] — **-a-bly**, adv. [8].

in-va'sion (ĭn-vā'zhŭn), n. 1. Act of invading. 2. The first attack of anything hurtful.

in-vec'tive (-vĕk'tĭv), n. [4] A violent attack with words ; hence, a severe or railing expression.

in-veigh' (ĭn-vā'), v. i. To declaim or rail ; use invectives; — with against. — **in-veigh'er**, n. [8].

in-vei'gle (-vē'g'l), v. t. [1] To lead astray as if blind ; entice ; insnare. — **in-vei'gler** (-glẽr), n.

in-vent' (-vĕnt'), v. t. 1. To frame by thought or imagination ; devise; contrive; as, to invent a yarn. 2. To discover, as by study or inquiry ; devise.

in-ven'tion (-vĕn'shŭn), n. 1. Act of inventing; esp., construction of something new. 2. That which is invented; as: **a** A contrivance. **b** A fiction ; falsehood. 3. Faculty of inventing.

in-ven'tive (-tĭv), a. [4] Able and apt to invent; ingenious; original. — **-ly**, adv. [8] — **-ness**, n. [8].

in-ven'tor (-tẽr), n. One who invents ; contriver.

in'ven-to-ry (ĭn'vĕn-tō-rĭ), n. ; pl. **-ries** (-rĭz). An itemized list of goods with their estimated worth. — v. t. [2] To make an inventory of.

in-verse' (ĭn-vûrs'; ĭn'vûrs), a. Opposite in order or effect; reversed ; inverted. — n. That which is inverse. — **-ly**, adv. [8].

in-ver'sion (ĭn-vûr'shŭn), n. Act of inverting; thing inverted.

in-vert' (-vûrt'), v. t. To turn upside down; reverse the position, order, or meaning of. ·

in-ver'te-brate (-vûr'tē-brȧt), a. Having no backbone.— n. An invertebrate animal.

in-vest' (-vĕst'), v. t. 1. To clothe or endow, as with office ; place in possession of rank, dignity, or estate. 2. To clothe, dress, or array. 3. Mil. To besiege. 4. To lay out (money) in business or other investment. — v.i. To make an investment.

in-ves'ti-gate (-vĕs'tĭ-gāt), v.t. [1] To follow up by inquiry or observation. — v. i. To make investigation. — **in-ves'ti-ga'tor** (-gā'tẽr), n. [8].

in-ves'ti-ga'tion (-gā'shŭn), n. Act or process of investigating. [2. Vestment.

in-ves'ti-ture (-vĕs'tĭ-tūr),n. 1. Act of investing.

in-vest'ment (-vĕst'mĕnt), n. 1. Act of investing. 2. A vestment. 3. The laying out of money for income or profit; the amount of money invested, or that in which money is invested.

in-ves'tor (-vĕs'tẽr), n. One who invests.

in-vet'er-a-cy (ĭn-vĕt'ẽr-ȧ-sĭ), n. State or quality of being inveterate.

in-vet'er-ate (-ȧt), a. [4] 1. Established by long continuance. 2. Confirmed ; habitual.

in-vid'i-ous (-vĭd'ĭ-ŭs), a. [4] Tending to excite ill will or envy; likely to give offense; unjustly discriminating. — **-ly**, adv. [8] — **-ness**, n. [8].

in-vig'or-ate (-vĭg'ŏr-āt), v. t. [1] To give vigor or life and energy to; refresh; animate.

in-vig'or-a'tion (-ā'shŭn), n. Act of invigorating.

in-vin'ci-bil'i-ty (ĭn-vĭn'sĭ-bĭl'ĭ-tĭ), n. Quality or state of being invincible.

in-vin'ci-ble (-vĭn'sĭ-b'l), a. [4] Incapable of being conquered ; insuperable. — **in-vin'ci-bly**, adv. [8]. [being inviolable.

in-vi'o-la-bil'i-ty (-vī'ŏ-lȧ-bĭl'ĭ-tĭ), n. Quality of

in-vi'o-la-ble (-vī'ŏ-lȧ-b'l), a. [4] Not violable ; not susceptible of hurt or harm ; sacred ; holy.

in-vi'o-late (-lȧt), a. 1. Not violated ; uninjured; unbroken. 2. Not profaned ; pure.

in-vis'i-bil'i-ty (-vĭz'ĭ-bĭl'ĭ-tĭ), n. State or quality of being invisible.

in-vis'i-ble (-vĭz'ĭ-b'l), a. [4] Not visible ; incapable of being seen. — n. An invisible person or thing; esp. (with the), God or the unseen world. — -**ness**, n. [8] — **in-vis'i-bly**, adv. [8].

in'vi-ta'tion (ĭn'vĭ-tā'shŭn), n. Act of inviting ; also, the expression by which one is invited.

in-vite' (-vīt'), v. t. [1] 1. To ask graciously to do or forbear some act. 2. To attract; tempt. 3. To give occasion for, or opening to. — **in-vit'er** (-vīt'ẽr), n. [8] — **in-vit'ing-ly**, adv. [8].

in'vo-ca'tion (ĭn'vŏ-kā'shŭn), n. 1. Act of invoking ; esp., prayer to a divine being. 2. Act of, or formula for, conjuring evil spirits.

in'voice (ĭn'vois), n. 1. A priced list of merchandise sent to a purchaser, consignee, etc. 2. The lot or set of goods as shipped or received. — v. t. [1] To make an invoice of ; insert in a priced list.

in-voke' (ĭn-vōk'), v. t. [1] 1. To call on for aid or protection; invite earnestly, as in prayer. 2. To call forth or upon by incantation ; conjure.

in-vol'u-cel (-vŏl'ŭ-sĕl), n. A secondary or small involucre.

---

chair ; go ; sing, iŋk ; then, thin ; nature, verdure ; yet ; zh = z in azure. Numbers refer to §§ in the Special Notes which, with Abbreviations, Signs, etc., precede the Vocabulary.

in′vo-lu′cre (ĭn′vŏ-lū′kẽr), *n. Bot.* In seed plants, a whorl or rosette of leaves, subtending or supporting a flower cluster or fruit. — **in′vo-lu′cral** (-lū′krăl), *a.*

Compound Umbel. *a* Involucre; *b b* Involucels.

in-vol′un-ta-ry (ĭn-vŏl′ŭn-tă-rĭ), *a.* [4] **1.** Not voluntary; not done willingly or by choice; unintentional. **2.** Designating, or concerned in, bodily action which is independent of the will. — **-ta-ri-ly,** *adv.* [8].

in′vo-lute (ĭn′vŏ-lūt), *a.* [4] **1.** Rolled inward, as a leaf, at the margin. **2.** Spiral.

in′vo-lu′tion (-lū′shŭn), *n.* **1.** Act of involving. **2.** That which is involved. **3.** Complication; entanglement; hence, something entangled.

in-volve′ (ĭn-vŏlv′), *v. t.* [1] **1.** To roll about, or infold, so as to conceal or obscure; envelop. **2.** To entwine; implicate; embarrass. **3.** To complicate, as in grammatical structure. **4.** To include or contain; imply. **5.** To occupy or absorb.

in-volve′ment, *n.* Act or process of involving; fact or state of being involved; embarrassment.

in-vul′ner-a-bil′i-ty (ĭn-vŭl′nẽr-à-bĭl′ĭ-tĭ), *n.* Quality or state of being invulnerable.

in-vul′ner-a-ble (ĭn-vŭl′nẽr-à-b′l), *a.* Not vulnerable. — **in-vul′ner-a-bly,** *adv.* [8].

in′ward (ĭn′wẽrd), **in′wards** (ĭn′wẽrdz), *adv.* **1.** Toward the interior. **2.** Into, or toward, the mind or thoughts; inwardly.

in′ward, *a.* [4] **1.** Being or placed within; inner. **2.** In the mind, heart, or soul; mental; spiritual. **3.** Proceeding inward.

in′ward-ly, *adv.* **1.** In the inner part or parts; internally. **2.** In spirit; secretly. **3.** Toward the center; inward.

in′ward-ness, *n.* **1.** Internal or true state; intrinsic nature. **2.** Quality or state of being inward or internal. **3.** Earnestness; spirituality.

in′wards (ĭn′wẽrdz), *adv.* Inward.

in-weave′ (ĭn-wēv′), *v. t.* [1] To weave in or together; interlace. [volve; infold.|

in-wrap′ (-răp′), *v. t.* To cover by wrapping; in-

in-wrought′ (ĭn-rŏt′; ĭn′rŏt′), *p. a.* Wrought or adorned; worked into any fabric.

i′o-dide (ī′ŏ-dīd; -dĭd), *n.* A compound of iodine with another element or radical.

i′o-dine (ī′ŏ-dīn; -dĭn), *n. Chem.* An element isolated as a shining, blackish gray, crystalline solid of chlorinelike odor.

i-o′do-form (ī-ō′dŏ-fôrm; ĭ-ŏd′ŏ-), *n.* A crystalline, volatile antiseptic, of pungent odor.

i′on (ī′ŏn), *n.* One of the electrically charged particles produced by the breaking up of some of the molecules of a gas or a substance in solution. Some of these particles bear a positive charge and some a negative charge. The process by which they are produced is called **i′on-i-za′tion** (-ī-zā′shŭn), *n.*

i-o′ta (ī-ō′tà), *n.* A very small quantity; jot.

ip′e-cac (ĭp′ē-kăk), *n.* A tropical South American creeping plant; also, the root, tincture, or extract, of this plant, used as an emetic.

i-ras′ci-bil′i-ty (ĭ-răs′ĭ-bĭl′ĭ-tĭ; ĭ-răs′-), *n.* Quality or state of being irascible.

i-ras′ci-ble (ĭ-răs′ĭ-b′l; ĭ-răs′-), *a.* [4] Hot-tempered; irritable. — **i-ras′ci-bly,** *adv.* [8].

i-rate′ (ī-rāt′; ī′rāt), *a.* [4] Angry; incensed.

ire (īr), *n.* Anger; wrath.

ire′ful (īr′fŏŏl), *a.* [4] Full of ire; irascible.

ir′i-des′cence (ĭr′ĭ-dĕs′ĕns), *n.* A rainbowlike play of colors, as in a soap bubble.

ir′i-des′cent (-ĕnt), *a.* [4] Having colors like the rainbow; prismatic; as, *iridescent* glass.

i-rid′i-um (ī-rĭd′ĭ-ŭm), *n. Chem.* A rare metal, resembling platinum, but harder, and brittle. It is an element and is one of the heaviest substances known.

i′ris (ī′rĭs), *n.; pl.* E. IRISES (-ĕs), L. IRIDES (Yr′ĭ-dēz; ĭ′rĭ-). **1.** The colored portion of the eye, surrounding the pupil. **2.** *Bot.* Any of a large genus (*Iris*) of plants, having large showy flowers; the fleur-de-lis.

I′rish (ī′rĭsh), *a.* Of, pertaining to, or characteristic of, Ireland or its inhabitants. — *n.* **1.** *Collective pl.* Natives or inhabitants of Ireland or their immediate descendants. **2.** The Irish language. [Irish birth.|

I′rish-man (-măn), *n.; pl.* -MEN (-mĕn). A man of

irk (ûrk), *v. t.* To weary or trouble; annoy; bore; — now chiefly impersonally with *it;* as, it *irks* me.

irk′some (-sŭm), *a.* [4] Wearisome; tedious. — **-ly,** *adv.* [8] — **-ness,** *n.* [8].

i′ron (ī′ŭrn), *n.* **1.** The commonest and most useful of the metals, malleable and ductile, strongly attracted by magnets, and readily oxidized (rusted) in moist air. **2.** An instrument, utensil, appliance, etc., of iron; as: **a** A harpoon. **b** A flatiron, etc. **c** *pl.* Iron fetters; handcuffs. — *a.* **1.** Of, or made of, iron. **2.** Like, or suggestive of, iron. — *v. t.* **1.** To furnish, arm, or cover with iron. **2.** To shackle with irons; fetter; handcuff. **3.** To smooth with an iron instrument, esp. a hot flatiron.

i′ron-clad′ (-klăd′), *a.* [4] Clad in iron; *Colloq.,* rigorous; exacting; as, an *ironclad* oath. — *n.* An ironclad or armored naval vessel. *Hist.*

i-ron′i-cal (ī-rŏn′ĭ-kăl), *a.* [4] Also **i-ron′ic** (-ĭk). **1.** Marked by irony. **2.** Given to the use of irony. — **-ly,** *adv.* [8] — **-ness,** *n.* [8].

i′ron-ware′ (ī′ŭrn-wâr′), *n.* Articles of iron.

i′ron-wood′ (-wŏŏd′), *n.* Any of certain trees with unusually hard wood; also, the wood itself.

i′ron-work′ (-wûrk′), *n.* **1.** Work in iron. **2.** [*pl.,* sometimes construed as *sing.*] A place where iron is smelted or is made into heavy work.

i′ro-ny (ī′rŏ-nĭ), *n.* **1. a** A sort of humor in which the intended meaning is the opposite of the literal sense of the words. **b** An ironical expression.

ir-ra′di-ate (ĭ-rā′dĭ-āt), *v. t.* [1] To throw rays of light on; illuminate. — *v. i.* To emit rays; be radiant; shine. — (-āt), *a.* Illuminated; irradiated.

ir-ra′di-a′tion (-ā′shŭn), *n.* An irradiating.

ir-ra′tion-al (ī-răsh′ŭn-ăl), *a.* [4] Not rational; as: **a** Not endowed with reason. **b** Not according to reason; absurd. — **ir-ra′tion-al-ly,** *adv.* [8].

ir-ra-tion-al′i-ty (-ăl′ĭ-tĭ), *n.* Quality or state of being irrational.

ir′re-claim′a-ble (ĭr′ē-klām′à-b′l), *a.* [4] Incapable of being reclaimed. — **-a-bly,** *adv.* [8].

ir-rec′on-cil′a-bil′i-ty (ĭr-rĕk′ăn-sĭl′ȧ-bĭl′ĭ-tĭ), n. Quality or state of being irreconcilable.

ir-rec′on-cil′a-ble (-sĭl′ȧ-b'l), a. [4] Not reconcilable; implacable; incompatible. — n. One that is irreconcilable. **—ness,** n. [8] **— -a-bly,** adv. [8].

ir′re-cov′er-a-ble (ĭr′ē-kŭv′ẽr-ȧ-b'l), a. Not capable of being recovered or rectified; irreparable; irretrievable. — **ir′re-cov′er-a-bly,** adv. [8].

ir′re-deem′a-ble (-dēm′ȧ-b'l), a. **1.** Not redeemable; esp., not convertible into specie at the holder's pleasure; — of paper money. **2.** Hopeless.

ir′re-du′ci-ble (-dū′sĭ-b'l), a. Not reducible.

ir-ref′ra-ga-ble (ĭ-rĕf′rȧ-gȧ-b'l),a. Not refragable; unanswerable; undeniable. — **-ga-bly,** adv. [8].

ir′re-fut′a-ble (ĭr′ē-fūt′ȧ-b'l; ĭ-rĕf′ū-tȧ-b'l), a. [4] Not to be refuted. — **-a-bly,** adv. [8].

ir-reg′u-lar (ĭ-rĕg′ū-lȧr), a. [4] Not regular; not straight; not uniform. — **-ly,** adv. [8].

ir-reg′u-lar′i-ty (-lăr′ĭ-tĭ), n. ; pl. -TIES (-tĭz). **1.** Quality or state of being irregular; that which is irregular. **2.** A breach of law, order, etc.

ir-rel′e-vance (ĭ-rĕl′ē-văns),**ir-rel′e-van-cy** (ĭ-rĕl′ē-văn-sĭ),n.; pl.-VANCES(-văn-sĕz),-VANCIES(-sĭz). Want of relevancy; also, that which is irrelevant.

ir-rel′e-vant (-ē-vănt), a. [4] Not relevant; not to the purpose; extraneous. — **-ly,** adv. [8].

ir′re-li′gion (ĭr′ē-lĭj′ŭn), n. State of being irreligious; want of religion; impiety.

ir′re-li′gious (-ŭs), a. [4] **1.** Destitute of religion; ungodly. **2.** Profane. **—-ly,** adv.

ir′re-me′di-a-ble (ĭr′ē-mē′dĭ-ȧ-b'l), a. Not remediable, incurable. — **ir′re-me′di-a-bly,** adv.

ir-rep′a-ra-ble (ĭ-rĕp′ȧ-rȧ-b'l), a. Not reparable; irretrievable, irremediable. — **-bly,** adv. [8].

ir′re-press′i-ble (ĭr′ē-prĕs′ĭ-b'l), a. [4] Not capable of being repressed or restrained. — **ir′re-press′i-bly,** adv. [8].

ir′re-proach′a-ble (-prōch′ȧ-b'l), a. Not reproachable; blameless. — **-ness,** n. [8] **—-a-bly,** adv. [8].

ir′re-sist′i-ble (-zĭs′tĭ-b'l), a. [4] That cannot be successfully resisted. — **ir′re-sist′i-bly,** adv. [8].

ir-res′o-lute (ĭ-rĕz′ō-lūt), a. [4] Not resolute; vacillating. — **-ly,** adv. [8] **— -ness,** n. [8].

ir-res′o-lu′tion (-lū′shŭn), n. Want of resolution.

ir′re-spec′tive (ĭr′ē-spĕk′tĭv), a. [4] Disregarding particular persons, conditions, etc. — **-ly,** adv.

ir′re-spir′a-ble (-spīr′ȧ-ble ; ĭ-rĕs′pĭ-rȧ-b'l), a. Unfit for respiration.

ir′re-spon′si-bil′i-ty (-spŏn′sĭ-bĭl′ĭ-tĭ), n. Want of responsibility. [sponsible.

ir′re-spon′si-ble (-spŏn′sĭ-b'l), a. [4] Not responsible.

ir′re-triev′a-ble (-trēv′ȧ-b'l),a. Not retrievable; irrecoverable. — **ir′re-triev′a-bly,** adv. [8].

ir-rev′er-ence (ĭ-rĕv′ẽr-ĕns), n. Want of reverence; an irreverent act or utterance.

ir-rev′er-ent (ĭ-rĕv′ẽr-ĕnt), a. [4] Not reverent; expressive of a want of veneration. — **-ly,** adv.

ir′re-vers′i-ble (ĭr′ē-vûr′sĭ-b'l), a. [4] Incapable of being reversed. — **-i-bly,** adv. [8].

ir-rev′o-ca-bil′i-ty (ĭ-rĕv′ō-kȧ-bĭl′ĭ-tĭ), n. Quality of being irrevocable.

ir-rev′o-ca-ble (ĭ-rĕv′ō-kȧ-b'l), a. [4] That cannot be revoked; unalterable. **—-bly,** adv. [8].

ir′ri-gate (ĭr′ĭ-gāt), v. t. & i. [1] To supply (land) with water by canals, etc., for nourishing plants.

ir′ri-ga′tion (-gā′shŭn), n. Act of irrigating.

ir′ri-ta-bil′i-ty (ĭr′ĭ-tȧ-bĭl′ĭ-tĭ),n.; pl.-TIES (-tĭz). Quality or state of being irritable.

ir′ri-ta-ble (ĭr′ĭ-tȧ-b'l), a. [4] Capable of being irritated. — **ir′ri-ta-bly,** adv. [8].

ir′ri-tant (-tănt), a. [4] Irritating. — n. That which irritates or excites or produces irritation.

ir′ri-tate (-tāt), v. t. [1] **1.** To excite impatience, anger, or displeasure in. **2.** To excite heat and redness in, as the skin ; bring into an abnormally excited state ; as, to irritate a wound, the nerves.

ir′ri-ta′tion (-tā′shŭn), n. An irritating; state of being irritated. [or irritate.

ir′ri-ta-tive (ĭr′ĭ-tȧ-tĭv), a. [4] Serving to excite

ir-rup′tion (ĭ-rŭp′shŭn), n. **1.** A bursting in. **2.** A sudden and violent inroad.

ir-rup′tive (-tĭv), a. [4] Rushing in or upon.

is (ĭz), v. i. 3d person sing. pres. indicative of BE.

i′sin-glass (ī′zĭn-glȧs), n. **1.** A very pure gelatin, chiefly from sturgeons' air bladders. **2.** Mica, esp. in thin sheets.

Is′lam (ĭs′lăm ; ĭz′- ; ĭs-läm′), n. **1.** Mohammedanism. **2.** The whole body of Mohammedans.

Is′lam-ism (-ĭz'm), n. Mohammedanism.

is′land (ī′lănd), n. **1.** A tract of land surrounded by water, and smaller than a continent. **2.** Something suggestive of an island in position. — v. t. To cause to become an island or like an island ; insulate. [of an island.

is′land-er (ī′lăn-dẽr), n. A native or inhabitant

isle (īl), n. An island; now, usually, a small island. Chiefly Poetic.— v. t. [1] To island.

is′let (ī′lĕt), n. A little island.

i′so-late (ī′sō-lāt; ĭs′ō-), v. t. [1] **1.** To place by itself ; insulate. **2.** In chemistry, to separate from all foreign substances.

i′so-la′tion (-lā′shŭn), n. Act of isolating, or state of being isolated : insulation ; loneliness.

i-sos′ce-les (ī-sŏs′ē-lēz), a. Geom. Having two equal sides ; — said of a triangle.

i′so-therm (ī′sō-thûrm), n. A line joining points on the earth's surface having the same temperature at a given time, or for a given period.

i′so-ther′mal (-thûr′măl), a. Having equal temperature ; of or pertaining to isotherms.

Is′ra-el-ite (ĭz′rȧ-ĕl-īt), n. A Hebrew ; Jew. — **Is′ra-el-it′ish** (-īt′ĭsh, a. [8].

is′su-ance (ĭsh′ū-ăns), n. Act of issuing.

is′sue (-ū), n. **1.** A passing or flowing out; egress; exit. **2.** Progeny ; offspring. **3.** That which issues; outcome; result. **4.** A point in debate ; the point at which a matter is ready for, or admits of, decision. **5.** Act of sending out ; delivery ; issuance. **6.** That which is issued, or sent out ; the quantity sent forth. — at, or in, issue, in controversy; in question. — v. i. **1.** To go, pass, or flow, out. **2.** To come out; sally forth. **3.** To proceed as from a source; be derived ; result ; end. **4.** To be given or sent out officially or publicly. — v. t. **1.** To send or let out; emit. **2.** To deliver, or give out. **3.** To send out officially . publish.

isth′mi-an (ĭs′mĭ-ăn), a. Of or pert. to an isthmus, as [cap.] the Isthmus of Panama.

isth′mus (-mŭs), n. A strip of land connecting two larger portions of land.

it (ĭt), pron. The neuter pronoun of the third person, corresponding to he and she, and having the

same plural (*they, their* or *theirs, them*). *It* is used:
1. As a substitute for any neuter noun or noun phrase in the nominative or the objective case. **2.** As a demonstrative; as, *it* is I; what is *it?* **3.** As an indefinite nominative ; as, *it* snows. **4.** As an indefinite object ; as, to foot *it* (i. e., to walk).

I-tal′ian (Ĭ-tăl′yăn), *a.* Of or pertaining to Italy or its people or their language. — *n.* **1.** A native of Italy. **2.** The language of the Italians.

I-tal′ic (-ĭk), *a.* **1.** Of or pertaining to Italy, esp. ancient Italy. **2.** [*l. c.*] Designating type in which the letters slope toward the right, as in *these words.* — *n.* [*l. c.*] An italic letter, character, or type, or such letters, etc., collectively.

i-tal′i-cize (-Ĭ-sīz), *v. t. & i.* [1] To print in italics ; use italics.

itch (Ĭch), *v. i.* **1.** To have an uneasy sensation in the skin, which inclines one to scratch the part affected. **2.** To have a constant desire; long. — *n.* **1.** An itching, contagious eruption of the skin; sensation in the skin due to the eruption, or a similar sensation. **2.** A constant irritating desire.

itch′y (Ĭch′Ĭ), *a.* [3] Having the itch, or an itching sensation ; of the nature of the itch.

i′tem (ī′tĕm), *adv.* Also;— introducing something additional or new. — *n.* **1.** An article ; separate particular ; detail. **2.** A separate piece of news ; a paragraph. [particulars.]

i′tem-ize (-īz), *v t.* [1] To state in items, or by

it′er-ate (Ĭt′ĕr-āt), *v. t.* [1] To repeat.

it′er-a′tion (-ā′shŭn), *n.* Repetition.

it′er-a-tive (Ĭt′ĕr-ă-tĬv), *a.* Repeating; repeated.

i-tin′er-a-cy (ī-tĬn′ĕr-ȧ-sĬ), *n.* Itinerancy (sense 1).

i-tin′er-an-cy (-ăn-sĬ), *n.* **1.** Act of itinerating ; state of being itinerant. **2.** A discharge of official duty involving frequent change of residence.

i-tin′er-ant (-ănt), *a.* [4] Traveling about a country ; going or preaching on a circuit ; wandering.

i-tin′er-a-ry (-ă-rĬ), *a.* **1.** Of or pert. to a journey or route. **2.** Itinerant. — *n.; pl.* -RIES (-rĬz). **1.** A route. **2.** Account of travels. **3.** Guidebook.

i-tin′er-ate (-āt), *v. i.* [1] To travel about or on a circuit, esp. to preach, lecture, etc.

its (Ĭts), *pron. & a.* Possessive case or possessive adjective of *it ;* of or belonging to it.

it′s (Ĭts). Contraction of *it is.*

it-self′ (Ĭt-sĕlf′), *pron.* An emphasized or reflexive form for the pronoun *it.*

I′ve (īv). Colloq. for *I have.*

i′vied (ī′vĬd), *a.* Overgrown with ivy.

i′vo-ry (ī′vō-rĬ), *n.; pl.* -RIES (-rĬz). **1.** The hard, creamy-white material composing the tusks of elephants; also, the similar material of tusks of other large mammals. **2.** Any article of ivory. **3.** An ivorylike substance.

i′vy (ī′vĬ), *n. ; pl.* IVIES (ī′vĬz). **1.** A well-known evergreen climbing shrub. **2.** Any of various plants more or less like the true ivy.

Ivy.

iz′zard (Ĭz′ȧrd), *n.* The letter *z.*

J

jab (jăb), *v. t. & i. ;* JABBED (jăbd) ; JAB′BING. To thrust abruptly with something sharp. — *n.* A jabbing. *Both Colloq.*

jab′ber (jăb′ĕr), *v. i. & t.* To talk rapidly, indistinctly, or unintelligibly; chatter. — *n.* A jabbering; gibberish ; chatter. — **jab′ber-er,** *n.* [8].

ja′bot′ (zhȧ′bō′), *n.* A trimming, as a ruffle on a shirt front, or lace for a dress front.

Jack (jăk), *n.* **1.** [*cap.*] A nickname for *John.* **2.** [*Often cap.*] A sailor. *Colloq.* **3.** *Playing Cards.* Any of the four knaves. **4 a** A contrivance to turn a spit. **b** A portable machine for exerting great force through a small distance. **5.** *Naval.* A small flag used as a signal, usually the same as the union (and called more fully *union jack*). — *v. t.* To move or lift by or as by a jack or jacks — usually with *up.*

jack′al (-ôl), *n.* Any of several wild dogs of the Old World.

American Jack.

jack′a-napes′ (-ȧ-nāps′), *n.* A coxcomb.

jack′ass′ (jăk′ăs′), *n.* **1.** A male ass ; a donkey. **2.** A blockhead ; ass. [crow family.]

jack′daw′ (jăk′dô′), *n.* A European bird of the

jack′et (jăk′ĕt), *n.* **1.** A short coat without skirts, usually with sleeves. **2.** Any of various coverings

or casings, esp. one to prevent heat radiation, as from a steam pipe. — *v. t.* To put a jacket on.

jack′knife′ (jăk′nīf′), *n.; pl.* JACKKNIVES. A large, strong pocket knife.

jack′-o′-lan′tern, *n.* **1.** An ignis fatuus. **2.** A lantern made of a pumpkin, or the like, so as to show features of a human face.

jack rabbit. Any of several large hares of western North America, with large ears and long hind legs.

jack′stone′ (-stōn′), *n.* One of the pieces used in playing a certain game; also, *pl.*, the game.

jack′straw′ (-strô′), *n.* One of a set of strips, as of wood, used in a certain game; also, *pl.*, the game.

Jac′o-bite (-ō-bīt), *n. Eng. Hist.* A partisan or adherent of James II. or of his descendants.

jade (jād), *n.* A compact stone, commonly green, capable of a fine polish.

jade, *n.* **1.** A horse; esp., a mean, vicious, or worn-out horse. **2.** A woman ; a disreputable woman. — *v. t. & i.* [1] To tire or wear out.

jae′ger (yā′gĕr ; jā′gĕr), *n.* Any of several rapacious, gull-like birds.

jag (jăg), *n.* A sharp projecting part; tooth; barb.

jag′ged (jăg′ĕd), *p. a.* [4] Having sharp notches; sharply pointed. — **-ly,** *adv.* — **-ness,** *n.*

jag′uar (jăg′wär; jȧ-gwär′), *n.* A large feline animal, ranging from Texas to Paraguay. It is marked with black spots.

jail (jāl), *n.* A prison, esp. one for persons held for

minor offenses or pending judicial proceedings.
— *v. t.* To confine in a jail. [criminal.|

jail′bird′ (-bûrd′), *n.* A prisoner in jail; a habitual

jail′er, *n.* Also **jail′or.** The keeper of a jail.

jam (jăm), *v. t.; * JAMMED (jămd) ; JAM′MING. **1.** To press closely or tightly; crowd; wedge in. **2.** To crush or bruise.—*v. i.* To become wedged or fixed; stick fast. — *n.* Act of jamming ; state of being jammed ; a crush. [with sugar.|

jam, *n.* A thick preserve made of fruit boiled

jamb (jăm), *n.* An upright piece forming the side of an opening, as a doorway.

jan′gle (jăŋ′g′l), *v. i.* [1] **1.** To talk idly ; chatter; gossip. **2.** To quarrel, wrangle. **3.** To sound discordantly, as bells out of tune. — *v. t.* To cause to jangle. — *n.* Act or sound of jangling.

jan′i-tor (jăn′ĭ-tẽr), *n.* **1.** A porter. **2.** One having the care of a building, offices, apartments, etc. — **jan′i-tress** (-trĕs), *n. fem.* [8].

Jan′u-a-ry (jăn′ū-ā-rĭ), *n.* The first month of the year, having 31 days.

ja-pan′ (já-păn′), *n.* **1.** A brilliant hard varnish or lacquer. **2.** Work varnished and figured in the Japanese manner. — *v. t.; * -PANNED (já-pănd′) ; -PAN′- NING. To cover with japan, or the like ; lacquer.

Jap′a-nese′ (jăp′á-nēz′ ; -nēs′), *a.* Of or pertaining to Japan, its inhabitants, or their language. — *n.* A native or inhabitant of Japan ; also, the language of the Japanese.

jar (jär), *n.* A deep, broad-mouthed vessel of earthenware or glass.

jar, *v. i.; * JARRED (järd) ; JAR′RING. **1.** To sound harshly; be discordant. **2.** To make a jarring sound, esp. by shaking; shake violently. **3.** To have a discordant effect. To clash; quarrel. — *v. t.* **1.** To cause to shake, esp. discordantly. **2.** To shock. — *n.* **1.** A harshly discordant sound; a shaking or vibration. **2.** A painful effect, as of discord; a shock. **3.** Clash, as of opinions; dispute.

‖ **jar′di-nière′** (zhär′dē′nyâr′), *n.* [F.] An ornamental stand or receptacle for plants, etc.

jar′gon (jär′gŏn), *n.* Unintelligible language.

jas′mine (jăs′mĭn), *n.* Any of various shrubby plants, bearing flowers, usually white or yellow, with a peculiar fragrance.

jas′per (jăs′pẽr), *n.* An impure quartz, of dull red, yellow, and other colors, used for vases, seals, etc.

jaun′dice (jän′dĭs; jôn′-), *n. Med.* A disease characterized by yellowness of the eyes, skin, etc. — *v. t.* [1] To affect with jaundice; make envious.

jaunt (jänt; jônt), *v. i.* To ramble, esp. for pleasure; stroll. — *n.* A short excursion for pleasure.

jaun′ty (jän′tĭ; jôn′-), *a.* [3] Having an air of easy unconcern or sprightliness. — **jaun′ti-ly** (-tĭ-lĭ), *adv.* [8] — **jaun′ti-ness,** *n.* [8].

jave′lin (jăv′lĭn; jăv′ē-), *n.* A kind of light spear.

jaw (jô), *n.* **1.** Either of the two parts of the face (upper and lower) that border the mouth and serve to open and close it. **2.** *pl.* Fig.: Mouth or entrance; as, the *jaws* of death. **3.** Something more or less suggestive of an animal's jaw.

jay (jā), *n.* A European bird allied to the magpies ; also, any of numerous related birds.

jazz (jăz), *n.* **a** A recent type of American music, esp. for dances, developed from ragtime. **b** A dance to jazz music. — *a.* Of or pertaining to jazz.

jeal′ous (jĕl′ŭs), *a.* **1.** Watchful in care; anxious. **2.** Disposed to suspect rivalry in matters of interest or affection. **3.** Demanding exclusive devotion.

jeal′ous-y (-ĭ), *n.; pl.* -OUSIES (-ĭz). Quality of being jealous. [*pl.*, a garment of it.|

jean (jēn ; jān), *n.* A kind of twilled cotton cloth;

jeer (jēr), *v. i. & t.* To utter, or to treat with, scoffing remarks ; taunt. — *n.* A jeering utterance.

Je-ho′vah (jĕ-hō′vá), *n.* God.

je-june′ (jĕ-jōōn′), *a.* [3] Void of interest; dry.

je-ju′num (-jōō′nŭm), *n.* The division of the small intestine between the duodenum and ileum.

jel′ly (jĕl′ĭ), *n. ; pl.* -LIES (-ĭz). A food preparation of a soft consistency due to its containing gelatin; similar preparation or substance. — *v. i. & t.* [2] To come, or to bring, to the consistency of jelly.

jel′ly-fish′ (-fĭsh′), *n.* Any of various marine invertebrates having a jellylike body.

jen′net (jĕn′ĕt), *n.* A small Spanish horse.

jeop′ard (jĕp′ẽrd), *v. t.* To jeopardize.

jeop′ard-ize (-är-dīz), *v. t.* [1] To expose to loss or injury ; risk ; jeopard.

jeop′ard-y (-dĭ), *n.* **1.** Hazard ; danger. **2.** *Law.* The danger that an accused person is subjected to when put on trial for a crime.

jerk (jûrk), *v. t. & i.* **1.** To give a short sharp thrust, push, pull, or twist. **2.** To throw with a short quick motion. — *n.* A sharp, suddenly arrested motion. [in the sun.|

jerk, *v. t.* To cut (meat) into long strips and dry

jer′kin (jûr′kĭn), *n.* A kind of jacket. *Now Dial.*

jerk′y (jûr′kĭ), *a.* [3] Moving by jerks and starts. — **jerk′i-ly,** *adv.* [8].

jer′sey (jûr′zĭ), *n.; pl.* -SEYS (-zĭz). A kind of knitted jacket ; hence, a close-fitting jacket or upper garment of an elastic fabric.

Jerusalem artichoke. = ARTICHOKE, 2.

jes′sa-mine (jĕs′á-mĭn), *n.* Var. of JASMINE.

jest (jĕst), *n.* **1.** A jeer; taunt; thing said or done in banter or raillery ; sport. **2.** Laughing-stock. — *v. i.* To joke ; make light of anything.

jest′er, *n.* **1.** A court "fool." **2.** One who jests.

jest′ing, *n.* Joking; pleasantry. — *p. a.* Sportive.

Je′sus (jē′zŭs), *n. Bible.* The son of Mary, and founder of the Christian religion. Cf. CHRIST.

jet (jĕt), *n.* **1.** A velvet-black mineral of the nature of coal, susceptible of a good polish. **2.** Velvet black. — *a.* **1.** Made of jet. **2.** Black as jet.

jet, *v. i.; * JET′TED ; JET′TING. To spout out in a stream ; spurt. — *n.* A spurt ; sudden gush.

jet′sam (jĕt′săm), *n.* Goods cast overboard to lighten a vessel in distress ; esp., such goods when washed ashore.

jet′ty (-ĭ), *n.; pl.* -TIES (-ĭz). **1.** A structure, as of wood or stone, extended into a sea, lake, etc., to influence the current or tide or to protect a harbor. **2.** A landing wharf or pier.

jet′ty, *a.* [3] Made of jet ; like jet in color.

Jew (jū ; jōō), *n.* A person of the Hebrew race, or one whose religion is Judaism.

jew′el (jū′ĕl ; jōō′ĕl), *n.* **1.** An ornament of gold, silver, or the like. **2.** A precious stone ; gem. **3.** An object of special affection; a precious thing. — *v. t.* [7] To adorn or furnish with jewels. [jewels or jewelry.|

jew′el-er (jū′ĕl-ẽr), *n.* A maker of, or a dealer in,

jew'el-ry (jū'ĕl-rĭ), *n.* Art or trade of the jeweler, also, jewels collectively.

Jew'ess (jū'ĕs), *n.* A female Jew.

Jew'ish, *a.* Of or pertaining to the Jews or Hebrews ; Hebrew.

jew's'–harp, *or* **jews'–harp**, *n.* A lyre-shaped instrument which, when held between the teeth, gives tones from a bent metal tongue struck by the finger.

jib (jĭb), *n. Naut.* A triangular sail, set forward of the foremast.

jib, *v. i.* Of an animal in harness, to move restively backward or sidewise ; refuse to go ; balk.

jibe(jīb),*v. i.* [1] To agree; harmonize. *Colloq., U. S.*

jif'fy (jĭf'ĭ), *n.* A moment ; instant. *Colloq.*

jig (jĭg), *n.* A brisk dance movement or a dance to it. — *v. t.* To sing, play, or dance as a jig. — *v. i.* **1.** To dance a jig. **2.** To move jerkily.

jig'ger (jĭg'ĕr), *n.* Any of certain mites which burrow under the skin. *Southern U. S.*

jilt (jĭlt), *n.* A woman who capriciously casts off a lover. — *v. t.* To cast off capriciously, as a lover.

Jim'son weed (jĭm's'n). A tall weed with white trumpet-shaped flowers. Cf. DATURA.

jin'gle (jĭŋ'g'l), *v. i. & t.* [1] **1.** To sound with clinking or tinkling sounds, as coins ; tinkle. **2.** To rime with a jingling effect. — *n.* **1.** A clinking or tinkling sound. **2.** A catchy repetition or correspondence of sounds in verse, or the verse itself.

jin'go (jĭŋ'gō), *n.; pl.* -GOES (-gōz). One who boastfully favors an aggressive foreign policy. — *a.* Of or pertaining to jingoes. — **jin'go-ism** (-ĭz'm), *n.*

jin-ni', jin-nee' (jĭ-nē'), *n.; pl.* JINN (jĭn). In Mohammedan belief, one of a class of supernatural beings, subject to magic control.

jin-rik'i-sha (jĭn-rĭk'ĭ-shä), *n.* Also **jin-rick'sha**. A small two-wheeled hooded Oriental vehicle drawn by a man or men.

jit'ney (jĭt'nĭ), *n.; pl.* -NEYS (-nĭz). **1.** Five cents; a "nickel." *Slang.* **2.** An automobile vehicle carrying passengers for (usu.) a five-cent fare. *Colloq.*

job (jŏb), *n.* **1.** A piece of work ; esp., any definite piece of work. **2.** A corrupt piece of official business. **3.** A situation or employment. *Colloq.* — *v. t.* To buy and sell as a broker or middleman. — *v. i.* **1.** To do odd pieces of work for hire; work by the piece. **2.** To do business as a jobber, or middleman.

job'ber (jŏb'ĕr), *n.* **1.** A worker by the job or on job work. **2.** A middleman.

job'ber-y (-ĭ), *n.* The conduct of a public office or trust for private gain ; official corruption.

jock'ey (jŏk'ĭ), *n.; pl.* -EYS (-ĭz). A professional rider of race horses. — *v. t.* **1.** To cheat. **2.** To treat or manipulate trickily. — *v. i.* To cheat; also, to maneuver skillfully for a legitimate advantage.

jo-cose' (jŏ-kōs'), *a.* [4] Given to jesting ; merry. — **-ly,** *adv.* [8] — **-ness, jo-cos'i-ty** (-kŏs'ĭ-tĭ), *n.*

joc'u-lar (jŏk'ū-lẽr), *a.* [4] **1.** Given to jesting; acting in jest. **2.** Said or done in joke; sportive. — **joc'-u-lar'i-ty** (-lăr'ĭ-tĭ), *n.* — **joc'u-lar-ly,** *adv.* [8].

joc'und (jŏk'ŭnd), *a.* [4] Feeling, or characteristic of, mirth ; merry ; gay. — **-ly,** *adv.* [8].

jog (jŏg), *v. t.* JOGGED (jŏgd) ; JOG'GING (jŏg'ĭng). **1.** To push, jostle, or nudge, esp. in order to rouse, warn, etc. **2.** To remind; call the attention of.

— *v. i.* To move by jogs or jolts, like those of a slow trot. — *n.* **1.** A slight shake; push ; jolt. **2.** A slow, steady walk, trot, etc. **3.** Any irregularity of line or surface, as in a wall.

jog'gle (-'l), *v. t. & i.* [1] To shake slightly; jog.

jog trot. A slow, regular, jolting gait; hence, a routine habit ; a slow, easy-going way.

John Bull. The English personified, or a typical Englishman.

john'ny-cake (jŏn'ĭ-kāk'), *n.* A kind of bread made of Indian corn meal, flour, eggs, milk, etc. *U. S.*

join (join), *v. t.* **1.** To unite; connect; couple; combine. **2.** a To associate one's self with; unite with. **b** To unite in marriage. **3.** To engage in. — *v. i.* To come together so as to be united.

join'er (-ẽr), *n.* **1.** One that joins. **2.** A mechanic who does the woodwork (as doors, stairs, etc.) necessary for the finishing of buildings.

join'er-y (-ĭ), *n.* Art, trade, or work of a joiner.

joint (joint), *n.* **1.** The part where two bones of an animal's body are joined, esp. so as to admit of motion. **2.** The place or part where two things or parts are joined. **3.** A part connected with another part by a joint (def. 1 & 2). **4.** Any large piece of meat as cut for roasting. — *a.* **1.** Combined; as, during their *joint* lives. **2.** Involving the united activity of, or shared by or affecting, two or more; as, *joint* action or ownership. — *v. t.* **1.** To unite by a joint or joints; fit together. **2.** To provide with a joint or joints; articulate. **3.** To disjoint.

joint'ly, *adv.* Together; unitedly; not separately.

joist (joist), *n.* Any of the small timbers laid horizontally in a building, to support the flooring, etc.

joke (jōk), *n.* **1.** Something witty or sportive; jest; witticism. **2.** A laughing stock. — *v. t.* [1] To make merry with ; make jokes on ; banter. — *v. i.* To do something as a joke.

jok'er (jōk'ẽr), *n.* **1.** One who jokes ; a jester. **2.** *Card Playing.* A card sometimes added to the pack, counting as a trump, usually the highest.

jol'li-fi-ca'tion (jŏl'ĭ-fĭ-kā'shŭn), *n.* A merry-making. *Colloq.*

jol'li-ty (jŏl'ĭ-tĭ), *n.; pl.* -TIES (-tĭz). State of being jolly.

jol'ly (jŏl'ĭ), *a.* [3] **1.** In high spirits; joyful; as, *jolly* over his good fortune. **2.** Full of life and mirth ; jovial ; merry. **3.** Expressing or inspiring mirth and gayety.

jol'ly–boat', *n.* A ship's boat of medium size.

jolt (jōlt), *v. i. & t.* To shake with short, abrupt risings and fallings, as a carriage on rough ground. — *n.* A sudden shock or jerk. — **-er,** *n.* [8].

jon'quil (jŏn'kwĭl; jŭn'-), *n.* A species of narcissus, with yellow or white fragrant flowers.

joss (jŏs), *n.* A Chinese household divinity ; Chinese idol.

joss stick. A reed covered with a paste, or a cylinder of the paste, burned as incense, etc.

Jonquil.

jos'tle (jŏs''l), *v. t. & i.* [1] To run against and shake; crowd against. — *n.* A crowding or bumping together, as in passing.

jot (jŏt), *n.* An iota; a point; tittle. — *v.t.; * JOT'TED, -TING. To set down; note.

jounce (jouns), *v. t. & i.* [1] To jolt; shake, esp. by rough riding or driving. — *n.* A jolt; shake.

jour'nal (jûr'năl), *n.* **1.** A diary; an account of daily transactions and events, as a daybook or a log book. **2.** A daily newspaper; hence, a periodical magazine. **3.** That portion of a rotating shaft, spindle, etc., that turns in a bearing.

jour'nal-ism (-ĭz'm), *n.* The business or profession of publishing, editing, or writing for, journals or newspapers. [nalism.]

jour'nal-ist (-ĭst), *n.* One whose profession is journal-

jour'nal-ize (-īz), *v. t.* [1] To enter or record in a journal, or book of records.

jour'ney (-nĭ), *n.; pl.* -NEYS (-nĭz). Travel or passage from one place to another. — *v. i.* To travel; go on a journey.

jour'ney-man (-măn), *n.; pl.* -MEN (-měn). One who has learned a trade and works, esp. by the day, for another.

joust (jŭst; jōost), *joust'er.* See 2d JUST, etc.

jo'vi-al (jō'vĭ-ăl), *a.* [4] Joyous; jolly; merry. — **al'i-ty** (-ăl'ĭ-tĭ), *n.* — **al-ly**, *adv.* [8].

jowl (jōl), *n.* A jaw, esp. under jaw. **2.** Cheek.

joy (joi), *n.* **1.** The emotion excited by acquisition or expectation of good; gladness; delight; happiness. **2.** That which causes joy. — *v. i.* To rejoice; be glad; exult. — *v. t.* To gladden.

joy'ful (joi'fŏŏl), *a.* [4] Full of joy; causing joy. — **joy'ful-ly**, *adv.* [8] — **joy'ful-ness**, *n.* [8].

joy'less, *a.* [4] Not having or causing joy; unenjoyable. — **ly**, *adv.* [8] — **ness**, *n.* [8].

joy'ous (-ŭs), *a.* [4] Glad; joyful; affording or inspiring joy. — **ly**, *adv.* [8] — **ness**, *n.* [8].

ju'bi-lant (jōō'bĭ-lănt), *a.* [4] Shouting with joy; exulting. [shouting ; exultation.]

ju'bi-la'tion (jōō'bĭ-lā'shŭn), *n.* A triumphant

ju'bi-lee (jōō'bĭ-lē), *n.* **1.** The 50th (usually) anniversary of an event, or its commemoration. **2.** A season or occasion of general joy. **3.** Jubilation.

Ju'da-ism (jōō'dá-ĭz'm), *n.* The religious doctrines and rites of the Jews.

judge (jŭj), *n.* **1.** The presiding officer, or magistrate, in a court of justice, who hears cases and decides questions in law. **2.** *pl.* [*cap.*] The seventh book of the Old Testament, called in full the Book of Judges. **3.** An umpire. **4.** One who has skill to decide on the merits or value of something; a connoisseur; critic. — *v. t. & i.* [1] **1.** To hear and determine as a judge; pass judgment on; also, to decree. **2.** To sit in judgment on; criticize. **3.** To determine by exercise of the judgment; esteem; think. — **judg'er** (jŭj'ēr), *n.* [8] — **judge'ship,** *n.*

judg'ment, judge'ment (jŭj'měnt), *n.* **1.** The pronouncing of a formal opinion or decision; opinion or decision given. **2.** *Law.* **a** Act of determining, as in courts, what is conformable to law and justice ; the decree or sentence of a court. **b** The obligation, esp. a debt, created by decree of court. **3.** A calamity regarded as sent by God. **4.** An opinion; estimate; decision. **5.** Power or faculty of judging wisely; good sense.

judgment, *or* **judgement, day.** [*Often caps.*] *Theol.* The day of God's or Christ's final judgment of mankind; doomsday.

ju'di-ca-to-ry (jōō'dĭ-ká-tō-rĭ), *n.; pl.* -RIES (-rĭz). **1.** A court of justice; tribunal. **2.** Administration of justice.

ju'di-ca-ture (-tŭr), *n.* **1.** The administration of justice. **2.** A court of justice; judges collectively. **3.** Right of judicial action; jurisdiction.

ju-di'cial (jōō-dĭsh'ăl), *a.* [4] **1.** Of or pertaining or appropriate to the administration of justice, courts of justice, or a judge thereof. **2.** Sanctioned, ordered, or enforced by a court. **3.** Fitted for judging or deciding. — **ju-di'cial-ly**, *adv.* [8].

ju-di'ci-a-ry (-ĭ-ă-rĭ), *a.* [4] Of or pertaining to courts, judges, or judicial procedure; judicial. — *n.* That branch of government in which judicial power is vested; courts or the judges collectively.

ju-di'cious (-ŭs), *a.* [4] Directed by sound judgment; wise; discreet; discerning. — **ly**, *adv.* [8] — **ness**, *n.* [8].

jug (jŭg), *n.* A pitcher or ewer; a deep vessel with a narrow mouth, and a handle on one side.

jug'gle (-'l), *v. i.* [1] **1.** To perform the tricks of a juggler. **2.** To practice artifice or imposture. — *v. t.* To perform juggling tricks with ; as, to *juggle* knives. — *n.* **1.** An act or piece of juggling. **2.** An imposture; deception.

jug'gler (-lẽr), *n.* **1.** One skilled in sleight of hand, or in feats of dexterity. **2.** Deceiver; trickster.

jug'gler-y (-ĭ), *n.; pl.* -GLERIES (-ĭz). **1.** Art or act of a juggler; sleight of hand. **2.** Trickery.

Ju'go-slav', *or* **Ju'go-Slav'** (yōō'gō-släv'), *n. & a.* See YUGOSLAV. — **slav'i-an** (-släv'ĭ-ăn), **-slav'ic** (-ĭk).

ju'gu-lar (jōō'gŭ-lár), *a.* Of or pertaining to the throat or neck. — *n.* Short for **jugular vein,** one of the large veins in the neck.

juice (jōōs), *n.* **1.** The fluid contents of plant or animal substance; *pl.*, all the fluids in the animal body. **2.** Any liquid extracted from a body.

juic'y (jōōs'ĭ), *a.* [3] Abounding with juice ; succulent. — **juic'i-ness** (-ĭ-něs), *n.* [8].

ju'jube (jōō'jōōb), *n.* **1.** The fruit of any of several trees of the Mediterranean region. **2.** A lozenge flavored with, or in imitation of, the jujube.

ju'jut'su (jōō'jōōt'sōō), *n.* The Japanese art of self-defense without weapons.

ju'lep (jōō'lĕp), *n.* A drink flavored with aromatic herbs ; as, a mint *julep.*

Ju-ly' (jōō-lī'), *n.; pl.* -LIES (-līz'). The seventh month of the year, having 31 days.

jum'ble (jŭm'b'l), *v. t. & i.* [1] To mix confusedly. — *n.* **1.** A mixture. **2.** A small sugared cake.

jump (jŭmp), *v. i.* **1.** To spring free from the ground; bound; leap. **2.** To pass abruptly as if by a leap. — *v. t.* **1.** To pass over or across by a spring or leap. **2.** To cause to jump. **3.** To seize suddenly or fraudulently, as a mining claim. — *n.* **1.** Act of jumping; leap; bound. **2.** Space cleared by a leap. **3.** A sudden involuntary movement; a start. — **jump'er,** *n.* [8].

jump'er (jŭm'pẽr), *n.* A loose outer jacket.

junc'tion (jŭnk'shŭn), *n.* **1.** Act of joining; state of being joined ; union ; coalition. **2.** Place or point of meeting, as of railroad lines.

---

chair; go; sing, iŋk; then, thin; nature, verdure; yet; zh = z in azure. Numbers refer to §§ in the Special Notes which, with Abbreviations, Signs, etc., precede the Vocabulary.

junc′ture (juŋk′tŭr), *n.* **1**. The line or point where, or that by which, two bodies are joined ; joint ; articulation ; seam. **2**. A point of time ; crisis.

June (jōōn), *n.*　The sixth month of the year, having thirty days.

jun′gle (jŭn′g'l), *n.*　An impenetrable thicket.

jun′ior (jōōn′yẽr), *a.* **1**. Younger. Abbr. *Jr.* or *jr.* **2**. Lower in standing or in rank ; later in office. **3**. Composed of juniors. — *n.* **1**. A younger person. **2**. One of a lower or later standing ; in American colleges and schools, one in the year next to the senior. — **jun-ior′i-ty** (jōōn-yŏr′ĭ-tĭ), *n.*

ju′ni-per (jōō′nĭ-pẽr), *n.* Any of various evergreen shrubs or small trees of the pine family.

junk (jŭŋk), *n.* *Naut.* Any of various vessels of Chinese and adjacent waters, having bluff lines, a very high poop, and an overhanging stem.

junk (jŭŋk),*n.* **1**. Pieces of old cordage used to make gaskets, mats, oakum, etc. **2**. Old metal, glass, paper, etc. **3**. Hard salted beef supplied to ships.

jun′ket (jŭn′kĕt),*n.* **1**. A cream cheese, or a dish of curds and cream, or of milk coagulated and flavored. **2**. A feast ; an outing or excursion. — *v. i. & t.* To feast; to go on or take a junket.

jun′ta (jŭn′tȧ),*n.* **1**. A council, tribunal, or committee, as in Spain, etc. **2**. A junto.

jun′to (-tō), *n.; pl.* -TOS (-tōz). A combination as for party intrigue ; faction ; clique.

Ju′pi-ter (jōō′pĭ-tẽr), *n.* *Astron.* The largest planet, and the brightest except Venus.

ju′ris-dic′tion (jōō′rĭs-dĭk′shŭn), *n.* **1**. Right or power to exercise judicial authority. **2**. Authority of a sovereign power to govern or legislate; authority. **3**. Sphere of authority.

ju′ris-pru′dence (-prōō′dĕns),*n.* **1**. The science or philosophy of law. **2**. Law, or a system of laws.

ju′rist (jōō′rĭst),*n.* One versed in the law.

ju′ror (jōō′rẽr), *n.* A member of a jury.

ju′ry (-rĭ), *n.; pl.* -RIES (-rĭz). **1**. *Law.* A body of men legally chosen to inquire into any matter of fact, and to render a verdict, according to the evidence. **2**. A committee to determine relative merit or award prizes at a competition.

ju′ry, *a.* *Naut.* For temporary use ; as, a *jury* mast.

ju′ry-man (-mȧn), *n.; pl.* -MEN (-mĕn). A juror.

just (jŭst), *a.* [3] **1**. Righteous ; violating no right or obligation ; fair ; impartial ; hence, deserved. **2**. Legally right ; lawful. **3**. Reasonable ; right ; due. — *adv.* **1**. Precisely ; exactly ; neither more nor less. **2**. Now, or but a moment ago. **3**. Barely ; only ; by a very little. **4**. Simply ; quite ; — intensive ; as, it is *just* splendid. *Colloq.*

just, *v. i.* To engage in a just ; tilt. — *n.* A combat on horseback between two knights with lances ; often, in *pl.*, a tournament. — **just′er**, *n.* [8].

jus′tice (jŭs′tĭs), *n.* **1**. Quality of being just. **2**. The principle or practice of just dealing ; rectitude. **3**. Uprightness ; fairness. **4**. The rendering to every one his due ; just treatment. **5**. Administration of law. **6**. A judge ; magistrate.

jus-ti′ci-ar (jŭs-tĭsh′ĭ-ȧr), **jus-ti′ci-ar-y** (-ȧ-rĭ),*n.* A high royal judicial officer.

jus′ti-fi′a-ble (jŭs′tĭ-fī′ȧ-b'l), *a.* [4] Capable of being justified, or shown to be just. — **jus′ti-fi′a-ble-ness**, *n.* [8] — **jus′ti-fi′a-bly**, *adv.* [8].

jus′ti-fi-ca′tion (-fĭ-kā′shŭn), *n.* A justifying ; also, that which justifies ; defense ; vindication. — **jus′ti-fi-ca-to-ry** (jŭs′tĭ-fĭ-kȧ-tō-rĭ ; jŭs-tĭf′ĭ-kȧ-tō-rĭ), *a.* [4] Tending or serving to justify.

jus′ti-fy (-fī), *v. t.* [2] **1**. To prove or show to be just; vindicate. **2**. To pronounce free from guilt or blame; exonerate. **3**. To adjust or arrange exactly.

just′ly (jŭst′lĭ), *adv.* In a just manner.

just′ness, *n.* Quality or state of being just.

jut (jŭt), *v. i.;* JUT′TED ; JUT′TING. To project beyond the main body ; protrude. — *n.* That which projects or juts ; a projection.

jute (jōōt), *n.* **1**. The glossy fiber of either of two East Indian plants, used for sacking, twine, etc. **2**. Either plant producing this fiber.

ju′ve-nile (jōō′vē-nĭl ; -nĭl), *a.* [4] **1**. Young ; youthful; immature or undeveloped. **2**. Of or pertaining to youth. — *n.* **1**. A young person or youth. **2**. A book for children.

jux′ta-po-si′tion (jŭks′tȧ-pŏ-zĭsh′ŭn), *n.* A placing or being placed side by side.

K

kai′ser (kī′zẽr), *n.* Emperor ; — a title, esp. [*cap.*] of German emperors.

kale, kail (kāl), *n.* **1**. Cole or colewort. **2**. A variety of cabbage with curled leaves.

ka-lei′do-scope (kȧ-lī′dō-skōp), *n.* An instrument containing loose pieces of colored glass, etc., and mirrors, arranged to show symmetrical forms when turned. — **ka-lei′do-scop′ic** (-skŏp′ĭk), *a.*

kal′so-mine (kăl′sŏ-mĭn). Var. of CALCIMINE.

kan′ga-roo′ (kăŋ′gȧ-rōō′), *n.; pl.* -ROOS (rōōz′). A large leaping animal of Australia, New Guinea, and adjacent islands, with very long and strong hind legs and tail, the female of which has a pouch underneath, in which the young are carried.

ka′o-lin (kā′ō-lĭn ; kä′-), *n.* A very pure white clay.

ka′ty-did′ (kā′tĭ-dĭd′), *n.* A large green insect allied to the grasshoppers.　　　　　[sealskin.]

kay′ak (kī′ăk), *n.* An Eskimo canoe, usually of

kedge (kĕj), *n.* Also **kedge anchor**. A small anchor, used in light work.

keel (kēl), *n.* **1**. A longitudinal timber (or, in an iron vessel, a combination of plates) extending along the middle of the bottom of a vessel. **2**. Something like, or suggestive of, a ship's keel. — *v. t. & i.* To turn up the keel of ; turn over.

keel′son (kĕl′sŭn),*n.* A strengthening structure in a ship above the keel and fixed to it.

keen (kēn), *a.* [3] **1**. Sharp ; having a fine edge or point. **2**. Sharply painful ; bitter ; cutting. **3**. Eager. **4**. Sharp ; acute ; — referring to sight, hearing, smell, etc. **5**. Acute of mind. — **ly**, *adv.* [8] — **ness**, *n.* [8].

keep (kēp), *v. t. ; pret. & p. p.* KEPT (kĕpt) ; *p. pr. & vb. n.* KEEP′ING. **1**. To observe (something prescribed or obligatory) ; perform, as duty ; celebrate. **2**. To preserve or maintain ; — variously, as : **a** To

āle, senâte, câre, ăm, *ă*ccount, ärm, åsk, sofȧ ; ēve, ĕvent, ēnd, recĕnt, makẽr ; īce, ĭll ; ōld, ŏbey, ôrb, ŏdd, sŏft, cŏnnect ; ūse, ūnite, ûrn, ŭp, circŭs ; fōōd, fŏŏt ; out, oil ;

preserve from danger, harm, or loss; guard. **b** To have the care of; tend. **c** To support. **d** To have in one's service. **e** To lodge or feed for pay. **f** To maintain a record of transactions, accounts, etc.; as, to *keep* books. **g** To have habitually for sale. **3.** To hold; retain; detain. **4.** To reserve; withhold; refrain from divulging. **5.** To remain or continue in; as, to *keep* one's room, etc. **6.** To conduct or carry on; manage. — *v. i.* **1.** To continue; stay. **2.** To last; endure; remain unimpaired or sweet. — *n.* **1.** Stronghold; fortress; castle; esp., the donjon of a medieval castle. **2.** Maintenance; support; as, the *keep* of a horse.

keep′er (kēp′ẽr), *n.* One that watches, guards, maintains, etc., as one in charge of a prison.

keep′ing (kēp′ĭng), *n.* **1.** Act of one who keeps; observance; custody; preservation. **2.** Maintenance; keep; support. **3.** Conformity; harmony.

keep′sake (kēp′sāk′), *n.* Something kept, or given to be kept, for the sake of the giver.

keg (kĕg), *n.* A small cask or barrel.

kelp (kĕlp), *n.* **1.** The ashes of seaweed. **2.** Any of various large brown seaweeds.

ken (kĕn), *n.* View; knowledge gained by observation; range of knowledge; as, beyond one's *ken*.

ken′nel (-ĕl), *n.* **1.** A house for a dog or dogs. Also, an establishment where dogs are bred; — often in *pl.* **2.** A pack of dogs.

kept (kĕpt), *pret. & p. p.* of KEEP.

ke·ram′ic (kē-răm′ĭk), -**ics.** Vars. of CERAMIC, etc.

ker′chief (kûr′chĭf), *n.* **1.** A cloth worn as a covering for the head. **2.** A handkerchief.

kerf (kûrf), *n.* The slit made in cutting or sawing.

ker′nel (kûr′nĕl), *n.* **1.** A whole grain or seed of a cereal, as of corn. **2.** Part of a seed within the husk, etc.; hence, the edible portion of a nut, etc. **3.** The central or vital part of anything; gist.

ker′o·sene (kĕr′ō-sēn′), *n.* An illuminating oil distilled from petroleum.

ker′sey (kûr′zĭ), *n.; pl.* -SEYS (-zĭz). A kind of woolen cloth, usually coarse and ribbed.

ker′sey·mere (-mēr), *n.* A kind of woolen cloth.

kes′trel (kĕs′trĕl), *n.* A small European falcon.

ketch (kĕch), *n. Naut.* A kind of strongly built, two-masted, fore-and-aft-rigged vessel.

ketch′up (kĕch′ŭp), *n.* Catchup.

ket′tle (kĕt′'l), *n.* A metallic vessel for boiling liquids; esp., a teakettle.

ket′tle-drum′ (-drŭm′), *n.* A drum with a hollow hemisphere of thin copper or brass for the body.

Kettledrum.

key (kē), *n.* A low island or reef.

key, *n.* **1.** An instrument to move the bolt of a lock. **2.** That which affords or prevents entrance, control, etc. Hence, that which serves to solve or explain. **3.** Something resembling a key (sense 1) in form or function; as, a watch *key*. **4.** In a piano, typewriter, etc., a lever, actuating the mechanism or regulating the action. **5.** *Music.* A system of tones based on their relation to a key-note, from which the system is named; as, the *key* of C major. **6.** Tone of voice; as, a plaintive *key*. — *v. t. Music.* To regulate the pitch of. Also fig., esp. with *up;* as, *keyed* up to a high pitch of excitement.

key′board′ (kē′bōrd′), *n.* Bank, row, or set of keys as of a piano, typewriter, linotype, etc.

keyed (kēd), *a.* **1.** Having keys, as a musical instrument. **2.** Fastened by a key or keystone. **3.** Set to a key, as a tune.

key′note′ (kē′nōt′), *n.* **1.** *Music.* The fundamental tone of a key. **2.** Fundamental fact or idea.

key′stone′ (-stōn′), *n. Arch.* The wedge-shaped piece at the center of the crown of an arch.

kha′ki (kä′kē), *a.* Dull brownish yellow or drab; — applied to cloth, originally a stout cotton cloth. — *n.* Any kind of khaki cloth or a uniform of it.

khe·dive′ (kĕ-dēv′), *n.* The title of the former Turkish viceroy in Egypt.

kick (kĭk), *v. i. & t.* **1.** To strike, thrust, or hit, with or as with the foot or feet. **2.** To object strenuously or grumblingly. **3.** Of a firearm, to recoil, or recoil against, when fired. — *n.* Act of one that kicks; esp., a blow with the foot.

kid (kĭd), *n.* **1.** A young goat. **2.** Flesh or skin of a kid; also, a thing made of such skin; as : **a** A kind of leather. **b** *pl.* Kid gloves.

kid′nap′ (kĭd′năp′), *v. t.* [7] To carry (any one) away by unlawful force.— **kid′nap′er** (-ẽr), *n.* [7].

kid′ney (kĭd′nĭ), *n.; pl.* -NEYS (-nĭz). Either of the pair of glandular organs that excrete urine.

kill (kĭl), *v. t.* **1.** To deprive of life; slay. **2.** To deprive of vital quality; destroy; neutralize. **3.** **a** To consume (time). **b** To defeat, as a bill. — **kill′er** (kĭl′ẽr), *n.*

kiln (kĭl; kĭln), *n.* A furnace or heated chamber for burning or heating something, as brick or lime.

kil′o·cy′cle (kĭl′ō-sī′k'l), *n. Radio.* Unit of frequency equal to 1000 cycles per second.

kil′o·gram (kĭl′ō-grăm), *n.* A thousand grams, equal to 2.2046 pounds avoirdupois.

kil′o·li′ter (-lē′tẽr), *n.* [6] A thousand liters, or a cubic meter.

kil′o·me′ter (-mē′tẽr), *n.* [6] One thousand meters (3,280.8 feet, 0.62137 mile).

kil′o·watt′ (-wŏt′), *n. Elec.* A unit of power equal to 1,000 watts. See WATT.

kilt (kĭlt), *n.* A kind of short plaited petticoat worn in the Scottish Highlands by men; any similar garment.

ki·mo′no (kĭ-mō′nō; *Jap.* kĭm′ō-nō), *n.; pl.* -NOS. A kind of loose Japanese gown, or one imitating it.

kin (kĭn), *n.* **1.** Relatives; kindred. **2.** Relationship; connection by birth. — *a.* [4] Kindred; related; akin.

kind (kīnd), *n.* **1.** A natural group, class, or division. **2.** A class; sort; description. — *a.* Disposed to do good; benevolent; sympathetic; gracious; as, a *kind* person; also, proceeding from, or marked by, kindness; as, a *kind* word.

kin′der·gar′ten (kĭn′dẽr-gär′t'n), *n.* A school for beginning the education of children by utilizing their normal aptitude for exercise, play, etc.

kind′-heart′ed (kīnd′här′tĕd), *a.* [7] Humane; sympathetic.

kin′dle (kĭn′d'l), *v. t.* [1] **1.** To set on fire; ignite; light. **2.** To inflame, as passions; incite. **3.** To light up as if with flame; cause to glow. — *v. i.* **1.** To take fire. **2.** To grow warm or animated. **3.** To become lighted up or glowing. — **kin′dler** (-dlẽr), *n.* [8].

kind'ly (kīnd'lĭ), *a.* [3] **1**. Humane; sympathetic; hence, benevolent; gracious. **2**. Favorable; mild; agreeable; beneficent. — *adv.* In a kind manner; affectionately with good will; agreeably; as, speak *kindly.* — **kind'li-ness** (-lĭ-nĕs), *n.* [8].

kind'ness (kīnd'nĕs), *n.* **1**. State or quality of being kind; beneficence. **2**. A kind act.

kin'dred (kĭn'drĕd), *n.* **1**. Relationship; affinity; kinship. **2**. *Collective pl.* The family or stock to which one belongs. — *a.* [4] Of the same family or race; related; cognate.

kine (kīn), *n. pl.* Cows. *Archaic or Poetic.*

kin'e-mat'ics (kĭn'ē-măt'ĭks; kī'nē-), *n.* *Physics.* Science of motions considered in themselves.

ki-net'ic (kĭ-nĕt'ĭk; kī-), *a.* *Physics.* Of, pertaining to, or due to, motion.

ki-net'ics (-ĭks), *n.* The branch of dynamics treating of the changes of motion produced by forces.

ki-ne'to-scope (kĭ-nē'tō-skōp; kī-), *n.* A machine for projecting moving pictures using a moving film carrying instantaneous views.

king (kĭng), *n.* **1**. A male sovereign; monarch. **2**. *pl.* [*cap.*] Two historical books in the Old Testament recording the reigns of Jewish kings. **3. a** *Chess.* The principal piece. **b** *Cards.* A card bearing a picture of a king. **c** *Checkers.* A man that has moved entirely across the board.

king'bird (kĭng'bûrd'), *n.* Any of several American flycatchers, noted for their pugnacity.

king'bolt (kĭng'bōlt'), *n.* A vertical bolt holding in place the forward axle of a vehicle.

king'dom (-dŭm), *n.* **1**. A state or territory subject to a king or queen; sphere of control; domain. **2**. A division of natural objects; as, the animal *kingdom.*

king'fish'er (-fĭsh'ẽr), *n.* Any of a family of birds, mostly crested, bright-colored, and having a long, stout, sharp bill.

king'ly (-lĭ), *a.* [3] Of or becoming a king; royal; sovereign; regal. — *adv.* In a kingly manner.

king'-post', *n.* *Carpentry.* An upright post connecting the apex and base of a triangular truss.

king'ship (kĭng'shĭp), *n.* **1**. State, office, or dignity of a king. **2**. Royal rule or government.

kink (kĭngk), *n.* A twist or loop in a rope, thread, etc. — *v. i.* To form a kink, as a rope or thread. — *v. t.* To cause to kink; make a kink in.

kink'y (kĭngk'ĭ), *a.* [3] Having kinks.

kins'folk' (kĭnz'fōk'), *n. pl.* Relatives; kindred.

kin'ship (kĭn'shĭp), *n.* Relationship.

kins'man (kĭnz'măn), *n.*; *pl.* -MEN. A relative. — **kins'wom'an** (-wŏom'ăn),*n.fem.*; *pl.* -WOMEN.

ki-osk' (kē-ŏsk'), *n.* **1**. A Turkish open summerhouse or pavilion. **2**. A similar structure used as a news stand, etc. [small beast.]

kip (kĭp), *n.* Hide or leather from a young or [small beast.]

kip'per (kĭp'ẽr), *v. t.* To cure, by salting, etc., and then drying or smoking; as, *kippered* herring.

kis'met (kĭs'mĕt), *n.* Fate. *Oriental.*

kiss (kĭs), *v. t. & i.* **1**. To touch or press with the lips, as a mark of greeting, forgiveness, etc. **2**. To touch gently or lightly. — *n.* **1**. A salute or caress with the lips. **2**. A gentle touch or contact. **3**. A small piece of confectionery. — **kiss'er**,*n.*[8].

kit (kĭt), *n.* **1**. A wooden vessel of various kinds. **2**. A set or collection of tools or implements.

kitch'en (kĭch'ĕn), *n.* **1**. A room appropriated to cookery. **2**. Cooking department; cuisine.

kitch'en-ette' (kĭch'ĕn-ĕt'), *n.* A room combining a very small kitchen and a pantry.

kite (kīt), *n.* **1**. Any of certain birds of the hawk family, mostly small or medium-sized, with long narrow wings. **2**. A contrivance to be flown in the air at the end of a string.

kith (kĭth), *n.* Familiar friends, neighbors, etc., collectively; by confusion, kindred or kin. *Archaic, except in kith and kin.*

kit'ten (kĭt'n), *n.* A young cat. — **-ish,** *a.* [4, 8].

klep'to-ma'ni-a (klĕp'tō-mā'nĭ-à), *n.* An insane propensity to steal.

klep'to-ma'ni-ac (-ăk),*n.*One having kleptomania.

knack (năk), *n.* **1**. A clever way of doing something; an ingenious device. **2**. Skill; dexterity.

knap'sack' (năp'săk'), *n.* A case of canvas or leather for carrying necessaries on the back.

knave (nāv), *n.* **1**. A boy or male servant or menial. *Archaic.* **2**. A tricky fellow; rogue. **3**. A playing card bearing the picture of a servant or a soldier; a jack.

knav'er-y (nāv'ẽr-ĭ), *n.*; *pl.* -ERIES (-ĭz). Practices of a knave; trickery; rascality. [—**-ness,** *n.*|

knav'ish (-ĭsh), *a.* [4] Like a knave. — **-ly,** *adv.*|

knead (nēd),*v. t.* **1**. To work and press into a mass, usually with the hands, as dough. **2**. To treat or form as by kneading.

knee (nē), *n.* **1**. The joint, or the region of the joint, in the middle part of the leg. **2**. Something suggestive of the bent knee.

knee'cap' (nē'kăp'), *n.* The patella.

kneed (nēd), *a.* Having (such) knees.

knee'–deep', *a.* Rising, or sunk, to the knees.

kneel (nēl), *v. i.*; KNELT (nĕlt) or KNEELED (nēld); KNEEL'ING. To fall or rest on the knees or a knee.

knee'pan' (nē'păn'), *n.* The patella; kneecap.

knell (nĕl), *v. i.* To summon or proclaim by or as by a knell.—*v. i.* To ring; esp., to toll at a death or a funeral. — *n.* The stroke of a bell, as at a death.

knelt (nĕlt), *pret. & p. p.* of KNEEL.

knew (nū), *pret.* of KNOW.

Knick'er-bock'er (nĭk'ẽr-bŏk'ẽr), *n.* **1**. A descendant of the old Dutch settlers of New York; hence, any New Yorker. **2**. [*l. c.*] *pl.* Short breeches gathered at the knee.

knick'knack' (-năk'), *n.* A trifle or toy.

knife (nīf), *n.*; *pl.* KNIVES (nīvz). A cutting instrument consisting of a thin blade fastened to a handle. — *v. t.* [1] To cut, stab, etc., with a knife.

knight (nīt), *n.* **1**. One devoted to the service of a lady as her attendant or champion. **2. a** In feudal times, a mounted man-at-arms; esp., one who was admitted to a special military rank and bound to chivalrous conduct. **b** In modern times, a man on whom knighthood has been conferred by a sovereign; in Great Britain, ranking next below a baronet, and having the title *Sir.* **3**. *Chess.* A certain piece usually bearing a horse's head. — *v. t.* To dub or create (one) a knight.

knight'-er'rant, *n.*; *pl.* KNIGHTS-ERRANT. A knight who traveled in search of adventures. — **knight'-er'rant-ry**, *n.*

knight'hood (nīt'hŏod), *n.* **1**. The rank or character of a knight. **2**. Body of knights.

āle, senāte, câre, ăm, ăccount, ärm, ȧsk, sofȧ; ēve, ĕvent, ĕnd, recĕnt, makẽr; īce, ĭll; ōld, ȯbey, ôrb, ŏdd, sŏft, cŏnnect; ūse, ŭnite, ûrn, ŭp, circŭs; fŏŏd, fŏŏt; out, oil;

knight'ly, *a.* [3] Of, pert. to, or becoming a knight; chivalrous.—*adv.* In a manner becoming a knight. — **-li-ness**, *n.* [8].

knit (nĭt), *v. t. ; pret. & p. p.* KNIT or KNIT'TED ; *p. pr. & vb. n.* KNIT'TING. **1.** To form, as a textile fabric, by interlacing yarn or thread in loops with needles. **2.** To bring or bind together as by knitting; unite firmly. **3.** To draw together; wrinkle. **4.** To bind by a social, legal, or similar tie ; also, to form (such a tie). — *v. i.* **1.** To weave by making knots or loops. **2.** To grow together.

knit'ting (nĭt'ĭng), *vb. n.* Action of one that knits, or the work or fabric made by one that knits.

knives (nīvz), *n., pl.* of KNIFE.

knob (nŏb), *n.* **1.** A rounded protuberance or mass; bunch; lump. **2.** A knoblike ornament or handle. **3.** A rounded hill, esp. an isolated one.

knob'by (-bĭ), *a.* [3] Abounding in knobs.

knock (nŏk), *v. i.* **1.** To strike a sharp or resounding blow, as with something hard or heavy or with the fist; rap; hit. **2.** To drive or be driven against something; collide. — *v. i.* To strike sharply or resoundingly, as with something hard or heavy ; beat ; hit. — *n.* An act of knocking; a blow ; rap.

knock'a-bout' (nŏk'ȧ-bout'), *n.* A kind of small yacht, with mainsail and jib, but no bowsprit.

knock'er (-ẽr), *n.* One that knocks; specifically, a kind of hammer hinged to a door, for knocking.

knock'-knee', *n.* A condition in which the knees touch each other in walking. — **knock'-kneed'**, *a.*

knoll (nōl), *n.* A small round hill ; mound.

knot (nŏt), *n.* **1. a** A lump or knob formed by interweaving the parts of a cord, rope, or other slender and flexible body. **b** Any tie or fastening formed with cord, rope, etc. **2.** Hence, fig.: **a** Something not easily solved ; a difficulty ; problem. **b** A bond ; tie ; specifically, the marriage tie. **3.** A bow, cockade, or epaulet. **4.** A cluster ; group. **5.** A knob ; lump ; esp., in a plant or tree, the hard lump at the point of insertion of a branch. **6.** *Naut.* **a** A division of the log line, showing the rate of a vessel's motion. **b** A unit of speed = one nautical mile (6,080.27 feet) an hour. **c** Loosely, in reference to speed, a nautical mile. — *v. t. ;* KNOT'TED ; -TING. **1.** To tie in or with, or form into, a knot. **2.** To unite closely or intricately. — *v. i.* To form knots ; tangle.

knot'ty (-ĭ), *a.* [3] **1.** Full of knots ; gnarled. **2.** Intricate; puzzling.— **knot'ti-ness** (-ĭ-nĕs), *n.*

knout (nout; nōōt), *n.* A kind of whip for flogging criminals. — *v. t.* To punish with the knout.

know (nō), *v. t.; pret.* KNEW(nū); *p. p.* KNOWN (nōn); *p. pr. & vb. n.* KNOW'ING. **1.** To perceive; recognize; recognize as distinct; distinguish. **2.** To perceive or apprehend as true; perceive with understanding and conviction. **3.** To be convinced or assured of. **4.** To have or acquire information about. **5.** To be acquainted with. **6.** To have practical knowledge or information of; be skilled in. — *v. i.* **1.** To have knowledge. **2.** To be certain or confident. — **know'er**, *n.* [8].

know'a-ble (nō'ȧ-b'l), *a.* [4] That may be known.

know'ing, *p. a.* [4] **1.** Informed; intelligent; as, a *knowing* dog. **2.** Artful; cunning; shrewd; as, a *knowing* look. — **know'ing-ly**, *adv.* [8].

knowl'edge (nŏl'ĕj), *n.* **1.** Familiarity from actual experience; practical skill. **2.** Acquaintance with fact; hence, scope of information. **3.** Act or state of knowing; clear perception of fact, truth, or duty. **4.** Enlightenment; learning.

known (nōn), *p. p.* of KNOW.

know'-noth'ing, *n.* An ignoramus.

knuck'le (nŭk'’l), *n.* **1.** A rounded prominence at a finger joint. **2.** The knee or hock joint of a quadruped, with the adjacent parts, used in cookery. **3.** Something shaped or projecting like a knuckle.— *v. i.* [1] To yield ; submit.

knurl (nûrl), *n.* A knot, knob, or nodule.

knurl'y (-lĭ), *a.* [3] Full of knurls.

ko'dak (kō'dăk), *n.* Kind of portable camera.

ko'la (kō'lȧ), *n.* The kola nut or extract from it.

kola nut. The nut of an African tree, cultivated in the West Indies and Brazil. It contains caffeine.

ko'peck (kō'pĕk), *n.* Also **ko'pek**. A small Russian copper coin, the 100th part of a ruble.

Ko-ran' (kō-rän'; kō'răn), *n.* The scriptures of the Mohammedans.

ko'sher (kō'shĕr), *a.* Ceremonially clean, according to Jewish law; — used of food, esp. meat.

ko-tow' (kō-tou'), *v. i.* Also **kow-tow'**. To kneel and knock the forehead on the ground in homage or worship. — *n.* Act of kotowing. *Both Chinese.*

kraal (kräl), *n.* **1.** A form of stockaded village of South African natives. **2.** A stockade or pen for live stock. *South Africa.*

Kriss Krin'gle (krĭs krĭn'g'l). Santa Claus.

ku'miss (kōō'mĭs), *n.* Also **ku'mys**. A fermented (or distilled) liquor made from milk.

L

L (ĕl); *pl.* L's or Ls (ĕlz). Something shaped like, or making a shape like, the letter L, esp. an extension to a main building at right angles to its length.

la (lä), *n. Music.* The sixth tone of the scale.

la'bel (lā'bĕl), *n.* A slip of silk, paper, parchment, metal, etc., affixed to anything, and indicating the contents, ownership, destination, etc. — *v. t.* [7] **1.** To affix a label to ; as, to *label* a package. **2.** To describe or designate as by a label ; tag.

la'bi-al (lā'bĭ-ăl), *a.* **1.** Of or pertaining to the lips. **2. a** Articulated mainly by the lips, as *b,*

p, m. **b** Modified by contraction of the lips, as ōō (fōōd), ō (ōld), etc. — *n.* A labial consonant.

la'bi-ate (lā'bĭ-āt), *a.* Having lips or liplike parts.

la'bi-o-den'tal (-ŏ-dĕn'tăl), *a.* Formed or articulated with the coöperation of the lips, or one lip, and the teeth, as *f* and *v.*— *n.* A labiodental consonant.

la'bor (-bẽr), *n.* [5] **1.** Toil ; exertion ; work. **2.** Hired workers, as a body or class. **3.** An act of laboring ; a work ; task. **4.** Travail ; childbirth. — *v. i.* **1.** To perform labor; work; toil. **2.** To be oppressed with difficulties or disease; move slowly, as under a burden; *Naut.,* to pitch or roll heavily.

---

chair; go; sing, iŋk; then, thin; nature, verdure; yet; zh = z in azure.   Numbers refer to §§ in the Special Notes which, with Abbreviations, Signs, etc., precede the Vocabulary.

lab'o-ra-to-ry (lăb'ŏ-rȧ-tŏ-rĭ), *n. ; pl.* -RIES (-rĭz). A place devoted to experimental study in natural science, or to testing, analyzing, or preparing drugs, chemicals, explosives, etc.

Labor Day. A legal holiday in most States of the U. S., usually the first Monday of September.

la'bored (lā'bĕrd), *p. a.* [5] Produced or done laboriously ; elaborate ; not easy or natural.

la'bor-er (-bĕr-ẽr), *n.* [5] One who labors ; esp., one who does physical labor or work that requires strength rather than skill.

la-bo'ri-ous (lȧ-bō'rĭ-ŭs), *a.* [4] **1**. Requiring labor ; toilsome. **2**. Diligent ; industrious. — **-ly,** *adv.* [8] — **-ness,** *n.* [8].

lab'y-rinth (lăb'ĭ-rĭnth), *n.* **1**. A place full of intricate passageways ; a maze. **2**. A bewildering state of things. **3**. The internal ear.

lab'y-rin'thi-an (-rĭn'thĭ-ăn), **lab'y-rin'thic** (-thĭk), *a.* [4] Labyrinthine. [tricate.]

lab'y-rin'thine (-thĭn), *a.* Like a labyrinth ; in-

lac (lăk), *n.* A resinous substance secreted by a certain scale insect. See SHELLAC, *n.*

lace (lās), *n.* **1**. A string, cord, or band, passing through holes, and used to draw and hold together opposite edges. **2**. An ornamental braid for trimming. **3**. An openwork fabric of fine threads, usually figured ; a delicate tissue of thread.— *v. t. & i.* [1] **1**. To fasten, unite, compress, adorn, or trim with or as with a lace. **2**. To beat.

lac'er-ate (lăs'ẽr-āt), *v. t.* [1] To tear ; rend ; mangle. Hence : To afflict ; harrow.

lac'er-a'tion (-ā'shŭn), *n.* **1**. Act of lacerating. **2**. A wound made by lacerating.

lach'ry-mal (lăk'rĭ-măl), *a.* Of or pert. to tears.

lach'ry-mose (-mōs), *a.* [4] Shedding tears.

lac'ing (lās'ĭng), *vb. n.* **1**. Action of one that laces. **2**. Something that laces.

lack (lăk), *n.* Deficiency ; want ; need.— *v. i.* **1**. To be wanting ; as, funds were *lacking*. **2**. To have need. — *v. t.* To be without; need.

lack'a-dai'si-cal (lăk'ȧ-dā'zĭ-kăl), *a.* [4] Affectedly languishing. — **-ly,** *adv.* — **-ness,** *n.* [8].

lack'ey (lăk'ĭ), *n. ; pl.* -EYS (-ĭz). A footman; valet.

la-con'ic (lȧ-kŏn'ĭk), *a.* [4] Expressing much in few words ; concise. — **la-con'i-cal-ly,** *adv.* [8].

lac'quer (lăk'ẽr), *n.* **1. a** A varnish consisting of a solution of shellac in alcohol. **b** Any of various varnishes with a resin as the base. **2**. A decorative article of wood coated with Japanese or other Oriental lacquer ; collectively, such work or articles.— *v. t.* To coat with lacquer ; varnish.

la-crosse' (lȧ-krŏs'), *n.* A game of ball, in which the ball is thrown, caught, and carried with long-handled rackets.

lac-ta'tion (lăk-tā'shŭn), *n.* The secretion of milk by the mammary gland ; act of giving suck.

lac'te-al (lăk'tē-ăl), *a.* **1**. Pert. to, consisting of, or like, milk ; milky. **2**. Conveying or containing chyle. — *n.* One of the lymphatics leading from the small intestine which convey chyle.

lac'tic (lăk'tĭk), *a.* Of or pertaining to milk ; as, *lactic* acid, formed in the souring of milk, etc.

lac'tose (lăk'tōs), *n.* A crystalline sugar, present in milk. Called also *milk sugar* or *sugar of milk.*

la-cu'na (lȧ-kū'nȧ), *n. ; pl.* L. -NÆ (-nē), E. -NAS (-nȧz). A blank space ; gap.

lad (lăd), *n.* A boy ; youth.

lad'der (lăd'ẽr), *n.* An appliance, consisting of two long side pieces joined at intervals by rungs, forming steps for ascent or descent.

lad'die (lăd'ĭ), *n.* A lad ; male sweetheart.

lade (lād), *v. t. ; pret.* LAD'ED (lād'ĕd); *p. p.* LAD'ED, LAD'EN (lād'n); *p. pr. & vb. n.* LAD'ING. **1**. To load ; put a burden on or in. **2**. To throw or lift in or out, with a ladle, dipper, etc. ; dip ; bail.

lad'ing (-ĭng), *n.* **1**. A loading. **2**. Load ; cargo.

la'dle (lā'd'l), *n.* A long-handled cuplike spoon or dipper used in lading or dipping. — *v. t.* [1] To take up and convey in a ladle.

la'dy (lā'dĭ), *n. ; pl.* -DIES (-dĭz). **1**. A woman having authority, of the same rank as a *lord.* **2**. A sweetheart. **3**. [*cap.*] The Virgin Mary ; — with *Our.* **4**. A woman of social distinction or position; a well-bred woman ; — the term corresponding to *gentleman.* **5**. [*cap.*] In England, a title prefixed to the names of women of certain ranks.

la'dy-bird' (-bûrd'),*n.* Also **la'dy-bug'** (-bŭg). Any of various small, often brightly colored beetles.

la'dy-like' (-līk'), *a.* [4] Like a lady.

la'dy-love' (-lŭv'), *n.* A sweetheart or mistress.

la'dy-ship (-shĭp), *n.* Rank or position of a lady; — used (when preceded by *her* or *your*) to designate or address one having the title of *Lady.*

la'dy's-slip'per (lā'dĭz-slĭp'ẽr), *n.* Also **la'dy-slip'per.** Any of various orchids, the flower of which suggests a slipper.

Lady's-slipper.

lag (lăg), *n.* A falling behind or retardation, as in a current.— *v. i. ;* LAGGED (lăgd); LAG'GING (lăg'ĭng). To move slowly; loiter.— **lag'ger,** *n.*

lager beer, *or* **lager** (lä'gẽr), *n.* A kind of beer made originally in Germany.

lag'gard (lăg'ȧrd), *a.* [4] Lagging ; loitering.— *n.* One who lags. — **-ly,** *adv.* [8].

la-goon' (lȧ-gōon'), *n.* A shallow channel or lake, esp. one near the sea.

la'ic (lā'ĭk), *n.* Layman.

laid (lād), *pret. & p. p.* of the verb LAY ; **lain** (lān), *p. p.* of the verb LIE.

lair (lâr), *n.* The bed or couch of a wild beast.

laird (lârd), *n.* A landholder. *Scot.*

la'i-ty (lā'ĭ-tĭ), *n.* **1**. The people, as distinguished from the clergy ; laymen. **2**. Those not of a certain profession.

lake (lāk), *n.* **1**. A purplish red pigment prepared from lac or cochineal ; also, the color of this pigment. **2**. Any of various related compounds.

lake, *n.* A considerable inland body of standing water ; also, an expanded part of a river.

la'ma (lä'mȧ), *n.* In Tibet, Mongolia, etc., a priest or monk of Lamaism (a form of Buddhism).

lamb (lăm), *n.* **1**. A young sheep. **2**. A person like a lamb, as in being innocent. **3**. Lamb's flesh.

lam'ben-cy (lăm'bĕn-sĭ), *n.* Quality or state of being lambent ; that which is lambent.

lam′bent (-bĕnt), *a.* [4] **1.** Playing or touching lightly, as over a surface; as, a *lambent* flame. **2.** Softly bright or radiant. — **-ly,** *adv.* [8].

lamb′kin (lăm′kĭn), *n.* A small or young lamb.

lam′bre-quin (lăm′brē-kĭn ; lăm′bĕr-), *n.* A drapery pendent from a shelf or window casing. *U. S.*

lame (lām), *a.* [3] **1.** Disabled in the leg or foot; crippled. **2.** Fig., halting; defective; as, a *lame* argument. — *v. t.* [1] To make lame; cripple. — **lame′ly,** *adv.* [8] — **lame′ness,** *n.* [8].

la-ment′ (lȧ-mĕnt′), *v. i.* To express or feel sorrow; weep; wail; mourn greatly. — *v. t.* To express deep sorrow for or about; mourn for; bewail. — *n.* **1.** Expression of grief or sorrow; lamentation. **2.** An elegy or dirge.

lam′en-ta-ble (lăm′ĕn-tȧ-b′l), *a.* [4] **1.** Mournful; expressing grief; doleful. **2.** Pitiable; deplorable. — **lam′en-ta-bly,** *adv.* [8].

lam′en-ta′tion (-tȧ′shŭn), *n.* **1.** Act of lamenting. **2.** [*cap.*] *pl.* A book of the Old Testament.

lam′i-na (lăm′ĭ-nȧ), *n. ; pl.* L. -NÆ (-nē), E. -NAS (-nȧz). A thin plate or scale ; a layer; flake.

lam′i-nar (-nȧr), *a.* Arranged in thin plates.

lam′i-nate (-nȧt), *a.* Shaped like, or made up of, a lamina or laminæ. — (-nāt), *v. t. & i.* [1] **1.** To divide into laminæ. **2.** To form, as metal, into a thin plate, as by rolling. **3.** To cover or construct with laminæ ; plate.

lam′i-na′tion (-nā′shŭn),*n.* Process of laminating; state of being laminated ; also, a lamina.

lamp (lămp), *n.* A vessel with a wick, for burning oil or the like to produce light; hence, any of various devices for producing light or heat ; as, an arc *lamp,* incandescent *lamp,* etc.

lamp′black′ (-blăk′), *n.* Fine soot from the smoke of carbonaceous substances, used as a pigment.

lam-poon′ (lăm-pōōn′), *n.* A personal satire in writing, usually malicious or abusive. — *v. t.* To make the subject of a lampoon. — **-er,** *n.* [8].

lam′prey (lăm′prĭ), *n.; pl.* -PREYS (-prĭz). Any of certain eel-like water animals having a large mouth without jaws, suited for sucking.

lance (làns), *n.* **1.** A weapon with a long shaft and a sharp steel head, carried by light cavalry. **2.** A soldier armed with a lance ; a lancer.

lance,*v. t.* [1] **1.** To pierce with or as with a lance. **2.** To open or cut with or as with a lancet.

lan′ce-o-late (lăn′sē-ō-lāt), *a.* Lance-shaped.

lanc′er (làn′sẽr), *n.* **1.** *a* One who lances. *b* A light cavalry soldier armed with the lance. **2.** *pl.* A set of quadrilles of a certain arrangement.

lan′cet (làn′sĕt), *n.* A surgical instrument, commonly pointed, used in opening abscesses, etc.

land (lănd), *n.* **1.** The solid part of the surface of the earth. **2.** Any part of the surface of the earth, as a country, estate, etc.; hence, a nation ; a people. **3.** Ground, esp. as to its situation, nature, or quality; soil. — *v. t.* **1.** To put on shore from a vessel ; disembark. **2.** To catch ; capture. **3.** To set down after conveying. — *v. i.* **1.** To disembark ; come to shore. **2.** To arrive ; alight.

lan′dau (lăn′dô ; -dou), *n.* A four-wheeled covered carriage with the top divided so that the vehicle can be used open or closed.

lan′dau-let′ (-dō-lĕt′), *n.* **1.** A small landau. **2.** An automobile with a top like that of a landau.

land′ed (lăn′dĕd), *a.* **1.** Owning land. **2.** Derived from land. [of land.|

land′hold′er (lănd′hōl′dẽr), *n.* A holder or owner

land′ing, *n.* **1.** Act of one that lands. **2.** A place for landing, as from a ship, a carriage, etc. **3.** A platform at the end of a flight of stairs.

land′la′dy (lănd′lā′dĭ), *n.; pl.* -DIES (-dĭz). **1.** A woman who has tenants. **2.** The mistress of an inn, lodging house, etc.

land′locked′ (-lŏkt′), *a.* [4] Inclosed, or nearly so, by land.

land′lord′ (-lôrd′), *n.* **1.** One who holds and lets real estate to another. **2.** Master of an inn, etc.

land′lub′ber (-lŭb′ẽr), *n.* *Naut.* A landsman ; hence, any one who is clumsy on shipboard.

land′mark′ (-märk′), *n.* **1.** A mark to designate the boundary of land. **2.** Any conspicuous object on land that serves as a guide.

land′own′er (lănd′ōn′ẽr), *n.* An owner of land.

land′scape (lănd′skāp), *n.* **1.** A portion of land comprehended in one view, esp. in its pictorial aspect. **2.** A picture representing natural scenery.

land′slide′ (-slīd′)) *n.* The slipping down of a **land′slip′** (-slĭp′)) mass of earth or rock on any steep slope ; the mass which slips down.

lands′man (lăndz′măn), *n.; pl.* -MEN (-mĕn). One who lives on the land ; — opposed to *seaman.*

land′ward (lănd′wẽrd), *adv.* Toward the land. — *a.* Lying or being toward the land.

land′wards (-wẽrdz). Var. of LANDWARD.

lane (lān),*n.* A narrow passageway or road, as between fences, hedges or buildings.

lang′syne′ (lăng′sīn′), *adv. & n.* Long since ; long ago. *Scot.*

lan′guage (lăn′gwåj), *n.* **1.** The body of words and forms of speech used by a considerable community. **2.** Any means of expressing feeling or thought. **3.** Form, manner, or style of expression, esp. verbal expression.

lan′guid (-gwĭd), *a.* [4] **1.** Drooping or flagging from exhaustion ; weak. **2.** Sluggish ; apathetic; listless. — **-ly,** *adv.* — **-ness,** *n.* [8].

lan′guish (-gwĭsh), *v. i.* **1.** To become languid ; to lose strength or animation. **2.** To droop or pine with longing.

lan′guish-ing, *p. a.* [4] **1.** Drooping ; pining, as with love or grief. **2.** Expressing sentimental feeling ; as, *languishing* eyes.

lan′guor (-gẽr ; -gwẽr), *n.* **1.** Languid state due to exhaustion. **2.** Listless indolence ; dreaminess.

lan′guor-ous (-ŭs), *a.* [4] Producing, or tending to produce, languor; characterized by languor.

lank (lăngk), *a.* [3] Slender and thin; lean; shrunken. — **lank′ness,** *n.* [8].

lank′y (-ĭ), *a.* [3] Lank. — **lank′i-ness,** *n.* [8].

lan′tern (lăn′tẽrn), *n.* **1.** Something inclosing and protecting a light, either portable or fixed. **2.** *Arch.* **a** An open structure on a roof, to give light and air to the interior. **b** A cupola or tower-like member crowning a larger one.

lan′yard (lăn′yȧrd), *n.* A short piece of rope or line, as for firing old-style cannon, etc.

lap (lăp), *n.* **1.** The loose or lower part of a coat or gown. **2.** The part of the clothing that lies on the knees, thighs, etc., as one sits; the part of the person so covered.

---

chair; go; sing, iŋk; then, thin; nature, verdure; yet; zh = z in azure. Numbers refer to §§ in the Special Notes which, with Abbreviations, Signs, etc., precede the Vocabulary.

lap (lăp), *v. t. & i. ; LAPPED* (lăpt); *LAP'PING.* **1.** To fold; bend and lay (over or on something); wrap (around something). **2.** To infold; hold as in the lap; cuddle. **3.** To lay or lie over or by the side of anything so as partly or wholly to cover it. — *n.* **1.** That part of a thing that overlaps another. **2.** One circuit around a race track.

lap, *v. i.* **1.** To take up liquid with the tongue. **2.** To make a sound as of taking up drink with the tongue. — *v. t.* **1.** To lick up with a quick motion of the tongue. **2.** Of water, to wash or splash gently. — *n.* Act or sound of lapping.

lap dog. A pet dog which may be held in the lap.

la-pel' (lá-pĕl'), *n.* That part of the front of a coat continuing the collar.   [as the lap holds.]

lap'ful (lăp'fŏŏl), *n. ; pl.* -FULS (-fŏŏlz). As much

lap'i-da-ry (lăp'ĭ-dā-rĭ), *n. ; pl.* -RIES (-rĭz). One who cuts, polishes, and engraves precious stones.

‖ **la'pis la'zu-li** (lā'pĭs lăz'ū-lī). [L.] A stone of a rich azure blue; also, its color.   [garment.]

lap'pet (lăp'ĕt), *n.* A loose fold or flap, as of a

lapse (lăps), *n.* **1.** A slip ; a fault ; a slight deviation from truth, accuracy, etc. **2.** A fall or apostasy. **3.** *Law.* The termination of a right through neglect to exercise it or failure of some contingency. **4.** A gliding ; a gradual passing. **5.** A falling into ruin or disuse, as a custom. — *v. i.* [1] **1.** To pass, fall, or slip by lapse. **2.** To fall into disuse or ruin. — **lapsed** (lăpst), *p. a.*

lap'wing' (lăp'wĭng'), *n.* An Old World plover, noted for its slow flight and wailing cry.

lar'board (lär'bōrd; -bĕrd), *n. Naut.* The port side. *Now Rare.* — **lar'board,** *a.*

lar'ce-ny (lär'sĕ-nĭ), *n.; pl.* -NIES (-nĭz). *Law.* The unlawful taking away of personal property with intent to deprive the rightful owner of it ; theft.

larch (lärch), *n.* Any of certain trees of the pine family, bearing small cones and having needlelike leaves that fall at the end of the growing season. Also, their wood.

lard (lärd), *n.* The fat of swine, esp. the fat from inside the body, melted down. — *v. t.* **1.** To enrich with bacon. **2.** To smear with lard or grease.

Branch of Larch (reduced) showing Leaves and mature Cones.

lard'er (lär'dẽr), *n.* A place where meat and other articles of food are kept.

large (lärj), *a.* [3] Having greater power, size, or the like than is usual ; big ; great. — *n.* Liberty ; freedom. *Obs.,* exc. in : **at large. a** Without restraint. **b** Of electors, representatives, etc., for the whole of a State. *U. S.* — **-ly,** *adv.* [8] — **-ness,** *n.* [8].

lar'gess (lär'jĕs), *n.* Also **lar'gesse.** Liberal giving ; a liberal gift.

‖ **lar'go** (lär'gō), *a. & adv.* [It.] *Music.* Slow or slowly ; — more so than *adagio.*

lar'i-at (lăr'ĭ-ăt), *n.* A lasso; also, a rope for picketing horses and mules.

lark (lärk), *n.* Any of various birds, as the English skylark or the American meadow lark.

lark, *v. i.* To sport; frolic. *Colloq.* — *n.* A frolic; a merry adventure. *Colloq.*

lark'spur (lärk'spûr), *n.* Any of a genus of plants, of the crowfoot family, many species of which are cultivated for their showy flowers.

lar'va (lär'vá), *n. ; L. pl.* -VÆ (-vē). *Zoöl.* The immature, wingless, often wormlike form (caterpillar, grub, etc.) in which most insects hatch from the egg. — **lar'val** (-văl), *a.*

la-ryn'ge-al (lá-rĭn'jê-ăl ; lär'ĭn-jē'ăl), *a.* Of or pertaining to, or used on, the larynx.

lar'yn-gi'tis (lär'ĭn-jī'tĭs), *n.* Inflammation of the larynx. — **lar'yn-git'ic** (-jĭt'ĭk), *a.*

lar'ynx (lär'ĭnks), *n. ; pl.* LARYNGES (lá-rĭn'jēz). The modified upper part of the trachea, or windpipe ; the organ of voice.

las-civ'i-ous (lă-sĭv'ĭ-ŭs), *a.* [4] Lewd ; lustful.

lash (lăsh), *n.* **1.** A stroke with a whip or anything pliant and tough. **2.** The thong or cord of a whip. **3.** A stroke of satire, sarcasm, or the like. **4.** An eyelash. — *v. t.* **1.** To whip ; scourge. **2.** To berate. — *v. i.* **1.** To rush ; dash. **2.** To ply the whip ; strike ; rebuke ; satirize.

lash, *v. t.* To bind with a cord, thong, or chain.

lash'ing, *n.* A cord, thong, etc., used in binding.

lass (lås), *n.* A girl ; sweetheart.

las'sie (lăs'ĭ), *n.* A lass. *Chiefly Scot.*

las'si-tude (lăs'ĭ-tūd), *n.* Debility ; weariness.

las'so (-ō), *n. ; pl.* -SOS (-ōz). A rope or long thong with a running noose, used to catch horses, etc. — *v. t.* To catch with a lasso. — **las'so-er,** *n.* [8].

last (lást), *n.* A wooden block shaped like the human foot, on which boots or shoes are formed.

last, *a.* **1.** Being or remaining after all others ; final, hindmost ; farthest. **2.** Most recent. **3.** Lowest in rank or degree. **4.** Most unlikely ; least fit. **5.** Conclusive ; final. **6.** Supreme; utmost.— *adv.* **1.** After all others ; at the end. **2.** At a time or on an occasion which is last. **3.** In conclusion. **4.** Finally; at last. — *n.* That which is last ; end.

last, *v. i.* To continue ; endure.

last'ing, *n.* **1.** Continuance; endurance. **2.** A durable woolen stuff, used for women's shoes, etc.

last'ing, *p. a.* [4] Existing or continuing a long while ; enduring. — **-ly,** *adv.* [8] — **-ness,** *n.* [8].

last'ly, *adv.* In conclusion; at last.

latch (lăch), *n.* A movable piece which holds a door or gate closed, though it be not bolted. — *v. t. & i.* To catch or fasten by means of a latch.

latch'et (lăch'ĕt), *n.* A string fastening a shoe.

late (lāt), *a. ; LATER* (lāt'ẽr), or LAT'TER (lăt'ẽr) LAT'EST (lāt'ĕst), or LAST (lást). **1.** Coming or doing after the usual or proper time; tardy. **2.** Far advanced toward the end or close. **3.** Lately deceased, or gone out of office. **4.** Recent. **5.** Continuing or doing until an advanced hour. — *adv.* **1.** After the usual, proper, or appointed time; after delay. **2.** Far in the night, day, week, etc. **3.** Not long ago. *Poetic.*

la-teen' (lá-tēn'), *a. Naut.* Designating, or pert. to, a peculiar rig common in the Mediterranean and adjacent waters. — **lateen sail,** a triangular sail extended by a long yard slung to the mast.

late'ly (lāt'lĭ), *adv.* Not long ago ; recently.

la'ten-cy (lā'tĕn-sĭ), *n.* Latent state or quality.

late'ness (lāt'nĕs), *n.* State or quality of being late.

la'tent (lā'tĕnt), *a.* [4] Not visible or apparent; hidden; concealed; dormant. — **-ly**, *adv.*

lat'er (lāt'ẽr), *a. & adv.*, *compar.* of LATE.

lat'er-al (lāt'ẽr-ăl), *a.* Of or pertaining to the side; situated at, directed toward, or coming from, the side. — **-ly**, *adv.* [8].

lat'est (lāt'ĕst), *a.* Superlative of LATE.

la'tex (lā'tĕks), *n. Bot.* A milky fluid found in certain cells, as of the milkweeds, spurges, etc.

lath (lȧth), *n.; pl.* LATHS (lȧthz). [4] A narrow strip of wood used as a groundwork to support plastering, etc. **2.** Laths collectively; lath work. — *v. t.* To cover or line with laths. — **lath'er**, *n.* [8].

lathe (lāth), *n.* A machine by which a piece of hard material is held and rotated while being shaped by a tool.

lath'er (lȧth'ẽr), *n.* **1.** Foam or froth made by agitation of a mixture of soap and water. **2.** Foam from profuse sweating. — *v. t.* To spread over with lather. — *v. i.* To form lather. — **-er**, *n.* [8].

Lat'in (lăt'ĭn), *a.* **1.** Of or pertaining to Latium, a country of ancient Italy, or its people, the Latins, or the language used by the Romans or Latins. **2.** Designating, or pertaining to, the peoples (French, Italian, Spanish, etc.) whose languages are descended from the Latin. — *n.* **1.** The language of ancient Latium and Rome. **2.** One of the people of ancient Latium or Rome.

Lat'in-ism (-ĭz'm), *n.* A Latin idiom.

Lat'in-ist, *n.* A Latin scholar.

lat'i-tude (lăt'ĭ-tūd), *n.* **1.** Freedom; independence. **2.** *Geog.* Distance, north or south, from the equator. **3.** A region or locality. **4.** *Astron.* More fully, **celestial latitude.** Angular distance of a heavenly body from the ecliptic.

lat'i-tu'di-nal (lăt'ĭ-tū'dĭ-năl), *a.* Of, pertaining to, or in the direction of, latitude.

lat'i-tu'di-na'ri-an (-nā'rĭ-ăn), *a.* [4] Tolerant of variations in opinions or doctrine, esp. in religion. — *n.* One who is broad and liberal, esp. in religious matters.

lat'ter (lăt'ẽr), *a.* **1.** More recent; later. **2.** Of two things, being the one mentioned second.

lat'ter-ly, *adv.* Lately; recently; at a later period.

lat'tice (lăt'ĭs), *n.* A kind of wood or metal network of strips; any window or gate having a lattice. — *v. t.* [1] **1.** To make a lattice of. **2.** To furnish with a lattice. [tices collectively].

lat'tice-work' (lăt'ĭs-wûrk'), *n.* A lattice, or lattices collectively.

laud (lôd), *n.* **1.** High commendation; praise. **2.** *pl.* A religious service, chiefly of praise. **3.** A hymn of praise. — *v. t.* To praise; celebrate; extol.

laud'a-bil'i-ty (lôd'á-bĭl'ĭ-tĭ), *n.* Quality of being laudable.

laud'a-ble (lôd'á-b'l), *a.* [4] Praiseworthy; commendable. — **-ness**, *n.* [8] — **-a-bly**, *adv.* [8].

lan'da-num (lô'dȧ-nŭm), *n.* Tincture of opium.

lau-da'tion (lô-dā'shŭn), *n.* Laud ; praise.

laud'a-to-ry (lôd'á-tô-rĭ), *a.* [4] Expressing praise.

laugh (lȧf), *v. i.* To show mirth, satisfaction, or derision, by laughter. — *n.* Act of laughing; the sound heard in laughing. — **laugh'er**, *n.* [8].

laugh'a-ble (lȧf'á-b'l), *a.* [4] Fitted to excite laughter. — **-ness**, *n.* — **laugh'a-bly**, *adv.* [8].

laugh'ing, *p. a.* Fit to be treated with laughter; — in phrases such as *this is no laughing matter.* —

laughing gas, nitrous oxide, used as an anæsthetic. It sometimes produces exhilaration and laughter.

laugh'ing-stock' (-stŏk'), *n.* An object of ridicule.

laugh'ter (-tẽr), *n.* The movement of the muscles of the face, esp. of the lips, with interrupted (often noisy) expulsion of air from the lungs, indicating merriment, satisfaction, or derision.

launch (länch; lônch), *v.t.* **1.** To throw, as a lance; hurl. **2.** To cause to slide into the water; set afloat. **3.** To send out; set going. — *v. i.* **1.** To move with force and swiftness; plunge. **2.** To set out, as on the sea; — often with *forth* or *out.* — *n.* **1.** Action or process of launching a vessel. **2.** *Naut.* **a** The largest boat of a ship of war. **b** Any open, or largely undecked, power boat.

laun'der (län'dẽr; lôn'-), *v. t.* To wash and iron. — **-der-er**, *n.* [8] — **-dress** (-drĕs), *n. fem.* [8].

laun'dry (-drĭ), *n.; pl.* -DRIES (-drĭz). **1.** A place where laundering is done. **2.** Articles sent to a laundry to be washed. *Colloq.*

lau're-ate (lô'rê-āt), *a.* [4] Crowned with laurel, as for poetic excellence. — *n.* One crowned with laurel ; a poet laureate. — **lau're-ate-ship'**, *n.*

lau'rel (lô'rĕl), *n.* **1.** Either of two species of trees or shrubs ; esp., the bay tree of southern Europe. Its foliage was used by the ancient Greeks as a mark of distinction. **2.** Any of various trees or shrubs resembling the true laurel. **3.** A crown of laurel ; hence, honor ; distinction ; — esp. in *pl.*

la'va (lä'vá), *n.* Fluid rock such as issues from a volcano, or such rock solidified.

lav'a-to-ry (lăv'á-tô-rĭ), *n.; pl.* -TORIES (-rĭz). **1.** A basin or other vessel for washing. **2.** A place for washing, as in hotels, schools, etc.

lave (lāv), *v. t.* [1] To wash ; bathe ; wash or flow along or against. — *v. i.* To bathe ; wash one's self.

lav'en-der (lăv'ĕn-dẽr), *n.* **1.** A European mint bearing spikes of lilac-purple flowers. **2.** The fragrant dried leaves and flowers of this plant. **3.** The color of lavender flowers.

lav'ish (lăv'ĭsh), *a.* [4] **1.** Expending or bestowing profusely; prodigal. **2.** Expended or produced profusely; excessive. — *v. t.* To squander. — **-er**, *n.* [8] — **-ly**, *adv.* [8] — **-ness**, *n.* [8].

law (lô), *n.* **1.** A binding custom or rule of conduct, or the whole body of such customs and rules; also, the regulation or state of society brought about by their enforcement. **2. a** *Legal science*: jurisprudence. **b** Trial under the laws; litigation. **c** The legal profession as a whole. **3.** In arts, works, games, etc., the rules of construction, or of procedure. **4.** *Science.* A statement of an order or relation of phenomena invariable under the given conditions.

law'ful (-fōōl), *a.* [4] **1.** Conformable to law; legitimate. **2.** Authorized or established by law. — **law'ful-ly**, *adv.* [8] — **-ness**, *n.* [8].

law'giv'er (-gĭv'ẽr), *n.* One who enacts a law.

law'less (lô'lĕs), *a.* [4] Without law; hence, not restrained or controlled by law; unruly; disorderly; licentious. — **-ly**, *adv.* [8] — **-ness**, *n.* [8].

law'mak'er (lô'māk'ẽr), *n.* A legislator; lawgiver.

lawn (lôn), *n.* A very fine linen (or sometimes cotton) fabric with a rather open texture.

lawn, *n.* Ground covered with fine grass kept closely mown.

lawn tennis. A variety of tennis, played in the open air on a court of turf or some even surface.

law'suit/ (lô'sūt/), n. A suit in law.

law'yer (lô'yẽr), n. One versed in the laws, or a practitioner of law, as an attorney, counselor, etc.

lax (lăks), a. [3] **1.** Not tense, firm, or rigid; loose; slack. **2.** Not strict or stringent; vague.

lax'a-tive (lăk'sá-tĭv), a. [4] Relieving from constipation. — n. A laxative medicine.

lax'i-ty (-sĭ-tĭ), n. State or quality of being lax.

lax'ly, adv. In a lax manner.

lax'ness, n. Laxity.

lay (lā), pret. of LIE, to recline.

lay, n. A song; a ballad.

lay, a. Of or pertaining to the laity.

lay, v. t.; LAID (lād); LAY'ING. **1.** To bring down, as with force. **2.** To calm; allay; suppress. **3.** To put or set down in a recumbent position; deposit. **4.** To bring forth and deposit (an egg or eggs). **5.** To wager; bet. **6.** To impose as a duty, burden, punishment, or the like. **7.** To impute; charge. **8.** To place; put. **9.** To coat; cover; spread. **10.** To cause to be in, or to place in, a given position or state. **11.** To present as true or valid, or for consideration; as, to lay claim. **12.** To prepare; arrange; as, to lay a table. — v. i. **1.** To lay eggs. **2.** To apply one's self vigorously; as, to lay to the oars. — n. The way in which a thing lies.

lay'er (lā'ẽr), n. **1.** One that lays. **2.** A stratum; one thickness, course, or fold. **3.** A shoot or branch of a plant, which for propagation is bent down and partly covered with earth.

lay figure. An adjustable model of the human body; hence, a mere puppet.

lay'man (lā'mán), n.; pl. -MEN (-mĕn). One of the laity; especially, one not of the clergy.

la'zar (lā'zar), n. A person, especially a beggar, infected with a pestilential disease; esp., a leper.

laz'a-ret'to (lăz'á-rĕt'ō), n.; pl. -TOS (-ōz). A hospital or pesthouse, esp. one for lazars or lepers.

la'zy (lā'zĭ), a. [3] Disinclined to action or labor; indolent; sluggish. — **la'zi-ly** (-ĭ-lĭ), adv. [8] — **la'zi-ness,** n. [8].

lea (lē), n. Pasture or grassland; meadow.

leach (lēch), v. t. **1.** To percolate (a liquid) through something, as ashes. **2.** To subject to the dissolving action of percolating liquid. **3.** To dissolve out by percolation.

lead (lĕd), n. **1.** A metallic element, heavy, pliable, and inelastic. **2.** An article of lead or an alloy of lead; as: **a** A plummet. **b** Print. A thin strip of metal to separate lines of type. **c** pl. Sheets of lead covering a roof; hence, a flat roof. Eng. **d** pl. Lead framing for panes, as in windows. **3.** A thin cylinder of graphite used in pencils. — v. t. **1.** To cover, line, or weight with lead. **2.** To fix (glass) in position with leads. **3.** Print. To place leads between the lines of.

lead (lēd), v. t.; LED (lĕd); LEAD'ING. **1.** To guide as with the hand. **2.** To show the way, esp. by going with; serve as a way for. **3.** To conduct or direct with authority. **4.** To precede and direct; to be chief among. **5.** To draw or direct by influence, good or bad; induce. **6.** To guide or constrain in a course; proceed along; pass; spend. **7.** To begin a game, round, or trick, with. — v. i.

1. To guide or conduct; be first. **2.** To be led; admit of being led. **3.** To tend or reach; take its course. — n. **1.** Action of one that leads; guidance; direction. **2.** Precedence; also, measure of precedence. **3.** Act or right of playing first in a game, round, or trick; card, suit, or piece so played. **4.** That which leads or acts as a guide. **5.** Mining. A lode.

lead'en (lĕd'n), a. [4] **1.** Made of lead; like lead. **2.** Heavy or dull; sluggish; spiritless.

lead'er (lēd'ẽr), n. One that leads; as: **1.** A guide; conductor. **2.** A chief; commander. **3.** A horse harnessed in front of others. **4.** A pipe to conduct water or other fluid. **5.** A chief article of trade, esp. one sold cheap to bring trade. **6.** A leading article. Chiefly Eng. — **lead'er-ship,** n.

lead'ing (lēd'ĭng), n. Action of one that leads; guidance. — p. a. Guiding; directing; foremost. — leading article, an editorial article of some prominence; a leader. — l. question, a question so framed as to suggest a certain answer.

leaf (lēf), n.; pl. LEAVES (lēvz). **1. a** One of the green expanded organs (foliage leaves) growing out of the stems of plants. **b** A petal; as, a rose leaf. Colloq. **2.** A part of a book or folded sheet containing two pages, one on each side. **3.** A part that slides or is hinged, as of shutters, doors, etc. **4.** A movable part of a table top. **5.** Metal or other substance in a thin sheet. — v. i. To produce leaves; leave.

leaf'age (lēf'ăj), n. Foliage.

leaf'let (lēf'lĕt), n. **1.** Bot. A division of a compound leaf. **2.** A small foliage leaf. **3.** Sheet of small pages folded, but not stitched.

Foliage Leaf.
b Blade; p Petiole, or Leafstalk; st Stipule.

leaf'stalk/ (-stôk/), n. Stem of a foliage leaf.

leaf'y (-ĭ), a. [3] Abounding in, or made of, leaves.

league (lēg), n. A measure of distance varying from 2.4 to 4.6 miles; ordinarily about 3 miles.

league, n. A covenant, as for mutual defense, etc.; also, the alliance so formed; a confederacy. — v. i. & t. [1] To unite in a league; confederate. — **lea'guer** (lē'gẽr), n. [8].

lea'guer, n. **1.** A camp, originally of a besieging army. Hist. **2.** A siege. — v. t. To besiege.

leak (lēk), n. **1.** A crack or hole which (contrary to intention) admits or lets out fluid. **2.** Act of leaking; leakage. **3.** Elec. A loss of electricity from imperfect insulation, or the point where it occurs. — v. i. To let fluid enter or escape (contrary to intention), as through a hole; also, to enter or escape in this manner, as a fluid.

leak'age (lēk'ăj), n. **1.** A leaking; a passage of fluid by a leak. **2.** That which leaks in or out.

leak'y (-ĭ), a. [3] Permitting water or other fluid to leak in or out. — **leak'i-ness** (-ĭ-nĕs), n. [8].

lean (lēn), v. i.; LEANED (lēnd), sometimes LEANT (lĕnt); LEAN'ING. **1.** To incline or bend so as to receive support. **2.** To incline or bend from the vertical. **3.** To incline in opinion or desire; tend; — with to, toward, etc. **4.** To rely for support, comfort, etc.; — with on or upon. — v. t. To cause to lean; incline; support or rest.

āle, senāte, câre, ăm, ăccount, ärm, àsk, sofȧ; ēve, ēvent, ĕnd, recĕnt, makẽr; īce, ĭll; ōld, ŏbey, ôrb, ŏdd, sŏft, cŏnnect; ūse, ŭnite, ûrn, ŭp, circŭs; fōŏd, foŏt; out, oil;

lean (lēn), *a.* **1.** Wanting flesh or fat; thin. **2.** Wanting fullness, richness, productiveness, etc.; scant. — *n.* Flesh that is chiefly muscle without fat. — **lean'ness,** *n.* [8].

lean'-to' (lēn'tōō'), *a.* Having only one slope or pitch; — of a roof. — *n.* A wing or extension with a lean-to roof.

leap (lēp), *v. i.;* LEAPED (lēpt) or, *Chiefly Poet.,* LEAPT (lĕpt); LEAP'ING (lēp'ĭng). **1.** To spring clear of the ground; jump; vault. **2.** To spring; bound; move swiftly. — *v. t.* **1.** To pass over by a leap or jump. **2.** To cause to leap. — *n.* **1.** Act of leaping; jump; spring; bound. **2.** A place that is, or must be, leaped over. — **leap'er,** *n.* [8].

leap'frog' (lēp'frŏg'), *n.* A play among boys, in which one stoops down and another leaps over him.

leapt (lĕpt), *pret. & p. p.* of LEAP. *Chiefly Poet.*

leap year. A year of 366 days. Years exactly divisible by 4, as 1912, are leap years except the last years of the centuries, as 1900, which are leap years only if exactly divisible by 400. See FEBRUARY.

learn (lûrn), *v. t.;* LEARNED (lûrnd) or LEARNT (lûrnt); LEARN'ING. **1.** To gain knowledge of, or skill in, by study or instruction; fix in the mind. **2.** To ascertain; hear. — *v. i.* To acquire knowledge or skill; receive instruction. — **learn'er,** *n.*

learn'ed (lûr'nĕd), *a.* [4] Of or pertaining to learning; marked by learning; erudite. — **-ly,** *adv.* [8].

learn'ing, *n.* Acquisition of knowledge or skill; knowledge or skill got by instruction or study.

lease (lēs), *v. t.* [1] **1.** To grant or convey by lease; let. **2.** To hold or take a lease of. — *n.* A contract by which one conveys real estate for life or for a term of years; also, the act of such conveyance or the term specified.

lease'hold' (lēs'hōld'), *n.* A tenure by lease, or the land held. — **lease'hold'er** (-hōl'dẽr), *n.* [8].

leash (lēsh), *n.* A thong or cord as for a dog. — *v. t.* To tie together or hold with a leash.

least (lēst), *a.* The superlative for *little.* Smallest, in size or degree; shortest; slightest; lowest. — *adv.* In the smallest or lowest degree.

leath'er (lĕth'ẽr), *n.* **1.** The skin of an animal tanned or otherwise dressed for use. **2.** Something made of leather.

leath'er-et (-ĕt), **leath'er-ette'** (lĕth'ẽr-ĕt'), *n.* A paper imitation of leather.

leath'ern (lĕth'ẽrn), *a.* Of or like leather.

leath'er-y (-ẽr-ĭ), *a.* Resembling leather; tough.

leave (lēv), *n.* **1.** Permission; leave of absence, as from military duty. **2.** A formal parting.

leave (lēv), *v. t.; pret. & p. p.* LEFT (lĕft); *p. pr. & vb. n.* LEAV'ING (lēv'ĭng). **1.** To allow or cause to remain; hence, to bequeath. **2.** To permit to be done, controlled, or the like, by another; hence, to commit; refer. **3.** To put, place, deposit, or the like. **4.** To withdraw or depart from. **5.** To desert; forsake; hence, relinquish. **6.** To cease from; stop. — *v. i.* To depart; set out.

leave (lēv), *v. i.* [1] To send out leaves; leaf.

leav'en (lĕv'n), *n.* **1.** Any substance used to produce fermentation; esp., a portion of fermenting dough reserved for this use; yeast. **2.** An admixture that modifies the whole. — *v. t.* **1.** To make light with leaven; cause to ferment. **2.** To mingle with a transforming element; imbue.

leaves (lēvz), *n., pl.* of LEAF.

leav'ing (lēv'ĭng), *vb. n.* Thing left; remnant; residue; — usually in *pl.*

lec'ture (lĕk'tŭr), *n.* **1.** A discourse; esp., a formal discourse for instruction. **2.** A reprimand. — *v. i.* [1] To deliver a lecture. — *v. t.* **1.** To deliver a lecture to; instruct by lectures. **2.** To reprimand. — **lec'tur-er** (-tŭr-ẽr), *n.* [8].

led (lĕd), *pret. & p. p.* of LEAD.

ledge (lĕj), *n.* **1.** A projecting ridge or raised edge; shelf. **2.** A ridge or reef of rock. **3.** A limited mass of rock bearing valuable mineral; a lode or vein.

ledg'er (lĕj'ẽr), *n. Bookkeeping.* A book in which a summary of accounts is preserved.

lee (lē), *n.* **1.** Shelter; a sheltered place, as a side protected from the wind. **2.** *Naut.* The quarter toward which the wind blows; that side, as of a ship, farthest from the point from which the wind blows. — *a. Naut.* Designating, or pertaining to, the lee, as of a ship; — opposed to *weather.* — **lee shore,** a shore on the lee side of a vessel.

leech (lēch), *n. Naut.* Either edge of a square sail; the after edge of any fore-and-aft sail.

leech, *n.* **1.** A physician or surgeon. *Archaic.* **2.** Any of numerous bloodsucking worms. **3.** One who clings to another to draw gain from him.

leek (lēk), *n.* A plant of the lily family, having a flavor resembling that of the onion, but stronger.

leer (lēr), *v. i.* To look askance or obliquely, esp. malignly. — *n.* A suggestive look of the eye.

lees (lēz), *n. pl.* Sediment, as in a cask of wine.

lee'ward (lē'wẽrd; *naut.* lū'ẽrd), *a. Naut.* Pert. to, or in the direction of, the lee. — *n.* The lee side; the lee. — *adv.* Toward the lee.

lee'way' (lē'wā'), *n.* **1.** *Naut.* The lateral drift of a ship to leeward. **2.** Margin or room for action or the like. *Colloq.*

left (lĕft), *pret. & p. p.* of LEAVE.

left, *a.* **1.** Designating, or pertaining to, that side of the body on which, in man, muscular action is generally weaker than on the other side. **2.** Situated to the left. — *n.* The part on the left side.

left'-hand', *a.* Situated on the left.

left'-hand'ed (-hăn'dĕd), *a.* [4] **1.** Having the left hand more serviceable than the right. **2.** Done, made with, or adapted to, the left hand instead of the right. **3.** Clumsy; awkward; unlucky; insincere. — **-ness,** *n.* [8].

leg (lĕg), *n.* **1.** A limb of an animal supporting the body; esp., that part of the limb between the knee and foot. **2.** Something like, or suggestive of, a leg. **3.** The part of a garment covering the leg.

leg'a-cy (lĕg'á-sĭ), *n.; pl.* -CIES (-sĭz). A gift of property, esp. personal property, by will.

le'gal (lē'găl), *a.* [4] **1.** Of, pertaining to, or based on, law. **2.** In conformity with law; lawful. — **legal tender,** money which a creditor is legally required to accept as payment. — **le'gal-ly,** *adv.* [8].

le-gal'i-ty (lē-găl'ĭ-tĭ), *n.* Conformity to law.

le'gal-ize (lē'găl-īz), *v. t.* [1] To make legal.

leg'ate (lĕg'āt), *n.* **1.** An ecclesiastic representing the Pope. **2.** Ambassador, envoy, or delegate.

leg'a-tee' (-á-tē'), *n.* One to whom a legacy is bequeathed.

le-ga'tion (lē-gā'shŭn), *n.* **1.** The commission of

one person to act for another. **2.** A delegate or envoy and his associates; embassy. **3.** The place of business or official residence of a diplomatic minister. **4.** The office and dignity of a legate.

|| **le-ga'to** (lā-gä'tō), *a. & adv.* [It.] *Music.* Connected without breaks between the tones.

leg'end (lĕj'ĕnd ; lē'jĕnd), *n.* **1.** An unauthentic story coming down from the past; a tradition. **2.** An inscription, motto, or title, as on a coin.

leg'end-a-ry (lĕj'ĕn-dä-rĭ),*a.* [4] Of or pertaining to a legend or legends.

leg'er-de-main' (-ēr-dĕ-mān'), *n.* Sleight of hand.

legged (lĕgd ; *in combination,* lĕg'ĕd or lĕgd), *a.* Having legs; as, a long-*legged* man.

leg'ging (lĕg'ĭng), *n.* Also **leg'gin.** A cover for the leg, like a long gaiter;—chiefly in *pl.*

leg'i-ble (lĕj'ĭ-b'l), *a.* [4] Capable of being read or deciphered; plain. — **leg'i-bil'i-ty** (lĕj'ĭ-bĭl'-ĭ-tĭ), **leg'i-ble-ness,** *n.* — **leg'i-bly,** *adv.* [8].

le'gion (lē'jŭn), *n.* **1.** *Roman Antiq.* A body of soldiers, varying from 3,300 to 6,000. **2.** An army. **3.** A multitude.

le'gion-a-ry (-ā-rĭ),*a.* Of or pert. to a legion.—*n.; pl.* -RIES (-rĭz.) A member of a legion.

leg'is-late (lĕj'ĭs-lāt), *v. i.* [1] To make or enact a law or laws. — *v. t.* To cause to be, become, go, pass, or the like, by legislation.

leg'is-la'tion (-lā'shŭn), *n.* Preparation and enactment of laws. Also, the laws thus enacted.

leg'is-la-tive (lĕj'ĭs-lā-tĭv), *a.* **1.** Making laws. **2.** Of or pert. to legislation or the legislature.

leg'is-la'tor (-lā'tẽr), *n.* One who makes laws for a state or community; a member of a legislature.

leg'is-la'ture (-tẙr), *n.* The body of persons in a state invested with power to make the laws.

le-git'i-ma-cy (lĕ-jĭt'ĭ-má-sĭ), *n.* State or quality of being legitimate.

le-git'i-mate (-māt), *a.* [4] **1.** Lawfully begotten. **2.** Accordant with law; lawful. **3.** Conforming to recognized principles or accepted rules or standards; logical; reasonable. — (-māt), *v. t.* [1] To make legitimate. — **-ly,** *adv.* [8].

le-git'i-ma'tion (-mā'shŭn), *n.* A making lawful.

leg'ume (lĕg'ūm ; lĕ-gūm'), *n.* **1.** The fruit or seed of a leguminous plant, as the pea, bean, etc., used for food. **2.** A leguminous plant. **3.** A pod usually opening into two parts, having seeds attached, as in the bean, pea, etc.

le-gu'mi-nous (lĕ-gū'mĭ-nŭs), *a.* Pertaining to, or of the nature of, legumes, as peas, beans, etc.

lei'sure (lē'zhẙr ; lĕzh'ẙr), *n.* Freedom from occupation or business; hence, convenience; ease. — *a.* Free; as, *leisure* hours.

lei'sure-ly, *a.* [4] Characterized by leisure; not hurried. — *adv.* In a leisurely manner. — **lei'sure-li-ness,** *n.* [8].

lem'ming (lĕm'ĭng), *n.* Any of several small [arctic rodents.

lem'on (lĕm'ŭn), *n.* **1.** A well-known, light-yellow, acid fruit related to the orange. **2.** The tree which bears this fruit. — *a.* Lemon-colored.

lem'on-ade' (-ād'), *n.* A beverage consisting of lemon juice mixed with water and sweetened.

le'mur (lē'mŭr), *n.* Any of numerous mammals allied to the monkeys, mostly native to Madagascar.

lend (lĕnd), *v. t.; pret. & p. p.* LENT (lĕnt) ; *p. pr. & vb. n.* LEND'ING. **1.** To allow the temporary use

of. **2.** To afford; grant. **3.** To devote or accommodate (one's self or itself) to. — *v. i.* To make a loan or loans. — **lend'er,** *n.* [8].

length (lĕngth), *n.* **1.** The longest, or longer, dimension of any object; extent from end to end. **2.** Extent in time, number, or quantity. **3.** Of a vowel or syllable, quantity as long or short. See LONG, *a.*, 4. **4.** A single piece or subdivision of a series. [come longer.|

length'en (lĕng'th'n), *v. t. & i.* To make or be-

length'ways' (lĕngth'wāz'), *adv.* Lengthwise.

length'wise' (lĕngth'wīz'), *adv. & a.* In the direction of the length; longitudinally.

length'y (lĕng'thĭ),*a.* [3] Having length; of discourse, long; prolix.— **-i-ly,** *adv.* — **-ness,**n. [8].

le'ni-ence (lē'nĭ-ĕns),*n.* Lenient action; clemency.

le'ni-en-cy (-ĕn-sĭ), *n.* Quality of being lenient.

le'ni-ent (lē'nĭ-ĕnt), *a.* [4] Mild; clement; merciful; not rigorous or severe.— **le'ni-ent-ly,** *adv.* [8].

len'i-tive (lĕn'ĭ-tĭv), *a.* [4] Soothing; easing.

len'i-ty (-tĭ), *n.; pl.* -TIES (-tĭz) State or quality of being lenient; also, a lenient act or action.

lens (lĕnz), *n.* **1.** **a** A piece of transparent substance having two opposite regular surfaces, both curved, or one curved and one plane, used for changing the direction of rays of light. **b** A combination of two or more simple lenses. **2.** In the eye, a transparent body of double convex form, which focuses the light rays on the retina.

Lent (lĕnt), *n.* A season of fasting, consisting of the 40 week days preceding Easter.

lent, *pret. & p. p.* of LEND.

Lent'en (lĕn't'n), *a.* [*Often l. c.*] Of or pertaining to, or suitable to, Lent.

len-tic'u-lar (lĕn-tĭk'ū-lår), *a.* [4] Resembling a lentil; of the form of a double convex lens.

len'til (lĕn'tĭl), *n.* [*Usually in pl.*] **1.** A plant of the bean family, cultivated for its flattened, lens-shaped edible seeds. **2.** A seed of this plant.

le'o-nine (lē'ō-nīn), *a.* [4] Pertaining to the lion.

leop'ard (lĕp'ẽrd), *n.* **1.** A ferocious cat of Asia and Africa;—called also *panther.* Its color is tawny or buff with black spots. **2.** The jaguar.

lep'er (lĕp'ẽr), *n.* A person affected with leprosy.

lep'ro-sy (-rō-sĭ), *n.* An infectious disease marked by affections of the skin, ulcerations, and disturbances of sensation. It is nearly always fatal.

lep'rous (-rŭs), *a.* [4] Infected with, or pertaining to, leprosy. [against the sovereign.|

lese maj'es-ty (lēz mǎj'ĕs-tĭ). *Law.* A crime

le'sion (lē'zhŭn), *n.* A hurt; injury.

less (lĕs), *a.; used as the comparative of* LITTLE. **1.** Smaller; not so great; not so much. **2.** Reduced by subtraction or omission; as, nine *less* three. — *adv.* Not so much; in a less degree. — *n.* **1.** A less amount. **2.** The inferior, younger, or smaller.

les-see' (lĕs-ē'), *n.* One to whom a lease is given.

less'en (lĕs'n), *v. t. & i.* **1.** To make or become less; reduce. **2.** To represent as less; disparage.

less'er (lĕs'ẽr), *a.* Smaller; inferior. — **Lesser Bear.** = URSA MINOR.

les'son (lĕs'n), *n.* **1.** A portion of Scripture read at divine service. **2.** A reading or exercise assigned for study. **3.** That which is learned or taught. **4.** A rebuke. — *v. t.* To teach; also, to rebuke.

les'sor (-ŏr; lĕs-ŏr'), *n.* One who leases to another.

lest (lĕst), *conj.* **1.** For fear that; that . . . not. **2.** That — after certain expressions denoting *fear* or *apprehension*.

let (lĕt), *v. t.* To hinder; impede; prevent. *Archaic.*

let, *n.* A retarding; hindrance. *Archaic*, except in *without let or hindrance.*

let, *v. t.; pret. & p. p.* LET; *p. pr. & vb. n.* LET'TING. **1.** To leave; abandon. *Archaic*, exc. with *alone* or *be.* **2.** To cause; make. *Obs.*, except in *let* (one) *know.* **3.** To permit; allow; as, *let* him go. **4.** To make escape, as a fluid; — chiefly *Obs.*, except in *to let blood*, to bleed. **5.** To lease; rent; give or assign, as a contract.

le'thal (lē'thăl), *a.* [4] Deadly; mortal; fatal.

le-thar'gic (lē-thär'jĭk), *a.* [4] Pertaining to, affected with, causing, or resembling, lethargy; dull.

leth'ar-gy (lĕth'ár-jĭ), *n.* **1.** Morbid drowsiness; profound sleep. **2.** A state of inaction or apathy.

let'ter (lĕt'ẽr), *n.* **1.** One of the characters used in writing or print to represent speech sounds. **2.** a A written or printed communication; an epistle. **b** *pl.* Literature; learning; erudition. **3.** Verbal expression; exact terms; literal statement. **4.** *Print.* A single type. — letter of credit, an order given by a banker at one place to enable a person to draw money at another place on the banker's guarantee of payment. — *v.t.* To mark with letters or words.

let'tered (-ẽrd), *p. a.* [4] **1.** Educated. **2.** Of or pertaining to learning or literature. **3.** Inscribed or marked with letters.   [letter paper.|

let'ter-head' (-ẽr-hĕd'), *n.* A heading printed on|

let'ter-ing, *n.* **1.** Act or business of making, or marking with, letters. **2.** The letters made.

let'ter-press' (-prĕs'), *n.* Print; — often used of reading matter in distinction from illustrations.

let'tuce (lĕt'ĭs), *n.* A garden plant of the chicory family, the leaves of which are used as salad.

leu'co-cyte (lū'kō-sīt), *n.* A white blood corpuscle.

Le-vant' (lē-vănt'), *n.* The countries washed by the eastern Mediterranean and adjacent waters.

Le-vant'ine (lē-văn'tĭn; lĕv'ăn-tĭn), *a.* Of or pertaining to the Levant.

lev'ee (lĕv'ĉ; lĕv-ē'), *n.* An embankment to prevent inundation; also, a landing place or quay. *Southern & Western U. S.*

lev-ee' (lĕ-vē'; lĕv'ĉ), *n.* **1.** A morning reception, esp. one held by a person of distinction. **2.** Any miscellaneous gathering of guests.

lev'el (lĕv'ĕl), *n.* **1. a** An instrument for finding, or adjusting by, a horizontal line or plane. **b** A measurement, with a level, of the difference in altitude of two points. **2.** Horizontal condition; uniform altitude. **·3.** A horizontal surface. — *a.* [3] **1.** Having no part higher than another. **2.** Horizontal. **3.** Even with anything else; of equal importance. **4.** Well-balanced; just; steady; as, a *level* head. *Colloq.* — *v. t.* [7] **1.** To make level, flat, or even. **2.** To bring to a horizontal position, as a gun; hence, to aim. **3.** To bring to a common level or plane. **4.** To bring to a lower level; overthrow; lower. **5.** *Surveying.* To find the heights of different points in (a piece of land), as with a surveyor's level. — *v. i.* **1.** To aim a gun, etc.; to direct the eye, mind, or effort to an object. **2.** To bring persons or things to a level. — **lev'el-er**, *n.* [7, 8] — **lev'el-ness**, *n.* [8].

le'ver (lē'vẽr; lĕv'ẽr), *n.* A bar used to exert force at one point of its length, by applying a force at a second point and thus turning the bar at a third (fixed) point called a *fulcrum.* — *v. t.* To raise, move, etc. with a lever.

le'ver-age (-åj), *n.* Action of a lever, or mechanical advantage gained by the lever.

le-vi'a-than (lē-vī'á-thăn), *n.* Something huge and formidable; — applied esp. to ships.

lev'i-ty (lĕv'ĭ-tĭ), *n.; pl.* -TIES (-tĭz). Lack of gravity; frivolity; flippancy.

lev'y (lĕv'ĭ), *n.* Act or process of levying or that which is levied. — *v. t.* [2] **1.** To raise or collect, as by assessment; as, to *levy* taxes or tribute. **2.** To raise or collect (as troops) for service. **3.** To wage (war). — *v. i.* To make a levy, as on property.

lewd (lūd), *a.* [3] Lustful; unchaste. — **lewd'ly**, *adv.* [8] — **lewd'ness**, *n.* [8].

lex'i-cog'ra-pher (lĕk'sĭ-kŏg'rá-fẽr),*n.* An author or compiler of a lexicon or dictionary.

lex'i-cog'ra-phy (lĕk'sĭ-kŏg'rá-fĭ), *n.* Art, process, or work of making a lexicon or dictionary. — **-co-graph'ic** (-kŏ-grăf'ĭk), **-i-cal** (-ĭ-kăl), *a.*

lex'i-con (lĕk'sĭ-kŏn), *n.* A dictionary, esp. one of Greek, Hebrew, or Latin.

li'a-bil'i-ty (lī'á-bĭl'ĭ-tĭ), *n.; pl.* -TIES (-tĭz). **1.** State or quality of being liable. **2.** That, as an obligation, for which one is liable. Specifically, *pl.*, all one's debts; — opposed to *assets.*

li'a-ble (lī'á-b'l), *a.* **1.** Bound in law or equity; responsible; answerable. **2.** Exposed to some undesirable contingency; — with *to.*

li'ar (lī'ẽr), *n.* A person who knowingly utters a falsehood; one who lies; an untruthful person.

li-ba'tion (lī-bā'shŭn),*n.* Act of pouring out a liquid, as wine, in honor of a deity; also, the liquid.

li'bel (lī'bĕl), *n.* **1.** *Law.* Any representation wrongfully published and tending to expose another to public hatred, contempt, or ridicule; also, the act of so publishing it. **2.** *Law.* In some jurisdictions, a written complaint beginning an action, and demanding relief. **3.** Any false and defamatory representation. — *v. t.* [7] To make or publish a libel against. — **li'bel-er**,*n.* [7, 8].

li'bel-ous (-ŭs), *a.* [4, 7] Including or involving a libel; defamatory. — **li'bel-ous-ly**, *adv.* [7,8].

lib'er-al (lĭb'ẽr-ăl), *a.* [4] **1.** Not servile or mean; esp., not narrowly restricted. **2.** Bestowing, or bestowed, in a large and noble way; generous; ample. **3.** Not strict or rigorous; free, as a translation. **4.** Broad-minded, not bigoted; independent in opinion; not conservative. — liberal arts, the branches of learning including the sciences, philosophy, history, etc. See ART, *n.*, 3. Hence, master of *arts* ; bachelor of *arts*, etc. — *n.* One who is liberal or favors liberality. — **-al-ly**, *adv.*

lib'er-al-ism (-ĭz'm), *n.* Liberal principles.

lib'er-al'i-ty (lĭb'ẽr-ăl'ĭ-tĭ), *n.; pl.* -TIES (-tĭz). Quality or state of being liberal.

lib'er-ate (-āt), *v. t.* [1] **1.** To release from restraint; free. **2.** To free from combination, as gases. — **lib'er-a'tor** (lĭb'ẽr-ā'tẽr), *n.* [8].

lib'er-a'tion (-ā'shŭn), *n.* A liberating; state of being liberated.

lib'er-tine (lĭb'ẽr-tĭn), *n.* A rake. — *a.* [4] Dissolute; profligate. — **lib'er-tin-ism** (-ĭz'm), *n.*

lib'er-ty (lĭb'ẽr-tĭ), *n. ; pl.* **-ties** (-tĭz). **1.** Freedom. **2.** Exemption from arbitrary or despotic control. **3.** Freedom from restraint; power to do as one pleases; state of being disengaged. **4.** A privilege or license in violation of propriety. **5.** Privilege; franchise; right or immunity.

li-bid'i-nous (lĭ-bĭd'ĭ-nŭs), *a.* [4] Lustful.

li-bra'ri-an (lī-brā'rĭ-ăn), *n.* One in charge of a library.

li'bra-ry (lī'brā-rĭ), *n.; pl.* **-ries** (-rĭz). **1.** A building devoted to books, or an establishment for their custody and control. **2.** A collection of books.

li-bret'to (lĭ-brĕt'ō), *n. ; pl.* E. **-tos** (-ōz), It. **-ti** (-tē). *Music.* The text of an opera or for an extended piece of music.

lice (līs), *n., pl.* of LOUSE.

li'cence. Var. of LICENSE.

li'cense (lī'sĕns), *n.* **1.** Authority or permission given to do or forbear any act. **2.** Any permitted unusual freedom of action. **3.** Excess of liberty; disregard of law or propriety. **4.** Deviation from strict fact, form, or rule by an artist or writer for the sake of effect.—*v. t.* [1] To permit or authorize, especially by formal license; give license to.

li-cen'ti-ate (lī-sĕn'shĭ-āt), *n.* One licensed to exercise a profession or calling, as medicine.

li-cen'tious (-shŭs), *a.* [4] **1.** Characterized by license; lawless; immoral. **2.** Lewd; lascivious. — **-ly,** *adv.* [8] — **-ness,** *n.* [8].

li'chen (lī'kĕn), *n.* One of a group of plants growing on rocks, bark, etc.

lick (lĭk), *n.* **1.** A stroke of the tongue in licking. **2.** A place where natural salt is found and where wild animals resort to lick it up. — *v. t.* **1.** To draw or pass the tongue over. **2.** To pass or play over or about, like a tongue, as flames.

lic'o-rice (lĭk'ō-rĭs), *n.* **1.** A European plant of the bean family, with spikes of blue flowers. **2.** The dried root of this plant or an extract from it.

lid (lĭd), *n.* **1.** That which covers the opening of a vessel, box, etc.; a movable cover. **2.** An eyelid.

lie (lī), *n.* A falsehood uttered or acted to deceive; hence, anything which misleads or deceives. — *v. i.;* LIED (līd) ; LY'ING (lī'ĭng). To tell or act a lie ; hence, to create a false impression.

lie, *v. i.; pret.* LAY (lā) ; *p. p.* LAIN (lān) ; *p. pr. & vb. n.* LY'ING. **1.** To rest extended on a support, as on the ground or a bed ; be stretched out. **2.** To be in a condition, esp. of inactivity, concealment, disuse, etc. **3.** To have direction; extend. **4.** To sojourn; lodge. *Archaic.* **5.** To be ; consist ; — with *in.*

lief (lēf), *adv.* Gladly; willingly ; — now only in, *had,* or *would, as lief, had,* or *would, liefer,* etc.

liege (lēj), *a.* **1.** Sovereign ; having authority or right to allegiance and service ; as, a *liege* lord. **2.** Bound to service and allegiance, as to a liege lord. — *n.* **1.** A liege lord. **2.** A liege subject.

liege man, *or* **liege'man** (lēj'măn), *n.; pl.* **-men** (-mĕn). A vassal ; hence, a devoted adherent.

li'en (lē'ĕn ; lēn), *n. Law.* A legal claim on property for satisfaction of a debt or duty.

lieu (lū), *n.* Place ; stead ; — chiefly in in lieu of.

lieu-ten'an-cy (lū-tĕn'ăn-sĭ ; *see* LIEUTENANT), *n.* Office, rank, or commission, of a lieutenant.

lieu-ten'ant (lū-tĕn'ănt ; *in British usage usually,*

in the U. S. occas., lĕf-tĕn'ănt), *n.* **1.** An officer who acts in place of an absent superior. **2. a** A commissioned officer in an army. See ARMY. **b** A commissioned officer in the British navy, ranking next below a commander. **c** A commissioned officer in the United States navy. See NAVY.

lieutenant colonel, general. See ARMY.

lieutenant commander. See NAVY.

lieutenant governor. A deputy governor ; also, an officer of a State, next in rank to the governor.

life (līf), *n. ; pl.* LIVES (līvz). **1.** The quality or state of being alive ; animate existence. **2.** A living being ; esp., a person; also, living beings or organisms collectively; as, animal *life.* **3.** An individual human existence; hence, a biography. **4.** The duration of a life. **5.** Way or manner of living. **6.** Animation ; spirit. **7.** That which imparts vigor or animation, or upon which success depends. **8.** The period of duration of anything, regarded as if having animate existence.

life belt. A life preserver in the form of a belt.

life'blood' (līf'blŭd'), *n.* Blood necessary to life.

life'boat' (-bōt'), *n.* A strong, buoyant boat for rescuing shipwrecked persons.

life buoy. A float, usually a buoyant ring, to support persons who have fallen into the water.

life'less, *a.* [4] Destitute of life ; hence, spiritless; dull. — **-ly,** *adv.* [8] — **-ness,** *n.* [8].

life'like' (līf'līk'), *a.* [4] Like a living being or a real object ; resembling life.

life'long' (-lŏng'), *a.* Lasting through life.

life preserver. A device, as a cork-filled jacket, to prevent drowning by buoying up the body.

life'time' (līf'tīm'), *n.* The duration of life.

lift (lĭft), *v. t.* **1.** To bring, or cause to move, up higher; raise; elevate. **2.** To exalt in rank, condition, estimation, spirits, etc. **3.** To steal. *Colloq.* **4.** To remove or take away (rightfully). — *v. i.* **1.** To try to raise something. **2.** To rise ; become or appear raised or elevated. — *n.* **1.** Act of lifting, or raising. **2.** Assistance, as by lifting; help. **3.** That which is lifted; also, the distance through which something is lifted. **4.** A hoisting machine ; elevator. — **lift'er,** *n.* [8].

lig'a-ment (lĭg'à-mĕnt), *n.* **1.** A bond; tie. **2.** *Anat.* A tough band of tissue serving to connect parts, as the extremities of bones.

lig'a-ture (lĭg'à-tŭr), *n.* **1.** Anything that binds; bandage; esp., in surgery, a thread or string for tying the blood vessels to prevent hemorrhage. **2.** *Music.* A tie ; slur; group of notes connected by a slur. **3.** *Printing.* A double character, as æ. — *v. t.* [1] To bind or furnish with a ligature.

light (līt), *n.* **1.** That by which objects are rendered visible, or by which we see. **2.** The sun's light; daylight; also, day; especially, dawn. **3.** That which furnishes light, as the sun, a candle, a lamp, etc. **4.** Mental or spiritual enlightenment, or its source. **5.** One who is noteworthy; a model or example. **6.** Visible state ; hence, state of exposure to public observation. **7.** Appearance due to the particular facts presented to view; as, to put things in the right *light.* **8.** *Paint.* The more illuminated part of a scene. — *a.* [3] **1.** Having light; not dark or obscure; bright. **2.** White or whitish; not of a deep shade; blond. — *v. t.; pret.*

& p. p. LIGHT′ED (-ĕd) or LIT (lĭt); p. pr. & vb. n. LIGHT′ING. **1**. To set fire to; ignite; kindle. **2**. To give light to; illuminate; hence, to cause to glow; animate; brighten; — often with *up*. **3**. To attend or conduct with a light. — *v. i.* **1**. To become ignited. **2**. To be illuminated; brighten; — usually with *up*.

light, *a.* [3] **1**. Having little, or comparatively little, weight; not heavy. **2**. Slight; not important. **3**. Not burdensome or severe. **4**. Easy to be digested. **5**. *Cookery.* Well leavened; not soggy or heavy; as, *light* biscuit. **6**. Not heavily burdened; as, *light* cavalry. **7**. Not burdened by care; happy. **8**. Active; nimble; swift. **9**. Trifling; frivolous. **10**. Dizzy; giddy; delirious. — *adv.* Lightly; cheaply; easily. — *v. i.; pret. & p. p.* LIGHT′ED (lĭt′ĕd) or LIT (lĭt); LIGHT′ING (lĭt′ĭng). **1**. To dismount, as from a horse; alight. **2**. To descend and rest, perch, or settle, as a bird. **3**. To come down suddenly and forcibly; fall, as a blow.

light′en (lĭt′'n), *v. t.* **1**. To relieve of a load; make lighter. **2**. To make less burdensome.

light′en (lĭt′'n), *v. i.* **1**. To grow lighter; brighten. **2**. To shine with or like lightning; — chiefly impersonal; as, it thunders and *lightens.*— *v. t.* To make light or clear; illuminate; brighten.

light′er (-ẽr), *n.* One that lights or kindles.

light′er, *n.* A barge, usually flat-bottomed, used in unloading or loading vessels not lying at wharves. — *v. t.* To convey by or as by a lighter.

light′er-age (-ăj), *n.* Price paid for lightering.

light′-foot′ed, *a.* [4] Having a light step; nimble.

light′-head′ed (-hĕd′ĕd), *a.* [4] **1**. Dizzy; delirious, as with fever. **2**. Thoughtless; frivolous.

light′-heart′ed, *a.* [4] Free from anxiety; gay; merry. — *ly*, *adv.* [8] — **-ness**, *n.* [8].

light′house′ (lĭt′hous′), *n.* A tower or other building with a light at the top, for guiding ships at sea or warning mariners.

light′ly (lĭt′lĭ), *adv.* **1**. With little weight or force; gently. **2**. In a small degree or quantity. **3**. Swiftly; nimbly. **4**. Without reason or care; indifferently; slightingly. **5**. Cheerfully; gayly.

light′-mind′ed, *a.* [4] Frivolous.

light′ness, *n.* State, quality, or degree of being illuminated or light.

light′ness, *n.* State or quality of being light, or not heavy; hence, buoyancy; levity; fickleness; nimbleness; airiness, etc.

light′ning (lĭt′nĭng), *n.* The flashing of light caused by a discharge of atmospheric electricity; hence, the discharge itself.

Light-
house.

lightning bug. A firefly.

lightning rod. A metal rod connected with the earth, as on a house to protect it from lightning.

light′ship′ (lĭt′shĭp′), *n.* A vessel with a light, moored off a dangerous place to warn sailors.

light′weight′ (lĭt′wāt′), *n.* One of less than average weight. — *a.* Light or deficient in weight.

lig′ne-ous (lĭg′nĕ-ŭs), *a.* [4] Of the nature of wood; woody.   [and bituminous coal.]

lig′nite (-nīt), *n.* A variety of coal between peat

lig′num-vi′tæ (-nŭm-vī′tē), *n.* A tropical American tree with hard, heavy wood; also, the wood.

lik′a-ble (līk′á-b'l), *a.* [4] Such as attracts liking.

like (līk), *a.* [3] **1**. Having the same, or nearly the same, appearance or characteristics; similar. **2**. Indicative of. **3**. Inclined toward.

☞ *Like* is used at will as a suffix with nouns to form adjectives; as, man*like*, like a man.

like (līk), *n.* That which is equal or similar to another; counterpart; copy; equal. — **the like**, something similar or of the same kind. — *adv. or prep.* **1**. To the same extent or in the same manner as. **2**. Likely; probably. *Rare,* except in *like enough, very like,* and (*Colloq.*) *as like as not.* — **like as**, in a like manner as; just as.

like, *v. t.* [1] To have a liking for; enjoy. — *n.* A liking; preference; fancy; — usually in *pl.*

like′li-hood (līk′lĭ-hŏŏd), *n.* Probability.

like′ly (-lĭ), *a.* [3] **1**. Appearing like truth; probable; credible. **2**. Such as to render something probable. **3**. Suitable. **4**. Promising. — *adv.* Probably.

lik′en (līk′'n), *v. t.* To represent as like; compare.

like′ness (līk′nĕs), *n.* **1**. State or quality of being like. **2**. Appearance; guise. **3**. A copy; portrait.

like′wise′ (-wīz′), *adv. & conj.* In like manner; also; moreover; too.

lik′ing (līk′ĭng), *n.* State of being pleased with a thing or person; hence, inclination; desire.

li′lac (lī′lăk), *n.* **1**. A shrub bearing large clusters of fragrant flowers; also, the flower. **2**. A light purplish color like that of the common lilac flower. — *a.* Of the color of the purplish lilac.

lilt (lĭlt), *n.* **1**. A lively, buoyant song or air. **2**. Rhythmical swing or movement. — *v. i. & t.* To sing a lilt; sing merrily.

lil′y (lĭl′ĭ), *n. ; pl.* **-IES** (-ĭz). Any plant, flower, or bulb of a certain genus of plants having scaly bulbs and showy funnel-shaped flowers. — **lily of the valley**, a low perennial herb bearing a raceme of very fragrant nodding bell-shaped white flowers.

limb (lĭm), *n.* **1**. A leg, arm, or wing. **2**. A large branch or bough of a tree. **3**. Something like, or suggestive of, a leg, arm, or branch.

limb, *n.* A border or edge, as of certain corollas, of the disk of a heavenly body, etc.

Turk's-cap
Lily.
Reduced.

limbed (lĭmd), *a.* Having limbs; — chiefly in combination; as, long-*limbed.*

lim′ber (lĭm′bẽr), *a.* [3] **1**. Easily bent; flexible; pliant. **2**. Supple; lithe. — *v. t.* To make limber. — **-ness**, *n.* [8].

lim′ber, *n. Mil.* The detachable fore wheels, axle, and pole of a gun carriage.

limb′less (lĭm′lĕs), *a.* Having no limbs.

lim′bo (lĭm′bō), *n.* A place or condition of restraint or confinement, or of neglect or oblivion.

lime (līm), *n.* A white, caustic substance (calcium oxide) obtained by calcining limestone, shells, etc.; — called also *quicklime.* — *v. t.* [1] To smear with a viscous substance; entangle; ensnare.

lime, *n.* The linden tree.

lime (līm), *n.* A tree related to the lemon and bearing a small, greenish yellow, very acid fruit.

lime′light′ (-līt′), *n.* A brilliant light produced by heating a piece of lime in an intensely hot flame ; — called also *calcium light.*

lime′stone′ (līm′stōn′), *n.* A rock, chiefly of calcium carbonate, yielding lime when burned.

lim′it (lĭm′ĭt), *n.* That which terminates, circumscribes, or confines ; bound ; border. — *v. t.* To set a limit to ; restrict.

lim′i-ta′tion (lĭm′ĭ-tā′shŭn), *n.* **1.** A limiting. **2.** That which limits ; restriction ; qualification.

lim′it-ed, *p. a.* [4] **1.** Confined within limits ; restricted. **2.** *Law.* Designating a government, as a monarchy, having constitutional limitations.

lim′it-less, *a.* Having no limits ; boundless.

limn (lĭm), *v. t.* To draw or paint, as a picture ; hence, to depict. — **lim′ner** (lĭm′nẽr), *n.* [8].

li′mou-sine′ (lē′mōō-zēn′), *n.* A kind of large automobile having a closed body for the passengers, and a driver's seat outside but covered with a roof.

limp (lĭmp), *a.* [3] Lacking stiffness ; flexible.

limp, *v. i.* To walk lamely. — *n.* A halt in one's walk ; act of limping.

lim′pet (lĭm′pĕt), *n.* A small shellfish with a low cone-shaped shell, found on rocky seacoasts.

lim′pid (-pĭd), *a.* [4] Clear ; translucent.

lim-pid′i-ty (lĭm-pĭd′ĭ-tĭ), *n.* Limpid quality.

limp′ly (lĭmp′lĭ), *adv.* In a limp manner.

limp′ness, *n.* State or quality of being limp.

linch′pin′ (lĭnch′pĭn′), *n.* A pin inserted in the end of an axletree to hold the wheel on.

lin′den (lĭn′dĕn), *n.* A large and handsome tree of various species, with heart-shaped leaves and yellow flowers ; the basswood.

line (līn), *v. t.* [1] **1.** To cover the inner surface of, as of a cloak. **2.** To put something in the inside of ; fill. **3.** To serve as the lining of.

line, *n.* **1.** A thread, cord, or rope ; esp., a strong slender cord. **2.** A threadlike mark, crease, or the like. **3.** A mark of division or outline ; hence, a limit ; boundary ; — often fig. **4. a** A circle of latitude or longitude. **b** The equator. **5.** *Math.* That which has length but not breadth or thickness. **6.** A straight line ; fig., agreement ; harmony. **7.** Lineament ; outline ; hence, plan ; method. **8.** A series, rank, or row of objects. Hence : **a** A verse of a poem. **b** A short letter ; a note. **c** *pl. Drama.* The spoken words of a play or a part. **9.** Conveyances plying regularly under one management, or a system of transportation. **10.** *Mil. & Nav.* **a** A trench ; rampart. **b** *pl.* Dispositions, as fortifications, made to cover extended positions. **c** A body of troops abreast. **d** The regular troops of an army or the purely combatant forces. **11.** A series of ancestors or descendants. **12.** Course of conduct, thought, occupation, or policy. **13.** A department of industry or activity. **14.** *Trade.* A supply of articles of the same general class. **15.** Course or direction ; hence, a road ; a railway. **16.** The connecting wire between telegraph or telephone stations. — *v. t.* [1] **1.** To represent by lines ; outline. **2.** To mark with a line or lines. **3.** To align, as troops. **4.** To place, or be, in a line along ; place a line along, as of trees along a street. — *v. i.* To form a line.

lin′e-age (lĭn′ē-âj), *n.* Descent in a line from a common ancestor ; race ; family.

lin′e-al (-ăl), *a.* **1.** Of or pert. to a line ; linear. **2.** In or consisting of a direct line of ancestry or descent. **3.** Hereditary. — **lin′e-al-ly,** *adv.* [8].

lin′e-a-ment (-á-mĕnt), *n.* One of the outlines or exterior features of a body or figure, esp. of the face ; distinctive feature ; — usually in *pl.*

lin′e-ar (-ē-ár), *a.* **1.** Of, pertaining to, or consisting of, a line or lines. **2.** Narrow ; threadlike.

lin′en (lĭn′ĕn), *n.* **1.** Thread or cloth of flax ; collectively, linen fabrics, articles of linen. **2.** Garments usually or chiefly of linen, esp. shirts, collars and cuffs. — *a.* Made of flax or linen.

lin′er (līn′ẽr), *n.* One who lines.

lin′er, *n.* A vessel of a regular line of vessels.

lin′ger (lĭng′gẽr), *v. i.* To delay ; loiter ; be slow in parting, going, coming, acting, etc.

‖ **lin′ge-rie′** (lăN′zh′-rē′), *n.* [F.] Linen goods ; linen or muslin underclothes, esp. of women.

lin′go (lĭng′gō), *n. ; pl.* -GOES (-gōz). Language ; dialect.

lin′gual (-gwăl), *a.* Of or pertaining to the tongue.

lin′guist (-gwĭst), *n.* One skilled in languages.

lin-guis′tic (lĭn-gwĭs′tĭk), *a.* Pert. to language

lin-guis′tics (-tĭks), *n.* The science of languages

lin′i-ment (lĭn′ĭ-mĕnt), *n.* A medicinal preparation thinner than an ointment, to rub on the skin.

lin′ing (līn′ĭng), *n.* **1.** That which lines, or is intended to line. **2.** Act of providing a lining.

link (lĭngk), *n.* A torch of tow, pitch, or the like.

link, *n.* **1.** A single ring of a chain. **2.** A tie ; bond. **3.** Something suggestive of a link of a chain. — *v. t. & i.* To unite with or as with a link.

links (lĭngks), *n. pl.* **1.** Gently rolling, sandy land. *Scot.* **2.** [Sometimes construed as a *sing.*] A golf course.

lin′net (lĭn′ĕt), *n.* A small Old World finch.

li-no′le-um (lĭ-nō′lē-ŭm), *n.* A floor cloth with a surface of hardened linseed oil and ground cork.

lin′o-type (lĭn′ō-tīp ; lĭn′ō-), *n.* A typesetting machine which casts each line of type in one piece.

lin′seed′ (lĭn′sēd′), *n.* Flaxseed (which see).

lin′sey-wool′sey (lĭn′zĭ-wōōl′zĭ), *n.* Coarse cloth of linen and wool, or cotton and wool.

lint (lĭnt), *n.* Linen scraped or otherwise made into a downy or fleecy substance for dressing wounds, etc. ; also, fluff from yarn or fabrics.

lin′tel (lĭn′tĕl), *n.* A horizontal beam, stone, or the like spanning an opening, as a door or window.

li′on (lī′ŭn), *n.* **1.** A large flesh-eating animal of Africa and southern Asia, belonging to the cat family, of a tawny yellowish color. The male has a dark shaggy mane. **2.** A person of celebrity made an object of social attentions.

li′on-ess (lī′ŭn-ĕs), *n.* Female lion.

li′on-ize (lī′ŭn-īz), *v. t.* [1] To treat or regard as a social " lion," or celebrity.

lip (lĭp), *n.* **1.** Either of the two fleshy folds which surround the mouth. **2.** An edge, as of a hollow vessel or cavity.

liq′ue-fac′tion (lĭk′wē-făk′shŭn), *n.* Act of liquefying ; state of being liquid.

liq′ue-fy (-fī), *v. t. & i.* [2] To reduce to a liquid.

liq′uid (lĭk′wĭd), *a.* [4] **1.** Flowing freely like water ; fluid ; neither solid nor gaseous. **2.** Smooth-

.ounding. **3.** *Phonetics.* Of consonant sounds, flowing; vowel-like, as the sounds of *l* and *r*. — **liquid measure.** See *Tables* in *Appendix.* — *n.* A liquid substance.

liq'ui-date (lĭk'wĭ-dāt), *v. t.* [1] **1.** To discharge; pay off, as a debt. **2.** To settle the accounts and distribute the assets of (a corporation or estate). — *v. i.* To liquidate one's debts or accounts.

liq'ui-da'tion (-dā'shŭn), *n.* A liquidating.

li-quid'i-ty (lĭ-kwĭd'ĭ-tĭ), *n.* State or quality of being liquid.

liq'uor (lĭk'ẽr), *n.* **1.** Any liquid. **2.** An alcoholic beverage, esp. if strong or distilled.

lisp (lĭsp), *v. i.* **1.** To substitute *th* for *s* or *z* in speaking. **2.** To speak imperfectly or falteringly. — *v. t.* To speak with a lisp. — *n.* Habit, act, or sound of lisping.

lis'som) (lĭs'ŭm), *a.* [4] Lithe; supple; flexi-
lis'some) ble; hence, nimble; agile. — **-ness,** *n.*

list (lĭst), *n.* **1.** A strip forming the border or selvage of cloth. **2.** A roll or catalogue, as of names. — *v. t.* **1.** To put a list, or border, on; cover with list, or strips of cloth. **2.** To enroll in a list or catalogue. — *v. i.* To enlist in the army or navy.

list, *v. i.* **1.** To please; suit; incline (to). *Archaic.* **2.** *Naut.* To careen; — said of a ship. — *n.* An inclination to one side; — mostly nautical.

list, *v. t. & i.* To hearken; listen (to). *Archaic.*

lis'ten (lĭs'n), *v. i.* To hearken; hence, to give heed; yield to advice. — **lis'ten-er,** *n.* [8].

list'less (lĭst'lĕs), *a.* [4] Having no desire or inclination; indifferent. — **-ly,** *adv.* — **-ness,** *n.*

lists (lĭsts), *n. pl.; rare in sing.* **1.** The barriers of a tilting field; hence, the field itself. **2.** A place of contest; an arena; — esp. in *to enter the lists.*

lit (lĭt), *pret. & p. p.* of LIGHT.

lit'a-ny (lĭt'á-nĭ), *n.; pl.* -NIES (-nĭz). A solemn supplication or prayer; esp., a form of prayer in which the clergy lead and the people respond.

li'ter (lē'tẽr), *n.* [6] A measure of capacity in the metric system, being a cubic decimeter. It equals .908 U. S. dry quart, or 1.0567 U. S. liquid quarts.

lit'o-ra-cy (lĭt'ẽr-á-sĭ), *n.* State of being literate.

lit'er-al (-ăl), *a.* [4] **1.** According to the "letter," or the natural or usual interpretation of the words employed; exact; precise. Hence, true to fact; not exaggerated; matter-of-fact; unimaginative. **2.** Of or pertaining to, or expressed by, letters. — **-ly,** *adv.* [8] — **-ness,** *n.* [8].

lit'er-a-ry (-á-rĭ), *a.* [4] **1.** Of or pertaining to letters, or literature. **2.** Versed in literature; occupied with literature as a profession.

lit'er-ate (-åt), *a.* [4] **1.** Instructed in letters; able to read and write. **2.** Literary. — *n.* A person who is literate. [letter.

‖ **lit'e-ra'tim** (lĭt'ē-rā'tĭm), *adv.* [L.] Letter for

lit'er-a-ture (lĭt'ẽr-á-tử̇r), *n.* **1.** Production of literary work, esp. as an occupation. **2.** Literary productions collective y, as all the writings of a country, notable for literary form or expression.

lith'arge (lĭth'ärj), *n.* A yellowish red oxide of lead used in making glass, etc.

lithe (lĭth), *a.* [3] Bending easily; pliant; limber. — **lithe'ness,** *n.* [8].

lithe'some (lĭth'sŭm), *a.* [4] Pliant; lissom.

lith'i-a (lĭth'ĭ-á), *n.* Oxide of lithium.

lith'i-um (-ĭ-ŭm), *n.* A soft, silver-white metal, the lightest known.

lith'o-graph (-ō-gráf), *v. t.* To produce, copy, or portray by lithography. — *n.* A lithographic print. — **li-thog'ra-pher** (lĭ-thŏg'rá-fẽr), *n.* [8].

lith'o-graph'ic (lĭth'ō-grăf'ĭk), *a.* Of, pertaining to, or made by, lithography.

li-thog'ra-phy (lĭ-thŏg'rá-fĭ), *n.* Art or process of putting writing or designs on stone (or zinc, aluminium, etc.) with a greasy material, and of producing prints therefrom.

lit'i-gant (lĭt'ĭ-gănt), *a.* [4] Disposed to, or engaged in, litigation. — *n.* Party to a lawsuit.

lit'i-gate (-gāt), *v. t.* [1] To make the subject of a lawsuit. — *v. i.* To carry on a contest at law.

lit'i-ga'tion (-gā'shŭn), *n.* A litigating; lawsuit.

li-ti'gious (lĭ-tĭj'ŭs), *a.* [4] **1.** Inclined to engage in lawsuits; contentious; quarrelsome. **2.** Of or pertaining to litigation.

lit'mus (lĭt'mŭs), *n.* A dyestuff got from certain lichens. It is turned red by acids and restored to its blue color by alkalies.

li'tre (lē'tẽr). Var. of LITER.

lit'ter (lĭt'ẽr), *n.* **1.** A couch with shafts, usually covered and curtained, for carrying passengers. **2.** A stretcher for carrying a sick or wounded person. **3.** Straw, hay, etc., used as bedding for animals. **4.** Things lying scattered about; scattered rubbish; disorder. **5.** The young, collectively, brought forth at one time, as by a sow. — *v. t.* **1.** To strew with scattered articles, as a room. **2.** To give birth to; — said of brutes. — *v. i.* To produce a litter.

lit'tle (lĭt'l), *a.; LESS, or LESS'ER; LEAST.* **1.** Small in size or extent; diminutive. **2.** Short in duration; brief. **3.** Small in quantity or degree. **4.** Small in dignity, power, or scope; not great **5.** Small in sympathies; narrow; mean; illiberal. — **Little Bear,** Ursa Minor. — *adv.* **1.** In a small quantity or degree; slightly. **2.** Not at all; — before verbs, as *think, imagine, know,* etc. — *n.* That which is little; a small amount, time, etc. — **lit'tle-ness,** *n.* [8].

lit'to-ral (-ō-răl), *a.* Of or pertaining to a shore especially of the sea. — *n.* A coastal region.

li-tur'gi-cal (lĭ-tûr'jĭ-kăl), *a.* Pertaining to, or of the nature of, a liturgy.

lit'ur-gy (lĭt'ûr-jĭ), *n.; pl.* -GIES (-jĭz). A form of public worship; a ritual.

liv'a-ble (lĭv'á-b'l), *a.* [4] **1.** Such as can be lived **2.** Suitable or pleasant to live in or with.

live (lĭv), *v. i.* [1] **1.** To be alive. **2.** To continue in life, existence, activity, or memory. **3.** To get a livelihood; subsist; — with *on* or *by.* **4.** To make one's home; dwell. **5.** To outlast danger; float. — *v. t.* To pass, or spend, as one's life.

live (līv), *a.* [3] **1.** Having, or full of, life; alive. **2.** Energetic or alert; wide awake. **3.** In a state of activity; as: **a** Burning; glowing. **b** *Engin.* Imparting power. **c** Having an electric current passing through, as a wire. **4.** Of color, bright; vivid. — live stock, horses, horned cattle, and other domestic animals kept for profit.

live'li-hood (līv'lĭ-hŏŏd), *n.* Means of supporting life; maintenance.

live'li-ly (-lĭ-lĭ), *adv.* In a lively manner.

live'li-ness, *n.* Quality of being lively.

live′long′ (lĭv′lŏng′), *a.* Whole; long in passing; — used of time.

live′ly (līv′lĭ), *a.* [3] **1.** Full of life; vigorous; active; animated. **2.** Enlivening. **3.** Vivid; brilliant. **4.** Responding quickly to outer forces; rebounding quickly. — *adv.* In a lively manner; briskly; vigorously.

liv′er (lĭv′ẽr), *n.* One that lives.

liv′er, *n.* In vertebrates, a large glandular organ which secretes bile and changes the blood, which passes through it.

liv′er-ied (-ĭd),*a.* Wearing a livery. See LIVERY, 1.

liv′er-wort′ (-wûrt′),*n.* **1.** Any of various plants resembling the mosses. **2.** The hepatica.

liv′er-y (-ĭ), *n.; pl.* -ERIES (-ĭz). **1.** The peculiar dress often worn by servants of a person of some fashion, or appropriated by any body of persons. **2. a** The feeding, stabling, and care of horses for pay; boarding of horses. **b** A livery stable. *U. S.*

livery stable. A stable where horses and vehicles are kept for hire, and where stabling is provided.

liv′id (lĭv′ĭd), *a.* [3] Black and blue; leaden.

liv′ing (-ĭng),*n.* **1.** State of one that lives. **2.** Manner or rule of life. **3.** Possibility of living, esp. comfortably. **4.** Means of living; livelihood. **5.** A benefice. *Eng.*

liv′ing (lĭv′ĭng), *p. a.* [4] **1.** Alive; that lives. **2.** Active; operative. **3.** Full of life; vivid.

liz′ard (lĭz′ãrd), *n.* Any of numerous small four-legged, long-bodied reptiles, with tapering tail, and scaly skin.

lla′ma (lä′mà), *n.* A South American animal allied to the camel, but smaller and with no hump.

lla′no (lä′nō; *Sp.* lyä′nō), *n.; pl.* -NOS (-nōz ; *Sp.* -nōs). An extensive plain. *Sp. Amer.*

lo (lō), *interj.* Look ! behold !

loach (lōch), *n.* Any of certain small Old World fresh-water fishes of the carp family.

load (lōd), *n.* **1.** That which is carried; a burden; hence, the quantity proper to carry, as in a cart. **2.** That which burdens the mind. **3.** The charge of a firearm. — *v. t.* **1.** To lay or put a load on or in. **2.** To place on or in something, as for carriage. **3.** To supply abundantly. **4.** To increase in weight, often fraudulently.— *v. i.* **1.** To give or receive a load. **2.** To insert the charge in a firearm. — **load′er**, *n.* [8].

load′stone′ (-stōn′),*n.* See MAGNETITE.

loaf (lōf), *n.; pl.* LOAVES (lōvz). A regularly shaped or molded mass of bread, cake, or sugar.

loaf, *v. i.* To spend time in idleness.

loaf′er (lōf′ẽr),*n.* One who loafs ; a lazy lounger.

loam (lōm), *n.* Earthy matter of clay and sand. Popularly, *loam* implies the presence of humus.

loam′y (-ĭ), *a.* [3] Consisting of, like, or partaking of the nature of, loam.

loan (lōn), *n.* **1.** A lending ; permission to use. **2.** That which one lends or borrows, esp. money. — *v. t. & i.* To lend. [sion.|

loath (lōth), *a.* [3] Filled with disgust or aver-

loathe (lōth), *v. t.* [1] To dislike greatly ; abhor.

loath′ing (-ĭng),*n.* Extreme disgust ; abhorrence.

loath′some (lōth′sŭm), *a.* [4] Fitted to cause loathing. — **-ly,** *adv.* [8] — **-ness,** *n.* [8].

loaves (lōvz), *n., pl.* of LOAF.

lo′bate (lō′bāt), *a.* [4] Lobed, as a leaf.

lob′by (lŏb′ĭ), *n.; pl.* -BIES (-ĭz). **1.** A passageway, esp. when serving also as a waiting room, etc. **2.** Persons, collectively, who lobby. — *v. i.* [2] To address or solicit members of a legislative body in the lobby or elsewhere with intent to influence their votes. — *v. t.* To urge or procure the passage of, as a bill, by lobbying. — **lob′by-ist,** *n.*

lobe (lōb), *n.* A somewhat rounded projection or division, esp. of an organ or part, as a leaf or ear.

lobed (lōbd), *a.* [4] Having lobes ; lobate.

lo-be′li-a (lō-bē′lĭ-à; -bēl′yà),*n.* Any of a certain genus (*Lobelia*) of plants having red, blue, or white flowers of very irregular form.

lob′lol′ly (lŏb′lŏl′ĭ), *n.* A pine of the southern United States having thick, flaky bark.

lob′ster (-stẽr), *n.* Any of various long-tailed shellfish used for food, esp. any of certain species having two enormous claws.

lo′cal (lō′kăl), *a.* [4] Pertaining to a particular place; characteristic of, or confined to, a particular place or places ; as, *local* customs.

lo′cal-ism (-ĭz′m), *n.* Affection for a particular place ; provincialism ; also, a local idiom or habit.

lo-cal′i-ty (lō-kăl′ĭ-tĭ), *n.; pl.* -TIES (-tĭz). **1.** Fact or state of being local. **2.** A place.

lo′cal-i-za′tion (lō′kăl-ĭ-zā′shŭn),*n.* Act of localizing, or fact of being localized.

lo′cal-ize (lō′kăl-īz), *v. t.* [1] To make local; fix in, or confine to, a definite place, or locality.

lo′cal-ly, *adv.* In a local manner.

lo′cate (lō′kāt), *v. t.* [1] **1.** To designate the site or place of, as a mining claim. **2.** To establish in a certain place; settle; place. **3.** To search for and discover the place of. **4.** To refer to a particular place. — *v. i.* To place one's self; settle. *Colloq.*

lo-ca′tion (lō-kā′shŭn),*n.* **1.** A locating. **2.** Situation ; place, as of residence or settlement.

loch (lŏk), *n.* A lake; also, a bay or arm of the sea, esp. when nearly landlocked. *Scot.*

lock (lŏk), *n.* **1.** A tress, or ringlet of hair; hence, *pl.*, the hair of the head. **2.** A bunch or tuft of wool, cotton, flax, or the like.

lock, *n.* **1.** A fastening, as for a door, operated by a key or by a combination. **2.** The apparatus of a firearm by which the charge is exploded. **3.** A locking or fastening together. **4.** An inclosure in a canal, river, dock, etc., with gates, used in raising or lowering boats from level to level. — *v. t.* **1.** To make fast with or as with a lock. **2.** To confine ; shut (in or out). **3.** To make fast or rigid, as by the engaging of parts. — *v. i.* **1.** To become locked. **2.** To interlock ; interlink.

lock′er (-ẽr), *n.* A drawer,compartment, chest, or closet, that may be locked. [hair.|

lock′et (-ĕt), *n.* A case for a miniature or lock of

lock′jaw′ (-jô′), *n.* A variety of tetanus in which the jaws are locked rigidly together.

lock′out′ (-out′),*n.* Refusal to give work to one's employees, used as a means of coercion.

lock′smith′ (-smĭth′), *n.* One who makes or mends locks.

lock′up′ (lŏk′ŭp′), *n.* A jail.

lo′co (lō′kō), *v. t.* To poison with loco weed; hence, *Colloq.*, to render insane or mad.

lo′co-mo′tion (lō′kō-mō′shŭn), *n.* Act or power of moving from place to place.

lo′co-mo′tive (-tĭv), *a.* Of or pertaining to loco-

motion, or power to change place. — *n.* A steam engine, or electric motor, for hauling cars on a railroad.

loco weed. Any of several herbs of the western United States causing a nervous disease in live stock feeding on them.

lo'cus (lō'kŭs), *n.; L. pl.* -CI (-sī). **1.** A place; locality. **2.** *Plane Geom.* A line or group of lines containing all and only such points in the plane as satisfy a given condition.

lo'cust (lō'kŭst), *n.* **1.** Any grasshopper having short antennæ; any of certain species that often travel in vast swarms and destroy vegetation. **2. a** A tree with pinnate leaves and white flowers; also, its hard durable wood. **b** The honey locust.

lo‑cu'tion (lō‑kū'shŭn), *n.* A particular or peculiar form of expression.

lode (lōd), *n.* A fissure in rock, filled with mineral; also, this body of mineral.

lode'star' (lōd'stär'), *n.* A star that leads; a guiding star; especially, the polestar.

lode'stone'. Var. of LOADSTONE.

lodge (lŏj), *n.* **1.** A small or temporary dwelling house; a hut; booth; tent; hence, any abode, as for a caretaker on an estate, etc. **2.** In some secret societies, the hall or meeting place of a local branch or the members composing it. **3.** The lair of an animal, as a beaver or otter. — *v. t.* [1] **1.** To provide quarters for, esp. temporarily. **2.** To shelter; entertain; also, to take as a lodger. **3.** To settle in a place; to fix. **4.** To place or vest, as authority in an agent. — *v. i.* **1.** To remain or dwell temporarily. **2.** To dwell; reside, esp. as a lodger. **3.** To come to a rest; stop and remain.

lodg'er (lŏj'ẽr), *n.* One that lodges; esp., one who occupies a hired room in another's house.

lodg'ing (-ĭng), *n.* **1.** Dwelling; esp., temporary abode; quarters. **2.** *pl.* A room or rooms in another's house, as a place of residence.

lodg'ment (-mĕnt), *n.* Act or manner of lodging; state of being lodged; also, material lodged.

loft (lŏft), *n.* **1.** A room or floor above another; esp., an attic room or an attic. **2.** An upper floor of a warehouse or business building, esp. when without partitions. *U. S.* **3.** A gallery in a church, hall, etc.; as, the organ *loft.*

loft'y (lŏf'tĭ), *a.* [3] **1.** Rising high; high; esp., having imposing height. **2.** Haughty; proud. **3.** Elevated in character, language, etc. — **loft'i‑ly** (-tĭ-lĭ), *adv.* [8] — **loft'i‑ness**, *n.* [8].

log (lŏg), *n.* **1.** A bulky piece or length of unshaped timber. **2.** *Naut.* An apparatus for measuring a ship's speed. **3.** The record of a ship's daily progress. — *v. t.; LOGGED* (lŏgd); LOG'GING (lŏg'ĭng). *Naut.* To enter in a log (sense 3). — *v. i.* To engage in cutting or transporting logs.

lo'gan‑ber'ry (lō'găn-bĕr'ĭ), *n.; pl.* -RIES (-ĭz). A hybrid between the raspberry and blackberry.

log'a‑rithm (lŏg'à-rĭth'm), *n.* One of a scheme of auxiliary numbers used to abridge arithmetical calculations by using addition and subtraction in place of multiplication and division.

log book, or **log'book'**, *n. Naut.* = LOG, *n.*, 3.

log'ger‑head' (lŏg'ẽr-hĕd'), *n.* **1.** A blockhead. **2.** A very large marine turtle. — **to be at logger‑heads**, to contend or quarrel.

log'gia (lŏj'à; lō'jĭ-à), *n.* A roofed open gallery.

log'ic (lŏj'ĭk), *n.* **1.** The science, art, or laws of exact reasoning or thinking. **2.** A treatise on logic. **3.** Reasoning; esp., sound reasoning. — **log'i‑cal** (-ĭ-kăl), *a.* — **log'i‑cal‑ly**, *adv.* [8].

lo‑gi'cian (lō-jĭsh'ăn), *n.* One skilled in logic.

log'roll'ing (lŏg'rōl'ĭng), *n.* A combining to assist another in consideration of assistance in return; — used of certain political methods. *Chiefly U. S.*

log'wood' (-wŏod'), *n.* The brownish heartwood of a Central American tree, much used in dyeing.

lo'gy (lō'gĭ), *a.* [3] Heavy or dull, esp. in motion or thought; as, a *logy* horse. *U. S.*

loin (loin), *n.* That part of the body, on either side, between hip bone and false ribs; — chiefly in *pl.*

loi'ter (loi'tẽr), *v. i.* To be slow in moving; saunter. — **loi'ter‑er**, *n.* [8].

loll (lŏl), *v. i.* **1.** Of the tongue, to hang out loosely. **2.** To move or recline lazily.

lol'li‑pop (lŏl'ĭ-pŏp), *n.* A kind of candy, often in the form of a lump on the end of a stick.

lo'ment (lō'mĕnt), *n.* A legume which breaks at maturity into one-seeded sections.

lone (lōn), *a.* [3] **1.** Without company; solitary; hence, lonesome. **2.** Unfrequented; lonely.

lone'ly, *a.* [3] **1.** Without company; alone; lone. **2.** Solitary; unfrequented. **3.** Lonesome. — **li‑ly** (-lĭ-lĭ), *adv.* [8] — **li‑ness**, *n.*

lone'some (-sŭm), *a.* [3] **1.** Secluded from society; unfrequented; solitary; hence, causing loneliness or depression. **2.** Conscious of, and depressed by, solitude. — **lone'some‑ly**, *adv.* [8] — **‑ness**, *n.* [8].

long (lŏng), *a.* **1.** Of considerable extent from end to end; not short. **2.** Of considerable extent in time; not brief; hence, tedious. **3.** Extended to (a specified) measure; as, a mile *long*. **4.** Of a relatively great duration; — said esp. of a vowel sound as compared with another called *short*. **5.** *Commerce.* Having a supply of stocks or goods; prepared for, or depending for a profit upon, an advance in prices. — **long measure**. See *Tables* in *Appendix.* —**l. ton**. See TON. — *adv.* **1.** For or during a long time. **2.** Throughout an extent of time indicated. **3.** At a point of duration far distant.

long, *v. i.* To feel a strong desire or craving.

long'boat' (lŏng'bōt'), *n.* The largest boat carried by a merchant sailing vessel.

lon‑gev'i‑ty (lŏn-jĕv'ĭ-tĭ), *n.* Length of life.

long'hand' (lŏng'hănd'), *n.* The characters used in ordinary writing; — opposed to *shorthand*.

long'ing (lŏng'ĭng), *n.* An eager desire.

lon'gi‑tude (lŏn'jĭ-tūd), *n.* **1.** *Geog.* Distance east or west measured by the angle between the meridian of a given place and a meridian of reference, as that of Greenwich, England. **2.** *Astron.* More fully, **celestial longitude**. The distance, in degrees, reckoned eastward on the ecliptic from the vernal equinox to the ecliptic meridian of any given point.

lon'gi‑tu'di‑nal (-tū'dĭ-năl), *a.* **1.** Of or pertaining to longitude or length. **2.** Placed or running lengthwise. — **‑ly**, *adv.* [8].

long'shore'man (lŏng'shōr'măn), *n.; pl.* -MEN (-mĕn). One employed about the wharves of a seaport, esp. in loading or unloading vessels.

long'‑sight'ed, *a.* [4] Far-sighted; sagacious.

---

long'–suf'fer-ing, *a.* [4] Bearing injuries or trials with patience. — *n.* Long patience of offense.

long'–wind'ed (lŏng'wĭn'dĕd), *a.* [4] Able to retain the breath a long time; hence, tediously long in speaking. — **-ly**, *adv.* [8] — **-ness**, *n.* [8].

look (lŏŏk), *v. i.* **1.** To direct the eyes for seeing. **2.** To direct the attention; give heed; take care. **3.** To expect. **4.** To turn, go, or resort (to). **5.** To appear. **6.** To face; front. — *v. t.* **1.** To give a look to. **2.** To influence or bring by looking. **3.** To express or manifest by a look. — *n.* **1.** Act of looking; glance. **2.** Expression of face; hence, personal aspect. **3.** Appearance; aspect.

look'er-on',*n.; pl.* LOOKERS-ON (-ĕrz-). A spectator.

look'ing-glass', *n.* A mirror.

look'out' (lŏŏk'out'), *n.* **1.** A watching for an object or event; also, the place from which such observation is made. **2.** One engaged in watching.

loom (lŏŏm), *v. i.* **1.** To appear above the surface of sea or land, or to appear enlarged, or distorted and indistinct; as, the ship *looms* large. **2.** To appear in an exaggerated or an impressively great form. — **n.** A looming appearance, shadow, etc.

loom, *n.* A frame or machine for interweaving yarn or threads into a fabric.

loon (lŏŏn), *n.* A rogue; also, a boor.

loon, *n.* Any of several fish-eating diving birds of northern regions.

loop (lŏŏp), *n.* **1.** A fold or doubling of a thread, rope, etc.; hence, a ring or fold forming a catch. **2.** A loop-shaped figure, course, bend, etc. — *v. t.* To make a loop or loops of or in; fasten with a loop or loops; — often with *up*. — *v. i.* To make a loop.

loop'hole' (-hōl'), *n.* **1.** A small opening, as in a wall or parapet, through which weapons may be discharged. **2.** A passage, or way of escape.

loose (lŏŏs), *a.* [3] **1.** Not fastened so as to be fixed, rigid, firm, or tight. **2.** Free, esp. from confinement. **3.** Not dense, close, or compact. **4.** Wanting in restraint; lax; also, dissolute; lewd. **5.** Wanting in precision or care. — *adv.* Loosely. — *v. t.* [1] **1.** To make or render loose; unbind, unpack, etc. **2.** To free from restraint or obligation; release. **3.** To relax; make less rigid, tight, or strict. — **-ly**, *adv.* [8] — **-ness**, *n.* [8].

loos'en (lŏŏs''n), *v. t.* **1.** To set or let loose; — now esp. in *to loosen* (one's) *tongue*. **2.** To make loose. — *v. i.* To become loose.

loot (lŏŏt), *n.* Plunder, esp. that taken in war. — *v. t. & i.* To plunder or sack, as a city; rob.

lop (lŏp), *v. t.;* LOPPED (lŏpt); LOP'PING. **1.** To hew branches or twigs from (a tree, vine, etc.); trim. **2.** To cut off or remove, as twigs from a tree.

lop, *v. i.* To hang down; droop.

lope (lōp), *v. i.* [1] To go or move with a lope. — *n.* An easy gait, resembling a canter.

lop'sid'ed (lŏp'sĭd'ĕd), *a.* [4] Leaning to one side, as from defect; hence, unsymmetrical.

lo-qua'cious (lō-kwā'shŭs), *a.* [4] Given to talking; garrulous. — **-ly**, *adv.* — **-ness**, *n.*

lo-quac'i-ty (lō-kwăs'ĭ-tĭ), *n.* Talkativeness.

lord (lôrd), *n.* **1.** One who has authority; a master; ruler. **2. a** A titled nobleman. *Eng.* **b** *pl.* [*cap.*], usually with *the*, the British House of Lords (see under HOUSE). **3.** [*cap.*] **a** The Supreme Being. **b** The Savior; Jesus Christ. —

the Lord's Day, Sunday. — the Lord's Prayer, the prayer which Jesus taught his disciples. *Matt.* vi. 9-13. — the Lord's Supper. **a** The supper partaken of by Jesus the night before his crucifixion. **b** The sacrament in commemoration of this; the Eucharist; the Holy Communion. — *v. i.* To play the lord; domineer; — esp. in *to lord it over*.

lord'ling (lôrd'lĭng), *n.* A little or petty lord.

lord'ly (-lĭ), *a.* [3] Suitable for, or resembling, a lord; as: **a** Grand; noble. **b** Haughty; insolent. — *adv.* In a lordly manner. — **lord'li-ness**, *n.* [8].

lord'ship (lôrd'shĭp), *n.* **1.** Rank or position of a lord; hence [usually *cap.* and with *his* or *your*], a title applied to a lord (cf. GRACE, *n.*, 4) or a judge (in Great Britain). **2.** Seigniory; domain; jurisdiction of a lord. **3.** Dominion; authority.

lore (lōr), *n.* Knowledge.

lor'gnette' (lôr'nyĕt'), *n.* **1.** An eyeglass or eyeglasses with a long handle. **2.** An opera glass.

lorn (lôrn), *a.* Forsaken; desolate; forlorn.

lose (lŏŏz), *v. t.;* *pret. & p. p.* LOST (lŏst); *p. pr. & vb. n.* LOS'ING (lŏŏz'ĭng). **1.** To bring to destruction; ruin; — chiefly in the passive. **2.** To suffer the loss of; to be deprived of. **3.** To fail to keep, sustain, or maintain. **4.** To fail to keep in sight or mind. **5.** To go astray from, as from a road. **6.** To waste; squander. **7.** To fail to gain, as a prize. **8.** To prevent from gaining or keeping. **9.** To cause or suffer (one's self, a person) to lose his way or bearings. — *v. i.* To suffer loss. — **los'er** (lŏŏz'ẽr), *n.* [8].

loss (lŏs), *n.* **1.** State or fact of being destroyed; ruin. **2.** Act or fact of suffering deprivation; esp., unintentional parting with something. **3.** Act or fact of failing to win, or utilize. **4.** That which is lost. — at a loss, puzzled; uncertain.

lost (lŏst), *p. a.* **1.** Ruined. **2.** Parted with; gone out of one's possession. **3.** Having wandered from, or unable to find, the way; also, no longer visible. **4.** Exclusively occupied with something; as, *lost* in thought. **5.** Not gained or won; also, wasted.

lot (lŏt), *n.* **1.** An object, such as a piece of paper, used in deciding something by chance. **2.** Use of lots as a means of deciding anything. **3.** Share; portion. **4.** Fortune; fate. **5.** A portion or plot of land. **6.** A separate portion; a number of objects collectively. — *v. t.* **1.** To form or divide into lots, as land. **2.** To allot; apportion.

loth. Var. of LOATH.

lo'tion (lō'shŭn), *n.* A medicinal liquid for bathing the skin or an injured or diseased part.

lot'ter-y (lŏt'ẽr-ĭ),*n.; pl.* LOTTERIES (-ĭz). A scheme for distributing prizes by lot, esp. such a scheme in which lots, or chances, are sold.

lo'tus (lō'tŭs), *n.* **1.** In Greek legend, the fruit of the lotus tree, which if eaten caused a state of dreamy contentment and forgetfulness. **2.** Any of several flowering water plants represented in ancient Egyptian and Hindu art. **3.** Any of a genus (*Lotus*) of the bean family having red, pink, or white flowers. — **lo'tus-eat'er**, *n.*

loud (loud), *a.* [3] **1.** Of sounds, intense; not low, soft, or subdued. **2.** Making a loud sound; noisy. **3.** Striking; outspoken. **4.** Offensively vivid or strong; unrefined. *Colloq.* — *adv.* With loudness; loudly. — **-ly**, *adv.* — **-ness**, *n.*

āle, senāte, câre, ăm, ăccount, ärm, àsk, sofá; ēve, ēvent, ĕnd, recĕnt, makẽr; īce, ĭll; ōld, ŏbey, ôrb, ŏdd, sŏft, cŏnnect; ūse, ŭnite, ûrn, ŭp, circŭs; fŏŏd, fŏŏt; out, oi̯l ;

lounge (lounj), *v. i.* [1] To move or act in a lazy or listless way; spend time lazily. — *n.* **1.** An idle gait or stroll; state of reclining indolently. **2.** A kind of sofa. — **loung'er** (loun'jẽr), *n.* [8].

louse (lous), *n. ; pl.* LICE (līs). **1.** Any of certain small, wingless insects, parasitic on animals. **2.** Any of various other parasitic insects, etc.

lous'y (louz'ĭ), *a.* [3] Infested with lice.

lout (lout), *n.* A clownish fellow; a bumpkin.

lout'ish, *a.* [4] Clownish; rude; awkward. — **lout'ish-ly**, *adv.* [8] — **-ness**, *n.* [8].

lov'a-ble (lŭv'á-b'l), *a.* [4] Worthy of love. — **lov'a-ble-ness**, *n.* [8] — **lov'a-bly**, *adv.* [8].

love (lŭv), *n.* **1.** A feeling of strong personal attachment; ardent affection. **2.** Strong liking; fondness. **3.** Tender and passionate affection for one of the opposite sex. **4.** The object of affection. **5.** [*cap.*] Cupid. — *v. t.* [1] **1.** To have or manifest love for. **2.** To take delight or pleasure in ; like. — *v. i.* To be in love.

love'less, *a.* Without love ; unloved or unloving.

love'lorn' (-lôrn'), *a.* [4] Forsaken by one's love.

love'ly (-lĭ), *a.* [3] **1.** Beautiful; esp., having a delicate beauty. **2.** Beautiful in character. — **love'-li ness**, *n.* [8].

lov'er (lŭv'ẽr), *n.* One who loves ; esp., one in love with one of the other sex.

lov'ing (lŭv'ĭng), *p. a.* [4] Feeling or expressing love. — **lov'ing-ly**, *adv.* [8].

low (lō), *v. i.* To make the calling sound of cattle; moo. — *n.* The calling sound made by cattle.

low (lō), *a.* [3] **1.** Having small elevation ; not high or tall. **2.** Below the normal level, surface, etc. **3.** Near the horizon. **4.** Of relatively little importance ; humble in station. **5.** Deficient, inferior, or unusually small in quantity, intensity, value, etc. **6.** Of sounds, etc.: a Not loud. **b** *Music.* Not high; depressed in pitch. **7.** Deficient or inferior in strength, energy, animation, or the like. **8.** Lacking high character ; mean ; base ; vulgar. **9.** Not advanced in organization, evolution, civilization, etc. — *adv.* **1.** In or to a low position. **2.** Near the horizon. **3.** In subjection, poverty, or disgrace. **4.** Humbly; meanly. **5.** Under the usual price. **6.** Not loudly; gently.

low'er (lou'ẽr), *v. i.* **1.** To frown. **2.** To be dark and threatening, as clouds. — *n.* A lowering look.

low'er (lō'ẽr), *a., compar.* of LOW.

low'er (lō'ẽr), *v. t.* **1.** To let descend by its own weight. **2.** To reduce the height of. **3.** To reduce in intensity, strength, or value ; as, to *lower* a price. — *v. i.* To become lower or less ; diminish.

low'er-most (lō'ẽr-mōst), *a.* Lowest.

low'land (-lănd), *n.* Low or level country.

low'ly (-lĭ), *a.* [3] **1.** Low in rank ; modest ; humble ; meek. **2.** Low in position or development. — *adv.* **1.** Meekly; modestly. **2.** In a low position, manner, or degree. — **li-ness**, *n.* [8].

low'ness, *n.* Quality or state of being low.

loy'al (loi'ăl), *a.* **1.** Faithful, as to the lawful government or to a friend; true. **2.** Of or showing loyalty; as, *loyal* expressions. — **-ly**, *adv.* [8].

loy'al-ist, *n.* One who adheres to his sovereign, or to the lawful authority, esp. in times of revolt.

loy'al-ty (-tĭ), *n.* State or quality of being loyal.

loz'enge (lŏz'ĕnj), *n.* **1.** A figure with four equal sides and oblique angles; diamond. **2.** A small tablet flavored and often medicated.

lub'ber (lŭb'ẽr), *n.* **1.** Big, awkward fellow. **2.** *Naut.* Unskilled seaman.

lub'ber-ly, *a. & adv.* [4] Like a lubber.

lu'bri-cant (lū'brĭ-kănt), *a.* [4] Lubricating. — *n.* That which lubricates, as oil, grease, etc.

lu'bri-cate (-kāt), *v. t.* [1] **1.** To make smooth or slippery. **2.** To apply a lubricant to. — **lu'-bri-ca'tor** (lū'brĭ-kā'tẽr), *n.* [8].

lu'bri-ca'tion (-kā'shŭn), *n.* A lubricating.

lu'cent (lū'sĕnt), *a.* [4] Shining ; bright; clear.

lu-cern', **lu-cerne'** (lū-sûrn'), *n.* Alfalfa.

lu'cid (lū'sĭd), *a.* [4] **1.** Shining; bright. **2.** Clear. **3.** Designating, or marked by, a sane or normal state of the faculties. — **-ly**, *adv.* — **-ness**, *n.*

lu-cid'i-ty (lū-sĭd'ĭ-tĭ), *n.* Lucid quality or state.

Lu'ci-fer (lū'sĭ-fẽr), *n.* **1.** The planet Venus, when it is the morning star. **2.** Satan ; — chiefly in *as proud as Lucifer*. **3.** [*l. c.*] A friction match.

luck (lŭk), *n.* **1.** That which happens to one seemingly by chance ; chance ; hap ; fortune, good or bad. **2.** Favorable fortune ; good luck.

luck'less, *a.* [4] Unfortunate.

luck'y (-ĭ), *a.* [3] **1.** Favored by luck; fortunate. **2.** Producing good by chance or unexpectedly. — **luck'i-ly**, *adv.* [8] — **luck'i-ness**, *n.* [8].

lu'cra-tive (lū'krá-tĭv), *a.* [4] Yielding profit, esp. financial profit. — **-ly**, *adv.* — **-ness**, *n.* [8].

lu'cre (lū'kẽr ; lōō'-), *n.* Gain in money or goods; profit ; riches ; — now in an ill sense.

lu'cu-bra'tion (lū'kū-brā'shŭn), *n.* **1.** Laborious study. **2.** That which is, or appears as if, produced by study or meditation in retirement ; — usu. in *pl.*

lu'di-crous (lū'dĭ-krŭs), *a.* [4] Adapted to excite laughter ; ridiculous. — **-ly**, *adv.* — **-ness**, *n.*

luff (lŭf), *n. Naut.* **a** The act of sailing a ship closer to the wind. **b** The forward or weather part of a fore-and-aft sail. — *v. i. Naut.* To turn the head of a vessel toward the wind.

lug (lŭg), *n.* **1.** A projecting part. **2.** A lugsail.

lug (lŭg), *v. t. & i. ;* LUGGED (lŭgd); LUG'GING. To pull, drag, or carry, esp. with difficulty.

lug'gage (-ãj), *n.* That which is lugged ; esp., a traveler's baggage.

lug'ger (-ẽr), *n.* Vessel with a lugsail or lugsails.

lug'sail' (lŭg'sāl'), *n.* A four-sided sail bent to a yard hanging obliquely on the mast.

lu-gu'bri-ous (lū-gū'brĭ-ŭs), *a.* [4] Mournful; doleful. — **-ly**, *adv.* [8] — **-ness**, *n.* [8].

luke'warm' (lūk'wôrm'), *a.* Moderately warm ; tepid ; indifferent. — **-ly**, *adv.* — **-ness**, *n.*

lull (lŭl), *v. t.* To cause to rest by soothing influences ; calm. — *v. i.* To become gradually calm. — *n.* A brief cessation of storm or confusion.

lull'a-by' (lŭl'á-bī'), *n. ; pl.* -BIES (-bīz'). A soothing refrain, as to quiet a baby.

lum-ba'go (lŭm-bā'gō), *n.* Rheumatic pain in the loins and the lower part of the back.

lum'bar (lŭm'bàr), *a.* Of or near the loins.

lum'ber (-bẽr), *n.* **1.** Old or refuse household stuff. **2.** Timber, esp. that sawed into boards, planks, etc. — *v. i.* **1.** To move as if burdened. **2.** To cut logs in the forest, or prepare timber for market. — *v. t.* **1.** To heap together in disorder. **2.** To fill or encumber with lumber.

---

chair; go; sing, iŋk; then, thin ; nature, verdure ; yet; zh = z in azure. Numbers refer to §§ in the Special Notes which, with Abbreviations, Signs, etc., precede the Vocabulary.

lum′ber-ing (lŭm′bẽr-ĭng), n. The business of cutting or getting timber or logs from the forest for lumber. — **lum′ber-man** (-măn), n.

lu′mi-na-ry (lū′mĭ-nă-rĭ), n.; pl. -RIES (-rĭz). A body that gives light, esp. a heavenly body.

lu′mi-nos′i-ty (-nŏs′ĭ-tĭ),n.; pl. -TIES (-tĭz). Quality or state of being luminous.

lu′mi-nous (lū′mĭ-nŭs), a. [4] **1**. Shining ; brilliant. **2**. Enlightened ; intelligent ; also, clear ; intelligible. — **-ly**, adv. [8] — **-ness**, n. [8].

lump (lŭmp), n. **1**. A piece or mass of indefinite or irregular shape. **2**. A swelling. **3**. A whole aggregation, collection, lot. — v. t. **1**. To make into a lump ; make lumps on or in. **2**. To unite in one body or sum. **3**. To speak of collectively. — v. i. To form into a lump ; become lumpy.

lump′ish, a. [4] Like a lump ; inert ; gross ; heavy ; dull. — **lump′ish-ly**, adv. [8] — **-ness**, n. [8].

lump′y (lŭm′pĭ), a. [3] Covered with, or full of, lumps. Hence, of water, rough ; choppy.

lu′na-cy (-sĭ), n.; pl. -CIES (-sĭz). **1**. Unsoundness of mind. **2**. Extravagant folly ; madness.

lu′nar (-når), a. **1**. Of or pertaining to the moon. **2**. Measured by the moon's revolutions.

lu′nate (lū′nāt), a. [4] Crescent-shaped.

lu′na-tic (-nå-tĭk), a. [4] **1**. Affected with lunacy; crazy. **2**. For insane persons; as, a lunatic asylum. — n. An insane person.

lu-na′tion (lū-nā′shŭn), n. Time between successive new moons, averaging 29 d., 12 h., 44 m., 2.9 s.

lunch (lŭnch), n. **1**. A luncheon. Colloq. **2**. Food for a lunch. — v. i. To take lunch.

lunch′eon (lŭn′chŭn), n. **1**. Food, or a light repast, taken between meals or as an irregular meal. **2**. A light repast between breakfast and dinner.

lung (lŭng), n. One of the (usually two) compound saclike organs forming the respiratory organ of air-breathing vertebrates.

lunge (lŭnj), n. **1**. A sudden thrust, as with a sword. **2**. A plunging forward; leap. — v.i.&t. [1] To make, cause to make, or move with, a lunge.

lu′pine (lū′pĭn), n. A plant, of the bean family, with handsome white, yellow, blue, or purple flowers ; also, its seed, used as food.

lurch (lûrch), n. A sudden roll of a ship ; hence, a swaying or staggering movement. — v. i. To roll or sway suddenly to one side.

lurch, n. Embarrassment ; discomfiture. Obs., except in to leave (one) in the lurch.

lurch′er (lûr′chẽr), n. One of a mongrel breed of dogs, often used by poachers. Brit.

lure (lūr), n. **1**. An allurement. **2**. A decoy or bait. — v. t. [1] To draw to the lure; allure; entice.

lu′rid (lū′rĭd), a. [4] **1**. Pale yellow ; ghastly pale ; wan ; dismal. **2**. Like glowing fire seen through smoke.—**-ly**, adv. [8] — **-ness**, n. [8].

lurk (lûrk), v. i. **1**. To lie hidden, as in ambush. **2**. To exist secretly. **3**. To move furtively.

lus′cious (lŭsh′ŭs), a. [4] **1**. Grateful to taste or smell, esp. from sweetness; delicious. **2**. Sweet to excess; cloying. — **-ly**, adv. [8] —**-ness**, n. [8].

lush (lŭsh), a. [3] **1**. Juicy or succulent ; luxuriant, as grass. **2**. Characterized by lush growth.

lust (lŭst), n. **1**. Sensuous, esp. sexual, desire. **2**. Longing desire; — usually in a bad sense; as, lust of gain.— v. i. To have lust ; — often with after.

lus′ter (lŭs′tẽr), n. [6] **1**. Fact or quality of shining with reflected light; shine or sheen; gloss. **2**. Brilliancy; glitter. **3**. A chandelier or the like.

lust′ful (lŭst′fŏol), a. [4] Full of, or excited by, lust ; characterized by lust.

lust′i-ly (lŭs′tĭ-lĭ), adv. In a lusty manner.

lust′i-ness, n. Robustness.

lus′tre. Var. of LUSTER.

lus′trous (-trŭs), a. [4] Having luster or sheen; shining ; hence, radiant ; illustrious.

lust′y (-tĭ), a. [3] Full of life and vigor; vigorous.

lute (lūt), n. A cement for sealing joints, vessels, or tubes, or for coating retorts, etc., when exposed to heat. — v. t. [1] To close, or cover, with lute.

lute, n. Music. A stringed instrument having a large pear-shaped body and played by plucking.

lux-u′ri-ance (lŭks-ū′rĭ-ăns; lŭg-zhōō′-), n. State or quality of being luxuriant; exuberance.

lux-u′ri-ant (-ănt), a. [4] Exuberant in growth; rank ; abundant ; profuse. — **-ly**, adv. [8].

lux-u′ri-ate (-āt), v. i. [1] To feed or live luxuriously ; to revel (in).

lux-u′ri-ous (-rĭ-ŭs), a. [4] Of, pertaining to, or ministering to, luxury.—**-ly**,adv. —**-ness**, n. [8].

lux′u-ry (lŭk′shŏō-rĭ), n.; pl. -RIES (-rĭz). **1**. Indulgence in costly gratifications of the tastes ; a mode of life marked by this. **2**. Anything which pleases the senses, and is also costly.

ly-ce′um (lī-sē′ŭm), n.; pl. E. -UMS (-ŭmz), L. -CEA (-á). **1**. An establishment for instruction by lectures. **2**. A literary and debating society.

lye (lī), n. A strong caustic alkaline solution, esp. that made from wood ashes.

ly′ing (lī′ĭng), p. pr. & vb. n. of LIE.

ly′ing-in′, n. Confinement in childbirth.

lymph (lĭmf), n. **1**. Pure water. Poetic. **2**. A fluid contained in the lymphatics. It consists chiefly of blood plasma and colorless corpuscles. **3**. A material exuded from inflamed blood vessels.

lym-phat′ic (lĭm-făt′ĭk), a. [4] **1**. Of, pertaining to, containing, or conveying, lymph. **2**. Designating or having a temperament lacking energy or animation.— n. Anat. A vessel containing or conveying lymph. [lymphatic gland.]

lymph′oid (lĭm′foid), a. Resembling lymph or a

lynch (lĭnch), v. t. To inflict punishment (now only death) upon, without the forms of law.

lynch law. Practice of inflicting summary punishment, esp. death, for crimes or offenses, without due process of law.

lynx (lĭnks), n. Any of certain wild cats having long legs, a stubby tail, and, often, tufted ears.

lynx′—eyed′, a. Having acute sight.

lyre (līr), n. Music. A stringed instrument of the harp class used by the ancient Greeks, esp. for accompanying song and recitation (see LYRIC).

Lyre.

lyr′ic (lĭr′ĭk), n. A lyric poem; a lyrical composition.

lyr′ic (lĭr′ĭk) { a. [4] **1**. Of or pertaining to a
lyr′i-cal (-ĭ-kăl) } lyre or harp. **2**. Suited to be sung to the lyre ; appropriate for song ; — used of poetry, generally in stanzas, expressive of the poet's feeling rather than of incident or events.—**lyr′i-cal-ly**, adv. [8].

āle, senāte, câre, ăm, ăccount, ärm, ȧsk, sofȧ ; ēve, ĕvent, ĕnd, recĕnt, makẽr; īce, ĭll ; ōld, ȯbey, ôrb, ŏdd, sŏft, cŏnnect ; ūse, ŭnite, ûrn, ŭp, circŭs; fŏŏd, fŏŏt; out, oil;

M

ma (mä), *n.* Mamma. *Colloq. or Childish.*

ma'am (mäm; mǎm), *n.* Madam. *Colloq.*

mac-ad'am (mǎk-ǎd'ǎm), *n.* **1.** Macadamized roadway or pavement. **2.** The broken stone used in macadamizing.

mac-ad'am-ize (-īz), *v. t.* [1] To construct or finish (a road) by putting a closely packed layer of small broken stone on a convex roadbed.

mac'a-ro'ni (mǎk'á-rō'nĭ), *n.; pl.* -NIS (-nĭz), or -NIES (-nĭz). **1.** A paste, chiefly of wheat flour dried in slender tubes, and used, when cooked, as food. While the same in composition as macaroni, *spaghetti* is smaller and solid and *vermicelli* solid and smaller still. **2.** *Hist.* An exquisite; dandy.

mac'a-roon' (-rōōn'), *n.* A small cake containing pounded almonds.

ma-caw' (má-kô'), *n.* Any of many very large, long-tailed, gaudy parrots of tropical America.

mace (mās), *n.* **1.** A heavy club, wholly or partly of metal and often spiked. **2.** A staff borne by, or carried before, certain officials.

mace, *n.* A kind of fragrant aromatic spice consisting of the dried outer covering of the nutmeg.

mac'er-ate (mǎs'ẽr-āt), *v. t.* [1] To soften by steeping in a liquid; as, to *macerate* food.

mac'er-a'tion (-ā'shŭn), *n.* A macerating.

ma-che'te (mä-chā'tā), *n.* A large heavy knife, used for cutting cane, etc. *Sp. America.*

Mach'i-a-vel'li-an (mǎk'ĭ-á-vĕl'ĭ-ǎn), *a.* Intriguing; crafty; cunning.

mach'i-nate (mǎk'ĭ-nāt), *v. i. & t.* [1] To plan; contrive; esp., to scheme to do harm; plot.

mach'i-na'tion (-nā'shŭn), *n.* Act of machinating; also, a hostile scheme; an artful plot.

ma-chine' (má-shēn'), *n.* **1.** A mechanical contrivance. **2.** A combination of mechanical parts serving to transmit and modify force and motion so as to do work. **3.** The body or leaders in a political party through which its activities are largely controlled. — *v. t.* [1] To shape or finish by the action of machinery.

ma-chin'er-y (má-shēn'ẽr-ĭ), *n.* **1.** Machines in general or collectively; also, the working parts of a machine. **2.** The agencies by which anything is kept in action or a desired result is obtained.

ma-chin'ist (-ĭst), *n.* A constructer of, or one skilled in, machines.

mack'er-el (mǎk'ẽr-ĕl), *n.* (See PLURAL, *n.*, *Note.*) An important food fish of the North Atlantic.

mackerel sky. A sky flecked with small white clouds. Cf. CIRRO-CUMULUS.

mack'in-tosh (mǎk'ĭn-tŏsh), *n.* A kind of waterproof outer garment.

ma'cron (mā'krŏn; mǎk'rŏn), *n. Gram. & Pron.* A short, straight, horizontal mark [‾] placed over vowels to denote long quantity.

☞ In this book the macron indicates the name sounds of vowels: *ā* in *dāme*, *ē* in *ēve*, *ī* in *īce*, *ō* in *ōld*, *ū* in *ūse.*

mad (mǎd), *a.;* MAD'DER (-ẽr); -DEST. **1.** Disordered in intellect; insane. **2.** Rashly foolish;

senseless. **3.** Frenzied; furious; *Colloq.*, angry; vexed. **4.** Carried away by desire or passion. **5.** Extravagantly gay. **6.** Rabid.

mad'am (mǎd'ǎm), *n.* A form of polite address to a lady; — for the plural the French *mesdames* is used in address or as a title.

ma'dame (má/dàm'; má-däm'; *often* mǎd'ǎm), *n.; pl.* MESDAMES (mā/dàm'). My lady; — a French title of courtesy for a married woman. Abbr. *Mme.*

mad'cap' (mǎd'kǎp'), *a.* [4] Inclined to wild or dangerous sports; wild. — *n.* A madcap person.

mad'den (-'n), *v. t. & i.* To make or become mad.

mad'der (-ẽr), *n.* **1.** A European herb with small yellowish flowers. **2.** The root of this plant, used in dyeing; also, a coloring matter prepared from it.

mad'ding (-ĭng), *p. a.* [4] Mad; raving; wild.

made (mād), *pret. & p. p. of* MAKE. Hence: *p. a.* Artificially produced or constructed.

Ma-dei'ra (má-dē'rá; má-dā'rá), *n.* Wine made on the island of Madeira.

‖ **ma'de-moi'selle'** (mǎd'mwá'zĕl'; mǎd'ē-mŏ-zĕl'; *colloq.* mǎm'zĕl'), *n.; pl.* MESDEMOISELLES (mā'd'-mwá'zĕl'). [F.] A French title of courtesy equivalent to the English *Miss.* Abbr. *Mlle.*

mad'ly (mǎd'lĭ), *adv.* In a mad manner; wildly.

mad'man (-mǎn), *n.; pl.* -MEN (-mĕn). A lunatic.

mad'ness, *n.* Insanity; folly; frenzy.

Ma-don'na (má-dŏn'á), *n.* **1.** The Virgin Mary. **2.** A picture or a statue of the Virgin Mary.

ma-dras' (má-drás'), *n.* A kind of fine cotton fabric.

mad'ri-gal (mǎd'rĭ-gǎl), *n.* **1.** A lyric, usually amorous and adapted to musical setting. **2.** *Music.* **a** An unaccompanied setting of such a poem in (usually) five or six parts. **b** Part song or glee.

mag'a-zine' (mǎg'á-zēn'), *n.* **1.** A storehouse or warehouse; esp., a place for keeping military stores. **2. a** The powder room in a fort or a ship. **b** A chamber in a gun for holding cartridges to be fed automatically to the piece. **3.** A periodical publication containing various articles.

ma-gen'ta (má-jĕn'tá), *n.* A dark red aniline dye; also, the purplish red color produced by it.

mag'got (mǎg'ŏt), *n.* **1.** A soft-bodied, grublike, footless larva of an insect, as that of the house fly. **2.** A whim. — **mag'got-y** (-ĭ), *a.* [4].

mag'ic (mǎj'ĭk), *n.* **1.** The art which pretends to produce effects by the aid of supernatural beings or by a mastery of secret forces in nature. **2.** The power brought into play by magic; hence, any seemingly secret power.

mag'ic (mǎj'ĭk), **mag'i-cal** (-ĭ-kǎl), *a.* [4] **1.** Of, pertaining to, or used in, magic. **2.** Seemingly due to magic; enchanting. — **magic lantern**, an optical instrument for throwing upon a screen, in a darkened room, pictures from slides placed in the focus of a lens. — **mag'i-cal-ly,** *adv.* [8].

ma-gi'cian (má-jĭsh'ǎn), *n.* A sorcerer; conjurer.

mag'is-te'ri-al (mǎj'ĭs-tē'rĭ-ǎl), *a.* [4] **1.** Of or pertaining to a master; authoritative; imperious. **2.** Of or pertaining to a magistrate, his office, or his duties. — **-ly,** *adv.* [8]. — **-ness,** *n.* [8].

mag'is-tra-cy (măj'ĭs-trá-sĭ), *n. ; pl.* -CIES (-sĭz). Office of a magistrate; magistrates collectively.

mag'is-trate (-trāt), *n.* A person having power as a public civil officer; as: **a** The official first in rank in a government. **b** An official of a class having summary, often criminal, jurisdiction.

mag'na-nim'i-ty (măg'ná-nĭm'ĭ-tĭ), *n.* Quality of being magnanimous.

mag-nan'i-mous (măg-năn'ĭ-mŭs), *a.* [4] **1.** Great of mind; raised above what is low or mean. **2.** Dictated by or exhibiting nobleness of soul. — **-ly**, *adv.* [8]. [ence, or distinction.]

mag'nate (măg'nāt), *n.* A person of rank, influ-

mag-ne'si-a (măg-nē'zhĭ-á, -zhá; -shĭ'á, -shá), *n. Chem.* Magnesium oxide, a light earthy white substance, used as a laxative.

mag-ne'si-um (-nē'zhĭ-ŭm; -shĭ'-ŭm), *n. Chem.* A silver-white metal, light and easily worked. It burns with a dazzling light.

mag'net (măg'nĕt), *n.* **1.** Loadstone. **2.** Any body which, like loadstone, has polarity and the property of strongly attracting iron and some other substances; esp., a mass of iron or steel having such properties artificially imparted.

mag-net'ic (măg nĕt'ĭk), *a.*. [4] **1.** Of or pert. to the magnet; possessing the properties of the magnet. **2.** Gifted with great personal attractiveness. — **magnetic needle**, a slender bar of magnetized steel which, when free to swing, as in a compass, indicates the direction of the earth's magnetism, and so approximately the north and south line.

mag'net-ism (măg'nĕt-ĭz'm), *n.* **1.** Property, quality, or state, of being magnetic; manifestation of the force in nature which is seen in a magnet. **2.** The science of magnetic phenomena. **3.** Power to attract others; personal attraction.

mag'net-ite (-īt), *n.* An iron oxide, strongly attracted by the magnet. It sometimes has the power to attract iron and is then called *loadstone*.

mag'net-iz'a-ble (-ĭz'á-b'l), *a.* Capable of being magnetized.

mag'net-i-za'tion (-ĭ-zā'shŭn), *n.* A magnetizing; also, degree to which a body is magnetized.

mag'net-ize (-ĭz), *v. t.* [1] **1.** To give magnetic properties to; convert into a magnet. **2.** To attract by magnetism; captivate. — **mag'net-iz'er** (-ĭz'ẽr), *n.* [8]. [nent magnets.]

mag-ne'to (măg-nē'tō), *n.* A dynamo with perma-

mag'net-o-e-lec'tric (măg'nĕt-ō-ē-lĕk'trĭk; măg-nē'tō-), *a.* — **-tric-al.** *a.* Pertaining to electricity developed by magnets. [being magnificent.]

mag-nif'i-cence (măg-nĭf'ĭ-sĕns), *n.* Quality of

mag-nif'i-cent (-sĕnt), *a.* [4] **1.** Marked by grandeur or splendor; imposing. **2.** Of ideas, language, etc.: Exalted ; noble. — **-ly**, *adv.* [8].

mag'ni-fy (măg'nĭ-fī), *v. t.* [2] **1.** To praise highly; extol. *Archaic.* **2.** To make great or greater; amplify ; enlarge, really or, as by a microscope, only apparently. **3.** To exaggerate. — *v. i.* To make objects appear larger, as a lens does. — **mag'ni-fi'er** (-fī'ẽr), *n.* [8].

mag-nil'o-quent (măg-nĭl'ō-kwĕnt), *a.* [4] Speaking pompously ; bombastic. — **-ly**, *adv.* [8].

mag'ni-tude (măg'nĭ-tūd), *n.* **1.** Greatness, as in size, position, importance, etc. **2.** Size, whether great or small. **3.** *Astron.* Degree of brightness.

mag-no'li-a (măg-nō'lĭ-á), *n.* Any of various trees (genus *Magnolia*) having aromatic bark and large fragrant white, pink, or purple flowers.

mag'pie (măg'pī), *n.* **1.** A bird, allied to the jays, having black-and-white plumage. **2.** A chatterer.

mag'uey (măg'wā ; *Sp.* mä-gā'ē̇), *n.* In general, any species of agave, esp. one yielding useful fiber; specif., the century plant.

Mag'yar (mŏd'yŏr), *n.* One of the dominant people of Hungary; also, their language.

ma-hog'a-ny (má-hŏg'á-nĭ), *n.* A tropical American tree with hard, dark wood ; also, the wood.

ma-hout' (má-hout'), *n.* The keeper and driver of an elephant. *East Indies.*

maid (mād), *n.* **1.** An unmarried girl or woman; a maiden; a virgin. **2.** A female servant.

maid'en (-'n), *n.* A maid. — *a.* **1.** Of or pertaining to a maiden. **2.** Virgin or virginal ; chaste ; unmarried. **3.** Fresh; untried. **4.** First; earliest.

maid'en-hair' (-hâr'), *n.*, *or* **maidenhair fern.** A fern with slender stipes and delicate fronds.

maid'en-hood (-hŏŏd), *n.* State or time of being a maiden; virginity. [**ness** (-lĭ-nĕs), *n.*]

maid'en-ly, *a.* Of or pert. to a maiden. — **-li-**|

maid'en-ly, *adv.* In a maidenlike manner.

mail (māl), *n.* **1.** A flexible fabric of linked metal rings for defensive armor. **2.** Hence, erroneously, armor or any defensive covering. — *v. t.* To arm with mail.

mail, *n.* **1.** a Matter, as letters, parcels, etc., conveyed under public authority from one post office to another. **b** The system of appliances used in the postal service. **2.** That which conveys mail, as a vehicle or person. — *v. t.* To deliver into the custody of the post office for transmission ; post; as, to *mail* a letter. *Chiefly U. S.*

mail'a-ble (-á-b'l), *a.* Lawful to mail, or post.

maim (mām), *v. t.* To mutilate ; cripple ; disable.

main (mān), *n.* **1.** Strength ; force; power. *Archaic,* except in *with might and main.* **2.** A broad stretch or expanse ; esp. : **a** Mainland. **b** Main or high sea. **3.** Chief part; essential point. **4.** A principal duct, pipe, or conduit. — *a.* **1.** Chief, first in size, rank, importance, etc. **2.** Sheer; utter. **3.** *Naut.* Connected with the mainmast.

main'land (-lănd), *n.* The continent; principal land ;—in general, opposed to *island*, or *peninsula.*

main'ly, *adv.* Principally ; chiefly.

main'mast (-màst), *n. Naut.* The mast regarded as the principal mast in a ship or other vessel.

main'sail' (măn'sāl' ; *naut.* măn's'l), *n. Naut.* The principal sail on the mainmast.

main'spring' (-sprĭng'), *n.* The principal spring in a mechanism, as in a watch; hence, chief motive.

main'stay' (-stā'), *n.* **1.** *Naut.* The stay from the top of the mainmast forward. **2.** Main support.

main-tain' (mān-tān' ; mĕn-), *v. t.* **1.** To hold or keep in any state, esp. in efficiency or soundness; keep up. **2.** To continue in or with ; carry on. **3.** To bear the expense of ; support. **4.** To keep possession of ; hold. **5.** To affirm; esp., to assert as true or as subject to proof; also, to support by argument. — **-a-ble**, *a.* [4]. — **-er**, *n.* [8].

main'te-nance (mān'tĕ-nǎns), *n.* **1.** Act of maintaining ; state of being maintained ; support, sustenance, defense, etc. **2.** Means of sustenance.

āle, senāte, câre, ăm, *ȧ*ccount, ärm, ȧsk, sofȧ; ēve, ĕvent, ĕnd, recĕnt, makẽr; īce, ĭll; ōld, ŏbey, ôrb, ŏdd, sŏft, cŏnnect; ūse, ŭnite, ûrn, ŭp, circŭs; fōōd, fŏŏt; out, oil;

maize (māz), *n.* Indian corn.

ma-jes'tic (mȧ-jĕs'tĭk), *a.* [4] Possessing or exhibiting majesty; grand. — **-ti-cal-ly,** *adv.* [8].

maj'es-ty (măj'ĕs-tĭ), *n.; pl.* -TIES (-tĭz). **1.** Sovereign dignity or authority; grandeur; exalted dignity. **2.** Hence [*cap.*], with a possessive, used as the title of a sovereign; as, His *Majesty.*

ma-jol'i-ca (mȧ-jŏl'ĭ-kȧ; -yŏl'-), *n.* A kind of pottery, with opaque glazing and showy decoration.

ma'jor (mā'jẽr), *a.* **1.** Greater in number, quantity, rank, etc.; as, the *major* part of the assembly. **2.** *Music.* Greater by a half step than the minor. — *n.* **1.** One of superior rank in a class. **2.** *Mil.* An officer next in rank above a captain. See ARMY.

ma'jor–do'mo (mā'jẽr-dō'mō), *n.; pl.* -DOMOS (-mōz). A head steward or palace official. Jocularly, a butler; steward.

major general. *Mil.* An officer of a certain rank, properly commanding a division. See ARMY.

ma-jor'i-ty (mȧ-jŏr'ĭ-tĭ), *n.; pl.* -TIES (-tĭz). **1.** Status of being of full legal age. **2.** The greater of two numbers regarded as parts of a whole; more than half of any total; also, the excess of this greater number over the remainder.

make (māk), *v. t.; pret. & p. p.* MADE (mād); *p. pr. & vb. n.* MAK'ING (māk'ĭng). **1.** To form, or cause to be; to prepare, manufacture, compose, or the like; as, to *make* bread; twice one *makes* two. **2. a** To form in the mind; as, to *make* plans. **b** To design; as to *make* a map. **c** To compute to be; as, he *made* the weight fifty pounds. **d** To signify; amount to; as, it *makes* no difference. **3.** To cause to exist; to create; as, to *make* a noise; to *make* laws. **4.** To cause to be or become; as, to *make* known; to *make* some one master. **5.** To assure the success of; as, he is a *made* man. **6.** To cause (to act in a certain way); as, they *made* him go away. **7.** To prepare or arrange; as to *make* a bed. **8.** To gain; acquire; get; as, to *make* money. **9.** To accomplish by going; also, to arrive at; as to *make* land. — *v. i.* **1.** To engage in the process of forming something, or to cause something to be formed; as, "*make* or mar." **2.** To cause something (understood) to assume a certain condition or to perform a certain action; as, to *make* fast; *make* ready. **3.** To act (in a certain manner); as, to *make* bold, merry, etc. **4.** To proceed; as, he *made* toward home. **5.** To increase; as, the snow *makes* fast.

☞ *Make* is often used intransitively in place of the passive; as, bolts are *making* in this shop.

make, *n.* **1. a** Structure; form. **b** Constitution; build. **2. a** Process of manufacture. **b** Output.

make'–be-lieve', *n.* A feigning to believe, as in children's play; a fiction. — *a.* Feigned; insincere.

mak'er (māk'ẽr), *n.* One that makes.

make'shift' (māk'shĭft'), *n.* Temporary expedient. — *a.* Shifty; serving as makeshift.

make'–up', *n.* **1.** The way in which anything is put together; as: **a** Way in which one is dressed, painted, etc., for a part, as on the stage. **b** Arrangement of type or of articles, headlines, etc. **2.** Constitution or composition of anything.

mal'a-chite (măl'ȧ-kīt), *n.* A carbonate of copper.

mal'ad-min'is-ter (măl'ăd-mĭn'ĭs-tẽr), *v. t.* To administer badly. [ministration.]

mal'ad-min'is-tra'tion (-trā'shŭn), *n.* Bad ad-

mal'a-droit' (măl'ȧ-droit'), *a.* [4] Clumsy; awkward; unskillful. — **-ly,** *adv.* [8] — **-ness,** *n.* [8].

mal'a-dy (măl'ȧ-dĭ), *n.; pl.* -DIES (-dĭz). A disease.

Mal'a-ga (-gȧ), *n.* A sweet, white Spanish grape.

mal'a-pert (măl'ȧ-pûrt), *a.* [4] Bold; impudent; saucy; pert. — *n.* A malapert person.

mal-ap'ro-pos' (măl-ăp'rȯ-pō'), *a.* [4] Unseasonable; out of place. — *adv.* Inappropriately.

ma-la'ri-a (mȧ-lā'rĭ-ȧ), *n.* **1.** Infected or noxious air; esp., an unhealthy exhalation from certain soils, as a marsh; miasma. **2.** A fever formerly attributed to such exhalations, but now to blood parasites transferred to man by mosquitoes.

ma-la'ri-al (-ăl), **ma-la'ri-ous** (-ŭs), *a.* Of or pertaining to, or infected by, malaria.

mal'con-tent' (măl'kŏn-tĕnt'),*a.*[4] Discontented, esp. with the government. — *n.* One who is malcontent.

male (māl), *a.* **1.** Designating, or of or pert. to, the sex which begets young. **2.** Masculine. — *n.* A male human being, animal, or plant.

mal'e-dic'tion (măl'ē-dĭk'shŭn),*n.* **1.** A proclaiming of evil against some one; a cursing; a curse. **2.** Slander. [fense; crime.]

mal'e-fac'tion (-făk'shŭn), *n.* An evil deed; of-

mal'e-fac'tor (-făk'tẽr), *n.* One guilty of a crime; a criminal. — **-fac'tress** (-trĕs), *n. fem.* [8].

ma-lev'o-lence (mȧ-lĕv'ȯ-lĕns), *n.* Quality of being malevolent.

ma-lev'o-lent (-lĕnt), *a.* [4] Disposed to injure others; showing ill will. — **-ly,** *adv.* [8].

mal-fea'sance (măl-fē'zǎns), *n.* Wrongdoing; specif., an illegal deed; official misconduct.

mal'for-ma'tion (măl'fôr-mā'shŭn), *n.* Irregular, abnormal, or wrong formation or structure.

mal'ice (măl'ĭs), *n.* **1.** Enmity of heart; malevolence. **2.** *Law.* State of mind shown by intent to commit an unlawful act.

ma-li'cious (mȧ-lĭsh'ŭs), *a.* [4] **1.** Indulging or exercising malice. **2.** Characterized by malice; arising from ill will. — **-ly,** *adv.* — **-ness,** *n.*

ma-lign' (-līn'), *a.* [3] **1.** Having an evil disposition; malevolent; malignant. **2.** Tending to injure; evil; baleful; sinister. — *v. t.* To speak evil of; slander; traduce. — **ma-lign'er,** *n.* [8].

ma-lig'nan-cy (-lĭg'nǎn-sĭ), *n.* State or quality of being malignant.

ma-lig'nant (-nǎnt), *a.* [4] **1.** In medicine, tending or threatening to produce death; virulent. **2.** Having a baleful influence; malign. **3.** Disposed to do harm or inflict suffering; malicious. — *n.* A malcontent. — **ma-lig'nant-ly,** *adv.* [8].

ma-lig'ni-ty (-nĭ-tĭ), *n.; pl.* -TIES (-tĭz). **1.** State or quality of being malignant; malignancy. **2.** A malignant act, feeling,event, etc.;— usually in *pl.*

ma-lign'ly (mȧ-līn'lĭ), *adv.* In a malign manner.

ma-lin'ger (-lĭŋ'gẽr), *v. i.* To feign illness or inability, in order to avoid duty, esp. military duty. — **ma-lin'ger-er,** *n.* [8].

mall (môl), *n.* **1.** A maul. **2.** A shaded walk.

mal'lard (măl'ẽrd), *n.* The male of the common wild duck; any wild duck of this species.

mal'le-a-bil'i-ty (măl'ē-ȧ-bĭl'ĭ-tĭ), *n.* Quality of being malleable.

mal'le-a-ble (-ē-ȧ-b'l), *a.* [4] Capable of being extended or shaped by hammering or rolling.

---

chair; go; sing, iŋk; then, thin; nature, verdure; yet; zh = z in azure. Numbers refer to §§ in the Special Notes which, with Abbreviations, Signs, etc., precede the Vocabulary.

mal′let (măl′ĕt), *n.* **1.** A small short-handled maul, used esp. for driving a tool, as a chisel. **2. a** The wooden hammerlike implement used to drive the balls in playing croquet. **b** A polo stick.

mal′low (-ō), *n.* Any of a genus of common wild plants, many very mucilaginous, with pink or purple flowers; also, any plant of the same family.

malm′sey (mäm′zĭ), *n.* A rich sweet wine, originally produced in Greece.

mal′nu-tri′tion (măl′nū-trĭsh′ŭn), *n.* Faulty nutrition.

mal-o′dor-ous (-ō′dẽr-ŭs), *a.* [4] Ill-smelling.

mal-prac′tice (-prăk′tĭs), *n.* Wrongful or negligent practice, as by a physician.

malt (môlt), *n.* Grain, generally barley, steeped in water until it has sprouted. — *v. t.* **1.** To convert or change into malt. **2.** To make or treat with malt.

Common Mallow, Flowering Shoot.

mal-treat′ (măl-trēt′), *v. t.* To treat ill; abuse.

mal-treat′ment (-mĕnt), *n.* Ill treatment; abuse.

mal′ver-sa′tion (măl′vẽr-sā′shŭn), *n.* Evil conduct; corruption or extortion in office.

mam-ma′ (mȧ-mä′; mä′mä), *n.* Also **ma-ma′.** Mother; — usually a child's word.

mam′ma (măm′ȧ), *n.; pl.* -MÆ (-ē). *Anat.* A glandular organ for secreting milk, characteristic of all mammals, but normally rudimentary in the male.

mam′mal (-ăl), *n.* One of the Mammalia.

Mam-ma′li-a (mă-mā′lĭ-ȧ), *n. pl.* *Zoöl.* The highest class of vertebrates, including man and all other animals that suckle their young.

mam-ma′li-an (mă-mā′lĭ-ăn), *a.* Of or pert. to, or characteristic of, the Mammalia, or mammals.

mam′ma-ry (măm′ȧ-rĭ), *a.* Of or pertaining to the mammæ, or breasts; as, the *mammary* gland.

mam′mon (-ŭn), *n.* In the Scriptures, riches; [*cap.*] the demon of greed; riches, personified.

mam′moth (-ŏth), *n.* A huge, extinct elephant with a long hairy coat and upwardly curving tusks. — *a.* [4] Very large; gigantic.

mam′my (măm′ĭ), *n.; pl.* -MIES (-ĭz). **1.** Mother; —a child's word. **2.** In the southern U.S., a negro nurse or old family servant.

man (măn), *n.; pl.* MEN (mĕn). **1.** A human being. **2.** The human race; mankind. **3.** The male human being; esp., an adult male person. **4.** With *a*: one, or any one, indefinitely. **5.** One having in a high degree the distinctive qualities of manhood; also, manliness. **6.** A husband. *Obs. or Dial.*, except in *man and wife.* **7.** An adult male servant or employee. **8.** One of the pieces in certain games, as chess or draughts (checkers). — *v. t.;* MANNED (mănd); MAN′NING. **1.** To supply with men, as for service. **2.** To make manly; brace up.

man′a-cle (măn′ȧ-k′l), *n.* A handcuff; a fetter; restraint; — usually in *pl.* — *v. t.* [1] To shackle.

man′age (-ăj), *v. t.* [1] **1.** To have under control and direction; administer; control; carry on. **2.** To bring around cunningly to one's plans. **3.** To contrive. — *v. i.* To direct affairs; administer.

man′age-a-ble (-ȧ-b'l), *a.* Such as can be managed. — **-ness**, *n.* [8] — **man′age-a-bly**, *adv.* [8].

man′age-ment (-mĕnt), *n.* **1.** Act or art of managing; administration; guidance; control. **2.** Judicious use of means to accomplish an end; cunning practice. **3.** Those collectively who manage an enterprise or interest; board of managers.

man′ag-er (-ȧ-jẽr), *n.* One who manages; director.

man′a-ge′ri-al (-ȧ-jē′rĭ-ăl), *a.* Of or pertaining to a manager.

man-da′mus (măn-dā′mŭs), *n.* *Law.* In the U. S., a writ issued by a superior court to an inferior court, or to some corporation or person, to enforce the performance of some public duty.

man′da-rin (măn′dȧ-rĭn), *n.* **1.** A Chinese public officer of one of the nine grades entitled to wear a button on the hat. **2.** [*cap.*] The dialect of Chinese used by the official classes; more widely, the chief dialect of China. **3.** A small Chinese species of orange.

man′date (-dāt), *n.* An authoritative command; injunction; order.

man′da-to-ry (măn′dȧ-tō-rĭ), *a.* [4] Containing, or of the nature of, a mandate; obligatory.

man′di-ble (-dĭ-b'l), *n.* A jaw; — chiefly of the jaws in beaked animals, as birds.

man′do-lin (-dô-lĭn), *n.* *Music.* An instrument of the lute kind, having a deep pear-shaped body.

man′drake (-drāk), *n.* **1.** A European herb of the nightshade family. **2.** The May apple. *U. S.*

man′drel (-drĕl), *n.* **1.** *Machinery.* An axis or spindle used to support work which is being operated on. **2.** A steel core around which metal, etc., may be cast or shaped.

mane (mān), *n.* The long heavy hair on the upper side of, or about, the neck of some quadrupeds, as the horse, lion, etc. — **maned** (mānd), *a.*

ma′nège′ (mȧ′nēzh′), *n.* Also **ma-nege′** (mȧ-nēzh′). **1.** A school of horsemanship; riding academy. **2.** Art of riding, driving, or training horses.

ma-neu′ver (mȧ-nōō′vẽr; -nū′vẽr), *n.* [6] **1.** A military or naval evolution. **2.** A stratagem; artifice. — *v. i.;* -VERED or -VRED (-vẽrd), -VER-ING (-vẽr-ĭng) or -VRING (-vrĭng). **1.** To execute a maneuver. **2.** To manage with address or art; scheme. — *v. t.* **1.** To cause to maneuver, as troops or ships. **2.** To put, get, make, draw, etc., by maneuvering. **3.** To manage with skill; manipulate. — **ma-neu′ver-er**, *n.* [8].

man′ful (măn′fŏŏl), *a.* [4] Manly; brave; resolute. — **-ly**, *adv.* — **-ness**, *n.*

man′ga-nese′ (măn′gȧ-nēs′; -nēz′), *n.* A hard, brittle metal having a grayish white color.

mange (mānj), *n.* A persistent contagious skin disease affecting various animals and sometimes man, caused by minute parasitic mites.

man′gel-wur′zel (măn′g'l-wûr′z'l), *n.* A large coarse variety of beet grown as fodder.

man′ger (mān′jẽr), *n.* A trough or open box in which fodder is placed for horses or cattle.

man′gle (măn′g'l), *v. t.* [1] **1.** To cut or hack with repeated strokes at random. **2.** To spoil, mutilate, or injure in making, doing, or performing.

man′gle, *n.* A machine for smoothing cloth by roller pressure. — *v. t.* [1] To smooth with a mangle, as damp linen. — **man′gler**, *n.* [8].

man'go (măŋ'gō), *n.; pl.* -GOES or -GOS (-gōz). An oblong yellowish tropical fruit; also, the tree.

man'grove (-grōv), *n.* A tropical tree or shrub with evergreen leaves and yellowish flowers.

man'gy (măn'jĭ), *a.* [3] **1.** Having, of the nature of, or caused by, the mange. **2.** Shabby; squalid.

man'hole' (măn'hōl'), *n.* A hole through which a man may get access to a drain, etc.

man'hood (-hŏŏd), *n.* **1.** State of being a man. **2.** Manly quality; courage. **3.** Men collectively.

ma'ni-a (mā'nĭ-à), *n.* **1.** Violent derangement of mind; insanity. **2.** Excessive excitement or enthusiasm; a "craze"; a "rage"; as, a stamp *mania*.

ma'ni-ac (-ăk), *a.* [4] **1.** Raving with madness; mad. **2.** Frantic; violent. — *n.* A madman.

ma-ni'a-cal (má-nī'á-kăl), *a.* [4] Maniac. — **ma-ni'a-cal-ly**, *adv.* [8].

man'i-cure (măn'ĭ-kūr), *n.* **1.** One who makes a business of taking care of people's hands, esp. their nails. **2.** The care of the hands and nails. — *v. t. & i.* [1] To care for (the hands and nails); care for the hands and nails of.

man'i-fest (-fĕst), *a.* [4] Evident to the senses, esp. the sight; obvious to the understanding.

man'i-fest, *n.* A list or invoice of a ship's cargo, to be exhibited at the customhouse. — *v. t.* **1.** To make appear distinctly; display; prove; evidence. **2.** To exhibit the manifest of, as of a cargo.

man'i-fes-ta'tion (-fĕs-tā'shŭn), *n.* **1.** A manifesting; display; revelation; disclosure. **2.** A public display made to show power and purpose.

man'i-fest-ly, *adv.* As is manifest; evidently.

man'i-fes'to (măn'ĭ-fĕs'tō), *n.; pl.* -TOES (-tōz). A public declaration, as of a sovereign, etc., showing his intentions, motives, etc.

man'i-fold (măn'ĭ-fōld), *a.* [4] **1.** Numerous and varied. **2.** Comprehending various features, kinds, functions, etc. — *n.* **1.** A copy made by manifolding. **2.** *Machinery.* A tube connecting two or more openings with one. — *v. t.* To make several copies of, esp. by the use of a kind of transfer paper. — **man'i-fold-ly**, *adv.* — **ness**, *n.*

man'i-kin (-kĭn), *n.* **1.** A little man; dwarf. **2.** A model of the human body.

Ma-nil'a (má-nĭl'á), *n.* [*Often l. c.*] Short for Manila hemp, the fiber of a Philippine species of banana, used for making ropes, textiles, paper, etc.

ma-nip'u-late (má-nĭp'ū-lāt), *v. t. & i.* [1] **1.** To treat, work, or operate with the hands, or by mechanical means, esp. with skill. **2.** To treat or manage with the mind, esp. skillfully. **3.** To control by management; treat artfully or fraudulently. **ma-nip'u-la'tion** (-lā'shŭn), *n.* A manipulating; skillful management. [manipulation.]

ma-nip'u-la-tive (-lā̇-tĭv), *a.* Of or pertaining to

ma-nip'u-la'tor (-lā'tẽr), *n.* One that manipulates.

man'kind', *n.* **1.** (măn'kīnd') The human race. **2.** (măn'kīnd') Men, as distinct from women.

man'like' (măn'līk'), *a.* [4] Like, or becoming to, a man; manly. — *adv.* Manfully.

man'ly (-lĭ), *a.* [3] Having qualities becoming to a man; manlike, esp. brave or noble; masculine. — **man'li-ness** (-lĭ-něs), *n.* [3].

man'na (măn'á), *n.* **1.** The food miraculously supplied to the Israelites in the wilderness. **2.** Something likened to the Biblical manna.

man'ner (măn'ẽr), *n.* **1.** Species; kind; sort. **2.** A way of acting; way; mode; habit; custom. **3.** Behavior; conduct; esp., *pl.*, social conduct or rules of conduct, as of a people or class; behavior.

man'ner-ism (-ẽr-ĭz'm), *n.* Excessive use of a peculiar style or manner, esp. in art or literature.

man'ner-less, *a.* Without manners; unmannerly.

man'ner-ly, *a.* [4] Showing good manners; civil. — *adv.* With good manners; politely.

man'nish (-ĭsh), *a.* [4] Resembling, suitable to, or characteristic of, a man; manlike; masculine. — **ly**, *adv.* [8] — **ness**, *n.* [8].

ma-nœu'vre, **-ver**, etc. Vars. of MANEUVER, etc.

man'-of-war', *n.; pl.* MEN-OF-WAR. A war vessel of a recognized navy.

man'or (măn'ẽr), *n.* In England, an amount of land, originally a feudal lordship, treated as a unit for certain administrative purposes.

ma-no'ri-al (má-nō'rĭ-ăl), *a.* Of or belonging to, or like, a manor.

man'sard roof (măn'särd). A roof having on all sides two slopes, the lower steeper than the upper.

manse (măns), *n.* A parsonage.

man'serv'ant (măn'sûr'vănt), *n.* A male servant.

man'sion (măn'shŭn), *n.* A large and stately residence.

man'slaugh'ter (-slô'tẽr), *n.* The killing of a human being, esp. unlawfully but without malice.

man'tel (măn't'l) or **man'tel-piece'** (-pēs'), *n.* The beam, stone, arch, or shelf, above a fireplace.

man-til'la (măn-tĭl'á), *n.* **1.** A woman's light cape. **2.** A kind of veil, covering a woman's head and shoulders; — worn in Spain, Mexico, etc.

man'tle (-t'l), *n.* **1.** A loose sleeveless overgarment; a cloak. **2.** A lacelike hood of some material hard to fuse which, placed over a flame, gives light by incandescence. — *v. t.* [1] To cover or envelop, as with a mantle; cloak. — *v. i.* **1.** To froth, cream, or the like, as cider. **2.** To be or become suffused with blood; flush; blush.

man'u-al (-ú-ăl), *a.* Of, done, made, or operated, by the hand or hands. — *n.* **1.** A small book; handbook. **2.** *Mil.* A prescribed exercise in the handling of a weapon. **3.** *Music.* An organ keyboard for the fingers. — **man'u-al-ly**, *adv.* [8].

man'u-fac'to-ry (măn'ú-făk'tō-rĭ), *n.; pl.* -RIES (-rĭz). A factory.

man'u-fac'ture (-tür), *n.* **1.** The making of wares or material products by hand or machinery. **2.** Anything manufactured. — *v.t.* [1] **1.** To make (products); produce by labor, esp. with division of labor and with machinery. **2.** To work into suitable forms for use. — **man'u-fac'tur-er**, *n.*

man'u-mis'sion (-mĭsh'ŭn), *n.* A manumitting.

man'u-mit' (-mĭt'), *v. t.; -*MIT'TED ; -MIT'TING. To release from slavery; free.

ma-nure' (má-nūr'), *v. t.* [1] To apply manure to; enrich, as land, by a fertilizer. — *n.* A fertilizer; esp., refuse of stables, dung of birds, etc.

man'u-script (măn'ú-skrĭpt), *a.* Written by hand. — *n.* **1.** A composition, esp. an author's copy of his work, in handwriting or typewriting. Abbr. *MS.*, pl. *MSS.* **2.** Writing, as opposed to print.

man'y (měn'ĭ), *a.* The comparative and superlative are supplied by *more, most.* Consisting of a great number; numerous.

man'y (mĕn'ĭ), *n. & pron.* A large number.

map (măp), *n.* A representation (usually flat) of the earth's surface or a part of it. — *v. t.;* MAPPED (măpt); MAP'PING. To represent by or on a map; indicate as on a map; sketch.

ma'ple (mā'p'l), *n.* Any of various well-known trees, or their wood, which is close-grained and hard. From the sap of some species sirup and sugar are made.

mar (mär), *v. t.;* MARRED (märd); MAR'RING. **1.** To damage greatly. **2.** To disfigure; deface.

mar'a-bou (mär'á-boō), *n.* **1.** A kind of large stork. **2.** One of the soft downy tail coverts or wing coverts of a marabou, used in millinery.

Mar'a-thon race (mär'á-thŏn). A long-distance race, esp. a foot race of about 25 miles.

ma-raud' (má-rôd'), *v. i.* To rove in quest of plunder; to plunder.

ma-raud'er (-ēr), *n.* A freebooter; plunderer.

mar'ble (mär'b'l), *n.* **1.** Any crystalline limestone capable of taking a polish or of being used for fine architectural work. **2.** A piece, slab, etc., of marble; a work of art, record, etc., of marble. **3. a** A little ball, orig. of marble, used as a plaything. **b** [In form marbles, construed as *sing.*] A child's game played with marbles. — *a.* **1.** Like or imitating marble; variegated or mottled. **2.** Like marble in being cold, hard, smooth, white, unfeeling, etc. — *v. t.* [1] To stain or variegate, like marble. [tier.

march (märch), *n.* A territorial border or fron-

march, *v. i.* **1.** To advance in step or in military order, as soldiers. **2.** To walk in a grave or steady manner. — *v. t.* To cause to march. — *n.* **1.** A marching, esp. of soldiers. **2.** Deliberate walk; steady progress. **3.** Distance passed over in marching. **4.** A regular, uniform step, used esp. by soldiers. **5.** A drumbeat or a piece of music suited to accompany marching. — **march'- er,** *n.* [8].

March, *n.* The third month, containing 31 days.

mar'chion-ess (mär'shŭn-ĕs), *n.* Wife or widow of a marquis; a lady of the rank of a marquis.

Mar-co'ni (mär-kō'nĭ), *a.* Pertaining to the system of wireless telegraphy used by Guglielmo *Marconi* (b. 1874). [message.

mar-co'ni-gram (-grăm), *n.* A Marconi wireless

mar-co'ni-graph (-grăf), *n.* The apparatus used in Marconi wireless telegraphy.

Mar'di gras' (mär'dē grä'). The day (Tuesday) before Lent begins; — in some cities, a day of merrymaking.

mare (mâr), *n.* The female of the horse kind.

mare's'-nest' (mârz'nĕst'), *n.* Something at first believed to be wonderful, but turning out to be imaginary. [butter; oleomargarine.

mar'ga-rine (mär'gá-rēn; -rĭn), *n.* Artificial

marge (märj), *n.* A margin. *Now Poetic.*

mar'gin (mär'jĭn), *n.* **1.** A border; edge; brink; verge; limit. **2.** A reserve, as of money, to meet unforeseen conditions. **3.** That part of a page outside of the main body of text. **4.** *Commerce.* **a** The difference between cost price and selling price. **b** A certain sum deposited with a broker by a speculative purchaser of stocks to secure the broker from loss on contracts.

mar'gin-al (mär'jĭ-năl), *a.* **1.** Pertaining to a margin. **2.** Written or printed in the margin.

mar'grave (-grāv), *n.* English equivalent of German *Markgraf*, a marquis.

mar'gra-vine (-grá-vēn), *n.* Wife of a margrave.

mar'gue-rite (mär'gē-rēt; mär'gē-rēt'), *n.* The daisy; oxeye daisy.

mar'i-gold (mär'ĭ-gōld), *n.* Any of several plants of the aster family having, commonly, large heads of yellow-rayed flowers; also, any of the flowers.

ma-rine' (má-rēn'), *a.* **1.** Of, pertaining to, or formed by or in, the sea. **2.** Of or pertaining to navigation of the sea; naval; nautical. **3.** Of or pertaining to the commerce of the sea; maritime; as, *marine* insurance. — *n.* **1.** Mercantile and naval shipping collectively. **2.** One, esp. a soldier, who serves on shipboard.

mar'i-ner (mär'ĭ-nēr), *n.* A seaman or sailor.

mar'i-o-nette' (mär'ĭ-ŏ-nĕt'), *n.* A puppet moved by strings or by hand.

mar'i-tal (mär'ĭ-tăl), *a.* **1.** Of or pertaining to a husband. **2.** Of or pertaining to marriage.

mar'i-time (-tĭm; -tīm), *a.* **1.** Bordering on, or living near, the ocean. **2.** Connected with the sea in respect to commerce; as, *maritime* affairs.

mar'jo-ram (mär'jŏ-rắm), *n.* Any of various mints.

mark (märk), *n.* The gold monetary unit, or (formerly) a silver coin, of Germany, worth 23.8 cents.

mark, *n.* **1.** A thing aimed at; a goal or target. **2.** A significant token; symptom; sign; esp., an indication of character; a trait. **3.** Limit or standard of action or fact. **4.** A visible sign, as a line, stain, scar, scratch. **5.** Note; distinction. — *v. t.* **1.** To put a mark on; affix a mark to. **2.** To bound, designate, indicate, or set apart by or as by a mark. **3.** To show as by a mark; manifest. **4.** To notice; observe; consider. — *v. i.* To notice; note. — **mark'er,** *n.* [8].

marked (märkt), *p. a.* [4] Having a mark; emphasized; conspicuous. — **ed-ly** (-ĕd-lĭ), *adv.* [8].

mar'ket (mär'kĕt), *n.* **1.** A meeting of people for traffic; the people at such a meeting. **2.** A place, as an open space in a town, or a large building, where a market is held, esp. where provisions are sold. **3.** The region in which any commodity can be sold. **4.** Opportunity for selling or buying commodities, or the price offered for them. — *v. i.* To deal in a market. — *v. t.* To expose for sale, or to sell, in a market; sell.

mar'ket-a-ble (mär'kĕt-á-b'l), *a.* [4] **1.** Fit to be offered for sale in a market. **2.** Of or pert. to buying or selling; current in the market.

marks'man (märks'măn), *n.* One who shoots at a mark; one who shoots well. — **ship,** *n.*

marl (märl), *n.* A crumbly deposit chiefly clay and calcium carbonate, used as a fertilizer.

mar'line (mär'lĭn), *n. Naut.* A small loosely twisted line of two strands, used for seizing.

mar'line-spike (-spīk'), *n.* Also **mar'lin-spike'.** *Naut.* A pointed tool used in splicing.

mar'ma-lade (mär'má-lād), *n.* A jamlike preserve of fruit pulp, as of orange, pear, etc.

mar'mo-set' (mär'mŏ-zĕt'), *n.* Any of numerous very small South and Central American monkeys.

mar'mot (-mŏt), *n.* Any of a genus of rodents including the woodchuck.

āle, senāte, câre, ăm, ăccount, ärm, ȧsk, sofȧ; ēve, évent, ĕnd, recĕnt, makēr; īce, ĭll; ōld, ȯbey, ôrb, ŏdd, sŏft, cŏnnect; ūse, ūnite, ûrn, ŭp, circŭs; fōōd, fŏŏt; out, oil;

ma-roon' (mȧ-rōōn'), *v. t.* To put (a person) ashore on a desolate island or coast and abandon him.

ma-roon', *n.* A dark brown chestnut color, or a dull red. — *a.* Of the above-named color.

mar'plot' (mär'plŏt'), *n.* One who, by officious interference, mars or frustrates a design or plot.

mar-quee' (mär-kē'), *n.* A large field tent.

mar'quet-ry (-kĕt-rĭ), *n.* Inlaid work, as in furniture.

mar'quis (-kwĭs), *n.* A nobleman of rank next above an earl or count. — **mar'quis-ate** (-ȧt), *n.*

mar-quise' (mär-kēz'), *n.* A marchioness.

mar'riage (mär'ĭj), *n.* **1.** The state or condition of being married; the relation existing between husband and wife; wedlock. **2.** Act of marrying, or rite used in marrying; a wedding. — **mar'riage-a-ble** (-ȧ-b'l), *a.* [8].

mar'row (-ō), *n.* **1.** A soft tissue which fills the cavities of most bones. **2. a** The choicest of food. **b** The source of animal vigor. **c** The inmost or essential part; essence. [ble marrow.]

mar'row-bone (-bōn'), *n.* A bone containing edi-

mar'row-fat (-ō-făt'), *n.* A large variety of pea.

mar'row-y (-ĭ), *a.* [4] Full of marrow; pithy.

mar'ry (-ĭ), *interj.* Indeed! in truth! *Archaic.*

mar'ry, *v. t.* [2] **1.** To unite in wedlock; join in matrimony. **2.** To dispose of in wedlock. **3.** To take as husband or wife; wed. — *v. i.* To enter into the connubial state; wed.

Mars (märz), *n. Astron.* One of the planets, next beyond the earth, conspicuous for its red light.

marsh (märsh), *n.* A tract of soft wet land; fen; swamp.

mar'shal (mär'shȧl), *n.* **1. a** Short for FIELD MARSHAL. **b** A general officer of the highest rank in various foreign armies. **2.** Any of various royal household officers of high rank. **3.** Any of various officers having police duties. — *v. t.* [7] **1.** To dispose in order. **2.** To usher, direct, or lead.

marsh mallow, *or* **marsh'mal'low** (märsh'-mǎl'ō), *n.* An herb of the mallow family. The root is used in confectionery and in medicine.

marsh marigold. A plant of the crowfoot family, with bright yellow flowers. See COWSLIP.

marsh'y (mär'shĭ), *a.* [3] Pert. to or like a marsh; boggy; as, *marshy* ground. — **marsh'i-ness**, *n.* [8].

mar-su'pi-al (mär-sū'pĭ-ǎl), *n. Zoöl.* Any of the order comprising the kangaroos, wombats, opossums, etc. Most of them have a pouch on the abdomen of the female serving to carry the young. — *a.* Having a pouch for carrying the young; of or pertaining to the marsupials.

Marsh Marigold.
Reduced.

mart (märt), *n.* A market.

mar'ten (mär'tĕn), *n.* **1.** Any of several slender flesh-eating mammals larger than the weasels, and frequenting trees. They are gray or brown above. **2.** The fur of the marten, more often called *sable.*

mar'tial (-shǎl), *a.* [4] **1.** Of, pertaining to, or suited for, war; warlike; as, *martial* music. **2.** Military; — opposed to *civil. Obs. or R.*, except in *court-martial*, etc. — **mar'tial-ly**, *adv.* [8].

mar'tin (-tĭn), *n.* Any of various swallows.

mar'ti-net (mär'tĭ-nĕt'; mär'tĭ-nĕt'), *n.* A strict disciplinarian ; — commonly deprecatory.

mar'tin-gale (mär'tĭn-gāl; mär'tĭn-), *n.* A strap connecting a horse's girth to the bit or reins so as to hold down his head.

mar'tyr (mär'tēr), *n.* **1.** One who suffers death for refusing to renounce his religion. **2.** One who sacrifices life, station, etc., for principle, or to sustain a cause. — *v. t.* To put to death for a belief, esp. Christianity.

mar'tyr-dom (-dŭm), *n.* Condition, death, or sufferings, of a martyr.

mar'vel (mär'vĕl), *n.* **1.** That which causes wonder or astonishment. **2.** Wonder; astonishment. — *v. i.* [7] To be struck with wonder.

mar'vel-ous (-ŭs), *a.* [4,7] Exciting marvel; astonishing. — **-ly**, *adv.* [8] — **-ness**, *n.* [8].

mas'cot (măs'kŏt), *n.* A person, animal, or thing supposed to bring good luck.

mas'cu-line (-kū-lĭn), *a.* [4] **1.** *Gram.* Of or pertaining to or designating the class of words that denote males. **2.** Having the qualities of a man ; virile ; of a woman, mannish.

mas'cu-lin'i-ty (-lĭn'ĭ-tĭ), *n.* State or quality of being masculine.

mash (măsh), *n.* **1.** Crushed malt, or meal of grain, steeped and stirred in hot water to form wort. **2.** A mixture of meal, bran, or the like, and hot water, fed warm to animals. **3.** A soft, pulpy mass of anything. — *v. t.* To convert into a mash ; reduce to a pulpy state ; crush.

mask (másk), *n.* **1.** A cover for the face, for disguise, protection, etc. **2.** A copy of a face molded in plaster, wax, etc. **3.** That which disguises or conceals. **4.** One wearing a mask; a masker. **5.** A masquerade ; a revel. **6.** An old form of play in which the actors wore masks. *v. t.* **1.** To cover, as the face, for concealment or defense. **2.** To disguise ; hide.

mask'er, *n.* One who wears a mask; one who appears in disguise at a masquerade.

ma'son (mā's'n), *n.* **1.** One who builds with stone, brick, etc., or prepares stone for building.

ma'son-ry (mā's'n-rĭ), *n.* **1.** Art or trade of a mason. **2.** That which is built by a mason; stonework.

masque (másk), *n.* Var. of MASK, nn., 5 & 6.

mas'quer-ade' (măs'kẽr-ād'), *n.* **1.** An assembly of masked persons, for dancing, etc. **2.** Acting under false pretenses; disguise. — *v. i.* [1] To frolic in disguise; make a show of being what one is not. — **mas'quer-ad'er** (-ād'ẽr), *n.* [8].

Mass (más), *n.* The service or liturgy of the Eucharist; the Lord's Supper;— now used chiefly of the Roman Catholic service.

mass, *n.* **1.** A quantity of matter cohering in one body, usually of considerable size. **2.** A large quantity, amount, or number ; a bulk. **3.** Bulk; size. **4.** The main body; as, the *mass* of men. — the masses, the populace, as contrasted with the higher classes. — *v. t. & i.* To form or collect into a mass; assemble.

mas'sa-cre (măs'á-kẽr), *n.* The atrocious killing of a considerable number of human beings. — *v. t.* [1] To make a massacre of; slaughter.

mas-sage' (má-säzh'), *n.* A method or the act of treating the body by rubbing, etc., as for remedial purposes. — *v. t.* [1] To treat by massage.

|| **mas'seur'** (má'sũr'), *n. masc.; pl.* -SEURS (-sũrz'; *F.* -sûr') ; || **mas'seuse'** (má'sũz'), *n. fem.; pl.* -SEUSES (*F.* -sũz'). [F.] One who practices massage.

mas'sive (măs'ĭv), *a.* [4] Forming, or consisting of, a large mass ; weighty ; bulky ; large ; ponderous; massy. — **-ly**, *adv.* [8] — **-ness**, *n.* [8].

mass meeting. A large or general assembly of people, as for discussion of a public question.

mass'y (măs'ĭ), *a.* [3] Bulky and heavy; massive.

mast (mást),*n.* Nuts collectively, as acorns, beechnuts, chestnuts, etc., esp. a food for hogs.

mast, *n.* **1.** A long pole or spar rising from the keel of a vessel or boat to sustain the yards, booms, sails, and rigging. **2.** Any upright pole.

mas'ter (más'tẽr), *n.* **1.** A man having another living being subject to his will. **2.** One who uses, or controls, anything inanimate. **3.** A victor, as in a contest. **4.** [When used as a title, *cap.*] A person holding a certain advanced academic degree; as, *Master* of Arts. **5.** One, esp. an artist, who has attained great skill. **6.** [*cap.*] A title prefixed to the name of boys or youths. **7.** *Law.* Any of various officers of court appointed to assist the judge. — *a.* Being master, or characteristic of a master; principal; controlling.— *v. t.* **1.** To become the master of; conquer; subdue. **2.** To become an adept in.

mas'ter-ful (-fŏŏl), *a.* [4] **1.** Inclined to play the master; domineering. **2.** Showing power or mastery; as, a *masterful* pen. — **-ful-ly**, *adv.* [8].

master key. A key adapted to open several locks differing somewhat from each other; — often fig.

mas'ter-ly, *a.* [4] Suitable to, or characteristic of, a master. — *adv.* With the skill of a master.

mas'ter-piece' (más'tẽr-pēs'), *n.* Anything done or made with extraordinary skill; a chef-d'œuvre.

mas'ter-ship, *n.* **1.** Status, office, or dignity of a master. **2.** Mastery; dominion. **3.** The knowledge or proficiency of a master.

mas'ter-y (más'tẽr-ĭ), *n.; pl.* -TERIES (-ĭz). **1.** The position of a master ; mastership. **2.** Superiority in war or competition; victory. **3.** Skill that makes one a master of a subject. [mast.|

mast'head' (mást'hĕd'), *n. Naut.* The top of a|

mas'tic (măs'tĭk), *n.* **1.** A gum or resin exuding from a certain tree found in Asia Minor. **2.** Any of various pasty cements.

mas'ti-cate (-tǐ-kāt), *v. t.* [1] To grind with or as with the teeth, and prepare for swallowing; chew. — **mas'ti-ca'tor** (-kā'tẽr), *n.* [8].

mas'ti-ca'tion (-kā'shŭn), *n.* A masticating.

mas'tiff (más'tǐf), *n.* One of a breed of large, powerful, smooth-coated dogs.

mas'to-don (măs'tó-dŏn), *n.* Any of numerous species of large extinct elephants.

mat (măt), *n.* **1.** A piece of coarse fabric made by weaving or plaiting. **2.** Anything growing thickly, or closely interwoven.— *v. t. & i. ; MAT-*TED (măt'ĕd); MAT'TING. To twine or felt together into, or like, a mat.

mat, *n.* **1.** A border serving as a frame or margin for a picture. **2.** A dead or dull finish, or roughened surface, as in gilding or painting.

mat'a-dor (măt'á-dōr; -dôr), *n.* Also **-dore.** The man appointed to kill the bull in bullfights.

match (măch), *n.* **1.** A fuse, as for firing an explosive. **2.** A short, slender piece of wood, etc., tipped with a mixture to produce fire.

match, *n.* **1.** A person or thing equal or similar to another. **2.** An exact counterpart. **3.** A pair suitably associated. **4.** A bringing or coming together of two parties for a contest, or the like. **5.** A matrimonial union. **6.** A candidate for matrimony. — *v. t.* **1.** To marry, esp. with reference to the suitability of the parties. **2.** To encounter as an antagonist, esp. successfully. **3.** To bring a match, or equal, against. **4.** To make or procure the equal of, or that which is like. — *v. i.* To be equal or similar, as in size or color.

match'less (măch'lĕs), *a.* Unequaled.

mate (māt), *n. & v. Chess.* Checkmate.

mate, *n.* **1.** A companion; comrade. **2.** A match; an equal. **3.** A husband or wife; also, one of a pair of animals. **4.** *Naut.* An officer in a merchant vessel, ranking next below the master.

mate, *v. t.* [1] **1.** To marry; of animals, to pair. **2.** To couple or associate as mate, or equal.— *v. i.* To be or become a mate or mates.

ma-te'ri-al (má-tē'rǐ-ăl), *a.* [4] **1.** Of or pertaining to matter; physical. **2.** Of solid or weighty character; of consequence; important; essential. **3.** Pertaining to or affecting man's physical nature ; bodily. — *n.* The substance or matter of which anything is made or may be made.

ma-te'ri-al-ism (-ĭz'm), *n.* **1.** In philosophy, any theory which considers the facts of the universe to be sufficiently explained by the existence and nature of matter. **2.** Tendency to give undue importance to material interests.

ma-te'ri-al-ist, *n.* **1.** An adherent of materialism. **2.** One absorbed in material interests.

ma-te'ri-al-is'tic (-ĭs'tĭk), *a.* Of or pertaining to materialism or materialists.

ma-te'ri-al'i-ty (-ăl'ĭ-tĭ), *n.; pl.* -TIES (-tĭz). Quality of being material; that which is material.

ma-te'ri-al-i-za'tion (-ĭ-zā'shŭn), *n.* Act of materializing, or state of being materialized.

ma-te'ri-al-ize (-tē'rǐ-ăl-īz), *v. t.* [1] **1.** To invest with material characteristics; to express through the medium of material objects. **2.** *Spiritualism.* To make (a spirit) visible in or as in material form. — *v. i.* To appear as a material form.

ma-te'ri-al-ly, *adv.* In a material manner; substantially; as, it aided *materially* to our comfort.

ma-ter'nal (má-tûr'năl), *a.* [4] **1.** Of or pertaining to a mother; motherly. **2.** Derived or received from, or connected through, one's mother. — **ma-ter'nal-ly**, *adv.* [8].

ma-ter'ni-ty (-nĭ-tĭ), *n.; pl.* -TIES (-tĭz). State or quality of being a mother; also, motherliness.

math'e-mat'i-cal (măth'ē-măt'ĭ-kăl), *a.* Of, pertaining to, or according to, mathematics ; hence, theoretically precise; accurate. — **-ly**, *adv.* [8].

math'e-ma-ti'cian (-má-tĭsh'ăn), *n.* One versed in mathematics.

math'e-mat'ics (-măt'ĭks), *n.* The science of the

āle, senăte, câre, ăm, ăccount, ärm, ásk, sofá; ēve, ĕvent, ĕnd, recĕnt, makẽr; īce, ĭll; ōld, ŏbey, ôrb, ŏdd, sŏft, cŏnnect; ūse, ŭnite, ûrn, ŭp, circŭs; fōōd, fŏŏt; out, oil;

relations between quantities or magnitudes and operations.

mat'i-née' (măt'Ĭ-nā'), *n.* A reception, or a musical or dramatic entertainment, held in the daytime.

mat'ins (-Ĭnz), *n. pl.* Morning service or worship.

mat'ri-ces (*pron.*, see MATRIX), *n.*, *pl.* of MATRIX.

mat'ri-cide (măt'rĬ-sīd; măt'trĬ-), *n.* **1.** The murder of a mother by her child. **2.** One who murders one's own mother. — **-cid'al** (-sĭd'ăl), *a.*

ma-tric'u-late (má-trĬk'ú-lāt), *v. t.* [1] To enroll; admit to membership by enrollment, as in a college or university. — *v. i.* To be matriculated.

ma-tric'u-la'tion (-lā'shŭn), *n.* A matriculating.

mat'ri-mo'ni-al (măt'rĬ-mō'nĬ-ăl), *a.* Of or pert. to marriage; conjugal; nuptial. — **-ly**, *adv.* [8].

mat'ri-mo-ny (măt'rĬ-mō-nĬ), *n.* Marriage.

ma'trix (mā'trĬks), *n. ; pl.* MATRICES (măt'rĬ-sēz ; *as Lat. properly* má-trī'sēz). That which gives form or origin to something inclosed within it, as a mold for casting.

ma'tron (-trŭn), *n.* **1.** A wife or a widow. **2.** A woman who manages the domestic economy of a public institution. — **ma'tron-al** (-ăl), *a.* [4].

ma'tron-ly (-lĬ), *a.* [4] Like, or befitting, a matron; hence, sedate; grave. — *adv.* Like a matron.

mat'ted (măt'ĕd), *p. a.* [4] **1.** Covered with a mat or mats. **2.** Tangled; as, *matted* hair.

mat'ter (-ẽr), *n.* **1.** That of which any physical object is composed; material. **2.** Pus. **3.** *Physics.* Whatever occupies space. **4.** Concern; affair; hence, indefinitely, a thing or things. **5.** Subject of action, discussion, feeling, complaint, or the like. **6.** Ground; cause; difficulty. **7.** Affair of consequence; significance; as, *no matter*, etc. **8.** Amount; quantity; — often indefinite; as, a *matter* of nine miles. **9.** *Printing.* Anything to be set in type; copy; also, type set up. — *v. i.* **1.** To be of importance. **2.** To form pus.

mat'ter-of-fact', *a.* [4] Adhering to facts; commonplace; dry.   [of straw, etc.

mat'ting (măt'Ĭng), *n.* Kind of carpeting made

mat'tock (-ŭk), *n.* An implement for digging, etc., of which the head has a blade like an adz and another like a narrow ax or a point like a pickax.

mat'tress (-rĕs), *n.* A bed stuffed with hair, moss, or the like, and tufted or otherwise fastened.

mat'u-rate (măt'ū-rāt), *v. t.* [1] To form pus.

mat'u-ra'tion (-rā'shŭn), *n.* Formation of pus.

ma-ture' (má-tūr'), *a.* [3] **1.** Full-grown; ripe ; fully developed. **2.** Completely worked out; perfected. **3.** Having run to the limit of its time; due, as a note. — **ma-ture'ly**, *adv.* [8]. — *v. t. & i.* [1] **1.** To bring or come to maturity; ripen; perfect. **2.** To become due, as a note.

ma-tu'ri-ty (-tū'rĬ-tĬ), *n.* **1.** Mature state or quality ; ripeness. **2.** A becoming due, as of a note.

ma-tu'ti-nal (má-tū'tĬ-năl; măt'ú-tī'năl), *a.* Of or pertaining to the morning; early.

maud'lin (môd'lĬn), *a.* [4] **1.** Tearfully or mawkishly sentimental. **2.** Drunk enough to be silly.

maul (môl), *n.* A heavy hammer or beetle. — *v. t.* To beat and bruise; handle roughly.

maul'stick' (môl'stĬk'), *n.* A stick used by painters as a rest for the hand while working.

maun'der (môn'dẽr; män'-), *v. i.* **1.** To move languidly or idly. **2.** To mutter; mumble.

mau'so-le'um (mô'sô-lē'ŭm), *n. ; pl.* E. **-leums** (-ŭmz), L. **-lea** (-á). A magnificent tomb.

mauve (mōv), *n.* A delicate purple or violet color.

mav'er-ick (măv'ẽr-Ĭk), *n.* An unbranded animal, esp. a motherless calf. *Western U. S.*

maw (mô), *n.* A stomach; in birds, the craw.

mawk'ish (môk'Ĭsh), *a.* [4] **1.** Apt to cause satiety or loathing; disgusting. **2.** Marked by sickly sentimentality. — **-ly**, *adv.* — **-ness**, *n.*

max-il'la (măk-sĬl'á), *n. ; pl.* **-læ** (-ē). *Anat.* A bone on either side of the face, which bears the upper teeth. — **max'il-la-ry** (măk'sĬ-lá-rĬ),*a.& n.*

max'im (măk'sĬm), *n.* A general truth or a sententious rule of conduct; esp., a proverbial saying embodying a moral or practical precept.

max'i-mal (măk'sĬ-măl), *a.* Highest; greatest.

max'i-mum (-mŭm), *n. ; pl.* L. **-ma** (-má), E. **-mums** (-mŭmz). The greatest quantity or value attainable in a given case ; the highest point or degree. — *a.* Greatest in quantity or highest in degree attainable or attained ; greatest allowed by law.

may (mā), *v. ; pres., sing., 1st & 3d pers.* MAY, *2d* MAY'EST (mā'ĕst), MAYST (māst), *pl.* MAY ; *pret.* MIGHT (mīt). Infinitive and participles now lacking, As auxiliary, with the infinitive without *to*, denoting : **a** Ability; as, no one *may* separate us ; — oftener expressed by *can.* **b** Opportunity; permission ; possibility ; as, he *may* go. **c** Desire or wish, as in prayer; as, *may* you live happily. **d** Contingency; as, though the chain *may* break.

May, *n.* The fifth month of the year, having 31 days.

May apple. An American herb of the barberry family or its edible, yellow, egg-shaped fruit.

may'be (mā'bĕ), *adv.* Perhaps.

May Day. The first day of May, sometimes celebrated by the crowning of a May queen with a garland, and by dancing about a Maypole.

May'flow'er (-flou'ẽr), *n.* **1.** In England, any of several plants flowering in May, as the hawthorn. **2.** The trailing arbutus. See ARBUTUS. *U. S.*

May fly. Any of various slender, delicate, short-lived insects with net-veined wings.

may'on-naise' (mā'ŏ-nāz'; F. má'yŏ'nâz'), *n.* A sauce of egg yolks beaten up with olive oil and seasoned.   [a city or borough.

may'or (mā'ẽr ; mâr), *n.* The chief magistrate of

may'or-al-ty (-ăl-tĬ), *n.* The office, or the term of office, of a mayor.

maze (māz), *n.* **1.** Confusion of thought; perplexity. **2.** A confusing network, as of paths.

ma-zur'ka (má-zûr'ká; -zoor'ká),*n.* A Polish dance in moderate triple time ; also, music for it.

ma'zy (mā'zĬ), *a.* [3] Perplexed with or as with turns and windings ; winding ; confusing. — **ma'zi-ly** (-zĬ-lĬ), *adv.* [8] — **ma'zi-ness**, *n.* [8].

me (mē), *pers. pron.* The objective (dative or accusative) case of *I.*   [and honey.

mead (mēd),*n.* A drink made by fermenting water

mead, *n.* A meadow. *Poetic.*

mead'ow (mĕd'ō), *n.* A piece of land devoted to grass; specif., low level grass land.

meadow lark. An American bird about the size of a robin, with yellow breast marked with black.

mea'ger (mē'gẽr), *a.* [3, 6] **1.** Having little flesh; thin ; lean. **2.** Destitute of richness, strength, or the like; poor. — **-ly**, *adv.* — **-ness**, *n.*

meal (mēl), *n*. **1**. Grain (esp. corn, rye, or oats) or pulse coarsely ground and unbolted. **2**. Any powdery substance resembling meal (sense 1).

meal (mēl), *n*. The food taken at a particular time; repast ; also, act or time of eating a meal.

meal'y (mēl'ĭ), *a*. [3] **1**. Having the qualities of meal; soft, dry, and easily crumbled; as, a *mealy* potato. **2**. Containing meal. —**i-ness**, *n*. [8].

meal'y-mouthed' (-mouthd'; -moutht'), *a*. [4] Using soft words ; timid of speech.

mean (mēn), *v. t. ; pret. & p. p.* MEANT (mĕnt) ; *p. pr. & vb. n.* MEAN'ING. **1**. To have in the mind as a purpose; intend; design. **2**. To intend (a remark or the like) to have a certain meaning; hence, to signify; denote. —*v. i.* To purpose or intend. *Rare*, except in *to mean well*, or *ill*.

mean, *a*. [3] **1**. Without distinction or eminence; common ; low. **2**. Without power or acumen ; ordinary. **3**. Of little value or account. **4**. Wanting dignity of mind; base. **5**. Closefisted; stingy.

mean, *a*. **1**. Occupying a middle position ; intermediate. **2**. *Math*. Average. — *n*. **1**. The middle point; hence, medium ; moderation; measure. **2**. *Math*. **a** A quantity having an intermediate value between several others of which it expresses the mean value ; usually, the one simple average (**arithmetical mean**) got by dividing the sum of the quantities by their number. **b** Often, the second or third term in a proportion of four terms. **3**. Intermediate agency ; instrument ; — usually in pl. form, with sing. sense and construction ; as, I was the *means* of this being done. **4**. *pl*. Resources ; wealth ; as, a man of *means*.

me-an'der (mē-ăn'dẽr), *n*. A winding, as of a stream ; hence, a winding course ; — usually in pl. — *v. i. & t*. To wind or turn in a course ; follow an intricate course; wander aimlessly or listlessly.

mean'ing (mēn'ĭng), *n*. **1**. That which is meant ; intent ; aim; object. **2**. Import ; sense. — *p. a*. Intending; also, expressive; significant. — **mean'-ing-less**, *a*. [8] — **-ly**, *adv*. [8].

mean'ly, *adv*. In a mean manner; poorly;ignobly.

mean'ness, *n*. **1**. State or quality of being mean. **2**. A mean act.

meant (mĕnt), *pret. & p. p.* of MEAN.

mean'time' (mēn'tīm'), *adv*. In the intervening time ; at the same time. — *n*. Intervening time.

mean'while' (-hwīl'), *n. & adv*. = MEANTIME.

mea'sles (mē'z'lz), *n.; pl.* in form, but used as *singular*. **1**. *Med*. A contagious disease, characterized by an eruption of red spots. **2** A disease of cattle and swine caused by the larvæ of a tapeworm ; also, *pl.*, the larvæ.

mea'sly (-zlĭ), *a*. [3] **1**. Of or pertaining to, or infected with, measles ; as, a *measly* rash. **2**. Containing larval tapeworms ; — said of meat.

meas'ur-a-ble (mĕzh'ûr-á-b'l), *a*. [4] Capable of being measured. — **meas'ur-a-bly**, *adv*. [8].

meas'ure (mĕzh'ûr), *n*. **1**. Act or process of ascertaining the extent, dimensions, or the like, of a thing ; measurement. **2**. An instrument for measuring. **3**. Size or quantity, determined by measuring. **4**. A unit of measurement. **5**. A system of measurement. **6**. Regulated division of movement, as in music, poetry, etc. **7**. *Arith*. An aliquot part. **8**. A step or definite part of a progressive course or policy; esp., a legislative

enactment proposed or adopted. — *v. t.* [1] **1**. To ascertain the extent of; estimate; value. **2**. To determine or lay off in measuring, as a given distance. **3**. To bring into comparison or competition (with). — *v. i.* **1**. To measure something. **2**. To result, or turn out, on being measured ; admit of being measured.

meas'ure-less, *a*. Immeasurable; immense.

meas'ure-ment (-ûr-mĕnt), *n*. **1**. Act or result of measuring; mensuration. **2**. Extent, size, capacity, amount, or quantity ascertained by measuring. **3**. A system of measures or measuring.

meat (mēt), *n*. **1**. Food in general ; esp., solid food ; hence, the edible part of anything ; as, the *meat* of a nut. **2**. Now esp., flesh used as food ; specif., flesh as distinguished from *fish* or *fowl*.

meat'y (mēt'ĭ), *a*. [3] Abounding in, or resembling, meat ; hence, pithy.

me-chan'ic (mē-kăn'ĭk), *a*. **1**. Pertaining to manual labor ; involving manual skill. **2**. Of or pertaining to a mechanic or an artisan, or the artisan class ; as, *mechanic* life. — *n*. One who practices any mechanic art; artisan.

me-chan'i-cal (-ĭ-kăl), *a*. [4] **1**. Of or pertaining to machinery or mechanism ; made by a machine or with tools. **2**. Done as if by a machine. **3**. Pertaining to, governed by, or accordant with, mechanics, or the laws of motion. — **-cal-ly**, *adv*. [8] — **-cal-ness**, *n*. [8].

mech'a-ni'cian (mĕk'á-nĭsh'ăn), *n*. One skilled in the construction of machines ; a machinist.

me-chan'ics (mē-kăn'ĭks), *n*. Applied mathematics treating of the action of forces on bodies.

mech'a-nism (mĕk'á-nĭz'm), *n*. **1**. The arrangement or relation of the parts of a machine. **2**. Mechanical operation or action.

med'al (mĕd'ăl), *n*. A piece, usually a disk, of metal bearing a device, etc., to commemorate some event or person, or to serve as a reward.

me-dal'lion (mē-dăl'yŭn), *n*. **1**. A large medal. **2**. Something resembling a large medal.

med'dle (mĕd'l), *v. i*. [1] To interest or concern one's self unnecessarily ; interfere ; — often followed by *with* or *in*. — **med'dler** (-lẽr), *n*. [8].

med'dle-some (mĕd'l-sŭm), *a*. [4] Given to meddling. — **-some-ly**,*adv*. [8] — **-some-ness**,*n*. [8].

me'di-a (mē'dĭ-á), *n*., *L. pl.* of MEDIUM.

me'di-al (mē'dĭ-ăl), *a*. **1**. Middle. **2**. Average; ordinary. — **me'di-al-ly**, *adv*. [8].

me'di-an (-ăn), *a*. Medial; middle.

me'di-ate (-āt), *a*. [4] Acting by or involving means, or intermediate agency ; not direct or immediate. — (-āt), *v. i*. [1] To interpose between parties to bring about a reconciliation. — *v. t*. To effect or settle by mediation.

me'di-a'tion (-ā'shŭn), *n*. Act of mediating.

me'di-a'tor (-ā'tẽr), *n*. One who mediates.

me'di-a-to-ry (mē'dĭ-á-tô-rĭ), *a*. [4] Of or pert. to mediation.   [herbs, as alfalfa.]

med'ic (mĕd'ĭk), *n*. Any of several cloverlike

med'i-cal (mĕd'ĭ-kăl), *a*. Of or pertaining to the science or art of medicine. — **-cal-ly**, *adv*. [8].

me-dic'a-ment (mē-dĭk'á-mĕnt; mĕd'ĭ-ká-mĕnt), *n*. A medicine ; a healing application.

med'i-cate (mĕd'ĭ-kāt), *v. t*. [1] To treat with medicine; cure. — **med'i-ca'tion** (-kā'shŭn), *n*.

me-dic'i-nal (mḗ-dĭs'ĭ-năl), *a.* [4] Curative; alleviative. — **me-dic'i-nal-ly,** *adv.* [8].

med'i-cine (mĕd'ĭ-sĭn; -s'n), *n.* **1.** The science and art dealing with the prevention, cure, or alleviation of disease. **2.** Any substance or preparation used in treating disease; remedy.

me'di-e'val (mē'dĭ-ē'văl; mĕd'ĭ-), *a.* Of, pertaining to, or characteristic of, the Middle Ages.

me'di-o'cre (mē'dĭ-ō'kẽr), *a.* [4] Of a middling quality; of but a moderate excellence; ordinary.

me'di-oc'ri-ty (-ŏk'rĭ-tĭ), *n.; pl.* -TIES (-tĭz). State of being mediocre. [To muse; reflect.]

med'i-tate (mĕd'ĭ-tāt), *v. t.* [1] To intend. — *v. i.*

med'i-ta'tion (-tā'shŭn), *n.* Act of meditating; thought; esp., close thought; reflection.

med'i-ta-tive (mĕd'ĭ-tā-tĭv), *a.* [4] Disposed to meditate; meditating. — **-ly,** *adv.* [8].

me'di-um (mē'dĭ-ŭm), *n.; pl.* E. -UMS (-ŭmz), L. -DIA (-ȧ). **1.** That which lies in the middle; mean. **2.** That by which a force acts or anything is done; means. **3.** Surrounding substance or element. **4.** One supposed to be capable of imparting knowledge derived from departed spirits. — *a.* Having a middle position or degree; medial.

med'lar (mĕd'lẽr), *n.* A small Asiatic tree of the apple family, widely cultivated; also, its fruit.

med'ley (-lĭ), *n.; pl.* -LEYS (-lĭz). **1.** A mixture; a hodgepodge; a jumble. **2.** *Music.* A composition of passages from different pieces.

me-dul'la (mė-dŭl'ȧ), *n. Anat.* **a** The marrow of bones. **b** The medulla oblongata (ŏb'lŏn-gā'tȧ), the lowest, or posterior, part of the brain.

meed (mēd), *n.* A reward of merit.

meek (mēk), *a.* [3] **1.** Mild of temper; patient; humble. **2.** Spiritless; easily cowed or imposed upon. — *adv.* Meekly. — **-ly,** *adv.* — **-ness,** *n.*

meer'schaum (mēr'shŏm; -shäm), *n.* **1.** A white claylike mineral, soft and very light. **2.** A tobacco pipe of this material.

meet (mēt), *v. t.; pret. & p. p.* MET (mĕt); *p. pr. & vb. n.* MEET'ING. **1.** To come upon. **2.** To come into proximity with. **3.** To come into connection with; join; intersect. **4.** To come within the perception or recognition of. **5.** To fight, cope, or grapple with; oppose. **6.** To experience; suffer. **7.** To equal; match; to discharge or pay, as a debt. — *v. i.* **1.** To come into contact or proximity, esp. by mutual approach; join. **2.** To assemble; congregate. **3.** To have an encounter or conflict. — *n.* Act of meeting; also, those who assemble. *Chiefly Sporting.*

meet, *a.* [3] Suitable; fit.

meet'ing, *n.* **1.** Act of persons or things that meet; as: **a** A duel. **b** An assembly. **c** An assembly for worship. **2.** A union or place of union; a junction. [ship; a church.]

meet'ing-house' (-hous'), *n.* A building for worship.

meet'ly, *adv.* Fitly; properly.

meg'a-phone (mĕg'ȧ-fōn), *n.* A device to magnify sound, as a very large funnel.

me'grim (mē'grĭm), *n.* **1.** A kind of sick or nervous headache. **2.** A fancy; whim; esp., in *pl.,* lowness of spirits; "the blues."

mel'an-cho'li-a (mĕl'ăn-kō'lĭ-ȧ), *n.* A kind of mental unsoundness characterized by extreme depression of spirits and delusions, or a case of this.

mel'an-chol'ic (-kŏl'ĭk), *a.* [4] Given to melancholy; depressed. — **-chol'i-cal-ly,** *adv.* [8].

mel'an-chol-y (mĕl'ăn-kŏl-ĭ),*n.; pl.* -CHOLIES (-ĭz). Depression of spirits; dejection. — *a.* [4] Characterized by, or expressive of, melancholy.

‖ **mê'lée'** (mā'lā'), *n.* A fight between combatants mingled in a confused mass; a fray.

mel'io-rate (mēl'yȯ-rāt), *v. t. & i.* [1] To make or become better; improve; make more tolerable.

mel'io-ra'tion (-rā'shŭn), *n.* Improvement.

mel-lif'lu-ence (mĕ-lĭf'lŏȯ-ĕns),*n.* Quality or state of being mellifluent; a flow of sweetness.

mcl-lif'lu-ent (-ĕnt), *a.* [4] Mellifluous.

mel-lif'lu-ous (-ŭs), *a.* [4] Flowing with or as with honey; smooth; honeyed. — **-ly,** *adv.* [8].

mel'low (mĕl'ō), *a.* [3] **1.** Soft or tender from ripeness. **2.** Soft; loamy, as soil. **3.** Soft; delicate; full and pure; — said of sound, color, etc. **4.** Well-matured; made sweet or gentle by maturity. — *v. t. & i.* To make or become mellow. — **-ness,** *n.* [8]. [organ.]

me-lo'de-on (mė-lō'dė-ŭn), *n.* A kind of small reed

me-lo'di-ous (-lō'dĭ-ŭs), *a.* [4] Containing, producing, or characterized by, melody. — **-ly,** *adv.* [8] — **ness,** *n.* [8]. [of melodies.]

mel'o-dist (mĕl'ō-dĭst), *n.* A composer or singer

mel'o-dra'ma (mĕl'ō-drä'mȧ; mĕl'ō-drā'mȧ), *n* Any romantic drama marked by sensational situations and a happy ending.

mol'o dra mat'ic (mĕl'ō-drȧ-măt'ĭk), *a.* [4] Of the nature of melodrama. — **mel'o-dra-mat'i-cal-ly,** *adv.*

mel'o-dy (mĕl'ō-dĭ),*n.; pl.* -DIES (-dĭz). **1.** An agreeable succession of sounds; musical quality. **2.** *Music.* **a** A rhythmical succession of single tones; a tune. **b** The chief voice part in a harmonic composition; the air.

mel'on (-ŭn),*n.* **1.** Muskmelon. **2.** Watermelon.

melt (mĕlt), *v. i. & t.; pret.& p. p.* MELT'ED, *Archaic p. p.* MOL'TEN (mōl't'n); *p. pr. & vb. n.* MELT'ING. **1.** To change from a solid to a liquid state, usually by heat. **2.** To dissolve; soften. **3.** To break up; vanish or cause to vanish by being dissipated. **4.** To become or render tender, mild, or gentle. **5.** To absorb or blend; merge insensibly. — **melt'-er,** *n.* [8].

mem'ber (mĕm'bẽr), *n.* **1.** A part or organ of the animal body; esp., a limb. *Archaic.* **2.** In botany, a part of a plant body. **3.** One of the persons composing a society, community, or party. **4.** A part of a whole; a unit in a series.

mem'ber-ship, *n.* **1.** State of being a member. **2.** The collective body of members, as of a society.

mem'brane (mĕm'brān), *n.* Any thin, soft, pliable sheet or layer of animal or vegetable tissue.

mem'bra-nous (-brȧ-nŭs), *a.* Pertaining to, consisting of, or resembling, membrane. — **membranous croup, laryngeal diphtheria.

me-men'to (mė-mĕn'tō), *n.; pl.* -TOS, -TOES (-tōz). A thing to awaken memory; reminder; souvenir.

mem'oir (mĕm'wŏr), *n.* **1.** *pl.* A history composed from personal experience; often, esp., an account of episodes in one's own life. **2.** A biography. **3.** A dissertation; *pl.,* the transactions or proceedings of a society.

mem'o-ra-bil'i-a (mĕm'ō-rȧ-bĭl'ĭ-ȧ), *n. pl.; sing.*

memorabile (-răb'ĭ-lē). Things worthy of remembrance or record ; also, the record of them.

mem'o-ra-ble (měm'ŏ-rā-b'l), *a.* [4] Worthy of remembrance or note. — **mem'o-ra-bly,** *adv.* [8].

mem'o-ran'dum (-răn'dŭm), *n.; pl.* E. -DUMS (-dŭmz), L. -DA (-dä). An informal record of something ; a note to help the memory.

me-mo'ri-al (mē-mō'rĭ-ăl), *a.* 1. Serving to preserve remembrance ; commemorative. 2. Of or pertaining to memory. — **Memorial Day,** a day (May 30 in the North, and of varying date in the Southern States) appointed for commemorating the dead soldiers and sailors of the Civil War. *U. S.* — *n.* 1. Anything intended to preserve the memory of a person or an event. 2. A statement of facts addressed to a government, a society, etc., often with a petition or remonstrance.

me-mo'ri-al-ize (-īz), *v. t.* [1] 1. To address or petition by a memorial. 2. To commemorate.

mem'o-rize (měm'ŏ-rīz), *v. t.* [1] To preserve the memory of ; esp., to learn by heart.

mem'o-ry (-rĭ), *n.; pl.* -RIES (-rĭz). 1. The act, capacity, or function of mentally reproducing and recognizing previous experience. 2. The sum total of a mind's experiences as actually or possibly remembered. 3. The time within which past events are remembered. 4. Any particular experience as remembered. 5. Remembrance.

men (měn), *n., pl.* of MAN.

men'ace (měn'ăs), *n.* A threat or threatening. — *v. t.* [1] To threaten. — *v. i.* [1] To act or talk in a threatening manner. — **men'ac-ing-ly,** *adv.* [8].

mé'nage' (mā'näzh'), **me-nage'** (mĕ-näzh'), *n.* 1. A household. 2. Housekeeping.

me-nag'er-ie (mē-năj'ĕr-ĭ ; mĕ-năzh'-), *n.* A collection of wild animals in cages, esp. for exhibition.

mend (měnd), *v. t. & i.* 1. To free from defects ; to alter (anything) for the better ; correct ; also, to repair. 2. To improve, better, or ameliorate. — *n.* Act or fact of mending or repairing ; also, a mended place. — **mend'er,** *n.* [8].

men-da'cious (měn-dā'shŭs), *a.* [4] Given to deception or falsehood ; lying. — **-ly,** *adv.* [8].

men-dac'i-ty (-dăs'ĭ-tĭ), *n.; pl.* -TIES (-tĭz). Quality of being mendacious.

men'di-can-cy (měn'dĭ-kăn-sĭ), *n.* Condition of being mendicant ; beggary ; begging.

men'di-cant (-kănt), *a.* Practicing beggary ; also, characteristic of a beggar. — *n.* A beggar.

men-ha'den (měn-hā'd'n), *n.* A fish of the herring family, used for making oil and fertilizer.

me'ni-al (mē'nĭ-ăl ; mēn'yăl), *a.* [4] Pertaining or appropriate to servants ; servile ; sordid ; low. — *n.* A domestic servant. — **me'ni-al-ly,** *adv.*

me-nin'ges (mē-nĭn'jēz), *n. pl. ; sing.* MENINX (mē'nĭnks). The three membranes which envelop the brain and spinal cord. [the meninges.]

men'in-gi'tis (měn'ĭn-jī'tĭs), *n.* Inflammation of

me-nis'cus (mē-nĭs'kŭs), *n.; pl.* L. -NISCI (-nĭs'ī), E.-CUSES (-kŭs-ĕz). A crescent ; a lens concave on one side and convex on the other.

men'su-ra-ble (měn'shoŏ-rā-b'l), *a.* Measurable.

men'su-ra'tion (-rā'shŭn), *n.* 1. Act or art of measuring. 2. The branch of applied geometry concerned with finding lengths, areas, and volumes from certain simple data of lines and angles.

men'tal (měn'tăl), *a.* Of or pertaining to the mind ; intellectual. — **men'tal-ly,** *adv.* [8].

men-tal'i-ty (měn-tăl'ĭ-tĭ), *n.* 1. Mental quality or power. 2. Mind considered as a characteristic.

men'thol (měn'thŏl ; -thōl), *n.* A white soothing substance obtained from oil of peppermint.

men'tion (-shŭn), *n.* A brief speaking or notice. — *v. t.* To specify, esp. by name ; refer to.

men'tion-a-ble, *a.* Fit to be mentioned.

men'tor (-tŏr), *n.* A wise and faithful counselor or monitor. [the dishes served.]

men'u (měn'ū; *F.* mĕ-nü'), *n.* A bill of fare ; also,

mer'can-tile (mûr'kăn-tĭl ; -tĭl), *a.* Of or pert. to merchants, or trade.

mer'ce-na-ry (mûr'sĕ-nă-rĭ), *a.* [4] 1. Acting or desirous merely for gain ; sordid. 2. Hired ; — now only of soldiers serving in a foreign army. — *n.; pl.* -RIES (-rĭz). A mercenary soldier.

mer'cer (mûr'sẽr), *n.* A dealer in textile fabrics, as silks or woolens. *Eng.*

mer'cer-ize (-īz), *v. t.* [1] To treat (cotton fiber or fabrics) with caustic alkali, causing the fiber to shrink and become stronger and more receptive of dyes, or sometimes, to assume a silky luster.

mer'chan-dise (-chăn-dīz), *n.* The objects of commerce ; wares ; goods.

mer'chant (-chănt), *n.* 1. One who traffics on a large scale, esp. abroad. 2. A retailer. *U. S.* — *a.* Of, pert. to, or used in, trade ; commercial

mer'chant-a-ble (-chăn-tá-b'l), *a.* [4] Marketable.

mer'chant-man (-chănt-măn), *n.; pl.* -MEN (-měn) A trading vessel.

mer'ci-ful (-sĭ-fool), *a.* [4] Full of mercy ; compassionate ; mild. — **-ly,** *adv.* [8] — **-ness,** *n.* [8].

mer'ci-less, *a.* [4] Destitute of mercy ; pitiless — **mer'ci-less-ly,** *adv.* [8] — **-less-ness,** *n.* [8]

mer-cu'ri-al (mẽr-kū'rĭ-ăl), *a.* [4] 1. Swift ; ac tive ; clever ; crafty. 2. Of or pertaining to, or due to the use of, mercury. — *n.* A drug contain ing mercury.

mer-cu'ric (-rĭk), **mer'cu-rous** (mûr'kŭ-rŭs ; mẽr kū'-), *a.* Of, pert. to, or containing, mercury.

Mer'cu-ry (mûr'kŭ-rĭ), *n.; pl.* -RIES (-rĭz). 1. *As tron.* The planet nearest to the sun. 2. [*l. c.*] A heavy silver-white metallic element ; quicksilver.

mer'cy (mûr'sĭ), *n.; pl.* -CIES (-sĭz). 1. Forbearance from inflicting harm, esp. in punishment ; clemency. 2. Compassionate treatment of the unfortunate. 3. Disposition to be merciful. 4. A merciful act, as of God.

mere (mēr), *n.* A lake or pool. *Archaic or Dial.*

mere, *a.; superl.* MER'EST (mēr'ĕst). Only this, and nothing else ; such, and no more ; simple.

mere'ly, *adv.* Not otherwise than ; simply.

mer'e-tri'cious (mẽr'ĕ-trĭsh'ŭs), *a.* [4] Alluring by false show ; tawdry. — **-ly,** *adv.* — **-ness,** *n.* [8].

merge (mûrj), *v. t. & i.* [1] To be, or to cause to be, swallowed up or absorbed.

merg'er (mûr'jẽr), *n.* An absorption of one estate or interest in another.

me-rid'i-an (mē-rĭd'ĭ-ăn), *a.* 1. Being at, or pertaining to, midday ; belonging to, or passing through, the highest point attained by a heavenly body in its diurnal course. 2. Highest ; culminating. — *n.* 1. Highest apparent point of a star or the sun. 2. Highest point, as of success.

3. *Geog.* A great circle on the earth passing through the poles and any given place, or, now usually, the half of such a circle included between the poles; as, the *meridian* of Greenwich.

me-rid′i-o-nal (mē-rĭd′ĭ-ō-năl), *a.* **1.** Southern. **2.** Of or pert. to a meridian.

me-ringue′ (mē-răng′), *n.* An icing; also, a small cake chiefly of sugar and beaten whites of eggs.

me-ri′no (mē-rē′nō), *a.* **1.** Designating, or pertaining to, a certain breed of fine-wooled sheep. **2.** Made of merino. — *n.; pl.* -NOS (-nōz). **1.** A merino sheep. **2.** A fine fabric of wool and cotton, orig. of merino wool. **3.** Kind of fine woolen yarn.

mer′it (mĕr′ĭt), *n.* **1.** Due reward or punishment (usually, reward). **2.** Quality, state, or fact of deserving well or ill. **3.** A praiseworthy quality, act, etc. — *v. t.* To earn; deserve.

mer′i-to′ri-ous (-ĭ-tō′rĭ-ŭs), *a.* [4] Deserving of reward or honor. — *-ly, adv.* [8] — *-ness, n.* [8].

mer′maid (mûr′mād), *n.* A fabled sea creature, typically with a woman's body and a fish's tail.

mer′man (-măn), *n.; pl.* -MEN. The male corresponding to a mermaid. [ing; mirth.]

mer′ri-ment (mĕr′ĭ-mĕnt), *n.* Act of merrymaking.

mer′ry (mĕr′ĭ), *a.* [3] **1.** Pleasing; delightful; also, amusing. *Archaic.* **2.** Laughingly gay; mirthful; sportive. — **mer′ri-ly** (-lĭ), *adv.* [8].

mer′ry-an′drew (-ăn′drōō), *n.* One whose business is to make sport for others; a buffoon; clown.

mer′ry-go-round′, *n.* Any of various revolving contrivances for amusement.

mer′ry-mak′ing (-māk′ĭng), *a.* Festive; jolly. — *n.* Festivity. — **mer′ry-mak′er,** *n.* [8].

me′sa (mā′sä), *n.* A table-land or plateau with an abrupt or steeply sloping side or sides.

mes′dames′ (mā′däm′), *n., pl.* of MADAM, MADAME.

mesh (mĕsh), *n.* **1.** One of the openings inclosed by the threads of network, or, *pl.*, the threads inclosing it. **2.** Network; a net. **3.** *Machinery.* Engagement of gear teeth; — chiefly in *in mesh.* — *v. t. & i.* **1.** To catch in meshes as of a net; to entangle. **2.** Of gear teeth, to engage.

mes-mer′ic (mĕz-mĕr′ĭk), *a.* Of, pertaining to, or induced by, mesmerism; hence, fascinating.

mes′mer-ism (mĕz′mĕr-ĭz′m), *n.* Hypnotism.

mes′mer-ist, *n.* A hypnotist.

mes′mer-ize (-īz), *v. t. & i.* [1] To hypnotize.

mess (mĕs), *n.* **1.** A quantity of food. **2.** A hodgepodge; hence, a muddle; botch. **3.** A group of persons who regularly eat together; also, the meal so taken. — *v. t.* To make a mess of; muddle. *Colloq.* — *v. i.* **1.** To take meals with a mess. **2.** To make a mess or muddle; also, to putter.

mes′sage (mĕs′āj), *n.* Any communication sent from one to another.

mes′sen-ger (mĕs′ĕn-jẽr), *n.* **1.** One who bears a message or does an errand. **2.** A forerunner.

Mes-si′ah (mē-sī′à), *n.* Also **-as.** The expected king and deliverer of the Hebrews; the Christ.

Mes′si-an′ic (mĕs′ĭ-ăn′ĭk), *a.* Of or pertaining to the Messiah.

mes′sieurs (mĕs′yẽrz; *F.* mā′syŭ′), *n., pl.* of MONSIEUR; — also (abbr. *Messrs.*) of E. *Mister* (*Mr.*).

mess′mate′ (mĕs′māt′), *n.* Associate in a mess.

mess′y (mĕs′ĭ), *a.* [3] Like a mess; disordered; untidy. — **mess′i-ness** (-ĭ-nĕs), *n.* [8].

mes-ti′zo (mĕs-tē′zō), *n. ; pl.* -zos (-zōz). A person of mixed blood, esp. Spanish and Indian.

met (mĕt), *pret. & p. p.* of MEET.

met′al (mĕt′ăl), *n.* **1.** Any of a class of substances usually fusible and opaque, good conductors of electricity, and of a peculiar luster. **2.** *Chem.* An elementary metal, as distinguished from an *alloy.* **3.** Material. Hence, temper; mettle.

me-tal′lic (mē-tăl′ĭk), *a.* Of, pertaining to, resembling, or of the nature of, a metal.

met′al-lif′er-ous (mĕt′ăl-ĭf′ĕr-ŭs), *a.* [4] Yielding or containing metal.

met′al-lur′gic (-lûr′jĭk), **met′al-lur′gi-cal** (-jĭ-kăl), *a.* Of or pertaining to metallurgy.

met′al-lur′gist (mĕt′ăl-lûr′jĭst), *n.* One skilled in, or practicing, metallurgy.

met′al-lur′gy (mĕt′ăl-lûr′jĭ), *n.* The science and art of preparing metals for use from their ores.

met′a-mor′phic (mĕt′à-môr′fĭk), *a.* Pertaining to metamorphism.

met′a-mor′phism (-fĭz′m), *n.* **1.** Metamorphosis. **2.** *Geol.* Change in the constitution of a rock, esp. a change due to pressure, heat, and water, and resulting in a more crystalline condition.

met′a-mor′phose (mĕt′à-môr′fōz; -fōs), *v. t.* [1] **1.** To transform; transmute. **2.** To subject to metamorphism or metamorphosis.

met′a-mor′pho-sis (-fō-sĭs), *n. ; pl.* -SES (-sēz). **1.** Change of form, structure, or substance; also, the form resulting from this. **2.** A marked change in the form of an animal after the embryonic stage, as when a tadpole changes to a frog.

met′a-phor (mĕt′à-fôr), *n.* A figure of speech by which a word or phrase literally denoting one kind of object or idea is applied to another to suggest a likeness; as in "the ship *plows* the sea."

met′a-phor′ic (-fôr′ĭk), *a.* Metaphorical.

met′a-phor′i-cal (-ĭ-kăl), *a.* Pertaining to, or comprising, a metaphor. — **i-cal-ly,** *adv.* [8].

met′a-phys′i-cal (-fĭz′ĭ-kăl), *a.* [4] **1.** Of or pert. to metaphysics; abstract, or hard to understand. **2.** Pertaining to, or having, the essential nature of reality. — **met′a-phys′i-cal-ly,** *adv.* [8].

met′a-phy-si′cian (mĕt′à-fĭ-zĭsh′ăn), *n.* One versed in metaphysics.

met′a-phys′ics (-fĭz′ĭks), *n.* That division of philosophy which includes the science of being and the theory of knowledge.

mete (mēt), *v. t.* [1] **1.** To measure. **2.** To allot; as, to *mete* out reward. — *v. i.* To measure. *Archaic*

me-temp′sy-cho′sis (mē-tĕmp′sĭ-kō′sĭs), *n. ; pl.* -CHOSES (-sēz). The passing of the soul at death into another body; transmigration of souls.

me′te-or (mē′tē-ôr), *n.* A meteoroid heated to incandescence by friction in passing through the earth's atmosphere; a shooting star.

me′te-or′ic (-ôr′ĭk), *a.* [4] **1.** Of or pertaining to a meteor or meteors. **2.** Like a meteor; flashing.

me′te-or-ite′ (mē′tē-ôr-īt′), *n.* A stony or metallic body fallen to earth from outer space. See METEOR.

me′te-or-oid′ (-oid′), *n.* One of the countless small bodies in the solar system, which become meteors on entering the earth's atmosphere.

me′te-or-o-log′i-cal (-ŏ-lŏg′ĭ-kăl), *a.* Of or pertaining to meteorology. [meteorology.]

me′te-or-ol′o-gist (-ŏl′ō-jĭst), *n.* A specialist in

---

chair; go; sing, iŋk; then, thin; nature, verdure; yet; zh = z in azure. Numbers refer to §§ in the Special Notes which, with Abbreviations, Signs, etc., precede the Vocabulary.

me'te-or-ol'o-gy (mē/tē-ŏr-ŏl/ŏ-jĭ), *n.* Physics treating of the atmosphere and its phenomena.

me'ter (mē/tẽr), *n.* One that measures; esp., an instrument for measuring, and usually for recording, the quantity measured; as, a gas *meter.*

me'ter (mē/tẽr), *n.* [6] **1.** Rhythmical arrangement of syllables or words in verse; rhythm. **2.** A measure of length, the basis of the metric system (which see), equal to 39.37 inches.

me-thinks' (mē-thĭnks/), *v. impers.; pret.* METHOUGHT/ (-thôt/). It seems to me. *Rare or Poet.*

meth'od (mĕth/ŭd), *n.* **1.** Mode of procedure; manner; way. **2.** Orderly arrangement; plan or design, as of an author.

me-thod'i-cal (mē-thŏd/ĭ-kăl), *a.* [4] Arranged, or habitually proceeding, according to method; systematic. — **-ly,** *adv.* [8].

me-thought' (mē-thôt/), *pret.* of METHINKS.

me-tic'u-lous (mē-tĭk/ū-lŭs),*a.* Unduly or excessively careful of small details. — **-ly,** *adv.* [8].

me-ton'y-my (mē-tŏn/ĭ-mĭ), *n.* A figure of speech which consists in substituting for the ordinary name of a thing the name of something that is closely related to it, or that is an attribute of it; as, " a good *table* " (that is, good *food*).

me'tre (mē/tẽr). Var. of METER.

met'ric (mĕt/rĭk), *a.* **1.** Relating to, or proceeding by, measurement. **2.** Of or pertaining to the meter (measure), or the metric system. **3.** = METRICAL, 1. — **metric system,** a decimal system of weights and measures. The basis is the *meter,* which is about 39.37 inches. — **m. ton,** a weight of 1,000 kilograms, or 2,204.6 pounds avoirdupois.

met'ri-cal (-rĭ-kăl), *a.* [4] **1.** Pert. to meter; arranged in meter. **2.** = METRIC, 1, 2.— **-ly,** *adv.* [8].

met'ro-nome (mĕt/rō-nōm), *n.* An instrument for marking exact time, esp. in music.

me-trop'o-lis (mē-trŏp/ŏ-lĭs), *n.; pl.* E. -LISES (-ēz). **1.** The chief or capital city of a country. **2.** A principal seat or center.

met'ro-pol'i-tan (mĕt/rŏ-pŏl/ĭ-tăn), *a.* [4] Of, pertaining to, or designating, a metropolis or metropolitan. — *n.* A bishop or archbishop who has oversight of the bishops of a province.

met'tle (mĕt/'l),*n.* Quality of temperament; spirit.

met'tle-some (-'l-sŭm), *a.* [4] Also **met'tled** (-'ld). Full of mettle, or spirit; fiery.

mew (mū), *n.* A sea gull.

mew, *v. t. & i.* To inclose, or confine, as in a cage.

mew (mū), *v. i.* To utter a cry like *mew,* as a cat. — *n.* The common cry of a cat.

mewl (mūl), *v. i. & t.* To cry weakly, as a baby.

Mex'i-can (mĕk/sĭ-kăn), *a.* Of or pertaining to Mexico or its people. — *n.* A native of Mexico.

mez'za-nine (mĕz/ȧ-nĭn; -nēn), *n.* Also **mezzanine** *floor or* **story.** A low story between two high ones.

|| **mez'zo**(mĕd/zō), *a.* [It.] *Music.* Mean; middling.

mez'zo-so-pra'no (-sō-prä/nō), *n. Music.* A voice between soprano and contralto.

mez'zo-tint (mĕd/zō-tĭnt; mĕz/ō-), *n.* **1.** A manner of engraving on copper or steel. **2.** An engraving so produced.

mi (mē), *n. Music.* The third tone of the scale.

mi-as'ma (mĭ-ăz/mȧ), *n.; pl.* -MATA (-mȧ-tȧ), E. -MAS (-mȧz). Infectious particles or germs floating in the air, or the air infected by them; malaria.

mi-as'mal (mĭ-ăz/măl), **mi'as-mat'ic** (mĭ/ăz-măt/-ĭk), *a.* [4] Containing, or caused by, miasma.

mi'ca (mī/kȧ), *n.* Any of a group of mineral silicates that readily separate into laminæ, or layers.

mice (mīs), *n., pl.* of MOUSE.

Mich'ael-mas (mĭk/ĕl-mȧs), *n.* The feast of the archangel Michael, Sept. 29th.

mi'crobe (mī/krōb), *n.* A microscopic organism; germ; popularly, one of the bacteria.

mi'cro-cosm (mī/krŏ-kŏz'm), *n.* A little world. Hence: Man, as an epitome of the great world.

mi-crom'e-ter (mī-krŏm/ē-tẽr), *n.* An instrument for measuring minute distances.

mi'cro-ör'gan-ism (mī/krŏ-ôr/găn-ĭz'm), *n.* Any organism of microscopic size; a microbe.

mi'cro-phone (mī/krŏ-fōn),*n.* An instrument to intensify feeble sounds or for transmitting sounds, esp. in radio broadcasting.

mi'cro-scope (mī/krŏ-skōp), *n.* Optical instrument for making enlarged images of minute objects.

mi'cro-scop'ic (-skŏp/ĭk), *a.* [4] **1.** = MICROSCOPICAL. **2.** Like a microscope; able to see minute objects. **3.** Visible only with a microscope.

mi'cro-scop'i-cal (-ĭ-kăl), *a.* [4] Of, pert. to, or conducted with, the microscope. — **mi'cro-scop'i-cal-ly,** *adv.* [uses the microscope.

mi-cros'co-pist (mī-krŏs/kŏ-pĭst), *n.* One who **mi-cros'co-py** (-pĭ), *n.* Use of the microscope.

mid (mĭd), *a.* **1.** Denoting the middle. **2.** Middle in position; — chiefly in combination.

mid (mĭd). Shortened form of AMID.

mid'day' (mĭd/dā/), *n.* Middle of the day; noon.

mid'dle (mĭd/'l), *a.* **1.** Equally distant from given extremes; mean. **2.** Intermediate; intervening; mediating. — **Middle Ages,** the period between ancient and modern times; — indefinitely applied, as from A. D. 476 to about 1400. Called also *Dark Ages.* — *n.* A middle point, part, or position.

mid'dle-aged' (mĭd/'l-ājd/), *a.* Being of an age between youth and old age.

mid'dle-man (-măn), *n.; pl.* -MEN (-mĕn). An agent or broker between two parties, esp. a dealer who buys of the producer and sells to the retailer.

mid'dling (-lĭng), *a.* Of middle or medium rank, state, size, or quality; moderate; mediocre. — *n. pl.* A combination of the coarser parts of ground wheat with the finest bran.

mid'dy (-ĭ), *n.; pl.* -DIES (-ĭz). Midshipman. *Colloq.*

midge (mĭj), *n.* Any very small gnat or fly.

midg'et (mĭj/ĕt), *n.* A very diminutive person.

mid'land (mĭd/lănd), *a.* Inland towns. — *n.* The interior region of a country; — usually in *pl.*

mid'most (-mōst), *a.* In the very middle.

mid'night (-nīt/), *n.* Twelve o'clock at night.

mid'rib' (-rĭb/), *n.* Central vein of a leaf blade.

mid'riff (mĭd/rĭf), *n.* Diaphragm (of the body).

mid'ship, *a.* Of or pert. to the middle of a ship.

mid'ship'man (mĭd/shĭp/măn),*n.; pl.* -MEN (-mĕn). In the United States navy, one of the rank next below a commissioned officer.

midst (mĭdst), *n.* **1.** The interior or central part or place; middle. **2.** The position or condition of being surrounded or beset; the press.

midst, *prep.* In the midst of; amidst.

mid'sum'mer (mĭd/sŭm/ẽr; mĭd/sŭm/ẽr), *n.* Middle of summer; esp., the summer solstice.

mid′way (mĭd′wā′), n. At a fair or exposition, a space devoted to the exhibition of curiosities, fantastic amusements, or the like. — (mĭd′wā′; mĭd′wā′), a. & adv. In the middle of the way or distance; halfway.

mid′wife (mĭd′wīf′), n.; pl. -WIVES (-wīvz). A woman who assists women in childbirth.

mid′win′ter (mĭd′wĭn′tēr; mĭd′wĭn′-), n. The middle of winter; esp., the winter solstice.

mien (mēn), n. Air; demeanor; carriage; bearing.

might (mīt), n. 1. Power; ability; efficacy; as, with all his might. 2. Great or superior strength, or power.

might, pret. of MAY.

might′y (-ĭ), a. [3] 1. Possessing might; potent; powerful. 2. Accomplished or marked by might. 3. Extraordinary; great. Chiefly Colloq. — adv. In a great degree; very. Chiefly Colloq. — **might′i-ly**, adv. [8] — **-i-ness**, n. [8].

mi′gnon-ette′ (mĭn′yŭn-ĕt′), n. A garden annual with fragrant greenish white flowers.

mi′grate (mī′grāt), v. i. [1] 1. To go from one country or region to another with a view to residence. 2. To pass periodically from one region or climate to another, as various birds.

mi-gra′tion (mī-grā′shŭn), n. Act of migrating.

mi′gra-to-ry (mī′grá-tō-rǐ), a. [4] 1. Migrating; or disposed to migrate. 2. Roving; nomad. 3. Of or pert. to migration.

mi-ka′do (mī-kä′dō), n. Popular title of the Emperor of Japan; — now little used by the Japanese.

milch (mĭlch), a. Giving milk; as, a milch cow.

mild (mīld), a. [3] Gentle; kind; soft; clement; moderate; temperate. — **-ly**, adv. — **-ness**, n.

mil′dew (mĭl′dū), n. A parasitic fungus or the whitish down or discoloration which it produces on plants, paper, clothing, etc. — v. t. & i. To affect, or be affected, with mildew.

mile (mīl), n. A measure of distance, equal to 5,280 feet (1,609.3 meters). The geographical, or nautical, mile is about 6,080 feet (1,853.25 meters).

mile′age (mīl′ăj), n. 1. An allowance for traveling expenses at a certain rate per mile. 2. Aggregate length or distance in miles.

mile′post′ (-pōst′), n. A post to indicate the distance in miles from a given point.

mile′stone′ (-stōn′), n. Stone serving as a milepost.

mil′i-tan-cy (mĭl′ĭ-tăn-sĭ), n. State of being militant; militant spirit.

mil′i-tant (mĭl′ĭ-tănt), a [4] Engaged in warfare; fighting; also, combative. — **-ly**, adv. [8].

mil′i-ta-rism (mĭl′ĭ-tá-rĭz′m), n. 1. A military condition; disposition to maintain strong armies. 2. The spirit that exalts military ideals.

mil′i-ta-ry (-rĭ), a 1. Of or pertaining to soldiers or war. 2. Done by soldiers; supported by armed force. — n. Soldiery; the army.

mil′i-tate (-tāt), v. i. [1] 1. To war; fight; contend. 2. Of things, to have weight or effect.

mi-li′tia (mī-lĭsh′á), n. A body of citizens enrolled for periodical military discipline, but called into active service only in emergencies.

mi-li′tia-man (-măn), n.; pl. -MEN. One who belongs to an organized militia.

milk (mĭlk), n. 1. The fluid secreted by the mammary glands of female mammals. 2. A liq-uid resembling milk, as the juice of the coconut, etc. — v. t. 1. To press or draw milk from. 2. To draw (milk) from the breast or udder. — v.i. To draw or to yield milk. — **milk′er**, n. [8].

milk′i-ness (mĭl′kĭ-nĕs), n. State of being milky.

milk′maid′ (mĭlk′mād′), n. A woman who milks cows or works in a dairy. [milk.

milk′man (-măn), n.; pl. -MEN. A man who sells

milk′sop′ (-sŏp′), n. An effeminate man.

milk sugar. Lactose.

milk tooth. One of the first set of teeth.

milk′weed′ (-wēd′), n. Any of several plants containing a milky, usually white, fluid.

milk′y (mĭl′kĭ), a. [3] Like milk. — Milky Way, a faintly luminous tract in the heavens, composed of stars and nebulous masses.

mill (mĭl), n. A money of account of the United States having the value of $\frac{1}{10}$ of a cent.

mill, n. 1. A building with machinery for grinding grain into flour; hence, a machine for grinding. 2. Any of various machines used in working up raw material. 3. An establishment with machinery by which manufacturing processes are carried on. — v. t. 1. To subject, as grain, to some process in a mill. 2. To make a raised border around or cut grooves across, the edges of (a coin).

mil′le-na-ry (mĭl′ē-ná-rĭ), a. Pertaining to a thousand, esp. a thousand years. — n. A thousand; a thousand years. [a millennium.

mil-len′ni-al (mĭ-lĕn′ĭ-ăl), a. Of or pertaining to

mil-len′ni-um (-ŭm), n.; pl. E. -NIUMS (-ŭmz), L. -NIA (-á). 1. A thousand years. 2. Esp., the thousand years (Rev. xx.), during which holiness is to be triumphant in the world.

mill′er (mĭl′ēr), n. 1. One who keeps or tends a mill, esp. a flour mill. 2. Any of various moths having wings appearing as if covered with dust.

mil′let (mĭl′ĕt), n. 1. An annual grass cultivated for its grain or cut for hay. 2. The grain.

mil′li-gram (mĭl′ĭ-grăm), n. One thousandth of a gram.

mil′li-li′ter (-lē′tēr), n. A thousandth of a liter.

mil′li-me′ter (-mē′tēr), n. [6] One thousandth of a meter, equal to .03937 of an inch.

mil′li-ner (mĭl′ĭ-nēr), n. One who makes, trims or deals in hats, bonnets, etc., for women.

mil′li-ner-y (-nēr-ĭ), n. 1. Articles made or sold by milliners. 2. Business or work of a milliner.

mil′lion (-yŭn), n. 1. The number of ten hundred thousand, or a thousand thousand, — written 1,000,000. 2. An indefinitely large number.

mil′lion-aire′ (-âr′), n. One whose wealth amounts to a million or millions of dollars, pounds, etc.

mil′lionth (mĭl′yŭnth), a. Coming last in a series of a million; also, forming one of a million equal parts into which a (whole) thing may be divided — n. A millionth part; millionth unit or object

mill race. The canal which conveys water to a mill wheel, or the current which drives the wheel

mill′stone′ (mĭl′stōn′), n. Either of two circular stones for grinding grain.

mill′wright′ (mĭl′rīt′), n. One whose occupation is to build mills, or to set up their machinery.

milt (mĭlt), n. The spleen.

milt, n. The male reproductive glands of fishes when filled with secretion, or the secretion itself.

mim'e-o-graph' (mĭm'ē-ō-gráf'), *n.* A kind of stencil copying device. — *v. t.* To duplicate or make with a mimeograph.

mi-met'ic (mĭ-mĕt'ĭk ; mī-), *a.* Imitative.

mim'ic (mĭm'ĭk), *a.* [4] Of the nature of, pert. to, or formed by, imitation or mimicry. — *n.* One that imitates or mimics. — *v. t.; -ICKED (-ĭkt); -ICK-ING.* **1.** To ridicule by imitation. **2.** To copy or imitate closely; ape; simulate. — **mim'ick-er,** *n.*

mim'ic-ry (-ĭk-rĭ), *n.; pl.* -RIES (-rĭz). **1.** Act, practice, or art of a mimic. **2.** Resemblance between some animals and other animals or the objects among which they live, affording some advantage, as concealment.

mi-mo'sa (mĭ-mō'sá; mĭ-; -zá), *n.* Any of many trees, shrubs, and herbs of warm regions, with clusters of white or pink flowers.

min'a-ret (mĭn'á-rĕt), *n.* A lofty tower attached to a mosque and surrounded by one or more balconies.

min'a-to-ry (-tō-rĭ), *a.* [4] Threatening.

mince (mĭns), *v. t.* [1] **1.** To cut or chop into very small pieces. **2.** To make little of; weaken the force of; utter mincingly. — *v. i.* **1.** To walk with short steps in a prim, affected way; act with affected delicacy. **2.** To talk or speak with affected elegance. — *n.* Minced meat; mincemeat.

mince'meat' (mĭns'mēt'), *n.* A mixture, chopped fine, of raisins, apples, suet, spices, etc., with or without meat, used to fill mince pies.

minc'ing-ly, *adv.* In an affectedly nice manner.

mind (mīnd), *n.* **1.** Remembrance. **2.** Consciousness; thought. **3.** Understanding; intellect; also, sanity. **4.** Mental disposition or mood; as: **a** Sentiment ; belief. **b** Choice ; intent ; will. — *v. t.* **1.** To turn the mind or attention to; as: **a** To heed; note. **b** To obey. **c** To attend strictly to. **2.** To be concerned about ; to object to ; dislike. **3.** To take care or charge of; tend. — *v. i.* **1.** To give heed; hence, to obey. **2.** To be concerned or troubled; care; — in negative constructions; as, never *mind.* **3.** To be careful or wary.

mind'ed (mīn'dĕd), *a.* Disposed; inclined.

mind'ful (mīnd'fŏŏl), *a.* [4] Bearing in mind; regardful; attentive. — **-ly,** *adv.* [8] — **-ness,** *n.* [8].

mine (mīn), *pron. & a.* Of me. See MY. *Mine* is now chiefly a possessive adj. pron., used : (1) attributively before a vowel or *h* or with a preceding vocative (*Archaic*) ; as, *mine* eyes; (2) with its noun apart or unexpressed ; as, a sister of *mine.*

mine, *n.* **1.** A place from which minerals, as ores, are got, as by digging. **2.** An ore deposit. **3.** A rich source; an abundant store. **4.** *Mil.* An excavation, or a case moored beneath or on the water, containing an explosive for the destruction of an enemy. — *v.i.* [1] **1.** To dig a mine; work in a mine. **2.** To burrow. **3.** *Mil.* To make a mine ; to lay mines, as in a harbor. — *v. t.* **1.** To dig in; remove the foundation of, as by digging; lay a mine under; undermine. **2.** To make by burrowing, esp. underground. **3.** To get, as metals, out of the earth by digging. **4.** To dig into for ore or metal.

min'er (mīn'ẽr), *n.* One who works in a mine.

min'er-al (mĭn'ẽr-ǎl), *a.* **1.** Of or pert. to, or of the nature of, a mineral or minerals; inorganic. **2.** Impregnated with minerals; as, *mineral* waters.

— *n.* **1.** Any chemical element or compound occurring naturally. **2.** *Mining.* Ore. **3.** Anything neither animal nor vegetable.

min'er-al'o-gy (-ǎl'ō-jĭ), *n.; pl.* -GIES (-jĭz). The science of minerals. — **min'er-al-og'i-cal** (-ǎl-ŏj'ĭ-kǎl), *a.* — **min'er-al'o-gist** (-ǎl'ō-jĭst), *n.*

min'gle (mĭng'g'l), *v. t.* [1] **1.** To combine or join by intermixture or diffusion ; mix ; associate or unite. **2.** To make or prepare by mixing; concoct. — *v. i.* To become mingled ; mix ; blend.

min'i-a-ture (mĭn'ĭ-á-tūr), *n.* **1.** Any very small painting, esp. a portrait, as on ivory. **2.** A representation on a small scale. — *a.* Being or represented on a small scale.

min'im (mĭn'ĭm), *n.* The smallest liquid measure, about a drop.

min'i-mal (-ĭ-mǎl), *a.* Least ; smallest.

min'i-mize (-mīz), *v. t.* [1] To reduce to the smallest part or proportion possible.

min'i-mum (mĭn'ĭ-mŭm), *n.; pl.* L. -MA (-má) ; E. -MUMS (-mŭmz). **1.** The least quantity or amount assignable, admissible, etc. **2.** The lowest point or amount reached. — *a.* Lowest or least.

min'ing (mīn'ĭng), *vb. n.* Act or business of constructing military mines, or of working ore mines.

min'ion (mĭn'yŭn), *n.* **1.** A favorite; idol; — now derogatory. **2.** A fawning or servile dependent or agent.

min'is-ter (-ĭs-tẽr), *n.* **1.** One to whom the executive head of a government intrusts the management of affairs of state. **2.** A representative of a government sent to a foreign government to transact diplomatic business. **3.** A pastor; clergyman. — *v. i.* **1.** To attend and serve; to perform service as a minister. **2.** To render aid.

min'is-te'ri-al (-tē'rĭ-ǎl), *a.* [4] **1.** Of or pertaining to ministry or service. **2.** Of or pertaining to the office of minister or the ministry. — **-ly,** *adv.*

min'is-te'ri-al-ist, *n.* A supporter of the ministry, or of the party in power.

min'is-tra'tion (-trā'shŭn), *n.* Act of ministering.

min'is-try (mĭn'ĭs-trĭ), *n.; pl.* -TRIES (-trĭz). **1.** Ministration; as, the *ministry* of angels. **2.** The office, duties, or functions of a minister. **3.** The clergy. **4.** The body of ministers of state.

mink (mĭngk), *n.* **1.** The fur, usually seal-brown, of the mink (def. 2). **2.** An animal related to the weasels, but larger, with partially webbed feet.

min'now (mĭn'ō), *n.* Any of various small fishes.

mi'nor (mī'nẽr), *a.* **1.** Inferior; less; smaller; as, of *minor* importance. **2.** *Music.* Less by a half step than the major. — *n.* A person of either sex under majority.

mi-nor'i-ty (mĭ-nŏr'ĭ-tĭ), *n.; pl.* -TIES (-tĭz). **1.** The smaller in number of two aggregates; — opposed to *majority.* **2.** Quality or state of being a minor.

min'ster (mĭn'stẽr), *n.* The church of a monastery; — often after the monastery has ceased to exist.

min'strel (-strĕl), *n.* **1.** A medieval musical entertainer. **2.** A poet; musician. *Poetic.* **3.** One of a troupe presenting negro melodies, jokes, etc., and usually blacked ; — called also *negro minstrels.*

min'strel-sy (-sĭ), *n.; pl.* -SIES (-sĭz). **1.** Practice or songs of minstrels. **2.** A body of minstrels.

mint (mĭnt), *n.* Any of various aromatic herbs having small pink or white flowers.

mint, *n.* **1.** A place where money is coined. **2.** A great supply of money; a vast sum. — *v. t.* To make by stamping; coin.

mint'age (mĭnt'tåj), *n.* **1.** Coinage. **2.** Cost of coining, or charge for coining.

min'u-end (mĭn'ū-ĕnd), *n. Arith.* The number or magnitude from which another is to be subtracted.

min'u-et' (mĭn'ū-ĕt'; mĭn'ū-ĕt), *n.* A kind of slow graceful dance, or music suited to such a dance.

mi'nus (mī'nŭs), *a.* **1.** *Math.* Less; decreased by; negative; as, a *minus* quantity. **2.** Deprived of; wanting. *Colloq.*—minus sign, the sign [—] indicating subtraction or a negative quantity.

min'ute (mĭn'ĭt), *n.* **1.** The sixtieth part of an hour or a degree; sixty seconds. **2.** A moment. **3. a** A memorandum, note, or draft, as of instructions. **b** *pl.* An official record of proceedings. — *v. t.* [1] To make a minute of.

mi-nute' (mĭ-nūt'; mī-), *a.* [3] **1.** Very small; little; slight. **2.** Of trivial importance; trifling. **3.** Marked by or attentive to small details.

mi-nute'ly (mĭ-nūt'lĭ ; mī-), *adv.* In a minute manner or degree ; exactly.

min'ute-man (mĭn'ĭt-măn), *n.; pl.* -MEN. *Amer. Hist.* One of a class of armed citizens who pledged themselves to take the field at a minute's notice, immediately previous to and during the War of Independence.

mi-nute'ness (mĭ-nūt'nĕs; mī-), *n.* Quality of being minute; as: **a** Extreme smallness. **b** Attention to minute details.

mi-nu'ti-a (mĭ-nū'shĭ-á), *n.; pl.* -TIÆ (-ē). A minute or minor detail; — chiefly in *pl.*

minx (mĭŋks), *n.* A pert girl; — commonly in playful sense.

mir'a-cle (mĭr'á-k'l), *n.* **1.** A wonderful thing; a marvel. **2.** An event or effect in the physical world deviating from the known laws of nature.

Minuteman

mi-rac'u-lous (mĭ-răk'ū-lŭs), *a.* [4] **1.** Of the nature of a miracle. **2.** Marvelous; wonderful. — **-ly,** *adv.* [8] — **-ness,** *n.* [8].

mi-rage' (mē-räzh'), *n.* An optical effect, as on ocean or desert, in which a reflected image is seen, commonly inverted, while the real object may or may not be in sight.

mire (mīr), *n.* Soft or deep mud, slush, or the like; also, dirt. — *v. t. & i.* [1] **1.** To sink or permit to stick fast in mire. **2.** To soil with mud or dirt.

mir'i-ness (mīr'ĭ-nĕs), *n.* Miry state or quality.

mir'ror (mĭr'ẽr), *n.* A looking-glass; any smooth substance that forms images by reflection. — *v. t.* To reflect, as in a mirror.

mirth (mûrth), *n.* Gladness or gayety, as shown by laughter; jollity. — **-ful** (-fool), *a.* [4] — **-ful-ly,** *adv.* [8] — **-ful-ness,** *n.* [8].

mir'y (mīr'ĭ), *a.* [3] **1.** Resembling, or of the nature of, mire; boggy; as, *miry* ground. **2.** Abounding or covered with mire; hence, dirty; filthy.

mis'ad-ven'ture (mĭs'ăd-vĕn'tụr), *n.* Mischance; ill luck; a mishap; accident; disaster.

mis'al-li'ance (-ă-lī'ăns), *n.* An improper or undesirable alliance, esp. in marriage.

mis'an-thrope (mĭs'ăn-thrōp), *n.* One who has aversion for or who distrusts his fellow men.

mis'an-throp'ic (-thrŏp'ĭk), **mis'an-throp'i-cal** (-ĭ-kăl), *a.* Of, pertaining to, or like a misanthrope. [thrope.

mis-an'thro-pist (mĭs-ăn'thrŏ-pĭst), *n.* A misanthrope.

mis-an'thro-py (-pĭ), *n.* Hatred of mankind.

mis-ap'pli-ca'tion (mĭs-ăp'lĭ-kā'shŭn), *n.* Act of misapplying.

mis'ap-ply' (mĭs'á-plī'), *v.t.* [2] To apply wrongly.

mis'ap-pre-hend' (mĭs-ăp'rē-hĕnd'), *v.t.* To misunderstand.

mis'ap-pre-hen'sion (-hĕn'shŭn), *n.* A misapprehending, or state of being misapprehended.

mis'ap-pro'pri-ate (mĭs'á-prō'prĭ-āt), *v. t.* [1] To appropriate or use wrongly or wrongfully.

mis'ap-pro'pri-a'tion, *n.* Act of misappropriating.

mis'be-have' (-bê-hāv'), *v. t. & i.* [1] To behave ill; — as *v. t.*, used with a reflexive pronoun.

mis'be-hav'ior (-hāv'yẽr), *n.* [5] Bad behavior.

mis-cal'cu-late (mĭs-kăl'kū-lāt), *v. t. & i.* [1] To calculate erroneously; misjudge. — **mis-cal'cu-la'tion** (-lā'shŭn), *n.*

mis-call' (mĭs-kôl'), *v. t.* To misname.

mis-car'riage (-kăr'ĭj), *n.* **1.** Mismanagement; failure. **2.** Failure to carry properly. **3.** Premature bringing forth of young.

mis-car'ry (-ĭ), *v. i.* [2] **1.** To fail of intended result. **2.** To suffer miscarriage (of young).

mis'cel-la'ne-ous (mĭs'ĕ-lā'nê-ŭs), *a.* [4] **1.** Mixed; consisting of diverse things. **2.** Having various qualities; many-sided; as, a *miscellaneous* writer. — **-ly,** *adv.* [8] — **-ness,** *n.* [8].

mis'cel-la-ny (mĭs'ĕ-lā-nĭ), *n.; pl.* -NIES (-nĭz). **1.** A mixture of various things, esp. of writings. **2.** *pl.* Miscellaneous treatises, studies, or the like, collected in one book.

mis-chance' (mĭs-chàns'), *n.* Ill luck; a mishap.

mis'chief (mĭs'chĭf), *n.* **1.** Harm; esp., trouble or vexation caused by some one; as, to make *mischief.* **2.** A cause or source of harm or vexation.

mis'chie-vous (mĭs'chĭ-vŭs), *a.* [4] Causing, or full of, mischief; injurious; esp., inclined to the causing of, or involving, petty injury or annoyance; naughty. — **-ly,** *adv.* [8] — **-ness,** *n.* [8].

mis'con-ceive' (mĭs'kŏn-sēv'), *v. t. & i.* [1] To conceive wrongly. [misconceiving.

mis'con-cep'tion (-sĕp'shŭn), *n.* Act or result of

mis'con-duct' (-dŭkt'), *v. t.* To conduct amiss.

mis-con'duct (mĭs-kŏn'dŭkt), *n.* Wrong or improper conduct; misbehavior.

mis'con-struc'tion (mĭs'kŏn-strŭk'shŭn), *n.* Act of misconstruing; wrong interpretation.

mis-con'strue (mĭs-kŏn'strōō ; mĭs'kŏn-strōō'), *v. t.* [1] To construe wrongly.

mis-count' (mĭs-kount'), *v. t. & i.* To count erroneously; miscalculate. — *n.* A wrong count.

mis'cre-ant (mĭs'krê-ănt), *n.* **1.** Villain; wretch. — *a.* [4] **1.** Infidel. *Archaic.* **2.** Villainous.

mis-date' (mĭs-dāt'), *v.t.* [1] To date erroneously.

mis-deal' (-dēl'), *v. t. & i. ; -*DEALT (-dĕlt); -DEAL-ING. To distribute wrongly, as cards. — *n.* Act of misdealing.

mis-deed' (-dēd'), *n.* An evil deed.

mis′de-mean′ (mĭs′dė-mēn′), v. t. To misbehave; — used reflexively. [a felony.]

mis′de-mean′or (-ẽr), n. [5] A crime less than

mis′di-rect′ (-dĭ-rĕkt′), v. t. To direct wrongly.

mis′di-rec′tion (-rĕk′shŭn), n. Wrong direction.

mis-do′ (mĭs-dōō′), v.t. & i.; for prin. parts see DO. To do wrongly or improperly. — **-er** (-ẽr), n. [8].

mis-do′ing (-ĭng), n. Wrongdoing, or a case of it.

mis′em-ploy′ (mĭs′ĕm-ploi′), v. t. To employ amiss. — **mis′em-ploy′ment** (-mĕnt), n.

mi′ser (mī′zẽr), n. A covetous person; esp., one having wealth who lives miserably to increase it.

mis′er-a-ble (mĭz′ẽr-à-b'l), a. [4] **1.** In a state of misery; wretched; as, she seems *miserable*; — often as a figure of speech. **2.** Causing misery, or discomfort; pitiably poor; as, a *miserable* lot. **3.** Pitiable; lamentable; as, a *miserable* failure. **4.** Wretchedly deficient; paltry; as, a *miserable* dinner. — **-bly**, adv. [8].

mi′ser-ly (mī′zẽr-lĭ), a. [4] Pertaining to, like, or characteristic of, a miser; very covetous.

mis′er-y (mĭz′ẽr-ĭ), n.; pl. -ERIES (-ĭz). **1.** A state of great distress; privation; poverty. **2.** A wretched circumstance; misfortune.

mis-fit′ (mĭs-fĭt′), n. **1.** Act or state of fitting badly. **2.** Something that fits badly, as a garment.

mis-for′tune (-fôr′tŭn), n. Bad fortune; mishap.

mis-give′ (mĭs-gĭv′), v. t. To give doubt and apprehension to; as, her heart *misgave* her.

mis-giv′ing, vb. n. A premonition of evil.

mis-gov′ern (-gŭv′ẽrn), v. t. To govern ill.

mis-gov′ern-ment (-mĕnt), n. A misgoverning.

mis-guid′ance (-gĭd′ăns), n. Wrong guidance.

mis-guide′ (-gīd′), v. t. [1] To guide wrongly.

mis-hap′ (-hăp′), n. Mischance.

mis′in-form′ (mĭs′ĭn-fôrm′), v. t. To give untrue or misleading information to.

mis′in-for-ma′tion (mĭs′ĭn-fŏr-mā′shŭn), n. A misinforming; incorrect information.

mis′in-ter′pret (mĭs′ĭn-tûr′prĕt), v. t. To interpret erroneously. — **mis′in-ter′pre-ta′tion** (-prė-tā′shŭn), n. [neously or unjustly.]

mis-judge′ (mĭs-jŭj′), v. t. & i. [1] To judge erro-

mis-judg′ment, mis-judge′ment (-jŭj′mĕnt), n. Wrong or unjust judgment. [lected; lose.]

mis-lay′ (-lā′), v. t. To lay in a place not recol-

mis-lead′ (-lēd′), v. t. To lead into a wrong way; lead astray; deceive. [tive; delusive.]

mis-lead′ing, p. a. [4] Leading astray; decep-

mis-man′age (-măn′åj), v.t. & i. [1] To manage ill. — **mis-man′ag-er**, n. [8].

mis-man′age-ment (-mĕnt), n. Wrong, bad, or bungling management.

mis-name′ (-nām′), v. t. [1] To name wrongly.

mis-no′mer (-nō′mẽr), n. **1.** An erroneous naming or designation. **2.** A wrong name.

mi-sog′y-nist (mĭ-sŏj′ĭ-nĭst), n. Hater of women.

mi-sog′y-ny (-nĭ), n. Hatred of women.

mis-place′ (mĭs-plās′), v. t. [1] To put in a wrong place or on an improper or unworthy object.

mis-play′ (-plā′), n. A wrong play.

mis-print′ (-prĭnt′), v. t. To print wrong or incorrectly. — n. A mistake in printing.

mis′pro-nounce′ (mĭs′prŏ-nouns′), v. t. & i. [1] To pronounce incorrectly. — **mis′pro-nun′ci-a′tion** (-nŭn′sĭ-ā′shŭn), n. ; -shĭ-ā′shŭn), n.

mis-quote′ (mĭs-kwōt′), v. t. & i. [1] To quote erroneously.

mis-read′ (-rēd′), v. t. To read amiss.

mis′rep′re-sent′ (mĭs-rĕp′rė-zĕnt′), v. t. & i. To represent falsely, improperly, or imperfectly. — **mis′rep′re-sen-ta′tion** (-zĕn-tā′shŭn), n.

mis-rule′ (-rōōl′), v. t. [1] To rule badly; misgovern. — n. Bad rule; hence, disorder; tumult.

miss (mĭs), n. ; pl. MISSES (mĭs′ĕz). **1.** [cap.] A title of courtesy prefixed to the name of an unmarried girl or woman. **2.** A young unmarried woman or a girl.

miss, v. t. **1.** To fail of hitting, meeting, finding, attaining, getting, receiving, seeing, hearing, perceiving, etc. **2.** To escape; avoid; — now *Dial.*, except with adverb; as, I just, or barely, *missed* being killed. **3.** To omit; fail or neglect to have, do, keep, attend, etc. **4.** To discover or feel the absence of; want. — v. i. **1.** To fail to hit; deviate. **2.** To fail; not to succeed. — n. Failure to hit.

mis′sal (mĭs′ăl), n. The book containing the service of the Mass.

mis-shape′ (mĭs-shāp′), v. t. [1] To shape ill.

mis-shap′en (-shāp′'n), p. a. [4] Having an ill shape; deformed.

mis′sile (mĭs′ĭl), a. Capable of being thrown or projected. — n. A weapon or object thrown, or to be thrown or projected, as a bullet or spear.

miss′ing (mĭs′ĭng), p. a. Absent; lost; gone.

mis′sion (mĭsh′ŭn), n. **1.** A sending, or being sent, by authority on some service or function. **2.** Persons sent; envoys. **3.** A body of missionaries; also, esp. pl., the organized effort to do missionary work. **4.** An organization for doing missionary work. **5.** A station or residence of missionaries. **6.** A messenger's or agent's charge; commission. **7.** That which one is destined or fitted to do; calling.

mis′sion-a-ry (-ă-rĭ), a. Of, pertaining to, or engaged in, missions. — n.; pl. -RIES (-rĭz). One sent on a mission; esp., one sent to spread religion.

mis′sive (mĭs′ĭv), n. A letter. — a. Specially sent or ready to be sent.

mis-spell′ (mĭs-spĕl′), v. t. To spell incorrectly.

mis-spend′ (-spĕnd′), v. i. To spend amiss.

mis-state′ (-stāt′), v. t. [1] To state wrongly.

mis-state′ment, n. A wrong statement.

mis-step′ (mĭs-stĕp′), n. A wrong step.

mist (mĭst), n. **1.** Visible watery vapor suspended in the atmosphere near the earth, or approaching the form of rain. **2.** Dimness of vision; a haze before the eyes. — v. t. To cover with or as with mist; dim. — v. i. To rain in very fine drops; form a mist; become blurred.

mis-take′ (mĭs-tāk′), v.t.; pret. MIS-TOOK′ (-tŏŏk′); p. p. -TAK′EN (-tāk′'n), p. pr. & vb. n. -TAK′ING (-tāk′ĭng). **1.** To take in a wrong sense; misunderstand, as a remark. **2.** To take erroneously, as one person or thing for another. — v. i. To make a mistake. — n. A misunderstanding.

Mis′ter (mĭs′tẽr), n. A title of courtesy prefixed to a man's name; as, *Mr.* Smith.

mist′i-ly (mĭs′tĭ-lĭ), adv. In a misty manner.

mis-time′ (mĭs-tīm′), v. t. [1] To time wrongly.

mist′i-ness (mĭs′tĭ-nĕs), n. State of being misty.

mis′tle-toe (mĭs′l-tō; mĭz′-), n. A parasitic

shrub with thick green leaves, small yellowish flowers, and waxy white berries.

mis-took' (mĭs-tŏŏk'), *pret. & obs. p. p.* of MISTAKE.

mis-treat' (mĭs-trēt'), *v. t.* To treat ill; abuse.

mis'tress (mĭs'trĕs), *n.* **1.** A woman having authority or ownership; female head of a family, etc. **2.** A woman skilled in anything. **3.** A sweetheart. **4.** A woman wrongfully living with, or supported by, a man. **5.** [*cap.*] A title of courtesy now superseded by the contracted forms, *Mrs.* (pronounced mĭs'ĭs *or* mĭs'ĭz), for a married, and *Miss*, for an unmarried, woman.

mis-trust' (-trŭst'), *n.* Want of confidence or trust. — *v. t. & i.* To suspect; distrust.

mis-trust'ful (-fŏŏl), *a.* Having mistrust.

mist'y (mĭs'tĭ), *a.* [3] **1.** Accompanied or marked by mist; blurred by mist. **2.** Dim; vague.

mis'un-der-stand' (mĭs'ŭn-dẽr-stănd'; mĭs-ŭn'-), *v. t. & i.* To misconceive; take in a wrong sense.

mis'un-der-stand'ing, *n.* **1.** Mistake of meaning; error. **2.** Disagreement; quarrel.

mis-us'age (mĭs-ūz'ăj; -ūs'ăj), *n.* Bad treatment; ill usage; abuse; misuse.

mis-use' (-ūs'), *n.* Wrong use; misapplication.

mis-use' (-ūz'), *v. t.* [1] **1.** To subject to misuse; to misapply. **2.** To abuse; treat ill.

mite (mīt), *n.* **1.** Any of numerous small crawling animals infesting animals, plants, etc. **2.** A small coin or sum of money. **3.** Anything very small; a bit; as, not a *mite* of good. *Colloq.*

mi'ter (mī'tẽr), *n.* [6] The official headdress of a bishop in the Roman Catholic Church since about A.D. 1000. — *v. t. & i.; -TERED or -TRED* (-tẽrd); *-TER-ING* (-tẽr-ĭng) *or -TRING* (-trĭng). **1.** To place a miter upon; hence, to raise to a bishopric. **2.** To fit in a miter joint.

miter, *or* **mitre, joint.** *Carp., etc.* A joint formed by pieces fitted on a line bisecting the angle of junction; sometimes, any bevel joint.

mit'i-gate (mĭt'ĭ-gāt), *v. t.* [1] To render mild or milder; soften; appease; lessen; moderate.

mit'i-ga'tion (mĭt'ĭ-gā'shŭn), *n.* Act of mitigating; alleviation. — **mit'i-ga-tive** (-gă-tĭv), *a.*

mi'tral (mī'trăl), *a.* Pertaining to or resembling a miter; *Anat.*, designating the cardiac valve (*mitral valve*) that prevents the blood in the left ventricle from returning to the auricle.

mitt (mĭt), *n.* A kind of glove without covering for the fingers, or with half fingers.

mit'ten (mĭt'ĕn), *n.* A covering for the hand having a separate sheath for the thumb only.

mix (mĭks), *v. t. & i.* **1.** To unite or blend into one mass, as by stirring together; mingle. **2.** To unite with in company; join; unite; associate. **3.** To form by mingling; compound; as, to *mix* a potion. — *n.* A mixing; mixture; *Colloq.*, a muddle or mess. — **mix'er**, *n.* [8].

mixed (mĭkst), *p. p. & p. a.* — **mixed number**, the sum of an integer and a fraction.

mix'ture (mĭks'tụ̄r), *n.* **1.** A mixing, as of ingredients. **2.** That which results from mixing. **3.** A mass of ingredients not chemically united.

miz'zen (mĭz'n), *n. Naut.* The aftermost of the fore-and-aft sails of a three-masted vessel; — called also *spanker.* **b** A mizzenmast. — *a. Naut.* Of or pertaining to the mizzenmast.

miz'zen-mast (-măst), *n. Naut.* The aftermost mast of a three-masted vessel, of a yawl, or of a ketch.

mne-mon'ic (nē-mŏn'ĭk), *a.* Assisting, or intended to assist, the memory; also, of or pertaining to mnemonics. [memory.]

mne-mon'ics (-ĭks), *n.* Art of developing the memory.

moan (mōn), *n.* A low prolonged sound, indicative of pain or grief. — *v. t. & i.* To utter a moan.

moat (mōt), *n.* A deep wide trench around a rampart, as of a castle, usually filled with water; a ditch. — *v. t.* To surround with or as with a moat.

mob (mŏb), *n.* **1.** The populace. **2.** The rabble; hence, a crowd, esp. a disorderly crowd. — *v. t.; MOBBED* (mŏbd); *MOB'BING.* To crowd about, as a mob does, and attack or annoy.

mo'bile (mō'bĭl; -bēl), *a.* [4] **1.** Movable; marked by ease of movement. **2.** Moving or flowing freely. **3.** Changing readily.

mo-bil'i-ty (mō-bĭl'ĭ-tĭ), *n.* State of being mobile.

mo'bil-i-za'tion (mō'bĭl-ĭ-zā'shŭn; mŏb'ĭ-), *n.* Act or process of mobilizing.

mo'bi-lize (mō'bĭ-līz; mŏb'ĭ-līz), *v. t.* [1] To assemble and put in a state of readiness for active service in war, as troops.

moc'ca-sin (mŏk'á-sĭn), *n.* **1.** A soft leather shoe, the sole and upper in one piece, as worn by American Indians. **2.** Any venomous snake of the genus including the copperhead.

mock (mŏk), *v. t.* **1.** To treat with scorn or contempt; deride; ridicule. **2.** To disappoint; deceive; delude. **3.** To imitate; mimic; esp., to deride by mimicry. — *v. i.* To make sport in contempt or in jest; scoff; jeer. — *n.* **1.** A jibe; jeer. **2.** Mockery; ridicule. — *a.* Sham; counterfeit. — **mock orange,** the syringa; also, any of various other plants. — **mock'er** (-ẽr), *n.* [8].

mock'er-y (mŏk'ẽr-ĭ), *n.; pl. -ERIES* (-ĭz). **1.** Insulting or contemptuous action or speech. **2.** A subject of derision. **3.** An insincere or contemptible imitation. **4.** Ridiculously useless action.

mock'ing, *p. pr. & vb. n.* of MOCK. — **mocking bird,** a common bird of the southern U. S. remarkable for its imitations of the notes of other birds.

mod'al (mōd'ăl), *a.* [4] **1.** Of or pertaining to a mode. **2.** *Gram.* Of or pertaining to mood; expressive of mode or manner.

mode (mōd), *n.* **1.** *Gram.* = MOOD. **2.** Manner of doing or being; way. **3.** A prevailing custom or style.

mod'el (mŏd'ĕl), *n.* **1.** A miniature representation of a thing. **2.** A copy; image. *Now Colloq.* **3.** A pattern of a thing to be made; hence, something worthy of imitation. **4.** A person that serves as an artist's pattern. — *a.* Serving, or that may serve, as a model. — *v. t.* [7] To form after a pattern; shape; fashion. — *v. i.* To make a pattern; design. — **mod'el-er,** *n.* [7, 8].

mod'er-ate (-ẽr-ăt), *a.* [4] Kept within due bounds; limited. — (-āt), *v. t.* [1] To render moderate; restrain or reduce from excess. — *v. i.* To become less violent, severe or intense. — **-ly,** *adv.* [8] — **-ness,** *n.* [8].

mod'er-a'tion (-ā'shŭn), *n.* Act of moderating; state or quality of being moderate; temperateness.

mod'er-a'tor (mŏd'ẽr-ā'tẽr), *n.* **1.** An arbitrator; mediator. **2.** A presiding officer.

mod′ern (mŏd′ẽrn), *a.* [4] Of or pert. to present or recent time. — *n.* **1.** A person of modern times. **2.** A person of modern views and tastes.

mod′ern-ism (-ẽr-nĭz′m), *n.* Modern practice; esp., a modern usage, characteristic, etc.

mod′ern-ist (-nĭst), *n.* An admirer of modern ways, fashions, schools of thought, etc.

mod′ern-ize (-nīz), *v. t.* [1] To render modern.

mod′est (-ĕst), *a.* [4] **1.** Placing a moderate or low estimate on one's own capabilities or merits. **2.** Appropriate to, or due to, absence of boldness, presumption, or arrogance. **3.** Observing the proprieties of sex; virtuous. — **-ly,** *adv.* [8].

mod′es-ty (-ĕs-tĬ), *n.* Quality of being modest.

mod′i-cum (-Ĭ-kŭm), *n.* A little; small quantity.

mod′i-fi-ca′tion (-fĬ-kā′shŭn), *n.* Act of modifying; modified state; as: **a** Limitation; qualification. **b** Partial alteration; result of being so altered.

mod′i-fy (mŏd′Ĭ-fī), *v. t.* [2] **1.** To limit or reduce in extent or degree; moderate. **2.** To change somewhat in form or qualities; alter somewhat. **3.** *Gram.* To limit or restrict the meaning of.

mod′ish (mŏd′Ĭsh), *a.* [4] According to the mode; fashionable; stylish. — **-ly,** *adv.* [8] — **-ness,** *n.* [8].

‖ **mo′diste′** (mō′dēst′), *n.* [F.] One who makes, or deals in, articles of fashion, esp. women's apparel.

mod′u-late (mŏd′ū-lāt), *v. t.* [1] To vary in tone. — *v. i.* *Music.* To pass from one key to another.

mod′u-la′tion (-lā′shŭn), *n.* Act of modulating or state of being modulated.

Mo-gul′ (mō-gŭl′), *n.* **1.** A Mongolian; esp., one of the Mongol conquerors of India or their descendants. **2.** [*l. c.*] A great personage; autocrat.

mo′hair′ (mō′hâr′), *n.* A fine fabric made from goat hair, or an imitation of it.

Mo-ham′med-an (mō-hăm′ĕd-ăn), *a.* Of or pertaining to Mohammed (570?-632) or Mohammedanism. — *n.* A follower of Mohammed.

Mo-ham′med-an-ism (-Ĭz′m), *n.* The religion or doctrines of Mohammed; Islam. Cf. KORAN.

moi′e-ty (moi′ê-tĬ), *n.; pl.* -TIES (-tĬz). **1.** A half. **2.** An indefinite part.

moil (moil), *v. i.* To work hard; drudge. — *n.* **1.** Drudgery. **2.** Disorder; confusion.

‖ **moire′** (mwär; mōr), *n.* [F.] A textile fabric watered by calendering; watered silk.

moist (moist), *a.* [3] Slightly wet; damp; humid; not dry. — **moist′ness,** *n.* [8].

mois′ten (mois′′n), *v. t.* To make moist or damp. — *v. i.* To become moist, as the eyes.

mois′ture (-tụr), *n.* That which moistens; exuding fluid; liquid in small quantity.

mo′lar (mō′lȧr), *a.* Grinding; as, a *molar* tooth. — *n.* A molar tooth. In man the three back teeth on each side of each jaw are molars.

mo-las′ses (mō-lăs′ĕz), *n.; pl.* MOLASSES. The dark sirup drained from sugar in manufacture.

mold (mōld), *n.* A fungous growth or discoloration produced on organic matter, esp. when damp or decaying. — *v. i. & t.* To become, or make, moldy.

mold, *n.* Soft, crumbly earth; esp., earth rich in organic matter, and hence suited to plant growth.

mold, *n.* **1.** The matrix, or cavity, from which anything takes its form; also, the body containing the cavity. **2.** That on or to which anything is molded or formed. — *v. t.* **1.** To mix or knead (esp.

dough) to a required consistency or shape. **2.** To shape; model; fashion. **3.** To form a mold of, as in sand, in which to make a casting. — **mold′a-ble,** *a.* [8] — **mold′er,** *n.* [8].

mold′er (mōl′dẽr), *v. i. & t.* To crumble into small particles; crumble away.

mold′ing, *n.* **1.** Act or process of shaping in or on a mold, or of making molds. **2.** Anything cast, or appearing as if cast, in a mold. **3.** A narrow surface, sunk or projecting, used for decoration.

mold′y (mōl′dĬ), *a.* [3] Overgrown with or containing mold; musty; as, *moldy* cheese.

mole (mōl), *n.* A spot or small permanent prominence on the human body, esp. a dark-colored one.

mole, *n.* Any of numerous small animals having minute eyes, small concealed ears, and very soft fur. They live almost entirely underground.

mole, *n.* A massive work of masonry or large stones, etc., laid in the sea, as for a breakwater.

mo-lec′u-lar (mō-lĕk′ū-lȧr), *a.* Pert. to, connected with, produced by, or consisting of, molecules.

mol′e-cule (mōl′ê-kūl; mŏl′ê-), *n.* **1.** A unit of matter, the smallest portion into which a substance can be conceived to be divided without being changed in character. **2.** Any minute particle.

mole′hill′ (mōl′hĬl′), *n.* A little ridge thrown up by moles; hence, a trifling obstacle, difficulty, etc.

mole′skin′ (-skĬn′), *n.* **1.** The skin of the mole used as fur. **2.** A fabric resembling moleskin (def. 1), or, *pl.*, garments, esp. trousers, of it.

mo-lest′ (mō-lĕst′), *v. t.* To interfere with hostilely or vexatiously.

mo′les-ta′tion (mō′lĕs-tā′shŭn; mŏl′ĕs-), *n.* Act of molesting; state of being molested; annoyance.

mol′li-fi-ca′tion (mŏl′Ĭ-fĬ-kā′shŭn), *n.* Act of mollifying, or state of being mollified.

mol′li-fy (mŏl′Ĭ-fī), *v. t.* [2] To allay, as rage; appease; calm. — **mol′li-fi′er** (-ẽr), *n.* [8].

mol′lusk (mŏl′ŭsk), *n.* One of the Mollusca, a large division of the animal kingdom including slugs, snails, mussels, clams, oysters, cuttlefishes, etc.

molt (mōlt), *v. i.* To shed or cast off the feathers, outer layer of the skin, or the like, which are replaced by new growth. — *v. t.* To cast off and renew. — *n.* The act or process of molting.

mol′ten (mōl′t′n), *p. a.* **1.** Melted, or fused, esp. by intense heat; — of metals, glass, etc. **2.** Made by melting and casting; as, a *molten* image.

mo-lyb′de-num (mō-lĬb′dē-nŭm), *n.* A metallic element of the chromium group, resembling iron.

mo′ment (mō′mĕnt), *n.* **1.** A minute portion of time; instant. **2.** Importance; consequence. **3.** Tendency, or measure of tendency, to produce motion.

mo′men-ta-ry (mō′mĕn-tȧ-rĬ), *a.* Continuing but a moment; transitory. — **ta-ri-ly** (-rĬ-lĬ), *adv.* [8].

mo-men′tous (mō-mĕn′tŭs), *a.* [4] Of moment; weighty. — **-ly,** *adv.* [8] — **-ness,** *n.* [8].

mo-men′tum (-tŭm), *n.; pl.* L. -TA (-tȧ), E. -TUMS (-tŭmz). **1.** *Mech.* The quantity of motion in a moving body, being proportioned to the mass multiplied by the velocity. **2.** Impetus.

mon′ad (mŏn′ăd; mō′năd), *n.* A unit; atom.

mon′arch (mŏn′ȧrk), *n.* **1.** A sole supreme ruler; also, the hereditary chief of a limited or constitutional monarchy. **2.** One likened to a sole ruler.

mo-nar′chal (mō-när′kăl), *a.* **1.** Of, pertaining

to, or suiting, a monarch; sovereign; regal. **2.** Of the nature of, or acting as, a monarch.

mo-nar'chi-al (-kĭ-ăl), *a.* Monarchic; monarchal.

mo-nar'chic (-kĭk)) *a.* [4] Of or pertain-
mo-nar'chi-cal (-kĭ-kăl)) ing to, or of the nature of, a monarch or monarchy; favoring a monarchy.

mon'arch-ist (mŏn'ár-kĭst), *n.* An advocate or supporter of monarchy or its principles.

mon'arch-y (mŏn'ár-kĭ), *n. ; pl.* -ARCHIES (-kĭz). **1.** The state or territory ruled by, or the government exercised by, a monarch. **2.** The system of government in which a single person is sovereign.

mon'as-ter-y (-ăs-tĕr-ĭ), *n. ; pl.* -TERIES (-ĭz). A house of religious retirement for persons under religious vows, esp. monks.

mo-nas'tic (mŏ-năs'tĭk), *a.* [4] **1.** Of or pert. to monasteries or their inmates. **2.** Secluded from worldly concerns and devoted to religion.

mo-nas'ti-cal (-tĭ-kăl), *a.* [4] Monastic.

mo-nas'ti-cism (-tĭ-sĭz'm), *n.* Monastic life, system, or rule. [week.]

Mon'day (mŭn'dă), *n.* The second day of the

mon'e-ta-ry (mŏn'ē-tă-rĭ ; mŭn'-), *a.* **1.** Of or pertaining to the coinage or currency. **2.** Of or pertaining to money; pecuniary.

mon'e-tize (-tīz), *v. t.* [1] To convert into money.

mon'ey (mŭn'ĭ), *n. ; pl.* -EYS (-ĭz), *or, esp. for* "*sums of money,*" MONIES. **1.** Metal, as gold, silver, or copper, coined or stamped, and issued as a medium of exchange. **2.** Any form or denomination of coin, certificate, or bank note, current as money. **3.** Wealth reckoned in terms of money. **4.** A sum or amount of money. — **money of account,** a denomination of money, used in accounts, for which there may, or may not, be an equivalent coin ; as, the mill is a *money of account.*

mon'eyed (mŭn'ĭd), *a.* [4] **1.** Wealthy. **2.** Consisting of, derived from, or due to, money.

money order. An order for payment of money.

Mon'gol (mŏn'gŏl), *a.* Mongolian. — *n.* One of the native race of Mongolia, mostly nomads.

Mon-go'li-an (mŏn-gō'lĭ-ăn), *a.* Designating, or pert. to, the yellow race, which includes the Chinese, Japanese, etc. — *n.* A member of the yellow race ; also, a Mongol.

mon'goose (mŏn'gōos), *n. ; pl.* -GOOSES (-ĕz). A mammal of India of the civet family, about the size of a ferret. It kills poisonous snakes.

mon'grel (mŭn'grĕl ; mŏn'-), *n.* The progeny resulting from the crossing of breeds; esp., a dog of no definable breed. — *a.* [4] Of or pert. to a mixed breed. [ing, as of danger.]

mo-ni'tion (mŏ-nĭsh'ŭn), *n.* An admonition; warn-

mon'i-tor (mŏn'ĭ-tẽr), *n.* **1.** One who admonishes. **2.** A pupil or student selected for special duties, usually disciplinary. **3.** A heavily armored war vessel, with low freeboard, having one or more revolving turrets. — **mon'i-tress,** *n. fem.* [8].

monk (mŭnk), *n.* One of a religious community of men living apart from the world and bound by vows of chastity, obedience, and poverty.

mon'key (mŭn'kĭ), *n. ; pl.* -KEYS (-kĭz). Any member of the highest order of mammals, except man and, usually, the lemurs ; esp., any of the smaller, longer-tailed forms (cf. APE).

monkey wrench. A wrench having a sliding jaw.

monk'ish (mŭn'kĭsh), *a.* [4] Monastic.

monks'hood (mŭnks'hŏŏd'), *n.* A plant of the crowfoot family, related to the wolfsbane.

mon'o-chro-mat'ic (mŏn'ō-krō-măt'ĭk), *a.* Of one color. [in a single color.]

mon'o-chrome (-krōm), *n.* Painting or drawing

mon'o-cle (-k'l), *n.* An eyeglass for one eye.

mon'o-dy (mŏn'ō-dĭ), *n.; pl.* -DIES (-dĭz). A species of poem in which a single mourner expresses lamentation ; also, a funeral song.

mo-nog'a-mous (mŏ-nŏg'á-mŭs), *a.* Upholding, or practicing, monogamy ; of or pert. to monogamy.

mo-nog'a-mist (-mĭst), *n.* One who advocates or practices monogamy.

mo-nog'a-my (-mĭ), *n.* Single marriage ; esp., marriage with but one person at the same time.

mon'o-gram (mŏn'ō-grăm), *n.* A character composed of letters interwoven or combined.

mon'o-graph (-gráf), *n.* A special treatise on a particular subject of limited range.

mon'o-lith (-lĭth), *n.* A single stone or block of stone, esp. one of large size, shaped into a pillar, statue, etc. — **mon'o-lith'ic** (-lĭth'ĭk), *a.*

mon'o-logue (-lŏg), *n.* **1.** A dramatic part or composition for a single performer. **2.** A soliloquy.

mon'o-ma'ni-a (-mā'nĭ-á), *n.* Derangement of mind upon a single subject only ; also, popularly, a "craze." — **mon'o-ma'ni-ac** (-ăk), *n.*

mon'o met'al lism (-mĕt'ăl ĭz'm), *n.* The legalized use of one metal only, as gold, as the standard of money values ; theory or practice of such use.

mo-no'mi-al (mŏ-nō'mĭ-ăl), *a.* Consisting of but a single term. — *n.* A monomial expression.

mon'o-plane (mŏn'ō-plān), *n.* An aëroplane having a single supporting plane.

mo-nop'o-list (mŏ-nŏp'ō-lĭst), *n.* One who has a monopoly, or who favors monopoly.

mo-nop'o-li-za'tion (-lĭ-zā'shŭn), *n.* Act of monopolizing ; state of being monopolized.

mo-nop'o-lize (-līz),*v. t.* [1] To gain a monopoly of.

mo-nop'o-ly (-lĭ), *n.; pl.* -LIES (-lĭz). **1.** Exclusive control of the supply of any commodity or service. **2.** Exclusive possession of anything. **3.** A company or combination having a monopoly. *Colloq.*

mon'o-rail (mŏn'ō-rāl'), *n.* A single rail serving as a track for a wheeled vehicle.

mon'o-syl-lab'ic (-sĭ-lăb'ĭk), *a.* Having but one syllable. [one syllable.]

mon'o-syl'la-ble (mŏn'ō-sĭl'á-b'l), *n.* A word of

mon'o-the-ism (-thē-ĭz'm), *n.* Belief that there is but one God. — **mon'o-the-ist,** *n.*

mon'o-tone (-tōn), *n.* **1.** Continuous utterance in one unvaried pitch. **2.** Monotony of style. **3.** Something uttered or written in one tone or strain or marked by monotonous recurrences.

mo-not'o-nous (mŏ-nŏt'ō-nŭs), *a.* [4] Uttered in one unvarying tone; marked by monotony; without change or variety. — **-ly,** *adv.* [8] — **-ness,** *n.* [8].

mo-not'o-ny (-nĭ), *n.* **1.** Sameness of tone or sound. **2.** Sameness, esp., irksome sameness.

mon'o-type (mŏn'ō-tīp), *n.* A machine that casts and sets individual types.

mon-sieur' (mē-syû'; m'syû'; m'syû'), *n. ; pl.* MESSIEURS (mā'syû'). [F.] Lit., my lord ; sir ; — the title [*cap.*] in France corresponding to the English *Mr.* Abbr., *sing., M.; pl.,* MM. or *Messrs.*

---

chair; go; sing, iŋk; then, thin; nature, verdure; yet; zh = z in azure. Numbers refer to §§ in the Special Notes which, with Abbreviations, Signs, etc., precede the Vocabulary.

mon-soon′ (mŏn-sōōn′), *n.* A periodic wind, esp. in the Indian Ocean and off the south coast of Asia. Also, the rainy season accompanying the southwest monsoon in India.

mon′ster (mŏn′stĕr), *n.* **1.** A fabulous or actually existing animal of strange or horrible form. **2.** Any huge animal or thing. **3.** An animal or plant departing greatly from the usual type. **4.** Anything monstrous; esp., a person of unnatural ugliness, wickedness, or cruelty; as, a *monster* of iniquity.

mon-stros′i-ty (mŏn-strŏs′ĭ-tĭ), *n.; pl.* -TIES (-tĭz). Monstrous quality or state; also, a monster.

mon′strous (mŏn′strŭs), *a.* [4] **1.** Deviating greatly from the natural form or character. **2.** Having the qualities or appearance of a monster. **3.** Huge; enormous. **4.** Hateful; horrible; dreadful. — **mon′strous-ly**, *adv.* [8].

month (mŭnth), *n.* **1.** One of the twelve portions (calendar *months*) into which the year is divided; also, a period of thirty days. **2.** *Astron.* A period (lunar *month*) of a complete revolution of the moon.

month′ly, *a.* **1.** Continued, or in, a month. **2.** Done, happening, published, etc., once a month, or every month. — *n.; pl.* -LIES (-lĭz). A publication appearing once a month. — *adv.* Once a month.

mon′u-ment (mŏn′ū-mĕnt), *n.* **1.** Something serving as a memorial; as: **a** A building, pillar, stone, or the like, erected in memory of the dead or of an event, etc. **b** Any lasting or notable instance. **2.** A boundary stone or the like.

mon′u-men′tal (-mĕn′tăl), *a.* [4] Of or pertaining to, suitable for, or serving as, a monument.

moo (mōō), *v. i.* To make the characteristic cry of a cow; low. — *n.* The lowing or low of a cow.

mood (mōōd), *n. Gram.* Distinction of form in a verb to express the manner in which the action or state it denotes is conceived.

mood, *n.* State or temper of mind; disposition.

mood′y (mōōd′ĭ), *a.* [3] **1.** Subject to moods of depression, bad temper, or the like; gloomy. **2.** Expressing moodiness or ill humor; as, a *moody* face. — **mood′i-ly**, *adv.* [8] — **mood′i-ness**, *n.* [8].

moon (mōōn), *n.* **1.** The satellite of the earth. **2.** A lunar month; a month; as, three *moons* ago. **3.** Any satellite, or secondary planet. **4.** Something shaped like the moon, esp. a crescent. — *v. i.* To wander, or gaze, about as if moonstruck.

moon′beam′ (-bēm′), *n.* A ray of moonlight.

moon′light′ (mōōn′līt′), *n.* The light of the moon.

moon′shine′ (-shīn′), *n.* **1.** Moonlight. **2.** Show without substance or reality; empty show. **3.** Liquor smuggled or illicitly distilled. *Colloq.*

moon′shin′er (-shīn′ĕr), *n.* A person engaged in illicit trade at night; *U. S.*, an illicit distiller. *Colloq.*

moon′stone′ (-stōn′), *n.* An ornamental stone, used in jewelry, having a peculiar luster somewhat suggestive of the pearl or opal.

moon′struck′ (mōōn′strŭk′), *a.* [4] Deranged through the supposed influence of the moon.

moor (mōōr), *n.* An extensive area of waste ground, esp. if covered with heather.

moor, *v. t.* To secure (a vessel) in a place, as by anchoring. — *v. i.* To be secured by being moored.

Moor, *n.* **1.** A native of Morocco. **2.** A Mohammedan of one of the native North African races or of Arabs settled in North Africa; esp., one of the

Saracenic invaders of Spain or their descendants.

moor′age (-ăj), *n.* Act of, or place for, mooring.

moor′ing, *vb. n.* **1.** That which serves to moor a vessel, as anchors, cables, etc.; — usually in *pl.* **2.** *pl.* Place where a vessel is or may be moored.

Moor′ish (mōōr′ĭsh), *a.* Of or pert. to the Moors.

moor′land (-lănd), *n.* A moor.

moose (mōōs), *n.* A large mammal of the deer family, inhabiting Canada and the northeastern United States. [— *a.* Debatable.]

moot (mōōt), *v. t.* To bring up for discussion.

moot court. A mock court.

mop (mŏp), *n.* **1.** An implement for washing floors, etc., made of cloth or yarn, fastened to a handle. **2.** Something likened to a mop, as a mass of hair. — *v. t.*; MOPPED (mŏpt); MOP′PING. To wipe with or as with a mop.

mop′board′ (-bōrd′), *n.* The baseboard of a room, extending round the walls and touching the floor.

mope (mōp), *v. i.* [1] To be dull and spiritless. — *n.* **1.** A dull, spiritless person. **2.** *pl.* Low spirits; "dumps." — **mop′ish** (mōp′ĭsh), *a.* [8].

mo-quette′ (mō-kĕt′), *n.* A kind of carpet or upholstery fabric having a velvety woolen pile.

mo-raine′ (mō-rān′), *n.* A mass of earth, stones, etc., carried and finally deposited by a glacier.

mor′al (mŏr′ăl), *a.* [4] **1.** Of or pert. to questions of right and wrong. **2.** Righteous; virtuous; just. **3.** Capable of being governed by, or of influencing, the sense of right. **4.** Virtual; as, a moral victory, an actual defeat regarded as a virtual victory. **5.** Serving to teach a moral. — **moral certainty**, a probability of so high a degree that it can be confidently acted upon. — *n.* **1.** Moral conduct or teachings; — usually in *pl.* **2.** The inner meaning, or lesson, of a fable, etc.

mo-rale′ (mō-răl′), *n.* Moral or mental condition; conduct, esp. as affected by zeal, spirit, hope, confidence, etc.; — used esp. of troops.

mor′al-ist (mŏr′ăl-ĭst), *n.* **1.** One who moralizes; a teacher or student of morals. **2.** One who practices moral duties or leads a moral life.

mo-ral′i-ty (mō-răl′ĭ-tĭ), *n.; pl.* -TIES (-tĭz). **1.** Moral quality; virtue. **2. a** Moral discourse or instruction. **b** A kind of allegorical play (popular esp. in the 16th century), in which actors personify faith, death, vice, etc. **3.** Moral practice or action; uprightness of life. **4.** Morals.

mor′al-ize (mŏr′ăl-īz), *v. t.* [1] **1.** To explain in a moral sense. **2.** To make moral. — *v. i.* To make moral reflections; draw moral lessons from events. — **mor′al-iz′er** (-īz′ĕr), *n.* [8].

mor′al-ly, *adv.* In a moral sense or manner.

mor′als (mŏr′ălz), *n. pl.* **1.** Science of right conduct; ethics. **2.** Moral principles or practice.

mo-rass′ (mō-răs′), *n.* A marsh; swamp; fen.

mor′bid (môr′bĭd), *a.* [4] **1.** Not sound and healthful; diseased; sickly; given to gloomy or unwholesome ideas. **2.** Relating to disease. — **-ly**, *adv.* [8] — **-ness**, *n.* [8]. [character.]

mor-bid′i-ty (môr-bĭd′ĭ-tĭ), *n.* Morbid state or

mor′dant (môr′dănt), *a.* [4] **1.** Biting; sarcastic; keen; as, *mordant* wit. — *n.* **1.** Any corrosive used in etching. **2.** Any substance which, by combining with a dyestuff to form an insoluble compound, produces in the fiber a fixed color.

āle, senāte, câre, ăm, ăccount, ärm, ȧsk, sofȧ; ēve, ĕvent, ĕnd, recĕnt, makēr; īce, ĭll; ōld, ȯbey, ôrb, ŏdd, sŏft, cȯnnect; ūse, ŭnite, ûrn, ŭp, circŭs; fōōd, fŏŏt; out, oil;

more (mōr), *a., compar.; positive wanting; superl.* **most** (mōst). **1.** Greater; superior; increased. **2.** Additional; other.— *n.* **1.** A greater quantity, amount, or number. **2.** An additional or greater amount. — *adv.* **1.** In or to a greater quantity or degree. **2.** Further; moreover.

mo-reen' (mô-rēn'), *n.* A coarse, stout woolen or woolen and cotton fabric, usually watered or with embossed figures.

more-o'ver (mōr-ō'vẽr), *adv.* Beyond what has been said; further; besides; also.

mor'ga-nat'ic (môr'gà-năt'ĭk), *a.* Of the nature of, or pertaining to, a form of marriage contracted by a man of high rank with a woman of inferior rank so that the wife and children do not take the husband's rank or inherit his property held in virtue thereof.

morgue (môrg), *n.* A place where bodies of persons found dead are exposed for identification.

mor'i-bund (mōr'ĭ-bŭnd), *a.* [4] In a dying state.

Mor'mon (môr'mŭn), *n.* A member of the Church of Jesus Christ of Latter-day Saints. They formerly practiced plural marriage.

morn (môrn), *n.* Morning. *Chiefly Poetic.*

morn'ing (môr'nĭng), *n.* Early part of the day.

morn'ing-glo'ry (-glō'rĭ), *n.; pl.* -ries (-rĭz). A twining plant with heart-shaped leaves and large funnel-shaped white, pink, or purple flowers.

mo-roc'co (mô-rŏk'ō), *n.; pl.* -cos (-ōz). A fine leather, commonly of goatskin tanned with sumac.

mo-rose' (mô-rōs'), *a.* [4] Sullen; ill-humored. —**ly**, *adv.* —**ness**, *n.* [8].

mor'phi-a (môr-fĭ-à), *n.* *Chem.* Morphine.

mor'phine (-fĭn; -fēn), *n.* The chief alkaloid of opium. It deadens pain and causes sleep.

mor-phol'o-gy (môr-fŏl'ō-jĭ), *n.* Biology dealing with the form and structure of animals and plants.

mor'row (môr'ō), *n.* **1.** Morning. *Archaic.* **2.** The day following. **3.** To-morrow.

mor'sel (môr'sĕl), *n.* **1.** A little bite or bit of food. **2.** A small piece; as, a *morsel* of clay.

mor'tal (môr'tăl), *a.* [4] **1.** Subject to death. **2.** Deadly; fatal; causing death, physical or spiritual. **3.** So severe as to be thought of as threatening death. **4.** Of or pertaining to death; deathly. **5.** Human. **6.** Wishing, or involving a wish, to kill.— *n.* A being that is subject to death; a human being; man. —**mor'tal-ly**, *adv.* [8].

mor-tal'i-ty (môr-tăl'ĭ-tĭ), *n.* **1.** Condition, quality, or nature of being mortal. **2.** The death of large numbers; esp., number or rate of deaths.

mor'tar (môr'tẽr), *n.* **1.** A strong bowl-like vessel in which substances are brayed with a pestle. **2.** A short light cannon used to throw shells of large caliber with low velocities and usually at very high angles. **3.** A building material made of lime, cement, or plaster of Paris, with sand and water. — *v. t.* To plaster or make fast with mortar.

mortar board. **1.** A small square board with a handle beneath, for holding mortar. **2.** A kind of academic cap. *Colloq.* See *Illust.*

Mortar Board, 2.

mort'gage (môr'găj), *n.* A conditional conveyance of property, as security for the payment of a debt, etc., to become void upon settlement of the obligation. — *v. t.* [1] **1.** *Law.* To convey by mortgage. **2.** To pledge; give as security.

mort'ga-gee' (-gà-jē'), *n.* The person to whom property is mortgaged.

mort'ga-gor' (môr'gà-jôr'; môr'găjēr'), *n.* Also **-gag-er** (môr'gă-jẽr). One who gives a mortgage.

mor'tice. [1] Var. of MORTISE.

mor'ti-fi-ca'tion (môr'tĭ-fĭ-kā'shŭn), *n.* **1.** A mortifying or state of being mortified; esp., *Med.*, gangrene. **2.** That which mortifies.

mor'ti-fy (môr'tĭ-fī), *v. t.* [2] To deaden by religious or other discipline, as the carnal affections; hence, to abase; humble. — *v. i.* To become affected with gangrene.

mor'tise (-tĭs), *n.* A cavity, hole, or the like, as in a timber, into or through which some other part fits or passes. — *v. t.* [1] **1.** To join or fasten securely; esp., to join or fasten by a tenon and mortise. **2.** To cut or make a mortise in.

mor'tu-a-ry (môr'tṳ-à-rĭ), *a.* Of or pertaining to the burial of the dead or death or mourning. — *n.; pl.* -ries (-rĭz). A place for the reception of the dead.

a Mortise, 1; b Tenon.

mo-sa'ic (mô-zā'ĭk), *n.* **1.** *Fine Arts.* A surface decoration made by inlaying small colored pieces in patterns. **2.** That which is so made; mosaic work. — *a.* Formed by, or resembling, mosaic.

Mos'lem (mŏz'lĕm; mŏs'-), *n.; pl.* MOSLEMS (-lĕmz), *or collectively* MOSLEM. A Mussulman; an orthodox Mohammedan.— *a.* Mohammedan.

mosque (mŏsk), *n.* A Mohammedan temple.

mos-qui'to (mŏs-kē'tō), *n.; pl.* -toes (-tōz). Any of certain two-winged insects, having a long proboscis adapted, in the females only, for puncturing the skin. Some species transmit the organisms that produce malaria, yellow fever, etc.

moss (môs), *n.* **1.** Any of various plants with small, leafy stems, growing on earth, on bark, etc. **2.** Any of various lichens; as, Iceland *moss.*

moss'y (môs'ĭ), *a.* [3] **1.** Overgrown or covered with or as with moss; as, a *mossy* bank. **2.** Resembling moss; as, *mossy* green. — **-i-ness** (-ĭ-nĕs), *n.*

most (mōst), *a. ; superl.* of MORE. **1.** Greatest in number, quantity, size, or extent;—often as superlative of *many, much;* nearly all; as, *most* men agree with him. **2.** Greatest in degree.— *n.* **1.** The greatest or largest quantity, amount, etc. **2.** [Construed as *pl.*] The greatest or largest number (of an aggregate). **3.** The utmost; greatest possible amount, value, degree, result, or the like. — *adv.* **1.** In the greatest degree or to the greatest extent. Placed before an adjective or adverb, *most* is used to form the superlative degree; as, *most* illustrious; *most* rapidly. **2.** Almost; nearly. *Now Colloq.*

most'ly (mōst'lĭ), *adv.* For the greatest part.

mote (mōt), *n.* A small particle, as of floating dust.

moth (môth), *n.; pl.* MOTHS (môthz). **1.** Any of many insects related to the butterflies but having a stouter body, smaller wings, and less brilliant colors. They usually fly at night. **2.** Loosely, any insect which feeds on woolens, furs, etc.

moth'er (mŭth'ẽr), n. A gelatin-like membrane that forms on alcoholic liquids which are turning to vinegar. Called also *mother of vinegar*.

moth'er, n. **1.** A female parent. **2.** Source of birth or origin. **3.** Used as a title of an abbess or the like. — v. t. To be or act as a mother to.

moth'er-hood (-hŏŏd), n. State of being a mother.

moth'er-in-law', n.; pl. MOTHERS-IN-LAW. Mother of one's husband or wife.

moth'er-less, a. Destitute of a living mother.

moth'er-ly, a. [4] Of, pertaining to, like, suitable for, or characteristic of, a mother; tender.

moth'er-of-pearl', n. The hard pearly inside layer of pearl oysters, river mussels, etc.

mother wit. Natural or native wit or sense.

mo'tion (mō'shŭn), n. **1.** Act, process, or state of changing place; movement. **2.** Mental act or impulse. **3.** A proposal, esp. a formal one in a deliberative body. **4.** pl. Movements; actions. — v. i. To gesture, as with the hand.— v. t. To direct or invite by a motion, as of the hand.

mo'tion-less, a. Without motion; being at rest.

motion picture. = MOVING PICTURE.

mo'tive (mō'tĭv), n. That which incites to action or moves the will. — a. Causing motion.

mot'ley (mŏt'lĭ), a. [3] **1.** Variegated in color. **2.** Composed of diverse parts; as, a *motley* crowd.

mo'tor (mō'tẽr), n. **1.** One that imparts motion. **2.** *Mach.* A machine that develops power; esp. : **a** An electric motor. **b** A small engine for an automobile, boat, etc. **3.** An automobile. — v. i. To ride in, or travel by, an automobile.

motor boat, *or* **mo'tor-boat'**, n. A boat propelled by a motor.

motor car, *or* **mo'tor-car'**, n. An automobile.

motor cycle, *or* **mo'tor-cy'cle**, n. A bicycle propelled by a motor.

mo'tor-ist, n. One who motors, esp. habitually.

mo'tor-ize (-īz), v. t. [1] To substitute motor-driven vehicles, or automobiles, for the horse-drawn vehicles of (a fire department, etc.).

mo'tor-man (-măn), n. A man who drives a motor; esp., the driver of an electric car or the like.

mot'tle (mŏt'l), v. t. [1] To mark with spots or blotches; spot; blotch.

mot'to (mŏt'ō), n.; pl. -TOES (-ōz). A sentence, phrase, or word inscribed on anything, as an escutcheon or a ring; also, a short pithy expression of a guiding principle; a maxim.

mould, mould'er, moult, etc. Vars. of MOLD, etc.

mound (mound), n. An artificial elevation of earth; rampart; also, a natural hillock or knoll.

mount (mount), n. A mountain; high hill; —now poetical, except in names; as, *Mount* Shasta.

mount, v. i. **1.** To rise; ascend. **2.** To get up (on something, as a platform); esp., to seat one's self on an animal for riding. **3.** To rise or increase in amount. — v. t. **1.** To ascend; climb; place or seat one's self on. **2.** To put or place (on something elevated). **3.** To cause to get on horseback. **4.** To put upon anything that sustains and fits for use or that preserves. — n. That on which a person or thing is mounted; esp., a saddle horse.

moun'tain (moun'tĭn), n. Any elevation higher than a hill, and often abrupt, but without great extent of surface at its summit.

mountain ash. Any of several trees having ash-like leaves and red berries.

moun'tain-eer' (-tĭ-nēr'), n. **1.** An inhabitant of a mountain region. **2.** A mountain climber.

moun'tain-ous (moun'tĭ-nŭs), a. [4] Containing, or abounding in, mountains; like a mountain.

moun'te-bank (moun'tē-bănk), n. **1.** One who publicly sells quack medicines. **2.** A charlatan.

mount'ing, n. **1.** Act of one that mounts. **2.** That which serves as a mount; setting.

mourn (mōrn), v. i. & t. To express or to feel sorrow; esp., to lament some one's death. — **mourn'er** (mōr'nẽr), n. [8].

mourn'ful (mōrn'fŏŏl), a. [4] Full of, expressing, or indicating, sorrow. — **mourn'ful-ly**, adv.

mourn'ing, vb. n. **1.** Act of sorrowing, esp. for a person's death; lamentation. **2.** Garb or emblems indicative of grief, esp. clothing of black.

mouse (mous), n.; pl. MICE (mīs). Any of numerous species of small rodents, esp. the common house mouse. — (mouz), v. i. [1] **1.** To hunt and catch mice. **2.** To hunt slyly or diligently. — **mous'er** (mouz'ẽr), n. [8].

mouth (mouth), n.; pl. MOUTHS (mouthz). **1.** The opening through which an animal receives food; also, the cavity containing the tongue and teeth. **2.** An opening suggestive of a mouth. **3.** A wry face; a grimace. — (mouth), v. t. **1.** To utter with a voice affectedly big or swelling; declaim. **2.** To seize with mouth or teeth. — v. i. To rant.

mouth'ful (mouth'fŏŏl), n.; pl. -FULS (-fŏŏlz). **1.** As much as the mouth holds, or as is put into the mouth at one time. **2.** A small quantity.

mouth'piece' (-pēs'), n. **1.** Something placed at or forming a mouth. **2.** The part of a musical or other instrument to which the mouth is applied. **3.** A spokesman; as, the *mouthpiece* of his party.

mov'a-ble (mŏŏv'à-b'l), a. **1.** Capable of being moved; not fixed or stationary. **2.** Changing from one date to another. — n. A thing capable of being moved, as an article of furniture.

move (mŏŏv), v. t. [1] **1.** To change the place or position of; shift. **2.** To set or keep in motion; stir; drive; actuate. **3.** To excite to action; impel. **4.** To arouse the feelings or passions of. **5.** To propose, esp. in a deliberative assembly. — v. i. **1.** To change place, position, or posture; stir; proceed; advance. **2.** To exercise one's activities. **3.** To act; begin to act. **4.** To change residence. **5.** To make an appeal, application, or the like; — used with *for*. — n. Act of moving; a movement.

move'ment (-měnt), n. **1.** A moving; change of place or position. **2.** A system of mechanism for transmitting or transforming motion, as in a watch. **3.** A series of acts tending toward some end. **4.** An act of evacuation of the bowels.

mov'er (mŏŏv'ẽr), n. One that moves.

mov'ie (mŏŏv'ĭ), n. A moving picture or a moving-picture show; also, in pl., with *the*, moving-picture shows as a class. *Slang or Colloq.*

mov'ing (-ĭng), p. a. [4] **1.** Changing place or posture; causing motion, movement, or action. **2.** Exciting movement of the mind; touching; pathetic.

āle, senāte, câre, ăm, ăccount, ärm, ȧsk, sofȧ; ēve, ĕvent, ĕnd, recĕnt, makẽr; īce, ĭll; ōld, ŏbey, ôrb, ŏdd, sŏft, cŏnnect; ūse, ūnite, ûrn, ŭp, circŭs; fŏŏd, fŏŏt; out, oil;

moving picture. A series of pictures thrown on a screen, so rapidly that the objects themselves seem to move (see KINETOSCOPE, CINEMATOGRAPH).

mow (mou), n. A heap or mass of hay or of sheaves of grain stowed in a barn ; also, the place in a barn for such stowing.— v. t. To lay, as hay, in a mow.

mow (mō, mou), v. i. To grimace.

mow (mō), v. t. ; pret. MOWED (mōd) ; p. p. MOWED or MOWN (mōn) ; p: pr. & vb. n. MOW′ING. **1.** To cut down, as grass. **2.** To cut the grass from.— v.i. To cut grass, etc. — **mow′er** (-ẽr), n. [8].

Mr. (mĭs′tẽr). Written form of the title Mister.

Mrs. (-ĭs ; -ĭz). Written form of the title Mistress.

much (mŭch), a. ; compar. MORE ; superl. MOST. Great in quantity, extent, or duration.— n. **1.** A great quantity. **2.** A thing uncommon or considerable. — adv. **1.** To a great degree or extent. **2.** Nearly ; almost ; as, they are much of an age.

mu′ci-lage (mū′sĭ-lăj), n. **1.** Bot. A gluey substance in certain plants. **2.** A solution, as of gum, in water, used to stick things together.

mu′ci-lag′i-nous (-lăj′ĭ-nŭs), a. [4] Of or pertaining to, or like, mucilage ; moist and sticky.

muck (mŭk), n. **1.** Moist dung ; manure. **2.** Decayed peat or black swamp earth. **3.** Filth ; dirt.

muck′rake′ (mŭk′rāk′), v. i. [1] To seek for, expose, or charge, esp. habitually, corruption on the part of public men and corporations. — **muck′rak′er**, n. [8].

muck′y (-ĭ), a. [3] Filthy with muck ; miry.

mu′cous (mū′kŭs), a. **1.** Of, pertaining to, or resembling, mucus. **2.** Secreting or containing mucus. — **mucous membrane**, Anat., the lining membrane of the passages and cavities of the body that communicate with the exterior.

mu′cus (mū′kŭs), n. A viscid, slippery secretion of mucous membranes, which it moistens.

mud (mŭd), n. Soft, wet earth ; mire.

mud′dle (mŭd′'l), v. t. [1] **1.** To cloud or stupefy ; stupefy with liquor. **2.** To mix confusedly ; make a mess of ; as, to muddle one's task.— v.i. To think or act in a confused, aimless way.— n. A state of confusion ; a mess. — **mud′dler** (-lẽr), n. [8].

mud′dy (-ĭ), a. [3] **1.** Abounding in mud ; smeared, dashed, or turbid with or as with mud. **2.** Not clear or bright ; cloudy. — v. t. [2] **1.** To soil with mud ; dirty. **2.** To cloud ; make dull. — **mud′di-ly**, adv. — **di-ness**, n. [8].

muff (mŭf), n. **1.** A soft, thick cover into which both hands may be thrust from the opposite ends to protect them from the cold. **2.** Colloq. **a** A stupid person. **b** A bungler. **3.** Baseball, failure to hold a ball in attempting to catch it. — v. t. & i. To handle awkwardly ; bungle.

muf′fin (mŭf′ĭn), n. A small light cake slightly sweetened, served hot for breakfast or tea.

muf′fle (-'l), n. Anything with which another thing is muffled. — v. t. [1] **1.** To wrap up so as to conceal or protect. **2.** To prevent seeing, hearing, or speaking, by wraps bound about the head. **3.** To deaden the sound of.

muf′fler (-lẽr), n. **1.** Anything used in muffling ; as : **a** A scarf for the throat. **b** A sort of veil or scarf for women. **2.** Mach. A device for deadening noises. [ing cup.]

mug (mŭg), n. A kind of earthen or metal drink-

mug′gy (mŭg′ĭ), a. [3] Warm, damp, and close ; as, muggy weather. — **mug′gi-ness** (-ĭ-nĕs), n.

mug′wump′ (-wŭmp′), n. An independent in politics. Political Cant, U. S.

mu-lat′to (mū-lăt′ō), n. ; pl. -TOES (-ōz). The off-spring of a white person and a negro.

mul′ber-ry (mŭl′bĕr-ĭ), n. ; pl. -RIES (-ĭz). Any of several trees bearing berrylike fruit, usually dark purple ; also, the fruit.

mulch (mŭlch ; mŭlsh), n. Any substance, as straw, used to protect the roots of plants from heat, cold, or drought. — v. t. To cover with mulch.

mulct (mŭlkt), n. A fine or penalty. — v. t. To fine ; deprive of, as by way of punishment.

mule (mūl), n. **1.** The offspring of a male ass and a mare. **2.** A very stubborn person. Colloq.

mu′le-teer′ (mū′lĕ-tēr′), n. A driver of mules.

mul′ish (mūl′ĭsh), a. [4] Like a mule ; hence, sullen ; stubborn. — **-ly**, adv. [8] — **-ness**, n. [8].

mull (mŭl), n. A thin, soft muslin.

mull, v. t. To heat, sweeten, and spice, as wine.

mul′lein (mŭl′ĭn), **mul′len** (-ĕn), n. A tall herb having coarse leaves, and flowers in dense spikes.

mul′let (mŭl′ĕt), n. Any of various fresh-water or salt-water fishes.

mul′lion (mŭl′yŭn), n. Arch. A vertical bar or pier between window lights, screens, etc.

mul′ti-fa′ri-ous (-tĭ-fā′rĭ-ŭs), a. [4] Having great diversity or variety ; diversified. — **-ly**, adv. [8] — **-ness**, n. [8]. [or shapes.]

mul′ti-form (-fôrm), a. [4] Having many forms

mul′ti-graph (mŭl′tĭ-gráf), n. A combined type-setting and printing machine. Trade-mark.

mul′ti-ple (-p'l), a. Containing more than one ; manifold.— n. Product of one number multiplied by another. [tiplied.]

mul′ti-pli′a-ble (-plĭ′á-b'l), a. That can be mul-

mul′ti-pli-cand′ (-plĭ-kănd′ ; mŭl′tĭ-plĭ-kănd′), n. Math. The number that is to be multiplied by another number called the multiplier.

mul′ti-pli-ca′tion (mŭl′tĭ-plĭ-kā′shŭn), n. **1.** Act or process of multiplying. **2.** Process of adding any given number or quantity a certain number of times ; commonly, the process of ascertaining by a briefer computation the result of such repeated additions. The sign of multiplication is ×, read multiplied by, or times.

mul′ti-plic′i-ty (-plĭs′ĭ-tĭ), n. Quality or state of being multiple, or various ; also, a multitude.

mul′ti-pli′er (mŭl′tĭ-plī′ẽr), n. **1.** One that multiplies or increases, as in number. **2.** Math. The number by which another number is multiplied.

mul′ti-ply (mŭl′tĭ-plī), v. t. [2] **1.** To increase in number. **2.** Math. To find the product of by multiplication.— v. i. **1.** To become greater in number. **2.** Math. To perform multiplication.

mul′ti-tude (-tūd), n. **1.** A crowd ; a large assembly. **2.** A great number of persons or things.

mul′ti-tu′di-nous (-tū′dĭ-nŭs), a. [4] Consisting of a multitude ; great in number, extent, or variety. — **-ly**, adv. [8] — **-ness**, n. [8].

mum (mŭm), a. [3] Silent. — interj. Be silent !

mum′ble (mŭm′b'l), v. i. & t. [1] **1.** To speak thickly or obscurely with the lips partly closed ; mutter. **2.** To chew softly with closed lips, or with little use of the teeth.— n. A mumbling.

mum′mer (mŭm′ẽr), *n.* A masker; buffoon.

mum′mer-y (-ĭ), *n.; pl.* -MERIES (-ĭz). **1.** Masking, as by mummers. **2.** Farcical show; ceremonies regarded as ridiculous, hypocritical, etc.

mum′mi-fy (mŭm′ĭ-fī), *v. t.* [2] To embalm and dry as a mummy; make into or like a mummy.

mum′my (mŭm′ĭ), *n.; pl.* -MIES (-ĭz). A corpse treated with preservatives after the manner of the ancient Egyptians.

mumps (mŭmps), *n. Med.* An infectious disorder marked by inflammation of the parotid glands.

munch (mŭnch), *v. t. & i.* To chew with a grinding, crunching sound, as a beast chews provender.

mun′dane (mŭn′dān), *a.* [4] Of or pertaining to the world; worldly; earthly. — **-ly,** *adv.* [8].

mu-nic′i-pal (mū-nĭs′ĭ-păl), *a.* **1.** Enjoying a local self-government; — said of a corporation such as a town, borough, or city. **2.** Of or pertaining to such a corporation; as, *municipal* buildings.

mu-nic′i-pal′i-ty (-păl′ĭ-tĭ), *n.; pl.* -TIES (-tĭz). A town, city, etc., having local self-government.

Lɯu-nif′i-cence (-nĭf′ĭ-sĕns), *n.* Quality or state of being munificent; lavish generosity.

mu-nif′i-cent (-nĭf′ĭ-sĕnt), *a.* [4] Very liberal in giving; lavish. — **-cent-ly,** *adv.* [8].

mu-ni′tion (mū-nĭsh′ŭn), *n.* Ammunition; also, stores and provisions; necessary equipment.

mu′ral (mū′răl), *a.* Of or pertaining to a wall; being on, in, or against a wall.

mur′der (mûr′dẽr), *n. Law.* The offense of unlawfully killing a human being with premeditated malice. — *v. t.* To commit murder. — **mur′der-er,** *n.* [8] — **-ess,** *n. fem.* [8].

mur′der-ous (-ŭs), *a.* [4] Of or pertaining to, or causing, murder or bloodshed; bloody; bloodthirsty. — **-ly,** *adv.* [8].

mu′ri-at′ic (mū′rĭ-ăt′ĭk), *a.* Pertaining to brine or salt. *Obs.,* exc. in **muriatic acid,** hydrochloric acid.

murk (mûrk), *n.* Darkness; gloom.

murk′y (mûr′kĭ), *a.* [3] Dark; obscure; gloomy. — **murk′i-ly** (-kĭ-lĭ), *adv.* [8] — **-i-ness,** *n.* [8].

mur′mur (mûr′mẽr), *n.* **1.** A low, confused, indistinct sound, as of running water. **2.** A low, muttered complaint. — *v. i. & t.* To make, or utter with or in, a murmur. — **-er,** *n.* [8].

mur′rain (mûr′ĭn), *n.* Any of several infectious diseases of cattle.

mus′cle (mŭs′′l), *n.* **1. a** An organ or mass of tissue whose special function is to exert physical .force. **b** The peculiar tissue of such an organ. **2.** Muscular strength or development. *Colloq.*

mus′cu-lar (mŭs′kṹ-lár), *a.* [4] **1.** Of or pert. to muscles. **2.** Having well-developed muscles; strong.

mus′cu-lar′i-ty (mŭs′kṹ-lär′ĭ-tĭ), *n.* State or quality of being muscular.

muse (mūz), *v. i. & t.* [1] To meditate; ponder. — *n.* Absorbing thought; hence, absence of mind.

Muse, *n.* **1.** *Class. Myth.* One of the nine sister goddesses of song and poetry, and of the arts and sciences; — often in *pl.* **2.** [*l. c.*] A peculiar power of, or inspiration to, poetry.

mu-se′um (mū-zē′ŭm), *n.* A building or part of a building for a collection of natural, scientific, or literary curiosities or objects of interest, or of works of art; also, the collection.

mush (mŭsh), *n.* **1.** Meal (esp. Indian meal) boiled in water. *U. S.* **2.** Anything soft and thick, like mush.

mush′room (mŭsh′rōōm), *n.* **1.** Any of various fleshy fungi; popularly, any edible fungus of this class. The poisonous species are commonly called *toadstools.* **2.** Something like, or suggestive of, a mushroom, as in rapidity of growth. — *a.* **1.** Of or pertaining to mushrooms. **2.** Resembling mushrooms, as in rapidity of growth.

mush′y (mŭsh′ĭ), *a.* [3] Like mush; good-naturedly weak and effusive; weakly sentimental.

mu′sic (mū′zĭk), *n.* **1.** Melody or harmony generally. **2.** The science or art of pleasing, expressive, or intelligible combination of tones.

mu′si-cal (mū′zĭ-kăl), *a.* [4] **1.** Of or pertaining to music. **2.** Having the pleasing qualities of music; melodious; harmonious. **3.** Fond of music. — **mu′si-cal-ly,** *adv.* [8].

mu′si-cale′ (-kȧl′), *n.* A social entertainment, usually private, devoted chiefly to music.

mu-si′cian (mū-zĭsh′ăn), *n.* One skilled in music; esp., a professional singer, musical performer, etc.

musk (mŭsk), *n.* **1.** A substance obtained from the male musk deer. It is used as the basis for many perfumes. **2.** The odor of musk.

musk deer. A small hornless deer of central Asia. The males have long upper canine teeth.

mus′kel-lunge (mŭs′kĕ-lŭnj; mŭs′kĕ-lŭnj′), *n.* A large pike of the Great Lakes region of North America.

Muskellunge. $\frac{1}{25}$

mus′ket (mŭs′kĕt), *n.* A hand firearm formerly carried by soldiers. [musket.]

mus′ket-eer′ (-ēr′), *n.* A soldier armed with a

mus′ket-ry (mŭs′kĕt-rĭ), *n.* **1.** Muskets, collectively. **2.** The fire of, or the art of firing, muskets.

musk′mel′on (mŭsk′mĕl′ŭn), *n.* The fruit of ɾ plant of the cucumber family; also, the plant.

musk ox. A hollow-horned hoofed quadruped of Greenland and northern North America.

musk′rat′ (mŭsk′răt′), *n.* A ratlike water animal of North America, yielding valuable fur.

musk′y (mŭs′kĭ), *a.* [3] Having an odor or taste of musk, or suggesting musk; scented with musk.

mus′lin (mŭz′lĭn), *n.* Any of various cotton cloths; as: **a** A very thin, fine, and soft plain cloth. **b** A stouter fabric, plain, printed, or dyed.

muss (mŭs), *n.* A state of disorder, or that which makes it, as rubbish. — *v. t.* **1.** To disarrange, as clothing. **2.** To mess. *All Colloq., U. S.*

mus′sel (-′l), *n.* Any of various bivalve mollusks.

must (mŭst), *n.* The expressed juice of the grape, or other fruit, before fermentation; new wine.

must, *v. t. & i.* To make or become musty.

must, *v. i. or auxiliary.* Used without inflection, as both *pres. & pret.* Infinitive and participles lacking. Am obliged, is obliged, are obliged, etc.

mus-tache′ (mŭs-tȧsh′), *n.* The beard growing on the upper lip; also, either side of this hair.

mus′tang (mŭs′tăng), *n.* The small, hardy, half-wild horse of Texas, New Mexico, etc.

mus′tard (mŭs′tȧrd), *n.* **1.** A plant of the cabbage family, with yellow flowers, and narrow pods. **2.** A pungent powder of ground mustard seed.

mus′ter (-tẽr), *v. t.* **1.** To assemble or gather, as troops, for roll call, parade, or the like. **2.** To summon together; collect and display.— *n.* **1.** An assembling or review of troops or a ship's company. **2.** The sum total of those assembled for muster; also, the roll of the men. **3.** Assemblage.

mus′ti-ness (-tĭ-nĕs), *n.* Musty state or quality.

mus′ty (mŭs′tĭ), *a.* [3] **1.** Moldy; sour. **2.** Spoiled by age; stale. [*mutable.*]

mu′ta-bil′i-ty (mū′tȧ-bĭl′ĭ-tĭ), *n.* Quality of being

mu′ta-ble (mū′tȧ-b'l), *a.* [4] **1.** Capable of, or subject to, mutation. **2.** Unstable; fickle.

mu-ta′tion (mū-tā′shŭn), *n.* Alteration in form or qualities.

mute (mūt), *a.* [3] **1.** Not speaking; silent; speechless. **2.** Incapable of speaking; dumb; also, unaccompanied by speech or sound. **3.** *Phon.* Not uttered; silent; also, produced with a complete momentary closure of some part of the oral passage;— said of certain letters, as *p, b, d, g, k, t.* — *n.* **1.** One who does not speak. **2.** *Phon.* A mute letter.— *ly, adv.* [8] — *-ness, n.* [8].

mu′ti-late (mū′tĭ-lāt), *v. t.* [1] **1.** To cut off or remove a limb or essential part of; maim. **2.** To destroy or remove a material part of, so as to render imperfect. — **mu′ti-la′tor** (-lā′tẽr), *n.* [8].

mu′ti-la′tion (-lā′shŭn), *n.* Act of mutilating.

mu′ti-neer′ (-tĭ-nēr′), *n.* One guilty of mutiny. — *v. i.* To mutiny.

mu′ti-nous (mū′tĭ-nŭs), *a.* [4] Disposed to, or marked by, mutiny. — **-ly,** *adv.* — **-ness,** *n.*

mu′ti-ny (-nĭ), *n.; pl.* -NIES (-nĭz). Insurrection against, or refusal to obey, constituted or rightful authority, esp. military or naval authority. — *v. i.* [2] To excite, or to be guilty of, mutiny.

mut′ter (mŭt′ẽr), *v. i.* To speak indistinctly or with a low voice and lips partly closed; to grumble; growl. — *n.* Obscure utterance; murmur.

mut′ton (mŭt′n), *n.* The flesh of sheep.

mu′tu-al (mū′tụ̄-ăl), *a.* **1.** Done or rendered by each (of two persons, things, etc.) to the other; reciprocal; interchanged; as a *mutual* promise. **2.** Possessed, experienced, or done by two or more at the same time; common; joint. — **-ly,** *adv.* [8].

mu′tu-al′i-ty (-ăl′ĭ-tĭ), *n.* Quality of being mutual.

muz′zle (mŭz′'l), *n.* **1.** The projecting jaws and nose of an animal. **2.** The mouth of a thing, as a gun. **3.** A fastening or covering (as a band or cage) for the mouth of an animal, to prevent eating or biting. — *v. t.* [1] To bind the muzzle of; fasten the mouth of; fig., to bind; gag.

my (mī), *pron. & a.* Of or belonging to me;— used attributively. Cf. MINE.

my-o′pi-a (mī-ō′pĭ-ȧ), *n. Med.* Nearsightedness.

my-op′ic (-ŏp′ĭk), *a.* Nearsighted.

myr′i-ad (mĭr′ĭ-ăd), *n.* **1.** The number of ten thousand. **2.** An immense or indefinitely large number; as, *myriads* of stars. — *a.* Innumerable.

myr′i-a-pod′ (-ȧ-pŏd′), *n.* Any of various vermiform animals, as the centipedes.

myrrh (mûr), *n.* A yellowish brown aromatic gum resin with a bitter, slightly pungent taste.

myr′tle (mûr′t'l), *n.* **1.** A shrub with evergreen leaves and white or rosy flowers, followed by black berries. **2.** The periwinkle. *U. S.*

my-self′ (mī-sĕlf′), *pron.; pl.* OURSELVES (oursĕlvz′). An emphasized form for *I* or *me.*

mys-te′ri-ous (mĭs-tē′rĭ-ŭs), *a.* [4] Of or pertaining to mystery; containing or implying a mystery; obscure. — *-ly, adv.* [8] — **-ness,** *n.* [8].

mys′ter-y (mĭs′tẽr-ĭ), *n.; pl.* -TERIES (-ĭz). A profound secret; something unknown or concealed; something beyond human comprehension.

mys′tic (mĭs′tĭk), *n.* A believer in mysticism.

mys′tic (mĭs′tĭk), *n.* A believer in mysticism.

mys′tic (mĭs′tĭk) } *a.* [4] **1.** Remote from or
mys′ti-cal (-tĭ-kăl) } beyond human comprehension; unknowable; mysterious. **2.** Pertaining to, or importing, mysticism; allegorical; emblematical. — **mys′ti-cal-ly,** *adv.* [8].

mys′ti-cism (-tĭ-sĭz′m), *n.* **1.** Mystic character or quality. **2.** The doctrine that reality or God may be known in an immediate insight differing from all ordinary sensation or reasoning.

mys′ti-fi-ca′tion (-fĭ-kā′shŭn), *n.* Act of mystifying, or state of being mystified.

mys′ti-fy (-fī), *v. t.* [2] **1.** To involve in mystery; make obscure. **2.** To puzzle; bewilder.

myth (mĭth), *n.* **1.** A legendary story, esp. one serving to explain some practice, belief, or the like, esp. in connection with religion. **2.** A person or thing whose existence is imaginary or not verifiable.

myth′ic (mĭth′ĭk) } *a.* [4] Of or relating to
myth′i-cal (-ĭ-kăl) } myths; fabulous; imaginary. — **myth′i-cal-ly,** *adv.* [8].

myth′o-log′ic (mĭth′ō-lŏj′ĭk), **-log′i-cal,** *a.* Of or pert. to mythology; mythical. — **-i-cal-ly,** *adv.* [8].

my-thol′o-gy (mĭ-thŏl′ō-jĭ), *n.; pl.* -GIES (-jĭz). **1.** The science treating of myths. **2.** A body of myths; esp., the collective myths of a people.

N

nab (năb), *v. t.; * NABBED (năbd); NAB′BING. To seize; catch suddenly; snatch. *Colloq.*

na′bob (nā′bŏb), *n.* **1.** A native deputy or viceroy in India during the Mogul dynasty (1526-1857). **2.** A very wealthy man.

na′dir (nā′dẽr), *n.* **1.** The point opposite the zenith. **2.** The lowest point. [*Colloq.,*]

nag (năg), *n.* A small riding horse; pony; *Colloq.,*

nag, *v. t. & i.;* NAGGED (năgd); NAG′GING (năg′ĭng). To annoy by persistent scolding or urging.

na′iad (nā′yăd; nī′ăd), *n.; L. pl.* NAIADES (nā′yȧ-dēz; nī′ȧ-). *Class. Myth.* One of the nymphs who lived in, and gave life to, lakes, rivers, and springs.

nail (nāl), *n.* **1.** The horny scale or plate on the fingers and toes of man, apes, etc. **2.** A slender, usually pointed piece of metal used esp. for driving into wood, etc. — *v. t.* **1.** To fasten with a nail or nails. **2.** To secure; bind; hold, as to a bargain; hence, to catch; trap.

nain′sook (nān′sook; năn′-), *n.* A sort of muslin.

---

chair; go; sing, iŋk; **then,** thin; nature, verdure; yet; zh = z in azure. Numbers refer to §§ in the Special Notes which, with Abbreviations, Signs, etc., precede the Vocabulary.

na-ïve (nä-ēv'), *a.* [4] Unaffectedly simple; ingenuous; artless. — **na-ïve'ly** (-lǐ), *adv.* [8].

∥ **na'ïve'té'** (ná/ēv'tā'), *n.* [F.] Quality or an instance of being naïve; ingenuousness; artlessness.

na'ked (nā/kĕd), *a.* [4] **1.** Having on no clothes or covering; nude; bare; uncovered. **2.** Destitute; bare of means. **3.** Defenseless; unprotected. **4.** Without concealment or disguise; plain. — **na'ked-ly**, *adv.* [8] — **na'ked-ness**, *n.* [8].

nam'by-pam'by (năm'bǐ-păm'bǐ), *a.* [4] Affectedly pretty; weakly sentimental. — *n.* Namby-pamby talk or writing, etc.

name (nām), *n.* **1.** The title by which any person or thing is known or designated. **2.** A descriptive appellation; epithet. **3.** Reputation; fame. — *v. t.* [1] **1.** To give a distinctive name to; entitle; call. **2.** To mention by name. **3.** To nominate; appoint; specify.

name'less, *a.* [4] **1.** Undistinguished; obscure. **2.** Anonymous; without a name. **3.** Unnamable; indescribable. — **-ness**, *n.* [8].

name'ly (nām'lǐ), *adv.* That is to say; to wit.

name'sake' (-sāk'), *n.* One that has the same name as another; esp., one named after another.

nan-keen' (năn-kēn'), *n.* A kind of brownish yellow cotton cloth.

nap (năp), *n.* Woolly or hairy surface of felt, cloth, etc.

nap, *v. i.*; NAPPED(năpt); NAP'PING. To have a short sleep; doze; be in a careless, unguarded state. — *n.* A short sleep; doze.

nape (nāp), *n.* The back part of the neck.

na'per-y (nā'pēr-ǐ), *n.* Household, esp. table, linen.

naph'tha (năf'thà), *n.* A volatile, inflammable petroleum product between gasoline and benzine.

nap'kin (năp'kǐn), *n.* A small towel or cloth, esp. one for wiping the fingers and lips at table.

na-po'le-on (nà-pō'lē-ŏn), *n.* A French gold coin of the value of 20 francs.

nar-cis'sus (när-sǐs'ŭs), *n.*; *pl.* E. -CISSUSES (-ĕz), L. -CISSI (-sǐs'ī). Any of various plants of a genus (*Narcissus*) including the daffodils and the jonquil.

nar-cot'ic (-kŏt'ǐk), *a.* [4] Having the properties of, or operating as, a narcotic. — *n.* A drug, as opium, which in moderate doses relieves pain and produces sleep.

Flower of Narcissus.

nar-rate' (nă-rāt'),*v. t.* [1] To tell; relate; detail.

nar-ra'tion (-rā'shŭn), *n.* **1.** Act of narrating; recital. **2.** That which is related; narrative; story.

nar'ra-tive (năr'à-tǐv), *n.* **1.** That which is narrated; story. **2.** Art or practice of narrating. — *a.* [4] Pert. to, or of the nature of, narration.

nar-ra'tor (nă-rā'tēr), *n.* One who narrates.

nar'row (năr'ō), *a.* [3] **1.** Of little breadth; not wide. **2.** Limited; circumscribed. **3.** Illiberal; bigoted. **4.** Meager; straitened. **5.** Close; near. — *n.* A narrow passage; a strait;—usually in *pl.* — *v. t. & i.* To lessen in breadth; contract; limit.

nar'row-ly (năr'ō-lǐ), *adv.* **1.** With minute scrutiny; closely; carefully. **2.** With little margin or space; barely. **3.** Not broadly; illiberally.

nar'row-mind'ed(-mīn'dĕd),*a.* Illiberal; bigoted.

nar'row-ness, *n.* Narrow condition or quality.

nar'whal (när'hwăl), *n.* A small arctic whale the male of which has a long ivory tusk.

Narwhal. ($\frac{1}{90}$)

na'sal (nā'zăl), *a.* [4] **1.** Of or pertaining to the nose. **2.** Marked by resonance in the nasal passage, as *m, n, ng.* — *n.* A nasal speech sound, as *m, n, ng.* — **na-sal'i-ty** (nà-zăl'ǐ-tǐ), *n.*

nas'cent(năs'ĕnt),*a.* Beginning to exist or to grow.

nas'ti-ly (năs'tǐ-lǐ), *adv.* In a nasty manner.

nas'ti-ness, *n.* Quality or state of being nasty.

nas-tur'tium (năs-tûr'shŭm), *n.* A pungent garden plant having red and yellow spurred flowers.

nas'ty (năs'tǐ), *a.* [3] **1.** Disgustingly dirty; foul. **2.** Morally filthy; obscene; indecent. **3.** Seriously harmful or dangerous; bad. **4.** Mean; dishonorable; ill-natured. *Colloq. in U. S.*

na'tal (nā'tăl), *a.* **1.** Native. **2.** Pertaining to, or dating from, one's birth.

na'tion (nā'shŭn), *n.* **1.** A people connected by ties of blood and generally having a common language, customs, etc. **2.** The body of inhabitants of a country united under a single government.

na'tion-al (năsh'ŭn-ăl), *a.* Of or pert. to a nation.

na'tion-al-ism (-ĭz'm),*n.* Devotion to, or advocacy of, national interests or national independence.

na'tion-al-ist, *n.* An advocate of nationalism.

na'tion-al'i-ty (-ăl'ǐ-tǐ), *n.; pl.* -TIES (-tǐz). **1.** State, quality, or relation of being, or belonging to, a nation; national character; political independence as a nation; statehood. **2.** A nation.

na'tion-al-i-za'tion (-ǐ-zā'shŭn), *n.* A nationalizing, or state of being nationalized.

na'tion-al-ize (năsh'ŭn-ăl-īz), *v. t.* [1] **1.** To make national; make a nation of. **2.** To vest the control, ownership, or the like, of in the nation.

na'tive (nā'tǐv), *a.* **1.** Born with one; inherent. **2.** That was the place of one's birth; as, *native* land, etc. **3.** Of minerals, etc., natural; not artificially prepared. **4.** Born in a particular place or country; as, *native* troops; — esp. of non-Caucasian peoples. **5.** Grown, produced, or originating in a particular place, region, or country. — *n.* One born in a place or country referred to; an animal, fruit, or vegetable native to a region.

na-tiv'i-ty (nà-tǐv'ǐ-tǐ), *n.; pl.* -TIES (-tǐz). **1.** Birth; the circumstances attending birth. **2.** [*cap.*] The birth of Christ.

nat'ty (năt'ǐ), *a.* [3] Trim; neat; tidy; spruce. — **nat'ti-ly** (-ǐ-lǐ), *adv.* [8] — **nat'ti-ness**, *n.* [8].

nat'u-ral (năt'ū-răl), *a.* [4] **1.** Of, from, or by, birth; innate; inborn. **2.** Born out of wedlock; illegitimate. **3.** In accordance with human nature. **4.** In accordance with, or determined by, nature; normal. **5.** Not artificial. **6.** True to nature; as, the portrait is *natural.* **7.** Pert. to nature, or the physical universe. **8.** In accordance with the circumstances of the case or with ordinary experience. **9.** *Music.* Having neither a flat nor a sharp for its signature; written without flats or sharps.— **natural history**, formerly, the study of animals, plants, minerals, and other natural objects. Now, commonly, the study of these subjects, esp. animals, in a more or less popular or superficial way. — *n. Music.* **a** A white key, as of a piano. **b** A character [♮] used to remove the effect of a sharp or flat preceding it. **c** A note or tone affected by a sign ♮. [ural history.]

nat'u-ral-ist (năt'ŭ-răl-ĭst), *n.* One versed in natural history.

nat'u-ral-is'tic (-ĭs'tĭk), *a.* [4] Natural; realistic.

nat'u-ral-i-za'tion (-răl-ĭ-zā'shŭn), *n.* A naturalizing ; state of being naturalized.

nat'u-ral-ize (năt'ŭ-răl-īz), *v. t.* [1] **1.** To confer the rights and privileges of a native subject or citizen on. **2.** To receive or adopt as native, natural, or vernacular. **3.** To acclimate.

nat'u-ral-ly, *adv.* In a natural manner.

nat'u-ral-ness, *n.* Natural state or quality.

na'ture (nā'tŭr), *n.* **1.** That which is the source or essence of life ; creative force. **2.** The universe. **3.** Kind ; sort. **4.** Natural endowment or essential character. **5.** The vital powers. **6.** The primitive condition of living beings ; hence, a natural or normal life.

naught (nôt), *n.* **1.** Nothing. **2.** The character 0 ; a cipher. — *a.* Of no account ; worthless.

naugh'ty (nô'tĭ), *a.* [3] Mischievous ; wayward ; disobedient ; — used of children or in sportive censure. — **naugh'ti-ly**, *adv.* [8] — **-ti-ness**, *n.* [8].

nau'se-a (nô'shē-à ; -sē-à), *n.* **1.** Seasickness ; hence, any sickness of the stomach with a desire to vomit ; qualm. **2.** Extreme disgust ; loathing.

nau'se-ate (-āt), *v. i.* [1] To become affected with nausea. — *v. t.* To affect with nausea ; sicken.

nau'seous (nô'shŭs ; -shē-ŭs), *a.* [4] Causing nausea ; disgusting. — **-ly**, *adv.* [8] — **-ness**, *n.* [8].

nau'ti-cal (nô'tĭ-kăl), *a.* [4] Pertaining to seamen, navigation, or ships. — **nautical mile.** See MILE. — **nau'ti-cal-ly**, *adv.* [8].

nau'ti-lus (-lŭs), *n. ; pl.* E. -LUSES (-ĕz), L. -LI (-lī). **1.** Any of several mollusks of the South Pacific and Indian oceans. **2.** The paper nautilus, related to the octopus and having eight arms.

na'val (nā'văl), *a.* [4] Of, pertaining to, possessing, or characteristic of, vessels of war or a navy.

nave (nāv), *n.* Block in the center of a wheel ; hub.

nave, *n.* The body, or main part, of a cruciform church, not including the aisles.

na'vel (nā'v'l), *n.* A depression in the middle of the abdomen. [of being navigable.]

nav'i-ga-bil'i-ty (năv'ĭ-gà-bĭl'ĭ-tĭ), *n.* Quality

nav'i-ga-ble (năv'ĭ-gà-b'l), *a.* [4] Capable of being navigated. — **nav'i-ga-ble-ness**, *n.* [8].

nav'i-gate (-gāt), *v. i.* [1] To journey by water ; sail or manage a vessel. — *v. t.* **1.** To sail over or on. **2.** To steer or direct in sailing.

nav'i-ga'tion (năv'ĭ-gā'shŭn), *n.* **1.** Act of navigating. **2.** Science or art of navigating, esp. of determining the position and course of vessels.

nav'i-ga'tor (năv'ĭ-gā'tẽr), *n.* One who navigates.

na'vy (nā'vĭ), *n. ; pl.* -VIES (-vĭz). **1.** A fleet of ships. **2.** The war vessels of a nation. **3.** The naval establishment of a nation, including yards, shops, men, ships, etc. Officers of the United States Navy rank as follows : admiral, vice admiral, rear admiral, commodore (only for retired officers), captain, commander, lieutenant commander, lieutenant, lieutenant junior grade, ensign.

nay (nā), *adv.* **1.** No. *Archaic.* **2.** Not only this but also. — *n.* Negative reply, vote, or voter.

neap (nēp), *a.* Designating the lowest tides (**neap tides**) in the lunar month. — *n.* A neap tide.

near (nēr), *adv.* [3] **1.** At, within, or to a little distance (in place or time). **2.** Within little ; almost ; nearly. **3.** Closely. — *a.* **1.** Closely related by blood. **2.** Close to one's interests, affection, etc. ; intimate. **3.** Not far distant ; close ; nigh. **4.** Closely following or imitating. **5.** Of animals, vehicles, etc., on the left. **6.** Direct ; short. **7.** Closefisted ; stingy. — *prep.* At or within little distance from ; close to or upon. — *v. i. & t.* To approach.

near'est (nēr'ĕst), *a., superlative* of NEAR.

near'ly, *adv.* In a near manner or degree.

near'ness, *n.* State or quality of being near.

near'sight'ed (-sīt'ĕd), *a.* Seeing distinctly at short distances only ; shortsighted. — **-ness**, *n.* [8].

neat (nēt), *a.* [3] **1.** Free from admixture or adulteration. **2.** Simple and becoming ; tasteful. **3.** Clever ; finished ; adroit. **4.** Orderly and cleanly ; tidy.

neat (nēt), *n. sing. & pl.* Cattle of the ox kind.

neat'ly (-lĭ), *adv.* In a neat manner.

neat'ness, *n.* State or quality of being neat.

neb (nĕb), *n.* The beak of a bird or tortoise ; bill.

neb'u-la (nĕb'ŭ-là), *n. ; pl.* -LÆ (-lē). A faint, cloudlike, luminous mass of gaseous matter situated at the distance of the stars. Very distant star clusters often appear like nebulæ.

neb'u-lar (-làr), *a.* Of or pert. to nebulæ ; hazy.

neb'u-los'i-ty (-lŏs'ĭ-tĭ), *n. ; pl.* -TIES (-tĭz). State or quality of being nebulous ; cloudiness.

neb'u-lous (nĕb'ŭ-lŭs), *a.* [4] **1.** Cloudy or cloudlike ; hazy ; — often fig. **2.** Of, or like, a nebula.

nec'es-sa-ry (nĕs'ĕ-sà-rĭ), *a.* [4] **1.** Impossible to be otherwise or to be done without ; indispensable. **2.** Not to be avoided ; inevitable. **3.** Acting from necessity or compulsion ; involuntary. — *n. ; pl.* -RIES (-rĭz). A requisite ; — chiefly in *pl.* — **nec'es-sa-ri-ly** (-rĭ-lĭ), *adv.* [8].

ne-ces'si-tate (nē-sĕs'ĭ-tāt), *v. t.* [1] To make necessary ; to force ; compel.

ne-ces'si-tous (-tŭs), *a.* [4] Needy ; indigent.

ne-ces'si-ty (-tĭ), *n. ; pl.* -TIES (-tĭz). **1.** Quality or state of being necessary. **2.** That which makes an act or an event unavoidable. **3.** Indigence ; want. **4.** That which is necessary ; — often in *pl.*

neck (nĕk), *n.* **1.** The part of an animal connecting the head and the trunk. **2.** A part of an object likened to an animal's neck ; as : **a** The slender part of a bottle, etc., or of various fruits. **b** A narrow stretch of land, as an isthmus. **c** A strait.

neck'cloth' (-klŏth'), *n.* A neckerchief.

neck'er-chief (-ẽr-chĭf), *n.* Kerchief for the neck.

neck'lace (-lås), *n.* A string of jewels, beads, etc., or a metal band or chain, worn round the neck.

neck'tie' (-tī'), *n.* A scarf or tie passing round the neck and tied in front.

nec-rol'o-gy (nĕk-rŏl'ŏ-jĭ), *n. ; pl.* -GIES (-jĭz). A list of the dead. [practices necromancy.]

nec'ro-man'cer (nĕk'rŏ-măn'sẽr), *n.* One who

nec'ro-man'cy (-sĭ), *n.* The pretended art of revealing the future by communication with spirits of the dead ; hence, magic ; enchantment.

---

chair ; go ; sing, ink ; then, thin ; nature, verdure ; yet ; zh = z in azure. Numbers refer to §§ in the Special Notes which, with Abbreviations, Signs, etc., precede the Vocabulary.

nec-rop'o-lis (nĕk-rŏp'ō-lĭs),*n.; pl.* -LISES (-lĭs-ĕz). A city of the dead; cemetery. *Chiefly Hist.*

nec-ro'sis (-rō'sĭs), *n.* Gangrene, esp. of bone.

nec'tar (nĕk'tär), *n.* **1.** *Classic Myth.* The drink of the gods; hence, any delicious beverage. **2.** A sweet liquid secreted by plant nectaries.

nec'tar-ine (nĕk'tär-ĭn; nĕk'tär-ēn'), *n.* A smooth-skinned variety of peach.

nec'ta-ry (nĕk'tá-rĭ), *n.; pl.* -RIES (-rĭz). The gland or part of a plant that secretes nectar.

‖**née** (nā), *p.p.* [F.] Born; — used in introducing a married woman's maiden family name; as, Madame de Staël, *née* Necker.

need (nēd), *n.* **1.** A state requiring supply or relief; necessity; lack of anything desired or useful. **2.** Poverty; destitution.— *v. t.* To be in need of; require.

need'ful (nēd'fŏŏl), *a.* [4] Necessary for supply or relief; requisite. —**ly,** *adv.* —**ness,** *n.* [8].

need'i-ness (nēd'ĭ-nĕs), *n.* State of being needy.

nee'dle (nē'd'l), *n.* **1.** A small pointed instrument for sewing, with an eyehole for thread. **2.** A slender rod used in knitting; also, a hooked instrument for crocheting, etc. **3.** Anything like, or suggestive of, a needle; as : **a** *Bot.* A needle-shaped leaf, esp. that of the pine. **b** The magnetic needle.

need'less (nēd'lĕs), *a.* [4] Not needed; unnecessary. —**need'less-ly,** *adv.* —**less-ness,** *n.* [8].

nee'dle-wom'an (nē'd'l-wŏŏm'ăn), *n.; pl.* -WOMEN (-wĭm'ĕn). A woman who does needlework.

nee'dle-work' (-wûrk'), *n.* Work done with a needle ; also, the occupation of sewing.

needs (nēdz), *adv.* Of necessity ; necessarily.

need'y (nēd'ĭ),*a.* [3] Poverty-stricken;necessitous.

ne'er (nâr ; năr), *adv.* Never ; — chiefly *Poetic.*

ne-fa'ri-ous (nē-fā'rĭ-ŭs),*a.* [4] Extremely wicked ; iniquitous.— **ly,** *adv.* [8] —**ness,** *n.* [8].

ne-ga'tion (-gā'shŭn),*n.* **1.** A denying ; denial ; — opp. of *affirmation.* **2.** Obliteration ; annihilation.

neg'a-tive (nĕg'á-tĭv), *a.* **1.** Expressing or implying negation; refusing assent. **2.** Not positive or direct. **3.** *Math., Physics, etc.* Designating a quantity to be subtracted ; minus. **4.** Designating, or pertaining to, a kind of electricity (see POSITIVE ELECTRICITY). **5.** *Photog.* Having the lights and shades of the original reversed. — *t.* **1.** A negative reply ; refusal of assent ; veto. **2.** That side of a question which denies or refuses. **3.** A word that expresses negation or denial ; as, *not, no.* **4.** *Photog.* A negative picture, usually for use in printing positive pictures. **5.** *Elec.* The negative plate of a cell. **6.** *Math.* A negative quantity or symbol. — *v. t.* [1] **1.** To refuse assent to. **2.** To pronounce against; reject by vote. **3.** To disprove.—**neg'a-tive-ly,***adv.* [8].

neg-lect' (nĕg-lĕkt'),*v. t.* To disregard ; as : **a** To omit to notice ; slight ; as, to *neglect* a rule. **b** To be remiss in attending to; as, to *neglect* a duty.— *n.* **1.** Act or fact of neglecting; state or fact of being neglected. **2.** Negligence.—**neg-lect'er,** *n.* [8].

neg-lect'ful (-fŏŏl), *a.* Careless ; negligent.

neg'li-gee' (nĕg'lĭ-zhā'; nĕg'lĭ-zhä'), *n.* Easy, or careless, attire ; undress.

neg'li-gence (nĕg'lĭ-jĕns),*n.* **1.** Quality or state of being negligent ; neglect ; disregard. **2.** Indifference as to appearance, manner, or style.

neg'li-gent (-jĕnt), *a.* [4] Guilty of neglect; heedless ; showing lack of attention. — **ly,** *adv.*

neg'li-gi-ble (-jĭ-b'l),*a.* [4] That may be neglected or disregarded. [being negotiated.|

ne-go'ti-a-ble (nē-gō'shĭ-á-b'l),*a.* [4] Capable of

ne-go'ti-ate (-āt), *v. t.* [1] **1.** To sell; as, to *negotiate* securities. **2.** To procure, or arrange for, by negotiating. — *v. i.* To have dealings with a view to coming to terms. —**ne-go'ti-a'tor** (-gō'shĭ-ā'tēr), *n.* [8].

ne-go'ti-a'tion (-ā'shŭn), *n.* Act of negotiating.

ne'gress (nē'grĕs), *n.* A female negro.

Ne'gro (nē'grō), *n.; pl.* -GROES (-grōz). **1.** A person of any of the black races of Africa. **2.** [*Usually l. c.*] A black man ; esp., a person having more or less Negro blood.— *a.* [*l. c.*] Of, pertaining to, or characteristic of, negroes ; black.

neigh (nā), *v. i.* Of a horse, to utter its cry; whinny. — *n.* The cry of a horse ; a whinny.

neigh'bor (nā'bẽr), *n.* [5] **1.** A person who lives near another. **2.** A person or thing near another. — *a.* Neighboring.— *v. t.* To adjoin ; be near to.

neigh'bor-hood (-hŏŏd), *n.* [5] **1.** State or fact of being neighbors; proximity. **2.** Vicinity ; region near; — usually with *of.* **3.** The people living near one another. **4.** A district, esp. with regard to the character of its inhabitants.

neigh'bor-ing, *p. a.* [5] Living or being near.

neigh'bor-ly, *a.* [5] Appropriate to the relation of neighbors ; friendly. —**li-ness,** *n.* [5, 8].

nei'ther (nē'thẽr ; nī'-), *a. & pron.* Not either ; not the one nor the other. — *conj.* **1.** Not either; — usually introducing the first of two or more coordinate clauses, those following beginning with *nor.* **2.** Nor yet ; also not.

Nem'e-sis (nĕm'ē-sĭs), *n. Gr. Relig.* A goddess of retributive justice.

ne-ol'o-gism (nē-ŏl'ō-jĭz'm),*n.* Use of a new word, words, or meanings ; a word or meaning so used.

ne-ol'o-gy (-jĭ), *n.; pl.* -GIES (-jĭz). Neologism.— **ne-ol'o-gist** (-jĭst), *n.* [elyte. **2.** A novice.|

ne'o-phyte (nē'ō-fīt),*n.* **1.** A new convert; pros-

ne-pen'the (nē-pĕn'thē),*n.* A potion or drug used to drown pain and sorrow. [or of a sister.|

neph'ew (nĕf'ū ; nĕv'ū), *n.* The son of a brother

ne-phri'tis (nē-frī'tĭs ; nĕf-rī'tĭs), *n. Med.* Inflammation of the kidneys ; Bright's disease.

nep'o-tism (nĕp'ō-tĭz'm),*n.* Favoritism to nephews and other relatives; bestowal of patronage by reason of relationship. —**ne-pot'ic** (nē-pŏt'ĭk), *a.*

Nep'tune (nĕp'tūn), *n.* The most remote known planet, except Pluto, of the solar system, about 2,792,000,000 miles distant from the sun.

nerve (nûrv), *n.* **1.** A sinew or tendon. *Obs. or R.,* exc. in *to strain every nerve,* that is, to put forth the utmost exertion. **2.** One of the cordlike bands of tissue that conduct the sensory and motor impulses. **3.** Mental strength ; coolness ; resolution. **4.** *pl.* An attack of acute nervousness. **5.** *Bot.*=VEIN.— *v. t.* [1] To give strength, vigor, or courage to.

nerve'less, *a.* [4] **1.** Destitute of strength or courage ; wanting vigor ; weak. **2.** Without nerves. — **nerve'less-ly,** *adv.* [8].

nerv'ine (nûr'vēn ; -vĭn), *a.* Soothing nervous excitement. — *n.* A nervine agent or tonic.

nerv′ous (nûr′vŭs), *a.* [4] **1.** Possessing or manifesting vigor of mind ; forcible ; spirited. **2.** Of, pertaining to, or affecting the nerves. **3.** Having the nerves diseased or easily excited ; excitable ; timid. — **nerv′ous-ly,** *adv.* [8] — **nerv′ousness,** *n.* [8].

nest (nĕst), *n.* **1.** The bed or receptacle prepared by a bird for its eggs and young. **2.** Any snug retreat. **3.** An abode ; haunt ; as, a *nest* of vice. **4.** The occupants or frequenters of a nest ; as, a *nest* of outlaws. **5.** A graduated series of boxes, bowls, etc., each fitting within the one next larger. — *v. t.* To form a nest for ; settle or place in or as in a nest. — *v. i.* To build or occupy a nest.

nes′tle (nĕs′'l), *v. i.* [1] **1.** To make and occupy a nest. **2.** To lie close and snug, as a bird in her nest.— *v. t.* **1.** To settle, shelter, or house, as in a nest. **2.** To move (a part of the body) against or into something as if nestling.

nest′ling (nĕst′lĭng ; nĕs′lĭng), *n.* A young bird which has not abandoned the nest.

net (nĕt), *n.* **1.** A fabric woven into meshes, esp. one used for catching fish, birds, etc. **2.** Anything designed to entrap after the manner of a net. — *v. t.;* NET′TED (-ĕd) ; NET′TING. **1.** To cover with or as with a net. **2.** To take or capture in or as in a net. **3.** To make into a net, as silk.

net, *a.* Clear of, or free from, all charges, deductions, etc.; as, *net* profit; *net* proceeds; *net* weight. — *v. t.* To produce or gain as·clear profit.

neth′er (nĕth′ẽr), *a.* Situated down or below; lying beneath ; lower ; under ; — opposed to *upper.*

neth′er-most (-mŏst), *a.* Lowest. [work.

net′ting (nĕt′ĭng), *n.* A piece of network ; a net-

net′tle (nĕt′'l), *n.* Any of various plants armed with prickles or stinging hairs. — *v. t.* [1] To whip or sting with or as with nettles ; to vex.

n ettle rash. *Med.* A kind of eruption on the skin.

net′work (nĕt′wûrk′), *n.* **1.** A fabric of intersecting threads, cords, or wires, with spaces, or meshes, between them. **2.** Any system of similarly crossing lines. [the nervous system.

neu′ral (nū′răl), *a.* Of or pertaining to a nerve or

neu-ral′gi-a (nū-răl′jĭ-á), *n.* *Med.* A very acute pain which follows the course of a nerve.

neu-ral′gic (-jĭk), *a.* Of or pert. to neuralgia.

neu′ras-the′ni-a (nū′răs-thē′nĭ-á ; nū-răs′the-nĭ′á), *n.* Nervous weakness or prostration. — **neu′ras-then′ic** (nū′răs-thĕn′ĭk), *a. & n.*

neu-ri′tis (nū-rī′tĭs), *n.* *Med.* Inflammation of a nerve or nerves. — **neu-rit′ic** (-rĭt′ĭk), *a.*

neu-rot′ic (nū-rŏt′ĭk), *a.* [4] *Med.* Of or pert. to the nerves ; nervous. — *n.* A neurotic person.

neu′ter (nū′tẽr), *a.* **1.** *Gram.* **a** Of neither masculine nor feminine gender. **b** Neither active nor passive ; intransitive ; as, a *neuter* verb. **2.** *Biol.* a Sexless. **b** Having imperfectly developed generative organs, as a worker bee or ant. — *n.* That which is neuter, as a word, insect, etc.

neu′tral (-trăl), *a.* [4] **1.** Not assisting either side. **2.** Of or pertaining to a neutral state or power. **3.** Neither one thing nor the other; indifferent. **4.** Free from admixture of color; as, a *neutral* gray. — *n.* A person, nation, etc., that is neutral.

neu-tral′i-ty (nū-trăl′ĭ-tĭ), *n.* Quality or state of being neutral.

neu′tral-i-za′tion (nū′trăl-ĭ-zā′shŭn), *n.* A neutralizing, or state of being neutralized.

neu′tral-ize (nū′trăl-īz), *v. t.* [1] To destroy the peculiar properties or opposite dispositions of ; make neutral; counteract; nullify.— **-iz′er,** *n.* [8].

neu′tral-ly (-lĭ), *adv.* In a neutral manner.

nev′er (nĕv′ẽr), *adv.* **1.** Not ever ; at no time. **2.** Not in any degree, or way, under any condition, etc. ; — in emphatic negation; as, *never* fear.

nev′er-more′ (-mōr′), *adv.* Never again.

nev′er-the-less′ (-thē-lĕs′), *adv. or conj.* Not the less ; notwithstanding ; yet.

new (nū), *a.* [3] **1.** Having existed but a short time ; recent ; not old. **2. a** Recently discovered; hence, strange; unfamiliar. **b** Other than the former, or old ; fresh. **3.** Not habituated; unaccustomed. — *adv.* Newly ; recently. — **New World,** the land of the Western Hemisphere.

new′com′er (nū′kŭm′ẽr), *n.* One lately come.

new′el (-ĕl), *n.* *Arch.* The upright about which the steps of a circular staircase wind ; hence, the post at the foot of a stairway, or one at a landing.

new′fan′gled (nū′făn′g'ld ; nū′făn′-), *a.* **1.** Inclined to novelties; given to new fashions. **2.** Newly made ; novel ; — used disparagingly.

New-found′land′ dog (nū-found′lănd). One of a breed of large dogs, originating in Newfoundland.

new′ly (nū′lĭ), *adv.* **1.** Lately ; recently ; as, *newly* wed. **2.** Anew ; afresh; as, *newly* painted.

new′mar′ket (nū′mär′kĕt ; nū′măr′kĕt), *n.* A long, closely fitting coat or cloak ; — called also **Newmarket coat.**

new′ness (-nĕs), *n.* Quality or state of being new.

news (nūz), *n.; pl.* in form, but commonly construed as *sing.* A report of a recent event; fresh information. [papers.

news′boy′, *n.* A boy who distributes or sells news-

news′mon′ger (-mŭn′gẽr), *n.* A dealer in news; one active in hearing and telling news.

news′pa′per (-pā′pẽr), *n.* A paper printed and distributed at stated intervals to convey news, etc.

newt (nūt), *n.* Any of various small salamanders, living in water during a part of their existence.

New Testament. See under TESTAMENT.

new year. The year approaching or just begun. — **new′-year′,** *a.,* or, more often, **new year′s** — New Year's Day, the first day of January. Often. *Colloq.,* New Year's.

next (nĕkst), *a., superl.* of NIGH (see NIGH). Nearest ; having nothing similar intervening ; immediately succeeding. — *adv.* **1.** In the time, place, or order nearest. **2.** On the first occasion to come.

nib (nĭb), *n.* **1.** A bill; beak. **2.** The point of a pen, or either of its divisions. **3.** A point ; prong.

nib′ble (nĭb′'l), *v. t. & i.* [1] To bite lightly or gently ; eat in small bits. — *n.* Act of nibbling ; a small or cautious bite. — **nib′bler** (-lẽr), *n.* [8].

nice (nīs), *a.* [3] **1.** Fastidious ; over-dainty ; finical ; also, refined ; cultured ; discriminating. **2.** Exacting ; scrupulous ; punctilious. **3.** Demanding, or marked by close discrimination, delicate, minute, or tactful treatment, etc. ; subtle ; fine. **4.** Delicately sensitive or discriminative ; minutely accurate ; precise ; exact. **5.** Pleasing, delightful, kind, considerate, etc. *Colloq.*

nice′ly, *adv.* In a nice manner.

nice′ness, *n.* Quality or character of being nice.

ni'ce-ty (nī'sĕ-tĭ), *n.; pl.* -TIES (-tĭz). **1.** A minute distinction, point, or detail. **2.** Delicacy or exactness of perception or discrimination; precision. **3.** Quality of demanding delicacy and accuracy of treatment. **4.** Fastidiousness.

niche (nĭch), *n.* A hollow or recess, generally in a wall, as for a statue.

nick (nĭk), *n.* **1.** A notch; slit. **2.** A broken or indented place in any edge or surface. **3.** The critical moment or point; as, in the *nick* of time. —*v. t.* **1.** To make a nick in; notch. **2.** To strike or grasp at the precise and proper point or time.

nick'el (nĭk″l), *n.* **1.** *Chem.* A hard, malleable, ductile metal of the iron group, resistant to oxidation. **2.** A coin of or containing nickel; esp., a five-cent piece. *Colloq., U. S.*

nick'name' (-nām″), *n.* **1.** A name given in derision or sportive familiarity. **2.** A familiar diminutive name, as " Bill " for "William." —*v. t.* [1] To give a nickname to.

nic'o-tine (nĭk′ō-tĭn; -tēn), *n.* A poisonous alkaloid, the active principle of tobacco.

niece (nēs), *n.* A daughter of one's brother or sister.

nig'gard (nĭg′ård), *n.* A close and covetous person; miser.—*a.* [4] Niggardly; stingy. —*ly, adv.* [8].

nig'gard-ly (-lĭ), *a.* [4] **1.** Meanly covetous or parsimonious; stingy. **2.** Characteristic of a niggard ; miserly. —**-li-ness** (-lĭ-nĕs), *n.* [8].

nigh (nī), *adv.* **1.** In or to a near situation or relationship; near. **2.** Almost; nearly. —*prep.* Near to; not remote or distant from.—*a.; * NIGH′ER (-ĕr); NIGH′EST, or NEXT (nĕkst). **1.** Not distant; near. **2.** Direct; short. **3.** Of domestic animals, vehicles, etc., on the left; near; as, the *nigh* wheel.

night (nīt), *n.* **1.** The time from sunset to sunrise, esp. when it is dark. **2.** Nightfall. **3.** The darkness of night ; — often used figuratively.

night'cap' (-kăp′), *n.* A cap or covering for the head, worn in bed or, formerly, in undress.

night'dress' (-drĕs′), *n.* A nightgown or, sometimes, other garments worn in bed.

night'fall' (nīt′fôl′), *n.* The close of the day.

night'gown' (-goun′), *n.* A light gown worn in bed.

night'in-gale (nīt′ĭn-gāl; nīt′ĭn-), *n.* Any of several Old World thrushes. The common British species is noted for the sweet song of the male.

night'ly (-lĭ), *a.* Of or pertaining to night ; happening, done, or used by night, or every night.

night'ly, *adv.* Every night ; also, at or by night.

night'mare' (nīt′mâr′), *n.* **1.** A female fiend formerly supposed to oppress people during sleep. **2.** A condition occurring in sleep characterized esp. by bad dreams.

night'shade' (nīt′shād′), *n.* **1.** A plant of the genus that includes the potato, esp. any of several poisonous species, as the belladonna, etc. **2.** The henbane. [man or boy.]

night'shirt' (nīt′shûrt′), *n.* A nightgown for a |

night'time' (-tīm′), *n.* The time from dusk to dawn.

|| **ni'hil** (nī′hĭl), *n.* [L.] Nothing; thing of no value.

ni'hil-ism (-hĭ-lĭz′m), *n.* **1.** A doctrine that denies any real ground of truth. **2.** [*cap.*] The doctrine of a Russian party proposing revolutionary reform, and resorting to terrorism and assassination. Hence, terrorism ; anarchism.

ni'hil-ist (-lĭst), *n.* An advocate of nihilism.

ni'hil-is'tic (-lĭs′tĭk), *a.* Of, pertaining to, or marked by, nihilism.

nil (nĭl), *n.* Nothing ; thing of no account.

nim'ble (nĭm′b′l), *a.* [3] **1.** Light and quick in motion; lively; swift. **2.** Of the mental faculties, alert; acute. — **nim'ble-ness,** *n.* [8] — **nim'bly** (nĭm′blĭ), *adv.* [8].

nim'bus (-bŭs), *n.; pl.* L. NIMBI (-bī), E. -BUSES (-ĕz). **1.** *Art.* A circle, disk, or any indication of radiant light around the head of a divinity, saint, or sovereign. **2.** A rain cloud, a cloud of uniform grayness often extending over the entire sky.

nine (nīn), *a.* Eight plus one. — *n.* **1.** The number greater by a unit than eight. **2.** A symbol denoting nine units, as 9 or ix. **3.** Something having as a feature nine units or members.

nine'pins', *n.* A bowling game played with nine wooden pins. Tenpins is a development of this.

nine'teen' (nīn′tēn′ ; nīn′tēn′), *a.* Nine plus ten. — *n.* **1.** The number greater by a unit than eighteen. **2.** A symbol denoting nineteen units, as 19 or xix.

nine'teenth' (nīn′tēnth′ ; nīn′tēnth′), *a.* Next in order after the eighteenth ; also, constituting one of nineteen equal parts into which a (whole) thing may be divided. — *n.* **1.** A nineteenth part. **2.** A nineteenth unit or object.

nine'ti-eth (nīn′tĭ-ĕth), *a.* Next in order after the eighty-ninth ; also, constituting one of ninety equal parts into which a (whole) thing may be divided. — *n.* **1.** A ninetieth part. **2.** A ninetieth unit or object.

nine'ty (-tĭ), *a.* Nine times ten. — *n.; pl.* -TIES (-tĭz). **1.** The product of nine times ten. **2.** A symbol for ninety units, as 90 or xc.

nin'ny (nĭn′ĭ), *n.; pl.* -NIES (-ĭz). A fool; simpleton.

ninth (nīnth), *a.* Next in order after the eighth ; also, constituting one of nine equal parts into which a (whole) thing may be divided. — *n.* **1.** A ninth part. **2.** A ninth unit or object.

nip (nĭp), *v. t.;* NIPPED· (nĭpt), NIP′PING (-ĭng). **1.** To catch tightly; pinch. **2.** To sever or remove by pinching or cutting with two meeting edges; clip. **3.** To stop; check, as in growth. *Now Rare,* exc. in *to nip in the bud.* **4.** To be numb or injure, as does cold.— *n.* **1.** A pinching ; pinch ; bite. **2.** A biting remark ; sarcasm ; rebuke. **3.** A check to vegetation due to cold or frost; hence, sharp cold. **4.** A small fragment or bit.

nip, *n.* A small draft, esp. of liquor ; a dram.

nip'per (nĭp′ĕr), *n.* **1.** One that nips. **2.** Any of various devices for nipping, as small pincers ; — usually in *pl.* **3.** One of the large claws of a crab or lobster.

nip'ple (-′l), *n.* **1.** The protuberance of a breast ; teat ; pap. **2.** Any small teatlike projection.

nit (nĭt), *n.* The egg of a louse or other parasitic insect ; also, the young insect.

ni'ter (nī′tĕr), *n.* [6] Saltpeter.

ni'trate (nī′trāt), *n.* **1.** A salt of nitric acid. **2.** Potassium nitrate or sodium nitrate, as a fertilizer.

ni'tric (-trĭk), *a.* Of, pertaining to, or containing, nitrogen. — **nitric acid,** a fuming corrosive liquid composed of hydrogen, nitrogen, and oxygen.

ni'trite (nī′trīt), *n.* A salt of nitrous acid.

āle, senáte, câre, ăm, *a*ccount, ärm, ȧsk, sofá ; ēve, ĕvent, ĕnd, recĕnt, makêr ; īce, ĭll ; ōld, ŏbey, ôrb, ŏdd, sŏft, cŏnnect ; ūse, ūnite, ûrn, ŭp, circ*u*s ; fōōd, fŏŏt ; out, oil ;

ni'tro-gen (nī'trṓ-jĕn), *n.* A colorless, tasteless, and odorless gas, forming about four fifths of the atmosphere by volume. It is an element.

ni-trog'e-nous (nī-trŏj'ĕ-nŭs), *a.* [4] Of, pertaining to, or containing, nitrogen.

ni'tro-glyc'er-in, -ine (nī'trṓ-glĭs'ēr-ĭn), *n.* A heavy, oily, explosive liquid, got by treating glycerin with a mixture of nitric and sulphuric acids.

ni'trous (nī'trŭs), *a.* Of, pertaining to, containing, or like, niter. — **nitrous acid**, an acid forming a series of salts (*nitrites*) but itself known only in solution. — **ɴ. oxide**, laughing gas.

nix (nĭks), *n.; pl.* ɴɪxᴇs (nĭk'sĕz). *Teut. Myth.* A water sprite.

nix'ie (nĭk'sĭ), *n.* A female water sprite.

no (nō), *adv.* **1.** Not ; — now only *Scot.*, or in expressions like *whether or no*. **2.** Not any; not at all. **3.** Not so ; — opposite of *yes.* — *n.; pl.* ɴoᴇs or ɴo's (nōz). **1.** Act of uttering *no;* a refusal by using *no.* **2.** A negative vote; *pl.*, those who vote in the negative. — *a.* Not any; not a.

no-bil'i-ty (nṓ-bĭl'ĭ-tĭ), *n.; pl.* -ᴛɪᴇs (-tĭz). **1.** Quality or state of being noble. **2.** Collectively, the nobles; in the United Kingdom, the peerage.

no'ble (nō'b'l), *a.* [3] **1.** Of persons, possessing eminence, elevation, dignity, or the like; illustrious; of deeds or acts, great; famous. **2.** Of high birth, rank, or station ; aristocratic. **3.** Magnanimous ; lofty; great. **4.** Grand, esp. in appearance; stately; imposing. **5.** Possessing very high or excellent qualities or properties. — **noble metals**, metals which do not oxidize in air, as gold, silver, platinum, etc. — *n.* A nobleman; in the United Kingdom, a peer. — **-ness,** *n.* [8].

no'ble-man (-măn), *n.; pl.* -ᴍᴇɴ (-mĕn), **no'ble-wom'an** (-wŏŏm'ăn), *n.; pl.* -ᴡoᴍᴇɴ (-wĭm'ĕn). A man (or woman) of noble rank; a peer (or peeress).

no'bly (nō'blĭ), *adv.* In a noble manner or degree.

no'bod-y (nō'bŏd-ĭ), *n.; pl.* -ʙoᴅɪᴇs (-ĭz). No person ; no one ; an insignificant person.

noc-tur'nal (nŏk-tûr'nặl), *a.* [4] **1.** Of, pertaining to, done, or occurring in, the night; — opposed to *diurnal.* **2.** Seeking food or active at night.

noc'turne (nŏk'tûrn; nŏk-tûrn'), *n.* **1.** *Music.* A night piece, or serenade, esp. a dreamy instrumental composition. **2.** *Paint.* A night scene.

nod (nŏd), *v. i. & t.* ; ɴoᴅ'ᴅᴇᴅ ; ɴoᴅ'ᴅɪɴɢ. **1.** To bow or incline the head in assent, salutation, etc., or involuntarily from drowsiness or sleep. **2.** To signify by nodding the head. **3.** To bend or incline the upper part downward or forward with a quick motion. — *n.* Act of one that nods.

nod'al (nō'dặl), *a.* Like or relating to a node.

nod'dle (nŏd'l), *n.* The head; pate. *Colloq.*

node (nōd), *n.* **1.** A knot; knob. **2.** *Bot.* Joint of a stem ; point of insertion of a leaf. **3.** *Astron.* Either of the two points where the orbit of a planet or comet intersects the ecliptic.

no'dose (nō'dōs; nṓ-dōs'), *a.* [4] Knotty; knobbed; also, *Bot. & Zoöl.*, having distinct nodes.

no-dos'i-ty (nṓ-dŏs'ĭ-tĭ), *n.; pl.* -ᴛɪᴇs (-tĭz). **1.** Knottiness. **2.** A knot; node. [or nodes.

nod'u-lar (nŏd'ṵ-lặr), *a.* Of or pert. to nodules.

nod'ule (nŏd'ṵl), *n.* A little knot or lump.

nog'gin (nŏg'ĭn), *n.* A small mug ; also, a small quantity of drink, usually a gill.

noise (noiz), *n.* **1.** Loud or confused shouting ; clamor. **2.** Any sound, esp. if without musical quality. — *v. t.* [1] To spread by rumor or report.

noise'less, *a.* [4] Making or causing no noise or stir; silent. — **-ly,** *adv.* [8]. — **-ness,** *n.* [8].

nois'i-ly (nois'ĭ-lĭ), *adv.* In a noisy manner.

nois'i-ness, *n.* Quality or state of being noisy.

noi'some (noi'sŭm), *a.* [4] **1.** Noxious; harmful; unwholesome. **2.** Offensive, esp. to the smell; disgusting. — **-ly,** *adv.* [8]. — **-ness,** *n.* [8].

nois'y (noiz'ĭ), *a.* [3] **1.** Making, or given to making, a noise. **2.** Marked by noise.

nom'ad (nŏm'ăd ; nō'măd), *n.* One of a wandering race or tribe. — *a.* [4] Roving.

no-mad'ic (nṓ-măd'ĭk), *a.* [4] Of, pertaining to, or characteristic of, nomads; wandering.

no'men-cla'ture (nō'mĕn-klā'tụ̍r), *n.* The system of names used in any science or art.

nom'i-nal (nŏm'ĭ-nặl), *a.* [4] **1.** Of, pertaining to, or of the nature of, a name or names. **2.** Existing in name only. — **nom'i-nal-ly,** *adv.* [8].

nom'i-nate (-nāt), *v. t.* [1] To name as a candidate for election or appointment; propose by name.

nom'i-na'tion (-nā'shŭn), *n.* Act of nominating; state or fact of being nominated.

nom'i-na-tive (nŏm'ĭ-nȧ-tĭv), *a.* *Gram.* Designating, or pertaining to, the case denoting the subject of a finite verb, a predicate noun referring to the subject, or a noun word in apposition with either. — *n.* The nominative case, or a word in it.

nom'i-na'tor (-nā'tẽr), *n.* One who nominates.

nom'i-nee' (-nē'), *n.* A person named, or designated, as for any office, duty, or position.

non-. A common prefix meaning *not*, being merely negative and generally less emphatic than *un-* and *in-*, which often imply an *opposite* thing or quality. Many compounds of *non-* are self-explaining, with the definitions of the prefix and the root word; as

non'ap-pear'ance	non-pay'ment
non'at-tend'ance	non'per-form'ance
non'-Chris'tian	non're-sist'ance
non'con-duct'ing	non're-sist'ant
non'es-sen'tial	non'sec-ta'ri-an
non'ful-fil'ment	non'sub-scrib'er
non'in'ter-course	non-tech'ni-cal
non'in-ter-fer'ence	non-un'ion
non'in'ter-ven'tion	non-ven'om-ous
non-par'ti-san	non-vo'cal

non'age (nŏn'ĕj ; nō'nặj), *n.* Legal minority.

non'a-ge-na'ri-an (nŏn'ȧ-jē-nā'rĭ-ặn),*n.* Between 90 and 100 years old. — *n.* One of such age.

nonce (nŏns), *n.* The particular or present (occasion, use, or purpose). [ing nonchalant.

non'cha-lance (nŏn'shȧ-lȧns),*n.* Quality of being nonchalant.

non'cha-lant (-lȧnt),*a.* Lacking in warmth of feeling, enthusiasm, or interest ; indifferent; careless.

non-com'bat-ant (nŏn-kŏm'băt-ặnt), *n.* Any person connected with a military or naval force whose duties do not include fighting, as a chaplain.

non'com-mis'sioned (nŏn-kŏ-mĭsh'ŭnd), *a.* Not having a commission. — **noncommissioned officer,** *Mil.,* an enlisted man appointed sergeant or corporal.

non'com-mit'tal (nŏn'kŏ-mĭt'ặl), *a.* [4] Marked by refusal to commit one's self ; indicating neither consent nor dissent. — **-tal-ly,** *adv.* [8].

non'con-duc'tor (nŏn'kŏn-dŭk'tẽr), *n.* A substance that is a very poor conductor of heat, electricity, sound, or the like; an insulator.

---

chair ; go ; sing, iŋk ; ᴛhen, thin ; nature, verdure ; yet ; zh = z in azure. Numbers refer to §§ in the Special Notes which, with Abbreviations, Signs, etc., precede the Vocabulary.

non'con-form'ist (nŏn'kŏn-fôr'mĭst), *n.* One who does not conform to an established church, esp. [*often cap.*] that of England ; a dissenter.

non'con-form'i-ty (-fôr'mĭ-tĭ), *n.* Neglect, failure, or refusal to conform ; esp., refusal or neglect to conform to an established church.

non'de-script(nŏn'dĕ-skrĭpt),*a.* [4] Not easily described ; of no particular class or kind. — *n.* A nondescript person or thing.

none (nŭn), *pron.* **1.** No one; not one. **2.** Not any. ☞ As subject, *none* with a plural verb is the commoner construction unless a singular idea is clearly intended.
— *adv.* Not at all ; in no way.

non-en'ti-ty (nŏn-ĕn'tĭ-tĭ), *n.; pl.* -TIES (-tĭz). **1.** A thing not existing, or existing in imagination only. **2.** A person or thing of little or no account.

non'ex-ist'ence (nŏn'ĕg-zĭs'tĕns), *n.* Absence of existence ; nonentity. — **non'ex-ist'ent,** *a.*

non'met'al (nŏn'mĕt'ăl ; nŏn-mĕt'ăl), *n. Chem.* An element not a metal, as phosphorus, oxygen, etc. —**non'me-tal'lic** (nŏn'mĕ-tăl'ĭk), *a.*

non'pa-reil' (nŏn'pȧ-rĕl'), *a.* Having no equal; peerless. — *n.* **1.** Something of unequaled excellence. **2.** A finch of the southern United States.

non'plus (nŏn'plŭs), *n.* A state in which no more can be said or done; quandary. —*v.t.* [7] To puzzle; to stop, or render helpless, by perplexity or the like.

non-res'i-dent (nŏn-rĕz'ĭ-dĕnt), *a.* Not residing in a particular place. — *n.* A nonresident person. — **non-res'i-dence** (nŏn-rĕz'ĭ-dĕns), *n.*

non'sense (nŏn'sĕns), *n.* **1.** That which is not sense, or has no sensible meaning ; absurdity. **2.** Trifles ; things of no importance or value.

non-sen'si-cal (nŏn-sĕn'sĭ-kăl), *a.* [4] Without sense ; absurd. —**-ly,** *adv.* [8] —**-ness,** *n.* [8].

non'suit' (nŏn'sūt'), *n. Law.* A judgment given against a plaintiff because of his failure to prosecute his case or to establish a prima facie case. — *v. t.* To subject to a nonsuit.

non-un'ion (nŏn-ūn'yŭn),*a.* **1.** Not connected with a trade-union. **2.** Not recognizing or favoring a trade-union. — **non-un'ion-ist,** *n.*

noo'dle (nōō'd'l), *n.* A simpleton ; blockhead.

noo'dle, *n.* A thin strip of dough made with flour and eggs, and used esp. in soups.

nook (nŏŏk), *n.* A corner formed by two walls, etc. ; recess ; secluded retreat.

noon (nōōn), *n.* **1.** Midday; twelve o'clock in the daytime. **2.** The highest point ; culmination.

noon'day' (nōōn'dā'), *n.* Midday; noon.

noon'ing, *n.* An intermission for food and rest at midday. *U. S.*

noon'tide' (-tīd'), *n.* Noon; midday.

noose (nōōs), *n.* **1.** A loop with a running knot, which binds the closer the more it is drawn.**2.**Fig.: A tie, bond, or snare. — *v. t.* [1] **1.** To secure by or as by a noose. **2.** To make a noose in or of.

nor (nôr), *conj.* A negative connective or particle, commonly introducing the second member or clause of a negative statement to continue the force of *not, no,* or the like, in the first member or clause, or following *neither* as a correlative.

norm (nôrm), *n.* A model ; type ; pattern.

nor'mal (nôr'măl),*a.* [4] **1.** *Geom.* According to a square or rule; perpendicular. **2.** Conformed to

a type or standard ; regular; natural. — **norma**, school, an institution for training teachers. — *n.* **1.** *Geom.* Any perpendicular. **2.** The ordinary or usual condition, degree, or the like; average mean. — **nor'mal-ly,** *adv.* [8].

Nor'man (nôr'măn), *a.* Of or pert. to Normandy or the Normans. — *n.* A native or inhabitant of Normandy ; originally, one of the Northmen who, in the 10th century, conquered the region, named after them, Normandy ; later, one of the mixed race which in 1066 conquered England (**Norman** Conquest).

Norse (nôrs), *a.* Of or pertaining to ancient Scandinavia or its language. — *n.* **1.** *Collective pl.* Scandinavians. **2.** The language of the Norse.

Norse'man (-măn), *n. ; pl.* -MEN (-mĕn). One of the ancient Scandinavians ; a Northman.

north (nôrth), *n.* **1.** That point of the compass which lies to the left of a person facing east ; the direction opposite south. **2.** Any country or region north of another ; as : [*cap.*] That part of the United States lying in general north of Mason and Dixon's line (the southern boundary of Pennsylvania) and the Ohio River. — *a.* Northern ; as : **a** Lying toward the north. **b** Proceeding or facing north. **c** Coming from the north ; as, the *north* wind. — North Star, the star of the Northern Hemisphere toward which the axis of the earth very nearly points ; polestar. — *adv.* Northward.

north'east' (nôrth'ēst'), *n.* Point or direction half-way between north and east ; northeast part or region. — *a.* Of or pertaining to, proceeding or facing toward, or (of the wind) blowing from, th**e** northeast. — *adv.* Toward the northeast.

north'east'er (nôrth'ēs'tẽr), *n.* Storm or wind from the northeast. [northeast.|

north'east'er-ly, *a. & adv.* To.vard or from the

north'east'ern (-tẽrn), *a.* Of, pertaining to, or being in, the northeast. [north.|

north'er (nôr'thẽr), *n.* A storm or wind from the

north'er-ly, *a.* Of or toward the north ; northern ; from the north. — *adv.* Toward the north.

north'ern (-thẽrn), *a.* [4] **1.** Of, pertaining to, or living or originating in, the north ; being in the north. **2.** [*cap.*] Of or pertaining to the North. *U. S.* **3.** Directed toward the north ; as, a *north-ern* course ; coming from the north ; as, a *northern* blast. — northern lights. See AURORA BOREALIS.

north'ern-er (-thẽr-nẽr), *n.* One born or living in the north, or [*cap.*] *U. S.,* the North.

north'ern-most(nôr'thẽn-mōst),*a.* Most northern.

North'man (nôrth'măn), *n. ; pl.* -MEN (-mĕn). An inhabitant of the north of Europe ; a Norseman.

north'-north'east', *a.,* **north'-north'west'**, *a.* See *points of the compass,* under POINT, *n.*

north'ward (nôrth'wẽrd), *adv.* Toward the north. — *a.* Situated, directed, or looking, northward. — *n.* The northward direction, point, or part.

north'ward-ly, *a.* Having a northern direction or situation ; blowing from the north. — *adv.* In a northern direction.

north'wards (nôrth'wẽrdz),*adv. & n.* Northward.

north'west' (-wĕst'), *n.* Point or direction half-way between north and west : northwest part or region. — *a.* Of, pertaining to, proceeding or facing toward, or (of the wind) blowing from, the northwest. — *adv.* Toward the northwest.

north′west′er (-wĕs′tẽr), *n.* A storm or wind from the northwest. [west.]

north′west′er-ly, *a.* Toward or from the north-

north′west′ern (-tẽrn), *a.* Of, pertaining to, or being in, the northwest; northwesterly.

Nor-we′gian (nŏr-wē′jăn), *a.* Of or pert. to Norway, its inhabitants, or language. — *n.* **1.** A native of Norway. **2.** Language of the Norwegians.

nose (nōz), *n.* **1.** That part of the face, or head, containing the nostrils. **2.** The smelling organ. **3.** Sense of smell; also, scent. **4.** Something like, or suggestive of, the nose, as the stem of a vessel. — *v. t.* [1] **1.** To smell; scent. **2.** To touch or rub with the nose. **3.** To make (one's way) by advancing the nose or front end. — *v. i.* **1.** To smell; sniff; scent. **2.** To pry or search curiously.

nose′gay (-gā′), *n.* A bunch of flowers; bouquet.

nos′tril (nŏs′trĭl), *n.* Either of the external openings of the nose.

nos′trum (-trŭm), *n.* **1.** A quack medicine. **2.** A pet scheme or remedy, as for some evil.

not (nŏt), *adv.* An adverbial particle expressing negation.

no′ta-bil′i-ty (nō′tá-bĭl′ĭ-tĭ), *n. ; pl.* -TIES (-tĭz). **1.** A person of note. **2.** Quality of being notable.

no′ta-ble (nō′tá-b'l), *a.* [4] Worthy of note or notice ; remarkable : hence, distinguished. — *n.* A person of note or distinction; a notability. — **no′-ta-ble-ness**, *n.* [8] — **no′ta-bly**, *adv.* [8].

no-ta′ri-al (nō-tā′rĭ-ăl), *a.* Of, pertaining to, or characteristic of, a notary ; done by a notary.

no′ta-ry (nō′tá-rĭ), *n. ; pl.* -RIES (-rĭz). A public officer who attests or certifies deeds, takes affidavits, etc. ; — usually called **notary public.**

no-ta′tion (nō-tā′shŭn), *n.* Act, process, or method of representing (numbers, quantities, etc.) by a system of marks, or signs; the system so used.

notch (nŏch), *n.* **1.** A V-shaped indentation ; a nick. **2.** A deep, close pass ; defile. *U. S.*—*v. t.* To cut or make notches in; also, to record or tally by or as by notches.

note (nōt), *n.* **1.** *Music.* **a** A character used to indicate a certain tone, esp. one showing by its form the relative length, and by its position the pitch, of a tone. **b** Inaccurately, a key, as of a pianoforte. **2.** A tone ; as, a joyous *note.* **3.** A cry, or sound, esp. of a bird. **4.** A sign ; distinctive mark or feature. **5.** A memorandum. **6.** An annotation. **7.** A short informal letter ; also, an official missive. **8.** A paper acknowledging a debt, and promising payment. **9.** Reputation ; fame ; distinction ; as, a person of *note.* **10.** Observation ; notice, heed. — *v. t.* [1] **1.** To notice or observe with care ; remark ; heed. **2.** To make a memorandum of. [memorandums.]

note′book (nōt′bŏŏk′), *n.* A book for notes or

not′ed (nōt′ĕd), *p. a.* [4] Well known by reputation or report; celebrated. — **-ly**, *adv.* — **-ness,** *n.*

note′wor′thy (-wûr′thĭ), *a.* [3] Worthy of notice; remarkable. — **-thi-ly** (-thĭ-lĭ), *adv.* [8].

noth′ing (nŭth′ĭng), *n.* **1.** Not anything ; no thing ; nought. **2.** What is of no significance. **3.** *Arith.* Absence of magnitude or quantity; also, a cipher. **4.** A thing of no account, value, or the like; a nobody. — *adv.* In no degree; not at all; in no wise.

noth′ing-ness, *n.* **1.** Nonexistence. **2.** Utter insignificance, worthlessness, or the like.

no′tice (nō′tĭs), *n.* **1.** Intelligence ; information; intimation or warning, esp. if formal **2.** A written or printed sign, announcement, or the like, communicating information or warning. **3.** Act of noting, remarking, or observing ; cognizance. **4.** Polite or favorable attention. — *v. t.* [1] **1.** To mention ; remark upon. **2.** To take notice or note of ; pay attention to.

no′tice-a-ble (-á-b'l), *a.* [4] Capable of being observed; worthy of notice.—**no′tice-a-bly,** *adv.* [8].

no′ti-fi-ca′tion (nō′tĭ-fĭ-kā′shŭn), *n.* **1.** An intimation; notice. **2.** The written or printed matter which gives notice, as an advertisement.

no′ti-fy (nō′tĭ-fī), *v. t.* [2] **1.** To give notice **of**; make known ; publish. **2.** To give notice to.

no′tion (-shŭn), *n.* **1.** Idea ; a theory, belief, or opinion. **2.** Inclination ; fancy. **3.** An ingenious device, any of various articles or wares, esp. small useful ones ; — usually in *pl. Colloq.*

no′tion-al (-ăl), *a.* [4] **1.** Consisting of, or conveying, notions or ideas. **2.** Given to visionary expectations ; fanciful ; as, a *notional* man.

no′to-ri′e-ty (nō′tó-rī′ē-tĭ), *n. ; pl.* -TIES (-tĭz). **1.** Quality or state of being notorious. **2.** A well-known or noted person.

no-to′ri-ous (nō-tō′rĭ-ŭs), *a.* [4] Generally known; well-known ; — now almost always implying evil or wickedness. — **no-to′ri-ous-ly,** *adv.* [8].

not′with-stand′ing (nŏt′wĭth-stăn′dĭng), *adv. & conj.* Nevertheless; yet; although. — *prep.* Without prevention from or by : in spite of.

nought (nôt), *n. Arith.* Nothing ; zero ; a naught.

noun (noun), *n. Gram.* A word used as the name of a person or thing, as John, Venice, stick.

nour′ish (nŭr′ĭsh), *v. t.* To supply with whatever promotes growth, development, etc.; feed; foster.

nour′ish-ment (-mĕnt), *n.* **1.** That which nourishes, food. **2.** A nourishing; nourished state.

nov′el (nŏv′ĕl), *a.* [4] New; not formerly known; of a new kind, unusual ; strange. — *n.* A fictitious prose narrative, of considerable length, portraying characters representative of real life.

nov′el-ette′ (nŏv′ĕl-ĕt′), *n.* A little or short novel.

nov′el-ist, *n.* A writer of a novel or novels.

nov′el-ty (nŏv′ĕl-tĭ), *n. ; pl.* -TIES (-tĭz). **1.** Quality or state of being novel ; newness ; freshness. **2.** Something novel, an innovation.

No-vem′ber (nō-vĕm′bẽr), *n.* The eleventh month of the year, having thirty days.

nov′ice (nŏv′ĭs), *n.* **1.** One who has entered a religious house on probation. **2.** One new in any business, profession, or calling ; beginner.

no-vi′ti-ate, no-vi′ci-ate (nō-vĭsh′ĭ-ăt), *n.* **1.** State or time of being a novice. **2.** A novice.

now (nou), *adv. & conj.* **1.** At the present time; at this moment. **2.** Hence : **a** In the time immediately to follow. **b** Very lately ; a moment ago; — chiefly in *just now.* **c** At the time spoken of or referred to. **3.** Chiefly as *conj.* : **a** With the force of *since, seeing that*; as, *now* (or *now that*) you have come, I'll go. **b** Simply marking or emphasizing transition of thought; as, come *now !* — **now and then,** at one time and another ; occasionally. — *n.* The present.

---

chair; go sing, ink; then, thin ; nature, verdure; yet; zh = z in azure. **Numbers refer to §§ in the Special Notes** which, with Abbreviations, Signs, etc., precede the Vocabulary.

now'a-days' (-ä-dāz'), *adv.* At the present time.

no'way' (nō'wā')) *adv.* In no manner or degree ;
no'ways' (-wāz')) not at all ; nowise.

no'where' (nō'hwâr'), *adv.* Not in or at any place.

no'wise' (-wiz'), *adv.* Noways.

nox'ious (nŏk'shŭs), *a.* [4] Hurtful; injurious ;
unwholesome. — **-ly**, *adv.* — **-ness**, *n.*

noz'zle (nŏz'l'), *n.* Any projecting vent ; a small
spout; nose; as : **a** A short tube forming the vent
of a hose. **b** A short outlet, or inlet, pipe.

nu'cle-at'ed (nū'klē-āt'ĕd), *a.* **1.** Having a nucleus. **2.** Clustered about a nucleus.

nu'cle-us (-ŭs), *n. ; pl.* E. **-cleuses** (-ĕz), L. **-clei**
(-ī). **1.** A center about which matter gath-
ers; kernel; core. **2.** *Biol.* A central mass in most
cells, regarded as essential to their growth.

nude (nūd), *a.* Bare; naked; unclothed. — *n.* A
nude figure; with *the*, the nude state.

nudge (nŭj), *v. t.* [1] To touch or push gently with
the elbow, as to call attention. — *n.* A gentle
push, poke, or jog, as with the elbow.

nu'di-ty (nū'dĭ-tĭ), *n. ; pl.* **-ties** (-tĭz). **1.** Quality or state of being nude. **2.** That which is nude.

nu'ga-to-ry (nū'gà-tō-rĭ), *a.* [4] **1.** Trifling; insignificant. **2.** Inoperative; ineffectual.

nug'get (nŭg'ĕt), *n.* A lump; esp., a native lump
of precious metal.

nui'sance (nū'sǎns), *n.* That which annoys or
gives trouble and vexation or that is offensive.

null (nŭl), *a.* [3] **1.** Of no legal or binding force;
invalid ; void. **2.** Of no consequence or value.

nul'li-fi-ca'tion (nŭl'ĭ-fĭ-kā'shŭn), *n.* Act of nul-
lifying ; state of being nullified.

nul'li-fy (nŭl'ĭ-fī), *v. t.* [2] **1.** To make null;
render invalid or void. **2.** To reduce to nothing;
destroy. — **nul'li-fi'er** (nŭl'ĭ-fī'ĕr), *n.* [8].

nul'li-ty (-tĭ), *n. ; pl.* **-ties** (-tĭz). **1.** State of
being null ; invalidity. **2.** That which is null.

numb (nŭm), *a.* [3] Benumbed; insensible. — *v. t.*
To deprive of sensation; make numb.

num'ber (nŭm'bĕr), *n.* **1.** Total or aggregate of
units. **2.** *pl.* [*cap.*] The fourth book of the Bible.
3. *pl.* Arithmetic. **4.** A numeral. **5.** One of a
numbered series ; esp., one of the issues of a
periodical. **6.** A considerable number ; many.
7. *Gram.* Distinction of a word as denoting or referring to one, or to more than one ; also, the form
indicating such distinction. **8.** *Poetry & Music.*
pl. Metrical groups of feet or periods; hence,
verse. — *v. t.* **1.** To count; enumerate. **2.** To
limit in number. **3.** To reckon as one of a collection, class, or company. **4.** To mark or distinguish by a number. **5.** To amount to; contain; comprise. — *v. i.* To count; reckon. — **num'ber-er**, *n.*

num'ber-less, *a.* Innumerable ; countless.

numb'ly, *adv.* In a numb manner.

numb'ness, *n.* Quality or state of being numb.

nu'mer-a-ble (nū'mẽr-à-b'l), *a.* [4] Capable of
being numbered, or counted.

nu'mer-al (-ăl), *n.* **1.** Expressing or denoting
number. **2.** Of or pertaining to number. — *n.* A
word, figure, or group of figures, used to express
a number.

nu'mer-a-ry (-à-rĭ), *a.* Of or pert. to numbers.

nu'mer-ate (-āt), *v. t.* [1] To number; divide off
and read according to the rules of numeration.

nu'mer-a'tion (-ā'shŭn), *n.* **1.** Act of numbering.
2. Act or art of reading or naming numbers.

nu'mer-a'tor (nū'mẽr-ā'tẽr), *n.* **1.** Part of a common fraction above the horizontal line, indicating
the number of parts taken. **2.** One that numbers.

nu-mer'i-cal (nū-mẽr'ĭ-kăl), *a.* [4] Of or pertaining to, or denoting, number; expressed by numbers, and not letters. — **nu-mer'i-cal-ly**, *adv.*

nu'mer-ous (nū'mẽr-ŭs), *a.* [4] Consisting of, or
containing, a great number of units ; pert. to great
numbers ; many. — *-ly*, *adv.* [8] — **-ness**, *n.*

nu'mis-mat'ic (nū'mĭz-măt'ĭk ; nū'mĭs-), *a.* Of
or pertaining to coins. [and medals.|

nu'mis-mat'ics (-ĭks), *n.* Science or study of coins

nu-mis'ma-tist (nū-mĭz'mà-tĭst ; nū-mĭs'-), *n.* A
specialist in numismatics.

num'skull' (nŭm'skŭl'), *n.* A blockhead. *Colloq.*

nun (nŭn), *n.* A woman under certain religious
vows, esp. one living in a convent.

nun'ci-o (nŭn'shĭ-ō), *n. ; pl.* **-cios** (-ōz). The
papal ambassador at a foreign court.

nun'ner-y (nŭn'ẽr-ĭ), *n.; pl.* **-neries** (-ĭz). A convent for nuns.

nup'tial (nŭp'shăl), *a.* Of or pert. to marriage.
— *n.* Marriage; wedding ; — now usually in *pl.*

nurse (nûrs), *n.* **1.** A person who nurses a child
or cares for an invalid. — *v. t.* [1] **1.** To nourish
(an infant) at the breast. **2.** To take care of (a
child or an invalid). **3.** To care tenderly. — *v. i.*
To suckle; of a child, to take the breast.

nurs'er-y (nûr'sẽr-ĭ), *n.; pl.* **-eries** (-ĭz). **1.** The
part of a house appropriated to the care of children. **2.** A place where young trees, shrubs, etc.,
are raised, esp. for sale. [child.|

nurs'ling (nûrs'lĭng), *n.* One that is nursed, as a

nur'ture (nûr'tụr), *n.* **1.** A nourishing or nursing. **2.** That which nourishes; food. — *v. t.* [1]
1. To nourish ; rear. **2.** To educate; bring up.

nut (nŭt), *n.* **1.** A dry fruit or seed having a hard
shell inclosing a kernel ; also, the kernel itself.
2. *Bot.* A one-seeded fruit, with a woody covering,
as the acorn, hazelnut, chestnut, etc. **3.** A perforated block (usually of metal), with an internal
screw thread, as for a bolt.

nut'gall' (-gôl'), *n.* Any nutlike gall.

nut'meg (-mĕg), *n.* The aromatic seed
of a certain tropical tree; also, the tree.

nu'tri-ent (nū'trĭ-ĕnt), *a.* [4] Nutritious. — *n.* A nutritious substance.

Nut, 3.

nu'tri-ment (-mĕnt), *n.* Nourishment; food.

nu-tri'tion (nū-trĭsh'ŭn), *n.* **1.** Act or process of
nourishing or being nourished. **2.** Nourishment.

nu-tri'tious (nū-trĭsh'ŭs), *a.* [4] Nourishing;
nutritive. — *-ly*, *adv.* [8] — **-ness**, *n.* [8].

nu'tri-tive (nū'trĭ-tĭv), *a.* [4] Of, pertaining to,
or concerned in, nutrition; nutritious.

nut'ting, *vb. n.* Act of gathering or seeking nuts.

nut'ty (nŭt'ĭ), *a.* [3] **1.** Abounding in or producing nuts. **2.** Having a flavor like that of nuts.

nux vom'i-ca (nŭks vŏm'ĭ-kà). The poisonous
seed of a certain Asiatic tree. Also, the tree.

nymph (nĭmf), *n.* **1.** *Class. Myth.* One of the inferior divinities of nature, represented as beautiful maidens. **2.** *Zoöl.* A chrysalis.

nymph'al (nĭm'făl)) *a.* Of or pertaining to
nym-phe'an (nĭm-fē'ăn)) a nymph or nymphs.

O

O (ō), *interj.* An exclamation used in calling or address, also in expressing pain, surprise, etc.

o' (ŏ ; ō), *prep.* Short for *of* or *on.* *Colloq.*

oaf (ōf), *n.* A changeling ; hence, a deformed or foolish child ; idiot. — **oaf'ish,** *a.* [8].

oak (ōk). *n.* **1. a** Any of a very large genus of trees and shrubs. The fruit is a rounded nut (acorn). **b** The wood of these trees. **2.** Any of various plants like, or suggestive of, the oak, as in foliage.

oak'en (ōk'ʼn), *a.* Of or pert. to oaks or oak.

oa'kum (ō'kŭm), *n.* Loose fiber picked from old hemp ropes ; — used to calk seams, stop leaks, etc.

oar (ōr), *n.* **1.** A long, slender wooden implement for propelling or steering a boat. **2.** An oarsman. — *v. t.* To propel with or as with oars.

oar'lock' (ōr'lŏk'), *n.* A rowlock.

oars'man (ōrz'măn), *n.; pl.* -MEN (-mĕn). A rower.

o-a'sis (ō-ā'sĭs; ō'ȧ-sĭs), *n.; pl.* -SES (-sēz). A fertile or green spot in a waste or desert.

oat (ōt), *n.* The grain or seed of a certain cereal grass, or the plant itself ; — commonly in *pl.*

oat'en (ōt'ʼn), *a.* **1.** Made of oat grain or of oatmeal. **2.** Made of an oat straw or stem.

oath (ōth), *n. ; pl.* OATHS (ōthz). **1.** A solemn appeal to God, or to something sacred by way of attesting truth or inviolability ; also, the statement supported by the oath. **2.** A blasphemous use of the name of the divine Being, or anything sacred.

oat'meal' (ōt'mēl'), *n.* Meal made of oats, or porridge made of such meal.

‖ **ob'bli-ga'to** (ŏb'blē-gä'tō), *a.* [It.] *Music.* Indispensable. — *n.* A more or less independent accompanying part, played by a single instrument.

ob'du-ra-cy (ŏb'dū-rȧ-sĭ), *n.* Quality or state of being obdurate.

ob'du-rate (ŏb'dū-rắt), *a.* [4] Hardened in feelings ; stubbornly wicked. — **-ly,** *adv.* [8].

o-be'di-ence (ō-bē'dĭ-ĕns), *n.* Act of obeying ; state of being obedient.

o-be'di-ent (-ĕnt), *a.* [4] Willing to obey ; submissive. — **-ly,** *adv.*

ɔ-bei'sance (ō-bā'săns), *n.* A bow or other bodily movement indicating respect or submission.

ob'e-lisk (ŏb'ê-lĭsk), *n.* **1.** A four-sided pillar, tapering as it rises, and ending in a pyramid. **2.** The mark of reference † ; — called also *dagger.*

o-bese' (ō-bēs'), *a.* [4] Very fat or fleshy.

o-bes'i-ty (-bēs'), *n.* Condition of being obese.

o-bey' (-bā'), *v. t.* **1.** To execute the commands of. **2.** To submit to the authority of. **3.** To yield to the impulse, power, or operation of. — *v. i.* To yield obedience.

o-bit'u-a-ry (-bĭt'ū-ȧ-rĭ),*a.* Of or pertaining to the death of a person or persons. — *n.; pl.* -RIES (-rĭz). A notice of a death, with a biographical sketch.

ob-ject' (ŏb-jĕkt'), *v. t.* To offer in opposition. — *v. i.* To make opposition ; also, to disapprove.

ob'ject (ŏb'jĕkt), *n.* **1.** Something visible or tangible ; a material thing. **2.** That which is set before the mind so as to be apprehended or known. **3.** That sought for ; end ; aim. **4.** *Gram.* A word,

phrase, or clause denoting that toward which a verb's action is directed, or that to which a preposition expresses some relation. The direct object of a verb denotes that which is immediately acted upon (as *ball,* in " throw me the ball ") ; an indirect object, that which is affected indirectly, as *me* in the example.

ob-jec'tion (ŏb-jĕk'shŭn), *n.* **1.** An objecting. **2.** That which is presented in opposition.

ob-jec'tion-a-ble (-ȧ-b'l), *a.* [4] Liable to objection; offensive. — **-ness,** *n.* [8] — **-a-bly,** *adv.* [8].

ob-jec'tive (ŏb-jĕk'tĭv), *a.* [4] **1.** Of or pertaining to an object. **2.** *Gram.* Pertaining to or designating the case denoting the relation of object (def. 4). — *n.* **1.** *Gram.* The objective case, or a word in it. **2.** The lens, or system of lenses, at the end of a telescope, microscope, etc., nearest the object. **3.** Something aimed at ; end. — **ob-jec'tive-ly,** *adv.* [8]. [objective.|

ob'jec-tiv'i-ty (ŏb'jĕk-tĭv'ĭ-tĭ), *n.* State of being|

ob-jec'tor (ŏb-jĕk'tĕr), *n.* One who objects.

ob-jur'gate (ŏb-jûr'gāt; ŏb'jûr-), *v. t.* [1] To chide; rebuke. — **ob'jur-ga'tion** (ŏb'jûr-gā'shŭn), *n.*

ob-jur'ga-to-ry (ŏb-jûr'gȧ-tō-rĭ), *a.* Expressing reproof. [poles.|

ob'late (ŏb'lāt ; ŏb-lāt'), *a.* [3] Flattened at the|

ob-la'tion (ŏb-lā'shŭn), *n.* **1.** Act of offering something to God or a god. **2.** A religious offering ; sacrifice. [or legal obligation.|

ob'li-gate (ŏb'lĭ-gāt), *v. t.* [1] To bind by moral|

ob'li-ga'tion (-gā'shŭn), *n.* **1.** *Law.* A bond with a penalty for nonfulfillment; hence, a formal agreement ; contract. **2.** Any duty imposed by law, promise, or contract, by social relations or by kindness, etc. **3.** State of being indebted for an act of favor ; also, the act itself ; as, to be under *obligation ;* his aid was a great *obligation.*

ob'li-ga-to-ry (ŏb'lĭ-gȧ-tō-rĭ ; ŏb-lĭg'ȧ-), *a.* [4] Imposing, or of the nature of, duty or obligation.

o-blige' (ō-blīj'), *v. t.* [1] **1.** To constrain ; put under obligation to do or forbear something. **2.** To bind by a favor rendered ; hence, to do a favor to ; accommodate. — **o-blig'er** (ō-blīj'ẽr), *n.*

ob-lique' (ŏb-lēk' ; -līk'), *a.* [3] Neither perpendicular nor horizontal ; slanting. — **oblique angle,** an acute or obtuse angle. — **-ly,** *adv.* — **-ness,** *n.*

ob-liq'ui-ty (-lĭk'wĭ-tĭ), *n.; pl.* -TIES (-tĭz). **1.** State of being oblique. **2.** Deviation from moral rectitude or sound thinking. [out ; efface.|

ob-lit'er-ate (-lĭt'ẽr-āt), *v. t.* [1] To erase or blot|

ob-lit'er-a'tion (ŏb-lĭt'ẽr-ā'shŭn), *n.* An obliterating, or state of being obliterated ; extinction.

ob-liv'i-on (-lĭv'ĭ-ŭn), *n.* **1.** A forgetting, or fact of having forgotten. **2.** State of being forgotten.

ob-liv'i-ous (-ŭs), *a.* [4] **1.** Forgetful. **2.** Causing forgetfulness. — **-ly,** *adv.* [8] — **-ness,** *n.* [8].

ob'long (ŏb'lŏng), *a.* Longer in one direction than in another, with sides parallel or nearly so. — *n.* An oblong figure, esp. when a rectangle.

ob'lo-quy (-lō-kwĭ),*n.; pl.* -QUIES (-kwĭz). **1.** Censorious speech ; blame. **2.** State of being under censure ; disgrace.

---

ob-nox'ious (ŏb-nŏk'shŭs), _a._ [4] Objectionable; odious. — **-ly**, _adv._ [8] — **-ness**, _n._ [8].

o'boe (ō'boi ; ō'bȯ-ā), _n._ One of the higher wind

Oboe.

instruments in the modern orchestra.

ob-scene' (ŏb-sēn'), _a._ [3] **1.** Foul; filthy. _Archaic._ **2.** Offensive to chastity or modesty; impure. — **ob-scene'ly**, _adv._ [8].

ob-scen'i-ty (-sĕn'ĭ-tĭ), _n.; pl._ -TIES (-tĭz). Obscene language or acts ; quality of being obscene.

ob'scu-ra'tion (ŏb'skū-rā'shŭn), _n._ Act of obscuring ; state of being obscured.

ob-scure' (ŏb-skūr'), _a._ [3] **1.** Shaded, or darkened; dim. **2.** Indistinctly seen; remote from observation. **3.** Not noticeable; humble. **4.** Not clear or distinct. **5.** Not easily understood; abstruse. — _v. t._ [1] To make obscure ; make dim. — **obscure'ly**, _adv._ [8] — **-ness**, _n._ [8].

ob-scu'ri-ty (ŏb-skū'rĭ-tĭ), _n.; pl._ -TIES (-tĭz). Quality or state of being obscure.

ob'se-quies (ŏb'sē-kwĭz), _n. pl._ Last duties rendered to one after death; funeral ceremonies.

ob-se'qui-ous (ŏb-sē'kwĭ-ŭs), _a._ [4] Servilely or meanly attentive; cringing; fawning. — **ob-se'-qui-ous-ly**, _adv._ [8] — **-ness**, _n._ [8].

ob-serv'a-ble (ŏb-zûr'vá-b'l), _a._ [4] **1.** That must or may be observed; as, forms _observable_ in social life. **2.** Capable of being observed.

ob-serv'ance (-vǎns), _n._ **1.** Act or practice of observing a rule, custom, or the like. **2.** An act or ceremony, as of worship; a form; practice; custom. **3.** Observation.

ob-serv'ant (-vǎnt), _a._ [4] Taking notice; observing ; watchful ; attentive ; heedful.

ob'ser-va'tion (ŏb'zẽr-vā'shǔn), _n._ **1.** Act, faculty, or habit of observing, or of recognizing and noting. Also, the information or record so obtained. **2.** Fact of being observed or seen. **3.** A remark.

ob-serv'a-to-ry (ŏb-zûr'vá-tô-rĭ), _n.; pl._ -RIES (-rĭz). **1.** A place equipped with instruments for observing natural, esp. astronomical, phenomena. **2.** A place or building affording a wide view.

ob-serve' (-zûrv'), _v. t._ [1] **1.** To take notice of by appropriate conduct; to keep ; comply with. **2.** To pay attention to; see. **3.** To say in a casual way; remark. — _v. i._ **1.** To take notice. **2.** To remark ; comment. — **ob-serv'er**, _n._ [8].

ob-serv'ing, _a._ [4] Observant. — **-ly**, _adv._ [8].

ob-sess' (ŏb-sĕs'), _v. t._ To beset or dominate ; — said of an evil spirit or a fixed idea.

ob-ses'sion (-sĕsh'ŭn), _n._ The fact or state of being obsessed; the persistent influence of a fixed idea.

ob-sid'i-an (ŏb-sĭd'ĭ-ăn), _n._ Volcanic glass, usually black or dark colored. [ing obsolete.

ob'so-les'cence (ŏb'sȯ-lĕs'ĕns), _n._ State of becom-

ob'so-les'cent (-ĕnt), _a._ Becoming obsolete.

ob'so-lete (ŏb'sȯ-lēt), _a._ No longer in use; fallen into disuse. [the way; obstruction.

ob'sta-cle (ŏb'stá-k'l), _n._ That which stands in

ob'sti-na-cy (ŏb'stĭ-ná-sĭ), _n.; pl._ -CIES (-sĭz). **1.** Firm and, usually, unreasonable adherence to an opinion or purpose; stubbornness. **2.** Quality or state of being difficult to remedy or relieve.

ob'sti-nate (-nǎt), _a._ [4] **1.** Pertinaciously adhering to an opinion. purpose, or course; stubborn. **2.** Not easily overcome. — **-ly**, _adv._ [8].

ob-strep'er-ous (ŏb-strĕp'ẽr-ŭs), _a._ [4] Noisy, esp. in opposition to control ; clamorous ; vociferous. — **-ly**, _adv._ [8] — **-ness**, _n._ [8].

ob-struct' (ŏb-strŭkt'), _v. t._ **1.** To block up; place an obstacle in, or fill with obstacles, as a way or passage. **2.** To be, or come, in the way of; impede ; retard. **3.** To cut off the sight of (an object). — **ob-struct'er**, **ob-struc'tor**, _n._ [8].

ob-struc'tion (-strŭk'shŭn), _n._ **1.** An obstructing; state of being obstructed. **2.** That which obstructs or impedes; hindrance ; barrier.

ob-struc'tion-ist, _n._ One who hinders progress; one who obstructs business.

ob-struc'tive (-tĭv), _a._ [4] Tending to obstruct.

ob-tain' (ŏb-tān'), _v. t._ To get hold of by effort ; gain possession of ; acquire; procure. — _v. i._ To become recognized or established; become or be prevalent or general. — **a-ble**, _a._ [8].

ob-trude' (ŏb-trōōd'), _v. t._ [1] To thrust impertinently upon another. — _v. i._ To thrust one's self upon a company or upon attention; intrude. — **ob-trud'er** (-trōōd'ẽr), _n._ [8].

ob-tru'sion (-trōō'zhŭn), _n._ Act of obtruding.

ob-tru'sive (-sĭv), _a._ [4] Disposed to obtrude; intrusive. — **-ly**, _adv._ [8] — **-ness**, _n._ [8].

ob-tuse' (ŏb-tūs'), _a._ [3] **1.** Not pointed or acute; blunt; — applied esp. to angles greater than a right angle. See ANGLE, _Illust._ **2.** Not having acute perceptions; stupid. — **-ly**, _adv._ — **-ness**, _n._ [8].

ob-verse' (ŏb-vûrs' ; ŏb'vûrs), _a._ **1.** Facing the observer ; — opp. of _reverse_. **2.** Having the base narrower than the top, as a leaf. — **-ly**, _adv._ [8].

ob'verse (ŏb'vûrs), _n._ The front or principal surface of anything ; esp., the side of a coin bearing the principal image or inscription.

ob'vi-ate (ŏb'vĭ-āt), _v. t._ [1] To meet or anticipate and dispose of. [being obviated.

ob'vi-a'tion (-ā'shŭn), _n._ Act of obviating; state of

ob'vi-ous (ŏb'vĭ-ŭs), _a._ [4] Easily seen or understood ; plain. — **-ly**, _adv._ — **-ness**, _n._

oc-ca'sion (ŏ-kā'zhŭn), _n._ **1.** A favorable opportunity; a timely chance. **2.** A contributory or incidental cause. **3.** Need; necessity; exigency. **4.** An occurrence. **5.** A special event or function. — _v. t._ To give occasion to ; cause.

oc-ca'sion-al (-ăl), _a._ [4] Of or pertaining to an occasion or occasions ; casual ; incidental ; as, _occasional_ remarks. — **-al-ly**, _adv._ [8].

oc'ci-dent (ŏk'sĭ-dĕnt), _n._ **1.** The west ; — opposed to _orient_. **2.** [_cap._] Europe as opposed to Asia and the Orient; also, the Western Hemisphere.

oc'ci-den'tal (-dĕn'tăl), _a._ Of, pertaining to, or situated in, the occident ; — opposed to _oriental_.

oc'ci-put (ŏk'sĭ-pŭt), _n.; L. pl._ OCCIPITA (ŏk-sĭp'ĭ-tá). _Anat._ The back part of the head or skull.

oc-cult' (ŏ-kŭlt'), _a._ [3] Hidden; secret; hence, mysterious or supernatural. — **-ly**, _adv._ [8].

oc'cul-ta'tion (ŏk'ŭl-tā'shŭn), _n._ _Astron._ The hiding from view of one heavenly body by another, as an eclipse of a star or planet by the moon.

oc'cu-pan-cy (ŏk'ū-pǎn-sĭ), _n._ Occupation (in sense 1).

oc'cu-pant (-pǎnt), _n._ One who occupies.

oc'cu-pa'tion (-pā'shŭn), *n.* **1.** Act or process of occupying; state of being occupied; occupancy; tenure. **2.** One's principal business in life; trade.

oc'cu-pi'er (ŏk'ū-pī'ẽr), *n.* One who occupies.

oc'cu-py (-pī), *v. t.* [2] **1.** To take or hold possession of; fill. **3.** To engage the service of; employ; busy. **2.** To take up the space or time of; fill. **3.** To engage the service of; employ; busy.

oc-cur' (ŏ-kŭr'), *v. i.; -CURRED* (-kŭrd'); *-CUR'RING* (-kŭr'ĭng). **1.** To present itself; appear; happen. **2.** To come to the mind; suggest itself.

oc-cur'rence (ŏ-kŭr'ĕns), *n.* A coming or happening; incident; event.

o'cean (ō'shăn), *n.* **1.** The whole body of salt water on the surface of the globe; the sea. **2.** One of the large bodies of water into which the great ocean is regarded as divided, as the Atlantic and Pacific *oceans.* **3.** An immense or limitless expanse or quantity; as, the *ocean* of eternity.

o'ce-an'ic (ō'shē-ăn'ĭk), *a.* Of or pertaining to, found in or about, or produced by, the ocean.

o'ce-lot (ō'sē-lŏt), *n.* An American cat, ranging from Texas to Patagonia, yellow or gray with markings of black.

o'cher (ō'kẽr), *n.* [6] An earthy ore of iron, usually red or yellow, used as a pigment.

o'-clock' (ŏ-klŏk'). Of (by) the clock.

oc'ta-gon (ŏk'tȧ-gŏn), *n.* Polygon of eight sides.

oc-tag'o-nal (ŏk-tăg'ō-năl), *a.* Eight-sided.

oc'ta-he'dral (ŏk'tȧ-hē'drăl), *a.* Having eight plane faces.

oc'ta-he'dron (-hē'drŏn), *n. Geom.* A solid having eight plane faces.

oc'tave (ŏk'tăv), *n. Music.* **a** An interval of eight diatonic steps. **b** The eighth tone in a scale, or one of successive eighth tones. **c** The harmonic combination of two tones an Octahedron. octave apart. **d** The notes comprised in this interval. — *a.* Consisting of eight; eight.

oc-ta'vo (ŏk-tā'vō; ŏk-tä'-), *n.; pl.* -vos (-vōz). A book of sheets folded each into eight leaves; hence, a size of book so made; — usually written 8vo or 8°. — *a.* Having eight leaves to a sheet.

Oc-to'ber (-tō'bẽr), *n.* The tenth month of the year, having thirty-one days.

oc'to-ge-na'ri-an (ŏk'tō-jē-nā'rĭ-ăn), *a.* Between eighty and ninety years old; of or pertaining to such age. — *n.* An octogenarian person.

oc'to-pus (ŏk'tō-pŭs; ŏk-tō'pŭs), *n.; pl.* E. *-PUSES* (-pŭs-ĕz); L. *-PI* (-tō'pī). **1.** Any of various eight-armed sea animals related to the squids and cuttlefishes. Most species are small, and inoffensive, but some are large. **2.** Something suggestive of an octopus; esp., a powerful and grasping organization with many branches.

oc'to-roon' (ŏk'tō-rōōn'), *n.* The offspring of a quadroon and a white person.

oc'u-lar (ŏk'ū-lȧr), *a.* **1.** Depending on, or perceived by, the eye; seeing or having seen. **2.** Of or pertaining to the eye or eyesight; visual.

oc'u-list (ŏk'ū-lĭst), *n.* An eye doctor.

odd (ŏd), *a.* [3] **1.** Not paired with another; without a mate. **2.** Not divisible by 2 without a remainder; — opposed to *even.* **3.** Left over after a definite round number has been taken or been mentioned; extra. **4.** Not belonging, or no longer belonging, to any particular set, group, or assortment. **5.** Unusual; singular.

odd'i-ty (ŏd'ĭ-tĭ), *n.; pl.* -TIES (-tĭz). **1.** Quality of being odd. **2.** That which is odd or peculiar.

odd'ly, *adv.* In an odd manner.

odd'ness, *n.* State of being odd; also, an oddity.

odds (ŏdz), *n. pl. & sing.* **1.** Difference in favor of one as against another; advantage; hence, excess of chances; probability. **2.** An equalizing allowance given to a contestant or opponent that is at a disadvantage; as, to give or take *odds.* **3.** Quarrel; dissension; — chiefly in *at* odds. — *odds and ends,* remnants; miscellaneous odd articles.

ode (ōd), *n.* A short poem expressive of noble sentiment with appropriate dignity of style.

o'di-ous (ō'dĭ-ŭs), *a.* [4] Deserving of or provoking hatred or repugnance. — **-ly,** *adv.* — **-ness,** *n.*

o'di-um (-ŭm), *n.* **1.** Hatred; state or fact of being hated; abhorrence; antipathy. **2.** The reproach attaching to what is hateful; opprobrium.

o-dom'e-ter (ō-dŏm'ē-tẽr), *n.* Instrument attached to a vehicle to measure distance traversed.

o'dor (ō'dẽr), *n.* [5] **1.** Any smell or scent, fragrant or otherwise. **2.** Repute; estimation; as, to be in bad *odor.* [usually, fragrant.]

o'dor-if'er-ous (-ĭf'ẽr-ŭs), *a.* [4] Yielding an odor; fragrant.

o'dor-less, *a.* Free from odor.

o'dor-ous (-ŭs), *a.* [4] Having an odor, esp. a sweet odor; fragrant. — **-ly,** *adv.* — **-ness,** *n.*

o'er (ōr), *prep. & adv.* For OVER. *Poetic or Dial.*

of (ŏv; *unaccented* ŏv), *prep.* **1.** From, as in origin, source, departure, deprivation, etc.; as, *of* noble blood; north *of,* etc.; to cure *of,* rid *of.* **2.** As a result of. **3.** Belonging or related to. **4.** Indicating composition, description, etc.; as, a throne *of* gold. **5.** About; concerning. **6.** During; in; on. *Obs. or Archaic & Colloq.,* except in *of late; of old,* etc.

off (ŏf), *adv.* Away so as not to be on, against, near, present, in existence, etc. *Naut.,* away from the land, shore, ship, or wind. — *off and on,* intermittently; now and then; also, alternately. — *a.* **1.** Away; gone. **2.** Of animals, vehicles, etc., on the right. **3.** Away from the fact, normal condition, or standard. **4.** Circumstanced, esp. materially; as, well *off.* — *prep.* **1.** Away from, as to departure, source, material, etc.; as, take it *off* the table. **2.** Not in condition for; as, *off* his feed **3.** *Naut.* To seaward of. — *interj.* Begone!

of'fal (ŏf'ăl), *n.* **1.** The waste parts of a butchered animal. **2.** Anything thrown away as worthless; carrion; refuse; rubbish; garbage.

off'cast (ŏf'kȧst'), *p. a.* Cast off; rejected. — *n.* One that is cast off or rejected.

off'-col'or, *a.* [5] **1.** Not of proper or natural color; below standard. **2.** Of doubtful propriety.

of-fence' Var. of OFFENSE.

of-fend' (ŏ-fĕnd'), *v. i.* To transgress the moral or divine law; sin. — *v. t.* **1.** *Biblical.* To cause to stumble; cause to sin or fall. *Obs.* **2.** To displease; make angry; affront. — **-er,** *n.* [8].

of-fense' (ŏ-fĕns'), *n.* **1.** Act of offending; state of being offended. **2.** Act of attacking; assault. **3.** Act of displeasing or affronting; state of being displeased, affronted, etc.; displeasure. **4.** A crime; sin; misdeed.

of-fen'sive (ŏ-fĕn'sĭv), a. [4] **1.** Making attack; pertaining to offense or attack; fitted for, or used in, attacking. **2.** Giving offense;insulting. **3.** Disagreeable; displeasing; disgusting.— n. State or posture of one who makes attack; aggressive attitude.— **-ly**, adv. [8] — **-ness**, n. [8].

of'fer (ŏf'ĕr), v.t. **1.** To present, as an act of worship; sacrifice. **2.** To tender; proffer. **3.** To propose; suggest. **4.** To try to inflict, make, or do; hence, to do, make, or give.— v.i. **1.** To present something in worship or devotion; sacrifice. **2.** To present itself; come to hand.— n. Act of offering or proposing; a proffer; proposal; bid.— **of'fer-er**, n. [8].

of'fer-ing, n. **1.** Act of one who offers; a proffering. **2.** That which is offered; a sacrifice; gift.

of'fer-to-ry (-tô-rĭ), n.; pl. -RIES (-rĭz). [Often cap.] Eccl. A passage sung, said, or played in connection with an offering, or that part of the service at which offerings are received. Hence, a collection of money taken at a religious service.

off'hand' (ŏf'hănd'), adv. Without previous study or preparation; extempore.

off'hand' (ŏf'hănd'), a. [4] Done or made offhand.

of'fice (ŏf'ĭs), n. **1.** Anything done for another; service. **2.** Special, proper, or assigned service, duty, or function; position of trust, as in the public service. **3.** A ceremony; rite. **4.** Eccl. Any prescribed service or form of worship. **5.** A place where professional business is transacted; the room or department in an establishment where the clerical work is done.

of'fi-cer (-sĕr), n. One who holds an office. — v.t. **1.** To furnish with officers. **2.** To command or direct as an officer.

of-fi'cial (ŏ-fĭsh'ăl), a. [4] Of, or pertaining to, holding, or derived from, an office; hence, authorized; authoritative. — n. One holding, or invested with, an office. — **of-fi'cial-ly**, adv. [8].

of-fi'cial-ism (-ĭz'm), n. Action characteristic of an official; also, strict adherence to office routine.

of-fi'ci-ate (-ĭ-āt), v.i. [1] To perform divine service; to act as an officer in performing a duty.

of-fic'i-nal (ŏ-fĭs'ĭ-năl; ŏf'ĭ-sī'năl), a. Kept in stock by apothecaries; — said of drugs.

of-fi'cious (ŏ-fĭsh'ŭs), a. [4] Volunteering one's services where they are neither asked nor needed; meddlesome. — **-ly**, adv. [8] — **-ness**, n. [8].

off'ing (ŏf'ĭng), n. That part of the sea, visible from the shore, where there is deep water; also, distance, or position at a distance, from the shore.

off'ish, a. [4] Shy or distant in manner. Colloq.

off'scour'ing (ŏf'skour'ĭng), n. Refuse; cast-off filth; — usually in pl.; as, offscourings of society.

off'set' (-sĕt'), n. **1.** Bot. A short lateral shoot, which takes root at the apex and develops a new individual. **2.** Something that counterbalances or compensates for something else. **3.** A ledge formed on the face of a wall by diminishing its thickness above. **4.** An abrupt bend, as in a pipe, to get by an obstruction.

off'set' (ŏf'sĕt'; ŏf'sĕt'), v.t.; OFF'SET'; OFF'SET'-TING. **1.** To set off; balance. **2.** To form an offset. — v.i. To proceed or project as an offset.

off'shoot' (ŏf'shoot'), n. A branch, shoot, or scion of a stem, family, race, etc.

off'shore' (ŏf'shōr'), a. **1.** Moving seaward, from the shore. **2.** Situated, or operating, offshore. — (ŏf'shōr'), adv. Out from the shore.

off'spring' (ŏf'sprĭng'), n. That which springs from something; produce; issue; progeny.

oft (ŏft), adv. Often. Archaic or Poetic.

of'ten (ŏf'n), adv. Frequently.

of'ten-times (-tīmz'), adv. Often.

o'gle (ō'g'l), v.t. [1] **1.** To view with amorous or inviting glances. **2.** To eye. — n. An amorous or coquettish glance or look.— **o'gler**, n. [8].

o'gre (ō'gĕr), n. A fabled man-eating monster; hence, a hideous or cruel man. — **o'gre-ish** (-ĭsh), a. [8] — **o'gress** (-grĕs), n. fem. [8].

oh (ō), interj. An exclamation expressing surprise, pain, sorrow, etc.— n.; pl. OH'S, OHS (ōz) The exclamation oh. Cf. O.

ohm (ōm), n. Elec. The practical unit of electrical resistance, being the resistance of a circuit in which a potential difference of one volt produces a current of one ampere.

oil (oil), n. **1.** Any of a large class of substances, usually liquid, of a smooth or greasy feel, burning easily, and soluble in ether, but not in water. **2.** Any substance of an oily consistency. **3.** Art. Oil color. — **oil of vitriol**. See SULPHURIC ACID. — v.t. To smear or lubricate with oil. — **oil'er**, n.

oil cake. A cake or mass of cottonseed, hempseed, etc., from which the oil has been expressed.

oil'cloth' (oil'klôth'), n. Cloth treated with oil or paint, and used for garments, floor covering, etc.

oil'i-ness (-nĕs), n. Quality or state of being oily.

oil'skin' (-skĭn'), n. **1.** Cloth made waterproof by oil. **2.** pl. Clothing or suit of oilskin.

oil'stone' (-stōn'), n. A whetstone used with oil.

oil'y (-ĭ), a. [3] **1.** Of, pertaining to, containing, or like, oil; unctuous. **2.** Covered with oil; greasy. **3.** Bland; fawning; as, an oily tongue.

oint'ment (oint'mĕnt), n. That which serves to anoint; an unguent.

o-ka'pi (ō-kä'pē), n. An African animal closely related to the giraffe.

Okapi. ⅛

o'kra (ō'krä; ōk'rä), n. A tall plant of the mallow family, widely cultivated in the South for its mucilaginous green pods; also, the pod or pods, used as a vegetable.

old (ōld), a.; OLD'ER (ōl'dĕr) or ELD'ER; OLD'EST or ELD'EST. **1.** Not young; advanced far in years or life. **2.** Of, pertaining to, or characteristic of, old age or the aged. **3.** Not new or fresh; long used; hence, worn out. **4.** Having (a certain) age; as, forty years old. **5.** Experienced. **6.** Longstanding; not new or modern. **7.** A colloquial term of familiarity or affection; as, Old England. **8.** Ancient; former; antiquated. — **Old Glory**, flag of the United States. Colloq. — **o. maid**. An elderly or confirmed spinster. — **O. Testament**. See under TESTAMENT. — **O. World**, the Eastern Hemisphere.

old (ōld), *n.* Old or former time ; as, days of *old*.

old'en (ōl'd'n), *a.* Old ; ancient.

old'–fash'ioned (ōld'făsh'ŭnd), *a.* Adhering to old customs or ideas.

old'–world', *a.* **1.** Of or pertaining to the old, or ancient, world. **2.** [In this sense written *Old World*.] Of, pertaining to, or characteristic of, the Old World, or Eastern Hemisphere.

o'le-ag'i-nous (ō'lē-ăj'ĭ-nŭs), *a.* [4] Oily ; unctuous. — **o'le-ag'i-nous-ness,** *n.* [8].

o'le-an'der (-ăn'dēr), *n.* An evergreen poisonous shrub with fragrant red or white flowers.

o'le-as'ter (-ăs'tēr), *n.* **1.** A shrub or small tree of southern Europe with fragrant yellow flowers and bitter olive-shaped fruit. **2.** The wild olive.

o'le-o-mar'ga-rine (-ō-mär'gȧ-rēn ; -rĭn : *often mispronounced* -mär'jēr-ēn), *n.* Also **-rin.** A butter substitute made largely from animal fats.

ol-fac'to-ry (ŏl-făk'tō-rĭ), *a. Anat.* Of or pertaining to the sense of smell ; as, an *olfactory* nerve.

ol'i-garch (ŏl'ĭ-gärk), *n.* A ruler in an oligarchy.

ol'i-gar'chy (-gär'kĭ), *n. ; pl.* -chies (-kĭz). Form of government in which the power is vested in a few ; state so governed ; also, the ruling few. — **ol'i-gar'chic** (-gär'kĭk), **-gar'chi-cal** (-kĭ-kăl), *a.*

ol'ive (ŏl'ĭv), *n.* **1.** A certain tree cultivated for its fruit ; also, the fruit, esteemed as a relish, esp. when green, and for its oil. **2.** An olive branch or wreath. **3.** Olive color. — *a.* **1.** Of a dark brownish or yellowish green like the unripe olive. **2.** Brownish yellow ; tawny, as a complexion.

olive branch. A branch of the olive tree, considered an emblem of peace.

O-lym'pi-an (ō-lĭm'pĭ-ăn), *a.* Pert. to Mount Olympus, home of the gods, in Thessaly, or to Olympia in the Peloponnesus, Greece, where the **Olympian** games were held every fourth year, from 776 B. C. (as claimed). The Greeks reckoned time in Olympiads, or periods of four years, from that date. The ancient games were revived in modified form in 1896 and are held internationally every four years, the first at Athens, in 1896.

O-lym'pic (-pĭk), *a.* Olympian.

om'e-let (ŏm'ē-lĕt ; ŏm'lĕt), *n.* Eggs beaten up with milk and, often, other ingredients, and fried.

o'men (ō'mĕn), *n.* An indication or action taken as a foreshowing ; foreboding ; augury. — *v. t.* To foreshow by signs or portents ; presage ; augur.

o-men'tum (ō-mĕn'tŭm), *n. ; pl.* -ta (-tȧ). *Anat.* A free fold of the peritoneum. The great **omentum** is attached to the stomach and transverse colon, the lesser o. connects the stomach and liver.

om'i-nous (ŏm'ĭ-nŭs), *a.* [4] Foreboding evil ; inauspicious. — **-ly,** *adv.* [8] — **-ness,** *n.* [8].

o-mis'sion (ō-mĭsh'ŭn), *n.* **1.** An omitting ; neglect to do something. **2.** That which is omitted.

o-mit' (ō-mĭt'), *v. t. ;* o-mit'ted, -ting. **1.** To leave out or unmentioned. **2.** To leave undone.

om'ni-bus (ŏm'nĭ-bŭs), *n.* A large heavy four-wheeled public vehicle ; a bus. — *a.* Pertaining to, or providing for, many things at once.

om-nip'o-tence (ŏm-nĭp'ō-tĕns), *n.* Omnipotent quality, state, or power ; [*cap.*] the Deity.

om-nip'o-tent (-tĕnt), *a.* Able in every way and for every work ; all-powerful. — *n.* One who is omnipotent ; [*cap.*, with *the*] God. — **-ly,** *adv.* [8].

om'ni-pres'ence (ŏm'nĭ-prĕz'ĕns), *n.* Quality of being omnipresent ; ubiquity. [at once.|

om'ni-pres'ent (-prĕz'ĕnt), *a.* Present everywhere

om-nis'cience (ŏm-nĭsh'ĕns), *n.* Quality of being omniscient ; hence, [*cap.*, with *the*] God.

om-nis'cient (-ĕnt), *a.* Having universal knowledge ; infinitely knowing or wise. — **-ly,** *adv.* [8].

om-niv'o-rous (ŏm-nĭv'ō-rŭs), *a.* Eating everything ; esp., *Zoöl.*, eating both animal and vegetable food. — **-ly,** *adv.* [8] — **-ness,** *n.* [8].

on (ŏn), *prep. On*, in general, refers to contact with or to support beneath ; as : **1.** Over and in contact with ; upon. **2.** In contact with (with or without support) ; as, a town *on* the river. **3.** In connection or activity with, in, or in respect of. **4.** Indicating a basis or ground of action, opinion, reliance, etc. **5.** In, or relating to, the region towards ; at. **6.** In, within, or during. **7.** Indicating state ; as, *on* fire, sale. **8.** Upon the occasion of. **9.** To or against. **10.** In reference or relation to ; about. — *on* to, *on'*to, *prep.*, upon ; on ; to ; — usually called colloquial.

on, *adv.* In or into a position, relation, or state denoted by *on*, prep., as of support, progress, etc.

once (wŭns), *adv.* **1.** One time and no more. **2.** At any one time ; ever ; — often equivalent to *if ever* or *whenever ;* as, *once* learned, never forgotten. **3.** At some one time ; — usually referring to the past ; formerly. — *n.* One time or occasion ; — in phrases ; as : at once. **a** Simultaneously. **b** Immediately. — **o. in a while,** occasionally. — **o. or** twice, a few times.

one (wŭn), *a.* **1.** Being a single unit, being, or thing ; individual. **2.** Denoting a person or thing indefinitely ; a certain. **3.** Denoting a particular thing or person ; — often in antithesis to *another, other*. **4.** Closely bound together ; united. **5.** Single in kind ; the same. — *n.* **1.** A single unit ; unity. **2.** A symbol for a unit, as 1 or 1. **3.** A single person or thing ; as, *one* by *one.* — *indef. pron.* **1.** (*pl.* ones (wŭnz).) A certain person or thing not specified ; a person or thing of the kind under consideration. **2.** Any person or thing whatever ; anybody.

one'ness (-nĕs), *n.* Singleness ; unity ; sameness.

on'er-ous (ŏn'ēr-ŭs), *a.* [4] Burdensome ; oppressive. — **-ly,** *adv.* [8] — **-ness,** *n.* [8].

one'self' (wŭn'sĕlf'), *pron.* A reflexive and emphatic form for the indefinite pronoun *one*.

one'–sid'ed (wŭn'sīd'ĕd), *a.* [4] Having, or occurring on, one side only ; having one side prominent or more developed ; hence, partial ; unfair.

on'ion (ŭn'yŭn), *n.* A plant of the lily family having a pungent edible bulb ; also, its bulb.

on'ly (ōn'lĭ), *a.* **1.** Alone in its or their class ; single. **2.** Alone because of superiority ; preëminent ; chief. — *adv.* **1.** Exclusively ; solely ; merely. **2.** Without there being others ; singly. *Obs. or R.*, exc. in only-begotten, begotten as the only child. — *conj.* Save or except (that).

on'rush' (ŏn'rŭsh'), *n.* A rushing onward.

on'set' (ŏn'sĕt'), *n.* An attack ; assault.

on'slaught' (-slôt'), *n.* A furious attack or assault.

on'to (ŏn'tōō), *prep.* See *on* to, under on, *prep.*

o'nus (ō'nŭs), *n.* A burden ; an obligation.

on'ward (ŏn'wērd), *a.* Moving forward ; forward.

---

chair ; go ; sing, iŋk ; then, thin ; nature, verdure ; yet ; zh = z in azure. Numbers refer to §§ in the Special Notes which, with Abbreviations, Signs, etc., precede the Vocabulary.

on′ward (ŏn′wẽrd), *adv.* **1.** Toward a point before or in front; forward. **2.** In an advanced position; in front.

on′wards (-wẽrdz). Var. of ONWARD, *adv.*

on′yx (ŏn′ĭks; ō′nĭks), *n.; pl.* ONYXES (-ĕz). Chalcedony in layers of different shades of color.

o′ö-lite (ō′ö-līt), *n.* A rock consisting of small round grains, usually carbonate of lime, resembling the roe of fish and cemented together.

ooze (ōōz), *n.* **1.** A decoction of oak bark, etc., used in tanning. **2.** Act of oozing; also, that which oozes. — *v. i.* [1] To percolate; exude; leak out slowly. Also fig.—*v.t.* To exude or give out slowly.

ooze (ōōz), *n.* Soft mud or slime.

oo′zy (ōō′zĭ), *a.* [3] **1.** Containing, or composed of, ooze; miry. **2.** Exuding moisture; slimy.

o-pac′i-ty (ō-păs′ĭ-tĭ), *n.* Quality or state of being opaque; obscurity or an instance of it.

o′pal (ō′păl), *n.* A form of silica, softer and lighter than quartz. The *precious*, or *noble*, *opal* is iridescent, and is valued as a gem.

o′pal-es′cence (-ĕs′ĕns), *n.* Opalescent quality.

o′pal-es′cent (-ĕs′ĕnt), *a.* [4] Giving forth a play of various colors, like an opal.

o-paque′ (ō-pāk′), *a.* [3] **1.** Not luminous; dark. **2.** Not admitting passage to light; not transparent. — *n.* That which is opaque. — **o-paque′ly**, *adv.* [8] — **o-paque′ness**, *n.* [8].

ope (ōp), *a. & v.* Open. *Poetic.*

o′pen (ō′p′n), *a.* [3] **1.** Not shut or closed; affording free ingress or egress. **2.** Hence: Free to be entered, visited, or used; also, available; disengaged. **3.** Of weather or season, not frosty or inclement. **4.** Uncovered; exposed; bare. Fig.: Liable; — with *to;* as, *open* to temptation. **5.** Not secret; public. **6.** Sincere; frank. **7.** Extended; expanded. **8.** Having openings, or the like. **9.** Accessible; — of a person: responsive; amenable; hence, generous. **10.** Not settled or adjusted. **11.** Permitted to hunters or fishermen; — of a season when game or fish may be lawfully taken. — *v. t.* **1.** To move (a gate, lid, etc.) from its shut position. **2.** To render clear for passage in or out. **3.** Hence: To render open or accessible for its especial purpose. **4.** To spread out; unfold or unroll. **5.** To make one or more openings in. **6.** To loosen or make less compact. **7.** To make more discerning; enlighten; enlarge, as the heart. **8.** To enter upon; begin. — *v. i.* **1.** To become open; unclose. **2.** To give access. **3.** To expand; fig., to become enlightened, as the mind. **4.** To become or be disclosed, as to view. **5.** To begin. — *n.* Open space, as land without trees or obstructions; open ocean, water, or air; — chiefly with *the.* — **o′pen-er**, *n.* [8].

o′pen–hand′ed, *a.* Generous; liberal.

o′pen–heart′ed, *a.* Candid; frank; generous.

o′pen-ing (ō′p′n-ĭng), *vb. n.* **1.** A making or becoming open. **2.** An open place or part; a breach; gap; hole; also, width; span. **3.** A thinly wooded space, without undergrowth, in a forest or grove. *U. S.* **4.** Act of beginning; first step or appearance. **5.** An opportunity.

o′pen-ly, *adv.* In an open manner.

o′pen-ness, *n.* Quality or state of being open.

o′pen-work′ (ō′p′n-wûrk′), *n.* Any work so made as to show openings through its substance.

|| **o′pe-ra** (ŏp′ĕ-rȧ), *n., pl.* of OPUS.

op′er-a (ŏp′ēr-ȧ), *n.* A drama wholly or mostly sung, with orchestral accompaniment and appropriate costumes, scenery, and action.

opera glass *or* **glasses.** A small telescope, usually binocular, with concave eye lenses.

op′er-ate (-āt), *v. i.* [1] **1.** To perform a work or labor; to act. **2.** To produce or take effect. **3.** To perform an operation or series of operations.—*v.t.* **1.** To produce as an effect; work. **2.** To put into, or to continue in, operation or activity; conduct.

op′er-at′ic (-ăt′ĭk), *a.* Of, pert. to, or like, opera.

op′er-a′tion (-ā′shŭn), *n.* **1.** Act, process, or effect of operating. **2.** Agency; exertion of power or influence. **3.** Mode of action or form of activity. **4.** State of being operative or in action. **5.** An act done as part of a plan. **6.** A surgical action on the living body, to produce a remedial effect, as in amputation, etc. **7.** *Math.* Some transformation to be made on quantities.

op′er-a-tive (ŏp′ēr-ȧ-tĭv), *a.* [4] **1.** Capable of acting; operating. **2.** Effective; efficacious. **3.** Involving, or having to do with, physical operations, as of the hands or of machines.— *n.* A mechanic; factory hand.

op′er-a′tor (ŏp′ēr-ā′tẽr), *n.* One that operates.

op′er-et′ta (ŏp′ēr-ĕt′ȧ), *n.; It. pl.* -TE (*It.* ō′pĕ-rĕt′tä). *Music.* A short, light, musical drama.

oph-thal′mi-a (ŏf-thăl′mĭ-ȧ), *n.* An inflammation of the membranes or coats of the eye.

oph-thal′mic (-mĭk), *a.* Of or pertaining to the eye.

o′pi-ate (ō′pĭ-āt), *n.* Any narcotic medicine containing, or derived from, opium.

o-pine′ (ō-pīn′), *v. t. & i.* [1] To have or express an opinion; think; suppose.

o-pin′ion (ō-pĭn′yŭn), *n.* **1.** That which is opined; a belief. **2.** A formal judgment by an expert.

o-pin′ion-at′ed (-āt′ĕd), *a.* [4] Stiff in adhering to one's own opinion; obstinate.

o′pi-um (ō′pĭ-ŭm), *n.* A powerful narcotic drug prepared from the juice of a species of poppy.

o-pos′sum (ō-pŏs′ŭm), *n.* An American animal, with a pouch beneath for carrying the young. When caught it feigns death.

op-po′nent (ŏ-pō′nĕnt),*a.* [4] Opposite; hence, adverse. — *n.* One who opposes; an adversary.

op′por-tune′ (ŏp′ŏr-tūn′), *a.* [4] Fit; ready; hence, seasonable; timely. — **-ly**, *adv.* — **-ness**, *n.*

op′por-tu′nism (ŏp′ŏr-tū′nĭz′m), *n.* The taking advantage, as in politics, of opportunities, often with little regard for principles or consequences.

op′por-tu′nist, *n.* One who practices opportunism.

op′por-tu′ni-ty (-nĭ-tĭ), *n.; pl.* -TIES (-tĭz). Fit or convenient time; chance.

op-pos′a-ble (ŏ-pōz′ȧ-b'l), *a.* Capable of being placed opposite something else.

op-pose′ (ŏ-pōz′), *v. t.* [1] **1.** To put or set in opposition; set against. **2.** To resist; confront. — **op-pos′er** (ŏ-pōz′ẽr), *n.* [8].

op′po-site (ŏp′ō-zĭt),*a.* **1.** Set over against; facing. **2.** Contrarily turned or moving. **3.** Diametrically different; contrary. — *n.* That which is opposed, or contrary. — **op′po-site-ly**, *adv.* [8] — **-ness**, *n.* [8].

op′po-si′tion (ŏp′ō-zĭsh′ŭn), *n.* **1.** Act of setting opposite, or the state of being so set. **2.** Resist-

---

ance. **3.** That which opposes; obstacle; in politics, the party opposed to the party in power.

op-press' (ŏ-prĕs'), *v. t.* **1.** Fig.: To weigh heavily on; weigh down; as, to be *oppressed* with care. **2.** To crush by abuse of power; tyrannize over.

op-pres'sion (-prĕsh'ŭn), *n.* **1.** Act of oppressing; state of being oppressed. **2.** That which oppresses; cruelty; tyranny.

op-pres'sive (ŏ-prĕs'ĭv), *a.* [4] **1.** Unreasonably burdensome; unjustly severe. **2.** Heavy; hard to be borne; as, *oppressive* heat. — **-ly,** *adv.* — **-ness,** *n.*

op-pres'sor (ŏ-prĕs'ẽr), *n.* One that oppresses.

op-pro'bri-ous (ŏ-prō'brĭ-ŭs), *a.* [4] **1.** Expressive of opprobrium; scurrilous. **2.** Infamous; despised; made hateful. — **-ly,** *adv.* [8] — **-ness,** *n.* [8].

op-pro'bri-um (-ŭm), *n.* **1.** Infamy; reproach mingled with contempt. **2.** Cause of disgrace.

op-pugn' (ŏ-pūn'), *v. t. & i.* To fight against; attack; resist; as, to *oppugn* a belief.

op'tic (ŏp'tĭk), *a.* **1.** Ocular. **2.** Relating to optics. — **optic nerve,** the nerve connecting the eye and the optic centers of the brain. — *n.* The eye.

op'ti-cal (ŏp'tĭ-kăl), *a.* **1.** Relating to optics. **2.** Relating to vision; optic. — **-ly,** *adv.* [8].

op-ti'cian (ŏp-tĭsh'ŭn), *n.* One who makes, or deals in, optical glasses and instruments.

op'tics (ŏp'tĭks), *n.* Science dealing with light and vision.

op'ti-mism (-tĭ-mĭz'm), *n.* **1.** Doctrine that everything is ordered for the best. **2.** Disposition to take the most hopeful view; — opp. to *pessimism.*

op'ti-mist (-tĭ-mĭst), *n.* One who looks on the bright side of things; — opposed to *pessimist.*

op'ti-mis'tic (-mĭs'tĭk), **op'ti-mis'ti-cal** (-tĭ-kăl), *a.* [4] Of or pertaining to optimism; hopeful. — **op'ti-mis'ti-cal-ly,** *adv.* [8].

op'ti-mum (ŏp'tĭ-mŭm), *n.* The best or most favorable condition for the growth of an organism.

op'tion (ŏp'shŭn), *n.* **1.** Act of choosing; choice. **2.** Power or right of choosing. **3.** That which is offered for choice, or which is chosen. **4.** A stipulated privilege, in some contracts, of demanding the fulfillment of the contract on any day within a specified limit. [pulsory.]

op'tion-al (-ăl), *a.* Involving an option; not com-

op'u-lence (-û-lĕns), *n.* Wealth; riches; affluence.

op'u-lent (-lĕnt), *a.* [4] Having large means; rich; hence, luxuriant, profuse, etc.

‖ **o'pus** (ō'pŭs), *n.; pl.* OPERA (ŏp'ĕ-rȧ). [L.] A work; esp., a musical composition.

or (ôr), *conj.* A coördinating conjunction that marks an alternative.

or'a-cle (ŏr'ȧ-k'l), *n.* **1.** *Class. Antiq.* The medium, as a priest, by which a god reveals divine knowledge; also, the place where the revelation is given. **2.** Response of an oracle to a question or petition. **3.** One who gives oracular decisions.

o-rac'u-lar (ô-răk'û-lȧr), *a.* [4] **1.** Of or pertaining to an oracle; forecasting the future. **2.** Resembling an oracle, as in solemnity, authority, or ambiguity. — **-ly,** *adv.* [8] — **-ness,** *n.* [8].

o'ral (ō'rȧl), *a.* **1.** Uttered by the mouth; spoken. **2.** Using speech or the lips; as, an *oral* teacher. **3.** Of or pertaining to the mouth. — **-ly,** *adv.* [8].

or'ange (ŏr'ĕnj), *n.* **1.** The large, globose fruit of an evergreen tree with oval leaves and fragrant white flowers; also, the tree. **2.** Any of several trees or fruits more or less resembling the orange. **3.** The color of the orange; reddish yellow. — *a.* Of or pertaining to an orange; of orange color.

o-rang'–u-tan' (ô-răng'ōō-tăn'; -tăng'; ō'răng-ō-rang'–ou-tang'} ōō'tăn), *n.* A manlike ape about two thirds as large as the gorilla.

o-ra'tion (ô-rā'shŭn), *n.* An elaborate discourse, esp. on some special occasion.

or'a-tor (ŏr'ȧ-tẽr), *n.* A public speaker, esp. one distinguished for skill and power.

or'a-tor'i-cal (-tŏr'ĭ-kăl), *a.* [4] Of or pertaining to an orator or oratory. — **-ly,** *adv.* [8].

or'a-to'ri-o (ŏr'ȧ-tō'rĭ-ō), *n.; pl.* -RIOS (-ōz). *Music.* A dramatic text or poem, usually on some Biblical theme, set to music, with orchestral accompaniment, but without action, scenery, or costume.

or'a-to-ry (ŏr'ȧ-tō-rĭ), *n.* Art of an orator.

or'a-to-ry, *n.; pl.* -RIES (-rĭz). A place of prayer; esp., a small chapel or room for private devotions.

orb (ôrb), *n.* **1.** A sphere; esp., a celestial sphere. **2.** A globe; *Poetic,* the eye. — *v. t. & i.* **1.** To form into a globe or disk. **2.** To encircle. *Poetic.*

or-bic'u-lar (ôr-bĭk'û-lȧr), *a.* Spherical; circular.

or'bit (ôr'bĭt), *n.* **1.** *Anat.* The eye socket. **2.** *Astron.* The path of a heavenly body in its revolution around another body.

or'bit-al (-bĭ-tăl), *a.* Of or pertaining to an orbit.

or'chard (ôr'chẽrd), *n.* An inclosure containing fruit trees; also, the trees collectively.

or'ches-tra (ôr'kĕs-trȧ), *n.* **1.** In a modern theater, etc., the space used by a company of instrumental performers. Also, the forward part, sometimes all, of the main floor in a theater. **2.** *Music.* A company of performers on various instruments, including esp. those of the viol class.

or-ches'tral (ôr-kĕs'trăl; ôr'kĕs-trăl), *a.* Of, suitable to, or performed by, an orchestra.

or'ches-tra'tion (ôr'kĕs-trā'shŭn), *n.* The arrangement of music for an orchestra.

or'chid (ôr'kĭd), *n.* Any plant of a family having entire sheathing leaves and usually showy flowers.

or-dain' (ôr-dān'), *v. t.* **1.** To invest with ministerial functions; introduce into the Christian ministry. **2.** To decree; destine; predestine.

or'de-al (ôr'dē-ăl; -dēl), *n.* **1.** A primitive means to determine guilt or innocence by imposing dangerous or painful tests supposed to be under superhuman control. **2.** Hence, any severe trial.

or'der (ôr'dẽr), *n.* **1.** A society of persons united by some common rule of obligation or honorary distinction; as: **a** A monastic society. **b** One of certain knightly fraternities. **2.** *Eccl.* **a** Any of the several grades or ranks of the Christian ministry. **b** The office or status of a person in the Christian ministry; — now usually in *pl.* and often with the epithet *holy.* **3.** A rank or class in society. **4.** A style of architecture. **5.** *Math.* Degree. **6.** *Biol.* A category of classification above the family. **7.** Regular arrangement; method; system. **8.** *Eccl.* A prescribed form of service, as for a rite. **9.** Customary mode of procedure; as, he raised a point of *order.* **10.** Conformity to law or decorum; public quiet. **11.** Condition in general; normal state. **12.** A rule or regulation; also, a command; direction. **13.** A commission to buy, sell, or supply goods, to furnish supplies, pay money, admit to a building, etc. — **in order to,** for the purpose of.—**on the o. of,** belonging to the class or kind of. — *v. t.* **1.** To regulate; dispose; direct; rule. **2.** To give an order for. **3.** To command. — *v. i.* To give orders or commands.

or'der-li-ness (ôr'dẽr-lĭ-něs), *n.* Orderly condition or quality.

or'der-ly, *a.* [4] **1.** In order; regular. **2.** Observant of order or rule; hence, obedient; quiet. **3.** Performed in good order; well-regulated. **4.** Keeping order; conveying orders.— *adv.* Methodically.— *n.; pl.* -LIES(-lĭz). **1.** *Mil.* A noncommissioned officer or soldier who attends a superior officer. **2.** A hospital attendant.

or'di-nal (ôr'dĭ-năl), *a.* **1.** Indicating order or succession. **2.** Of or pert. to an order, as of plants, etc. — *n.* **1.** [*Often cap.*] A book containing certain church services. **2.** An ordinal number, as first, second, etc.

or'di-nance (-năns), *n.* **1.** That which is decreed or ordained, as by God or fate. **2.** Established rule; esp., any public rule or law. **3.** A prescribed practice; *Eccl.,* an established rite or ceremony.

or'di-na-ri-ly, *adv.* In an ordinary manner.

or'di-na-ry (ôr'dĭ-nā-rĭ), *a.* [4] **1.** According to established order; regular. **2.** Common; usual. **3.** Of common rank, quality, or ability; not distinguished; commonplace. — *n.* **1.** That which is ordinary, as in use or character. **2.** A meal served at a fixed price; a table d'hôte meal.

or'di-na'tion (-nā'shŭn),*n.* Act of ordaining; state of being ordained; the conferring of holy orders.

ord'nance (ôrd'năns), *n.* **1.** Military supplies. **2.** Cannon; artillery.

or'dure (ôr'dụr), *n.* Filth; dung; excrement.

ore (ōr), *n.* A native mineral containing metal or metallic constituents.

or'gan (ôr'găn), *n.* **1.** *Music.* A wind instrument consisting of one or more sets of pipes, sounded by compressed air from bellows, and played by means of one or more keyboards. **2.** *Biol.* A part or structure in an animal or plant adapted to perform some specific function, as the heart, kidney, etc. **3.** An instrument, medium, or faculty by which an action is performed. **4.** A medium of communication, as a newspaper.

or'gan-die (ôr'găn-dĭ),*n.* A kind of fine thin muslin, plain or figured, used for dresses.

or'gan-dy

or-gan'ic (ôr-găn'ĭk), *a.* [4] **1.** Of or pertaining to an organ or a system of organs. **2.** Pertaining to, or derived from, living organisms. **3.** Pertaining to, or inherent in, a certain organization or structure; constitutional.— **or-gan'i-cal-ly,** *adv.*

or'gan-ism (ôr'găn-ĭz'm), *n.* **1.** Organization. **2.** *Biol.* Any animal or plant. **3.** Something likened to a physical organism; *as,* the social *organism.*

or'gan-ist (-ĭst), *n.* A player on the organ.

or'gan-i-za'tion (-ĭ-zā'shŭn),*n.* **1.** Act or process of organizing. **2.** State or manner of being organized; organic structure. **3.** Any organic whole.

or'gan-ize (ôr'găn-īz), *v. t.* [1] **1.** To make organic ; as, certain plants are highly *organized.* **2.** To arrange or constitute in interdependent parts; systematize. — **-iz'er** (-īz'ẽr), *n.* [8].

or'gy (ôr'jĭ), *n.; pl.* -GIES (-jĭz). **1.** *Gr. & Rom Antiq.* Secret rites marked by wild revelry;—usually in *pl.* **2.** Drunken revelry.

o'ri-el (ō'rĭ-ĕl), *n.* *Arch.* A bay window, esp. one polygonal in plan.

o'ri-ent (ō'rĭ-ĕnt), *a.* **1.** Eastern; Oriental. *Now Poetic.* **2.** Bright; lustrous ;—of superior pearls and gems. **3.** Rising, as the sun. — *n.* **1.** The east. *Poetic.* **2.** [*Usually cap.*] The East; esp., the countries immediately east of the Mediterranean. — (-ĕnt), *v. t.* **1.** To cause to point toward the east ; define the position of in relation to the east. **2.** To put in a correct position or relation.

O'ri-en'tal (ō'rĭ-ĕn'tăl), *a.* [4] Pertaining to the Orient, or East; Eastern.— *n.* A member of any of the native races of the Orient.

O'ri-en'tal-ism (-ĭz'm), *n.* Any trait, style, custom, etc., peculiar to Orientals.

O'ri-en'tal-ist, *n.* One versed in Oriental languages, literature, etc.

o'ri-en-tate/ (ō'rĭ-ĕn-tāt/; ō'rĭ-ĕn'tāt), *v. t.* [1] To orient.— *v. i.* To move or turn toward the east.

o'ri-en-ta'tion (-ĕn-tā'shŭn), *n.* Act or process of orienting; as : **a** The placing of a church or temple so that the altar shall be at the east end. **b** Act of facing eastward, as in worship.

or'i-fice (ôr'ĭ-fĭs), *n.* A mouth or aperture.

or'i-gin (-jĭn), *n.* **1.** The first existence or beginning; birth; hence, parentage; ancestry. **2.** That from which anything primarily proceeds.

o-rig'i-nal (ô-rĭj'ĭ-năl), *a.* [4] **1.** Of or pert. to the origin or beginning; primitive; primary. **2.** Not copied or reproduced; novel; fresh. **3.** Independent and creative; inventive.— *n.* **1.** That of which something else is a copy. **2.** An eccentric person. [being original.|

o-rig'i-nal'i-ty (-năl/ĭ-tĭ), *n.* Quality or state of

o-rig'i-nal-ly, *adv.* **1.** By virtue of origin ; primarily. **2.** At the time of origin; at first.

o-rig'i-nate (ô-rĭj'ĭ-nāt), *v. t.* [1] To give an origin to ; produce as new. — *v. i.* To have origin; begin to exist or act. — **o-rig'i-na'tor,** *n.* [8].

o-rig'i-na'tion (-nā'shŭn), *n.* An originating, or state of being originated; origin.

o'ri-ole (ō'rĭ-ōl), *n.* **1.** Any of various black and yellow birds, esp. the European golden oriole. **2.** Any of various American birds, as the *Baltimore oriole, orchard oriole,* etc., colored similarly to the golden oriole, and, like it, building hanging nests.

Golden Oriole.

$\frac{1}{6}$

O-ri'on (ō-rī'ŏn), *n.* A large and bright constellation on the celestial equator, represented on astronomical charts by the figure of a man.

or'i-son (ôr'ĭ-zŭn), *n.* A prayer. *Archaic.*

or'mo-lu (ôr'mō-lōō), *n.* A kind of brass in imitation of gold.

or'na-ment (-nȧ-mĕnt), *n.* Anything that adorns or adds beauty to ; a decoration or adornment.

or'na-ment (ôr'nȧ-mĕnt; ôr'nȧ-mĕnt/), *v. t.* To adorn; deck; embellish.

or′na-men′tal (-mĕn′tăl), a. [4] Serving to ornament; marked by ornament. — **-ly**, adv. [8].

or′na-men-ta′tion (-mĕn-tā′shŭn), n. **1.** Act of ornamenting. **2.** That which ornaments.

or-nate′ (ŏr-nāt′; ŏr′nāt), a. [4] Elaborately adorned. — **-ly**, adv. [8] — **-ness**, n. [8].

or′ni-tho-log′i-cal (ŏr′nĭ-thŏ-lŏj′ĭ-kăl), a. Of or pertaining to ornithology. [ornithology.]

or′ni-thol′o-gist (-thŏl′ŏ-jĭst), n. One skilled in

or′ni-thol′o-gy (-thŏl′ŏ-jĭ), n. Zoölogy of birds.

o′ro-tund (ō′rŏ-tŭnd; ŏr′ŏ-), a. [4] Full, clear, and strong; — of the voice. Also, bombastic.

or′phan (ŏr′făn), n. A child bereaved by death of both father and mother, or, less commonly, of either parent. — a. Bereaved by death of parents. — v. t. To deprive of a parent or of parents.

or′phan-age (-āj), n. **1.** State of being an orphan. **2.** An institution for the care of orphans.

or′ris (ŏr′ĭs), n. A variety of iris, or its fragrant rootstock.

or′tho-dox (ŏr′thŏ-dŏks), a. [4] **1.** Sound in opinion or doctrine; hence, holding the Christian faith as formulated in the church creeds; — opp. to *heretical* and *heterodox*. **2.** Approved; conventional

or′tho-dox′y (-dŏk′sĭ), n.; pl. **-DOXIES** (-sĭz). Orthodox character; orthodox belief or practice.

or-thog′ra-pher (ŏr-thŏg′ra-fẽr), n. One versed in orthography; one who spells correctly.

or′tho-graph′ic (ŏr′thŏ-grăf′ĭk) } a. Of or pert.
or′tho-graph′i-cal (-ĭ-kăl) } to orthography; correct in spelling. — **-i-cal-ly**, adv. [8].

or-thog′ra-phy (ŏr-thŏg′rá-fĭ), n. **1.** Art of correct spelling. **2.** Grammar treating of letters and spelling. [to orthopedics.]

or′tho-pe′dic (ŏr′thŏ-pē′dĭk; -pĕd′ĭk), a. Pert.
or′tho-pe′dics (-pē′dĭks), n. Correction or prevention of deformities, esp. in children.

or′to-lan (ŏr′tŏ-lăn), n. **1.** A European bunting (bird), about six inches long. It is netted and fattened for a table delicacy. **2. a** A kind of rail (bird). **b** The bobolink. U. S.

o′ryx (ō′rĭks; ŏr′ĭks), n. Any of several large African antelopes.

O′sage or′ange (ō′sāj). A tree allied to the mulberry; also, its yellow apple-shaped fruit.

ɔs′cil-late (ŏs′ĭ-lāt), v. i. [1] **1.** To swing backward and forward like a pendulum. **2.** To fluctuate between fixed limits. — **os′cil-la′tor**, n.

os′cil-la′tion (ŏs′ĭ-lā′shŭn), n. An oscillating.

ɔs′cil-la-to-ry (ŏs′ĭ-lá-tŏ-rĭ), a. Oscillating.

ɔs′cu-late (ŏs′kŭ-lāt), v. t. & i. [1] To kiss.

os′cu-la′tion (-lā′shŭn), n. Act of osculating.

os′cu-la-to-ry (ŏs′kŭ-lá-tŏ-rĭ), a. Of or pertaining to kissing; kissing.

o′sier (ō′zhẽr), n. **1.** Any of various willows the pliable twigs of which are used for basketry, etc. **2.** Any of several American dogwoods.

os′prey (ŏs′prā), n. A large fish-eating hawk.

os′se-ous (-ē-ŭs), a. Composed of bone; bony.

os′si-fi-ca′tion (-ĭ-ff-kā′shŭn), n. **1.** State of being ossified. **2.** That which is ossified, as a bone.

os′si-fy (-fĭ), v. i. or t. [2] To change into bone.

os-ten′si-ble (ŏs-tĕn′sĭ-b'l), a. [4] Professed; apparent. — **os-ten′si-bly**, adv. [8].

os′ten-ta′tion (ŏs′tĕn-tā′shŭn), n. Unnecessary show; pretentious parade.

os′ten-ta′tious (-shŭs), a. [4] Marked by, or fond of, ostentation; pretentious. — **-ly**, adv. [8]

os′te-o-path (ŏs′tĕ-ŏ-păth), n. A practitioner of osteopathy.

os′te-o-path′ic (-păth′ĭk), a. Pert. to osteopathy.

os′te-op′a-thist (-ŏp′á-thĭst), n. An osteopath.

os′te-op′a-thy (-thĭ), n. A method of treating diseases by manipulating the bones, nerves, blood vessels, and other tissues.

ost′ler (ŏs′lẽr), n. A stableman; hostler.

os′tra-cism (ŏs′trá-sĭz'm), n. **1.** Gr. Antiq. A method of temporary banishment by popular vote. **2.** Exclusion by general consent from common privileges, favor, etc.; as, social *ostracism*.

os′tra-cize (-sīz), v. t. [1] To exile, banish, or exclude, by ostracism.

os′trich (-trĭch), n. A swift-footed African bird, the largest existing bird, attaining a weight of 300 lbs. Its wings are useless for flight.

oth′er (ŭth′ẽr), a. **1.** (That) which remains of two, as distinguished from that which is specified; (the) remaining. **2.** Second. Obs., except in: every other, every second or alternate. **3.** Additional, different. — adv. Otherwise. — pron.; pl. OTHERS (-ẽrz). **1.** One or ones remaining; part remaining; — the substantive use of OTHER, a., 1. **2.** A different or additional one; — the substantive use of OTHER, a., 3. — conj. Or; either.

oth′er-wise′ (ŭth′ẽr-wiz′), adv. **1.** In another way, or in other ways; contrarily. **2.** In different circumstances. **3.** In other respects. — a. Different.

ot′tar (ŏt′ár), **ot′to** (ŏt′ō). Vars. of ATTAR.

ot′ter (-ẽr), n. Any of several aquatic, fish-eating, fur-bearing mammals allied to the martens.

Ot′to-man (ŏt′ō-măn), a. Of or pertaining to the Turks. — n.; pl. **-MANS** (-mănz). **1.** A Turk. **2.** [l.c.] A stuffed seat without a back.

ought (ŏt), v. Orig. pret., later also p. p. of OWE; now only an auxiliary in the pret. form, except in the illiterate "had ought." To be bound or obliged, as by duty or moral obligation, or by what is necessary, fit, or naturally to be expected.

ought (ŏt), n. & adv. Aught; anything; at all.

ounce (ouns), n. **1.** A weight of various values; as: **a** In avoirdupois weight, the sixteenth of a pound (437½ grains or 28.35 grams). **b** In troy and apothecaries' weight, the twelfth of a pound (480 grains or 31.1 grams). **2.** = FLUID OUNCE. **3.** Fig.: A small quantity; as, an *ounce* of sense.

ounce (ouns), n. **1.** A leopardlike cat inhabiting the mountains of Asia. **2.** Any of various other feline animals, esp. the jaguar; — often so called.

our (our), pron. & a. Of or belonging to us.

ours (ourz), pron. & a. The form of the possessive pronoun *our* that is used with no governed noun following; as, this world of *ours*.

our-selves′ (our-sĕlvz′), pron. An emphasized form for *we, us*. The singular **our-self′** is used chiefly in regal or formal style.

oust (oust), v. t. To eject; turn out; drive out.

out (out), adv. Outside of, or away from within, a space; from the interior, or beyond the limits or boundary; not in. Hence: **1.** Away from a usual, or particular place. **2.** Beyond possession, control, or occupation. **3.** Beyond the limit of existence, continuance, or supply; to a conclusion;

---

completely. **4.** Beyond the limits of concealment, privacy, constraint, etc. **5.** Beyond the bounds of what is true, reasonable, proper, etc.; in error; in the wrong; in disagreement, opposition, etc. **—** *n.* One that is out; as: **a** One out of office; — generally in *pl.* **b** A place or space outside; a corner; — chiefly fig. in *ins and outs.* **—** *interj.* **1.** Begone! away! **2.** Expressing grief, horror, or indignation;—often in *out upon* or *on* (a person).

out'-and-out', *a.* Thoroughgoing; complete.

out-bid' (-bǐd'), *v. t.;* for prin. parts see BID. To exceed or surpass in bidding.

out'bound' (out'bound'), *a.* Outward bound.

out'break' (out'brāk'), *n.* A bursting forth.

out'build'ing (out'bǐl'dǐng), *n.* A building near, and subordinate to, a main house; an outhouse.

out'burst' (-bûrst'), *n.* An outbreak.

out'cast' (out'kȧst'), *n.* One who is cast out; an exile; hence, a vagabond. **—** *a.* [4] Cast out; rejected; thrown away; hence, exiled; degraded.

out-class' (out-klȧs'), *v. t.* To excel or surpass.

out'come' (out'kŭm'), *n.* Result; consequence.

out'crop' (-krŏp'), *n. Geol. & Mining.* **a** The coming out of a stratum to the surface of the ground. **b** That part of a stratum which appears at the surface. **—** *v. i.* To come out to the surface of the ground, as strata.

out'cry' (-krī'), *n.* **1.** A loud cry; clamor. **2.** An auction; the crying of wares for sale in the streets.

out-dis'tance (-dĭs'tȧns), *v. t.* [1] To outstrip.

out-do' (-dōō'), *v. t.;* for prin. parts see DO. To excel; surpass. [out of doors.]

out'door' (out'dōr'), *a.* Being, belonging, or done

out'doors' (out'dōrz'; out'dōrz'), *adv.* Out of the house; out of doors. **—** (out'dōrz'), *n.* The world out of doors.

out'er (out'ẽr), *a.* Being on the outside; exterior; external; — opposed to *inner.*

out'er-most (out'ẽr-mōst), *a.* Farthest outward.

out-face' (out-fās'), *v. t.* [1] To face or look (one) out of countenance; also, to brave; defy.

out'field' (out'fēld'), *n.* **1.** An outlying field. **2.** *Baseball.* **a** The part of the field beyond the diamond, or infield. **b** The players in the outfield. **—** out'field'er, *n.* [8]. [fit'ter, *n.* [8].]

out'fit' (-fǐt), *n.* A fitting out; equipment. **—** out'-

out-flank' (out-flăŋk'), *v. t. Mil.* To go, extend, or be, beyond the flank of; turn the flank of.

out'flow' (-flō'), *n.* A flowing out.

out-gen'er-al (-jĕn'ẽr-ȧl), *v. t.* [7] To exceed in generalship; surpass in military skill.

out-go' (-gō'), *v. t.* To go beyond; surpass; outdo.

out'go' (out'gō'), *n.; pl.* -GOES (-gōz'). That which goes out; that which is paid out; outlay.

out'go'ing, *a.* Going out; departing. **—** *n.* **1.** A going out. **2.** That which goes out.

out-grow' (out-grō'), *v. t.* **1.** To surpass in growing. **2.** To grow out of or away from.

out'growth' (out'grōth'), *n.* That which grows out of, or proceeds from, anything; an offshoot.

out'house' (out'hous'), *n.* An outbuilding.

out'ing, *n.* A going out; esp., an excursion.

out'land-er (out'lăn-dẽr), *n.* A foreigner or alien.

out-land'ish (out-lăn'dǐsh), *a.* [4] **1.** Unfamiliar; strange; hence, barbarous; uncouth. **2.** Remote. **—** -ly, *adv.* [8] **—** ness, *n.* [8].

out-last' (-lȧst'), *v. t.* To exceed in duration.

out'law' (out'lô'), *n.* **1.** One excluded from the benefit or protection of the law. **2.** A lawless person; a fugitive from the law. **—** *v. t.* **1.** To deprive of the benefit or protection of law; proscribe. **2.** To remove from legal jurisdiction or enforcement; as, to *outlaw* a debt.

out'law'ry (out'lô'rĭ), *n.; pl.* -RIES (-rĭz). Act of outlawing; state of being outlawed.

out'lay' (out'lā'), *n.* **1.** A laying out, or expending. **2.** That which is expended; expenditure.

out'let (out'lĕt), *n.* A passage out; exit; vent.

out'line (-līn'), *n.* **1. a** The line that marks the outer limits of an object or figure; contour; — commonly in *pl.* **b** The style of drawing in which contours are unshaded. **c** A sketch in outline. **2.** A preliminary sketch in words; rough draft. **—** *v. t.* [1] **1.** To draw the outline of. **2.** To sketch out as by an outline.

out-live' (out-lǐv'), *v. t.* [1] To live longer than.

out'look' (out'lŏŏk'), *n.* **1.** A lookout. **2.** The view had by one looking out; scope of vision; prospect.

out'ly'ing (-lī'ǐng), *a.* Lying or being at a distance from the central part or main body; remote.

out-num'ber (-nŭm'bẽr), *v. t.* To exceed in number.

out'-of-door', *a.* Being out of the house; outdoor.

out'post' (-pōst'), *n.* A post or station at a distance from an army, or the troops stationed there.

out-pour' (-pōr'), *v. t. & i.* To pour out.

out'pour', *n.* A pouring out; outflow.

out'put' (out'pŏŏt'), *n.* **1.** The product of one or more mines, machines, mills, etc., in a given time. **2.** Hence, yield of any commodity.

out'rage (-rāj), *n.* Injurious and wanton wrong; gross violation of right or decency. **—** *v. t.* [1] **1.** To treat with violence or abuse. **2.** To ravish.

out-ra'geous (out-rā'jŭs), *a.* [4] Of the nature of outrage or an outrage; excessive; violent; atrocious. **—** -ly, *adv.* [8] **—** -ness, *n.* [8].

out-rank' (-răŋk'), *v. t.* To exceed in rank.

|| ou'tré' (ōō'trā'), *a.* [F.] Extravagant; bizarre.

out-ride' (out-rīd'), *v. t.* To surpass in riding.

out'rid'er (out'rĭd'ẽr), *n.* A mounted servant attending a carriage.

out'rig'ger (-rĭg'ẽr), *n.* **1.** Any projecting spar, or the like, as from a ship's mast. **2.** *Naut.* **a** An extended support for a rowlock. **b** A device attached to the side of a boat to prevent upsetting.

out'right' (out'rīt'; out'rīt'), *adv.* **1.** Forthwith; at once. **2.** Wholly; entirely.

out'right' (out'rīt'), *a.* [4] **1.** Proceeding straight ahead. **2.** Straightforward; out-and-out.

out-run' (-rŭn'), *v. t.* To outstrip; go beyond.

out'set' (-sĕt'), *n.* A setting out or beginning.

out-shine' (-shīn'), *v. t.* To excel in splendor.

out'side' (out'sīd'; out'sīd'), *adv. or prep.* On or to the outside or exterior (of); without.

out'side' (out'sīd'), *a.* **1.** Of, on, or pertaining to, the outside; external; exterior. **2.** Reaching the extreme limit, as to extent, quantity, etc.; as, an *outside* estimate. *Colloq.* **3.** Situated or done beyond or outside of certain limits.

out'side' (out'sīd'; out'sīd'), *n.* **1.** The external, or surface, part. **2.** The space without an inclosure; the outer side, as of a door. **3.** The limit; utmost; as, in a week, at the *outside. Colloq.*

out'sid'er (out'sīd'ẽr), *n.* One outside; esp., one not belonging to the party, etc., spoken of.

out'skirt' (out'skûrt'), *n.* A part remote from the center; — usually in *pl.*; as, the *outskirts* of a town.

out'spo'ken (out'spō'k'n; out'spō'k'n), *a.* [4] Speaking, or spoken, freely or boldly. — **-ly,** *adv.* [8] — **-ness,** *n.* [8]. [or unpaid.]

out-stand'ing, *a.* That stands out; uncollected

out-stretch' (-strĕch'), *v. t.* To stretch out.

out-strip' (-strĭp'), *v. t.* **1.** To go faster than; leave behind. **2.** Hence, to excel.

out-vote' (out-vōt'), *v. t.* To outnumber in voting.

out'ward (out'wẽrd), *a.* [4] **1.** Out; outer; exterior. **2.** Of or pertaining to the physical character; external; hence, formal.

out'ward (-wẽrd)] *adv.* **1.** In an outward **out'wards** (-wẽrdz)] sition or direction; on or to the outside; out; as, a ship *outward* bound. **2.** Outwardly; externally; hence, apparently; publicly.

out'ward-ly, *adv.* In regard to external or physical character or action; in respect of appearance.

out-wear' (-wâr'), *v. t.*; for prin. parts see WEAR. **1.** To wear out; consume by wearing. **2.** To outlast. **3.** To outlive; outgrow.

out-weigh' (-wā'), *v. t.* To exceed in weight.

out-wit' (-wĭt'), *v. t.* To surpass in cunning; get the better of by cunning.

out'work' (out'wûrk'), *n. Fort.* A minor defense beyond the main body of a work, as a rifle pit.

out-worn' (-wōrn'), *pret. & p. p.* of OUTWEAR.

o'va (ō'vȧ), *n., Lat. pl.* of OVUM.

o'val (ō'văl), *a.* Having the figure of an egg, with one end broader than the other; also, popularly, elliptical. — *n.* A body or figure oval in shape.

Oval.

o'va-ry (ō'vȧ-rĭ), *n.; pl.* -RIES (-rĭz). **1.** *Anat. & Zoöl.* The female organ in which ova or eggs are produced. **2.** *Bot.* An enlarged (usually the basal) portion of the pistil.

o'vate (ō'vāt), *a.* **1.** Oval. **2.** *Bot.* Egg-shaped.

o-va'tion (ō-vā'shŭn), *n.* An enthusiastic popular reception or tribute.

ov'en (ŭv''n), *n.* A chamber or structure for baking, heating, or drying, esp., now, in a stove.

o'ver (ō'vẽr), *prep.* **1.** Above, or higher than. **2.** More than. **3.** Upon the surface of; upon. **4.** Throughout or during the time of. **5.** Across; from side to side of. — *adv.* **1.** To the other side; across. Also, on the opposite side. **2. a** From inside to outside across the brim; as, a cup running *over.* **b** Away from the perpendicular; as, to fall *over.* **c** So as to bring the under side to or toward the top. **3.** In excess of a certain quantity or limit. **4.** From beginning to end; throughout. **5.** At an end. **6.** Again. — **over and above.** In addition to; more than; besides. — **o. and over,** repeatedly. — *a.* Upper; higher; superior; also, excessive; surplus.

o'ver-alls' (-ôlz'), *n. pl.* Loose trousers worn over others to protect them.

o'ver-arch' (-ärch'), *v. t. & i.* To arch over.

o'ver-awe' (-ô'), *v. t.* [1] To restrain by awe.

o'ver-bal'ance (-bǎl'ȧns), *v. t.* [1] **1.** To exceed equality with; outweigh. **2.** To cause to lose balance. — *n.* Excess of weight or value.

o'ver-bear' (-bâr'), *v. t.*; *.* **1.** To bear down, as by

excess of weight, force, etc.; overcome; suppress. **2.** To domineer over. — *v. i.* To be too prolific.

o'ver-bear'ing, *a.* [4] Arrogant; domineering.

o'ver-board' (ō'vẽr-bōrd'), *adv.* Over the side of a ship; from a ship into or in the water.

o'ver-bur'den (-bûr'd'n), *v. t.* To load with too great weight or too much care, etc.

o'ver-cap'i-tal-ize (-kǎp'ĭ-tǎl-īz), *v. t.* [1] To fix the capital value of at more than its real value.

o'ver-cast' (-kàst'), *v. t.*; *.* **1.** To cast or cover over; hence, to cloud; darken. **2.** (*pron.* ō'vẽr-kàst') To take long, loose stitches over (the raw edges of a seam) to prevent raveling; sew over and over.

o'ver-charge' (ō'vẽr-chärj'), *n.* **1.** An excessive load. **2.** An excessive charge in an account.

o'ver-charge' (-chärj'), *v. t.* [1] **1.** To charge or load too heavily; fill too full. **2.** To charge excessively in price. [with clouds.]

o'ver-cloud' (-kloud'), *v. t. & i.* To overspread

o'ver-coat' (ō'vẽr-kōt'), *n.* A coat worn over the other clothing; greatcoat; topcoat.

o'ver-come' (-kŭm'), *v. t.*; *.* **1.** To get the better of, surmount; conquer. — *v. i.* To be victorious.

o'ver-do' (-dōō'), *v. t.*; *.* **1.** To do too much; exaggerate. **2.** To overtask; exhaust. **3.** To cook too much, as meat. — *v. i.* To do too much.

o'ver-dose' (ō'vẽr-dōs'), *n.* An excessive dose.

o'ver-draw' (-drô'), *v. t.* **1.** To exaggerate. **2.** *Banking.* To make drafts upon in excess of the drawer's balance; as, to *overdraw* an account.

o'ver-due' (ō'vẽr-dū'; ō'vẽr-dū'), *a.* [4] Delayed beyond the proper time of arrival or payment, etc.

o'ver-eat' (-ēt'), *v. t. & i.*; *.* To eat to excess.

o'ver-es'ti-mate (-ĕs'tĭ-māt), *v. t.* [1] To estimate too highly. — **o'ver-es'ti-mate** (-māt), *n.*

o'ver-feed' (-fēd'), *v. t. & i.*; *.* To feed to excess.

o'ver-flow' (ō'vẽr-flō'), *n.* **1.** A flowing over; inundation. **2.** A superabundance; as, an *overflow* of population. **3.** An outlet for surplus liquid.

o'ver-flow' (-flō'), *v. t.* **1.** To flow over; inundate. **2.** To flow over the brim of; also, to cause to overflow. — *v. i.* **1.** To flow over the bounds. **2.** To be filled to running over.

o'ver-gar'ment (-gär'mĕnt), *n.* An outer garment.

o'ver-grow' (-grō'), *v. t.*; *.* **1.** To grow over; cover with growth or herbage. **2.** To outgrow. — *v. i.* To grow to excess. — **o'ver-growth',** *n.*

o'ver-hand' (-hǎnd'), *a.* **1.** Down from above, as a blow. **2.** Grasping with the palm downward, or inward toward the body. — (ō'vẽr-hǎnd'; ō'vẽr-hǎnd'), *adv.* In an overhand manner.

o'ver-hang' (-hǎng'), *v. t. & i.*; *.* To hang over; jut or project over (something); impend.

o'ver-hang', *n.* A projection; also, extent of projection, as of a roof, or of the stern of a vessel.

o'ver-haul' (ō'vẽr-hôl'), *v. t.* **1.** To haul or drag over; hence, to examine thoroughly for correction or repair. **2.** *Chiefly Naut.* To gain on; overtake.

o'ver-head' (-hĕd'), *adv.* Above one's head; aloft.

o'ver-head' (ō'vẽr-hĕd'), *a.* **1.** Operating or situated above or overhead. **2.** Passing over the head.

o'ver-hear' (-hēr'), *v. t.*; *.* **1.** To hear (something) not intended to be heard or not addressed to one. **2.** To hear (a speaker) whose remarks are not addressed to one or not intended for one.

o'ver-joy' (-joi'), *v. t.* To make extremely joyful.

---

chair; go; sing, iŋk; then, thin; nature, verdure; yet; zh = z in azure. Numbers refer to §§ in the Special Notes which, with Abbreviations, Signs, etc., precede the Vocabulary.

* For principal parts see the main verb.

o′ver-land′(ō′vẽr-lănd′),a. Being, or accomplished, over the land. — *adv.* By, upon, or across, land.

o′ver-lap′ (-lăp′), *v. t. & i. ; *. To extend over a part of ; extend over and beyond.

o′ver-lay′ (-lā′), *v. t. ; *. To lay or spread over or across ; superimpose ; cover.

o′ver-lie′ (-lī′), *v. t. ; *. To lie over or on.

o′ver-load′ (-lōd′), *v. t.* To load or fill to excess.

o′ver-look′ (-lŏŏk′), *v. t.* **1.** To look down on ; hence, to rise above ; overtop. **2.** To supervise ; watch over. **3.** To look over and beyond (anything) without seeing it ; hence, to pass over without notice, censure, or punishment.

o′ver-lord′ (ō′vẽr-lôrd′), *n.* A lord over another.

o′ver-mas′ter (más′tẽr), *v. t.* To overpower.

o′ver-match′ (-măch′), *v.t.* To be more than equal to or a match for ; hence, to vanquish.

o′ver-much′ (ō′vẽr-mŭch′; ō′vẽr-mŭch′), *a.* Too much. — *adv.* (*pron.* ō′vẽr-mŭch′). Too much.

o′ver-night′ (ō′vẽr-nīt′), *adv.* In the evening before ; also, during the night.

o′ver-pay′ (-pā′), *v. t. ; *. **1.** To pay too much to. **2.** To pay more than (a just or due amount).

o′ver-plus (ō′vẽr-plŭs), *n.* A surplus ; excess.

o′ver-pow′er (-pou′ẽr), *v. t.* **1.** To excel or exceed in power ; vanquish ; subdue. **2.** To affect intensely or overwhelmingly.

o′ver-pro-duc′tion (-prō-dŭk′shŭn), *n.* Excessive production ; supply beyond the demand.

o′ver-rate′ (-rāt′), *v. t.* To rate too highly

o′ver-reach′ (-rēch′), *v. t.* **1.** To reach above or beyond. **2.** To miss by reaching too far. **3.** To get the better of ; outwit ; cheat.

o′ver-read′y (ō′vẽr-rĕd′ĭ), *a.* Too ready.

o′ver-ride′ (-rīd′), *v. t. ; *. **1.** To ride over ; trample down. **2.** To set aside ; as, to *override* a veto. **3.** To ride too much, as a horse.

o′ver-rule′ (-rōōl′), *v. t.* **1.** To rule or decide to the contrary of or against. **2.** To bring over, as by persuasion. — *v. i.* To be superior in ruling ; also, to prevail by influence, character, etc.

o′ver-run′ (-rŭn′), *v. t. ; *. **1.** To run over, as in the manner of a fluid, rapid growth, etc. ; overspread. **2.** To run down ; invade and occupy ; infest. **3.** To run or go beyond. — *v. i.* To flow over or by something ; extend beyond limits.

o′ver-see′ (-sē′), *v. t. ; *. To look over ; inspect ; superintend. — -**se′er**(ō′vẽr-sē′ẽr;ō′vẽr-sē′ẽr),*n.*[8].

o′ver-set′ (-sĕt′), *v. t. ; *. **1.** To tip over ; upset. **2.** To cause to fall, or to fail ; subvert. — *v. i.* To turn, or to be turned, over ; upset.

o′ver-shad′ow (-shăd′ō), *v. t.* **1.** To throw a shadow, or shade, over ; darken ; obscure. **2.** Figuratively. To dominate ; be more important than.

o′ver-shoe′ (ō′vẽr-shōō′), *n.* A shoe worn over another for protection ; esp., an India-rubber shoe.

o′ver-shoot′ (-shōōt′), *v. t. ; *. **1.** To shoot over or beyond. **2.** Hence, to exceed. — *v. i.* To fly or shoot above or beyond the mark.

o′ver-shot′ (ō′vẽr-shŏt′), *p. a.* Moved by water flowing over from above. See *Illust.*

Overshot Wheel.

o′ver-sight′ (-sīt′), *n.* **1.** Watchful care ; superintendence. **2.** An overlooking ; omission or error due to inadvertence.

o′ver-skirt′ (ō′vẽr-skûrt′), *n.* An outer skirt.

o′ver-sleep′ (ō′vẽr-slēp′),*v.i.;*. To sleep too long.

o′ver-spread′ (-sprĕd′), *v. t.* [1] To spread over.

o′ver-state′ (-stāt′), *v. t.* To state too strongly.

o′ver-step′ (-stĕp′), *v. t. & i. ; *. To step over or beyond ; transgress.

o′ver-stock′ (-stŏk′), *v. t.* To supply to excess.

o′vert (ō′vẽrt), *a.* [3] Open to view ; manifest.

o′ver-take′ (ō′vẽr-tāk′), *v. t. ; *. **1.** To come or catch up with. **2.** To come upon suddenly or unexpectedly ; surprise.

o′ver-throw′ (-thrō′), *v. t. ; *. **1.** To overturn ; upset. **2.** To cause to fall or to fail.

o′ver-throw′ (ō′vẽr-thrō′), *n.* Act of overthrowing ; state of being overthrown.

o′ver-time′ (-tīm′), *n.* Time beyond a limit ; esp., extra working time. — *adv.* After the proper or regular time.

o′vert-ly (ō′vẽrt-lĭ), *adv.* Publicly ; openly.

o′ver-top′ (-tŏp′), *v. t.* **1.** To rise or tower above. **2.** To go beyond ; transcend ; obscure.

o′ver-train′ (-trān′), *v. t.* To train to excess.

o′ver-ture (ō′vẽr-tụr), *n.* **1.** A proposal ; offer. **2.** *Music.* An orchestral composition introductory to an oratorio, opera, etc.

o′ver-turn′ (-tûrn′), *v. t.* To turn over ; overthrow. — *v. i.* To turn over ; esp., to upset or capsize.

o′ver-turn′ (ō′vẽr-tûrn′), *n.* Act of overturning, or state of being overturned.

o′ver-ween′ing (-wēn′ĭng), *a.* [4] Unduly confident ; arrogant ; also, exaggerated.

o′ver-whelm′ (-hwĕlm′), *v. t.* To cover over completely, as by a great wave ; submerge ; engulf ; hence, fig., to crush ; bury ; oppress, etc., overpoweringly. — **-ing**, *p. a.* — **-ing-ly**, *adv.* [8].

o′ver-work′ (-wûrk′), *v. t. ; *. To cause to work too much or too long ; as, to *overwork* a horse. — *v. i.* To work beyond one′s strength.

o′ver-work′ (ō′vẽr-wûrk′; ō′vẽr-wûrk′), *n.* Work beyond the usual or stipulated amount.

o′ver-wrought′ (-rôt′), *p. a.* **1.** Wrought upon to excess ; too excited. **2.** Overworked. **3.** Overdone.

o-vip′a-rous (ō-vĭp′à-rŭs), *a.* Producing eggs that hatch after being expelled from the body.

o′void (ō′void), *a.* Resembling an egg in shape ; ovate. — *n.* An ovoid body.

o′vum (ō′vŭm), *n. ; pl.* L. OVA (-và) ; E. OVUMS. *Biol.* An egg cell, or egg, in the widest sense.

owe (ō), *v. t. ;* OWED (ōd), OW′ING (ō′ĭng). **1.** To be under an obligation to restore, pay, or render (something) in return ; be indebted to. **2.** To have or bear (a certain feeling) ; as, to *owe* a grudge. **3.** To be indebted for. — *v. i.* To be in debt.

ow′ing (ō′ĭng), *p. p. & a.* **1.** Indebted ; also, owed. **2.** Had or experienced as an effect, result, etc.

owl (oul), *n.* Any of certain birds of prey distinguished by large head and eyes, and nocturnal habits. — **owl′ish**, *a.* [8].

owl′et (-ĕt), *n.* A small or young owl.

own (ōn), *a.* Belonging to one′s self or itself ; peculiar ; — after a possessive case or pronoun, as *my, our, your, his, her, its, their,* to intensify the idea of interest or ownership.

āle, senāte, cāre, ăm, ăccount, ärm, ȧsk, sofȧ ; ēve, ĕvent, ĕnd, recĕnt, makẽr ; īce, ĭll ; ōld, ȯbey, ôrb, ŏdd, sŏft, cŏnnect ; ūse, ŭnite, ûrn, ŭp, circŭs ; fŏŏd, fŏŏt ; out, oil ;

* For principal parts see the main verb.

own, *v. t.* To possess; have as property. **2.** To admit. — *v. i.* To confess; — with *to*.

own'er (ōn'ẽr), *n.* One who owns; a proprietor.

own'er-ship, *n.* State or fact of being an owner.

ox (ŏks), *n.; pl.* OXEN (ŏk's'n). **1.** The domestic animal of the cattle kind, esp. an adult castrated male (cf. BULL, STEER). **2.** Any of various animals related to the domestic ox.

ox-al'ic (ŏks-ăl'ĭk), *a. Chem.* Designating a poisonous acid existing in oxalis and in other plants.

ox'a-lis (ŏks'ȧ-lĭs), *n. Bot.* Any of a large genus of plants, the wood sorrels, having compound leaves and white, pink, purple, or yellow flowers.

ox'bow' (ŏks'bō'), *n.* A U-shaped frame embracing an ox's neck as a collar.

ox'eye' (ŏks'ī'), *n.* Any of several composite plants having heads with a conspicuous disk and marginal rays; esp., an oxeye daisy.

oxeye daisy. 1. = DAISY, 2. **2.** Any plant of a certain genus having showy yellow-rayed flowers.

Ox'ford (-fẽrd), *n.* An article named after Oxford, Eng.; esp., short for Oxford shoe, a low, laced shoe.

ox'i-da'tion (ŏk'sĭ-dā'shŭn), *n.* Act or process of oxidizing; state or result of being oxidized.

ox'ide (ŏk'sīd; -sĭd), *n. Chem.* A compound of oxygen with an element or radical.

ox'i-dize (ŏk'sĭ-dīz), *v. t.* [1] *Chem.* To combine with oxygen. — *v. i.* To become oxidized. — **ox'-i-diz'er** (ŏk'sĭ-dīz'ẽr), *n.* [8].

ox'y-gen (ŏk'sĭ-jĕn), *n.* A tasteless, odorless gas occurring in the air, of which it forms about 21 per cent by volume. It is an element.

ox'y-gen-ate (-jĕn-āt), *v. t.* [1] To combine or mix with oxygen; oxidize. — **-a'tion** (-ā'shŭn), *n.*

oys'ter (ois'tẽr), *n.* A common shellfish, much used as food, with a rough irregular hinged shell in two parts, found in shallow water along seacoasts.

oyster plant. Salsify.

o'zone (ō'zōn), *n. Chem.* A dense form of oxygen, used as a sterilizing and bleaching agent.

P

pab'u-lum (păb'ů-lŭm), *n.* Food; nourishment.

pace (pās), *n.* **1.** A step. **2.** The length of a step in walking. **3.** Gait. **4.** Specifically, a gait of the horse in which the legs on the same side are moved at the same time. **5.** Rate of movement; speed. — *v. i.* [1] **1.** To move with slow or measured steps. **2.** To move at a pace, as a horse. — *v. t.* **1.** To walk over with measured tread. **2.** To measure by paces. **3.** To develop or guide the pace of.

pac'er (pās'ẽr), *n.* One (esp. a horse) that paces.

pach'y-derm (păk'ĭ-dûrm), *n.* **1.** A thick-skinned animal, as the elephant, hippopotamus, etc. **2.** An unfeeling person. — **pach'y-der'ma-tous** (-dûr'mȧ-tŭs), *a.*

pa-cif'ic (pȧ-sĭf'ĭk), *a.* [4] Peaceful; peaceable. — **-ly**, *adv.* [8].

pa-cif'i-cal (-ĭ-kăl), *a.* Pacific. — **-ly**, *adv.* [8].

pa-cif'i-cate (-kāt), *v. t.* [1] To pacify.

pac'i-fi-ca'tion (păs'ĭ-fĭ-kā'shŭn; pȧ-sĭf'ĭ-kā'-), *n.* Act or process of pacifying; state of being pacified.

pa-cif'i-ca-to-ry (pȧ-sĭf'ĭ-kȧ-tō-rĭ), *a.* Tending to make peace; conciliatory.

pac'i-fism (păs'ĭ-fĭz'm), *n.* The spirit or temper which opposes militarism and advocates international arbitration. — **pac'i-fist** (păs'ĭ-fĭst), *n.*

pac'i-fy (păs'ĭ-fī), *v. t.* [2] To make to be at peace; appease; calm; soothe. — **pac'i-fi'er** (-fī'ẽr), *n.*

pack (păk), *v. t.* To select or make up fraudulently, to secure a certain result; as, to *pack* a jury.

pack, *n.* **1.** A bundle prepared to be carried, esp. on the back. **2.** A number or quantity of associated or similar persons or things; as: **a** A gang. **b** A number of animals, as dogs or wolves, hunting or kept together. **c** A full set of playing cards. **3.** A large area of floating pieces of ice driven together. — *v. t.* **1.** To make a pack of; put or arrange in a pack. **2.** To crowd together. **3.** To fill closely or to repletion; crowd. **4.** *Mech.* To render impervious, as by filling with suitable material, as a joint. **5.** To load with a pack. **6.** To form into a pack, as hounds, cards, or ice. **7.** To cause to go or depart, esp. peremptorily or suddenly; — often with *off.* — *v. i.* **1.** To make up packs, bales, or bundles. **2.** To gather into packs; crowd together. **3.** To admit of being stowed, as for transportation or storage. **4.** To depart, esp. in haste; — generally with *off.*

pack'age (păk'ăj), *n.* **1.** Act or process of packing. **2.** A bundle; a parcel.

pack animal. An animal used in carrying packs.

pack'er (păk'ẽr), *n.* One who packs; esp., *U. S.*, a wholesale provision dealer who packs his wares for a distant or future market.

pack'et (păk'ĕt), *n.* **1.** A small pack or little bundle. **2.** *Naut.* A vessel conveying mails, passengers, and goods, and having fixed sailing days.

pack'ing, *n.* **1.** Act or process of one that packs. **2.** Any material used to pack, fill up, or make close.

pack'sad'dle (păk'săd'l), *n.* A saddle made for supporting the load on a pack animal.

pack'thread' (-thrĕd'), *n.* Strong thread or twine.

pact (păkt), *n.* An agreement; a compact.

pad (păd), *n.* Dull sound of footfalls or of a staff.

pad, *n.* **1.** A cushion or cushionlike mass. **2.** A tablet or block of many sheets of paper. **3.** A floating leaf of a water plant, esp. of a water lily. *U. S.* — *v. t.* **1.** To stuff; furnish with padding. **2.** To expand (a writing or speech) with needless matter.

pad'ding, *n.* **1.** Act of one that pads, or stuffs. **2.** The material with which anything is padded.

pad'dle (păd'l), *n.* **1.** A broad-bladed implement used without a fixed fulcrum to propel and steer canoes and other boats. **2.** One of the broad boards at the circumference of a water wheel or paddle wheel. **3.** An implement for stirring, mixing, beating clothes, etc. — *v. i.* [1] **1.** To use a paddle for propelling one on or through the water. **2.** To row easily or gently. — *v. t.* **1.** To propel or move with or as with a paddle or paddles.

pad'dle, *v. i.* **1.** To move the feet or wade about in shallow water or the like. **2.** To toddle.

paddle wheel. A wheel with paddles around its circumference, used to propel a vessel.

---

chair; go; sing, iṅk; then, thin; nature, verdure; yet; zh = z in azure. Numbers refer to §§ in the Special Notes which, with Abbreviations, Signs, etc., precede the Vocabulary.

pad′dock (păd′ŭk), n. **1.** A small inclosure, esp. one for pasture, adjoining a stable or house. **2.** An inclosure near the stables, esp. at a race course, in which horses are exercised, etc.

pad′dy (păd′ĭ), n. In commerce, unhusked rice, growing or cut; by extension, rice in general.

pad′lock′ (păd′lŏk′), n. A portable lock having a shackle jointed or pivoted at one end. — v. t. To fasten with or as with a padlock.

‖ **pa′dre** (pä′drā), n.; pl. Sp. & Pg. -DRES (-drās); It. -DRI (-drē). [Sp., Pg., & It.] A priest or monk; — used in Spain, Portugal, Italy, etc.

‖ **pa-dro′ne** (pä-drō′nā), n.; pl. It. -NI (-nē), E. -NES (-nāz). [It.] A patron; master; proprietor; specif., an Italian employment agent, as in America.

pæ′an (pē′ăn), n. A song of praise, triumph, etc.

pa′gan (pā′găn), n. **1.** A heathen. **2.** An irreligious person. — a. [4] Of or pertaining to pagans; heathen; heathenish.

pa′gan-ism (-ĭz′m), n. State of being pagan.

page (pāj), n. Formerly, a youth training for knighthood, who acted as attendant of his master and mistress, or a youth attending a person of high degree, esp. at courts; now, a youth for errands, waiting on the door, etc., also, U. S., a boy to wait on the members of a legislature.

page (pāj), n. One side of a leaf of a book, etc. — v. t. [1] To mark or number the pages of.

pag′eant (păj′ĕnt; pā′jĕnt), n. **1.** A showy display; unsubstantial pomp. **2.** An elaborate exhibition or spectacle, esp. a stately or showy procession.

pag′eant-ry (-rĭ), n. Pageants collectively; pomp.

pag′i-na′tion (păj′ĭ-nā′shŭn), n. Act or process of paging a book, etc.; page numbering.

pa-go′da (pá-gō′dá), n. A towerlike, storied structure, usually a temple, or a memorial, of the kind frequent in India, China, and Japan.

paid (pād), p. a. **1.** Receiving pay; hired. **2.** Delivered to discharge an obligation; discharged, as a debt.

pail (pāl), n. A vessel for holding or carrying liquids, commonly circular, having a bail, and often a cover. —

pail′ful (pāl′fŏŏl), n.; pl. -FULS (-fŏŏlz).

pain (pān), n. **1.** Punishment for crime; penalty. Obs., exc. in phrases, as "on pain of death." **2.** A distressing feeling due to derangement of functions, disease, or bodily injury. **3.** Distressing uneasiness of mind; grief. **4.** pl. Labor; toilsome effort; as, he took great pains.

Pagoda.

pain′ful (pān′fŏŏl), a. [4] **1.** Full of, or affected with, pain; grievous. **2.** Requiring toil; difficult.

— **pain′ful-ly**, adv. [8] — **pain′ful-ness**, n. [8].

pain′less, a. [4] Free from pain; without pain.

— **pain′less-ly**, adv. [8] — **-ness**, n. [8].

pains′tak′ing (pānz′tāk′ĭng), a. [4] Taking pains; careful in doing; assiduous. — **-ly**, adv. [8].

paint (pānt), v. t. **1. a** To form a representation of, as on a canvas, by applying paints. **b** To make (a picture or design) with pigments. **2.** To ornament by painting. **3.** To describe vividly; depict. **4.** To apply paint to; color. — v. i. **1.** To practice the art of painting. **2.** To color one's face in order to beautify it. — n. **1.** A preparation of a

pigment, as with oil, for application to a surface; also, the pigment alone, or a cake of it. **2.** Pigment, as rouge, etc., for the face or body. —

paint′er, n. [8].

paint′er (pān′tẽr), n. The cougar or puma.

paint′er, n. A rope for fastening a boat.

paint′ing, vb. n. **1.** Act of one who paints. **2.** The art of depicting objects or scenes in color on a surface with pigments; also, a painted picture, design, etc.

pair (pâr), n.; pl. PAIRS. **1.** Two things of a kind, suited to each other, and intended to be used together. **2.** A thing composed of two corresponding pieces. **3.** Two persons or animals of opposite sexes consorting together. **4.** Two of a sort; a couple; a brace. **5.** Two members of opposite parties or opinion who mutually agree not to vote on a given question; also, the arrangement thus made. **6.** A set; — now only in a pair of stairs or steps. — v. t. To unite, arrange, or match so as to form a pair or couple; mate. — v. i. **1.** To form a pair; match; suit. **2.** To unite in a pair; couple; mate.

pa-ja′mas (pá-jä′máz), n. Var. of PYJAMAS.

pal (păl), n. A mate; chum; accomplice. Slang.

pal′ace (păl′ås), n. **1.** The official residence of a sovereign, also, Eng., of an archbishop or bishop. **2.** A large, stately, or splendid house or building.

pal′a-din (-á-dĭn), n. One of the twelve peers or companions of Charlemagne; hence, fig., a knight-errant; a distinguished champion.

pal′an-quin′ (păl′ăn-kēn′), n. In India, China, etc., an inclosed litter. [taste; savory.

pal′at-a-ble (păl′ăt-á-b'l), a. [4] Agreeable to the

pal′a-tal (-á-tăl), a. **1.** Of or pertaining to the palate. **2.** Phon. Formed or articulated between the tongue and the palate, esp. the hard palate; as, k in key. — n. A palatal sound or its symbol.

pal′ate (-ăt), n. **1.** The roof of the mouth. The front part is the hard palate, the back part is the soft palate, or velum. **2.** The sense of taste.

pa-la′tial (pá-lā′shăl), a. [4] Of, pertaining to, or of the nature of, a palace; magnificent.

pal′a-tine (păl′á-tĭn; -tĭn), a. Possessing royal privileges; as, a count, earl, or county palatine.

pa-la′ver (pá-lä′vẽr; -lăv′ẽr), n. Talk; esp., profuse, idle, or beguiling talk. — v. i. To talk profusely, idly, or beguilingly.

pale (pāl), a. [3] **1.** Wanting in color; dusky white; ashen. **2.** Not bright or brilliant; faint. — v. i. & t. [1] To turn pale; lose color or luster.

pale, n. **1.** A stake; pointed slat, as for fencing; picket. **2.** An inclosure; also, limits; bounds. — v. t. [1] To inclose with or as with pales; fence.

pale′ness, n. State or quality of being pale.

pa′le-on-tol′o-gist (pā′lē-ŏn-tŏl′ŏ-jĭst), n. One versed in paleontology.

pa′le-on-tol′o-gy (-jĭ), n. The science dealing with the life of past geological periods, as shown by fossil remains of animals and plants.

pal′ette (păl′ĕt), n. A painter's tablet, with thumb hole at one end, on which to lay and mix pigments.

pal′frey (pôl′frĭ; păl′-), n. A saddle horse for the road, esp. a small one for ladies.

pal′imp-sest (păl′ĭmp-sĕst), n. A parchment, tablet, etc., which has been used two or more times, the earlier writing being erased.

āle, senāte, câre, ăm, ăccount, ärm, ȧsk, sofȧ; ēve, ĕvent, ĕnd, recĕnt, makēr; īce, ĭll; ōld, ōbey, ôrb, ŏdd, sŏft, cŏnnect; ūse, ŭnite, ûrn, ŭp, circŭs; fŏŏd, fŏŏt; out, oil;

pal'ing (pāl'ĭng), *n.* Wood for making pales; pales collectively; a fence.

pal'i-sade' (păl'ĭ-sād'), *n.* **1.** A fence of pales or stakes, as for defense. **2.** A long, strong stake, pointed at the top, used with others to set in the ground as a defense. **3.** A line of bold cliffs;— usually in *pl.* ; as, the *Palisades* of the Hudson. — *v. t.* [1] To inclose or furnish with palisades.

pall (pôl), *n.* A heavy cloth, as of black velvet, over a coffin, hearse, or tomb.

pall, *v. i.* To become dull and spiritless; lose strength, life, interest, etc.; as, the work soon *palled.* — *v. t.* To satiate; cloy, as the appetite.

pall'bear'er (pôl'bâr'ẽr), *n.* One of those who attend the coffin at a funeral.

pal'let (păl'ĕt), *n.* Small, mean bed; bed of straw.

pal'let (păl'ĕt), *n. Mach.* A click or pawl driving or regulating a ratchet wheel, as in a watch.

pal'li-ate (-ĭ-āt), *v. t.* [1] **1.** To reduce in violence; mitigate. **2.** To extenuate; excuse.

pal'li-a'tion (-ā'shŭn), *n.* A palliating; state of being palliated.

pal'li-a-tive (păl'ĭ-ā-tĭv), *a.* [4] Serving to palliate. — *n.* That which palliates.

pal'lid (-ĭd), *a.* [4] Deficient in color; pale; wan. — -**ly,** *adv.*[8] — -**ness,** *n.* [8].

pal'lor (păl'ŏr), *n.* Quality or state of being pale.

palm (päm), *n.* **1.** The part of the hand, on the side opposite the knuckles, between the bases of the fingers and the wrist. **2.** A lineal measure, usually reckoned at 3 inches or 4 inches. — *v. t.* **1.** To manipulate with, or conceal in, the palm. **2.** To impose by fraud;— usually with *off.*

palm, *n.* **1.** Any of various plants, mainly tropical, mostly trees with tall columnar trunks bearing a crown of gigantic leaves. **2.** A leaf of the palm, borne as a symbol of victory or rejoicing. **3.** Any symbol of triumph; also, victory; triumph.

pal'mate (păl'māt), *a.* **1.** Having the shape of the hand with fingers spread, as a leaf. **2.** Having the toes united by a web, as in swimming birds. — **pal'mat-ed,** *a.* — **pal'mate-ly,** *adv.* [8].

palm'er (päm'ẽr), *n.* One who palms ; a conjurer.

palm'er, *n.* A wandering religious votary, esp. one who bore a palm branch as a token of having visited the Holy Land.

pal-met'to (păl-mĕt'ō), *n. ; pl.* -TOS, -TOES (-ōz). Any of several palms, of the West Indies and the southern United States, having fan-shaped leaves.

palm'ist (päm'ĭst), *n.* An adept in palmistry.

palm'is-try (päm'ĭs-trĭ), *n.* Art or practice of telling fortunes, or of judging character, etc., by the features of the palm of the hand.

Palm Sunday. The Sunday next before Easter.

palm'y (päm'ĭ), *a.* [3] **1.** Bearing, or derived from, palms. **2.** Flourishing; prosperous.

pal'pa-bil'i-ty (păl'pá-bĭl'ĭ-tĭ), *n.* Quality of being palpable; that which is palpable.

pal'pa-ble (păl'pá-b'l), *a.* [4] **1.** Capable of being touched or felt; tangible. **2.** Easily perceptible by one or more of the senses; noticeable. — -**ness,** *n.* [8] — **pal'pa-bly,** *adv.* [8].

pal'pi-tate (-pĭ-tāt), *v. i.* [1] To pulsate violently; — esp. of the heart. [throbbing.

pal'pi-ta'tion (-tā'shŭn), *n.* A rapid pulsation; a

pal'pus (păl'pŭs), *n.; L. pl.* -PI (-pī). An append-

age, usually an organ of touch or taste, attached to a mouth part, as in insects, crustaceans, etc.

pal'sy (pôl'zĭ), *n.; pl.* -SIES (-zĭz). Paralysis. — *v. t.* [2] To paralyze.

pal'ter (-tẽr), *v. i.* **1.** To act insincerely ; equivocate. **2.** To haggle; traffic. — -**er,** *n.* [8].

pal'try (-trĭ),*a.* [3] Comtemptible; pitiful.— **pal'tri-ly** (-trĭ-lĭ), *adv.* — **pal'tri-ness,** *n.*

pam'pas (păm'páz), *n. pl.* Vast treeless plains, south of the Amazon valley, esp. in Argentina.

pam'per (-pẽr), *v. t.* To treat indulgently.

pam'phlet (-flĕt), *n.* A book of a few sheets of printed matter, commonly with a paper cover.

pan (păn), *n.* **1.** A vessel or dish for domestic uses, commonly broad and shallow, and often open. **2. a** Either of the receptacles in a balance. **b** A vessel for washing out gold, tin, etc., in mining. **c** In old guns, the hollow part of the lock to receive the priming. **3.** Hardpan. — *v. t. ;* PANNED (pănd); PAN'NING. To wash, cook, or treat in a pan. — *v. i.* **1.** *Mining.* **a** To wash earth, gravel, etc., in a pan. **b** To yield gold in panning. **2.** To yield a result ; turn out ;— with *out. Colloq.*

pan'a-ce'a (păn'á-sē'á), *n.* A remedy for all diseases ; a cure-all.

Pan'a-ma' hat (păn'á-mä'), *or* **pan'a-ma',** *n.* A fine hand-plaited hat made, in South and Central America, of the young leaves of a palmlike tree.

Păn'-A-mer'i-can, *a.* Of or pertaining to both North and South America or all Americans.

pan'cake' (păn'kāk'), *n.* A griddlecake; flapjack.

pan'cre-as (păn'krē-ăs ; păn'-), *n.* A large gland discharging into the intestine. Its secretion, the pancreatic juice, acts on all classes of food.

pan'de-mo'ni-um (păn'dē-mō'nĭ-ŭm), *n.* **1.** [*cap.*] The abode of demons ; loosely, hell. **2.** A den of riotous vice ; also, wild uproar.

pan'der (păn'dẽr), *n.* **1.** A go-between in love intrigues. **2.** A minister to the lusts of others.— *v. i.* To act as pander; cater; as, to *pander* to low taste.

pane (pān), *n.* A panel; hence, a compartment of a window, door, etc., consisting of one sheet of glass in a frame; the sheet of glass so set.

pan'e-gyr'ic (păn'ē-jĭr'ĭk), *n.* An oration or writing in praise of some person or event; laudation. — **pan'e-gyr'i-cal** (-ĭ-kăl), *a.* [4].

pan'e-gyr'ist (păn'ē-jĭr'ĭst), *n.* A eulogist.

pan'el (păn'ĕl), *n.* **1.** A list of persons summoned as jurors; hence, the whole jury. **2.** A compartment, portion, or section of a wall, ceiling, or other surface, as of a door or window. **3.** A thin flat piece of wood on which a picture is painted; also, the picture. — *v. t.* [7] To furnish, fit, or adorn with paneling.

pang (păng), *n.* **1.** A paroxysm of extreme pain. **2.** A sudden sharp attack of any emotion.

pan'ic (păn'ĭk), *a.* Of, pertaining to, or coming from, a panic. — *n.* **1.** A sudden, overpowering fright, esp. one that is groundless. **2.** A sudden widespread fright concerning financial affairs. — **pan'ick-y** (-ĭ-kĭ), *a.* [4].

pan'i-cle (-ĭ-k'l), *n. Bot.* Strictly, a compound raceme; popularly, any pyramidal, loosely branched flower cluster.

pan'ic-strick'en, -struck', *a.* Struck with panic.

pan'nier (păn'yẽr ; -ĭ-ẽr), *n.* **1.** A basket carried on the back by a horse or a person. **2.** A framework to expand a woman's skirts at the hips.

pan'o-plied (păn'ŏ-plīd), *a.* Dressed in panoply.

pan'o-ply (-ŏ-plĭ), *n.; pl.* -PLIES (-plĭz). **1.** A full suit of plate armor. **2.** Anything protecting completely, or forming a bright, splendid covering.

pan'o-ra'ma (păn'ŏ-rä'mä), *n.* **1.** A picture presenting a view of objects from or as from a central point. **2.** A picture exhibited a part at a time, by being unrolled. **3.** A scene that passes continuously before one. **4.** An unobstructed view in every direction ; hence, a comprehensive presentation of a subject. [a panorama.

pan'o-ram'ic (-răm'ĭk), *a.* Pertaining to, or like,

pan'sy (păn'zĭ), *n.; pl.* -SIES (-zĭz). A garden plant and flower, a species of violet.

pant (pănt ; pȧnt), *v. i.* **1.** To breathe quickly or in a labored manner, as from exertion. **2.** To long eagerly ; yearn. — *v. t.* To gasp ; — with *out* or *forth*. — *n.* A gasp. Also, a puff of an engine.

pan'ta-lets' (păn'tȧ-lĕts'), *n. pl.* Long, loose, frilled drawers formerly worn by women and girls.

pan'ta-loon' (-lōōn'), *n.* **1.** In pantomimes, a buffoon. **2.** *pl.* Trousers.

pan'the-ism (păn'thē-ĭz'm), *n.* The doctrine that the universe, taken as a whole, is God.

pan'the-ist (-ĭst), *n.* One who holds to pantheism.

pan'the-is'tic (-ĭs'tĭk), **pan'the-is'ti-cal** (-tĭ-kăl), *a.* [4] Of or pertaining to pantheism.

pan'the-on (păn-thē'ŏn; păn'thē-ŏn), *n.* **1.** A temple dedicated to all the gods; esp. [*cap.*], the building so called at Rome. **2.** A building where rest the famous dead of a nation, as Westminster Abbey.

pan'ther (păn'thẽr), *n.* **1.** The leopard. **2.** In America, the cougar; also, the jaguar.

pan'to-mime (păn'tŏ-mīm), *n.* **1.** A dramatic performance in, or chiefly in, dumb show (i. e., without words). **2.** Dumb show of any sort.

pan'to-mim'ic (-mĭm'ĭk), *a.* Of or pertaining to pantomime.

pan'try (păn'trĭ), *n. ; pl.* -TRIES (-trĭz). A room or closet for bread and other provisions.

pap (păp), *n.* A soft food for infants or invalids.

pa-pa' (pȧ-pä' ; pȧ'pä), *n.* Father ; — a child's word.

pa'pa-cy (pā'pȧ-sĭ), *n.* **1.** The office of the Pope of Rome. **2.** The popes collectively. **3.** The Roman hierarchy.

pa'pal (-pȧl), *a.* **1.** Of or pertaining to the Pope of Rome; as, the *papal* crown. **2.** Of or pertaining to the Roman Catholic Church; as, *papal* ritual.

pa-paw' (pȧ-pô'; pô'pô'), *n.* **1.** The papaya ; also, the tree that bears it. **2.** The oblong yellowish fruit, with a sweetish bananalike pulp, of a tree of the central and southern United States.

pa-pa'ya (pä-pä'yä), *n.* The edible fruit of a palmlike tropical American tree.

pa'per (pā'pẽr), *n.* **1.** A substance made in thin sheets or leaves from rags, straw, bark, wood, or other fibrous material. **2.** A sheet, leaf, or piece of paper (def. 1). **3.** A document or legal instrument; a writing, as an essay. **4.** Hence : Short for commercial paper, negotiable paper, including bills of exchange, promissory notes, checks, etc. **5.** A newspaper ; a journal. **6.** Decorated coverings for walls, made of paper. — *v. t.* To furnish with paper ; as, to *paper* a room.

paper hangings. Wall paper.

paper money. Government notes, bank notes, etc., that circulate as a substitute for coin.

pa'per-y (-ĭ), *a.* [4] Like paper, as in consistency.

‖ **pa'pe-terie'** (pȧ'pĕ-trē'), *n.* [F.] A case or box with paper and writing materials.

‖ **pa'pier'–mâ'ché'** (pȧ'pyä'mä'shā' ; pȧ'pyä-mä'-shā), *n.* [F.] A hard strong substance made of a paper pulp mixed with size, rosin, or the like.

pa-pil'la (pȧ-pĭl'ȧ), *n.; L. pl.* -LÆ (-ē). Any small nipplelike projection or part, as on the tongue.

pa'pist (pā'pĭst), *n.* A Roman Catholic ; — used disparagingly. [American Indian parents.

pa-poose' (pȧ-pōōs'), *n.* A young child of North

pap'pose (păp'ōs ; pȧ-pōs'), *a. Bot.* Furnished with, or of the nature of, a pappus.

pap'pus (păp'ŭs), *n. ; L. pl.* PAPPI (-ī). *Bot.* Any appendage or tuft of appendages crowning the ovary or fruit in certain seed plants.

pa'pri-ka (pä'prē-kä), *n.* The dried ripened fruit of various peppers; also, the mildly pungent red condiment prepared from it.

pa-py'rus (pȧ-pī'rŭs), *n. ; L. pl.* -RI (-rī). **1.** A tall sedge, native of the Nile region. **2.** The pith of this plant, sliced and pressed into a writing material by the ancients. **3.** A writing on papyrus ; esp., *pl.*, written scrolls of papyrus.

par (pär), *n.* **1.** The established value of the currency of one country expressed in that of another using the same standard of value. **2.** Equality of the nominal and market values of securities. **3.** Equality as to value, condition, or circumstances.

par'a-ble (păr'ȧ-b'l), *n.* A comparison ; esp., a fictitious narrative embodying a moral.

Papyrus.

pa-rab'o-la (pȧ-răb'ŏ-lȧ), *n. ; pl.* -OLAS (-lȧz). *Geom.* A conic section, the intersection of a cone with a plane parallel to its side.

par'a-bol'ic (păr'ȧ-bŏl'ĭk), *a.* [4] **1.** Of the nature of, or expressed by, a parable ; allegorical. **2.** *Geom.* Like, or relating to, a parabola.

par'a-bol'i-cal (-ĭ-kăl), *a.* [4] Parabolic.

par'a-chute (păr'ȧ-shōōt), *n.* An umbrella-like device for making a descent, as from a balloon.

pa-rade' (pȧ-rād'), *n.* **1.** Pompous display. **2.** *Mil.* **a** The ceremonial formation of a body of troops for inspection or review. **b** The area on which troops regularly assemble for parade. **3.** Any march or procession, esp. a formal one. **4.** Place where people promenade ; those who parade. — *v. t.* [1] **1.** To exhibit ostentatiously. **2.** To assemble and form, as troops for review; marshal. **3.** To march over or through. — *v. i.* **1.** To walk in public with ostentation. **2.** To assemble in military order for evolutions and inspection. — **rad'er**, *n.*

par'a-digm (păr'ȧ-dĭm ; -dīm), *n.* **1.** An example or pattern. **2.** *Gram.* An example of a conjugation or declension, showing a word in all its inflectional forms.

āle, senāte, câre, ăm, ăccount, ärm, ȧsk, sofȧ ; ēve, ėvent, ėnd, recėnt, makēr ; īce, ĭll ; ōld, ŏbey, ôrb, ŏdd, sŏft, cŏnnect ; ūse, ŭnite, ûrn, ŭp, circŭs ; fōōd, fŏŏt ; out, oil ;

par'a-dise (-dīs), n. **1.** [cap.] The garden of Eden. See EDEN. **2.** The abode of sanctified souls after death. **3.** A place of bliss; a state of happiness.

par'a-dox (păr'ă-dŏks), n. **1.** An assertion or sentiment seemingly contradictory, or opposed to common sense, but possibly true. **2.** A statement actually self-contradictory or false.

par-a-dox'i-cal (-dŏk'sĭ-kăl), a. [4] Of the nature of a paradox. — **-ly,** adv. [8] — **-ness,** n. [8].

par'af-fin (păr'ă-fĭn), n. A waxy inflammable substance produced in distilling wood, lignite, coal, etc., and occurring also in the earth.

par'a-gon (păr'ă-gŏn), n. A model or type of excellence or perfection; as, a paragon of beauty.

par'a-graph (păr'ă-gráf), n. **1.** A character [¶ or ℗] used in manuscripts and printing, to indicate a paragraph (sense 2, below), and as a reference mark. **2.** A distinct subdivision of a discourse, chapter, or writing. **3.** An item, remark, or quotation forming one paragraph. — v. t. **1** To write a paragraph about. **2.** To divide into paragraphs.

par'al-lel (-lĕl), a. **1.** Geom. Lying or extended in the same direction, and in all parts equally distant. **2.** Having the same direction or tendency; like in essential parts. — n. **1.** A parallel line, curve, or surface. **2.** Conformity; similarity. **3.** A tracing of similarity. **4.** Anything equal to or resembling another; a counterpart. **5.** Geog. One of the imaginary circles on the earth, parallel to the equator, marking latitude. — v. t. **1.** To place or set so as to be parallel to something else. **2.** To equal; match.

par'al-lel'e-pi'ped (-lĕl'ĕ-pī'pĕd), n. A 6-sided prism whose faces are parallelograms.

par'al-lel-ism (păr'ă-lĕl-Iz'm), n. Parallel quality or state; precise correspondence.

par'al-lel'o-gram (-lĕl'ŏ-grăm), n. A quadrilateral with opposite sides parallel.

pa-ral'y-sis (pă-răl'ĭ-sĭs), n.; pl. -SES (-sēz). Med. Loss or impairment of function in any part of the body, esp., loss of the power of voluntary motion, or of sensation.

par'a-lyt'ic (păr'ă-lĭt'ĭk), a. Of, pertaining to, resembling, or affected with, paralysis. — n. A person affected with paralysis.

par'a-lyze (păr'ă-liz), v. t. [1] **1.** To affect with paralysis. **2.** To unnerve; render ineffective.

par'a-mount (-mount), a. Higher or highest in rank or jurisdiction; chief; superior.

par'a-mour (-mōor), n. One who takes the place, without possessing the rights, of a husband or wife.

par'a-pet (păr'ă-pĕt), n. **1.** Fort. A rampart, or elevation of earth, stone, etc., to protect soldiers. **2.** A low wall, or similar barrier, as a railing.

par'a-pher-na'li-a (-fẽr-nā'lĭ-ă), n. pl. **1.** Personal belongings. **2.** Furnishings or apparatus.

par'a-phrase (păr'ă-frăz), n. A free rendering of a text, etc., giving the meaning in another form. — v. t. & i. [1] To express, interpret, or translate in, or to make, a paraphrase.

par'a-site (-sīt), n. **1.** A hanger-on; sycophant. **2.** Biol. A plant or animal living in, on, or with, some other living organism (called its host) at whose expense it obtains its food, or the like.

par'a-sit'ic (-sĭt'ĭk), **par'a-sit'i-cal** (-ĭ-kăl), a. Of the nature of a parasite.

par'a-sol' (-sŏl'), n. A light portable sunshade.

par'boil' (păr'boil'), v. t. To boil partially.

par'cel (-sĕl), n. **1.** Law. A portion; part. **2.** A bundle; package. — v. t. [7] **1.** To divide and distribute by parts or portions. **2.** To make up into parcels. [ing with parcels.]

parcel post. That branch of a postal service dealing with parcels.

parch (pärch), v. t. **1.** To burn the surface of; roast over the fire, as dry grain. **2.** To shrivel with heat. — v. i. To become dry and hot.

parch'ment (-mĕnt), n. **1.** The skin of an animal, as a lamb or goat, prepared for writing on; also, paper imitating it. **2.** A document on parchment.

pard (pärd), n. A leopard. Archaic or Poetic.

par'don (păr'dŭn; -d'n), v. t. **1.** To free from penalty for a fault. **2.** To remit the penalty of; forgive. **3.** To excuse. — n. **1.** A pardoning; forgiveness. **2.** An official warrant of remission of penalty. **3.** Excuse or toleration. — **par'don-er,** n. [8].

par'don-a-ble (-ă-b'l), a. [4] Excusable.

pare (pâr), v. t. [1] **1.** To cut or shave off the superficial substance or ends of. **2.** To cut or shave, as the outside part, from anything.

par'e-gor'ic (păr'ĕ-gŏr'ĭk), n. A medicine that eases pain; esp., camphorated tincture of opium.

pa-ren'chy-ma (pă-rĕn'kĭ-mă), n. Bot. The tissue making up the bulk of the substance of leaves (apart from veins), the pulp of fruits, etc.

par'ent (păr'ĕnt), n. **1.** A father or a mother. **2.** That which produces; source; author.

par'ent-age (-ĕn-tăj), n. **1.** Descent from parents; birth. **2.** State or fact of being a parent.

pa-ren'tal (pă-rĕn'tăl), a. Of, pertaining to, or characteristic of, a parent. — **-ly,** adv. [8].

pa-ren'the-sis (-thĕ-sĭs), n.; pl. -SES (-sēz). **1.** A word, phrase, or sentence, by way of comment or explanation, inserted in, or attached to, a sentence grammatically complete without it. **2.** One of the curved lines, ( ), inclosing a parenthetic word or phrase. Also, these curves collectively.

par'en-thet'ic (păr'ĕn-thĕt'ĭk), **-i-cal** (-ĭ-kăl), a. [4] **1.** Of the nature of a parenthesis. **2.** Using or containing parentheses. — **-i-cal-ly,** adv. [8].

par-he'li-on (pär-hē'lĭ-ŏn), n.; L. pl. -LIA (-lĭ-ă). A mock sun in the form of a bright light, often tinged with color, sometimes near the sun, and sometimes opposite to it. Cf. SUN DOG.

pa'ri-ah (pä'rĭ-ă; păr'ĭ-ă; pă-rī'ă), n. **1.** A member of a certain low caste of southern India. **2.** An outcast; one despised by society.

par'ing (pâr'ĭng), n. **1.** Act of paring. **2.** That which is pared off; as, potato parings.

par'ish (păr'ĭsh), n. **1.** The district committed to one pastor. Brit. **2.** The members of a parish collectively. **3.** A local church; loosely, the territory in which the members live.

pa-rish'ion-er (pă-rĭsh'ŭn-ẽr), n. One who belongs to, or is connected with, a parish.

Pa-ri'sian (-rĭzh'ăn; -rĭz'ĭ-ăn), a. Of or pert. to Paris (in France). — n. A native of Paris.

par'i-ty (păr'ĭ-tĭ), n. **1.** Equality; close correspondence. **2.** Equality in purchasing power between different kinds of money at a given ratio.

park (pärk), n. **1.** A tract of land, either ornamentally laid out or kept in its natural state, as for game, riding, or, esp., recreation. **2.** A space occupied by assembled military animals, wagons, supplies, etc.; also, the objects themselves.— *v. t.* **1.** To inclose in or as in a park. **2.** To bring together in a park or compact body. — *v. i.* To halt a vehicle and leave it standing; hence, *Slang*, to leave something any place.

par'lance (pär'lǎns), *n.* Conversation; debate or parley; now, esp.: Way of speaking; language.

par'ley (pär'lĭ), *n.; pl.* -LEYS (-lĭz). Oral conference, esp. with an enemy.— *v. i.* To confer, esp. orally with an enemy.

par'lia-ment (pär'lĭ-měnt), *n.* **1.** A formal conference of representatives, esp. those of a nation or people empowered to make laws. **2.** [*Often cap.*] The assembly constituting the legislature of Great Britain and some other countries.

par'lia-men-ta'ri-an (-měn-tā'rĭ-ǎn), *n.* One versed in parliamentary rules and usages.

par'lia-men'ta-ry (pär'lĭ-měn'tà-rĭ), *a.* **1.** Of, pert. to, or done by, Parliament. **2.** According to the rules and usages of deliberative bodies.

par'lor (pär'lẽr), *n.* [5] A room primarily for conversation, for reception of guests, etc.

pa-ro'chi-al (pà-rō'kĭ-ǎl), *a.* [4] **1.** Of or pertaining to a parish. **2.** Narrow; provincial.

pa-ro'chi-al-ism (pà-rō'kĭ-ǎl-ĭz'm), *n.* Quality or state of being parochial.

par'o-dy (pär'ō-dĭ), *n.; pl.* -DIES (-dĭz). A mimicry of the style or sentiment of an author; travesty; also, a burlesque of a musical composition. — *v. t.* [2] To burlesque.— **par'o-dist** (pär'ō-dĭst), *n.*

pa-role' (pà-rōl'), *n.* Word of promise; esp., promise of a prisoner to fulfill stated conditions, in consideration of, usually, release from captivity. — *v. t.* [1] To release (a prisoner) on parole.

pa-rot'id (pà-rŏt'ĭd), *a.* Designating, pertaining to, or in the region of, a salivary gland below and in front of the ear. — *n.* The parotid gland.

par'ox-ysm (pär'ŏk-sĭz'm), *n.* **1.** *Med.* A fit, attack, or increased acuteness of a disease, usually periodic. **2.** A sudden and violent action or emotion.— **par'ox-ys'mal** (-sĭz'mǎl), *a.*

par-quet' (pär-kā'; -kĕt'), *n.* **1.** A flooring, esp. of parquetry. **2.** The lower floor of a theater, esp. the part from the orchestra to the parquet circle; — called also, esp. in U. S., *orchestra.*

parquet circle. That part of the lower floor of a theater with seats at the rear of the parquet.

par'quet-ry (pär'kĕt-rĭ), *n.* Wooden inlay or mosaic work, used esp. for floors.

par'ra-keet (pär'à-kēt), *n.* Any of certain parrots, esp. those of small size and with a long tail.

par'ri-cide (pär'ĭ-sīd), *n.* **1.** One who murders a close relation, as a father or mother. **2.** Act or crime of a parricide. — **-cid'al** (-ĭ-sīd'ǎl), *a.*

par'rot (-ŭt), *n.* A bird of the order including the parrakeets, cockatoos, macaws, etc., distinguished esp. by a stout, hooked bill.

par'ry (pär'ĭ), *v. t.* [2] **1.** To ward off, as a blow. **2.** To evade; as, he *parried* my questions.— *v. i.* To ward off or evade something. — *n.; pl.* -RIES (-ĭz). A warding off of a thrust or blow.

parse (pärs), *v. t.* [1] To analyze and describe grammatically, as a word or sentence.

par'si-mo'ni-ous (pär'sĭ-mō'nĭ-ŭs), *a.* [4] Showing parsimony; frugal to excess. — **-ly**, *adv.* [8].

par'si-mo-ny (pär'sĭ-mō-nĭ), *n.* Closeness in expenditure; stinginess; penuriousness.

pars'ley (pärs'lĭ), *n.* A garden herb, the leaves of which are used to flavor soups, as a garnish, etc.

pars'nip (-nĭp), *n.* A plant allied to the carrot; also, its long tapering root, poisonous in the wild state, but made edible and palatable by cultivation.

par'son (pär's'n), *n.* **1.** The rector of a parochial church. **2.** Any clergyman. *Colloq.*

par'son-age (-åj), *n.* The house appropriated by a parish for the minister.

part (pärt), *n.* **1.** One of the portions into which anything is divided; a piece. **2.** Hence: **a** One of several like quantities, numbers, etc., of which anything is composed; as, an ounce is the sixteenth *part* of a pound. **b** *pl.* Abilities; talents; as, a man of *parts.* **3.** Share; lot; interest; duty; office; as, each did his *part.* **4.** A particular character acted or to be acted in a play. **5.** *Music.* In music arranged for several voices or instruments, a particular voice or instrument, or the individual score for it. **6.** Quarter; region; — usually in *pl.*; as, in foreign *parts.* **7.** One of the opposing parties or sides in a conflict or a controversy.— **part of speech**, a word classed according to the kind of idea or relation it denotes in the sentence. The parts of speech are eight: noun, adjective, pronoun, verb, adverb, preposition, conjunction, interjection.

part (pärt), *v. t.* **1.** To divide or separate into distinct parts. **2.** To disunite; sunder. **3.** To hold apart; separate, as combatants.— *v. i.* **1.** To be broken or divided into parts or pieces; break. **2.** To go away; to quit each other. **3.** To give up a connection; as, to *part* with a friend. **4.** To separate.

par-take' (pär-tāk'), *v. i.; for prin. parts see* TAKE. **1.** To take a part in common with others; participate; share. **2.** To take or receive a portion (of). — *v. t.* To take a part in.— **par-tak'er**, *n.* [8].

part'ed (pär'tĕd), *p. a.* Divided; cleft.

par-terre' (pär-târ'), *n.* An ornamental arrangement of flower beds or plots.

par'tial (-shǎl), *a.* [4] **1.** Inclined to one party more than the other; biased. **2.** Having a liking (for). **3.** Of, pertaining to, affecting, or constituting, a part only; as, **partial payment:** **a** A payment in part on a bond or other obligation. **b** *pl.* That branch of arithmetic which treats of the computation of the amount due on a bond or other obligation on which one or more partial payments have been made.— **par'tial-ly**, *adv.* [8].

par'ti-al'i-ty (pär'shĭ-ǎl'ĭ-tĭ; -shǎl'-), *n.* **1.** Quality or state of being partial. **2.** A special liking.

par-tic'i-pant (pär-tĭs'ĭ-pǎnt), *a.* Sharing. — *n.* A participator; sharer.

par-tic'i-pate (-pāt), *v. i. & t.* [1] To have a share in common with others; partake; share; — with *with* (a person), or *in* (a thing).— **-pa'tor**, *n.* [8].

par-tic'i-pa'tion (-pā'shŭn), *n.* A participating.

par'ti-cip'i-al (pär'tĭ-sĭp'ĭ-ǎl), *a.* Having the nature and use of, or formed from, a participle. — **par'ti-cip'i-al-ly**, *adv.* [8].

par'ti-ci-ple (pär'tĭ-sĭ-p'l), *n.* *Gram.* A word partaking of the nature of both verb and adjective. The English verb has two participles: (1) the *present*, ending in -*ing*; as, *writing*; (2) the *past* or *passive*, ending usually in -*ed*, -*d*, -*t*, -*en*, or -*n*.

āle, senāte, câre, ăm, ȧccount, ärm, ȧsk, sofȧ; ēve, ĕvent, ēnd, recĕnt, makĕr; īce, ĭll; ōld, ŏbey, ôrb, ŏdd, sŏft, cŏnnect; ūse, ŭnite, ûrn, ŭp, circŭs; fōod, fŏot; out, oil;

par'ti-cle (-k'l), *n.* **1.** A minute portion of matter; a bit. **2.** Any very small portion. **3.** *Gram.* A subordinate word never inflected (a preposition, conjunction, interjection); an element having a distinct meaning, but used only in composition; as, *-ward* in back*ward*, *-ly* in love*ly*.

par-tic'u-lar (pär-tĭk'ū-lȧr), *a.* [4] **1.** Relating to a portion of anything; separate; specific. **2.** Of or pert. to a single person, class, or thing; not general; personal. **3.** Noteworthy; special. **4.** Concerned with, or attentive to, details; hence, nice; fastidious. — *n.* A separate member of a class, or part of a whole; individual fact, or item.

par-tic'u-lar'i-ty (pär-tĭk'ū-lȧr'ĭ-tĭ), *n.; pl.* -TIES (-tĭz). **1.** State or quality of being particular. **2.** That which is particular.

par-tic'u-lar-ize (-tĭk'ū-lȧr-īz), *v. t.* [1] To give as a particular, or as the particulars; mention particularly. — *v. i.* To mention or attend to particulars; be circumstantial, as in a story.

par-tic'u-lar-ly, *adv.* **1.** In a particular manner; individually; severally. **2.** Especially.

part'ing (pär'tĭng), *p. a.* **1.** That parts: **a** Departing; fig., dying. **b** Dividing. **2.** Given, etc., when departing; farewell; as, a *parting* kiss. — *vb. n.* **1.** A parting; division; separation. **2.** Place of division or separation. **3.** A leave-taking.

par'ti-san, **par'ti-zan**, *n.* A devoted adherent. — *a.* Adherent, esp. blindly, to a party or faction. — **par'ti-san-ship'**, *n.*

par-ti'tion (pär-tĭsh'ŭn), *n.* **1.** A parting; separation; division. **2.** That which divides or separates; esp., an interior wall dividing a house, inclosure, etc. — *v. t.* **1.** To divide into parts or shares, as an estate. **2.** To divide, as a house, into distinct parts by lines, walls, etc.

par'ti-tive (pär'tĭ-tĭv), *a.* Serving to part or divide into parts; *Gram.*, denoting a part. — *n.* *Gram.* A word expressing partition or denoting a part. — **par'ti-tive-ly**, *adv.* [8].

par'ti-zan. Var. of PARTISAN.

part'ly, *adv.* In part; not wholly.

part'ner (pärt'nẽr), *n.* **1.** An associate; sharer; companion. **2.** **a** A husband or a wife. **b** Either of a couple who dance together.

part'ner-ship, *n.* **1.** State of being a partner; association; participation. **2.** *Law.* **a** The relation between persons who have contracted to join in business and share the profit between them. **b** The association of persons thus joined for business; company; firm.

par-took' (pär-tŏŏk'), *pret.* of PARTAKE.

par'tridge (pär'trĭj), *n.* **1.** Any of certain Old World stout-bodied game birds akin to the domestic fowl. **2.** Hence, any of various similar birds, esp., in North America, the ruffed grouse.

partridge berry. An American trailing evergreen plant with a scarlet berry.

Partridge Berry.

par'ty (pär'tĭ), *n.; pl.* -TIES (-tĭz).

1. A body of persons forming one side in a contest, etc.; esp., one of the parts into which a people is divided on public questions; as, the Democratic *party.* **2.** A detachment, as of troops. **3.** A company of persons, esp. for social enjoyment, etc.; as, a dinner *party.* **4.** A person, or one of two or more persons, or a body of persons, forming a side in an affair; as, a *party* to a contract.

par'ty-col'ored, *a.* [5] Colored with different tints; variegated. [properties.]

party wall. A wall which divides two adjoining

par've-nu (pär'vĕ-nū'; *F.* pär'vē-nü'), *n. masc.;* **-nue** (-nū'; *F.* -nü') *n. fem.; pl.* -NUS (-nūz'; *F.* -nü'); *F. fem. pl.* -NUES (-nūz'; *F.* -nü'). One who has risen, as by wealth, above the station in which he was born; an upstart. *Usually Derogatory.*

pas'chal (păs'kăl), *a.* Of or pertaining to Passover or Easter; as, *paschal* eggs.

pa-sha' (pȧ-shä'; păsh'ä), *n.* **1.** [*Usually cap.*] A title (placed after the name) given to officers of rank in Turkey. **2.** A person bearing the title.

pass (pȧs), *n.* **1.** A passageway; road; route; esp., a defile through mountains.

pass, *n.* **1.** Act of passing; passage. **2.** State of things; condition. **3.** Permission or license to pass, or to go and come. **4.** A thrust or lunge, as in fencing. **5.** Transference of objects by sleight of hand or the like. **6.** A movement of the hand over, before, or along anything, as by a mesmerist. — *v. i.; pret.* PASSED (pȧst); *p. p* PASSED, PAST; *p. pr. & vb. n.* PASS'ING. **1.** To go; move; proceed. **2.** To circulate, as money; gain general acceptance, as a fact. **3.** To undergo transition or conversion. **4.** *Law.* To be conveyed or transferred, as by will or deed, as an estate **5.** To be exchanged; be done; as, few words *passed.* **6.** To go away; depart; also, to die. **7.** To force or make one's way. **8.** To go unheeded or unchallenged. **9.** To receive legislative sanction; be enacted. **10.** To go through any test successfully. **11.** To render a verdict or judgment. **12.** *Fencing.* To make a pass; thrust. **13.** *Cards.* To decline to play a round, or to decline a privilege, as of making the trump. — *v. t.* **1.** **a** To go by, beyond, over, through, or the like; cross; traverse. **b** To go successfully or satisfactorily through, as a trial, test, etc. **c** To go beyond; surpass. **2. a** To cause or enable to pass, or go. **b** To cause to, or let, pass or elapse; spend; — said of time. **c** To cause or allow to advance; esp., to give official sanction to; ratify; enact, as a bill. **d** To hand or deliver, as from one to another; to put in circulation, as money. **e** To express, as an opinion; as, to *pass* sentence or one.

pass'a-ble (pȧs'ȧ-b'l), *a.* [4] **1.** Capable of being passed, as a road, or penetrated, as a forest. **2.** Generally receivable; current. **3.** Admissible; moderate; fairly good. — **-a-bly**, *adv.*

pas'sage (păs'ăj), *n.* **1.** Act of passing; transit. **2.** Transition; lapse; course; progress. **3** Right, liberty, or permission to pass. **4.** Of a measure or law: Enactment; sanction. **5.** A means of passing a way; course; a pass; a hall, corridor, lobby, vestibule, etc. **6.** A mutual act or transaction; interchange, as of vows, blows, etc.; encounter **7.** A portion of something, as of a discourse.

pas'sage-way' (păs'ăj-wā'), n. = PASSAGE, 5.

pass book. a *Banking.* Depositor's book in which is entered a record of his deposits and withdrawals. **b** A customer's book in which a storekeeper enters a record of goods bought on credit.

passe-men'terie (păs-měn'trĭ; F. päs'män'trē'), n. Trimmings, esp. of braids, cords, beads, etc.

pas'sen-ger (păs'ĕn-jẽr), n. **1.** A wayfarer. *Now Rare,* exc. in *foot passenger.* **2.** A traveler by an established conveyance, as by boat, train, etc.

‖ **passe' par'tout'** (päs' pär'tōo'). [F.] In picture framing, a piece of cardboard, wood, or the like with its center cut out to receive the picture.

pass'er (pás'ẽr), n. One who passes.

pass'er–by', n. ; pl. PASSERS-. One who passes by.

pass'ing (pás'ĭng), a. **1.** Going by, beyond, through, or away. **2.** Fleeting. **3.** Made, given, etc., in passing; cursory. — n. **1.** Act of one that passes. **2.** A means of passing ; a ford.

pas'sion (păsh'ŭn), n. **1.** A suffering of inflicted pain; esp. : [*Often cap.*] The suffering of Christ on the cross, or, often, His sufferings between the Lord's Supper and His death. **2.** Intense emotion ; often, rage or love; also, enthusiasm ; eager desire. **3.** *pl.* The emotions collectively.

pas'sion-ate (-ăt), a. [4] **1.** Capable or susceptible of passion; easily excited, esp. to anger. **2.** Affected with, or marked by, passion; ardent. **3.** Affected with love. — **-ly**, adv [8] — **-ness**, n. [8].

passion flower. A flower or plant of a genus of herbs or shrubs, many of them climbers, with showy blossoms of white, red, purple, etc.

pas'sion-less, a. [4] Void of passion ; calm.

Passion Week. The week before Easter.

pas'sive (păs'ĭv), a. [4] **1.** Not active, but acted on or receiving impressions. **2.** *Gram.* Designating, or pert. to : **a** The form or voice of a transitive verb which makes its grammatical subject the actual object of its action, as in *I am taught.* **b** Verbs which assert that the subject is acted upon ; — disting. from *active* and *neuter.* **3.** Submissive; unresisting. — n. *Gram.* The passive voice. — **-ly**, adv. [8].

Passion Flower.

pas'sive-ness, pas-siv'i-ty (pă-sĭv'ĭ-tĭ), n. Quality or state of being passive.

pass'-key', n. A master key; also, a private key.

pass'o'ver (pás'ō'vẽr), n. **1.** [*cap.*] An annual feast of the Jews, instituted (*Ex.* xii.) to commemorate the sparing of the Israelites in Egypt when God smote the firstborn of the Egyptians. **2.** The sacrifice offered at the feast of the Passover.

pass'port (păs'pōrt), n. **1.** An official document permitting one to pass or travel about unmolested. **2.** That which secures admission or acceptance.

pass'word' (păs'wûrd'), n. A word to be uttered by one before he is allowed to pass ; watchword.

past (påst), a. **1.** Of or pertaining to a former time or state ; gone by ; elapsed ; last ; foregoing. **2.** *Gram.* Expressive of time gone by ; as, the *past* tense.— **past master.** a One who has held the office of master, as in a lodge of Freemasons. **b** An adept. — n. **1.** A former time or state. **2.** Past

life or history ; esp. a past career unknown **3.** *Gram.* The past tense. — adv. By ; beyond. — prep. Beyond, as time, position, power, etc.

paste (påst), n. **1.** Dough; esp., dough prepared with shortening for pastry. **2.** A soft mixture, esp. an adhesive one of flour and water. **3.** A kind of glass used to make imitation gems ; also, an imitation gem so made. — v. t. [1] To unite with, or cover by or as by, paste.

paste'board' (-bōrd'), n. A stiff material made by pasting together sheets of paper.

pas'tel (păs'tĕl ; păs-tĕl'), n. **1.** A kind of paste made by grinding pigments and mixing with gum water ; also, a crayon made of this. **2.** A drawing in pastel ; art of drawing with pastels.

past'er (pās'tẽr), n. **1.** One who pastes. **2.** A gummed paper to be pasted on or over something.

Pas'teur-i-za'tion (păs'tẽr-ĭ-zā'shŭn; păs-tûr'-), n. A process for preventing or checking fermentation in fluids, by heating them to 131°–158°F.

Pas'teur-ize (păs'tẽr-īz; păs-tûr'-), v. t. [1] To subject to Pasteurization.

pas'til (păs'tĭl) } n. **1.** A small cone or mass **pas-tille'** (păs-tēl') } of aromatic paste, used for fumigating, deodorizing, etc. **2.** A lozenge.

pas'time' (pás'tīm'), n. That which amuses, and serves to make time pass agreeably ; amusement ; diversion ; recreation.

pas'tor (-tẽr), n. A priest ; a minister.

pas'tor-al (păs'tẽr-ăl), a. [4] **1.** Of or pertaining to shepherds or rural life and scenes. **2.** Relating to the pastor of a church. — n. **1.** A poem, drama, etc., describing pastoral life. **2.** A pastoral picture or scene. — **pas'tor-al-ly**, adv. [8].

pas'tor-ate (-ăt), n. Office, state, jurisdiction, or tenure of office of a pastor ; also, a body of pastors

pas'try (pās'trĭ), n. ; pl. -TRIES (-trĭz). Articles of food made of paste, with a crust of paste.

pas'tur-age (pás'tṳr-ăj), n. **1.** A pasturing ; the grazing of cattle. **2.** Grazing ground; pasture.

pas'ture (-tṳr), n. Growing grass or grass land for sheep, cattle, etc., to feed upon ; pasturage. — v. i. [1] To feed on growing grass ; graze. — v. t. [1] To feed. *Obs.,* exc. : To put out to pasture; graze. **2.** To eat in grazing ; graze.

past'y (pās'tĭ), a. [3] Like paste, as in color, softness, stickiness.— **past'i-ness** (-tĭ-nĕs), n. [8].

past'y, n. ; pl. -TIES (-tĭz). A pie, usually of meat, with a paste crust, and often baked without a dish.

pat (păt), v. t. ; PAT'TED ; -TING. To strike, esp. gently, with a flat surface, with the hand, or the like. — n. **1.** A light blow, as with the fingers ; a tap. **2.** A small mass, as of butter, shaped by pats. **3.** The sound of a pat or tap, as of bare feet.

pat, a. ; PAT'TER (-ẽr) ; PAT'TEST. That hits the object or mark or suits the purpose or occasion; fit ; apt. — adv. Aptly ; opportunely ; readily.

patch (păch), n. **1.** A piece of cloth sewed on a garment to repair or strengthen it. **2.** A small piece of black silk or court-plaster stuck on the face, as to heighten beauty. **3.** A small piece of ground or of something on it ; a tract ; plot. **4.** A small piece ; a scrap. — v t. **1.** To provide, mend, strengthen, adorn, etc., with or as with a patch or patches ; often, esp. with *up*, to repair clumsily **2.** To make of patches joined together, as by sewing; arrange or put together hastily or insecurely; piece. — **patch'er,** *n.* [8].

patch'work' (păch'wûrk'), *n.* Work of pieces sewed together, esp. pieces of various colors and figures; hence, a jumble; hodgepodge.

pate (pāt), *n.* The head or the crown of the head.

pa-tel'la (pă-těl'ă), *n.; L. pl.* -LÆ (-ē). *Anat.* A thick, flat, triangular, movable bone, forming the anterior point of the knee; kneepan; kneecap.

pat'ent (păt'ĕnt; pā'tĕnt; *in sense 3,* usually pā'tĕnt), *a.* [3] **1.** Open to public perusal; — said of a document conferring a privilege or the like; as, letters *patent.* **2.** Appropriated or protected by letters patent; patented. **3.** Open; evident; manifest. — **patent leather,** a kind of leather having a hard, smooth, glossy, usually black, surface. — *n.* **1.** An official document conferring a right or privilege. **2.** A writing securing to an inventor, for a term of years, the exclusive right to make, use, and vend his invention; also, the monopoly or right so granted. **3.** The subject matter protected by a patent. **4.** An instrument making a conveyance or grant of public lands; the land so conveyed. — *v. t.* **1.** To grant, or grant to, by patent. **2.** To secure by patent; as, to *patent* an invention.

pat'ent-a-ble(-*ă*-b'l), *a.* Capable of being patented.

pat'ent-ee' (păt'ĕn-tē'), *n.* One to whom a grant is made, or a privilege secured, by patent.

pa'ter-fa-mil'i-as (pā'tẽr-fă-mĭl'ĭ-ăs), *n.* The father or head of a family.

pa-ter'nal (pă-tûr'năl), *a.* [4] **1.** Of or pertaining to a father; fatherly. **2.** Received or derived from a father, as an estate. **3.** Related through the father; as, a *paternal* aunt. — **-ly,** *adv.* [8].

pa-ter'nal-ism (-ĭz'm), *n.* The attempt to supply the needs or regulate the conduct of a nation or community in the same way as a father does those of his children.

pa-ter'ni-ty (-nĭ-tĭ), *n.* **1.** Fatherhood. **2.** Derivation or descent from a father; male parentage.

pa'ter-nos'ter (pā'tẽr-nŏs'tẽr; păt'ẽr-), *n.* **1.** The Lord's Prayer, esp. in its Latin form. **2.** A bead on a rosary, indicating that a paternoster is to be said; also, a rosary.

path (páth), *n.; pl.* PATHS (páthz). **1.** A beaten way; footway. **2.** A way or track in which anything moves; also, a course or way of life, thought, etc.

pa-thet'ic (pă-thĕt'ĭk), *a.* [4] Affecting or moving the tender emotions, especially pity or grief. — **-i-cal-ly,** *adv.* [8].

path'find'er (pàth'fīn'dẽr), *n.* One who discovers a way or path; an explorer.

path'less (páth'lĕs), *a.* Having no path or paths.

path'o-gen'ic (păth'ŏ-jĕn'ĭk), *a.* [4] Causing, or relating to the causation of, disease.

path'o-log'ic (păth'ŏ-lŏj'ĭk), **-log'i-cal** (-ĭ-kăl), *a.* [4] Of or pert. to pathology. — **-i-cal-ly,** *adv.* [8].

pa-thol'o-gist (pă-thŏl'ŏ-jĭst), *n.* One skilled in, or a student of, pathology.

pa-thol'o-gy (pă-thŏl'ŏ-jĭ), *n.; pl.* -GIES (-jĭz). **1.** The science treating of diseases. **2.** The condition of an organ, tissue, or fluid due to disease.

pa'thos (pā'thŏs), *n.* That quality which excites pity, sympathy, or tender sorrow.

path'way' (páth'wā'), *n.* A way which is, or serves as, a path; a footpath; any path or course.

pa'tience (pā'shĕns), *n.* State or quality of being patient; perseverance.

pa'tient (pā'shĕnt), *a.* [4] **1.** Undergoing pains, trials, etc., without complaint. **2.** Lenient; forbearing. **3.** Expectant with calmness, or without discontent; composed. **4.** Persevering. **5.** Enduring or able to endure; — with *of.* — *n.* A person under medical or surgical treatment. — **pa'tient-ly,** *adv.* [8].

pa'tois' (pă'twä'; păt'wä), *n.* An illiterate or provincial form of speech; dialect.

pa'tri-arch (pā'trĭ-ärk), *n.* **1.** The father and ruler of a family or tribe; — esp. in Biblical history before Moses. **2.** A venerable old man.

pa'tri-ar'chal (-är'kăl), *a.* Of or pertaining to, like, or characteristic of, a patriarch or patriarchs.

pa-tri'cian (pă-trĭsh'ăn), *a.* [4] **1.** Of or pert. to patricians. **2.** Aristocratic; not plebeian. — *n.* A noble by right of birth or privilege.

pat'ri-mo'ni-al (păt'rĭ-mō'nĭ-ăl), *a.* Pertaining to a patrimony; hereditary, as an estate.

pat'ri-mo-ny (păt'rĭ-mŏ-nĭ), *n.; pl.* -NIES (-nĭz). **1.** A heritage derived from one's father or other ancestor. **2.** An endowment of a church, etc.

pa'tri-ot (pā'trĭ-ŏt; păt'rĭ-), *n.* One who loves his country and zealously supports it.

pa'tri-ot'ic (-ŏt'ĭk), *a.* [4] Inspired by, or full of, patriotism. — **pa'tri-ot'i-cal-ly,** *adv* [8].

pa'tri-ot-ism (-ŏt-ĭz'm), *n.* Love of country.

Patriots' Day. A legal holiday in Massachusetts and Maine, April 19 (battle of Lexington).

pa-trol' (pă-trōl'), *v. i. & t.; -*TROLLED' (-trōld'); -TROL'LING. To go the rounds of, or traverse as for guarding. — *n.* A going of the rounds by a guard to insure greater security; also, the guard.

pa-trol'man (-măn), *n.; pl.* -MEN (-mĕn). One who patrols; a policeman who patrols a certain beat.

pa'tron (pā'trŭn), *n.* **1.** One who protects or supports; defender. **2.** A regular customer. **3.** A guardian saint; a tutelary deity.

pat'ron-age (păt'rŭn-ăj; pā'trŭn-), *n.* Act, office, aid, etc., of a patron.

pa'tron-ess (pā'trŭn-ĕs), *n.* A female patron.

pat'ron-ize (păt'rŭn-īz; pā'trŭn-), *v. t.* [1] **1.** To act as patron toward; protect; favor; aid. **2.** To treat with condescension. *Disparaging.* — **pat'ron-iz'er** (-īz'ẽr), *n.* [8] — **pat'ron-iz'ing-ly,** *adv.* [8].

pat'ro-nym'ic (păt'rŏ-nĭm'ĭk), *n.* A modification of an ancestor's name borne by a descendant; as, *Johnson,* the son of John; also, the family name.

pa-troon' (pă-troon'), *n.* Certain landed proprietors under the old Dutch governments of New York and New Jersey.

pat'ten (păt'ĕn), *n.* Any of various kinds of footgear, as a wooden shoe or clog, or a kind of overshoe, that raise the wearer off the ground.

pat'ter (-ẽr), *v. i. & t.* **1.** To say rapidly or mumblingly; mumble. **2.** To chatter; jabber. — *n.* **1.** The cant of thieves, etc.; jargon; lingo. **2.** Hence, glib talk; chatter. *Cant or Colloq.*

pat'ter, *v. i.* To strike or move with a quick succession of pats. — *n.* A pattering; a quick succession of slight sounds; as, a *patter* of rain.

pat'tern (-ẽrn), *n.* **1.** Anything proposed or designed for imitation; a model. **2.** Form of dec-

oration; design. Also, form of natural marking.
3. A specimen; sample; esp., a model example.
4. A length of cloth sufficient for a garment. *U. S.*
— *v. t.* To make or design by, from, or after a pattern; copy.

pat'ty (păt'ĭ), *n.; pl.* PATTIES (-ĭz). A small pasty.

pau'ci-ty (pô'sĭ-tĭ), *n.;pl.* -TIES (-tĭz). **1.** Fewness; a small number. **2.** Smallness of quantity; insufficiency.   [tents; abdomen.

paunch (pänch; pônch), *n.* The belly and its con-

pau'per (pô'pẽr), *n.* **1.** One without means except from charity. **2.** A very poor person.

pau'per-ism (-ĭz'm), *n.* State of being a pauper; also, paupers collectively.

pau'per-ize (-īz), *v. t.* [1] To make a pauper of.

pause (pôz), *n.* **1.** A temporary stop or rest; interruption; cessation. **2.** Temporary inaction; hesitation. **3.** a *Gram.* In writing and printing, a punctuation point. **b** A break or paragraph in writing. — *v. i.* [1] To make a pause; stop; cease for a time; delay.

pave (pāv), *v. t.* [1] **1.** To lay or cover with stone, brick, etc. **2.** To make smooth or easy; prepare; — with *way;* as, to *pave* the way for another.

pave'ment (pāv'ment), *n.* That with which anything is paved; a paved road, sidewalk, etc.

pa-vil'ion (pȧ-vĭl'yŭn), *n.* **1.** A tent; esp., a large peaked tent raised on posts. **2.** A single light building of a decorative character.

pav'ing (pāv'ĭng), *n.* **1.** Act or process of laying a pavement. **2.** A pavement or material for it.

paw (pô), *n.* The foot of a quadruped having claws. — *v. t. & i.* **1.** To strike or touch with or as with a paw; hence, to handle fondly or rudely. *Colloq.* **2.** To scrape or beat with the fore foot.

pawl (pôl), *n.* A pivoted tongue, or sliding bolt, on one part of a machine, adapted to fall into notches on another part, as a ratchet wheel, so as to permit motion in one direction only.

pawn (pôn), *n.* Any of 16 chessmen of least value.

pawn, *n.* **1.** A surety or pledge; gage. **2.** State of being pledged. — *v. t.* To give or deposit as security, as for a loan; pledge. — -**er,** *n.* [8].

pawn'bro'ker (-brō'kẽr), *n.* One whose business is lending money on pledged personal property.

pawn'shop' (pôn'shŏp'), *n.* A pawnbroker's shop.

pay (pā), *v. t.;* PAID (pād), or, *Obs.,* exc. in sense 6, PAYED; PAY'ING. **1.** To satisfy (another person) for service rendered, property delivered, etc.; compensate. **2.** To requite according to merit. **3.** To discharge, as a debt, by giving or doing what is due. **4.** To give or offer, with no implied obligation. **5.** To be profitable to. **6.** To pass out, as a rope; — with *out* or *away.*— *v. i.* **1.** To give a recompense; make payment. **2.** To make or secure suitable return for expense or trouble; be worth the effort or pains required; — *n.* Act of paying, state of being paid, or that which is paid; payment.

pay'a-ble (pā'ȧ-b'l), *a.* That may, can, or should be paid; justly due.   [is to be, paid.

pay-ee' (pā-ē'), *n.* The one to whom money is, or

pay'er (pā'ẽr), *n.* One that pays; esp., the person by whom a bill or note has been, or should be, paid.

pay'mas'ter (pā'mȧs'tẽr), *n.* One who pays, esp. as an officer of a government, corporation, etc.

pay'ment (pā'mĕnt), *n.* Act of paying; that which is paid; pay; recompense; requital.

pea (pē), *n.; pl.* PEAS (pēz) or, esp. collectively, PEASE (pēz). The well-known seed of a vine allied to the bean, in common cultivation; also, the plant.

peace (pēs), *n.* A state of quiet; freedom from disturbance; calm; esp.: **a** Public quiet, order, and security. **b** Harmony between persons or nations.

peace'a-ble (pēs'ȧ-b'l), *a.* [4] Being in or at peace; disposed to peace. — -**ness,** *n.* — -**a-bly,** *adv.*

peace'ful (-fŏŏl), *a.* [4] **1.** Pacific; peaceable; as, *peaceful* words. **2.** Possessing or enjoying peace; quiet; tranquil; as, a *peaceful* country. — -**ly,** *adv.* [8] — -**ness,** *n.* [8].

peace'mak'er (-māk'ẽr), *n.* One that makes peace.

peach (pēch), *n.* The well-known fruit, a drupe, of a low tree of the plum family; also, the tree.

pea'cock' (pē'kŏk'), *n.* The male of a certain large bird related to the barnyard fowl, well-known for its splendid plumage. It has long covering feathers (coverts) above the true tail feathers. In common usage the female (strictly **pea'hen'**) is also called peacock.

pea'fowl' (pē'foul'), *n.* The peacock or peahen.

pea'hen' (-hĕn'), *n.* Female peafowl.

pea'-jack'et, *n.* A thick loose double-breasted woolen coat, worn esp. by sailors.

peak (pēk), *v. i.* To grow thin or peaked.

peak, *n.* **1.** The sharp end or pointed top of anything. **2. a** The projecting front part of a cap or the like. **b** The top, or one of the tops, of a mountain, or range, ending in a point; often, the whole mountain, esp. when isolated. **3.** *Naut.* The upper aftermost corner of a fore-and-aft sail.

peaked (pēkt; pēk'ĕd), *a.* [4] **1.** Pointed; as, a *peaked* roof. **2.** (*pron. usually* pēk'ĕd). Having sharpness of figure or features; thin. *Colloq.*

peal (pēl), *n.* **1.** A set of bells or a series of changes rung on a set of bells. **2.** A loud sound or succession of sounds, as of thunder. — *v. i.* To give out peals; resound. — *v. t.* To noise abroad.

pea'nut (pē'nŭt), *n.* A trailing plant of the bean family, widely cultivated in warm regions, whose pods ripen underground; also, its nutlike seed.

pear (pâr), *n.* The fleshy fruit of a tree related to the apple; also, the tree.

pearl (pûrl), *n.* **1.** A small, hard, smooth body formed within the shell of the pearl oyster and certain other shellfish as a growth around some foreign substance (as a grain of sand). It is used as a gem. **2.** The color of a fine pearl; a pale bluish gray. **3.** Mother-of-pearl.

pearl'ash' (pûrl'ásh'), *n.* See POTASH.

pearl'y (pûr'lĭ), *a.* [3] Abounding in or resembling pearls or pearl; also, of the color of pearl.

peas'ant (pĕz'ănt), *n.* A farmer of the working class in European countries; farm laborer.

peas'ant-ry (-rĭ), *n.* Peasants collectively.

pease (pēz), *n.* Plural of PEA (which see).

peat (pēt), *n.* A carbonaceous substance formed by partial decomposition in water of various plants, esp. certain mosses. It is used as fuel.

peb'ble (pĕb''l), *n.* A small stone rounded by the action of water. — *v. t.* [1] To grain (leather) so as to produce an irregularly indented surface.

peb'bly (-lĭ), *a.* [3] Full of pebbles; pebbled.

āle, senᾱte, cȃre, ăm, ăccount, ärm, ȧsk, sofȧ; ēve, ĕvent, ĕnd, recᴇnt, makᴇr; īce, ĭll; ōld, ȯbey, ôrb, ŏdd, sŏft, cŏnnect; ūse, ūnite, ûrn, ŭp, circᵫs; fōōd, fŏŏt; ᴏut, oil;

pe-can' (pē-kăn'; -kän'), n. A species of hickory of the southern U. S.; also, its nut.

pec'ca-dil'lo (pĕk'ȧ-dĭl'ō), n.; pl. -LOS or -LOES (-ōz). A petty fault. [piglike mammal.]

pec'ca-ry (-rĭ), n.; pl. -RIES (-rĭz). An American

peck (pĕk), n. **1.** The fourth part of a bushel; a dry measure of eight quarts. **2.** A great deal.

peck (pĕk), v. t. **1.** To strike with the beak. **2.** To make (a hole), with or as with a beak. **3.** To strike with a pick or other sharp instrument, esp. with repeated quick movements. — v. i. **1.** To make strokes with the beak; pick. **2.** To pick up food with the beak.—n. **1.** Act of pecking; a quick, sharp stroke. **2.** The mark made by pecking.

peck'er (-ẽr), n. **1.** An instrument for pecking, as a pick. **2.** One that pecks.

pec'to-ral (pĕk'tō-rȧl), a. **1.** Of, or pertaining to, the breast, or chest. **2.** Relating to, or good for, diseases of the chest or lungs. — n. **1.** Something worn on the breast. **2.** A medicine for diseases of the chest organs, as the lungs.

pec'u-late (pĕk'ū-lāt), v. i. & t. [1] To steal or misappropriate moneys intrusted to one's care; embezzle. — **pec'u-la'tor** (-lā'tẽr), n. [8].

pec'u-la'tion (-lā'shŭn), n. Act or practice of peculating; embezzlement.

pe-cu'liar (pē-kūl'yȧr), a. [4] **1.** One's own; belonging to an individual; particular; special. **2.** Singular; queer. — **-ly**, adv. [8].

pe-cu'li-ar'i-ty (pē-kū'lĭ-ăr'ĭ-tĭ), n. pl.; -ITIES (-Ĭ-tĭz). Quality or state of being peculiar; that which is peculiar; also, a singularity; odd trait.

pe-cu'ni-a-ry (-kū'nĭ-ȧ-rĭ), a. Consisting of or relating to money; monetary; as, a *pecuniary* reward.

ped'a-gog'ic (pĕd'ȧ-gŏj'ĭk) } a. Of or pertain-
ped'a-gog'i-cal (-Ĭ-kȧl) } ing to a pedagogue; concerned with pedagogics.

ped'a-gog'ics (-ĭks), n. Science of teaching.

ped'a-gogue (-gŏg), n. A teacher of children; a schoolmaster, esp. a dogmatic or pedantic one.

ped'a-go'gy (pĕd'ȧ-gō'jĭ; -gŏj'ĭ), n. **1.** Pedagogics. **2.** Instruction or discipline.

ped'al (pĕd'ȧl or, esp. in Anat. & Zoöl., pē'dȧl), a. Of or pertaining to the foot or feet.

ped'al (pĕd'ȧl), n. A lever acted on by the foot; treadle. — v. t. & i. [7] To work the pedals of.

ped'ant (-ȧnt), n. One with book learning or the like who lacks ability to make proper use of his knowledge or overrates mere knowledge.

pe-dan'tic (pē-dăn'tĭk), a. [4] Of, pert. to, characteristic of, or like, a pedant. — **-ti-cal-ly**, adv.

ped'ant-ry (pĕd'ȧnt-rĭ), n.; pl. -RIES (-rĭz). **1.** The acts, style, etc., of a pedant; excessive emphasis of trivial details, etc. **2.** An instance of this.

ped'dle (pĕd'l), v. i. [1] **1.** To travel about with wares for sale. **2.** To do a small business. — v. t. To sell from place to place; hawk; deal out in small quantities.

ped'dler (-lẽr), n. One who peddles; a hawker.

ped'es-tal (pĕd'ĕs-tȧl), n. The support or foot of a column, and hence of a statue, vase, lamp, etc.

pe-des'tri-an (pē-dĕs'trĭ-ȧn), a. [4] **1.** Going or performed on foot. **2.** Of or pert. to walking; hence, slow or dull. — n. A walker; a foot traveler.

pe-des'tri-an-ism (-ĭz'm), n. Act, art, or practice of a pedestrian.

ped'i-cel (pĕd'ĭ-sĕl), n. Bot. **a** Any slender stalk, esp. one supporting a fruiting organ. **b** In seed plants, a flower stalk bearing a single flower.

ped'i-gree (pĕd'ĭ-grē), n. A record of ancestry; line of ancestors; descent, also, notable descent

ped'i-ment (-mĕnt), n. Originally, in classical architecture, the triangular space forming the gable of a roof; hence, a similar form used as a decoration over porticoes, doors, etc.

pe-dom'e-ter (pē-dŏm'ē-tẽr), n. An instrument to record distance covered in walking.

pe-dun'cle (pē-dŭn'k'l), n. Bot. A flower stalk.

peek (pēk), v. i. To look slyly, or with the eyes half closed; peep. — n. A glance; peep.

peel (pēl), v. t. **1.** To strip off the skin, bark, or rind of; sometimes, to pare. **2.** To strip or tear off, as the bark of a tree, etc. — v. i. To lose the skin, bark, or rind; come off as the skin, bark, or rind does. — n. Skin or rind of a fruit.

peep (pēp), v. i. **1.** To cry, as a young chick, a mouse, etc.; cheep. **2.** To speak with a small thin voice. — n. The sound of one that peeps.

peep, v. i. **1.** To peer through or as through a crevice. **2.** To begin to come from or as if from concealment; emerge partially. — n. **1.** Act of peeping; a slight look; esp., a furtive, peering glance. **2.** The first glance or appearance.

peep'er, n. One that peeps. [intently.]

peer (pēr), v. i. To look narrowly, curiously, or

peer, n. **1.** One of the same rank, quality, etc.; an equal; match. **2.** A nobleman; a member of one of the five degrees of the British nobility, namely, duke, marquis, earl, viscount, baron.

peer'age (pēr'ăj), n. **1.** The body of peers; also, the rank or dignity of a peer. **2.** A record of the peers of the realm, with genealogy, etc.

peer'ess, n. The wife of a peer; a woman ennobled in her own right, or by right of marriage.

peer'less, a. Having no peer, or equal; matchless.

pee'vish (pē'vĭsh), a. [4] **1.** Habitually fretful or complaining. **2.** Showing ill nature or temper.

peg (pĕg), n. **1.** A small pointed piece, as of wood, used for fastening or for closing a hole; pin; plug. **2.** A projecting piece of wood or metal to hold things, as coats, or to mark a boundary, or the like; — sometimes fig. **3.** A step; degree. — v. t.; PEGGED (pĕgd); PEG'GING (pĕg'ĭng). **1.** To put a peg in; fasten with pegs. **2.** To indicate by pegs. — v. i. To work diligently; — usually with on, at, or away.

pel'age (pĕl'ăj), n. The covering, or coat, of a mammal, as of wool, fur, or hair.

pe-lag'ic (pē-lăj'ĭk), a. Of or pertaining to the ocean; — esp. applied to organisms living at the surface, away from the coast.

Pelican

pelf (pĕlf), n. **1.** Stolen property. **2.** Money; lucre.

pel'i-can (pĕl'ĭ-kȧn), n. Any of certain large, web-footed birds, with a pouch on the lower jaw in which food (fish) is caught.

pe-lisse' (pĕ-lēs'), *n.* A long outer garment, originally of fur or fur-lined.

pel-lag'ra (pĕ-lăg'rȧ; -lā'grȧ), *n.* A skin disease, caused by a microbe, accompanied by disturbance of the digestive and nervous systems.

pel'let (pĕl'ĕt), *n.* A round small body; a little ball, esp. of food, medicine, etc.

pell'—mell', pell/mell' (pĕl'mĕl'), *adv.* **1.** In utter confusion. **2.** In furious haste; vehemently.

pel-lu'cid (pĕ-lū'sĭd), *a.* [4] Being transparent; hence, easy to understand, as an author's thought.

pelt (pĕlt), *n.* An undressed skin of a sheep, goat, or fur-bearing animal.

pelt, *v. t.* To strike with something thrown or driven. — *v. i.* **1.** To throw or strike strongly and repeatedly. **2.** To beat; drive. — *n.* Act of pelting; also, a blow as with something thrown.

pel'tate (pĕl'tāt), *a.* Shield-shaped, as a leaf with stem attached to the lower surface.

pelt'ry (pĕl'trĭ), *n.; pl.* -RIES (-trĭz). Pelts, or skins collectively; furs; also, *pl.*, kinds of pelts.

pel'vic (pĕl'vĭk), *a.* Pertaining to, or in the region of, the pelvis. — *pelvic arch or girdle, Anat.*, the bony arch formed by the hip bones.

pel'vis (-vĭs), *n.; L. pl.* PELVES (-vēz). *Anat.* The basin-like structure formed by the hip bones, coccyx, and sacrum.

pem'mi-can (pĕm'Ĭ-kăn), *n.* A preparation of dried lean meat, fat, and sometimes, dried fruit.

pen (pĕn), *n.* **1.** A small inclosure for animals. **2.** Any small place of confinement or storage. — *v. t.;* PENNED (pĕnd) or PENT (pĕnt); PEN'NING. To shut in or as in a pen; coop up; inclose.

pen, *n.* An instrument with a split point for writing with fluid ink; also, such a pen and its holder. — *v. t.;* PENNED (pĕnd); PEN'NING. To write.

pe'nal (pē'nȧl), *a.* Of or pertaining to punishment or penalties; as, a *penal* code.

pe'nal-ize (-īz), *v. t.* [1] To put a penalty on.

pen'al-ty (pĕn'ȧl-tĭ), *n.; pl.* -TIES (-tĭz). **1.** Penal retribution; punishment. **2.** A forfeit to which a person binds himself in default of fulfilling stipulations; forfeiture; fine.

pen'ance (-ȧns), *n.* Action performed to show penitence and as reparation for sin.

pence (pĕns), *n., pl.* of PENNY.

‖**pen'chant** (päN'shäN'; pĕn'chănt), *n.* [F.] Strong mental leaning or attraction; strong inclination.

pen'cil (pĕn'sĬl), *n.* **1.** A brush, esp. a fine one, used by artists. **2.** A slender cylinder of black lead, colored chalk, slate, etc., commonly incased in wood, for drawing or writing. **3.** An aggregate of rays, as of light, esp. when diverging or converging. — *v. t.* [7] To sketch, write, or mark with or as with a pencil.

pend'ant (pĕn'dȧnt), *n.* Something which hangs or depends, esp. as an ornament.

pend'en-cy (-dĕn-sĬ), *n.* **1.** State of being pendent. **2.** State of being undetermined; suspense.

pend'ent (-dĕnt), *a.* [4] **1.** Supported from above; suspended. **2.** Jutting over; overhanging. **3.** Undetermined; pending.

pend'ing, *p. a.* Not yet decided; as, a *pending* suit. — *prep.* During; during the pendency of.

pen'du-lous (pĕn'dū-lŭs), *a.* [4] Loosely pendent; hanging. — **-ly**, *adv.* [8] — **-ness**, *n.* [8].

pen'du-lum (-lŭm), *n.; pl.* -LUMS (-lŭmz). A body suspended from a fixed point and free to swing.

pen'e-tra-bil'i-ty (pĕn'ĕ-trȧ-bĬl'Ĭ-tĬ), *n.* Quality of being penetrable. [being penetrated.|

pen'e-tra-ble (pĕn'ĕ-trȧ-b'l), *a.* [4] Capable of

pen'e-trate (pĕn'ĕ-trāt), *v. t.* [1] **1.** To enter into; pierce. **2.** To pervade; permeate. **3.** To move deeply. **4.** To pierce into by the mind; understand. — *v. i.* To pass into or through something; pierce; also, to affect the feelings.

pen'e-trat'ing (-trāt'Ĭng), *p. a.* [4] **1.** Sharp; penetrative. **2.** Acute; discerning; sagacious.

pen'e-tra'tion (-trā'shŭn), *n.* **1.** Act or process of penetrating. **2.** Sharp discernment; sagacity.

pen'e-tra-tive (pĕn'ĕ-trȧ-tĬv), *a.* [4] **1.** Tending to penetrate; piercing. **2.** Acute; sagacious.

pen'guin (pĕn'gwĬn; pĕn'-), *n.* Any of certain flightless aquatic birds of the Southern Hemisphere, with flipperlike wings.

pen-in'su-la (pĕn-Ĭn'sȧ-lȧ), *n.* A portion of land nearly surrounded by water; also, any piece of land jutting out into the water.

pen-in'su-lar (-lȧr), *a.* Of or pert. to a peninsula.

pen'i-tence (pĕn'Ĭ-tĕns), *n.* State or fact of being penitent; sorrow for sins or faults.

pen'i-tent (-tĕnt), *a.* [4] Feeling sorrow for sins or offenses; repentant. — *n.* **1.** A penitent person. **2.** One undergoing penance. — **-ly**, *adv.*

pen'i-ten'tial (-tĕn'shȧl), *a.* Of or pertaining to penitence or penance.

pen'i-ten'tia-ry (-shȧ-rĬ), *a.* **1.** Of or pertaining to penance. **2.** Used for punishment, discipline, and reformation. **3.** Making one liable to punishment in a penitentiary. *U. S.* — *n.; pl.* -RIES (-rĬz). House of correction in which offenders are confined, usually at labor.

pen'knife' (pĕn'nĬf'), *n.* A small pocketknife.

pen'man (-măn), *n.; pl.* -MEN (-mĕn). One who uses the pen; a writer.

pen'man-ship, *n.* Art or practice of using the pen in writing; style or manner of writing.

pen'nant (-ănt), *n. Naut.* **a** A flag usually long and narrow. **b** Any small flag used for decorating, signaling, or the like.

pen'ni-less (pĕn'Ĭ-lĕs), *a.* Without a penny; extremely poor. [2. Any flag or banner.|

pen'non (-ŭn), *n.* **1.** A long triangular flag.

pen'ny (pĕn'Ĭ), *n.; pl.* -NIES (-Ĭz), for a number of coins, or PENCE (pĕns), for amount in pennies. **1.** An English coin, now of bronze, worth 1⁄12 of a shilling, or 2.03 cents U. S. **2.** A cent. *Colloq., U. S.* **3.** A sum of money; as, a pretty *penny*.

pen'ny-roy'al (-roi'ăl), *n.* A perennial mint with pungently aromatic leaves.

pen'ny-weight' (pĕn'Ĭ-wāt'), *n.* A troy weight of 24 grains, or 1⁄20 of an ounce (1.55517 grams).

pen'ny-wise', *a.* Wise in small matters; saving small sums while losing larger.

pe-nol'o-gy (pē-nŏl'ō-jĬ), *n.* The study of punishment for crime; the science that treats of the management of prisons and reformatories.

pen'sile (pĕn'sĬl), *a.* [4] **1.** Hanging; pendent. **2.** Having or building a hanging nest.

pen'sion (-shŭn), *n.* **1.** A stated allowance made to one retired from service. **2.** A payment regularly made to one not an employee, as for good will. — *v. t.* To grant a pension to.

pen'sion-a-ry (pĕn'shŭn-ā-rĭ), *n.; pl.* -RIES (-rĭz). A pensioner; often, a hireling.

pen'sion-er (-ẽr), *n.* One in receipt of a pension.

pen'sive (-sĭv), *a.* [4] **1.** Dreamily or somewhat sadly thoughtful; musing. **2.** Expressing or suggesting thoughtfulness with sadness. — **pen'sive-ly**, *adv.* [8] — **pen'sive-ness**, *n.* [8].

pent (pĕnt), *p. a.* [3] Penned or shut up; confined.

pen'ta-gon (pĕn'tȧ-gŏn), *n.* A plane figure having five angles and five sides.

pen-tag'o-nal (pĕn-tăg'ō-năl), *a.* Having five corners or angles.

pen-tam'e-ter (pĕn-tăm'ē-tẽr), *n.* A poetic verse of five feet. — *a.* Having five metrical feet.

pen-tath'lon (-tăth'lŏn), *n.* In modern sports, a contest of five events : running broad jump, throwing the javelin, 200-meter run, throwing the discus, and a 1500-meter run.

Pen'te-cost (-tē-kŏst), *n.* **1.** A solemn festival of the Jews, celebrated the fiftieth day after the second day of the Passover. **2.** Whitsunday.

pent'house' (pĕnt'hous'), *n.* A shed or roof attached to, and sloping from, a wall or building.

pe'nult (pē'nŭlt; pē-nŭlt'), **pe-nul'ti-ma** (pē-nŭl'-tĭ-mȧ), *n.* The last syllable but one of a word.

pe-nul'ti-mate (-mȧt), *a.* Last but one; as, the *penultimate* syllable. — *n.* The penult.

pe-num'bra (-nŭm'brȧ), *n.* The space of partial illumination, as in an eclipse, between the umbra, or perfect shadow, and the full light.

pe-nu'ri-ous (-nū'rĭ-ŭs), *a.* [4] Stingy; miserly. — **pe-nu'ri-ous-ly**, *adv.* [8] — **ous-ness**, *n.* [8].

pen'u-ry (pĕn'ū-rĭ), *n.* Poverty; destitution.

pe'on (pē'ŏn), *n.* A common laborer of any kind; — often, in reference to Latin America, esp. Mexico, implying bondage, as for debt.

pe'on-age (-ăj), *n.* State of being a peon; also, a system of using peon labor.

pe'o-ny (pē'ō-nĭ), *n.; pl.* -NIES (-nĭz). A plant of the crowfoot family, having divided leaves and large handsome flowers; also, the flower.

peo'ple (pē'p'l), *n. sing. & pl.; in* sense of a particular body of persons, *pl.* PEOPLES. **1.** A body of persons united by a common character, culture, or sentiment. **2.** A race, tribe, or nation. **3.** The persons of a particular group. **4.** The populace. **5.** Persons indefinitely. — *v. t.* [1] To populate.

pep'per (pĕp'ẽr), *n.* **1.** A strong spice, or seasoning, made from dried berries of several East Indian plants. **2.** Any plant yielding pepper (def. 1), esp. the common, or black, pepper, a climbing shrub. — *v. t.* **1.** To season with or as with pepper. **2.** To shower missiles on.

pep'per-grass' (-grȧs'), *n.* A kind of cress.

pep'per-mint (-mĭnt), *n.* **1.** A pungent mint; also, its oil or essence. **2.** A peppermint lozenge.

pepper tree. A tree with red berrylike drupes, much cultivated as a shade tree in California.

pep'per-y (pĕp'ẽr-ĭ), *a.* [4] **1.** Of or pert. to pepper; pungent. **2.** Hot-tempered; choleric.

pep'sin (-sĭn), *n.* A ferment secreted in the stomach, one of the chief active principles of gastric juice; also, a digestive preparation from it.

pep'tic (-tĭk), *a.* [4] **1.** Pertaining to gastric digestion. **2.** Of or pertaining to pepsin.

per (pŭr), *prep.* Through; by means of; by.

per'ad-ven'ture (pŭr'ăd-vĕn'tŭr; pŭr'-), *adv. & conj.* **1.** Perhaps; it may be. **2.** If; supposing.

per-am'bu-late (pĕr-ăm'bū-lāt), *v. t.* [1] To walk through or over. — *v. i.* To walk about; stroll.

per-am'bu-la'tor (-ăm'bū-lā'tẽr), *n.* A low carriage for a child; baby carriage.

per-cale' (pẽr-kāl'; pẽr'kȧl'), *n.* A fine, smooth-finished cotton fabric, often printed.

per-ceive' (pẽr-sēv'), *v. t.* [1] **1.** To obtain knowledge of through the senses; see, hear, or feel. **2.** To apprehend by the mind; discern.

per cent (sĕnt). By the hundred; in the hundred; — used of proportions, rates of interest, etc.

per-cent'age (pẽr-sĕn'tȧj), *n.* A certain rate per cent; allowance, duty, rate of interest, or commission on a hundred; loosely, a part or proportion.

per cen'tum (pŭr sĕn'tŭm). Per cent.

per-cep'ti-bil'i-ty (pẽr-sĕp'tĭ-bĭl'ĭ-tĭ), *n.* Capability of being perceived.

per-cep'ti-ble (pẽr-sĕp'tĭ-b'l), *a.* [4] That may be perceived. — **per-cep'ti-bly**, *adv.* [8].

per-cep'tion (-shŭn), *n.* The act or experience of the mind by which it gains knowledge of objects or ideas; faculty of perceiving. [perception.]

per-cep'tive (-tĭv), *a.* [4] Of or pertaining to perch (pûrch), *n.* **1.** A certain rather small, spiny-finned, fresh-water fish. **2.** Any of numerous similar fishes, many marine.

perch, *n.* **1.** A horizontal pole or other support for birds to roost on; hence, any elevated seat or station. **2.** A measure equal to a rod. — *v. i.* To alight, as a bird; sit or rest on a perch. — *v. t.* To place or set on or as on a perch.

per-chance' (pẽr-chȧns'), *adv.* **1.** By chance. **2.** Perhaps; possibly.

per'co-late (pûr'kō-lāt), *v. t. & i.* [1] **1.** To filter, as a liquor. **2.** To ooze through; permeate.

per'co-la'tion (-lā'shŭn), *n.* Act or process of percolating. [kind of coffeepot.]

per'co-la'tor (-lā'tẽr), *n.* One that percolates.

per-cus'sion (pẽr-kŭsh'ŭn), *n.* **1.** Act of striking smartly on or against. **2.** The effect of violent collision; vibratory shock.

percussion cap. A small metallic cap or cup, as on a cartridge, containing a special powder exploded by the sharp blow of the hammer of the gun.

per-di'tion (pẽr-dĭsh'ŭn), *n.* Entire loss; ruin; esp., utter loss of final happiness in a future state.

per'e-gri-nate (pĕr'ē-grĭ-nāt), *v. i. & t.* [1] To travel; journey. — **per'e-gri-na'tion** (-nā'shŭn), *n.*

per'emp-to-ry (pẽr'ĕmp-tō-rĭ; pẽr-ĕmp'-), *a.* [4] **1.** Taking away a right of action, debate, etc. Hence, conclusive; absolute. **2.** Admitting no denial or refusal; imperative. **3.** Positive in opinion; stubborn; also, dictatorial. — **per'emp-to-ri-ly** (-rĭ-lĭ), *adv.* [8] — **ri-ness**, *n.* [8].

per-en'ni-al (pẽr-ĕn'ĭ-ăl), *a.* [4] **1.** Lasting or continuing through the year. **2.** Unceasing; enduring. **3.** *Bot.* Continuing more than two years. — *n.* *Bot.* A perennial plant. — **ly**, *adv.* [8].

per'fect (pûr'fĕkt), *a.* [4] **1.** Having all the properties naturally belonging to it; complete; sound; right; faultless; righteous, etc. **2.** Utter; down-

---

chair; go; sing, iŋk; then, thin; nature, verdure; yet; zh = z in azure. Numbers refer to §§ in the Special Notes which, with Abbreviations, Signs, etc., precede the Vocabulary.

right. *Colloq.* — **perfect tense**, *Gram.*, a tense denoting an act or state as completed at the time of speaking. — *n. Gram.* The perfect tense.

per'fect (pŭr'fĕkt ; pẽr-fĕkt'), *v. t.* To make perfect ; finish ; complete. — **per'fect-er**, *n.* [8].

per-fect'i-bil'i-ty (pẽr-fĕk'tĭ-bĭl'ĭ-tĭ), *n.* Quality or state of being perfectible, esp. morally.

per-fect'i-ble (pẽr-fĕk'tĭ-b'l), *a.* [4] Capable of becoming, or being made, perfect.

per-fec'tion (-shŭn), *n.* **1.** Quality or state of being perfect, or complete. **2.** A quality completely excellent. **3.** A perfect thing or person.

per'fect-ly (pŭr'fĕkt-lĭ), *adv.* In a perfect manner ; rightly ; correctly ; also, completely.

per'fect-ness, *n.* Perfect quality or state.

per-fer'vid (pẽr-fûr'vĭd), *a.* [4] Very fervid.

per-fid'i-ous (-fĭd'ĭ-ŭs), *a.* [4] **1.** Guilty of perfidy ; false to trust. **2.** Involving, or marked by, perfidy. — **-ly**, *adv.* [8].

per'fi-dy (pûr'fĭ-dĭ), *n. ; pl.* -DIES (-dĭz). Breach of faith or allegiance ; faithlessness ; treachery.

per'fo-rate (pûr'fō-rāt), *v. t. & i.* [1] To pierce through ; to make a hole through.

per'fo-ra'tion (-rā'shŭn), *n.* **1.** A perforating. **2.** A hole made by boring, punching, or the like.

per'fo-ra'tor (pûr'fō-rā'tẽr), *n.* One that perforates ; an instrument for perforating.

per-force' (pẽr-fōrs'), *adv.* By necessity.

per-form' (-fôrm'), *v.t.* **1.** To execute (anything) ; accomplish ; do. **2.** To discharge ; fulfill. **3.** To render, as a play ; act on the stage, as a part. — *v.i.* To do or accomplish something ; esp., to act a part, or to play on a musical instrument.

per-form'ance (-fôr'mǎns), *n.* **1.** Act of performing ; execution ; achievement. **2.** A thing done ; esp., an action of a public character. — **-er**, *n.* [8].

per-fume' (-fūm'), *v. t.* [1] To fill with an agreeable odor, as of incense, flowers, etc. ; scent.

per'fume (pûr'fūm ; pẽr-fūm'), *n.* **1.** A pleasant odor ; fragrance ; aroma. **2.** A fluid preparation used for scenting.

per-fum'er (pẽr-fūm'ẽr), *n.* **1.** One that perfumes. **2.** One whose trade is to make or sell perfumes.

per-fum'er-y (-ĭ), *n. ; pl.* -ERIES (-ĭz). A perfume, or perfumes in general.

per-func'to-ry (-fŭŋk'tō-rĭ), *a.* [4] Done or acting mechanically and as a matter of routine ; careless. — **per-func'to-ri-ly**, *adv.* — **-ri-ness**, *n.*

per'go-la (pûr'gō-lá), *n.* An arbor or trellis treated architecturally.   [be.

per-haps' (pẽr-hǎps'), *adv.* By chance ; it may

pe'ri (pē'rĭ), *n. ; pl.* -RIS (-rĭz). *Persian Myth.* A kind of elf or fairy descended from fallen angels.

per'i-anth (pĕr'ĭ-ǎnth), *n.* The external envelope of a flower ; the floral leaves collectively.

per'i-car'di-ac (-kär'dĭ-ǎk), **-di-al** (-ǎl), *a.* Of or pert. to the pericardium ; situated around the heart.

per'i-car'di-um (-kär'dĭ-ŭm), *n. ; L. pl.* -DIA (-á). The sac of serous membrane inclosing the heart.

per'i-carp (pĕr'ĭ-kärp), *n. Bot.* The ripened and variously modified walls of the ovary.

per'i-gee (pĕr'ĭ-jē), *n.* That point in the orbit of the moon nearest to the earth ; — opp. to *apogee*.

per'i-he'li-on (-hē'lĭ-ŏn), *n. ; L. pl.* -LIA. *Astron.* That point of the orbit of a planet or comet nearest to the sun ; — opposed to *aphelion*.

per'il (pĕr'ĭl), *n.* Danger ; exposure to injury or destruction. — *v. t.* [7] To expose to danger.

per'il-ous (-ĭ-lŭs), *a.* [4] Full of, attended with, or involving, peril ; dangerous. — **-ly**, *adv.* [8].

per-im'e-ter (pẽr-ĭm'ē-tẽr), *n. Geom.* The whole outer boundary of a body or figure, or its measure.

pe'ri-od (pē'rĭ-ŏd), *n.* **1.** A portion of time determined by some recurrence, as by the completion of a revolution of a planet. **2.** A certain series of years, months, days, etc. ; cycle ; age ; era ; epoch. **3.** The completion of a series of events, or act ; limit ; bound. **4.** *Rhet.* A period. **5.** a The full pause closing a complete sentence. **b** The point [.] that marks the end of a complete declarative sentence, or of an abbreviated word.

pe'ri-od'ic (pē'rĭ-ŏd'ĭk), *a.* [4] **1.** Of, pert. to, or performed in, a period, or revolution, of a heavenly body. **2.** Acting, happening, or appearing, at fixed intervals ; recurring ; intermittent.

pe'ri-od'i-cal (pē'rĭ-ŏd'ĭ-kǎl), *a.* **1.** = PERIODIC. **2.** Published or appearing with a fixed interval (more than one day) between the issues or numbers ; — said of magazines, etc. Also, of or pertaining to such publications. — *n.* A periodical publication. — **pe'ri-od'i-cal-ly**, *adv.* [8].

per'i-os'te-um (pĕr'ĭ-ŏs'tē-ŭm), *n. ; L. pl.* -TEA (-á). *Anat.* Tissue which closely covers all bones except where they are enveloped by cartilage.

pe-riph'er-al (pē-rĭf'ẽr-ǎl), *a.* Of or pert. to, or constituting, a periphery ; hence, *Anat.*, external.

pe-riph'er-y (-ĭ), *n. ; pl.* -ERIES (-ĭz). **1.** The line bounding a rounded surface ; hence, the surface of any body. **2.** *Geom.* The circumference or perimeter of a circle, ellipse, etc.

per'i-phras'tic (pĕr'ĭ-frǎs'tĭk), *a.* [4] Using two or more words in place of one. — **-ti-cal-ly**, *adv.*

por'i-scope (pŏr'ĭ-skōp), *n.* An optical instrument, consisting essentially of a tube having reflecting prisms at its upper and lower ends, often used on submarines to afford a view over the water when the boat is submerged, and on land to enable one to see over or around an obstacle, etc.

per'ish (pĕr'ĭsh), *v. i.* To be destroyed ; hence, to waste away ; pass away ; die.

per'ish-a-ble (-á-b'l), *a.* [4] Liable to perish.

per'i-stal'sis (-ĭ-stǎl'sĭs), *n.* Peristaltic action.

per'i-stal'tic (pĕr'ĭ-stǎl'tĭk), *a. Physiol.* Designating, or pert. to, the wormlike wave motion of the intestines which forces their contents onward.

per'i-style (pĕr'ĭ-stĭl), *n. Arch.* A range of columns with their entablature, etc. ; esp., a system of roof-supporting columns round a court or building.

per'i-to-ne'um (-tō-nē'ŭm), *n. ; L. pl.* -NEA (-á). The membrane lining the abdominal cavity.

per'i-to-ni'tis (-nī'tĭs), *n. Med.* Inflammation of the peritoneum.

per'i-wig (pĕr'ĭ-wĭg), *n.* A wig.

per'i-win'kle (-wĭŋ'k'l), *n.* Any of various mostly small mollusks, with a short thick spiral shell.

per'i-win'kle, *n.* A kind of trailing evergreen herb with blue or white flowers.

per'jure (pûr'jŭr), *v. t.* [1] To make guilty of perjury ; — used reflexively. — **per'jur-er**, *n.* [8.]

per'ju-ry (-jû-rĭ), *n. ; pl.* -RIES (-rĭz). False swearing ; voluntary violation of an oath or vow.

perk (pûrk), *v. i.* **1.** To behave jauntily or smartly.

āle, senāte, câre, ăm, ăccount, ärm, åsk, sofá ; ēve, ĕvent, ĕnd, recĕnt, makĕr ; īce, ĭll ; ōld, ŏbey, ôrb, ŏdd, sŏft, cŏnnect ; ūse, ŭnite, ûrn, ŭp, circŭs ; fōōd, fŏŏt ; out, oil ;

2. To become erect, brisk, or lively ;—usually with *up*. — *v. t.* To make trim or smart.

per'ma-nence (pûr'má-nĕns), *n.* Quality or state of being permanent.

per'ma-nen-cy (-nĕn-sĭ), *n.; pl.* -CIES (-sĭz). **1.** Permanence. **2.** One that is permanent.

per'ma-nent (-nĕnt), *a.* [4] Continuing in the same state ; abiding ; fixed ; stable. — **-ly**, *adv.* [8].

per'me-a-bil'i-ty (pûr'mē-á-bĭl'ĭ-tĭ), *n.* Quality of being permeable. [being permeated.]

per'me-a-ble (pûr'mē-á-b'l), *a.* [4] Capable of

per'me-ate (-āt), *v. t. & i.* [1] **1.** To pass through the pores or interstices of ; as, water *permeates* sand. **2.** To enter and spread through ; pervade.

per'me-a'tion (-ā'shŭn), *n.* Act of permeating.

per-mis'si-ble (pĕr-mĭs'ĭ-b'l), *a.* [4] Allowable.

per-mis'sion (-mĭsh'ŭn), *n.* Act of permitting ; formal consent.

per-mis'sive (-mĭs'ĭv), *a.* [4] **1.** Permitting ; granting liberty. **2.** Permitted ; tolerated.

per-mit' (-mĭt'), *v. t. ; -*MITTED ; -MITTING. **1.** To consent to ; tolerate. **2.** To grant (one) express license to do an act ; authorize. — *v. i.* To grant permission ; allow.

per'mit (pûr'mĭt), *n.* Warrant ; license.

per'mu-ta'tion (pûr'mū-tā'shŭn), *n.* **1.** Interchange. **2.** *Math.* Any one of all possible arrangements of a number of objects in a series ; transposition of the objects to effect such arrangements.

per-ni'cious (pĕr-nĭsh'ŭs), *a.* [4] Destructive ; ruinous ; injurious ; hurtful. — **-ly**, *adv.* [8].

per'o-ra'tion (pĕr'ō-rā'shŭn), *n.* The concluding part or summing up of a discourse.

per-ox'ide (pĕr-ŏk'sĭd, -sĭd), *n. Chem.* **a** An oxide containing more oxygen than some other oxide of the same element. **b** Peroxide of hydrogen.

per'pen-dic'u-lar (pûr'pĕn-dĭk'ū-lᾱr), *a.* Exactly upright or vertical ; *Geom.*, at right angles to a given line or surface. — *n.* **1.** A line at right angles to the plane of the horizon or, *Geom.*, to another line or surface. **2.** Upright position. — **per'pen-dic'u-lar-ly**, *adv.* [8].

ad Perpendicular Line ; *bc* Horizontal Line.

per'pen-dic'u-lar'i-ty (-lăr'ĭ-tĭ), *n.* State of being perpendicular.

per'pe-trate (pûr'pē-trāt), *v. t.* [1] To do or commit ; — usually in a bad sense ; as, to *perpetrate* a crime. — **-tra'tor** (-trā'tẽr), *n.* [8].

per'pe-tra'tion (-trā'shŭn), *n.* Act of perpetrating ; also, the thing perpetrated.

per-pet'u-al (pĕr-pĕt'ū-ăl), *a.* Continuing for an unlimited time ; continuous. — **-ly**, *adv.* [8].

per-pet'u-ate (-āt), *v. t.* [1] To make perpetual.

per-pet'u-a'tion (pĕr-pĕt'ū-ā'shŭn), *n.* A making perpetual ; permanent continuation.

per'pe-tu'i-ty (pûr'pē-tū'ĭ-tĭ), *n. ; pl.* -TIES (-tĭz). **1.** Quality or state of being perpetual. **2.** Something that is perpetual. **3.** Endless time.

per-plex' (pĕr-plĕks'), *v. t.* To trouble with ambiguity, suspense, or anxiety ; confuse.

per-plexed' (-plĕkst'), *p. a.* [4] Doubtful ; puzzled ; bewildered.

per-plex'i-ty (-plĕk'sĭ-tĭ), *n. ; pl.* -TIES (-tĭz). **1.** Quality or state of being perplexed ; also, an instance of this state. **2.** That which perplexes.

per'qui-site (pûr'kwĭ-zĭt), *n.* An incidental gain or profit in addition to regular salary or wages.

per'ry (pĕr'ĭ), *n.* A cider made from pears.

per'se-cute (pûr'sē-kūt), *v. t.* [1] To harass, esp., to afflict or kill because of belief or religion.

per'se-cu'tion (-kū'shŭn), *n.* **1.** Act or practice of persecuting. **2.** State of being persecuted.

per'se-cu'tor (-tẽr), *n.* One who persecutes.

Per'seus (pûr'sūs ; -sē-ŭs), *n. Astron.* A northern constellation between Taurus and Cassiopeia.

per'se-ver'ance (pûr'sē-vēr'ăns), *n.* Act of persevering ; persistence ; steadfastness ; constancy.

per'se-vere' (pûr'sē-vēr'), *v. i.* To persist in any business or enterprise undertaken.

per'si-flage' (pĕr'sĭ-fläzh' ; pûr'sĭ-fläzh), *n.* Frivolous or bantering talk ; light raillery.

per-sim'mon (pĕr-sĭm'ŭn), *n.* A tree bearing small white flowers, and a plumlike fruit ; the fruit.

per-sist' (-sĭst'), *v. i.* **1.** To continue steadfastly. **2.** To endure or remain.

per-sist'ence (-sĭs'tĕns), **per-sist'en-cy** (-tĕn-sĭ), *n.* Quality or state of being persistent.

per-sist'ent (-sĭs'tĕnt), *a.* [4] **1.** Inclined to persist ; having staying qualities. **2.** Existing continuously ; enduring. — **-ly**, *adv.* [8].

per'son (pûr'sŭn ; -s'n), *n.* **1.** A human being. **2.** The bodily form of a human being ; outward appearance. **3.** Individual personality. **4.** *Gram.* One of the three relations (speaker, one spoken to, and another spoken of, called respectively the *first, second,* and *third person*) underlying discourse, distinguished by certain pronouns and, in many languages, by inflection of the verb.

per'son-age (-ᾱj), *n.* **1.** A distinguished person hence, any person. **2.** Character assumed or represented, as in a play.

per'son-al (-ăl), *a.* [4] **1.** Of or pertaining to a particular person ; not general. **2.** Done in person direct from one person to another. **3.** Pertaining to the person, or body. **4.** Relating to a person, esp. in an offensive manner. **5.** *Gram.* Denoting person ; as, a *personal* pronoun. **6.** *Law.* Designating estate or property that consists of things temporary or movable ; as, *personal* estate — *personal pronoun*, *Gram.*, one of the substantive pronouns (as *I, thou, he, she, it*), expressing a distinction of person. — **per'son-al-ly**, *adv.* [8].

per'son-al'i-ty (-ăl'ĭ-tĭ), *n. ; pl.* -TIES (-tĭz). **1.** Quality or state of being personal, or of being a person **2.** That which constitutes distinction of person individuality. **3.** A personal being ; a person **4.** Quality of relating to a particular person, esp disparagingly or hostilely. **5.** A personal remark esp. one of a disparaging nature ; — usually in *pl*

per'son-al-ty (pûr'sŭn-ăl-tĭ), *n. ; pl.* -TIES (-tĭz) Personal property.

per'son-ate (-āt), *v. t.* [1] To assume the character of ; act the part of. — **a'tor** (-ā'tẽr), *n.* [8].

per'son-a'tion (-ā'shŭn), *n.* A personating.

per-son/i-fi-ca'tion (pĕr-sŏn'ĭ-fĭ-kā'shŭn), *n.* **1.** Act of personifying ; that which personifies. **2.** A figure of speech in which an inanimate object or abstract idea is endowed with personal attributes.

per-son'i-fy (pĕr-sŏn'ĭ-fĭ), *v. t.* [2] **1.** To regard treat, or represent as a person. **2.** To be the embodiment of ; impersonate ; typify.

per'son'nel' (pĕr'sŏ'nĕl'; pŭr'sŏ-nĕl'), *n.* The body of persons in some (esp. public) service.

per-spec'tive (pĕr-spĕk'tĭv), *n.* **1.** Art or science of representing, on a surface, objects as they actually appear to the eye. **2.** The appearance of objects to the eye as affected by distance. — *a.* Pert. to the art of perspective.

per'spi-ca'cious (pûr'spĭ-kā'shŭs), *a.* [4] Of acute vision; mentally keen. — **-ly,** *adv.* [8].

per'spi-cac'i-ty (-kăs'ĭ-tĭ), *n.* Acuteness of sight or discernment.   [spicuous; lucidity.

per'spi-cu'i-ty (-kū'ĭ-tĭ), *n.* Quality of being perspicuous.

per-spic'u-ous (pĕr-spĭk'û-ŭs), *a.* [4] Clear to the understanding. — **-ly,** *adv.* [8] — **ness,** *n.* [8].

per'spi-ra'tion (pûr'spĭ-rā'shŭn), *n.* **1.** Act or process of perspiring. **2.** Moisture given out in minute drops through the pores of the skin; sweat.

per-spir'a-to-ry (pĕr-spīr'ȧ-tȯ-rĭ), *a.* Of, pert. to, or producing, perspiration; as, *perspiratory* glands.

per-spire' (pĕr-spīr'), *v. i. & t.* [1] *Physiol.* To excrete, esp. fluids, through the skin; sweat.

per-suade' (-swād'), *v.t.* [1] To induce (a person) to believe or do something; convince. — **persuad'a-ble,** *a.* [8] — **per-suad'er,** *n.* [8].

per-sua'si-bil'i-ty (pĕr-swā'sĭ-bĭl'ĭ-tĭ), *n.* Quality of being persuasible.   [persuasion.

per-sua'si-ble (pĕr-swā'sĭ-b'l), *a.* [4] Open to

per-sua'sion (-zhŭn), *n.* **1.** Act of persuading. **2.** Power of persuading; persuasiveness. **3.** State of being persuaded. **4.** A creed or belief.

per-sua'sive (-sĭv), *a.* [4] Tending to persuade. — *n.* That which persuades. — **per-sua'sive-ly,** *adv.* [8] — **ness,** *n.* [8].

pert (pûrt), *a.* [3] Indecorously free, or presuming; bold. — **pert'ly,** *adv.* [8] — **pert'ness,** *n.* [8].

per-tain' (pĕr-tān'), *v. i.* **1.** To belong; have connection with, or dependence on, something. **2.** To have relation to something.

per'ti-na'cious (pûr'tĭ-nā'shŭs), *a.* [4] Holding obstinately to any opinion or design; resolute; obstinate. — **-ly,** *adv.* [8] — **ness,** *n.* [8].

per'ti-nac'i-ty (pûr'tĭ-năs'ĭ-tĭ), *n.* Quality or state of being pertinacious.

per'ti-nence (-nĕns)   } *n.* Quality or state of

per'ti-nen-cy (-nĕn-sĭ) } being pertinent; fitness.

per'ti-nent (-nĕnt), *a.* Related to the subject or matter in hand; apposite; relevant. — **-ly,** *adv.* [8].

per-turb' (pĕr-tûrb'), *v. t.* To disturb greatly; trouble; disquiet; derange.   [turbing.

per'tur-ba'tion (pûr'tŭr-bā'shŭn), *n.* Act of per-

pe-ruke' (pĕ-rōōk'), *n.* A wig; periwig.

pe-rus'al (pĕ-rōōz'ăl), *n.* Act of perusing.

pe-ruse' (pĕ-rōōz'), *v. t.* [1] To read through or carefully; read.   [the whole of.

per-vade' (pĕr-vād'), *v. t.* [1] To spread through

per-va'sion (-vā'zhŭn), *n.* Act of pervading.

per-va'sive (-vā'sĭv), *a.* [4] Tending or having power to pervade. — **-ly,** *adv.* [8] — **ness,** *n.* [8].

per-verse' (-vûrs'), *a.* [3] **1.** Turned away from the right; wicked. **2.** Obstinate in the wrong; stubborn. **3.** Wayward; petulant; as, a *perverse* child. — **-ly,** *adv.* [8] — **ness,** *n.* [8].

per-ver'sion (-vûr'shŭn), *n.* A perverting; state of being perverted; a perverted form of something.

per-ver'si-ty (-sĭ-tĭ), *n.; pl.* -TIES (-tĭz). Quality or state of being perverse; perverseness.

per-ver'sive (-vûr'sĭv), *a.* Tending to pervert.

per-vert' (-vûrt'), *v. t.* To lead away from uprightness; corrupt; misinterpret designedly.

per'vert (pûr'vĕrt), *n.* One perverted.

per-vert'i-ble (pĕr-vûr'tĭ-b'l), *a.* [4] Capable of perversion.   [permeable. — **ness,** *n.*

per'vi-ous (pûr'vĭ-ŭs), *a.* [4] Admitting passage;

pe'so (pā'sō), *n.; pl.* -SOS (-sōz; *Sp.* -sōs). **1.** The Mexican dollar, par value 49.846 cents. **2.** A monetary unit and silver coin of the Philippines, worth $0.50. Symbol, ₽ (used like $); as, ₽100.

pes'si-mism (pĕs'ĭ-mĭz'm), *n.* **1.** The doctrine that the pains of life overbalance its happiness. **2.** A disposition to take the least hopeful view.

pes'si-mist (-mĭst), *n.* One who looks on the dark side of things.

pes'si-mis'tic (-mĭs'tĭk), *a.* [4] Of, pertaining to, or marked by, pessimism; gloomy. — **pes'si-mis'ti-cal-ly,** *adv.* [8].

pest (pĕst), *n.* **1.** A pestilence. **2.** Something that is troublesome or destructive; a nuisance.

pes'ter (pĕs'tĕr), *v. t.* To harass with petty vexations; annoy; worry; tease. — **pes'ter-er,** *n.* [8].

pest'house (pĕst'hous'), *n.* A house or hospital for persons infected with any pestilential disease.

pes-tif'er-ous (pĕs-tĭf'ẽr-ŭs), *a.* [4] **1.** Pest-bearing. **2.** Pernicious; vicious. — **-ly,** *adv.*

pes'ti-lence (pĕs'tĭ-lĕns), *n.* Any contagious or infectious epidemic disease that is virulent and devastating; esp., bubonic plague.

pes'ti-lent (-lĕnt), *a.* [4] **1.** Deadly; poisonous. **2.** Pernicious. **3.** Annoying. — **-ly,** *adv.* [8].

pes'ti-len'tial (-lĕn'shăl), *a.* [4] **1.** Producing pestilence. **2.** Morally destructive or harmful.

pes'tle (pĕs''l), *n.* Implement for breaking or braying substances in a mortar.

pet (pĕt), *n.* **1.** An animal kept to pet. **2.** A person specially cherished and indulged; a darling. — *a.* Petted; indulged; cherished. — *v. t.;* PET'TED; -TING. To play with fondly; fondle; indulge.

pet, *n.* A fit of peevishness or ill humor.

pet'al (pĕt'ăl), *n.* One of the leaves of a corolla.

pet'i-ole (pĕt'ĭ-ōl), *n. Bot.* A leafstalk; the slender stem of a foliage leaf. See LEAF, *Illust.*

‖ **pe-tite'** (pĕ-tēt'), *a.* [F.] Small; little; esp., of a woman or girl, of small size or trim figure.

pe-ti'tion (pĕ-tĭsh'ŭn), *n.* A formal supplication, entreaty, or request; a prayer. — *v. t.* To pray; entreat; request. — *v. i.* To make a petition. — **pe-ti'tion-er,** *n.* [8].   [sea birds.

pet'rel (pĕt'rĕl), *n.* Any of numerous long-winged

pet'ri-fac'tion (pĕt'rĭ-făk'shŭn), *n.* **1.** Act or process of petrifying. **2.** A thing petrified.

pet'ri-fac'tive (-tĭv), *a.* [4] **1.** Able to cause petrifaction. **2.** Pert. to, or marked by, petrifaction.

pet'ri-fi-ca'tion (-fĭ-kā'shŭn), *n.* Petrifaction.

pet'ri-fy (pĕt'rĭ-fī), *v. t.* [2] **1.** To convert (organic matter) into stone or stonelike substance. **2.** To benumb or stupefy, as with fear. — *v. i.* To become petrified.

pet'rol (pĕt'rŏl; -rōl), *n.* Gasoline. *British.*

pe-tro'le-um (pĕ-trō'lĕ-ŭm), *n.* Rock oil, a dark brown or greenish inflammable liquid, which at certain points exists in the upper strata of the earth. Petroleum is refined by distillation, yielding gasoline, benzine, kerosene, paraffin, etc.

pet'ti-coat (pĕt'ĭ-kōt), *n.* A skirt worn by women, girls, or young children ; now, an underskirt.

pet'ti-fog (-fŏg), *v. i. ;* -FOGGED (-fŏgd) ; -FOG'GING (-fŏg'ĭng). To do a petty law business, esp. in a tricky way. — **pet'ti-fog'ger** (-fŏg'ẽr), *n.* [8].

pet'tish (pĕt'ĭsh), *a.* [4] Fretful ; peevish. — **-ly**, *adv.* [8] — **-ness**, *n.* [8].

pet'ty (pĕt'ĭ), *a.* [3] Of small importance ; inconsiderable ; also, inferior ; subordinate. — **pet'ti-ly** (-ĭ-lĭ), *adv.* [8] — **pet'ti-ness**, *n.* [8].

pet'u-lance (pĕt'ū-lăns), *n.* Capricious ill humor.

pet'u-lan-cy (-lăn-sĭ), *n.* Petulance.

pet'u-lant (-lănt), *a.* [4] Capriciously fretful. — **pet'u-lant-ly**, *adv.*

pe-tu'ni-a (pē-tū'nĭ-à), *n.* Any of a genus of herbs of the nightshade family, with funnel-shaped corollas. [seats in a church.

pew (pū), *n.* One of the long, fixed benches or

pe'wee (pē'wē), *n.* A phœbe.

pe'wit (pē'wĭt ; pū'ĭt), *n.* **1.** The lapwing. **2.** The European black-headed gull. **3.** A pewee.

pew'ter (pū'tẽr), *n.* **1.** Any of various alloys having tin as a chief constituent. **2.** Utensils made of pewter. [carriage.

pha'ē-ton (fā'ē-tŏn), *n.* A kind of four-wheeled

phag'o-cyte (făg'ō-sīt), *n.* Any leucocyte, or white blood corpuscle, that absorbs or destroys waste and harmful material, bacteria, etc.

pha'lanx (fā'lănks ; făl'ănks), *n. ; pl.* E. -LANXES (-lănk-sĕz), L. -LANGES (fá-lăn'jēz). **1.** *Antiq.* A compact body of heavy-armed infantry, originally of the Greeks. **2.** Any body of persons, animals, or things in close order or massed. **3.** One of the digital bones of the hand or foot.

phan'tasm (făn'tăz'm), *n.* **1.** A product of phantasy ; as : **a** A mental image of a real object. **b** A phantom. **2.** Apparition of a person, living or dead, in a place where his body is known not to be.

phan-tas'ma-go'ri-a (făn-tăz'má-gō'rĭ-à), *n.* A medley or shifting series of imaginary figures, illusive images, or real appearances.

phan-tas'mal (făn-tăz'măl), *a.* [4] Of the nature of, or like, a phantasm ; spectral ; illusive.

phan'ta-sy (făn'tá-sĭ), *n. ; pl.* -SIES (-sĭz). Power of creating mental images ; an image so created.

phan'tom (-tŭm), *n.* **1.** An apparition ; phantasm ; illusion. **2.** Visible semblance.

Phar'i-sa'ic (făr'ĭ-sā'ĭk) } *a.* **1.** Of or pertaining to the Pharisees.
Phar'i-sa'i-cal (-sā'ĭ-kăl) } **2.** [*l. c.*] Self-righteous ; hypocritical.

Phar'i-see (făr'ĭ-sē), *n.* **1.** A member of a sect among the ancient Jews, noted for strict regard for outward forms and for pretensions to superior sanctity. **2.** [*l. c.*] One who is pharisaical.

phar'ma-ceu'tic, phar'ma-ceu'ti-cal (fär'má-sū'tĭ-kăl), *a.* Of, pertaining to, or using, pharmacy.

phar'ma-ceu'tics (-tĭks), *n.* Pharmacy.

phar'ma-cist (fär'má-sĭst), **phar'ma-ceu'tist** (-sū'tĭst), *n.* One skilled in pharmacy ; druggist.

phar'ma-co-pœ'ia (-kō-pē'yá), *n.* **1.** A book describing drugs. **2.** A collection or stock of drugs.

phar'ma-cy (fär'má-sĭ), *n. ; pl.* -CIES (-sĭz). **1.** Art or practice of preparing drugs, and of dispensing medicines. **2.** A drug store ; apothecary's shop.

pha-ryn'ge-al (fá-rĭn'jē-ăl ; făr'ĭn-jē'ăl), *a.* Pertaining to, or in the region of, the pharynx.

phar'ynx (făr'ĭnks), *n.; L. pl.* -RYNGES (fá-rĭn'jēz). *Anat.* The part of the alimentary canal between the cavity of the mouth and the esophagus.

phase (fāz), *n.* **1.** *Astron.* A particular appearance or state in a regularly recurring cycle of changes, as of the moon. **2.** Any of different and varying appearances of an object or thing.

phea's'ant (fĕz'ănt), *n.* **1.** Any of numerous large, long-tailed, brilliantly colored birds allied to the domestic fowls. **2.** Any of various birds likened to a pheasant, as, *Southern U. S.*, the ruffed grouse.

phe-nac'e-tin (fē-năs'ē-tĭn), *n.* A compound used in medicine principally as a febrifuge.

phe'nol (fē'nŏl ; -nōl), *n. Chem.* A crystalline substance, derived from coal tar, etc. ; — popularly called *carbolic acid.* It is a caustic poison, and, in weak solution, is used as an antiseptic.

phe-nom'e-na (fē-nŏm'ē-ná), *n., pl.* of PHENOMENON.

phe-nom'e-nal (-năl), *a.* [4] Of the nature of, or pert. to, a phenomenon or phenomena. — **-ly**, *adv.*

phe-nom'e-non (-nŏn), *n. ; L. pl.* -ENA (-ná). **1.** Any observable fact or event. **2.** Something unaccountable or very notable or exceptional.

phi'al (fī'ăl), *n.* A vial.

phil'an-throp'ic (fĭl'ăn-thrŏp'ĭk), *a.* Of or pertaining to philanthropy ; benevolent ; humane.

phil'an-throp'i-cal (-thrŏp'ĭ-kăl), *a.* Philanthropic. — **phil'an-throp'i-cal-ly**, *adv.* [8].

phi-lan'thro-pist (fĭ-lăn'thrō-pĭst), *n.* One who practices philanthropy.

phi-lan'thro-py (-pĭ), *n. ; pl.* -PIES (-pĭz). **1.** Love to mankind ; desire and readiness to do good to all men. **2.** Philanthropic act, agency, or the like.

phi-lat'e-list (fĭ-lăt'ē-lĭst), *n.* Stamp collector.

phi-lat'e-ly (fĭ-lăt'ē-lĭ), *n.* The collection of postage stamps. [harmony or music.

phil'har-mon'ic (fĭl'här-mŏn'ĭk), *a.* [4] Loving

phi-lip'pic (fĭ-lĭp'ĭk), *n.* Any invective discourse.

Phil'ip-pine (fĭl'ĭ-pĭn ; -pēn), *a.* Of or pertaining to the Philippine Islands or their inhabitants.

Phi-lis'tine (fĭ-lĭs'tĭn ; fĭl'ĭs-tĭn), *n.* A person lacking, and indifferent to, liberal culture and refinement. — *a.* Uncultured ; prosaic.

phil'o-log'i-cal (fĭl'ō-lŏj'ĭ-kăl), *a.* Of or pert. to philology. [devoted to, philology.

phi-lol'o-gist (fĭ-lŏl'ō-jĭst), *n.* One skilled in, or

phi-lol'o-gy (fĭ-lŏl'ō-jĭ), *n.* The study of language, esp. as a science ; linguistic science.

phil'o-pe'na (-pē'ná), *n.* A gift made as a forfeit in a social game variously played ; also, the game.

phi-los'o-pher (fĭ-lŏs'ō-fẽr), *n.* **1.** One versed in, or devoted to, philosophy. **2.** One who meets or regards all changes of fortune calmly.

phil'o-soph'ic (fĭl'ō-sŏf'ĭk) } *a.* [4] Of, pert. to,
phil'o-soph'i-cal (-sŏf'ĭ-kăl) } or versed in, philosophy ; hence, rational ; unruffled. — **-ly**, *adv.*

phi-los'o-phize (fĭ-lŏs'ō-fīz), *v. i.* [1] To reason like a philosopher. — **phi-los'o-phiz'er**, *n.* [8].

phi-los'o-phy (-fĭ), *n. ; pl.* -PHIES (-fĭz). **1.** The knowledge of phenomena as explained by, and resolved into, causes and reasons, powers and laws. **2.** Practical wisdom ; equanimity.

phil'ter (fĭl'tẽr), *n.* [6] A potion, drug, or charm supposed to excite love ; loosely, any magic potion.

phle-bot'o-my (flē-bŏt'ō-mĭ), *n. Med.* Act or practice of opening a vein to let blood.

---

chair ; go ; sing, ink ; then, thin ; nature, verdure ; yet ; zh = z in azure. Numbers refer to §§ in the Special Notes which, with Abbreviations, Signs, etc., precede the Vocabulary.

phlegm (flĕm), *n.* **1.** Thick stringy mucus, esp. in the respiratory passages. **2.** Sluggishness of temperament; apathy; also, coolness; self-possession.

phleg-mat′ic (flĕg-măt′ĭk), *a.* [4] Sluggish; apathetic; cool; composed.

phleg-mat′i-cal (-ĭ-kăl), *a.* Phlegmatic. — **phleg-mat′i-cal-ly**, *adv.* [8].

phlo′ĕm (flō′ĕm), *n.* *Bot.* That part of a bundle of vascular fibers which is composed of thin-walled cells placed end to end (containing protoplasm and nutritive material) with adjacent cells and parenchyma ; bast tissue.

phlox (flŏks), *n.* Any of a large genus (*Phlox*) of handsome American herbs, commonly cultivated.

phœ′be (fē′bē), *n.* Any of several flycatchers.

phone (fōn), *n. & v.* Abbrev. for TELEPHONE. *Colloq.*

pho-net′ic (fō-nĕt′ĭk), *a.* [4] **1.** Of or pert. to the voice, or its use ; of or pertaining to speech sounds. **2.** Representing sounds, esp. speech sounds.

pho-net′i-cal (-ĭ-kăl), *a.* Phonetic. — **-ly**, *adv.* [8].

pho′ne-ti′cian (fō′nē-tĭsh′ăn), *n.* One versed in phonetics.

pho-net′ics (fō′nĕt′ĭks), *n.* The doctrine or science of sounds, esp. of speech sounds, including their representation by phonetic symbols.

phon′ic (fŏn′ĭk; fō′nĭk), *a.* Of, pertaining to, or of the nature of, sound, usually of vocal sounds.

phon′ics (fŏn′ĭks; fō′nĭks), *n.* Science of sound; usually, the science of speech sounds; phonetics.

pho′no-graph (fō′nō-gráf), *n.* An instrument for recording and reproducing speech, music, etc.

pho′no-graph′ic (fō′nō-gráf′ĭk), **-graph′i-cal** (-ĭ-kăl), *a.* **1.** Of, pertaining to, or based on, phonography. **2.** Of, pertaining to, or done by, the phonograph. — **pho′no-graph′i-cal-ly**, *adv.* [8].

pho-nog′ra-phy (fō-nŏg′rȧ-fĭ), *n.* **1.** A description of the human voice, or of speech sounds. **2.** Art of phonetic writing ; esp., the shorthand system invented by Isaac Pitman (1813–97), or a derived system.— **pho-nog′ra-pher** (-fẽr), *n.* [8].

pho′no-log′ic (fō′nō-lŏj′ĭk), **pho′no-log′i-cal** (-ĭ-kăl), *a.* Of or pertaining to phonology.

pho-nol′o-gy (-nŏl′ō-jĭ), *n.* **1.** The science of speech sounds. **2.** That part of grammar which treats of the sounds of a language.

phos′phate (fŏs′fāt), *n.* **1.** *Chem.* A salt of phosphoric acid. **2.** Any material containing chemical phosphates and used for fertilizer.

phos′phor-esce′ (-fŏr-ĕs′), *v. i.* [1] To exhibit phosphorescence.

phos′phor-es′cence (-ĕs′ĕns), *n.* State, property, or act, of emitting light without sensible heat, as shown by phosphorus ; also, light so produced.

phos′phor-es′cent (fŏs′fŏr-ĕs′ĕnt), *a.* [4] Exhibiting phosphorescence.

phos-phor′ic (fŏs-fŏr′ĭk), *a.* **1.** *Chem.* Of, pert. to, or like, phosphorus. **2.** Phosphorescent.

phos′phor-ous (fŏs′fŏr-ŭs; fŏs-fō′rŭs), *a.* *Chem.* Of, pertaining to, or like, phosphorus.

phos′phor-us (fŏs′fŏr-ŭs), *n.* *Chem.* A waxy yellowish substance, poisonous, inflammable, and ill-smelling, that glows faintly in moist air.

pho′to-en-grav′ing (fō′tō-ĕn-grāv′ĭng), *n.* A photomechanical process for reproducing pictures, etc.; also, a print so made.

pho′to-graph (fō′tō-gráf), *n.* A picture or likeness

obtained by or as by photography.— *v. t.* To take a picture or copy of by or as by photography. — **pho-tog′ra-pher** (fō-tŏg′rȧ-fẽr), *n.* [8].

pho′to-graph′ic (fō′tō-grăf′ĭk), *a.* **1.** Of or pertaining to photography. **2.** Faithfully or minutely accurate. — **pho′to-graph′i-cal-ly**, *adv.* [8].

pho-tog′ra-phy (fō-tŏg′rȧ-fĭ), *n.* Art or process of producing images on sensitized surfaces by the chemical action of light.

pho′to-gra-vure′ (fō′tō-grȧ-vūr′ ; -grā′vŭr), *n.* A process for making prints from an intaglio plate prepared photographically; also, a print so made.

pho′to-me-chan′i-cal (-mē-kăn′ĭ-kăl), *a.* Pertaining to or designating any process of producing pictures or copies by mechanical printing from a photographically prepared plate.

pho-tom′e-ter (fō-tŏm′ē-tẽr), *n.* An instrument for measuring the intensity of light.

phrase (frāz), *n.* **1.** A brief expression; *Gram.*, two or more words having in the sentence the force of a single part of speech ; as, an adverbial *phrase*. **2.** A short, pithy expression. **3.** A form of speech ; expression. — *v. t.* [1] To express in words, esp. in appropriate words.

phra′se-ol′o-gy (frā′zē-ŏl′ō-jĭ), *n.* Manner of expression ; diction ; language ; style.

phren′o-log′i-cal (frĕn′ō-lŏj′ĭ-kăl), *a.* Of or pertaining to phrenology. [phrenology.]

phre-nol′o-gist (frē-nŏl′ō-jĭst), *n.* One versed in

phre-nol′o-gy (frē-nŏl′ō-jĭ), *n.* The theory that mental faculties and traits of character are shown by the shape of the skull; also, the system of faculties and their localization based on this theory.

phthi′sis (thī′sĭs), *n.* *Med.* A wasting of the tissue ; usually, tuberculosis.

phy-lac′ter-y (fĭ-lăk′tẽr-ĭ), *n.; pl.* -TERIES (-ĭz). **1.** A small box, containing slips inscribed with certain scriptural passages. Two such boxes are worn by orthodox Jews during prayer, one on the head and one on the left arm. **2.** An amulet.

phyl′lox-e′ra (fĭl′ŏk-sē′rȧ), *n.* Any of a genus (*Phylloxera*) of plant lice related to the aphids.

phy′lum (fī′lŭm), *n.; L. pl.* -LA (-lȧ). *Biol.* A primary division of plants and animals.

phys′ic (fĭz′ĭk), *n.* **1.** Art of healing diseases ; practice of medicine. **2.** An internal medicine. **3.** A cathartic.— *v. t.; -*ICKED (-ĭkt) ; -ICK-ING. To treat with physic; esp., to purge.

phys′i-cal (-ĭ-kăl), *a.* **1.** Of or pert. to nature or the laws of nature ; material. **2.** Of or pert. to natural science. **3.** Of or pert. to the body; bodily. — **physical geography**, geography treating of the exterior physical features and changes of the earth, in land, water, and air. — **-i-cal-ly**, *adv.*

phy-si′cian (fĭ-zĭsh′ăn), *n.* One skilled in physic, or the art of healing ; a doctor of medicine.

phys′i-cist (fĭz′ĭ-sĭst), *n.* A specialist in physics.

phys′ics (-ĭks), *n.* The science of phenomena of inanimate matter involving no chemical changes.

phys′i-og′no-mist (-ĭ-ŏg′nō-mĭst), *n.* One skilled in physiognomy.

phys′i-og′no-my (-ŏg′nō-mĭ), *n. ; pl.* -MIES (-mĭz). **1.** Art of discovering mental traits from the cast, or expression, of the face, as denoting character. **2.** General appearance or aspect of a thing.

phys′i-og′ra-phy (-ĭ-ŏg′rȧ-fĭ), *n.* **1.** A description of nature or of natural phenomena, objects, or products. **2.** Physical geography.

phys′i-o-log′ic (fĭz′ĭ-ō-lŏj′ĭk), *a.* Physiological.

phys′i-o-log′i-cal (-ĭ-kăl), *a.* Of or pertaining to physiology.

phys′i-ol′o-gist (-ŏl′ō-jĭst), *n.* One versed in physiology.

phys′i-ol′o-gy (-jĭ), *n.; pl.* -GIES (-jĭz). **1.** Biology dealing with life or living organisms; — distinct from *anatomy.* **2.** A treatise on this science.

phy-sique′ (fĭ-zēk′), *n.* Physical or bodily structure, constitution, or appearance.

pi, pie (pī). *Print.* Type confusedly mixed or disarranged. — *v. t. ;* PIED (pīd) ; PIE′ING. To mix or disarrange type.

pi′a ma′ter (pī′à mā′tēr). The innermost of the three membranes investing brain and spinal cord.

pi′a-nis′si-mo (pē′à-nĭs′ĭ-mō; pyä-nēs′sē-mō), *a. & adv. Music.* Very soft. Abbr. *pp.*

pi-an′ist (pĭ-ăn′ĭst; pē′à-nĭst), *n.* A performer, esp. a skilled performer, on the piano.

pia′no (pyä′nō), *a. & adv. Music.* Soft. Abbr. *p.*

pi-an′o (pĭ-ăn′ō), **pi-an′o-for′te** (-fōr′tā ; -fōrt′), *n. Music.* A keyboard instrument, giving its tones from steel wires struck by hammers.

pi-az′za (pĭ-ăz′à); *It. pron.* pyät′sä), *n. ; It. pl.* PIAZZI (pyät′sē). **1.** A large open square in an Italian town. **2.** By extension, an arcaded and roofed gallery; whence, in *U. S.,* a veranda.

pi′broch (pē′brŏk), *n.* A kind of Scottish Highland bagpipe music, usually martial.

pic′a-yune′ (pĭk′à-yōon′), *n.* **1.** A small coin. *U. S.* **2.** A trifle; a bit. *Colloq.*

pic′ca-lil′li (pĭk′à-lĭl′ĭ), *n.* A pickle, orig. East Indian, of chopped vegetables and hot spices.

pic′co-lo (pĭk′ō-lō), *n. Music.* A small flute, pitched an octave higher than the ordinary flute.

pick (pĭk), *n.* A heavy pointed iron tool with a wooden handle ; a pickax.

pick, *v. t.* **1.** To use a pointed instrument on ; strike or strike at with a pointed implement. **2.** To clear of, or free from, something with or as with a pointed instrument or by plucking or tearing. **3.** To pull or tear away, esp. with the fingers; gather. **4.** To eat daintily or mincingly. **5.** To choose; select. **6.** To make or find occasion for intentionally; as, to *pick* a quarrel. **7.** To steal the contents of ; rob ; — in *to pick one's pocket, purse,* etc. **8.** To open (a lock) by or as by a wire. **9.** To pull or pluck (the strings of a musical instrument).

pick (pĭk), *v. i.* **1.** To eat daintily or by morsels ; nibble. **2.** To search carefully ; choose with care. **3.** To pilfer ; — in the phrase *pick and steal.* — *n.* **1.** Act of picking ; blow with a pointed instrument. **2.** Act of selecting ; choice ; also, the choicest or best. [shoulders.]

pick′a-back′ (pĭk′à-băk′), *adv.* On the back or

pick′a-nin′ny (-nĭn′ĭ), *n. ; pl.* -NIES (-ĭz). A negro or colored child.

pick′ax′, pick′axe′ (-ăks′), *n.* Pick or mattock.

picked (pĭkt), *p. a.* **1.** Carefully selected; chosen; as, *picked* men. **2.** Purposely caused ; sought ; — said of a quarrel.

pick′er (pĭk′ēr), *n.* One that picks.

pick′er-el (-ĕl), *n.* The pike ; esp., any of several smaller species of the pike family.

pick′et (pĭk′ĕt), *n.* **1.** A pointed or sharpened stake or pale, as for making fences. **2.** *Mil.* A detached body of soldiers, or a soldier, serving to guard an army from surprise. **3.** A person posted by a labor organization at a place affected by a strike. — *v. t.* **1.** To fasten, fence, or fortify with pickets, or pointed stakes ; palisade. **2.** To tether to or as to a picket. **3.** *Mil.* **a** To guard by picket. **b** To post as a picket. **4.** To post pickets at or near. See PICKET, *n.,* 3.

pick′ing (-ĭng), *n.* **1.** Act of one that picks. **2.** That which is or may be picked or picked up; a scrap ; *pl.,* portions picked up or out.

pick′le (pĭk′l), *n.* **1.** Brine or vinegar for preserving food ; also, an article of food, or (usually in *pl.*) food, so preserved. **2.** A difficult situation; predicament ; as, to be in a *pickle.* Now *Colloq.* — *v. t.* [1] To preserve, season, or steep in pickle.

pick′pock′et (pĭk′pŏk′ĕt), *n.* One who steals purses or other articles from pockets.

pic′nic (pĭk′nĭk), *n.* An excursion or outdoor pleasure party in which the members partake of refreshments carried, usually, by themselves. — *v. i. ;* -NICKED (-nĭkt) ; -NICK-ING (-nĭ-kĭng). To go on, or hold, a picnic ; eat in picnic fashion. — **pic′nick-er** (-nĭ-kēr), *n.* [8].

pic-to′ri-al (pĭk-tō′rĭ-ăl), *a.* [4] Pert. to, or of the nature of, a picture ; graphic. — **-ly,** *adv.*

pic′ture (pĭk′tụr), *n.* **1.** A representation, esp. as a work of art, produced by painting, drawing, engraving, photography, etc **2.** A transitory visible image. **3.** A likeness or copy; embodiment; as, he is the *picture* of grief. — *v. t.* [1] **1.** To represent in a picture ; depict. **2.** To describe graphically. **3.** To imagine.

pic′tur-esque′ (pĭk′tụr-ĕsk′), *a.* [4] **1.** Forming, or fitted to form, a picture. **2.** Possessing quaint, rugged, or homely charm, as disting. from beauty or sublimity. — **-ly,** *adv.* [8] — **-ness,** *n.* [8].

pidg′in, pi′geon (pĭj′ĭn ; -ŭn), *n.* Chinese corruption of *business;* — chiefly in **pidgin English,** the jargon, mainly of English words arranged after Chinese syntax, used in the East between foreigners and the Chinese.

pie (pī), *n.* An article of food consisting of a pastry crust with any of various kinds of filling.

pie, *n.* A magpie.

pie, *n.* **1.** = PI. *Brit.* **2.** A jumble ; chaos ; mess.

pie′bald′ (pī′bôld′), *a.* Of different colors, esp. white and black ; mottled ; party-colored.

piece (pēs), *n.* **1.** A fragment; a part separated; portion. **2.** A distinct or limited part or quantity; a bit. **3.** A quantity, as a length, weight, or size, usually fixed, in which various articles or products are made or put up. **4.** A single object or individual (of a class or group). **5.** A firearm, as a rifle or cannon. — *v. t.* [1] **1.** To enlarge, complete, or repair, by adding a piece or pieces; patch. **2.** To make up or mend by joining pieces ; unite.

piece′meal′ (pēs′mēl′), *adv.* **1.** Piece by piece ; little by little ; by degrees. **2.** In pieces.

piece′work′ (pēs′wûrk′), *n.* Work done or paid for by the piece or job. — **piece′work′er,** *n.* [8].

pied (pīd), *a.* Party-colored; piebald.

pied′mont (pēd′mŏnt), *a.* In physical geography, lying or formed at the base of mountains.

---

pie'plant' (pī'plănt'), *n.* Garden rhubarb. *U. S.*

pier (pēr), *n.* **1.** A support for a bridge span. **2.** A supporting pillar, or structure, as of an arch or lintel. **3.** A narrow piece of wall between two openings. **4.** An auxiliary mass of masonry to stiffen a wall. **5.** A breakwater or mole ; hence, any similar structure for use as a landing place, a promenade, etc., or to protect or form a harbor.

pierce (pērs), *v. t.* [1] **1.** To run into or through as a pointed instrument does ; stab. **2.** To perforate. **3.** To force a way into or through. **4.** To penetrate with the eye or mind ; discern.— *v. i.* To make a way (into or through something) ; enter ; penetrate.

pier glass. A large high mirror, as, orig., a narrow one designed to occupy the pier, or wall space between windows.

pi'e-ty (pī'ĕ-tĭ), *n. ; pl.* -TIES (-tĭz). **1.** Quality or state of being pious ; godliness ; devoutness. **2.** A pious act, observance, or characteristic.

pig (pĭg), *n.* **1.** A young swine ; also, any swine. **2.** *Metal.* A casting, as of iron or lead, run directly from the smelting furnace into a troughlike mold. — *v. i. ;* PIGGED (pĭgd) ; PIG'GING. To farrow.

pi'geon (pĭj'ŭn), *n.* A well-known stout-bodied, short-legged bird.

pi'geon-hole' (-hōl'), *n.* **1.** Small recess for pigeons. **2.** A small open compartment in a desk, case, or the like, for letters, documents, etc.— *v. t.* [1] To place in or as in a pigeonhole ; lay aside ; shelve.

pig'gin (pĭg'ĭn), *n.* A small wooden pail or tub with an upright stave as handle.

pig'gish (pĭg'ĭsh), *a.* [4] Like a pig ; greedy ; stubborn ; filthy.— **-ly,** *adv.* [8] — **-ness,** *n.* [8].

pig'-head'ed (-hĕd'ĕd), *a.* Stupidly obstinate.

pig'ment (pĭg'mĕnt), *n.* A coloring matter ; specifically : **a** Any powder prepared as a paint by mixture with some vehicle in which it is insoluble. **b** *Biol.* Any of various coloring matters in animals and plants, esp. in a cell or tissue.

pig'men-ta-ry (pĭg'mĕn-tä-rĭ), *a.* Of, pertaining to, producing, or containing, pigment.

pig'skin' (-skĭn'), *n.* **1.** Skin of a pig or leather made of it. **2.** *Colloq.* **a** A saddle. **b** A football.

pig'tail' (-tāl'), *n.* A queue, as that worn by the Chinese.

pike (pīk), *n.* A long and slender, greedy, freshwater food fish. Cf. PICKEREL.

pike, *n.* A turnpike road.

pike, *n.* A military weapon, formerly common, consisting of a long wooden shaft with steel point.

pike'staff' (pīk'stàf'), *n.* A staff with a spike at the end, to keep the user from slipping.

pi-las'ter (pĭ-lăs'tẽr), *n.* An upright architectural member, rectangular in plan, structurally a pier, but treated as a column, with capital, shaft, and base.

pil'chard (pĭl'chàrd), *n.* The sardine, or some related fish.

pile (pīl), *n.* **1.** Hair ; esp., fine soft hair. **2.** Nap on a fabric ; esp., thick nap, as of velvet.

pile, *n.* **1.** A mass of things heaped together, esp. more or less regularly ; a heap. **2. a** A large number, quantity, etc. *Colloq., U. S.* **b** A large building, or mass of buildings.— *v. t.* [1] **1.** To heap up, as in a pile. **2.** To cover with heaps or in

great abundance ; fill.— *v. i.* To form a pile ; accumulate.

pile (pīl), *n.* A large stake or pointed timber, driven into the earth, as to support a foundation ; any post or pillar similarly used. — *v. t.* [1] To drive or sink piles into ; support with piles.

piles (pīlz), *n. pl. Med.* Hemorrhoids.

pil'fer (pĭl'fēr), *v. i. & t.* To practice petty theft ; filch. — **pil'fer-er** (-ẽr), *n.* [8].

pil'grim (pĭl'grĭm), *n.* **1.** A journeyer ; wayfarer. *Rhetorical.* **2.** One who travels to some holy place as a devotee. **3.** *pl.* [*cap.*] *U. S. Hist.* The Puritans who founded Plymouth Colony, Massachusetts ; — called also *Pilgrim Fathers.*

pil'grim-age (-grĭ-mäj), *n.* **1.** Journey of a pilgrim ; long and weary journey. **2.** Life, regarded as a journey.

pill (pĭl), *n.* **1.** A medicine in a little ball, or small round mass, to be taken whole. **2.** A pellet.

pil'lage (pĭl'āj), *n.* **1.** Act of pillaging or plundering, esp. in war ; plunder. **2.** Spoil ; booty. — *v. t. & i.* [1] To strip of money or goods by open violence ; plunder. — **pil'lag-er** (-ā-jẽr), *n.*

pil'lar (-àr), *n.* **1.** A firm, upright, detached support, slender or narrow in proportion to its height ; any upright support, as a bedpost ; also, a column or shaft standing alone, as for a monument. **2.** Something like a pillar ; a main support.

pil'lion (-yŭn), *n.* A kind of light saddle ; also, a pad put behind a man's saddle, as for a woman.

pil'lo-ry (-ō-rĭ), *n. ; pl.* -RIES (-rĭz). A device for publicly punishing offenders, consisting of a frame having holes for the head and hands. — *v. t.* [2] **1.** To set in, or punish with, the pillory. **2.** To expose to public scorn ; as, to *pillory* a politician.

pil'low (pĭl'ō), *n.* **1.** Anything used to support one's head when reposing ; esp., a sack filled with feathers or other soft material. **2.** Any of various things likened to a pillow. — *v. t. & i.* To rest, lay, or support, on or as on a pillow.

pil'low-case' (-kās'), *n.* A removable case or covering, usually of white linen or cotton, for a pillow.

pi'lose (pī'lōs), *a.* [4] Covered with hair ; hairy.

pi'lot (pī'lŭt), *n.* **1.** One who steers a vessel ; helmsman. **2.** One qualified to conduct vessels into and out of a port, or in certain waters. **3.** One qualified to fly a balloon, airship, or flying machine. **4.** A guide. **5.** = COWCATCHER. — *v. t.* **1.** To direct the course of, as of a ship. **2.** To guide, as through dangers or difficulties.

pi'lot-age (-āj), *n.* **1.** Act or business of piloting. **2.** The compensation made or allowed to a pilot.

pilot biscuit, pilot bread. Ship biscuit.

pi-men'to (pĭ-mĕn'tō), *n.; pl.* -TOS (-tōz). Allspice, or the allspice tree.

pim'per-nel (pĭm'pẽr-nĕl), *n.* A plant of the primrose family, with scarlet, white, or purple flowers which close at the approach of bad weather.

pim'ple (pĭm'p'l), *n.* Any small pointed elevation of the skin ; pustule.— **pim'pled** (-p'ld), *a.* [4].

pim'ply (-plĭ), *a.* [4] Pimpled.

pin (pĭn), *n.* **1.** A peg, bolt, etc., used to fasten articles together, or to hang something on. **2. a** A small pointed and headed piece of wire, for fastening clothing, etc. **b** A larger pointed instrument ; as, hat*pin,* scarf*pin,* etc. **3.** An ornament, as a badge, fastened to the clothing by a pin. — *v. t.*; **PINNED** (pĭnd); **PIN'NING.** To fasten, join, secure, or transfix, by or as by a pin.

pin'a-fore' (pĭn'ȧ-fōr'), *n.* A sleeveless overdress worn esp. by children or girls to protect the dress.

‖ **pince'-nez'** (păns'nā'), *n. sing. and pl.* [F.] Eyeglasses kept on the nose by a spring.

pin'cers (pĭn'sērz), *n. pl.* An instrument having two handles and two grasping jaws working on a pivot, used for gripping things.

pinch (pĭnch), *v. t.* **1.** To squeeze, as between the finger and thumb. **2.** To squeeze or compress painfully. **3.** To afflict; distress; make waste or shrunken, etc. — *v. i.* **1.** To compress; squeeze. **2.** To be niggardly. — *n.* **1.** Act of pinching; a nip. **2.** As much as may be taken between the finger and thumb; a bit. **3.** Pressure; pain; stress. **4.** An emergency; a strait. — **pinch'er,** *n.*

pinch'beck (-bĕk), *n.* An alloy of copper and zinc, used to imitate gold. — *a.* Sham; cheap.

pinch'ers (pĭn'chērz), *n. pl.* Pincers.

pine (pīn), *v. i.* [1] **1.** To languish; lose vigor or flesh, esp. under distress or anxiety; droop. **2.** To languish with desire; long intensely.

pine, *n.* **1.** A cone-bearing tree of many species, and having needle-shaped leaves (**pine needles**). **2.** Wood of the pine. **3.** Pineapple.

pine'ap'ple (pīn'ăp''l), *n.* A tropical plant having rigid spiny-margined leaves, and bearing a short stalk with a dense oblong head of small rudimentary flowers. **2.** The edible juicy fruit of this plant.

pin'feath'er (pĭn'fĕth'ēr), *n.* A little feather just coming out of the skin (as of a fowl) and still inclosed in the horny sheath which is later cast off.

pin'hole' (-hōl'), *n.* A hole made by or as by a pin.

pin'ion (pĭn'yŭn), *n. Mach.* A cogwheel with a small number of teeth, designed to gear with a larger wheel or with a rack.

pin'ion, *n.* **1.** The terminal part of a bird's wing. **2.** A wing. **3.** A feather; quill. — *v. t.* To disable or restrain by binding the arms, esp. to the body.

pink (pĭngk), *v. t.* **1.** To pierce with small holes; cut the edge of, as cloth, in small scallops. **2.** To pierce or prick, as with a sword.

pink, *n.* **1.** Any of various herbs, some of which as the carnations, are cultivated for their flowers. **2.** A thing supremely excellent; the highest type. **3.** A color resulting from mixture of red with white. — *a.* Of the color called *pink.*

pink eye. A kind of contagious inflammation of the eye, marked by redness of the eyeball.

pin money. Money allowed by a man to his wife for her private purposes.

pin'nace (pĭn'ăs), *n.* **1.** A light sailing vessel. *Hist. or Poetic.* **2.** Any of various ship's boats.

pin'na-cle (-ȧ-k'l), *n.* **1.** A small turret, generally ending in a small spire. **2.** A lofty peak. **3.** The highest point.

pin'nate (-āt), *a.* Featherlike; having parts arranged along two sides of an axis; as, a *pinnate* leaf. See *Illust.*

pi'no-chle, pi'no-cle (pē'nŏ-k'l; pĭn'-ŏ-), *n.* A game at cards; also, a certain combination in it.

Pinnate Leaf.

pi-ñon' (pē-nyōn'; pĭn'yŏn), *n.* Any of various pines producing an edible nutlike seed; also, the seed itself.

pint (pīnt), *n.* A measure of capacity; half a quart; four gills. Abbr., *pt.* [as of a hinge.

pin'tle (pĭn't'l), *n.* A (usually upright) pivot pin, **pin'to** (-tō), *a.* Piebald; mottled.

pin'y (pīn'ĭ), *a.* [3] **1.** Abounding in pines. **2.** Of, pertaining to, or characteristic of, pine; pinelike.

pi'o-neer' (pī'ŏ-nēr'), *n.* **1.** *Mil.* One of the soldiers detailed to make roads, etc. **2.** One who goes before, preparing the way for others.

pi'ous (pī'ŭs), *a.* [4] **1.** Showing faith in the Deity; reverential; religious; dutiful. **2.** Practiced under pretext of religion.— **pi'ous-ly,** *adv.*

pip (pĭp), *n.* A small seed, as of an apple.

pip, *n.* A contagious disease of chickens.

pipe (pīp), *n.* **1.** A tubular wind instrument of reed, wood, etc., as an oboe. **2.** The bagpipe; — usually in *pl.* **3.** The voice, esp. the singing voice; the peeping whistle or note of a bird, insect, etc. **4.** A long tube or hollow body, as to conduct water, steam, etc. **5. a** A tube with a small bowl used for smoking tobacco or other substances. **b** A pipeful of what is smoked. **6.** A large cask of varying capacity, used esp. for wine and oil; also, its volume, reckoned as two hogsheads. — *v. t.* [1] **1.** To play on a pipe, etc. ; to utter in the shrill tone of a pipe. **2.** To furnish or equip with pipes, as a building. — *v. i.* **1.** To play on or sound a pipe. **2.** To emit, or have, a shrill sound like that of a pipe.

pip'er (pīp'ēr), *n.* One who plays on a pipe.

pip'ing (pīp'ĭng), *n.* **1.** Action of one that pipes; also, the music or sound of one that pipes. **2.** Pipes collectively. **3.** A small cord covered with cloth, used as a dress trimming.

pip'it (pĭp'ĭt), *n.* Any of various small birds resembling the lark, and singing on the wing.

pip'kin (-kĭn), *n.* A small earthen pot; a piggin.

pip'pin (-ĭn), *n.* Any of numerous varieties of apple.

pi'quan-cy (pē'kăn-sĭ), *n.* Piquant quality.

pi'quant (-kănt), *a.* [4] Stimulating to the taste, curiosity, etc.; tart; pungent. —-**ly,** *adv.* [8].

pique (pēk), *n.* A feeling of hurt or resentment due to a slight or injury, esp. to one's pride. — *v. t.* [1] **1.** To anger by wounding the pride of; nettle. **2.** To stimulate; prick; as, to *pique* curiosity. **3.** To pride or value, — reflexively.

pi-qué' (pē-kā'), *n.* A heavy ribbed or figured cotton fabric.

pi-quet' (pē-kĕt'), *n.* A certain game at cards.

pi'ra-cy (pī'rȧ-sĭ), *n.; pl.* -**CIES** (-sĭz). **1.** Robbery on the high seas. **2.** Any unauthorized appropriation and reproduction of another's work.

pi'rate (pī'rȧt), *n.* **1.** One who commits piracy. **2.** An armed vessel engaged in piracy. — *v. i. & t.* [1] To play the pirate; commit piracy upon.

pi-rat'ic (pī-răt'ĭk), *a.* Piratical.

pi-rat'i-cal (-ĭ-kăl), *a.* Of, pertaining to, or like, a pirate or piracy. — **pi-rat'i-cal-ly,** *adv.* [8].

pir'ou-ette' (pĭr'ōō-ĕt'), *n.* A whirling or turning on the toes. — *v. i.* [1] To perform a pirouette.

pis'ca-to-ry (pĭs'kȧ-tō-rĭ), *a.* Also **pis'ca-to'-ri-al** (pĭs-kȧ-t···'rĭ-ȧl). Of or pert. to fishes or fishing.

pis/ci-cul/ture (pĭs/ĭ-kŭl/tụr), *n.* Fish culture.

pish (pĭsh), *interj. & n.* Exclamation of contempt.

pis-ta/chi-o (pĭs-tā/shĭ-ō ; pĭs-tä/-), *n.* **1.** A small tree of southern Europe and Asia Minor. **2.** Its seed, used for flavoring. [flower.]

pis/til (pĭs/tĭl), *n.* The seed-bearing organ of a

pis/til-late (-tĭ-lāt), *a.* Having or producing a pistil or pistils; having pistils but no stamens.

pis/tol (-tŭl), *n.* A firearm for use with one hand.

pis/ton (pĭs/tŭn), *n. Mach.* A sliding piece moved by, or moving against, fluid pressure, usually a short cylinder moving in a cylinder.

pit (pĭt), *n.* The hard stone of a drupe. *U. S.*

pit, *n.* **1.** A cavity or hole in the ground. **2.** A pitfall for wild beasts; hence, a trap; snare. **3.** Hades; hell, or a part of it; — with *the.* **4.** A surface depression or hollow. **5.** In England, the cheaper part of the theater, behind the stalls. **6.** *Commerce.* That part of the floor of some exchanges devoted to a special branch of business; as, the wheat *pit. U. S.*—*v.t.;* PIT/TED (-ĕd); PIT/TING. **1.** To put into a pit or hole. **2.** To form pits in.

pit/a-pat/ (pĭt/á-păt/), *adv.* With quick succession of beats.—*n.* A light, repeated sound; a patter.

pitch (pĭch), *n.* **1.** A black or dark sticky substance got as a residue in distilling tar, etc., and occurring naturally as asphalt. **2.** The resin from certain pines. — *v. t.* To smear or cover over with or as with pitch.

pitch, *v. t.* **1.** To place and set up or erect. **2.** To set in order or arrange, as for battle. *Archaic,* except in p. p.; as, a *pitched* battle. **3.** To fix at a certain pitch or level, as the voice. **4.** To throw, hurl, or toss. — *v. i.* **1.** To fix one's choice; decide. **2.** To plunge or fall, esp. forward. **3.** *Naut.* To plunge so that the bow and stern alternately rise and fall, as a ship. **4.** *Baseball.* To throw the ball to the batsman; act as pitcher. — *n.* **1.** Act of pitching, or throwing. **2.** Act of plunging downward; esp., the pitching of a vessel in a head sea. **3.** A point or peak; extreme; acme; as, the *pitch* of merriment. **4.** A slope; declivity. **5.** *Mechanics.* Distance apart of two things, esp. in a series, as from center to center of adjacent gear teeth. **6.** Highness or lowness of sound or of a tone.

pitch/blende (pĭch/blĕnd/), *n.* A brown to black mineral with pitchlike luster.

pitch/er (-ẽr), *n.* A vessel for holding and pouring liquids, usually with a handle.

pitch/er, *n.* One who pitches.

pitcher plant. Any plant with leaves wholly or partially modified into cuplike appendages.

pitch/fork/ (pĭch/fôrk/), *n.* A fork used in pitching hay, grain, etc.

pitch/y (-ĭ), *a.* [3] **1.** Resembling pitch. **2.** Abounding in, or smeared with, pitch. **3.** Dark as pitch; as, *pitchy* night. —**-i-ness** (-ĭ-nĕs), *n.* [8].

pit/e-ous (pĭt/ē-ŭs), *a.* [4] **1.** Evincing pity; tender. **2.** Fitted to excite pity or sympathy; miserable; lamentable. —**-ly,** *adv.* [8] —**-ness,** *n.* [8].

pit/fall (pĭt/fôl/), *n.* A trap for birds, beasts, or men; esp., a pit with the opening masked.

pith (pĭth), *n.* **1.** The loose spongy tissue occupying the center of the stem in certain plants. **2.** The soft interior of a bone, feather, etc. **3.** Concentrated force; vigor.

pith/y (pĭth/ĭ), *a.* [3] **1.** Of or abounding in pith. **2.** Having nervous energy; forceful; as, *pithy* remarks. — **pith/i-ly** (-ĭ-lĭ), *adv.* [8]—**-i-ness,** *n.*

pit/i-a-ble (pĭt/ĭ-à-b'l), *a.* [4] **1.** Exciting pity. **2.** Arousing pitying contempt. —**-bly,** *adv.*

pit/i-ful (-fŏŏl), *a.* [4] **1.** Full of pity; compassionate. **2.** Piteous; lamentable. **3.** Paltry. — **-ly,** *adv.* [8] —**-ness,** *n.* [8].

pit/i-less, *a.* [4] Destitute of pity; merciless. — **pit/i-less-ly,** *adv.* [8] — **pit/i-less-ness,** *n.* [8]

pit/tance (pĭt/ăns), *n.* A small portion, quantity, or allowance, esp. of money.

pit/y (pĭt/ĭ), *n.; pl.* PITIES (-ĭz). **1.** A feeling for the sufferings of others; compassion. **2.** A reason or cause of pity, grief, or regret. — *v. t.* [2] To feel pity for; sympathize with.

piv/ot (pĭv/ŭt), *n.* A point, fixed pin, etc., on the end of which something turns; — often fig. — *v. t. & i.* To furnish with, or turn on, a pivot or pivots.

pix/y } (pĭk/sĭ), *n.; pl.* PIXIES (-sĭz). *Folklore.* A
pix/ie } fairy.

pla/ca-bil/i-ty (plā/ká-bĭl/ĭ-tĭ), *n.* Quality or state of being placable.

pla/ca-ble (plā/ká-b'l), *a.* [4] Capable of being pacified. — **-ness,** *n.* — **pla/ca-bly,** *adv.*

plac/ard (plăk/ärd ; plȧ-kärd/), *n.* A notice to be posted in a public place; a poster; bill.

pla-card/ (plȧ-kärd/ ; plăk/ärd), *v. t.* **1.** To post placards on or in. **2.** To announce by placards. **3.** To post as a placard. [conciliate.]

pla/cate (plā/kāt; plăk/āt), *v. t.* [1] To appease;

place (plās), *n.* **1.** An open space, or square, in a city or town. **2.** Space: a Room. **b** Region; locality. **3.** A portion of space occupied by, reserved for, or vacated by, a body. **4.** A building set apart for a special purpose. **5.** *Arith.* The position of a figure relative to others of a series. **6.** Order of priority, advancement, dignity, etc.; esp., social position ; high rank ; grade ; status; also, function. **7.** Ordinal relation; as, in the first *place.* — *v. t.* [1] **1.** To put in a certain place. **2.** To identify by connecting with some place, time, circumstance, etc.

plac/er (plăs/ẽr), *n. Mining.* A place where gold is got by washing; a deposit of sand, gravel, or the like containing particles of valuable mineral.

plac/id (plăs/ĭd), *a.* [3] Calm ; peaceful ; quiet. — **-ly,** *adv.* — **-ness,** *n.* [being placid.]

pla-cid/i-ty (plȧ-sĭd/ĭ-tĭ), *n.* Quality or state of

plack/et (plăk/ĕt), *n.* The opening or slit in a petticoat or skirt for convenience in putting it on.

pla/gi-a-rism (plā/jĭ-á-rĭz'm; plā/jȧ-), *n.* Act of plagiarizing ; also, plagiarized matter.

pla/gi-a-rist (-rĭst), *n.* One who plagiarizes.

pla/gi-a-rize (-rĭz), *v. t. & i.* [1] To steal and use as one's own (the ideas, words, etc., of another).

pla/gi-a-ry (-rĭ), *n.; pl.* -RIES (-rĭz). **1.** A plagiarist. **2.** Plagiarism.

plague (plāg), *n.* **1.** Any afflictive evil. **2.** A nuisance. *Colloq.* **3.** Any malignant, esp. infectious, disease, esp., an acute infectious fever. — *v. t.* [1] **1.** To smite or afflict with disease, or evil. **2.** To vex ; harass.

plaice (plās), *n.* Any of various flatfishes.

plaid (plăd; *Scot.* plād), *n.* **1.** A rectangular cloth, usually of tartan, worn by both sexes in

Scotland in place of a cloak. **2.** Any goods of the pattern of a plaid; a checkered cloth or pattern.

plain (plān), *a.* [3] **1.** Flat; plane (which see). **2.** Open; clear; as, in *plain* sight. **3.** Open to the mind; manifest; also, candid. **4.** Not intricate; simple, as a pattern. **5.** Without ornament or decoration; not rich; simple; as, *plain* clothes; *plain* food. **6.** Not highly born, or gifted. **7.** Without beauty; homely. — *adv.* In a plain manner; clearly. — *n.* **1.** Level land. **2.** *pl.* Broad tracts of almost treeless level country; prairie. — **-ly,** *adv.* [8] — **-ness,** *n.* [8].

plaint (plānt), *n.* **1.** Lamentation. **2.** Complaint.

plain'tiff (plān'tĭf), *n. Law.* One who commences a personal suit for an injury to his rights.

plain'tive (-tĭv), *a.* [4] Expressive of sorrow or melancholy. — **-ly,** *adv.* [8] — **-ness,** *n.* [8].

plait (plăt; plĕt; *in sense 2 of n. & v. commonly* plāt), *n.* **1.** A doubling back, as of cloth on itself; a pleat. **2.** A braid, as of hair. — *v. t.* **1.** To fold, esp. in plaits; as, to *plait* a ruffle. **2.** To interweave the strands of; braid.

plan (plăn), *n.* **1.** A draft or form, properly one drawn on a plane, as a map; esp., a top view. **2.** A method of procedure or arrangement; a scheme. — *v. t. & i.; PLANNED* (plănd); *PLAN'NING.* **1.** To form a plan of; draft. **2.** To scheme; devise.

plane (plān), *n., or* **plane tree.** Any of several trees with large palmately lobed leaves, and flowers in round heads.

plane, *a.* Without elevations or depressions; level; flat; *Math.,* involving only planes.

☞ In science, plane (instead of *plain*) is generally used to designate a flat or level surface. — *n.* **1.** A surface in which, if any two points are taken, the straight line that joins them lies wholly in that surface. **2.** A flat or level material surface. **3.** Level; stage of development; grade.

plane, *n. Joinery.* A tool for smoothing wood, etc. — *v. t.* [1] **1.** To make smooth or even, esp. with a plane. **2.** To efface; remove. — *v. i.* To work with a plane.

plan'er (-ēr), *n.* One that planes, esp. a machine.

plan'et (plăn'ĕt), *n. Astron.* Any body, except a comet or a meteoroid, that revolves about the sun.

plan'et-a-ry (-ā-rĭ), *a.* **1.** Of or pert. to a planet or the planets. **2.** Erratic; wandering.

plank (plăngk), *n.* **1.** A heavy thick board. **2.** Timber in planks. **3.** *Politics.* An article in a party platform; as, a tariff *plank.* — *v. t.* To cover, floor, or lay with planks.

plan'ner (plăn'ēr), *n.* One who plans; a projector.

plant (plănt), *n.* **1.** Any member of the lower of the two groups of living organisms; a vegetable. **2.** a The machinery, apparatus, fixtures, etc., sometimes also the real estate, used in carrying on a trade or industrial business. **b** Equipment of any institution, as a college. — *v. t.* **1.** To put or set in the ground for growth, as a seed or a young tree. **2.** To set firmly, as in or on the ground; fix. **3.** To implant, as a passion, idea, etc. **4.** To stock with something, esp. plants.

plan'tain (plăn'tăn; -tĭn), *n.* Any of a genus of weeds bearing spikes of minute greenish flowers.

plan'tain, *n.* A species of banana.

plan-ta'tion (plăn-tā'shŭn), *n.* **1.** A group, usually large, of plants or trees under cultivation. **2.** A place planted; esp., in the southern U. S., West Indies, etc., an estate cultivated by resident laborers.

plant'er (plăn'tēr), *n.* **1.** One that plants. **2.** One who owns or cultivates a plantation.

plan'ti-grade (plăn'tĭ-grād), *a. Zoöl.* Walking on the sole with the heel touching the ground, as do bears and man. — *n.* A plantigrade animal.

plant louse. Any of certain small insects that live on plants and suck their juices; an aphid.

plaque (plăk), *n.* Any flat, thin piece, as of metal, used, as on a wall, for ornament.

plash (plăsh), *v. i. & t.* To splash. — *n.* A splash.

plash, *n.* A pool; puddle.

plash'y (-ĭ), *a.* [3] Plashing; splashing.

plash'y, *a.* [3] Abounding with puddles.

plas'ma (plăz'mà), *n.* The watery part of blood, lymph, or milk.

plas'ter (plås'tēr), *n.* **1.** *Med.* An application harder than ointment, spread on linen, silk, or the like, and applied to the body. **2.** A pasty composition, as of lime, water, and sand, hardening on drying, used for coating walls, etc. **3.** Short for plaster of Paris, a white powdery substance formed by calcining gypsum. — *v. t.* **1.** To cover or smear with plaster. **2.** To conceal, as with plaster. — **plas'ter-er,** *n.* [8].

plas'ter-ing, *vb. n.* **1.** Act of applying plaster. **2. a** A covering of plaster. **b** = PLASTER, *n.,* 2.

plas'tic (plăs'tĭk), *a.* [4] **1.** Giving form. **2.** Pert. to molding or modeling; — said of sculpture, ceramics, etc. **3.** Capable of being molded or modeled, as clay; impressionable.

plas-tic'i-ty (plăs-tĭs'ĭ-tĭ), *n.* Plastic quality.

plat (plăt), *v. t.; PLAT'TED; -TING.* To braid; plait.

plat, *n.* **1.** A plot of ground. **2.** A diagram or map *U. S.* — *v. t.* To make a plat of; plot.

plate (plāt), *n.* **1.** A flat thin piece, esp. of uniform thickness. **2.** A flat, smooth piece of metal on which anything is engraved or etched, as for printing; hence, an impression from an engraving. **3.** *Photog.* A sensitized sheet of glass, metal, etc. **4.** Domestic vessels, utensils, etc., esp. such as platters, etc., of gold or silver. **5.** Metallic ware which is plated. **6.** A shallow, usually circular, vessel from which food is eaten; hence, a plateful — *v. t.* [1] **1.** To cover or overlay with gold, silver, or other metal. **2.** To overlay with metal plates or armor plate.

pla-teau' (plà-tō'), *n.; pl.* E. **-teaus** (-tōz'), F. **-teaux** (*F.* -tō'; *E.* -tōz'). A broad, relatively elevated tract of land; a table-land.

plate'ful (plāt'fŏŏl), *n.; pl.* **-fuls** (-fŏŏlz). Enough to fill a plate; contents of a filled plate.

plat'form (plăt'fôrm'), *n.* **1.** A level, usually raised, surface; a flooring, for speakers, etc. **2.** A declaration of principles on which a party stands.

plat'i-na (plăt'ĭ-nà; plà-tē'nà), *n.* Platinum.

plat'ing (plāt'ĭng), *n.* **1.** Art or process of covering anything with a plate, plates, or a coating of metal. **2.** A coating of metal or of metal plates.

plat'i-num (plăt'ĭ-nŭm), *n.* A precious metal; a heavy, silver-white element, ductile, malleable, very infusible, and able to resist most chemicals.

plat'i-tude (-tūd), *n.* **1.** Quality of being flat, dull, or commonplace. **2.** A commonplace.

Pla-ton'ic (plȧ-tŏn'ĭk), *a.* Pert. to Plato or his philosophy. — **Platonic love,** spiritual love.

pla-toon' (plȧ-toon'), *n.* A subdivision of a company, troop, etc., commanded by a lieutenant.

plat'ter (plăt'ẽr), *n.* One that plats, or braids.

plat'ter, *n.* A large dish for serving meat, etc.

plat'y-pus (-ĭ-pŭs), *n.* The duckbill. [applause.

plau'dit (plô'dĭt),*n.* Act of applauding; a round of |

plau'si-bil'i-ty (plô'zĭ-bĭl'ĭ-tĭ), *n.; pl.* -TIES (-tĭz). Quality or state of being plausible; also, something plausible.

plau'si-ble (plô'zĭ-b'l), *a.* [4] **1.** Superficially fair, reasonable, or valuable; specious; as, a *plausible* excuse. **2.** Fair-spoken; as, a *plausible* man. — **plau'si-bly,** *adv.* [8].

play (plā), *v. i.* **1.** To move, operate, or have effect in a lively or brisk and irregular, or alternating manner, or in a jet or stream. **2.** To busy or exercise one's self for diversion; sport; frolic. **3.** To dally; toy. **4.** To take part in a game. **5.** To act; behave. **6.** To perform on an instrument of music; to operate so as to give music. **7.** To act on or as on the stage; perform. — *v. t.* **1.** To operate; work. **2.** To make to play; cause to ripple, vibrate, change rapidly, etc. **3.** To do; perform; execute. **4.** To engage in (a game, etc.). **5.** To treat, practice, or deal with, in sport, jest, etc. **6.** To contend against in a game; also, to use, as a contestant, in a game. **7.** To perform or execute (music). **8.** To perform music upon. **9.** To act or perform (a play, or in or as in a play). — *n.* **1.** Brisk and vigorous physical action or exercise. **2.** Brisk handling, using, or plying. **3.** Brisk motion or change of movement, action, or effect. **4.** Action; activity. **5.** Freedom, room, or scope for motion or action. **6.** Amusement; sport; frolic. **7.** Fun; jest. **8.** Dealing; conduct. *Obs.,* exc. in *fair play, foul play.* **9.** Conduct of a game; also, a point in play; turn to play. **10.** Gambling. **11.** Performance of a dramatic piece. **12.** A drama.

‖ **pla'ya** (plä'yä),*n.* [Sp.] A beach; shore; in Texas, New Mexico,and Arizona,a broad,level spot,where water temporarily accumulates after rains.

play'er (plā'ẽr), *n.* One that plays.

play'fel'low (-fĕl'ō), *n.* A playmate.

play'ful (-fŏŏl), *a.* [4] Full of play; sportive; merry. — **play'ful-ly,** *adv.* [8] — **ness,** *n.* [8].

play'house (-hous'), *n.* A theater.

play'ing, *p. pr. & vb. n.* of PLAY. — **playing card,** any of the cards composing a pack divided into four suits (hearts, diamonds, clubs, spades).

play'mate (-māt'), *n.* A companion in play.

play'thing (-thĭng'), *n.* Thing to play with; toy.

play'wright (-rīt'), *n.* A writer of plays.

pla'za (plä'zȧ), *n.* A public square.

plea (plē), *n.* **1.** That which is alleged in defense or excuse; excuse; apology. **2.** An entreaty.

plead (plēd), *v. i. ; pret. & p. p.* PLEAD'ED (-ĕd), *Colloq.* PLEAD (plĕd) *or* PLED ; *p. pr. & vb. n.* PLEAD'ING (plēd'ĭng). **1.** *Law.* To make a plea, or conduct a cause, in court. **2.** To argue for or against a thing. **3.** To entreat or appeal earnestly. — *v. t.* **1.** To discuss and defend or excuse by arguments. **2.** To allege or cite in, or by way of, a defense or excuse. — **er** (-ẽr), *n.* [8].

plead'ing, *n.* *Law.* The successive statements by which the plaintiff sets forth his cause, and the defendant his defense; — usually in *pl.*

pleas'ant (-ănt), *a.* [3] **1.** Pleasing; agreeable. **2.** Having pleasing manners, behavior, or appearance; agreeable. — **ly,** *adv.* — **ness,** *n.*

pleas'ant-ry (plĕz'ănt-rĭ), *n. ; pl.* -RIES (-rĭz). **1.** An agreeable playfulness in conversation; fun. **2.** A humorous act or speech ; a joke; jest.

please (plēz), *v. i.* [1] **1.** To afford or give pleasure: be agreeable. **2.** To be pleased or willing; like; choose. — *v. t.* **1.** To give pleasure to; gratify. **2.** To be the will or pleasure of; — used impersonally; as, *please* God.

pleas'ing, *p. a.* [4] Giving pleasure; agreeable.

pleas'ur-a-ble (plĕzh'ŭr-ȧ-b'l), *a.* [4] Pleasant; gratifying. — **pleas'ur-a-bly,** *adv.* [8].

pleas'ure (-ŭr), *n.* **1.** State of gratification; delight; joy. **2.** Amusement; sport; frivolous or dissipating enjoyment; hence, gratification of the senses. **3.** Will; choice. **4.** A delight, joy.

pleat (plēt), *n.* A fold (of cloth, etc). = PLAIT, *n.,*1. — *v. t.* To fold (cloth, etc.). = PLAIT, *v. t.,* 1.

ple-be'ian (plē-bē'yăn ; -ăn), *a.* [4] Of or pertaining to the common people; vulgar; common. — *n.* A plebeian person. [the people. |

pleb'i-scite (plĕb'ĭ-sīt), *n.* A vote or decree of |

plec'trum (plĕk'trŭm), *n. ; pl.* L. -TRA (-trȧ), E. -TRUMS (-trŭmz). A small instrument, as of ivory, used in playing the lyre, mandolin, etc.

pledge (plĕj), *n.* **1.** A security for the performance of an act ; a guarantee. **2.** A toast ; a health. **3.** A promise or agreement to do or forbear something. **4.** State of being given or held as a security.— *v. t.* [1] **1.** To give as a pledge; pawn. **2.** To bind by or as by a pledge. **3.** To drink the health of; toast. — **pledg'er,** *n.* [8].

Ple'ia-des (plē'yȧ-dēz), *n. pl.* *Astron.* A conspicuous cluster of stars in the constellation Taurus.

ple'na-ry (plē'nȧ-rĭ ; plĕn'ȧ-), *a.* Full ; complete.

plen'i-po-ten'ti-a-ry (plĕn-ĭ-pȯ-tĕn'shĭ-ȧ-rĭ), *n.; pl.* -RIES (-rĭz). One, esp. a diplomatic agent, invested with full power to transact business. — *a.* Containing or conferring full power; unlimited.

plen'i-tude (plĕn'ĭ-tūd), *n.* Fullness.

plen'te-ous (-tē-ŭs), *a.* [4] **1.** Plentiful; copious. **2.** Yielding abundance. — **ly,** *adv.* — **ness,** *n.*

plen'ti-ful (-tĭ-fŏŏl), *a.* [4] **1.** Yielding or containing plenty. **2.** Marked by, or existing in, plenty; copious. — **ful-ly,** *adv.* — **ness,** *n.*

plen'ty (-tĭ), *n. ; pl.* -TIES (-tĭz). **1.** Full supply; an abundance. **2.** Abundance; copiousness.

ple'o-nasm (plē'ȯ-năz'm), *n.* Redundancy of language; a case of it, or the redundant expression.

ple'o-nas'tic (-năs'tĭk), *a.* [4] Pert. to or marked by, pleonasm; redundant. [excess. |

pleth'o-ra (plĕth'ȯ-rȧ), *n.* State of being too full; |

ple-thor'ic (plē-thŏr'ĭk ; plĕth'ȯ-rĭk), *a.* [4] Marked by plethora; copious; bombastic.

pleu'ra (plŏŏ'rȧ), *n. ; L. pl.* -RÆ (-rē). The delicate serous membrane lining each half of the thorax and folded back over the surface of the lung of the same side. — **pleu'ral** (-răl), *a.*

pleu'ri-sy (-rĭ-sĭ), *n.* Inflammation of the pleura.

plex'us (plĕk'sŭs), *n.; L. pl.* PLEXUS. A network, esp. of blood vessels or nerves.

āle, senāte, câre, ăm, ȧccount, ärm, ȧsk, sofȧ ; ēve, ĕvent, ĕnd, recĕnt, makēr; īce, ĭll ; ōld, ȯbey, ôrb, ŏdd, sŏft, cŏnnect ; ūse, ūnite, ûrn, ŭp, circŭs; fōōd, fŏŏt ; out, oil ;

pli′a-bil′i-ty (plī′ȧ-bǐl′ĭ-tǐ), *n.* Pliable quality.
pli′a-ble (plī′ȧ-b'l), *a.* [4] **1.** Flexible; pliant. **2.** Easily influenced; as, a *pliable* youth. — **-ness,** *n.* [8] — **-a-bly,** *adv.* [8].
pli′an-cy (plī′ȧn-sǐ), *n.* Quality of being pliant.
pli′ant (-ȧnt), *a.* [4] **1.** Flexible; pliable; as, a *pliant* rod. **2.** Easily influenced; compliant; as, a *pliant* will. — **-ly,** *adv.* [8].
pli′er (plī′ẽr), *n.* **1.** One that plies. **2.** [*pl.*] Small pincers with long jaws.
plight (plīt), *n.* Condition; state; — now usually qualified as bad.
plight, *v. t.* **1.** To put in danger of forfeiture; pledge; — never applied to property or goods. **2.** To bind by a pledge; betroth.
plinth (plĭnth), *n.* **1.** *Arch.* The lowest member of a base, as of a column. **2.** A block serving as a base for a statue, vase, etc.
plod (plŏd), *v. i.;* PLOD′DED; -DING. **1.** To walk heavily; trudge. **2.** To toil monotonously; drudge. — *v. t.* To walk slowly or heavily along. — **plod′der** (plŏd′ẽr), *n.* [8].
plot (plŏt), *n.* **1.** A small area of ground; a plat. **2.** A ground plan; a diagram. **3.** The plan or main story of a literary composition. **4.** Any secret scheme; a conspiracy; intrigue. — *v. t.;* PLOT′TED; -TING. **1.** To make a plot, map, or plan, of (something). **2.** To scheme; contrive, esp. secretly. — *v. i.* To form a plot; conspire. — **plot′ter,** *n.* [8].
plough (plou). Var. of PLOW.
plov′er (plŭv′ẽr), *n.* (See PLURAL, *n.,* note). Any of certain shore birds which differ from the sandpipers in having a stouter build and a short bill.
plow (plou), *n.* **1.** An implement for making a furrow in, and turning up, the earth, as in tilling it. **2.** Any implement

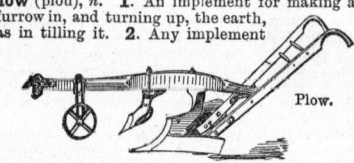

Plow.

suggestive of a plow. — *v. t.* To turn up with or as with a plow. — *v. i.* **1.** To use a plow; till with a plow; to admit of plowing. **2.** To move or cut as a plow does.
plow′boy′ (-boi′), *n.* A boy that leads or guides a team in plowing; a young rustic.
plow′man (-mǎn), *n.; pl.* -MEN (-měn). **1.** One who plows; a husbandman. **2.** A rustic.
plow′share′ (-shâr′), *n.* The share of a plow.
pluck (plŭk), *v. t.* **1.** To pull or pick off or out; pick. **2.** To pull; drag; — with *out, off, up,* etc. **3.** To jerk; twitch; hence, to twang. **4.** To pull off the feathers, hair, etc., of. — *v. i.* To twitch sharply; tug; — usually with *at.* — *n.* **1.** Act of plucking; a pull; twitch; tug. **2.** State of being plucked. **3.** That which is plucked. **4.** The heart, liver, and lungs of an animal killed for food. **5.** Spirit; courage; resolution. *Colloq.*
pluck′y (plŭk′ĭ), *a.* [3] Having pluck; resolute. — **pluck′i-ly** (-ĭ-lĭ), *adv.* [8]. Both *Colloq.*
plug (plŭg), *n.* **1.** Any piece used to stop or fill

a hole; stopple. **2. a** A piece of conducting material for insertion between conductors to make an electrical connection. **b** A cake of pressed tobacco. — *v. t.;* PLUGGED (plŭgd); PLUG′GING (-ĭng). To make tight or secure by a plug.
plum (plŭm), *n.* **1.** The well-known fruit of any of various species of a tree allied to the peach; also, the tree. **2.** A raisin, esp. one used in cooking. **3.** A good or choice thing of its kind.
plum′age (plōōm′ȧj), *n.* The entire clothing of feathers of a bird.
plumb (plŭm), *n.* A weight, as of lead, attached to a line, and used to indicate a vertical direction; a plummet. — *v. t.* **1.** To sound, adjust, or test with a plumb; fig., test; sound.
plumb (plŭm), *a.* Vertical. — *adv.* Vertically.
plum-ba′go (plŭm-bā′gō), *n.* Graphite.
plumb bob. The bob, or weight, of a plumb line.
plumb′er (plŭm′ẽr), *n.* An artisan who works in lead, zinc, tin, etc.; esp., one who furnishes, fits, or repairs water pipes, water-closets, etc.
plumb′ing (plŭm′ĭng), *n.* **1.** Act of using a plumb. **2.** Art of working in lead, now, esp. as a plumber. **3.** Plumber's work; system of pipes for water, sewage, etc., in a building.
plumb line. 1. Line suspending a weight (plumb bob), to determine verticality. **2.** Sounding line.
plume (plōōm), *n.* **1.** A feather; also, an ornamental tuft of feathers. **2.** A feather, group of feathers, tuft of hair, etc., worn as an ornament, as on a helmet. — *v. t.* [1] **1.** To provide or adorn with plumes or plumage. **2. a** To dress the feathers of (itself); — said of a bird. **b** To pride; congratulate (one's self).
plum′met (plŭm′ĕt), *n.* A plumb; also, a plumb rule; hence, a test or criterion.
plump (plŭmp), *a.* [3] **1.** Well rounded or filled out; chubby; fat. **2.** Blunt; direct. — **-ness,** *n.* [8].
plump, *v. i. & t.* To drop, fall, sink, or come in contact, suddenly or heavily. — *n.* A sudden or heavy fall; also, the sound made by such a fall. *Colloq.* — *adv.* **1.** With a sudden or heavy drop. **2.** Straight down; vertically. **3.** Directly; bluntly.
plun′der (plŭn′dẽr), *v. t.* **1.** To rob; pillage. **2.** To take (goods, valuables, etc.) by force or wrongfully. — *v. i.* To commit robbery or spoliation. — *n.* **1.** Act of plundering, as in war; pillaging. **2.** Pillage; spoil. — **plun′der-er,** *n.* [8].
plunge (plŭnj), *v. t.* [1] **1.** To thrust or force, as into liquid or a cavity; immerse; submerge. — *v. i.* **1.** To thrust or cast one's self, as into water; penetrate, sink, or enter, suddenly. **2.** To throw one's self headlong. — *n.* **1.** A place for plunging or diving. **2.** Act of plunging.
plung′er (plŭn′jẽr), *n.* **1.** One that plunges; a diver. **2.** *Mach.* A piston, as in a force pump.
plu′per′fect (plōō′pûr′fĕkt; plōō′pûr′fĕkt), *a. Gram.* Past perfect; — applied to the tense expressing an action or event as completed at or before a given past time. — *n.* The pluperfect tense; also, a verb or verb form denoting it.
plu′ral (plōō′rǎl), *a.* Relating to or containing more than one; designating two or more; as, a *plural* word; — opposed to *singular.* — *n. Gram.* The plural number or form; a word in that form. ☞ Some nouns, as *trout, carp, plover,* etc., are

used without change of form to denote more than one individual, but take the plural *-s* to denote more than one species: thus, a dozen *trout;* but, the *trouts* of Wisconsin. Many names of tribes, races, etc., are more or less commonly used either without change for the plural or with the form in *-s.*

plu-ral′i-ty (plōō-răl′ĭ-tĭ), *n.; pl.* -TIES (-tĭz). **1.** State of being plural; also, state of being numerous; a multitude. **2.** The majority. **3.** *U.S. Politics.* Excess of votes over those for any other (esp. the next) candidate for an office.

plus (plŭs), *a. Math.* More; to be added; positive, in distinction from negative; — opposed to *minus.* — plus sign, *Math.*, the sign +, denoting addition, or a positive quantity. — *n.* **1.** The plus sign; — opposed to *minus.* **2.** An added quantity.

plush (plŭsh), *n.* A textile fabric with a nap longer and softer than that of velvet.

Plu′to (plōō′tō), *n. Astron.* The most remote known planet, ab. 4,650,000,000 m. from the sun.

plu-toc′ra-cy (-tŏk′rȧ-sĭ), *n.* Rule or dominion of wealth or the rich; also, a body of plutocrats.

plu′to-crat (plōō′tō-krăt), *n.* One who has power due to wealth. — **plu′to-crat′ic** (-krăt′ĭk), *a.* [4].

plu′vi-al (plōō′vĭ-ȧl), *a.* [4] **1.** Of or pertaining to rain. *Rare.* **2.** *Geol.* Caused by rain.

ply (plī), *n.* A fold; plait; a turn or twist, as of yarn; as, two-*ply,* i. e., a fold of two thicknesses.

ply, *v. t.* [2] **1.** To use or wield diligently. **2.** To work at steadily; urge importunately. — *v. i.* **1.** To apply one's self. **2.** To go back and forth.

pneu-mat′ic (nṳ-măt′ĭk), *a.* **1.** Of, pertaining to, or using, air or wind; pertaining to pneumatics. **2. a** Moved or worked, as a tool, by pressure of air. **b** Adapted for holding compressed air; inflated with air. **3.** Fitted with pneumatic tires.

pneu-mat′ics (-ĭks), *n.* Physics treating of the mechanical properties of air and other gases.

pneu-mo′ni-a (nṳ-mō′nĭ-ȧ), *n. Med.* Inflammation of the lungs.

poach (pōch), *v. t.* **1.** To cook (an egg) by breaking it into boiling water. **2.** To trespass on, esp. for game or fish; steal (game). — *v. i.* To trespass; take illegally game or fish. — **er,** *n.* [8].

pock (pŏk), *n.* A pustule in smallpox or a similar disease; a spot like, or left by, such a pustule.

pock′et (pŏk′ĕt), *n.* **1.** A bag or pouch carried by a person; esp., a small bag inserted in a garment; hence, purse; money. **2.** A cavity or receptacle. — *v. t.* **1.** To put in or as in a pocket. **2.** To take (money, etc.), esp. secretly or fraudulently. **3.** To receive (an affront, etc.) quietly.

pock′et-book′ (-bŏŏk′), *n.* A small case for carrying papers, money, etc., in the pocket.

pock′et-knife′ (-nīf′), *n.* Knife with folding blades for carrying in the pocket.

pock′mark′ (-märk′), *n.* A mark due to smallpox.

pod (pŏd), *n. Bot.* A seed vessel; esp., a legume, as of the pea or bean. — *v. i.;* POD′DED; POD′DING. To produce pods.

Pod.

po′em (pō′ĕm), *n.* A piece of poetry; — opposed to *prose.* [*chaic or Poetic.*

po′e-sy (pō′ē-sĭ), *n.; pl.* -SIES (-sĭz). Poetry. *Archaic or Poetic.*

po′et (pō′ĕt), *n.* An author of, or one skilled in making, poetry. — **po′et-ess,** *n. fem.* [8].

po′et-as′ter (pō′ĕt-ăs′tẽr), *n.* Petty poet; rimester.

po-et′ic (pō-ĕt′ĭk) } *a.* [4] Of, pertaining to, or **po-et′i-cal** (-ĭ-kȧl) } proper to, poets or poetry; imaginative or rhythmical. — **cal-ly,** *adv.* [8].

po′et-ry (pō′ĕt-rĭ), *n.* Embodiment in rhythmical language, usually metrical, of beautiful thought, imagination, or emotion; also, poems collectively.

poign′an-cy (poin′ȧn-sĭ; -yȧn-sĭ), *n.* Quality or state of being oignant.

poign′ant (-ȧn-; -yȧnt), *a.* [4] **1.** Keen; piercing; pungent. **2.** Severe; keen. — **ly,** *adv.*

‖ **poi′lu′** (pwȧ′lü′), *n.* [F.] A French soldier. *Slang.*

poin-set′ti-a (poin-sĕt′ĭ-ȧ), *n.* A plant of the spurge family, with large scarlet flower-like leaves surrounding small greenish-yellow flowers.

point (point), *n.* **1.** Tapering sharp end, as of a needle, finger, etc. **2.** Something having a tapering end, as a promontory or cape, etc. **3.** The chief feature, as of an argument, etc.; a distinct feature. **4.** The hole or mark made by a point, as of a needle; a spot; speck. **5.** A mark used in punctuation; punctuation mark. **6.** A mere spot indicated or supposed; *Math.*, that which has neither parts nor extent, but position only. **7.** A place considered as to position only; spot; locality. **8.** A unit, as in scoring, in quoting prices of stocks, etc. **9.** A position or condition attained; a step; stage. **10.** An end aimed at; object. **11.** Fine lace. — points of the compass, the 32 divisions in a compass card, being the four marking east, west, north, and south, called *cardinal points,* and the rest named from their respective directions, as N. by E., N N E., N E. by N., N E., etc. — *v. t.* **1.** To punctuate. **2.** To furnish with a point; give point or force to, as to a remark. **3.** To indicate the position or direction of, as with the finger; indicate; — esp. with *out.* **4.** To indicate (game) by a fixed look and position; — said of certain dogs. **5.** To direct (at, to, or upon); aim. — *v. i.* **1.** To direct something, as a finger, at an object; also, to hint (at); allude (to); — with *at* or *to.* **2.** To point game. **3.** To face; look; aim.

point′-blank′ (point′blăŋk′), *adv.* In a point-blank manner. — *a.* **1.** Aimed directly toward the mark. **2.** Direct; unqualified.

point′ed (poin′tĕd), *a.* [4] **1.** Having a point or points. **2.** Sharp, direct, or pithy; terse. — **ly,** *adv.* [8] — **ness,** *n.* [8].

point′er (-tẽr), *n.* **1.** One that points or points out; as: **a** The hand of a timepiece, etc. **b** An item of private information; a hint. *Colloq.*

Pointer.

2. One of a breed of hunting dogs that point game. **3.** *pl.* [*cap.*] Two stars in the Great Bear, the line between which points nearly to the North Star.

point′less (point′lĕs), *a.* [4] Without a point.

poise (poiz), *n.* **1.** State of being balanced; balance. **2.** The bearing or carriage of the body or head. **3.** Suspension of motion due to exact balance. — *v. t.* [1] To make steady or stable; balance. — *v. i.* To hang or be held in equilibrium.

āle, senāte, câre, ăm, ăccount, ärm, ȧsk, sofȧ; ēve, ĕvent, ĕnd, recĕnt, makẽr; īce, ĭll; ōld, ȯbey, ôrb, ŏdd, sŏft, cŏnnect; ūse, ŭnite, ûrn, ŭp, circŭs; fōōd, fŏŏt; out, oil;

poi′son (poi′z'n), *n.* **1.** Any agent which, introduced into the animal organism, may produce a morbid, noxious, or deadly effect. **2.** That which taints or destroys moral purity or character. — *v. t. & i.* **1.** To infect or impregnate with poison. **2.** To injure or kill by poison. **3.** To corrupt; vitiate; pervert. — **-er**, *n.* [8].

poison ivy. Any of several American sumacs with trifoliolate leaves, greenish flowers, and white berries, the herbage being poisonous to the touch.

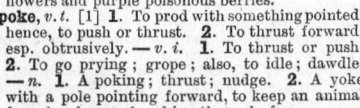

poi′son-ous (poi′z'n-ŭs), *a.* [4] Having the qualities or effects of poison; venomous. — **-ly**, *adv.*

poke (pōk), *n.* A coarse American herb with white
Poison Ivy.
flowers and purple poisonous berries.

poke, *v. t.* [1] **1.** To prod with something pointed; hence, to push or thrust. **2.** To thrust forward, esp. obtrusively. — *v. i.* **1.** To thrust or push. **2.** To go prying; grope; also, to idle; dawdle. — *n.* **1.** A poking; thrust; nudge. **2.** A yoke with a pole pointing forward, to keep an animal from leaping, or breaking through, fences.

poke, *n.* A projecting brim or front of a woman's bonnet; a bonnet (**poke bonnet**) with such a brim.

pok′er (pōk′ẽr), *n.* That which pokes or is used in poking, as a metal rod used in stirring a fire.

pok′er, *n.* A gambling game at cards.

poke′weed′ (pōk′wēd′), *n.* The poke.

pok′y (-ĭ), *a.* [3] Slow; dull; petty.

po′lar (pō′lär), *a.* **1.** Of or pertaining to a pole, as of the earth; lying near, or proceeding from, one of the poles. **2.** Likened to the poles of a magnet; opposite in action. — **polar bear**, a large white bear of arctic regions.

po-lar′i-ty (pō-lăr′ĭ-tĭ), *n.* **1.** Quality or state of having magnetic poles; polarization. **2.** Particular state (positive or negative) with reference to the two poles or to polarization.

po′lar-i-za′tion (pō′lär-ĭ-zā′shŭn), *n.* **1.** Act of polarizing; state of being polarized, or of having poles. **2.** *Elec.* The weakening of a battery current due chiefly to deposition of hydrogen on the negative electrode.

po′lar-ize (pō′lär-īz), *v. t.* [1] To give polarity to; bring into a state of polarization.

pole (pōl), *n.* **1.** Either extremity of an axis of a sphere, esp. of the earth's axis. **2.** One of the opposite or contrasted parts in which certain forces are manifested, as in a magnet or battery.

pole, *n.* **1.** A long, slender piece of wood. **2.** A measure of length or surface; a rod. — *v. t.* [1] To act on with a pole, as in pushing a boat.

Pole, *n.* A native or inhabitant of Poland.

pole′cat′ (-kăt′), *n.* **1.** A European animal of which the ferret is a variety. **2.** A skunk. *U. S.*

po-lem′ic (pō-lĕm′ĭk), *a.* [4] Of or pert. to controversy; controversial. — *n.* **1.** A controversialist. **2.** A controversy.

po-lem′i-cal (-ĭ-kăl), *a.* [4] Polemic.

po-lem′ics (-ĭks), *n.* Art or practice of disputation or controversy, esp. of religious controversy.

pole′star′ (pōl′stär), *n.* **1.** The North Star. **2.** A guide; a controlling principle; also, a lodestar.

po-lice′ (pō-lēs′), *n.* **1.** The department of government charged with enforcement of the laws and maintenance of public order, etc. **2.** [*Commonly a collective pl.*] The body of civil officials and officers in this department. — *v. t.* [1] To protect or keep in order by or as by police.

po-lice′man (-măn), *n.; pl.* -MEN (-mĕn). A member of a body of police; a constable. — **po-lice′wom′an** (-wŏŏm′ăn), *n. fem.*

pol′i-cy (pŏl′ĭ-sĭ), *n.; pl.* -CIES (-sĭz). **1.** Wisdom in managing affairs; shrewdness. **2.** Procedure based on material interest; worldly wisdom. **3.** A settled course of procedure or conduct.

pol′i-cy, *n.* A certificate of insurance.

Pol′ish (pōl′ĭsh), *a.* Of or pert. to Poland or its inhabitants. — *n.* The language of the Poles.

pol′ish (pŏl′ĭsh), *v. t.* **1.** To make smooth and glossy, usually by friction. **2.** To make elegant, cultured, or polite; refine. — **pol′ish-er**, *n.* — *v. i.* To become polished. — *n.* **1.** Act or process of polishing. **2.** A smooth, glossy surface; a luster. **3.** Refinement; elegance; as, a man of *polish.* **4.** Anything used to produce a gloss.

po-lite′ (pō-līt′), *a.* [3] Marked by refinement or culture; courteous; civil. — **-ly**, *adv.* [8].

po-lite′ness, *n.* Quality of being polite.

pol′i-tic (pŏl′ĭ-tĭk), *a.* [4] **1.** Political; as, the body *politic.* **2.** Sagacious in promoting a policy; prudent; in a bad sense, artful; cunning. **3.** Pertaining to or promoting a policy.

po-lit′i-cal (pō-lĭt′ĭ-kăl), *a.* **1.** Of or pertaining to polity, or politics. **2.** Having, or conforming to, a system of government. **3.** Having to do with control of the appointment or action of those who govern. **4.** Of or pert. to those who make a business or profession of politics. — **-ly**, *adv.* [8]. — **political economy**, economics.

pol′i-ti′cian (pŏl′ĭ-tĭsh′ăn), *n.* One devoted to politics.

pol′i-tic-ly (pŏl′ĭ-tĭk-lĭ), *adv.* With policy.

pol′i-tics (-tĭks), *n.* **1.** The science and art of government. **2.** Direction of the affairs of public policy or of political parties; hence, political affairs, principles, or the like.

pol′i-ty (-tĭ), *n.; pl.* -TIES (-tĭz). **1.** Form or constitution of the government of a state, church, etc. **2.** A politically organized community; a state.

pol′ka (pōl′kä), *n.* A round dance of Polish origin, in two-part time; also, the music for it.

poll (pōl), *n.* **1.** The head; skull; esp., the back or back and top of the head. **2.** A list of individuals, as for taxing or voting. **3.** The casting or recording of votes, as of the registered electors; also, the number of such votes cast. **4.** A place for voting; — usually in *pl.* **5.** A poll tax. — *v. t.* **1.** To cut off or cut short the hair, wool, horns, top, etc., or the like, of. **2.** To enroll; receive and register the votes of. **3.** To register or deposit, as a vote; also, to call forth, as votes.

pol′lack (pŏl′ăk), *n.* Any of several marine fishes of the cod family, valued as food.

pol′lard (-ärd), *n.* **1.** A hornless animal (sheep, cow, etc.). **2.** A tree cut back to the trunk to promote the growth of a dense head of foliage.

polled (pōld), *a.* Without horns.

pol'len (pŏl'en), *n.* The powdery fertilizing substance formed in the anther of seed plants.

pol'li-na'tion (-ĭ-nā'shŭn), *n. Bot.* The transfer of pollen from the stamens to the pistils.

pol'li-wog (pŏl'ĭ-wŏg), *n.* A tadpole.

poll tax (pōl). A tax of so much per head or person.

pol-lute' (pŏ-lūt'), *v. t.* [1] To make impure; defile; profane. — **pol-lut'er** (-lūt'er), *n.* [8].

pol-lu'tion (pŏ-lū'shŭn), *n.* Act of polluting, or state of being polluted; defilement.

po'lo (pō'lō), *n.* **1.** A game resembling hockey, with the players on horseback. **2.** A similar game played by skaters.

po'lo-naise' (pō'lō-nāz'; pŏl'ō-), *n.* **1.** An article of dress for women, consisting of a waist and drapery in one piece worn over a separate skirt. **2.** A certain Polish dance, or the music for it.

pol-troon' (pŏl-trōōn'), *n.* An arrant coward.

pol-troon'er-y (-ẽr-ĭ), *n.* Cowardice.

po-lyg'a-la (pŏ-lĭg'à-là), *n.* Any of many plants (genus *Polygala*), often having showy flowers.

po-lyg'a-mist (-à-mĭst), *n.* One who practices polygamy. [polygamy. — **-ly**, *adv.*

po-lyg'a-mous (-mŭs), *a.* Pert. to, or marked by, |

po-lyg'a-my (-mĭ), *n.* State of having plurality of wives or (rarely) husbands at the same time.

pol'y-glot (pŏl'ĭ-glŏt), *a.* **1.** Containing, or made up of, several languages. **2.** Versed in several languages. — *n.* **1.** One who speaks or writes several languages. **2.** A book in several languages.

pol'y-gon (-gŏn), *n. Geom.* A figure having many sides, esp. one of more than four sides.

po-lyg'o-nal (pŏ-lĭg'ō-nǎl), *a.* Having the form of a polygon.

pol'y-he'dral (pŏl'ĭ-hē'drǎl), *a.* Having many faces, as a solid; relating to a polyhedron.

pol'y-he'dron (pŏl'ĭ-hē'drŏn), *n.; pl.* E. **-drons** (-drŏnz), L. **-dra** (-drà). *Geom.* A figure or solid formed by many faces or planes.

Pol'y-ne'sian (-nē'shǎn; -zhǎn), *a.* Of or pertaining to Polynesia or the Polynesians. — *n.* A member of any of several brown races of Oceania.

pol'y-no'mi-al (-nō'mĭ-ǎl), *n. Algebra.* An expression of two or more terms, as $a^2 - 2ab + b^2$. — *a. Chiefly Math.* Containing many terms.

pol'yp (pŏl'ĭp), *n. Zoöl.* An invertebrate having typically a hollow cylindrical body, and a mouth surrounded by tentacles, as the sea anemone, the coral, etc. See CORAL, *Illust.*

pol'y-pus (pŏl'ĭ-pŭs), *n.; L. pl.* **-pi** (-pī). A kind of tumor of the mucous membrane, as in the nose.

pol'y-syl-lab'ic (-sĭl-lăb'ĭk)) *a.* Having many, **pol'y-syl-lab'i-cal** (-ĭ-kǎl)) esp., having more than three, syllables.

pol'y-syl'la-ble (-sĭl'à-b'l), *n.* A polysyllabic word.

pol'y-tech'nic (-tĕk'nĭk), *a.* Pertaining to many arts and sciences; — applied esp. to schools.

pol'y-the-ism (pŏl'ĭ-thē-ĭz'm), *n.* The doctrine of, or belief in, a plurality of gods.

pol'y-the-ist (-ĭst), *n.* A believer in polytheism.

pol'y-the-is'tic (-ĭk), *a.* Of or pertaining to polytheism.

pom'ace (pŭm'ás), *n.* Substance of apples crushed in cider making; anything crushed to a pulp.

po-ma'ceous (pō-mā'shŭs), *a.* **1.** Of the nature of a pome. **2.** Of or pertaining to apples.

po-made' (pō-mād'; -mäd'), *n.* Scented ointment.

po-ma'tum (pō-mā'tŭm), *n.* Pomade.

pome (pōm), *n. Bot.* The characteristic fruit of the apple family.

pome-gran'ate (pŏm-grăn'ăt), *n.* The fruit of a certain tropical Asiatic tree, resembling the orange, but having a crimson pulp; also, the tree.

pom'mel (pŭm'el), *n.* **1.** A knob, as on the hilt of a sword or the like. **2.** The knoblike protuberance at the front and top of a saddlebow. — *v. t.* [7] To beat soundly, as with the pommel of a sword; hence, to beat with the fists.

po'mo-log'i-cal (pō'mō-lŏj'ĭ-kǎl), *a.* Of or pertaining to pomology. [pomology.

po-mol'o-gist (pō-mŏl'ō-jĭst), *n.* An expert in |

po-mol'o-gy (pō-mŏl'ō-jĭ), *n.* Science and practice of fruit growing.

pomp (pŏmp), *n.* **1.** A show of magnificence; sometimes, esp. in the *pl.*, vain display. **2.** A procession marked by magnificent display.

pom'pa-dour (pŏm'pá-dōōr ; colloq. -dōr), *n.* A mode of dressing the hair.

pom'pon (pŏm'pŏn), *n.* An ornamental ball, as of ribbon or feathers, wool, etc.

pom-pos'i-ty (pŏm-pŏs'ĭ-tĭ), *n.* Pompous quality.

pom'pous (pŏm'pŭs), *a.* [4] Marked by excessive self-importance. — **-ly**, *adv.* — **-ness**, *n.* [8].

pon'cho (pŏn'chō), *n.; pl.* **-chos** (-chōz). A kind of cloak like a blanket with a slit for the head.

pond (pŏnd), *n.* A small body of still water.

pon'der (pŏn'dẽr), *v. t. & i.* To weigh in the mind; deliberate; meditate. — **pon'der-er**, *n.* [8].

pon'der-a-ble (-à-b'l), *a.* [4] Capable of being weighed; having weight.

pon'der-os'i-ty (-ŏs'ĭ-tĭ), *n.; pl.* **-ties** (-tĭz). Quality or state of being ponderous.

pon'der-ous (-ŭs), *a.* [4] **1.** Heavy; massive **2.** Heavy in spirit; dull. — **-ly**, *adv.* — **-ness**, *n*

pone (pōn), *n.* A kind of johnnycake. *U. S.*

pon-gee' (pŏn-jē'; pŏn'jē'), *n.* A thin soft fabric of silk from India or China.

pon'iard (pŏn'yárd), *n.* A kind of dagger.

pon'ti-fex (pŏn'tĭ-fĕks), *n.; pl.* PONTIFICES (pŏn-tĭf'ĭ-sēz). A high priest; pontiff.

pon'tiff (-tĭf), *n.* **1.** A high priest. **2.** A bishop, esp., the Pope.

pon-tif'i-cal (pŏn-tĭf'ĭ-kǎl), *a.* Of or pertaining to a pontiff; esp., papal. — *n. pl.* The vestments and other insignia of a pontiff. — **-ly**, *adv.* [8].

pon-tif'i-cate (-kǎt), *n.* State, office, or term of office of a pontiff.

pon-toon' (pŏn-tōōn'), *n.* A flat-bottomed boat; esp., *Mil.*, a boat or float used as one of the supports of a temporary bridge (pontoon bridge).

po'ny (pō'nĭ), *n.; pl.* **-nies** (-nĭz). A small horse; esp., a horse of any of certain small stocky breeds.

poo'dle (pōō'd'l), *n.* One of a breed of very intelligent medium-sized dogs with thick, curly hair.

pooh (pōō ; pōōh), *interj.* Pshaw! nonsense !

pooh'—pooh' (-pōō'), *v. t.* To make light of.

pool (pōōl), *n.* **1.** A small body of (usually fresh) water; also, a reservoir. **2.** A puddle.

pool, *n.* **1.** The stake played for in certain games. **2.** A kind of billiards. **3.** In a joint gambling venture, the total amount staked; the combination of persons in such a venture. **4.** A combination of

---

the interests of different persons made to further a joint undertaking; also, the persons. — *v. t.* To contribute to a common fund, on the basis of a mutual division of profits or losses. — *v. i.* To combine with others in a pool.

poop (poōp), *n. Naut.* **a** The stern of a vessel. *Now Rare.* **b** A deck above the spar, or open, deck abaft the mizzen, sometimes over a cabin.

poor (poōr), *a.* [3] **1.** Wanting in money or goods; needy. **2.** Destitute of some normal or desirable quality; as: **a** Scanty; inadequate. **b** Lean; emaciated. **c** Feeble. Also, mean-spirited. **d** Barren; — said of land. **e** Unfavorable; unfortunate. **f** Wanting in elegance. **3.** Worthy of pity or sympathy. *Colloq.* — **-ly**, *adv.* [8] — **-ness**, *n.* [8].

poor'house' (poōr'hous'), *n.* An almshouse.

pop (pŏp), *n.* **1.** A small sharp explosive report. **2.** A shot from a firearm. **3.** An effervescing beverage, usually not intoxicating. — *v. i.;* POPPED (pŏpt); POP'PING. **1.** To make a pop, or sharp, quick sound. **2.** To go, enter, or issue forth with a quick, sudden movement. **3.** To burst open with a pop, esp. when heated. — *v. t.* **1.** To thrust, push, or put, suddenly. **2.** To cause to pop, or burst open, by heat. — *adv.* Like a pop; suddenly.

pop corn. Corn, or maize, of a kind that pops readily; also, the corn when popped.

pope (pōp), *n.* [*Often cap., esp. when used of a particular pope.*] The (or a) bishop of Rome, the head of the Roman Catholic Church.

pope'dom (-dŭm), *n.* Papacy.

pop'er-y (pōp'ĕr-ĭ), *n.* Papal doctrines and practices; — used as a term of reproach.

pop'gun' (pŏp'gŭn'), *n.* A toy gun which shoots, with a popping noise, by compression of air.

pop'in-jay (-ĭn-jā), *n.* A person likened to a parrot, as a talkative coxcomb.

pop'ish (pōp'ĭsh), *a.* Of or pert. to the Roman Catholic Church; — used as a term of reproach.

pop'lar (pŏp'lår), *n.* Any of certain trees with handsome foliage. [and worsted.|

pop'lin (-lĭn), *n.* A corded fabric, usually of silk|

pop'per (pŏp'ĕr), *n.* One that pops.

pop'py (-ĭ), *n.; pl.* -PIES (-ĭz). Any of various species of bristly-hairy herbs with showy flowers.

pop'u-lace (pŏp'ù-lås), *n.* The common people.

pop'u-lar (pŏp'ù-lår), *a.* [4] **1.** Of or pert. to the common people. **2.** Suitable to the public in general; as: **a** Easy to understand; plain. **b** Cheap. **3.** Beloved or approved by the people.

pop'u-lar'i-ty (pŏp'ù-lăr'ĭ-tĭ), *n.* Quality or state of being popular. [making popular.|

pop'u-lar-i-za'tion (-lår-ĭ-zā'shŭn), *n.* Act of

pop'u-lar-ize (-ĭz), *v. t.* [1] To make popular.

pop'u-lar-ly, *adv.* In a popular manner.

pop'u-late (pŏp'ù-lāt), *v. t.* [1] To inhabit or furnish with inhabitants; to people.

pop'u-la'tion (-lā'shŭn), *n.* **1.** The number of people of a country or section. **2.** A populating.

pop'u-lous (-lŭs), *a.* [4] Abounding in people; thickly inhabited. — **-ly**, *adv.* [8] — **-ness**, *n.* [8].

por'ce-lain (pôr'sê-lån; pôrs'lån), *n.* A fine, white earthenware; — called also *china*, or *chinaware*.

porch (pôrch), *n.* **1.** A covered entrance to a building. **2.** A veranda. [swine.|

por'cine (pôr'sĭn; -sĭn), *a.* [4] Of or pert. to

por'cu-pine (-kŭ-pīn), *n.* Any of certain animals related to the woodchuck, having sharp, barbed spines or quills.

pore (pōr), *v. i.* [1] To look or gaze intently, esp. in reading; also, to meditate or ponder intently.

pore, *n.* A minute opening, as in the skin.

por'gy (pôr'gĭ), *n.; pl.* -GIES (-gĭz). The scup, or any of several other marine food fishes.

pork (pōrk), *n.* The flesh of swine, used for food.

pork'er (pōr'kĕr), *n.* A swine, esp. if fattened.

po-ros'i-ty (pô-rŏs'ĭ-tĭ), *n.; pl.* -TIES (-tĭz). **1.** Quality or state of being porous. **2.** A pore.

po'rous (pō'rŭs), *a.* [4] Full of pores or tiny holes through which fluids may pass; as, *porous* earthenware. — **po'rous-ness**, *n.* [8].

por'phy-ry (pôr'fĭ-rĭ), *n.; pl.* -RIES (-rĭz). An igneous rock, dark red or purple in color, variegated by crystals of feldspar.

por'poise (pôr'pŭs), *n.* **1.** Any of various sea animals of the whale kind, about five to eight feet long. **2.** Popularly, either of two kinds of dolphin.

por'ridge (pôr'ĭj), *n.* A broth or thin pudding made by boiling meal or legumes in water or milk.

por'rin-ger (-ĭn-jêr), *n.* A dish, as a bowl or cup, from which porridge, broth, etc., may be eaten.

port (pōrt), *n.* A strong wine, usually dark red.

port, *n.* **1.** A harbor; haven. **2.** Place to which vessels may resort to discharge or receive cargo.

port, *n.* **1.** A gate; portal. *Archaic.* **2.** *Naut.* A porthole, esp., one through which cannon may be discharged; also, the cover for a porthole. **3.** *Mechanics.* An opening for inlet or outlet of a fluid.

port, *n.* Carriage; bearing; demeanor.

port, *n. Naut.* The left side of a vessel (looking from the stern toward the bow). Also used adjectively. — *v. t. Naut.* To turn or put to the port side of a vessel; — used mainly of the helm.

port'a-bil'i-ty (pōr'tà-bĭl'ĭ-tĭ), *n.* Quality of being portable. [borne; easily transported.|

port'a-ble (pōr'tà-b'l), *a.* [4] Capable of being|

por'tage (pōr'tăj), *n.* Act or process of carrying, esp. boats, goods, etc., overland between navigable waters; also, the route traversed.

por'tal (-tăl), *n.* A door, gate, or entrance.

port-cul'lis (pōrt-kŭl'ĭs), *n.* A grating at the gateway of a fortress, to be let down to prevent entrance.

‖ **porte'-co-chère'** (pōrt'kô-shâr'), *n.* [F.] **1.** A large gateway allowing vehicles to drive into a court. **2.** Erroneously, a carriage porch. *U. S.*

‖ **porte'mon'naie'** (pōrt'mô'nĕ'; *Anglicized* pōrt'-mŭn'ĭ), *n.* [F.] A small pocketbook or purse.

por-tend' (pōr-tĕnd'), *v. t.* To indicate (events, etc.) as in the future; foretoken; — now esp. of unfavorable signs. [omen.|

por'tent (pōr'tĕnt), *n.* That which portends; an|

por-ten'tous (pōr-tĕn'tŭs), *a.* [4] **1.** Of or pertaining to a portent. **2.** Prodigious; as, a *portentous* effort. — **-ly**, *adv.* [8] — **-ness**, *n.* [8].

por'ter (pōr'tĕr), *n.* **1.** A doorkeeper. **2.** An attendant on a sleeping car or parlor car. *U. S.*

porter, *n.* **1.** A carrier; one who carries luggage, etc., for hire. **2.** A kind of dark heavy beer.

por'ter-age (-åj), *n.* Work or charge of a porter.

port-fo'li-o (pōrt-fō'lĭ-ō; -fōl'yō), *n.* **1.** A portable case for holding loose papers, prints, etc. **2.** The office and functions of a minister of state.

port′hole′ (pōrt′hōl′), *n.* *Naut.* An opening in a vessel's side ; a port.

por′ti-co (pōr′tĭ-kō), *n.; pl.* -COES or -COS (-kōz). *Arch.* A colonnade, usually at an entrance of a building.

‖ **por′tière′** (pŏr′tyâr′), *n.* [F.] A curtain hanging at a doorway.

por′tion (pōr′shŭn), *n.* **1.** A part of anything. **2.** An allotted part ; share. — *v. t.* **1.** To divide into portions. **2.** To endow with a portion. — **-less** (-lĕs), *a.* [8].

port′li-ness (pōrt′lĭ-nĕs), *n.* Quality or state of being portly. [ing ; imposing ; stout.

port′ly (pōrt′lĭ), *a.* [3] Having a dignified bearing ;

port-man′teau (pōrt-măn′tō), *n.; pl.* -TEAUS (-tōz), -TEAUX (-tōz). An oblong traveling bag or case, hinged so that it opens like a book. *Chiefly Brit.*

por′trait (pōr′trāt), *n.* A pictorial representation of a person, esp. of the face ; a likeness, esp. one from life. [of making portraits.

por′trai-ture (-trā-tŭr), *n.* Act, practice, or art

por-tray′ (pŏr-trā′), *v. t.* **1.** To represent by drawing, painting, etc. ; delineate ; depict. **2.** To describe in words ; represent dramatically. — **-er,** *n.*

por-tray′al (-ăl), *n.* Act, process, or result of portraying ; esp., verbal or graphic description.

por′tress (pōr′trĕs), *n.* A female doorkeeper.

Por′tu-guese (pōr′tu̇-gēz ; -gĕs), *a.* Of or pertaining to Portugal or its inhabitants. — *n.* **1.** *sing. & pl.* One of the people, or the people, of Portugal. **2.** The Portuguese language.

pose (pōz), *v. t.* [1] To puzzle ; nonplus.

pose, *v. t.* **1.** To lay down ; propound. **2.** To place in a fixed position ; arrange posture and drapery of. — *v. i.* To assume a studied attitude ; affect a certain character. — *n.* Attitude of a person, esp. as assumed for effect.

pos′er (pōz′ẽr), *n.* That which poses, or puzzles.

pos′er, *n.* One who poses for effect.

po-si′tion (pŏ-zĭsh′ŭn), *n.* Manner or place in which anything is placed or disposed. Hence : **a** Mental attitude. **b** Station ; hence, proper place. **c** Relative place or standing ; hence, employment.

pos′i-tive (pŏz′ĭ-tĭv), *a.* [4] **1.** Definitely or formally laid down or imposed ; hence, explicit ; definite ; also, *Colloq.*, downright ; absolute. **2.** Confident ; certain. **3.** Having reality ; real ; actual ; concrete. **4.** *Math.* Plus ; not negative. **5.** Designating, or pertaining to, the kind of electricity (**positive electricity**) induced in glass when rubbed with silk, as distinguished from the (*negative*) electricity of the silk. **6.** *Photog.* Corresponding with the original in position of lights and shades. **7.** *Gram.* Designating, or pertaining to, the degree denoted by an adjective or adverb in its simple form. — *n.* That which is positive ; as : **a** *Gram.* The positive degree, or a form denoting it. **b** A positive quantity, electrode, picture, etc. — **pos′i-tive-ly,** *adv.* [8] — **pos′i-tive-ness,** *n.* [8].

pos′se (pŏs′ē), *n.* A company ; force ; esp., a body (called in full **posse comitatus**) of inhabitants summoned by the sheriff to his aid.

pos-sess′ (pŏ-zĕs′), *v. t.* **1.** To have and hold as property ; own. **2.** To have as a property, attribute, etc. ; have. **3.** To gain ; seize ; win. **4.** To keep in control ; — said of one's self, one's feelings,

etc. **5.** To enter into and influence powerfully. **6.** To put in possession ; make the owner or holder of.

pos-ses′sion (pŏ-zĕsh′ŭn), *n.* **1.** Act or state of possessing ; fact or state of being possessed. **2.** Thing possessed ; *pl.*, property ; wealth.

pos-ses′sive (-zĕs′ĭv), *a.* *Gram.* Designating, or pertaining to, the case (**possessive case**), denoting ownership, origin, etc., or a pronoun or construction, as with *of*, having the same force ; designating the relation so denoted. — *n.* The possessive case, or a word in that case, as, *Homer's, his,* etc.

pos-ses′sor (-ẽr), *n.* One who possesses ; owner.

pos′set (pŏs′ĕt), *n.* A beverage of hot milk curdled as by ale, wine, etc., often with spices, etc.

pos′si-bil′i-ty (pŏs′ĭ-bĭl′ĭ-tĭ), *n.; pl.* -TIES (-tĭz). **1.** Quality or state of being possible. **2.** That which is possible.

pos′si-ble (pŏs′ĭ-b'l), *a.* **1.** Capable of being or becoming ; potential. **2.** Not contrary to the nature of things ; free to happen or not. **3.** That may be true. — **-bly** (-blĭ), *adv.* [8].

post (pōst), *n.* **1.** *Mil.* The station or patrol of a soldier or sentry. **2.** A station ; position, place, or office, esp. one assigned. **3.** The place at which a body of troops is stationed, or the troops there. **4.** A trading station. — *v. t.* To station ; place.

post, *n.* A mail or the mail. *Chiefly British.* — *v. i.* To travel with post horses ; hence, to hasten. — *v. t.* **1.** To dispatch by the post ; mail. **2.** *Bookkeeping.* To transfer (an entry or item), as from journal or daybook to ledger ; also, to enter (an item) in a book. **3.** To inform ; as, he is well *posted*. *Colloq.* — *adv.* With post horses ; hence, at full speed.

post, *n.* A piece of timber, metal, or the like, fixed firmly upright, esp. as a support ; pillar. — *v. t.* **1.** To affix to a post, wall, etc. ; placard. **2.** To publish or advertise by or as by the use of a placard. **3.** To enter (a name) on a posted list. **4.** To placard, as a wall.

post′age (pōs′tǎj), *n.* Charge for conveyance of anything by public post.

postage stamp. A government stamp to be put on articles sent by mail, in payment of postage.

post′al (pōs′tǎl), *a.* Of or pertaining to the post office or mail service. — **postal card. a** A card, with postage stamp printed on it. **b** = POST CARD, 2.

post card, *or* **post′card′,** *n.* **1.** A postal card. *British.* **2.** A private card admitted to the mails when bearing an adhesive postage stamp.

post chaise. A carriage for traveling post.

post′date′ (pōst′dāt′), *v. t.* [1] To date after the real time, or time of making, as a check.

post′er (pōs′tẽr), *n.* **1.** One who posts bills. **2.** A bill or placard, often decorative.

pos-te′ri-or (pŏs-tē′rĭ-ẽr), *a.* **1.** Coming after another ; later. **2.** Situated behind or toward the hinder end ; hinder. — *n. pl.* The buttocks.

pos-te′ri-or′i-ty (-ŏr′ĭ-tĭ), *n.* State of being later or subsequent. [ture generations.

pos-ter′i-ty (-tĕr′ĭ-tĭ), *n.* **1.** Descendants. **2.** Future

pos′tern (pōs′tẽrn), *n.* A back door or gate ; a private entrance or way. *Obsolescent.*

post-grad′u-ate (pōst-grăd′u̇-ât), *a.* Of, pertaining to, or designating, studies pursued after graduation. — *n.* A student pursuing such studies.

---

post'haste' (pōst'hāst'), *adv. & a.* With great speed; very hastily; speedy.

post'hu-mous (pŏs'tŭ-mŭs; pŏst'hū-mŭs), *a.* **1.** Born after the death of the father, as a son. **2.** Published after the death of the author. **3.** Being, arising, or continuing after one's death.

pos-til'ion (pōs-tĭl'yŭn), *n.* One who rides the near horse of the first pair, or of a pair, drawing a coach or chaise, to act as a guide or driver.

post'lude (pōst'lūd), *n. Music.* A voluntary (esp. an organ voluntary) at the end of a service.

post'man (pōst'mǎn), *n.; pl.* -MEN. One who carries letters, etc.; a letter carrier.

post'mark' (-märk'), *n.* Any mark officially put on mail, as the date or the cancellation. — *v. t.* To put a postmark on. [post office.]

post'mas'ter (-mȧs'tẽr), *n.* One in charge of a [post office.]

post'me-rid'i-an (-mė-rĭd'ĭ-ăn), *a.* Coming after the sun has passed the meridian; of the afternoon.

║post me-ri'di-em (mė-rĭd'ĭ-ĕm). [L.] After noon. Abbr. *P. M.* or *p. m.*

post'mis'tress, *n.* Mistress of a post office.

║post mor'tem (mȯr'tĕm). [L.] After death.

post'-mor'tem, *a.* **1.** Occurring or made after death, as an examination of a body. **2.** Of or pertaining to a post-mortem examination. — *n.* A post-mortem examination.

post-na'tal (-nā'tǎl), *a.* Subsequent to birth.

post office. **1.** A government system or department for forwarding mail matter. **2.** An office where mail is received and distributed.

post'paid' (pōst'pād'), *a.* With postage prepaid.

post-pone' (pōst-pōn'), *v. t.* [1] To defer to a future or later time; put off.

post-pone'ment (-mĕnt), *n.* Act of postponing.

post'script (pōst'skrĭpt), *n.* A paragraph added to a letter after it is concluded; an addition appended to a completed book or composition.

pos'tu-late (pŏs'tṵ-lāt), *n.* Something assumed as a basis of reasoning. — (-lāt), *v. t.* [1] To affirm without proof; assume.

pos'ture (pŏs'tṵr), *n.* **1.** Relative arrangement of parts; bearing; attitude. **2.** State or situation. — *v.t.* [1] To put into, or cause to assume, a posture. — *v. i.* To pose. — **pos'tur-er** (-ẽr), *n.* [8].

po'sy (pō'zĭ), *n.; pl.* -SIES (-zĭz). **1.** A brief sentiment or motto. *Archaic.* **2.** A flower; bouquet; nosegay. *Archaic or Colloq.*

pot (pŏt), *n.* **1.** A metallic or earthen vessel of rounded form. **2.** A pot (vessel) with its contents. — *v. t.; pot'TED; -TING.* **1.** To place in or as in a pot or pots. **2.** To shoot for the pot, that is, for cooking. **3.** To secure; win; bag. *Colloq.*

po'ta-ble (pō'tȧ-b'l), *a.* [4] Drinkable. — *n.* In *pl.:* Something drinkable.

pot'ash' (pŏt'ăsh'), *n.* Potassium carbonate, a white salt made from wood ashes, etc., and used in making soap, glass, etc.

po-tas'si-um (pȯ-tǎs'ĭ-ŭm), *n. Chem.* A soft, light, silver-white metal of the alkali group.

po-ta'tion (pȯ-tā'shŭn), *n.* **1.** A drinking; draft. **2.** A drink; beverage.

po-ta'to (-tō), *n.; pl.* -TOES (-tōz). **1.** The sweet potato. **2.** The edible starchy tuber of an American plant of the nightshade family; also, the plant.

potato beetle. The potato bug.

potato bug. A black-and-yellow striped beetle which feeds on the leaves of the potato.

po'tence (pō'tĕns), *n.* Potency.

po'ten-cy (pō'tĕn-sĭ), *n.; pl.* -CIES (-sĭz). Quality or state of being potent; power; efficiency; capability.

po'tent (pō'tĕnt), *a.* [4] Having great power; mighty; powerful.

po'ten-tate (-tĕn-tāt), *n.* One who possesses great power or sway, as a monarch.

po-ten'tial (pȯ-tĕn'shǎl), *a.* **1.** Existing in possibility only; latent. **2.** *Gram.* Expressive of possibility; as, the *potential* mood. — *n.* **1.** A possibility; potentiality. **2.** *Gram.* The potential mood. **3.** *Elec.* The degree of electrification as referred to some standard.

po-ten'ti-al'i-ty (-shĭ-ăl'ĭ-tĭ), *n.; pl.* -TIES (-tĭz). Potential quality or state: a Potency. **b** Possibility, not actuality; also, an instance of this.

po-ten'tial-ly, *adv.* In a potential manner.

po'tent-ly, *adv.* In a potent manner.

poth'er (pŏth'ẽr), *n.* Bustle; bother. — *v. t.* To harass and perplex; fuss; worry.

pot'herb' (pŏt'ûrb'; -hûrb'), *n.* Any plant whose leaves or stems are boiled for food, as spinach.

pot'house' (pŏt'hous'), *n.* An alehouse.

pot'hunt'er (-hŭn'tẽr), *n.* A hunter who shoots anything that will help to fill his bag, without regard to the rules of sport. — **hunt'ing**, *n. & a.*

po'tion (pō'shŭn), *n.* A draft; dose.

pot'luck' (pŏt'lŭk'), *n.* Whatever may chance to be in the pot, or may be provided for a meal.

pot'pie' (pŏt'pī'), *n.* A meat pie boiled in a pot.

pot'pour'ri' (pō'pŏŏ'rē'), *n.* A medley or mixture.

pot shot. A shot fired simply to fill the pot; a shot taken under conditions suggesting such a shot.

pot'tage (pŏt'ȧj), *n.* A dish of vegetables, or vegetables and meat; a thick soup.

pot'ter (-ẽr), *n.* One who makes earthen vessels.

pot'ter, *v. i.* Also, and in U. S., usually, **put'ter** (pŭt'ẽr). To trifle; dawdle. — *n.* Act or habit of pottering. — **-er,** *n.* [8].

pot'ter-y (-ĭ), *n.; pl.* -TERIES (-ĭz). **1.** A place where earthen vessels are made. **2.** Art of the potter. **3.** Ware made from clay, etc., molded and hardened by heat; esp., the coarser ware so made.

pouch (pouch), *n.* **1.** A small bag or sack. **2.** *Zoöl.* A sac or bag, esp. one for carrying the young.

poul'ter-er (pōl'tẽr-ẽr), *n.* A dealer in poultry.

poul'tice (-tĭs), *n.* A soft composition applied to sores, etc. — *v. t.* [1] To apply a poultice to.

poul'try (pōl'trĭ), *n.* Domestic fowls.

pounce (pouns), *n.* A powder formerly used to keep ink from spreading on paper.

pounce, *n.* The claw, or talon, of a bird of prey.

pounce, *v. i.* **1.** To swoop down; come down suddenly and seize. **2.** To spring or come suddenly. — *n.* A pouncing; sudden swoop or spring.

pound (pound), *n.* An inclosure for confining stray animals. — *v. t.* To confine in or as in a pound.

pound, *n.; pl.* POUNDS (poundz), collectively POUND or POUNDS. **1.** A unit of weight; esp., the *avoirdupois pound* of 7,000 grains (divided into 16 oz.), or the *troy pound* of 5,760 grains (divided into 12 oz.). Abbr. *lb.;* in plural, *lbs.* **2.** The gold monetary unit of Great Britain, equal to 20 shillings, or $4.8665 U. S. money. Symbol, £.

---

chair; go; sing, iŋk; then, thin; nature, verdure; yet; zh = z in azure. Numbers refer to §§ in the Special Notes which, with Abbreviations, Signs, etc., precede the Vocabulary.

pound (pound), *v. t.* **1.** To reduce to powder or pulp by beating, as with a pestle. **2.** To strike heavily or repeatedly ; beat ; pommel. — *v. i.* **1.** To beat ; make a sound of heavy blows. **2.** To walk, etc., with heavy steps. — *n.* Act of pounding.

pound'er (poun'dẽr), *n.* **1.** A thing weighing a pound. **2.** A thing having, or having to do with, a (specified) weight in pounds ; as, a twelve-*pound-er*, i. e., a cannon firing a twelve-pound shell.

pound'er, *n.* One that pounds.

pour (pōr), *v. t. & i.* To send or issue in or as in a stream or flood ; emit, discharge, or escape, freely. — *n.* A pouring ; heavy downpour. — **-er**, *n.* [8].

pout (pout), *v. i.* To thrust out the lips, as in sullenness. — *v. t.* To protrude (the lips). — *n.* A pouting protrusion of the lips ; *pl.*, a fit of sullenness.

pout'er (-ẽr), *n.* **1.** One that pouts. **2.** One of a breed of pigeons having a crop which they dilate.

pov'er-ty (pŏv'ẽr-tĭ), *n.* **1.** Quality or state of being poor or indigent ; need ; destitution. **2.** Any deficiency in what constitutes richness ; dearth.

pov'er-ty–strick'en, *a.* Very poor or destitute.

pow'der (pou'dẽr), *n.* **1.** Substance in fine dry particles ; dust. **2.** Any of various solid explosives, as gunpowder. — *v. t.* **1.** To sprinkle with powder. **2.** To sprinkle like powder. **3.** To pulverize. — *v. i.* **1.** To be reduced to powder. **2.** To use cosmetic powder.

pow'der-y (-dẽr-ĭ), *a.* **1.** Resembling powder ; as, *powdery* snow. **2.** Sprinkled with powder ; dusty.

pow'er (-ẽr), *n.* **1.** Ability to act ; faculty of doing or performing something. **2.** Exerted energy ; vigor ; force. **3.** Control ; authority ; influence. **4.** *Law.* Authority, capacity, or right ; esp., delegated authority. **5.** A government exercising control or possessing international influence. **6.** *Math.* The product arising from the continued multiplication of a number into itself. **7.** *Mechanics.* The rate at which mechanical energy is exerted. **8.** *Optics.* The degree to which a lens, mirror, or any optical instrument magnifies.

power boat. A boat driven by an engine ; esp., a motor boat.

pow'er-ful (-fŏŏl), *a.* [4] Full of or having power ; potent ; influential. — **-ly**, *adv.* [8].

pow'er-less, *a.* [4] Destitute of power ; unable to produce effect. — **-ly**, *adv.* [8] — **-ness**, *n.* [8].

pow'wow' (pou'wou'), *n.* **1.** Among North American Indians, a ceremony for the cure of diseases, etc. ; also, a conference of Indians. **2.** Any assembly likened to an Indian powwow. *U. S.*

pox (pŏks), *n.* *Med.* Any of various diseases marked by pustules or eruptions ; as, small*pox*.

prac'ti-ca-bil'i-ty (prăk'tĭ-kȧ-bĭl'ĭ-tĭ), *n. ; pl.* **-TIES** (-tĭz). Quality or state of being practicable.

prac'ti-ca-ble (prăk'tĭ-kȧ-b'l), *a.* [4] **1.** Capable of being put into practice, done, or accomplished. **2.** Usable ; passable. — **-ca-bly**, *adv.* [8].

prac'ti-cal (-kăl), *a.* [4] **1.** Of or pert. to practice or action. **2.** Available or valuable in practice or action. **3.** Given or disposed to action, as opposed to speculation, etc. **4.** That is such in practice or effect ; virtual.

prac'ti-cal'i-ty (-kăl'ĭ-tĭ), *n.* Quality or state of being practical ; practicalness. [way.

prac'ti-cal-ly (prăk'tĭ-kăl-ĭ), *adv.* In a practical

prac'tice, prac'tise (-tĭs), *v. t.* [1] **1.** To do, carry on, act, or exercise ; to do or perform often or habitually. **2.** To follow or work at, as a profession, etc. **3.** To perform repeatedly, for proficiency. **4.** To teach by practice ; train. — *v. i.* **1.** To act ; operate. **2.** To act or do something habitually. **3.** To exercise a profession, esp. medicine or law. **4.** To perform certain acts often, for proficiency.

prac'tice, *n.* **1.** Actual performance or application of knowledge. **2.** Repeated or customary action ; habit ; custom. **3.** *Law.* The established method of conducting proceedings. **4.** Systematic exercise for instruction or discipline ; also, proficiency, etc., so acquired. **5.** The exercise of any vocation.

prac-ti'tion-er (-tĭsh'ŭn-ẽr), *n.* One engaged in the practice of a profession, esp. law or medicine.

præ'tor, pre'tor (prē'tŏr), *n.* *Roman Hist.* A magistrate next to the consul in rank.

præ-to'ri-an, pre-to'ri-an (prē-tō'rĭ-ăn), *a.* Of or pertaining to a Roman prætor.

prag-mat'ic (prăg-măt'ĭk)) *a.* [4] **1.** Busy ; esp.,
prag-mat'i-cal (-ĭ-kăl)) meddling. **2.** Conceited ; dogmatic. **3.** Practical ; matter-of-fact ; *Philos.*, dealing with practical values or consequences. — **-ly**, *adv.* [8] — **-ness**, *n.* [8].

prag'ma-tism (prăg'mȧ-tĭz'm), *n.* **1.** Pragmatic quality or state. **2.** *Philos.* The doctrine that the whole meaning of a conception lies in its practical consequences, esp. in its bearing upon conduct.

prag'ma-tist (-tĭst), *n.* One who is pragmatic ; as : **a** A busybody. **b** An adherent of pragmatism.

prai'rie (prâ'rĭ ; prâr'ĭ), *n.* A meadow tract ; esp., an extensive tract of level or rolling land in the Mississippi Valley, with a deep fertile soil.

prairie chicken. A grouse of the western prairies.

prairie dog. An American burrowing animal related to the woodchucks.

praise (prāz), *v. t.* [1] **1.** To express approval of, applaud. **2.** To proclaim the goodness and greatness of (God, or a

Prairie Dog.

deity) ; glorify, esp. in worship or song. — *n.* Act of praising ; state of being praised.

praise'wor'thy (-wûr'thĭ), *a.* [4] Worthy of praise. — **-wor'thi-ly**, *adv.* [8] — **-ness**, *n.* [8].

prance (prȧns), *v. i.* [1] **1.** To spring from the hind legs, or move by so doing, as a horse. **2.** To swagger. — *n.* Act of prancing ; a prancing movement. — **pranc'er** (prȧn'sẽr), *n.* [8].

prank (prănk), *v. t.* To dress showily ; adorn ; deck. — *v. i.* To make ostentatious show.

prank, *n.* A gay or sportive action or trick ; a frolic.

prate (prāt), *v. i. & t.* [1] To talk, esp. much and idly ; chatter ; babble. — *n.* Act of prating ; chatter. — **prat'er** (prāt'ẽr), *n.* [8].

prat'tle (prăt'l), *v. i. & t.* [1] To prate ; esp., to talk or say artlessly, like a child. — *n.* Trifling talk or chatter ; babble. — **prat'tler** (-lẽr), *n.* [8].

prawn (prôn), *n.* Any of numerous small shrimplike shellfish, used as food.

pray (prā), *v. t.* **1.** To entreat ; implore. *Archaic.*

2. To ask earnestly for; supplicate for. — *v. i.* To make earnest request or entreaty; offer prayer to a deity as a religious act. — **pray'er** (prā'ẽr), *n.* [8].

prayer (prâr), *n.* **1.** Act or practice of praying; supplication. **2.** The offering of adoration, confession, supplication, thanksgiving, etc., to God. **3.** The form of words used in praying. **4.** [*Often in pl.*] A form of religious service consisting largely of prayers. **5.** That prayed for.

prayer book. A book of devotional prayers.

prayer'ful (-fŏŏl), *a.* [4] Given to prayer.

preach (prēch), *v. i.* **1.** To proclaim, esp. the gospel; deliver a sermon. **2.** To give serious advice, as on morals. — *v. t.* **1.** To proclaim or urge in or as in a sermon. **2.** To deliver or pronounce, as a sermon. — **preach'er**, *n.* [8].

preach'ment (-mĕnt), *n.* Act of preaching, or that which is preached; esp., a tedious discourse.

pre'am'ble (prē'ăm'b'l), *n.* Prefatory statement.

pre-ca'ri-ous (prē-kā'rĭ-ŭs), *a.* [4] **1.** Depending on the will of another; uncertain. **2.** Taken for granted; unfounded. **3.** Insecure; dubious. — *ly, adv.* — *ness, n.* [8].

pre-cau'tion (prē-kô'shŭn), *n.* **1.** Previous caution or care. **2.** A measure taken beforehand to ward off evil or secure good or success.

pre-cau'tion-a-ry (-ā-rĭ), *a.* Of the nature of a precaution.   [in rank, order, etc.

pre-cede' (-sēd'), *v. t. & i.* [1] To be or go before

pre-ced'ence (-ĕns), *n.* Act or state of preceding.

pre-ced'en-cy (-ĕn-sĭ), *n.* Precedence.

prec'e-dent (prĕs'ē-dĕnt), *n.* Something done or said that may serve as an example or rule to authorize or justify a subsequent act of like kind.

pre-cen'tor (prē-sĕn'tŏr), *n.* A leader of the singing of a choir or congregation.

pre'cept (prē'sĕpt), *n.* Any commandment, instruction, or order for conduct, esp. moral conduct; a working rule or direction.

pre-cep'tor (prē-sĕp'tẽr), *n.* One who gives precepts; esp., the master of a school; a teacher.

pre-cep'tress (-sĕp'trĕs), *n.* A female preceptor.

pre'cinct (prē'sĭŋkt), *n.* **1.** An inclosure bounded by walls or other limits or by an imaginary line; esp., *pl.*, environs. **2.** A boundary or limit. **3.** A district within certain boundaries, esp. one for governmental purposes, as for police control.

pre'cious (prĕsh'ŭs), *a.* [4] **1.** Of great price or value; costly. **2.** Of great worth morally or spiritually; d e a r; as, *precious* recollections. **3.** Downright; arrant; as, a *precious* fool. *Colloq.* — **precious metals**, gold, silver, and platinum. — **pre'cious-ly**, *adv.* [8] — *ness, n.* [8].

prec'i-pice (prĕs'ĭ-pĭs), *n.* A very steep or overhanging place, as the face of a cliff; a cliff.

pre-cip'i-tance (prē-sĭp'ĭ-tăns), *n.* Precipitancy.

pre-cip'i-tan-cy (-tăn-sĭ), *n.* Quality or state of being precipitant, or precipitate; rashness.

pre-cip'i-tant (-tănt), *a.* [4] **1.** Falling or rushing headlong. **2.** Very sudden or unexpected; abrupt; hasty. — *ly, adv.* [8].

pre-cip'i-tate (-tāt), *a.* [4] **1.** Acting with unwise haste; overhasty. **2.** Done without due deliberation; hurried. **3.** Falling or rushing with steep descent. **4.** Very sudden or abrupt. — (-tāt), *v. t. & i.* **1.** To throw or dash headlong, as from a

precipice. **2.** To cause to move, act, etc., very rapidly. **3.** To separate as a precipitate. — *n.* A substance separated from a solution by chemical action, or by heat or cold. — *ly, adv.* [8].

pre-cip'i-ta'tion (-tā'shŭn), *n.* A precipitating; that which is precipitated, as rain or snow.

pre-cip'i-tous (-tŭs), *a.* **1.** Steep like a precipice; consisting of, or marked by, precipices. **2.** Falling very quickly; rapid. — *ly, adv.* — *ness, n.*

pre-cise' (prē-sīs'), *a.* [3] **1.** Definite; exact; distinct. **2.** Strictly conforming to rule or usage; punctilious; scrupulous; nice; sometimes, overnice. — *ly, adv.* [8] — *ness, n.* [8].

pre-ci'sian (-sĭzh'ăn), *n.* One rigidly or ceremoniously exact in observing rules or forms.

pre-ci'sion (-ĭn), *n.* Quality or state of being precise; exactness; accuracy; definiteness.

pre-clude' (-klōōd'), *v. t.* [1] **1.** To put a barrier before; close; hinder; stop. **2.** To prevent or obviate by anticipation.

pre-clu'sion (-klōō'zhŭn), *n.* Act of precluding.

pre-clu'sive (-sĭv), *a.* [4] Preventive.

pre-co'cious (-kō'shŭs), *a.* [4] Prematurely developed; pertaining to, or indicative of, premature development. — *ly, adv.* [8] — *ness, n.* [8].

pre-coc'i-ty (-kŏs'ĭ-tĭ), *n.* Quality or state of being precocious; also, one that is precocious.

pre'con-ceive' (prē'kŏn-sēv'), *v. t.* [1] To conceive, or form an opinion of, beforehand.

pre'con-cep'tion (-sĕp'shŭn), *n.* Act of preconceiving; a conception or opinion previously formed.

pre'con-cert' (-sûrt'), *v. t.* To arrange beforehand and indicates approach.   [cursor.

pre-cur'sor (prē-kûr'sẽr), *n.* One that precedes

pre-cur'so-ry (-sō-rĭ), *a.* Of the nature of a pre-

pre-da'cious (prē-dā'shŭs), *a.* [4] Living by preying on other animals; predatory.

pred'a-to-ry (prĕd'à-tō-rĭ), *a.* [4] **1.** Of, pertaining to, or marked by, plundering. **2.** Predacious.

pred'e-ces'sor (prĕd'ē-sĕs'ẽr; prē'dē-), *n.* One that has preceded another in any state, position, office, etc.   [ordain.

pre-des'ti-nate (prē-dĕs'tĭ-nāt), *v. t.* [1] To fore-

pre-des'ti-na'tion (-ĭnā'shŭn), *n.* **1.** A predestinating; state of being predestined; fate; destiny. **2.** In theology, the foreordaining of men to everlasting happiness or misery.

pre-des'tine (-dĕs'tĭn), *v. t.* [1] To predestinate.

pre'de-ter'mi-na'tion (prē'dē-tûr'mĭ-nā'shŭn), *n.* A determination in advance, or beforehand.

pre'de-ter'mine (prē'dē-tûr'mĭn), *v. t. & i.* To determine beforehand.   [predicated.

pred'i-ca-ble (prĕd'ĭ-ká-b'l), *a.* That may be

pre-dic'a-ment (prē-dĭk'à-mĕnt), *n.* Condition; situation; esp., an unfortunate or trying position.

pred'i-cate (prĕd'ĭ-kāt), *v. t.* [1] **1.** To proclaim; declare. **2.** a To assert to be a quality, attribute, or property (of). b To imply; connote. — *v. i.* To affirm something of another thing; assert. — (-kāt), *a.* **1.** Predicated. **2.** *Gram.* Belonging to the predicate. — *n.* **1.** That which is affirmed or denied of a subject. **2.** *Gram.* The word or words in a proposition or sentence which express what is said of the subject.

pred'i-ca'tion (-kā'shŭn), *n.* Act of predicating; affirmation; assertion.

pred′i-ca-tive (prĕd′ĭ-kā-tĭv), *a.* Expressing affirmation; predicating. — **pred′i-ca-tive-ly**, *adv.*

pre-dict′ (prē-dĭkt′), *v.t. & i.* To tell beforehand; foretell; prophesy; presage.—**pre-dic′tor** (-tēr),*n.*

pre-dic′tion (-dĭk′shŭn), *n.* Act of predicting; that which is foretold; a prophecy.

pre′di-lec′tion (prē′dĭ-lĕk′shŭn; prĕd′ĭ-), *n.* A previous liking ; favorable prepossession.

pre-dis-pose′ (prē′dĭs-pōz′), *v. t.* [1] To dispose or incline beforehand ; give a tendency to.

pre-dis′po-si′tion (prē-dĭs′pŏ-zĭsh′ŭn), *n.* Act of predisposing. [being predominant.

pre-dom′i-nance (prē-dŏm′ĭ-năns), *n.* Quality of

pre-dom′i-nant (-nănt) *a.* Having ascendancy over others; prevailing; prevalent.—**-ly**. *adv.* [8].

pre-dom′i-nate (-nāt) *v. i.* [1] To be superior in number, strength, influence, or authority.

pre-ĕm′i-nence (-ĕm′ĭ-nĕns), *n.* Quality or state of being preëminent ; distinction above others.

pre-ĕm′i-nent (-nĕnt), *a.* Eminent above others; superior, as in excellence. — **-nent-ly**, *adv.* [8].

pre-ĕmpt′ (-ĕmpt′), *v.t. & i.* To settle on (public land) with a right of preëmption ; to take by preemption. — **pre-ĕmp′tor** (-ĕmp′tŏr), *n.* [8].

pre-ĕmp′tion (-ĕmp′shŭn), *n.* Act or right of purchasing before others.

preen (prēn), *v. t. & i.* To trim or dress with the beak, as the feathers;— of birds.

pre′ĕx-ist′ (prē′ĕg-zĭst′), *v. i.* To exist before.

pre′ĕx-ist′ence (-zĭs′tĕns), *n.* Previous existence.

pre′ĕx-ist′ent (-zĭs′tĕnt),*a.* Existing previously.

pref′ace (prĕf′ăs), *n.* Something spoken or written as introductory to a book, or the like. — *v. i.* [1] To make, speak, write, etc., a preface. —*v. t.* **1.** To introduce by a preface. **2.** To be preliminary to.

pref′a-to-ry (-ă-tō-rĭ), *a.* Pertaining to, or of the nature of, a preface; introductory ; preliminary.

pre′fect (prē′fĕkt), *n.* **1.** In ancient Rome, any of various high officials or magistrates. **2.** A president or chief magistrate or official.

pre′fec-ture (prē′fĕk-tṳr), *n.* Office, jurisdiction, period of office, or official residence, of a prefect.

pre-fer′ (prē-fûr′), *v. t. ; -ferred′** (-fûrd′); **-fer′-ring. 1.** To exalt; promote. *Now Rare.* **2.** To bring, put, or set forward or before one; present; proffer. **3.** To set above or before something else in estimation, favor, honor, etc.

pref′er-a-ble (prĕf′ẽr-ȧ-b′l), *a.* [4] Worthy to be preferred; more desirable.—**pref′er-a-ble-ness**, *n.* [8] — **pref′er-a-bly**, *adv.* [8].

pref′er-ence (-ĕns), *n.* **1.** Act of preferring; state of being preferred. **2.** That which is preferred.

pref′er-en′tial (-ĕn′shăl), *a.* Of, or of the nature of, preference; giving or having a preference.

pre-fer′ment (prē-fûr′mĕnt), *n.* **1.** Act of preferring; state of being advanced; promotion. **2.** A position, appointment, or office of honor or profit.

pre-fig′ure (-fĭg′ṳr), *v.t.* [1] **1.** To show, suggest, or announce beforehand by a type or figure. **2.** To imagine beforehand. — **pre-fig′u-ra′tion**, *n.*

pre-fix′ (prē-fĭks′), *v. t.* To put or fix before, or at the beginning of, another thing.

pro′fix (prē′fĭks), *n.* That which is prefixed; esp., one or more letters or syllables added at the beginning of a word to modify its meaning.

preg′nan-cy (prĕg′năn-sĭ), *n.* State of being pregnant ; of the mind, fertility ; inventiveness.

preg′nant (-nănt), *a.* [4] **1.** Being with young. **2.** Full of ideas; fertile; inventive. *Archaic.* **3.** Heavy with significance or issue; weighty.

pre-hen′sile (prē-hĕn′sĭl), *a.* [4] Adapted for grasping ; as, the *prehensile* tail of a monkey.

pre′his-tor′ic (prē′hĭs-tŏr′ĭk), *a.* Of or pertaining to the period before written history begins.

pre-judge′ (prē-jŭj′), *v. t.* To judge before full and sufficient examination; judge beforehand.

pre-judg′ment (-mĕnt), *n.* Act of prejudging.

prej′u-dice (prĕj′ŏŏ-dĭs), *n.* **1.** Injury due to some judgment or action of another, as in disregard of a person's right;— now chiefly in phrases, as *to the prejudice of.* **2.** Judgment or opinion formed beforehand; esp.,an opinion unfavorable to anything without sufficient reason. — *v. t.* [1] **1.** To injure by some judgment or action; hence, to hurt; damage; as, to *prejudice* a cause. **2.** To cause to have prejudice; as, to *prejudice* a juryman.

prej′u-di′cial (-dĭsh′ăl), *a.* [4] Injurious; hurtful; damaging; detrimental. — **-ly**, *adv.* [8].

prel′a-cy (prĕl′ȧ-sĭ), *n.; pl.* **-cies** (-sĭz). **1.** Office or dignity of a prelate. **2.** Prelates collectively.

prel′ate (-ăt), *n.* One of superior rank and authority in the service of the church, as a bishop.

pre-lim′i-na-ry (prē-lĭm′ĭ-nä-rĭ),*a.* Introductory; prefatory. — *n.; pl.* **-ries** (-rĭz). That which is introductory or preparatory.

prel′ude (prĕl′ūd; prē′lūd), *n.* An introductory performance, action, event, etc., preparing for a more important matter; preface; esp., *Music,* a strain, section, or movement introducing the theme or chief subject, as of a fugue, etc.

pre-lude′ (prē-lūd′ *or, esp. in ref. to music,* prĕl′-ūd. prē′lūd), *v. t.* [1] **1.** To serve as a prelude to; introduce. **2.** To play as a prelude ; play a prelude to. — **lud′er**, *n.* [8].

pre′ma-ture′ (prē′mȧ-tūr′; prē′mȧ-tūr), *a.* [4] Happening, arriving, or performed before the proper or usual time. — **-ly**, *adv.* — **-ness**, *n.*

pre′ma-tu′ri-ty (prē′mȧ-tū′rĭ-tĭ), *n.* Quality or state of being premature.

pre-med′i-tate (prē-mĕd′ĭ-tāt), *v. t. & i.* [1] To revolve in the mind, or deliberate, beforehand.

pre-med′i-ta′tion (-tā′shŭn), *n.* Act of premeditating ; forethought ; planning.

pre′mi-er (prē′mĭ-ẽr; prēm′yẽr), *a.* **1.** First in position, rank, or importance; chief. **2.** First in time; earliest. — *n.* A prime minister; more generally, a chief officer.

pre′mi-er-ship′, *n.* Office of a premier.

prem′ise (prĕm′ĭs), *n.* **1.** *Logic.* A proposition stated or assumed as leading to a conclusion; either of the first two propositions of a syllogism. **2.** *pl. Law.* The property conveyed in a deed; real estate ; a piece of land or a building.

pre-mise′ (prē-mīz′), *v. t.* [1] To set forth beforehand, or as introductory ; offer previously, as in explanation.— *v. i.* To make a premise.

pre′mi-um (prē′mĭ-ŭm), *n.* **1.** A reward or recompense ; a prize to be won in a competition. **2.** Something offered or given for the loan of money ; bonus. **3.** The consideration given for a contract of insurance. **4.** A sum above the par

---

āle, senāte, câre, ăm, ăccount, ärm, ȧsk, sofȧ; ēve, ĕvent, ĕnd, recēnt, makēr; īce, ĭll; ōld, ŏbey, ôrb, ŏdd, sŏft, cŏnnect; ūse, ŭnite, ûrn, ŭp, circŭs; fōōd, fŏŏt; out, oil;

value of anything. **5.** The excess in purchasing power of one form of money over another of the same nominal value, as of gold dollars over paper.

pre'mo-ni'tion (prē'mŏ-nĭsh'ŭn), *n.* **1.** Previous warning; as, a *premonition* of winter. **2.** A feeling or forewarning as to what will occur; as, a *premonition* of danger.

pre-mon'i-to-ry (prē-mŏn'ĭ-tō-rĭ), *a.* Giving previous warning or notice.

pre-oc'cu-pa'tion (prē-ŏk'ū-pā'shŭn), *n.* Act of preoccupying; state of being preoccupied.

pre-oc'cu-py (-pī), *v. t.* [2] **1.** To occupy before another, as a country. **2.** To engage, occupy, or engross the attention of, beforehand.

prep'a-ra'tion (prĕp'à-rā'shŭn), *n.* **1.** Act of preparing. **2.** State of being prepared; readiness. **3.** That which makes ready or prepares the way. **4.** That which is prepared, as an ointment.

pre-par'a-tive (prē-păr'd-tĭv), *a.* [4] Tending or serving to prepare, or make ready; preparatory. — *n.* A preparation. —**tive-ly**, *adv.* [8].

pre-par'a-to-ry (-tō-rĭ), *a.* [4] **1.** Preparing, or serving to prepare, the way for something. **2.** Being prepared, as by training or instruction.

pre-pare' (-pâr'), *v. t.* [1] **1.** To fit or adapt for a particular purpose; make ready. **2.** To make; compound. — *v. i.* To make ready. **2.** To get ready. — **pre-par'er** (-pâr'ēr), *n.* [8].

pre-pay' (prē-pā'), *v. t.* To pay, or to pay the charge on, in advance. — **pre-pay'ment** (-mĕnt), *n.*

pre-pense' (prē-pĕns'), *a.* Premeditated; as, malice *prepense.*

pre-pon'der-ance (-pŏn'dēr-ăns), *n.* Quality or state of being preponderant; an outweighing.

pre-pon'der-ant (-ănt), *a.* Superior in influence, force, etc.; predominant. — **-ly**, *adv.* [8].

pre-pon'der-ate (-āt), *v. i.* [1] To exceed in weight; fig., to exceed in influence, power, etc.

prep'o-si'tion (prĕp'ō-zĭsh'ŭn), *n. Gram.* A word generally having a fundamental meaning of position, direction, time, means, or other abstract relation, used to connect a noun or a pronoun (which it usually precedes), in an adjectival or adverbial sense, with some other word; as, a bridge *of* iron.

prep'o-si'tion-al (-ăl), *a.* Of, or pertaining to, or of the nature of, a preposition.

pre'pos-sess' (prē'pŏ-zĕs'), *v. t.* To preoccupy, as the mind, so as to shut out other things; hence, to induce to a favorable opinion beforehand.

pre'pos-sess'ing, *p. a.* [4] Tending to invite favor; attractive. [of mind; bias.]

pre'pos-ses'sion (-pŏ-zĕsh'ŭn), *n.* Preoccupation

pre-pos'ter-ous (prē-pŏs'tēr-ŭs), *a.* [4] Contrary to nature, reason, or common sense; utterly foolish; absurd. — **-ly**, *adv.* [8] —**ness**, *n.* [8].

pre-req'ui-site (prē-rĕk'wĭ-zĭt), *a.* Previously required; necessary to a proposed end. — *n.* Something prerequisite.

pre-rog'a-tive (prē-rŏg'à-tĭv), *n.* A prior or exclusive right or privilege.

pres'age (prĕs'āj; prē'sāj), *n.* **1.** An omen. **2.** A presentiment; foreboding. **3.** Foreknowledge.

pre-sage' (prē-sāj'), *v. t.* [1] **1.** To portend; foreshow. **2.** To foretell; predict. — *v. i.* To utter or make a prediction; to have a presentiment.

pres'by-ter (prĕz'bĭ-tēr; prĕs'-), *n.* **1.** An elder

in the early church. **2.** A priest. **3.** A member of a presbytery.

pres'by-te'ri-an (-ăn), *a.* Of or pertaining to a presbyter or presbyters. — *n.* [*cap.*] A member of a presbyterian church.

pres'by-ter-y (prĕz'bĭ-tĕr-ĭ; prĕs'-), *n.; pl.* **-TER-IES** (-ĭz). **1.** In presbyterian churches, a tribunal consisting of ministers and laymen. **2.** The jurisdiction of a presbyter or of a presbytery. **3.** Part of a church reserved for officiating priests.

pre'sci-ence (prē'shĭ-ĕns; prĕsh'ĭ-), *n.* Foreknowledge; foresight. [seeing.]

pre'sci-ent (-ĕnt), *a.* [4] Foreknowing; fore-

pre-scribe' (prē-skrīb'), *v. t.* [1] **1.** To lay down authoritatively as a guide, direction, or rule of action. **2.** *Med.* To designate or order the use of as a remedy. — *v. i.* **1.** To give directions. **2.** *Med.* To write or give prescriptions. — **-scrib'er** (-ēr), *n.* [8]. [rection; rule.]

pre'script (prē'skrĭpt), *n.* Thing prescribed; di-

pre-scrip'tion (prē-skrĭp'shŭn), *n.* **1.** A prescribing; thing prescribed; direction. **2.** *Med.* A written direction for the preparation and use of a medicine; also, the medicine. **3.** *Law.* Establishment of a claim of title by long use and enjoyment; right or title so acquired.

pre-scrip'tive (-tĭv), *a.* Consisting in, acquired by, pertaining to, or arising from, prescription.

pres'ence (prĕz'ĕns), *n.* **1.** Act, fact, or state of being present. **2.** The immediate vicinity of a person; proximity. **3.** The whole of one's personal qualities; personality. **4.** Mien; bearing. — *presence of mind,* control or alertness of the mental faculties, esp. in emergency.

pres'ent (-ĕnt), *a.* **1.** Being before, in view, or at hand. **2.** Now existing, or in process. **3.** Immediate; instant. **4.** *Gram.* Denoting, or pertaining to, time that now is; as, the *present* tense. — *n.* **1.** Present time. **2.** Present occasion or affair. **3.** *pl. Law.* Present letters or instrument, as a deed, a lease, or other writing. **4.** *Gram.* A present tense, or a verb form denoting it.

pre-sent' (prē-zĕnt'), *v. t.* **1.** To bring or introduce into the presence of some one; introduce (a person) to another. **2.** To exhibit. **3.** To offer as a gift. **4.** To make a gift to. **5.** To deliver.

pres'ent (prĕz'ĕnt), *n.* Anything presented or given; a gift. [of being presentable.]

pre-sen'ta-bil'i-ty (prē-zĕn'tà-bĭl'ĭ-tĭ), *n.* State

pre-sent'a-ble (prē-zĕn'tà-b'l), *a.* [4] Capable of being presented; hence, suitable to appear.

pres'en-ta'tion (prĕz'ĕn-tā'shŭn), *n.* Act of presenting; that which is presented.

pre-sent'er (prē-zĕn'tĕr), *n.* One who presents.

pre-sen'ti-ment (-sĕn'tĭ-mĕnt; -zĕn'-), *n.* A feeling or expectation as to what will occur; foreboding.

pres'ent-ly (prĕz'ĕnt-lĭ), *adv.* **1.** At once. **2.** Soon; shortly; before long.

pre-sent'ment (prē-zĕnt'mĕnt), *n.* **1.** Presentation. **2.** A setting forth to view; representation.

pre-serv'a-ble (-zûr'và-b'l), *a.* Capable of being preserved.

pres'er-va'tion (prĕz'ēr-vā'shŭn), *n.* Act or process of preserving; state of being preserved.

pre-serv'a-tive (prē-zûr'và-tĭv), *a.* [4] Tending to preserve. — *n.* A preservative agent.

pre-serve′ (prĕ-zûrv′), *v. t.* [1] **1.** To defend from injury; protect; save. **2.** To save from decay, as by the use of sugar, salt, etc.; as, to *preserve* fruit. **3.** To maintain. — *v. i.* To make preserves. — *n.* **1.** That which is preserved. ·*Obs.*, except of fruit, etc.; esp., fruit cooked with sugar; — usually in *pl.* **2.** A place in which game, fish, etc., are preserved. — **pre-serv′er,** *n.* [8].

pre-side′ (prĕ-zīd′), *v. i.* [1] **1.** To occupy the place of authority or control, as of chairman. **2.** To exercise superintendence, guidance, or control.

pres′i-den-cy (prĕz′ĭ-dĕn-sĭ), *n.; pl.* -DENCIES (-sĭz). **1.** Function or action of one who presides. **2.** Office, or term of office, of president. **3.** One of three great divisions of British India.

pres′i-dent (-dĕnt), *n.* One who presides; a head; as: **a** A presiding officer. **b** [*Often cap.*] The chief executive officer of a modern republic.

pres′i-den′tial (-dĕn′shăl), *a.* Of or pertaining to a president or presidency; as, a *presidential* election.

pre-sid′er (prĕ-zīd′ẽr), *n.* One who presides.

press (prĕs), *v. t.* To force into service; impress.

press, *v. t.* **1.** To act on, with a continuous force, as by weight; compress. **2.** To squeeze out the juice or contents of; squeeze out, or express. **3.** To constrain; force; compel. **4.** To entreat earnestly; urge. **5.** To seek or solicit strongly. **6.** To emphasize. **7.** To hasten; urge on. — *v. i.* **1.** To push or crowd with steady force. **2.** To move on with urging and crowding; hurry. — *n.* **1.** Act of pressing forward; a crowding. **2.** A crowd; throng. **3.** Urgent demands of business. **4.** A machine by which any substance is pressed or stamped; hence, a printing press. Also, the place containing a press or presses. **5.** Printed publications collectively, esp. newspapers and periodicals. **6.** An upright closet or cupboard. — **press′er,** *n.* [8].

press gang, *or* **press′gang′,** *n.* A detachment to force men into military, or esp. naval, service.

press′ing, *a.* [4] Urgent; exacting. — -**ly,** *adv.* [8].

press′man (prĕs′măn), *n.; pl.* -MEN (-mĕn). One who manages a press, esp. a printing press.

pres′sure (prĕsh′ûr), *n.* **1.** A pressing; compression. **2.** A constraining force or impulse. **3.** Affliction; distress; burden. **4.** Urgency. **5.** Action of a force against some opposing force.

pres′ti-dig′i-ta′tion (-tĭ-dĭj′ĭ-tā′shŭn), *n.* Sleight of hand; legerdemain; juggling. — **pres′ti-dig′i-ta′tor** (-dĭj′ĭ-tā′tẽr), *n.* [8].

pres-tige′ (prĕs-tēzh′; prĕs′tĭj), *n.* Weight, influence, or force derived from past success, etc.

pres′to (prĕs′tō), *adv.* Quickly; suddenly.

pre-sum′a-ble (prĕ-zūm′á-b'l), *a.* [4] Such as may be presumed to be true. — **-a-bly,** *adv.* [8].

pre-sume′ (-zūm′), *v. t.* [1] **1.** To take upon one's self; esp., to do without authority; venture. **2.** To take for granted; infer. **3.** To raise a presumption of or that. — *v. i.* To venture, go, or act, by assuming leave or authority; take liberties.

pre-sump′tion (-zŭmp′shŭn), *n.* **1.** Act of venturing beyond due bounds; arrogance; effrontery. **2.** Act of taking for granted; belief on incomplete proof. **3.** Ground for presuming; probable evidence. **4.** That which is presumed.

pre-sump′tive (-tĭv), *a.* [4] Based on presumption or probability; probable. — **-ly,** *adv.* [8].

pre-sump′tu-ous (-tū̇-ŭs), *a.* [4] **1.** Full of presumption; arrogant. **2.** Founded on presumption. — **-ly,** *adv.* — **-ness,** *n.* [8].

pre′sup-pose′ (prē′sŭ-pōz′), *v. t.* To suppose or assume beforehand.

pre′sup′po-si′tion (prē-sŭp′ō-zĭsh′ŭn), *n.* Act of presupposing; that which is presupposed.

pre-tend′ (prĕ-tĕnd′), *v. t.* **1.** To represent, esp. falsely; feign. **2.** To put forward as a reason, pretext, or excuse. — *v. i.* **1.** To lay claim to something. **2.** To make believe; feign.

pre-tend′er, *n.* One who pretends; one who claims a title (to something); a dissembler.

pre-tense′, pre-tence′ (prĕ-tĕns′), *n.* **1.** A claiming; claim made; pretension. **2.** A holding out to others something false or feigned; deception. **3.** False or hypocritical show, etc.; pretext.

pre-ten′sion (prĕ-tĕn′shŭn), *n.* **1.** Act of pretending; also, quality of being pretentious. **2.** A claim made (true or false).

pre-ten′tious (-shŭs), *a.* [4] Full of pretension. — **-ly,** *adv.* [8] — **-ness,** *n.* [8].

pret′er-it (prĕt′ẽr-ĭt), *a. Gram.* Past; — applied esp. to a tense or form denoting an action or state as bygone, without reference to duration. — *n.* The preterit tense, or a preterit word or form.

pre′ter-mit′ (prē′tẽr-mĭt′), *v. t. ;* -MIT′TED; -TING. To pass by; omit; disregard.

pre′ter-nat′u-ral (prē′tẽr-năt′ṳ-răl), *a.* [4] Beyond, or different from, what is natural; irregular; abnormal. — **-nat′u-ral-ly,** *adv.* [8].

pre′text (prē′tĕkst; prĕ-tĕkst′), *n.* That which is assumed to conceal a purpose or condition; pretense; disguise.

pre′tor, pre-to′ri-an. Vars. of PRÆTOR, PRÆTORIAN.

pret′ti-ly (prĭt′ĭ-lĭ), *adv.* In a pretty manner.

pret′ti-ness, *n.* Quality or state of being pretty.

pret′ty (prĭt′ĭ), *a.* [3] **1.** Pleasing by delicacy or grace; pleasing, but not grand. **2.** Pleasing to the mind; entertaining. **3.** Good; fine; — often ironical. **4.** Moderately large. — *adv.* In some degree; rather.

pret′zel (prĕt′sĕl), *n.* A kind of salted biscuit.

pre-vail′ (prĕ-vāl′), *v. i.* **1.** To gain the victory; triumph. **2.** To have effect, power, or influence. **3.** To persuade; induce ; — with *on, upon,* etc.

pre-vail′ing, *p. a.* **1.** Having superior force or influence; efficacious. **2.** Prevalent.

prev′a-lence (prĕv′á-lĕns), *n.* Quality or condition of being prevalent.

prev′a-lent (-lĕnt), *a.* Most generally received, current, adopted, or practiced; also, widespread; prevailing. — **-ly,** *adv.* [8].

pre-var′i-cate (prĕ-văr′ĭ-kāt), *v. i.* [1] To deviate from the truth; quibble. — **pre-var′i-ca′tor** (-văr′ĭ-kā′tẽr), *n.* [cating.

pre-var′i-ca′tion (-kā′shŭn), *n.* Act of prevari-

pre-vent′ (-vĕnt′), *v. t.* To intercept; hinder; frustrate. — **pre-vent′er** (prĕ-vĕn′tẽr), *n.* [8].

pre-vent′a-ble (-vĕn′tá-b'l), **pre-vent′i-ble** (-tĭ-b'l), *a.* [8] Capable of prevention.

pre-ven′tion (prĕ-vĕn′shŭn), *n.* Act of preventing; also, that which prevents; preventive.

pre-ven′tive (-tĭv), *a.* [4] Tending or serving to prevent. — *n.* That which prevents; *Med.*, something to prevent disease. — **-ly,** *adv.* [8].

---

pre'vi-ous (prē'vĭ-ŭs), *a.* Going before in time ; prior. — **-ly**, *adv.* [8].

pre-vi'sion (prē-vĭzh'ŭn), *n.* Foresight.

prey (prā), *n.* Any animal seized by another to be devoured ; hence, a person given up or seized as a victim. — *v. i.* To pillage ; plunder ; take food by violence ; affect injuriously.

price (prīs), *n.* **1.** Value ; worth. **2.** The quantity of one thing, usually money, that is exchanged or demanded in barter or sale for another. **3.** Reward ; recompense ; as, the *price* of industry.

price, *v. t.* [1] To set a price on ; value.

price'less, *a.* Of inestimable worth ; invaluable.

prick (prĭk), *n.* **1.** A sharp thing ; a pointed instrument. **2.** A pricking, or sensation of being pricked ; a stinging pain. **3.** A puncture ; point ; dot ; a minute wound. — *v. t.* **1.** To pierce slightly with something pointed. **2.** To ride cr guide with spurs ; spur ; urge. **3.** To pain or sting, as with remorse. **4.** To mark or outline by pricking, as a pattern. **5.** To denote by a puncture ; hence, to choose ; mark. **6.** To raise or erect, as the ears of an animal in listening. — *v. i.* **1.** To be prickly. **2.** To feel a sharp pain, as by puncture ; tingle. **3.** To spur onward ; esp., to ride fast. *Archaic.* **4.** To point upward ; be erect.

prick'er (-ẽr), *n.* One that pricks ; prickle.

prick'le (-'l), *n.* A small, sharp point ; a spine, thorn, or the like. — *v. t.* [1] **1.** To prick slightly, as with prickles. **2.** To cover with pricks or dots.

prick'ly (prĭk'lĭ), *a.* [3] **1.** Full of prickles ; armed or covered with prickles. **2.** Pricking ; stinging. — **prickly pear,** a kind of flat-jointed prickly cactus, often used as food for cattle ; its pear-shaped edible fruit. — **-li-ness** (-lĭ-nĕs), *n.*

pride (prīd), *n.* **1.** Quality or state of being proud ; as : **a** Excessive self-esteem ; conceit. **b** Lofty self-respect ; a reasonable or justifiable feeling of elation. **2.** Proud behavior ; arrogance ; disdain. **3.** That of which one is proud. **4.** Highest pitch ; prime. *Archaic.* **5.** Show ; ostentation ; glory. — *v. t.* [1] To indulge in pride ; — reflexive.

priest (prēst), *n.* **1.** One set apart or authorized to perform religious or sacred functions. **2.** A person ordained to the Christian ministry ; minister.

priest'ess, *n.* A female priest.

priest'hood (prēst'hŏod), *n.* **1.** Office or character of a priest. **2.** Priests collectively.

priest'ly, *a.* Of or pertaining to a priest or priests.

prig (prĭg), *n.* One narrowly and self-consciously engrossed in his own attainments. — **prig'gish** (-ĭsh), *a.* [8] — **-ly,** *adv.* [8] — **-ness,** *n.* [8].

prim (prĭm), *a.;* PRIM'MER (-ẽr) ; -MEST. Formally neat or precise ; stiffly decorous or nice.

pri'ma-cy (prī'må-sĭ), *n.; pl.* -CIES (-sĭz). **1.** State of being first, as in time, rank, etc. ; preëminence. **2.** Office, rank, or character of a primate.

pri'ma don'na (prē'må dŏn'å). A principal female singer in an opera or concert organization.

‖ **pri'ma fa'ci-e** (prī'må fā'shĭ-ē). [L.] At first view ; on the first appearance.

pri'mage (prī'mȧj), *n.* A small charge for use of ropes, etc., in unloading goods from a vessel.

pri'mal (prī'mǎl), *a.* **1.** Primary ; original. **2.** Principal ; chief. [ner ; in the first place.]

pri'ma-ri-ly (-må-rĭ-lĭ), *adv.* In a primary man-

pri'ma-ry (-rĭ), *a.* **1.** First in order ; primitive ; original. **2.** First in dignity or importance ; chief ; principal. **3.** First, as preparatory to something higher. **4.** *Zoöl.* Designating the principal quills of a bird's wing. **5.** *Elec.* In an induction coil or transformer, pertaining to or designating the inducing current or its circuit.

pri'ma-ry (prī'må-rĭ), *n.; pl.* -RIES (-rĭz). **1.** That which stands first in order, rank, or importance. **2.** A meeting of voters at which the first steps are taken toward nominating candidates. *U. S.* **3.** One of the principal feathers or quills of a bird's wing. **4.** *Elec.* A primary coil.

pri'mate (prī'māt), *n.* **1.** A bishop of a see which ranks first in a province. **2.** One of the Primates.

Pri-ma'tes (prī-mā'tēz), *n. pl.* The highest order of mammals, including man and the apes, monkeys, marmosets, and lemurs.

prime (prīm), *a.* **1.** Primary ; original. **2.** First in rank, dignity, etc. ; chief. **3.** First in excellence. **4.** *Math.* **a** Divisible by no number except itself and unity. **b** Having no common divisor but 1; — used with *to* ; as, 4 is *prime* to 9. — **prime minister,** responsible head of a ministry or executive government, esp. of a monarchical government; — *n.* **1.** The first part; earliest stage; hence, dawn. spring. **2. a** Spring of life; youth. **b** The period, in human life, of highest or full health, strength, or beauty. **3.** That which is first in quality; best part. — *v.t.* [1] **1.** To prepare for firing, as a firearm, by supplying with a firing charge. **2.** Hence: **a** *Chiefly Mechanics.* To put into a working condition by performing a necessary preliminary operation on. **b** To prepare; post; coach; as, to *prime* a witness. — **prim'er** (prĭm'ẽr), *n.* [8].

prim'er (prĭm'ẽr), *n.* A small book for teaching children to read ; any small book of elementary principles. [ages; primitive; primal.]

pri-me'val (prī-mē'vǎl), *a.* Belonging to the first

prim'ing (prīm'ĭng), *n.* **1.** Act of one that primes something. **2. a** The powder or other material used to fire a charge. **b** *Paint.* The first coating of color, size, or the like, laid on a surface.

prim'i-tive (prĭm'ĭ-tĭv), *a.* [4] **1.** Pertaining to the beginning or origin, or to early times. **2.** Characterized by the style, rudeness, etc., of early times; old-fashioned. **3.** Original as opposed to derivative ; primary ; radical. — *n.* An original or primary word. — **-ly,** *adv.* [8] — **-ness,** *n.* [8].

prim'ly, *adv.* In a prim or precise manner.

prim'ness, *n.* Quality or state of being prim.

pri'mo-gen'i-ture (prī'mō-jĕn'ĭ-tụr), *n.* **1.** State of being a first-born child. **2.** *Law.* An exclusive right of inheritance belonging to the first-born.

pri-mor'di-al (prī-môr'dĭ-ǎl), *a.* First in order; earliest. — **-ly,** *adv.* [8].

prim'rose' (prĭm'rōz'), *n.* Any of a genus of well-known plants with showy flowers.

prince (prĭns), *n.* **1.** The one of highest rank ; a sovereign. **2.** The son of a sovereign, or other member of a royal family. **3.** One very eminent in a class or profession.

prince'dom (prĭns'dŭm), *n.* The jurisdiction, sovereignty, rank, or estate of a prince.

prince'ly (prĭns'lĭ), *a.* [4] **1.** Of or relating to a prince. **2.** Befitting a prince.

---

chair ; go ; sing, iŋk ; then, thin ; nature, verdure ; yet ; zh = z in azure. Numbers refer to §§ in the Special Notes which, with Abbreviations, Signs, etc., precede the Vocabulary.

prin′cess (prĭn′sĕs), *n.* **1.** A female having the rank of a prince. **2.** The daughter or granddaughter of a sovereign; loosely, a female member of a royal family. **3.** The consort of a prince.

prin′ci-pal (-sĭ-păl), *a.* Highest in rank, authority, importance, degree, etc.; chief; main. — *n.* **1.** A leader or head. **2.** A capital sum placed at interest. **3.** A chief officer, as of a school.

prin′ci-pal′i-ty (-păl′ĭ-tĭ), *n.; pl.* -TIES (-tĭz). **1.** Supreme station or power; sovereignty. **2.** Territory or jurisdiction of a prince.

prin′ci-pal-ly (prĭn′sĭ-păl-ĭ), *adv.* In a principal manner; primarily; chiefly; mainly.

prin′ci-pal-ship′, *n.* Office of a principal.

prin′ci-ple (-p′l), *n.* **1.** A source; origin; ultimate element, or cause. **2.** An original faculty or endowment. **3.** A fundamental or general truth. **4.** A general or settled rule or ground of action; a law of conduct.

prink (prĭngk), *v. i.* To dress or arrange one's self for show or affectedly. — *v. t.* To dress up.

print (prĭnt), *v. t.* **1.** To fix or impress, as a mark, character, idea, etc., into or on something. **2.** To stamp something in or on. **3.** To stamp or impress with characters, patterns, or the like, transferred by pressure from plates, types, etc.; also, to publish in print. **4.** To form in characters like those of type (other than script). **5.** *Photog.* To take (a copy, a positive picture, etc.) from a negative, etc. — *v. i.* **1.** To take impressions of type, electrotypes, engravings, etc. **2.** To publish a book, article, music, or the like. **3.** To make characters like those used in type (other than script). — *n.* **1.** A line, character, figure, or indentation, made by pressure. **2.** A stamp or die for molding. **3.** That which receives an impression, as from a mold. **4.** Printed letters; impression from type. **5.** Hence, printed matter; esp., a printed publication. **6.** An impression, as from an engraved plate. **7.** A cloth, esp. calico, figured by stamping. **8.** A photographic copy made on a sensitized surface.

print′er (prĭn′tẽr), *n.* One who prints or works at printing ; a typesetter or a pressman.

print′ing, *n.* Act, art, or business of a printer.

pri′or (prī′ẽr), *a.* Preceding in time or order ; antecedent. — *n.* The superior or ruler of a priory; also, the coadjutor of an abbot. [nuns.]

pri′or-ess, *n.* A woman superior of a priory of

pri-or′i-ty (prī-ŏr′ĭ-tĭ), *n.* State of being prior.

pri′o-ry (prī′ō-rĭ), *n.; pl.* -RIES (-rĭz). A religious house next below an abbey.

prism (prĭz′m), *n.* **1.** *Geom.* A solid whose bases or ends are similar, equal, and parallel polygons, the faces being parallelograms. **2.** *Optics.* A transparent body in the form of a 3-faced prism (def. 1).

pris-mat′ic (prĭz-măt′ĭk), *a.* **1.** Of, pertaining to, or like, a prism. **2.** Formed by a prism ; resembling the colors of light refracted by a prism.

pris′on (prĭz′′n), *n.* **1.** A place or state of confinement. **2.** A place for the confinement of criminals.

Prism.

pris′on-er (prĭz′′n-ẽr), *n.* A person under arrest, or in custody ; a captive. [earliest period.]

pris′tine (prĭs′tĭn ; -tĭn), *a.* Belonging to the

prith′ee (prĭth′ē), *interj.* Corruption of *pray thee.*

pri′va-cy (prī′vá-sĭ), *n.; pl.* -CIES (-sĭz). **1.** Seclusion. **2.** A place of seclusion. **3.** Secrecy.

pri′vate (prī′vät), *a.* [4] **1.** Of or concerning an individual person, company, or interest; personal; not public. **2.** Sequestered; secret; secluded; solitary. **3.** Not invested with public office. **4.** Not publicly known. — *n.* **1.** Privacy; retirement. *Obs.*, exc. in *in private.* **2.** *Mil.* A soldier below the grade of a noncommissioned officer.

pri′va-teer′ (-vá-tēr′), *n.* **1.** An armed private vessel commissioned to war against an enemy. **2.** The commander, or one of the crew, of a privateer. — *v. i.* To cruise in or as a privateer. — **pri′va-teers′man** (-tērz′măn), *n.*

pri′vate-ly (prī′vät-lĭ), *adv.* In a private manner.

pri-va′tion (prī-vā′shŭn), *n.* **1.** A depriving ; deprivation. **2.** State of being without something required. **3.** Loss or absence of a quality.

priv′a-tive (prĭv′á-tĭv), *a.* [4] **1.** Causing privation ; depriving. **2.** Consisting in the absence of something; negative. **3.** *Gram.* Denoting privation or negation ; giving a negative force to a word. — *n.* That which is privative ; *Gram.*, a privative prefix or suffix.

priv′et (prĭv′ĕt), *n.* An ornamental European shrub of the olive family, much planted for hedges.

priv′i-lege (-ĭ-lĕj), *n.* A right or immunity granted as a peculiar advantage or favor. — *v. t.* [1] To grant some particular right or exemption to.

priv′i-ly (-ĭ-lĭ), *adv.* In a privy manner ; secretly.

priv′i-ty (-tĭ), *n.; pl.* -TIES (-tĭz). **1.** Privacy , secrecy. **2.** Joint knowledge of a private concern.

priv′y (-ĭ), *a.* [3] **1.** Not public; private. **2.** Private; secluded. **3.** Secretly aware. — *n.; pl.* PRIV-IES (-ĭz). A small building for defecation.

prize (prīz), *n.* **1.** Something captured. **2.** Anything striven for or worth striving for. **3.** Something striven for in competition.

prize, *v. t.* [1] **1.** To value highly; esteem. **2.** To make a prize of; seize as a prize, as a vessel.

pro (prō), *adv.* For, on, or in behalf of, the affirmative side ; — in contrast with *con.* — pro and con, for and against. — *n.* A person, argument, etc., on the affirmative side.

prob′a-bil′i-ty (prŏb′á-bĭl′ĭ-tĭ), *n.; pl.* -TIES (-tĭz). **1.** State of being probable. **2.** Something probable.

prob′a-ble (prŏb′á-b′l), *a.* [4] **1.** Supported by evidence, but leaving some room for doubt; likely. **2.** Giving ground for belief, but not proving. — **prob′a-bly** (-blĭ), *adv.* [8].

pro′bate (prō′bāt), *n.* *Law.* Official proof, esp. of an instrument offered as a will.

pro-ba′tion (prō-bā′shŭn), *n.* **1.** Act of proving ; also, proof. **2.** Any proceeding designed to ascertain truth, determine character, etc.

pro-ba′tion-al (-ăl), *a.* Probationary.

pro-ba′tion-a-ry (-ă-rĭ), *a.* Serving for trial.

pro-ba′tion-er (-ẽr), *n.* One under probation.

pro′ba-tive (prō′bá-tĭv), *a.* [4] Serving for, or pertaining to, trial or proof.

probe (prōb), *v. t.* [1] **1.** To examine with a probe. **2.** To examine thoroughly. — *n.* *Surgery.* A slender instrument for examining a cavity.

prob′i-ty (prŏb′ĭ-tĭ ; prō′bĭ-), *n.* Tried virtue or integrity ; uprightness.

prob'lem (prŏb'lĕm), *n.* **1.** A matter difficult of solution. **2.** *Math.* Anything required to be done.

prob'lem·at'ic (-ăt'ĭk) } *a.* Of the nature of a
prob'lem·at'i·cal (-ĭ-kăl) } problem , uncertain.

pro·bos'cis (prŏ-bŏs'ĭs), *n.; L. pl.* -BOSCIDES (-ĭ-dēz). **1.** The trunk of an elephant; also, a long and flexible snout in other animals, as in a tapir. **2.** *Zoöl.* Any of various tubular processes of the head of animals, as of the mosquito.

pro·ce'dure (prŏ-sē'dụr), *n.* **1.** *Law.* The mode of conducting litigation. **2.** An action in a course of conduct ; a proceeding.

pro·ceed' (prŏ-sēd'), *v.i.* **1.** To go forward or onward ; advance; continue. **2.** To issue or come forth as from a source; come (from). **3.** To go on in an orderly or regulated manner. **4.** *Law.* To carry on a legal proceeding. — (prŏ'sēd), *n.* [*Now only in pl.*] That which results or accrues from some possession or transaction ; esp., the amount realized from a sale.

pro·ceed'ing, *n.* **1.** Act of one who proceeds ; a measure or step in a course of business ; a transaction. **2.** *Law.* **a** *pl.* Course of procedure in an action at law. **b** Any step in litigation. **3.** *pl.* The published record of the action taken, addresses read, etc., at the meetings of a society.

proc'ess (prŏs'ĕs *or*, *esp. in British usage*, prō'sĕs), *n.* **1.** Act of proceeding ; progress ; advance. **2.** A series of actions, motions, or events ; an operation or series of operations leading to some result. **3.** *Law.* Any writ or other writing by which a court exercises its jurisdiction. **4.** *Anat.* Any marked projecting part.

pro·ces'sion (prŏ-sĕsh'ŭn), *n.* **1.** Regular, orderly, or ceremonial progress. **2.** Action of issuing forth. **3.** That which is moving onward in an orderly manner, esp. a train of persons, as of mourners.

pro·ces'sion·al (-ăl), *a.* Pert. to a procession. — *n.* A hymn sung during a church procession.

pro·claim' (-klām'), *v.t.* To make known by public announcement. — **pro·claim'er**, *n.* [8].

proc'la·ma'tion (prŏk'lá-mā'shŭn), *n.* Act of proclaiming; publication; also, the thing proclaimed.

pro·cliv'i·ty (prŏ-klĭv'ĭ-tĭ), *n.; pl.* -TIES (-tĭz). Inclination; propensity.

pro·con'sul (prŏ-kŏn'sŭl), *n.* *Roman Antiq.* An officer who discharged the duties of a consul ; a governor of, or military commander in, a province.

pro·con'sul·ship, *n.* Office of proconsul.

pro·cras'ti·nate (prŏ-krăs'tĭ-nāt), *v.t. & i.* [1] To put off from day to day ; defer ; postpone. — **·na'tor** (-nā'tĕr), *n.* [8]. [nating ; delay.

pro·cras'ti·na'tion (-nā'shŭn), *n.* A procrasti-

pro'cre·ate (prō'krē-āt), *v. t.* [1] To generate and produce ; beget. — **pro'cre·a'tor** (-ā'tĕr), *n.* [8].

pro'cre·a'tion (-ā'shŭn), *n.* Act of procreating.

pro'cre·a'tive (prō'krē-ā'tĭv), *a.* Having power to beget ; generative. — **·ness**, *n.* [8].

proc'tor (prŏk'tĕr), *n.* An officer in a university, etc., who enforces order. — **·ship**, *n.*

pro·cur'a·ble (prŏ-kūr'á-b'l), *a.* Capable of being procured.

proc'u·ra'tion (prŏk'ū-rā'shŭn), *n.* **1.** A power of attorney ; a proxy. **2.** A procuring.

pro·cure' (prŏ-kūr'), *v. t.* [1] **1.** To bring into possession ; get. **2.** To contrive.

pro·cure'ment (-mĕnt), *n.* Act of procuring.

prod (prŏd), *n.* **1.** A pointed thing for pricking or puncturing, as a goad. **2.** A prick, punch, or poke. — *v. t. ;* PROD'DED ; PROD'DING. To thrust a prod into ; to goad or incite. — **prod'der**, *n.* [8].

prod'i·gal (prŏd'ĭ-găl), *a.* [4] Given to prodigality ; recklessly profuse. — *n.* A spendthrift.

prod'i·gal'i·ty (-găl'ĭ-tĭ), *n.; pl.* -TIES (-tĭz). Extravagance, or an extravagant act, in expenditure, esp. of money ; waste; loosely, profuse liberality.

prod'i·gal·ly, *adv.* In a prodigal manner.

pro·di'gious (prŏ-dĭj'ŭs), *a.* [4] Extraordinary in bulk, extent, quantity, or degree ; vast ; immense. — **·ly**, *adv.* [8] — **·ness**, *n.* [8].

prod'i·gy (prŏd'ĭ-jĭ), *n. ; pl.* -GIES (-jĭz). Anything so extraordinary as to excite astonishment.

pro·duce' (prŏ-dūs'), *v. t.* [1] **1.** To bring forward; exhibit ; show. **2.** To bring forth; bear; yield. **3.** To give rise to ; bring about. **4.** To manufacture ; make. — *v. i.* To yield appropriate offspring, crops, effects, etc.

prod'uce (prŏd'ūs), *n.* That which is produced ; yield ; esp., farm products.

pro·duc'er (prŏ-dūs'ēr), *n.* One who produces, esp. an agriculturist or a manufacturer.

pro·duc'i·ble (-ĭ-b'l), *a.* Capable of being produced.

prod'uct (prŏd'ŭkt), *n.* **1.** Anything produced, as by growth, labor, chemical reaction, etc. **2.** *Math.* The number resulting from the multiplication together of two or more numbers.

pro·duc'tion (prŏ-dŭk'shŭn), *n.* **1.** Act of producing. **2.** That which is produced.

pro·duc'tive (-tĭv), *a.* [4] **1.** Having the quality or power of producing ; also, fertile. **2.** Producing ; causing to exist. — **·ly**, *adv.* — **·ness**, *n.* [8].

pro'em (prō'ĕm), *n.* Preface. [ing.

prof'a·na'tion (prŏf'á-nā'shŭn), *n.* Act of profan-

pro·fane' (prŏ-fān'), *a.* [4] **1.** Not sacred or holy **2.** Treating sacred things irreverently , irreverent ; blasphemous. — *v. t.* [1] **1.** To treat with abuse, irreverence, or contempt (something regarded as sacred) ; desecrate. **2.** To put to a wrong or unworthy use ; debase. — **·ly**, *adv.* [8] — **·ness.** *n.* [8] — **pro·fan'er** (-fān'ēr), *n.* [8].

pro·fan'i·ty (-făn'ĭ-tĭ), *n.; pl.* -TIES (-tĭz). **1.** Quality or state of being profane ; irreverence ; esp., blasphemy. **2.** Profane language or acts.

pro·fess' (prŏ-fĕs'), *v. t.* **1.** To declare openly as one's belief, action, etc. ; avow ; acknowledge. **2.** To set up a claim of ; pretend. **3.** To pretend to knowledge of. — *v. i.* To avow ; make a public declaration. — **·ed·ly** (-ĕd-lĭ), *adv.* [8].

pro·fes'sion (-fĕsh'ŭn), *n.* **1.** A professing ; open declaration ; avowal. **2.** That which one professes ; esp., religious faith openly avowed. **3.** That of which one professes knowledge ; vocation ; calling:— applied esp. to theology, law, and medicine. **4.** Those engaged in a calling, collectively.

pro·fes'sion·al (-ăl), *a.* [4] **1.** Of or pert. to a profession or calling. **2.** **a** Engaged in by professionals. **b** Engaging in a profession for gain. — *n.* One who engages in anything professionally ; — opposed to *amateur.* — **·ly**, *adv.* [8].

pro·fes'sion·al·ism (-ĭz'm), *n.* The following of a profession, sport, etc., for livelihood or gain.

pro·fes'sor (prŏ-fĕs'ēr), *n.* **1.** One who professes

his opinions, esp. in religion. **2.** One who publicly teaches any branch of learning; esp., a lecturing or teaching officer in a college.

pro′fes-so′ri-al (prŏ′fĕ-sō′rĭ-ăl), a. [4] Of or pertaining to a professor. — **-so′ri-al-ly**, adv. [8].

pro-fes′sor-ship (prŏ-fĕs′ẽr-shĭp), n. Office, duties, or position of an academic professor.

prof′fer (prŏf′ẽr), v. t. To offer for acceptance. — n. An offer. [proficient.]

pro-fi′cien-cy (prŏ-fĭsh′ĕn-sĭ), n. Quality of being

pro-fi′cient (-ĕnt), n. One well skilled; an expert. — a. [4] Well-skilled; versed. — **-ly**, adv. [8].

pro′file (prŏ′fīl; -fēl), n. **1.** An outline or contour. **2.** A human] ad seen or depicted in a side view.

prof′it (prŏf′ĭt), n. **1.** Accession of good; valuable results;] nefit; gain. **2.** Excess of returns or income over expenditure in a given transaction, etc. — v. t. **1.** To gain advantage; improve; gain; advance. **2.** To be of use; do or bring good. — v. t. To be of service to; benefit.

prof′it-a-ble (-ȧ-b'l), a. [4] Yielding profit; lucrative. — **-ness**, n. [8] — **prof′it-a-bly**, adv. [8].

prof′it-eer′ (-ĭ-tēr′), n. One who makes what is considered an unreasonable profit, as by taking advantage of a public need in time of war. — **-it-eer′**, v. i.

prof′it-less, a. Without profit. [profligate.]

prof′li-ga-cy (prŏf′lĭ-gȧ-sĭ), n. Quality of being

prof′li-gate (-gȧt), a. [4] Broken down in rectitude, principle, virtue, or decency; dissolute. — n. A profligate person. — **prof′li-gate-ly**, adv. [8].

pro-found′ (prŏ-found′), a. [3] **1.** Opening or reaching to a great depth; deep. **2.** Intellectually deep; thorough. **3.** Deeply felt; intense. **4.** Bending low, as showing deep respect, etc. **5.** Coming from a depth; deeply drawn. — **-ly**, adv. [8] — **-ness**, n. [8].

pro-fun′di-ty (-fŭn′dĭ-tĭ), n.; pl. -TIES (-tĭz). **1.** Quality or state of being profound; depth. **2.** That which is profound or deep.

pro-fuse′ (-fūs′), a. [3] **1.** Pouring forth liberally, as esp. money or gifts; prodigal. **2.** Done, given, etc., with great liberality; very abundant or copious. — **-ly**, adv. [8] — **-ness**, n. [8].

pro-fu′sion (-fū′zhŭn), n. **1.** Quality or state of being profuse. **2.** Abundance; copious supply.

pro-gen′i-tor (prŏ-jĕn′ĭ-tẽr), n. A lineal ancestor.

prog′e-ny (prŏj′ē-nĭ), n. Offspring.

prog-no′sis (prŏg-nō′sĭs), n. Med. Forecast of the course and termination of a disease.

prog-nos′tic (-nŏs′tĭk), a. Indicating something future by signs or symptoms. — n. **1.** A sign indicating a future event; omen. **2.** A prediction.

prog-nos′ti-cate (-tĭ-kāt), v. t. [1] To foretell from signs or symptoms; predict.

prog-nos′ti-ca′tion (-kā′shŭn), n. Act of prognosticating. [ticates.]

prog-nos′ti-ca′tor (-kā′tẽr), n. One who prognos-

pro′gram, pro′gramme (prō′grăm), n. **1.** A brief outline of the order form, or of the subjects of, any public exercise, performance, etc. **2.** Hence, the selections or features of a performance collectively. **3.** A plan of future procedure.

prog′ress (prŏg′rĕs or, esp. British, prō′grĕs), n. **1.** A moving or going forward; an advance. **2.** Growth, development, or course. [proceed.]

pro-gress′ (prŏ-grĕs′), v. i. To make progress;

pro-gres′sion (prŏ-grĕsh′ŭn), n. **1.** Act of progressing. **2.** Course; passage; also, lapse of time.

pro-gres′sive (-grĕs′ĭv), a. [4] **1. a** Moving forward; advancing; increasing. **b** Advancing by successive stages or degrees. **2.** Tending to progress; favoring progress. — Progressive party, U. S. Politics, the party organized in 1912 under the leadership of Theodore Roosevelt. — n. **1.** One who is progressive, esp. in political policy. **2.** [cap.] A member of the Progressive party. U. S. — **-ly**, adv. — **-ness**, n. [8].

pro-hib′it (-hĭb′ĭt), v. t. **1.** To hinder; prevent. **2.** To forbid by authority; interdict.

pro′hi-bi′tion (prō′hĭ-bĭsh′ŭn), n. **1.** Act of prohibiting; interdict. **2.** The forbidding by law of the sale and, sometimes, the manufacture of alcoholic liquors as beverages.

pro′hi-bi′tion-ist, n. One who favors prohibition (in sense 2). — **pro′hi-bi′tion-ism** (-ĭz′m), n.

pro-hib′i-tive (prŏ-hĭb′ĭ-tĭv), a. Prohibitory.

pro-hib′i-to-ry (-tô-rĭ), a. Serving to prohibit.

pro-ject′ (prŏ-jĕkt′), v. t. **1.** To throw or cast forward; shoot forth. **2.** To contrive; scheme. **3.** Geom. To throw forward (as a point, line, etc.) so as to depict on a given surface. — v. i. To extend forward; jut.

proj′ect (prŏj′ĕkt), n. That which is projected or designed; a scheme; plan.

pro-jec′tile (prŏ-jĕk′tĭl), a. **1.** Projecting or impelling forward. **2.** Caused by impulse or projection; impelled forward. — n. A body projected by exterior force; a missile, as for a firearm.

pro-jec′tion (-shŭn), n. **1.** Act of projecting. **2.** A jutting out; also, a part that projects. **3.** A scheming or planning. **4.** Geom. Act or process of projecting on a surface; the picture so formed.

pro-jec′tor (-tẽr), n. One who forms projects.

pro′le-ta′ri-an (prō′lĕ-tā′rĭ-ăn; prŏl′ĕ-), a. Of or pertaining to the proletarians. — n. **1.** One of the poorest and lowest class in a community or state. **2.** One of the wage-earning class.

pro′le-ta′ri-at (-ăt), n. Proletarians collectively.

pro-lif′ic (prŏ-lĭf′ĭk), a. [4] **1.** Producing young or fruit abundantly. **2.** Serving to produce, esp. abundantly. — **pro-lif′i-cal-ly**, adv. [8].

pro′lix (prō′lĭks; prŏ-lĭks′), a. [4] **1.** Unduly prolonged or drawn out; wordy; as, a prolix speech; prolix writing. **2.** Using more words than necessary; wordy, as a prolix speaker or writer. —

pro-lix′i-ty (prŏ-lĭk′sĭ-tĭ), n. [a drama, etc.]

pro′logue (prō′lŏg; prŏl′ŏg), n. A preface, as to

pro-long′ (prŏ-lông′), v. t. **1.** To extend in space or length. **2.** To lengthen in time; draw out.

pro′lon-ga′tion (prō′lŏn-gā′shŭn), n. **1.** Act of prolonging. **2.** A part added by prolonging.

prom′e-nade′ (prŏm′ē-nād′), n. **1.** A walk, esp. in a public place, for pleasure, display, or exercise. **2.** A public walk. **3.** A large ball or dance. — v. i. [1] To take a promenade.

prom′i-nence (prŏm′ĭ-nĕns), n. **1.** Quality or state of being prominent; conspicuousness. **2.** A protuberance. [Prominence.]

prom′i-nen-cy (-nĕn-sĭ), n.; pl. -CIES (-sĭz).

prom′i-nent (-nĕnt), a. [4] **1.** Projecting beyond the surface. **2.** Distinctly manifest. **3.** Standing out from the crowd; eminent. — **-ly**, adv. [8].

pro'mis-cu'i-ty (prŏ'mĭs-kū'ĭ-tĭ ; prŏm'ĭs-), *n. ; pl.* -TIES (-tĭz). Mixture of kinds or classes.

pro-mis'cu-ous (prŏ-mĭs'kū-ŭs), *a.* [4] **1.** Mingled; confused. **2.** Distributed or applied indiscriminately. — **-ly**, *adv.* — **-ness**, *n.*

prom'ise (prŏm'ĭs), *n.* **1.** A declaration which gives an assurance of something to be done or forborne; an engagement. **2.** A cause or ground for hope, expectation, or assurance, esp. of success or distinction. **3.** That which is promised. — *v. t.* [1] **1.** To engage to do or forbear something; covenant. **2.** To afford reason to expect; foretoken. — *v. i.* **1.** To give assurance by or as by a promise. **2.** To give ground for expectations. — **prom'is-er** (prŏm'ĭs-ẽr), **prom'i-sor** (prŏm'ĭ-sôr), *n.* [8]. [ise is made.

prom'is-ee' (prŏm'ĭs-ē'), *n.* One to whom a promise is made.

prom'is-ing, *p. a.* [4] Giving promise; affording hope or assurance. — **prom'is-ing-ly**, *adv.* [8].

prom'is-so-ry (-rĭ), *a.* Containing a promise. — **promissory note,** a written promise to pay on demand or at a fixed time a certain sum of money to, or to order of, a specified person or to bearer.

prom'on-to-ry (prŏm'ŭn-tō-rĭ), *n. ; pl.* -TORIES (-rĭz). A high point of land or rock projecting into the sea ; a headland.

pro-mote' (prŏ-mōt'), *v. t.* [1] **1.** To contribute to the growth or prosperity of; further; encourage. **2.** To exalt in station or rank; advance.

pro-mot'er (-mōt'ẽr), *n.* **1.** One that promotes; encourager. **2.** One who initiates the organization of a company, the sale of bonds, stock, etc.

pro-mo'tion (-mō'shŭn), *n.* Act of promoting; state of being promoted, as in rank ; preferment.

pro-mo'tive (-tĭv), *a.* [4] Tending to promote.

prompt (prŏmpt), *a.* [3] **1.** Ready and quick to act. **2.** Done or rendered readily or immediately. — *v. t.* **1.** To assist or induce the action of ; instigate; incite. **2.** To suggest; dictate. **3.** To remind ; esp., to remind (an actor, speaker, etc.) of words or topics forgotten. — **prompt'er** (prŏmp'-tẽr), *n.* [8] — **-ly**, *adv.* [8] — **-ness**, *n.* [8].

promp'ti-tude (prŏmp'tĭ-tūd), *n.* Quality of being prompt.

pro-mul'gate (prŏ-mŭl'gāt), *v. t.* [1] **1.** To make known by open declaration. **2.** To publish abroad with intent to gain adherents to. — **pro'mul-ga'tor** (prŏ'mŭl-gā'tẽr ; prŏm'ŭl-), *n.* [8].

pro'mul-ga'tion (prŏ'mŭl-gā'shŭn ; prŏm'ŭl-), *n.* A promulgating ; publication.

prone (prōn), *a.* [3] **1.** Bending forward ; inclined; hence, humble. **2.** Lying on the belly, or face downwards. **3.** Inclined ; disposed ; — of the mind or affections, usually in an ill sense; as, *prone* to mischief. — **prone'ness**, *n.* [8].

prong (prŏng), *n.* A sharp point or sharp-pointed instrument, as the tine of a fork.

prong'horn' (-hôrn'), *n.* An antelope-like ruminant of the treeless parts of the western United States.

pro-nom'i-nal (prŏ-nŏm'ĭ-nǎl), *a.* Belonging to, or of the nature of, a pronoun.

pro'noun (prō'noun), *n.* Gram. Lit., a word used instead of a noun, or name ; one of a small group of words used to stand in place of, or to refer to, words or expressions denoting persons or things, as, *he, she, it, you,* etc.

pro-nounce' (prŏ-nouns'), *v. t.* [1] **1.** To utter articulately ; speak with the proper sound and accent. **2.** To utter officially or solemnly; deliver. **3.** To speak or utter rhetorically. **4.** To declare. — *v.i.* To give a pronunciation; articulate. — **-a-ble**, *a.* [8] — **-nounc'er** (-noun'sẽr), *n.* [8].

pro-nounced' (prŏ-nounst'), *p. a.* [4] Strongly marked; decided.

pro-nounce'ment (-nouns'mĕnt), *n.* A pronouncing ; a declaration ; formal announcement.

pro-nun'ci-a'tion (prŏ-nŭn'sĭ-ā'shŭn ; -shĭ-ā'-shŭn), *n.* Act or mode of pronouncing.

proof (proof), *n.* **1.** Any effort or process designed to establish or discover a fact or truth ; test ; trial ; check. **2.** Quality or state of having been proved or tried. **3.** Convincing evidence; demonstration. **4.** *Print.* A trial impression, as from type. — *a.* **1.** Firm or successful in resisting. **2.** Used in proving or testing, or serving as a proof. **3.** Being of a certain standard ; as, *proof* spirit.

proof reader. *Print.* One who reads, and marks corrections in, proofs. Hence, **proof reading.**

prop (prŏp), *v. t. ;* PROPPED (prŏpt) ; PROP'PING. To support by placing something under or against or by being placed under or against ; sustain. — *n.* That which props ; a support ; a stay.

prop'a-gan'da (prŏp'à-găn'dá), *n.* **1.** Any organization or plan for spreading a particular doctrine. **2.** The doctrine or principles thus propagated.

prop'a-gan'dism (-dĭz'm), *n.* Art, practice, or system of propagating tenets or principles.

prop'a-gan'dist (-dĭst), *n.* One devoted to any system of propagandism.

prop'a-gate (prŏp'á-gāt), *v. t.* [1] **1.** To cause to continue or multiply by generation. **2.** To extend the action of ; diffuse ; transmit. **3.** To spread from person to person ; disseminate. — *v. i.* To reproduce by generation, or, in plants, by seeds, cuttings, etc. — **-ga'tor** (-gā'tẽr), *n.* [8].

prop'a-ga'tion (-gā'shŭn), *n.* Act of propagating.

pro-pel' (prŏ-pĕl'), *v. t. ;* -PELLED (-pĕld') ; -PEL'-LING. To impel forward or onward; drive; push.

pro-pel'ler (-ẽr), *n.* One that propels; esp., a screw propeller. [ural inclination ; bent.

pro-pen'si-ty (-pĕn'sĭ-tĭ), *n.; pl.* -TIES (-tĭz). Natural or essential constitution ; peculiar. **2.** Befitting one's nature; appropriate. **3.** Conforming to the best usage; correct. **4.** Pertaining to or designating one individual only. **5.** Rightly called or considered. — *proper fraction,* *Arith.,* a fraction in which the numerator is less than the denominator. — **p.** *noun* or *name,* Gram., a name distinguishing an individual from others of the same class ; — opp. to *common noun* ; as, *John, Boston.*

prop'er-ly, *adv.* Suitably ; fitly ; strictly ; rightly.

prop'er-ty (-tĭ), *n.; pl.* -TIES (-tĭz). **1.** A quality or attribute belonging to a thing ; a distinctive quality; peculiarity. **2.** The exclusive right to possess, enjoy, and dispose of, a thing ; ownership. **3.** Thing owned ; estate.

proph'e-cy (prŏf'ē-sĭ), *n.;pl.* -CIES (-sĭz). Function or declaration of a prophet.

proph'e-sy (-sī), *v. t.* [2] **1.** To utter with divine inspiration. **2.** To foretell. — *v. i.* **1.** To declare or foretell as a prophet. — **proph'e-si'er**, *n.* [8].

proph'et (prŏf'ĕt), *n.* **1.** One inspired by God to speak in His name, announcing future events. **2.** One who foretells events. **3.** [*cap.*] *pl.*: with *the.* Certain books of the Old Testament. — **proph'et-ess,** *n. fem.* [8] — the Prophet, Mohammed.

pro-phet'ic (prō-fĕt'ĭk) } *a.* [4] Of or pertaining to
pro-phet'i-cal (-ĭ-kăl) } a prophet or prophecy; predictive ; — with *of.* — **-phet'i-cal-ly,** *adv.* [8].

pro'phy-lac'tic (prō'fĭ-lăk'tĭk ; prŏf'ĭ-), *a.* [4] *Med.* Defending from disease. — *n.* A prophylactic medicine. [place, time, or blood.]

pro-pin'qui-ty (prō-pĭn'kwĭ-tĭ), *n.* Nearness in

pro-pi'ti-ate (-pĭsh'ĭ-āt), *v. t.* [1] To appease and render favorable ; conciliate.

pro-pi'ti-a'tion (-ā'shŭn), *n.* Act of propitiating.

pro-pi'ti-a-to-ry (prō-pĭsh'ĭ-ȧ-tô-rĭ), *a.* [4] Having the power to make propitious; expiatory.

pro-pi'tious (prō-pĭsh'ŭs), *a.* **1.** Favorably disposed; gracious; helpful. **2.** Favorable; fortunate. — **-ly,** *adv.* [8] — **-ness,** *n.* [8].

pro-por'tion (-pōr'shŭn), *n.* **1.** The relation in magnitude, quantity, or degree of one to another; ratio. Loosely : Size; *pl.,* dimensions. **2.** Harmonic relation of one part to another; symmetry. **3.** One's share of a whole distributed by rule; lot. **4.** *Math.* Equality of ratios, as $\frac{1}{2} = \frac{3}{6}$, or $1 : 2 = 3 : 6$; also, the method (the *rule of three*) of finding the fourth term of such a proportion when three terms are known. — *v. t.* **1.** To adjust in a suitable proportion. **2.** To form with symmetry.

pro-por'tion-al (-ăl), *a.* **1.** Having a due proportion; being in suitable proportion. **2.** *Math.* Having the same or a constant ratio. — **-ly,** *adv.* — *n. Math.* Any term in a proportion.

pro-por'tion-ate (-ăt), *a.* Proportional. — (-āt), *v. t.* [1] To make proportional. — **-ly,** *adv.*

pro-pos'al (-pōz'ăl), *n.* **1.** Act of proposing; presentation. **2.** That which is proposed ; offer.

pro-pose' (-pōz'), *v. t.* [1] **1.** To offer for consideration or adoption. **2.** To purpose; intend. — *v. i.* **1.** To scheme; design. **2.** To offer; esp., to offer one's self in marriage. — **pos'er** (-pōz'ẽr), *n.*

prop'o-si'tion (prŏp'ŏ-zĭsh'ŭn), *n.* **1.** That which is proposed; proposal. **2.** Any expression in which some quality, state, or relation is asserted of some being or fact. **3.** *Math.* A formal statement of a truth to be demonstrated (a *theorem*), or of an operation to be performed (a *problem*).

pro-pound' (prō-pound'), *v. t.* To offer for consideration ; set forth ; put. — **pro-pound'er,** *n.* [8].

pro-pri'e-ta-ry (-prī'ē-tā-rĭ), *n. ; pl.* -RIES (-rĭz). **1.** A proprietor; owner. **2.** A body of proprietors. — *a.* Belonging or pertaining to a proprietor.

pro-pri'e-tor (-tẽr), *n.* Owner. — **-tress,** *n. fem.*

pro-pri'e-ty (prō-prī'ē-tĭ), *n. ; pl.* -TIES (-tĭz). Quality or state of being proper ; fitness.

pro-pul'sion (-pŭl'shŭn), *n.* Act of propelling.

pro-pul'sive (-sĭv), *a.* [4] Tending, or having power, to propel; urging.

‖**pro ra'ta** (prō rā'tȧ). [L.] In proportion; according to share, interest, or liability of each.

pro'ro-ga'tion (prō'rō-gā'shŭn), *n.* A proroguing.

pro-rogue' (prō-rōg'), *v. t.* [1] To end the session of (a parliament) by order of the crown.

pro-sa'ic (prō-zā'ĭk), *a.* [4] Dull ; commonplace ; prosy. — **-sa'i-cal-ly,** *adv.* — **-i-cal-ness,** *n.* [8].

pro-sce'ni-um (-sē'nĭ-ŭm), *n. ; L. pl.* -NIA (-ȧ). *Theater.* The stage in front of the curtain; sometimes, the curtain and its framework.

pro-scribe' (prō-skrīb'), *v. t.* [1] **1.** To outlaw. **2.** To denounce and condemn ; prohibit.

pro-scrip'tion (-skrĭp'shŭn), *n.* **1.** Act of proscribing; outlawry. **2.** State of being proscribed.

pro-scrip'tive (-tĭv), *a.* Of, pertaining to, or consisting in, proscription. — **-ly,** *adv.* [8].

prose (prōz), *n.* **1.** Ordinary language, as in speaking or writing ; — opposed to *verse.* **2.** Dull discourse. — *a.* Pert. to, or composed of, prose. — *v. t. & i.* [1] To write or talk in prose or prosily.

pros'e-cute (prŏs'ē-kūt), *v. t.* [1] **1.** To follow or pursue with a view to reach, execute, or accomplish ; carry on. **2.** *Law.* **a** To seek to get or enforce by legal process. **b** To proceed against judicially, esp. for a crime. — *v. i.* To institute and carry on a legal suit ; sue. — **-cu'tor** (-kū'tẽr), *n.*

pros'e-cu'tion (-kū'shŭn), *n.* A prosecuting.

pros'e-lyte (prŏs'ē-līt), *n.* A new convert, esp. to some religion. — *v. t. & i.* [1] To convert or win over from one belief or party to another.

pros'e-ly-tism (-lĭ-tĭz'm), *n.* The making of proselytes, or converts.

pros'i-ly (prōz'ĭ-lĭ), *adv.* In a prosy manner.

pros'i-ness (-nĕs), *n.* Prosy quality; dullness.

pro-slav'er-y (prō-slāv'ẽr-ĭ), *a.* Favoring slavery.

pros'o-dist (prŏs'ō-dĭst), *n.* An expert in prosody.

pros'o-dy (-dĭ), *n.* That part of grammar treating of the quantity of syllables, of accent, and of the laws of versification or metrical composition.

pros'pect (prŏs'pĕkt), *n.* **1.** That which is seen; view; scene. **2.** Relative aspect; outlook. **3.** Act of looking forward; anticipation. **4.** That which is hoped for; expectation. — *v. t. & i.* To explore for something, as gold. — **pro-spec'ter** (prō-spĕk'tẽr), **pros'pec-tor** (prŏs'pĕk-tẽr), *n.*

pro-spec'tive (prō-spĕk'tĭv), *a.* **1.** Looking forward in time; acting with foresight. **2.** That is in prospect; expected. — **-ly,** *adv.* [8].

pro-spec'tus (-tŭs), *n.* A preliminary statement of a plan or scheme, affording a view of its nature.

pros'per (prŏs'pẽr), *v. t.* To render successful. — *v. i.* To succeed; thrive. [prosperous.]

pros-per'i-ty (prŏs-pĕr'ĭ-tĭ), *n.* State of being

pros'per-ous (prŏs'pẽr-ŭs), *a.* [4] **1.** Favorable; as, a *prosperous* wind. **2.** Making gain, or increase; successful; as, a *prosperous* voyage. — **-ly,** *adv.* [8].

pros'ti-tute (prŏs'tĭ-tūt), *v. t.* [1] To devote to base or unworthy purposes.

pros'ti-tu'tion (-tū'shŭn), *n.* Act of prostituting.

pros'trate (-trāt), *a.* **1.** Lying with the body extended ; stretched out. **2.** Lying at another's mercy; powerless. **3.** Lying in a lowly or suppliant posture. — *v. t.* [1] **1.** To lay flat; level ; fell. **2.** To overthrow ; destroy ; ruin. **3.** To throw (one's self) down in humility or adoration. **4.** To deprive of strength. — **-tra-tor** (-trā-tẽr), *n.* [8].

pros-tra'tion (prŏs-trā'shŭn), *n.* Act of prostrating; state of being prostrate; great depression.

pros'y (prōz'ĭ), *a.* [3] **1.** Of or pertaining to prose; like prose. **2.** Dull; tedious.

pro'te-an (prō'tē-ăn; prō-tē'ăn), *a.* Readily assuming different shapes or forms.

pro-tect' (prō-tĕkt'), *v. t.* **1.** To shield from danger or injury; defend; guard. **2.** *Econ.* To foster by a protective tariff.

pro-tec'tion (-tĕk'shŭn), *n.* **1.** Act of protecting. **2.** That which protects; a defense. **3.** A passport. **4.** The imposition of duties on imported goods for the benefit of domestic producers.

pro-tec'tion-ism (-ĭz'm), *n.* The doctrine or policy of protection (def. 4). [tion.]

pro-tec'tion-ist, *n. Econ.* One who favors protec-

pro-tec'tive (-tĭv), *a.* [4] **1.** Affording protection. **2.** Of or pertaining to protection (def. 4).

pro-tec'tor (-tĕr), *n.* One that protects; defender; guardian; patron.— **pro-tec'tress**, *n. fem.* [8].

pro-tec'tor-ate (-tŏr-āt), *n.* **1.** Government by a protector; also, the rank or office of a protector. **2.** The relation of one state to another, which it protects and partly controls; also, the authority exercised, or the country so protected.

‖ **pro'té'gé'** (prō'tā'zhā'), *n. masc.; pl.* PROTÉGÉS (-zhāz'). [F.] One under the care and protection of another. — ‖ **pro'té'gée'** (-zhā'), *n. fem.; pl.* -GÉES (-zhāz').

pro-te-id (prō'tē-ĭd), *n.* Any of a class of complex substances present in all living cells and necessary in animal diet.

pro'te-in (-ĭn), *n.* Proteid.

pro-test' (prō-tĕst'), *v. t.* **1.** To declare solemnly; affirm. **2.** To make a certain formal written declaration to protect the holder of a dishonored bill of exchange or note. — *v. i.* To make a solemn declaration, esp. a written one, expressive of opposition or condemnation. [is protested.]

pro'test (prō'tĕst), *n.* A protesting; that which

prot'es-tant (prŏt'ĕs-tănt), *n.* One who protests; esp. [*cap.*], any Christian not of the Roman Catholic Church or the Greek Church. — *a.* **1.** Making a protest. **2.** [*cap.*] Of or pertaining to Protestants or their faith and practice.

prot'es-tant-ism (-ĭz'm), *n.* **1.** Quality or state of being protestant. **2.** [*cap.*] State of being a Protestant; Protestant religion.

prot'es-ta'tion (prŏt'ĕs-tā'shŭn), *n.* Act of protesting; public avowal; solemn declaration, esp. of dissent.

pro-test'er (prō-tĕs'tĕr), *n.* One who protests.

pro'to-col (prō'tō-kŏl), *n.* An original copy, draft, minute, or record; esp., *Diplomacy*, a preliminary memorandum, often a basis for a final treaty.

pro'to-mar'tyr (-mär'tĕr), *n.* The first martyr in any cause, esp. Stephen, the first Christian martyr.

pro'to-plasm (prō'tō-plăz'm), *n. Biol.* The essential substance of the cell body and nucleus of cells of animals and plants, regarded as the only form of matter in which life is manifested. — **pro'to-plas'mic** (-plăz'mĭk), *a.*

pro'to-type (-tīp), *n.* An archetype; pattern.

pro-tract' (prō-trăkt'), *v. t.* **1.** To draw out, usually in time; continue; prolong. **2.** To draw with scale and protractor; plot.

pro-trac'tion (-trăk'shŭn), *n.* A protracting.

pro-trac'tive (-tĭv), *a.* Drawing out or prolonging.

pro-trac'tor (-trăk'tĕr), *n.* **1.** One that protracts, or causes protraction. **2.** An instrument for laying down and measuring angles on paper. See *Illust.*

Common Protractor.

pro-trude' (-trōōd'), *v. t. & i.* [1] To thrust out; project.

pro-tru'sile (-sĭl), *a.* Capable of being protruded.

pro-tru'sion (-trōō'zhŭn), *n.* A protruding; state of being protruded; that which protrudes.

pro-tru'sive (-sĭv), *a.* [4] Tending to thrust forward.

pro-tu'ber-ance (-tū'bĕr-ăns), *n.* That which is protuberant; a prominence; fact or state of being protuberant. [ing; swelling.]

pro-tu'ber-ant (-ănt), *a.* [4] Prominent; bulg-

proud (proud), *a.* [3] **1.** Feeling or manifesting pride; as: **a** Arrogant; haughty. **b** Having proper self-respect or self-esteem. **c** Exulting (in); elated;—often with *of.* **2.** Arising from, or produced by, pride. **3.** Giving reason for pride; splendid; admirable. — **proud'ly**, *adv.* [8].

prov'a-ble (prōōv'a-b'l), *a.* That may be proved.

prove (prōōv), *v. t.* [1] **1.** To try, as by experiment or by a standard; test. **2.** To establish or ascertain by argument or evidence; demonstrate. **3.** To establish the genuineness or validity of; verify. **4.** To know by trial; experience. — *v. i.* To be found by experience, trial, or result.

prov'en (prōōv'n), *p. p. or p. a.* Proved.

prov'en-der (prŏv'ĕn-dĕr), *n.* Dry food for domestic animals, as hay, oats, etc.; feed.

prov'er (prōōv'ĕr), *n.* One that proves.

prov'erb (prŏv'ĕrb), *n.* **1.** An old and common saying; a maxim; saw; adage. **2.** *pl.* [*cap.*] The Book of Proverbs.—**Book of Proverbs,** a book of the Old Testament, containing wise maxims.

pro-ver'bi-al (prō-vûr'bĭ-ăl), *a.* [4] **1.** Mentioned in, or of the nature of, a proverb; well-known. **2.** Of or pert. to proverbs.— **-ly**, *adv.* [8].

pro-vide' (-vīd'), *v. t.* [1] **1.** To look out for in advance; procure beforehand; prepare. **2.** To supply; afford. **3.** To furnish; supply. **4.** To stipulate. — *v. i.* To procure means in advance.

pro-vid'ed (-vīd'ĕd), *conj.* On condition; if;— usually followed by *that.*

prov'i-dence (prŏv'ĭ-dĕns), *n.* **1.** Foresight; care; esp., divine foresight, care, or guidance; hence [*cap.*], God. **2.** A manifestation of God's care over his creatures. **3.** Prudence; economy.

prov'i-dent (-dĕnt), *a.* [4] Providing for the future; foreseeing; frugal; thrifty.— **-ly**, *adv.* [8].

prov'i-den'tial (-dĕn'shăl), *a.* [4] Effected by, or referable to, divine direction; opportune; fortunate. — **prov'i-den'tial-ly**, *adv.* [8].

pro-vid'er (prō-vīd'ĕr), *n.* One who provides.

prov'ince (prŏv'ĭns), *n.* **1.** A country or region dependent on a distant authority. **2.** A portion of a country, esp. one outside the capital or largest city. **3.** A department of knowledge or activity. **4.** Office; sphere.

pro-vin'cial (prō-vĭn'shăl), *a.* [4] **1.** Of or pert. to a province. **2.** Characteristic of a province; hence, rude; also, narrow. — *n.* One who is provincial or is from a province. — **-ly**, *adv.* [8].

pro-vin'cial-ism (-ĭz'm), *n.* **1.** Provincial quality or characteristic; as: **a** Attachment to local ideas, etc.; hence, narrowness. **b** A word or mannerism peculiar to a province or remote district.

pro-vi'sion (-vĭzh'ŭn), *n.* **1.** Act of providing; preparation. **2.** That which is provided; esp.,

---

chair; go; sing, iŋk; then, thin; nature, verdure; yet; zh = z in azure. Numbers refer to §§ in the Special Notes which, with Abbreviations, Signs, etc., precede the Vocabulary.

a stock of food; food; — often in *pl.* **3.** A stipulation; proviso. — *v. t.* To supply with provisions.

pro-vi'sion-al (prŏ-vĭzh'ŭn-ăl), *a.* Of the nature of a provision, esp. for the time being; temporary. — **-al-ly,** *adv.* [stipulation.]

pro-vi'so (-vī'zō), *n.; pl.* -sos (-zōz). A conditional

pro-vi'so-ry (-zō-rĭ), *a.* **1.** Of the nature of, or containing. a proviso; conditional. **2.** Provisional.

prov'o-ca'tion (prŏv'ŏ-kā'shŭn), *n.* Act of provoking to anger; annoyance; incitement.

pro-voc'a-tive (prŏ-vŏk'ȧ-tĭv; -vō'kȧ-tĭv), *a.* [4] Serving to provoke or stimulate. — *n.* That which provokes. — **-ly,** *adv.* [8] — **-ness,** *n.* [8].

pro-voke (prŏ-vōk'), *v. t.* [1] **1.** To move; arouse. **2.** To cause; instigate; excite. **3.** To incite or incense to action (a faculty or passion); hence, to irritate; offend. — **pro-vok'er,** *n.* [8].

prov'ost (prŏv'ŭst; *also, esp. in mil. terms,* prō'vō, prŏ-vō'), *n.* A superintendent; as: **a** The head of any of various colleges. **b** The head of certain churches or of some cathedral chapters.

prow (prou), *n.* The bow of a vessel.

prow'ess (prou'ĕs), *n.* **1.** Distinguished bravery; valor. **2.** A brave or valorous act or feat.

prowl (proul), *v. t. & i.* To rove about stealthily, esp. for prey. — *n.* Act of prowling. — **-er,** *n.*

prox'i-mate (prŏk'sĭ-māt), *a.* Nearest; next immediately preceding or following. — **-ly,** *adv.* [8].

prox-im'i-ty (prŏk-sĭm'ĭ-tĭ), *n.* Quality or state of being next; immediate nearness

prox'i-mo (prŏk'sĭ-mō), *adv.* In or of the next month after the present; as, on the 3d *proximo.* Abbr. *prox.* Cf. INSTANT, *a.; ULTIMO.*

prox'y (prŏk'sĭ), *n.; pl.* PROXIES (-sĭz). **1.** Authority to act for another; agency. **2.** A person authorized to act for another. **3.** A writing authorizing another to act in the signer's stead.

prude (prood), *n.* A woman of excessive, esp. affected, modesty or propriety.

pru'dence (proo'dĕns), *n.* Quality or state of being prudent; discretion; also, economy; frugality.

pru'dent (-dĕnt), *a.* [4] **1.** Sagacious in adapting means to ends; discreet; sensible; dictated by prudence. **2.** Provident. — **pru'dent-ly,** *adv.*

pru-den'tial (proo-dĕn'shăl), *a.* [4] **1.** Proceeding from, or marked by, prudence; discreet. **2.** Exercising prudence; advisory. — **-ly,** *adv.*

prud'er-y (prood'ẽr-ĭ), *n.; pl.* -ERIES (-ĭz). Quality of being prudish; extreme or affected modesty.

prud'ish (prood'ĭsh), *a.* [4] Like a prude.

prune (proon), *n.* A plum; now, any plum that may be, or has been, dried without fermentation.

prune, *v. t. & i.* [1] **1.** To cut off the superfluous parts, branches, or shoots of; trim; as, to *prune* trees. **2.** To cut off or out, as useless parts. — **prun'er** (proon'ẽr), *n.* [8].

pru'ri-ence (proo'rĭ-ĕns) } *n.* Quality or state of
pru'ri-en-cy (-ĕn-sĭ) } being prurient.

pru'ri-ent (-ĕnt), *a.* [4] Itching; impure in thought or desire; lustful. — **pru'ri-ent-ly,** *adv.* [8].

Prus'sian (prŭsh'ăn), *a.* Of or pert. to Prussia or its people. — *n.* One of the people of Prussia.

pry (prī), *n.* A lever for prying. — *v. t.* [2] To raise or move, or pull (apart), or attempt to do so, with a pry or lever. [peep; peer.]

pry, *v. i.* To look closely; inspect impertinently;

psalm (säm), *n.* A sacred song or poem. Hence [*Often cap.*] One of the hymns comprising a certain book (**the Psalms**) of the Old Testament.

psalm'ist (säm'ĭst), *n.* An author of a psalm or psalms; — chiefly used [*cap.*], with *the,* of David.

psalm'o-dist (säm'ŏ-dĭst; săl'mŏ-), *n.* One who sings or composes psalms.

psalm'o-dy (-dĭ), *n.* Act or art of singing psalms; also, psalms collectively, or a collection of psalms.

Psal'ter (sôl'tẽr), *n.* The Book of Psalms.

pseu'do (sū'dŏ), *a.* False; counterfeit; — often used as a prefix, **pseudo-.**

pseu'do-nym (sū'dŏ-nĭm), *n.* A fictitious name.

pseu-don'y-mous (sū-dŏn'ĭ-mŭs), *a.* Bearing or using a fictitious name, as a work or an author.

pshaw (shô; pshô), *interj. & n.* An exclamation expressive of contempt, disdain, dislike, etc.

psy'chic (sī'kĭk) } *a.* **1.** Of or pertaining to
psy'chi-cal (-kĭ-kăl) } the soul. **2.** Of or pertaining to the mind; mental. — **-cal-ly,** *adv.* [8].

psy'cho-log'ic (sī'kŏ-lŏj'ĭk) } *a.* Of or pertaining
psy'cho-log'i-cal (-ĭ-kăl) } to psychology. — **psy'cho-log'i-cal-ly,** *adv.* [8].

psy-chol'o-gist (sī-kŏl'ŏ-jĭst), *n.* One versed in psychology. [and functions.]

psy-chol'o-gy (-jĭ), *n.* Science of mind, its nature,

psy-chop'a-thy (sī-kŏp'ȧ-thĭ), *n.* Mental disease. — **psy'cho-path'ic** (sī'kŏ-păth'ĭk), *a.*

ptar'mi-gan (tär'mĭ-găn), *n.* Any of various species of grouse of northern and mountainous regions.

pto'ma-ine (tō'mȧ-ĭn; -ēn; *colloq.* tō'mān), *n.* Also **pto'ma-in.** Any of certain substances (alkaloids) found in decaying animal and vegetable matter, some of which are very poisonous.

pu'ber-ty (pū'bẽr-tĭ), *n.* The earliest age at which a person can beget or bear children.

pu-bes'cence (pū-bĕs'ĕns), *n.* **1.** Quality or state of being pubescent. **2.** *Biol.* A covering of soft hairs.

pu-bes'cent (-ĕnt), *a.* **1.** Arrived at puberty. **2.** Hairy; downy; as, *pubescent* leaves.

pub'lic (pŭb'lĭk), *a.* [4] **1.** Of or pertaining to the people at large. **2.** Open to the knowledge or view of all; common. — *n.* The general body of mankind; a nation, etc.; the people.

pub'li-can (-ĭ-kăn), *n.* **1.** *Roman Antiq.* A farmer of public revenues. **2.** An innkeeper. *Brit.*

pub'li-ca'tion (-kā'shŭn), *n.* **1.** Act of publishing; state of being published; proclamation. **2.** That which is published, esp. a book, pamphlet, etc.

pub'li-cist (pŭb'lĭ-sĭst), *n.* One versed in the laws of nations; also, a writer on politics.

pub-lic'i-ty (pŭb-lĭs'ĭ-tĭ), *n.* Quality or state of being public, or open to common knowledge.

pub'lic-ly (pŭb'lĭk-lĭ), *adv.* **1.** Without concealment; openly. **2.** In respect of the community.

pub'lic-spir'it-ed, *a.* [4] Having or showing a disposition to advance the interest of the community.

pub'lish (-lĭsh), *v. t.* **1.** To make public; divulge. **2.** To expose for sale, distribution, etc.; esp., to print and to issue from the press, as a book. — **er,** *n.*

puck'er (pŭk'ẽr), *v. t. & i.* To gather into small folds or wrinkles; — often with *up.* — *n.* A fold; wrinkle; a collection of folds.

pud'ding (pood'ĭng), *n.* **1.** A piece of intestine stuffed with seasoned chopped meat or the like.

2. A soft kind of food, variously made, as of flour, milk, eggs, etc., commonly served as a dessert.

pud′dle (pŭd′l), *n.* A small pool of dirty water.

pud′dling (-lĭng), *n.* Process of converting cast iron into wrought iron by intense heat and frequent stirring in the presence of oxidizing agents.

pudg′y (pŭj′ĭ), *a.* [3] Short and stout. — **pudg′i-ness.** *n.* [8].

pueb′lo (pwĕb′lō), *n.; pl.* -LOS (-lōz). **1.** An Indian village of Arizona and adjacent regions, built of stone or adobe in the form of a communal house. **2.** [*cap.*] An Indian of a pueblo.

pu′er-ile (pū′ēr-ĭl), *a.* [4] Childish.

pu′er-il′i-ty (-ĭl′ĭ-tĭ), *n.; pl.* -TIES (-tĭz). **1.** Quality of being puerile. **2.** That which is puerile.

puff (pŭf), *n.* **1.** A sudden and single emission of breath; a slight gust; whiff. **2.** Any of various light objects; as: **a** A kind of pastry. **b** A soft ball or pad for applying powder to the skin or hair. **c** A soft, loose roll of hair. **3.** Exaggerated praise, esp. in a public journal. *Colloq.* — *v. i.* **1.** To blow in, or to emit, a puff or puffs. **2.** To breathe quick and hard, as a runner. **3.** To be inflated; as, a blister *puffs* up. — *v. t.* **1.** To blow, drive, or inflate with a puff; to puff at. **2.** To swell, as with pride; — often with *up*. **3.** To praise exaggeratedly. **4.** To arrange in puffs, as the hair.

puff′ball (pŭf′bôl), *n.* Any of various ball-shaped fungi that emit ripe spores in a smokelike cloud.

puf′fin (-ĭn), *n.* Any of several sea birds of the auk family.

puff′i-ness, *n.* Quality or state of being puffy.

Puffin. (⅛)

puff′y (pŭf′ĭ), *a.* [3] **1.** Swollen with air, or any soft matter. **2.** Inflated; bombastic. **3.** Gusty.

pug (pŭg), *n.* One of a breed of small, pet dogs.

pu′gil-ism (pū′jĭl-ĭz′m), *n.* The practice of boxing, or fighting with the fists.

pu′gil-ist (-lĭst), *n.* A prize fighter; boxer.

pu′gil-is′tic (-lĭs′tĭk), *a.* Pert. to pugilism.

pug-na′cious (pŭg-nā′shŭs), *a.* [4] Disposed to fight; fighting. — **-ly,** *adv.* [8] — **-ness,** *n.* [8].

pug-nac′i-ty (-năs′ĭ-tĭ), *n.* Inclination to fight.

pug nose. A nose turning upward at the tip, usually short and thick. — **pug′-nosed′** (-nōzd′), *a.*

pu′is-sance (pū′ĭs-săns; pū-ĭs′-), *n.* Power; force.

pu′is-sant (-sănt), *a.* [4] Powerful; strong.

pule (pūl), *v. i.* [1] To whimper; whine.

pull (pŏŏl), *v. t.* **1.** To exert force on so as to cause, or tend to cause, motion toward oneself; draw; move or operate in this way. **2.** To gather with the hand; pluck. — *n.* **1.** Act of pulling; also, the force so exerted; a tug. **2.** A knob, cord, etc., for pulling or operating something by pulling. **3.** Influence; advantage. *Colloq. or Slang.*

pull′er (pŏŏl′ēr), *n.* One that pulls.

pul′let (pŏŏl′ĕt), *n.* A young hen.

pul′ley (pŏŏl′ĭ), *n. ; pl.* -LEYS (-ĭz). **1.** A small wheel with a grooved rim, used to change the direction of a pulling force or to increase an applied force, esp. in lifting. **2.** Any wheel used to transmit power by means of a band, belt, etc.

Pull′man car *or* **Pull′man** (pŏŏl′măn), *n.* A sleeping or day car of superior equipment, made or run by the Pullman Co. [**2.** Having lungs.

pul′mo-na-ry (pŭl′mō-nă-rĭ), *a.* **1.** Pert. to lungs.

pulp (pŭlp), *n.* The fleshy or pithy part of a vegetable or animal body, organ, or part, as the flesh of a fruit, the pith of a plant stem, etc.; hence, any moist soft mass of undissolved matter.

pul′pit (pŏŏl′pĭt), *n.* A place, usually elevated, in a church, where the clergyman stands while preaching or conducting the service. [wood pulp.

pulp′wood (pŭlp′wŏŏd′), *n.* Wood used for making

pulp′y (pŭl′pĭ), *a.* [3] Like pulp; consisting of pulp; esp., fleshy, succulent. — **pulp′i-ness,** *n.*

pul′sate (pŭl′sāt), *v. i.* [1] To throb, as a pulse; beat, as the heart.

pul-sa′tion (pŭl-sā′shŭn), *n.* **1.** Act of pulsating. **2.** A single beat, throb, or impulse.

pulse (pŭls), *n.* The seeds of such plants as the pea, bean, etc., used as food; also, any of the plants that yield these seeds.

pulse, *n.* **1.** The throbbing in the arteries due to the contractions of the heart. **2.** A beat or stroke; vibration. — *v. i.* [1] To beat, as the arteries; pulsate; throb. — **pulse′less,** *a.* [8]. [verizing.

pul′ver-i-za′tion (pŭl′vēr-ĭ-zā′shŭn), *n.* A pul-

pul′ver-ize (pŭl′vēr-īz), *v. t. & i.* [1] To reduce, or be reduced, to powder or dust, as by grinding, etc. — **pul′ver-iz′er** (-īz′ēr), *n.* [8].

pu′ma (pū′mà), *n.* The cougar.

pum′ice (pŭm′ĭs), *n.* A highly spongy or porous volcanic glass, used, esp. powdered, as an abrasive.

pump (pŭmp), *n.* A low shoe with plain upper, a thin sole, and, in those for men, a low heel.

pump, *n.* Any of numerous machines for raising, transferring, or compressing liquids or gases, or for rarefying gases. — *v. t.* **1.** To raise with a pump, as water, etc. **2.** To draw water, air, or the like, from ; free from water, etc., with a pump. **3.** Fig. : To draw out, as information or secrets, by persistent questioning. **4.** To operate by a handle or lever, as if by a pump handle. — *v. i.* To work, raise water, etc., with a pump.

pump′kin (pŭmp′kĭn; *colloq. and commonly* pŭn′kĭn), *n.* A certain gourdlike fruit widely cultivated ; also, the vine producing it.

Suction Pump, viewed in section. *A C* Cylinder or Barrel ; *A B* Pipe; *H* Handle : *P* Bucket or Piston ; *R* Rod ; *v v* Valves.

pun (pŭn), *n.* A play on words of the same sound but different meanings or on different applications of a word. — *v. i.* To make puns.

punch (pŭnch), *n.* A beverage of wine or distilled liquor and water, milk, tea, or the like.

punch, *v. t.* To thrust or strike, esp. with the fist. — *n.* A quick thrust or blow, as with the fist.

punch, *n.* A tool for perforating, indenting, etc.: a die. — *v. t.* To perforate, stamp, drive, or make with an instrument by pressure or by a blow.

punch′eon (pŭn′chŭn), *n.* A kind of large cask.

punc-til′i-o (pŭnk-tĭl′ĭ-ō), *n. ; pl.* -IOS (-ĭ-ōz). A nice point of exactness in conduct, form, etc.

---

chair; go; sing, iŋk; then, thin; nature, verdure; yet; zh = z in azure. **Numbers refer to §§ in the Special Notes which, with Abbreviations, Signs, etc., precede the Vocabulary.**

punc·til'i-ous (pŭnk-tĭl'ĭ-ŭs), *a.* [4] Exact in conduct or etiquette. — **-ly**, *adv.* — **-ness**, *n.*

punc'tu-al (pŭnk'tū̇-ăl), *a.* [4] Appearing or done at, or adhering exactly to, an appointed time; prompt. — **-ly**, *adv.* [being punctual.

punc'tu-al'i-ty (-ăl'ĭ-tĭ), *n.* Quality or state of

punc'tu-ate (-āt), *v. t.* [1] To separate (written matter) into sentences, clauses, etc., by punctuation marks. — *v. i.* To use punctuation marks.

punc'tu-a'tion (-ā'shŭn), *n.* Act of punctuating. — punctuation marks, the period, colon, semicolon, comma, interrogation mark, exclamation mark, parentheses, dash, and brackets.

punc'ture (pŭnk'tû̇r), *n.* **1.** Act of puncturing. **2.** A hole made by a point, as of a pin. — *v. t.* [1] To make a puncture in. [pungent.

pun'gen-cy (pŭn'jĕn-sĭ), *n.* Quality of being

pun'gent (-jĕnt), *a.* [4] **1.** Causing a sharp sensation; biting. **2.** Caustic; — said of speech, etc.

pun'ish (pŭn'ĭsh), *v. t.* **1.** To impose punishment on; chasten. **2.** To inflict a penalty for (an offense) on the offender. **3.** To deal with roughly or harshly. *Colloq. or Slang.* — *v. i.* To inflict punishment. — **pun'ish-er**, *n.* [8].

pun'ish-a-ble, *a.* Capable of being punished.

pun'ish-ment (-mĕnt), *n.* **1.** Act of punishing; pain or loss suffered by a person because of doing wrong. **2.** Severe or rough treatment. *Colloq. or Slang.* [punishment.

pu'ni-tive (pū'nĭ-tĭv), *a.* Of or pertaining to

punk (pŭnk), *n.* **1.** Wood so decayed as to serve for tinder. **2.** Artificial tinder.

pun'ster (pŭn'stĕr), *n.* One addicted to punning.

punt (pŭnt), *n.* **1.** A narrow, flat-bottomed boat with square ends, usually propelled with a pole. **2.** *Football.* Act of punting the ball. — *v. t.* **1.** To propel, as a punt, by pushing with a pole. **2.** *Football.* To kick (the ball) before it touches the ground, when let fall from the hands. — *v. i.* **1.** To propel a punt. **2.** To punt a football.

punt'er (pŭn'tĕr), *n.* One who punts.

pu'ny (pū'nĭ), *a.* [3] Imperfectly developed; insignificant; petty. — **pu'ni-ness** (-nĭ-nĕs), *n.*

pup (pŭp), *n.* A young dog or seal.

pu'pa (pū'på), *n.; L. pl.* PUPÆ (-pē). *Zoöl.* The intermediate form assumed by certain insects between the larval stage and the beginning of the adult stage, as of a butterfly.

pu'pal (-pǎl), *a.* Of or pertaining to a pupa.

pu'pil (-pĭl), *n.* The small opening in the middle of the eye, which looks like a black spot and contracts and expands according to the degree of light.

pu'pil, *n.* A youth of either sex under an instructor or tutor.

pu'pil-age (-ĕj), *n.* State or period of being a pupil.

pup'pet (pŭp'ĕt), *n.* **1.** A small image in human form; doll. **2.** A similar figure, often jointed, moved by the hand or by strings or wires; marionette. **3.** One acting as another wills; a tool.

pup'py (pŭp'ĭ), *n.; pl.* -PIES (-ĭz). **1.** A young dog. **2.** A silly fop. *Contemptuous.* — **-ish**, *a.* [8].

pur, purr (pûr), *v. i.;* PURRED (pûrd) PUR'RING. To utter a low, murmuring sound, as a cat does when pleased. — *n.* Sound made by one that purs.

pur'blind' (pûr'blīnd'), *a.* [4] Almost blind; dimsighted. — **-ly**, *adv.* [8] — **-ness**, *n.* [8].

pur'chas-a-ble (-chǎs-á-b'l), *a* [4] Capable of being purchased ; hence, venal ; corrupt.

pur'chase (-chǎs), *v. t.* [1] To get by paying money or its equivalent ; buy. — *n.* **1.** Acquisition for a price ; buying. **2.** That which is acquired ; now, specif., that obtained for a price. **3.** Any mechanical hold or advantage applied to the raising of heavy bodies, as by a lever or tackle ; also, the apparatus or device used. — **pur'chas-er**, *n.* [8].

pure (pūr), *a.* [3] **1.** Separate from all foreign matter ; clear ; unmixed. **2.** Free from defilement ; innocent ; chaste. **3.** Genuine ; perfect. **4.** Abstract ; theoretic ; as, *pure* mathematics ; — distinguished from *applied*.

‖ **pu·rée'** (pü'rā'), *n.* [F.] A dish made by reducing boiled food to a pulp ; esp., a soup with thickening so treated.

pure'ly (pūr'lĭ), *adv.* In a pure manner.

pure'ness, *n.* State or quality of being pure.

pur-ga'tion (pûr-gā'shŭn), *n.* Act of purging.

pur'ga-tive (pûr'gå-tĭv), *a.* [4] That purges. — *n. Med.* A purging medicine ; cathartic.

pur'ga-to'ri-al (-tō'rĭ-ǎl), *a.* Of or pertaining to purgatory ; expiatory.

pur'ga-to-ry (-tō-rĭ), *n.* [*Often cap.*] *R. C. Church.* A state or place of purification after death where certain offenses may be expiated.

purge (pûrj), *v. t.* [1] **1.** To cleanse; purify. **2.** To clear of guilt, or moral defilement. **3.** To remove in cleansing ; wash away. **4.** To act on as a purgative. — *v. i.* **1.** To become pure, as by clarification. **2.** To have or produce frequent stools. — *n.* **1.** A purging ; purgation. **2.** That which purges; esp., a purgative. — **purg'er** (pûr'jĕr), *n.*

pu'ri-fi-ca'tion (pū'rĭ-fĭ-kā'shŭn), *n.* Act of purifying ; cleansing.

pu'ri-fy (pū'rĭ-fī), *v. t.* [2] To make or become pure ; as : **a** To free from foreign elements or matter. **b** To free from guilt or defilement. — **pu'ri-fi'er** (-fī'ẽr), *n,* [8].

pur'ism (pûr'ĭz'm), *n.* Rigid purity or nicety, esp. in language ; also, an instance of this.

pur'ist, *n.* A stickler for purity, esp. in language.

pu'ri-tan (pū'rĭ-tǎn), *n.* **1.** One who is extremely scrupulous in his religious life. **2.** [*cap.*] One who, in the 16th and 17th centuries, advocated simpler forms of faith and worship than those established by law. — *a.* [*cap.*] Of, pertaining to, or characteristic of, the Puritans.

pu·ri-tan'ic (-tǎn'ĭk) } *a.* [4] **1.** [*cap.*] Of or
pu·ri-tan'i-cal (-ĭ-kǎl) } pertaining to the Puritans, or their doctrines. **2.** Precise and very scrupulous in observance of religious requirements and in the manner of living ; strict.

Pu'ri-tan-ism (pū'rĭ-tǎn-ĭz'm), *n.* The doctrines or practice of, or like those of, Puritans.

pu'ri-ty (-tĭ), *n.* Condition of being pure ; freedom from foreign or contaminating matter.

purl (pûrl), *v. i.* To eddy ; swirl ; murmur, as a brook. — *n.* **1.** A circle made by a fluid in motion; eddy. **2.** A gentle murmur, as of purling water.

pur'lieu (pûr'lū), *n.* Environs ; outskirts of a city or town ; neighborhood ; now, esp., a poor, mean, or squalid section or quarter.

pur-loin' (pûr-loin'), *v. t. & i.* To steal ; filch.

pur'ple (pûr'p'l), *n.* **1.** A color formed by a combination of red and blue. **2.** Cloth dyed purple; a purple robe emblematic of rank or authority. **3.** Imperial or regal rank or power; also, *Colloq.*, exalted station; great wealth. — *v. t. & i.* [1] To make or become purple. — *a.* Showing the color purple.

pur'plish (-plĭsh), *a.* Somewhat purple.

pur'port (pûr'pōrt; pûr-pōrt'), *v. t.* To mean or seem to mean. — (pûr'pōrt), *n.* Meaning.

pur'pose (-pŭs), *v. t. & i.* [1] To propose, as an aim, to one's self; intend; design; resolve. — *n.* **1.** Aim; design; intention. **2.** The object, effect, or result aimed at, intended, or attained. — **pur'pose-less**, *a.* [8].

pur'pose-ful (-fŏŏl), *a.* [4] **1.** Having an aim in view. **2.** Serving a purpose; not aimless.

pur'pose-ly, *adv.* With purpose; intentionally.

purr (pûr), *v. i. & n.* Variant of PUR.

purse (pûrs), *n.* **1.** A small bag or pouch, esp. to carry money in; a pocketbook. **2.** A treasury; finances; money. **3.** A sum offered as a prize, or collected as a present. — *v. t.* [1] **1.** To put into a purse. **2.** To contract into folds or wrinkles; pucker.

purse'–proud', *a.* [4] Proud because of wealth.

purs'er (pûr'sẽr), *n.* A clerk on a passenger vessel who keeps the accounts.

purs'lane (pûrs'lăn), *n.* A common succulent herb, used as a potherb, etc.

pur-su'ance (pŭr-sū'ăns), *n.* **1.** Act of pursuing. **2.** State of being pursuant; consequence.

pur-su'ant (-sū'ănt), *a.* Done in consequence (of anything); hence, according; — with *to*. — *adv.* Agreeably; conformably.

pur-su'ant-ly, *adv.* Pursuant.

pur-sue' (-sū'), *v. t.* [1] **1.** To follow with a view to overtake; chase. **2.** To seek; use or adopt measures to obtain. **3.** To proceed along, for some end or object; follow. **4.** To be engaged in. — *v. i.* To go in pursuit. — **pur-su'er** (-ẽr), *n.*

pur-suit' (-sūt'), *n.* **1.** Act of pursuing. **2.** One's business or occupation.

pur'sy (pûr'sĭ), *a.* [3] Short of breath and, usually, fat; hence, fat and, often, short.

pu'ru-lence (pū'rŏŏ-lĕns), **-len-cy** (-lĕn-sĭ), *n.* Quality or state of being purulent; also, pus.

pu'ru-lent (pū'rŏŏ-lĕnt), *a.* [4] Consisting of pus; attended with suppuration.

pur-vey' (pûr-vā'), *v. t. & i.* To furnish or provide, as provisions.

pur-vey'ance (-ăns), *n.* Act of providing.

pur-vey'or (-ẽr), *n.* One who purveys; caterer.

pur'view (pûr'vū), *n.* **1.** The body, or the scope, of a statute. **2.** Range of vision; outlook.

pus (pŭs), *n.* The opaque creamy matter produced in suppuration.

push (pŏŏsh), *v. t.* **1.** To press against in order to impel; move or endeavor to move by pressure. **2.** To press or urge forward; prosecute; extend; as, to *push* the war into the interior. **3.** To bear hard on; put to straits; as, *pushed* for funds. — *v. i.* **1.** To press with steady force. **2.** To press forward, esp. with energy or haste. — *n.* **1.** A thrust; shove. **2.** Aggressive energy or enterprise. *Colloq.* — **push'er**, *n.* [8]. — **push'ing**, *p. a.*

pu'sil-la-nim'i-ty (pū'sĭ-lȧ-nĭm'ĭ-tĭ), *n.* Quality or state of being pusillanimous; cowardice.

pu'sil-lan'i-mous (-lăn'ĭ-mŭs), *a.* [4] **1.** Weak or mean in spirit; cowardly. **2.** Evincing, due to, or marked by, weakness of spirit or cowardice; as, *pusillanimous* counsels. — **-ly**, *adv.* [8].

puss (pŏŏs), **puss'y** (-ĭ), *n.* A cat; — pet name.

pus'sy (pŭs'ĭ), *a.* [3] Full of, or like, pus.

pus'tu-lar (pŭs'tṵ-lȧr), *a.* **1.** Of or pert. to pustules. **2.** Covered with pustulelike prominences.

pus'tule (-tṵl), *n.* A small elevation of the cuticle with inflamed base, containing pus; pimple.

pus'tu-lous (-lŭs), *a.* Pustular.

put (pŏŏt), *v. t.; pret. & p. p.* PUT; *p. pr. & vb. n.* PUT'TING. **1.** To push; thrust; as, to *put* a knife into. **2.** To throw or cast, esp. with a certain pushing overhand motion; as, to *put* the shot. **3.** To drive or force; incite; urge; constrain. **4.** To bring to a (given) position, place, or condition; place; lay; cause to experience; — usually with *in*, *to*, *on*, etc.; as, to *put* to flight. **5.** To attribute; assign; as, to *put* a wrong construction on an act. **6.** To set before one for judgment, acceptance, or rejection; as, to *put* a question. — *v. i.* To go; take one's course; — with *for*, *back*, *in*, *to*, etc. — *n.* Act of putting; a thrust; push; throw.

pu'ta-tive (pū'tȧ-tĭv), *a.* Reputed; supposed.

pu'tre-fac'tion (pū'trḗ-făk'shŭn), *n.* Act or process of putrefying; putrefied condition.

pu'tre-fac'tive (-tĭv), *a.* Of, pertaining to, or causing, putrefaction.

pu'tre-fy (pū'trḗ-fī), *v. t. & i.* [2] To render or become putrid; cause to rot. [trescent.

pu-tres'cence (pū-trĕs'ĕns), *n.* State of being pu-

pu-tres'cent (-ĕnt), *a.* Becoming putrid; rotting.

pu'trid (pū'trĭd), *a.* [4] **1.** Decomposed; rotten; as, *putrid* flesh. **2.** Indicating, or proceeding from, decay; as, a *putrid* smell. — **-ness**, *n.* [8].

pu-trid'i-ty (pū-trĭd'ĭ-tĭ), *n.* Quality or state of being putrid; also, putrid matter.

putt (pŭt), *n.* *Golf.* A stroke made on a putting green to play the ball into the hole. — *v. i.* To make a putt.

put'ter (pŭt'ẽr), Var. of POTTER, *v.*

put'ter (pŏŏt'ẽr), *n.* One who puts something.

putt'ing green (pŭt'ĭng). *Golf.* The green, or plot of smooth turf, surrounding a hole.

put'ty, *n.* A common cement made, usually, of whiting and boiled linseed oil. — *v. t.* [2] To cement or stop with putty.

puz'zle (pŭz''l), *n.* **1.** A thing that perplexes; a difficult problem or question; esp., a toy, contrivance, etc., designed to test ingenuity. **2.** Perplexity; as, to be in a *puzzle*. — *v. t.* [1] **1.** To perplex; confuse. **2.** To solve by thought or ingenuity; — with *out*. — **puz'zler** (-lẽr), *n.* [8] — *v. i.* To work at a puzzle.

pyg'my (pĭg'mĭ), *n.; pl.* -MIES (-mĭz). Also **pig'my**. A dwarf; a short, insignificant person. — *a.* Dwarfish; very small.

py-ja'mas (pĭ-jä'măz; pĭ-), *or*, *chiefly U. S.*, **pa-ja'mas** (pȧ-jä'máz), *n. pl.* A suit, consisting of loose trousers or drawers and a jacket, for wear in the dressing room and during sleep.

py-lor'ic (pī-lŏr'ĭk), *a.* Of or pert. to the pylorus.

py-lo′rus (pĭ-lō′rŭs; pī-), *n.; pl.* -RI (-rī). The opening from the stomach into the intestine.

pyr′a-mid (pĭr′ă-mĭd), *n.* **1.** In geometry, a figure having for its base a plane polygon and for its sides several triangles with a common vertex and with their bases forming the sides of the base. **2.** Anything, esp. an edifice, of the shape of a pyramid (in sense 1); specifically, such an edifice as was used for tombs in ancient Egypt.

Pyramids.

py-ram′i-dal (pĭ-răm′ĭ-dăl), *a.* Of, pert. to, or in the form of, a pyramid.

pyr′a-mid′ic (pĭr′ă-mĭd′ĭk), **pyr′a-mid′i-cal** (-ĭ-kăl), *a.* Pyramidal.

pyre (pīr), *n.* A funeral pile; a combustible heap on which the dead are burned.

py′rite (pī′rīt; pĭr′īt), *n.* *Min.* Iron pyrites, a yellow mineral with a brilliant metallic luster.

py-ri′tes (pĭ-rī′tēz), *n.* *Min.* Any of several metallic-looking sulphides, as pyrite.

pyr′o-la (pĭr′ō-lă), *n.* Any of a genus (*Pyrola*) of short-stemmed herbs with evergreen leaves and racemes of white, pink, or purple flowers.

py′ro-tech′nic (pī′rō-tĕk′nĭk), **py′ro-tech′ni-cal** (-nĭ-kăl), *a.* Of or pertaining to pyrotechnics.

py′ro-tech′nics (pī′rō-tĕk′nĭks; pĭr′ō-), *n.* Art of making fireworks; a display of fireworks.

py′ro-tech′nist (-nĭst), *n.* A maker of fireworks.

py′thon (pī′thŏn), *n.* Any of various large nonvenomous snakes, closely related to the boas; any large snake, as a boa.

pyth′o-ness (pĭth′ō-nĕs), *n.* A woman supposed to be possessed or inspired by a soothsaying spirit.

pyx (pĭks), *n.* *R. C. Ch.* Receptacle in which the Host is reserved.

Pyx.

Q

quack (kwăk), *v. i.* **1.** Of a duck, to utter its characteristic cry. **2.** To utter a cry similar to a duck's. — *n.* The duck's cry, or a sound like it.

quack, *n.* **1.** A boastful pretender to medical skill. **2.** A charlatan. — *a.* Pertaining to quacks or quackery; pretending to cure diseases.

quack′er-y (kwăk′ĕr-ĭ), *n.* Acts, arts, or pretensions, of a quack; charlatanry.

quad (kwŏd), *n.* *Print.* A quadrat.

quad′ran′gle (kwŏd′răn′g'l), *n.* **1.** *Geom.* A plane figure having four angles and four sides. **2.** A rectangular inclosure, esp. when bounded by buildings.

quad-ran′gu-lar (kwŏd-răn′gŭ-lăr), *a.* Having four angles and four sides.

quad′rant (kwŏd′rănt), *n.* **1.** *Geom.* The quarter of a circle, an arc of 90°; also, the area bounded by a quadrant and two radii. **2.** An instrument for measuring altitudes.

quad′rat (kwŏd′răt), *n.* *Print.* A block of type metal lower than the letters, — used in spacing.

quad-rat′ic (kwŏd-răt′ĭk), *a.* **1.** Square. **2.** *Algebra.* Marked by terms of second degree as the highest; as, a *quadratic* equation, in which the highest power of the unknown quantity is a square.

quad-rat′ics (-ĭks), *n.* Algebra treating of quadratic equations.

quad-ren′ni-al (-rĕn′ĭ-ăl), *a.* **1.** Comprising, or lasting through, 4 years. **2.** Occurring once in 4 years.

quad′ri-lat′er-al (kwŏd′rĭ-lăt′ĕr-ăl), *a.* Having four sides and four angles. — *n.* *Geom.* A plane figure of four sides and four angles; a quadrangle.

Quadrilateral.

qua-drille′ (kwă-drĭl′), *n.* Square dance of five figures, in ⅜ and ⅔ time, for four couples; music for it.

quad-ril′lion (kwŏd-rĭl′yŭn), *n.* The number denoted by a unit with 15 zeros annexed in French and American notation, or 24 in English.

quad-roon′ (-rōōn′), *n.* Offspring of a mulatto and a white person; person of ¼ negro blood.

quad′ru-ped (kwŏd′rōō-pĕd), *a.* Having four feet. — *n.* An animal having four feet. — **-ped′al**, *a.*

quad′ru-ple (-p'l), *a. & adv.* Fourfold. — *n.* A sum or amount four times as great as another. — *v. t. & i.* [1] To multiply or be multiplied by four; increase fourfold.

quad′ru-plet (-plĕt), *n.* A collection of four of one kind; esp., *pl.*, four children born at one birth.

quad′ru-plex (-plĕks), *a.* Fourfold.

quad-ru′pli-cate (kwŏd-rōō′plĭ-kāt), *v. t.* [1] To quadruple. — (-kăt), *a.* Fourfold; esp., *Math.*, raised to the 4th power. — **quad-ru′pli-ca′tion**, *n.*

quaff (kwăf), *v. t. & i.* To drink copiously.

quag′ga (kwăg′á), *n.* **1.** A South African wild ass allied to the zebras, exterminated in the 19th century. **2.** Erroneously, a zebra.

quag′gy (-ĭ), *a.* [3] Like a quagmire; boggy.

quag′mire′ (-mīr′), *n.* Soft, miry land, which yields under foot.

quail (kwāl), *v. i.* To sink under trial or prospect of danger; lose heart; shrink; cower.

quail, *n.; pl.* QUAIL or QUAILS (see PLURAL, *n.*). **1.** A migratory Old World game bird, allied to the pheasant. **2.** In America, any of several small game birds, most of which are called also *partridge*. In northern and eastern U.S., the bobwhite.

European Quail.

quaint (kwānt), *a.* [3] **1.** Curious and fanciful; affected. **2.** Strange, esp. old-fashioned, but pleasing in character, appearance, etc. — **quaint′ly**, *adv.* — **-ness**, *n.* [8].

quake (kwāk), *v. i.* [1] **1.** To shake, vibrate, or quiver, as soft, wet land. **2.** To shake with fear,

---

āle, senāte, câre, ăm, ăccount, ärm, àsk, sofȧ; ēve, ĕvent, ēnd, recĕnt, makēr; īce, ĭll; ōld, ŏbey, ôrb, ŏdd, sŏft, cŏnnect; ūse, ŭnite, ûrn, ŭp, circŭs; fōōd, fŏŏt; out, oil;

cold, anger, or the like. — *n.* A shaking or trembling, esp. an earthquake.

Quak'er (kwāk'ẽr), *n.* See FRIEND, *n.*, 4.

qual'i-fi-ca'tion (kwŏl'ĭ-fĭ-kā'shŭn), *n.* **1.** Act of qualifying; state of being qualified. **2.** That which qualifies; requisite capacity or possession.

qual'i-fied (kwŏl'ĭ-fīd), *p. a.* **1.** Fitted; competent; fit. **2.** Limited or modified.

qual'i-fy (-fī), *v. t.* [2] **1.** To modify; limit. **2.** To soften; abate. **3.** To fit, as for office. — *v. i.* To be or become fit or competent. — **-fi'er** (-fī'ẽr), *n.*

qual'i-ta-tive (-tă-tĭv), *a.* Relating to quality; — often opposed to *quantitative.* — **-ly**, *adv.* [8].

qual'i-ty (-tĭ), *n.; pl.* -TIES (-tĭz). **1.** A property, characteristic, or attribute. **2.** Proper or essential being; character; nature; kind. **3.** Special or temporary character. **4. a** Excellence of character. **b** An accomplishment. **c** Superior birth or station; high rank. **5.** *Acoustics.* Timbre.

qualm (kwäm), *n.* **1.** A sudden attack of illness or pain, esp. of nausea. **2.** A sudden misgiving. **3.** A scruple of conscience. — **qualm'ish**, *a.* [8].

quan'da-ry (kwŏn'dá-rĭ), *n.; pl.* -RIES (-rĭz). A state of perplexity or doubt; a dilemma.

quan'ti-ta-tive (-tĭ-tă-tĭv), *a.* **1.** Estimated or estimable by quantity. **2.** Of or pert. to quantity.

quan'ti-ty (-tĭ), *n.; pl.* -TIES (-tĭz). **1.** The being so much with reference to a possible more or less. **2.** Amount or portion; bulk; extent, etc. **3.** An indefinite, usually a considerable, amount.

quar'an-tine (kwŏr'ăn-tēn), *n.* **1.** The term during which an arriving ship suspected of infection is restrained from intercourse with the shore; hence, such restraint, or the measures taken to enforce it; also, the place where prohibited vessels are stationed. Now, any forced stoppage of travel or intercourse on account of disease. **2.** A restraint upon the transportation of animals, plants, or goods that are possible carriers of disease or other pest. — *v. t.* [1] To subject to quarantine.

quar'rel (kwŏr'ĕl), *n.* A breach of concord; disagreement; esp., an angry dispute; altercation. — *v. i.* [7] **1.** To find fault; cavil. **2.** To have a difference or misunderstanding. **3.** To dispute angrily or violently. — **quar'rel-er**, *n.* [7, 8].

quar'rel-some (-sŭm), *a.* [4] Apt or disposed to quarrel. — **-ly**, *adv.* [8] — **-ness**, *n.* [8].

quar'ry (kwŏr'ĭ), *n.; pl.* -RIES (-ĭz). The object of the chase; game; esp., game hunted with hawks.

quar'ry, *n.* An excavation, esp. an open one, for obtaining stone. — *v. t.* [2] **1.** To dig or take from or as from a quarry. **2.** To make a quarry in.

quart (kwôrt), *n.* A measure of capacity, both in dry and in liquid measure; one fourth of a gallon; one eighth of a peck; 2 pints. Abbr. *qt.*

quar'ter (kwôr'tẽr), *n.* **1.** A fourth part; as: **a** The fourth part of a hundredweight. **b** Eight bushels, ¼ of a ton; — as in measuring grain. **c** One fourth of a year. **d** A fourth of an hour; hence, the moment marking this. **e** Twenty-five cents, ¼ of a dollar; also, a silver coin of this value. **2.** *Naut.* The after part of a vessel's side. **3.** One limb of a quadruped with the adjacent parts. **4.** One of the four parts into which the horizon is regarded as divided; region; direction. **5.** A district or locality. **6. a** Proper station; assigned position. **b** [*Usu-*

ally pl.] Place of lodging or temporary residence; shelter. **7.** *Mil.* Clemency shown in sparing the life of an enemy. — *a.* Consisting of, or equal to, a quarter. — *v. t.* **1.** To divide into four equal parts. **2.** Hence, to divide into parts. **3.** To shelter; esp., to assign (soldiers) to a place of shelter. **4.** To quarter-saw.

quarter day. A day on which quarterly payments, as rent, become due.

quar'ter-deck', *n.* *Naut.* That part of the spar, or upper, deck abaft the mainmast.

quar'ter-ly (-tẽr-lĭ), *adv.* By quarters; once in a quarter of a year. — *a.* **1.** Containing, or consisting of, a quarter. **2.** Recurring during, or at the end of, each quarter. — *n.; pl.* -LIES (-lĭz). A periodical work published quarterly.

quar'ter-mas'ter (-más'tẽr), *n.* **1.** *Mil.* A commissioned officer charged with providing quarters, clothing, etc., for troops. **2.** *Naut.* A petty officer who attends the helm, etc.

quar'tern (-tẽrn), *n.* A fourth; quarter; as, a fourth of a pint; a gill.

quar'ter-saw', *v. t.* To saw (a log) into quarters and then into lumber, so as to show the grain to advantage, etc.

quar'ter-staff' (-tẽr-stàf'), *n.; pl.* -STAVES (-stāvz'; -stävz'). A long staff formerly used as a weapon.

quar-tet' (kwôr-tĕt'), *n.* **1.** *Music.* **a** A composition in four parts, each for a single performer. **b** The set of four performers of such music. **2.** A group of four.

quar'to (kwôr'tō), *a.* Having four leaves (eight pages) to the sheet; of the size of a quarto. — *n.; pl.* -TOS (-tōz). A book of a nearly square form, commonly 9½ by 12 inches. Abbr. 4*to* or 4°.

quartz (kwôrts), *n.* A form of silica occurring in hexagonal crystals, also in crystalline masses, etc., and in granite, sand, etc.

quash (kwŏsh), *v. t.* *Law.* To abate or annul.

quash, *v. t.* To suppress; crush out; quell.

qua'si (kwā'sī). As if; as though; in a manner.

quas'si-a (kwŏsh'ĭ-á), *n.* A bitter tonic drug from the wood of any of several tropical American trees.

quat'rain (kwŏt'rān), *n.* A stanza of four lines, usually riming alternately.

qua'ver (kwā'vẽr), *v. i.* To tremble; shake; esp., to cause the voice to vibrate. — *v. t.* To utter with quavers; esp., to sing with trills or quavers. — *n.* A shake, or rapid and tremulous vibration, as of the voice.

quay (kē), *n.* A solid landing place, as of masonry, made at the side of a navigable body of water.

quea'sy (kwē'zĭ), *a.* [3] Inclined to nausea.

queen (kwēn), *n.* **1.** The wife of a king. **2.** A female monarch. **3.** A woman eminent in power or attractions; — also used of cities, countries, etc. **4.** The fully developed female of social bees, ants, etc., whose function is reproduction. **5.** The most powerful piece in chess. **6.** A playing card bearing the picture of a queen.

queen'ly (kwēn'lĭ), *a.* [3] Like, becoming, or suitable to, a queen. — *adv.* In a queenly manner.

queen mother. A queen dowager who is mother of the reigning king or queen.

queer (kwēr), *a.* [3] **1.** Differing in some odd way from the ordinary; singular; peculiar. **2.** Suspi-

cious; questionable. *Colloq.* **3.** Qualmish; faint.
— **queer'ly**, *adv.* [8] — **queer'ness**, *n.* [8].

quell (kwĕl), *v. t.* **1.** To overpower; subdue; suppress. **2.** To quiet; allay; calm. — **-er**, *n.* [8].

quench (kwĕnch), *v. t.* **1.** To extinguish; make an end of, **2.** To cool suddenly, as heated metal. — **-a-ble**, *a.* [8] — **-er**, *n.* [8] — **-less**, *a.* [8].

quer'ist (kwē'rĭst), *n.* One who queries.

quer'u-lous (kwĕr'ṓṓ-lŭs), *a.* [4] **1.** Apt to find fault; habitually complaining. **2.** Fretful; whining. — **quer'u-lous-ly**, *adv.* — **-ness**, *n.*

que'ry (kwē'rĭ), *n.* ; *pl.* -RIES (-rĭz). **1.** A question; an inquiry. **2.** An interrogation point [?]. — *v. t. & i.* [2] To inquire into; ask; question.

quest (kwĕst), *n.* A seeking; search; adventure; in medieval romance, a knightly expedition, as that in search of the Holy Grail (see GRAIL); also, the knights engaged in the expedition.

ques'tion (kwĕs'chŭn), *n.* **1.** Act of asking; interrogation; inquiry. **2.** Discussion; debate; hence, objection; doubt. **3.** Investigation, esp. a judicial one. **4.** That which is asked; query. **5.** Hence, a subject of or for investigation or debate. — *v. i.* To ask questions; inquire. — *v. t.* **1.** To examine by queries. **2.** To doubt. **3.** To call in question; dispute. — **ques'tion-er**, *n.* [8].

ques'tion-a-ble (-á-b'l), *a.* [4] Liable to be called in question; problematical. — **-a-bly**, *adv.*

ques'tion-naire' (-âr'), *n.* A set of questions for submission to a number of persons, as in giving instruction to pupils, in investigations, etc.

queue (kū), *n.* A pigtail. = 1st CUE, *n.*, 1.

quib'ble (kwĭb'l), *n.* A shift or turn from the point in question; an evasion; equivocation. — *v. i.* [1] To evade the point in question; equivocate.

quick (kwĭk), *a.* [3] **1.** Living; animate. *Archaic.* **2.** Characterized by life or animation. **3.** Speedy; hasty. **4.** Impatient; passionate. **5.** Taking place rapidly or briefly. **6.** Sensitive; ready. — *adv.* Quickly. — *n.* The life; a vital part; the sensitive living flesh; part of a finger or toe to which the nail is attached.

quick'en (-'n), *v. t.* **1.** To make alive; revive; excite; stimulate. **2.** To hasten; accelerate. — *v. i.* **1.** To come to life. **2.** To move with increased rapidity. — **quick'en-er**, *n.* [8].

quick'lime' (-līm'), *n.* Unslaked lime. See LIME.

quick'ly, *adv.* In a quick manner; speedily.

quick'ness, *n.* Quality or state of being quick.

quick'sand' (-sănd'), *n.* Sand easily yielding to pressure; esp., a mass of loose sand mixed with water into which a person or object readily sinks.

quick'set' (-sĕt'), *n.* **1.** A cutting, esp. when set for a hedge; hawthorn. **2.** A hedge or thicket.

quick'sil'ver (-sĭl'vẽr), *n.* Mercury, the metal.

quick'step' (-stĕp'), *n.* A spirited march, esp. one in military quick time.

quid (kwĭd), *n.* A piece suitable to be chewed; cud.

quid'di-ty (kwĭd'ĭ-tĭ), *n.* ; *pl.* -TIES (-tĭz). **1.** The essence of a thing. **2.** A trifling nicety; quibble.

quid'nunc' (-nŭŋk'), *n.* One curious to know everything going on; a gossip.

qui-es'cence (kwī-ĕs'ĕns), *n.* State or quality of being quiescent.

qui-es'cent (-ĕnt), *a.* [4] At rest; still; dormant. — **qui-es'cent-ly**, *adv.* [8].

qui'et (kwī'ĕt), *a.* [3] **1.** In a state of rest or calm; still; hushed. **2.** Not excited or anxious; calm; placid. **3.** Not turbulent; gentle. **4.** Not showy; modest. **5.** Enjoyed in peace and relaxation. — *n.* State or quality of being quiet, or in repose; stillness; peace. — *v. t.* To stop motion in; still; silence; calm. — *v. i.* To become still; — often with *down.* — **qui'et-er** (kwī'ĕt-ẽr), *n.* [8] — **qui'et-ly**, *adv.* [8] — **qui'et-ness**, *n.* [8].

qui'e-tude (kwī'ē-tūd), *n.* Repose; tranquillity.

qui-e'tus (kwī-ē'tŭs), *n.* Final acquittance, as from debt or obligation; hence, death.

quill (kwĭl), *n.* **1.** A large stiff feather; also, the hollow barrel or tube of a feather. **2.** A pen for writing made from a quill. **3.** A spine of the hedgehog or porcupine.

quilt (kwĭlt), *n.* **1.** A bed coverlet of two thicknesses of material with a filling of wool, cotton, etc. **2.** Anything quilted or like a quilt. — *v. t.* **1.** To fill or wad like a quilt. **2.** To stitch or sew in layers, usually with some soft, thick substance between. — *v. i.* To make quilted work. — **quilt'er**, *n.* [8].

quince (kwĭns), *n.* The applelike fruit of a tree or shrub of the apple family; also, the tree.

qui'nine (kwī'nīn; kwĭ-nēn'), *n.* A bitter alkaloid got from the bark of species of cinchona.

quin-quen'ni-al (kwĭn-kwĕn'ĭ-ăl), *a.* Occurring once in five years, or at the end of every five years; also, lasting five years. — *n.* A quinquennial event.

quin'sy (kwĭn'zĭ), *n.* Suppurative tonsillitis.

quin'tal (-tăl), *n.* A hundredweight.

quin-tes'sence (kwĭn-tĕs'ĕns), *n.* Pure or concentrated essence; hence, the most perfect representative of certain things, persons, qualities, etc.

quin-tet' (kwĭn-tĕt'), *n.* **1.** *Music.* A composition for five voices or instruments; also, the set of five performers. **2.** Any set of five.

quin'tu-ple (-tŭ-p'l), *a.* Multiplied by five. — *v. t. & i.* [1] To make, or to become, five times as much.

quip (kwĭp), *n.* **1.** A smart, sarcastic turn or jest; gibe; witty sally. **2.** A quibble. **3.** A droll or eccentric action; also, something odd or strange.

quire (kwīr), *n.* A collection of 24 (sometimes 25) sheets of paper of the same size and quality.

Quir'i-nal (kwīr'ĭ-năl; kwĭ-rī'năl), *n.* One of the seven hills of Rome. On it is the residence of the ruling house of Italy. Hence, fig., the secular government of Italy, as distinguished from the "Vatican," or papal government. — **Quir'i-nal**, *a.*

quirk (kwûrk), *n.* **1.** A sudden turn, twist, or curve, as of the pen in writing; a flourish. **2.** A quibble; equivocation. **3.** A quip; a conceit.

quirt (kwûrt), *n.* A kind of riding whip.

quit (kwĭt), *v. t.* ; *pret. & p. p.* QUIT or QUIT'TED; *p. pr. & vb. n.* QUIT'TING. **1.** To discharge, as an obligation; requite; repay. **2.** To conduct; acquit; — used reflexively. *Archaic.* **3.** To have done with; stop; leave; forsake; yield. — *v. i.* **1.** To go away; also, to stop. — *a.* Released from obligation.

quit'claim' (kwĭt'klām'), *n.* *Law.* A release or relinquishment of a claim; a deed of release.

quite (kwīt), *adv.* **1.** Completely; wholly; entirely. **2.** Positively; really; also, loosely, to a considerable extent or degree; as, it is *quite* near.

quits (kwĭts), *a.* Even or equal (with another) by having returned or repaid something.

quit′tance (kwĭt′ăns), *n.* **1.** Discharge from a debt or an obligation. **2.** Recompense; requital.

quit′ter (-ẽr), *n.* One that quits, or shirks, or gives up tamely; hence, a coward.

quiv′er (kwĭv′ẽr), *v. i.* To shake or move with slight and tremulous motion; tremble; shiver.—*n.* Act, fact, or state of quivering; a tremor.

quiv′er, *n.* A sheath for arrows.— **-ered** (-ẽrd), *a.*

‖**qui vive′** (kē vēv′). [F.] The challenge of a French sentinel; — used like the English : "Who goes there?" — **to be on the qui vive**, to be on the alert.

quix-ot′ic (kwĭk-sŏt′ĭk), *a.* [4] Romantic to extravagance; absurdly chivalric. — **quix-ot′i-cal-ly** (-ĭ-kăl-ĭ), *adv.* [8]. [or thought.]

quix′ot-ism (kwĭk′sŏt-ĭz′m), *n.* Quixotic action

quiz (kwĭz), *n.; pl.* QUIZZES (-ĕz). **1.** One who quizzes others. **2.** A hoax; jest. **3.** A quizzing. — *v. t.;* QUIZZED (kwĭzd); QUIZ′ZING. **1.** To ridicule; banter; question closely. **2.** To examine or coach by questions. *U. S.* — **quiz′zer** (-ẽr), *n.*

quiz′zi-cal (-ĭ-kăl), *a.* [4] Comical; odd; queer. — **quiz′zi-cal-ly**, *adv.* [8].

quoin (koin; kwoin), *n.* **1.** *Arch.* Originally, a solid exterior angle; now, one of the selected pieces of material for a corner. **2.** A wedgelike piece.

quoit (kwoit; koit), *n.* **1.** A flattened ring-shaped piece of iron to be pitched at an object in play. **2.** *pl.* The game so played.

quon′dam (kwŏn′dăm), *a.* Former; sometime.

quo′rum (kwō′rŭm), *n.* Such a number of members of any body as is, when duly assembled, legally competent to transact business.

quo′ta (kwō′tȧ), *n.; pl.* -TAS (-tȧz). A (certain) proportional part or share.

quot′a-ble (kwōt′ȧ-b′l), *a.* [4] Capable or worthy of being quoted.

quo-ta′tion (kwō-tā′shŭn), *n.* **1.** Act of quoting, or citing. **2.** That which is quoted, or cited. **3.** *Commerce.* The naming of the current price of any security or commodity; also, the price named.

quotation mark. A mark used to indicate the beginning or end of a quotation. In general English usage two inverted commas ["] are used at the beginning, and two apostrophes ["] at the end, but a quotation within a quotation is generally set off by single marks, as, "The youth replies, 'I will!'"

quote (kwōt), *v. t.* [1] **1.** To name, repeat, or adduce, as a passage from an author, by way of authority or illustration; cite. **2.** To cite a passage from; cite. **3.** *Commerce.* To name the current price of. — **quot′er** (-ẽr), *n.* [8].

quoth (kwōth), *v. t.* Said; spoke; uttered; — used in the first and third persons in the preterit, and always followed by its nominative. *Archaic.*

quo′tient (kwō′shĕnt), *n.* *Arith.* The number resulting from the division of one number by another.

R

rab′bet (răb′ĕt), *n.* A groove cut in the edge or face of a timber, etc., to receive another member, as a panel.— *v. t.* **1.** To cut a rabbet in. **2.** To unite the edges of, as boards, in a rabbet joint.

rab′bi (răb′ī; -ĭ), *n.; pl.* -BIS or -BIES (ĭz; -ĭz). Master; — a Jewish title for a doctor of the law. — **rab-bin′ic** (ră-bĭn′ĭk), **-bin′i-cal** (-ĭ-kăl), *a.*

rab′bit (răb′ĭt), *n.* A small burrowing animal of the hare family, of which the wild form is grayish brown in color. — *v. i.* To hunt or kill rabbits.

rab′ble (răb′′l), *n.* A tumultuous crowd; a mob.

rab′id (răb′ĭd), *a.* [4] **1.** Furious; raging. **2.** Extreme in opinion; as, a *rabid* partisan. **3.** Affected with rabies; mad. — **-ly**, *adv.* [8]. — **-ness**, *n.*

ra′bi-es (rā′bĭ-ēz), *n.* Hydrophobia.

rac-coon′ (ră-kōōn′), *n.* A small, flesh-eating animal of North America, living largely in trees and active at night. It is chiefly gray, with a bushy, ringed tail.

race (rās), *n.* **1.** Career; course of life. **2.** A contest of speed. **3.** A strong or rapid current of water, or its channel. — *v. i.* **1.** To go swiftly, esp. in competition. **2.** To run too fast under a diminished load, as an engine. — *v. t.* **1.** To cause to contend in a race. **2.** To run a race with.

race, *n.* **1.** The descendants of the same ancestor; a family, tribe, or people; breed; as, the human *race*. **2.** State of being one of a particular race.

ra-ceme′ (rȧ-sēm′; rā-), *n.* *Bot.* A flower cluster with flowers attached at intervals to an elongated axis by slender stalks, as in the currant. — **rac′e-mose** (răs′ē-mōs), *a.*

rac′er (rās′ẽr), *n.* One that races.

ra′cial (rā′shăl), *a.* Of or pert. to a race.— **-ly**, *adv.*

rac′i-ly (rās′ĭ-lĭ), *adv.* In a racy manner or style.

rac′i-ness (-nĕs), *n.* Fact or quality of being racy.

rack (răk), *v. i.* To go with a rack; pace; — said of a horse.— *n.* A certain gait of a horse; as : a = PACE, *n.*, 4. **b** = SINGLE-FOOT. — **rack′er**, *n.* [8].

rack, *n.* Wreck. *Rare,* except in *rack and ruin.*

rack, *n.* Thin, flying, broken clouds.

rack, *n.* **1.** A framework to hold fodder for cattle, etc. **2.** A framework on or in which articles are kept or displayed. **3.** A machine for torturing by stretching the body. **4.** A bar with teeth on one face for gearing with those of a pinion, worm, etc. — *v. t.* **1.** To stretch or strain; stretch on the rack (sense 3). **2.** To torment; torture.

Rack and Pinion.

rack′et (răk′ĕt), *n.* **1.** A kind of light bat having a netting stretched in a frame. **2.** *pl.* A game played with ball and rackets in a four-walled court.

rack′et, *n.* **1.** Confused, clattering noise; din; noisy talk or sport. **2.** A scheme for extorting money under veiled threat of damage, etc. *Slang.* — **rack′et-eer′** (răk′ĕt-ēr′), *n. & v. i.*

rac′quet (răk′ĕt). Var. of RACKET, a bat.

rac′y (rās′ĭ), *a.* [3] **1.** Having a strong flavor indicating origin, as a wine. **2.** Vigorous or spirited; as, a *racy* narrative.

ra′di-al (rā′dĭ-ăl), *a.* Of or pert. to a radius or ray; consisting of or like radii or rays. — **-ly**, *adv.* [8].

ra′di-ance (-ăns), **ra′di-an-cy** (-ăn-sĭ), *n.* State or quality of being radiant; vivid brightness.

ra′di-ant (rā′dĭ-ănt), a. [4] **1.** Emitting rays of light; beaming; as, the *radiant* sun. **2.** Beaming with joy, hope, or the like; as, a *radiant* face. **3.** *Physics.* Emitted or transmitted by radiation; as, *radiant* energy; *radiant* heat.

ra′di-ate (-āt), v. i. [1.] **1.** To emit rays; shine. **2.** To issue in or as in rays, or direct lines, as heat. — v. t. To emit in rays, as heat.

ra′di-a′tion (-ā′shŭn), n. **1.** Act or process of radiating. **2.** That which is radiated; radiant energy.

ra′di-a′tor (-ā′tēr), n. One that radiates; as: **a** A device for heating the surrounding air by radiation. **b** A device for cooling a contained liquid, as water, by radiation; as, the *radiator* of an automobile.

rad′i-cal (răd′ĭ-kăl), a. [4] **1.** Of or pertaining to the root; hence, thoroughgoing; extreme. **2.** *Math.* Of or pertaining to a root. **3.** [*Often cap.*] Of or pertaining to radicals in politics. — **radical sign**, *Math.*, the sign √, put before an expression to denote that its root is to be extracted. — n. **1.** A root, or radical part. **2.** [*Often cap.*] In politics, one who advocates radical changes, esp. for equalizing social conditions. **4.** *Alg.* A radical expression; the radical sign. — **-ly**, *adv.* [8] — **ness**, n. [8].

rad′i-cal-ism (-ĭz′m), n. The doctrines or principles of radicals; also, radical quality.

ra′di-i, n., *pl.* of RADIUS.

ra′di-o (rā′dĭ-ō), a. Of or pertaining to, employing, or operated by, radiant energy, especially that of electric waves; hence, pertaining to, or employed in, radiotelegraphy or radiotelephony. — n.; *pl.* -DIOS (-ōz). A radiotelegraph or radiotelephone, or a radiotelegram. *Colloq.*

ra′di-o-ac′tive (rā′dĭ-ō-ăk′tĭv), a. [4] Spontaneously emitting rays consisting (at least in part) of material particles, as does radium. — **ra′di-o-ac-tiv′i-ty**, n.

ra′di-o-graph (rā′dĭ-ō-gráf) n. A picture produced by Röntgen rays. — v. t. To make a radiograph of. — **ra′di-og′ra-phy** (-ŏg′rá-fĭ), n.

Radiograph.

ra′di-o-tel′e-gram (rā′dĭ-ō-tĕl′ē-grăm), n. A message transmitted by radiotelegraph.

ra′di-o-tel′e-graph (-gráf), n. A wireless telegraph. — **ra′di-o-te-leg′ra-phy**, n. — **graph′ic**, a.

ra′di-o-tel′e-phone (-fōn), n. Wireless telephone. — **-te-leph′o-ny** (-tĕ-lĕf′ō-nĭ), n.

rad′ish (răd′ĭsh), n. The spicy root of a common garden plant; also, the plant.

ra′di-um (rā′dĭ-ŭm), n. An intensely radioactive metal found in minute quantities in pitchblende.

ŗa′di-us (rā′dĭ-ŭs), n.; *pl.* -DII (-ī). **1.** *Geom.* A right line extending from the center of a circle or sphere to the circumference or surface. **2.** The thicker and shorter bone of the forearm.

raf′fi-a (răf′ĭ-ȧ), n. A kind of palm fiber.

raf′fle (răf′′l), n. A kind of lottery. — v. i. [1] To engage in a raffle. — v. t. To dispose of by means of a raffle. — **raf′fler** (-lēr), n. [8].

raft (ràft), n. A float of logs, etc., fastened together. — v. t. To transport on or as a raft.

raft′er (ràf′tēr), n. A sloping timber of a roof.

rag (răg), n. **1.** A waste piece of cloth; shred; tatter. **2.** [*Usually in pl.*] Mean or tattered attire.

rag′a-muf′fin (răg′ȧ-mŭf′ĭn), n. A fellow, esp. a disreputable fellow, who wears ragged clothing.

rage (rāj), n. **1.** Violent passion or feeling; anger; fury; frenzy. **2.** The subject of eager desire. **3.** Enthusiasm, esp. at its height. — v. i. **1.** To be furious with anger. **2.** To act with fury. **3.** To prevail without restraint, as a violent disease.

rag′ged (răg′ĕd), a. [3] **1.** Rough; jagged. **2.** Unfinished; irregular. **3.** Worn into tatters. **4.** Wearing ragged clothes. — **-ly**, *adv.* — **-ness**, n.

rag′man (-măn), n. A man who deals in rags.

ra-gout′ (rȧ-gōō′), n. A highly seasoned stew.

rag′time′ (răg′tīm′), n. Syncopated time, as in negro melodies, or music in this time. *Colloq.*

raid (rād), n. **1.** A sudden invasion, esp. by mounted men. **2.** An attack or invasion, to make arrests, seize property, or plunder. *Colloq. U. S.* — v. t. To make a raid on or into. — **raid′er**, n. [8].

rail (rāl), n. Any of certain wading birds related to the cranes, but smaller, prized as game birds.

rail (rāl), v. i. To use insolent and reproachful language; scoff; — with *at* or *against*.

rail (rāl), n. **1.** A bar of timber or metal extending from one support to another as a guard or barrier, or as a support. **2.** A fence; a railing **3.** A bar, as of steel, of any of various forms, forming a track for wheeled vehicles, etc. — v. t. To provide with, or inclose within, rails or railing.

rail′ing, n. **1.** A barrier consisting of rails and supports. **2.** Rails. [cule; banter.

rail′ler-y (răl′ēr-ĭ; răl′-), n. Good-natured ridi-

rail′road (rāl′rōd′), n. **1.** A permanent road or way having a line or lines of rails providing a track for cars; such a road or line together with the lands, buildings, rolling stock, etc., pertaining thereto. — v. t. **1.** To transport by railroad. *U. S.* **2.** To send or put through rapidly. *Colloq., U. S.*

rail′way′ (-wā′), n. **1.** A railroad. **2.** Any line of rails providing a runway for wheels.

rai′ment (rā′mĕnt), n. Clothing; garments.

rain (rān), n. **1.** Water falling in drops from the clouds. **2.** A shower or continued fall of, or as of, rain. — v. i. **1.** To fall as or like rain. **2.** To send down rain. — v. t. **1.** To pour down. **2.** To yield or shed copiously.

rain′bow′ (rān′bō′), n. A bow or arc exhibiting the several colors of the spectrum, and formed opposite the sun by refraction and reflection of the sun's rays in drops of rain, or in spray, mist, etc.

rain′fall′ (-fôl′), n. A fall or descent of rain; amount of water fal ing in rain, snow, etc.

rain′y (rān′ĭ), a. [3] Abounding with rain; wet; showery. — **rain′i-ness** (-ĭ-nĕs), n. [8].

raise (rāz), v. t. [1] **1.** To cause to rise up; awaken; arouse. **2.** To cause to arise, grow up, or come into being, as: **a** To build up; erect. **b** To bring to get together; collect. **c** To breed; grow. **d** To utter. **3.** To heighten; intensify. **4.** To cause to rise or become light, as bread. **5.** To end, as if by lifting away, as a siege. — **rais′er**, n. [8].

Charlotte

rai′sin (rā′z′n), *n.* A dried grape of a special type.

ra′jah, ra′ja (rä′jà), *n.* In India, originally, a prince or king ; later, also, a chief or dignitary.

rake (rāk), *v. i.* [1] To incline from a perpendicular. — *n.* Inclination from the perpendicular.

rake, *n.* An implement, with projecting pegs or prongs, for gathering hay, spreading earth, etc. — *v. t.* [1] **1.** To collect, scrape, etc., with or as with a rake. **2.** To collect; scrape together. **3.** To search through; ransack. **4.** *Mil.* To sweep with shot ; esp., to fire along the length of.

rake, *n.* A dissolute man ; debauchee ; roué.

rak′ish (rāk′ĭsh), *a.* [4] Like a rake, or roué, in character, looks, or the like.

rak′ish, *a.* **1.** *Naut.* Having a smart appearance indicative of speed. **2.** Showy ; dashing. — **rak′ish-ly,** *adv.* — **rak′ish-ness,** *n.*

ral′ly (răl′ĭ), *v. t.* [2] **1.** To collect and bring to order, as troops in confusion ; reunite. **2.** To revive ; rouse. — *v. i.* **1.** To assemble in order ; unite in action ; also, to renew order or united effort. **2.** To revive ; recover strength. — *n.* ; *pl.* -LIES (-ĭz). **1.** Act or process of rallying. **2.** A mass meeting. *Colloq., U. S.*

ral′ly, *v. t.* To attack with raillery ; banter.

ram (răm), *n.* **1.** A male sheep. **2.** An engine of war used for battering. — *v. t. ;* RAMMED (rămd) ; RAM′MING. **1.** To butt or strike against violently. **2.** To fill by pounding or driving.

ram′ble (răm′b′l), *n.* An excursion or stroll merely for recreation. — *v. i.* [1] **1.** To go from place to place without definite object. **2.** To talk or write discursively. **3.** To extend or grow at random. — **-bler,** *n.* [8] — **-bling,** *a. & n.*

ram′i-fi-ca′tion (-ĭ-fĭ-kā′shŭn), *n.* **1.** Act or process of ramifying. **2.** A small branch or offshoot. **3.** A division ; subordinate part.

ram′i-fy (răm′ĭ-fī), *v. t. & i.* [2] To divide or spread out into branches or ramifications.

ram′mer (răm′ẽr), *n.* One that rams or drives.

ra′mose (rā′mōs ; rà-mōs′), *a.* Having branches.

ra′mous (rā′mŭs), *a.* **1.** Ramose. **2.** Pertaining to or like branches.

ramp (rămp), *v. i.* **1.** To stand or advance with forelegs or arms raised as if in menace ; to rage. **2.** To rush about wildly. — *n.* Act of ramping.

ramp′age (răm′pāj ; răm′pāj′), *n.* Violent or riotous behavior ; a state of excitement or passion.

ram-pa′geous (răm-pā′jŭs), *a.* Unruly ; rampant.

ramp′an-cy (răm′păn-sĭ), *n.* Quality or state of being rampant ; exuberance ; extravagance.

ram′pant (-pănt), *a.* [4] **1.** Ramping ; rearing up with forelegs or paws extended. **2.** Threatening, extravagant, or unrestrained in action, etc. **3.** Exuberant ; unchecked. — **-ly,** *adv.* [8].

ram′part (răm′pärt), *n.* **1.** *Fort.* A broad embankment round a place, on which the parapet is raised. **2.** A defense or bulwark.

ram′rod′ (-rŏd′), *n.* The rod used in ramming home the charge in a muzzle-loading firearm.

ram′shack-le (-shăk–′l), *a.* [4] Rickety.

ran (răn), *pret. & obs. p. p.* of RUN.

ranch (rănch), *n.* **1.** An establishment, with its estate, for the grazing and rearing of horses, cattle, or sheep. **2.** A large farm.

ranch′er (rănch′ẽr), **ran-che′ro** (rän-chā′rō), *n. ;*

pl. -ROS (-rōz). A herdsman employed on a ranch; also, sometimes, the owner.

ranch′man (rănch′măn), *n.* A rancher.

ran′cho (rän′chō), *n. ; pl.* -CHOS (-chōz). A ranch. *Southwestern U. S.*

ran′cid (răn′sĭd), *a.* [4] Having a rank smell or taste, as of old oil. — **ran′cid-ness,** *n.* [8].

ran-cid′i-ty (răn-sĭd′ĭ-tĭ), *n.* Quality or state of being rancid. [malice.]

ran′cor (răn′kẽr), *n.* [5] Deep-seated enmity or [malice.]

ran′cor-ous (-ŭs), *a.* [4] Full of rancor.

ran′dom (răn′dŭm), *n.* A haphazard course or progress ; — chiefly in : **at random,** without definite direction or method ; aimlessly. — *a.* [4] Going by chance ; left to chance ; haphazard ; aimless.

rang (răng), *pret.* of RING, *v. t. & i.*

range (rānj), *v. t.* [1] **1.** To set in a row or rows. **2.** To place (as one's self) among others in a line ; hence, to espouse a cause, etc. **3.** To dispose or arrange systematically ; classify. **4.** To rove over, through, or along. — *v. i.* **1.** To rove at large ; wander ; roam, as cattle. **2.** To have, or extend in, a certain direction ; trend ; run. — *n.* **1.** A series of things in a line. **2.** A line of direction. **3.** A region where cattle may pasture. **4.** Extent or space taken in or covered ; reach ; scope. **5.** A form of cooking stove. **6.** In the public land system, a row of townships. *U. S.* **7.** The region throughout which a plant or animal naturally lives. **8.** a The distance to which a projectile is, or may be, propelled. Also, distance of the target from the gun. **b** A place where shooting is practiced.

rang′er (rān′jẽr), *n.* **1.** The keeper of a royal park or forest. *Eng.* **2.** One that ranges ; as : **a** A rover ; wanderer. **b** One of a body of mounted troops. **c** In America, a warden who patrols tracts of forest.

rang′y (rān′jĭ), *a.* [3] Adapted for ranging ; long-limbed and long-bodied ; — chiefly of animals.

rank (răngk), *a.* [3] **1.** Luxuriant or coarse in growth. **2.** Producing luxuriantly ; very (or too) rich. **3.** Rancid. **4.** Extreme ; gross.

rank, *n.* **1.** A row ; line ; range ; series ; tier. **2.** *Mil.* **a** A line of soldiers ranged side by side ;— opposed to *file.* **b** *pl.* An army ; the forces. **c** *pl.* The privates as distinguished from officers. **3.** A social class ; an order. **4.** Grade of official standing. **5.** Degree of excellence ; status ; grade. **6.** Eminence ; distinction. — *v. t.* **1.** To arrange in a line or row or in ranks; set in a regular formation. **2.** To classify. **3.** To outrank. *U. S.* — *v. i.* To be ranged ; have a certain grade, etc.

ran′kle (răng′k′l), *v. i.* [1] To fester ; also, to produce a festering or inflamed effect ; — esp. fig.

rank′ly (răngk′lĭ), *adv.* In a rank manner.

rank′ness, *n.* Quality of being rank.

ran′sack (răn′săk), *v. t.* To search thoroughly.

ran′som (-sŭm), *n.* Redemption of a captive by paying a price ; the price paid or demanded. — *v. t.* **1.** To redeem from captivity by paying a price. **2.** To deliver ; redeem. — **ran′som-er** (-ẽr), *n.*

rant (rănt), *v. i.* To be noisy and bombastic in talk or declamation. — *n.* Ranting speech; bombast. — **rant′er** (răn′tẽr), *n.* [8] — **rant′ing-ly,** *adv.* [8].

rap (răp), *v. t. & i. ;* RAPPED (răpt) ; RAP′PING. **1.** To strike quickly and smartly. **2.** To utter sharply ; — with *out.* — *n.* A quick, smart blow.

---

chair; go; sing, ink; then, thin; nature, verdure; yet; zh = z in azure. Numbers refer to §§ in the Special Notes which, with Abbreviations, Signs, etc., precede the Vocabulary.

ra-pa′cious (rá-pā′shŭs), a. [4] **1.** Given to plunder; seizing by force; predacious. **2.** Avaricious; grasping. — **-ly**, adv. [8] — **-ness**, n. [8].

ra-pac′i-ty (rá-pás′ĭ-tĭ), n. Rapaciousness.

rape (rāp), n. A plant allied to the cabbage and turnip, grown for seeds and herbage.

rape, n. **1.** A seizing and carrying away by force; robbery. **2.** Violation by force.

rap′id (răp′ĭd), a. [4] **1.** Very swift. **2.** Advancing with speed; done quickly. **3.** Quick in execution; as, a rapid penman. — n. A part of a river where the current flows swiftly, but without waterfall; — usually in pl. — **rap′id-ly**, adv. [8].

ra-pid′i-ty (rá-pĭd′ĭ-tĭ), n. Rapid quality or state.

ra′pi-er (rā′pĭ-ẽr), n. A straight two-edged sword with narrow blade, chiefly for thrusting.

rap′ine (răp′ĭn), n. A plundering; spoliation.

rap-scal′lion (răp-skăl′yŭn), n. A rascal.

rapt (răpt), p. a. [4] **1.** Seized and transported up or away. **2.** Transported with delight, etc.; enraptured. **3.** Deeply engrossed, as in meditation.

rap′ture (răp′tụr), n. **1.** Transport; ecstasy. **2.** An expression of ecstasy; a rhapsody.

rap′tur-ous (-tụr-ŭs), a. [4] Feeling or expressing rapture; ecstatic. — **rap′tur-ous-ly**, adv. [8].

rare (râr), a. [3] Not thoroughly cooked; underdone; — used of meat.

rare, a. [3] **1.** Not dense; tenuous. **2.** Not frequent; unusual. **3.** Uncommon in nature; unusually excellent.

rar′e-fac′tion (răr′ē-făk′shŭn; râr′ē-), n. Act or process of rarefying; state of being rarefied.

rar′e-fy (răr′ē-fī; râr′-), v. t. & i. [2] To make or become rare, or less dense; — opposed to condense.

rare′ly (râr′lĭ), adv. **1.** Seldom; not often. **2.** Finely; with rare skill. **3.** In an exceptional degree.

rare′ness, n. State or quality of being rare.

rar′i-ty (răr′ĭ-tĭ; râr′-), n.; pl. -TIES (-tĭz). **1.** Quality, state, or fact of being rare; as: **a** Rareness; thinness. **b** Uncommonness; infrequency; hence, unusual excellence. **2.** That which is rare.

ras′cal (răs′kăl), n. A mean, trickish fellow; a rogue; knave; — often jocular.

ras-cal′i-ty (răs-kăl′ĭ-tĭ), n.; pl. -TIES (-tĭz). The character or action of a rascal; knavery.

ras′cal-ly (răs′kăl-ĭ), a. [4] Of, pertaining to, or characteristic of, a rascal; mean; base.

rash (răsh), n. A fine eruption on the body.

rash, a. [3] **1.** Overhasty in counsel or action; precipitate; reckless; — opp. to prudent. **2.** Due to too much haste or too little reflection; as, a rash word.

rash′er, n. A thin slice of bacon or ham.

rash′ly, adv. In a rash manner.

rash′ness, n. Quality of being rash.

rasp (răsp), v. t. **1.** To rub or file with something rough, as a rasp. **2.** Fig.: To grate harshly on; irritate. — v. i. To grate or scrape. — n. A kind of coarse file with raised points instead of lines.

rasp′ber-ry (răz′bĕr-ĭ), n.; pl. -RIES (-ĭz). The fruit of any of various brambles; also, the plant bearing it.

rat (răt), n. Any of certain rodents allied to the mice, but larger. — v. i.; RAT′TED (-ĕd); -TING. To catch or hunt rats.

rat′a-ble (rāt′á-b'l), a. Capable of being rated, or appraised.

ratch′et (răch′ĕt), n. **1.** A pawl, click, or detent, to act on a ratchet wheel. **2.** A mechanism composed of ratchet wheel and pawl.

ratchet wheel. Mach. A wheel having teeth with which a reciprocating pawl engages.

rate (rāt), v. t. & i. [1] To chide; scold vehemently.

rate, n. **1.** Quantity, amount, or degree of a thing measured per unit of something else; proportional amount. **2.** A fixed ratio; proportion; also, a charge or price fixed by a ratio, scale, or standard. **3.** Relative condition or quality; rank; class; kind. **4.** A tax on property; — usually in pl. — v. t. **1.** To appraise; value. **2.** To consider; regard. **3.** To settle the relative rank, position, class, or quality of. — v. i. To be classed; have rank.

a Ratchet Wheel; b Reciprocating Lever; c Click, Pawl, or Ratchet, for communicating motion; d Pawl, for preventing backward motion.

rath′er (răth′ẽr), adv. **1.** More properly, reasonably, or truly; hence, instead. **2.** More than not; somewhat. **3.** More readily or willingly.

rat′i-fi-ca′tion (răt′ĭ-fĭ-kā′shŭn), n. Act of ratifying; state of being ratified.

rat′i-fy (răt′ĭ-fī), v. t. [2] To approve and sanction; confirm; establish. — **-fi′er** (-fī′ẽr), n. [8].

rat′ing (rāt′ĭng), p. pr. & vb. n. of RATE. Hence: n. Classification according to grade; rank; class.

ra′ti-o (rā′shĭ-ō;rā′shō), n. Fixed relation of number, quantity, or degree; rate; proportion; as, in the ratio of 2 to 3.

ra′tion (rā′shŭn), n. An allowance of provisions, esp. daily to a soldier or a sailor.

ra′tion-al (răsh′ŭn-ăl), a. [4] **1.** Having reason or understanding; reasoning. **2.** Of or pert. to reason; as, the rational faculty. **3.** Agreeable to reason; sensible; as, rational conduct.

ra′tion-al-ism (răsh′ŭn-ăl-ĭz′m), n. The doctrine or system of those who base their religious opinions on reason, rather than revelation. — **-al-ist**, n.

ra′tion-al-is′tic (-ĭs′tĭk), a. Characterized by, or inclined to, rationalism.

ra′tion-al′i-ty (-ăl′ĭ-tĭ), n.; pl. -TIES (-tĭz). Quality or state of being rational; reasonableness.

ra′tion-al-ly, adv. In a rational manner.

rat′line, rat′lin (răt′lĭn), n. Naut. One of the small cross ropes attached to the shrouds to serve as steps. [arsenic.]

rats′bane (răts′bān′), n. Rat poison; esp., white

rat-tan′ (ră-tăn′), n. **1. a** Any of certain climbing palms with remarkably long stems. **b** A portion of one of these stems. **2.** A rattan cane or switch.

rat′ter (răt′ẽr), n. One that catches rats, esp. a dog.

rat′tle (răt′'l), v. i. [1] **1.** To make a quick succession of sharp noises; clatter. **2.** To talk rapidly and idly. Colloq. **3.** To move or go with a rattling noise. — v. t. **1.** To cause to make a rattling sound. **2.** To say, perform, etc., briskly; as, he rattled off his lesson. **3.** To disconcert. Colloq. — n. A rapid succession of sharp, clattering sounds.

2. An instrument (as a toy, etc.) for making a rattling sound. 3. Racket; esp., noisy, rapid talk.

rat'tler (-lẽr), n. 1. One that rattles. 2. Rattlesnake.

rat'tle-snake' (-'l-snāk'), n. Any of certain venomous American snakes having horny joints at the end of the tail which rattle sharply when shaken.

rau'cous (rô'kŭs), a. [4] Hoarse; harsh; rough; as, a _raucous_ voice. — **rau'cous-ly**, adv. [8].

rav'age (răv'ăj), n. Desolation by violence; waste. — v. t. [1] To lay waste. — **-er**, n. [8].

rave (rāv), v. i. [1] To talk or act wildly; rage.

rav'el (răv''l), v. i. [7] 1. To entangle. 2. To unweave or unknit. 3. Fig., to disentangle; as, to _ravel_ a meaning. — v. i. To become raveled.

rav'en (răv'n), v. t. To devour with great eagerness. — v. i. To prey with rapacity; to be greedy.

ra'ven (rā'v'n), n. A glossy black bird of the crow kind. — a. Jet black.

rav'en-ing (răv''n-ĭng), p. a. Greedily devouring; greedy; grasping.

rav'en-ous (-ŭs), a. [4] Greedy; very hungry; eager for prey. — **-ly**, adv.

ra-vine' (ra-vēn'), n. A depression worn by running water; gorge.

Raven.

$\frac{1}{17}$

rav'ing (rāv'ĭng), p. a. Talking or acting wildly; delirious; as, a _raving_ lunatic.

rav'ish (răv'ĭsh), v. t. 1. To seize and carry away by violence. 2. To transport with joy or delight. 3. To violate. — **rav'ish-er**, n. [8].

rav'ish-ment, n. 1. Rapture. 2. Violation.

raw (rô), a. [3] 1. Not cooked. 2. In the natural state or nearly so; unrefined. 3. Crude; immature; as, _raw_ judgment. 4. Deprived of skin; galled; as, a _raw_ spot. 5. Disagreeably damp or cold. — **raw'ly**, adv. [8] — **-ness**, n. [8].

raw'boned' (rô'bōnd'), a. [4] Lean; gaunt.

raw'hide' (rô'hīd'), n. Untanned cattle skin; also, a whip of untanned hide.

ray (rā), n. Any of numerous fishes having the body very flat up and down and expanded laterally.

ray (rā), n. 1. A line of light or other form of radiant energy. 2. A thin line like a ray; esp., one of a number diverging from a center. 3. _Bot._ A raylike part of a flower. 4. _Zoöl._ One of the rods that support the membrane in a fish's fin. — v. i. to emit rays; radiate. — **ray'less**, a.

ray'on (rā'ŏn), n. A glossy fiber resembling silk, made from cellulose; also the woven fiber.

raze (rāz), v. t. [1] 1. To cut or wound slightly; graze. 2. To erase. 3. To lay level with the ground; overthrow; destroy; as, to _raze_ a city.

ra'zor (rā'zẽr), n. A keen-edged instrument used in shaving the face or head.

re (rā), n. _Music._ The second tone of the scale.

re-. A prefix denoting: 1. _Back;_ as in _recline_, refuge, _recall_, etc. 2. _Again_ (indicating that an action is repeated or is a restoration to a former state). In this sense _re-_ is so widely used and so

well understood that definition of many of its formations is needless. Some of these words are:

re'ad-just'
re'ap-pear'
re'ap-point'
re'ar-range'
re'as-sem'ble
re'as-sert'
re'as-sume'
re-bind'
re-born'
re-build'
re-charge'
re-clothe'
re'com-mit'
re-con'quer
re-con-sid'er
re'con-sid'er-a'tion
re'con-struct'
re'con-vey'
re'ē-lect'

re'ē-lec'tion
re'ēm-bark'
re-ēn-act'
re-ēn-act'ment
re'ēn-gage'
re'ēn-list'
re'ēx-am'i-na'tion
re'ēx-am'ine
re-fash'ion
re-fas'ten
re-gild'
re-kin'dle
re-lay'
re-lease'
re-live'
re-load'
re-make'
re-nom'i-nate
re-num'ber

re-oc'cu-py
re-or'der
re-paint'
re-peo'ple
re-phrase'
re-plant'
re'pos-sess'
re-pur'chase
re-read'
re-seat'
re-set'
re-shape'
re-spell'
re-state'
re-state'ment
re-take'
re-tell'
re-vis'it
re-write'

reach (rēch), v. t. 1. To stretch out, as a limb. 2. To pass to another. 3. To touch or seize, esp. with the hand. 4. To extend to. 5. To arrive at; come to; attain. 6. To hit or touch with a missile. 7. To influence. — v. i. 1. To stretch out the hand or arm, esp. as if to touch or grasp something. 2. To strain after something. 3. To extend. 4. To get or make its way (to a place, etc.); also, of a gun, sound, or the like, to carry; of the eye, to see. — n. 1. Act of reaching or stretching out. 2. Power of reaching; hence, power of seizing, touching, etc., or, esp., extent of such power. 3. Power of attainment. 4. A straight or level stretch. — **read'er**, n. [8].

re-act' (rē-ăkt'), v. t. To perform a second time.

re-act' (rē-ăkt'), v. i. 1. To return an impulse; resist action by an opposite force. 2. To respond to a stimulus. 3. To act in a contrary direction or manner.

re-ac'tion (-ăk'shŭn), n. 1. _Mechanics._ The force which a body opposes to a force acting upon it. 2. Reciprocal or return action or influence. 3. Chemical change; a chemical process or its result. 4. An action induced by vital resistance to some other action. 5. A counter tendency or contrary movement.

re-ac'tion-a-ry (-ă-rĭ), a. [4] Of, pertaining to, characterized by, or favoring, reaction. — n.; pl. **-aries** (-rĭz). One who favors reaction; esp., one who seeks to undo political progress.

read (rēd), v. t.; pret. & p. p. READ (rĕd); p. pr. & vb. n. READ'ING (rēd'ĭng). 1. To interpret (as a riddle, etc.); hence, to foresee; foretell. 2. To go over, esp. understandingly, as characters or words. 3. To learn of by perusal. 4. Hence, to discern by observation of signs. 5. To attribute (a meaning, explanation, etc.) to what is read. 6. To register; indicate, as do a thermometer, etc. 7. To make a special study of, as by perusing books. — v. i. 1. To perform the act of reading. 2. To learn by reading; — usually with _of_. 3. To have import; admit of interpretation. 4. To study, esp. by reading. 5. To appear in writing or print.

read (rĕd), p. a. Versed in books.

read'a-ble (rēd'á-b'l), a. [4] 1. Legible. 2. Worth reading; interesting. — **read'a-ble-ness**, n.

read'er (-ẽr), n. 1. One who reads. 2. A book for instruction and practice in reading.

---

read′i-ly (rĕd′ĭ-lĭ), *adv.* **1.** Without delay or objection; cheerfully. **2.** Quickly; easily.

read′i-ness, *n.* **1.** State of being ready; preparation; willingness. **2.** Ease or facility of performance.

read′ing (rĕd′ĭng), *n.* **1.** Act of one who reads; perusal; recital. **2.** A public recital; also, a lecture. **3.** Study of books. **4.** Form in which anything is written; version. **5.** Written or printed matter to be read. **6.** Manner of rendering something written; interpretation. **7.** That which is indicated, as on the scale of a barometer.

read′y (rĕd′ĭ), *a.* [³] **1.** Prepared for immediate action or use. **2.** Immediately liable; likely. **3.** Prepared in mind; willing; disposed. **4.** Quick; dexterous; also, prompt. **5.** At hand; available.

read′y–made′ (rĕd′ĭ-mād′), *a.* Made beforehand, in anticipation of need; not made to order.

re-a′gent (rē-ā′jĕnt), *n. Chem.* Any substance which, from its capacity for certain reactions, is used in detecting or examining other substances.

re′al (rē′ăl), *a.* [4] **1.** *Law.* Of or pertaining to things themselves; pertaining to, or consisting of, immovable property (*real estate* or *real property*), as lands or tenements; — opposed to *personal.* **2.** Actual; existing inherently. **3.** Genuine.

re′al-ism (-ĭz′m), *n.* In art and literature, fidelity to nature or to real life. — **re′al-ist,** *n.*

re′al-is′tic (-ĭs′tĭk), *a.* [4] Of or pert. to, or after the manner of, realism or realists. — **ti-cal-ly,** *adv.*

re-al′i-ty (rē-ăl′ĭ-tĭ), *n.* ; *pl.* **-ties** (-tĭz). **1.** State or quality of being real. **2.** That which is real.

re′al-iz′a-ble (rē′ăl-īz′à-b′l), *a.* Capable of being realized.

re′al-i-za′tion (-ĭ-zā′shŭn), *n.* **1.** A realizing; state of being realized. **2.** An instance or product of realizing.

re′al-ize (rē′ăl-īz), *v. t.* [1] **1.** To make real; hence, to accomplish. **2.** To cause to seem real. **3.** To conceive as real; apprehend clearly. **4.** To convert into money. **5.** To obtain by plans and efforts; gain. Of property, to bring, as by sale. — *v. i.* To convert property into money.

re′al-ly (rē′ăl-ĭ), *adv.* In a real manner.

realm (rĕlm), *n.* **1.** A kingdom. **2.** Hence, province; region; domain; as, the *realm* of fancy.

re′al-ty (rē′ăl-tĭ), *n.* Real estate or property.

ream (rēm), *n.* A quantity of paper, 20 quires, or 480 sheets (now often 500 sheets).

ream, *v. t.* To enlarge or shape with a reamer.

ream′er (rēm′ẽr), *n.* Any of various cutting tools used with a revolving motion to enlarge or shape a hole.

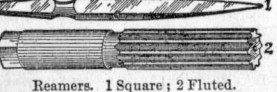

Reamers. 1 Square ; 2 Fluted.

re-an′i-mate (rē-ăn′ĭ-māt), *v. t.* [1] To animate anew; revive.

reap (rēp), *v. t.* **1.** To cut (grain, etc.); gather, as a harvest, by cutting. **2.** To obtain or receive as a reward, or as the fruit of labor. **3.** To clear of a crop by reaping. — *v. i.* To reap something. — **reap′er,** *n.* [8].

rear (rēr), *n.* **1.** The part of an army, fleet, or force which is behind the rest. **2.** Back part.

3. Space or position behind, or at the back. — *a.* Being at the back; hindmost. — **rear admiral.** See NAVY, *n.,* 3.

rear, *v. t.* **1.** To raise or set up. **2.** To erect by building; construct. **3.** To elevate; raise. **4.** To breed and raise; also, to cause to grow, as plants. **5.** To bring up to maturity; foster; instruct. — *v. i.* To rise up, esp. on the hind legs.

rear′most (rēr′mōst), *a.* Farthest in the rear.

rear′ward (-wẽrd), *a. & adv.* At or toward the rear.

rea′son (rē′z′n), *n.* **1.** A motive causing or confirming a belief, or leading to an action or course of action; a cause; as, I have *reasons* for believing as I do. **2.** The power of thinking out things; intellect. **3.** Sanity; sense; also, a sane or sound view or consideration. **4.** Right thinking; as, to bring one to *reason.* — *v. i.* **1.** To hold discussion or argument; hence, to discourse; converse. **2.** To think in logical forms. — *v. t.* **1.** To consider; seek by reasoning; — with *what, why,* etc. **2.** To debate; discuss. **3.** To persuade, or affect by reasoning. — **rea′son-er,** *n.* [8].

rea′son-a-ble (-à-b′l), *a.* [4] **1.** Having the faculty of reason; rational. **2.** Governed by reason; just; rational. **3.** Not excessive. — **-ness,** *n.* [8] — **-a-bly,** *adv.* [8].

rea′son-ing (rē′z′n-ĭng), *n.* **1.** Act of one who reasons. **2.** Reasons arranged and developed.

re′as-sur′ance (rē′ă-shōōr′ăns), *n.* Renewed assurance. [store confidence to.'

re-as-sure′ (-shōōr′), *v. t.* [1] To assure anew; to re-

re-bate′ (rē-bāt′), *v. t.* [1] To deduct from; allow a discount to. — **re-bat′er,** *n.* [8].

re-bate′ (rē-bāt′; rē′bāt), *n.* Deduction; abatement ; remission or payment back.

re-bel′ (rē-bĕl′), *v. i.* ; -BELLED′ (-bĕld′); -BEL′LING. **1.** To renounce, and resist by force, the authority of one's ruler or government. **2.** To revolt.

reb′el (rĕb′ĕl), *a.* [4] Of, pert. to, or characteristic of, rebels or rebellion. — *n.* One who rebels or is in rebellion.

re-bel′lion (rē-bĕl′yŭn), *n.* **1.** Act of rebelling; revolt; as, the *rebellion* of the nobles. **2.** Open resistance to, or defiance of, any authority.

re-bel′lious (-yŭs), *a.* [4] **1.** Engaged in rebellion; disposed to rebel; insubordinate. **2.** Resisting treatment or operation; refractory; as, a *rebellious* disease. — **-ly,** *adv.* [8] — **-ness,** *n.* [8].

re-bound′ (rē-bound′), *v. i.* To spring back on collision or impact. — *n.* Act of rebounding.

re-buff′ (rē-bŭf′), *n.* **1.** A brusque refusal; snub. **2.** A repulse. — *v. t.* To administer a rebuff to.

re-buke′ (-būk′), *v. t.* [1] To reprimand; reprove; censure. — *n.* A sharp reproof.

re′bus (rē′bŭs), *n.* ; *pl.* -BUSES (-ĕz). Representation of words and phrases by pictures of objects the names of which resemble the words or their syllables; hence, a riddle made up of such pictures.

re-but′ (rē-bŭt′), *v. t. & i.* ; -BUT′TED; -TING. To contradict or oppose by argument, etc.; refute.

re-but′tal (rē-bŭt′ăl), *n.* Act of rebutting.

re-cal′ci-trant (rē-kăl′sĭ-trănt), *a.* [4] Showing opposition; refractory. — **-trance** (-trăns), *n.*

re-call′ (rē-kôl′), *v. t.* **1.** To call or summon back. **2.** To call back to mind; recollect. **3.** To revoke; annul; retract. — *n.* **1.** Act of recalling, or a signal used to recall, or summon back. **2.** The right or procedure by which a public official may be removed from office by popular vote.

re-cant′ (-kănt′), *v. t. & i.* To withdraw or repudiate formally (opinions formerly expressed); to retract. — **-er,** *n.* [8].

re′can-ta′tion (rē′kăn-tā′shŭn), *n.* A recanting.

re′ca-pit′u-late (rē′kȧ-pĭt′ū̇-lāt), *v. t. & i.* [1] To repeat or restate briefly; summarize.

re′ca-pit′u-la′tion (-lā′shŭn), *n.* Act of recapitulating; a concise summary or repetition.

re′ca-pit′u-la-to-ry (-pĭt′ū̇-lȧ-tō-rĭ), *a.* [4] Of the nature of, or containing, recapitulation.

re-cap′ture (rē-kăp′tŭr), *n.* **1.** Recovery by capture. **2.** That which is recaptured. — *v. t.* [1] To capture again.

re-cast′ (rē-kȧst′), *v. t.* To mold or cast anew.

re-cede′ (rē-sēd′), *v. i.* [1] **1.** To move back or away; retreat; retire; as, the water *receded.* **2.** To withdraw a claim, pretension, or proposal.

re-cede′ (rē-sēd′), *v. t.* To cede back.

re-ceipt′ (rē-sēt′), *n.* **1.** A formula according to which things are to be taken or combined; a recipe. **2.** That which is received, in distinction from what is expended; — usually in *pl.* **3.** Act of receiving; reception. **4.** A writing acknowledging the receiving of goods or money.

re-ceipt′ (rē-sēt′), *v. t.* To put a receipt on; as, to *receipt* a bill. — *v. i.* To give a receipt. *U. S.*

re-ceiv′a-ble (rē-sēv′ȧ-b'l), *a.* **1.** Capable of being, or that must be, received. **2.** Such that payment should be had; as, bills *receivable.*

re-ceive′ (-sēv′), *v. t.* [1] **1.** To take, as something that is offered, sent, paid, or the like; accept. **2.** To permit to enter, as into one's house; hence, to greet. **3.** To admit; hence, to hold. **4.** To get, acquire; hence, to experience. **5.** To support; catch; bear. — *v. i.* **1.** To be a recipient. **2.** To receive visitors.

re-ceiv′er (rē-sēv′ẽr), *n.* **1.** One that receives. **2.** *Law.* A person appointed to receive, and hold in trust, property under litigation.

re-ceiv′er ship, *n.* Office of receiver (in sense 2).

re′cent (rē′sĕnt), *a.* [4] Of late origin, existence, or occurrence. — **-ly,** *adv.* **ness,** *n.* [8].

re-cep′ta-cle (rē-sĕp′tȧ-k'l), *n.* That which serves to receive and contain something; a repository.

re-cep′tion (rē-sĕp′shŭn), *n.* **1.** Act of receiving; state of being received; admission. **2.** Act or manner of receiving, esp. visitors; an occasion of receiving guests. **3.** Acceptance.

re-cep′tive (-tĭv), *a.* [4] Able or inclined to take in or contain. — **-ly,** *adv.* [8] **-ness,** *n.* [8].

re′cep-tiv′i-ty (rē′sĕp-tĭv′ĭ-tĭ; rē′sĕp-), *n.* Quality or state of being receptive.

re-cess′ (rē-sĕs′; rē′sĕs), *n.* **1.** Suspension of business for a brief time. **2.** A retired place; as, wooded *recesses.* **3.** An alcove, niche, or the like.

re-ces′sion (rē-sĕsh′ŭn), *n.* A ceding back.

re-ces′sion (rē-sĕsh′ŭn), *n.* Act or fact of receding or retiring; withdrawal; retirement.

re-ces′sion-al (-ăl), *a.* Of or pertaining to recession. — *n.* A recessional hymn, a hymn sung during the recession of the clergy and choir from the chancel to the robing room.

re-ces′sive (-sĕs′ĭv), *a.* Tending to go back.

rec′i-pe (rĕs′ĭ-pē), *n. ; pl.* **-pes** (-pēz). A formula for some combination or preparation; a receipt.

re-cip′i-ent (rē-sĭp′ĭ-ĕnt), *n.* A receiver; as, a *recipient* of honors. — *a.* [4] Receiving; receptive.

re-cip′ro-cal (-rŏ-kăl), *a.* **1.** Done by each to the other; mutual. **2.** Mutually interchangeable; also, complementary. **3.** *Gram.* Expressive of mutual action or relation; as, a *reciprocal* pronoun (*each other, one another*). — *n.* **1.** That which is reciprocal to another thing. **2.** *Math.* Quotient of unity divided by any quantity. — **-ly,** *adv.*

re-cip′ro-cate (-kāt), *v. i.* [1] **1.** To move forward and backward alternately; act interchangeably; alternate. **2.** To make a return for something done or given. — *v. t.* **1.** To cause to move back and forth. **2.** To give and receive in return mutually; also, to return; requite.

re-cip′ro-ca′tion (-kā′shŭn), *n.* Act or state of reciprocating.

rec′i-proc′i-ty (rĕs′ĭ-prŏs′ĭ-tĭ), *n.* **1.** State of being reciprocal; mutual action and reaction. **2.** *International Trade.* That relation or policy as to trade, etc., between countries under which each grants special advantages to the other.

re-cit′al (rē-sīt′ăl), *n.* **1.** Act of reciting; rehearsal. **2.** A telling in detail; narration; story. **3.** *Music.* A performance by one person.

rec′i-ta′tion (rĕs′ĭ-tā′shŭn), *n.* **1.** Act of reciting. **2.** Delivery before an audience of something memorized; also, that which is delivered. **3.** A repeating of a lesson by pupils before a teacher.

rec′i-ta-tive′ (-tȧ-tēv′), *n.* *Music.* A kind of musical recitation; also, music for such recitation. — *a.* Of or pert. to, or in the style of, recitative.

re-cite′ (rē-sīt′), *v. t. & i.* [1] **1.** To repeat, as a lesson. **2.** To tell over. — **re-cit′er,** *n.* [8].

reck (rĕk), *v. i.* *Archaic or Poetic.* **1.** To take heed, care; mind. **2.** To be of account; matter. — *v. t.* **1.** To care for; heed. **2.** To concern.

reck′less (rĕk′lĕs), *a.* [4] Rashly negligent; utterly heedless. — **-ly,** *adv.* [8] **-ness,** *n.* [8].

reck′on (rĕk′'n), *v. t.* **1.** To count; enumerate; also, to compute. **2.** To estimate by rank or quality; esteem. **3.** To conclude; hence, to think; suppose. — *v. i.* **1.** To make an enumeration or computation. **2.** To come to an accounting; settle. **3.** To depend; rely; — with *on.* **4.** To think; suppose. *Colloq.* — **-er,** *n.* [8].

reck′on-ing, *n.* Act of one who reckons; calculation; esp. **a** Settlement of obligations, liabilities, etc. **b** The calculation of a ship's position.

re-claim′ (rē-klām′), *v. t.* **1.** To rescue from being wild, waste, etc. **2.** To reform. **3.** To demand the return of as a right. — **-a-ble,** *a.* [8] — **-er,** *n.* [8].

rec′la-ma′tion (rĕk′lȧ-mā′shŭn), *n.* Act or process of reclaiming.

re-cline′ (rē-klīn′), *v. t. & i.* [1] To lean; incline; place in, assume, or be in, a recumbent position.

re-cluse′ (rē-klōōs′), *a.* [4] Secluded from society. — *n.* One who lives recluse.

re-clu′sion (-klōō′zhŭn), *n.* Act of becoming, or state of being, a recluse; also, imprisonment.

rec′og-ni′tion (rĕk′ŏg-nĭsh′ŭn), *n.* Act of recognizing; state of being recognized; formal avowal.

re-cog′ni-zance (rē-kŏg′nĭ-zȧns; rē-kŏn′ĭ-), *n.* *Law.* An obligation of record entered into before some court of record or magistate, with condition to do some particular act.

rec'og-nize (rĕk'ŏg-nīz),*v.t.* [1] **1.** To avow knowledge of; consent to admit, hold, etc. **2.** To acknowledge formally. **3.** To know again; identify as previously known. **4.** To acknowledge acquaintance with, as by salutation. **5.** To show appreciation of (services, etc.). — **-niz'a-ble** (-nĭz'á-b'l), *a.* [8] — **-niz'er,** *n.* [8].

re-coil' (rė-koil'), *v. i.* **1.** To retreat; draw back. **2.** To draw back, as from anything repugnant, alarming, etc.; shrink. **3.** To rebound; spring back; as, a cannon *recoils.* **4.** To return to or as to the source. — *n.* **1.** A starting or falling back; rebound; shrinking. **2.** State of having recoiled.

re'col-lect' (rē'kŏ-lĕkt'),*v.t.* **1.** To collect again, as something scattered; also, to gather; rally; recover. **2.** To compose (one's self).

rec'ol-lect' (rĕk'ŏ-lĕkt'), *v. t.* **1.** To call to mind; remember. **2.** Reflexively, to compose (one's self); recover command of (one's self).

rec'ol-lec'tion (-lĕk'shŭn), *n.* **1.** Act or power of calling to mind. **2.** That which is recollected.

rec'om-mend' (rĕk'ŏ-mĕnd'), *v. t.* **1.** To commit; consign **2.** To commend to favorable notice. **3.** To make acceptable; attract favor to. **4.** To advise. — **-er,** *n.* [8].

rec'om-men-da'tion (-mĕn-dā'shŭn), *n.* **1.** Act of recommending. **2.** That which commends to favor; as, a letter of *recommendation.*

rec'om-mend'a-to-ry (rĕk'ŏ-mĕn'dá-tō-rǐ), *a.* [2] Serving to recommend; also, advisory.

rec'om-pense (rĕk'ŏm-pĕns),*v.t.* [1] **1.** To render an equivalent to, for service, loss, etc.; compensate. **2.** To give compensation for; atone for. — *n.* Compensation; requital; reward.

rec'on-cil'a-ble (rĕk'ŏn-sīl'á-b'l), *a.* [4] Capable of being reconciled. — **rec'on-cil'a-bly,** *adv.* [8].

rec'on-cile (-sīl),*v.t.* [1] **1.** To cause to be friendly again. **2.** To adjust, as a quarrel; settle. **3.** To bring to acquiescence or content. **4.** To m'ke consistent. — **rec'on-cil'er** (-sīl'ẽr), *n.* [8].

rec'on-cile'ment (-sīl'mĕnt), *n.* Reconciliation.

rec'on-cil'i-a'tion (-sīl'ĭ-ā'shŭn), *n.* Act of reconciling; state of being reconciled.

rec'on-dite (rĕk'ŏn-dīt), *a.* [4] **1.** Hidden; abstruse; obscure. **2.** Dealing in things abstruse; profound. — **-ly,** *adv.* [8] — **-ness,** *n.* [8].

re-con'nais-sance, re-con'nois-sance (rḗ-kŏn'ĭ-săns), *n.* A reconnoitering; preliminary survey.

rec'on-noi'ter (rĕk'ŏ-noi'tẽr), *v. t.* [1, 6] To examine with the eye; make a preliminary examination or survey of, esp. for military or engineering operations. — *v. i.* To make a reconnoissance.

re'con-struc'tion (rē'kŏn-strŭk'shŭn), *n.* Act of constructing or organizing again.

re'con-struc'tive (-tǐv), *a.* Constructing, or tending to construct, again; as, a *reconstructive* policy.

re-cord' (rḗ-kôrd'), *v. t.* To commit to writing, printing, inscription, or the like; register; enroll.

rec'ord (rĕk'ôrd; -ŏrd), *n.* **1.** A recording or being recorded; reduction to writing as evidence. **2.** Esp. : **a** An official writing recording public acts. **b** An authentic official copy of a document. **3.** Testimony. *Archaic.* **4.** Something written or transcribed to perpetuate a knowledge of events.

5. a The cylinder or disk used to reproduce sounds in phonographs, etc. **b** The perforated paper roll of an automatic piano player, etc. **6.** The known facts in the course of anything, as in a man's career. **7.** That which has been recorded as publicly achieved in any kind of competitive sport; also, the best of such achievements.

re-cord'er (rḗ-kôr'dẽr), *n.* **1.** The chief judicial officer of some cities and boroughs. **2.** One who records, esp. officially. **3.** A recording apparatus.

rȯ-count' (rḗ-kount'), *v. t.* To count again. — (rḗ-kount'; rḗ'kount), *n.* A counting again.

re-count' (rḗ-kount'), *v. t.* To tell over; relate.

re-coup' (rḗ-kōōp'),*v.t.* [1] **1.** To get compensation for; as, to *recoup* a loss. **2.** To reimburse; indemnify.

re-course' (rḗ-kōrs'), *n.* **1.** Resort or application for assistance. **2.** A person or thing resorted to.

re-cov'er (rḗ-kŭv'ẽr), *v. t.* **1.** To get again; esp , to regain, as lost property. **2.** *Law.* To gain as a compensation, or return; obtain title to by a judicial decision. **3.** To make up for; retrieve. **4.** To rescue; deliver. — *v. i.* **1.** To regain health after sickness; to regain a former (good) state. **2.** *Law.* To obtain judgment in one's favor in a suit for something. — **-a-ble** (-á-b'l), *a.* [4].

re-cov'er-y (-Ĭ), *n. ; pl. -ERIES* (-Ĭz). A recovering.

rec're-an-cy (-ăn-sĬ), *n.* Quality of being recreant.

rec're-ant (rĕk'rḗ-ănt), *a.* [4] **1.** Craven. **2.** Apostate; false; unfaithful. — *n.* **1.** A cowardly wretch. **2.** A deserter; apostate.

re'—cre-ate' (rē'krḗ-āt'), *v. t.* [1] To create anew.

rec're-ate (rĕk'rḗ-āt), *v. t.* [1] To give fresh life to; refresh; divert. — *v. i.* To take recreation.

re'—cre-a'tion (rē'krḗ-ā'shŭr,), *n.* A creating anew.

rec're-a'tion (rĕk'rḗ-ā'shŭn), *n.* Act of recreating; state of being recreated; refreshment; diversion.

rec're-a-tive (rĕk'rḗ-ȧ-tĬv), *a.* [4] Tending to recreate; amusing. [accuse in return.

re-crim'i-nate (rḗ-krĬm'Ĭ-nāt), *v. i. & t.* [1] To recriminate; a counter accusation.

re-crim'i-na'tion (rḗ-krĬm'Ĭ-nā'shŭn), *n.* Act of recriminating; a counter accusation.

re-crim'i-na-tive (-nȧ-tĬv), *a.* Recriminatory.

re-crim'i-na-to-ry (-nȧ-tō-rĬ), *a.* [4] Having the quality of recrimination; retorting accusation.

re'cru-des'cence (rē'krōō-dĕs'ĕns), *n.* State or fact of breaking out again, as of a disease.

re'cru-des'cent (-ĕnt), *a.* Breaking out again, as a disease or rebellion.

re-cruit' (rḗ-krōōt'), *v. t.* **1.** To supply with new men, as an army; also, to muster; raise. **2.** To reinvigorate. — *v. i.* **1.** To enlist new soldiers. **2.** To gain new supplies of anything wasted; gain health. — *n. Mil.* A newly enlisted soldier.

re-cruit'ment(-mĕnt),*n.* **1.** Reinforcement. **2.** Act of recruiting. [parallelogram.

rec'tan'gle (rĕk'tăn'g'l),*n. Geom.* A right-angled

rec-tan'gu-lar (rĕk-tăn'gû-lár), *a.* Having one or more right angles. [fying.

rec'ti-fi-ca'tion (rĕk'tĬ-fĬ-kā'shŭn), *n.* A rectification.

rec'ti-fy (rĕk'tĬ-fī),*v.t.* [2] **1.** To make or set right amend. **2.** To refine or purify. — **-fi'er,** *n.* [8].

rec'ti-lin'e-al (-lĬn'ḗ-ăl), *a.* = RECTILINEAR.

rec'ti-lin'e-ar (-ár), *a.* **1.** Straight. **2.** Formed or bounded by straight lines.

rec'ti-tude (rĕk'tĬ-tūd),*n.* Rightness of principle or practice; uprightness; integrity.

āle, senāte, câre, ăm, *ă*ccount, ärm, ȧsk, sofᴀ; ēve, ĕvent, ĕnd, recĕnt, makēr; īce, ĭll; ōld, ȯbey, ôrb, ŏdd, sŏft, cŏnnect; ūse, ŭnite, ûrn, ŭp, circᴜs; fōōd, fŏŏt; out, oil;

rec′tor (rĕk′tẽr), *n.* **1.** A clergyman in charge of a parish. **2.** Head of a university, school, etc.

rec′to-ry (rĕk′tō-rĭ), *n. ; pl.* -ries (-rĭz). **1.** A benefice held by a rector. *Eng.* **2.** A rector's house.

rec′tum (-tŭm), *n. ; L. pl.* -ta (-tà). *Anat.* The terminal part of the intestine. [recumbent.]

re-cum′ben-cy (rē-kŭm′bĕn-sĭ), *n.* State of being

re-cum′bent (-bĕnt), *a.* [4] Leaning ; reclining ; lying. — **re-cum′bent-ly,** *adv.* [8].

re-cu′per-ate (-kū′pẽr-āt), *v. t.* [1] To recover ; regain ; also, to restore to health. — *v. i.* To recover health. — **re-cu′per-a′tion** (-ā′shŭn), *n.*

re-cu′per-a-tive (-kū′pẽr-á-tĭv), *a.* [4] Of or pertaining to recuperation ; tending to recovery.

re-cur′ (rē-kûr′), *v. i. ;* -curred (-kûrd′); -cur′ring. **1. a** To go or come back in thought or discourse. **b** To come again to mind ; come up again for consideration. **2.** To occur again, as a fever.

re-cur′rence (-kûr′ĕns), *n.* A recurring ; state of being recurrent ; return ; resort ; recourse.

re-cur′rent (-ĕnt), *a.* [4] Returning from time to time ; recurring, as fever.

re-curved′ (-kûrvd′), *p. a.* Curved in a direction opposite to the usual one ; as, *recurved* petals.

rec′u-san-cy (rĕk′û-zăn-sĭ ; rē-kū′-), *n.* State of being recusant or a recusant ; nonconformity.

rec′u-sant (rĕk′û-zănt), *a.* [4] Refusing, as to submit. — *n.* A dissenter ; nonconformist.

red (rĕd), *a. ;* red′der (-ẽr); red′dest. **1.** Having, or characterized by, the color of red. **2.** [*cap.*] Revolutionary.

red, *n.* **1.** The color of blood ; a tint or hue resembling that color. **2.** A red pigment or dye. **3.** [*cap.*] An extreme anarchist ; Bolshevik.

red′bird′ (rĕd′bûrd′), *n.* Any of various red birds.

red′breast′ (rĕd′brĕst′), *n.* The robin.

red corpuscle. One of the colored corpuscles of the blood, which contain the hæmoglobin and carry oxygen to the tissues.

red′den (rĕd′′n), *v. t. & i.* [1] To make or become red or reddish ; flush ; blush.

red′dish (-ĭsh), *a.* Somewhat red.

re-deem′ (rē-dēm′), *v. t.* **1.** To buy back ; hence, to recover, as pledged property. **2.** To ransom or liberate as from captivity. **3.** In theology, to deliver from the bondage of sin and its penalties. **4.** To fulfill, as a promise. **5.** To make amends for. — **re-deem′a-ble,** *a.* [8].

re-deem′er (-ẽr), *n.* One who redeems ; specif. [*cap.*], Christ.

re-demp′tion (rē-dĕmp′shŭn), *n.* A redeeming ; state of being redeemed ; deliverance ; salvation.

re-demp′tive (-tĭv), *a.* [4] Tending to redeem.

re-demp′to-ry (-tō-rĭ), *a.* [4] Redemptive.

red′-hot′, *a.* **1.** Of a red heat. **2.** Excited ; furious.

re-din′te-grate (rē-dĭn′tē-grāt), *v. t.* [1] To make whole again ; restore. — **-gra′tion** (-grā′shŭn), *n.*

red′ness, *n.* Quality or state of being red.

red′o-lence (rĕd′ô-lĕns), *n.* Quality of being redolent ; sweetness of scent ; fragrance.

red′o-lent (-lĕnt), *a.* [4] Diffusing odor or fragrance ; odorous ; — usually with *of.*

re-dou′ble (rē-dŭb′'l), *v. t. & i.* [1] To double again ; — esp. in *to double* and *redouble.*

re-dou′ble (rē-), *v. i. & t.* [1] To double in size, amount, or degree.

re-doubt′ (rē-dout′), *n. Fort.* **a** In permanent works, a work within an outwork. **b** A small inclosed work, commonly temporary.

re-doubt′a-ble (-á-b'l), *a.* [4] Formidable ; dread ; worthy of respect. — **-ness,** *n.* [8].

re-doubt′ed, *p. a.* [4] Formidable ; dread.

re-dound′ (rē-dound′), *v. i.* To flow back as an effect ; hence, to conduce ; contribute ; result.

red pepper. A very hot pungent powder made from the fruits or seeds of several tropical herbs of the nightshade family.

re-dress′ (rē-drĕs′), *v. t.* **1.** To set right, as a wrong ; repair, as an injury ; remedy. **2.** To make amends to. — *n.* **1.** Reparation of wrong ; amends. **2.** A redressing ; correction ; — with *of.* — **-er,** *n.* [8].

red′skin′ (rĕd′skĭn′), *n.* A North American Indian.

red′start′ (rĕd′stärt′), *n.* **1.** A European singing bird allied to the nightingale. **2.** A fly-catching warbler of North America.

American Redstart.

red tape. Tape used in public offices ; hence, official formality and delay. — **red′-tape′,** *a.*

re-duce′ (rē-dūs′), *v. t.* [1] **1.** *Med.* To restore to its proper place or condition, as a displaced part. **2.** To bring into a certain order, or classification. **3.** *Arith.* To change the denominations of (a quantity) or the form of (an expression) without changing the value. **4.** To bring to a certain condition by grinding ; reduce to. **5.** *Chem.* To bring to the metallic state by removal of nonmetallic elements. **6.** To lower ; degrade. **7.** To conquer. — **re-duc′er** (-ẽr), *n.* [8] — **re-duc′i-ble** (-ĭ-b'l), *a.* [4, 8]. [being reduced.]

re-duc′tion (rē-dŭk′shŭn), *n.* A reducing ; state of

re-dun′dance (-dŭn′dăns), *n.* Redundancy.

re-dun′dan-cy (-dăn-sĭ), *n.* **1.** Quality of being redundant ; excess. **2.** That which is redundant.

re-dun′dant (-dănt), *a.* [4] **1.** Exceeding what is natural or necessary ; superabundant. **2.** Characterized by redundance ; pleonastic. — **-ly,** *adv.*

re-du′pli-cate (rē-dū′plĭ-kāt), *a.* Double ; doubled. — (-kāt), *v. t.* [1] To redouble ; repeat.

re-du′pli-ca′tion (-kā′shŭn), *n.* A reduplicating.

re-du′pli-ca-tive (-kā-tĭv), *a.* Of or pertaining to reduplication ; reduplicate.

red′wood′ (-wòòd′), *n.* **1.** Any of various trees having reddish wood. **2. a** A very large Californian timber tree of the pine family. **b** The handsome brownish red wood of this tree.

re-ēch′o (rē-ĕk′ō), *v. t. & i.* To echo back ; reverberate. — *n.* An echo of an echo ; reverberation.

reed (rēd), *n.* **1.** Any of various bamboo-like grasses or their slender, often jointed, stems. **2.** A growth or mass of reeds. **3.** A musical instrument made of the hollow joint of a plant. **4.** *Music.* A thin, elastic tongue, vibrated by an air current, as in a clarinet.

reed′bird′ (-bûrd′), *n.* The bobolink. *Local, U. S.*

reed′y (rēd′ĭ), *a.* [3] **1.** Abounding in reeds ; made of or like a reed or reeds. **2.** Of the quality of a reed instrument in tone. — **reed′i-ness,** *n.*

reef (rēf), *n.* A ridge of rocks or sand at or near the surface of the water.

reef, *n. Naut.* That part of a sail taken in or let out to regulate the size. — *v. t. & i. Naut.* To reduce (a sail) by rolling or folding up part of it.

reef'er (rēf'ẽr), *n.* A heavy close-fitting, usually double-breasted, jacket.

reek (rēk), *n.* **1.** Smoke. *Scot. & Dial. Eng.* **2.** Vapor; steam; an exhalation; a disagreeable fume or smell. — *v. i.* To emit vapor; to fume.

reek'y (-ĭ), *a.* [3] **1.** Emitting reek. **2.** Smoky.

reel (rēl), *n.* **a** A lively dance of the Scottish Highlanders. **b** Music suited for this dance.

reel, *n.* A revolvable device on which yarn, cordage, is wound. — *v. t.* **1.** To wind on a reel. **2.** To draw by reeling; as, to *reel* a fish in.

reel, *v. i.* **1.** To turn round and round; whirl; to be giddy; be in a whirl. **2.** To walk, sway, or move unsteadily. — *n.* Act or motion of reeling or staggering.

re'ën-force' (rē'ĕn-fōrs'), *v. t.* [1] To strengthen with new force; esp., to strengthen with additional troops or ships.

re'ën-force'ment (-mĕnt), *n.* **1.** Act of reënforcing; state of being reënforced. **2.** That which reënforces; esp., *pl.*, additional troops or ships.

re-ën'ter (-ĕn'tẽr), *v. t. & i.* To enter again.

re-ën'trant (rē-ĕn'trănt), *a.* Directed inward.

re-ën'try (-trĭ), *n.* A second or new entry.

re'ës-tab'lish (rē'ĕs-tăb'lĭsh), *v. t.* To establish again. — **re'ës-tab'lish-ment,** *n.*

reeve (rēv), *n.* Female of the ruff (sandpiper).

reeve, *v. t.; pret. & p. p.* ROVE (rōv), REEVED (rēvd) *p. pr. & vb. n.* REEV'ING. *Naut.* To pass, as the end of a rope, through a hole in a block, around a cleat, etc.

re'ëx-port' (rē'ĕks-pōrt'), *v. t.* To export again, as what has been imported.

re-ëx'port (rē-ĕks'pōrt), *n.* Reëxportation; something reëxported; — chiefly in *pl.*

re-ëx'por-ta'tion (-pŏr-tā'shŭn), *n.* The act of reexporting.

re-fec'tion (rē-fĕk'shŭn), *n.* Refreshment, esp. after hunger or fatigue; repast; lunch.

re-fec'to-ry (-tō-rĭ), *n.; pl.* -RIES (-rĭz). A dining hall in a convent; a room for refreshment.

re-fer' (-fûr'), *v. t.; -*FERRED (-fûrd'); -FER'RING. **1.** To assign, as to a class, cause, source, motive. **2.** To send or direct elsewhere, as for aid, information, decision, etc.; submit to another. — *v. i.* **1. a** To have relation or reference; relate. **b** To direct attention; make reference. **2. a** To have recourse; apply. **b** To direct inquiry for information, as in respect of one's integrity, etc.

ref'er-a-ble (rĕf'ẽr-à-b'l),*a.* That may be referred.

ref'er-ee' (-ē'), *n.* One to whom a thing is referred for settlement.

ref'er-ence (rĕf'ẽr-ĕns), *n.* **1.** A referring; state of being referred. **2.** Relation; respect. **3. a** That which alludes to something. **b** A specific direction of the attention, as to a book; also, the book referred to. **4.** One that is referred to; as: **a** One of whom inquiries can be made as to another. **b** A written statement of the qualifications of an employee given by the employer. *U. S.*

ref'er-en'dum (-ĕn'dŭm), *n.; pl.* -DA (-dă). The

referring of measures already passed upon by the legislative body to the body of voters, or electorate, for approval or rejection; also, the right so to pass on laws, or the vote by which this is done.

re-fer'ri-ble (rē-fûr'ĭ-b'l), *a.* Referable.

re-fine' (rē-fīn'), *v. t.* [1] **1.** To reduce to a fine or pure state. **2.** To purify from what is coarse, vulgar, etc. — *v. i.* **1.** To become pure. **2.** To affect nicety or subtlety. **3.** To improve in fineness.

re-fined' (-fīnd'), *p. a.* [4] Freed from impurities, alloy, etc.; cultured; free from vulgarity.

re-fine'ment (-fīn'mĕnt), *n.* **1.** Act of refining; state of being refined. **2.** Elegance; culture.

re-fin'er (rē-fīn'ẽr), *n.* One that refines.

re-fin'er-y (-ĭ), *n.; pl.* -ERIES (-ĭz). A place for the refining of, esp., metals, oil, or sugar.

re-fit' (-fĭt'), *v. t.;* for prin. parts see FIT. To fit for use again; restore after damage. — *v. i.* To get refitted; obtain fresh supplies or equipment.

re-flect' (-flĕkt'), *v. t.* **1.** To bend or throw back, esp. after striking. **2.** To give back an image. **3.** To bring or cast as a result. — *v. i.* **1.** To throw or turn back the thoughts (upon anything); contemplate. **2.** To cast reproach, discredit, etc. **3.** To throw back light, heat, etc. — **er,** *n.* [8].

re-flect'ed (rē-flĕk'tĕd), *p. a.* **1.** Coming indirectly, or from another. **2.** Mirrored.

re-flec'tion (-flĕk'shŭn), *n.* **1.** Act of reflecting; state of being reflected; esp., return of light, heat, sound, etc., from surfaces. **2.** That which is produced by reflection, as: **a** Reflected light or heat. **b** A reflected image. **3.** Act of bending, turning, or folding back. **4.** Reproach cast; imputation. **5.** Mental consideration of some suggested idea. **6.** A thought or opinion formed after contemplation.

re-flec'tive (-tĭv), *a.* [4] **1.** Throwing back images, light, etc., as a mirror. **2.** Deliberative; thoughtful; as, a *reflective* mind. — **-ly,** *adv.* [8].

re-flec'tor (-tẽr), *n.* One that reflects.

re'flex (rē'flĕks), *a.* [4] **1.** Bent, turned, or directed back; of light, etc., reflected. **2.** *Physiol.* Pert. to, or produced by, stimulus or excitation without any necessary intervention of consciousness; as, *reflex* action. — *n.* **1.** Reflection; reflected light or color. **2.** A reflection. **3.** An involuntary movement due to reflex action.

re-flex' (rē-flĕks'), *v. t.* To bend back; reflect.

re-flex'ive (-flĕk'sĭv), *a. Gram.* **a** Denoting an action that is directed back on the agent or subject. **b** Referring back to the subject; as, a *reflexive* pronoun (in English, those ending in *-self*).—*n.* A reflexive pronoun or verb. — **-ly,** *adv.*

re'flux (rē'flŭks), *n.* A flowing back; ebb.

re-for'est (rē-fŏr'ĕst), *v. t. & i.* To replant with trees. — **re-for'est-a'tion** (-ĕs-tā'shŭn), *n.*

re-form' (rē-fôrm'), *v. t.* To amend or improve by change of form, by removal of faults or abuses, etc.; correct; improve.—*v. i.* To amend or correct one's character or habits. — *n.* Amendment of what is defective, vicious, etc., or a case of it.

ref'or-ma'tion (rĕf'ŏr-mā'shŭn), *n.* **1.** Act of reforming; change from worse to better. **2.** [*cap.*] The religious movement beginning early in the 16th century and resulting in the formation of the Protestant churches.

āle, senăte, câre, ăm, ăccount, ärm, àsk, sofá; ēve, ĕvent, ĕnd, recĕnt, makẽr; īce, ĭll; ōld, ŏbey, ôrb, ŏdd, sŏft, cŏnnect; ūse, ŭnite, ûrn, ŭp, circŭs; fōōd, fŏŏt; out, oil;

re-form′a-tive (rĕ-fôr′mȧ-tĭv), a. [4] Tending to reform; reformatory.

re-form′a-to-ry (-tô-rĭ), a. [4] Tending to, or intended for, reformation. — n.; pl. -RIES (-rĭz). A penal institution for promoting the reformation of young offenders.

re-form′er (-fôr′mĕr), n. **1.** One who effects or urges a reform. **2.** A leader of the Reformation.

re-fract′ (-frăkt′), v. t. To subject (rays of light, heat, etc.) to refraction.

re-frac′tion (-frăk′shŭn), n. Deflection of a ray of light, sound, etc., in passing obliquely from a medium into another in which its velocity is different, as from air into water.

re-frac′tive (-tĭv), a. [4] Serving or able to refract; pertaining or due to refraction.

re-frac′tor (-tĕr), n. Anything that refracts.

re-frac′to-ry (-tô-rĭ), a. [4] **1.** Obstinate; unmanageable. **2.** Resisting ordinary treatment; difficult to fuse, reduce, or the like. — **-to-ri-ly** (-rĭ-lĭ), adv. — **-ri-ness**, n.

sl Ray of Light in straight line; *spr* Ray of Light refracted ; *Qq* Perpendicular ; *rpq* Angle of Refraction.

re-frain′ (-frān′), v. i. To hold back or aloof; forbear; abstain.

re-frain′, n. The burden of a song; a phrase or verse which recurs at the end of each stanza.

re-fran′gi-bil′i-ty (-frăn′gĭ-bĭl′ĭ-tĭ), n. Property of being refrangible. [ing refracted.|

re-fran′gi-ble (-frăn′jĭ-b'l), a. [4] Capable of be-

re-fresh′ (-frĕsh′), v. t. **1.** To make fresh again; restore strength to. **2.** To renew (the memory).

re-fresh′ment (-mĕnt), n. **1.** Act of refreshing; state of being refreshed ; restoration of strength, spirit, vigor, etc. **2.** That which refreshes; esp. (chiefly in pl.), food or drink.

re-frig′er-ant (-frĭj′ĕr-ănt), a. [4] Cooling; allaying heat or fever.— n. That which makes cool; as: **a** A medicine to allay fever. **b** Any substance, as ice, ammonia, etc., used in reducing temperatures.

re-frig′er-ate (-āt), v. t. [1] To cool or freeze.

re-frig′er-a′tion (-ā′shŭn), n. Action or process of refrigerating. [to cool; cooling.|

re-frig′er-a-tive (rĕ-frĭj′ĕr-ȧ-tĭv), a. [4] Tending

re-frig′er-a′tor (-ā′tĕr), n. A box or room for keeping food, etc., cool, usually by means of ice.

re-frig′er-a-to-ry (-ȧ-tô-rĭ), a. [4] Refrigerative.

ref′uge (rĕf′ūj), n. **1.** Shelter or protection from danger or distress. **2.** One that protects from danger, distress, or calamity; an asylum.

ref′u-gee′ (rĕf′ū-jē′), n. One who flees for safety, esp. to a foreign power or country.

re-ful′gence (rĕ-fŭl′jĕns), n. Refulgent quality.

re-ful′gen-cy (-jĕn-sĭ), n. Refulgence.

re-ful′gent (-jĕnt), a. [4] Radiant; brilliant. — **re-ful′gent-ly**, adv. [8] — **-ness**, n. [8].

re-fund′ (rē-fŭnd′), v. t. To fund again or anew.

re-fund′ (rē-fŭnd′), v. t. & i. To give back; repay.

re-fus′al (-fūz′ăl), n. **1.** Act of refusing. **2.** The right to refuse or take before others; option.

re-fuse′ (-fūz′), v. t. & i. [1] **1.** To decline to accept; reject. **2.** To decline to submit to; decline to do or deny. — **re-fus′er** (rē-fūz′ĕr), n.

ref′use (rĕf′ūs), a. [4] Refused; rejected; worthless. — n. Worthless matter; rubbish.

ref′u-ta′tion (rĕf′ū-tā′shŭn), n. Act of refuting.

re-fute′ (rē-fūt′), v. t. [1] To disprove; prove to be false or erroneous. — **re-fut′a-ble** (-ȧ-b'l), a.

re-gain′ (-gān′), v. t. **1.** To gain anew; recover. **2.** To get back to; reach again.

re′gal (rē′găl), a. [4] Pert. or suitable to a king; royal; stately; splendid. — **re′gal-ly**, adv.

re-gale′ (rĕ-gāl′), v. t. [1] To entertain or feast sumptuously; refresh. — v. i. To feast.

re-ga′li-a (rē-gā′lĭ-ȧ), n. pl. **1.** Emblems or insignia of royalty, as the crown, etc. **2.** Decorations or insignia of an office or order.

re-gal′i-ty (-găl′ĭ-tĭ), n.; pl. -TIES (-tĭz). Royalty.

re-gard′ (rē-gärd′), v. t. **1.** To keep in view; view; observe; gaze upon. **2.** To take into account; consider. **3.** To esteem; care for. **4.** To heed; respect. **5.** To look upon; hold; consider. **6.** To relate to; concern. — v. i. To look attentively; gaze; also, to heed.— n. **1.** A look; glance; gaze. **2.** Consideration; heed; care. **3.** Respect; affection.

re-gard′ful (-gärd′fŏŏl), a. [4] Heedful; observant; respectful. — **-ly**, adv. — **-ness**, n.

re-gard′ing, prep. Concerning; respecting.

re-gard′less, a. Having no regard; careless.

re-gat′ta (-găt′ȧ), n.; pl. -TAS (-ȧz). A rowing or sailing race or races.

re′gen-cy (rē′jĕn-sĭ), n.; pl. -CIES (-sĭz). **1.** Office of ruler; dominion; government. **2.** Esp., office, jurisdiction, or dominion of a regent, or of a body of regents; deputed government. **3.** A body of regents. **4.** Period during which a regent governs.

re-gen′er-a-cy (rē-jĕn′ĕr-ȧ-sĭ), n. State of being regenerate.

re-gen′er-ate (-āt), a. [4] **1.** In theology, spiritually reborn; become Christian. **2.** Restored; reformed; redeemed. — (-āt), v. t. [1] **1.** In theology, to cause to be spiritually reborn. **2.** To generate or produce anew; give new life, strength, or vigor to. — **re-gen′er-a′tion** (-ā′tĕr), n.

re-gen′er-a′tion (-ā′shŭn), n. Act of regenerating.

re-gen′er-a-tive (-ȧ-tĭv), a. [4] Of or pertaining to regeneration; tending to regenerate.

re′gent (rē′jĕnt), a. Acting as regent; as, queen *regent.*— n. **1.** One who rules during the minority, absence, or disability of the sovereign. **2.** One of a governing board, as of certain universities.

reg′i-cid′al (rĕj′ĭ-sĭd′ăl), a. [4] Pertaining to regicide or a regicide; disposed to regicide.

reg′i-cide (rĕj′ĭ-sīd), n. **1.** One who kills a king, esp. his own king. **2.** The killing of a king.

‖**ré′gime′** (rā′zhēm′),**re-gime′**(rā-),n.[F.*régime.*] Mode of rule or management; prevailing system.

reg′i-men (rĕj′ĭ-mĕn), n. **1.** A governing; administration. **2.** *Med.* A systematic course of diet, etc.

reg′i-ment (-mĕnt), n. *Mil.* An organized body of soldiers under a colonel.

reg′i-men′tal (-mĕn′tăl), a. Belonging to, or concerning, a regiment. — **-tals**, n. pl. Military dress.

re′gion (rē′jŭn), n. **1.** A large tract of land; district; tract. **2.** A part or division of the body.

re′gion-al (-ăl), a. Of or pertaining to a region.

reg′is-ter (rĕj′ĭs-tĕr), n. A registrar.

reg′is-ter, n. **1.** A written account or record; a book containing regular entries of items or details;

also, an entry therein.   **2.** The compass of a voice or instrument.   **3.** A device to admit or exclude heated air, or to regulate ventilation.   **4.** That which registers, or records. — *v. t.*   **1.** To enter in a *register*; record formally; enroll; as, to *register* a name.   **2.** To record; indicate; as, the thermometer *registers* 70°. — *v. i.*   **1.** To enroll one's name in a register.   **2.** To correspond exactly.

reg′is-trar (rĕj′ĭs-trär), *n.* One who registers; an official recorder, or keeper of records.

reg′is-tra′tion (-trā′shŭn), *n.* Act or fact of registering; a registry; enrollment.

reg′is-try (rĕj′ĭs-trĭ), *n.; pl.* -TRIES.   **1.** Registration.   **2.** Place where a register is kept.   **3.** Register.

reg′nant (rĕg′nănt), *a.* [4]   **1.** Ruling; as, queen *regnant*.   **2.** Prevalent; as, a *regnant* custom.

re′gress (rē′grĕs), *n.* A retrogression.

re-gress′ (rē-grĕs′), *v. i.* To go back; return.

re-gres′sion (-grĕsh′ŭn), *n.* Return; retrogression.

re-gres′sive (-grĕs′ĭv), *a.* [4] Moving back.

re-gret′ (-grĕt′), *v. t.; -*GRET′TED*; -*TING*. To experience regret on account of; grieve at.— *n.*   **1.** Pain or distress of mind on account of something past, with a wish that it had been different.   **2.** An expression of regret;— usually in *pl.*

re-gret′ful (rē-grĕt′fŏol), *a.* [4] Full of regret; repining. — **re-gret′ful-ly**,*adv.* [8] — **-ful-ness**,*n.* [8] — **re-gret′ta-ble** (-á-b'l), *a.* [8].

reg′u-lar (rĕg′ū-lår), *a.* [4]   **1.** Belonging to a religious order.   **2.** Conformed to some established rule, law, principle, or type; symmetrical.   **3.** Governed by rule; uniform in course, practice, or occurrence; orderly; methodical.   **4.** In conformity with established usages, rules, or discipline; duly authorized or qualified.— *n.* One of the regular clergy or army.— **reg′u-lar-ly**, *adv.*

reg′u-lar′i-ty (rĕg′ū-lăr′ĭ-tĭ), *n.* State or quality of being regular.

reg′u-late (rĕg′ū-lāt), *v. t.*   **1.** To adjust or control by rule, method, or laws.   **2.** To put in good order; make regular.   **3.** To adjust, esp. so as to work accurately, as a clock.

reg′u-la′tion (-lā′shŭn), *n.*   **1.** A regulating; state of being regulated.   **2.** A rule or law.   [ulate.

reg′u-la-tive (rĕg′ū-lā-tĭv), *a.* [4] Tending to regulate.

reg′u-la′tor (-lā′tẽr), *n.*   **1.** One that regulates.   **2.** A clock, or other timepiece, used as a standard.

re-gur′gi-tate (rē-gûr′jĭ-tāt), *v. t. & i.* [1] To pour or cast back or out again, esp. from the stomach; eructate. — **-gi-ta′tion** (rē-gûr′jĭ-tā′shŭn), *n.*

re′ha-bil′i-tate (rē′há-bĭl′ĭ-tāt), *v. t.* [1] To reinstate; to put or bring into good repute again. — **re′ha-bil′i-ta′tion** (-tā′shŭn), *n.*

re-hash′ (rē-hăsh′), *v. t.* To hash over again; restate in a new form. — (rē-hăsh′, rē′hăsh′), *n.* A rehashing; something served again in a new form.

re-hears′al (rē-hûr′săl), *n.* A rehearsing; recital.

re-hearse′ (-hûrs′), *v. t.* [1]   **1.** To repeat, as a statement; recite aloud formally; enumerate.   **2.** To drill in preparation for a public performance. — *v. i.* To recite something for practice. — **-er**, *n.*

‖ **Reich** (rīk), *n.* [G.] **a** Formerly the German Empire (1871–1919). **b** Since 1919, Germany, a federated republic.

reign (rān), *n.* Royal authority; sovereignty; also, time during which a sovereign rules. — *v. i.* **1.** To

rule with sovereign power or authority; hold sway.   **2.** Hence, to prevail, as fear, a plague, etc.

re′im-burse′ (rē′ĭm-bûrs′), *v. t.* [1]   **1.** To pay back; repay.   **2.** To restore, or to pay an equivalent, to.

re′im-burse′ment (-mĕnt), *n.* A reimbursing.

rein (rān), *n.*   **1.** The strap of a bridle, fastened to the bit, to govern a horse; — usually in *pl.*   **2.** A means of guiding or controlling; curb; restraint; — usually in *pl.* — *v. t.* To check or direct by the reins; to restrain; check; guide.

re′in-car′nate (rē′ĭn-kär′nāt), *v. t.* To incarnate, or embody in flesh, anew. — **re′in-car-na′tion** (-kär-nā′shŭn), *n.*

rein′deer (rān′dēr′), *n.* Any of several species of deer of northern Europe, Asia, and America.

re′in-force′ (rē′ĭn-fōrs′). Var. of REËNFORCE.

reins (rānz), *n. pl. Archaic.*   **1.** Kidneys; loins.   **2.** Seat of the feelings or affections.

re′in-state′ (rē′ĭn-stāt′), *v. t.* [1] To place again (in possession, or in a former state); reëstablish.

re′in-state′ment (-mĕnt), *n.* A reinstating.

re-is′sue (-ĭsh′ū), *v. t.* [1] To issue again.— *n.* A second or repeated issue.

re-it′er-ate (rē-ĭt′ẽr-āt), *v. t.* [1] To repeat; say or do over again or repeatedly.

re-it′er-a′tion (-ā′shŭn), *n.* A reiterating.

re-ject′ (rē-jĕkt′), *v. t.*   **1.** To refuse to acknowledge, receive, etc.; decline to accept.   **2.** To cast off; throw away, as useless, etc.; discard.   **3.** To refuse to grant or consider. — **re-ject′er, re-jec′tor** (-jĕk′tẽr), *n.*   [being rejected.|

re-jec′tion (-jĕk′shŭn), *n.* A rejecting; state of

re-joice′ (-jois′), *v. t.* [1] To give joy to; gladden. — *v. i.* To feel joy.

re-join′ (-join′), *v. t. & i.*   **1.** To join again.   **2.** To say as a rejoiner.

re-join′der (-dẽr), *n.* An answer to a reply; an answer; reply.   [young or vigorous again.|

re-ju′ve-nate (rē-jōō′vē-nāt), *v. t.* [1] To make

re-ju′ve-na′tion (-nā′shŭn), *n.* A rejuvenating.

re-ju′ve-nes′cence (-nĕs′ĕns),*n.* Renewal of youth.

re-ju′ve-nes′cent (-nĕs′ĕnt),*a.* [4] Rejuvenating.

re-lapse′ (rē-lăps′), *v. i.* [1] To slip or fall back into a former state or practice, as from convalescence. — *n.* A relapsing; state of having relapsed.

re-late′ (rē-lāt′), *v. t.* [1]   **1.** To recount; narrate.   **2.** To connect; establish a relation between.— *v. i.* To pertain; refer; — with *to*. — **re-lat′ed** (-lāt′ĕd), *p. a.* [4] — **re-lat′er** (-ẽr), *n.* [8].

re-la′tion (-lā′shŭn), *n.*   **1.** Act of relating, or telling; recital; narration.   **2.** State of being related or of referring; connection.   **3.** Reference; respect; — esp. in *in relation to.*   **4.** Connection by blood or affinity; kinship.   **5.** A relative; kinsman; kinswoman.   **6.** State of mutual or reciprocal interest; also, *pl.,* dealings; affairs.

re-la′tion-ship, *n.* The state of being related.

rel′a-tive (rĕl′á-tĭv), *a.* [4]   **1.** *Gram.* Referring to an antecedent, as a pronoun or adverb.   **2.** Having relation; referring; pertaining; relevant.   **3.** Comparative; not absolute.   **4.** Dependent for signification on relation to something else. — *n.*   **1.** *Gram.* A relative pronoun.   **2.** A person connected with another by blood or (loosely) by affinity; a relation. — **-tive-ly**, *adv.* [8].

āle, senâte, câre, ăm, ăccount, ärm, àsk, sofá ; ēve, ĕvent, ĕnd, recĕnt, makēr ; īce, ĭll ; ōld, ŏbey, ôrb, ŏdd, sŏft, cŏnnect ; ūse, ûnite, ûrn, ŭp, circŭs ; fōod, fŏot ; out, oil ;

rel'a-tiv'i-ty (-tĭv'ĭ-tĭ), *n.* State of being relative.

re-la'tor (rē-lā'tēr), *n.* One that relates; a relater.

re-lax' (-lăks'), *v. t.* [1] **1.** To make lax; slacken; loosen. **2.** To make less severe, rigorous, or tense; abate. — *v. i.* **1.** To become lax, weak, or loose. **2.** To remit attention or effort.

re'lax-a'tion (rē'lăk-sā'shŭn; rĕl'ăk-), *n.* A relaxing; recreation.

re-lay' (rē-lā'; rē'lā), *n.* **1.** A supply (as of dogs, horses, men, etc.) arranged beforehand for successive relief. **2.** *Elec.* An electromagnetic device by which the opening or closing of one circuit opens or closes a more powerful one.

re-lease' (rē-lēs'), *v. t.* [1] **1.** *Law.* To remit. **2.** To set free. **3.** To relieve, as from pain, penalty, etc. — *n.* **1.** Deliverance or relief from care, pain, trouble, etc. **2.** Discharge from obligation or responsibility. **3.** Act of liberating or freeing.

rel'e-gate (rĕl'ē-gāt), *v. t.* [1] To exile; banish; hence, to remove, usually to a worse position.

rel'e-ga'tion (rĕl'ē-gā'shŭn), *n.* Act of relegating.

re-lent' (rē-lĕnt'), *v. i.* To become less hard, harsh, cruel, or the like; to become compassionate.

re-lent'less, *a.* [4] Unmoved by sympathy; unyielding; unpitying. — **-ly**, *adv.* [8] — **-ness**, *n.*

rel'e-vance (rĕl'ē-văns), *n.* Quality or state of being relevant; pertinency; applicability.

rel'e-van-cy (-văn-sĭ), *n.* Relevance.

rel'e-vant (-vănt), *a.* [4] Bearing upon, or applying to, the case in hand. — **-ly**, *adv.* [8].

re-li'a-ble (rē-lī'á-b'l), *a.* [4] Fit to be relied on; trustworthy. — **re-li'a-bil'i-ty** (-bĭl'ĭ-tĭ), *n.* — **re-li'a-bly**, *adv.*

re-li'ance (-ăns), *n.* **1.** Act of relying; confidence. **2.** Anything on which to rely; dependence.

re-li'ant (-ănt), *a.* [4] Confident; trusting.

rel'ic (rĕl'ĭk), *n.* An object, as a piece of the cross, a bone of a martyr, etc., which remains as a sacred memorial. **2.** Something that remains; survival; trace; as, a *relic* of other days.

rel'ict (rĕl'ĭkt), *n.* A widow or widower.

re-lief' (rē-lēf'), *n.* **1.** Act of relieving; state of being relieved; removal of any evil or burden. **2.** Release from duty. **3.** That which or one who gives aid or comfort. **4.** In sculpture, the projection of figures, etc., from a background; a work of art so produced. **5.** *Phys. Geog.* The elevations or inequalities of a land surface.

re-lieve' (-lēv'), *v. t.* [1] **1.** To raise or remove, as anything that depresses; alleviate; mitigate. **2.** To give ease, comfort, consolation, or succor to. **3.** To release from a post, station, or duty. **4.** To ease of any burden, wrong, or oppression. **5.** To set off by contrast. **6.** To remove the monotony of, as by contrast. — **re-liev'a-ble**, *a.* [8].

re-li'gion (-lĭj'ŭn), *n.* The outward act or form by which men indicate recognition of a god or gods to whom obedience and honor are due; the feeling or expression of human love, fear, or awe of some superhuman or overruling power; a system of faith and worship. [religion.]

re-li'gion-ist, *n.* One devoted or attached to a

re-li'gious (-lĭj'ŭs), *a.* [4] **1.** Possessing, or conforming to, religion; pious; godly. **2.** Bound by monastic vows. **3.** Of or pertaining to religion. **4.** Scrupulous; strict. — **-ly**, *adv.* [8].

re-lin'quish (-lĭŋ'kwĭsh), *v. t.* **1.** To withdraw from; abandon. **2.** To give up, as a right.

re-lin'quish-ment (-mĕnt), *n.* A relinquishing.

rel'i-qua-ry (rĕl'ĭ-kwá-rĭ), *n.; pl.* -RIES (-rĭz). A casket, shrine, etc., in which relics are kept.

rel'ish (rĕl'ĭsh), *n.* **1.** A taste or flavor, esp. one characteristic and pleasing. **2.** A taste for; liking; appetite. **3.** Something taken with food to render it more palatable; a condiment. — *v. t.* **1.** To give a relish, or flavor, to. **2.** To taste or eat with pleasure; like or care for. — *v. i.* To have a relish; be appetizing.

re-luc'tance (rē-lŭk'tăns), *n.* State or quality of being reluctant; repugnance; aversion.

re-luc'tant (-tănt), *a.* [4] Disinclined; loath; unwilling. — **re-luc'tant-ly**, *adv.* [8].

re-ly' (rē-lī'), *v. i.* [2] To rest with confidence; trust; depend; — with *on*.

re-main' (rē-mān'), *v. i.* **1.** To be left after another, or a part, or others have been removed, destroyed, or subtracted. **2.** To be left as not included or comprised. **3.** To stay behind while others withdraw. **4.** To endure; continue. — *n.* **1.** The portion remaining; esp.: a A fragment; relic; remainder; — chiefly in *pl.* b *pl.* A dead body; relics. **2.** *pl.* Works, esp. unpublished literary works left by a person when he dies.

re-main'der (-dẽr), *n.* **1.** Residue; remnant. **2.** That which is left after any deduction.

re-mand' (rē-mánd'), *v. t.* To recommit; send back. — *n.* A remanding; state of being remanded.

re-mark' (rē-märk'), *v. t.* **1.** To notice; observe. **2.** To state; say. — *n.* Act of remarking or noticing; a casual observation or statement.

re-mark'a-ble (-mär'ká-b'l), *a.* [4] Worthy of being remarked or noticed; uncommon; extraordinary. — **-ble-ness**, *n.* [8] — **-bly**, *adv.* [8].

re-me'di-a-ble (-mē'dĭ-á-b'l), *a.* [4] Capable of being remedied.

re-me'di-al (-ăl), *a.* [4] Affording remedy.

rem'e-di-less (rĕm'ē-dĭ-lĕs; rē-mĕd'ĭ-lĕs), *a.* [4] Beyond remedy; incurable; irreparable.

rem'e-dy (rĕm'ē-dĭ), *n.; pl.* -DIES (-dĭz). **1.** That which relieves or cures a disease. **2.** That which corrects or counteracts an evil; corrective; cure. — *v. t.* [2] To apply a remedy to; cure; correct.

re-mem'ber (rē-mĕm'bẽr), *v. t.* **1.** To have (an idea) come into the mind again; recollect. **2.** To hold in mind; as, *remember* to go. **3.** To recall to the mind of another; as, *remember* me to him. — *v. i.* To exercise or have the power of memory.

re-mem'brance (-brăns), *n.* **1.** Act of remembering; recollecting. **2.** State of being remembered. **3.** Power or faculty of remembering; hence, period over which one's memory extends. **4.** A reminder; memento; souvenir. **5.** *pl.* Greetings recalling or betokening friendship.

re-mind' (rē-mīnd'), *v. t.* To put (one) in mind (of something). — **re-mind'er** (-ẽr), *n.* [8].

rem'i-nis'cence (rĕm'ĭ-nĭs'ĕns), *n.* **1.** Act or power of recalling experiences. **2.** That which is remembered; a narration of experience.

rem'i-nis'cent (-ĕnt), *a.* [4] **1.** Pertaining to, or marked by, reminiscence. **2.** Recalling to mind.

re-miss' (rē-mĭs'), *a.* [4] Negligent; careless; hence, lacking earnestness or activity; slow.

---

re·mis'sion (rĕ-mĭsh'ŭn), n. Act or fact of remitting; as: **a** Pardon. **b** Relinquishment of a claim, debt, etc. **c** Diminution of intensity; abatement.

re·miss'ness, n. The quality of being remiss.

re·mit' (rĕ-mĭt'), v. t. ; -MIT'TED ; -MIT'TING. **1.** To forgive, as sin ; pardon. **2.** To refrain from inflicting or enforcing; as, to *remit* a penalty. **3.** To send, esp. to a distance, as money due. — v. i. **1.** To abate. **2.** To send money, as in payment.

re·mit'tal (-mĭt'ăl), n. Remission, as of a penalty.

re·mit'tance (-ăns), n. Transmittal of money, etc.; also, the thing, esp. money, remitted.

re·mit'tent (-ĕnt), a. [4] Remitting or abating; having remissions. — n. A remittent fever.

re·mit'ter (-ẽr), n. One that remits.

rem'nant (rĕm'nănt), n. Residue ; remainder.

re·mod'el (rĕ-mŏd'ĕl), v. t. [7] To model anew.

re·mon'strance (rĕ-mŏn'străns), n. Act of remonstrating; protest ; expostulation.

re·mon'strant (-strănt), a. Remonstrating; tending to remonstrate. — n. One that remonstrates.

re·mon'strate (-strāt), v. t. [1] To state or plead in protest. — v. i. To protest ; expostulate.

re·morse' (rĕ-môrs'), n. Tormenting distress excited by a sense of guilt ; repentant regret.

re·morse'ful (-fŏŏl), a. [4] Full of, or affected with, remorse. —**-ly**, adv. [8] —**-ness**, n. [8].

re·morse'less (rĕ-môrs'lĕs), a. [4] Being with·at remorse; pitiless. —**-ly**, adv. [8] —**-ness**, n. [8].

re·mote' (-mōt'), a. [3] **1.** Far away ; distant. **2.** Not connected or closely related; not obvious; as, a *remote* resemblance.—**-ly**, adv. —**-ness**, n.

re·mount' (rĕ-mount'), v. t. & i. To mount again. — n. A fresh horse. [being removed.]

re·mov'a·ble (rĕ-mōŏv'ȧ-b'l), a. Admitting of

re·mov'al (-ăl), n. A removing; a being removed.

re·move' (-mōŏv'), v. t. [1] **1.** To move away; cause to change the place of ; displace ; shift. **2.** To take or put away. — v. i. To depart. — **1.** Transfer of one's business or belongings from one location to another. **2.** Distance, space, or interval through which anything is removed ; hence, a step ; degree; as, but one *remove* from the presidency. — **re·mov'er** (-mōŏv'ẽr), n. [8].

re·mu'ner·ate (rĕ-mū'nẽr-āt), v. t. [1] To pay an equivalent for or to; compensate; repay ; pay.

re·mu'ner·a'tion (-ā'shŭn), n. Act or fact of remunerating ; also, that which remunerates.

re·mu'ner·a·tive (rĕ-mū'nẽr-ȧ-tĭv), a. [4] Serving to remunerate ; profitable.

ren'ais·sance' (rĕn'ĕ-säns'; rĕ-nā'săns ; F. rĕ-nĕ'-säns'), n. **1.** [cap.] **a** The revival (14th–16th century) of classical art and learning in Europe, marking the transition from medieval to modern times. **b** The style of art which then prevailed. **2.** A revival, or a state or period of marked improvement, along any line, esp. in art.

re'nal (re'năl), a. Of or pert. to the kidneys.

re·nas'cence (rĕ-năs'ĕns), n. **1.** State or fact of being renascent. **2.** [cap.] = RENAISSANCE, 1.

re·nas'cent (-ĕnt), a. Springing again into being or vigor ; being born again, or reproduced.

ren·coun'ter (rĕn-koun'tẽr), n. **1.** A hostile meeting, esp. a casual one. **2.** A personal contest, as in debate. **3.** A meeting, esp. a casual meeting; as, a lucky *rencounter* with a friend.

rend (rĕnd), v. t. ; RENT (rĕnt); REND'ING. **1.** To part, tear off, or take away, by force. **2.** To separate into parts with force ; tear asunder; split. — v. i. To be rent ; split ; tear. — **-er**, n. [8].

ren'der (rĕn'dẽr), v. t. **1.** To give or inflict in return or requital. **2.** To give; deliver; transmit. **3.** To yield ; surrender. **4.** To state ; deliver; as, to *render* an account. **5.** To furnish, as aid. **6.** To pay as due, esp. as tribute, etc. **7.** To cause to be or become; as, to *render* a fortress secure. **8.** To represent or depict ; to interpret or perform ; as, to *render* a song, rôle, etc. **9.** To translate. **10.** To melt down; extract or clarify by melting; as, to *render* lard.

ren'dez·vous (rän'dĕ-vōō), n.; pl. -vous. **1.** A place appointed for a meeting. **2.** A meeting by appointment. — v. i. & t. ; -VOUSED (-vōōd) ; -VOUS'ING (-vōō'ĭng). To meet, esp. by appointment.

ren·di'tion (rĕn-dĭsh'ŭn), n. **1.** Act of rendering; esp., surrender. **2.** Translation ; version.

ren'e·gade (rĕn'ĕ-gād), n. **1.** An apostate. **2.** A deserter; turncoat ; traitor.

ren'e·ga'do (-gā'dō), n.; pl. -DOES (-dōz). Renegade.

re·new' (rĕ-nū'), v. t. [1] **1.** To make new again; restore. **2.** To begin again ; resume ; as, to *renew* one's efforts. **3.** To revive; reëstablish; rebuild. — v. i. **1.** To become new. **2.** To begin again.

re·new'a·ble (-ȧ-b'l), a. Capable of being renewed.

re·new'al (-ăl), n. A renewing; a being renewed.

ren'net (rĕn'ĕt), n. The contents of the stomach of an unweaned calf or other animal, or the lining membrane of the stomach, used to curdle milk.

re·nounce' (rĕ-nouns'), v. t. [1] **1.** To give up, abandon, or resign. **2.** To repudiate; as, to *renounce* one's son. — **re·nounc'er** (-noun'sẽr), n. [8].

re·nounce'ment (-mĕnt), n. A renouncing.

ren'o·vate (rĕn'ō-vāt), v.t. [1] To make over; repair. — **ren'o·va'tor** (-vā'tẽr), n. [8].

ren'o·va'tion (-vā'shŭn), n. Act or process of renovating, or state of being renovated.

re·nown' (rĕ-noun'), n. Celebrity; fame.

re·nowned' (rĕ-nound'), a. [4] Famous.

rent (rĕnt), pret. & p. p. of REND.

rent, n. An opening made by rending or tearing.

rent, n. Periodical payment for the use of property. — v. t. **1.** To take and hold under an agreement to pay rent ; pay rent for; as, to *rent* a house from an owner. **2.** To grant possession of for rent; lease; as, to *rent* a house to a tenant. — v. i. To be leased or let. — **rent'er**, n. [8].

rent'al (rĕn'tăl), n. The amount of a rent or rents.

re·nun'ci·a'tion (rĕ-nŭn'sĭ-ā'shŭn; -shĭ-ā'shŭn), n. Act of renouncing.

re·or'gan·i·za'tion (rĕ-ôr'găn-ĭ-zā'shŭn), n. Act of reorganizing, or state of being reorganized.

re·or'gan·ize (rĕ-ôr'găn-īz), v. t. & i. [1] To organize again or anew. — **-iz'er** (-īz'ẽr), n. [8].

rep (rĕp), n. A ribbed fabric of silk or wool, or both.

re·pair' (rĕ-pâr'), v. i. To go ; betake one's self.

re·pair', v. t. **1.** To restore to a sound state after decay, injury, etc. **2.** To remedy, heal, make right, or mend; as, to *repair* a loss. **3.** To make amends for (an injury, etc.) by an equivalent ; as, to *repair* an injustice. — n. **1.** Act of repairing; state of being repaired; restoration. Also, an instance or result of such restoration;— often in pl.

---

2. Condition as to soundness, etc.; as, in good *repair*. — **re-pair'a-ble**, *a.* [8] — **-er**, *n.* [8].

rep'a-ra-ble (rĕp'á-rá-b'l), *a.* [4] Capable of being repaired or made good.

rep'a-ra'tion (-rā'shŭn), *n.* **1.** Act of repairing or restoring, etc., or state of being repaired or restored. **2.** Act of making amends for a wrong, etc.

rep'ar-tee' (rĕp'ár-tē'), *n.* A clever, ready, and witty reply; clever retorts collectively.

re-pass' (rē-pȧs'), *v. t. & i.* To pass again.

re-past' (rē-pȧst'), *n.* Food; a meal; feast.

re-pay' (rē-pā'), *v. t.; -*PAID* (-pād'); -*PAY'ING*. **1.** To pay back; pay back to; as, to *repay* money or a creditor. **2.** To give or do something for, in requital. **3.** To recompense, as a kindness. — *v. i.* To make payment or requital. — **-a-ble**, *a.* [8].

re-pay'ment (-mĕnt), *n.* A repaying.

re-peal' (-pēl'), *v. t.* To recall, as a statute ; rescind. — *n.* Revocation. — **-a-ble** (-á-b'l), *a.*

re-peat' (-pēt'), *v. t.* **1.** To say or utter again. **2.** To make or do again. **3.** To say over from memory ; recite; also, to utter after another. — *v. i.* To say or do what has been said or done. — **re-peat'ed-ly** (rē-pēt'ĕd-lĭ), *adv.* [8].

re-peat'er (-ẽr), *n.* One that repeats or is repeated ; as : **a** A watch which, on pressure of a spring, strikes the time. **b** A small arm firing several shots without reloading.

re-pel' (-pĕl'), *v. t. ; -*PELLED* (-pĕld') ; -*PEL'LING. **1.** To drive back; repulse. **2.** *Physics.* To force, or tend to force, apart by mutual action at a distance; — opp. to *attract.* **3.** To cause aversion in. — *v. i.* To exercise repulsion ; cause aversion.

re-pel'lent (rē-pĕl'ĕnt), *a.* [4] Repelling.

re-pent' (rē-pĕnt'), *v. i. & t.* **1.** To feel penitence or regret for past conduct. **2.** To change the mind with regard to one's conduct, from regret or dissatisfaction. — **re-pent'er**, *n.* [8].

re-pent'ance (-pĕn'tȧns), *n.* Act of repenting, or state of being penitent; esp., contrition.

re-pent'ant (-tȧnt), *a.* [4] **1.** Penitent. **2.** Expressing or showing repentance. — **-ly**, *adv.* [8].

rep'er-toire (rĕp'ẽr-twär', or ‖ rĕ'pẽr'toire' (*F.* rȧ'pĕr'twär'), *n.* [F.] A list of dramas, operas, parts, etc., ready for performance ; a repertory.

rep'er-to-ry (rĕp'ẽr-tō-rĭ), *n.; pl.* -RIES (-rĭz). **1.** A repository; storehouse. **2.** A repertoire.

rep'e-ti'tion (-ē-tĭsh'ŭn), *n.* **1.** Act of repeating; iteration; reiteration. **2.** Act of reciting, as something learned ; also, recital ; mention.

re-pine' (rē-pīn'), *v. i.* [1] To feel depressing discontent; complain. — **re-pin'er** (-pīn'ẽr), *n.*

re-place' (rē-plās'), *v. t.* [1] **1.** To place again; restore to a former place. **2.** To take the place of; supply the want of. **3.** To refund; repay; restore. — **-place'a-ble**, *a.* [8] — **-plac'er**, *n.* [8].

re-place'ment (-mĕnt), *n.* Act of replacing, or fact of being replaced.

re-plen'ish (rē-plĕn'ĭsh), *v. t.* To fill again; stock anew; refill. — **re-plen'ish-er** (-ẽr), *n.* [8].

re-plen'ish-ment (-mĕnt), *n.* **1.** That which replenishes. **2.** Act or process of replenishing.

re-plete' (-plēt'), *a.* [4] Filled, esp. abundantly.

re-ple'tion (-plē'shŭn), *n.* Act of making, or state of being, replete, esp. in *excess* ; surfeit.

re-plev'in (-plĕv'ĭn), *n. Law.* **a** The return to,

or recovery by, a person of goods taken from him upon giving security to try the matter in court and return the goods if defeated. **b** The writ by, or the action in, which goods are thus recovered. — *v. t.* To take or get back by replevin.

rep'li-ca (rĕp'lĭ-kȧ), *n.* A copy, as of a statue, esp. by the maker of the original.

re-ply' (rē-plī'), *v. i.* [2] **1.** To answer in words; respond; rejoin. **2.** To do something as a response to something done. — *v. t.* To return as an answer. — *n.; pl.* -PLIES (-plīz'). Answer; response.

re-port' (rē-pōrt'), *v. t.* **1.** To give an account of; relate ; tell. **2.** To repeat, as something heard, or said ; hence, to make minutes of, as a speech ; also, to prepare an account of. **3.** To state formally. **4.** To prefer a charge of misconduct against (one) to a superior. — *v. i.* **1.** To make or furnish a report. **2.** To present one's self, as for service. — *n.* **1.** Common talk; rumor; hence, fame; reputation. **2.** An official statement of facts. **3.** An account, as of a speech, judicial decision, etc., as for publication. **4.** An explosive noise.

re-port'er (rē-pōr'tẽr), *n.* One who makes reports, esp. one who reports events, etc., for a newspaper.

re-pose' (-pōz'), *v. t.* [1] To place, rest, or set (trust, hope, etc.); — with *in.*

re-pose' (rē-pōz'), *v. t.* To lay at rest ; rest. — *v. i.* **1.** To lie or be at rest ; rest. **2.** To lie ; recline. — *n.* State of reposing ; rest. — **re-pose'ful**, *a.*

re-pos'i-to-ry (rē-pŏz'ĭ-tō-rĭ), *n.; pl.* -RIES (-rĭz). Place where things are stored; depository.

rep're-hend' (rĕp'rē-hĕnd'), *v. t.* To blame; censure.

rep're-hen'si-ble (-hĕn'sĭ-b'l), *a.* [4] Deserving reprehension. — **-ness**, *n.* [8] — **-si-bly**, *adv.* [8].

rep're-hen'sion (-shŭn), *n.* Act of reprehending ; reproof ; reprimand. — **rep're-hen'sive** (-sĭv), *a.*

rep're-sent' (rĕp're-zĕnt'), *v. t.* **1.** To bring clearly before the mind ; present. **2.** To state in order to affect action or judgment. **3.** To portray or depict; exhibit. **4.** To act the part of ; personate. **5.** To typify; also, to symbolize. **6.** To stand in the place of; speak and act in behalf of.

rep're-sen-ta'tion (-zĕn-tā'shŭn), *n.* **1.** A likeness, picture, model, or other reproduction. **2.** A dramatic production or performance. **3.** Act of setting forth by statement, account, etc.; sometimes, a protest. **4.** Fact of representing another, or state of being represented by another. **5.** Delegates of a constituency, collectively.

rep're-sent'a-tive (-zĕn'tȧ-tĭv), *a.* [4] **1.** Representing or portraying ; as, a picture *representative* of a battle. **2.** Pertaining to, or founded on, representation of a larger body of persons (esp. the whole people) by delegates ; as, America has a *representative* government. **3.** Serving as an example ; typical. — *n.* One who or that which represents ; as : **a** An example ; specimen. **b** An agent or deputy ; esp., one who represents a community in a legislature or lawmaking body ; a member of the lower house in Congress, or in a State legislature.

re-press' (rē-prĕs'), *v. t.* **1.** To check; curb, as a desire. **2.** To press back; quell; subdue.

re-pres'sion (-prĕsh'ŭn), *n.* A repressing.

re-pres'sive (-prĕs'ĭv), *a.* [4] Having power or tending to repress; as, a *repressive* measure.

re-prieve' (rĕ-prēv'), v. t. [1] To postpone execution of sentence on; respite; as, to *reprieve* a prisoner.—*n.* A reprieving; temporary delay in execution, esp. of the death sentence; the order or warrant for such a delay.

rep'ri-mand (rĕp'rĭ-mȧnd), n. A severe reproof. — *v. t.* To reprove severely or formally.

re'print' (rē'prĭnt'; rē-prĭnt'), n. A new impression of a printed work; esp., a facsimile copy.

re-print' (rē-prĭnt'), v. t. To print or impress again; esp., to print another edition of.

re-pris'al (rĕ-prīz'ăl), n. 1. *International Law.* The resorting to force, short of war, to procure redress, orig. by seizing property or persons; also, an instance of this. 2. Any retaliation, as,esp.in war, by infliction of punishment or death on prisoners.

re-proach' (rĕ-prōch'), v. t. To charge with a fault; rebuke; censure. — *n.* 1. A cause of blame, censure, disgrace, or discredit; hence, disgrace or the like. 2. Censure, rebuke, or blame. — **-a-ble** (-ȧ-b'l), a. [8] — **-er,** n. [8].

re-proach'ful (-fōol), a. [4] Expressing or containing reproach or censure. — **-ful-ly,** adv. [8].

rep'ro-bate (rĕp'rȯ-bāt), a. [4] Abandoned; depraved; — said of persons. — *n.* A depraved, vicious, or unprincipled person; a scoundrel. — *v. t.* [1] To disapprove of; condemn; reject.

rep'ro-ba'tion (rĕp'rȯ-bā'shŭn), n. Act of reprobating; state of being reprobated.

re'pro-duce' (rē'prȯ-dūs'), v. t. [1] To produce again; as: **a** To produce again by generation or the like. **b** To repeat. **c** To make an image, a copy, etc., of; portray. **d** To present or exhibit again; as, to *reproduce* a witness. — *v. i.* To reproduce its kind. — **-duc'er** (-dūs'ẽr), n.

re'pro-duc'tion (-dŭk'shŭn), n. 1. Act or process of reproducing. 2. *Biol.* The process by which plants and animals give rise to offspring. 3. That which is reproduced or revived.

re'pro-duc'tive (rē'prȯ-dŭk'tĭv), a. [4] Of or pert. to reproduction. — **-ness,** n. [8].

re-proof' (rē-prōof'), n. Censure; blame; rebuke.

re-prov'a-ble (rē-prōov'ȧ-b'l), a. [4] Deserving reproof or censure.

re-prov'al (-prōov'ăl), n. Reproof.

re-prove' (-prōov'), v. t. [1] To chide as blameworthy; censure. — **re-prov'er** (-prōov'ẽr), n. [8] — **re-prov'ing-ly,** adv. [8].

rep'tile (rĕp'tĭl), a. [4] 1. Creeping. 2. Groveling; low; malignant; as, *reptile* meanness. 3. Of the nature of, or pertaining to, reptiles. — n. 1. Any of a class of air-breathing vertebrates including alligators, crocodiles, lizards, snakes, and turtles. 2. A groveling, mean, or despicable person.

rep-til'i-an (-tĭl'ĭ-ăn), a. & n. Reptile.

re-pub'lic (rē-pŭb'lĭk), n. A state in which the sovereign power resides in a certain body of the people, and is exercised by representatives elected by, and responsible to, them; a commonwealth; also, the form of government of such a state.

re-pub'lic-an (-lĭ-kăn), a. Of or pertaining to, or consonant with or favoring the principles of, a republic. — Republican party, *U. S. Politics,* one of the existing great parties, organized in 1856. — n. 1. One who favors a republican government. 2. [*cap.*] Member of the Republican party. *U. S.*

re-pub'lic-an-ism (-ĭz'm), n. Republican spirit, principles, or government.

re-pub'li-ca'tion (-lĭ-kā'shŭn), n. A republishing.

re-pub'lish (rē-pŭb'lĭsh), v. t. To publish anew.

re-pu'di-ate (rē-pū'dĭ-āt), v. t. [1] 1. To divorce (one's wife). 2. To cast off; renounce; reject. 3. To refuse to acknowledge or to pay; disclaim. — **re-pu'di-a'tor** (rē-pū'dĭ-ā'tẽr), n. [8].

re-pu'di-a'tion (-ā'shŭn), n. Act of repudiating, or fact of being repudiated.

re-pug'nance (-pŭg'năns), n. A strong antagonism; aversion; antipathy; disgust.

re-pug'nant (-nănt), a. [4] 1. Inconsistent; contradictory; contrary. 2. Distasteful; offensive; repulsive; as, a *repugnant* face. — **-ly,** adv. [8].

re-pulse' (-pŭls'), v. t. [1] 1. To repel; beat or drive back. 2. To repel by discourtesy, coldness, or denial; rebuff. — *n.* 1. Act of repelling; state of being repelled. 2. Denial; rebuff.

re-pul'sion (-pŭl'shŭn), n. 1. A repulsing; state of being repulsed. 2. A feeling of aversion; repugnance. 3. *Physics.* Act of repelling, or the force with which bodies repel one another.

re-pul'sive (-sĭv), a. [4] 1. Serving or able to repulse, or drive back. 2. Forbidding; repellent. 3. Causing aversion; offensive; disgusting. — **-ly,** adv. [8] — **-ness,** n. [8].

rep'u-ta-ble (rĕp'ū-tȧ-b'l), a. [4] Having, or worthy of, good repute; esteemed; estimable. — **-bly,** adv. [8].

rep'u-ta'tion (-tā'shŭn), n. 1. Estimation in which one is held; repute. 2. Good reputation, good name; as, a man of *reputation.*

re-pute' (rē-pūt'), v. t. [1] To consider; esteem; — usually in passive. — *n.* 1. Character; reputation, good or bad. 2. Good reputation.

re-put'ed (-pūt'ĕd), p. a. Having the reputation of being something specified. — **-ly,** adv. [8].

re-quest' (-kwĕst'), n. 1. Act of asking for something desired; expression of desire; solicitation. 2. That which is asked for. 3. A state of being asked for or sought after; demand. — *v. t.* 1. To ask for (something); solicit. 2. To ask (one) to do something; as, to *request* one to go.

re'qui-em (rē'kwĭ-ĕm; rĕk'wĭ-), n. 1. *R. C. Ch.* A Mass for the repose of a departed soul or souls or the music for such a service. 2. Any grand musical service or hymn in honor of the dead.

re-quire' (rĕ-kwīr'), v. t. [1] 1. To demand or enjoin; exact. 2. To need; call for.

re-quire'ment (-mĕnt), n. 1. Act of requiring; demand; also, that which is required; essential condition. 2. That which is required or necessary.

req'ui-site (rĕk'wĭ-zĭt), a. [4] Required by the nature of things, or by circumstances; necessary. — *n.* That which is required, necessary, or indispensable. — **req'ui-site-ness,** n. [8].

req'ui-si'tion (-zĭsh'ŭn), n. 1. An authoritative or formal demand or application; as, a *requisition* for troops, money, etc. 2. State of being demanded or put to use. — *v. t.;* -si'TIONED (-zĭsh'ŭnd); -si'TION-ING. 1. To make a requisition for; demand. 2. To make a requisition on.

re-quit'al (rē-kwīt'ăl), n. Act of requiting; also, that which requites; recompense; retaliation.

re-quite' (rē-kwīt'), v. t. [1] 1. To repay (as ɛ

benefit or injury); make return for. **2**. To repay (as a person) for a benefit or for an injury. — **re-quit'er**, *n*. [8].

rere'dos (rēr'dŏs), *n*. A screen or partition wall, usually ornamental, behind an altar.

re-scind' (rĕ-sĭnd'), *v. t*. To cancel; revoke, as a decision; esp., to repeal or make void, as a law.

re-scis'sion (-sĭzh'ŭn), *n*. Act of rescinding.

re'script (rē'skrĭpt), *n*. **1**. Decree or edict, as of the Pope. **2**. An official or authoritative order.

res'cue (rĕs'kū), *v. t*. [1] To free from confinement, violence, danger, or evil. — *n*. Act of rescuing. — **res'cu-er**, *n*. [8].

re-search' (rĕ-sûrch'), *n*. **1**. A searching for something with care or diligence. **2**. Careful or critical examination in seeking facts or principles; as, scientific *research*. — **re-search'er**, *n*. [8].

re-sem'blance (rĕ-zĕm'blăns), *n*. Quality or state of resembling; similarity.

re-sem'ble (-b'l), *v. t*. [1] To be like or similar to.

re-sent' (rĕ-zĕnt'), *v. t*. To feel, express, or exhibit indignant displeasure at.

re-sent'ful (-fŏŏl), *a*. [4] Full of, or caused or marked by, resentment. — **-ful-ly**, *adv*. [8].

re-sent'ment (-mĕnt), *n*. Indignant displeasure because of something regarded as a wrong.

res'er-va'tion (rĕz'ẽr-vā'shŭn), *n*. **1**. A keeping back, or concealing; that which is kept back. **2**. A reserving or keeping, esp. for one's self. **3**. Limiting condition. **4**. A tract of public land reserved for special use. *U. S*.

re-serve' (rĕ-zûrv'), *v. t*. [1] **1**. To keep in store, as for future use. **2**. To keep back; not to deliver. — *n*. **1**. That which is reserved; store. **2**. *Mil*. **a** [*Usually in pl.*] Troops reserved from action to be ready as a reënforcement or relief. **b** Military or naval forces not in active service. **3**. A tract of public land set apart for some purpose; a reservation. **4**. Act of reserving; that which is reserved; reservation. **5**. Self-restraint.

re-served' (-zûrvd'), *p. a*. [4] **1**. Restrained in words or actions. **2**. Set aside for future use. — **re-serv'ed-ly** (-zûr'vĕd-lĭ), *adv*. [8]. — **re-serv'ed-ness**, *n*. [8].

res'er voir (rĕz'ẽr-vwôr), *n*. **1**. A place where anything, esp. water, is kept in store. **2**. A reserve; a store.

re-side' (rĕ-zīd'), *v. i*. [1] **1**. To dwell permanently or for a considerable time. **2**. To be present; inhere; be as an attribute or element.

res'i-dence (rĕz'ĭ-dĕns), *n*. **1**. Act or fact of residing in a place for some time. **2**. The place or house where one resides; dwelling place.

res'i-den-cy (-dĕn-sĭ), *n.; pl*. -CIES (-sĭz). The official residence of, or the territory subject to, a resident (in sense 2).

res'i-dent (-dĕnt), *a*. Residing. — *n*. **1**. One who resides in a place. **2**. The representative of a government in a protectorate of it.

res'i-den'tial (-dĕn'shăl), *a*. [4] Pertaining to, or connected with, residence or residences.

re-sid'u-al (rĕ-zĭd'ū-ăl), *a*. Residuary.

re-sid'u-a-ry (-zĭd'ū-ă-rĭ), *a*. Pertaining to or constituting, a residue, residuum, or remainder.

res'i-due (rĕz'ĭ-dū), *n*. That which remains after a part is taken or designated; remnant; remainder.

re-sid'u-um (rĕ-zĭd'ū-ŭm), *n.; pl*. -UA (-á). That which remains; residue.

re-sign' (rĕ-zīn'), *v. t*. To yield to another; surrender. — *v. i*. To surrender a position.

res'ig-na'tion (rĕz'ĭg-nā'shŭn), *n*. **1**. Act or fact of resigning; surrender. **2**. State of being resigned; patient submission.

re-signed' (rĕ-zīnd'), *p. a*. [4] Submissive; yielding; acquiescent. — **re-sign'ed-ly** (-zīn'ĕd-lĭ), *adv*. [8] — **re-sign'ed-ness**, *n*. [8].

re-sil'i-ence (-zĭl'ĭ-ĕns), *n*. Act or capacity of rebounding, or springing back; elasticity.

re-sil'i-en-cy (-ĕn-sĭ), *n*. Resilience.

re-sil'i-ent (-ĕnt), *a*. [4] **1**. Rebounding; recoiling; returning to the original position or shape. **2**. Possessing power of recovery; elastic; buoyant.

res'in (rĕz'ĭn), *n*. Any of various solid or semisolid organic substances, chiefly vegetable, soluble in ether, alcohol, etc., but not in water; esp., rosin. — **res'in-ous** (rĕz'ĭ-nŭs), *a*. [4].

re-sist' (rĕ-zĭst'), *v. t*. **1**. To withstand. **2**. To strive against. — *v. i*. To make opposition; offer resistance. — **re-sist'er**, *n*. [8].

re-sist'ance (-zĭs'tăns), *n*. **1**. Act or capacity of resisting; opposition. **2**. *Physics*. Any opposing force. **3**. *Elec*. The opposition of a substance to the passage through it of an electric current.

re-sist'ant (-tănt), *a*. [4] Making resistance.

re-sist'i-ble (-tĭ-b'l), *a*. [4] That can be resisted.

re-sist'less, *a*. [4] **1**. Irresistible. **2**. Having no power to resist; unresisting. — **-ly**, *adv*. [8].

res'o-lute (rĕz'ô-lūt), *a*. [4] Having a fixed purpose; firm. — **-ly**, *adv*. — **-ness**, *n*. [8].

res'o-lu'tion (-lū'shŭn), *n*. **1**. Act or process of reducing to simpler form or to component parts. **2**. Act of determining; resoluteness; also, that which is decided on. **3**. A formal expression of the opinion or will of an assembly, adopted by vote.

re-solv'a-ble (rĕ-zŏl'vá-b'l), *a*. Capable of being resolved.

re-solve' (rĕ-zŏlv'), *v. t*. [1] **1**. To separate (into component parts or elements). **2**. To change or convert by resolution or formal vote. **3**. To answer or solve, as a problem; explain; clear up. **4**. To declare or decide by a formal vote. — *v. i*. **1**. To disintegrate; be reduced, as by dissolving or analysis. **2**. To form a purpose or resolution; determine. — *n*. **1**. That which has been resolved on, or determined. **2**. Resolute quality; determination.

res'o-nance (rĕz'ô-năns), *n*. Act of resounding by reflection of sound or by sympathetic vibration.

res'o-nant (-nănt), *a*. [4] Returning, or capable of returning, sound; resounding; echoing back; as, *resonant* eloquence. — **-ly**, *adv*. [8].

re-sort' (rĕ-zôrt'), *v. i*. **1**. To go; repair. **2**. To have recourse. — *n*. **1**. That to which, or a person to whom, one resorts for help. **2**. Act of going; recourse. **3**. Habitual or general going or visiting. **4**. A place frequented.

re-sound' (rĕ-sound'), *v. t. & i*. To sound again.

re-sound' (rĕ-zound'), *v. i*. **1**. To be filled with sound; ring. **2**. To be echoed. — *v. t*. To reëcho.

re-source' (-sōrs'), *n*. **1**. That resorted to for supply or support. **2**. *pl*. Funds; available means. **3**. Ability to meet a situation. — **-ful** (-fŏŏl), *a*. [8] — **-ful-ness**, *n*. [8].

---

re-spect' (rĕ-spĕkt'), v. t. **1.** To relate to; be concerned with. **2.** To consider worthy of esteem; hence, to refrain from obtruding upon. — n. **1.** Relation; relationship; reference; regard. **2.** A point regarded; a particular; detail. **3.** Regard; consideration. **4.** Favor; partiality; discrimination. **5.** Esteem; deferential regard; honor. **6.** pl. Expressions of respect or deference. **-er,** n. [8].

re-spect'a-bil'i-ty (-spĕk'tȧ-bĭl'ĭ-tĭ), n. Quality or state of being respectable.

re-spect'a-ble (-spĕk'tȧ-b'l), a. [4] **1.** Worthy of respect; of good repute. **2.** Considerable; also, moderate, in size, excellence, or number. **3.** Decent in behavior or character; also, presentable. **— re-spect'a-ble-ness,** n. [8] **— re-spect'a-bly,** adv. [8].

re-spect'ful (-spĕkt'fŏŏl), a. [4] Full of, or characterized by, respect. **-ly,** adv. **-ness,** n. [8].

re-spect'ing (rĕ-spĕk'tĭng), prep. With regard to; concerning.

re-spec'tive (-spĕk'tĭv), a. Particular; several.

re-spec'tive-ly, adv. As relating to each.

re-spir'a-ble (rĕ-spīr'ȧ-b'l; rĕs'pĭ-rȧ-b'l), a. [4] Suitable to breathe; adapted for respiration.

res'pi-ra'tion (rĕs'pĭ-rā'shŭn), n. Act or process of respiring, or breathing, by which an animal takes in oxygen and gives off the products formed by oxidation in the tissues.

res'pi-ra'tor (rĕs'pĭ-rā'tẽr), n. A device covering the mouth or nose to prevent inhalation of noxious substances.

re-spir'a-to-ry (rĕ-spīr'ȧ-tŏ-rĭ; rĕs'pĭ-rȧ-), a. Physiol. Of or pertaining to respiration.

re-spire' (rĕ-spīr'), v. t. & i. [1] To breathe.

res'pite (rĕs'pĭt), n. **1.** A putting off; postponement; delay. **2.** Temporary intermission of labor, etc. **— v. t.** [1] To give a respite to.

re-splend'ence (rĕ-splĕn'dĕns), n. Brilliant luster; brightness; splendor.

re-splend'en-cy (-dĕn-sĭ), n. Resplendence.

re-splend'ent (-dĕnt), a. [4] Shining with brilliant luster; splendid. **-ly,** adv. [8].

re-spond' (-spŏnd'), v. i. **1.** To answer; reply. **2.** To act in response.

re-spond'ent (-spŏn'dĕnt), a. [4] Answering; responsive. — n. One who makes reply; a defendant.

re-sponse' (-spŏns'), n. A responding; answer; responsive act or feeling.

re-spon'si-bil'i-ty (-spŏn'sĭ-bĭl'ĭ-tĭ), n.; pl. -TIES (-tĭz). **1.** State of being responsible, as for an obligation. **2.** That for which one is accountable.

re-spon'si-ble (-spŏn'sĭ-b'l), a. [4] **1.** Liable to respond; accountable. **2.** Able to respond for one's conduct, etc.; trustworthy. **3.** Involving responsibility. **-ness,** n. [8] **-si-bly,** adv. [8].

re-spon'sive (-sĭv), a. [4] Ready or inclined to respond. **-ly,** adv. [8] **-ness,** n. [8].

rest (rĕst), n. **1.** Repose; sleep; slumber. **2.** Freedom from activity; quiet; tranquillity. **3.** Peace of mind or spirit. **4.** A place where one may rest; abode; stopping place. **5.** Music. **a** Silence in music. **b** A character that stands for such silence. **6.** A short pause in reading. **7.** That on which anything rests or leans for support. — v. i. **1.** To get repose by lying down; sleep; also, to be dead. **2.** To cease from action or exertion; be

still. **3.** To lie; be fixed. **4.** To trust; depend; also, to be founded; — usually with on. — v. t. **1.** To give rest to; refresh by repose; lay or place at rest. **2.** To place or lay; lean; settle. **3.** To base; ground, as a hope.

rest (rĕst), n. With the, that which is left after removal of a part; remainder; the others. — v. i. To be left; remain.

res'tau-rant (rĕs'tô-rănt), n. Public eating house.

rest'ful (rĕst'fŏŏl), a. [4] Giving, or characterized by, rest. **-ly,** adv. [8] **-ness,** n. [8].

res'ti-tu'tion (rĕs'tĭ-tū'shŭn), n. Act of restoring; restoration; indemnification.

res'tive (rĕs'tĭv), a. [4] **1.** Obstinate in refusing to move forward; intractable. **2.** Uneasy; restless. **-ly,** adv. [8] **-ness,** n. [8].

rest'less, a. [4] **1.** Deprived of rest; uneasy. **2.** Not affording rest. **3.** Never resting; unquiet. **4.** Eager for change; discontented. **-ly,** adv. [8] **-ness,** n. [8].

res'to-ra'tion (rĕs'tŏ-rā'shŭn), n. **1.** Act of restoring. **2.** That which is restored.

re-stor'a-tive (rĕ-stŏr'ȧ-tĭv), a. [4] Of or pertaining to restoration; having power to restore. — n. Something that restores, as to health.

re-store' (rĕ-stōr'), v. t. [1] **1.** To give back; return. **2.** To bring back to the former or original state; repair. **— re-stor'er,** n. [8].

re-strain' (-strān'), v. t. **1.** To check; curb. **2.** To limit; restrict. **— re-strain'er,** n. [8].

re-strain'a-ble (-ȧ-b'l), a. That can be restrained.

re-straint' (-strānt'), n. **1.** Act, process, or means of restraining. **2.** State of being restrained.

re-strict' (-strĭkt'), v. t. To restrain within bounds.

re-stric'tion (-strĭk'shŭn), n. **1.** That which restricts; limitation. **2.** Act of restricting; state of being restricted.

re-stric'tive (-tĭv), a. [4] Serving or tending to restrict. **— re-stric'tive-ly,** adv. [8].

re-sult' (rĕ-zŭlt'), v. i. **1.** To arise as a consequence; follow; end; — followed by from or in. — n. That which results; consequence; effect.

re-sult'ant (-zŭl'tănt), a. Resulting or issuing; following as a consequence. — n. That which results.

re-sume' (-zūm'), v. t. [1] **1.** To assume or take again; put on anew. **2.** To enter upon, or begin, again. **3.** To take up again; go back to using. — v. i. To begin again.

ré'su'mé' (rā'zü'mā'), n. [F.] A summary.

re-sump'tion (rĕ-zŭmp'shŭn), n. Act of resuming.

re-surge' (rĕ-sûrj'), v. i. To rise again. **— sur'gence** (-sûr'jĕns), n. **— sur'gent** (-jĕnt), a.

res'ur-rect' (rĕz'ŭ-rĕkt'), v. t. To raise from the dead; reanimate; bring to view again.

res'ur-rec'tion (-rĕk'shŭn), n. **1.** The rising again from the dead. **2.** Restoration; revival.

res'ur-rec'tion-ist, n. **1.** One who steals dead bodies from the grave, etc., usually for dissection. **2.** One who restores, revives, or the like.

re-sus'ci-tate (rĕ-sŭs'ĭ-tāt), v. t. & i. [1] To revive, esp. from apparent death or unconsciousness.

re-sus'ci-ta'tion (-tā'shŭn), n. Restoration to life.

re-sus'ci-ta-tive (-tȧ-tĭv), a. [4] Tending to resuscitate; revivifying.

ret (rĕt), v. t. To soak or expose to moisture in order to soften or season, as flax, hemp, etc.

re'tail (rē'tāl), *n.* The sale of commodities in small quantities ; — opposed to *wholesale.* — *a.* Done at retail; engaged in retailing commodities.

re-tail' (rē-tāl'; rē'tāl), *v. t.* **1.** To sell in small quantities or to the consumer. **2.** To tell again or to many. — *v. i.* To sell at retail. — *-er, n.* [8].

re-tain' (rē-tān'), *v. t.* **1.** To keep in possession, use, etc.; keep. **2.** To employ (as a lawyer) by paying a preliminary fee. **3.** To remember.

re-tain'er (-ēr), *n.* **1.** One that retains. **2.** One retained in service; adherent. *Hist. or Archaic.*

re-tain'er, *n.* Act of a client by which he engages the services of a lawyer, etc.; also, the fee paid.

re-tal'i-ate (rē-tăl'ĭ-āt), *v. t. & i.* [1] To return the like for; return evil for evil.

re-tal'i-a'tion (-ā'shŭn), *n.* Act of retaliating.

re-tal'i-a-tive (rē-tăl'ĭ-à-tĭv), *a.* [4] Retaliatory.

re-tal'i-a-to-ry (rē-tăl'ĭ-à-tō-rĭ), *a.* [4] Tending to, of the nature of, or involving, retaliation.

re-tard' (-tärd'), *v. t.* **1.** To make slow ; delay ; hinder. **2.** To put off; postpone. — *n.* Retardation ; delay. — **re-tard'er,** *n.*

re'tar-da'tion (rē'tär-dā'shŭn), *n.* Act of retarding ; hindrance ; obstruction.

retch (rěch *or, esp. in British usage,* rěch), *v. i.* To make an effort to vomit ; strain, as in vomiting.

re-ten'tion (rē-těn'shŭn), *n.* **1.** Act of retaining; state of being retained. **2.** Act of retaining, or ability to retain, things in the mind ; memory.

re-ten'tive (-tĭv), *a.* [4] Tending, or having power, to retain. — **-ness,** *n.* [cent.]

ret'i-cence (rět'ĭ-sĕns), *n.* Quality of being reticent.

ret'i-cen-cy (-sĕn-sĭ), *n.* Reticence.

ret'i-cent (-sĕnt), *a.* [4] Inclined to keep silent; uncommunicative. — **ret'i-cent-ly,** *adv.* [8].

re-tic'u-lar (rē-tĭk'ū-lȧr), *a.* [4] Having the form of a net or of network.

re-tic'u-late (-lāt), *a.* Resembling network; netted. — (-lāt), *v. t. & i.* To divide or mark so as to resemble network. [being reticulated.]

re-tic'u-la'tion (-lā'shŭn), *n.* Quality or state of

ret'i-cule (rět'ĭ-kūl), *n.* A small bag, orig. of network, carried by women as a workbag or pocket.

re'ti-form (rē'tĭ-fôrm), *a.* Having the form of a net.

ret'i-na (rět'ĭ-nȧ), *n.* The membrane of the eye which receives the image of vision and is connected with the brain by the optic nerve.

ret'i-nue (-nū), *n.* The body of retainers who follow a distinguished person ; train of attendants.

re-tire' (rē-tīr'), *v. t.* [1] **1.** To withdraw ; remove. **2.** To withdraw from circulation, or from the market. **3.** To cause to retire. — *v. i.* **1.** To retreat. **2.** To withdraw. **3.** To go to bed. **4.** To withdraw from office, etc.

re-tired' (-tīrd'), *p. a.* [4] **1.** Secluded ; quiet. **2.** Withdrawn from active duty or business.

re-tire'ment (rē-tīr'mĕnt), *n.* **1.** A retiring ; state of being retired. **2.** A place of seclusion; retreat.

re-tir'ing (-tīr'ĭng), *p. a.* [4] Reserved; shy.

re-tort' (-tôrt'), *v. t.* **1.** To cast, or hurl, back (accusation, censure, etc.). **2.** To make a like reply to. — *v. i.* To return an argument or a charge; make a severe reply. — *n.* A quick, sharp reply, esp. one that counters a statement.

re-tort', *n.* A vessel in which substances are distilled or decomposed by heat.

re-touch' (rē-tŭch'), *v. t.* To touch again; rework, in order to improve.

re-trace' (rē-trās'), *v. t.* To trace again or back.

re-tract' (-trăkt'), *v. t. & i.* **1.** To draw back or in. **2.** To withdraw.

re-trac'tile (-trăk'tĭl), *a.* [4] Capable of being drawn back or in, as the claws of a cat.

re-trac'tion (-shŭn), *n.* **1.** Withdrawal of something advanced, claimed, said, or done. **2.** Act of retracting ; state of being retracted.

re-trac'tive (-tĭv), *a.* Serving to retract; of the nature of or involving a retraction.

re-trac'tor (-tēr), *n.* One that retracts.

re-treat' (-trēt'), *n.* **1.** Act of withdrawing, as from danger. **2.** The retiring of troops or ships from the presence of an enemy; a signal for so doing. **3.** Place to which any one retires ; refuge; asylum. **4.** An asylum for the insane, inebriates, etc. — *v. i.* To make a retreat; withdraw.

re-trench' (rē-trěnch'), *v. t.* **1.** To cut down ; lessen ; reduce. **2.** To cut off; remove. — *v. i.* To make retrenchments; economize.

re-trench'ment (-mĕnt), *n.* Act or process of retrenching ; reduction ; curtailment.

re-tri'al (rē-trī'ȧl), *n.* A second trial.

ret'ri-bu'tion (rět'rĭ-bū'shŭn), *n.* That which is given in compensation ; esp., fitting punishment.

re-trib'u-tive (rē-trĭb'ū-tĭv), *a.* [4] Of or pertaining to, or involving, retribution or repayment.

re-trib'u-to-ry (-tō-rĭ), *a.* [4] Retributive.

re-triev'a-ble (rē-trēv'à-b'l), *a.* Capable of being retrieved.

re-triev'al (-ăl), *n.* Act of retrieving.

re-trieve' (-trēv'), *v. t.* [1] **1.** To find and bring in (killed or wounded game). **2.** To recover ; regain. **3.** To restore ; revive. **4.** To make good ; repair. — *v. i.* To retrieve game.

re-triev'er (-trēv'ẽr), *n.* One that retrieves; esp., one of a certain breed of dogs used for retrieving.

re'tro-act' (rē'trō-ăkt' ; rět'rō-), *v. i.* To act backward, In return, or in opposition ; to act so as to affect something done in the past. — **re'tro-ac'tion** (-ăk'shŭn), *n.* — **re'tro-ac'tive** (-tĭv), *a.*

re'tro-cede' (rē'trō-sēd' ; rět'rō-), *v. t.* [1] To cede or grant back. [back ; recede.]

re'tro-cede (rět'rō-sēd ; rē'trō-), *v. i.* [1] To go

re'tro-ces'sion (rē'trō-sĕsh'ŭn ; rět'rō-), *n.* Act of retroceding ; recession.

re'tro-ces'sion, *n.* A ceding back.

ret'ro-grade (rět'rō-grād ; rē'trō-), *a.* [4] **1.** Directed, moving, or tending backward, or contrary to the previous direction. **2.** Declining from a better to a worse state. — *v. i.* [1] **1.** To go, move, or appear to move, in a retrograde direction; recede. **2.** To decline from better to worse.

re'tro-gres'sion (rē'trō-grěsh'ŭn ; rět'rō-), *n.* Act of retrograding. [or tending to retrograde.]

re'tro-gres'sive (-grěs'ĭv), *a.* [4] Retrograding]

ret'ro-spect (rět'rō-spěkt ; rē'trō-), *n.* A looking back ; contemplation or review of the past.

ret'ro-spec'tion (-spěk'shŭn), *n.* Act or faculty of looking back on things past ; a retrospect.

ret'ro-spec'tive (-tĭv), *a.* [4] Looking backward, esp. in thought; directed to the past. — **-ly,** *adv.* [8].

‖**re-trous-sé'** (rē-trōō'sā'), *a.* [F.] Turned up ; — said chiefly of the nose.

---

chair ; **go** ; **sing, ink** ; **then, thin** ; **nature, verdure** ; **yet** ; **zh = z** in **azure**. **Numbers refer to §§ in the Special Notes which, with Abbreviations, Signs. etc., precede the Vocabulary.**

re-turn' (rē-tûrn'), *v. i.* **1.** To go or come back again to a place or condition. **2.** To go back or revert in thought, narration, or argument. **3.** To come back, as in possession; revert, as an estate. **4.** To reply; respond. — *v. t.* **1.** To bring, carry, send, or turn, back; restore. **2.** To produce in return; yield. **3.** To report, or bring back and make known. **4.** To render, as an account, to a superior; report officially. **5.** To send in reply; say in response. **6.** To repay; respond to similarly. — *n.* **1.** A returning, or coming back, to or from a place or condition. **2.** The profit on, or advantage from, labor, a loan, etc.; — in *pl.*, proceeds; results. **3.** An account; formal report. **4.** Act of returning something. **5.** That which returns or is returned.

re-turn'a-ble (-tûr'nà-b'l), *a.* **1.** Required to be returned. **2.** Admitting of being returned.

re-un'ion (rē-ūn'yŭn), *n.* **1.** Reuniting; state of being reunited. **2.** An assembling of persons who have been separated; as, a family *reunion.*

re'u-nite' (rē'ū-nīt'), *v. t. & i.* [1] To unite again.

re-vamp' (rē-vămp'), *v. t.* To patch up again.

re-veal' (rē-vēl'), *v. t.* **1.** To make known; unveil; disclose. **2.** To communicate by supernatural instruction or agency. — **re-veal'er,** *n.* [8].

re-veil'le (rē-vāl'yà; *in U. S. service* rĕv'ĕ-lē' or rĕv'ĕ-lā'), *n.* A signal, by bugle or drum, at about sunrise, summoning soldiers or sailors to duty.

rev'el (rĕv'ĕl), *v. i.* [7] **1.** To take part in a revel or revels. **2.** To take great or intense delight or satisfaction (in); as, to *revel* in music. — *n.* Riotous or noisy festivity or merrymaking; carousal.

rev'e-la'tion (-ē-lā'shŭn), *n.* **1.** Act of revealing; disclosure; also, that which is revealed. **2.** [*cap.*] The last book of the Bible; the Apocalypse.

rev'el-er (rĕv'ĕl-ẽr), *n.* [7] One who revels.

rev'el-ry (rĕv'ĕl-rĭ), *n.* Boisterous merrymaking.

re-venge' (rē-vĕnj'), *v. t.* [1] To inflict harm or injury in return for; avenge. — *n.* **1.** Act of revenging; vengeance. **2.** An opportunity of getting satisfaction. — **re-veng'er,** *n.* [8].

re-venge'ful (-fŏŏl), *a.* [4] Full of, or prone to, revenge; vindictive; vengeful. — **-ness,** *n.* [8].

rev'e-nue (rĕv'ē-nū), *n.* **1.** Return from an investment; income. **2.** The yield of taxes, rents, etc., which a state, city, etc., collects for public use.

re-ver'ber-ant (rē-vûr'bēr-ănt), *a.* [4] Reverberating; resonant.

re-ver'ber-ate (-āt), *v. t.* [1] To drive back; repel; echo, as sound; reflect, as light. — *v. i.* **1.** To rebound; recoil. **2.** To resound; echo.

re-ver'ber-a'tion (-ā'shŭn), *n.* Act of reverberating; reflection; echo.

re-ver'ber-a-tive (-vûr'bēr-à-tĭv), *a.* [4] Of the nature of reverberation; tending to reverberate.

re-ver'ber-a-to-ry (-à-tō-rĭ), *a.* [4] Acting by reverberation; forced back or diverted, as flame.

re-vere' (rē-vēr'), *v. t.* To regard with reverence.

rev'er-ence (rĕv'ẽr-ĕns), *n.* **1.** Profound respect mingled with fear and affection; veneration. **2.** A token of respect or veneration; an obeisance. **3.** One entitled to be revered; — a designation used of or to clergymen, with *his* or (*Obsoles.*) *your.*

rev'er-ence (rĕv'ẽr-ĕns), *v. t.* [1] To salute with a reverence; regard or treat with reverence.

rev'er-end (-ĕnd), *a.* [4] **1.** Worthy of reverence; revered; — a title of respect given to clergymen. **2.** Of, pert. to, or characteristic of, the clergy.

rev'er-ent (-ĕnt), *a.* [4] Disposed to revere; reverential; deeply respectful. — **-ly,** *adv.* [8].

rev'er-en'tial (-ĕn'shăl), *a.* [4] Proceeding from or expressing reverence; reverent. — **-ly,** *adv.*

rev'er-ie (rĕv'ẽr-ĭ), *n.; pl.* -ERIES (-ĭz). Deep or abstracted musing; daydream.

re-ver'sal (rē-vûr'săl), *n.* A reversing; overthrow.

re-verse' (-vûrs'), *a.* Turned back; opposite. — *n.* **1.** A direct opposite or contrary. **2.** The back; — opposed to *obverse.* **3.** Misfortune; a check; defeat. — *v. t.* [1] **1.** To turn upside down. **2.** To revoke; annul. **3.** To turn completely about in position or direction; transpose. **4.** To cause to go or move oppositely. — *v. i.* To turn or move oppositely, as in waltzing. — **-ly,** *adv.*

re-vers'i-ble (-sĭ-b'l), *a.* **1.** Capable of being reversed or reversing. **2.** Finished on both sides.

re-ver'sion (-vûr'shŭn), *n.* **1.** *Law.* The returning of an estate to the grantor or his heirs, by operation of law after termination of the grant. **2.** Right of succession or future possession or enjoyment. **3.** A return toward an ancestral type.

re-ver'sion-a-ry (-â-rĭ), *a.* Of, pertaining to, or of the nature of, a reversion.

re-vert' (-vûrt'), *v. i.* To return; go back; recur.

rev'er-y. Var. of REVERIE.

re-vet'ment (rē-vĕt'mĕnt), *n.* A facing of stone, concrete, or the like, to sustain an embankment; also, a retaining wall.

re-view' (rē-vū'), *v. t.* **1.** To view, examine, or study again. **2.** To examine critically. **3.** To look back on. — *v. i.* To write reviews; be a reviewer. — *n.* **1.** Judicial reëxamination, as of the proceedings of a lower court. **2.** An inspection, as of troops, by a higher officer. **3.** A lesson studied or recited a second time. **4.** A criticism. — **re-view'er** (-ẽr), *n.* [8].

re-vile' (-vīl'), *v. t.* [1] To use abusive language toward; rail at. — *v. i.* To use abusive language; rail. — **re-vil'er** (-vil'ẽr), *n.* [8].

re-vis'al (-vīz'ăl), *n.* Act of revising; revision.

re-vise' (-vīz'), *v. t.* [1] To look over or reëxamine for correction. — *n.* Review; revision. — **re-vis'er** (rē-vīz'ẽr), **re-vi'sor** (-vī'zẽr), *n.* [8].

re-vi'sion (-vĭzh'ŭn), *n.* **1.** A revising. **2.** A revised form or version.

re-viv'al (rē-vīv'ăl), *n.* **1.** Act of reviving: state of being revived; restoration. **2.** A religious awakening; a meeting or series of meetings for rousing interest in religion.

re-viv'al-ist, *n.* Promoter of religious revivals.

re-vive' (-vīv'), *v. i.* [1] To return to consciousness or life; recover life, vigor, or strength. — *v. t.* **1.** To restore to consciousness or life. **2.** To invigorate again. **3.** To recover from neglect or disuse; restore. **4.** To renew; reawaken; refresh. — **re-viv'er,** *n.* [8].

re-viv-i-fi-ca'tion (rē-vĭv'ĭ-fĭ-kā'shŭn), *n.* Renewal or restoration of life; revival.

re-viv'i-fy (-vĭv'ĭ-fī), *v. t. & i.* [2] To revive.

rev'o-ca-ble (rĕv'ô-kà-b'l), *a.* Capable of being revoked. [peal; withdrawal.

rev'o-ca'tion (-kā'shŭn), *n.* Act of revoking; re-

āle, senāte, cāre, ăm, ăccount, ärm, ȧsk, sofȧ; ēve, ĕvent, ĕnd, recĕnt, makẽr; īce, ĭll; ōld, ȯbey, ôrb, ŏdd, sŏft, cŏnnect; ūse, ŭnite, ûrn, ŭp, circŭs; fōŏd, fŏŏt; out, oil;

re-voke' (rĕ-vōk'), *v. t.* [1] To annul by recalling; repeal; rescind. — *v. i.* *Card Playing.* To fail to follow suit when able, in violation of the rules. — *n.* *Card Playing.* Act of revoking.

re-volt' (rĕ-vōlt'; -vŏlt'), *n.* Act of revolting; esp., rebellion; insurrection. — *v. t.* To affect with disgust or loathing; nauseate. — *v. i.* **1.** To renounce allegiance; rebel. **2.** To be disgusted, or grossly offended. — **re-volt'er** (-vōl'tĕr; -vŏl'tĕr), *n.* [8].

rev'o-lu'tion (rĕv'ō-lū'shŭn), *n.* **1.** Rotation. **2.** Of a heavenly body, act of going round in an orbit, or elliptic course; also, apparent movement around the earth. **3.** Completion of a course, as of years; circuit. **4.** Radical change. **5.** Overthrow or renunciation of one government, and substitution of another, by the governed.

rev'o-lu'tion-a-ry (-ā-rĭ), *a.* [4] Of or pert. to a revolution. — *n.* A revolutionist.

rev'o-lu'tion-ist, *n.* One engaged in a revolution.

rev'o-lu'tion-ize (-īz), *v. t.* [1] To change fundamentally; subject to a revolution.

re-volve' (rĕ-vŏlv'), *v. t.* [1] **1.** To turn over in the mind; cogitate. **2.** To cause to move or turn around; rotate. — *v. i.* **1.** To move around or turn, as in an orbit or about an axis; rotate. **2.** To pass in cycles; recur. — **re-volv'a-ble**, *a.* [8].

re-volv'er (rĕ-vŏl'vĕr), *n.* A repeating pistol having a revolvable cylinder with several cartridge chambers.

re-vul'sion (rĕ-vŭl'shŭn), *n.* A sudden or strong reaction, reversion, or change. [revulsion.]

re-vul'sive (-sĭv), *a.* [4] Causing, or tending to.

re-ward' (-wôrd'), *v. t.* **1.** To give as a reward. **2.** To make a return, or give a reward, to (a person) or for (a service, etc.); requite; recompense. — *n.* **1.** That which is given in return for good or evil done or received; recompense. **2.** Remuneration for services. — **-er**, *n.* [8].

re-word' (rĕ-wûrd'), *v.t.* To restate in other words.

rhap-sod'ic (răp-sŏd'ĭk), **rhap-sod'i-cal** (-ĭ-kăl), *a.* [4] Like a rhapsody. [dizes.]

rhap'so-dist (răp'sō-dĭst), *n.* One who rhapso-

rhap'so-dize (-dīz), *v. t.* [1] To recite as a rhapsody. — *v. i.* To utter rhapsodies.

rhap'so-dy (-dĭ), *n.; pl.* -DIES (-dĭz). **1.** An utterance or writing marked by emotionalism and lack of connection and soundness. **2.** *Music.* An irregular instrumental composition.

rhe'o-stat (rē'ō-stăt), *n.* *Elec.* Any contrivance for regulating a current by means of (usually) variable resistances.

rhet'o-ric (rĕt'ō-rĭk), *n.* **1.** The art of expressive speech or of discourse, esp. the art of literary composition. **2.** Artificial elegance of language.

rhe-tor'i-cal (rĕ-tŏr'ĭ-kăl), *a.* [4] Of, pert. to, or exhibiting, rhetoric; oratorical. — *ly*, *adv.* [8].

rhet'o-ri'cian (rĕt'ō-rĭsh'ăn), *n.* **1.** One versed in rhetoric. **2.** An eloquent writer or speaker.

rheum (rōōm), *n.* A watery discharge, esp. from the eyes or nose; hence, a cold; catarrh. *Archaic.*

rheu-mat'ic (rōō-măt'ĭk), *a.* [4] Of, pertaining to, affected with, or causing, rheumatism.

rheu'ma-tism (rōō'mà-tĭz'm), *n.* A painful constitutional disease. It attacks joints, muscles, etc.

rhine'stone' (rīn'stōn'), *n.* A colorless brilliant stone made of paste, — used in cheap jewelry.

rhi-noc'er-os (rī-nŏs'ẽr-ŏs), *n.* Any of certain large, thick-skinned animals of Africa and Asia, with a heavy, upright horn (in some species, two horns) on the snout.

rhi'zome (rī'zōm), *n.* *Bot.* Any underground rootlike stem sending leafy shoots from the upper surface and roots from the lower side; a rootstock.

rho'do-den'dron (rō-dō-dĕn'drŏn), *n.* Any of a genus of evergreen shrubs, bearing handsome white, pink, crimson, or rose-purple flowers.

rhomb'ic (rŏm'bĭk), *a.* Rhomb-shaped.

rhom'boid (rŏm'boid), *n.* A parallelogram with oblique angles and the adjacent sides unequal.— *a.* Shaped like a rhombus or a rhomboid.

rhom-boi'dal (rŏm-boi'dăl), *a.* Shaped more or less like a rhomboid.

rhom'bus (rŏm'bŭs), *n.* An equilateral parallelogram, usually one having its angles oblique.

rhu'barb (rōō'bärb), *n.* Any of certain tall, coarse herbs with large leaves. The fleshy, acid leafstalks of the common species are used in cookery.

rhyme (rīm), *n.*, **rhym'er** (rīm'ẽr), **rhyme'ster** (rīm'stẽr). See RIME, etc.

rhythm (rĭth'm; rĭth'm), *n.* Movement, esp. in language or music, marked by some regular recurrence, as of accent.

rhyth'mic (rĭth'mĭk; rĭth'-), *a.* [4] Rhythmical.

rhyth'mi-cal (-mĭ-kăl), *a.* [4] Pert. to, of the nature of, or marked by, rhythm. — *ly*, *adv.* [8].

rib (rĭb), *n.* **1.** *Anat.* One of the elastic arches of bone which form the chief part of the chest wall. In man there are twelve on each side. **2.** Something likened to a rib; as : **a** One of the primary veins of a leaf. **b** A strengthening or shaping timber, bar, rod, etc. **c** A prominent ridge in cloth. — *v. t.*; RIBBED (rĭbd); RIB'BING. To furnish, strengthen, or mark with ribs or ridges.

rib'ald (rĭb'ăld), *a.* [4] Low, coarse, or abusive; esp., blasphemous or indecent in language.

rib'ald-ry (-rĭ), *n.* Ribald acts or words.

rib'bon (rĭb'ŭn), *n.* **1.** A fillet or narrow woven fabric, commonly of silk or velvet, for trimming, etc. **2.** A strip or shred; as, sails torn to *ribbons.* — *v. t.* To adorn with ribbons; — chiefly in p. p.

rice (rīs), *n.* A cereal grass cultivated in warm climates; also, its grain.

rice'bird' (-bûrd'), *n.* The bobolink. *Southern U. S.*

rich (rĭch), *a.* [3] **1.** Abounding in material possessions; wealthy. **2.** Abundant; copious; bountiful. **3.** Productive or fertile; fruitful. **4.** Sumptuous; costly. **5.** Abounding in superior or pleasing qualities; — esp. of food or drink which is highly seasoned, abounds in fat, etc. **6. a** Of colors, not faint or delicate; vivid. **b** Full and mellow in tone. — *ly*, *adv.* — *ness*, *n.*

rich'es (rĭch'ĕz), *n. pl.;* originally a *sing.* Wealth.

rick (rĭk), *n.* A large stack, as of straw or hay, in the open air.

rick'ets (-ĕts), *n. pl.* A children's disease marked by defective nutrition and changes in the bones.

rick'et-y (-ĕt-ĭ), *a.* [4] **1.** Affected with rickets. **2.** Feeble in the joints; shaky; weak.

ric'o-chet' (rĭk'ō-shā'; -shĕt'), *n.* A glancing rebound or skipping, as of a projectile along the ground or water.— *v. i.* [7] To skip with a glancing rebound or rebounds, as a projectile.

rid (rĭd), *v. t. ;* RID *or* RID′DED ; RID′DING. To free; disencumber; — with *of.* — to be, *or* get, rid of, to be or become free from; as, *to get rid of* a nuisance.

rid′dance (rĭd′ăns), *n.* **1.** Act of ridding or freeing; removal. **2.** The being or getting rid of something; also, that of which one gets rid.

rid′den (-′n), *p. p.* of RIDE.

rid′dle (-′l), *n.* A coarse sieve. — *v. t.* [1] **1.** To sift with a riddle. **2.** To pierce with holes.

rid′dle, *n.* A puzzling question ; enigma. — *v. t.* [1] To explain ; unriddle. — *v. i.* To speak ambiguously or enigmatically.

ride (rīd), *v. i. ; pret.* RODE (rōd) ; *p. p.* RID′DEN (rĭd′′n) ; *p. pr. & vb. n.* RID′ING (rīd′ĭng). **1.** To be carried on or as on the back of an animal, esp. a horse. **2.** To be borne in or on a vehicle. **3.** To float; of a vessel, to float at anchor or when moored. **4.** To be borne along. **5.** To support and carry one; as, the carriage *rides* easy. — *v. t.* **1.** To sit on and control so as to be carried. **2.** To control or manage, esp. autocratically. **3.** To make; perform, do, or traverse, by riding. **4.** To cause to ride. — *n.* Act or fact of riding.

rid′er (rīd′ẽr), *n.* **1.** One that rides. **2.** A clause annexed to a legislative bill.—**rid′er-less,** *a.* [8].

ridge (rĭj), *n.* **1.** The back, or top of the back, of an animal. **2.** A range, or the upper part of a range, of hills or mountains. **3.** A raised line or strip, as of ground, or as on metal, cloth, etc. **4.** The intersection of two surfaces forming a salient angle. — *v. t. & i.* [1] To form into, or extend in, a ridge or ridges; furnish or mark with ridges.

ridge′pole′ (-pōl′), *n.* The highest horizontal timber in a roof, receiving the rafters.

ridg′y (-ĭ), *a.* [3] Having a ridge or ridges.

rid′i-cule (rĭd′ĭ-kūl), *n.* Remarks designed to excite laughter with a degree of contempt for the subject of the remarks. — *v. t.* [1] To treat with ridicule ; laugh at disparagingly.

ri-dic′u-lous (rĭ-dĭk′ū-lŭs), *a.* [4] Fitted to excite ridicule. —**ly,** *adv.* [8] —**ness,** *n.* [8].

rife (rīf), *a.* [3] **1.** Prevalent; existing generally; current. **2.** Abounding; replete; — usually with *with.*

riff′raff′ (rĭf′răf′), *n.* **1.** Rubbish. **2.** The rabble

ri′fle (rī′f′l), *v. t.* [1] **1.** To seize and bear away by force. **2.** To rob; pillage; strip.

ri′fle, *v. t.* [1] To groove (a gun barrel) internally with spiral channels to insure greater accuracy of fire. — *n.* A firearm having the barrel rifled, esp. such a firearm fired from the shoulder.

ri′fle-man (rī′f′l-măn), *n. ; pl.* -MEN (-měn). A soldier armed with, or one skilled in using, a rifle.

ri′fler (rī′flẽr), *n.* One who rifles ; a robber.

rift (rĭft), *n.* An opening made by riving; cleft; fissure. — *v. t. & i.* To cleave; rive; split.

rig (rĭg), *v. t. ;* RIGGED (rĭgd) ; RIG′GING (rĭg′ĭng). **1.** To fit the rigging of (a vessel) to the masts, spars, etc.; fit shrouds, stays, etc., to (a mast, spar, etc.). **2.** To fit up; equip. **3.** To dress; clothe, esp. in an odd manner. — *n.* **1.** The distinctive shape, number, and arrangement of sails and masts of a type of vessel. **2.** Dress ; esp., odd or fanciful clothing. *Colloq.* **3.** Anything rigged up; outfit.

rig′ger (rĭg′ẽr), *n.* One who rigs; esp., one whose occupation is fitting the rigging of ships.

rig′ging (-ĭng), *n.* **1.** *Naut.* Ropes, etc., that support or adjust spars and sails. **2.** Tackle; gear.

right (rīt), *a.* **1.** Straight; not crooked. **2.** Upright; erect from a base; not oblique. **3.** Conformed to justice : just; upright; — now rarely used of persons. **4.** Fit; suitable; proper. **5.** Correct; true. **6.** Well; in good condition. **7.** Designed to be placed or worn outward. **8.** Designating, or pert. to, that side of the body usually stronger than the other side; — opposed to *left.* — **right angle,** the angle bounded by two lines perpendicular to each other. See ANGLE, *Illust.* — r. **triangle,** a triangle one of whose angles is a right angle.

right, *adv.* **1.** In a right line; directly. **2.** According to right; righteously. **3.** In a suitable or desired manner. **4.** Truly; correctly. **5.** Exactly; precisely. *Chiefly Colloq.* **6.** Very.

right, *n.* **1.** That which is right or correct ; esp., obedience to duty or authority. **2.** That, as a power or privilege, to which one has a just or lawful claim. **3.** The side or part on or toward the right side (see RIGHT, *a.*, 8).

right, *v. t.* **1.** To bring or restore to the proper position or state. **2.** To do justice to ; relieve from wrong. — *v. i.* To recover the proper or natural condition or position ; become upright.

right′-an′gled (-ăŋ′g′ld), *a.* Containing a right angle or right angles. See ANGLE, *Illust.*

right′eous (rī′chŭs), *a.* [4] Doing, or according with, that which is right ; just ; upright ; equitable. — **right′eous-ly,** *adv.* [8].

right′eous-ness, *n.* **1.** Quality or state of being righteous. **2.** The quality of being rightful or just.

right′er (rīt′ẽr), *n.* One who sets right.

right′ful (-fŏŏl), *a.* [4] **1.** Consonant to justice ; just. **2.** Having a right or just claim according to law. **3.** Belonging or possessed by right. —**ly,** *adv.* [8] —**ness,** *n.* [8].

right′-hand′, *a.* **1.** Being on the right hand. **2.** Of, pertaining to, or done with, the right hand. **3.** Chiefly relied on; as, a *right-hand* man.

right′-hand′ed, *a.* **1.** Using the right hand more easily than the left. **2.** Rotating in the same direction as the hands of a watch seen from in front.

right′ly, *adv.* **1.** According to justice; uprightly. **2.** Properly; fitly. **3.** Correctly; exactly.

right′ness, *n.* Quality or state of being right.

rig′id (rĭj′ĭd), *a.* [4] **1.** Firm; stiff; inflexible. **2.** Not lax; strict. —**ly,** *adv.* — **ness,** *n.* [8].

ri-gid′i-ty (rĭ-jĭd′ĭ-tĭ), *n.* State of being rigid.

rig′ma-role (rĭg′mà-rōl), *n.* A succession of confused or foolish statements ; rambling discourse.

rig′or (rĭg′ẽr), *n.* [5] **1.** (*pron.* rī′gŏr, rĭg′ŏr). *Med.* A convulsive shuddering or tremor, as in the chill preceding a fever. **2.** Quality of being unyielding or inflexible ; severity ; harshness.

rig′or-ous (-ŭs), *a.* [4] **1.** Characterized by rigor. **2.** Harsh; severe. —**ly,** *adv.* —**ness,** *n.* [8].

rill (rĭl), *n.* A very small brook; streamlet.

rim (rĭm), *n.* A border or margin, usually of something curving. — *v. t. ;* RIMMED (rĭmd) ; RIM′MING. To furnish with a rim.

rime (rīm), *n.* White frost ; hoarfrost.

rime (rīm), *n.* **1.** A composition in verse having correspondence of terminal sounds. Hence, riming verse. **2. a** The correspondence of terminal sounds in two or more words or verses. **b** One of two or more words thus corresponding in sound. — *v. i.* [1] **1.** To make rimes, or verses. **2.** To end in rime.— *v. t.* **a** To put into rime. **b** To compose (rimed verse). **c** To make (words) rime.

rim′er (rīm′ēr), *n.* One who makes rimes.

rime′ster (rīm′stēr), *n.* A mere rimer.

rim′y (rīm′ĭ), *a.* [3] Covered with rime; frosty.

rind (rīnd), *n.* An external coat, as skin or bark.

rin′der-pest (rĭn′dēr-pĕst), *n.* A contagious disease of neat cattle, less often of sheep and goats.

ring (rĭng), *v. t.; pret.* RANG (răng) or RUNG (rŭng); *p. p.* RUNG; *p. pr. & vb. n.* RING′ING. **1.** To cause to sound, esp. by striking, as a metallic body. **2.** To make (a sound), as by ringing a bell. **3.** To announce, proclaim, etc., by or as by ringing. — *v. i.* **1.** To sound, as a bell or sonorous body. **2.** To sound sonorously or vibrantly. **3.** To resound. **4.** To ring a bell, as a summons. **5.** To be filled with report or talk. — *n.* A sound made by or as by a vibrating metal.

ring (rĭng), *n.* **1.** A circle, or a circular line; a circular band or hoop; a band, esp. of precious metal, to be worn, usually on the finger. **2.** A race course, usually circular; hence, an arena or area for competition or display. **3.** A combination of persons for a selfish, often corrupt, purpose. — *v. t.* **1.** To surround with a ring; encircle. **2.** To provide with a ring or rings.

ring′dove′ (-dŭv′), *n.* A European pigeon having a whitish patch on each side of the neck.

ring′er (-ēr), *n.* One that rings.

ring′lead′er (-lēd′ēr), *n.* A leader in some improper enterprise, as riot, mutiny, conspiracy, etc.

ring′let (rĭng′lĕt), *n.* **1.** A small ring. **2.** A curl of hair, esp. a long one.

ring′worm′ (-wûrm′), *n.* A contagious skin affection causing a ring-shaped eruption.

rink (rĭnk), *n.* An inclosed sheet of ice for skating; hence, a covered inclosure for roller skating.

rinse (rĭns), *v. t.* [1] To wash lightly; cleanse with water after washing. — **rins′er**, *n.* [8].

ri′ot (rī′ŭt), *n.* **1.** Disorderly behavior; uproar; tumult. **2.** Profligate living; revelry. **3.** A tumultuous disturbance of the public peace by an unlawful assembly of three or more persons.— *v. i.* To engage in a riot; act riotously. — **ri′ot-er**, *n.*

ri′ot-ous (-ŭs), *a.* [4] Involving, or engaging in, riot; as: **a** Wanton; profligate. **b** Seditious; tumultuous. — **-ly,** *adv.* [8] — **-ness,** *n.* [8].

rip (rĭp), *v. t.; pret.* RIPPED (rĭpt); RIP′PING. **1.** To divide or separate by cutting or tearing; tear off or out by violence. **2.** To saw (wood) lengthwise of the grain. — *v. i.* To become torn apart. — *n.* A rent made by ripping; a tear.

ri-pa′ri-an (rī-pā′rī-ăn; rĭ-), *a.* Of, pert. to, or living on, the bank of a river, or other body of water.

ripe (rīp), *a.* [3] **1.** Ready for reaping or gathering; mature. **2.** Like ripened fruit in ruddiness and plumpness. **3.** Advanced to the state best for use; mellow. **4.** Mature; perfected. **5.** Ready for action; prepared.— **-ly,** *adv.* [8]— **-ness,** *n.* [8].

rip′en (rīp′'n), *v. i. & t.* **1.** To grow or make ripe; mature. **2.** To come to perfection.

rip′per (rĭp′ēr), *n.* One that rips; a ripping tool.

rip′ple (-'l), *v. i. & t.* To become or make fretted or dimpled on the surface, as of water running over rough shallows. — *n.* **1.** The dimpling of the surface of ruffled water; a wavelet; undulation. **2.** A sound such as is made by rippling water.

rip′ply (-lĭ), *a.* [3] Marked by ripples.

rip′rap′ (-răp′), *n.* A foundation or sustaining wall of stones thrown together without fitting; also, stones so used.

rip′saw′ (-sô′), *n.* A saw used for cutting wood in the direction of the grain.

rise (rīz), *v. i.; pret.* ROSE (rōz); *p. p.* RIS′EN (rĭz′'n); *p. pr. & vb. n.* RIS′ING (rīz′ĭng). **1.** To move from a lower position to a higher; ascend. **2.** To emerge above the horizon, as the sun. **3.** To have a beginning; originate. **4.** To increase in size, force, interest, value, etc. **5.** To become hostile; rebel. **6.** To attain to a better position; be promoted. **7.** To ascend from the grave.

rise (rīz; rĭs), *n.* **1.** Act of rising; state of being risen; ascent. **2.** Distance through which anything rises. **3.** A piece of land higher than its surroundings. **4.** Spring; source; origin, as of a river. **5.** Increase; advance, as of price, value, etc. **6.** Increase of sound, as of a voice.

ris′er (rīz′ēr), *n.* **1.** One who rises, esp. from bed; — chiefly in *early riser*, etc. **2.** *Arch.* The upright piece of a step, from tread to tread.

ris′i-bil′i-ty (rĭz′ĭ-bĭl′ĭ-tĭ), *n.; pl.* -TIES (-tĭz). **1.** The quality of being risible. **2.** *pl.* A person's sensibilities to what seems ridiculous.

ris′i-ble (rĭz′ĭ-b'l), *a.* [4] **1.** Having the faculty of laughing. **2.** Laughable. **3.** Used in, or pert. to, laughter. — *n. pl.* Risibilities (sense 2).

risk (rĭsk), *n.* Hazard; peril; exposure to loss or injury. — *v. t.* **1.** To expose to risk; hazard. **2.** To incur the risk or danger of. —**-er,** *n.* [8].

risk′y (rĭs′kĭ), *a.* [3] Attended with risk.

rite (rīt), *n.* **1.** Act of performing divine or solemn service; a solemn observance. **2.** A prescribed form of service; liturgy.

rit′u-al (rĭt′ṳ-ăl), *a.* Of or pertaining to rites or a ritual. — *n.* **1.** Established form of worship; religious ceremonial. **2.** Hence, a code of ceremonies observed. — **rit′u-al-ly,** *adv.* [8].

rit′u-al-ism (-ĭz′m), *n.* Adherence to a ritual. — **rit′u-al-ist** (-ĭst), *n. & a.* — **-is′tic,** *a.* [8].

ri′val (rī′văl), *n.* One of two or more striving to reach or get that which one only can possess; competitor. — *a.* Having the same pretensions or claims; standing in competition. — *v. t.* [7] **1.** To stand or strive in competition with. **2.** To strive to equal or excel; emulate ;— often implying success.

ri′val-ry (-rĭ), *n.; pl.* -RIES (-rĭz). A rivaling; state of being a rival.

rive (rīv), *v. t.; pret.* RIVED (rīvd); *p. p.* RIVED or RIV′EN (rĭv′'n); *p. pr. & vb. n.* RIV′ING (rīv′ĭng). To rend asunder; split; cleave.

riv′er (-ēr), *n.* A natural stream of water larger than a brook or a creek.

riv′et (rĭv′ĕt), *n.* A headed pin or bolt of metal, used to unite two or more pieces by passing it through them and heading the plain end. — *v. t.* To fasten with a rivet; hence, to fasten firmly.

riv′u-let (rĭv′ṳ-lĕt), *n.* A small stream or brook.

roach (rōch), *n.* A cockroach.

---

chair; go; sing, iŋk; ǂhen, thin; nature, verdure; yet; zh = z in azure. Numbers refer to §§ in the Special Notes which, with Abbreviations, Signs, etc., precede the Vocabulary.

roach (rōch), *n.* **1.** A European fish of the carp family. **2.** Any of various similar fishes.

road (rōd), *n.* A place, less inclosed than a *harbor*, where ships may ride at anchor;— often in *pl.*

road, *n.* An open way or public passage for vehicles, persons, and animals; highway.

road′bed′ (rōd′bĕd′), *n.* **1.** In railroads, the bed on which the superstructure (ties, rails, etc.) rests. **2.** In common roads, the whole material laid in place and ready for travel.

road′stead (-stĕd), *n.* = 1st ROAD.

road′ster (rōd′stẽr), *n.* **1.** A horse used for pleasure or for light work on ordinary roads. **2.** A fairly powerful automobile for use on common roads, usually seating two passengers.

road′way′ (-wā′), *n.* A road, esp. the traveled part.

roam (rōm), *v. i.* To wander with no certain aim; rove. — *v. t.* To range or wander over.— **-er**, *n.*

roan (rōn), *a.* Bay, chestnut, or red, with gray or white thickly interspersed;— of a horse. — *n.* **1.** The color of a roan horse; a roan horse. **2.** A kind of leather imitating ungrained morocco.

roar (rōr), *v. i. & t.* **1. a** To bellow, as does a lion or bull. **b** To cry loudly, as in distress or anger. **2.** To make a loud, confused sound. **3.** To laugh out loud and continuously. — *n.* A loud, deep cry; loud, confused sound. — **-er**, *n.* [8].

roast (rōst), *v. t.* Primarily, to cook by exposure before a fire; also, to cook (as meat) in a close oven. — *v. i.* To undergo the process of being roasted. — *n.* **1.** A piece of meat roasted or suitable for roasting. **2.** Act or process of roasting. — *a.* Roasted; as, *roast* beef. — **roast′er**, *n.* [8].

rob (rŏb), *v. t. ;* ROBBED (rŏbd); ROB′BING. **1.** To take something away from by force; steal from. **2.** To deprive of, or withhold from, unjustly or injuriously; defraud. — *v. i.* To commit robbery.

rob′ber (rŏb′ẽr), *n.* One who robs. [of robbing.]

rob′ber-y (-ĭ), *n.; pl.* -BERIES (-ĭz). Act or practice

robe (rōb), *n.* **1.** An outer garment of a flowing, elegant style ; *pl.*, dress ; costume. **2.** A skin of an animal used as a wrap. *U. S.* — *v. t. & i.* [1] To put on a robe or robes ; dress ; array.

rob′in (rŏb′ĭn), *n.* **1.** A small European bird of the thrush family, with back brownish olive and throat and breast yellowish red. **2.** In North America, a kind of large thrush with breast and underparts dull reddish.

rob′ot (rŏb′ŏt), *n.* Any one of a number of artificially manufactured persons, mechanically efficient, but devoid of sensibility.

a American Robin.
b European Robin.

ro-bust′ (rō-bŭst′), *a.* [4] Having or evincing strength or vigorous health ; strong ; vigorous ; sturdy ; hearty. — **-ness**, *n.* [8].

rock (rŏk), *v. t. & i.* **1.** To sway or move backward and forward; vibrate. **2.** To move as in a cradle; hence, to quiet, as by rocking. — *n.* A rocking.

rock, *n.* **1.** A large concreted mass of stony material; also, broken pieces of such masses. **2.** *Geol.* Any mineral matter occurring in large quantities; also, a particular mass of it. **3.** The striped bass.

rock crystal. = CRYSTAL, *n.*, 1.

rock′er (rŏk′ẽr), *n.* **1.** One who rocks a cradle, etc. **2.** Either of the curving pieces on which a chair, etc., rocks; also, a rocking-chair. **3.** Any of various devices that work with a rocking motion.

rock′et (-ĕt), *n.* A well-known kind of firework.

rock′i-ness (-ĭ-nĕs), *n.* State of being rocky.

rock′ing-chair′, *n.* A chair mounted on rockers.

rock′ing-horse′, *n.* A toy horse on rockers.

rock oil. Petroleum.

rock′y (-ĭ), *a.* [3] **1.** Full of rocks ; consisting of rocks. **2.** Like a rock ; hard ; unfeeling.

ro-co′co (rō-kō′kō), *n.* A florid style of ornamentation popular in the 17th and 18th centuries.

rod (rŏd), *n.* **1.** A straight and slender stick or bar; as : **a** An instrument of punishment. **b** A scepter. **c** A staff for measuring. **2.** A measure of length; 5½ yards, or 16½ feet, or 5.029 meters.

rode (rōd). Pret. of RIDE.

ro′dent (rō′dĕnt), *a.* [4] **1.** Gnawing ; biting. **2.** Of or pertaining to rodents. — *n.* Any of an order (*Rodentia*) comprising the gnawing mammals, as rats, mice, squirrels, beavers, etc.

ro′de-o (rō′dē-ō), *n.* [Sp.] An entertainment presenting features of cowboy life.

rod′o-mon-tade′ (rŏd′ô-mŏn-tād′ ; -täd′), *n.* Vain boasting ; brag ; rant.

roe (rō), *n.* The roe deer.

roe, *n.* The eggs of fishes.

roe′buck (bŭk), *n.* The male roe deer.

roe deer. A small deer of Europe and Asia.

Roent′gen rays. See RÖNTGEN RAYS.

rogue (rōg), *n.* **1.** A knave ; cheat. **2.** In playful use, one who is mischievous or frolicsome.

ro′guer-y (rō′gẽr-ĭ), *n.; pl.* -GUERIES (-ĭz). **1.** Practices of a rogue. **2.** Playful mischievousness.

ro′guish (rō′gĭsh), *a.* [4] **1.** Knavish. **2.** Playfully mischievous. — **-ly**, *adv.* — **-ness**, *n.* [8].

roil (roil), *v. t.* **1.** To render turbid by stirring, as a spring. **2.** To ruffle ; vex. — **roil′y**, *a.* [3].

roist′er (rois′tẽr), *v. i.* To bluster or swagger.

roist′er-er (-ẽr), *n.* A blustering bully or reveler.

rôle (rōl), *n.* An actor's part in a drama.

roll (rōl), *v. t.* **1.** To revolve by turning over and over. **2.** To move, or cause to be moved, on rollers. **3.** To wrap round on itself or on something else. **4.** To drive or impel as if rolling. **5.** To press or level with a roller, as a field. — *v. i.* **1.** To turn over and over. **2.** To move or be moved on wheels. **3.** To have an undulating form, as land. **4.** To incline first to one side and then to the other, as a ship. **5.** To move, as waves, with alternate swell and depression. **6.** To make a heavy rising and falling or rumbling noise. — *n.* **1.** Act of rolling; state of being rolled. **2.** A roller; revolving cylinder. **3.** Something rolled up, as a scroll. Hence, a register; list. **4.** A reverberatory sound. **5.** A swell or undulation on a surface.

roll′er (rōl′ẽr), *n.* **1.** One that rolls ; esp. : **a** A

lindrical body for rotating, pressing, etc.; a roll.
b A small wheel, as of a caster. **2.** One of a series of long, heavy waves.

roller skate. A skate with wheels instead of a runner. Hence, **roller skating.**

rol'lic (rŏl'ĭk), *v. i.;* -LICKED (-ĭkt); -LICK-ING. To romp in a joyous, careless manner; frolic; sport.

roll'ing (rōl'ĭng), *n.* **1.** Act of one that rolls. **2.** A rolling sound, as of thunder. — *a.* **1.** Moving like one that rolls. **2.** Having undulations, as land. **3.** Of or pert. to rolling; as, a *rolling* mill.

roll'ing-pin' (rōl'ĭng-pĭn'), *n.* A cylinder, as of wood or glass, for rolling out paste or dough.

Ro'man (rō'măn), *a.* **1.** Of, pertaining to, like, or derived from, Rome or the Roman people. **2.** Of or pertaining to the Roman Catholic Church. **3.** [*Usually l. c.*] Designating type, or the characters, of that form of the Roman alphabet commonly used in print;— distinguished from *italic.* — **Roman Catholic,** of, pertaining to, or designating, the Church of Rome, of which the Pope is the head. Also, a member of this church. — **R. nose,** a nose somewhat aquiline. — *n.* **1.** A native, inhabitant, or citizen of Rome. **2.** [*Usually l. c.*] Roman type or letters. **3.** *pl.* The Epistle to the Romans, in the New Testament.

ro-mance' (rō-măns'), *n.* **1.** A fictitious tale; esp., a sort of novel characterized by adventure, surprising incident, etc. **2.** An act, or a series of acts or happenings, like those of romances. **3.** A dreamy, imaginative habit of mind; as, a girl full of *romance.* **4.** A fictitious tale. — *v. i.* [1] **1.** To write or tell romances; indulge in extravagant stories. **2.** To indulge in romantic fancies. — **ro-manc'er** (rō-măn'sẽr), *n.* [8].

Ro'man-esque' (rō'măn-ĕsk'), *a.* Pertaining to or designating a style of architecture developed between the classical Roman and Gothic periods.

ro-man'tic (rō-măn'tĭk), *a.* [4] **1.** Of or pertaining to romance; hence, fanciful; extravagant. **2.** Entertaining ideas suited to a romance. **3.** Characterized by picturesque strangeness or variety.

ro-man'ti-cism (-tĭ-sĭz'm), *n.* Romantic principles or characteristics; conformity to the romantic style. — **ro-man'ti-cist** (-sĭst), *n.*

romp (rŏmp), *v. i.* To play boisterously. — *n.* **1.** A person, esp. a girl, who romps. **2.** Boisterous play or frolic; rough sport.

Rönt'gen rays (rŭnt'gĕn; rĕnt'-). *Physics.* Rays produced when cathode rays strike on the surface of a solid, as the wall of the vacuum tube. They penetrate many opaque substances and act on photographic plates.

Diagram showing use of Röntgen Rays. *i* Induction Coil; *t* Vacuum Tube; *p* Photographic Plate.

They were called *X rays* by their discoverer, W. K. Röntgen.

rood (rōōd), *n.* **1.** A cross or crucifix; esp., in churches, a large crucifix at the entrance of the chancel. **2.** A square measure equal to ¼ of an acre, or 40 square rods.

roof (rōōf), *n.* **1.** The cover of a building. **2.** That which resembles, or corresponds to, the roof of a house; as, the *roof* of a cave. — *v. t.* To cover with or as with a roof.

roof'ing, *n.* **1.** Act of covering with a roof. **2.** Materials for, or of, a roof.

roof'less, *a.* Having no roof or shelter.

rook (rōōk), *n.* *Chess.* A piece moving parallel to the sides of the board across any number of unoccupied squares.

rook, *n.* A common European crowlike bird.

rook'er-y (rōōk'ẽr-ĭ), *n.; pl.* -ERIES (-ĭz). **1.** The breeding place of a colony of rooks; also, the rooks. Also, a breeding place of other gregarious birds, as herons, penguins, etc., or of seals. **2.** A dilapidated building with many occupants; cluster of mean buildings.

room (rōōm), *n.* **1.** Extent of space, great or small; compass; esp., unobstructed space. **2.** An apartment or chamber. **3.** Possibility of admission; opportunity; as, *room* for doubt. — *v. i.* To occupy a room or rooms. *U. S.*

room'er (rōōm'ẽr), *n.* A lodger. *U. S.*

room'mate' (-māt'), *n.* Companion with whom one rooms.

room'y (rōōm'ĭ), *a.* [3] Having ample room; spacious. — **-i-ly** (-ĭ-lĭ), *adv.* [8] — **-i-ness,** *n.* [8].

roost (rōōst), *n.* A perch; a place for roosting. — *v. i.* To rest, or sleep, as fowls on a roost; perch.

roost'er (rōōs'tẽr), *n.* Male domestic fowl; cock.

root (rōōt), *v. i.* To turn up earth with the snout, as swine. — *v. t.* To dig up or out with the snout.

root, *n.* **1.** *Bot.* In the higher plants, a portion, commonly underground, of the plant body provided with a growing point and serving as an organ of absorption and aëration, a food reservoir, or a support. **2.** Popularly, any underground part of a plant. **3.** That which resembles a root, as:
a An ancestor or progenitor; an early race. **b** The part of an organ by which it is attached; as, the *root* of a tooth. **c** *Philol.* A primitive word form. **d** A cause; source. **e** The bottom; fundamental part. **f** *Math.* A quantity which, taken as a factor a number of times (indicated by the index), produces another quantity; thus, 3 is a second *root* of 9, since $3 \times 3 = 9$. — *v. i.* **1.** To fix the root; take root and begin to grow. **2.** To be or become firmly fixed or established. — *v. t.* **1.** To plant and fix deeply in or as in the earth; implant firmly; establish; as, a *rooted* dislike. **2.** To tear up by the root; eradicate.

Root, 1. *aa* Crown; *bb* Main Root; *cc* Rootlets.

root'let (rōōt'lĕt), *n.* A small root.

root'stock' (rōōt'stŏk'), *n.* A rhizome.

rope (rōp), *n.* **1.** A large, stout cord of twisted or braided strands. **2.** A row or string of things united by braiding, twining, etc.; as, a *rope* of onions. **3.** A sticky or glutinous formation in a liquid. — *v. t.* [1] **1.** To bind, fasten, or tie with a rope. **2.** To divide off by a rope; as, to *rope* off a space. **3.** To lasso (a steer, etc.). *Colloq.*

rop'y (rōp'ĭ), *a.* [3] Forming sticky threads, etc.; stringy; as, a *ropy* sirup. — **rop'i-ness,** *n.* [8].

ror'qual (rôr'kwăl), *n.* Any of certain whales having a large vertical fin on the back.

ro'sa-ry (rō'zá-rĭ), *n.; pl.* -RIES (-rĭz). *R. C. Ch.* A series of prayers to be recited in order; also, a string of beads for counting prayers.

rose (rōz), *pret.* of RISE.

rose (rōz), *n.* **1.** A well-known, widely cultivated, beautiful and fragrant flower of many varieties, usually pink, red, white, or yellow in color; also, the plant or bush (**rose'bush'**) that bears this flower. **2.** A rosette. **3.** The color of a rose; pink or light crimson.

ro'se-ate (rō'zê-āt), *a.* [4] Tinged with rose color.

rose'bud' (rōz'bŭd'), *n.* Flower bud of a rose.

rose'ma-ry (rōz'mā-rĭ), *n.; pl.* -RIES (-rĭz). A fragrant Old World evergreen shrub.

ro-sette' (rṓ-zĕt'), *n.* An ornament in the form of a rose.

rose'wood' (rōz'wŏŏd'), *n.* A tropical cabinet wood of a dark red color, streaked with black.

ros'i-ly (rōz'ĭ-lĭ), *adv.* In a rosy manner.

ros'in (rŏz'ĭn), *n.* The hard, commonly amber-colored resin left after distilling off the oil from crude turpentine. — *v. t.* To rub with rosin.

ros'i-ness (rōz'ĭ-nĕs), *n.* Rosy color.

ros'ter (rŏs'tẽr), *n.* **1.** *Mil. & Nav.* A roll or list of officers or enlisted men, subject to certain assignments for duty. **2.** Hence, any roll or list.

ros'trum (-trŭm), *n.; pl. L.* -TRA (-trá), E. -TRUMS (-trŭmz). A stage for public speaking; platform.

ros'y (rōz'ĭ), *a.* [3] **1.** Resembling a rose; rose-colored; blushing. **2.** Bright; hopeful.

rot (rŏt), *v. i.;* ROT'TED, -TING. To decompose; decay. — *v. t.* To cause to rot. — *n.* Process of rotting; decay; that which is rotten.

Ro-ta'ri-an (rṓ-tā'rĭ-ăn), *n.* A member of any of a large number of clubs (**Rotary Clubs**) having the same constitution. Their motto is "Service."

ro'ta-ry (rō'tá-rĭ), *a.* Turning, as a wheel, on its axis; having parts that rotate; rotatory.

ro'tate (rō'tāt), *v. i. & t.* [1] To turn, as a wheel, round an axis; revolve.

ro-ta'tion (rṓ-tā'shŭn), *n.* **1.** Act of rotating. **2.** Any return or succession in a series; recurrence; as, the *rotation* of the seasons.

ro'ta-to-ry (rō'tá-tṓ-rĭ), *a.* [4] **1.** Of, pertaining to, or producing, rotation; rotary. **2.** Going or following in rotation or succession.

rote (rōt), *n.* A customary course; routine. *Obs.,* except in: by rote, mechanically; esp., by memory of the mere words.

rot'ten (rŏt'ʼn), *a.* [3] **1.** Having rotted; putrid; decayed; hence, fetid. **2.** Unsound, as if rotted; not firm; as, *rotten* iron. — **rot'ten-ness,** *n.* [8].

rot'ten-stone' (-stŏn'), *n.* A decomposed siliceous limestone, used for polishing.

ro-tund' (rṓ-tŭnd'), *a.* [4] **1.** Round or rounded out. **2.** Rounded; full and flowing, as speech.

ro-tun'da (-tŭn'dá), *n.* **1.** A round building, esp. one covered by a dome. **2.** A large round room.

ro-tun'di-ty (-dĭ-tĭ), *n.; pl.* -TIES (-tĭz). State of being rotund; of speech, full and flowing.

‖ rou-é' (rŏŏ-ā'), *n.* [F.] A debauchee; rake.

rouge (rŏŏzh), *n.* **1.** A red powder used in polishing, as a pigment, etc. **2.** Any of various cosmetics used to redden the cheeks or lips. — *v. i. & t.* [1] To tint with rouge, as the cheeks.

rough (rŭf), *a.* [3] **1.** Having an uneven surface; not smooth or plain; shaggy. **2.** Coarse; unrefined; harsh; rude; discordant; grating. **3.** Boisterous; tempestuous. **4.** Crude or unfinished; hastily or carelessly done or made. — *n.* **1.** A coarse, rude fellow; rowdy; ruffian. **2.** That which is rough. — *v. t.* **1.** To roughen. **2.** To shape, make, or dress, roughly.

rough'en (-ʼn), *v. t. & i.* To make or become rough.

rough'hew' (-hū'), *v. t.* **1.** To hew (timber, etc.) roughly. **2.** To give the first form or shape to.

rough'ly, *adv.* In a rough manner.

rough'ness, *n.* Quality or state of being rough.

rough'rid'er (rŭf'rīd'ẽr), *n.* One who breaks horses to the saddle or who rides little-trained horses. Specif. [*cap.*], one of the 1st U. S. Volunteer Cavalry in the Spanish-American War. *Colloq.*

rough'shod' (-shŏd'), *a.* Shod with calked shoes.

rou-lette' (rŏŏ-lĕt'), *n.* **1.** A gambling game, in which a rotating disk, or wheel, is used. **2.** Any of various toothed wheels or disks variously used.

round (round), *a.* [3] **1.** Spherical or circular, as a ball. **2.** Circular in cross section; esp., cylindrical, as a gun barrel. **3.** Having a curved outline or form. **4.** Full; complete; — of numbers; as, a *round* dozen; also, approximate; as, in *round* numbers. **5.** Full; large; liberal in size or amount; as, a *round* sum. **6.** Free and vigorous in motion; as, a *round* pace. **b** Uttered or emitted with a full tone; as, a *round* voice. **c** Outspoken; plain and direct; as, a *round* oath. **7.** Complete; rounded; as, a *round* trip, that is, a trip which brings the traveler back to the starting point.

round (round), *n.* **1.** Anything round, as a circle, globe, or ring. **2.** A circular dance. **3.** A course ending where it began; a circuit; beat. **4.** A cycle of changes, events, acts, etc. **5.** A course of action, conduct, etc., performed by a number of persons in turn, or, loosely, simultaneously or nearly so. **6.** *Mil.* **a** One shot discharged by each soldier, gun, or cannon of a command. **b** Ammunition for one shot by each soldier, etc. **7.** A rung of a ladder; a round stick similarly placed, as in a chair.

round, *adv.* **1.** On all sides; around. **2.** Circularly. **3.** In circumference; as, a ball 10 inches *round.* **4.** By, in, or through a circuit or cycle. **5.** In the vicinity; around.

round, *prep.* **1.** On every side of; around; about. **2.** About or past in a circular course.

round, *v. t.* **1.** To make round. **2.** To complete; finish; — often with *out.* **3.** To fill out to roundness or fullness; — often with *off* or *out.* **4.** To go round; go about (a corner or point). — **to round up. a** To collect (cattle) by riding around them and driving them in. **b** To gather in, as scattered persons. — *v. i.* **1.** To grow round, rotund, full, complete, or perfect. **2.** To turn round; wheel about.

round'a-bout' (-à-bout'), a. [4] Circuitous. — n. A kind of short jacket.

roun'de-lay (roun'dē-lā), n. A song in which a simple strain is often repeated.

Round'head' (round'hĕd'), n. In the reign of Charles I. and later, a Puritan; — derisively so called because the Puritans wore the hair short.

round'house' (-hous'), n. **1.** Naut. A cabin on the after part of the quarter-deck. **2.** A house for locomotive engines, built round a turntable.

round'ish, a. Somewhat round.

round'ly, adv. In a round manner.

round'ness, n. Quality or state of being round.

round'-shoul'dered (-shōl'dĕrd), a. [4] Having the shoulders stooping or projecting.

rounds'man (roundz'măn), n. A police officer, below a sergeant, who makes rounds of inspection.

round'-up', n. Act or process of collecting cattle by riding around them and driving them in; also, the men and horses collectively that do this.

rouse (rouz), n. Carousal; drinking bout.

rouse, v. t. & i. **1.** To start from a covert. **2.** To wake or awake from sleep or repose. **3.** To excite, or be roused, to activity. **4.** To stir up; agitate. — n. Signal for rousing. — -er, n. [8].

roust'a-bout' (roust'à-bout'), n. A wharf laborer or deck hand, esp. on a river steamboat. U. S.

rout (rout), v. i. **1.** To root, search, or rummage. — v. t. **1.** To root up. **2.** To scoop out.

rout, n. **1.** A tumultuous crowd; mob; hence, the rabble. **2.** State of being disorganized and put to flight; as, the rout of an army. **3.** A fashionable assembly, esp. in the evening. Archaic. — v. t. To put to flight in disorder; defeat utterly.

route (rōōt), n. The course or way which is, or is to be, traveled. — v. t. [1] To forward or transport by a certain route.

rou-tine' (rōō-tēn'), n. A regular course of action; customary or mechanical procedure.

rove (rōv), v. t. [1] To draw out and twist slightly, as slivers of wool or cotton, before spinning.

rove, v. i. To wander. — v. t. To wander over.

rov'er (rōv'ẽr), n. **1.** A pirate. **2.** A wanderer.

row (rou), n. A noisy quarrel; brawl. Colloq.

row (rō), v. t. **1.** To propel (a boat) with oars. **2.** To transport in a boat propelled with oars. — v. i. **1.** To use an oar or oars in rowing a boat. **2.** To be moved by oars; as, the boat rows easily. — n. Act of rowing; a trip in a rowboat.

row (rō), n. **1.** A series in a continued line; a rank; file. **2.** A line of houses close together; street with houses so placed; as, Park Row.

row'boat' (rō'bōt'), n. A boat for rowing.

row'dy (rou'dĭ), n.; pl. -dies (-dĭz). One who engages in rows, or in rough behavior; a rough. — -di-ness (dĭ-nĕs), n. [8] — -dy-ish, a. [8].

row'dy-ism (-ĭz'm), n. Conduct of a rowdy.

row'el (rou'ĕl), n. A little toothed wheel on a spur. — v. t. [7] To prick with a rowel.

row'en (rou'ĕn), n. A second-growth crop.

row'er (rō'ẽr), n. One who rows a boat.

row'lock (rō'lŏk; colloq. rŭl'ŭk), n. A device serving as the fulcrum for an oar.

roy'al (roi'ăl), a. [4] **1.** Kingly; of or pert. to a king or sovereign; regal. **2.** Established or chartered by the crown; as, the Royal Society. **3.** Characteristic of or befitting a king. — n. See sail, Illust.

roy'al-ism (-ĭz'm), n. The principles of monarchical government; adherence to royalty.

roy'al-ist, n. An adherent of royalty.

roy'al-ly (roi'ăl-ĭ), adv. In a royal manner.

roy'al-ty (-tĭ), n.; pl. -ties (-tĭz). **1.** Royal status, station, birth, etc.; kingship. **2.** The person of a king or royal person; collectively, royal persons. **3.** Kingly quality or nature; greatness; generosity. **4. a** A share of the product or profit (as of a mine, forest, etc.) paid by the user to the owner of the property. **b** A compensation paid to an inventor, author, etc. for the use of his invention, work, etc.

rub (rŭb), v. t.; rubbed (rŭbd); rub'bing. **1.** To subject (a body) to pressure and friction. **2.** To scour or polish by rubbing; — often with up or off. **3.** To move (a body) with pressure and friction along a surface. — v. i. To grate; to fret or chafe with friction. — n. **1.** A rubbing; friction. **2.** That which rubs; hindrance; esp., a difficulty; a pinch. **3.** Something grating to the feelings, as sarcasm.

rub'ber (rŭb'ẽr), n. **1.** One that rubs; as: **a** An instrument used in rubbing. **b** An eraser, esp. of caoutchouc. **2.** In some games, as whist, the odd game when there is a tie; also, a contest determined by the winning of two out of three games. **3.** Caoutchouc, or India rubber, esp. in a commercial form. **4.** An India rubber overshoe. Colloq.

rub'bish (rŭb'ĭsh), n. Waste or rejected matter.

rub'ble (-'l), n. Rough broken stones, bricks, etc., used in coarse masonry; also, the masonry.

ru'bi-cund (rōō'bĭ-kŭnd), a. [4] Ruddy; red.

ru'ble (-b'l), n. Monetary unit of Russia, worth 51.5 cents; a silver coin of this value.

ru'bric (-brĭk), n. **1.** A part of a written or printed work colored red. Hence: **a** The title of a statute or law; — originally written in red. **b** A direction for the conduct of a church service, in liturgical books. **2.** A section heading of a discourse, etc.

ru'by (-bĭ), n.; pl. -bies (-bĭz). **1.** A precious stone, a red crystallized variety of corundum. **2.** The color of the ruby; carmine.

ruche (rōōsh), n. A plaited or fluted strip of lace, net, etc., used for a collar or cuff, or as a trimming.

ruch'ing (rōōsh'ĭng), n. A ruche, or ruches collectively; also, material for making ruches.

ruck (rŭk), n. Throng; crowd, esp. of ordinary or common persons or things; ordinary run.

rud'der (rŭd'ẽr), n. **1.** A flat piece hinged vertically at the stern of a vessel to steer with. **2.** An analogous part used to steer a balloon, flying machine, etc. — rud'der-less, a. [8].

rud'di-ly (-ĭ-lĭ), adv. In a ruddy manner.

rud'di-ness, n. Quality or state of being ruddy.

rud'dy (-ĭ), a. [3] **1.** Red, or reddish. **2.** Having a healthy reddish color; as, ruddy cheeks.

rude (rōōd), a. [3] **1.** Characterized by roughness; rough; harsh; severe. **2.** Lacking delicacy or refinement; uncultured; impudent. **3.** Unskillful; raw; ignorant. **4.** Rugged; sturdy; vigorous. — rude'ly, adv. [8] — rude'ness, n. [8].

ru'di-ment (rōō'dĭ-mĕnt),n.[*Chiefly in pl.*] **1.** That which is undeveloped ; fundamental principle ; unfinished beginning. **2.** An element or first principle of any art or science.

ru'di-men'ta-ry (-mĕn'tá-rĭ), *a.* [4] Of or pertaining to rudiments ; undeveloped ; immature.

rue (rōō), *n.* A shrubby yellow-flowered plant with a heavy odor and bitter taste.

rue, *v. t.* To regret extremely ; suffer remorse for ; as, to *rue* a sin ; *rue* the day. — *n.* Regret.

rue'ful (-fōōl), *a.* [4] **1.** Lamentable ; pitiable. **2.** Expressing sorrow, pity, or regret ; sorrowful. — **rue'ful-ly,** *adv.* [8] — **rue'ful-ness,** *n.* [8].

ruff (rŭf), *n.* Card Playing. Act of trumping. — *v. i. & t.* To trump.

ruff, *n.* **1.** A kind of muslin or linen collar plaited, crimped, or fluted. **2.** *Zoöl.* A fringe of 2d Ruff, l. hairs or feathers around or on the neck. **3.** A species of sandpiper of Europe and Asia. The female is called *reeve.*

ruffed (rŭft), *a.* Furnished with a ruff. — **ruffed** grouse, a North American grouse ; — often called *partridge* in the North and *pheasant* in the South.

ruf'fi-an (rŭf'ĭ-ăn ; rŭf'yăn), *n.* A cruel, brutal fellow. — *a.* Brutal ; cruel. — **-ly,** *a.* [4].

ruf'fi-an-ism (-ĭz'm), *n.* Action or conduct of a ruffian ; ruffianly qualities.

ruf'fle (rŭf''l), *v. t.* [1] **1.** To make into a ruff ; draw into plaits, or folds ; also, to furnish with ruffles. **2.** To erect in or like a ruff, as feathers. **3.** To make rough or uneven. **4.** To agitate mentally ; disturb ; vex. — *n.* A strip, as of lace, plaited or gathered, and used as a trimming ; a frill.

ru'fous (rōō'fŭs), *a.* Yellowish or brownish red.

rug (rŭg), *n.* A piece of thick fabric with a heavy nap for floor covering, etc. ; also, a fur mat, etc. ; also, a heavy woolen coverlet or traveling wrap.

Rug'by (rŭg'bĭ), *n.* A kind of football game, originally played at Rugby school, England.

rug'ged (rŭg'ĕd), *a.* [4] **1.** Irregular ; rough ; unkempt ; shaggy. **2.** Seamed ; wrinkled. **3.** Harsh ; rude ; unpolished. — **-ly,** *adv.* — **-ness,** *n.*

ru'in (rōō'ĭn), *n.* **1.** Such change as destroys anything or impairs effectiveness ; destruction ; overthrow. **2.** That which causes, or the act of causing, such destruction or impairment ; ruination. **3.** That which is fallen down and become worthless from injury or decay ; esp., *pl.*, the remains of a ruined house, city, etc. **4.** State of decay or worthlessness. — *v. t. & i.* To bring, fall, go, or come to ruin.

ru'in-a'tion (rōō'ĭ-nā'shŭn), *n.* Act of ruining, or state of being ruined.

ru'in-ous (-ĭ-nŭs), *a.* [4] **1.** Ruined ; dilapidated. **2.** Causing, or tending to, ruin ; destructive. — **-ly,** *adv.* [8] — **ru'in-ous-ness,** *n.* [8].

rule (rōōl), *n.* **1.** A prescribed guide for conduct ; regulation. **2.** A governing direction or precept ; controlling principle. **3.** Systematic method or practice ; usual course. **4.** Act of ruling ; administration of law ; authority. **5.** A straight strip used in drawing, etc. ; a ruler. — rule of three.

See PROPORTION, 4. — *v. t.* [1] **1.** To control ; govern ; manage. **2.** To control by influence, etc. ; guide. **3.** To mark with lines guided by a ruler. — *v. i.* **1.** To exercise supreme authority. **2.** *Law.* To lay down a rule or order of court ; decide an incidental point.

rul'er (rōōl'ẽr), *n.* **1.** One who rules ; one who exercises authority, as a sovereign. **2.** A strip of wood, metal, etc., with a smooth edge, used as a guide in drawing lines ; a rule.

rul'ing (rōōl'ĭng), *n.* **1.** Ruled lines. **2.** *Law.* A judicial decision, esp. one on a point of law.

rum (rŭm), *n.* **1.** An alcoholic liquor distilled from molasses. **2.** Alcoholic liquor in general. *Colloq.*

rum'ble (rŭm'b'l), *v. i.* [1] To make a low, heavy, rolling sound. — *v. t.* To utter or give forth with a rumbling sound. — *n.* **1.** A low, heavy, continuous sound like that of heavy wagons or of thunder. **2.** A seat behind the body of a vehicle.

ru'mi-nant (rōō'mĭ-nănt), *a.* [4] **1.** Chewing the cud ; of or pertaining to the ruminants. **2.** Meditative. — *n.* Any of a division of hoofed mammals including those that chew the cud, as the oxen, sheep, goats, antelopes, giraffes, deer, and camels.

ru'mi-nate (-nāt), *v. i.* [1] **1.** To chew the cud. **2.** To meditate ; ponder ; reflect. — *v. t.* **1.** To chew over again. **2.** To ponder.

ru'mi-na'tion (-nā'shŭn), *n.* **1.** Action of chewing the cud. **2.** Meditation.

ru'mi-na-tive (rōō'mĭ-nā-tĭv), *a.* [4] Meditative.

rum'mage (rŭm'áj), *n.* A thorough search by rummaging. — *v. t. & i.* [1] To search thoroughly by turning over or removing goods, etc. ; ransack.

ru'mor (rōō'mẽr), *n.* [5] **1.** A popular report ; common talk ; notoriety ; reputation. **2.** A story current without known authority for its truth. — *v. t.* To tell by rumor.

rump (rŭmp), *n.* The tail end of an animal.

rum'ple (rŭm'p'l), *v. t. & i.* [1] To wrinkle ; crumple ; muss. — *n.* A fold.

rum'pus (-pŭs), *n.* Disturbance ; fracas. *Colloq.*

run (rŭn), *v. i. ; pret.* RAN (răn) *or* RUN ; *p. p.* RUN ; *p. pr. & vb. n.* RUN'NING. **1.** To move swiftly, smoothly, or with quick action, as a stream, wagon, etc. ; hasten. **2.** To move rapidly by springing steps so that for an instant in each step neither foot touches the ground ; — disting. from *walking.* **3.** To go or move (in some particular way), as a spreading or climbing plant, an engine, a railroad train, a melting solid, a spreading color in cloth, etc. **4.** To extend or reach (in space or time), as a ditch, a railroad track, the memory, etc. **5.** To be in force or in activity ; have or take effect. **6** To pass from one state to another ; as, to *run* in debt. **7.** To discharge pus, as a sore.

run, *v. t.* **1.** To cause to run, as an engine, a horse, a candidate, a metal, a boundary line, etc. **2.** To perform by or as by running. **3.** To incur, as a risk. **4.** To discharge ; emit. **5.** To flow with. **6.** To sew, as a seam, continuously.

run, *n.* **1.** Act of running. **2. a** Continuation or course. **b** A continuing urgent demand, as on a bank for money. **c** *Games, etc.* The making of a number of successful shots, strokes, or the like, successively, or the score so made. **3.** A brook ; watercourse. **4. a** Distance covered, or amount of work turned out in a special course, time, or operation. **b** A range of ground for feeding stock, etc. **5.** A trip or course. **6.** In baseball and cricket, the score unit, made by running over a prescribed course. **7.** Freedom to go about at will.

run′a-bout′ (rŭn′à-bout′), n. A kind of light wagon, automobile, or motor boat.

run′a-gate (-gāt), n. A fugitive; wanderer.

run′a-way′ (-wā′), n. **1.** A fugitive. **2.** Act of running away, esp. of a horse or team. — a. **1.** Fleeing. **2.** Accomplished by elopement.

rung (rŭng), pret. & p. p. of RING.

rung (rŭng), n. A crosspiece of a ladder; round.

run′let (rŭn′lĕt), **run′nel** (-ĕl), n. A rivulet.

run′ner (-ẽr), n. **1.** One that runs, as a racer. **2.** Either of the pieces on which a sled or sleigh slides; the blade of a skate. **3.** Bot. **a** A slender prostrate branch which roots at the joints or end. **b** A plant which spreads by this method.

runt (rŭnt), n. **1.** An animal unusually small of its kind. **2.** A person of small or stunted growth.

run′way′ (rŭn′wa′), n. **1.** The beaten path made by animals, esp. deer, in going to and from their feeding grounds. **2.** A way or track for wheeled vehicles, etc.

ru-pee′ (rōō-pē′), n. The principal silver coin of British India, valued at 1s. 4d. (32.4 cents).

rup′ture (rŭp′tŭr), n. **1.** A breaking apart; state of being broken apart. **2.** Breach of peace; open hostility; war. **3.** Med. Hernia. — v. t. & i. [1] To cause a rupture of or in.

ru′ral (rōō′rǎl), a. [4] Of or pertaining to the country or country life ; rustic. — **-ly**, adv. [8].

ruse (rōōz), n. An artifice; trick; fraud; deceit.

rush (rŭsh), n. **1.** Any of various aquatic or marsh-growing plants, having cylindrical, often hollow, stems. **2.** A mere trifle ; as, not worth a rush.

rush, v. i. & t. **1.** To move, push, or urge forward with impetuosity or violence. **2.** To act or do with undue haste and eagerness. **3.** To make an onset on ; charge ; carry by assault. — n. **1.** Act of rushing; a sudden tumultuous movement. **2.** That which causes unusual activity; as, a rush of work. Colloq. — **rush′er** (rŭsh′ẽr), n.

rush′y (-ĭ), a. [3] Abounding with rushes; made of, or consisting of, rushes.

rusk (rŭsk), n. **1.** A light, soft bread, often crisped in an oven; also, a kind of sweet biscuit. **2.** Bread or cake browned in an oven.

rus′set (rŭs′ĕt), a. Reddish brown ; also, yellowish brown. — n. **1.** A russet color. **2.** Cloth or clothing of a russet color; esp., homespun. **3.** A kind of winter apple of a russet color.

Rus′sian (rŭsh′ǎn), a. Of or pertaining to Russia, its inhabitants, or language. — n. **1.** One of the people of Russia ; esp., a member of the Slavic-speaking race or races of Russia. **2.** The chief Slavic language of Russia.

rust (rŭst), n. **1.** The reddish coating of hydroxide formed on iron, as upon exposure to moist air; also, a coating produced on other metals by corrosion. **2.** Bot. **a** Any of numerous minute parasitic fungi causing discoloration of the tissues. **b** The disease caused by such fungi; also, brown or reddish discoloration of vegetation or fruit. — v. i. & t. To affect or be affected with rust.

rus′tic (rŭs′tĭk), a. [4] **1.** Of or pert. to the country; rural. **2.** Awkward; rough. **3.** Befitting the country ; plain ; simple. — n. An inhabitant of the country, esp. one who is rough or simple.

rus′ti-cal (-tĭ-kǎl), a. Rustic. — **-ly**, adv.

rus′ti-cate (-tĭ-kāt), v. i. [1] **1.** To go into, or reside in, the country. **2.** To spend a period of rustication as a punishment. — v. t. **1.** To compel to reside in the country. **2.** To punish by requiring temporary absence, as from a college.

rus′ti-ca′tion (-kā′shǎn), n. Act of rusticating ; state of being rusticated. [being rustic.]

rus-tic′i-ty (rŭs-tĭs′ĭ-tĭ), n. Quality or state of

rust′i-ly (rŭs′tĭ-lĭ), adv. In a rusty way or manner.

rust′i-ness (-nĕs), n. Condition of being rusty.

rus′tle (rŭs′′l), v. i. [1] To make a rustle. — v. t. To cause to rustle, as leaves. — n. A quick succession or confusion of small sounds, like those of shaking leaves. — **rus′tler** (-lẽr), n. [8].

rust′y (rŭs′tĭ), a. [3] **1.** Covered or affected with, or resembling, rust. **2.** Rust-colored.

rut (rŭt), n. A track worn by a wheel ; groove in which anything runs. — v. t. To make a rut or ruts in ; as, the road was badly rutted.

ru′ta-ba′ga (rōō′tà-bā′gà), n. A kind of turnip commonly with a large elongated yellowish root.

ruth′less (rōōth′lĕs), a. [4] Cruel ; pitiless. — **ruth′less-ly**, adv. [8] — **-ness**, n. [8].

rut′ty (rŭt′ĭ), a. [3] Full of ruts, as a road.

rye (rī), n. **1.** A hardy perennial cereal grass, cultivated as a food grain. **2.** The grain of this plant. **3.** Whisky distilled from rye grain.

S

Sab′ba-ta′ri-an (săb′à-tā′rĭ-ǎn), a. Of or pert. to the tenets of Sabbatarians. — n. **1.** One who keeps the seventh day of the week as holy. **2.** One who favors a strict observance of the Sabbath.

Sab′bath (săb′àth), n. **1.** In the Jewish calendar, the seventh day of the week, now generally called Saturday, observed by Jews and some Christians as a day of rest and worship (see Ex. xx. 8–11). **2.** Sunday; — often so called by Christians.

sab-bat′ic (să-băt′ĭk), a. Sabbatical.

sab-bat′i-cal (-ĭ-kǎl), a. Of, pert. to, or like, the Sabbath. — sabbatical year, every seventh year, allowed for rest, etc., as to professors in some colleges.

sa′ber (sā′bẽr), n. [6] A form of sword, usually with a curved blade. It is the typical cavalry arm. — v. t. To strike, cut, or kill, with a saber.

sa′ble (-b'l), n. **1.** A small flesh-eating animal related to the martens. See MARTEN. **2.** Fur of the sable. **3.** Color of sable ; black. **4.** A mourning garment ; — gen. in pl. — a. [4] Dark; black.

‖sa′bot′ (sȧ′bō′), n. [F.] A wooden shoe.

Sable. ($\frac{1}{12}$)

‖ **sa'bo'tage'** (sȧ/bŏ/täzh/), n. [F.] Malicious waste or destruction of an employer's property by workmen during labor troubles.

sac (săk), n. A baglike part of an animal or plant.

sac'cha-rin (săk/ȧ-rĭn), n. A coal-tar product several hundred times sweeter than cane sugar.

sac'cha-rine (săk/ȧ-rĭn; -rĭn), a. [4] Of, pertaining to, like, or producing, sugar; sweet.

sac'er-do'tal (săs/ĕr-dō/tăl), a. [4] Priestly.

sac'er-do'tal-ism (-ĭz'm), n. System, spirit, or character, of a priesthood; devotion to a priesthood.

sa'chem (sā/chĕm), n. A chief in some tribes of American Indians.

sa'chet' (sȧ/shā/), n. A scent bag, or perfumed pad.

sack (săk), n. Formerly, any of various strong white wines from southern Europe.

sack, n. The plundering of a captured place; pillage; ravage. — v. t. To pillage after capture.

sack, n. 1. A bag; a large pouch. 2. A kind of short loosely fitting coat; as, a flannel *sack*. — v. t. To put in a sack; bag. — **sack'ful**, n.

sack'cloth' (săk/klŏth/), n. Sacking; — anciently worn as a sign of mourning, penitence, etc.

sack'ing, n. Coarse cloth for making sacks.

sac'ra-ment (săk/rȧ-mĕnt), n. 1. One of the solemn religious ceremonies, as baptism, the Eucharist, etc., enjoined by Christ or by the church. 2. [*Often cap.*] The Eucharist; also, R. C. Ch., usually with *blessed* or *holy*, the consecrated Host.

sac'ra-men'tal (-mĕn/tăl), a. [4] Of, pertaining to, or of the nature of, a sacrament.

sa'cred (sā/krĕd), a. 1. Set apart to religious use; not profane, or common. 2. Relating to religion. 3. Not to be profaned or violated; inviolable. — **-ly**, adv. — **-ness**, n.

sac'ri-fice (săk/rĭ-fīs; -fiz), n. 1. An offering to a deity of animal or vegetable life or of food, incense, or the like. 2. Anything consecrated and offered to God or to a divinity. 3. Destruction, surrender, or loss made or incurred for the sake of something; also, the thing sacrificed.

sac'ri-fice (-fiz; -fis), v. t. [1] 1. To make an offering of; offer in sacrifice. 2. To give up for the sake of something. — v. i. To offer or make a sacrifice. — **sac'ri-fic'er**, n. [8].

sac'ri-fi'cial (-fĭsh/ăl), a. [4] Of or pertaining to sacrifice. — **sac'ri-fi'cial-ly**, adv. [8].

sac'ri-lege (săk/rĭ-lĕj), n. The sin or crime of violating sacred things.

sac'ri-le'gious (-lē/jŭs), a. [4] Violating sacred things; impious. — **-ly**, adv. [8] — **-ness**, n. [8].

sac'ris-tan (săk/rĭs-tăn), n. A church officer in charge of the sacristy; also, a sexton.

sac'ris-ty (-tĭ), n.; pl. -TIES (-tĭz). A room in a church for the sacred utensils, vestments, etc.

sa'crum (sā/krŭm), n. That part of the spine forming a part of the pelvis.

sad (săd), a.; SAD/DER (-ĕr); -DEST. 1. Dull; dark; somber; — of colors. 2. Affected with grief; downcast; mournful. 3. Inspiring melancholy or mournfulness. 4. Causing sorrow; grievous.

sad'den (săd/'n), v. t. & i. To make or become sad.

sad'dle (-'l), n. 1. A seat for a rider on a horse's back, a bicycle, etc. 2. A piece of meat consisting of the upper back portion of an animal. 3. *Geog.* A ridge connecting two higher elevations.

— v. t. [1] 1. To put a saddle on. 2. To fix as a charge or burden on; load.

sad'dle-bag' (-băg/), n. A pouch, usually one of a pair, attached to a saddle, to carry small articles.

sad'dle-bow' (-bō/), n. The arch in the front, or the pieces forming the front, of a saddle.

sad'dler (săd/lĕr), n. One who makes saddles and other horse furniture.

sad'dler-y (-ĭ), n.; pl. -DLERIES (-ĭz). The trade, the articles of trade, or the shop, of a saddler.

sad'dle-tree' (-'l-trē/), n. The frame of a saddle.

Sad'du-cee (săd/ū-sē), n. One of a sect, among the ancient Jews, which denied the resurrection, the existence of angels, etc.

sad'i'ron (săd/ī/ŭrn), n. A flatiron.

sad'ly (-lĭ), adv. In a sad manner or way.

sad'ness, n. Quality or state of being sad.

safe (sāf), a. [3] 1. Free from harm or risk; unhurt; whole. 2. Conferring safety; trustworthy. 3. Incapable of doing harm; in secure custody.

safe, n. A place or receptacle for safe-keeping; as: **a** A box, now of steel, for valuables. **b** A box to keep anything separate; as, a match *safe*.

safe'-con'duct (-kŏn/dŭkt), n. That which assures a safe passage; convoy; guard; passport.

safe'guard' (sāf/gärd/), n. 1. Defense; protection. 2. A safe-conduct. — v. t. To guard; protect.

safe'-keep'ing, n. A preserving in safety; care

safe'ly, adv. In a safe manner.

safe'ness, n. Quality or state of being safe.

safe'ty (sāf/tĭ), n. State of being safe.

safety valve. Automatic escape or relief valve; as, the *safety valve* of a steam boiler, which is set so as to open when the pressure reaches a certain point. Hence, fig., a means of relief from worry.

saf'fron (săf/rŭn), n. 1. The dried orange-colored stigmas of a species of crocus. They are used for flavoring and coloring. 2. The color of saffron (sense 1). — a. Deep orange-yellow.

sag (săg), v. i.; SAGGED (săgd); SAG/GING (săg/ĭng). 1. To sink or lean by weight or under pressure. 2. To lose firmness or elasticity; droop; flag. — n. Fact, state, or degree of sagging.

sa'ga (sä/gȧ; sā/gȧ), n.; pl. -GAS (-găz). A medieval Scandinavian narrative of legend or history.

sa-ga'cious (sȧ-gā/shŭs), a. [4] Of keen penetration and judgment; farsighted; shrewd; wise. — **-ly**, adv. — **-ness**, n. [gacious.]

sa-gac'i-ty (sȧ-găs/ĭ-tĭ), n. Quality of being sa-

sag'a-more (săg/ȧ-mōr), n. A tribal chief among certain of the American Indians.

sage (sāj), n. 1. A half-shrubby, aromatic mint, used to flavor meats, etc. 2. The sagebrush.

sage (sāj), a. [3] 1. Wise; sagacious. 2. Proceeding from wisdom; well judged; shrewd. — n. A profoundly wise man. — **-ly**, adv. — **-ness**, n.

sage'brush' (sāj/brŭsh/), n. Any of several American low, hoary, strongly scented shrubs of the aster family, of the western alkali plains.

sag'it-tate (săj/ĭ-tāt), a. Shaped like the barbed head of an arrow; as, a *sagittate* leaf.

sa'go (sā/gō), n. A granulated starch from the trunk of various East Indian palms.

sa'hib (sä/ĭb), n. [*Usually cap.*] The title used by natives when speaking to or of a European gentleman; sir; master; as, Baker *Sahib*. *India.*

said (sĕd), *pret. & p. p.* of SAY. Hence: *p. a.* Before-mentioned; already spoken of.

sail (sāl), *n.* **1.** An extent of canvas or other fab-

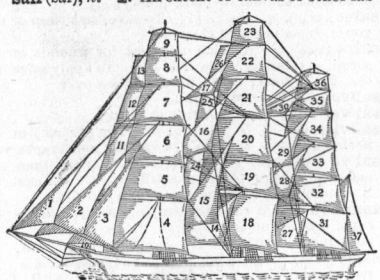

Full-rigged Ship under All Plain Sail. 1 Flying Jib; 2 Jib; 3 Fore-topmast Staysail; 4 Foresail; 5 Lower Fore-topsail; 6 Upper Fore-topsail; 7 Fore-topgallant Sail; 8 Fore Royal; 9 Fore Skysail; 10 Lower Studding Sail (never on the main); 11 Fore-topmast Studding Sail; 12 Fore-topgallant Studding Sail; 13 Foreroyal Studding Sail; 14 Main Staysail; 15 Main-topmast Staysail; 16 Main-topgallant Staysail; 17 Main-royal Staysail; 18 Mainsail; 19 Lower Main Topsail; 20 Upper Main Topsail; 21 Main-topgallant Sail; 22 Main Royal; 23 Main Skysail; 24 Main-topmast Studding Sail; 25 Main-topgallant Studding Sail; 26 Main-royal Studding Sail; 27 Mizzen Staysail; 28 Mizzen-topmast Staysail; 29 Mizzen-topgallant Staysail; 30 Mizzenroyal Staysail; 31 Mizzen Sail; 32 Lower Mizzen Topsail; 33 Upper Mizzen Topsail; 34 Mizzen-topgallant Sail; 35 Mizzen Royal; 36 Mizzen Skysail; 37 Spanker.

ric by means of which the wind is used to propel a vessel. **2.** Something suggestive of a sail, as the acting surface of the arm of a windmill. **3.** A sailing vessel; craft; also, sailing vessels collectively. **4.** A journey or excursion on the water. — *v. i.* **1.** To be impelled by the action of wind on sails; hence, to be impelled on water by steam, etc. **2.** To move or glide in a manner suggestive of a sailing boat, as a bird through the air. **3.** To be conveyed in a vessel on water; pass by water. **4.** To begin a voyage.— *v. t.* **1.** To sail upon or through. **2.** To direct or manage the motion of; as, to *sail* a vessel.

sail'boat (sāl'bōt'), *n.* A boat usually propelled by a sail; — seldom applied to large vessels.

sail'or (-ẽr), *n.* **1.** One who sails; mariner; technically, a common seaman. **2.** A kind of straw hat with a flat top and brim.

sail'or-ly, *a.* [4] Characteristic of a sailor.

saint (sānt), *n.* **1.** One sanctified or consecrated; a holy or godly person. **2.** One of the blessed dead in heaven. **3.** One canonized by the church. Abbr. *St.* — *v. t.* To make a saint of; canonize. — St. Val'en-tine's Day (văl'ĕn-tīnz), Feb. 14. — St. Vi'tus's dance (vī'tŭs-ĭz), chorea.

Saint Ber-nard' (bẽr-närd'). One of a breed of large, handsome dogs noted for sagacity.

saint'ed (sān'tĕd), *p. a.* [4] **1.** Sacred. **2.** Canonized. **3.** Entered into heaven; — a euphemism for *dead;* as, my *sainted* mother.

saint'ly, *a.* [3] Like a saint. — **-li-ness,** *n.* [8].

Saint Nich'o-las (nĭk'ō-làs). Patron saint of Russia, and of seafarers, virgins, and children. The name of Saint Nicholas, as bearer of presents on Christmas Eve, has been corrupted to *Santa Claus.*

sake (sāk), *n.* Cause; concern; motive; account; — chiefly in *for the sake of*, *for his sake,* etc.

sa-laam' (sà-läm'), *n.* An Oriental salutation; obeisance. — *v. i. & t.* To salute with a salaam.

sal'a-bil'i-ty (sāl'à-bĭl'ĭ-tĭ), *n.* Salable quality.

sal'a-ble (sāl'à-b'l), *a.* [4] Capable of being sold; marketable.— **sal'a-ble-ness,** *n.* [8].

sa-la'cious (sà-lā'shŭs), *a.* [4] Lustful. — **sa-la'-cious-ly,** *adv.* [8] — **-ness,** *n.* [8].

sal'ad (sāl'ǎd), *n.* **1.** A preparation of herbs, vegetables, or fruit, often with meat, fish, egg, etc., usually with a dressing, as of salt, vinegar, oil, and pepper. **2.** Herbs or vegetables for salad (sense 1).

sal'a-man'der (sāl'à-mǎn'dẽr), *n.* Any of numerous harmless amphibians superficially resembling lizards, but having a soft, moist skin. They were formerly fabled to be able to live in fire.

sal'a-ry (sāl'à-rĭ), *n. ; pl.* -RIES (-rĭz). A regular payment made for services; stipend.— *v. t.* [2] To pay a salary to; attach a salary too.

sale (sāl), *n.* **1.** Act or fact of selling. **2.** Opportunity of selling; as, ready *sale.* **3.** Auction.

sale'a-ble. Var. of SALABLE.

sal'e-ra'tus (sāl'ē-rā'tŭs), *n.* Baking soda, or sodium bicarbonate.

sales'man (sālz'mǎn), *n. ; pl.* -MEN (-mĕn) One whose occupation is to sell goods.

sales'man-ship, *n.* Art or skill of a salesman.

sales'wom'an (-wŏom'ǎn), *n. ; pl.* -WOMEN (-wĭm'ĕn). A woman whose occupation is to sell goods.

sal'i-cyl'ic acid (sāl'ĭ-sĭl'ĭk). A white crystalline acid, used as an antiseptic.

sa'li-ence (sā'lĭ-ĕns), *n.* **1.** Quality or state of being salient. **2.** A projection.

sa'li-en-cy (-ĕn-sĭ), *n.* Salience.

sa'li-ent (sā'lĭ-ĕnt), *a.* [4] **1.** Leaping; bounding; jumping. **2.** Prominent; conspicuous; as, *salient* traits. **3.** Projecting outwardly; as, a *salient* angle; —opposed to *reëntrant.* — **-ly,** *adv.* [8].

sa'line (sā'lĭn), *a.* [4] **1.** Consisting of salt, or containing salt. **2.** Of, pert. to, or like, salt; salty; as, a *saline* taste.— *n.* **1.** A salt spring. **2.** *Med.* A salt of potassium, sodium, lithium, or magnesium.

sa-lin'i-ty (sà-lĭn'ĭ-tĭ), *n.* Degree of saltness.

sa-li'va (sà-lī'và), *n.* The secretions of the glands discharging into the mouth; spit.

sal'i-va-ry (sāl'ĭ-vā-rĭ), *a.* Of or pert. to saliva.

sal'i-vate (-vāt), *v. t.* [1] To produce an excess of saliva, as with mercury.

sal'i-va'tion (-vā'shŭn), *n.* Process of salivating.

sal'low (sāl'ō), *n.* **1.** Any European broad-leaved species of willow. **2.** A willow twig or rod.

sal'low, *a.* [3] Yellowish; of a pale, yellowish, sickly color; — usually of the skin, etc.— *v. t.* To make sallow. — **-ish,** *a.* [8] — **-ness,** *n.* [8].

sal'ly (-ĭ), *n. ; pl.* -LIES (-ĭz). **1.** A rushing or bursting forth; esp., *Mil.*, a sudden rush (out) upon besiegers. **2.** A flight of fancy, wit, etc.; witticism.— *v. i.* [2] To rush out; come out suddenly, as troops to attack besiegers.

salm'on (săm'ŭn), *n.* (See PLURAL, *n.*, *Note.*) **1.** Any of certain large marine food fishes living near northern coasts and ascending rivers to spawn. **2.** A yellowish red, like the color of the salmon's flesh. — *a.* Of this color.

‖ **sa'lon'** (să/lôn'), *n.; pl.* -LONS (-lôn'). [F.] **1.** An apartment for reception of company; hence, a fashionable assemblage. **2.** An apartment for exhibition of works of art; hence, the exhibition.

sa-loon' (să-loon'), *n.* **1.** A spacious apartment for reception of company or for works of art. **2.** A public room for specific uses; as, the *saloon* of a steamer (i. e., the main cabin); an eating *saloon.* **3.** A barroom; grogshop. *U. S.*

sal'si-fy (săl/sĭ-fĭ), *n.* A European plant, of the chicory family, with heads of purple-rayed flowers. Its edible root is often called *oyster plant.*

salt (sôlt), *n.* **1.** Sodium chloride, used to season food, as a preservative, etc. **2.** *Chem.* Any of a class of compounds formed when the acid hydrogen of an acid is replaced by a metal or a metal-like radical. **3.** *pl.* Any mineral salt used to move the bowels. **4.** A saltcellar. **5.** Piquancy; wit; sense; as, Attic *salt.* **6.** A sailor; — usually qualified by *old. Colloq.* — *a.* [3] **1.** Of, relating to, or containing, salt; prepared or preserved with, or tasting of, salt. **2.** Overflowed with, or growing in, salt water; as, *salt* grass. — *v. t.* **1.** To add salt to; preserve with salt. **2.** To supply with salt; as, to *salt* cattle.

salt'cel-lar (sôlt/sĕl-ẽr), *n.* A vessel for holding salt at table.

salt'ish, *a.* Somewhat salt; salty.

salt'ness, *n.* Quality or state of being salt.

salt'pe'ter (sôlt/pē'tẽr), *n.* [6] **1.** Potassium nitrate; niter. It is a strong oxidizer, used in explosives, matches, as a food preservative, flux, etc. **2.** Chile saltpeter (sodium nitrate).

salt rheum. Any of various eruptions of the skin, esp. those of eczema. *Colloq., esp. U. S.*

salt'y (sôl/tĭ), *a.* [3] Somewhat salt; saltish.

sa-lu'bri-ous (să-lū/brĭ-ŭs), *a.* [4] Favorable to health. — **ness,** *n.* [8].

sa-lu'bri-ty (-tĭ), *n.* Quality of being salubrious.

sal'u-ta-ry (săl/ū-tă-rĭ), *a.* [4] **1.** Healthful; as, a *salutary* exercise. **2.** Beneficial; advantageous. — **-ri-ly** (-rĭ-lĭ), *adv.* [8] — **ri-ness,** *n.* [8].

sal'u-ta'tion (-tā/shŭn), *n.* Act of saluting; also, that which is uttered or done in saluting.

sa-lu'ta-to'ri-an (să-lū/tă-tō/rĭ-ăn), *n.* The student (commonly second highest in rank) who delivers the salutatory. Cf. VALEDICTORIAN. *U. S.*

sa-lu'ta-to-ry (-lū'tă-tô-rĭ), *a.* Expressing salutations; — applied esp. to the oration introducing the exercises at commencement, in some colleges and schools. *U. S.* — *n.; pl.* -RIES (-rĭz). A salutatory oration. *U. S.*

sa-lute' (-lūt'), *v. t.* [1] **1.** To address with courteous expressions of good will; greet. **2.** To compliment by an act, as by a bow, a kiss, etc. **3.** *Mil. & Nav.* **a** To honor by a discharge of cannon, by dipping colors, etc. **b** To show deference to by assuming a prescribed position; as, to *salute* an officer. — *v. i.* To make a salute. — *n.* Act of saluting. — **sa-lut'er** (-lūt'ẽr), *n.* [8].

sal'vage (săl/văj), *n.* Act of saving a vessel or goods from peril; also, the property so saved, or recompense paid for the saving of it.

sal-va'tion (săl-vā/shŭn), *n.* **1.** Act of saving or delivering from evil. **2.** In theology, deliverance from sin and its consequences.

salve (sălv), *v. t. & i.* [1] To save, as a ship or goods, from perils of the sea.

salve (säv), *n.* A thick ointment for wounds or sores; — often fig. — *v. t.* [1] **1.** To apply salve to. **2.** To heal; cure; soothe; gloss over.

sal've (săl/vē), *interj.* Hail!

sal'ver (săl/vẽr), *n.* A tray or waiter.

sal'vi-a (-vĭ-à), *n.* Any of a genus (*Salvia*) of herbs or shrubs, the sages, of varying appearance.

sal'vo (-vō), *n.; pl.* -vos (-vōz). **1.** Simultaneous discharge of pieces of artillery. Cf. VOLLEY. **2.** Combined shouts or cheers of a crowd.

sam'a-ra (săm/à-rà; să-mā/rà), *n.* A dry, indehiscent, usually one-seeded, winged fruit.

same (sām), *a.* **1.** Being not another or other; identical. **2.** Not differing in kind; like in quality or qualities; equal. **3.** Just mentioned, or about to be mentioned; as, this *same* man.

a Double Samara of Maple ; *b* Samara of Elm.

same'ness (sām/nĕs), *n.* **1.** State of being the same; identity. **2.** Want of variety; monotony.

Sa-mo'an (så-mō'ăn), *a.* Of or pert. to the Samoa Islands, or their inhabitants. — *n.* A native of the Samoa Islands ; the language of the Samoans.

sam'o-var (săm/ō-vär), *n.* A metal urn used, originally in Russia, to heat water for making tea.

samp (sămp), *n.* Coarse hominy. *U. S.*

sam'ple (săm/p'l), *n.* A part of anything presented as evidence of the quality of the whole ; a specimen. — *v. t.* [1] To take or to test a sample or samples of.

sam'pler (-plẽr), *n.* **1.** A piece of needlework made as a sample of skill. **2.** One who examines samples, or by samples.

san'a-tive (săn/à-tĭv), *a.* [4] Healing; sanatory.

san'a-to'ri-um (-tō'rĭ-ŭm), *n.; pl.* L. -RIA (-å), E. -RIUMS (-ŭmz). **1.** A health resort. **2.** An establishment for treatment of the sick; sanitarium.

san'a-to-ry (săn/à-tō-rĭ), *a.* [4] Conducive to health ; healing ; curative.

sanc'ti-fi-ca'tion (săŋk'tĭ-fĭ-kā/shŭn), *n.* Act of sanctifying ; state of being sanctified.

sanc'ti-fied (săŋk/tĭ-fīd), *p. a.* [4] Made holy.

sanc'ti-fy (-fī), *v.t.* [2] **1.** To free from sin; purify. **2.** To make holy ; set apart to holy use ; hallow. **3.** To give sanctity or sanction to. — **-fi'er** (-ẽr), *n.*

sanc'ti-mo'ni-ous (-mō'nĭ-ŭs), *a.* [4] Making a show of sanctity; hypocritically devout. — **sanc'-ti-mo'ni-ous-ly,** *adv.* [8] — **ness,** *n.* [8].

sanc'ti-mo-ny (săŋk/tĭ-mō-nĭ), *n.* Assumed or pretended holiness; hypocritical devoutness.

sanc'tion (-shŭn), *n.* Solemn ratification; confirmation ; approbation. — *v. t.* To ratify; confirm.

sanc'ti-ty (-tĭ-tĭ), *n.; pl.* -TIES (-tĭz). **1.** State or quality of being sacred or holy; holiness. **2.** Sacredness; solemnity ; as, the *sanctity* of an oath.

sanc'tu-a-ry (-tụ̆-å-rĭ), *n.; pl.* -RIES (-rĭz). **1.** A con secrated and sacred place. **2.** A sacred and in-violable place of refuge ; asylum.

sanc'tum (-tŭm), n. A sacred place ; place of retreat or for personal use ; as, an editor's *sanctum*.

sand (sănd), n. **1.** A loose material consisting of fine grains, resulting from the wearing away of rocks. **2.** [Also **sands**.] A tract, region, or deposit, of sand ; beach. **3.** The sand in an hourglass, or a grain of it. — *v. t.* To sprinkle or mix with sand.

san'dal (săn'dăl), n. **1.** Kind of shoe covering the sole of the foot only. **2.** Kind of fancy slipper or shoe. **3.** A kind of rubber overshoe cut very low.

san'dal-wood' (-dăl-wŏŏd'), or **san'dal,** n. The close-grained, fragrant wood of any of certain Oriental trees ; any tree furnishing this wood.

sand'bag' (sănd'băg'), n. A bag of sand, as for use as ballast, as a club, etc. — *v. t.* ; for prin. parts see BAG. To hit or stun with a sandbag.

sand'glass' (sănd'glás'), n. An hourglass measuring time by the running of sand.

sand'i-ness, n. Quality or state of being sandy.

sand'pa'per (sănd'pā'pēr), n. Paper coated on one side with sand, used for smoothing and polishing. — *v. t.* To smooth or polish with sandpaper.

sand'pip'er (-pīp'ēr), n. Any of numerous small shore birds distinguished from the plovers chiefly by the longer bill.

sand'stone' (-stōn'), n. A rock consisting of consolidated sand.

sand'wich (-wĭch), n.
Two pieces of bread having a layer of meat, cheese, or the like, between them. — *v.t.* To make into a sandwich ; also, to insert something between things that are unlike it.

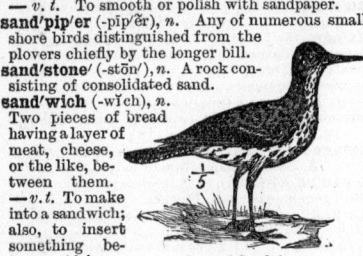

Spotted Sandpiper.

sand'y (săn'dĭ), a. [3] **1.** Consisting of or containing sand ; full of sand ; covered with sand. **2.** Like, or suggestive of, sand ; as a Unstable ; not firm. **b** Yellowish red ; as, *sandy* hair.

sane (sān), a. [3] **1.** Mentally sound. Of the mind, acting rationally. **2.** Proceeding from a sound mind ; as, a *sane* criticism. — **sane'ly,** adv.

sang (săng), pret. of SING.

‖ **sang'–froid'** (säN'frwä'), n. [F.] Freedom from agitation ; coolness in difficulty ; composure.

san'gui-na-ry (săn'gwĭ-nă-rĭ), a. [4] **1.** Consisting of blood. **2.** Attended with bloodshed ; bloody. **3.** Bloodthirsty. — **san'gui-na-ri-ly,** adv. [8] — **san'gui-na-ri-ness,** n. [8].

san'guine (-gwĭn), a. [4] **1.** Red, like blood ; ruddy. **2.** Marked by abundant and active circulation of blood ; hence, cheerful ; hopeful. **3.** Warm ; ardent ; confident ; as, *sanguine* of success. — **-ly,** adv. [8] — **-ness,** n. [8].

San'he-drin (săn'hḕ-drĭn)) n. *Jewish Antiq.*
San'he-drim (săn'hḕ-drĭm)) Council ; esp., Great Sanhedrin, supreme council of 71 members.

san'i-ta'ri-um (-ĭ-tā'rĭ-ŭm), n.; pl. E. -RIUMS (-ŭmz), L. -RIA (-ȧ). A sanatorium, esp. in sense 2.

san'i-ta-ry (săn'ĭ-tă-rĭ), a. [4] Of or pertaining to health ; hygienic.

san'i-ta'tion (-tā'shŭn), n. Science of sanitary conditions ; use of sanitary measures ; hygiene.

san'i-ty (săn'ĭ-tĭ), n. State or quality of being sane ; soundness or health of mind.

sank (săŋk), pret. of SINK.

sans (sănz ; F. säN), prep. Without ; deprived or destitute of. *Archaic.*

San'ta Claus (săn'tȧ klôz). See SAINT NICHOLAS.

sap (săp), n. **1.** The juices of a plant. **2.** Any vital fluid ; vigor ; vitality. **3.** Sapwood.

sap, v.t.; SAPPED (săpt) ; SAP'PING. **1.** To dig under the foundations of ; undermine. **2.** To unsettle ; weaken. — n. *Mil.* An approach made by besiegers, in the form of a narrow trench with its head protected by the earth dug up.

sa'pi-ence (sā'pĭ-ĕns), n. Wisdom ; — often in irony. [— **-ly,** adv.

sa'pi-ent (-ĕnt), a. [4] Wise ; — often in irony.

sap'less (săp'lĕs), a. Without sap or vigor.

sap'ling (-lĭng), n. **1.** A young tree. **2.** A youth.

sap'o-na'ceous (-ṓ-nā'shŭs), a. [4] Soapy.

sa-pon'i-fi-ca'tion (sȧ-pŏn'ĭ-fĭ-kā'shŭn), n. Act or result of converting into soap. [soap.

sa-pon'i-fy (-ĭ-fī), v.t. & i. [2] To convert into

sap'per (săp'ēr), n. One (esp. a soldier) who saps.

sap'phire (săf'īr), n. **1.** A pure variety of corundum ; esp., a blue transparent variety, prized as a gem. **2.** The color of the gem ; bright blue.

sap'py (săp'ĭ), a. [3] **1.** Abounding with sap ; juicy. **2.** Foolish ; silly. — **sap'pi-ness,** n. [8].

sap'wood' (-wŏŏd'), n. The soft, recently formed, and living wood between bark and heartwood.

Sar'a-cen (săr'ȧ-sĕn), n. Anciently, an Arab ; later, a Mohammedan hostile to the Crusaders.

Sar'a-cen'ic (-sĕn'ĭk), a. Of or pertaining to the Saracens ; as, *Saracenic* architecture.

sar'casm (săr'kăz'm), n. A bitter taunt ; also, bitter and contemptuous irony

sar-cas'tic (sär-kăs'tĭk), a. [4] Marked by, or of the nature of, sarcasm ; given to the use of sarcasm. — **sar cas'ti-cal-ly,** adv. [8].

sar-coph'a-gus (sär-kŏf'ȧ-gŭs), n. ; pl. L. -GI (-jī), E. -GUSES (-gŭs-ĕz). A coffin or tomb of stone.

sar-dine' (sär-dēn' ; sär'dēn), n. Any of several small fishes of the herring kind suitable for preserving in oil for food.

sar-don'ic (sär-dŏn'ĭk), a. [4] Strained ; forced ; hence, sneering ; bitterly sarcastic ; — only of laughter, a smile, etc. — **-don'i-cal-ly,** adv. [8].

sar'do-nyx (sär'dṓ-nĭks), n. A kind of onyx.

sar'sa-pa-ril'la (sär'sȧ-pȧ-rĭl'ȧ), n. **1.** Any of various tropical American species of smilax. **2.** The dried roots of any of these, mildly tonic.

sash (săsh), n. ; pl. SASHES (-ĕz) or, collectively, SASH. Frame of a glazed window or door.

sash, n. A scarf or band worn about the waist or over the shoulder ; belt ; girdle. — **-less,** a. [8].

sas'sa-fras (săs'ȧ-frăs), n. Any of a genus of American trees of the laurel family ; also, the aromatic bark of the root.

sat (săt), pret. of SIT.

Sa'tan (sā'tăn), n. In theology, the great adversary of man ; the Devil.

sa-tan'ic (sȧ-tăn'ĭk), or **sa-tan'i-cal** (-ĭ-kăl), a. [4]

Of, pertaining to, or resembling, Satan; devilish; infernal. — **sa-tan′i-cal-ly,** *adv.* [8].

satch′el (săch′ĕl), *n.* A small bag for carrying papers, books, or small articles; a hand bag.

sate (sāt), *v. t.* [1] To satiate; glut; surfeit.

sa-teen′ (să-tēn′), *n.* A fabric of cotton or wool, with a satiny surface.

sat′el-lite (săt′ĕ-līt), *n.* **1.** An attendant to a prince; a fawning dependent. **2.** *Astron.* An attendant body, revolving about a larger one; a moon.

sa′ti-a-ble (sā′shĭ-á-b′l), *a.* That may be satiated.

sa′ti-ate (sā′shĭ-āt), *a.* [4] Filled to satiety; glutted. — (-āt), *v. t.* [1] To satisfy the appetite or desire of; sate; also, to surfeit; glut.

sa′ti-a′tion (sā′shĭ-ā′shŭn), *n.* Satiety.

sa-ti′e-ty (sá-tī′ĕ-tĭ), *n.* State of being satiated.

sat′in (săt′ĭn), *n.* A kind of glossy silk fabric.

sat′i-net′ (săt′ĭ-nĕt′), *n.* **1.** A kind of satin or imitation satin. **2.** A kind of cloth of cotton warp and woolen filling.

sat′in-wood′ (săt′ĭn-wŏŏd′), *n.* An East Indian tree or its yellowish wood, with satiny luster.

sat′in-y (-ĭ), *a.* [4] Resembling satin; glossy.

sat′ire (săt′ir), *n.* **1.** A literary composition, originally in verse, holding up abuses, vice, etc., to ridicule. **2.** Biting wit; sarcasm.

sa-tir′ic (sá-tĭr′ĭk) } *a.* [4] Pertaining to, of the
sa-tir′i-cal (-I-kăl) } nature of, or using, satire. — **sa-tir′i-cal-ly,** *adv.* [8].

sat′i-rist (săt′ĭ-rĭst), *n.* One who satirizes.

sat′i-rize (-ĭ-rīz), *v. t.* [1] To subject to satire.

sat′is-fac′tion (-ĭs-făk′shŭn), *n.* **1.** Act of satisfying; state of being satisfied. **2.** That which serves to satisfy.

sat′is-fac′to-ry (-tŏ-rĭ), *a.* [4] Giving satisfaction; esp., relieving the mind from uncertainty. — **-ri-ly** (-rĭ-lĭ), *adv.* [8]. — **-ri-ness,** *n.* [8].

sat′is-fy (săt′ĭs-fī), *v. t.* [2] **1.** To gratify fully; content. **2.** To give what is due to. **3.** To discharge, as a debt; pay off; requite. **4.** To assure; convince. — *v. i.* To give or afford satisfaction.

sa′trap (sā′trăp; săt′răp), *n.* **1.** The governor of a province in ancient Persia. **2.** A petty ruler.

sa′trap-y (sā′trá-pĭ), *n.* Government or jurisdiction of a satrap.

sat′u-rate (săt′ṵ-rāt), *v. t.* [1] To cause to become completely penetrated or soaked; fill fully; as, to *saturate* a sponge with water; treat (with something) till no more can be taken up, as water with salt.

sat′u-ra′tion (-rā′shŭn), *n.* Act or process of saturating; state of being saturated. [of the week.]

Sat′ur-day (săt′ũr-dā), *n.* Seventh and last day

Sat′urn (-ũrn), *n.* *Astron.* The planet next in size to Jupiter, and next more remote from the sun, remarkable for its encircling rings.

Saturn.

sat′ur-na′li-a (-ũr-nā′lĭ-á), *n. pl.* A period or occasion of riotous indulgence. — **-li-an,** *a.*

sat′ur-nine (săt′ũr-nīn), *a.* [4] Heavy; grave; gloomy; — opposed to *mercurial.*

sat′yr (săt′ĕr; sā′tĕr), *n.* **1.** [*Often cap.*] *Class. Myth.* A sylvan deity or demigod, part man and part horse or goat, given to riotous merriment and lust. **2.** A lewd man.

sauce (sôs), *n.* **1.** A condiment or composition of appetizing ingredients eaten with food as a relish; esp., a dressing for meat, fish, puddings, etc. **2.** Stewed or preserved fruit. **3.** Sauciness. *Colloq.* — *v. t.* [1] **1.** To season; flavor. **2.** To be saucy to. *Colloq.*

sauce′pan (-păn′), *n.* A small metallic vessel with a handle, for use in stewing; stewpan.

sau′cer (sô′sẽr), *n.* **1.** Small dish to hold a cup. **2.** Something shaped like a saucer.

sau′cy (sô′sĭ), *a.* [3] Impudent; pert. — **sau′ci-ly** (sô′sĭ-lĭ), *adv.* [8] — **sau′ci-ness,** *n.* [8].

sauer′kraut (sour′krout′), *n.* Cabbage cut fine and allowed to ferment in a brine made of its own juice with salt.

saun′ter (sän′tẽr; sôn′-), *v. i.* To wander about idly; stroll. — *n.* A sauntering. — **-er,** *n.* [8].

sau′ri-an (sô′rĭ-ăn), *n.* Any of a group of reptiles including the lizards, and formerly the crocodiles, etc. — *a.* [4] Of or pert. to the saurians; lizardlike.

sau′sage (sô′sáj), *n.* Meat (esp. pork) minced, seasoned, and, commonly, inclosed in a skin.

sav′age (săv′áj), *a.* [3] **1.** Wild; rugged; as, a *savage* wilderness. **2.** Wild; untamed; uncultivated; as, *savage* beasts. **3.** Uncivilized; rude; as, *savage* manners. **4.** Cruel; inhuman; brutal. — *n.* **1.** A person untaught, uncivilized, or without cultivation. **2.** A person of brutal cruelty. — **-ly,** *adv.* [8] — **-ness,** *n.* [8].

sav′age-ry (-rĭ), *n.; pl.* **-ries** (-rĭz). **1.** Savageness. **2.** Savage disposition or action; barbarity.

sa-van′na (sá-văn′á), *n.* A treeless plain; an open, level region, esp. as in Florida.

|| **sa′vant′** (sȧ′vän′), *n.; pl.* SAVANTS (*F.* sȧ′vän′). [*F.*] A man of learning.

save (sāv), *v. t.* [1] **1.** To make safe; rescue. **2.** In theology, to deliver from sin and its penalty. **3.** To lay up; hoard. **4.** To obviate the necessity or occurrence of; spare; as, to *save* one labor. — *v. i.* To avoid expense; prevent waste.

save, *prep. or conj.* Except; excepting.

sav′er (sāv′ẽr), *n.* One that saves.

sav′ing (sāv′ĭng), *p. a.* [4] That saves; as: **a** Preserving; rescuing. **b** Economizing; frugal. **c** Making reservation or exception. — *vb. n.* **1. a** Preservation from danger or loss. **b** Economy in outlay; reduction in cost. **2.** That which is saved; esp., *pl.*, sums saved, and kept unexpended. — *prep. or conj.* With the exception of; except.

sav′ings bank (sāv′ĭngz). A bank which receives small sums for deposit at compound interest.

sav′ior (sāv′yẽr), *n.* [5] **1.** One who saves, or delivers. **2.** [*cap.*] Jesus Christ.

sa′vor (sā′vẽr), *n.* [5] **1.** Taste and odor; flavor; relish; scent. **2.** Specific flavor or quality; essential property. — *v. i.* **1.** To have a taste or smell; — with *of.* **2.** To partake of the quality or nature; smack. — *v. t.* **1.** To season. **2.** To taste with pleasure; relish; appreciate. — **-less,** *a.* [5, 8]. [used in cooking.]

sa′vor-y (sā′vẽr-ĭ), *n.* A European mint, much

sa'vor-y (-Ĭ), *a.* [4, 5] **1.** Pleasing to taste or smell. **2.** Pleasing morally; reputable. — **sa'vor-i-ly** (-Ĭ-lĬ), *adv.* [5, 8] — **-i-ness**, *n.* [5, 8].

saw (sô), *pret.* of SEE.

saw, *n.* A saying; proverb; maxim.

saw, *n.* A common tool with teeth on the edge. — *v. t.*; *pret.* SAWED (sôd); *p. p.* SAWED or SAWN (sôn). **1.** To cut with a saw. **2.** To form by cutting with a saw. **3.** To make motions suggesting those made with a saw. — *v. i.* **1.** To use a saw. **2.** To cut, as a saw. **3.** To be cut with a saw.

saw'buck' (sô'bŭk'), *n.* A sawhorse. *U. S.*

saw'dust' (-dŭst'), *n.* Dust made by sawing.

saw'er (sô'ẽr), *n.* One who saws.

saw'fish' (-fĭsh'), *n.* Any of several large shark-like fishes having a long, flat snout with stout, toothlike structures along each edge.

saw'horse' (-hôrs'), *n.* A rack on which wood is laid for sawing by hand.

saw'mill' (-mĭl'), *n.* A mill for sawing up logs.

sawn (sôn), *p. p.* of SAW.

saw'yer (sô'yẽr), *n.* One who saws wood.

sax'horn' (săks'hôrn'), *n.* *Music.* Any of a family of brass wind instruments with valves.

sax'i-frage (săk'sĬ-frāj), *n.* Any of various plants, chiefly perennial, with white or yellow flowers.

sax'o-phone (-ō-fōn), *n.* *Music.* A keyed wind instrument having the reed mouthpiece of a clarinet.

say (sā), *v. t.*; *pret. & p. p.* SAID (sĕd); *p. pr. & vb. n.* SAY'ING. Indic. pr. 3d person sing., SAYS (sĕz). **1.** To express in words; tell; speak; declare. **2.** To repeat; recite. **3.** To announce as a decision or opinion; assert. **4.** To suppose; — in the imperative, as, he had, *say* a dollar. — *v.i.* To speak; express an opinion. — *n.* **1.** That which is said or to be said; a speech. *Obs.*, except in *to have one's say*, etc. **2.** One's turn or right to speak or decide in an affair. *Colloq.* — **say'er**, *n.* [3].

say'ing, *n.* That which is said; statement; aphorism; proverb.

scab (skăb), *n.* **1.** An incrustation over a sore, wound, etc. **2.** Mange, esp. on sheep. **3.** *Hort.* Any of various fungous diseases of cultivated plants, usually indicated by crustlike spots.

scab'bard (skăb'ȧrd), *n.* A sheath for a sword, dagger, etc. — *v. t.* To put into a scabbard.

scab'by (skăb'Ĭ), *a.* [3] Affected with scabs or the scab. — **-bi-ly** (-Ĭ-lĬ), *adv.* [8] — **-bi-ness**, *n.* [8].

scaf'fold (skăf'ōld),*n.* A platform,as for exhibiting or supporting something, or for executing a criminal. — *v. t.* To furnish or uphold with a scaffold.

scaf'fold-ing, *n.* A scaffold or system of scaffolds; materials for scaffolds.   [grace. *Colloq.*

scal'a-wag (skăl'ȧ-wăg), *n.* A scamp; scape-

scald (skōld), *v. t.* **1.** To burn with hot liquid or steam. **2.** To cause to come to a boil. **3.** To subject to the action of a boiling liquid. — *n.* A burn by hot liquid or steam.

scald (skōld; skäld), *n.* An ancient Scandinavian poet; a Norse reciter of heroic poems.

scale (skāl), *n.* The dish of a balance; hence, usually in *pl.*, the balance itself; an instrument for weighing. — *v. t.* [1] **1.** To weigh in scales; measure; compare. **2.** To have a weight of; weigh.

scale, *n.* **1.** A small, flattened, bony or horny plate forming part of the external covering of an animal, as a fish. **2.** Any layer or leaf like, or suggestive of, a fish scale; a flake; a scab. **3.** A hard incrustation. — *v.t. & i.* **1.** To clear of scales or scale. **2.** To come off in thin layers.

scale, *n.* **1.** Anything graduated, esp. when used as a measure; esp.: a A series of spaces marked by lines, representing proportionately larger distances; as, a *scale* of miles for a map. b A basis for a numeral system. **2.** *Music.* A series of tones ascending or descending in pitch according to a scheme of intervals. **3.** Gradation; graded system. **4.** Proportion in dimensions between a drawing, map, plan, or the like, and what it represents. — *v. t.* **1.** To climb by or as by a ladder; clamber up. **2.** To reduce according to a fixed scale. — *v. i.* To ascend; mount. — **scal'er**, *n.*

scale insect. Any of numerous small but very prolific insects which suck the juices of plants.

soa-lene' (skȧ-lēn'), *a.* *Geom.* a Having the sides and angles unequal;— said of a triangle. b Oblique.

scal'i-ness (skāl'Ĭ-nĕs), *n.* Scaly quality or state

scal'lop (skŏl'ŭp), *n.* **1.** Any of numerous marine bivalve mollusks with the shell usually radially ribbed and the edge wavy. **2.** One of a series of segments of circles joined at their extremities and forming an edge, as of certain laces. — *v. t.* **1.** To mark or cut the edge or border of into scallops. **2.** *Cookery.* To prepare with crumbs of bread or cracker, and bake.

scalp (skălp), *n.* The part of the skin of the head usually covered with hair. — *v. t.* To deprive of the scalp.   [knife with a thin blade.

scal'pel (skăl'pĕl), *n.* *Surgery.* A small, straight

scalp'er (skăl'pẽr), *n.* One that scalps.

scal'y (skāl'Ĭ), *a.* [3] **1.** Covered with or abounding with scales. **2.** Resembling scales.

scamp (skămp), *n.* A rascal; rogue; worthless fellow. — *v. t.* To perform hastily or imperfectly.

scam'per (skăm'pẽr), *v. i.* To run or move in a quick, hurried manner; hasten away. — *n.* A scampering; hasty flight. — **scam'per-er**, *n.* [8].

scan (skăn), *v. t.*; SCANNED (skănd); SCAN'NING. **1.** To go through, as a verse in poetry, foot by foot. **2.** To examine point by point; scrutinize. — *v. i.* To conform to metrical rules.

scan'dal (skăn'dȧl), *n.* **1.** Injury to reputation, or rumor or general comment causing it. **2.** Heedless or malicious defamatory talk. **3.** That which causes scandal.

scan'dal-ize (-īz), *v. t.* [1] To horrify or shock by some action considered immoral or improper.

scan'dal-ous (-ŭs), *a.* [4] Involving scandal; disgraceful; opprobrious; defamatory. — **-ly**, *adv.* [8] — **scan'dal-ous-ness**, *n.* [8].

scan'sion (skăn'shŭn), *n.* Act of scanning verse.

scant (skănt),*a.* [3] **1.** Scarcely sufficient; meager. **2.** Having a small or insufficient supply. — *v. t.* To limit; stint. — **-ly**, *adv.* — **-ness**, *n.*

scant'ling (skănt'lĬng), *n.* A piece of timber of small cross-sectional area, as a stud.

Saxophone.

scant'y (skăn'tĭ), a. [3] **1.** Small; not abundant; as, a *scanty* crop. **2.** Insufficient; scant; as, a *scanty* supply. — **scant'i-ly,** adv. [8] — **-i-ness,** n. [8].

scape (skāp), n. *Bot.* A flower stalk arising at or below the surface of the ground, as in the tulip.

scape'goat' (skāp'gōt'),n. A person or thing bearing blame for others. [less ; a scamp.

scape'grace' (-grās'), n. One who is wild or reckless.

scap'u-la (skăp'ū-lä), n. ; pl. L. -LÆ (-lē), E. -LAS (-lȧz). The shoulder blade.

scap'u-lar(-lȧr),a. Of or pert. to the shoulder blade.

scar (skär), n. **1.** A mark remaining after a wound or ulcer is healed. **2.** A mark where a fallen leaf was attached. — v. t. & i.; SCARRED (skärd); SCAR'-RING. To mark with or form a scar or scars.

scar, n. A steep rock or cliff on a mountain side.

scar'ab (skăr'ȧb), n. **1.** A kind of beetle, esp. the one sacred in ancient Egypt. **2.** A representation of the scarab, used as an amulet, etc.

scarce (skârs), a. [3] Deficient in quantity; hence, infrequent ; rare. — adv. Scarcely. — **scarce'-ness,** n. [8]. [but just.

scarce'ly (skârs'lĭ), adv. With difficulty; barely;

scar'ci-ty (skâr'sĭ-tĭ), n. Quality or state of being scarce; deficiency; dearth; hence, rareness.

scare (skâr), v. t. [1] To frighten ; strike with sudden fear. — v. i. To be scared. *Colloq.* — n. Fright or a fright. *Colloq.*

scare'crow' (-krō'), n. **1.** An object, usually suggesting a human figure, set up to frighten crows, etc., away from crops ; hence, anything terrifying without danger. **2.** A person in rags and tatters.

scarf (skärf), n. ; pl. SCARFS (skärfs), sometimes SCARVES (skärvz). **1.** A broad band of fabric worn loosely over the shoulders or about the neck, sometimes over the head or around the waist. **2.** A cravat with falling ends.

scarf'skin' (skärf'skĭn'), n. The epidermis.

scar'i-fi-ca'tion(skăr'ĭ-fĭ-kā'shŭn),n.A scarifying.

scar'i-fy (skăr'ĭ-fī),v. t. [2] **1.** To scratch or cut the skin of ; esp., *Med.*, to make small incisions in for drawing blood without opening a large vein. **2.** To lacerate, as the feelings. — **fi'er,** n. [8].

scar'la-ti'na (skär'lä-tē'nä), n. Scarlet fever.

scar'let (skär'lĕt), n. **1.** A deep bright red tinged with orange or yellow ; a vivid red. **2.** Scarlet cloth. — a. Of the color called scarlet. — scarlet fever, an acute contagious disease marked by fever, sore throat, and a scarlet rash.

scarp (skärp), n. *Fort.* The inner side of the ditch. — v. t. To cut down vertically, or nearly so.

scathe (skāth), n. Harm; damage ; injury ; hurt; misfortune. *Archaic.*—v. t. [1] **1.** To do harm to; injure; damage; hurt. **2.** To injure by fire; scorch; blast. *Literary.* — **scathe'less** (-lĕs), a. [8].

scath'ing (skāth'ĭng), p. a. [4] Injuring, as by blasting or burning ; hence, bitterly severe ; as, a *scathing* rebuke. — **scath'ing-ly,** adv. [8].

scat'ter (skăt'ẽr), v. t. & i. **1.** To dissipate ; disperse; dispel. **2.** To strew; throw about loosely.— **scat'ter-er,** n. [8].

scav'en-ger (skăv'ĕn-jẽr), n. One employed to clean streets and carry off filth ; also, any animal that devours refuse, etc.

scene (sēn), n. **1.** One of the slides, or other devices, used to give an appearance of reality to a

play ; pl., stage scenery. **2.** A division of a drama, usually a division of an act. **3.** The place, circumstances, etc., in which anything occurs. **4.** One of a series of actions and events. **5.** An exhibition of strong feeling, esp. between persons. **6.** A landscape ; view ; prospect.

scen'er-y (sēn'ẽr-ĭ), n. **1.** The painted scenes or hangings of a stage, with their accessories. **2.** The general aspect of a landscape.

sce'nic (sē'nĭk; sĕn'ĭk), a. [4] **1.** Of or pertaining to the stage; dramatic. **2.** Of or pertaining to scenery ; affording attractive scenery.

scent (sĕnt), v. t. **1.** To smell ; hence, to get or have an inkling of. **2.** To fill with odor. — n. **1.** Odor; smell; fragrance. **2.** A sweet-smelling, aromatic extract; perfume. **3.** The odor left by an animal in passing; hence, course of pursuit. **4.** Sense of smell. — **scent'less,** a. [8].

scep'ter (sĕp'tẽr), n. A staff or baton borne by a sovereign as an emblem of authority.

scep'tic (skĕp'tĭk), **scep'ti-cal,** etc. Vars. of SKEPTIC, SKEPTICAL, etc.

sched'ule (skĕd'ūl), n. A formal list; catalogue; inventory. — v. t. [1] To form into, or place in, a schedule.

scheme (skēm), n. **1.** A systematic plan. **2.** A plan or theory of action ; design ; project. —v.t. & i. [1] To plan; design; plot; contrive. — **schem'er** (skēm'ẽr), n. [8]. [Scepter.

|| **scher'zo** (skĕr'tsō), n. ; It. pl. -ZI (-tsē). [It.] *Music.* A playful movement, usually taking the place of the old minuet in a sonata or a symphony.

Schick test (shĭk). *Med.* A test in which the injection of a diluted diphtheria toxin indicates whether the patient is immune.

schism (sĭz'm), n. **1.** Division ; esp., formal division or separation in the church; offense of seeking to cause such division. **2.** A schismatic body.

schis-mat'ic (sĭz-măt'ĭk), a. [4] Of, pert. to, or characteristic of, schism. — n. One who creates or takes part in schism. — **-i-cal** (-ĭ-kăl), a. [4].

schist (shĭst), n. A crystalline rock that readily splits into slabs or sheets.

schol'ar (skŏl'ẽr), n. **1.** One who attends a school ; pupil; student. **2.** One who holds a scholarship. **3.** A learned person.

schol'ar-ly (skŏl'ẽr-lĭ), a. [4] Like, or characteristic of, a scholar ; learned.

schol'ar-ship, n. **1.** Character or qualities of a scholar ; learning. **2.** A foundation for the support of a student.

scho-las'tic (skō-lăs'tĭk), a. [4] Pertaining to a scholar or school. [— v. i. To swim in shoals.

school (skōōl), n. Of fish, etc., a shoal ; company.

school, n. **1.** A place for instruction ; also, the institution or body of teachers and learners in such a place. **2.** The body of pupils in a school ; as, a small *school.* **3.** A sect or denomination in philosophy, theology, science, medicine, etc. In the United States, schools are classified as: (1) elementary schools, covering the first eight years or grades; (2) secondary s., including high schools and private schools immediately preparatory to college. — v. t. **1.** To educate in a school. **2.** To discipline; train.

āle, senāte, câre, ăm, ȧccount, ärm, ȧsk, sofȧ ; ēve, ĕvent, ĕnd, recĕnt, makẽr ; īce, ĭll ; ōld, ŏbey, ôrb, ŏdd, sŏft, cŏnnect ; ūse, ŭnite, ûrn, ŭp, circŭs ; fōōd, fŏŏt ; out, oil ;

school'book' (-bŏŏk'), *n.* Book for use in schools.

school'boy' (-boi'), *n.* Boy belonging to a school.

school'fel'low (-fĕl'ō), *n.* An associate in school.

school'girl' (-gûrl'), *n.* Girl belonging to a school.

school'house' (-hous'), *n.* A building for a school.

school'ing, *n.* **1.** Instruction in school; act of teaching. **2.** Discipline; reproof; reprimand. **3.** Pay for instruction.

school'mas'ter (-más'tẽr), *n.* A master of a school; a man who teaches a school.

school'mate' (-māt'), *n.* A companion at school.

school'mis'tress (-mĭs'trĕs), *n.* A woman who teaches a school. [are taught.]

school'room' (-rŏŏm'), *n.* A room in which pupils

schoon'er (skŏŏn'ẽr), *n.* A fore-and-aft rigged vessel, having two or more masts. See SAIL, *Illust.*

schot'tish } (shŏt'ĭsh),*n.* A dance similar to the
schot'tische } polka; also, the music for it.

sci-at'ic (sī-ăt'ĭk), *a.* Of or pertaining to the hip; in the region of, or affecting, the hip.

sci-at'i-ca (-ĭ-ká), *n. Med.* Neuralgia of the sciatic nerve, which runs down the back of the thigh.

sci'ence (sī'ĕns), *n.* **1.** Knowledge, as of principles or facts. **2.** Knowledge systematized and formulated with reference to general truths or general laws. **3.** Esp., such knowledge relating to the physical world. **4.** Any branch of systematized knowledge.

sci'en-tif'ic (-ĕn-tĭf'ĭk), *a.* [4] **1.** Of, pertaining to, or used in, science. **2.** Agreeing with, or depending on, science. **3.** Having a knowledge of science, or of a science. **— i-cal-ly,** *adv.* [8].

sci'en-tist (sī'ĕn-tĭst), *n.* One learned in science, esp. natural science.

scim'i-tar } (sĭm'ĭ-tẽr), *n.* Oriental saber
scim'i-ter } with a much curved blade.

scin-til'la (sĭn-tĭl'á), *n.* A spark; atom; — used only fig. of evidence, truth, etc.

scin'til-late (sĭn'tĭ-lāt), *v. i.* [1] **1.** To emit sparks; spark. **2.** To sparkle or twinkle.

scin'til-la'tion (-lā'shŭn), *n.* **1.** Act of scintillating. **2.** A spark or flash emitted in scintillating.

sci'on (sī'ŭn), *n.* **1.** Any bud, shoot, or other portion of a plant capable of propagation; such a part removed and prepared for grafting. **2.** A descendant. [or splitting; fission.]

scis'sion (sĭzh'ŭn; sĭsh'-),*n.* A cutting, dividing,

scis'sors (sĭz'ẽrz),*n. pl.* A cutting instrument like shears, but smaller; — often *pair of scissors.*

scle-ro'sis (sklē-rō'sĭs), *n.; pl.* -ROSES (-sēz). *Med.* Morbid hardening of a tissue or structure.

scle-rot'ic (-rŏt'ĭk), *a.* **1.** *Anat.* Designating, or pertaining to, the dense white outer coat of the eyeball. **2.** *Med.* Affected with sclerosis. **—** *n.* The sclerotic coat of the eye.

scoff (skŏf), *n.* An expression or object of scorn, derision, or contempt. **—** *v. i.* To manifest contempt by derisive acts or language;—often with *at.* **—** *v. t.* To treat with derision; mock at. **— scoff'er,** *n.* [8] **— scoff'ing-ly,** *adv.* [8].

scold (skōld), *v. i. & t.* To find fault, esp. noisily or rudely; chide or rebuke harshly. **—** *n.* One who scolds, esp. habitually.

sconce (skŏns), *n.* **1.** A small fort or redoubt; hence, a shelter or protective screen. **2** The head; skull. *Colloq.* **3.** A bracket candlestick, or group of candlesticks, secured to a wall. **—** *v. t.* [1] To ensconce; imprison.

scone (skōn), *n.* A cake of barley, wheat, or oatmeal, often baked on a griddle. *Scot.*

scoop (skŏŏp), *n.* **1.** A large ladle. **2.** A deep shovel, or similar implement for dipping or shoveling; as, a flour *scoop.* **3.** A basinlike cavity; hollow. **4.** Act of scooping. **—** *v. t.* **1.** To take out or up with a scoop. **2.** To make hollow; dig out.

scoot (skŏŏt), *v. i. & t.* To dart. **—** *n.* An act of scooting, or darting. *Both Colloq.*

scope (skōp), *n.* **1.** Range or extent of view, intent, action, etc. **2.** Room or opportunity for free outlook, aim, or action; liberty.

scor-bu'tic (skôr-bū'tĭk), *a. Med.* Of, pertaining to, or like, scurvy; diseased with scurvy.

scorch (skôrch), *v. t.* To parch by heat or burn superficially. **—** *v. i.* **1.** To be burnt on the surface. **2.** To go at great speed on a cycle or in a motor vehicle. *Colloq.* **— scorch'er,** *n.* [8].

score (skōr), *n.* **1.** A notch or incision, esp. one made as for keeping account. **2.** An account so kept; any account; indebtedness. **3.** The number of points gained in a contest. **4.** *Music.* The draft of a composition, with the parts for all the instruments or voices. **5.** The number twenty; hence, in *pl.*, a large number. **—** *v. t.* [1] **1.** To mark with lines, scratches, or notches, esp. for keeping account. **2.** To set down; record; charge. **3.** To gain for addition to the score, as points in a game; hence, to win; as, to *score* a success. **—** *v. i.* **1.** To keep the score in a game. **2.** To make or count a point or points, as in a game; tally; also, to win or have the advantage. **— scor'er,** *n.* [8].

sco'ri-a (skō'rĭ-á), *n.; L. pl.* -RIÆ (-ē). Refuse from melting of metals, reduction of ores, etc.; dross; slag; also, cellular, slaggy lava; — usually in *pl.*

sco'ri-a'ceous (-ā'shŭs), *a.* Of or pert. to scoria.

scorn (skôrn), *n.* Extreme contempt; disdain. **—** *v. t.* To hold in, or reject with, scorn; disdain. **—** *v. i.* To scoff. **— scorn'er,** *n.* [8].

scorn'ful (skôrn'fŏŏl), *a.* [4] Full of scorn; disdainful. **— scorn'ful-ly,** *adv.* **—ful-ness,** *n.*

scor'pi-on (-ŭn), *n.* Any of numerous insects allied to the spiders, having a narrow tail with a venomous sting at the tip.

scot (skŏt), *n.* A tax or contribution; fine.

Scot, *n.* A native or inhabitant of Scotland.

Scotch (skŏch),*a.* Scottish.**—** **1.** *Collective pl.* Natives or inhabitants of Scotland or their immediate descendants; the Scots. **2.** *sing.* The dialect or dialects of English spoken by the people of Scotland.

scotch, *v. t.* To cut superficially; wound; score. **—** *n.* A slight cut or incision; notch; score.

Scotch'man (-mán), *n.; pl.* -MEN (-mĕn). A Scot.

sco'ter (skō'tẽr), *n.* Any of several sea ducks.

scot'-free', *a.* Without payment of scot; untaxed; hence, unhurt; clear; safe.

Scots (skŏts), *a.* Scottish; Scotch.

Scots'man (skŏts'mán), *n.* A Scotchman.

Scot'tish (-ĭsh), *a.* Of or pert. to the inhabitants of Scotland, their country, or language; Scotch.

---

scoun'drel (skoun'drĕl), *n.* A mean, worthless fellow; rascal; villain. — *a.* [4] Low; base; mean. — **scoun'drel-ly**, *a.* [4].

scour (skour), *v. i.* To run swiftly; range in pursuit. — *v. t.* To pass over swiftly; also, to go over thoroughly in or as if in search.

scour, *v. t.* **1.** To make clean and bright by friction. **2.** To cleanse by rubbing or scrubbing. **3.** To remove as if by rubbing; esp., to carry off or sweep away, as a flood. **4.** To purge. — *v. i.* **1.** To clean anything by hard rubbing or friction. **2.** Of cattle, to have diarrhea. — *n.* Act or fact of scouring. — **scour'er**, *n.* [8].

scourge (skûrj), *v. t. & i.* [1] **1.** To whip; lash; flog. **2.** To punish or afflict severely. — *n.* **1.** A lash or whip, esp. as used for chastising human beings. **2.** A means of inflicting punishment or suffering; hence, a punishment; also, a cause of calamity or affliction. — **scourg'er** (skûr'jẽr), *n.*

scout (skout), *v. t.* To reject with contempt; treat with ridicule. — *v. i.* To scoff; mock.

scout, *n.* **1.** One sent out to gain and bring in tidings, or to reconnoiter. **2.** A boy scout. See BOY SCOUT. — *v. i.* To go about to explore a region or to get information of the movements of an enemy; reconnoiter. — *v. t.* To reconnoiter.

scow (skou), *n.* A large flat-bottomed boat having broad, square ends.

scowl (skoul), *v. i.* To wrinkle the brows, as in frowning; look sullen, angry, or threatening. — *n.* A wrinkling of the brows; a frown.

scrab'ble (skrăb'b'l), *v. i.* [1] To scrape, paw, or scratch with the hands; scramble. — *v. t.* To gather hastily as by clutching. — *n.* A scrabbling.

scrag (skrăg), *n.* Any of various lean and tough things, as the back of the neck, esp. in a sheep.

scrag'gly (-lĭ), *a.* [3] Irregular; jagged; ragged.

scrag'gy (-ĭ), *a.* [3] **1.** Rough with irregular points. **2.** Scrawny. — **-gi-ness**, *n.* [8].

scram'ble (skrăm'b'l), *v. i.* [1] **1.** To move or climb with struggling use of hands and feet or knees; scrabble. **2.** To struggle with others for something on the ground; struggle with others for something. — *v.t.* To collect by scrambling. — *n.* A scrambling. — **scram'bler**, *n.* [8]. — scrambled eggs, eggs of which the whites and yolks are stirred together while cooking.

scrap (skrăp), *n.* **1.** Something scraped off; a bit; fragment. **2.** A fragment of something written or printed; a brief excerpt. **3.** *pl.* The crisp substance that remains after trying out animal fat; as, pork *scraps*. **4.** *sing.* or *pl.* Scrap metal. — *a.* In the form of scraps or fragments; valuable only as raw material; as, *scrap* metal.

scrap'book' (-book'), *n.* A blank book in which pictures, clippings, etc., may be pasted.

scrape (skrāp), *v. t.* [1] **1. a** To rub over the surface of with a sharp or rough instrument; to grate harshly over. **b** To remove in this way. **2.** To collect by or as by a process of scraping. **3.** To draw harshly or roughly over a surface. — *v. i.* **1.** To scrape anything; also, to rub harshly or gratingly. **2.** To occupy one's self with getting goods, esp. money, laboriously. **3.** To draw back the foot along the ground or floor when making a bow. — *n.* **1.** Act or sound of scraping. **2.** A

disagreeable predicament; difficulty. — **scrap'er** (skrāp'ẽr), *n.* [8].

scrap'ple (skrăp''l), *n.* An article of food made by boiling together scraps of meat, usually pork, with herbs and flour or Indian meal. *U. S.*

scrap'py (-ĭ), *a.* [3] Consisting of scraps.

scratch (skrăch), *v. t.* **1.** To rub and tear or mark the surface of with something sharp or ragged; scrape. **2.** To rub so as to allay itching, or the like. **3.** To cancel or expunge as by drawing a line through. **4.** To dig with the claws. — *v. i.* **1.** To use the claws or nails in tearing, wounding, digging, etc. **2.** To rub one's head, back, etc., with something rough. **3.** To gather money by hard work and hoarding. — *n.* **1.** A break or mark made by scratching. **2.** A slight, superficial wound. **3.** The starting line in a race. **4.** A test or proof of courage; as, to come up to the *scratch*. — **scratch'er**, *n.* [8].

scrawl (skrôl), *v. t. & i.* To draw or mark awkwardly; write carelessly; scribble. — *n.* Unskillful or careless writing. — **scrawl'er**, *n.* [8].

scraw'ny (skrô'nĭ), *a.* [3] Meager; thin; bony. Chiefly *U. S.* — **scraw'ni-ness** (-nĭ-nĕs), *n.* [8].

screak (skrēk), *v. i.* To emit a shrill sound; screech; creak. — *n.* A creaking; screech.

scream (skrēm), *v. i.* To cry out with a shrill voice; utter a sudden, sharp outcry, as in fright, pain, anger, etc. — *v. t.* To utter as or with a scream. — *n.* Act or sound of screaming.

screech (skrēch), *v. i.* To utter a harsh, shrill cry; shriek. — *v.t.* To utter as or with a screech. — *n.* A harsh, shrill cry, as of acute pain or terror.

screed (skrēd), *n.* A long tirade on any subject.

screen (skrēn), *n.* **1.** Anything in the nature of a protective partition or curtain. **2.** A surface on which an image is thrown by a magic lantern, etc. **3.** A coarse sieve. — *v. t.* **1.** To shelter; protect; conceal. **2.** To sift through a screen. — **screen'er**, *n.* [8].

screw (skrōō), *n.* **1.** A common mechanical device consisting in its simplest form of a continuous spiral rib or "thread" with the cylindrical shank from which it projects. Also, the corresponding part into which this external screw fits and advances. **2.** Hence, anything containing such a device; as, a wood *screw*. **3.** A screw propeller. **4.** A turn of or as of a screw. — *v. t.* **1.** To turn, as a screw; press, fasten, make firm, move, etc., by means of a screw. **2.** To turn as by a screw. **3.** To force as by pressure of screws; as, to *screw* up courage. **4.** To practice extortion on. **5.** To twist; distort. — *v. i.* **1.** To turn as or like a screw. **2.** To practice extortion or oppression.

screw driver, *or* **screw'driv'er**, *n.* A tool for turning screws so as to drive them into place.

screw propeller. A device consisting of a central hub with radiating blades forming part of two or more spiral surfaces, used to propel steamships, boats, airships, etc.

scrib'ble (skrĭb''l), *v. t.* [1] To write hastily or carelessly. — *v. i.* To scrawl; make meaningless marks. — *n.* Hasty or careless writing; scrawl. — **scrib'bler** (-lẽr), *n.* [8].

scribe (skrīb), *n.* **1.** One who writes; esp., an

official or public writer. **2.** *Jewish Religion &* *Hist.* A doctor or teacher of the law.— *v. t.* [1] To write or mark on. — **scrib′er** (skrīb′ẽr), *n.*

scrim (skrĭm), *n.* A kind of light, coarse cotton or linen fabric.

scrim′mage (skrĭm′åj), *n.* A confused struggle.

scrimp (skrĭmp), *v. t.* **1.** To be sparing of. **2.** To put on short allowance.— *v. i.* To be niggardly.

scrimp′y (skrĭm′pĭ), *a.* [3] Scanty.— **scrim′pi-ness,** *n.* [8]. *Both Colloq.*

scrip (skrĭp), *n.* Small bag; wallet. *Archaic.*

scrip, *n.* **1.** A writing, as a certificate, memorandum, or list. **2.** A small piece or scrap of paper. **3.** A document used as evidence that the holder is entitled to receive something; such documents collectively.   [writing.

script (skrĭpt), *n.* Written characters; style of

Scrip′tur-al (skrĭp′tụr-ăl), *a.* [4] Pertaining to, contained in, or according to, the Scriptures.

scrip′ture (-tụr), *n.* **1.** [*cap.*] The books of the Old and the New Testament, or of either of them; the Bible;— usually in *pl.* **2.** Any sacred writing.

scrive′ner (skrĭv′nẽr; skrĭv′n̵-ẽr), *n.* A professional writer; one who d:..ws contracts, etc.

scrof′u-la (skrŏf′ụ-là), *n. Med.* A tuberculous condition with enlargement and degeneration of the lymphatic glands, esp. those of the neck.

scrof′u-lous (-lŭs), *a.* Pertaining to scrofula.

scroll (skrōl), *n.* **1.** A roll of paper or parchment. **2.** Something, as an ornament, in form resembling a roll of paper, esp. one partly unrolled.

scroll saw. A ribbonlike saw stretched in a frame, adapted for sawing curved outlines.

scrub (skrŭb), *v. t. & i.;* SCRUBBED (skrŭbd); SCRUB′BING. To rub hard in washing; wash with rubbing. — *n.* **1.** Act or process of scrubbing. **2.** A drudge. **3.** Vegetation consisting of dwarf or stunted shrubs. **4.** Anything undersized, mean, or inferior.— *a.* **1.** Undersized; mean; inferior. **2.** *Sports.* Composed of individuals without previous practice together.— **scrub′ber,** *n.* [8].

scrub′by (skrŭb′ĭ), *a.* [3] **1.** Like scrub; stunted; paltry. **2.** Having much scrub, or underbrush.

scruff (skrŭf), *n.* The nape of the neck.

scrunch (skrŭnch), *v. t. & i.* To crunch; crush; squeeze. — *n.* Act or sound of scrunching.

scru′ple (skrōō′p'l), *n.* **1.** A minute portion; small part. **2.** A weight of 20 grains or ⅓ of a dram,— used by apothecaries. **3.** Hesitation from difficulty in determining what is right or proper. — *v. i. & t.* [1] To have scruples.

scru′pu-los′i-ty (skrōō′pụ-lŏs′ĭ-tĭ), *n.; pl.* -TIES (-tĭz). Quality or state of being scrupulous.

scru′pu-lous (skrōō′pụ-lŭs), *a.* [4] Full of or having scruples; inclined to scruple; careful; punctilious. — **-ly,** *adv.* [8] —**-ness,** *n.* [8].

scru′ti-nize (skrōō′tĭ-nīz), *v. t. & i.* [1] To examine closely.   [inspection.

scru′ti-ny (-nĭ), *n.* Close examination; minute

scud (skŭd), *v. i.;* SCUD′DED; -DING. **1.** To move or run swiftly. **2.** *Naut.* To sail swiftly, or to run, before a gale. — *n.* **1.** Act of scudding. **2.** Light clouds or spray driven swiftly by the wind.

scuff (skŭf), *v. i. & t.* To walk with a scraping movement; scuffle.

scuf′fle (skŭf′'l), *v. i.* [1] **1.** To struggle or fight

at close quarters and confusedly. **2.** To shuffle. — *n.* A scrambling struggle. — **-fler,** *n.* [8].

scull (skŭl), *n.* **1.** A small rowboat. **2.** One of a pair of short oars for one person. **3.** An oar used at the stern to propel a boat. — *v. t. & i.* To propel (a boat) with a scull or sculls.— **scull′er,** *n.* [8].

scul′ler-y (skŭl′ẽr-ĭ), *n.; pl.* -LERIES (-ĭz). A small room attached to a kitchen, in which dishwashing and other dirty work is done.

scul′lion (skŭl′yŭn), *n.* A kitchen menial.

scul′pin (-pĭn), *n.* Any of numerous spiny, large-headed, broad-mouthed sea fishes.

sculp′tor (skŭlp′tẽr), *n.* One who sculptures; one who designs works of sculpture.— **sculp′tress** (-trĕs), *n. fem.*

sculp′tur-al (-tụr-ăl), *a.* Of or pert. to sculpture.

sculp′ture (-tụr) *n.* Act or art of sculpturing. — *v. t.* [1] To form with the chisel or other tool on, in, or from, wood, stone, metal, etc.

scum (skŭm), *n.* **1.** A film or layer of floating matter risen to or formed on, the surface of liquids. **2.** Refuse; low people; as, the *scum* of the earth.

scup (skŭp), *n.* A common food fish, of the Atlantic coast.

scup′per (-ẽr), *n. Naut.* One of the holes at a vessel's side to carry off water from the deck.

scurf (skûrf), *n.* Thin dry scales or scabs on the body, esp. on the scalp; dandruff.

scurf′y (skûr′fĭ), *a.* [3] Covered with scurf.

scur′rile (skûr′ĭl), *a.* [4] Also **-ril.** Scurrilous.

scur-ril′i-ty (skŭ-rĭl′ĭ-tĭ), *n.; pl.* -TIES. Quality of being scurrile; also, a scurrilous remark or act.

scur′ril-ous (skûr′ĭ-lŭs), *a.* [4] **1.** Using or given to using indecent language. **2.** Containing low indecency or abuse. — **-ly,** *adv.* — **-ness,** *n.*

scur′ry (skûr′ĭ), *v. i.* [2] To hasten away or along; scamper. — *n.* Act of scurrying.

scur′vy (skûr′vĭ), *a.* [3] Mean; low; contemptible. — **scur′vi-ly,** *adv.* [8] — **scur′vi-ness,** *n.* [8].

scur′vy, *n. Med.* A disease marked by debility, livid spots, spongy and bleeding gums, etc.

scu′tate (sku′tāt), *a.* Peltate.

scutch′eon (skŭch′ŭn). Var. of ESCUTCHEON.

scu′ti-form (sku′tĭ-fôrm), *a.* Shield-shaped.

scut′tle (skŭt′'l), *n.* A utensil for carrying coal.

scut′tle, *v. i.* [1] To run swiftly or hurriedly; scurry. — *n.* A quick pace; scurry.

scut′tle, *n.* **1.** A small opening with a lid; as: **a** *Naut.* A small opening or hatchway in a vessel's deck, side, or bottom. **b** An opening in a roof. **2.** The lid covering such opening. — *v. t.* To cut a hole or holes through the bottom, deck, or sides of (a vessel), esp. in the bottom, to sink her.

scythe (sīth), *n.* An agricultural implement, consisting of a handle and long curved blade attached at an angle, for mowing by hand.

sea (sē), *n.* **1.** One of the larger bodies of salt water, less than an ocean. **2.** A large inland body of water, esp. salt. **3.** The ocean as a whole. **4.** The swell of the ocean, etc., in or following a high wind; as, there was a high *sea.*

sea anemone. Any of numerous, usually solitary, and often large and beautifully colored, polyps.

sea′board′ (sē′bōrd′), *n.* The seacoast.

sea bread. Ship biscuit.

sea′coast′ (sē′kōst′), *n.* The coast of the sea.

sea dog. 1. A seal. **2.** An old sailor. *Colloq.*

sea'far'er (sē'fâr'ẽr), *n.* A mariner.

sea'far'ing (-ĭng), *a.* Following the sea.

sea'go'ing (sē'gō'ĭng), *a.* **1.** Adapted for use on the open sea; as, a *seagoing* tug. **2.** Seafaring.

sea'-green', *a.* Of a bluish green color.

sea gull. Any gull frequenting the sea.

sea horse. 1. A fabulous marine creature, half horse and half fish. **2.** a A walrus. **b** Any of various small fishes, with head suggestive of that of a horse. [VIKING.]

sea king. A Norse pirate chief of royal blood. See [seal]

seal (sēl), *n.* A flesh-eating sea animal, of va-

Seal. ($\frac{1}{50}$)

rious species, chiefly of the colder regions, hunted for its fur, hide, etc. — *v. i.* To hunt seals.

seal, *n.* **1.** An impression made on wax or the like; also, that which bears the impression. **2.** Stamp for making an impression in wax, etc. **3.** That which seals or secures; pledge; guaranty. **4.** Wax or a wafer placed on a letter, etc. — *v. t.* **1.** To affix a seal to, or mark with a seal; authenticate; ratify. **2.** To give under or as under seal. **3.** To fasten with a seal. **4.** To shut close; keep secret. **5.** To determine irrevocably. **6.** To close up the chinks, crevices, etc., of, as with plaster.

seal brown. The rich, dark-brown color of the fur of the seal after it has been dyed.

seal'er (sēl'ẽr), *n.* One who seals; esp., an officer who tests and certifies weights and measures.

seal'er, *n.* A mariner or vessel that hunts seals.

sealing wax. A resinous compound, plastic when warm, used to seal letters, documents, etc.

sea lion. Any of several large Pacific seals.

seal'skin' (sēl'skĭn'), *n.* The skin of a seal, esp. of one of a certain species (**fur seal**) after removal of the coarse outer hair; also, a garment of it.

seam (sēm), *n.* **1.** The line formed by sewing together pieces of cloth, etc. **2.** A line of junction. **3.** *Geol.* A layer or stratum, as of coal. **4.** A scar. — *v. t.* **1.** To form a scam upon or of; sew together. **2.** To line; scar; as, his face was *seamed.*

sea'man (sē'măn), *n.; pl.* -MEN. A sailor.

sea'man-ship, *n.* The skill of a good seaman.

seam'less, *a.* Without a seam.

seam'stress (sēm'strĕs), *n.* A needlewoman.

seam'y (sēm'ĭ), *a.* [3] Having, containing, or showing seams, esp. in the rough; hence, more or less disreputable; as, the *seamy* side of life.

sé'ance (sā'äns; sā'äns'), *n.* **1.** A session. **2.** A meeting to receive spirit communications.

sea'plane (sē'plān'), *n.* An airplane designed to rise from and land on the water.

sea'port (sē'pōrt'), *n.* A port, harbor, or town, on the seashore, accessible to seagoing vessels.

sear (sēr), *a.* [3] Withered;— esp. of vegetation.

sear, *v. t.* **1.** To wither; dry up. **2.** To burn (the surface, as of flesh) to dryness and hardness. **3.** Fig., to make callous or unfeeling.

search (sûrch), *v. t.* **1.** To look over or through, in order to find something; examine; explore. **2.** To inquire after; seek;— usually with *out.* **3.** To probe. **4.** To examine; try; test. — *v. i.* To seek; make inquiry or examination; investigate. — *n.* Act of searching; quest. — **-a-ble** (sûr'chȧ-b'l), *a.* [8] — **search'er,** *n.* [8].

search'light' (sûrch'līt'), *n.* A swiveled apparatus for projecting a powerful beam of light.

search warrant. *Law.* A warrant authorizing a search of a house, etc., as for stolen goods.

sea'scape (sē'skāp), *n.* A picture of a sea scene.

sea serpent. A serpent-like monster often said to have been seen at sea, but never proved to exist.

sea'shore' (sē'shōr'), *n.* The shore along the sea.

sea'sick' (-sĭk'), *a.* [4] Affected with seasickness.

sea'sick'ness, *n.* Nausea, prostration, etc., caused by the pitching or rolling of a vessel.

sea'side' (sē'sīd'), *n.* The seashore.

sea'son (sē'z'n), *n.* **1.** One of the divisions of the year, as spring, summer, autumn, and winter. **2.** A period of the year set off as by special activity. **3.** The suitable, fitting, or natural time or occasion. **4.** A while; esp., a relatively short period. — *v. t.* **1.** To fit or adapt for use or a given condition; as: **a** To habituate; inure. **b** To cure, as timber; mature. **2.** To render palatable; give zest or relish to; spice. **3.** To moderate; temper. — *v. i.* To become fit for use or adapted to a condition; to become acclimated, cured, etc.

sea'son-a-ble (-ȧ-b'l), *a.* [4] Opportune; in keeping with the season. — **sea'son-a-ble-ness,** *n.* — **sea'son-a-bly,** *adv.* [or the seasons.

sea'son-al (-ăl), *a.* Of or pertaining to a season]

sea'son-ing, *n.* **1.** Act or process by which anything is seasoned. **2.** That which is added to give zest or relish, as salt, spices, etc.; condiment.

seat (sēt), *n.* **1.** The place, part, or thing on which one sits; hence, anything made to sit in or on, as a chair. **2.** Location; site; residence. **3.** A right to sit; sitting; also, place of sitting. **4.** Way of sitting. — *v. t.* **1.** To place on a seat; cause to sit. **2.** To cause to occupy a post, site, or situation. **3.** To furnish with seats. **4.** To repair the seat of.

sea urchin. A marine animal of ball-shaped form having a thin, brittle, spiny shell.

sea wall. A wall or embankment to resist encroachments of the sea.

sea'ward (sē'wẽrd), *a.* Directed or situated toward the sea. — *adv.* Toward the sea.

sea'wards (-wẽrdz), *adv.* Seaward.

sea'way (sē'wā'), *n. Naut.* **a** A way over the sea; open sea. **b** A rough sea;—chiefly in *in a seaway.*

sea'weed', *n.* Plant or plants growing in the sea.

sea'wor'thy (sē'wûr'thĭ), *a.* [4] Fit for a sea voyage; able to stand rough weather at sea. — **sea'wor'thi-ness,** *n.* [8].

se-ba'ceous (sē-bā'shŭs), *a. Physiol.* Of, pertaining to, or secreting, fat; like fat.

se'cant (sē'kănt), *a.* Cutting. — *n. Geom.* A line that cuts another. See CIRCLE, *Illust.*

se-cede' (sē-sēd'), *v. i.* [1] To withdraw from fellowship; esp., to withdraw from a political or religious body. — **se-ced'er** (-sēd'ẽr), *n.* [8].

se-ces'sion (-sĕsh'ŭn), *n.* Act of seceding; esp. [*often cap.*], *U.S.*, the withdrawal of a State from the Union. as that of 11 States in 1860-61.——**ist,** *n.*

se-clude' (-klōōd'),*v. t.* [1] To shut up apart from others; place in solitude.　　　　[state.

se-clu'sion (-klōō'zhŭn), *n.* A secluding; secluded

se-clu'sive (-sĭv), *a.* [4] Tending to seclude.

sec'ond (sĕk'ŭnd), *a.* **1.** Immediately after the first in place or time; hence, occurring again; another;other. **2.** Next to the first in value, power, rank, etc.; secondary;subordinate ;inferior. **3.** Of the same kind as another. **4.** *Music.* Lower in pitch; rendering a part of lower pitch. — *n.* **1.** One that is second. **2.** One who attends another to support and aid him, as in a duel; a backer; assistant. **3.** *Music.* The second part in a concerted piece; alto. — *v. t.* **1.** To act as the second of; assist; support. **2.** In parliamentary practice, to support, as a motion, by adding one's voice to that of the mover or proposer. — **-er,** *n.* [8].

sec'ond (sĕk'ŭnd), *n.* The sixtieth part of a minute of time,or of angular measure.

sec'ond-a-ry (sĕk'ŭn-dă-rĭ),*a.* **1.** Next below the first in importance ; being in or of second place, rank, degree, etc. **2.** *Elec.* See PRIMARY, *a.* — secondary school. See SCHOOL. — *n.; pl.* -RIES (-rĭz). *Zoöl.* Any of the quill feathers arising from the inside segment of a bird's wing.—**-ri-ly,** *adv.*

sec'ond-hand' (-ŭnd-hănd'), *a.* **1.** Not original; received from another; not new. **2.** Of, pertaining to, or dealing in, secondhand merchandise.

sec'ond-ly, *adv.* In the second place.

sec'ond-rate', *a.* Of the second size, rank, etc.

sec'ond-sight', *n.* Power of discerning what is not visible or of foreseeing events; clairvoyance.

se'cre-cy (sē'krē-sĭ), *n. ; pl.* -CIES (-sĭz). **1.** Quality or state of being hidden; seclusion; privacy. **2.** Quality of being secretive; closeness.

se'cret (sē'krĕt), *a.* [4] **1.** Hidden; concealed. **2.** a Inscrutable; occult. **b** Secluded. — secret service, a government detective service. — *n.* **1.** Something studiously concealed. **2.** A mystery. **3.** A hidden cause. **4.** Secrecy. *Rare,* exc. in: in secret, in a private place; in secrecy. — **-ly,** *adv.*

sec're-ta'ri-al (sĕk'rē-tā'rĭ-ăl), *a.* Of or pertaining to a secretary.

sec're-ta'ri-at (sĕk'rē-tā'rĭ-ăt), *n.* The office of a secretary; the body of secretaries in an office.

sec're-ta-ry (sĕk'rē-tā-rĭ), *n.; pl.* -TARIES (-rĭz). **1.** One who attends to orders, letters, etc., for an organization or an individual. **2.** An officer of state in charge of a department. **3.** A writing desk. — **-ship'**, *n.*

se-crete' (sē-krēt'), *v. t.* [1] **1.** To keep secret or hidden; hide; conceal. **2.** *Physiol.* To produce and emit; as, the liver *secretes* bile.

se-cre'tion (-krē'shŭn), *n.* **1.** Act or process of secreting. **2.** That which is secreted.

se-cre'tive (-tĭv), *a.* [4] Tending to keep secret; marked by, or disposed to, secrecy. — **-ness,** *n.* [8].

se-cre'to-ry (sē-krē'tō-rĭ), *a. Physiol.* Secreting ; pertaining to, or promoting, secretion.

sect (sĕkt), *n.* Those attached to a certain opinion or opinions ; esp., a religious denomination.

sec-ta'ri-an (sĕk-tā'rĭ-ăn), *a.* [4] Of or pert. to a sect or sects. — *n.* One of a sect. — **-ism,** *n.*

sec'ta-ry (sĕk'tā-rĭ), *n. ; pl.* -RIES (-rĭz). A sectarian ; member of a sect, esp. of a dissenting sect.

sec'tile (sĕk'tĭl), *a.* [4] Capable of being cut.

sec'tion (-shŭn), *n.* **1.** Act of cutting ; separation by cutting. **2.** A part cut off, or so conceived of ; portion ; slice ; as : **a** A subdivision. **b** A distinct part of a country, people, community, class, etc. **c** See TOWNSHIP, 3. **3.** The representation of anything as it would appear if cut through by a plane.

sec'tion-al (-ăl), *a.* [4] **1.** Of or pertaining to a section or district; local. **2.** Consisting of sections ; divisible into sections.

sec'tion-al-ism (-ĭz'm), *n.* Devotion to local interests ; sectional feeling, prejudice, etc.

sec'tor (-tĕr), *n.* The figure bounded by two radii and the included arc of a circle. See CIRCLE, *Illust.*

sec'u-lar (-ŭ-lắr), *a.* [4] **1.** Of or pert. to this world; temporal ; worldly. **2.** Not bound by monastic vows or rules. — **-ly,** *adv.* [8].

sec'u-lar-ism (-lắr-ĭz'm), *n.* **1.** Secularity; secular spirit. **2.** Tenets or principles of secularists.

sec'u-lar-ist (-ĭst), *n.* One who rejects religious faith and worship ; also, one who opposes church intervention in education and other civil affairs.

sec'u-lar'i-ty (-lắr'ĭ-tĭ), *n.* State of being secular.

sec'u-lar-ize (sĕk'ŭ-lắr-īz), *v. t.* [1] To render secular; as : **a** To free from monastic vows or rules. **b** To transfer from ecclesiastical to temporal use, as a building. **c** To make worldly.

se-cure' (sē-kūr'), *a.* [3] **1.** Free from fear, care, or anxiety ; confident. **2.** Confident in opinion; certain ; sure. **3.** Not exposed to danger ; safe. **4.** Free from uncertainty ; assured. — *v. t.* [1] **1.** To guard ; protect ; make safe. **2.** To put beyond hazard of losing; assure; insure. **3.** To make fast ; close or confine effectually. **4.** To get; acquire certainly. — **se-cure'ly,** *adv.* [8].

se-cu'ri-ty (-kū'rĭ-tĭ), *n.; pl.* -TIES (-tĭz). **1.** Condition or quality of being secure. **2.** That which secures or makes safe; as : **a** Something given or pledged to make certain the fulfillment of an obligation, etc. **b** One who becomes surety for another. **3.** An evidence of debt or of property.

se-dan' (-dăn'), *n.* **1.** *Also* **sedan chair.** A portable chair or covered vehicle for carrying a single person, usually borne on poles by two men. **2.** An automobile with inclosed body of one compartment seating 4 to 7 persons, including the driver.

se-date' (-dāt'), *a.* [3] Undisturbed by passion or emotion ; calm. — **-ly,** *adv.* — **-ness,** *n.* [8].

sed'a-tive (sĕd'ă-tĭv), *a.* [4] Tending to make calm; soothing. — *n.* A sedative agent or remedy.

sed'en-ta-ry (-ĕn-tā-rĭ), *a.* [4] **1.** Stationary. **2.** Accustomed to sit much. **3.** Marked by or requiring much sitting. — **-ri-ly,** *adv.* — **-ri-ness,** *n.* [8].

sedge (sĕj), *n.* Any of various grasslike herbs, growing in dense tufts in marshes.　　　[sedge.

sedg'y (-ĭ), *a.* [3] Overgrown or fringed with

sed'i-ment (sĕd'ĭ-mĕnt), *n.* Matter which settles to the bottom from a liquid ; settlings ; dregs.

sed'i-men'ta-ry (-mĕn'tă-rĭ), *a.* [4] Of, pert. to, or containing, sediment.

se-di'tion (sē-dĭsh'ŭn), *n.* Conduct tending to treason, but without an overt act ; excitement of rebellion against constituted authority.

se-di'tious (-ŭs), *a.* [4] Of or pert. to sedition.

se-duce' (sē-dūs'), *v. t.* [1] To lead aside or astray, esp. from duty; corrupt. — **se-duc'er**, *n.* [8].

se-duc'tion (-dŭk'shŭn), *n.* **1.** Act of seducing. **2.** That which seduces; allurement.

se-duc'tive (-tĭv), *a.* [4] Tending to seduce: alluring; tempting. — **-ly**, *adv.* [8] — **-ness**, *n.* [8].

sed'u-lous (sĕd'ū̇-lŭs), *a.* [4] Diligent in application or pursuit. — **-ly**, *adv.* — **-ness**, *n.* [8].

see (sē), *n.* The seat or center of authority of a bishop; rank, office, authority, etc., of a bishop (in the case of Rome, the Pope or papal court).

see, *v. t.; pret.* SAW (sô); *p. p.* SEEN (sēn); *p. pr. & vb. n.* SEE'ING. **1.** To perceive with the eye; behold; view. **2.** To perceive mentally; discern; comprehend. **3.** To take care or heed; make sure. **4.** To escort; wait upon. **5.** To call upon; visit. **6.** To receive a call from; receive. **7.** To learn by observation or experience. — *v. i.* **1.** To have or use the sense of sight. **2.** To have intellectual sight; know; discern. **3.** To be attentive; take care; — usually with *to*. **4.** To look. *Obs.*, exc. as imperative or interjection: Look! behold!

seed (sēd), *n.; pl.* SEED *or* SEEDS (sēdz), (see PLURAL, *n.*, *Note*). **1. a** *Bot.* In flowering plants, the part, consisting of the embryo and one or more coverings, which separates from the parent plant and by germination produces a new individual like the parent. **b** Popularly, any small seedlike fruit. **2.** Progeny; descendants. **3.** That from which anything springs; source. — *v. t.* **1.** To sow. **2.** To extract the seeds from. — *v. i.* To go to seed; produce seed. — **seed'er**, *n.* [8].

seed'i-ness (-ĭ-nĕs), *n.* Seedy quality or state.

seed leaf. A cotyledon.

seed'less, *a.* Without seed.

seed'ling (-lĭng), *n.* **1.** A plant grown from seed. **2.** Any young tree under three feet in height.

seeds'man (sēdz'măn), *n.* **1.** A sower. **2.** A dealer in seeds.

seed'time (sēd'tīm'), *n.* Season for sowing.

seed'y (sēd'ĭ), *a.* [3] **1.** Abounding with seeds; bearing seeds; having run to seed. **2.** Shabby; as, a *seedy* coat; also, spiritless. *Colloq.*

see'ing, *n.* Sight; vision.

see'ing, *conj.* (orig. a *p. pr.*). In view of the fact (that); since; because.

seek (sēk), *v. t.; pret. & p. p.* SOUGHT (sôt); *p. pr. & vb. n.* SEEK'ING. **1.** To go in search of; look for. **2.** To inquire for; ask for. **3.** To try to acquire or gain; aim at. **4.** To try to reach or come to; go to. **5.** To try; attempt; — with an infinitive. **6.** To search; explore. — *v. i.* To make search or inquiry. — **seek'er**, *n.* [8].

seem (sēm), *v. i.* **1.** To look to be; appear. **2.** To appear to one's own mind.

seem'ing, *p. a.* Having a semblance. — *n.* Appearance; semblance. — **-ly**, *adv.* [8].

Seedling. 1 Primary Root; 2 Rootlet; 3 Root Hairs; 5 Cotyledon; 6 Stem; 7 7 True Leaves.

seem'ly (sēm'lĭ), *a.* [3] Suited to the object, occasion, purpose, or character. — *adv.* Becomingly. — **seem'li-ness** (-lĭ-nĕs), *n.* [8].

seen (sēn), *p. p.* of SEE.

seep (sēp), *v. i.* To ooze; percolate slowly.

seep'age (sēp'åj), *n.* Act or process of seeping; oozing; also, seeping fluid.

se'er (sē'ẽr; sēr), *n.* **1.** One that sees. **2.** (*pron.* sēr, sē'ẽr). One who foresees or foretells events.

seer'suck'er (sēr'sŭk'ẽr), *n.* A light linen, or cotton, fabric, usually striped and puckered.

see'saw' (sē'sô'), *n.* A children's pastime in which they move up and down on opposite ends of a balanced plank; also, the plank so used. — *v.i. & t.* To move up and down or to and fro.

seethe (sēth), *v. t. & i.; pret.* SEETHED (sēthd); *p. p.* SEETHED; *Now R.* SOD'DEN (sŏd'n); *p. pr. & vb. n.* SEETH'ING. To boil; steep; surge or foam up.

seg'ment (sĕg'mĕnt), *n.* **1.** Any of the parts into which a body naturally separates or is divided; part cut off; a section. **2.** *Geom.* A part cut off from a figure by a line or plane; esp., that part of a circular area cut off by a chord. See CIRCLE, *Illust.*

seg're-gate (sĕg'rē̇-gāt),*a.* [4] Separate.— (-gāt), *v. t.* [1] To separate or set apart.

seg're-ga'tion (-gā'shŭn), *n.* Act of segregating, or state of being segregated.

seign'ior (sēn'yẽr), *n.* A lord; gentleman.

seign'ior-age (-åj), *n.* Something claimed or taken by sovereign prerogative, as a charge on bullion brought to a mint to be coined; the difference between the cost of a mass of bullion and the value as money of the pieces coined from it.

seign'ior-y (-ĭ), *n.; pl.* -IORIES (-ĭz). Power, authority, or jurisdiction of a seignior; domain.

seine (sān; sēn), *n.* *Fishing.* A large net, one edge provided with sinkers and the other with floats. — *v. t. & i.* [1] To fish with a seine.

seis'mic (sīs'mĭk; sīz'-), *a.* Of, pertaining to, or caused by, an earthquake.

seis'mi-cal (-mĭ-kăl), *a.* Seismic. [mometer.]

seis'mo-graph (-mȯ-gráf), *n.* A recording seismograph.

seis'mo-graph'ic (-grăf'ĭk), *a.* Of, pertaining to, or indicated by, a seismograph or seismography.

seis-mog'ra-phy (sīs-mŏg'ra-fĭ; sīz-), *n.* A description of earthquakes; seismology.

seis-mol'o-gist (-mŏl'ȯ-jĭst), *n.* A specialist in seismology.

seis-mol'o-gy (-jĭ), *n.* The science of earthquakes and attendant phenomena.

seis-mom'e-ter (-mŏm'ē̇-tẽr), *n.* An instrument for measuring the direction, duration, and force of earthquakes.

seize (sēz), *v. t.* [1] **1.** To take possession of by force. **2.** To lay hold of suddenly or forcibly; reach and grasp; clutch. **3.** To grasp with the mind. — *v. i.* To take, or take possession, suddenly or forcibly; grasp; clutch; — with *on* or *upon*. — **seiz'a-ble** (-å-b'l), *a.* [8] — **seiz'er**, *n.* [8].

seiz'ing (sēz'ĭng), *p. pr. & vb. n.* of SEIZE. Hence: *n.* *Naut.* Act of fastening together or lashing with small rope; also, the cord or lashing so used.

sei'zure (sē'zhŭr), *n.* **1.** Act of seizing; state of being seized. **2.** Sudden attack, as of a disease; fit.

sel'dom (sĕl'dŭm), *adv.* Rarely; not often.

se-lect' (sē̇-lĕkt'), *a.* [4] **1.** Taken from a larger number by preference; hence, of special excellence; choice; exclusive; as, a *select* club. **2.** Nice in choosing. — *v. t.* To take by preference.

se-lec′tion (-lĕk′shŭn), *n.* **1.** A selecting; state of being selected. **2.** Thing selected; collection of things chosen. [tion; selecting.]

se-lec′tive (-tĭv), *a.* [4] Of or pertaining to selec-

se-lect′man (-lĕkt′măn), *n.; pl.* -MEN (-mĕn). In New England (except in Rhode Island), one of a board of town officers, chosen annually.

se-lec′tor (sĕ-lĕk′tẽr), *n.* One that selects.

se-le′ni-um (sē-lē′nĭ-ŭm), *n. Chem.* A nonmetallic element, resembling tellurium chemically.

self (sĕlf), *a.* **1.** Same; very; identical. *Archaic,* exc. in *selfsame.* **2.** Having its own or a single nature or character, as in color, composition, etc.; as, *self*-colored. — *n.; pl.* SELVES (sĕlvz). **1.** An individual regarded as having personality. **2.** Personal interest or advantage; selfishness.

self′-act′ing, *a.* Acting of itself; automatic.

self′-as-ser′tion, *n.* Assertion of one's individuality; insistence on one's claims or rights.

self′-as-ser′tive, *a.* Disposed to self-assertion.

self′-col′ored, *a.* [5] Of a single color.

self′-com-mand′, *n.* Self-control.

self′-com-pla′cen-cy, *n.* Self-complacent state.

self′-com-pla′cent, *a.* [4] Self-satisfied.

self′-con-ceit′, *n.* An overweening opinion of one's own powers, merits, etc.

self′-con-ceit′ed, *a.* [4] Having self-conceit.

self′-con′fi-dence, *n.* A being confident of one's own strength or powers. [—**-ly,** *adv.* [8].]

self′-con′fi-dent, *a.* [4] Having self-confidence.

self′-con′scious, *a.* [4] Conscious of one's self as an object of the observation of others. — **-ly,** *adv.* [8] — **-ness,** *n.* [8].

self′-con-tained′, *a.* [4] **1.** Reserved; not communicative. **2.** Showing self-control.

self′-con-trol′, *n.* Control of one's self.

self′-de-fense′, *or* **self′-de-fence′,** *n.* Act of defending one's own person, property, or reputation.

self′-de-ni′al, *n.* Denial of self or of one's own desires; unselfishness. — **-de-ny′ing,** *a.*

self′-es-teem′, *n.* Self-respect or self-conceit.

self′-ev′i-dent, *a.* [4] Evident without proof or reasoning. — **self′-ev′i-dent-ly,** *adv.* [8].

self′-gov′ern-ing, *a.* That governs itself.

self′-gov′ern-ment, *n.* **1.** Self-control. **2.** Government by joint action of the people constituting a civil body; also, state of being so governed.

self′-im-por′tant, *a.* Having an exaggerated idea of one's own importance or merit.

self′-in-dul′gence, *n.* Indulgence of one's appetites, desires, etc. [tites, desires, etc.]

self′-in-dul′gent, *a.* [4] Indulging one's appe-

self′-in′ter-est, *n.* Private interest.

self′ish (sĕl′fĭsh), *a.* [4] Caring unduly for one's self; putting one's own comfort, etc., before that of others. — **-ly,** *adv.* [8] — **-ness,** *n.* [8].

self′-love′, *n.* Love of one's self; tendency to seek one's own happiness, benefit, or advantage.

self′-made′, *a.* [4] Having risen from poverty or obscurity unaided, esp. without pecuniary aid.

self′-pit′y, *n.* Pity of one's self.

self′-pos-sessed′, *a.* [4] Having or exhibiting control or command over one's powers.

self′-pos-ses′sion, *n.* Self-control; composure.

self′-pres′er-va′tion, *n.* Preservation of one's self from destruction, injury, loss, etc.

self′-reg′is-ter-ing, *a.* Registering automatically.

self′-re-li′ance, *n.* Reliance on one's own powers.

self′-re-li′ant, *a.* [4] Having self-reliance.

self′-re-proach′, *n.* Reproaching of one's self.

self′-re-spect′, *n.* Respect for one's self.

self′-re-straint′, *n.* Restraint over self.

self′-right′eous (-rī′chŭs), *a.* [4] Righteous in one's own esteem; pharisaical. — **-ness,** *n.* [8].

self′-sac′ri-fice, *n.* Sacrificing of one's self or one's interest.

self′same′ (sĕlf′sām′), *a.* Precisely the same.

self′-sat′is-fac′tion, *n.* Satisfaction with one's self, etc. [or one's actions, etc.]

self′-sat′is-fied, *a.* [4] Satisfied with one's self

self′-seek′er, *n.* One who seeks only, or unduly, his own interest, advantage, or pleasure.

self′-seek′ing, *a.* [4] Seeking one's own interest; selfish. — *n.* Selfishness.

self′-styled′, *a.* Styled or called by one's self.

self′-suf-fi′cien-cy (-sŭ-fĭsh′ĕn-sĭ), *n.* State or quality of being self-sufficient.

self′-suf-fi′cient (-ĕnt), *a.* [4] **1.** Sufficient in or for one's self or itself; able to satisfy one's own needs. **2.** Having an overweening self-confidence.

self′-will′, *n.* One's own will, esp. when opposed to that of others; obstinacy.

self′-willed′, *a.* [4] Having self-will; obstinate.

sell (sĕl), *v. t.; pret. & p. p.* SOLD (sōld); *p. pr. & vb. n.* SELL′ING. **1.** To transfer (property) for a consideration. **2.** To make a matter of bargain and sale, esp. in breach of duty, trust, or the like; betray. — *v. i.* **1.** To sell commodities. **2.** To be sold; as, corn *sells* high. — **sell′er,** *n.* [8].

Selt′zer (sĕlt′sẽr), *n.,* or **Seltzer water.** An effervescing mineral water from Germany; also, an artificially carbonated water imitating it.

sel′vage (sĕl′vĕj), *n.* Edge of a woven fabric, so formed as to prevent raveling.

selves (sĕlvz), *n., pl. of* SELF.

sem′a-phore (sĕm′a-fōr), *n.* A signal telegraph; apparatus for signaling by the disposition of lanterns, flags, oscillating arms, etc.

sem′blance (-blăns), *n.* **1.** Image; likeness; form. **2.** Seeming; outward show; as, the *semblance* of virtue. **3.** Resemblance; similarity.

se-mes′ter (sĕ-mĕs′tẽr), *n.* A period of six months; esp., either of the two terms into which the period of instruction is divided in many colleges, etc.

sem′i-an′nu-al (sĕm′ĭ-ăn′ū-ăl), *a.* Half-yearly. — **sem′i-an′nu-al-ly,** *adv.* [8].

sem′i-cir′cle (-sûr′k'l), *n.* A half circle.

sem′i-cir′cu-lar (-sûr′kū-lẽr), *a.* Having the form of, or pertaining to, a semicircle.

sem′i-cir-cum′fer-ence (-sẽr-kŭm′fẽr-ĕns), *n.* Half of a circumference.

sem′i-co′lon (sĕm′ĭ-kō′lŏn), *n. Punctuation.* The mark [;] indicating a separation between parts of a sentence more distinct than that marked by a comma. [A semifluid substance.]

sem′i-flu′id (-flōō′ĭd), *a.* Imperfectly fluid. — *n.*

sem′i-liq′uid (-lĭk′wĭd), *a.* Half liquid; semifluid. — *n.* A semiliquid substance.

sem′i-month′ly (-mŭnth′lĭ), *a.* Coming or made

twice in a month. — *n.* Something done or made every half month, esp. such a periodical.

sem'i-nar' (sĕm'ĭ-när'), *n.* A group of students engaged, under an instructor, in original research.

sem'i-na-ry (sĕm'ĭ-nă-rĭ), *n. ; pl.* -RIES (-rĭz). **1.** A place where a thing originates and develops. **2.** A place of education, as a school of a high grade, an academy, or college. **3.** = SEMINAR.

sem'i-sol'id (sĕm'ĭ-sŏl'ĭd), *a.* Imperfectly solid.

Sem'ite (sĕm'ĭt), *n.* One of a Caucasian race represented by the Jews, etc.

Se-mit'ic (sĕ-mĭt'ĭk), *a.* Of or pertaining to the Semites or the family of languages spoken by them.

sem'i-tone' (sĕm'ĭ-tōn'), *n. Music.* Lit., half a tone; the tone at a half step; the half step itself.

sem'i-vow'el (-vou'ĕl), *n.* A sound intermediate between a vowel and a consonant, or partaking of the nature of both, as that of English *w* or *y.*

sem'i-week'ly (-wēk'lĭ), *a.* Coming, or made, or done, once every half week. — *n.* That which comes or happens once every half week, esp. such a periodical. — *adv.* At intervals of half a week.

sem'pi-ter'nal (sĕm'pĭ-tûr'năl), *a.* Everlasting.

sen'ate (sĕn'ăt), *n.* An assembly with the highest deliberative or legislative functions; as: **a** *Ancient Rome.* The supreme council of the state. **b** [*cap.*] The upper and smaller branch of various legislatures, as of France, the U. S., etc.

sen'a-tor (-á-tẽr), *n.* A member of a senate.

sen'a-to'ri-al (-á-tō'rĭ-ăl), *a.* **1.** Of, pertaining to, or befitting, a senator or a senate. **2.** Entitled to elect a senator; as, *senatorial* districts. *U. S.*

sen'a-tor-ship' (-), *n.* Office or dignity of a senator.

send (sĕnd), *v. t.;* SENT (sĕnt); SEND'ING. To cause to go; dispatch; impel. — *v. i.* To dispatch an agent or messenger or a message. — **send'er,** *n.*

sen'es-chal (sĕn'ĕ-shăl), *n.* The bailiff, steward, or major-domo of a great medieval lord, holding high military command.

se'nile (sē'nĭl; -nĭl), *a.* [4] Of, pertaining to, or proceeding from, old age or its infirmities.

se-nil'i-ty (sĕ-nĭl'ĭ-tĭ), *n.* Old age or its infirmity.

sen'ior (sēn'yẽr), *a.* **1.** Elder; — often used (abbr. *Sr.*) after a personal name to indicate the older of two bearing it. **2.** Superior in dignity, rank, or office. **3.** Of or pert. to the final year of the course in American colleges, high schools, etc. — *n.* **1.** A person older than another. **2.** One older in office or prior in grade. **3.** An aged person. **4.** A student in the senior year. [being senior.]

sen-ior'i-ty (sēn-yŏr'ĭ-tĭ), *n.* Quality or state of ‖ **se-ñor'** (sā-nyōr'), *n.; pl.* SEÑORES (-nyō'rās), ‖ **se-ño'ra** (-nyō'rä), *n.,* ‖ **se'ño-ri'ta** (sā'nyō-rē'tä), *n.* [Sp.] Spanish titles of courtesy corresponding respectively to the English *Mr.* or *sir, Mrs.* or *madam,* and *Miss;* also, a gentleman, lady, young lady.

sen-sa'tion (sĕn-sā'shŭn), *n.* **1.** A feeling produced by an external object (stimulus). **2.** Any feeling; esp., a more or less indefinite bodily feeling. **3.** A state of excited interest or feeling, or its cause.

sen-sa'tion-al (-ăl), *a.* [4] **1.** Of or pertaining to sensation or sensationalism. **2.** Melodramatic; emotional; as, a *sensational* novel. — **-ly,** *adv.* [8].

sen-sa'tion-al-ism (-ĭz'm), *n.* The practice or methods of sensational writing or speaking.

sense (sĕns), *n.* **1.** Meaning; import. **2.** Perception through the intellect; discernment. **3.** Sound perception and reasoning; also, that which is sound, or reasonable; rational meaning. **4.** Moral perception or appreciation. **5.** The faculty of receiving mental impressions through certain organs (**sense organs**) of the body; also, any particular faculty of sensation; as, the **five senses** (sight, smell, hearing, taste, and touch). **6.** That which is felt or is held as a sentiment or opinion; judgment. — *v. t.* [1] To get the meaning of ; understand ; realize. *Colloq., U. S.*

sense'less (sĕns'lĕs), *a.* [4] Destitute of, deficient in, or contrary to, sense; as: **a** Insensible. **b** Without intelligence; stupid. **c** Nonsensical.

sen'si-bil'i-ty (sĕn'sĭ-bĭl'ĭ-tĭ), *n.; pl.* -TIES (-tĭz). **1.** Ready discernment. **2.** Capacity of emotion or feeling; delicacy of feeling. **3.** State or quality of being sensible, or able to feel or perceive. **4.** Delicacy of an instrument; sensitiveness.

sen'si-ble (sĕn'sĭ-b'l), *a.* [4] **1.** Capable of being perceived. **2.** Capable of receiving impressions from external objects. **3.** Perceiving, or having perception ; cognizant ; satisfied ; persuaded. **4.** Possessing sense or reason; marked by good or common sense; wise. — **sen'si-bly,** *adv.*

sen'si-tive (-tĭv), *a.* [4] **1.** Having sense or feeling; impressible by external objects. **2.** Having quick and acute sensibility; highly susceptible; easily affected. **3.** Readily affected or changed by certain agents. — **sensitive plant,** a species of mimosa. — **-ly,** *adv.* [8].

sen'si-tive-ness, *n.* State of being sensitive.

sen'si-tize (-tīz), *v. t.* [1] *Chem. & Photog.* To render sensitive. — **sen'si-tiz'er** (-tīz'ẽr), *n.*

sen'so-ry (sĕn'sō-rĭ), *a.* [4] **1.** Of or pert. to sensation; — esp. applied to nerves carrying to a nerve center impulses resulting in sensation. **2.** Of the nature of sensation; pertaining to sense.

sen'su-al (sĕn'shōō-ăl), *a.* [4] **1.** Not spiritual or intellectual ; carnal ; fleshly. **2.** Devoted to the pleasures of sense ; voluptuous; sometimes, lewd.

sen'su-al-ism (-ĭz'm), *n.* Sensuality.

sen'su-al-ist, *n.* One who is sensual.

sen'su-al'i-ty (-ăl'ĭ-tĭ), *n.* State of being sensual.

sen'su-al-ly, *adv.* In a sensual manner.

sen'su-ous (-ŭs), *a.* [4] **1.** Of or pert. to the senses; addressing the senses. **2.** Easily affected through the senses. **3.** Of the nature of sensation or of sense imagery. — **-ly,** *adv.* — **-ness,** *n.*

sent (sĕnt), *pret. & p. p.* of SEND.

sen'tence (sĕn'tĕns), *n.* **1.** An opinion; hence, a decision; determination; judgment. **2.** *Gram.* A combination of words complete as expressing a thought, and in writing marked at the close by a period, interrogation point, or exclamation point. — *v. t.* [1] To pass or pronounce judgment on; doom. — **sen'tenc-er** (-tĕn-sẽr), *n.*

sen-ten'tious (sĕn-tĕn'shŭs), *a.* [4] **1.** Terse; pithy. **2.** Abounding in sayings, axioms, or maxims. — **-ly,** *adv.* [8] — **-ness,** *n.* [8].

sen'ti-ent (sĕn'shĭ-ĕnt; -shĕnt), *a.* **1.** Having the power of sensation and perception. **2.** Experiencing sensation. — *n.* A sentient being. — **-ly,** *adv.*

sen'ti-ment (sĕn'tĭ-mĕnt), *n.* **1.** Feeling; sensibility; tender susceptibility. **2.** A mental attitude, thought, or judgment prompted by feeling. **3.** Refined feeling; delicate sensibility. **4.** Opinion; notion. **5.** A maxim, saying, or toast.

sen'ti-men'tal (-měn'tăl), *a.* [4] **1.** Of the nature of, or marked by, sentiment. **2.** Affectedly or excessively tender or emotional. — *ly, adv.*

sen'ti-men'tal-ism (-ĭz'm), *n.* Sentimentality.

sen'ti-men'tal-ist, *n.* One who has or affects sentiment or sentimentality. [being sentimental.

sen'ti-men-tal'i-ty (-měn-tăl'ĭ-tĭ), *n.* Quality of

sen'ti-nel (sěn'tĭ-něl), *n.* A watch, or guard; a soldier set to guard against surprise; sentry.

sen'try (sěn'trĭ), *n.; pl.* -TRIES (-trĭz). **1.** A sentinel. **2.** Guard; watch, as by a sentinel.

se'pal (sē'păl; sĕp'ăl), *n. Bot.* A leaf or division of the calyx. [being separable.

sep'a-ra-bil'i-ty (sĕp'à-rà-bĭl'ĭ-tĭ), *n.* Quality of

sep'a-ra-ble (sĕp'à-rà-b'l), *a.* Capable of being separated. — *ness, n.* [8] — *ra-bly, adv.* [8].

sep'a-rate (-rāt), *v.t.* [1] **1.** To disunite; divide. **2.** To intervene; lie between. — *v.i.* **1.** To part; become disunited. **2.** To come apart; divide. — (-rät), *a.* **1.** Divided; separated. **2.** Unconnected; distinct. **3.** Particular; single. — *ly, adv.* [8] — *ness, n.* [8].

sep'a-ra'tion (-rā'shŭn), *n.* **1.** A separating; state of being separated. **2.** *Law.* **a** Divorce. **b** A cessation of cohabitation between husband and wife.

sep'a-ra-tist (sĕp'à-rà-tĭst),*n.* One who withdraws, esp. from a church. [aration.

sep'a-ra-tive (-tĭv), *a.* [4] Tending to cause sep-

sep'a-ra'tor (-rā'tẽr), *n.* One that separates, as an apparatus for separating cream from milk.

se'pi-a (sē'pĭ-à), *n.* **1.** Any of various species of cuttlefish. **2.** A brown pigment prepared from the ink of cuttlefishes. Also, the color of this pigment.

se'poy (sē'poi), *n.* A native of India employed as a soldier by a European power.

sep'sis (sĕp'sĭs), *n. Med.* Poisoning due to decaying material in the blood; blood poisoning.

Sep-tem'ber (sĕp-tĕm'bẽr), *n.* The ninth month of the year, containing thirty days.

sep'te-na-ry (sĕp'tē-nà-rĭ), *a.* **1.** Consisting of, or relating to, seven. **2.** Septennial.

sep-ten'ni-al (sĕp-tĕn'ĭ-ăl), *a.* Lasting seven years; also, happening once in every seven years.

sep'tic (sĕp'tĭk), *a.* [4] Of or pertaining to sepsis.

sep'ti-cæ'mi-a (sĕp'tĭ-sē'mĭ-à), *n. Med.* A poisoned condition due to sepsis; blood poisoning.

sep'tu-a-ge-na'ri-an (sĕp'tṳ-à-jĕ-nā'rĭ-ăn), *n.* A person who is from 70 to 79 years of age.

sep'tum (sĕp'tŭm), *n.; L. pl.* -TA (-tà). Any dividing wall, partition, etc., esp. in an organism.

sep'ul-cher (sĕp'ŭl-kẽr), *n.* [6] A grave; tomb; burial vault. — *v.t.* To bury; inter.

se-pul'chral (sē-pŭl'krăl), *a.* [4] **1.** Of or pertaining to burial or the grave. **2.** Unnaturally low and grave; — esp. of the voice. **3.** Gloomy.

sep'ul-ture (sĕp'ŭl-tụr), *n.* Burial; interment.

se'quel (sē'kwĕl), *n.* **1.** That which follows; continuation. **2.** Consequence; effect; result.

se'quence (sē'kwĕns), *n.* **1.** State of being sequent; succession. **2.** An effect; result. **3.** Order of events in time; as, in chronological *sequence*.

se'quent (-kwĕnt), *a.* **1.** Following; succeeding. **2.** Consequent; as, *sequent* punishment.

se-ques'ter (sē-kwěs'tẽr), *v.t.* To cause to retire or withdraw into obscurity; seclude; to separate.

se-ques'tered (-tẽrd), *p.a.* [4] Retired; secluded.

se-ques'trate (-trāt), *v.t.* [1] To sequester.

se'ques-tra'tion (sē'kwĕs-trā'shŭn; sěk'wĕs-), *n.* Act of separating, or state of being separated.

se-quoi'a (sē-kwoi'à), *n.* Either of two trees of California, the "big tree" and the redwood, constituting a genus (*Sequoia*) of the pine family.

se-ragl'io (sē-răl'yō; sē-răl'-), *n.; pl.* It. -RAGLI (-yē); E. -RAGLIOS (-yōz). A harem.

ser'aph (sĕr'ăf), *n.; pl.* E. -APHS (-ăfs), Heb. SER-APHIM (-à-fĭm). One of an order of celestial beings.

se-raph'ic (sē-răf'ĭk), *a.* [4] Of, pert. to, or be fitting, a seraph; angelic. — *i-cal-ly, adv.*

Serb (sûrb), *n. & a.* Serbian.

Ser'bi-an (sûr'bĭ-ăn), *a.* Of or pert. to Serbia.— *n.* One of the people of Serbia; also, their language.

sere (sēr), *a.* [3] Dry; withered. See SEAR.

ser'e-nade' (sĕr'ē-nād'), *n. Music.* **a** A Music as sung or played in the open air at night, esp. for gallantry, under the windows of ladies. **b** A piece of music suitable for such performance. — *v.t. & i.* [1] To entertain with a serenade; perform a serenade. — **ser'e-nad'er** (-nād'ẽr), *n.* [8].

se-rene' (sē-rēn'), *a.* [3] **1.** Bright; clear **2.** Calm; placid. — *ly, adv.* — *ness, n.* [8].

se-ren'i-ty (-rěn'ĭ-tĭ), *n.* Serene quality or state

serf (sûrf), *n.* A slave; now, usually, a person bound to the soil and subject to its owner.

serf'age (sûr'fàj), **serf'dom** (sûrf'dŭm), *n.* State, quality, or fact of being a serf.

serge (sûrj), *n.* A twilled fabric of wool or silk.

ser'gean-cy (sär'jěn-sĭ), *n.; pl.* -CIES (-sĭz). Office or function of a sergeant.

ser'geant (-jěnt), *n.* **1.** = SERGEANT AT ARMS. **2.** *Mil.* A noncommissioned officer next above a corporal. — sergeant at arms, an officer, as of a legislative body, who preserves order, etc.

se'ri-al (sē'rĭ-ăl), *a.* Of, pertaining to, or arranged in, a series, rank, or row; appearing in successive parts or numbers. — *n.* **1.** A serial publication. **2.** A tale, or other writing, published in successive numbers of a periodical. — **se'ri-al-ly**, *adv.* [8].

‖ **se'ri-a'tim** (-ā'tĭm), *adv.* [L.] In a series; serially.

se'ries (sē'rēz; sē'rĭ-ēz), *n. sing. & pl.* A succession of things or events connected by a like relation

se'ri-ous (sē'rĭ-ŭs), *a.* [4] **1.** Grave in disposition; earnest. **2.** Important; weighty. **3.** Attended with danger. — *ly, adv.* — *ness, n.* [8].

ser'mon (sûr'mŭn), *n.* **1.** A public religious discourse grounded on Scripture. **2.** A serious address, a lecture on conduct or duty; — often depreciatory.

ser'mon-ize (-īz), *v.i. & t.* [1] To compose or deliver sermons; preach or preach to.— *iz'er,n.* [8].

se'rous (sē'rŭs), *a. Physiol.* **a** Thin; watery; like serum. **b** Of or pertaining to serum.

ser'pent (sûr'pĕnt), *n.* **1.** A snake, esp. a large one. **2.** A subtle, treacherous person; esp., Satan.

ser'pen-tine (sûr'pĕn-tīn; -tĭn), *a.* [4] Like a serpent; subtle; winding; tortuous; sinuous.

ser'pen-tine, *n.* A mineral or rock, usually dull green, and often marked like a serpent's skin.

ser'rate (sĕr'āt), **ser'rat-ed** (-āt-ĕd), *a.* Notched or toothed on the edge, like a saw.

ser-ra'tion (sě-rā'shŭn), *n.* **1.** Condition of being serrate. **2.** A serrate formation. **3.** One of the teeth in a serrate margin.

ser′ry (sĕr′ĭ), *v. t.* To crowd; compact; — chiefly in **ser′ried** (-ĭd), *p. a.* ; as, *serried* ranks.

se′rum (sē′rŭm), *n. ; pl.* E. -RUMS (-rŭmz) ; L. -RA (-rȧ). The watery residue of an animal fluid after coagulation; esp. : **a** Blood serum. **b** Whey.

serv′ant (sûr′vȧnt), *n.* **1.** One employed by another, esp. for menial offices. **2.** *Law.* An agent subject to control of his principal.

serve (sûrv), *v. t.* [1] **1.** To work for ; be in the employment of, as an inferior, domestic, slave, helper, etc. ; in a religious sense, to obey and worship. **2.** To wait upon, as at table or in a shop. **3.** To bring forward, arrange, or distribute, as food. **4.** To perform the duties belonging to; labor for ; hence, to benefit. **5.** To be sufficient for ; satisfy. **6. a** To answer; be of use to. **b** To avail; be a means to. **7.** To suffice; satisfy. **8.** To treat; act toward. **9.** To work; operate. **10.** *Law.* **a** To deliver, or execute. **b** To make legal service on (a person). **11.** To pass or spend, as time; as, to *serve* a term in prison. **12.** To furnish; supply. **13.** In various games, as tennis, etc., to put (the ball) in play by delivering it by a stroke to one's opponent. — *v. i.* **1.** To be or act as a servant or a slave. **2.** To perform domestic offices; prepare and dish up food, etc. **3.** To do duty as a soldier, etc. **4.** To be of use; answer; suit. **5.** To put the ball in play, as in tennis, etc.

serv′er (sûr′vẽr), *n.* **1.** One who serves ; specif., *Eccl.*, one who assists the officiating priest. **2.** That which serves ; tray for dishes; salver.

Ser′vi-an (-vĭ-ăn), *a. & n.* Var. of SERBIAN.

serv′ice (-vĭs), *n.* **1.** Act or occupation of serving. **2.** Labor done for another ; duty done or required. **3.** An office of devotion; rite. **4.** Official function; military or naval duty; hence, a branch of employment with an organization of its own, esp. under a government. **5.** Advantage conferred; benefit. **6.** A set of articles for a particular use. **7.** *Law.* Act of bringing to notice; execution of any writ or process. **8.** Act or means of supplying some general demand.

serv′ice-a-ble (-ȧ-b'l), *a.* [4] **1. a** Doing service; beneficial ; advantageous. **b** Capable of, or fit for, performance of duty. **2.** Lasting well in use. — **-a-ble-ness,** *n.* [8] — **-a-bly,** *adv.* [8].

ser′vi-ette′ (sûr′vĭ-ĕt′), *n. ; pl.* -ETTES (-ĕts′). A table napkin.

ser′vile (sûr′vĭl), *a.* [4] **1.** Slavish; consisting of slaves. **2.** Held in subjection. **3.** Like a slave; meanly submissive. — **-ly,** *adv.* — **-ness,** *n.* [8].

ser-vil′i-ty (sẽr-vĭl′ĭ-tĭ), *n.* Quality or state of being servile.

ser′vi-tor (sûr′vĭ-tẽr), *n.* A servant ; attendant.

ser′vi-tude (-tūd), *n.* **1.** Condition of a slave; bondage. **2.** Penal service. **3.** Condition of a servant or servitor ; menial service.

ses′a-me (sĕs′ȧ-mē), *n.* An East Indian annual plant or its flattish seeds, which yield an oil.

ses′sile (-ĭl), *a.* Attached directly by the base; not raised on a stalk; as, a *sessile* leaf.

ses′sion (sĕsh′ŭn), *n.* The sitting, or time of sitting, of a court, legislature, etc.

set (sĕt), *v. t. ; pret. & p. p.* SET; *p. pr. & vb. n.*

SET′TING. 1. To cause to sit ; place. **2.** To put (a fowl) on eggs to hatch them, or to put (eggs) into a nest to be hatched. **3.** To cause to be (in a condition, etc.). **4.** To fix firmly. **5.** To make unyielding or obstinate. **6.** To put into a desired position or condition; adjust. **7.** To adapt (words to music, or music to words). **8.** To appoint; fix, as a time, a price. **9.** To adorn, as a ring with jewels. **10.** To establish ; prescribe ; assign. **11.** *Print.* To compose; arrange (type) in words, lines, etc.

set (sĕt), *v. i.* **1.** To pass below the horizon. Hence, to sink; pass away. **2.** To plant. **3.** *Hort.* To be fixed for growth; develop as the result of fertilization; — applied to fruits. **4.** To become fixed or rigid; harden. **5.** To flow; tend. **6.** To begin to move ; start. **7.** To indicate the position of game ; — said of a dog. See SETTER, *n.*, 2. **8.** To apply one's self.

set, *p. a.* [4] **1.** Fixed in position; rigid. **2.** Firm; obstinate. **3.** Regular ; formal. Hence, prescribed. **4.** Formed; made; built; as, a heavy-*set* man.

set, *n.* **1.** Act of setting, as of a heavenly body; hence, close. **2.** *Hort.* **a** A young plant or rooted cutting ready to set out. **b** A small tuber, bulb, corm, etc. **3.** A number of things of the same kind ordinarily used or classed together; as : **a** A group (of persons) ; clique. **b** A series of games, as in lawn tennis. **4.** Direction or course. **5.** Form; build; also, carriage; pose.

set′back′ (sĕt′băk′), *n.* A setting back; reverse.

set′-off′, *n.* **1.** Thing set off against another thing ; offset. **2.** *Law.* Discharge of a debt by setting against it a distinct claim of the debtor.

se′ton (sē′tŭn), *n.* *Med.* A few threads, horsehairs, or the like, introduced beneath the skin to form an issue, or artificial ulcer; also, the issue.

se′tose (sē′tōs ; sē-tōs′), *a.* [4] Bristly.

set-tee′ (sĕ-tē′), *n.* A long seat with a back.

set′ter (sĕt′ẽr), *n.* **1.** One that sets; as, a type*setter*, etc. **2.** One of a breed of hunting dogs having long wavy coats.

set′ting (-ĭng), *n.* **1.** Act of one that sets. **2.** Something inserted. **3.** That in which something is set. **4.** The eggs incubated by a fowl at one time.

set′tle (-'l), *n.* A bench, esp. a high-backed one.

set′tle, *v. t.* [1] **1.** To place in a permanent condition ; establish. **2.** To quiet ; calm. **3.** To determine, as something in doubt. **4.** To adjust, as a dispute ; pacify. **5.** To adjust, as accounts ; liquidate. **6.** Hence, to pay (a bill, etc.). *Colloq.* **7. a** To put in order; arrange. **b** To reduce to order or good behavior. *Colloq.* **8.** To clear (a liquid) of dregs, etc., by causing them to sink. **9.** To cause to sink; lower. **10.** To render close or compact ; make dry and firm, as soil or a road. **11.** To colonize ; people. — *v. i.* **1.** To become fixed or permanent. **2.** To fix one's residence. **3.** To clarify by depositing matter held in suspension, as wine. **4.** To sink ; descend gradually, as soil. **5.** To become calm. **6.** To decide ; determine. **7.** To adjust differences or accounts; come to an agreement.

set′tle-ment (-mĕnt), *n.* **1.** Act of settling; state of being settled. **2.** That which settles, or is set tled, established, or fixed. **3.** A settled place of abode; a colony. **4.** *Law.* A disposition of property for the benefit of some one.

set'tler (-lẽr), *n.* One who settles; a colonist.

set'tling (-lĭng), *n.* **1.** Act of one that settles. **2.** *pl.* Lees; dregs; sediment.

sev'en (sĕv'n), *a.* One more than six. — *n.* **1.** The number greater by a unit than six; seven units or objects. **2.** A symbol for seven units, as 7 or vii. **3.** Something having as an essential feature seven units or members.

sev'en-teen' (sĕv'n-tēn'; -tēn'),*a.* One more than sixteen. — *n.* **1.** The number greater by one than sixteen; seventeen units or objects. **2.** A symbol for seventeen units, as 17 or xvii.

sev'en-teenth' (sĕv'n-tēnth'; sĕv'n-tēnth'), *a.* Next after the sixteenth; constituting one of seventeen equal parts into which a (whole) thing may be divided. — *n.* **1.** A seventeenth part. **2.** A seventeenth unit or object.

sev'enth (sĕv'nth), *a.* Next after the sixth; constituting one of seven equal parts into which a (whole) thing may be divided. — *n.* **1.** A seventh part. **2.** A seventh unit or object. — **sev'-enth-ly,** *adv.* [8].

sev'en-ti-eth (-'n-tĭ-ĕth), *a.* Next after the sixty-ninth; constituting one of seventy equal parts into which a (whole) thing may be divided. — *n.* **1.** A seventieth part. **2.** A seventieth unit or object.

sev'en-ty (-tĭ), *a.* One more than sixty-nine. — *n.*; *pl.* -TIES (-tĭz). **1.** Sum of 7 tens; seventy units or objects. **2.** A symbol for seventy units, as 70 or lxx.

sev'er (-ẽr), *v. t. & i.* **1.** To separate, as one from another; divide; part, esp. by cutting, rending, etc. **2.** To cut or break open or apart; disjoin.

sev'er-al (-ăl), *a.* **1.** Individual; single; separable. **2.** Diverse; various. **3.** Consisting of more than two, but not many. — **sev'er-al-ly,** *adv.* [8].

sev'er-al-ty (-tĭ), *n.* State of being separate.

sev'er-ance (-ăns), *n.* A severing; separation.

se-vere' (sẽ-vēr'), *a.* [3] **1.** Serious in feeling or manner; grave; austere. **2.** Very strict; harsh; rigorous. **3.** Rigidly methodical; not using needless ornament, etc. **4.** Sharp; distressing; extreme. **5.** Difficult to be endured; rigorous. — **-ly,** [8] *adv.* — **-ness,** *n.* [8].

se-ver'i-ty (sẽ-vēr'ĭ-tĭ), *n.* Severe quality or state.

sew (sō), *v. t.; pret.* SEWED (sōd); *p. p.* SEWED, SEWN (sōn); *p. pr. & vb. n.* SEW'ING. To unite or fasten by stitches. — *v.i.* To work with needle and thread.

sew'age (sū'ăj), *n.* Contents of a sewer or drain; refuse liquids or matter carried off by sewers.

sew'er (sō'ẽr), *n.* One that sews, or stitches.

sew'er (sū'ẽr), *n.* An artificial, usually subterranean, conduit to carry off water and waste.

sew'er-age (-ăj), *n.* **1.** Removal of sewage by sewers. **2.** System of sewers. **3.** Sewage.

sewn (sōn), *p. p.* of SEW.

sex (sĕks), *n.* **1.** Character of being male or female, or of pertaining to the distinctive function of the male or female. **2.** One of the two divisions of organisms distinguished as male and female. — **the sex,** the female sex; women, in general.

sex'a-ge-na'ri-an (sĕks'ȧ-jē-nā'rĭ-ăn),*a.* Between

sixty and seventy years old; of or pertaining to such age. — *n.* A sexagenarian person.

sex-en'ni-al (sĕks-ĕn'ĭ-ăl), *a.* Lasting, or happening once in, six years. — *n.* A sexennial event.

sex'less, *a.* Without sex; neuter. — **-ness,** *n.* [8].

sex'tant (sĕks'tănt), *n.* Instrument for measuring angular distances, esp. for observing altitudes at sea to ascertain latitude and longitude.

sex-tet' (-tĕt'), *n.* *Music.* A composition for six voices or instruments; the six performers of such a piece.

sex'to-dec'i-mo (sĕks'tō-dĕs'ĭ-mō), *a.* Having 16 leaves to a sheet. — *n.; pl.* -MOS (-mōz). A book of sheets each folded into 16 leaves; a size of book so made; — usually written 16*mo*, or 16°.

sex'ton (-tŭn), *n.* An officer of a church, who takes care of the church building, rings the bell, etc.

sex'tu-ple (sĕks'tŭ-p'l), *a.* Sixfold.

sex'u-al (sĕk'shŭ-ăl), *a.* Pertaining to sex or the sexes. — **sex'u-al-ly,** *adv.* [8].

sex'u-al'i-ty (-ăl'ĭ-tĭ), *n.* Quality or state of being distinguished by sex.

shab'by (shăb'ĭ), *a.* [3] **1.** Torn or much worn. **2.** Clothed with worn or seedy garments. **3.** Mean; despicable; as, *shabby* treatment. — **shab'bi-ly,** *adv.* [8] — **shab'bi-ness,** *n.* [8].

shack (shăk), *n.* A hut; shanty. *Colloq.*

shack'le (shăk''l), *n.* **1.** A manacle; fetter; — usually in *pl.* **2.** That which prevents free action, as if by fetters. **3.** Any of various fastening devices, as a link for coupling cars. — *v. t.* [1] To bind or fasten with a shackle; chain.

shad (shăd), *n. sing. & pl.* An American food fish of the herring family.

shad'bush' (-bŏosh'), *n.* Any of various American shrublike trees bearing edible berrylike pomes.

shad'dock (-ŭk), *n.* A citrous fruit with a finely flavored pulp; also, the tree that bears this fruit. The grapefruit is a variety of shaddock.

shade (shād), *n.* **1.** Comparative obscurity owing to interception of the rays of light. **2.** Darkness; obscurity. **3.** A retired or secluded place. **4.** That which intercepts, or shelters from, the sun's direct rays; screen. **5.** Disembodied soul; spirit; ghost. **6.** Depth of a color, as darker or lighter. **7.** A minute difference, variation, or degree, as of thought, expression, etc. — *v. t.* [1] **1.** To shelter; screen. **2.** To obscure; dim. **3.** To paint in obscure colors; darken. **4.** To mark with gradations of light or color. — *v. i.* To undergo or exhibit minute difference or variation, as of color, meaning, etc. — **shade'less,** *a.* [8].

shad'i-ness (-ĭ-nĕs), *n.* Shady quality or state.

shad'ow (shăd'ō), *n.* **1.** Shade within defined limits; partial darkness in a space from which rays are cut off by a body, or any image thus made on an intersecting surface. **2.** Darkness; obscurity. **3.** A shaded or darker portion of a picture. **4.** A reflected image, as in water. **5.** An imperfect and faint representation; indistinct image. **6.** A small degree; shade; as, a *shadow* of doubt. — *v. t.* **1.** To cut off light from; shade. **2.** To mark with gradations of light or color; shade. **3.** To represent faintly, mystically, etc. **4.** To darken; cast a gloom over. **5.** To follow and watch closely, esp. secretly. — **shad'ow-er,** *n.* [8].

---

shad′ow-y (shăd′ō-ĭ), *a.* [4] **1.** Full of or causing shade or shadow. **2.** Obscure; dim; vague; as, the *shadowy* past. **3.** Unsubstantial; unreal.

shad′y (shād′ĭ), *a.* [3] **1.** Abounding in shade; also, causing shade. **2.** Questionable; of doubtful morality; corrupt. *Colloq.*

shaft (shȧft), *n.* **1.** Slender stem of an arrow; handle of a spear, etc.; an arrow; a spear. **2.** Hence: **a** A long, slender part, esp. when cylindrical, as the stalk of a plant, midrib of a feather, thill of a vehicle, etc., body of an architectural column (see COLUMN, *Illust.*) and hence, a column. **b** *Machinery.* A bar to support rotating pieces, or to transmit power by rotation. **3.** A well-like excavation. **4.** A passage for air or light.

shag (shăg), *n.* **1.** Coarse hair, wool, etc. **2.** Long, coarse nap of cloth; hence,a cloth having such a nap.

shag′bark (shăg′bärk′), *n.* Any of several species of rough-barked hickory.

shag′gy (-ĭ), *a.* [3] **1.** Rough with or as with long hair or wool. **2.** Thick and rough, tangled, or irregular in surface, as hair. — **-gi-ness,** *n.* [8].

sha-green′ (shȧ-grēn′), *n.* A kind of untanned leather, covered with granulations.

shah (shä), *n.* The title of the ruler in certain Eastern countries, esp. Persia.

shake (shāk), *v. t.* ; *pret.* SHOOK (shŏŏk); *p. p.* SHAK′EN (shāk′n); *p. pr. & vb. n.* SHAK′ING. **1.** To vibrate quickly or violently; make to tremble or shiver. **2.** To move from firmness; cause to waver. **3.** *Music.* To give a tremulous tone to; trill. **4.** To cause to be, become, go, move, etc., by agitating; — generally with *off, out,* etc. — *v. i.* **1.** To tremble; quake. **2.** *Music.* To make a trill. — *n.* **1.** Act, motion, or result of shaking, etc. **2.** *Music.* A rapid alternation of a principal tone with another of one degree above or below; a trill.

shak′er (-ẽr),*n.* **1.** One that shakes, or with which something is shaken. **2.** [*cap.*] One of a religious celibate sect, popularly so named from movements in dancing, which forms a part of their worship.

shak′i-ly (shāk′ĭ-lĭ), *adv.* In a shaky manner.

shak′i-ness, *n.* Shaky quality or state.

shak′o (shăk′ō), *n.* ; *pl.* -OES (-ōz) A kind of stiff military cap or headdress.

shak′y (shāk′ĭ), *a.* [3] **1.** Liable to shake. **2.** Easily shaken; unsound. **3.** Questionable; uncertain; unreliable. *Colloq.*

shale (shāl), *n.* A kind of rock in thin layers, formed by consolidation of clay, mud, or silt.

shall (shăl), *v. auxiliary* followed by the infinitive with the *to* omitted; *pres., sing. 1st & 3d pers.* SHALL, *2d,* SHALT, *pl.* SHALL; *pret.* SHOULD. Infinitive and participles lacking. Am (is, are, etc.) obliged; must. Hence, am (is, are, etc.) to; — forming future-tense phrases. See also SHOULD. *Shall,* when used in the 2d or 3d person, regularly indicates that the speaker predicts or promises some one else's action, and hence is expressive of authority or compulsion on the speaker's part; as in, you *shall* go. In the 1st person *shall* expresses simply futurity; as in, I *shall* be glad to see you.

shal′lop (shăl′ŭp), *n.* A kind of light open boat.

shal-lot′ (shȧ-lŏt′), *n.* A kind of small onion.

shal′low (shăl′ō), *a.* [3] **1.** Not deep; shoal. **2.** Superficial. — *n.* A shoal. — **-ly,** *adv.* — **-ness,**

shalt (shălt), *2d pers. sing. pres.* of SHALL.

shal′y (shāl′ĭ), *a.* [3] Containing or like shale.

sham (shăm), *n.* That which deceives expectation; a fraud; imposture; humbug. — *a.* False; counterfeit; unreal. — *v. t. & i.* ; SHAMMED (shămd) SHAM′MING. To feign; as, to *sham* illness.

sham′ble (-b'l), *v. i.* [1] To walk unsteadily; shuffle along. — *n.* Act of shambling.

sham′bles, *n. pl.,* often construed as *sing.* A slaughterhouse ; fig., a place of carnage.

shame (shām), *n.* **1.** Painful sense of guilt or impropriety. **2.** Reproach incurred; dishonor; contempt. **3.** Cause of shame; a disgrace. — *v. t.* [1] **1.** To put to shame; dishonor; disgrace. **2.** To make ashamed; humiliate; mortify. **3.** To bring or drive (a person) by shame.

shame′faced′ (shām′fāst′), *a.* [4] Easily confused or embarrassed ; diffident ; bashful.

shame′ful (-fŏŏl), *a.* [4] **1.** Bringing shame or disgrace ; disgraceful. **2.** Exciting shame; indecent. — **shame′ful-ly,** *adv.* — **-ful-ness,** *n.* [8].

shame′less, *a.* [4] **1.** Insensible to shame; brazen. **2.** Indecent; impudent. — **-ly,** *adv.* — **-ness,** *n.*

sham′my (shăm′ĭ), *n.* = CHAMOIS.

sham-poo′ (shăm-pŏŏ′), *v. t.* To subject (the scalp) to washing and rubbing; also, to shampoo the scalp of (a person). — *n.* Act or process of shampooing.

sham′rock (shăm′rŏk), *n.* A three-leaved plant used as a national emblem by the Irish, — as white clover, black medic, or wood sorrel.

shang-hai′ (shăng-hī′), *v. t.* To drug, intoxicate, or render insensible, and ship as a sailor; — usually in order to secure advance money or a premium.

Shamrock. *a* Wood Sorrel; *b* White Clover; *c* Black Medic.

shank (shăngk), *n.* **1. a** The lower part of the leg ; the part between the knee and the ankle. **b** In beef cattle, the lower part of either hind leg (cf. SHIN). **2.** The entire leg. **3.** That part of a tool, etc., connecting the acting part with a handle or holder.

shan′t (shȧnt ; shánt). Shall not. *Colloq.*

shan′ty (shăn′tĭ), *n.; pl.* -TIES. A rough hut.

shape (shāp),*n.* **1.** External appearance; figure; form. **2.** That which has form or figure ; a figure. **3.** Form of embodiment, as in words; concrete embodiment. **4.** Condition; state. *Colloq.* **5.** Form; way; manner. **6.** A model; pattern; mold. — *v. t.* [1] **1.** To form; create; give proper form or figure to. **2.** To adapt, as to a purpose; adjust. **3.** To design ; plan.

shape′less, *a.* [4] Destitute of shape or regular form; misshapen. — **-ly,** *adv.* [8] — **-ness,** *n.* [8].

shape′ly (shāp′lĭ),*a.* [3] Well-formed; symmetrical. — **shape′li-ness** (-lĭ-nĕs), *n.* [8].

shard (shärd), *n.* **1.** A fragment, as of an earthern vessel. **2.** A beetle's wing cover.

share (shâr), *n.* The bottom part of a plow, which cuts the ground ; plowshare.

share, *n.* **1.** A certain quantity; portion ; division. **2.** Part allotted or belonging to one of a number owning together any property or interest. **3.** Any of a certain number of equal portions into which any property is divided. — *v. i. & t.* [1] **1.** To divide and distribute in portions ; apportion ; divide. **2.** To partake of, experience, or enjoy, with others. — **shar′er** (shâr′ẽr), *n.* [8].

share′hold′er (-hōl′dẽr), *n.* A holder of a share or shares.

shark (shärk), *n.* **1.** Any of numerous voracious fishes, esp. abundant in warm seas. **2.** A rapacious person; sharper. *Colloq.*

sharp (shärp), *a.* [3] **1.** Having a very thin edge or fine point; keen. **2.** Terminating in a point or edge; not obtuse or rounded. **3.** Well-defined; sharp-cut; distinct, as a shadow. **4.** Affecting the senses, or feelings, as if pointed or cutting, as : of taste, pungent, acid, or sour; of sound, piercing or shrill; of pain, etc., severe ; of language, cutting, biting. **5.** *Music.* **a** High in pitch; acute. **b** Raised a semitone in pitch. **c** Above true pitch. **6.** Of keen perception ; penetrating. **7.** Very attentive; vigilant. **8.** Eager; keen. **9.** Fierce; violent; impetuous. **10.** Shrewd or close in dealing. **11.** Composed of hard, angular grains; gritty. **12.** Steep; abrupt. — *adv.* In a sharp manner. — *n. Music.* A sharp tone or note; also, a character [♯] on a degree of the staff, indicating a pitch a half step higher than that of the degree alone. — *v. t. & i. Music.* To make or become sharp.

sharp′en (shär′p′n), *v. t. & i.* To make or become sharp. [gains; a swindler.

sharp′er (shär′pẽr), *n.* One who cheats in bar-|

sharp′ly, *adv.* In a sharp manner.

sharp′ness, *n.* Quality of being sharp.

sharp′shoot′er (shärp′shoot′ẽr), *n.* One skilled in shooting, esp. with a rifle; a good marksman.

shat′ter (shăt′ẽr), *v. t.* **1.** To break at once into pieces ; rend into splinters. **2.** To disorder; derange; impair. — *v. i.* To break into fragments.

shave (shāv), *v. t. ; pret.* SHAVED (shāvd) ; *p. p.* SHAVED *or* SHAV′EN (shāv′′n); *p. pr. & vb. n.* SHAV′-ING (shāv′ĭng). **1.** To cut or pare, as by the sliding movement of a razor ; cut off (hair) close to the skin with a razor. **2.** To cut off thin slices from. **3.** To skim along or near the surface of. — *v. i.* To remove hair with a razor; be hard and severe in a bargain ; practice extortion ; cheat. — *n.* **1.** A thin slice ; shaving. **2.** Act of shaving, esp. the beard. **3.** A narrow escape. *Colloq.* **4.** Any of various woodworking tools for shaving.

shave′ling (shāv′lĭng), *n.* A man shaved; in contempt, a monk, priest, friar, or the like.

shav′er (shāv′ẽr), *n.* **1.** One who shaves. **2.** A sharper. **3.** A fellow; boy ; youngster. *Colloq.*

shav′ing (-ĭng), *n.* That which is shaved off ; thin slice or strip pared off with a plane, or the like.

shawl (shôl), *n.* A square or oblong outer garment used to cover the neck and shoulders.

she (shē), *pron. ; sing. nom.* SHE ; *poss.* HER (hûr) *or* HERS (hûrz); *obj.* HER. **1.** The female previously referred to. **2.** A woman; a female person or animal ; as, a *she*-bear.

sheaf (shēf), *n. ; pl.* SHEAVES (shēvz). **1.** A bundle of the stalks and ears of grain. **2.** A bundle, as of arrows sufficient to fill a quiver. — *v. t.* To gather and bind into a sheaf ; make into sheaves.

shear (shēr), *v. t. ; pret.* SHEARED (shērd) ; *p. p.* SHEARED *or* SHORN (shŏrn); *p. pr. & vb. n.* SHEAR′-ING. **1.** To cut, clip, or sever something from, esp. wool from sheep. **2.** To cut off; clip. — *n.* A machine for shearing metal. — **shear′er**, *n.* [8].

shears (shērz), *n. pl.* Any of various instruments consisting of two blades so fastened together that the edges slide one by the other, used for cutting cloth, etc.; large scissors. Also, any of various machines for cutting metals.

shear′wa′ter (shēr′wô′tẽr), *n.* Any of numerous long-winged oceanic birds, allied to the petrels.

sheath (shēth), *n.; pl.* SHEATHS (shēthz). **1.** A case for a sword, knife, etc.; scabbard. **2.** A covering structure or part as of a leaf, insect, etc.

sheathe (shēth), *v. t.* [1] To put into, or fit, furnish, or cover with, a sheath or sheathing.

sheath′ing (shēth′ĭng), *n.* **1.** Act of one who sheathes. **2.** That which sheathes; an outside covering, or material for it.

sheave (shēv), *n.* A grooved wheel, as of a pulley.

sheave, *v. t.* [1] To gather and bind into sheaves.

sheaves (shēvz), *n., pl.* of SHEAF & SHEAVE.

shed (shĕd), *n.* A slight structure for shelter or storage, as for a wagon or airplane or for wood.

shed, *v. t.; pret.* SHED; SHED′DING. **1.** To throw off; give or pour forth ; emit. **2.** To cast or throw off, as hair, feathers, or shell; let fall. — *v. i.* To shed a covering, envelope, etc.

sheen (shēn), *n.* Brightness; splendor.

sheen′y (-ĭ), *a.* [3] Beautiful; bright; shining.

sheep (shēp), *n. sing. & pl.* (See PLURAL, *n.*) **1.** Any of various cud-chewing animals related to the goats, esp. the domestic variety, kept for its flesh (mutton), wool, and skin. **2.** Leather of sheepskin.

sheep′fold (shēp′fōld′), *n.* A pen for sheep.

sheep′ish, *a.* [4] Like a sheep; bashful; timorous to excess; silly. — **-ly**, *adv.* [8] — **-ness**, *n.* [8].

sheep′skin′ (-skĭn′), *n.* The skin of a sheep, or leather from it ; formerly, parchment.

sheer (shēr), *a.* [3] **1.** Very thin or transparent; — of fabrics. **2.** Obvious; downright; as, *sheer* folly. **3.** Vertical; perpendicular. — *adv.* Completely; quite; also, steeply up and down.

sheer, *v. i.* To turn aside; swerve; — of a ship.

sheet (shēt), *n.* **1.** A large, broad, thin piece, as of paper, cloth, etc. **2.** A single piece of any of the various sizes of cut paper. **3.** A newspaper, etc.; in *pl.*, the unbound leaves of a book. **4.** A broad expanse or surface, as of water or flame.

sheet, *n. Naut.* [*Often in pl.*] A rope or chain which regulates the angle at which a sail is set.

sheet anchor. **1.** *Naut.* A large anchor, formerly the heaviest carried. **2.** Anything regarded as the best hope, reliance, or refuge.

sheet′ing, *n.* **1.** Act of forming into sheets. **2.** Cloth for bed sheets.

sheik (shēk; shāk), *n.* Lit., elder; chief; — a title of respect among Mohammedans.

shek′el (shĕk′′l), *n.* Ancient Hebrew weight and, later, coin.

shel′drake′ (shĕl′drāk′), *n.* Any of various ducks.

shelf (shĕlf), *n. ; pl.* SHELVES (shĕlvz). A thin, flat, usually long and narrow, piece set horizontally, as on a wall, to set things on ; a ledge.

shell (shĕl), *n.; pl.* SHELLS *or*, in sense 3 **d**, usually

---

collectively, **SHELL**. **1.** A hard outside covering, as of a fruit, animal, egg, etc. **2.** Tortoise shell. **3.** Something suggestive of, or likened to, a shell; as : **a** Any slight hollow structure ; framework. **b** Outside covering, lit. or fig.; husk. **c** A light racing boat. **d** A hollow projectile for cannon, containing an explosive to burst it. **e** A case holding the charge for breech-loading small arms. — *v. t.* **1.** To remove the shell of ; take out of the shell, pod, etc. **2.** To separate the kernels of (Indian corn, wheat, oats, etc.) from the cob, ear, or husk. **3.** To bombard. — *v. i.* **1.** To fall off, as a shell, crust, etc. **2.** To cast the shell ; fall out of the pod or husk.

shel·lac′ (shĕ-lăk′; shĕl′ăk), *n.* A purified form of lac largely used in varnishes. — *v. t.;* -LACKED′ (shĕ-lăkt′; shĕl′ăkt) ; -LACK′ING (shĕ-lăk′ĭng; shĕl′-ăk-ĭng). To coat or treat with shellac.

shell′fish (shĕl′fĭsh′), *n.* Any animal (not a vertebrate) that lives in the water and has a shell for its outer covering, as the oyster, clam, or lobster.

shell′y (shĕl′ĭ), *a.* [3] **1.** Abounding in shells. **2.** Of, pertaining to, or of the nature of, a shell.

shel′ter (-tẽr), *n.* **1.** That which covers or defends; protection; refuge. **2.** State of being covered and protected. — *v. t.* **1.** To be a shelter for; shield; protect. **2.** To take or betake to cover, or safety. — *v. i.* To take shelter. — **shel′ter-er,** *n.*

shelve (shĕlv), *v. i.* [1] To incline ; slope.

shelve, *v. t.* [1] **1.** To furnish with shelves. **2.** To place on a shelf ; hence, to put aside ; dismiss.

shep′herd (shĕp′ẽrd), *n.* A herder of sheep; fig., a pastor. — *v. t.* To tend, guard, lead, or drive as a shepherd. — **shep′herd-ess,** *n. fem.* [8].

sher′bet (shũr′bĕt), *n.* **1.** An Oriental beverage of diluted fruit juice. **2.** A water ice.

sher′iff (shĕr′ĭf), *n.* The chief executive officer of a shire or county, esp. charged with execution of the laws and preservation of the peace.

sher′ry (shĕr′ĭ), *n. ; pl.* -RIES (-ĭz). A still, dry, light-colored wine made especially in Spain.

shib′bo-leth (shĭb′ō-lĕth), *n.* Criterion ; test ; watchword. See *Judges* xii.

shield (shēld), *n.* **1.** A broad piece of defensive armor carried on the arm or by the hand. **2.** One that protects or defends; defense; shelter. **3.** *Her.* The escutcheon or field for bearings in coats of arms. — *v. t. & i.* To cover with or as with a shield; to serve as a shield ; defend.

shift (shĭft), *v. t.* **1.** To move or remove ; transfer. **2.** To exchange ; change. — *v. i.* **1.** To change position, etc.; move ; veer. **2.** To use expedients ; contrive ; manage. **3.** To practice indirection or evasion. — *n.* **1.** Act of shifting; as: **a** Change; substitution. **b** A turn; an expedient; trick. **2.** Something changed or used in alternation ; esp.: **a** A change of clothes. **b** A woman's chemise. **3.** The change of one set of workmen for another; turn of work ; set of workers who work in turn. —

shift′er (shĭft′tẽr), *n.* [8].

shift′less (shĭft′lĕs), *a.* [4] Lacking in expedients ; hence, lazy ; thriftless. — **-ness**, *n.* [8].

shift′y (shĭf′tĭ), *a.* [3] Full of shifts ; fertile in expedients; tricky. — **shift′i-ness** (-tĭ-nĕs),*n.* [8].

shil-la′lah (shĭ-lā′là), *n.* A cudgel. *Irish.*

shil′ling (shĭl′ĭng), *n.* A British silver coin and money of account, equal to twelve pence (24⅓ cents U. S.), or 1-20th of a pound sterling. Abbr., *s.*

shil′ly-shal′ly (-ĭ-shăl′ĭ),*adv.* In an irresolute or hesitating manner. — *v. i.* [2] To hesitate; trifle. — *n.* Irresolution ; trifling. — *a.* Hesitating.

shi′ly (shī′lĭ). Var. of SHYLY.

shim′mer (shĭm′ẽr), *v. i.* To shine with a faint, tremulous light ; glimmer. — *n.* A glimmer.

shin (shĭn), *n.* **1.** The front part of the leg below the knee. **2.** In beef cattle, the lower part of the fore leg. — *v. i. ;* SHINNED (shĭnd) ; SHIN′NING. To climb (esp. a pole, tree, etc.) by alternately embracing with the arms or hands and the legs ; — often with *up.* *Colloq.* — *v. t.* To shin up (a tree, pole, etc.). *Colloq.*

shine (shīn), *v. i. ; pret. & p. p.* SHONE (shōn ; shŏn), *Archaic or R.* SHINED (shīnd) ; *p. pr. & vb. n.* SHIN′-ING (shīn′ĭng). **1.** To emit rays of light; beam with radiated or reflected light ; gleam. **2.** To be conspicuous or distinguished. — *v. t.* **1.** To cause to shine. **2.** [In this sense the pret. *shined* is common.] To make bright; polish. *Colloq.* — *n.* **1.** Quality or state of emitting light; illumination. **2.** Splendor ; luster ; sheen, as of silk. **3.** A polish ; gloss. **4.** Sunshine.

shin′er (shīn′ẽr), *n.* **1.** One that shines. **2.** Any of numerous small silvery fishes.

shin′gle (shĭn′g'l), *n.* **1.** One of the thin oblong pieces of wood used to cover roofs, etc. **2.** A sign or signboard, as of a lawyer's office. *Colloq.* — *v. t.* [1] **1.** To cover with shingles. **2.** To cut (the hair) so that the ends lie like shingles; cut (the hair) short. — **shin′gler** (shĭn′glẽr), *n.* [8].

shin′gle, *n.* Coarse gravel; small roundish stones, as on the seashore.

shin′gles (-g'lz), *n.* An acute, inflammatory skin disease, of nervous origin.

shin′ing (shīn′ĭng), *a.* [4] **1.** Emitting or reflecting light, esp. steadily; radiant. **2.** Splendid ; brilliant. — **-ly,** *adv.* [8].

shin′ny (shĭn′ĭ), *n.* A kind of hockey.

shin′y (shīn′ĭ), *a.* [3] **1.** Bright; clear; unclouded ; as, a *shiny* day. **2.** Polished; glossy.

ship (shĭp), *n.* **1.** Any large seagoing vessel. **2.** *Naut.* A square-rigged vessel with three (rarely four) masts. **3.** In general, any water craft or vessel, esp. one not propelled by oars, paddles, etc. — *v.t.;* SHIPPED (shĭpt); SHIP′PING. **1.** To put or receive on board a ship, or other vessel, for transportation ; send by water. **2.** To commit to any conveyance for transportation. **3.** To send away ; get rid of. *Colloq.* **4.** To engage for service on a ship, as seamen. **5.** To put (oars, the tiller, etc.) in place for use. — *v. i.* **1.** To engage to serve on a vessel, as a seaman. **2.** To embark on a ship.

ship biscuit. Hard biscuit prepared for use on shipboard ; hard-tack ; pilot bread.

ship′board′ (shĭp′bōrd′), *n.* A ship's side; — now chiefly in: on shipboard, on board ship.

ship′ment (-mĕnt), *n.* Act of shipping goods for transportation ; also, the goods.

ship′per (shĭp′ẽr), *n.* One who ships goods.

ship′ping, *n.* **1.** Act or business of one who ships goods. **2.** Vessels generally ; tonnage.

ship′shape′ (shĭp′shāp′),*a.* [4] Arranged as befits a ship ; tidy. — *adv.* In a shipshape manner.

ship'worm' (-wûrm'), *n.* Any of certain burrowing marine mollusks destructive to wooden ships, the piles of wharves, etc.

ship'wreck' (-rĕk'), *n.*
1. The destruction or loss of a vessel, as by sinking or grounding. **2.** A wrecked ship, or its parts; wreckage.—*v. t.* To cause to suffer shipwreck; wreck.

ship'wright' (-rīt'), *n.* A builder or repairer of vessels.

ship'yard' (-yärd'), *n.* A place where ships are built or repaired.

Shipworm; Section of Wood containing its Burrows.

shire (shīr; shēr), *n.* In Great Britain, a county.

shirk (shûrk), *v. t. & i.* To evade meanly, unfaithfully, or by fraud. — *n.* One who shirks.

shirr (shûr), *v. t. Sewing.* To run parallel lines of stitches and draw them up so as to gather the material between.—*n.* A gather made by shirring.

shirt (shûrt), *n.* A loose undergarment for the upper part of the body.

shirt'ing, *n.* Cloth suitable for making shirts.

shiv'er (shĭv'ẽr), *n.* A fragment or splinter;— chiefly in *pl.* — *v. t. & i.* To splinter; shatter.

shiv'er, *v. i.* To tremble; quiver; shake, as from cold or fear. — *n.* A shivering.

shoal (shōl), *n.* A crowd, esp. of fish.

shoal, *a.* [3] Having little depth; shallow. — *n.*
1. A place where a body of water is shallow ; a shallow. **2.** A bank or bar making the water shoal.

shoal'y (-ĭ), *a.* [3] Full of shoals.

shock (shŏk), *n.* A conical pile of sheaves of grain set up in the field. — *v. t. & i.* To collect, or make up, into shocks.

shock, *v. t.* **1.** To give a shock to; cause to shake; hence, to encounter with violence. **2.** To strike with surprise, terror, horror, or disgust. **3.** To subject (the body) to an electrical discharge. — *n.*
1. A blow, impact, concussion, or violent shake or jar. **2.** A sudden agitation of the sensibilities or the cause of it. **3.** *Med.* A sudden depression of vitalities marking a profound impression on the nervous system; as, surgical *shock*. **4.** A stroke of paralysis. *Colloq.* **5.** *Physiol.* Effect caused by discharge of electricity through the animal system.—*-er*, *n.* [8].

shock, *n.* A thick, bushy mass, as of hair.

shod (shŏd), *pret. & p. p.* of SHOE.

shod'dy (shŏd'ĭ), *n.* **1.** A fibrous material got by shredding refuse woolen or cotton goods. **2.** A cloth entirely or largely of shoddy ; an inferior person or thing claiming superiority.— *a.* [3] Wholly or in part of shoddy; hence, *Colloq.*, sham.

shoe (shōō), *n. ; pl.* SHOES (shōōz). **1.** The ordinary outer covering for the human foot. **2.** A thing suggestive of a shoe; as: **a** A metal plate to protect an animal's hoof. **b** The part of a brake which presses on a wheel. **c** The outer casing of a pneumatic automobile tire. — *v. t.; pret. & p. p.* SHOD (shŏd) ; *p. pr. & vb. n.* SHOE'ING. **1.** To furnish with a shoe or shoes. **2.** To protect by adding a plate, rim, ferrule, etc.

shoe'horn' (-hôrn'), *n.* A curved piece, as of horn, to aid in slipping on a shoe.

shoe'mak'er (shōō'māk'ẽr), *n.* A maker of shoes.

sho'er (shōō'ẽr), *n.* One who shoes.

shone (shōn ; shŏn), *pret. & p. p.* of SHINE.

shoo (shōō), *interj.* Begone! away!—used esp. in frightening away fowls.

shook (shŏok), *pret.* of SHAKE.

shook (shŏok), *n.* **1.** A set of staves sufficient for one cask, barrel, etc. **2.** A set of parts of boxes, or piece of furniture, ready to be put together.

shoot (shōōt), *v. t.; pret. & p. p.* SHOT (shŏt) ; *p. pr. & vb. n.* SHOOT'ING. **1.** To send out or forth, esp. rapidly or suddenly; to cast ; throw; emit ; discharge. **2.** To let fly, or project, with force from a bow, gun, or the like. **3.** To discharge (a gun, etc.). **4.** To hit, kill, or wound with a missile. **5.** To pass rapidly along, through, over, or under. **6.** To color in streaks or patches ;— esp. in *p. p.*; as, silk *shot* with silver.—*v. i.*
1. To drive or rush swiftly. **2.** To dart with a piercing sensation ; as, *shooting* pains. **3.** To bud; sprout. **4.** To cause a bow, gun, etc., to discharge a missile. **5.** To discharge a missile, as a bow, gun, etc.—*n.* **1.** **a** A shooting match. **b** A hunt. **2.** A sending out of new growth; also, the new growth.

shoot'er (shōōt'ẽr), *n.* One that shoots.

shooting star. = METEOR.

shop (shŏp), *n.* **1.** A building or apartment where goods are retailed ; store. **2.** A place where mechanics or artisans work. **3.** [*Often in pl.*] Any factory.—*v. i.; pret.* SHOPPED (shŏpt); SHOP'PING. To visit shops in order to buy or inspect goods.— **shop'per**, *n.* [8]. [shop.]

shop'keep'er, *n.* A trader who sells goods in a|

shop'lift'er (-lĭf'tẽr), *n.* One who steals from a shop, esp. under pretense of buying.

shop'worn' (-wôrn'), *a.* [4] Somewhat worn or marred by having been kept in a shop.

shore (shōr), *n.* A prop placed against or beneath. — *v. t.* [1] To support by a shore; prop.

shore, *n.* The land bordering a body, esp. a large body, of water ; the coast.

shorn (shōrn), *p. p.* of SHEAR.

short (shŏrt), *a.* [3] **1.** Not long; of brief length ; not tall. **2.** Not extended in time ; brief. **3.** Curt; abrupt; uncivil. **4.** Not prolonged in utterance, as a vowel or syllable. **5.** Not coming up to a measure, requirement, limit, or the like; deficient. **6.** Less than ;—with *of.* **7.** Insufficiently supplied ;—usually with *of* or *in.* **8.** Not having at the time of sale goods or property that one has sold ;—usually with *of* or *in* ; as, to be *short* of wheat. **9.** Easily broken ; crisp ; crumbly ; as, *short* pastry. — **short ton.** See TON. — *n.* **1.** Something that is short. **2.** *pl.* Securities or other commodities that have been sold short ; also, dealers who have sold short. **3.** *pl.* The part of milled grain next finer than the bran; sometimes, middlings. — *adv.* In a short manner.

short'age (shŏr'tāj), *n.* A deficiency or deficit.

short'cake' (shŏrt'kāk'), *n.* **1.** A crisp, short breakfast or tea cake. **2.** A similar, thicker cake split and spread with sweetened fruit; also, a sweetened layer cake spread with fruit.

short circuit. *Elec.* A circuit through a small resistance, esp. one acting as a shunt to a circuit of larger resistance. — **short'-cir'cuit,** *v. t. & i.*

short'com'ing (shôrt'kŭm'ĭng; shôrt'kŭm'ĭng), *n.* A failing; neglect in performance of duty.

short'en (shôr't'n), *v. t.* **1.** To make short or shorter; abridge. **2.** To make brittle, as pastry, with butter, lard, etc. — *v. i.* To become short or shorter. — **short'en-er,** *n.* [8].

short'en-ing (shôr't'n-ĭng; shôrt'nĭng), *n.* **1.** Act of making or becoming short or shorter. **2.** That which renders pastry short, or crumbly, as lard.

short'hand' (shôrt'hǎnd'), *n.* A rapid method of writing by substituting characters, abbreviations, or symbols, for letters, words, etc.; stenography.

short'-lived' (-lĭvd'), *a.* Having a short life.

short'ly, *adv.* **1.** In a short or brief time or manner. **2.** In few words; briefly. **3.** Abruptly; curtly.

short'ness, *n.* Quality or state of being short.

short'sight'ed (shôrt'sĭt'ĕd), *a.* **1.** Nearsighted. **2.** Lacking foresight. — **-ly,** *adv.* — **-ness,** *n.*

short'stop' (-stŏp'), *n.* In baseball, a player stationed in the field between second and third base.

short'-wind'ed (-wĭn'dĕd), *a.* Having a quick, difficult respiration, or unable to make much violent exertion without having such respiration.

shot (shŏt), *pret. & p. p. of* SHOOT.

shot, *n.; pl.* SHOT *or* SHOTS (shŏts). **1.** A missile, esp. for firearms; esp., a solid projectile for artillery. **2.** A small pellet of lead, for killing game. **3. a** The flight of a missile, or the distance to which it is thrown. **b** Fig., reach; range; as, within ear*shot*. **4.** A marksman. **5.** Act of shooting; discharge of a firearm, etc. **6.** A stroke in certain games, as billiards.

shote (shōt), *n.* A young hog.

shot'gun' (shŏt'gŭn'), *n.* A smooth bore gun, for firing shot at short range.

should (shŏod), *pret.* of SHALL. As auxiliaries *should* and *would* are used: **1.** To express action, etc., as impending in the past; as in, I said that I *should* go. **2.** [In this sense the choice between *should* and *would* resembles that between *shall* and *will*. See SHALL.] To form the conditional mood; as, if I had not fallen I *should* not have been hurt. **3.** To express moral obligation; as, if you are not sorry you *should* be.

shoul'der (shōl'dẽr), *n.* **1.** The projecting part of the human body formed by the bones and muscles where the arm joins the trunk. **2.** A projection, or part suggestive of the human shoulder. **3.** The upper joint of the fore leg and adjacent parts of an animal, dressed for market. — *v. t. & i.* **1.** To push with the shoulder; jostle. **2.** To take upon the shoulder or shoulders; assume the burden of.

shoulder blade. The flat bone of the shoulder, to which the humerus is articulated; the scapula.

shoulder strap. A strap worn on or over the shoulder, esp., *Mil. & Nav.*, a narrow one worn with certain uniforms by officers as a badge of rank.

shout (shout), *v. i.* To utter a sudden and loud cry. — *v. t.* To utter with a shout. — *n.* A loud burst of voice or voices; a vehement outcry.

shove (shŭv), *v. t.* [1] To push; thrust; push along. — *v. i.* To move off, along, or onward by pushing or jostling. — *n.* Act of shoving; push.

shov'el (shŭv''l), *n.* A scooplike implement used to lift and throw earth, coal, grain, etc. — *v. t.* [7] To take up and throw with a shovel.

shov'el-er (-ẽr), *n.* [7] **1.** One that shovels. **2.** A broad-billed river duck.

show (shō), *v. t.; pret.* SHOWED (shōd); *p. p.* SHOWN (shōn) *or* SHOWED; *p. pr. & vb. n.* SHOW'ING. **1.** To exhibit or present to view; display. **2.** To tell; disclose; reveal. **3.** To direct; guide. **4.** To make apparent or clear. **5.** To bestow; confer. — *v. i.* **1.** To present an appearance; look. **2.** To be noticeable. **3.** To make an appearance; become visible. — *n.* **1.** Act of showing; exhibition. **2.** That which is shown; display; exhibition. **3.** Parade; pomp. **4.** Semblance; appearance. **5.** Deceitful appearance; pretense. **6.** Indication; sign.

show case. A glass case to display and protect shopkeepers' wares, articles in museums, etc.

show'er (shō'ẽr), *n.* One that shows or exhibits.

show'er (shou'ẽr), *n.* **1.** A brief fall of rain or of sleet, hail, or, rarely, snow. **2.** That which resembles a shower. — *v. t.* **1.** To wet copiously. **2.** To bestow or scatter in abundance. — *v. i.* To fall in or as in a shower.

show'er-y (-ĭ), *a.* [4] **1.** Raining in, or abounding with, showers. **2.** Of, pert. to, or resembling, a shower or showers. — **show'er-i-ness,** *n.* [8].

show'i-ly (shō'ĭ-lĭ), *adv.* In a showy manner.

show'i-ness, *n.* Quality or state of being showy.

show'ing, *n.* An exhibition of something; also, a presentation of some fact, condition, or the like.

show'man (shō'mǎn), *n.; pl.* -MEN (-mĕn). One who exhibits, or aids in exhibiting, a show.

shown (shōn), *p. p.* of SHOW.

show'y (shō'ĭ), *a.* [3] Making a show; ostentatious; gaudy; gorgeous; sumptuous.

shrank (shrǎngk), *pret.* of SHRINK.

shrap'nel (shrăp'nĕl), *n., sing. & pl.* A shell containing small round projectiles.

shred (shrĕd), *n.* A long, narrow piece cut or torn off; strip; fragment. — *v. t.; pret. & p. p.* SHRED *or* SHRED'DED; *p. pr. & vb. n.* SHRED'DING. To cut or tear into shreds.

shrew (shrōō), *n.* **1.** A scolding or brawling woman; termagant. **2.** Any of numerous small molelike mammals with very small eyes.

shrewd (shrōōd), *a.* [3] **1.** Biting; keen; harsh. **2.** Artful; wily; cunning. **3.** Clever in practical affairs; sagacious; keen. — **-ly,** *adv.* — **-ness,** *n.*

shrew'ish (shrōō'ĭsh), *a.* [4] Like a shrew; scolding. — **-ly,** *adv.* [8] — **-ness,** *n.* [8].

shriek (shrēk), *v. i.* To utter a sharp, shrill sound or cry; scream, as in sudden fright, or anguish. — *v. t.* To utter in or with a shriek or shrieks. — *n.* A sharp, shrill outcry; scream.

shrift (shrĭft), *n.* **1.** Act of shriving. **2.** Confession to a priest, esp. by a dying penitent, and consequent absolution.

shrike (shrīk), *n.* Any of various birds, including the *butcher birds*, which feed chiefly on insects but sometimes kill small birds, mice, etc.

shrill (shrĭl), *a.* [3] Sharp and piercing in tone or sound; acute. — *v. i. & t.* To emit, or sound with, or utter in, a sharp, piercing sound or tone.

shrill'ness, *n.* Quality of being shrill.

āle, senāte, câre, ăm, ăccount, ärm, ȧsk, sofȧ; ēve, ĕvent, ĕnd, recĕnt, makẽr; īce, ĭll; ōld, ȯbey, ôrb, ŏdd, sŏft, cŏnnect; ūse, ŭnite, ûrn, ŭp, circŭs; fōōd, fŏŏt; out, oil;

shril'ly (shrĭl'lĭ), *adv.* In a shrill manner.

shrimp (shrĭmp), *n.* **1.** Any of numerous small, mostly marine, crustaceans. Many are used as food. **2.** A little wrinkled or puny person.

shrine (shrīn), *n.* **1.** A case or box for sacred relics. **2.** Tomb of a saint. **3.** Place consecrated to some deity or saint. — *v. t.* [1] To enshrine.

shrink (shrĭŋk), *v. i.; pret.* SHRANK (shrăŋk) or SHRUNK (shrŭŋk); *p. p.* SHRUNK or (chiefly as *p. a.*) SHRUNK'EN (shrŭŋk'n); *p. pr. & vb. n.* SHRINK'ING. **1.** To contract in compass or extent. **2.** To withdraw or retire, as from danger. — *v. t.* To cause to shrink. — *n.* A shrinking.

shrink'age (-ăj), *n.* Act or amount of shrinking.

shrive (shrīv), *v. t. & i.; pret.* SHRIVED (shrīvd), SHROVE (shrōv), *p. p.* SHRIV'EN (shrĭv'n), SHRIVED; *p. pr. & vb. n.* SHRIV'ING. **1.** To hear the confession of; absolve. **2.** To make one's confession; as, to *shrive* oneself.

shriv'el (shrĭv'l), *v. i. & t.* [7] To draw into wrinkles; shrink.

shroud (shroud), *n.* **1.** The dress for the dead. **2.** That which covers like a shroud. **3.** *Naut.* One of the lateral, supporting ropes leading, usually in pairs, from the masthead. — *v. t.* To cover with a shroud; hide; veil.

shrove (shrōv), *pret.* of SHRIVE.

shrub (shrŭb), *n.* A beverage made from some acid fruit juice, as lemon or raspberry, and sugar, sometimes with spirit.

shrub, *n.* A woody-stemmed perennial plant smaller than a tree and having several stems arising at or near the ground; a bush.

shrub'ber-y (shrŭb'ẽr-ĭ), *n.; pl.* -BERIES (-ĭz). **1.** Shrubs collectively. **2.** A plantation of shrubs.

shrub'by (shrŭb'ĭ), *a.* [3] Full of shrubs; of the nature of, or like, a shrub. — **shrub'bi-ness**, *n.* [8].

shrug (shrŭg), *v. t. & i.;* SHRUGGED (shrŭgd); SHRUG'GING (-ĭng). To draw up or contract (the shoulders), esp. in dislike, doubt, etc. — *n.* Act of shrugging.

shrunk'en (shrŭŋk'n), *a.* [4] Shriveled.

shuck (shŭk), *n.* A shell, husk, or pod; outer covering of a nut. — *v. t.* To deprive of the shucks.

shud'der (shŭd'ẽr), *v. i.* To tremble involuntarily; shiver; quake. — *n.* A shuddering.

shuf'fle (shŭf'l), *v. t.* [1] **1.** To shove one way and another. **2.** To mix or rearrange by pushing or shoving, as the cards in a pack. **3.** To remove or introduce by artificial confusion. **4.** To move or perform with a shuffle. — *v. i.* **1.** To shove. **2.** To shuffle cards. **3.** To change position; shift ground; equivocate. **4.** To proceed awkwardly or with difficulty. **5.** To move in a slovenly, dragging manner. — *n.* **1.** Act of shuffling. **2.** A trick; artifice. **3.** A slovenly, dragging motion or gait. — **shuf'fler**, *n.* [8].

shun (shŭn), *v. t.;* SHUNNED (shŭnd); SHUN'NING. To avoid; keep clear of; escape from; eschew.

shunt (shŭnt), *v. t.* **1.** To turn to one side; shift; esp., *Chiefly Eng.*, to switch (a car or train). **2.** *Elec.* To provide with, or place on, a shunt. — *v. i.* To go or turn aside or off. — *n.* **1.** A shunting. **2. a** *Railroads.* A switch. *Chiefly Eng.* **b** *Elec.* A conductor joining two points in a circuit to form a parallel circuit. — **shunt'er**, *n.* [8].

shut (shŭt), *v. t.; pret. & p.p.* SHUT; *p. pr. & vb. n.*

SHUT'TING. 1. To close to ingress or egress. **2.** To forbid entrance into; bar. **3.** To preclude; exclude. **4.** To fold together; close up parts of.

shut'ter (shŭt'ẽr), *n.* **1.** One that shuts. **2.** A movable cover for a window; blind. **3.** A removable cover, lid, slide, or gate, for closing an aperture.

shut'tle (-'l), *n.* **1.** An instrument used in weaving for shooting the woof thread between the warp threads. **2.** The sliding thread holder in a sewing machine, or a device for a similar purpose.

shut'tle-cock' (-kŏk'), *n.* A cork, stuck with feathers, to be struck by a battledore for sport; also, the sport.

shy (shī), *v. t. & i.* To throw sidewise with a jerk; fling. — *n.; pl.* SHIES (shīz). A side throw; fling.

shy (shī), *a.; * SHI'ER (shī'ẽr) or SHY'ER; SHI'EST or SHY'EST. **1.** Easily frightened; timid. **2.** Bashful; coy. **3.** Wary; suspicious.

Shuttlecock.

shy, *v. i.* [2] To start suddenly aside through fright or suspicion; — said esp. of horses. — *n.; pl.* SHIES (shīz). A sudden start aside.

shy'ly, *adv.* In a shy manner.

shy'ness, *n.* Quality or state of being shy.

shy'ster (shī'stẽr), *n.* A trickish knave; esp., a knavish lawyer. *U. S.*

si (sē). *Music.* The seventh tone of the scale.

Si-be'ri-an (sī-bē'rĭ-ăn), *a.* Of or pertaining to Siberia. — *n.* A native or inhabitant of Siberia.

sib'i-lance (sĭb'ĭ-lăns), *n.* Sibilant quality.

sib'i-lant (sĭb'ĭ-lănt), *a.* Making, uttered with, or representing, a hissing sound; hissing, as, *s, z, sh,* and *zh.* — *n.* A sibilant sound or letter.

sib'yl (sĭb'ĭl), *n.* A prophetess; female seer.

sib'yl-line (sĭb'ĭl-līn; -lĭn), *a.* [4] **1.** Pertaining to sibyls. **2.** Prophetic; mysterious; occult.

‖ **sic** (sĭk), *adv.* [L.] Thus; — sometimes inserted [*sic*] to note that an expression, spelling, etc., is just as given.

sick (sĭk), *a.* [3] **1.** Affected with disease; ill; indisposed. **2.** Having, or attended by, nausea. **3.** Disordered; impaired; perturbed. **4.** Pining; languishing. **5.** Disgusted; surfeited; — with *of.* **6. a** Indicative of sickness; as, a *sick* look. *Colloq.* **b** Designed for, or put to, the use of a sick person; as, a *sick* bed.

sick'en (sĭk'n), *v. t. & i.* To make or become sick.

sick'ish, *a.* [4] **1.** Somewhat sick, or nauseated. **2.** Somewhat sickening. — **-ly**, *adv.* — **-ness**, *n.*

sick'le (-'l), *n.* An agricultural implement consisting of a curved metal blade with a handle.

sick'ly (-lĭ), *a.* [3] **1.** Somewhat sick; ailing. **2.** Characteristic or indicative of sickness. **3.** Marked by or producing disease. **4. a** Sickening. **b** Mawkish; disgusting. **5.** Appearing as if sick; languid; pale. — **-li-ness** (-lĭ-nĕs), *n.* [8].

sick'ness, *n.* **1.** Diseased condition; ill-ness. **2.** A malady; disease; ailment. **3.** Nausea.

Sickle.

side (sīd), *n.* **1.** The margin, edge, or border of a surface; esp., one of the longer as distinguished from the shorter edges (*ends*). **2.** One of the surfaces that limit a solid, esp. one of the longer surfaces; a face. **3. a** A longitudinal half of the body, or that which pertains to such a half; as, a *side* of beef. **b** The right or left part of the trunk of the body. **4.** A body of advocates or partisans; party. **5.** A line of descent through one parent. **— a. 1.** Of or pertaining to a side, or the sides; lateral. **2.** Indirect; oblique; incidental; as, a *side* issue. **— v. i.** [1] To embrace the opinions, or take the part, of one as opposed to another or others; — usually with *with*.

side'board (sīd'bōrd'), *n.* A piece of dining-room furniture for holding articles of table service.

side'ling (-lǐng), *adv.* Sidelong; laterally; obliquely.— *a.* [4] **1.** Directed or moving sidewise; as, a *sideling* blow. **2.** Inclining to one side; sloping.

side'long' (sǐd'lŏng'), *adv.* **1.** Laterally; obliquely. **2.** On the side. — *a.* Lateral; oblique.

si-de're-al (sī-dē'rĕ-ǎl), *a.* Relating to the stars or constellations; astral.

side'sad'dle (sǐd'sǎd'l), *n.* A woman's saddle on which the rider sits with both feet on the same side of the horse.

side'track' (sǐd'trǎk'), *v.t. Railroads.* To transfer to a siding from a main line. — *n.* A siding.

side'walk' (-wôk'), *n.* A walk for foot passengers at the side of a street or road; foot pavement.

side'way' (-wā'), *adv.* Sideways.— *a.* Sidelong.

side'ways' (-wāz'), *adv.* Sidewise.

side'wise' (-wīz'), *adv.* On or toward one side.

sid'ing (sǐd'ǐng), *n. Railroads.* A short track connected with the main track.

si'dle (sī'd'l), *v. i.* [1] To go or move with one side foremost; move sidewise.

siege (sēj), *n.* **1.** A seat. *Archaic.* **2.** The besetting of a fortified place by an army; a besieging; beleaguering; investment. Hence, continued attempt to gain possession.

si-en'na (sǐ-ĕn'ȧ), *n.* An earthy substance, brownish yellow when raw and orange-red or reddish brown when burnt, much used as a pigment.

si-er'ra (-ĕr'ȧ), *n.* A range of mountains rising in peaks which give it an irregular outline.

si-es'ta (sǐ-ĕs'tȧ), *n.* A midday or after-dinner nap.

sieve (sǐv), *n.* A utensil with meshes for separating the coarser particles of a substance from the finer ones.

sift (sǐft), *v. t.* **1.** To separate with or as with a sieve. **2.** To pass through or as through a sieve. **3.** To examine critically or minutely; as, to *sift* the evidence. — **sift'er,** *n.* [8].

A form of Sieve.

sigh (sī), *v. i.* **1.** To make a deep, audible respiration, esp. from fatigue, grief, sorrow, etc. **2.** Hence, to lament; grieve; yearn. **3.** To make a sound like sighing, as wind. — *n.* Act of sighing. — **sigh'er,** *n.* [8].

sight (sīt), *n.* **1.** Power or act of seeing; vision; view. **2.** That which is seen; a spectacle; something worth seeing. **3.** Visibility; open view; range of vision. **4. a** Inspection. **b** Insight; opportunity for investigation. **5.** A device to guide the eye, as in aiming a firearm. **6.** An aim or observation taken by means of a sight or sights.— *v. t.* **1.** To get sight of; see. **2.** To look at through or as through a sight. **3.** To direct by means of a sight or sights; as, to *sight* a rifle.— *v. i.* To take aim by a sight.

sight'less, *a.* Wanting sight; blind.

sight'ly (sīt'lǐ), *a.* [3] Pleasing the sight.— **sight'li-ness** (-lǐ-nĕs), *n.* [8].

sight'-see'ing, *a.* Engaged in seeing sights.— *n.* Act of seeing sights. — **-se'er** (-sē'ẽr), *n.* [8].

sign (sīn), *n.* **1.** That by which anything is represented; mark; token. **2.** An event considered as showing divine will; a miracle; omen; portent. **3.** An action or gesture expressive of a thought, command, or wish. **4.** A lettered board or the like to advertise a business, etc. **5.** *Astron.* One of the 12 divisions of the zodiac. **6.** *Math.* A character indicating the relation of quantities, or an operation performed on them. — *v. t.* **1.** To mark with a sign, esp. the sign of the cross. **2.** To represent by a sign; signify. **3.** To affix a signature to. **4.** To assign or convey formally; — usually with *away*. **5.** To engage by securing the signature of.— *v. i.* **1.** To make a sign or signal. **2.** To write one's name, esp. in token of assent.

sig'nal (sǐg'nǎl), *n.* A sign made to give notice of something, as of a command or danger.— *a.* [4] Noticeable; extraordinary. — *v. t. & i.* [7] **1.** To communicate or to notify by a signal or signals. — **sig'nal-er,** *n.* [7,8] — **-ly,** *adv.* [8].

sig'nal-ize (-īz), *v. t.* [1] **1.** To make signal, or noteworthy. **2.** To point out carefully or distinctly.

sig'na-to-ry (sǐg'nȧ-tō-rǐ), *a.* Joining in a signature. — *n.; pl.* -RIES (-rǐz). A signer.

sig'na-ture (-tŭr), *n.* **1.** A person's name written with his own hand; autograph. **2.** *Music.* **a** The sign (one or more sharps or flats) placed after the clef at the beginning of a staff to designate the key. **b** A sign placed after the key signature to indicate the time.

sign'er (sīn'ẽr), *n.* One who signs.

sig'net (sǐg'nĕt), *n.* **1.** A seal. **2.** Impression made by or as by a seal.

sig-nif'i-cance (sǐg-nǐf'ǐ-kǎns), *n.* **1.** Quality of being significant; meaning, import. **2.** Importance.

sig-nif'i-can-cy (-kǎn-sǐ), *n.* Significance.

sig-nif'i-cant (-kǎnt), *a.* [4] Fitted or designed to signify something; having a meaning; full of meaning; expressive or suggestive.— **-ly,** *adv.* [8].

sig'ni-fi-ca'tion (sǐg'nǐ-fǐ-kā'shǔn), *n.* **1.** A signifying. **2.** Things signified.

sig-nif'i-ca-tive (-nǐf'ǐ-kȧ-tǐv), *a.* [4] Significant.

sig'ni-fy (sǐg'nǐ-fī), *v. t.* [2] **1.** To show by a sign; make known; express. **2.** To mean; import. — *v. i.* To have meaning; matter.

‖ **si'gnor** (sē'nyôr), *n.* [It.] **1.** See SIGNORE. **2.** A lord or gentleman, esp. an Italian of note or rank.

‖ **si-gno're** (sē-nyô'rā), *n.; pl.* -RI (-rē). ‖ **si-gno'ra** (-rä), *n.; pl.* -RE (-rā). ‖ **si'gno-ri'na** (sē'nyô-rē'nä), *n.; pl.* -RINE (-nä). [It.] Italian titles of courtesy corresponding respectively to the English *Mr.* or *sir*, *Mrs.* or *madam*, and *Miss;* also, a gentleman, lady, young lady. Before a man's name *signor* is used. [guidepost].

sign'post' (sīn'pōst'), *n.* Post for a sign or signs; [guidepost].

si'lage (sī'lāj), *n.* Fodder, usually finely cut, preserved by compressing it, as in a silo, while green.

si'lence (sī'lĕns), *n.* **1.** State of keeping or being silent; muteness. **2.** Absence of mention. **3.** Absence of sound or noise; absolute or general stillness. — *interj.* Be silent! — *v. t.* [1] **1.** To compel to silence; stop the noise of. **2.** *Mil.* To cause to cease hostile firing, esp. by return fire. **3.** To put to rest; quiet.

si'lenc-er (-lĕn-sẽr), *n.* One that silences, as the muffler of a gas engine, or a device for a gun.

si'lent (sī'lĕnt), *a.* **1.** Making no utterance; mute; taciturn. **2.** Free from sound or noise; still. **3.** a Unuttered; unexpressed. **b** *Pron.* Not pronounced; as *e* in *fire*. — **silent partner,** one whose partnership is kept from the public. —**-ly,** *adv.* [8] — **-ness.** *n.* [8].

si-le'si-a (sī-lē'shĭ-à; -shà), *n.* **1.** A kind of linen cloth. **2.** A twilled cotton fabric.

si'lex (sī'lĕks), *n.* Silica; quartz; flint.

sil'hou-ette' (sĭl'ōō-ĕt'), *n.* An outline figure of an object filled in, usually with black; a profile of this kind, as in a shadow. — *v. t.* [1] To represent by, or project so as to form, a silhouette; — chiefly in p. p.

sil'i-ca (sĭl'ĭ-kà), *n.* Silicon dioxide, occurring naturally as quartz and opal.

sil'i-cate (-kāt), *n. Chem.* A salt of any of the silicic acids.

si-li'ceous (sĭ-lĭsh'ŭs), *a.* [4] Pertaining to, containing, or like, flint or silica.

si-lic'ic (-lĭs'ĭk), *n. Chem.* Pert. to, derived from, or containing, silica or silicon.

sil'i-con (sĭl'ĭ-kŏn), *n.* A nonmetal abundant (combined) in nature. It is, next to oxygen, the chief elementary constituent of the earth's crust.

silk (sĭlk), *n.* **1.** A fine, strong, lustrous fiber produced by various insect larvæ, usually to form a cocoon; esp., that of silkworms, used for weaving into fabrics; also, thread or fabric made of it. **2.** The silky styles on an ear of Indian corn.

silk'en (sĭl'k'n), *a.* [4] **1.** Of or pert. to silk; silky; soft; smooth. **2.** Dressed in silk; luxurious.

silk'i-ness (sĭl'kĭ-nĕs), *n.* Silky quality or state.

silk'worm' (sĭlk'wûrm'), *n.* The larva of any of certain moths, which spins a strong silk in forming its cocoon.

Silkworm. *a* Larva; *b* Pupa; *c* Adult Female; *d* Adult Male.

silk'y (sĭl'kĭ), *a.* [3] Pertaining to silk; silken.

sill (sĭl), *n.* A horizontal piece forming the lowest member of a frame or supporting a structure.

sil'la-bub (sĭl'à-bŭb), *n.* A dish of wine or cider with milk, forming a soft curd; also, sweetened cream flavored with wine and beaten to a stiff froth.

sil'ly (sĭl'ĭ), *a.* [3] **1.** Weak in intellect; foolish; witless; simple. **2.** Unwise; absurd; stupid. — **sil'li-ly** (-ĭ-lĭ), *adv.* [8]. — **sil'li-ness,** *n.* [8].

si'lo (sī'lō), *n.; pl.* -LOS (-lōz). A pit or vat for green fodder to be converted into silage.

One form of Silo, partly in section.

silt (sĭlt), *n.* Mud or fine earth suspended in water;

a deposit of such mud or earth. — *v. t. & i.* To choke or obstruct with silt.

silt'y (sĭl'tĭ), *a.* [3] Full of or resembling silt.

sil'va, syl'va (sĭl'và), *n.; pl.* E. -VAS (-vàs), L. -VÆ (-vē). The forest trees of a region, collectively, or a description of them.

sil'van, syl'van (-văn), *a.* [4] Of or pertaining to woods or groves.

sil'ver (sĭl'vẽr), *n.* **1.** One of the precious metals, white in color, used for coins, ornaments, silverware, etc. **2.** Silver coin; money. **3.** Silverware. **4.** The color of silver. — *a.* **1.** Made of silver. **2.** Silvery; white. **3.** Giving a clear, ringing sound; silvery. — *v. t.* **1.** To coat with or as with silver. **2.** To make white like silver.

sil'ver-smith' (-smĭth'), *n.* Worker in silver.

sil'ver-ware' (-wâr'), *n.* Silver dishes, vases, etc.

sil'ver-y (-ĭ), *a.* [4] **1.** Resembling silver. **2.** Covered with silver. **3.** Soft and clear in sound.

sim'i-an (sĭm'ĭ-ăn), *a.* [4] Apelike. — *n.* Any monkey or ape, esp. manlike (anthropoid) ape.

sim'i-lar (-làr), *a.* [4] **1.** Nearly corresponding; having a general likeness. **2.** *Geom.* Having the same shape, differing only in size and position; — said of figures. — **sim'i-lar-ly,** *adv.* [8].

sim'i-lar'i-ty (-lăr'ĭ-tĭ), *n.; pl.* -TIES (-tĭz). Quality or state of being similar; likeness.

sim'i-le (sĭm'ĭ-lē), *n.; pl.* -LES (-lēz). A figure of speech which likens two different things in one or more aspects; an imaginative comparison.

si-mil'i-tude (sĭ-mĭl'ĭ-tūd), *n.* **1.** Similarity. **2.** Simile. **3.** That which is similar; facsimile.

sim'mer (sĭm'ẽr), *v. i. & t.* To boil gently; cook in liquid heated almost or just to boiling.

sim'o-ny (sĭm'ō-nĭ), *n.* Traffic in what is sacred; act of buying or selling ecclesiastical preferment.

si-moom' (sĭ-mōōm'), *n.* A hot, dry, violent, dust-laden wind that blows in Arabia, Syria, etc.

sim'per (sĭm'pẽr), *v. i.* To smile in a silly or affected manner. — *n.* A silly smile; smirk.

sim'ple (-p'l), *a.* [3] **1.** Single; uncompounded; uncombined; elementary; esp., *Bot.*, having only one blade, or not compound, as a leaf. **2.** Free from intricacy; easy to understand or solve; plain. **3.** Unadorned; plain; not luxurious. **4.** Of low degree; humble. **5.** Sincere; artless; straightforward. **6. a** Having only moderate understanding; hence, weak in intellect; foolish; silly. **b** Proceeding from ignorance, weakness of mind, etc. **7.** Mere; as, the *simple* truth. — *n.* **1.** Something not mixed or compounded. **2.** A medicinal plant. — **sim'ple-ness,** *n.* [8].

sim'ple-ton (-p'l-tŭn), *n.* A foolish or silly person.

sim-plic'i-ty (sĭm-plĭs'ĭ-tĭ), *n.; pl.* -TIES (-tĭz). **1.** Quality or state of being simple; clearness; plainness. **2.** Artlessness. **3.** Lack of sagacity.

sim'pli-fi-ca'tion (sĭm'plĭ-fĭ-kā'shŭn), *n.* Act or process of simplifying.

sim'pli-fy (sĭm'plĭ-fī), *v. t.* [2] To make simple; show an easier way of doing, making, etc.

sim'ply (sĭm'plĭ), *adv.* **1.** In a simple manner or state; merely. **2.** Plainly. **3.** Foolishly.

sim'u-late (-ū-lāt), *a.* Feigned; pretended. — (-lāt), *v. t.* [1] To counterfeit; feign; imitate.

sim'u-la'tion (-lā'shŭn), *n.* A feigning.

si'mul-ta'ne-ous (sī'mŭl-tā'nē-ŭs; sĭm'ŭl-), *a.* Ex-

---

isting, happening, or done, at the same time. — **si'-mul-ta'ne-ous-ly**, *adv.* [8] —**ness**, *n.* [8].

sin (sĭn), *n.* **1.** Transgression of the law of God; iniquity. **2.** An offense ; misdemeanor. — *v. i. ;* SINNED (sĭnd) ; SIN'NING. To violate the divine law by transgression or neglect ; violate any rule of duty. — *v. t.* To do or commit sinfully ; to commit (a sin).

since (sĭns), *adv.* **1. a** From a definite past time until now. **b** Subsequent to a certain past time and before the present. **2.** In the time past ; before this or now ; ago. — *prep.* From the time of ; subsequently to ; after. — *conj.* **1.** From and after the time when. **2.** Seeing that ; because.

sin-cere' (sĭn-sēr'), *a.* [3] Genuine ; true ; real. — **sin-cere'ly**, *adv.* [8] —**ness**, *n.* [8].

sin-cer'i-ty (-sēr'ĭ-tĭ), *n.* Sincere quality or state.

si'ne-cure (sī'nĕ-kūr), *n.* Any office or position requiring little or no responsibility or service.

||si'ne di'e (sī'nē dī'ē). [L.] Without day ; without appointing a day for reassembling ; finally.

sin'ew (sĭn'ū), *n.* **1.** A tendon. **2.** Strength ; nervous energy.

sin'ew-y (-ŭ-ĭ), *a.* [4] **1.** Pert. to, consisting of, or like, a sinew or sinews. **2.** Nervous ; vigorous.

sin'ful (-fool), *a.* [4] Tainted with sin ; wicked ; unholy. — **sin'ful-ly**, *adv.* [8] —**ful-ness**, *n.* [8].

sing (sĭng), *v. i. ; pret.* SANG (săng) *or* SUNG (sŭng) ; *p. p.* SUNG ; *p. pr. & vb. n.* SING'ING. **1.** To utter vocal sounds with musical changes or variations in pitch or tone. **2.** To produce harmonious or pleasing sounds, as a brook. **3.** To make a small, shrill sound. **4.** To hum ; ring. **5.** To relate or celebrate something in poetry. — *v. t.* **1.** To utter with musical changes or variations. **2.** To chant ; intone. **3.** To celebrate in song or in verse. **4.** To express enthusiastically ; as, to *sing* one's praises. **5.** To dispatch, force, influence, etc., by or as by song ; as, to *sing* a child to sleep.

singe (sĭnj), *v. t. ; pret. & p. p.* SINGED ; *p. pr.* SINGEING. **1.** To burn superficially ; scorch. **2.** To remove the nap of (cloth), or the down of (a fowl, etc.), by burning. — *n.* A burning of the surface ; slight burn. — **sing'er** (sĭn'jĕr), *n.*

sing'er (sĭng'ẽr); *n.* One that sings.

sin'gle (sĭn'g'l), *a.* **1.** One only ; individual ; separate. **2.** Alone ; without company or aid. **3.** Unmarried. **4.** Performed by one, or one on each side. **5.** Simple ; sincere ; artless. **6.** Having only the normal number of petals or rays ; not double ; as, a *single* rose. — *v. t.* [1] To select (one) from among a number ; usually with *out* or *from.* — *n.* A single thing ; unit ; one.

sin'gle-foot', *n.* A horse's gait in which each foot strikes singly, with alternately one and two feet on the ground.

sin'gle-hand'ed, *a.* Unassisted ; managed or done by one person or with one hand.

sin'gle-heart'ed, *a.* [4] Free from duplicity.

sin'gle-mind'ed, *a.* Guileless ; single-hearted.

sin'gle-ness, *n.* Quality or state of being single.

sin'gle-stick' (-stĭk'), *n.* A stick used for hitting and fencing ; the sport of fencing with such sticks.

sin'gle-tree' (-trē'), *n.* A whippletree.

sin'gly (sĭn'glĭ), *adv.* **1.** Individually ; severally. **2.** As or by a single individual or unit.

sing'song' (sĭng'sŏng'), *n.* **1.** Verse marked by monotonous cadence ; doggerel. **2.** A monotonously rhythmical tone. — *a.* [4] Having a monotonous cadence or rhythm.

sin'gu-lar (sĭng'gŭ-lär), *a.* [4] **1.** *Gram.* Denoting one person or thing ; as, the *singular* number. **2.** Separate from others ; alone ; hence : **a** Unique ; unparalleled. **b** Unusual ; strange. **c** Eminent ; exceptional. **d** Odd ; whimsical. — *n.* *Gram.* The singular number or form, or a word in that form. — **sin'gu-lar-ly**, *adv.* [8].

sin'gu-lar'i-ty (-lär'ĭ-tĭ), *n. ; pl.* -TIES (-tĭz). **1.** Quality or state of being singular. **2.** A singular person, thing, act, etc. ; peculiarity.

sin'is-ter (sĭn'ĭs-tẽr), *a.* [4] **1.** On the left ; left. **2.** Unfavorable ; evil. **3.** Wrong ; dishonest ; corrupt. **4.** Indicating lurking evil or harm.

sink (sĭngk), *v. i. ; pret.* SANK (săngk), *or* SUNK (sŭngk) ; *p. p.* SUNK (*Obs.* SUNK'EN ; — now used as *adj.*) ; *p. pr. & vb. n.* SINK'ING. **1.** To fall ; descend lower and lower ; go under or to the bottom (of water, etc.). **2. a** To fail in strength. **b** To decline ; degenerate. **c** To fall in pitch or tone. **3.** To enter so as to impress lastingly ; as, the story *sank* into his mind. — *v. t.* **1.** To cause to sink ; immerse ; lower ; hence, to degrade ; debase ; destroy. **2.** To suppress ; ignore. **3.** To excavate downward, as a well. — *n.* **1.** A drain ; cesspool. **2.** A shallow vessel connected with a drain. **3.** A slight depression of the land, esp. one with no outlet or with one underneath ; — called also *sink hole.*

sink'er, *n.* One that sinks ; weight, as on fishline.

sink'ing (sĭngk'ĭng), *n.* Act of one that sinks. — **sinking fund**, the aggregate of monies set apart to extinguish a debt by accumulation of interest.

sin'less (sĭn'lĕs), *a.* [4] Free from sin.

sin'ner (-ẽr), *n.* One who sins ; transgressor.

Sinn Fein (shĭn fān). A political movement in Ireland aiming at independence and home rule. Also, those Irish people as a body who adhere to the policy of Sinn Fein.

sin'u-ate (sĭn'ū-āt), *a.* [4] *Bot.* Having the margin wavy with strong indentations ; — of leaves.

sin'u-os'i-ty (-ŏs'ĭ-tĭ), *n. ; pl.* -TIES (-tĭz). **1.** Sinuous quality or state. **2.** That which is sinuous.

sin'u-ous (sĭn'ū-ŭs), *a.* [4] **1.** Winding. **2.** *Bot.* Sinuate. — **ly**, *adv.* [8] —**ness**, *n.* [8].

sip (sĭp), *v. t. ; pret.* SIPPED (sĭpt) ; *p. pr. & vb. n.* SIP'PING. To drink little by little. — *v. i.* To take a sip or sips. — *n.* **1.** Act of sipping. **2.** A small draft taken with the lips.

si'phon (sī'fŏn), *n.* A pipe or tube bent to form two legs of unequal length, by which a liquid can be transferred to a lower level over an intermediate elevation by atmospheric pressure. — *v. t.* To convey, or draw off, by a siphon.

sir (sûr), *n.* **1.** A title prefixed [*cap.*] to the Christian name of a knight or a baronet. **2.** A respectful title used in addressing a man without using his name.

a Siphon, through which water flows from the Dish *b.*

sire (sīr), *n.* **1.** A title of respect formerly used in addressing superiors, now only in addressing a sovereign. **2.** A male progenitor ; father ; — often in composition, as in grand*sire*. **3.** The male parent of a beast, esp. of a horse or dog. — *v. t.* [1] To beget ; — used esp. of stallions.

si'ren (sī'rĕn),*n.* **1.** An enticing,dangerous woman. **2.** A kind of compressed-air fog signal.

Sir'i-us (sĭr'ĭ-ŭs), *n.*   The Dog Star.

sir'loin' (sûr'loin'), *n.*   The upper and choicer part of a loin of beef, that is, of a cut extending from the last ribs to the rump.

si-roc'co (sĭ-rŏk'ō), *n. ; pl.* -cos (-ōz). **1.** A hot, dust-laden wind from the African desert which, blowing northward over the Mediterranean, often becomes moist and oppressive when it reaches the shores of southern Europe. **2.** Any warm, moist wind from the south that causes a warm wave.

sir'rah (sĭr'ȧ), *n.*   A term of address (usually to a man or boy) used in anger, contempt, etc.

sir'up, syr'up (sĭr'ŭp), *n.*   Any concentrated, more or less sticky, solution of sugar in water.

sir'up-y, syr'up-y (-ŭp-ĭ), *a.* [4]   Like sirup.

sis'ter (sĭs'tẽr), *n.*   **1.** A female considered in her relation to another having the same parents (**whole sister**), or one parent in common (**half sister**). **2.** A woman closely associated with another or others, as in the same sisterhood, order, etc.

sis'ter-hood (-hŏŏd), *n.*   **1.** State or relation of being a sister ; office or duty of a sister. **2.** Sisters, collectively ; a society or order of women.

sis'ter-in-law', *n. ; pl.* SISTERS-IN-LAW.   Sister of one's husband or wife ; also, wife of one's brother.

sis'ter-ly, *a.*   Like or becoming a sister.

sit (sĭt), *v. i.; pret.* SAT (săt); *p.p.* SAT; *p. pr. & vb. n.* SIT'TING.   **1.** To rest on the haunches or buttocks. **2.** To perch ; rest with the feet drawn up, as birds. **3.** To be situated; lie, rest, or bear. **4.** To fit. **5.** To cover and warm eggs for hatching, as a fowl; incubate. **6.** To occupy a place as a member of an official body. **7.** To hold a session. **8.** To pose, as for one's picture. — *v. t.*   To sit on, as a horse.

site (sīt), *n.*   Place where anything is, or is to be, fixed ; situation ; local position.

sit'ter (sĭt'ẽr), *n.*   One that sits.

sit'ting, *n.*   **1.** Act or posture of one that sits. **2.** A seat in a church, theater, etc. **3.** A session, as of a court. **4.** Incubation ; also, number of eggs incubated by a fowl at one time. — *a.* **1.** Being in the state or position of one that sits. **2.** Pert. to, or used for, sitting; as, a *sitting* room.

sit'u-at-ed (sĭt'ṷ-āt'ĕd), *a.*   Having a site ; located.

sit'u-a'tion (-ā'shŭn), *n.*   **1.** Manner or position in which an object is placed ; locality ; site. **2.** Position as regards conditions and circumstances; state. **3.** Position of employment; office.

sitz bath (sĭtz).   A tub in which one bathes in a sitting posture; also, a bath so taken.

six (sĭks), *a.*   One more than five. — *n.* **1.** The number greater by a unit than five ; six units or objects. **2.** A symbol for six units, as 6 or vi. **3.** Something having as an essential feature six units or members.

six'pence (-pĕns), *n. ; pl.* -PENCES (-sĕz).   The sum of six pence ; an English silver coin of this value.

six'teen' (sĭks'tēn' ; sĭks'tēn'), *a.*   Fifteen and one more. — *n.* **1.** The number greater by a unit than fifteen ; sixteen units or objects. **2.** A symbol for sixteen units, as 16 or xvi.

six-teen'mo (sĭks-tēn'mō), *n. ; pl.* -MOS (-mōz). = SEXTODECIMO.

six'teenth' (sĭks'tēnth'; sĭks'tēnth'), *a.*   **1.** Next in order after the fifteenth. **2.** Constituting one of sixteen equal parts into which any (whole) thing is divided.— *n.*   A sixteenth part, unit, or object.

sixth (sĭksth), *a.*   **1.** Next in order after the fifth. **2.** Constituting one of six equal parts into which any (whole) thing is divided. — *n.*   A sixth part, unit, or object.

six'ti-eth (sĭks'tĭ-ĕth), *a.*   **1.** Next in order after the fifty-ninth. **2.** Constituting one of sixty equal parts into which any (whole) thing is divided. — *n.*   A sixtieth part, unit, or object.

six'ty (sĭks'tĭ), *a.*   One more than fifty-nine ; six times ten. — *n. ; pl.* -TIES (-tĭz). **1.** Product of six times ten ; sixty units or objects. **2.** A symbol for sixty units, as 60 or lx.

siz'a-ble (sīz'ȧ-b'l), *a.* [4]   Of suitable size; usually, of considerable size. — **siz'a-ble-ness**, *n.* [8] — **siz'a-bly** (-blĭ), *adv.* [8].

size (sīz), *n.*   A glutinous material for glazing paper, etc. — *v. t.* [1]   To cover or prepare with size.

size, *n.*   **1.** Extent of surface or volume ; magnitude. **2.** A conventional relative measure of dimension, as for shoes, gloves, etc. — *v. t.*   To adjust or arrange according to size.

siz'ing (sīz'ĭng), *n.*   Size (glutinous material).

siz'zle (sĭz'l), *v. i.* [1]   To hiss ; shrivel up with a hissing sound. — *n.*   A hissing sound, as of something frying.   *Both Colloq.*

skate (skāt), *n.*   *Zoöl.* Any of numerous rays.

skate (skāt), *n.*   **1.** A metallic runner with a frame fitting the sole of a shoe, for gliding on ice. **2.** A roller skate. — *v. i.* [1]   To glide on skates.

skat'er (skāt'ẽr), *n.*   One who skates.

skein (skān), *n.*   A quantity of yarn, thread, silk, etc., put up after it is taken from the reel.

skel'e-ton (skĕl'ē-tŭn), *n.*   **1.** The bones collectively ; bony framework of an animal body. **2.** Framework or outline of anything.

skep'tic (skĕp'tĭk), *n.*   One whose attitude is critical or is marked by doubt. — *a.*   Skeptical.

skep'ti-cal (-tĭ-kăl), *a.* [4]   Of or pertaining to a skeptic or skepticism. — **skep'ti-cal-ly**, *adv.* [8].

skep'ti-cism (-tĭ-sĭz'm), *n.*   **1.** A doubting state of mind; incredulity. **2.** Unbelief in Christianity.

sketch (skĕch), *n.*   **1.** An outline ; rough draft; a slight preliminary draft. **2.** A simply constructed literary composition, as a short story. — *v. t.*   To outline ; make a rough draft of. — *v. i.*   To make a sketch or sketches. — **sketch'er**, *n.* [8].

sketch'book', *n.*   A book of or for sketches.

sketch'y (-ĭ), *a.* [3]   Like a sketch ; rough.

skew (skū),*a.* [3] **1.** Turned or twisted to one side; — chiefly technical. **2.** Not symmetrical. — *n.*   A twist; turn; distortion.

skew'er (skū'ẽr), *n.*   A long pin of wood or metal for keeping meat in form while roasting. — *v. t.*   To fasten with or as with a skewer.

ski (skē), *n.; pl.* SKI (skē) or SKIS (skēz).   One of a pair of long strips of wood bound one on each foot for gliding over snow. — *v. i.*   To use ski.

ski'a-graph (skī'ȧ-gråf), **sci'a-graph** (sī'ȧ-), *n.* A shadowlike image or picture made on a sensitive surface, esp. by Röntgen rays.   Cf. RADIOGRAPH.

---

chair; go; sing, ink; then, thin; nature, verdure; yet; zh = z in azure.   Numbers refer to §§ in the Special Notes which, with Abbreviations, Signs, etc., precede the Vocabulary.

skid (skĭd), *n.* **1.** A clog placed under a wheel to prevent its turning. **2.** A bar, rail, etc., used in pairs to form a way on which something may be slid or rolled, as from a truck. **3.** Act of skidding. — *v. t.; skid´ded; -ding.* To check, drag, etc., with or on skids. — *v. i.* **a** To slide without rotating; — said of a wheel. **b** To slip sideways on the road; — said esp. of an automobile.

skiff (skĭf), *n.* A light rowboat.

skill (skĭl), *n.* Knowledge of, and expertness in, execution or performance; practical ability in art, science, etc.; expertness; aptitude; dexterity.

skilled (skĭld), *a.* [4] Having skill.

skil´let (skĭl´ĕt), *n.* A kind of small metal vessel with a handle, for cooking.

skill´ful (-fŏŏl), *a.* [4] Having or displaying skill; expert. — **skill´ful-ly**, *adv.* — **skill´ful-ness**, *n.*

skim (skĭm), *a.* Skimmed; as, *skim* milk.

skim, *v. t.; skimmed* (skĭmd); *skim´ming.* **1.** To clear (a liquid) from scum or floating substance; also, to take off by skimming. **2.** To pass swiftly or lightly over. **3.** To read or examine superficially and rapidly. **4.** To skip or ricochet. — *v. i.* **1.** To pass lightly or hastily; glide along evenly and smoothly, esp. near the surface. **2.** To skip or ricochet over a surface, as of water.

skim´mer (-ẽr), *n.* **1.** One that skims; esp., a utensil for skimming liquids. **2.** Any of several long-winged marine birds allied to the terns.

skimp (skĭmp), *v. t.* To slight; do carelessly; also, to scrimp. — *v. i.* To be parsimonious. — *a.* Scanty; meager. — **skim´py** (skĭm´pĭ), *a.* [3] *All Dial. or Colloq.*

skin (skĭn), *n.* **1.** The outer surface covering of the body of man and animals. **2.** The surface covering of an animal as separated from the body; as, a sheep*skin.* **3.** A vessel of skin to hold liquids. **4.** Outermost layer; rind, peel, etc. — *v.t.; skinned* (skĭnd); *skin´ning.* To strip the skin from; flay; hence, to peel; strip off.

skin´flint (-flĭnt´), *n.* A penurious person; niggard.

skin´ner (skĭn´ẽr), *n.* One that skins or flays.

skin´ny (skĭn´ĭ), *a.* [3] **1.** Of the nature of skin. **2.** Lean; emaciated. — **skin´ni-ness** (-ĭ-nĕs), *n.*

skip (skĭp), *v. i.; skipped* (skĭpt); *skip´ping.* **1.** To move with leaps and bounds; move with light dancing motion; caper. **2.** To pass from point to point omitting the intervals, as in writing, speaking, etc.; pass without notice or attention; — often with *over.* **3.** To ricochet. — *v.t.* **1.** To leap lightly over; as to *skip* rope. **2.** To pass over or by without notice; omit; as, to *skip* a page. **3.** To cause to ricochet. *Colloq.*

skip (skĭp), *n.* **1.** A light leap or bound. **2.** A passing over or neglecting; omission.

skip´per (skĭp´ẽr), *n.* One that skips, as a cheese maggot or any of various small mothlike insects.

skip´per (skĭp´ẽr), *n.* The master of a fishing or small trading vessel, or, *Colloq.*, of any vessel.

skir´mish (skûr´mĭsh), *v. i.* To engage in a skirmish. — *n.* **1.** A slight fight in war, usually incidental to larger movements. **2.** A slight contest. — **skir´mish-er** (-ẽr), *n.* [8].

skirt (skûrt), *n.* **1.** The lower, hanging part of a coat, dress, etc.; esp., a separate outer garment for women or girls, covering the body from the waist down; also, a petticoat. **2.** On a saddle, the pendent side flaps. **3.** Border; margin. — *v. t.* To run along the edge of. — *v. i.* To be on, or move along, the edge or border. — **skirt´er**, *n.* [8].

skit (skĭt), *n.* A short literary composition, esp. one involving humor or satire; a sketch (sense 2).

skit´tish (skĭt´ĭsh), *a.* [4] **1.** Marked by levity or liveliness. **2.** Easily excited or frightened. **3.** Fickle; tricky; deceptive. **4.** Coy; shy. — **-ly**, *adv.* — **-ness**, *n.* [8].

skit´tles (-'lz), *n. pl.* A game played by throwing disks at pins. [thin layers.

skive (skīv), *v. t.* [1] To cut off, as leather, in [skiv´er** (skĭv´ẽr), *n.* A leather made of the hair side of a split sheepskin. [sneakingly.

skulk (skŭlk), *v. i.* To hide, or get out of the way,

skulk (skŭlk)) *n.* One that skulks; hence, an
skulk´er (-ẽr)) idle, good-for-nothing fellow.

skull (skŭl), *n.* The skeleton of the head of a vertebrate; the cranium and parts united with it.

skull´cap (skŭl´kăp´), *n.* A close-fitting cap; esp., a light brimless cap for indoor wear.

skunk (skŭnk), *n.* A common mammal of temperate North America, allied to the weasels. It ejects a very offensive secretion when attacked.

sky (skī), *n.; pl.* skies (skīz). **1.** The upper atmosphere; the region of clouds, storms, etc.; — often in *pl.* **2.** The heavens; firmament. **3.** Heaven.

sky´lark (skī´lärk´), *n.* The common Old World lark, noted for its song.

Skunk. (1/12)

sky´lark´, *v. i.* To frolic boisterously.

sky´light (-līt´), *n.* A window in a roof, etc.

sky´rock´et (-rŏk´ĕt), *n.* A rocket that ascends, and explodes high in the air.

sky´sail (skī´sāl´; *naut.* skī´s'l), *n. Naut.* The highest sail on full-rigged ships. See SAIL, *Illust.*

sky´scrap´er (-skrāp´ẽr), *n.* A very tall building.

sky´ward (skī´wẽrd), *a. & adv.* Toward the sky.

sky´wards (-wẽrdz), *adv.* Toward the sky.

slab (slăb), *n.* **1.** A thick plate or slice of anything. **2.** The outside piece, sawed from a log.

slack (slăk), *a.* [3] **1.** Slow. **2.** Sluggish. **3.** Remiss; inattentive. **4.** Inactive; dull. **5.** Lax; not tense. — *n.* The part of anything (as a rope) that hangs loose. — *adv.* Slackly. — **slack´ness**, *n.*

slack (slăk), *n.* Small coal; culm.

slack (slăk)) *v. i. & t.* To slow down; to loosen;
slack´en (-'n)) relax; retard; abate; slake.

slack´er (-ẽr), *n.* One who shirks a duty or responsibility, esp. to his country in time of war, as by attempting to evade military duty.

slack´ly, *adv.* In a slack manner.

slag (slăg), *n.* **1.** The dross or scoria of a metal; cinder. **2.** The scoria of a volcano.

slain (slān), *p. p.* of SLAY.

slake (slāk), *v. t. & i.* [1] **1.** To allay; quench; as, to *slake* thirst. **2.** To mix (lime) with water.

slam (slăm), *v.t. & i.;* SLAMMED (slămd); SLAM'MING. **1.** To shut violently, bang. **2.** To put in or on some place, or strike, forcibly and noisily. — *n.* Act of slamming, or the noise so made.

slan'der (slăn'dẽr), *n.* Defamation, oral or written. — *v.t.* To utter slander against. — **er,** *n.* [8].

slan'der-ous (-*ŭs*), *a.* [4] **1.** Given to or uttering slander. **2.** Containing, or of the nature of, slander. — **-ly,** *adv.* [8] — **-ness,** *n.* [8].

slang (slăng), *n.* Language consisting either of new words or phrases or of ordinary words or phrases in arbitrary senses, and having a conventional, but vulgar or inelegant, use. — **slang'i-ly** (-ĭ-lĭ), *adv.* [8] — **slang'i-ness,** *n.* [8].

slang'y (slăng'ĭ), *a.* [3] Of or pert. to slang.

slank (slăngk), *pret. & p. p.* of SLINK.

slant (slȧnt), *v. i. & t* To turn or incline from a right line or a level; to slope. — *n.* A slanting direction or plane. — *a.* Oblique.

slap (slăp), *n.* A blow, esp. one from or as from the open hand; also, a rebuff; insult. — *v. t.;* SLAPPED (slăpt); SLAP'PING. **1.** To subject to a slap. **2.** To put or place with force. *Colloq.*

slap'dash' (-dăsh'), *a.* [4] Carelessly violent or impetuous. — *adv.* In a slapdash manner. *Colloq.*

slash (slăsh), *v. t.* To cut by sweeping, esp. random, strokes; gash. — *v. i.* To strike violently and at random, esp. with or as with an edged instrument. — *n.* **1.** Act of slashing, or a cut so made; gash. **2.** A stroke with a whip. — **er,** *n.* [8].

slat (slăt), *n.* A thin, narrow bar of wood or metal.

slate (slāt), *n.* **1.** A fine-grained rock that splits readily into thin layers. **2.** A color like that of common slate; dark bluish gray. **3.** A prepared piece of slate, esp. for roofing or for a writing tablet. **4.** A list of candidates, officers, etc., devised beforehand. *Polit. Cant.* — *v. t.* **1.** To cover with slate. **2.** To register (as on a slate) for an appointment. *Polit. Cant.* — **slat'er** (slāt'ẽr), *n.*

slat'tern (slăt'ẽrn), *n.* A slovenly woman.

slat'tern ly, *a.* [4] Slovenly; untidy. — *adv.* In a slatternly manner.

slat'y (slāt'ĭ), *a.* [3] Of the nature of, or like, slate.

slaugh'ter (slô'tẽr), *n.* Act of killing; as: **a** Car nage. **b** Act of butchering for market. — *v. t.* **1.** To kill, esp. ruthlessly or in large numbers. **2.** To butcher. — **slaugh'ter-er,** *n.* [8].

slaugh'ter-house' (-hous'), *n.* A building where beasts are butchered for the market.

Slav (släv; slăv), *n.* A person speaking a Slavic language as his native tongue. The Slavs include the Russians, Poles, Serbians, etc.

slave (slāv), *n.* **1.** A person held in bondage; bondsman. **2.** One who has lost control of himself, as to vice, lust, etc. **3.** A drudge. — *v. i.* [1] To labor as a slave; drudge; toil.

slav'er (slāv'ẽr), *n.* A slave ship or trader.

slav'er (slăv'ẽr), *v. i.* To let spittle, etc., run from the mouth. — *v. t.* To smear or soil with saliva. — *n.* Saliva driveling from the mouth.

slav'er-y (slāv'ẽr-ĭ), *n.* **1.** The condition of a slave; bondage. **2.** The institution of holding slaves. **3.** A condition like that of a slave. **4.** Drudgery.

Slav'ic (slăv'ĭk; släv'ĭk), *a.* Of or pertaining to the Slavs or their languages. — *n.* The group of allied languages dominant in eastern Europe.

slav'ish (släv'ĭsh), *a.* [4] Of, pert. to, or befitting, a slave; servile. — **slav'ish-ly,** *adv.* [8].

slaw (slô), *n.* Sliced cabbage served as a salad.

slay (slā), *v. t.; pret.* SLEW (slōō); *p. p.* SLAIN (slān); *p. pr. & vb. n.* SLAY'ING. To put to death by violence; destroy. — **slay'er,** *n.*

slea'zy (slē'zĭ; slā'zĭ), *a.* [3] Wanting firmness, as of texture; flimsy. — **slea'zi-ness** (-zĭ-nĕs), *n.* [8].

sled (slĕd), *n.* **1.** A sledge. **2.** A small vehicle with runners for sliding on snow or ice. — *v. t.;* SLED'DED; SLED'DING. To convey on a sled.

sledge (slĕj), *n.* A strong vehicle with low runners, or one made of plank slightly turned up at one end without runners, for transporting loads, esp. on snow or ice; a sled. — *v. i. & t.* [1] To travel or convey in a sledge or sledges.

sledge, *n.,* or **sledge hammer.** A large hammer, usually wielded with both hands.

sleek (slēk), *a.* [3] Smooth; glossy. — *v. t.* To make smooth. — **-ly,** *adv.* — **-ness,** *n.*

sleep (slēp), *v. i.; pret. & p. p.* SLEPT (slĕpt); *p. pr. & vb. n.* SLEEP'ING. **1.** To be or pass time in the condition of repose called sleep; slumber. **2. a** To lie dormant. **b** To be dead. — *v. t.* To spend, use up, or get rid of, in or by sleep; — with *away, off.* — *n.* **1.** A natural, temporary and periodical, diminution or virtual cessation of consciousness. **2.** Rest or repose; often, fig., death.

sleep'er, *n.* **1.** One who sleeps; a drone, or lazy person; one who is dead. **2.** A railroad sleeping car. *Colloq., U. S.* **3.** A beam, etc., used, on or near the ground, to support a structure, etc.

sleep'i-ly (-ĭ-lĭ), *adv.* In a sleepy manner.

sleep'i-ness, *n.* Quality or state of being sleepy.

sleep'ing, *p. pr. & vb. n.* of SLEEP. — **sleeping car,** a railroad car with berths for sleeping.

sleep'less (slēp'lĕs), *a.* [4] Having no sleep or rest. — **sleep'less-ly,** *adv.* [8] — **-ness,** *n.* [8].

sleep'walk'er (-wôk'ẽr), *n.* A somnambulist.

sleep'walk'ing, *n.* Walking in one's sleep.

sleep'y (slēp'ĭ), *a.* [3] Drowsy; inclined to sleep; dull; lazy; sluggish; inducing sleep.

sleet (slēt), *n.* Fine, driving, icy particles, often with rain. — *v. i.* To shower sleet. [sleet.]

sleet'y (-ĭ), *a.* [3] Consisting of, or marked by,

sleeve (slēv), *n.* **1.** The part of a garment covering an arm only. **2.** *Mach.* A tubular part designed to fit over another part. — **sleeve'less,** *a.*

sleigh (slā), *n.* A vehicle on runners used to transport persons or goods on snow or ice.

sleigh'ing, *n.* **1.** Act of riding in a sleigh. **2.** State of the snow or ice enabling the use of sleighs.

sleight (slīt), *n.* A sly artifice; a scheme; trick; dexterity; skill. — **sleight of hand,** a trick or tricks requiring skillful manipulation; legerdemain.

slen'der (slĕn'dẽr), *a.* [3] **1.** Small or narrow in proportion to the length or height; slim. **2.** Weak; feeble; slight. **3.** Moderate; small. **4.** Spare; frugal. — **-ly,** *adv.* [8] — **-ness,** *n.* [8].

slept (slĕpt), *pret. & p. p.* of SLEEP.

slew (slōō), *pret.* of SLAY.

slice (slīs), *n.* A thin, broad piece, esp. one cut off. — *v. t.* [1] **1.** To cut into slices; cut a slice from. Also *fig.* **2.** To remove as a slice; cut off.

slick (slĭk), *a.* [3] Sleek. *Chiefly Dial. or Colloq.* — *v. t.* To make sleek; sleek.

slick'er (slĭk'ẽr), n. A long, loose waterproof coat, esp. one of oilskin. *U. S.*

slide (slīd), v. i.; pret. SLID (slĭd); p. p. SLID'DEN (slĭd'n), SLID; p. pr. & vb. n. SLID'ING (slīd'ĭng). **1.** To move freely along a surface, as on snow or ice, with little friction; glide. **2.** To move or go easily, quietly, quickly, or secretly. — v. t. **1.** To cause to slide along a surface. **2.** To pass or put quietly or imperceptibly; slip. — n. **1.** Act of sliding. **2.** That on which anything moves by sliding. **3.** Something that operates by sliding. **4.** The descent of a mass of earth, etc., down a declivity. **5.** A plate of glass on which is a picture or an object to be projected by a stereopticon or examined with a microscope. — **slid'er** (slīd'ẽr), n.

sli'er (slī'ẽr), **sli'est.** See SLY.

slight (slīt), a. [3] **1.** Slender; frail. **2.** Unimportant; paltry; feeble. — v. t. To disregard as insignificant; as: **a** To treat (a person) with intentional neglect. **b** To perform (as work) carelessly and inadequately. — n. A slighting; esp., an intentional neglect of courtesy due.

slight'ly, adv. In a slight manner or degree.

slight'ness, n. Quality or state of being slight.

sli'ly (slī'lĭ). Var. of SLYLY.

slim (slĭm), a.; SLIM'MER (-ẽr); -MEST. **1.** Frail; slight; unsubstantial. **2.** Slender. **3.** Small in numbers, etc.; sparse; as, a *slim* attendance. — **-ly**, adv. [8] — **-ness**, n. [8].

slime (slīm), n. **1.** Soft, moist earth or clay; sticky mud. **2.** Any dirty substance that is moist, soft, and sticky.

slim'y (slīm'ĭ), a. [3] Of or pertaining to, or like, slime. — **slim'i-ly**, adv. [8] — **-i-ness**, n. [8].

sling (slĭng), n. A drink composed of spirit (usually gin) sweetened.

sling, v. t.; pret. SLUNG (slŭng), Archaic SLANG (slăng); p. p. SLUNG; p. pr. & vb. n. SLING'ING. **1.** To throw with a sling. **2.** To throw; hurl; cast. **3.** To place in a sling or slings for hoisting, etc.; also, to hoist, etc., by slings; as, to *sling* a cask. **4.** To suspend by or as by a sling. — n. **1.** An instrument for throwing stones, etc., usually consisting of a short strap with two strings fastened to its ends. **2.** Act or motion of hurling with or as with a sling; a throw. **3.** A contrivance to suspend something; as: **a** A bandage put around the neck to support the arm or hand. **b** A loop, as of rope, to suspend something. — **sling'er**, n.

slink (slĭngk), v. i.; pret. SLUNK (slŭngk); p. p. SLUNK; p. pr. & vb. n. SLINK'ING. To steal off or away; sneak.

slip (slĭp), v. i.; SLIPPED (slĭpt); SLIP'PING. **1.** To slide; hence, to move smoothly; glide. **2.** To lose one's footing. **3.** To err; fall into error. **4.** To move or start out of place with a sliding motion. **5.** To go, move, etc., in a quiet or furtive manner; steal; — with *off*, *away*, etc. **6.** To pass away or escape. — v. t. **1.** To cause to slip; slide. **2.** To omit to seize, as an advantage. **3.** To cause to slip or slide off. **4.** To let loose, as in pursuit of game. — n. **1.** Act of slipping; fig., a sudden mishap. **2.** An inadvertent fault; error; blunder; a slight offense. **3.** *Hort.* A cutting or scion. **4.** A strip. **5.** A space for vessels to lie in between wharves or in a dock. *U. S.*

slip'knot' (slĭp'nŏt'), n., or **slip knot.** A knot which slips along the cord around which it is made.

slip'per (slĭp'ẽr), n. **1.** One that slips. **2.** A kind of light shoe, easily slipped on or off.

slip'per-y (-ẽr-ĭ), a. [4] **1.** Allowing anything to slip; having a smooth or slimy surface. **2.** Untrustworthy; tricky. — **slip'per-i-ness**, n.

slippery elm. An American elm whose inner bark is slippery when moist, and pleasant to the taste and smell; also, the bark, often used in medicine.

slip'shod' (slĭp'shŏd'), a. [4] **1.** Wearing shoes or slippers down at the heel. **2.** Slovenly.

slit (slĭt), v. t.; pret. & p. p. SLIT or SLIT'TED; p. pr. & vb. n. SLIT'TING. **1.** To cut lengthwise; cut into long strips. **2.** To make a slit in or on. — n. A long cut; narrow opening. — **slit'ter**, n. [8].

sliv'er (slĭv'ẽr), v. t. To cut into long, thin pieces. — v. i. To split; have slivers split off. — n. A sharp, slender fragment; splinter.

slob'ber (slŏb'ẽr), v. i. To slaver. — v. t. To wet by slobbering. — n. Slaver. — **-er**, n. [8].

slo'gan (slō'găn), n. A rallying or battle cry.

sloop (sloop), n. A vessel having one mast and a fore-and-aft rig consisting of at least a boom-and-gaff mainsail and a jib.

slop, n. **1.** Liquid spilled or thrown about. **2.** Mean, esp. weak, drink or liquid food; — usually in *pl.* **3.** *pl.* Dirty refuse water. — v. t. & i.; SLOPPED (slŏpt); SLOP'PING. **1.** To spill or be spilled, as a liquid. **2.** To soil with liquid spilled.

slope (slōp), n. **1.** A sloping line or direction. **2.** An acclivity or a declivity. **3.** The part of a continent descending toward an ocean. — v. t. & i. [1] To incline, esp. from the horizontal; slant.

slop'py (slŏp'ĭ), a. [3] **1.** Wet so as to spatter easily; wet as if spattered. **2.** Slovenly; careless. *Colloq.* — **-pi·ly**, adv. — **-pi-ness**, n. [8].

slop'shop' (-shŏp'), n. A shop where cheap clothes are sold.   [cheap clothing.|

slop'work' (-wûrk'), n. The manufacture of

s!ot (slŏt), n. Track of a deer; hence, any trail.

slot, n. An aperture, now esp. a narrow one. — v. t.; SLOT'TED; SLOT'TING. To cut a slot in.

sloth (slōth; slŏth), n. **1.** Laziness; indolence. **2.** Any of several slow-moving animals of tropical America that live mostly in trees.

sloth'ful (-fool), a. [4] Addicted to sloth; lazy; indolent. — **-ly**, adv. — **-ness**, n. [8].

slouch (slouch), n. **1.** A hanging of the head; ungainly gait. **2.** An awkward fellow.

slouch, v. i. **1.** To droop, as the head. **2.** To walk, etc., in a careless, ungainly manner.

slouch'y (-ĭ), a. [3] Slouching in gait or attitude.

slough (slŭf), n. **1.** The skin, esp. the cast-off skin, of a serpent, etc. **2.** The dead mass separating from a foul sore, etc. — v. i. **1.** To separate as dead matter from living tissues. **2.** To be shed or cast off, as the skin; of the animal, to shed its skin. — v. t. To cast off; discard.

slough (slou), n. A place of deep mud or mire.

slough'y (slŭf'ĭ), a. [3] Like slough.

slough'y (slou'ĭ), a. [3] Full of sloughs; miry.

slov'en (slŭv'n), n. One habitually negligent, esp. in dress; one lazy and slipshod.

slov'en-ly, a. [3] Having the habits of a sloven; slipshod. — **slov'en-li-ness** (-lĭ-nĕs), n. [8].

---

slov'en-ly, *adv.* In a slovenly manner.

slow (slō),*a.* [3] **1.** Moving at a low speed. **2.** Not happening in a short time; gradual. **3.** Not quick; sluggish. **4.** Not hasty or precipitate. **5.** Behind in time, as a watch. **6.** Stupid; dull. **7.** Such as to hinder rapid movement, etc.— *adv.* Slowly. — *v. t.* To render slow; delay.— *v. i.* To go slower; — often with *up* or *down.* — **-ly,** *adv.* [8] — **-ness,** *n.* [8].

slow match. A slow-burning fuse.

sloyd (sloid), *n.* A system of training in the use of tools and materials.

sludge (slŭj), *n.* Mud; mire; slush; sleet.

slue (slōō), *v. t. & i.* [1] To turn about a fixed point, usually the center or axis; twist.

slug (slŭg), *n.* **1.** A slow-moving, slimy, snail-like animal, usually having no shell. **2.** Any smooth, soft larva of a moth, which creeps like a snail or slug. **3.** A rough piece of metal, esp. one used as a missile; a small bullet for air guns, etc. — *v. t.;* SLUGGED (slŭgd); SLUG'GING (-ĭng). To strike heavily, esp. with the fist. *Slang.*

slug'gard (slŭg'ård), *n.* One habitually lazy and inactive; a drone.— *a.* [4] Sluggish; lazy.

slug'gish (slŭg'ĭsh), *a.* [4] **1.** Idle and lazy, esp. habitually; slothful; dull. **2.** Slow; inert.— **slug'gish-ly,** *adv.* [8] — **-ness,** *n.* [8].

sluice (slōōs), *n.* **1.** An artificial passage for water, with a gate to regulate the flow; a floodgate. **2.** A channel through which anything flows. **3.** A long, inclined trough, or flume, for washing gold-bearing earth. — *v. t.* [1] **1.** To draw off by a sluice. **2.** To let water upon through a sluice.

slum (slŭm), *n.* A foul street of a city, esp. one with a slovenly, often vicious, population; a low neighborhood; — usually in *pl.* — *v. i.;* SLUMMED (slŭmd); SLUM'MING. To visit or frequent slums. *Colloq.*— **slum'mer** (-ẽr), *n.* [8].

slum'ber (-bẽr), *v. i.* **1.** To sleep. **2.** To be in a state of negligence or inactivity.— *n.* Sleep, esp. light sleep; doze. — **-er,** *n.* [8] — **-less,** *a.* [8].

slum'ber-ous (-ŭs), *a.* [4] Also **slum'brous** (-brŭs). **1.** Inducing sleep. **2.** Sleepy; drowsy.

slump (slŭmp), *n.* A falling or declining, esp. suddenly and markedly; a falling off; as, a *slump* in prices. *Colloq.* — *v. i.* **1.** To fall or sink suddenly, as into a bog, etc. **2.** To undergo a slump. *Colloq.*

slung (slŭng), *pret. & p. p.* of SLING.

slung shot. A small mass of metal or stone fixed on a thong or the like, for use as a weapon.

slunk (slŭngk), *pret. & p. p.* of SLINK.

slur (slûr), *v. t.;* SLURRED (slûrd); SLUR'RING (-ĭng). **1.** To soil, as by smearing. **2.** To pass over lightly; slight. **3.** To pronounce indistinctly. **4.** *Music.* **a** To perform (successive tones of different pitch) in a legato manner. **b** To mark with a slur.— *n.* **1.** A mark or stain; hence, a stigma. **2.** A slighting remark; innuendo. **3.** *Music.* **a** A curved line [⌣ or ⌢], connecting notes to be sung to the same syllable or performed without a break. **b** The combination of slurred tones.

slush (slŭsh), *n.* A mixture of snow and water.

slush'y (-ĭ), *a.* [3] Abounding in or like slush.

slut (slŭt), *n.* **1.** A slattern. **2.** A bitch.

slut'tish (slŭt'ĭsh), *a.* [4] Like a slut; untidy.
— **slut'tish-ly,** *adv.* [8] — **-tish-ness,** *n.* [8].

sly (slī), *a.; *SLI'ER (slī'ẽr) or SLY'ER; SLI'EST or SLY'-EST. **1.** Artful; crafty; marked by artful secrecy; subtle. **2.** Lightly artful; roguish.

sly'ly, sli'ly (slī'lĭ), *adv.* In a sly manner.

sly'ness, *n.* Quality or state of being sly.

smack (smăk), *n.* A sailing vessel, esp. a sloop or cutter, used chiefly in coasting and fishing.

smack, *n.* **1.** Taste or flavor, esp. a slight one, savor. **2.** A smattering. **3.** A loud kiss. **4.** A quick, sharp noise, as of the lips when suddenly separated. **5.** A quick, smart blow; a slap.— *v. i.* **1.** To have a smack, or savor, of anything. **2.** To suggest by its quality; as, his talk *smacked* of cant. **3.** To make a noise by separation of the lips. — *v. t.* **1.** To make a smack (of the lips). **2.** To strike so as to make a sharp noise.

smack'ing, *p. a.* Making a sharp, brisk sound, hence, brisk; lively.

small (smôl), *a.* [3] **1.** Relatively little in size. **2.** Little, or not large, in number, duration, value, etc. **3.** Trivial; insignificant. **4.** Of little strength. **5.** Petty; mean. — **-ness,** *n.* [8].

small arms, arms carried on the person; now, generally, only portable firearms.— **s. talk,** light or trifling conversation.

small'pox' (smôl'pŏks'), *n.* A contagious febrile disease, with a peculiar pustular eruption.

smart (smärt), *v. i.* **1.** To feel or cause a pungent local pain. **2.** To feel sharp pain or grief; suffer. — *v. t.* To cause to smart.— *n.* **1.** A quick, pungent pain; a pricking local pain. **2.** Sharp pain of mind. — *a.* [3] **1.** Causing smart; stinging. **2.** Vigorous; sharp. **3.** Brisk; fresh. **4.** Witty; esp., cheaply witty. **5.** Active; capable; shrewd. **6. a** Of persons, articles of dress, etc., fashionable; in the mode. **b** Elegantly or showily dressed.

smart'ly (smärt'lĭ), *adv.* In a smart manner.

smart'ness (smärt'nĕs), *n.* Smart quality or state.

smash (smăsh), *v. t.* **1.** To dash to pieces; crush. **2.** To destroy utterly; shatter.— *v. i.* **1.** To go to pieces suddenly, as from collision. **2.** To move or be propelled violently against something.— *n.* **1.** A smashing; *Colloq.,* a severe collision. **2.** Ruin; wreck. *Colloq.* — **-er,** *n.* [8].

smat'ter (smăt'ẽr), *n.* Superficial knowledge.

smat'ter-er (-ẽr),*n.* One who has only a smattering.

smat'ter-ing, *n.* A slight, shallow knowledge.

smear (smēr), *n.* A blot or blotch; daub.— *v. t.* To overspread with anything greasy or sticky; daub.

smell (smĕl), *v. t.* **1.** To perceive or become aware of through the nose; get the scent of. **2.** To detect, perceive, or investigate, as if by the sense of smell; — often with *out.* — *v. i.* **1.** To have an odor or scent; — often with *of;* as, to *smell* of smoke. **2.** To savor or smack. **3.** To exercise the sense of smell; — *Colloq.,* with *of.* — *n.* **1.** The sense by which certain qualities of substances are perceived through the nose. **2.** A sensation of odor, scent, perfume, etc.; odor; scent; as, the *smell* of flowers. **3.** An act or instance of smelling. — **smell'er,** *n.* [8].

smell'y (smĕl'ĭ), *a.* [3] Unpleasantly odorous.

smelt (smĕlt), *n.* Any of certain small fishes closely resembling the trout in general structure.

smelt, *v. t.* To melt or fuse, as ore, in order to separate and refine the metal; reduce; refine.

smelt′er (smĕl′tẽr), *n.* A smelting furnace or establishment, or a man who owns or runs one.

smi′lax (smī′lăks), *n.* **1.** *Bot.* Any of various plants (genus *Smilax*), usually woody vines, often with sharp prickles. **2.** A species of asparagus grown in greenhouses for decorative purposes.

smile (smīl), *v. i.* [1] **1.** To have, produce, or exhibit a smile. **2.** To look joyous. **3.** To be propitious; favor. — *n.* **1.** A facial expression marked esp. by an upward curving of the corners of the mouth. **2.** Favor; propitiousness. **3.** Gay or joyous appearance. — **smil′er** (smīl′ẽr), *n.*

smirch (smûrch), *v. t.* To smear; to make dirty; soil; sully. — *n.* A smutch; smear; stain.

smirk (smûrk), *v. i.* To smile in an affected or conceited way; simper.—*n.* An affected smile; simper.

smite (smīt), *v. t.; pret.* SMOTE (smōt); *p. p.* SMIT′-TEN (smĭt′'n), SMIT; *p. pr. & vb. n.* SMIT′ING (smīt′ĭng). **1.** To strike, esp. heavily. **2.** To blast; hence, to afflict; chasten. **3.** To strike or affect with passion or emotion. **4.** To bring distress or grief to; trouble. **5.** To affect with the force and abruptness of a blow.— *v. i.* **1.** To strike, esp. heavily. *Archaic.* **2.** To act like a sudden blow.

smith (smĭth), *n.* One who forges with the hammer; a worker in metals.

smith′y (-ĭ), *n.; pl.* SMITHIES (-ĭz). The workshop of a smith, esp. a blacksmith.

smit′ten (smĭt′'n), *p. p. & p. a.* of SMITE.

smock (smŏk), *n.* **1.** A chemise; shift. **2.** A smock frock.— *v. t.* To clothe in a smock.

smock frock. A coarse, long, loose shirt, worn over the other dress by farm laborers in Europe.

smoke (smōk), *n.* **1.** The gaseous products of burning materials, made visible by carrying small particles of carbon, which settle as *soot.* **2.** Any visible fumes. **3.** Something unsubstantial or ephemeral, as idle talk. **4.** Act or fact of smoking, esp. tobacco. — *v. i.* [1] **1.** To emit or exhale smoke. **2.** To smoke a pipe, cigar, etc. — *v. t.* **1.** To apply smoke to; disinfect, cure, etc., by smoke. **2.** To fill or scent with smoke. **3.** To subject to the action of smoke, as for driving out, stupefying, etc. **4.** To inhale and puff out the smoke of, as tobacco.

smoke′less, *a.* Making or having no smoke.

smok′er (smōk′ẽr), *n.* **1.** One that smokes. **2.** A smoking car or compartment. *Colloq.* **3.** A gathering for smoking and social intercourse. *Colloq.*

smoke′stack′ (smōk′stăk′), *n.* A chimney; esp., a pipe serving as a chimney, as of a locomotive.

smok′y (smōk′ĭ), *a.* [3] **1.** Emitting smoke, esp. in large quantities or offensively. **2.** Like, or of the color of, smoke. **3.** Filled with smoke; thick; hazy. **4.** Tarnished with smoke.

smol′der (smōl′dẽr), *v. i.* **1.** To burn and smoke without flame. **2.** To exist in suppressed activity.

smooth (smōōth), *a.* [3] **1.** Not rough; even. **2.** Evenly spread or arranged; sleek. **3.** Without lumps or with perfect blending of the elements. **4.** Without hair. **5.** Gently flowing; unruffled; calm. **6.** Fluent; even. **7.** Bland; mild; soothing; suave. **8.** Without jarring, or jolting. — *adv.* Smoothly.— *v. t.* **1.** To make smooth or even. **2.** To make easy. **3.** To free from harshness; make flowing. **4.** To palliate; gloze. **5.** To quiet; soften, esp. with blandishments.

smooth′bore′, *or* **smooth′-bore′,** *a.* *Firearms.* Having a smooth bore ; — disting. from *rifled.*

smooth′faced′ (-fāst′), *a.* **1.** Beardless; clean-shaven. **2.** Smooth, or bland, in expression.

smooth′ly, *adv.* In a smooth manner.

smooth′ness, *n.* Smooth quality or state.

smote (smōt), *pret. (& rare p. p.)* of SMITE.

smoth′er (smŭth′ẽr), *n.* **1.** That which smothers or stifles, as smoke, fog, etc. **2.** A state of smoldering or of suppression.— *v. t.* **1.** To suffocate or stifle. **2.** To stifle; deprive of air by a thick covering, as of ashes. **3.** To suppress; conceal.— *v. i.* **1.** To be suffocated or stifled. **2.** To be suppressed or deprived of vent, as wrath.

smudge (smŭj), *n.* **1.** A thick or suffocating smoke. **2.** A smutch; smear. — *v. t.* [1] **1.** To smoke with a smudge. **2.** To smutch; smear.

smudg′y (smŭj′ĭ), *a.* [3] Discolored with or as with smudge. — **smudg′i-ness** (-ĭ-nĕs), *n.* [8].

smug (smŭg), *a.* [3] Primly or affectedly neat, nice, or proper, as in dress ; of or pert. to a self-satisfied, and affectedly or primly proper, character.

smug′gle (smŭg′'l), *v. t. & i.* [1] **1.** To import or export secretly and contrary to law or without paying duties imposed by law. **2.** To convey or introduce secretly. — **smug′gler** (-lẽr), *n.* [8].

smug′ly, *adv.* In a smug manner.

smug′ness, *n.* Quality or state of being smug.

smut (smŭt), *n.* **1.** Soot; also, a smutch. **2.** A fungous disease of plants ; any fungus producing it. **3.** Obscene language.— *v. t.; smut′ted; smut′-ting.* To stain or taint with smut. — *v. i.* **1.** To be affected by smut. **2.** To give off smut.

smutch (smŭch), *n.* A dark or dirty spot; smudge. — *v. t.* To blacken, as with smoke, soot, etc.

smutch′y, *a.* [3] Stained; smudged.

smut′ty (smŭt′ĭ), *a.* [3] **1.** Soiled or tainted with smut. **2.** Obscene; indecent. — **smut′ti-ness,** *n.*

snack (snăk), *n.* **1.** Share; part. *Obs.*, except in to go snacks, i. e., to share. *Colloq.* **2.** A slight, hasty repast. *Colloq.*

snaf′fle (snăf′'l), *n.* A kind of jointed bridle bit without curb. Called also *snaffle bit.*

snag (snăg), *n.* **1.** A stump of a branch lopped off; a rough branch broken off. **2.** A tooth projecting beyond the rest; a broken or decayed tooth. **3.** A tree or branch fixed in the bottom of navigable water and dangerous to boats.

snag′gy (snăg′ĭ), *a.* [3] Full of snags.

snail (snāl), *n.* Any of numerous small, slow-moving animals having a shell, esp. the common kind which lives on land and has a spiral shell.

snake (snāk), *n.* Any of numerous limbless, very slender reptiles; serpent.

snak′y (snāk′ĭ), *a.* [3] **1.** Pert. to, or like a snake. **2.** Sly; deceitful. **3.** Abounding in snakes.

snap (snăp), *v. t. ;* SNAPPED (snăpt) ; SNAP′PING. **1.** To snatch, or seize suddenly, esp. with the teeth; hence, to bite. **2.** To break short, as brittle substances. **3.** To crack, as a whip. **4.** To shut or close down with a sharp sound. **5.** To take an instantaneous photograph of.— *v. i.* **1.** To grasp sharply or snatch (at anything), as with the teeth; — usually with *at.* **2.** To break short or suddenly. **3.** To give forth a sharp, cracking noise; crack, as blazing wood. **4.** Of a firearm, to make a sharp sound by the falling of the hammer; hence, to miss fire. **5.** Of the eyes, to flash, as in anger. — *n.* **1.** Act of snatching, or seizing suddenly, as with the teeth. **2.** A sudden breaking of something brittle or tense; also, the sharp sound of such breaking. **3.** A sudden, sharp blow. **4.** A sharp, abrupt sound, as the crack of a whip. **5.** A small catch held by a spring. **6.** Briskness; vigor; energy. *Colloq.* **7.** A sudden severe spell of (cold) weather. **8.** A thin, crisp cake, usually small and flavored with ginger. — *a.* Done or made quickly and without deliberation; as, a *snap* decision. *Colloq.*

snap′drag′on (snăp′drăg″ǎn), *n.* Any of several garden plants having showy flowers.

snap′per (snăp′ẽr), *n.* **1.** One that snaps. **2.** Any of numerous active flesh-eating fishes, of warm seas.

snap′pish (-ĭsh), *a.* [4] **1.** Apt to snap at persons or things. **2.** Apt to speak sharply or testily; also, tart; peevish. — **-ly,** *adv.* [8] — **-ness,** *n.* [8].

snap′py (-ĭ), *a.* [3] **1.** Snappish. *Colloq.* **2.** Full of snap, or life and briskness. *Colloq., U.S.*

snap′shot′ (-shŏt′), *n.* **1.** Commonly **snap shot.** **a** A quick offhand shot. **b** Act of taking a snapshot (sense 2). **2.** An instantaneous photograph made without posing.

snare (snâr), *n.* **1.** A contrivance for catching birds, etc.; a trap; gin. **2.** Anything by which one is entangled and got into trouble. — *v. t.* To catch with a snare. — **snar′er,** *n.* [8].

snarl (snärl), *v. t. & i.* To involve in knots; entangle, or become entangled; complicate. — *n.* A tangled knot of hair, thread, or the like.

snarl, *v. i.* To growl; grumble. — *v. t.* To utter or express with a snarl or by snarling. — *n.* A growl; a surly or peevish expression. — **snarl′er,** *n.* [8].

snarl′y (snär′lĭ), *a.* [3] Snarling; ill-natured.

snatch (snăch), *v. t.* To seize abruptly, or without ceremony. — *v. i.* To try to seize something suddenly; — often with *at.* — *n.* **1.** A hasty catching or seizing; a grab. **2.** A short period. **3.** A small piece or fragment; scrap. — **snatch′er,** *n.* [8].

snatch′y (snăch′ĭ), *a.* [3] Interrupted; spasmodic.

sneak (snēk), *v. i.* **1.** To creep or steal (away or about) furtively. **2.** To act furtively and cowardly. — *n.* **1.** A sneaking fellow. **2.** Act of sneaking. — **sneak′er,** *n.* [8].

sneak′ing, *a.* [4] **1.** Cowardly; furtive. **2.** Of feelings, etc., concealed; shamefaced.

sneak′y (snēk′ĭ), *a.* [3] Like a sneak.

sneer (snēr), *v. i.* **1.** To show contempt by curling the lip, etc. **2.** To speak contemptuously or derisively. — *v. t.* **1.** To utter with a sneer. **2.** To affect or effect by sneering. — *n.* **1.** Act of sneering. **2.** A change of countenance showing contempt. **3.** Verbal insinuation of contempt. — **-er,** *n.* [8] — **-ing-ly,** *adv.* [8].

sneeze (snēz), *v. i.* [1] To make a sudden, violent, spasmodic, and audible expiration of breath, through the nose. — *n.* Act or fact of sneezing.

snell (snĕl), *n.* A short line, as of gut, etc., by which a fishhook is attached to a longer line.

snick′er (snĭk′ẽr), *v. i.* To laugh in a partly suppressed manner; giggle. — *n.* A half-suppressed, broken laugh; giggle.

sniff (snĭf), *v. i.* To draw air audibly up the nose; snuff, as in contempt. — *v. t.* **1.** To draw in

through the nose. **2.** To scent; smell. — *n.* Act or sound of sniffing; that which is sniffed.

snip (snĭp), *v. t.;* SNIPPED (snĭpt); -PING. To cut off at one stroke, as with shears; nip. — *n.* **1.** A single cut, as with shears; a clip. **2.** A bit cut off.

snipe (snĭp), *n. sing. & pl.* (See PLURAL, *n.*) Any of certain shore birds related to the woodcocks. — *v. i. & t.* **1.** To shoot or hunt snipe. **2.** To shoot at (usually detached men of an enemy's forces) at long range.

snip′py (snĭp′ĭ), *a.* [3] Fragmentary; cut short.

sniv′el (snĭv′'l), *v. i.* [7] **1.** To run at the nose. **2.** To snuffle. **3.** To cry or whine with snuffling; hence, to lament whiningly.

snob (snŏb), *n.* One who regulates his attitude toward people according to their wealth, station, etc.

snob′ber-y (-ẽr-ĭ), *n.* Snobbish conduct.

snob′bish (-ĭsh), *a.* [4] Of or pert. to a snob.

snore (snōr), *v. i.* [1] To breathe during sleep with a rough noise. — *n.* Act or noise of snoring.

snort (snôrt), *v. i.* To force air audibly through the nose, as high-spirited horses. — *v. t.* To utter with, or express by, a snort. — *n.* A snorting.

snout (snout), *n.* The long, projecting nose of a beast, as of a swine; muzzle; nozzle.

snout beetle. Any of various beetles in which the head is usually produced into a beak.

snow (snō), *n.* Watery particles congealed into white or transparent crystals or flakes in the air and falling or fallen to the earth. — *v. i.* To fall in or as snow; — used impersonally; as, it *snows.* — *v. t.* **1.** To shower down like snow. **2.** To cover, or shut in, with snow; — with *in, up, under,* or *over.*

snow′ball′ (-bôl′), *n.* A round mass of snow pressed or rolled together. — *v. t.* To pelt with snowballs. — *v. i.* To throw snowballs.

snow′bird′ (-bûrd′), *n.* Any of numerous small American finches.

snow′-blind (-blīnd′), *a.* [4] Having defective vision caused by the glare of snow. — **-ness,** *n.* [8].

snow′-bound (-), *a.* Shut in or blockaded by snow.

snow′drift′ (snō′drĭft′), *n.* Bank of drifted snow.

snow′drop′ (-drŏp′), *n.* An early-flowering bulbous plant, with nodding white flowers; also, its flower.

snow′fall′ (-fôl′), *n.* A fall of snow; amount of snow that falls in a single storm or given period.

snow′flake′ (-flāk′), *n.* A flake of snow.

snow′plow′, snow′plough′ (snō′plou′), *n.* A contrivance to clear away snow from roads, etc.

snow′shoe′ (-shōō′), *n.* A slight frame of wood, strung with rawhide, worn under the shoe to prevent sinking in soft snow.

Snowshoe.

snow′y (-ĭ), *a.* [3] **1.** Abounding or covered with snow. **2.** White like snow; as, *snowy* hair.

snub (snŭb), *v. t.;* SNUBBED (snŭbd); SNUB′BING. **1.** To check or rebuke with a tart, sarcastic remark. **2.** To neglect or slight (a person) designedly. — *n.* A check or rebuke; an intended slight. — *a.* [3] Short and turned up; — said of the nose.

snuff (snŭf), *n.* The charred part of a candle wick. — *v. t.* To crop the snuff of, as a candle.

snuff, *v. t.* **1.** To draw in, or inhale, forcibly

through the nose; sniff. **2.** To perceive by smelling; scent; smell. **3.** To sniff in order to examine; — said of dogs, etc. — *v. i.* To inhale through the nose noisily and forcibly; sniff inquiringly. — *n.* **1.** Act of snuffing. **2.** Tobacco pulverized to be taken into the nose.

snuff'er (snŭf'ẽr), *n.* **1.** One who snuffs. **2.** *pl.* A device for snuffing a candle.

snuf'fle (-'l), *v. i.* [1] To breathe through the nose noisily, as in whimpering. — *n.* **1.** Act or sound of snuffling. **2.** A nasal twang.

snug (snŭg), *a.* [3] **1.** Trim; tidy; sheltered; cozy. **2.** Close; concealed. **3.** Fitting closely.

snug'ger-y (snŭg'ẽr-ĭ), *n.* A snug, cozy place.

snug'gle (-'l), *v. i.* [1] To move one way and the other to get close; cuddle; nestle. — *v. t.* To draw close, as for comfort; cuddle.

snug'ly (-lĭ), *adv.* In a snug manner.

snug'ness, *n.* Snug quality or state.

so (sō), *adv.* **1.** In that manner, degree, or state; as indicated or implied; as, *so* goes the song. **2.** In like manner or degree; in such manner; to such degree; as, he is not *so* old as I am. **3.** For that reason; thus; as, obey the laws, *so* shalt thou prosper. **4.** Thereabouts; more or less; as, only a pa⁀ṛe or *so*. — so as, so that. — so that. **a** In order that. **b** Provided that. — *conj.* **1.** Provided or on condition that; if; as, I am content *so* you are satisfied. **2.** So that; in such a way that; — with clause of purpose or result; as, he was sick, *so* they were quiet.

soak (sōk), *v. t.* **1.** To saturate in a fluid; steep. **2.** To drench. **3.** To draw in by pores or small passages. **4.** To saturate; wet through. — *v. i.* **1.** To become saturated. **2.** To enter (into something) by pores or small passages. — *n.* **1.** A soaking; state of being soaked. **2.** Liquid in which anything is soaked. — **soak'er,** *n.* [8].

soap (sōp), *n.* A cleansing agent soluble in water, made, usually, by action of alkali on fat. — *v. t.* To rub or wash over with soap.

soap'stone' (-stōn'), *n.* A kind of soft stone with a soapy feel; a variety of talc; steatite.

soap'y (-ĭ), *a.* [3] Like soap; soft and smooth; smeared with soap. — **-i-ness** (-ĭ-nĕs), *n.* [8].

soar (sōr), *v. i.* **1.** To fly aloft, as a bird; mount on or as on wings. **2.** To be exalted in thought, or spirits. — *n.* Act of soaring; upward flight.

sob (sŏb), *v. i.; soed;* SOBBED (sŏbd); SOB'BING. To sigh with a sudden heaving of the breast; weep with a convulsive catching of the breath. — *n.* Act or sound of sobbing.

so'ber (sō'bẽr), *a.* [3] **1.** Not drunk; also, temperate in the use of liquor. **2.** Temperate or moderate in thought or action; self-controlled. **3.** Not proceeding from or attended with passion; calm. **4.** Serious; solemn; grave. — *v. t. & i.* To make or become sober. — **-ly,** *adv.* — **-ness,** *n.*

so-bri'e-ty (sō-brī'ē-tĭ), *n.* Sober quality or state.

‖ **so'bri'quet'** (sō'brē'kā' ; sō'brĭ-kā), *n.* [F.] An assumed name; nickname.

so'–called' (sō'kôld'), *a.* Commonly named (but with doubtful propriety); thus termed.

so'cia-bil'i-ty (sō'shá-bĭl'ĭ-tĭ), *n.* Sociable quality.

so'cia-ble (sō'shá-b'l), *a.* [4] **1.** Inclined to, or adapted for, society; social. **2.** Marked by friendly

and, esp., informal meeting and conversation. — *n.* A gathering; informal reception. *Colloq., U. S.* — **-ble-ness,** *n.* [8] — **so'cia-bly,** *adv.* [8].

so'cial (sō'shăl), *a.* [4] **1.** Of or pertaining to companionship or persons associated in friendly intercourse. **2.** Disposed to companionship; sociable. **3.** Of or pertaining to society or a social organism. **4. a** *Bot.* Naturally growing in groups or masses. **b** *Zoöl.* Living in more or less organized communities; as, *social* ants, etc.

so'cial-ism (-ĭz'm), *n.* A political and economic theory of social reorganization, the essential feature of which is governmental control of economic activities, to the end that competition shall give way to coöperation and the opportunities of life and the rewards of labor shall be equitably apportioned.

so'cial-ist (-ĭst), *n.* An advocate of socialism.

so'cial-ist, *a.* Socialistic.

so'cial-is'tic (-ĭs'tĭk), *a.* [4] Pertaining to, or of the nature of, socialism; relating to socialists.

so'cial-ly, *adv.* In a social manner.

so-ci'e-ty (sō-sī'ē-tĭ), *n.; pl.* -TIES (-tĭz). **1.** The relationship of men associated in any way; companionship; fellowship; company. **2.** A number or body of persons associated for mutual or joint usefulness, pleasure, or profit; an association. **3.** The more cultivated or fashionable portion of any community. [to sociology.]

so'ci-o-log'i-cal (sō'shĭ-ō-lŏg'ĭ-kăl), *a.* Of or pert.

so'ci-ol'o-gy (-ŏl'ō-jĭ), *n.* Science of the constitution, phenomena, and growth of society. — **so'ci-ol'o-gist** (-jĭst), *n.*

sock (sŏk), *n.* **1.** A stocking with a short leg.

sock'et (sŏk'ĕt), *n.* Any hollow thing or place which receives and holds something else.

sod (sŏd), *n.* That layer of the soil which is filled with the roots of grass, herbs, etc.; turf; sward; also, a piece of it cut or pulled off; a turf. — *v. t.;* SOD'DED; SOD'DING. To cover with sod.

so'da (sō'dà), *n.* **1.** A strong alkaline salt used in making soap, glass, etc.; sodium carbonate; — called also *washing soda; sal soda.* **2.** A white crystalline substance of a slight alkaline taste; bicarbonate of soda; — called also *baking,* or *cooking, soda; saleratus.* **3.** Sodium. **4.** Soda water.

soda fountain. An apparatus with delivery tubes, faucets, etc., for drawing soda water. *U. S.*

so-dal'i-ty (sō-dăl'ĭ-tĭ), *n.; pl.* -TIES (-tĭz). A fraternity; a brotherhood.

soda water. A beverage of water charged with carbon dioxide and flavored.

sod'den (sŏd'n), *a.* [4] **1.** Soaked; saturated. **2.** Not well cooked; heavy, as bread. **3.** Appearing as if soaked or seethed; esp., showing effects of habitual intemperance. — **-ness,** *n.* [8].

so'di-um (sō'dĭ-ŭm), *n.* A waxy, silver-white metal of the alkali group, occurring always combined, as in common salt, borax, etc.

so-ev'er (sō-ĕv'ẽr). A word used in composition with *who, what, where, when, how,* etc., and indicating any out of all possible or supposable persons, things, places, times, ways, etc.

so'fa (sō'fà), *n.* A kind of long seat, usually upholstered and having a back and arms.

soft (sôft), *a.* [3] **1.** Easily impressed, molded, or cut; also, malleable. **2.** Susceptible; easily

---

āle, senāte, câre, ăm, ăccount, ärm, ȧsk, sofȧ; ēve, ĕvent, ĕnd, recĕnt, makẽr; īce, ĭll; ōld, ȍbey, ôrb, ŏdd, sôft, cŏnnect; ūse, ŭnite, ûrn, ŭp, circŭs; fōod, fŏot; out, oil;

affected; esp., gentle; kind; tender. **3.** Not rough or harsh, as to the touch, sight, or hearing; delicate. **4.** Expressing gentleness, tenderness, etc., mild, courteous; kind. **5.** Gentle in action; easy. **6. a** Weak; effeminate. **b** Simple; foolish. *Colloq.* **c** With muscles not hardened by exercise. *Colloq.* **d** Of beverages, not alcoholic. *Colloq.* **7.** Marked by the lack of certain salts which prevent lathering : — said of water. **8.** Of consonants, sibilant or spirant (as *g* in *gem*, *c* in *cent*, etc.). — *adv.* Softly; gently; quietly. — *interj.* Be quiet! hold! stop! — **soft′ly**, *adv.* — **soft′ness**, *n.* [8]. [or softer.

sof′ten (sôf′'n), *v. t. & i.* To make or become soft

sog′gy (sŏg′Ĭ), *a.* [3] Heavy and wet; sodden.

soil (soil), *v. t.* To feed (stock) with fresh grass or green food cut for them.

soil, *n.* **1.** The loose surface material of the earth in which plants grow. **2.** Firm land; earth. — *v. t.* To enrich with soil or muck.

soil, *v. t.* **1.** To foul; dirty; defile. **2.** To stain or mar, as with disgrace; sully. — *v. i.* To become soiled or dirty. — *n.* **1.** Fact of being soiled; soiling; a soiled place; stain. **2.** Filth; sewage; dung; manure.

soil′ure (soil′ŭr), *n.* A soiling; a stain; pollution.

∥ **soi·rée′** (swä′rā′), *n.* [F.] An evening party.

so′journ (sō′jŭrn; sō·jûrn′), *v. i.* To dwell temporarily; tarry. — *n.* A temporary residence or stay. — **so′journ-er**, *n.* [8].

sol (sŏl), *n.* The sun.

sol (sōl), *n. Music.* The fifth tone of the scale.

sol′ace (sŏl′ås), *n.* Comfort in grief; relief; consolation. — *v. t.* [1] **1.** To cheer in grief or calamity; console. **2.** To allay; soothe. **3.** To divert; cheer ; — sometimes reflexive.

so′lar (sō′lär), *a.* **1.** Of, pertaining to, or from, the sun. **2.** Determined by the sun; as, the *solar* year. — **solar plexus**, *Anat.*, a nervous plexus behind the stomach. — **s. system**, the sun with the celestial bodies revolving round it.

sold (sōld), *pret. & p. p.* of SELL.

sol′der (sŏd′ẽr), *n.* **1.** A metal or alloy used, when melted, to join metallic surfaces. **2.** Something which unites or cements. — *v. t.* **1.** To join with solder. **2.** Fig., to mend; patch up.

sol′dier (sōl′jẽr), *n.* **1.** One engaged in military service. **2.** An enlisted man, as distinguished from a commissioned officer; sometimes, a private. — *v. i.* **1.** To serve as a soldier. **2.** To make a pretense of working, while doing only enough to escape punishment or discharge. *Colloq.*

sol′dier-ly, *a.* [4] Like or befitting a soldier.

sol′dier-y (-Ĭ), *n.* A body of soldiers; soldiers collectively.

sole (sōl), *n.* Any of certain flatfishes with small mouth and small close-set eyes.

sole, *n.* **1.** The under surface of the foot. **2.** The bottom of a shoe, boot, etc. — *v. t.* [1] To furnish with a sole.

sole, *a.* Single; only.

sol′e-cism (sŏl′ė-sĬz′m; sō′lė-), *n.* **1.** A deviation from the idiom of a language or from the rules of syntax ; loosely, any minor blunder in speech. **2.** Any impropriety or unfitness.

sole′ly (sōl′lĬ), *adv.* Singly; alone.

sol′emn (sŏl′ĕm), *a.* [4] **1.** Marked with religious rites and pomps; sacred. **2.** Serious; grave. **3.** Inspiring serious thought; impressive.

so-lem′ni-ty (sŏ-lĕm′nĬ-tĬ), *n. ; pl.* -TIES (-tĬz). **1.** A religious or ritual ceremony ; hence, any ceremony, celebration, or formal festivity. **2.** Seriousness ; gravity. **3.** Awe or reverence.

sol′em-ni-za′tion (sŏl′ĕm-nĬ-zā′shŭn), *n.* Act of solemnizing ; celebration.

sol′em-nize (sŏl′ĕm-nīz), *v. t.* [1] To perform with solemn ceremonies or legal formality.

sol′emn-ly (-ĕm-lĬ), *adv.* In a solemn manner.

sol′emn-ness, *n.* Solemn quality or state.

so-lic′it (sŏ-lĬs′Ĭt), *v. t.* **1.** To ask earnestly; petition. **2.** To seek ; plead for. — *v. i.* To make solicitation.

so-lic′i-ta′tion (-Ĭ-tā′shŭn), *n.* **1.** Act of soliciting ; importunity. **2.** Excitement ; allurement.

so-lic′i-tor (sŏ-lĬs′Ĭ-tẽr), *n.* **1.** One who solicits. **2.** *Law.* **a** In England, one admitted to practice law (but not to plead) in any court. **b** The law officer of a city, government, etc. — **so-lic′i-tor-ship**, *n.* — **so-lic′i-tress** (-trĕs), *n. fem.* [8].

so-lic′it-ous (-Ĭ-tŭs), *a.* [4] Eager to obtain or to avoid something ; anxious ; apprehensive. — **so-lic′i-tous-ly**, *adv.* [8] — **ness**, *n.* [8].

so-lic′i-tude (-Ĭ-tūd), *n.* State of being solicitous.

sol′id (sŏl′Ĭd), *a.* [3] **1.** Capable of resisting, up to a certain limit, forces tending to deform , not liquid or gaseous. **2.** Not hollow, full of matter. dense. **3.** Cubic ; as, a *solid* foot. **4.** Compact ; hard ; firm; stable. **5.** Entirely of one substance, formation, kind, color, etc. **6.** Sound ; strong. **7.** Trustworthy ; reliable; weighty ; real; genuine. **8.** Complete ; entire ; unbroken ; as, a *solid* hour. *Colloq.* — *n.* **1.** A solid substance or body. **2.** A magnitude having three dimensions.

sol′i-dar′i-ty (sŏl′Ĭ-dăr′Ĭ-tĬ), *n.* An entire union or consolidation of interests and responsibilities.

so-lid′i-fi-ca′tion (sŏ-lĬd′Ĭ-fĬ-kā′shŭn), *n.* Act of solidifying, or state of being solidified.

so-lid′i-fy (sŏ-lĬd′Ĭ-fī), *v. t. & i.* [2] To make or become solid or compact ; to embody concretely.

so-lid′i-ty (-tĬ), *n.* **1.** Solid state or quality ; hardness; massiveness. **2.** Moral firmness; truth.

sol′id-ly, *adv.* In a solid manner.

sol′id-ness, *n.* Solid quality or state.

so-lil′o-quize (sŏ-lĬl′ō-kwīz), *v. i.* [1] To utter a soliloquy. [talking to one's self.

so-lil′o-quy (-kwĬ), *n. ; pl.* -QUIES (-kwĬz). Act of

sol′i-taire′ (sŏl′Ĭ-târ′), *n.* **1.** A single diamond or (sometimes) other gem set alone. **2.** A game (as at cards) which one person can play alone.

sol′i-ta-ry (sŏl′Ĭ-tă-rĬ), *a.* [4] **1.** Living or being by one's self or by itself; single. **2.** Not frequented; remote ; retired ; lonely; desolate ; deserted ; — of places, etc. **3.** Single; sole. — **sol′i-ta-ri-ly** (-rĬ-lĬ), *adv.* [8] — **ri-ness**, *n.* [8].

sol′i-tude (sŏl′Ĭ-tūd), *n.* **1.** State of being alone, or remote from society. **2.** A solitary place.

so′lo (sō′lō), *n. ; pl.* E. SOLOS (-lōz), It. -LI (·lē). An air, strain, or a whole piece, played or sung by one person, with or without accompaniment.

so′lo-ist, *n.* One who sings or plays a solo.

Sol′o-mon′s-seal′ (sŏl′ō-mŭnz-), *n.* Any of several plants allied to the lily of the valley.

sol'stice (sŏl'stĭs), n. Point in the ecliptic, or time (about June 21 and Dec. 21), at which the sun is farthest from the equator, north or south. — **sol-sti'tial** (sŏl-stĭsh'ăl), a.

sol'u-bil'i-ty (sŏl-ū-bĭl'ĭ-tĭ), n.; pl. -TIES (-tĭz). Quality of being soluble.

sol'u-ble (sŏl'ū-b'l), a. [4] 1. Susceptible of being dissolved in a fluid. 2. Susceptible of being solved; solvable. — **sol'u-ble-ness**, n. [8].

so-lu'tion (sŏ-lū'shŭn), n. 1. Separation of the parts of any body; disruption. 2. Disintegration. 3. Act or process of solving a problem. 4. Act or process by which a substance (solid, liquid, or gaseous) is absorbed into a liquid ; the resulting liquid. [ing solvable.

solv'a-bil'i-ty (sŏl'vă-bĭl'ĭ-tĭ), n. Quality of being solvable.

solv'a-ble (sŏl'vă-b'l), a. [4] Susceptible of being solved, resolved, or explained. — **-ness**, n. [8].

solve (sŏlv), v. t. [1] To clear up (what is obscure or difficult) ; explain ; settle. — **solv'er**, n. [8].

sol'ven-cy (sŏl'vĕn-sĭ), n. Solvent state or quality.

sol'vent (-vĕnt), a. [4] 1. Able to dissolve. 2. Able to pay all just debts. — n. A liquid capable of, or used in, dissolving something.

som'ber (sŏm'bẽr), a. [6] 1. Dull ; gloomy. 2. Melancholy ; grave ; depressing. — **som'ber-ly**, adv. [6, 8] — **som'ber-ness**, n. [6,8].

som-bre'ro (-brā'rō), n. ; pl. -ROS (-rōz). A kind of broad-brimmed hat, usually of felt.

some (sŭm), a. 1. A certain ; one ; — indicating a person, thing, etc., as not designated specially. 2. Being a certain (indefinite) portion or number ; as, some wine. 3. About ; more or less ; — used adverbially before a numeral ; as, some eighty houses. — pron. A certain (indefinite) quantity, portion, or number, as distinguished from the rest.

Sombrero.

some'bod-y (sŭm'bŏd-ĭ), n.; pl. -BODIES (-ĭz). 1. A person unknown or not certainly known; some person. 2. A person of importance.

some'how' (-hou'), adv. In one way or another.

som'er-sault (sŭm'ẽr-sôlt), n. A leap or fling in which a person turns his heels over his head.

som'er-set (-sĕt), n. A somersault.

some'thing (sŭm'thĭng), n. 1. Some thing ; a certain indefinite thing. 2. A thing or a person of importance. — adv. In some degree; somewhat.

some'time' (-tīm'), adv. 1. At a past time indefinitely referred to ; once ; formerly. 2. Once in a while ; sometimes. 3. At one time or other hereafter. — a. Having been formerly ; former; late.

some'times' (-tīmz'), adv. At times ; now and then ; occasionally.

some'what' (-hwŏt'), n. A part, more or less. — adv. In some degree or measure ; a little.

some'where' (-hwâr'), adv. In or to a place unknown or not specified ; in one place or another.

som-nam'bu-lism (sŏm-năm'bū-lĭz'm), n. A state in which one asleep walks or performs other actions appropriate to the waking state. — **-list**, n.

som-nif'er-ous (-nĭf'ẽr-ŭs), a. [4] Inducing sleep.

som'no-lence (sŏm'nō-lĕns), n. Sleepiness.

som'no-lent (-lĕnt), a. [4] Sleepy ; drowsy.

son (sŭn), n. 1. A human male considered with reference to his parents or either of them ; a male descendant ; a man of a given country, faith, etc. 2. A son-in-law. 3. [cap.] (Commonly with the) Jesus Christ, called the Son of God, and the Son of man.

so'nan-cy (sō'năn-sĭ), n. Sonant quality or state.

so'nant (sō'nănt), a. Phon. Uttered with voice or vocal sound, as distinguished from mere breath sound ; voiced ; vocal. — n. A sonant sound.

so-na'ta (sŏ-nä'tà), n. Music. A kind of extended composition for one or two instruments.

song (sŏng), n. 1. That which is sung ; singing ; vocal music. 2. A lyrical poem adapted to vocal music ; a ballad ; poem. 3. Poetical composition; poetry ; verse; as, heroic song. 4. Music. A musical setting for a lyric poem or ballad.

song'ster (sŏng'stẽr), n. 1. One skilled in singing. — chiefly of birds. 2. A book of popular songs.

song'stress (-strĕs), n. A female singer.

son'–in–law', n. ; pl. SONS-IN-LAW. The husband of one's daughter.

son'net (sŏn'ĕt), n. A certain verse form consisting of 14 lines running according to a prescribed scheme ; also, a poem in this form. — **-eer'**, n.

so-nor'i-ty (sŏ-nŏr'ĭ-tĭ), n. Sonorous quality.

so-no'rous (sŏ-nō'rŭs), a. [4] 1. Resonant. 2. Loud or full in sound. 3. Impressive in sound. — **-ly**, adv. [8] — **-ness**, n. [8].

son'ship (sŭn'shĭp), n. The relation of a son.

soon (sōon), adv. 1. In a short time ; also, shortly after any time specified or understood ; as, soon after sunrise. 2. Early. 3. Promptly ; quickly; also, easily. 4. Readily; willingly.

soot (sŏot ; sŏot), n. A black substance formed by combustion and adhering to chimneys or pipes conveying smoke; the fine powder, chiefly carbon, which colors smoke. — v. t. To cover with soot.

sooth (sōoth), n. Truth; reality; — chiefly in in sooth.

soothe (sōoth), v. t. [1] 1. To quiet; calm. 2. To soften; assuage ; allay. — **sooth'er**, n. [8].

sooth'say'er (sōoth'sā'ẽr), n. One who foretells events. — **sooth'say'ing**, n.

soot'y (sŏot'ĭ; sōot'ĭ), a. [3] 1. Pertaining to or producing soot ; soiled with soot. 2. Having a dark brown or black color like soot. — **-i-ness**, n. [8].

sop (sŏp), n. 1. Something dipped or steeped in a liquid. 2. Something given to pacify. — v. t.; SOPPED (sŏpt) ; SOP'PING. 1. To steep or dip in a liquid. 2. To soak up ; as, to sop up water.

soph'ism (sŏf'ĭz'm), n. A plausible but fallacious argument.

soph'ist (-ĭst), n. One who uses clever and plausible, but misleading, reasoning.

so-phis'tic (sŏ-fĭs'tĭk) } a. [4] Of or pertaining to **so-phis'ti-cal** (-tĭ-kăl) } a sophist or sophistry; fallaciously subtle. — **so-phis'ti-cal-ly**, adv. [8].

so-phis'ti-cate (-tĭ-kāt), v. t. [1] 1. To make artificial ; deprive of simplicity. 2. To delude.

so-phis'ti-ca'tion (-kā'shŭn), n. A sophisticating.

soph'ist-ry (sŏf'ĭs-trĭ), n.; pl. -TRIES (-trĭz). Plausible but misleading reasoning.

soph'o-more (-ō-mōr), n. A student in the second year of a four-year college course. Now U. S.

soph'o-mor'ic (-mŏr'ĭk), **-i-cal** (-ĭ-kăl), a. Like a sophomore; inflated in style or manner. U. S.

so′por(sō′pŏr), *n.* Profound or lethargic sleep.

so′po-rif′ic(sō′pē-rĭf′ĭk; sŏp′ō-), *a.* [4] Causing, or tending to cause, sleep. — *n.* A narcotic.

sop′py(sŏp′ĭ), *a.* [3] Soaked or saturated; wet.

so-pra′no(sō-prä′nō), *n.; pl.* E. -NOS (-nōz), It. -NI (-nē). *Music.* **a** The treble; the highest quality of voice. **b** A part for such a voice. **c** A singer, esp. a woman, with a treble voice.

sor′cer-er(sôr′sẽr-ẽr), *n.* A practicer of sorcery; magician; wizard. — **sor′cer-ess**, *n. fem.* [8].

sor′cer-ous(-ŭs),*a.* [4] Of or pertaining to sorcery.

sor′cer-y (-ĭ), *n.; pl.* SORCERIES (-ĭz). The use of magic; necromancy; witchcraft.

sor′did(-dĭd),*a.* [4] **1.** Vile; base; gross. **2.** Meanly avaricious. — **-ly**, *adv.* — **-ness**, *n.*

sore(sōr),*a.* [3] **1.** Sensitive to pain from pressure; tender. **2.** Distressed mentally; pained; irritable; sensitive. **3.** Distressing; vexatious; severe; violent; extreme. — *n.* A place where the skin and flesh are ruptured or bruised so as to be tender or painful. — *adv.* Sorely.

sore′ly(sōr′lĭ), *adv.* In a sore manner.

sore′ness, *n.* Quality or state of being sore.

sor′ghum(sôr′gŭm), *n.* A cereal grass cultivated as a fodder or grain plant or for making molasses.

so-ror′i-ty(sō-rŏr′ĭ-tĭ), *n.; pl.* -TIES (-tĭz). A society or club of girls or women.

so-ro′sis(sō-rō′sĭs), *n.* A woman's club.

sor′rel (sŏr′ĕl), *a.* Yellowish or reddish brown. — *n.* **1.** A sorrel color. **2.** A sorrel animal.

sor′rel, *n.* Any of various plants with sour juice.

sor′ri-ly (sŏr′ĭ-lĭ), *adv.* In a sorry manner.

sor′ri-ness, *n.* Quality or state of being sorry.

sor′row(sŏr′ō), *n.* **1.** Distress of mind due to loss or disappointment; unhappiness; sadness; regret. **2.** A cause of grief or sadness; trouble; affliction. — *v. i.* To feel sorrow; grieve. — **sor′row-er**, *n.*

sor′row-ful (-fŏŏl), *a.* [4] Full of, expressive of, marked by, or inducing, sorrow. — **sor′row-ful-ly**, *adv.* [8] — **-ful-ness**, *n.* [8].

sor′ry (-ĭ), *a.* [3] **1.** Grieved for loss; feeling sorrow. **2.** Melancholy; dismal, mournful. **3.** Poor; pitiful; contemptible; mean; as, a *sorry* excuse.

sort (sôrt), *n.* **1.** A group having the same or similar characteristics; a kind, class, order, or species. **2.** Way; fashion; manner. **3.** Character; quality; nature. *Colloq.* — *v. t.* To place, rank, separate, or select according to sort, kind, class, etc. — **sort′a-ble**, *a.* — **sort′er**, *n.*

sor′tie (sôr′tē), *n. Mil.* A sally of troops from a besieged place against the besiegers.

so′-so′ } (sō′sō′), *a.* Middling; passable. — *adv.*
so′—so′ } Tolerably. *Both Chiefly Colloq.*

sot (sŏt), *n.* A habitual drunkard.

sot′tish(sŏt′ĭsh),*a.* [4] Like a sot; doitish; very foolish; drunken. — **-ly**, *adv.* [8] — **-ness**,*n.* [8].

sou (sŏŏ), *n.; pl.* SOUS (sŏŏz; *F.* sŏŏ). The French bronze 5-centime piece, worth about a cent.

sou-brette′ (sŏŏ-brĕt′), *n. Theat.* Originally, in comedies, an intriguing lady's maid; hence, a coquettish maidservant or frivolous young woman; an actress who plays such a part.

‖**souf-flé′** (sŏŏ′flā′; sŏŏ′flā), *a.* [F.] Often **-flée′**. *Cookery.* Filled with air by beating, and baked.

‖**souf-flé′** (sŏŏ′flā′; sŏŏ′flā), *n.* A delicate, spongy dish of eggs, milk, flour, etc.

sough (sŭf; sou), *n.* A hollow moaning, as of the wind; sigh. — *v. i.* To make a sough; sigh.

sought (sôt), *pret. & p. p.* of SEEK.

soul (sōl), *n.* **1.** That which is conceived to be the essence of individual, esp. psychical, life. **2.** Man's moral and emotional nature; hence, effective expression of emotion. **3.** The seat of real life, action, etc.; animating or essential part. **4.** The leader; inspirer. **5.** Courage; spirit; fervor. **6.** A person; as, not a *soul* was there.

soul′ful (sōl′fŏŏl), *a.* [4] Full of deep feeling.

soul′less (-lĕs), *a.* [4] Having no soul, or no nobleness of mind or feeling. — **-less-ness**, *n.* [8].

sound (sound), *a.* [3] **1.** Free from flaw, defect, or decay. **2.** Healthy; not diseased. **3.** Firm; strong; safe; trustworthy. **4.** Founded in truth or right; right. **5.** Morally good or honorable; orthodox. **6.** Thorough. **7.** Not broken or troubled; — of sleep. **8.** Legal; valid.

sound, *n.* A fish's air bladder.

sound, *n.* A long passage (larger than a strait) of water connecting two larger bodies.

sound, *v. t.* **1.** To measure the depth of, esp. by line and plummet. **2.** To find or seek the thoughts, motives, etc., of. — *v. i.* To sound water.

sound, *n.* **1.** Sensation or a sensation usually having as its source a body set in vibration, so that waves from it stimulate the auditory nerve. **2.** A particular tone or noise. **3.** Distance within which a certain noise may be heard. — *v. i.* **1.** To make a noise or sound. **2.** To be conveyed in sound; be spread. **3.** To convey a certain impression, or to have a certain import, when heard. — *v. t.* **1.** To cause to sound. **2.** To cause to exist as a sound. **3.** To indicate by a sound. **4.** To celebrate by or as by sounds. — **sound′er**, *n.*

sound′ing, *n.* **1.** Act of one that sounds. **2.** *Naut.* **a** Measurement by sounding, or the depth so ascertained. **b** *pl.* Any place or part of a body of water where a hand sounding line will reach bottom.

sound′less, *a.* [4] Silent; noiseless.

sound′ly, *adv.* In a sound manner.

sound′ness, *n.* Sound quality or state.

soup (sŏŏp), *n.* A liquid food usually made by boiling meat or vegetables, or both, in water; broth.

sour (sour), *a.* [4] **1.** Acid; tart; changed so as to be acid, rancid, or musty; turned. **2.** Distasteful; unpleasant; also, cross; morose. — **-ish**, *a.* **sour**, *v. t. & i.* To make or become sour.

source (sōrs), *n.* **1.** A spring; fountainhead. **2.** Origin; first cause; as, the *source* of ideas.

sour′ly, *adv.* In a sour manner.

sour′ness, *n.* Sour quality or state.

souse (sous), *n.* **1.** Act of sousing. **2.** Pickle made with salt. **3.** Something steeped in pickle. — *v. t.* [1] **1.** To pickle. **2.** To plunge or immerse in any liquid. **3.** To drench.

south (south), *n.* **1.** The cardinal point directly opposite the north. **2.** A region relatively farther south than another; esp. [*cap.*]: That part of the United States south of Mason and Dixon's line (southern boundary of Pennsylvania) and the Ohio River, corresponding in general to the former slaveholding States. — *a.* Situated at the south, or in a southern direction; proceeding toward, or coming from, the south; southern.—*adv.* Toward, or in, the south; of the wind, from the south.

south′east′ (south′ēst′; *colloq.* sou′-), *n.* Point or direction halfway between south and east.—*a.* Of or pertaining to, proceeding or facing toward, or (of wind) blowing from, the southeast.—*adv.* Toward, or from, the southeast.

south′east′er (-ēs′tẽr), *n.* Storm or wind from the southeast. [southeast.|

south′east′er-ly, *a. & adv.* Toward or from the|

south′east′ern (-ēs′tẽrn), *a.* Southeasterly.

south′er-ly (sŭth′ẽr-lĭ), *a.* Of or pertaining to the south; southern.—*adv.* From the south.

south′ern (sŭth′ẽrn), *a.* 1. Of or pertaining to, or situated in or toward, the south; proceeding from or toward the south. 2. [*cap.*] Of or pertaining to the South. *U. S.*

south′ern-er (-ẽr-nẽr), *n.* An inhabitant or native of the south, esp. [*cap.*] of the southern U. S.

south′ern-most (-ẽrn-mōst), *a.* Farthest south.

south′ron (sŭth′rŭn), *n.* A southerner.

south′-south′east′, *a.*, **south′-south′west′**, *a.* See *points of the compass*, under POINT, *n.*

south′ward (south′wẽrd), *adv.* Toward the south. — *a.* Situated, directed, or looking, southward. — *n.* The southward direction, point, or part.

south′ward-ly, *a.* Having a southern direction or situation; blowing from the south. — *adv.* In a southern direction.

south′west′ (south′wĕst′; *colloq.* sou′-), *n.* Point or direction halfway between south and west; southwest part or region.—*a.* Of, pertaining to, proceeding or facing toward, or (of the wind) blowing from, the southwest; toward or from the southwest.—*adv.* Toward or from the southwest.

south′west′er (-wĕs′tẽr), *n.* Often, esp. in nautical use, **sou′-west′er.** 1. A storm or strong wind from the southwest. 2. A waterproof hat, with a flap at the back, worn in stormy weather.

south′west′er-ly, **south′west′ern** (-tẽrn), *a.* Toward or from the southwest.

sou′ve-nir′ (sōō′vĕ-nēr′; sōō′vĕ-nēr), *n.* That which serves as a reminder; memento; keepsake.

sov′er-eign (sŏv′ẽr-ĭn; sŭv′-), *a.* [4] 1. Supreme; paramount. 2. Supreme in position or power. 3. Independent of and unlimited by, any other. 4. Excellent; effectual, as a remedy. — *n.* 1. A person, body of men, or state, sovereign in authority. 2. A British gold coin worth one pound sterling ($4.8665).

sov′er-eign-ty (sŏv′ẽr-ĭn-tĭ; sŭv′-), *n.; pl.* -TIES (-tĭz). Quality or state of being sovereign; power, right, or status of a sovereign; dominion.

||**so′viet′** (sō′vyĕt′), *n.* In Russia, a council; specif., [*often cap.*] any of the various elected governing bodies of the Union of Socialist Soviet Republics, established by the revolution of 1917 and by a constitution adopted in 1918. Hence, any of various similar radically socialistic bodies elsewhere.

sow (sou), *n.* The adult female of swine.

sow (sō), *v. t.; pret.* SOWED (sōd); *p. p.* SOWN (sōn) or SOWED; *p. pr. & vb. n.* SOW′ING. 1. To scatter, as seed, on the earth for growth. 2. To scatter seed on, in, or over. 3. To disseminate. — *v. i.* To scatter seed for growth. —*-er, n.* [8].

soy (soi), *n.* 1. A Chinese and Japanese liquid sauce for fish, etc., made of fermented beans. 2. The soy bean, an Asiatic herb, or its white seed.

spa (spä), *n.* A mineral spring; a locality or resort containing mineral springs.

space (spās), *n.* 1. That which is characterized by dimension (esp. three mutually perpendicular dimensions), boundlessness, and indefinite divisibility. 2. A small portion of space (sense 1); distance; interval; expanse. 3. Quantity of time; interval; duration. 4. *Music.* A degree, or open place, of the staff. — *v. t.* [1] To place at intervals; arrange with spaces between.

spa′cious (spā′shŭs), *a.* [8] 1. Vast in extent; roomy. 2. Large in scale; expansive.

spade (spād), *n.* 1. A digging implement adapted for being pushed into the ground with the foot. 2. Something like a spade (sense 1); hence, one of a suit (called *spades*) of playing cards marked by black figures resembling a pointed spade. — *v. t.* [1] To dig with a spade. — **spad′er** (spād′ẽr), *n.*

spa′dix (spā′dĭks), *n.; l. pl.* SPADI-CES (spā-dī′sēz). *Bot.* A spike with a fleshy axis, usually inclosed in a spathe.

spa-ghet′ti (spȧ-gĕt′ĭ), *n.* A variety of macaroni. See MACARONI.

α Spathe, b Spadix (bearing flowers at c) of Jack-in-the-pulpit.

spake (spāk). A pret. of SPEAK.

span (spăn), *n.* 1. The space from the end of the thumb to the end of the little finger when extended; 9 inches. 2. **a** A limited or brief space of time. **b** Spread or extent between abutments or supports; also, the portion of anything thus extended. 3. A pair of horses, mules, etc., driven together.—*v. t.;* SPANNED (spănd) ; SPAN′NING. To spread, stretch, or extend, over or across, as an arch.

span′gle (spăn′g'l), *n.* A small plate, as of shining metal; any sparkling bit. — *v. t.* [1] To set or sprinkle with or as with spangles.

Span′iard (spăn′yȧrd), *n.* A native of Spain.

span′iel (spăn′yĕl), *n.* Any of numerous breeds of long-haired dogs.

Span′ish (-ĭsh), *a.* Of or pertaining to Spain, the Spaniards, or their language. — *n.* 1. The chief language of Spain. 2. *pl.* The people of Spain.

spank (spăngk), *v. t.* To strike, or to strike the buttocks of, as with the open hand. — *n.* A slap, as on the buttocks.

spank′er (spăngk′ẽr), *n.* 1. One that spanks. 2. *Naut.* The fore-and-aft sail on the after mast of a square-rigged vessel, or the fourth mast of a schooner.

spank′ing, *p. a.* [4] Moving with a quick, lively pace ; loosely, dashing ; lively ; of wind, brisk. — *n.* One that spanks.

span′ner (spăn′ẽr), *n.* One that spans.

span′-new′, *a.* Quite new ; brand-new.

spar (spär), *n.* Any of various nonmetallic minerals, usually cleavable and somewhat lustrous.

spar, *n.* A mast, yard, boom, etc.—*v. t.;* SPARRED (spärd); SPAR′RING. To equip with spars.

spar, *v. i.* To box with fists, esp. scientifically. — *n.* A contest at sparring; a boxing match.

spar deck. The upper deck of a vessel.

āle, senāte, cãre, ăm, ăccount, ärm, ȧsk, sofȧ; ēve, ėvent, ĕnd, recĕnt, makẽr; īce, ĭll; ōld, ȯbey, ôrb, ŏdd, sŏft, cŏnnect; ūse, ũnite, ûrn, ŭp, circŭs; fo͞od, fo͝ot; out, oil;

spare (spâr), *v. t.* [1] **1.** To refrain from ; forbear. **2.** To use frugally or stintingly. **3.** To deprive one's self of : do without ; part with. **4.** To forbear to destroy or punish. — *v. i.* **1.** To be frugal or saving. **2.** To refrain from inflicting harm. — *a.* [3] **1.** Scanty. **2.** Lean ; gaunt. **3.** Superfluous ; also, held in reserve ; as, *spare* time, or cash. — **spare'ly**, *adv.* — **-ness**, *n.* [8].

spare'rib' (spâr'rĭb'), *n.* A cut of pork, consisting of ribs somewhat closely trimmed of meat.

spark (spärk), *n.* **1.** A small particle of fire or ignited substance emitted by a burning body, or remaining in one almost extinguished, or produced by the impact of hard bodies. **2.** Anything like, or suggestive of, such a particle, as in brilliancy, etc. **3.** That which may be kindled into flame or action. **4.** *Elec.* The light accompanying a sudden disruptive discharge, as across an air space. — *v. i.* *Elec.* To produce sparks.

spark, *n.* **1.** A brisk, showy, gay man. **2.** A lover. — *v. i. & t.* To play the spark, or beau. *Colloq.*

spar'kle (spär'k'l), *n.* A little spark ; scintillation. — *v. i. & t.* [1] **1.** To emit or cause (sparks) ; scintillate ; twinkle. **2.** To effervesce, as wine. — **spar'kler** (-klẽr), *n.* [8].

spark plug. In most internal-combustion engines with electric ignition, a plug, screwed into the cylinder head, arranged so that a current makes a spark inside the cylinder. [finches.

spar'row (spăr'ō), *n.* Any of numerous small **sparrow hawk.** **1.** Any of various small hawks. **2.** A small American falcon.

spar'ry (spär'ĭ), *a.* [3] Of or like spar.

sparse (spärs), *a.* [3] Of few and scattered elements ; scanty. — **sparse'ly**, *adv.* — **-ness**, *n.*

Spar'tan (spär'tăn), *a.* Of or pert. to ancient Sparta, in Greece, ruled by a people noted for hardihood and valor ; hence, hardy ; undaunted. — *n.* A citizen of Sparta ; a person of great fortitude.

spasm (spăz'm), *n.* **1.** *Med.* An involuntary and unnatural muscular contraction. **2.** A sudden, violent, and temporary effort, emotion, etc.

spas-mod'ic (spăz-mŏd'ĭk), *a.* [4] **1.** *Med.* Of, pertaining to, or affected or marked by a spasm or spasms. **2.** Acting fitfully ; jerky ; intermittent. **spas-mod'i-cal** (-ĭ-kăl), *a.* [4] Spasmodic. — **spasmod'i-cal-ly**, *adv.* [8].

spat (spăt), *n.* A light blow ; slap. Hence, a petty quarrel, esp. verbal. — *v. t. ;* SPAT'TED ; -TING. To slap. — *v. i.* To dispute ; quarrel. *All Colloq.*

spat, *n.* A young oyster or other bivalve mollusk ; such young collectively. — *v. i.* To emit spawn.

spat, *pret.* of SPIT.

spat, *n.* A kind of short gaiter ; — chiefly in *pl.*

spathe (spāth), *n.* *Bot.* The large sheathing leaf or pair of leaves inclosing a spike of small flowers.

spa'tial (spā'shăl), *a.* [4] Of or pertaining to space. — **spa'tial-ly**, *adv.* [8].

spat'ter (spăt'ẽr), *v. t.* **1.** To splash with liquid ; soil by splashing. **2.** To scatter by splashing. — *n.* **1.** Act or noise of spattering. **2.** A drop or splash on something ; a spot due to spattering.

spat'u-la (spăt'ů-lȧ), *n.* A flexible knifelike implement for spreading paints, drugs, etc.

spav'in (spăv'ĭn), *n.* A disease of the hock of horses, marked by a bony enlargement.

spav'ined (-ĭnd), *a.* Affected with spavin.

spawn (spôn), *v. t. & i.* **1.** To produce or deposit (spawn). **2.** To bring forth ; generate or be generated ; — in contempt. — *n.* **1.** The eggs of fishes, oysters, etc. **2.** Any product or offspring ; — in contempt. [male animal.

spay (spā), *v. t.* To remove the ovaries of (a female animal).

speak (spēk), *v. i. ; pret.* SPOKE (spōk), *Archaic* SPAKE (spāk) ; *p. p.* SPO'KEN (spō'k'n) ; *p. pr. & vb. n.* SPEAK'ING. **1.** To utter words with the ordinary voice. **2.** To express opinions. **3.** To utter a discourse, or the like. **4.** To make mention. **5.** To convey ideas, etc., as if by utterance. — *v. t.* **1.** To utter by speaking ; express orally. **2.** To tell or express in words. **3.** To use, or be able to use, in talk or conversation ; talk ; as, to *speak* French. **4.** To address ; accost ; hail ; as, to *speak* a vessel.

speak'er (-ẽr), *n.* One who speaks ; as : **a** One who gives a discourse or address. **b** One who speaks for others ; esp., a presiding officer.

speak'er-ship, *n.* Office of speaker.

speak'ing, *p. a.* **1.** Uttering speech. **2.** Seeming capable of speech ; lifelike. — *n.* Act of uttering words ; also, public declamation. — **-ly**, *adv.* [8].

spear (spēr), *n.* **1.** A weapon with long shaft and sharp head or blade for thrusting or throwing. **2.** A spearman. **3.** A sharp-pointed, barbed instrument for stabbing fish. **4.** A shoot, as of grass. — *v. t.* To pierce or strike with a spear.

spear'man (-măn), *n. ; pl.* -MEN. One, esp. a soldier, armed with a spear.

spear'mint' (-mĭnt'), *n.* The common garden mint.

spe'cial (spĕsh'ăl), *a.* [4] **1.** Of or pert. to or constituting a species or sort. **2.** Pertaining or confined to a single thing or class of things ; limited. **3.** Of an unusual quality ; extraordinary. — **spe'cial-ly**, *adv.*

spe'cial-ist (-ĭst), *n.* One devoted to some special branch of learning or art or business.

spe'ci-al'i-ty (spĕsh'ĭ-ăl'ĭ-tĭ), *n. ; pl.* -TIES (-tĭz). = SPECIALTY, 2 & 3.

spe'cial-i-za'tion (spĕsh'ăl-ĭ-zā'shŭn), *n.* A specializing, or state of being specialized.

spe'cial-ize (-īz), *v. t.* [1] To apply to a specific use ; — chiefly in *p. p.* — *v. i.* To pursue a special kind of action or development ; concentrate one's efforts on a particular subject. — **iz'er** (-īz'ẽr), *n.*

spe'cial-ly, *adv.* In a special manner.

spe'cial-ty (-tĭ), *n. ; pl.* -TIES (-tĭz). **1.** A special feature or characteristic. **2.** An article to which special attention is devoted. **3.** A branch of learning, art, or business to which one especially devotes one's self.

spe'cie (spē'shĭ), *n.* Coin ; hard money.

spe'cies (spē'shēz ; -shĭ-ēz), *n. sing. & pl.* **1.** A sort ; kind ; variety ; class. **2.** *Biol.* A class or group lower than a genus or subgenus and above a subspecies or variety ; a distinct kind or sort of animal or plant.

spe-cif'ic (spē-sĭf'ĭk), *a.* [4] **1.** Of, pertaining to, or constituting, a species. **2.** Definite ; explicit. **3.** *Med.* **a** Preventing or curing a disease by a peculiar adaptation. **b** Of a disease, due to a particular minute organism or virus. — *n.* Something that is specific ; esp., a specific remedy. See SPECIFIC, *a.*, 3 **a.** — **spe-cif'i-cal-ly** (-ĭ-kăl-ĭ), *adv.*

---

chair; go; sing, iŋk; then, thin; nature, verdure; yet; zh = z in azure. Numbers refer to §§ in the Special Notes which, with Abbreviations, Signs, etc., precede the Vocabulary.

spec'i-fi-ca'tion (spĕs'ĭ-fĭ-kā'shŭn), *n.* A designation or statement of particulars ; particular mention ; also, a single article, item, or particular.

spec'i-fy (spĕs'ĭ-fī), *v. t.* [2] To mention or name in a specific or explicit manner.

spec'i-men (-mĕn), *n.* A part, or one of a number, intended to show the kind and quality of the whole ; a sample.

spe'ci-os'i-ty (spē'shĭ-ŏs'ĭ-tĭ), *n. ; pl.* -TIES (-tĭz). **1.** Quality or state of being specious. **2.** That which is specious.

spe'cious (spē'shŭs), *a.* [4] Apparently right ; superficially, but not actually, fair, just, or correct. — **spe'cious-ly**, *adv.* [8] — **-ness**, *n.* [8].

speck (spĕk), *n.* **1.** A small spot ; stain ; blemish. **2.** A small piece or object ; bit ; particle. — *v. t.* To produce specks on or in.

speck'le (spĕk''l), *n.* A little speck or spot. — *v.t.* [1] To mark with speckles ; speck ; spot.

spec'ta-cle (spĕk'tá-k'l), *n.* **1.** Something exhibited to view, esp. as unusual ; a noteworthy sight. **2.** *pl.* A device to aid vision, consisting of two lenses supported by a frame with a bridge over the nose and bows passing over the ears.

spec-tac'u-lar (spĕk-tăk'ū-lár), *a.* [4] Of, pertaining to, or of the nature of, a spectacle, or show ; imposing. — **-ly**, *adv.* [beholds.|

spec-ta'tor (spĕk-tā'tẽr), *n.* One who looks on or

spec'ter (spĕk'tẽr), *n.* [6] An apparition ; ghost.

spec'tra (spĕk'trá), *n.*, *L. pl.* of SPECTRUM.

spec'tral (-trăl), *a.* [4] **1.** Of, like, or pert. to, a specter ; ghostly ; as, a *spectral* form. **2.** Of, pert. to, or made by, a spectrum. — **-ly**, *adv.* [8].

spec'tro-scope (-trŏ-skōp), *n.* An optical instrument for forming and examining spectra.

spec'tro-scop'ic (-skŏp'ĭk), **-scop'i-cal** (-ĭ-kăl), *a.* Of, pertaining to, or produced by, a spectroscope. — **spec'tro-scop'i-cal-ly**, *adv.* [8].

spec-tros'co-py (spĕk-trŏs'kō-pĭ ; spĕk'trŏ-skō'pĭ), *n.* Study of spectra ; use of the spectroscope.

spec'trum (spĕk'trŭm), *n. ; L. pl.* -TRA (-trá). An image formed when a beam of light is decomposed (as by means of a prism) so that its rays are arranged as in the rainbow.

spec'u-late (-û-lāt), *v.i.* [1] **1.** To ponder a subject in its different aspects and relations ; meditate ; theorize. **2.** To enter into a business venture in order to profit by a change in market value ; often, to engage in hazardous business transactions for the chance of unusually large profit.

spec'u-la'tion (-lā'shŭn), *n.* Faculty, act, process, or product of speculating.

spec'u-la-tive (spĕk'û-lā-tĭv), *a.* [4] Of or pert. to, given to, involving, formed by, or engaged in, speculation. — **-ly**, *adv.*[8] — **-ness**, *n.* [8].

spec'u-la'tor (-lā'tẽr), *n.* One who speculates.

sped (spĕd), *pret. & p. p.* of SPEED.

speech (spēch), *n.* **1.** Faculty of uttering articulate sounds or words ; power of speaking. **2.** Act or manner of speaking ; oral utterance. **3.** That which is spoken ; talk. **4.** A public discourse ; oration ; harangue. **5.** A language ; tongue.

speech'less, *a.* **1.** Destitute or deprived of speech. **2.** Not speaking ; silent ; dumb. **3.** Not orally expressed. — **-ly**, *adv.* [8] — **-ness**, *n.* [8].

speed (spēd), *n.* **1.** Prosperity in an undertak-

ing ; success. *Archaic.* **2.** Act or state of moving swiftly ; swiftness ; rapidity ; also, rate of motion ; velocity. — *v. i. ; pret. & p. p.* SPED (spĕd), SPEED'ED, *p. pr. & vb. n.* SPEED'ING. **1.** *Archaic.* **a** To experience any fortune, good or ill. **b** To succeed ; prosper. **2.** To hasten ; move with celerity. — *v. t.* **1.** To promote ; further ; aid ; favor. **2.** To send forth or away ; dismiss. **3.** To dispatch with celerity ; hasten ; hurry. — **speed'er**, *n.*

speed-om'e-ter (spēd-ŏm'ē-tẽr), *n.* An instrument for indicating speed or velocity.

speed'way' (spēd'wā'), *n.* A course where fast driving, as of horses or motor cars, is allowed.

speed'y (-ĭ), *a.* [3] Marked by speed. — **speed'i-ly**, *adv.* [8] — **-ness**, *n.* [8].

spell (spĕl), *n.* **1. a** The relief of one person by another in any work or duty. **b** A period of work, duty, etc. ; a turn ; also, a rest from work. **2.** Any relatively short period ; as, a cold *spell*.

spell (spĕl), *n.* A spoken word or formula of words supposed to have magic power ; an incantation. — *v. t. ;* SPELLED (spĕld) or SPELT (spĕlt) ; SPELL'ING. **1.** To name, write, or print in order the letters of, esp. the proper letters. **2.** To constitute ; to signify ; import ; as, such an act *spells* ruin. — *v. i.* To form words with letters, esp. the proper letters.

spell'bind' (spĕl'bīnd'), *v. t. ;* -BOUND' ; -BIND'ING. To bind or hold by or as by a spell or charm ; fascinate ; charm. — **spell'bind'er**, *n.* [8].

spell'bound' (-bound'), *a.* [4] Bound by or as by a spell ; fascinated.

spell'er, *n.* **1.** One who spells. **2.** Spelling book.

spell'ing, *n.* Act of one who spells ; orthography. — **spelling book**, a book with exercises for teaching pupils to spell.

spelt (spĕlt), *pret. & p. p.* of SPELL.

spelt, *n.* A variety of wheat having loose ears, the grains being triangular in cross section.

spel'ter (spĕl'tẽr), *n.* Zinc.

spend (spĕnd), *v. t. ; pret. & p. p.* SPENT (spĕnt) ; *p. pr. & vb. n.* SPEND'ING. **1.** To consume by using ; expend. **2.** To consume wastefully ; squander. **3.** To pass, as time. — *v. i.* **1.** To expend, consume, use, or waste something. **2.** To waste or wear away ; lose force or strength. — **spend'er**, *n.* [8].

spend'thrift' (spĕnd'thrĭft'), *n.* One who spends money improvidently. — *a.* [4] Prodigal.

spent (spĕnt), *p. a.* [4] Exhausted ; worn out.

sper'ma-ce'ti (spũr'má-sē'tĭ ; -sĕt'ĭ), *n.* A waxy solid which separates from sperm oil, and is used in making candles, cosmetics, etc.

sperm oil. A fatty oil found as a liquid, with spermaceti, in the head of the sperm whale.

sperm whale. A large whale of the warmer parts of all oceans. Its head has a large closed cavity, containing fluid spermaceti and sperm oil.

spew (spū), *v. t. & i.* To eject from the stomach ; vomit ; cast forth ; eject.

spher'al (sfēr'ăl), *a.* [4] Of, pert. to, or like, a sphere ; symmetrical ; harmonious.

sphere (sfēr), *n.* **1.** *Geom.* A body or space bounded by one surface all points of which are equally distant from a point within called its *center.* **2.** Any globe or globular body, esp. a celestial one ; an orb. **3.** *Astron.* The apparent surface of the heavens. **4.** Circuit or range; compass; province. **5.** Rank; social position.

spher'ic (sfĕr'ĭk), a. Spherical.

spher'i-cal (-ĭ-kăl), a. **1.** Like a sphere; globular. **2.** Of or pertaining to a sphere.

sphe-ric'i-ty (sfē-rĭs'ĭ-tĭ), n. Roundness.

sphe'roid (sfē'roid), n. A figure having nearly the form of a sphere; esp., a figure made by revolving an ellipse about one of its axes.

sphe-roi'dal (sfē-roi'dăl), a. Having the form of a spheroid.

spher'ule (sfĕr'ōōl), n. A little sphere.

sphinx (sfĭnks), n.; pl. E. SPHINXES (sfĭnk'sĕz), L. SPHINGES (sfĭn'jēz). **1.** Gr. Myth. A monster having (typically) a lion's body, wings, and the head and bust of a woman. **2.** A sphinxlike person; one who is puzzling or difficult to understand.

spice (spīs), n. **1.** Any of certain aromatic or pungent vegetable condiments, as pepper, cinnamon, nutmeg, etc. **2.** That which gives zest or pungency. — v. t. [1] To season with spices; make spicy.

spic'i-ly (spīs'ĭ-lĭ), adv. In a spicy manner.

spic'i-ness (-ĭ-nĕs), n. Spicy quality or state.

spick'-and-span', a. New and fresh.

spic'ule (spĭk'ūl), n. A minute, slender, pointed body; a needlelike body.

spic'y (spīs'ĭ), a. [3] **1.** Flavored with or containing spice or spices; fragrant; aromatic. **2.** Producing, or abounding with, spices. **3.** Piquant; pungent; racy; as, a spicy debate.

spi'der (spī'dĕr), n. **1.** A crawling animal having four pairs of walking legs and a body with but two main parts. **2.** A kind of frying pan.

spig'ot (spĭg'ŭt), n. A pin or peg used to stop the vent in a cask; also, the plug of a faucet or cock; also, sometimes, U. S., a faucet or cock.

spike (spīk), n. **1.** An ear of grain. **2.** Bot. A form of flower cluster in which the flowers are closely set along the axis, as in the plantain.

spike, n. Any of various pointed, usually slender, objects or projections; a kind of very large nail. — v. t. [1] **1.** To fasten or furnish with spikes. **2.** To disable (a cannon) temporarily by plugging the vent.   [as in grasses.]

spike'let (spīk'lĕt), n. Bot. A secondary spike,

spike'nard (-nård), n. A fragrant ointment of the ancients.

spile (spīl), n. **1.** A small plug to stop a vent. **2.** A spout inserted in a tree to conduct sap. U. S. **3.** A large stake used as a support; a pile.

spil'ing (spīl'ĭng), n. Spiles collectively.

spill (spĭl), n. A slender piece; as: **a** A peg for plugging a hole. **b** A metallic rod or pin. **c** A small roll of paper, or slip of wood, for lighting.

spill (spĭl), v. t.; SPILLED (spĭld) or SPILT (spĭlt); SPILL'ING. **1.** To cause or allow to fall, flow, or run out, esp. so as to be lost, wasted, etc.; hence, to lose, or suffer to be scattered. **2.** To shed (blood). — v. i. To fall or run out or over and thus, usually, be lost or wasted. — n. Act of spilling; state of being spilled; that which is spilled.

spin (spĭn), v. t.; pret. SPUN (spŭn); p. p. SPUN; p. pr. & vb. n. SPIN'NING. **1.** To draw out and twist into threads. **2.** To form, as a thread of silk or a web, by expelling viscous fluid; — said of spiders, silkworms, etc. **3.** To form or produce by a slow process; — usually with out; as, to spin out a story. **4.** To turn round rapidly; whirl; twirl; as, to spin a top. — v. i. **1.** To make yarn or thread from fiber by drawing and twisting. **2.** To form a thread, as a spider. **3.** To whirl, as a top. **4.** To move swiftly, as on a bicycle. Colloq. — n. Act of spinning.

spin'ach (spĭn'ăj; -ĕch), n. Also **spin'age** (-ăj). A potherb of the same family as the beet.

spi'nal (spī'năl), a. Anat. Of, pertaining to, or near, the backbone. — **spinal column**, the series of small bones or vertebræ forming the backbone; the spine. — **s. cord**, the thick cord of nervous tissue protected by the spinal column.

spin'dle (spĭn'd'l), n. **1. a** In hand spinning, a round stick, tapering toward each end, used to twist and hold the yarn. **b** The long rod or pin in spinning wheels or machines by which the thread is twisted, and on which it is wound. **2.** A pin or rod suggestive of a spindle (sense 1).

spin'dle-leg'ged (-lĕg'ĕd; -lĕgd'), **-shanked'** (-shănkt'), a. [4] Having long, slender legs.

spin'dle-shanks (-shănks'), n. 1. pl. Long, slender shanks or legs. **2.** Construed as a sing. A spindle-shanked person.

spin'dling (-dlĭng), a. [4] Long and slender, or disproportionately tall and slender.

spine (spīn), n. **1.** A stiff, sharp process on a plant or animal. **2.** The backbone; spinal column.

spin'el (spĭn'ĕl; spĭ-nĕl'), n. A hard mineral of various colors. The red variety is the gem **spinel ruby**.

spine'less (spīn'lĕs), a. **1.** Having no spine; invertebrate; fig., without backbone or courage; cowardly. **2.** Without spines.

spin'et (spĭn'ĕt; spĭ-nĕt'), n. Music. An obsolete instrument resembling a harpsichord, but smaller.

spin'na-ker (spĭn'ă-kẽr), n. A large triangular sail used when running before the wind.

spin'ner (-ẽr), n. One that spins.

spin'ner-et (-ĕt), n. Zoöl. An organ for producing silk from the secretion of the silk glands.

spin'ning, p. pr. & vb. n. of SPIN. — **spinning wheel**, machine for spinning wool, cotton, etc., into yarn or thread, in which a wheel drives a single spindle.

spi'nose (spī'nōs; spī-nōs'), a. [4] Full of, or armed with, spines.

spi'nous (spī'nŭs), a. [4] Like a spine; spinose.

spin'ster (spĭn'stĕr), n. **1.** A woman who spins. **2.** An unmarried woman.

spin'y (spĭn'ĭ), a. [3] Having spines; thorny.

spi-ræ'a (spī-rē'à), n. Any of several shrubs of the rose family, some of which are cultivated.

spi'ral (spī'răl), a. **1.** Winding round a center or pole and gradually receding from it. **2.** Helical, like the thread of a screw. — n. **1.** A curve of spiral form. **2.** A helix. — **-ly**, adv. [8].

spi'rant (-rănt), n. A fricative consonant; as, f, s, sh.

spire (spīr), n. **1.** A spiral; curl. **2.** The upper part of a spiral shell.

Spinning Wheel, for Yarn.

Spiral.

spire (spīr), *n.* **1.** Slender blade or stalk, as of grass. **2.** A tapering roof surmounting a tower or structure; loosely, a steeple.

spir′it (spĭr′ĭt), *n.* **1.** The breath of life; life, or the life principle. **2.** The soul. **3.** [*cap.*] A part of the divine nature; the Holy Spirit. **4.** Any supernatural being; specter; ghost; sometimes, a sprite; fairy. **5.** Temper or disposition of mind; mood; — often in *pl.*; as, to be in good *spirits*. **6.** Liveliness, energy, vivacity, courage, etc.; as, to act with *spirit*. **7.** Animating principle; intent; real meaning; as, the *spirit* of a law. **8. a** A liquid produced by distillation. **b** *Pharm.* A solution in alcohol of a volatile principle. — *v. t.* To convey rapidly and secretly; kidnap; — often with *away* or *off.*

spir′it-ed, *a.* [4] **1.** Animated; full of vigor; lively. **2.** Having (such) a spirit; — used in composition; as, high-*spirited.* — **-ly,** *adv.* [8] — **-ness,** *n.* [8].

spir′it-less, *a.* [4] Without spirit. — **-ly,** *adv.* [8].

spir′it-u-al (-ĭt-ū̇-ăl), *a.* [4] **1.** Of or pert. to spirit or the spirit; incorporeal. **2.** Of, pert. to, or like, the soul; pure; holy. **3.** Of or pert. to sacred things or the church. — *n.* A kind of religious song in use among Negroes of the southern United States.

spir′it-u-al-ism (-ĭz′m), *n.* **1.** The doctrine that all that exists is spirit; idealism. **2.** A belief or doctrine that departed spirits hold intercourse with mortals, esp. through a medium.

spir′it-u-al-ist, *n.* A believer in spiritualism. — **spir′it-u-al-is′tic** (-ĭs′tĭk), *a.* [4].

spir′it-u-al′i-ty (-ĭt-ū̇-ăl′ĭ-tĭ), *n.; pl.* -TIES (-tĭz). **1.** Quality or state of being spiritual. **2.** That which belongs to the church, to an ecclesiastic in his official capacity, or to religion.

spir′it-u-al-ize (spĭr′ĭt-ū̇-ȧl-īz), *v. t.* [1] To render spiritual. — **-i-za′tion** (-ĭ-zā′shŭn), *n.*

spir′it-u-al-ly, *adv.* In a spiritual manner.

‖ **spi′ri′tu′el′** (spē′rē′tü′ĕl′), *a. masc.*) [F.] Like
‖ **spi′ri′tu′elle′** (-ĕl′), *a. fem.* } a spirit; refined; ethereal; also, sprightly; bright; witty.

spir′it-u-ous (spĭr′ĭt-ū̇-ŭs), *a.* [4] Containing, or of the nature of, alcoholic spirit.

spi-rom′e-ter (spī-rŏm′ē-tẽr), *n.* An instrument for measuring the breathing capacity of the lungs.

spit (spĭt), *n.* **1.** A slender, pointed rod to hold roasting meat. **2.** A narrow point of land running out into a body of water. — *v. t.;* SPIT′TED (-ĕd); SPIT′TING. To thrust a spit through; impale.

spit, *v. t.; pret. & p. p.* SPIT or SPAT (spăt); *p. pr. & vb. n.* SPIT′TING. **1.** To eject from the mouth. **2.** To eject; throw out; belch. — *v. i.* To eject saliva. — *n.* Spittle; saliva; act of spitting.

spite (spīt), *n.* Ill will; petty malice; rancor. — **in spite of,** or **spite of,** in defiance or contempt of; notwithstanding. — *v. t.* [1] To do despite to; treat maliciously; shame; mortify.

spite′ful (spīt′fŏŏl), *a.* [4] Filled with or showing spite; malicious. — **-ly,** *adv.* [8] — **-ness,** *n.* [8].

spit′ter (spĭt′ẽr), *n.* One who spits.

spit′tle (spĭt′'l), *n.* Saliva; spit.

spit-toon′ (spĭ-tōͦn′), *n.* A receptacle for spit.

spitz dog (spĭts). One of a breed of dogs with long silky hair, bushy tail, and sharp muzzle.

splash (splăsh), *v. t.* **1.** To strike and dash about (water, mud, etc.). **2.** To bespatter. — *v. i.* **1.** To dash about water, mud, etc. **2.** To fall or strike with a splash. — *n.* **1.** Liquid splashed. **2.** Noise made in splashing. **3.** A blotch.

splash′er (-ẽr), *n.* One that splashes; that which is splashed, or keeps off splashes.

splash′y (splăsh′ĭ), *a.* [3] **1.** Wet and muddy; slushy. **2.** Of or resembling splashes or blotches.

splay (splā), *v. t.* **1.** To spread or open out. **2.** To make slanting, as the side of a window, etc. — *n.* **1.** Spread; expansion. **2.** *Arch.* A slant or bevel.

splay′foot′ (splā′fŏŏt′), *n.; pl.* -FEET. A foot abnormally flattened and spread out.

spleen (splēn), *n.* **1.** A ductless gland (that is, one having no duct for excretion) in the abdomen of most vertebrates. It was formerly believed to be the seat of the emotions or passions. **2.** Anger; latent spite; ill humor; malice.

splen′did (splĕn′dĭd), *a.* [4] **1.** Possessing or displaying splendor; shining; brilliant; showy; gorgeous. **2.** Grand; glorious. — **splen′did-ly,** *adv.*

splen′dor (-dẽr), *n.* [5] **1.** Great brightness; brilliancy. **2.** Magnificence; pomp; glory.

sple-net′ic (splē-nĕt′ĭk), *a.* [4] **1.** Splenic. **2.** Affected with spleen; spiteful; fretful. — *n.* One affected with spleen or having a diseased spleen.

splice (splīs), *v. t.* [1] **1.** To unite, as two ropes, or parts of a rope, by interweaving the strands. **2.** To unite, as spars, timbers, etc., by a lap joint. — *n.* A joining or junction made by splicing.

splint (splĭnt), *n.* **1.** A piece split off; splinter. **2.** *Surg.* An appliance, as of wood, to hold or protect an injured part. **3.** A thin strip of wood interwoven with others to make a basket, etc.

splin′ter (splĭn′tẽr), *v. t. & i.* To split, or to become split, into long, thin pieces. — *n.* A thin piece split off lengthwise. [ters.

splin′ter-y (-ĭ), *a.* [4] Consisting of or like splin-

split (splĭt), *v. t. & i.;* SPLIT; SPLIT′TING. **1.** To divide lengthwise; rive. **2.** To burst; rend; tear asunder. **3.** To divide into parts or factions, as a political party; break up. — *n.* **1.** A crack, rent, or fissure. **2.** A breach or separation. — *a.* Divided; cleft. — **split′ter,** *n.* [8].

splotch (splŏch), *n. & v. t.* Spot; blotch.

splotch′y (-ĭ), *a.* [3] Marked with splotches.

splurge (splûrj), *n.* **A** showy display. *Colloq.* — *v. i.* [1] To make a splurge. *Colloq.*

splut′ter (splŭt′ẽr), *v. i. & t.* To sputter. — *n.* Confusion, as of hasty speaking. *Both Colloq.*

spoil (spoil), *v. t.;* SPOILED (spoild) or SPOILT (spoilt); SPOIL′ING. **1.** To plunder; rob. **2.** To impair; vitiate; destroy; ruin. **3.** To impair the disposition of (a person). — *v. i.* To become corrupted; decay. — *n.* **1.** That which is taken by violence or after a contest; booty; loot. **2.** Public offices and all the income, fees, etc., that go with them, regarded as belonging to a successful party or faction, to be bestowed for its own advantage; — usually in *pl.* **3.** An object for plundering; prey. — **spoil′er,** *n.* [8].

Spire, 2.

āle, senāte, câre, ăm, *ȧ*ccount, ärm, ȧsk, sof*ȧ*; ēve, ĕvent, ĕnd, recĕnt, makẽr; īce, ĭll; ōld, ōbey, ôrb, ŏdd, sôft, cŏnnect; ūse, ūnite, ûrn, ŭp, circ*ŭ*s; fōͦod, fŏŏt; out, oil;

spoke (spōk), *pret.* of SPEAK.

spoke (spōk), *n.* **1.** One of the small bars inserted in the hub, or nave, of a wheel and supporting the rim or felly. **2.** Rung of a ladder. **3.** A bar to prevent a wheel from turning, as in going down hill.

spo'ken (spō'k'n), *p. p.* of SPEAK.

spoke'shave (spōk'shāv'), *n.* A tool, with a blade like that of a plane and handles on each side.

spokes'man (spōks'măn), *n. ; pl.* -MEN (-měn). A speaker for another or others.

spo'li·ate (spō'lĭ-āt), *v. t. & i.* [1] To plunder; pillage; despoil. — **spo'li·a'tor** (-ā'tẽr), *n.* [8].

spo'li·a'tion (-ā'shŭn), *n.* A plundering; robbery.

sponge (spŭnj), *n.* **1.** The mass of horny fibers forming the internal skeleton of certain fixed marine animals. Also, the animal producing it. **2.** One who lives on others; parasite. **3.** Raised dough. **4.** A long-handled brush, or swab, for cleaning the bore of a cannon. — *v. t.* [1] **1.** To cleanse, wipe, or wet with a sponge. **2.** To erase or wipe out with or as with a sponge; efface ; — with *out, off*, etc. **3.** To absorb or take up with or as with a sponge. **4.** To get by imposition or mean arts without cost. — *v. i.* **1.** To absorb, as does a sponge. **2.** To get a living, a meal, etc., meanly at the expense of another. **3.** To gather, or fish for, sponges. — **spong'er** (-ẽr), *n.* [8].

spon'gy (spŭn'jĭ), *a.* [3] Like a sponge ; soft and full of cavities. — **spon'gi·ness** (-jĭ-něs), *n.* [8].

spon'son (spŏn'sŭn), *n.* A projection from a ship's side, to act as a bearing or protection for some part.

spon'sor (-sẽr), *n.* **1.** One who binds himself to answer for another's default. **2.** A godparent.

spon'ta·ne'i·ty (spŏn'tå-nē'ĭ-tĭ), *n. ; pl.* -TIES (-tĭz). Quality or state of being spontaneous.

spon·ta'ne·ous (spŏn-tā'nē-ŭs), *a.* [4] **1.** Proceeding from natural feeling or tendency, without constraint. **2.** Proceeding from, or acting by, internal impulse or energy or natural law, without external force or cause; as, *spontaneous* combustion. — **-ly**, *adv.* [8] — **-ness**, *n.* [8].

spook (spook), *n.* A spirit; ghost; apparition; hobgoblin. *Now Humorous.*

spook'ish, spook'y (-ĭ), *a.* **1.** Like a spook. **2.** Haunted. **3.** Suggestive of, or due to, spooks.

spool (spool), *n.* A cylinder with a rim or ridge at each end, to wind thread on. — *v. t.* To wind on a spool.

spoon (spoon), *n.* **1.** A utensil having a small shallow bowl, with a handle, used esp. in cooking or eating. **2.** Something suggestive of a spoon (sense 1). — *v. t.* To take up in a spoon.

spoon'bill' (-bĭl'), *n.* Any of several wading birds having the bill greatly expanded.

spoon'ful (-fŏŏl), *n. ; pl.* -FULS (-fŏŏlz). As much as a spoon can contain.

spoor (spoor), *n.* The track or trail of a wild animal. — *v. i. & t.* To follow or track by a spoor.

spo·rad'ic (spŏ-răd'ĭk), *a.* [4] Occurring singly or in scattered instances ; separate ; single.

spo·rad'i·cal (-ĭ-kăl), *a.* [4] Sporadic. — **-ly**, *adv.*

spore (spōr), *n.* Any of various primitive reproductive bodies produced by plants.

sport (spōrt), *n.* **1.** Pastime; amusement. **2.** A diversion of the field, esp. an athletic game ; also, any of various similar games usually played under cover. **3. a** Pleasantry. **b** Mockery; derision. **4.** One interested in sports, esp. for gambling; a flashy, cheap person. *Colloq.* — *v. i.* **1.** To play; frolic. **2.** To engage in sports. **3.** To trifle.

sport'ful (-fŏŏl), *a.* [4] **1.** Full of sport ; frolicsome. **2.** Done in jest; sportive.

spor'tive (spōr'tĭv), *a.* [4] Frolicsome; playful; merry. — **-ly**, *adv.* [8] — **-ness**, *n.* [8].

sports'man (spōrts'măn), *n. ; pl.* -MEN (-měn). One who pursues sports, esp. of the field, as hunting, fishing, racing, etc.; one who is fair and generous in sports. — **sports'man-like, sports'man-ly**, *a.* — **sports'man-ship**, *n.*

spot (spŏt), *n.* **1.** A mark or blot; stain; blemish. **2.** A small part differing, as in color, from the main part. **3.** A small extent of space ; a place. — **on**, or **upon, the spot,** immediately; before moving. — *v. t.;* SPOT'TED; -TING. **1.** To mark in or with spots; stain. **2.** To blemish. **3.** To mark or note so as to insure recognition; hence, to recognize; detect. *Cant.* — *v. i.* To become stained with spots. — *a.* Lit., being on the spot ; hence : *Commerce.* **a** On hand for immediate delivery after sale ; as, *spot* wheat. **b** Paid on delivery; as, *spot* cash.

spot'less, *a.* [4] Without a spot; unspotted. — **-ly**, *adv.* [8] — **-ness**, *n.* [8].

spot'ter (-ẽr), *n.* One that spots.

spot'ty (-ĭ), *a.* [3] Full of, or marked with, spots.

spouse (spouz), *n.* Either one of a married couple.

spout (spout), *v. t.* **1.** To throw out forcibly and abundantly, as liquids, esp. in a jet or stream. **2.** To utter pompously. — *v. i.* **1.** To issue with violence, as a liquid through a narrow opening. **2.** To eject material in a jet. **3.** To utter a speech, esp. pompously. — *n.* **1.** That through which anything spouts. **2.** A jet, as of liquid. — **spout'er**, *n.*

sprain (sprān), *v. t.* To weaken by sudden and excessive exertion or strain. — *n.* **1.** Act of spraining. **2.** Condition caused by spraining.

sprang (sprăng), *pret.* of SPRING.

sprat (sprăt), *n.* Any of several small herrings.

sprawl (sprôl), *v. i.* **1.** To move awkwardly or spread the limbs carelessly, while lying down. **2.** To spread irregularly, as vines. — *v. t.* To cause to sprawl. — *n.* Act or posture of sprawling.

spray (sprā), *n.* A branch with small branches bearing foliage or flowers.

spray, *n.* **1.** Liquid flying in small drops or particles. **2.** An instrument for producing or applying a spray (def. 1). — *v. t. & i.* **1.** To scatter in spray; discharge spray. **2.** To throw spray on; as, to *spray* a tree. — **spray'er**, *n.* [8].

spread (sprĕd), *v.t. ; pret. & p.p.* SPREAD; *p.pr. & vb. n.* SPREAD'ING. **1.** To scatter; distribute or extend over a surface; strew. **2.** To stretch forth; extend. **3.** To divulge; disseminate ; publish. **4.** To cover or overlay. **5.** To set forth ; record. **6.** To push or force apart. — *v.i.* To become spread. — *n.* **1.** Extension; diffusion; expansion. **2.** Extent ; compass ; expanse. **3.** A cloth to cover a table or bed. — **spread'er**, *n.* [8].

spree (sprē), *n.* **1.** A frolic. **2.** Drunken debauch. — *v. i. ;* SPREED (spred) SPREE'ING. To carouse.

sprig (sprĭg), *n.* A small shoot or twig.

spright'ly (sprīt'lĭ), *a.* [3] Having animation; lively ; brisk ; gay. — **-li·ness** (-lĭ-něs), *n.* [8].

spring (sprĭng), *v. i. ; pret.* SPRANG (sprăng) or SPRUNG (sprŭng) ; *p. p.* SPRUNG ; *p. pr. & vb. n.* SPRING'NG. **1.** To leap ; bound. **2.** To start or rise suddenly ; dart ; shoot. **3.** To recoil. **4.** To bend ; warp, as a plank. **5.** To shoot up, out, or forth. **6.** To tower ; rise, as a spire.— *v. t.* **1.** To cause to spring. **2.** To produce or disclose suddenly or unexpectedly. **3.** To crack ; split ; also, to bend or strain so as to weaken, as a mast. **4.** To explode, as a mine. **5.** To bend by force. **6.** To leap over.— *n.* **1.** Act of springing, as a leap, jump, etc. **2.** Season of the year when plants begin to vegetate, usually including March, April, and May in the North temperate zone. **3.** A source of supply, esp. of a stream ; an issue of water from the earth. **4.** An elastic body or device that recovers its original shape when released after being distorted. **5.** Cause ; origin ; motive. **6.** Elastic power or force.

spring'bok' (-bŏk'), **spring'buck'** (-bŭk'), *n.* A South African gazelle noted for springing lightly into the air. [to catch small game.]

springe (sprĭnj), *n.* A noose fastened to a spring

spring'er (sprĭng'ēr), *n.* **1.** One that springs. **2.** *Arch.* The bottom stone of one end of an arch.

spring'halt (sprĭng'hôlt'), *n.* Stringhalt.

spring'i-ness (-ĭ-nĕs), *n.* Springy quality or state.

spring'tide' (sprĭng'tīd'), **spring'time'** (-tīm'), *n.* Season of spring.

spring'y (-ĭ), *a.* [3] **1.** Like a spring ; elastic. **2.** Abounding with springs of water ; wet ; spongy.

sprin'kle (sprĭn'k'l), *v. t.* [1] **1.** To scatter so as to make fall in drops or particles. **2.** To scatter on or over in small drops or particles.— *v. i.* **1.** To sprinkle something. **2.** To rain lightly in scattered drops. — *n.* A sprinkling ; esp., a slight rain. —

sprin'kler (-klēr), *n.* [8].

sprint (sprĭnt), *v. i.* To run at top speed.— *n.* A short run at top speed. — **sprint'er**, *n.* [8].

sprit (sprĭt), *n. Naut.* A small pole or spar which crosses a fore-and-aft sail diagonally.

sprite (sprīt), *n.* **1.** A ghost ; spirit. **2.** Elf ; fairy.

sprit'sail' (sprĭt'sāl'; *naut.* -s'l), *n.* A sail extended by a sprit.

sprock'et (sprŏk'ĕt), *n.* **1.** A tooth, as on a wheel (sprocket wheel) shaped so as to engage with a chain. **2.** A sprocket wheel.

sprout (sprout), *v. i.* To germinate, as seed ; form new shoots. — *v. t.* To cause to sprout. — *n.* The shoot of a plant.

spruce (sprōōs), *n.* A kind of evergreen tree of the pine family, or its wood. — *a.* [3] **1.** Neat and dapper ; smart ; trim. **2.** Overnice.— *v. t. & i.* [1] To dress smartly ; give or restore a look of neatness to ; — often with *up. Now Colloq.* — **spruce'ly**, *adv.* [8] —**ness**, *n.* [8].

sprung (sprŭng), *pret. & p. p.* of SPRING.

spry (sprī), *a. ;* SPRI'ER or SPRY'ER ; SPRI'EST or SPRY'EST. Nimble ; active. *Colloq. & Dial.*

spud (spŭd), *n.* A sharp, narrow spade, esp. for digging up large-rooted weeds.

spume (spūm), *n.* Froth ; foam ; scum.— *v. i.* [1] To froth ; foam.

spu'mous (spū'mŭs), **spum'y** (spūm'ĭ), *a.* Consisting of, containing, or covered with, spume.

spun (spŭn), *pret. & p. p.* of SPIN.

spunk (spŭnk), *n.* **1.** Punk. **2.** Spirit ; mettle ; anger. *Colloq.* — *v. i.* To kindle. *Colloq.*

spunk'y (spŭnk'ĭ), *a.* [3] Full of spunk ; mettlesome ; also, touchy. *Colloq.*

spur (spûr), *n.* **1.** A pointed implement secured to a rider's heel to urge the horse. **2.** A goad to action ; an incitement. **3.** A spine, esp. the spine on a cock's leg. **4.** A ridge or lesser elevation that extends laterally from a mountain, or range of mountains. **5.** A short branch of railway track. — *v. t. ;* SPURRED (spûrd) ; SPUR'RING. **1.** To prick with spurs ; incite ; stimulate ; instigate. **2.** To put spurs on.—*v. i.* To spur on one's horse ; hasten.

spurge (spûrj), *n.* Any of numerous species of plants, mostly shrubby and yielding bitter juice.

spu'ri-ous (spū'rĭ-ŭs), *a.* [4] Not proceeding from the true source ; not genuine ; counterfeit ; false ; fictitious. —**ly**,*adv.* [8]—**ness**, *n.* [8].

spurn (spûrn), *v. t.* **1.** To kick ; drive back or away as with the foot. **2.** To reject with disdain.

spurt (spûrt), *v. i.* To gush out ; spout forth ; jet. — *v. t.* To expel, as a liquid, in a jet ; squirt. — *n.* A sudden gushing forth, as of liquor ; a jet.

spurt, *n.* A sudden increased exertion for a short time, as in an emergency.— *v. i.* To make a spurt.

spur wheel. *Mach.* The simplest form of toothed wheel, having teeth parallel to the axis.

sput'ter (spŭt'ēr), *v. i. & t.* **1.** To spit small, scattered particles, as in slovenly and rapid speaking ; splutter. **2.** To utter words hastily and indistinctly. **3.** To throw out anything, as jets of steam, with a noise as of one sputtering, as green wood burning. — *n.* **1.** Act of sputtering.

Spur Wheel.

2. Confused and excited speech ; hence, fuss ; ado. — **sput'ter-er**, *n.* [8].

spu'tum (spū'tŭm), *n. ; L. pl.* SPUTA (-tả). Spittle.

spy (spī), *v. t.* [2] **1.** To discover at a distance, or in a state of concealment ; espy. **2.** To discover by close search. **3.** To explore ; inspect secretly ; — usually with *out.* — *v. i.* **1.** To scrutinize. **2.** To watch secretly ; — with *on* or *upon.* — *n. ; pl.* SPIES (spīz). **1.** One who watches, esp. secretly or furtively, the conduct of others. **2.** One who, clandestinely or on false pretenses, obtains or seeks information in the zone of operations of a belligerent, with intent to communicate it to the enemy.

spy'glass' (-glàs'), *n.* A small telescope.

squab (skwŏb), *a.* [4] **1.** Fat ; short and thick. **2.** Recently hatched ; as, a *squab* pigeon.— *n.* **1.** A nestling pigeon or similar bird. **2.** Short, fat person.

squab'ble (skwŏb''l), *v. i.* [1] To quarrel noisily ; wrangle. — *n.* A noisy dispute ; wrangle. — **squab'bler** (-lēr), *n.* [8].

squad (skwŏd), *n.* **1.** *Mil.* A small party of men grouped for drill, inspection, etc. **2.** Any small group of individuals engaged in a common effort.

squad'ron (skwŏd'rŭn), *n.* **1.** Any body of men in regular formation ; esp. : *Mil.* A division of a cavalry regiment. **2.** *Nav.* A division of a fleet.

squal'id (skwŏl'ĭd), *a.* [4] Dirty through neglect. — **-ly**, *adv.* — **-ness**, *n.* [8].

squall (skwôl), *n.* A sudden violent gust, often with rain or snow. — *v. i.* To blow a squall.

squall, *v. i. & t.* To cry out or scream violently. — *n.* A harsh piercing cry.— **squall'er**, *n.* [8].

squall'y (skwôl'ĭ), *a.* [3] Abounding with or threatening squalls. [condition.|

squal'or (skwŏl'ôr), *n.* Miserable and unkempt

squan'der (skwŏn'dẽr), *v. t. & i.* To spend lavishly or wastefully. — **squan'der-**er, *n.*

square (skwâr), *n.* **1.** A parallelogram having four equal sides and four right angles. **2.** An area of four sides bounded by streets, or the distance along one side of it. **3.** An open place or area, as at the meeting of streets. **4.** An instrument having at least one right angle and two or more straight edges, used to lay out or test square work. **5.** The product of a number or quantity multiplied by itself. — *v. t.* [1] **1.** To form with four equal sides and four right angles. **2.** To compare with, or reduce to, a standard; adjust. **3.** To make even; balance; settle. **4.** To multiply (a number or a quantity) by itself. — *v. i.* To accord, conform, or agree; fit; — usually followed by *with*.— *a.* [3] **1.** Having four equal sides and four right angles. **2.** Forming a right angle. **3.** Squared; as, a *square* foot. **4.** Having a broad shape with angular outlines. **5.** Exactly adjusted ; hence, just ; exact; honest. **6.** Even; leaving no balance. **7.** Of a meal, etc., substantial; satisfying. *Colloq.* **8.** Straightforward; absolute; unequivocal. — **square'ly**, [8] *adv.* — **square'ness**, *n.* [8].

square'-rigged' (-rĭgd'), *a. Naut.* Having the principal sails extended on yards suspended horizontally at the middle; — disting. from *fore-and-aft*.

squash (skwŏsh), *n.* The fruit of any of several vines of the cucumber family ; also, the vine.

squash, *v. t. & i.* To beat or press, or to be pressed, into pulp or a flat mass; crush. *Colloq.* — *n.* **1.** Something soft and easily crushed. **2.** A sudden fall or shock of a heavy, soft body. **3.** A crushed mass. **4.** A game much like rackets.

squash'y, *a.* [3] Soft; esp., soft and wet. — **squash'i-ness**, *n.* [8].

squat (skwŏt), *v. i.; squat'ted or squat; squat'ting.* **1.** To sit down upon the hams or heels. **2.** To settle on land without right or title ; to settle on public land with a view to acquiring title. — *a.; -ter ; -test.* **1.** Sitting on the hams or heels. **2.** Short and thick.— *n.* The posture of one that squats. — **squat'ter**, *n.* [8].

squat'ty (skwŏt'ĭ), *a.* [3] Squat ; thickset.

squaw (skwô), *n.* A female; a woman; — used with reference to North American Indians.

squawk (skwôk), *v. i.* To utter a harsh, abrupt scream, as a fowl.— *n.* Act or noise of squawking.

squeak (skwēk), *v. i.* To utter or make a squeak. — *v. t.* To cause to squeak.— *n.* A sharp, shrill, usually short, cry or sound. — **squeak'er**, *n.*

squeak'y (-ĭ), *a.* [3] Squeaking. — **-i-ly**, *adv.*

squeal (skwēl), *v. i.* To utter a squeal. — *n.* A shrill, somewhat prolonged cry. — **-er**, *n.* [8].

squeam'ish (skwēm'ĭsh), *a.* [4] Inclined to be sick at the stomach; qualmish ; hence, fastidious. — **squeam'ish-ly**, *adv.* [8] — **-ness**, *n.* [8].

squeeze (skwēz), *v. t.* [1] **1.** To exert pressure on opposite sides or parts of ; compress. **2.** To force,

gain, or procure by or as by pressure. — *v. i.* To press ; crowd. — *n.* A squeezing ; pressure. — **squeez'er** (skwēz'ẽr), *n.* [8].

squelch (skwĕlch), *v. t.* To quell or crush; discomfit; disconcert. *Colloq.*

squib (skwĭb), *n.* **1.** A paper tube or ball filled with gunpowder. **2.** A brief witty or sarcastic writing or speech ; lampoon.

squid (skwĭd), *n.* Any of numerous ten-armed sea animals related to the cuttlefishes, having a long, tapered body, and only a small internal shell.

squill (skwĭl), *n.* A plant of the lily family, the bulb of which is used in medicine; also, its bulb.

squint (skwĭnt), *a.* [3] **1.** Looking obliquely or askance. **2.** Cross-eyed. — *v. i.* **1.** To see or look obliquely or askance; also, to look or peer with eyes partly closed. **2.** To be cross-eyed. — *n.* **1.** A squinting. **2.** Strabismus.

squire (skwīr), *n.* **1.** = esquire. **2.** A male attendant on a great personage. — *v. t.* To attend as a squire.

squirm (skwûrm), *v. i.* To twist about with contortions like an eel or a worm; wriggle; writhe.

squir'rel (skwûr'ĕl; skwĭr'-), *n.* Any of various small, slender, graceful, gnawing animals, with a long bushy tail, living mostly in trees.

squirt (skwûrt), *v. t. & i.* To eject, or come forth, in a jet from a narrow orifice. — *n.* **1.** Act of squirting; also, an instrument, as a syringe, for squirting a liquid. **2.** A jet. — **-er**, *n.* [8].

stab (stăb), *v. t.; stabbed* (stăbd); *stab'bing.* To pierce with a pointed weapon ; thrust (a pointed weapon, etc.). — *v. i.* To thrust or give a wound with a pointed weapon. — *n.* A thrust of, or a wound made by, a pointed weapon. — **stab'ber**, *n.*

sta-bil'i-ty (stà-bĭl'ĭ-tĭ), *n.* State or quality of being stable.

sta'bi-lize (stā'bĭ-līz; stăb'ĭ-), *v. t.* [1] To make stable; esp., *Aëronautics,* to maintain the equilibrium of (a flying machine, etc.) by means of fixed surfaces. — **sta'bi-liz'er** (-līz'ẽr), *n.* [8].

sta'ble (stā'b'l), *n.* A building for beasts to lodge and feed in. — *v. t. & i.* [3] To lodge in a stable.

sta'ble, *a.* [3] **1.** Firmly established; not easily overthrown. **2.** Steady in purpose. **3.** Durable; abiding. — **-ness**, *n.* — **sta'bly** (-blĭ), *adv.* [8].

stac-ca'to (stà-kä'tō), *a.* [4] *Music.* Disconnected; cut short or apart by gaps of silence.

stack (stăk), *n.* **1.** A large pile of hay, grain, straw, or the like. **2.** A more or less orderly pile or heap. **3.** A number of flues in one structure, rising above the roof; any chimney. **4.** A fixed rack or set of racks for books. — *v. t.* To pile up.

sta'di-um (stā'dĭ-ŭm), *n.; L. pl.* -dia (-à). **1.** *Gr. Antiq.* A course for foot races, with tiers of seats for spectators. **2.** A similar modern structure, with its inclosure, for athletic games, etc.

staff (stàf), *n.* A plaster used for temporary ornamental buildings.

staff, *n.; pl.* in senses 1–2, staves (stāvz; stävz) or staffs (stàfs); in senses 3–4, staffs. **1.** A pole or stick. **2.** *Music.* The five horizontal lines, with their spaces, on which music is written; — called also *stave.* **3.** *Mil.* An establishment of officers having no command but administrative and executive duties. **4.** A body of assistants to a manager.

stag (stăg), *n.* The adult male of certain large deers.

stage (stāj), *n.* **1.** An elevated platform, esp. one on which an orator may speak, a play may be presented, etc. **2.** A scaffold; staging. **3.** The theater; the drama; also, theatrical profession. **4.** A place of rest on a road; a station. **5.** A stagecoach. **6.** The distance between two places of rest on a road; hence, a degree of advance in a journey or in any pursuit, process, etc. — *v. t.* [1] To exhibit on or as on a stage.

stage′coach (stāj′kōch′), *n.* A coach that runs regularly between stations.

stag′er (stāj′ẽr), *n.* One who has long acted on the stage of life ; — usually with *old.*

stag′ger (stăg′ẽr), *v. i.* To reel to one side and the other, as if about to fall; sway ; totter. — *v. t.* **1.** To cause to reel or totter. **2.** To cause to doubt, waver, or hesitate. — *n.* **1.** A reeling or tottering movement of the body. **2.** *pl.* A disease, as of horses, attended by reeling or falling. — **stag′ger-er**, *n.* [8].

stag′ing (stāj′ĭng), *n.* **1.** Scaffolding. **2.** Business of running stagecoaches; also, act of journeying in stagecoaches. **3.** Act or art of putting a play on the stage. [stagnant.]

stag′nan-cy (stăg′năn-sĭ), *n.* [1] State of being **stag′nant** (stăg′nănt), *a.* [4] **1.** Not flowing; foul from want of motion, as a pool. **2.** Not active or brisk; dull ; as, business is *stagnant.*

stag′nate (-nāt), *v. i.* [1] To be or become stagnant.

stag-na′tion (-nā′shŭn), *n.* State of being stagnant.

stag′y (stāj′ĭ), *a.* [3] Theatrical ; — used depreciatively. — **stag′i-ness** (-ĭ-nĕs), *n.* [8].

staid (stād), *pret. & p. p.* of STAY, *v. t.* Hence, *a.* [3] Sober; grave; steady ; sedate. — **staid′ly**, *adv.*

stain (stān), *v. t.* **1.** To discolor with foreign matter; foul; spot. **2.** To dye. **3.** To spot with guilt or infamy; soil; tarnish. — *v. i.* To give or receive a stain. — *n.* **1.** A discoloration, esp. by foreign matter; a spot. **2.** A dye or pigment used in staining. **3.** Taint of guilt ; also, cause of reproach; shame. — **stain′er**, *n.* [8] — **stain′less**, *a.* [8].

stair (stâr), *n.* **1.** Any step of a series for ascending or descending. **2.** A series of steps from one level to another ; — commonly in *pl.*

stair′case′ (stâr′kās′), *n.* A flight of stairs with the supporting framework, casing, balusters, etc.

stair′way′ (stâr′wā′), *n.* A staircase.

stake (stāk), *n.* **1.** A pointed piece, as of wood, driven or to be driven into the ground. **2.** A post to which a person is bound to be burned; hence, death by such burning. **3.** That which is staked, or hazarded, for gain or loss. **4.** The prize set in any contest; — often in *pl.* **5.** A property or interest involved. — *v. t.* **1.** To fasten or support with stakes. **2.** To mark the limits of by stakes; — with *out* or *off.* **3.** To wager ; venture.

sta-lac′tite (stá-lăk′tĭt), *n.* A pendent stonelike deposit in a cave, like an icicle, left by the evaporation of water containing a mineral solution.

sta-lag′mite (stá-lăg′mīt), *n.* A deposit more or less like an inverted stalactite, formed by water containing lime dropping on the floor of a cavern.

stale (stāl), *a.* [3] **1.** Vapid or tasteless from age. **2.** Not fresh. **3.** Trite; commonplace. **4.** Impaired in vigor or energy by prolonged activity.

— *v. t.* [1] To make stale or common ; destroy the charm or freshness of. — *v. i.* To become or grow stale ; wear out. — **stale′ness**, *n.* [8].

stalk (stôk), *n.* **1.** Stem, or main axis, of a plant. **2.** *Bot.* A supporting organ, as a petiole. **3.** Something like, or suggestive of, the stalk of a plant.

stalk, *v. i.* **1.** To approach game stealthily or under cover. **2.** To walk with lofty, haughty, or pompous bearing. — *v. t.* To approach, as game, under cover or by stealth. — *n.* **1.** A stately or haughty step or walk. **2.** Act or process of stalking game. — **stalk′er**, *n.* [8].

stalk′ing-horse′, *n.* **1.** A horse, or a figure like a horse, behind which a hunter stalks game. **2.** A mask ; pretense.

stall (stôl), *n.* **1.** A stable; esp., a compartment for one animal. **2.** A small booth in which business is conducted. **3.** A seat in the choir of a church. **4.** In a theater, a seat in the forward part of the orchestra. *Eng.* — *v. t.* **1.** To put or keep in a stall. **2.** To mire; stop contrary to desire. — *v. i.* To stick fast, as in mire ; stop contrary to desire.

stall′fed′ (-fĕd′), *a.* Fed or fattened in a stall or on dry fodder.

stal′lion (stăl′yŭn), *n.* A male horse not castrated.

stal′wart (stôl′wẽrt; stôl′-), *a.* *[4] Stout; strong; sturdy ; also, brave. — **-ly**, *adv.* — **-ness**, *n.* [8].

sta′men (stā′mĕn), *n.; pl.* -MENS (-mĕnz). In seed plants, that organ of the flower which gives rise to the male fertilizing cell.

stam′i-na (stăm′ĭ-ná), *n.* Staying power; endurance. [a stamen or stamens.]

stam′i-nal (-năl), *a.* Of, pert. to, or consisting of,

stam′i-nate (-nāt), *a.* *Bot.* Having or producing stamens ; esp., having stamens but no pistils.

stam′mer (-ẽr), *v. i. & t.* To speak with involuntary stops or hesitations ; stutter. — *n.* Act of stammering; defective utterance. — **-er**, *n.* [8].

stamp (stămp), *v. t.* **1.** To crush; pulverize, as ore. **2.** To strike or beat forcibly with the bottom of the foot. **3.** To bring down (the foot) forcibly and noisily. **4.** To impress or imprint with a mark; fix deeply or indelibly. **5.** To cut out, bend, or indent with a stamp, die, etc. **6.** To indicate as by a mark or stamp; mark; distinguish. **7.** To put a stamp on. — *v. i.* To strike the foot forcibly and noisily downward. — *n.* **1.** Act of stamping. **2.** That which stamps; as : **a** An instrument for making imprints, as a die. **b** A heavy pestle for crushing ores. **3.** The mark, impression, design, or the like, made by stamping. **4.** An official mark, seal, or slip of paper set on things, as to evidence the payment of a tax or dues. **5.** A distinctive nature or sign ; as, the *stamp* of genius. **6.** Make; cast; form; character. — **stamp′er**, *n.*

stam-pede′ (stăm-pēd′), *n.* A wild, headlong scamper, or running away, of a number of animals; hence, a sudden flight, or a sudden unconcerted acting together of a number, as from some common impulse. — *v. i.* [1] **1.** To run away in a panic. **2.** To act together suddenly and unconcertedly. — *v. t.* To cause to stampede.

stanch (stánch; stănch), *v. t.* To stop or check the flow of; stop the flow of blood from. — *a.* **1.** Watertight; sound; firm. **2.** Loyal;steadfast. — **stanch′ly**, *adv.* [8] — **-ness**, *n.* [8].

stan′chion (stăn′shŭn), *n.* An upright bar, post, prop, or support.

stand (stănd), *v. i.; pret. & p. p.* STOOD (stŏŏd); *p. pr. & vb. n.* STAND′ING. **1.** To take, or be at rest in, an upright position. **2.** To take or have one's stand; hence, be situated or located. **3.** To remain unchanged or unimpaired; endure; last. **4.** To assume and maintain a position, as with reference to a course of action; be fixed or steadfast. **5.** To have or maintain a relative position, order, or rank in or as in a graded scale. **6.** To be in some particular state. **7.** To be a candidate. **8.** *Naut.* To hold a course at sea; sail (in a specified direction). **9.** To measure when erect on the feet.

stand, *v. t.* **1.** To set upright; cause to stand. **2.** To endure; sustain; tolerate; bear; withstand. **3.** To submit to; suffer; abide. **4.** To be at the expense of; pay for. *Colloq.*

stand, *n.* **1.** Act of standing. **2.** A stop, esp. for defense or resistance. **3.** A place where one stands; station. **4. a** The place where a witness testifies. **b** A raised platform whence any outdoor spectacle may be viewed. **5.** A stall or booth for business. **6.** A small table; also, something on or in which anything may be placed for support. **7.** The relative number of plants growing on a given area.

stand′ard (stăn′dȧrd), *n.* **1.** An emblematic figure; loosely, a banner. **2.** That which is established as a rule for measuring or as a model or example; criterion; test. **3.** An upright support. — *a.* **1.** Being, or according with, a standard for comparison and judgment. **2.** Having a recognized value.

stand′ard‑i‑za′tion (stăn′dȧr‑dĭ‑zā′shŭn), *n.* A standardizing. [to a standard.

stand′ard‑ize (stăn′dȧr‑dīz), *v. t.* [1] To reduce

stand′ing, *p. a.* **1.** Upright or erect. **2.** Not flowing; stagnant, as water. **3.** Established by law, custom, or the like; settled. **4.** Not movable; fixed. — **standing army**, a permanent army of paid soldiers. — *n.* **1.** Act of one that stands or comes to a stand. **2.** Place to stand in; station. **3.** Condition in society; position; reputation. **4.** Maintenance of position or condition; duration.

stand′pipe (stănd′pīp′), *n.* A high vertical pipe or reservoir for water, used to produce a constant pressure in a supply system.

stand′point (‑point′), *n.* A position from which objects or principles are viewed and judged.

stand′still′ (‑stĭl′), *n.* Stop; state of rest.

stank (stăngk), *pret.* of STINK.

stan′za (stăn′zȧ), *n.; pl.* ‑ZAS. A group of verses forming a division of a poem.

sta′ple (stā′p'l), *n.* **1.** Principal commodity of traffic; chief product. **2.** A chief constituent or item. **3.** Unmanufactured or raw material. **4.** The fiber of wool, cotton, flax, etc **5.** A loop of iron or wire with two points to be driven into wood, etc., to hold a hook, pin, etc. — *a.* **1.** Established in commerce; settled. **2.** Regularly produced in large quantities.

star (stär), *n.* **1.** Any of those heavenly bodies which are visible as apparently fixed points of light; — in popular usage extended to include also the planets. **2.** In astrology, a star, esp. a planet, supposed to influence fortune; hence, destiny; fortune. **3.** A conventional figure having five or more points, representing a star. **4.** An asterisk [*]. **5.** A person of brilliant and attractive qualities; *Theat.*, the principal member of a company. — *v. t.;* STARRED (stärd); STAR′RING. **1.** To set or adorn with stars or spangles. **2.** To mark with an asterisk. — *v. i.* To be brilliant or prominent; *Theat.*, to act as a star.

star′board (stär′bōrd;‑bẽrd), *n. Naut.* The right side of a vessel (looking from the stern toward the bow). Also used adjectively. — *v. t. Naut.* To turn or put to the starboard side of a vessel; — used mainly of the helm.

starch (stärch), *n.* **1.** A well-known white, tasteless carbohydrate. **2.** A paste made of starch (def. 1), for stiffening linen. **3.** A stiff, formal manner; stiffness. — *v. t.* To stiffen with starch.

starch′y (stär′chĭ), *a.* [3] Consisting of or resembling starch; hence, stiff; precise.

stare (stâr), *v. i.* [1] **1.** To gaze fixedly, as through wonder, impudence, etc. **2.** To be conspicuous. — *v. t.* To gaze at. — *n.* Act of staring; a fixed look, as suggesting wonder, impudence, etc. —

star′er (stâr′ẽr), *n.* [8].

star′fish (stär′fĭsh′), *n.* (See PLURAL, *n.*) Any of numerous marine animals having a body of radially disposed arms or rays, usually five in number.

stark (stärk), *a.* [3] **1.** Stiff; rigid; as, *stark* in death. **2.** Sheer; utter; as, *stark* folly. — *adv.* Wholly; quite; as, *stark* mad.— **stark′ly**, *adv.* [8].

star′less (stär′lĕs), *a.* Without stars.

star′light (‑līt′), *n.* The light given by the stars. — *a.* Lighted by the stars, or by the stars only.

star′ling (‑lĭng), *n.* A bird of dark brown (in summer, greenish black) plumage, spotted with yellowish white.

star′lit (stär′lĭt′), *a.* Starlight.

starred (stärd), *p. a.* **1.** Adorned with stars. **2.** Affected in fortune by the stars. *Obs.* exc. in comp.; as, ill*-starred*. **3.** Marked with an asterisk.

star′ry (stär′ĭ), *a.* [3] **1.** Of or pert. to the stars. **2.** Consisting of, or proceeding from, the stars; stellar. **3.** Shining like stars; sparkling.

start (stärt), *v. i.* **1.** To move suddenly and quickly; dart; spring. **2.** To give an involuntary twitch or spring, as in sudden surprise, pain, joy, etc. **3.** To set out; begin. **4.** To become somewhat displaced or loosened. — *v. t.* **1.** To cause to start; rouse. **2.** To cause to move or act; set going. **3.** To displace or loosen; dislocate. **4.** To tap and begin drawing from; as, to *start* a cask. — *n.* **1.** Act of starting; sudden involuntary motion, as from surprise, fear, etc. **2.** A spasmodic and brief effort or action. **3.** A sudden, capricious impulse; a sudden leap or dash. **4.** The beginning, as of a journey or a course of action. **5.** A lead at the beginning of a competition. — **start′er**, *n.* [8].

star′tle (stär′t'l), *v. i.* [1] To move suddenly as in surprise, fear, alarm, etc. — *v. t.* To excite by sudden alarm, surprise, etc.; frighten suddenly. — **star′tler**, *n.* [8].

star‑va′tion (stär‑vā′shŭn), *n.* Act of starving; state of being starved.

starve (stärv), *v. i.* [1] To perish with or as with

hunger ; suffer extreme hunger. — *v. t.* To kill with hunger ; to distress or subdue by famine.

starve'ling (stärv'lĭng), *n.* One that pines or is thin from lack of nutriment. — *a.* [4] Starving.

state (stāt), *n.* **1.** Mode or condition of being ; condition. **2.** Condition as to wealth, social position, etc.; standing ; rank ; status. **3.** Condition of living ; esp., elaborate style ; hence, formal dignity, pomp, etc. **4.** A body of people occupying a definite territory and politically organized under one government. **5.** [*Often cap.*] Any of a number of commonwealths, or bodies politic, constituting a sovereign state (in sense 4) by federation, as in the United States. **6.** The territory or the government of a state (in sense 4 or 5). — *v. t.* [1] **1.** To set ; fix ; as, to *state* a time. **2.** To tell ; recite ; narrate ; as, to *state* one's opinion.

state'craft' (stāt'kráft'), *n.* State management.

state'house' (-hous'), *n.*, or **state house.** The building in which a State legislature sits. *U. S.*

state'ly (-lĭ), *a.* [3] Evincing state, or lofty dignity. — **state'ly**, *adv.* — **-li-ness** (-lĭ-něs), *n.*

state'ment (-měnt), *n.* **1.** Act of stating. **2.** That which is stated ; narrative ; abstract of an account.

state'room' (stāt'rōōm'), *n.* An individual apartment on a vessel or a railroad car.

states'man (stāts'măn), *n. ; pl.* -MEN (-měn). A man who shows unusual wisdom in treating great public matters.

states'man-like, *a.* [4] Befitting a statesman.

states'man-ly, *a.* [4] Statesmanlike.

states'man-ship, *n.* Qualifications or skill of a statesman.

stat'ic (stăt'ĭk) } *a.* **1.** Acting by mere weight
stat'i-cal (-ĭ-kǎl) } without motion. **2.** Pertaining to bodies at rest. — **-ly,** *adv.* [8].

stat'ics (stăt'ĭks), *n.* Mechanics treating of the equilibrium of forces.

sta'tion (stā'shŭn). *n.* **1.** Place where anything stands ; place where a force is assembled, as in readiness for duty. **2.** A regular stopping place, as on a railroad. **3.** Situation ; position ; location. **4.** Social standing ; rank. — *v. t.* To appoint or assign ; place ; set.

sta'tion-a-ry (stā'shŭn-ā-rĭ), *a.* **1.** Fixed ; not moving ; stable ; as, a *stationary* engine. **2.** Not changing state or condition.

sta'tion-er (-ẽr), *n.* One who sells writing materials.

sta'tion-er-y (-ẽr-ĭ), *n.* Writing materials.

sta-tis'ti-cal (stă-tĭs'tĭ-kǎl), *a.* [4] Of or pertaining to statistics. — **sta-tis'ti-cal-ly,** *adv.* [8].

stat'is-ti'cian (stăt'ĭs-tĭsh'ăn), *n.* One versed in, or engaged in compiling, statistics.

sta-tis'tics (stă-tĭs'tĭks), *n.* **1.** (*sing.*) Systematic compilation of facts or instances for general inferences. **2.** (*pl.*) Classified facts, esp. those facts which can be stated in numbers.

stat'u-a-ry (stăt'ū-ā-rĭ), *n. ; pl.* -ARIES (-rĭz). **1.** One who makes statues. **2.** Art of making statues. **3.** Statues collectively.

stat'ue (stăt'ū), *n.* The sculptured or modeled likeness of a living being, in the full form on all sides, as in marble or bronze.

stat'u-esque' (-ěsk'), *a.* [4] Resembling a statue, as in massive or formal dignity. — **-ly,** *adv.* [8].

stat'u-ette' (-ět'), *n.* A small statue.

stat'ure (stăt'ūr), *n.* Natural height of an animal, esp. man.

sta'tus (stā'tŭs), *n.* **1.** The condition of a person in relation to others, as fixed by law. **2.** State or rank of a person. **3.** Position of affairs.

stat'ute (stăt'ūt), *n.* Something laid down or declared as fixed or established, esp. as a rule or law ; esp., a law enacted by a legislature ; an act.

stat'u-to-ry (stăt'ū-tō-rĭ), *a.* Enacted, constituted, or imposed, by statute.

staunch (stänch). Var. of STANCH.

stave (stāv), *n.* **1.** A stick ; cudgel ; staff. **2.** Any of a number of strips forming the sides, covering, or lining of something, as a cask. **3. a** A metrical portion ; stanza ; staff. **b** *Music.* = STAFF, 2. — *v. t. ; pret. & p. p.* STAVED (stāvd) or STOVE (stōv); *p. pr. & vb. n.* STAV'ING (stāv'ĭng). **1.** To break in a stave or the staves of ; break a hole in. **2.** To furnish with staves. **3.** To keep at a distance ; drive away ; — usually with *off.*

staves (stāvs), *n., pl.* of STAFF (see STAVE), STAVE.

stay (stā), *n.* **1.** A rope, now usually of wire, supporting a mast. **2.** A guy rope or the like.

stay (stā), *v. t. ; pret. & p. p.* STAYED (stād) or STAID (stād) ; *p. pr. & vb. n.* STAY'ING. **1.** To prop ; support. **2.** To satisfy for a time, as the stomach by food ; sustain. **3.** To stop ; check ; also, to hinder ; postpone. **4.** To fasten with stays, as a mast. — *v. i.* **1.** To cease from action or motion ; delay ; remain. **2.** To stand still ; not to retreat. — *n.* **1.** A support. **2.** *pl.* A corset. **3.** A hindrance. **4.** A halt ; stand ; stop. **5.** Continuance in a place ; sojourn. — **-er,** *n.* [8].

stay'sail' (stā'sāl' / *naut.* stā's'l), *n.* Any sail on a stay, as the triangular sails set between masts.

stead (stěd), *n.* **1.** Advantage ; service ; avail. **2.** Place or room which another had, has, or might have. Cf. INSTEAD.

stead'fast (stěd'fást), *a.* **1.** Firmly fixed or established. **2.** Constant ; unswerving. — **stead'fast-ly,** *adv.* [8] — **-ness,** *n.* [8].

stead'i-ly (-ĭ-lĭ), *adv.* In a steady manner.

stead'i-ness (-něs), *n.* Quality of being steady.

stead'y (-ĭ), *a.* [3] **1.** Firm in position ; fixed. **2.** Constant ; not fickle or wavering. **3.** Of a vessel, keeping nearly upright in a seaway. **4.** Sober. *Colloq.* — *v. t. & i.* [2] To make, or become, steady. [broiling, etc.]

steak (stāk), *n.* A slice of meat, esp. of beef, for

steal (stēl), *v. t. ; pret.* STOLE (stōl) ; *p. p.* STO'LEN (stō'l'n) ; *p. pr. & vb. n.* STEAL'ING. **1.** To take feloniously ; take without right and with intent to keep wrongfully. **2.** To appropriate to one's self furtively. **3.** To move stealthily. **4.** To accomplish in a concealed or unobserved manner. — *v. i.* **1.** To commit theft. **2.** To move furtively. — *n.* An act of stealing. — **steal'er** (-ẽr), *n.* [8].

stealth (stělth), *n.* Secret procedure or action.

stealth'y (stěl'thĭ), *a.* [3] Acting or done by stealth ; furtive ; sly. — **stealth'i-ly** (-thĭ-lĭ), *adv.* [8] — **stealth'i-ness,** *n.* [8].

steam (stēm), *n.* **1.** The invisible vapor of boiling water. **2.** The mist formed by condensation of water vapor. — *v. i.* **1.** To emit steam. **2.** To rise or pass off as vapor. **3.** To move by the agency of steam. — *v. t.* To expose to steam.

āle, senāte, câre, ăm, *ă*ccount, ärm, ȧsk, sofȧ ; ēve, ĕvent, ĕnd, recĕnt, makẽr ; īce, ĭll ; ōld, ŏbey, ôrb, ŏdd, sŏft, cŏnnect ; ūse, ûnite, ûrn, ŭp, circŭs ; fōōd, fŏŏt ; out, oil ;

steam'boat' (-bōt'), *n.* A boat propelled by steam.

steam engine. An engine worked by steam.

steam'er (stēm'ẽr), *n.* **1.** Any of various machines driven by steam, as a steamboat. **2.** A vessel in which articles are subjected to steam.

steam'ship' (-shǐp'), *n.* A ship propelled by steam.

steam'y (stēm'ǐ), *a.* [3] Consisting of or resembling steam; full of steam; vaporous; misty.

ste'a-tite (stē'ȧ-tīt), *n.* A massive variety of talc.

sted'fast, -ly, etc. Vars. of STEADFAST, etc.

steed (stēd), *n.* A horse; esp., a spirited horse.

steel (stēl), *n.* **1.** A variety of iron combined with a small portion of carbon and intermediate between cast iron and wrought iron, very tough and, when tempered, hard and elastic; now, also, ingot iron, or nearly pure iron made by fusion processes. **2.** An instrument or implement of steel. — *v. t.* **1.** To overlay, point, or edge, with steel. **2.** To make hard or strong, insensible or obdurate.

steel'y (stēl'ǐ), *a.* [3] **1.** Made of or consisting of steel. **2.** Resembling steel, as in hardness, color, etc.

steel'yard (-yärd, *colloq.* stǐl'yẽrd), *n.* A form of lever balance for weighing a body suspended from the shorter arm, the longer arm being graduated for the counterpoise; — often in *pl.*

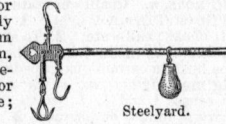
Steelyard.

steep (stēp), *v. t.* To soak; esp., to extract the essence of by soaking, as in water below the boiling point; fig., to imbue with. — *v. i.* To be steeped.

steep, *a.* [3] Having a side or slope departing widely from the horizontal; precipitous. — *n.* A precipitous place.

stee'ple (stē'p'l), *n.* A tall structure, usually topped with a spire, surmounting a church roof.

stee'ple-chase' (-chās'), *n.* A race across country between horsemen; hence, a race over a prescribed course obstructed by hedges, walls, etc.

steep'ly, *adv.* In a steep manner.

steep'ness, *n.* Quality of being steep.

steer (stēr), *n.* A young castrated male of the ox kind, or, in the western U. S., one of any age.

steer, *v. t.* To direct the course of; guide; direct. — *v. i.* **1.** To direct a vessel in its course. **2.** To take a direction; obey the helm.

steer'age (stēr'ăj), *n.* **1.** Act of steering. **2.** *a* Effect of the helm on a ship. *b* The part of a vessel occupied by passengers paying the smallest fare.

steer'age-way' (-wā'), *n. Naut.* A rate of motion sufficient to make a vessel answer the helm.

steers'man (stērz'măn), *n.; pl.* -MEN (-měn). One who steers; helmsman.

stel'lar (stěl'ȧr), *a.* Pert. to stars; astral; starry.

stel'late (stěl'āt) } *a.* Pointed or radiated like a

stel'lat-ed (-āt-ĕd) } star.

stem (stěm), *n.* **1.** The main axis or trunk of a tree or other plant; stalk; stock. **2.** Something like, or suggestive of, the stem of a plant. **3.** The piece to which the sides of a ship or boat are secured in the bow; the prow. **4.** That part of an inflected word not changed by inflection. — *v. t.; STEMMED (stěmd); STEM'MING.* To remove the stem or stems from.

stem, *v. t.* **1.** To stop; dam up; as, to *stem* a river. **2.** Of a vessel, to make headway against.

stench (stěnch), *n.* A stink.

sten'cil (stěn'sǐl), *n.* A thin sheet, as of metal, so perforated that when it is laid on a surface and color is applied, a certain figure is made. — *v. t.* [7] To mark or paint with a stencil.

sten'o-graph (-ȯ-grȧf), *n.* A production of stenography. — *v. t.* To write or report by stenography.

ste-nog'ra-pher (stē-nŏg'rȧ-fēr), **ste-nog'ra-phist** (-fĭst), *n.* A writer of shorthand.

sten'o-graph'ic (stěn'ȯ-grăf'ĭk), **-i-cal,** *a.* Of, pert. to, or using, stenography. — **-i-cal-ly,** *adv.*

ste-nog'ra-phy (stē-nŏg'rȧ-fĭ), *n.* Art of writing in shorthand, by using abbreviations or characters for whole words; shorthand. [loud.|

sten-to'ri-an (stěn-tō'rĭ-ăn), *a.* [4] Extremely|

step (stěp), *v. i.; STEPPED (stěpt); STEP'PING.* **1.** To move the feet as in walking. **2.** To go on foot; walk, esp. a short distance. **3.** To walk slowly, gravely, or resolutely. — *v. t.* **1.** To set or place, as the foot. **2.** *Naut.* To fix the foot of in its step and so erect (a mast). **3.** To measure (a distance) by stepping. — *n.* **1.** A movement made by one removal of the foot; a pace; hence, in *pl.*, progress by or as by stepping. **2.** A rest for the foot in ascending or descending, as a stair; a degree. **3.** Space passed over by one movement of the foot in walking or running. **4.** A footstep; footprint. **5.** Gait; manner of walking; also, footfall. **6.** Proceeding; measure; action; an act. **7.** *Music.* **a** A degree (line or space) of the scale or staff. **b** Any interval between two contiguous degrees of the scale or staff. **8.** *Naut.* A frame, block, or platform supporting the bottom of a mast.

step'broth'er (stěp'brŭth'ẽr), *n.* Son of one's step-parent by a former marriage.

step'child' (-chīld'), *n.* Child of one's wife or husband by a former marriage.

step'daugh'ter (-dô'tēr), *n.* Daughter of one's wife or husband by a former marriage.

step'fa'ther (-fä'thẽr), *n.* Husband of one's mother by a subsequent marriage.

step'lad'der (stěp'lăd'ēr), *n.* A portable set of steps, usually with a hinged back frame.

step'moth'er (-mŭth'ẽr), *n.* The wife of one's father by a subsequent marriage. [mother.|

step'-par'ent (-pâr'ĕnt), *n.* A stepfather or step-|

steppe (stěp), *n.* One of the vast tracts in southeastern Europe or in Asia, level and without forests.

step'ping-stone', *n.* **1.** A stone projecting above water or mud, on which to step in walking. **2.** A means of progress or advancement.

step'sis'ter (-sǐs'tẽr), *n.* A daughter of one's step-parent by a former marriage.

step'son' (-sŭn'), *n.* A son of one's husband or wife by a former marriage.

stere (stēr), *n.* A cubic meter.

ster'e-op'ti-con (stēr'ē-ŏp'tĭ-kŏn; stē'rē-), *n.* A lantern for projecting pictures, as photographs, upon a screen by means of an intense light.

ster'e-o-scope' (stěr'ē-ȯ-skōp'; stē'rē-), *n.* An optical instrument with two eyeglasses producing the effect of solidity or relief by combining the images of two pictures taken from points a little way apart. — **ster'e-o-scop'ic** (-skŏp'ĭk), *a.*

ster'e-o-type' (stĕr'ė-ō-tīp ; stē'rĕ-), n. A plate made by taking a mold of a printing surface and making from this a cast in type metal. — v. t. [1] **1.** To make stereotype plates of. **2.** To fix in lasting, esp. conventional, form. — **-typ'er,** n.

ster'e-o-typ'y (stĕr'ė-ō-tīp'ĭ ; stē'rĕ- ; -ŏt'ĭ-pĭ), n. Art or process of making stereotype plates.

ster'ile (stĕr'ĭl), a. [4] **1.** Producing little or no crop; barren; as, *sterile* land. **2.** Incapable of reproduction; as, a *sterile* plant or seed. **3.** Free from disease germs; as, a *sterile* instrument.

ste-ril'i-ty (stė-rĭl'ĭ-tĭ), n. State of being sterile.

ster'i-li-za'tion (stĕr'ĭ-lĭ-zā'shŭn), n. A sterilizing; also, state of being sterile.

ster'i-lize (stĕr'ĭ-lĭz), v. t. [1] To make sterile (esp. in sense 3). — **ster'i-liz'er** (-līz'ẽr), n. [8].

ster'ling (stûr'lĭng), n. Standard of fineness of lawful British coin. — a. **1.** Pert. to the standard British money. **2.** Of full value ; genuine.

stern (stûrn), a. [3] **1.** Having a certain hardness or severity of nature or aspect; severe; grim; austere. **2.** Proceeding from, or characteristic of, such a nature or aspect. **3.** Stout; resolute; firm; unyielding. — **stern'ly,** adv. — **stern'ness,** n.

stern, n. The after end of a ship or boat.

ster'nal (stûr'năl), a. Of or pert. to the sternum.

ster'num (stûr'nŭm), n.; pl. L. -NA (-nȧ), E. -NUMS (-nŭmz). Anat. A flat narrow bone situated in the middle of the front of the chest. Seven pairs of ribs and the collar bones are connected with it.

stern'way' (stûrn'wā'), n. Movement of a ship backward.

ster'to-rous (stûr'tō-rŭs), a. Characterized by a deep snoring, as in apoplexy; hence, hoarsely breathing. — **ster'to-rous-ly,** adv.

steth'o-scope (stĕth'ō-skōp), n. Med. An instrument applied esp. to the chest, to convey to the ear sounds produced in the body.

ste've-dore' (stē'vĕ-dōr'), n. One whose occupation is to load and unload vessels in port.

stew (stū), v. t. & i. **1.** To boil slowly ; seethe. **2.** To worry. Colloq. — n. **1.** A dish prepared by stewing. **2.** Worry. Colloq.

stew'ard (stū'ẽrd), n. **1.** One who directs affairs; manager, as of an estate. **2.** One who supervises the provision and distribution of food, as in a club; esp., on a ship, one who superintends the culinary affairs,etc.; also,a waiter or a caretaker of the state-rooms. **3.** A fiscal agent. — **-ess,** n. fem. [8].

stew'ard-ship, n. Office or functions of a steward.

stew'pan' (stū'păn'), n. A pan for stewing.

stick (stĭk), n. **1.** A shoot taken from a tree or shrub. **2.** A stem or branch of a tree taken for fuel or timber. **3.** Any long and relatively slender piece of wood. **4.** Something long and slender. **5.** Adhesive tendency.

stick, v. t.; pret. & p. p. STUCK(stŭk); p. pr. & vb. n. STICK'ING. **1.** To pierce with a pointed implement; stab ; kill by piercing. **2.** To cause to penetrate. **3.** To push; thrust; poke. **4.** To fasten by thrusting in. **5.** To set with something pointed. **6.** To fix on a pointed implement; impale. **7.** To attach by causing to adhere ; in general, to place.

stick, v. i. **1.** To adhere. **2.** To hold fast; cling. **3.** To be fixed by or as by piercing. **4.** To be thrust or put; protrude ; — commonly with up, out,

through, etc. **5.** To be prevented from going farther. **6.** To hesitate ; scruple.— **stick'er,** n. [8].

stick'i-ness (-ĭ-nĕs), n. Sticky quality or state.

sticking plaster. An adhesive plaster for closing wounds, etc.

stick'le (stĭk'l), v. i. [1] **1.** To contend pertinaciously on insufficient grounds. **2.** To hesitate.

stick'le-back' (-băk'), n. Any of numerous small, scaleless, nest-building fishes having two or more free dorsal spines.

stick'ler (-lẽr), n. One who stickles, or obstinately contends, esp. for some trifling thing.

stick'y (-ĭ), a. [3] Adhesive ; gluey. — **-i-ly,** adv.

stiff (stĭf), a. [3] **1.** Not easily bent; rigid; firm. **2.** Not liquid; thick and tenacious. **3.** Tense; taut. **4.** Not moving with ease; not limber. **5.** Not natural and easy; constrained. **6.** Of a breeze, current, or the like, having force not easily opposed; strong. **7.** Strong ; — of a beverage. **8.** Difficult.

stiff'en (stĭf'n), v. t. & i. To make or become stiff or stiffer.

stiff'ly, adv. In a stiff manner.

stiff'ness, n. Quality or state of being stiff.

sti'fle (stī'f'l), v. t. & i. [1] **1.** To stop the breath of; choke ; suffocate. **2.** To stop; extinguish.

sti'fle, n., or **stifle joint.** The joint next above the hock in certain quadrupeds, esp. horses.

stig'ma (stĭg'mȧ), n.; pl. E. -MAS (-mȧz), chiefly in senses 1 and 4; L. -MATA (-mȧ-tȧ). **1.** Any mark of infamy or disgrace. **2.** Med. A red speck on the skin. **3.** A mark or sign of defect, taint, etc. **4.** Bot. That part of the pistil which receives the pollen grains, and on which they germinate.

stig-mat'ic (stĭg-măt'ĭk), a. [4] Of the nature of, or marked with, a stigma or stigmata.

stig'ma-ti-za'tion (stĭg'mȧ-tĭ-zā'shŭn), n. A stigmatizing, or state of being stigmatized.

stig'ma-tize (stĭg'mȧ-tīz), v. t. [1] To set a mark of disgrace on; describe opprobriously.

stile (stīl), n. A step, or set of steps, for passing a fence or wall; also, a turnstile.

sti-let'to (stĭ-lĕt'ō), n.; pl. -TOS (-ōz). **1.** A kind of dagger. **2.** Instrument for making eyelet holes.

still (stĭl), a. [3] **1.** Motionless; quiet. **2.** Not disturbed; calm. **3.** Silent; hushed. **4.** Comparatively quiet or silent; soft; low. **5.** Not sparkling or effervescent; — of wines. — adv. **1.** Always; constantly. **2. a** To this or that time. **b** In the future as now and before. **c** After that. **3.** In an increasing or additional degree ; even more. **4.** Notwithstanding ; nevertheless. — v. t. **1.** To stop, as physical motion or agitation. **2.** To appease; calm ; quiet; allay. **3.** To silence. — **still'y** (stĭl'lĭ), adv.

still, n. **1.** A vessel or apparatus for distilling liquids, esp. alcoholic liquors ; a retort. **2.** A distillery. — v. t. To expel spirit from by heat; distill.

still'born' (-bôrn'), a. Dead at the birth.

still'ness (stĭl'nĕs), n. Quiet; silence.

still'y (stĭl'ĭ), a. Still; calm. Rare.

stilt (stĭlt), n. One of two poles with a support to raise the foot above the ground in walking.

Stilts.

stilt′ed, *p. a.* [4] Elevated as if on stilts; hence, pompous; also, stiffly formal. — **-ness**, *n.* [8].

stim′u-lant (stĭm′ū-lănt), *a.* Serving to stimulate; esp., producing increased vital action. — *n.* That which stimulates: esp., an alcoholic drink.

stim′u-late (stĭm′ū-lāt), *v. t.* [1] **1.** To excite as with a goad; rouse; spur on. **2.** To excite the activity of (a nerve or a muscle), as by electricity. **3.** To arouse by an intoxicating, esp. an alcoholic, beverage. — *v. i.* To act as a stimulant or stimulus. — **stim′u-la′tor** (-lā′tẽr), *n.* [8].

stim′u-la′tion (-lā′shŭn), *n.* A stimulating, or state of being stimulated; quickened activity.

stim′u-la-tive (stĭm′ū-lā-tĭv), *a.* [4] Able or tending to stimulate. — *n.* That which stimulates.

stim′u-lus (-lŭs), *n.; L. pl.* -LI (-lī). **1.** A goad. **2.** Something that rouses the mind or spirits; an incentive. **3.** That which excites a temporary increase of vital action, as of a nerve or muscle.

sting (stĭng), *v. t.; pret. & p. p.* STUNG (stŭng); *p. pr. & vb. n.* STING′ING (stĭng′ĭng). **1.** To prick painfully; as: **a** To wound with a poisonous sting; as, bees *stung* him. **b** To affect with sharp quick pain or smart. **2.** To incite as with a sting. — *v. i.* **1.** To use, or wound with, a sting. **2.** To give a keen burning pain or smart; — also fig.; as, his conscience *stung*. — *n.* **1.** *Zoöl.* Any of various sharp organs of offense and defense, esp. when connected with a poison gland. **2.** *Bot.* A stinging hair, as of a nettle. **3.** Act of stinging; also, a wound or pain caused by a sting. — **sting′er**, *n.*

stin′gi-ly (stĭn′jĭ-lĭ), *adv.* In a stingy manner.

stin′gi-ness, *n.* Stingy quality or state.

sting′y (stĭng′ĭ), *a.* [3] Stinging; able to sting.

stin′gy (stĭn′jĭ), *a.* [3] **1.** Meanly avaricious; miserly. **2.** Scanty; as, a *stingy* crop.

stink (stĭngk), *v. i.; pret.* STANK (stăngk), STUNK (stŭngk); *p. p.* STUNK; *p. pr. & vb. n.* STINK′ING. To emit a disgusting odor. — *n.* A disgusting odor; stench.

stint (stĭnt), *v. t.* To limit; restrict to a scant allowance. — *v. i.* To be sparing or frugal. — *n.* **1.** Restraint; limitation; also, limit; bound. **2.** Quantity or task assigned; as, a daily *stint*.

stipe (stīp), *n. Bot.* A short stalk or support, as a mushroom stem or fern-leaf petiole.

sti′pend (stī′pĕnd), *n.* Settled pay for services.

sti-pen′di-a-ry (stī-pĕn′dĭ-ă-rĭ), *a.* Receiving pay. — *n.; pl.* -RIES (-rĭz). One who receives a stipend.

stip′u-late (stĭp′ū-lāt), *a.* Furnished with stipules.

stip′u-late (-lāt), *v. i.* [1] To agree to do or forbear anything; bargain; contract. — *v. t.* To arrange definitely; specify (something).

stip′u-la′tion (-lā′shŭn), *n.* A stipulating; an agreement; also, that which is stipulated.

stip′u-la′tor (stĭp′ū-lā′tẽr), *n.* One who stipulates.

stip′ule (-ūl), *n.* One of the pair of appendages at the base of the leaf in many plants.

a Stipule of Common Pea.

stir (stûr), *v. t.; stirred* (stûrd); STIR′RING. **1.** To change the place of; move. **2.** To disturb the relative position of the constituent particles of, as a liquid, by moving something about in it. **3.** To rouse; excite or incite; stimulate. — *v. i.* **1.** To move. **2.** To be in motion; to be active. **3.** To be stirred. — *n.* Act or result of stirring; agitation; activity. — **stir′rer** (-ẽr), *n.* [8].

stir′ring (stûr′ĭng), *p. a.* [4] **1.** Active; lively. **2.** Rousing; inspiring; as, a *stirring* song.

stir′rup (stĭr′ŭp; stûr′ŭp), *n.* A kind of ring attached to a saddle, to support a rider's foot.

stitch (stĭch), *n.* **1.** A local, sharp and sudden pain, esp. in the back or side. **2. a** In sewing, a single pass of a needle, or the loop so made. **b** A single turn of the thread round the needle in knitting, etc.; a link, or loop, of yarn. **c** A particular arrangement of stitches or method of stitching. **3.** Any least part of a fabric or dress. *Colloq.* — *v. t.* **1.** To form stitches in. **2.** To unite by stitches. — *v. i.* To practice stitching; sew. — **stitch′er** (stĭch′ẽr), *n.* [8].

stith′y (stĭth′ĭ; stĭth′ĭ), *n.; pl.* STITHIES (-ĭz). A smithy; a forge.

sti′ver (stī′vẽr), *n.* A Dutch coin of small value (now about 2 cents); hence, a trifle.

stoat (stōt), *n.* The European ermine, esp. in the brown summer coat; also, any ermine or weasel.

stock (stŏk), *n.* **1.** A wooden post; stump; block of wood. **2.** The part in which other parts are inserted, or to which they are attached; as, a gun-*stock*. **3.** Stalk or trunk of a plant. **4.** The stem or plant in which a graft is inserted; also, any plant from which cuttings are taken. **5. a** Original progenitor. **b** Line of descent; lineage; family. **6.** *pl.* A frame with holes for confining the feet, or the feet and hands, of offenders. **7.** *pl.* The frame on which a ship rests while building. **8.** A debt or fund due to individuals for money loaned. **9.** The capital of a company or corporation in transferable shares. **10. a** The capital employed in a business. **b** A merchant's or manufacturer's store of goods; hence, store; supply. **11.** Raw material; as, paper *stock*. **12.** A liquid or jelly containing juices, etc., extracted by cooking, used in making soup, gravy, etc. **13.** Domestic animals collectively; — called also *live stock.* **14.** A close-fitting wide band or cravat for the neck. **15.** Any of various fragrant-flowered garden plants with woody stem. — *v. t.* **1.** To lay up; store; as, to *stock* grain. **2.** To provide with stock or requisites. — *a.* Used for constant service; kept in stock; as, a *stock* sermon. — *v. i.* To put in stock, or supplies; — often with *up.*

stock-ade′ (stŏk-ād′), *n.* **1.** *Mil.* A line of stout posts or timbers forming a barrier. **2.** An inclosure made with posts and stakes. — *v. t.* [1] To surround, fortify, or protect, with a stockade.

stock′bro′ker (stŏk′brō′kẽr), *n.* A broker who deals in stocks. — **stock′bro′king** (-kĭng), *n.*

stock company. *Commerce.* A corporation the capital of which is represented by stock (sense 9).

stock exchange. a An exchange for the sale and purchase of stocks, bonds, etc. **b** An association of stockbrokers who meet and transact business by recognized forms, regulations, and usages.

---

stock′hold′er (stŏk′hōl′dẽr), *n.* One who is a holder or proprietor of stock or stocks.

stock′i-ness, *n.* Stocky quality or state.

stock′i-net′ (-ĭ-nĕt′), *n.* An elastic textile fabric, used for stockings, undergarments, etc.

stock′ing (stŏk′ĭng), *n.* A close-fitting covering for the foot and leg, usually knit or woven.

stock′job′ber(-jŏb′ẽr),*n.* One who deals in stocks.

stock′job′bing, *n.* The business of a stockjobber.

stock′man (stŏk′măn), *n.; pl.* -MEN (-mĕn). One owning, or in charge of, live stock; a ranchman.

stock′-still′, *a.* Still as a stock, or post.

stock′y (stŏk′ĭ), *a.* [3] Short and thick.

stock′yard′ (-yärd′), *n.* A yard for live stock; esp., an inclosure with stables, pens, sheds, etc.

stodg′y (stŏj′ĭ), *a.* [3] Thick; heavy; lumpish.

sto′gy (stō′gĭ), *n.; pl.* -GIES (-gĭz). **1.** A brogan. **2.** A cheap cigar of cylindrical form.

sto′ic (stō′ĭk), *n.* One apparently indifferent to pleasure or pain.

sto′ic (stō′ĭk) *a.* [4] Showing indifference to
sto′i-cal (-ĭ-kăl) pain or pleasure; impassive. — **sto′i-cal-ly,** *adv.* [8] — **-ness,** *n.* [8].

sto′i-cism (stō′ĭ-sĭz′m), *n.* Indifference to pain or pleasure; impassiveness.

stoke (stōk), *v. t.* [1] To poke, as a fire; tend, as a fire or furnace; supply with fuel. — *v. i.* To stoke a fire or furnace.—**stok′er** (stōk′ẽr), *n.* [8].

stoke′hold′ (-hōld′), *n.* Space in front of a boiler of a ship from which the furnaces are fed; also, a boiler room. — **stoke′hole′,** *n.*

stole (stōl), *n.* **1.** A loose garment reaching to the feet. **2.** A long narrow band, esp. of silk, worn over the shoulders by bishops and priests.

stole, *pret.,* **sto′len** (stō′l′n), *p. p.,* of STEAL.

stol′id (stŏl′ĭd), *a.* [3] Having or expressing little or no sensibility; impassive. — **stol′id-ly,** *adv.* [8] — **stol′id-ness,** *n.* [8].

sto-lid′i-ty (stō-lĭd′ĭ-tĭ),*n.* Stolid quality or state.

stom′ach (stŭm′ŭk), *n.* **1.** In man and animals, the cavity or pouch within the body into which the food goes after it is swallowed and in which most of the earlier stages of digestion take place. **2.** The abdomen. **3.** Appetite; desire. —*v.t.* To bear without disgust; put up with.

stom′ach-er (-ŭk-ẽr; -á-chẽr), *n.* An ornamental covering for the breast.

sto-mach′ic (stō-măk′ĭk), *a.* **1.** Pertaining to the stomach. **2.** Strengthening to the stomach.

stone (stōn), *n.* **1.** Hard, compact mineral substance other than metal: **a** A small piece of rock or one of moderate size. **b** Rock as a material, esp. for building. **2.** A gem. **3. a** A small hard mass such as sometimes forms in the kidneys, bladder, or gall bladder. **b** The hard covering of the kernel in a drupe or any hard, stone-like seed; as, a peach *stone*. **4.** A unit of weight, now legally 14 pounds in Great Britain. — *v. t.* [1] **1.** To pelt or kill with stones. **2.** To remove the stones or seeds of. — *a.* Made of stone or stoneware.

stone′-blind′, *a.* As blind as a stone.

stone fruit. A drupe.

stone′ware′ (-wâr′), *n.* A species of coarse potter's ware, glazed and baked.

stone′work′ (-wûrk′), *n.* Work made of stone.

ston′y (stōn′ĭ), *a.* [3] **1.** Abounding in stone or

stones. **2.** Pert. to, or characteristic of, stone; inflexible; pitiless; cold; as, a *stony* heart. — **ston′i-ly** (-ĭ-lĭ), *adv.* [8] — **ston′i-ness,** *n.* [8].

stood (stŏŏd), *pret. & p. p.* of STAND.

stool (stōōl), *n.* A stock or parent plant; esp., the stump or root which throws out shoots. — *v. i.* To form a stool; to tiller, as grain.

stool, *n.* **1.** A single seat without a back. **2.** Evacuation of the bowels. **3.** A pole or the like to which a bird, as a pigeon, is fastened as a decoy.

stool pigeon. 1. A pigeon used to decoy others. **2.** A person used as a decoy; police spy.

stoop (stōōp), *v. i.* **1.** To bend or lean forward and downward. **2.** To condescend. **3.** To yield; submit.— *v. t.* To bend (as the body) forward and downward. — *n.* **1.** A habitual forward bend of the back and shoulders. **2.** Condescension.

stoop (stōōp), *n.* A porch, platform, or small veranda, at a house door. *U. S.*

stop (stŏp), *v. t.; pret. & p. p.* STOPPED (stŏpt), STOPT (*Chiefly Poetic*); *p. pr. & vb. n.* STOP′PING. **1.** To close, as an aperture, by filling or obstructing; hence, to stanch (a wound). **2.** To obstruct; render impassable. **3.** To arrest the progress or motion of; cause to cease; suppress. — *v. i.* **1.** To cease to go on; halt. **2.** To stay; tarry. *Colloq.* — *n.* **1.** Act of stopping; state of being stopped. **2.** That which stops. **3.** *Music.* **a** A contrivance for regulating the pitch of an instrument. **b** A graduated set of organ pipes or reeds of like kind and tone quality. **4.** A mark of punctuation. **5.** A mute consonant. See MUTE, *a.,* 3.

stop′cock′ (stŏp′kŏk′), *n.* A cock, tap, or faucet.

stop′-gap′ (stŏp′găp′), *n.* That which closes or fills up an opening; hence, a temporary expedient.

stop′page (stŏp′ăj), *n.* Act of stopping, or arresting motion or action; also, state of being stopped.

stop′per (-ẽr), *n.* One that stops, closes, plugs, etc. —*v. t.* To close or secure with a stopper.

stop′ple (stŏp′′l), *n. & v. t.* [1] Stopper.

stor′age (stōr′ăj), *n.* **1.** Act of storing; state of being stored; safe-keeping of goods in a depository. **2.** Space for the safe-keeping of goods, or the price charged therefor.

storage battery. A battery for generating electricity by the reversal of chemical reactions previously produced in it by an electric current.

store (stōr), *n.* **1.** That which is accumulated; source from which supplies may be drawn; reserve fund. **2.** *pl.* Articles, esp. of food, accumulated for a special object; supplies. **3.** An abundance; great amount. **4.** A storehouse; warehouse. **5.** A place where goods are kept for sale; a shop. — *v. t.* [1] **1.** To furnish; provide; supply. **2.** To collect a supply; lay away. **3.** To deposit, as in a storehouse.

store′house′ (stōr′hous′), *n.* Building for storing goods, esp. provisions; warehouse; store.

store′keep′er (-kēp′ẽr), *n.* A shopkeeper. *U. S.*

store′room′ (-rōōm′), *n.* Room for storing things.

sto′ried (stō′rĭd), *a.* Having (such or so many) stories; as, a two-*storied* house.

sto′ried, *p. a.* Celebrated in story or history.

stork (stôrk), *n.* Any of various large wading birds allied to the herons.

storm (stôrm), *n.* **1.** A disturbance of the atmosphere attended by wind, rain, snow, hail, sleet, or thunder and lightning. **2.** Vehement or passionate outbreak. **3.** A determined assault on a fortified place. — *v. i.* **1.** To blow with violence; also, to rain, hail, snow, or the like, usually violently ; — used impersonally ; as, it *storms.* **2.** To rage. — *v. t.* To attack, and attempt to take, by sudden assault.

storm'y (stôr'mĭ), *a.* [3] **1.** Marked by, or pertaining to, a storm ; tempestuous. **2.** Turbulent, violent ; passionate. — **storm'i-ly** (-mĭ-lĭ), *adv.* — **storm'i-ness** (-mĭ-nĕs), *n.*

sto'ry (stō'rĭ), *n. ; pl.* -RIES (-rĭz). A set of rooms on one floor ; a floor ; space between two floors.

sto'ry, *n.* **1.** A connected narration of past events; history. **2. a** An account of some incident. **b** A report ; a statement. **c** An anecdote. **3.** In literature, a narrative in prose or verse ; a tale, esp. fictitious. **4.** A fib ; falsehood. *Colloq.*

sto'ry-tell'er, *n.* A teller of stories.

stoup (stoop), *n.* **1.** A small vessel for liquids. **2.** A basin for holy water at a church entrance.

stout (stout), *a.* [3] **1.** Strong and firm of character ; brave ; bold ; resolute. **2.** Physically strong ; sturdy ; tough. **3.** Bulky; stocky; corpulent. — *n.* A strong malt liquor, esp. porter.

stout'ly, *adv.* In a stout manner.

stout'ness, *n.* Quality or state of being stout.

stove (stōv), *pret. & p. p.* of STAVE.

stove (stōv), *n.* Any of various apparatus, commonly of iron, for heating and cooking.

stow (stō), *v. t.* **1.** To arrange compactly ; pack. **2.** To arrange anything compactly in.

stow'age (stō'ăj), *n.* **1.** Act or method of stowing ; also, room for stowing. **2.** That which is stowed. **3.** Money paid for stowing goods.

stow'a-way' (stō'ă-wā'), *n.* One who hides on a vessel or railroad train to obtain a free passage.

stra-bis'mus (strá-bĭz'mŭs), *n.* Eye affection in which the optic axes cannot be directed to the same object ; cross-eye. — **stra-bis'mic** (-mĭk), *a.*

strad'dle (străd'l), *v. i.* [1] To stand, sit, or walk with legs wide apart ; sit astride.— *v. t.* To stand or sit astride of. — *n.* **1.** A straddling. **2.** Distance between the feet or legs of one straddling.

strag'gle (străg'l), *v. i.* [1] **1.** To wander from the direct course ; stray. **2.** To become separated from others of its kind ; be, become, or occur as if, dispersed. — **strag'gler** (-lẽr), *n.* [8].

strag'gly (străg'lĭ), *a.* [4] Straggling.

straight (strāt), *a.* [3] **1.** Having an invariable direction : not curved or crooked. **2.** Conforming to justice and rectitude; upright. **3.** Direct; unbroken. **4.** Properly ordered or arranged. — *adv.* Directly ; rightly ; straightway.

straight'en (-'n), *v. t.* To make straight ; put in order.— *v. i.* To become straight.— **-er,** *n.* [8].

straight'for'ward (-fôr'wẽrd), *a.* [4] Proceeding in a straight course or manner ; hence, honest ; frank. — **straight'for'ward-ly, straight'for'ward,** *adv.* — **-for'ward-ness,** *n.* [8].

straight'ly, *adv.* In a straight manner.

straight'ness, *n.* Straight quality or state.

straight'way' (-wā'), *adv.* Immediately.

strain (strān), *n.* **1.** Race ; stock ; descent ; family. **2. a** Hereditary character. **b** A trace ;

a streak. **3.** Sort, kind. **4. a** The burden, tone, manner, of a song, book, etc. **b** Mood ; temper. **5.** A melody, tune, or air. **6.** A song ; a poem.

strain, *v. t.* **1.** To draw tight; stretch. *Archaic.* **2.** To force ; constrain. **3.** To act upon so as to cause change of form or volume, as forces on a beam to bend it. **4.** To exert to the utmost. **5.** To distort from its true sense or meaning. **6.** To injure by stretching or by exertion of force, or by overexertion or overuse. **7.** To squeeze ; hug. **8.** To put through a strainer ; filter. — *n.* **1.** Act of straining ; state of being strained. **2.** *Mech.* **a** Distortion due to stress or force. **b** Stress, thrust, or force. [sieve or filter.]

strain'er (-ẽr), *n.* One that strains, as (esp.) a

strait (strāt), *a.* [3] **1.** Narrow. **2.** Tight; close. **3.** Strict; scrupulous. **4.** Embarrassed; hampered. — *n.* **1.** Passageway connecting two large bodies of water. **2.** Perplexity or distress ; difficulty ; need ; — often in *pl.*

strait'en (strāt'n), *v. t.* **1.** To make strait; confine. **2.** To afflict, as with difficulty ; embarrass.

strait'-laced' (-lāst'), *a.* [4] **1.** Laced tightly; wearing tight stays. **2.** Unusually strict in manners, morals, or opinion.

strait'ly, *adv.* In a strait manner.

strait'ness, *n.* Strait quality or state.

strake (strāk), *n. Shipbuilding.* One breadth of planks or plates forming a continuous strip on the bottom or sides of a vessel.

strand (strănd), *n.* Any of the twists, or strings, of a rope ; also, a single filament. — *v. t.* **1.** To break a strand of (a rope). **2.** To form (a rope, etc.) by uniting strands.

strand, *n.* A shore, esp. of the ocean. *Poetic.* — *v. t. & i.* To run aground.

strange (strānj), *a.* [3] **1.** Of or pert. to another or others ; belonging to others. **2.** Not before known, heard, or seen ; unfamiliar. **3.** Novel ; extraordinary ; queer. **4.** Reserved ; distant in deportment ; shy or coy. **5.** Unaccustomed ; inexperienced. — **-ly,** *adv.* — **-ness,** *n.*

stran'ger (strān'jẽr), *n.* One who is strange; as: **a** A foreigner. **b** A visitor or intruder. **c** A person with whom one is unacquainted.

stran'gle (străn'g'l), *v. t.* [1] **1.** To choke to death by compressing the throat. **2.** To stifle or suffocate. **3.** To suppress; repress.— *v. i.* To be strangled, or suffocated. — **stran'gler** (-glẽr), *n.*

stran'gu-late (-gu-lāt), *v. t.* [1] To compress, esp., *Med.,* so as to stop circulation ; strangle.

stran'gu-la'tion (-lā'shŭn), *n.* A strangling; strangulating; state of being strangled or strangulated.

strap (străp), *n.* **1.** A narrow strip, esp. of leather, for use as a fastening. **2.** Something resembling a strap (sense 1). — *v. t.;* STRAPPED (străpt); STRAP'-PING. **1.** To beat with a strap. **2.** To secure with a strap. **3.** To sharpen on a strap.

strap'ping, *a.* [4] Tall; strong; large. *Colloq.*

stra'ta (strā'tá), *n., L. pl.* of STRATUM.

strat'a-gem (străt'á-jĕm), *n.* A trick in war for deceiving the enemy ; artifice ; deceptive device.

stra-te'gic (strá-tē'jĭk; -tē'jīk) } *a.* [4] Of, pert. **stra-te'gi-cal** (-tē'jĭ-kăl; -tē'jĭ-) } to, or effected or marked by, strategy. — **-gi-cal-ly,** *adv.* [8].

strat'e-gist (străt'ē-jĭst), *n.* A master of strategy.

strat'e-gy (străt'ĕ-jĭ), *n.* **1.** The science or art of projecting and directing great military movements. **2.** Use of stratagem.

strat/i-fi-ca'tion (străt/ĭ-fĭ-kā'shŭn), *n.* Act or process of stratifying ; state of being stratified.

strat'i-fy (străt'ĭ-fĭ), *v. t. & i.* [2] To arrange or form in strata, or layers. [(-fāmz). A layer.

stra'tum (strā'tŭm), *n.; pl.* L. -TA (-tȧ), E. -TUMS

stra'tus (strā'tŭs), *n.* A cloud form marked by horizontal extension and low altitude.

straw (strô), *n.* **1.** A stalk or stem of grain or pulse. **2.** Stalks of grain after threshing.

straw'ber-ry (strô'bĕr-ĭ), *n. ; pl.* -RIES (-ĭz). The edible red fruit of any of various stemless herbs, or the plant that bears it.

stray (strā), *v. i.* **1.** To wander ; deviate. **2.** To roam ; go astray.— *a.* **1.** Gone astray ; wandering. **2.** Incidental ; unrelated. — *n.* **1.** Any domestic animal wandering at large or lost. **2.** A person or thing that strays.

streak (strēk), *n.* A line or long mark ; stripe ; vein.— *v. t.* To form streaks in or on ; stripe.

streak'y (strēk'ĭ), *a.* [3] Marked with streaks. — **streak'i-ly,** *adv.* [8] — **-i-ness,** *n.* [8].

stream (strēm), *n.* **1.** A current or course of water or other fluid. **2.** A steady flow, as of air ; a beam or column of light. **3.** Current ; drift. — *v. i.* **1.** To issue or flow in a stream. **2.** To pour out, or emit, a stream or streams. **3.** To issue, shoot, or pass swiftly, as light, a comet, etc. **4.** To stretch out at length, or in a line, often wavy ; as, *streaming* hair. — *v. t.* To cause to stream.

stream'er (-ẽr), *n.* That which streams out, as a flag, esp. a long, narrow one, or a column of light.

stream'let (-lĕt), *n.* A small stream ; rivulet ; rill.

stream'line (-līn'), *n.* The path of any particle in a fluid flowing smoothly and with the least possible resistance. [or village.

street (strēt), *n.* A thoroughfare, esp. in a city

street car. A car, usually a passenger car, running through the public streets, usually on rails. *U. S.*

strength (strĕngth), *n.* **1.** Quality or state of being strong ; ability to do or to bear ; force ; power. **2.** Power to resist force ; solidity or toughness. **3.** Power of resisting attacks ; impregnability. **4.** Intensity ; vehemence ; vigor. **5.** Force as measured in numbers. **6.** Legal or moral force.

strength'en (strĕng'th'n), *v. t. & i.* To make, grow, or become, stronger. — **strength'en-er,** *n.* [8]. [being strenuous.

stren'u-os'i-ty (strĕn'ŭ-ŏs'ĭ-tĭ), *n.* Quality of

stren'u-ous (strĕn'ŭ-ŭs), *a.* [4] **1.** Eagerly pressing or urgent ; zealous ; ardent. **2.** Marked by zealous energy. — **-ly,** *adv.* [8] — **-ness,** *n.* [8].

stress (strĕs), *v. t.* **1.** To subject to mechanical stress. **2.** To accent or emphasize. — *n.* **1.** Pressure ; strain ; hence, urgency ; importance ; significance. **2.** *Mech.* Mutual force or action between contiguous parts of a body, due to external force. **3.** Force of utterance of words, or syllables, increasing their relative loudness ; accent.

stretch (strĕch), *v. t.* **1.** To reach out ; extend. **2.** To draw out ; expand ; distend. **3.** To make tense ; strain. **4.** To cause to reach or continue, as from one point to another. **5.** To extend too far ; exaggerate. — *v. i.* **1.** To spread ; reach.

2. To extend or spread one's self or one's limbs. **3.** To bear extension without breaking. — *n.* **1.** Act of stretching ; state of being stretched. **2.** A continuous line, surface, or period. **3.** Extent to which anything may be stretched.

stretch'er (strĕch'ẽr), *n.* **1.** One that stretches. **2.** A timber or rod used as a tie, esp. when horizontal. **3.** A litter, usually of canvas stretched on a frame, for carrying the disabled or dead.

strew (strōō), *v. t. ; pret. & p. p.* STREWED (strōōd ; strōd) ; *p. p.* STREWN (strōōn ; strōn) ; *p. pr. & vb. n.* STREW'ING. **1.** To scatter ; as, to *strew* seed in beds. **2.** To cover by or as by scattering something over ; also, to be dispersed over as if scattered.

stri'ate (strī'āt) ⎱ *a.* [4] Marked with parallel
stri'at-ed (-āt-ĕd) ⎰ lines or bands.

stri-a'tion (strī-ā'shŭn), *n.* State of being striated ; arrangement of parallel lines or bands.

strick'en (strĭk'n), *p. p.* of STRIKE. Hence : *p. a.* [4] **1.** Smitten ; wounded. **2.** Worn out.

strict (strĭkt), *a.* [3] **1.** Drawn close ; tight ; also, tense. **2.** Exact ; precise ; hence, rigid in interpretation ; without exception or deviation. **3.** Rigorous. — **strict'ly,** *adv.* — **strict'ness,** *n.*

stric'ture (strĭk'tūr), *n.* **1.** An adverse criticism. **2.** A morbid contraction of any passage of the body.

stride (strīd), *v. i. ; pret.* STRODE (strōd) ; *p. p.* STRID'DEN (strĭd'n) ; *p. pr. & vb. n.* STRID'ING (strĭd'ĭng). To walk or run with long steps. — *v. t.* **1.** To pass over at a step. **2.** To bestride. — *n.* Act of striding ; also, a long step.

stri'dent (strī'dĕnt), *a.* [4] Harsh-sounding ; grating ; shrill. — **stri'dent-ly,** *adv.* [8].

strid'u-late (strĭd'ủ-lāt),*v. i.* To make a shrill, creaking noise, as crickets. — **-la'tion** (-lā'shŭn), *n.*

strid'u-lous (-lŭs), *a.* [4] Making a shrill, creaking sound. [conflict ; fight ; contest.

strife (strīf), *n.* **1.** Emulation. **2.** Contention ;

strike (strīk), *v. t. ; pret.* STRUCK (strŭk) ; *p. p.* STRUCK, or STRICK'EN (strĭk'n) ; *p. pr. & vb. n.* STRIK'ING (strīk'ĭng). **1.** To hit ; smite. **2.** To strike against ; collide with. **3.** To give or inflict, as a blow. **4.** To impel, as with a blow ; dash. **5.** To cause or produce as by a stroke. **6.** To cause to ignite by friction. **7.** To impress with a die ; mint ; coin. **8.** To thrust in. **9.** To affect sensibly in a particular manner, as with wonder. **10.** To cause to sound, esp. by strokes ; indicate by sounding. **11.** To make and ratify, as a bargain. **12.** To lower, as a flag. **13.** To efface, cancel, or the like ; — usually with *from, off*, or *out.* **14.** To assume (a posture, etc.).— *v. i.* **1.** To advance ; proceed. **2.** To come upon something suddenly. **3.** To give or aim a blow. **4.** To hit ; collide. **5.** To sound by percussion ; as, the clock *strikes.* **6.** To lower a flag in token of respect or in surrender. **7.** To quit work in order to obtain or resist a change in conditions of employment. See STRIKE, *n.,* 2. **8.** *Hort.* To take root. — *n.* **1.** A striking. **2.** A stopping of work by workmen to obtain more pay, shorter hours, etc. **3.** A sudden finding of rich ore in mining ; any sudden success, esp. financial. — **strik'er** (strīk'ẽr), *n.* [8].

strike breaker. A workman who takes the place of a striker ; also, one supplying such workmen.

āle, senåte, câre, ăm, *ă*ccount, ärm, ȧsk, sofȧ ; ēve, ĕvent, ĕnd, recĕnt, makēr; īce, ĭll ; ōld, ŏbey, ôrb, ŏdd, sôft, cŏnnect ; ūse, ûnite, ûrn, ŭp, circ*ŭ*s ; fōōd, fŏŏt; out, oil ;

strik'ing (strīk'ĭng), *a.* [4] Very noticeable; re-markable.— **strik'ing-ly**, *adv.* [8].

string (strĭng), *n.* **1.** A small cord or the like, used esp. for tying things. **2.** A thread or cord strung with a number of objects; hence, a line or series of things arranged on or as on a thread. **3.** The cord of a musical instrument, as a piano, violin, etc., or of a bow. **4.** A fiber, as of a plant. — *v. t.*; *pret.* STRUNG (strŭng); *p. p.* STRUNG; *p. pr. & vb. n.* STRING'ING (strĭng'ĭng). **1.** To furnish with strings. **2.** To make tense. **3.** To thread on a string. **4.** To deprive of strings; as, to *string* beans. **5.** To tie, hang up, or the like, with a string. **6.** To extend or stretch like a string. — *v. i.* **1.** To form into a string or strings. **2.** To move or progress in a string, or series.

stringed (strĭngd), *a.* Having strings, as a musi-cal instrument. [stringent.]

strin'gen-cy (strĭn'jĕn-sĭ), *n.* Quality of being

strin'gent (strĭn'jĕnt), *a.* [4] **1.** Restrictive; rigid. **2.** Tight; having little available money.— **strin'gent-ly**, *adv.* [8] — **-ness**, *n.* [8].

string'er (strĭng'ẽr), *n.* **1.** One who strings. **2.** *Mech.* A long horizontal timber to connect up-rights, support a floor, or the like.

string'halt (-hôlt'), *n.* A spasmodic affection of a horse's hind legs.

string'piece' (-pēs'), *n.* A long timber in a con-struction, esp. a principal one, usually horizontal.

string'y (-ĭ), *a.* [3] **1.** Consisting of strings; fibrous; as, a *stringy* root. **2.** Ropy; viscid; as, *stringy* sirup. — **string'i-ness** (-ĭ-nĕs), *n.* [8].

strip (strĭp), *v. t.*; *pret.* STRIPPED (strĭpt); STRIP'PING. **1.** To deprive; divest; plunder (a person, building, etc.); to deprive, as of a covering; to skin; peel. **2.** To milk dry, as a cow. **3.** To pull or tear off, as a covering; remove; hence, to plunder, as jewels, etc.— *v. i.* To undress.— *n.* A narrow or relatively long piece; as, a *strip* of cloth.

stripe (strīp), *n.* **1.** A line, or long narrow divi-sion of anything. **2.** A strip attached to something of a different color or material. **3.** A long, nar-row discoloration of the skin made by the blow of a lash; hence, such a blow. **4.** Distinctive color; type; sort.— *v. t.* [1] To make stripes upon.

strip'ling (strĭp'lĭng), *n.* A youth; lad.

strive (strĭv), *v. i.*; *pret.* STROVE (strōv); *p. p.* STRIV'EN (strĭv'n); *p. pr. & vb. n.* STRIV'ING (strĭv'-ĭng). **1.** To make efforts; labor hard. **2.** To con-tend; battle.— **striv'er** (strĭv'ẽr), *n.* [8].

strob'ile (strŏb'ĭl), *n.* A cone, as of the fir, or any fruit resembling such a cone; esp., the matured cat-kin, or dense flower cluster, of the hop. See HOP.

strode (strōd), *pret.* of STRIDE.

stroke (strōk), *n.* **1.** Act of striking; impact; blow. **2.** A sudden action suggesting a blow; hence, the result of such action; esp., any sudden attack, as of disease. **3.** A vigorous effort to accomplish something, or the thing so accomplished. **4.** The sound of striking, esp. of a clock. **5.** One of a series of movements to effect passage through or on a resisting medium; as, the *stroke* of a swimmer. **6.** The rower nearest the stern. **7.** A movement, as with an implement; as, a pen *stroke*; also, a mark made by such a stroke. **8.** *Mach.* Movement, in either direction, as of a piston.— *v. t.* [1]

1. To rub gently. **2.** To row as stroke of (a row-boat).

stroll (strōl), *v. i.* To wander on foot; rove; saun-ter.— *n.* A strolling; ramble.— **stroll'er**, *n.*

strong (strŏng), *a.* [3] **1.** Having great power to act; vigorous. **2.** Having ability to bear or endure; hale; robust. **3.** Having great resources, as of wealth, numbers, etc. **4.** Of specified number; as, ten thousand *strong.* **5.** Forceful. **6.** Intense; concentrated. **7.** Moving with rapidity or force. **8.** Ardent; zealous. **9.** Containing much alcohol. **10.** Solid; tough. **11.** Well established. **12.** *Gram.* Pertaining to or designating a verb which forms its preterit by variation in the root vowel, and the past participle (usually) by addition of -*en*, as in *strive*, *strove*, *striven*. **13.** Offensive; rank. *Colloq.*

strong'hold' (-hōld'), *n.* A fort; place of security.

strong'ly, *adv.* In a strong manner.

strop (strŏp), *n.* A strap; esp., a strap for sharp-ening a razor.— *v. t.*; STROPPED (strŏpt); STROP'-PING. To sharpen on a strop.

strove (strōv), *pret.* of STRIVE.

struck (strŭk). See STRIKE.

struc'tur-al (strŭk'tụr-ăl), *a.* Of or pertaining to structure or a structure.— **-ly**, *adv.* [8].

struc'ture (strŭk'tụr), *n.* **1.** Manner of building; construction. **2.** Something built; a building. **3.** Arrangement of parts, organs, tissues, etc.

strug'gle (strŭg''l), *v. i.* [1] To put forth great ef-forts; strive; contend.— *n.* **1.** A violent effort or exertion. **2.** Contest; strife.— **-gler** (-lẽr), *n.* [8].

strum (strŭm), *v. t. & i.*; STRUMMED (strŭmd); STRUM'MING. To play on a stringed instrument un-skillfully or carelessly.— *n.* Act of strumming.

strung (strŭng), *pret. & p. p.* of STRING.

strut (strŭt), *v. i.*; STRUT'TED (-ĕd); STRUT'TING. To walk with a lofty, proud gait or with affected dignity.— *n.* **1.** A strutting. **2.** *Arch.* Any bar or piece for resisting pressure endwise.

strych'nine (strĭk'nĭn; -nēn), *n.* Also **strych'nin**. A poisonous alkaloid got from various plants, as nux vomica, and used as a heart stimulant.

stub (stŭb), *n.* **1.** Tree stump. **2.** The short blunt remnant of something. **3.** In a check book, etc., a part of each leaf fastened to the back for memo-randa of deposits and withdrawals. **4.** Something short and blunt.— *v. t.*; STUBBED (stŭbd); STUB'-BING. To strike, as the toes, against a stone, etc.

stub'ble (stŭb''l), *n.* The stumps of grain, left in the ground, as after reaping.

stub'bly (-lĭ), *a.* [3] Covered with stubble.

stub'born (-ẽrn), *a.* [3] **1.** Resolute in mental attitude; inflexible; esp., obstinate. **2.** Performed or practiced persistently or obstinately. **3.** Diffi-cult to manage; refractory.— **stub'born-ly**, *adv.* [8]— **stub'born-ness**, *n.* [8].

stub'by (stŭb'ĭ), *a.* [3] **1.** Abounding with stubs. **2.** Short, thick, and stiff, as bristles.

stuc'co (stŭk'ō), *n.*; *pl.* -COES, -COZ (-ōz). Plaster for coating walls; esp., a fine plaster for inside dec-oration.— *v. t.* To cover or decorate with stucco.

stuck (stŭk), *pret. & p. p.* of STICK.

stud (stŭd), *n.* **1.** A collection of horses for breed-ing, racing, riding, etc. **2.** The place where a stud is kept, esp. for breeding. **3.** A studhorse.

stud, *n.* **1.** *Building.* A small scantling; esp., one of the uprights for lath-and-plaster partitions. **2.** A kind of nail with a large head; boss. **3.** A buttonlike device, used for ornament, etc. — *v. t.;* stud′ded; stud′ding. To supply with studs.

stud′ding sail (sāl; *naut.* stŭn′s'l). A sail set at the side of a principal square sail in free winds.

stu′dent (stū′dĕnt), *n.* **1.** A person engaged in study; scholar. **2.** An attentive and systematic observer. [kept for breeding.

stud′horse′ (stŭd′hôrs′), *n.* A stallion, esp. one

stud′ied (stŭd′ĭd), *a.* [4] **1.** Made the subject of study. **2.** Premeditated; designed. —**ly**, *adv.* —**ness**, *n.* [room of an artist.

stu′di-o (stū′dĭ-ō), *n. ; pl.* -dios (-ōz). The work-

stu′di-ous (-ŭs), *a.* [4] **1.** Given to study. **2.** Diligent in attention. —**ly**, *adv.* —**ness**, *n.* [8].

stud′y (stŭd′ĭ), *n. ; pl.* studies (-ĭz). **1.** Application of the mind to books, etc., in order to acquire knowledge. **2.** Act or process of acquiring knowledge of a particular subject. **3.** Earnest and reasoned effort. **4.** Meditation. **5.** A branch of learning. **6.** A preliminary sketch. **7.** *Music.* A piece for special practice. **8.** A room devoted esp. to study. — *v. i.* [2] **1.** To apply the mind to books or learning. **2.** To fix the mind closely on a subject ; ponder. —*v. t.* To apply the mind to.

stuff (stŭf), *n.* **1.** Material out of which anything is to be or may be made ; hence, any material. **2.** Elemental part ; essence. **3.** Goods, esp. domestic goods. **4.** Woven material not made into garments. — *v. t.* **1.** To fill by crowding ; cram. **2.** To fill the cavity of (as a turkey, a skin) with a particular material. **3.** To put fraudulent votes into (a ballot box). *U. S.* **4.** To thrust or crowd in ; pack. — *v. i.* To feed gluttonously ; cram.

stuff′ing, *n.* Act or process of, or that which is used for, filling anything.

stuff′y (stŭf′ĭ), *a.* [3] Ill-ventilated ; close. — **stuff′i-ness** (-ĭ-nĕs), *n.* [8].

stul′ti-fi-ca′tion (stŭl′tĭ-fĭ-kā′shŭn), *n.* A stultifying, or state of being stultified.

stul′ti-fy (stŭl′tĭ-fī), *v. t.* [2] To make foolish.

stum′ble (stŭm′b'l), *v. i.* [1] **1.** To trip in walking, etc. **2.** To walk unsteadily ; hence, to act or perform blunderingly. **3.** To fall into sin or error. **4.** To come or happen without design. — *n.* **1.** A trip in walking or running. **2.** A blunder. —**bler** (-blẽr), *n.* [8] —**bling-ly**, *adv.* [8].

stum′bling-block′ (stŭm′blĭng-blŏk′), *n.* Any cause of stumbling, perplexity, or error.

stump (stŭmp), *n.* **1.** The part of a tree or plant remaining in the earth after the stem is cut off. **2.** The portion, as of a limb remaining after the rest is removed. **3.** A platform for political speaking ; hence, public speaking, esp. political. — *v. i.* To walk heavily and stiffly.

stump′y (stŭm′pĭ), *a.* [3] **1.** Abounding in stumps. **2.** Short and thick ; stubby. *Colloq.*

stun (stŭn), *v. t. ;* stunned (stŭnd) ; stun′ning. **1.** To make senseless or dizzy, as by a blow. **2.** To overpower or confound with noise. — *n.* Condition of being stunned ; also, that which stuns.

stung (stŭng), *pret. & p. p.* of sting.

stunk (stŭngk), *pret. & p. p.* of stink.

stunt (stŭnt), *n.* A feat. *Colloq.*

stunt, *v. t.* To hinder from normal growth; dwarf; cramp ; check. — *n.* A check in growth.

stu′pe-fac′tion (stū′pē-făk′shŭn), *n.* Act of stupefying ; state of being stupefied.

stu′pe-fy (stū′pē-fī), *v. t.* [2] To make stupid, dull, or torpid. — **stu′pe-fi′er** (-fī′ẽr), *n.* [8].

stu-pen′dous (stū-pĕn′dŭs), *a.* [4] Amazing, esp. in magnitude. —**ly**, *adv.* —**ness**, *n.* [8].

stu′pid (stū′pĭd), *a.* [3] **1.** Very dull ; stupefied. **2.** Foolish. **3.** Resulting from or evincing mental dullness ; dull. —**ly**, *adv.* —**ness**, *n.* [8].

stu-pid′i-ty (stū-pĭd′ĭ-tĭ), *n.* Quality or state of being stupid. [nution of sensibility.

stu′por (stū′pŏr), *n.* Suspension or great dimi-

stur′dy (stûr′dĭ), *a.* [3] **1.** Resolute ; firm. **2.** Strong; robust. —**di-ly**, *adv.* —**di-ness**, *n.*

stur′geon (-jŭn), *n.* Any of certain large fishes, living in fresh and salt waters of the north temperate zone. The roe is made into caviar and the air bladder into isinglass.

stut′ter (stŭt′ẽr), *v. i. & t.* To hesitate or stumble in uttering words ; stammer. — *n.* Act of stuttering ; a stammer. — **stut′ter-er** (-ẽr), *n.* [8].

sty (stī), *n. ; pl.* sties (stīz). A pen for swine.

sty, *n. ; pl.* sties. Also **stye.** *Med.* An inflamed swelling on the edge of the eyelid.

style (stīl), *n.* **1.** An instrument used by the ancients in writing on waxed tablets ; also, any similar instrument. **2.** The gnomon of a sun dial. **3.** Mode of expressing thought in language. **4.** Distinctive mode of construction or execution in any art or product. **5.** Manner of acting or performing. **6.** Fashionable elegance. **7.** Title ; mode of address. **8.** A mode of reckoning time ; a calendar. **9.** *Bot.* A prolongation of the ovary, commonly bearing the stigma at its apex. — *v. t.* [1] To entitle ; name or call.

styl′ish (stīl′ĭsh), *a.* [4] Highly fashionable ; modish. — **styl′ish-ly**, *adv.* [8] —**ness**, *n.* [8].

styl′ist (-ĭst), *n.* One who is a master or a model of style, esp. in writing or speaking.

sty′lo-graph (stī′lō-gráf), *n.* A stylographic pen.

sty′lo-graph′ic (-grăf′ĭk), *a.* Of, pertaining to, or used in, a mode of writing by means of a style, etc.— **stylographic pen**, a pen having a conical point and with a reservoir in the handle for ink.

sty′lus (stī′lŭs), *n.* = style, *n.,* 1.

styp′tic (stĭp′tĭk), *a.* [4] Astringent ; stopping bleeding. — *n.* A styptic medicine.

sua′sion (swā′zhŭn), *n.* Persuasion.

sua′sive (-sĭv), *a.* [4] Persuasive.

suave (swāv; swäv), *a.* [3] Blandly pleasing ; gracious ; bland. — **suave′ly**, *adv.* [8].

suav′i-ty (swăv′ĭ-tĭ; swä′vĭ-tĭ), *n.* Agreeableness ; pleasant urbanity.

sub-ac′id (sŭb-ăs′ĭd), *a.* Slightly acid.

sub-al′tern (sŭb-ôl′tẽrn), *a.* Subordinate ; *Mil.,* being below the rank of captain. — *n.* A commissioned military officer below a captain.

sub-a′que-ous (sŭb-ā′kwē-ŭs), *a.* Being under water ; adapted for use under water.

sub′-base′, *n. Arch.* The lowest member of a base when divided horizontally.

sub-con′scious (sŭb-kŏn′shŭs), *a.* Of the nature of mental operation, but not present in consciousness. —**ly**, *adv.* [8] —**ness**, *n.* [8].

sub'con'tract (sŭb'kŏn'trăkt), *n.* A contract under, or subordinate to, a previous contract.

sub'cu-ta'ne-ous (sŭb'kŭ-tā'nē-ŭs), *a.* Situated under the skin. [again.

sub'di-vide' (-dĭ-vīd'), *v. t. & i.* [1] To divide

sub'di-vi'sion (-dĭ-vĭzh'ŭn), *n.* **1.** Act of subdividing. **2.** A part of a thing made by subdividing.

sub-due' (sŭb-dū'), *v. t.* [1] **1.** To bring under; conquer; vanquish. **2.** To overcome, as by persuasion. **3.** To destroy the force of, as of a fever. **4.** To reduce; hence, to soften. — **du'er**, *n.* [8].

sub'fam'i-ly (sŭb'făm'ĭ-lĭ), *n.* A category below a family and above a genus.

sub'ge'nus (-jē'nŭs), *n.* A category below a genus and above a species.

sub'ject (sŭb'jĕkt), *a.* [4] **1.** Under the power or dominion of another. **2.** Exposed; liable; prone. **3.** Being under the contingency (of); exposed (to);—with *to*; as, *subject* to approval.— *n.* **1.** One under the authority, control, or influence of another. **2.** One subject to a monarch or ruler; one who owes allegiance. **3.** That concerning which anything is said or done; theme; topic. **4.** *Gram.* The word or word group denoting that of which anything is affirmed.

sub-ject' (sŭb-jĕkt'), *v. t.* **1.** To bring under control; subdue. **2.** To expose; make liable; cause to undergo; — with *to*.

sub-jec'tion (-jĕk'shŭn), *n.* A subjecting; state of being subject, obedient, or submissive.

sub-jec'tive (-tĭv), *a.* [4] **1.** Of the nature of, or pertaining to, a subject. **2.** Esp., pertaining to, or derived from, one's own consciousness, in distinction from external observation. — *-ly, adv.*

sub'jec-tiv'i-ty (sŭb'jĕk-tĭv'ĭ-tĭ), *n.* Subjective quality, state, or nature.

subject matter. Subject of thought or study.

sub-join' (sŭb-join'), *v. t.* To add after something, esp. something said or written; append.

sub'ju-gate (sŭb'jŏŏ-gāt), *v. t.* [1] To conquer by force; subdue. — **-ga'tor**, *n.* [8].

sub'ju-ga'tion (-gā'shŭn), *n.* A subjugating, or state of being subjugated.

sub-junc'tive (sŭb-jŭŋk'tĭv), *a. Gram.* Designating, or pertaining to, that mood of a verb expressing the action or state not as a fact, but only as a contingent and dependent mental conception. — *n.* The subjunctive mood.

sub'king'dom (sŭb'kĭng'dŭm), *n.* A primary division of a kingdom, now usually called a *phylum.*

sub-let' (sŭb-lĕt'), *v. t. & i.; -let'*; -let'ting. To lease to another (the one leasing being a tenant).

sub'li-mate (sŭb'lĭ-māt), *v. t.* [1] **1.** To cause to sublime. **2.** To refine and exalt; elevate. — *a.* **1.** Sublimated. **2.** Refined; elevated. — (-măt), *n. Chem.* A product obtained by subliming.

sub'li-ma'tion (-mā'shŭn), *n.* Act, process, or product of sublimating or subliming.

sub-lime' (sŭb-līm'), *a.* [3] **1.** Lifted up; high. *Archaic.* **2.** Exalted. **3.** Producing a sense of elevated beauty, grandeur, etc. — *n.* That which is sublime; — with *the.* — *v. t.* [1] **1.** *Chem.* To cause to sublime; purify. **2.** To exalt; refine. — *v. i. Chem.* To pass from the solid to the gaseous state, and again condense to solid form, without apparently liquefying. — *-ly, adv.* — *-ness, n.* [8].

sub-lim'i-nal (-lĭm'ĭ-năl), *a.* Subconscious.

sub-lim'i-ty (-I-tĭ), *n.; pl.* -ties (-tĭz). **1.** Sublime quality or state. **2.** That which is sublime.

sub-lu'nar (sŭb-lū'nár) } *a.* Situated beneath

sub'lu-na-ry (sŭb'lū-nā-rĭ) } the moon; mundane.

sub'ma-rine' (-má-rēn'), *a.* Being, acting, growing, or used, under water in the sea. — *n.* A submarine, esp. torpedo, boat.

sub-merge' (sŭb-mûrj'), *v. t.* [1] **1.** To put under water; plunge. **2.** To cover with water; inundate. — *v. i.* To become submerged.

sub-mer'gence (-mûr'jĕns), *n.* Submersion.

sub-mer'sion (-mûr'shŭn), *n.* A submerging, or state of being submerged.

sub-mis'sion (-mĭsh'ŭn), *n.* **1.** Act of submitting; esp., yielding to power or authority. **2.** State of being submissive; obedience; compliance.

sub-mis'sive (-mĭs'ĭv), *a.* [4] Inclined or ready to submit; yielding; humble. — *-ly, adv.* — *-ness, n.*

sub-mit' (-mĭt'), *v. t.; -mit'ted (-ĕd); -mit'ting. **1.** To yield to power, will, or authority. **2.** To commit to the discretion or judgment of another; refer. **3.** To offer as an opinion, or affirm. — *v. i.* **1.** To yield; surrender. **2.** To be subject or submissive.

sub-nor'mal (-nôr'măl), *a.* [4] Below the normal.

sub-or'di-nate (sŭb-ôr'dĭ-nát), *a.* [4] **1.** Placed in a lower order, class, or rank. **2.** Inferior in order, nature, importance, etc. — *n.* One that is subordinate. — (-nāt), *v. t.* [1] **1.** To place in a lower order or class. **2.** To make subject or subservient. — **sub-or'di-nate-ly**, *adv.* — *-ness, n.*

sub-or'di-na'tion (-nā'shŭn), *n.* Act of subordinating; quality or state of being subordinate.

sub-orn' (sŭb-ôrn'), *v. t. Law.* To procure (another) to commit perjury. — **sub-orn'er**, *n.* [8].

sub'or-na'tion (sŭb'ôr-nā'shŭn), *n.* Act of suborning.

sub-pe'na. Var. of subpœna.

sub-pœ'na (sŭb-pē'ná), *n. Law.* A writ or process commanding the person designated in it to attend court or appear, under a penalty for failure. — *v. t. Law.* To serve or summon with a subpœna.

sub-scribe' (sŭb-skrīb'), *v. t.* [1] **1.** To write underneath; sign (one's name) to a document. **2.** To sign with one's own hand; consent to (something written) by writing one's name beneath. **3.** To promise to give by writing one's name with the amount. — *v. i.* **1.** To sign one's name to a document. **2.** To give consent to something written, by signing; hence, to assent; agree. **3.** To promise, or to agree to take and pay for, something by subscribing one's name. — **sub-scrib'er** (-skrīb'ẽr), *n.* [8].

sub-scrip'tion (sŭb-skrĭp'shŭn), *n.* **1.** Act of subscribing. **2.** That which is subscribed.

sub'se-quence (sŭb'sē-kwĕns), **-quen-cy** (-kwĕn-sĭ), *n.* Act or state of being subsequent.

sub'se-quent (-kwĕnt), *a.* Succeeding; following; as, *subsequent* events. — *-ly, adv.* [8].

sub-serve' (sŭb-sûrv'), *v. t.* [1] To serve subordinately or instrumentally; promote.

sub-ser'vi-ence (-sûr'vĭ-ĕns), **sub-ser'vi-en-cy** (-ĕn-sĭ), *n.* Quality or state of being subservient.

sub-ser'vi-ent (-sûr'vĭ-ĕnt), *a.* [4] **1.** Fitted or disposed to subserve; subordinate. **2.** Servile; truckling. — *-ly, adv.* [8] — *-ness, n.* [8].

sub-side′ (sŭb-sīd′), v. i. [1] **1.** To sink to the bottom; settle, as lees. **2.** To tend downward; descend; sink. **3.** To fall into a state of quiet; abate.

sub-sid′ence (-sīd′ĕns; sŭb′sĭ-dĕns), n. Act or process of subsiding.

sub-sid′i-a-ry (sŭb-sĭd′ĭ-ā-rĭ), a. [4] **1.** Furnishing aid; auxiliary; tributary. **2.** Of or pert. to a subsidy. — n.; pl. -RIES (-rĭz). One that contributes aid or supplies; assistant; auxiliary.

sub′si-dize (sŭb′sĭ-dīz), v. t. [1] To furnish or aid with a subsidy.

sub′si-dy (-dĭ), n.; pl. -DIES (-dĭz). **1. a** A sum granted by one state to another. **b** A government grant to assist a private enterprise; a subvention. **2.** Any gift made by way of financial aid.

sub-sist′ (sŭb-sĭst′), v. i. **1.** To continue; to exist. **2.** To be; exist. **3.** To be maintained with food and clothing. — v. t. To support with provisions.

sub-sist′ence (-sĭs′tĕns), n. **1.** Act or condition of subsisting; existence. **2.** Means of support; livelihood. **3.** State of being inherent in some thing, fact, or the like.

sub′soil′ (sŭb′soil′), n. The bed of weathered material which underlies the soil proper, or surface soil. — v. t. To break up the subsoil of.

sub′spe′cies (-spē′shēz; -shĭ-ēz), n. Biol. A subdivision of a species.

sub′stance (sŭb′stăns), n. **1.** That which underlies all outward manifestations; that which is real; real essence. **2.** The most important element in any existence; main part; purport. **3.** Body; matter; material of a thing; hence, solidity; firmness. **4.** Material possessions.

sub-stan′tial (sŭb-stăn′shăl), a. [4] **1.** Of or pert. to substance; material. **2.** Not imaginary; real; true. **3.** Having good substance; strong; solid. **4.** Possessed of goods; moderately wealthy. **5.** That is such in the main. **6.** Considerable; large.— n. That which is substantial. —ly, adv. —ness, n.

sub-stan′ti-al′i-ty (-shĭ-ăl′ĭ-tĭ), n. Quality or state of being substantial; materiality.

sub-stan′ti-ate (sŭb-stăn′shĭ-āt), v. t. [1] To establish the existence or truth of; verify, as a charge.

sub-stan′ti-a′tion (-shĭ-ā′shŭn), n. A substantiating; proof.

sub′stan-tive (sŭb′stăn-tĭv), a. [4] **1.** Betokening existence; as, the substantive verb; that is, the verb to be. **2.** Pertaining to or constituting the essential part or principles; as, the law substantive. — n. Gram. A noun or name. — ly, adv. [8].

sub′sti-tute (sŭb′stĭ-tūt), n. One put in place of another. — v. t. [1] To put in the place of another.

sub′sti-tu′tion (-tū′shŭn), n. Act of substituting.

sub-stra′tum (sŭb-strā′tŭm), n.; pl., L. -TA (-tä); E. -TUMS (-tŭmz). **1.** That which is laid or spread under. **2.** The subsoil.

sub-struc′ture (-strŭk′tụ̄r), n. An under structure; groundwork.

sub-tend′ (sŭb-tĕnd′), v. t. To extend under, or be opposite to; as, a chord subtends an arc.

sub′ter-fuge (sŭb′tẽr-fūj), n. A device, plan, or the like, for escape or concealment; artifice.

sub′ter-ra′ne-an (-ā′nē-ăn) } a. [4] Being under
sub′ter-ra′ne-ous (-ŭs) } the surface of the earth; hence, hidden; secret.

sub′tile (sŭb′tĭl; sŭt′′l), a. [3] Subtle. Now R. — -ly, adv. [8] —ness, n. [8].

sub′til-ize (-īz), v. t. [1] To make subtle; refine.

sub′til-ty (-tĭ), n. Subtlety. [a book.]

sub′ti′tle (sŭb′tī′t′l), n. A secondary title, as of]

sub′tile (sŭt′′l), a. [3] **1.** Thin; tenuous; delicate. **2.** Skillfully or cunningly devised; ingenious; crafty; sly. **3.** Nicely discriminating; discerning; shrewd; penetrating. **4.** Skillful; expert.—**sub′tle-ness,** n. [8].

sub′tle-ty (-tĭ), n.; pl. -TIES (-tĭz). **1.** Quality of being subtle. **2.** Something subtle.

sub′tly (sŭt′lĭ), adv. In a subtle manner.

sub-tract′ (sŭb-trăkt′), v. t. To take away, as a part from the whole or one number from another; deduct. — -er, n. [8]. [of subtracting.]

sub-trac′tion (-trăk′shŭn), n. Act or operation]

sub-trac′tive (-tĭv), a. Tending or able to subtract.

sub′tra-hend′ (sŭb′trȧ-hĕnd′), n. Math. The quantity to be subtracted.

sub-trop′ic (-trŏp′ĭk) } a. Of, pert. to, or desig-
sub-trop′i-cal (-ĭ-kăl) } nating, the regions [sub-
trop′ics (-ĭks)] bordering on the tropical zone.

sub′urb (sŭb′ûrb), n. An outlying part of a city or town. [characteristic of, suburbs.]

sub-ur′ban (sŭb-ûr′băn), a. Of, pert. to, or]

sub-ven′tion (sŭb-vĕn′shŭn), n. **1.** Support; help. **2.** A government aid; subsidy.

sub-ver′sion (sŭb-vûr′shŭn), n. A subverting, or state of being subverted; utter ruin.

sub-ver′sive (-vûr′sĭv), a. [4] Tending to subvert.

sub-vert′ (-vûrt′), v. t. **1.** To overturn from the foundation; ruin utterly. **2.** To pervert; corrupt. — **sub-vert′er,** n. [8] — -vert′i-ble, a. [8].

sub′way′ (sŭb′wā′), n. An underground way.

suc-ceed′ (sŭk-sēd′), v. t. **1.** To come after; follow. **2.** To come next after; hence, to take the place of. — v. i. **1.** To come after; follow; hence, to come next in possession; —often with to. **2.** To ascend the throne after the removal or death of the occupant. **3.** To obtain the object desired; be successful. — **suc-ceed′er,** n. [8].

suc-cess′ (-sĕs′), n. **1.** Favorable termination of anything attempted. **2.** A thing or person achieving success. Colloq.

suc-cess′ful (-fŏŏl), a. [4] Resulting in success; having success. — **-ful-ly,** adv. — **-ful-ness,** n.

suc-ces′sion (-sĕsh′ŭn), n. **1.** Act of succeeding; sequence. **2.** Act or right of succeeding to a throne. **3.** A series of persons or things that follow according to some established rule. **5.** A series of descendants; lineage; race; descent.

suc-ces′sion-al (-ăl), a. [4] Of or pert. to a succession; consecutive. — -ly, adv. [8].

suc-ces′sive (-sĕs′ĭv), a. [4] Following in order or in uninterrupted course; consecutive. — -ly, adv. [8] — -ness, n. [8].

suc-ces′sor (-sĕs′ẽr), n. One that succeeds.

suc-cinct′ (sŭk-sĭnkt′), a. [4] Compressed; concise; terse. — -ly, adv. [8] — -ness, n. [8].

suc′cor (sŭk′ẽr), v. t. [5] To help or relieve in difficulty or want. — n. Aid; help; relief.

suc′co-tash (-ŏ-tăsh), n. Beans and corn of maize boiled together.

suc′cu-lence (-ū-lĕns), **suc′cu-len-cy** (-lĕn-sĭ), n. Quality or condition of being succulent.

āle, senāte, câre, ăm, ăccount, ärm, ȧsk, sofȧ; ēve, évent, ênd, recênt, makẽr; īce, ĭll; ōld, ȯbey, ôrb, ŏdd, sŏft, cŏnnect; ūse, ŭnite, ûrn, ŭp, circŭs; fōŏd, fŏŏt; out, oil;

suc′cu-lent (-ŭ-lĕnt), a. [4] Juicy.

suc-cumb′ (sŭ-kŭm′), v. i. To yield; submit.

such (sŭch), a. **1.** Of that or the like kind; like; similar. **2.** Having the quality or character specified or implied. **3.** The same; — with *as*. **4.** Certain; as, *such* a one. — *pron.* Such a person or thing; such persons or things.

suck (sŭk),v.t. **1.** To draw (a liquid)by the mouth. **2.** To draw liquid from by the mouth. **3.** To draw by any process like sucking; inhale; absorb. — v. i. **1.** To draw something by producing a vacuum. **2.** To draw milk from the breast or udder. — n. Act or opportunity of sucking; suction.

suck′er (-ēr), n. **1.** One that sucks. **2.** Suckling; a sucking animal. **3.** Any of numerous fresh-water fishes that suck in food, or have mouths suggestive of sucking. **4.** In various animals, an organ for sucking or adhering. **5.** A shoot from the roots or lower part of the stem of a plant.

suck′le (sŭk′'l), v. t. [1] To give suck to. — v. i. To nurse; suck.

suck′ling (-lĭng), n. Unweaned offspring.

suc′tion (sŭk′shŭn), n. Act of drawing, as a fluid, by exhausting the air. [ble of; sucking.

suc-to′ri-al (sŭk-tō′rĭ-ǎl), a. Fitted for, or capa-

sud′den (sŭd′'n; -ĕn), a. [3] **1.** Happening or coming unexpectedly; rapid and unforeseen. **2.** Hastily prepared, made, done, etc.; quick; rapid. — n. An unexpected occurrence. *Obs.*, exc. in all of a sudden, etc., suddenly. — **-ly**, *adv.* — **-ness**, n.

su′dor-if′er-ous (sū′dŏr-ĭf′ẽr-ŭs), a. [4] Producing or secreting sweat.

su′dor-if′ic (sū′dŏr-ĭf′ĭk), a. [4] Causing sweat. — n. A sudorific medicine.

suds (sŭdz), n. pl. Soapy water, esp. when frothy.

sue (sū), v. t. [1] **1.** To seek after; woo. **2.** *Law.* **a** To seek justice or right from by legal process. **b** To proceed with (an action); to take legal action upon (a claim).— v. i. **1.** To make request (for); plead. **2.** *Law.* To take legal proceedings in court.

suède (swād; *F.* swĕd), n. Undressed kid.

su′et (sū′ĕt), n. The hard fat about the kidneys and loins in beef and mutton.

suf′fer (sŭf′ẽr), v. t. **1.** To feel or endure (pain, annoyance, etc.); submit to with distress or grief. **2.** To experience. **3.** To allow; permit; tolerate. — v. i. **1.** To undergo pain of body or mind. **2.** To sustain loss or damage. **3.** To undergo punishment, esp. of death. — **suf′fer-er**, n. [8].

suf′fer-a-ble (-ȧ-b'l), a. [4] Endurable.

suf′fer-ance(-ǎns),n. **1.** Patient endurance; long-suffering. **2.** Toleration; permission; leave.

suf′fer-ing, *vb. n.* of SUFFER. The bearing of pain, inconvenience, or loss; also, a pain endured.

suf-fice′ (sŭ-fīs′; -fīz′), v. t. [1] To satisfy; content. — v. i. To be enough or adequate.

suf-fi′cien-cy (sŭ-fĭsh′ĕn-sĭ), n. **1.** Quality of being sufficient, or adequate; adequacy. **2.** Qualification for any purpose. **3.** Adequate substance or means. **4.** Conceit; self-confidence.

suf-fi′cient (-ĕnt), a. [4] Enough; equal to the need. — **-ly**, *adv.* [8].

suf′fix (sŭf′ĭks), n. A letter, letters, or syllable or syllables added to the end of a word to modify the meaning. [tach as a suffix.

suf-fix′ (sŭ-fĭks′), v. t. To annex to the end; at-

suf′fo-cate (sŭf′ō-kāt), v. t. [1] **1.** To kill by stopping respiration; stifle. **2.** To extinguish by depriving of air, as fire. — v. i. To be suffocated.

suf′fo-ca′tion (-kā′shŭn), n. Act of suffocating, or state of being suffocated. [to stifle.

suf′fo-ca-tive (sŭf′ō-kā-tĭv), a. Tending or able

suf′fra-gan (sŭf′rȧ-gǎn), a. Assistant; as, a *suffragan* bishop. — n. A suffragan bishop.

suf′frage (-rȧj), n. **1.** A vote; assent. **2.** Right or act of voting in political matters.

suf′fra-gette′ (sŭf′rȧ-jĕt′), n. A woman who advocates woman's suffrage. *Cant.*

suf′fra-gist (sŭf′rȧ-jĭst), n. **1.** A voter. **2.** An advocate of suffrage; as, a woman *suffragist*.

suf-fuse′ (sŭ-fūz′), v. t. [1] To overspread, as with a fluid, tinge, or tint.

suf-fu′sion (-fū′zhŭn), n. **1.** A suffusing, or state of being suffused. **2.** That which suffuses.

sug′ar (shŏŏg′ẽr), n. **1.** A well-known sweet carbohydrate, derived chiefly from a tall, perennial, jointed tropical grass (**sugar cane**) and from the large white roots of a variety of beet (**sugar beet**). **2.** Any of a class of sweet carbohydrates, as glucose, lactose, etc.— sugar of milk. = LACTOSE. — v. t. **1.** To sweeten, cover, or sprinkle with sugar. **2.** To sweeten (something distasteful), as by soft words. — v. i. To form or make sugar.

sugar loaf. **1.** A loaf or mass of refined sugar, usually cone-shaped, now rarely made. **2.** Something shaped like a sugar loaf, as a hat or a hill.

sugar maple. A hard maple of the eastern United States. Its sap is the chief source of maple sugar.

sug′ar-plum′ (shŏŏg′ẽr-plŭm′), n. A sweetmeat.

sug′ar-y (-ĭ), a. [4] Like sugar; sweet; honeyed.

sug-gest′ (sŭg-jĕst′), v. i. To present (a matter, problem, etc.), usually indirectly, to the mind; intimate; hint.— **sug-gest′er**, n. [8].

sug-ges′tion (-jĕs′chŭn), n. **1.** A suggesting; presentation of an idea, esp. indirectly. **2.** That which is suggested; intimation.

sug-ges′tive (-jĕs′tĭv), a. [4] **1.** Tending to suggest; stimulative of thought. **2.** Suggesting, or tending to suggest, what is improper, etc.; as, a *suggestive* play. — **-ly**, *adv.* [8].— **-ness**, n. [8].

su′i-cid′al (sū′ĭ-sĭd′ǎl), a. [4] Pertaining to, or of the nature of, suicide.— **su′i-cid′al-ly**, *adv.* [8].

su′i-cide (sū′ĭ-sīd), n. Act of taking one's own life voluntarily and intentionally; self-murder. — n. One guilty of self-murder.

suit (sūt), n. **1.** Act of suing; entreaty; solicitation; esp., wooing. **2.** *Law.* An action or process in a court; legal application to a court for justice. **3.** *Playing Cards.* One of the four sets of cards in a pack. **4.** A number of things used together; a set. Often, short for *suit of clothes*.— v. t. **1.** To fit; adapt; accommodate. **2.** To be fitted or adjusted to accord with; befit. **3.** To please; satisfy. — v. i. To agree; accord; correspond.

suit′a-bil′i-ty (sūt′ȧ-bĭl′ĭ-tĭ), n. Suitable quality.

suit′a-ble (sūt′ȧ-b'l), a. [4] Capable of suiting; proper. — **-ness**, n. — **suit′a-bly**, *adv.* [8].

suite(swēt),n. **1.** A retinue, or company of attendants, as on a person of rank. **2.** A connected series or succession of objects.

suit′or (sūt′ẽr), n. One who sues; esp.: **a** A wooer; lover. **b** *Law.* A party in a suit.

sulk (sŭlk), *v. i.* To be sulky or sullen.—*n.* State of being sulky; sulky mood or humor; — often in *pl.*

sulk'i-ly (sŭl'kĭ-lĭ), *adv.* In a sulky manner.

sulk'i-ness (sŭl'kĭ-nĕs), *n.* Quality or state of being sulky; sullenness; moroseness.

sulk'y (sŭl'kĭ), *a.* [3] Moodily silent; morose.

sulk'y, *n. ; pl.* SULKIES (-kĭz). A light two-wheeled carriage for one person.

sul'len (sŭl'ĕn), *a.* [3] **1.** Disposed to be alone; gloomily silent; morose. **2.** Gloomy; dismal; melancholy. — **-ly**, *adv.* — **-ness**, *n.* [8].

sul'ly (-ĭ), *v. t.* [2] To soil; tarnish; stain; defile. — *v. i.* To become soiled; tarnish.— *n. ; pl.* -LIES (-ĭz). Soil; stain. [acid.

sul'phate (sŭl'fāt), *n.* *Chem.* A salt of sulphuric

sul'phide (-fīd; -fĭd), *n.* *Chem.* A binary compound of sulphur.

sul'phur (sŭl'fŭr), *n.* *Chem.* A nonmetallic element occurring native and combined. It burns in air with a flame and suffocating odor.

sul'phu-rate (-fū-rāt), *v. t.* [1] To sulphuret.

sul-phu're-ous (sŭl-fū'rē-ŭs), *a.* [4] Sulphurous.

sul'phu-ret (sŭl'fū-rĕt), *v. t.* [7] To combine or impregnate with sulphur.

sul-phu'ric (sŭl-fū'rĭk), *a.* Of, pertaining to, or containing, sulphur, esp. in a higher valence. — **sulphuric acid**, a heavy, corrosive, oily liquid, early made from green vitriol, whence the name *oil of vitriol*.

sul'phur-ous (sŭl'fŭr-ŭs ; sŭl-fū'rŭs), *a.* [4] Of, pertaining to, or containing, sulphur, esp. in a lower valence; like sulphur; fig., heated; fiery.

sul'phur-y (sŭl'fŭr-ĭ), *a.* [4] Resembling sulphur.

sul'tan (sŭl'tăn ; *Ar.* sŏŏl-tän′), *n.* A ruler or sovereign, esp. of a Mohammedan state; esp. [*often cap.*], a sovereign of the former Turkish Empire.

sul-ta'na (sŭl-tä'nà), *n.* The wife or, sometimes, the mother, sister, or daughter, of a sultan.

sul'tan-ate (sŭl'tăn-āt), *n.* The rule, dominion, territory, or office, of a sultan.

sul'tan-ess (sŭl'tăn-ĕs), *n.* A sultana.

sul'try (sŭl'trĭ), *a.* [3] **1.** Oppressively hot. **2.** Very hot and moist, or close and oppressive, as air. — **sul'tri-ly**, *adv.* [8] — **-tri-ness**, *n.* [8].

sum (sŭm), *n.* **1.** The aggregate of two or more numbers, magnitudes, or the like; amount. **2.** A quantity of money or currency. **3.** Maximum amount; utmost degree; height; as, the *sum* of earthly bliss. **4.** *Arith.* A problem; an example. — *v. t. ;* SUMMED (sŭmd) ; SUM'MING. **1.** To cast up, as a column of figures ; add together; — usually with *up*. **2.** To condense; recapitulate briefly ; — usually with *up*. — *v. i.* To recapitulate ; — usually with *up*.

su'mac (sū'măk ; shŏō'măk), *n.* **1.** Any of a large genus of shrubs or small trees many species of which are poisonous. Also, the wood of any species. **2.** A material used in tanning and dyeing, made from various species of sumac.

sum'ma-rize (sŭm'à-rīz), *v. t.* [1] To tell in, or reduce to, a summary; present briefly.

sum'ma-ry (-rĭ), *a.* [4] **1.** Formed into a sum; summed up; compact; concise. **2.** Done without delay or formality.— **sum'ma-ri-ly** (-rĭ-lĭ), *adv.* [8] — **-ri-ness**, *n.* [8].

sum'ma-ry, *n. ; pl.* -RIES (-rĭz). An abstract, abridgment, or compendium.

sum-ma'tion (sŭm-ā'shŭn), *n.* Act of summing or adding ; addition ; also, an aggregate.

sum'mer (sŭm'ẽr), *n.* In any region, the season of the year in which the sun shines most directly; the warmest period of the year. — *v. i.* To pass the summer ; as, to *summer* in Europe.

sum'mer-house/ (-hous′), *n.* A rustic covered structure in a garden or park.

sum'mer-y (-ĭ), *a.* Of, pert. to, or like, summer.

sum'mit (sŭm'ĭt), *n.* The top; highest point.

sum'mon (sŭm'ŭn), *v. t.* **1.** To call, bid, or send for. **2.** To notify or command to come or appear, as in court. **3.** To rouse or excite. — **-er** (-ẽr), *n.*

sum'mons (-ŭnz), *n. ; pl.* -MONSES (-ŭn-zĕz). Act of summoning ; a call by authority to appear or attend ; a citation or warning to appear in court.

sump'ter (sŭmp'tẽr), *n.* An animal, esp. a horse, that carries burdens. [or expenditure.

sump'tu-a-ry (-tụ̄-ȧ-rĭ), *a.* Relating to expense

sump'tu-ous (-ŭs), *a.* [4] Involving large expense; luxurious. — **-ly**, *adv.* [8] — **-ness**, *n.* [8].

sun (sŭn), *n.* **1.** The heavenly luminary the light of which constitutes day; the member of the solar system round which the earth and other planets revolve. **2.** Any heavenly body like our sun. **3.** Sunshine. — *v. t. ;* SUNNED (sŭnd) ; SUN'NING. To expose to the sun's rays; warm or dry in the sun.

sun'beam/ (sŭn'bēm′), *n.* A ray of sunshine.

sun'bon'net (-bŏn′ĕt), *n.* A projecting bonnet worn as a protection against the sun.

sun'burn/ (-bûrn′), *n.* Inflammation of the skin, from exposure to the sun's rays; tan. — *v.t. & i.* To burn or discolor by the sun; tan.

Sun'day (-dȧ), *n.* The first day of the week, widely observed as a day of rest and of religious worship; the Christian Sabbath.

sun'der (sŭn'dẽr), *v. t.* To disunite; part ; divide; sever. — *n.* A separation into parts ; division.

sun'dew/ (-dū′), *n.* Any of a genus of herbs, having viscid glands on their leaves, by means of which they capture and digest small insects.

sun'di'al (-dī′ȧl), *n.* An instrument to show the time of day by the shadow of a gnomon, or style.

sun dog, *or* **sun'dog**/, *n.* A parhelion.

sun'down/ (sŭn'doun′), *n.* Sunset.

sun'dries (-drĭz), *n. pl.* Sundry small things.

sun'dry (-drĭ), *a.* Several ; divers ; various.

sun'fish/ (-fĭsh′), *n.* **1.** A remarkable marine fish having a deep body truncated behind, high dorsal and anal fins, and a fringelike caudal fin. **2.** Any of certain perchlike fresh-water fishes, having, usually, brilliant metallic coloration.

sun'flow'er (-flou′ẽr), *n.* Any of a genus of plants, of the aster family, with large yellow flowers.

sung (sŭng), **sunk** (sŭnk), *pret. & p. p.* of SING, SINK.

sunk'en (sŭnk′'n), *a.* Sunk; esp., lying on the bottom of a body of water. [*n.* [8].

sun'less, *a.* Without sun; dark.— **sun'less-ness**,

sun'light/ (sŭn'lĭt′), *n.* The light of the sun.

sun'ny (sŭn′ĭ), *a.* [3] **1.** Of or pertaining to, or like, the sun; shining ; bright ; cheerful ; genial. **2.** Exposed to the sun. — **sun'ni-ly**, *adv.* [8] — **sun'ni-ness**, *n.* [8].

sun'rise/ (sŭn'rīz′), *n.* **1.** The first appearance, or the rising, of the sun above the horizon ; the time of such appearance. **2.** The east.

āle, senāte, cáre, ăm, ắccount, ärm, ȧsk, sofȧ ; ēve, ĕvent, ĕnd, recĕnt, makẽr; īce, ĭll; ōld, ŏbey, ôrb, ŏdd, sŏft, cŏnnect; ūse, ŭnite, ûrn, ŭp, circŭs; fŏŏd, fŏŏt; out, oil;

sun'set' (sŭn'sĕt'), n. **1.** The descent of the sun below the horizon; the time of such descent; evening. **2.** The west.

sun'shade' (-shād'), n. Anything used as a protection from sunshine, as a sun umbrella.

sun'shine' (-shīn'), n. **1.** The sun's direct rays, the place where they fall, or the warmth and light which they give. **2.** Anything having a warming and cheering influence.— **sun'shin'y** (-ĭ), a.

sun spot, or **sun'spot'**, n. One of the dark spots that appear periodically on the sun's surface.

sun'stroke' (sŭn'strōk'), n. An affection, often fatal, due to exposure to the sun or excessive heat.

sup (sŭp), v.t.; SUPPED (sŭpt); -PING. To take (liquid) into the mouth with the lips; sip. — n. A small mouthful of liquid; a sip. — v. i. **1.** To sip. **2.** To eat the evening meal; take supper.

su'per-a-bound' (sū'pẽr-á-bound'), v. i. To be superabundant.

su'per-a-bun'dance (-bŭn'dăns), n. Excess.

su'per-a-bun'dant (-bŭn'dănt), a. [4] Abounding greatly or to excess; redundant.— **-ly**, adv.[8].

su'per-add' (-ăd'), v. t. To add over and above.

su'per-an'nu-ate (-ăn'ū-āt), v. t. [1] **1.** To impair or disqualify on account of age or infirmity; — chiefly in p. p. **2.** To retire and pension because of old age or infirmity. — **su'per-an'nu-a'-tion** (-ā'shŭn), n.

su-perb' (sū-pûrb'), a. [3] **1.** Grand, magnificent; stately. **2.** Rich; elegant.— **su-perb'ly**, adv. [8].— **su-perb'ness**, n. [8].

su'per-car'go (sū'pẽr-kär'gō), n. An officer in a merchant ship in charge of the commercial concerns of the voyage.

su'per-cil'i-ous (sū'pẽr-sĭl'ĭ-ŭs), a. [4] Lofty with pride, haughtily contemptuous.— **su'per-cil'i-ous-ly**, adv. [8] — **-ness**, n. [8].

su'per-er'o-gate (-ĕr'ō-gāt), v. i. [1] To do more than duty requires.

su'per-er'o-ga'tion (-gā'shŭn), n. The performance of more than duty requires.

su'per-e-rog'a-to-ry (-ē-rŏg'á-tō-rĭ), a. [4] Of the nature of supererogation; superfluous.

su'per-fi'cial (-fĭsh'ăl), a. [4] **1.** Of or pert. to the superficies, or surface; lying on, or near, the surface; shallow. **2.** Reaching or comprehending only what is obvious or apparent; not profound or thorough.— **-ly**, adv. — **-ness**, n. [8].

su'per-fi'ci-al'i-ty (-ĭ-ăl'ĭ-tĭ), n.; pl. -TIES (-tĭz). Quality or state of being superficial; also, a superficial quality, character, or the like.

su'per-fi'ci-es (-fĭsh'ĭ-ēz), n. The surface.

su'per-fine (sū'pẽr-fīn), a. **1.** Very fine; extra fine. **2.** Very subtle or delicate; too nice; as, superfine tastes. — **-fine'ness**, n. [8].

su'per-flu'i-ty (-flōō'ĭ-tĭ), n.; pl. -ITIES (-tĭz). State of being, or that which is, superfluous.

su-per'flu-ous (sū-pûr'flōō-ŭs), a. [4] In excess of what is wanted or is sufficient; excessive. — **su-per'flu-ous-ly**, adv. — **-ness**, n. [8].

su'per-hu'man (sū'pẽr-hū'măn), a. [4] Above or beyond what is human; sometimes, divine.

su'per-im-pose' (-ĭm-pōz'), v. t. [1] To lay or impose on something else.

su'per-in-cum'bent (sū'pẽr-ĭn-kŭm'bĕnt), a. Lying or resting on something else.

su'per-in-duce' (-dūs'), v. t. [1] To bring in, or on, as an addition to something.

su'per-in-tend' (-tĕnd'), v. t. To have charge and oversight of; supervise.

su'per-in-tend'ence (-tĕn'dĕns), n. Act of superintending; supervision; oversight, direction.

su'per-in-tend'en-cy (-tĕn'dĕn-sĭ), n. Office or term of office of a superintendent.

su'per-in-tend'ent (-dĕnt), a. Overseeing, superintending. — n. One who superintends.

su-pe'ri-or (sū-pē'rĭ-ẽr), a. **1.** More elevated in place or position; higher, upper. **2.** Higher in rank or office; more exalted. **3.** Higher or greater in excellence. **4.** Beyond the power or influence of. **5.** Affecting superiority.— n. **1.** One who surpasses another, as in rank or ability. **2.** Head of a monastery, convent, or the like.— **su-pe'ri-or-ly**, adv. [8].

su-pe'ri-or'i-ty (sū-pē'rĭ-ŏr'ĭ-tĭ), n. Quality or state of being superior.

su-per'la-tive (sū-pûr'lá-tĭv), a. **1.** Surpassing all other; supreme. **2.** Gram. Expressing the highest (or, with least, the lowest) degree or amount of the quality, manner, etc., denoted by an adjective or an adverb; as, highest, most pleasant, least bright.— n. **1.** The utmost degree, **2.** Gram. The superlative degree; also, a form denoting it. — **-ly**, adv. — **-ness**, n. [8].

su-per'nal (sū-pûr'năl), a. **1.** Being in a higher place or region. **2.** Celestial; heavenly.

su'per-nat'u-ral (sū'pẽr-năt'ū-răl), a. [4] Beyond or exceeding the powers or laws (i. e., observed sequences) of nature; miraculous.— **-ly**, adv. [8].

su'per-nu'mer-a-ry (-nū'mẽr-á-rĭ), a. [4] **1.** Exceeding the stated, prescribed, usual, or required number or quantity; superfluous. — n.; pl. -RIES (-rĭz). **1.** A supernumerary person or thing **2.** In theaters, one not a regular actor who appears in mob scenes, spectacles, etc.

su'per-pose' (-pōz'), v. t. [1] To lay (on or upon). — **su'per-po-si'tion** (-pô-zĭsh'ŭn), n.

su'per-scribe' (-skrīb'), v. t. [1] To write or engrave (anything) on the top or surface, write a name, address, or the like, on the outside or cover of (anything).

su'per-scrip'tion (-skrĭp'shŭn), n. **1.** Act of superscribing. **2.** That which is superscribed; inscription; an address on a letter, envelope, etc.

su'per-sede' (-sēd'), v. t. [1] **1.** To come or be placed in the room of; replace. **2.** To supplant. — **-sed'er** (-sēd'ẽr), n. [8].

su'per-so'dure (-sē'dūr), n. Act of superseding.

su'per-ses'sion (-sĕsh'ŭn), n. Act of superseding, or state of being superseded.

su'per-sti'tion (-stĭsh'ŭn), n. **1.** An excessive reverence for, or fear of, that which is unknown **2.** A belief, act, or practice, esp. of a religious nature, regarded as irrational or injurious; false religion. **3.** Such beliefs, etc., collectively.

su'per-sti'tious (-ŭs), a. [4] Of, pert. to, proceeding from, or marked by, superstition. — **su'per-sti'tious-ly**, adv. [8] — **-tious-ness**, n. [8].

su'per-struc'ture (-strŭk'tūr), n. An edifice or a part of a structure considered in relation to that on which it rests; a building above the basement.

su'per-vene' (-vēn'), v. i. [1] To come as something additional or extraneous; occur with reference to something else; be added or follow closely.

su'per-vise' (sū'pẽr-vīz'), *v. t.* [1] To superintend; oversee. [superintendence.]

su'per-vi'sion (-vĭzh'ŭn), *n.* Act of overseeing; [superintendence.]

su'per-vi'sor (-vī'zẽr), *n.* One who supervises.

su'per-vi'so-ry (-zō-rĭ), *a.* Pert. to supervision.

su-pine' (sū-pīn'; sū'pīn), *a.* [4] **1.** Lying on the back, or with the face upward. **2.** Mentally or morally inert; listless. — **-ly,** *adv.* — **-ness,** *n.*

su'pine (sū'pīn), *n.* A verbal noun, esp. one in Latin having two cases, accusative and ablative.

sup'per (sŭp'ẽr), *n.* The evening meal; the last meal of the day when dinner is not the last.

sup-plant' (sŭ-plȧnt'), *v. t.* To remove or displace, as by stratagem; esp., to supersede. — **-er,** *n.* [8].

sup'ple (sŭp''l), *a.* [4] **1.** Pliant; flexible. **2.** Yielding; compliant; submissive. **3.** Bending to the humor of others; obsequious. — *v. t. & i.* [1] To make or become supple. — **-ness,** *n.*

sup'ple-ment (sŭp'lē-mĕnt), *n.* That which completes something already organized, arranged, or set apart; esp., a continuation of a book or paper to make good deficiencies. — (-mĕnt), *v. t.* To fill or supply by additions; add to.

sup'ple-men'tal (-mĕn'tăl), **-men'ta-ry** (-mĕn'tȧ-rĭ), *a.* [4] Serving to supply what is lacking.

sup'pli-ance (sŭp'lĭ-ăns), *n.* Supplication.

sup'pli-ant (-ănt), *a.* [4] **1.** Asking earnestly and submissively. **2.** Expressing supplication. — *n.* One who supplicates. — **-ly,** *adv.* [8].

sup'pli-cant (sŭp'lĭ-kănt), *a.* [4] Entreating; asking submissively. — *n.* One who supplicates.

sup'pli-cate (-kāt), *v. t.* [1] **1.** To entreat for; implore. **2.** To address in prayer. — *v. i.* To make supplication.

sup'pli-ca'tion (-kā'shŭn), *n.* Act of supplicating; humble petition; entreaty; solicitation.

sup'pli-ca-to-ry (-kȧ-tō-rĭ), *a.* [4] Supplicating.

sup-ply' (sŭ-plī'), *v. t.* [2] **1.** To furnish with what is wanted or needed; replenish. **2.** To give or provide; furnish. **3.** To make up for, or repair, as a vacancy or loss; to fill temporarily. — *n.; pl.* **-PLIES** (-plīz'). **1.** Act of supplying. **2.** That which supplies a want; esp., the daily food, etc., of an army; stores; — chiefly in *pl.* **3.** Quantity of any article offered at a given price.

sup-port' (sŭ-pōrt'), *v. t.* **1.** To bear the weight or stress of; uphold; sustain. **2.** To endure; bear; undergo; suffer; tolerate. **3.** To encourage; aid; help. **4.** To maintain; provide for. **5.** To enable to continue; carry on. **6.** To verify, substantiate. — *n.* **1.** Act or operation of supporting. **2.** One that supports.

sup-port'a-ble (-pōrtȧ-b'l), *a.* [4] Capable of being supported; endurable. — **-bly,** *adv.* [8].

sup-port'er (-pōr'tẽr), *n.* One that supports.

sup-pos'a-ble (-pōz'ȧ-b'l), *a.* [4] Capable of being supposed. — **sup-pos'a-bly,** *adv.* [8].

sup-pos'al (-pōs'ăl), *n.* Supposition.

sup-pose' (-pōz'), *v. t.* [1] **1.** To assume tentatively as proved or true. **2.** To receive as true; imagine; believe; think. **3.** To imply. — *v. i.* To conjecture; think; opine. — **sup-pos'er,** *n.* [8].

sup-posed' (-pōzd'), *p. a.* Accepted as true; imagined; — often implying falsity. — **-ly,** *adv.*

sup'po-si'tion (sŭp'ō-zĭsh'ŭn), *n.* **1.** Act of supposing or assuming something, as for argument; assumption. **2.** Opinion or belief without sufficient evidence; conjecture; hypothesis.

sup'po-si'tion-al (-ăl), *a.* [4] Hypothetical. — **sup'po-si'tion-al-ly,** *adv.* [8].

sup-pos'i-ti'tious (sŭ-pŏz'ĭ-tĭsh'ŭs), *a.* [4] Fraudulently substituted; spurious. — **-ly,** *adv.* [8].

sup-pos'i-to-ry (-pŏz'ĭ-tō-rĭ), *n.; pl.* **-RIES** (-rĭz). An easily fusible, medicated preparation for introduction into the rectum, etc.

sup-press' (-prĕs'), *v. t.* **1.** To overpower and crush; subdue; quell. **2.** To keep in; restrain from utterance or vent. **3.** To conceal; prevent publication or revelation of. **4.** To stop; check; restrain. — **sup-press'er, sup-pres'sor** (-ẽr), *n.*

sup-pres'sion (sŭ-prĕsh'ŭn), *n.* Act of suppressing; overthrow. [suppress.]

sup-pres'sive (sŭ-prĕs'ĭv), *a.* [4] Tending to [suppress.]

sup'pu-rate (sŭp'ū-rāt), *v. i.* [1] To generate pus.

sup'pu-ra'tion (-rā'shŭn), *n.* **1.** Act or process of suppurating. **2.** Pus. [suppurate.]

sup'pu-ra-tive (sŭp'ū-rā-tĭv), *a.* Tending to [suppurate.]

su'pra-mun'dane (sū'prȧ-mŭn'dān), *a.* Being above the world; celestial.

su-prem'a-cy (sū-prĕm'ȧ-sĭ), *n.* Supreme state, authority, or power.

su-preme' (-prēm'), *a.* **1.** Highest in authority or power. Hence: a Dominant; overruling. b Holding, or pert. to, the highest rank. **2.** Highest in degree. — **-ly,** *adv.* **-ness,** *n.* [8].

su'rah (sōō'rȧ; sū'rȧ), *n.* Soft twilled silk fabric.

sur'base (sûr'bās'), *n.* *Arch.* A molding at the top of the base of a pedestal, wall, etc.

sur-cease' (sûr-sēs'), *n.* Cessation; stop; end.

sur-charge' (-chärj'), *v. t.* [1] To overload; overcharge. — *n.* An overcharge; excessive burden.

sur'cin'gle (sûr'sĭn'g'l), *n.* A belt or girth to bind a saddle, blanket, etc., on a horse's back.

surd (sûrd), *a.* *Phon.* Uttered, as an element of speech, without voice, or vocal tone; voiceless; as, *f, p, s,* etc. — *n.* *Phon.* A surd element of speech.

sure (shŏŏr), *a.* [3] **1.** Assured in mind; knowing, believing, trusting, etc., with certainty. **2.** Admitting of no doubt, condition, etc.; indubitable. **3.** Entirely trustworthy or dependable; reliable. **4.** Firmly established; fixed; stable. **5.** Destined; certain; — followed by *to.* — *adv.* Surely.

sure'–foot'ed, *a.* [4] Not liable to stumble or fall.

sure'ly (shŏŏr'lĭ), *adv.* **1.** In a sure or certain manner; certainly. **2.** Without danger; securely.

sure'ness, *n.* Quality or state of being sure.

sure'ty (shŏŏr'tĭ), *n.; pl.* **-TIES** (-tĭz). **1.** State of being sure; certainty. **2.** That which makes sure; esp., security against loss or damage. **3.** *Law.* One liable for the debt, default, or miscarriage of another. **4.** A sponsor.

sure'ty-ship (-shĭp), *n.* The state of being surety; obligation of a surety. [the shore.]

surf (sûrf), *n.* The swell of the sea breaking on [the shore.]

sur'face (sûr'fȧs), *n.* The exterior of anything that has length and breadth; a face of a solid, esp. the upper one; outside. — *v. t.* [1] To give a surface to; esp., to make smooth or plain.

sur'feit (sûr'fĭt), *n.* **1.** Excess, esp. in eating and drinking. **2.** Fullness and oppression of the sys-

tem; satiety. — *v. t.* To produce surfeit in; cloy; — often reflexive. — *v. i.* To indulge to satiety.

surge (sûrj), *n.* **1.** A billow; a great, rolling swell of water; also, such swells collectively. **2.** The motion of, or that caused by, a wave; sweep; rush. — *v. i.* [1] To swell; rise high and roll.

sur'geon (sûr'jŭn), *n.* One who practices surgery.

sur'ger-y (sûr'jẽr-ĭ), *n.* Art or practice of healing by manual operation; science which treats of mechanical or operative remedial measures.

sur'gi-cal (-jĭ-kăl), *a.* Of or pertaining to surgeons or surgery. — **sur'gi-cal-ly**, *adv.* [8].

sur'ly (sûr'lĭ), *a.* [3] Gloomily morose; ill-natured, abrupt, and rude. — **sur'li-ly** (-lĭ-lĭ), *adv.* [8] — **sur'li-ness**, *n.* [8].

sur-mise' (sŭr-mīz'), *n.* A thought based on scanty evidence; suspicion. — *v. t.* [1] To imagine or infer on slight grounds; guess.

sur-mount' (-mount'), *v. t.* **1.** To rise above; overtop. **2.** To conquer; overcome. — **sur-mount'a-ble**, *a.* [8] — **sur-mount'er**, *n.* [8].

sur'name' (sûr'nām'), *n.* A name or appellation added to the baptismal, or Christian, name, and become a family name. — *v. t.* To call by a surname; give a surname to.

sur-pass' (sŭr-pàs'), *v. t.* To exceed. — **-a-ble**, *a.*

sur-pass'ing, *p. a.* [4] Eminently excellent.

sur'plice (sûr'plĭs), *n.* An outer vestment of white linen worn (chiefly) by certain clergy.

sur'plus (-plŭs), *n.* That which remains when use or need is satisfied; excess. — *a.* Being or constituting a surplus; more than sufficient.

sur'plus-age (-åj), *n.* Surplus; excess.

sur-pris'al (sŭr-prīz'ăl), *n.* Surprise.

sur-prise' (-prīz'), *v. t.* [1] **1.** To come upon or attack unexpectedly. **2.** To take unawares. **3.** To strike with wonder, astonishment, or confusion, by something sudden, unexpected, or remarkable. — *n.* **1.** Act of coming upon, or taking, unawares; surprisal. **2.** State of being surprised; astonishment. **3.** Anything sudden and unexpected, esp. when causing astonishment.

sur-ren'der (sŭ-rĕn'dẽr), *n.* A yielding one's person or a thing into the power of another. — *v. t.* **1.** To yield to the power of another; give up on compulsion or demand. **2.** To give up possession of; yield; relinquish. **3.** To yield to any influence, emotion, etc.; — used reflexively. — *v. i.* To give up to the power of another; yield.

sur'rep-ti'tious (sŭr'ĕp-tĭsh'ŭs), *a.* [4] Done or made by stealth, or without authority. — **-ly**, *adv.*

sur'rey (sûr'ĭ), *n.; pl.* -REYS (-ĭz). A kind of four-wheeled, two-seated pleasure carriage.

Surrey.

sur'ro-gate (-ö-gåt), *n.* A judicial officer who has jurisdiction over the probate of wills, etc.

sur-round' (sŭ-round'), *v. t.* **1.** To inclose on all sides; encompass. **2.** To inclose, as a body of troops, so as to cut off retreat; invest, as a city.

sur-round'ings, *n. pl.* The things which surround or environ; external conditions, etc.

sur-tout' (sŭr-tōōt'; -tōō'), *n.* A man's overcoat, esp. when long and close-fitting.

sur-veil'lance (sûr-vāl'yăns; -ăns), *n.* Oversight.

sur'vey' (-vā'), *v. t.* **1.** To inspect; look over or about, as from a height. **2.** To scrutinize. **3.** To examine with reference to condition, situation, value, etc. **4.** To make a survey of.

sur'vey (sûr'vā; sŭr-vā'), *n.* **1.** Act, process, or result of surveying; examination. **2.** Operation of finding and delineating the contour, dimensions, position, etc., of any part of the earth's surface; also, a measured plan and description of any place, or of a road or line through it.

sur-vey'ing, *n.* Act, occupation, or science of making surveys (sense 2).

sur-vey'or (-ẽr), *n.* **1.** One who makes a survey. **2.** *Customs.* An officer charged with ascertaining the quantity, condition, and value of imports. *U. S.*

sur-viv'al (-vīv'ăl), *n.* **1.** Act or fact of surviving; an outliving. **2.** One that survives or outlasts.

sur-vive' (-vīv'), *v. t.* [1] To live beyond the life or existence of; outlive; outlast. — *v. i.* To remain alive or existent. — **sur-viv'or** (-ẽr), *n.* [8].

sus-cep'ti-bil'i-ty (sŭ-sĕp'tĭ-bĭl'ĭ-tĭ), *n.; pl.* -TIES (-tĭz). **1.** State of being susceptible. **2.** Sensibility, sensitiveness; — often in *pl.*

sus-cep'ti-ble (-sĕp'tĭ-b'l), *a.* [4] **1.** Capable of being changed or influenced; readily acted on; — with *of* or *to*. **2.** Capable of mental or emotional impression; sensitive. — **-ness**, *n.* — **-bly**, *adv.*

sus-cep'tive (-tĭv), *a.* Susceptible.

sus-pect' (sŭs-pĕkt'), *v. t.* **1.** To imagine to be, occur, happen, etc.; surmise. **2.** To imagine to be guilty, without proof. **3.** To doubt; mistrust; distrust. — *v. i.* To suspect anything; be suspicious. — *n.* One suspected; now, a person suspected of crime.

sus-pend' (-pĕnd'), *v. t.* **1.** To attach to something above; hang; hence, to hold as if by hanging. **2.** To cause to cease for a time; stay. **3.** To hold in an undetermined or undecided state. **4.** To debar temporarily (from a privilege, office, etc.). — *v. i.* To cease temporarily from operation, esp., to stop payment; — of a business concern.

sus-pend'er (-pĕn'dẽr), *n.* **1.** One that suspends. **2.** One of two bands to support the trousers; — usually in *pl.*

sus-pense' (-pĕns'), *n.* **1.** State of being suspended. **2.** State of uncertainty, usually with anxiety or expectation. **3.** Cessation; pause.

sus-pen'sion (-pĕn'shŭn), *n.* **1.** Act of suspending; state of being suspended; esp., temporary delay, interruption, or cessation. **2.** Stoppage of payment; failure; — of a business concern. **3.** State of a solid when its particles are mixed with, but undissolved in, a fluid.

suspension bridge. A bridge having its roadway suspended, usually by rods, from a freely hanging cable or cables.

sus-pen'so-ry (sŭs-pĕn'sô-rĭ), *a.* Suspended; also, fitted or serving to suspend. — *n.; pl.* -RIES (-rĭz). That which holds up, as a truss or bandage.

sus-pi'cion (-pĭsh'ŭn), *n.* **1.** Act or fact of suspecting; mistrust. **2.** Slight degree; suggestion; hint; as, a *suspicion* of sarcasm in one's remarks. *Colloq.*

---

chair; go; sing, iŋk; **then**, thin; nature, verdure; yet; zh = z in azure. Numbers refer **to §§** in the Special Notes which, with Abbreviations, Signs, etc., precede the Vocabulary

sus-pi'cious (sŭs-pĭsh'ŭs), *a.* [4] **1.** Inclined to suspect; distrustful. **2.** Showing suspicion. **3.** Questionable. — **-ly,** *adv.*[8] — **-ness,** *n.* [8].

sus-tain' (sŭs-tān'), *v. t.* **1.** To bear up; uphold; support. **2.** To keep from sinking, as in despondency, etc. **3.** To maintain or keep up, as a conversation, an effort, etc. **4.** To maintain; support. **5.** To aid; comfort; relieve. **6.** To suffer; bear; undergo. **7.** To bear up under. **8.** To allow, support, or admit, as valid. **9.** To prove; maintain. — **sus-tain'a-ble,** *a.* [8] — **-er,** *n.* [8].

sus'te-nance (sŭs'tĕ-nǎns),*n.* **1.** Support. **2.** That which supports life; provisions.

sut'ler (sŭt'lẽr), *n.* One who follows an army and sells provisions, liquors, etc., to the troops.

sut-tee' (sŭ-tē'), *n.* A Hindu widow cremated on her husband's funeral pile; also, such cremation.

su'ture (sū'tụ̄r), *n.* **1.** Act of sewing. **2.** The seam or seamlike line along which things are sewed or united, as parts of a garment, or, *Anat.*, the line of joining or closure between the bones of the skull, etc., or any similar line of union.

su'ze-rain (-zē-rǎn), *n.* **1.** Feudal superior or lord. **2.** A state that exercises political control over another state in relation to which it is sovereign.

su'ze-rain-ty (-tĭ), *n. ; pl.* **-ties** (-tĭz). The dominion, authority, or relation of a suzerain.

swab (swŏb), *n.* **1.** A kind of mop. **2.** A bit of sponge, cloth, or the like, for applying medicaments, etc. — *v. t.;* SWABBED (swŏbd); SWAB'-BING. To clean with or as with a swab; mop.

swab'ber (-ẽr), *n.* **1.** One who swabs. **2.** A swab.

swad'dle (swŏd'l), *v. t.* [1] To bind as with a bandage; swathe; — esp. of infants. — **swaddling band, cloth,** *or* **clout,** a band or cloth wrapped round an infant, esp. a newborn infant.

swag (swăg), *n.* Booty; plunder. *Cant or Slang.*

swage (swāj), *n.* A tool for shaping metal work, by striking with a hammer or sledge. — *v. t.* [1] To shape with a swage.

swag'ger (swăg'ẽr), *v. i.* **1.** To walk with a conceited strut; walk and act pompously. **2.** To brag noisily; bluster. — *n.* Act or manner of one who swaggers. — **swag'ger-er,** *n.* [8].

swain (swān), *n.* A young rustic, esp. a country gallant or lover.

swal'low (swŏl'ō), *n.* **1.** Any of numerous small long-winged birds noted for their graceful flight. **2.** Any of certain swifts resembling swallows.

swal'low, *v. t.* **1.** To take through the gullet into the stomach. **2.** To take in or absorb; ingulf; engross. **3.** To retract; recant. **4.** To put up with; bear patiently. — *v. i.* To perform the act of swallowing something. — *n.* **1.** Act of swallowing. **2.** As much as is swallowed at once. — **swal'low-er,** *n.* [8].

swal'low-tailed' (-tāld'),*a.* Having a forked tail like that of a swallow.

swam (swăm), *pret.* of SWIM.

swamp (swŏmp),*n.* Wet, spongy land; marshy ground. — *v. t.* **1.** To plunge

American Barn Swallow. (⅓)

or sink into a swamp. **2.** To cause (a boat) to fill with water. **3.** To overwhelm. — *v. i.* **1.** To sink or stick in a swamp; become involved in insuperable difficulties. **2.** To founder; sink; be ruined.

swamp'y (swŏm'pĭ), *a.* [3] Consisting of swamp.

swan (swŏn), *n.* **1.** Any of certain aquatic birds related to but larger than the geese. **2.** A sweet singer, or a poet noted for grace and melody.

swan's'-down' (swŏnz'-doun'), *or* **swans'-down',** *n.* **1.** The fine, soft feathers of the swan. **2.** A soft, thick cloth of wool mixed with silk or cotton.

swan song. The fabled death song of the swan.

swap (swŏp), *v. t. & i. ;* SWAPPED (swŏpt) ; SWAP'-PING. Exchange; barter. *Colloq. & Dial.*

sward (swôrd), *n.* Grassy surface of land ; turf. — *v. t. & i.* To cover, or be covered, with sward.

swarm (swôrm),*n.* **1.** A large number or multitude, as of insects, esp. when in motion. **2.** A great number of honeybees, with a queen, emigrating from a hive to start a new colony; loosely, a colony of honeybees settled permanently in a hive. — *v. i.* **1.** To depart from a hive and emigrate in a body to form a new colony; — of bees. **2.** To appear or collect in a crowd, like bees ; throng together. **3.** To be thronged with beings in motion. — *v. t.* To crowd or throng.

swart (swôrt), *a.* [8] Dark-hued ; swarthy.

swarth'y (swôr'thĭ ; -thĭ), *a.* [3] Dark-hued ; swart. — **-i-ness,** *n.* [8].

swash (swŏsh), *v. i.* **1.** To move with or as with a splashing sound; splash. **2.** To bluster; brag. — *v. t.* To dash or splash about, as water. — *n.* **1.** A splashing of a liquid against something, or the noise due to it. **2.** A narrow channel of water within a sand bank, or between a sand bank and the shore.

swash'buck'ler (-bŭk'lẽr), *n.* A swaggerer.

swas'ti-ka, swas'ti-ca (swäs'tĭ-kä), *n.* A kind of symbol or ornament (see *Illust.*)

swath (swŏth ; swôth), *n.* **1.** A line of grass or grain cut and thrown together by the scythe. **2.** The whole sweep of a scythe or a machine in mowing, or the path cut in one course.

Typical Swastika.

swathe (swāth), *v. t.* [1] To bind with a band, bandage, or the like; also, to wrap (a bandage, band, or the like) about something. — *n.* A bandage ; band. — **swath'er** (swāth'ẽr), *n.* [8].

sway (swā), *v. t.* **1.** To wield with the hand ; swing. **2.** To cause to incline to one side or from side to side; turn aside. **3.** To influence or direct; govern; guide. — *v. i.* **1.** To lean; incline. **2.** To swing from side to side; oscillate; fluctuate. — *n.* **1.** Act of swaying. **2.** Influence, weight, or authority that inclines to one side. **3.** Rule; dominion; control.

swear (swâr),*v. i.; pret.* SWORE (swōr);*p. p.* SWORN (swōrn); *p. pr. & vb. n.* SWEAR'ING. **1.** To utter a solemn declaration, with an appeal to God for its truth. **2.** To make a promise, threat, vow, etc., on oath; vow. **3.** *Law.* To give evidence or state on oath. **4.** To use the name of God or sacred things profanely; curse. — *v. t.* **1.** To affirm with a solemn appeal to God for the truth of the declaration. **2.** To make (a promise, threat, etc.) or oath; vow. **3.** *Law.* To bind by an oath; administer an oath to. — **swear'er** (-ẽr), *n.* [8].

sweat (swĕt), *v. i.; pret. & p. p.* SWEAT or SWEAT'ED; *p. pr. & vb. n.* SWEAT'ING. **1.** To give off moisture through the pores of the skin; perspire. **2.** To condense moisture in drops on the surface, as a pitcher of water on a hot day. *Colloq.* **3.** To work hard; drudge. — *v. t.* **1.** To cause to perspire. **2.** To exude. **3.** To wet with perspiration. **4.** To extort property or labor from by exaction or oppression, as by a system (the **sweating system**) of taking advantage of the necessities of employees to overwork them. — *n.* **1.** Perspiration. **2.** Act of sweating; state of one who sweats. **3.** Hard work; drudgery. **4.** Moisture issuing from any substance; as, the *sweat* of hay in a stack.

sweat'er (swĕt'ẽr), *n.* One that sweats; as: **a** A sudorific. **b** A kind of thick woolen jersey.

sweat'shop' (-shŏp'), *n.* A workroom where employees are sweated (see SWEAT, *v. t.,* 4).

sweat'y (swĕt'ĭ), *a.* [3] **1.** Moist with sweat. **2.** Consisting of or like sweat. **3.** Causing sweat; laborious; toilsome; as, a *sweaty* task.

Swede (swēd), *n.* **1.** One of the people of Sweden. **2.** [*Often l. c.*] A rutabaga.

Swed'ish (swēd'ĭsh), *a.* Of or pertaining to Sweden, its inhabitants, or their language. — *n.* **1.** The language of Sweden. **2.** [Collective *pl.*] The inhabitants of Sweden.

sweep (swēp), *v. i.; pret. & p. p.* SWEPT (swĕpt); *p. pr. & vb. n.* SWEEP'ING. **1.** To move or pass with swiftness or force, as if brushing something. **2.** To move with stateliness or dignity. **3.** To pass over anything comprehensively. **4.** To clean rooms, etc., by brushing with or as with a broom. — *v. t.* **1.** To drive or carry along or off by or as by brushing. **2.** To pass a broom or the like across in order to clean. **3.** To brush against, pass over, or draw along with, or as with a brushing motion. **4.** To pass over, or traverse searchingly, as with the eye. — *n.* **1.** Act of sweeping; also: **a** A clearing out or away. **b** Act of viewing or surveying comprehensively; also, the region so viewed. **2.** Motion of a sweeping nature. **3.** A bend; curve. **4.** *Naut.* A long oar. **5.** A chimney sweeper. **6.** A long pole pivoted to the top of a post, to raise and lower a bucket for drawing water. — **sweep'er,** *n.* [8].

sweep'ing (swēp'ĭng), *n.* **1.** Act of one that sweeps. **2.** *pl.* Things collected by sweeping.

sweep'ing, *p. a.* [4] **1.** Moving swiftly and violently; of great range or scope. **2.** That sweeps or cleans with or as with a broom. —**-ly,** *adv.* [8].

sweep'stake' (swēp'stāk'), *n.* A winning of all the stakes or prizes by one contestant.

sweep'stakes' (-stāks'), *n.* **1.** = SWEEPSTAKE. **2.** *sing.* or *pl.* The whole stake on an event, esp. on a horse race. **3.** A race for a sweepstakes.

sweet (swēt), *a.* [3] **1. a** Having an agreeable taste or flavor as of sugar; sugary. **b** Having a fresh taste; fresh; as, *sweet* milk. **2.** Pleasing; agreeable; melodious; attractive; kindly. **3.** Pure and salubrious; not salt or salted; fresh. **4.** Containing sugar; not dry; — of fermented liquors. — **sweet alyssum,** an annual plant, of the cress family, with clusters of small fragrant white flowers. —

s. fern. a Any of several ferns. **b** A small shrub having aromatic fernlike leaves. — **s. flag,** a plant having long flaglike leaves and a pungent rootstock. — **s. potato,** a tropical American vine of the morning-glory family; also, its sweet mealy root, used as a vegetable. — **s. William,** a species of pink having small flowers of many colors in dense clusters. — *n.* **1.** Quality of being sweet; sweetness. **2.** That which is sweet to the taste; esp., confectionery, preserves, etc.; — usually in *pl.* **3.** That which is pleasing to the mind or the senses. **4.** A loved one; darling. — *adv.* Sweetly.

sweet'bread' (-brĕd'), *n.* The pancreas of an animal (esp. a calf or a lamb) used for food.

sweet'bri'er (-brī'ẽr), *n.* A European rose with stout prickles and single pink flowers; eglantine.

sweet'en (swēt'n), *v. t. & i.* To make or become sweet. — **sweet'en-er,** *n.* [8].

sweet'en-ing (-ĭng), *n.* **1.** The act of making sweet. **2.** That which sweetens.

sweet'heart' (swēt'härt'), *n.* One beloved.

sweet'ish, *a.* Somewhat sweet. —**-ness,** *n.* [8].

sweet'ly, *adv.* In a sweet manner.

sweet'meat' (-mēt'), *n.* Fruit preserved with sugar, as peaches, nuts, etc.; — usually in *pl.*

sweet'ness, *n.* Quality or state of being sweet.

swell (swĕl), *v. i.; pret.* SWELLED (swĕld); *p. p.* SWELLED or SWOL'LEN (swōl'n); *p. pr. & vb. n.* SWELL'ING. **1.** To increase; grow larger; dilate. **2.** To bulge out. **3.** To be puffed up with or as with some emotion. — *v. t.* **1.** To increase the size, importance, value, or the like, of. **2.** To puff up; inflate. **3.** To augment gradually in loudness, as a tone. — *n.* **1.** Act of swelling; increase in bulk, force, value. **2.** A rounded elevation, as of land **3.** A long, rolling undulation of the open sea loosely, a billow; surge. **4.** *Music.* A gradual increase and decrease of the loudness or volume of sound; also, the sign for this (<>). **5.** A fashionable man. *Colloq.*

swell'ing, *n.* **1.** Act of that which swells; state of being swollen. **2.** A prominence; esp., *Med.,* a morbid protuberance or enlargement.

swel'ter (swĕl'tẽr), *v. i.* To perspire profusely; also, to be faint from heat.

swel'ter-ing, *p. a.* [4] **1.** Sultry; oppressively hot. **2.** Faint from heat.

swept (swĕpt), *pret. & p. p.* of SWEEP.

swerve (swûrv), *v. i.* [1] **1.** To go out of a straight line; deflect; turn aside. **2.** To depart from what is established; deviate. — *v. t.* To turn aside. — *n.* A swerving; a turning aside.

swift (swĭft), *a.* [3] **1.** Moving with great speed; fleet; rapid. **2.** Happening or accomplished with rapidity. **3.** Quick; alert; prompt. **4.** Brief, short. — *adv.* Swiftly. — *n.* Any of numerous small, dull-colored birds, allied to the humming birds, but superficially resembling swallows.

swift'ly (-lĭ), *adv.* In a swift manner.

swift'ness, *n.* Quality or state of being swift.

swig (swĭg), *v. t. & i.;* SWIGGED (swĭgd); SWIG'GING. To drink in long drafts; gulp. — *n.* A long draft or drink. *Both Dial. or Colloq.*

swill (swĭl), *v. t. & i.* **1.** To drink or swallow greedily; guzzle. **2.** To fill, esp. with drink. — *n.* A semiliquid food for animals, esp. swine, composed of refuse food, mixed with water, etc.

swim (swĭm), v. i. ; pret. SWAM (swăm) or SWUM (swŭm); p. p. SWUM; p. pr. & vb. n. SWIM'MING. To be dizzy ; also, to reel or appear to reel.

swim, v. i. (for prin. parts see SWIM, to be dizzy). **1.** To move or propel one's self in water, as with hands and feet, fins, etc. **2.** To glide smoothly and quietly. **3.** To float, as on water. **4.** To abound; be plentifully supplied. — v. t. **1.** To cross, or to move over or on, by swimming. **2.** To cause to swim ; as, to swim a horse. — n. Act of swimming; also, a swimming motion. — **mer** (-ẽr), n. [8].

swin'dle (swĭn'd'l), v. t. & i. [1] To cheat or defraud. — n. Act or process of swindling ; a cheat.

swin'dler (-dlẽr), n. One who swindles ; cheat.

swine (swīn), n. sing. & pl. (See PLURAL.) Any animal of the hog kind; — chiefly used collectively.

swine'herd' (-hûrd'), n. A keeper of swine.

swing (swĭng), v. i. ; pret. & p. p. SWUNG (swŭng); p. pr. & vb. n. SWING'ING (swĭng'ĭng). **1.** To sway ; esp., to oscillate. **2.** To turn on or as on a pivot or hinge. **3.** To progress with a loose, free, swaying action. **4.** To use, or sway in, a swing. See SWING, n., 5. — v. t. **1.** To hang or suspend. **2.** To cause to swing or move to and fro. See SWING, n., 5. **3.** To hang on a pivot or hinges or between end supports. **4.** To cause to move around as on a pivot or hinges ; also, to wield ; brandish. — n. **1.** Act or process of swinging. **2.** Arc or extent through which an object swings. **3.** Tendency ; also, free scope. **4.** That which swings or is swung. **5.** An apparatus, commonly a suspended loop or rope carrying a seat, on which one may sit and swing.

swin'ish (swīn'ĭsh), a. [4] Pert. to, like, or befitting, swine ; beastly. — **ly**, adv. — **ness**, n.

swipe (swīp), n. A strong blow given with a sweeping motion. — v. t. To give a swipe to.

swirl (swûrl), v. i. To move with an eddying or whirling motion ; whirl. — v. t. To cause to swirl, or whirl. — n. A whirling motion ; eddy ; whirl.

swish (swĭsh), v. t. & i. To wave, sway, or move, making the noise represented by the word "swish." — n. A rustling sound.

Swiss (swĭs), a. Of or pertaining to Switzerland or the Swiss. — n. sing. A native or inhabitant of Switzerland ; also, pl., collectively, the people of Switzerland.

switch (swĭch), n. **1.** A small, flexible twig or rod. **2.** A tress of false hair. **3.** Railroads. a A movable part of a rail, or movable parts of opposite rails, for transferring cars from one track to another. b Act of switching. **4.** Elec. A device for shifting a current to another circuit, or for making and breaking a circuit. — v. t. **1.** To strike with a switch ; whip. **2.** To swing or whisk. **3.** To turn or shift by means of a switch. — **er**, n.

switch'back' (-băk'), n. An arrangement of zigzag railroad tracks for lessening the grade up a steep hill.

switch'board' (swĭch'bōrd'), n. Elec. An apparatus consisting of panels bearing a collection of switches so arranged that various circuits may be connected or combined.

switch'man (-măn), n. ; pl. -MEN (-mĕn). One who attends to a switch or switches.

swiv'el (swĭv'l), n. A part that turns on or as on

a headed bolt or pin ; a compound link one part of which turns on a headed bolt, pin, or the like, in the other part, so as to permit rotation. — v. i. [7] To swing or turn, as on a pin or pivot.

Swivel, in Chain.

swoll'en (swōl'n), p. p. of SWELL. [cope.

swoon (swōōn), v. i. To faint. — n. A faint ; syn-

swoop (swōōp), v. t. **1.** To sweep suddenly down on and seize ; catch while on the wing. **2.** To seize or catch up in any sudden sweeping manner. — v. i. To descend swiftly with closed wings upon prey, as a hawk ; pounce. — n. Act of coming down upon and seizing something.

sword (sōrd), n. **1.** A weapon having a long and usually pointed blade with a cutting edge or edges. **2.** Dissension; conflict; war.

sword'fish' (sōrd'fĭsh'), n. An oceanic food fish, the bones of the upper jaw of which form a sword-like beak.

Swordfish.

sword'play' (-plā'), n. Fencing ; a sword fight.

swords'man (sōrdz'măn), n. ; pl. -MEN (-mĕn). One skilled in using a sword ; fencer.

swore (swōr), pret. of SWEAR.

sworn (swōrn), p. p. of SWEAR.

swum (swŭm), pret. & p. p. of SWIM.

swung (swŭng), pret. & p. p. of SWING.

syc'a-more (sĭk'à-mōr), n. **1.** In the Bible, a fig tree bearing a sweet and edible fruit. **2.** In England, a kind of maple. **3.** The plane tree. U. S.

syc'o-phan-cy (sĭk'ȯ-făn-sĭ), n. Servile flattery

syc'o-phant (-fănt), n. A parasite ; flatterer.

syc'o-phan'tic (-făn'tĭk), a. [4] Pert. to, or characteristic of, a sycophant; servilely courting favor.

sy'e-nite (sī'ē-nīt), n. An igneous rock chiefly of feldspar, with some hornblende, etc.

syl-lab'ic (sĭ-lăb'ĭk), -i-cal (-ĭ-kăl), a. Of or pert to a syllable or syllables. — **syl-lab'i-cal-ly**, adv

syl-lab'i-fi-ca'tion (-ĭ-fĭ-kā'shŭn), n. Act of dividing into syllables. [vide into syllables.

syl-lab'i-fy (sĭ-lăb'ĭ-fī), v. t. [2] To form or di-

syl'la-ble (sĭl'à-b'l), n. **1.** An elementary sound, or a combination of such sounds, uttered with a single impulse of the voice, and constituting a word or a part of a word. **2.** In writing and printing, a part of a word separated from the rest.

syl'la-bus (-bŭs), n. ; pl. E. -BUSES (-ĕz), L. -BI (-bī). An abstract giving the heads or main subjects of a book, course of study, etc.; compendium.

syl'lo-gism (sĭl'ȯ-jĭz'm), n. A logical scheme or analysis of a formal argument, consisting of (1) a major premise, (2) a minor premise, and (3) a conclusion. Thus: (1) All sinners deserve punishment. (2) AB is a sinner. (3) Therefore, AB deserves punishment. — **syl'lo-gis'tic** (-jĭs'tĭk), a.

sylph (sĭlf), n. **1.** An imaginary being inhabiting the air. **2.** A slender, graceful woman.

syl'va (sĭl'và). Var. of SILVA.

syl'van (-văn), a. [4] Abounding in forests; woody ; rural ; rustic. See SILVAN.

sym'bol (sĭm'bŏl), *n.* **1.** A visible sign of an idea or a quality, or of another object; an emblem. **2.** A letter, sign, or the like, representing something, as an operation in mathematics, etc.

sym-bol'ic (sĭm-bŏl'ĭk) } *a.* [4] Of, pert. to, or of
sym-bol'i-cal (-ĭ-kăl) } the nature of, a symbol or symbols. — **-i-cal-ly,** *adv.* — **-cal-ness,** *n.*

sym'bol-ism (sĭm'bŏl-ĭz'm), *n.* Representation by means of symbols. [symbols.]

sym'bol-ist, *n.* One who advocates or employs

sym'bol-i-za'tion (-ĭ-zā'shŭn), *n.* A symbolizing.

sym'bol-ize (sĭm'bŏl-īz), *v.i.* [1] To use symbols or symbolism. — *v. t.* **1.** To regard or treat as symbolic. **2.** To represent by a symbol or symbols.

sym-met'ric (sĭ-mĕt'rĭk), *a.* [4] Symmetrical.

sym-met'ri-cal (sĭ-mĕt'rĭ-kăl), *a.* [4] Involving or exhibiting symmetry; regular; even. — **sym-met'ri-cal-ly,** *adv.* [8] — **-cal-ness,** *n.* [8].

sym'me-try (sĭm'ē-trĭ), *n.* **1.** A harmonious relation of parts. **2.** Correspondence of form, dimensions, or parts on opposite sides of an axis, etc.

sym'pa-thet'ic (sĭm'pá-thĕt'ĭk), *a.* [4] **1.** Feeling, or inclined to, sympathy; congenial. **2.** Due to, or expressive of, sympathy. — **-i-cal-ly,** *adv.*

sym'pa-thize (sĭm'pá-thīz), *v. i.* [1] **1.** To feel or show sympathy; be affected sympathetically. **2.** To agree; accord. — **-thiz'er** (-thĭz'ẽr), *n.*

sym'pa-thy (-thĭ), *n.; pl.* **-THIES** (-thĭz). **1.** Fellow feeling. **2.** An agreement of inclinations causing persons to be congenial. **3.** A tendency of things to unite or to act on each other.

sym-phon'ic (sĭm-fŏn'ĭk), *a.* [4] **1.** Relating to harmony of sound; also, sounded alike. **2.** Of, pertaining to, or in the manner of, a symphony.

sym-pho'ni-ous (-fō'nĭ-ŭs), *a.* [4] **1.** Agreeing in sound; harmonious. **2.** Symphonic. — **-ly,** *adv.* [8].

sym'pho-ny (sĭm'fō-nĭ), *n.; pl.* **-NIES** (-nĭz). **1.** A consonance or harmony of sounds. **2.** *Music.* A kind of elaborate orchestral composition.

sym-po'si-um (sĭm-pō'zĭ-ŭm), *n.; pl.* **-POSIA** (-ȧ). **1.** A convivial gathering, esp. one marked by free interchange of ideas. **2.** A collection of essays by different authors treating a common topic.

symp'tom (sĭmp'tŭm), *n.* **1.** A perceptible change in the body or its functions, indicating disease, or the kind of disease. **2.** A sign; indication.

symp'tom-at'ic (-ăt'ĭk), **-at'i-cal** (-ĭ-kăl), *a.* [4] **1.** Indicative. **2.** According to symptoms.

syn'a-gogue (sĭn'á-gŏg), *n.* A local assembly of Jews organized chiefly for public worship; also, the place primarily used for religious worship.

syn'chro-nism (sĭn'krō-nĭz'm), *n.* **1.** Simultaneousness. **2.** The tabular arrangement of historical events and personages according to dates.

syn'chro-nize (-nīz), *v. i.* [1] To agree in time; be synchronous. — *v. t.* **1.** To assign to the same date or period. **2.** To cause to agree in time, as a clock. — **-niz'er** (-nīz'ẽr), *n.* [8].

syn'chro-nous (-nŭs), *a.* Happening at the same time; simultaneous. — **-ly,** *adv.* [8].

syn'co-pate (sĭn'kō-pāt), *v. t.* [1] To affect or modify by syncope or syncopation.

syn'co-pa'tion (-pā'shŭn), *n.* A syncopating; as: **a** *Gram.* Syncope. **b** *Music.* The beginning of a tone on an unaccented part of a measure, and continuing it through the time of the following accent.

syn'co-pe (sĭn'kō-pē), *n.* **1.** *Gram.* Elision of one or more letters or sounds from the middle of a word; as in *e'er* for *ever*. **2.** *Med.* A fainting.

syn'dic (sĭn'dĭk), *n.* **1.** A magistrate. **2.** A business agent of a corporation or body of men.

syn'di-cal-ism (-dĭ-kăl-ĭz'm), *n.* The theory, plan, or practice of trade-union action which aims to gain control of the means and processes of production by the general strike, sabotage, or even revolutionary violence. — **syn'di-cal-ist,** *n.*

syn'di-cate (-dĭ-kăt), *n.* **1.** A body of syndics. **2.** An association of persons officially authorized to act in some matter. **3.** An association or group of persons who combine to carry out, on their own account, a project. — (-kāt), *v. t.* [1] **1.** To combine or form into, or manage as, a syndicate. **2.** To acquire or control for or by a syndicate. — *v. i.* To unite in a syndicate.

syn'od (sĭn'ŭd), *n.* **1.** A church council. **2.** An assembly, council, or meeting.

syn-od'ic (sĭ-nŏd'ĭk), *a.* Synodical.

syn-od'i-cal (-ĭ-kăl), *a.* Of, or pert. to, a synod.

yn'o-nym (sĭn'ō-nĭm), *n.* One of two or more words (of the same language) having the same or nearly the same meaning.

yn-on'y-mous (sĭ-nŏn'ĭ-mŭs), *a.* Having the character of a synonym. — **-ly,** *adv.* [8].

syn-on'y-my (-mĭ), *n.; pl.* **-MIES** (-mĭz). **1.** Quality of being synonymous. **2.** A system or collection of synonyms; also, the study of synonyms.

syn-op'sis (-nŏp'sĭs), *n.; pl.* **-OPSES** (-sēz). A general view of a whole; abstract; syllabus.

syn-op'tic (-tĭk), *a.* Affording a general view of a whole, or of its principal parts.

syn-op'ti-cal (-tĭ-kăl), *a.* Synoptic. — **-ly,** *adv.*

syn-tac'tic (sĭn-tăk'tĭk), *a.* Of, pertaining to, or according to the rules of, syntax.

syn-tac'ti-cal (-tĭ-kăl), *a.* Syntactic. — **-ly,** *adv.*

syn'tax (sĭn'tăks), *n.* *Gram.* Sentence structure; due arrangement of words in sentences in their mutual relations, according to established usage.

syn'the-sis (sĭn'thē-sĭs), *n.; pl.* **-SES** (-sēz). Composition, or the putting of things together.

syn-thet'ic (sĭn-thĕt'ĭk), *a.* Of, pert. to, or consisting in, synthesis; — contrasted with *analytic.*

syn-thet'i-cal (-ĭ-kăl),'*a.* Synthetic. — **-ly,** *adv.*

sy-rin'ga (sĭ-rĭŋ'gȧ), *n.* A garden shrub having white or cream-colored flowers; mock orange.

syr'inge (sĭr'ĭnj), *n.* An instrument for injecting liquids, cleansing wounds, etc. — *v. t.* [1] To inject or wash by means of a syringe.

syr'up (sĭr'ŭp). Var. of SIRUP.

sys'tem (sĭs'tĕm), *n.* **1.** A combination of objects united as an organic whole. **2.** An assemblage of objects arranged after a method or plan. **3.** A scheme for interrelating things. **4.** Regular method or order; orderliness. **5.** The body considered as a functional unit.

sys'tem-at'ic (-ăt'ĭk), *a.* [4] **1.** Of or pert. to a system. **2.** Methodical. — **-at'i-cal-ly,** *adv.*

sys'tem-a-ti-za'tion (-ȧ-tĭ-zā'shŭn), *n.* Act of systematizing, or state of being systematized.

sys'tem-a-tize (sĭs'tĕm-ȧ-tīz), *v. t.* [1] To reduce to system or method; methodize.

sys-tem'ic (sĭs-tĕm'ĭk), *a.* *Physiol.* Of or taining to the body as a whole.

---

chair; go; sing, iŋk; then, thin; nature, verdure; yet; zh = z in azure. Numbers to §§ in the Special Notes which, with Abbreviations, Signs, etc., precede the Voca'

T

tab (tăb), *n.* **1.** A small flap, tag, or the like, as to a garment. **2.** Account; as, to keep *tab*. *Colloq.*

tab'ard (tăb'ẽrd), *n.* **1.** A kind of coarse short outer coat. **2.** A kind of mantle worn by knights, over the armor. **3.** A herald's official garment, a mantle blazoned with his lord's arms.

ta-bas'co (tȧ-băs'kō), *n.* A pungent sauce of capsicum berries.

tab'by (tăb'ĭ), *n.; pl.* -BIES (-ĭz). **1.** A kind of silk, usually called *watered silk.* **2.** A brindled cat; popularly, any domestic cat. — *a.* Brindled.

tab'er-na-cle (tăb'ẽr-nȧ-k'l), *n.* **1.** A temporary habitation; tent. **2.** *Jewish Antiq.* A tent carried through the wilderness, in the Exodus, as a place of sacrifice and worship. *Ex.* xxvi. **3.** A Jewish temple. **4.** A church with a very large auditorium. **5.** A small cell or receptacle to hold a holy or precious thing.

ta'ble (tā'b'l), *n.* **1.** A smooth flat surface or thin slab. **2.** An article of furniture having a smooth flat top fixed on legs. **3.** Food put on a table to be eaten; fare. **4.** The company assembled round a table. **5.** A condensed tabulated statement. **6.** Any collection and arrangement in condensed form of statistics, mathematical data, etc. — *v. t.* [1] **1.** To lay or place on a table, as money. **2.** To lay (a motion, etc.) on the table.

tab'leau (tăb'lō; tä/blō'), *n.; pl.* -LEAUX (tăb'lōz; tä/blō'), sometimes, E., -LEAUS (-lōz). A vivid representation; picture; esp., a representation of some scene by the appropriate grouping of persons.

∥ **ta'ble d'hôte'** (tä/b'l' dōt'); *pl.* TABLES D'HÔTE (tä/b'l'). **1.** A common table for guests at a hotel. **2.** A meal served in a restaurant at a fixed price.

ta'ble-land' (tā'b'l-lănd'), *n.* A plateau.

ta'ble-spoon' (tā'b'l-spoon'), *n.* The largest spoon in common use at table.

ta'ble-spoon'ful (-fool), *n.; pl.* -FULS (-foolz). As much as a tablespoon will hold.

tab'let (tăb'lĕt), *n.* **1.** A small flat surface or slab; esp., a flat piece on which to write, draw, etc. **2.** One of a set of leaves or sheets fastened together and used for memoranda, etc.; also, such a set; a collection of sheets of paper, like a pad, but fastened at the top only. **3.** A somewhat flat cake or piece.

ta-boo' (tȧ-boo'), *a.* **1.** Set apart or sacred by religious custom; subject to a taboo. **2.** Forbidden by social usage. — *n.* **1.** A sacred decree prohibiting the use of certain things or the performance of certain actions, as among the Polynesians. **2.** The system of prohibitions based on the principle of taboo. — *v. t.* To prohibit by taboo.

ta'bor (tā'bẽr), *n.* [5] A small drum used as an accompaniment to a pipe or fife; a timbrel.

tab'o-ret (tăb'ō-rĕt), **tab'ou-ret** (tăb'ŏō-), *n.* **1.** A small tabor. **2.** A seat without arms or back; a stool; also, a small stand of similar form.

tab'u-lar (tăb'ū-lȧr), *a.* **1.** Having the form of, or pertaining to, a table. **2.** Derived from, or computed by, the use of tables.

tab'u-late (-lāt), *v. t.* [1] **1.** To shape with a flat surface. **2.** To form into a table, or synopsis; reduce to tables. — **tab'u-la'tor** (-lā'tẽr), *n.* [8].

tab'u-la'tion (-lā'shŭn), *n.* Act of tabulating.

tac'it (tăs'ĭt), *a.* Done or made in silence; implied, but not expressed; silent. — **tac'it-ly**, *adv.* [8].

tac'i-turn (-tûrn), *a.* [4] Habitually silent; not talkative. — **-ly**, *adv.* [8].

tac'i-tur'ni-ty (-tûr'nĭ-tĭ), *n.* Habitual silence, or reserve in speaking.

tack (tăk), *n.* **1.** A small, short, sharp-pointed nail, usually having a broad, flat head. **2.** *Naut.* The direction of a vessel in regard to the trim of her sails; as, on starboard *tack*, she has the wind on her starboard side. Hence, the run of a vessel on one tack or a change from starboard to port tack or vice versa. **3.** A course or method of action; as, to change one's *tack*. — *v. t.* **1.** To fasten or attach by tacks. **2.** Hence, to attach or fasten in a slight or hasty manner. **3.** *Naut.* To change the direction of (a vessel) when sailing close-hauled, by putting the helm alee and shifting the sails. — *v. i.* *Naut.* To tack a vessel; also (of a vessel), to have her tack changed. See TACK, *v. t.*, 3, & *n.*, 2. — **tack'er**, *n.* [8].

tack'le (tăk'l), *n.* **1.** An assemblage of ropes and pulleys for hoisting or pulling. **2.** Apparatus; equipment; gear. **3.** Act of tackling, or seizing and holding; a grasp; hold. — *v. t.* [1] **1.** To seize; grapple. **2.** To undertake to do, conquer, etc. *Colloq.*

tact (tăkt), *n.* Nice discernment of the best course of action under given conditions; ability to deal with others without offending; address.

tact'ful (tăkt'fool), *a.* [4] Full of tact. — **-ly** *adv.* [8]. — **-ness**, *n.* [8].

tac'ti-cal (tăk'tĭ-kăl), *a.* [4] Of or pertaining to military or naval tactics; pertaining to, or marked by, planning or maneuvering.

tac-ti'cian (tăk-tĭsh'ăn), *n.* One versed in tactics.

tac'tics (tăk'tĭks), *n.* **1.** Art of handling or using troops or ships in battle or in the presence of the enemy. **2.** Hence, method of procedure; esp., adroit devices or expedients to accomplish an end.

tac'tile (tăk'tĭl), *a.* [4] **1.** Of or pertaining to the organs or sense of touch. **2.** Tangible.

tac-til'i-ty (tăk-tĭl'ĭ-tĭ), *n.* Tactile quality or state.

tact'less, *a.* Without tact. — **-ly**, *adv.* — **-ness**, *n.*

tac'tu-al (tăk'tụ-ăl), *a.* [4] Of or pert. to touch; derived from, or producing the sensation of, touch.

tad'pole' (tăd'pōl'), *n.* The very young form of frogs, toads, etc., during which they have a long tail and live in the water.

tael (tāl), *n.* **1.** A weight of eastern Asia, varying from 1 to 2½ ounces avoirdupois. **2.** A Chinese money of account, the value of a tael of silver.

taf'fe-ta (tăf'ē-tȧ), **taf'fe-ty** (tăf'ē-tĭ), *n.* Any of various kinds of silk or linen goods.

taff'rail (tăf'rāl), *n.* The rail around a ship's stern.

taf'fy (tăf'ĭ), *n.* A candy made of molasses or brown sugar boiled down, often with butter.

tag (tăg), *n.* **1.** A slight flap, tab, etc., forming an appendage; card or label for appending to a package; a loose end, rag, or tatter. **2.** A metallic binding or point at the end of a string or lace, to stiffen it.—*v. t.;* TAGGED (tăgd); TAG'GING. **1.** To fit with, or as if with, a tag or tags; attach a tag, or label, to. **2.** To follow closely after. *Colloq.* —*v. i.* To follow closely. *Colloq.*

tag, *n.* A child's game in which one runs after others until he touches, or "tags," one of them. —*v. t.* To touch in or as in the game of tag.

tail (tāl), *a. Law.* Limited; abridged; entailed. —*n. Law.* Limitation; abridgment; entail.

tail, *n.* **1.** The rear end, or a process or prolongation of the rear end, of the body of an animal. **2.** An appendage suggestive of the tail of an animal. **3.** The back, last, lower, or inferior part; end; rear.—*v. t.* To furnish with a tail; also, to follow like a tail.—*v. i.* To form a tail.

tail'ings, *n. pl.* The refuse or residue separated out in various operations, as in threshing.

tai'lor (tā'lẽr), *n.* One whose occupation is to cut out and make outer garments.—*v. i.* To follow the business of a tailor.—**tai'lor-ess,** *n. fem.* [8].

tailor bird. Any of numerous Asiatic, East Indian, and African birds, of the warbler group, which stitch leaves to support and hide their nests.

taint (tānt), *v. t.* To imbue with something odious or poisonous; hence, to infect; poison; corrupt. —*v. i.* To become tainted, as meat.—*n.* **1.** A spot or stain; esp., blemish; touch of disgrace. **2.** A corrupting tinge or trace; infection.

take (tāk), *v. t.; pret.* TOOK (tŏŏk); *p. p.* TAK'EN (tāk'n); *p. pr. & vb. n.* TAK'ING (tāk'ĭng). **1.** To lay hold of, as in grasping, seizing, catching, capturing, adhering to, or the like. **2.** To receive into one's hold, possession, etc., by a voluntary act, as in eating, purchasing, choosing, etc. **b** To assume, adopt, undertake, or the like. **3.** To derive or obtain (from a source). **4.** To remove from life. **5.** To charm or attract. **6.** To require; demand. **7.** To receive; accept; admit. **8.** To contract by infection. **9.** To regard; consider. **10.** To observe, fix upon, or ascertain. **11.** To make a picture, photograph, or the like, of. *Colloq.* **12.** To do, make, etc. ;—with an object denoting movement or action.

take, *v. i.* **1.** To lay hold; fix upon anything. **2.** To resort; go ;—usually with *to.* **3.** To take effect; operate; act. **4.** To charm; prove attractive or pleasing. *Colloq.*—*n.* **1.** Act of taking. **2.** That which is taken, as fish caught at one haul.—**tak'er** (tāk'ẽr), *n.* [8].

take'-off', *n.* An imitation; esp., a caricature.

tak'ing (tāk'ĭng), *n.* **1.** Act of one that takes. **2.** That which is taken or received.—*a.* [4] **1.** Alluring; attractive. *Colloq.* **2.** Infectious; contagious.—**-ly,** *adv.* [8] — **-ness,** *n.* [8].

talc (tălk), *n.* A soft mineral of which soapstone and French chalk are varieties.

talc'ose (tăl'kōs ; tăl-kōs'), **talc'ous** (tăl'kŭs), *a.* Composed of, containing, or resembling, talc.

tale (tāl), *n.* **1.** That which is told; account; story. **2.** A libelous report or piece of evil gossip. **3.** A reckoning by numbers; a count; enumeration. **4.** A sum.

tale'bear'er (-bâr'ẽr), *n.* **One** who officiously or maliicously spreads gossip, scandal, etc.

tale'bear'ing, *a.* Tattling.—*n.* Act of a talebearer.

tal'ent (tăl'ĕnt), *n.* **1.** An ancient weight and money unit. Estimated money values of the talent are: Hebrew, gold, $32,640; Hebrew, silver, $2,176; Attic, silver, $1,446. **2.** Superior intelligence and ability; faculty. Cf. GENIUS, 5. **3.** Collectively, persons of ability or skill.

tal'ent-ed, *a.* [4] Having talent or talents; gifted.

ta'ler (tä'lẽr). Var. of THALER.

tales'man (tālz'măn), *n.; pl.* -MEN. *Law.* One summoned to fill up a panel for a particular trial.

tale'tell'er (tāl'tĕl'ẽr), *n.* A talebearer; telltale.

tale'tell'ing, *a.* Talebearing.—*n.* Talebearing.

tal'is-man (tăl'ĭs-măn; tăl'ĭz-), *n.; pl.* -MANS (-mănz). A charm; amulet; as, a stone, ring, or the like with mystic figures or characters engraved on it.—**tal'is-man'ic** (-măn'ĭk), *a.*

talk (tôk), *v. t.* **1.** To deliver in speech; utter. **2.** To discourse about; discuss. **3.** To speak (a language) freely. **4.** To affect or effect by talking. —*v. i.* **1.** To speak; esp., to express by spoken words; converse. **2.** To communicate by any means; express ideas, as by speech.—*n.* **1.** Act of talking; speech; esp., familiar converse; conversation. **2.** Report; rumor. **3.** Empty verbiage. **4.** Subject of discourse; theme for conversation, gossip, etc. **5.** A conference or council.

talk'a-tive (tôk'ȧ-tĭv), *a.* [4] Given to talking; loquacious.—**-ly,** *adv.* [8]—**-ness,** *n.* [8].

talk'er, *n.* One that talks; often, a babbler.

talk'ie (tôk'ĭ), *n.* A moving picture accompanied by reproduced speech or sound.

talk'ing, *a.* That talks; able to utter words; also, talkative.—*n.* Discourse; converse.

tall (tôl), *a.* [3] **1.** High of stature. **2.** Of a given height ; as, five feet *tall.*

tall'ness, *n.* Quality of being tall.

tal'low (tăl'ō), *n.* The suet or fat of sheep, oxen, etc., extracted by melting ; any fat resembling it. —*v. t.* To grease or smear with tallow.

tal'low-y (-ĭ), *a.* [4] Like tallow; greasy.

tal'ly (tăl'ĭ), *n. ; pl.* -LIES (-ĭz). **1.** Formerly, a piece of wood on which notches were cut as marks of number or account. **2.** Any account or score kept by notches or marks, esp. one kept in duplicate. **3.** A notch, mark, or score made on or in a tally. **4.** A number as a unit of computation. —*v. t.* [2] To register on or in a tally; score. —*v. i.* To correspond.   [pleasure coach.]

tal'ly-ho' (-hō'), *interj. & n.* A kind of four-in-hand

tal'on (tăl'ŭn), *n.* Claw, esp. of a bird of prey.

ta'lus (tā'lŭs), *n.* Rock débris at the base of a cliff.

tam'a-ble (tăm'ȧ-b'l), *a.* [4] That can be tamed.

tam'a-rack (tăm'ȧ-răk), *n.* Any of several American larches.

tam'a-rind (-rĭnd), *n.* A tropical tree bearing edible legumes or pods having an acid pulp.

tam'a-risk (-rĭsk), *n.* Any of a large genus (*Tamarix*) of Old World tropical shrubs or small trees.

tam'bour (tăm'bōōr), *n.* **1.** A military drum. **2.** A circular frame for embroidering.

tam'bou-rine' (tăm'bōō-rēn'), *n.* A small drum; esp., a shallow one-headed drum with loose metallic disks, or jingles, at the sides.

---

tame (tām), *a.* [3] **1.** Reduced from native wildness; domesticated. **2.** Subdued; also, harmless; gentle; as, *tame* behavior. **3.** Deficient in spirit, interest, etc.; dull; insipid. — *v. t.* [1] **1.** To reduce from a wild to a domestic state; make gentle, tractable, etc. **2.** To deprive of spirit, courage, etc.; subdue. — **-ly**, *adv.* — **-ness,** *n.* [8].

tam-o'-shan'ter (tăm'ŏ-shăn'tēr), *n.* A Scottish cap with a round, somewhat flat top wider than the headband and, usually, a tassel in the center.

tamp (tămp), *v. t.* **1.** In blasting, to plug (a drilled hole), as with clay, to prevent misdirection of the force of the blast. **2.** To drive in or down by a succession of light or medium blows; as, to *tamp* earth. — **tamp'er** (tăm'pēr), *n.* [8].

tam'per (tăm'pēr), *v. i.* **1.** To meddle ; try trifling or foolish experiments ; — commonly with *with.* **2.** To meddle so as to alter a thing ; esp., to make changes without right. **3.** To deal unfairly, esp. by bribery.

tan (tăn), *n.* **1.** Tanbark. **2.** A yellowish brown color, like that of tan (sense 1). **3.** A brown color imparted to the skin by exposure to the sun. — *a.* Of the color of tan ; yellowish brown. — *v. t. ;* TANNED (tănd) ; TAN'NING. **1.** To convert (a skin) into leather, usually by soaking in an infusion of oak bark. **2.** To make brown, as by exposure to sun. — *v. i.* To become tanned.

tan'a-ger (tăn'á-jēr), *n.* Any of numerous American birds allied to the finches. They are mainly unmusical. The males usually are bright-colored.

tan'bark' (-bärk'), *n.* Any bark rich in tannin, bruised or cut into small pieces, and used in tanning. Spent tanbark is used for circus rings, etc.

tan'dem (-dĕm), *adv.* One after or behind another; — of two or more things so arranged, esp. of horses so driven. — *a.* Consisting of two arranged tandem. — *n.* **1.** A team of horses harnessed one behind the other. **2.** A tandem bicycle, or one with seats for two, one behind the other.

tang (tăng), *n.* A projecting shank, prong, tongue, or the like, forming part of an object, as of a file, knife, etc., and serving to secure it to another.

tang, *n.* **1.** A strong or offensive taste, esp. of something foreign to the thing itself. **2.** A sharp specific flavor ; as, a *tang* of dialect.

tang, *n. & v. t. & i.* Twang.

tan'gen-cy (tăn'jĕn-sĭ), *n.* State of being tangent.

tan'gent (-jĕnt), *n. Geom.* A tangent line, curve, or surface. See CIRCLE, *Illust.* — *a.* Touching ; esp., *Geom.*, meeting a curve or surface at only one point, and not cutting it if produced; — said of a straight line, curve, or surface.

tan-gen'tial (tăn-jĕn'shăl), *a.* Pert. to a tangent.

tan'ger-ine (tăn'jēr-ēn; tăn'jēr-ēn'), *n.* An orange resembling the mandarin.

tan'gi-bil'i-ty (tăn'jĭ-bĭl'ĭ-tĭ), *n.* Tangibleness.

tan'gi-ble (tăn'jĭ-b'l), *a.* [4] **1.** Capable of being touched; palpable. **2.** Real; substantial; evident. — **-ble-ness,** *n.* [8] — **-bly,** *adv.* [8].

tan'gle (tăng'g'l), *v. t.* [1] **1.** To intertwine confusedly ; entangle. **2.** To involve ; insnare ; as, to be *tangled* in lies. — *v. i.* To be or become entangled. — *n.* **1.** A confused knot, as of hair or threads. **2.** State of perplexity; muddle.

tan'go (tăn'gō; *Sp.* tän'gō), *n. ; pl.* TANGOS (-gōz).

A difficult dance in two-part time marked by posturing and a great variety of steps.

tank (tăngk), *n.* **1.** A pond, pool, or small lake. **2.** A large basin, cistern, or vessel of any kind ; a receptacle for liquids ; as, **a** swimming *tank.* **3.** A kind of self-propelling engine of destruction consisting of a casing of heavy armor plates mounted on a tractor and armed with guns.

tank'ard (tăngk'árd), *n.* A large drinking vessel.

tan'ner (tăn'ēr), *n.* One who tans hides.

tan'ner-y (-ĭ), *n. ; pl.* -NERIES (-ĭz). A place where tanning is carried on.

tan'nic acid (tăn'ĭk). A strongly astringent acid, got from gallnuts, sumac, tea, etc.; — called also **tannin.** It is used in dyeing, tanning, etc.

tan'ning (tăn'ĭng), *n.* **1.** Art or process by which a skin is tanned. **2.** A browning, as of the skin, by exposure to the sun or weather.

tan'sy (-zĭ), *n.* Any of various plants of the aster family. The common tansy is very bitter.

tan'ta-lize (tăn'tá-līz), *v. t.* [1] To tease by keeping something desired in view but just out of reach. — **-liz'er** (-līz'ēr), *n.* [8].

tan'ta-mount' (-mount'), *a.* Equivalent.

tan'trum (tăn'trŭm), *n.* A fit of ill temper. *Colloq.*

tap (tăp), *v. t. ;* TAPPED (tăpt) or TAPT ; TAP'PING. **1.** To strike or rap lightly. **2.** To give a light blow or blows with. **3.** To put a tap (sense 2 below) on (a shoe, boot, etc.). — *v. i.* To strike or rap lightly. — *n.* **1.** A light blow or rap. **2.** A piece of leather fastened on the bottom of a boot or shoe in repairing. **3.** *pl.* A signal, by drum, bugle, or trumpet, for extinguishing all lights in soldiers' or sailors' quarters, going to bed, and silence.

tap, *n.* **1.** A hole or pipe through which liquor is drawn. **2.** A cock or faucet. *Chiefly British.* **3.** A plug, or spile, to stop a hole, as in a cask; spigot. **4.** Liquor drawn through a tap ; hence, a certain kind or quality of liquor ; also, a barroom ; bar. *Colloq.* **5.** A tool for forming an internal screw. — **on tap,** ready to be drawn, as ale. — *v. t.* **1.** To pierce (a cask, tree, etc.) so as to let out, or draw off, a fluid. **2.** To let out by piercing, or by drawing a plug from, the containing vessel. **3.** To draw from (anything) in any analogous way.

tape (tāp), *n.* **1.** A narrow woven fillet or band. **2. a** A tapeline. **b** The paper strip of a printing telegraph, ticker, etc. **c** *Sports.* A string stretched at the finishing line and broken by the winner.

tape'line' (-līn'), *n.* A tape or strip, now often of steel, marked with linear dimensions.

ta'per (tā'pēr), *n.* **1.** A small wax candle ; a long wick coated with wax. **2.** Gradual diminution of thickness in an elongated object. — *a.* Regularly narrowed toward a point ; conical. — *v. i. & t.* To become or make gradually smaller toward one end ; grow gradually less.

tap'es-try (tăp'ĕs-trĭ), *n. ; pl.* -TRIES (-trĭz). A fabric worked on a warp of thread, originally by hand, the designs being usually pictorial. — *v. t.* [2] To furnish or adorn with or as with tapestry.

tape'worm' (tāp'wûrm'), *n.* Any of numerous long, flat, segmented worms, parasitic when adult in the intestines, esp. of man.

tap'i-o'ca (tăp'ĭ-ō'ká), *n.* A coarsely granular preparation of cassava starch.

āle, senāte, câre, ăm, ẵccount, ärm, ȧsk, sofȧ; ēve, ĕvent, ѐnd, recѐnt, makĕr; īce, ĭll; ōld, ȯbey, ôrb, ŏdd, sŏft, cŏnnect; ūse, ûnĭte, ûrn, ŭp, circŭs; fōōd, fŏŏt; out, oil;

ta′pir (tā′pēr), *n.* A hoofed mammal, chiefly of South or Central America, somewhat like a swine, but more nearly related to the rhinoceros, having a short flexible proboscis. It is chiefly nocturnal, shy, and gentle.

ta′pis (tā′pĭs; tăp′ĭs ; tȧ·pē′), *n.* Tapestry ; formerly, the cover of a council table. — **on**, *or* **upon**, **the tapis** (*pron. in this use perh. more often as F.* tȧ·pē′), on the table, or under consideration.

tap′per (tăp′ēr), *n.* One that taps.

tap′pet (tăp′ĕt), *n. Mach.* A lever or projection which, by intermittent contact with some other piece, causes a particular motion.

tap′root′ (-rōōt′), *n.* A primary root which grows straight downward, giving off small lateral roots.

tap′ster (tăp′stēr), *n.* One who taps liquors.

tar (tär), *n.* A sailor ; seaman.

tar, *n.* A thick, brown to black, sticky liquid got by distilling wood, coal, etc. — *v. t. ;* TARRED (tärd) ; TAR′RING. To smear with or as with tar.

ta-ran′tu-la (tȧ-răn′tụ̇-lȧ), *n.* Any of several large venomous spiders.

tar′dy (tär′dĭ), *a.* [3] **1.** Moving slowly ; slow. **2.** Late ; dilatory. — **tar′di-ly** (-dĭ-lĭ), *adv.* [8] — **tar′di-ness**, *n.* [8].

tare (târ), *n.* **1.** In the Bible, a weed ; — supposed to be the darnel. **2.** Any of several vetches.

tare, *n. Com.* A deduction of weight made as an allowance for the weight of a container or vehicle.

tar′get (tär′gĕt), *n.* **1.** A kind of small round shield or buckler. **2.** A mark to shoot at. **3.** An object of remarks, criticisms, etc. ; a butt.

tar′iff (tär′ĭf), *n.* **1.** A schedule, system, or scheme of duties imposed by a government on exports or, esp., imports. **2.** The duty, or rate of duty, imposed in a tariff (sense 1) ; as, the *tariff* on wool. **3.** Any schedule or system of rates, charges, etc.

tar′la-tan (tär′lȧ-tăn), *n.* A kind of thin, stiff, transparent muslin used for dresses, caps, etc.

tarn (tärn), *n.* Small mountain lake or pool.

tar′nish (tär′nĭsh), *v. t.* To dull the luster of ; sully ; stain. — *v. i.* To lose luster ; become dull. — *n.* Quality or state of being tarnished.

tar-pau′lin (tär-pô′lĭn), *n.* **1.** Canvas waterproofed with tar, paint, or the like. **2.** A hat or coat of, or covered with, tarpaulin.

tar′pon (tär′pŏn), *n.* A marine fish common on the coast of Florida and among the West Indies. It becomes about six feet long. Its flesh is poor.

tar′ry (-ĭ), *a.* [3] Of, covered with, or like, tar.

tar′ry (tăr′ĭ), *v. i.* [2] **1.** To abide at or in a place ; stay ; lodge ; wait. **2.** To delay ; loiter ; as, we had no time to *tarry.* — **tar′ri-er** (-ĭ-ēr), *n.* [8].

tar′sal (tär′săl), *a.* Of or pertaining to the tarsus. — *n.* A tarsal bone or cartilage.

tar′sus (-sŭs), *n.; pl.* -SI (-sī). **1.** *Anat.* The ankle. Also, the group of small bones supporting this part. **2.** The shank of a bird's leg.

tart (tärt), *a.* [3] **1.** Sharp to the taste ; sour. **2.** Severe ; sharp ; as, a *tart* reply.

tart (tärt), *n.* A small pie, or shell of pastry filled with jelly, custard, fruit, or the like.

tar′tan (tär′tăn), *n.* Woolen cloth, checkered or marked with narrow crossbars of various colors.

tar′tar (tär′tär), *n.* **1.** A substance, essentially a potassium salt of an acid (**tartaric acid**), existing in grape juice and deposited in wine casks as a crust ; esp., a refined product, distinguished from *cream of tartar*, got by further purification. **2.** A concretion which often incrusts the teeth.

Tar′tar, *n.* **1.** Var. of TATAR. **2.** [*Often l. c.*] A person of a keen, irritable temper. **3.** [*l. c.*] A person who proves too strong for an assailant ; — esp. in *to catch a tartar*.

tar-tar′ic (tär-tăr′ĭk), *a.* Of or pertaining to tartar ; derived from tartar ; as, *tartaric* acid.

tart′ly, *adv.* In a tart manner.

tart′ness (tärt′nĕs), *n.* Quality of being tart.

task (tȧsk), *n.* Labor, work, or study imposed, often in a definite quantity ; undertaking ; work. — *v. t.* To impose a task on ; to strain ; burden.

task′mas′ter (tȧsk′mȧs′tēr), *n.* One who imposes a task, or burdens another with labor ; overseer.

task′work′, *n.* Forced work ; also, piecework.

tas′sel (tăs′′l), *n.* **1.** A pendent ornament, ending in a tuft of threads, etc. **2.** Something like, or suggestive of, a tassel, as the flower cluster of some plants ; esp., the flower cluster at the top of the stalk of Indian corn, or maize. — *v. i.* [7] To put forth tassels, as corn or maize ; as, the corn has begun to *tassel.* — *v. t.* To adorn with, or make into, tassels.

taste (tāst), *v. t.* [1] **1.** To ascertain the relish or flavor of by taking a little into the mouth. **2.** To eat or drink a little of, as for testing. **3.** To partake of ; experience. — *v. i.* **1.** To try food or drink with the mouth ; eat or drink a little only. **2.** To have a certain flavor or particular quality. **3.** To have perception, experience, or enjoyment ; partake ; — often with *of.* — *n.* **1.** Act of tasting with the mouth. **2.** Quality of any substance as perceived by the taste organs ; savor ; flavor. **3.** *Physiol.* The one of the five senses by which certain properties of bodies (called their *taste*) are ascertained by contact with certain organs of the mouth. **4.** Intellectual relish ; liking ; fondness. **5.** Power of appreciating beauty, order, etc. **6.** Manner as to what is pleasing, refined, or good usage. **7.** A little piece tasted ; a bit.

taste′ful (tāst′fōōl), *a.* [4] **1.** Savory. **2.** Having, exhibiting, or conforming to good taste. — **taste′ful-ly**, *adv.* [8] — **taste′ful-ness**, *n.* [8].

taste′less, *a.* [4] **1.** Having no taste ; insipid. **2.** Not manifesting, or not conscious of what is, good taste ; not in good taste. — **-ness**, *n.* [8].

tast′er (tās′tēr), *n.* **1.** One who tastes. **2.** That in which or by means of which anything is tasted.

tast′y (tās′tĭ), *a.* [3] **1.** Having, or showing, good taste. *Colloq.* **2.** Pleasing to the palate ; as, a *tasty* meal. — **-i-ly** (-tĭ-lĭ), *adv.* [8] — **-i-ness,** *n.* [8]

tat (tăt), *v. t. ;* TAT′TED ; -TING. Also **tatt**. To make by tatting. — *v. i.* To work at tatting.

Ta′tar (tä′tär), *n.* A member of any of numerous mixed tribes, inhabiting parts of Russia and of central and eastern Asia. — *a.* Of or pertaining to the Tatars.

tat′ter (tăt′ēr), *n.* A rag or a part torn and hanging ; — usually in *pl.* — *v. t. & i.* To make or become ragged.

tat′ter-de-mal′ion (-dĕ-māl′yŭn), *n.* Ragamuffin.

tat′tered (tăt′ērd), *p. a.* [4] **1.** Ragged ; torn into shreds. **2.** Clad in ragged clothes.

---

chair; go; sing, iŋk ; then, thin; nature, verdure; yet; zh = z in azure. Numbers refer to §§ in the Special Notes which, with Abbreviations, Signs, etc., precede the Vocabulary.

tat′ting (tăt′ĭng), *n.* A lace made from thread wound on a shuttle; also, act or process of making it.

tat′tle (-'l), *v. i.* [1] **1.** To chatter. **2.** To tell tales or secrets. — *v. t.* To utter or disclose by tattling. — *n.* Idle talk. — **tat′tler**(-lẽr), *n.* [8].

tat-too′ (tă-tōō′), *n. Mil. & Nav.* A call sounded on drum and fife, trumpet, or bugle, shortly before taps, giving notice to repair to quarters.

tat-too′, *v. t.* To mark or color (the skin) indelibly by pricking in coloring matter. — *n.* A mark or figure formed by tattooing. — **tat-too′er,** *n.* [8].

tat-too′ing, *n.* Marks or designs tattooed on flesh.

taught (tôt), *pret. & p. p.* of TEACH.

taunt (tänt; tônt), *v. t.* To reproach severely or insultingly; jeer at. — *n.* Sarcastic reproach. — **taunt′er,** *n.* — **taunt′ing-ly,** *adv.* [8].

tau′rine (tô′rĭn; -rĭn), *a.* Of or pert. to a bull.

taut (tôt), *a.* [3] **1.** *Chiefly Naut.* Tight; tensely stretched; as, a *taut* hawser. **2.** Snug; tidy.

tau-tog′ (tô-tŏg′), *n.* A food fish of the Atlantic coast of the United States, allied to the cunner.

tau′to-log′i-cal (tô′tô-lŏj′ĭ-kăl), *a.* [4] Using tautology; repetitious. — **-log′i-cal-ly,** *adv.* [8].

tau-tol′o-gy (tô-tŏl′ô-jĭ), *n. ; pl.* -GIES (-jĭz). A repetition of the meaning in other words ; needless repetition, as in "audible to the ear."

tav′ern (tăv′ẽrn), *n.* A house where liquors are sold to be drunk on the premises ; also, esp. in rural districts of the United States, a hotel.

taw (tô), *n.* A marble to be used as a shooter ; also, a game at marbles. *Colloq. & Dial.*

taw, *v. t.* To dress and prepare, as skins of sheep, goats, etc., by softening and bleaching with alum, salt, and other agents. — **taw′er,** *n.* [8].

taw′dry (tô′drĭ), *a.* [3] Showy, without taste or elegance; cheap and gaudy. — **taw′dri-ly,** *adv.* [8] — **-dri-ness,** *n.* [8]. [things tanned.]

taw′ny (tô′nĭ), *a.* [3] Dull yellowish brown, like

tax (tăks), *n.* **1.** A charge; esp., a charge imposed for public use. **2.** A burdensome duty or charge. — *v. t.* **1.** To subject to the payment of a tax or taxes; also, to lay any burden or demand on; task. **2.** To charge; accuse; also, to censure.

tax′a-ble (tăk′să-b'l), *a.* Liable to be taxed.

tax-a′tion (tăk-sā′shŭn), *n.* Act of taxing.

tax′i (tăk′sĭ), *n.* Short for TAXICAB.

tax′i *or* **tax′y** (tăk′sĭ), *v. i. ;* TAX′IED (-sĭd) ; -I-ING *or* -Y-ING (-sĭ-ĭng). *Aviation.* To travel along the ground or on the water under the machine's own power ;— said of an airplane or a seaplane. [taximeter.]

tax′i-cab′ (tăk′sĭ-kăb′), *n.* A cab fitted with a

tax′i-der′mist (tăk′sĭ-dûr′mĭst), *n.* One skilled in, or one who practices, taxidermy.

tax′i-der′my (-dûr′mĭ), *n.* Art of stuffing and mounting skins of animals, in lifelike form.

tax-im′e-ter (-sĭm′ê-tẽr), *n.* Instrument for automatically showing the fare due in a taxicab.

tea (tē), *n.* **1.** A shrub cultivated in China, Japan, India, etc., for its leaves. **2.** The dried leaves of this plant, from which a beverage is made by infusion ; also, the beverage. **3.** Any of various plants more or less like tea; also, an infusion of their leaves. **4.** A light meal, in the afternoon, at which tea is commonly served ; hence, supper.

teach (tēch), *v. t. ; pret. & p. p.* TAUGHT (tôt) ; *p. pr. & vb. n.* TEACH′ING. **1.** To make to know how. **2.** To instruct. **3.** To impart the knowledge of ; give lessons in. **4.** To make aware by experience, etc. ; inform ; tell ; to cause to know. — *v. i.* To give instruction. — **teach′er,** *n.*

teach′a-ble (-à-b'l), *a.* [4] Capable of being taught; esp., quick to learn; docile. — **-ness,***n.*[8].

teach′ing, *n.* Act or business of instructing; also, that which is taught.

tea′cup′ (tē′kŭp′), *n.* Cup for tea ; teacupful.

tea′cup′ful (-fōōl), *n. ; pl.* -FULS (-fōōlz). As much as a teacup can hold ; enough to fill a teacup.

teak (tēk), *n.* A tall East Indian timber tree; also, its hard, yellowish brown wood.

tea′ket′tle (tē′kět′'l), *n.* A kettle, usually with a handle and spout, for boiling water for tea, etc.

teal (tēl), *n.* Any of certain small river ducks.

team (tēm), *n.* **1.** A group or brood of young, esp. of ducks. **2.** Two or more horses or other beasts harnessed. Hence, often, the animals with their harness and attached vehicle. **3.** A number of persons associated together, esp. for contest.

team′ster (tēm′stẽr), *n.* One who drives a team.

team′work′ (-wûrk′), *n.* **1.** Work done with a team. **2.** Work done by associates, subordinating personal prominence to general efficiency.

tea′pot′ (tē′pŏt′), *n.* A vessel with a spout, in which tea is made and from which it is served.

tear (tēr), *n.* **1.** A drop of the saline fluid secreted by the lachrymal gland. **2.** Something in the form of a tear (sense 1) ; as, a *tear* of balsam.

tear (târ), *v. t. ; pret.* TORE (tōr) ; *p. p.* TORN (tōrn) ; *p. pr. & vb. n.* TEAR′ING. **1.** To separate parts of, or pull apart, by force ; rend ; lacerate. **2.** To disrupt ; distress sharply. **3.** To make, effect, etc., by or as by tearing. **4.** To remove by force. — *v. i.* **1.** To separate on being pulled; be rent. **2.** To move or act with violence, excited haste, etc.— *n.* A tearing ; state of being torn ; a rent.

tear′drop′ (tēr′drŏp′), *n.* A tear.

tear′ful (tēr′fōōl), *a.* [4] Abounding with tears; weeping. — **-ly,** *adv.* [8] — **-ness,** *n.* [8].

tease (tēz), *v. t.* [1] **1.** To disentangle and lay parallel, as fibers ; comb or card, as wool or flax. **2.** To teasel. **3.** To vex or annoy by petty requests, or by jests and raillery ; plague; beg. — *n.* **1.** Act of teasing. **2.** One that teases. *Colloq.*

tea′sel (tē′z'l), *n.* **1.** Any of a certain genus of prickly herbs having blue or lilac flowers in dense, oblong heads, esp. a variety, the fuller's **teasel,** the flower head of which is covered with stiff, hooked bracts. **2.** A flower head of the fuller's teasel, used, when dried, to raise a nap on woolen cloth ; any substitute for this. — *v. t.* [7] To subject to the action of teasels.

teas′er (tēz′ẽr), *n.* One that teases.

tea′spoon′ (tē′spōōn′), *n.* The ordinary spoon used to stir tea, coffee, etc.

tea′spoon′ful (-fōōl), *n. ; pl.* -FULS (-fōōlz). Enough to fill a teaspoon.

teat (tēt), *n.* One of the nipples through which milk is drawn from the breast or udder.

tech′nic (těk′nĭk), *n.* **1.** The style of performance in any art ; technical skill. **2.** = TECHNICS.

tech′ni-cal (-nĭ-kăl), *a.* [4] Of or pertaining to,

or appropriate to, the useful or mechanic arts, or any art, science, business, etc. — **-ly**, *adv.* [8].

tech/ni·cal/i·ty (-kăl/ĭ-tĭ), *n. ; pl.* -TIES (-tĭz). **1.** Quality or state of being technical. **2.** That which is technical, esp. in terminology or method.

tech/nics (tĕk/nĭks), *n.* The science or doctrine of an art or of arts in general, esp. the mechanical or industrial arts; also, technic; technique.

tech/nique/ (tĕk/nēk/), *n.* Technic (in sense 1).

tech/no·log/ic (tĕk/nō-lŏj/ĭk), **tech/no·log/i·cal** (-ĭ-kăl), *a.* Of or pertaining to technology.

tech·nol/o·gist (tĕk-nŏl/ō-jĭst), *n.* One skilled in technology.

tech·nol/o·gy (tĕk-nŏl/ō-jĭ), *n.* **1.** Industrial science. **2.** Terminology of arts, sciences, etc.

tech/y (tĕch/ĭ), *a.* [3] Peevish; fretful; irritable.

ted (tĕd), *v. t.; TED/DED ; TED/DING.* To spread or scatter, for drying, as new-mown grass.

ted/der (-ẽr), *n.* One, esp. a machine, that teds.

te/di·ous (tē/dĭ-ŭs ; tēd/yŭs), *a.* [4] Tiresome ; wearisome. — **-ly**, *adv.* [8] — **-ness**, *n.* [8].

te/di·um (tē/dĭ-ŭm), *n.* Wearisomeness.

tee (tē), *n.* **1.** Mark aimed at in various games, as curling. **2.** *Golf.* Place from which the ball is struck in starting for a hole. — *v. t. ; TEED* (tēd); *TEE/ING.* To place (the ball) on a tee.

teem (tēm), *v. i.* To be prolific; abound.

teens (tēnz), *n. pl.* The years of one's age of which the numbers have the termination *-teen.*

tee/ter (tē/tẽr), *v. i. & t. & n.* Seesaw. *U. S.*

teeth (tēth), *n., pl.* of TOOTH.

teethe (tēth), *v. i.* [1] To grow teeth.

teeth/ing (tēth/ĭng), *n.* The cutting of teeth.

tee·to/tal (tē-tō/tăl), *a.* **1.** Entire ; total. *Colloq.* **2.** Of or pertaining to total abstinence from intoxicating drink. — **tee·to/tal·ly**, *adv.* [8].

tee·to/tal·er (-ẽr), *n.* [7] One who abstains totally from intoxicating drink.

tee·to/tal·ism (-ĭz'm), *n.* Principle or practice of abstaining from intoxicating drink.

tee·to/tum (-tŭm), *n.* A child's toy, somewhat like a top, twirled by the fingers. [graph.]

tel/e·gram (tĕl/ē·grăm), *n.* A message by telegraph.

tel/e·graph (-gráf), *n.* Any apparatus or process for communication (esp. by means of electrical transmission) at a distance. — *v. t. & i.* To send or communicate by telegraph; also, to send a telegram to (a person).

te·leg/ra·pher (tē-lĕg/rá-fẽr; tĕl/ē-gráf/ẽr),*n.* One who sends telegraphic messages.

tel/e·graph/ic (tĕl/ē-grăf/ĭk), *a.* Of or pert. to the telegraph. — **tel/e·graph/i·cal·ly**, *adv.* [8].

te·leg/ra·phist (tē-lĕg/rá-fĭst; tĕl/ē-gráf/ĭst), *n.* One skilled in telegraphy ; a telegrapher.

te·leg/ra·phy (tē-lĕg/rá-fĭ), *n.* Art or practice of making or using telegraphs.

tel/e·path/ic (tĕl/ē-păth/ĭk),*a.* Of,pert. to,or communicated by, telepathy. — **-i·cal·ly**, *adv.*

te·lep/a·thy (tē-lĕp/á-thĭ), *n.* Affection of one mind by the thoughts or emotions of another without communication through ordinary channels of sensation.

tel/e·phone (tĕl/ē-fōn),*n.* An instrument for reproducing sounds, esp. speech, at a distance. — *v. t. & i.* [1] To send, communicate, or speak to, by telephone.

tel/e·phon/ic (-fŏn/ĭk), *a.* Conveying sound to a distance; also, of or pertaining to the telephone.

te·leph/o·ny (tē-lĕf/ō-nĭ ; tĕl/ē-fō/nĭ), *n.* Art or process of reproducing sounds at a distance.

tel/e·scope (tĕl/ē-skōp), *n.* An optical instrument used to aid the eye or camera in viewing or photographing distant objects, as the heavenly bodies. — *v. i. & t.* [1] To slide, or force a way, one within another, as do sections of a small telescope.

tel/e·scop/ic (-skŏp/ĭk), *a.* [4] **1.** Of or pertaining to, or seen or discoverable only by, a telescope. **2.** Farseeing ; as, a *telescopic* eye. **3.** Having the power of extension by joints sliding one within another. — **tel/e·scop/i·cal·ly**, *adv.* [8].

tel/e·vi/sion (tĕl/ē·vĭzh/ŭn), *n.* Apparatus for transmitting and reproducing a distant view (esp. of moving persons) by turning light rays into electrical rays and turning these back into light rays.

tell (tĕl), *v. t. ; pret. & p. p. TOLD* (tōld); *p. pr. & vb. n.* TELL/ING. **1.** To mention one by one; enumerate ; reckon ; number. **2.** To relate in detail; narrate ; recount. **3.** To make known; disclose; reveal. **4.** To inform; report to. **5.** To order; request; direct. **6.** To ascertain by observing ; find out; decide. **7.** To assure emphatically. — *v. i.* **1.** To give an account; make report. **2.** To take effect; have a marked effect.

tell/er (tĕl/ẽr), *n.* **1.** One who tells, or relates; informer; narrator; describer. **2. a** One appointed to count the votes in a legislative body, assembly, etc. **b** A bank officer who receives and counts money paid in, and pays money out on checks.

tell/ing (tĕl/ĭng), *p. a.* [4] Effective.

tell/tale/ (-tāl/), *n.* **1.** A talebearer; informer. **2.** Any of various things that serve to give information or warning. — *a.* [4] **1.** Talebearing. **2.** Disclosing; betraying; as, a *telltale* blush.

tel·lu/ri·um (tĕ-lū/rĭ-ŭm), *n. Chem.* A rare element related to sulphur and selenium. [ness.|

te·mer/i·ty (tē-mĕr/ĭ-tĭ), *n.* Rashness ; heedless-|

tem/per (tĕm/pẽr), *v. t.* **1.** To regulate, esp. by moderating; soften; mollify. **2.** To moisten and stir to a proper consistency, as clay for brick, etc. **3.** To bring (steel, glass, etc.) to a proper degree of hardness and toughness. — *v. i.* To be tempered. — *n.* **1.** Mixture, esp. due or just mixture of qualities. **2.** Disposition or frame of mind. **3.** Composure ; equanimity. **4.** Heat of mind; proneness to anger. **5.** The state of a metal, glass, etc., esp. as to hardness and toughness.

tem/per·a·ment (-á·mĕnt), *n.* **1.** The physical and mental character of an individual; habitual disposition. **2.** Act of tempering, or modifying. — **-men/tal** (-mĕn/tăl), *a.* [4] — **-ly**, *adv.* [8].

tem/per·ance (tĕm/pẽr·ăns), *n.* Habitual moderation in the indulgence of the appetites and passions; esp., in the use of intoxicants.

tem/per·ate (-ăt), *a.* [4] **1.** Moderate; not excessive; as: **a** Moderate in indulging the appetites or the passions. **b** Exhibiting self-control; restrained. **2.** Mild in climate or temperature. — **-ly**, *adv.* [8] — **-ness**, *n.* [8].

tem/per·a·ture (tĕm/pẽr·á·tụr), *n.* Condition as to heat or cold ; degree of heat or cold.

tem/pered (-pẽrd), *a.* Having (such) a temper ; — chiefly in composition, as, sweet-*tempered.*

---

tem′pest (těm′pĕst), *n.* **1.** A furious storm. **2.** Any violent tumult, commotion, or agitation.

tem-pes′tu-ous (těm-pěs′tŭ-ŭs), *a.* [4] Stormy; violent. — **tem-pes′tu-ous-ly,** *adv.* [8] — **tem-pes′tu-ous-ness,** *n.* [8].

tem′plate (-plāt), **-plet** (-plĕt), *n.* A pattern or mold used as a guide in mechanical work.

tem′ple (těm′p′l), *n.* The flattened space on either side of the forehead.

tem′ple, *n.* **1.** An edifice for worship. **2.** A Christian edifice for public worship; a church.

tem′po (těm′pō), *n.; It. pl.* -PI (-pē). *Music.* Time; rate of movement.

tem′po-ral (-pŏ-rǎl), *a.* [4] Of or pert. to the temple or temples of the head.

tem′po-ral, *a.* **1.** Of, pertaining to, or limited by, time. **2.** Pert. to the present life; secular; transitory. **3.** Civil or political. — **-ly,** *adv.*

tem′po-ral′i-ty (-răl′ĭ-tĭ), *n.; pl.* -TIES (-tĭz). State or quality of being temporary.

tem′po-ra-ry (těm′pŏ-rā-rĭ), *a.* [4] Lasting for a time only; not permanent. — **tem′po-ra-ri-ly** (-rĭ-lĭ), *adv.* [8] — **tem′po-ra-ri-ness,** *n.* [8].

tem′po-rize (-rīz), *v. i.* [1] To comply with time or occasion; to yield to circumstances so as to gain time; to trim. — **tem′po-riz′er** (-rīz′ẽr), *n.*

tempt (těmpt), *v. t.* **1.** *Archaic.* **a** To test; make trial of. **b** To provoke; defy. **2.** To incite. **3.** To lead, or try to lead, into evil.

temp-ta′tion (těmp-tā′shŭn), *n.* **1.** Act of tempting. **2.** State of being tempted, or enticed to evil. **3.** That which tempts, esp. to evil.

tempt′er (těmp′tẽr), *n.* One who tempts or entices; esp. [*cap.*], with *the,* the Devil.

tempt′ress (těmp′trĕs), *n.* A woman who tempts.

ten (těn), *a.* One more than nine; twice five; — a cardinal number. — **Ten Commandments,** the Decalogue, or summary of God's commands (*Ex.* xx. 1-18). — *n.* **1.** The number greater by one than nine; ten units or objects. **2.** A symbol for ten units, as 10 or X. **3.** Something having as an essential feature ten units or members.

ten′a-bil′i-ty (těn′ȧ-bĭl′ĭ-tĭ), *n.* Tenableness.

ten′a-ble (těn′ȧ-b′l), *a.* [4] Capable of being held, maintained, or defended.

ten′a-ble-ness, *n.* Quality of being tenable.

te-na′cious (tê-nā′shŭs), *a.* [4] **1.** Holding fast; inclined to hold fast; — chiefly with *of.* **2.** Apt to retain; retentive. **3.** Cohesive; tough. **4.** Viscous; sticky. — **-ly,** *adv.* [8] — **-ness,** *n.* [8].

te-nac′i-ty (tê-năs′ĭ-tĭ), *n.* Quality or state of being tenacious; also, cohesiveness.

ten′an-cy (těn′ăn-sĭ), *n.; pl.* -CIES (-sĭz). **1.** A holding of lands or tenements; tenure, as under a lease. **2.** The period of a tenant's possession.

ten′ant (těn′ănt), *n.* **1.** One who holds or possesses real estate by any kind of right; also (as correlative to *landlord*) one in temporary possession of lands or tenements of another. **2.** Occupant. — *v. t.* To hold, occupy, or possess, as a tenant.

ten′ant-a-ble (-ȧn-tȧ-b′l), *a.* Fit to be tenanted.

ten′ant-ry (těn′ănt-rĭ), *n.; pl.* -RIES (-rĭz). The body of tenants on an estate.

tend (těnd), *v. t.* To attend; care for; watch; guard. — *v. i.* To serve; — with *on* or *upon.*

tend, *v. i.* **1.** To move in a certain direction; —

usually with *to* or *toward.* **2.** To be directed or have a tendency to any end, object, or purpose.

tend′ance (těn′dăns), *n.* Attention; care.

tend′en-cy (těn′děn-sĭ), *n.; pl.* -CIES (-sĭz). Direction or course toward anything; drift.

tend′er (těn′dẽr), *n.* **1.** One who tends. **2.** *Naut.* **a** A supply vessel employed to attend other vessels. **b** A rowboat carried or towed by a larger vessel, for landing passengers, etc. **3.** A car attached to a locomotive to carry fuel and water.

ten′der, *n.* **1.** An offer, as of money or service to satisfy an obligation. **2.** Thing offered; esp., money offered in payment. — *v. t.* **1.** To make a tender of. **2.** To offer.

ten′der, *a.* [3] **1.** Easily impressed, broken, cut, masticated, or the like. **2.** Delicate; not hardy; weak. **3.** Very susceptible or sensitive as to pain, to emotions, etc. **4.** Susceptible to love, kindness, etc.; sympathetic; compassionate. **5.** Adapted to a delicate or sensitive constitution or character; gentle. **6.** Expressive of the softer feelings; loving; affectionate. **7.** Considerate, as of one's feelings.

ten′der-foot′ (těn′dẽr-fŏŏt′), *n.; pl.* -FEET (-fēt′). A new-comer in a rough or newly settled region, esp. when not inured to hardship. *Slang or Colloq.*

ten′der-heart′ed, *a.* [4] Having great sensibility; susceptible, esp. to love or pity.

ten′der-loin′ (-loin′), *n.* A strip of tender flesh under the short ribs, in beef or pork.

ten′der-ly (-lĭ), *adv.* In a tender manner.

ten′der-ness, *n.* Quality or state of being tender.

ten′di-nous (těn′dĭ-nŭs), *a.* Of or pert. to a tendon; full of tendons; sinewy.

ten′don (-dŭn), *n.* *Anat.* A tough cord or band of dense, inelastic, white fibrous tissue uniting a muscle with some other part; a sinew.

ten′dril (-drĭl), *n.* A slender, leafless organ of climbing plants, serving as a means of attachment.

ten′e-ment (-ê-měnt), *n.* **1.** Real property held of another. **2. a** A dwelling house; esp.: (1) A house for renting. (2) A tenement house. **b** An apartment, or suite of rooms, used by one family.

tenement house. A dwelling house for renting, esp. one of the poorer sort divided into separate apartments, or tenements, for families.

ten′et (těn′ĕt), *n.* Any opinion, principle, dogma, belief, or doctrine, held as true; as, religious *tenets.*

ten′nis (-ĭs), *n.* **1.** A game played with a ball struck with a racket in an inclosed court; — called also, in the U. S., *court tennis.* **2.** = LAWN TENNIS.

ten′on (-ŭn), *n.* A projection for insertion into a mortise to make a joint. — *v. t.* **1.** To cut or fit for insertion into a mortise. **2.** To unite by or as by a tenon.

ten′or (-ẽr), *n.* **1.** General tendency; course; career. **2.** General drift of thought; purport; intent. **3.** *Music.* **a** The higher of the two ordinary kinds of voices of adult males; the part in the harmony adapted to this voice. **b** One who sings the tenor, or the instrument that plays it. — *a. Music.* Of or pertaining to the tenor.

ten′pins′ (těn′pĭnz′), *n.* A bowling game resembling ninepins, but played with ten pins. *U. S.*

tense (těns), *n. Gram.* Modification of verbal form to express distinctions of time; one of the forms which a verb takes, by inflection or by adding auxiliary words, to indicate such distinctions.

tense, *a.* [3] Stretched tight; rigid; — often fig.; as, a *tense* moment.— **-ly,** *adv.* [8]— **-ness,** *n.* [8].

ten′sile (těn′sĭl), *a.* [4] **1.** Of or pert. to tension. **2.** Capable of tension; ductile; as, *tensile* wire.

ten′sion (-shŭn), *n.* **1.** A stretching; state of being stretched or strained. **2. a** Strain of mind or intensity of feeling. **b** A condition of strain. **3.** A device to produce a tension, or pull, as in a sewing machine.

ten′sor (-sŏr), *n.* A muscle that stretches a part.

tent (těnt), *n.* A portable lodge or shelter of skins or cloth stretched over a pole or poles, or the like.— *v. i. & t.* To lodge as in a tent; encamp.

ten′ta-cle (těn′tȧ-k′l), *n.* **1.** Any of the long, slender "feelers" around the mouth or on the head of some fishes, insects, etc.; an antenna. **2.** A sensitive hair or filament on a plant.

ten′ta-tive (-tȧ-tĭv), *a.* [4] Of or pertaining to a trial or attempt; experimental. — **-ly,** *adv.* [8].

tent′ed, *a.* **1.** Covered with, sheltered by, or provided with, a tent or tents; as, a *tented* field. **2.** Formed or shaped like a tent.

ten′ter (těn′tẽr), *n.* A frame for stretching cloth by tenterhooks, to prevent shrinking, etc., in drying.— *v. t.* To hang or stretch, as on tenters.

ten′ter-hook′ (-hook′), *n.* One of the row of sharp hooked nails set on a tenter to hold the cloth.

tenth (těnth), *a.* **1.** Next in order after the ninth. **2.** Being one of ten equal parts into which a (whole) thing may be divided.— *n.* **1.** A tenth part. **2.** A tenth unit or object.

te-nu′i-ty (tė-nū′ĭ-tĭ), *n.* Tenuous quality or state.

ten′u-ous (těn′ů-ŭs), *a.* [4] **1.** Thin; slender; flimsy. **2.** Rare; subtile; not dense; — of fluids.

ten′ure (-ûr), *n.* Act, right, or manner, of holding, as real estate, properly of a superior; period for which anything is had and enjoyed.

te′pee (tē′pē; tē′pĕ′), *n.* An American Indian tent.

tep′id (těp′ĭd), *a.* [3] Moderately warm; lukewarm; — chiefly used of liquids. — **-ness,** *n.* [8].

te-pid′i-ty (tė-pĭd′ĭ-tĭ), *n.* Tepid state or quality.

ter-cen′te-na-ry (tûr-sěn′tė-nȧ-rĭ), *a.* Including, or relating to, a term of 300 years.— *n.; pl.* -RIES (-rĭz). The 300th anniversary of any event.

ter′gi-ver-sate′ (tûr′jĭ-vẽr-sāt′), *v. i.* [1] To shift; evade; shuffle; also, to desert; apostatize.

ter′gi-ver-sa′tion (-sā′shŭn), *n.* Act of tergiversating; shifting; subterfuge; evasion; desertion.

term (tûrm), *n.* **1.** Limit; bound; end. **2.** A limited or definite extent of time, esp.: **a** One of the periods of instruction in the school year. **b** The period for which a court is held. **3.** *Logic.* One of the three component parts of a syllogism. **4.** A word or expression, esp. one peculiar to a science, art, etc. **5.** *pl.* Stipulations; conditions. **6.** *pl.* **a** Mutual relationship; footing. **b** Agreement. **7.** *Math.* Any of the members of a proportion or ratio. — *v. t.* To apply a term to; call.

ter′ma-gan-cy (tûr′mȧ-găn-sĭ),*n.* Termagant quality or state.

ter′ma-gant (-gȧnt), *n.* A turbulent, brawling woman. — *a.* [4] Tumultuous; quarrelsome.

ter′mi-na-ble (tûr′mĭ-nȧ-b′l), *a.* Capable of being, or liable to be, terminated; limitable.

ter′mi-nal (-nȧl), *a.* **1.** Of or pert. to the end, extremity, boundary, or terminus. **2.** Pertaining to a railroad terminal. **3.** Of or pertaining to a term, or fixed period of time.— *n.* **1.** Terminating part; end. **2.** The end of a line of railroad, with the switches, stations, sheds, etc. — **-ly,** *adv.*

ter′mi-nate (-nāt), *v. t.* [1] **1.** To set a limit to; bound. **2.** To put an end to; end.— *v. i.* To be limited in space or time; end.

ter′mi-na′tion (-nā′shŭn), *n.* **1.** Act of terminating. **2.** That which ends, limits, or bounds. **3.** *Gram.* Ending of a word; a final syllable or letter; esp., the part added to a stem in inflection.

ter′mi-na-tive (tûr′mĭ-nā-tĭv), *a.* [4] Tending or serving to terminate; terminating; definitive.

ter′mi-no-log′i-cal (-nō-lŏj′ĭ-kȧl), *a.* Pertaining to terminology.

ter′mi-nol′o-gy (-nŏl′ō-jĭ), *n.* The technical or special terms used in a business, art, science, etc.

ter′mi-nus (tûr′mĭ-nŭs), *n.; L. pl.* -NI (-nī). **1.** A boundary; limit. **2.** Termination; end; limit; final goal. **3.** Either end of a railroad line; also, the station, or the town or city, at that place.

ter′mite (-mīt), *n.* A white ant. See WHITE ANT.

tern (tûrn),*n.* Any of numerous birds of the gull family, mostly

Common Tern.

smaller than the true gulls.

ter′na-ry (tûr′nȧ-rĭ), *a.* Proceeding by threes; consisting of three. — *n.; pl.* -RIES. The number three; a triad. [in threes.]

ter′nate (-nāt), *a.* Consisting of threes; arranged [in threes.]

ter′race (těr′ås), *n.* A raised level or platform of earth, often one of a series arranged one above the other on a slope. — *v. t.* [1] To form into, or furnish with, a terrace or terraces.

ter′ra cot′ta (těr′ȧ kŏt′ȧ). **1.** Hard-baked pottery, esp. that of a brownish red or yellowish red color. **2.** A color like that of terra cotta (def. 1).

ter′ra-pin (těr′ȧ-pĭn), *n.* Any of various edible turtles living in fresh or brackish water.

ter-rene′ (tĕ-rēn′), *a.* Terrestrial; earthly.

ter-res′tri-al (-rĕs′trĭ-ăl), *a.* **1.** Earthly;—opposed to *celestial.* **2.** Representing, or consisting of, the earth. **3.** Consisting of land, in distinction from water. **4.** Of or inhabiting the land, or ground, in distinction from trees, water, etc.

ter′ri-ble (těr′ĭ-b′l), *a.* [4] **1.** Adapted, or likely, to excite terror; dreadful. **2.** Excessive; extreme. *Colloq.* — **-ness,** *n.* — **ter′ri-bly,** *adv.*

ter′ri-er (-ẽr), *n.* A dog of any of certain breeds differing much in shape, coat, etc., but generally small, vivacious, and courageous.

ter-rif′ic (tĕ-rĭf′ĭk), *a.* [4] Exciting, or adapted to excite, great fear or dread; terrible.

ter′ri-fy (těr′ĭ-fī), *v. t.* [2] To frighten greatly.

ter′ri-to′ri-al (-tō′rĭ-ȧl), *a.* **1.** Of or pertaining to territory or land. **2.** Limited to a certain district. **3.** [*cap.*] Of or pertaining to all or any one of the Territories of the United States, or any similar district. — **ter′ri-to′ri-al-ly,** *adv.* [8].

ter′ri-to-ry (těr′Ĭ-tṓ-rĬ), *n. ; pl.* -RIES (-rĬz). **1.** A large extent of land; region; district. **2.** Extent of land and waters belonging to, or under the jurisdiction of, a prince, state, or government, or any given portion of it. **3.** Any definite portion of the area of a state considered by itself; esp. [*cap.*], in the U. S., a portion of the country, as Alaska and Hawaii, not included within any State.

ter′ror (-ẽr), *n.* Extreme fear; violent dread; fright; also, the cause of such fear.

ter′ror-ism (těr′ẽr-Ĭz′m), *n.* A terrorizing; state of being terrorized; a mode of governing, or of opposing government, by intimidation.

ter′ror-ist, *n.* An advocate of terrorism.

ter′ror-i-za′tion (-Ĭ-zā′shŭn), *n.* Act of terrorizing, or state of being terrorized.

ter′ror-ize (-īz), *v. t.* [1] To impress with terror; coerce by intimidation. — **-iz′er** (-īz′ẽr), *n.* [8].

terse (tûrs), *a.* [3] Elegantly concise ; pithy; succinct. — **terse′ly**, *adv.* [8] — **terse′ness**, *n.* [8].

ter′tian (tûr′shăn), *a. Med.* Occurring every third day reckoning inclusively (i. e., every other day). — *n. Med.* A tertian disease, esp. fever.

ter′ti-a-ry (tûr′shĬ-ȧ-rĬ; -shả-rĬ), *a.* Of the third formation, order, or rank.

tes′sel-late (těs′ē-lāt), *v. t.* [1] To form into squares or checkers; lay with checkered work.

tes′sel-la′tion (-lā′shŭn), *n.* Act of tessellating; also, the mosaic work so formed.

test (těst), *n.* **1.** A critical examination or decisive trial. **2. a** Means of trial. **b** That with which anything is compared for proof of genuineness; standard. **3.** *Chem.* A procedure or reaction used to distinguish any particular substance or constituent; also, the reagent used. — *v. t.* **1.** To put to the test or proof; try. **2.** *Chem.* To examine or try, as by a reagent.

tes′ta-ment (těs′tȧ-měnt), *n.* **1.** A solemn covenant. *Obs.*, exc. : [*cap.*] **a** Either of the two main divisions of the Bible, called *Old Testament* and *New Testament.* **b** The New Testament. *Colloq.* **2.** *Law.* A will ; — chiefly in the tautological expression *last will* and *testament.*

tes′ta-men′ta-ry (těs′tȧ-měn′tȧ-rĬ), *a.* Of or pert. to a will, or the administration of a will.

tes′tate (těs′tāt), *a. Law.* Having made and left a testament, or will ; as, a person dying *testate.*

tes-ta′tor (těs-tā′tŏr), *n.* A man who leaves a valid will, or testament, at his death.

tes-ta′trix (-trĬks), *n.* A female testator.

test′er (těs′tẽr), *n.* One that tests.

tes′ter (těs′tẽr), *n.* A canopy, as over a bed.

tes′ti-fy (-tĬ-fī), *v. i.* [2] **1.** To make a solemn declaration; give testimony. **2.** To serve as an indication of. — *v. t.* **1.** To bear witness to ; affirm or declare solemnly ; declare or make known freely or publicly. — **tes′ti-fi′er** (-fī′ẽr), *n.* [8].

tes′ti-ly (-lĬ), *adv.* In a testy manner.

tes′ti-mo′ni-al (těs′tĬ-mō′nĬ-ăl), *n.* **1.** A certificate in favor of one's character, conduct, ability, etc. **2.** A token of regard or admiration, of obligation or the like.

tes′ti-mo-ny (těs′tĬ-mō-nĬ), *n. ; pl.* -NIES (-nĬz). **1** A solemn declaration or affirmation made to establish some fact. **2.** Affirmation; declaration.

tes′ti-ness (-nĕs), *n.* Quality or state of being testy.

tes′ty (těs′tĬ), *a.* [3] Fretful; easily irritated.

tet′a-nus (tět′ȧ-nŭs), *n.* A specific disease marked by prolonged contractions of the voluntary muscles, esp. of the lower jaw. Cf. LOCKJAW.

‖ **tête′-à-tête′** (tāt′ȧ-tāt′; tĕ′tȧ-tāt′), *n.* [F.] **1.** Private conversation, or a familiar interview, between two persons. **2.** A short sofa or the like to seat two persons, esp. facing each other.

‖ **tête′ à tête′**. [F.] Face to face; privately; familiarly ; — said of two persons.

teth′er (tĕth′ẽr), *n.* A rope, chain, or the like, by which an animal is fastened to restrict its range. — *v. t.* To confine by a tether.

tet′ra-he′dral (tět′rȧ-hē′drăl), *a.* Pertaining to a tetrahedron.

tet′ra-he′dron (-drŏn), *n.; pl.* E. -HEDRONS (-drŏnz), L. -HEDRA (-drȧ). A polyhedron of four faces.

Tetrahedron.

tet-ram′e-ter (tět-răm′ē-tẽr), *n.* A verse of four measures.

te′trarch (tē′trärk ; tět′rärk), *n. Classical Antiq.* A governor of the fourth part of a Roman province; also, a subordinate prince or petty king.

tet′rarch-y (tět′rär-kĬ), *n.* The district, office, or jurisdiction, of a tetrarch.

tet′ter (tět′ẽr), *n.* Any of various skin diseases marked by eruptions, as ringworm and shingles.

text (těkst), *n.* **1.** The words and sentences of an author as originally written. **2.** A passage of Scripture, esp. one chosen as the subject of a sermon. **3.** Topic ; theme. **4.** The main body of printed or written matter on a page.

text′book′ (-bŏŏk′), *n.* A manual of instruction.

tex′tile (těks′tĬl), *a.* **1.** Of or pert. to weaving. **2.** Woven or capable of being woven. — *n.* **1.** A woven fabric. **2.** A material for weaving.

tex′tu-al (-tũ-ăl), *a.* [4] Of, pertaining to, contained in, or based on, the text, as of the Scriptures; also, verbal or literal.

tex′ture (-tũr), *n.* **1.** Characteristic disposition of interwoven threads, filaments, etc. **2.** Disposition of the smaller parts ; minute structure.

tha′ler (tä′lẽr), *n. sing. & pl.* A German silver coin worth three marks (71.4 cents).

than (thăn), *conj.* A particle indicating the second member of a comparison, used after adjectives and adverbs expressing comparison or diversity.

thane (thān), *n. Early Eng. Hist.* Originally, a servant ; attendant ; hence, one of a class of free attendants on a lord, answering to the knight and baron of later times.

thank (thăngk), *v. t.* To express gratitude to.

thank′ful (thăngk′fŏŏl), *a.* [4] Feeling or expressing thanks. — **-ly**, *adv.* [8] — **-ness**, *n.* [8].

thank′less, *a.* [4] **1.** Not acknowledging favors; ungrateful. **2.** Not obtaining or deserving thanks. — **-ly**, *adv.* [8] — **-ness**, *n.* [8]. [tude.]

thanks (thăngks), *n. pl.* The expression of grati-

thanks′giv′ing (thăngks′gĬv′Ĭng; thănks′gĬv′Ĭng), *n.* **1.** Act of rendering thanks. **2.** A formula expressing gratitude, esp. for divine mercies. **3. a** A public acknowledgment of divine goodness and mercies. **b** A day set apart for making this ; esp. [*cap.*], Thanksgiving Day. *U. S.*

āle, senāte, câre, ăm, ăccount, ärm, ȧsk, sofȧ ; ēve, ĕvent, ĕnd, recĕnt, makẽr ; īce, ĭll ; ōld, ȯbey, ôrb, ŏdd, sŏft, cŏnnect ; ūse, ŭnite, ûrn, ŭp, circŭs ; fŏŏd, fŏŏt ; out, oil ;

Thanks'giv'ing Day (thăngks'gĭv'ĭng). In the United States, a day (usually the last Thursday of November) set apart each year for thanksgiving.

that (thăt), *pron. & a.* A pronominal word used: **1.** As a demonstrative pronoun (*pl.* THOSE): The person, thing, or idea mentioned, indicated, or understood from the situation or context; as, what noise was *that?* **2.** As an adjective (*pl.* THOSE), with the same demonstrative force as the pronoun; as, a yard wide and of twice *that* length. **3.** As a relative pronoun, equivalent to *who* or *which*, either sing. or pl.; as, the man *that* we now see. Present usage generally favors *who* or *which* when the relative clause conveys a qualification simply additional or parenthetic, and *that* when it is definitely restrictive. — *conj. That* is used: **1.** To introduce a clause employed as object or subject of a verb, or to introduce a purpose, consequence, result, or effect, or a clause denoting time. **2.** To introduce a sentence or clause expressing a wish, cause of surprise, indignation, etc. — *adv.* To such a degree; so; as, she did n't go *that* far. *Colloq.*

thatch (thăch), *n.* A covering material, of straw, rushes, reeds, or leaves, for a roof, grain stack, etc.; also, a covering of such material. — *v. t.* To cover with or as with thatch, as a roof. — **thatch'er**, *n.*

thaw (thô), *v. i.* **1.** To melt, dissolve, or become fluid or semifluid; — said of a frozen substance. Also, to have its frozen contents melted ; as, the pipe *thawed.* **2.** To become so warm as to melt ice and snow; — used with *it*, referring to the weather. **3.** Fig., to be freed from coldness or reserve. — *v. t.* To cause to thaw. — *n.* **1.** Act or process of thawing. **2.** A condition of the weather caused by a rise of temperature above freezing point.

the (thē, *when emphatic or alone;* thĕ *or* thĭ *unaccented before a vowel, as in "the egg;"* thĕ, *unaccented before a consonant, as in "the man"*), *definite article.* A demonstrative word used esp. before a noun to particularize its meaning. — *adv.* By that; by so much; on that account; — used before comparatives; as, *the* more, *the* merrier.

the'a-ter (thē'á-tēr), *n.* [6] **1.** A construction or edifice for dramatic performances. **2.** A place where events, esp. of importance, are enacted; as, the *theater* of war. **3.** The drama.

the-at'ri-cal (thē-ăt'rĭ-kăl), *a.* [4] Also **the-at'-ric** (-rĭk), *a.* [4] Of or pert. to a theater or dramatic representations; histrionic; hence, artificial; "stagy." — **the-at'ri-cal-ly**, *adv.* [8].

the-at'ri-cals (-kălz), *n. pl.* Dramatic performance, esp. when produced by amateurs.

thee (thē), *pers. pron.* The objective (dative or accusative) case of *thou.*

theft (thĕft), *n.* Act of stealing; larceny.

the'ine (thē'ĭn ; -ēn), *n.* See CAFFEINE.

their (thâr), *pron. & a.* Of or belonging to them; — used as possessive of *they*, or as a possessive adj.

theirs (thârz), *pron.* Form of the possessive *their* used absolutely, that is, without a following noun.

the'ism (thē'ĭz'm), *n.* Belief in a god or gods.

the'ist, *n.* A believer in a god or gods.

the-is'tic (thē-ĭs'tĭk), **the-is'ti-cal** (-tĭ-kăl), *a.* [4] Of or pertaining to theism or a theist.

them (thĕm), *pers. pron.* Objective case of *they.*

the-mat'ic (thē-măt'ĭk), *a.* Of or pert. to a theme.

theme (thēm), *n.* **1.** A subject or topic of discourse. **2.** A brief dissertation or essay; esp., a school composition. **3.** *Music.* A melodic subject.

them-selves' (thĕm-sĕlvz'), *pron.* Emphasized form for *they, them* ; — *pl.* of *himself, herself*, and *itself.*

then (thĕn), *adv.* **1.** At that time. **2.** Soon afterward, or immediately; next. **3.** At another time; later. — *a.* Then being. — *conj.* In that case.

thence (thĕns), *adv.* From that place or time.

thence'forth' (thĕns'fôrth'; thĕns'fōrth), *adv.* From that time forward.

thence'for'ward (thĕns'fôr'wĕrd), *adv.* Onward from that place or, esp., time.

the-oc'ra-cy (thē-ŏk'rá-sĭ), *n. ; pl.* -CIES (-sĭz). **1.** Government by direction of God; rule by priests as representing the word of God. **2.** A state so governed.

the-o-crat'ic (thē'ó-krăt'ĭk), **-crat'i-cal** (-ĭ-kăl), *a.* [4] Of or pertaining to, or being, a theocracy.

the-od'o-lite (-ŏd'ó-līt), *n.* Surveying instrument for measuring horizontal and vertical angles.

the'o-lo'gi-an (thē'ó-lō'jĭ-ăn), *n.* A person well versed in theology, esp. Christian theology.

the'o-log'i-cal (-lŏj'ĭ-kăl), *a.* Of or pertaining to theology. — **the'o-log'i-cal-ly**, *adv.* [8].

the-ol'o-gy (thē-ŏl'ó-jĭ), *n. ; pl.* -GIES (-jĭz). Science of God or of religion; divinity.

the'o-rem (thē'ó-rĕm), *n.* **1.** That which is established as a principle or law. **2.** *Math.* A general statement capable of being proved.

the'o-ret'ic (-rĕt'ĭk), *a.* Theoretical.

the'o-ret'i-cal (-ĭ-kăl), *a.* [4] Pertaining to theory ; speculative ; not practical. — **-ly**, *adv.* [8].

the'o-rist (-rĭst), *n.* One who theorizes.

the'o-rize (thē'ó-rīz), *v. i.* [1] To form a theory or theories; speculate. — **-riz'er** (-rĭz'ēr), *n.* [8].

the'o-ry (-rĭ), *n. ; pl.* -RIES (-rĭz). **1.** The general or abstract principles of any science or art. **2.** Apprehension or analysis of a given set of factors in their ideal relations to one another. **3.** A general principle offered to explain phenomena.

the'o-soph'ic (thē'ó-sŏf'ĭk), *a.* Theosophical.

the'o-soph'i-cal (-ĭ-kăl), *a.* Of or pertaining to theosophy. — **the'o-soph'i-cal-ly**, *adv.* [8].

the-os'o-phist (thē-ŏs'ó-fĭst), *n.* An adherent of theosophy.

the-os'o-phy (-fĭ), *n. ; pl.* -PHIES (-fĭz). **1.** Any system of philosophy or mysticism which proposes to reveal a knowledge of God by extraordinary spiritual illumination. **2.** Doctrines and beliefs of a modern school or sect following, in the main, the philosophy and mysticism of India.

ther'a-peu'tic (thĕr'á-pū'tĭk), *a.* [4]. Pertaining to the healing art; curative.

ther'a-peu'tics (-tĭks), *n.* Science of the discovery and application of remedies for diseases.

ther'a-py (thĕr'á-pĭ), *n.* Therapeutics.

there (thâr), *adv.* **1.** In or at that place. **2.** Into or to that place; thither. **3.** At that point, stage, etc. **4.** In that matter, relation, respect, etc.

there'a-bout' (thâr'á-bout')) *adv.* **1.** Near that

there'a-bouts' (-bouts')) place. **2.** Near that number, degree, or quantity; nearly.

there-aft'er (thâr-áf'tēr), *adv.* **1.** After that; afterward. **2.** According to that; accordingly.

there-at' (thâr-ăt'), *adv.* **1.** At that place; there. **2.** At that occurrence; on that account.

there-by' (thâr-bī'), *adv.* **1.** By that ; by that means. **2.** Connected with that. **3.** Near by.

there-for' (thâr-fôr'), *adv.* For that or this.

there'fore (thâr'fōr'), *adv. & conj.* For that or this reason ; on that account.

there-from' (thâr-frŏm'), *adv.* From this or that.

there-in' (-ĭn'), *adv.* **1.** In or into that or this place, time, or thing. **2.** In that particular.

there-of' (-ŏv' ; -ŏf'), *adv.* **1.** Of that, this, or it. **2.** From that or this ; therefrom.

there-on' (-ŏn'), *adv.* On that or this.

there-to' (-tōō'), *adv.* To that or this.

there'to-fore (thâr'tōō-fōr'), *adv.* To that time.

there'un-to' (thâr'ŭn-tōō'), *adv.* Thereto.

there'up-on' ('-ŭ-pŏn'), *adv.* **1.** Thereon. **2.** Therefore. **3.** Immediately after that ; at once.

there-with' (thâr-wĭth' ; -wĭth'), *adv.* **1.** With that or this. **2.** At the same time ; thereupon.

there'with-al' (thâr'wĭth-ôl'), *adv.* **1.** Over and above ; besides. **2.** With that or this.

ther'mal (thûr'măl), *a.* [4] Of or pertaining to heat ; warm ; hot ; as, *thermal* waters.

ther'mic (thûr'mĭk), *a.* Thermal.

ther-mom'e-ter (thĕr-mŏm'ē-tēr), *n.* Any device for measuring relative temperature, commonly by means of the expansion or contraction of mercury or alcohol as indicated by its rise and fall within a slender tube.

☞ In the Fahrenheit thermometer the freezing and boiling points of water are marked respectively 32 and 212 degrees ; in the centigrade thermometer the corresponding points are 0 (zero) and 100. To reduce degrees centigrade to degrees Fahrenheit, multiply by $\frac{9}{5}$ and add 32°.

ther'mo-met'ric (thûr'mŏ-mĕt'rĭk), *a.* Of or pert. to a thermometer. — **-ri-cal** (-rĭ-kăl), *a.*

ther'mo-si'phon (-sī'fŏn), *a.* Designating a water-cooling system for internal-combustion engines in which the circulation is due to the difference in weight between hot and cold water.

ther'mo-stat (thûr'mŏ-stăt), *n.* An automatic device to regulate temperature.

the-sau'rus (thē-sô'rŭs), *n. ; L. pl.* -SAURI (-rī). A treasury or storehouse ; hence, a repository, esp. of words, as a dictionary.

these (thēz), *pron.* Plural of *this.*

the'sis (thē'sĭs), *n. ; pl.* THESES (-sēz). **1.** A proposition ; esp., a position or proposition which a person advances and offers to maintain by argument. **2.** An essay or dissertation, esp. by a candidate for a diploma or degree.

thew (thū), *n.* A muscle ; sinew ; — usually in *pl. ; hence, pl.,* muscular power ; strength ; resolution.

they (thā), *pers. pron. pl. ; poss.* THEIRS (thârz) ; *obj.* THEM (thĕm). The plural of *he, she,* or *it.*

thick (thĭk), *a.* [3] **1.** Of relatively great depth or extension from one surface to its opposite. **2.** Measuring in the third dimension (length and breadth being the other two), or from one surface to its opposite. **3.** Closely set ; dense ; numerous ; abundant. **4.** Having, or being of, relatively great density or consistency. **5.** Not clear ; turbid, muddy, or foggy. **6.** Dull ; stupid ; dense. **7.** Indistinct ; muffled ; dull ; as, a *thick* voice. **8.** Intimate ; familiar. *Colloq.* — *n.* Thickest part, or time when anything is thickest. — *adv.* Thickly.

thick'en (thĭk'n), *v. t. & i.* To make or become thick. [liquid or the like).]

thick'en-ing, *n.* Something used to thicken (a

thick'et (thĭk'ĕt), *n.* A dense growth of shrubbery ; a thick grove or coppice.

thick'ly, *adv.* In a thick manner.

thick'ness, *n.* Quality or state of being thick.

thick'set' (thĭk'sĕt'), *a.* [4] **1.** Closely placed ; as, a *thickset* hedge. **2.** Stout and short of body. **3.** Set or studded thickly. — *n.* A thicket.

thief (thēf), *n. ; pl.* THIEVES (thēvz). One who steals, esp. stealthily ; one who commits theft.

thieve (thēv), *v. t. & i.* [1] To steal.

thiev'er-y (thēv'ẽr-ĭ), *n.* Stealing ; theft.

thiev'ish, *a.* [4] **1.** Given to stealing. **2.** Of, pertaining to, or like, a thief ; stealthy ; sly ; as, *thievish* propensities. — *-ly, adv.* [8] — *-ness, n.* [8].

thigh (thī), *n.* The leg from the knee up.

thill (thĭl), *n.* Either of the two shafts between which a horse is hitched to a vehicle.

thim'ble (thĭm'b'l), *n.* **1.** A kind of cap, or sometimes a broad ring, used in sewing to protect the finger when pushing the needle. **2.** *Mech.* A more or less thimble-shaped appendage or fixture.

thim'ble-ber'ry (-bẽr'ĭ), *n. ; pl.* -RIES (-ĭz). Any of several American raspberries.

thin (thĭn), *a. ;* THIN'NER (-ẽr) ; -NEST. **1.** Of relatively little depth ; not thick. **2.** Of small diameter ; slender ; fine. **3.** Of little density or thickness. **4.** Not close or abundant ; scanty. **5.** Wanting substance, strength, or richness. **6.** Wanting in volume ; not full ; as, a *thin* voice. **7.** Slim ; spare ; lean. — *v. t. & i. ;* THINNED (thĭnd) ; THIN'NING. To make or become thin or thinner.

thine (thīn), *pron. & a.* Of or pert. to thee. See THY *Thine* is superseded in ordinary language by *your. Thine* is used before a vowel as, *thine* eye.

thing (thĭng), *n.* **1.** Whatever exists as a separate entity. **2. a** An act or occurrence ; event ; deed **b** A creature, an object, or a material. **c** *pl.* Personal belongings ; esp., clothes. **d** Anything with out life ; inanimate object ; — distinguished from a *person* or living *creature.* **3.** A particular ; item, bit ; whit.

think (thĭngk), *v. i. ; pret. & p. p.* THOUGHT (thôt), *p. pr. & vb. n.* THINK'ING. **1.** To reflect ; ponder ; meditate. **2.** To form an idea (of) ; conceive (of), as, *think* of me as safe. **3.** To call to mind ; remember ; — with *of ;* as, he didn't *think* of that. **4.** To purpose ; intend ; — with *of ;* as, he *thinks* of returning. **5.** To have an opinion or feeling ; as, I *think* it will rain. — *v. t.* **1.** To conceive ; imagine **2.** To believe ; consider. — **think'er,** *n.*

thin'ly, *adv.* In a thin manner.

thin'ness, *n.* Quality or state of being thin.

third (thûrd), *a.* **1.** Next in order after the second. **2.** Constituting one of three equal parts into which a (whole) thing is divided. — *n.* Quotient of a unit divided by three ; one of three equal parts. — **-ly,** *adv.*

thirst (thûrst), *n.* **1.** A sensation of dryness in the mouth and throat, with a craving for liquids, or the condition producing it. **2.** Eager desire after anything ; a longing. — *v. i.* To feel thirst

thirst'y (thûrs'tĭ), *a.* [3] **1.** Feeling thirst **2.** Deficient in moisture ; dry ; as, a *thirsty* land. — **thirst'i-ly** (-tĭ-lĭ), *adv.* [8] —**-i-ness,** *n.* [8]

thir'teen' (thûr'tēn'; thûr'tēn'), *a.* Ten and three. — *n.* **1.** Number greater by three than ten; thirteen units or objects. **2.** A symbol for thirteen units, as 13 or xiii.

thir'teenth' (thûr'tēnth'; thûr'tēnth'), *a.* **1.** Next in order after the twelfth. **2.** Constituting one of thirteen equal parts into which a (whole) thing is divided. — *n.* **1.** A thirteenth part. **2.** A thirteenth unit or object.

thir'ti-eth (thûr'tĭ-ĕth), *a.* **1.** Next in order after the twenty-ninth. **2.** Constituting one of thirty equal parts into which a (whole) thing is divided. — *n.* **1.** A thirtieth part. **2.** A thirtieth unit or object.

thir'ty (-tĭ), *a.* Three times ten; one more than twenty-nine. — *n.; pl.* -TIES (-tĭz). **1.** Sum of three tens; thirty units or objects. **2.** A symbol for thirty units, as 30 or xxx.

this (thĭs), *pron. & a.; pl.* THESE (thēz). A demonstrative word, referring particularly to what is present or near.

this'tle (thĭs''l), *n.* Any of various prickly plants of the aster family. Also (with qualifying word), any of numerous other prickly plants.

this'tly (thĭs'lĭ), *a.* [4] **1.** Resembling a thistle; prickly. **2.** Full of, or abounding in, thistles.

thith'er (thĭth'ẽr), *adv.* **1.** To that place. **2.** To that point, end, or result. — *a.* Farther.

thith'er-ward (-wẽrd), **thith'er-wards** (-wẽrdz), *adv.* Toward that place; in that direction.

thole (thōl), *n.* A pin set in the gunwale of a boat to serve as a fulcrum for the oar.

thong (thŏng), *n.* A strip of leather.

tho-rac'ic (thō-răs'ĭk), *a.* Of or pert. to the thorax.

tho'rax (thō'răks), *n.* **1.** The part of the body between the neck and the abdomen, containing the heart, lungs, etc. **2.** In insects, the middle of the three chief divisions of the body.

tho'ri-um (-rĭ-ŭm), *n. Chem.* A somewhat rare metallic element, the oxide of which, tho'ri-a (-ä), a white earthy substance, is used in gas mantles.

thorn (thôrn), *n.* **1.** A stiff, sharp-pointed outgrowth on the stem or other part of a plant, as on the rose; a spine; prickle. **2.** Fig., a source of distress. **3.** Any thorn-bearing shrub or small tree.

thorn apple. Any of certain poisonous plants of the nightshade family. Cf. DATURA.

thorn'y (thôr'nĭ), *a.* [3] **1.** Full of thorns; spiny. **2.** Like, or characteristic of, a thorn.

thor'ough (thûr'ō), *a.* [4] Thoroughgoing; fully executed; complete.

thor'ough-bred' (-brĕd'), *a.* [4] **1.** Of animals, bred from the best blood through a long line; pureblooded. **2.** Of persons, having characteristics like, or suggestive of, those of thoroughbred animals. — *n.* A thoroughbred animal, esp. a horse.

thor'ough-fare' (thûr'ō-fâr'), *n.* A place or way for passing or travel; a passage through; a public road or street open at both ends.

thor'ough-go'ing (-gō'ĭng), *a.* [4] Going through, or to the end or bottom; thorough; extreme.

thor'ough-ly, *adv.* In a thorough manner.

thor'ough-ness, *n.* Thorough quality or state.

those (thōz), *pron.* Pl. of *that.* See THAT.

thou (thou), *pron.; sing.:* nom. THOU; poss. THY

(thī) or THINE (thīn); *obj.* THEE (thē); *pl.:* nom. YOU (yōō); *poss.* YOUR (yōōr) or YOURS (yōōrz); *obj.* YOU. The personal pronoun of the 2d person singular, in the nominative case; the subject pronoun denoting the person addressed. It is used chiefly in solemn or poetical style.

though (thō), *conj.* **1.** Granting or supposing that; notwithstanding that. **2.** In case that; if; — usually with *as.* **3.** In spite of that; notwithstanding; yet. — *adv.* However; for all that; — a familiar use.

thought (thôt), *n.* **1.** Act or state of thinking; reflection; cogitation. **2. a** Consideration; heed; care. **b** Solicitude; anxious care. *Obs. or Dial.* **c** Meditation; as, lost in *thought.* **3.** The understanding; intellect. **4.** That which is thought; an idea; a judgment. **5.** A little; trifle.

thought, *pret. & p. p.* of THINK.

thought'ful (-fŏŏl), *a.* [4] **1.** Full of thought; contemplative. **2.** Marked by, or concerned with, thought. **3.** Attentive; careful; heedful. **4.** Mindful of others; kind. — **-ly,** *adv.* — **-ness,** *n.* [8].

thought'less, *a.* [4] **1.** Destitute of thoughts. **2.** Careless; heedless. — **-ly,** *adv.* — **-ness,** *n.* [8].

thou'sand (thou'zănd), *n.* **1.** The number of ten hundred. **2.** Indefinitely, a great number. **3.** A symbol for one thousand units; as, 1,000 or M. — *a.* Consisting of ten hundred; indefinitely, great in number. — **-sandth** (-zăndth), *a. & n.*

thrall (thrôl), *n.* **1.** A slave; bondman. **2.** Thralldom; bondage. [age; servitude.

thrall'dom, thral'dom (-dŭm), *n.* Slavery; bondage.

thrash (thrăsh), **thresh** (thrĕsh), *v. t.* **1.** To beat; flog. *Colloq.* **2.** To beat out grain from, as wheat stalks; beat off, as oat kernels. — *v. i.* **1.** To thresh grain or the like. **2.** To move violently; toss about. ☞ Both *thrash* and *thresh* are in use in all the meanings, but *thresh* is now chiefly used of beating out grain, *thrash* in the other senses.

thrash'er, thresh'er, *n.* **1.** One that thrashes or threshes. **2.** Also **thrasher,** *or* **thresher, shark.**

Thrasher Shark.

A large shark said to drive together or kill with its great tail the small fish on which it feeds. **3.** Any of numerous long-tailed thrushlike birds.

thread (thrĕd), *n.* **1.** A small twist of flax, cotton, silk, or other fiber, drawn out. **2.** A filament, or fiber, also, a fine line, as of gold or silver. **3.** *Mech.* The projecting helical rib of a screw. **4.** Something running through the entire course of a thing and serving to connect its parts, as a line of thought. — *v. t.* **1.** To pass a thread through the eye of, as a needle. **2.** To put on a thread; string, as beads. **3.** To pass through (a narrow or intricate way); make (one's way), esp. carefully, through obstacles. **4.** *Mech.* To form a thread on or in. — **thread'er,** *n.* [8].

thread'bare' (-bâr'), *a.* [4] **1.** Worn to the thread; having the nap worn off. **2.** Worn out; trite; hackneyed. **3.** Wearing threadbare clothes; shabby.

thread'y (-ĭ), *a.* [4] **1.** Like a thread; as: stringy; fibrous; slender; viscid; ropy; thin (of the voice).

threat (thrĕt), *n.* Menace; threatening.

---

chair; go; sing, iṅk; then, thin; nature, verdure; yet; zh = z in azure. Numbers refer to §§ in the Special Notes which, with Abbreviations, Signs, etc., precede the Vocabulary.

threat'en (thrĕt''n), v. t. **1.** To utter threats against; menace. **2.** To give signs of the approach of (evil); portend. — v. i. **1.** To use threats. **2.** To have a threatening appearance. — **-er**, n. [8].

three (thrē), a. One more than two ; — a cardinal numeral. — n. **1.** The number greater by a unit than two ; three units or objects. **2.** A symbol for three units, as 3 or iii. **3.** Something having as an essential feature three units or members.

three'fold' (-fōld'), a. Consisting of three ; thrice repeated ; triple. — adv. Thrice ; triply.

three'-ply', a. Consisting of three distinct parts, as of three webs interwoven.

thren'o-dy (thrĕn'ō-dĭ), n. ; pl. -DIES (-dĭz). A song of lamentation ; a dirge or funeral song.

thresh (thrĕsh), v. t. & i. See THRASH. — **-er**, n.

thresh'old (thrĕsh'ōld), n. **1.** The plank, stone, or piece of timber which lies under a door; sill of a door; hence, an entrance. **2.** Entrance; outset.

threw (thrōō), pret. of THROW.

thrice (thrīs), adv. **1.** Three times. **2.** In a three-fold manner or degree ; hence, repeatedly; fully.

thrift (thrĭft), n. **1.** Economical management; frugality. **2.** Any of a certain genus of plants, esp. one bearing heads of pink or white flowers.

thrift'less, a. [4] Without thrift; improvident. — **thrift'less-ly**, adv. [8] — **-ness**, n. [8].

thrift'y (thrĭf'tĭ), a. [3] **1.** Given to or showing thrift ; saving. **2.** Thriving by industry and frugality ; prosperous. **3.** Growing vigorously ; thriving. — **-i-ly**, adv. [8] — **-i-ness**, n. [8].

thrill (thrĭl), v. t. To affect emotionally as if by something that pierces ; penetrate and pervade with feeling. — v. i. **1.** To pierce, as an emotion or experience ; penetrate. **2.** To feel a tingling or shivering sensation. **3.** To move or act tremulously ; vibrate ; tremble. — n. A sensation as of being thrilled ; tremulous excitement.

thrips (thrĭps), n. Any of numerous small insects, most species of which feed on plant juices.

thrive (thrīv), v.i.; pret. THROVE (thrōv) or THRIVED (thrīvd) ; p. p. THRIVED or THRIV'EN (thrĭv''n); p. pr. & vb. n. THRIV'ING (thrīv'ĭng). **1.** To prosper by thrift. **2.** To be successful or flourishing. **3.** To grow vigorously or luxuriantly; flourish.

throat (thrōt), n. **1.** The part of the neck in front of the vertebral column ; the passage through it. **2.** An entrance, passageway, or narrowed place.

throat'y (-ĭ), a. [3] Guttural ; — of sounds.

throb (thrŏb), v. i. ; THROBBED (thrŏbd) ; THROB'-BING. To pulsate ; vibrate ; palpitate. — n. A beat, or pulsation, as of the heart.

throe (thrō), n. Extreme pain ; anguish ; agony.

throne (thrōn), n. **1.** A chair of state ; esp., a royal seat on a dais with a canopy, as of a prince, bishop, etc. **2.** Sovereign power and dignity.

throng (thrŏng), n. **1.** An assembled multitude of persons ; a crowd. **2.** A great number; host. — v. i. & t. To crowd together; fill; crowd.

throt'tle (thrŏt''l), n. **1.** The throat or windpipe. Now Chiefly Dial. **2.** Short for THROTTLE VALVE. — v. t. [1] **1.** To choke; strangle. **2.** To obstruct the flow of, as steam to an engine.

throttle valve. A valve for regulating supply, as of steam, gas, or air, to an engine.

through (thrōō), prep. **1.** From end to end of, or from side to side of ; into at one point and out of at another. **2.** From the beginning to the end of. **3.** By way of. **4.** By means or reason of ; in consequence of. **5.** Over the whole surface or extent of; throughout. **6.** Among or in the midst of ; — denoting passage. — adv. **1.** From one end or side to the other ; throughout. **2.** From beginning to end. **3.** To the end ; at an end. — a. Going or extending from one place to another without change or interruption; as, a through train.

through-out' (-out'), prep. Quite through; in every part of. — adv. In every part ; everywhere.

throve (thrōv), pret. of THRIVE.

throw (thrō), v. t. ; pret. THREW (thrōō); p. p. THROWN (thrōn); p. pr. & vb. n. THROW'ING. **1.** To twist filaments of, as silk, so as to form one thread. **2.** To fling, cast, or hurl. **3.** To cause to fall ; cast down. **4.** To shed ; cast. **5.** To bring forth; produce; bear. **6.** To cast, as dice; venture at dice. — v. i. To cast, hurl, or fling. — n. **1.** A throwing, hurling, or flinging ; a cast. **2.** A cast of dice ; a venture ; risk. **3.** Distance to which a missile is thrown ; as, a stone's throw. **4.** Mech. Stroke, or travel, of a crank, eccentric, etc. — **throw'er**, n. [8].

thrum (thrŭm), n. **1.** Weaving. **a** One of the ends of weavers' warp threads. **b** The fringelike row of such threads on the loom when the web has been cut free. **c** Any soft, short threads, tufts, or fringes. **2.** Any loose, coarse yarn waste ; — chiefly in pl. **3.** pl. Tufts, or short pieces, of rope yarn. — v. t. ; THRUMMED (thrŭmd) ; THRUM'MING. To furnish with, or make of, thrums ; tuft ; fringe.

thrum, v. i. & t. To play (a stringed instrument) rudely, monotonously, or listlessly. — n. A monotoncus sound, as of thrumming.

thrush (thrŭsh), n. **1.** An ulcerous affection of the mouth, fauces, etc., common in babies. **2.** An affection of the feet in certain animals.

thrush, n. Any of many small or medium-sized birds, typically plainly colored, but sometimes spotted below.

thrust (thrŭst), v. t. & i. ; pret. & p. p. THRUST ; p. pr. & vb. n. THRUST'ING. **1.** To push or drive with force ; impel ; shove. **2.** To stab ; pierce ; — usually with through. — n. **1.** A violent push or drive; a stab. **2.** Force or pressure of one thing against another.

thud (thŭd), n. A dull heavy sound ; a thump.

thug (thŭg), n. A ruffian ; assassin.

thumb (thŭm), n. **1.** The first digit of the human hand, opposable to the other fingers. **2.** The part of a glove or mitten that covers the thumb. — v. t. **1.** To handle awkwardly, as a musical instrument. **2.** To soil or wear with the thumb.

thumb'screw' (thŭm'skrōō'), n. A screw having the head so that it may be turned by the thumb and forefinger.

thump (thŭmp), n. A blow or knock, as with something blunt or heavy ; heavy fall ; also, the sound made by such a blow or fall. — v. t. & i. To strike with something thick or heavy, or so as to cause a dull or heavy sound; pound; of the heart, to beat heavily. — **thump'er**, n. [8].

thun'der (thŭn'dẽr), n. **1.** The sound following a flash of lightning. **2.** A startling or impressive utterance of threat, denunciation, censure, etc.

āle, senăte, câre, ăm, ăccount, ärm, ásk, sofά ; ēve, ĕvent, ĕnd, recĕnt, makẽr ; īce, ĭll ; ōld, ŏbey, ôrb, ŏdd, sŏft, cŏnnect ; ūse, ŭnite, ûrn, ŭp, circŭs ; fōōd, fŏŏt ; out, oil .

thun′der, *v. i.* **1.** To produce thunder. **2.** To give forth a sound likened to thunder. **3.** To utter violent denunciation.— *v. t.* To emit or utter with a noise of or as of thunder.

thun′der-bolt′ (thŭn′dẽr-bōlt′), *n.* **1.** A single discharge of lightning with accompanying thunder. **2.** Something like, or suggestive of, thunder in being sudden and awful, destructive, or startling.

thun′der-clap′ (-klăp′), *n.* A crash of thunder.

thun′der-cloud′ (-kloud′), *n.* An electrically charged cloud, producing lightning and thunder.

thun′der-er (-ẽr), *n.* One that thunders.

thun′der-ous (-ŭs), *a.* [4] Producing thunder; also, making a noise like thunder. — **-ly**, *adv.* [8].

thun′der-stroke′ (-strōk′), *n.* A stroke by or as by lightning, with the attendant thunder.

thun′der-struck′ (-strŭk′), *p. a.* Astonished; amazed.

Thurs′day (thŭrz′dă), *n.* Fifth day of the week.

thus (thŭs), *adv.* **1.** In this or that manner. **2.** To this degree or extent; so far. **3.** Consequently.

thwack (thwăk), *v. t. & n.* Whack; bang; thrash.

thwart (thwôrt), *a.* [3] Tranverse; oblique.— *adv.* Athwart. — *n.* A rower's seat across a boat. — *v. t.* To oppose or baffle, as a purpose; contravene; hence, to frustrate or defeat.

thy (thī), *pron. & a.* Of or belonging to thee;—used attributively. [family.]

thyme (tīm), *n.* Any of various plants of the mint family.

thy-self′ (thī-sĕlf′), *pron.* An emphasized form for *thou* or *thee.*

ti-a′ra (tī-ā′rá; tē-ä′rá), *n.* **1.** The Pope's triple crown. **2.** A crown-like head ornament; a coronet.

tib′i-a (tĭb′ĭ-á), *n.; pl.* -LÆ (-ē). The inner of the two bones of the leg or hind limb between knee and ankle.

tib′i-al (-ăl), *a.* Of or pert. to a tibia.

tic (tĭk), *n.* *Med.* A habitual convulsive motion of certain muscles, esp. of the face; twitching.

Tiara, 1.

tick (tĭk), *n.* The case of a bed, mattress, etc., containing the filling.

tick, *n.* Any of numerous bloodsucking parasites.

tick, *v. i.* To make a small, repeated noise, esp. one like that of a watch. — *v. t.* To mark, note, or check, by a tick, or small mark. — *n.* **1.** A light, repeated, sound of or as of tapping. **2.** Any small mark to direct attention.

tick′er, *n.* One that ticks; esp., a telegraphic receiving instrument that automatically prints off news.

tick′et (-ĕt), *n.* **1.** A small piece of paper, cardboard, or the like, serving as a notice, certificate, or token, esp. of a right, as of admission, etc. **2.** *Politics.* A list of candidates, esp. of one party, to be voted for; ballot.— *v. t.* **1.** To distinguish or mark by a ticket. **2.** To furnish with a ticket.

tick′le (tĭk′'l), *v. t.* [1] **1.** To touch lightly so as to produce a peculiar thrilling sensation. **2.** To please; amuse.— *v. i.* **1.** To feel or to excite a sense of being tickled. — *n.* A tickling; a light touch on a sensitive part.— **tick′ler** (-lẽr), *n.* [8].

tick′lish (-lĭsh), *a.* [4] **1.** Sensitive to tickling. **2.** Insecure; unstable. **3.** Critical or dubious. — **-ly**, *adv.* — **-ness**, *n.* [8]. [tides.]

tid′al (tīd′ăl), *a.* Pert. to, caused by, or having,

tide (tīd), *n.* **1.** Time; season. **2.** The alternate rise and fall of the surface of the ocean occurring twice in each lunar day (24 h. 51 m.). **3.** Stream; flood. **4.** Tendency or direction of causes, influences, or events.— *v. t.* [1] To carry or help along as by a tide.

tide′wa′ter (tīd′wô′tẽr), *n.* Water affected by the tide; hence, broadly, the seaboard.

ti′di-ly (tī′dĭ-lĭ), *adv.* In a tidy manner.

ti′di-ness, *n.* Quality or state of being tidy.

ti′dings (tī′dĭngz), *n. pl.* News: intelligence.

ti′dy (tī′dĭ), *a.* [3] **1.** Orderly; neat. **2.** Considerable in size, amount, etc. *Colloq.*— *v. t. & i.* [2] To make tidy. — *n.; pl.* -DIES. A partial covering to protect the back of a chair, etc.

tie (tī), *v. t.; pret. & p. p.* TIED (tīd); *p. pr. & vb. n.* TY′ING. **1.** To fasten by drawing through or around, and knotting, a band, cord, etc. **2.** To form a knot in. **3.** To form (a knot); interlace; knit. **4.** To join firmly; connect. **5.** To restrict. **6.** *Music.* To unite, as notes, by a tie. **7.** To make or have an equal score with, in a contest. — *n.; pl.* TIES (tīz). **1.** A knot; fastening. **2.** A knot of ribbon, hair, or the like, often ornamental. **3.** Short for NECKTIE. **4.** A bond; an obligation, moral or legal. **5.** A beam, post, or rod to hold parts together. **6.** *Music.* A curved line joining two notes of the same pitch, to denote a single tone of the time value of the two. **7.** Equality in a contest.

tier (tẽr), *n.* A row or rank.

tiff (tĭf), *n.* A fit of anger; petty quarrel. *Colloq.*

ti′ger (tī′gẽr), *n.* A large Asiatic flesh-eating animal of the cat family, of a tawny color transversely striped with black.

tiger cat. Any of certain wild cats of moderate size having marks or patches of different colors.

ti′ger-ish, *a.* [4] Of or like a tiger; fierce.

tight (tīt), *a.* [3] **1.** Firmly held together; compact; firm. **2.** Impervious; not leaky. **3.** Fitting close, usually too close. **4.** Taut; tense. **5.** Scarce; dear; as, *tight* money; stringent. — **-ly**, *adv.* — **-ness**, *n.* [or tighter.]

tight′en (-'n), *v. t. & i.* To make or become tight.

tights (tīts), *n. pl.* Garments fitting close to the skin, usually for the lower part of the body and the legs, worn esp. by acrobats, gymnasts, etc.

ti′gress (tī′grĕs), *n.* A female tiger.

til′de (tĭl′dĕ; *Sp.* tēl′dā), *n.* The diacritical mark used in cañon, año (Sp., year), são (Port., saint), etc.

tile (tīl), *n.* **1.** A plate, or thin piece, of baked clay, stone, etc., for roofing, floors, etc. **2.** Pipe made of cement or pottery. **3.** Tiles collectively. — *v. t.* [1] To cover with or as with tiles.

till (tĭl), *n.* A drawer or tray; a money drawer.

till, *prep.* To; as far as; until;—now only as to time. — *conj.* To the time that or when; until.

till, *v. t.* To plow, sow, dress, raise crops from, etc.; cultivate. — *v. i.* To cultivate soil.

till′a-ble (-á-b'l), *a.* Capable of being tilled.

till′age (-ăj), *n.* The cultivation of land.

till′er (-ẽr), *n.* One who tills.

till′er, *n.* A sprout; shoot; a sucker. — *v. i.* To put forth new shoots from the root.

till′er, *n.* A lever for turning a rudder.

tilt (tĭlt), *n.* **1.** A canopy; awning; esp., a tent. **2.** A cloth covering of a cart, boat, stall, etc.

---

chair; go; sing, iṇk; then, thin; nature, verdure; yet; zh = z in azure. Numbers refer to §§ in the Special Notes which, with Abbreviations, Signs, etc., precede the Vocabulary.

tilt (tĭlt), v. i. **1.** To lean; fall partly over; tip. **2.** To ride or charge, and thrust with a lance. — v. t. **1.** To slope; incline; tip. **2.** To point or thrust, as a lance. — n. **1.** Slope. **2.** A military exercise on horseback in which the combatants tilt at each other, or at a mark. — **-er**, n. [8].

tilth (tĭlth), n. **1.** Tillage. **2.** Land tilled.

tim'ber (tĭm'bẽr), n. **a** Wood suitable for use in building, etc. **b** A dressed piece of wood, esp. one of comparatively large size. — v. t. To furnish with timber; — chiefly in p. p., *timbered*.

tim'bre (tĭm'bẽr ; F. tăn'br'), n. *Music.* The quality of tone distinguishing voices or instruments.

time (tīm), n. **1.** That in which events are distinguished with reference to before and after ; duration. **2.** A particular point or period of duration. **3.** A period in history ; age ; era ; — often in *pl.* **4.** Duration of one's life ; lifetime. **5.** A fixed or inevitable point of time, esp. that for death. **6.** A portion of time considered as to the effect of what takes place during it ; — often in *pl.* ; as, *times* are dull. **7.** Reckoning, or way of reckoning, the passing of time. **8.** Repetition ; — often in *pl.*; as, ten *times*. **9.** *Music.* **a** The grouping of successive rhythmic beats into equal measures ; — called also *meter*, and *rhythm*. **b** The tempo, or speed at which a piece or passage moves.

time, v. t. [1] **1.** To bring, perform, etc., at a particular season or time. **2.** To regulate as to time. **3.** To ascertain or record the time of. **4.** To measure, as in music. — v. i. To keep or beat time ; move in time.

time'-hon'ored, a. [4, 5] Honored, or worthy of honor, because of age; as, a *time-honored* custom.

time'keep'er (tīm'kēp'ẽr), n. One that marks, measures, regulates, or determines, the time.

time'ly (tīm'lĭ), a. [3] Seasonable; opportune. — adv. Early ; soon ; also, opportunely. — **-li-ness**, n. [8].   [a chronometer.

time'piece' (pēs'), n. A device to measure time ;

time'serv'er (-sûr'vẽr), n. Timeserving person.

time'serv'ing, a. [4] Obsequiously complying with the spirit of the times, or with the humors of those in power; temporizing ; truckling.— n. Timeserving conduct.

time'-ta'ble, n. A tabular statement of the time at which, or within which, things are to take place.

tim'id (tĭm'ĭd), a. [3] Wanting courage to meet danger ; timorous ; shy.— **-ly**, adv.— **-ness**, n.

ti-mid'i-ty (tĭ-mĭd'ĭ-tĭ), n. Quality or state of being timid.

tim'or-ous (tĭm'ẽr-ŭs), a. [4] **1.** Fearful of danger. **2.** Indicating, or caused by, timidity.— **-ly**, adv. — **-ness**, n. [8].

tim'o-thy, n. Also **timothy grass.** A grass with long cylindrical spikes, grown for hay.

tin (tĭn), n. **1.** A soft white metal, malleable at ordinary temperatures, but brittle when heated. **2.** Tin plate. **3.** A can, pan, etc., of tin plate. — v.t.; TINNED (tĭnd) ; TIN'NING. **1.** To cover with tin or tin plate. **2.** To pack in tins ; can. *Chiefly Brit.*

tinc'ture (tĭnk'tụr), n. **1.** Color; tint. **2.** *Pharm.* A solution of medicinal substance in alcohol.— v.t. [1] **1.** To tinge. **2.** To imbue ; impregnate.

tin'der (tĭn'dẽr), n. Something very inflammable, esp. for kindling fire from a spark.

tine (tīn), n. A tooth or spike, as of a fork; prong

tinge (tĭnj), v. t.; TINGED (tĭnjd) ; TINGE'ING *or* TING'ING (tĭn'jĭng). To imbue slightly with a color; tint ; to impregnate with something different or foreign. — n. Tincture ; flavor ; touch.

tin'gle (tĭn'g'l), v. i. [1] To feel or cause a thrilling or stinging sensation, as from cold, a slap, a shrill sound, etc. — n. A tingling sensation.

tink'er (tĭnk'ẽr), n. **1.** A mender of kettles, pans, etc., esp. an itinerant one. **2.** A person skilled in various kinds of small mechanical work.— v. t. **1.** To mend, esp. metal wares. **2.** To mend unskillfully or temporarily. — v. i. **1.** To act as a tinker. **2.** To work at anything in a bungling manner.

tin'kle (tĭn'k'l), v. i. [1] To make or emit small, quick, sharp, metallic sounds; clink. — v. t. To cause to tinkle. — n. A tinkling sound.

tin'ny (tĭn'ĭ), a. [3] Pert. to, or like, tin.

tin plate. Thin sheet iron or steel coated with tin.

tin'sel (tĭn'sĕl), n. **1.** A shining metallic or metalcoated material used to produce a glittering appearance. **2.** Something shining and gaudy; showy pretense.— v. t. [7] To adorn with tinsel.

tin'smith' (-smĭth'), n. Worker in tin or tin plate.

tint (tĭnt), n. A slight coloring; as : **a** Any pale tinge. **b** A light variety of a color. Loosely, hue; shade.— v. t. To tinge.

tin'tin-nab'u-la'tion (tĭn'tĭ-năb'ũ-lā'shŭn), n. The ringing of bells.   [thin iron plate.

tin'type' (tĭn'tīp'), n A photograph taken on a

tin'ware' (tĭn'wâr'), n. Articles of tin plate.

ti'ny (tī'nĭ), a. [3] Very small or diminutive.

tip (tĭp), n. **1.** The point, extremity, or top part, of something. **2.** An end piece or part, as a cap, nozzle, or ferrule.— v. t.; TIPPED (tĭpt) ; TIP'PING. To form or place a tip upon; cover the tip of.

tip (tĭp), v. t. **1.** To strike lightly; tap. **2.** To make incline; slant; tilt. **3.** To give a tip, or fee, to. *Colloq.*— v. i. **1.** To fall on, or incline to, one side ; tilt. **2.** To give a tip, or fee. *Colloq.* — n. **1.** A light touch or blow ; tap. **2.** Secret information, esp. as to the chances of a future event. *Colloq.* **3.** A small gift or fee, esp. to a servant.

tip'pet (tĭp'ĕt), n. **1.** A long hanging part, as on a sleeve, cape, or hood. **2.** A scarf or scarflike garment, to cover the neck, or neck and shoulders.

tip'ple (tĭp''l), v. i. [1] To indulge in intoxicating drinks habitually and often.— v. t. To drink, as liquor, frequently or by sips, esp. too often.— n. Liquor ; drink. — **tip'pler** (-lẽr), n. [8].

tip'sy (-sĭ), a. [3] Rendered weak or foolish by liquor.— **tip'si-ly**, adv.— **tip'si-ness**, n. [8].

tip'toe' (tĭp'tō'), n.; pl. -TOES (-tōz'). The tip, or end, of a toe; also, the ends of the toes, collectively. — a. **1.** Being on tiptoe ; exalted. **2.** Cautious; stealthy. — adv. Expectantly ; eagerly. — v. i.; TIP'TOED (-tōd) ; TIPTOEING. To go on tiptoe.

tip'top' (-tŏp'), n. The very top ; acme ; the best. — (tĭp'tŏp'), a. Most excellent; first-rate. *Colloq.*

ti-rade' (tĭ-rād'; tĭ'rād), n. A long-drawn speech or declamatory passage, esp. of censure or abuse.

tire (tīr), n. A band forming the tread of a wheel of a vehicle.— v. t. [1] To furnish with a tire.

tire, v. t. To become weary.— v. t. To decrease or wear out the strength, patience, or interest of.

tire'less (tīr'lĕs), a. [4] Untiring.— **-ly**, adv. [8].

tire′some (tīr′sŭm), *a.* [4] Wearisome; tedious. —**tire′some-ly**,*adv.*[8]—**tire′some-ness**,*n.*[8].

tis′sue (tĭsh′ū),*n.* **1.** A woven fabric. **2.** A fine transparent silk stuff; any light gauzy fabric. **3.** *Biol.* An aggregate of cells, with their inter-cellular substance, forming one of the structural materials of a plant or animal. **4.** Web; texture; series; as, a *tissue* of lies. **5.** Tissue paper.

tissue paper. A very thin gauzelike paper.

tit (tĭt), *n.* A titmouse; also, esp. with a qualifying term, any of various other small birds.

tit, *n.* A tap; — in **tit** for **tat,** blow for blow.

ti-tan′ic(tī-tăn′ĭk),*a.* [4] Enormous; superhuman.

tit′bit′ (tĭt′bĭt′),*n.* A choice morsel.

tithe (tĭth), *n.* **1.** A tenth; small part. **2.** A tenth paid as a voluntary contribution, a tax, etc.

tith′ing (tĭth′ĭng), *n.* A taking tithes; a tithe.

tit′il-late (tĭt′ĭ-lāt), *v. t. & i.* [1] To tickle; excite pleasurably. [of being titillated.]

tit′il-la′tion (-lā′shŭn), *n.* A titillating, or state

tit′lark′ (-lärk′), *n.* A pipit.

ti′tle (tī′t′l), *n.* **1.** The distinctive designation of a book, poem, statute, etc.; heading. **2.** A descriptive name; epithet. **3.** A personal appellation of dignity, distinction, or rank. **4.** A claim or right. **5.** Legal right to the possession of property, esp. real property: also, the instrument which is evidence of such right. — *v. t.* [1] To call by a title; name; entitle.

ti′tled (tī′t′ld), *a.* Having a title, esp. of nobility.

ti′tle-page′, *n.* Page of a book bearing the title.

tit′mouse (tĭt′mous′), *n.; pl.* -MICE (-mīs′). Any of numerous small birds with, generally, gray, black, and white plumage.

tit′ter (tĭt′ẽr), *v. i.* To laugh with restraint, or without much noise, as in affectation or embarrassment; giggle. — *n.* Restrained laugh; giggle.

tit′tle (tĭt′′l), *n.* **1.** A diacritical mark over a letter or word. Cf. TILDE. **2.** A particle; jot.

tit′tle-tat′tle, *n.* Idle, trifling talk; esp., gossip.

tit′u-lar (tĭt′ū-lär), *a.* **1.** Pert. to or having a title. **2.** Existing in title or name only. — *n.* A person holding a title of office, esp. without obligation to perform its duties. — **-lar-ly,** *adv.* [8].

tit′u-la-ry (-lả-rĭ), *a.* Titular.

to (tōō ; *unemphatic*, tŏŏ), *prep.* Primarily *to* denotes the relation of approach and arrival, making its governed word denote the terminus. Hence: **1.** *To* indicates that toward which there is movement, tendency, or position, with or without arrival. **2.** *To* connects transitive verbs with their indirect object. **3.** *To* is used with, or as the sign of, the infinitive mood. **4.** Hence *to* may denote or imply : **a** Effect; consequence. **b** Opposition. **c** Accord. **d** Comparison. **e** Addition; union. **f** Accompaniment. — *adv.* **1.** To the matter or business in hand. **2.** To or at the normal position.

toad (tōd), *n.* Any of many tailless, leaping animals, living usually on land, but at certain seasons also in the water. They eat insects, worms, etc.

European Toad.

toad′eat′er (-ēt′ẽr), *n.* A toady.

toad′stool′ (-stōōl′),*n.* Any of various fungi having an umbrella-shaped cap ; a mushroom, esp. (popularly) a poisonous one.

toad′y (tōd′ĭ), *n.; pl.* TOADIES (-ĭz). A slavish flatterer; toadeater.—*v.t. & i.* [2] To fawn upon.

toad′y-ism (-ĭz′m), *n.* The behavior of a toady.

toast (tōst), *v. t. & i.* **1.** To dry and brown by the heat of a fire. **2.** To warm thoroughly. **3.** To drink to the health of or in honor of ; drink toasts. — *n.* **1.** Sliced bread toasted. **2. a** One whose health is drunk, or anything in honor of which persons drink; a sentiment drunk to. **b** Act of proposing, or of drinking in honor of, a toast. — **-er,** *n.* [8].

toast′mas′ter (tōst′mȧs′tẽr), *n.* At a banquet, one who presides and announces the toasts.

to-bac′co (tŏ-băk′ō),*n.; pl.* -COS (-ōz). **1.** A certain American plant of the nightshade family. **2.** Its leaves as prepared and used for smoking or chewing, or as snuff.

to-bac′co-nist (-ŏ-nĭst), *n.* A dealer in tobacco.

to-bog′gan (-bŏg′ăn), *n.* A kind of sled made of a thin board or boards curved up at one end — *v. i.* To coast or slide on or as on a toboggan.

toc′sin (tŏk′sĭn), *n.* An alarm bell, or its ringing.

to-day′ (tŏŏ-dā′), *adv.* **1.** On this day. **2.** At the present time; nowadays. — *n.* The present day, time, or age.

tod′dle (tŏd′′l), *v. i.* [1] To walk with short tottering steps, as a child. — **tod′dler** (-lẽr),*n.* [8].

tod′dy (-ĭ), *n.; pl.* -DIES (-ĭz). A mixture of spirit and hot water sweetened.

to-do′ (tŏŏ-dōō′), *n.* Bustle ; stir ; ado. *Colloq.*

toe (tō), *n.* **1.** A terminal member or digit of the foot. **2.** The fore part or end of the foot, or the part of a shoe or stocking covering it; — opposed to *heel.* — *v. t. ;* TOED (tōd) ; TOE′ING. To touch, reach, or drive with the toes.

to′ga (tō′gȧ), *n. ; pl.* E. -GAS (-gȧz), L. -GÆ (-jē). *Roman Antiq.* The loose outer garment worn by citizens in public.

to-geth′er (tŏŏ-gĕth′ẽr), *adv.* **1.** In company, conjunction, or concert. **2.** With each other ; mutually. **3.** In or into union, junction, contact, or the like. **4.** In uninterrupted succession; consecutively.

tog′ger-y (tŏg′ẽr-ĭ), *n.* Clothes, esp. of a particular kind. *Colloq.*

tog′gle (-′l), *n.* **1.** *Naut.* A pin or bolt fixed transversely in an eye of a rope or chain to be secured to a loop, bight, or ring. **2.** *Mach.* A toggle joint, or a device having one.

toggle joint. *Mach.* A device consisting of two bars joined together end to end but not in line, so that when a force is applied to the knee, tending to straighten the arrangement, the bars exert an endwise pressure. [*Slang.*]

togs (tŏgz), *n. pl.* Clothes ; toggery. *Colloq. or*

toil (toil), *n.* A net or snare ; as, in the *toils.*

toil, *v. i.* **1.** To exert strength with pain and fatigue ; labor. **2.** To go or travel with toil. — *n.* **1.** Labor with pain and fatigue. **2.** A piece of toil ; a labor. — **toil′er,** *n.* [8].

toi′let (toi′lĕt),*n.* Also **toi-lette** (toi-lĕt′ ; *F.* twȧ′lĕt′). **1.** A dressing table. **2.** Act or process of dressing, including bathing, etc. ; attire ; dress. **3.** A lavatory, usually with a water-closet. *U. S.*

toilet water. A perfumed liquid for the toilet.

toil′some (toil′sŭm), *a.* [4] Laborious; wearisome. — **toil′some·ly**, *adv.* [8] — **ness**, *n.* [8].

to′ken (tō′k'n), *n.* **1.** Something given or shown as a symbol of authority, good faith, etc. **2.** A memento; souvenir. **3.** A symbol; sign. **4.** A piece of currency issued at a face value in excess of its real value.

told (tōld), *pret. & p. p.* of TELL.

tol′er·a·ble (tŏl′ẽr-à-b'l), *a.* [4] **1.** Endurable; supportable. **2.** Moderately good or agreeable. — **ness**, *n.* [8] — **tol′er·a·bly**, *adv.* [8].

tol′er·ance (-ăns), *n.* **1.** Quality or state of being tolerant. **2.** Act of tolerating.

tol′er·ant (tŏl′ẽr·ănt), *a.* [4] Inclined to tolerate; forbearing. — **tol′er·ant·ly**, *adv.* [8].

tol′er·ate (-āt), *v. t.* [1] **1.** To bear; endure. **2.** To suffer to be, or to be done, without hindrance; allow; put up with.

tol′er·a′tion (-ā′shŭn), *n.* Act of tolerating; esp., recognition of the right of private judgment, chiefly as to religious matters; tolerance.

toll (tōl), *v. t.* **1.** To cause to sound, as a bell, with strokes slowly and uniformly repeated. **2.** To strike (the hour); also, to ring a toll for; as, to *toll* a departed friend. **3.** To call, summon, or notify, by tolling. — *v. i.* To sound, as a bell, with strokes uniformly repeated at intervals, as during funerals. — *n.* The sound of a tolling bell.

toll, *n.* **1.** A tax paid for some liberty or privilege, as of passing over a road or bridge. **2.** A compensation taken for services, as for conveyance or for grinding grain. — *v. t.* To collect as toll.

toll′bar′, toll′gate′, toll′house′, *n.* A bar, gate, or house, where toll is taken.

toll bridge. A bridge at which toll is charged.

to·lu′ (tō-lōō′), *n.,* or **tolu balsam.** A fragrant balsam got from a South American tree.

tom′a·hawk (tŏm′à-hôk), *n.* The light war ax used by the North American Indians. — *v. t.* To cut, strike, or kill, with a tomahawk.

to·ma′to (tò-mā′tō; -mä′tō), *n.; pl.* -TOES (-tōz). Any of various plants of the nightshade family or their pulpy edible fruit.

tomb (tōōm), *n.* A grave, chamber, vault, or monument, for the dead. — *v. t.* To place in a tomb.

tom′boy′ (tŏm′boi′), *n.* A romping girl; hoyden.

tomb′stone′ (tōōm′stōn′), *n.* A gravestone.

tom′cat′ (tŏm′kăt′), *n.* A male cat.

tom′cod′ (-kŏd′), *n.* Any of several small fishes resembling the common codfish, except in size.

tome (tōm), *n.* A volume forming part of a larger work; also, any book; esp., a ponderous volume.

tom′fool′er·y (tŏm′fōōl′ẽr-ĭ), *n.* Foolish or ridiculous trifling; nonsense.

to·mor′row (tōō-mŏr′ō), *adv.* On the morrow. — *n.* The day after the present.

tom′-tom′ (tŏm′tŏm′), *n.* A kind of drum used in Oriental countries.

ton (tŏN), *n.* [F.] Fashion; style.

ton (tŭn), *n.* A large weight, usually divided into twenty hundredweight. Esp.: **a** The weight of 2,240 pounds avoirdupois, often called long ton. **b** The weight of 2,000 pounds, often called short ton. **c** A metric ton (2,204.6 pounds). [nality.]

ton′al (tōn′ăl), *a.* Of or pertaining to tone or to-

to·nal′i·ty (tō-năl′ĭ-tĭ), *n.* Tonal quality; esp., *Music,* the principle of key in music.

tone (tōn), *n.* **1.** Sound, or a sound considered as of a certain character; as, a low *tone.* **2.** a A musical sound; — opposed to *noise.* **b** *Music.* A whole step, as distinguished from a *semitone.* **3.** Inflection or modulation of the voice. **4.** *Physiol.* Healthy state. **5.** Tenor; character; spirit; as, the *tone* of his remarks. **6.** In , painting, the general effect of light and shade together with color. **7.** Color quality proper; — called also *hue.* Also, a gradation of color, either a hue, or a tint or shade; as, a gray *tone.* — *v. t.* **1.** To give tone, or a particular tone, to. **2.** *Photog.* To bring, as a print, to a required color, usually by treatment with a chemical reagent. — *v. i.* **1.** To assume a tone. **2.** To harmonize in color.

tongs (tŏngz), *n. pl.* Any of numerous instruments, usually two-legged, for holding or gripping something; — called also *pair of tongs.*

Tongs. 1 Common Fire; 2 Horseshoer's; 3 Pipe.

tongue (tŭng), *n.* **1.** An organ of the mouth, serving as the chief organ of taste and in man also as an organ of speech. **2.** a Utterance; discourse; sometimes, fluency of expression. **b** Manner or quality of utterance. **c** A language. **3.** A part like, or suggestive of, an animal's tongue; as: **a** The flap of leather under the lacing of a shoe. **b** A bell clapper. **c** The movable pin in a buckle. **d** A reed in a musical instrument. **e** The pole of a vehicle. **f** A jet of flame.

tongue′less, *a.* **1.** Having no tongue. **2.** Mute.

tongue′-tie′, *n.* Impeded motion of the tongue due (esp.) to shortness of the connecting membrane beneath the tongue. — **tongue′-tied′** (-tīd′), *a.*

ton′ic (tŏn′ĭk), *a.* [4] **1.** Of or pertaining to tones or sounds. **2.** Pertaining to or increasing tension; hence, increasing strength. **3.** Increasing the strength or tone of the system — *n.* **1.** *Music.* Keynote. **2.** *Med.* A tonic medicine.

to·night′ (tōō-nīt′), *adv.* On this present or coming night. — *n.* The present or coming night.

ton′nage (tŭn′âj), *n.* **1.** *Naut.* **a** The weight of goods carried in a vessel. **b** Cubical content, burden, or capacity, in tons. **c** A charge per ton on cargo. **2.** Amount of shipping estimated in tons.

ton′neau′ (tŏ′nō′; tŭn-ō′), *n.; pl.* -NEAUX (*F.* tŏ′nō′; *E.* tŭn-ōz′). In an automobile, an after-body having sides closing in a seat or seats, and entered by a door now usually at the side; also, the whole body of an automobile of this style. Cf. LIMOUSINE.

ton′sil (tŏn′sĭl), *n.* One of a pair of masses of tissue at the back of the mouth.

ton′sil·li′tis (tŏn′sĭ-lī′tĭs), *n.* *Med.* Inflammation of the tonsils or of a tonsil.

ton·so′ri·al (tŏn-sō′rĭ-ăl), *a.* Of or pert. to a barber or his work; — generally affected or humorous.

ton′sure (tŏn′shŭr), *n.* Act of clipping the hair, or of shaving the crown, of the head, as of a person entering the priesthood; also, state of being shorn; shaven crown of an ecclesiastic.

too (tōō), *adv. & conj.* **1.** Over; more than enough; as, *too* long; — used also as a mere intensive; as, I am only *too* glad. **2.** Likewise; also.

took (tŏŏk). Pret. of TAKE.

tool (tōōl), *n*. **1.** An instrument of manual operation, as a hammer, saw, plane, file, etc.; an implement. **2.** *Mach*. The cutting or shaping part in a machine; also, a machine for shaping metal in any way. **3.** A person used as an instrument by another person ; — a word of reproach. — *v. t.* To shape, form, or finish with a tool.

toot (tōōt), *v. i.* **1.** To blow a horn or the like. **2.** To utter a similar sound, as do certain birds. **3.** To give forth a toot or toots, as a horn. — *v. t.* To cause (a horn, etc.) to sound. — *n.* A sound made by tooting. — **toot′er**, *n.* [S].

tooth (tōōth), *n.; pl.* TEETH (tēth). **1.** In most vertebrates, one of the hard bony appendages of the jaws. **2.** A projection like, or suggestive of, the tooth of an animal. **3.** Discriminating taste ; also, fondness for a (certain) kind of food ; as, a sweet *tooth*. — *v. t.* To furnish with teeth; indent.

tooth′ache′ (-āk′), *n.* Pain in a tooth or the teeth.

toothed (tōōtht), *a.* Provided with teeth.

tooth′less (tōōth′lĕs), *a.* Having no teeth.

tooth′pick′ (tōōth′pĭk′), *n.* An instrument to remove substances lodged between the teeth.

tooth′some (-sŭm), *a.* [4] Pleasing to the taste.

top (tŏp), *n.* A child's toy having a point on which it is made to spin.

top, *n.* **1.** A crowning tuft, as of hair on the head. **2.** The crown; head. **3.** Upper end, edge, or part; summit ; cover, as of a carriage ; lid. **4.** Highest degree ; acme. **5.** Highest rank; most honorable position. **6.** *Naut*. A platform surrounding the head of the lower mast, serving to spread the topmast rigging, and afford a standing place. — *a.* Of or pert. to the top; highest ; foremost. *Colloq*. — *v. t. ;* TOPPED (tŏpt) ; -PING. **1.** To cover on the top; be at the top of; cap; crown. **2.** To rise to, reach, or go over, the top of ; surmount. **3.** To excel ; surpass. **4.** To remove the top of ; prune.

to′paz (tō′păz), *n.* **1.** A mineral, often in transparent prismatic crystals, commonly yellow in color. **2.** The yellow sapphire (Oriental topaz).

top′-boot′, *n.* A high boot, often with a light-colored leather band around the upper part.

top′coat′ (tŏp′kōt′), *n.* An outer coat ; overcoat.

top′er (tōp′ẽr), *n.* Drunkard ; sot.

top′gal′lant (tŏp′găl′ănt ; *naut*. tŏ-găl′ănt), *a. Naut*. Next above the topmast ; designating, or pertaining to, the spars next above the topmasts. See SAIL, *Illust.* — *n.* A topgallant mast or sail.

top′-heav′y (tŏp′hĕv′ĭ), *a.* [4] Having the top part too heavy for the lower. — **-i-ness** (-nĕs), *n.*

top′ic (tŏp′ĭk), *n.* The subject of any distinct portion of a discourse, argument, or composition; also, the general or main subject ; a theme.

top′i-cal (-ĭ-kăl), *a.* [4] **1.** Of or pertaining to a place ; limited; local, or designed for local application. **2.** Of or pert. to a topic or topics ; dealing with topics, esp. current topics.— **-ly**, *adv.* [8].

top′knot′ (tŏp′nŏt′), *n.* A crest, knot, or tuft of feathers, hair, or wool on the top of the head.

top′mast (-mȧst), *n.* Second mast from the deck.

top′most (-mōst), *a.* Highest ; uppermost.

to-pog′ra-pher (tŏ-pŏg′rȧ-fẽr), *n.* One skilled in topography ; one who describes a particular place.

top′o-graph′ic (tŏp′ō-grăf′ĭk), *a.* Topographical.

top′o-graph′i-cal (-ĭ-kăl), *a.* Pert. to topography.

to-pog′ra-phy (tŏ-pŏg′rȧ-fĭ), *n.* **1.** Description, esp. exact and scientific description, of place or region. **2.** *Geog.* Configuration of a surface.

top′ple (tŏp′'l), *v. i.* [1] **1.** To fall forward; tumble. **2.** To jut out or overhang, as if about to fall ; beetle. — *v. t.* To overturn.

top′sail′ (tŏp′sāl′ ; *naut.* -s′l), *n.* In a square-rigged vessel, the sail next above the lowermost sail on a mast ; in a fore-and-aft-rigged vessel, the sail above, sometimes on, the gaff.

top′sy–tur′vy (tŏp′sĭ-tûr′vĭ), *adv.* Upside down ; in confusion. — *a.* [4] Being upside down ; confused. — *n.* A topsy-turvy state.

toque (tōk), *n.* **1.** A former kind of round cap. **2.** A woman's small round hat with no brim.

torch (tôrch), *n.* **1.** A stick of resinous wood, piece of tow soaked with tallow, etc., to be lighted, generally to carry in the hand. **2.** A kind of lamp attached to a pole for carrying.

torch′light′ (tôrch′līt′), *n.* Light of a torch.

tore (tōr), *pret. & dial. p. p.* of TEAR.

tor′ment (tôr′mĕnt), *n.* **1.** That which gives pain, misery, or the like. **2.** Anguish; torture.

tor-ment′ (tôr-mĕnt′), *v. t.* **1.** To torture. **2.** To pain; distress; afflict. **3.** To tease; harass. *Colloq*. — **tor-men′tor**, *n.* [8].

torn (tōrn), *p. p.* of TEAR.

tor-na′do (tôr-nā′dō), *n.; pl.* -DOES. **1.** A form of squall off the west coast of Africa. **2.** A funnel-shaped cloud, like a waterspout, sand column, or dust whirl, with violent eddies and whirls of wind, progressing in a narrow path for many miles.

tor-pe′do (tôr-pē′dō), *n.; pl.* -DOES (-dōz). **1.** An electric ray (fish). **2.** An engine or machine for blowing up ships, esp. a dirigible, self-propelling, cigar-shaped, submarine missile carrying an explosive charge. **3.** Any inclosed charge of an explosive; as: **a** *Railroading*. A kind of signal cartridge placed on a rail. **b** A kind of firework which explodes when thrown against a hard object. — *v. t.* To attack with, or destroy by, a torpedo.

torpedo boat. A vessel for discharging torpedoes; esp., such a small swift vessel carrying light guns.

tor′pid (tôr′pĭd), *a.* [4] **1.** In a state of torpor; dormant. **2.** Dull; sluggish. — **-ly**, *adv.* — **-ness**, *n.*

tor-pid′i-ty (tôr-pĭd′ĭ-tĭ), *n.* Torpid state.

tor′por (tôr′pŏr), *n.* **1.** Loss of motion or feeling ; dormancy ; numbness. **2.** Dullness; apathy.

tor′rent (tôr′ĕnt), *n.* **1.** A violent stream. **2.** A violent or rapid flow; flood, as of abuse.

tor-ren′tial (tŏ-rĕn′shȧl), *a.* [4] **1.** Pert. to or like a torrent. **2.** Suggestive of a torrent, as impassioned speech. — **-ly**, *adv.* [8].

tor′rid (tôr′ĭd), *a.* [4] **1.** Exposed to heat, esp. of the sun ; arid and hot. **2.** Burning ; parching.

tor′sion (tôr′shŭn), *n.* A turning or twisting; state of being twisted. — **tor′sion-al** (-ăl), *a.*

tor′so (tôr′sō), *n. ; pl.* E. -SOS (-sōz), It. -SI (-sē). The trunk of a human body; hence, the trunk of a statue, esp. of one mutilated of head and limbs.

tort (tôrt), *n.* Any wrongful act (not involving a breach of contract) for which a civil, as distinguished from a criminal, action can be brought.

tor′toise (tôr′tŭs; -tĭs), *n.* A turtle ; esp., a land or fresh-water turtle.

---

chair; go; sing, iŋk; then, thin; nature, verdure; yet; zh = z in azure. Numbers refer to §§ in the Special Notes which, with Abbreviations, Signs, etc., precede the Vocabulary.

tor'tu-os'i-ty (tôr'tū-ŏs'ĭ-tĭ), *n.; pl.* -TIES (-tĭz). **1.** Tortuous state. **2.** A bend; twist; winding.

tor'tu-ous (tôr'tū-ŭs), *a.* [4] **1.** Bent in different directions; twisted; winding. **2.** Not straightforward; devious. — **-ly,** *adv.* — **-ness,** *n.* [8].

tor'ture (tôr'tŭr), *n.* **1.** Act or process of inflicting severe pain. **2.** Extreme pain; torment. — *v. t.* [1] To put to torture; to punish with torture. — **tor'tur-er,** *n.* [8].

To'ry (tō'rĭ), *n.; pl.* -RIES (-rĭz). **1.** *Eng. Politics.* A member of the party of conservatism, now called the *Conservative* party, as opposed to the progressive party, formerly the *Whig,* now the *Liberal,* party. **2.** *Amer. Hist.* One who, in the time of the Revolution, favored yielding to Great Britain. — *a.* Of or pert. to Tories.

toss (tŏs), *v. t.;* TOSSED (tŏst); TOSS'ING. **1.** To throw with the palm of the hand upward, or to throw upward; pitch. **2.** To lift or throw up with a sudden motion; as, to *toss* the head. **3.** To heave up and down or to tumble about. **4.** To agitate; disturb. — *v. i.* **1.** To toss something; fling; pitch. **2.** To fling one's self about. **3.** To be tossed, as a ship by the waves. — *n.* Act of tossing; a pitch; fling.

tot (tŏt), *n.* Anything small; often, a little child.

to'tal (tō'tăl), *a.* **1.** Whole; undivided; entire. **2.** Complete; utter; absolute; as, a *total* failure. — *n.* The whole; whole sum or amount. — *v. t.* [7] To ascertain the sum or total of; add. — *v. i.* To be in its totality; amount to.

to-tal'i-ty (tō-tăl'ĭ-tĭ), *n.* **1.** Quality of being total or a total. **2.** The whole sum; the entirety.

to'tal-ly, *adv.* In a total manner; completely.

tote (tōt), *v. t.* [1] To carry or bear, esp. on the person. — **tot'er** (tōt'ẽr), *n.* [8] *Both Colloq., U. S.*

to'tem (tō'těm), *n.* Among savages, as the American Indians, a natural kind or class, esp. of animals conceived as having an intimate relationship to a group of human beings, usually a clan; also, a symbol or representation of this. — **-ism,** *n.*

tot'ter (tŏt'ẽr), *v. i.* **1.** To shake as if about to fall, as a building; waver. **2.** To walk with short, unsteady steps; stand unsteadily.

tou-can' (tōō-kăn'; tōō'kăn), *n.* Any of many fruit-eating birds of tropical America, having a very large, but light and thin, beak.

touch (tŭch), *v. t.* **1.** To perceive by the sense of feeling. **2.** To come in contact with; esp., to extend the hand or foot or a cane, stick, or the like, so as to reach or rest on. **3.** To be in contact with. **4.** To bring into contact (with something). **5.** To come to; reach; attain. **6.** To disturb; meddle with; also, to attack; harm or distress. **7.** To allude to or speak of, esp. lightly. **8.** To relate to; concern. **9.** To strike, or play on, as a musical instrument. **10.** To take, as food; partake of. **11.** To have effect upon; as, a file will not *touch* this steel. **12.** To infect or affect slightly by or as by contact. **13.** To move mentally or emotionally; as: **a** To melt; soften. **b** To irritate or sting, as with ridicule.

touch, *v. i.* **1.** To be in contact. **2.** To make an incidental stop at a point on shore, when on a voyage; — with *at.* **3.** To treat anything in discourse, esp. slightly or casually; — esp. with *on* or *upon.*

touch, *n.* **1.** Act or fact of touching; state of being touched; contact. **2.** Accord; harmony. **3.** The sense by which pressure, as on the skin, is perceived. **4.** A light stroke or tap. **5.** Sensation conveyed through contact; feel. **6.** A stroke, esp. a light one, as with pen or brush; effect so produced; as, a *touch* of color. **7. a** A light attack, as of fever. **b** A small quantity; dash. **8.** Feature; trait; quality. **9.** Distinctive manner, method, or skill. **10.** *Music.* Manner of touching the keys, as of a piano. — **touch'er,** *n.* [8]. [touched.]

touch'a-ble (tŭch'á-b'l), *a.* [4] Capable of being

touch'down' (-doun'), *n. Football.* The act of touching the ball down behind the opponents' goal.

touch'i-ness, *n.* Touchy quality or state.

touch'ing (-ĭng), *p. a.* [4] Affecting; moving; pathetic. — *prep.* Concerning. — **-ly,** *adv.* [8] — **-ness,** *n.* [8].

touch'stone' (-stōn'), *n.* **1.** A black siliceous stone used to test the purity of gold and silver by the streak left on the stone when rubbed by the metal. **2.** Any test or criterion of a thing's qualities.

touch'wood' (-wŏŏd'), *n.* Decayed wood, also dried fungi, used for tinder; spunk; punk.

touch'y (-ĭ), *a.* [3] Peevish; irritable; irascible.

tough (tŭf), *a.* [3] **1.** Flexible without brittleness. **2.** Able to endure strain or hardship; strong. **3.** Sticky; tenacious; as, *tough* clay. **4.** Stubborn. **5.** Very hard to influence; *Colloq.,* vicious. **6.** Hard to overcome or the like; as, a *tough* job. *Colloq.* — *n.* A vicious person; a rowdy. *Colloq. U. S.* — **-ly,** *adv.* [8] — **-ness,** *n.* [8].

tough'en (tŭf'n), *v. i. & t.* To grow or make tough.

tour (tōōr), *n.* **1.** A journey in a circuit, esp. a short one from place to place. **2.** A prolonged journey. — *v. i.* To make a tour. — *v. t.* To make a tour of or through.

tour'ing, *p. pr. & vb. n.* of TOUR. — **touring** car, an automobile designed for touring; esp., a roomy car of the tonneau type for five or more passengers.

tour'ist (tōōr'ĭst), *n.* One who makes a tour.

tour'ma-line (-má-lĭn), *n.* A mineral, commonly black; also blue, red, green, brown, and (rarely) colorless. When transparent it is used as a gem.

tour'na-ment (tōōr'ná-měnt; tûr'-), *n.* **1.** A contest or knightly sport (esp. of the 12th–14th centuries) in which mounted armored combatants contended, usually, with blunted lances or swords. **2.** Any trial of skill in which many contend in a series of contests.

tour'ney (tōōr'nĭ; tûr'nĭ), *n.* A tournament. — *v. i.* To perform in a tournament; tilt; just.

tour'ni-quet (tōōr'nĭ-kět), *n. Surg.* A device for arresting bleeding.

tou'sle (tou'z'l), *v. t.* [1] To put into disorder; tumble; dishevel. *Colloq. or Dial.*

tow (tō), *n.* The coarse and broken part of flax or hemp separated by the hatchel or swingle.

tow, *v. t.* To draw or pull along after, esp. through the water by a rope. — *n.* **1.** A towing; state of being towed. **2.** That which is towed, as a barge. — *n.* A towline.

tow'age (tō'ăj), *n.* Act of, or price paid for, towing.

to'ward (tō'ẽrd; tōrd), **to'wards** (tō'ẽrdz; tōrdz), *prep.* **1.** In the direction of, literally or figuratively. **2.** Approaching to; close upon.

āle, senāte, câre, ăm, *à*ccount, ärm, ȧsk, sofá; ēve, ėvent, ěnd, recēnt, makẽr; īce, ĭll; ōld, ȯbey, ôrb, ŏdd, sôft, cŏnnect; ūse, ūnite, ûrn, ŭp, circ*u*s, fōōd, fŏŏt; out, oil;

to'ward (tō'ẽrd ; tōrd), *a.* Ready; apt; docile.
to'wards (tō'ẽrdz ; tōrdz), *prep.* = TOWARD.
tow'boat' (tō'bōt'), *n.* A vessel for towing other vessels; a tug. [wet.]
tow'el (tou'ĕl), *n.* A cloth for drying anything
tow'el-ing, *n.* [7] Cloth for towels.
tow'er (tou'ẽr), *n.* **1.** A structure typically higher than its diameter, or relatively high by position, either isolated or appended to a larger structure. **2.** A citadel; fortress; defense. — *v. i.* To rise and overtop other objects ; to be lofty; soar.
tow'er-ing (-ẽr-ĭng), *p. a.* [4] **1.** Lofty; as, a *towering* height. **2.** Extreme; violent, as rage.
town (toun), *n.* **1.** Any large collection of houses and buildings ; esp., one not incorporated as a city; any large closely populated place;— often, usually with *the,* contrasted with the country. **2.** Townspeople ; the citizens or qualified voters of a town.
town hall. A public hall or building belonging to a town, used for public offices, etc.
town'house' (toun'house'), *n.* A town hall.
towns'folk' (tounz'fōk'), *n. pl.* Townspeople.
town'ship (toun'shĭp), *n.* **1.** In the United States, a primary unit of local government. **2.** In surveys of United States public lands, a division of territory six miles square, divided into 36 *sections* each one mile square. **3.** In Canada, one of the subdivisions of a county.
towns'man (tounz'măn), *n. ; pl.* -MEN (-mĕn). **1.** An inhabitant of a town. **2.** A fellow citizen. **3.** In New England, a selectman.
towns'peo'ple (-pē'p'l), *n. pl.* People of a town.
tow'path' (tō'pàth'), *n.* A path traveled in towing boats ; — called also *towing path.*
tox'ic (tŏk'sĭk), *a.* [4] Of or pertaining to poison.
tox-ic'i-ty (tŏk-sĭs'ĭ-tĭ), *n.* Poisonousness.
tox'i-co-log'i-cal (tŏk'sĭ-kō-lŏj'ĭ-kăl), *a.* Of or pertaining to toxicology.
tox'i-col'o-gy (-kŏl'ō-jĭ), *n.* Science treating of poisons, their antidotes, etc. — -o-gist (-jĭst), *n.*
tox'in (tŏk'sĭn), *n.* *Chem.* Any of a class of toxic substances formed as secretion products of vegetable and animal organisms.
toy (toi), *n.* **1.** A plaything, esp. for a child. **2. a** Something diminutive like a plaything. **b** A trifle. — *v. i.* To trifle; play ; dally lovingly.
trace (trās), *n.* One of two straps, chains, etc., of a harness, attaching a horse to a vehicle ; a tug.
trace, *v. t.* [1] **1. a** To mark out; draw ; sketch. **b** To form, as letters; write carefully. **c** To copy, as a drawing, by marking lines on a transparent sheet superimposed. **2.** To make marks, letters, tracery, etc., on. **3. a** To follow, as a track; track. **b** To follow the course or position of. **c** To follow the development or progress of; as, to *trace* a genealogy. — *v. i.* To go ; follow a track, trail, etc. — *n.* **1.** A mark left by a thing passing; footprint; track; trail; vestige. **2.** A very small amount. — **trac'er** (trās'ẽr), *n.* [8].
trace'a-ble (-á-b'l), *a.* Capable of being traced.
trac'er-y (trās'ẽr-ĭ), *n.; pl.* -ERIES (-ĭz). Ornamental work with branching or crossing lines.
tra'che-a (trā'kē-á ; trá-kē'á), *n. ; L. pl.* -CHEÆ (-ē). In vertebrates, the windpipe.
trac'ing (trās'ĭng), *n.* **1.** Act of one that traces. **2.** That which is traced, or marked out.

track (trăk), *n.* **1.** An impression left by the foot; a trace ; vestige. **2.** Mark left by something that has passed; as, a wheel *track.* **3. a** A road ; path. **b** A course laid out for racing, etc. **c** A metal way for wheeled vehicles, esp., for a railroad or railway. — *v. t.* **1.** To follow the tracks of; trace. **2.** To traverse. **3.** To make tracks upon or with. — -less, *a.*
track'age (-ăj), *n. Railroads.* **a** Lines of track, collectively. **b** Right to use tracks of another road.
tract (trăkt), *n.* A treatise or written discourse, generally short, esp. on practical religion.
tract, *n.* **1.** Duration; lapse (of time); extent. **2.** An expanse; an area. **3.** *Anat.* A system of parts or organs serving some special purpose.
trac'ta-bil'i-ty (trăk'tá-bĭl'ĭ-tĭ), *n.* Quality of being tractable.
trac'ta-ble (trăk'tá-b'l), *a.* [4] Capable of being easily handled; as : **a** Readily wrought, as gold. **b** Easily led or managed. — **-ness**, *n.* — **-ta-bly**, *adv.*
trac'tile (-tĭl), *a.* [4] Capable of being drawn out.
trac'tion (-shŭn), *n.* Act of drawing a body along a surface; as, steam *traction.*
trac'tive (-tĭv), *a.* [4] Serving to draw; pulling.
trac'tor (-tŏr), *n.* One that draws or pulls something ; specif., an automobile used esp. for drawing or hauling something, as a vehicle, plow, etc.
trade (trād), *n.* **1.** A course ; course of action. *Obs.,* exc. in *trade wind* (See in Vocab.). **2.** Any occupation or employment pursued as a calling; business ; occupation ; esp., mechanical employment. **3.** Act or business of exchanging commodities by barter or sale; commerce. **4.** Those engaged in the same line of business, esp. in *the trade.* **5.** A bargain. **6.** *pl.* The trade winds.
trade, *v. i. & t.* [1] **1.** To buy and sell; traffic as a business. **2.** To participate in a sale or exchange.
trade'-mark', *n.* A distinguishing mark used by a manufacturer or merchant on his goods.
trad'er (trād'ẽr), *n.* **1.** One engaged in trade; a merchant. **2.** A vessel engaged in trading.
trades'man (trādz'măn), *n. ; pl.* -MEN (-mĕn). One who trades ; a shopkeeper.
trade'-un'ion (trād'ūn'yŭn, *or* **trades'-un'ion** (trādz'-), *n. ; pl.* TRADE- *or* TRADES-UNIONS. A voluntary association of working people organized to further or maintain their rights and interests.
trade wind. A wind blowing steadily in one course, or *trade,* easterly toward the equator.
tra-di'tion (trá-dĭsh'ŭn), *n.* Oral delivery or transmission of information, opinions, practices, customs, etc., esp. from ancestors to posterity; also, that which is so transmitted.
tra-di'tion-al (-ăl), *a.* [4] Of or pertaining to or derived from tradition. — **-ly**, *adv.* [8].
tra-di'tion-a-ry (-á-rĭ), *a.* [4] Traditional.
tra-duce' (trá-dūs'), *v. t.* [1] To expose wrongfully to contempt or shame; calumniate ; vilify; defame ; slander. — **tra-duc'er** (-dūs'ẽr), *n.* [8].
traf'fic (trăf'ĭk), *n.* **1.** Interchange of commodities by barter or by sale; commerce; trade. **2.** The business done on a railway, steamboat line, etc., as measured by the number of passengers or the amount of freight carried. — *v. i.;* -FICKED (-ĭkt); -FICK-ING. To barter ; trade ; deal, often meanly or mercenarily. — **traf'fick-er**, *n.* [8].

---

tra-ge′di-an (tra̍-jē′dĭ-ăn), *n.* **1.** A writer of tragedy. **2.** An actor or player of tragedy.

‖ **tra′gé′dienne′** (tra̍/zha̍/dyĕn′; *E.* tra̍-jē′dĭ-ĕn′), *n.* [F.] An actress who plays tragedy.

trag′e-dy (trăj′ĕ-dĭ), *n.; pl.* -DIES (-dĭz). **1.** A dramatic or other literary composition depicting a serious story, in which, typically, the leading character is brought to a catastrophe. **2.** A fatal and mournful event; any tragic event.

trag′ic (trăj′ĭk), *a.* [4] Of or pert. to, or of the nature of, tragedy. [-ness, *n.*

trag′i-cal (-ĭ-kăl), *a.* [4] Tragic. — -ly, *adv.* —

trag′i-com′e-dy (-ĭ-kŏm′ĕ-dĭ), *n.* A drama or composition partaking of both tragedy and comedy and not having a fatal issue. — **trag′i-com′ic** (-ĭk), *a.*

trail (trāl), *v. t.* **1.** To draw or drag, as on the ground. **2.** To hunt by the track, or trail. — *v. i.* **1.** To hang down or to be drawn along, as the train of a dress. **2.** To follow after. **3.** To grow to a considerable length, esp. when slender and creeping, as a plant. **4.** To follow a trail. **5.** To move along leisurely. — *n.* **1.** Something drawn or dragged behind. **2.** **a** A track or scent left by man or beast. **b** A footpath or track worn through a wilderness. — **trail′er** (-ẽr), *n.* [8].

train (trān), *v. t.* **1.** To trail; drag. **2.** To bring to a desired state or condition by instruction, practice, or guidance. **3.** To prepare for a test or contest, as by dieting and practice. **4.** To lead or direct the growth of (a plant). **5.** To aim or point at an object; bring to bear. — *v. i.* **1.** To drill or teach. **2.** To prepare one's self for a performance, test, or contest, as by exercise, diet, etc.; drill. **train,** *n.* **1.** That which is drawn along in the rear of, or after, something, as a part of a gown that trails behind. **2.** A body of attendants; retinue; suite. **3.** A procession; company. **4.** A succession of connected things; as, a *train* of thoughts. **5.** A connected line of cars, etc., on a railroad. **6.** Process; course; order. **7.** A line of gunpowder laid to lead fire to a charge.

train′er (trān′ẽr), *n.* One who trains; esp., one who trains men, horses, etc., for exercises requiring agility and strength.

train oil. Oil from the whale or other sea animal.

trait (trāt; *Brit. commonly* trā), *n.* **1.** A stroke; a touch; — used fig.; as, a *trait* of humor. **2.** A distinguishing feature; peculiarity; characteristic.

trai′tor (trā′tẽr), *n.* One who betrays a confidence or trust; esp., one who betrays his country.

trai′tor-ous (-ŭs), *a.* [4] **1.** Guilty or capable of treason; treacherous; faithless. **2.** Of the nature of treason. — -ly, *adv.* [8] —-ness, *n.* [8].

trai′tress (-trĕs), *n.* A female traitor.

tra-jec′to-ry (tra̍-jĕk′tō-rĭ), *n.; pl.* -RIES (-rĭz). The curve which a body describes in moving through space, as a ball when thrown.

tram (trăm), *n.* **1.** **a** A boxlike wagon running on a tramway in a mine. **b** A passenger car of a street railway. *Eng.* **2.** Short for TRAMCAR, TRAMWAY, as on a street railway (*Brit.*), or in a mine.

tram′car′ (-kär′), *n.* A tram running on rails, as on a street railway (*Brit.*), or in a mine.

tram′mel (-ĕl), *n.* **1.** A kind of net to catch birds, fishes, etc. **2.** Something impeding activity, progress, or freedom, as a net or shackle; restraint; check. — *v. t.* [7] To confine; hamper; shackle.

tramp (trămp), *v. t.* **1.** To tread on forcibly and repeatedly; trample. **2.** To travel through on foot. *Colloq.* — *v. i.* **1.** To walk, step, or tread, esp. heavily. **2.** To travel about on foot. — *n.* **1.** A foot journey or excursion. **2.** One who walks from place to place, idly or seeking employment; vagrant. **3.** The sound of the foot or feet striking the earth. **4.** *Naut.* A vessel taking a cargo when and where it offers and to any port. — **tramp′er,** *n.*

tram′ple (trăm′p'l), *v. t.* [1] To tread under foot; tread down. — *v. i.* To tread rapidly and forcibly, or as in contempt. — *n.* Act or sound of trampling. — **tram′pler** (-plẽr), *n.* [8].

tram′way′ (-wā′), *n.* A way or track for trams.

trance (tràns), *n.* **1.** A state in which the soul seems to have passed out of the body or to be rapt into visions; ecstasy. **2.** *Med.* A prolonged profound or abnormal sleep, from which the patient cannot easily be aroused. [disturbed.

tran′quil (trăn′kwĭl), *a.* [4] Quiet; calm; unc

tran′quil-ize (-īz), *v. t. & i.* [1, 7] To render or become tranquil; make calm and peaceful.

tran-quil′li-ty (trăn-kwĭl′ĭ-tĭ; trăn-), *n.* Quality or state of being tranquil; calmness; composure.

tran′quil-ly, *adv.* In a tranquil manner.

trans-act′ (trăns-ăkt′; trăn-zăkt′), *v. t.* To carry through; do; perform; manage.

trans-ac′tion (trăns-ăk′shŭn), *n.* **1.** The doing or performing of any affair; management. **2.** That which is done; affair. **3.** *pl.* Records, as of the proceedings of a society; proceedings.

trans′at-lan′tic (trăns′ăt-lăn′tĭk), *a.* Lying or belonging beyond, or crossing, the Atlantic Ocean.

tran-scend′ (trăn-sĕnd′), *v. t.* **1.** To rise above or beyond; overpass. **2.** To excel; exceed.

tran-scend′ence (-sĕn′dĕns) ‖ *n.* Quality or state of

tran-scend′en-cy (-dĕn-sĭ) ‖ being transcendent.

tran-scend′ent (-sĕn′dĕnt), *a.* [4] Superior or supreme; surpassing. — -ly, *adv.* [8].

tran′scen-den′tal (trăn′sĕn-dĕn′tăl), *a.* [4] **1.** Transcendent. **2.** In philosophy, going beyond human experience; intuitive or spiritual. **3.** Fancifully speculative. — -ly, *adv.* [8].

tran′scen-den′tal-ism (-ĭz'm), *n.* *Philos.* The going beyond human experience to ascertain the fundamental principles of knowledge. — **tran′scen-den′tal-ist,** *n.*

tran-scribe′ (trăn-skrīb′), *v. t.* [1] **1.** To write a copy of; copy. **2.** *Music.* To make a transcription of. — **tran-scrib′er** (-skrīb′ẽr), *n.* [8].

tran′script (trăn′skrĭpt), *n.* **1.** That which has been transcribed. **2.** A copy of any kind; imitation.

tran-scrip′tion (trăn-skrĭp′shŭn), *n.* **1.** Act or process of transcribing. **2.** A copy; transcript. **3.** *Music.* An arrangement of a composition for an instrument or voice other than that for which it was originally written; adaptation.

tran′sept (trăn′sĕpt), *n.* The part of a cross-shaped church crossing at right angles to the greatest length, between the nave and the apse or choir.

trans-fer′ (trăns-fûr′), *v. t.; pl.* -FERRED′ (-fûrd′); -FER′RING. **1.** To convey from one place or person to another. **2.** To make over the possession or control of, as a title to land. — **-fer′rer,** *n.* [8].

trans′fer (trăns′fûr), *n.* **1.** A transferring; state of being transferred. **2.** That which is transferred.

trans-fer'a-ble (trăns-fûr'ȧ-b'l), *a.* **1.** Capable of being transferred. **2.** Negotiable, as stocks.

trans'fer-ence (trăns'fẽr-ĕns; trăns-fûr'ĕns), *n.* Act of transferring; conveyance; transfer.

trans-fig'u-ra'tion (trăns-fĭg'ū-rā'shŭn), *n.* A change of form or appearance; esp. [*cap.*], the supernatural change in the personal appearance of Christ on the mount (*Matt.* xvii. 1–9).

trans-fig'ure (-fĭg'ūr), *v. t.* [1] **1.** To change form or appearance; transform. **2.** To change to something exalted and glorious.

trans-fix' (-fĭks'), *v. t.* To pierce through; impale.

trans-form' (-fôrm'), *v. t.* **1.** To change in form; change in outward shape or semblance. **2.** To change into another substance; transmute. **3.** To change in nature, disposition, heart, etc.; convert. — *v. i.* To be or become transformed. — **-er,** *n.*

trans'for-ma'tion (trăns'fŏr-mā'shŭn), *n.* A transforming, or state of being transformed.

trans-fuse' (-fūz'), *v. t.* [1] **1.** To pour, as liquid, out of one vessel into another. **2.** To transfer, as blood, from the veins or arteries of one person or animal to those of another.

trans-fu'sion (-fū'zhŭn), *n.* **1.** Act or operation of transfusing. **2.** A gradual commingling.

trans-gress' (trăns-grĕs'), *v. t.* **1.** To overstep (a limit or rule). **2.** To break or violate, as a law. — *v. i.* To offend against a law; sin. — **transgres'sor** (-grĕs'ẽr), *n.* [8].

trans-gres'sion (-grĕsh'ŭn), *n.* Act of transgressing; esp., violation of a law of rectitude; sin.

tran'sience (trăn'shĕns), **tran'sien-cy** (-shĕn-sĭ), *n.* Quality or state of being transient.

tran'sient (trăn'shĕnt), *a.* [4] **1.** Transitive; passing over (to). **2.** Fleeting; brief. **3.** Staying for a short time; not regular. *Colloq.* — *n.* One that is transient; esp., *Colloq., U. S.*, a transient guest or boarder. — **-ly,** *adv.* [8].

trans'it (trăn'sĭt), *n.* **1.** Passage through or over; transition. **2.** Act or process of causing to pass; conveyance. **3.** *Astron.* a Passage of a heavenly body over the meridian of a place, or through the field of a telescope. **b** Passage of a body across the disk of a larger one. **4.** An instrument mounted on three legs, used by surveyors to measure angles; a kind of theodolite.

tran-si'tion (trăn-sĭzh'ŭn), *n.* Passage from one place, state, or act to another; change.

tran-si'tion-al (-ăl), *a.* [4] Of or pert. to transition; as, in a *transitional* stage. — **-ly,** *adv.* [8].

tran'si-tive (trăn'sĭ-tĭv), *a.* **1.** Having power to make a transit, or passage. **2.** *Gram.* Expressing an action as ending in or passing over to a direct object; as, a *transitive* verb: for example, he *holds* the book. — **tran'si-tive-ly,** *adv.* [8].

tran'si-to-ry (-tō-rĭ), *a.* [4] Continuing only for a short time. — **-to-ri-ly** (-rĭ-lĭ), *adv.* [8] — **-ri-ness,** *n.* [8]. [being translated.]

trans-lat'a-ble (trăns-lāt'ȧ-b'l), *a.* Capable of

trans-late' (-lāt'), *v. t.* [1] **1.** To remove from one place, condition, etc., to another; transfer. **2.** To render into another language. — **trans-la'tor** (-lā'tẽr), *n.* [8]. [lating.]

trans-la'tion (-lā'shŭn), *n.* Act or result of trans-

trans-lit'er-ate (-lĭt'ẽr-āt), *v. t.* [1] To express in the characters of another alphabet.

trans-lit'er-a'tion (-ā'shŭn), *n.* A transliterating.

trans-lu'cence (-lū'sĕns), **trans-lu'cen-cy** (-sĕn-sĭ), *n.* Partial transparency.

trans-lu'cent (-sĕnt), *a.* [4] Transmitting light without allowing objects to be distinctly seen.

trans'mi-grate (trăns'mĭ-grāt), *v. i.* [1] **1.** To migrate from one country or jurisdiction to another. **2.** To undergo transmigration.

trans'mi-gra'tion (trăns'mĭ-grā'shŭn), *n.* **1.** Migration from one country to another. **2.** The passing of the soul at death into another body.

trans-mis'si-ble (trăns-mĭs'ĭ-b'l), *a.* Capable of being transmitted.

trans-mis'sion (-mĭsh'ŭn), *n.* **1.** Act of transmitting; state of being transmitted. **2.** The gear for transmitting the power from the engine of an automobile to the live axle.

trans-mis'sive (-mĭs'ĭv), *a.* [4] Capable of transmitting, or of being transmitted; also, transmitted.

trans-mit' (-mĭt'), *v. t. ; -mit'ted, -ting.* **1.** To cause to pass over or through; transfer; pass on. **2.** To suffer to pass through; conduct.

trans-mit'tal (-ăl), *n.* Transmission.

trans-mit'ter (trăns-mĭt'ẽr), *n.* One that transmits; esp., that portion of a telegraphic or telephonic instrument by which a message is sent.

trans-mit'ti-ble (-ĭ-b'l), *a.* Transmissible.

trans-mut'a-ble (-mūt'ȧ-b'l), *a.* Capable of being transmuted. [muting.]

trans'mu-ta'tion (trăns'mū-tā'shŭn), *n.* A trans-

trans-mute' (-mūt'), *v. t.* [1] To change from one nature, form, or substance, into another. — **trans-mut'er** (-mūt'ẽr), *n.* [8].

tran'som (trăn'sŭm), *n.* **1.** A transverse beam or piece, as a horizontal crossbar in a window, over a door, etc. **2.** A window above a door or another window, built on, and commonly hinged to, a transom. *Chiefly U. S.*

trans-par'en-cy (trăns-pâr'ĕn-sĭ), *n.; pl.* **-cies** (-sĭz). **1.** Quality or state of being transparent. **2.** That which is transparent; esp., a picture or the like shown by light shining through it.

trans-par'ent (-ĕnt), *a.* [4] **1.** Transmitting light so that bodies can be distinctly seen through; diaphanous; pellucid. **2.** Open in texture so as to admit the passage of light, as a veil. **3.** Perspicuous; clear, as a statement. — **-ly,** *adv.* [8].

tran'spi-ra'tion (trăn'spĭ-rā'shŭn), *n.* Act or process of transpiring, as in exhalation.

tran-spire' (-spīr'), *v. i.* [1] **1.** To pass off as vapor; exhale. **2.** To emerge from secrecy; become known. — *v. t.* To excrete, as vapor; exhale; perspire.

trans-plant' (trăns-plănt'), *v. t.* To remove and plant or settle in another place. — **-er,** *n.* [8].

trans'plan-ta'tion (trăns'plăn-tā'shŭn), *n.* A transplanting; state of being transplanted.

trans-port' (-pōrt'), *v. t.* **1.** To carry from one place to another; transfer. **2.** To banish. **3.** To carry away or overcome with emotion; ravish.

trans'port (trăns'pōrt), *n.* **1.** Transportation; conveyance. **2.** A vessel used in transportation, esp. of soldiers. **3.** Vehement emotion; rapture.

trans'por-ta'tion (-pŏr-tā'shŭn), *n.* Act of transporting; state of being transported; conveyance.

trans-port'er (-pōr'tẽr), *n.* One that transports.

trans-pos'al (-pōz'ăl), *n.* Transposition.

trans-pose' (trăns-pōz'), *v. t.* [1] **1.** To change the relative place or order of. **2.** To change the natural order of, as words. **3.** *Music.* To change the key of.

trans'po-si'tion (trăns'pŏ-zĭsh'ŭn), *n.* Act of transposing; state of being transposed.

tran'sub-stan'ti-a'tion (trăn'sŭb-stăn'shĭ-ā'shŭn), *n.* In theology, the change of the bread and wine of the Eucharist into the body and blood of Christ, as held by Roman Catholics.

trans-ver'sal (trăns-vûr'săl), *a.* Transverse.— *n. Geom.* A line that intersects any system of lines.

trans-verse' (-vûrs'), *a.* Lying or being across.

trans-verse' (trăns-vûrs'; trăns'vûrs), *n.* Anything transverse or athwart. — **-ly**, *adv.* [8].

trap (trăp), *v. t. ;* TRAPPED (trăpt) ; TRAP'PING. To ornament; adorn.— *n. pl.* Goods; luggage. *Colloq.*

trap, *n.* Any of various dark-colored rocks.

trap, *n.* **1.** A device or contrivance that shuts suddenly, as with a spring, for taking game, etc. **2.** Fig. : A stratagem ; snare. **3.** A bend or chamber in a drain pipe, which prevents the passage of sewer gas. **4.** A wagon; esp., a light two-wheeled carriage. *Colloq.* — *v. t.* **1.** To catch in a trap; take by stratagem. **2.** To provide with a trap or traps. — *v. i.* To set traps for game.

trap'door' (trăp'dōr'), *n.* A lifting or sliding door covering an opening in a roof or floor.

tra-peze' (tra-pēz'), *n.* A short horizontal bar suspended by two parallel ropes, one at each end.

tra-pe'zi-um (-pē'zĭ-ŭm), *n. ; pl.* E. -ZIUMS (-ŭmz), L. -ZIA (-â). *Geom.* A plane figure formed by 4 straight lines of which no two are parallel.

trap'e-zoid (trăp'ē-zoid), *n. Geom.* A plane four-sided figure with two parallel sides.

trap'per (trăp'ẽr), *n.* One who traps ; esp., one who traps animals for their furs.

trap'pings (-ĭngz), *n. pl.* Ornamental housings for a horse ; hence, ornaments; dress.

trash (trăsh), *n.* **1.** Worthless stuff ; rubbish. **2.** A worthless person ; also, rabble ; riffraff.

trash'y (trăsh'ĭ), *a.* [3] Like trash ; worthless.

trav'ail (trăv'ăl), *v. i.* **1.** To toil. *Archaic.* **2.** To suffer the pangs of childbearing.— *n.* **1.** Labor; toil. *Now Rare.* **2.** The labor of childbearing. **3.** Agony ; racking pain; as, a soul in *travail.*

trav'el (trăv'ĕl), *v. i.* [7] **1.** To pass; go; move. **2.** To go to a distant place ; journey.— *v. t.* To journey over or through ; traverse. — *n.* **1.** Act of traveling ; passage; movement. **2.** *Mach.* Motion, esp. reciprocating motion ; also, length of stroke, as of a piston. **3.** A journey ; journeying.

trav'el-er (-ĕl-ẽr), *n.* [7] One that travels.

trav'erse (-ẽrs), *a.* Lying across ; transverse. — *adv.* Across; crosswise. — *v. t.* [1] **1.** To lay crosswise ; cause to cross. **2.** To cross in opposition ; thwart. **3.** To cross in traveling. **4.** To survey carefully. **5.** To deny formally. — *v. i.* To move across or over ; to cross to and fro. — *n.* **1.** Something that traverses, or crosses. **2.** Something that crosses, thwarts, or obstructs. **3.** Act of traversing, or crossing ; also, a passage across.

trav'es-ty (-ĕs-tĭ), *n. ; pl.* -TIES (-tĭz). A burlesque translation or imitation ; also, any grotesque likeness.— *v. t.* [2] To represent so as to make ridiculous ; burlesque.

trawl (trôl), *v. i. & t.* To fish or catch with a trawl ; also, to troll.— *n.* **1.** A long fishing line, anchored at the ends, having many short lines bearing hooks. **2.** A large bag net dragged at the bottom in sea fishing. — **trawl'er** (-ẽr), *n.* [8].

tray (trā), *n.* A shallow receptacle ; esp., a flat plate, as of tin or silver, with a low rim.

treach'er-ous (trĕch'ẽr-ŭs), *a.* [4] **1.** Using or involving treachery ; traitorous. **2.** Deceiving; untrustworthy.— **-ly**, *adv.* [8] — **-ness**, *n.* [8].

treach'er-y (-ĭ), *n. ; pl.* -ERIES (-ĭz). Violation of allegiance or of faith and confidence; perfidy.

trea'cle (trē'k'l), *n.* Molasses.

tread (trĕd), *v. i. ; pret.* TROD (trŏd) ; *p. p.* TROD'-DEN (trŏd'n), TROD ; *p. pr. & vb. n.* TREAD'ING. **1.** To set the foot ; step. **2.** To press or be set down on or as on the ground. **3.** To walk; go on foot.— *v. t.* **1.** To step or walk on. **2.** To beat or press with the feet. **3.** To execute by dancing, walking, or the like. **4.** To trample ; subdue.— *n.* **1.** A step or stepping ; footstep. **2.** Manner of stepping; gait. **3.** a The upper horizontal part of a step. **b** The part of a wheel that bears on the road or rail, or the corresponding part of a rail. **4.** In a bird's egg, the small mass of protoplasm, on the yolk, from which the embryo develops.

trea'dle (trĕd'l), *n.* A swiveling or lever device pressed by the foot to operate a machine.— *v. i.* [1] To operate a treadle.

tread'mill' (-mĭl'), *n.* A mill worked by treading.

trea'son (trē'z'n), *n.* **1.** Betrayal of any trust or confidence ; treachery. **2.** The offense of attempting to overthrow the government of the state to which one owes allegiance, or (in monarchies) to kill or to injure the sovereign or any of his family.

trea'son-a-ble (-á-b'l), *a.* [4] Of or pert. to or involving treason.— **-ness**, *n.* — **-a-bly**, *adv.* [8].

treas'ure (trĕzh'ûr), *n.* **1.** Money, jewels, etc., hoarded up. **2.** A hoard. **3.** A thing of great worth. — *v. t.* [1] To lay up ; hoard ; cherish.

treas'ur-er (-ûr-ẽr), *n.* One in charge of a treasure or treasury, or of collected funds.

treas'ure-trove' (-trōv'), *n. Law.* Money, bullion, etc., found hidden, the owner being unknown.

treas'ur-y (trĕzh'ûr-ĭ), *n. ; pl.* -IES (-ĭz). **1.** A place in which stores of wealth are deposited; esp., a place where revenues, esp. public revenues, are deposited, kept, and disbursed. **2.** Department of a government which has charge of the finances.

treasury note. *U. S. Finance.* A currency note or bill issued from the Treasury Department.

treat (trēt), *v. t.* **1.** To deal with or handle. **2.** To subject to some action, as of a chemical reagent. **3.** To care for medicinally or surgically. **4.** To pay the expenses of as a compliment or expression of regard, etc.— *v. i.* **1.** To handle a subject or topic. **2.** To negotiate. **3.** To pay a person's expenses as an expression of regard, etc.— *n.* **1.** Entertainment given by one who treats. **2.** That which affords gratification.— **treat'er**, *n.* [8].

trea'tise (trē'tĭs), *n.* A written composition on a particular subject. [treating.]

treat'ment (trēt'mĕnt), *n.* Act or manner of

trea'ty (trē'tĭ), *n. ; pl.* -TIES (-tĭz). An agreement made by negotiation ; esp., a nagreement, league, or contract between two or more states or sovereigns.

āle, senāte, câre, ăm, *ă*ccount, ärm, ȧsk, sof*ȧ*; ēve, ĕvent, ĕnd, recĕnt, makẽr; īce, ĭll; ōld, ȯbey, ôrb, ŏdd, sŏft, cŏnnect; ūse, ŭnite, ûrn, ŭp, circ*ŭ*s; fŏŏd, fŏŏt; out, oil;

tre'ble (trĕb'l), *a.* **1.** Threefold; triple. **2.** *Music.* **a** Acute; sharp. **b** Performing, or pertaining to, the highest part.— *n.* *Music.* **1.** Highest of the four voice parts or music for it; soprano. **2.** A singer or instrument rendering this.— *v. t. & i.* [1] To increase threefold. — **tre'bly** (trĕb'lĭ), *adv.* [8].

tree (trē), *n.* **1.** A woody perennial plant having a single main stem (trunk), commonly exceeding 10 feet in height. **2.** Piece of timber, or a thing commonly made of timber; — chiefly in composition. **3.** Something suggestive of a tree. — *v. t.;* TREED (trēd); TREE'ING. To drive up a tree.

tree fern. A fern having a woody trunk.

tree frog, *or* **tree toad.** Any of various small froglike or toadlike animals that live in trees.

tree'less, *a.* Destitute of trees.

tree'nail' (trē'nāl'; *Colloq.,* trĕn'l, trŭn'l), *n.* A wooden pin, made of dry timber so as to swell in its hole when moistened.

tre'foil (trē'foil), *n.* **1.** The clover. **2.** *Arch.* A leaflike ornament of three parts, or foils.

Trefoils, 2.

trek (trĕk), *v.i.;* TREKKED (trĕkt); TREK'KING. **1.** To draw a load, as do oxen. **2.** To travel, esp. by ox wagon and to a new home; migrate. — *n.* Act of trekking. *All Chiefly South Africa.*

trel'lis (trĕl'ĭs), *n.* A structure or frame of latticework. — *v. t.* To provide with a trellis.

trel'lis-work', *n.* Latticework.

trem'ble (trĕm'b'l), *v. i.* [1] **1.** To shake involuntarily, as with fear, cold, etc. **2.** To quaver or shake, as sound; be tremulous. — *n.* An involuntary shaking or quivering.— **-bler** (-blĕr), *n.* [8].

tre-men'dous (trē-mĕn'dŭs), *a.* [4] **1.** Fitted to excite trembling fear; dreadful. **2.** Arousing wonderment or awe; marvelously great.— **-ly,** *adv.*

trem'o-lo (trĕm'ō-lō), *n.* Rapid fluttering reiteration of a tone or chord without apparent breaks.

tre'mor (trē'mŏr; trĕm'ŏr), *n.* A trembling; a shivering; a quivering or vibratory motion.

trem'u-lous (trĕm'ū-lŭs), *a.* [4] Trembling; quivering. — **-ly,** *adv.* [8] — **-ness,** *n.* [8].

trench (trĕnch), *v. t.* **1.** To cut furrows or ditches in. **2.** *Mil.* To intrench.— *v. i.* To intrench; encroach.— *n.* A long, narrow cut in the earth; ditch.

trench'an-cy (trĕn'chăn-sĭ), *n.* Trenchant quality.

trench'ant (-chănt), *a.* [4] **1.** Fitted to cut; cutting; sharp. **2.** Keen; biting; as, *trenchant* wit.

trench'er (-chĕr), *n.* A wooden plate or platter on which to carve or serve food. *Obs. or Hist.*

trend (trĕnd), *v. i.* To have or take a particular direction; tend. — *n.* Inclination; tendency.

trep'i-da'tion (trĕp'ĭ-dā'shŭn), *n.* **1.** A vibration; trembling. **2.** Trembling agitation; fright.

tres'pass (trĕs'pás), *v. i.* **1.** *Law.* To commit a trespass. **2.** To intrude; encroach. **3.** To injure or annoy another; transgress voluntarily any divine law or any duty; offend; sin.— *n.* **1.** Any offense done to another. **2.** Any voluntary transgression of the moral law or of duty; sin. **3.** An unlawful act of violence (however slight) against another's person or property. — **tres'pass-er,** *n.*

tress (trĕs), *n.* A braid, lock, or curl of hair.

tres'tle (trĕs'l), *n.* **1.** A kind of stool or horse, usually a horizontal piece with three or four braced legs. **2.** A braced frame for supporting a table top, etc. **3.** A braced framework of timbers, piles, or steelwork, for supporting a road, etc.

tres'tle-tree' (-trē'), *n.* *Naut.* A strong bar, usually one of two, to support the crosstrees, etc.

tres'tle-work' (-wûrk'), *n.* The system of connected trestles supporting a viaduct, pier, etc.

tret (trĕt), *n.* *Commerce.* An allowance to purchasers for waste or refuse, after tare is deducted.

tri'ad (trī'ăd), *n.* A union or group of three, esp. of three closely related persons or things.

tri'al (trī'ăl), *n.* **1.** Act of trying or testing; test. **2.** State of being tried, or tested. **3.** A misfortune or affliction. **4.** *Law.* The formal judicial examination of the matter in issue in a cause to determine the issue.

tri'an'gle (trī'ăng'g'l), *n.* **1.** *Geom.* A figure bounded by three lines and containing, therefore, three angles. **2.** *Music.* An instrument, usually made of a rod of steel bent to form a triangle, open at one angle, and sounded by being struck.

tri-an'gu-lar (trī-ăng'gū-lår), *a.* Of, relating to, or consisting of, a triangle or three parts.

tri-an'gu-late (-lāt), *v. t.* [1] **1.** To divide into triangles, esp. for surveying purposes. **2.** To make triangular, or three-cornered.— **tri-an'gu-la'tion** (-lā'shŭn), *n.*

trib'al (trīb'ăl), *a.* Of, pertaining to, or characteristic of, a tribe or tribes; as, *tribal* customs.

tribe (trīb), *n.* **1.** A social group comprising a series of families, clans, or generations, descended from the same ancestor, together with slaves, dependents, etc. **2.** A division or class composed of individuals having some common characteristic.

trib'u-la'tion (trīb'ū-lā'shŭn), *n.* A state of distress or affliction, or its cause; a trouble.

tri-bu'nal (trī-bū'năl), *n.* **1.** The seat of a judge **2.** A court of justice. [stand.

trib'une (trīb'ūn), *n.* A raised platform, seat, or]

trib'une, *n.* *Roman Hist.* Any of various magistrates, esp. of certain ones (tribunes of the people) chosen to protect the plebeian citizen from the arbitrary action of patrician magistrates.

trib'u-ta-ry (trīb'ū-tá-rĭ), *a.* [4] **1.** Paying tribute to another; subject; subordinate. **2.** Paid or owed as tribute. **3.** Contributory; of streams, affluent. — *n.;* *pl.* -RIES (-rĭz). **1.** A ruler or state that pays tribute to a conqueror. **2.** A stream flowing into a larger stream or into a lake.

trib'ute (-ūt), *n.* **1.** A stated payment from one ruler or state to another, as an acknowledgment of submission, for peace and protection, or by virtue of a treaty. **2.** A personal contribution or tax; impost; duty. **3.** Any personal contribution, as of praise, service, etc.

trice (trīs), *v. t.* [1] To haul up or in and secure with a small rope. *Chiefly Naut.* — *n.* A very short time; instant; — now only in *in a trice.*

tri'ceps (trī'sĕps), *n.* The three-headed extensor muscle at the back of the upper arm.

tri-chi'na (trĭ-kī'ná), *n.; L. pl.* -NÆ (-nē). A small slender worm which is parasitic in the muscles of man, the hog, and many other animals.

trich'i-no'sis (trĭk'ĭ-nō'sĭs), *n.* Disease caused by trichinæ in the intestines and the muscles.

---

trick (trĭk), *n.* **1.** An artifice; crafty or deceitful contrivance or procedure. **2. a** A dexterous or ingenious feat fitted to puzzle or amuse; also, a knack; dexterity. **b** An illusion or deception, likened to that caused by sleight of hand; as, a *trick* of the eyesight. **3.** A prank. **4.** A mannerism. **5.** *Card Playing.* The cards played in one round, collectively. — *v. t.* **1.** To deceive by cunning; cheat. **2.** To dress; adorn, esp. fancifully.

trick'er-y (-ĕr-ĭ), *n.; pl.* -ERIES (-ĭz). Act or practice of tricking; artifice; fraud.

trick'i-ly (trĭk'ĭ-lĭ), *adv.* In a tricky manner.

trick'i-ness, *n.* Quality or state of being tricky.

trick'ish, *a.* [4] Given to, or marked by, tricks or trickery; knavish. — **-ly,** *adv.* [8] — **-ness,** *n.* [8].

trick'le (trĭk'l), *v. i.* [1] To flow in a small stream; run in drops; also, to drip, as a spout. — *n.* Act or state of trickling; also, that which trickles.

trick'ster (-stẽr), *n.* One who tricks; a cheat.

trick'y (trĭk'ĭ), *a.* [3] Trickish; shifty; deceptive.

tri'col'or (trī'kŭl'ẽr), *n.* [5] The French national banner, blue, white, and red, in vertical stripes.

tri-cus'pid (trī-kŭs'pĭd), *a.* Having three cusps; as, the **tricuspid valve,** which prevents reflux of blood from right ventricle to right auricle.

tri'cy-cle (trī'sĭ-k'l), *n.* A light three-wheeled vehicle to be propelled by treadles or hand levers; also, a three-wheeled motor cycle.

tri'dent (-dĕnt), *n.* *Class. Myth.* A three-pronged spear, the attribute of Neptune, god of the sea.

tri-den'tate (-dĕn'tāt)) *a.* Having three teeth or
tri-den'tat-ed (-tăt-ĕd)) points.

tried (trīd), *pret. & p. p.* of TRY. Hence: *a.* [4] Proved; tested; faithful; trustworthy.

tri-en'ni-al (trī-ĕn'ĭ-ăl), *a.* **1.** Continuing three years. **2.** Occurring every three years. — *n.* **1.** Something that occurs once in three years, or that lasts three years. **2.** The third anniversary of an event. — **tri-en'ni-al-ly,** *adv.* [8].

tri'er (trī'ẽr), *n.* One that tries.

tri'fid (trī'fĭd), *a.* Three-cleft; divided part way to the base into three lobes with narrow sinuses.

tri'fle (-f'l), *n.* A thing of little value or importance; a paltry affair, object, etc. — a trifle, a little; slightly. — *v. i.* [1] **1.** To act or talk jestingly, or with levity. **2.** To amuse one's self lightly; toy; as, to *trifle* with a watch chain. — *v. t.* To spend in trifling or on trifles. — **tri'fler** (-flẽr), *n.* [8].

tri'fling (-flĭng), *a.* [4] **1.** Shallow; frivolous. **2.** Trivial. — **-ly,** *adv.* [8]. [2. Trifoliolate.]

tri-fo'li-ate (trī-fō'lĭ-āt), *a.* **1.** Three-leaved.

tri-fo'li-o-late (-ō-lāt), *a.* Having three leaflets.

trig (trĭg), *a.; ;* TRIG'GER (-ẽr); TRIG'GEST. Trim; neat; spruce; smart.

trig'ger (trĭg'ẽr), *n.* A piece for releasing a catch; esp., *Firearms,* the part of a lock moved by the finger to release the cock.

trig'o-no-met'ric (trĭg'ō-nō-mĕt'rĭk), **-met'ri-cal** (-rĭ-kăl), *a.* Of or pertaining to trigonometry.

trig'o-nom'e-try (trĭg'ō-nŏm'ĕ-trĭ), *n. ; pl.* -TRIES (-trĭz). Mathematics treating of the relations between the sides and angles of triangles.

tri'graph (trī'grȧf), *n.* A combination of three letters representing one sound, as *-eau* in *beau.*

tri-lat'er-al (trī-lăt'ẽr-ăl), *a.* *Geom.* Having three sides. — **tri-lat'er-al-ly,** *adv.* [8].

tri-lit'er-al (-lĭt'ẽr-ăl), *a.* Consisting of three letters. — *n.* A triliteral word.

trill (trĭl), *v. t.* To impart the quality of a trill to. — *v. i.* To utter trills or a trill; quaver. — *n.* **1.** A quavering consonantal sound, as *r* in many languages. **2.** *Music.* = SHAKE, *n.,* **2.** **3.** A sound likened to a musical trill.

tril'lion (trĭl'yŭn), *n.* The number denoted by a unit with 12 zeros annexed (in French and American notation) or with 18 zeros (in English notation). — **tril'lionth** (-yŭnth), *n. & a.*

tril'li-um (-ĭ-ŭm), *n.* Any of various plants (genus *Trillium*) having short rootstocks and an erect stem bearing a whorl, or verticil, of three leaves and a large solitary flower.

tri-lo'bate (trī-lō'bāt), *a.* Having three lobes.

tril'o-gy (trĭl'ō-jĭ), *n.; pl.* -GIES (-jĭz). A series of three dramas or, by extension, three literary or musical compositions, each essentially complete in itself, but all so interrelated as to form one theme.

trim (trĭm), *v. t. ;* TRIMMED (trĭmd); TRIM'MING. **1.** To make neat or trim; dispose; adjust. **2.** To make trim, neat, ready, or right by cutting, clipping, or the like. **3.** To decorate; adorn; embellish. **4.** *Naut.* **a** To adjust to a proper balance, as a boat. **b** To arrange for sailing; as, to *trim* the sails. — *v. i.* **1.** *Naut.* Of a vessel, to assume, or, of a person, to cause a vessel to assume, a certain position, or *trim,* in the water. **2.** To balance; esp., to maintain a middle position between parties or the like so as to appear to favor each or to be neutral.

trim, *n.* **1.** Order- condition. **2.** *Naut.* **a** State of a ship or her cargo, ballast, masts, etc., in reference to her readiness and fitness for sailing. **b** Position of a vessel in the water, esp. in reference to the horizontal plane. **3.** Condition as to equipment, furnishings, dress, etc.; dress; gear.

trim, *a. ;* TRIM'MER (-ẽr); TRIM'MEST. Neat and compact or well ordered. — **trim'ly,** *adv.* [8] — **trim'mer** (-ẽr), *n.* [8] — **trim'ness,** *n.* [8].

trim'ming (-ĭng), *n.* **1.** Act of one who trims. **2.** That which serves to trim, etc. **3.** *pl.* Parts or pieces removed by trimming.

tri'nal (trī'năl), **trine** (trīn), *a.* Threefold; triple.

trin'i-ty (trĭn'ĭ-tĭ), *n. ; pl.* -TIES (-tĭz). **1.** [*cap.*] In theology, union of three persons (the Father, Son, and Holy Ghost) in one Godhead. **2.** A triad.

trin'ket (trĭn'kĕt), *n.* **1.** A small ornament, as a jewel. **2.** A thing of little value; trifle; toy.

tri-no'mi-al (trī-nō'mĭ-ăl), *n.* *Math.* An expression consisting of three terms, connected by the sign plus (+) or minus (—) or both.

tri'o (trē'ō; trī'ō), *n. ; pl.* TRIOS (-ōz). **1.** Three collectively ; a set of three. **2.** *Music.* A composition for three solo parts or three instruments.

trip (trĭp), *v. i. ;* TRIPPED (trĭpt) ; TRIP'PING. **1.** To move with light, quick steps; skip. **2.** To make a false step; stumble. **3.** To offend in manners, morals, or the like; slip; err. — *v. t.* **1.** To perform lightly or nimbly, as a dance. **2.** To cause to stumble. **3.** To detect in a misstep, error, or the like. **4.** *Mach.* To release, let fall, or set free, as a weight or spring. — *n.* **1.** A quick, light step. **2.** A journey; an excursion or jaunt. **3.** A false step ; a misstep ; stumble ; an error ; mis-

take. 4. A stroke or catch by which one, esp. a wrestler, causes his antagonist to lose footing. **5.** *Mach.* Act of tripping; also, a pawl or other device for tripping a catch or detent.

tri-par'tite (trĭ-pär'tĭt; trĭp'ȧr-), *a.* **1.** Divided into three parts. **2.** Having three corresponding parts or copies. **3.** Made between three parties. — **tri'par-ti'tion** (trī'pär-tĭsh'ŭn; trĭp'ȧr-), *n.*

tripe (trīp), *n.* A part of the stomach of a ruminant, esp. of the ox kind, used as food.

tri-pet'al-ous (trī-pĕt'ȧl-ŭs), *a.* Having three petals.

trip hammer. *Mach.* A massive tilt hammer raised by cams, used esp. for working iron.

Trip Hammer. *a* Lever, or Helve, pivoted at *b*; *c* Hammer Head; *d* Anvil; *f* Shaft carrying Collar *e* with Cams for lifting the Hammer Head; *g* Prop to hold up the Hammer when not in use.

triph'thong (trĭf'thŏng), *n.* A combination of three distinct vowel sounds uttered with one effort of articulation, as -*oya*- in *loyal;* improperly, a trigraph.

tri'ple (trĭp'l), *a.* **1.** Consisting of three, usually united; threefold. **2.** Three times repeated; treble. — *v. t. & i.* [1] To make or increase threefold.

trip'let (-lĕt), *n.* **1.** Three of a kind or three united. **2.** *Poetry.* Three verses, or lines, riming together. **3.** *Music.* Three notes sung or played in the time of two or four. **4.** One of three children or offspring born at one birth. *Colloq.*

tri'plex (trī'plĕks; trĭp'lĕks), *a.* Having three parts; triple. — *n. Music.* Triple time or measure.

trip'li-cate (trĭp'lĭ-kåt), *a.* Threefold. — *n.* A third thing corresponding to two others of the same kind. (-kåt), *v. t.* [1] To triple.

trip'li-ca'tion (trĭp'lĭ-kā'shŭn), *n.* Act of tripling.

tri'pod (trī'pŏd), *n.* **1.** A utensil on three feet or legs. **2.** A three-legged stand, as for a camera.

trip'ping (trĭp'ĭng), *p. a.* Nimble; stepping agilely. — **trip'ping-ly,** *adv.* [8].

tri-sect' (trī-sĕkt'), *v. t.* To cut or divide into three parts, esp., *Geom.,* three equal parts.

tri-sec'tion (-sĕk'shŭn), *n.* Division into three parts, esp., *Geom.,* three equal parts.

tri-syl'la-ble (trī-sĭl'ȧ-b'l; trī-), *n.* A word of three syllables. — **tris'yl-lab'ic** (trĭs'ĭ-lăb'ĭk), *a.*

trite (trīt), *a.* [3] Worn or hackneyed; stale; commonplace. — **trite'ly,** *adv.* [8] — **ness,***n.* [8].

trit'u-rate (trĭt'ụ-råt), *v. t.* [1] To rub or grind; masticate. **2.** To pulverize. — *n.* A triturated substance.   [of being triturated.]

trit'u-ra'tion (-rā'shŭn),*n.* A triturating, or state

tri'umph (trī'ŭmf), *n.* **1.** Joy or exultation for success. **2.** Victory; conquest. — *v. i.* **1.** To celebrate victory or success; exult. **2.** To obtain victory; prevail.   [umph, in a triumph.]

tri-um'phal (trī-ŭm'fȧl), *a.* Of, pertaining to, or tri-um'phant (-ŭm'fȧnt), *a.* [4] **1.** Rejoicing for or celebrating victory; exultant; as, a *triumphant* shout. **2.** Victorious. — **ly,** *adv.* [8].

tri-um'vir (trī-ŭm'vẽr), *n.; pl.* L. **-viri** (-vĭ-rī), E. **-virs** (-vẽrz). *Roman Antiq.* One of three men united in public office or authority.

tri-um'vi-rate (-vĭ-råt), *n.* **1.** Office or term of a triumvir. **2.** Government, or term of government, by three in coalition. **3.** A coalition of three in office or authority. **4.** A group of three.

tri'une (trī'ūn), *a.* Being three in one; — used of unity of the Trinity in the Godhead.

triv'et (trĭv'ĕt), *n.* A three-legged stand; tripod.

triv'i-al (-ĭ-ăl), *a.* [4] Trifling; petty; paltry. — **-ly,** *adv.* [8] — **ness,** *n.* [8].

triv'i-al'i-ty (-ăl'ĭ-tĭ), *n.; pl.* **-ties** (-tĭz). **1.** Quality or state of being trivial. **2.** A trifle.

tri'week'ly (trī'wēk'lĭ), *a.* Occurring or appearing every three weeks or three times a week — *adv.* Thrice a week.

tro'che (trō'kē), *n.* Medicinal tablet or lozenge.

trod (trŏd), **trod'den** (trŏd'n). See TREAD.

troll (trōl), *n. German Folklore.* A supernatural being, conceived sometimes as a dwarf, sometimes as a giant, fabled to inhabit caves, hills, etc.

troll, *v. t.* **1. a** To sing the parts of in succession. **b** To sing loudly or freely. **2.** To troll for or in; as, to *troll* a lake. — *v. i.* **1.** To take part in trolling a song. **2.** To fish, esp. by drawing the hook along or through the water. — *n.* A song sung in parts successively. — **troll'er,** *n.* [8].

trol'ley (trŏl'ĭ), *n.; pl.* **-leys** (-ĭz). **1.** A truck running on an overhead rail or track and supporting a suspended load. **2.** *Elec. Railroads.* **a** The grooved wheel pressed upwards in rolling contact with the overhead wire to take off the current; any similar device. **b** An electric car; a trolley car.

trom'bone (trŏm'bōn), *n. Music.* A powerful brass instrument of the trumpet kind.

Trombone.

troop (trōōp), *n.* **1.** A collection of people or formerly, also, of things; a company; number. **2.** Soldiers collectively; an armed force; — usually in *pl.* **3.** *Mil.* A division of a cavalry squadron commanded by a captain. — *v. i.* **1.** To move or gather in crowds or troops. **2.** To go forward, off, or away. — *v. t.* To unite with, or form into, a troop or troops.

troop'er (-ẽr), *n.* A cavalryman or his horse.

troop'ship (trōōp'shĭp'), *n.* A military transport.

trope (trōp), *n. Rhetoric.* The use of an expression in a figurative sense; a figure of speech.

tro'phy (trō'fĭ), *n.; pl.* **-phies** (-fĭz). **1.** Anything taken and preserved as a memorial of victory, as arms, flags, etc. **2.** Something regarded as evidence of conquest. **3.** A memorial; memento.

trop'ic (trŏp'ĭk), *n.* **1.** *Astron.* Either of the two small circles of the celestial sphere, one on each side of, and parallel to, the equator, at a distance of 23½°, reached by the sun at its greatest declination north and south. The northern circle is called the *tropic of Cancer,* and the southern the *tropic of Capricorn.* **2. a** Either of the two parallels of terrestrial latitude corresponding to the celestial tropics. **b** *pl.* The region between or near these parallels, marked by its torrid climate, luxuriant vegetation, etc. — *a.* [4] Tropical.

trop'i-cal (trŏp'ĭ-kăl), *a.* [4] **1.** Of, pertaining

chair; go; sing, iŋk; then, thin; nature, verdure; yet; zh = z in azure. Numbers refer to §§ in the Special Notes which, with Abbreviations, Signs, etc., precede the Vocabulary.

to, or characteristic of, the tropics. **2.** Figurative; metaphorical. — **trop′i-cal-ly,** *adv.* [8].

trot (trŏt), *v. i. & t.; * TROT′TED; -TING. **1.** To ride, drive, or move, at a trot. **2.** To run; jog; hurry. — *n.* **1.** A gait of the horse and other quadrupeds in which the legs move in pairs, diagonally, but not quite simultaneously. **2.** A jogging pace.

troth (trŏth; trōth), *n.* **1.** Faith; fidelity; as, plighted *troth.* **2.** Truth; verity. **3.** Betrothal. *Archaic.* — *v. t.* To pledge; betroth.

trot′ter (trŏt′ẽr), *n.* **1.** One that trots, esp. a race horse. **2.** The foot of an animal, esp. as food.

trou′ba-dour (troo′bȧ-door), *n.* One of a class of lyric poets who flourished from the 11th century to the end of the 13th, in the south of France.

trou′ble (trŭb′′l), *v. t.* [1] **1.** To disturb; agitate. **2.** To worry; perplex; inconvenience. — *v. i.* To take trouble or pains. — *n.* **1.** State of being troubled; uneasiness; annoyance. **2.** That which causes annoyance, etc. **3.** Exertion; labor; pains. **4.** A condition of ill health or physical distress. — **trou′bler** (trŭb′lẽr), *n.* [8].

trou′ble-some (-′l-sŭm), *a.* [4] Giving trouble; disturbing; vexatious. — **-ly,** *adv.* — **-ness,** *n.*

trou′blous (trŭb′lŭs), *a.* [4] **1.** Full of trouble; troubled. **2.** Causing trouble; turbulent.

trough (trŏf), *n.* **1.** Any of various receptacles; esp., a long shallow vessel, as for water or fodder. **2.** Any long channel, as between waves.

trounce (trouns), *v. t.* [1] To beat; whip; flog.

troupe (troop), *n.* A company, esp. of actors.

trou′sers (trou′zẽrz), *n. pl.* An outer garment of men or boys, extending from waist to knee or ankle, and covering each leg separately.

trous′seau′ (troo′sō′), *n.* A bride's personal outfit, as of clothes, jewelry, etc.

trout (trout), *n.* (See PLURAL.) Any of certain fresh-water game fishes of the salmon family, having finely flavored flesh.

trow (trō), *v. i. & t.* To think; suppose. *Archaic.*

trow′el (trou′ĕl), *n.* Any of various hand implements for spreading, shaping, and smoothing loose or plastic material, as mortar; also, an implement for taking up and setting out small plants, etc.

troy (troi), *a.* Pert. to or designating the system of weights (**troy weight**) for gold, silver, etc.
1 pound (*lb.*) = 12 ounces (0.82286 lb. av. or 373.2419 g.); 1 ounce (*oz.*) = 20 pennyweights (1.09714 oz. av. or 31.1035 g.); 1 pennyweight (*dwt.*) = 24 grains (0.87771 dr. av. or 1.5552 g.).
The troy pound = 5,760 grains. See MEASURES, WEIGHTS, ETC., in *Appendix.* — *n.* Troy weight.

tru′an-cy (troo′ăn-sǐ), *n.* Act or habit of playing truant; state of being truant.

tru′ant (-ănt), *n.* One who stays away from business or duty, esp. from school without leave. — *a.* [4] Idle, and shirking duty.

truce (troos), *n.* **1.** *Mil.* A suspension of arms by agreement; armistice. **2.** Respite; brief quiet.

truck (trŭk), *n.* **1.** A small wheel. **2.** Any of numerous wheeled vehicles for transporting heavy articles. **3.** A swiveling frame with one or more pairs of wheels, to carry and guide one end of a locomotive, of a car, etc. — *v. t.* To transport on a truck or trucks.

truck, *v. t. & i.* To exchange; to barter; to traffic. — *n.* **1.** Small commodities; esp., *U. S.*, vegeta-

bles raised for market; as, garden *truck.* **2.** Small articles of little value; hence, rubbish. *Colloq.*

truck′age (trŭk′ȧj), *n.* Money paid for conveyance on a truck; freight; conveyance by trucks.

truck′le (-′l), *v. i.* [1] To yield slavishly to another; show servility. — **truck′ler** (-lẽr), *n.*

truck′le-bed′ (trŭk′′l-bĕd′), *n.* A trundle-bed.

truck′man, *n.* One who drives a truck, or who conveys goods on a truck.

truc′u-lence (trŭk′ū̇-lẽns; troo′kū̇-), **-len-cy** (-lĕn-sǐ), *n.* Quality or state of being truculent.

truc′u-lent (trŭk′ū̇-lĕnt; troo′kū̇-), *a.* [4] Fierce; savage; ferocious. — **-ly,** *adv.* [8].

trudge (trŭj), *v. i.* [1] To walk, esp. wearily.

true (troo), *a.* [3] **1.** Faithful to friends, promises, etc.; loyal. **2.** Actual; genuine. **3.** Conformable to fact; correct. **4.** Truthful. **5.** Conformable to a standard, rule, or pattern; exact; correct. **6.** Legitimate; rightful. **7.** To be relied on; certain. — **t. skin,** the derma, or cutis. — *adv.* In accordance with truth; truly. — *n.* State of being true or accurate; — used in *in true, out of true,* etc.

true′ness, *n.* Quality of being true.

truf′fle (trŭf′′l; troo′f′l; troo′f′l), *n.* Any of various subterranean fungi, esteemed as a delicacy.

tru′ism (troo′ĭz′m), *n.* A self-evident truth.

tru′ly (troo′lǐ), *adv.* **1.** In a true manner; as, to state facts *truly.* **2.** In fact; in reality; in truth.

trump (trŭmp), *n.* A trumpet, or trumpet sound.

trump, *n. Card Playing.* One of a suit any card of which takes any card of the other suits; also the suit itself; — usually in *pl.* — *v. i.* To play a trump card when one of another suit has been led. — *v. t.* To take or play upon by trumping.

trump, *v. t.* To impose unfairly. *Rare.* — **to trump up,** to devise or concoct, as a charge, unfairly.

trump′er-y (trŭm′pẽr-ǐ), *n.; pl.* -ERIES (-ǐz). A thing deceptively showy; hence, rubbish; trash. — *a.* [4] Deceptively showy; worthless.

trump′et (trŭm′pĕt), *n.* **1.** *Music.* A wind instrument consisting of a long metallic tube, commonly once or twice curved, ending in a bell. **2.** A sound as of a trumpet; esp., an elephant's cry. **3.** A trumpet-shaped instrument to direct or intensify sounds; as, an ear *trumpet.* — *v. t.* To publish by or as by sound of trumpet; noise abroad; proclaim. — *v. i.* To sound like a trumpet; utter a trumpetlike cry, as elephants.

trump′et-er (-ẽr), *n.* One that trumpets.

trun′cate (trŭn′kāt), *v. t.* [1] To cut off; lop.

trun′cat-ed (-kāt-ĕd), *a.* Cut off or cut short, truncate. — **truncated** cone *or* **pyramid,** *Geom.,* part left of a cone or pyramid whose vertex is cut off by a plane.

Truncated Pyramid.

trun-ca′tion (trŭn-kā′shŭn), *n.* A truncating, or state of being truncated.

trun′cheon (trŭn′shŭn), *n.* **1.** A short staff; spear shaft; club. *Archaic.* **2.** A baton, or staff of command.

trun′dle (-d′l), *n.* **1.** A little wheel; caster. **2.** A kind of truck. **3.** A trundle-bed. — *v. t. & i.* [1] **1.** To roll on little wheels. **2.** To revolve; as, to *trundle* a hoop.

trun′dle-bed′, *n.* A low bed, usually on trundles, that can be pushed under a higher bed.

trunk (trŭŋk), *n.* **1.** The main stem, or body, of

a tree. **2.** The body of an animal or a man, apart from head and limbs. **3.** The main body of anything having branches, etc. **4.** A proboscis, esp. of an elephant. **5.** *pl.* Close-fitting short breeches, worn by athletes, swimmers, etc. **6.** A box or chest to contain clothes or other goods, as those of a traveler. — *a.* Designating, or pertaining to, a main railroad or other main line.

trun'nion (trŭn'yŭn), *n.* Either of two opposite projecting pivots, journals, or gudgeons, to support a cannon, a large crucible, etc.

truss (trŭs), *v. t.* **1.** To pack into a bundle; to bundle. **2.** To bind, tie, or fasten; tighten and fasten; skewer. **3.** To support by a truss; strengthen, as a girder, by a brace or braces.— *n.* **1.** A bundle; pack; package. **2.** *Surg.* A bandage or apparatus used in cases of hernia, etc. **3.** *Arch. & Engin.* An assemblage of members, as beams, bars, rods, etc., forming a rigid framework.

trust (trŭst), *n.* **1.** Assured reliance on another's integrity, veracity, justice, etc.; confidence; faith. **2.** Assured anticipation; hope. **3.** Person or thing on which confidence is reposed. **4.** Custody; care; charge. **5.** Credit given. **6.** That which is committed or intrusted to one, as a duty, task, or office. **7.** A property interest held for another's benefit. **8.** A business organization or combination consisting of a number of firms or corporations, esp. one formed mainly to regulate the supply and price of commodities, etc. — *v. t.* **1.** To place confidence in; rely on. **2.** To give credence to; believe. **3.** To hope or expect confidently. **4.** To invest with a trust; intrust. **5.** To commit, or consign, as to one's care; confer as a trust. **6.** To venture confidently; risk. **7.** To give credit to; sell to (one) in confidence of future payment. — *v. i.* **1.** To have trust; confide; rely. **2.** To be confident; hope. — *a.* Held in trust. — **trust'er**, *n.* [§].

trus-tee' (trŭs-tē'), *n.* A person holding property in trust. — **trus-tee'ship** (-shĭp), *n.*

trust'ful (trŭst'fŏol), *a.* [§] Full of trust; confiding. — **trust'ful-ly**, *adv.* [§] — **-ful-ness**, *n.* [§].

trust'wor'thy (-wûr'thĭ), *a.* [§] Worthy of trust. — **trust'wor'thi-ness** (-thĭ-nĕs), *n.* [§].

trust'y (trŭs'tĭ), *a.* [§] Justly deserving confidence; trustworthy; reliable; as, a *trusty* servant. — **trust'i-ly**, *adv.* [§] — **trust'i-ness**, *n.* [§].

truth (trŏoth), *n.*; *pl.* TRUTHS (trŏothz; trŏoths). Quality or state of being true; hence: **1.** Fidelity; constancy. **2.** Sincerity. **3.** Conformity to fact or reality. **4.** That which is true.

truth'ful (-fŏol), *a.* [§] Full of, or habitually speaking, truth; veracious. — **-ly**, *adv.* — **-ness**, *n.*

try (trī), *v. t.* [§] **1.** To purify or refine, as metals; to melt out, as oil, lard, etc.; render. **2.** To test, prove, or make trial of. **3.** To settle; determine, as by contest. **4.** *Law.* To investigate judicially; conduct the trial of. **5. a** To use or test experimentally. **b** To experiment or practice on. **c** To subject to trials; afflict. **6.** To essay; attempt. **7.** To strain. — *v. i.* **1.** To endeavor. **2.** To prove; make trial. — *n.*; *pl.* TRIES (trīz). Act of trying; attempt; experiment; trial.

try'ing, *a.* [§] Adapted to try; severe; grievous.

try'sail' (trī'sāl'; *Naut.*, trī's'l), *n.* *Naut.* A fore-

and-aft sail, bent to a gaff, hoisted on a lower mast or a small mast close abaft a lower mast.

try'-square', *n.* An instrument for laying off right angles and testing work for squareness.

tryst (trĭst; trīst), *n.* An appointment to meet; a meeting; also, an appointed place of meeting.

tsar (tsär), **tsa-ri'na** (tsä-rē'na). See CZAR, etc.

tset'se (tsĕt'sĕ), *n.* An African fly which transmits a parasite that causes a disease of cattle, etc.

tub (tŭb), *n.* **1.** An open wooden vessel formed with staves, bottom, and hoops. **2.** Amount which a tub will hold. **3.** A vessel to contain water for tubbing; act or process of tubbing. *Colloq.* — *v. t.;* TUBBED (tŭbd); TUB'BING. **1.** To plant or set in a tub. **2.** To wash or bathe in a tub.

tu'ba (tū'bá), *n.* A large form of saxhorn.

tube (tūb), *n.* **1.** A hollow cylinder; pipe. **2.** A tunnel for an underground railway; *Colloq.*, the railway itself. *Chiefly Eng.* — *v. t.* [1] To furnish with, or inclose in, a tube.

tu'ber (tū'bẽr), *n.* *Bot.* A short fleshy underground stem or shoot bearing modified buds, or "eyes," as the potato.

tu'ber-cle (-k'l), *n.* **1.** A small knoblike prominence, esp. on an animal or plant. **2.** *Med.* A small rounded morbid growth; esp., the specific lesion of tuberculosis.

tu-ber'cu-lar (tū-bûr'kũ-lãr), *a.* [4] Of, pertaining to, or like, a tubercle or tubercles; having tubercles; *Med.*, marked by tubercles; tuberculous.

tu-ber'cu-lo'sis (-lō'sĭs), *n.* *Med.* An infectious disease due to a bacillus and marked by the production of tubercles; esp., this disease when seated in the lungs; pulmonary phthisis; consumption.

tu-ber'cu-lous (-bûr'kũ-lŭs), *a.* [4] Tubercular; hence, *Med.*, affected with tuberculosis.

tu'ber-ose (tū'bẽr-ōs), *a.* Tuberous.

tube'rose' (tūb'rōz'; tū'bẽr-ōs'), *n.* A bulbous plant bearing a spike of fragrant white flowers.

tu'ber-ous (tū'bẽr-ŭs), *a.* [4] **1.** Covered with knobby or wartlike prominences. **2.** *Bot.* Consisting of, bearing, or like, a tuber or tubers.

tub'ing (tūb'ĭng), *n.* **1.** Act of making tubes. **2.** A series of tubes; tubes collectively; a length or piece of a tube; material for tubes.

tu'bu-lar (tū'bũ-lãr), *a.* Having the form of a tube, or pipe; containing, or provided with, tubes.

tuck (tŭk), *v. t.* **1.** To draw, turn, or gather up; make snug or close by or as by folding or gathering. **2.** To put or press into or as into a snug, close place. **3.** To cover closely or neatly, as with bedclothes. **4.** To make a tuck or tucks in. — *n.* A sewed fold made for decoration or shortening.

tuck'er (tŭk'ẽr), *n.* **1.** One that tucks; esp., an instrument for making tucks. **2.** A strip, as of linen or lace, folded across the breast, or attached to the gown at the neck.

Tues'day (tūz'dā), *n.* The third day of the week.

tu'fa (tōō'fà), *n.* **1.** A porous rock formed as a deposit from springs or streams. **2.** A rock composed of the finer kinds of volcanic detritus.

tuft (tŭft), *n.* **1.** A small cluster of elongated flexible parts or outgrowths, as hairs, arising close together. **2.** A cluster; clump; as, a *tuft* of plants. — *v. t.* To separate into, or adorn with, tufts.

tuft'y (tŭf'tĭ), *a.* [3] Abounding with tufts.

---

tug (tŭg), *v. t. & i.;* TUGGED (tŭgd); TUG'GING (tŭg'ĭng). To pull or draw with great effort. — *n.* **1.** A laborious pulling or straining; hence, a supreme effort. **2.** *Naut.* A small, powerful steam vessel for towing. **3.** A trace of a harness; a rope, chain, etc., used in pulling something along. — *tug of war.* **a** A sport in which several men pull on a rope against an equal number. **b** Hence, any violent contest.

tu-i'tion (tū-ĭsh'ŭn), *n.* Instruction; fee for instruction.

tu'lip (tū'lĭp), *n.* Any of various plants of the lily family, having a large showy flower; also, a flower or bulb of the plant.

tulip tree. A tall tree, of the magnolia family, having large, tuliplike red and yellow flowers. Its timber is *whitewood*.   [fabric.|

tulle (tōōl; *F.* tül), *n.* A thin, fine silk netlike

tum'ble (tŭm'b'l), *v. i.* [1] **1.** To roll over, or to and fro; roll or toss about. **2.** To fall suddenly and violently. **3.** To move, go, come, pass, etc., in a hasty, disorderly manner. **4.** To perform acrobatic feats, such as somersaults, springs, etc. — *v. t.* **1.** To turn over; turn or throw about. **2.** To disturb; rumple; disorder. **3.** To throw down or roll over. — *n.* Act of tumbling.

tum'bler (-blĕr), *n.* **1.** One that tumbles; esp., an acrobat. **2.** Any of various receptacles in which objects are tumbled, as for polishing, etc. **3.** A movable obstruction in a lock, which must be adjusted to a particular position, as by a key, before the bolt can be thrown. **4.** A drinking glass without a foot or stem.

tum'brel (-brĕl), **tum'bril** (-brĭl), *n.* A cart.

tu'me-fac'tion (tū'mē-fāk'shŭn), *n.* A swelling or enlargement; puffiness; a tumor.

tu'me-fy (tū'mē-fī), *v. t. & i.* [2] To swell.

tu'mid (tū'mĭd), *a.* [4] **1.** Swollen, enlarged, or distended. **2.** Protuberant. **3.** Swelling in sound or sense; pompous; inflated; bombastic; as, a *tumid* style. — *ly, adv.* [8] — *ness, n.* [8].

tu-mid'i-ty (tū-mĭd'ĭ-tĭ), *n.* Tumid quality or state.

tu'mor (tū'mĕr), *n.* [5] A morbid swelling or growth, not inflammatory, in any part of the body.

tu'mult (-mŭlt), *n.* **1.** Agitation of a multitude, usually with uproar and confusion of voices. **2.** Violent agitation, with confusion of sounds. **3.** Irregular or confused motion; high excitement.

tu-mul'tu-ous (tū-mŭl'tū-ŭs), *a.* [4] Full of or marked by tumult; turbulent; as, a *tumultuous* meeting. — *ly, adv.* [8] — *ness, n.* [8].

tu'mu-lus (tū'mū-lŭs), *n. ; pl.* -LI (-lī). An artificial hillock or mound, as over a grave.

tun (tŭn), *n.* **1.** A large cask. **2.** Hence, the capacity of a tun as a varying liquid measure (formerly legal at 252 wine gallons).

tun'dra (tōōn'drà), *n.* One of the level or undulating treeless plains of Arctic regions.

tune (tūn), *n.* **1.** *Music.* **a** A melody; air. **b** State or capacity of giving tones of proper pitch. **2.** Order; harmony; right mood. — *v. t.* [1] **1.** To adjust (a voice or instrument) to a given musical pitch or temperament. **2.** To attune. **3.** To utter musically. **4.** *Elec.* To bring (a circuit) into tune with another. — *v. i.* To sound in harmony.

tune'ful (-fŏŏl), *a.* [4] Harmonious; melodious. — *tune'ful-ly, adv.* [8] — *tune'ful-ness, n.* [8].

tune'less, *a.* [4] **1.** Without tune; inharmonious. **2.** Silent; as, *tuneless* harps.

tun'er (tūn'ĕr), *n.* One that tunes.

tung'sten (tŭng'stĕn), *n.* *Chem.* A rare element of the chromium group, isolated as a hard, brittle, white or gray metal.

tu'nic (tū'nĭk), *n.* **1.** *Roman Antiq.* An undergarment worn by both sexes, girdled at the waist. **2.** Any similar garment worn by ancient or Oriental peoples; any of various loose-fitting garments.

tun'nel (tŭn'ĕl), *n.* **1.** A smoke flue. **2.** A subterranean passageway, esp. one horizontal and open at both ends. — *v. t.* [7] **1.** To form into or like a tunnel. **2.** To make an opening, or a passageway, through or under. — *v. i.* To make a tunnel. — *tun'nel-er, n.* [7, 8].

tun'ny (-ĭ), *n. ; pl.* -NIES (-ĭz). Any of several oceanic fishes of the mackerel family. The great tunny sometimes weighs over 1,000 pounds.

tu'pe-lo (tū'pē-lō), *n. ; pl.* -LOS (-lōz). A North American tree having red berries and hard wood.

tur'ban (tûr'băn), *n.* **1.** A headdress for men, worn in the Levant and by most male Mohammedans, consisting of a cap, with a sash or scarf wound about it. **2.** Any headdress like a turban (def. 1). **3.** A kind of hat, with no brim or with the brim turned up close to the crown, worn by women and children.

tur'bid (-bĭd), *a.* [4] **1.** Having the lees or sediment disturbed; loosely, muddy; not clear. **2.** Disturbed; confused. — *ly, adv.* — *ness, n.* [8].

One form of Turban, 1.

tur-bid'i-ty (-ĭ-tĭ), *n.* Turbid quality or state.

tur'bine (-bĭn; -bĭn), *n.* A rotary motor turned by a current of water or steam, acting usually on a series of curved vanes on a central spindle.

tur'bot (-bŏt), *n.* A large European flounder.

tur'bu-lence (-bū-lĕns), *n.* Quality or state of being turbulent; tumult; disorder; commotion.

tur'bu-lent (-lĕnt), *a.* [4] **1.** Violently agitated; tumultuous. **2.** Disposed to disorder; restless. **3.** Producing commotion; seditious. — *ly, adv.*

tu-reen' (tū-rēn'), *n.* A deep vessel to hold soup.

turf (tûrf), *n.* **1.** The upper stratum of earth and vegetable mold filled with the roots of grass and other small plants ; sod ; also, a sod. **2.** Peat, esp. when prepared for fuel. — *v. t.* To cover with turf.

turf'y, *a.* [3] Abounding with, or like, turf.

tur-ges'cence (tûr-jĕs'ĕns), *n.* Act of swelling, or state of being turgescent.   [gid; swelling.|

tur-ges'cent (tûr-jĕs'ĕnt), *a.* [4] Becoming turgid|

tur'gid (tûr'jĭd), *a.* [4] **1.** Distended abnormally; swollen; bloated. **2.** Swelling in style or language; pompous. — *ly, adv.* [8] — *ness, n.* [8].

tur-gid'i-ty (tûr-jĭd'ĭ-tĭ), *n.* Turgid quality or state.

Turk (tûrk), *n.* **1.** A native or inhabitant of Turkey. **2.** A Mohammedan, esp. one living in Turkey.

tur'key (tûr'kĭ), *n. ; pl.* -KEYS (-kĭz). A large American bird of the pheasant family, widely domesticated; also, an allied wild species.

āle, senāte, câre, ăm, ăccount, ärm, àsk, sofà ; ēve, ĕvent, ĕnd, recĕnt, makĕr; īce, ĭll ; ōld, ŏbey, ôrb, ŏdd, sŏft, cŏnnect ; ūse, ŭnite, ûrn, ŭp, circŭs ; fōōd, fŏŏt ; out, oil

turkey buzzard. A vulture common in South and Central America and in the southern U. S.

Turk'ish (tûr'kĭsh), *a.* Of or pert. to Turkey or the Turks. — *n.* The language spoken by Turks.

tur'moil (tûr'moil), *n.* Harassing labor; trouble; loosely, worrying confusion; turbulence.

turn (tûrn), *v. t.* **1.** To cause to revolve about or as about a center; rotate. **2. a** To revolve mentally; ponder. **b** To perform or execute by revolving, as a somersault. **3.** To form in a lathe; hence, to fashion; adapt. **4.** To reverse in position. **5.** To cause to have another, or a certain, course, direction, or inclination; deflect. **6.** To devote; apply. **7.** To change the form, quality, aspect, or effect, of; convert. Specifically: To ferment; curdle, etc.; as, to *turn* milk. **8.** To distress; esp., to sicken; nauseate. **9.** To derange; unsettle. **10.** To make a turn about or around (something).

turn, *v. i.* **1.** To move about or as about an axis; revolve; whirl; wheel. **2.** To hinge; depend. **3.** To take a different direction or tendency; be deflected. **4. a** To change one's course of action, policy, etc. **b** To incline in the other direction; — of scales. **c** To change from ebb to flow, or from flow to ebb; — of the tide. **5.** To be changed or transformed. Specifically: **a** To become acid, rancid, or putrid; to sour, as milk. **b** To become giddy or dizzy. **c** Of the stomach, to be nauseated. **6.** To result; issue.

turn, *n.* **1.** Act of turning; revolution; rotation. **2.** Change of direction or tendency, or the point at which such change occurs; also, a bend. **3.** A nervous start or shock. *Colloq.* **4.** A short walk, ride, or drive. **5.** An incidental or opportune deed. **6.** Alternate time, occasion, or opportunity. **7.** A special occasion or exigency. **8.** Special ability or aptitude; bent. **9.** Particular form, cast, or style; shape; fashion; appearance. **10.** A twist or coil.

turn'buck'le (tûrn'bŭk'l), *n.* A loop or sleeve with a screw thread at one end and a swivel at the other to tighten a rod, stay, etc.

One form of Turnbuckle.

turn'coat' (-kōt'), *n.* A deserter; renegade.

turn'er (tûr'nẽr), *n.* **1.** One that turns. **2.** One who forms articles with a lathe.

tur'nip (tûr'nĭp), *n.* The edible root of either of two plants of the mustard family; also, either plant.

turn'key (tûrn'kē'), *n.; pl.* -KEYS (-kēz'). One in charge of the keys of a prison; warder.

turn'out' (-out'), *n.* **1.** A coming forth. **2.** A gathering of persons. *Colloq.* **3.** An equipage. *Colloq.* **4.** *Railroads.* A siding. **5.** Yield; output.

turn'o'ver (-ō'vẽr), *n.* **1.** Act or result of turning over. **2.** A small pie or tart having a crust turned over on itself. — *a.* That can be turned over; made with a part turned over.

turn'pike' (-pīk'), *n.* A tollgate; turnpike road.

turnpike road. A road that has or formerly had turnpikes, or tollgates, established by law.

turn'spit' (-spĭt'), *n.* One that turns a spit.

turn'stile' (-stīl'), *n.* **1.** Orig., a post with four arms pivoted on the top, set in a passageway. **2.** A similar device, as at a doorway, to register the number of persons passing.

turn'ta'ble (-tā'b'l), *n.* A revolvable platform.

tur'pen-tine (tûr'pen-tīn), *n.* **1.** A semifluid or fluid resin derived from any of various coniferous trees, used in mixing varnishes, paints, etc., and also in medicine. **2.** Popularly, oil of turpentine.

tur'pi-tude (-pĭ-tūd), *n.* Inherent baseness; shameful wickedness; depravity. [blue gem.]

tur-quoise' (tûr-koiz'; tûr'kwoiz), *n.* A bright, merely ornamental structure at an angle of a building.

tur'ret (tûr'ĕt), *n.* **1.** *Arch.* A little tower, often a merely ornamental structure at an angle of a building. **2.** *Nav.& Mil.* A towerlike structure, armored and usually revolving, containing heavy guns.

tur'tle (tûr't'l), *n.* Any of a group of reptiles having the trunk inclosed in a shell of bony plates, usually covered externally with horny shields.

tur'tle-dove' (-dŭv'), *n.* Any of various Old World wild doves, esp. a certain one noted for its plaintive cooing and affectionate disposition.

tush (tŭsh), *n.* A tusk; a horse's canine.

tush, *interj.* An exclamation used to check or rebuke, or in contempt.

tusk (tŭsk), *n.* **1.** In the elephant, walrus, wild boar, etc., a projecting and greatly enlarged tooth. **2.** Hence, any long, protruding tooth.

tus'sle (tŭs''l), *v. i.* [1] To scuffle, as in sport wrestle. — *n.* A struggle; scuffle.

tus'sock (tŭs'ŭk), *n.* A tuft, as of grass, twigs. etc.; esp., a dense tuft or bunch of grass or sedge

tut (tŭt), *interj.* Be still! hush!

tu'te-lage (tū'tē-lāj), *n.* **1.** Act of guarding **2.** State of being under a guardian or tutor.

tu'te-lar (-lär), *a.* [4] **1.** Having the guardianshi₁ of a person or a thing. **2.** Of or pert. to a guardian

tu'te-la-ry (-lā-rĭ), *a.* Tutelar.

tu'tor (tū'tẽr), *n.* One in charge of the instruc of another. — *v. t.* To teach; instruct. — *v. i.* To do the work of a tutor.

tut'ti-frut'ti (tōōt'tē-frōōt'tē), *n.* A confection consisting of different kinds of preserved fruits. — *a.* Flavored with, or containing, various fruits.

twad'dle (twŏd''l), *v. i. & t.* [1] To talk idly or nonsensically; prate; gabble. — *n.* Silly talk.

twain (twān), *a. & n.* Two. *Chiefly Poetic.*

twang (twăng), *v. i. & t.* To sound with a twang. — *n.* **1.** A harsh, ringing sound, as of a plucked bowstring. **2.** A sharp vibrant nasal tone.

tweak (twēk), *v. t.* To pinch and pull with a sudden jerk and twist. — *n.* A sharp pinch or twist.

tweed (twēd), *n.* A soft fabric for men's wear. esp. of wool.

tweez'ers (twēz'ẽrz), *n. pl.* A small pincerlike implement for grasping or extracting something.

twelfth (twĕlfth), *a.* **1.** Next in order after the eleventh. **2.** Constituting one of twelve equal parts of a (whole) thing. — *n.* **1.** A twelfth part. **2.** A twelfth unit or object.

twelve (twĕlv), *a.* One more than eleven. — *n.* **1.** The number next after eleven; twelve units or objects; a dozen. **2.** A symbol for twelve units. as 12 or xii.

twelve'mo (-mō), *a. & n.* = DUODECIMO.

twelve'month' (-mŭnth'), *n.* A year.

twen'ti-eth (twĕn'tĭ-ĕth), *a.* **1.** Next in order after the nineteenth. **2.** Constituting one of twenty equal parts into which a (whole) thing may be divided. — *n.* A twentieth part, unit, or object,

---

twen'ty (twĕn'tĭ), *a.* Twice ten. — *n.; pl.* -TIES (-tĭz). **1.** The number next after nineteen; twenty units or objects; a score. **2.** A symbol for twenty units, as 20 or xx.

twice (twis), *adv.* **1.** Two times; once and again. **2.** Doubly; in twofold quantity or degree.

twid'dle (twĭd'l), *v. t. & i.* [1] To twirl, esp. idly, as one's thumbs; to trifle.

twig (twĭg), *n.* A small shoot or branch.

twi'light (twi'lit'), *n.* The light perceived before the rising, and after the setting, of the sun. — *a.* **1.** Of or pertaining to the twilight. **2.** Imperfectly illuminated; shaded; obscure.

twill (twĭl), *v. t.* To weave so as to produce a twill. — *n.* **1.** An appearance of diagonal lines or ribs in textile fabrics. **2.** A fabric woven with a twill.

twin (twĭn), *a.* Made up of two distinct, nearly related, and equal members; double; twofold; consisting of, or being, twins. **2.** Being a twin; as, a *twin* brother. — *n.* One of two persons or things closely related by ties of birth, resemblance, etc.; esp., one of two produced at a birth.

twine (twin), *n.* **1.** Strong thread of strands twisted together. **2.** A twining round; an entwining. — *v. t.* [1] **1.** To twist together. **2.** To wind, wreathe, or coil. **3.** To wind about; entwine. — *v. i.* **1.** To intertwine. **2.** To wind; coil.

twinge (twĭnj), *v. i.* [1] To have a sharp, sudden pain. — *n.* A sharp, sudden pain.

twin'kle (twĭn'k'l), *v. i.* [1] **1.** To wink or blink rapidly; — said of eyes or eyelids. **2.** To shine with an intermittent light; sparkle; scintillate. **3.** To appear rapidly at intervals. — *n.* **1.** A quick motion of the eye; a wink. **2.** A brief flash or gleam. **3.** The time of a wink; a twinkling.

twin'kling (-klĭng), *n.* **1.** Act of one that twinkles; twinkle. **2.** Scintillation. **3.** A moment.

twirl (twûrl), *v. t. & i.* To whirl round. — *n.* **1.** A twirling. **2.** A twist; convolution.

twist (twĭst), *v. t. & i.* **1.** To unite by winding one thread or the like round another. **2.** To wreathe; twine; wind. **3.** To wrench; turn; contort. — *n.* **1.** Thing formed by twisting; kind of sewing silk. **2.** Act or state of being twisted. — **er**, *n.* [8].

twit (twĭt), *v. t.; * TWIT'TED; -TING. To reproach or upbraid, esp. by reminding of a fault, etc.

twitch (twĭch), *v. t. & i.* To pull with a short quick motion; to move jerkily or spasmodically. — *n.* **1.** Act of twitching. **2.** A short spasmodic contraction of fibers or muscles.

twit'ter (twĭt'ẽr), *v. i.* **1.** To make a succession of small, tremulous, intermittent noises, as birds. **2.** To have a slight trembling of the nerves. — *n.* Act, sound, or sensation of twittering.

'twixt (twĭkst). For BETWIXT. *Poet. or Colloq.*

two (tōō), *a.* One and one; twice one. — *n.* **1.** The number next greater than one; two units or objects. **2.** A symbol for two units, as 2 or ii.

two'-edged' (-ĕjd' ; -ĕj'ĕd), *a.* Having two edges, or an edge on each side; as, a *two-edged* sword.

two'fold' (-fōld'), *a.* Double; duplicate. — *adv.* In a double degree; doubly.

two'-hand'ed, *a.* **1.** Having two hands. **2.** Used with two hands. **3.** Ambidextrous.

two'pence (tŭp'ĕns; tōō pĕns *only if two words*), *n.* The sum of two pence.

two'pen-ny (tŭp'ĕn-ĭ ; *cf.* TWOPENCE), *a.* Of the value of twopence; hence, cheap; mean.

two'-step (tōō'stĕp'), *n.* A kind of round dance in march or polka time.

ty'ing (ti'ĭng), *p. pr. & vb. n.* of TIE.

tym-pan'ic (tĭm-păn'ĭk), *a.* **1.** Like a drum or drumhead. **2.** *Anat.* Of or pert. to the tympanum.

tym'pa-num (tĭm'pá-nŭm),*n.,pl.* E. -NUMS (-nŭmz), L. -NA (-ná). **a** The middle ear. **b** Eardrum.

type (tip), *n.* **1.** The mark or impression of something; stamp; sign; emblem. **2.** A figure or representation of something to come; a symbol. **3.** That which serves or may serve as an example, pattern, or model; that which has characteristics common to a number of individuals; a model; standard. **4.** *Print.* **a** A rectangular block, usually of metal, having its face so shaped as to produce, by printing, a letter, figure, etc. **b** Such blocks, or the letters or characters impressed, collectively.

type (tip), *v. t.* [1] **1.** To produce a copy of; represent; typify. **2.** To typewrite. *Colloq.*

type'set'ter (tip'sĕt'ẽr), *n.* One that sets type; a compositor; a machine for setting type.

type'set'ting, *n.* Act or process of setting type.

type'write' (tip'rit'), *v. t. & i.* To write with a typewriter.

type'writ'er (-rit'ẽr), *n.* **1.** A machine for writing in characters similar to those produced by printers' types. **2.** One who operates a typewriter.

type'writ'ing (-rit'ĭng), *n.* Act of using a typewriter; also, a print made with a typewriter.

ty'phoid (ti'foid), *a. Med.* Of, pertaining to, or like, typhus. — *n.* Typhoid fever. — **typhoid fever**, an infectious febrile, often fatal, disease due to a bacillus introduced with food or drink.

ty-phoon' (ti-fōōn'), *n.* A violent whirlwind.

ty'phus (ti'fŭs), *n. Med.* A contagious fever marked by great prostration, disorder of the brain, and eruption of red spots on the body.

typ'i-cal (tĭp'ĭ-kál), *a.* [4] **1.** Of the nature of a type or symbol; emblematic. **2.** Characteristic; representative; as, a *typical* Yankee. — **ly**, *adv.* [8]. — **ness**, *n.* [8].

typ'i-fy (-fi), *v. t.* [2] **1.** To represent by an image, model, or resemblance; prefigure. **2.** To embody the essential or salient characteristics of.

typ'ist (tip'ĭst), *n.* One who operates a typewriter.

ty-pog'ra-pher (ti-pŏg'rá-fẽr), *n.* A printer.

ty'po-graph'ic (ti'pŏ-grăf'ĭk), **-i-cal** (-ĭ-kál), *a.* Of or pert. to typography. — **i-cal-ly**, *adv.*

ty-pog'ra-phy (ti-pŏg'rá-fĭ), *n.* Art of printing with type.

ty-ran'ni-cal (ti-răn'ĭ-kál), *a.* [4] Of or pert. to a tyrant; despotic. — **ly**, *adv.* [8].

tyr'an-nize (tĭr'ă-niz), *v. i.* [1] To act the tyrant; rule oppressively. — *v. t.* To treat tyrannically.

tyr'an-nous (-nŭs), *a.* [4] Tyrannical; despotic.

tyr'an-ny (tĭr'ă-nĭ), *n. ; pl.* -NIES (-nĭz). **1.** The government or authority of a tyrant. **2.** Despotic exercise of power. **3.** A tyrannical act.

ty'rant (ti'rănt), *n.* **1.** An absolute ruler; a sovereign unrestrained by law. **2.** A monarch, or other ruler or master, who exercises absolute power oppressively. [learning; novice.]

ty'ro (ti'rō), *n. ; pl.* -ROS (-rōz). A beginner in

tzar (tsär), **tza-ri'na** (tsä-rē'ná). See CZAR, etc.

U

u-biq′ui-tous (ŭ-bĭk′wĭ-tŭs), *a.* Existing everywhere at the same time ; omnipresent. — **u-biq′-ui-tous-ly**, *adv.* [8] — **-tous-ness**, *n.* [8].

u-biq′ui-ty (-tǐ), *n.* Omnipresence.

U′-boat′, *n.* A German or Austrian submarine.

ud′der (ŭd′er), *n.* A pendent mammary gland having teats, as in cows.

ug′li-ness (ŭg′lĭ-nĕs), *n.* Quality of being ugly.

ug′ly (ŭg′lĭ), *a.* [1]. **1.** Offensive to the sight; unsightly; repulsive. **2.** Ill-natured; quarrelsome.

u-kase′ (ū-kās′), *n.* **1.** In Russia, formerly, a proclamation or imperial order, having the force of law. **2.** Hence, any official decree.

u′ku-le′le (ū′kōō-lā′lĕ), *n.* A kind of small guitar with four strings, used originally in Hawaii.

ul′cer (ŭl′sĕr), *n.* A sore, usually on the surface of the body, that discharges pus.

ul′cer-ate (-āt), *v. t. & i.* [1] To make, be, or become, ulcerous. — **ul′cer-a′tion** (-ā′shŭn), *n.*

ul′cer-ous (ŭl′sĕr-ŭs), *a.* **1.** Having the nature or character of an ulcer. **2.** Ulcerated.

ul′na (ŭl′nà), *n.; pl.* -NÆ (-nē). The inner of the two bones of the forearm. — **ul′nar** (-når), *a.*

ul′ster (ŭl′stĕr), *n.* A long, loose overcoat, originally made of frieze from Ulster, Ireland.

ul-te′ri-or (ŭl-tē′rĭ-ĕr), *a.* **1.** Situated beyond, or on the farther side. **2.** Further ; more remote ; beyond what is manifest. — **ly**, *adv.* [8].

ul′ti-ma (ŭl′tĭ-mà), *n.* Last syllable of a word.

ul′ti-mate (-māt), *a.* **1.** Farthest; most remote; extreme. **2.** Last ; final. **3.** Incapable of further analysis ; elemental. — **ul′ti-mate-ly**, *adv.*

ul′ti-ma′tum (-mā′tŭm), *n.; pl.* E. -TUMS (-tŭmz) L. -TA (-tà). A final proposition, or condition.

‖ **ul′ti-mo** (ŭl′tĭ-mō), *adv.* [L.] In or of the month preceding the present. Abbr. *ult.* Cf. PROXIMO.

ul′tra (-trà), *a.* [4] Extreme ; extravagant.

ul′tra-ma-rine′ (-mà-rēn′), *n.* A pigment, or coloring matter, of a characteristic pure blue color, made originally from lapis lazuli.

ul′tra-mon′tane (-mŏn′tān), *a.* [4] Beyond the mountains, esp. the Alps. — *n.* A dweller beyond the mountains; esp., one who lives south of the Alps; a supporter of papal supremacy.

um′bel (ŭm′bĕl), *n. Bot.* An arrangement of flowers on the stem in which the flower stems appear to spring from the same point, and form a flat or rounded flower cluster. — **um′bel-late** (-āt), *a.*

um′ber (ŭm′bĕr), *n.* A brown earth valued as a pigment. — *a.* Of, pert. to, or like umber; dark brown; dusky.

um′bra (ŭm′brà), *n.; pl.* -BRÆ (-brē). **1.** A shade; shadow; *Optics*, a complete shadow ; — disting. from *penumbra*. **2.** *Astron.* **a** The conical shadow projected from a planet or satellite, on the side away from the sun, within which a spectator could see no portion of the sun's disk. **b** The central dark portion of a sun spot.

Umbel.

um′brage (ŭm′brāj), *n.* Suspicion of injury or wrong; offense; resentment.

um-bra′geous (ŭm-brā′jŭs), *a.* [4] Forming or affording a shade, or being shaded; shady; as, *umbrageous* foliage. — **ly**, *adv.* [8] — **ness**, *n.* [8].

um-brel′la (-brĕl′à), *n.* A shade, screen, or guard carried in the hand as a shelter from rain, sun, etc.

um′pire (ŭm′pīr), *n.* A person to whose sole decision a controversy or question is referred ; esp., one chosen to rule on the plays of a game. — *v. t.* **1.** To decide as umpire; arbitrate.

un-. A common prefix meaning, usually, *not*, *in-*, *non-*. For other senses see PREFIXES and SUFFIXES.

☞ *Un-* with this value may be attached to almost any adjective or adverb, and (though less freely) to nouns, from which it is desired to form a corresponding negative (see the *Note* under NON-). The number of such compounds of self-evident meaning is practically unlimited, and only those most important, or involving some difficulty, are here defined.

un-a′ble (ŭn-ā′b'l), *a.* Not able; incapable.

un′ac-count′a-ble (ŭn′à-koun′tà-b'l), *a.* [4] Not accountable ; inexplicable. — **a-bly**, *adv.* [8].

un′ac-cus′tomed (-kŭs′tŭmd), *a.* [4] **1.** Not used; not habituated. **2.** Not usual ; uncommon.

un′ad-vised′ (ŭn′ăd-vīzd′), *a.* [4] Not advised ; esp., indiscreet or rash; inconsiderate.

un′af-fect′ed (ŭn′ă-fĕk′tĕd), *a.* [4] Not affected ; simple ; sincere. — **ly**, *adv.* [8] — **ness**, *n.* [8].

u′na-nim′i-ty (ū′nà-nĭm′ĭ-tĭ), *n.* Quality or state of being unanimous.

u-nan′i-mous (ŭ-năn′ĭ-mŭs), *a.* **1.** Being of one mind ; agreeing. **2.** Formed with the agreement and consent of all. — **ly**, *adv.* — **ness**, *n.*

un-apt′ (ŭn-ăpt′), *a.* [4] Inapt; not accustomed and not likely. — **ly**, *adv.* [8] — **ness**, *n.* [8].

un′as-sum′ing (ŭn′ă-sūm′ĭng), *a.* [4] Not assuming; modest. [able. **2.** Not voidable.|

un′a-void′a-ble (-void′à-b'l), *a.* **1.** Not avoid-

un′a-wares′ (-wârz′)) *adv.* Without design or **un′a-ware′** (-wâr′) } preparation; unexpectedly.

un-backed′ (ŭn-băkt′), *a.* **1.** Never mounted by a rider; unbroken. **2.** Unaided.

un-bal′anced (-băl′ånst), *a.* [4] **1.** Not balanced. **2.** Out of equilibrium; deranged, as the mind.

un-bar′ (-bär′), *v. t. & i.; -*BARRED′ (-bärd′) ; *-BAR-*RING. To remove a bar or bars from ; unbolt; open.

un′be-com′ing (ŭn′bĕ-kŭm′ĭng), *a.* [4] Not becoming; unfit; indecorous; improper. — **un′be-com′ing-ly**, *adv.* [8] — **ness**, *n.* [8].

un′be-lief′ (-lēf′), *n.* **1.** The withholding of belief ; incredulity; skepticism. **2.** Disbelief, esp of divine revelation.

un′be-liev′er (-lēv′ẽr), *n.* **1.** One who does not believe ; skeptic. **2.** A disbeliever ; infidel.

un-bend′ (ŭn-bĕnd′), *v. t.; -*BENT′ (-bĕnt′); -BEND′-ING. **1.** To free from flexure ; make, or allow to become, straight ; loosen; relax. **2.** *Naut.* To unfasten, as sails, from the spars or stays. — *v. i.* **1.** To cease to be bent. **2.** To relax in severity, stiffness, etc. ; become affable.

---

chair; go; sing, iŋk; **t**hen, thin; nature, verdure; yet; zh = z in azure. Numbers refer to §§ in the Special Notes which, with Abbreviations, Signs, etc., precede the Vocabulary.

un-bend'ing (ŭn-bĕnd'ĭng), a. [4] Not bending; unyielding; inflexible; resolute. — **-ly**, adv.

un-bind' (-bīnd'), v. t.; for prin. parts see BIND. To remove a band from; untie; unfasten; loose.

un-bolt' (-bōlt'), v. t. To withdraw a bolt from; unfasten; unbar; open.— **un-bolt'ed**, a.

un-bolt'ed, a. Not bolted, or sifted.

un-born' (-bôrn'), a. Not born; future.

un-bos'om (-bŏoz'ŭm), v. t. & i. To disclose, as secrets; confess; —often used reflexively.

un-braid' (-brād'), v. t. To separate the strands of; undo, as a braid.

un-bri'dle (-brī'd'l), v. t. [1] To free or loose from the bridle.

un-bri'dled (-d'ld), a. [4] Not confined by the bridle; hence, unrestrained.

un-buck'le (-bŭk'l), v. t. To loose the buckle of.

un-bur'den (-bûr'd'n), v. t. Also **un-bur'then** (-th'n). To relieve from a burden; also, to throw off, as a burden.

un-but'ton (-bŭt''n), v. t. To loose the buttons of; unfasten in this way.

un-called'-for', a. [4] Not called for; gratuitous.

un-can'ny (-kăn'ĭ), a. [3] Not canny; hence, unearthly; mysterious; weird. — **-ni-ly** (-ĭ-lĭ), adv. [8] — **-ni-ness**, n. [8].

un-cer'tain (-sûr'tĭn), a. [4] Not certain; as: **1.** Not having certain knowledge; not assured. **2.** Not known; indefinite; problematical. **3.** Not sure; fallible. **4.** Irresolute; untrustworthy; variable. — **-ly**, adv. [8] —**-ness**, n. [8].

un-cer'tain-ty (-tĭ), n.; pl. -TIES (-tĭz). Quality or state of being uncertain; something uncertain.

un-chain' (-chān'), v. t. To free from chains or (fig.) slavery; let loose.

un-char'i-ta-ble (-chăr'ĭ-tá-b'l), a. [4] Not charitable; censorious.— **-ness**, n.— **-ta-bly**, adv. [8].

un-chaste' (ŭn-chāst'), a. [4] Not chaste; as: **a** Not continent; lewd. **b** Not chaste in style.

un-chris'tian (-krĭs'chăn), a. [4] Not Christian; heathen; contrary to Christianity; barbarous.

un'ci-al (ŭn'shĭ-ăl; -shăl), a. Pert. to or designating a kind of letters used in ancient manuscripts. — n. An uncial letter, writing, etc.

NON hABEMUS REGEM

NISI CAESAREM

Uncial Letters from a Latin Bible.

un-civ'il (-sĭv'ĭl), a. [4] Not civil; discourteous; rude. — **un-civ'il-ly**, adv. [8].

un-civ'i-lized (-ĭ-līzd), a. Not civilized; savage.

un-clasp' (ŭn-klåsp'), v. t. To loose the clasp of; to open, as something fastened with a clasp.

un'cle (ŭn'k'l), n. The brother of one's father or mother; also, one's aunt's husband.

un-clean' (ŭn-klēn'), a. [3] **1.** Not clean; dirty. **2.** Ceremonially or morally impure. —**-ness**, n.

un-clean'ly (-klĕn'lĭ), a. [3] Not cleanly; filthy; also, unchaste.—**un-clean'li-ness** (-lĭ-nĕs), n. [8].

un-close' (-klōz'), v. t. & i. [1] To open; disclose.

un-clothe' (-klōth'), v. t. To strip of clothing.

un-coil' (-koil'), v. t. To unwind the coils of.

un-com'fort-a-ble (-kŭm'fẽr-tá-b'l), a. [4] Not comfortable; as: **a** Feeling discomfort; uneasy. **b** Causing discomfort; unpleasant.

un-com'mon (-kŏm'ŭn), a. [3] Not common; unusual; rare; hence, remarkable; strange.

un-com'pro-mis'ing (ŭn-kŏm'prŏ-mīz'ĭng), a. [4] Unyielding; inflexible. — **-ly**, adv. [8].

un'con-cern' (ŭn'kŏn-sûrn'), n. Want of concern; freedom from solicitude; indifference.

un'con-cerned' (-sûrnd'), a. [4] Not concerned; indifferent.— **un'con-cern'ed-ly**, adv. [8].

un'con-di'tion-al (-dĭsh'ŭn-ăl), a. [4] Not conditional or limited; absolute.—**-ly**, adv. [8].

un-con'scion-a-ble (ŭn-kŏn'shŭn-á-b'l), a. [4] **1.** Not conscionable; unreasonable. **2.** Not guided or controlled by conscience. — **-a-bly**, adv. [8].

un-con'scious (-shŭs), a. [4] Not conscious. Also, with of, not aware.—**-ly**, adv. —**-ness**, n.

un-con'sti-tu'tion-al (-stĭ-tū'shŭn-ăl), a. [4] Not constitutional; contrary to the constitution. — **un-con'sti-tu'tion-al'i-ty** (-ăl'ĭ-tĭ), n.

un-cork' (-kôrk'), v. t. To draw a cork from.

un-cou'ple (ŭn-kŭp''l), v. t. [1] To loose, as dogs, from their couples, or leashes; also, to disconnect.

un-couth' (-kōoth'), a. [3] Awkwardly strange; awkward; boorish. —**-ly**, adv. — **-ness**, n. [8].

un-cov'er (-kŭv'ẽr), v. t. & i. **1.** To take the cover from. **2.** To divest of, or to remove, the hat or cap; bare the head of. **3.** To show openly; disclose.

unc'tion (ŭngk'shŭn), n. **1.** Act of anointing, esp. medicinally, or as a symbol of consecration. **2.** Thing used for anointing; unguent; hence, anything soothing. **3.** That quality in language, address, etc., which expresses or excites fervent emotion; also, unctuousness.

unc'tu-ous (ŭngk'tū-ŭs), a. [4] **1.** Of the nature or quality of an unguent or ointment; oily; greasy. **2.** Bland; suave; also, fervid; esp., insincerely suave or gushing; as, an unctuous speech. —**-ly**, adv. [8] —**-ness**, **unc'tu-os'i-ty** (-ŏs'ĭ-tĭ), n.

un-daunt'ed (ŭn-dän'tĕd; -dôn²-), a. [4] Not daunted; fearless; intrepid. —**-ly**, adv. [8].

un'de-ceive' (ŭn'dĕ-sēv'), v. t. [1] To free from deception, fraud, fallacy, or mistake.

un'de-ni'a-ble (ŭn'dĕ-nī'á-b'l), a. [4] **1.** Incapable of denial; indisputable. **2.** Unquestionably excellent. Colloq. —**-bly**, adv. [8].

un'der (ŭn'dẽr), prep. **1.** Below or beneath, with the idea of being covered; at a point or position lower than; — opposed to over; as, under a tree; under water. **2.** Hence: **a** Weighed upon; oppressed or controlled by; as, under a heavy load; under oath. **b** Beneath, as sustaining, receiving, or undergoing something; as, under discussion; under a charge. **c** Falling short of; hence, at, with, or for, less than; as, to sell a horse under 60 dollars. **d** Beneath, with reference to category, etc.; as, under this head. **e** Beneath, with reference to cover, pretext, etc. — adv. In a lower position, or in a subordinate condition; as, to bring under; go under. —a. Lower in position, intensity, rank, or degree; subordinate; — esp. in composition.

un'der-bid' (-bĭd'), v. t.; for prin. parts see BID. To offer to contract, sell, or do, for a less price than.

un'der-bred' (ŭn'dẽr-brĕd'), a. [4] **1.** Not of pure breed; as, an underbred dog. **2.** Ill-bred.

un'der-brush' (-brŭsh'), n. Shrubs, small trees, etc., growing beneath large trees in a forest.

un'der-clothes' (-klōthz'), *n. pl.* Clothes worn under others, esp. next the skin.

un'der-cloth'ing (-klōth'ĭng), *n.* Underclothes.

un'der-cur'rent (-kŭr'ĕnt), *n.* **1.** A current below the upper currents or surface of water, etc. **2.** A tendency of feeling, opinion, etc., more or less hidden.

un'der-done' (ŭn'dẽr-dŭn'; ŭn'dẽr-dŭn'), *p. a.* Cooked for an insufficient time; rare.

un'der-feed' (-fēd'), *v. t. ;* for prin. parts see FEED. To feed too little.

un'der-foot' (-fŏŏt'), *adv.* Under the feet.

un'der-gar'ment (ŭn'dẽr-gär'mĕnt), *n.* Garment to wear under another, esp. under outer clothing.

un'der-go' (-gō'), *v. t. ;* for prin. parts see GO. To be subjected to ; bear up against ; endure ; suffer.

un'der-grad'u-ate (-grăd'ů-āt), *n.* A member of a university or of a college who has not taken his first degree.

un'der-ground' (ŭn'dẽr-ground'), *n.* Place or space beneath the surface of the ground. — *a.* **1.** Being below the surface of the ground ; subterranean. **2.** Secret. *Colloq.* — *adv.* Beneath the surface of the earth.

un'der-growth' (-grōth'), *n.* Underbrush.

un'der-hand' (-hănd'), *a.* [4] **1.** Secret ; sly ; hence, mean ; unfair. **2.** *Baseball, Cricket, etc.* Done, as pitching, with the hand lower than the shoulder, or, as bowling, with the whole movement of the arm approximately in a vertical plane below the shoulder. — *adv.* In an underhand manner ; secretly ; unfairly.

un'der-hand'ed, *a.* [4] Underhand ; clandestine. —**un'der-hand'ed-ly,** *adv.* [8] —**ness,** *n.* [8].

un'der-lay' (-lā'), *v. t. ;* for prin. parts see LAY. **1.** To lay beneath ; put under. **2.** To raise or support by something laid under, as a cut, plate, or the like, for printing.

un'der-lay', *n. Printing.* A thickness of paper or the like placed under type, etc., to bring it to the right height for printing.

un'der-let' (-lĕt'), *v. t. ;* -LET' ; LET'TING. To sublet.

un'der-lie' (-lī'), *v. t. ;* for prin. parts see LIE. **1.** To lie or be situated under. **2.** To be at the basis of; form the foundation of, as of a theory or an argument.

un'der-line' (-līn'), *v. t.* [1] To underscore.

un'der-ling (ŭn'dẽr-lĭng), *n.* An inferior person ; a subordinate. [damental.

un'der-ly'ing (-lī'ĭng), *a.* [4] Lying under ; fun-

un'der-mine' (-mīn'), *v. t.* [1] **1.** To excavate beneath ; form a mine under ; sap. **2.** Hence, fig., to weaken or overthrow secretly, underhandedly, or insidiously. —**min'er** (-mīn'ẽr), *n.* [8].

un'der-most (ŭn'dẽr-mōst), *a.* Lowest, as in place, rank, etc. [neath ; below ; under.

un'der-neath' (-nēth' ; -nēth'), *adv. & prep.* Be-

un'der-pay' (-pā'), *v. t. ;* for prin. parts see PAY. To pay inadequately.

un'der-pin' (-pĭn'), *v. t. ;* -PINNED (-pĭnd') ; -PIN'-NING. **1.** To lay stones, masonry, etc., under for a support, as of a building to be erected. **2.** To support by a foundation ; hence, fig., to prop.

un'der-score' (-skōr'), *v. t.* [1] To draw a mark or line under. — *n.* An underscored line.

un'der-sell' (-sĕl'), *v. t. ;* for prin. parts see SELL. To sell at a lower price than.

un'der-shirt' (ŭn'dẽr-shûrt'), *n.* A shirt worn next the skin, under another shirt.

un'der-shot' (ŭn'dẽr-shŏt'), *a.* **1.** Having the lower incisor teeth projecting beyond the upper ones when the mouth is closed, as a bulldog. **2.** Moved by water passing beneath ; — said of a water wheel.

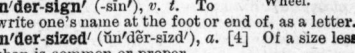

Undershot Water Wheel.

un'der-shrub' (-shrŭb'), *n.* A low shrub.

un'der-sign' (-sīn'), *v. t.* To write one's name at the foot or end of, as a letter.

un'der-sized' (ŭn'dẽr-sīzd'), *a.* [4] Of a size less than is common or proper.

un'der-skirt' (-skûrt'), *n.* A petticoat.

un'der-slung' (-slŭng'), *a.* Of an automobile body, suspended from the springs in such a manner that the frame of the chassis is below the axles.

un'der-stand' (-stănd'), *v. t. ;* for prin. parts see STAND. **1.** To apprehend the meaning of ; comprehend. **2.** To be apprised of ; learn. **3.** To suppose to mean ; interpret ; explain. **4.** To assume. — *v. i.* **1.** To have the use of the intellectual faculties. **2.** To be informed.

un'der-stand'ing, *p. a.* [4] Knowing ; intelligent. — *n.* **1.** Knowledge ; discernment ; comprehension. **2.** Agreement of opinion ; adjustment of differences. **3.** Power to understand ; the intelligence. —**-ly,** *adv.* [8].

un'der-state' (-stāt'), *v. t. & i.* [1] To state less strongly, or as less, than the truth warrants.

un'der-stood' (-stŏŏd'), *pret. & p. p.* of UNDERSTAND.

un'der-stud'y (ŭn'dẽr-stŭd'ĭ), *v. t. & i.* [2] *Theater.* To study another actor's part, in order to be his substitute in an emergency. — *n.* One prepared to act another's part.

un'der-take' (-tāk'), *v. t. ;* for prin. parts see TAKE. **1.** To take upon one's self ; enter upon ; set about. **2.** To enter into stipulations to perform or to execute ; contract. — *v. i.* To promise ; guarantee.

un'der-tak'er (-tāk'ẽr), *n.* **1.** One who undertakes something. **2.** (*pron.* ŭn'dẽr-tā'kẽr ; ŭn'-dẽr-tāk'ẽr) One who takes charge of funerals.

un'der-tak'ing (-tāk'ĭng), *n.* **1.** Act of one who undertakes anything ; specif., the business of an undertaker (sense 2). **2.** Thing undertaken ; enterprise. **3.** A guarantee.

un'der-tone' (-tōn'), *n.* **1.** A low or subdued tone or utterance. **2.** A subdued color.

un'der-took' (-tŏŏk'), *pret.* of UNDERTAKE.

un'der-tow' (-tō'), *n.* The current beneath the surface that sets seaward or along the beach.

un'der-val'u-a'tion (-văl'ů-ā'shŭn), *n.* An undervaluing ; a rate or value below the real worth.

un'der-val'ue (-văl'ū), *v. t.* [1] To value below the real worth ; esteem lightly.

un'der-vest' (ŭn'dẽr-vĕst'), *n.* An undershirt.

un'der-waist' (-wāst'), *n.* A waist for wear under another.

un'der-wear' (ŭn'dẽr-wâr'), *n.* Underclothes.

un'der-went' (-wĕnt'), *pret.* of UNDERGO.

un'der-work' (-wûrk'), *v. t. ;* for prin. parts see WORK. **1. a** To expend too little work upon. **b** To exact too little work from. **2.** To do like work

chair ; go ; sing, ink ; then, thin ; nature, verdure ; yet ; zh = z in azure. Numbers refer to §§ in the Special Notes which, with Abbreviations, Signs, etc., precede the Vocabulary.

at a less price than. —*v. i.* To do less work than is proper.

un′der-world′ (ŭn′dẽr-wûrld′), *n.* **1.** Hades. **2.** The antipodes. **3.** The lower, debased, or criminal portion of humanity.

un′der-write′ (-rīt′), *v. t.;* for prin. parts see WRITE. **1.** To write under something else; subscribe. **2.** To write one's name under, or set one's name to (a policy of insurance), and thereby become answerable for a designated loss or damage, esp. on marine property. **3.** To agree to purchase on a fixed date at a fixed price (bonds or shares to be issued). — *v. i.* To do the business of an underwriter.

un′der-writ′er (ŭn′dẽr-rīt′ẽr), *n.* One who underwrites a policy of insurance, a loan, etc.

un′de-sign′ing (ŭn′dē-zīn′ĭng), *a.* [4] Having no artful or fraudulent purpose; sincere; simple.

un-did′ (-dĭd′), *pret.* of UNDO.

un-do′ (ŭn-dōō′), *v. t.;* for prin. parts see DO. **1.** To reverse, as something done; annul; bring to naught. **2.** To unfasten; loose; untie; hence, to unravel; solve. **3.** To bring to ruin, disaster, or destruction. — **un-do′er,** *n.* [8] — **un-do′ing,** *n.*

un-done′ (-dŭn′), *p. p.* of UNDO.

un-done′, *a.* Not performed; neglected.

un-doubt′ed (-dout′ĕd), *a.* [4] Not doubted, or called in question; indubitable. — **-ly,** *adv.* [8].

un-dress′ (-drĕs′), *v. t. & i.* To divest of clothes, ornaments, or covering.

un′dress (ŭn′drĕs′; ŭn-drĕs′), *n.* A loose, informal dress; ordinary, as disting. from full, dress.

un-due′ (ŭn-dū′; ŭn′dū), *a.* [4] **1.** Not due; not yet owing. **2.** Not right; not lawful or legal. **3.** Not agreeable to a rule or standard, or to duty.

un′du-late (ŭn′dụ̇-lāt), *v. t. & i.* [1] To move backward and forward, or up and down, in waves.

un′du-la′tion (-lā′shŭn), *n.* **1.** An undulating. **2.** A wavy appearance or outline; waviness.

un′du-la-to-ry (ŭn′dụ̇-lȧ-tō-rĭ), *a.* [4] Of or pertaining to undulation; wavelike.

un-earth′ (-ûrth′), *v. t.* To drive or draw from the earth; exhume; hence, bring to light; disclose.

un-earth′ly, *a.* [3] Not terrestrial; supernatural; hence, weird; appalling. — **-earth′li-ness,** *n.*

un-eas′y (-ēz′ĭ), *a.* [3] **1.** Restless; disturbed by pain, anxiety, etc. **2.** Not easy in manner; constrained; awkward. **3.** Occasioning want of ease; disagreeable. — **un-eas′i-ly** (-ēz′ĭ-lĭ), *adv.* [8] — **un-eas′i-ness** (-ĭ-nĕs), *n.* [8].

un-e′qual (ŭn-ē′kwȧl), *a.* [4] **1.** Not equal; not of the same size, quantity, strength, talents, age, station, etc. **2.** Ill-balanced or ill-matched. **3.** Not uniform; irregular; uneven. **4.** Not adequate or sufficient; — with *to.* — **-ly,** *adv.* [8].

un-e′qualed (-kwȧld), *a.* [4, 7] Not equaled; unmatched; unparalleled; unrivaled; surpassing.

un′e-quiv′o-cal (ŭn′ē-kwĭv′ō-kȧl), *a.* [4] Not equivocal; clear; sincere; plain.

un-e′ven (ŭn-ē′v'n), *a.* [3] **1.** Not even; not level; not uniform; rough. **2.** Not equal; not of equal length. **3.** Not divisible by two without a remainder; odd. — **-ly,** *adv.* [8] — **-ness,** *n.* [8].

un′ex-am′pled (ŭn′ĕg-zȧm′p'ld; -zȧm′p'ld), *a.* [4] Having no example or similar case; unprecedented.

un′ex-cep′tion-a-ble (ŭn′ĕk-sĕp′shŭn-ȧ-b'l), *a.*

[4] Not liable to any exception or objection; beyond reproach. — **-ble-ness,** *n.* [8] — **-a-bly,** *adv.*

un′ex-pect′ed (-ĕks-pĕk′tĕd), *a.* [4] Not expected; sudden. — **-ly,** *adv.* [8] — **-ness,** *n.* [8].

un-fail′ing (ŭn-fāl′ĭng), *a.* [4] Not failing; not liable to fail; inexhaustible; sure. — **-ly,** *adv.* [8].

un-fair′ (-fâr′), *a.* [3] Not fair; disingenuous; dishonest; unjust. — **-ly,** *adv.* [8] — **-ness,** *n.* [8].

un-faith′ful (ŭn-fāth′fŏŏl), *a.* [4] **1.** Not faithful; not observant of promises, duty, etc. **2.** Inaccurate; untrustworthy. — **un-faith′ful-ly,** *adv.* [8] — **un-faith′ful-ness,** *n.* [8].

un-fas′ten (-fȧs′'n), *v. t. & i.* To loose.

un-fa′vor-a-ble (-fā′vẽr-ȧ-b'l), *a.* [4, 5] Not favorable; not propitious; adverse.

un-feel′ing (-fēl′ĭng), *a.* [4] **1.** Destitute of feeling; insensible; insensate. **2.** Cruel; hardhearted. — **-ly,** *adv.* [8] — **-ness,** *n.* [8].

un-feigned′ (-fānd′), *a.* [4] Not feigned; sincere.

un-fet′ter (-fĕt′ẽr), *v. t.* To loose from fetters or from restraint. [complete; imperfect.

un-fin′ished (-fĭn′ĭsht), *a.* [4] Not finished; in-

un-fit′ (-fĭt′), *v. t.; -FIT′TED ; -FIT′TING.* To disable; incapacitate; disqualify.

un-fledged′ (-flĕjd′), *a.* [4] Not fledged; hence, not fully developed; immature.

un-fold′ (-fōld′), *v. t. & i.* **1.** To open the folds of; expand; open. **2.** To lay open to view; disclose.

un-for′tu-nate (-fôr′tụ̇-nȧt), *a.* [4] Not fortunate; unsuccessful; attended with misfortune. — *n.* An unfortunate person. — **-ly,** *adv.* [8].

un-found′ed (-foun′dĕd), *a.* [4] **1.** Not founded or established. **2.** Having no foundation; baseless.

un-friend′ly (-frĕnd′lĭ), *a.* [3] **1.** Hostile. **2.** Not favorable. — **un-friend′li-ness,** *n.* [8].

un-frock′ (-frŏk′), *v. t.* To deprive of a frock; hence, to deprive of priestly rank or privilege.

un-furl′ (-fûrl′), *v. t. & i.* To loose from a furled state; unfold.

un-gain′ly (-gān′lĭ), *a.* [3] Clumsy; uncouth. — *adv.* In an ungainly manner. — **un-gain′li-ness** (-lĭ-nĕs), *n.* [8]. [unbind.

un-gird′ (-gûrd′), *v. t.* To loose the girdle of ;

un-god′ly (-gŏd′lĭ), *a.* [3] Not godly; wicked; sinful. — **un-god′li-ness,** *n.* [8].

un-gov′ern-a-ble (-gŭv′ẽr-nȧ-b'l), *a.* [4] Not capable of being governed or restrained; unbridled.

un-gra′cious (-grā′shŭs), *a.* [4] **1.** Not gracious; uncivil; rude. **2.** Offensive; unpleasing.

un-grate′ful (-grāt′fŏŏl), *a.* [3] **1.** Not grateful; not thankful for favors. **2.** Unpleasing; disagreeable. — **-ly,** *adv.* [8] — **-ness,** *n.* [8].

un′guent (ŭn′gwĕnt), *n.* Lubricant or salve for sores, burns, etc.; ointment.

un′gu-late (ŭn′gụ̇-lāt), *n. Zoöl.* Any of a group (*Ungulata*) consisting of the hoofed mammals. They are mostly large, and nearly all eat plants only. — *a.* Hoofed; of or pertaining to the ungulates. [profane; unholy.

un-hal′lowed (ŭn-hăl′ōd), *a.* [4] Not consecrated;

un-hand′ (-hănd′), *v. t.* To loose from the hand.

un-hand′y (-hăn′dĭ), *a.* [3] Clumsy; awkward.

un-hap′py (-hăp′ĭ), *a.* [3] **1.** Not happy or fortunate; unlucky. **2.** Sad; sorrowful. **3.** Marked by infelicity; calamitous; inappropriate. — **un-hap′pi-ly** (-ĭ-lĭ), *adv.* [8] — **-pi-ness,** *n.* [8].

un-heard′ (-hûrd′), *a.* Not heard; not heeded.

un-hinge′ (-hĭnj′), *v. t.* [1] **1.** To take from the hinges. **2.** To displace. **3.** To render unstable.

un-hitch′ (-hĭch′), *v. t.* To free from being hitched.

un-ho′ly (-hō′lĭ), *a.* [3] Not holy; profane; impious. — **-ho′li-ly,** *adv.* [8] — **-li-ness,** *n.* [8].

un-hook′ (-hŏŏk′), *v. t. & i.* To loose, or become loosed, from a hook.

un-horse′ (-hôrs′), *v. t.* To throw from a horse.

u′ni-cel′lu-lar (ū′nĭ-sĕl′ū-lȧr), *a. Biol.* Having, or consisting of, a single cell.

u′ni-corn (ū′nĭ-kôrn), *n.* A fabulous animal with one horn.

u′ni-fi-ca′tion (-fĭ-kā′shŭn), *n.* A unifying; state of being unified.

u′ni-form (ū′nĭ-fôrm), *a.* [4] **1.** Having always the same form, manner, or degree; homogeneous. **2.** Of the same form with others; consonant; as, buildings of *uniform* style. — *n.* A dress of a particular style or fashion worn by persons in the same service, etc. — *v. t.* To clothe with a uniform. — **-ly,** *adv.* [8].

Unicorn, in British Royal Coat of Arms.

u-ni-form′i-ty (-fôr′mĭ-tĭ), *n.* Quality or state of being uniform.

u′ni-fy (ū′nĭ-fī), *v. t.* [2] To cause to be one or uniform; unite.

u′ni-lat′er-al (ū′nĭ-lăt′ẽr-ȧl), *a.* One-sided; being on, or affecting, but one side.

un′im-peach′a-ble (ŭn′ĭm-pēch′ȧ-b'l), *a.* [4] Not impeachable; not to be called in question.

un′ion (ūn′yŭn), *n.* **1.** Act of uniting two or more things into one; state of being so united; junction; combination. **2.** That which is united, or made one; something formed by combination or coalition; a confederation; as: **a** = TRADE-UNION, 1. **b** A device emblematic of union, used on a national flag or ensign. **4.** Any of various devices for connecting parts, as of a machine, of a pipe, etc.

un′ion-ism (-ĭz′m), *n.* Principle or sentiment of union.

un′ion-ist, *n.* One who advocates or promotes union.

un′ion-ize (-īz), *v. t.* [1] To cause to become a member of, or subject to the rules of, a trade-union.

union jack. *Naval.* A jack consisting of the union of the national ensign. See JACK.

u-nique′ (ū-nēk′), *a.* Being without a like or equal; single in kind or excellence; unequaled; sole. — **u-nique′ly,** *adv.* [8] — **ness,** *n.* [8].

u′ni-son (ū′nĭ-sŭn; -zŭn), *n.* **1.** Harmony; agreement; concord; union. **2.** *Music.* A identity in pitch. **b** State of sounding at the same pitch.

u′nit (ū′nĭt), *n.* **1.** A single thing or person, or a group taken as an individual member of a number of groups. **2.** a *Arith.* The least whole number; one. **b** An amount or quantity taken as a standard of measurement.

U′ni-ta′ri-an (ū′nĭ-tā′rĭ-ȧn), *n.* [*Also l. c.*] One who denies the doctrine of the Trinity, believing God to exist only in one person. — **U′ni-ta′ri-an-ism** (-ĭz′m), *n.*

u′ni-ta-ry (ū′nĭ-tȧ-rĭ), *a.* **1.** Of or pert. to a unit or units; relating to unity. **2.** Of the nature of a unit; not divided.

u-nite′ (ū-nīt′), *v. t.* [1] **1.** To put together so as to make one; combine; connect. **2.** To join by a legal or moral bond. — *v. i.* **1.** To become one; combine; coalesce; grow together. **2.** To join in an act.

u′ni-ty (ū′nĭ-tĭ), *n.; pl.* **-TIES** (-tĭz). **1.** State of being one; oneness. **2.** Concord; harmony. **3.** *Math.* Any definite quantity, or aggregate of quantities taken as one, or for which 1 is made to stand in calculation.

u′ni-valve (ū′nĭ-vălv), *n. Zoöl.* A mollusk shell of one piece; also, any mollusk with such a shell; specifically, any gastropod. — *a.* Having one valve only, as a gastropod shell.

u′ni-ver′sal (ū′nĭ-vûr′sȧl), *a.* [4] **1.** Of or pertaining to the universe; general. **2.** Constituting, or considered as, a whole; entire. — **universal coupling. u. joint,** *Mach.,* any joint or coupling permitting swiveling or turning at any angle within certain limits.

U′ni-ver′sal-ism (-ĭz′m), *n.* The doctrine or belief that all men will eventually be saved, or restored to holiness and happiness.

Universal Joint.

U′ni-ver′sal-ist (-ĭst), *n.* One who believes in Universalism.

u′ni-ver-sal′i-ty (-vẽr-săl′ĭ-tĭ), *n.; pl.* **-TIES** (-tĭz). Quality or state of being universal.

u′ni-ver′sal-ly, *adv.* In a universal manner.

u′ni-verse (ū′nĭ-vûrs), *n.* All created things as constituting one system; the world; creation.

u′ni-ver′si-ty (ū′nĭ-vûr′sĭ-tĭ), *n.; pl.* **-TIES** (-tĭz). An institution for teaching and study in the higher branches of learning.

un-just′ (ŭn-jŭst′), *a.* [4] Contrary to justice; wrongful. — **-ly,** *adv.* [8] — **-ness,** *n.* [8].

un-kempt′ (-kĕmpt′), *a.* [4] Not combed; disheveled; hence, rough. — **un-kempt′ness,** *n.* [8].

un-kind′ (-kīnd′), *a.* [3] Wanting in kindness; cruel; harsh. — **-ly,** *adv.* [8] — **-ness,** *n.* [8].

un-lace′ (-lās′), *v. t.* [1] To loose, open, or unfasten by undoing or loosening a lacing.

un-law′ful (-lô′fŏŏl), *a.* [4] **1.** Not lawful; contrary to law. **2.** Illegitimate. — **un-law′ful-ly,** *adv.* [8] — **un-law′ful-ness,** *n.* [8].

un-learn′ (-lûrn′), *v. t.* To forget (what has been learned); also, to learn the contrary of.

un-learn′ed (-lûr′nĕd), *a.* [4] **1.** Not learned; illiterate. **2.** (*pron.* -lûrnd′) Not gained by study; not known. **3.** Not exhibiting learning.

un-less′ (-lĕs′), *conj.* If not; supposing that not; if it be not; were it not that. [illiterate.

un-let′tered (ŭn-lĕt′ẽrd), *a.* [4] Not lettered;

un-like′ (-līk′), *a.* [4] Not like; dissimilar; diverse.

un-like′ly, *a.* [3] **1.** Not likely; improbable. **2.** Not having prospect of success; likely to fail.

un-lim′ber (-lĭm′bẽr), *v. t. & i.* To detach the limber from (a gun).

un-lim′it-ed (ŭn lĭm′ĭ-tĕd), *a.* [4] **1.** Not limited; unrestricted. **2.** Undefined; indefinite.

un-load′ (-lōd′), *v. t.* **1.** To take the load or cargo from. **2.** Fig., to relieve from anything onerous. **3.** To remove or discharge, as a cargo.

un-lock' (ŭn-lŏk'), *v. t.* **1.** To unfasten, as what is locked. **2.** To open; undo; hence, to disclose.

un-loose' (-lōōs'), *v. t. & i.;* -LOOSED' (-lōōst'); -LOOS'ING. To loosen.

un-loos'en (-'n), *v. t.* To loosen.

un-luck'y (-lŭk'ĭ), *a.* [3] **1.** Not lucky; unfortunate. **2.** Bringing bad luck; inauspicious. — **un-luck'i-ly** (-ĭ-lĭ), *adv.* [8] — **-i-ness,** *n.* [8].

un-make' (-māk'), *v. t.;* for prin. parts see MAKE. To deprive of being; uncreate.

un-man' (-măn'), *v. t.;* for prin. parts see MAN. To deprive of manly courage; make womanish.

un-man'ner-ly (-măn'ẽr-lĭ), *a.* [4] Not mannerly; rude. — *adv.* Uncivilly. — **-li-ness** (-lĭ-nĕs), *n.*

un-mask' (-măsk'), *v. t.* To strip of a mask or disguise; expose. — *v. i.* To put off a mask.

un-mean'ing (-mēn'ĭng), *a.* [4] **1.** Having no meaning. **2.** Senseless; expressionless.

un-mer'ci-ful (-mûr'sĭ-fōōl), *a.* [4] Not merciful; cruel. — **-ly,** *adv.* [8] — **-ness,** *n.* [8].

un'mis-tak'a-ble (ŭn'mĭs-tāk'á-b'l), *a.* [4] Not mistakable; clear; evident. — **-a-bly,** *adv.* [8].

un-nat'u-ral (-năt'ŭ-răl), *a.* [4] Not natural; contrary to nature. — **-ly,** *adv.* — **-ness,** *n.* [8].

un-nec'es-sa-ry (-nĕs'ē-sā-rĭ), *a.* Not necessary; useless; needless. — **-sa-ri-ly** (-rĭ-lĭ), *adv.* [8].

un-nerve' (-nûrv'), *v. t.* [1] To deprive of nerve, force, strength, etc. [innumerable.

un-num'bered (-nŭm'bẽrd), *a.* Not numbered;

un-pack' (ŭn-păk'), *v. t.* To separate and remove, as things packed; open and remove the contents of.

un-par'al-leled (-păr'ă-lĕld), *a.* [4] Having no parallel, or equal; unequaled; unmatched.

un-par'lia-men'ta-ry (-pär'lĭ-mĕn'tá-rĭ), *a.* [4] Contrary to the practice of parliamentary usage.

un-pin' (-pĭn'), *v. t.;* -PINNED' (-pĭnd'); -PIN'NING. To remove the pin or pins from; unfasten.

un-pleas'ant (-plĕz'ănt), *a.* [3] Not pleasant; offensive. — **-ly,** *adv.* [8] — **-ness,** *n.* [8].

un-prec'e-dent-ed (-prĕs'ē-dĕn-tĕd), *a.* [4] Having no precedent; novel; new. — **-ly,** *adv.* [8].

un-prej'u-diced (-prĕj'ōō-dĭst), *a.* [4] Not prejudiced; as **: a** Impartial. **b** Unimpaired, as a right.

un'pre-med'i-tat'ed (ŭn'prē-mĕd'ĭ-tāt'ĕd), *a.* [4] Not premeditated. — **-ly,** *adv.* [8].

un-prin'ci-pled (ŭn-prĭn'sĭ-p'ld), *a.* [4] Being without principle, esp. right moral principle.

un-ques'tion-a-ble (-kwĕs'chŭn-á-b'l), *a.* [4] Not questionable. — **un-ques'tion-a-bly,** *adv.* [8].

un-qui'et (-kwī'ĕt), *a.* [3] Not quiet; disturbed; also, disturbing. — **un-qui'et-ly,** *adv.* [8].

un-rav'el (-răv''l), *v. t.* [7] **1.** To disentangle. **2.** To solve. — *v. i.* To become unraveled.

un-read'y (ŭn-rĕd'ĭ), *a.* [3] Not ready or prepared; not prompt; slow. — **-read'i-ness,** *n.* [8].

un-rea'son-a-ble (ŭn-rē'z'n-á-b'l), *a.* [4] Not reasonable. — **-ness,** *n.* [8] — **-a-bly,** *adv.* [8].

un're-served' (ŭn'rē-zûrvd'), *a.* [4] Not reserved; as **: a** Unrestricted. **b** Frank; open. — **un're-serv'ed-ly** (-zûr'vĕd-lĭ), *adv.* [8] — **-ed-ness,** *n.* [8].

un-rest' (-rĕst'), *n.* Want of rest or repose.

un-rid'dle (-rĭd''l), *v. t.* [1] To read the riddle of.

un-right'eous (-rī'chŭs), *a.* [4] **1.** Not righteous; wicked. **2.** Unjust. — **-ly,** *adv.* — **-ness,** *n.*

un-ri'valed (-rī'văld), *a.* [4, 7] Having no rival; without a competitor; peerless.

un-roll' (ŭn-rōl'), *v. t.* **1.** To open (what is rolled). **2.** Fig., to display. — *v. i.* To become unrolled.

un-rul'y (-rōōl'ĭ), *a.* [3] Not submissive to rule or restraint; turbulent. — **un-rul'i-ness,** *n.* [8].

un-sad'dle (-săd''l), *v. t.* [1] **1.** To strip of a saddle. **2.** To unhorse.

un-sa'vor-y (-sā'vẽr-ĭ), *a.* [5] **1.** Not savory; insipid; tasteless. **2.** Unpleasant to taste or smell; fig., morally offensive.

un-say' (-sā'), *v. t.;* for prin. parts see SAY. To recant, recall, or retract.

un-screw' (-skrōō'), *v. t.* To loose from screws; also, to loosen or withdraw (a screw) by turning it.

un-scru'pu-lous (-skrōō'pū-lŭs), *a.* [4] Not scrupulous; unprincipled. — **-ly,** *adv.* — **-ness,** *n.* [8].

un-seal' (-sēl'), *v. t.* To break or remove the seal of; to open, as what is sealed.

un-search'a-ble (-sûr'chá-b'l), *a.* [4] Not searchable; inscrutable.

un-sea'son-a-ble (-sē'z'n-á-b'l), *a.* [4] Not seasonable; untimely. — **-ble-ness,** *n.* — **-bly,** *adv.* [8].

un-seat' (-sēt'), *v. t.* To displace from one's seat; specif., to deprive of one's seat in a legislature.

un-seem'ly (-sēm'lĭ), *a.* [3] Not seemly; unbecoming; indecent. — *adv.* In an unseemly manner. — **un-seem'li-ness** (-lĭ-nĕs), *n.* [8].

un-seen' (-sēn'), *a.* Not seen; invisible.

un-set'tle (-sĕt''l), *v. t. & i.* [1] To move or loosen from a settled state; unfix; disorder.

un-sex' (-sĕks'), *v. t.* To deprive of sex, or of qualities becoming one's sex; — esp. of a woman.

un-shack'le (-shăk''l), *v. t.* [1] To loose from shackles or bands; set free from restraint.

un-sheathe' (-shēth'), *v. t.* [1] To take from the sheath, or scabbard, as a sword.

un-ship' (-shĭp'), *v. t.;* -SHIPPED' (-shĭpt'); -SHIP'-PING. **1.** To take out of a ship or vessel. **2.** To remove or detach, as an oar, from its proper place.

un-sift'ed (-sĭf'tĕd), *a.* Not sifted; hence, not critically examined; untried.

un-'kill'ful (-skĭl'fōōl), *a.* Also **un-skil'ful.** [4] Not skillful; awkward. — **-ly,** *adv.* — **-ness,** *n.* [8].

un'so-phis'ti-cat'ed (ŭn'sō-fĭs'tĭ-kāt'ĕd), *a.* [4] Not sophisticated. — **-ness,** *n.* [8].

un-sound' (-sound'), *a.* [3] Not sound; infirm. — **un-sound'ness,** *n.* [8].

un-speak'a-ble (-spēk'á-b'l), *a.* [4] Not speakable; inexpressible; unutterable; also, unspeakably bad. — **un-speak'a-bly,** *adv.* — **-a-ble-ness,** *n.*

un-spot'ted (ŭn-spŏt'ĕd), *a.* [4] Not spotted; free from spot or stain, esp. moral stain; immaculate.

un-sta'ble (-stā'b'l), *a.* [4] Not stable; unsteady.

un-string' (-strĭng'), *v. t.;* for prin. parts see STRING. **1.** To deprive of a string or strings; also, to take from a string. **2.** To loosen the string or strings of. **3.** To relax the tension of; loosen.

un-strung' (-strŭng'), *p. a.* [4] **1.** Deprived of a string or strings; also, having the strings loosened. **2.** Relaxed; weakened; as, *unstrung* nerves.

un'sub-stan'tial (ŭn'sŭb-stăn'shăl), *a.* [4] Wanting matter or substance; visionary; flimsy. — **-ti-al'i-ty** (-shĭ-ăl'ĭ-tĭ), *n.* — **-tial-ly,** *adv.* [8].

un-tan'gle (-tăng'g'l), *v. t.* [1] To loose from tangles or intricacy; disentangle.

un-think'ing (-thĭnk'ĭng), *a.* [4] **1.** Thoughtless. **2.** Not indicating thought. — **-ly,** *adv.* [8].

un-ti'dy (-tī'dĭ), *a.* [3] Careless; slovenly.

un-tie' (-tī'), *v. t. ;* for prin. parts see TIE. **1.** To loosen, as something knotted. **2.** To free from restraint. — *v. i.* To become untied.

un-til' (-tĭl'), *prep.* To ; up to ; till ; — in reference to time. — *conj.* As far as ; to the place or degree that ; esp., to the time that ; till.

un-time'ly (-tīm'lĭ), *a.* [4] Not timely ; premature. — *adv.* Inopportunely ; prematurely.

un-tir'ing (-tīr'ĭng), *a.* [4] Not becoming tired or exhausted ; unwearied.

un'to (ŭn'tōō), *prep.* To. *Now Archaic or Formal.*

un-told' (ŭn-tōld'), *a.* **1.** Not told ; not revealed. **2.** Not counted ; hence, vast.

un-to'ward (ŭn-tō'ẽrd ; -tôrd'), *a.* **1.** Froward ; perverse. **2.** Inconvenient ; vexatious ; unfortunate. — **un-to'ward-ly,** *adv.* — **ness,** *n.* [8].

un-tried' (-trīd'), *a.* [4] Not tried ; not tested.

un-true' (-trōō'), *a.* [3] Not true ; as : **a** False ; contrary to fact. **b** Not accordant with a standard. **c** Not faithful ; disloyal.

un-truth' (-trōōth'), *n.* **1.** Quality of being untrue. **2.** That which is untrue ; a falsehood.

un-used' (-ūzd'), *a.* [4] **1.** Not used. **2.** Unaccustomed.

un-u'su-al (ŭn-ū'zhŭ-ăl), *a.* [4] Not usual ; unaccustomed ; uncommon. — **un-u'su-al-ly,** *adv.* [8].

un-ut'ter-a-ble (-ŭt'ẽr-á-b'l), *a.* [4] Unspeakable. — **un-ut'ter-a-bil'i-ty,** *n.* — **a-bly,** *adv.* [8].

un-var'nished (-vär'nĭsht), *a.* [4] Not varnished ; hence, not embellished ; as, the *unvarnished* truth.

un-veil' (-vāl'), *v. t.* To remove a veil from ; reveal. — *v. i.* To remove a veil ; reveal one's self.

un-war'rant-a-ble (-wŏr'ăn-tá-b'l), *a.* [4] Not warrantable ; indefensible. — **a-bly,** *adv.* [8].

un-weave' (-wēv'), *v. t. ;* for prin. parts see WEAVE. To unfold ; ravel.

un-well' (-wĕl'), *a.* [4] Not well ; indisposed.

un-wield'y (-wēl'dĭ), *a.* [3] Not easily wielded ; unmanageable from bulk or weight. — **i-ness,** *n.*

un-will'ing (-wĭl'ĭng), *a.* [4] Not willing ; loath. — **un-will'ing-ly,** *adv.* [8] — **ness,** *n.* [8].

un-wind' (-wīnd'), *v. t. ;* UN-WOUND' (-wound') ; -WIND'ING. To wind off ; loose, as what is wound. — *v. i.* To be, or admit of being, unwound.

un-wise' (-wīz'), *a.* [3] Not wise ; injudicious ; foolish. — **wis'dom,** *n.* — **wise'ly,** *adv.* [8].

un-wit'ting (-wĭt'ĭng), *a.* [4] Not knowing ; unconscious ; ignorant. — **un-wit'ting-ly,** *adv.* [8].

un-wont'ed (-wŭn'tĕd), *a.* [4] **1.** Not wonted ; unaccustomed ; unused. **2.** Uncommon ; unusual ; rare. — **un-wont'ed-ly,** *adv.* [8] — **ness,** *n.* [8].

un-wor'thy (ŭn-wûr'thĭ), *a.* [3] Not worthy. — **un-wor'thi-ly** (-thĭ-lĭ), *adv.* — **thi-ness,** *n.*

un-writ'ten (-rĭt'n), *a.* **1.** Not written ; oral ; traditional. **2.** Containing no writing ; blank.

un-yoke' (-yōk'), *v. t. & i.* [1] **1.** To loose or become free from or as from a yoke. **2.** To part ; disjoin.

up (ŭp), *adv.* **1.** In or toward a higher position ; above ; aloft. **2.** At, toward, or to, any point thought of as higher. **3.** Into being or action ; in action ; as, to set *up* vibrations. **4.** Not short of, back of, less advanced than, away from, or the like. **5.** To or in a state of completion ; wholly ; quite ; as, to burn *up*. Also, to or at an end : as, his time is *up*. **6.** Aside ; by ; as, to lay *up* riches. — *prep.*

To a higher place on or along ; toward, near, or **at,** the top of. — *a.* Upward ; as, an *up* grade. — *n.* State of being up ; prosperity ; — in *ups and downs.*

up-braid' (ŭp-brād'), *v. t.* **1.** To reproach with something wrong or disgraceful. **2.** To chide.

up'growth' (ŭp'grōth'); *n.* Process of growing up ; development ; also, that which grows up.

up-heav'al (ŭp-hēv'ăl), *n.* An upheaving ; **state** of being upheaved.

up-heave' (-hēv'), *v. t.* [1] To heave or lift up from beneath ; raise. — *v. i.* To rise.

up-held' (-hĕld'), *pret. & p. p.* of UPHOLD.

up-hill' (-hĭl'), *adv.* Upwards on or as on a hill.

up'hill' (ŭp'hĭl'), *a.* [4] Ascending ; laborious.

up-hold' (ŭp-hōld'), *v. t.* **1.** To hold up ; raise. **2.** To keep erect ; support ; maintain. **3.** To **aid** by approval or encouragement ; back. — **-er,** *n.*

up-hol'ster (-hōl'stẽr), *v. t.* To furnish (rooms, furniture, etc.) with hangings, coverings, etc. — **up-hol'ster-er** (-ŭp-hōl'stẽr-ẽr), *n.*

up-hol'ster-y (-ĭ), *n. ; pl.* -TERIES (-ĭz). Furniture or interior fittings, as hangings, cushions, etc. [taining; maintenance.]

up'keep' (ŭp'kēp'), *n.* Act of keeping up, or main-

up'land (-lănd), *n.* High land ; ground elevated above the lowlands along rivers, near the sea, etc.

up-lift' (ŭp-lĭft'), *v. t.* To lift or raise aloft ; elevate.

up'lift' (ŭp'lĭft'), *a.* Elevation.

up-on' (ŭ-pŏn'), *prep.* On.

up'per (ŭp'ẽr), *a. ; comp.* of UP. Higher ; superior. — *n.* Vamp of a shoe.

up'per-most (-mōst), *a.* Highest in place, position, rank, power, or the like.

up-raise' (ŭp-rāz'), *v. t.* [1] To raise up.

up-rear' (-rēr'), *v. t.* To rear up ; raise ; erect.

up'right' (ŭp'rīt'), *a.* [4] **1.** Erect in position ; vertical, or nearly so. **2.** Having rectitude ; honest ; just. — *n.* Something standing upright, as **a** timber. — **-ly,** *adv.* — **ness,** *n.* [8].

up-rise' (ŭp-rīz'), *v. i. ;* for prin. parts see RISE. **1.** To rise, as from sleep. **2.** To swell up, as **a** river. **3.** To have an upward inclination ; ascend.

up-ris'ing (ŭp-rīz'ĭng), *n.* **1.** Act of rising ; also, a steep place ; ascent. **2.** An insurrection.

up'roar' (ŭp'rōr'), *n.* Great tumult ; clamor.

up-roar'i-ous (ŭp-rōr'ĭ-ŭs), *a.* [4] Making, or accompanied by, uproar, or noise and tumult. — **up-roar'i-ous-ly,** *adv.* [8] — **ness,** *n.* [8].

up-root' (-rōōt'), *v. t.* To tear up by the roots.

up-set' (-sĕt'), *v. t. ; pret. & p. p.* UP-SET' or -SET'-TED ; *p. pr. & vb. n.* -SET'TING. **1.** To overturn ; overthrow. **2.** To discompose ; disturb. *Colloq.* — *v. i.* To become upset.

up'set', *n.* Act of upsetting ; state of being upset.

up'shot' (-shŏt'), *n.* Final issue ; conclusion.

up'side' (-sīd'), *n.* The upper side or part. — **up**side down, with the upper part undermost ; hence, in confusion ; topsy-turvy.

up-stairs' (ŭp-stârz'), *adv.* Up the stairs ; in or toward an upper story.

up'stairs' (ŭp'stârz'), *a.* Being above stairs. — *n.* The part above the ground story.

up-start' (ŭp-stärt'), *v. i.* To start up.

up'start' (ŭp'stärt'), *n.* A person who has risen suddenly, esp. when presuming on his success. — *a.* Suddenly raised to prominence.

---

chair; go; sing, iŋk; then, thin; nature, verdure; yet; zh = z in azure. Numbers refer to §§ in the Special Notes which, with Abbreviations, Signs, etc., precede the Vocabulary.

up-turn' (ŭp-tûrn'), *v. t. & i.* To turn up.

up'ward (ŭp'wẽrd), *adv.* Also **up'wards** (-wẽrdz). **1.** In a direction from lower to higher. **2.** Toward the source or origin. **3.** Toward a higher, or greater, age, degree, etc. **4.** Indefinitely more; over. — *a.* Directed upward.

u-ra'ni-um (ū-rā'nĭ-ŭm), *n. Chem.* A hard, nickel-white metal. It is radioactive. See RADIUM.

U'ra-nus (ū'rȧ-nŭs), *n. Astron.* A planet between Saturn and Neptune.

ur'ban (ûr'bȧn), *a.* Of or pert. to a city or town.

ur-bane' (ûr-bān'), *a.* [3] Courteous; polite; suave. — **ur-bane'ly**, *adv.* [8]. [bane.

ur-ban'i-ty (-băn'ĭ-tĭ), *n.* Quality of being urbane.

ur'chin (ûr'chĭn), *n.* A pert or roguish child, esp. such a boy; boy; youngster.

urge (ûrj), *v. t.* [1] **1.** To force onward; press; push; drive. **2.** To press the mind or will of; importune. **3.** To present in an earnest or pressing manner. — *v. i.* To declare or press earnestly a statement, argument, or the like.

ur'gen-cy (ûr'jĕn-sĭ), *n.* Quality of being urgent.

ur'gent (ûr'jĕnt), *a.* [4] Urging; pressing; calling for immediate attention. — **ly**, *adv.* [8].

u'ri-nal (ū'rĭ-nȧl), *n.* A vessel for urine; place for urinating.

u'ri-na-ry (ū'rĭ-nȧ-rĭ), *a.* Of or pertaining to urine or the organs for excreting and removing it. — *n.; pl.* -RIES (-rĭz). A urinal.

u'ri-nate (-nāt), *v. i.* [1] To discharge urine.

u'rine (ū'rĭn), *n. Physiology.* A fluid excretion from the kidneys. [or pedestal.

urn (ûrn), *n.* A vessel, usually a vase with a foot

Ur'sa (ûr'sȧ), *n. Astron.* Ursa Major or Ursa Minor (see below). — **Ursa Major**, the Great Bear, a northern constellation containing the stars which form the *Dipper*, including the *Pointers*. — **U. Minor**, the Little Bear (or Little Dipper), the constellation including the North Star.

ur'sine (ûr'sĭn; -sĭn), *a.* Pert. to, or like, a bear.

us (ŭs), *pron.* Objective case of *we*.

us'a-ble (ūz'ȧ-b'l), *a.* [4] That can be used. — **us'a-ble-ness**, *n.* [8].

us'age (ūz'ăj; ūs'ăj), *n.* **1.** Act or mode of using; treatment. **2.** Long-continued practice. **3.** Customary use or employment.

use (ūz), *v. t.* [1] **1.** To make use of; employ. **2.** To practice, esp. customarily. **3.** To behave toward; treat. **4.** To accustom; inure; — chiefly in p. p. — *v. i.* To be wont or accustomed; — now obsolete or archaic in the present tense.

use (ūs), *n.* **1.** Act of employing anything; employment. **2.** Occasion or need to employ. **3.** Utility; advantage. **4.** Continued practice; usage.

use'ful (ūs'fŏŏl), *a.* [4] Full of use; serviceable; having utility; advantageous. — **ly**, *adv.* [8].

use'ful-ness (-nĕs), *n.* Quality of being useful.

use'less (-lĕs), *a.* [4] Being of no use; unserviceable; ineffectual. — **ly**, *adv.* [8] — **ness**, *n.* [8].

us'er (ūz'ẽr), *n.* One that uses.

ush'er (ŭsh'ẽr), *n.* A doorkeeper; hence, one who escorts persons to seats in a church, theater, etc. — *v. t.* To announce; escort; show in.

u'su-al (ū'zhŭ-ăl), *a.* [4] Ordinary, common. — **ly**, *adv.* [8] — **ness**, *n.* [8].

u'su-rer (ū'zhŭ-rẽr), *n.* One who lends money at a usurious rate of interest.

u-su'ri-ous (ū-zū'rĭ-ŭs; ū-zhŏŏ'-), *a.* [4] Taking, involving, or practicing, usury.

u-surp' (ū-zûrp'), *v. t.* To seize and keep by force or without right. — *v. i.* To be, or act as, a usurper; encroach. — **u'sur-pa'tion** (ū'zŭr-pā'shŭn), *n.* — **u-surp'er** (ū-zûr'pẽr), *n.* [8].

u'su-ry (ū'zhŭ-rĭ), *n.* **1.** An exorbitant rate of interest; esp., *Law*, interest in excess of a legal rate. **2.** The taking, or practice of taking, usury.

u-ten'sil (ū-tĕn's'l), *n.* An instrument or vessel, esp. one used in a kitchen or dairy.

u'ter-ine (ū'tẽr-ĭn), *a.* Of or pert. to the uterus.

u'ter-us (-ŭs), *n.; L. pl.* UTERI (-ī). In female mammals, an organ for containing, and usually for nourishing, the young before birth; the womb.

u-til'i-ta'ri-an (ū-tĭl'ĭ-tā'rĭ-ăn), *a.* [4] Of, pertaining to, or consisting in, utility.

u-til'i-ty (ū-tĭl'ĭ-tĭ), *n.; pl.* -TIES (-tĭz). **1.** Quality or state of being useful. **2.** A useful thing.

u'til-ize (ū'tĭl-īz), *v. t.* [1] To make useful; make use of. — **u'til-i-za'tion** (-ĭ-zā'shŭn), *n.*

ut'most (ŭt'mōst), *a.* **1.** Situated at the farthest point or extremity; most distant; extreme; last. **2.** Of the greatest or highest degree, quantity, etc. — *n.* The most possible; farthest limit.

u-to'pi-a (ū-tō'pĭ-ȧ), *n.* A place or state of ideal or imaginary perfection. [tions.

u-to'pi-an (-ȧn), *a.* Involving imaginary perfec-

ut'ter (ŭt'ẽr), *a.* Complete; total; absolute.

ut'ter, *v. t.* **1.** To put in circulation, as money, esp. counterfeit notes or coins. **2.** To give expression to; speak. — **ut'ter-a-ble** (-ȧ-b'l), *a.* [8].

ut'ter-ance (-ăns), *n.* **1.** Act of uttering; esp., vocal expression. **2.** That which is uttered.

ut'ter-ly, *adv.* In an utter manner; fully; totally.

ut'ter-most (-mōst), *a. & n.* Utmost.

u'vu-la (ū'vū-lȧ), *n.* The pendent fleshy lobe in the middle of the soft palate.

ux-o'ri-ous (ŭk-sō'rĭ-ŭs; ĭg-zō'-), *a.* [4] Excessively or dotingly fond of, or submissive to, a wife. — **ux-o'ri-ous-ly**, *adv.* [8] — **ness**, *n.* [8].

V

va'can-cy (vā'kăn-sĭ), *n.; pl.* -CIES (-sĭz). **1.** Quality or state of being vacant; emptiness; also, idleness; listlessness. **2.** Vacant thing; as: **a** Empty space. **b** An unoccupied office or position.

va'cant (-kănt), *a.* [4] **1.** Without contents; empty. **2.** Free from business or care; unemployed; as, *vacant* hours. **3.** Not occupied by an incumbent, etc. **4.** Empty of thought or reflection; as, a *vacant* stare. — **ly**, *adv.* [8].

va'cate (vā'kāt), *v. t.* [1] **1.** To make vacant; leave empty. **2.** To annul; make void. — *v. i.* To vacate anything; *Colloq.*, to leave.

va-ca'tion (vȧ-kā'shŭn), *n.* **1.** Act of vacating. **2.** Intermission of employment, etc.; holiday.

āle, senâte, câre, ăm, *ă*ccount, ärm, ȧsk, sofȧ; ēve, ĕvent, ēnd, recĕnt, makẽr; īce, ĭll; ōld, ŏbey, ôrb, ŏdd, sŏft, cŏnnect; ūse, ŭnite, ûrn, ŭp, circŭs; fŏŏd, fŏŏt; out, oil;

vac'ci-nate (văk'sĭ-nāt), v. t. [1] To inoculate with a vaccine, as that of cowpox, to prevent an attack of smallpox. — **vac'ci-na'tion**, n.

vac'cine (văk'sĭn; -sēn), a. **1.** Pertaining to, or derived from, cows. **2.** Pertaining to cowpox. — n. **1.** The virus of cowpox, used in vaccination. **2.** Any substance for preventive inoculation.

vac'il-late (văs'ĭ-lāt), v. i. [1] To hesitate or waver in mind, as between two opinions; waver.

vac'il-la'tion (-lā'shŭn), n. A vacillating.

va-cu'i-ty (vă-kū'ĭ-tĭ), n.; pl. -TIES (-tĭz). **1.** Emptiness; a void; vacuum. **2.** Vacancy of mind.

vac'u-ous (văk'ū-ŭs), a. [4] Empty; void; vacant.

vac'u-um (-ŭm), n.; pl. E. -UUMS (-ŭmz), L. -UA (-ȧ). A space entirely devoid of matter; hence, a space artificially exhausted to a high degree.

vacuum tube. A sealed tube containing highly rarefied air or other gas, for examination of the electric discharge between metallic electrodes. Special vacu..n tubes, resembling incandescent lamps, are used in radio, as for detectors.

vag'a-bond (văg'ȧ-bŏnd), a. [4] **1.** Moving from place to place without any settled home; leading a wandering life. **2.** Of, pertaining to, or characteristic of, a vagabond; as, a vagabond life. — n. One who wanders about with no fixed dwelling; vagrant; tramp; Colloq., a worthless person; rascal.

vag'a-bond'age (-bŏn'dăj), n. State of a vagabond; idle wandering.

va-ga'ry (vă-gā'rĭ), n.; pl. -RIES (-rĭz). A whim.

va'gran-cy (vā'grăn-sĭ), n. State or fact of being a vagrant; vagabondage.

va'grant (-grănt), a. [4] **1.** Moving about without certain object; wandering without settled habitation. **2.** Of, pert. to, or characteristic of, a vagrant; vagabond; erratic; as, a vagrant nature. — n. A vagabond. — **ly**, adv. [8].

vague (văg), a. [3] **1.** Not clearly defined, grasped, etc.; hazy; as, a vague idea. **2.** Not confirmed; uncertain. **3.** Not thinking, seeing, etc., clearly. — **vague'ly**, adv. — **ness**, n. [8].

vain (văn), a. [3] **1.** Without value or importance; empty; idle; trifling. **2.** Without force or efficacy; futile; as, a vain attempt. **3.** Proud of petty things, or of trifling attainments; conceited. **4.** Showy; ostentatious.

vain'glo'ri-ous (văn'glō'rĭ-ŭs), a. [4] Boastful. — **vain'glo'ri-ous-ly**, adv. [8] — **ness**, n. [8].

vain'glo'ry (-rĭ), n. Excessive vanity over one's own performances, attainments, etc.

vain'ly (-lĭ), adv. In a vain or futile manner.

vale (vāl), n. A valley. Chiefly Poetic.

val'e-dic'tion (văl'ē-dĭk'shŭn), n. A farewell.

val'e-dic-to'ri-an (-dĭk-tō'rĭ-ăn), n. One who makes a valedictory address; esp., in American colleges, etc., the student of the graduating class who delivers the valedictory at commencement.

val'e-dic'to-ry (-dĭk'tō-rĭ), a. Bidding farewell; suitable or designed for an occasion of leave-taking. — n.; pl. -RIES (-rĭz). A valedictory oration.

va'lence (vā'lĕns), n. Chem. The degree of combining power of an element (or radical).

va'len-cy (vā'lĕn-sĭ), n.; pl. -CIES. Valence.

val'en-tine (văl'ĕn-tīn), n. A sweetheart chosen on St. Valentine's Day; also, a sentimental or a comic missive sent for St. Valentine's Day.

va-le'ri-an (vă-lē'rĭ-ăn), n. Any of a large genus of perennial herbs, the dried rootstock and roots of one species of which constitute a drug used as a mild tonic and stimulant; also, the drug.

val'et (văl'ĕt ; văl'ā), n. A manservant who attends a man, taking care of his clothes, etc.

val'e-tu'di-na'ri-an (văl'ē-tū'dĭ-nā'rĭ-ăn), a. [4] Of infirm health; sickly. — n. An invalid.

val'e-tu'di-na-ry (-tū'dĭ-nă-rĭ), a. [4] Infirm ; sickly; valetudinarian. — n. A valetudinarian.

val'iant (văl'yănt), a. [4] **1.** Intrepid ; brave ; courageous. **2.** Performed with valor or bravery ; heroic. — **val'iant-ly**, adv. [8] — **ness**, n. [8].

val'id (văl'ĭd), a. [4] **1.** Founded on truth or fact; sound; as, a valid argument. **2.** Law. Having legal force or authority.

val'i-date (văl'ĭ-dāt), v. t. [1] To render valid.

va-lid'i-ty (vă-lĭd'ĭ-tĭ), n. Quality or state of being valid.

val'id-ly (văl'ĭd-lĭ), adv. In a valid manner.

va-lise' (vă-lēs'), n. Traveling bag ; hand bag.

val'ley (văl'ĭ), n. ; pl. -LEYS (-ĭz). A depression, usually with outlet, between hills or mountains.

val'or (văl'ēr), n. [5] Strength of mind in braving danger ; bravery ; courage, esp. in fighting.

val'or-ous (-ŭs), a. [4] Possessing, exhibiting, or characteristic of, valor ; brave. — **ly**, adv. [8].

val'u-a-ble (-ū-ȧ-b'l), a. [4] **1.** Commanding or worth a good price. **2.** Of considerable worth in any respect; precious; as, a valuable friend. — n. A possession or thing of value, esp. a small thing, as a jewel ; — usually in pl.

val'u-a'tion (-ā'shŭn), n. **1.** Act of valuing ; appraisement. **2.** Estimated value.

val'ue (văl'ū), n. **1.** Worth ; excellence ; utility. **2. a** Purchasing power. **b** Proper, or legitimate, price. **3.** Precise signification ; import. **4.** Music. Relative length or duration of a tone or note. **5.** Art. **a** That property of a color by which it is distinguished as light or dark ; also, a neutral tone. **b** The relation of one part or detail in a picture to another with respect to light and shade. **6.** A valuable consideration. — v. t. [1] **1.** To estimate the value of ; appraise. **2.** To regard highly ; esteem ; prize. — **val'u-er**, n. [8].

valve (vălv), n. **1.** A door ; esp., one of a pair of folding doors. **2.** Mech. Any device for regulating or directing the flow of a liquid, gas, etc. **3.** Anat. A structure which temporarily closes a passage or opening, or permits flow in one direction only. **4.** One of the distinct pieces, usually hinged, composing the shell of clams, oysters, etc.

val'vu-lar (văl'vū-lár), a. **1.** Of or pertaining to a valve or valves. **2.** Containing, or opening by, valves ; serving as a valve.

vamp (vămp), n. **1.** The part of a shoe above the sole and welt, and in front of the ankle seam ; an upper. **2.** Any piece added to an old thing to make it look new. — v. t. To provide with a new vamp; patch ; —often with up. — **er**, n. [8].

vam'pire (văm'pīr), n. **1.** A soul or reanimated body of a dead person superstitiously believed to suck the blood of sleeping persons. **2.** One who preys on others; extortioner; bloodsucker. **3.** Also **vampire bat.** Any of certain bats popularly (in most cases incorrectly) supposed to suck blood.

van(văn), *n.* The front of an army, fleet, etc. ; the front or those at the front of any movement.

van, *n.* A large covered wagon.

va-na'di-um (vȧ-nā'dĭ-ŭm), *n.* A silver-white metal found in small quantities combined in various ores and clays. It is an element.

Van'dal (văn'dăl), *n.* [*Often l. c.*] One who willfully destroys or mars anything beautiful, as a work of art. — **van'dal-ism** (-ĭz'm), *n.*

vane (vān), *n.* **1.** A movable contrivance attached to an elevated object to show which way the wind blows ; weathercock. **2.** Anything flat attached to an axis to be moved by the wind ; as, the *vane* of a windmill.

van'guard (văn'gärd'), *n. Mil.* The troops who march in front of an army ; the van, or forefront.

va-nil'la (vȧ-nĭl'ȧ), *n.* **1.** *Bot.* Any of a genus (*Vanilla*) of tropical American climbing plants of the orchid family. **2. a** The long podlike capsules of any of various species of Vanilla. **b** A flavoring extract made from the capsules.

van'ish (văn'ĭsh), *v. i.* **1.** To become invisible ; disappear. **2.** To be lost ; pass away.

van'i-ty (-ĭ-tĭ), *n. ; pl.* -TIES (-tĭz). **1.** Quality or state of being vain, or empty ; emptiness ; futility. **2.** An empty pride in one's personal appearance, attainments, etc. ; conceit. **3.** That which is vain or unsubstantial ; empty pleasure ; idle show.

van'quish (văn'kwĭsh), *v. t.* **1.** To conquer or subdue in battle ; overpower, as an enemy. **2.** To defeat in any contest, as in argument ; get the better of. — **-a-ble**, *a.* [8] — **-er**, *n.* [8].

van'tage (văn'tăj), *n.* Superior situation or opportunity ; advantage ; vantage ground.

vantage ground. Superiority of state or place.

vap'id (văp'ĭd), *a.* [4] Having lost its life and spirit ; flat ; dull ; spiritless. — **vap'id-ly**, *adv.* [8] — **vap'id-ness**, *n.* [8].

va-pid'i-ty (vȧ-pĭd'ĭ-tĭ), *n.* Vapid quality or state.

va'por (vā'pẽr), *n.* [5] **1.** Any visible diffused substance floating in the air, as smoke, fog, etc. **2.** *Physics.* Any substance in the gaseous state, thought of with some reference to the liquid or solid form. **3.** Something unsubstantial or transitory. — *v. i.* To pass off in vapor ; emit vapor or fumes. — **va'por-er** (-ẽr), *n.* [5, 8].

va'por-ish (vā'pẽr-ĭsh), *a.* [4, 5] Full of vapors ; vaporous. — **va'por-ish-ness**, *n.*

va'por-i-za'tion (vā'pẽr-ĭ-zā'shŭn, văp'ŏ-rĭ-), *n.* A vaporizing ; state of being vaporized.

va'por-ize (vā'pẽr-īz), *v. t. & i.* [1] To convert or change into vapor. — **-iz'er** (-īz'ẽr), *n.* [8].

va'por-ous (vā'pẽr-ŭs), *a.* [4] **1.** Having the form or nature of vapor. **2.** Full of vapors, or exhalations. **3.** Producing vapors ; flatulent. **4.** Unreal ; vain. — **-ly**, *adv.* [8] — **-ness**, *n.* [8].

va'por-y (vā'pẽr-ĭ), *a.* [4, 5] Full of, or of the nature of, a vapor or vapors ; vaporous.

¶ **va-que'ro** (vä-kā'rō), *n. ; pl.* -ROS (-rōz ; *Sp.* -rōs). [Sp.] A herdsman ; cowboy.

va'ri-a-bil'i-ty (vā'rĭ-ȧ-bĭl'ĭ-tĭ), *n.* Quality or state of being variable.

va'ri-a-ble (vā'rĭ-ȧ-b'l), *a.* [4] **1.** Having the capacity or characteristic of varying ; changeable. **2.** Liable to vary ; fickle ; unsteady. — *n.* **1.** That which is variable. **2.** *Math.* A quantity that may

increase or decrease, or the symbol for it. — **-ble-ness**, *n.* [8] — **-bly**, *adv.* [8].

va'ri-ance (-ȧns), *n.* **1.** Act of varying ; state of being variant ; variation. **2.** Difference that produces dispute or controversy ; disagreement.

va'ri-ant (-ȧnt), *a.* [4] Varying in form, etc., from something of the same general kind ; different. — *n.* Something that differs in form from another thing, though essentially the same. Abbr. *Var.*

va'ri-a'tion (-ā'shŭn), *n.* **1.** Act of varying ; a partial change ; modification. **2.** Extent or degree to which a thing varies. **3.** *Gram.* Inflection. **4.** *Music.* Repetition of a theme or melody with embellishments or modifications. — **va'ri-a'tion-al** (-ăl), *a.*

va'ri-col'ored (vā'rĭ-kŭl'ẽrd), *a.* [4, 5] Having various colors. [as a vein.

var'i-cose (văr'ĭ-kōs), *a.* [4] Irregularly swollen,

va'ried (vā'rĭd), *p. a.* [4] **1.** Changed ; altered. **2.** Various ; diverse. **3.** Variegated.

va'ri-e-gate (vā'rĭ-ē-gāt), *v. t.* [1] To diversify in external appearance, esp. with different colors.

va'ri-e-ga'tion (-gā'shŭn), *n.* Diversity of colors.

va-ri'e-tal (vȧ-rī'ē-tăl), *a.* Pert. to a variety.

va-ri'e-ty (-tĭ), *n. ; pl.* -TIES (-tĭz). **1.** State or quality of being various or varied ; diversity. **2.** That which is various ; as : **a** A collection of different things. **b** Something differing from others of the same general kind ; sort. **c** A group of animals or plants distinguished from similar groups only by characters too slight to constitute it a species.

va-ri'o-la (vȧ-rī'ō-lȧ), *n.* The smallpox.

va'ri-o-loid (vā'rĭ-ō-loid ; văr'ĭ-), *a.* Resembling smallpox ; pertaining to varioloid. — *n.* A modified mild form of smallpox, or variola.

va'ri-ous (vā'rĭ-ŭs), *a.* **1.** Different ; diverse ; several ; manifold. **2.** Changeable ; uncertain. **3.** Having varied characteristics ; many-sided ; also, variegated ; diversified. — **-ly**, *adv.* [8] — **-ness**, *n.* [8].

var'let (vär'lĕt), *n.* A low fellow ; scoundrel ; knave. *Archaic.*

var'nish (-nĭsh), *v. t.* **1.** To lay varnish on ; cover with varnish. **2.** To gloss over. — *n.* **1.** A sticky liquid which when spread becomes a hard lustrous coating. **2.** That which resembles varnish by its gloss. **3.** Outside show ; gloss. — **-er**, *n.* [8].

va'ry (vā'rĭ), *v. t.* [2] **1.** To alter in form, appearance, substance, position, etc.; modify. **2.** To make different, or change from one another. **3.** To diversify ; as, to *vary* one's diet. **4.** *Music.* To embellish with variations. — *v. i.* **1.** To alter or be altered ; be modified. **2.** To differ ; be different, unlike, or diverse. **3.** To deviate ; swerve. **4.** To alternate.

vas'cu-lar (văs'kŭ-lȧr), *a. Biol.* Of or pert. to a vessel or vessels for the conveyance of a fluid, as (in animals) blood or lymph, or (in plants) sap.

vase (vās ; vâz ; *or, esp. Brit.,* väz), *n.* A vessel, usually rounded, and of greater depth than width, chiefly ornamental.

vas'e-line (văs'ē-lĭn ; -lēn), *n.* A translucent, jellylike substance obtained as a residue in the purification of crude petroleum.

vas'sal (-ăl), *n.* **1.** *Early Law.* One who placed himself under the protection of another as his lord ;

later, a feudal tenant. **2.** A subject; servant; bondman. — *a.* [4] Like a vassal; servile.

vas'sal-age (-ǎj), *n.* State or relation of a vassal.

vast (vȧst), *a.* [3] Of great extent; immense; very great. — **-ly,** *adv.* [8] — **-ness,** *n.* [8].

vast'y (vȧs'tĬ), *a.* Vast; immense. *Archaic.*

vat (vǎt), *n.* A large vessel, cistern, or tub.

Vat'i-can (vǎt'Ĭ-kăn), *n.* **1.** The Pope's palace, at Rome, including museums, library, etc. **2.** The papal authority or government. Cf. QUIRINAL.

va-tic'i-nate (vȧ-tĬs'Ĭ-nāt), *v. i. & t.* [1] To prophesy; foretell. — **va-tic'i-na'tion** (-nā'shŭn), *n.*

vaude'ville (vōd'vĬl; *F.* vōd'vēl'), *n.* Entertainment consisting of successive separate performances of songs, dances, acrobatic feats, etc.

vault (vȯlt), *n.* **1.** An arched structure of masonry, usually forming a ceiling or roof, but sometimes carrying a separate roof, a floor, staircase, or the like. **2.** A room or space covered by a vault (def. 1), esp. when underground; a room, commonly of steel, for the safe-keeping of valuables. **3.** The sky. — *v. t.* To form or cover with a vault; arch.

vault, *n.* A leap or bound; esp. : **a** The leap of a horse; a curvet. **b** A leap made by aid of the hands or of a pole. — *v. i. & t.* To leap; spring, esp. by aid of the hands or a pole.

vault'er, *n.* One who vaults.

vaunt (vänt; vônt), *v. i.* To brag. — *v. t.* To boast of. — *n.* A boast; brag. — **-er,** *n.* [8] — **-ing-ly,** *adv.* [8].

veal (vēl), *n.* Calf's flesh used for food.

ve-dette' (vė-dĕt'), *n. Mil.* A mounted sentinel stationed in advance of the pickets.

veer (vēr), *v. i. & t.* To change direction; shift.

veg'e-ta-ble (vĕj'ė-tȧ-b'l), *a.* Of or pertaining to plants; having the nature of, or produced by, plants; consisting of plants. — *n.* A plant; in common usage, a plant cultivated for food.

veg'e-tal (-tǎl), *a.* Pertaining to vegetables, or the vegetable kingdom; vegetable.

veg'e-ta'ri-an (-tā'rĬ-ăn), *n.* One who holds that plants afford the only proper food for man. — *a.* Of or pert. to vegetarians; also, consisting wholly of vegetables. — **-ism** (-Ĭz'm), *n.*

veg'e-tate (vĕj'ė-tāt), *v. i.* [1] **1.** To grow after the fashion of plants. **2.** To lead a passive existence without exertion of body or mind.

veg'e-ta'tion (-tā'shŭn), *n.* **1.** Act or process of vegetating. **2.** Vegetable life; plants in general.

veg'e-ta-tive (vĕj'ė-tȧ-tĬv), *a.* **1.** Of or pertaining to, or capable of, vegetation; that vegetates. **2.** Having the power to produce growth in plants. — **veg'e-ta-tive-ly,** *adv.* [8] — **-ness,** *n.* [8].

ve'he-mence (vē'hė-mĕns; vē'ė-), *n.* Quality or state of being vehement.

ve'he-ment (-mĕnt), *a.* [4] **1.** Acting with great force; furious; violent. **2.** Very ardent, eager, or urgent; passionate. — **-ly,** *adv.* [8].

ve'hi-cle (vē'hĬ-k'l, vē'Ĭ-), *n.* **1.** That in or on which a thing is carried; a carriage. **2.** That which is used as the instrument of conveyance or communication; as: **a** *Pharm.* A substance in which medicine is taken. **b** *Paint.* Liquid medium, as oil, in which a pigment is applied.

ve-hic'u-lar (vė-hĬk'ů-lạr), *a.* Of or pertaining to a vehicle; also, serving as a vehicle.

veil (vāl), *n.* **1.** A fabric hung up, or spread out, to hide an object; curtain; esp., a piece of gauzy stuff worn to hide or protect the face. **2.** A cover; disguise; mask; pretense. — *v. t.* **1.** To cover with a veil. **2.** To cover; hide; mask.

veiled (vāld), *a.* Covered by a veil; hidden.

veil'ing, *n.* A veil; gauzy material, as for veils.

vein (vān), *n.* **1.** One of the system of tubular vessels which carry the blood to the heart. **2.** One of the radiating or branching ribs forming the framework of a plant or of an insect's wing. **3. a** A crack in rock filled by mineral matter. **b** A lode. **c** A bed; as, a *vein* of coal. **4.** A streak or wave appearing in wood, marble, etc. **5.** Anything distinctive considered as running through something else; a strain; as, a satirical *vein.* — *v. t.* To form, fill, or cover, with veins.

vein'ing, *n.* A system or pattern of veins.

vein'let, *n.* A small vein.

vein'y (vān'Ĭ), *a.* [3] Full of veins; veined.

veldt (fĕlt; vĕlt), *n.* In South Africa, a tract not forested or one thinly forested; grass country.

vel'lum (vĕl'ŭm), *n.* A fine parchment, usually of calfskin; hence, a vellum manuscript; loosely, a kind of paper or cotton cloth in imitation of vellum parchment.

ve-loc'i-pede (vė-lŏs'Ĭ-pēd), *n.* Any of various relatively light vehicles propelled by the rider or riders; esp., an early form of bicycle or tricycle.

ve-loc'i-ty (-Ĭ-tĬ), *n.; pl.* -TIES (-tĬz). Quickness of motion; rate of motion; swiftness; speed; celerity; rapidity; — chiefly of inanimate things.

ve-lours' (vė-lōōr'), *n.* Any of various textile fabrics having a pile like that of velvet.

ve'lum (vē'lŭm), *n.; pl.* VELA (-lȧ). A membrane or membranous partition; esp., the soft palate.

vel'ure (vĕl'ūr),*n.* Velvet or some fabric resembling it, esp. one of linen, silk, or jute, used as drapery.

vel'vet (vĕl'vĕt), *n.* A silk fabric having a short thick pile of erect threads. — *a.* [4] Like, or suggestive of, velvet; velvety.

vel'vet-een' (vĕl'vĕ-tēn'), *n.* **1.** A kind of cloth, usually of twilled cotton, imitating velvet. **2.** A velvety fabric of mixed silk and cotton.

vel'vet-y (-Ĭ), *a.* [4] Velvetlike; soft and smooth.

ve'nal (vē'nǎl), *a.* [4] **1.** That may be bought; purchasable; as, *venal* services; — used esp. of that which is base or degrading. **2.** Originating in, or marked by, venality. — **-ly,** *adv.* [8].

ve-nal'i-ty (vė-nǎl'Ĭ-tĬ), *n.* Venal quality or state.

ve-na'tion (-nā'shŭn), *n.* The arrangement or system of veins; veins collectively.

vend (vĕnd), *v. t. & i.* To make an object of trade, esp. by hawking or peddling.

vend-ee' (vĕn-dē'), *n.* One to whom a thing is vended, or sold; — chiefly in legal usage.

vend'er (vĕn'dẽr), *n.* One that vends; vendor.

ven-det'ta (vĕn-dĕt'ȧ), *n.* Feud for blood revenge.

vend'i-ble (vĕn'dĬ-b'l), *a.* [4] Salable; marketable. — *n.* A vendible article; — usually in *pl.*

vend'or (vĕn'dŏr; *in contrast with vendee often* vĕn-dôr'), *n.* A vender; seller; — chiefly legal.

ven-due' (vĕn-dū'), *n.* A public sale by auction.

ve-neer' (vė-nēr'), *v. t.* To overlay or plate, as wood, with a thin layer of a finer or more valuable kind; hence, to coat or face so as to give a superior surface. Also fig.— n. **1.** The thin leaf or layer used in veneering. **2.** Mere outward show.

ven′er-a-ble (vĕn′ẽr-á-b'l), a. [4] **1.** Worthy of veneration; — generally implying advanced age. **2.** Rendered sacred by associations.

ven′er-ate (vĕn′ẽr-āt), v. t. [1] To have veneration for; reverence; revere.— **-a′tor** (-ā′tẽr), n.

ven′er-a′tion (-ā′shŭn), n. **1.** Act of venerating; state of being venerated. **2.** Worship.

ve′ne-sec′tion (vē′nē-sĕk′shŭn), n. Act or practice of opening a vein to let blood.

venge′ance (vĕn′jăns), n. Punishment in return for an injury or offense; retribution; also, passionate or unrestrained revenge.

venge′ful (vĕnj′fŏŏl), a. [4] Revengeful.— **venge′-ful-ly,** adv. [8].— **venge′ful-ness,** n. [8].

ve′ni-al (vē′nĭ-ăl), a. [4] Capable of being forgiven; not heinous. — **ve′ni-al-ly,** adv. [8]

ve′ni-al′i-ty (-ăl′ĭ-tĭ), n. Quality of being venial.

ven′i-son (vĕn′ĭ-z'n), n. The flesh of an animal of the deer kind.

ven′om (vĕn′ŭm), n. **1.** The poisonous matter which certain animals, as serpents, scorpions, bees, etc., secrete and communicate by biting or stinging. **2.** That which poisons, embitters, or blights.

ven′om-ous (-ŭs), a. [4] **1.** Full of venom; poisonous. **2.** Mischievous; malignant; spiteful. — **-ly,** adv. [8] — **-ness,** n. [8].

ve′nous (vē′nŭs), a. Of or pert. to a vein or veins.

vent (vĕnt), n. **1.** A small aperture; a hole or opening for passage or escape, as of a fluid. **2.** Ordnance. The opening at the breech of a gun through which fire is communicated to the powder. **3.** Outlet, as from confinement; hence, utterance, expression.— v. t. **1.** To let out at a vent; give outlet to. **2.** To utter; express; publish. **3.** To furnish with a vent; make a vent in.

ven′ti-late (vĕn-tĭ-lāt), v. t. [1] **1.** To cause fresh air to circulate through (a room, mine, etc.). **2.** To give vent to; utter. — **ven′ti-la′tor,** n. [8].

ven′ti-la′tion (-lā′shŭn), n. Act of ventilating; state of being ventilated.

ven′tral (vĕn′trăl), a. Of or pert. to the belly.

ven′tri-cle (-trĭ-k'l), n. Anat. Either of the two lower chambers of the heart, which deliver blood to the arteries.

ven-tril′o-quism (vĕn-trĭl′ŏ-kwĭz′m), n. Act or art of speaking in such a way that the voice appears to come from a source other than the speaker's vocal organs. [ventriloquism.]

ven-tril′o-quist (-kwĭst), n. One who practices ventriloquism.

ven-tril′o-quize (-kwĭz), v. i. [1] To practice ventriloquism.

ven-tril′o-quy (-kwĭ), n. Ventriloquism.

ven′ture (vĕn′tụr), n. **1.** An undertaking of chance or danger; a hazard; risk; business speculation. **2.** The thing put to hazard; stake; risk. — v. t. [1] **1.** To expose to hazard; risk. **2.** To undertake the risk of; brave; dare. **3.** To put or send on a venture, as a business speculation.— v. i. **1.** To hazard one's self; dare. **2.** To make a venture; run a risk. — **ven′tur-er,** n. [8].

ven′ture-some (-sŭm), a. [4] Venturous; daring. — **-ly,** adv. [8] —**-ness,** n. [8].

ven′tur-ous (-tụr-ŭs), a. [4] Daring; bold. — **-ly,** adv. [8] —**-ness,** n. [8].

ven′ue (vĕn′ū), n. Law. The place or county in which the alleged events from which an action arises took place; also, the place from which the jury is taken, and where the trial is held.

Ve′nus (vē′nŭs), n. Astron. The most brilliant of the planets, second in order from the sun.

ve-ra′cious (vē-rā′shŭs), a. [4] **1.** Observant of truth; truthful. **2.** Characterized by truth; true; as, a veracious story. — **ve-ra′cious-ly,** adv. [8].

ve-rac′i-ty (vē-răs′ĭ-tĭ), n. Quality or state of being veracious, or true; truthfulness.

ve-ran′da (-răn′dá), **-dah,** n. An open gallery or portico, usually roofed, attached to a building.

verb (vûrb), n. Gram. A word which affirms or predicates something; the part of speech expressing action or mode of being.

ver′bal (vûr′băl), a. **1.** Of or pert. to words; esp., dealing with words rather than with the ideas to be conveyed. **2.** Expressed in words, esp. spoken words; hence, spoken; oral; not written. **3.** Word for word; literal. **4.** Gram. Of or pertaining to a verb; derived directly from a verb. — **ver′bal-ly,** adv. [8].

ver-ba′tim (vẽr-bā′tĭm), adv. Word for word; in the same words; verbally.

ver-be′na (-bē′ná), a. A garden plant of numerous varieties, with large flowers of various colors.

ver′bi-age (vûr′bĭ-áj), n. Verbosity; wordiness.

ver-bose′ (vẽr-bōs′), a. [4] Abounding in words; prolix; wordy. —**-ly,** adv. —**-ness,** n.

ver-bos′i-ty (-bŏs′ĭ-tĭ), n. ; pl. -TIES (-tĭz). State or quality of being verbose; wordiness.

ver′dan-cy (vûr′dăn-sĭ), n. Verdant quality.

ver′dant (-dănt), a. [4] **1.** Covered with growing plants or grass; green; fresh. **2.** Unripe in knowledge or judgment. Colloq. — **-ly,** adv.

ver′dict (vûr′dĭkt), n. **1.** Law. The finding or decision of a jury on the matter submitted in trial. **2.** Decision; judgment.

ver′di-gris (-dĭ-grēs), n. **1.** A green or greenish blue pigment and drug, formed by action of acetic acid on copper. **2.** A green or bluish rust on copper, brass, or bronze. Colloq.

ver′dure (-dụr), n. Greenness, esp. of vegetation; also, green vegetation. — **-less,** a. [8].

verge (vûrj), n. **1.** A rod or staff carried as an emblem of authority or symbol of office. **2.** A border, limit, or boundary; edge or brink. **3.** An inclosing or encircling thing, as a ring.— v. i. **1.** To be on the verge. **2.** To tend; incline.

ver′ger (vûr′jẽr), n. One who carries a verge; as: **a** An attendant on a bishop, a dean, etc. Eng. **b** An official who takes care of a church building.

ver′i-fi′a-ble (vẽr′ĭ-fī′á-b'l), a. Capable of being verified. [confirmation.]

ver′i-fi-ca′tion (-fĭ-kā′shŭn), n. Act of verifying;

ver′i-fy (vẽr′ĭ-fī), v. t. [2] **1.** To prove to be true; confirm; substantiate. **2.** To authenticate.

ver′i-ly (-lĭ), adv. **1.** In very truth; in fact; certainly. **2.** Truly; really; as, I verily believe.

ver′i-sim′i-lar (-sĭm′ĭ-lảr), a. [4] Having the appearance of truth; probable. — **-ly,** adv. [8].

ver′i-si-mil′i-tude (-sĭ-mĭl′ĭ-tūd), n. Quality or state of being verisimilar.

ver′i-ta-ble (vẽr′ĭ-tả-b'l), a. Agreeable to truth or to fact; actual; true. — **ver′i-ta-bly,** adv. [8].

ver'i-ty (-tǐ), *n. ; pl.* -TIES (-tǐz). **1.** Quality of being true; reality. **2.** That which is true.

ver'mi-cel'li (-mē-sěl'ǐ; -chěl'ǐ), *n.* See MACARONI.

ver-mic'u-lar (vĕr-mǐk'ū-lár), *a.* Vermiculate.

ver-mic'u-late (-lāt),*v.t.* [1] To form or work, as by inlaying, with irregular lines or impressions resembling tracks of worms.

ver-mic'u-late (-lāt), *a.* Wormlike in shape; covered with elevations or markings suggestive of worms or worm tracks.

ver-mic'u-la'tion (-lā'shǔn), *n.* **1.** A vermiculate marking, or ornamentation. **2.** Act or art of vermiculating.

ver'mi-form (vûr'mǐ-fôrm),*a.* Resembling a worm. — *vermiform appendix, Anat.*, a narrow, blindly ending tube three or four inches long which extends from the cæcum. Cf. APPENDICITIS.

ver'mi-fuge (-fūj), *n. Med.* A medicine or substance that expels worms from animal bodies.

ver-mil'ion (vĕr-mǐl'yǔn), *n.* **1.** A brilliant red pigment. **2.** A red color like the pigment.

ver'min (vûr'mǐn), *n. sing. & pl. ;* chiefly as *pl.* A noxious animal, or esp. such animals collectively, when of small size. Flies, lice, bedbugs, fleas, rats, mice, etc., are classed as *vermin.*

ver'min-ous (vûr'mǐ-nǔs), *a.* [4] Of or pert. to vermin; infested by vermin.

wer-nac'u-lar (vĕr-năk'ū-lár), *a.* Of or pertaining to one's native speech. — *n.* One's mother tongue; often, the common mode of expression in a locality, or, by extension, in a trade, etc.

ver'nal (vûr'nǎl), *a.* [4] **1.** Of or pert. to the spring. **2.** Belonging to youth.

ver'sa-tile (vûr'sá-tǐl), *a.* [4] Turning with ease from one thing to another. [tile.]

ver'sa-til'i-ty (-tǐl'ǐ-tǐ), *n.* State of being versatile.

verse (vûrs), *n.* **1. a** A poetic line consisting of a certain number and disposition of metrical feet (see FOOT, *n.*, 6). **b** Metrical arrangement and language; versification; poetry. **c** A piece of poetry. **2.** A short division of any composition.

versed (vûrst), *a.* [4] Acquainted or familiar from experience, study, practice, etc.; skilled.

ver'si-cle (vûr'sǐ-k'l). *n.* A short verse or sentence said or sung by a priest or minister, and followed by a response from the people.

ver'si-fi-ca'tion (-fǐ-kā'shǔn), *n.* Act, process, or art of versifying; metrical composition.

ver'si-fy (-fǐ),*v. i.* [2] To make verses. — *v. t.* **1.** To render into metrical form. **2.** To relate, describe, or compose in verse. — **ver'si-fi'er** (-fī'ẽr), *n.*

ver'sion (-shǔn), *n.* **1** A translation; esp., a translation or rendering of the Bible or a part of it. **2.** An account from a particular point of view.

ver'sus (vûr'sǔs), *prep.* Against ; — used chiefly in legal or in sporting language. Abbr. *v.* or *vs.*

ver'te-bra (vûr'tĕ-brá), *n. ; L. pl.* -BRÆ (-brē). One of the segments composing the spinal column.

ver'te-bral (-brǎl), *a.* Of or pert. to a vertebra, vertebræ, or the spine; composed of vertebræ.

ver'te-brate (-brāt), *a.* Having a backbone, or spinal column. — *n.* One of a division of animals (*Vertebrata*) containing those with a backbone.

ver'tex (-tĕks), *n. ; pl.* E. -TEXES (-tĕk-sĕz), L. -TICES (-tǐ-sēz). Highest point; top; apex.

ver'ti-cal (-tǐ-kǎl), *a.* **1.** Of or pert. to the vertex;

directly overhead. **2.** Perpendicular; upright; plumb. — *n.* A vertical line or plane. — **ver'ti-cal'i-ty** (-kǎl'ǐ-tǐ), *n.* — **ver'ti-cal-ly**, *adv.* [8].

ver'ti-cil (vûr'tǐ-sǐl), *n.* A whorl.

ver-tig'i-nous (vẽr-tǐj'ǐ-nǔs), *a.* [4] **1.** Turning round; rotary. **2.** Affected with vertigo; giddy; dizzy. **3.** Causing, or tending to cause, dizziness.

ver'ti-go (vûr'tǐ-gō), *n. ; pl.* E. -GOES (-gōz). Dizziness, or swimming of the head; giddiness.

verve (vûrv), *n.* Vivacity of imagination ; spirit.

ver'y (vĕr'ǐ), *a.* [3] **1.** Absolute; utter. **2.** Identical; same. **3.** Used intensively in sense of *even, even the;* as, the *very* birds stopped singing. — *adv.* In a high degree; exceedingly.

ves'i-cate (vĕs'ǐ-kāt), *v. t.* [1] *Med.* To blister.

ves'i-ca'tion (-kā'shǔn), *n. Med.* Process of vesicating; a blister.

ves'i-ca-to-ry (vĕs'ǐ-ká-tō-rǐ), *a. Med.* Tending to raise a blister. — *n. Med.* A blistering application or plaster. [blister; bleb.]

ves'i-cle (ĭ-k'l), *n.* A small bladderlike vessel ;

ves'per (vĕs'pẽr), *n.* **1.** The evening. *Poetic.* **2.** [*cap.*] The evening star; Venus as evening star. **3.** A vesper prayer, hymn, or service; a vesper bell. — *a.* Of or pertaining to the evening or the service of vespers.

ves'pers (-pẽrz), *n. pl.* Evening service or worship; also, in some Protestant churches, a service, largely musical, on Sunday afternoon.

ves'sel (vĕs'ĕl), *n.* **1.** A hollow or concave utensil or receptacle, as a barrel, bottle, kettle, cup, bowl, etc. **2.** Any craft for navigation of the water ; usually, one larger than a rowboat. **3.** *Anat.* A tube or canal in which a fluid is contained and circulated, as an artery, vein, etc.

vest (vĕst), *n.* **1.** A waistcoat. *Colloq.* **2.** A body garment or part of a garment for women, as a facing to the front of a bodice. **3.** A knitted or woven undershirt, esp. one for women. — *v. t.* **1.** To clothe with or as with a vestment or garment; hence, to encompass. **2.** To clothe (with authority, power, or the like) ; invest ; endow. **3.** To trust or commit to another ; — often with *in ;* as, powers *vested* in the courts. — *v. i.* To become vested; be fixed; take effect or pass, as a title.

ves'tal (-tǎl), *a.* [4] **1.** Of or pert. to Vesta, the Roman goddess of the hearth and its fire. **2.** Pertaining to or befitting a vestal. — *n.* **1.** *Roman Relig.* A virgin consecrated to Vesta and to her service. **2.** A virgin ; also, a nun.

vest'ed (vĕs'tĕd), *a.* **1.** Clothed ; robed, esp. in a ceremonial costume. **2.** *Law.* That has become a consummated right ; as, *vested* interests.

ves'ti-bule (vĕs'tǐ-būl), *n.* **1.** A passage, hall, or chamber between the outer door and the interior of a building ; a porch, or entrance into a house. **2.** An inclosed entrance to a passenger car.

ves'tige (-tǐj), *n.* A trace or visible sign left by something lost, perished, or absent; remains.

vest'ment (vĕst'mĕnt), *n.* **1.** A covering; garment; esp., a robe of ceremony or office. **2.** Any garment worn besides the ordinary dress by the clergy or their assistants in divine service.

ves'try (vĕs'trǐ), *n. ; pl.* -TRIES (-trǐz). **1.** *Eccl.* **a** A sacristy. **b** A room within, or a building attached to, a church building and used as a chapel, Sunday-school room, etc. **2.** A body of persons who administer the affairs of a parish.

ves′try-man (vĕs′trĭ-măn), *n.; pl.* -MEN (-mĕn). One of a vestry (sense 2).

ves′ture (vĕs′tụ̄r), *n.* **1.** That with which one is clothed. **2.** A covering.

vetch (vĕch), *n.* Any of various leguminous plants, some valuable for fodder.

vet′er-an (vĕt′ẽr-ăn), *a.* [4] **1.** Grown old in experience ; long practiced, esp. in military life. **2.** Of, pertaining to, or characteristic of, a veteran ; as, with *veteran* skill. — *n.* One long exercised in any service or art, esp. in war.

vet′er-i-na′ri-an (-ĭ-nā′rĭ-ăn), *n.* One who treats diseases and injuries of domestic animals.

vet′er-i-na-ry (vĕt′ẽr-ĭ-nā-rĭ), *a.* Of or pert. to the art of treating the injuries and diseases of domestic animals.— *n.; pl.* -RIES (-rĭz). A veterinarian.

ve′to (vē′tō), *n. ; pl.* -TOES (-tōz). **1.** An authoritative prohibition ; interdiction. **2.** A right or power of the chief executive of a government to prevent legislative enactment. **3.** Act of vetoing. — *v. t.* To prohibit ; negative ; esp., to exercise the right of veto.— **ve′to-er**, *n.* [8].

vex (vĕks), *v. t.* **1.** To disquiet ; disturb. **2.** To agitate ; discuss ; dispute ;— chiefly in *vexed question*, *point*, etc. **3.** To annoy or anger by petty provocations ; irritate ; harass ; afflict.

vex-a′tion (vĕk-sā′shŭn), *n.* **1.** A vexing ; state of being vexed ; trouble ; irritation. **2.** A cause of trouble or disquiet ; affliction.

vex-a′tious (-shŭs), *a.* [4] **1.** Causing vexation. **2.** Full of vexation, trouble, or disquiet ; disturbed ; as, a *vexatious* life.— **-ly**, *adv.* [8] — **-ness**, *n.* [8].

vi′a (vī′ȧ), *prep.* By the way of.

vi′a-ble (vī′ȧ-b'l), *a.* Capable of living,— said of a newly born infant.

vi′a-duct (-dŭkt), *n.* A bridge, esp. one on narrow masonry arches, having high supporting piers, for carrying a road over a valley, etc. Also, a steel structure of short spans on high steel towers.

vi′al (vī′ăl), *n.* A small bottle ; a phial.

vi′and (vī′ănd), *n.* An article of food ;— chiefly in *pl.*, provisions; food; fare.

vi-at′i-cum (vī-ăt′ĭ-kŭm), *n.* The Eucharist, when given to a person supposedly dying.

vi′brant (vī′brănt), *a.* [4] Vibrating; sounding as a result of vibrating; resonant; resounding.

vi′brate (-brāt), *v. t.* [1] To set in vibration.— *v. i.* **1.** To move to and fro, as a pendulum ; swing ; oscillate. **2.** To be in a state of vibration. **3. a** To thrill; throb. **b** To waver; fluctuate.

vi-bra′tion (vī-brā′shŭn), *n.* Act of vibrating.

vi-bra′tion-al (-ăl), *a.* Of or pert. to vibration.

vi′bra-tor (vī′brā-tẽr), *n.* One that vibrates, as a hammer between a contact piece and an electromagnet to make and break an electric circuit.

vi′bra-to-ry (vī′brȧ-tō-rĭ), *a.* [4] Consisting in, or causing, vibration; vibrating.

vic′ar (vĭk′ẽr), *n.* **1.** An ecclesiastic representing the Pope or an ordinary bishop;— with a qualifying word, as in *vicar-general*. **2.** The priest of a parish the tithes of which are owned by a layman. *Eng.* **3.** *Prot. Epis. Ch.* A clergyman who is the head of a chapel only ; also, a bishop's deputy in charge of a church or mission.

vic′ar-age (vĭk′ẽr-åj), *n.* The benefice, residence, or office or function, of a vicar. *Chiefly Brit.*

vi-ca′ri-ous (vī-kā′rĭ-ŭs), *a.* **1.** Deputed ; delegated. **2.** Acting for another. **3.** Performed or suffered in place of another.— **-ly**, *adv.* [8] — **-ness**, *n.* [8].

vice (vīs), *n.* **1.** A moral fault or failing ; esp., immoral conduct or habit. **2.** State of being given up to evil conduct or habits. **3.** Error; fault; also, blemish.

vi′ce (vī′sē), *prep.* In the place of; in the stead of.

vice (vīs), *a.* Denoting a person who in certain cases may assume the office of a superior whose title is the same as that qualified by *vice*, or the office of such a person; also, denoting a deputy, or the office of a deputy; as, *vice* president.

vice-ge′rent (vīs-jē′rĕnt), *a.* Having delegated power ; acting in the place of another. — *n.* An officer deputed to exercise the powers of another.

vice′re′gal (-rē′găl), *a.* Of or pertaining to a viceroy or viceroyalty.

vice′roy (vīs′roi), *n.* A governor who rules as representative of a king or sovereign.

vice′roy′al-ty (-roi′ăl-tĭ), *n.* The dignity, office, or jurisdiction of a viceroy.

∥ **vi′ce ver′sa** (vī′sē vûr′sȧ). [L.] The relations being reversed.

vic′i-nage (vĭs′ĭ-nåj), *n.* Neighborhood; vicinity.

vi-cin′i-ty (vī-sĭn′ĭ-tĭ), *n.; pl.* -TIES (-tĭz). **1.** Nearness; proximity. **2.** A region about, near, or adjacent ; neighborhood.

vi′cious (vĭsh′ŭs), *a.* [4] **1.** Addicted to vice, or immorality ; depraved ; wicked. **2.** Characterized by vice, or defect ; faulty. **3.** Impure ; noxious. **4.** Not well tamed or broken. — **-ly**, *adv.* [8] — **-ness**, *n.* [8].

vi-cis′si-tude (vī-sĭs′ĭ-tūd), *n.* Irregular change; revolution; mutation; as, *vicissitudes* of fortune.

vic′tim (vĭk′tĭm), *n.* **1.** A living being sacrificed in a religious rite. **2.** One injured, destroyed, or sacrificed, in the pursuit of an object, at the hands of another, or from disease, accident, etc.

vic′tim-ize (-īz), *v. t.* [1] To make a victim of ; dupe; cheat.

vic′tor (-tẽr), *n.* Winner; conqueror.

Victoria.

vic-to′ri-a (vĭk-tō′rĭ-ȧ), *n.* **1.** *Bot.* A water lily (genus *Victoria*), native of Guiana and Brazil, with leaves often over 6 feet in diameter, and with rose-white flowers 12–18 inches across ;— called also **vic-to′ri-a re′gi-a** (rē′jĭ-ȧ). **2.** A kind of low, four-wheeled pleasure carriage with a top.

vic-to′ri-ous (-ŭs), *a.* [4] **1.** Having gained victory ; conquering. **2.** Of, pert. to, or symbolic of, victory. — **-ly**, *adv.* [8] — **-ness**, *n.* [8].

vic′to-ry (vĭk′tŏ-rĭ), *n. ; pl.* -RIES (-rĭz). The overcoming of an enemy or antagonist; triumph.

vict′ual (vĭt′'l), *n.* Food ;— [chiefly in *pl.*], food for human beings, esp. when prepared for eating;

viands. *Now Chiefly Colloq. or Dial.* — *v. t.* [7] To provide or store with food.

vict'ual-er (-'l-ẽr ; -lẽr), *n.* [7] One who furnishes victuals or provisions; esp., an inn-keeper.

vi-cu'ña (vĭ-kōōn'yä), *n.* **1.** A wild animal of the Andes from Ecuador to Bolivia, allied to the llama and alpaca. **2.** For **vicuña cloth**, a soft fabric of vicuña wool, or an imitation of it.

Vicuña.

vie (vī), *v. i.,* VIED (vīd) ; VY'ING (vī'ĭng). To strive for superiority; contend.

view (vū), *n.* **1.** Act of seeing; sight; look; survey. **2.** Mental survey. **3.** Power of seeing; range of vision. **4.** That which is seen; scene; prospect. **5.** A picture of a scene; sketch. **6.** Mode of looking at anything; opinion. **7.** That which is kept in sight as an object. — *v. t.* To see; behold; esp., to look at or consider attentively; inspect. — **view'er,** *n.* [8].

vig'il (vĭj'ĭl), *n.* **1.** Abstinence from sleep; wakefulness. **2.** A watching; watch. **3.** Devotional watching; in *pl.,* evening or nocturnal devotions. **4.** A religious service on the eve of a feast.

vig'i-lance (-ĭ-lăns), *n.* Quality or state of being vigilant; watchfulness; caution.

vig'i-lant (-lănt), *a.* [4] Alertly watchful; alert; circumspect; wary. — **vig'i-lant-ly,** *adv.* [8].

vig'i-lan'te (-lăn'tē), *n.* A member of a committee organized to suppress crime, when the ordinary processes of law are considered inadequate. *U. S.*

vi-gnette' (vĭn-yĕt'), *n.* **1.** A small decorative design or illustration of a book. **2.** Any engraving, etc., which shades off gradually. — *v. t.* [1] To make a vignette of. — **vi-gnet'ter** (-ẽr), *n.* [8].

vig'or (vĭg'ẽr), *n.* [5] Active strength or force, as of body or mind; effective energy or power.

vig'or-ous (-ŭs), *a.* [4] **1.** Having vigor; strong; robust. **2.** Exhibiting strength, bodily or mental; powerful; energetic. — **-ly,** *adv.* — **-ness,** *n.*

vi'king (vī'kĭng; vē'-), *n.* One of the pirate Northmen who plundered the coasts of Europe in the 8th–10th centuries.

vile (vīl), *a.* [3] **1.** Of small account; low; mean; base. **2.** Morally base; impure; evil. **3.** Unclean; repulsive. — **-ly,** *adv.* [8] — **-ness,** *n.* [8].

vil'i-fi-ca'tion (vĭl'ĭ-fĭ-kā'shŭn), *n.* Act of vilifying or defaming; abuse.

vil'i-fy (vĭl'ĭ-fī), *v. t.* [2] To degrade by report; defame; traduce. — **vil'i-fi'er** (-fī'ẽr), *n.* [8].

vil'la (vĭl'ȧ), *n.* A somewhat pretentious rural or suburban residence.

vil'lage (-åj), *n.* Any small aggregation of houses in the country, less than a town.

vil'lag-er (-å-jẽr), *n.* An inhabitant of a village.

vil'lain (-ĭn), *n.* In sense 1 now usually **vil'lein. 1.** One of a class of feudal serfs. **2.** One capable or guilty of great crimes; scoundrel; knave.

vil'lain-ous (-ŭs), *a.* [4] **1.** Befitting a villain; evil. **2.** Mean; wretched. — **-ly,** *adv.* — **-ness,** *n.*

vil'lain-y (-ĭ), *n.; pl.* -LAINIES (-ĭz). **1.** Quality or state of being villainous, or evil; depravity. **2.** A villainous act; crime.

vil'lous (-ŭs), *a.* [4] Covered with fine hairs. *Colloq.*

vin'di-cate (vĭn'dĭ-kāt), *v. t.* [1] To support or maintain as true or correct against denial, censure, etc. ; sustain; justify. — **-ca'tor** (-tẽr), *n.*

vin'di-ca'tion (-kā'shŭn), *n.* Act of vindicating; state of being vindicated. [Vindicatory.]

vin-dic'a-tive (-dĭk'ȧ-tĭv; vĭn'dĭ-kā-tĭv), *a.* [4]

vin'di-ca-to-ry (vĭn'dĭ-kȧ-tō-rĭ), *a.* [4] Tending or serving to vindicate; justificatory.

vin-dic'tive (vĭn-dĭk'tĭv), *a.* [4] Disposed to revenge; retaliatory. — **-ly,** *adv.* — **-ness,** *n.*

vine (vīn), *n.* **1.** A grapevine. **2.** Any climbing, trailing, or creeping plant; also, its stem.

vin'e-gar (vĭn'ē-gẽr), *n.* A sour liquid got by fermentation of alcoholic liquids, as cider. — **gar-y,** *a.*

vine'yard (vĭn'yȧrd), *n.* Plantation of grapevines.

vi'nous (vī'nŭs), *a.* Of, pertaining to, or like, wine.

vin'tage (vĭn'tȧj), *n.* **1.** Act or time of gathering grapes, or making wine. **2.** A season's produce of grapes or, now usually, of wine.

vin'tag-er (-tȧ-jẽr), *n.* A gatherer of grapes.

vint'ner (vĭnt'nẽr), *n.* A wine seller or wine merchant, esp. at wholesale.

vi'ol (vī'ŏl), *n.* Any of a class of medieval musical instruments from which the violin was developed.

vi-o'la (vē-ō'lä ; vī-), *n.* An instrument of the violin class, intermediate in size and compass between the violin and violoncello.

vi'o-la-ble (vī'ō-lȧ-b'l), *a.* That may be violated.

vi'o-late (vī'ō-lāt), *v. t.* [1] **1.** To treat roughly or harshly; abuse. **2.** To profane; desecrate. **3.** To infringe on ; disturb ; also, to disregard, as a promise. **4.** To ravish. — **vi'o-la'tor,** *n.* [8].

vi'o-la'tion (-lā'shŭn), *n.* Act of violating, or state of being violated.

vi'o-la-tive (vī'ō-lȧ-tĭv), *a.* [4] Violating; tending to violate.

vi'o-lence (vī'ō-lĕns), *n.* **1.** Strength or energy actively displayed or exerted ; force ; impetuosity; vehemence. **2.** Profanation; outrage; assault.

vi'o-lent (vī'ō-lĕnt), *a.* [4] **1.** Moving, acting, or characterized, by extreme and sudden, or improper, force ; furious ; vehement. **2.** Marked by, or due to, strong mental excitement; passionate. **3.** Produced or effected by force. **4.** Great; extreme. — **-ly,** *adv.*

vi'o-let (-lĕt), *n.* **1.** Any of a large genus (*Viola*) of low plants whose flowers are purple, yellow, or white, often (as in the pansy) variegated with some other color. **2.** The color of the common violet; bluish purple. — *a.* Of the color violet.

vi'o-lin' (-lĭn'), *n.* **1.** The modern treble instrument developed from the viol. It is made of carefully selected wood and has four strings that are played with a bow. It is the most important instrument in the modern orchestra. **2.** A violin player.

vi'o-lin'ist (-ĭst), *n.* A player on the violin.

vi'o-lon-cel'list (vē'ō-lŏn-chĕl'ĭst; vī'ō-lŏn-sĕl'-), *n.* A player on the violoncello; — often shortened to *cellist,* '*cellist.*

vi'o-lon-cel'lo (-chĕl'ō ; -sĕl'ō), *n.; pl.* -LOS (-ōz). A bass violin; — often shortened to *cello* or '*cello.*

vi′per (vī′pẽr), *n.* **1.** Any of certain Old World venomous snakes; an adder. **2.** A malignant person. — **vi′per-ish**, *a.* [4,8].

vi′per-ine (-pẽr-ĭn ; -ĭn), *a.* [4] Of or pertaining to a viper.

vi′per-ous (-*ŭs*), *a.* [4] Malignant; venomous.

vi-ra′go (vĭ-rā′gō; vĭ-), *n.; pl.* -goes (-gōz). A turbulent woman; termagant; vixen.

vir′e-o (vĭr′ē-ō), *n.; pl.* -os (-ōz). Any of certain small American song birds.

vir′gin (vûr′jĭn), *n.* **1.** An unmarried woman; a maid. **2.** [*cap.*] The Virgin Mary. — *a.* [4] **1.** Being a virgin; chaste; maidenly; modest. **2.** Pure; undefiled. **3.** Undisturbed; fresh.

vir′gin-al (-ĭ-nǎl), *a.* [4] Of, pert. to, or befitting, a virgin.

vir′gin-al, *n.* A small rectangular spinet, without legs, popular in the 16th and 17th centuries.

Vir-gin′i-a (vẽr-jĭn′ĭ-*ȧ*), *n.* One of the United States. — **Virginia creeper**, a North American climbing plant having bluish black berries; — called also *woodbine*.

vir-gin′i-ty (-ĭ-tĭ), *n.* Quality or state of being virgin; maidenhood.

Virgin Mary. The mother of Jesus.

vir′ile (vĭr′ĭl; vī′rĭl), *a.* [4] **1.** Having the nature or qualities of a man. **2.** Masterful; forceful. **3.** Manly vigor; power.

vi-ril′i-ty (vĭ-rĭl′ĭ-tĭ; vī-), *n.* **1.** Quality or state of being virile; manliness. **2.** Manly vigor; power.

vir′tu-al (vûr′tụ̇-ǎl), *a.* **1.** Of or relating to a real force or energy; potential; as, a *virtual* cause. **2.** Being in effect, but not in fact. — **-ly,** *adv.*

vir′tue (vûr′tụ̇), *n.* **1.** Active quality or power; energy; potency; efficacy. **2.** Excellence; merit. **3.** Moral excellence; rectitude; morality. Also, a particular moral excellence. **4.** Chastity; purity.

vir′tu-os′i-ty (-tụ̇-ŏs′ĭ-tĭ), *n.; pl.* -ties. Quality or state of being a virtuoso; skill of a virtuoso.

vir′tu-o′so (vĭr′tŏō-ō′sō; vûr′-), *n.; pl.* E. -sos (-sōz), It. -si (-sē). **1.** One skilled in, or having a taste for, the fine arts, curios, etc. **2.** One who excels in technic, esp. in the performing of music.

vir′tu-ous (vûr′tụ̇-*ŭs*), *a.* [4] Having or exhibiting virtue. — **-ly,** *adv.* [8] — **-ness,** [8].

vir′u-lence (vĭr′ōō-lĕns), *n.* Quality or state of being virulent; malignancy.

vir′u-len-cy (-lĕn-sĭ), *n.* Virulence.

vir′u-lent (-lĕnt), *a.* [4] **1.** Extremely poisonous or venomous. **2.** Bitter in enmity. — **-ly,** *adv.*

vi′rus (vī′rŭs), *n.* **1.** *Med.* The poison or contagion of an infectious disease; also, vaccine virus. **2.** Anything that poisons the mind or the soul.

vis′age (vĭz′ĭj), *n.* Face, countenance, or look, esp. of a human being; aspect.

vis′aged (-ĭjd), *a.* Having (such) a visage;—usually in composition; as, " grim-*visaged* war."

‖ **vis′-à-vis′** (vē′zȧ-vē′), *adv. & a.* [F.] Face to face. — *n.* One face to face with another.

vis′cer-a (vĭs′ẽr-*ȧ*), *n. pl.* The internal organs, esp. the heart, liver, intestines, etc.

vis′cer-al (-ǎl), *a.* Of or pertaining to the viscera.

vis′cid (vĭs′ĭd), *a.* [4] Sticking or adhering and having a ropy or glutinous consistency; viscous.

vis-cid′i-ty (vĭ-sĭd′ĭ-tĭ), *n.* Quality or state of being viscid; stickiness. [being viscous.]

vis-cos′i-ty (vĭs-kŏs′ĭ-tĭ), *n.* Quality or state of

vis′count′ (vī′kount′), *n.* A nobleman next below an earl or count and next above a baron. — **vis′-count′ess** (vī′koun′tĕs), *n. fem.* [8].

vis′coun′ty (vī′koun′tĭ), **vis′count′cy** (-kount′sĭ), *n.* Rank or office of a viscount.

vis′cous (vĭs′kŭs), *a.* [4] Adhesive; sticky; viscid.

vise (vīs), *n.* Any of various devices having two jaws closed by a screw, lever, etc., to hold work.

‖ **vi-sé′** (vē-zā′), *n.* [F.] An official indorsement on a passport or other document. — *v. t.* To examine and mark with a visé. [quality.]

vis′i-bil′i-ty (vĭz′ĭ-bĭl′ĭ-tĭ), *n.* Visible state or]

vis′i-ble (vĭz′ĭ-b'l), *a.* Capable of being seen; perceptible; apparent. — **-ness,** *n.* — **vis′i-bly,** *adv.*

vi′sion (vĭzh′ŭn), *n.* **1.** The sense by which light and color are apprehended. **2.** Act or power of perceiving mental images. **3.** Thing seen; object of sight. **4.** Apparition ; phantom.

vi′sion-a-ry (-ā-rĭ), *a.* [4] **1.** Of or pertaining to a vision or visions. **2.** Dreamy; imaginative. **3.** Fanciful; impracticable. — *n.; pl.* -ries (-rĭz). One who sees visions; one who is not practical.

vis′it (vĭz′ĭt), *v. t.* **1.** To make a visit to. **2.** To come to or upon with purpose to reward, punish, or the like. — *v. i.* To make a visit; be a guest. — *n.* **1.** A short stay of business, friendship, etc. **2.** Act of going to view, inspect, or attend.

vis′it-ant (-ĭ-tȧnt), *n.* One who visits; a guest; visitor. — *a.* Visiting.

vis′it-a′tion (-tā′shŭn), *n.* **1.** Act of visiting; state of being visited; a visit. **2.** Special dispensation, esp. of divine wrath; judgment.

vis′i-tor (vĭz′ĭ-tẽr), *n.* One who makes a visit.

vis′or, viz′or (vĭz′ẽr; vī′zẽr), *n.* **1.** The front piece of a helmet, esp. an upper piece, arranged so as to lift or open. **2.** Projecting front piece of a cap.

vis′ta (vĭs′tȧ), *n.* **1.** A view, or prospect, commonly through or along an avenue, as of trees. **2.** A mental view; as, *vistas* of memory.

vis′u-al (vĭzh′ū-ǎl), *a.* **1.** Of or pert. to, or used in, sight. **2.** That can be seen; visible. — **-ly,** *adv.*

vis′u-al-i-za′tion (vĭzh′ū-ǎl-ĭ-zā′shŭn), *n.* The power, act, or result of visualizing.

vis′u-al-ize (-īz), *v. t. & i.* [1] To make visual, or visible; esp., to form a mental image of.

vi′tal (vī′tǎl), *a.* [4] **1.** Of or relating to life. **2.** Contributing or essential to life. **3.** Containing life; living. **4.** Fundamental; essential.

vi-tal′i-ty (vī-tǎl′ĭ-tĭ), *n.* Vital force or animation; hence, power of enduring.

vi′tal-ize (vī′tǎl-īz), *v. t.* [1] To endow with life, or vitality. — **vi′tal-iz′er** (vī′tǎl-iz′ẽr), *n.* [8].

vi′tal-ly (-tǎl-ĭ), *adv.* In a vital manner.

vi′tals (-tǎlz), *n. pl.* Organs most necessary for life; esp., heart, lungs, and brain.

vi′ta-min (vī′tȧ-mĭn; vĭt′ȧ-), *n.* Any of a group of substances needed for the proper nourishment of the body, one or more of which occur in most foods in their natural state.

vi′ta-scope (vī′tȧ-skōp), *n.* A cinematograph.

vi′ti-ate (vĭsh′ĭ-āt), *v. t.* [1] **1.** To make vicious or faulty; contaminate; spoil. **2.** To render ineffective, invalidate. — **vi′ti-a′tion** (-ā′shŭn), *n.*

vit′i-cul′ture (vĭt′ĭ-kŭl′tụ̇r), *n.* The cultivation of the vine; grape culture. — **vit′i-cul′tur-al** (-kŭl′tụ̇r-ǎl), *a.* — **vit′i-cul′tur-ist** (-ĭst), *n.*

āle, senāte, câre, ăm, ŭccount, ärm, àsk, sof*ȧ*; ēve, ĕvent, ĕnd, recĕnt, makẽr; īce, ĭll; ōld, ŏbey, ôrb, ŏdd, sŏft, cŏnnect; ūse, ŭnite, ûrn, ŭp, circ*ŭs*; fŏŏd, fŏŏt; out, oil;

vit′re-ous (vĭt′rē-ŭs), *a.* [4] **1.** Glassy. **2.** Of, pert. to, or derived from, glass.

vit′ri-fi-ca′tion (vĭt′rĭ-fĭ-kā′shŭn), *n.* Act, art, or process of vitrifying; state of being vitrified.

vit′ri-fy (vĭt′rĭ-fī), *v.t.* [2] To convert into, or cause to resemble, glass by heat and fusion.— *v.i.* To become glass. — **-fi′a-ble** (-fī′à-b'l), *a.* [8].

vit′ri-ol (-ŭl), *n. Chem.* **a** A sulphate of any of various metals, as copper (**blue vitriol**), iron (**green vitriol**), zinc (**white vitriol**). **b** Oil of vitriol.

vit′ri-ol′ic (-ŏl′ĭk), *a.* [4] Of or pertaining to vitriol; caustic; biting; as, a *vitriolic* temper.

vi-tu′per-ate (vĭ-tū′pĕr-āt), *v.t.* [1] To berate.

vi-tu′per-a′tion (-ā′shŭn), *n.* Act of vituperating; wordy abuse; railing.

vi-tu′per-a-tive (-tū′pĕr-à-tĭv), *a.* [4] Uttering censure; abusive; railing. — **-tive-ly**, *adv.* [8].

vi-va′cious (vĭ-vā′shŭs; vī-), *a.* [4] Lively in temper or conduct; sprightly. — **-ly**, *adv.* [8].

vi-vac′i-ty (-văs′ĭ-tĭ), *n.; pl.* -TIES (-tĭz). Quality or state or being vivacious; animation.

viv′id (-ĭd), *a.* [3] **1.** Having the appearance of vigorous life or freshness; animated; brilliant; intense. **2.** Lively; active; as, a *vivid* imagination. — **-ly**, *adv.* [8] — **-ness**, *n.* [8].

viv′i-fy (vĭv′ĭ-fī), *v.t.* [2] To endue with life.

vi-vip′a-rous (vĭ-vĭp′à-rŭs), *a.* Producing living young (instead of eggs); — opp. to *oviparous.*

viv′i-sect′ (vĭv′ĭ-sĕkt′; vĭv′ĭ-sĕkt), *v.t. & i.* To perform vivisection on; dissect alive.

viv′i-sec′tion (-sĕk′shŭn), *n.* The dissection of, or operation on, a living animal for investigation.

vix′en (vĭk′s'n), *n.* **1.** A she-fox. **2.** A shrewish, ill-tempered woman. — **vix′en-ish**, *a.* [8].

vi-zier′ (vĭ-zēr′), *n.* Also **vi-zir′** (vĭ-zēr′). A high executive officer of various Mohammedan countries, esp. of Turkey; a minister of state.

viz′or. Var. of VISOR.

vo-cab′u-la-ry (vō-kăb′ū-lȧ-rĭ), *n.; pl.* -RIES (-rĭz). **1.** A list or collection of words, usually alphabetically arranged and explained or defined; a dictionary or lexicon. **2.** Stock of words used in a language, or by a class, individual, etc.

vo′cal (vō′kăl), *a.* **1.** Of or pertaining to the voice or speech. **2.** Uttered by the voice; oral. — **vocal cords**, either of two pairs of folds of mucous membrane which project into the cavity of the larynx.

vo′cal-ist (vō′kăl-ĭst), *n.* A singer.

vo′cal-ize (vō′kăl-īz), *v.t.* [1] **1.** To form into voice. **2.** To change into, or use as, a vowel. — *v.i.* To utter vocal sounds, as in singing. — **vo′cal-i-za′tion** (-ĭ-zā′shŭn), *n.*

vo′cal-ly, *adv.* In a vocal manner; orally.

vo-ca′tion (vō-kā′shŭn), *n.* Regular or appropriate employment; calling; occupation; profession.

vo-ca′tion-al (-ăl), *a.* Of or pert. to vocation.

voc′a-tive (vŏk′à-tĭv), *a.* Of or pertaining to, or used in, calling; esp., *Gram.*, designating, or pertaining to, the case denoting that which is addressed. — *n. Gram.* The vocative case.

vo-cif′er-ate (vō-sĭf′ẽr-āt), *v.i. & t.* [1] To cry out loudly; bawl; clamor.

vo-cif′er-a′tion (-ā′shŭn), *n.* Outcry; clamor.

vo-cif′er-ous (vō-sĭf′ẽr-ŭs), *a.* [4] Making a loud outcry; clamorous. — **-ly**, *adv.* — **-ness**, *n.* [8].

vogue (vōg), *n.* **1.** The way or fashion of people at

any period; style; mode; as, a word now in *vogue.* **2.** Popular repute or acceptation for a time.

voice (vois), *n.* **1.** Sound uttered by the mouth, esp. of human beings, in speech or song; *Phon.*, vocal sound of the kind or quality heard in vowels and in such consonants as *b, v, d*, etc.; tone; — distinguished from mere *breath* (as in *f, sh*, etc.) and from *whisper.* **2.** Faculty or power of utterance; speech. **3.** Any sound like, or suggestive of, vocal utterance. **4.** Expressed wish, choice, or opinion; also, the right to express a wish, choice, or opinion. **5.** *Gram.* Distinction of form in a verb, to indicate the relation of the subject of the verb to the action which the verb expresses; also, the relation so indicated; as, the active and passive *voices.*— *v.t.* [1] **1.** To give voice or expression to; utter; announce; divulge. **2.** *Phon.* To utter with voice. See VOICE, *n.*, 1.

voiced (voist), *a.* **1.** Furnished with a voice; — usually in combination; as, sweet-*voiced.* **2.** *Phon.* Uttered with voice; sonant; vocal; — said esp. of certain consonants, as *b, d, g, m*, etc., contrasted with the voiceless *p, t, k*, etc.

voice′less, *a.* **1.** Having no voice, utterance, or vote; mute. **2.** *Phon.* Surd. Cf. VOICED, *a.*, 2.

void (void), *a.* [3] **1.** Empty; vacant. **2.** Having no incumbent; unoccupied; — of offices, etc. **3.** Destitute; wanting;—usually with *of.* **4.** Not producing effect; useless; null.—*n.* That which is void; a vacuum. — *v.t.* **1.** To make or leave void, or empty; clear; vacate. **2.** To throw or send out; evacuate; discharge. **3.** To annul; nullify.

vol′a-tile (vŏl′à-tĭl), *a.* [4] **1.** Evaporating or vaporizing readily. **2.** Light-hearted; airy; lively; also, changeable; fickle. — **-ness**, *n.* [8].

vol′a-til′i-ty (-tĭl′ĭ-tĭ), *n.; pl.* -TIES (-tĭz). Quality or state of being volatile; volatileness.

vol′a-til-i-za′tion (-tĭl-ĭ-zā′shŭn), *n.* Act or process of volatilizing.

vol′a-til-ize (vŏl′à-tĭl-īz), *v.t. & i.* [1] To render or become volatile; exhale or evaporate.

vol-can′ic (vŏl-kăn′ĭk), *a.* [4] Of, pertaining to, or produced by, a volcano or volcanic agencies.

vol-ca′no (vŏl-kā′nō), *n.; pl.* -NOES or -NOS (-nōz). A vent in the earth's crust from which hot rock, steam, etc., issue; also, a hill or mountain composed wholly or in part of the ejected material.

vo-li′tion (vō-lĭsh′ŭn), *n.* **1.** Act of willing or choosing. **2.** Power of willing; will.

vo-li′tion-al (-ăl), *a.* Of or pertaining to volition.

vol′ley (vŏl′ĭ), *n.; pl.* -LEYS (-ĭz). **1.** A flight of missiles; simultaneous discharge of a number of missiles. **2.** A burst or emission of many things at once; as, a *volley* of oaths. — *v.t. & i.* To discharge, or be discharged, in or as in a volley.

vol′plane′ (vŏl′plān′), *n.* A glide to earth in a flying machine with power shut off. — *v.i.* [1] To glide in a flying machine.

volt (vōlt), *n. Elec.* The unit of electromotive force; that electromotive force which, if steadily applied to a conductor having a resistance of one ohm, will produce a current of one ampere.

volt′age (vōl′tăj), *n. Elec.* Electric potential or potential difference expressed in volts.

vol-ta′ic (vŏl-tā′ĭk), *a.* Of or pertaining to current electricity; galvanic.

volt′me′ter (vōlt′mē′tēr), *n.* *Elec.* Any instrument for measuring in volts the differences of potential between points of an electrical circuit.

vol′u-bil′i-ty (vŏl′ū-bĭl′ĭ-tĭ), *n.* Quality or state of being voluble.

vol′u-ble (vŏl′ū-b′l), *a.* [4] Characterized by ease and smoothness of utterance; glib. — **vol′u-ble-ness,** *n.* — **vol′u-bly,** *adv.* [8].

vol′ume (vŏl′ūm), *n.* **1.** Any collection of printed sheets bound together; a book. **2.** Space occupied, as measured by cubic inches, feet, etc.; a mass; bulk. **3.** *Music.* Fullness or quantity of tone.

vo-lu′mi-nous (vŏ-lū′mĭ-nŭs), *a.* [4] **1.** Of great volume, or bulk. **2.** Consisting of many volumes, or books. **3.** Having written much, or produced many volumes. — **ly,** *adv.*— **-ness,** *n.*

vol′un-ta-ry (vŏl′ŭn-tă-rĭ), *a.* [4] **1.** Proceeding from the will; produced in or by an act of choice. **2.** Unconstrained; spontaneous; free. **3.** Done by design or intention; intentional. **4.** Of or pert. to the will; subject to the will. **5.** Able to will; free.— **-ri-ly,** *adv.*— **-ri-ness,** *n.* — *n. ; pl.* -RIES (-rĭz). **1.** A voluntary action or piece of work. **2.** *Music.* An organ solo played before, during, or after, divine service.

vol′un-teer′ (-tēr′), *n.* One who voluntarily enters into, or offers himself for, a service, esp. military service. — *a.* Of or pert. to volunteers; voluntary. — *v. t.* To offer or bestow voluntarily. — *v. i.* To enter into, or offer one's self for, any service voluntarily.

vo-lup′tu-a-ry (vŏ-lŭp′tu̇-à-rĭ), *n.; pl.* -RIES (-rĭz). A person who is voluptuous (sense 2).

vo-lup′tu-ous (-ŭs), *a.* [4] **1.** Ministering or pertaining to sensuous or sensual gratification. **2.** Given to, or spent in, enjoyment of luxury, pleasure, or sensual gratification. — **ly,** *adv.* [8] — **ness,** *n.* [8]. [ment.

vo-lute′ (-lūt′), *n.* A spiral scroll-shaped ornament.

vom′it (vŏm′ĭt), *n.* That which is vomited.— *v. i.* **1.** To eject the contents of the stomach by the mouth; spew. **2.** To be ejected or emitted.—*v. t.* **1.** To throw up; spew. **2.** To eject violently from any hollow place; belch forth.

voo′doo (vōō′dōō; vōō-dōō′), *n.* **1.** = VOODOOISM. **2.** One who practices voodooism; negro sorcerer. — *a.* Of or pertaining to voodooism or a voodoo.

voo′doo-ism (-ĭz′m), *n.* A form of superstition and sorcery among negroes, esp. in Haiti.

vo-ra′cious (vō-rā′shŭs), *a.* [4] Greedy in eating; ravenous; rapacious. — **vo-ra′cious-ly,** *adv.*

vo-rac′i-ty (-răs′ĭ-tĭ), *n.* Voracious quality.

vor′tex (vôr′tĕks), *n.; pl.* E. -TEXES (-tĕk-sĕz), L. VORTICES (-tĭ-sēz). A whirlpool; eddy.

vo′ta-ress (vō′tà-rĕs), *n.* A woman votary.

vo′ta-ry (-rĭ), *a.* Consecrated by a vow or promise; devoted; promised. — *n.; pl.* -RIES (-rĭz). One devoted or consecrated by a vow or promise.

vote (vōt), *n.* **1.** A wish, choice, or judgment, of a person or a body of persons, formally expressed, as by a ballot; also, the right to such expression of wish, etc.; suffrage. **2.** That by means of which a vote (sense 1) is expressed, as a ballot, etc. **3.** Votes collectively; as, the Prohibition *vote.* — *v. i.* [1] To signify the wish, choice, or will, as by ballot, etc.; cast or give a vote. — *v. t.* **1.** To enact, grant, determine, effect, etc., by formal vote. **2.** To declare by general opinion or common consent, as if by a vote. *Colloq.*

vot′er (vōt′ēr), *n.* One who votes.

vo′tive (vō′tĭv), *a.* Given in fulfillment of a vow; consecrated by a vow. — **ly,** *adv.* [8].

vouch (vouch), *v. t.* To warrant; answer for. — *v. i.* To bear witness; as, to *vouch* for one.

vouch′er, *n.* **1.** One who vouches, or attests, anything, or who acts as a surety. **2.** A book, paper, or the like, which serves to vouch the truth of something; esp., a receipt showing payment.

vouch-safe′ (vouch-sāf′), *v. t.* [1] To condescend to grant; bestow. — *v. i.* To condescend; deign.

vow (vou), *n.* A solemn promise, esp. one made to God or a deity. — *v. t. & i.* **1.** To bind one's self by a vow. **2.** To asseverate; swear.

vow′el (vou′ĕl), *n.* A voiced, or sometimes a whispered, vocal sound without the audible friction or stoppage characteristic of a consonant. Also, a letter or character representing such a sound. In English, the written vowels are *a, e, i, o, u,* and sometimes *w* and *y.* — *a.* Of or pert. to a vowel.

voy′age (voi′ăj), *n.* A passage or journey by water, esp. to a distant place. — *v. i.* [1] To make a voyage; travel. — *v. t.* To pass over. — *n.* [8].— **-ag-er** (-ă-jẽr), *n.* [8].

vul′can-ite (vŭl′kăn-ĭt), *n.* Hard rubber produced by vulcanizing with much sulphur.

vul′can-i-za′tion (-ĭ-zā′shŭn), *n.* Process of imparting to caoutchouc, gutta-percha, etc., greater elasticity, durability, or hardness by heating or other treatment with sulphur.

vul′can-ize (vŭl′kăn-īz), *v. t.* [1] To subject to vulcanization. — **vul′can-iz′er** (-īz′ẽr), *n.* [8].

vul′gar (-găr), *a.* [4] **1.** Of or pertaining to the common people; ordinary; plebeian; hence, vernacular. **2.** Lacking refinement; low ; coarse.

vul′gar-ism (vŭl′găr-ĭz′m), *n.* **1.** Grossness; rudeness; vulgarity. **2.** A vulgar phrase or expression, or one used only in colloquial speech.

vul-gar′i-ty (vŭl-găr′ĭ-tĭ), *n. ; pl.* -TIES (-tĭz). Quality or state of being vulgar; coarseness.

vul′gar-ize (vŭl′găr-īz), *v. t. & i.* [1] To make vulgar. — **vul′gar-i-za′tion** (-ĭ-zā′shŭn), *n.*

vul′gar-ly, *adv.* In a vulgar manner.

vul′ner-a-bil′i-ty (vŭl′nẽr-à-bĭl′ĭ-tĭ), *n.* Quality or state of being vulnerable.

vul′ner-a-ble (vŭl′nẽr-à-b′l), *a.* [4] **1.** Capable of being wounded. **2.** Liable to injury.

vul′ner-a-ry (-ă-rĭ), *a.* [4] Used for, or useful in, healing wounds. — *n.* A vulnerary remedy.

vul′pine (-pĭn; -pĭn), *a.* [4] Like a fox ; crafty.

vul′ture (-tūr), *n.* Any of certain large birds allied to the eagles, but with weaker claws, and head usually naked. They subsist chiefly on carrion.

vy′ing (vī′ĭng), *p. pr. & vb. n.* of VIE.

āle, senāte, cāre, ăm, ăccount, ärm, ȧsk, sofá; ēve, ĕvent, ĕnd, recĕnt, makēr; īce, ĭll; ōld, ŏbey, ôrb, ŏdd, sŏft, cŏnnect; ūse, ŭnite, ûrn, ŭp, circŭs; fōōd, fŏŏt; out, oil;

W

wab'ble (wŏb'l), *v. i.* [1] To move unsteadily from side to side; hence, to vacillate; waver. — *n.* A rocking or oscillating motion, as of a wheel not hung true. — **wab'bly** (-lĬ), *a.* [8].

wad (wŏd), *n.* **1.** A little mass, as of hay or tow. **2.** A soft plug to retain a charge of powder. **3.** A soft mass, esp. of fibrous substance, to stop an aperture, etc. — *v. t.;* WAD'DED (wŏd'ĕd); WAD'DING. **1.** To form into a wad. **2.** To insert a wad into; also, to pad or stuff.

wad'ding (wŏd'ĭng), *n.* Wads collectively, or material for making wads.

wad'dle (-'l), *v. i.* [1] To walk with short steps, swaying from side to side, like a duck; toddle. — *n.* Act of waddling. — **wad'dler** (-lẽr), *n.* [8].

wade (wād), *v. i.* [1] **1.** To move by stepping in or through a medium, as water. **2.** To proceed with labor. — *v. t.* To cross by wading. — **wad'er**, *n.*

wa'fer (wā'fẽr), *n.* **1.** A thin cake or biscuit. **2.** A thin cake of unleavened bread used in the Eucharist in certain churches. **3.** An adhesive disk of dried paste, etc., or of paper, used as a seal.

waf'fle (wŏf'l), *n.* A crisped indented batter cake cooked in a **waffle iron.**

waft (wȧft), *v. t.* To cause to move by the impulse of waves, as of air. — *n.* **1.** Act of wafting. **2.** A wave or current ; puff ; gust.

wag (wăg), *v. t.;* WAGGED (wăgd) ; WAG'GING (wăg'ĭng). To sway or swing shortly, esp. from side to side, with jerky or quick turns. — *v. i.* To move one way and the other. — *n.* One full of sport and humor ; a wit.

wage (wāj), *v. t.* [1] To engage in, as a contest ; carry on, as a war. — *n.* That which is paid for services ; hire ; pay; — chiefly in *pl.*

☞ The plural form *wages* was formerly often, and is still sometimes, construed as a singular.

wa'ger (wā'jẽr), *n.* **1.** That which is risked on an uncertain event ; a stake; bet. **2.** Act of wagering, or betting ; a bet; as, to make a *wager.* — *v. t. & i.* To stake ; bet. — **wa'ger-er**, *n.* [8].

wa'ges (wā'jĕz), *pl.* of WAGE, *n.* (See WAGE, *n.,* *Note.*) Pay given for labor at short stated intervals, as distinguished from a salary or fee.

wag'ger-y (wăg'ẽr-ĭ), *n.; pl.* -GERIES (-ĭz). Manner or action of a wag; mischievous merriment.

wag'gish (-ĭsh), *a.* [4] **1.** Like a wag ; frolicsome. **2.** Done in sport ; sportive. —**-ly**, *adv.* —**-ness**, *n.* [8]. [waggling.|

wag'gle (wăg'l), *v. i. & t.* [1] To wag. — *n.* A|

wag'on (wăg'ŭn), *n.* A kind of four-wheeled vehicle, esp. one used for freight or merchandise.

wag'on-er (-ẽr), *n.* One who drives a wagon.

wag'on-ette' (-ĕt'), *n.* A kind of passenger wagon with two facing side seats.

wag'tail' (wăg'tāl'), *n.* Any of numerous birds having a long tail habitually jerked up and down.

waif (wāf), *n.* **1.** Something found, or without an owner. **2.** A homeless wanderer ; castaway.

wail (wāl), *v. t. & i.* To lament; mourn. — *n.* Lamentation ; mournful sound. — **-er**, *n.* [8].

wain'scot (-skŏt ; -skŏt), *n.* A wooden lining of an interior wall, usually paneled. — *v. t.* [7] To line with or as with boards or paneled work.

waist (wāst), *n.* **1.** The part of the body between the thorax and hips. **2.** A garment, or that part of a garment, which covers the body from shoulders to waist. **3.** Part of a vessel's deck between the quarter-deck and forecastle.

waist'band' (wāst'bănd'; -bǎnd), *n.* The band, as of a skirt, which encompasses the waist.

waist'coat (wāst'kŏt; *colloq.* wĕs'kŭt),*n.* A sleeveless garment for men, worn under the coat ; vest.

wait (wāt), *v. i.* **1.** To be in expectation ; — usually with *for.* **2.** To stay in expectation, as till the arrival of some person or event. **3.** To act as attendant or servant, esp. at table; serve. — *v. t.* To stay for; await. — *n.* **1.** Ambush. *Obs.,* exc. in *to lie in wait.* **2.** Act of waiting ; delay; also, interval of waiting.

wait'er (-ẽr), *n.* **1.** One who waits for or awaits something. **2.** An attendant ; servant in attendance, esp. at table. **3.** A tray for dishes, etc.

wait'ress (-rĕs), *n.* A female attendant at table.

waive (wāv), *v. t.* [1] To give up claim to; forgo.

waiv'er (wāv'ẽr), *n.* *Law.* Act of waiving or relinquishing something, as a right.

wake (wāk), *n.* Track left by a vessel in the water.

wake, *v. i.;* WAKED (wākt) or WOKE (wōk); WAK'-ING (wāk'ĭng). **1.** To be awake ; also, to keep watch or vigil. **2.** To be roused from sleep; awake. **3.** To be excited or roused up. **4.** To become alive again; undergo resurrection. — *v. t.* **1.** To rouse from sleep; awake. **2.** To arouse; excite. **3.** To revive. **4.** To watch with at night, as a dead body; hold a wake over. — *n.* **1.** State of forbearing sleep, esp. for solemn or festive purposes ; a vigil. **2.** The sitting up with a dead body, often attended with a degree of festivity, chiefly among the Irish.

wake'ful (-fŏŏl), *a.* [4] Not sleeping; indisposed to sleep; vigilant. —**-ly**, *adv.* [8] —**-ness**, *n.* [8].

wak'en (-'n), *v. i. & t.* To wake. — **wak'en-er**, *n.*

wale (wāl), *n.* **1.** A streak made on the skin by a rod or whip. **2.** *pl. Shipbuilding.* Certain strakes of the outside planking of a vessel.

walk (wôk), *v. i.* **1.** To roam. *Obs.,* except: To go restlessly about, as a somnambulist or a specter. **2.** To move along on foot ; go without running. **3.** To behave ; conduct one's self. — *v. t.* **1.** To pass through, over, or upon; traverse. **2.** To cause to walk. — *n.* **1.** Act or manner of walking; gait; stroll. **2.** Habitual or proper place or sphere of action. **3.** Place where one walks, or for walking. **4.** Pasture land ; range. — **walk'er**, *n.* [8].

walk'out' (-out'), *n.* A labor strike. *Colloq., U.S.*

wall (wôl), *n.* **1.** A work or structure, as of stone or brick, for security or inclosure. **2.** A defense; rampart ; *pl.,* fortifications. **3.** Inside surface of a room, cavity, or vessel, as of a boiler. — *v. t.* To inclose, fill, or defend, with or as with a wall.

wal'la-by (wŏl'ȧ-bĬ), *n.; pl.* -BIES (-bĬz). Any of various small or medium-sized kangaroos.

wal'let (wŏl'ĕt), n. **1.** A bag; knapsack; pack. **2.** A pocket-book, esp. one of some size.

wall'-eye' (wôl), n. **1.** An eye, as of a horse, with whitish iris. **2.** Any of various fishes with prominent eyes. — **wall'-eyed'**, a. [4].

wall'flow'er (-flou'ẽr), n. **1.** A perennial plant, of the cabbage family, with yellow or orange flowers. **2.** A person who remains by the wall, as a spectator at a dance. *Colloq.*

wal'low (wŏl'ō), v. i. To roll one's self about, as in mire. — n. **1.** Act of wallowing. **2.** A place to which an animal comes to wallow.

wall paper. Paper for walls of rooms.

wal'nut (wŏl'nŭt), n. The nut of any of a genus of well-known trees of the north temperate zone; also, the tree or its timber.

wal'rus (wŏl'rŭs), n. A large Arctic marine mammal, valuable for its tusks, skin, and blubber.

Walrus.

waltz (wôltz), n. A kind of round dance in triple time; also, music for this dance, or its time. — v. i. To dance a waltz. — **er**, n. [8].

wam'pum (wŏm'pŭm ; wŏm'-), n. Beads of shell used by the North American Indians as money.

wan (wŏn), a. ; WAN'NER ; WAN'NEST. Looking pale and worn; pale; pallid.

wand (wŏnd), n. A small stick ; rod; baton.

wan'der (wŏn'dẽr), v. i. **1.** To ramble about without any definite course; stroll. **2.** To stray off ; deviate. **3.** To be delirious; rave. — v. t. To wander over or through. — n. Act of wandering; ramble. — **er** (-ẽr), n. [8].

wan'der-ing, p. pr. & vb. n. of WANDER.

wane (wān), v. i. [1] To be diminished; decrease; — esp. of the moon. — n. **1.** Decrease; decline. **2.** The apparent decrease of the illuminated part of the moon from full to new.

wan'ly (wŏn'lǐ), adv. In a wan manner.

wan'ness, n. State or quality of being wan.

want (wŏnt; wŏnt), n. **1.** State of being without anything ; dearth. **2.** Absence of necessaries ; poverty. **3.** Thing needed. — v. t. **1.** To be without; lack. **2.** To need ; require. **3.** To feel need of; desire; crave. — v. i. **1.** To be absent, deficient, or lacking ; fail ; — often impersonal with *of*. **2.** To be destitute ; lack.

want'ing, a. Absent; lacking; missing.

wan'ton (wŏn'tŭn), a. [4] **1.** Not disciplined ; loose ; playful. **2.** Loose morally; dissolute. **3.** Reckless ; malicious. — n. A wanton person. — v. i. To ramble or frolic without restraint. — v. t. To waste wantonly. — **ly**, adv. — **ness**, n.

wap'i-ti (wŏp'ĭ-tĭ; wăp'-), n. The American elk.

war (wôr), n. **1.** State of using violence against another; a contest by force between estates. **2.** State of opposition or contest; hostility; contention; as, a *war* of words. — v. i. ; WARRED (wôrd); WAR'RING. To make or wage war.

war'ble (wôr'b'l), v. t. & i. [1] **1.** To trill; carol. **2.** To sound in a tremulous or softly melodious manner. — n. Act of warbling.

war'bler (-blẽr). n. **1.** One that warbles; singer; songster. **2.** Any of numerous singing birds, mostly small and bright-colored.

ward (wôrd), v. t. **1.** To guard. **2.** To keep under care or watch. **3.** To fend ; repel.

ward, n. **1.** Act of guarding; watch; guard; guardianship. **2.** Confinement under guard. **3.** A person under guard or protection ; esp., a person under the protection of a court because of some incapacity. **4.** A division ; as : **a** A district of a town or city. **b** A division of a hospital. **5.** A projecting ridge in a lock casing or keyhole ; also, a corresponding notch in a key.

ward'en (wôr'd'n), n. A keeper ; guardian ; guard ; as : **a** A chief keeper, as of a prison. **b** A churchwarden. — **ward'en-ship**, n.

ward'er (wôr'dẽr), n. One who wards, or keeps.

ward'robe' (wôrd'rōb'), n. **1.** A portable closet for clothes. **2.** Wearing apparel.

ward'room' (-rōom'), n. *Naut.* In a war vessel, the living quarters of the commissioned officers above the rank of ensign, excluding the captain.

ward'ship (-shĭp), n. **1.** Guardianship. **2.** State of being under a guardian; pupilage.

ware (wâr), a. Aware ; conscious.

ware, n. Articles of merchandise ; goods ; — now usually in *pl.*, exc. in composition ; as, glass*ware.*

ware'house' (wâr'hous'), n. A storehouse.

war'fare' (wôr'fâr'), n. Military operations between enemies ; war ; strife; struggle.

war horse. A horse used in war ; a charger.

wa'ri-ly (wā'rĭ-lĭ), adv. In a wary manner.

wa'ri-ness (-nĕs), n. Quality of being wary.

war'like' (wôr'līk'), a. [4] **1.** Fit for, or fond of, war. **2.** Of or relating to war ; soldierly. **3.** Threatening war; belligerent ; hostile.

war'lock (-lŏk), n. A witch or wizard ; also, a magic spell; incantation. *Archaic.*

warm (wôrm), a. [3] **1.** Having heat, or a sensation of heat, esp. in a moderate degree ; not cold. **2.** Sending out or imparting warmth. **3.** Subject to little or no cold weather. **4.** Passionate; sprightly ; ardent ; excitable. — v. t. & i. **1.** To render or become warm. **2.** To make or become ardent, animated, or interested; — often with *up*. — **warm'ly**, adv. [8] — **warm'ness**, n. [8].

warmth (wôrmth), n. Quality of being warm.

warn (wôrn), v. t. **1.** To put on guard ; caution. **2.** To notify in advance; notify or summon by authority ; bid. **3.** To admonish ; advise. — **er**, n.

warn'ing, n. **1.** Previous notice; caution; admonition. **2.** That which warns. **3.** A summons.

warp (wôrp), v. t. & i. **1.** To turn or twist out of shape. **2.** To turn from a proper course; pervert; swerve. **3.** To move (a vessel, etc.) by hauling on a line, or warp, attached to another object.

warp, n. **1.** The threads lengthwise in a loom, crossed by the woof. **2.** A rope used in warping a vessel. **3.** State of being warped or twisted.

war'rant (wŏr'ănt), n. **1.** That which vouches for anything ; guaranty ; security. **2.** Authorization; right. **3.** A writ giving authority, as to make an arrest. — v. t. **1.** To make secure; guarantee safety to; to give to (one) authority or power to do something. **2.** To give a warrant or warranty to ; secure by a warranty. **3.** To support by authority; justify; sanction. — **war'rant-er** (-tẽr), **war'ran-tor'** (-tôr'), n. [8].

war'rant-a-ble (-ăn-tȧ-b'l), a. [4] Capable of being warranted; justifiable. — **-a-bly**, adv. [8].

warrant officer. A noncommissioned army or navy officer.

war'ran-ty (-ăn-tǐ), n.; pl. -TIES (-tǐz). 1. Law. An engagement that a certain fact regarding the subject of a contract is, or shall be, as it is declared or promised to be. 2. Authority; justification.

war'ren (wŏr'ĕn), n. A piece of ground for breeding rabbits, etc.; a place abounding in rabbits.

war'rior (wŏr'yẽr), n. A man engaged or experienced in war or in military life; soldier.

wart (wôrt), n. A small, usually hard, tumor on the skin. [a wart.]

wart'y (wôr'tǐ), a. [3] 1. Having warts. 2. Like

wa'ry (wā'rǐ), a. [3] 1. Cautious of danger or deception. 2. Characterized by caution.

was (wŏz). A verb form supplying the first and third persons singular of the verb be, in the indicative mood, preterit (imperfect) tense. See BE.

wash (wŏsh), v. t. 1. To cleanse by dipping, rubbing, or scrubbing in water. 2. To cover with water; wet; flow against or over. 3. To waste or abrade by the force of water in motion. 4. To remove by or as by the action of water. 5. To tint lightly and thinly. 6. To overlay with a thin deposit of metal. — v. i. 1. To perform the act of ablution. 2. To clean anything by washing it. 3. To move with a lapping or swashing sound, as waves. 4. To bear, as do some fabrics, without injury the operation of being washed. 5. To be eroded by water, as a beach, etc. — n. 1. Act of washing. 2. A collection of articles being or to be washed. 3. The flow, dash, or sound of a body of water, as a wave. 4. That with which anything is washed; as, a face wash. 5. A thin coat of water color. — a. Capable of being washed without injury. Colloq. — **wash'a-ble** (-ȧ-b'l), a. [8].

wash'er (wŏsh'ẽr), n. 1. One that washes. 2. A ring or a perforated plate used to distribute pressure (as of a nut), to prevent play, etc. 3. A machine or apparatus for washing, as clothes.

wash'ing, n. 1. Act of one who washes. 2. The clothes washed, or to be washed, at one time; wash.

wash'out' (wŏsh'out'), n. Washing out of earth, etc., as by a freshet; also, a place washed out.

wasp (wŏsp), n. Any of numerous insects generally with slender body and (in workers and females) a formidable sting.

wasp'ish, a. [4] Resembling a wasp; as: **a** Having a slender waist; of the waist, slender. **b** Quick to resent affront; irascible. — **-ly**, adv. [8] — **-ness**, n. [8].

wast (wŏst). A verb form supplying the second person singular of the verb be, in the indicative mood, preterit (imperfect) tense. Cf. WAS.

wast'age (wās'tȧj), n. Loss by use, decay, evaporation, leakage, or the like; waste.

waste (wāst), a. [4] 1. Desolate; desert; dreary. 2. Unproductive; worthless; refuse. — v. t. [1] 1. To lay waste; devastate. 2. To wear away; impair or diminish gradually. 3. To spend unnecessarily; squander. — v. i. To lose bulk, strength, value, etc., gradually. — n. 1. That which is

waste, or desolate; desert; wilderness. 2. A wasting; thing wasted. 3. That which has no value for the main purpose of manufacture; refuse.

waste'ful (-fŏŏl), a. [4] 1. Occasioning waste; destructive. 2. Wasting what is valuable; prodigal. — **-ly**, adv. [8] — **-ness**, n. [8].

wast'er (wās'tẽr), n. One that wastes.

watch (wŏch), v. i. 1. To be awake; keep vigil. 2. To be attentive; be on the lookout. 3. To be expectant; wait. — v. t. 1. To tend; have in keeping. 2. To give heed to; keep in view. — n. 1. A keeping awake to guard, protect, etc.; vigil. 2. Vigilant attention; vigilance. 3. A watchman or watchmen; sentry; guard. 4. Time during which a guard does duty. 5. Naut. **a** An allotted time, usually four hours, for duty. **b** That part of the officers and crew who manage a vessel during the same watch. 6. A timepiece to be carried in the pocket.

watch'case' (wŏch'kās'), n. The case of a watch.

watch'dog' (wŏch'dŏg'), n. A dog kept to watch and guard premises or property.

watch'er (-ẽr), n. One who watches.

watch'ful (-fŏŏl), a. [4] Full of vigilance; attentive; cautious. — **-ly**, adv. [8] — **-ness**, n. [8].

watch'mak'er, n. A maker or repairer of watches.

watch'man (-măn), n.; pl. -MEN (-mĕn). A guard; sentinel; esp., one who guards a building.

watch'word' (-wûrd'), n. 1. A secret word used as a countersign; password. 2. A rallying cry.

wa'ter (wô'tẽr), n. 1. A fluid compound consisting of hydrogen and oxygen. 2. Hence: **a** Rain. **b** A wave; flood; — usually in the pl. **c** A lake, river, sea, or stream. 3. Any liquid suggestive of water. 4. The limpidity and luster of a precious stone. 5. A kind of wavy lustrous pattern, as of silk. — v. t. 1. To moisten, sprinkle, or soak with or as with water; irrigate. 2. To cause or allow to drink. 3. To diversify with wavelike lines, as silk. 4. To add water to; dilute. — v. i. 1. To shed, secrete, or fill with, water or liquid matter. 2. To get, or take in, water; drink water.

water buck. A large antelope of Central Africa.

wa'ter-clos'et, n. A closet with a hopper flushed with water, for defecation; also, the hopper.

water color. Painting. **a** A pigment applied with water. **b** A picture or design in water colors.

wa'ter-course' (-kōrs'), n. A stream of water.

water cress, or **wa'ter-cress'**, n. A cress, used for salad, growing usually in running water.

wa'ter-fall' (-fôl'), n. A fall, or very steep descent, of the water of a stream; cascade; cataract.

wa'ter-fowl' (-foul'), n. Any bird that frequents rivers, lakes, etc., or the sea; esp., a swimming bird; collective pl., swimming, esp. game, birds.

water ice. = ICE, n., 2.

watering place. 1. A place where water may be obtained. 2. A place where there are medicinal springs, or a resort for bathing, boating, etc.

water jacket. A casing holding water, or through which water circulates to cool the interior.

water lily. Any of many aquatic plants many of which bear showy flowers; also, the flower.

Water Lily. (⅛)

wa′ter-logged′ (wŏ′tẽr-lŏgd′), *a.* [4] Filled or saturated with water, so as to be heavy or loglike.

wa′ter-man (-măn), *n.* A man who manages or rows a boat.

wa′ter-mark′ (-märk′), *n.* **1.** A mark indicating the height of water. **2.** A marking produced in paper during manufacture.

wa′ter-mel′on (-mĕl′ŭn), *n.* The fruit of a plant of the cucumber family; also, the plant.

water power. The power of water used to drive machinery; a fall of water which may be so used.

wa′ter-proof′ (wŏ′tẽr-proof′), *a.* [4] Impervious to water. — *n.* Something waterproof, as a kind of cloak. — *v. t.* To make waterproof.

wa′ter-shed′ (-shĕd′), *n.* **1.** A dividing ridge between two drainage areas. **2.** The region or area drained by a river or lake; drainage area.

wa′ter-side′ (-sīd′), *n.* The land bordering water.

wa′ter-soak′, *v. t.* To fill the interstices of with water; soak in water.

wa′ter-spout′ (wŏ′tẽr-spout′), *n.* A slender funnel-shaped cloud extending from a cumulus cloud down to a cloud of spray torn up by whirling winds from the surface of water.

wa′ter-tight′, *a.* So tight as to be waterproof.

water tower. 1. A tower serving as a reservoir. **2.** A fire-extinguishing apparatus having a pipe which can be raised to various heights.

wa′ter-way′ (wŏ′tẽr-wā′), *n.* A way or channel for water; also, a navigable body of water.

water wheel. A wheel rotated by direct action of water.

wa′ter-works′ (-wûrks′), *n. pl.* A hydraulic apparatus or system by which water is supplied.

wa′ter-y (-ĭ), *a.* [4] **1.** Of or pertaining to water. **2.** Containing or discharging water; wet; tearful. **3.** Like, or suggestive of, water. **4.** Soft; soggy.

watt (wŏt), *n. Physics.* A unit of power equal to the rate of work represented by a current of one ampere under a pressure of one volt.

wat′tle (wŏt′'l), *n.* **1.** A twig or flexible rod; also, a framework of such rods. **2.** A naked, fleshy process hanging from the chin or throat of a bird or reptile. — *v. t.* [1] **1.** To bind, fence, etc., with wattles. **2.** To interweave, as twigs.

wat′tled (-'ld), *a.* Furnished with wattles.

watt′me′ter (wŏt′mē′tẽr), *n. Elec.* An instrument for measuring electric power in watts.

wave (wāv), *v. i.* [1] **1.** To move like a wave; undulate; flutter. **2.** To be moved to and fro as a signal; signal in this way. **3.** To bend up and down like a wave; as, *waving* hair. — *v. t.* **1.** To swing; brandish. **2.** To give an undulating form or surface to. **3.** To signal by a waving motion. — *n.* **1.** A ridge or swell on the surface of a liquid, as of the sea. **2.** *Physics.* A vibrational disturbance propagated through a body or elastic medium, as in transmission of sound, light, etc. **3.** An undulation. **4.** A waving or undulating motion.

wave′let (-lĕt), *n.* A little wave; ripple.

wa′ver (wā′vẽr), *v. i.* **1.** To move to and fro; wave; hence, to reel; also, to flicker. **2.** To be unsettled in opinion; vacillate. — *n.* A wavering. — *-er*, *n.* [8].

wav′y (wāv′ĭ), *a.* [3] **1.** Rising or swelling in waves. **2.** Moving to and fro with an undulating motion. — **wav′i-ly**, *adv.* — **-i-ness**, *n.* [8].

wax (wăks), *v. i.* **1.** To increase in size; grow. **2.** To pass from one state to another gradually.

wax, *n.* **1.** Beeswax. **2.** Any of various substances resembling beeswax. — *v. t.* To treat with wax.

wax′en (wăk′s'n), *a.* [4] Made of, or covered with, wax; waxlike; hence, soft; yielding.

wax′i-ness (-sĭ-nĕs), *n.* State of resembling wax.

wax myrtle. An evergreen shrub or tree bearing small berries (bayberries) coated with a white wax.

wax′wing′ (wăks′wĭng′), *n.* Any of certain birds with showy crest and velvety plumage.

wax′work′ (-wûrk′), *n.* **1.** Work in wax; esp., a wax figure or figures in imitation of living beings. **2.** *pl.* An exhibition of such figures.

wax′y (wăk′sĭ), *a.* [3] **1.** Resembling wax. **2.** Made of, or abounding in, wax.

way (wā), *n.* **1.** Direction of motion, progress, etc.; route. **2.** A road, street, or path. **3.** Distance. **4.** A moving; passage; journey. **5.** Manner; method. **6.** Means of attaining anything; device; plan. **7.** An aspect or feature; respect; — with *in.* **8.** Regular course; habitual method of life or action. **9.** Resolved mode of action or conduct. **10.** *Naut.* Progress; headway. **11.** *pl. Shipbuilding.* The inclined structure upon which a vessel is built.

way′bill′ (wā′bĭl′), *n.* A document describing, and giving shipping directions for, goods transported by a railroad or steamer.

way′far′er (-fâr′ẽr), *n.* A traveler, esp. on foot.

way′far′ing, *p. a.* Traveling, esp. on foot.

way′lay′ (wā′lā′; wā′lā′), *v. t.;* for prin. parts see LAY. To lie in wait for in the way, esp. with a view of seizing, robbing, or killing. — *-er*, *n.* [8].

way′side′ (wā′sīd′), *n.* The side or edge of the way.

way station. An intermediate station between principal stations, esp. on a railroad. *U. S.*

way train. A train which stops at way stations.

way′ward (wā′wẽrd), *a.* [4] **1.** Taking one's own way; disobedient. **2.** Fluctuating; irregular. — **-ly**, *adv.* [8] — **-ness**, *n.* [8].

way′worn′ (wā′wōrn′), *a.* [4] Wearied by traveling.

we (wē), *pron.; pl.* of I; *poss.* OUR (our) or OURS (ourz); *obj.* US (ŭs). See I. The personal pronoun of the 1st person pl., nominative case. *We* is used in place of the singular *I* by kings and other sovereigns, and often editorially or by writers as being less personal or egotistical.

weak (wēk), *a.* [3] **1.** Lacking in strength, power, or force. **2.** Not possessing mental or moral strength, etc.; simple; foolish. **3.** *Gram.* Pertaining to or designating a verb or its conjugation which forms the preterit and past participle by adding to the present tense the suffix *-ed, -d,* (or *-t*) ; as in *spell, spelled* (or *spelt*) ; *abate, abated ; feel, felt.* [or weaker.

weak′en (wēk′'n), *v. t.* To make or become weak

weak′fish′ (-fĭsh′), *n.* Any of several marine food fishes with very tender flesh.

weak′ling (-lĭng), *n.* A weak or feeble creature.

weak′ly (-lĭ), *adv.* In a weak manner; feebly.

weak′ly, *a.* [3] Not strong; weak.

weak′ness, *n.* **1.** Quality or state of being weak. **2.** A fault; defect.

weal (wēl), *n.* A sound, healthy, or prosperous state; well-being; prosperity. *Archaic or Rhet.*

weald (wēld), *n.* A wold; an open country.

wealth (wĕlth), *n.* Large possessions; affluence.

wealth'y (wĕl'thĭ), *a.* [3] Having wealth; rich.

wean (wēn), *v. t.* **1.** To accustom (a child or young animal) to feed otherwise than by nursing. **2.** To alienate, as from some object of desire.

weap'on (wĕp'ŭn), *n.* **1.** An instrument of combat, as a gun, sword, shield, etc. **2.** Any means by which one contends against another.

wear (wâr), *v. t.*; *pret.* WORE (wōr); *p. p.* WORN (wōrn); *p. pr. & vb. n.* WEAR'ING. **1.** To carry or bear upon the person. **2.** To bear; carry; show; as, she *wears* a smile. **3.** To use up by wearing (in sense 1); hence, to consume, waste, or exhaust gradually. **4.** To cause or make by friction or wasting. **5.** *Naut.* To cause to go about, as a vessel, so that its bow is turned away from the wind.—*v. i.* **1.** To endure use; last under use. **2.** To be wasted, consumed, or diminished by use;—often with *out*, *off*, *on*, etc.—*n.* **1.** A wearing, or state of being worn; use. **2.** That which is worn; style of dress; fashion. **3.** Result of wearing or use.—**wear'er** (wâr'ẽr), *n.* [8].

wea'ri-ly (wē'rĭ-lĭ), *adv.* In a weary manner.

wea'ri-ness (-nĕs), *n.* State of being weary.

wea'ri-some (-sŭm), *a.* [4] Causing weariness; tiresome; tedious; irksome.—**-ly**, *adv.*—**-ness**, *n.*

wea'ry (-rĭ), *a.* [3] **1.** Fatigued; tired. **2.** Having one's patience or liking exhausted;—esp. with *of*. **3.** Expressing weariness.—*v. i. & t.* [2] To become or make weary.

wea'sel (-z'l), *n.* Any of certain small flesh-eating animals related to the minks and polecats.

weath'er (wĕth'ẽr), *n.* State of the atmosphere as to heat or cold, calm or storm, etc.—*v. t.* **1.** To expose to the air; season, dry, injure, or alter in any way by exposure to air. **2.** *Naut.* **a** To pass to the windward of. **b** To make headway against or come safely through (a storm).—*v. i.* To endure or alter under atmospheric influences. —*a.* *Naut.* Windward;—opposed to *lee*.

weath'er-beat'en, *a.* [4] Beaten, worn, or toughened, by the weather.

weath'er-board' (-bōrd'), *n.* *Arch.* A board adapted to form lapped joints with boards above and below so as to shed water; a clapboard.—*v. t.* To nail boards on so as to lap one over another.

weath'er-cock' (-kŏk'), *n.* A vane, often in the figure of a cock, showing the direction of the wind.

weath'er-glass' (-glàs'), *n.* An instrument to indicate the state of the atmosphere, as a barometer.

weave (wēv), *v. t.*; *pret.* WOVE (wōv); *p. p.* WO'VEN (wō'v'n), WOVE; *p. pr. & vb. n.* WEAV'ING. **1.** To unite, as threads, so as to form a texture (as cloth). **2.** To form, as cloth, by interlacing threads.—*v. i.* **1.** To make cloth, etc., by interlacing yarns, threads, etc. **2.** To become interwoven.—*n.* A particular method or pattern of weaving.

weav'er (wēv'ẽr), *n.* One who weaves.

web (wĕb), *n.* **1.** That which is woven, esp. in a loom; a textile fabric, esp. a whole piece of cloth. **2.** *Engin.* A plate or thin portion, often between stiffening ribs or flanges. **3.** A cobweb. **4.** A membrane uniting the toes of many water birds and amphibians.—*v. t.*; WEBBED (wĕbd); WEB'BING. To unite or surround with a web; envelop.

web'bing (wĕb'ĭng), *n.* **1.** Membrane forming a web, as of a bird's foot. **2.** A stout, woven tape.

web'foot (wĕb'fŏŏt'), *n.*; *pl.* -FEET. **1.** A foot having the toes joined by a web (sense 4). **2.** Any web-footed animal.—**web'-foot'ed**, *a.*

wed (wĕd), *v. t.*; *pret.* WED'DED; *p. p.* WED'DED or WED; *p. pr. & vb. n.* WED'DING. **1.** To marry; espouse. **2.** To join in marriage; give in wedlock. **3.** To attach firmly or indissolubly.—*v. i.* To contract matrimony; marry.

wed'ding (-ĭng), *n.* **1.** Nuptial ceremony; a marriage. **2.** An anniversary of a wedding (sense 1); as, a golden *wedding* (fiftieth anniversary).

wedge (wĕj), *n.* A piece, as of wood or metal, tapering to a thin edge, used in splitting wood, rocks, etc., in raising heavy bodies, etc.—*v. t.* [1] **1.** To cleave or separate with or as with a wedge; rive. **2.** To force or drive as a wedge is driven; crowd. **3.** To fasten with a wedge.

wed'lock (wĕd'lŏk), *n.* Matrimony.

Wednes'day (wĕnz'dā), *n.* Fourth day of the week.

wee (wē), *a.* [3] Very small; little.

weed (wēd), *n.* A garment;—now chiefly in *pl.*, and used esp. of a widow's mourning garments.

weed, *n.* Any unsightly, useless, or injurious plant. —*v. t.* To free from weeds, or from anything like, or suggestive of, weeds;—often with *out*.

weed'y (wēd'ĭ), *a.* [3] **1.** Abounding with weeds; full of weeds. **2.** Like a weed.

week (wēk), *n.* A period of seven days, usually reckoned as beginning with Sunday.

week day. Any day of the week except Sunday.

week'-end', *n.* End of the week; esp., the period from Saturday noon (or Friday night) to Monday.

week'ly (wēk'lĭ), *a.* Coming, happening, or done, once a week.—*n.*; *pl.* -LIES (-lĭz). A publication issued weekly.—*adv.* Once a week.

ween (wēn), *v. i. & t.* To suppose; believe. *Archaic.*

weep (wēp), *v. i.*; *pret.* WEPT (wĕpt); WEEP'ING. To show grief or other passion by shedding tears; to cry.—*v. t.* **1.** To shed tears for; hence, to lament; bewail. **2.** To shed, as tears.—**weep'er**, *n.*

weep'ing, *p. a.* [4] **1.** That weeps; crying. **2.** Having drooping branches;—of some trees.

wee'vil (wē'v'l), *n.* Any of numerous beetles the larvæ of which destroy nuts, fruit, grain, etc.

weft (wĕft), *n.* In weaving, the woof.

weigh (wā), *n.* *Naut.* A corruption of WAY;—used only in *under weigh*.

weigh, *v. t.* **1.** To raise; lift. *Obs. or R.*, except in *to weigh anchor*. **2.** To ascertain the weight of. **3.** To ponder; balance.—*v. i.* **1.** To have a certain weight. **2.** To have weight, or importance. **3.** To bear heavily.—**weigh'er**, *n.* [8].

weight (wāt), *n.* **1.** Quality of being heavy; that property by which bodies tend toward the center of the earth. **2.** Quantity of heaviness. **3.** Pressure; burden; load. **4.** Importance; consequence; influence. **5.** A mode of estimating weight or mass. **6.** A ponderous mass; something heavy. **7.** A definite mass of metal or the like used in weighing. **8.** A unit of weight.—*v. t.* To put a weight or weights upon; make heavy.

weight'y (wāt'ĭ), *a.* [3] **1.** Having much weight; heavy; burdensome. **2.** Important; momentous; influential.—**-i-ly**, *adv.*—**-i-ness**, *n.* [8].

---

chair; go; sing, ink; then, thin; nature, verdure; yet; zh = z in azure. Numbers refer to §§ in the Special Notes which, with Abbreviations, Signs, etc., precede the Vocabulary.

weir (wēr), *n.* **1.** A dam in a river to stop and raise the water, for conducting it to a mill, forming a pond for fish, etc. **2.** A kind of fence set in a stream, channel, etc., for taking fish.

weird (wērd), *a.* [3] **1.** Of, pertaining to, or dealing with, fate or the Fates. **2.** Of or pert. to witchcraft; unearthly; uncanny. — **-ness**, *n.* [8].

wel′come (wĕl′kŭm), *a.* [4] **1.** Received gladly into one's presence or companionship. **2.** Giving pleasure; grateful. **3.** Free or willingly permitted. — *n.* Cordial greeting to, or reception of, a guest or newcomer. — *v. t.* [1] To receive gladly; make welcome. — **wel′com-er**, *n.* [8].

weld (wĕld), *v. t.* **1.** To press or beat, as the ends of two iron bars, into intimate union, usually while softened by heat. **2.** To unite closely. — *v. i.* To be, or be capable of being, welded. — *n.* State of being welded; also, a welded joint.

wel′fare′ (wĕl′fâr′), *n.* State of faring, or doing, well; condition of health, happiness, etc.

wel′kin (-kĭn), *n.* The vault of heaven; the sky.

we′ll (wēl). Short for *we will* or *we shall.*

well (wĕl), *n.* **1.** A spring; fountain. **2.** A pit or hole sunk into the earth to reach a supply of water or other fluid. **3.** A source of supply.— *v. i. & t.* To issue or pour forth from or as from a well.

well, *adv.; compar.* BET′TER (bĕt′ẽr); *superl.* BEST (bĕst). **1.** In such manner as is desirable or pleasing; satisfactorily; favorably. **2.** In a good or proper manner; rightly; worthily. **3.** To a proper or suitable degree; abundantly. **4.** To the full degree or extent; fully.

well (wĕl), *a.* **1.** Good or desirable; fortunate; proper; — now only predicative; as, it is *well* for him. **2.** Being in health; sound. **3.** Being in satisfactory condition or circumstances.

well′-be′ing, *n.* State of being well; welfare.

well′-born′, *a.* Born of a good family.

well′-bred′, *a.* **1.** Having good breeding; refined; cultivated. **2.** Of good breed, as an animal.

well′-nigh′ (wĕl′nī′), *adv.* Almost; nearly.

well′spring′ (-sprĭng′), *n.* A source of continual supply.

well′-to-do′ (-tŏŏ-dōō′), *a.* [4] Prosperous.

Welsh (wĕlsh), *a.* Of or pertaining to Wales or its inhabitants. — **Welsh rabbit,** a dish made of melted cheese, etc., poured over toasted bread.

welt (wĕlt), *n.* **1.** A border or edge. **2.** A narrow strip of leather between the upper and the sole of a shoe. — *v. t.* To furnish with a welt.

wel′ter (wĕl′tẽr), *v. i.* To tumble about or wallow, as a hog in mire; to roll about in; be soaked with. — *n.* Act or motion of weltering; confusion.

wench (wĕnch), *n.* **1.** A girl; maiden. *Archaic.* **2.** A maidservant. [in, *to wend one's way.*

wend (wĕnd), *v. t. & i.* To go; proceed on; — esp.

went (wĕnt), *pret. & p. p.* of WEND. *Obs.,* except as preterit of *go.* See GO.

wept (wĕpt), *pret. & p. p.* of WEEP.

were (wûr; wâr), *pret. indic. pl.,* and *pret. subj. sing. & pl.,* of BE. See BE.

were′wolf′ (wēr′wŏŏlf′; wĕr′-), *n.; pl.* -WOLVES (-wŏŏlvz′). *Folklore.* A person transformed into a wolf or a person who can assume a wolf's form.

wert (wûrt), *2d pers. sing. pret. subj.* of BE. *Archaic.*

west (wĕst), *n.* **1.** The direction of sunset. **2.** [*cap.*]

Regions, countries, or peoples, lying to the west; esp.: **a** The Western Hemisphere, or the New World. **b** *U. S.* Formerly, that part of the United States west of the Allegheny Mountains; now, commonly, the whole region west of the Mississippi River, esp. that north of Arkansas, etc.— *a.* Lying or proceeding toward or at the west; coming from the west, as a wind.— *adv.* To or toward the west.

west′er-ly (wĕs′tẽr-lĭ), *a. & adv.* Situated, directed, or moving toward the west; of winds, blowing from the west. [2. [*cap.*] Occidental.]

west′ern (-tẽrn), *a.* **1.** Of or pert. to the west.

west′ern-er (-tẽr-nẽr), *n.* A native or inhabitant of the west, esp. [*cap.*] of the Western U. S.

west′ward (wĕst′wẽrd), *a.* Lying or facing toward the west.— *adv.* Also **west′wards** (-wẽrdz). Toward the west. — **west′ward-ly**, *adv.* [8].

wet (wĕt), *a.; wet′ter* (-ẽr); WET′TEST. **1.** Consisting of, or covered or soaked with, water or other liquid. **2.** Rainy. **3.** Favoring the sale of intoxicating liquor. *Slang.* — **wet nurse,** a nurse who suckles a child. — *n.* **1.** Water or wetness; moisture. **2.** Rainy weather; rain. **3.** One opposed to prohibition. — *v. t.;* WET or WET′TED; WET′TING. To make wet. — **wet′ness,** *n.* [8].

weth′er (wĕth′ẽr), *n.* A castrated ram.

whack (hwăk), *v. t. & i.* To strike with a whack. *Colloq.* — *n.* A smart or resounding blow. *Colloq.*

whale, *n.* Any of numerous great sea animals which are true air-breathing, warm-blooded mammals. — *v. i.* [1] To engage in whale fishing.

whale′back′ (hwāl′băk′), *n.* A freight steamer having a very convex upper deck.

whale′bone′ (-bōn′), *n.* An elastic, horny substance from the upper jaw of certain whales.

whal′er (hwāl′ẽr), *n.* A vessel or person employed in the pursuit or taking of whales.

wharf (hwôrf), *n.; pl.* WHARVES (hwôrvz) or WHARFS (hwôrfs). A structure built on the shore of a harbor, river, canal, etc., so that vessels may lie close alongside to load and unload; a pier.

wharf′age (hwôr′fáj), *n.* **1.** Fee or duty paid for use of a wharf. **2.** Wharves collectively.

wharf′in-ger (-fĭn-jẽr), *n.* Wharf owner.

what (hwŏt), *pron. & a.* A pronominal word used both substantively and adjectively, as singular or plural. It is: **1.** An interrogative used in asking questions referring to the nature or identity of something; as, *what* is this? **2.** An exclamatory word; as, *what* a man! **3.** A compound relative, equivalent to *that which, those who, those which,* or *the . . . which,* etc.; as, you may have *what* (= that which) is left. **4.** An indefinite relative: Whatever; whatsoever. **5.** An indefinite pronoun; — now only in such phrases as *I tell you what,* where *what* is elliptical for *what I think,* etc.

what, *adv.* **1.** How? in what respect? **2.** In part; somewhat; — followed by a preposition, esp. by *with;* as, *what* with hunger and *what* with toil he was almost dead. — *conj.* **1.** As much as; so far as. **2.** That; — in *but what.*

what-ev′er (hwŏt-ĕv′ẽr), *pron.* All that; no matter what; — indefinite relative used substantively or adjectively; as, *whatever* its cost.

what′not′ (hwŏt′nŏt′), *n.* Piece of furniture with shelves, as for bric-a-brac.

āle, senāte, câre, ăm, *ă*ccount, ärm, ȧsk, sofȧ; ēve, ĕvent, ĕnd, recĕnt, makĕr; īce, ĭll; ōld, ȯbey, ôrb, ŏdd, sŏft, cȯnnect; ūse, ŭnite, ûrn, ŭp, circŭs; fŏŏd, fŏŏt; out, oil;

what'so-ev'er (-sō-ĕv'ĕr), *pron. & a.* Whatever.

wheat (hwēt), *n.* A well-known cereal grain; also, the grass that yields it.

wheat'en (hwēt'n), *a.* Made of wheat.

whee'dle (hwē'd'l), *v. t. & i.* [1] **1.** To coax; flatter. **2.** To get by flattery or coaxing.

wheel (hwēl), *n.* **1.** A disk, or a circular frame or body, capable of turning on a central axis. **2.** Something like, or suggestive of, a wheel (def. 1); as : **a** *Naut.* A circular frame with handles, for controlling the rudder. **b** An obsolete instrument of torture. **3.** A turn; revolution; rotation. **4.** *pl.* Fig.: Moving power or elements; that which imparts or directs motion or activity. — *v. t.* **1.** To convey or move on wheels, or in a wheeled vehicle. **2.** To turn; revolve. **3.** To make or perform in a circle. — *v. i.* **1.** To turn on or as on an axis or about a center; revolve. **2.** To roll forward.

wheel'bar'row (hwēl'băr'ō), *n.* A small vehicle with handles and (usually) one wheel.

wheeled (hwēld), *a.* Having a wheel or wheels.

wheel'wright' (-rīt'), *n.* A man who makes or repairs wheels and wheeled vehicles.

whooze (hwēz), *v. i.* [1] To breathe hard and with audible piping or whistling. — *n.* A piping or whistling sound caused by difficult respiration.

wheez'y (hwēz'ĭ), *a.* [3] Wheezing. [mollusks.

whelk (hwĕlk), *n.* Any of numerous large marine

whelm (hwĕlm), *v. t.* To overwhelm; engulf.

whelp (hwĕlp), *n.* The young of a dog or of certain beasts of prey. — *v. i. & t.* To bear whelps.

when (hwĕn), *adv.* **1.** At what time; — used interrogatively. **2.** At, during, or after the time that. **3.** At which time; the time at which; as, I know *when* he will come. **4.** While; whereas; although; — as an adverbial conj. **5.** Which time; then; — elliptically as a noun.

whence (hwĕns), *adv.* From what place; hence, from what or which source, origin, or the like.

whence'so-ev'er (hwĕns'sō-ĕv'ĕr), *adv. & conj.* From what place, cause, or source soever.

when-ev'er (hwĕn-ĕv'ĕr), *adv. & conj.* At whatever time.

when'so-ev'er (hwĕn'sō-ĕv'ĕr), *adv. & conj.* At what time soever; whenever.

where (hwâr), *adv.* **1.** At or in what or which place, situation, or circumstances. **2.** To what or which place; whither. **3.** From what place or source. — *conj.* Whereas.

where'a-bout' (-à-bout'), *adv. & n.* Whereabouts.

where'a-bouts' (-à-bouts'), *adv.* **1.** About where; near what or which place; as, *whereabouts* did you meet him? **2.** Concerning which or about which. — *n. sing.* The place where a person or thing is.

where-as' (hwâr-ăz'), *conj.* **1.** Considering that; it being the case that; since. **2.** When in fact; while on the contrary; the case being that.

where-at' (-ăt'), *adv.* **1.** At which; upon which; whereupon. **2.** At what; — used interrogatively.

where-by' (-bī'), *adv.* **1.** By which; — used relatively. **2.** By what; how; — used interrogatively.

where'fore (hwâr'fōr), *adv. & conj.* **1.** For which reason; so. **2.** For what reason; why.

where-in' (hwâr-ĭn'), *adv.* **1.** In which; in which place, thing, time, respect, etc.; — used relatively. **2.** In what; — used interrogatively.

where-of' (-ŏv'), *adv.* **1.** Of which or whom; — used relatively. **2.** Of what; — used interrogatively.

where-on' (-ŏn'), *adv.* **1.** On which; — used relatively. **2.** On what; — used interrogatively.

where'so-ev'er (hwâr'sō-ĕv'ĕr), *adv.* In or to whatsoever place; wherever.

where-to' (-tōō'), *adv.* **1.** To which; — used relatively. **2.** To what; to what place or end.

where'up-on' (hwâr'ŭ-pŏn'), *adv.* **1.** Upon which; in consequence of, or after, which; whereon; — used relatively. **2.** Whereon; — interrogatively.

wher-ev'er (hwâr-ĕv'ĕr), *adv.* At, to, in, or (with *from*) from, whatever place; wheresoever.

where-with' (hwâr-wĭth'; -wĭth') ⎱ *adv.* **1.** With
where'with-al' (hwâr'wĭth-ôl') ⎰ which; —
relative. **2.** With what; — interrogative.

where'with-al', *n.* Also, **where-with'**. That with which anything can be purchased or done.

wher'ry (hwĕr'ĭ), *n.; pl.* -RIES (-ĭz). A long light rowboat; also, a large light barge or fishing boat.

whet (hwĕt), *v. t.;* WHET'TED ; WHET'TING. **1.** To sharpen by rubbing. **2.** To make keen or eager. — *n.* **1.** Act of whetting. **2.** That which whets.

wheth'er (hwĕth'ĕr), *pron. & a.* Which (of two); which one (of two); — used interrogatively and relatively. *Archaic.* — *conj.* A particle used to indicate a following alternative. Its correlative is *or* or *whether*.

whet'stone' (hwĕt'stōn'), *n.* A stone for whetting edge tools.

whey (hwā), *n.* The watery part of milk, separated from the curd, as in cheese making. — **whey'ey,** *a.*

which (hwĭch), *pron.* **1.** An interrogative pronoun, used to ask for or concerning one or moi of a number; as, *which* man is it? **2.** A relative pronoun, used : **a** For *who* or *whom*, of persons. *Archaic.* **b** Of animals, things, or ideas, its antecedent being sometimes a phrase or clause. **3.** A compound relative or indefinite pronoun, standing for *any one which, whichever, that which, those which, the . . . which,* etc.

which-ev'er (hwĭch-ĕv'ĕr) ⎱ *pron. & a.* Whether
which'so-ev'er (-sō-ĕv'ĕr) ⎰ one or another; whether one or the other.

whiff (hwĭf), *n.* **1.** A quick puff or slight gust of air, esp. one conveying some odor. **2.** A sudden expulsion of tobacco smoke or the like from the mouth. **3.** An inhalation of tobacco smoke or the like. — *v. t. & i.* **1.** To expel in a whiff or whiffs. **2.** To convey by or as by a whiff.

whif'fle (hwĭf'l), *v. i.* [1] **1.** To blow unsteadily or in gusts; — of the wind. **2.** To vacillate.

whif'fle-tree' (-'l-trē'), *n.* A whippletree.

Whig (hwĭg), *n.* **1.** *Eng. Politics.* One of a political party which became the Liberal party. **2.** *Amer. Hist.* **a** A supporter of the American Revolution. **b** One of a political party formed about 1834 in opposition to the Democrats. — *a.* Of, pertaining to, or consisting of, Whigs.

Whig'gish, *a.* Of or pertaining to Whigs.

while (hwīl), *n.* **1.** A space of time. **2.** Time used in doing something; labor; pains; — only in *worth,* or *worth one's. while.* — *conj.* **1.** During the time that; as long as. **2.** At the same time that; — often used like *although; as, while* young he is wise. — *v. t.* [1] To cause to pass (away), esp. agreeably.

whiles (hwīlz), *adv.* Sometimes; at times. *Scot.* — *conj.* While. *Archaic or Dial.*

whi'lom (hwī'lŭm), *a.* Former; sometime.

whilst (hwīlst), *adv. & conj.* While.

whim (hwĭm), *n.* A capricious notion; a fancy.

whim'per (-pẽr), *v. i.* To cry with a low, whining, broken sound. — *n.* A low, whining, broken cry.

whim'sey (hwĭm'zĭ), *n.; pl.* -SEYS (-zĭz) ; -SIES (-zĭz). A whim; freak; caprice.

whim'si-cal (-zĭ-kăl), *a.* [4] **1.** Full of whims. **2.** Odd; queer; fantastic.— **-ly,** *adv.* **—ness,** *n.*

whim'si-cal'i-ty (-kăl'ĭ-tĭ), *n.* Whimsical quality or state; also, usually *pl.,* anything whimsical.

whim'sy (-zĭ), *n.; pl.* -SIES. Var. of WHIMSEY.

whin (hwĭn), *n.* Gorse; furze.

whine (hwīn), *v. i. & t.* [1] To utter, or utter with a low plaintive nasal or prolonged sound; also, to complain. — *n.* Act or sound of whining. — **whin'er,** *n.* [8].

whin'ny (hwĭn'ĭ), *v. i.* [2] To utter a neigh; neigh. — *n.; pl.* -NIES (-ĭz). A neigh.

whip (hwĭp), *v. t.; WHIPPED* (hwĭpt) *or WHIPT; WHIP'PING.* **1.** To move, take, or the like, suddenly and forcibly ; — usually with *into, out, up, off,* etc. **2.** To strike with a whip or lash. **3.** To beat, as eggs, into a froth. **4.** To conquer; defeat. *Colloq.* **5.** To overlay (a cord, rope, etc.) with other cords going round and round it. **6.** To wind, wreathe, or bind, about something. **7.** To gather (a fabric) by overcasting loosely and drawing up the thread. — *v. i.* **1.** To start, turn, go, pass, etc., suddenly; whisk. **2.** To thrash about like the lash of a whip. — *n.* **1.** An instrument consisting usually of a lash attached to a handle. **2.** One who handles a whip. **3.** A lifting device consisting of a block and a rope. — **whip'per** (hwĭp'ẽr), *n.* [8].

whip'cord' (hwĭp'kôrd'), *n.* A kind of hard cord, sometimes used for making whiplashes.

whip'per-snap'per (-ẽr-snăp'ẽr),*n.* A diminutive, insignificant, or presumptuous person. *Colloq.*

whip'lash' (hwĭp'lăsh'), *n.* The lash of a whip.

whip'ple-tree' (-'l-trē'), *n.* Pivoted or swinging bar to which the traces of a harness are fastened.

whip'poor-will' (-pōōr-wĭl'),*n.* A nocturnal bird of eastern America.

whip'saw' (-sô'), *n.* A long narrow ripsaw.

whip'stock' (-stŏk'), *n.* A whip handle.

whir (hwûr), *v. i.; WHIRRED* (hwûrd) ; *-RING.* To move, fly, or revolve, quickly with a whir. — *n.* A buzzing or whizzing sound due to rapid motion.

whirl (hwûrl), *v. t.* **1.** To rotate or revolve rapidly. **2.** To remove or carry quickly, with a revolving motion.— *v. i.* **1.** To revolve or rotate rapidly. **2.** To move, go, pass, etc., swiftly. — *n.* **1.** Rapid rotation or revolution. **2.** Something that whirls.

whirl'i-gig' (hwûr'lĭ-gĭg'), *n.* **1.** A child's toy that whirls. **2.** A merry-go-round.

whirl'pool' (hwûrl'pōōl'), *n.* A vortex of water; water whirling round so as to produce a depression or cavity, into which objects may be drawn.

whirl'wind' (-wĭnd'), *n.* A violent windstorm having an inward spiral motion with a central upward current, and usually rapid progression.

whisk (hwĭsk), *n.* **1.** Act of whisking; a sudden puff or whiff. **2.** A small bunch of grass, straw, twigs, hair, etc., esp. such a bunch for brushing; hence, a small brush or broom. — *v. t.* **1.** To sweep or brush with a light rapid motion. **2.** To move, pass, carry, etc., with a quick sweeping motion.— *v. i.* To move nimbly and quickly.

whisk'er (hwĭs'kẽr), *n.* **1.** [*Chiefly in pl.*] The beard on the sides of the face, on the chin, or on both. **2.** A hair of the beard. **3.** A long hair or bristle near the mouth of a cat, rat, etc.

whis'ky } (hwĭs'kĭ),*n.; pl.* WHISKIES, WHISKEYS.
whis'key } A distilled alcoholic liquor made from grain or from potatoes.

whis'per (-pẽr), *v. i.* **1.** To speak softly, or under the breath. **2.** To make a low sibilant sound. — *v. t.* **1.** To say under the breath ; mention privately. **2.** To speak to in a whisper, as in privacy. — *n.* **1.** A low soft sibilant utterance. **2.** A secret or private utterance, etc. **3.** A low rustling sound. — **whis'per-er,** *n.* [8].

whist (hwĭst), *interj.* Be silent ! be still ! hush ! — *a.* Silent. — *n.* A well-known card game.

whis'tle(hwĭs''l),*v.i.*[1] **1.** To make a kind of shrill musical sound by forcing the breath through the teeth or contracted lips. **2.** To make a sound like a whistle. — *v. t.* **1.** To form or utter by whistling, as a tune. **2.** To signal by a whistle. — *n.* **1.** A sound made by or as by whistling. **2.** An instrument in which air, steam, etc., produces a (usually) shrill sound. — **whis'tler** (-lẽr), *n.* [8].

whit (hwĭt), *n.* A bit; jot; iota.

white (hwīt), *a.* [3] **1.** Of the color of pure snow or sunlight; — opp. to *black* or *dark.* **2. a** Having a light-colored skin ; of the Caucasian race. **b** Wanting in color; pale; wan. **c** Gray or hoary, as the hair. **3.** Spotless; unblemished; pure. — *n.* **1.** Whiteness; — opp. to *black.* **2.** Something white or nearly so; as : **a** A white pigment. **b** Egg albumen. **c** The white part of the eyeball. **d** A person with a white skin. — *v. t.* [1] **1.** To whiten; bleach. **2.** To gloss over.

white ant. Any of numerous pale-colored, softbodied social insects ; a termite.

white'bait' (-bāt'), *n.* The young of any of several species of herrings. [foam.|

white'cap' (-kăp'), *n.* A wave crest breaking into

white corpuscle. One of a class of colorless corpuscles, having a nucleus and capable of change of shape and of locomotion, that form a constituent of the blood. They destroy bacteria, etc.

white'fish' (hwīt'fĭsh'), *n.* Any of several freshwater fishes, of the salmon family, valued as food.

white flag. A flag of truce.

white lead (lĕd). **1.** A heavy white substance consisting of lead carbonate, chiefly used as a pigment **2.** Native lead carbonate.

white'-liv'ered, *a.* [4] Having a pale look; feeble; hence, cowardly.

whit'en (-'n), *v. i. & t.* To become or make white.

white'ness (hwīt'nĕs), *n.* **1.** Quality or state of being white. **2.** Paleness. **3.** Purity; cleanness.

white'wash' (-wŏsh'), *n.* Any liquid composition for whitening. — *v. t.* **1.** To whiten with whitewash. **2.** To gloss over. — **white'wash'er,** *n.* [8].

white'wood' (-wŏŏd'), *n.* Any of numerous trees having white or light-colored wood; also,the wood.

whith'er (hwĭth'ẽr), *adv.* **1.** To what place; — interrogative. **2.** To what or which place;— relative.

whith′er-so-ev′er (-sŏ-ĕv′ẽr), *adv.* To whatever place.

whit′ing (hwīt′ĭng), *n.* **1.** Any of various marine food fishes. **2.** A preparation of chalk.

whit′ish (hwĭt′ĭsh), *a.* Somewhat white.

whit′low (hwĭt′lō), *n.* An inflammation (usually suppurative) of a finger or toe ; felon.

whit′tle (hwĭt′'l), *v. t. & i.* [1] To pare or cut with or as with a knife.

whiz, whizz (hwĭz), *v. i. ;* whizzed (hwĭzd) ; whiz′zing. To hum, whir, or hiss like a speeding arrow, ball, etc. — *v. t.* To cause to whiz ; rotate very rapidly. — *n.* A whirring sound.

who (hōō), *pron. ; possess.* whose (hōōz) ; *object.* whom (hōōm). A substantive pronoun, either singular or plural. It is used : **1.** As an interrogative : What or which person or persons? **2.** As a simple relative ; — properly used of persons (corresponding to *which* as applied to things). *Whose* is sometimes used of anything to avoid an awkward construction with *of which.* **3.** As a compound or indefinite relative, with its antecedent implied : Whoever ; the person or persons that.

whoa (hwō), *interj.* Stop ! stand ! hold !

who-ev′er (hōō-ĕv′ẽr), *pron.* Whatever person ; whosoever ; he or she who.

whole (hōl), *a.* **1.** Possessing, or being in a state of, health and soundness ; well ; sound ; hence, healed. **2.** Not broken ; unimpaired. **3.** Complete ; entire. — **whole brother.** See BROTHER. — **w. note,** *Music,* a semibreve. — **w. number,** *Math.,* an integer. — *n.* **1.** The entire thing ; totality. **2.** System ; as, an organic *whole.* — **whole′ness,** *n.* [8].

whole′-heart′ed, *a.* Sincere ; also energetic.

whole′sale′ (hōl′sāl′), *n.* Sale of goods by the piece or in large quantity ; — disting. from *retail.* — *a.* [4] **1.** Pert. to, or engaged in, trade by wholesale. **2.** Extensive and indiscriminate.

whole′some(-sŭm),*a.* [3] **1.** Salubrious. **2.** Characteristic of bodily health. **3.** Promoting, or characteristic of, health of mind, etc. ; sound ; as, *wholesome* advice. — **-ly,** *adv.* [8] — **-ness,** *n.* [8].

whol′ly (hōl′lĭ ; hōl′ĭ), *adv.* In a whole or complete manner ; entirely ; exclusively ; fully.

whom (hōōm), *pron.* Objective of *who.*

whom′so-ev′er (-sŏ-ĕv′ẽr), *pron.* Objective of *whosoever.*

whoop (hōōp), *v. i.* **1.** To utter a whoop, or loud cry ; shout ; halloo ; hoot. **2.** To make a whoop (in sense 3, below). — *n.* **1.** A shout or cry, as of war, pursuit, enthusiasm, etc. **2.** A hoot, or cry. **3.** The characteristic noisy taking in of the breath which follows a fit of coughing in whooping cough. — **whooping cough,** an infectious disease, characterized by a convulsive cough and a whoop.

whorl (hwûrl ; hwôrl), *n.* **1.** *Bot.* A circle of radiating leaves, flowers, or flower clusters. **2.** *Zoöl.* One of the volutes, or turns, of a univalve shell.

whor′tle-ber′ry (hwûr′t'l-bĕr′ĭ), *n.; pl.* -RIES (-ĭz). The huckleberry.

whose (hōōz), *pron.* The possessive of *who,* and sometimes of *which.* See under WHO, 2.

whose′so-ev′er (-sŏ-ĕv′ẽr), *pron.* Possessive of *whosoever.*

who′so (hōō′sō), *pron.* Whoever.

who′so-ev′er (hōō′sŏ-ĕv′ẽr), *pron.* Whoever.

why (hwī), *adv.* **1.** For what cause, reason, or purpose ; on what account ; wherefore ; — used interrogatively and as a relative. **2.** For which ; on account of which ; — used relatively.

wick (wĭk), *n.* A cord, tape, tube, etc., of fibers, which draws up a steady supply of the oil in lamps, the melted tallow or wax in candles, etc.

wick′ed (wĭk′ĕd), *a.* [3] **1.** Evil ; addicted to vice or sin ; iniquitous. **2.** Mischievous ; roguish. *Colloq.* — **-ly,** *adv.* — **-ness,** *n.*

wick′er (-ẽr), *n.* **1.** A small pliant twig or osier ; withe. **2.** Wickerwork, or a piece of wickerwork. — *a.* Made of, or covered with, wickerwork.

wick′er-work′ (-wûrk′),*n.* A texture of osiers, etc.

wick′et (wĭk′ĕt), *n.* **1.** A small gate or door, esp. in a larger gate or door. **2.** *Cricket.* Either of the two frameworks at which the ball is pitched.

wide (wīd), *a.* [3] **1.** Of a specified measure in a direction at right angles to that of length. **2.** Having considerable extent between the sides ; broad. **3.** Spacious ; extensive. **4.** Expanded ; distended. **5.** Roomy ; ample. **6.** Of large scope ; comprehensive. **7.** Far from a point aimed at.— *adv.* **1.** To a great distance ; widely. **2.** So as to form a large opening. — **-ly,** *adv.* — **-ness,** *n.* [8].

wide′-a-wake′, *a.* Fully awake ; keen ; alert.

wid′en (wīd′'n), *v. t. & i.* To make or become wide or wider ; expand. [ducks.

widg′eon (wĭj′ŭn),*n.* Any of several fresh-water

wid′ow (wĭd′ō), *n.* A woman who has lost her husband by death, and has not married again. — *v. t.* To bereave of a husband. *Usually in p. p.*

wid′ow-er (wĭd′ō-ẽr), *n.* A man who has lost his wife by death, and has not married again.

wid′ow-hood (-hŏŏd), *n.* State of being a widow ; time during which a woman is a widow.

width (wĭdth), *n.* Extent sidewise ; breadth.

wield (wēld), *v. t.* **1.** To direct by influence or authority ; manage ; sway. **2.** To use with full command or power ; as, to *wield* a sword. — **-er,** *n.*

wife (wīf), *n.; pl.* WIVES (wīvz). **1.** A woman. *Rare,* except in composition ; as, fish*wife.* **2.** A woman united to a man in lawful wedlock ; spouse ; — correlative of *husband.* — **wife′hood,** *n.*

wife′ly, *a.* [3] Befitting, like, or pert. to, a wife.

wig(wĭg),*n.* Artificial covering of hair for the head.

wig′an (wĭg′ăn), *n.* A canvaslike cotton fabric, used to stiffen parts of garments.

wig′gle (wĭg′'l), *v. i. & t.* [1] To move to and fro with a quick jerky motion ; wag ; wriggle. *Colloq.*

wig′gler (-lẽr), *n.* One that wiggles ; specif., the larva or pupa of the mosquito.

wight (wīt), *n.* A person ; being ; — chiefly jocose.

wig′wag′ (wĭg′wăg′),*v. t. & i. ;* -WAGGED′ (-wăgd′) ; -WAG′GING (-wăg′ĭng). **1.** To move to and fro ; wag. **2.** *Mil. & Nav.* To signal by means of a flag, or portable light, waved according to a code.

wig′wam (wĭg′wŏm), *n.* An Indian hut, formed of poles overlaid with bark, rush mats, or hides.

wild (wīld), *a.* [3] **1.** Living in a state of nature ; not tamed or domesticated ; as, a *wild* animal. **2.** Not cultivated ; as, *wild* cherry. **3.** Not inhabited or cultivated. **4.** Savage ; uncivilized ; rude. **5.** Ungoverned ; boisterous. **6.** Visionary ; crazy. **7.** Indicating strong emotion. **8.** Wide of the mark. — *n.* A wilderness ; waste. — *adv.* Wildly.

wild'cat' (wĭld'kăt'), *a.* **1.** Not sound or safe; reckless; irresponsible. **2.** Of trains, etc., running without control or contrary to orders.

wil'der·ness (wĭl'dĕr-nĕs), *n.* **1.** A tract uncultivated and uninhabited by human beings; a wild; waste. **2.** A confusing multitude or mass; as, a *wilderness* of flowers.

wild'fire' (wĭld'fīr'), *n.* An inflammable composition hard to quench. [its fruit.]

wild'ing (wīl'dĭng), *n.* An uncultivated plant or

wild'ly (wĭld'lĭ), *adv.* In a wild manner.

wild'ness, *n.* Quality or state of being wild.

wile (wĭl), *n.* A sly artifice; a beguiling trick.—*v. t.* [1] To lure; entice; beguile; allure.

wil'ful (wĭl'-), **-ly, -ness.** Vars. of WILLFUL, etc.

wil'i·ly (wĭl'ĭ-lĭ), *adv.* In a wily manner.

wil'i·ness (-nĕs), *n.* Wily quality or state.

will (wĭl), *n.* **1.** Wish or desire. **2.** What is wished by another. Hence, a request, command, or decree. **3.** Power coupled with desire or intention; as, a man of iron *will*. **4.** Act or experience of willing. **5.** Power of choosing. **6.** *Law.* The legal declaration of a person's mind as to the disposition of his property after his death.—with a will, with willingness and zeal ; heartily. —*v. t.*; WILLED (wĭld); WILL'ING. **1.** To determine by an act of choice; ordain; decree. **2.** To influence by one's will, as through hypnotism. **3.** To give, dispose of, or direct, by will or testament.—*v. i.* To exercise volition; choose; decide; decree.

will, *v. t. & auxiliary; pret.* WOULD (wo̅o̅d) *; p. p.* WOULD. **1.** As *v. t.* : Wish ; desire ;—now chiefly in the form *would* (which see). **2.** As *auxiliary*, followed by the infinitive without *to* (see also WOULD) : **a** Am (is, are, etc.) willing or desirous to, or, emphatically, determined to. Hence, simply, am (is, are, etc.) to ;—forming future-tense phrases. See SHALL. **b** Am (is, are, etc.) accustomed to.—*v. i.* To be willing; wish.

will'ful, wil'ful (wĭl'fo̅o̅l), *a.* [4] **1.** Voluntary; intentional ; as, *willful* murder. **2.** Obstinate ; perverse. —**-ly,** *adv.* —**-ness,** *n.*

will'ing, *a.* [4] **1.** Favorably disposed in mind; desirous ; ready. **2.** Ready to act ; prompt to do, give, etc. **3.** Done, given, etc., without reluctance; voluntary. —**-ly,** *adv.* — **-ness,** *n.* [8].

will'-o'-the-wisp' (-ŏ-thḗ-wĭsp'), *n.* Ignis fatuus.

wil'low (wĭl'ō), *n.* Any of various trees or shrubs having pliable shoots; also, their wood.

wil'low-y (-ŏ-ĭ), *a.* [4] **1.** Abounding with willows. **2.** Willowlike ; pliant ; flexible ; graceful.

wilt (wĭlt), *v. i.* To lose freshness and become flaccid ; droop. —*v. t.* To cause to droop or languish.

wilt, 2d *pers. sing.* of WILL.

wil'y (wĭl'ĭ), *a.* [3] Full of wiles; crafty.

wim'ple (-p'l), *n.* A covering of silk, linen, etc., for the neck, chin, and sides of the face, worn by nuns.—*v. t.* [1] **1.** To clothe with a wimple. **2.** To plait, or fold ; to cause to ripple or undulate. —*v. i.* To lie in folds; also, to ripple.

win (wĭn), *v. i.; pret. & p. p.* WON (wŭn) *; p. pr. & vb. n.* WIN'NING. **1.** To gain the victory; prevail. **2.** To succeed by effort in reaching a specified place or state; get.—*v. t.* **1.** To get by labor; gain ; obtain. **2.** To gain in competition or contest; also, to come off victor in. **3.** To achieve by

effort. **4.** To come to by effort; reach. **5.** To persuade ; allure ; gain the favor of.

wince (wĭns), *v. i.* [1] To shrink, as from a blow, or from pain; flinch. —*n.* Act of wincing.

winch (wĭnch), *n.* **1.** A crank with a handle for giving motion to a machine, grindstone, etc. **2.** Any of various devices to turn or strain something forcibly, as a form of windlass.

wind (wīnd), *v. t.; pret. & p. p.* WOUND (wound) *; p. pr. & vb. n.* WIND'ING (wīn'dĭng). **1.** To turn completely or repeatedly, esp. about something fixed; twist; twine; coil. **2.** To infold; entwine. **3.** To introduce sinuously or stealthily. **4.** To hoist or haul by a rope, etc., pulled by a machine. —*v. i.* **1.** To move in a sinuous course. **2.** To make one's way by stealthy or indirect methods. **3.** To coil; twine. —*n.* A winding ; turn ; bend.

wind (wĭnd; *poet. or rhetorical,* wīnd), *n.* **1.** Air naturally in motion. **2.** Air artificially put in motion; as, the *wind* of a bellows. **3.** Air impregnated with a scent, as of game; scent; as, to get *wind* of. **4.** Power of respiration; breath. **5.** Mere talk. **6.** Gas in the stomach or bowels.

wind (wĭnd), *v. t.; pret. & p. p.* WOUND *; p. pr. & vb. n.* WIND'ING. To blow; sound, as a horn, by blowing.

wind'age (wĭn'dāj), *n.* **1.** *Gun.* Deflection of a projectile by the wind. **2.** *Naut.* The surface exposed by a vessel to the wind. [wind.]

wind'break' (wĭnd'brāk'), *n.* A shelter from the

wind'fall' (wĭnd'fôl'), *n.* **1.** Something blown down by the wind, as fruit. **2.** An unexpected legacy or other gain. [being windy.]

wind'i·ness (wĭn'dĭ-nĕs), *n.* Quality or state of

wind instrument (wĭnd). *Music.* An instrument sounded by wind, esp. by the breath.

wind'lass (wĭnd'lăs), *n.* Any of various machines for hoisting or hauling, as by turning a crank.

wind'mill' (-mĭl'), *n.* A mill operated by wind.

win'dow (wĭn'dō), *n.* **1.** An opening in the wall of a building to admit light and air. **2.** *Arch.* The shutter, casement, sash, or other framework, which closes a window opening. —*v. t.* To furnish with a window or windows.

Windmill. *a a* Sails ; *b* Vane to bring Windmill into the wind.

wind'pipe' (wĭnd'pīp'), *n.* The trachea.

wind'row' (wĭnd'rō'), *n.* **1.** A row of hay raked up before being heaped into cocks ; also, any similar row for drying, as of sheaves of grain. **2.** A windswept line or row, as of dry leaves or dust.

wind'ward (-wĕrd), *n.* Point or side from which the wind blows;—opp. to *leeward*.—*a.* On the side toward the windward. — *adv.* Toward the wind.

wind'y (wĭn'dĭ), *a.* [3] **1.** Consisting of wind; accompanied or characterized by wind ; swept by wind. **2.** Flatulent. **3.** Bombastic ; boastful. *Colloq.*

wine (wĭn), *n.* **1.** The fermented juice of grapes. **2.** The fermented juice of any fruit or plant, used as a beverage. —*v. t. & i.* [1] To supply or treat with wine, or to drink wine.

wing (wĭng), n. **1.** An organ of aërial flight; one of the appendages by means of which birds, bats, and insects fly. **2.** Passage by flying; flight. **3.** A part of a building projecting from the main part. **4.** Either half (right or left) of a main supporting surface (or "plane") of an airplane. — v. t. **1.** To furnish with wings. **2.** To effect or achieve by wings. **3.** To fly through. **4.** To wound in the wing; wound. — v. i. To fly.

wing/less, a. Without wings.

wink (wĭnk), v. i. **1.** To close and open the eyelids quickly; blink. **2.** To avoid seeing or noting, as if by shutting the eyes; connive; — usually with at. **3.** To flicker; twinkle. — v. t. **1.** To cause (the eyes) to wink. **2.** To effect by winking. — n. **1.** Act of winking, esp. with one eye; a hint thus given. **2.** Time required for a single wink; instant. **3.** A sparkle; gleam. — **wink/er**, n.

win/ner (wĭn/ẽr), n. One that wins.

win/ning (wĭn/ĭng), n. **1.** Act of one that wins. **2.** That which one wins; — often in pl.

win/now (wĭn/ō), v. t. **1.** To drive off the chaff from by wind; fan. **2.** To separate or sift. **3.** To scatter by wind. — v. i. To separate chaff from grain by fanning.

win/some (-sŭm), a. [3] **1.** Causing joy or pleasure; winning. **2.** Cheerful; merry; gay; lighthearted. — **win/some-ly**, adv. — **-ness**, n. [8].

win/ter (-tẽr), n. The coldest season; cold weather. — v. i. To pass the winter. — v. t. To keep, feed, or manage during the winter.

win/ter-green/ (-grēn/), n. An evergreen herb, of the heath family, bearing red berries called *check-erberries*. The leaves yield oil of wintergreen.

win/ter-y (-ĭ), a. [4] Wintry.

win/try (wĭn/trĭ), a. [3] Of or pert. to winter.

win/y (wĭn/ĭ), a. [3] Pert. to, or like, wine.

wipe (wīp), v. t. [1] **1.** To rub lightly, or with something soft, for cleaning. **2.** To draw, pass, or the like, for rubbing or cleaning. **3.** To rub off; obliterate. — n. Act of rubbing, esp. to clean.

wip/er (wīp/ẽr), n. One that wipes.

wire (wīr), n. **1.** A thread or very slender rod of metal, usually round. **2.** A telegraph wire or cable; *Colloq.*, the telegraph system or a telegram. — v. t. & i. [1] **1.** To provide with wire, or to use wire on. **2.** To telegraph. *Colloq.*

wire/less (wīr/lĕs), a. Having no wire or wires; esp., *Elec.*, designating, or pert. to, a method of telegraphy, telephony, etc., by means of electric waves without wire connections.

wir/y (-ĭ), a. [3] **1.** Made of, or like, wire. **2.** Tough and sinewy. — **wir/i-ness** (-ĭ-nĕs), n. [8].

wis/dom (wĭz/dŭm), n. **1.** Quality of being wise; sagacity. **2.** Erudition; learning.

wisdom tooth. The back tooth of the full set on each half of each jaw in man, appearing from the 17th to the 21st year, or later.

wise (wīz), a. [3] **1.** Discerning and judging soundly concerning what is true or false, proper or improper; sagacious. **2.** Dictated or guided by wisdom. **3.** Having knowledge; learned. — **-ly**, adv.

wise (wīz), n. Way of being or acting; manner; fashion. *Rare*, exc. in *in any wise*, *in no wise*, etc.

wise/a-cre (wīz/ā-kẽr), n. A pretender to wisdom; hence, in contempt, a simpleton; dunce.

wish (wĭsh), v. i. To desire; long; — usually with an infinitive or *for*. — v. t. **1.** To long for; crave; desire. **2.** To invoke or desire in favor of, or against, any one. — n. **1.** Eager desire; longing. **2.** Expression of desire; request. **3.** Object of desire. — **wish/er**, n. [8].

wish/bone/ (wĭsh/bōn/), n. The forked bone in front of the breastbone in most birds.

wish/ful (-fool), a. [4] Having desire; longing; wistful. — **-ly**, adv. [8] — **-ness**, n. [8].

wisp (wĭsp), n. Small bunch, as of hay or straw.

wist (wĭst), pret. of WIT, know.

wis-ta/ri-a (wĭs-tā/rĭ-à), n. Any of various climbing shrubs cultivated for their purple flowers.

wist/ful (wĭst/fool), a. [4] **1.** Longing; wishful. **2.** Meditative; pensive. — **-ly**, adv. — **-ness**, n.

wit (wĭt), v. t. & i. To know; learn; — now only in *to wit*, namely.

wit, n. **1.** Mind; intellect; sense. **2.** A mental faculty, or power; — chiefly in pl. **3.** The perception or expression of associations between ideas or words not usually connected, such as to produce an amusing surprise; power of such perception or expression. **4.** A witty person.

witch (wĭch), n. **1.** One regarded as having supernatural or magical power by compact with an evil spirit, esp. the Devil; — chiefly or only of women. **2.** A hag. **3.** A bewitching, or fascinating, woman or girl. *Colloq.* — v. t. To bewitch; fascinate.

witch/craft/ (wĭch/kräft/), n. **1.** Practices or art of witches; sorcery. **2.** Witchery.

witch/er-y (wĭch/ẽr-ĭ), n.; pl. -ERIES (-ĭz). Fascination; irresistible influence.

witch/-ha/zel, n. **1.** A shrub having hazel-like leaves. **2.** An extract of the bark of this plant.

with (wĭth), prep. *With* means, or is used to indicate: **1.** Against; in opposition to. *Obs.*, except after *fight, contend, vie*, etc., or in composition, as in *with*stand, *witha*l. **2.** Contact, association, or connection. **3.** Because or by reason of; by the agency of.

with-al/ (wĭth-ôl/), adv. Together with this; likewise; moreover; at the same time; also. *Archaic.* — prep. With; — put after its object. *Archaic.*

with-draw/ (-drô/), v. t.; for prin. parts see DRAW. **1.** To take back or away; draw back. **2.** To recall or retract. — v. i. To retire; retreat; recede.

with-draw/al (-ăl), n. Act of withdrawing.

withe (wĭth; wĭth), n. A flexible twig or branch used as a band.

with/er (wĭth/ẽr), v. i. & t. **1.** To dry or shrivel up; fade. **2.** To decay; decline; languish.

with/ers (-ẽrz), n. pl. Ridge between the shoulder bones of the horse and some other animals.

with-hold/ (wĭth-hōld/), v. t. & i.; for prin. parts see HOLD. **1.** To hold back or in; restrain; refrain from action. **2.** To refrain from granting, etc.; as, to *with*hold consent.

with-in/ (-ĭn/), adv. **1.** In the inner part; inwardly. **2.** In the house; indoors. — prep. **1.** In the interior part of; inside of. **2.** In the limits or compass of.

with-out/ (-out/), adv. **1.** On or at the outside; outwardly. **2.** Outdoors. **3.** With the lack or absence of something indicated. — prep. **1.** At or on the outside of. **2.** Beyond ; as, *without* dispute. **3.** Not with ; as : **a** In absence of ; as, *without* delay. **b** Exclusive of. — **without day.** = SINE DIE.

with-stand' (-stănd'), *v. t. & i. ; -STOOD' ; -STAND'-ING.* To stand against, esp. successfully ; oppose.

with'y (wĭth'ĭ ; wĭth'ĭ), *a.* [3] Like a withe.

wit'less (wĭt'lĕs), *a.* [4] Void of wit ; foolish.

wit'ness (-nĕs), *n.* **1.** Attestation of a fact or an event ; testimony. **2.** One who testifies. **3.** That which serves as evidence or proof. **4.** One who has personal knowledge of anything. — *v. t.* **1.** To act as a witness of. **2.** To testify to. **3.** To give evidence of. **4.** To see or know by personal presence. — *v. i.* To testify.

wit'ted (-ĕd), *a.* Having wit, or understanding.

wit'ti-cism (wĭt'ĭ-sĭz'm), *n.* A witty saying.

wit'ti-ly (wĭt'ĭ-lĭ), *adv.* In a witty manner.

wit'ti-ness, *n.* Quality of being witty.

wit'ting-ly (-ĭng-lĭ), *adv.* Knowingly.

wit'ty (wĭt'ĭ), *a.* [3] **1.** Possessing wit (in sense 3) ; sometimes, sarcastic. **2.** Marked by wit.

wives (wīvz), *n., pl.* of WIFE.

wiz'ard (wĭz'ärd), *n.* A magician ; sorcerer.

wiz'ard-ry (-rĭ), *n.* Sorcery ; magic.

wiz'en (-'n), **wiz'ened** (-'nd), *a.* [4] Shriveled.

wo, wo'be-gone', etc. Vars. of WOE, etc.

woad (wōd), *n.* Plant formerly grown for the blue dyestuff yielded by its leaves ; also, the dyestuff.

woe (wō), *n.* Grief ; misery ; a heavy calamity.

woe'be-gone' (wō'bē-gŏn'), *a.* [4] Overwhelmed with woe ; woeful ; hence, indicating woe.

woe'ful, wo'ful (-fŏŏl), *a.* [4] **1.** Full of woe ; sad. **2.** Bringing or pertaining to, woe. — **-ly**, *adv.* [8] — **-ness**, *n.* [8]. [without woods.

wold (wōld), *n.* A plain or a low hill ; a region

wolf (wŏŏlf), *n. ; pl.* WOLVES (wŏŏlvz). Any of certain large doglike carnivores.

wolf'ish (wŏŏl'fĭsh), *a.* [4] Like a wolf.

wolf'ram (wŏŏl'frăm ; wŏlf'-), *n.* Tungsten.

wolfs'bane' (wŏŏlfs'bān'), *n.* Aconite.

wol'ver-ene' (wŏŏl'vẽr-ēn'), *n.* A carnivorous mammal, with shaggy fur ; glutton.

wol'ver-ine' (-ēn'). Var. of WOLVERENE. *U. S.*

wolves (wŏŏlvz), *n., pl.* of WOLF.

wom'an (wŏŏm'ăn),*n.;pl.* WOMEN (wĭm'ĕn). **1.** An adult female person. **2.** Womankind.

wom'an-hood (-hŏŏd), *n.* **1.** State of being a woman. **2.** Womankind.

wom'an-ish, *a.* [4] Suitable to or like a woman ; — usually disparaging.

wom'an-kind (-kīnd'), *n.* Women collectively.

wom'an-like (-līk'), *a.* [4] Womanly.

wom'an-ly, *a.* [4] Befitting or like a woman. — **-li-ness**, *n.* [8] — **wom'an-ly**, *adv.*

womb (wŏŏm), *n.* The uterus.

wom'bat (wŏm'băt), *n.* A burrowing Australian marsupial, resembling a small bear.

wom'en (wĭm'ĕn), *n., pl.* of WOMAN.

won (wŭn), *pret. & p. p.* of WIN.

won'der (wŭn'dẽr), *n.* **1.** A cause of surprise or astonishment ; marvel ; prodigy. **2.** The emotion excited by novelty or by something strange or extraordinary.—*v. i. & t.* **1.** To be affected with surprise ; marvel. **2.** To feel doubt and curiosity.

won'der-ful (-fŏŏl), *a.* [4] Adapted to excite wonder ; marvelous. — **-ly**, *adv.* [8] — **-ness**, *n.* [8].

won'der-land' (-lănd'), *n.* A land of wonders.

won'der-ment (-mĕnt), *n.* Surprise.

won'drous (wŭn'drŭs), *adv.* Wonderfully. — *a.* [4] Wonderful. — **-ly**, *adv.* — **-ness**, *n.* [8].

won't (wōnt ; wŭnt). A colloquial contraction of *woll not*, obs. var. of *will not.*

wont (wŭnt ; wōnt), *a.* Accustomed ; used ; — with an infinitive. — *n.* Custom ; habit. — *v. i.* To be accustomed. — *v. t.* To accustom.

wont'ed, *p. a.* (4] Accustomed ; usual.

woo (wŏŏ), *v. t. & i.* **1.** To solicit in love ; to court. **2.** To invite or beseech importunately ; seek.

wood (wŏŏd), *n.* **1.** A dense growth of trees ; forest ; grove ; — often in *pl.* **2.** The hard fibrous substance of trees or shrubs beneath the bark. **3.** Timber ; lumber ; firewood. **4.** Something made of wood. — *v. t.* To supply with wood.

wood'bine' (wŏŏd'bīn'), *n.* **1.** Any of several honeysuckles. **2.** The Virginia creeper. *U. S.*

wood'chuck' (-chŭk'), *n.* A burrowing animal of N. America, 15 to 18 inches long, brownish, grayish, and reddish in color ; the groundhog.

Woodchuck.

wood'cock' (-kŏk'), *n.* A gamebird with long bill and prominent eyes.

wood'craft' (-kráft'), *n.* Skill in what pertains to the woods, esp. in hunting, trapping, etc.

wood'cut' (-kŭt') *n.* An engraving on wood ; also, a print from such an engraving.

wood'en (wŏŏd'n), *a.* [3] **1.** Made or consisting of wood. **2.** Stiff ; awkward ; spiritless ; stupid.

wood'land (-lănd ; -lănd'), *n.* Land covered with wood, or trees ; forest. — **wood'land-er**, *n.* [8].

wood'man (-măn), *n. ; pl.* -MEN (-mĕn). **1.** A forester. **2.** One who cuts down trees.

wood'peck'er (wŏŏd'pĕk'ẽr), *n.* A bird having a chisel-like bill used to drill into wood for insects.

woods'man (wŏŏdz'măn), *n. ; pl.* -MEN (-:nĕn). A woodman, esp. one who lives in the forest.

wood sorrel. An oxalis, esp. the white-flowered, stemless species.

wood'work' (wŏŏd'wûrk'), *n.* Work of wood.

wood'y (wŏŏd'ĭ), *a.* [3] **1.** Abounding with wood or woods. **2.** Of, containing, or like, wood.

woo'er (wŏŏ'ẽr), *n.* One who woos ; a suitor.

woof (wŏŏf), *n.* **1.** The threads that cross the warp in a fabric ; weft ; filling. **2.** Texture ; cloth.

wool (wŏŏl), *n.* **1.** The soft and curled, or crisped, covering or coat of domesticated sheep and some other animals. **2.** Something like wool.

wool'en, wool'len (wŏŏl'ĕn), *a.* **1.** Made or consisting of wool. **2.** Of or pertaining to wool or woolen cloths. — *n.* Fabric made of wool.

wool'gath'er-ing (-găth'ẽr-ĭng), *n.* Indulgence in vagrant fancies. — *a.* Idly fanciful.

wool'ly (wŏŏl'ĭ), *a.* [3] Consisting of, like, or clothed with, wool. — **wool'li-ness** (-nĕs), *n.* [8].

word (wûrd), *n.* **1.** That which is said ; esp., a brief expression. **2.** Statement ; affirmation ; promise. **3.** Tidings ; information ; — only in *sing.* **4.** A

āle, senāte, câre, ăm, ăccount, ärm, ȧsk, sofȧ; ēve, ĕvent, ĕnd, recĕnt, makēr; īce, ĭll; ōld, ȯbey, ôrb, ŏdd, sŏft, cŏnnect; ūse, ûnite, ûrn, ŭp, circŭs; tŏŏd, fŏŏt; out, oil;

password; also, command. **5.** Talk; discourse; — chiefly in *pl.* **6.** *pl.* Verbal contention; dispute. **7.** An articulate sound or combination of sounds symbolizing an idea; also, its written or printed symbol. **8. a** The Scriptures. **b** [*cap.*] The second person in the Trinity before incarnation. — *v. t.* To express in words; phrase.

word'ing, *n.* Expression in words; phrasing.

word'y (wûr'dĭ), *a.* [3] **1.** Consisting of words; verbal. **2.** Using many words, esp. more than are necessary. — **word'i-ly** (-ĭ-lĭ), *adv.* [8] — **word-i-ness,** *n.* [8].

work (wûrk), *n.* **1.** Physical or mental effort directed to an end; toil; labor; also, employment; occupation. **2.** Task; duty. **3.** Deed; achievement. **4. a** Thing produced by mental labor, as a book or piece of art. **b** Embroidery; needlework. **c** *pl.* Structures such as docks, bridges, fortifications, etc. **5.** A place where industrial labor is carried on. **6.** *pl.* The working parts of a mechanism, as of a clock. **7.** Manner of working. — *v. i.*, *pret. & p. p.* WORKED (wûrkt), or WROUGHT (rôt); *p. pr. & vb. n.* WORK'ING. **1.** To exert one's self for a purpose; labor; toil. **2.** To operate or act; be effective. **3.** To move, progress, etc., laboriously or slowly; — with *out, into, up, through,* etc. **4.** To ferment, as a liquid. — *v. t.* **1.** To fashion; shape; make. **2.** To bring to pass; cause; do; as, to *work* havoc. **3.** To operate; manage; set or keep in motion. **4.** To cause to labor or toil. **5.** To carry on one's occupation in, through, etc. **6.** To make, effect, or bring into some condition, by or as if by labor; as, to *work* one's self free. **7.** To make or ornament by needlework; embroider. **8.** To solve, as a problem. **9.** To influence; prevail on. **10.** To excite; provoke.

work'a-day' (wûr'ká-dā'), *a.* [4] Pertaining to working days; laboring; hence, prosaic.

work'day' (-dā'), *n.* A day for work as disting. from Sunday, festivals, etc. — *a.* Workaday.

work'er (wûr'kĕr), *n.* One that works.

work'house' (wûrk'hous'), *n.* **1.** Workshop. **2.** In England, a poorhouse. **3.** A house of correction in which petty offenders are confined at labor. *U.S.*

work'ing-man (-măn), *n.; pl.* -MEN (-mĕn). A laboring man; a manual laborer.

work'man (wûrk'măn), *n.; pl.* -MEN (-mĕn). A man employed in labor; esp., a skilled laborer.

work'man-like', *a. & adv.* Befitting a workman, esp. a skillful one.

work'man-ship, *n.* **1.** Art or skill of a workman. **2.** That which is effected or produced; work.

work'peo'ple (-pē'p'l), *n. pl.* Laboring people.

work'ta'ble (-tā'b'l), *n.* A table for holding working materials and implements.

work'wom'an (-wŏom'ăn), *n. ; pl.* -WOMEN. A woman who works, esp. at manual labor.

world (wûrld), *n.* **1.** The universe. **2.** The earth; hence, mankind; the public. **3.** A state of existence; sphere of life and action. **4.** Individual experience; career, or course of life. **5.** The social customs, practices, and interests of men; as, to know the *world*. **6.** A great number or quantity. **7.** A part or section of the earth.

world'ling (wûrld'lĭng), *n.* A person devoted to this world and its enjoyments.

world'ly, *a.* [3] Of or pertaining to this world; of or pert. to the concerns of this life as distinguished from those of the life to come. — **world'li-ness** (-lĭ-nĕs), *n.* [8] — **world'ly,** *adv.* [8].

world'ly-wise', *a.* [4] Wise as to this world.

worm (wûrm), *n.* **1.** Any of numerous small, slender, creeping or crawling animals, usually having soft, naked, and limbless bodies. **2.** *pl.* Any disorder due to parasitic worms, as in the intestines. **3.** A spiral or wormlike thing, as a screw thread, etc. **4.** See WORM WHEEL. — *v. i.* To move, go, or work slowly and insidiously. — *v.t.* To work, effect, remove, draw, etc., by slow and secret means.

worm'-eat'en (-ēt''n), *a.* [4] Eaten, or eaten into, by a worm or worms.

worm gear. *Mach.* **a** A worm wheel. **b** A gear of a worm and worm wheel working together.

worm wheel. A cogwheel to gear with a short revolving screw called a *worm*.

worm'wood' (-wŏod'), *n.* **1.** A plant, of the aster family, bitter, and tonic. **2.** Something bitter; bitterness. [with, or like, worms.]

worm'y (wûr'mĭ), *a.* [3] Containing, abounding

worn (wôrn), *p. p.* of WEAR.

worn'-out', *a.* Exhausted or used up by wear.

wor'ri-some (-sŭm), *a.* [4] Inclined to worry or fret; also, causing worry.

wor'ry (wûr'ĭ), *v. t.* [2] **1.** To harass with or as with continual snapping or biting; also, to tear or mangle with the teeth. **2.** To harass with importunity, or with care and anxiety. — *v. i.* To feel or express great care and anxiety; fret. — *n.; pl.* -RIES (-ĭz). **1.** Act of worrying. **2.** Undue solicitude; anxiety. — **wor'ri-er** (-ĭ-ẽr), *n.*

worse (wûrs), *a.*, *comparative* of BAD. Bad, ill, evil, or corrupt, in a greater degree; less good; also, more sick. — *adv.* In a worse degree or manner. — *n.* That which is worse.

wor'ship (wûr'shĭp), *n.* **1.** Reverence, adoration, or homage paid to God, a god, or a sacred object. **2.** A title of honor. — *v. t.* [7] To pay divine honors to; adore; idolize. — *v. i.* To perform acts of homage or adoration; esp., to perform religious service. — **ship-er,** *n.* [7, 8].

wor'ship-ful (-fŏol), *a.* [4] **1.** Entitled to worship, reverence, or high respect. **2.** Honorable; esteemed; — in formal address. — **ful-ly,** *adv.* [8].

worst (wûrst), *a.*, *superlative* of BAD. Bad, evil, or pernicious in the highest degree. See WORSE. — *adv.* To the extreme degree of badness or inferiority. — *n.* That which is most bad or evil. — *v. t.* To get the better of; defeat; discomfit.

wor'sted (wŏos'tĕd; wŏor'stĕd), *n.* **1.** Well-twisted yarn of long-staple wool; also, cloth made from such yarn. **2.** Soft woolen yarn, untwisted or lightly twisted, used in knitting and embroidery.

wort (wûrt), *n.* Any plant or herb; esp., a potherb; — chiefly in combination; as, cole*wort*.

wort, *n.* An infusion of malt unfermented, or in process of fermentation.

worth (wûrth), *a.* **1.** Deserving of; meriting. **2.** Equal in value to. **3.** Having possessions equal to. — *n.* **1.** The quality or qualities of a thing rendering it valuable or useful; value; hence, price. **2.** Excellence; virtue; as, a man of *worth*.

---

wor'thi-ly (wûr′thĭ-lĭ), *adv.* In a worthy manner.

wor'thi-ness (-nĕs), *n.* Quality of being worthy.

worth'less (wûrth′lĕs), *a.* [4] Destitute of worth; useless; mean. — **-ly**, *adv.* [8] — **-ness**, *n.* [8].

wor'thy (wûr′thĭ), *a.* [3] **1.** Having worth or excellence. **2.** Meriting; fit. — *n.; pl.* -THIES (-thĭz). A person of great worth or desert.

wot (wŏt), *1st & 2d pers. sing. pres.* of WIT, to know. *Archaic or Scot. & Dial. Eng.*

would (wŏŏd), *pret. & (obs.) p. p.* of WILL, *v. t.* & of 2d WILL, *v. i.* For use of *would* as auxiliary, see SHOULD. Special uses of *would* are: a In expressions of desire or wish; as, I *would* I were young again. b In expressing what might be expected; as, that *would* make talk.

wound (wound), *pret. & p. p.* of 1st & 3d WIND.

wound (wŏŏnd ; wound), *n.* **1.** An injury by which the skin is divided; a stab, cut, or laceration. **2.** An injury or hurt to feelings, reputation, etc. — *v. t.* To pain. — *v. i.* To inflict a wound.

wove (wōv), *pret. & occasional p. p.* of WEAVE.

wo'ven (wō′v'n), *p. p.* of WEAVE. [shore.

wrack (răk), *n.* Marine vegetation cast up on the

wraith (rāth), *n.* An apparition of a living person in his exact likeness ; apparition ; specter.

wran'gle (răn′g'l), *v. i.* [1] To argue ; dispute ; brawl. — *n.* An angry dispute ; noisy quarrel.

wran'gler (răn′glẽr), *n.* One who wrangles.

wrap (răp), *v. t. ;* WRAPPED (răpt) or WRAPT ; WRAP′PING. **1.** To wind or roll together ; fold. **2.** To cover by winding or folding ; infold ; — often with *up.* **3.** To inclose in a package ; do up ; — usu. with *up.* — *n.* An article of dress to be wrapped round the person ; — used. in *pl.*, for furs, shawls, etc.

wrap'per (-ẽr), *n.* **1.** One that wraps, or folds. **2.** Envelope ; covering. **3.** A loose outer garment.

wrath (răth ; râth ; *or, esp. in British usage,* rŏth), *n.* Violent anger ; rage ; ire.

wrath'ful (-fŏŏl), *a.* [4] Full of wrath ; very angry. — **-ly**, *adv.* — **-ness**, *n.*

wreak (rēk), *v. t.* To execute in vengeance or passion ; inflict.

wreath (rēth), *n. ; pl.* WREATHS (rēthz). **1.** Something twisted or intertwined into circular shape ; as, a *wreath* of flowers. **2.** A garland ; chaplet.

wreathe (rēth), *v. t. & i.* [1] To entwine ; infold.

wreck (rĕk), *n.* **1.** That which has been wrecked or is in ruin. **2.** Destruction or injury of anything by violence ; ruin. — *v. t.* To shipwreck ; to bring wreck or ruin on by violence. — **-er**, *n.* [8].

wreck'age (-ăj), *n.* A wrecking ; state of being wrecked ; also, thing wrecked ; remains of a wreck.

wren (rĕn), *n.* Any of various small singing birds.

wrench (rĕnch), *n.* **1.** A violent twist. **2.** A sprain. **3.** A tool for turning nuts, etc. — *v. t.* **1.** To wrest or force by violence. **2.** To strain ; sprain.

wrest (rĕst), *v. t.* **1.** To turn ; twist ; extort by violence. **2.** To distort. — *n.* **1.** Act of wresting. **2.** A key to tune a stringed musical instrument.

wres'tle (rĕs′'l), *v. i.* [1] **1.** To grapple. **2.** To struggle ; strive earnestly. — *n.* A wrestling bout ; struggle. — **wres'tler** (-lẽr), *n.* [8].

wretch (rĕch), *n.* A wretched person.

wretch'ed, *a.* [4] **1.** Very miserable ; unhappy.

2. Despicable. **3.** Unsatisfactory. — **-ly**, *adv.* [8] — **-ness**, *n.* [8].

wrig'gle (rĭg′'l), *v. i. & t.* [1] To squirm. — *n.* Act of wriggling. — **-gler** (-lẽr), *n.* [8].

wright (rīt), *n.* A workman ; artificer, esp. in wood ; — chiefly in composition, as in ship*wright.*

wring (rĭng), *v. t. ; pret. & p. p.* WRUNG (rŭng) ; *p. pr. & vb. n.* WRING′ING. **1.** To twist and compress. **2.** To torture. **3.** To extract or get by twisting and compressing ; extort. — **-er**, *n.* [8].

wrin'kle (rĭng′k'l), *n.* A small ridge ; crease. — *v. t.* [1] To make a wrinkle or wrinkles in. — *v. i.* To be or become wrinkled.

wrin'kly (-klĭ), *a.* [3] Wrinkled ; puckered.

wrist (rĭst), *n.* The joint, or the region of the joint, between the hand and the arm.

wrist'band (rĭst′bănd ; *colloq.* rĭz′-), *n.* The band of a sleeve, as of a shirt, covering the wrist.

wrist'let (rĭst′lĕt), *n.* A band worn around the wrist, esp. to protect from cold.

writ (rĭt), *Archaic pret. & p. p.* of WRITE.

writ, *n.* **1.** A writing ; scripture ; as, in Holy *Writ.* **2.** A judicial or official order under seal.

write (rīt), *v. t. ;* WROTE (rōt) ; *p. p.* WRIT′TEN (rĭt′'n) ; *Archaic pret. & p. p.* WRIT (rĭt) ; *p. pr. & vb. n.* WRIT′ING (rīt′ĭng). **1.** To set down, as legible characters ; to trace (characters, or words, etc.) on a surface ; inscribe. **2.** To compose. **3.** To record ; imprint. — **to write off,** *Bookkeeping,* to take off the books or to cancel. — *v. i.* **1.** To form characters to represent sounds or ideas. **2.** To express ideas in written words ; compose. **3.** To send, or communicate by, letters. — **writ'er** (rĭt′ẽr), *n.*

writhe (rĭth), *v. t. & i.* [1] To twist ; esp., to twist or turn so as to distort. [one who writes.

writ'ing (rīt′ĭng), *n.* Act, art, or production of

writ'ten (rĭt′'n), *p. p.* of WRITE.

wrong (rŏng), *a.* **1.** Out of order ; amiss. **2.** Not morally right ; perverse. **3.** Not legal ; not just or equitable. **4.** Not according to truth or fact ; incorrect ; false. **5.** Not suitable to an end or object ; not according to intention or purpose. **6.** Designed to be worn or placed inward. — *adv.* In a wrong manner. — *n.* That which is wrong ; evil ; an injury ; trespass. — *v. t.* **1.** To do wrong to ; harm. **2.** To represent erroneously. — **-er**, *n.*

wrong'do'er (rŏng′dōō′ẽr ; rŏng′dōō′ẽr), *n.* One who does wrong. — **wrong'do'ing**, *n.*

wrong'ful (-fŏŏl), *a.* [4] Full of wrong ; injurious ; unjust. — **-ly**, *adv.* [8] — **-ness**, *n.* [8].

wrong'ly, *adv.* In a wrong manner.

wrong'ness, *n.* State or quality of being wrong.

wrote (rōt). Pret. of WRITE.

wroth (rŏth), *a.* Full of wrath ; angry.

wrought (rŏt), *pret. & p. p.* of WORK. Hence : *a.* Worked ; elaborated. — **wrought iron,** a very tenacious, malleable iron which cannot be hardened by sudden cooling.

wrung (rŭng), *pret. & p. p.* of WRING.

wry (rī), *a.* [3] **1.** Turned to one side ; contorted ; as, a *wry* mouth. **2.** Distorted, as in meaning ; perverted. — **wry'ly**, *adv.* [8] — **wry'ness**, *n.* [8].

wry'neck (rī′nĕk′), *n.* A bird having a peculiar manner of writhing its head and neck.

āle, senăte, câre, ăm, *ă*ccount, ärm, ȧsk, sofȧ ; ēve, ĕvent, ĕnd, recĕnt, makẽr ; īce, ĭll ; ōld, ōbey, ôrb, ŏdd, sŏft, cŏnnect ; ūse, ŭnite, ûrn, ŭp, circŭs ; fōōd, fŏŏt ; out, oil ;

X

X rays. The Röntgen rays ;—so called because of their enigmatical character, *X* being used in mathematics to indicate an unknown quantity.

xan′thic (zăn′thĭk), *a.* Pertaining to, or tending toward, a yellow color.

xe′bec (zē′bĕk), *n. Naut.* A kind of Mediterranean vessel, usually three-masted.

xen′on (zĕn′ŏn; zē′nŏn), *n.* A heavy, inert gas.

xy′lem (zī′lĕm), *n. Bot.* Woody tissue.

xy-loph′a-gous (zĭ-lŏf′à-gŭs), *a. Zoöl.* Eating, boring in, or destroying, wood ; — said esp. of certain insect larvæ, crustaceans and mollusks.

xy′lo-phone (zī′lō-fōn), *n. Music.* An instrument consisting of a series of graduated wooden bars and sounded by striking with two small wooden hammers.

Xylophone.

Y

yacht (yŏt), *n. Naut.* A vessel larger than a rowboat, used either for pleasure or as a vessel of state. — *v. i.* To sail, cruise, or race in a yacht.

yacht′ing, *n.* Sailing for pleasure in a yacht.

yachts′man (yŏts′măn), *n.; pl.* -MEN (-mĕn). One who owns or sails a yacht.

yak (yăk), *n.* A large, long-haired, wild or domesticated ox of central Asia.

yam (yăm), *n.* **1.** The edible, starchy tuberous root of a climbing plant of various species, used as a staple food in tropical climates ; also, the plant. **2.** The sweet potato. *Southern U. S.*

yank (yăngk), *n.* A strong jerk or twitch. *Colloq.* — *v. t.* To pull quickly or twitch strongly. *Colloq.*

Yan′kee (yăn′kē), *n.* A native of New England or of the Northern States ; sometimes, among foreigners, any inhabitant of the United States ; — a nickname. — *a.* Of or pert. to the Yankees.

yap (yăp ; yáp), *n.* A snappish bark ; yelp. *Scot.* or *Dial.* — *v. i.* To bark snappishly ; yelp. *Scot.* or *Dial.*

yard (yärd), *n.* **1.** A measure of length equal to 3 feet, or 36 inches (0.9144 meter). Abbr.; *yd., yds. yds.* **2.** *Naut.* A long spar to support and extend a square sail, lateen sail, or lugsail.

yard, *n.* **1.** An inclosure before or about a house, barn, etc. **2.** An inclosure where work or business is carried on ; as, a brick*yard.*

yard′arm′ (yärd′ärm′), *n. Naut.* Either end of a square-rigged vessel's yard.

yard′stick′ (-stĭk′), *n.* A measuring stick three feet in length.

yarn (yärn), *n.* **1.** Spun wool ; woolen thread ; thread. **2.** A story, esp. one told by a sailor. *Colloq.* — *v. i.* To tell yarns. *Colloq.*

yar′row (yăr′ō), *n.* A strong-scented plant, of the aster family, having small white flowers.

yat′a-ghan (yăt′à-găn), *n.* A long knife, or short saber, common among Mohammedans.

yaw (yô), *v. i. & t. Naut.* To steer wild ; deviate, as when struck by a sea ; — of a ship. — *n.* A deviation from a straight course in steering.

yawl (yôl), *n. Naut.* **a** A ship's small boat. **b** A fore-and-aft rigged vessel with a small mast at the stern.

yawn (yôn), *v. i.* **1.** To open the mouth, esp. involuntarily through drowsiness, dullness, or fatigue ; gape. **2.** To gape ; open wide, as a chasm. — *n.* A yawning.

ye (yē), *pron.* The personal pronoun of the 2d person, used : **1.** As nominative *pl.*, originally its only construction. **2.** As objective (accusative or dative) *pl.* **3.** As nominative or objective *sing.* ☞ *Ye* is now superseded by *you*, except in solemn or poetical style, and in dialect.

yea (yā). An affirmative adverbial particle, used (def. 3) also as a conjunction, now archaic, and superseded in senses 1 and 3 by *yes*, except in solemn usage : **1.** Yes. **2.** Indeed ; truly ; — introducing a sentence or clause. **3.** More than this ; not only so, but; — used to mark the addition of something more emphatic. — *n.* An affirmative reply or vote ; one who votes in the affirmative.

year (yēr), *n.* **1.** The time of one apparent revolution of the sun around the ecliptic ; the period of the earth's revolution round the sun (**astronomical year**), or 365 days, 5 hours, 48 minutes, 45.51 seconds. **2.** A period of 365 days, in leap year, 366 days, beginning January 1 (the **calendar**, or **civil**, **year**).

year′book′ (yēr′book′), *n.* A book published yearly ; annual report or summary.

year′ling (-lĭng), *n.* An animal one year old, or in the second year of its age. — *a.* A year old.

year′ly, *a.* Happening or coming every year; annual. — *adv.* Annually. [sire.]

yearn (yûrn), *v. i.* To be filled with longing desire.

yeast (yēst), *n.* **1.** A substance, consisting of cells of minute fungi, appearing as a froth or sediment in saccharine liquids, as fruit juices, etc. It is used in making alcoholic liquors, esp. beer, and, in baking, as a means of leavening. **2.** Spume, or foam.

yeast′y (yēs′tĭ), *a.* [3] Resembling, or consisting of, yeast.

yell (yĕl), *v. i. & t.* To cry out or utter with a loud and sharp noise ; shriek ; shout. — *n.* **1.** A sharp and loud hideous outcry. **2.** A shout or cheer.

yel′low (yĕl′ō), *a.* [3] Of the color yellow ; of the color of gold, sulphur, etc. — *n.* **1.** The most luminous color of the spectrum, lying between orange and green. **2.** Any pigment or dye that colors yellow. — *v. t. & i.* To make or become yellow.

---

chair; go; sing, ink; then, thin; nature, verdure; yet; zh = z in azure. Numbers refer to §§ in the Special Notes which, with Abbreviations, Signs, etc., precede the Vocabulary.

yel'low-bird' (yĕl'ō-bûrd'), *n.* **1.** The American goldfinch. **2.** The yellow warbler. *Local, U. S.*

yellow fever. *Med.* An acute, infectious, often fatal, febrile disease, marked by jaundice, vomiting, etc. It is transmitted by mosquitoes.

yel'low–ham'mer (-hăm'ẽr), *n.* **1.** A European finch. The male is marked with bright yellow. **2.** The flicker. *U. S.*

yel'low-ish, *a.* Somewhat yellow.

yellow jack. **1.** The yellow fever. **2.** The quarantine flag.

yellow jacket. Any of several American social wasps, having the body partly bright yellow.

yel'low-ness, *n.* Yellow quality or state.

yelp (yĕlp), *v. i.* To utter a sharp, quick cry, as a dog. — *n.* A sharp, quick cry; a bark.

yen (yĕn), *n. sing. & pl.* The monetary unit of Japan; also, a gold or a silver coin of this value. It is worth about 49.8 cents.

yeo'man (yō'măn), *n. ; pl.* -MEN (-mĕn). A petty freeholder; small landowner. *Chiefly Eng.*

yeo'man-ry (-rĭ), *n.* Yeomen collectively.

yes (yĕs). An affirmative adverbial particle, denoting : **1.** Aye ; yea ; it is so ; — opposed to *no.* **2.** More than this; what is more; — used to mark the addition of something more emphatic.

yes'ter (yĕs'tẽr), *a.* Of or pertaining to yesterday. *Rare,* except in combination, as in **yestereve, yestereven,** the evening of yesterday. *Archaic.*

yes'ter-day (yĕs'tẽr-dā), *n.* The day next before the present. — *adv.* On yesterday.

yes'ter-night' (-nīt'), *adv.* On the night last past. *Archaic.* — *n.* The night last past. *Archaic.*

yet (yĕt), *adv.* **1.** As soon as now; hitherto. **2.** Continuing; still. **3.** In addition; further; still; as, this makes his offense *yet* blacker. **4.** Before all is done; eventually. **5.** Although such is the case. — *conj.* **1.** Nevertheless; however; but. **2.** Although; though.

yew (yōō), *n.* A large European coniferous tree with dark green foliage; also, its fine-grained wood.

Yid'dish (yĭd'ĭsh), *n.* A German dialect developed under Hebrew and Slavic influence, used by German and other Jews.

yield (yēld), *v. t.* **1.** To give in return for labor, or to produce as interest on what is invested; pay. **2.** To produce; furnish; give forth. **3.** To give; grant; afford. **4.** To give up, as a thing claimed; surrender; relinquish. **5.** To admit as true; concede; acknowledge. — *v. i.* **1.** To produce; bear. **2.** To give way; submit; surrender. **3.** To give place, as to a superior; give precedence. — *n.* Amount yielded; product. — **yield'er**, *n.* [S].

yo'del } (yō'd'l), *v. t. & i.* [7, 1] To sing with **yo'dle** } sudden changes from natural to falsetto voice. — *n.* A song so sung. — **yo'del-er** (yō'd'l-ẽr), **yo'dler** (yō'dlẽr), *n.* [S].

yo'gi (yō'gē), *n.* A Hindu ascetic.

yo'icks (yō'ĭks; yoiks), *interj.* *Hunting.* A cry of encouragement to the hounds in fox hunting.

yoke (yōk), *n.* **1.** A bar or frame of wood by which two draft animals, esp. oxen, are joined at the heads or necks for working together. **2.** A band or shaped piece cut to fit the shoulders or

hips to support hanging parts of a garment. **3.** Fig. : That which connects or binds; tie; bond. **4.** A mark or emblem of subjection, servitude, etc. ; hence, servitude; bondage. **5.** *sing. & pl.* Two animals yoked together ; a couple ; a pair that work together. — *v. t.* [1] **1.** To put a yoke on; as, to *yoke* oxen; join in or with a yoke. **2.** To couple ; join; link; fig., to marry.

yoke'fellow (yōk'fĕl'ō), *n.* A mate ; spouse.

yo'kel (yō'k'l), *n.* A plowboy ; rustic.

yolk (yōk ; yōlk), *n.* **1.** The yellow spheroidal mass of food material in the egg of a bird or reptile. **2.** A greasy substance in sheep's wool.

yon (yŏn), *a. & adv.* Yonder. *Chiefly Poetic.*

yon'der (yŏn'dẽr), *adv.* At or in that (indicated and more or less distant) place. — *a.* Being at a distance within, or conceived of as within, view.

yore (yōr), *n.* Time long past; — now only in the phrase of yore, of old time ; long ago.

you (yōō), *pron. ; poss.* YOUR (yōōr) or YOURS (yōōrz) ; *dat. & obj.* YOU. A personal pronoun of the second person, indicating the person or persons addressed, and used as a nominative or objective plural (replacing *ye*), and as a nominative or objective singular (replacing *thou, thee,* but taking, as subject, a plural verb).

young (yŭng), *a.* [3] **1.** Being in the first or early period of life, growth, or existence. **2.** Youthfully fresh in body, mind, or feeling. **3.** Immature ; inexperienced. **4.** Of or pert. to youth. — *n.* The offspring of animals.

young'ling (-lĭng), *n.* A young person ; also, a young animal, plant, etc. — *a.* Young ; youthful.

young'ster (yŭng'stẽr), *n.* A young person; youth.

your (yōōr), *pron. & a.* Of or belonging to you ; — used as the possessive case of *you,* or as a possessive adjective.

yours (yōōrz), *pron. & a.* The form of the possessive *your* used when the governing noun does not follow; as, the book is *yours.*

your-self' (yōōr-sĕlf'), *pron. ; pl.* -SELVES (-sĕlvz'). An emphasized form for *ye, you.*

youth (yōōth), *n. ; pl.* YOUTHS (yōōths ; yōōthz) or, *collectively,* YOUTH. **1.** Quality or state of being young ; youthfulness. **2.** The part of life that succeeds to childhood. **3.** A young person ; esp., a young man. **b** Collective *pl.* Young people.

youth'ful (yōōth'fōōl), *a.* [4] **1.** Possessing youth; young. **2.** Of or pertaining to the early part of life; suitable to youth. **3.** Fresh; vigorous. — **-ly**, *adv.* [8] — **-ness**, *n.* [8].

yowl (youl), *n.* A loud, long, mournful cry, as of a dog ; a howl. — *v. i.* To utter a yowl ; to howl.

yuc'ca (yŭk'á), *n.* A plant, of the lily family, having long, pointed, often rigid leaves on a woody stem. It bears a large cluster of white blossoms.

Yu'go-slav', or **Ju'go-slav'** (yōō'gō-släv'), *n.* A native or inhabitant of Yugoslavia. — **Yu'go-slav'i-an** (-släv'ĭ-ăn), **Yu'go-slav'ic** (-släv'ĭk), *a.*

yule (yōōl), *n.* Christmas or Christmastide. — **yule log,** log formerly put with ceremony on the hearth on Christmas Eve, as the foundation of the fire.

yule'tide' (-tīd'), *n.* Christmastide.

āle, senãte, câre, ăm, ăccount, ärm, àsk, sofá; ēve, ĕvent, ênd, recĕnt, makêr; īce, ĭll; ōld, ŏbey, ôrb, ŏdd, sôft, cŏnnect; ūse, ûnite, ûrn, ŭp, circŭs; fōōd, fŏŏt; out, oil;

Z

za'ny (zā'nĭ), *n.; pl.* -NIES (-nĭz). **1.** A clown; buffoon; jester. **2.** A simpleton.

zeal (zēl), *n.* Ardor in pursuit of anything; enthusiasm; fervor.

zeal'ot (zĕl'ŭt), *n.* One who is zealous in any cause; esp., one who is a fanatical partisan.

zeal'ot-ry (-rĭ), *n.* Excess of zeal.

zeal'ous (zĕl'ŭs), *a.* [4] Filled with, marked by, or due to, zeal. — **-ly**, *adv.* [8]. — **-ness**, *n.* [8].

ze'bra (zē'brà), *n.* An African animal of the horse family, with black or blackish stripes on a white or buff ground.

ze'bu (zē'bū), *n.* A species of ox domesticated in India, China, the East Indies, etc. It usually has short horns and a large hump over the shoulders.

zed (zĕd), *n.* The letter Z; — usual name in England.

ze'nith (zē'nĭth), *n.* **1.** That point of the heavens vertically above one; — opposed to *nadir*. **2.** Greatest height; summit; culmination.

zeph'yr (zĕf'ēr), *n.* **1.** The west wind; any soft, gentle breeze. **2.** For zephyr yarn, a fine soft yarn or worsted for knitting and embroidery.

Zep'pe-lin (zĕp'ĕ-lĭn), *n.* A dirigible balloon of the rigid type, often of great size: — so called from Count von Zeppelin, of Germany.

ze'ro (zē'rō), *n.; pl.* -ROS or -ROES (-rōz). **1.** *Arith.* A cipher; nothing. **2.** The point from which the graduation of a scale, as of a thermometer, begins. **3.** Lowest point; nothingness. **4.** Also zero hour. *Mil.* Hour at which a previously planned movement is started. Called *H hour* in U. S. service.

zest (zĕst), *n.* **1.** Something that gives a pleasant taste or relish; also, the relish or taste as imparted; piquancy. **2.** Keen enjoyment; gusto.

zig'zag' (zĭg'zăg'), *n.* One of a series of short sharp turns or angles in a course; also, something characterized by such a series, as a path, pattern, etc. — *a.* Having zigzags. — *adv.* In or by a zigzag path or course. — *v. t. & i.;* -ZAGGED' (-zăgd'); -ZAG'GING (-zăg'ĭng). To form or move with zigzags; make or be zigzag.

zinc (zĭnk), *n.* A bluish white metal, but little affected by air and moisture. — *v. t.;* ZINCKED or -ZINCED (zĭnkt); ZINCK'ING or ZINC'ING (zĭnk'ĭng). To treat or coat with zinc.

zinck'y, zink'y (zĭnk'ĭ), **zinc'ous** (-ŭs), *a.* Pert. to, containing, or appearing like, zinc.

Zi'on (zī'ŏn), *n.* **1.** A hill in Jerusalem, where the temple was. **2. a** The theocracy, or church of God. **b** The heavenly Jerusalem.

Zi'on-ism (-ĭz'm), *n.* Among modern Jews, a theory or plan for colonizing Jews in Palestine.

Zi'on-ist, *n.* An advocate of Zionism.

zir'con (zûr'kŏn), *n.* A mineral containing the element zirconium, usually occurring in square brown or grayish prisms or pyramids.

zir-co'ni-um (zẽr-kō'nĭ-ŭm), *n. Chem.* An element found in zircon, from which it has been separated as a black powder and as a white crystalline metallic substance.

zith'er (zĭth'ẽr), *n.* A musical instrument, with 30 to 40 strings, played with a plectrum.

zo'di-ac (zō'dĭ-ăk), *n. Astron.* An imaginary belt in the heavens including the paths of the moon and the principal planets and, as its middle line, the ecliptic. See SIGN, *n.*, 5.

zo-di'a-cal (zō-dī'à-kăl), *a.* Pertaining to the zodiac; within the zodiac; as, *zodiacal* planets.

zone (zōn), *n.* **1.** An encircling band, stripe, or girdle. **2.** Any of five great divisions of the earth's surface as to latitude and temperature; the **torrid** zone, extending 23° 28' on each side of the equator, from tropic to tropic; two **temperate**, or **variable**, zones, between the tropics and the polar circles, which are 23° 27' from the poles; two **frigid zones**, between the polar circles and poles. **3.** An area or region taken as distinct from adjoining parts; as, on the Isthmus of Panama, the Canal *Zone*.

zoo (zoō), *n.* A zoölogical garden or collection.

zo-ög'ra-phy (zō-ŏg'rà-fĭ), *n.* A description of animals, their forms and habits.

zo'ö-log'i-cal (zō'ô-lŏj'ĭ-kăl), *a.* Of or pertaining to zoölogy, or the science of animals.

zo-öl'o-gist (zō-ŏl'ô-jĭst), *n.* One versed in zoölogy.

zo-öl'o-gy (zō-ŏl'ô-jĭ), *n.; pl.* -GIES (-jĭz). Science of animals; biology dealing with animals.

zoom (zoōm), *v. i. Aviation.* To climb for a short time at an angle greater than that which can be maintained in steady flight. — *n.* Any sudden increase in the upward slope of the path of flight.

Zo'ro-as'tri-an (zō'rō-ăs'trĭ-ăn), *a.* Of or pert. to Zoroaster (flourished ab. 1000 B. C.) ancient Persian prophet, or the religion, Zo'ro-as'tri-an-ism, founded by him. — *n.* A follower of Zoroaster.

Zou-ave' (zoō-äv'), *n.* One of a body of infantry in the French service wearing a brilliant uniform of peculiar cut; hence, a member of any body of soldiers adopting a similar dress and form of drill.

zounds (zoundz), *interj.* An old oath.

‖ **Zwie'back'** (tsvē'bäk') *n.* [G.] [*Often l. c.*] Kind of biscuit or rusk baked in a loaf and afterwards cut and toasted.

zyme (zīm), *n.* A ferment; esp., *Med.*, the cause of a zymotic disease.

zy-mot'ic (zī-mŏt'ĭk), *a.* **1.** Of, pert. to, or caused by, fermentation. **2.** *Med.* Designating any infectious or contagious disease.

---

chair; go; sing, ink; then, thin; nature, verdure; yet; zh = z in azure. Numbers refer to §§ in the Special Notes which, with Abbreviations, Signs, etc., precede the Vocabulary.

GEOGRAPHICAL AND BIOGRAPHICAL NAMES

In the **geographical entries** are given the location of each place, height of mountains, length of rivers, population of cities and countries (*in nearest thousands; thus, p. 300 = population 300,000*), area, and the name of the nation having jurisdiction, where this information is of interest.

In the **biographical entries** are given (*in parentheses*) the dates of birth and death, or the date of death (indicated by **d.**) where this alone is known, or the date of the person's greatest activity (indicated by **fl.,** *flourished*) where more precise data are lacking. In the case of rulers and, often, holders of other high offices are given the date of accession, and the date of the end of the reign or term of office where this is not the same as the date of death.

The following **abbreviations** need explanation. For others, see page x.

Each entry is given the most approved **spelling** and **pronunciation.**

ab. about.	*Du.* Dutch.	*Minn.* Minnesota.	*rep., repub.* republic.
adm. admiral.	*E* east; eastern.	*Miss.* Mississippi.	*R. I.* Rhode Island.
Afr. Africa.	*E.* East; Eastern.	*Mo.* Missouri.	*riv.* river.
Ala. Alabama.	*Egypt.* Egyptian.	*mod.* modern.	*Rom.* Roman.
Am. America; -can.	*emp.* emperor.	*Mont.* Montana.	*Russ.* Russia; -an.
arch. archipelago.	*eng.* engineer.	*mt.* mountain.	*S* south; southern.
Ariz. Arizona.	*Eur.* Europe.	*N* north; northern.	*S. South;* Southern.
Ark. Arkansas.	*Fed.* Federation.	*N. North;* Northern.	*S. C.* South Carolina.
astron. astronomer.	*Fla.* Florida.	*nav.* navigator.	*Scot.* Scotland.
Atl. Atlantic.	*Fr.* France; French.	*N. C.* North Carolina.	*S. Dak.* South Dakota.
au., auth. author.	*ft.* feet.	*N. Dak.* North Dakota.	*sec.* secretary.
b. born.	*ftd.* fortified.	*Nebr.* Nebraska.	*Sp.* Spain.
bat. battle.	*Ga.* Georgia.	*Neth.* Netherlands.	*spt.* seaport.
B. C. British Columbia.	*gen.* general.	*Nev.* Nevada.	*St.* Saint.
Belg. Belgium.	*Ger.* German; Germany.	*N. H.* New Hampshire.	*statesm.* statesman.
Bib. Biblical.	*gov.* governor.	*N. J.* New Jersey.	*sub.* suburb; suburbs.
bor. borough.	*Gr.* Greece.	*N. Mex.* New Mexico.	*Sw.* Sweden.
Br., Brit. British.	*Gr. Br.* Great Britain.	*nr.* near.	*Switz.* Switzerland.
Bulg. Bulgaria.	*hist.* historian.	*N. S. W.* New South	*Tenn.* Tennessee.
Calif. California.	*Ill.* Illinois.	Wales.	*ter.* territory.
Can. Canada.	*incl.* including.	*N. Y.* New York.	*Tex.* Texas.
cath. cathedral.	*Ind.* Indian; Indiana.	*N. Z.* New Zealand.	*tn.* town.
cen. central.	*Ir.* Irish.	*oc., ocs.* ocean; oceans.	*trib.* tributary.
cent. century.	*Ire.* Ireland.	*Okla.* Oklahoma.	*Turk.* Turkish.
cml. commercial.	*isl.* island.	*Ont.* Ontario.	*univ.* university.
co. county.	*Jap.* Japan; Japanese.	*Ore.* Oregon.	*Va.* Virginia.
col. colony.	*Kans.* Kansas.	*p.* population.	*vil.* village.
Colo. Colorado.	*kdm.* kingdom.	*Pa.* Pennsylvania.	*vol.* volcano.
Conn. Connecticut.	*kg.* king.	*Pac.* Pacific.	*Vt.* Vermont.
Dan. Danish.	*Ky.* Kentucky.	*pen.* peninsula.	*W* west; western.
D. C. District of Co-	*La.* Louisiana.	*Phil. isls.* Philippine is-	*W. West;* Western.
lumbia.	*m.* miles.	lands.	*Wash.* Washington.
Del. Delaware.	*Mass.* Massachusetts.	*philos.* philosopher.	*W. I.* West Indies.
depend. dependency.	*Md.* Maryland.	*polit.* politician.	*Wis.* Wisconsin.
dipl. diplomat.	*Me.* Maine.	*poss.* possession.	*W. Va.* West Virginia.
disc. discoverer.	*Medit.* Mediterranean.	*pres.* president.	*Wyo.* Wyoming.
dist. district.	*Mex.* Mexico.	*prot.* protectorate.	□ square miles.
div. division.	*Mich.* Michigan.	*prov.* province.	✻ capital.
dram. dramatist.	*min.* minister.	*pseud.* pseudonym.	

A

Aachen (ä′kĕn), *Fr.* **Aix-la-Chapelle** (ĕks′-là-shà′-pĕl′; ĕs′-), city, Rhine Prov. Prussia, p. 146.

Aberdeen (ăb′ẽr-dēn′), city, E Scot. p. 159; univ.

Abyssinia (ăb′ĭ-sĭn′ĭ-à), *or* **Ethiopia,** country, E Afr. 350,000 □ p. ab. 11,500, ✻ Addis Ababa.

Aconcagua (ä′kŏn-kä′gwä), mt. NW Argentina, 23,080 ft.; highest in W. Hemisphere.

Adams (ăd′ămz), John. 2d pres. of U. S. in 1797-

āle, senāte, cãre, ăm, ăccount, ärm, ȧsk, sofȧ; ēve, ĕvent, ĕnd, recĕnt, makẽr; īce, ĭll; ōld, ōbey, ôrb, ŏdd, sŏft, cŏnnect; ūse, ŭnite, ûrn, ŭp, circŭs; fōōd, fŏŏt; out, oil; chair; go; sing, iŋk; then, thin; nature, verdure; yet; zh = z in azure. Numbers refer to §§ in the Special Notes which, with Abbreviations, Signs, etc., precede the Vocabulary.

(530)

1801 (1735–1826). —, John Quincy. Son of John. 6th pres. of U. S. in 1825–29 (1767–1848).

Addison (-ĭ-sŭn), Joseph. Eng. essayist (1672–1719).

Adelaide (-ĕ-lād), city, ✳ of S. Australia, p. 255.

Aden (ä'dĕn; ā'-), spt. and ter. SW Arabia, p. 57; Br. —, **Gulf of**, bet. S Arabia and coast of Africa.

Adirondacks (ăd'ĭ-rŏn'dăks), mts. NEN. Y. 5,344 ft.

Adriatic Sea (ā'drĭ-ăt'ĭk), arm of Medit. E of Italy.

Ægean Sea (ē-jē'ăn), bet. Asia Minor and Greece.

Æschylus (ĕs'kĭ-lŭs). Greek poet (B. C. 525–456).

Æsop (ē'sŏp). Greek writer of fables (fl. B. C. 560?).

Afghanistan (ăf-găn'ĭ-stän'), monarchy, W Asia, 245,000 ☐ p. 6,380, ✳ Kabul.

Africa (ăf'rĭ-kȧ), continent, 11,622,000 ☐ p. 142,000.

Agra (ä'grä), div. and city, N Br. India, p. city 186.

Ahmedabad (ä'mĕd-ä-bäd'), city, W India, p. 274.

Akron (ăk'rŭn), city, NE Ohio, p. 208.

Alabama (ăl'ȧ-băm'ȧ; -bä'mȧ), S state U. S. 51,-998 ☐ p. 2,348, ✳ Montgomery. Abbr. *Ala.*

Alaric (ăl'ȧ-rĭk). King of Visigoths, conquered Rome (376?–410).

Alaska (ȧ-lăs'kȧ), ter. of U. S., NW N. Am. 590,884 ☐ p. 55, ✳ Juneau; bought from Russia in 1867.

Albania (ăl-bā'nĭ-ȧ), country, Europe, bet. Yugoslavia & Greece, 14,000 ☐ p. 832, ✳ Tirana.

Albany (ôl'bȧ-nĭ), city, ✳ of N. Y. in E, p. 113.

Albert (ăl'bĕrt) **I.** King of Belgium fr. 1909 (1875–). [cen. Africa, 2,064 ☐.

Albert, Lake, or **Albert Nyanza** (nyän'zä), lake,

Aleppo (ȧ-lĕp'ō), city, N Syria, Asia, p. 140.

Alexander (ăl'ĕg-zän'dĕr). *The Great.* Kg. of Macedonia fr. B. C. 336 (B. C. 356–323). [445.

Alexandria (-drĭ-ȧ), Medit. spt. city, Egypt, p.

Alfonso (ăl-fŏn'sō) **XIII.** King of Spain, 1902–31 (1886–). [fr. 871 (849–901).

Alfred (ăl'frĕd). *The Great.* Kg. of W. Saxons

Algeria (ăl-jē'rĭ-ȧ), Fr. col. N Afr. 222,180 ☐ p. 5,802.

Algiers (-jērz'), spt. ✳ of Algeria, p. 207.

Allahabad (äl'ȧ-hä-bäd'), div. & city (p. 157), N Br. India. [Md. Va. & W. Va.

Allegheny Mountains (ăl'ĕ-gā'nĭ), ranges in Pa.

Alps (ălps), mt. system, S cen. Europe: highest, Mont Blanc. [Ger.; ceded to Fr. 1919.

Alsace-Lorraine (ăl-säs'-lō'rän'), former ter. W

Altai (äl-tī'), mts. cen. Asia; highest, 14,890 ft.

Amazon (ăm'ȧ-zŏn), riv. Brazil, ab. 3,500 m.; largest in world.

Amsterdam (ăm'stĕr-dăm), spt. Neth. p. 647.

Amundsen (ä'mŭn-sĕn), Roald. Norwegian discoverer of South Pole, Dec. 14, 1911 (1872–1928).

Amur (ä-mōōr'), riv. E Asia, 2,700 m. long.

Anatolia (ăn'ȧ-tō'lĭ-ȧ), part of Turkey in Asia.

Andes (ăn'dēz), mt. system, W S. Am. 23,080 ft.

Andorra (än-dôr'rä), small country, Europe, bet. Fr. & Sp. p. 5. [4,119; Port. col.

Angola (ăn-gō'lȧ), country, W Afr. 484,800 ☐ p.

Angora (-gō'rȧ), *anc.* ANCY'RA, city, Asia Minor, Turkey in Asia, ✳ of Turkey, p. 35.

Annam (ăn'năm'), or **Anam** (ä-näm'), native kdm. Indo-China, 39,758 ☐ p. 5,731, ✳ Hué; Fr. prot.

Annapolis (ȧ-năp'ō-lĭs), city, ✳ of Md. p. 11; U. S. Naval Academy.

Anne (ăn). Queen of England fr. 1702 (1665–1714).

Antarctic Continent (ănt-ärk'tĭk), land around

the S. Pole, ab. 5,000,000 ☐. — **Ocean,** S of antarctic circle. (See ANTARCTIC, in *Dict.*)

Antilles (ăn-tĭl'ēz), **Greater & Lesser,** isl. groups, West Indies. [1914.

Antwerp (ănt'vwĕrp), city, N Belg. p. 323; siege,

Apennines (ăp'ĕ-nīnz), mt. chain, cen. Italy, 9,585 ft.

Appalachian Mountains (ăp'ȧ-lăch'ĭ-ăn; -lā'-chĭ-ăn), mt. system, E N. Am. 6,711 ft.

Arabia (ȧ-rā'bĭ-ȧ), great pen. SW Asia, ab. 1,200,-000 ☐ p. 5,000. [Arabia.

Arabian Sea (-ăn), part of Ind. oc. bet. India &

Aral Sea (är'ăl), inland sea, SW Russ. in Asia.

Ararat (ăr'ȧ-răt), mt. in Armenia, ab. 17,000 ft.

Arc, Jeanne d' (zhän därk'). See JOAN OF ARC.

Arctic Ocean (ärk'tĭk), ocean around North Pole.

Argentina (är'jĕn-tē'nä), or **Argentine Republic,** republic, S S. Am. 1,153,119 ☐ p. 7,885, ✳ Buenos Aires. [statesm. & gen. (d. B. c. 468?).

Aristides (ăr'ĭs-tī'dēz). *The Just.* Athenian

Aristotle (ăr'ĭs-tŏt''l). Greek philos. (B. c. 384–22).

Arizona (ăr'ĭ-zō'nȧ), state, SW U. S. 113,956 ☐ p. 334, ✳ Phoenix. Abbr. *Ariz.*

Arkansas (är'kăn-sô), riv. 2,000 m. a W trib. of the Miss. — state, S cen. U. S. 53,335 ☐ p. 1,752, ✳ Little Rock. Abbr. *Ark.*

Armenia (är-mē'nĭ-ȧ), *Bib.* MINNI (mĭn'ī), anc. country, W Asia; now divided between Russia, Turkey, & Persia. [(1822–88).

Arnold (är'nŭld), Matthew. Eng. poet & essayist

Arthur (är'thŭr). Legendary Br. kg. (fl. 5th or 6th cent.). —, Chester Alan. 21st pres. of the U. S. in 1881–85 (1830–86).

Ashanti (ȧ-shän'tē), native kingdom, Br. W. Afr. p. 407; dependency of Gold Coast colony.

Asia (ā'shȧ; -zhȧ), largest continent, 17,000,000 ☐ p. ab. 900,000.

Asia Minor, or **Anatolia,** pen. Turkey, W Asia, bet. Black & Medit. seas, 199,272 ☐ p. 10,427.

Assyria (ȧ-sĭr'ĭ-ȧ), anc. empire, W Asia.

Astrakhan (ăs'trȧ-kăn'), city, SE Russia, p. 123.

Asunción (ä-sōōn'syōn'), ✳ of Paraguay, p. 100.

Athens (ăth'ĕnz), city, ✳ of Greece, in SE, p. 293.

Atlanta (ăt-lăn'tȧ), city, ✳ of Georgia, in N. p. 201.

Atlantic Ocean (-tĭk), separating America fr. Europe & Africa. [15,000 ft.

Atlas Mountains (ăt'lăs), system, NW Afr. ab.

Attica (ăt'ĭ-kȧ), anc. div. & state of E Greece.

Attila (ăt'ĭ-lȧ). King of the Huns (406?–53).

Auckland (ôk'lȧnd), spt. N N. Z., p. with sub. 158.

Augsburg (ouks'bŏŏrk), city, SW Bavaria, p. 155.

Augusta (ô-gŭs'tȧ), city, ✳ of Maine, in S, p. 14.

Augustine (ô-gŭs'tĭn; ô'gŭs-tĭn), St. Apostle of the Eng. (d. 604). —, St. A bishop of ancient Numidia, in N Africa (354–430).

Augustus (ô-gŭs'tŭs). *Octavianus.* 1st Roman emp. fr. B. c. 27 (B. c. 63–A. D. 14).

Aurelian (-rē'lĭ-ăn). Rom. emp. fr. 270 (212?–275).

Austin (ôs'tĭn), city, ✳ of Tex. p. 35; Univ. of Tex.

Australasia (ôs'trȧl-ā'shȧ; -zhȧ), part, sometimes all, of Oceania.

Australia (ôs-trā'lĭ-ȧ; -trāl'yȧ), isl. continent bet. Indian & Pacific ocs. 2,948,366 ☐ p. 5,223. —, **Commonwealth of,** Br. col. consisting of Australia continent & Tasmania; 2,974,581 ☐ p. 5,436; with Ter. of Papua, 3,065,121 ☐ p. 5,714; ✳ Canberra.

---

chair; go; sing, iŋk; then, thin; nature, verdure; yet; zh = z in azure. Numbers refer to §§ in the Special Notes which, with Abbreviations, Signs, etc., precede the Vocabulary.

Austria (ôs'trĭ-à), repub. cen. Europe, 32,369 □ p. 6,536, ✳ Vienna.

Azerbaijan (ä'zĕr-bä-ê-jän'), repub. Transcaucasian Fed. W Asia, 33,970 □ p. 2,097, ✳ Baku.

Azores (à-zōrz'), isls. N Atlantic oc. p. 243; Port.

B

Babylon (băb'ĭ-lŏn), anc. city of Babylonia.

Babylonia (-lō'nĭ-à), anc. country in Euphrates valley, SW Asia. [music (1685–1750).|

Bach (bäk), Johann Sebastian. Ger. composer of

Bacon (bā'k'n), Francis, Baron Verulam, Viscount St. Albans. Eng. philos. & statesm. (1561–1626).

Baden (bä'dĕn), state, SW Ger. 5,819 □ p. 2,209.

Bagdad (băg'dăd), cml. city, cen. Mesopotamia, SW Asia, ✳ of Irak, p. 250.

Bahama Islands (bà-hā'mà), group NE of Cuba, 4,404 □ p. 53, ✳ Nassau; Br. colony.

Bahia (bä-ē'à), spt. city, E Brazil, p. 283.

Baikal (bī-käl'), lake, S Siberia, Asia, 13,200 □.

Baku (bà-kōō'), spt. ✳ of Azerbaijan, Asia, p. 250.

Balearic Islands (băl'ê-ăr'ĭk), group ✳ Sp. prov. in Medit. 1,936 □ p. 351.

Balkan Mountains (bôl'kăn; bàl-kän'), Serbia to Black sea, 9,610 ft. — **Peninsula**, SE Europe.

Balkan States, Yugoslavia, Roumania, Bulgaria, Albania, Greece, & Turkey in Europe, — states of the Balkan pen. [of Baltic states.|

Baltic Sea (bôl'L .), N of Germany & Poland & W

Baltic States, Esthonia, Latvia, & Lithuania, on E shore of Baltic sea; sometimes, also, Finland.

Baltimore (bôl'tĭ-mōr), city, cen. Md. p. 734.

Baluchistan (bà-lōō'chĭ-stän'), country, E of S Persia, 134,638 □ p. 800, ✳ Kalat. [1850).|

Balzac, de (dĕ bäl'zàk'), Honoré. Fr. au. (1799–

Bangkok (băng'kŏk'), city, ✳ of Siam, p. 629.

Barbados (bär-bā'dōz), British island and colony, West Indies, 166 □ p. 156. [Egypt.|

Barbary (bär'bà-rĭ), region in N Africa, W of|

Barcelona (bär'sē-lō'nà), spt. NE Spain, p. 706.

Basel (bä'zĕl), Fr. **Bâle** (bäl), city, N Switz. p. 136.

Basra or **Busrah** (büs'rà), tn. S Mesopotamia, p. 166. [Indies, p. 254.|

Batavia (bà-tā'vĭ-à), spt. NW Java, ✳ of Du. East|

Baton Rouge (băt'ŭn rōōzh'), city, ✳ of La. in SE, on Miss. riv. p. 22.

Bavaria (bà-vā'rĭ-à), state, S Germany, 29,506 □ p. 7,140, ✳ Munich.

Bechuanaland (bĕch'ōō-ä'nà-lănd'), Brit. prot. cen. S. Afr. 275,000 □ p. 153.

Becket, à (à bĕk'ĕt), Thomas. Archbishop of Canterbury (1118?–70).

Beecher (bē'chĕr), Henry Ward. Am. preacher (1813–87). [composer (1770–1827).|

Beethoven, van (vän bā'tō-vĕn), Ludwig. Ger.|

Beirut (bā'rōōt'), spt. Syria, p. 180.

Belem (bá-lĕn'), or **Pará** (pä-rä'), spt. Brazil, p. 236.

Belfast (bĕl-fàst'), city, ✳ of N. Ireland, p. 393.

Belgian Congo, col. of Belgium, S cen. Afr. 909,654 □ p. 8,508, ✳ Leopoldville.

Belgium (bĕl'jĭ-ŭm), kdm. W Europe, 11,752 □ p. 7,637, ✳ Brussels.

Belgrade (bĕl'grād'), city, ✳ of Serbia & of Yugoslavia, on Danube riv. p. 112. [198.|

Benares (bĕn-ä'rĕz), city on Ganges, Br. India, p.

Bengal (bĕn-gôl'), prov. Br. India, 78,699 □ p. 46,696, ✳ Calcutta. —, **Bay of**, part of Indian oc. bet. India & Indo-China.

Bergen (bĕr'gĕn), spt. city on Atl. oc. Norway, p. 91.

Bering Sea (bē'rĭng), S of Bering strait. — **Strait**, bet. Alaska & Siberia, 36 m. wide.

Berlin (bŭr'lĭn'; G. bĕr-lēn'), city, ✳ of Prussia & of Ger. p. 1,903; Greater Berlin, p. 3,804; univ.

Bermuda (bĕr-mū'dà), isls. N Atl. p. 23, ✳ Hamilton; Br. colony. [(1091–1153).|

Bernard (bûr'nàrd; bĕr-närd'), Saint. Fr. abbot|

Berne or **Bern** (bĕrn), city, ✳ of Switz. in W, p. 105.

Bessarabia (bĕs'à-rā'bĭ-à), div. E Roumania, 17,146 □ p. 2,725, ✳ Kishinev; form. a part of Russia in Europe.

Birkenhead (bûr'kĕn-hĕd), bor. W Eng. p. 146.

Birmingham (-mĭng-ăm), city, cen. Eng. p. 919. — (-ăm; -hăm), city, cen. Ala. p. 179.

Biscay, Bay of (bĭs'kā), part of Atl. W of France & N of Spain.

Bismarck (bĭz'märk), city, ✳ of N. Dak. p. 7.

Bismarck-Schönhausen, von (fôn bĭs'märk-shūn'hou'zĕn), Otto E. L., Prince. Bismarck. Ger. statesman (1815–98). [Asia, 168,500 □.|

Black, or **Euxine** (ūk'sīn), **Sea**, bet. Eur. &|

Blanc, Mont (mŏn'blän'), highest of Alps; 15,781 ft.

Bœotia (bē-ō'shĭ-à), dist. & anc. repub. E Greece.

Bogotá (bō'gō-tä'), city, ✳ of Colombia, p. 160.

Bohemia (bō-hē'mĭ-à), form. kdm. now prov. W Czechoslovakia, 20,098 □ p. 6,665.

Boise (boi'zā), city, ✳ of Idaho, in SW, p. 21.

Bolivar (bŏl'ĭ-vär), Simon. S. Am. patriot (1783– 1830). [✳✳ La Paz & Sucre.|

Bolivia (bō-lĭv'ĭ-à), S. Am. rep. 514,155 □ p. 2,890,|

Bologna (-lōn'yà), city, N Italy, p. 205; univ.

Bombay (bŏm-bā'), western presidency of Br. India, 123,541 □ p. 19,348. — its ✳, chief spt. of W India, on Bombay isl. in Arabian sea, p. 1,176.

Bonaparte (bō'nà-pärt). Corsican family, esp. Napoleon I. & her brothers: Jérôme, Kg. of Westphalia (1784–1860); Joseph, Kg. of Naples & Spain (1768–1844); Louis, Kg. of Holland (1778– 1846); Lucien (1775–1840). See NAPOLEON.

Bonheur (bō'nûr'), Rosa. Fr. painter of animals (1822–99). [93.|

Booth (bōōth), Edwin Thomas. Am. actor (1833–|

Bordeaux (bôr'dō'), spt. city, SW France, p. 267.

Borgia (bôr'jä). It. family, esp. Pope Alexander VI. & his children: Cesare, cardinal & soldier (1476–1507); Lucrezia, Duchess of Ferrara (1480–1519).

Borneo (-nê-ō), isl. Malay arch. 289,843 □ p. 2,459.

Bosnia and Herzegovina (bŏz'nĭ-à, hĕr'tsĕ-gō-vē'nà), prov. W cen. Yugoslavia, 19,678 □ p. 1,890, ✳ Sarajevo. [mara seas.|

Bosporus (bŏs'pō-rŭs), strait bet. Black & Mar-|

Boston (bŏs'tŭn), spt. city, ✳ of Mass. in E, p. 748.

Bothnia, Gulf of (bŏth'nĭ-à), N part of Baltic sea.

Bradford (brăd'fĕrd), bor. N Eng. p. 286.

Brahmaputra (brä'mà-pōō'trà), riv. Tibet & India, 1,800 m.

Bratislava (brä'tĭ-slä'và), Ger. **Pressburg** (prĕs'-bŏŏrk), city, S Czechoslovakia, on Danube, p. 93.

Brazil, United States of (brà-zĭl'), rep. S. Am. 3,275,528 □ p. 30,636, ✳ Rio de Janeiro.

Bremen (brä'mĕn; brĕm'ĕn), port, NW Ger. p. 270.

āle, senâte, câre, ăm, ăccount, ärm, àsk, sofà; ēve, ĕvent, ĕnd, recĕnt, makĕr; īce, ĭll; ōld, ōbey, ôrb, ŏdd, sôft, cŏnnect; ūse, ŭnite, ûrn, ŭp, circŭs; fōōd, fŏŏt; out, oil;

Breslau (brĕs'lou), city, Silesia, Prussia, p. 528.

Bridgeport (brĭj'pōrt), city, SW Conn. p. 144.

Bridges (brĭj'-ĭz), Robert, Sir. Eng. poet laureate (1844–). [p. 210.

Brisbane (brĭz'bân), spt. ✳ of Queensland, in SE, N Fr. p. 73. [1,328.

Bristol (brĭs'tŭl), city, W Eng. on Avon riv. p. 377.

British America, Canada, Newfoundland, & Labrador; sometimes, all Br possessions in America.

— Columbia, Pacific prov. Can. 355,855 ☐ p. 523, ✳ Victoria. **— East Africa,** ter. E Afr. incl. Kenya, Uganda, & Zanzibar prot.; also sometimes Tanganyika Ter. **— Empire,** the United Kingdom of Gr. Britain & N Ireland & its possessions. **— Guiana,** Br. col. N S. Am. 89,480 ☐ p. 307, ✳ Georgetown. **—India,** Br. col. embracing greater part of India (incl. Burma), 1,093,074 ☐ p. 247.003, ✳ Delhi. **— Isles,** Gr. Br., Ire. & adjacent isls. 121,582 ☐ p. 47,308. **— North Borneo,** Br. prot. NE Borneo, 31,106 ☐ p. 208. ✳ Sandakan. **— West Africa,** Br. poss. in W Afr.: Nigeria, Gambia, Gold Coast, & Sierra Leone cols. & Togo & Cameroons mandates.

Brontë (brŏn'tĕ), three sisters, Eng. authors: Anne (1820–49); Charlotte, *Mrs. A. B. Nicholls* (1816–55); Emily Jane (1818–48).

Bronx, The (brŏŋks), bor. N New York city, p. 732.

Brooklyn (brŏŏk'lĭn), bor. of N. Y city, p. 2,018.

Browning (broun'ĭng), Robert. Eng. poet (1812–89). **—** his wife, Elizabeth Barrett. Eng. poet (1806–61).

Bruce, de (dĕ brōōs'), Robert. *Robert Bruce.* Liberator, & king fr. 1306, of Scot. (1274–1329).

Brussels (brŭs'ĕlz), city, ✳ of Belgium, p. 157, with sub. 685. [1925].

Bryan (brī'ăn), Wm. Jennings. Am. polit. (1860–1878). [(1838–1922).

Bryant (brī'ănt), William Cullen Am. poet (1794–1878).

Bryce (brīs), James, 1st Viscount. Eng. statesm. & amb. to the U. S. in 1857–61 (1791–1868).

Buchanan (bŭ-kăn'ăn; bū-), James. 15th pres. of the U. S. in 1857–61 (1791–1868).

Bucharest (bōō'kȧ-rĕst'), city, ✳ of Roumania, in S, p. 309. [N, p. 1,185.

Budapest (bōō'dȧ-pĕst'), city, ✳ of Hungary, in

Buddha (bōōd'ȧ). See in *Dict.*

Buenos Aires (bwā'nōs ī'rās), city, ✳ of Argentina, on Plata river, p. 1,733; largest in S. Am.

Buffalo (bŭf'ȧ-lō), city & lake port, W N. Y. p. 507

Bulgaria (bŏŏl-gā'rĭ-ȧ), kingdom, SE Europe, 39,841 ☐ p. 4,861, ✳ Sofia.

Bunyan (bŭn'yăn), John. Eng. author (1628–88).

Burgundy (bûr'gŭn-dĭ), former Fr. kingdoms. dukedom, & province.

Burke (bûrk), Edmund. Br. statesman (1729–97).

Burma (bûr'mȧ), prov. E Br. India, 230,839 ☐ p. 13,212, ✳ Rangoon

Burns (bûrnz), Robert. Scot. poet (1759–96).

Burroughs (bŭr'ōz), John. Am. au. (1837–1921).

Byron (bī'rŭn), George Gordon Byron, 6th Lord. Eng. poet (1788–1824). [Constantinople.]

Byzantium (bĭ-zăn'shĭ-ŭm), anc. city on site of

C

Cabot (kăb'ŭt), John. It. disc. under Eng. flag of N. Am. cont. 1497 (ab. 1451–aft. 1498). **—** his son, Sebastian. Eng. navigator (1472?–1557).

Cæsar (sē'zȧr), (Gaius) Julius. Roman general & statesm. (B. C. 100–44). [p. 791.

Cairo (kī'rō), ✳ of Egypt, nr. right bank of Nile, [p. 791.

Calais (kăl'ā; *F.* kȧ'lĕ'), city, on Strait of Dover, N Fr. p. 73. [1,328.

Calcutta (kăl-kŭt'ȧ), city, ✳ of Bengal, in S, p.

Calhoun (kăl-hōōn'), John Caldwell. Am. statesman (1782–1850).

California (kăl'ĭ-fôr'nĭ-ȧ), Pacific state, U. S. 158,297 ☐ p. 3,427, ✳ Sacramento. Abbr. *Calif.*

Calvin (kăl'vĭn), John. Fr. reformer (1509–64).

Cambodia (kăm-bō'dĭ-ȧ), kingdom, Indo-China, 57,900 ☐ p. 2,403, ✳ Pnompenh; Fr.

Cambridge (kām'brĭj), bor. E Eng. p. 59; univ. — city, E Mass. p. 110; Harvard univ.

Camden (kăm'dĕn), city & riv. port, W N. J. p. 116.

Cameroons (kăm'ĕr-ōōnz'), or **Kamerun** (-ōōn'), form. Ger. prot. W Afr. now Br. & Fr. mandates.

Canada, Dominion of (kăn'ȧ-dȧ), Br. poss. N N. Am. 3,684,723 ☐ p. 8,788, ✳ Ottawa. [U. S.]

Canal Zone, strip 10 m. wide, across Panama; to

Canary Islands (kȧ-nā'rĭ), group in Atlantic off NW Afr. 2,808 ☐ p. 488; prov. of Spain.

Canberra (kăn'bĕr-ȧ), city, in Fed. Ter., since 1927 ✳ of Australian Commonwealth, SE N. S. W.

Canton (kăn-tŏn'), city, ✳ of Kwangtung prov. S China, p. 900. [mark (994?–1035).

Canute (kȧ-nūt'). King of Eng. fr. 1017, & of Denmark (994?–1035).

Cape of Good Hope, prov. of Union of S. Afr. 276,966 ☐ p. 2,783, ✳ Cape Town.

Cape Town or **Capetown,** spt. city, ✳ of Cape of Good Hope prov., legislative seat of Union of S. Afr. p. 207.

Cape Verde Islands (vûrd), in Atlantic oc. W of N Afr. 1,487 ☐ p. 148; Portuguese.

Caracas (kä-rä'käs), ✳ of Venezuela, in N, p. 92.

Cardiff (kär'dĭf), spt. city, SE Wales, p. 200.

Caribbean Sea (kăr'ĭ-bē'ăn), bet. W. Indies & S. America. [1881.

Carlyle (kär-līl'), Thomas. Scot. author (1795–

Carnegie (kär-nĕg'ĭ), Andrew. Scot.-Am. capitalist and philanthropist (1837–1919).

Carpathian Mountains (kär-pā'thĭ-ăn), Europe, bet. Poland & Czechoslovakia, 800 m. long; highest, 8,737 ft.

Cartagena (kär'tȧ-jē'nȧ), spt. SE Spain, p. 102.

Carthage (kär'thâj), anc. city & state, N Africa, occupying nearly the site of mod. Tunis; founded by Phœnicians; destroyed by Romans, B. C. 146.

Caruso (kä-rōō'zō), Enrico. It. tenor (1873–1921).

Cascade Range (kăs-kād'), mts. Oregon, Wash., & B. C.; highest Mt. Rainier, Wash. 14,408 ft.

Caspian Sea (kăs'pĭ-ăn), inland salt lake, 760 m. long, bet. Europe & Asia; ab.85 ft. below sea level.

Cassel or **Kassel** (käs'ĕl), city, SW Prussia, p. 162.

Castile (kăs-tēl'), former kingdom, cen. Spain.

Catania (kä-tä'nyä), city, NE Sicily, p. 255; univ.

Catherine (kăth'ĕr-ĭn) **I.** Empress of Russia. Wife of Peter the Great (d. 1727). **— II.** *The Great.* Empress of Russia. Wife of Peter III. (1729–96).

Cato (kā'tō), Marcus Porcius. Either of two Roman patriots: *The Elder* (B. C. 234–149); *The Younger* (B. C. 95–46).

Caucasia (kô-kā'shȧ), or **Caucasus** (kô'kȧ-sŭs),

region of Caucasus mts. S Soviet Russia, Eur. & Asia. See TRANSCAUCASIAN FEDERATION.

Caucasus (kô′ká-sŭs), mts. bet. Black & Caspian seas, Russia; 18,526 ft. [It. statesm. (1810–61).]

Cavour, di (dē ká′vōōr′), Camillo Benso, Count.

Cawnpore (kôn′pōr′), city, N Br. India, p. 216.

Caxton (kăks′tŭn), Wm. Earliest Eng. printer (1422?–91).

Celebes (sĕl′ê-bēz), isl. Dutch E. Indies, 69,255 □.

Central America, S part of North America, bet. Mexico & S. America.

Cervantes Saavedra, de (dä thĕr-vän′täs sä′ä-vā′-drä; E. sĕr-văn′tēz), Miguel. Sp. author. Don Quixote. (1547–1616.)

Ceylon (sê-lŏn′), isl. in Indian ocean, 60 m. SE of India, 25,331 □ p. 4,505; Br. col.

Chaldea (kăl-dē′á), anc. region, SW Asia.

Champlain, Lake (shăm-plān′), bet. N. Y. & Vt. 125 m. long; bat. Sept. 11, 1814. [p. 500.]

Changchowfu (chäng′chō′fōō′), city, SE China.

Changsha (chäng′shä′), * of Hunan, China, p. 250.

Channel Islands, Br. isls. in Eng. channel. 75 □ p. 90.

Charlemagne (shär′lê-mān), **Charles the Great,** or **Charles I.** King of the Franks fr. 768; Emp. of the West fr. 800 (742–814).

Charles (chärlz) **I.** Charles Stuart. King of England fr. 1625 (1600–49). — his son, **C. II.** King of Eng. fr. 1660 (1630–85). — **V.** Holy Roman emp. (1519–56) & king of Spain as C. I. 1516–56 (1500–58).

Charleston (chärlz′tŭn), spt. SE S. C. p. 68. — city, * of W. Va. in W, p. 40.

Chatham (chăt′dm), Earl of. See PITT, William.

Chaucer (chô′sĕr), Geoffrey. Eng. poet (1340?–1400).

Chemnitz (kĕm′nĭts), city, S Germany, p. 304.

Chengtu (chŭng′tōō′), * of Szechwan, China, p. 450.

Chersonese (kŭr′sô-nēz ; -nēs), or **Chersonesus, The** (-nē′sŭs). See GALLIPOLI. [m. long.

Chesapeake Bay (chĕs′á-pēk), in Md. & Va. 200

Cheyenne (shī-ĕn′), city, * of Wyoming, p. 14.

Chicago (shĭ-kô′gō), city, NE Ill., p. 2,702.

Chile (chē′lä), or **Chili** (chĭl′ĭ), repub. SW S. Am. 289,721 □ p. 3,755, * Santiago. [20,498 ft.]

Chimborazo (chĭm′bô-rä′zō), mt. in Ecuador,

China (chī′ná), country, form. empire, repub. fr. Jan. 1912, consisting of China proper (" 18 provs."), 1,532,795 □ p. 316,000, & Manchuria, Mongolia, Sinkiang, & Tibet; total, 4,278,352 □ p. 342,639, * Nanking. — **Sea,** part of Pacific oc. fr. Japan to S Malay pen.

Choate (chōt), Joseph H. Am. lawyer & dipl. (1832–1917). [poser (1809–49).

Chopin (shô′păN′), Frédéric F. Polish-Fr. com-

Chosen (chō′sĕn′). See KOREA.

Christiania (krĭs-tyä′nê-ä), former name of Oslo (ôs′lō), * of Norway. [B. C. 106–43).

Cicero (sĭs′ĕr-ō), Marcus Tullius. Roman statesm.

Cilicia (sĭ-lĭsh′ĭ-á), anc. country, SE Asia Minor.

Cincinnati (sĭn′sĭ-năt′ĭ), city, S Ohio, p. 401.

Clay (klä), Henry. Am. statesman (1777–1852).

Clemenceau (klä′män′sō′), Georges. French statesman (1841–1929).

Clemens (klĕm′ĕnz), Samuel Langhorne. Mark Twain. Am. humorist (1835–1910). [69–30).

Cleopatra (klē′ô-pä′trá). Queen of Egypt (B. C.

Cleveland (klēv′lănd), city, NE Ohio, p. 797. — Grover. 22d (1885–89) & 24th (1893–97) pres. of the U. S. (1837–1908).

Cochin China (kō′chĭn), Fr. col. in Indo-China, 22,000 □ p. 3,795, * Saigon.

Coleridge (kōl′rĭj), Samuel Taylor. Eng. poet (1772–1834).

Cologne (kô-lōn′), city, W Prussia, p. 634.

Colombia (kô-lôm′bê-ä), republic, NW S. Am. 40,846 □ p. 5,855, * Bogotá.

Colombo (-lôm′bō), spt. * of Ceylon, p. 249.

Colorado (kŏl′ô-rä′dō), state, W cen. U. S. 103,948 □ p. 940, * Denver. Abbr. Colo. — **River,** riv., Colo., Utah, & Ariz. ab. 1,450 m.; Grand Canyon.

Columbia (kô-lŭm′bĭ-á), city, * of S. C. p. 38. — riv. of Ore., Wash., & Br. Columbia, 1,400 m.

Columbus (-lŭm′bŭs), city, * of Ohio, in cen. part, p. 237. — , Christopher. Genoese discoverer of America (1451–1506).

Concord (kŏn′kôrd), city, * of N. H. in S cen. part, p. 22. [B. C. 551–478).

Confucius (kŏn-fū′shĭ-ŭs). Chinese philosopher

Congo (kŏn′gō), riv. 2,500–3,000 m. cen. & W Afr. to Atl. oc. — **Free State.** See BELGIAN CONGO.

Connecticut (kŏ-nĕt′ĭ-kŭt), state, NE U. S. A. 4,965 □ p. 1,381, * Hartford. Abbr. Conn.

Constantine (kŏn′stăn-tĭn) **I.** The Great. Rom. emp. fr. 323 (272–337).

Constantinople (kŏn-stăn′tĭ-nō′p'l), off. Turk. **Istanbul** (ē′stän-bōōl′), city on the Bosporus, Turkey in Eur.; form. * of Turkey, p. with sub. 1,000.

Cook (kōōk), James, Capt. Eng. nav. (1728–79).

Coolidge (kōōl′ĭj), Calvin. 30th pres. of the U. S. 1923–29 (1872–   ).

Cooper (kōō′pĕr), James Fenimore. Am. auth. (1789–1851). [mark, p. 561, with sub. 710.

Copenhagen (kō′pĕn-hā′gĕn), spt. city, * of Den-

Copernicus (kô-pûr′nĭ-kŭs), Nikolaus. Prussian astronomer (1473–1543).

Córdoba (kôr′dô-vä), city, cen. Argentina, p. 156.

Cork (kôrk), city, S Irish Free State, p. 77.

Corneille (kôr′nā′y′), Pierre. Fr. poet (1000–84).

Corsica (kôr′sĭ-ká), Fr. isl. SE of France, 3,368 □ p. 282.

Cortes, Sp. **Cortés** (kôr-tās′), Hernando or Hernán Sp. conqueror of Mex. (1485–1547).

Costa Rica (kŏs′tá rē′ká), repub. S Cen. Am 23,000 □ p. 468, * San José. [19,613 ft.

Cotopaxi (kō′tô-păk′sê), vol. Andes mts. Ecuador;

Coventry (kŭv′ĕn-trĭ), city, cen. Eng. p. 128.

Cracow (krä′kō), city, S Poland, p. 182.

Crete (krēt), or **Candia** (kăn′dĭ-á), isl. E Medit. 3,547 □ p. 345, * Canea ; to Greece. [56.

Crimea (krī-mē′á ; krī-), pen. S Russia ; war; 1854–

Croatia (krô-ä′shĭ-á), prov. NW Yugoslavia, 16,920 □ p. 2,740, * Zagreb.

Cromwell (krŏm′wĕl), Oliver. Eng. gen. & statesm. Lord Protector fr. 1653 (1599–1658).

Croydon (kroi′dŭn), bor. SE Eng. p. 191.

Cuba (kū′bá), isl. S of Fla. with adjacent isls. 44,164 □ p. 2,889 ; a republic, * Havana.

Curie (kü′rē′), Pierre (1859–1906), & his wife, Marie Sklodowska (1867–   ). Fr. scientists; Radium.

Curtis (kûr′tĭs), Charles. Am. lawyer. 31st vice pres. of U. S. fr. 1929 (1860–   ).

Cyprus (sī′prŭs), isl. E Medit. 3,584 □ p. 311; Br.

āle, senāte, câre, ăm, ŏccount, ärm, ásk, sofá; ēve, évent, ĕnd, recĕnt, makĕr; īce, ĭll; ōld, ŏbey, ôrb, ŏdd, sŏft, cŏnnect; ūse, ŭnite, ûrn, ŭp, circŭs; fōōd, fŏŏt; out, oil;

Cyrus (sī'rŭs). *The Elder* or *the Great*. King of Persia (d. B. C. 529).

Czechoslovakia (chĕk'ô-slô-vä'kĭ-à), repub. cen. Eur. 54,241 ☐ p. 13,610, ✳ Prague; form. part of Austria-Hungary.

D

Dagestan (dä'gĕs-tän'), repub. SE Soviet Russia, Eur. 13,730 ☐ p. 798, ✳ Petrovsk.

Dahomey (dä-hō'mä), col. Fr. W. Afr. 42,460 ☐.

Dairen (dī'rĕn'), *Chinese* **Talien** (tä'lĭ-ĕn'), *form.* **Dalny** (dál'y'-nĭ), spt. S Manchuria, p. 105; Jap.

Dallas (dăl'ás), city, NE Tex. p. 159.

Damascus (dá-măs'kŭs), city, ✳ of Syria, p. 170.

Dante Alighieri (dän'tĕ; *It.* dän'tä ä'lĕ-gyá'rē). *Dante.* It. poet (1265–1321). [sea.

Danube (dăn'ūb), riv. cen. Eur. 1,750 m. to Black

Danzig, Free City of (dän'tsĭk), ter. on Baltic, 754 ☐ p. 365, & spt. in ter. p. 195.

Dardanelles (där'dá-nĕlz'), *anc.* HELLESPON'TUS, strait bet. the Ægean and the Sea of Marmara.

Darius (dá-rī'ŭs) **I.** Persian king fr. B. C. 521 (B. C. 558–486).

Darling, riv. SE Australia, 1,160 m. to Murray riv.

Darwin (där'wĭn), Charles Robert. Eng. naturalist (1809–82).

Dayton (dā'tŭn), city, SW Ohio, p. 153.

Dead Sea, salt lake, 370 ☐, S Palestine.

Defoe (dĕ-fō'), Daniel. Eng. author (1661?–1731).

Delaware (dĕl'á-wâr), Atl. state, U. S. 2,370 ☐ p. 223, ✳ Dover. Abbr. *Del.*

Delhi (dĕl'ē), city, N India, ✳ of Br. India, p. 304.

Demosthenes (dē-mŏs'thē-nēz). Greek orator (B. C. 384–22).

Denmark (dĕn'märk), kdm. NW Eur. 16,605 ☐ p. 3,268, ✳ Copenhagen. [256; univ.

Denver (-vēr), city, ✳ of Colo. in N cen. part, p.

De Quincey (dĕ kwĭn'sĭ), Thomas. Eng. author (1785–18.9).

Derby (dûr'bĭ; där'-), bor. cen. Eng. p. 130.

Des Moines (dē moin'), city, ✳ of Iowa, p. 126; univ. (1499?–1542).

De Soto (dē sō'tô), Hernando. Spanish explorer

Detroit (dē-troit'), city, SE Michigan, p. 994.

Dickens (dĭk'ĕnz), Charles. Eng. auth. (1812–70)

Diogenes (dī-ŏj'ĕ-nēz). Greek philosopher (B. C. 412?–323?).

Disraeli (dĭz-rā'lĭ), Benj., Earl of Beaconsfield. Eng. statesman and author (1804–81).

District of Columbia, on Potomac riv. U. S. 70 ☐ p. 438. Abbr. *D. C.* [sea.

Dnieper (nē'pēr), riv. SW Russia, 1,300 m. to Black

Dominican Republic (dô-mĭn'ĭ-kán), *or* **Santo Domingo,** E part of Haiti isl. 19,332 ☐ p. 897, ✳ Santo Domingo.

Don (dŏn), riv. SE Russia, 1,300 m. long. [1930).

Doyle (doil), Arthur Conan, Sir. Br. author (1859–

Drake (drāk), Francis, Sir. Eng. adm. 1540?–96).

Dresden (drĕz'dĕn), ✳ of Saxony, Germany, p. 588.

Dryden (drī'dĕn), John. Eng. poet (1631–1700).

Dublin (dŭb'lĭn), city, ✳ of Ir. Free State, p. 427.

Duluth (dŏ-lōōth'), port on Lake Superior, NE Minn. p. 99.

Dumas (dü'mä'), Alexandre. Fr. auth. (1802–70).
— his son, Alexandre. Dram. & au. (1824–95).

Dundee (dŭn-dē'), spt. E Scot. p. 168. [146.

Durban (dûr'bǎn), spt. Natal, Union of S. Afr. p.

Düsseldorf (düs'ĕl-dôrf), city. W Prussia, p. 407.

Dutch East Indies, possessions of Netherlands in Malay arch. 733,642 ☐ p. 49,351, ✳ Batavia. —
Guiana, col. S. Am. 46,060 ☐ p. 113, ✳ Paramaribo. [Eur. ab. 1,100 m.

Dvina (dvē-nä'), *or* **Dwina** (dwē'ná),riv. N Russia,

E

East Indies, a name applied, somewhat vaguely, to India, Indo-China, and the Malay archipelago.

Ecuador (ĕk'wá-dôr), rep. NW S. Am. 116,000 to 276,000 ☐ p. 2,000, ✳ Quito.

Edinburgh (ĕd'ĭn-bûr-ô), ✳ of Scot. in SE, p. 420.

Edison (-ĭ-sŭn), Thomas Alva. Am. inventor (1847–1931).

Edward. Seven kings of Eng.: **I.** *Longshanks.* Kg. fr. 1272 (1239–1307); **II.** fr. 1307 (1284–1327); **III.** fr. 1327 (1312–77); **IV.** in 1461–70 & 1471–83 (1442–83); **V.** in 1483 (1470–83); **VI.** fr. 1547 (1537–53); **VII.** fr. 1901 (1841–1910).

Egypt (ē'jĭpt), kdm. NE Afr. 350,000 ☐, settled 12,023 ☐ p. 12,751, ✳ Cairo.

Ekaterinodar (yĕ-kà'tyĕ-rē'nô-där'), *or* **Krasnodar** (kräs'nô-där'), city, SE Russia, Eur. p. 143.

Ekaterinoslav (-slái'), city, E cen. Ukraine, p. 164.

Elbrus (ĕl'brōōs), *or* **Elbruz,** Caucasus mt. 18,526 ft.; highest in Eur.

Eliot (ĕl'ĭ-ŭt), Charles William. Am. educator (1834–1926). —, George. Pseud. of *Mary Ann Evans* (*Lewes*) (*Cross*). Eng. auth. (1819–80).

Elizabeth (ē-lĭz'á-bĕth). Queen of Eng. fr. 1558 (1533–1603). [(1803–82).

Emerson (ĕm'ēr-sŭn), Ralph Waldo. Am. philos.

England (ĭŋ'glánd), div. of Gr. Br. S of Scot. & E of Wales, 50,874 ☐ p. 35,679, ✳ London.

English Channel, bet. Eng. & France, 20 to 100 m.

Epictetus (ĕp'ĭk-tē'tŭs). Roman philosopher (60?–120?). [270).

Epicurus (-ĭ-kū'rŭs). Greek philos. (B. C. 342–

Erie (ē'rĭ), city, NW Pa. on Lake Erie, p. 102. —
Canal, fr. Lake Erie at Buffalo to Hudson riv. at Albany; 363 m. —, **Lake,** Great Lake, bet. U. S. & Ontario, Can. 9,968 ☐. [menia, p. 90.

Erivan (ĕr'ē-vän'), city, ✳ of Soviet repub. of Ar-

Essen (ĕs'ĕn), city, Rhine Prov. Prussia, p. 439.

Esthonia (ĕs-thō'nĭ-à), repub. on Baltic, 16,955 ☐ p. 1,109, ✳ Revel. [mod. Abyssinia.

Ethiopia (ē'thĭ-ō'pĭ-á), anc. country, Africa, incl.

Etna (ĕt'ná), volcano, NE Sicily, 10,755 ft. high.

Euclid (ū'klĭd) of Alexandria. Gr. mathematician (fl. B. C. 300).

Euphrates (û-frā'tēz), riv. 1,600 m. Armenia through Kurdistan & Mesopotamia to Tigris.

Euripides (û-rĭp'ĭ-dēz). Gr. poet (B. C. 480–406).

Europe (ū'rŭp), continent, 3,872,000 ☐ p. 476,000.

Everest, Mount (ĕv'ēr-ĕst), Himalayan mt.; highest in world; 29,002 ft.

F

Falkland Islands (fôk'lǎnd), in S Atl. oc. 7,3C0 ☐ p. 3, ✳ Stanley; Br. colony.

Fall River, city, SE Mass. p. 120.

Faraday (făr′ȧ-dā), Michael. Eng. chem. (1791–1867).

Faroe (fâr′ō), isls. N Atl. 537 □ p. 21; Danish.

Farragut (făr′ȧ-gŭt), David Glasgow. American admiral (1801–70).

Ferdinand (fûr′dĭ-nănd) **II.** of Aragon fr. 1479 & **V.** of Castile fr. 1474. *The Catholic*. Founder of Sp. monarchy (1452–1516).

Ferrara (fĕr-rä′rä), city, N Italy, p. 107.

Fielding (fēl′dĭng), Henry. Eng. auth. (1707–54).

Fiji Islands (fē′jē), S Pacific, 7,435 □ p.157; Br.col.

Fillmore (fĭl′mōr), Millard. 13th pres. of the U. S. in 1850–53 (1800–74).

Finland (fĭn′lănd), country, N Eur. form. in NW Russ. 145,685 □ p. 3,367, ✳ Helsingfors.

Fiske (fĭsk), John. Am. hist. & philos. (1842–1901).

Fiume (fyōō′mȧ), spt. NE Italy, 8 □ p. 50.

Flanders (flăn′dẽrz), coast region of W Eur. chiefly in Belgium & France.

Florence (flŏr′ĕns), city, Italy, p. 247.

Florida (flŏr′ĭ-dȧ), SE state of U. S. 58,666 □ p. 968, ✳ Tallahassee. Abbr. *Fla.*

Foch (fŏsh), Ferdinand. Fr. marshal (1851–1929).

Foochow (fōō′chō′), ✳ of Fukien prov. China, p. 624. [turer (1863–).

Ford (fōrd), Henry. Am. automobile manufac-|

Formosa (fŏr-mō′sȧ), *or* **Taiwan** (tī′wän′), isl. in China sea; 13,888 □ p.3,654; Jap. possession.

Fort Worth (wûrth′), city, NE Tex. p. 106.

Fox (fŏks), Charles James. Eng. statesman (1749–1806).

France (frȧns), republic, form. empire & kdm. W Europe. 212,659 □ p. 39,210, ✳ Paris.

Francis (frăn′sĭs), *or* **Francis of Assisi** (äs-sē′zē), Saint. It. friar (1182–1226). — **I.** Kg. of Fr. fr. 1515 (1494–1547).

Francis Joseph I. Emp. of Austria fr. 1848, crowned king of Hungary 1867 (1830–1916).

Frankfort (frăŋk′fŭrt). ✳ of Ky. p. 10.

Frankfurt am Main (frăŋk′fōōrt äm mīn′), city, SW Prussia, p. 433. [90].|

Franklin (frăŋk′lĭn), Benj. Am. statesman (1706–|

Frederick (frĕd′ẽr-ĭk) **II.** *The Great*. Kg. of Prussia fr. 1740 (1712–86).

French, Daniel Chester. Am. sculptor (1850–1931).

French Equatorial Africa, Fr. poss. W Afr., Congo riv. to the Sahara, 982,049 □ p. 2,846. — **Guiana** (gē-ä′nȧ), Fr. col. in N S. Am. 32,000 □ p. 44, ✳ Cayenne. — **Indo-China,** Fr. depend. SE Asia, incl. Cochin China, Cambodia, Annam, Tonkin, & Laos; 256,878 □ p. 19,747, ✳ Hanoï. — **West Africa,** Fr. poss. comprising Senegal, Dahomey, Ivory Coast, Fr. Guinea, Fr. Sudan, Ter. of the Niger, Upper Volta, & Mauritania: ✳ Dakar.

Froissart (frwä′sär′; *Eng.* froi′särt), Jean. Fr. chronicler (1337?–1410?).

Fuji (fōō′jē), *or* **Fujiyama** (-yä′mȧ), mt. S cen. Honshu, Japan, 12,390 ft. [p. 95.|

Fukuoka (-kōō-ō′kä), city, N Kyushu isl. Japan,|

G

Galápagos (gä-lä′pȧ-gōs), isl. group, 2,870 □; to Ecuador. [tria, now chiefly in S Poland.|

Galicia (gȧ-lĭsh′ĭ-ȧ), form. crownland, NE Aus-|

Galilee (găl′ĭ-lē), *or* **Tiberias, Sea of** (tī-bē′rĭ-ȧs), *or* **Gennesaret, Lake of** (gĕ-nĕs′ȧ-rĕt), lake in N Palestine; 14 m. long.

Galilei (gä′lĕ-lā′ē), known by his Christian name, **Galileo** (găl′ĭ-lē′ō). It. astron. (1564–1642).

Gallipoli (gȧ-lĭp′ō-lē), *anc.* CHERSONE′SUS, pen. bet. the Dardanelles & Ægean sea. [1524).

Gama, da (dä gä′mä), Vasco. Port. nav. (1469?–|

Gandhi (gän′dē), Mohandas Karamchand. Hindu reformer (1869–   ). [Bengal.|

Ganges (găn′jēz), riv. N India, 1,557 m. to Bay of|

Garfield (gär′fēld), James Abram. 20th pres. of the U. S. in 1881 (1831–81). [(1807–82).|

Garibaldi (gä′rē-bäl′dē), Giuseppe. It. patriot|

Geneva (jĕ-nē′vȧ), city, SW Switzerland, p. 136. —, **Lake of,** bet. Switz. & France.

Genoa (jĕn′ō-ȧ), spt. NW Italy, p. 299.

George (jôrj), 5 kings of Great Brit. & Ireland: **I.** fr. 1714 (1660–1727); **II.** fr. 1727 (1683–1760); **III.** fr. 1760 (1738–1820); **IV.** fr. 1820 (1762–1830); **V.** fr. 1910 (1865–   ).

Georgia (jôr′jĭ-ȧ; -jä), state, SE U. S. 59,265 □ p. 2,896, ✳ Atlanta. Abbr. *Ga.* — Soviet repub. Transcaucasia, Asia, 25,760 □ p. 2,372, ✳ Tiflis.

German East Africa. See TANGANYIKA TERRITORY.

Germany (jûr′mȧ-nĭ), repub. cen. Eur. comprising 18 states, 182,271 □ p. 59,858, ✳ Berlin.

Ghent (gĕnt), city, W Belgium, p. 166.

Gibbon (gĭb′ŭn), Edward. Eng. hist. (1737–94).

Gibraltar (jĭ-brôl′tȧr), town & ftd. rock, S Iberian pen. p. 22; Br. —, **Strait of,** joins Medit. to Atl.

Gladstone (glăd′stŭn), William Ewart. Eng. statesman (1809–98).

Glasgow (glăs′gō; -kō), city, W Scotland, p. 1,034.

Gobi (gō′bē), desert, cen. Asia, 500,000 □.

Goethe, von (fŏn gû′tē), Johann Wolfgang. Ger. author (1749–1832).

Gold Coast, Br. col. W Afr. 23,490 □ p. 1,173, ✳ Akkra; & prot. 55,160 □ p. 937.

Goldsmith, Oliver. Br. author (1728–74).

Good Hope, Cape of, promontory of S Africa.

Gordon (gôr′dŭn), Charles George. *Chinese Gordon.* Eng. soldier (1833–85).

Göteborg (yû′tĕ-bôr′y′), city, SW Sweden, p. 227.

Granada (grȧ-nä′dȧ), city, S Spain, p. 104.

Grand Canyon, valley of Colo. riv. NW Ariz. 217 m. long, 8–15 m. wide, over 1 m. deep.

Grande, Rio (rē′ō grän′dä), either of two rivs. of Brazil. — See RIO GRANDE.

Grand Rapids, city, SW Michigan, p. 138.

Grant (grănt), Ulysses Simpson (*orig.* Hiram Ulysses), Am. gen., & 18th pres. of the U. S. in 1869–77 (1822–85).

Gray, Thomas. Eng. poet (1716–71).

Graz *or* **Gratz** (gräts), ✳ of Styria, Austria, p. 158.

Great Britain (brĭt′'n), isl. comprising England, Scotland, & Wales, 88,745 □ p. 42,768.

Great Lakes, Lakes Superior, Huron, Michigan, Erie, and Ontario.

Great Salt Lake, Utah, 80 m. long, 20–35 m. wide.

Great Slave Lake, in N.W. Ters. Can. 300 m. long.

Greece (grēs), *Gr.* **Hellas** (hĕl′ȧs), repub. S Europe, 47,191 □ p. 5,071, ✳ Athens.

Greeley (grē′lĭ), Horace. Am. journalist (1811–72).

Greenland (grēn′lănd), isl. NE of N. Am. 827,275 □; Danish colony, 46,740 □ p. 14.

āle, senāte, câre, ăm, ȧccount, ärm, ȧsk, sofȧ; ēve, ĕvent, ĕnd, recĕnt, makẽr; īce, ĭll; ōld, ȯbey, ôrb, ŏdd, sŏft, cŏnnect; ūse, ŭnite, ûrn, ŭp, circŭs; fōōd, foot; out, oil;

Greenwich (grĭn′ĭj), part of London. See in *Dict.*

Gregory (grĕg′ō-rĭ). Name of 16 popes, esp.: **I.,** Saint. *The Great.* Pope fr. 590 (540?–604); **VII.,** Saint. Pope fr. 1073 (1020?–85).

Grimm (grĭm), Jakob L. K. (1785–1863), & Wilhelm K. (1786–1859), brothers. Ger. philologists.

Guam (gwäm), largest of Marianas, 210 ☐ p. 13, ✲ Agaña; U. S.

Guatemala (gwä′tä-mä′lȧ), rep. NW Cen. Am. 48,290 ☐ p. 2,005. — its ✲ p. 91.

Guiana (gē-ä′nȧ), region, N S. Am. incl. Brit. Fr. and Du. Guiana.

Guinea (gĭn′ĭ), coast region, W Afr. fr. Senegal riv. to S. W. Afr. —, **Gulf of,** on W coast Africa.

Gulf Stream, warm ocean current of the N Atl. issuing from the Gulf of Mexico.

Gustavus (gŭs-tā′vŭs). Name of 5 kings of Sweden, esp.: **I.** Vasa, king fr. 1523 (1496–1560); **V.** fr. 1907 (1858–). — **Adolphus** *or* **Gustavus II.** fr. 1611 (1594–1632).

Gutenberg (gōō′tĕn-bĕrk), Johannes. Ger. inventor of printing from movable types (1397?–1468).

H

Haakon (hō′kôn) **VII.** King of Norway fr. 1905 (1872–). [138].

Hadrian (hā′drĭ-ăn). Roman emperor fr. 117 (76–138).

Hague, The (häg), city, ✲ of Neth. in SW, p. 360.

Haiti (hā′tĭ), W. Ind. isl. 29,536 ☐ p. 3,400. — repub. in W part of isl. 10,204 ☐ p. 2,031, ✲ Port-au-Prince. [145.]

Hakodate (hä′kŏ-dä′tȧ), ✲ of Hokkaido, Japan, p.

Halifax (hăl′ĭ-făks), bor. N Eng. p. 99. — ✲ of Nova Scotia, p. 58.

Hamburg (hăm′bûrg), free city & state. N Germany; state 168 ☐ p. 1,050; city, p. 986.

Hamilton (hăm′ĭl-tŭn), city, S Ontario, Can. p. 114. —, Alexander. Am. statesman (1757–1804).

Hancock (hăn′kŏk), John. Am. statesm. (1737–93).

Handel (hăn′dĕl), George Frederick. Ger. composer (1685–1759). [350.]

Hangchow (häng′chō′), ✲ of Chekiang, China, p.

Hankow (hän′kō), city, Hupeh prov. China, p. 826.

Hannibal (hăn′ĭ-bȧl). Carthaginian gen. (B. C. 247–183). [p. 120.]

Hanoi (hä′noi′), city, Tonkin, ✲ of Fr. Indo-China.

Hanover (hăn′ō-vẽr), city, W Prussia, p. 393.

Harding (här′dĭng), Warren Gamaliel. 29th pres. of the U. S. in 1921–23 (1865–1923).

Hardy (-dĭ), Thomas. Eng. auth. (1840–1928).

Harold (hăr′ŭld). English kings: **I.** *Harefoot.* From 1035 (d. 1040); **II.** in 1066 (1022?–66).

Harrisburg (-bûrg), city, ✲ of Pa. in S, p. 76.

Harrison (hăr′ĭ-sŭn), Benjamin. Grandson of W. H. 23d pres. of U. S. in 1889–93 (1833–1901). —, William Henry. 9th pres. of U. S. in 1841 (1773–1841). [1902].

Harte (härt), Francis Bret. Am. author (1836–).

Hartford (härt′fẽrd). city, ✲ of Conn. in N, p. 138.

Harun-al-Rashid (hä-rōōn′-är-rȧ-shēd′; *Eng.* -ăl-răsh′ĭd). Caliph of Bagdad fr. 786 (766?–809).

Havana (hȧ-văn′ȧ), spt. ✲ of Cuba, p. 364.

Havre (hä′vẽr), spt. N France, p. 163.

Hawaii (hä-wi′ē), largest of Hawaiian isls. 4,015 ☐ p. 65. — *or* **Hawaiian Islands** (-yȧn), group,

N Pacific, 6,449 ☐ p. 256, ✲ Honolulu; U. S. ter. [(1804–64).]

Hawthorne (hô′thôrn), Nathaniel. Am. novelist.

Hay (hā), John. Am. auth. & statesm. (1838–1905).

Haydn (hā′d′n; *G.* hī′-), Joseph. Austrian composer (1732–1809).

Hayes (hāz), Rutherford Birchard. 19th pres. of the U. S. in 1877–81 (1822–93). [p. 90.]

Hebrides (hĕb′rĭ-dēz), isls. W of N Scot. 3,000 ☐ p. 89.

Heine (hī′nĕ), Heinrich. Ger. poet (1797–1856).

Hejaz *or* **Hedjaz** (hĕ-jäz′), kdm. NW Arabia, 170,-000 ☐ p. 900, ✲ Mecca.

Helena (hĕl′ē-nȧ), city, ✲ of Montana, in W, p. 12.

Hellespont (hĕl′ĕs-pŏnt), *anc.* HELLESPON′TUS. = DARDANELLES.

Helsingfors (hĕl′sĭng-fôrs′), spt. ✲ of Finland in SW, p. 198. [Switz.]

Helvetia (hĕl-vē′shĭ-ȧ), anc. country, most of mod.

Henry (hĕn′rĭ), Patrick. Am. statesman (1736–99). — Eight kings of England, esp.: **III.** fr. 1216 (1207–72); **VII.** fr. 1485 (1457–1509); **VIII.** fr. 1509 (1491–1547). — Four kings of France, esp.: **IV.** *Of Navarre,* fr. 1589 (1553–1610).

Herod (hĕr′ŭd). *The Great.* Kg. of the Jews (B. C. 62?–4). [425?.]

Herodotus (hē-rŏd′ō-tŭs). Gr. hist. (B. C. 484?–)

Herschel (hûr′shĕl), William, Sir. German in Eng. (1738–1822); his son, Sir J. F. Wm. (1792–1871). Astronomers.

Herzegovina (hĕr′tsĕ-gō-vē′nä). See BOSNIA.

Hesse (hĕs), state, SW Ger. p. 1,291, ✲ Darmstadt.

Highlands, The, N & W Scot. incl. Hebrides.

Hildebrand (hĭl′dē-brănd), St. See GREGORY VII.

Himalaya (hĭ-mä′lȧ-yȧ), mt. system bet. India & Tibet; 29,002 ft. (Everest) highest in world.

Hindenburg, von (fôn hĭn′dĕn-bōͦrk), Paul. Ger. general & 2d pres. of Ger. fr. 1925 (1847–).

Hindu Kush (hĭn′dōō kōōsh′), mt. range, over 20,000 ft. NE Afghanistan. [dian peninsula.]

Hindustan (hĭn′dōō-stän′). Persian name of In-

Hispania (hĭs-pā′nĭ-ȧ; hĭs-pä′-), ancient name of Iberian pen., now sometimes (esp. poet.) Spain.

Hokkaido (hŏk′kī′dō), *form.* **Yezo** (yĕz′ō), isl. N of Honshu, Jap. 35,654 ☐ p. 2,359, ✲ Hakodate.

Holland. See NETHERLANDS. [(1809–94).]

Holmes (hōmz), Oliver Wendell. Am. author.

Homer (hō′mẽr). Epic poet of Gr. (fl. ab. 9th cent. B. C.). [p. 662, ✲ Tegucigalpa.]

Honduras (hŏn-dōō′rȧs), rep. Cen. Am. 44,275 ☐

Hongkong (hŏng′kŏng′), Br. isl. & col. S China; isl. 32 ☐, with leased ter. 391 ☐ p. 625, ✲ Victoria. [on S coast of Oahu isl. p. 83.]

Honolulu (hŏ′nō-lōō′lōō; hŏn′ō-), spt. ✲ of Hawaii,

Honshu (hŏn′shōō), *or* **Hondo** (-dō), largest isl. of Japan, 88,879 ☐ p. 41,808.

Hoover (hōō′vẽr), Herbert Clark. 31st pres. of U. S. fr. 1929 (1874–).

Horace (hŏr′ȧs). Latin poet (B. C. 65–8).

Horn, Cape, on isl., S extremity of South America.

Houston (hūs′tŭn), city, E Tex. p. 138. [1920].

Howells (hou′ĕlz), William Dean. Am. au. (1837–).

Hudson (hŭd′sŭn), Henry. Eng. nav. (d. 1611). —, riv. E N.Y. 350 m. to N.Y. bay. — **Bay,** inland sea, E Canada. — **Strait,** bet. Hudson bay and Atl. oc. [fr. 1930 (1862–).]

Hughes (hūz), Charles Evans. Chief just. of U. S.

Hugo (hū'gō), Victor, Viscount. Fr. poet, dram. & novelist (1802–85).

Hungary (hŭn'gá-rĭ), monarchy, cen. Eur. 35,790 ☐ p. 7,946, ✻ Budapest.

Huron, Lake (hū'rŏn), Great Lake, bet. Mich. & Ontario, 23,200 ☐.

Huxley (hŭks'lĭ), Thomas Henry. Eng. biologist (1825–95). [2,700 m. to Yellow sea.

Hwang or **Hwang Ho** (hwäng'hō'), riv. N China,

I J

Iberian Peninsula (ī-bē'rĭ-ăn), Spain & Portugal.

Iceland (īs'lănd), Dan. isl. N Atl. 39,709 ☐ p. 95, ✻ Reykjavik. [✻ Boise.

Idaho (ī'dá-hō), state, NW U. S. 83,888 ☐ p. 432,

Illinois (ĭl'ĭ-noi'; -noiz'), state, N cen. U. S. 56,665 ☐ p. 6,485, ✻ Springfield. Abbr. *Ill.*

India (ĭn'dĭ-á), S Asia, S of Himalaya mts.: Br. India (incl. Burma), 1,093,074 ☐ p. 247,003; native states, 709,555 ☐ p. 71,939; total, 1,805,- 332 ☐ p. 318,942, ✻ Delhi.

Indiana (-ăn'á), N cen. state, U. S. 36,354 ☐ p. 2,930, ✻ Indianapolis. Abbr. *Ind.*

Indianapolis (-ăn-ăp'ō-lĭs), city, ✻ of Indiana, in cen. part, p. 314. [tralia.

Indian Ocean, S of Asia, E of Afr., & W of Aus-

Indo-China (ĭn'dō-), or **Farther India,** SE pen. of Asia. See FRENCH INDO-CHINA. [sea.

Indus (ĭn'dŭs), riv. NW India, 2,000 m. to Arabian

Iowa (ī'ō-wá), state, N cen. U. S. 56,147 ☐ p. 2,404, ✻ Des Moines.

Irak or **Iraq** (ē'räk'), kdm. SW Asia, 143,250 ☐ p. 2,849, ✻ Bagdad; Br. mandate.

Iran (ē'rän'; *Eng.* ī-răn'), native name of Persia.

Ireland (īr'lănd), one of the Br. Isles & form. div. of United Kingdom, 32,535 ☐ p. 4,390; now IRISH FREE STATE & NORTHERN IRELAND.

Irish Free State, self-governing state of Br. Empire, S & cen. Ire. 27,084 ☐ p. 3,140, ✻ Dublin.

Irrawaddy (ĭr'á-wŏd'ĭ), riv. Burma, 1,250 m. to Bay of Bengal. [Russia.

Irtish or **Irtysh** (-tish'), riv. 2,300 m. to Ob riv.

Irving (ûr'vĭng), Henry, Sir. Eng. actor (1838– 1905). —, Washington. Am. author (1783–1859).

Isabella (ĭz'á-bĕl'á) **I.** *The Catholic.* Queen of Castile & León (1451–1504).

Israel (ĭz'rá-ĕl), anc. kdm. N. Palestine.

Istanbul. Turk. official name of Constantinople.

Italy (ĭt'á-lĭ), kdm. S Eur. 117,982 ☐ p. 40,123, ✻ Rome.

Jackson (jăk'sŭn), Andrew. Am. gen. & 7th pres. U. S. in 1829–37 (1767–1845). —, Thomas J. *Stonewall Jackson.* Confederate gen. (1824–63).

Jamaica (já-mā'ká), isl. West Indies, 4,450 ☐ p. 858, ✻ Kingston; Br. colony.

James (jāmz). Seven kings of Scotland, esp.: **VI.** fr. 1567, kg. of Eng. (as **James I.**) fr. 1603 (1566– 1625) ; **VII.** fr. 1685, kg. of Eng. (as **James II.**) in 1685–88 (1633–1701).

Jamestown (-toun), form. vil. E Va.; 1st success- ful Eng. settlement (1607) in U. S.

Japan (já-păn'), *Jap.* **Nippon** (nĭp'pŏn') or **Nihon** (nē'hŏn'), empire, isls. E of Japan sea, 148,856 ☐ p. 55,963, ✻ Tokyo; with depend. (Korea, For- mosa, Karafuto, etc.) 261,910 ☐ p. 76,987.

Java (jä'vá), most important isl. of Du. E. Indies, with Madura, 50,745 ☐ p. 34,984, ✻ Batavia.

Jefferson (jĕf'ēr-sŭn), Thomas Am. statesm. 3d pres. of U. S. in 1801–9 (1743–1826). — **City,** ✻ of Mo. in cen. part, p. 14. [N. Y. city, p. 298.

Jersey City (jûr'zĭ), city & port, NE N. J. opp.

Jerusalem (jē-rōō'sá-lĕm), ✻ of Palestine, p. 63.

Joan of Arc (jōn ŭv ärk'; jō-än'), *Fr.* **Jeanne d'Arc** (zhän'därk'). Fr. heroine (1412–31).

Joffre (zhŏf'ĭr'), Joseph Jacques Césaire. French marshal (1852–1931). [Transvaal, p. 288.

Johannesburg (yō-hän'ĕs-bûrg), chief cml. tn.

John (jŏn). *Lackland.* King of Eng. fr. 1199 (1167?–1216).

Johnson (jŏn'sŭn), Andrew. 17th pres. of U. S. in 1865–69 (1808–75). —, Samuel. Eng. lexicogra- pher & author (1709–84).

Jones (jōnz), John Paul. Orig. name *John Paul.* Am. naval officer b. in Scot. (1747–92).

Jonson (jŏn'sŭn), Ben. Eng. dram. (1573?–1637).

Jordan (jôr'dăn), riv. Palestine, 200 m. to Dead sea.

Judah (jōō'dá), anc. kingdom, S Palestine.

Judea or **Judæa** (jōō-dē'á), S div. of Palestine.

Jugoslavia, Jugo-Slavia. See YUGOSLAVIA.

Justinian (jŭs-tĭn'ĭ-ăn). *The Great.* Byzantine emp. fr. 527 (483–565).

Jutland (jŭt'lănd), Dan. pen. 11,444 ☐ p. 1,498.

K

Kabul (kä'bōōl), ✻ of Afghanistan, in E, p. 150.

Kaifeng (kī'fŭng'), city, NE China, p. 223.

Kamchatka (kăm-chăt'ká), pen. prov. E Siberia, Soviet Russia, Asia, 502,415 ☐ p. 42.

Kansas (kăn'zás), state, cen. U. S. 82,158 ☐ p. 1,769, ✻ Topeka. Abbr. *Kans.* — **City,** city, E Kans. p. 101. — **City,** city, W Mo. p. 324.

Kant (känt), Immanuel. Ger. philos. (1724–1804).

Karachi (ká-rä'chē), spt. ✻ of Sind, W Br. India, p. 217. [☐ p. 106; Japanese.

Karafuto (kä'rá-fōō'tō), S part of Sakhalin, 13,935

Karakoram Mountains (-kō'rŭm), range, Kash- mir, India; highest, Godwin-Austen, 28,250 ft.

Karelia (ká-rē'lĭ-á), repub. NW Soviet Russia, Eur. 28,890 ☐ p. 144, ✻ Petrozavodsk.

Karlsruhe (kärls'rōō'ĕ), ✻ of Baden, Ger. p. 136.

Kashmir or **Cashmere** (kăsh'mēr'), native state, NW India, 84,258 ☐ p. 3,321, ✻ Srinagar.

Kattegat or **Cattegat** (kăt'ē-găt'), arm of North sea bet. Sweden & Jutland; 40–70 m. wide.

Keats (kēts), John. Eng. poet (1795–1821).

Kentucky (kĕn-tŭk'ĭ), state, E cen. U. S. 40,598 ☐ p. 2,417, ✻ Frankfort. Abbr. *Ky.*

Kenya (kē-nyä'; kĕn'yá), Brit. col. & prot. E Afr., form. E. Afr. Prot. 200,000 ☐ p. 2,376, ✻ Nairobi.

Kharkov (kär'kôf), city, ✻ of Ukraine, Eur. p. 284.

Kiel (kēl), ftd. spt. N Prussia, on Baltic, p. 205.

Kiev (kē'yĕf), city, cen. Ukraine, Europe, p. 366.

Kilimanjaro (kĭl'ē-män-jä'rō), mt. Tanganyika Ter. Afr. 19,450 ft.; highest in Africa. [(1819–75).

Kingsley (kĭngz'lĭ), Chas. Eng. divine & auth.

Kingston upon Hull (kĭngz'tŭn), spt. city, N Eng. p. 287.

Kipling (kĭp'lĭng), Rudyard. Eng. author (1865– [p. 5,059, ✻ Orenburg.

Kirghiz Republic (kĭr-gēz'), repub. Soviet Russia, SE Eur. & W Asia, 843,640 ☐

āle, senåte, câre, ăm, ăccount, ärm, ásk, sofá; ēve, ĕvent, ĕnd, recĕnt, makẽr; īce, ĭll; ōld, ŏbey, ôrb, ŏdd, sŏft, cŏnnect; ūse, ŭnite, ûrn, ŭp, circŭs; fōōd, fŏŏt; out, oil;

Kitchener of Khartoum (kĭch′ĕn-ẽr), Horatio H. Kitchener, 1st Earl. Eng. gen. (1850–1916).

Klondike (klŏn′dĭk), region, NW Canada; gold.

Kobe (kō′bĕ), spt. city, S Honshu, Japan, p. 609.

Königsberg (kū′nĭks-bĕrK), * of E. Prussia, p. 261.

Korea, *or* **Chosen** (kô-rē′ā, chō′sĕn′), form. kingdom, ter. of Japan, 85,231 □ p. 17,264, * Seoul.

Kublai Khan (kōo′blī kän′). Founder of Mongol dynasty, China (1216?–1294).

Kurdistan (kōor′dĭ-stän′), region, Turkey, Mesopotamia, & Persia, ab. 74,000 □ p. 2,500.

Kurile Islands (kōo′rĭl), *Jap.* **Chishima** (chē′-shē′mä), group N Pacific oc.; 6,068 □ p. 15; Jap.

Kyoto *or* **Kioto** (kyō′tō), city, SW Honshu, Japan, p. 591. [SW, 17,075 □ p. 8,730.

Kyushu (kyōō′shōō′), one of main isls. of Japan, in

L

Labrador (lăb′rȧ-dôr′; lăb′rȧ-dôr), pen. E Br. N. Am. ab. 530,000 □ p. 7. — E part of this pen. dependency of Newfoundland, 110,000 □ p. 4.

Lafayette, de (dĕ lä′fā-yĕt′), Marie Joseph Paul, Marquis. Fr. gen. & statesman (1757–1834).

La Fontaine, de (lȧ fôn′tĕn′), J. Fr. writer of fables (1621–95). [282.

Lahore (lȧ-hōr′), * of Punjab, NW Br. India, p.

Lamb (lăm), Charles. Eng. essayist (1775–1834).

Lanchowfu (län′chō′fōō′), * of Kansu, China, p. 500. [1802–73).

Landseer (lănd′sēr), Edwin H., Sir. Eng. artist

Lansing (lăn′sĭng), city, * of Mich. in S cen. p. 57.

La Paz (lä päs′), city, a * of Bolivia, p. 107.

Lap′land, region N Norway & Sw. & NW Russia, Europe. [explorer (1643–87).

La Salle, de (dĕ lȧ säl′), René Robert, Sieur. Fr.

Latin America, Spanish America (which see) and Brazil (a Portuguese-speaking country).

Latvia (lăt′vĭ-ȧ), repub. of Europe, on Baltic, S of Esthonia, 25,000 □ p. 1,851, * Riga.

Lebrun (lĕ-brŭn′), Albert François. Pres. of France fr. 1932 (1871–). [70).

Lee (lē), Robert Edward. Confederate gen. (1807–

Leeds (lēdz), city, N Eng. p. 458.

Leeward Islands (lē′wĕrd), part of West Indies.

Leicester (lĕs′tẽr), mfg. bor. cen. Eng. p. 234.

Leiden *or* **Leyden** (lī′dĕn), city, W Neth. p. 61; univ.; siege, 1573–74. [604.

Leipzig *or* **Leipsic** (līp′sĭk), city, Saxony, Ger. p.

Lemberg (lĕm′bĕrk), city, SE Poland, p. 219.

Lena (lē′nȧ), riv. Siberia, 2,860 m. to Arctic oc.

Lenin (lĕn′ĭn), Nikolay. Russ. Bolshevist leader & pres. (1870–1924).

Leningrad (-grȧd), city, former * of Russia, in NW part, p. 1,067; form. St. Petersburg & Petrograd. Renamed in 1924 after the death of Lenin.

Leo (lē′ō). Name of 13 popes: **I.,** Saint. *The Great,* fr. 440 (390?–461); **XIII.** fr. 1878 (1810–1903).

Levant (lĕ-vănt′), E shores of Medit. sea. [25.

Lhasa *or* **Lassa** (läs′ȧ), sacred city, * of Tibet, p.

Liberia (lī-bē′rĭ-ȧ), negro rep. W Afr. 40,000 □ p. 1,500, * Monrovia.

Libya (lĭb′ĭ-ȧ), name given to Africa by anc. Greeks. — It. depend. N Afr. 406,000 □ p. 1,000.

Liége (lē-ĕzh′), city, E Belgium, p. 167; univ.

Lille, *form.* **Lisle** (lēl), city, N Fr. p. 201; univ.

Lima (lē′mä), * of Peru, near coast, p. 176; univ.

Lincoln (lĭŋ′kŭn), * of Nebr. p. 55. —, Abraham. 16th pres. of the U. S. in 1861–65 (1809–65).

Lisbon (lĭz′bŭn), city & port, * of Port. p. 490.

Lithuania (lĭth′û-ā′nĭ-ȧ), rep. on Baltic, N of Poland, 21,037 □ p. 2,900, * Kovno.

Little Rock, city, * of Arkansas, p. 65.

Liverpool (lĭv′ẽr-pōol), spt. NW Eng. p. 803.

Livingstone (lĭv′ĭng-stŭn), David. Scot. explorer (1813–73). [59–A. D. 17).

Livy (-ĭ). *Titus Livius.* Roman historian (B. C.

Lloyd George (loid′ jôrj′), David. Eng. liberal politician; prime minister 1916–22 (1863–).

Łódź (lōōj), *or* **Lodz** (lôdz), city, W Poland, p. 452.

Loire (lwär), riv. in Fr. 625 m. to Bay of Biscay.

Lombardy (lŏm′bȧr-dĭ), div. N It. 9,333 □ p. 5,243.

London (lŭn′dŭn), city, * of England & of the Brit. Empire, on Thames riv. 117 □ p. 4,483; "Greater London," p. 7,476; oldest part, "the City," p. 14. [poet (1807–82).

Longfellow (lŏng′fĕl′ō), Henry Wadsworth. Am.

Longs Peak, Rocky mts. N Colo. 14,255 ft. high.

Los Angeles (lôs ăn′gĕl-ĕs; lôs ăn′jĕl-ĕs), city, S Calif. p. 577.

Louis (lōō′ĭs; lōō′ĭ). Name of 18 kings of France, esp.: **IX.,** Saint, fr. 1226 (1215–70); **XIV.** *Le Grand* (*the Great*), fr. 1643 (1638–1715); **XV.** fr. 1715 (1710–74); **XVI.** fr. 1774 (1754–93). —

Napoleon. See NAPOLEON III.

Louisiana (lōō-ē′zē-ăn′ȧ), state, S U. S. 48,506 □ p. 1,799, * Baton Rouge. Abbr. *La.* [p. 235.

Louisville (lōō′ĭs-vĭl; lōō′ĭ-), city, Ky. on Ohio riv.

Lowell (lō′ĕl), city, NE Mass. p. 113. —, James Russell. Am. author (1819–91).

Loyola, de (dĕ lō-yō′lä; lŏi-ō′lȧ), Ignatius. Sp. founder of Jesuits (1491–1556). [siege, 1857.

Lucknow (lŭk′nou′), city, N British India, p. 241;

Luther (lōō′thẽr), Martin. Leader of Ger. Reformation (1483–1546).

Luxemburg (lŭk′sĕm-bûrg), independent grand duchy, E of Belgium, 909 □ p. 264. — its * p. 46.

Luzon (lōō-zŏn′), chief isl. Phil. isls. 40,814 □ p. 3,799. [France, p. 562.

Lyon (lĭ′ŭn; *F.* lē′ôN′), *or* **Lyons** (lĭ′ŭnz), city, SE

M

Macaulay (mȧ-kô′lĭ), Thomas Babington. Baron Macaulay. Eng. hist. & statesm. (1800–59).

MacDonald (măk-dŏn′ăld), James Ramsay. Eng. labor prime minister, 1924,1929– (1866–).

Macedonia (măs′ē-dō′nĭ-ȧ), *or* **Macedon,** anc. country, N of Greece; now divided among Serbia, Bulgaria, & Greece. [& writer (1469–1527).

Machiavelli (mä′kyä-vĕl′lē), Niccolò. It. statesm.

McKinley (mȧ-kĭn′lĭ), Wm. 25th pres. of U. S. fr. 1897 (1843–1901). —, **Mt.,** Alaska, highest in N. Am. 20,300 ft.

Madagascar (măd′ȧ-găs′kȧr), large isl. E. of S Afr. 224,721 □ p. 3,382, * Antananarivo; Fr. colony.

Madeira (mȧ-dē′rȧ; *Pg.* mä-dā′rä), riv. 2,100 m. W Brazil to Amazon. — **Islands,** Port. group W of Morocco, 314 □ p. 185, * Funchal.

Madison (măd′ĭ-sŭn), city, * of Wis. in S cen. part, p. 38. —, James. 4th pres. of the U. S. in 1809–17 (1751–1836).

---

chair; go; sing, iŋk; then, thin; nature, verdure; yet; zh = z in azure. Numbers refer to §§ in the Special Notes which, with Abbreviations, Signs, etc., precede the Vocabulary.

Madras (mȧ-dràs'), spt. ✳ of Madras prov. E Br. India, p. 527. [p. 729.]

Madrid (mȧ-drĭd'), city, ✳ of Spain, in cen. part,

Magdeburg (mäg'dĕ-bōōrK), city, ✳ of Saxony prov., Prussia, p. 286.

Magellan (mȧ-jĕl'ȧn), Fernando. Port. nav. (1480?–1521). —, **Strait of,** in S S. America.

Mahomet. See MOHAMMED. [Augusta.]

Maine (mān), state, NE U. S. 33,040 ☐ p. 768, ✳|

Mainz (mīnts), *or* **Mayence** (mȧ'yäNs'), city, Hesse, Germany, on Rhine, p. 108.

Malacca *or* **Malakka** (mȧ-lăk'ȧ), **Strait of,** bet. Malay pen. & Sumatra.

Málaga (mä'lä-gä; mäl'ȧ-gȧ), spt. S Spain, p. 150.

Malay Archipelago, *or* **Malaysia** (mȧ-lā'shȧ), the largest of isl. groups, SE of Asia.

Malay Peninsula, extreme S Asia, 70,000 ☐.

Malay States, Br. protectorate, Malay pen., 51,003 ☐ p. 2,449.

Malta (môl'tȧ), isl. (95 ☐) & Br. col. (122 ☐ civil p. 225), Medit. sea, ✳ Valletta.

Manchester (măn'chĕs-tēr), city, W Eng. p. 731.

Manchuria (-chōō'rĭ-ȧ), Chinese depend. E of Mongolia & Chihli, 363,700 ☐ p. 15,000, ✳ Mukden.

Mandalay (măn'dȧ-lā), N Burma, p. 149.

Manhattan (-hăt'ȧn), bor., part of N. Y. city, p. 2,284, occupying island of same name, 13½ m. long. [p. 285.]

Manila (mȧ-nĭl'ȧ), city, W Luzon, ✳ of Phil. isls.|

Mannheim (män'hīm) city, SW Germany, p. 230.

Marconi (mär-kō'nī), Guglielmo. It. electrician (1874–)

Marlborough (märl'bŏ-rȧ; môl'brȧ), John Churchill, Duke of. Eng. general (1650–1722).

Marlowe (mär'lō), Julia. Am. actress (1866–).

Marmara, Sea of (-mȧ-rȧ), in Turkey bet. Europe & Asia. [75.]

Marquette (mär-kĕt'), Jacques. Fr. expl. (1637–

Marrakesh (mȧr-rä'kĕsh), *or* **Morocco** (mô-rŏk'ō), tn. W Morocco, p. 140; a ✳ of the sultanate.

Marseille (mȧr'sā'y'), *or* **Marseilles** (mär-sālz'), spt. SE Fr. p. 586. [1801 (1755–1835).]

Marshall (mär'shȧl), John. U. S. chief justice fr.|

Martinique (mär'tĭ-nēk'), isl. Lesser Antilles, 385 ☐ p. 244, ✳ Fort-de-France; Fr. colony.

Mary (mā'rĭ) **I.** "*Bloody Mary.*" Queen of Eng. fr. 1553 (1516–58). — **II.** Joint Br. sov. fr. 1689 with William III. (1662–94). — **Stuart.** Queen of Scots, 1542–67 (1542–87); beheaded.

Maryland (mĕr'ĭ-lȧnd), a middle Atl. state, U. S. 12,327 ☐ p. 1,450, ✳ Annapolis. Abbr. *Md.*

Massachusetts (măs'ȧ-chōō'sĕts), state, NE U. S. 8,266 ☐ p. 3,852, ✳ Boston. Abbr. *Mass.*

Matterhorn (mät'ĕr-hôrn), mt. Alps, Switz. & It. 14,780 ft.

Mauna Loa (mou'nä lō'ä), vol. Hawaii isl. 13,675 ft.

Mecca (mĕk'ȧ), city, ✳ of Hejaz, Arabia, p. 70.

Medici, de' (dā mĕd'ē-chē), Catherine, queen of Henry II. of France (1519–89). —, Lorenzo I. *The Magnificent* (1449–92.)

Mediterranean Sea (mĕd'ĭ-tēr-ā'nē-ȧn), inclosed by Europe, Asia, & Africa, 2,330 m. long. [sea.]

Mekong (mā'kŏng'), riv. 2,600 m. Tibet to China|

Melbourne (mĕl'bûrn), ✳ of Victoria, Australia, p. 795. [treas., 1921–32 (1855–).]

Mellon (-ŭn), Andrew W. Am. banker. Sec. of|

Memphis (mĕm'fĭs), anc. city & ✳ of anc. Egypt.
— city & riv. port, SW Tenn. p. 162.

Mendelssohn-Bartholdy (mĕn'dĕl-sōn-bär'tōl'dē'), Felix. Ger. Jewish musical composer (1809–47).

Mesopotamia (mĕs'ō-pō-tā'mĭ-ȧ), region bet. Euphrates & Tigris, nearly corresponding to IRAK.

Messina (mĕ-sē'nȧ), city, E Sicily, p. 177; earthquake, 1908. —, **Strait of,** bet. Sicily & Italy.

Mexico (mĕk'sĭ-kō), repub. S N. Am. 767,198 ☐ p. 16,800. — city, its ✳, cen. Mex. p. 500. —, **Gulf of,** on SE coast of N. Am. 1,000 m. E to W.

Michelangelo (mī'kĕl-ăn'jĕ-lō *It.* mē'kĕl-än'jä-lō). It. painter, sculptor, & poet (1475–1564).

Michigan (mĭsh'ĭ-gȧn), state, N cen. U. S. 57,980 ☐ p. 3,668, ✳ Lansing. Abbr. *Mich.* —, **Lake,** Great Lake, bet. Mich. & Wis. 22,336 ☐.

Milan (mĭl'ȧn; mĭ-lăn'), city, N Italy, p. 701; cath.

Milton (mĭl'tŭn), John. Eng. poet (1608–74).

Milwaukee (-wô'kē), city, SE Wis. p. 457. [933.]

Mindanao (mĭn'dä-nä'ō), isl. Phil. isls. 36,906 ☐ p.|

Minneapolis (mĭn'ē-ăp'ō-lĭs), city, E Minn. p. 381.

Minnesota (-sō'tȧ), state, N cen. U. S. 84,682 ☐ p. 2,387, ✳ St. Paul. Abbr. *Minn.*

Mississippi (mĭs'ĭ-sĭp'ĭ), riv. 2,500 m. Minn. to G. of Mex.; length headwaters Missouri riv. to Gulf, 4,200 m. — state, SE U. S. 46,865 ☐ p. 1,791, ✳ Jackson. Abbr. *Miss.*

Missouri (mĭ-sōō'rĭ; -zōō'rĭ), riv. U. S. 3,000 m. Rocky mts. to Mississippi riv. — state, cen. U. S. 69,420 ☐ p. 3,404, ✳ Jefferson City. Abbr. *Mo.*

Mohammed (mō-hăm'ĕd). Founder of Islam (570?–632).

Molière (mō'lyâr'). French dramatist (1622–73).

Moluccas (mō-lŭk'ȧz), isls. bet. Celebes & New Guinea, 30,168 ☐ p. 427; Dutch.

Mongolia (mŏŋ-gō'lĭ-ȧ), Chin. depend. N & NW of China, 1,367,600 ☐ p. 2,500; chief city, Urga.

Monroe (mŭn-rō'), James. 5th pres. of the U. S. in 1817–25 (1758–1831).

Montaigne, de (mŏn-tān'; *F.* dĕ mŏN'tȧn'y'), Michel E. Fr. author (1533–92).

Montana (mŏn-tăn'ȧ; -tä'nȧ), state, NW U. S. 146,997 ☐ p. 549, ✳ Helena. Abbr. *Mont.*

Montenegro (mŏn'tā-nā'grō; -nē'grō), form. kdm. now prov. S Yugoslavia, 3,733 ☐ p. 200, ✳ Cetinje.

Montevideo (mŏn'tē-vĭd'ē-ō), spt. ✳ of Uruguay, p. 351. [Mex. fr. 1503 (1480?–1520).]

Montezuma (-zōō'mä) **II.** Last Aztec emp. of|

Montgomery (mŏnt-gŭm'ēr-ĭ), city, ✳ of Ala. p. 43.

Montpelier (-pĕl'yēr), ✳ of Vermont, p. 7.

Montreal (mŏnt'rē-ôl'), city, S Quebec, Can. p. 619.

Morea (mō-rē'ȧ), S pen. of Greece.

Morocco (mō-rŏk'ō), sultanate, NW Afr. 230,920 ☐ p. 6,000, chief ✳ Rabat; Fr. & Sp. — See MARRAKESH. [1872.]

Morse (môrs), Samuel F. B. Am. inventor (1791–|

Moscow (mŏs'kō), city, cen. Russia, ✳ of Soviet Russia & Union of Russ. Soviet repubs. p. 1,543.

Motley (mŏt'lĭ), John L. Am. hist. (1814–77).

Mount Vernon (vûr'nŭn), homestead and burial place of George Washington, on Potomac, Va. 15 m. below Washington, D. C.

Mozart (mō'zärt), Wolfgang A. Austrian composer of music (1756–91). [158; bat. 1905.]

Mukden (mōōk'dĕn'), ✳ of Manchuria, in S, p.|

Munich (mū'nĭk), ✳ of Bavaria, p. 631; univ.

āle, senāte, câre, ăm, ȧccount, ärm, ȧsk, sofȧ; ēve, ĕvent, ĕnd, recĕnt, makēr; īce, ĭll; ōld, ŏbey, ôrb, ŏdd, sŏft, cŏnnect; ūse, ŭnite, ûrn, ŭp, circŭs; fōōd, fŏŏt; out, oil;

Murray (mŭr'ĭ), chief riv. of Australia, 1,500 m.
Mussolini (mōōs'sŏ-lē'nē), Benito. Premier of Italy fr. 1922 (1883–   ).
Mustafa Kemal (mōōs'tä-fä kĕ-mäl') (Pasha). Turk. leader; pres. of Turkey fr. 1924 (1879–   ).

N O

Nagasaki (nä'gà-sä'kē),spt. W Kyushu, Jap. p. 177.
Nanchang (nän'chäng'), city, SE China, p. 750.
Nanking (năn'kĭng'), ✳ of Kiangsu and since 1928 ✳ of China, p. 393.   [(1861–1930)].
Nansen (nän'sĕn), Fridtjof. Norw. Arctic explorer|
Nantes (nänts; F. nänt), city, NW France, p. 184.
Naples (nā'p'lz), city, W coast of S Italy, p. 770.
Napoleon (nà-pō'lē-ŭn) I. Napoleon Bonaparte. Emp. of the French 1804–1815 (1769–1821). —
  III. Louis Napoleon. Emp. of the Fr. in 1852–70 (1808–73).
Nashville (năsh'vĭl), ✳ of Tenn. in N cen. p. 118.
Natal (nà-täl'), prov. of Union of S. Afr. 35,284 ☐ p. 1,429, ✳ Pietermaritzburg.
Nebraska (nē-brăs'kà), state, W cen. U. S. 77,520 ☐ p. 1,296, ✳ Lincoln. Abbr. Nebr.
Nelson (nĕl'sŭn), Horatio. Viscount Nelson of the Nile. Eng. admiral (1758–1805).
Nero (nē'rō). Roman emperor fr. 54 (37–68).
Netherlands (nĕth'ẽr-lăndz), or Holland (hŏl'ănd), kdm. W Eur. 12,582 ☐ p. 6,831, ✳ The Hague.   [✳ Carson City. Abbr. Nev.|
Nevada (nē-vä'dà), state, W U. S. 110,690 ☐ p. 77,|
Newark (nū'ẽrk), city, NE New Jersey, p. 415.
New Bedford (nū bĕd'fẽrd), spt. SE Mass. p. 121.
Newcastle (nū'kàs''l), city, NE Eng. p. 275.
Newfoundland (nū'fŭnd-lănd'; nū'fŭnd-lănd'), isl. E N. Amer. 42,734 ☐ p. 259, ✳ St. John's; br.
New Guinea (gĭn'ĭ), or Papua (pä'pōō-ä; păp'-ū-à), large isl. N of Australia, 305,900 ☐ p. 950.
New Hampshire (hămp'shĭr), state, NE U. S. 9,341 ☐ p. 443, ✳ Concord. Abbr. N. H.
New Haven (hā'v'n), spt. S Conn. p. 163; Yale univ.   [Trenton. Abbr. N. J.|
New Jersey, state, E U. S. 8,224 ☐ p. 3,156, ✳|
New Mexico, state, SW U. S. 122,634 ☐ p. 360, ✳ Santa Fe. Abbr. N. Mex.
New Orleans (ôr'lē-ănz), city, SE La. p. 387; bat. 1815; chief cotton market, U. S. A.; univs.
New South Wales, state, SE Australia, 309,432 ☐ p. 2,100, ✳ Sydney.   [1727).|
Newton (nū'tŭn), Isaac, Sir. Eng. scientist (1642–|
New York, state, NE U. S. 49,204 ☐ p. 10,385, ✳ Albany. Abbr. N. Y. —city, SE N. Y. p. 5,620.
New Zealand (zē'lănd), Br. col. S Pac. oc. with depend. 103,861 ☐ p. 1,232, ✳ Wellington.
Niagara (nī-ăg'à-rà), falls, in Niagara riv. bet. Lakes Erie & Ontario, 158 ft. on Canadian side, 167 ft. on American.   [☐ p. 638, ✳ Managua.|
Nicaragua (nĭk'à-rä'gwà),repub. Cen. Am. 51,660|
Nice (nēs), spt. SE Fr. p. 156; resort.   [Guinea.|
Niger (nī'jẽr), riv. W Afr. 2,600 m. to Gulf of|
Nigeria (nī-jē'rī-à), Br. col. & prot. W Afr. 335,700 ☐ p. 18,071, ✳ Lagos.
Nightingale (nīt'ĭn-gāl; nīt'ĭn-), Florence. Eng. philanthropist and nurse (1820–1910). [Medit.|
Nile (nīl), riv. E Afr., 3,473 m. Lake Victoria to|
Nineveh (nĭn'ē-vĕ), anc. city, ✳ of Assyria.

Ningpo (nĭng'pō'), spt. E China, p. 450.
Nizhni Novgorod (nyĭzh'nyē nôv'gŏ-rŏt), city, cen. Russia, p. 112.
Norfolk (nôr'fŏk), spt. SE Va. p. 116.
North America, cont. 9,300,000 ☐ p. 145,000.
North Carolina, S Atl. state, U. S. 52,426 ☐ p. 2,559, ✳ Raleigh. Abbr. N. C.
North Dakota, state, NW U. S. 70,837 ☐ p. 647, ✳ Bismarck. Abbr. N. Dak.
Northern Ireland, div. of United Kingdom. N Ireland, 5,451 ☐ p. 1,250, ✳ Belfast.
North Sea, arm of Atl. E of Gr. Brit.
Norway (nôr'wā), kingdom, NW Europe, 124,964 ☐ p. 2,650, ✳ Oslo (Christiania).
Nottingham (nŏt'ĭng-ăm), bor. cen. Eng. p. 263.
Nova Scotia (nō'và skō'shyà), form. Acadia, mar- itime prov. E Can. 21,428 ☐ p. 525, ✳ Halifax.
Nova Zembla (zĕm'blà), isl. group Eur., N. of Russia.
Nuremberg (nū'rĕm-bûrg), city, Bavaria, p. 353.
Oakland (ōk'lănd), city, W Calif. p. 216.
Ob (ŏp), riv. W Siberia, 3,200 m. to Arctic oc.
Oceania (ō'shē-ăn'ĭ-à), or Oceanica (-ĭ-kà), col- lective name for lands of the cen. & W Pacific.
Odessa (ō-dĕs'à), spt. SW Ukraine, p. 435.
Ohio (ō-hī'ō), riv. 963 m. fr. Pittsburgh, Pa. to Miss. riv. at boundary of Ill. & Ky. — NE cen. state, U. S. 41,040 ☐ p. 5,759, ✳ Columbus.
Oklahoma (ō'klà-hō'mà), state, SW U. S. 70,057 ☐ p. 2,028, ✳ Oklahoma City, p. 91. Abbr. Okla.
Omaha (ō'mà-hô'), city, E Nebr. p. 192.
Oman (ō-män'), country, SE Arabia, 82,000 ☐ p. 500, ✳ Muscat.   [& Ont. prov. Canada.|
Ontario, Lake, (ŏn-tā'rĭ-ō), Great Lake, bet. N. Y.|
Oporto (ō-pôr'tō), city & port, NW Portugal, p. 203.
Orange (ŏr'ĕnj), riv. S Africa 1,100 m. to Atl. oc.
Orange Free State, prov. of U. of S. Afr. 50,389 ☐ p. 629, ✳ Bloemfontein.   [☐ p. 783, ✳ Salem.|
Oregon (ŏr'ē-gŏn), Pacific state, NW U. S. 96,699|
Orinoco (ō'rī-nō'kō), riv. Venez. 1,550 m. to Atl. oc.
Orkney Islands (ôrk'nĭ), group N of Scot.
Osaka (ō'zä'kä), spt. W Honshu, Japan, p. 1,253.
Oslo (ōs'lō), spt. ✳ of Norway, p. 258.   [p. 108.|
Ottawa (ŏt'à-wà), city, NE Ontario, ✳ of Canada,|
Ovid (ŏv'ĭd). Roman poet (B. C. 43–A. D. 17).

P

Pacific Ocean, from Am. W to Asia & Australia.
Paderewski (pä'dĕ-rĕf'skē), Ignace Jan. Polish pianist; premier of Poland in 1919 (1860–   ).
Padua (păd'ū-à), city, NE Italy, p. 109.
Palermo (pä-lûr'mō), spt. N Sicily, p. 400.
Palestine (păl'ĕs-tīn), Bib. Canaan (kā'năn), country, W Asia, 9,000 ☐ p. 757, ✳ Jerusalem.
Panama (păn'à-mä'), rep. Cen. Am. bet. Costa Rica & Colombia, 32,380 ☐ p. 434, ✳ Panama (p. 67). —, Isthmus of, narrowest part (30 m. wide) of Am. continent; canal built by U. S.
Papua (pä'pōō-à; păp'ū-à). See New Guinea.—,
  Territory of, SE New Guinea, 90,540 ☐ p. 277; to Australia.
Paraguay (păr'à-gwā; pä'rä-gwī'), rep. bet. Brazil & Argentina, 97,722 ☐ p. 1,000, ✳ Asunción.
Paraná (pä'rä-nä'), riv. S. Am. 2,720 m. S Brazil to Plata riv.

Paris (păr′ĭs), city. ✲ of Fr. in N, p. 2,906. [93].|

Parkman (pärk′măn), Francis. Am. hist. (1823–|

Parnassus (pär-năs′ŭs), mt. cen. Greece, 8,065 ft.

Patagonia (păt′à-gō′nĭ-à), name of region in S S. Am., now part of Argentina.

Paterson (păt′ẽr-sŭn), city, NE N. J. p. 136.

Patrick (-rĭk), Saint. Apostle and patron saint of Ireland (373?– 463?)

Peary (pē′rĭ), Robert Edwin. Am. naval officer, discovered North Pole, April 6, 1909 (1856–1920).

Peking (pē′kĭng′), city, former ✲ of China, in NE, p. 934, with sub. 1,300; changed to **Peiping** (pē′ĭ-pĭng′) in 1928. [Morea.|

Peloponnesus (pĕl′ô-pŏ-nē′sŭs), anc. name of the |

Penn (pĕn), William. Eng. Quaker, founder of Pennsylvania (1644–1718).

Pennsylvania (-sĭl-vā′nĭ-à), middle Atl. state, U. S. 45,126 ☐ p. 8,720, ✲ Harrisburg. Abbr. *Pa.* or *Penn.* [B. C. 495?–429).|

Pericles (pĕr′ĭ-klēz). Greek statesman & orator|

Pernambuco (pẽr′năm-bōō′kŏ), *or* **Recife** (rā-sē′fā), spt. E Brazil, p. 239.

Perry (pĕr′ĭ), Matthew C. (1794–1858), & his bro Oliver H. (1785–1819). American commodores.

Pershing (pûr′shĭng), John Joseph. Am. general (1860–).

Persia (pûr′shà ; -zhà), kingdom, SW Asia, 628,000 ☐ p. 10,000, ✲ Teheran. [✲ Lima.|

Peru (pē-rōō′), rep. W S. Am. 722,461 ☐ p. 5,550,|

Peter (pē′tẽr) **I.** *The Great.* Czar of Russ. fr. 1682 (1672–1725). **— the Hermit.** Preacher of 1st crusade (d. 1115).

Petrograd (pĕt′rŏ-grăd). See LENINGRAD.

Phidias (fĭd′ĭ-ăs). Gr. sculptor (B. C. 500?–432?).

Philadelphia (fĭl′à-dĕl′fĭ-à), city, SE Pa. p. 1,824.

Philip (fĭl′ĭp) **II.** Kg. of Macedon fr. B. C. 359 (B. C. 382–336). **—II.** Kg. of Sp. fr. 1556(1527–98).

Philippine Islands (fĭl′ĭ-pēn; -pĭn), group SE of Asia, 114,400 ☐ p. 10,314, ✲ Manila; to U. S.

Phœnicia (fē-nĭsh′ĭ-à), anc. country, W Syria, ✲ Tyre. [1853–57 (1804–69).|

Pierce (pērs), Franklin. 14th pres. of the U. S. in|

Pikes Peak (pīks), mt. Rocky mts. Colo. 14,108 ft.

Pitt (pĭt), William, 1st Earl of Chatham (1708–78), & his son, William (1759–1806). Eng. statesmen.

Pittsburgh (pĭts′bûrg), city, SW Pa. p. 588.

Pius (pī′ŭs), **XI.** Pope fr. 1922 (1857–).

Pizarro (pĭ-zär′rŏ; *Sp.* pē-thär′rŏ), Francisco. Sp. conqueror of Peru (1471 *or* 1475–1541).

Plata (plä′tä), estuary bet. Argentina & Uruguay.

Plato (plā′tŏ). Gr. philosopher (B. C. 427–347).

Pliny (plĭn′ĭ). *The Elder.* Roman naturalist & writer (23–79). — his nephew, *The Younger.* Roman writer (62?–114?). [120?).|

Plutarch (plōō′tärk). Greek biographer (46?–|

Plymouth (plĭm′ŭth), spt. SW Eng. p. 210.

Po (pō), riv. N Italy, 418 m. to Adriatic sea.

Poe (pō), Edgar Allan. Am. poet & au. (1809–49).

Poland (pō′lănd), former kingdom, cen. Europe, now repub. 146,821 ☐ p. 27,092, ✲ Warsaw.

Pole, North, reached by Peary, April 6, 1909. — **South,** by Amundsen, Dec. 14, 1911.

Polk (pōk), James Knox. 11th pres. of U. S. in 1845–49 (1795–1849). [1323).|

Polo (pō′lŏ), Marco. Venetian traveler (1254–|

Pompey (pŏm′pĭ). Rom. gen. (B. C. 106–48).

Popocatepetl (pō-pō′kä-tā′pĕt′l), volcano, S Mex. 17,876 ft.

Portland (pōrt′lănd), riv. port, NW Oregon, p. 258.

Porto Rico (pōr′tŏ rē′kŏ), from 1932 officially **Puerto Rico.** See PUERTO RICO.

Portsmouth (pōrts′mŭth), spt. bor. S Eng. p. 247.

Portugal (pōr′tū̇-gǎl), form. kingdom, since Oct. 5, 1910, rep., W Iberian pen. 34,254 ☐ p. 5,546, ✲ Lisbon; with Azores & Madeira isls. 35,490 ☐ p. 6,041. [☐ p. 3,120, ✲ Lourenço Marques.|

Portuguese East Africa, Port. col. SE Afr. 426,712|

Potomac (pô-tō′măk), riv. W. Va. Md. & Va. 450 m.

Prague (präg), ✲ of Czechoslovakia, in NW, p. 676; univ. [(1796–1859).|

Prescott (prĕs′kŭt), Wm. Hickling. Am. hist.|

Pretoria (prē-tō′rĭ-à), ✲ of Transvaal prov. & of Union of S. Afr. p. 74. [238; univ.|

Providence (prŏv′ĭ-dĕns), spt. ✲ of R. I. in N, p.|

Prussia (prŭsh′à), state, N Ger. over ⅗ of Germany, 113,746 ☐ p. 36,696, ✲ Berlin.

Ptolemy (tŏl′ē-mĭ). Gr.-Egypt. astronomer & geographer (fl. 2d cent.).

Puerto Rico (pwẽr′tŏ rē′kŏ), W. I. isl. E of Haiti, 3,435 ☐ p. 1,300, ✲ San Juan; to U. S.

Punjab (pŭn-jäb′), prov. NW Br. India, 99,222 ☐ p. 20,685, ✲ Lahore; with native states, 135,773 ☐ p. 25,101.

Pyrenees (pĭr′ē-nēz), mt. chain bet. Fr. & Sp. 11,165 ft. [582–507?).|

Pythagoras (pĭ-thăg′ō-răs). Greek philos. (B. C.|

Q R

Quebec (kwē-bĕk′), city, E Can. a riv. port, p. 95; captured 1759. [Long Isl. 108 ☐ p. 469.|

Queens, bor. of N. Y. city, E of Brooklyn bor. on|

Queensland (kwēnz′lănd), state, NE Australia. 670,500 ☐ p. 758, ✲ Brisbane.

Rainier, Mount (rä-nēr′), peak, W Wash. 14,408 ft.

Raleigh (rô′lĭ), ✲ of N. C. in cen. part, p. 24. —, Walter, Sir. Eng. nav. & courtier (1552–1618).

Rangoon (răn-gōōn′), port, ✲ of Burma,in S,p.342.

Raphael (răf′à-ĕl ;). It. painter (1483–1520).

Reading (rĕd′ĭng), city, SE Pa. p. 108.

Red River, Tex. 1,200 m. to Mississippi riv. La.

Red Sea, inland sea, bet. Arabia & Egypt, 1,450 m.

Reims *or* **Rheims** (rēmz), city, NE Fr. p. 77; cath.

Rembrandt (rĕm′brănt). Du. painter (1606–69).

Revel (rĕv′ĕl; *Russ.* rĕ′vĕl-y′), *Esthonian* **Tallinn** (tăl′lĭn), ftd. spt. ✲ of Esthonia, in NW, p. 130.

Reynolds (rĕn′ŭlz), Joshua, Sir. Eng. painter (1723–92).

Rhine (rīn), riv. 810 m. Switz. to North sea.

Rhode Island (rōd), state (the smallest), NE U. S. 1,248 ☐ p. 604, ✲ Providence. Abbr. *R. I.*

Rhodes (rōdz), Cecil John. Eng. statesm. in S. Afr. (1853–1902). [444,575 ☐ p. 1,812.|

Rhodesia (rô-qē′zhĭ-à), Br. ter. N of Transvaal,|

Rhone (rōn), riv. 504 m. Switz. to Medit. sea, Fr.

Richard (rĭch′ärd). Three kings of England: **I.** *Cœur de Lion,* fr. 1189 (1157–99) ; **II.** fr. 1377–1399 (1367–1400) ; **III.** fr. 1483 (1452–85).

Richelieu, de (dē̇ rē′shĕ-lyü′; *Angl.* rĕsh′ē-lōō′), Duke. Fr. cardinal & statesm. (1585–1642).

Richmond (rĭch′mŭnd), bor. Staten isl. part of N. Y. city, p. 117. — ✲ of Va. in E cen. part, p. 172.

Riga (rē'gà), city & port, ✳ of Latvia, in N cen. part, p. 300.   [1916].

Riley (rī'lǐ), James Whitcomb. Am. poet (1853–

Rio de Janeiro (rē'ō dā zhà-nā'rō), spt. city, ✳ of Brazil, on SE coast, p. 1,158.

Rio Grande (grän'dā), riv. 1,800 m. Colo. to Gulf of Mex., partly bet. U. S. & Mex.

Riviera (rē-vyä'rä). beautiful coast region along Medit. sea, SE Fr. & NW It.; winter resorts.

Roberts (rŏb'ẽrts), Frederick Sleigh.   1st Earl Roberts. Br. field marshal (1832–1914).

Robespierre, de (dē rō'bĕs-pyâr'), Maximilien Marie I. Fr. revolutionist (1758–94).

Rochester (rŏch'ĕs-tẽr), city, W N. Y. p. 296.

Rocky Mountains, mt. system, Mex. to Arctic oc.

Rome (rōm), ✳ of Italy, in W cen. part. p. 637.

Roosevelt (rō'zĕ-vĕlt; *almost* rōz'vĕlt), Theodore. 26th pres. of the U. S. in 1901–09 (1858–1919).

Root (rōōt), Elihu. Am. statesman (1845–   ).

Rosario (rō-sä'rē-ō), riv. port, E Argentina, p. 260.

Rotterdam (rŏt'ẽr-dăm'), city, SW Neth. p. 506.

Rouen (rwän), city, N France, p. 124 ; carib.

Roumania *or* **Rumania** (rōō-mā'nǐ-à), kingdom, E Europe, 122,282 ☐ p. 17,393, ✳ Bucharest.

Rousseau (rōō'sō'), Jean Jacques.   Fr. philosopher (1712–78).   [(1577–1640).

Rubens (rōō'bĕnz), Peter Paul. Flemish painter

Ruhr (rōōr), min. & industrial region, valley of Ruhr riv. W Prussia, Germany, E of Rhine.

Ruskin (rŭs'kǐn), John. Eng. author (1819–1900).

Russia (rŭsh'à), Union of Soviet repubs. E Eur. & N & W Asia, 8,166,130 ☐ p. 131,546, ✳ Moscow. **—, Soviet,** federal repub. chief part of Union, 7,893,360 ☐ p. 98,226.

S

Saar Region (zär), *or* **The Saar,** *Fr.* **Sarre** (sàr), valley of Saar riv. (84 m.) bet. NE Fr. & SW Ger. 743 ☐ p. 653; under League of Nations; coal.

Sacramento (săk'rà-mĕn'tō), city, ✳ of Calif. in N cen. part, p. 66

Sahara (sà-hä'rà), desert N Afr. 3,500,000 ☐.

Saint Gaudens (sânt gô'dĕnz), Augustus. Irish-American sculptor (1848–1907)

Saint Helena (hĕ-lē'nà), Br. isl. S Atl. oc. 47 ☐ p. 4, ✳ Jamestown; Napoleon's exile, 1815–21.

Saint Kitts (sânt kǐts'), *or* **Saint Christopher** (krǐs'tō-fẽr), isl. Leeward group, Br. W. Indies, 68 ☐ p. 22, ✳ Basseterre.

Saint Lawrence (lô'rĕns), riv. 760 m. Lake Ontario to Gulf of St. Lawrence. **—, Gulf of,** in E Can.

Saint Louis (lōō'ǐs; -ǐ), city, E Mo. p. 773.

Saint Paul (pôl'), city, on Miss. riv. ✳ of Minn. in SE, p. 235.

Saint Petersburg (pē'tẽrz-bûrg). See LENINGRAD.

Sakhalin (sà'kà-lēn'), isl. NE asia ; N part Russ. 14,668 ☐ p. 34; S part Jap. (see KARAFUTO).

Salem (sā'lĕm), city, ✳ of Oregon, in NW, p. 18.

Salonika (sä'lō-nē'kà), spt. NE Gr. p. 170.

Salt Lake City, city, ✳ of Utah, in N, p. 118.

Salvador (săl'và-dōr'), republic, Pacific coast, Cen. America, 13,176 ☐ p. 1,526, ✳ San Salvador.

Samoa (sä-mō'à), isl. group S cen. Pacific oc.; to U. S. (77 ☐ p. 8) & to N. Z. (1,210 ☐ p. 38).

San Antonio (săn ăn-tō'nǐ-ō), city, S Tex. p. 161.

San Francisco (săn frăn-sǐs'kō), spt. Calif. p. 507.

San Juan (săn hwän'), ✳ of Porto Rico, in N, p. 71.

Santa Fe (săn'tà fā'), ✳ of New Mex. in N cen. part, p. 7; founded ab. 1605.

Santiago (săn'tē-ä'gō), ✳ of Chile, in S, p. 507.

Santo Domingo (săn'tō dō-mǐn'gō). See DOMINICAN REPUBLIC.   [579.

São Paulo (souN' pou'lōō), spt. city, S Brazil, p. 188. [p. 890.

Saratov (sä-rä'tôf), city, SE Russ. p. 188. [p. 890.

Sardinia (sär-dǐn'ǐ-à), It. isl. Medit. sea, 9,299 ☐

Saxony (săk'sǔn-ǐ), state, E cen Ger. 5,789 ☐ p. 4,663, ✳ Dresden. — prov. cen. Prussia, 9,757 ☐ p. 3,129, ✳ Magdeburg.

Scandinavia (skăn'dǐ-nā'vǐ-à), pen. of Norway & Sweden.   [(1759–1805).

Schiller, von (fôn shǐl'ẽr), Johann C. F. Ger. poet.

Scipio (sǐp'ǐ-ō). *Africanus Major.* Rom. gen. (B. C. 237–183?). — *Africanus Minor.* Rom. gen. (B. C. ab. 185–129). [p. 4,882, ✳ Edinburgh.

Scotland (skŏt'lănd), N div. of Gr. Brit. 30,405 ☐

Scott, Walter, Sir. Scot. au. & poet (1771–1832).

Scranton (skrăn'tǔn), city, NE Pa. p. 138.

Seattle (sē-ăt'l), city & port, W Wash. p. 315.

Seine (sān), riv. France, 480 m. to Eng. channel.

Seoul (sē-ōōl'), ✳ of Korea, p. 247.

Serbia (sûr'bǐ-à), form. Balkan kdm. now div. of Yugoslavia, 36,937 ☐ p. 4,130, ✳ Belgrade.

Seville (sĕv'ǐl; sē-vǐl'), city, SW Spain, p. 206.

Shakespeare (shāk'spẽr), William. Eng. poet & dramatist (1564–1616).

Shanghai (shăng'hä'ǐ), port, E China, p. 953.

Shasta, Mount (shăs'tà), peak, N Calif. 14,380 ft.

Shaw (shô), George Bernard. Ir. dram. (1856–   ).

Sheffield (shĕf'ēld), city, N Eng. p. 491.

Shelley (shĕl'ǐ), Percy Bysshe. Eng. poet (1792–1822).   [(1831–88)

Sheridan (shĕr'ǐ-dǎn), Philip Henry. Am. gen.

Sherman (shûr'mǎn), Wm. Tecumseh. Am. gen. (1820–91).

Siam (sī-ăm'), kingdom, SE Asia, 194,580 ☐ p. 9,221, ✳ Bangkok.   [1,000.

Sianfu (sē'än-foo'), ✳ of Shensi prov. N China, p.

Siberia (sī-bē'rǐ-à), popularly, all N Asia; politically, part of this region, a div. of Soviet Russia, 3,406,000 ☐ p. 10,769.   [4,304.

Sicily (sǐs'ǐ-lǐ), It. isl. largest in Medit. 9,935 ☐ p.

Sierra Leone (sǐ-ĕr'à lē-ō'nē), Br. col. (4,000 ☐ p. 85, ✳ Freetown) & prot. (27,000 ☐ p. 1,456), W Afr.   [   ).

Sims (sǐmz), William Sowden. Am. adm. (1858–

Sinai (sī'nǐ), pen. N end Red sea; to Egypt.

Singapore (sǐŋ'gà-pōr'), spt. ✳ of Straits Settlements & of Br. Malaya, p. 350.

Sinkiang (sǐn'kyäng'), Chinese prov. bet. Mongolia & Tibet, 550,579 ☐ p. 2,500, ✳ Kuldja.

Smyrna (smûr'nà), spt. W Turkey in Asia, p. 300.

Society Islands, in S Pacific oc. 637 ☐ p. 15; Fr.

Socrates (sŏk'rà-tēz). Greek philosopher (B. C. 469–399).   [p. 154.

Sofia (sō'fē-yà; *Eng.* sō-fē'à), ✳ of Bulgaria, in W.

Solomon Islands, S Pac. oc. 15,300 ☐ p. 190; chiefly Br. prot.; NW part in Australian mandate.

Solon (sō'lǒn). Greek lawgiver (B. C. 639?–559).

Somaliland (sō-mä'lē-lănd'), ter. bet. equator & Gulf of Aden, E Afr.; Fr., Br., & It.   [406].

Sophocles (sŏf'ō-klēz). Gr. tragic poet (B. C. 496?–

South Africa, Union of, Br. colony comprising Cape of Good Hope, Natal, Transvaal, & Orange Free State provs. 473,089 □ p. 6,929, ✳ Pretoria.

South America, continent, ab. 7,500,000 □ p. 62,700.

Southampton (southămp′tŭn), spt. S Eng. p. 161.

South Australia, state, Australia, 380,070 □ p. 495, ✳ Adelaide.   [Columbia. Abbr. *S. C.*

South Carolina, S Atl. state, 30,989 □ p. 1,684, ✳|

South Dakota, state, NW U. S. 77,615 □ p. 637, ✳ Pierre. Abbr. *S. Dak.*

Spain (spān), republic (from 1931), SW Europe, 194,800 □ p. 21,959, ✳ Madrid.

Spanish America, S. Am. (exc. Brazil & the Guianas), Cen. Am. (exc. Br. Honduras), Mexico, Cuba, Puerto Rico, & Domin. Repub. Cf. LATIN AMERICA.   [99).|

Spenser (spĕn′sẽr), Edmund. Eng. poet (1552?–

Spitsbergen (spĭts′bûr′gĕn), isl. group N of Norway.

Spokane (spō′kăn′), city, E Wash. p. 104.

Springfield (sprĭng′fĭeld), city, ✳ of Ill. in cen. p. 59.
— city, on Conn. riv. S Mass. p. 130.   [p. 142.

Srinagar (srē′nŭ-gûr′), ✳ of Kashmir, NW India,|

Stanley (stăn′lĭ), Henry M., Sir. Eng. explorer. (1841–1904).   [p. 233.

Stettin (shtĕ-tēn′), spt. ✳ of Pomerania, Prussia,|

Stevenson (stē′-vĕn-sŭn), Robert Louis. Scot. writer (1850–94).   [SE, p. 422.|

Stockholm (stŏk′hōlm), spt. ✳ of Sweden, in

Stoke on Trent, bor. cen. Eng. p. 240; pottery.

Straits Settlements, Br. col. mostly in S Malay pen. & adjacent isls. 1,600 □ p.884, ✳ Singapore.

Strasbourg (sträs′bōōr′; *Eng.* străs′bûrg), *Ger.* **Strassburg** (shträs′bŏŏrk), city, NE Fr. p. 167.

Stuart (stū′ẽrt). Scot. & Eng. royal family.

Stuttgart (shtŏŏt′gärt), ✳ of Württemberg, p. 324.

Stuyvesant (stī′vĕ-sănt), Peter. Last gov. of New Netherland (1602–82).

Sudan (sōō-dän′), region, Afr. S of Sahara. **—, Anglo-Egyptian,** E end Sudan region, S of Egypt, 1,-014,000 □ p.5,850, ✳ Khartoum; Br. & Egyptian.

Suez (sōō-ĕz′; sōō′ĕz), **Isthmus of,** joins Asia & Africa; ship canal (**Suez Canal**) 100 m. long.

Sumatra (sōō-mä′trà), large isl. S of Malay pen. with adjacent isls. 176,967 □ p. 6,075; Dutch.

Sumner (sŭm′nẽr), Chas. Am. statesm. (1811–74).

Superior, Lake, Great Lake, bet. U. S. & Canada.

Susquehanna (sŭs′kwē-hăn′à), riv. in N. Y. Pa. & Md. 420 m. to Chesapeake bay.

Sweden (swē′dĕn), kdm. N Eur. 173,035 □ p. 5,904, ✳ Stockholm.

Swift (swĭft), Jonathan. *Dean Swift.* Eng. dean & satirist, b. in Ireland (1667–1745).

Switzerland (swĭt′zẽr-lănd), republic, cen. Europe, 15,941 □ p. 3,880, ✳ Berne.   [suburbs, 906.|

Sydney (sĭd′nĭ), spt. ✳ of N. S. Wales, p. with|

Syracuse (sĭr′à-kūs′; -kūs′), city, cen. N. Y. p. 172.

Syria (-ĭ-à), country, W Asia, E of Medit. sea, 60,000 □ p. 3,000, ✳ Damascus; Fr. mandate.

T

Tabriz (tä-brēz′), city, NW Persia, p. 200.

Taft (tàft), Wm. Howard. 27th pres. of U. S. 1909–13. Ch. justice, Sup. Court fr. 1921 (1857–1930).

Tallinn. See REVEL.

Tamerlane (tăm′ẽr-lān′). Mongol conqueror (1333?–1405).

Tanganyika (tăn′găn-yē′kà), lake, cen. Afr. 400 m.

long. **— Territory,** ter. E Afr. 365,000 □ p.4,123; Br. mandate; form. Ger. E. Africa.

Tasmania (tăz-mā′nĭ-à), isl. & state of Australia, S of the mainland, 26,214 □ p. 214, ✳ Hobart.

Taylor (tā′lẽr), Zachary. Am. gen. & 12th pres. of the U. S. fr. 1849 (1784–1850).

Teheran (tĕ-h′rän′), ✳ of Persia, in N, p. 220.

Tennessee (tĕn′ĕ-sē′), state, SE cen. U. S. 42,022 □ p. 2,338, ✳ Nashville. Abbr. *Tenn.*

Tennyson (tĕn′ĭ-sŭn), Alfred, first Baron Tennyson. Eng. poet (1809–92).

Texas (tĕk′săs), state, SW U. S. 265,896 □ p.4,663, ✳ Austin; largest state in union. Abbr. *Tex.*

Thackeray (thăk′ẽr-ĭ), William Makepeace. Eng. auth. (1811–63).

Thames (tĕmz), riv. S Eng. 210 m. to North sea.

Thessaly (thĕs′à-lĭ), region (anc. div.), N Greece.

Thoreau (thō′rō), Henry David. Am. author (1817–62).

Thrace (thrās), anc. country & Rom. prov. now in Bulgaria, Gr. & Turkey in Europe.

Tiberius (tī-bē′rĭ-ŭs). Rom. emp. fr. A. D. 14 (B. C. 42–A. D. 37).

Tibet (tĭ-bĕt′; tĭb′ĕt), country, Chinese depend., SW of China proper, 465,000 □ p. 3,500, ✳ Lhasa.

Tientsin (tĕ-ĕn′tsĕn′), city, ✳ of Chihli prov. China, p. 800.

Tiflis (tyĕ-flyĕs′), ✳ of Georgia & of Transcaucasian Fed. Asia, p. 347.   [1,150 m.|

Tigris (tī′grĭs), riv. Turkey in Asia & Mesopotamia,|

Tirol *or* **Tyrol** (tĭr′ŏl; *G.* tē-rōl′), Alpine prov. W Austria, 4,790 □ p. 306, ✳ Innsbruck.

Titian (tĭsh′ăn). It. painter (1477–1576).

Titicaca, Lake (tē′tē-kä′kä), bet. S Peru & Bolivia.

Titus (tī′tŭs). Roman emp. fr. 79 (40–81).

Tokyo *or* **Tokio** (tō′kĕ-ō), ✳ of Japan, p. (1920) 2,173; earthquake & fire, Sept. 1, 1923.

Toledo (tō-lē′dō), city & port, NW Ohio, p. 243.

Tonkin (tŏn′kĭn′) *or* **Tongking** (tŏng′kĭng′), prot. Fr. Indo-China, 40,530 □ p. 6,850, ✳ Hanoi.

Topeka (tô-pē′kà), ✳ of Kansas, in NE, p. 50.

Toronto (-rŏn′tō), ✳ of Ontario, Canada, p. 522.

Toulouse (tōō′lōōz′), city, S Fr. p. 175.   [117).|

Trajan (trā′jăn). Roman emp. fr. 98 (52 *or* 53–|

Transcaucasian Federation (trăns′kô-kā′shăn; -kăsh′ăn), republic, Russia, S of Caucasus mts. 74,970 □ p. 5,684, ✳ Tiflis.

Transvaal (-väl′), prov. U. of S. Afr. 110,450 □ p. 2,088, ✳ Pretoria.

Trenton (trĕn′tŭn), ✳ of N. J. p. 119; bat. 1776.

Trieste (trē-ĕst′), *or* **Triest,** spt. NE It. p. 240.

Trinidad (trĭn′ĭ-dăd′), isl. off coast of Venezuela 1,862 □ p. 339; Br.

Tripoli (trĭp′ō-lĭ), form. Turk country, N Afr.; now ✳ Tripoli; Ital.   [fr. 1918–25 (1879– |

Tripolitania (trē′pô-lē-tä′nyä), dist. W Libya,|

Trotsky (trŏt′skē), Leon. Russ. soviet min. of war|

Troy (troi), anc. ruined city, NW Asia Minor.

Tunis (tū′nĭs), country, N Afr. 49,030 □ p. 2,095 Fr. prot. **—** its ✳ p. 172.

Turin (tū′rĭn ; tû-rĭn′), city, NW It. p. 500.

Turkestan (tōōr′kĕ-stän′), region, cen. Asia.

Turkey (tûr′kĭ), *form.* **Ottoman Empire** (ŏt′ô-măn), repub. in SE Eur. & SW Asia, 296,420 □ p. 15.008, ✳ Angora.

Twain (twān), Mark. Pseud. of CLEMENS, S. L.

Tyler (tī′lẽr), John. 10th pres. of the U. S. in 1841–45 (1790–1862).

Tyre (tīr), anc. spt. ✳ of Phœnicia; modern SUR.

U V W

Uganda (ōō-gän'dä), country, cen. Afr. 110,300 □ p. 3,066; Br. protectorate.

Ukraine (ū'krān), repub. in Union of Russ. Soviet repubs. SE Eur. 174,510 □ p. 26,002, ❋ Kharkov.

Ulster (ŭl'stĕr), form. prov. N Ireland, 8,567 □ p. 1,579; divided bet. Irish Free State & N. Ire.

United Kingdom of Great Britain & Northern Ireland, isl. kdm. of NW Eur. composed of Gr. Brit. (England, Wales, Scotland) & N. Ireland, 94,498 □ p. 44,168, ❋ London.

United States of America, federal repub. N. Am.; 48 states & fed. dist.; continental U. S. 3,026,789 □ p. 105,828; with Alaska & Hawaii, 3,624,122 □ p. 106,139; with all possessions, 3,742,903 □ p. 117,823; ❋ Washington.

Ural Mountains (ū'răl), E Russia, chiefly in Eur.

Uruguay (ū'rōō-gwä; ōō'rōō-gwī'), rep. S of Brazil, 72,153 □ p. 1,495, ❋ Montevideo. [Lake City.

Utah (ū'tô), state, W U. S. 84,990 □ p. 449, ❋ Salt

Utrecht (-trĕkt), city, Neth. p. 138; treaty, 1713.

Valencia (vȧ-lĕn'shĭ-ȧ; -shä), spt. E Spain, p. 247.

Valparaiso (văl'pȧ-rī'sō; -zō), spt. Chile, p. 182.

Van Buren (văn bū'rĕn), Martin. 8th pres. of the U. S. in 1837–41 (1782–1862).

Vancouver (văn-kōō'vĕr), isl. off coast of Br. Columbia, 16,400 □. — spt. SW B. C. p. 117.

Vatican City (văt'ĭ-kăn), ind. papal state, part of Rome, Italy, on rt. bank of Tiber; created 1929.

Velásquez (vä-läs'kāth), Diego Rodríguez. Sp. painter (1599–1660). [□ p. 2,412, ❋ Caracas.

Venezuela (vĕn'ē-zwē'lä), rep. N S. Am. 393,-874

Venice (vĕn'ĭs), coast city, NE Italy, p. 165.

Vergil (vûr'jĭl). Rom. poet (B. C. 70–19).

Vermont (vĕr-mŏnt'), state, NE U. S. 9,564 □ p. 352, ❋ Montpelier. Abbr. *Vt.* [69 (9–79).

Vespasian (vĕs-pā'zhĭ-ăn). Roman emperor fr.

Vesuvius (vē-sū'vĭ-ŭs), volcano, E of Naples bay, 4,267 ft. [ ).

Victor Emmanuel III. Kg. of It. fr. 1900 (1869–

Victoria (vĭk-tō'rĭ-ȧ), state, SE Australia, 87,884 □ p. 1,532, ❋ Melbourne. — spt. ❋ of Hongkong, p. 323. — Queen of Gr. Brit. & Ire. fr. 1837 & Empress of India fr. 1876 (1819–1910). — **Falls,** in Zambezi riv. S. Rhodesia.—, *or* **Victoria Nyanza** (nyän'zä), largest lake in Africa, in E, 26,828 □

Vienna (vē-ĕn'ä), *Ger.* **Wien** (vēn), city, ❋ of Austria, on Danube riv. p. 1,841.

Virginia (vĕr-jĭn'ĭ-ȧ), state, E U. S. 42,627 □ p. 2,309, ❋ Richmond. Abbr. *Va.*

Virgin Islands (U. S.), W. I. isls. of St. Thomas, St. Croix, & St. John, 132 □ p. 26, ❋ St. Thomas.

Volga (vŏl'gȧ), riv. Russ. in Eur. 2,300 m. to Caspian sea. [pop. 2,207.

Wales (wālz), principality, W of Eng., 7,466 □

Warsaw (wôr'sô), ❋ of Poland, on Vistula, p. 931.

Washington (wŏsh'ĭng-tŭn), state, NW U. S. 69,127 □ p. 1,357, ❋ Olympia. Abbr. *Wash.* — city, D. C. ❋ of U. S. p. 438.—, George. 1st pres. of the U. S. in 1789–97 (1732–99). [6,293 ft.

Washington, Mount, highest of White mts. N. H.

Watt (wŏt), James. Scot. inventor (1736–1819).

Webster (wĕb'stĕr), Daniel. Am. statesman (1782–1852). —, Noah. Am. lexicographer (1758–1843).

Wellington (wĕl'ĭng-tŭn), ❋ of N. Z. p. 107. —, Arthur Wellesley, Duke of. Br. gen. (1769–1852).

Western Australia, state, Australia, 975,920 □ p. 332, ❋ Perth.

West Indies (ĭn'dĭz), Atl. isls. bet. Fla. & S. Am.

West Virginia, state, E U. S. 24,170 □ p. 1,464, ❋ Charleston. Abbr. *W. Va.* [ft.

White Mountains, in N cen. N. H.; highest, 6,293

White Russia, repub. in Russ. Soviet Union, W Russia, Eur. 23,290 □ p. 1,634, ❋ Minsk.

White Sea, gulf, NW Russia in Europe.

Whitman (hwĭt'măn), Walt. Am. poet (1819–92).

Whitney, Mount (hwĭt'nĭ), mt. E cen. Calif. 14,502 ft.; highest in U. S. [92).

Whittier (-ĭ-ĕr), John Greenleaf. Am. poet (1807–

Wight, Isle of (wīt), isl. S coast Eng. 147 □ p. 95.

William (wĭl'yăm) **I.** *The Conqueror.* Kg. of Eng. fr. 1066 (1027 *or* '28–87). — **III.** Kg. of Eng. Scot. & Ire. fr. 1689 (1650–1702). — **I.** Kg. of Prussia fr. 1861 & Ger. emp. fr. 1871 (1797–1888.) — **II.** Kg. of Prussia & Ger. emp. 1888–1918; abdicated (1859–   ).

Williams (wĭl'yămz), Roger. Eng. colonist in America; founder of Rhode I. (1604?–1683).

Wilmington (wĭl'mĭng-tŭn), city, N Del. p. 110.

Wilson (-sŭn), Woodrow. 28th pres. of the U. S. in 1913–21 (1856–1924).

Windward Islands, S part of Lesser Antilles, W. I.

Winnipeg (wĭn'ĭ-pĕg), city, ❋ of Manitoba, p. 179.

Wisconsin (wĭs-kŏn'sĭn), state, N U. S. 56,066 □ p. 2,632, ❋ Madison. Abbr. *Wis.*

Worcester (wōōs'tĕr), city, cen. Mass. p. 180.

Wordsworth (wûrdz'wûrth), Wm. Eng. poet (1770–1850). [□ p. 2,519, ❋ Stuttgart.

Württemberg (vür'tĕm-bĕrk), state, SW Ger. 7,532

Wycliffe (wĭk'lĭf), John. Eng. reformer (d. 1384).

Wyoming (wī-ō'mĭng), state, W U. S. 97,914 □ p. 194, ❋ Cheyenne. Abbr. *Wyo.*

X Y Z

Xavier (zăv'ĭ-ĕr), Francis, Saint. Sp. Jesuit & missionary (1506–52). [434?–355?).

Xenophon (zĕn'ō-fŏn). Greek hist. & gen. (B. C.

Xerxes (zûrk'sēz), Kg. of Persia fr. B. C. 486 (d. B. C. 465). [□ p. 301.

Yakutsk (yȧ-kōōtsk'), repub. E Siberia, 1,457,070

Yangtze (yäng'tsĕ'), riv. cen. China, 3,200 m. to Pac. oc.

Yellow Sea, inlet, Pac. oc. on NE coast of China.

Yellowstone, lake in Y. Nat'l Park, 140 □. — riv. Wyo. to Missouri riv. 600 m.; falls 110 & 310 ft.

Yellowstone National Park, mostly in NW Wyo. 3,348 □. [Arctic ocean.

Yenisei (yĕ'nĕ-sĕ'ē), riv. cen. Siberia, 3,000 m. to

Yokohama (yō'kō-hä'mä), spt. E Japan, p. (1920) 423; earthquake & fire, Sept. 1, 1923.

Yonkers (yŏn'kĕrz), city, SE New York, p. 100.

Yosemite Falls, (yō-sĕm'ĭ-tē), series of falls, total height, 2,526 ft., in **Yosemite National Park,** E cen. Calif. 1,125 □.

Youngstown (yŭngz'toun), city, NE Ohio, p. 132.

Yugoslavia *or* **Jugoslavia** (yōō'gō-slä'vĭ-ä), kdm. SE Eur. 96,134 □ p. 12,017, ❋ Belgrade.

Yukon (yōō'kŏn), riv. Can. & Alaska, 2,300 m. to N Pac. oc. [Rhodesia to Indian oc.

Zambezi (zăm-bē'zĭ), riv. 1,600 m. E Angola &

Zanzibar (zăn'zĭ-bär'; zän'-), isl. E Afr. 640 □ p. 114; Br. prot. — spt. its ❋ p. 35.

Zoroaster (zō'rō-ăs'tĕr). Founder of anc. Persian religion (fl. ab. 1000 B. C.).

Zuider Zee (zī'dĕr zā'), gulf of North sea, Neth.

Zurich (zōō'rĭk) city, ❋ N Switz. p. 207,

MEASURES, WEIGHTS, METRIC SYSTEM, MONEY, DECIMAL EQUIVALENTS, ETC.

Long Measure

12 inches (in.)	= 1 foot (ft.)
3 feet	= 1 yard (yd.)
5½ yards or 16½ feet	= 1 rod (rd.) or pole (p.)
40 rods	= 1 furlong (fur.)
8 furlongs or 1760 yards	= 1 mile (mi.)

Surveyors' Measure

7.92 inches	= 1 link (li.)
100 links or 66 feet	= 1 chain (ch.)
10 chains	= 1 furlong (fur.)
80 chains	= 1 mile (mi.)

The *engineer's chain* is 100 feet long, with links one foot long.

Square Measure (Area)

144 square inches (sq. in.)	= 1 square foot (sq. ft.)
9 square feet	= 1 square yard (sq. yd.)
30¼ square yards	= 1 square rod (sq. rd.)
160 square rods	= 1 acre (A.)

Surveyors' Measure (Area)

625 square links (sq. li.)	= 1 square rod (sq. rd.)
16 square rods	= 1 square chain (sq. ch.)
10 square chains	= 1 acre (A.)
640 acres	= 1 square mile (sq. mi.) or 1 section (sec.)
36 square miles	= 1 township (tp.)

Cubic Measure (Volume)

1728 cubic inches (cu. in.)	= 1 cubic foot (cu. ft.)
27 cubic feet	= 1 cubic yard (cu. yd.)

(for measuring wood, etc.)

16 cubic feet	= 1 cord foot (cd. ft.) or 4 ft. x 4 ft. x 1 ft.
8 cord feet	= 1 cord (cd.) or 4 ft. x 4 ft. x 8 ft.

Time Measure

60 seconds (sec.)	= 1 minute (min.)
60 minutes	= 1 hour (hr.)
24 hours	= 1 day (da.)
7 days	= 1 week (wk.)
30 days (commonly)	= 1 calendar month (mo.)
365 days or 12 calendar months	= 1 common year (yr.)
366 days	= 1 leap year
100 years	= 1 century

Every year whose number is divisible by 4 without a remainder is a *leap year*, excepting the full centuries, which to be leap years must be divisible by 400 without a remainder; 1900, therefore, is not a leap year.

Angular Measure (Longitude, Etc.)

60 seconds (″)	= 1 prime minute (′)
60 minutes	= 1 degree (°)
360 degrees	= 1 circle

Longitude and Time

1 second of longitude (″)	= $\frac{1}{15}$ sec. of time
1 minute ″ ″ (′)	= 4 sec. of time
1 degree ″ ″ (°)	= 4 min. of time
15 degrees ″ ″	= 1 hour
360 degrees ″ ″	= 24 hours

Dry Measure (Grain, Fruit, Etc.)

2 pints (pt.)	= 1 quart (qt.)
8 quarts	= 1 peck (pk.)
4 pecks	= 1 bushel (bu.) = 2150.42 cu. in.

Liquid Measure

4 gills (gi.)	= 1 pint (pt.)
2 pints	= 1 quart (qt.)
4 quarts	= 1 gallon (gal.) = 231 cu. in.
63 gallons	= 1 hogshead (hhd.)

The *barrel* is usually taken to be 31½ gallons; in some States, 32 gallons. The *imperial gallon* contains 277.274 cubic inches.

Apothecaries' Measure (Drugs, Etc.)

60 minims or drops (♏)	= 1 fluid dram (f ℥)
8 fluid drams	= 1 fluid ounce (f ℥)
16 fluid ounces	= 1 pint (*octarius*) (O.)
8 pints	= 1 gallon (*congius*) (C.)

Avoirdupois Weight (Ordinary Commodities)

16 drams (dr.)	= 1 ounce (oz.)
16 ounces or 7000 grains	= 1 pound (lb.)
14 pounds	= 1 stone (st.)
100 (in Eng. 112) pounds	= 1 hundredweight (cwt.)
2000 pounds or 20 hundredweights	= 1 short ton (s. t.)
2240 pounds or 20 hundredweights	= 1 long ton (l. t.)

Troy Weight (Precious Metals, Jewels, Etc.)

3.2 grains (gr.)	= 1 carat (car.)
24 grains	= 1 pennyweight (dwt.)
20 pennyweights	= 1 ounce (oz.)
12 ounces or 5760 grains	= 1 pound (lb.)

Apothecaries' Weight (Drugs, Etc.)

20 grains (gr.)	= 1 scruple (℈)
3 scruples	= 1 dram (ℨ)
8 drams	= 1 ounce (℥)
12 ounces	= 1 pound (lb)

Numbers

12 units	= 1 dozen (doz.)
12 dozen	= 1 gross (gr.)
12 gross	= 1 great gross
20 units	= 1 score

Paper

24 sheets	= 1 quire (qr.)
20 quires	= 1 ream (rm.)

METRIC MEASURES

NOTE. The metric system, a decimal system of measures and weights, originated in France shortly after the French Revolution, being fixed by law in 1799 and made compulsory in 1801. It is now used for almost all scientific purposes in the United States and Great Britain, and its use is required by law in the majority of civilized countries.

Decimal fractions of the primary units are designated by the Latin prefixes *deci-* (10th), *centi-* (100th), *milli-* (1000th); decimal multiples are denoted by the Greek prefixes *deca-* (10 times), *hecto-* (100 times), *kilo-* (1000 times), *myria-* (10,000 times).

The most commonly used names are italicized.

Measures of Length

10 *millimeters* (mm.)	= 1 *centimeter* (cm.)	= 0.3937 in.
10 centimeters	= 1 decimeter (dm.)	= 3.937 in.
10 decimeters	= 1 *meter* (m.)	= 39.37 in.
10 meters	= 1 decameter (Dm.)	= 393.7 in.
10 decameters	= 1 hectometer (hm.)	= 328 ft. 1 in.
10 hectometers	= 1 *kilometer* (km.)	= 0.62137 mi.
10 kilometers	= 1 myriameter (Mm.)	= 6.2137 mi.

The *micron* (μ) is one millionth of a meter or one thousandth of a millimeter.

Measures of Surface

100 *sq. millimeters* (mm².)	= 1 *sq. centimeter* (cm².)	
100 sq. centimeters	= 1 sq. decimeter (dm².)	
100 sq. decimeters	= 1 *sq. meter* (m².)	
100 sq. meters	= 1 sq. decameter (Dm².)	
100 sq. decameters	= 1 sq. hectometer (hm².)	
100 sq. hectometers	= 1 *sq. kilometer* (km².)	

Land Measure

1 sq. meter (m².)	= 1 centiare (ca.)	= 1,550 sq. in.
100 centiares or 100 m².	= 1 *are* (a.)	= 119.6 sq. yds.
100 ares or 10,000 m².	= 1 *hectare* (ha.)	= 2.471 acres.

The *square kilometer* is used in topographical work on a large scale, or in recording areas for maps and charts. *Hectare* is used for field measurements, analogous to our *acre*. For city lots and the like *are* is generally used.

Measures of Capacity

The standard unit of capacity is the *liter*, equal to 1 cubic decimeter or 0.908 dry quarts or 1.0567 liquid quarts.

10 milliliters (ml.)	= 1 *centiliter* (cl.)
10 centiliters	= 1 deciliter (dl.)
10 deciliters	= 1 *liter* (l.)
10 liters	= 1 decaliter (Dl.)
10 decaliters	= 1 *hectoliter* (hl.)
10 hectoliters	= 1 kiloliter (kl.)

Measures of Volume

The standard unit of volume is the *cubic meter*, equal to 1.308 cubic yards.

1000 *cu. millimeters* (mm³.)	= 1 *cu. centimeter* (cm³.)
1000 cu. centimeters	= 1 cu. decimeter (dm³.)
1000 cu. decimeters	= 1 *cu. meter* (m³.), or 1 stere (st.)

Stere is used in regard to firewood. 1 stere = 0.2759 cord; 1 *decistere* = $\frac{1}{10}$ stere; 1 decastere = 10 steres.

Weights

The standard unit of weight is the *gram*, equal to 15.432 grains.

10 *milligrams* (mg.)	= 1 *centigram* (cg.)	= 0.1543 gr.
10 centigrams	= 1 decigram (dg.)	= 1.5432 gr.
10 decigrams	= 1 *gram* (g.)	= 15.432 gr.
10 grams	= 1 decagram (Dg.)	= 0.3527 oz.
10 decagrams	= 1 hectogram (hg.)	= 3.5274 oz.
10 hectograms	= 1 *kilogram* or *kilo* (kg.)	= 2.2046 lbs.
10 kilograms	= 1 myriagram (Mg.)	= 22.046 lbs.
10 myriagrams	= 1 quintal (q.)	= 220.46 lbs.
10 quintals or 1000 kg.	= 1 *metric ton* (t.)	= 2204.6 lbs.

Metric Equivalents of Common Units

inch	= 2.54 cm.	minim	= 0.059 ml.
foot	= 0.3048 m.	gill	= 0.118 l.
yard	= 0.9144 m.	liquid quart	= 0.9464 l.
rod	= 5.029 m.	dry quart	= 1.101 l.
mile	= 1.6093 km.	gallon	= 3.785 l.
sq. inch	= 6.452 cm².	peck	= 8.809 l.
sq. foot	= 0.0929 m².	bushel	= 35.24 l.
sq. yard	= 0.836 m².	oz. avdp.	= 28.35 g.
acre	= 0.4046 ha.	lb. avdp.	= 0.4536 kg.
sq. mile	= 259 ha. or 2.5899 km².	ton, long	= 1.0161 t.
		ton, short	= 0.9072 t.
cu. inch	= 16.39 cm³.	grain	= 0.0648 g.
cu. foot	= 0.0283 m³.	oz. troy	= 31.103 g.
cu. yard	= 0.7645 m³.	lb. troy	= 0.3732 kg.
fathom	= 1.829 m.	cord	= 3.623 m³.

Decimal Equivalents of Common Fractions

EIGHTHS		THIRDS	SIXTHS
$\frac{1}{8}=.125$	$\frac{5}{8}=.625$	$\frac{1}{3}=.33\dot{3}$	$\frac{1}{6}=.166\dot{6}$
$\frac{1}{4}=.25$	$\frac{3}{4}=.75$		
$\frac{3}{8}=.375$	$\frac{7}{8}=.875$	$\frac{2}{3}=.66\dot{6}$	$\frac{5}{6}=.833$
$\frac{1}{2}=.5$			

NINTHS		FIFTHS	TENTHS
$\frac{1}{9}=.11\dot{1}$	$\frac{5}{9}=.55\dot{5}$	$\frac{1}{5}=.2$	$\frac{1}{10}=.1$
$\frac{2}{9}=.22\dot{2}$	$\frac{7}{9}=.77\dot{7}$	$\frac{2}{5}=.4$	$\frac{3}{10}=.3$
$\frac{4}{9}=.44\dot{4}$	$\frac{8}{9}=.88\dot{8}$	$\frac{3}{5}=.6$	$\frac{7}{10}=.7$
		$\frac{4}{5}=.8$	$\frac{9}{10}=.9$

Percentages and their Fractional Equivalents

PER CENT	FRACTIONAL EQUIVALENT	PER CENT	FRACTIONAL EQUIVALENT
$2\frac{1}{2}\%$	$\frac{1}{40}$	25%	$\frac{1}{4}$
5%	$\frac{1}{20}$	$33\frac{1}{3}\%$	$\frac{1}{3}$
10%	$\frac{1}{10}$	40%	$\frac{2}{5}$
$12\frac{1}{2}\%$	$\frac{1}{8}$	50%	$\frac{1}{2}$
$16\frac{2}{3}\%$	$\frac{1}{6}$	$66\frac{2}{3}\%$	$\frac{2}{3}$
20%	$\frac{1}{5}$	75%	$\frac{3}{4}$

Money

COUNTRY	UNIT	SYMBOL	VALUE
United States	dollar	$	$1.00
Argentina	peso oro	$ m/1	$0.965
Austria	krone	Kr.	$0.203
Belgium	franc	Fr.	$0.193
Brazil	milreis	1$000	$0.546
Canada	dollar	$	$1.00
Chile	peso oro	P.	$0.365
Czechoslovakia	krone	Kr.	$0.203
France	franc	Fr.	$0.193
Germany	mark	M.	$0.238
Great Britain	pound (sterling)	£	$4.8665
Greece	drachma	Dr.	$0.193
Hungary	krone	Kr.	$0.203
India	rupee	Re., Rs.	$0.487
Italy	lira	L.	$0.193
Japan	yen	Yen	$0.498
Mexico	peso	P.	$0.498
Netherlands	gulden	Gld.	$0.402
Philippines	peso	₱	$0.50
Poland	zloty	Zl.	$0.193
Portugal	escudo	Es.	$1.08
Russia	ruble	R.	$0.515
Sweden	krona	Kr.	$0.268
Turkey	piaster	Pi.	$0.044
Venezuela	bolivar	Bol.	$0.193
Yugoslavia	dinar	Din.	$0.193

FOREIGN COINAGE

Great Britain

4 farthings = 1 penny = $0.0203
12 pence = 1 shilling = $0.2433
20 shillings = 1 pound or sovereign = $4.8665
21 shillings = 1 guinea (= $5.11 (obsolete as a coin)
Silver coins: — Threepence, sixpence, shilling, florin (= 2 shillings), half crown (= 2½ shillings).
Gold coins: — Half sovereign, sovereign.

Canada

100 cents = 1 dollar = $1.00
Silver coins: — 5, 10, 25, 50 cents; 1 dollar.
Gold coins: — 5, 10 dollars.

France, Belgium, Switzerland, Monaco

100 centimes = 1 franc = $0.193
Silver coins: — 50 centimes (also, in France, 20 centimes); 1, 2, 5 francs.
Gold coins: — 10 francs in France and Switzerland; 20 francs in France, Belgium, Switzerland, and Monaco; 100 francs in Monaco.

Italy, Greece, Spain, Yugoslavia, Roumania, Bulgaria, Finland

The French standard is adopted under different names.

In Italy, 100 centesimi = 1 lira
In Greece, 100 lepta = 1 drachma
In Spain, 100 centimos = 1 peseta
In Yugoslavia, 100 paras = 1 dinar
In Roumania, 100 bani = 1 leu
In Bulgaria, 100 stotinki = 1 lev
In Finland, 100 penni = 1 markka

Germany *

100 pfennigs = 1 mark = $0.238
Silver coins: — 50 pfennigs; 1, 2, 3, 5 marks.
Gold coins: — 10, 20 marks.

Austria, Hungary, Czechoslovakia *

100 heller = 1 krone = $0.203
Silver coins: — 1, 2, 5 kronen.
Gold coins: — 10, 20, 100 kronen.

Russia

100 kopecks = 1 ruble
10 rubles = 1 chervonetz = $5.146
Silver coins — 10, 15, 20, 50 kopecks; 1 ruble.

Norway

100 öre = 1 krone = $0.268
Silver coins: — 10, 25, 50 öre; 1 krone, 2 kroner.
Gold coins: — 5, 10, 20 kroner.

Sweden

100 öre = 1 krona = $0.268
Silver coins: — 10, 25, 50 öre; 1 krona, 2 kronor.
Gold coins: — 5, 10, 20 kronor.

Denmark

100 öre = 1 krone = $0.268
Silver coins: — 10, 25 öre; 1 krone, 2 kroner.
Gold coins: — 10, 20 kroner.

* At present (1925) in these countries the currency is almost entirely paper money.

Successful Teachers Agree

that to do the best school work pupils need

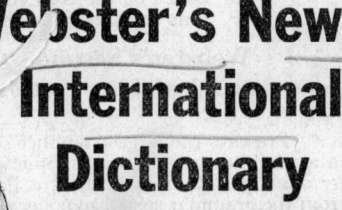

Webster's New International Dictionary

—*the Merriam Webster*

When questions arise in the history recitation, in language work, in spelling, or about noted people, places, foreign words, synonyms, pronunciation, new words, flags, state seals, etc., do you suggest that the **New International** is a universal question answerer and contains just the information desired?

Dr. Suzzalo says: "Training children to a competent and ready use of the dictionary and fixing the habit of consulting it is one of the main duties that the school can perform for a student."

Constantly Improved and Kept Up to Date.
More than 407,000 Vocabulary Terms. 12,000 Biographical Entries.
New Gazetteer, 32,000 Subjects. 6000 Illustrations. 2700 Pages.

The One Great Standard Authority

It is the **Standard** of the Federal and State Courts. The **Standard** of the Government Printing Office. The **Basis** of nearly all the schoolbooks in the country. **Indorsed** by State School Superintendents. **Universally recommended** by Statesmen, College Presidents, Educators and Authors. Adhered to as **Standard** by over 99% of the Newspapers. **All States** that have adopted a large dictionary as standard have selected the New International.

The above cannot be said of any other book.   Get The Best.

CAUTION: Look for the circular trade-mark Write for specimen pages, FREE.

G. & C. Merriam Co., Springfield, Mass., U. S. A.